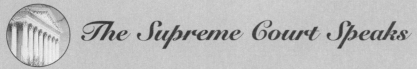

The Supreme Court Speaks

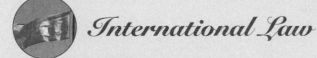

International Law

Fourth Edition

Contemporary Business and E–Commerce Law

Legal, Global, Digital, and Ethical Environment

Henry R. Cheeseman

Clinical Professor of Business Law
Director of the Legal Studies Program
Marshall School of Business
University of Southern California

Prentice Hall

Upper Saddle River, New Jersey 07458

Library of Congress Cataloging-in-Publication Data

Cheeseman, Henry R.
  Contemporary business and e-commerce law : legal, global, digital, and ethical
environment / Henry R. Cheeseman.—4th ed.
    p. cm.
  Rev. ed. of: Contemporary business law, 3rd ed. ©2000.
  Includes bibliographical references and index.
  ISBN 0-13-034852-X (alk. paper)
  1. Business law—United States—Cases.   I. Cheeseman, Henry R. Contemporary
business law.   II. Title.
KF889.C46 2003
346.7307—dc21

Acquisitions Editor: David Parker
Editor-in-Chief: Jeff Shelstad
Assistant Editor: Ashley Keim
Media Project Manager: Anthony Palmiotto
Executive Marketing Manager: Debbie Clare
Managing Editor (Production):   Judy Leale
Production Editor: Cindy Spreder
Production Assistant: Dianne Falcone
Permissions Supervisor: Suzanne Grappi
Associate Director, Manufacturing: Vinnie Scelta
Production Manager: Arnold Vila
Manufacturing Buyer: Diane Peirano
Design Manager: Patricia Smythe
Art Director: Janet Slowik
Interior Design: Jill Little
Cover Design: Jill Little
Cover Illustration/Photo: Salem Kreiger
Illustrator (Interior):   UG/GGS Information Services, Inc.
Manager, Print Production: Christy Mahon
Page Formatter: Ashley Scattergood
Composition: UG/GGS Information Services, Inc.
Full-Service Project Management: Evelyn Podsiadlo and Terri O'Prey,
  UG/GGS Information Services, Inc.
Printer/Binder: Courier-Kendallville

Pearson Education LTD.
Pearson Education Australia PTY, Limited
Pearson Education Singapore, Pte. Ltd
Pearson Education North Asia Ltd
Pearson Education, Canada, Ltd
Pearson Educación de Mexico, S.A. de C.V.
Pearson Education-Japan
Pearson Education Malaysia, Pte. Ltd

10 9 8 7 6 5 4 3
ISBN 0-13-034852-X

Dedication

*This book is dedicated
to the victims of the terrorist attack on the
World Trade Center in New York,
and their families and loved ones, to the police,
firefighters, and other rescuers, and to the women
and men of the U. S. armed forces who for centuries
have protected the freedoms we hold so dear.*

Contents in Brief

$\mathcal{C}$ontents

Preface

—To the Students—

Each semester, as I stand up in front of a new group of business majors in my business law class I am struck by the thought that, cases and statutes aside, I know two very important things that they have yet to learn. The first is that I draw as much from them as they do from me. Their youth, enthusiasm, questions, and even the doubts a few of them hold about the relevance of law to their futures, fuel my teaching. They don't know that every time they open their minds to look at a point from a new perspective or critically question something they have taken for granted, I get a wonderful reward for the work that I do.

The other thing I know is that both teaching and learning the law are all about stories. The stories I tell provide the framework on which students will hang everything they learn about the law in my class. It is my hope that long after the facts about the specific language of the cases and statutes have faded, they will retain that framework. Several years from now, "unintentional torts" may draw only a glimmer of recognition with business managers who learn about them as students in my class this year. However, they will likely recall the story of the woman who sued McDonald's for serving her coffee that was too hot and caused her injuries. The story sticks and gives students the hook on which to hang the concepts.

I remind myself of these two facts every time I sit down to work on writing and revising **Contemporary Business and E-Commerce Law,** as well. My goal is to present the law in a way that will spur students to ask questions, to go beyond rote memorization. Business law is an evolving outgrowth of its environment, and that environment keeps changing. In addition to the social, ethical, and international contexts I have incorporated in previous editions of **Contemporary Business and E–Commerce Law,** this edition adds coverage and emphasis on electronic commerce and entrepreneurship as two vital catalysts to the law and a key part of its environment.

It is my wish that my commitment to these goals shines through in this labor of love, and I hope you have as much pleasure in using it as I have had in creating it for you.

Henry Cheeseman

Making the Most of the Fourth Edition

These new chapters and boxes feature coverage of the latest acts which include: The Anticybersquatting Act, The Uniform Computer Information Transactions Act (UCITA), The Digital Millennium Copyright Act, The NET Act, The American Inventor's Protection Act, The Federal Electronic Signatures Act, and all other relevant federal and state laws and cases governing the Internet and E-Commerce.

E-Commerce & Information Technology

Two new chapters are dedicated to coverage of the Internet, e-commerce, and the law.

- **Chapter 14** Intellectual Property and Internet Law
- **Chapter 15** Electronic Commerce and Information Technology Licensing

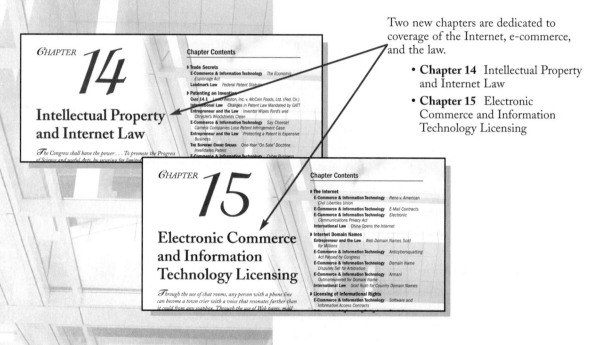

Over 50 **E-Commerce and Information Technology** boxes focus on the legal issues businesses face as they either launch new Internet ventures or rise to the challenge of incorporating online technologies into their existing business models.

The Entrepreneur and the Law

Chapter 27, Entrepreneurship, Franchising, and Licensing, recognizes the explosion of entrepreneurial ventures as an important factor in contemporary American business and investigates the legal issues unique to them.

CHAPTER

27

Entrepreneurship, Franchising, and Licensing

Commerce never really flourishes so much, as when it is delivered from the guardianship of legislators and ministers.
—William Godwin
Enquiry Concerning Political Justice (1798)

Chapter Objectives

After studying this chapter, you should be able to:

1. Describe the role of entrepreneurs in starting and operating businesses.

2. List and describe the forms of conducting domestic

Entrepreneur and the Law

THE ENTREPRENEURIAL SPIRIT: THE CREATION OF AMAZON.COM

In 1994, Jeff Bezos, the son of a Cuban immigrant to the United States, had made it big. After graduating from Princeton University, he had gone on to Wall Street where he worked for a hedge fund. But Bezos saw an even greater opportunity: online commerce. So he quit his job, jumped in the car with his wife, MacKenzie, and headed west. While she drove, he typed on his laptop computer. Bezos drew up a list of 20 products that he figured he could sell online but then narrowed it to two—books and music. Bezos settled on books for two reasons. First, there are more to sell (about 1.3 million books in print versus 300,000 music titles). Second, the Goliaths of publishing seemed less imposing than the six record companies that dominated music; there were thousands of bookstores, the largest being Barnes & Noble with 12 percent of the industry's $25 billion annual sales.

After checking out Colorado and Oregon, Bezos and his wife settled in Seattle, Washington. They rented a house, hired four employees, and started Amazon.com out of their garage. Bezos and his family incorporated the business, sold some stock to friends and other investors, and kept the rest of the stock for themselves. Bezos took a traditional business—bookselling—online. He reasoned that books were fungible—everyone sold the same product—and that a portion of a traditional bookseller's cost represented the real estate on which the store sat. So Bezos lined up a distribution center in Oregon and began taking orders in cyberspace. Amazon.com sold its first book in July 1995.

customers and getting the Amazon.com brand name to be recognized by over one-quarter of Americans. Like most start-ups, Amazon.com needed more seed money. Undeterred by the company's unprofitability, the venture capitalist firm Kleiner Perkins Caufield & Byer put up $10 million for preferred stock, which represented a 15 percent stake in Amazon.com

Following on the heels of its book-selling success, Amazon.com began selling other products over the Internet, including CDs, videos, gifts, greeting cards, and thousands of other items. Amazon.com entered the world of online auctions; linked with other companies selling pet supplies, drugstore goods, and more; and agreed to pay fees of 4 to 8 percent to other Web site owners who linked a purchaser to Amazon.com. Purchasers pay Amazon.com by credit card, submitted over the telephone or the Web, and the transaction is guarded by encryption. Amazon.com offers one-click ordering, which lets buyers store credit cards and addresses after their first purchase.

After several years of operation and quick growth, Amazon.com needed more money to reach its goals. In May 1997, Amazon.com went public, raising over $40 million by selling stock for $18 per share. The price of Amazon.com doubled on the first day of trading and reached $200 per share over the next year before retreating. Bezos became a billionaire before the age of 34. Bezos and his family own about 40 percent of Amazon.com. In the span of less than five years, Bezos had taken his business plan and created the

---

Over 40 **Entrepreneur and the Law** boxes examine the legal implications of entrepreneurial successes and failures.

International Law

Chapter 6, International and Comparative Law, is devoted exclusively to coverage of international laws, courts, the World Trade Organization (WTO), regional economic organizations (EU and NAFTA), and dispute resolution.

CHAPTER

6

International and Comparative Law

International law, or the law that governs between nations, has at times been like the common law within states, a twilight existence during which it is bardly distinguishable from morality or justice, till at length the imprimatur of a court attests its jural quality.
—Justice Cardozo
New Jersey v. Delaware, 291 U.S. 361, 54 S.Ct. 407, 78 L.Ed. 847 (1934)

Chapter Objectives

After studying this chapter, you should be able to:

1. Describe the federal government's power under the Foreign Commerce and Treaty Clauses of the U.S.

But Mexico decided to exploit its unique position and sought an even bigger deal. After much negotiations, in November 1999 Mexico signed an international trade agreement with the 15-member European Union (EU). This

directly export goods more cheaply to the EU. The new trade pact with the EU assures that Mexico, already the world's eighth-largest trading country, will continue the growth in its industrial-export economy.

THE WORLD TRADE ORGANIZATION (WTO)

In 1995, the **World Trade Organization (WTO)** was created as part of the Uruguay Round of trade negotiations on the *General Agreement on Tariffs and Trade (GATT)*. GATT is a multilateral treaty that establishes trade agreements and limits tariffs and trade restrictions among its more than 130 member nations.

The WTO is an international organization located in Geneva, Switzerland. WTO members have entered into many trade agreements among themselves, including international agreements on investments, sale of goods, provision of services, intellectual property, licensing, tariffs, subsidies, and the removal of trade barriers.

World Trade Organization (WTO)
An international organization of more than 130 member nations created to promote and enforce trade agreements among member nations.

International Law

CHINA JOINS THE WORLD TRADE ORGANIZATION (WTO)

For the past 50 years, China and the United States have pursued divergent paths. China became the world's largest Communist country and the United States the leading

democracy. China maintained its agricultural base, while the United States pursued industrialization. China's businesses were state-owned, while those in the United States were

---

More than 40 **International Law** boxes provide students the opportunity to draw comparisons between the American legal system and those of other countries.

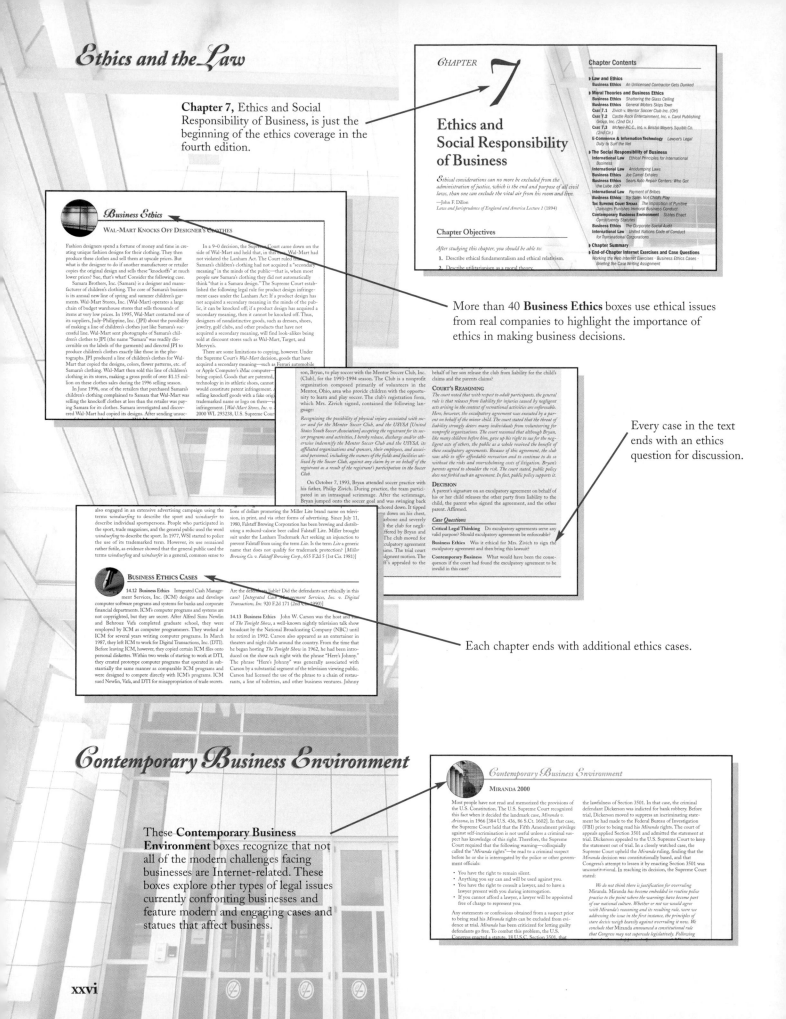

Ethics and the Law

Chapter 7, Ethics and Social Responsibility of Business, is just the beginning of the ethics coverage in the fourth edition.

More than 40 **Business Ethics** boxes use ethical issues from real companies to highlight the importance of ethics in making business decisions.

Every case in the text ends with an ethics question for discussion.

Each chapter ends with additional ethics cases.

Contemporary Business Environment

These **Contemporary Business Environment** boxes recognize that not all of the modern challenges facing businesses are Internet-related. These boxes explore other types of legal issues currently confronting businesses and feature modern and engaging cases and statues that affect business.

Cases

The new edition offers you and your students the perfect balance of case presentation with a mix of recent Supreme Court decisions and traditional cases. Each chapter includes 3 to 5 interesting cases with three follow-up discussion questions at the end of each case to promote active learning.

M.A. Mortenson Company, Inc. v. Timberline Software Corporation
970 P. 2d 803 (1999)
Court of Appeals of Washington

CASE 15.1

BACKGROUND AND FACTS
The Timberline Software Corporation (Timberline) produces software programs that are used by contractors to prepare bids to do work on construction projects. The M.A. Mortenson Company (Mortenson), a contractor, had been using Timberline software for some time without any problem. In 1993, Timberline introduced an advanced version of its bidding software program called *Precision*. Mortenson, as the licensee, entered into a license agreement with Timberline, the licensor, to license the use of the Precision software. Timberline delivered the software to Mortenson and a Timberline representative installed the software on Mortenson's computer. The software license agreement contained the following terms, which were printed on the outside of the envelope in which the software disks were packaged and on the inside cover of the user's manual, and they also appear on the introductory computer screen each time the software program is executed:

Carefully read the following terms and conditions before using the programs. Use of the programs indicates your acknowledgement that you have read this license, understand it, and agree to be bound by its terms and conditions. If you do not agree to these terms and conditions, promptly return the programs and user manuals to the place of purchase and your purchase price will be refunded. You agree that your use of the program acknowledges that you have read this license, understand it, and agree to be bound by its terms and conditions.

Limitation of remedies and liability neither Timberline nor anyone else who has been involved in the creation, production or

tions of remedies clause was unconscionable and therefore unenforceable. The trial court granted summary judgment to Timberline and dismissed the lawsuit. Mortenson appealed.

ISSUE
Was the limitation of remedies clause in the Timberline software license unconscionable?

COURT'S REASONING
The court stated that although Mortenson makes much of the fact that Timberline never mentioned the license agreement or any of its terms during the negotiations, the negotiations between the parties involved only the number of copies and the price. The court held that the terms of the present license agreement are part of the contract as formed between the parties. The court further found that Mortenson's installation and use of the software manifested its assent to the terms of the license and that it was bound by all of the terms of that license that were not found to be illegal or unconscionable.

Whether a limitation on consequential damages is unconscionable is a question of law. Considering all the circumstances surrounding the transaction in this case, the court held that the limitations clause was not unconscionable. The introductory screen warned that use of the program was subject to a license. This warning placed Mortenson on notice that use of the software was governed by a license. Mortenson had reasonable opportunity to learn

---

Lakin v. Senco Products, Inc.
925 P.2d 107 (1996)
Court of Appeals of Oregon

CASE 18.7

BACKGROUND AND FACTS
Senco Products, Inc. (Senco), manufactures and markets a variety of pneumatic nail guns, including the SN325 nail gun, which discharges 3.25 inch nails. The SN325 uses special nails designed and sold by Senco. The SN325 will discharge a nail only if two trigger mechanisms are activated; that is, the user must both squeeze the nail gun's finger trigger and press the nail gun's muzzle against a surface, activating the bottom trigger or safety. The SN325 can fire up to nine nails per second if the trigger is continuously depressed and the gun is bounced along the work surface, constantly reactivating the muzzle safety/trigger.

On December 1, 1990, John Lakin was using a Senco SN325 nail gun to help build a new home. When attempting to nail two-by-fours under the eaves of the garage, Lakin stood on tiptoe and raised a two-by-four over his head. As he held the board in position with his left hand and the nail gun in his right hand, he pressed the nose of the SN325 up against the board, depressed the safety, and pulled the finger trigger to fire the nail into the board. The gun fired the first nail and then, in a phenomenon known as "double firing," immediately discharged an unintended second nail that struck the first nail. The gun recoiled violently backward toward Lakin and, with Lakin's finger still on the trigger, came into contact with his cheek. That contact activated the safety/trigger, causing the nail gun to fire a third nail. This third nail went through Lakin's cheekbone and into his brain.

The nail penetrated the frontal lobe of the right hemisphere of Lakin's brain, blocked a major artery, and caused extensive tissue damage. Lakin was unconscious for several days and ultimately underwent multiple surgeries. He suffers permanent brain damage and is unable to perceive information from the left hemisphere of the brain. He also suffers partial paralysis of the left side of his body. Lakin has undergone a radical personality change and is prone to violent outbursts. He is unable to obtain employment. Lakin's previously warm and loving relationship with his wife and four children has been permanently altered. He can no longer live with his family and instead resides in a supervised group home for brain-injured persons. Lakin and his wife sued Senco for strict liability based

on design defect. The trial court found Senco liable and awarded $3.6 million to Lakin, $457,000 to his wife, and $4 million in punitive damages against Senco. Senco appealed.

ISSUE
Is Senco liable to Lakin for strict liability based on a design defect in the SN325 that allowed it to double fire?

COURT'S REASONING
Evidence showed that the SN325 could double fire within 15 firings. The court found that Senco could have changed production so as to maintain its profitability and simply modified an existing nail gun to shoot longer nails without engaging in additional design work. The longer nails in that model would not double fire, which it did. The court concluded that the SN325 could have been modified with a more sensitive finger trigger that would have made the nail gun less prone to the risk-utility analysis, the court held that the SN325 was defectively designed. The court stated that Senco could not effectively address the SN325's double firing. Senco was conscious and was motivated, at least in part by a profit motive." The court upheld the compensatory and punitive damage award.

DECISION AND REMEDY
The court of appeals applied the risk-utility analysis and held that the SN325 was defectively designed by Senco. It upheld the award of damages to Lakin and his wife.

Case Questions

Critical Legal Thinking Do you think that the nine-nail-per-second SN325 outweighs the risk of injury?

Business Ethics Did Senco act in an ethical manner by selling safety factors when it designed, manufactured, and sold the SN325 nail gun?

Contemporary Business Do you think punitive damages was warranted in this case?

Crashworthiness Doctrine

Often, when an automobile is involved in an accident, the driver

---

The Supreme Court Speaks

PGA Tour Must Allow Disabled Golfer to Use a Golf Cart

PGA Tour, Inc. v. Martin
U.S., 121 S.Ct. 1879 (2001), 2001 U.S. Lexis 415,WL
Supreme Court of the United States

BACKGROUND AND FACTS
The PGA Tour, Inc., is a nonprofit entity that sponsors professional golf tournaments. The PGA has adopted a set of rules that apply to its golf tour. One rule requires golfers to walk the golf course during PGA-sponsored tournaments. Casey Martin is a talented amateur golfer who won many Oregon junior events, and the state championship as a high school senior. He played on the Stanford University golf team and won the 1994 National Collegiate Athletic Association (NCAA) championship.

Martin has been afflicted with Klippel-Trenaunay-Weber Syndrome, a degenerative circulatory disorder that obstructs the flow of blood from his right leg to his heart. The disease is progressive and has atrophied his right leg. Walking causes him pain, fatigue, and anxiety, with significant risk of hemorrhaging. Martin is an individual with a disability as defined by the Americans with Disabilities Act of 1990 (ADA). When Martin turned professional, he qualified for the PGA Tour. He made a request to use a golf cart while playing in PGA tournaments. When the PGA denied his requests, Martin sued the PGA in violation of the ADA for not making reasonable accommodations for his disability. The district court sided with Martin and ordered the PGA to permit Martin to use a golf cart. The court of appeals affirmed. The U.S. Supreme Court agreed to hear the appeal.

SUPREME COURT ISSUE
Does the Americans with Disabilities Act of 1990 require the PGA Tour, Inc. to accommodate Casey Martin, a disabled professional golfer, by permitting him to use a golf cart while playing in PGA sponsored golf tournaments?

IN THE LANGUAGE OF THE U.S. SUPREME COURT
Stevens, Justice In this case, the narrow dispute is whether allowing Martin to use a golf cart, despite the walking requirement that applies to the PGA Tour tournaments, is a modification that would "fundamentally alter the nature" of those events.

As an initial matter, we observe that the use of carts is not itself inconsistent with the fundamental character of the game of golf. From early on, the use of the game has been that woods

started appearing with increasing regularity on American golf courses in the 1950s. Today they are everywhere. And they are encouraged. For one thing, they often speed up play, and for another, they are great revenue producers.

The force of petitioner PGA Tour's argument is, first of all, mitigated by the fact that golf is a game in which it is impossible to guarantee that all competitors will play under exactly the same conditions or that an individual's ability will be the sole determinant of the outcome. For example, changes in the weather may produce harder greens and more head winds for the tournament leader than for his closest pursuers. A lucky bounce may save a shot or two. Whether such happenstance events are more or less probable than the likelihood that a golfer afflicted with Klippel-Trenaunay-Weber Syndrome would one day qualify for the PGA Tour, they at least demonstrate that pure chance may have a greater impact on the outcome of elite golf tournaments than the fatigue resulting from the enforcement of the walking rule. The District Court credited the testimony of a professor in physiology and expert on fatigue, who calculated the calories expended in walking a golf course (about five miles) to be approximately 500 calories—"nutritionally—less than a Big Mac."

DECISION AND REMEDY
The U.S. Supreme Court held that the Americans with Disabilities Act of 1990 requires that the PGA Tour, Inc. accommodate Casey Martin, a disabled professional golfer, by allowing him to use a golf cart while competing in PGA sponsored professional golf tournaments. The judgment of the court of appeals is affirmed.

CASE QUESTIONS

Critical Legal Thinking Do you agree with the U.S. Supreme Court's decision? Will the decision open a "flood-gate" of similar lawsuits?

Business Ethics Was Casey Martin just asking for "fairness," or was he asking for an advantage when competing in professional golf tournaments?

Contemporary Business Is the PGA Tour a lucrative busi-

In the revision, we've introduced a new feature called **The Supreme Court Speaks** boxes that showcase recent Supreme Court cases with legal reasoning, the actual language of the court.

Plus, students will also have the benefit of a variety of traditional cases that are summarized in the author's words.

---

broadly interpreted by the federal courts, particularly the U.S. Supreme Court. States have also enacted antidiscrimination laws.

This chapter discusses federal and state equal opportunity in employment laws.

EQUAL EMPLOYMENT OPPORTUNITY COMMISSION (EEOC)

The **Equal Employment Opportunity Commission (EEOC)** is the federal agency responsible for enforcing most federal antidiscrimination laws. The members of the EEOC are appointed by the President. The EEOC is empowered to conduct investigations, interpret the statutes, encourage conciliation between employees and employers, and bring suit to enforce the law. The EEOC can also seek injunctive relief.

employment
The right of all employees and job applicants (1) to be treated without discrimination and (2) to be able to sue employers if they are discriminated against.

Equal Employment Opportunity Commission (EEOC)
The federal administrative agency responsible for enforcing most federal antidiscrimination laws.

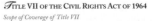

Landmark Law

TITLE VII OF THE CIVIL RIGHTS ACT OF 1964

After substantial debate, Congress enacted the **Civil Rights Act of 1964. Title VII** of the Civil Rights Act of 1964 (entitled the **Fair Employment Practices Act**) was intended to eliminate job discrimination based on the following *protected classes: (1) race, (2) color, (3) religion, (4) sex, or (5) national origin*. As amended by the **Equal Employment Opportunity Act of 1972**, Section 703(a)(2) of the Title VII provides in pertinent part that

It shall be an unlawful employment practice for an employer
(1) to fail or refuse to hire or to discharge any individ-

ual, or otherwise to discriminate against any individual with respect to his compensation, terms, conditions, or privileges of employment, because of such individual's race, color, religion, sex, or national origin; or
(2) to limit, segregate, or classify his employees or applicants for employment in any way which would deprive or tend to deprive any individual of employment opportunities or otherwise adversely affect his status as an employee, because of such individual's race, color, religion, sex, or national origin.

TITLE VII OF THE CIVIL RIGHTS ACT OF 1964

Scope of Coverage of Title VII

Title VII applies to (1) employers with 15 or more employees, (2) all employment agencies, (3) labor unions with 15 or more members, (4) state and local governments and their agencies, and (5) most federal government employment. Indian tribes and tax-exempt private clubs are expressly excluded from coverage.[1]

Title VII prohibits discrimination in hiring, decisions regarding promotion or demotion, payment of compensation and fringe benefits, availability of job training and appren-

Title VII of the Civil Rights Act of 1964 (Fair Employment Practices Act)
Intended to eliminate job discrimination based on five protected classes: race, color, religion, sex, or national origin.

Landmark Law

There are over **30 new Landmark Law** boxes that describe major federal and state statutes that have been enacted that have significant impact on business. Examples include: "Title VII of the Civil Rights Act of 1964," "Racketeer Influenced and Corrupt Organizations Act (RICO)," "The Securities Exchange Act of 1934," "Americans with Disabilities Act of 1990," etc…

Additional Support for Student Success

Exhibits help clarify legal formats and documents that may be foreign to students.

Margin notes include a running glossary of terms, business briefs, and relevant historical quotes.

Concept Summaries appear periodically within each chapter to give students a chance to pause and be sure they have mastered the preceding material.

At the end of each chapter, **Working the Web** exercises require students to work through interactive web-based activities. **Critical Legal Thinking Cases** at the end of each chapter encourage the application of students' analytical skills, and **Briefing the Case Writing Assignments** give students experience in briefing cases.

Promissory Notes

promissory note
A two-party negotiable instrument that is an unconditional written promise by one party to pay money to another party.

A **promissory note** (or **note**) is an unconditional written promise by one party to pay money to another party [UCC 3-104(e)]. It is a two-party instrument (see Exhibit 19.3), not an order to pay. Promissory notes usually arise when one party borrows money from another. The note is evidence of (1) the extension of credit and (2) the borrower's promise to repay the debt.

Exhibit 19.3 *A Promissory Note*

PROMISSORY NOTE

maker of a note
The party who makes the promise to pay (borrower).

payee of a note
The party to whom the promise to pay is made (lender).

time note

The party who makes the promise to pay is the **maker** of the note (i.e., the borrower). The party to whom the promise to pay is made is the **payee** (i.e., the lender). A promissory note is a negotiable instrument that the payee can freely transfer to other parties.

The parties are free to design the terms of the note to fit their needs. For example, notes can be payable at a specific time (**time note**) or on demand (**demand note**). Notes can be...

CONCEPT SUMMARY TYPES OF INTELLECTUAL PROPERTY PROTECTED BY FEDERAL LAW

Type	Subject Matter	Term
Patent	Inventions (e.g., machines; processes; compositions of matter; designs for articles of manufacture; and improvements to existing machines, processes). Invention must be 1. Novel 2. Useful 3. Nonobvious Public use doctrine: Patent will not be granted if the invention was used in public for more than one year prior to the filing of the patent application.	Patents on articles of manufacture and processes: 20 years; design patents: 14 years.
Copyright	Tangible writing (e.g., books, magazines, newspapers, lectures, operas, plays, screenplays, musical compositions, maps, works of art, lithographs, photographs, postcards, greeting cards, motion pictures, newsreels, sound recordings, computer programs, and mask works fixed to semiconductor chips). Writing must be the original work of the author. Fair use doctrine: It permits use of copyrighted material without consent for limited uses (e.g., scholarly work, parody or satire, and brief quotation in news reports).	Individual registrant: life of author plus 70 years. Business registrant: for the shorter of either (1) 120 years from the date of creation or (2) 95 years from the date of first publication.
Trademark	Marks (e.g., name, symbol, word, logo, or device).	Original registration: 10 years.

End-of-Chapter Internet Exercises and Case Questions

www *Working the Web Internet Exercises*

ACTIVITIES

1. Trade Secrets: Research the web to determine if your state has adopted the Uniform Trade Secrets Act. Visit the Trade Secrets Home Page at **www.execpc.com/~mhallign**.

2. Trademarks: **www.uspto.gov** contains information about the federal trademark registration system. Find your analogous state trademark site. See also Marksonline—free trademark search and domain name search—**www.marksonline.com**.

3. Copyrights: **www.uspto.gov** contains information about the federal copyright registration system. Does the most recent copyright law require authors to use the copyright notice on printed material in order to protect it from infringement?

4. What is the current duration of a U.S. Patent? What was the duration of a U.S. Patent under previous law and why was it changed? See Patents: **www.uspto.gov**

5. International protection of intellectual property: Visit **www.wipo.int** and outline the process for international registration of a patent.

---

1. Trade Secrets: Research the web to determine if your state has adopted the Uniform Trade Secrets Act. Visit the Trade Secrets Home Page at **www.execpc.com/~mhallign**.

2. Trademarks: **www.uspto.gov** contains information about the federal trademark registration system. Find your analogous state trademark site. See also Marksonline—free trademark search and domain name search—**www.marksonline.com**.

about the federal copyright registration system. Does the most recent copyright law require authors to use the copyright notice on printed material in order to protect it from infringement?

4. What is the current duration of a U.S. Patent? What was the duration of a U.S. Patent under previous law and why was it changed? See Patents: **www.uspto.gov**

5. International protection of intellectual property: Visit **www.wipo.int** and outline the process for international registration of a patent.

CRITICAL LEGAL THINKING CASES

14.1 Trade Secret CRA-MAR Video Center, Inc., sells electronic equipment and videocassettes, as does its competitor, Koach's Sales Corporation. Both CRA-MAR and Koach's purchased computers from Radio Shack. CRA-MAR used the computer to store customer lists, movie lists, personnel files, and financial records. Because the computer was new to CRA-MAR, Randall Youts, Radio Shack's salesman and programmer, agreed to modify CRA-MAR's programs when needed, including the customer list program. At one point, CRA-MAR decided to send a mailing to everyone on its customer list. The computer was unable to perform the function, so Youts took the disks containing the customer lists to the Radio Shack store to work on the program. Somehow Koach's came into possession of CRA-MAR's customer lists and did advertising mailings to the parties on the lists. When CRA-MAR discovered this fact, it sued Koach's, seeking an injunction against any further use of its customer lists. Is a customer list a trade secret that can be protected from misappropriation? [*Koach's Sales Corp. v. CRA-MAR Video Center, Inc.*, 478 N.E.2d 110 (Ind. App. 1985)]

14.2 Trade Secret Acuson Corporation, a Delaware corporation, and Aloka Co., Ltd., a Japanese company, are competitors who both manufacture ultrasonic imaging equipment, a widely used medical diagnostic tool. The device uses sound waves to produce moving images of the inside of a patient's body, which a computer processes into an image that is displayed on a video monitor. Acuson's unit provides finer resolution than Aloka's unit. Both companies have sold many units to hospitals and medical centers. In November 1985, Aloka decided to purchase an Acuson unit. Aloka had another company make the actual purchase because it was concerned that Acuson would not sell

---

BRIEFING THE CASE WRITING ASSIGNMENT

Read the following case, which has been excerpted from the court's opinion, and brief the case.

Feist Publications, Inc. v. Rural Telephone Service Co., Inc.,
499 U.S. 340, 111 S.Ct. 1282, 113 L.ED.2D 358 (1991)
U.S. Supreme Court

O'Conner, Justice

Rural Telephone Service Company is a certified public utility that provides telephone service to several communities in northwest Kansas. It is subject to a state regulation that requires all telephone companies operating in Kansas to issue annually an updated telephone directory. Accordingly, as a condition of its monopoly franchise, Rural publishes a typical telephone directory, consisting of white pages and yellow pages. The white pages list in alphabetical order the names of Rural's subscribers, together with their towns and telephone numbers. The yellow pages list Rural's business subscribers alphabetically by category and feature classified advertisements of various sizes. Rural distributes its directory free of charge to its subscribers, but earns revenue by selling yellow pages advertisements.

Feist Publications, Inc., is a publishing company that specializes in area-wide telephone directories. Unlike a typical directory, which covers only a particular calling area, Feist's area-wide directories cover a much

Rural sued for copyright infringement in the District Court for the District of Kansas taking the position that Feist, in compiling its own directory, could not use the information contained in Rural's white pages. The District Court granted summary judgment to Rural, explaining that "courts have consistently held that telephone directories are copyrightable" and citing a string of lower court decisions. In an unpublished opinion, the Court of Appeals for the Tenth Circuit affirmed "for substantially the reasons given by the district court."

This case concerns the interaction of two well-established propositions. The first is that facts are not copyrightable; the other, that compilations of facts generally are. The key to resolving the tension lies in understanding why facts are not copyrightable. To qualify for copyright protection, a work must be original to the author. Original, as the term is used in copyright, means only that the work was independently created by the author (as opposed to copied from other works), and that it possesses at least some minimal degree of creativity.

Originality is a constitutional requirement. The source of Congress' power to enact copyright laws is Article I, §8, Cl. 8, of the Constitution, which authorizes Congress to "secure for limited Timers to Authors . . . the exclusive Right to their respective Writings." It is this bedrock principle of copyright that mandates the law's seemingly disparate treatment of facts and factual compilations. No one may claim originality as to facts. This is because facts do not owe their origin to

An Integrated Supplements Package

*T*o ensure consistency of style, approach, and coverage among the key print supplements, these critical pieces were created by a single author team working in conjunction with Henry Cheeseman.

The ***Instructor's Manual*** provides bulleted chapter outlines and reviews, answers to text questions and cases, and video discussion as well as lecture suggestions linked directly to PowerPoint slides.

PowerPoint slides provide complete lecture support.

The ***Study Guide*** includes the same bulleted outline found in the ***Instructor's Manual*** along with a variety of objective questions and critical thinking legal essays to effectively reinforce the concepts introduced in the corresponding text chapter.

The ***Test Item File*** contains over 30 percent new questions to this edition and closely mirrors the content stressed in the ***Instructor's Manual*** and ***Study Guide.***

Prentice Hall's New Companion Web Site

The **Surfing for Success** in Legal Studies Internet guide covers frequently asked questions and offers concrete discipline-specific advice on navigating the Internet. It is available free to your students and is updated annually.

The Business Law Custom Video Series provides ten 5-10 minute segments designed to foster discussion on key business law topics. Each segment revolves around the activities of a single company and its employees, suppliers, customers, and other associates.

Prentice Hall's Companion Web Site (www.prenhall.com/cheeseman) lets students log on to have a dialogue with their peers, talk to a tutor, take a quiz with immediate feedback, and review real and hypothetical cases designed to illustrate major topics from each chapter—all with the click of a mouse.

www.prenhall.com/cheeseman

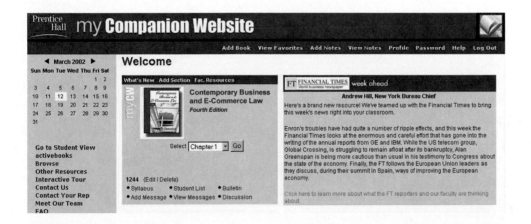

Acknowledgments

$\mathcal{W}$hen I first began writing this book, I was a solitary figure researching cases in the law library and writing text at my desk. As time passed, others entered upon the scene—editors, research assistants, reviewers, production personnel—and touched the project and made it better. Although my name appears on the cover of this book, it is no longer mine alone. I humbly thank the following persons for their contributions to this project.

The Professionals at Prentice Hall

For this fourth edition of *Contemporary Business and E-Commerce Law*, a special group of people from Prentice Hall have come together: Cindy Spreder, production editor who was a joy to work with through the patient task of shepherding the manuscript from first manuscript pages to the final bound book; Debbie Clare, executive marketing manager, who is the most creative marketing person in the industry and who has more energy than anyone I know; Janet Slowik, art director, whose design suggestions I accepted wholeheartedly; David Parker, acquisitions editor, who brought new insight and wonderful suggestions for new features for this edition; and Jerome Grant, president of Prentice Hall Business Publishing, whose influence is a very important part of this revision.

The Supplements Team

Ashley Keim, assistant editor, is in charge of producing the extensive supplements that support this fourth edition of *Contemporary Business and E-Commerce Law*. The supplements themselves have been produced by a remarkable team of authors: John T. Ballantine Jr., professor of business law, School of Business, University of Colorado; Rhonda Carlson, lecturer, University of Denver School of Law; Ed Gac, professor of business law, School of Business, University of Colorado; and Dawn Swink, College of Business, Minnesota State University. I have worked closely with this team in producing the Instructor's Manual, Study Guide, Test Item File, and PowerPoint slides to support this edition. Anthony Palmiotto, media project manager, has been in charge of putting together the Prentice Hall Web site to support this edition.

The Prentice Hall "family" has come together and produced a book and supplements package that I believe is the best available. My success is theirs, and theirs mine. They are my friends.

The Reviewers

I would like to particularly thank the following reviewers, who have spent considerable time and effort reviewing the manuscript, and whose comments, suggestions, and criticisms are seen in the final project.

A. David Austill	Union University
John J. Balek	Morton College
Laura Barelman	Wayne State College
Denise Bartles	Missouri Western State College
Weldon Blake	Bethune Cookman College
Patricia Defrain	Glendale College

Margaret Dillard	Ivy State College and Mary Baldwin College
Joe D. Dillsaver	Northeastern State University
Michael Engber	Truman State University
C. Kerry Fields	University of Southern California
Edward J. Gac	University of Colorado at Boulder
Nancy Gallo	Sussex County Community College
Jeane Gohl-Noice	Parkland College
Janine S. Hiller	Virginia Polytech Institute
William C. Marrs	Morton College
Greg McCann	Stetson University
Ann McClure	Fort Hayes State University
Margaret Zonia Morrison	Webster University
James Muck	Milwaukee Area Technical College
Sheldon Pollack	University of Delware
Louise Regelein	Washington State University
William Rutledge	Macomb Community College
Scott Sandstrom	College of the Holy Cross
Allen J. Simonson	Montclair State University
Lou Ann Simpson	Drake University
Denise Smith	Missouri Western State College
Maurice Tonissi	Quinsigamond Community College
James E. Walsh	Tidewater Community College
Clark Wheeler	Santa Fe Community College
John Wrieden	Florida International University

My family: My parents—Henry B. and Florence, deceased; my twin brother Gregory; my sister Marcia. In memory of Mike Martin, Ketchum, Idaho.

The students at the Marshall School of Business at the University of Southern California. Their spirit, energy, and joy is contagious, and I love teaching them (and as important, they teaching me).

While writing the Preface, I have thought about the thousands of hours I have spent researching, writing, and preparing this manuscript. I loved every minute, and the knowledge gained has been sufficient reward for the endeavor.

I hope this book and its supplementary materials will serve you as well as they have served me.

Henry R. Cheeseman

With joy and sadness,
emptiness and fullness,
honor and humility,
I surrender the fruits of this labor

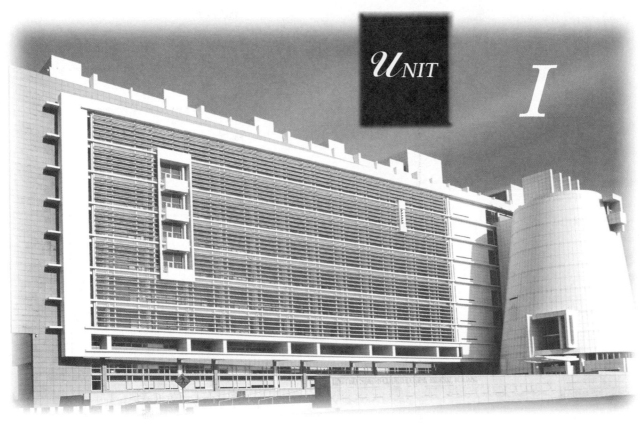

Central Islip Courthouse, Central Islip, N.Y.

The Legal, E-Commerce, and Global Environment

CHAPTER

1

Legal, Business, and E-Commerce Environment

Where there is no law, there is no freedom.

—John Locke
Second Treatise of Government, Sec. 57

Chapter Objectives

After studying this chapter, you should be able to:

1. Define *law* and describe the functions of law.

2. Describe the flexibility of the law and its applications to modern e-commerce.

3. List and describe the schools of jurisprudential thought.

4. Explain the development of the U.S. legal system.

5. Explain how English common law was adopted in the United States.

6. List and describe the sources of law in the United States.

7. Define the doctrine of *stare decisis*.

8. Describe the international civil law legal system used in some other countries.

9. Describe the development of e-commerce and Internet law.

10. Apply critical legal thinking in analyzing judicial decisions.

Chapter Contents

Every society makes and enforces laws that govern the conduct of the individuals, businesses, and other organizations that function within it. In the words of Judge Learned Hand, "Without law we cannot live; only with it can we insure the future which by right is ours. The best of men's hopes are enmeshed in its success."[1]

Although the law of this country is primarily based on English common law, other legal systems, such as Spanish and French civil law, also influenced it. The sources of law in this country are the U.S. Constitution, state constitutions, federal and state statutes, ordinances, administrative agency rules and regulations, executive orders, and judicial decisions by federal and state courts.

Businesses that are organized in the United States are subject to its laws. They are also subject to the laws of other countries in which they operate. Businesses organized in other countries must obey the laws of the United States when doing business here. In addition, businesspeople owe a duty to act ethically in the conduct of their affairs, and businesses owe a responsibility not to harm society.

This chapter discusses the nature and definition of law, the history and sources of law, and "critical legal thinking" as applied by the U.S. Supreme Court in deciding an actual case.

Let every American, every lover of liberty, every well-wisher to his posterity, swear by the blood of the Revolution never to violate in the least particular the laws of the country, and never to tolerate their violation by others.

Abraham Lincoln
Speech January 27, 1837

$\mathcal{W}$HAT IS LAW?

The law consists of rules that regulate the conduct of individuals, businesses, and other organizations within society. It is intended to protect persons and their property from unwanted interference from others. In other words, the law forbids persons from engaging in certain undesirable activities.

Consider the following passage:

A lawyer without history or literature is a mechanic, a mere working mason: if he possesses some knowledge of these, he may venture to call himself an architect.

Sir Walter Scott
Guy Mannering, Ch. 37 (1815)

> *Hardly anyone living in a civilized society has not at some time been told to do something or to refrain from doing something, because there is a law requiring it, or because it is against the law. What do we mean when we say such things? Most generally, how are we to understand statements of the form "x is law"? This is an ancient question. In his Memorabilia (I, ii), Xenophon reports a statement of the young Alcibiades, companion of Socrates, who in conversation with the great Pericles remarked that "no one can really deserve praise unless he knows what a law is."*

> *At the end of the 18th century, Immanuel Kant wrote of the question "What is law?" that it "may be said to be about as embarrassing to the jurist as the well-known question 'What is truth?' is to the logician."[2]*

$\mathcal{E}$-$\mathcal{C}$ommerce & $\mathcal{I}$nformation $\mathcal{T}$echnology

STUDENTS PLUG INTO THE INTERNET AND THE LAW

Every year millions of students arrive on college campuses and unpack an array of items—clothes, books, furniture, decorations, and their computers. College students used to be judged by the size of their stereo speakers; today it is their computer and their Internet savvy. Ninety percent of college students now own personal computers.

The Internet has revolutionized campus life. Computer kiosks abound around college campuses, occupying more space in libraries, dorm rooms, and hallways of athletic departments. Traditional libraries have become obsolete for many students as they conduct almost all of their research online. More than 70 percent of college students check out the Web daily, while others communicate through e-mail, pick up course assignments, download course notes, and socialize online. Current university and college students are wired to modern technology and will lead their parents,

employers, and sometimes even their professors into the new world of high technology. Today's college students are the leaders of the e-generation.

Universities and colleges are now rated on not only how well they are connected with alumni, but also on how well they are connected to computer technology. Some universities have installed software that allows their students to sit anywhere on campus with their laptops and "plug" into the school's computers. The computer is no longer just a study tool; it has become totally integrated into the lives of college students. The new generation of students study online, shop online, and even date online.

With this new technology comes one other thing that a student should know about: e-commerce and Internet law. The use of new computer technology has developed rapidly. For example, purchase of goods and items over the Internet is exploding. How is the contract formed? What about signatures? Is a purchaser's credit card information protected? What laws protect privacy over the Internet? can an Internet user crack a wrapper and use certain software? What criminal laws apply to fraud over the Internet? The number of legal questions pertaining to this new technology is endless.

To help the student understand his or her legal rights and duties, this business law book fully integrates e-commerce and Internet law. Through this total integration of e-commerce and Internet law, a student will not only learn traditional business law topics, but will also be well versed in his or her legal rights while using the Internet.

Definition of Law

law

That which must be obeyed and followed by citizens subject to sanctions or legal consequences; a body of rules of action or conduct prescribed by controlling authority, and having binding legal force.

The concept of **law** is very broad. Although it is difficult to state a precise definition, *Black's Law Dictionary* gives one that is sufficient for this text:

> Law, in its generic sense, is a body of rules of action or conduct prescribed by controlling authority, and having binding legal force. That which must be obeyed and followed by citizens subject to sanctions or legal consequences is a law.[3]

Functions of the Law

Commercial law lies within a narrow compass, and is far purer and freer from defects than any other part of the system.

Henry Peter Brougham
House of Commons,
February 7, 1828

The law, in its majestic equality, forbids the rich as well as the poor to sleep under bridges.

Anatole France

The law is often described by the function it serves within a society. The primary *functions* served by the law in this country are:

1. Keeping the peace, which includes making certain activities crimes.
2. Shaping moral standards (e.g., enacting laws that discourage drug and alcohol abuse).
3. Promoting social justice (e.g., enacting statutes that prohibit discrimination in employment).
4. Maintaining the status quo (e.g., passing laws preventing the forceful overthrow of the government).
5. Facilitating orderly change (e.g., passing statutes only after considerable study, debate, and public input).
6. Facilitating planning (e.g., well-designed commercial laws allow businesses to plan their activities, allocate their productive resources, and assess the risks they take).
7. Providing a basis for compromise (approximately 90 percent of all lawsuits are settled prior to trial).
8. Maximizing individual freedom (e.g., the rights of freedom of speech, religion, and association granted by the First Amendment to the U.S. Constitution).

Business Ethics

FAIRNESS OF THE LAW

On the whole, the American legal system is one of the most comprehensive, fair, and democratic systems of law ever developed and enforced. Nevertheless, some misuses and oversights of our legal system—including abuses of discretion and mistakes by judges and juries, unequal applications of the law, and procedural mishaps—allow some guilty parties to go unpunished.

In *Standefer v. United States*[4] the Supreme Court *affirmed* (let stand) the criminal conviction of a Gulf Oil Corporation executive for aiding and abetting the bribery of an Internal

Revenue Service agent. The agent had been acquitted in a separate trial. In writing the opinion of the Court, Chief Justice Burger stated, "This case does no more than manifest the simple, if discomforting, reality that different juries may reach different results under any criminal statute. That is one of the consequences we accept under our jury system."

1. Do you think the law is fair? Or as fair as it can be?
2. Can you site an instance where you believe the law was not applied fairly?

Business Brief

Laws cannot be written in advance to anticipate every dispute that could arise in the future. Therefore, general principles are developed to be applied by courts and juries to individual disputes. This flexibility in the law leads to some uncertainty in predicting results of lawsuits.

Flexibility of the Law

U.S. law evolves and changes along with the norms of society, technology, and the growth and expansion of commerce in the United States and the world. The following quote by Judge Jerome Frank discusses the value of the adaptability of law.

> The law always has been, is now, and will ever continue to be, largely vague and variable. And how could this be otherwise? The law deals with human relations in their most complicated aspects. The whole confused, shifting helter-skelter of life parades before it—more confused than ever, in our kaleidoscopic age.

Men have never been able to construct a comprehensive, eternalized set of rules anticipating all possible legal disputes and formulating in advance the rules which would apply to them. Situations are bound to occur which were never contemplated when the original rules were made. How much less is such a frozen legal system possible in modern times?

The constant development of unprecedented problems requires a legal system capable of fluidity and pliancy. Our society would be straightjacketed were not the courts, with the able assistance of the lawyers, constantly overhauling the law and adapting it to the realities of ever-changing social, industrial, and political conditions; although changes cannot be made lightly, yet rules of law must be more or less impermanent, experimental and therefore not nicely calculable.

Much of the uncertainty of law is not an unfortunate accident; it is of immense social value.[5]

> *Two things most people should never see made: sausages and laws.*
>
> *An old saying*

Landmark Law

BROWN V. BOARD OF EDUCATION

One of the main attributes of American law is its *flexibility*. It is generally responsive to cultural, technological, economic, and social changes. For example, laws that are no longer viable—such as those that restricted the property rights of women—are often repealed.

Sometimes it takes years before the law reflects the norms of society. Other times, society is led by the law. The Supreme Court's landmark decision in *Brown v. Board of Education* [347 U.S. 483, 74 S.Ct. 686, 98 L.Ed 873 (1954)] is an example of the law leading the people. The Court's decision overturned the old "separate but equal" doctrine that condoned separate schools for black children and white children.

Contemporary Business Environment

FEMINIST LEGAL THEORY

In the past, the law treated men and women unequally. For example, women were denied the right to vote, could not own property if they were married, were unable to have legal abortions, and could not hold the same jobs as men. The enactment of statutes and the interpretation of constitutional provisions by the courts have changed all of these things. The Nineteenth Amendment gave women the right to vote. States have repealed constraints on the ability of women to own property. The famous U.S. Supreme Court decision in *Roe v. Wade*, 410 U.S. 959 (1973), gave women the constitutional right to an abortion.

Title VII of the Civil Rights Act of 1964 prohibits employment discrimination based on sex. In addition, the equal protection clause of the U.S. and state constitutions provides that women cannot be treated differently from men (and vice versa) by the government unless some imperative reason warrants different treatment.

But is it enough for women to be treated like men? Should the female perspective be taken into account when legislators and judges develop, interpret, and apply the law? A growing body of scholarship known as **feminist legal theory** or **feminist jurisprudence**, is being created around just such a theory.

The so-called "battered woman's syndrome" illustrates how this type of theory works. It has been introduced into evidence to prove self-defense in homicide cases where a woman is accused of killing her husband or another male. This defense asserts that sustained domestic violence against a woman may justify such a murder. Although this defense has been rejected by many courts, some courts have recognized battered woman's syndrome as a justifiable defense.

Some other areas of the law where a woman's perspective might differ from a man's include male-only combat rules in the military, rights to privacy, family law, child custody, surrogate motherhood, job security for pregnant women, rape, sexual assault, abortion, and sexual harassment. Even the traditional "reasonable man standard," so prevalent in American law, is being attacked as being gender-biased.

SCHOOLS OF JURISPRUDENTIAL THOUGHT

The philosophy or science of the law is referred to a **jurisprudence**. There are several different philosophies about how the law developed. They range form the classical natural theory to modern theories of law and economics and critical legal studies. Legal

jurisprudence
The philosophy or science of law.

philosophers can generally be grouped into the major categories discussed in the paragraphs that follow.

The Natural Law School

The **Natual Law School** of jurisprudence postulates that the law is based on what is "correct." Natural law philosophers emphasize a **moral theory of law**—that is, law should be based on morality and ethics. Natural law is "discovered" by man through the use of reason and choosing between good and evil. Documents such as the U.S. Constitution, the Magna Carta, and the United Nations Charter reflect this theory.

The Historical School

The **Historical School** of jurisprudence believes that the law is an aggregate of social traditions of customs that have developed over the centuries. It believes that changes in the norms of society will gradually be reflected in the law. To these legal philosophers, the law is an evolutionary process. Thus, historical legal scholars look to past legal decisions (precedent) to solve contemporary problems.

The Analytical School

The **Analytical School** of jurisprudence maintains that the law is shaped by logic. Analytical philosophers believe results are reached by applying principles of logic to the specific facts of the case. The emphasis is on the logic of the result rather than on how the result is reached.

The Sociological School

The **Sociological School** of jurisprudence asserts that the law is a means of achieving and advancing certain sociological goals. The followers of this philosophy, who are known as *realists*, believe that the purpose of law is to shape social behavior. Sociological philosophers are unlikely to adhere to past law as precedent.

The Command School

The philosophers of the **Command School** of jurisprudence believe that the law is a set of rules developed, communicated, and enforced by the ruling party rather than a reflection of the society's morality, history, logic, or sociology. This school maintains that the law changes when the ruling class changes.

The Critical Legal Studies School

The **Critical Legal Studies School** proposes that legal rules are unnecessary and are used as an obstacle by the powerful to maintain the status quo. Critical legal theorists (the "*Crits*") argue that legal disputes should be solved by applying arbitrary rules that are based on broad notions of what is "fair" in each circumstance. Under this theory, subjective decision making by judges would be permitted.

Human beings do not ever make laws; it is the accidents and catastrophes of all kinds happening in every conceivable way that make law for us.

Plato
Laws IV.709

Law must be stable and yet it cannot stand still

Roscoe Pound
Interpretations of Legal History
(1923)

The law is not a series of calculating machines where definitions and answers come tumbling out when the right levers are pushed.

William O. Douglas
The Dissent, A Safeguard of
Democracy (1948)

 *Contemporary Business Environment*

THE LAW AND ECONOMICS SCHOOL OF JURISPRUDENTIAL THOUGHT

Should free market principles, like the supply-and-demand and cost-benefit theories, determine the outcome of lawsuits and legislation? U.S. Court of Appeals Judge Richard Posner thinks so, and so do a growing number of other judges and legal theorists. These people are members of the **Law and Economics School** (or the "Chicago School") of jurisprudence, which had its roots at the University of Chicago.

According to the Law and Economics School, which is unofficially headed by Judge Posner, promoting market efficiency should be the central goal of legal decision making. In the area of antitrust law, for example, law and economics theorists would not find corporate mergers and takeovers to be illegal simply because they resulted in market domination. Instead, they would find this practice to be illegal only if it rendered the overall market less efficient.

Focusing on cold economic categories like market efficiency may seem appropriate when making decisions in cases that involve businesses. However, proponents of law and economics theory use this type of analysis in cases involving everything from freedom of religion to civil rights. For example, in a 1983 dissenting opinion, Judge Posner suggested that the practice of appointing counsel, free of charge, to prisoners who bring civil rights cases should be abolished. If a prisoner cannot find a lawyer who will take the case on a contingency fee basis, it probably means that the case is not worth bringing. Naysayers warn that the morality of certain rights and liberties must be safeguarded even if it is unpopular or costly from an economic point of view.

CONCEPT SUMMARY   SCHOOLS OF JURISPRUDENTIAL THOUGHT

School	Philosophy
Natural Law	Postulates that law is based on what is "correct." It emphasizes a moral theory of law—that is, law should be based on morality and ethics.
Historical	Believes that law is an aggregate of social traditions and customs.
Analytical	Maintains that law is shaped by logic.
Sociological	Asserts that the law is a means of achieving and advancing certain sociological goals.
Command	Believes that the law is a set of rules developed, communicated, and enforced by the ruling party.
Critical Legal Studies	Maintains that legal rules are unnecessary and that legal disputes should be solved by applying arbitrary rules based on fairness.
Law of Economics	Believes that promoting market efficiency should be the central concern of legal decision making.

HISTORY OF AMERICAN LAW

When the American colonies were first settled, the English system of law was generally adopted as the system of jurisprudence. This was the foundation from which American judges developed a common law in America.

English Common Law

English **common law** was law developed by judges who issued their opinions when deciding a case. The principles announced in these cases became *precedent* for later judges deciding similar cases. The English common law can be divided into cases decided by the law courts, equity courts, and merchant courts.

common law

Developed by judges who issued their opinions when deciding a case. The principles announced in these cases became precedent for later judges deciding similar cases.

Law Courts   Prior to the Norman Conquest of England in 1066, each locality in England was subject to local laws as established by the lord or chieftain in control of the local area. There was no countrywide system of law. After 1066, William the Conqueror and his successors to the throne of England began to replace the various local laws with one uniform system of law. To accomplish this, the king or queen appointed loyal followers as judges in all local areas. These judges were charged with administering the law in a uniform manner in courts that were called **law courts**. Law at this time tended to emphasize form (legal procedure) over the substance (merit) of the case. The only relief available at law courts was a monetary award for damages.

law court

A court that developed and administered a uniform set of laws decreed by the kings and queens after William the Conqueror; legal procedure was emphasized over merits at this time.

Chancery (Equity) Courts   Because of the unfair results and the limited remedy available in the law courts, a second set of courts—the **Court of Chancery** (or **equity court**)—was established. These courts were under the authority of the Lord Chancellor. Persons who believed that the decision of the law court was unfair or that the law court could not grant an appropriate remedy could seek relief in the Court of Chancery. The Chancery Court inquired into the merits of the case, rather than emphasizing legal procedure. The Chancellor's remedies were called *equitable remedies* because they were shaped to fit each situation. Equitable order and remedies of the Court of Chancery took precedence over the legal decisions and remedies of the law courts.

Court of Chancery

Court that granted relief based on fairness. Also called equity court.

Merchant Court

The separate set of courts established to administer the "law of merchants."

Merchant Courts As trade developed in the Middle Ages, the merchants who traveled about England and Europe developed certain rules to solve their commercial disputes. These rules, known as the "law of merchants" or the **Law Merchant,** were based upon common trade practices and usage. Eventually, a separate set of courts was established to administer these rules. This court was called the **Merchant Court.** In the early 1900s, the Merchant Court was absorbed into the regular law court system of England.

International Law

ADOPTION OF ENGLISH COMMON LAW IN AMERICA

All the states except Louisiana base their legal systems primarily on the English *common law.* Because of its French heritage, Louisiana bases its law on the *civil law* (see discussion of international legal systems later in this chapter). Elements of California and Texas law, as well as other southwestern states, are rooted in civil law.

In the United States, the law, equity, and merchant courts have been merged. Thus, most U.S. courts permit the aggrieved party to seek both law and equitable orders and remedies.

The importance of common law to the American legal system is described in the following excerpt from Justice Douglas's opinion in the 1841 case of *Penny v. Little* [4 Ill. 301 (IL 1841)]:

The common law is a beautiful system, containing the wisdom and experiences of ages. Like the people it ruled and protected, it was simple and crude in its infancy and became enlarged, improved, and polished as the nation advanced in civilization, virtue, and intelligence. Adapting itself to the conditions and circumstances of the people and relying upon them for its administration, it necessarily improved as the condition of the people was elevated. The inhabitants of this country always claimed the common law as their birthright, and at an early period established it as the basis of their jurisprudence.

Red bus, London *The legal system of most states in the United States is primarily based on the English common law. Some state legal systems, because of their French and Spanish heritage, reflect the European civil law as well.*

International Law

THE CIVIL LAW SYSTEM

One of the major legal systems that has developed in the world in addition to the Anglo-American common law system is the **Romano-Germanic civil law system.** This legal system, which is commonly called the **civil law,** dates to 450 B.C., when Rome adopted the Twelve Tables, a code of laws applicable to the Romans. A compilation of Roman law, called the

Corpus Juris Civilis (the Body of Civil Law), was completed in A.D. 534. Later, two national codes—the French Civil Code of 1804 (the Napoleonic Code) and the German Civil Code of 1896—became models for countries that adopted civil codes.

In contrast to the Anglo-American common law, where laws are created by the judicial system as well as by congressional legislation, the Civil Code and parliamentary statutes that expand and interpret it are the sole sources of the law in most civil law countries. Thus, the adjudication of a case is simply the application of the code or the statutes to a particular set of facts. In some civil law countries, court decisions do not have the force of law.

Today, Austria, Belgium, Greece, Indochina, Indonesia, Japan, Latin America, the Netherlands, Poland, Portugal, South Korea, Spain, Sub-Saharan Africa, Switzerland, and Turkey follow the civil law.

SOURCES OF LAW IN THE UNITED STATES

In more than 200 years since the founding of this country and the adoption of the English common law, the lawmakers of this country have developed a substantial body of law. The *sources of modern law* in the United States are discussed in the paragraphs that follow.

Constitutions

The **Constitution of the United States of America** is the *supreme law of the land.* This means that any law—whether federal, state, or local—that conflicts with the U.S. Constitution is unconstitutional and, therefore, unenforceable.

The principles enumerated in the Constitution are extremely broad since the founding fathers intended them to be applied to evolving social, technological, and economic conditions. The U.S. Constitution is often referred to as a "living document" because it is so adaptable.

The U.S. Constitution established the structure of the federal government. It created the following three branches of government and gave them the following powers:

- **Legislative (Congress)**   Power to make (enact) the law.
- **Executive (President)**   Power to enforce the law.
- **Judicial (Courts)**   Power to interpret and determine the validity of the law.

Powers not given to the federal government by the Constitution are reserved for the states. States also have their own constitutions. These are often patterned after the U.S. Constitution, although many are more detailed. State constitutions establish the legislative, executive, and judicial branches of state government and establish the powers of each branch. Provisions of state constitutions are valid unless they conflict with the U.S. Constitution or any valid federal law.

Constitution of the United States of America
The supreme law of the United States.

The Constitution of the United States is not a mere lawyers' document: it is a vehicle of life, and its spirit is always the spirit of the age.

Woodrow Wilson
Constitutional Government in
the United States *69 (1927)*

The Constitution of the United States of America establishes the structure of the federal government, delegates powers to the federal government, and guarantees certain fundamental rights.

Treaties

treaty

A compact made between two or more nations.

The U.S. Constitution provides that the president, with the advice and consent of the Senate, may enter into **treaties** with foreign governments. Treaties become part of the supreme law of the land. With increasing international economic relations among nations, treaties will become an even more important source of law that will affect business in the future.

International Law

ANTARCTIC TREATY (SELECTED PROVISIONS)

The Governments of Argentina, Australia, Belgium, Chile, the French Republic, Japan, New Zealand, Norway, the Union of South Africa, the Union of Soviet Socialist Republics, the United Kingdom of Great Britain and Northern Ireland, and the United States of America, have agreed as follows:

Article I. Antarctica shall be used for peaceful purposes only. There shall be prohibited, inter alia, *any measures of a military nature, such as the establishment of military bases and fortifications, the carrying out of military maneuvers, as well as the testing of any type of weapons.*

Article II. Freedom of scientific investigation in Antarctica and cooperation toward that end, as applied during the International Geophysical Year, shall continue, subject to the provisions of the present treaty.

Article III. In order to promote international cooperation in scientific investigation in Antarctica, as provided for in Article II of the present treaty, the contracting parties agree that, to the greatest extent feasible and practicable:

(a) information regarding plans for scientific programs in Antarctica shall be exchanged to permit maximum economy and efficiency of operations;

(b) scientific personnel shall be exchanged in Antarctica between expeditions and stations;

(c) scientific observations and results from Antarctica shall be exchanged and made freely available.

Article IV. Nothing contained in the present treaty shall be interpreted as a renunciation by any contracting party of previously asserted rights of or claims to territorial sovereignty in Antarctica.

Article V. Any nuclear explosions in Antarctica and the disposal there of radioactive waste material shall be prohibited.

Article VI. The provisions of the present treaty shall apply to the area south of 60° South Latitude, including all ice shelves, but nothing in the present treaty shall prejudice or in any way affect the rights, or the exercise of the rights, of any state under international law with regard to the high seas within that area.

Article VII. In order to promote the objectives and ensure the observance of the provisions of the present treaty, each contracting party whose representatives are entitled to participate in the meetings referred to in Article IX of the treaty shall have the right to designate observers to carry out any inspection provided for by the present Article.

Article IX. Representatives of the Contracting Parties named in the preamble to the present treaty shall meet at the city of Canberra within two months after the date of entry into force of the treaty, and thereafter at suitable intervals and places, for the purpose of exchanging information, consulting together on matters of common interest pertaining to Antarctica, and formulating and considering, and recommending to their governments, measures in furtherance of the principles and objectives of the treaty.

Article X. Each of the Contracting Parties undertakes to exert appropriate efforts, consistent with the Charter of the United Nations, to the end that no one engages in any activity in Antarctica contrary to the principles or purposes of the present treaty.

Codified Law

statute

Written law enacted by the legislative branch of the federal and state governments that establishes certain courses of conduct that must be adhered to by covered parties.

Statutes are written laws that establish certain courses of conduct that must be adhered to by covered parties. The U.S. Congress is empowered by the Commerce Clause and other provisions of the U.S. Constitution to enact *federal statutes* to regulate foreign and interstate commerce. Federal statutes include antitrust laws, securities laws, bankruptcy laws, labor laws, equal employment opportunity laws, environmental protection laws, consumer protection laws, and such. State legislatures enact *state statutes*. State statutes include corporation laws, partnership law, workers' compensation laws, the Uniform Commercial Code, and the like. The statutes enacted by the legislative branches of the federal and state governments are organized by topic into code books. This is often called *codified law.*

State legislatures often delegate lawmaking authority to local government bodies, including cities and municipalities, counties, school districts, water districts, and such. These governmental units are empowered to adopt **ordinances**. Examples of ordinances are traffic laws, local building codes, and zoning laws. Ordinances are also codified.

ordinances

Laws enacted by local government bodies such as cities and municipalities, counties, school districts, and water districts.

U.S. Congress, Washington, DC
The U.S. Congress, which is a bicameral system made up of the U.S. Senate and the U.S. House of Representatives, creates federal law by enacting statutes. Each state has two senators and is allocated a certain number of representatives based on population.

Contemporary Business Environment

AMERICAN INDIAN GAMBLING REGULATORY STATUTE

The Commerce Clause in the U.S. Constitution grants the federal government the power to deal with the American Indian tribes. Pursuant to this power, the federal government has enacted many statutes granting rights to and regulating commerce with the American Indian nations.

In 1988, Congress enacted the **Indian Gaming Regulatory Act (IGRA)** [25 U.S.C. §2701]. The IGRA is a federal statute that authorizes Native American Indian tribes to conduct various gambling operations—including casino-style gambling—if the state permits such gambling for the Indians. Most states have entered into compacts that permit American Indian tribes to conduct gambling on Indian reservation lands. American Indian gambling casinos have been erected in most states and now provide a substantial income to members of the American Indian tribes that operate the gaming casinos.

Contemporary Business Environment

REGULATIONS AND ORDER OF ADMINISTRATIVE AGENCIES

The legislative and executive branches of federal and state governments are empowered to establish **administrative agencies** to enforce and interpret statutes enacted by Congress and state legislatures. Many of these agencies regulate business. For example, Congress has created the Securities and Exchange Commission (SEC) and the Federal Trade Commission (FTC), among others.

Congress or the state legislatures usually empower these agencies to adopt **administrative rules and regulations** to interpret the statutes that the agency is authorized to enforce. These rules and regulations have the force of law. Administrative agencies usually have the power to hear and decide disputes. Their decisions are called *orders*. Because of their power, administrative agencies are often informally referred to as the "fourth branch" of government."

Executive Orders

executive order

An order issued by a member of the executive branch of the government.

The executive branch of government, which includes the president of the United States and state governors, is empowered to issue **executive orders**. This power is derived from express delegation from the legislative branch and is implied from the U.S. Constitution and state constitutions. For example, in 1993, President Clinton issued an executive order that lifted the so-called "gag" rule forbidding abortion counseling in federally funded family planning clinics.

E-Commerce & Information Technology

EXECUTIVE ORDER PROTECTS ENCRYPTION TECHNOLOGY

Encryption technology permits a computer user to basically put a lock around his or her computer information to protect it from being discovered by others. Encryption technology is like a lock on a house: Without the lock in place unwanted persons can easily enter the house and steal its contents; with the lock in place it is more difficult to enter and take the house's contents. Encryption software serves a similar function in that it lets a computer user scramble information so that only those who have the encryption code can enter the database and discover the information.

Software companies in the United States led the development of encryption technology. For years, however, the U.S. government permitted American software companies to sell their encryption software domestically but prohibited the export of the most powerful encryption technology to foreigners. The U.S. government worried that powerful encryption and data-scrambling technology would fall into the hands of criminals and terrorists who would use it to

protect their illegal and clandestine activities. Based on this fear, the Clinton administration issued an executive order that prohibited the export of much of the most powerful encryption technology developed in the United States. These export restrictions remained in effect during most of the 1990s.

In September 1999, after much lobbying by software companies located in the United States, the Clinton administration changed its export policy to allow the export of the most powerful American-made encryption technology. The export rule was changed because criminals and terrorists could obtain similar data-scrambling technology from software producers in other countries. Therefore the American policy prohibiting the export of encryption technology to foreigners was no longer effective. The Clinton administration's export controls on encryption technology were lifted for all countries except Iran, Iraq, Syria, Sudan, North Korea, and Cuba, countries that have a history of terrorist activities.

Judicial Decisions

judicial decision

A decision about an individual lawsuit issued by federal and state courts.

When deciding individual lawsuits, federal and state courts issue **judicial decisions**. In these written opinions the judge or justice usually explains the legal reasoning used to decide the case. These opinions often include interpretations of statutes, ordinances, administrative regulations, and the announcement of legal principles used to decide the case. Many court decisions are printed (reported) in books that are available in law libraries.

precedent

A rule of law established in a court decision. Lower courts must follow the precedent established by higher courts.

***The Doctrine of* Stare Decisis**   Based on the common law tradition, past court decisions become **precedent** for deciding future cases. Lower courts must follow the precedent established by higher courts. That is why all federal and state courts in the United States must follow the precedents established by U.S. Supreme Court decisions.

The courts of one jurisdiction are not bound by the precedent established by the courts of another jurisdiction, although they may look to each other for guidance. For example, state courts of one state are not required to follow the legal precedent established by the courts of another state.

stare decisis

Latin: "To stand by the decision." Adherence to precedent.

Adherence to precedent is called *stare decisis* ("to stand by the decision"). The doctrine of *stare decisis* promotes uniformity of law within a jurisdiction, makes the court system more efficient, and makes the law more predictable for individuals and businesses. A court may later change or reverse its legal reasoning if a new case is presented to it and change is warranted. The doctrine of *stare decisis* is discussed in the following excerpt from Justice Musmanno's decision in *Flagiello v. Pennsylvania.*[6]

Without stare decisis, *there would be no stability in our system of jurisprudence.* Stare decisis *channels the law. It erects lighthouses and flies the signal of safety. The ships of jurisprudence must follow that well-defined channel which, over the years, has been proved to be secure and worthy.*

The Supreme Court Speaks

Warrantless Search of a Home with a Thermo Imaging Device Is an Unconstitutional Search

Kyllo v. United States,
121 S.Ct. 2038 (2001)
Supreme Court of the United States

BACKGROUND AND FACTS

In 1992, government agents suspected that marijuana was being grown in the home of Danny Kyllo, which was part of a triplex building in Florence, Oregon. Indoor marijuana growth typically requires high-intensity lamps. In order to determine whether an amount of heat was emanating from Kyllo's home consistent with the use of such lamps, federal agents used a thermal imager to scan the triplex. Thermal imagers detect infrared radiation and produce images of the radiation. The scan of Kyllo's home, which was performed from an automobile on the street, showed that the roof over the garage and a side wall of Kyllo's home were "hot." The federal agents concluded that Kyllo was using halide lights to grow marijuana in his house. The agents used this scanning evidence to obtain a search warrant authorizing a search of Kyllo's home. During the search, the agents found an indoor growing operation involving more than 100 marijuana plants.

Kyllo was indicted for manufacturing marijuana, a violation of federal criminal law. Kyllo moved to suppress the imaging evidence and the evidence it lead to, arguing that it was an unreasonable search that violated the Fourth Amendment to the U.S. Constitution. The trial court disagreed with Kyllo and let the evidence be introduced and considered at trial. Kyllo then entered a conditional guilty plea and appealed the trial court's failure to suppress the challenged evidence. The court of appeals affirmed. The U.S. Supreme Court granted certiorari to hear the appeal.

SUPREME COURT ISSUE

Is the use of a thermal-imaging device aimed at a private home from a public street to detect relative amounts of heat within the home a "search" within the meaning of the Fourth Amendment?

IN THE LANGUAGE OF THE U.S. SUPREME COURT

Scalia, Justice *At the very core of the Fourth Amendment stands the right of a man to retreat into his own home and there be free from unreasonable government intrusion. With few exceptions, the question whether a warrantless search of a home is reasonable and*

hence constitutional must be answered no. On the other hand, the lawfulness of warrantless visual surveillance of a home has still been preserved. In fact we have held that visual observation is no "search" at all. We have applied the test on different occasions in holding that aerial surveillance of private homes and surrounding areas does not constitute a search. California v. Ciraolo, 476 U.S. 207, 213, 106 S. Ct. 1809 (1986) and Florida v. Riley, 488 U.S. 445, 109 S. Ct. 693 (1989).

The present case involves officers on a public street engaged in more than naked-eye surveillance of a home. The question we confront today is what limits there are upon this power of technology to shrink the realm of guaranteed privacy. We think that obtaining by sense-enhancing technology any information regarding the interior of the home that could not otherwise have been obtained without physical intrusion into a constitutionally protected area. This assures preservation of that degree of privacy against government that existed when the Fourth Amendment was adopted. On the basis of this criterion, the information obtained by the thermal imager in this case was the product of a search.

DECISION AND REMEDY

The U.S. Supreme Court held that the use of a thermal-imaging device aimed at a private home from a public street to detect relative amounts of heat within the home is a "search" within the meaning of the Fourth Amendment. The Supreme Court reversed and remanded the case for further proceedings.

CASE QUESTIONS

Critical Legal Thinking Is the Fourth Amendment's prohibition against unreasonable search and seizures an easy standard to apply? Explain.

Business Ethics Did the police act ethically in obtaining the evidence in this case? Did Kyllo act ethically in trying to suppress the evidence?

Contemporary Business How can the government catch entrepreneurs such as Kyllo? Explain.

Priority of Law in the United States

As mentioned previously, the U.S. Constitution and treaties take precedence over all other laws. Federal statutes take precedence over federal regulations. Valid federal law takes precedence over any conflicting state or local law. State constitutions rank as the highest state law. State statutes take precedence over state regulations. Valid state law takes precedence over local laws.

CONCEPT SUMMARY SOURCES OF LAW IN THE UNITED STATES

Source of Law	Description
Constitutions	The U.S. Constitution establishes the federal government and enumerates its powers. Powers not given to the federal government are reserved to the states. State constitutions establish state governments and enumerate their powers.
Treaties	The president, with the advice and consent of the Senate, may enter into treaties with foreign countries.
Codified law: Statutes and ordinances	Statutes are enacted by Congress and state legislatures. Ordinances are enacted by municipalities and local government agencies. They establish courses of conduct that must be followed by covered parties.
Administrative agency rules and regulations	Administrative agencies are created by the legislative and executive branches of government. They may adopt rules and regulations that regulate the conduct of covered parties.
Executive orders	Issued by the president and governors of states, executive orders regulate the conduct of covered parties.
Judicial decisions	Courts decide controversies. In doing so, a court issues decisions that state the holding of the case and the rationale used by the court in reaching that decision.

Business Ethics

NIKE CLEANS UP ITS ACT IN VIETNAM

Nike produces basketball, running, and other athletic shoes that it sells in the United States and worldwide. Nike, with over 40 percent of the athletic shoe market, has basketball great Michael Jordan as its pitchman. The majority of Nike's shoes are produced by subcontractors located in some of the poorest countries of the world. In 1997, Nike faced a public relations and ethical nightmare: It was being charged with selling shoes made by slave and child laborers who worked in horrid conditions.

In Vietnam, where Nike has 12 percent of its shoes manufactured, subcontractors worked employees eight hours per day, six days per week, and paid them as little as $40 per month in wages. These workers, who were mostly women in their 20s, worked under terrible conditions. They were subject to hot and noisy working environments, exposed to toxic chemicals and fumes, and were mistreated by the managers. Workers were hit for not working fast enough or for talking, were made to run in stifling heat or lick the factory floor if they did not do what the managers told them to do, and were subject to sexual harassment. These conditions were brought to light not by Nike but by humanitarian organizations. After first vehemently denying the allegations, Nike backed down and agreed to improve the working conditions at its subcontractors in Vietnam.

Nike took the following steps:

- Required many managers at the subcontractors to be fired for their abusive conduct.
- Reduced toxic petroleum-based compounds used in making Nike shoes.
- Banned its subcontractors from paying below Vietnam's minimum wage of $45 per month.
- Installed Nike managers in the subcontractors' plants to monitor working conditions.
- Opened the manufacturing plants to outside inspectors.

Nike states that it has taken the necessary steps to prohibit and prevent abuses by its subcontractors in Vietnam and that its decision to have its shoes made in Vietnam is an economic one. Critics contend that Nike is outsourcing the production of its shoes to workers in poor countries that do not have the same worker protections as provided in the United States. They cite the fact that Michael Jordan's payment of $25 million from Nike exceeds the wages of all 35,000 persons who work for Nike's subcontractors in Vietnam.

CHAPTER SUMMARY

What Is Law? p. 3

Law	*Law* is a body of rules of action or conduct that has binding legal force. Laws must be obeyed by citizens subject to sanction or legal consequences.
Functions of the Law	1. Keep the peace 2. Shape moral standards 3. Promote social justice 4. Maintain the status quo 5. Facilitate orderly change 6. Facilitate planning 7. Provide a basis for compromise 8. Maximize individual freedom
Flexibility and Fairness of the Law	1. *Flexibility.* The law must be flexible to meet social, technological, and economic changes in the United States and the world. 2. *Fairness.* Although the American legal system is one of the fairest and most democratic systems of law, abuses of process and mistakes in the application of the law do occur.

Schools of Jurisprudential Thought, p. 5

Schools of Juriprudential Thought	1. *Natural Law School.* Postulates that law is based on what is "correct." It emphasizes a moral theory of law—that is, law should be based on morality and ethics. 2. *Historical School.* Believes that law is an aggregate of social traditions and customs. 3. *Analytical School.* Maintains that law is shaped by logic. 4. *Sociological School.* Asserts that the law is a means of achieving and advancing certain sociological goals. 5. *Command School.* Believes that the law is a set of rules developed, communicated, and enforced by the ruling party. 6. *Critical Legal Studies* (the Crits). Maintains that legal rules are unnecessary and that legal disputes should be solved by applying arbitrary rules based on fairness. 7. *Law and Economics School.* Believes that promoting market efficiency should be the central concern of legal decision making.

History of American Law, p. 7

Foundation of American Law	The English law (judge-made law) forms the basis of the legal systems of most states in this country. Louisiana bases its law on the French civil code.

Sources of Law in the United States, p. 9

Sources of Law in the United States	1. *Constitutions.* The U.S. Constitution establishes the federal government and enumerates its powers. Powers not given to the federal government are reserved to the states. State constitutions establish state governments and enumerate their powers. 2. *Treaties.* The president, with the advice and consent of the Senate, may enter into treaties with foreign countries. 3. *Codified Law, Statues* are enacted by the federal Congress and state legislatures. *Ordinances* are passed by municipalities and local government bodies. They establish courses of conduct that must be followed by covered parties. 4. *Administrative agency regulations and orders.* Administrative agencies are created by the legislative and executive branches of government. They may adopt administrative regulations and issue orders. 5. *Executive orders.* Issued by the president and governors of states. They regulate the conduct of covered parties. 6. *Judicial decisions.* Federal and state courts decide controversies. In doing so, they issue decisions that state the holding of each case and the reasoning used by the court in reaching its decision.
Doctrine of *Stare Decisis*	*Stare decisis.* Doctrine that provides for the adherence to precedent. *Stare decisis* means "to stand by the decision."

END-OF-CHAPTER INTERNET EXERCISES AND CASE QUESTIONS

Working the Web Internet Exercises

ACTIVITIES

Visit the Web sites listed below for more information about the topics covered in this chapter:

1. For a broad overview of legal history visit **jurist.law.pitt.edu/sg_hist.htm**.

2. To better understand the conceptual differences between law versus equity see **www.law.cornell.edu/topics/equity/html**.

3. For a working definition of basic legal categories visit common law: *The Columbia Encyclopedia*, Sixth Edition, 2201 at **www.bartleby.com/65/co/commonla.html**.

4. The Law, Commerce and Technology Center, University of Washington Law, provides online information about Internet issues, biotechnology, electronic commerce, and technology news in the northwest. Visit **www.law.washington.edu/lct/**.

5. Check out the latest developments at the Business Law—Committee on Cyberspace Law Home Page. Visit **www.abanet.org/buslaw/cyber/home.html**.

6. An ongoing series of publications and seminars can be found at the Online Education—Berkman Center for Internet and Society **www.cyber.harvard.edu/online**.

CRITICAL LEGAL THINKING CASES

1.1 Fairness and Flexibility of the Law   In 1909, the state legislature of Illinois enacted a statute called the "Woman's 10-Hour Law." The law prohibited women who were employed in factories and other manufacturing facilities from working more than 10 hours per day. The law did not apply to men. W. C. Ritchie & Co., an employer, brought a lawsuit that challenged the statute as being unconstitutional in violation of the Equal Protection Clause of the Illinois constitution. In upholding the statute, the Illinois Supreme Court stated,

It is known to all men (and what we know as men we cannot profess to be ignorant of as judges) that woman's physical structure and the performance of maternal functions place her at a great disadvantage in the battle of life; that while a man can work for more than 10 hours a day without injury to himself, a woman, especially when the burdens of motherhood are upon her, cannot; that while a man can work standing upon his feet for more than 10 hours a day, day after day, without injury to himself, a woman cannot; and that to require a

woman to stand upon her feet for more than 10 hours in any one day and perform severe manual labor while thus standing, day after day, has the effect to impair her health, and that as weakly and sickly women cannot be mothers of vigorous children.

We think the general consensus of opinion, not only in this country but in the civilized countries of Europe, is, that a working day of not more than 10 hours for women is justified for the following reasons: (1) the physical organization of women, (2) her maternal function, (3) the rearing and education of children, (4) the maintenance of the home; and these conditions are, so far, matters of general knowledge that the courts will take judicial cognizance of their existence.

Surrounded as women are by changing conditions of society, and the evolution of employment which environs them, we agree fully with what is said by the Supreme Court of Washington in the Buchanan *case; "Law is, or ought to be, a progressive science."*

Is the statute fair? Would the statute be lawful today? Should the law be a "progressive science"? [*W. C.Ritchie & Co. v. Wayman, Attorney for Cook County, Illinois* 91 N.E. 695 (IL 1910)]

BUSINESS ETHICS CASES

1.2 Business Ethics   In 1975, after the war in Vietnam, the U.S. government discontinued draft registration for men in this country. In 1980, after the Soviet Union invaded Afghanistan, President Jimmy Carter asked Congress for funds to reactivate draft registration. President Carter suggested that both males and females be required to

register. Congress allocated funds only for the registration of males. Several men who were subject to draft registration brought a lawsuit that challenged the law as being unconstitutional in violation of the Equal Protection Clause of the U.S. Constitution. The U.S. Supreme Court upheld the constitutionality of the draft registration law, reasoning as follows:

The question of registering women for the draft not only received considerable national attention and was the subject of wide-ranging public debate, but also was extensively considered by Congress in hearings, floor debate, and in committee. The foregoing clearly establishes that the decision to exempt women from registration was not the "accidental by-product of a traditional way of thinking about women."

This is not a case of Congress arbitrarily choosing to burden one of two similarly situated groups, such as would be the case with an all-black or all-white, or an all-Catholic or all-Lutheran, or an all-Republican or all-Democratic registration. Men and women are simply not similarly situated for purposes of a draft or registration for a draft.

Justice Marshall dissented, stating that "The Court today places its imprimatur on one of the most potent remaining public expressions of 'ancient canards about the proper role of women.' It upholds a statute that requires males but not females to register for the draft, and which thereby categorically excludes women from a fundamental civic obligation. I dissent."

Was the decision fair? Has the law been a "progressive science" in this case? Is it ethical for males, but not females, to have to register for the draft? [*Rostker, Director of the Selective Service v. Goldberg*, 453 U.S. 57, 101 S.Ct. 2646, 69 L.Ed.2d 478 (1981)]

ENDNOTES

1. *The Spirit of Liberty*, 3d ed (New York: Alfred A. Knopf, 1960).
2. "Introduction," *The Nature of Law: Readings in Legal Philosophy*, ed. M.P. Golding (New York: Random House, 1966).
3. *Black's Law Dictionary*, 5th ed (St. Paul, MN: West, 1979).
4. 447 U.S. 10, 100 S.Ct. 1999, 64 L.Ed.2d 689 (1980).
5. *Law and the Modern Mind* (New York: Brentano's, 1930).
6. 208 A.2d 193 (PA 1965).

*C*RITICAL *L*EGAL *T*HINKING

Judges apply *legal reasoning* in reaching a decision in a case. That is, the judge must specify the issue presented by the case, identify the key facts in the case and the applicable law, and then apply the law to the facts to come to a conclusion that answers the issue presented. This process is called **critical legal thinking**. Skills of analysis and interpretation are important in deciding legal cases.

critical legal thinking

The process of specifying the issue presented by a case, identifying the key facts in the case and applicable law, and then applying the law to the facts to come to a conclusion that answers the issue presented.

Key Terms   Before you embark upon the study of law, you should know the following key legal terms.

- **Plaintiff**   The party who originally brought the lawsuit.
- **Defendant**   The party against whom the lawsuit has been brought.
- **Petitioner** or **Appellant**   The party who has appealed the decision of the trial court or lower court. The petitioner may be either the plaintiff or defendant, depending on who lost the case at the trial court or lower court level.
- **Respondent** or **Appellee**   The party who must answer the petitioner's appeal. The respondent may be either the plaintiff or defendant, depending upon which party is the petitioner. In some cases, both the plaintiff *and* the defendant may disagree with the trial court's or lower court's decision, and both parties may appeal the decision.

Briefing a Case   It is often helpful for a student to "brief" a case in order to clarify the legal issues involved and to gain a better understanding of the case.

The procedure for briefing a case is as follows. The student must summarize, or brief, the court's decision in no more than 400 words (some professors may shorten or lengthen this limit). The assignment's format is highly structured, consisting of five parts, each of which is numbered and labeled:

Part	Maximum Words
1. Case name and citation	25
2. A summary of the key facts in the case	125
3. The issue presented by the case, stated as a one-sentence question answerable only by *yes* or *no*	25
4. The court's resolution of the issue (the "holding")	25
5. A summary of the court's reasoning justifying the holding	200
Total words	400

case brief

A summary of each of the following items of a case:

1. Case name and citation

2. Key facts

3. Issue presented

4. Holding of the court

5. Court's reasoning

Briefing a case consists of making a summary of each of the following items of the case.

1. **Case Name and Citation**
   The name of the case should be placed at the beginning of each briefed case. The case name usually contains the names of the parties to the lawsuit. Where there are multiple plaintiffs or defendants, however, some of the names of the parties may be omitted from the case name. Abbreviations are also often used in case names.
       The case citation, which consists of a number plus the year in which the case was decided, such as "121 S.Ct. 1879 (2001)," is set forth below the case name. The case citation identifies the book in the law library in which the case may be found. For example, the case in the above citation may be found in volume 121 of the *Supreme Court Reporter* page 1879. The name of the court that decided the case should be set forth below the case name for the case.

2. **Summary of the Key Facts in the Case**
   The important facts of a case should be stated briefly. Extraneous facts and facts of minor importance should be omitted from the brief. The facts of the case can usually be found at the beginning of the case, but not necessarily. Important facts may be found throughout the case.

3. **Issue Presented by the Case**
   It is crucial in the briefing of a case to identify the issue presented to the court to decide. The issue on appeal is most often a legal question, although questions of fact are sometimes the subject of an appeal. The issue presented in each case is usually quite specific and should be asked in a one-sentence question that is answerable only by a *yes* or *no*. For example, the issue statement,

"Is Mary liable?" is too broad. A more proper statement of the issue would be, "Is Mary liable to Joe for breach of the contract made between them based on her refusal to make the payment due on September 30?"

4. **Holding**

The "holding" is the decision reached by the present court. It should be *yes* or *no*. The holding should also state which party won.

5. **Summary of the Court's Reasoning**

When an appellate court or supreme court issues a decision, which is often called an *opinion*, the court will normally state the reasoning it used in reaching its decision. The rationale for the decision may be based on the specific facts of the case, public policy, prior law, or other matters. In stating the reasoning of the court, the student should reword the court's language into the student's own language. This summary of the court's reasoning should pick out the meat of the opinions and weed out the nonessentials.

BRIEFING THE CASE WRITING ASSIGNMENT

The following is an excerpted decision by the Supreme Court of the United States. The case is presented in the language of the Supreme Court. Following the case is a *Brief of the Case* using the previous model.

Case name, Citation, and Court	**PGA TOUR, Inc. v. Martin 121 S.Ct. 1879, 149 L.Ed.2d 904 (2001) 2001 U.S. LEXIS 4115 U.S. Supreme Court**
Opinion of the Court	***OPINION, STEVEN, JUSTICE*** *This case raises two questions concerning the application of the Americans with Disabilities Act of 1990 [42 U.S.C. § 12101 et seq.] to a gifted athlete: first, whether*
Issue	*the Act protects access to professional golf tournaments by a qualified entrant with a disability; and second, whether a disabled contestant may be denied the use of a golf cart because it would "fundamentally alter the nature" of the tournaments to allow him to ride when all other contestants must walk.*
Facts	*Petitioner PGA TOUR, Inc., a nonprofit entity formed in 1968, sponsors and cosponsors professional golf tournaments conducted on three annual tours. About 200 golfers participate in the PGA TOUR; about 170 in the NIKE TOUR; and about 100 in the SENIOR PGA TOUR. PGA TOUR and NIKE TOUR tournaments typically are four-day events, played on courses leased and*
Petitioner: PGA TOUR Inc.	*operated by petitioner. The revenues generated by television, admissions, concessions, and contributions from cosponsors amount to about $300 million a year, much of which is distributed in prize money. The "Conditions of Competition and Local Rules," often described as the "hard card," apply specifically to petitioner's professional tours. The hard cards for the PGA TOUR and NIKE TOUR required players to walk the golf course during tournaments, but not during open qualifying rounds. On the SENIOR PGA TOUR, which is limited to golfers age 50 and older, the contestants may use golf carts. Most seniors, however, prefer to walk.*
Respondent: Casey Martin	*Casey Martin is a talented golfer. As an amateur, he won 17 Oregon Golf Association junior events before he was 15, and won the state championship as a high school senior. He played on the Stanford University golf team that won the 1994 National Collegiate Athletic Association (NCAA) championship. As a professional, Martin qualified for the NIKE TOUR in 1998 and 1999, and based on his 1999 performance, qualified for the PGA TOUR in 2000. In the 1999 season, he entered 24 events, made the cut 13 times, and had six top-10 finishes, coming in second twice and third once.*
	Martin is also an individual with a disability as defined in the Americans with Disabilities Act of 1990 (ADA or Act). Since birth he has been afflicted with Klippel-Trenaunay-Weber Syndrome, a degenerative circulatory disorder that obstructs the flow of blood from his right leg back to his heart. The disease is progressive; it causes severe pain and has atrophied his right leg. During the latter part of his college career, because of the progress of the disease, Martin could no longer walk an 18-hole golf course. Walking not only caused him pain, fatigue, and anxiety, but also created a significant risk of hemorrhaging, developing blood clots, and fracturing his tibia so badly that an amputation might be required.

When Martin turned pro and entered petitioner's Qualifying-School, the hard card permitted him to use a cart during his successful progress through the first two stages. He made a request, supported by detailed medical records, for permission to use a golf cart during the third stage. Petitioner refused to review those records or to waive its walking rule for the third stage. Martin therefore filed this action.

District Court's Decision
994 F.Supp. 1242
[District: Oregon (1998)]

At trial, petitioner PGA TOUR did not contest the conclusion that Martin has a disability covered by the ADA, or the fact that his disability prevents him from walking the course during a round of golf. Rather, petitioner asserted that the condition of walking is a substantive rule of competition, and that waiving it as to any individual for any reason would fundamentally alter the nature of the competition. Petitioner's evidence included the testimony of a number of experts, among them some of the greatest golfers in history. Arnold Palmer, Jack Nicklaus, and Ken Venturi explained that fatigue can be a critical factor in a tournament, particularly on the last day when psychological pressure is at a maximum. Their testimony makes it clear that, in their view, permission to use a cart might well give some players a competitive advantage over other players who must walk.

The judge found that the purpose of the rule was to inject fatigue into the skill of shot-making, but that the fatigue injected "by walking the course cannot be deemed significant under normal circumstances." Furthermore, Martin presented evidence, and the judge found, that even with the use of a cart, Martin must walk over a mile during an 18-hole round, and that the fatigue he suffers from coping with his disability is "undeniably greater" than the fatigue his able-bodied competitors endure from walking the course. As a result, the judge concluded that it would "not fundamentally alter the nature of the PGA Tour's game to accommodate him with a cart." The judge accordingly entered a permanent injunction requiring petitioner to permit Martin to use a cart in tour and qualifying events.

Court of Appeals Decision
204 F.3d 994
[9th Circuit (2000)]

The Court of Appeals concluded that golf courses remain places of public accommodation during PGA tournaments. On the merits, because there was no serious dispute about the fact that permitting Martin to use a golf cart was both a reasonable and a necessary solution to the problem of providing him access to the tournaments, the Court of Appeals regarded the central dispute as whether such permission would "fundamentally alter" the nature of the PGA TOUR or NIKE TOUR. Like the District Court, the Court of Appeals viewed the issue not as "whether use of carts generally would fundamentally alter the competition, but whether the use of a cart by Martin would do so." That issue turned on "an intensively fact-based inquiry," and, the court concluded, had been correctly resolved by the trial judge. In its words, "all that the cart does is permit Martin access to a type of competition in which he otherwise could not engage because of his disability."

Federal Statute
Being Interpreted

Congress enacted the ADA in 1990 to remedy widespread discrimination against disabled individuals. To effectuate its sweeping purpose, the ADA forbids discrimination against disabled individuals in major areas of public life, among them employment (Title I of the Act), public services (Title II), and public accommodations (Title III). At issue now is the applicability of Title III to petitioner's golf tours and qualifying rounds, in particular to petitioner's treatment of a qualified disabled golfer wishing to compete in those events.

U.S. Supreme Court's
Reasoning

It seems apparent, from both the general rule and the comprehensive definition of "public accommodation," that petitioner's golf tours and their qualifying rounds fit comfortably within the coverage of Title III, and Martin within its protection. The events occur on "golf courses," a type of place specifically identified by the Act as a public accommodation. Section 12181(7)(L). In this case, the narrow dispute is whether allowing Martin to use a golf cart, despite the walking requirement that applies to the PGA TOUR, the NIKE TOUR, and the third stage of the Qualifying-School, is a modification that would "fundamentally alter the nature" of those events.

As an initial matter, we observe that the use of carts is not itself inconsistent with the fundamental character of the game of golf. From early on, the essence of the game has been shot-making—using clubs to cause a ball to progress from the teeing ground to a hole some distance away with as few strokes as possible. Golf carts started appearing with increasing regularity on American golf courses in the 1950s. Today they are everywhere. And they are encouraged. For one thing, they often speed up play, and for another, they are great revenue producers. There is nothing in the rules of golf that either forbids the use of carts or penalizes a player for using a cart.

Petitioner, however, distinguishes the game of golf as it is generally played from the game that it sponsors in the PGA TOUR, NIKE TOUR, and the last stage of the Qualifying-School—golf at the "highest level." According to petitioner, "the goal of the highest-level competitive athletics is to assess and compare the performance of different competitors, a task that is meaningful only if the competitors are subject to identical substantive rules." The waiver of any possibly "outcome-affecting" rule for a contestant would violate this principle and therefore, in petitioner's view, fundamentally alter the nature of the highest level athletic event. The walking rule is one such rule, petitioner submits, because its purpose is "to inject the element of fatigue into the skill of shot-making," and thus its effect may be the critical loss of a stroke. As a consequence, the reasonable modification Martin seeks would fundamentally alter the nature of petitioner's highest level tournaments.

The force of petitioner's argument is, first of all, mitigated by the fact that golf is a game in which it is impossible to guarantee that all competitors will play under exactly the same conditions or that an individual's ability will be the sole determinant of the outcome. For example, changes in the weather may produce harder greens and more head winds for the tournament leader than for his closest pursuers. A lucky bounce may save a shot or two. Whether such happenstance events are more or less probable than the likelihood that a golfer afflicted with Klippel-Trenaunay-Weber Syndrome would one day qualify for the NIKE TOUR and PGA TOUR, they at least demonstrate that pure chance may have a greater impact on the outcome of elite golf tournaments than the fatigue resulting from the enforcement of the walking rule.

Further, the factual basis of petitioner's argument is undermined by the District Court's finding that the fatigue from walking during one of petitioner's 4-day tournaments cannot be deemed significant. The District Court credited the testimony of a professor in physiology and expert on fatigue, who calculated the calories expended in walking a golf course (about five miles) to be approximately 500 calories—"nutritionally less than a Big Mac." What is more, that energy is expended over a 5-hour period, during which golfers have numerous intervals for rest and refreshment. In fact, the expert concluded, because golf is a low intensity activity, fatigue from the game is primarily a psychological phenomenon in which stress and motivation are the key ingredients. And even under conditions of severe heat and humidity, the critical factor in fatigue is fluid loss rather than exercise from walking. Moreover, when given the option of using a cart, the majority of golfers in petitioner's tournaments have chosen to walk, often to relieve stress or for other strategic reasons. As NIKE TOUR member Eric Johnson testified, walking allows him to keep in rhythm, stay warmer when it is chilly, and develop a better sense of the elements and the course than riding a cart. As we have demonstrated, the walking rule is at best peripheral to the nature of petitioner's athletic events, and thus it might be waived in individual cases without working a fundamental alteration.

Holding and Remedy

Under the ADA's basic requirement that the need of a disabled person be evaluated on an individual basis, we have no doubt that allowing Martin to use a golf cart would not fundamentally alter the nature of petitioner's tournaments. As we have discussed, the purpose of the walking rule is to subject players to fatigue, which in turn may influence the outcome of tournaments. Even if the rule does serve that purpose, it is an uncontested finding of the District Court that Martin "easily endures greater fatigue even with a cart than his able-bodied competitors do by walking." The purpose of the walking rule is therefore not compromised in the slightest by allowing Martin to use a cart. A modification that provides an exception to a peripheral tournament rule without impairing its purpose cannot be said to "fundamentally alter" the tournament. What it can be said to do, on the other hand, is to allow Martin the chance to qualify for and compete in the athletic events petitioner offers to those members of the public who have the skill and desire to enter. That is exactly what the ADA requires. As a result, Martin's request for a waiver of the walking rule should have been granted.

The judgment of the Court of Appeals is affirmed. It is so ordered.

Dissenting Opinion

DISSENTING OPINION, SCALIA, JUSTICE *In my view today's opinion exercises a benevolent compassion that the law does not place it within our power to impose. The judgment distorts the text of Title III, the structure of the ADA, and common sense. I respectfully dissent.*

The Court, for its part, assumes that conclusion for the sake of argument, but pronounces respondent to be a "customer" of the PGA TOUR or of the golf courses on which it is played. That seems to me quite incredible. The PGA TOUR is a professional sporting event, staged for the entertainment of a live and TV audience. The professional golfers on the tour are no more "enjoying" (the statutory term) the entertainment that the tour provides, or the facilities of the golf courses on which it is held, than professional baseball players "enjoy" the baseball games in which they play or the facilities of Yankee Stadium. To be sure, professional ballplayers participate in the games, and use the ball fields, but no one in his right mind would think that they are customers of the American League or of Yankee Stadium. They are themselves the entertainment that the customers pay to watch. And professional golfers are no different. A professional golfer's practicing his profession is not comparable to John Q. Public's frequenting "a 232-acre amusement area with swimming, boating, sunbathing, picnicking, miniature golf, dancing facilities, and a snack bar."

Having erroneously held that Title III applies to the "customers" of professional golf who consist of its practitioners, the Court then erroneously answers—or to be accurate simply ignores—a second question. The ADA requires covered businesses to make such reasonable modifications of "policies, practices, or procedures" as are necessary to "afford" goods, services, and privileges to individuals with disabilities; but it explicitly does not require "modifications that would fundamentally alter the nature" of the goods, services, and privileges. Section 12182(b)(2)(A)(ii). In other words, disabled individuals must be given access to the same goods, services, and privileges that others enjoy.

A camera store may not refuse to sell cameras to a disabled person, but it is not required to stock cameras specially designed for such persons. It is hardly a feasible judicial function to decide whether shoe stores should sell single shoes to one-legged persons and if so at what price, or how many braille books the Borders or Barnes and Noble bookstore chains should stock in each of their stores. Eighteen-hole golf courses, 10-foot-high basketball hoops, 90-foot baselines, 100-yard football fields—all are arbitrary and none is essential. The only support for any of them is tradition and (in more modern times) insistence by what has come to be regarded as the ruling body of the sport—both of which factors support the PGA TOUR's position in the present case. One can envision the parents of a Little League player with attention deficit disorder trying to convince a judge that their son's disability makes it at least 25 percent more difficult to hit a pitched ball. (If they are successful, the only thing that could prevent a court order giving the kid four strikes would be a judicial determination that, in baseball, three strikes are metaphysically necessary, which is quite absurd.)

Agility, strength, speed, balance, quickness of mind, steadiness of nerves, intensity of concentration—these talents are not evenly distributed. No wild-eyed dreamer has ever suggested that the managing bodies of the competitive sports that test precisely these qualities should try to take account of the uneven distribution of God-given gifts when writing and enforcing the rules of competition. And I have no doubt Congress did not authorize misty-eyed judicial supervision of such a revolution. The year was 2001, and "everybody was finally equal." K. Vonnegut, Harrison Bergeron, *in* Animal Farm and Related Readings *129 (1997).*

*B*RIEF OF CASE: *PGA TOUR, INC. V. MARTIN*

1. **Case Name, Citation, and Court**
   PGA TOUR, Inc. v Martin
   121 S.Ct. 1879, 2001 LEXIS 415 (2001)
   U.S. Supreme Court
2. **Key Facts**
   A. PGA TOUR, Inc. is a nonprofit organization that sponsors professional golf tournaments.
   B. The PGA establishes rules for its golf tournaments. A PGA rule requires golfers to walk the golf course and not use golf carts.
   C. Casey Martin is a professional golfer who suffers from Klippel-Trenaunay-Weber Syndrome, a degenerative circulatory disorder that atrophied Martin's right leg and causes him pain, fatigue, and anxiety when walking.
   D. When Martin petitioned the PGA to use a golf cart during golf tournaments, the PGA refused.
   E. Martin sued the PGA, alleging discrimination against a disabled individual in violation of the Americans with Disabilities Act of 1990, a federal statute.
3. **Issue**
   Does the Americans with Disabilities Act require the PGA to accommodate Martin by permitting him to use a golf cart while playing in PGA tournaments?
4. **Holding**
   Yes. The Supreme Court held that the PGA must allow Martin to use a golf cart when competing in PGA golf tournaments. Affirmed.
5. **Court's Reasoning**
   The Supreme Court held that:
   A. Martin was disabled and covered by the act.
   B. Golf courses are "public accommodations" covered by the act.
   C. The use of golf carts is not a fundamental character of the game of golf.
   D. Other than the PGA rule, there is no rule of golf that forbids the use of golf carts.
   E. It is impossible to guarantee all players in golf will play under the exact same conditions, so allowing Martin to use a golf cart gives him no advantage over other golfers.
   F. Martin, because of his disease, will probably suffer more fatigue playing golf using a golf cart than other golfers will suffer without using a cart.
   G. The PGA's "walking rule" is only peripheral to the game of golf and not a fundamental part of golf.
   H. Allowing Martin to use a golf cart will not fundamentally alter the PGA's highest-level professional golf tournaments.

2

Judicial and Alternative Dispute Resolution

I was never ruined but twice; once when I lost a lawsuit, and once when I won one.

—Voltaire

Chapter Objectives

After studying this chapter, you should be able to:

1. Describe and compare the state court systems and the federal court system.

2. Apply a cost-benefit analysis for bringing and defending a lawsuit.

3. Explain how a justice is chosen for the U.S. Supreme Court.

4. Explain subject matter jurisdiction and venue of federal and state courts.

5. Describe how jurisdiction of courts applies to Web site operators.

6. Describe the pretrial litigation process.

7. Describe how e-filings are used in court.

8. Describe how a case proceeds through trial and how a trial court decision is appealed.

9. Compare the Japanese and American legal systems.

10. Explain the use of arbitration and other nonjudicial methods of alternative dispute resolution.

Chapter Contents

There are two major court systems in the United States: (1) the federal court system and (2) the court systems of the 50 states and the District of Columbia. Each of these systems has jurisdiction to hear different types of lawsuits. The process of bringing, maintaining, and defending a lawsuit is called **litigation**. Litigation is a difficult, time-consuming, and costly process that must comply with complex procedural rules. Although it is not required, most parties employ a lawyer to represent them when they are involved in a lawsuit.

Several forms of *nonjudicial* dispute resolution have developed in response to the expense and difficulty of bringing a lawsuit. These methods, collectively called **alternative dispute resolution**, are being used more and more often to resolve commercial disputes.

This chapter discusses the various court systems, the jurisdiction of courts to hear and decide cases, the litigation process, and alternative dispute resolution.

The law, wherein, as in a magic mirror, we see reflected, not only our own lives, but the lives of all men that have been! When I think on this majestic theme, my eyes dazzle.

Oliver Wendell Holmes
The Law, *Speeches* 17 (1913)

*T*HE STATE COURT SYSTEMS

Each state and the District of Columbia has a separate court system. Most state court systems include the following: *limited-jurisdiction trial courts, general-jurisdiction trial courts, intermediate appellate courts*, and a *supreme court*.

We're the jury, dread our fury!
William S. Gilbert
Trial by Jury

Limited-Jurisdiction Trial Court

State **limited-jurisdiction trial courts**, which are sometimes referred to as **inferior trial courts**, hear matters of a specialized or limited nature. For example, in many states, traffic courts, juvenile courts, justice-of-the-peace courts, probate courts, family law courts, and courts that hear misdemeanor criminal law cases and civil cases involving lawsuits under a certain dollar amount are examples of such courts. Because these courts are trial courts, evidence can be introduced and testimony given. Most limited-jurisdiction courts keep a record of their proceedings. Their decisions usually can be appealed to a general-jurisdiction court or an appellate court.

Many states have also created **small claims courts** to hear civil cases involving small dollar amounts (e.g., $5,000 or less). Generally, the parties must appear individually and cannot have a lawyer represent them. The decisions of small claims courts are often appealable to general-jurisdiction trial courts or appellate courts.

limited-jurisdiction trial court
A court that hears matters of a specialized or limited nature.

small claims court
A court that hears civil cases involving small dollar amounts.

General-Jurisdiction Trial Court

Every state has a **general-jurisdiction trial court**. These courts are often referred to as **courts of record** because the testimony and evidence at trial are recorded and stored for future reference. They hear cases that are not within the jurisdiction of limited-jurisdiction trial courts, such as felonies, civil cases over a certain dollar amount, and so on. Some states divide their general-jurisdiction courts into two divisions, one for criminal cases and

general-jurisdiction trial court
A court that hears cases of a general nature that are not within the jurisdiction of limited-jurisdiction trial courts. Testimony and evidence at trial are recorded and stored for future reference.

Courthouse, St. Louis Missouri
State courts hear and decide the majority of cases in this country.

another for civil cases. Evidence and testimony are given at general-jurisdiction trial courts. The decisions handed down by these courts are appealable to an intermediate appellate court or the state supreme court, depending on the circumstances.

Intermediate Appellate Court

intermediate appellate court

An intermediate court that hears appeals from trial courts.

In many states, **intermediate appellate courts** (also called **appellate courts** or courts of appeal) hear appeals from trial courts. They review the trial court record to determine if there have been any errors at trial that would require reversal or modification of the trial court's decision. Thus, the appellate court reviews either pertinent parts or the whole trial court record from the lower court. No new evidence or testimony is permitted. The parties usually file legal *briefs* with the appellate court stating the law and facts that support their positions. Appellate courts usually grant a brief oral hearing to the parties. Appellate court decisions are appealable to the state's highest court. In less populated states that do not have an intermediate appellate court, trial court decisions can be appealed directly to the state's highest court.

Highest State Court

state supreme court

The highest court in a state court system; it hears appeals from intermediate state courts and certain trail courts.

Each state has a highest court in its court system. Most states call this highest court the **supreme court**. The function of a state supreme court is to hear appeals from intermediate state courts and certain trial courts. No new evidence or testimony is heard. The parties usually submit pertinent parts of or the entire lower court record for review. The parties also submit legal briefs to the court and are usually granted a brief oral hearing. Decisions of state supreme courts are final, unless a question of law is involved that is appealable to the U.S. Supreme Court.

Exhibit 2.1 portrays a typical state court system.

*E*XHIBIT **2.1**   *A Typical State Court System*

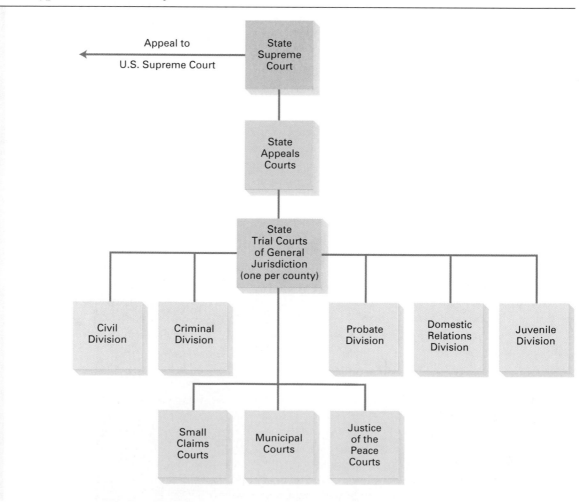

Entrepreneur and the Law

SPECIALIZED COURTS HEAR COMMERCIAL DISPUTES

In most states, business and commercial disputes are heard by the same judges who hear and decide criminal, landlord-tenant, matrimonial, medical malpractice, and other non-business related cases. The one major exception to this standard has been the state of Delaware, where a special Chancery Court hears and decides business litigation. The court, which deals mainly with cases involving corporate governance disputes, has earned a reputation for its expertise in handling and deciding corporate matters. Perhaps the existence of this special court and a corporation code that tends to favor corporate management are the primary reasons that more than 60 percent of the corporations listed on the New York Stock Exchange are incorporated in Delaware.

New York is one state that is following Delaware's lead in this area. New York has designated four courts within its general court system to hear commercial disputes. These courts, which began operating in 1993, hear contract, sales, insurance, unfair competition, libel, and slander, shareholder, business-related tort, and other commercial cases. Other states are expected to establish courts that specialize in commercial matters in the near future.

Businesses tend to favor special commercial courts because the judges presiding over them are expected to have the expertise to handle complex commercial lawsuits. The courts are also expected to be more efficient in deciding business related cases, thus saving time and money for the parties.

THE FEDERAL COURT SYSTEM

Article III of the United States Constitution provides that the federal government's judicial power is vested in one "Supreme Court." This court is the **U.S. Supreme Court**. The Constitution also authorizes Congress to establish "inferior" federal courts. Pursuant to this power Congress has established special federal courts, the U.S. District courts, and the U.S. courts of appeal. Federal judges are appointed for life by the president with the advice and consent of the Senate (except bankruptcy court judges, who are appointed for 14-year terms).

Special Federal Courts

The **special federal courts** established by Congress have limited jurisdiction. They include the following courts:

- **U.S. Tax Court** Hears cases involving federal tax laws.
- **U.S. Claims Court** Hears cases brought against the United States.
- **U.S. Court of International Trade** Hears cases involving tariffs and international commercial disputes.
- **U.S. Bankruptcy Court** Hears cases involving federal bankruptcy laws.

U.S. District Courts

The **U.S. district courts** are the federal court system's trial courts of general jurisdiction. There is at least one federal district court in each state and the District of Columbia, although more populated states have more than one district court. The geographical area served by each court is referred to as a *district*. There are presently 96 federal district courts. The federal district courts are empowered to impanel juries, receive evidence, hear testimony, and decide cases. Most federal cases originate in federal district courts.

U.S. Courts of Appeals

The **U.S. courts of appeals** are the federal court system's intermediate appellate courts. There are 13 circuits in the federal court system. The first 12 are geographical. Eleven are designated by a number, such as the "First Circuit," "Second Circuit," and so on. The geographical area served by each court is referred to a *circuit*. The twelfth circuit court is located in Washington, DC, and is called the "District of Columbia Circuit."

As appellate courts, these courts hear appeals from the district courts located in their circuit as well as from certain special courts and federal administrative agencies. The courts

Pieces of evidence, each by itself insufficient, may together constitute a significant whole and justify by their combined effect a conclusion.

Lord Wright
Grant v. Australian
Knitting Mills, Ltd. (1936)

special federal courts
Federal courts that hear matters of specialized or limited jurisdiction.

U.S. district courts
The federal court system's trial courts of general jurisdiction.

U.S. courts of appeals
The federal court system's intermediate appellate courts.

review the record of the lower court or administrative agency proceedings to determine if there has been any error that would warrant reversal or modification of the lower court decision. No new evidence or testimony is heard. The parties file legal briefs with the court and are given a short oral hearing. Appeals are usually heard by a three-judge panel. After a decision is rendered by the three-judge panel, a petitioner can request a review *en banc* by the full court.

The thirteenth court of appeals was created by Congress in 1982. It is called the **Court of Appeals for the Federal Circuit** and is located in Washington, DC.[1] This court has special appellate jurisdiction to review the decisions of the Claims Court, the Patent and Trademark Office, and the Court of International Trade. This court was created to provide uniformity in the application of federal law in certain areas, particularly patent law.

Exhibit 2.2 shows the 13 federal circuit courts of appeals.

Court of Appeals for the Federal Circuit

A court of appeals in Washington, DC, that has special appellate jurisdiction to review the decisions of the Claims Court, the Patent and Trademark Office, and the Court of International Trade.

*Ɛ*XHIBIT 2.2   *The Thirteen Federal Judicial Circuits*

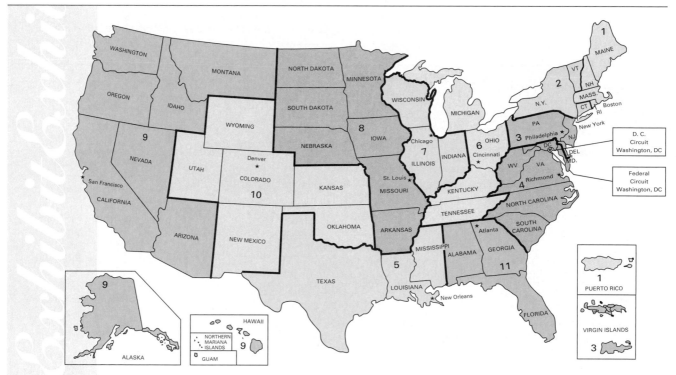

The U.S. Supreme Court

U.S. Supreme Court

The Supreme Court was created by Article III of the U.S. Constitution. The Supreme Court is the highest court in the land. It is located in Washington, DC.

The highest court in the land is the **Supreme Court of the United States**, located in Washington, DC. The Court is composed of nine justices who are nominated by the president and confirmed by the Senate. The president appoints one justice as *chief justice*, responsible for the administration of the Supreme Court. The other eight justices are *associate justices*.

The Supreme Court, which is an appellate court, hears appeals from federal circuit courts of appeals and, under certain circumstances, from federal district courts, special federal courts, and the highest state courts. No evidence or testimony is heard. As with other appellate courts, the lower court record is reviewed to determine whether there has been an error that warrants a reversal or modification of the decision. Legal briefs are filed, and the parties are granted a brief oral hearing. The Supreme Court's decision is final.

The federal court system is illustrated in Exhibit 2.3.

*𝓔*XHIBIT 2.3 *The Federal Court System*

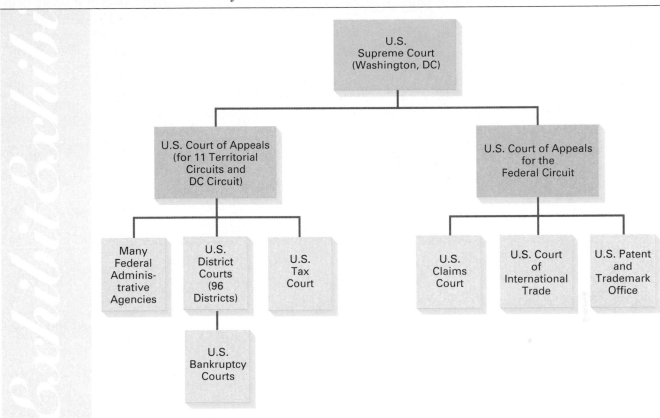

Decisions by the U.S. Supreme Court

The U.S. Constitution gives Congress the authority to establish rules for the appellate review of cases by the Supreme Court, except in the rare case where mandatory review is required. Congress has given the Supreme Court discretion to decide what cases it will hear.[2]

A petitioner must file a **petition for certiorari** asking the Supreme Court to hear the case. If the Court decides to review a case, it will issue a **writ of certiorari**. Because the Court issues only about 150 to 200 opinions each year, writs are granted only in cases involving constitutional and other important issues.

Each justice of the Supreme Court, including the chief justice, has an equal vote. The Supreme Court can issue the following types of decisions:

- **Unanimous Decision** If all of the justices voting agree as to the outcome and reasoning used to decide the case, it is a unanimous opinion. Unanimous decisions are precedent for later cases.
- **Majority Decision** If a majority of the justices agrees to the outcome and reasoning used to decide the case, it is a majority opinion. Majority decisions are precedent for later cases.
- **Plurality Decision** If a majority of the justices agrees to the outcome of the case, but not as to the reasoning for the reaching outcome, it is a plurality opinion. A plurality decision settles the case but is not precedent for later cases.
- **Tie Decision** Sometimes the Supreme Court sits without all nine justices being present. This could happen because of illness, conflict of interest, or a justice not having been confirmed to fill a vacant seat on the Court. If there is a tie vote, the lower court decision is affirmed. Such votes are not precedent for later cases.

A justice who agrees with the outcome of a case, but not the reason proffered by other justices, can issue a *concurring opinion* that sets forth his or her reasons for deciding the case. A justice who does not agree with a decision can file a *dissenting opinion* that sets forth the reasons for his or her dissent.

petition for certiorari

A petition asking the Supreme Court to hear one's case.

writ of certiorari

An official notice that the Supreme Court will review one's case.

Sancho: *But if this is hell, why do we see no lawyers?*

Clarindo: *They won't receive them, lest they bring lawsuits here.*

Sancho: *If there are no lawsuits here, hell's not so bad.*

Lope de Vega
The Star of Seville, Act 3, Scene 2

Supreme Court of the United States *The highest court in the land is the Supreme Court of the United States, located in Washington, DC. The Supreme Court's decisions are precedent for all the other courts in the country. In Bush v. Gore 531 U.S. 98 (2000) the Supreme Court decided that George W. Bush had been elected President of the United States.*

Contemporary Business Environment

I'LL TAKE YOU TO THE U.S. SUPREME COURT!—NOT!

As textbooks say, in the United States you can appeal your legal case all the way to the U.S. Supreme Court. In reality, however, the chance of ever having your case heard by the highest court is slim to none.

Each year, over 7,000 petitioners pay the $300 filing fee to ask the Supreme court to hear their case. In addition, these petitioners usually pay big law firms from $30,000 to $100,000 or more to write the appeal petition. In recent years, the Supreme Court has only accepted fewer than 100 of theses cases for full review each term.

Each of the nine Supreme Court justices has three law clerks—recent law school graduates usually chosen from the elite law schools across the country—who assist them. The justices rarely read the appellate petitions but instead delegate this task to their law clerks. The clerks then write a short memorandum discussing the key issues raised by the appeal and recommend to the justices whether they should grant or deny a review. The justices meet once a week to discuss what cases merit a review. The votes of four justices are necessary to grant an appeal and schedule an oral argument before the Court ("rule of four"). Written opinions by the justices are usually issued many months later.

So what does it take to win a review by the Supreme Court? The U.S. Supreme Court usually decides to hear cases involving major constitutional questions such as freedom of speech, freedom of religion, and due process. The Court, therefore, rarely decides day-to-day legal issues as breach of contract, tort liability, or corporations law unless it involves a more important constitutional or federal law question. Often it requires that there be a "split" in the circuit courts of appeal, that is, several circuit courts have decided the legal issue differently. The Supreme Court's ruling resolves the split among the circuit courts.

So the next time you hear someone say, "I'll take you to the U.S. Supreme Court!" just say, "Not!".

Jurisdiction of Federal and State Courts

federal question

A case arising under the U.S. Constitution, treaties, or federal statutes and regulations.

diversity of citizenship

A case between (1) citizens of different states, (2) a citizen of a state and a citizen or subject of a foreign country, and (3) a citizen of a state and a foreign country where a foreign country is the plaintiff.

Article III, Section 2, of the U.S. Constitution sets forth the jurisdiction of federal courts. Federal courts have *limited jurisdiction* to hear cases involving:

1. **Federal Questions**   Cases arising under the U.S. Constitution, treaties, and federal statutes and regulations. There is no dollar-amount limit on federal question cases that can be brought in federal court.[3]

2. **Diversity of Citizenship**   Cases between (a) citizens of different states, (b) a citizen of a state and a citizen or subject of a foreign country, and (c) a citizen of a state and foreign country where the foreign country is the plaintiff. A corporation is considered to be a citizen of the state in which it is incorporated and in which it has its principal place of business. The reason for providing diversity of citizenship jurisdiction was to prevent state court bias against nonresi-

dents. The federal court must apply the appropriate state's law in deciding the case. The dollar amount of the controversy must exceed $75,000.[4] If this requirement is not met, action must be brought in the appropriate state court.

Federal courts have **exclusive jurisdiction** to hear cases involving federal crimes, antitrust, bankruptcy, patent and copyright cases, suits against the United States, and most admiralty cases. State courts cannot hear these cases.

exclusive jurisdiction
Jurisdiction held by only one court.

State and federal courts have **concurrent jurisdiction** to hear cases involving diversity of citizenship and federal questions over which federal courts do not have exclusive jurisdiction (e.g., cases involving federal securities laws). If a case involving concurrent jurisdiction is brought by a plaintiff in state court, the defendant can remove the case to federal court. If a case does not qualify to be brought in federal court, it must be brought in the appropriate state court.

concurrent jurisdiction
Jurisdiction shared by two or more courts.

Exhibit 2.4 illustrates the jurisdiction of federal and state courts.

Ɛxhibit 2.4 *Jurisdiction of Federal and State Courts*

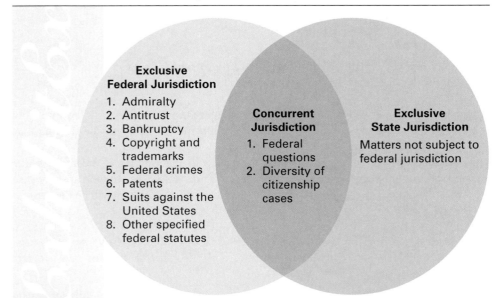

Exclusive Federal Jurisdiction
1. Admiralty
2. Antitrust
3. Bankruptcy
4. Copyright and trademarks
5. Federal crimes
6. Patents
7. Suits against the United States
8. Other specified federal statutes

Concurrent Jurisdiction
1. Federal questions
2. Diversity of citizenship cases

Exclusive State Jurisdiction
Matters not subject to federal jurisdiction

ℒandmark ℒaw

THE PROCESS OF CHOOSING A SUPREME COURT JUSTICE

In an effort to strike a balance of power between the executive and legislative branches of government, Article II, Section 2 of the U.S. Constitution give the president the power to appoint Supreme Court justices "with the advice and consent of the senate." In recent years, however, many conservative and liberal critics have charged that this process has become nothing more than a political tennis match in which the hapless nominee is the ball.

Some of the most notorious fights over Supreme Court nominations in U.S. history took place during the Reagan administration. President George Bush was given the chance to cast a conservative shadow over the Court's decisions when Justice Thurgood Marshall retired in 1991. Marshall,

who served 24 years, was one of the most liberal members of the Court. Also, he had been the only black person to serve on the Supreme Court. In 1991, Bush nominated Clarence Thomas, a black conservative serving as a judge of the U.S. court of appeals in the District of Columbia, to replace Marshall. Thomas grew up in rural Georgia and graduated from Yale Law School. After a heated political debate, Clarence Thomas was confirmed by the U.S. Senate with a 52–48 vote in October 1991.

The election of Bill Clinton as president swung the pendulum back to the Democrats. President Clinton got an early opportunity to nominate a candidate when Justice Byron R. White, a Democrat-appointed member of the Court, retired.

President Clinton nominated Judge Ruth Bader Ginsburg to serve on the Supreme Court. Justice Ginsburg was considered a moderate liberal. Ginsburg was approved by a bipartisan vote of the Senate and took office for the Supreme Court's 1993–1994 term. She is the second woman to serve on the Court, joining Sandra Day O'Connor, who was nominated by President Ronald Reagan. Ginsburg is also the first Jewish person to serve on the Court since Justice Abe Fortas resigned in 1969.

In January 2001, George W. Bush was inaugurated as the president of the United States. This was after over one month of legal battles between Mr. Bush, the Republican Party's candidate, and then Vice President Al Gore, the Democratic Party's candidate. It was only after a decision by the United States Supreme Court concerning the recounting of votes in the state of Florida that Mr. Bush was elected by the Electoral College to be president.

𝒯HE JURISDICTION OF COURTS

Not every court has the authority to hear all types of cases. First, to bring a lawsuit in a court the plaintiff must have *standing to sue*. In addition, the court must have *jurisdiction* to hear the case, and the case must be brought in the proper *venue*. These topics are discussed in the following paragraphs.

Standing to Sue

standing to sue
The plaintiff must have some stake in the outcome of the lawsuit.

To bring a lawsuit, a plaintiff must have **standing to sue**. This means that the plaintiff must have some stake in the outcome of the lawsuit.

Consider This Example   Linda's friend Jon is injured in an accident caused by Emily. Jon refuses to sue. Linda cannot sue Emily on Jon's behalf because she does not have an interest in the result of the case.

A few states now permit investors to invest money in a lawsuit for a percentage return of any award or judgment. Courts hear and decide actual disputes involving specific controversies. Hypothetical questions will not be heard and trivial lawsuits will be dismissed.

Jurisdiction

jurisdiction
The authority of a court to hear a case.

A court must have **jurisdiction** to hear and decide a case. There are two types of jurisdiction: (1) subject matter jurisdiction and (2) in personam, in rem, or quasi in rem jurisdiction.

subject matter jurisdiction
Jurisdiction over the subject matter of a lawsuit.

1. **Subject Matter Jurisdiction**   To hear and decide a case, a court must have **subject matter jurisdiction** over the subject matter of the case. Some courts have only limited jurisdiction. For example, federal courts have jurisdiction to hear only certain types of cases (discussed later in this chapter). Certain state courts, such as probate courts and small claims courts, can hear only designated types of cases. If a court does not have subject matter jurisdiction, it cannot hear the case.

in personam jurisdiction
Jurisdiction over the parties to a lawsuit.

service of process
A summons is served on the defendant to obtain personal jurisdiction over him or her.

2. **In Personam, in Rem, and Quasi in Rem Jurisdiction**   Jurisdiction over the person is called **in personam jurisdiction**, or **personal jurisdiction**. A *plaintiff*, by filing a lawsuit with a court, gives the court in personam jurisdiction over themselves. The court must also have in personam jurisdiction over the *defendant*, which is usually obtained by having that person served a summons within the territorial boundaries of the state (i.e., **service of process**). Service of process is usually accomplished by personal service of the summons and complaint on the defendant. If this is not possible, alternative forms of notice such as mailing of the summons or publication of a notice in a newspaper may be permitted. A corporation is subject to personal jurisdiction in the state in which it is incorporated, has its principal office, and is doing business. A party who disputes the jurisdiction of a court can make a *special appearance* in that court to argue against imposition of jurisdiction. Service of process is not permitted during such an appearance.

in rem jurisdiction
Jurisdiction to hear a case because of jurisdiction over the property of the lawsuit.

A court may have jurisdiction to hear and decide a case because it has jurisdiction over the property of the lawsuit. This is called **in rem jurisdiction** ("jurisdiction over the thing"). For example, a state court would have jurisdiction to hear a dispute over the ownership of a piece of real estate located within the state. This is so even if one or more of the disputing parties live in another state or states.

Sometimes a plaintiff who obtains a judgment against a defendant in one state will try to collect the judgment by attaching property of the defendant that is located in another state. This is permitted under **quasi in rem**, or **attachment jurisdiction**.[5]

Long-Arm Statutes   In most states, a state court can obtain jurisdiction over persons and businesses located in another state or country through the state's **long-arm statute**. These statutes extend a state's jurisdiction to nonresidents who were not served a summons within the state. The nonresident must have had some *minimum contact* with the state.[6] In addition, the maintenance of the suit must uphold the traditional notions of fair play and substantial justice.

The exercise of long-arm jurisdiction is generally permitted over nonresidents who have (1) committed torts within the state (e.g., caused an automobile accident in the state), (2) entered into a contract either in the state or that affects the state (and allegedly breached the contract), or (3) transacted other business in the state that allegedly caused injury to another person.

Parties to a contract may include a **forum-selection clause** that designates a certain court to hear any dispute concerning nonperformance of the contract.

quasi in rem jurisdiction

Jurisdiction allowed a plaintiff who obtains a judgment in one state to try to collect the judgment by attaching property of the defendant located in another state.

long-arm statute

A statute that extends a state's jurisdiction to nonresidents who were not served a summons within the state.

forum-selection clause

Contract provision that designates a certain court to hear any dispute concerning nonperformance of the contract.

The Supreme Court Speaks

Forum-Selection Clause in Contract Upheld

Carnival Cruise Lines, Inc. v. Shute,
499 U.S. 585, 111 S.Ct. 1522, 113 L.Ed.2d 622 (1991)
Supreme Court of the United States

BACKGROUND AND FACTS

Mr. and Mrs. Shute, residents of the State of Washington, purchased passage for a seven-day cruise on the *Tropicale* a cruise ship operated by the Carnival Cruise Lines, Inc. (Carnival). They paid the fare to the travel agent, who forwarded the payment to Carnival's headquarters in Miami, Florida. Carnival prepared the tickets and sent them to the Shutes. Each ticket consisted of five pages, including contract terms. The ticket contained a forum-selection clause that designated the state of Florida as the forum for any lawsuits arising under or in connection with the ticket and cruise. The Shutes boarded the *Tropicale* in Los Angeles, which set sail for Puerto Vallarta, Mexico. While the ship was on its return voyage and in international waters off the Mexican coast, Mrs. Shute was injured when she slipped on a deck mat during a guided tour of the ship's galley. Upon return to Washington, she filed a negligence lawsuit against Carnival in U.S. district court in Washington seeking damages. Carnival filed a motion for summary judgment contending that the lawsuit could be brought only in a court located in the state of Florida. The district court granted Carnival's motion. The court of appeals reversed, holding that Mrs. Shute could sue Carnival in Washington. Carnival appealed to the U.S. Supreme Court.

SUPREME COURT ISSUE

Is the forum-selection clause in Carnival Cruise Lines' ticket enforceable?

IN THE LANGUAGE OF THE U.S. SUPREME COURT

Blackmun, Justice As an initial matter, we do not adopt the court of appeals' determination that a nonnegotiated forum-selection clause in a form ticket contract is never enforceable simply because it is not the subject of bargaining. Including a reasonable forum clause in form contract of this kind may well be permissible for several reasons: First, a cruise line has a special interest in limiting the fora in which it potentially could be subject to suit. Because a cruise ship typically carries passengers from many locales, it is not unlikely that a mishap on a cruise could subject the cruise line to litigation in several different fora.

Additionally, a clause establishing the forum for dispute resolution has the salutary effect of dispelling any confusion where suits arising from the contract must be brought and defended, sparing litigants the time and expense of pretrial motions to determine the correct forum, and conserving judicial resources that otherwise would be devoted to deciding those motions. Finally, it stands to reason that passengers who purchase tickets containing a forum clause like that at issue in this case benefit in form of reduced fares reflecting the savings that the cruise line enjoys by limiting the fora in which it may be sued.

DECISION AND REMEDY

The forum-selection clause in Carnival's ticket is fair and reasonable and therefore enforceable against Mrs. Shute. If she wishes to sue Carnival, she must do so in a court in the state of Florida, not in a court in the State of Washington. The

U.S. Supreme Court reversed the decision of the court of appeals.

CASE QUESTIONS

Critical Legal Thinking   Should forum-selection clauses be enforced? Why or why not?

Business Ethics   Did Carnival Cruise Lines act ethically by placing the forum-selection clause in their tickets?

Contemporary Business   Do forum-selection clauses serve any legitimate business purpose? Explain.

Venue

venue

A concept that requires lawsuits to be heard by the court with jurisdiction that is nearest the location in which the incident occurred or where the parties reside.

Venue requires lawsuits to be heard by the court with jurisdiction nearest the location in which the incident occurred or where the parties reside.

Consider This Example   Harry, a Georgia resident, commits a felony crime in Los Angeles County, California. The California Superior Court located in Los Angeles is the proper venue because the crime was committed there, the witnesses are probably from the area, and so on.

Occasionally, pretrial publicity may prejudice jurors located in the proper venue. In such cases, a *change of venue* may be requested so that a more impartial jury can be found. The courts generally frown upon *forum shopping* (i.e., looking for a favorable court without a valid reason).

 *E-Commerce & Information Technology*

OBTAINING PERSONAL JURISDICTION IN CYBERSPACE

Obtaining personal jurisdiction over a defendant located in another state has always been a difficult issue for the courts located in one state to reach out and make people in another state come to court and defend themselves. To make sure this is not overly burdensome, the U. S. Supreme Court has held that out-of-state defendants must have had certain "minimum contacts" with the state before they are made to answer to a lawsuit there [*International Shoe Co. v. Washington*, 326 U.S. 310, 66 S.Ct. 154 (1945)]. Today, with the advent of the Internet and the ability of persons and businesses to reach millions of people in other states electronically, the application of the *International Shoe* minimum contacts standard is even more difficult.

Several courts have decided cases involving the reach of a state's long-arm statute to obtain jurisdiction over someone in another state because of his or her Internet activities. In one case, Zippo Manufacturing Company (Zippo) sued Zippo Dot Com, Inc. (Dot Com) in federal district court in Pennsylvania. Zippo manufactures its well known line of Zippo tobacco lighters in Bradford, Pennsylvania, and sells them worldwide. Dot Com, a California corporation with its principal place of business and its servers located in Sunnyvale, California, operates an Internet Web site that transmits information and sexually explicit material to its subscribers. Three thousand of Dot Com's 140,000 paying subscribers worldwide are located in Pennsylvania. Zippo sued Dot Com in federal district court in Pennsylvania for

trademark infringement. Dot Com alleged that it was not subject to personal jurisdiction in Pennsylvania. The district court applied the *International Shoe* "minimum contacts" standard and held that Dot Com was subject to personal jurisdiction under the Pennsylvania long-arm statute and ordered Dot Com to defend itself there. [*Zippo Manufacturing Company v. Zippo Dot Com, Inc.*, 952 F.Supp. 1119 (W.D.Pa. 1997)]

In another case, the court held that maintaining a passive Web site that merely provides advertising and other information is not sufficient to draw the Web site operator into another state's courts. The case involved Circus Circus Hotel (Circus Circus) a hotel and casino located in Las Vegas, Nevada, which maintains an Internet Web site advertising its services. Janice and Robert Decker, two New Jersey residents, brought a lawsuit against Circus Circus in federal district court in New Jersey for alleged personal injuries suffered at the Las Vegas hotel. On Circus Circus's motion, the district court dismissed the action, finding that Circus Circus's passive Web site did not subject it to personal jurisdiction in New Jersey even though its advertisements were seen by the Deckers in New Jersey. The court held that mere Internet advertising, without selling products or services over the Internet, does not meet *International Shoe's* minimum contacts standard necessary to haul a defendant into court. [*Decker v. Circus Circus Hotel*, 49 F.Supp.2d 743 (D.N.J. 1999)]

Courts will be faced with thousands of lawsuits that involve the issue of when a state's long-arm statute can reach into cyberspace and make an out-of-state Web site owner respond to a lawsuit in that state. The *International Shoe* "minimum contacts" standards is in for a whole new application.

Entrepreneur and the Law

COST-BENEFIT ANALYSIS OF A LAWSUIT

In most civil lawsuits each party is responsible for paying its own attorney's fees, whether the party wins or loses. This is called the "American rule." The court can award attorney's fees to the winning party if a statute so provides, the parties have so agreed (e.g., in a contract), or the losing party has acted maliciously or pursued a frivolous case.

An attorney in a civil lawsuit can represent the plaintiff on an hourly, project, or contingency fee basis. Hourly fees usually range from $75 to $500 per hour, depending on the type of case, the expertise of the lawyer, and the locality of the lawsuit. Under a *contingency fee arrangement*, the lawyer receives a percentage of the amount recovered for the plaintiff upon winning or settling the case. Contingency fees normally range from 20 to 50 percent of the award or settlement, with the average being about 35 percent. Lawyers for defendants in lawsuits are normally paid on an hourly basis.

The choice of whether to bring or defend a lawsuit should be analyzed like any other business decision. This includes performing a **cost-benefit analysis** of the lawsuit. For the plaintiff, it may be wise not to sue. For the defendant, it may be wise to settle. The following factors should be considered in deciding whether to bring or settle a lawsuit:

- The probability of winning or losing.
- The amount of money to be won or lost.
- Lawyers' fees and other costs of litigation.
- Loss of time by managers and other personnel.
- The long-term effects on the relationship and reputations of the parties.
- The amount of prejudgment interest provided by law.
- The aggravation and psychological costs associated with a lawsuit.
- The unpredictability of the legal system and the possibility of error.
- Other factors peculiar to the parties and lawsuit.

THE PRETRIAL LITIGATION PROCESS

The bringing, maintaining, and defense of a lawsuit are generally referred to as the **litigation process**, or **litigation**. The pretrial litigation process can be divided into the following major phases: *pleadings*, *discovery*, *dismissals and pretrial judgments*, and *settlement conference*. Each of these phases is discussed in the paragraphs that follow.

The Pleadings

The paperwork that is filed with the court to initiate and respond to a lawsuit is referred to as the **pleadings**. The major pleadings are the *complaint*, the *answer*, the *cross-complaint*, and the *reply*.

Complaint and Summons   To initiate a lawsuit, the party who is suing (**plaintiff**) must file a **complaint** with the proper court. The complaint must name the parties to the lawsuit, allege the ultimate facts and law violated, and contain a "prayer for relief" for a remedy to be awarded by the court. The complaint can be as long as necessary, depending on the case's complexity. A sample complaint appears in Exhibit 2.5.

Once a complaint has been filed with the court, the court issues a **summons**. A summons is a court order directing the defendant to appear in court and answer the complaint. The complaint and summons are served on the defendant by a sheriff, other government official, or a private process server.

litigation

The process of bringing, maintaining, and defending a lawsuit.

pleadings

The paperwork that is filed with the court to initiate and respond to a lawsuit.

plaintiff

The party who files the complaint.

complaint

The document the plaintiff files with the court and serves on the defendant to initiate a lawsuit.

summons

A court order directing the defendant to appear in court and answer the complaint.

*𝒺*XHIBIT **2.5** *A Sample Complaint*

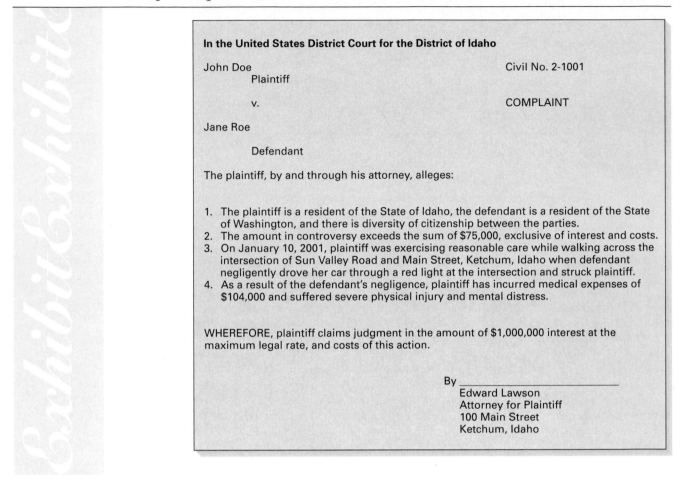

In the United States District Court for the District of Idaho

John Doe   Civil No. 2-1001
       Plaintiff

       v.   COMPLAINT

Jane Roe

       Defendant

The plaintiff, by and through his attorney, alleges:

1. The plaintiff is a resident of the State of Idaho, the defendant is a resident of the State of Washington, and there is diversity of citizenship between the parties.
2. The amount in controversy exceeds the sum of $75,000, exclusive of interest and costs.
3. On January 10, 2001, plaintiff was exercising reasonable care while walking across the intersection of Sun Valley Road and Main Street, Ketchum, Idaho when defendant negligently drove her car through a red light at the intersection and struck plaintiff.
4. As a result of the defendant's negligence, plaintiff has incurred medical expenses of $104,000 and suffered severe physical injury and mental distress.

WHEREFORE, plaintiff claims judgment in the amount of $1,000,000 interest at the maximum legal rate, and costs of this action.

By _____
       Edward Lawson
       Attorney for Plaintiff
       100 Main Street
       Ketchum, Idaho

---

answer

The defendant's written response to the plaintiff's complaint that is filed with the court and served on the plaintiff.

Business Brief

Some complaints in complicated cases exceed 100 pages.

cross-complaint

Filed by the defendant against the plaintiff to seek damages or some other remedy.

reply

Filed by the original plaintiff to answer the defendant's cross-complaint.

intervention

The act of others to join as parties to an existing lawsuit.

Answer   The defendant must file an **answer** to the plaintiff's complaint. The defendant's answer is filed with the court and served on the plaintiff. In the answer, the defendant admits or denies the allegations contained in the plaintiff's complaint. A judgment will be entered against a defendant who admits all of the allegations in the complaint. The case will proceed if the defendant denies all or some of the allegations. If the defendant does not answer the complaint, a *default judgment* is entered against him or her. A default judgment establishes the defendant's liability. The plaintiff then has only to prove damages.

In addition to answering the complaint, a defendant's answer can assert *affirmative defenses*. For example, if a complaint alleges that the plaintiff was personally injured by the defendant, the defendant's answer could state that he or she acted in self-defense. Another affirmative defense would be an assertion that the plaintiff's lawsuit is barred because the *statute of limitations* (time within which to bring the lawsuit) has expired.

Cross-Complaint and Reply   A defendant who believes that he or she has been injured by the plaintiff can file a **cross-complaint** against the plaintiff in addition to an answer. In the cross-complaint, the defendant (now the *cross-complainant*) sues the plaintiff (now the *cross-defendant*) for damages or some other remedy. The original plaintiff must file a **reply** (answer) to the cross-complaint. The reply, which can include affirmative defenses, must be filed with the court and served on the original defendant.

Intervention and Consolidation   If other persons have an interest in a lawsuit, they may **intervene** and become parties to the lawsuit. For instance, a bank that has made a secured loan on a piece of real estate can intervene in a lawsuit between parties who are litigating ownership of the property.

If several plaintiffs have filed separate lawsuits stemming from the same fact situation against the same defendant, the court can **consolidate** the cases into one case if it would not cause undue prejudice to the parties. Suppose for example, that a commercial airplane crashes, killing and injuring many people. The court could consolidate all of the lawsuits against the defendant airplane company.

consolidation

The act of a court to combine two or more separate lawsuits into one lawsuit.

E-Commerce & Information Technology

E-FILINGS IN COURT

When litigation ensues, the clients, lawyers, and judges involved in the case are usually buried in paper. These papers include pleadings, interrogatories, documents, motions to the court, briefs, and memorandums; the list goes on and on. By the time a case is over, reams of paper are stored in dozens, if not hundreds, of boxes. In addition, court appearances, no matter how small the matter, must be made in person. For example, lawyers often wait hours for a 10-minute scheduling or other conference with the judge. The time it takes to drive to and from court also has to be taken into account, which in an urban area may amount to hours.

Some forward-thinking judges and lawyers envision a day when the paperwork and hassle are reduced or eliminated in a "virtual courthouse." The technology is currently available for implementing electronic filing—**e-filing**—of pleadings, briefs, and other documents related to a lawsuit. E-filing would include using CD-ROMs for briefs, scanning evidence and documents into a computer for storage and retrieval, and e-mailing correspondence and documents to the court and the opposing counsel. Scheduling and other conferences with the judge or opposing counsel could be held via telephone conferences and e-mail.

Some courts have instituted e-filing. For example, in the Manhattan bankruptcy court, e-filing is now mandatory. Other courts around the world are doing the same. Companies such as Microsoft, West Group, and LEXIS-NEXIS have developed systems to manage e-filings of court documents.

Some court personnel are resisting the advancement of the electronic courthouse because they perceive it as a means of reducing personnel needs and court funding. Some lawyers are resisting e-filing because they have to learn how to deal with new technology and because it might reduce their billable hours when they no longer get paid for shuffling paper or sitting and waiting to appear before a judge. But eventually—albeit slowly—courts and lawyers will be brought into this new technological age.

Statute of Limitations

A **statute of limitations** establishes the period during which a plaintiff must bring a lawsuit against a defendant. If a lawsuit is not filed within this time period, the plaintiff loses his or her right to sue. A statute of limitations begins to "run" at the time the plaintiff first has the right to sue the defendant (e.g., when the accident happens, or when the breach of contract occurs).

Federal and state governments have established statutes of limitation for each type of lawsuit. Most are from one to four years, depending on the type of lawsuit. For example, a one-year statute of limitation is common for ordinary negligence actions. Thus, if on July 1, 2000, Otis negligently causes an automobile accident in which Cha-Yen is injured, Cha-Yen has until July 1, 2001, to bring a negligence lawsuit against Otis. If she waits longer than that, she loses her right to sue him.

In the following case, the court held that the statute of limitations barred the plaintiff's lawsuit.

statute of limitations

A statute that establishes the period during which a plaintiff must bring a lawsuit against a defendant.

Norgart v. the Upjohn Company

21 Cal.4th 383, 87 Cal.Rpt. 2nd 453 (1999)

Supreme Court of California

CASE 2.1

FACTS AND BACKGROUND

Kristi Norgart McBride lived with her husband in Santa Rosa, California. Kristi suffered from manic-depressive mental illness (now called bipolar disorder). In this disease, the person cycles between manic (ultrahappy, expansive, extrovert) episodes to depressive episodes. The disease is often treated with prescription drugs. In April 1984, Kristi attempted suicide. A psychiatrist prescribed an antianxiety drug. In May 1985, Kristi attempted suicide again by overdosing on drugs. The doctor prescribed Halcion, a hypnotic drug, and added Darvocet-N, a mild narcotic analgesic. On October 16, 1985, after descending into a severe depression, Kristi committed suicide by overdosing on Halcion and Darvocet-N. On October 16, 1991, exactly six years after Kristi's death, Leo and Phyllis Norgart, Kristi's parents, filed a lawsuit against the Upjohn Company, the maker of Halcion, for wrongful death based on Upjohn's alleged failure to warn of the unreasonable dangers of taking Halcion. The trial court granted Upjohn's motion for summary judgment based on the fact that the one-year statute of limitations for wrongful death actions had run out. The court of appeals reversed, and Upjohn appealed to the Supreme Court of California.

ISSUE
Is the plaintiff's action for wrongful death barred by the one-year statute of limitations?

COURT'S REASONING
The court noted that the statute of limitations is the collective term commonly applied to a great number of acts that prescribe the periods beyond which a plaintiff may not bring a cause of action. It has a purpose to protect defendants from the stale claims of dilatory plaintiffs. It has as a related purpose to stimulate plaintiffs to assert fresh claims against defendants in a diligent fashion. The court
stated that under the statute of limitations, a plaintiff must bring a cause of action from wrongful death within one year of accrual—that means that the date of accrual of a cause of action for wrongful death is the date of death. The court concluded that the Norgarts had to bring the cause of action for wrongful death within one year of accrual. The court stated, "They did not do so. Pursuant to this rule, the Norgarts were too late, exactly five years too late."

DECISION
The Supreme Court of California held that the defendant, the Upjohn Company, was entitled to judgment as a matter of law based on the fact that the one-year statute of limitations for wrongful death actions had run out, thus barring the plaintiff's lawsuit. Reversed.

Case Questions

Critical Legal Thinking   What is the public policy behind having statutes of limitations? What is the public policy against having such statutes? Which policy should dominate and why?

Business Ethics   Was it ethical for the Upjohn Company to avoid facing the merits of the lawsuit by asserting the one-year statute of limitations?

Contemporary Business   What are the business implications for having statutes of limitations?

Discovery

The legal process provides for a detailed pretrial procedure called **discovery**. During discovery, both parties engage in various activities to discover facts of the case from the other party and witnesses prior to trial. Discovery serves several functions, including preventing surprise, allowing parties to thoroughly prepare for trial, preserving evidence, saving court time, and promoting the settlement of cases. The major forms of discovery are as follows:

discovery

A legal process during which both parties engage in various activities to discover facts of the case from the other party and witnesses prior to trial.

1. **Depositions**   A **deposition** is the oral testimony given by a party or witness prior to trial. The person giving the deposition is called the **deponent**. The *parties* to the lawsuit must give their depositions, if called upon by the other party to do so. The deposition of a *witness* can be given voluntarily or pursuant to a subpoena (court order). The deponent can be required to bring documents to the deposition. Most depositions are taken at the office of one of the attorneys. The deponent is placed under oath and then asked oral questions by one or both of the attorneys. The questions and answers are recorded in written form by a court reporter. Depositions can also be videotaped. The deponent is given an opportunity to correct his or her answers prior to signing the deposition. Depositions are used to preserve evidence (e.g., if the deponent is deceased, ill, or not otherwise available at trial) and impeach testimony given by witnesses at trial.

deposition

Oral testimony given by a party or witness prior to trial. The testimony is given under oath and is transcribed.

deponent

Party who gives his or her deposition.

2. **Interrogatories**   **Interrogatories** are written questions submitted by one party to a lawsuit to another party. The questions can be very detailed. In addition, it might be necessary to attach certain documents to the answers. A party is required to answer the interrogatories in writing within a specified time period (e.g., 60 to 90 days). An attorney usually helps with the preparation of the answers. The answers are signed under oath.

interrogatories

Written questions submitted by one party to another party. The questions must be answered in writing within a stipulated time.

3. **Production of Documents**   Often, particularly in complex business cases, a substantial portion of the lawsuit may be based on information contained in documents (e.g., memoranda, correspondence, company records, and such). One party to a lawsuit may request that the other party produce all documents that are relevant to the case prior to trial. This is called **production of documents**. If the documents sought are too voluminous to be moved, are in permanent storage, or would disrupt the ongoing business of the party who is to produce them, the requesting party may be required to examine the documents at the other party's premises.

production of documents

Request by one party to another party to produce all documents relevant to the case prior to the trial.

4. **Physical and Mental Examination**   In cases that concern the physical or mental condition of a party, a court can order the party to submit to certain **physical or mental examinations** to determine the extent of the alleged injuries. This would occur, for example, where the plaintiff has been injured in an accident and is seeking damages for physical injury and mental distress.

physical or mental examination

A court may order another party to submit to a physical or mental examination prior to trial.

Business Ethics

CALENDARS ORDERED INTO THE DAYLIGHT

Most executives keep some form of calendar that contains lists of things to do, where to be, and "what I've done" notes. If a calendar contains business-related information exclusively, it is discoverable by the prosecution in a criminal case. If the calendar is personal in nature, its owner can shield it from discovery under the Fifth Amendment's self-incrimination privilege. What if an executive's calendar contains both business and personal information? Is it discoverable or not? The court had to decide this issue in the following case.

John Doe I and John Doe II are two executives of a company that is the subject of an ongoing grand jury investigation into possible illegal price fixing in a certain industry. Both executives kept calendars that contained both business and personal notes. The grand jury sought production of the calendars, but the executives refused to produce them, alleging Fifth Amendment protection. After examining the evidence, the district court determined that the calendars were corporate in nature and ordered them disclosed. The court also issued an order holding the executives in contempt for their failure to turn over their calendars. The executives appealed.

The court of appeals decided that where a calendar contains a mixture of business and personal notes, a multifactor approach should be applied to determine if they are discoverable. The court will look at ownership, preparation, access,

content, purpose, and ratio of business to personal entries in determining whether a document is corporate or personal in nature. This balancing test asks, What is the essential nature of the document? No single factor is dispositive, and the final determination whether the calendar is business or personal in nature is a question of fact.

Applying this multifactor approach to the instant case, the court found that the executives' calendars contained a majority of business-related entries. There were notes concerning business travel, job-related "to do" lists, and compensation at work. The court found that the executives' self-serving affidavits to the contrary were not credible. The court of appeals stated, "In the totality of these circumstances, the district court's conclusion that the daytimers were prepared, maintained, and used for business, not personal purposes, is not clearly erroneous." The court held that the executives' calendars were discoverable and were not protected by the Fifth Amendment's privilege against self-incrimination. [*In Re Grand Jury Proceedings*, 55 F3d. 1012 (1995)]

1. Is asserting the Fifth Amendment privilege against self-incrimination an ethical act? Explain.
2. Why do you think the executives asserted the Fifth Amendment privilege in this case?

Dismissals and Pretrial Judgments

There are several **pretrial motions** that parties to a lawsuit can make to try to dispose of all or part of a lawsuit prior to trial. The two major pretrial motions are:

1. **Motion for Judgment on the Pleadings**   A **motion for judgment on the pleadings** can be made by either party once the pleadings are complete. This motion alleges that if all of the facts presented in the pleadings are true, the party making the motion would win the lawsuit when the proper law is applied to these facts. In deciding this motion, the judge cannot consider any facts outside the pleadings.
2. **Motion for Summary Judgment**   The trier of the fact (i.e., the jury, or, if there is no jury, the judge) determines factual issues. A **motion for summary judgment** asserts that there are no factual disputes to be decided by the jury and that the judge should apply the relevant law to the undisputed facts to decide the case. Motions for summary judgment, which can be made by either party, are supported by evidence outside the pleadings. Affidavits from the parties and witnesses, documents (e.g., a written contract between the parties), depositions, and such are common forms of evidence. If, after examining the evidence, the court finds no factual dispute, it can decide the issue or issues raised in the summary judgment motion. This may dispense with the entire case or with part of the case. If the judge finds that a factual dispute exists, the motion will be denied and the case will go to trial.

Settlement Conference

Federal court rules and most state court rules permit the court to direct the attorneys or parties to appear before the court for a **pretrial hearing**, or **settlement conference**. One of the major purposes of such hearings is to facilitate the settlement of the case. Pretrial conferences are often held informally in the judge's chambers. If no settlement is reached, the pretrial hearing is used to identify the major trial issues and other relevant factors. More than 90 percent of all cases are settled before they go to trial.

pretrial motion

A motion a party can make to try to dispose of all or part of a lawsuit prior to trial.

motion for judgment on the pleadings

Motion that alleges that if all the facts presented in the pleadings are taken as true, the party making the motion would win the lawsuit when the proper law is applied to these asserted facts.

motion for summary judgment

Motion that asserts that there are no factual disputes to be decided by the jury; if so, the judge can apply the proper law to the undisputed facts and decide the case without a jury. These motions are supported by affidavits, documents, and deposition testimony.

pretrial hearing

A hearing before the trial in order to facilitate the settlement of a case. Also called a *settlement conference*.

Contemporary Business Environment

FORD EXPLORER SUV ROLLOVER LAWSUIT SETTLED FOR $22 MILLION

Approximately 90 percent of civil lawsuits are settled prior to trial. Settlements are reached when both parties believe that a trial provides too much risk of loss and the amount of the settlement is reasonable in light of that risk. Consider the settlement in the following case. On June 23, 1992, Nabil Boury was driving a 1992 Ford Explorer SUV on the Eisenhower Expressway in Chicago with five passengers in the vehicle. When another car clipped the Explorer on the driver's-side rear wheel well, the Explorer immediately rolled over. By the time it came to rest, the Explorer had rolled over three times, ejecting several of the passengers. Boury's sister and another teenager were killed, Boury's cousin lost vision in one eye, and another passenger was rendered a quadriplegic; Boury and his mother suffered minor injuries.

After the accident, the injured persons and the estates of the two deceased teenagers sued Ford Motor Company in a product liability lawsuit, alleging that there was a defect in the design of the Explorer SUV that caused it to roll over. The plaintiffs sued Michelin Tire Corporation, alleging that the Michelin tires on the SUV were inappropriate for the vehicle and that Michelin had not warned of this fact. The plaintiffs sued Packey Webb Ford, the car dealer that sold the Explorer, for putting Michelin tires on the SUV in a size and type specifically contrary to the warnings in the Ford owner's manual. The plaintiffs also sued Cassidy Tire Company, the distributor of the Michelin tires.

Several months before the case was to proceed to trial in the fall of 2001, the parties reached settlement. Ford agreed to pay $8 million, Packey Webb $10.5 million, Cassidy Tire $3 million, and Michelin Tire $500,000. The plaintiffs reached a separate agreement as to how to divide the settlement proceeds. This is just one example of the hundreds of thousands of civil lawsuits that are settled every year. [*Boury v. Ford Motor Company*, Cook County Circuit Court, Illinois (2001)]

---

trier of fact

The jury in a jury trial; the judge where there is not a jury trial.

trial briefs

Documents submitted by the parties' attorneys to the judge that contain legal support for their side of the case.

THE TRIAL

Pursuant to the Seventh Amendment to the U.S. Constitution, a party to an action at law is guaranteed the right to a *jury trial* in cases in federal court.[7] Most state constitutions contain a similar guarantee for state court actions. If either party requests a jury, the trial will be by jury. If both parties waive their right to a jury, the trial will be without a jury. The judge sits as the **trier of fact** in nonjury trials. At the time of trial, the parties usually submit **trial briefs** to the judge that contain legal support for their side of the case.

Contemporary Business Environment

PHASES OF A TRIAL

Trials are usually divided into the following phases:

1. **Jury Selection**   The pool of the potential jurors is usually selected from voter or automobile registration lists. Individuals are selected to hear specific cases through the process called **voir dire** ("to speak the truth"). Lawyers for each party and the judge can ask prospective jurors questions to determine if they would be biased in their decision. Biased jurors can be prevented from sitting on a particular case. Once the appropriate number of jurors is selected (usually 6 to 12 jurors), they are *impaneled* to hear the case and are sworn in. The trial is ready to begin. A jury can be *sequestered* (i.e., separated from family, etc.) in important cases. Jurors are paid minimum fees for the service.

2. **Opening Statements**   Each party's attorney is allowed to make an **opening statement** to the jury. In opening statements, attorneys usually summarize the main factual and legal issues of the case and describe why they believe their client's position is valid. The information given in this statement is not considered as evidence.

3. **The Plaintiff's Case**   Plaintiffs bear the **burden of proof** to persuade the trier of the fact of the merits of their case. This is called the **plaintiff's case**. The plaintiff's attorney will call witnesses to give testimony. After a witness has been sworn in, the plaintiff's attorney examines (i.e., questions) the witness. This is called *direct examination*. Documents and other evidence can be introduced through each witness. After the plaintiff's attorney has completed his or her questions, the defendant's attorney can question the witness. This is called *cross-examination*. The defendant's attorney can ask questions only about the subjects that were brought up during the direct examination. After the defendant's attorney completes his or her questions, the plaintiff's attorney can ask questions of the witness. This is called *redirect examination*. The defendant's attorney can then again ask questions of the witness. This is called *recross examination*.

4. **The Defendant's Case**   The **defendant's case** proceeds after the plaintiff has concluded his or her case. The defendant's case must (1) rebut the plaintiff's evidence, (2) prove any affirmative defenses asserted by the defendant, and (3) prove any allegations contained in the defendant's cross-complaint. The defendant's witnesses are examined in much the same way as the plaintiff's attorney cross-examines each witness. This is followed by redirect and recross examination.

5. **Rebuttal and Rejoinder**   After the defendant's attorney has completed calling witnesses, the plaintiff's attorney can call witnesses and put forth evidence to rebut the defendant's case. This is called a *rebuttal*. The defendant's attorney can call additional witnesses and introduce other evidence to counter the rebuttal. This is called the *rejoinder*.

6. **Closing Arguments**   At the conclusion of the evidence, each party's attorney is allowed to make a **closing argument** to the jury. Both attorneys try to convince the jury to render a verdict for their client by pointing out the strengths in the client's case and the weaknesses in the other side's case. Information given by the attorneys in their closing statements is not evidence.

7. **Jury Instructions**   Once the closing arguments are completed, the judge reads **jury instructions** (or **charges**) to the jury. These instructions inform the jury about what law to apply when they decide the case. For example, in a criminal trial the judge will read the jury the statutory definition of the crime charged. In an accident case, the judge will read the jury the legal definition of *negligence*.

8. **Jury Deliberation**   The jury then retires to the jury room to deliberate its findings. This can take from a few minutes to many weeks. After deliberation, the jury assesses penalties in criminal cases.

9. **Entry of Judgment**   After the jury has returned its verdict, in most cases the judge will enter **judgment** to the successful party based on the verdict. This is the official decision of the court. The court may, however, overturn the verdict if it finds bias or jury misconduct. This is called a **judgment notwithstanding the verdict** or **judgment n.o.v.** or **j.n.o.v.** In a civil case, the judge may reduce the amount of monetary damages awarded by the jury if he or she finds the jury to have been biased, emotional, or inflamed. This is called *remittitur*. The trial court usually issues a *written memorandum* setting forth the reasons for the judgment. This memorandum, together with the trial transcript and evidence introduced at trial, constitutes the permanent *record* of the trial court proceeding. In the following case, the court was asked to grant a judgment notwithstanding the verdict.

Ferlito v. Johnson & Johnson Products, Inc.

771 F.Supp. 196 (1991)
United States District Court, E.D. Michigan

CASE 2.2

FACTS AND BACKGROUND
Susan and Frank Ferlito were invited to a Halloween party. They decided to attend as Mary (Mrs. Ferlito) and her little lamb (Mr. Ferlito). Mrs. Ferlito constructed a lamb costume for her husband by gluing cotton batting manufactured by Johnson & Johnson Products, Inc. (JJP), to a suit of long underwear. She used the same cotton batting to fashion a headpiece, complete with ears. The costume covered Mr. Ferlito from his head to his ankles, except for his face and hands, which were blackened with paint. At the party, Mr. Ferlito attempted to light a cigarette with a butane lighter. The flame passed close to his left arm, and the cotton batting ignited. He suffered burns over one-third of his body. The Ferlitos sued JJP to recover damages, alleging that JJP failed to warn them of the ignitability of cotton batting. The jury returned a verdict for Mr. Ferlito in the amount of $555,000 and for Mrs. Ferlito in the amount of $70,000. JJP filed a motion for judgment notwithstanding the verdict (j.n.o.v.).

ISSUE
Should defendant JJP's motion for j.n.o.v. be granted?

COURT'S REASONING
If, after reviewing the evidence, the court is of the opinion that reasonable minds could not come to the result reached by the jury, then the motion for j.n.o.v. should be granted. At trial, both plaintiffs testified that they knew that cotton batting burns when exposed to flame. The court stated, "Because both plaintiffs were already aware of the danger, a warning by JJP would have been superfluous." Mrs. Ferlito testified that the idea for the costume was hers alone. As described on the product's package, its intended uses are for cleansing, applying medications, and infant care. The court concluded, "Plaintiffs' showing that the product may be used on occasion in classrooms for decorative purposes failed to demonstrate the forseeability of an adult male encapsulating himself from head to toe in cotton batting and then lighting up a cigarette."

DECISION
The trial court granted defendant JJP's motion for j.n.o.v. By doing so, the court vacated the verdict entered by the jury in favor of Mr. and Mrs. Ferlito.

Case Questions

Critical Legal Thinking   Should trial courts have the authority to enter a j.n.o.v., or should jury verdicts always be allowed to stand? Explain your answer.

Business Ethics   Did the Ferlitos act ethically in suing JJP in this case? Were they responsible for their own injuries?

Contemporary Business   What would have been the business implications had JJP been found liable?

THE APPEAL

appeal

The act of asking an appellate court to overturn a decision after the trial court's final judgment has been entered.

appellant

The appealing party in an appeal. Also known as *petitioner*.

appellee

The responding party in an appeal. Also known as *respondent*.

Business Brief

Trial court decisions are overturned on appeal only if there has been an error of law or the decision is not supported by the evidence.

In a civil case, either party can **appeal** the trial court's decision once a *final judgment* is entered. Only the defendant can appeal in a criminal case. The appeal is made to the appropriate appellate court. A *notice of appeal* must be filed within a prescribed time after judgment is entered (usually within 60 or 90 days). The appealing party is called the **appellant**, or **petitioner**. The responding party is called the **appellee**, or **respondent**. The appellant is often required to post a bond (e.g., one-and-one-half-times the judgment) on appeal.

The parties may designate all or relevant portions of the trial record to be submitted to the appellate court for review. The appellant's attorney may file an *opening brief* with the court that sets forth legal research and other information to support his or her contentions on appeal. The appellee can file a *responding brief* answering the appellant's contentions. Appellate courts usually permit a brief oral argument at which each party's attorney is heard.

An appellate court will reverse a lower court decision if it finds an *error of law* in the record. An error of law occurs if the jury was improperly instructed by the trial court judge, prejudicial evidence was admitted at trial when it should have been excluded, prejudicial evidence was obtained through an unconstitutional search and seizure, and the like. An appellate court will not reverse a *finding of fact* unless such finding is unsupported by the evidence or is contradicted by the evidence.

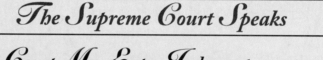

The Supreme Court Speaks

Appellate Court May Enter Judgment Against Jury-Verdict Winner

Weisgram v. Marley Company,
528 U.S. 440, 120 S.Ct. 1011 (2000)
Supreme Court of the United States

BACKGROUND AND FACTS

On December 30, 1993, Bonnie Weisgram died from carbon monoxide poisoning from a fire at her home. Her son, Chad Weisgram, brought a wrongful death tort action against Marley Company to recover damages, alleging that a defect in the electric baseboard heater manufactured by Marley had caused the fire and his mother's death. At trial, over Marley's objections, Weisgram introduced the evidence from three expert (paid-for) witnesses. The jury returned a verdict against Marley. Marley requested judgment as a matter of law, asserting that the expert testimony was unreliable and therefore inadmissible. The court of appeals agreed with Marley, finding that the expert witnesses' testimony was speculative and not scientifically sound. The court of appeals granted judgment as a matter law for Marley and refused to grant Weisgram's motion for a new trial. Weisgram appealed to the U.S. Supreme Court.

SUPREME COURT ISSUE

Can an appellate court enter judgment as a matter of law against a jury-verdict winner if it determines on appeal that evidence was erroneously admitted at trial and concludes that the other properly admitted evidence is not sufficient to constitute a submissible case?

IN THE LANGUAGE OF THE U.S. SUPREME COURT

Ginsburg, Justice Our decision is guided by Federal Rule of Civil Procedure 50, which governs the entry of judgment as a matter of law. Courts of appeals should be constantly alert to the trial judge's firsthand knowledge of witnesses, testimony, and issues; in other words, appellate courts should give due consideration to the first-instance decision maker's "feel" for the overall case. But the court of appeals has authority to render the final decision. If, in the particular case, the appellate tribunal determines that the district court is better positioned to decide whether a new trial, rather than judgment for defendant, should be ordered, the court of appeals should return the case to the trial court for such an assessment. But if, as in the instant case, the court of appeals concludes that further proceedings are unwarranted because the loser on appeal has had a full and fair opportunity to present the case, including arguments for a new trial, the appellate court may appropriately instruct the district court to enter judgment against the jury-verdict winner.

DECISION AND REMEDY

The U.S. Supreme Court held that an appellate court may enter judgment as a matter of law against a jury-verdict winner if it determines that evidence was erroneously admitted at trial and that other properly admitted evidence is not sufficient to remand the case for a new trial.

CASE QUESTIONS

Critical Legal Thinking Is the testimony of expert witnesses important at many types of trials? Give some examples.

Business Ethics Can an expert witness be found to testify for almost anyone, plaintiff or defendant, at trial? Why or why not?

Contemporary Business What implications does the Supreme Court's opinion have for business?

The Great Wall, China
The uniform application of the law will increase in China since it has joined the World Trade Organization (WTO) and opened its markets to international competition.

ALTERNATIVE DISPUTE RESOLUTION

The use of the court system to resolve business and other disputes can take years and cost thousands, if not millions, of dollars in legal fees and expenses. In commercial litigation, the normal business operations of the parties are often disrupted. To avoid or lessen these problems, businesses are increasingly turning to methods of **alternative dispute resolution (ADR)** and other aids to resolving disputes. The most common form of ADR is *arbitration*. Other forms of ADR are *mediation, conciliation, minitrial, fact-finding*, and a *judicial referee*.

alternative dispute resolution (ADR)

Methods of resolving disputes other than litigation.

Arbitration

In **arbitration**, the parties choose an impartial third party to hear and decide the dispute. This neutral party is called the *arbitrator*. Arbitrators are usually selected from members of the American Arbitration Association (AAA) or another arbitration association. Labor union agreements, franchise agreements, leases, and other commercial contracts often contain **arbitration clauses** that require disputes arising out of the contract to be submitted to arbitration. If there is no arbitration clause, the parties can enter into a *submission agreement* whereby they agree to submit a dispute to arbitration after the dispute arises.

Evidence and testimony are presented to the arbitrator at a hearing held for this purpose. Less formal evidentiary rules are usually applied in arbitration hearings than at court. After the hearing, the arbitrator reaches a decision and enters an *award*. The parties often agree in advance to be bound by the arbitrator's decision and award. If the parties have not so agreed, the arbitrator's award can be appealed to court. The court gives great deference to the arbitrator's decision.

Congress enacted the **Federal Arbitration Act** to promote the arbitration of disputes.[8] About half of the states have adopted the **Uniform Arbitration Act**. This act promotes the arbitration of disputes at the state level. Many federal and state courts have instituted programs to refer legal disputes to arbitration or another form of alternative dispute resolution.

arbitration

A form of ADR in which the parties choose an impartial third party to hear and decide the dispute.

arbitration clause

A clause in contracts that requires disputes arising out of the contract to be submitted to arbitration.

Business Brief

Litigation is expensive and time-consuming. Businesses should consider ADR to solve their disputes.

Landmark Law

THE FEDERAL ARBITRATION ACT

The **Federal Arbitration Act (FAA)** was originally enacted in 1925 to reverse the long-standing judicial hostility to arbitration agreements that had existed as English common law and had been adopted by American courts. The act provides that arbitration agreements involving commerce are valid, irrevocable, and enforceable contracts, unless some grounds exist at law or equity (e.g., fraud, duress) to revoke them. The FAA permits one party to obtain a court order to compel arbitration if the other party has failed, neglected, or refused to comply with an arbitration agreement.

Since the FAA's enactment, the courts have wrestled with the problem of which types of disputes should be arbitrated. Breach of contract cases, tort claims, and such are clearly candidates for arbitration if there is a valid arbitration agreement. In addition, the U.S. Supreme Court has enforced arbitration agreements that call for the resolution of disputes arising under federal statutes. For example, in *Shearson/American Express, Inc. v. McMahon,* 482 U.S. 220 (1987), and *Rodriquez de Quijas v. Shearson/American Express, Inc.,* 490 U.S. 4777 (1990), the Court held that certain civil claims arising under federal securities laws and the Racketeer Influenced and Corrupt Organizations Act (RICO) were arbitrative. In these cases, the Court enforced arbitration

clauses contained in customer agreements with the securities firm.

In another case, *Gilmer v. Interstate/Johnson Lane Corporation,* Ill. S.Ct. 1647 (1991), the Supreme Court upheld an arbitration clause in an employment contract. In that case, a 62-year-old employee who was dismissed from his job sued his employer for alleged age discrimination in violation of the federal Age Discrimination in Employment Act (ADEA). The employer countered with a motion to compel arbitration. The Supreme Court upheld the motion and stated, "By agreeing to arbitrate a statutory claim, a party does not forgo the substantive rights afforded by the statute, it only submits to their resolution in an arbitral, rather than a judicial, forum."

The Court did not find any reason to revoke the contract. There was no indication that the employee was coerced or defrauded into agreeing to the arbitration clause at issue in the case.

Because the Supreme Court has placed its imprimatur on the use of arbitration to solve employment disputes, it is likely that such clauses will appear in more employment contracts. Critics contend that this gives the advantage to employers. Employers argue that arbitration is the only way to combat skyrocketing jury verdicts.

The Supreme Court Speaks

Arbitration Clause in Employment Contract Is Enforceable

Circuit City Stores, Inc. v. Adams,
121 S.Ct. 1302 (2001)
Supreme Court of the United States

BACKGROUND AND FACTS
In October 1995, Saint Clair Adams was hired as a sales counselor by Circuit City Stores, Inc., a national retailer of consumer electronics. Adams signed an employment contract that included the following arbitration clause:

I agree that I will settle any and all previously unasserted claims, disputes or controversies arising out of or relating to my application or candidacy for employment, employment and/or cessation of employment with Circuit City, exclusively by final and binding arbitration before a neutral Arbitrator. By way of example only, such claims include claims under federal, state, and local statutory or com-

mon law, such as the Age Discrimination in Employment Act, Title VII of the Civil Rights Act of 1964, the Americans with Disabilities Act, the law of contract and the law of tort.

Two years later Adams filed an employment discrimination lawsuit against Circuit City in court. Circuit City sought to enjoin the court proceeding and to compel arbitration, pursuant to the Federal Arbitration Act (FAA). The district court granted Circuit City's request. The court of appeals reversed, holding that employment contracts are not subject to arbitration. The U.S. Supreme Court granted certiorari to hear the appeal.

SUPREME COURT ISSUE
Are employment contracts, other than those of exempted transportation workers, subject to arbitration if a valid arbitration agreement has been entered into between the parties?

IN THE LANGUAGE OF THE U.S. SUPREME COURT
Kennedy, Justice Congress enacted the FAA in 1925. As the Court has explained, the FAA was a response to hostility of American courts to the enforcement of arbitration agreements, a judicial disposition inherited from then-long-standing English practice. To give effect to this purpose, the FAA compels judicial enforcement of a wide range of written arbitration agreements. The FAA's coverage provision, Section 2, provides that "a written provision in any contract evidencing a transaction involving commerce to settle by arbitration a controversy thereafter arising out of such contract or transaction, or the refusal to perform the whole or any part thereof, shall be valid, irrevocable, and enforceable, save upon such grounds as exist at law or in equity for the revocation of any contract."

The instant case, of course, involves not the basic coverage authorization under Section 2 of the Act, but the exemption from coverage under Section 1. The exemption clause provides the Act shall not apply "to contracts of employment of seamen, railroad employees, or any other class of workers engaged in foreign or interstate commerce. In sum, the text of the FAA forecloses the construction of Section 1 followed by the Court of Appeals in the case under review, a construction which would exclude all employment contracts from the FAA. The text of Section 1 precludes interpreting the exclusion provision to defeat the language of Section 2 as to all employment contracts. Section 1 exempts from the FAA only contracts of employment of transportation workers.

DECISION AND REMEDY
The U.S. Supreme Court held that the exemption of Section 1 of the Federal Arbitration Act only exempts employment contracts of transportation workers from arbitration. All other employment contracts, including the one in this case between Circuit City and Adams, are subject to arbitration if a valid arbitration agreement has been executed. Reversed and remanded.

CASE QUESTIONS
Critical Legal Thinking How do you think transportation workers became exempted from arbitration under the Federal Arbitration Act?

Business Ethics Is it ethical for employers to include arbitration clauses in employment contracts?

Contemporary Business Who do you think benefits most from arbitration clauses in employment contracts, employers or employees? Why?

Mediation and Conciliation
In **mediation**, the parties choose a neutral third party to act as the *mediator* of the dispute. Unlike an arbitrator, a mediator does not make a decision or award. Instead, the mediator acts as a conveyor of information between the parties and assists them in trying to reach a settlement of the dispute. A mediator often meets separately with each of the parties. A settlement agreement is reached if the mediator is successful. If not, the case proceeds to trial. In a **conciliation**, the parties choose an interested third party, the *conciliator*, to act as the mediator.

mediation
A form of ADR in which the parties choose a *neutral* third party to act as the mediator of the dispute.

conciliation
A form of mediation in which the parties choose an *interested* third party to act as the mediator.

Minitrial
A *minitrial* is a session, usually lasting a day or less, in which the lawyers for each side present their cases to representatives of each party who have authority to settle the dispute. In many cases, the parties hire a neutral person (e.g., a retired judge) to preside over the minitrial. Following the presentations, the parties meet to try to negotiate a settlement.

A lawyer without history or literature is a mechanic, a mere working mason: if he possesses some knowledge of these, he may venture to call himself an architect.
Sir Walter Scott
Guy Mannering, Ch. 37 (1815)

Fact-Finding
Fact-finding is a process whereby the parties hire a neutral person to investigate the dispute. The *fact-finder* reports his or her findings to the adversaries and may recommend a basis for settlement.

Judicial Referee
If the parties agree, the court may appoint a *judicial referee* to conduct a private trial and render a judgment. Referees, who are often retired judges, have most of the powers of a trial judge, and their decisions stand as a judgment of the court. The parties usually reserve their right to appeal.

International Law

COMPARISON OF THE JAPANESE AND AMERICAN LEGAL SYSTEMS

Businesses often complain that there are too many lawyers and too much litigation in the United States. There are currently more than 900,000 lawyers and over 20 million lawsuits per year in this country. On the other hand, in Japan, a country with about half the population, there are only 20,000 lawyers and little litigation. Why the difference?

Much of the difference is cultural: Japan nurtures the attitude that confrontation should be avoided. Litigious persons in Japan are looked down upon. Thus, companies rarely do battle in court. Instead, they opt for private arbitration of most of their disputes. Other differences are built into the legal system itself. For example, there is only one place to go to become a *bengoshi,* or lawyer, in Japan–the government-operated National Institute for Legal Training. Only 2 percent of 35,000 applicants are accepted annually, and only 400 new *bengoshi* are admitted to Japan's exclusive legal club per year.

There are other obstacles, too. For example, no class actions or contingency fee arrangements are allowed.

Plaintiffs must pay their lawyers a front fee of up to 8 percent of the damages sought, plus a nonrefundable filing fee to the court of one-half of 1 percent of the damages. To make matters even more difficult, no discovery is permitted. Thus, plaintiffs are denied access before trial to an opponent's potential evidence, and even if the plaintiff wins the lawsuit, damage awards are low.

Some experts argue that Japan has more legal practitioners than statistics revel. For example, there are approximately 5,000 non*bengoshi* patent specialists who perform services similar to U.S. patent attorneys. Another 50,000 licensed tax practitioners offer services similar to U.S. tax attorneys. Many non*bengoshi* legal experts handle tasks such as contract negotiation and drafting. In addition, sales personnel and front-line managers often act as problem solvers.

The Japanese bias against courtroom solutions remains strong. The current system is designed to save time and money and to preserve long-term relationships.

CHAPTER SUMMARY

The State Court Systems, p. 25

State Court Systems	1. *Limited-jurisdiction trial court.* State courts that hear matters of a specialized or limited nature (e.g., misdemeanor criminal matters, traffic tickets, civil matters under a certain dollar amount). Many states have created small claims courts that hear small-dollar-amount civil cases (e.g., under $3,000) where the parties cannot be represented by lawyers.
	2. *General-jurisdiction trial court.* State courts that hear cases of a general nature that are not within the jurisdiction of limited-jurisdiction trial courts.
	3. *Intermediate appellate court.* State courts that hear appeals from state trial courts. The appellate court reviews the trial court record in making its decision: No new evidence is introduced at this level.
	4. *Highest state court.* Each state has a highest court in its court system. This court hears appeals from appellate courts, and where appropriate, trial courts. This court reviews the record in making its decision: No new evidence is introduced at this level. Most states call this court the supreme court.

The Federal Court System, p. 27

Federal Court System	1. *Special federal courts.* Federal courts that have specialized or limited jurisdiction. They include:
	a. *U.S. tax court.* Hears cases involving federal tax laws.
	b. *U.S. claims court.* Hears cases brought against the United States.
	c. *U.S. Court of International Trade.* Hears cases involving tariffs and international commercial disputes.
	d. *U.S. bankruptcy courts.* Hear cases involving federal bankruptcy law.
	2. *U.S. districts courts.* Federal trial courts of general jurisdiction that hear cases not within the jurisdiction of specialized courts. There is at least one U.S. district court per state: More populated states have several district courts. The area served by one of these courts is called a *district.*
	3. *U.S. courts of appeals.* Intermediate federal appellate courts that hear appeals from district courts located in their circuit, and in certain instances from special federal courts and federal administrative agencies. There are 12 geographical circuits in this country. Eleven serve areas that are comprised of several states, while another is located in Washington, DC. A thirteenth circuit court—the *Court of Appeals for the Federal Circuit*—is located in Washington, DC., and reviews patent, trademark, and international trade cases.

4. *U.S. Supreme Court.* Highest court of the federal court system. It hears appeals from the circuit courts and, in some instances, from special courts and U.S. district courts. The Court, which is located in Washington, DC, is composed of nine justices, one of whom is named chief justice.
5. *Decisions by the U.S. Supreme Court.*
   a. *Writ or certiorari.* To have a case heard by the U.S. Supreme Court, a petitioner must file a *petition for certiorari* with the Court. If the Court decides to hear the case, it will issue a *writ of certiorari.*
   b. Voting by the U.S. Supreme Court:
      i. *Unanimous decision.* All of the justices agree as to the outcome and reasoning used to decide the case. The decision becomes precedent.
      ii. *Majority decision.* A majority of the justices agrees as to the outcome and reasoning used to decide the case. The decision becomes precedent.
      iii. *Plurality decision.* A majority of the justices agrees to the outcome but not the reasoning. The decision is not precedent.
      iv. *Tie decision.* If there is a tie vote, the lower court's decision stands. The decision is not precedent.
      v. *Concurring opinion.* A justice who agrees as to the outcome of the case but not the reasoning used by other justices may write a concurring opinion setting forth his or her reasoning.
      vi. *Dissenting opinion.* A justice who disagrees with the outcome of a case may write a dissenting opinion setting forth his or her reasoning for dissenting.

Jurisdication of Federal and State Courts

1. *Jurisdiction of federal courts.* Federal courts may hear the following cases:
   a. *Federal question.* Cases arising under the U.S. Constitution, treaties, and federal statutes and regulations. There is no dollar-amount limit in federal question cases.
   b. *Diversity of citizenship.* Cases between (i) citizens of different states and (ii) citizens of a state and a citizen or subject of a foreign country. Federal courts must apply the appropriate state law in such cases. The controversy must exceed $50,000 for the federal court to hear the case.
2. *Jurisdiction of state courts.* State courts hear some cases that may be heard by federal courts.
   a. *Exclusive jurisdiction.* Federal courts have exclusive jurisdiction to hear cases involving federal crimes, antitrust and bankruptcy, patent and copyright cases, suits against the United States, and most admiralty cases. State courts may not hear these matters.
   b. *Concurrent jurisdiction.* State courts have concurrent jurisdiction to hear cases involving diversity of citizenship cases and federal question cases over which the federal courts do not have exclusive jurisdiction. The defendant may have the case removed to federal court.

The Jurisdiction of Courts, p. 32

Standing to Sue, Jurisdiction and Venue

1. *Standing to sue.* To bring a lawsuit, the plaintiff must have some stake in the outcome of the lawsuit.
2. *Subject matter jurisdiction.* The court must have jurisdiction over the subject matter of the lawsuit. Each court has limited jurisdiction to hear only certain types of cases.
3. *In personam jurisdiction* (or *personal jurisdiction*). The court must have jurisdiction over the parties to a lawsuit. The plaintiff submits to the jurisdiction of the court by filing the lawsuit there. Personal jurisdiction is obtained over the defendant by serving that person *service of process.*
4. *In rem jurisdiction.* A court may have jurisdiction to hear and decide a case because it has jurisdiction over the property at issue in the lawsuit (e.g., real property located in the state).
5. *Quasi in rem jurisdiction* (or *attachment jurisdiction*) A plaintiff who obtains a judgment against a defendant in one state may utilize the court system of another state to attach property of the defendant's located in the second state.
6. *Long-arm statutes.* Permit a state to obtain personal jurisdiction over an out-of-state defendant as long as the defendant had the requisite minimum contact with the state. The out-of-state defendant may be served process outside the state in which the lawsuit has been brought.
7. *Venue.* A case must be heard by the court that has jurisdiction nearest to where the incident at issue occurred or where the parties reside. A *change of venue* will be granted if prejudice would occur because of pretrial publicity or another reason.
8. *Forum-selection clause.* A clause in a contract that designates the court that will hear any dispute that arises out of the contract.

The Pretrial Litigation Process, p. 35

Pleadings

Paperwork that initiates and responds to a lawsuit. Pleadings include:
1. *Complaint.* Filed by the plaintiff with the court and served with a *summons* on the defendant. It sets forth the basis of the lawsuit.
2. *Answer.* Filed by the defendant with the court and served on the plaintiff. It usually denies most allegations of the complaint.

	3. *Cross-complaint.* Filed and served by the defendant if he or she countersues the plaintiff. The defendant is the *cross-complainant* and the plaintiff is the *cross-defendant.* The cross-defendant must file and serve a *reply* (answer).
	4. *Intervention.* A person who has an interest in a lawsuit may intervene and become a party to the lawsuit.
	5. *Consolidation.* Separate cases against the same defendant arising from the same incident may be consolidated by the court into one case if it would not cause prejudice to the parties.
Discovery	The pretrial litigation process for discovering facts of the case from the other party and witnesses. Discovery consists of:
	1. *Depositions.* Oral testimony given by a *deponent,* either a party or witness. Depositions are transcribed.
	2. *Interrogatories.* Written questions submitted by one party to the other party. They must be answered within a specified period of time.
	3. *Production of documents.* A party to a lawsuit may obtain copies of all relevant documents from the other party.
	4. *Physical and mental examination.* These examinations of a party are permitted upon order of the court where injuries are alleged that could be verified or disputed by such examination.
Dismissals and Pretrial Judgments	1. *Motion for summary judgment on the pleadings.* Alleges that if all facts as pleaded are true, the moving party would win the lawsuit. No facts outside the pleadings may be considered.
	2. *Motion for summary judgment.* Alleges that there are no factual disputes, so the judge may apply the law and decide the case without a jury. Evidence outside the pleadings may be considered (e.g., affidavits, documents, depositions).
Settlement Conference	Conference prior to trial between the parties in front of the judge to facilitate the settlement of the case. Also called *pretrial hearing.* If a settlement is not reached, the case proceeds to trial.

The Trial, p. 40

Phases of a Trial	1. *Jury selection.* Done through a process called *voir dire.* Biased jurors are dismissed and replaced.
	2. *Opening statements.* Made by the parties' lawyers. Are not evidence.
	3. *The plaintiff's case.* The plaintiff bears the burden of proof. The plaintiff calls witnesses and introduces evidence to try to prove his or her case.
	4. *The defendant's case.* The defendant calls witnesses and introduces evidence to rebut the plaintiff's case and to prove affirmative defenses and cross-complaints.
	5. *Rebuttal and rejoinder.* The plaintiff and defendant may call additional witnesses and introduce additional evidence.
	6. *Closing arguments.* Made by the parties' lawyers. Are not evidence.
	7. *Jury instructions.* Judge reads instructions to the jury as to what law they are to apply to the case.
	8. *Jury deliberation.* Jury retires to the jury room and deliberates until it reaches a *verdict.*
	9. *Entry of judgment.* The judge may:
	a. Enter the verdict reached by the jury as the court's *judgment.*
	b. Grant a motion for *judgment n.o.v.* if the judge finds the jury was biased. This means that the jury's verdict does not stand.
	c. Order *remittitur* (reduction) of any damages awarded if the judge finds the jury to have been biased or emotional.

The Appeal p. 42

Appeal	Both parties in a civil suit and the defendant in a criminal trial may appeal the decision of the trial court. *Notice of appeal* must be filed within a specified period of time. The appeal must be made to the appropriate appellate court.

Alternative Dispute Resolution p. 43

Alternative Dispute Resolution (ADR)	*Nonjudicial* means of solving legal disputes. ADR usually saves time and money of costly litigation.

Types of ADR

1. *Arbitration.* An impartial third party, called the arbitrator, hears and decides the dispute. The arbitrator makes an award. The award is appealable to a court if the parties have not given up this right. Arbitration is designated by the parties pursuant to:
   a. *Arbitration clause.* Agreement contained in a contract stipulating that any dispute arising out of the contract will be arbitrated.
   b. *Submission agreement.* Agreement to submit a dispute to arbitration after the dispute arises.
2. *Mediation.* A neutral third party, called a *mediator*, assists the parties in trying to reach a settlement of their dispute. The mediator does not make an award.
3. *Conciliation.* An interested third party, called a *conciliator*, assists the parties in trying to reach a settlement of their dispute. The conciliator does not make an award.
4. *Minitrial.* A short session in which the lawyers for each side present their cases to representatives of each party who have the authority to settle the dispute.
5. *Fact-finding.* the parties hire a neutral third person, called a *fact-finder*, to investigate the dispute and report his or her findings to the adversaries.
6. *Judicial referee.* With consent of the parties, the court appoints a judicial referee (usually a retired judge or lawyer) to conduct a private trial and render a judgment. The judgment stands as the judgment of the court and may be appealed to the appropriate appellate court.

End-of-Chapter Internet Exercises and Case Questions

Working the Web Internet Exercises

ACTIVITIES

1. Go to **www.adr.org/rules/ethics/code.html** and study the rules of the ethics for arbitrators. How do they compare with rules of professional conduct for attorneys?

2. At the International Chamber of Commerce Web site **www.iccwbo.org/court/english/news_archives/2001/adr.asp** you will find information about rules and procedures for settlement of international commercial disputes. Under what circumstances would you advise a client to elect ICC arbitration rules as compared to AAA rules?

3. Go to the U.S. Supreme Court site **www.supremecourtus.gov**. Find a case from your state that recently has been appealed to the Court. Outline the procedural steps involved in the process.

4. **Guide.lp.findlaw.com/10fedgov/judicial/appeals_courts.html** contains links to each of the federal judicial circuits. Find your own jurisdiction and review the cases available there. What is the oldest case you can find? The most recent? Compare your search results with the same two questions looking at state court cases available in your state.

CRITICAL LEGAL THINKING CASES

2.1 Federal Questions   Nutrilab, Inc., manufactures and markets a product known as "Starch Blockers." The purpose of the product is to block the human body's digestion of starch as an aid in controlling weight. On July 1, 1982, the U.S. FDA classified Starch Blockers as a drug and requested that they be removed from the market until the FDA approved of their use. The FDA claimed that it had the right to classify new products as drugs and prevent their distribution until their safety is determined. Nutrilab disputes the FDA's decision and wants to bring suit to halt the FDA's actions. Do the federal courts have jurisdiction to hear this case? [*Nutrilab, Inc. v. Schweiker*, 713 F.2d 335 (7th Cir. 1983)]

2.2 Diversity of Citizenship   James Clayton Allison, a resident of the state of Mississippi, was employed by the Tru-Amp Corporation as a circuit-breaker tester. As part of his employment, Allison was sent to inspect, clean, and test a switch gear located at the South Central Bell Telephone Facility in Brentwood, Tennessee. One August 26, 1988, he attempted to remove a circuit breaker manufactured by ITE Corporation (ITE) from a bank of breakers, when a portion of the breaker fell off. The broken piece fell behind a switching bank and, according to Allison, caused an electrical fire and explosion. Allison was severely burned in the accident. Allison brought suit against ITE in a Mississippi state court, claiming more than $50,000 in damages. Can this suit be removed to federal court? [*Allison v. ITE Imperial Corp.*, 729 F. Supp. 45 (S.D. Miss. 1990)]

2.3 In Personam Jurisdiction Saul and Elaine Mozuck borrowed money from the Peoples Trust Company of Bergen County and cosigned a promissory note promising to repay the money. When Peoples Trust contacted the Mozucks about payment, they denied liability on the ground that the bank improperly filled in the due date on the note. Peoples Trust filed suit against the Mozucks in a New Jersey state court. A process server went to the Mozucks' home in New Jersey to serve the summons. The process server rang the bell at the home, and a woman appeared at an upstairs window. The process server asked her if she was Mrs. Mozuck, and the woman replied in the affirmative. When the process server identified himself, the woman denied that she was Mrs. Mozuck and refused to come out to the house. The process server told the woman that he would leave the papers in the mailbox if she refused to open the door. When the woman did not reappear, the process server placed the summons in the mailbox and left. Is the service of process good? [*Peoples Trust Co. v. Mozuck*, 236 A.2d. 630 (N.J.Super. 1967)]

2.4 Long-Arm Statute Sean O'Grady, a professional boxer, was managed by this father, Pat. Sean was a contender for the world featherweight title. On January 30, 1978, Pat entered into a contract with Magna Verde Corporation, a Los Angeles–based business, to copromote a fight between Sean and the current featherweight champion. The fight was scheduled to take place on February 5, 1978, in Oklahoma City, Oklahoma. To promote the fight Pat O'Grady scheduled a press conference for January 30, 1978. At the conference, Pat was involved in a confrontation with a sportswriter named Brooks. He allegedly struck Brooks in the face. Brooks brought suit against Pat O'Grady and Magna Verde Corporation in an Oklahoma state court. Court records showed that the only contact Magna Verde had had with Oklahoma was that a few of its employees had taken several trips to Oklahoma in January 1978 to plan the title fight. The fight was never held. Oklahoma has a long-arm statute. Magna Verde was served by mail and made a special appearance in Oklahoma state court to argue that Oklahoma does not have jurisdiction over it. Does Oklahoma have jurisdiction over Magna Verde Corporation? [*Brooks v. Magna Verde Corp.*, 619 P.2d 1271 (Okla.App. 1980)]

2.5 Minimum Contacts The National Enquirer, Inc., is a Florida corporation with its principal place of business in Florida. It publishes the *National Enquirer*, a national weekly newspaper with a total circulation of more than 5 million copies. About 600,000 copies, almost twice the level of the next highest state, are sold in California. On October 9, 1979, the *Enquirer* published an article about Shirley Jones, an entertainer. Jones, a California resident, filed a lawsuit in California state court against the *Enquirer* and its president, who was a resident of Florida. The suit sought damages for alleged defamation, invasion of privacy, and intentional infliction of emotional distress. Are the defendants subject to suit in California? [*Calder v. Jones*, 465 U.S. 783, 104 S.Ct. 1482, 79 L.Ed.2d 804 (1984)]

2.6 Service of Process On May 9, 1983, attorneys for Ronald Schiavone filed a lawsuit against *Fortune* magazine in U.S. district court in New Jersey. The complaint claimed that *Fortune* had defamed Schiavone in a cover story entitled "The Charges Against Reagan's Labor Secretary," which appeared in the May 31, 1982, issue of the magazine. The complaint named *Fortune* as the defendant. *Fortune*, however, is only a trademark owned by Time, Incorporated, a New York corporation. Time, Incorporated, refused to accept service of the complaint because it had not been named as a defendant. Has there been proper service of process? [*Schiavone v. Fortune*, 477 U.S. 21, 106 S.Ct. 2379, 91 L.Ed.2d 18 (1986)]

2.7 Summary Judgment Captain Conrad was a pilot for Delta Airlines. In 1970, Conrad was forced to resign by the airline. He sued, alleging that he was discharged due to his prounion activities and not because of poor job performance, as claimed by Delta. During discovery, a report written by a Delta flight operations manager was produced that stated: "More than a few crew members claimed that Conrad professed to being a leftist-activist. His overactivity with the local pilots' union, coupled with inquiries regarding company files to our secretary, lead to the conclusion that potential trouble will be avoided by acceptance of his resignation." Conrad claims that the report is evidence of the antiunion motivation for his discharge. Delta made a summary judgment motion to the trial court. Should its summary judgment motion be granted? [*Conrad v. Delta Airlines, Inc.*, 494 F.2d. 914 (7th Cir. 1974)]

2.8 Physical Examination Robert Schlagenhauf worked as a bus driver for the Greyhound Corporation. One night the bus he was driving rear-ended a tractor-trailer. Seven passengers on the bus who were injured sued Schlagenhauf and Greyhound for damages. The complaint alleged that Greyhound was negligent for allowing Schlagenhauf to drive a bus when it knew that his eyes and vision "were impaired and deficient." The plaintiffs petitioned the court to order Schlagenhauf to be medically examined concerning these allegations. Schlagenhauf objected to the examination. Who wins? [*Schlagenhauf v. Holder*, 379 U.S. 104,85 S.Ct. 234, 13 L.Ed.2d 152 (1964)]

2.9 Deposition Haviland & Company filed suit against Montgomery Ward & Company in U.S. district court claiming that Ward used the trademark "Haviland" on millions of dollars worth of merchandise. As the owner of the mark, Haviland & Company sought compensation from Ward. Ward served notice to take the deposition of Haviland & Company's president, William D. Haviland. The attorneys for Haviland told the court that Haviland was 80 years old, lived in Limoses, France, and was too ill to travel to the United States for the deposition. Haviland's physician submitted an affidavit confirming these facts. Must Haviland give his deposition? [*Haviland & Co. v. Montgomery Ward & Co.*, 31 F.R.D. 578 (S.D.N.Y. 1962)]

2.10 Interrogatories Cine Forty-Second Street Theatre Corporation operates a movie theater in New York City's Times Square area. Cine filed a lawsuit against Allied Artists Pictures Corporation alleging that Allied Artists and local theater owners illegally attempted to prevent Cine from opening its theater in violation of federal antitrust law. The suit also alleged that once Cine opened the theater, the defendants conspired with motion picture distributors to prevent cine from exhibiting first-run, quality films. Attorneys for Allied Artists served a set of written questions concerning the lawsuit on Cine. Does Cine have to answer these questions? [*Cine Forty-Second Street Theatre Corp. v. Allied Artists Pictures Corp.*, 602 F.2d 1062 (2d Cir. 1979)]

2.11 Judgment N.O.V. On November 9, 1965, Mr. Simblest was driving a car that collided with a fire engine at an intersection in Burlington, Vermont. The accident occurred on the night on which a power blackout left most of the state without lights. Mr. Simblest, who was injured in the accident, sued the driver of the fire truck for damages. During the trial, Simblest testified that when he entered the intersection, the traffic light was green in his favor. All of the other witnesses testified that the traffic light had gone dark at least 10 minutes before the accident. Simblest testified that the accident was caused by the fire truck's failure to use any warning lights or sirens. Simblest's testimony was contradicted by four witnesses who testified that the fire truck had used both its lights and sirens. The jury found that the driver of the fire truck had been negligent and rendered a verdict for Simblest. The defense made a motion for judgment n.o.v. Who wins? [*Simblest v. Maynard*, 427 F.2d 1 (2d Cir. 1970)]

2.12 Arbitration AMF Incorporated and Brunswick Corporation both manufacture electric and automatic bowling center equipment. In 1983 the two companies became involved in a dispute over whether Brunswick had advertised certain automatic scoring devices in a false and deceptive manner. The two parties settled the dispute by signing an agreement that any future problems between them involving advertising claims would be submitted to the National Advertising Council for arbitration. In March 1985, Brunswick advertised a new product, Armor Plate 3000, a synthetic laminated material used to make bowling lanes. Armor Plate 3000 competed with wooden lanes produced by AMF. Brunswick's advertisements claimed that bowling centers could save up to $500 per lane per year in maintenance and repair costs if they switched from wooden lanes to Armor Plate 3000. AMF disputed this claim and requested arbitration. Is the arbitration agreement enforceable? [*AMF Incorporated v. Brunswick Corp.*, 621 F.Supp. 456 (E.D.N.Y. 1985)]

2.13 Delegation Doctrine The Federal Communications Commission (FCC) is a federal administrative agency that is empowered to enforce the federal Communication Act of 1934. This act, as amended, gives the FCC power to regulate broadcasting on radio and television. In *United States v. Midwest Video Corporation*, 406 U.S. 649 (1972), the U.S. Supreme Court held that the FCC also has the power to regulate cable television operators that have 3,500 or more subscribers to (1) develop a 20-channel capacity; (2) make four channels available for use by public, educational, local, government, and leased-access users; (3) make equipment available for those utilizing these public-access users; and (4) limit the fees cable operators could charge for their services. Do these rules exceed the statutory authority of the FCC? [*Federal Communications Commission v. Midwest Video Corporation*, 440 U.S. 689, 99 S.Ct. 1435, 59 L.Ed.2d 692 (1979)]

BUSINESS ETHICS CASES

2.14 Business Ethics One day Joshua Gnaizda, a three-year-old, received what he (or his mother) thought was a tantalizing offer in the mail from Time, Inc. The front of the envelope contained a see-through window that revealed the following statement: "Joshua Gnaizda, I'll give you this versatile new calculator watch free just for opening the envelope before Feb. 15, 1985." Beneath the offer was a picture of the calculator watch itself. When Joshua's mother opened the envelope, she realized that the see-through window had not revealed the full text of Time's offer. Not viewable through the see-through window were the following words: "And mailing this Certificate today." The certificate required Joshua to purchase a subscription to *Fortune* Magazine in order to receive the free calculator watch. Joshua (through his father, a lawyer) sued Time in a class action, seeking compensatory damages in an amount equal to the value of the calculator watch and $15 million in punitive damages. The trial court dismissed the lawsuit as being too trivial for the court to hear. Joshua appealed. Should Joshua be permitted to maintain his lawsuit against Time Inc.? Did Time act ethically? Should Joshua's father have sued for $15 million? [*Harris v. Time, Inc.*, 191 C.A.3d 449, 237 Cal. Rptr. 584 (Cal. App. 1987)]

2.15 Business Ethics Dennis and Francis Burnham were married in 1976 in West Virginia. In 1977, the couple moved to New Jersey, where their two children were born. In July 1987, the Burnhams decided to separate. Mrs. Burnham, who intended to move to California, was to have custody of the children. Mr. Burnham agreed to file for divorce on the grounds of "irreconcilable differences." In October 1987, Mr. Burnham threatened to file for divorce in New Jersey on the grounds of "desertion." After unsuccessfully demanding that Mr. Burnham adhere to the prior agreement, Mrs. Burnham brought suit for divorce in California state court in early January 1988. In late January, Mr. Burnham visited California on a business trip. He then visited his children in the San Francisco Bay area, where his wife resided. He took the older child to San Francisco for the weekend. Upon returning the child to Mrs. Burnham's home, he was served with a court summons and a copy of Mrs. Burnham's divorce petition. He then returned to New Jersey. Mr. Burnham made a special appearance in the California court and moved to quash the service of process. Did Mr. Burnham act ethically in trying to quash the service of process? Did Mrs. Burnham act ethically in having Mr. Burnham served on his visit to California? Is the service of process good? [*Burnham v. Superior Court of California*, 495 U.S. 604, 110 S.Ct. 2105, 109 L.Ed.2d 631 (1990)]

BRIEFING THE CASE WRITING ASSIGNMENT

Read the following case, which has been excerpted from the court's opinions. Review and brief the case.

Gnazzo v. G.D. Searle & Co.
973 F.2d 136 (1992)
U.S. Court of Appeals for the Second Circuit

Pierce, Circuit Judge

On November 11, 1974, Gnazzo had a CU-7 intrauterine devise (IUD) inserted in her uterus for contraceptive purposes. The IUD was developed, marketed and sold by G.D. Searle & Co. (Searle). When Gnazzo's deposition was taken, she stated that her doctor had informed her that "insertion would hurt, but not for long," and that she "would have uncomfortable and probably painful periods for the first three to four months." On October 11, 1975, Gnazzo found it necessary to return to her physician due to excessive pain and cramping. During this visit she was informed by her doctor that he thought she had Pelvic Inflammatory Disease (PID). She recalled that he stated that the infection was possibly caused by venereal disease or the use of the IUD. The PID was treated with antibiotics and cleared up shortly thereafter. Less than one year later, Gnazzo was again treated with antibiotics. Gnazzo continued using the IUD until it was finally removed in December of 1977.

Following a laparoscopy in March of 1989, Gnazzo was informed by a fertility specialist that she was infertile because of PID-induced adhesions resulting from her prior IUD use. Subsequent to this determination, and at the request of her then-attorneys, Gnazzo completed a questionnaire dated May 11, 1989. In the response to the following question, "When and why did you first suspect that your IUD had caused you any harm?," Gnazzo responded "Sometime in 1981" and explained: "I was married in April 1981 so I stopped using birth control so I could get pregnant—nothing ever happened (of course), then I started hearing and reading about how damaging IUD's could be. I figured that was the problem; however, my marriage started to crumble so I never pursued the issue."

On May 4, 1990, Gnazzo initiated the underlying action against Searle. In an amended complaint, she alleged that she had suffered injuries as a result of her use of the IUD developed by Searle. Searle moved for summary judgment on the ground that Gnazzo's claim was time-barred by Connecticut's three-year statute of limitations for product liability actions. Searle argued, inter alia, that Gnazzo knew in 1981 that she had suffered harm caused by her IUD. Gnazzo contended that her cause of action against Searle accrued only when she learned from the fertility specialist that the IUD had caused her PID and subsequent infertility.

In a ruling dated September 18, 1991, the district court granted Searle's motion for summary judgment on the ground that Gnazzo's claim was time-barred by the applicable statute of limitations. In reaching this result, the court determined that Connecticut law provided no support for Gnazzo's contention that she should not have been expected to file her action until she was told of her infertility and the IUD's causal connection. This appeal followed.

On appeal, Gnazzo contends that the district court improperly granted Searle's motion for summary judgment because a genuine issue of material fact exists as to when she discovered, or reasonably should have discovered, her injuries and their casual connection to the defendant's alleged wrongful conduct. Summary judgment is appropriate when there is no genuine issue as to any material fact and the moving party is entitled to judgment as a matter of law. We consider the record in the light most favorable to the non-movant. However, the non-movant "may not rest upon the mere allegations of denials of her pleading, but must set forth specific facts showing that there is a genuine issue for trial."

Under Connecticut law, a product liability claim must be brought within "three years from the date when the injury is first sustained or discovered or in the exercise of reasonable care should have been discovered." In Connecticut, a cause of action accrues when a plaintiff suffers actionable harm. Actionable harm occurs when the plaintiff discovers or should discover, through the exercise of reasonable care, that he or she has been injured and that the defendant's conduct caused such injury.

Gnazzo contends that "the mere occurrence of a pelvic infection or difficulty in becoming pregnant does not necessarily result in notice to the plaintiff of a cause of action." Thus, she maintains that her cause of action did not accrue until 1989 when the fertility specialist informed her both that she was infertile and that this condition resulted from her previous use of the IUD.

Under Connecticut law, however, "the statute of limitations begins to run when the plaintiff discovers some form of actionable harm, not the fullest manifestation thereof. Therefore, as Gnazzo's responses to the questionnaire indicate, she suspected "sometime in 1981" that the IUD had caused her harm because she had been experiencing trouble becoming pregnant and had "started hearing and reading about how damaging IUD's could be and had figured that was the problem." Thus, by her own admission, Gnazzo had recognized, or should have recognized, the critical link between her injury and the defendant's causal connection to it. In other words she had "discovered or should have discovered through the exercise of reasonable care, that she had been injured and that Searle's conduct caused such injury." However, as Gnazzo acknowledged in the questionnaire, she did not pursue the "issue" at the time because of her marital problems. Thus, even when viewed in the light most favorable to Gnazzo, the nonmoving party, we are constrained to find that she knew by 1981 that she had "some form of actionable harm." Consequently, by the time she commenced her action in 1990, Gnazzo was time-barred by the Connecticut statute of limitations.

Since we have determined that Gnazzo's cause of action commenced in 1981, we need not address Searle's additional contention that Gnazzo's awareness in 1975 of her PID and her purported knowledge of its causal connection to the IUD commenced the running of the Connecticut statute of limitations at that time.

We are sympathetic to Gnazzo's situation and mindful that the unavoidable result we reach in this case is harsh. Nevertheless, we are equally aware that "it is within Connecticut General Assembly's constitutional authority to decide when claims for injury are to be brought. Where a plaintiff has failed to comply with this requirement, a court may not entertain the suit." The judgment of the district court is affirmed.

ENDNOTES

1. Federal Courts Improvement Act of 1982. Pub. L. 97-164, 96 Stat. 25, 28 U.S.C. § 1292 and § 1295.

2. Effective September 25, 1988, mandatory appeals were all but eliminated except for reapportionment cases and cases brought under the Civil Rights and Voting Rights Acts, antitrust laws, and the Presidential Election Campaign Fund Act.

3. Prior to 1980, there was a minimum dollar amount controversy requirement of $10,000 to bring a federal question action in federal court. this minimum amount was eliminated by the Federal Question Jurisdictional Amendment Act of 1980, Public Law 96-486.

4. The amount was raised from $50,000 to $75,000 by the 1996 Federal Courts Improvement Act.

5. Under the Full Faith and Credit Clause of the U.S. Constitution, a judgment of a court in one state must be given "full faith and credit" by the courts of another state. Article IV, Section 1.

6. *International Shoe Co. v. Washington*, 326 U.S. 310, 66 S.Ct. 154, 90 L.Ed. 95 (1945).

7. There is no right to a jury trial for actions in equity (e.g., injunctions, specific performance).

8. 9 U.S.C. §§ 1 et seq.

CHAPTER

3

Constitutional Law for Commerce and Information Technology

The nation's armor of defense against the passions of men is the Constitution. Take that away, and the nation goes down into the field of its conflicts like a warrior without armor.

—Henry Ward Beecher
Proverbs from Plymouth Pulpit, 1887

Chapter Objectives

After studying this chapter, you should be able to:

1. Describe the concept of federalism and the doctrine of separation of powers.

2. Define and apply the Supremacy Clause of the U.S. Constitution.

3. Describe the treaty power of the federal government.

4. Explain the federal government's authority to regulate foreign commerce.

5. Explain the federal government's authority to regulate interstate commerce.

6. Explain how speech is protected by the First Amendment.

7. Describe how the Internet is protected by the Freedom of Speech Clause.

8. Describe constitutional limits on e-commerce.

9. Desribe substantive and procedural due process.

10. Explain the doctrine of equal protection.

Chapter Contents

Prior to the American Revolution, each of the 13 original colonies operated as a separate sovereignty under the rule of England. In September 1774, representatives of the colonies met as a Continental Congress. In 1776, the colonies declared independence from England and the American Revolution ensued.

This chapter examines the major provisions of the U.S. Constitution and the amendments that have been adopted to the Constitution. Of particular importance, this chapter discusses how these provisions affect the operations of business in this country. The Constitution, with amendments, is set forth as an Appendix to this chapter.

The Constitution of the United States is not a mere lawyers' document: It is a vehicle of life, and its spirit is always the spirit of the age.

Woodrow Wilson
Constitutional Government in
the United States *69 (1927)*

*B*ASIC CONSTITUTIONAL CONCEPTS

The **U.S. Constitution** is a unique document that provides rights and protections to individuals and businesses. Some important constitutional concepts are discussed in the following paragraphs.

U.S. Constitution

The fundamental law of the United States of America. It was ratified by the states in 1788.

Landmark Law

THE CONSTITUTION OF THE UNITED STATES OF AMERICA

In 1778, the Continental Congress formed a *federal government* and adopted the **Articles of Confederation**. The Articles of Confederation created a federal Congress composed of representatives of the 13 new states. The Articles of Confederation was a particularly weak document that gave limited power to the newly created federal government. For example, it did not provide Congress with the power to levy and collect taxes, to regulate commerce with foreign countries, or to regulate interstate commerce among the states.

The **Constitutional Convention** was convened in Philadelphia in May 1787. The primary purpose of the Convention was to strengthen the federal government. After substantial debate, the delegates agreed to a new **U.S.**

Constitution. The Constitution was reported to Congress in September 1787. State ratification of the Constitution was completed in 1788. Many amendments, including the **Bill of Rights**, have been added to the Constitution since that time.

The U.S. Constitution serves two major functions:

1. It creates the three branches of the federal government (i.e., the executive, legislative, and judicial branches) and allocates powers to these branches.
2. It protects individual rights by limiting the government's ability to restrict those rights.

The Constitution itself provides that it may be amended to address social and economic changes.

Federalism and Delegated Powers

Our country's form of government is referred to as **federalism**. That means that the federal government and the 50 state governments share powers.

When the states ratified the Constitution, they *delegated* certain powers to the federal government. They are called **enumerated powers**. The federal government is authorized to deal with national and international affairs. Any powers that are not specifically delegated to the federal government by the Constitution are reserved to the state governments. State governments are empowered to deal with local affairs.

federalism

The U.S. form of government; the federal government and the 50 state governments share powers.

enumerated powers

Certain powers delegated to the federal government by the states.

The Doctrine of Separation of Powers

As mentioned previously, the federal government is divided into three branches:

1. Article I of the Constitution established the **legislative branch** of government. This branch is bicameral; that is, it consists of the Senate and the House of Representatives. Collectively, they are referred to as *Congress*.[1] Each state has two senators. The number of representatives to the House of Representatives is determined according to the population of each state. The current number of representatives is determined from the 2000 census.
2. Article II of the Constitution establishes the **executive branch** of government by providing for the election of the president and vice president. The president is not elected by popular vote but instead is selected by the *electoral college*, whose representatives are appointed by state delegations.[2]
3. Article III establishes the **judicial branch** of the government by establishing the Supreme Court and providing for the creation of other federal courts by Congress.[3]

legislative branch

The part of the government that consists of Congress (the Senate and the House of Representatives).

executive branch

The part of the government that consists of the President and Vice President.

judicial branch

The part of the government that consists of the Supreme Court and other federal courts.

Checks and Balances

Certain **checks and balances** are built into the Constitution to ensure that no one branch of the federal government becomes too powerful. Some of the checks and balances in our system of government are

1. The judicial branch has authority to examine the acts of the other two branches of government and determine whether these acts are constitutional.[4]
2. The executive branch can enter into treaties with foreign governments only with the advice and consent of the Senate.
3. The legislative branch is authorized to create federal courts and determine their jurisdiction and to enact statutes that change judicially made law.

Business Brief

Checks and balances is the way the U.S. Constitution prevents any one of the three branches of the government from becoming too powerful.

The United States is the world's leading democracy. The country, however, has had many blemishes on its citizens' constitutional rights. For example, during World War II Japanese Americans were involuntarily placed in camps. During the McCarthy hearings of the 1950s, citizens who were Communists or associated with Communists were "blackballed" from their occupations, most notably in the film industry. It was not unit the mid-1960s that equal opportunity laws outlawed discrimination in the workplace based on race and sex.

THE SUPREMACY CLAUSE

The **Supremacy Clause** establishes that the federal Constitution, treaties, federal laws, and federal regulations are the supreme law of the land.[5] State and local laws that conflict with valid federal law are unconstitutional. The concept of federal law taking precedence over state or local law is commonly called the **preemption doctrine**.

Congress may expressly provide that a particular federal statute *exclusively* regulates a specific area or activity. No state or local law regulating the area or activity is valid if there is such a statute. More often, though, federal statutes do not expressly provide for exclusive jurisdiction. In these instances, state and local governments have *concurrent jurisdiction* to regulate the area or activity. However, any state or local law that "directly and substantially" conflicts with valid federal law is preempted under the Supremacy Clause.

Supremacy Clause

A clause of the U.S. Constitution that establishes that the federal Constitution, treaties, federal laws, and federal regulations are the supreme law of the land.

preemption doctrine

The concept that federal law takes precedence over state or local law.

The Supreme Court Speaks

Supremacy Clause Downs Conflicting State Law

Capital Cities Cable, Inc. v. Crisp, Director, Oklahoma Alcoholic Beverage Control Board,
467 U.S. 691, 104 S.Ct. 2694 (1984)
Supreme Court of the United States

BACKGROUND AND FACTS

The Federal Communications Act (Act) authorized the Federal Communications Commission (FCC) to regulate television and radio broadcasts in this country. The FCC adopted a regulation that requires cable television operators to transmit all signals "in full, without deletion or alteration of any portion," including commercials. A provision in the Oklahoma state constitution prohibited the advertising of alcoholic beverages within the state. Many out-of-state cable broadcasts contain alcoholic beverage commercials. When the director of the Oklahoma Alcoholic Beverage Control Board (Board) threatened to criminally prosecute cable operators that televised out-of-state alcoholic beverage commercials in the state, Capital Cities Cable, Inc. and other cable operators sued the Board, alleging that the Oklahoma law was preempted by federal law. The U.S. court of appeals reversed. The cable operators appealed to the U.S. Supreme Court.

SUPREME COURT ISSUE
Is the provision in the Oklahoma constitution that prohibits advertising of alcoholic beverage commercials by cable operators preempted by federal law?

IN THE LANGUAGE OF THE U.S. SUPREME COURT
Brennan, Justice *Under the Supremacy Clause, the enforcement of a state regulation may be preempted by federal law when compliance with both state and federal law is impossible, or when the state law stands as an obstacle to the accomplishment and execution of the full purposes and objectives of Congress.*

The Oklahoma advertising ban plainly conflicts with specific federal regulations. Consequently, those Oklahoma cable operators required by federal law to carry out-of-state broadcast signals in full, including any alcoholic beverage commercials, are *subject to criminal prosecution under Oklahoma law as a result of their compliance with federal regulations. Since the Oklahoma law, by requiring deletion of a portion of these out-of-state signals, compels conduct that federal law forbids, the state ban clearly stands as an obstacle to the accomplishment and execution of the full purposes and objectives of the federal regulatory scheme.*

DECISION AND REMEDY
The U.S. Supreme Court held that the provision in the Oklahoma constitution directly and substantially conflicted with a valid federal regulation and was therefore unconstitutional under the Supremacy Clause of the U.S. Constitution.

CASE QUESTIONS

Critical Legal Thinking   Should federal law preempt state and local law? Why or why not?

Business Ethics   Should law, such as Oklahoma's ban on alcoholic beverage advertising on television, be used to promote a moral view?

Contemporary Business   What would have been the economic consequences to cable operators if the Oklahoma law in this case had been upheld?

The Supreme Court Speaks

State Law Tort Action Preempted by Federal Law

Geier v. American Honda Motor Company, Inc.,
120 S.Ct. 1913 (2000)
Supreme Court of the United States

BACKGROUND AND FACTS
The United States Department of Transportation is the federal administrative agency responsible for administering and enforcing federal traffic safety laws, including the National Traffic and Motor Vehicle Safety Act of 1966. Pursuant to this act, in 1987 the Department of Transportation adopted a Federal Motor Vehicle Safety Standard that required automobile manufacturers to equip 10 percent of their 1987 vehicles with passive restraints, including automatic seat belts or air bags.

In 1992, Alexis Geier, driving a 1987 Honda Accord automobile in the District of Columbia, collided with a tree and was seriously injured. The car was equipped with manual shoulder and lap belts that Geier had buckled up at the time of the accident; the car was not equipped with air bags, however. Geier sued the car's manufacturer, the American Honda Motor Company, Inc., alleging that American Honda had negligently and defectively designed the car because it lacked a driver's side air bag, thus violating the District of Columbia's

tort law. The trial court dismissed Geier's lawsuit, finding that the District of Columbia's tort law conflicted with the federal passive restraint safety standard and was therefore preempted under the Supremacy Clause of the U.S. Constitution. The court of appeals affirmed. Geier appealed to the U.S. Supreme Court, which granted review.

SUPREME COURT ISSUE
Does the federal passive restraint safety standard preempt the District of Columbia's common law tort action in which the plaintiff claims that the defendant American Honda, which was in compliance with the federal standard, should nonetheless have equipped the 1987 automobile with air bags.

IN THE LANGUAGE OF THE U.S. SUPREME COURT
Breyer, Justice *In effect, the petitioner Geier's tort action depends upon his claim that the manufacturer had a duty to install an air bag when it manufactured the 1987 Honda Accord. Such a state*

law—i.e., a rule of state tort law imposing such a duty—by its terms would have required manufacturers of all similar cars to install air bags rather than other passive restraint systems, such as automatic belts or passive interiors. It would have required all manufacturers to have installed air bags in respect to the entire District of Columbia-related portion of their 1987 new car fleet, even though the federal safety standard at that time required only 10 percent of a manufacturer's nationwide fleet be equipped with any passive restraint device at all. Regardless, the language of the federal passive restraint standard is clear enough: The federal standard sought a gradually developing mix of alternative passive restraint devices for safety-related reasons. The rule of state tort law for which petitioner Geier argues would stand as an "obstacle" to the accomplishment of that objective. And the federal statute foresees the application of ordinary principles of preemption in cases of actual conflict. Hence the tort action is preempted.

DECISON AND REMEDY

The U.S. Supreme Court held that the federal passive restraint safety standard preempted petitioner Geier's tort lawsuit under the District of Columbia's law against American Honda.

CASE QUESTIONS

Critical Legal Thinking   What would be the consequences if there were no Supremacy Clause? Explain.

Business Ethics   Do you think American Honda owed a duty to equip all of its 1987 vehicles with air bags even though federal law did not require this?

Contemporary Business   Do laws ever protect—rather than harm—businesses? Do you think defendant American Honda would say "There are too many laws" in this case?

Business Ethics

CIGARETTE COMPANIES ASSERT SUPREMACY CLAUSE

Business people often complain that there are too many laws. In some cases business executives actually like a law because it works in their favor, however. Consider the following case. Rose Cipollone began smoking cigarettes in 1942, when she was 17 years old. She continued to smoke between one and two packs of cigarettes per day until the early 1980s. Cipollone first smoked Chesterfield cigarettes, manufactured by Liggett Group, Inc. She then switched to L&M filter cigarettes, also made by Liggett Group. Cipollone subsequently switched to Virginia Slims cigarettes manufactured by Phillip Morris, Inc. Finally, she smoked Parliament cigarettes, also made by Phillip Morris.

In 1981, Cipollone was diagnosed with lung cancer. Even though her doctor advised her to quit smoking, she was unable to do so. Cipollone continued to smoke heavily until June 1982 when her lung was removed, but even after that she smoked in secret. She only stopped smoking in 1983, after she had become terminally ill with cancer. On August 1, 1983, she sued those cigarette manufacturers for personal injuries. Cipollone died on October 21, 1984, but her heir continued to prosecute the case.

In 1965 the Congress enacted the Federal Cigarette Labeling and Advertising Act, which required cigarette manufacturers to place on cigarette packages a warning of the dangers of smoking. The act requires one of the following warning labels, which must be rotated ever quarter, to be placed on each cigarette package after the words "SURGEON GENERAL'S WARNING":

1.   *Smoking Causes Lung Cancer, Heart Disease, Emphysema, and May Complicate Pregancy.*
2.   *Cigarette Smoke Contains Carbon Monoxide.*
3.   *Quitting Smoking Now Greatly Reduces Serious Risks to Your Health.*

4.   *Smoking by Pregnant Women May Result in Fetal Injury, Premature Birth, and Low Birth Weight.*

The cigarette company defendants argued that the warnings on cigarette packages—which are mandated by the Federal Cigarette Labeling and Advertising Act—preempted Cipollone's state tort action against them.

The U.S. Supreme Court held that the federal act preempted Cipollone's state law claims based on failure to warn of the dangers of smoking. The Court held that the Federal Cigarette Labeling and Advertising Act was a valid federal law that, under the Supremacy Clause of the U.S. Constitution, took precedent over conflicting state law failure to warn claims.

The Supreme Court did, however, rule that the act did not bar lawsuits against cigarette companies for claims based on fraudulent misrepresentation or conspiracy among cigarette companies to misrepresent or conceal material facts about the dangers of cigarette smoking. Therefore, if they can prove fraud—that is, intentional conduct whereby the cigarette companies knew of the dangers of cigarette smoking and either lied to the public or concealed this information—smokers can win against cigarette companies. The Supreme Court reversed the court of appeals and allowed Cipollone's heirs to proceed against the defendants on this issue. Worn down, Cipollone's heirs dropped the lawsuit after this U.S. Supreme Court ruling. [*Cipollone v. Liggett Group, Inc.*, 112 S.Ct. 2608 (1992)]

1.   Do you think cigarette companies knew of the dangers of smoking during the period that Cipollone smoked? Did they conceal this information from her?
2.   What would be the economic consequences if courts held cigarette companies liable to injured smokers? Who would gain? Who would suffer?

THE COMMERCE CLAUSE

The **Commerce Clause** of the U.S. Constitution grants Congress the power "to regulate commerce with foreign nations, and among the several states, and with Indian tribes."6 Because this clause authorizes the federal government to regulate commerce, it has a greater impact on business than any other provision in the Constitution. Among other things, this clause is intended to foster the development of a national market and free trade among the states.

Commerce Clause

A clause of the U.S. Constitution that grants Congress the power "to regulate commerce with foreign nations, and among the several states, and with Indian tribes."

The Supreme Court Speaks

Treaty with the Chippewa Indian Nation Enforced

Minnesota v. Mille Lacs Band of Chippewa Indians,
119 S.Ct. 1187 (1999)
Supreme Court of the United States

BACKGROUND AND FACTS
When the Constitution was ratified by the original thirteen colonies in 1788, it delegated to the federal government the exclusive power to regulate commerce with Indian tribes. At that time, the area making up the United States of America was substantially occupied by dozens of American Indian nations. During the next one hundred years, as the colonists migrated westward, the federal government represented the United States in dealing with the American Indians and entered into many treaties with Indian nations. One such treaty was with the Chippewa Indians in 1837 whereby they sold land located in the Minnesota Territory to the United States. The treaty provided: "The privilege of hunting, fishing, and gathering wild rice, upon the lands, the rivers and the lakes included in the territory ceded, is guaranteed to the Indians." The state of Minnesota was admitted to the Union in 1858.

In 1990, the Mille Lacs Band of the Chippewa nation of American Indians sued the state of Minnesota seeking declaratory judgment that they retained the hunting, fishing, and gathering rights provided in the 1837 treaty and an injunction to prevent Minnesota from interfering with those rights. The state of Minnesota argued that its admission to the Union in 1858 extinguished those rights. The district court and court of appeals held in favor of the Chippewa Indians. The U.S. Supreme Court agreed to hear the appeal.

SUPREME COURT ISSUE
Are the hunting, fishing, and gathering rights guaranteed to the Chippewa Indians in the 1837 treaty still valid and enforceable?

IN THE LANGUAGE OF THE U.S. SUPREME COURT
The state of Minnesota argues that the Chippewa's rights under the 1837 treaty were extinguished when Minnesota was admitted to the Union in 1858. In making this argument, the state faces an uphill battle. Congress may abrogate Indian treaty rights, but it must clearly express its intent to do so. There is no such clear evidence of congressional intent to abrogate the Chippewa Treaty rights here. The relevant statute—Minnesota's enabling act—provides in relevant part: "The state of Minnesota shall be one, and is hereby declared to be one, of the United States of America, and admitted into the Union on an equal footing with the original states in all respects whatever."

This language, like the rest of the act, makes no mention of Indian treaty rights.

DECISION AND REMEDY
The U.S. Supreme Court held that the hunting, fishing, and gathering rights provided to the Chippewa Indians in the 1837 treaty with the United States of America were valid and enforceable and had not been extinguished when Minnesota was admitted to the union.

CASE QUESTIONS

Critical Legal Thinking Do the American Indians have any legal claim to the lands that now comprise the United States of America? Discuss.

Business Ethics Did the state of Minnesota act ethically in arguing that the Chippewa Indians' hunting, fishing, and gathering rights had been extinguished? Why do you think the state argued this?

Contemporary Business Does the Supreme Court's decision have any effects on either American Indian or non-Indian businesses located in Minnesota? Explain.

Federal Regulation of Interstate Commerce

The Commerce Clause also gives the federal government the authority to regulate **interstate commerce**. Originally, the courts interpreted this clause to mean that the federal government could only regulate commerce that moved *in* interstate commerce. The modern rule, however, allows the federal government to regulate activities that *affect* interstate commerce.

interstate commerce

Commerce that moves between states or that affects commerce between states.

Business Brief

The federal government may regulate:
1. *Interstate* commerce that crosses state borders.
2. *Intrastate* commerce that affects interstate commerce.

The American Constitution is, so far as I can see, the most wonderful work ever struck off at a given time by the brain and purpose of man.

W.E. Glastone
Kin Beyond Sea (1878)

Under the **effects on interstate commerce test**, the regulated activity does not itself have to be in interstate commerce. Thus, any local (*intrastate*) activity that has an effect on interstate commerce is subject to federal regulation. Theoretically, this test subjects a substantial amount of business activity in the United States to federal regulation.

For example, in the famous case of *Wickard, Secretary of Agriculture v. Filburn*,[7] a federal statute limited the amount of wheat that a farmer could plant and harvest for home consumption. Filburn, a farmer, violated the law. The U.S. Supreme Court upheld the statute on the grounds that it prevented nationwide surpluses and shortages of wheat. The Court reasoned that wheat grown for home consumption would affect the supply of wheat available in interstate commerce.

In several recent cases, the U.S. Supreme Court held that the federal government had enacted statutes beyond its interstate commerce clause powers. For example, in *United States v. Lopez*, the Supreme Court invalidated the Gun-Free School Zone Act, a federal statute that made it a crime to knowingly possess a firearm in a school zone.[8] The Court found that there was no commercial activity that was being regulated.

The Supreme Court Speaks

Federal Statute Upheld as Proper Regulation of Interstate Commerce

Reno, Attorney General of the United State v. Condon, Attorney General of South Carolina,
120 S.Ct. 666 (2000)
Supreme Court of the United States

BACKGROUND AND FACTS
State motor vehicle departments (DMVs) register automobiles and issue drivers' licenses. State DMVs require automobile owners and drivers to provide personal information, which includes a person's name, address, telephone number, vehicle description, Social Security number, medical information, and a photograph, as a condition for registering an automobile or obtaining a driver's license. Many states DMVs sold this personal information to individuals, advertisers, and businesses. These sales generated significant revenues for the states.

After receiving thousands of complaints from individuals whose personal information had been sold, the Congress of the United States enacted the Driver's Privacy Protection Act of 1994 (DPPA) [18 U.S.C. §§ 2721-2775]. This federal statute prohibits a state from selling the personal information of a person unless the state obtains that person's affirmative consent to do so. South Carolina sued the United States, alleging that the federal government exceeded its authority under the Commerce Clause by adopting the DPPA. The district court and the court of appeals held for South Carolina. The U.S. Supreme Court granted review.

SUPREME COURT ISSUE
Was the Driver's Privacy Protection Act properly enacted pursuant to the interstate commerce clause power granted to the federal government by the U.S. Constitution?

IN THE LANGUAGE OF THE U.S. SUPREME COURT
Rehnquist, Chief Justice The United States asserts that the DPPA is a proper exercise of Congress's authority to regulate interstate

commerce under the Commerce Clause. The United States bases its Commerce Clause argument on the fact that the personal, identifying information that the DPPA regulates is a thing in interstate commerce, and that the sale or release of that information in interstate commerce is therefore a proper subject of congressional regulation. We agree with the United States' contention.

The motor vehicle information which the States have historically sold is used by insurers, manufacturers, direct marketers, and others engaged in interstate commerce to contact drivers with customized solicitations. The information is also used in the stream of interstate commerce by various public and private entities for matters related to interstate motoring. Because drivers' information is, in this context, an article of commerce, its sale or release into the interstate stream of business is sufficient to support congressional regulation.

DECISION AND REMEDY
The U.S. Supreme Court held that Congress had the authority under the Commerce Clause to enact the federal Driver's Privacy Protection Act.

CASE QUESTIONS

Critical Legal Thinking   How often do you think one government (the federal government) saves people from the intrusiveness of another government (state or local government)?

Business Ethics   Was it ethical for the states to sell the personal information of automobile owners and drivers?

Contemporary Business   Who were the winners from this decision? Who were the losers?

The Supreme Court Speaks

Federal Violence Against Women Act Found Lacking "Interstate Commerce" Connection

United States v. Morrison,
529 U.S. 598, 120 S.Ct. 1740 (2000)
2000 U.S. Lexis 3422
Supreme Court of the United States

BACKGROUND AND FACTS

Christy Brzonkala enrolled at Virginia Polytechnic Institute (Virginia Tech) in the fall of 1994. In September 1994, Brzonkala met Antonio Morrison and James Crawford, who were both students at Virginia Tech and members of the varsity football team. Brzonkala alleges that, within 30 minutes of meeting Morrison and Crawford, they assaulted and repeatedly raped her. Brzonkala alleges that this attack caused her to become severely emotionally disturbed and depressed, and she withdrew from the university. In December 1995, Brzonkala brought a civil lawsuit in district court to recover damages against Morrison and Crawford as provided in Section 13981 of the Violence Against Women Act of 1994, a federal statute. In the statute, Congress stated that it had enacted the statute pursuant to the power granted it by the Commerce Clause of the U.S. Constitution. The defendants alleged that Section 13981 was invalid because the activity it regulated did not involve interstate commerce, and therefore Congress lacked the authority to enact the statute. The district court and court of appeals agreed with the defendants and dismissed the case. The U.S. Supreme Court accepted the appeal of the case.

SUPREME COURT ISSUE

Is Section 13981 of the Violence Against Women Act of 1994, which provides a civil cause of action to recover damages, valid as a proper exercise of Congress's Commerce Clause power?

IN THE LANGUAGE OF THE U.S. SUPREME COURT

Every law enacted by Congress must be based on one or more of its powers enumerated in the Constitution. Due respect for the decisions of a coordinate branch of Government demands that we invalidate a congressional enactment only upon a plain showing that Congress has exceeded its constitutional bounds. The proper resolution of the present case is clear. Gender-motivated crimes of violence are not, in any sense of the phrase, economic activity. While we need not adopt a categorical rule against aggregating the effects of any noneconomic activity in order to decide this case, thus far in our nation's history our cases have upheld Commerce Clause regulation of intrastate activity only where that activity is economic in nature.

DECISION AND REMEDY

The U.S. Supreme Court held that Congress lacked constitutional authority under the Commerce Clause to enact Section 13981 of the Violence Against Women Act because the activity it regulated did not constitute interstate commerce. The judgment of the court of appeals was affirmed.

CASE QUESTIONS

Critical Legal Thinking   Do you agree with the reasoning of the Supreme Court that there was no interstate commerce regulated in this case?

Business Ethics   What state law civil and criminal remedies does Brzonkala have against the defendants?

State and Local Government Regulation of Business—State "Police Power"

The states did not delegate all power to regulate business to the federal government. They retained the power to regulate *intrastate* and much interstate business activity that occurs within their borders. This is commonly referred to as states' **police power**.

Police power permits states (and, by delegation, local governments) to enact laws to protect or promote the *public health, safety, morals, and general welfare.* This includes the authority to enact laws that regulate the conduct of business. Zoning ordinances, state environmental laws, corporation and partnership laws, and property laws are enacted under this power.

State and local laws cannot **unduly burden interstate commerce.** If they do, they are unconstitutional because they violate the Commerce Clause. For example, if the federal government has chosen not to regulate an area that it has the power to regulate (*dormant Commerce Clause*), but the state does regulate it, the state law cannot unduly burden interstate commerce.

police power
The power of states to regulate private and business activity within their borders.

Business Brief
States may enact laws that protect or promote the public health, safety, morals, and general welfare as long as the law does not unduly burden interstate commerce.

Business Brief
State and local governments may regulate:
1. *Intrastate* commerce.
2. *Interstate* commerce not exclusively regulated by the federal government.

The Supreme Court Speaks

State Law Imposes Undue Burden on Interstate Commerce

Fort Gratiot Sanitary Landfill, Inc. v. Michigan Department of Natural Resources,
112 S.Ct. 2019 (1992)
Supreme Court of the United States

BACKGROUND AND FACTS

In 1988, the state of Michigan added the Waste Import Restrictions to its Solid Waste Management Act. These restrictions prohibited privately owned landfills in the state from accepting solid wastes (e.g., garbage, rubbish, sludges, and industrial waste) from any source outside the county in which the landfill was located unless the county expressly permitted it. Fort Gratiot Sanitary Landfill, Inc. (Fort Gratiot), submitted an application to the county government to allow it to accept up to 1,750 tons per day of out-of-state solid waste. The county rejected the application. Fort Gratiot sued the county and state, alleging that the Waste Import Restrictions created an undue burden on interstate commerce in violation of the Commerce Clause of the U.S. Constitution. The U.S. district court concluded that the restrictions did not create an undue burden on interstate commerce. The U.S. court of appeals agreed. The U.S. Supreme Court granted review.

SUPREME COURT ISSUE

Do Michigan's Waste Import Restrictions violate the Commerce Clause?

IN THE LANGUAGE OF THE U.S. SUPREME COURT

Stevens, Justice *Solid waste, even if it has no value, is an article of commerce. The Commerce Clause thus imposes some constraints on Michigan's ability to regulate these transactions. The "negative" or "dormant" aspect of the Commerce Clause prohibits states from advancing their own commercial interests by curtailing the movement of articles of commerce, either into or out of the state.*

Michigan and St. Clair County assert that the Waste Import Restrictions are necessary because they enable individual counties to make adequate plans for the safe disposal of future waste. Although accurate forecasts about the volume and compositions of future waste flows may be an indispensable part of a comprehensive waste disposal plan, Michigan could attain that objective without discriminating between in- and out-of-state waste. Michigan could, for example, limit the amount of waste that landfill operators may accept each year.

The Waste Import Restrictions enacted by Michigan authorize each of its 83 counties to isolate itself from the national economy. The Court has consistently found parochial legislation of this kind to be constitutionally invalid.

DECISION AND REMEDY

The Supreme Court held that the Waste Import Restrictions created an undue burden on interstate commerce in violation of the Commerce Clause of the U.S. Constitution.

CASE QUESTIONS

Critical Legal Thinking   Do you think some states will "export" their wastes to other states rather than provide landfills within their own boundaries?

Business Ethics   Is it ethical for a state to prohibit wastes from other states to be dumped within its boundaries? Was the state of Michigan acting in "good faith"?

Contemporary Business   What effect will the Supreme Court's ruling have on landfill operators? Would your answer be different if the restriction had been found constitutional?

E-Commerce & Information Technology

FEDERAL TELECOMMUNICATIONS ACT PREEMPTS STATE AND LOCAL LAWS

Congress enacted the **Federal Telecommunications Act of 1996 (FTA)** to increase competition within the telecommunications industry. In addition to deregulating the telephone industry, the FTA prohibits state and local governments from blocking freedom of entry into the burgeoning telecommunications industry. To accomplish this goal, **Section 253** of the FTA prohibits any state or local government laws that "prohibit or have the effect of prohibiting the ability of any entity to provide any interstate or intrastate telecommunications service." Because the FTA is federal law, under the Supremacy Clause of the U.S. Constitution, it preempts any state or local law that conflicts with its provisions. Consider the following case.

Prince George's County, Maryland, enacted a county ordinance that required telecommunications firms to obtain a franchise from the county to use its rights-of-way, imposed a $5,000 applications fee, charged 3 percent of the franchisee's gross revenues, and gave the county sole discretion to deny the franchise. Bell Atlantic-Maryland, Inc. (Bell Atlantic), a telecommunications company, sued Prince George's County in federal district court, alleging that the county ordinance violated the FTA and was preempted by the Supremacy Clause.

The court agreed with plaintiff Bell Atlantic. The court held that the county's ordinance went way beyond the county's authority to recover legitimate cost of maintaining the county's rights-of-way and instead was a general revenue-raising tax statute. The court also determined that the local government did not have the authority to keep out telecommunications companies because that authority was granted by Congress to the Federal Communications Commission (FCC), a federal administrative agency that oversees telecommunications for the nation. The Supreme Court concluded that the county's ordinance was preempted by FTA. [*Bell Atlantic-Maryland, Inc. v. Prince George's County, Maryland,* 49 F.Supp.2d 805 (D.Md.1999)]

International Law

FOREIGN COMMERCE CLAUSE

The Commerce Clause of the U.S. Constitution gives the federal government the exclusive power to regulate commerce with foreign nations. Direct and indirect regulation of *foreign commerce* by state or local governments that discriminates against foreign commerce violates the Foreign Commerce Clause and is therefore unconstitutional.

Consider the Following Examples The state of Michigan is the home of General Motors Corporation, Ford Motor Company, and Chrysler Corporation, the three largest automobile manufacturers in the United States. Suppose the Michigan state legislature enacts a law that imposes a 100 percent tax on any automobile imported from a foreign country that is sold in Michigan but does not impose the same tax on domestic automobiles sold in Michigan. The Michigan tax violates the Foreign Commerce Clause and is therefore unconstitutional and void. If, on the other hand, Michigan enacts a law that imposes a 100 percent tax on all automobiles sold in Michigan, domestic and foreign, the law does not discriminate against foreign commerce and therefore does not violate the Foreign Commerce Clause. The federal government could enact a 100 percent tax on all foreign automobiles but not domestic automobiles sold in the United States and that law would be valid, however.

Landmark Law

THE BILL OF RIGHTS

In 1791, the 10 amendments that are commonly referred to as the **Bill of Rights** were approved by the states and became part of the U.S. Constitution. The Bill of Rights guarantees certain fundamental rights to natural persons and protects these rights from intrusive government action. Most of these rights have also been found applicable to so-called artificial persons (i.e., corporations).

In addition to the Bill of Rights, 17 other amendments have been added to the Constitution. These amendments cover a variety of things. For instance, they have abolished slavery, prohibited discrimination, authorized a federal income tax, given women the right to vote, and specifically recognized that persons 18 years of age and older have the right to vote.

Originally, the Bill of Rights limited intrusive action by the *federal government* only. Intrusive actions by state and local governments were not limited until the **Due Process Clause of the Fourteenth Amendment** was added to the Constitution in 1868. The Supreme Court has applied the **incorporation doctrine** and held that most of the fundamental guarantees contained in the Bill of Rights are applicable to state and local government action. The amendments to the Constitution that are most applicable to business are discussed in the paragraphs that follow.

THE BILL OF RIGHTS AND BUSINESS

The Bill of Rights provide certain freedoms and protections to individuals and businesses. The most important of these rights are discussed in the following paragraphs.

Freedom of Speech

One of the most honored freedoms guaranteed by the Bill of Rights is the **freedom of speech** of the First Amendment. Many other constitutional freedoms would be meaningless without it. The First Amendment's Freedom of Speech Clause protects speech only, not conduct. The U.S. Supreme Court places speech into three categories: (1) *fully protected*, (2) *limited protected*, and (3) *unprotected speech*.

Fully Protected Speech   **Fully protected speech** is speech that the government cannot prohibit or regulate. Political speech is an example of such speech. For example, the government could not enact a law that forbids citizens from criticizing the current administration. The First Amendment protects oral, written, and symbolic speech.

Homeless Poets' Wall, Downtown Los Angeles The Free Speech Clause of the First Amendment to the Constitution of the United States of America guarantees free speech rights. These rights have been defined by decisions of the Supreme Court of the United States.

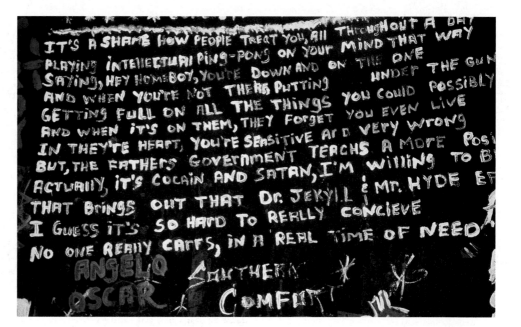

The Supreme Court Speaks

Federal "Signal Bleed" Statute Violates Playboy's Free Speech Rights

United States v. Playboy Entertainment Group, Inc.,
529 U.S. 803, 120 S.Ct. 1878 (2000)
Supreme Court of the United States

BACKGROUND AND FACTS

Many entertainment companies, including Playboy Entertainment Group, Inc., produce and distribute sexually explicit adult entertainment features for transmission over cable televi-sion stations. These shows are usually offered on a pay-per-view subscription service. Cable operators provide viewers with a converter box that attaches to the television set that scrambles these sexually explicit materials so they can only be viewed by subscribers who pay the subscription fee. However, with today's analog television sets, there often occurs "signal bleed" of either a blurred visual image or muted audio transmission of these materials. Digital television eliminates the signal bleed problem, but it will be years before digital technology becomes prevalent.

To address the signal bleed problem, Congress enacted Section 505 of the Telecommunications Act of 1996, which requires cable operators not to transmit sexually explicit materials during the hours from 6:00 A.M. to 10:00 P.M. if the signal bleed problem can occur. Thus, in this instance cable operators could not make their sexually explicit adult entertainment available for 16 hours each day.

Playboy Entertainment Group, Inc., a cable operator of Playboy Television and Spice, two adult entertainment cable television networks, sued the federal government alleging that Section 505 violated its free speech rights guaranteed by the U.S. Constitution. The district court declared Section 505 unconstitutional. The court found it feasible to allow cable operators to block individual cable boxes in the home, so therefore Section 505 was an overly broad restriction on content-based speech. The U.S. Supreme Court agreed to hear the case on direct appeal.

SUPREME COURT ISSUE

Is Section 505 an overly broad restriction on content-based speech that violates the free speech rights of Playboy Entertainment Group, Inc.?

IN THE LANGUAGE OF THE U.S. SUPREME COURT

Kennedy, Justice As this case has been litigated, the programming is not alleged to be obscene; adults have a constitutional right to view it.

The speech in questions is defined by its content; and the statute which seeks to restrict it is content based. Section 505 applies only to channels primarily dedicated to "sexually explicit adult programming or other programming that is indecent." The overriding justification for the regulation is concern for the effect of the subject matter on young viewers.

The effect of the federal statute on the protected speech is now apparent. It is evident that the only reasonable way for a substantial number of cable operators to comply with the letter of Section 505 is to "time channel", which silences the protected speech for two-thirds of the day in every home in a cable service area, regardless of the presence or likely presence of children or of the wishes of the viewers. According to the District Court, 30 to 50 percent of all adult programming is viewed by households prior to 10 P.M., when the safe-harbor period begins. To prohibit this much speech is a significant restriction of communication between speakers and willing adult listeners, communication which enjoys First Amendment protection.

Cable systems have the capacity to block unwanted channels on a household-by-household basis. Targeted blocking enables the Government to support parental authority without affecting the First Amendment interests of speakers and willing listeners—listeners for whom, if the speech is unpopular or indecent, the privacy of their own homes may be the optimal place of receipt. Simply put, targeted blocking is less restrictive than banning, and the Government cannot ban speech if targeted blocking is a feasible and effective means of furthering its compelling interests. If a less restrictive means is available for the Government to achieve its goals, the Government must use it.

DECISON AND REMEDY

The U.S. Supreme Court held that Section 505 was an overly broad restriction on legal content-based speech and was therefore an unconstitutional violation of free speech rights. The judgment of the district court was affirmed.

CASE QUESTIONS

Critical Legal Thinking Do you think that Section 505 was an overly broad restriction on free speech rights? Why or why not?

Business Ethics Why do you think Congress enacted Section 505 rather than require each home to choose to individually block the challenged programming?

Contemporary Business What economic consequences did the Supreme Court's ruling have for Playboy Entertainment and other adult entertainment cable companies?

Limited Protected Speech The Supreme Court has held that certain types of speech have only *limited protection* under the First Amendment. The government cannot forbid this type of speech, but it can subject this speech to **time, place, and manner restrictions**. The following types of speech are accorded limited protection:

Offensive Speech **Offensive speech** is speech that offends many members of society. (It is not the same as obscene speech, however.) The Supreme Court has held that offensive speech may be restricted by the government under time, place, and manner restrictions. For example, the Federal Communications Commission (FCC) can regulate the use of offensive language on television by limiting such language to time periods when children would be unlikely to be watching (e.g., late at night).

offensive speech
Speech that is offensive to many members of society. It is subject to time, place, and manner restrictions.

Commercial Speech **Commercial speech**, such as advertising, was once considered unprotected by the First Amendment. The Supreme Court's landmark decision in *Virginia State Board of Pharmacy v. Virginia Citizens Consumer Council, Inc.*[9] changed this rule. In that case, the Supreme Court held that a state statute prohibiting a pharmacist from adver-

commercial speech
Speech used by businesses, such as advertising. It is subject to time, place, and manner restrictions.

tising the price of prescription drugs was unconstitutional because it violated the Freedom of Speech Clause. However, the Supreme Court held that commercial speech is subject to proper time, place, and manner restrictions. For example, a city could prohibit billboards along its highways for safety and aesthetic reasons as long as other forms of advertising (e.g., print media) was available.

The Supreme Court Speaks

Casino Advertising Is Protected Commercial Speech

Greater New Orleans Broadcasting Association, Inc. v. United States,
119 S.Ct.1923 (1999)
Supreme Court of the United States

BACKGROUND AND FACTS
The state of Louisiana permits licensed gambling casinos. Section 1304 of the Federal Communications Act, a federal statute, and Federal Communication Commission (FCC) rules, prohibit the broadcast of gambling and lottery information and advertisements over radio and television. The Greater New Orleans Broadcasting Association, Inc., an association of radio and television station owners, sued the federal government, alleging that Section 1304 and the FCC rules violated their commercial free speech rights as guaranteed by the First Amendment to the U.S. Constitution. The district court and the court of appeals sided with the federal government. The U.S. Supreme Court agreed to hear the appeal.

SUPREME COURT ISSUE
Do Section 1304 and the FCC rules violate the petitioner association members' commercial free speech rights.

IN THE LANGUAGE OF THE U.S. SUPREME COURT
Stevens, Justice All parties to this case agree that the messages petitioners wish to broadcast constitute commercial speech. Their content is not misleading and concerns lawful activities, private casino gambling in Louisiana. In addition, petitioners' broadcasts presumably would disseminate accurate information as to the operation

of market competitors, such as pay-out ratios, which can benefit listeners by informing their consumption choices and fostering price competition. Thus, even if the broadcasters' interest in conveying these messages is entirely pecuniary, the interests of, and benefit to, the audience may be broader.

DECISION AND REMEDY
The U.S. Supreme Court held that Section 1304 and the FCC rules restrictions on the broadcast on radio and television of casino gambling information and advertisements violate the petitioner association members' commercial free speech rights as guaranteed by the First Amendment to the U.S. Constitution.

CASE QUESTIONS
Critical Legal Thinking   What was the federal government's purpose in restricting casino advertising on radio and television? Explain.

Business Ethics   What are the social implications of gambling? Should all gambling be outlawed? Should all forms of gambling be legal?

Contemporary Business   What are the economic implications of the U.S. Supreme Court's ruling? Explain.

The Supreme Court Speaks

The Government Cannot Compel Commercial Speech

United States Department of Agriculture v. United Foods, Inc.,
U.S.(?), 121 S.Ct. (2001) 2001 U.S. Lexis 4904
Supreme Court of the United States

BACKGROUND AND FACTS
In 1990, Congress enacted the Mushroom Promotion, Research, and Consumer Information Act. This federal statute authorizes

the U.S. Department of Agriculture, a federal administrative agency, to impose, through representatives, a mandatory financial assessment upon the handlers and sellers of fresh mushrooms in an amount not to exceed on cent (1c) per pound of mushrooms produced or imported. The assessment is used to pay for generic advertising to promote mushroom sales. In 1996, United Foods, Inc., a mushroom producer and importer, refused to pay its mandatory assessment as required by the statute, arguing that the forced subsidy for generic advertising violated its First Amendment free speech rights. The administrative law judge (ALJ) at the U.S. Department of Agriculture and the district court held against United Foods. The court of appeals reversed, and the U.S. Supreme Court granted review to hear the case.

SUPREME COURT ISSUE

Does the forced subsidy for generic advertising of mushrooms mandated by the federal Mushroom Promotion, Research, and Consumer Information Act violate the Free Speech Clause of the First Amendment to the Constitution?

IN THE LANGUAGE OF THE U.S. SUPREME COURT

A quarter of a century ago, the Court held that commercial speech, usually defined as speech that does no more than propose a commercial transaction, is protected by the First Amendment. The question in this case is whether the government may underwrite and sponsor speech with a certain viewpoint using special subsidies exacted from a designated class of persons, some of whom object to the idea being advanced. Just as the First Amendment may prevent the government from prohibiting speech, the Amendment may prevent the government from compelling individuals to express certain views, or from compelling certain individuals to pay subsidies for speech to which they object. The fact that the speech is in aid of a commercial purpose does not deprive United Foods, Inc. of all First Amendment protection. First Amendment concerns apply here because of the

requirement that producers subsidize speech with which they disagree.

It is true that the party who protests the assessment here is required simply to support speech by others, not to utter the speech itself. We conclude, however, that the mandated support is contrary to the First Amendment principles.

DECISION AND REMEDY

The U.S. Supreme Court held that the federal Mushroom Promotion, Research, and Consumer Information Act that requires mushroom handlers to pay a mandatory assessment for the generic advertising of mushrooms violates the commerce speech rights of United Foods, Inc., and is therefore unconstitutional.

CASE QUESTIONS

Critical Legal Thinking In its Opinion, the U.S. Supreme Court stated: "Just as the First Amendment may prevent the government from prohibiting speech, the Amendment may prevent the government from compelling individuals to express certain views." Is one violation as bad as the other? Comment.

Business Ethics Was it ethical for United Foods, Inc. to refuse to pay its assessment? Why do you think United Foods refused to pay its assessment?

Contemporary Business What are the business and economic consequences of the U.S. Supreme Court's decision? What would be the consequences if the Supreme Court had ruled in favor of the government?

Unprotected Speech The Supreme Court has held that the following types of speech are **unprotected speech**; they are not protected by the First Amendment and may be totally forbidden by the government:

unprotected speech

Speech that is not protected by the First Amendment and may be forbidden by the government.

1. Dangerous speech (including such things as yelling "fire" in a crowded theater when there is no fire).
2. Fighting words that are likely to provoke a hostile or violent response from an average person.[10]
3. Speech that incites the violent or revolutionary overthrow of the government; the mere abstract teaching of the morality and consequences of such action is protected.[11]
4. Defamatory language.[12]
5. Child pornography.[13]
6. Obscene speech.[14]

The definition of **obscene speech** is quite subjective. One Supreme Court justice stated, "I know it when I see it."[15] In *Miller v. California*, the Supreme Court determined that speech is obscene when

obscene speech

Speech that (1) appeals to the prurient interest, (2) depicts sexual conduct in a patently offensive way, and (3) lacks serious literary, artistic, political, or scientific value.

1. The average person, applying contemporary community standards, would find that the work, taken as a whole, appeals to the prurient interest.
2. The work depicts or describes, in a patently offensive way, sexual conduct specifically defined by the applicable state law.
3. The work, taken as a whole, lacks serious literary, artistic, political, or scientific value.[16]

States are free to define what constitutes obscene speech. Movie theaters, magazine publishers, and so on are often subject to challenges that the material they display or sell are obscene and therefore not protected by the First Amendment.

The Freedom of Speech Clause of the First Amendment to the U.S. Constitution protects the right to engage in political speech.

Contemporary Business Environment

RAP MUSIC: WHEN IS IT OBSCENE?

Every older generation believes that the music young people are listening to is louder and more obnoxious than the music they listened to during their youth. Today, this criticism goes even further: Some people are accusing modern music of being obscene. Consider the following case.

A Florida statute outlaws the production, distribution, or sale of any obscene thing, including a recording. Skyywalker Records, Inc. (Skyywalker), is a Florida corporation head-quartered in Miami, Florida. Luther Campbell, Mark Ross, David Hobbs, and Chris Wongwon constitute a rap group known as 2 LIVE CREW. Campbell is president, secretary, sole shareholder, and sole director of Skyywalker. In 1989, the group released the *As Nasty as They Wanna Be* (Nasty) record album. Public sales totaled approximately 1.7 million copies in various formats. The lyrics and titles to many of the songs explicitly refer to sexual conduct. A Florida judge issued an order finding that the recording was obscene. The Sheriff's Department distributed the order to music stores to warn the stores as a matter of courtesy rather than make initial arrests. The warnings were effective: Within days, all retail stores in Broward County ceased offering the Nasty recording for sale.

Skyywalker and members of 2 LIVE CREW brought a declaratory relief action against Broward County Sheriff Nicholas Navarro, seeking an injunction. The trial court judge found the music to be obscene and held for the sheriff. The judge stated:

This is a case between two ancient enemies: Anything Goes and Enough Already. Justice Oliver Wendell Holmes, Jr., observed in Schenck v. United States, *249 U.S. 47 (1919), that the First Amendment is not absolute and that it does not permit one to yell "Fire" in a crowded theater. Today, this court decides whether the First Amendment absolutely permits one to yell another "F" word anywhere in the community when combined with graphic sexual descriptions.*

The appellate court reversed, however [*Skyywalker Records, Inc., v. Navarro,* 960 F.2d 134 (11th Cir. 1992)].

Other courts presented with the same issue could reach a different result. Musicians, singers, and other performers face uncertainty as to whether their work is obscene. Work that is found to be obscene loses its constitutional protection.

E-Commerce & Information Technology

BROAD FREE SPEECH RIGHTS GRANTED IN CYBERSPACE

Once or twice a century a new medium comes along that presents new problems for applying freedom of speech rights. This time it is the Internet. In 1996 Congress enacted the **Telecommunication Act** to regulate telecommunications, including the Internet. Two provisions of this federal statute restricted the ability of cyberspace operators from transmitting certain images. These two provisions were:

- **Computer Decency Act**   This part of the statute made it a felony to knowingly make "indecent" or "patently offensive" materials available on computer systems, including the Internet, to persons under 18 years of age.
- **Signal Bleed Provision**   This provision of the statute required cable operators to either limit programming on cable channels to the hours between 10:00 P.M. and 6:00 A.M. or to scramble sexually explicit channels in full.

The act provided for fines, prison terms, and loss of licenses for anyone convicted of violating the terms of these provisions. Immediately, cyberspace providers and users filed lawsuits challenging these provisions of the act as violating their free speech rights granted under the First Amendment to the Constitution. Proponents of the act countered that these provisions were necessary to protect children from indecent materials. The plaintiffs won both cases at trial, and the U.S. Supreme Court granted review to decide the free speech issues.

The Supreme Court also came down on the plaintiffs' side in each case. The Court overturned the Computer Decency Act, finding that the terms "indecent" and "patently offensive" were too vague to define and criminally enforce. The Court decided that the signal bleed provisions imposed an overly broad illegal content-based restriction on speech. In both cases, the Supreme Court reasoned that limiting the content on the Internet to what is suitable for a child resulted in unconstitutional limiting of adult speech. The Court noted that children are far less likely to trip over indecent material on the Internet than on TV or radio because the information must be actively sought out on the Internet. The Court also stated that parents can regulate their children's access to the Internet and can install blocking and filtering software programs to protect their children from seeing adult materials.

The Supreme Court declared emphatically that the Internet must be given the highest possible level of First Amendment free speech protection, greater than that accorded to TV and radio. The Court concluded that the Internet allows an individual to reach an audience of millions at almost no cost, setting it apart from TV, radio, and print media, which are prohibitively expensive to use. The Supreme Court stated, "As the most participatory form of mass speech yet developed, the Internet deserves the highest protection from government intrusion." The Court also reasoned that because the Internet is a global medium, even if the challenged provisions of the act were upheld, there would be no way to prevent indecent material from flowing over the Internet from abroad. [*Reno v. American Civil Liberties Union*, 117 S.Ct. 2329 (1997); *United States v. Playboy Entertainment Group, Inc.*, 120 S.Ct. 1878 (2000)]

Freedom of Religion

The U.S. Constitution requires federal, state, and local governments to be neutral toward religion. The First Amendment actually contains two separate religion clauses. They are:

1. **The Establishment Clause**   The **Establishment Clause** prohibits the government from either establishing a state religion or promoting one religion over another. Thus, it guarantees that there will be no state-sponsored religion. The Supreme Court used this clause as its reason for ruling that an Alabama statute that authorized a one-minute period of silence in school for "meditation or voluntary prayer" was invalid.[17] The Court held that the statute endorsed religion.

2. **The Free Exercise Clause**   The **Free Exercise Clause** prohibits the government from interfering with the free exercise of religion in the United States. Generally, this clause prevents the government from enacting laws that either prohibit or inhibit individuals from participating in or practicing their chosen religion. For example, in *Church of Lukumi Babalu Aye, Inc. v. City of Hialeah, Florida*,[18] the U.S. Supreme Court held that a city ordinance that prohibited ritual sacrifices of animals (chickens) during church services violated the Free Exercise Clause. Of course, this right to be free from government intervention in the practice of religion is not absolute. For example, human sacrifices are unlawful and are not protected by the First Amendment.

Establishment Clause

A clause to the First Amendment that prohibits the government from either establishing a state religion or promoting one religion over another.

Free Exercise Clause

A clause to the First Amendment that prohibits the government from interfering with the free exercise of religion in the United States.

Freedom of Religion *The* **Establishment Clause** *prohibits the government from establishing a state religion or promoting one religion over another; the* **Free Exercise Clause** *prohibits the government from interfering with the free exercise of religion.*

The Supreme Court Speaks

The Establishment Clause Violated by Student-led Prayer

Santa Fe Independent School District v. Jane and John Doe,
120 S.Ct. 2266 (2000)
Supreme Court of the United States

BACKGROUND AND FACTS

The Santa Fe Independent School District is a political subdivision of the state of Texas that operates the Santa Fe High School, a public high school. The school district adopted a policy that permitted the students of the high school to elect a student who would give invocations over the public loud speaker system at all football games during the football season. The invocations were religious in nature, invoking Jesus Christ and the Lord, as well as Christian beliefs. Several students (designated the Does so that their identity would be kept secret) sued the school district alleging that this football game policy violated the Establishment Clause of the U.S. Constitution and was therefore unconstitutional. The district court upheld the school district's policy if it only permitted nonproselytizing prayer. The court of appeals held that the football prayer policy was unconstitutional. The U.S. Supreme Court granted review.

SUPREME COURT ISSUE

Does the school district's policy permitting student-led prayer at football games violate the Establishment Clause?

IN THE LANGUAGE OF THE U.S. SUPREME COURT

Stevens, Justice The first Clause in the First Amendment to the Federal Constitution provides that "Congress shall make no law respecting an establishment of religion, or prohibiting the free exercise thereof." The Fourteenth Amendment imposes those substantive limitations on the legislative power of the States and their political sub-divisions. In this case the School District first argues that this principle is inapplicable to its October policy because the messages are private student speech, not public speech. We are not persuaded that the pregame invocations should be regarded as "private speech."

Granting only one student access to the stage at a time does not, of course, necessarily preclude a finding that a school has created a limited public forum. Here, Santa Fe's student election system ensures that only those messages deemed "appropriate" under the School District's policy may be delivered. That is, the majoritarian process implemented by the School District guarantees, by definition, that minority candidates will never prevail and that their views will be effectively silenced. This student election does nothing to protect minority views but rather places the students who hold such views at the mercy of the majority.

The choice between whether to attend these games or to risk facing a personally offensive religious ritual is in no practical sense an easy one. The Constitution, moreover, demands that the school may not force this difficult choice upon these students. Thus, nothing in the Constitution as interpreted by this Court prohibits any public school student from voluntarily praying at any time before, during, or after the schoolday. But the religious liberty protected by the

Constitution is abridged when the State affirmatively sponsors the particular religious practice of prayer.

DECISION AND REMEDY

The U.S. Supreme Court held that the school district's policy permitting student-led prayer at high school football games violated the Establishment Clause of the U.S. Constitution and therefore must be struck down as unconstitutional.

CASE QUESTIONS

Critical Legal Thinking What is the purpose of the Establishment Clause? Explain.

Business Ethics Do you think that the school district was attempting to force the majority of the students' religious beliefs on other students?

CONCEPT SUMMARY   FREEDOM OF RELIGION

Clause	Description
Establishment Clause	Prohibits the government from either establishing a government-sponsored religion or promoting one religion over other religions.
Free Exercise Clause	Prohibits the government from enacting laws that either prohibit or inhibit individuals from participating in or practicing their chosen religion.

OTHER CONSTITUTIONAL CLAUSES AND BUSINESS

The **Fourteenth Amendment** was added to the U.S. Constitution in 1868. Its original purpose was to guarantee equal rights to all persons after the Civil War. The provisions of the Fourteenth Amendment prohibit discriminatory and unfair action by the government. Several of these provisions—namely the *Equal Protection Clause*, the *Due Process Clause*, and the *Privileges and Immunities Clause*—have important implications for business.

The Equal Protection Clause

The **Equal Protection Clause** provides that a state cannot "deny to any person within its jurisdiction the equal protection of the laws." Although this clause expressly applies to state and local government action, the Supreme Court has held that it also applies to federal government action.

This clause prohibits state, local, and federal governments from enacting laws that classify and treat "similarly situated" persons differently. Artificial persons, such as corporations, are also protected. Note that this clause is designed to prohibit invidious discrimination; it does not make the classification of individuals unlawful per se.

The Supreme Court has adopted three different standards for reviewing equal protection cases. They are:

1. **Strict Scrutiny Test** Any government activity or regulation that classifies persons based on a *suspect class* (i.e., **race**) is reviewed for lawfulness using a **strict scrutiny test**. Under this standard, most government classifications of persons based on race are found to be unconstitutional. For example, a government rule that permitted persons of one race, but not of another race, to receive government benefits would violate this test.

2. **Intermediate Scrutiny Test** The lawfulness of government classifications based on *protected classes* other than race (such as **sex** or **age**) are examined using an **intermediate scrutiny test**. Under this standard, the courts determine whether the government classification is "reasonably related" to a legitimate government purpose. For example, a rule prohibiting persons over a certain age from serving in military combat would be lawful, but a rule prohibiting persons over a certain age from acting as government engineers would not be.

3. **Rational Basis Test** The lawfulness of all government classifications that do not involve suspect or protected classes is examined using a **rational basis test**. Under this test, the courts will uphold government regulation as long as there is a justifiable reason for the law. This standard permits much of the government regulation of business. For example, providing government subsidies to farmers but not to other occupations is permissible.

Fourteenth Amendment

Amendment that was added to the U.S. Constitution in 1868. It contains the Due Process, Equal Protection, and Privileges and Immunities clauses.

Equal Protection Clause

A clause that provides that a state cannot "deny to any person within its jurisdiction the equal protection of the laws."

strict scrutiny test

Test that is applied to classifications based on race.

intermediate scrutiny test

Test that is applied to classifications based on protected classes other than race (e.g., sex or age).

rational basis test

Test that is applied to classifications not involving a suspect or protected class.

The Supreme Court Speaks

Equal Protection Clause Protects Against Government Discrimination

Village of Willowbrook v. Olech,
528 U.S. 562, 120 S.Ct. 1073 (2000),
2000 U.S. Lexis 1540
Supreme Court of the United States

BACKGROUND AND FACTS

Grace Olech, who owned real property in the Village of Willowbrook, asked the Village to connect her property to the municipal water supply. The Village conditioned the connection requiring Olech to grant the Village a 33-foot easement across her property. Olech cited evidence that the Village only required a 15-foot easement from other real property owners seeking access to the Village's water supply. Olech claimed that the Village's demand for an additional 18-foot easement from her was irrational and arbitrary, and was actually motivated by ill will resulting from her previous filing of an unrelated, successful lawsuit against the Village. Olech sued the Village claiming that the Village's action violated the Equal Protection Clause of the U.S. Constitution. The district court dismissed the lawsuit, but the court of appeals reversed, allowing Olech to sue. The U.S. Supreme Court granted certiorari to hear the case.

SUPREME COURT ISSUE

Can a party of one qualify as a "class" to bring a lawsuit alleging a violation of the Equal Protection Clause of the U.S. Constitution?

IN THE LANGUAGE OF THE U.S. SUPREME COURT

Our cases have recognized successful Equal Protection Clause claims brought by a "class of one," where the plaintiff alleges that she has been intentionally treated differently from others similarly situated and that there is no rational basis for the difference in treatment. We have explained that the purpose of the Equal Protection Clause of the Fourteenth Amendment is to secure every person within the State's jurisdiction against intentional and arbitrary discrimination, whether occasioned by express terms of a statute or by its improper execution through duly constituted agents. That reasoning is applicable to this case. Olech's complaint can fairly be construed as alleging that the Village intentionally demanded a 33-foot easement as a condition of connecting her property to the municipal water supply where the Village required only a 15-foot easement from other similarly situated property owners.

DECISION AND REMEDY

The U.S. Supreme Court held that Olech, a "class of one," may pursue an Equal Protection Clause claim against the Village of Willowbrook.

CASE QUESTIONS

Critical Legal Thinking   What does the Equal Protection Clause protect persons from? Which one of the following tests would be applied in analyzing the legality of the Village of Willowbrook's action?

1. Strict scrutiny test
2. Intermediate scrutiny test
3. Rational basis test

Business Ethics   Do you think Olech was discriminated against by the Village? Was this a violation of the Equal Protection Clause?

Contemporary Business   Can government laws or decisions treat classes of businesses or industries differently without violating the Equal Protection Clause? If so, give an example.

Due Process Clause

Due Process Clause

A clause that provides that no person shall be deprived of "life, liberty, or property" without due process of the law.

The Fifth and Fourteenth Amendments to the U.S. Constitution both contain a **Due Process Clause**. These clauses provide that no person shall be deprived of "life, liberty, or property" without due process of the law. The Due Process Clause of the Fifth Amendment applies to federal government action; that of the Fourteenth Amendment applies to state and local government action. It is important to understand that the government is not prohibited from taking a person's life, liberty, or property. However, the government must follow due process to do so. There are two categories do due process: *substantive* and *procedural*.

substantive due process

Requires that government statutes, ordinances, regulations, or other laws be clear on their face and not overly broad in scope.

Substantive Due Process   This category of due process requires that government statutes, ordinances, regulations, or other laws be clear on their face and not overly broad in scope. The test of whether substantive due process is met is whether a "reasonable person" could understand the law to be able to comply with it. Laws that do not meet this test are declared *void for vagueness*. Suppose, for example, that a city ordinance made it illegal for persons to wear "clothes of the opposite sex." Such an ordinance would be held unconstitutional as void for vagueness because a reasonable person could not clearly determine whether his or her conduct violates the law.

Procedural Due Process   This form of due process requires that the government must give a person proper *notice* and *hearing* of the legal action before that person is deprived of his or her life, liberty, or property. The government action must be fair. For example, if the government wants to take a person's home by eminent domain to build a highway, the government must (1) give the homeowner sufficient notice of its intention and (2) provide a hearing. Under the **Just Compensation Clause** of the Fifth Amendment, the government must pay the owner just compensation for taking the property.

procedural due process

Requires that the government must give a person proper notice and hearing of the legal action before that person is deprived of his or her life, liberty or property.

CONCEPT SUMMARY   DUE PROCESS

Type of Due Process	Description
Substantive due process	Requires government laws to be clear and not overly broad. The test is whether a reasonable person could understand the law.
Procedural due process	Requires the government to give a person proper notice and hearing before depriving that person of his or her life, liberty, or property.

Business Ethics

WHEN ARE PUNITIVE DAMAGES TOO BIG?

Punitive damages are damages that can be awarded to plaintiffs in civil cases. These damages are assessed against defendants who have engaged in fraud, intentional misconduct, or other egregious conduct. They are intended to (1) punish the defendant, (2) deter the defendant from similar conduct in the future, and (3) set an example for others. Punitive damages are awarded in addition to actual damages.

U.S. businesses have argued for years that the award of punitive damages has gotten out of hand. They point to hundreds of multimillion-dollar punitive damage awards to back up their claim. Plaintiffs, on the other hand, argue that punitive damages serve a useful purpose and that without them businesses could engage in reprehensible conduct with impunity.

The U.S. Supreme Court addressed the issue of punitive damages in *BMW of North America, Inc. v. Gore* [517 U.S. 559, 116 S.Ct 1589 (U.S.)]. In that case, Dr. Ira Gore, Jr., purchased a black BMW sports sedan for $40,470 from an authorized BMW dealer. Later, Dr. Gore discovered that several panels on the car had been repainted by BMW because of damage suffered while the car was being transported from Germany to the United States. BMW failed to disclose this fact to Dr. Gore when he purchased the car.

Dr. Gore sued BMW for fraud. The jury found BMW liable and awarded Dr. Gore $4,000 in compensatory damages and $4 million in punitive damages. The Alabama

Supreme Court reduced the punitive damages to $2 million. BMW appealed to the U.S. Supreme Court.

In a 5–4 decision, the Supreme Court found that the punitive damage was "grossly excessive" and therefore violated the Due Process Clause of the U.S. Constitution. The Court based its determination on the fact that the harm was purely economic, the repainting had no effect on the car's performance, BMW's conduct evinced no reckless disregard for the health and safety of others, and the amount of the punitive damages— 500 times actual damages—was excessive. The Supreme Court remanded the case to the Alabama supreme court for a determination of reasonable punitive damages. On remand, the award was reduced to $50,000 by the Alabama court.

The business community hailed the *BMW v. Gore* decision as a necessary limitation on oppressive and excessive awards of punitive damages by juries. Plaintiffs' lawyers and consumer groups argue that the case reduces an important lever against businesses that engage in unethical and illegal conduct.

1. What purposes are served by the award of punitive damages?
2. Do you think that the specter of punitive damage awards forces companies to act more ethically?
3. Should punitive damages be awarded to charities or other worthy causes rather than to the plaintiff?

The Privileges and Immunities Clause

The purpose of the U.S. Constitution is to promote nationalism. If the states were permitted to enact laws that favored their residents over out-of-state residents, the concept of nationalism would be defeated. Both Article IV of the Constitution and the Fourteenth Amendment contain a **Privileges and Immunities Clause** that prohibits states from enacting laws that unduly discriminate in favor of their residents. For example, a state cannot enact a law that prevents residents of other states from owning property or businesses in that state. Only invidious discrimination is prohibited. Thus, state universities are permitted to charge out-of-state residents higher tuition than instate residents. Note that this clause applies only to citizens; corporations are not protected.

Privileges and Immunities Clause

A clause that prohibits states from enacting laws that unduly discriminate in favor of their residents.

International Law

CONSTITUTION OF THE PEOPLE'S REPUBLIC OF CHINA

**CHAPTER TWO
THE FUNDAMENTAL RIGHTS AND DUTIES OF CITIZENS
[SELECTED PROVISIONS]**

ARTICLE 33
All citizens of the People's Republic of China are equal before the law.

ARTICLE 34
All citizens of the People's Republic of China who have reached the age of 18 have the right to vote and stand for election, regardless of ethnic status, race, sex, occupation, family background, religious belief, education, property status or length of residence, except persons deprived of political rights according to law.

ARTICLE 35
Citizens of the People's Republic of China enjoy freedom of speech, of the press, of assembly, of association, of procession and of demonstration.

ARTICLE 36
Citizens of the People's Republic of China enjoy freedom of religious belief. No state organ, public organization or individual may compel citizens to believe in, or not to believe in, any religion; nor may they discriminate against citizens who believe in, or do not believe in, any religion.

ARTICLE 40
Freedom and privacy of correspondence of citizens of the People's Republic of China are protected by law. No organization or individual may, on any ground, infringe upon citizens' freedom and privacy of correspondence, except in cases where, to meet the needs of state security or of criminal investigation, public security or procuratorial organs are permitted to censor correspondence in accordance with procedures prescribed by law.

ARTICLE 41
Citizens of the People's Republic of China have the right to criticize and make suggestions regarding any state organ or functionary.

ARTICLE 48
Women in the People's Republic of China enjoy equal rights with men in all spheres of life, in political, economic, cultural, social and family life.

ARTICLE 54
It is the duty of citizens of the People's Republic of China to safeguard the security, honor and interests of the motherland; they must not commit acts detrimental to the security, honor and interests of the motherland.

CHAPTER SUMMARY

Basic Constitutional Concepts p. 55

The U.S. Constitution	The Constitution consists of 7 articles and 26 amendments. It establishes the three branches of the federal government, enumerates their powers, and provides important guarantees of individual freedom. The Constitution was ratified by the states in 1788.

Basic Constitutional Concepts	1. *Federalism.* The Constitution created the federal government. The federal government and the 50 state governments share powers in this country.
	2. *Delegated powers.* When the states ratified the Constitution, they delegated certain powers to the federal government. These are called *enumerated powers.*
	3. *Reserved powers.* Those powers not granted to the federal government by the Constitution are reserved to the states.
	4. *Separation of powers.* Each branch of the federal government has separate powers. These powers are:
	  a. Legislative branch—power to make the law.
	  b. Executive branch—power to enforce the law.
	  c. Judicial branch—power to interpret the law.
	5. *Checks and balances.* Certain checks and balances are built into the Constitution to ensure that no one branch of the federal government becomes too powerful.

The Supremacy Clause p. 56

The Supremacy Clause	Stipulates that the U.S. Constitution, treaties, and federal law (statutes and regulations) are the *supreme law of the land.* State or local laws that conflict with valid federal law are unconstitutional. This is called the *preemption doctrine.*

The Commerce Clause p. 59

The Commerce Clause	1. *Commerce Clause.* Authorizes the federal government to regulate commerce with foreign nations, among the states, and with Indian tribes. 2. *Interstate commerce.* Under the broad *effects test,* the federal government may regulate any activity (even intrastate commerce) that *affects* interstate commerce. 3. *Undue burden on interstate commerce.* Any state or local law that causes an undue burden on interstate commerce is unconstitutional as a violation of the Commerce Clause.

The Bill of Rights and Business, p. 64

The Bill of Rights	Consists of the first 10 amendments to the Constitution. They establish basic individual rights. The Bill of Rights was ratified in 1791.

Freedom of Speech	1. *Freedom of Speech Clause.* Clause of the First Amendment that guarantees that the government shall not infringe on a person's right to speak. Protects oral, written, and symbolic speech. This right is not absolute—that is, some speech is not protected and other speech is granted only limited protection.
	2. *Fully protected speech.* Speech that cannot be prohibited or regulated by the government.
	3. *Limited protected speech.* The following types of speech are granted only limited protection under the Freedom of Speech Clause—that is, they are subject to governmental *time, place, and manner restrictions.*
	  a. Offensive speech
	  b. Commercial speech
	4. *Unprotected speech.* The following speech is not protected by the Freedom of Speech Clause:
	  a. Dangerous speech
	  b. Fighting words
	  c. Speech that advocates the violent overthrow of the government
	  d. Defamatory language
	  e. Child pornography
	  f. Obscene speech

| **Freedom of Religion** | There are two religion clauses in the First Amendment. They are:
 1. *Establishment Clause.* Prohibits the government from establishing a state religion or promoting religion.
 2. *Free Exercise Clause.* Prohibits the government from interfering with the free exercise of religion. This right is not absolute: for example, human sacrifices are forbidden. |

Other Constitutional Clauses and Business, p. 71

Equal Protection Clause	*Equal Protection Clause.* Prohibits the government from enacting laws that classify and treat "similarly situated" persons differently. This standard is not absolute. The U.S. Supreme Court has applied the following tests to determine if the Equal Protection Clause has been violated: 1. *Strict scrutiny test.* Applies to *suspect classes* (e.g., race and national origin). 2. *Intermediate scrutiny test.* Applies to other *protected classes* (e.g., sex and age). 3. *Rational basis test.* Applies to government classifications that do not involve a suspect or protected class.
Due Process Clause	*Due Process Clause.* Provides that no person shall be deprived of "life, liberty, or property" without due process. There are two categories of due process: 1. *Substantive due process.* Requires that laws be clear on their face and not overly broad in scope. Laws that do not meet this test are *void for vagueness.* 2. *Procedural due process.* Requires that the government give a person proper *notice* and *hearing* before that person is deprived of his or her life, liberty, or property. An owner must be paid *just compensation* if the government takes his or her property.
Privileges and Immunities Clause	Prohibits states from enacting laws that unduly discriminate in favor of their residents over residents of other states.

END-OF-CHAPTER INTERNET EXERCISES AND CASE QUESTIONS

Working the Web Internet Exercises

ACTIVITIES

Visit **www.infoctr.edu/fwl**, the Web site for the Federal Law Locator. Try the following:

1. Check on the product safety record for selected products at the U.S. Consumer Product Safety Commission site. For example, *CPSC, Burger King Corporation Announce Voluntary Recall of Pokemon Ball.*

2. Find and compare the U.S. Constitution to the Washington State Constitution **www.access.wa.gov**. How are they similar? How are they different?

3. Locate the municipal code for your city. Find the law on loitering in public places. Is it constitutional?

4. Find and review the USA Patriot Act of 2001. Is it constitutional?

CRITICAL LEGAL THINKING CASES

3.1 Separation of Powers   In 1951, a dispute arose between steel companies and their employees about the terms and conditions that should be included in a new labor contract. At the time, the United States was engaged in a military conflict in Korea that required substantial steel resources from which to make weapons and other military goods. On April 4, 1952, the steelworkers' union gave notice of a nationwide strike called to begin at 12:01 A.M. on April 9. The indispensabil- ity of steel as a component in weapons and other war materials led President Dwight D. Eisenhower to believe that the pro- posed strike would jeopardize the national defense and that gov- ernmental seizure of the steel mills was necessary in order to ensure the continued availability of steel. Therefore, a few hours before the strike was to begin, the president issued Executive Order 10340, which directed the secretary of commerce to take possession of most of the steel mills and keep them running. The steel companies obeyed the order under protest and brought proceedings against the president. Was the seizure of the steel mills constitutional? [*Youngstown Co. v. Sawyer, Secretary of Commerce*, 343 U.S. 579, 72 S.Ct. 863, 96 L.Ed. 2d 1153 (1952)]

3.2 Preemption Doctrine Article 1, Section 8, clause 8 of the U.S. Constitution grants Congress the power to enact laws to give inventors the exclusive right to their discoveries. Pursuant to this power, Congress enacted federal patent laws that establish the requirements to obtain a patent. Once a patent is granted, the patent holder has exclusive rights to use the patent. Bonito Boats, Inc. developed a hull design for a fiberglass recreational boat that it marketed under the trade name Bonito Boats Model 5VBR. The manufacturing process involved creating a hardwood model that was sprayed with fiberglass to create a mold. The mold then served to produce the finished fiberglass boats for sale. Bonito did not file a patent application to protect the utilitarian or design aspects of the hull or the manufacturing process. After the Bonito 5VBR was on the market for six years, the Florida legislature enacted a statute prohibiting the use of a direct molding process to duplicate unpatented boat hulls and forbade the knowing sale of hulls so duplicated. The protection afforded under the state statute was broader than that provided for under the federal patent statute. Subsequently, Thunder Craft Boats, Inc. produced and sold boats made by the direct molding process. Bonito sued Thunder Craft under Florida law. Is the Florida statute valid? [*Bonito Boats, Inc. v. Thunder Craft Boats, Inc.*, 489 U.S. 141, 109 S.Ct. 971, 103 L.Ed.2d 118 (1989)]

3.3 Commerce Clause The Heart of Atlanta Motel, located in the state of Georgia, has 216 rooms available to guests. The motel is readily accessible to interstate highways 75 and 85 and to state highways 23 and 41. The motel solicits patronage from outside the state of Georgia through various national advertising media, including magazines of national circulation, and it maintains more than 50 billboards and highway signs within the state. Approximately 75 percent of the motel's registered guests are from out of state. Congress enacted the Civil Rights Act of 1964, which made it illegal for public accommodations to discriminate against guests based on their race. Prior to that, the Heart of Atlanta Motel had refused to rent rooms to blacks. After the act was passed, it alleged that it intended to continue not to rent rooms to blacks. The owner of the motel brought an action to have the Civil Rights Act of 1964 declared unconstitutional, alleging that Congress, in passing the act, had exceeded its powers to regulate commerce under the Commerce Clause of the U.S. Constitution. Who wins? [*Heart of Atlanta Motel v. United States*, 379 U.S. 241, 85 S.Ct. 348, 13 L.Ed.2d 258 (1964)]

3.4 Commerce and Supremacy Clause In 1972, Congress enacted a federal statute, called the Ports and Waterways Safety Act, that established uniform standards for the operation of boats on inland waterways in the United States. The act coordinated its provisions with those of foreign countries so that there was a uniform body of international rules that applied to vessels that traveled between countries. Pursuant to the act, a federal rule was adopted that regulated the design, length, and size of oil tankers,

some of which traveled the waters of the Puget Sound area in State of Washington. Oil tankers from various places entered Puget Sound to bring crude oil to refineries located in Washington. In 1975, the State of Washington enacted a statute that established different designs, smaller lengths, and smaller sizes for oil tankers serving Puget Sound than allowed by the federal law. Oil tankers used by the Atlantic Richfield Company (ARCO) to bring oil into Puget Sound met the federal standards but not the state standards. ARCO sued to have the state statute declared unconstitutional. Who wins? [*Ray, Governor of Washington v. Atlantic Richfield Co.*, 435 U.S. 151, 98 S.Ct. 988, 55 L.Ed.2d 179 (1978)]

3.5 Undue Burden on Interstate Commerce Most trucking firms, including Consolidated Freightways Corporation, use 65-foot-long "double" trailer trucks to ship commodities on the highway system across the United States. Almost all states permit these vehicles on their highways. The federal government does not regulate the length of trucks that can use the nation's highways. The state of Iowa enacted a statute that restricts the length of trucks that can use highways in the state to 55 feet. This means that if Consolidated wants to move goods through Iowa it must either use smaller trucks or detach the double trailers and shuttle them through the state separately. Its only other alternative is to divert its 65-foot doubles around Iowa. Consolidated filed suit against Iowa alleging that the state statute is unconstitutional. Is it? [*Kassel v. Consolidated Freightways Corporation*, 450 U.S. 662, 101 S.Ct. 1309, 57 L.Ed.2d 580 (1981)]

3.6 Privileges and Immunities Clause During the 1970s, a period of a booming economy in Alaska, many residents of other states moved there in search of work. Construction work on the Trans-Alaska Pipeline was a major source of employment. In 1972, the Alaska legislature enacted an act entitled the "Local Hire" Statute. This act required employers to hire Alaska residents in preference to nonresidents. Is this statute constitutional? [*Hicklin v. Orbeck, Commissioner of the Department of Labor of Alaska*, 437 U.S. 518, 98 S.Ct. 2482, 57 L.Ed.2d 397 (1978)]

3.7 Offensive Speech Satiric humorist George Carlin recorded a 12-minute monologue entitled "Filthy Words" before a live audience in a California theater. He began referring to "the words you couldn't say on the public airwaves—the ones you definitely couldn't say, ever." He proceeded to list those words and repeat them over and over again in a variety of colloquialisms. At about 2:00 P.M. on October 30, 1973, a New York radio station owned by Pacifica Foundation broadcast the "Filthy Words" monologue. A man who heard the broadcast while driving with his young son complained to the FCC, the federal administrative agency in charge of granting radio licenses and regulating radio broadcasts. The FCC administers a statute that forbids the use of any offensive language on the radio. The FCC found that Carlin's monologue violated this law and censured the Pacifica Foundation for playing the monologue. Can the FCC prohibit Pacifica Foundation from playing the Carlin monologue on the radio? [*Federal Communications Commission v. Pacifica Foundation*, 438 U.S. 726, 98 S.Ct. 3026, L.Ed.2d 1073 (1978)]

3.8 Commercial Speech The city of San Diego, California, enacted a city zoning ordinance that prohibited outdoor advertising display signs—including billboards. On-site signs at a business location were exempted from this rule. The city based the restriction on traffic safety and aesthetics. Metromedia, Inc., a company that is in the business of leasing commercial billboards to advertisers, sued the city of San Diego, alleging that the zoning ordinance is unconstitutional. Is it? [*Metromedia, Inc. v. City of San Diego*, 453 U.S. 490, 101 S.Ct. 2882, 69 L.Ed.2d 800 (1981)]

3.9 Freedom of Religion Eddie C. Thomas, a Jehovah's Witness, was initially hired to work in a roll factory at Blaw-Knox Company. The function of the department was to fabricate sheet steel for a variety of industrial uses. On his application, Thomas listed that he was a Jehovah's Witness. Approximately one year later, the roll foundry closed and Blaw-Knox transferred Thomas to a department that fabricated turrets for military tanks. On the first day at his new job, Thomas realized that the work he was doing violated his religious beliefs because it was weapon-related. Because there were no other jobs available, Thomas quit and filed for unemployment compensation. The state of Indiana denied his claim on the ground that Thomas quit his job for personal reasons. Thomas sued, alleging that the government's denial of unemployment benefits violated his right to freedom of religion. Who wins? [*Thomas v. Review Board of the Indiana Employment Security Division*, 450 U.S. 707, 101 S.Ct. 1425, 67 L.Ed.2d 624 (1981)]

3.10 Substantive Due Process On February 20, 1978, the village of Hoffman Estates, Illinois, enacted an ordinance regulating drug paraphernalia. The ordinance made it unlawful for any person "to sell any items, effect, paraphernalia, accessory or thing which is designed or marketed for use with illegal cannabis or drugs as defined by Illinois Revised Statutes, without obtaining a license therefore." The license fee was $150. A violation was subject to a fine of not more than $500. The Flipside, a retail store located in the village, sold a variety of merchandise, including smoking accessories, clamps, roach clips, scales, water pipes, vials, cigarette rolling papers, and other items. On May 30, 1978, instead of applying for a license, Flipside filed a lawsuit against the village, alleging that the ordinance was unconstitutional as a violation of substantive due process because it was overly broad and vague. Who wins? [*Village of Hoffman Estates v. Flipside, Hoffman Estates, Inc.*, 455 U.S. 489, 102 S.Ct. 1186, 71 L.Ed.2d. 362 (1982)]

3.11 Equal Protection Clause The state of Alabama enacted a statute that imposed a tax on premiums earned by insurance companies. The statute imposed a 1 percent tax on domestic insurance companies (i.e., insurance companies that were incorporated in Alabama and had their principal office in the state). The statute imposed a 4 percent tax on the premiums earned by out-of-state insurance companies that sold insurance in Alabama. Out-of-state insurance companies could reduce the premium tax by 1 percent by investing at least 10 percent of their assets in Alabama. Domestic insurance companies did not have to invest any of their assets in Alabama. Metropolitan Life Insurance Company, an out-of-state insurance company, sued the state of Alabama, alleging that the Alabama statute violated the Equal Protection Clause of the U.S. Constitution. Who wins? [*Metropolitan Life Insurance Co. v. Ward, Commissioner of Insurance of Alabama*, 470 U.S. 689, 105 S.Ct. 1676, 84 L.Ed.2d 751 (1985)]

BUSINESS ETHICS CASES

3.12 Business Ethics The "Raiders" are a professional football team and a National Football League (NFL) franchise. Each NFL franchise is independently owned. Al Davis is an owner and the managing general partner of the Raiders. The NFL establishes schedules, negotiates television contracts, and otherwise promotes NFL football, including conducting the "Super Bowl" each year. The Raiders play home and away games against other NFL teams.

Up until 1982, the Raiders played their home games in Oakland, California. The owners of the Raiders decided to move the team from Oakland to Los Angeles, California, to take advantage of the greater seating capacity of the Los Angeles Coliseum, the larger television market of Los Angeles, and other economic reasons. The renamed team was to be known as the "Los Angeles Raiders." The city of Oakland brought an eminent domain proceeding in court to acquire the Raiders as a city-owned team. Can the city of Oakland acquire the Raiders through eminent domain? Is it socially responsible for a professional sports team to move to another location? [*City of Oakland,*

California v. Oakland Raiders, 174 C.A.3d 414, 220 Cal. Rptr. 153 (Cal.App. 1985)]

3.13 Business Ethics In 1989, Congress enacted the Flag Protection Act, which made it a crime to knowingly mutilate, deface, physically defile, burn, or trample the U.S. flag. The law provided for fines and up to one year in prison upon conviction [18 U.S.C. § 700]. Certain individuals set fire to several U.S. flags on the steps of the U.S. Capitol in Washington, DC, to protest various aspects of the federal government's foreign and domestic policy. In a separate incident, other individuals set fire to a U.S. flag to protest the act's passage. All of these individuals were prosecuted for violating the act. The district courts held the act unconstitutional in violation of the defendants' First Amendment free speech rights and dismissed the charges. The government appealed to the U.S. Supreme Court, which consolidated the two cases. Who wins? Does the flag burner exhibit any morals? [*United States v. Eichman*, 496 U.S. 310, 110 S.Ct. 2404, 110 L.Ed.2d 287 (1990)]

BRIEFING THE CASE WRITING ASSIGNMENT

Read the following case, which has been excerpted from the court's opinions. Review and brief the case.

Lee v. Weisman
112 S.CT. 2649 (1992)
United States Supreme Court

Kennedy, Justice

Deborah Weisman graduated from Nathan Bishop Middle School, a public school in Providence, at a formal ceremony in June 1989. She was about 14 years old. For many years it has been the policy of the Providence School committee and the Superintendent of Schools to permit principals to invite members of the clergy to give invocations and benedictions at middle school and high school graduations. Many, but not all, of the principals elected to include prayers as part of the graduation ceremonies. Acting for himself and his daughter, Deborah's father, Daniel Weisman, objected to any prayers at Deborah's middle school graduation, but to no avail. The school principal, petitioner Robert E. Lee, invited a rabbi to deliver prayers at the graduation exercises for Deborah's class. Rabbi Leslie Gutterman, of the Temple Beth El in Providence, accepted.

It has been the custom of Providence school officials to provide invited clergy with a pamphlet entitled "Guidelines for Civic Occasions," prepared by the National Conference of Christians and Jews. The Guidelines recommended that public prayers at nonsectarian civic ceremonies be composed with "inclusiveness and sensitivity," though they acknowledge that "prayer of any kind may be inappropriate on some civic occasions." The principal gave Rabbi Gutterman the pamphlet before the graduation and advised him the invocation and benediction should be nonsectarian.

Deborah's graduation was held on the premises of Nathan Bishop Middle School on June 29, 1989. Four days before the ceremony, Daniel Weisman, in his individual capacity as a Providence taxpayer and as next friend of Deborah, sought a temporary restraining order in the United States District Court for the District of Rhode Island to prohibit school officials from including an invocation or benediction in the graduation ceremony. The court denied the motion for lack of adequate time to consider it. Deborah and her family attended the graduation, where the prayers were recited. In July 1989, Daniel Weisman filed an amended complaint seeking a permanent injunction barring petitioners, various officials of the Providence public schools, from inviting the clergy to deliver invocations and benedictions at future graduations.

The case was submitted on stipulated facts. The District Court held that petitioners' practice of including invocations and benedictions in public school graduations violated the Establishment Clause of the First Amendment, and it enjoined petitioners from continuing the practice. The court applied the three-part Establishment Clause test. Under the test, to satisfy the Establishment Clause a governmental practice must (1) reflect a clearly secu-lar purpose; (2) have a primary effect that neither advances nor inhibits religion; and (3) avoid excessive government entanglement with religion. On appeal, the United States Court of Appeals for the First Circuit affirmed.

These dominant facts mark and control the confines of our decision: State officials direct the performance of a formal religious exercise at promotional and graduation ceremonies for secondary schools. Even for those students who object to the religious exercise, their attendance and participation in the state-sponsored religious activity are in a fair and real sense obligatory, though the school district does not require attendance as a condition for receipt of the diploma.

The controlling precedents as they relate to the prayer and religious exercise in primary and secondary public schools compel the holding here that the policy of the city of Providence is an unconstitutional one. It is beyond dispute that, at a minimum, the Constitution guarantees that government may not coerce anyone to support or participate in religion or its exercise, or otherwise act in a way which "establishes a state religion or religious faith, or tends to do so."

We are asked to recognize the existence of a practice of nonsectarian prayer within the embrace of what is known as the Judeo-Christian tradition, prayer which is more acceptable than one which, for example, makes explicit references to the God of Israel, or to Jesus Christ, or to a patron saint. If common ground can be defined which permits once conflicting faiths to express the shared conviction that there is an ethic and a morality which transcend human invention, the sense of community and purpose sought by all decent societies might be advanced. But though the First Amendment does not allow the government to stifle prayers which aspire to these ends, neither does it permit the government to undertake that task for itself.

The sole question presented is whether a religious exercise may be conducted at a graduation ceremony in circumstances where, as we have found, young graduates who object are induced to conform. No holding by this Court suggests that a school can persuade or compel a student to participate in a religious exercise. That is being done here, and it is forbidden by the Establishment Clause of the First Amendment.

For the reasons we have stated, the judgment of the Court of Appeals is affirmed.

Scalia, Justice (joined by Rehnquist, White, and Thomas) dissenting, expressed the view that (1) the establishment of religion clause should not have been interpreted so as to invalidate a longstanding American tradition of nonsectarian prayer at public school graduations, (2) graduation invocations and benedictions involve no psychological coercion of students to participate in religious exercises, (3) the only coercion that is forbidden by the establishment of religion clause is that which is backed by a threat of penalty, and (4) the middle school principal did not direct or control the content of the prayers in questions, and thus there was no pervasive government involvement with religious activity.

ENDNOTES

1. To be elected to Congress, an individual must be a U.S. citizen, either naturally born or granted citizenship. To serve in the Senate, a person must be 30 years of age or older. To serve in the House of Representatives, a person must be 25 years of age or older.

2. To be president, a person must be 35 years of age or older and a natural citizen of the United States. By amendments to the Constitution (Amendment XXII), a person can serve only two full terms as president.

3. Federal court judges and justices are appointed by the president with the consent of the Senate.

4. The principle that the U.S. Supreme Court is the final arbiter of the U.S. Constitution evolved from *Marbury v. Madison*, 1 Cranch 137 (1803). In that case, the Supreme Court held that a judiciary statute enacted by Congress was unconstitutional.

5. Article VI, Section 2.

6. Article I, Section 8, clause 3.

7. 317 U.S. Ill., 63 S.Ct. 82 (1942).

8. 115 S.Ct. 1624 (1995).

9. 425 U.S. 748, 96 S.Ct. 1817 (1976).

10. *Chaplinsky v. New Hampshire.* 315 U.S. 568, 62 S.Ct. 766 (1942).

11. *Brandenburg v. Ohio.* 395 U.S. 444, 89 S.Ct. 1827 (1969).

12. *Beauharnais v. Illinois.* 343 U.S. 250, 72 S.Ct. 725 (1952).

13. *New York v. Ferber.* 458 U.S. 747, 102 S.Ct. 3348 (1982).

14. *Roth v. United States.* 354 U.S. 476, 77 S.Ct. 1304 (1957).

15. Justice Stewart in *Jacobellis v. Ohio.* 378 U.S. 184, 84 S.Ct. 1676 (1963).

16. 413 U.S. 15, 93 S.Ct. 2607 (1973).

17. *Wallace v. Jaffree*, 472 U.S. 38, 105 S.Ct. 2479 (1985).

18. 113 S.Ct. 2217 (1993).

The Constitution of the United States of America

We the People of the United States, in Order to form a more perfect Union, establish Justice, insure domestic Tranquility, provide for the common defense, promote the general Welfare, and secure the Blessings of Liberty to ourselves and our Posterity, do ordain and establish this Constitution for the United States of America.

ARTICLE I

Section 1. All legislative Powers herein granted shall be vested in a Congress of the United States, which shall consist of a Senate and House of Representatives.

Section 2. The House of Representatives shall be composed of Members chosen every second Year by the People of the several states, and the Electors in each State shall have the Qualifications requisite for Electors of the most numerous Branch of the State Legislature.

No Person shall be a Representative who shall not have attained to the Age of twenty five Years, and been seven Years a Citizen of the United States, and who shall not, when elected, be an Inhabitant of that State in which he shall be chosen.

Representatives and direct Taxes shall be apportioned among the several states which may be included within this Union, according to their respective Numbers, which shall be determined by adding to the whole Number of free Persons, including those bound to Service for a Term of Years, and excluding Indians not taxed, three fifths of all other Persons. The actual Enumeration shall be made within three Years after the first Meeting of the Congress of the United States, and within every subsequent Term of ten Years, in such Manner as they shall by Law direct. The number of Representatives shall not exceed one for every thirty Thousand, but each State shall have at Least one Representative; and until such enumeration shall be made, the State of New Hampshire shall be entitled to chuse three, Massachusetts eight, Rhode Island and Providence Plantations one, Connecticut five, New York six, New Jersey four, Pennsylvania eight, Delaware one, Maryland six, Virginia ten, North Carolina five, South Carolina five, and Georgia three.

When vacancies happen in the Representation from any State, the Executive Authority thereof shall issue Writs of Election to fill such vacancies.

The House of Representatives shall chuse their Speaker and other Officers; and shall have the sole Power of Impeachment.

Section 3. The Senate of the United States shall be composed of two Senators from each State, chosen by the Legislature thereof, for six Years; and each Senator shall have one Vote.

Immediately after they shall be assembled in Consequence of the first Election, they shall be divided as equally as may be into three Classes. The Seats of the Senators of the first Class shall be vacated at the Expiration of the second Year, of the second Class at the Expiration of the fourth Year, and the third Class at the Expiration of the sixth Year, so that one third may be chosen every second Year; and if Vacancies happen by Resignation, or otherwise, during the Recess of the Legislature of any State, the Executive thereof may make temporary Appointments until the next meeting of the Legislature, which shall then fill such Vacancies.

No person shall be a Senator who shall not have attained to the Age of thirty Years, and been nine Years a Citizen of the United States, and who shall not, when elected, be an Inhabitant of that State for which he shall be chosen.

The Vice President of the United States shall be President of the Senate, but shall have no Vote, unless they be equally divided.

The Senate shall chuse their other Officers, and also a President pro tempore, in the Absence of the Vice President, or when he shall exercise the Office of President of the United States.

The Senate shall have the sole power to try all Impeachments. When sitting for that Purpose, they shall be an Oath or Affirmation. When the President of the United States is tried, the Chief Justice shall preside: And no Person shall be convicted without the Concurrence of two thirds of the Members present.

Judgment in Cases of Impeachment shall not extend further than to removal from Office, and disqualification to hold and enjoy any Office of honor, Trust or Profit under the United States: but the Party convicted shall nevertheless be liable and subject to Indictment, Trial, Judgment and Punishment, according to Law.

Section 4. The Times, Places and Manner of holding Elections for Senators and Representatives, shall be prescribed in each State by the Legislature thereof: but the Congress may at any time by Law make or alter such Regulations, except as to the Places of chusing Senators.

The Congress shall assemble at least once in every Year, and such Meeting shall be on the first Monday in December, unless they shall by Law appoint a different day.

Section 5. Each House shall be the Judge of the Elections, Returns and Qualifications of its own Members, and a Majority of each shall constitute a Quorum to do Business; but a smaller Number may adjourn from day to day, and may be authorized to compel the Attendance of absent Members, in such Manner, and under such Penalties as each House may provide.

Each House may determine the Rules of its Proceedings, punish its Members for disorderly Behaviour, and, with the Concurrence of two thirds, expel a Member.

Each House shall keep a Journal of its Proceedings, and from time to time publish the same, excepting such Parts as may in their Judgment require Secrecy; and the Yeas and Nays of the Members of either House on any question shall, at the Desire of one fifth of those Present, be entered on the Journal.

Neither House, during the Session of Congress, shall, without the Consent of the other, adjourn for more than three days, nor to any other Place than that in which the two Houses shall be sitting.

Section 6. The Senators and Representatives shall receive a Compensation for their Services, to be ascertained by Law, and paid out of the Treasury of the United States. They shall in all Cases, except Treason, Felony and Breach of the Peace, be privileged from Arrest during their Attendance at the Session of their respective Houses, and in going to and returning from the same; and for any Speech or Debate in either House, they shall not be questioned in any other Place.

No Senator or Representative shall, during the Time for which he was elected, be appointed to any civil Office under the Authority of the United States, which shall have been created, or the Emoluments whereof shall have been encreased during such time; and no Person holding any Office under the United States, shall be a Member of either House during his Continuance in Office.

Section 7. All Bills for raising Revenue shall originate in the House of Representatives; but the Senate may propose or concur with Amendments as on other Bills.

Every Bill which shall have passed the House of Representatives and the Senate, shall, before it become a Law, be presented to the President of the United States; If he approve he shall sign it, but if not he shall return it, with his Objections to that House in which it shall have originated, who shall enter the Objections at large on their Journal, and proceed to reconsider it. If after such Reconsideration two thirds of that House shall agree to pass the Bill, it shall be sent, together with the Objections, to the other House, by which it shall likewise be reconsidered, and if approved by two thirds of that House, it shall become a Law. But in all such Cases the Votes of both Houses shall be determined by Yeas and Nays, and the Names of the Persons voting for and against the Bill shall be entered on the Journal of each House respectively. If any Bill shall not be returned by the President within ten Days (Sundays excepted) after it shall have been presented to him, the Same shall be a Law, in like Manner as if he had signed it, unless the Congress by their Adjournment prevent its Return, in which Case it shall not be a Law.

Every Order, Resolution, or Vote to which the Concurrence of the Senate and House of Representatives may be necessary (except on a question of Adjournment)

shall be presented to the President of the United States; and before the Same shall take Effect, shall be approved by him, or being disapproved by him, shall be repassed by two thirds of the Senate and House of Representatives, according to the Rules and Limitations prescribed in the Case of a Bill.

Section 8. The Congress shall have Power to lay and collect Taxes, Duties, Imposts and Excises, to pay the Debts and provide for the common Defence and general Welfare of the United States; but all Duties, Imposts and Excises shall be uniform throughout the United States;

To borrow Money on the credit of the United States;

To regulate Commerce with foreign Nations, and among the several States, and with the Indian Tribes;

To establish an uniform Rule of Naturalization, and uniform Laws on the subject of Bankruptcies throughout the United States;

To coin Money, regulate the Value thereof, and of foreign Coin, and fix the Standard of Weights and Measures;

To provide for the Punishment of counterfeiting the Securities and current Coin of the United States;

To establish Post Offices and post Roads;

To promote the Progress of Science and useful Arts, by securing for limited Times to Authors and Inventors the exclusive Right to their respective Writings and Discoveries;

To constitute Tribunals inferior to the supreme Court;

To define and punish Piracies and Felonies committed on the high Seas, and Offenses against the Law of Nations;

To declare War, grant Letters of Marque and Reprisal, and make Rules concerning Captures on Land and Water;

To raise and support Armies, but no Appropriation of Money to that Use shall be for a longer Term than two Years;

To provide and maintain a Navy;

To make Rules for the Government and Regulation of the land and naval Forces;

To provide for calling forth the Militia to execute the Laws of the Union, suppress Insurrections and repel Invasions;

To provide for organizing, arming, and disciplining, the Militia, and for governing such Part of them as may be employed in the Service of the United States, reserving to the States respectively, the Appointment of the Officers, and the Authority of training the Militia according to the discipline prescribed by Congress;

To exercise exclusive Legislation in all Cases whatsoever, over such District (not exceeding ten Miles square) as may, by Cession of particular States, and the Acceptance of Congress, become the Seat of the Government of the United States, and to exercise like Authority over all Places purchased by the Consent of the Legislature of the State in which the Same shall be, for the Erection of Forts, Magazines, Arsenals, dock-Yards, and other needful Buildings;—And

To make all Laws which shall be necessary and proper for carrying into Execution the foregoing Powers, and all other Powers vested by this Constitution in the Government of the United States, or in any Department or Officer thereof.

Section 9.   The Migration or Importation of such Persons as any of the States now existing shall think proper to admit, shall not be prohibited by the Congress prior to the Year one thousand eight hundred and eight, but a Tax or Duty may be imposed on such Importation, not exceeding ten dollars for each Person.

The Privilege of the Writ of Habeas Corpus shall not be suspended, unless when in Cases of Rebellion or Invasion the public Safety may require it.

No Bill of Attainder or ex post facto Law shall be passed.

No Capitation, or other direct, Tax shall be laid, unless in Proportion to the Census or Enumeration herein before directed to be taken.

No Tax or Duty shall be laid on Articles exported from any State.

No Preference shall be given by any Regulation of Commerce or Revenue to the Ports of one State over those of another; nor shall Vessels bound to, or from, one State, be obliged to enter, clear, or pay Duties in another.

No Money shall be drawn from the Treasury, but in Consequence of Appropriations made by Laws; and a regular Statement and Account of the Receipts and Expenditures of all public Money shall be published from time to time.

No Title of Nobility shall be granted by the United States: And no Person holding any Office of Profit or Trust under them, shall, without the Consent of the Congress, accept of any present, Emolument, Office, or Title, of any kind whatever, from any King, Prince, or foreign State.

Section 10.   No State shall enter into any Treaty, Alliance, or Confederation; grant Letters of Marque and Reprisal; coin Money; emit Bills of Credit; make any Thing but gold and silver Coin a Tender in Payment of Debts; pass any Bill of Attainder, ex post facto Law, or Law impairing the Obligation of Contracts, or grant any Title of Nobility.

No State shall, without the Consent of the Congress, lay any Imposts or Duties on Imports or Exports, except what may be absolutely necessary for executing its inspection Laws: and the net Produce of all Duties and Imposts, laid by any State on Imports or Exports, shall be for the Use of the Treasury of the United States; and all such Laws shall be subject to the Revision and Controul of the Congress.

No State shall, without the Consent of Congress, lay any Duty of Tonnage, keep Troops, or Ships of War in time of Peace, enter into any Agreement or Compact with another State, or with a foreign Power, or engage in War, unless actually invaded, or in such imminent Danger as will not admit of delay.

ARTICLE II

Section 1.   The executive Power shall be vested in a President of the United States of America. He shall hold his Office during the Term of four Years, and, together with the Vice President, chosen for the same Term, be elected, as follows:

Each State shall appoint, in such Manner as the Legislature thereof may direct, a Number of Electors, equal to the whole Number of Senators and Representatives to which the State may be entitled in the Congress: but no Senator or Representative, or Person holding an Office of Trust or Profit under the United States, shall be appointed an Elector.

The Electors shall meet in their respective States, and vote by Ballot for two Persons, of whom one at least shall not be an Inhabitant of the same State with themselves. And they shall make a list of all the Persons voted for, and of the Number of Votes for each; which List they shall sign and certify, and transmit sealed to the Seat of the Government of the United States, directed to the President of the Senate. The President of the Senate shall, in the presence of the Senate and House of Representatives, open all the Certificates, and the Votes shall be counted. The Person having the greatest Number of Votes shall be the President, if such Number be a Majority of the whole Number of Electors appointed; and if there be more than one who have such Majority, and have an equal Number of Votes, then the House of Representatives shall immediately chuse by Ballot one of them for President; and if no Person have a Majority, then from the five highest on the List the said House shall in like Manner chuse the President. But in chusing the President, the Votes shall be taken by States, the Representation from each State having one Vote; A quorum for this Purpose shall consist of a Member or Members from two thirds of the States, and a Majority of all the States shall be necessary to a Choice. In every Case, after the Choice of the President, the Person having the greatest Number of Votes of the Electors shall be the Vice President. But if there should remain two or more who have equal Votes, the Senate shall chuse from them by Ballot the Vice President.

The Congress may determine the Time of Chusing the Electors, and the Day on which they shall give their Votes; which Day shall be the same throughout the United States.

No Person except a natural born Citizen, or a Citizen of the United States, at the time of the Adoption of this Constitution, shall be eligible to the Office of President; neither shall any Person be eligible to that Office who shall not have attained to the Age of thirty five Years, and been fourteen Years a Resident within the United States.

In Case of the Removal of the President from Office, or of his Death, Resignation, or Inability to discharge the Powers and Duties of the said Office, the Same shall devolve on the Vice President, and the Congress may by Law provide for the Case of Removal, Death, Resignation or Inability, both of the President and Vice President, declaring what Officer shall then act as President, and such Officer shall act accordingly, until the Disability be removed, or a President shall be elected.

The President shall, at stated Times, receive for his Services, a Compensation, which shall neither be increased nor diminished during the Period for which he shall have been elected, and he shall not receive within that Period any other Emolument from the United States, or any of them.

Before he enter on the Execution of his Office, he shall take the following Oath or Affirmation:—"I do solemnly swear (or affirm) that I will faithfully execute the Office of President of the United States, and will to the best of my Ability, preserve, protect and defend the Constitution of the United States."

Section 2. The President shall be Commander in Chief of the Army and Navy of the United States, and of the Militia of the several States, when called into the actual Service of the United States; he may require the Opinion, in writing, of the principal Officer in each of the executive Departments, upon any Subject relating to the Duties of their respective Offices, and he shall have Power to grant Reprieves and Pardons for Offences against the United States, except in Cases of Impeachment.

He shall have Power, by and with the Advice and Consent of the Senate, to make Treaties, provided two thirds of the Senators present concur; and he shall nominate, and by and with the Advice and Consent of the Senate, shall appoint Ambassadors, other public Ministers and Consuls, Judges of the supreme Court, and all other Officers of the United States, whose Appointments are not herein otherwise provided for, and which shall be established by Law: but the Congress may by Law vest the Appointment of such inferior Officers, as they think proper, in the President alone, in the Courts of Law, or in the Heads of Departments.

The President shall have Power to fill up all Vacancies that may happen during the Recess of the Senate, by granting Commissions which shall expire at the End of their next Session.

Section 3. He shall from time to time give to the Congress Information of the State of the Union, and recommend to their Consideration such Measures as he shall judge necessary and expedient; he may, on extraordinary Occasions, convene both Houses, or either of them, and in Case of Disagreement between them, with Respect to the Time of Adjournment, he may adjourn them to such Time as he shall think proper; he shall receive Ambassadors and other public Ministers; he shall take Care that the Laws be faithfully executed, and shall Commission all the Officers of the United States.

Section 4. The President, Vice President and all civil Officers of the United States, shall be removed from Office on Impeachment for, and Conviction of, Treason, Bribery, or other high Crimes and Misdemeanors.

*A*RTICLE III

Section 1. The judicial Power of the United States, shall be vested in one supreme Court, and in such inferior Courts as the Congress may from time to time ordain and establish. The Judges, both of the supreme and inferior Courts, shall hold their Offices during good Behaviour, and shall, at Times, receive for their Services, a Compensation, which shall not be diminished during their Continuance in Office.

Section 2. The judicial Power shall extend to all Cases, in Law and Equity, arising under this Constitution, the Laws of the United States, and Treaties made, or which shall be made, under their Authority;—to all Cases affecting Ambassadors, other public Ministers and Consuls;—to all Cases of admiralty and maritime Jurisdiction;—to Controversies to which the United States shall be a Party;—to controversies between two or more States;—between a State and Citizens of another State;—between Citizens of different States;—between Citizens of the same State claiming Lands under Grants of different States, and between a State, or the Citizens thereof, and foreign States, Citizens or Subjects.

In all Cases affecting Ambassadors, other public Ministers and Consuls, and those in which a State shall be Party, the supreme Court shall have original Jurisdiction. In all the other Cases before mentioned, the supreme Court shall have appellate Jurisdiction, both as to Law and Fact, with such Exceptions, and under such Regulations as the Congress shall make.

The Trial of all Crimes, except in Cases of Impeachment, shall be by Jury; and such Trial shall be held in the State where the said Crimes shall have been committed; but when not committed within any State, the Trial shall be at such Place or Places as the Congress may by Law have directed.

Section 3. Treason against the United States, shall consist only in levying War against them, or in adhering to their Enemies, giving them Aid and Comfort. No Person shall be convicted of Treason unless on the Testimony of two Witnesses to the same overt Act, or on Confession in open Court.

The Congress shall have Power to declare the Punishment of Treason, but no Attainder of Treason shall work Corruption of Blood, or Forfeiture except during the Life of the Person attainted.

*A*RTICLE IV

Section 1. Full Faith and Credit shall be given in each State to the public Acts, Records, and judicial Proceedings of every other State. And the Congress may by general Laws prescribe the Manner in which such Arts, Records, and Proceedings shall be proved, and the Effect thereof.

Section 2. The Citizens of each State shall be entitled to all Privileges and Immunities of Citizens in the several States.

A person charged in any State with Treason, Felony, or other Crime, who shall flee from Justice, and be found in another State, shall on Demand of the executive Authority of the State from which he fled, be delivered up, to be removed to the State having Jurisdiction of the Crime.

No Person held to Service or Labour in one State, under the Laws thereof, escaping into another, shall, in Consequence of any Law or Regulation therein, be discharged from such Service or Labour, but shall be delivered up on Claim of the Party to whom such Service or Labour may be due.

Section 3.   New States may be admitted by the Congress into this Union; but no new state shall be formed or erected within the Jurisdiction of any other State; nor any State be formed by the Junction of two or more States, or Parts of States, without the Consent of the Legislatures of the States concerned as well as of the Congress.

The Congress shall have Power to dispose of and make all needful Rules and Regulations respecting the Territory or other Property belonging to the United States; and nothing in this Constitution shall be so construed as to Prejudice any Claims of the United States, or of any particular State.

Section 4.   The United States shall guarantee to every State in this Union a Republican Form of Government, and shall protect each of them against Invasion; and on Application of the Legislature, or of the Executive (when the Legislature cannot be convened) against domestic Violence.

ARTICLE V

The Congress, whenever two thirds of both Houses shall deem it necessary, shall propose Amendments to this Constitution, or, on the Application of the Legislatures of two thirds of the several States, shall call a Convention for proposing Amendments, which, in either Case, shall be valid to all Intents and Purposes, as Part of this Constitution, when ratified by the Legislatures of three fourths of the several States, or by Conventions in three fourths thereof, as the one or the other Mode of Ratification may be proposed by the Congress; Provided that no Amendment which may be made prior to the Year One thousand eight hundred and eight shall in any Manner affect the first and fourth Clauses in the Ninth Section of the first Article; and that no State, without its Consent, shall be deprived of its equal Suffrage in the Senate.

ARTICLE VI

All Debts contracted and Engagements entered into, before the Adoption of this Constitution, shall be as valid against the United States under this Constitution, as under the Confederation.

This Constitution, and the Laws of the United States which shall be made in Pursuance thereof; and all Treaties made, or which shall be made, under the Authority of the United States, shall be the supreme Law of the Land; and the Judges in every State shall be bound thereby, any Thing in the Constitution or Laws of any State to the Contrary notwithstanding.

The Senators and Representatives before mentioned, and the Members of the several State Legislatures, and all executive and judicial Officers, both of the United States and of the Several States, shall be bound by Oath or Affirmation, to support this Constitution; but no religious Test shall ever be required as a Qualification to any Office or public Trust under the United States.

ARTICLE VII

The Ratification of the Conventions of nine States, shall be sufficient for the Establishment of this Constitution between the States so ratifying the Same.

AMENDMENT I [1791]

Congress shall make no law respecting an establishment of religion, or prohibiting the free exercise thereof; or abridging the freedom of speech, or the press; or the right of the people peaceably to assemble, and to petition the Government for a redress of grievances.

AMENDMENT II [1791]

A well regulated Militia, being necessary to the security for a free State, the right of the people to keep and bear Arms, shall not be infringed.

AMENDMENT III [1791]

No Soldier shall, in time of peace be quartered in any house, without the consent of the Owner, nor in time of war, but in a manner to be prescribed by law.

AMENDMENT IV [1791]

The right of the people to be secure in their persons, houses, papers, and effects, against unreasonable searches and seizures, shall not be violated, and no Warrants shall issue, but upon probable cause, supported by Oath or Affirmation, and particularly describing the place to be searched, and the persons or things to be seized.

AMENDMENT V [1791]

No person shall be held to answer for a capital, or otherwise infamous crime, unless on a presentment or indictment of a Grand Jury, except in cases arising in the land or naval forces, or in the Militia, when in actual service in time of War or public danger; nor shall any person be subject for the same offense to be twice put in jeopardy of life or limb; nor shall be compelled in any criminal case to be a witness against himself, nor be deprived of life, liberty, or property, without due process of law; nor shall private property be taken for public use, without just compensation.

*A*MENDMENT VI [1791]

In all criminal prosecutions, the accused shall enjoy the right to a speedy and public trial, by an impartial jury of the State and district wherein the crime shall have been committed, which district shall have been previously ascertained by law, and to be informed of the nature and cause of the accusation; to be confronted with the Witnesses against him; to have compulsory process for obtaining witnesses in his favor, and to have the Assistance of counsel for his defence.

*A*MENDMENT VII [1791]

In suits at common law, where the value in controversy shall exceed twenty dollars, the right of trial by jury shall be preserved, and no fact tried by a jury, shall be otherwise re-examined in any Court of the United States, than according to the rules of the common law.

*A*MENDMENT VIII [1791]

Excessive bail shall not be required, nor excessive fines imposed, nor cruel and unusual punishments inflicted.

*A*MENDMENT IX [1791]

The enumeration in the Constitution, of certain rights, shall not be construed to deny or disparage others retained by the people.

*A*MENDMENT X [1791]

The powers not delegated to the United States by the Constitution, nor prohibited by it to the States, are reserved to the States respectively, or to the people.

*A*MENDMENT XI [1798]

The judicial power of the United States shall not be construed to extend to any suit in law or equity, commenced or prosecuted against one of the United States by Citizens of another State, or by Citizens or Subjects of any Foreign State.

*A*MENDMENT XII [1804]

The Electors shall meet in their respective states and vote by ballot for President and Vice-President, one of whom, at least, shall not be an inhabitant of the same state with themselves; they shall name in their ballots the person voted for as President, and in distinct ballots the person voted for as Vice-President, and they shall make distinct lists of all persons voted for as President, and of all persons voted for as Vice-President, and of the number of votes for each, which lists they shall sign and certify, and transmit sealed to the seat of the government of the United States, directed to the President of the Senate;—The President of the Senate shall, in the presence of the Senate and House of Representatives, open all the certificates and the votes shall then be counted;—The person having the greatest number of votes for President, shall be the President, if such number be a majority of the whole number of Electors appointed; and if no person have such majority, then from the persons having the highest numbers not exceeding three on the list of those voted for as President, the House of Representatives shall choose immediately, by ballot, the President. But in choosing the President, the votes shall be taken by states, the representation from each state having one vote; a quorum for this purpose shall consist of a member or members from two-thirds of the states, and a majority of all the states shall be necessary to a choice. And if the House of Representatives shall not choose a President whenever the right of choice shall devolve upon them, before the fourth day of March next following, then the Vice-President shall act as President, as in the case of the death or other constitutional disability of the President. The person having the greatest number of votes as Vice-President, shall be the Vice-President, if such number be a majority of the whole number of Electors appointed, and if no person have a majority, then from the two highest numbers on the list, the Senate shall choose the Vice-President; a quorum for the purpose shall consist of two-thirds of the whole number of Senators, and a majority of the whole number shall be necessary to a choice. But no person constitutionally ineligible to the office of President shall be eligible to that of the Vice-President of the United States.

*A*MENDMENT XIII [1865]

Section 1. Neither slavery nor involuntary servitude, except as a punishment for crime whereof the party shall have been duly convicted, shall exist within the United States, or any place subject to their jurisdiction.

Section 2. Congress shall have power to enforce this article by appropriate legislation.

*A*MENDMENT XIV [1868]

Section 1. All persons born or naturalized in the United States, and subject to the jurisdiction thereof, are citizens of the United States and of the State wherein they reside. No State shall make or enforce any law which shall abridge the privileges or immunities of citizens of the United States; nor shall any State deprive any person of life, liberty, or property, without due process of law; nor deny to any person within its jurisdiction the equal protection of the laws.

Section 2. Representatives shall be appointed among the several States according to their respective numbers, counting the whole number of persons in each State, excluding Indians not taxed. But when the right to vote at any election for the choice of electors for President and Vice President of the United States, Representatives in Congress, the Executive and Judicial officers of a State, or the members of the Legislature thereof, is denied to any of the male inhabitants of such State, being twenty-one years of age, and citizens of the United States, or in any way abridged, except for participation in rebellion, or other crime, the basis of representation therein shall be reduced in the proportion which the number of such male citizens shall bear to the whole number of male citizens twenty-one years of age in such State.

Section 3.   No person shall be a Senator or Representative in Congress, or elector of President and Vice President, or hold any office, civil or military, under the United States, or under any State, who, having previously taken an oath, as a member of Congress, or as an officer of the United States, or as a member of any State legislature, or as an executive or judicial officer of any State, to support the Constitution of the United States, shall have engaged in insurrection or rebellion against the same, or given aid or comfort to the enemies thereof. But Congress may by a vote of two-thirds of each House, remove such disability.

Section 4.   The validity of the public debt of the United States, authorized by law, including debts incurred for payment of pensions and bounties for services in suppressing insurrection or rebellion, shall not be questioned. But neither the United States nor any State shall assume or pay any debt or obligation incurred in aid of insurrection of rebellion against the United States, or any claim for the loss or emancipation of any slave; but all such debts, obligations and claims shall be held illegal and void.

Section 5.   The Congress shall have power to enforce, by appropriate legislation, the provisions of this article.

AMENDMENT XV [1870]

Section 1.   The right of citizens of the United States to vote shall not be denied or abridged by the United States or by any State on account of race, color, or previous condition of servitude.

Section 2.   The Congress shall have power to enforce this article by appropriate legislation.

AMENDMENT XVI [1913]

The Congress shall have power to lay and collect taxes on incomes, from whatever source derived, without apportionment among the several States, and without regard to any census or enumeration.

AMENDMENT XVII [1913]

The Senate of the United States shall be composed of two Senators from each State, elected by the people thereof, for six years; and each Senator shall have one vote. The electors in each State shall have the qualifications requisite for electors of the most numerous branch of the State legislatures.

When vacancies happen in the representation of any State in the Senate, the executive authority of each State shall issue writs of election to fill such vacancies; *Provided*, That the legislature of any State may empower the executive thereof to make temporary appointments until the people fill the vacancies by election as the legislature may direct.

This amendment shall not be so construed as to affect the election or term of any Senator chosen before it becomes valid as part of the Constitution.

AMENDMENT XVIII [1919]

Section 1.   After one year from the ratification of this article the manufacture, sale, or transportation of intoxicating liquors within, the importation thereof into, or the exportation thereof from the United States and all territory subject to the jurisdiction thereof for beverage purposes is hereby prohibited.

Section 2.   The Congress and the several States shall have concurrent power to enforce this article by appropriate legislation.

Section 3.   This article shall be inoperative unless it shall have been ratified as an amendment to the Constitution by the legislatures of the several States, as provided in the Constitution, within seven years from the date of the submission hereof to the States by the Congress.

AMENDMENT XIX [1920]

The right of citizens of the United States to vote shall not be denied or abridged by the United States or by any State on account of sex.

Congress shall have power to enforce this article by appropriate legislation.

AMENDMENT XX [1933]

Section 1.   The terms of the President and Vice President shall end at noon on the 20th day of January, and the terms of Senators and Representatives at noon on the 3d day of January, of the years in which such terms would have ended if this article had not been ratified; and the terms of their successors shall then begin.

Section 2.   The Congress shall assemble at least once in every year, and such meeting shall begin at noon on the 3d day of January, unless they shall by law appoint a different day.

Section 3. If, at the time fixed for the beginning of the term of the President, the President elect shall have died, the Vice President elect shall become President. If a President shall not have been chosen before the time fixed for the beginning of his term, or if the President elect shall have failed to qualify, then the Vice President elect shall act as President until a President shall have qualified; and the Congress may by law provide for the case wherein neither a President elect nor a Vice President elect shall have qualified, declaring who shall then act as President, or the manner in which one who is to act shall be selected, and such person shall act accordingly until a President or Vice President shall have qualified.

Section 4. The Congress may by law provide for the case of the death of any of the persons from whom the House of Representatives may choose a President whenever the right of choice shall have devolved upon them, and for the case of the death of any of the persons from whom the Senate may choose a Vice President whenever the right of choice shall have devolved upon them.

Section 5. Sections 1 and 2 shall take effect on the 15th day of October following the ratification of this article.

Section 6. This article shall be inoperative unless it shall have been ratified as an amendment to the Constitution by the legislatures of three-fourths of the several States within seven years from the date of its submission.

AMENDMENT XXI [1933]

Section 1. The eighteenth article of amendment to the Constitution of the United States is hereby repealed.

Section 2. The transportation or importation into any State, Territory, or possession of the United States for delivery or use therein of intoxicating liquors, in violation of the laws thereof, is hereby prohibited.

Section 3. This article shall be inoperative unless it shall have been ratified as an amendment to the Constitution by conventions in the several States, as provided in the Constitution, within seven years from the date of the submission hereof to the States by the Congress.

AMENDMENT XXII [1951]

Section 1. No person shall be elected to the office of the President more than twice, and no person who has held the office of President, or acted as President, for more than two years of a term to which some other person was elected President shall be elected to the office of the President more than once. But this Article shall not apply to any person holding the office of President when this article was proposed by the Congress, and shall not prevent any person who may be holding the office of President, or acting as President, during the term within which this Article

becomes operative from holding the office of President, or acting as President during the remainder of such term.

Section 2. This article shall be inoperative unless it shall have been ratified as an amendment to the Constitution by the legislatures of three-fourths of the several States within seven years from the date of its submission to the States by the Congress.

AMENDMENT XXIII [1961]

Section 1. The District constituting the seat of government of the United States shall appoint in such manner as the Congress may direct:

A number of electors of President and Vice President equal to the whole number of Senators and Representatives in Congress to which the District would be entitled if it were a State, but in no event more than the least populous State; they shall be in addition to those appointed by the States, but they shall be considered, for the purposes of the election of President and Vice President, to be electors appointed by a State; and they shall meet in the District and perform such duties as provided by the twelfth article of amendment.

Section 2. The Congress shall have power to enforce this article by appropriate legislation.

AMENDMENT XXIV [1964]

Section 1. The right of citizens of the United States to vote in any primary or other election for President or Vice President, for electors for President or Vice President, or for Senator or Representative in Congress, shall not be denied or abridged by the United States or any State by reason of failure to pay any poll tax or other tax.

Section 2. The Congress shall have power to enforce this article by appropriate legislation.

AMENDMENT XXV [1967]

Section 1. In case of the removal of the President from office or of his death or resignation, the Vice President shall become President.

Section 2. Whenever there is a vacancy in the office of the Vice President, the President shall nominate a Vice President who shall take office upon confirmation by a majority vote of both Houses of Congress.

Section 3. Whenever the President transmits to the President pro tempore of the Senate and the Speaker of the House of Representatives his written declaration that he is unable to discharge the powers and duties of his office, and until he transmits to them a written declaration to the contrary, such powers and duties shall be discharged by the Vice President as Acting President.

Section 4. Whenever the Vice President and a majority of either the principal officers of the executive departments or of such other body as Congress may by law provide, transmit to the President pro tempore of the Senate and the Speaker of the House of Representatives their written declaration that the President is unable to discharge the powers and duties of his office, the Vice President shall immediately assume the powers and duties of the office as Acting President.

Thereafter, when the President transmits to the President pro tempore of the Senate and the Speaker of the House of Representatives his written declaration that no inability exists, he shall resume the powers and duties of his office unless the Vice President and a majority of either the principal officers of the executive department or of such other body as Congress may by law provide, transmit within four days to the President pro tempore of the Senate and the Speaker of the House of Representatives their written declaration that the President is unable to discharge the powers and duties of his office. Thereupon Congress shall decide the issue, assembling within forty-eight hours for that purpose if not in session. If the Congress, within twenty-one days after receipt of the latter written declaration, or, if Congress is not in session, within twenty-one days after Congress is required to assemble, determines by two-thirds vote of both Houses that the President shall continue to discharge the same as Acting President; otherwise, the President shall resume the powers and duties of his office.

AMENDMENT XXVI [1971]

Section 1. The right of citizens of the United States, who are 18 years of age or older, to vote, shall not be denied or abridged by the United States or any State on account of age.

Section 2. The Congress shall have the power to enforce this article by appropriate legislation.

AMENDMENT XXVII [1992]

No law, varying the compensation for the services of the Senators and Representatives, shall take effect, until an election of Representatives shall have intervened.

CHAPTER 4

Intentional Torts, Negligence, and Strict Liability

Negligence is not actionable unless it involves the invasion of a legally protected interest, the violation of a right. Proof of negligence in the air, so to speak, will not do.

—C.J. Cardozo
Palsgraf v. Long Island Railroad Co. (1928)

Chapter Objectives

After studying this chapter, you should be able to:

1. List and describe intentional torts against persons and against property.

2. Define the tort of false imprisonment and apply merchant protection statutes.

3. Describe the torts of invasion of privacy and misappropriation of the right to publicity.

4. List and explain the elements necessary to prove negligence.

5. Apply special negligence doctrines such as negligence per se, negligent infliction of emotional distress, and *res ipsa loquitur*.

6. Describe the business torts of unfair competition and disparagement.

7. Describe and list the elements to prove the tort of fraud.

8. Define racketeering under the civil RICO statute and the remedies that are awarded to successful plaintiffs.

9. Explain when punitive damages are awarded with the tort of bad faith.

10. Describe and apply the doctrine of strict liability.

Chapter Contents

▶ **Intentional Torts Against Persons**
Contemporary Business Environment   *Wal-Mart Shopper Wins $3.2 Million*
E-Commerce & Information Technology   *AOL Left off the Hook for User's Defamation*
CASE 4.1   *White v. Samsung Electronics America, Inc. (9th Cir.)*
Contemporary Business Environment   *Sound-Alike Commits Tort of Misappropriation of Publicity*
CASE 4.2   *Roach v. Stern (NY)*

▶ **Intentional Torts Against Property**
Entrepreneur and the Law   *Liability for Frivolous Lawsuits*

▶ **Unintentional Torts (Negligence)**
Contemporary Business Environment   *Ouch! The Coffee's Too Hot!*
CASE 4.3   *Fischer v. Pepsi Cola Bottling Company of Omaha, Inc.*
Contemporary Business Environment   *Is a Singer Liable When Someone Acts upon His Lyrics?*
CASE 4.4   *Estrada v. Aeronaves de Mexico, S.A. (9th Cir.)*

▶ **Special Negligence Doctrines**

▶ **Defenses Against Negligence**
CASE 4.5   *Cheong v. Antablin (CA)*

▶ **Business Torts**
Business Ethics   *Hallmark Greeted by an Unfair Competition Lawsuit*
Business Ethics   *Used-Car Dealer Punished for Fraud*
CASE 4.6   *Gourley v. State Farm Mutual Automobile Insurance Co. (CA)*

▶ **Strict Liability**
CASE 4.7   *Klein v. Pyrodyne Corporation (WA)*
International Law   *Israeli Tort Law*

▶ **Chapter Summary**

▶ **End-of-Chapter Internet Exercises and Case Questions**
Working the Web Internet Exercises · Critical Legal Thinking Cases · Business Ethics Cases · Briefing the Case Writing Assignment

90

Tort is the French word for a "wrong." Tort law protects a variety of injuries and provides remedies for them. Under tort law, an injured party can bring a *civil lawsuit* to seek compensation for a wrong done to the party or to the party's property. Many torts have their origin in common law. The courts and legislatures have extended tort law to reflect changes in modern society.

Tort damages are monetary damages that are sought from the offending party. They are intended to compensate the injured party for the injury suffered. They may consist of past and future medical expenses, loss of wages, pain and suffering, mental distress, and other damages caused by the defendant's tortious conduct. If the victim of a tort dies, his or her beneficiaries can bring a *wrongful death action* to recover damages from the defendant. *Punitive damages*, which are awarded to punish the defendant, may be recovered in intentional tort and strict liability cases. Other remedies, such as injunctions, may be available, too.

This chapter discusses various tort laws, including intentional torts, negligence, and strict liability.

INTENTIONAL TORTS AGAINST PERSONS

The law protects a person from unauthorized touching, restraint, or other contact. In addition, the law protects a person's reputation and privacy. Violations of these rights are actionable as torts. ***Intentional torts against the person*** are discussed in the paragraphs that follow.

Assault

Assault is (1) the threat of immediate harm or offensive contact or (2) any action that arouses reasonable apprehension of imminent harm. Actual physical contact is unnecessary. Threats of future harm are not actionable. For example, suppose a 6-foot-5-inch, 250-pound male makes a fist and threatens to punch a 5-foot, 100-pound woman. If the woman is afraid that the man will physically harm her, she can sue him for assault. If she is a black-belt karate champion and laughs at the threat, there is no assault because the threat does not cause any apprehension.

Battery

Battery is unauthorized and harmful or offensive physical contact with another person. Basically, the interest protected here is each person's reasonable sense of dignity and safety. For example, intentionally hitting someone is considered battery because it is harmful. Note that there does not have to be direct physical contact between the victim and the perpetrator. If an injury results, throwing a rock, shooting an arrow or a bullet, knocking off a hat, pulling a chair out from under someone, and poisoning a drink are all instances of actionable battery. The victim need not be aware of the harmful or offensive contact (e.g., it may take place while the victim is asleep). Assault and battery often occur together, although they do not have to (e.g., the perpetrator hits the victim on the back of the head without any warning).

Transferred Intent Doctrine   Sometimes a person acts with the intent to injure one person but actually injures another. The *doctrine of transferred intent* applies to these situations. Under this doctrine, the law transfers the perpetrator's intent from the target to the actual victim of the act. The victim can then sue the defendant.

False Imprisonment

The intentional confinement or restraint of another person without authority or justification and without that person's consent constitutes **false imprisonment**. The victim may be restrained or confined by physical force, barriers, threats of physical harm, or the perpetrator's false assertion of legal authority (i.e., *false arrest*). A threat of future harm or moral pressure is not considered false imprisonment. The false imprisonment must be complete. For example, merely locking one door to a building when other exits are not locked is not false imprisonment. A person is not obliged to risk danger or an affront to his or her dignity by attempting to escape.

Business Brief

Merchant protection statutes allow merchants to stop, detain, and investigate suspected shoplifters without being held liable for false imprisonment if (1) there are reasonable grounds for the suspicion, (2) suspects are detained for only a reasonable time, and (3) investigations are conducted in a reasonable manner.

Merchant Protection Statutes Shoplifting causes substantial losses to merchants each year. Almost all states have enacted **merchant protection statutes**, also known as the **shopkeeper's privilege**. These statutes allow merchants to stop, detain, and investigate suspected shoplifters without being held liable for false imprisonment if

1. There are reasonable grounds for the suspicion,
2. Suspects are detained for only a reasonable time, and
3. Investigations are conducted in a reasonable manner.

Contemporary Business Environment

WAL-MART SHOPPER WINS $3.2 MILLION

On Christmas Eve 1995, LaShawna Goodman went to a local Wal-Mart store in Opelika, Alabama, to do some last minute holiday shopping. She brought along her two young daughters and a telephone she had purchased earlier at Wal-Mart to exchange. She presented the telephone and receipt to a Wal-Mart employee, who took the telephone. Unable to find another telephone she wanted, Goodman retrieved the previously purchased telephone from the employee, bought another item, and left. Outside, Ms. Goodman was stopped by Wal-Mart security personnel and was accused of stealing the phone. Goodman offered to show the Wal-Mart employees the original receipt, but the Wal-Mart employees detained her and called the police. Ms. Goodman was handcuffed in front of her children. Wal-Mart filed criminal charges against Ms. Goodman.

At the criminal trial, Ms. Goodman was acquitted of all charges. Now it was Ms. Goodman's turn: She filed a civil lawsuit against Wal-Mart Stores, Inc., to recover damages for falsely accusing her of stealing the telephone. She presented

evidence as outlined above. Wal-Mart asserted the defense that it was in its rights to have detained Ms. Goodman as it did and to prosecute Ms. Goodman based on its investigation. Wal-Mart asserted that the merchant protection statute protected its actions in this case. Wal-Mart alleged that it had reasonable grounds to suspect Ms. Goodman of shoplifting, that it conducted the investigation in a reasonable manner, and that it had sufficient grounds to have Ms. Goodman prosecuted criminally based on its investigation.

But the jury did not accept Wal-Mart's plea that it had acted reasonably. The jury rejected Wal-Mart's defenses, including the shopkeeper's privilege and its allegations that it had not maliciously prosecuted her. The jury determined that Ms. Goodman should be awarded $200,000 in compensatory damages for her suffering. The jury then decided that Wal-Mart had acted so badly in this case that it tacked on $3 million in punitive damages in its award to Ms. Goodman just to teach Wal-Mart a lesson. [*Goodman v. Wal-Mart* (AL 1999)]

defamation of character

False statement(s) made by one person about another. In court, the plaintiff must prove that (1) the defendant made an untrue statement of fact about the plaintiff and (2) the statement was intentionally or accidentally published to a third party.

slander

Oral defamation of character.

libel

A false statement that appears in a letter, newspaper, magazine, book, photograph, movie, video, and so on.

Landmark Law

In *New York Times v. Sullivan*, the U.S. Supreme Court held that public officials cannot recover for defamation unless they can prove that the defendant acted with *actual malice*.

Defamation of Character

A person's reputation is a valuable asset. Therefore, every person is protected from false statements made by others during his or her lifetime. This protection ends upon a person's death. The tort of **defamation of character** requires a plaintiff to prove that (1) the defendant made an *untrue statement of fact* about the plaintiff and (2) the statement was intentionally or accidentally *published* to a third party. In this context publication simply means that a third person heard or saw the untrue statement. It does not just mean appearance in newspapers, magazines, or books.

The name for an oral defamatory statement is **slander**. A false statement that appears in a letter, newspaper, magazine, book, photograph, movie, video, and the like is called **libel**. Most courts hold that defamatory statements in radio and television broadcasts are considered libel because of the permanency of the media.

The publication of an untrue statement of fact is not the same as the publication of an opinion. The publication of opinions is usually not actionable. For example, the statement "My lawyer is lousy" is an opinion. Because defamation is defined as an untrue statement of fact, truth is an absolute defense to a charge of defamation.

Public Figures as Plaintiffs In *New York Times Co. v. Sullivan*,[1] the U.S. Supreme Court held that *public officials* cannot recover for defamation unless they can prove that the defendant acted with "actual malice." Actual malice means that the defendant made the false statement knowingly or with reckless disregard of its falsity. This requirement has since been extended to *public figure* plaintiffs such as movie stars, sports personalities, and other celebrities.

E-Commerce & Information Technology

AOL LEFT OFF THE HOOK FOR USER'S DEFAMATION

Under the common law concept of defamation, publishers of newspapers, magazines, newsletters, and such are liable for defamatory statements made by writers whose material appear in these publications. A distributor of defamatory material, such as a newsstand that sells a magazine that contains a defamatory statement, is liable for defamation if it has knowledge of the defamation yet still sells the publication. But these common law doctrines of *publisher* and *distributor* liability pose particular problems for Internet providers.

Many firms, such as America Online, Inc. (AOL), provide interactive computer services to which tens of millions of users worldwide subscribe to gain access to the Internet. Users may transfer information privately via e-mail or may communicate publicly by posting messages on bulletin boards. But what if a user transfers a defamatory statement over the Internet using an online provider's service? Should the online provider be held liable for defamation as a publisher or distributor of the information?

Congress expressly addressed this issue by passing **Section 230 of the Communications Decency Act of 1996,** which states, "No provider or user of an interactive computer service shall be treated as the publisher or speaker of any information provided by another information content provider" [47 U.S.C. § 230 (c) (1)]. By its plain language, Section 230 creates a federal statutory immunity against liability of online service providers for defamatory statements made by users of its services. This policy recognizes that interactive service providers have millions of users and that the specter of imposing tort liability on service providers for defamatory statements of users would impose a chilling effect on free speech.

The court applied Section 230 in *Zeran v. America Online, Inc.* In that case, some unidentified AOL user posted a message on an AOL bulletin board advertising T-shirts featuring offensive and tasteless slogans relating to the bombing of the federal building in Oklahoma City. Those interested in purchasing the shirts were instructed to call "Ken" at Ken Zeran's home number in Seattle, Washington. Zeran received a high volume of calls, including angry and derogatory messages, as well as death threats. Zeran sued AOL for defamation. The trial court applied Section 230 and held that AOL was immune from liability and dismissed the case. The court of appeals affirmed. [*Zeran v. America Online, Incorporated*, 129 F.3d 327 (4th Cir. 1997)]

Misappropriation of the Right to Publicity

Each person has the exclusive legal right to control and profit from the commercial use of his or her name and personality during his or her lifetime. This is a valuable right, particularly to well-known persons such as sports figures and movie stars. Any attempt by another person to appropriate a living person's name or identify for commercial purposes is actionable. The wrongdoer is liable for the **tort of misappropriation of the right to publicity** (also called the **tort of appropriation**). In such cases, the plaintiff can (1) recover the unauthorized profits made by the offending party and (2) obtain an injunction against further unauthorized use of his or her name or identity. Many states provide that the right to publicity survives a person's death and may be enforced by the deceased's heirs.

tort of misappropriation of the right to publicity

An attempt by another person to appropriate a living person's name or identity for commercial purposes.

In the following case, the court found that there had been a misappropriation of the right to publicity.

White v. Samsung Electronics America, Inc.

971 F.2d 1395 (1992)
United States Court of Appeals, Ninth Circuit

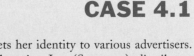

BACKGROUND AND FACTS

Vanna White is the hostess of *Wheel of Fortune*, one of the most popular game shows in television history. An estimated 40 million people watch the program daily. Capitalizing on her fame, White markets her identity to various advertisers. Samsung Electronics America, Inc. (Samsung), distributes various electronics products in the United States. Samsung and its advertising agency, David Deutsch Associates, Inc.,

(Deutsch), devised a series of advertisements that followed the same theme. Each depicted a current item of popular culture and a Samsung electronics product. The advertisements were set in the twenty-first century to convey the message that the Samsung product would still be in use at that time.

The advertisement that prompted the current dispute was for Samsung videocassette recorders. The ad depicted a robot that was outfitted to resemble White. The set in which the robot was posed was instantly recognizable as the *Wheel of Fortune* game show set, and the robot's stance was one for which White is famous. The caption of the ad read: "Longest-running game show. 2012 A.D." Defendants referred to the ad as the "Vanna White" ad. White did not consent to the ads and was not paid. White sued Samsung and Deutsch to recover damages for alleged misappropriation of her right to publicity. The district court granted defendants' motions for summary judgment. White appealed.

ISSUE

Did White properly plead the claim of misappropriation of the right to publicity?

COURT'S REASONING

The individual aspects of the advertisement in the present case say little. Viewed together, though, they leave little doubt about whom the celebrity is that the ad is meant to depict. Although the female-shaped robot was dressed exactly the way Vanna White dresses at times, so do many other women. The look-alike robot is

in the process of turning a block letter on a gameboard, but similarly attired Scrabble-playing women may do this as well. But the robot is standing on what looks to be the *Wheel of Fortune* game show set, and Vanna White is the only one who dresses like this and turns letters on the *Wheel of Fortune* game show. Indeed, the defendants themselves referred to their ad as the "Vanna White" ad. Television exposure created Vanna White's marketable celebrity value. The court stated, "The law protects the celebrity's sole right to exploit this value whether the celebrity has achieved her fame out of rare ability, dumb luck, or a combination thereof."

DECISION

The court of appeals held that the law of misappropriation of the right of publicity had been properly pleaded by White under the facts of this case. The court reversed and remanded the case. The case went to trial, and in January 1994 the jury awarded Vanna White $403,000 in damages.

Case Questions

Critical Legal Thinking Should the right to publicity be a protected right? Why or why not?

Business Ethics Did Samsung act ethically in using Vanna White's celebrity status without getting her permission or paying her?

Contemporary Business Sometimes the worth of a celebrity's publicity goes up in value after his or her death. Can you think of any examples?

Contemporary Business Environment

SOUND-ALIKE COMMITS TORT OF MISAPPROPRIATION OF PUBLICITY

Tom Waits is a professional singer, songwriter, and actor of some renown. He has a raspy, gravelly singing voice, described by one fan as "like how you'd sound if you drank a quart of bourbon, smoked a pack of cigarettes, and swallowed a pack of razor blades." Waits has recorded more than 17 albums and has played to sold-out audiences throughout the United States, Canada, Europe, Japan, and Australia. Waits follows a strict personal policy against doing commercials.

When Frito-Lay, Inc., which is in the business of manufacturing, distributing, and selling prepared and packaged food products, decided to introduce a new product, SalsaRio Doritos corn chips, it hired Tracy-Locke, Inc., an advertising agency, to help develop a marketing campaign. Tracy-Locke found inspiration in a 1976 Waits song, "Step Right Up." The agency wrote a commercial that echoed the rhyming word play of the Waits song. Only one problem remained: Since Waits refused to do commercials, who would sing the song in the commercial?

Tracy-Locke auditioned many singers, but none could imitate Waits's gravelly style. Finally, the agency found Stephen Carter, a professional musician who did Tom Waits imitations. Carter had performed Waits's songs as part of his band's repertoire for over 10 years, and he had perfected an imitation of Waits's voice.

The commercial, which was recorded with Frito-Lay's authorization, was broadcast on more than 250 radio stations located in 61 markets nationwide. After Waits heard the commercial during an appearance on a Los Angeles radio station, he sued Frito-Lay and Tracy-Locke. Waits claimed misappropriation of the right to publicity. The jury found in Waits's favor and awarded him $375,000 in compensatory damages and $2 million in punitive damages. The defendants appealed.

The court of appeals affirmed the judgment, holding that voice misappropriation is a form of the tort of misappropriation of the right to publicity. The court stated, "We recognize that when voice is a sufficient indicia of a celebrity's identity, the right to publicity protects against its imitation for commercial purposes without the celebrity's consent." The court found that the award of punitive damages was warranted because the defendants acted with malice and conscious disregard toward Waits by recording and broadcasting the commercial that pirated his voice.

Waits's victory is expected to make advertisers and their agencies think twice before producing "sound-alike" commercials that misappropriate a celebrity's vocal style. [*Waits v. Frito-Lay, Inc.*, 978 F2d 1093 (9th Cir. 1992)]

Invasion of the Right to Privacy

The law recognizes each person's right to live his or her life without being subjected to unwarranted and undesired publicity. A violation of this right constitutes the tort of **invasion of the right to privacy**. Examples of this tort include reading someone else's mail, wiretapping, and such. In contrast to defamation, the fact does not have to be untrue. Therefore, truth is not a defense to a charge of invasion of privacy. If the fact is public information, there is no claim to privacy. However, a fact that was once public (e.g., the commission of a crime) may become private after the passage of time.

Placing someone in a "false light" constitutes an invasion of privacy. For example, sending an objectionable telegram to a third party and signing another's name would place the purported sender in a false light in the eyes of the receiver. Falsely attributing beliefs or acts to another can also form the basis of a lawsuit.

invasion of the right to privacy

A tort that constitutes the violation of a person's right to live his or her life without being subjected to unwarranted and undesired publicity.

Intentional Infliction of Emotional Distress

In some situations, a victim may suffer mental or emotional distress without first being physically harmed. The Restatement (Second) of Torts provides that a person whose *extreme and outrageous* conduct intentionally or recklessly causes severe emotional distress to another is liable for that emotional distress.[2] This is called the tort of **intentional infliction of emotional distress**, or the **tort of outrage**. The plaintiff must prove that the defendant's conduct was "so outrageous in character and so extreme in degree as to go beyond all possible bounds of decency, and to be regarded as atrocious and utterly intolerable in a civilized society."[3] An indignity, an annoyance, rough language, or an occasional inconsiderate or unkind act does not constitute outrageous behavior. However, repeated annoyances or harassment coupled with threats are considered "outrageous."

The tort does not require any publication to a third party or physical contact between the plaintiff and defendant. For example, a credit collection agency making harassing telephone calls to a debtor every morning between 1:00 and 5:00 A.M. is outrageous conduct.

The mental distress suffered by the plaintiff must be severe. Many states require that this mental distress be manifested by some form of physical injury, discomfort, or illness, such as nausea, ulcers, headaches, or miscarriage. This requirement is intended to prevent false claims. Some states have abandoned this requirement. The courts have held that shame, humiliation, embarrassment, anger, fear, and worry constitute severe mental distress. The tort of intentional infliction of emotional distress was asserted in the following case.

intentional infliction of emotional distress

A tort that says a person whose extreme and outrageous conduct intentionally or recklessly causes severe emotional distress to another person is liable for that emotional distress. Also known as the *tort of outrage*.

Roach v. Stern
675 N.Y.S.2d 133 (1998)
Supreme Court, Appellate Division, New York

CASE 4.2

BACKGROUND AND FACTS

Howard Stern is a famous television talk-show host who emcees an irreverent daily show on the radio. The show is syndicated by Infinity Broadcasting, Inc. (Infinity), and is listened to by millions of people across the country. Deborah Roach, a self-described topless dancer and cable-access television host, was a perennial guest on the Howard Stern radio show. She was famous for her stories about encounters with aliens. Roach died of a drug overdose at the age of 27. Roach's sister, Melissa Driscoll, had Roach's body cremated and gave a portion of the remains to Roach's close friend Chaunce Hayden. Driscoll said she did so with the understanding that Hayden would "preserve and honor said remains in an appropriate and private manner."

On July 18, 1995, Hayden brought a box containing Roach's cremated remains to Stern's radio show. Hayden said she did so as a memorial to Roach because "the only happiness

Debbie had was the Howard Stern show." Thereafter, Stern, Hayden, and other participants in the broadcast played with Roach's ashes and made crude comments about the remains. The radio show was videotaped and later broadcast on a national cable television station. Roach's sister and brother sued Stern, Infinity, and Hayden to recover damages for intentional infliction of emotional distress. The trial court dismissed the complaint. The plaintiffs appealed.

ISSUE

Have the plaintiffs sufficiently pleaded a cause of action to recover damages for the intentional infliction of emotional distress?

COURT'S REASONING

The court stated that to impose liability for intentional infliction of emotional distress, "the conduct complained of must be so outrageous in character, and so extreme in degree, as to be beyond all possible bounds of decency, and to be regarded as atrocious, and utterly intolerable in a civilized community." The court noted that the element of outrageous conduct is rigorous and difficult to satisfy and that its purpose is to filter out trivial complaints and ensure that the claim of severe emotional distress is genuine. The court decided that a jury could reasonably conclude that the manner in which Roach's remains were handled for entertainment purposes went beyond the bounds of decent behavior. The court reinstated the plaintiff's complaint.

DECISION AND REMEDY

The court held that the complaint and the facts of the case as pleaded sufficiently stated a cause of action to recover

damages for intentional infliction of emotional distress. Reversed.

Case Questions

Critical Legal Thinking Should the tort of intentional infliction of emotional distress be recognized by the law? What difficulties arise in trying to apply this tort?

Business Ethics Was Stern's and the other participants' conduct on the radio show tasteless? Did it amount to "outrageous conduct" for which legal damages should be awarded?

Contemporary Business If Stern and Infinity are found liable, will a chilling effect on future broadcasts result?

INTENTIONAL TORTS AGAINST PROPERTY

> Law must be stable and yet it cannot stand still.
>
> *Roscoe Pour*
> Interpretations of Legal History
> (1929)

There are two general categories of property: real property and personal property. *Real property* consists of land and anything permanently attached to that land. *Personal property* consists of things that are movable, such as automobiles, books, clothes, pets, and such. The law recognizes certain torts against real and personal property. These torts are discussed in the paragraphs that follow.

Trespass to Land

trespass to land
A tort that interferes with an owner's right to exclusive possession of land.

Interference with an owner's right to exclusive possession of land constitutes the tort of **trespass to land**. There does not have to be any interference with the owner's use or enjoyment of the land; the ownership itself is what counts. Thus, unauthorized use of another person's land is trespass even if the owner is not using it. Actual harm to the property is not necessary.

Examples of trespass to land include entering another person's land without permission, remaining on the land of another after permission to do so has expired (e.g., a guest refuses to leave), or causing something or someone to enter another's land (e.g., one person builds a dam that causes another person's land to flood). A person who is pushed onto another's land or enters that land with good reason is not liable for trespass. For example, a person may enter onto another person's land to save a child or a pet from harm.

Trespass to and Conversion of Personal Property

trespass to personal property
A tort that occurs whenever one person injures another person's personal property or interferes with that person's enjoyment of his or her personal property.

The tort of **trespass to personal property** occurs whenever one person injures another person's personal property or interferes with that person's enjoyment of his or her personal property. The injured party can sue for damages. For example, breaking another's car window is trespass to personal property.

conversion of personal property
A tort that deprives a true owner of the use and enjoyment of his or her personal property by taking over such property and exercising ownership rights over it.

Depriving a true owner of the use and enjoyment of his or her personal property by taking over such property and exercising ownership rights over it constitutes the tort of **conversion of personal property**. Conversion also occurs when someone who originally is given possession of personal property fails to return it (e.g., fails to return a borrowed car). The rightful owner can sue to recover the property. If the property was lost or destroyed, the owner can sue to recover its value.

Entrepreneur and the Law

LIABILITY FOR FRIVOLOUS LAWSUITS

Entrepreneurs and others often believe they have a reason to sue someone to recover damages or other remedies. If the plaintiff has a reason to bring the lawsuit and does so, but the

plaintiff does not win the lawsuit, he or she does not have to worry about being sued by the person whom he or she sued. A losing plaintiff does have to worry about being sued by the defendant in a second lawsuit for **malicious prosecution** if certain elements are met, however.

In a lawsuit for malicious prosecution, the original defendant sues the original plaintiff. In this second lawsuit, which is a *civil* action for damages, the original defendant is the plaintiff and the original plaintiff is the defendant. The courts do not look favorably on malicious prosecution lawsuits because they feel they inhibit the original plaintiff's incentive to sue. Thus, to succeed in a malicious prosecution lawsuit, the courts require the plaintiff to prove all of the following:

- The plaintiff in the original lawsuit (now the defendant) instituted or was responsible for instituting the original lawsuit.

- There was no *probable cause* for the first lawsuit; that is, it was a frivolous lawsuit.
- The plaintiff in the original action brought it with *malice*. [Caution: This is a very difficult element to prove.]
- The original lawsuit was terminated in favor of the original defendant (now the plaintiff).
- The current plaintiff suffered injury as a result of the original lawsuit.

A successful case of malicious prosecution involves proof of malicious conduct, which is an intentional tort. Therefore, punitive damages can be awarded in a malicious prosecution case. The moral of the story is simple: Make sure you have probable cause for instituting an action before bringing a lawsuit.

$\mathcal{U}$NINTENTIONAL TORTS (NEGLIGENCE)

Under the doctrine of **unintentional tort**, commonly referred to as **negligence**, a person is liable for harm that is the *foreseeable consequence* of his or her actions. Negligence is defined as "the omission to do something which a reasonable man would do, or doing something which a prudent and reasonable man would not do."[4]

unintentional tort or negligence

A doctrine that says a person is liable for harm that is the foreseeable consequence of his or her actions.

Consider This Example   A driver who causes an automobile accident because he or she fell asleep at the wheel is liable for any resulting injuries caused by his or her negligence.

Few of us can pass one of these familiar roadside markers without thinking about the pain and suffering of the occupants of the vehicle, let alone their surviving loved ones.

Elements of Negligence

To be successful in a negligence lawsuit, the plaintiff must prove that (1) the defendant owed a *duty of care* to the plaintiff, (2) the defendant *breached* this duty of care, (3) the plaintiff suffered *injury*, and (4) the defendant's negligent act *caused* the plaintiff's injury. Each of these elements is discussed in the paragraphs that follow.

Duty of Care   To determine whether a defendant is liable for negligence, it must first be ascertained whether the defendant owed a **duty of care** to the plaintiff. Duty of care refers to the obligation we all owe each other—that is, the duty not to cause any unreasonable harm or risk of harm. For example, each person owes a duty to drive his or her car carefully, not to push or shove on escalators, not to leave skateboards on the sidewalk, and the like. Businesses owe a duty to make safe products, not to cause accidents, and so on.

Negligence is the omission to do something which a reasonable man would do, or doing something which a prudent and reasonable man would not do.

B. Alderson Blyth v. Brimingham Waterworks Co. *(1856)*

duty of care

The obligation we all owe each other not to cause any unreasonable harm or risk of harm.

Business Brief

Domino's Pizza canceled its 30-minute delivery guarantee after juries concluded in several cases that Domino's drivers, trying to meet this deadline, negligently caused accidents.

The courts decide whether a duty of care is owed in specific cases by applying a *reasonable person standard*. Under this test, the courts attempt to determine how an *objective, careful, and conscientious person would have acted in the same circumstances*, and then measure the defendant's conduct against this standard. The defendant's subjective intent ("I did not mean to do it") is immaterial in assessing liability. Certain impairments do not affect the reasonable person standard. For example, there is no reasonable alcoholics standard.

Defendants with a particular expertise or competence are measured against a *reasonable professional standard*. This standard is applied in much the same way as the reasonable person standard. For example, a brain surgeon is measured against a reasonable brain surgeon standard, rather than a lower reasonable doctor standard. Children are generally required to act as a *reasonable child* of similar age and experience would act.

breach of the duty of care

A failure to exercise care or to act as a reasonable person would act.

Breach of Duty   Once a court finds that the defendant actually owed the plaintiff a duty of care, it must determine whether the defendant breached this duty. A **breach of the duty of care** is the failure to exercise care. In other words, it is the failure to act as a reasonable person would act. A breach of this duty may consist of either an action (e.g., throwing a lit match on the ground in the forest and causing a fire) or a failure to act when there is a duty to act (e.g., a firefighter who refuses to put out a fire). Generally, passersby are not expected to rescue others gratuitously to save them from harm.

Contemporary Business Environment

OUCH! THE COFFEE'S TOO HOT!

Studies have shown that people care less about how good their coffee tastes than if it is hot. So restaurants, coffee shops, and other sellers make their coffee hot. McDonald's, however, discovered that it was in hot water for making their coffee *too* hot. Consider this case.

Stella Liebeck, and 81-year-old resident of Albuquerque, New Mexico, visited a "drive-through" window of a McDonald's restaurant with her grandson. Her grandson, the driver of the vehicle, placed the order. When it came, he handed a hot cup of coffee to Liebeck. As her grandson drove away from the drive-through window, Liebeck took the lid off the coffee cup she held in her lap. The coffee spilled all over Liebeck, who suffered third-degree burns on her legs, groin, and buttocks. She required medical treatment, was hospitalized, and suffers permanent scars from the incident.

Liebeck sued McDonald's for selling coffee that was too hot and for failing to warn her of the danger of the hot coffee it served. McDonald's rejected Liebeck's pretrial offer to settle the case for $300,000. At trial, McDonald's denied that it had been negligent and asserted that Liebeck's own negligence— opening a hot coffee cup on her lap—caused her injuries. The jury heard evidence that McDonald's enforces a quality-control rule that requires its restaurants and franchises to serve coffee at 180 to 190 degrees Fahrenheit. Evidence showed that this was 10 to 30 degrees hotter than coffee served by competing restaurant chains, and approximately 40 to 50 degrees hotter than normal house-brewed coffee.

Based on this evidence, the jury concluded that McDonald's acted recklessly and awarded Liebeck $200,000 compensatory damages (reduced by $40,000 for her own negligence), and $2.7 million punitive damages. After the trial court judge reduced the amount of punitive damages to $480,000, the parties reached an out-of-court settlement for an undisclosed amount. Because of this case, McDonald's and other purveyors of coffee have reduced the temperature at which they sell coffee and have placed warnings on their coffee cups.

injury

The plaintiff must suffer personal injury or damage to his or her property to recover monetary damages for the defendant's negligence.

Injury to Plaintiff   Even though a defendant's act may have breached a duty of care owed to the plaintiff, this breach is not actionable unless the plaintiff suffers **injury**. For example, a business's negligence causes an explosion and fire to occur at its factory at night. No one is injured and there is no damage to the neighbors' property. The negligence is not actionable.

The damages recoverable depend on the effect of the injury on the plaintiff's life or profession. Suppose two men injure their hands when a train door malfunctions. The first man is a professional basketball player. The second is a college professor. The first man can recover greater damages.

In the following case, the court held the defendant liable for the injuries caused to the plaintiff.

Fischer v. Pepsi Cola Bottling Company of Omaha, Inc.
972 F.2d 906 (1992)
United States Court of Appeals, Eighth Circuit

CASE 4.3

BACKGROUND AND FACTS
On March 4, 1987, Robert J. Fischer was in Omaha, Nebraska, attending a seminar and was a guest at the Red Lion Inn. At the end of the seminar's first day, Fischer took a swim in the inn's pool. Following his swim, Fischer stopped to purchase a soda from a vending machine on the inn's eleventh floor. The machine was owned and operated by Pepsi Cola Bottling Company of Omaha, Inc., (Pepsi). Fischer was still wearing his wet swimming trunks and was barefoot. As he inserted his money into the vending machine, an electrical current passed through his body.

After Fischer reported the accident, a service technician inspected the machine and found that the power cord connecting the rear of the machine to the electrical socket was resting underneath the machine's metal cabinet. He noticed that the power cord's metal conducting wires were exposed and came into contact with the machine's cabinet. After the accident, Fischer suffered pain while having sexual relations with his wife and became impotent. According to expert testimony, Fischer's impotence resulted from the electrical shock. He sued Pepsi for damages for alleged negligence in not inspecting and correcting the problem with the vending machine. The trial court found in favor of Fischer and awarded him $324,000. Pepsi appealed.

ISSUE
Is Pepsi liable for negligence?

COURT'S REASONING
Evidence showed that the machine in question was part of a group of approximately 10,000 machines owned and operated by Pepsi. Pepsi received one or two complaints a month that a vending machine was causing electrical shocks. The court of appeals held that Pepsi owed a duty to inspect its vending machines for the defect that electrocuted customers and breached that duty by failing to do so. The court stated, "For a supplier to be liable for failing to exercise reasonable care, it is not necessary for the supplier to know that a particular chattel is dangerous. Where the chattel supplied is part of a lot, it is sufficient that the supplier knows some of the chattels in the lot are dangerous."

DECISION AND REMEDY
The court of appeals held that Pepsi had been negligent for failing to inspect the vending machine and correct the problem associated with electrical shocks caused by the machine. Affirmed.

Case Questions

Critical Legal Thinking   Should the law recognize the type of injury claimed in this case? Is it hard to prove (or disprove) the injury alleged?

Business Ethics   Was it ethical for Pepsi to deny liability in this case?

Contemporary Business   How could Pepsi have protected itself from liability in this case?

Causation   A person who commits a negligent act is not liable unless this act was the **cause** of the plaintiff's injuries. Courts have divided causation into two categories—*causation in fact* and *proximate cause*—and require each to be shown before the plaintiff may recover damages.

1. **Causation in Fact**   The defendant's negligent act must be the **causation in fact** (or **actual cause**) of the plaintiff's injuries. For example, suppose a corporation negligently pollutes the plaintiff's drinking water. The plaintiff dies of a heart attack unrelated to the polluted water. Although the corporation has acted negligently, it is not liable for the plaintiff's death. There was a negligent act and an injury but there was no cause-and-effect relationship between them. If instead, the plaintiff had died from the pollution, there would have been causation in fact, and the polluting corporation would have been liable. If two (or more) persons are liable for negligently causing the plaintiff's injuries, both (or all) can be held liable to the plaintiff if each of their acts is a substantial factor in causing the plaintiff's injuries.

causation

A person who commits a negligent act is not liable unless his or her act was the cause of the plaintiff's injuries. The two types of causation that must be proven are (1) *causation in fact* (*actual cause*) and (2) *proximate cause* (*legal cause*).

causation in fact or actual cause

The actual cause of negligence. A person who commits a negligent act is not liable unless causation in fact can be proven.

proximate cause or legal cause

A point along a chain of events caused by a negligent party after which this party is no longer legally responsible for the consequences of his or her actions.

Ethics Brief

A negligent party who is found to be the actual cause but not the proximate cause of the plaintiff's injuries is not liable.

Landmark Law

The doctrine of proximate cause was defined in the *Palsgraf v. Long Island Railroad Company* case.

2. **Proximate Cause**   Under the law, a negligent party is not necessarily liable for all damages set in motion by his or her negligent act. Based on public policy, the law establishes a point along the damage chain after which the negligent party is no longer responsible for the consequences of his or her actions. This limitation on liability is referred to as **proximate cause** (or **legal cause**). The general test of proximate cause is *forseeability*. A negligent party who is found to be the actual cause—but not the proximate cause—of the plaintiff's injuries is not liable to the plaintiff. Situations are examined on a case-by-case basis.

The landmark case establishing the doctrine of proximate cause is *Palsgraf v. Long Island Railroad Company*.[5] Helen Palsgraf was standing on a platform waiting for a passenger train. The Long Island Railroad Company owned and operated the trains and employed the station guards. As a man carrying a package wrapped in a newspaper tried to board the moving train, railroad guards tried to help him. In doing so, the package was dislodged from the man's arm, fell to the railroad tracks, and exploded. The package contained hidden fireworks. The explosion shook the railroad platform, causing a scale located on the platform to fall on Palsgraf, injuring her. She sued the railroad for negligence. Justice Cardoza denied her recovery, finding that the railroad was not the proximate cause of her injuries.

Contemporary Business Environment

IS A SINGER LIABLE WHEN SOMEONE ACTS UPON HIS LYRICS?

Many people, particularly youths, are influenced by singers, musicians, sports figures, movie stars, and other celebrities. Some listeners, readers, or watchers will be moved to love; others to tears; some to creativity, spirituality, or fear. But what happens when a person is so moved by a song, a movie, or a book that he or she commits a crime or engages in other dangerous conduct? Is the songwriter, singer, author, scriptwriter, or movie company liable for this conduct? This question was posed to the court in *McCollum v. CBS, Inc., and Osbourne.*

John "Ozzie" Osbourne is a well-known singer of rock-and-roll music and has become a cult figure. The words and music of his songs demonstrate a preoccupation with unusual, antisocial, and even bizarre attitudes and beliefs, often emphasizing such things as satanic worship, the mocking of religious beliefs, death, and suicide. CBS Records (CBS) produced and distributed Osbourne's albums.

On Friday night, October 26, 1984, John Daniel McCollum (John) listened over and over again to certain music recorded by Osbourne. He was a 19-year-old youth who had a problem with alcohol abuse as well as serious emotional problems. John was in his bedroom using headphones to listen to the final side of Osbourne's two-record album, *Speak to the Devil*, when he placed a .22 caliber handgun next to his right temple and took his own life.

One of the songs that John had been listening to was called "Suicide Solution." Three of the verses of the song stated:

Wine is fine but whiskey's quicker
Suicide is slow with liquor
Take a bottle drown your sorrows

Then it floods away tomorrows
Made your bed, rest your head
But you lie there and moan
Suicide is the only way out
Don't you know what it's really about
Ah know people
You really know where it's at
You got it
Why try, why try
Get the gun and try it
Shoot, shoot, shoot

John's relative, Jack McCollum, and John's estate sued Ozzie Osbourne and CBS for negligence, alleging that the lyrics of Osbourne's music incited John to commit suicide. When the trial court dismissed the action, the plaintiffs appealed. The appellate court held that although Osbourne's lyrics might have been an actual cause of John's suicide, they were not the proximate cause of the suicide. The court stated:

John's tragic self-destruction, while listening to Osbourne's music, was not a reasonably foreseeable risk or consequence of defendant's remote artistic activities. It is simply not acceptable to a free and democratic society to impose a duty upon performing artists to limit and restrict their creativity in order to avoid the dissemination of ideas in artistic speech that may adversely affect emotionally troubled individuals. Such a burden would quickly have the effect of reducing and limiting artistic expression to only the broadest standard of taste and acceptance and the lowest level of offense, provocation, and controversy.

[McCollum v. CBS, Inc., and Osbourne, 202 Cal.App.3d 989, 249 Cal.Rptr. 187 (Cal.App. 1988)]

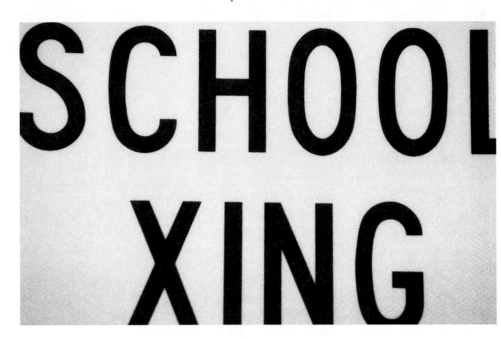

Local laws reduce speed limits, and drivers owe a heightened duty of care in school zones.

Negligent Infliction of Emotional Distress

Some jurisdictions have extended the tort of emotional distress to include the **negligent infliction of emotional distress**. The most common examples of this involve bystanders who witness the injury or death of a loved one that is caused by another's negligent conduct. The bystander, even though not personally physically injured, can sue the negligent party for his or her own mental suffering under this tort.

Generally, to be successful in this type of case, the plaintiff must prove that (1) a relative was killed or injured by the defendant, (2) the plaintiff suffered severe emotional distress, and (3) the plaintiff's mental distress resulted from a sensory and contemporaneous observance of the accident. Some states require that the plaintiff's mental distress be manifested by some physical injury; other states have eliminated this requirement.

In the following case, plaintiff recovered damages for negligent infliction of emotional distress.

negligent infliction of emotional distress

A tort that permits a person to recover for emotional distress caused by the defendant's negligent conduct.

No court has ever given, nor do we think ever can give, a definition of what constitutes a reasonable or an average man.

Lord Goddard C.J.R. v. McCarthy *(1954)*

Estrada v. Aeronaves de Mexico, S.A.
967 F.2d 1421 (1992)
United States Court of Appeals, Ninth Circuit

CASE 4.4

BACKGROUND AND FACTS

On the morning of August 31, 1986, Theresa Estrada left her home near Cerritos, California, to go shopping at a nearby grocery store. She left her husband at home reading the newspaper, and her three children were still in bed. Returning from the store, Estrada saw, heard, and felt a big explosion. Within minutes, she maneuvered her way through burning homes, cars, and debris to find her home engulfed in flames. Her husband and children died in the house. Although she did not know it at the time, an Aeromexico passenger airplane had crashed into her home after colliding with a privately owned plane. Estrada suffered severe emotional distress from the incident. She sued Aeromexico, the owner of the private plane, and the U.S. government for the wrongful death of her

family. Aeromexico was found not responsible for the accident. The jury found the private pilot 50 percent liable and the United States 50 percent liable because air traffic controllers had failed to detect the private plane's intrusion into commercial airspace and to give a traffic advisory to the Aeromexico flight. The jury awarded Estrada $5.5 million for the death of her family and $1 million for negligent infliction of emotional distress. The U.S. government appealed the $500,000 judgment against it for negligent infliction of emotional distress.

ISSUE

Was Estrada entitled under the law to recover damages for negligent infliction of emotional distress?

COURT'S REASONING

The court stated that a plaintiff may recover damages for emotional distress caused by observing the negligently inflicted injury of a third person if, but only if, said plaintiff: (1) is closely related to the injury victim; (2) is present at the scene of the injury-producing event at the time it occurs and is then aware that it is causing injury to the victim; and (3) as a result suffers serious emotional distress—a reaction beyond that which would be anticipated in a disinterested witness and which is not an abnormal response to the circumstances.

The court found that Estrada clearly satisfied the first and third requirements. The second requirement is the one at issue here. The Government argued that Estrada was neither present at the scene of the injury-producing event nor aware that it was causing injury to her family. The court held the plaintiff need not visually perceive the injury while it is being inflicted. The district court concluded that the disaster was still occurring while Mrs. Estrada was driving to her home and after she arrived to see her house in flames. The injury-producing event was the fire. The court correctly found that Estrada knew her husband and children were being injured by the fire. The court found that Estrada understandably experienced great emotional distress as a result of watching helplessly as flames engulfed her home and burned her family to death.

DECISION AND REMEDY

The court of appeals held that Estrada had established the elements necessary to recover damages for the negligent infliction of emotional distress.

Case Questions

Critical Legal Thinking   Should the law recognize the doctrine of negligent infliction of emotional distress? Should the elements be expanded so that they are easier to meet?

Business Ethics   Did the U.S. government act ethically in arguing against paying Mrs. Estrada the award assessed by the jury?

Contemporary Business   What economic effects does the doctrine of negligent infliction of emotional distress have on businesses?

Professional Malpractice

professional malpractice

The liability of a professional who breaches his or her duty of ordinary care.

Professionals, such as doctors, lawyers, architects, accountants, and others, owe a duty of ordinary care in providing their services. This duty is known as the *reasonable professional standard*. A professional who breaches this duty of care is liable for the injury his or her negligence causes. This liability is commonly referred to as **professional malpractice**. For example, a doctor who amputates a wrong leg is liable for *medical malpractice*. A lawyer who fails to file a document with the court on time, causing the client's case to be dismissed, is liable for *legal malpractice*. An accountant who fails to use reasonable care, knowledge, skill, and judgment when providing auditing and other accounting services to a client is liable for *accounting malpractice*.

Professionals who breach this duty are liable to their patients or clients. They may also be liable to some third parties.

SPECIAL NEGLIGENCE DOCTRINES

The courts have developed many *special negligence doctrines*. The most important of these are discussed in the paragraphs that follow.

Negligence Per Se

negligence per se

Tort where the violation of a statute or ordinance constitutes the breach of the duty of care.

Statutes often establish duties owed by one person to another. The violation of a statute that proximately causes an injury is **negligence per se**. The plaintiff in such an action must prove that (1) a statute existed, (2) the statute was enacted to prevent the type of injury suffered, and (3) the plaintiff was within a class of persons meant to be protected by the statute.

Every unjust decision is a reproach to the law or the judge who administers it. If the law should be in danger of doing injustice, then equity should be called in to remedy it. Equity was introduced to mitigate the rigour of the law.

Lord Denning, M. R.
Re Vandervell's Trusts (1974)

Consider This Example   Most cities have an ordinance that places the responsibility for fixing public sidewalks in residential areas on the homeowners whose homes front the sidewalk. A homeowner is liable if he or she fails to repair a damaged sidewalk in front of his or her home and a pedestrian trips and is injured because of the damage. The injured party does not have to prove that the homeowner owed the duty, because the statute establishes that.

Res Ipsa Loquitur

If a defendant is in control of a situation where a plaintiff has been injured and has superior knowledge of the circumstances surrounding the injury, the plaintiff might have difficulty proving the defendant's negligence. In such a situation, the law applies the doctrine of *res ipsa loquitur* (Latin for "the thing speaks for itself"). This doctrine raises a presumption of negligence and switches the burden to the defendant to prove that he or she was not negligent. *Res ipsa loquitur* applies in cases where the following elements are met:

1. The defendant had exclusive control of the instrumentality or situation that caused the plaintiff's injury.
2. The injury would not have ordinarily occurred "but for" someone's negligence.

res ipsa loquitur

Tort where the presumption of negligence arises because (1) the defendant was in exclusive control of the situation and (2) the plaintiff would not have suffered injury but for someone's negligence. The burden switches to the defendant(s) to prove they were not negligent.

Consider These Examples   Haeran goes in for major surgery and is given anesthesia to put her to sleep during the operation. Sometime after the operation it is discovered that a surgical instrument had been left in Haeran during the operation. She suffers severe injury because of the left-in instrument. Haeran would be hard pressed to identify which doctor or nurse had been careless and left the instrument in her body. In this case, the court can apply the doctrine of *res ipsa loquitur* and place the presumption of negligence on the defendants. Any defendant who can prove he or she did not leave the instrument in Haeran escapes liability; any defendant who does not disprove his or her negligence is liable. Other typical *res ipsa loquitur* cases involve commercial airplane crashes, falling elevators, and the like.

Pier, Santa Monica, California
Would the doctrine of res ipsa loquitur *apply if the roller-coaster broke, causing injury to the rider?*

Good Samaritan Laws

In the past, liability exposure made many doctors, nurses, and other medical professionals reluctant to stop and render aid to victims in emergency situations, such as highway accidents. Almost all states have enacted **Good Samaritan laws** that relieve medical professionals from liability for injury caused by their ordinary negligence in such circumstances. Good Samaritan laws protect medical professionals only from liability for their *ordinary negligence*, not for injuries caused by their gross negligence or reckless or intentional conduct. Most Good Samaritan laws protect licensed doctors and nurses and laypersons who have been certified in CPR. Laypersons not trained in CPR are not generally protected by Good Samaritan statutes—that is, they are liable for injuries caused by their ordinary negligence in rendering aid.

Good Samaritan law

Statute that relieves medical professionals from liability for ordinary negligence when they stop and render aid to victims in emergency situations.

Consider This Example   Sam is injured in an automobile accident and is unconscious in his automobile alongside the road. Doctor Pamela Heathcoat, who is driving by the scene of the accident, stops, pulls Sam from the burning wreckage, and administers first aid. In doing so, Pamela negligently breaks Sam's shoulder. If Pamela's negligence is ordinary negligence, she is not liable to Sam because the Good Samaritan law protects her from liability; if Pamela was grossly negligent or reckless in administering aid to Sam, she is liable to him for the injuries she caused. It is a question of fact for the jury to decide whether a doctor's conduct was ordinary negligence or gross negligence or recklessness. If Cathy, a layperson not trained in CPR, had rendered aid to Sam and caused Sam injury because of her ordinary negligence, the Good Samaritan law would not protect her and she would be liable to Sam.

Dram Shop Acts

Dram Shop Act

Statute that makes taverns and bartenders liable for injuries caused to or by patrons who are served too much alcohol.

Many states have enacted **Dram Shop Acts** that make a tavern and bartender civilly liable for injuries caused to or by patrons who are served too much alcohol. The alcohol must be either served in sufficient quantity to make the patron intoxicated or served to an already intoxicated person. Both the tavern and the bartender are liable to third persons injured by the patron and for injuries suffered by the patron. They are also liable for injuries caused by or to minors served by the tavern, regardless of whether the minor is intoxicated.

Guest Statutes

guest statute

Statute that provides that if a driver of a vehicle voluntarily and without compensation gives a ride to another person, the driver is not liable to the passenger for injuries caused by the driver's ordinary negligence.

Many states have enacted **guest statutes** that provide that if a driver voluntarily and without compensation gives a ride in a vehicle to another person (e.g., a hitchhiker), the driver is not liable to the passenger for injuries caused by the driver's ordinary negligence. However, if the passenger pays compensation to the driver, the driver owes a duty of ordinary care to the passenger and will be held liable. The driver is always liable to the passenger for wanton and gross negligence, for example, injuries caused because of excessive speed.

Fireman's Rule

Under the **fireman's rule**, a fireman who is injured while putting out a fire may not sue the party whose negligence caused the fire. This rule has been extended to policemen and other government workers. The bases for this rule are (1) people might not call for help if they could be held liable; (2) firemen, policemen, and other such workers receive special training for their jobs; and (3) these workers have special medical and retirement programs paid for by the public.

"Danger Invites Rescue" Doctrine

"danger invites rescue" doctrine

Doctrine that provides that a rescuer who is injured while going to someone's rescue can sue the person who caused the dangerous situation.

The law recognizes a **"danger invites rescue" doctrine**. Under this doctrine, a rescuer who is injured while going to someone's rescue can sue the person who caused the dangerous situation. For example, a passerby who is injured while trying to rescue children from a fire set by an arsonist can bring a civil suit against the arsonist.

Social Host Liability

social host liability

Rule that provides that social hosts are liable for injuries caused by guests who become intoxicated at a social function. States vary as to whether they have this rule in effect.

Several states have adopted the **social host liability** rule. This rule provides that a social host is liable for injuries caused by guests who are served alcohol at a social function (e.g., a birthday party, a wedding reception, etc.) and later cause injury because they are intoxicated. The injury may be to a third person or to the guest himself. The alcohol served at the social function must be the cause of the injury. A few states have adopted statutes that relieve social hosts from such liability.[6]

Liability of Landowners

Owners and renters of real property owe certain duties to protect visitors from injury while on the property. A landowner's and tenant's liability generally depends on the status of the visitor. Visitors fall into the following categories:

1. **Invitees and Licensees**   An *invitee* is a person who has been expressly or impliedly invited onto the owner's premises for the *mutual benefit* of both parties (e.g., guests invited for dinner, the mail carrier, and customers of a business). A licensee is a person who, *for his or her own benefit*, enters onto the premises with the express or implied consent of the owner (e.g., the Avon representative, encyclopedia salesperson, Seventh-Day Adventists). An owner owes a **duty of ordinary care** to invitees and licensees. An owner is liable if he or she negligently causes injury to an invitee or licensee. For example, a homeowner is liable if she leaves a garden hose across the walkway on which an invitee or a licensee trips and is injured.

2. **Trespassers**   A *trespasser* is a person who has no invitation, permission, or right to be on another's property. Burglars are a common type of trespasser. Generally, an owner does not owe a duty of ordinary care to a trespasser. For example, if a trespasser trips and injures himself on a

duty of ordinary care

The duty an owner owes an invitee or a licensee to prevent injury or harm when the invitee or licensee steps on the owner's premises.

bicycle the owner negligently left out, the owner is not liable. An owner does owe a **duty not to willfully or wantonly injure a trespasser**. Thus, an owner cannot set traps to injure trespassers.

A few states have eliminated the invitee-licensee-trespasser distinction. These states hold that owners and renters owe a duty of ordinary care to all persons who enter upon the property.

Liability of Common Carriers and Innkeepers

The common law holds common carriers and innkeepers to a higher standard of care than most other businesses. Common carriers and innkeepers owe a **duty of utmost care**—rather than a duty of ordinary care—to their passengers and guests. For example, innkeepers must provide security for their guests. The concept of utmost care is applied on a case-by-case basis. Obviously, a large hotel must provide greater security to guests than a "mom-and-pop" motel. Some states and cities have adopted specific statutes and ordinances relating to this duty.

DEFENSES AGAINST NEGLIGENCE

A defendant in a negligence lawsuit may raise several defenses to the imposition of liability. These defenses are discussed in the following paragraphs.

Superseding or Intervening Event

Under negligence, a person is liable only for foreseeable events. Therefore, an original negligent party can raise a **superseding** (or **intervening**) **event** as a defense to liability. For example, assume that an avid golfer negligently hits a spectator with a golf ball, knocking the spectator unconscious. While lying on the ground waiting for an ambulance to come, the spectator is struck by a bolt of lightning and killed. The golfer is liable for the injuries caused by the golf ball. He is not liable for the death of the spectator, however, because the lightning bolt was an unforeseen intervening event.

Assumption of the Risk

If a plaintiff knows of and voluntarily enters into or participates in a risky activity that results in injury, the law recognizes that the plaintiff assumed, or took on, the risk involved. Thus, the defendant can raise the defense of **assumption of the risk** against the plaintiff. This defense assumes that the plaintiff (1) had knowledge of the specific risk and (2) voluntarily assumed that risk. For example, under this theory, a race-car driver assumes the risk of being injured or killed in a crash. Assumption of the risk was raised as a defense in the following case.

duty not to willfully or wantonly injure

The duty an owner owes a trespasser to prevent intentional injury or harm to the trespasser when the trespasser is on his or her premises.

duty of utmost care

A duty of care that goes beyond ordinary care that says common carriers and innkeepers have a responsibility to provide security to their passengers or guests.

superseding event

A defendant is not liable for injuries caused by a superseding or intervening event for which he or she is not responsible.

assumption of the risk

A defense a defendant can use against a plaintiff who knowingly and voluntarily enters into or participates in a risky activity that results in injury.

Cheong v. Antablin
16 Cal.4th 1063, 68 Cal. Rptr.2d 859 (1997)
Supreme Court of California

CASE 4.5

BACKGROUND AND FACTS
On April 11, 1991, Wilkie Cheong and Drew R. Antablin, longtime friends and experienced skiers, skied together at Alpine Meadows, a resort near Tahoe City, California. While skiing, Antablin accidentally collided with Cheong, causing injury to him. Cheong sued Antablin to recover damages for negligent skiing. The trial court granted Antablin's motion for summary judgment, holding that the doctrine of assumption of risk barred Cheong's claim and dismissed the lawsuit. The court of appeals affirmed. Cheong appealed to the California Supreme Court.

ISSUE
Does the doctrine of assumption of risk bar recovery?

COURT'S REASONING
As a general rule, persons have a duty to use due care to avoid injuring others. The supreme court held that this general rule does not apply to coparticipants in a sport where dangerous conditions or conduct are an inherent risk of the sport. The court stated: "Courts should not hold a sports participant liable to a coparticipant for ordinary careless conduct committed during the sport because in the heat of an active sporting event a participant's normal energetic conduct often includes accidentally careless behavior. Vigorous participation in such sporting events likely would be chilled if legal liability were to be imposed on a participant on the basis of his or her ordinary careless conduct."

The court noted that the defense of assumption of risk does not apply where a sports participant intentionally injures another player or engages in reckless conduct outside the range of the ordinary activity involved in the sport. The court found that Antablin negligently caused the skiing collision and had not engaged in intentional or reckless conduct.

DECISION AND REMEDY

The state supreme court held that the doctrine of assumption of risk barred recovery in this case.

Case Questions

Critical Legal Thinking Do you think the law should recognize the doctrine of assumption of risk? Why or why not?

Business Ethics Should Cheong have sued Antablin? Discuss.

Contemporary Business Should the doctrine of assumption of risk be applied as a defense when spectators are injured at professional sports events? Explain.

Contributory Negligence

contributory negligence

A doctrine that says a plaintiff who is partially at fault for his or her own injury cannot recover against the negligent defendant.

Under the common law doctrine of **contributory negligence**, a plaintiff who is partially at fault for his or her own injury cannot recover against the negligent defendant. For example, suppose a driver who is driving over the speed limit negligently hits and injures a pedestrian who is jaywalking. Suppose the jury finds that the driver is 80 percent responsible for the accident and the jaywalker is 20 percent responsible. The pedestrian suffered $100,000 in injuries. Under the doctrine of contributory negligence, the pedestrian cannot recover any damages from the driver.

There is one major exception to the doctrine of contributory negligence: The defendant has a duty under the law to avoid the accident if at all possible. This rule is known as the *last clear chance rule*. For example, a driver who sees a pedestrian walking across the street against a "Don't Walk" sign must avoid hitting him or her if possible. When deciding cases involving this rule, the courts consider the attentiveness of the parties and the amount of time each has to respond to the situation.

Comparative Negligence

comparative negligence

A doctrine under which damages are apportioned according to fault.

As seen, the application of the doctrine of contributory negligence could reach an unfair result where a party only slightly at fault for his or her injuries could not recover from an otherwise negligent defendant. Many states have replaced the doctrine of contributory negligence with the doctrine of **comparative negligence**. Under this doctrine, damages are apportioned according to fault. When the comparative negligence rule is applied to the previous example, the result is much fairer. The plaintiff-pedestrian can recover 80 percent of his damages (or $80,000) from the defendant-driver. This is an example of *pure comparative negligence*. Several states have adopted *partial comparative negligence*, which provides that a plaintiff must be less than 50 percent responsible for causing his or her own injuries to recover under comparative negligence; otherwise, contributory negligence applies.

𝒞ONCEPT SUMMARY   CONTRIBUTORY AND COMPARATIVE NEGLIGENCE COMPARED

Situation	Doctrine	Liability of the Defendant
Defendant liable for causing injury to plaintiff, but plaintiff partially at fault for causing his own injuries.	Contributory negligence	Defendant not liable exception: Last clear chance rule
	Comparative negligence 1. Pure comparative negligence	Defendant liable for plaintiff's injuries according to fault
	2. Partial comparative negligence a. Plaintiff less than 50 percent responsible b. Plaintiff 50 percent or more responsible	Defendant liable for plaintiff's injuries according to fault Defendant not liable

BUSINESS TORTS

Although many of the torts previously discussed are committed by or against businesses, certain other torts commonly involve businesses. Several of these torts are discussed in the following paragraphs.

Entering Certain Businesses and Professions Without a License

There are government restrictions and prohibitions on the freedom of entry into certain businesses and professions. These restrictions are intended to protect the public from unqualified practitioners and to promote the efficient operation of the economy.

For example, a person cannot simply erect a television or radio transmitter and start broadcasting: The Federal Communications Commission grants television and radio station licenses for assigned frequencies. In addition, many occupations, such as lawyers, physicians, dentists, real estate brokers, hairdressers, and the like, require state licenses. In some states, even palm readers and astrologists must be licensed. To obtain the necessary license, and applicant must (1) meet certain educational requirements and (2) demonstrate a certain level of proficiency in the subject matter through examination, experience, or both. Entry into these industries or professions without permission subjects the violator to various civil and criminal penalties. In many states, a licensed professional can bring an action to prevent an unlicensed person from practicing.

Unfair Competition

In most situations, competitors are free to compete vigorously, even if that means that someone is driven out of business or sustains severe losses. However, competitors may not engage in illegal **unfair competition** or **predatory practices**.

The common law tort of **palming off** is one of the oldest forms of unfair competition. This tort usually occurs when one company tries to "palm off" its products as those of a rival. For example, if a company implied that it was affiliated with International Business Machines (IBM) by selling computers under the IBM label, it would be liable for the business tort of palming off.

To prove the tort of palming off, the plaintiff must prove that (1) the defendant used the plaintiff's logo, symbol, mark, and so on and (2) there is a likelihood of confusion as to the source of the product. Actual consumer confusion need not be shown. The key element is whether consumers are likely to be confused as to the origin of the copied product.

He that's cheated twice by the same man, is an accomplice with the Cheater.

Thomas Fuller
Gnomologia *(1732)*

Business Brief

A license must be obtained from the government to enter certain industries, such as banking and broadcasting, and to practice certain professions, such as law and medicine.

unfair competition

Competition that violates the law.

palming off

Unfair competition that occurs when a company tries to pass one of its products as that of a rival.

Business Ethics

HALLMARK GREETED BY AN UNFAIR COMPETITION LAWSUIT

Imitation may be a form of flattery. In a business setting, however, it may constitute unfair competition. Consider the following case.

Susan Polis Schutz and Stephen Schutz own Hartford House, Ltd., which does business under the trade name Blue Mountain Art. Blue Mountain is in the greeting card business. In 1981 and 1983, Blue Mountain introduced two lines of cards entitled "AireBrush Feelings" and "WaterColor Feelings," respectively. The cards contained nonoccasion emotional messages concerning love and personal relationships superimposed on soft airbrush and watercolor artwork. The cards were printed on high-quality, uncoated, textured

art paper and contained lengthy free-verse poetry with many letters and words printed in hand-lettered calligraphy. The cards were a commercial success.

Hallmark Cards, Inc., which has produced and marketed greeting cards for 75 years, is the giant of the greeting card industry. In 1986, Hallmark introduced a line of cards called "Personal Touch." Like Blue Mountain's cards, the cards were done in soft watercolors that conveyed emotional messages about personal relationships in free-verse poetry. Hallmark mounted an intense effort to capture the emotionally expressive nonoccasion greeting card market and designed and marketed its Personal Touch cards to appeal to the same type of consumer who purchased Blue Mountain's cards.

Blue Mountain sued Hallmark for the tort of unfair competition. It alleged that Hallmark's Personal Touch line of greeting cards was deceptively and confusingly similar to Blue Mountain's and infringed upon the trade dress of Blue Mountain's AireBrush Feelings and WaterColor Feelings lines.

The U.S. district court issued an injunction that prohibited Hallmark from selling or distributing its Personal Touch cards. The court held that Hallmark had engaged in unfair competition by infringing upon Blue Mountain's distinctive trade dress of its lines of cards. The court determined that

there was a likelihood of confusion among card purchasers as to the source of Blue Mountain's two lines and Hallmark's Personal Touch line. The court of appeals affirmed. The court stated, "It is Blue Mountain's specific artistic expression, in combination with other features to produce an overall Blue Mountain look, that is being protected." [*Hartford House, Ltd. v. Hallmark Cards, Incorporated*, 846 F.2d 1268 (10th Cir. 1988)]

1. Did Hallmark act ethically in this case?
2. Should trade dress be protected? Why or why not?
3. Do you think Hallmark engaged in unfair competition in this case?

Disparagement

Business firms rely on their reputation and the quality of their products and services to attract and keep customers. That is why state unfair-competition laws protect businesses from disparaging statements made by competitors or others. A disparaging statement is an untrue statement made by one person or business about the products, services, property, or reputation of another business.

To prove **disparagement**, which is also called **product disparagement**, **trade libel**, or **slander of title**, the plaintiff must show that the defendant (1) made an untrue statement about the plaintiff's products, services, property, or business reputation; (2) published this untrue statement to a third party; (3) knew the statement was not true; and (4) made the statement maliciously (i.e., with intent to injure the plaintiff).

False Advertising

Companies often engage in comparative advertising in which they compare the qualities of their products to those of competitors. Truthful comparative advertising is lawful. However, untruthful comparative advertising constitutes disparagement of product and false and misleading advertising in violation of **Section 43(a) of the Lanham Act**,[7] a federal statute.

Section 43(a) prohibits false and misleading advertising. Under this act, private parties may obtain injunctions and recover damages from competitors who make disparaging or false or misleading statements about the plaintiff's products.

Intentional Misrepresentation (Fraud)

One of the most pervasive business torts is **intentional misrepresentation**. This tort is also known as **fraud** or **deceit**. It occurs when a wrongdoer deceives another person out of money, property, or something else of value. A person who has been injured by an intentional misrepresentation can recover damages from the wrongdoer. The elements required to find fraud are

1. The wrongdoer made a false representation of material fact.
2. The wrongdoer had knowledge that the representation was false and intended to deceive the innocent party.
3. The innocent party justifiably relied on the misrepresentation.
4. The innocent party was injured.

Item 2 above, which is called **scienter**, includes situations where the wrongdoer recklessly disregards the truth in making a representation that is false. Intent or recklessness can be inferred from the circumstances.

Ethics Brief

Companies that engage in comparative advertising must be able to substantiate their claims of superiority over a rival's products or services.

intentional misrepresentation

Intentionally defrauding another person out of money, property, or something else of value.

There are some frauds so well conducted that it would be stupidity not to be deceived by them.

C. C. Colton
Lacon Vol. 1 (1820)

Business Ethics

USED-CAR DEALER PUNISHED FOR FRAUD

On December 11, 1992, Charles Forshey did what millions of people in this country have done—bought a used vehicle from a used-car dealership. Forshey brought two older vehicles he owned, traded them in for a value of $3,100 added some cash, and purchased a used 1983 three-quarter ton Chevrolet Suburban truck for $5,995 from Carr Chevrolet, Inc. in Oregon. Forshey bought the vehicle "as-is," which means that the dealership disclaimed any warranties as to quality.

Shortly after the purchase, Forshey noticed that the Suburban was missing all of its emission control equipment. Through library research, he learned that the engine had a distributor coil that did not belong to the year and engine he thought he had bought. He learned later that the 1983 Suburban had a 1981 engine. He also noticed that the vehicle identification numbers (VIN) were not on the door, transmission, or glove box. Forshey took the vehicle to an environmental agency and was told that it did not have the required smog control equipment and that the vehicle could not be brought into compliance because of the difference in age between the vehicle and the engine. Forshey conducted his own title search and found that the truck had been stolen at some previous time in California and stripped of its parts.

After discovering this information, Forshey tried to return the truck to the dealer and recover his two vehicles and the cash he paid. The dealer told Forshey that he had purchased the Suburban "as-is" and it was his problem. The dealer told Forshey that he could not have his trade-in vehicles back because they had been sold (they had not) and he could not get a refund of the $3,100 trade-in value because the dealer would not reimburse him. Exasperated, Forshey sued the dealership for fraud.

At trial, evidence proved that the vehicle had a rear-wheel alignment; the driver's door was misaligned, was a different color, and had been replaced; the dashboard came from a different vehicle; the VIN number had been cut out of the glove box and the door; the VIN number had been ground off the the transmission; the engine was not the original; the odometer had been tampered with; and the truck had been heavily reconditioned. The dealership denied any knowledge of these facts, however. The trial court disagreed. The jury returned a verdict in favor of Forshey, awarded him $11,496 in compensatory damages and $1 million in punitive damages.

On appeal, the dealership argued that the "as-is" clause saved it from liability. The court of appeals rejected this argument, stating that an "as-is" clause saves a seller from being liable for normal features—that is, the engine fails because of honestly disclosed miles—but does not save a seller who concealed facts from the buyer and who has engaged in fraud. The court of appeals changed the award of punitive damages to $300,000 and warded the plaintiff $55,468 to cover his attorney's fees. The court stated that this award would "accomplish the legitimate state interest in punishing the defendant and deterring its future misconduct." [*Forshey v. Carr Chevrolet, Inc.*, 965 P.2d 440 (Oregon, 1998)]

1. How reprehensible was the dealership's conduct? Was this conduct ethical?
2. Should an "as-is" clause shield the seller from liability? Why or why not?
3. Was the award of punitive damages sufficient in this case?

Intentional Interference With Contractual Relations

A party to a contract may sue any third person who intentionally interferes with the contract and causes that party injury. The third party does not have to have acted with malice or bad faith. This tort, which is known as the tort of **intentional interference with contractual relations**, usually arises when a third party induces a contracting party to breach the contract with another party. The following elements must be shown:

1. A valid, enforceable contract between the contracting parties
2. Third-party knowledge of this contract
3. Third-party inducement to breach the contract

A third party can contract with the breaching party without becoming liable for this tort if a contracting party has already breached the contract. This is because the third party cannot be held to have induced a preexisting breach.

Breach of the Implied Covenant of Good Faith and Fair Dealing

Several states have held that a **covenant of good faith and fair dealing** is implied in certain types of contracts. Under this covenant, the parties to a contract not only are held to the express terms of the contract but also are required to act in "good faith" and deal fairly in all

intentional interference with contractual relations

A tort that arises when a third party induces a contracting party to breach the contract with another party.

covenant of good faith and fair dealing

Under this implied covenant, the parties to a contract not only are held to the express terms of the contract but also are required to act in "good faith" and deal fairly in all respects in obtaining the objective of the contract.

respects in obtaining the objective of the contract. A breach of this implied covenant is a tort for which tort damages are recoverable. This tort, which is sometimes referred to as the **tort of "bad faith,"** is an evolving area of the law.

Punitive Damages

punitive damages

Damages that are awarded to punish the defendant, to deter the defendant from similar conduct in the future, and to set an example for others.

Generally, **punitive damages** are not recoverable for breach of contract. They are recoverable, however, for certain *tortious* conduct. This includes fraud, intentional conduct, or other egregious conduct. Punitive damages are in addition to actual damages and may be kept by the plaintiff. Punitive damages are awarded to punish the defendant, to deter the defendant from similar conduct in the future, and to set an example for others.

The court found a bad faith tort in the following case and awarded punitive damages.

Gourley v. State Farm Mutual Automobile Insurance Co.
227 Cal.App.3d 1099, 265 Cal.Rptr. 634 (1990)
California Court of Appeals

CASE 4.6

BACKGROUND AND FACTS
In late 1981, Julie Gourley was a passenger in an automobile that was struck by an out-of-control vehicle driven by an uninsured drunk driver. Gourley, who was not wearing a seat belt at the time of the accident, suffered a fractured right shoulder when she struck some portion of her vehicle's interior. Gourley made a claim under the uninsured motorist coverage in her automobile policy with State Farm Mutual Automobile Insurance Company (State Farm). Medical evidence showed that Gourley had some permanent disability and a limited range of motion, suffered residual pain, and might require surgery in the future. She demanded the policy limit of $100,000. In September 1982, State Farm's attorney, Barry Allen, advised Gourley that State Farm would contest the proximate cause of the injuries based upon Gourley's failure to wear her seat belt. Evidence showed that under California law the seat belt issue was not a defense. State Farm offered a settlement of $20,000. Gourley refused it. When Gourley reduced her demand to $60,000, State Farm responded with a counteroffer of $25,000. Because the parties could not reach a settlement, the case went to arbitration. In October 1984, the arbitrator awarded Gourley $88,137, which State Farm promptly paid. Gourley sued State Farm for breach of the implied covenant of good faith and fair dealing in handling the claim and sought actual damages for emotional distress and punitive damages. The jury awarded her $15,765 in actual damages and $1,576,000 in punitive damages. State Farm appealed.

ISSUE
Did State Farm's conduct amount to a bad faith tort for which punitive damages could be awarded?

COURT'S REASONING
The court noted that there is an implied covenant in every insurance contract that the insurer will do nothing to impair the insured's right to receive the benefit of the contractual bargain—that the insurer will promptly pay to the insured all sums due

under the contract. A major motivation for the purchase of insurance is the peace of mind that claims will be paid promptly. When an insurer unreasonably refuses to pay benefits due, it frustrates that motivation and a cause of action in tort arises. Withholding benefits is unreasonable if it is without proper cause. In determining proper cause, the interests of the insured must be given at least as much consideration as those of the insurer.

The court held that in this case the jury could reasonably find "intentional" bad faith. The testimony of the expert witness and the arbitrator's award provided ample basis to conclude State Farm intentionally made settlement offers that it knew were inadequate. Gourley presented substantial evidence that State Farm adopted a "stonewall" or "see-you-in-court" attitude as exhibited by grossly insufficient offers to settle. The evidence was sufficient to support the jury's finding of bad faith. The court stated that to support an award of punitive damages, the plaintiff must show "oppression, fraud, or malice." The court concluded that there was ample evidence to support an award of punitive damages. The court stated, "While there is always some concern that plaintiffs not receive a windfall as a result of punitive damages, their major purpose remains punishment and deterrence."

DECISION AND REMEDY
The appellate court held that State Farm's actions in not settling the claim under the policy limits by asserting an illegal defense (failure of Gourley to wear a seat belt) constituted bad faith. Affirmed.

Case Questions

Critical Legal Thinking Should the law recognize the doctrine of bad faith tort? Why or why not?

Business Ethics Does an insurer act unethically whenever it refuses to settle a claim under the policy limits? Do you think State Farm acted unethically in this case?

Contemporary Business What effect will the recognition of bad faith torts associated with contracts have on businesses such as insurance companies? Explain.

Civil RICO

In an effort to combat organized crime, Congress enacted the **Racketeer Influenced and Corrupt Organizations Act (RICO)**.[8] The act outlaws a pattern of "racketeering activity," including arson, counterfeiting, gambling, dealing in narcotics, bribery, embezzlement, mail and wire fraud, and other enumerated criminal activities. (For a discussion of criminal RICO, see Chapter 5.)

Persons injured by a RICO violation can bring a private civil action against the violator. RICO permits recovery only for injury to business or property. Recovery for personal injury is not permitted under RICO. The plaintiff can sue to recover **treble damages** (three times actual loss), plus attorney fees.[9] A defendant in a civil RICO case does not have to first be found guilty of criminal RICO.[10]

Because by definition commercial fraud is a racketeering activity, many fraud cases are now being brought as RICO cases. Thus, insurance companies, banks, and other businesses are being sued in RICO treble damage actions.

STRICT LIABILITY

Strict liability is another category of torts. Strict liability is *liability without fault.* That is, a participant in a covered activity will be held liable for any injuries caused by the activity even if he or she was not negligent. This doctrine holds that (1) there are certain activities that can place the public at risk of injury even if reasonable care is taken, and (2) the public should have some means of compensation if such injury occurs.

Strict liability was first imposed for *abnormally dangerous activities*, such as crop dusting, blasting, fumigation, burning fields, storage of explosives, and keeping wild animals as pets. In the following case, the court applied the doctrine of strict liability to a dangerous activity.

Racketeer Influenced and Corrupt Organizations Act (RICO)

Federal statute that authorizes civil lawsuits against defendants for engaging in a pattern of racketeering activities.

treble damages

Civil damages three times actual damages may be awarded to persons whose business or property is injured by a RICO violation.

strict liability

Liability without fault.

Business Brief

Whereas intentional torts and negligence require the defendant to have been at fault, strict liability imposes liability without the defendant's having been at fault.

Klein v. Pyrodyne Corporation

810 P.2d 917 (1991)
Supreme Court of Washington

CASE 4.7

BACKGROUND AND FACTS

Pyrodyne Corporation (Pyrodyne) is a licensed fireworks-display company that contracted to display fireworks at the Western Washington State Fairgrounds in Puyallup, Washington, on July 4, 1987. During the fireworks display, one of the mortar launchers discharged a rocket on a horizontal trajectory parallel to the earth. The rocket exploded near a crowd of onlookers, including Danny Klein. Klein's clothing was set on fire, and he suffered facial burns and serious injury to his eyes. Klein sued Pyrodyne for strict liability to recover for his injuries. Pyrodyne asserted that the Chinese manufacturer of the fireworks was negligent in producing the rocket and therefore Pyrodyne should not be held liable. The trial court applied the doctrine of strict liability and held in favor of Klein. Pyrodyne appealed.

ISSUE

Is the conducting of public fireworks displays an abnormally dangerous activity that justifies the imposition of strict liability?

COURT'S REASONING

Section 519 of the Restatement (Second) of Torts provides that any party carrying on an "abnormally dangerous activity" is strictly liable for ensuing damages. The public display of

fireworks fits this definition. The court stated: "Any time a person ignites rockets with the intention of sending them aloft to explode in the presence of large crowds of people, a high risk of serious personal injury or property damage is created. That risk arises because of the possibility that a rocket will malfunction or be misdirected." Pyrodyne argued that its liability was cut off by the Chinese manufacturer's negligence. The court rejected this argument, stating, "Even if negligence may properly be regarded as an intervening cause, it cannot function to relieve Pyrodyne from strict liability."

DECISION AND REMEDY

The Washington Supreme Court held that the public display of fireworks is an abnormally dangerous activity that warrants the imposition of strict liability. Affirmed.

Case Questions

Critical Legal Thinking Should the law recognize the doctrine of strict liability? What is the public policy underlying the imposition of liability without fault?

Business Ethics Did Pyrodyne act ethically in denying liability in this case?

Contemporary Business Does the doctrine of strict liability increase the cost of doing business? Explain.

International Law

ISRAELI TORT LAW

David Ben Gurion proclaimed the establishment of the State of Israel on May 14, 1948. Historically, the Jewish people have been governed by biblical law. With the advent of a national state, secular laws were developed and coexist with religious law. One of the laws developed by the State of Israel was *tort* law. Israeli tort law is based on the theory that monetary compensation is awarded to promote justice and to ensure fair compensation when a tort occurs.

American tort law allows juries almost unlimited discretion to evaluate injuries and award damages. Under Israeli tort law, there is no right to trial by jury. Instead, all actions are tried by a panel of three judges or three laypeople who decide both questions of fact and law. In essence, they are closer to arbitrators than judges.

Also, under Israeli tort law, all damages awarded must be assessed under one of these categories of damages:

1. *Medical expenses (ripui)* actually incurred and those expected to be incurred in order to cure the victim or return him or her as close as possible to a preinjury state.
2. *Loss of earnings (shevet)* incurred during the time of the victim's injury and recovery.
3. *Loss of income (nezek)* for the long-term decrease in the victim's market value as a worker and skills he or she will never recover.
4. *Pain and suffering (tza'ar)* for short-term pain and suffering incurred at the time of the injury and their immediate consequences.
5. *Embarrassment (boshet)* for long-term pain and suffering caused from such things as permanent disfigurement, emotional distress, and such.

Israeli law limits the assessment of noneconomic damages (categories 4 and 5) to cases of willful, intentional, or grossly negligent infliction of harm.

Medical malpractice is one area of tort law where the American and Israeli systems differ. Under American law, doctors are liable for their negligent conduct unless a Good Samaritan law relieves them of liability. Jewish law goes one step further. It excuses doctors from liability for their negligence in most situations. This is based on the public policy that the fear of such liability would otherwise discourage people from going into the medical profession.

Chapter Summary

Intentional Torts Against Persons, p. 91

Intentional Torts Against Persons	1. *Assault.* Threat of immediate harm or offensive contact, or any action that arouses reasonable apprehension of imminent harm.
	2. *Battery.* The unauthorized and harmful or offensive physical contact with another person.
	a. *Transferred intent doctrine.* If a person intends to injure one person but actually harms another person, the law transfers the perpetrator's intent from the target to the actual victim.
	3. *False imprisonment.* Intentional confinement or restraint of another person without authority or justification and without that person's consent.
	a. *Merchant protection statutes.* Permit businesses to stop, detain, and investigate suspected shoplifters (and not be held liable for false imprisonment) if the following requirements are met:
	i. There are reasonable grounds for the suspicion.
	ii. Suspects are detained for only a reasonable time.
	iii. Investigations are conducted in a reasonable manner.
	4. *Defamation of character.* The defendant makes an untrue statement of fact about the plaintiff that is published to a third party. Truth is an absolute defense.
	a. Types of defamation:
	i. *Slander.* Oral defamation
	ii. *Libel.* Written defamation
	b. *Public figure plaintiffs.* Must prove the additional element of *malice.*
	5. *Misappropriation of the right to publicity.* Appropriating another person's name or identity for commercial purposes without that person's consent. Also called the tort of appropriation.
	6. *Invasion of privacy.* Unwarranted and undesired publicity of a private fact about a person. The fact does not have to be untrue. Truth is not a defense.

7. *Intentional infliction of emotional distress.* Extreme and outrageous conduct intentionally or recklessly done that causes severe emotional distress. Some states require that the mental distress be manifested by physical injury. Also known as the *tort of outrage.*
8. *Malicious prosecution.* A successful defendant in a prior lawsuit can sue the plaintiff if the first lawsuit was frivolous.

Intentional Torts Against Property, p. 96

Intentional Torts Against Property	1. *Trespass to land.* Interference with a landowner's right to exclusive possession of his or her land. 2. *Trespass to personal property.* A person injures another person's personal property or interferes with that person's enjoyment of his or her property. 3. *Conversion of personal property.* Taking over another person's personal property and depriving him or her of the use and enjoyment of the property.

Unintentional Torts (Negligence), p. 97

Negligence	"The omission to do something which a reasonable man would do, or doing something which a prudent and reasonable man would not do."

Elements of Negligence	To establish negligence, the plaintiff must prove:
	 1. The defendant owed a *duty of care* to the plaintiff.
	 2. The defendant *breached this duty.*
	 3. The plaintiff suffered *injury.*
	 4. The defendant's negligent act *caused* the plaintiff's injury. Two types of causation must be shown:
	   a. *Causation in fact (or actual cause).* The defendant's negligent act was the actual cause of the plaintiff's injury.
	   b. *Proximate cause (or legal cause).* The defendant is liable only for the *foreseeable* consequences of his negligent act.

Negligent Infliction of Emotional Distress	*Negligent infliction of emotional distress.* A person who witnesses a close relative's injury or death may sue the negligent party who caused the accident to recover damages for any emotional distress suffered by the bystander. To recover for *negligent infliction of emotional distress,* the plaintiff must prove: 1. A relative was killed or injured by the defendant. 2. The plaintiff suffered severe emotional distress. 3. The plaintiff's mental distress resulted from a sensory and contemporaneous observance of the accident. Some states require that the mental distress be manifested by physical injury.
Professional Malpractice	Doctors, lawyers, architects, accountants, and other professionals owe a duty of ordinary care in providing their services. They are judged by a *reasonable professional standard.* Professionals who breach this duty are liable to clients and some third parties for *professional malpractice.*

Special Negligence Doctrines, p. 102

Special Negligence Doctrines	1. *Negligence per se.* A statute or ordinance establishes the duty of care. A violation of the statute or ordinance constitutes a breach of this duty of care. 2. *Res ipsa loquitur.* A presumption of negligence is established if the defendant had exclusive control of the instrumentality or situation that caused the plaintiff's injury and the injury would not have ordinarily occurred but for someone's negligence. The defendants may rebut this presumption. 3. *Good Samaritan laws.* Relieve doctors and other medical professionals from liability for ordinary negligence when rendering medical aid in emergency situations. 4. *Dram Shop Acts.* State statutes that make taverns and bartenders liable for injuries caused to or by patrons who are served too much alcohol and cause injury to themselves or others. 5. *Guest statutes.* Provide that a driver of a vehicle is not liable for ordinary negligence to passengers he or she gratuitously transports. The driver is liable for gross negligence. 6. *Fireman's rule.* Firemen, policemen, and other government employees who are injured in the performance of their duties cannot sue the person who negligently caused the dangerous situation that caused the injury. 7. *"Danger invites rescue" doctrine.* A person who is injured while going to someone's rescue may sue the person who caused the dangerous situation.

8. *Social host liability.* Some states make social hosts liable for injuries caused by guests who are served alcohol at a social function and later cause injury because they are intoxicated.
9. *Liability of landowners.* Landowners (and tenants) owe the following duties to persons who come upon their property:
    a. *Invitees.* Duty of ordinary care
    b. *Licensees.* Duty of ordinary care
    c. *Trespassers.* Duty not to willfully and wantonly injure trespassers
10. *Liability of common carriers and innkeepers.* Owe a *duty of utmost care*, rather than the duty of ordinary care, to protect their passengers and patrons from injury.

Defenses Against Negligence, p. 105

Defenses Against Negligence

1. *Superseding event.* An intervening event caused by another person that caused the plaintiff's injuries that relieves the defendant from liability.
2. *Assumption of the risk.* A defendant is not liable for the plaintiff's injuries if the plaintiff had knowledge of a specific risk and voluntarily assumed that risk.
3. *Plaintiff partially at fault.* States have adopted one of the following two rules that affect a defendant's liability if the plaintiff had been partially at fault for causing his or her own injuries:
    a. *Contributory negligence.* A plaintiff cannot recover anything from the defendant.
    b. *Comparative negligence.* Damages are apportioned according to the parties' fault. Also called *comparative fault.*

Business Torts, p. 107

Business Torts

1. *Entering business without a license.* The law requires that persons obtain a license from the government prior to entering certain businesses or professions.
2. *Palming off.* A company passes off its products or services as those of another company.
3. *Disparagement.* An untrue statement about the products, services, property, or reputation of a business. Also called *product disparagement, trade libel,* or *slander of title.*
4. *False advertising.* Section 43(a) of the Lanham Act, a federal law, prohibits false and misleading advertising. State laws also prohibit false and misleading advertising.
5. *Intentional misrepresentation.* A wrongdoer defrauds another person out of money, property, or something else of value. Also known as *fraud* or *deceit.* The following elements must be shown:
    a. The wrongdoer made a false representation of material fact.
    b. The wrongdoer had knowledge that the representation was false and intended to deceive the innocent party.
    c. The innocent party justifiably relied on the misrepresentation.
    d. The innocent party was injured.
6. *Intentional interference with contractual relations.* A third party intentionally interferes with another party's contract and induces the other party to that contract to breach it, causing the nonbreaching party injury.
7. *Breach of the implied covenant of good faith and fair dealing.* A party to a contract does not act in good faith or fails to deal fairly in achieving the object of the contract. This duty is only implied in certain contracts (e.g., insurance contracts). Also called the *tort of bad faith.*
8. *Civil RICO.* Federal law that outlaws engaging in a pattern of racketeering activity such as arson, bribery, embezzlement, fraud, and other enumerated crimes. A private plaintiff who is injured in his or her business or property may recover *treble damages* from the wrongdoer in a civil lawsuit.

Tort Damages

1. *Actual damages.* Include compensation for personal injury, pain and suffering, emotional distress, and other injuries caused by the defendant's tortious conduct.
2. *Punitive damages.* Recoverable against a defendant for intentional or egregious conduct. Awarded to punish the defendant, to deter the defendant from similar conduct in the future, and to set an example for others. The plaintiff may keep these damages.

Strict Liability, p. 111

Strict Liability

Liability is assessed on defendants without regard to fault. Applies to *abnormally dangerous activities* and certain products.

END-OF-CHAPTER INTERNET EXERCISES AND CASE QUESTIONS

Working the Web Internet Exercises

ACTIVITIES

1. Find a state court case opinion relating to intentional torts. See, for example, a state-based plaintiffs' trial lawyers association site **www.wstla.org**, or at the national level, The Association of Trial Lawyers of America **www.atla.org**, or the ABA Tort and Insurance Practice Section **www.abanet.org/tips/thebrief.html**.

2. Find a medical malpractice case. For the viewpoint of the defense, see **www.dri.org** For the insurance industry's view, see **www.ircweb.org**.

Check the following site as a starting point for the questions 3 to 5: **www.law.cornell.edu/topics/torts.html**.

3. Find a state court case that establishes the rule in your jurisdiction on Social Host Liability.

4. Find the statute in your jurisdiction that contains the Good Samaritan Rule.

5. Find the statute in your jurisdiction that contains the Innkeepers Liability Law.

CRITICAL LEGAL THINKING CASES

4.1 Intentional Tort On September 16, 1975, the Baltimore Orioles professional baseball team was at Boston's Fenway Park to play the Boston Red Sox. Ross Grimsley was a pitcher for the visiting Baltimore club. During one period of the game, Grimsley was warming up in the bull pen, throwing pitches to a catcher. During this warm-up, Boston spectators in the stands heckled Grimsley. After Grimsley had completed warming up and the catcher had left from behind the plate in the bull pen, Grimsley wound up as if he were going to throw the ball in his hand at the plate, then turned and threw the ball at one of the hecklers in the stand. The ball traveled at about 80 miles an hour, passed through a wire fence protecting the spectators, missed the heckler that Grimsley was aiming at and hit another spectator, David Manning, Jr., causing injury. Manning sued Grimsley and the Baltimore Orioles. Are the defendants liable [*Manning v. Grimsley*, 643 F.2d 20 (1st Cir. 1981)]

4.2 Merchant Protection Statute At about 7:30 P.M. on September 8, 1976, Deborah A. Johnson entered a Kmart store located in Madison, Wisconsin, to purchase some diapers and several cans of motor oil. She took her small child along to enable her to purchase the correct size diapers, carrying the child in an infant seat that she had purchased at Kmart two or three weeks previously. A large Kmart price tag was still attached to the infant seat. Johnson purchased the diapers and oil and some children's clothes. She was in a hurry to leave because it was 8:00 P.M., her child's feeding time, and she hurried through the checkout lane. She paid for the diapers, the oil, and the clothing. Just after leaving the store she heard someone ask her to stop. She turned around and saw a Kmart security officer. He showed her a badge and asked her to come back into the store, which she did. The man stated, "I have reason to believe that you have stolen this car seat." Johnson explained that she had purchased the seat previously. She demanded to see the manager, who was called to the scene. When Johnson pointed out that the seat had cat hairs, food crumbs, and milk stains on it, the man said "I'm really sorry, there's been a terrible mistake. You can go." Johnson looked at the clock when she left, which read 8:20 P.M. Johnson sued Kmart for false imprisonment. Is Kmart liable? [*Johnson v. Kmart Enterprises, Inc.*, 297 N.W.2d 74 (Wis.App. 1980)]

4.3 Defamation Dorchen Leidholdt is a New Yorker who is a vigorous opponent of pornography. She is a founding member of the organization Women Against Pornography, has given public speeches against pornography, and has debated opponents in the national media. Larry Flynt Publications is a California corporation that owns *Hustler* magazine. *Hustler* regularly includes a monthly column in which some personage whose activities *Hustler* opposes is vilified in graphic terms. *Hustler's* June 1985 issue featured Leidholdt in the column. The article criticizes Leidholdt and her fellow antipornographers in scatological terms, employing such phrases as a "pus bloated walking sphincter," "sexually repressed," "hating men, hating sex, and hating themselves," and "this frustrated group of sexual fascists." The article was accompanied by a small photograph of Leidholdt's face superimposed over the buttocks of a bent-over naked man. Leidholdt sued *Hustler* for defamation. Who wins? [*Leidholdt v. Larry Flynt Publications*, 860 F.2d 890 (9th Cir. 1988)]

4.4 Right to Privacy On December 15, 1956, Marvin Briscoe and another man hijacked a truck in Danville, Kentucky. They were caught and convicted, and Briscoe served a term in prison. After release from prison, Briscoe established a life of respectability. In 1967, *Reader's Digest* published an article entitled "The Big Business of Hijacking," stating that the looting of trucks had reached a rate of more than $100 million per year. Without indicating that the Briscoe hijacking had occurred 11 years earlier, the article contained the following sentence: "Typical of many beginners, Marvin Briscoe and another man stole a 'valuable-looking' truck in Danville, Ky., and then fought a gun battle with the local police, only to learn that they had hijacked four bowling pin spotters." After publication of the article, Briscoe brought an action for damages against Reader's Digest Association, Inc., for the intentional tort of invasion of the right of privacy. The complaint alleged that as a result of the *Readers' Digest* publication, the plaintiff's 11-year-old daughter, as well as the plaintiff's friends, learned of his criminal record for the first time and thereafter scorned and abandoned him. Did Briscoe's compliant state a cause of action for invasion of the right to privacy? [*Briscoe v. Reader's Digest Association, Inc.*, 4 Cal.2d 529,93 Cal. Rptr.866 (CA 1971)]

4.5 Trespass A.C. Wade operated a liquor store in Cordele, Georgia. Because the store had been burglarized on several occasions and money had been stolen from a cigarette vending machine, Wade booby-trapped the machine with dynamite with the intent to scare away thieves when they tried to steal money from the vending machine. Robert McKinsey, a 16-year-old, was killed when the dynamite attached to the vending machine exploded when McKinsey was burglarizing the liquor store. Mrs. Ella McKinsey, Robert's mother, although admitting her son was committing a crime at the time he was killed, brought action for damages against Wade for the wrongful death of her son. Who wins? [*McKinsey v. Wade*, 220 SE.2d 30 (GA 1975)]

4.6 Negligence In January 1984, George Yanase was a paying guest at the Royal Lodge-Downtown Motel in San Diego, California. Yanase was a member of the Automobile Club of Southern California. The Auto Club publishes a "Tourbook" in which it lists hotels and motels and rates the quality of their services, including the cleanliness of rooms, quality of the restaurant, level of personal service, and the like. Yanase had selected the Royal from the Tourbook. On the night of his stay at the Royal, Yanase was shot in the parking lot adjacent to the motel and died as a result of his injuries. Yanase's widow sued the Auto Club for negligence. Is the Auto Club liable? [*Yanase v. Automobile Club of Southern California*, 212 Cal.App.3d 468, 260 Cal.Rptr. 513 (Cal.App. 1989)]

4.7 Causation In February 1973, W. L. Brown purchased a new large Chevrolet truck from Days Chevrolet. The truck had been manufactured by General Motors Corporation. On March 1, 1973, and employee of Brown's was operating the truck when it ceased to function in rush-hour traffic on Interstate Highway 75 in the Atlanta suburbs. A defect within the alternator caused a complete failure of the truck's electrical system. The defect was caused by General Motors' negligence in manufacturing the truck. When the alternator failed to operate, the truck came to rest in the right-hand lane of two north-bound lanes of freeway traffic. Because of the electrical failure, no blinking lights could be used to warn traffic of the danger. The driver, however, tried to

motion traffic around the truck. Some time later when the freeway traffic had returned to normal, the large Chevrolet truck was still motionless on the freeway. At approximately 6:00 P.M. a panel truck approached the stalled truck in the right-hand lane of traffic at freeway speed. Immediately behind the panel truck, Mr. Davis, driving a Volkswagen fastback, was unable to see the stalled truck. At the last moment the driver of the panel truck saw the stalled truck and swerved into another lane to avoid it. Mr. Davis drove his Volkswagen into the stalled truck at freeway speed, causing his death. Mr. Davis's wife brought a wrongful death action based on negligence against General Motors. Was there causation linking the negligence of the defendant to the fatal accident? [*General Motors Corporation v. Davis*, 233 S.E.2d 835, Ga.App. 1977)]

4.8 Negligence Per Se On March 21, 1980, Julius Ebanks set out from his home in East Elmhurst, Queens, New York, en route to his employment in the downtown district of Manhattan. When Ebanks reached the Bowling Green subway station, he boarded an escalator owned and operated by the New York City Transit Authority. While the escalator was ascending, Ebanks's left foot became caught in a two-inch gap between the escalator step on which he was standing and the side wall of the escalator. Ebanks was unable to free himself. When he reached the top of the escalator he was thrown to the ground, fracturing his hip and suffering other serious injuries. The two-inch gap exceeded the three-eighths-inch standard required by the city's building code. Ebanks sued the Transit Authority to recover damages for his injuries. Who wins? [*Ebanks v. New York City Transit Authority*, 70 N.Y.2d 621, 518 N.Y.S.2d 776 (N.Y.App. 1986)]

4.9 *Res Ipsa Loquitur* Elsie Mack was admitted as a patient to the Lydia E. Hall Hospital for a surgical procedure for the treatment of rectal cancer. Dr. Joseph Jahr was the surgeon in charge of the operation. An anesthesiologist, nurses, and other hospital personnel assisted with the operation. An electrical instrument called an electrocoagulator was used during the surgery to coagulate Mack's blood vessels and stop the bleeding. A component part of the electrocoagulator known as a grounding pad was placed on Mack's left thigh and remained there throughout the surgery. While under anesthesia, Mack sustained third-degree burns on the side of her left thigh during the course of surgery. This was because the pad came in full contact with Mack's skin tissue. When the grounding pad was removed at the conclusion of the operation, a burn more than $\frac{1}{2}$ inch deep and over 2 inches in diameter was discovered where the pad had been. The burn was excised along with the nerves and a $2\frac{3}{4}$-inch scar remains. Mack sued the hospital, Dr. Jahr, and other medical personnel to recover damages caused by their negligence. Does the doctrine of *res ipsa loquitur* apply to this lawsuit? [*Mack v. Lydia E. Hall Hospital*, 503 N.Y.S.2d 131 (N.Y.Sup.Ct. 1986)]

4.10 Liability of Landowners George and Beverly Wagner own a 1.6-acre parcel of land upon which they operate "Bowag Kennels," which caters to training, boarding, and caring for show dogs. The property is entirely surrounded by land owned by Reuben Shiling and W. Dale Hess. In August 1964, Shiling and Hess granted the Wagners an easement right-of-way over their land that connected the kennel to Singer Road, a public road. Singer Road is a rural, unlit two-lane road running through a wooded area. The right-of-way is an unpaved, unlit, narrow road that crosses an uninhabited wooded area leading to the Bowag Kennels. On numerous occasions, unauthorized motorcyclists drove upon the right-of-way. On several occasions, the bikers had loud parties along the right-of-way. In September 1982, the Wagners stretched a large metal chain between two poles at the entrance of the right-of-way. The Wagners testified that they marked the chain with reflectors and signs. Just before midnight on October 2, 1982, William E. Doehring, Jr., and his passenger, Kelvin Henderson, drove their motorcycle off Singer Road and turned onto the right-of-way. The motorcycle they were riding was not equipped with a headlight and the riders were not wearing helmets. Doehring and Henderson had not been granted permission by the Wagners or Shiling or Hess to use the right-of-way. The motorcycle struck the chain, and the riders were thrown off. Doehring died several hours later at a hospital. Doehring's father filed a wrongful death and survival action against the Wagners. Who wins? [*Wagner v. Doehring*, 553 A.2d 684 (Md.App. 1989)]

4.11 Social Host Liability David Andres was a 19-year old student at Northeast Missouri State University. He was a member of Alpha Kappa Lambda Fraternity and lived in the fraternity house. During the evening of December 11, 1979, and the early morning hours of December 12, 1979, the fraternity sponsored a mixer at its house with the Delta Zeta Sorority at which alcoholic beverages were furnished without restriction as to age. Missouri's lawful age for drinking alcoholic beverages was 21. Andres was observed drinking before, during, and following the mixer. During the early morning hours of December 12, he was sitting at the bar in the fraternity house, matching straight shots of whiskey with a fraternity brother. After watching them for some time, another fraternity brother took the bottle from them. Several fraternity brothers helped Andres into the television room, where a pillow and blanket were obtained for him. He was left to "sleep it off" on the television room floor. At about 10:00 A.M. on December 12, when Andres could not be wakened, he was taken to a local hospital but could not be revived. The autopsy showed Andres's blood level measured 0.43 percent, and the cause of death was acute alcohol intoxication with aspiration. Andres's parents brought a wrongful death action against the fraternity. Who wins? [*Andres v. Alpha Kappa Lambda Fraternity*, 730 S.W. 2d 547 (MO 1987)]

4.12 Liability of Common Carrier The Southern California Rapid Transit District (RTD) is a public common carrier that operates public buses throughout the Los Angeles area. Carmen and Carla Lopez were fare-paying passengers on an RTD bus when a group of juveniles began harassing them and other passengers. When the bus driver was notified of this problem, he failed to take any precautionary measures and continued to operate the bus. The juveniles eventually physically assaulted Carmen and Carla, who were injured. The RTD was aware of a history of violent attacks on its bus line. Carmen and Carla sued the RTD to recover damages for their injuries. Who wins? [*Lopez v. Southern California Rapid Transit District*, 40 Cal.3d 780, 221 Cal.Rptr. 840 (CA 1985)]

4.13 Emotional Distress Virginia Rulon-Miller began working for International Business Machines Corporation (IBM) in 1967. Over the course of several years she was promoted to a marketing-representative position, selling typewriters and office equipment in San Francisco's financial district. She became one of the most successful salespersons in the office and received money prizes and awards for her work. She also received the highest merit rating an employee could receive under the IBM rating system. In 1976, Rulon-Miller met Matt Blum, who was an account manager for IBM. They began dating shortly thereafter and became involved in a romantic relationship. This fact was widely known at IBM. In 1977, Blum left IBM to work at QXY, a competitor of IBM. Rulon-Miller and Blum continued their relationship. About one year later, Phillip Callahan, who was Rulon-Miller's immediate manager, called her into his office. He told her that her dating Blum constituted a "conflict of interest," told her to stop dating Blum, and told her he would give her a "couple of days to a week" to think about it. The next day, however, Callahan called Rulon-Miller in again and told her he had "made up her mind for her" and dismissed her. Rulon-Miller suffered severe emotional distress because of this incident. She sued IBM for intentional infliction of emotional distress. Who wins? [*Rulon-Miller v. International Business Machines Corporation*, 162 Cal.App.3d 241, 208 Cal.Rptr. 524 (Cal.App.1985)]

4.14 Emotional Distress On August 10, 1983, Gregory and Demetria James, brother and sister, were riding their bicycles north on 50th Street in Omaha, Nebraska. Spaulding Street intersects 50th Street. A garbage truck owned by Watts Trucking Service, Inc., and driven by its employee, John Milton Lieb, was backing up into the intersection of 50th and Spaulding Streets. The truck backed into the intersection, went through a stop sign, and hit and ran over Demetria, killing her. Gregory helplessly watched the entire accident but was not in danger himself. As a result of watching his sister's peril, Gregory suffered severe emotional distress. Gregory sued Watts and Lieb to recover damages for his emotional distress. Who wins? [*James v. Watts Trucking Service, Inc.*, 375 N.W. 2d 109 (NE 1985)]

4.15 Defense On the night of June 13, 1975, the New York Yankees professional baseball team played the Chicago White Sox at Shea Stadium, New York. Elliot Maddox played center field for the Yankees that night. It had rained the day before, and the previous night's game had been canceled because of bad weather. On the evening of June 13 the playing field was still wet, and Maddox commented on this fact several times to the club's manager but continued to play. In the ninth inning, when Maddox was attempting to field a ball in center field, he slipped on a wet spot, fell, and injured his right knee. Maddox sued the City of New York who owned Shea Stadium, the Metropolitan Baseball Club, Inc., as lessee, the architect, the consulting engineer, and the American League. Maddox alleged that the parties were negligent in causing the field to be wet, and that the injury ended his professional career. Who wins? [*Maddox v. City of New York*, 496 N.Y.S.2d 726 (N.Y.App. 1985)]

4.16 Palming Off Stiffel Company designed a pole lamp (a vertical tube that can stand upright between the floor and ceiling of a room with several lamp fixtures along the outside of it). Pole lamps proved to be a decided commercial success. Soon after Stiffel brought them on the market, Sears, Roebuck, & Company put a substantially identical pole lamp on the market. The Sears retail price was about the same as Stiffel's wholesale price. Sears used its own name on the lamps it sold. Stiffel sued Sears for unfair competition, alleging that Sears had engaged in the tort of palming off. Is Sears liable for palming off? [*Sears, Roebuck & Co. v. Stiffel Co.,* 376 U.S. 225, 84 S.Ct. 1131, 12 L.Ed.2d 87 (1964)]

4.17 Disparagement Robin Williams, a comedian, did a comedy performance at the Great American Music Hall, a San Francisco nightclub. During the performance he told a joke that contained the following words: "Whoa—White Wine. This is a little wine here. If it's not wine it's been through somebody already. Oh—There are White wines, there are Red Wines, but why are there no Black wines like: Rege. It goes with fish, meat, any damn thing it wants to. I like my wine like I like my women, ready to pass out." Audio versions of the performance were distributed by Polygram Records, Inc., and a video version was shown on Home Box Office (HBO). David H. Rege, who sells and distributes assorted varieties of "Rege" brand wines from his San Francisco store, Rege Cellars, sued Williams, Polygram, and HBO for disparagement of his products and business (trade libel). Are the defendants liable for disparagement? [*Polygram Records, Inc. v. Superior Court,* 170 Cal.App.3d 543, 216 Cal.Rptr. 252 (Cal. App. 1985)]

BUSINESS ETHICS CASES

4.18 Business Ethics Radio station KHJ was a successful Los Angeles broadcaster of rock music that commanded a 48 percent market share of the teenage audience in the Los Angeles area. KHJ was owned and operated by RKO General, Inc. In July 1973, KHJ inaugurated a promotion entitled "The Super Summer Spectacular." As part of this promotion, KHJ had a disc jockey known as "The Real Don Steele" ride around the Los Angeles area in a conspicuous red automobile. Periodically KHJ would announce to its radio audience Steele's location. The first listener to thereafter locate Steele and answer a question received a cash prize and participated in a brief interview on the air with Steele. On July 16, 1973, one KHJ broadcast identified Steele's next destination as Canoga Park. Robert Sentner, 17 years old, heard the broadcast and immediately drove to Canoga Park. Marsha Baime, 19 years old, also heard the broadcast and drove to Canoga Park. By the time Sentner and Baime located Steele, someone else had already claimed the prize. Without the knowledge of the other, Sentner and Baime each decided to follow Steele to the next destination and be first to "find" him.

Steele proceeded onto the freeway. For the next few miles Sentner and Baime tried to jockey for position closest to the Steele vehicle, reaching speeds of up to 80 miles per hour. There is no evidence that the Steele vehicle exceeded the speed limit. When Steele left the freeway at the Westlake off ramp, Sentner and Baime tried to follow. In their attempts to do so, they knocked another vehicle driven by Mr. Weirum into the center divider of the freeway, where it overturned. Mr. Weirum died in the accident. Baime stopped to report the accident, Sentner, after pausing momentarily to relate the tragedy to a passing police officer, got back into his car, pursued and successfully located Steele, and collected the cash prize. The wife and children of Mr. Weirum brought a wrongful death negligence action against Sentner, Baime, and RKO General. Who wins? Did RKO General, Inc. act responsibly in this case? [*Weirum v. RKO General, Inc.,* 15 Cal.3d 40, 123 Cal.Rptr. 468 (CA 1975)]

4.19 Business Ethics Guy Portee, a seven-year-old, resided with his mother in an apartment building in Newark, New Jersey. Edith and Nathan Jaffee owned and operated the building. On the afternoon of May 22, 1976, Guy became trapped in the building's elevator between its outer door and the wall of the elevator shaft. When someone activated the elevator, the boy was dragged up to the third floor. Another child who saw the accident ran to seek help. Soon afterward, Renee Portee, the boy's mother, and officers of the Newark Police Department arrived. The officers worked for four and one-half hours trying to release the boy, during which time the mother watched as her son moaned, cried out, and flailed his arms. The police contacted the Atlantic Elevator Company, which was responsible for the installation and maintenance of the elevator, and requested the company to send a mechanic to assist in the effort to free the boy. Apparently no one came. The boy suffered multiple bone fractures and massive internal hemorrhaging. He died while still trapped, his mother a helpless observer.

After her son's death, Renee became severely distressed and seriously self-destructive. On March 24, 1979, she attempted to take her own life. She survived and the wound was repaired by surgery, but she has since required considerable physical therapy. She has received extensive counseling and psychotherapy to help overcome the mental and emotional problems associated with her son's death. Renee sued the Jaffees and Atlantic to recover damages for her emotional distress. Who wins? Did either of the defendants act unethically in this case? [*Portee v. Jaffee,* 417 A.2d 521 (NJ 1980)]

4.20 Business Ethics Rosina Crisci owned an apartment building in which Mrs. DiMare was a tenant. One day while Mrs. DiMare was descending a wooden staircase on the outside of the apartment building, she fell through the staircase and was left hanging 15 feet above the ground until she was saved. Crisci had a $10,000 liability insurance policy on the building from the Security Insurance Company of New Haven, Connecticut. Mrs. DiMare sued Crisci and Security for

$400,000 for physical injuries and psychosis suffered from the fall. Prior to trial, Mrs. DiMare agreed to take $10,000 in settlement of the case. Security refused this settlement offer. Mrs. DiMare reduced her settlement offer to $9,000, of which Crisci offered to pay $2,500. Security again refused to settle the case. The case proceeded to trial and the jury awarded Mrs. DiMare and her husband $110,000. Security paid $10,000 pursuant to the insurance contract, and Crisci had to pay the difference.

Crisci, a widow of 70 years of age, had to sell her assets, became dependent on her relatives, declined in physical health, and suffered from hysteria and suicide attempts. Crisci sued Security for tort damages for breach of the implied covenant of good faith and fair dealing. Who wins? Did Security Insurance Company act ethically in this case? [*Crisci v. Security Insurance Company of New Haven, Connecticut,* 426 P.2d 173, 66 Cal.App.2d 425, 58 Cal.Rptr. 13 (Cal. App. 1967)]

BRIEFING THE CASE WRITING ASSIGNMENT

Read the following case, which has been excerpted from the court's opinion. Review and brief the case.

Braun v. Soldier of Fortune Magazine, Inc.
968 F.2d 1110 (1992)
U.S. Court of Appeals for the Eleventh Circuit

Anderson, Circuit Judge

In January 1985, Michael Savage submitted a personal service advertisement to Soldier of Fortune (SOF). After several conversations between Savage and SOF's advertising manager, Joan Steel, the following advertisement ran in the June 1985 through March 1986 issues of SOF:

GUN FOR HIRE: 37-year-old professional mercenary desires jobs. Vietnam Veteran. Discrete [sic] and very private. Bodyguard, courier, and other special skills. All jobs considered. Phone (615) 436-9785 (days) or (615) 436-4335 (nights), or write: Rt. 2, Box 682 Village Loop Road, Gatlinburg, TN 37738.

Savage testified that, when he placed the ad, he had no intention of obtaining anything but legitimate jobs. Nonetheless, Savage stated that the overwhelming majority of the 30 to 40 phone calls a week he received in response to his ad sought his participation in criminal activity such as murder, assault, and kidnapping. The ad also generated at least one legitimate job as a bodyguard, which Savage accepted.

In late 1984 or early 1985, Bruce Gastwirth began seeking to murder his business partner, Richard Braun. Gastwirth enlisted the aid of another business associate, John Horton Moore, and together they arranged for at least three attempts on Braun's life, all of which were unsuccessful. Responding to Savage's SOF ad, Gastwirth and Moore contacted him in August 1985 to discuss plans to murder Braun. On August 26, 1985, Savage, Moore, and another individual, Sean Trevor Doutre, went to Braun's suburban Atlanta home. As Braun and his sixteen-year-old son Michael were driving down the driveway, Doutre stepped in front of Braun's car and fired several shots into the car with a MAC 11 automatic pistol. The shots hit Michael in the thigh and wounded Braun as well. Braun managed to roll out of the car, but Doutre walked over to Braun and killed him by firing two more shots into the back of his head as Braun lay on the ground.

On March 31, 1988, appellees Michael and Ian Braun filed this diversity action against appellants in the United States District Court for the Middle District of Alabama, seeking damages for the wrongful death of their father. Michael Braun also filed a separate action seeking recovery for the personal injuries he received at the time of his father's death. The district court consolidated these related matters.

Trial began on December 3, 1990. Appellees contended that, under Georgia law, SOF was liable for their injuries because SOF negligently published a personal service advertisement that created an unreasonable risk of the solicitation and commission of violent criminal activity, including murder. To show that SOF knew of the likelihood that criminal activity would result from placing an ad like Savage's, appellees introduced evidence of newspaper and magazine articles published prior to Braun's murder which described links between SOF and personal service ads and a number of criminal convictions including murder, kidnapping, assault, extortion, and attempts thereof. Appellees also presented evidence that, prior to SOF's acceptance of Savage's ad, law enforcement officials had contacted SOF staffers on two separate occasions in connection with investigations of crimes.

In his trial testimony, SOF president Robert K. Brown denied having any knowledge of criminal activity associated with SOF's personal service ads at any time prior to Braun's murder in August 1985. Both Jim Graves, a former managing editor of SOF, and Joan Steel, the advertising manager who accepted Savage's advertisement, similarly testified that they were not aware of other crimes connected with SOF ads prior to running Savage's ad. Steel further testified that she had understood the term "Gun for Hire" in Savage's ad to refer to a "bodyguard or protection service-type thing," rather than to any illegal activity.

The jury returned a verdict in favor of appellee and awarded compensatory damages on the wrongful death claim in the amount of $2,000,000. The jury also awarded appellee Michael Braun $375,000 in compensatory damages and $10,000,000 in punitive damages for his personal injury claim.

To prevail in an action for negligence in Georgia, a party must establish the following elements:

(1) A legal duty to conform to a standard of conduct raised by the law for the protection of others against unreasonable risks of harm, (2) a breach of this standard, (3) a legally attributable causal connection between the conduct and the resulting injury, and (4) some loss or damage flowing to the plaintiff's legally protected interest as a result of the alleged breach of the legal duty. To the extent that SOF denies that a publisher owes any duty to the public when it publishes personal service ads, its position is clearly inconsistent with Georgia law. We believe, however, that the crux of SOF's argument is not that it had no duty to the public, but that as a matter of law, there is a risk to the public when a publisher prints an "unreasonable" advertisement only if the ad openly solicits criminal activity.

SOF further argues that imposing liability on publishers for the advertisements they print indirectly threatens core, non-commercial speech to which the Constitution accords its full protection. Supreme Court cases discussing the limitations the First Amendment places on state defamation law indicate that there is no constitutional infirmity in Georgia law holding publishers liable under a negligence standard with respect to the commercial advertisements they print. Past Supreme Court decisions indicate, however, that the negligence standard that the First Amendment permits is a "modified" negligence standard. The Court's decisions suggest that Georgia law may impose tort liability on publishers for injury caused by the advertisements they print only if the ad on its face, without the need to investigate, makes it apparent that there is a substantial danger of harm to the public.

We conclude that the First Amendment permits a state to impose upon a publisher liability for compensatory damages for negligently publishing a commercial advertisement where the ad on its face, and without the need for investigation, makes it apparent that there is a substantial danger of harm to the public. The absence of a duty requiring publishers to investigate the advertisements they print and the requirement that the substance of the ad itself must warn the publisher of a substantial danger of harm to the public guarantee that the burden placed on publishers will not impermissibly chill protected commercial speech.

Our review of the language of Savage's ad persuades us that SOF had a legal duty to refrain from publishing it. Savage's advertisement (1) emphasized the term "Gun for Hire," (2) described Savage as a "professional mercenary," (3) stressed Savage's willingness to keep his assignments confidential and "very private," (4) listed legitimate jobs involving the use of a gun—bodyguard and courier—followed by a reference to Savage's "other special skills," and (5) concluded by stating that Savage would consider "all jobs." The ad's combination of sinister terms makes it apparent that there was a substantial danger of harm to the public. The ad expressly solicits all jobs requiring the use of a gun. When the list of legitimate jobs—i.e., bodyguards and courier—is followed by "other special skills" and "all jobs considered," the implication is clear that the advertiser would consider illegal jobs. We agree with the district court that "the language of this advertisement is such that, even though couched in terms not explicitly offering criminal services, the publisher could recognize the offer of criminal activity as readily as its readers obviously did." We find that the jury had ample grounds for finding that SOF's publication of Savage's ad was the proximate cause of Braun's injuries.

For the foregoing reasons, we AFFIRM the district court's judgment.

ENDNOTES

1. 376 U.S. 254, 84 S.Ct. 710 (1964).
2. *Restatement (Second) of Torts*, Section 46.
3. *Restatement (Second) of Torts*, Section 46, comment d.
4. Justice B. Anderson, *Blyth v. Birmingham Waterworks Co.*, 11 Exch. 781, 784 (1856).
5. 248 N.Y. 339, 162 N.E. 99 (1928).
6. For example, see Cal. Civil Code, Section 1714(c).
7. 15 U.S.C.§ 1125(a).
8. 18 U.S.C.§§1961–1968.
9. 18 U.S.C. § 1964(c).
10. *Sedima, S.P.R.L. v. Imrex Co., Inc.*, 473 U.S. 479, 105 S.Ct. 3275, 87 L.Ed.2d 346 (1985).

CHAPTER

5

Business and Online Crimes

It is better that ten guilty persons escape, than that one innocent suffer.

—Sir William Blackstone
Commentaries on the Laws of England (1809)

Chapter Objectives

After studying this chapter, you should be able to:

1. Distinguish between felonies and misdemeanors.

2. Define and list the essential elements of a crime.

3. Describe criminal procedure, including arrest, indictment, arraignment, and the criminal trial.

4. List and describe crimes against persons and property.

5. Define major white-collar crimes, such as embezzlement and bribery.

6. Explain the elements necessary to find criminal fraud.

7. Describe the scope of the Racketeer Influenced and Corrupt Organizations Act (RICO).

8. Explain the constitutional safeguards provided by the Fourth, Fifth, Sixth, and Eighth Amendments to the U.S. Constitution.

9. Explain the scope of the Foreign Corrupt Practices Act.

10. List and describe laws involving computer and Internet crimes.

Chapter Contents

Business Brief

In the United States, a person accused of a crime is *presumed innocent until proven guilty.* The government has the burden of proving that the accused is guilty of the crime charged.

For members of society to peacefully coexist and commerce to flourish, people and their property must be protected from injury by other members of society. Federal, state, and local governments' **criminal laws** are intended to accomplish this by providing an incentive for persons to act reasonably in society and imposing penalties on persons who violate them.

The United States has one of the most advanced and humane criminal law systems in the world. It differs from any other criminal law systems in several respects. A person charged with a crime in the United States is *presumed innocent until proven guilty.* The *burden of proof* is on the government to prove that the accused is guilty of the crime charged. Further, the accused must be found guilty "beyond a reasonable doubt." Conviction requires unanimous jury vote. Under many other legal systems, a person accused of a crime is presumed guilty unless the person can prove he or she is not. A person charged with a crime in the United States is also provided with substantial constitutional safeguards during the criminal justice process.

This chapter discusses the definition of a crime, criminal procedure, crimes affecting business, white-collar crime, computer crime, inchoate crime, criminal penalties, and constitutional safeguards afforded criminal defendants.

DEFINITION OF A CRIME

A **crime** is defined as any act done by an individual in violation of those duties that he or she owes to society and for the breach of which the law provides that the wrongdoer shall make amends to the public. Many activities have been considered crimes through the ages, whereas other crimes are of recent origin.

crime

A crime is a violation of a statute for which the government imposes a punishment.

Penal Codes and Regulatory Statutes

Statutes are the primary source of criminal law. Most states have adopted comprehensive **penal codes** that define in detail the activities considered to be crimes within their jurisdiction and the penalties that will be imposed for their commission. A comprehensive federal criminal code defines federal crimes.[1] In addition, state and federal regulatory statutes often provide for criminal violations and penalties. The state and federal legislatures are continually adding to the list of crimes.

penal codes

A collection of criminal statutes.

The penalty for committing a crime may consist of the imposition of a fine, imprisonment, both, or some other form of punishment (e.g., probation). Generally, imprisonment is imposed to (1) incapacitate the criminal so he or she will not harm others in society, (2) provide a means to rehabilitate the criminal, (3) deter others from similar conduct, and (4) inhibit personal retribution by the victim.

Parties to a Criminal Action

In a criminal lawsuit, the government (not a private party) is the **plaintiff**. The government is represented by a lawyer called the *prosecutor*. The accused is the **defendant**. The accused is represented by a *defense attorney*. If the accused cannot afford a defense lawyer, the government will provide one free of charge.

Business Brief

The plaintiff in a criminal trial is the government.

Classification of Crimes

All crimes can be classified in one of the following categories.

felony

The most serious type of crime; inherently evil crime. Most crimes against the person and some business-related crimes are felonies.

Felonies   **Felonies** are the most serious kinds of crimes. Felonies include crime that are *mala in se*, that is, inherently evil. Most crimes against the person (e.g., murder, rape, and the like) and certain business-related crimes (e.g., embezzlement and bribery) are felonies in most jurisdictions. Felonies are usually punishable by imprisonment. In some jurisdictions, certain felonies (e.g., first-degree murder) are punishable by death. Federal law[2] and some state laws require mandatory sentencing for specified crimes. Many statutes define different degrees of crimes (e.g., first-, second-, and third-degree murder). Each degree earns different penalties.

The White House, Washington, DC *The White House, located in Washington, DC, is the home of the president of the United States. The U.S. Department of Justice which is part of the executive branch of the federal government, prosecutes federal crimes.*

Misdemeanors **Misdemeanors** are less serious than felonies. They are crimes *mala prohibita*; that is, they are not inherently evil but are prohibited by society. Many crimes against property, such as robbery, burglary, and violations of regulatory statutes, are included in this category. Misdemeanors carry lesser penalties than felonies. They are usually punishable by fine and/or imprisonment for one year or less.

> **misdemeanor**
>
> A less serious crime; not inherently evil but prohibited by society. Many crimes against property are misdemeanors.

Violations Crimes such as traffic violations, jaywalking, and such are neither felonies nor misdemeanors. These crimes, which are called **violations**, are generally punishable by a fine. Occasionally, a few days of imprisonment are imposed.

> **violation**
>
> A crime that is neither a felony nor a misdemeanor that is usually punishable by a fine.

Essential Elements of a Crime

The following two elements must be proven for a person to be found guilty of most crimes:

1. **Criminal Act** The defendant must have actually performed the prohibited act. The actual performance of the criminal act is called the ***actus reus*** (guilty act). Killing someone without legal jurisdiction is an example of *actus reus*. Sometimes, the omission of an act constitutes the requisite *actus reus*. For example, a crime has been committed if a taxpayer who is under a legal duty to file a tax return fails to do so. However, merely thinking about committing a crime is not a crime because no action has been taken.

> ***actus reus***
>
> "Guilty act"—the actual performance of the criminal act.

2. **Criminal Intent** To be found guilty of a crime, the accused must be found to have possessed the requisite state of mind (i.e., specific or general intent) when the act was performed. This is called the ***mens rea*** (evil intent). *Specific intent* is found where the accused purposefully, intentionally, or with knowledge commits a prohibited act. *General intent* is found where there is a showing of recklessness or a lesser degree of mental culpability. The individual criminal statutes state whether the crime requires a showing of specific or general intent. Juries may infer an accused's intent from the facts and circumstances of the case. There is no crime if the requisite *mens rea* cannot be proven. Thus, no crime is committed if one person accidentally injures another person.

> ***mens rea***
>
> "Evil intent"—the possession of the requiste state of mind to commit a prohibited act.

Some statutes impose criminal liability based on **strict** or **absolute liability**. That is, a finding of *mens rea* is not required. Criminal liability is imposed if the prohibited act is committed. Absolute liability is often imposed by regulatory statutes, such as environmental laws.

> **strict or absolute liability**
>
> Standard for imposing criminal liability without a finding of *mens rea* (intent).

Criminal Acts as the Basis for Tort Actions

An injured party may bring a *civil tort action* against a wrongdoer who has caused the party injury during the commission of a criminal act. Civil lawsuits are separate from the government's criminal action against the wrongdoer. In many cases, a person injured by a criminal act will not sue the criminal to recover civil damages. This is because the criminal is often *judgment proof*—that is, the criminal does not have the money to pay a civil judgment.

> **Business Brief**
>
> The same act may be the basis for both a criminal lawsuit and a civil lawsuit.

CONCEPT SUMMARY   CIVIL AND CRIMINAL LAW COMPARED

Issue	Civil Law	Criminal Law
Party who brings the action	The plaintiff	The government
Trial by jury	Yes, except actions for equity	Yes
Burden of proof	Preponderance of the evidence	Beyond a reasonable doubt
Jury vote	Judgment for plaintiff requires specific jury vote (e.g., 9 of 12 jurors)	Conviction requires unanimous jury vote
Sanctions and penalties	Monetary damages and equitable remedies (e.g., injunction, specific performance)	Imprisonment, capital punishment, fine, probation

Business Ethics

SHOULD CRIME PAY?

To satisfy the public's seemingly endless thirst for tales of crime, publishers have eagerly paid large sums of money to acquire criminal defendants' rights to tell their sensational stories. Convicted murderers Caryl Chessman, Juan Corona, James Earl Ray, Sirhan Sirhan, and other convicted felons, such as the Watergate burglars, have all reaped substantial profits from selling the publication rights to their stories.

Beginning in the late 1970s, however, the public's distaste at rewarding crime fueled the passage by state legislatures of laws that prevented enterprising criminals from pocketing megabucks from selling their stories. Many of these so-called Son of Sam laws, which were passed by 40 states, were patterned on New York's statute. New York's law was enacted in 1977 while New York City's "Son of Sam" killer held the population hostage by continuing a highly publicized killing spree despite one of the most intense manhunts in the city's history.

To preclude the Son of Sam and other criminals from cashing in on crime, the New York law required publishers and movie companies to deposit any profits earned by criminals with the state's victim's compensation agency. If there was a conviction, the money went to the victim or the victim's heir. If the accused was acquitted, the money was used to pay the defense attorney's bill and any remainder was paid to the defendant.

The enactment of Son of Sam statutes quieted the public's outcry. However, the statutes were challenged by criminals and publishers as an unconstitutional abridgment of free-speech rights. In 1991, the U.S. Supreme Court agreed that the Son of Sam laws were unconstitutional. In a case brought by publisher Simon & Schuster, which had published a book by a convicted criminal, the Supreme Court held that the Son of Sam law violated the Freedom of Speech Clause of the U.S. Constitution.

Opponents of this decision argue that the potential of lucrative book and movie contracts will provide an incentive for people to commit heinous crimes. They also continue to argue that "crime should not pay." Proponents of the U.S. Supreme Court's decision assert that even criminals should be accorded full free-speech rights guaranteed by the Constitution. [*Simon & Schuster, Inc. v. Members of the New York State Crime Victim's Board*, 112 S.Ct. 501 (1991)]

1. Should a person who commits a crime be permitted to profit from that crime?
2. Will the U.S. Supreme Court's decision lead to more or fewer crimes? Explain.
3. Is it ethical for publishers, movie companies, and other entertainment firms to pay criminals for their stories?

CRIMINAL PROCEDURE

The magnitude of a crime is proportionate to the magnitude of the injustice which prompts it. Hence, the smallest crimes may be actually the greatest.

Aristotle
The Rhetoric, Bk. 1, Ch. XIV

The court procedure for initiating and maintaining a criminal action is quite detailed. It includes both pretrial procedures and the actual trial.

Pretrial Criminal Procedure

Pretrial criminal procedure consists of several distinct stages, including *arrest*, *indictment* or *information*, *arraignment*, and *plea bargaining*.

Arrest   Before the police can arrest a person for the commission of a crime, they usually must obtain an **arrest warrant** based upon a showing of "probable cause." *Probable cause* is defined as the substantial likelihood that the person either committed or is about to commit a crime. If there is no time for the police to obtain a warrant (e.g., if the police arrive during the commission of a crime, when a person is fleeing from the scene of the crime, or when it is likely that evidence will be destroyed), the police may still arrest the suspect. *Warrantless arrests* are also judged by the probable cause standard.

After a person is arrested, he or she is taken to the police station to be "booked." Booking is the administrative proceeding for recording the arrest, fingerprinting, and so on.

Indictment or Information   Accused persons must be formally charged with a crime before they can be brought to trial. This is usually done by the issuance of a *grand jury indictment* or a *magistrate's information statement.*

Evidence of serious crimes, such as murder, is usually presented to a *grand jury*. Most grand juries comprise between 6 and 24 citizens who are charged with evaluating the evidence presented by the government. Grand jurors sit for a fixed period of time, such as one year. If the grand jury determines that there is sufficient evidence to hold the accused for trial, it issues an **indictment**. Note that the grand jury does not determine guilt. If an indictment is issued, the accused will be held for later trial.

For lesser crimes (e.g., burglary, shoplifting, and such), the accused will be brought before a *magistrate* (judge). A magistrate who finds that there is enough evidence to hold the accused for trial will issue an **information**.

The case against the accused is dismissed if neither an indictment nor an information is issued.

Arraignment   If an indictment or information is issued, the accused is brought before a court for an **arraignment** proceeding during which the accused is (1) informed of the charges against him or her and (2) asked to enter a **plea**. The accused may plead *guilty, not guilty,* or *nolo contendere*. A plea of *nolo contendere* means that the accused agrees to the imposition of a penalty but does not admit guilt. A *nolo contendere* plea cannot be used as evidence of liability against the accused at a subsequent civil trial. Corporate defendants often enter this plea. The government has the option of accepting a *nolo contendere* plea or requiring the defendant to plead guilty or not guilty.

arrest warrant
A document for a person's detainment based upon a showing of probable cause that the person committed the crime.

indictment
The charge of having committed a crime (usually a felony), based on the judgment of a grand jury.

information
The charge of having committed a crime (usually a misdemeanor), based on the judgment of a judge (magistrate).

arraignment
A hearing during which the accused is brought before a court and is (1) informed of the charges against him or her and (2) asked to enter a plea.

The Supreme Court Speaks

Warrantless Arrest Pursuant to a Minor Criminal Offense Is Permitted

Atwater v. Lago Vista, Texas
121 S.Ct. 1536 (2001)
Supreme Court of the United States

BACKGROUND AND FACTS
Texas law requires that front-seat drivers and passengers must wear seat belts, and that a driver must secure any small child riding in front. In March 1997, Gail Atwater was driving her pickup truck in Lago Vista, Texas, with her three-year-old son and five-year-old daughter in the front seat. None of them was wearing a seat belt. Bart Turek, a Lago Vista police officer, observed the seat-belt violation and pulled Atwater over. A friend of Atwater's arrived at the scene and took charge of the children. Turek handcuffed Atwater, placed her in his squad car, and drove her to the police station. Atwater was booked, her "mug shot" was taken, and she was placed in a jail cell for about one hour until she was released on a $310 bond. Atwater ultimately pleaded no contest to the misdemeanor seat-belt offenses and paid a $50 fine. Atwater sued the City of Lago Vista and the police officer for compensatory and punitive damages for allegedly violating her Fourth Amendment right to be free from unreasonable seizure. The district court ruled against Atwater and the court of appeals affirmed. The U.S. Supreme Court granted certiorari to hear the appeal.

SUPREME COURT ISSUE

Does the Fourth Amendment permit police to make a warrantless arrest pursuant to a minor criminal offense?

IN THE LANGUAGE OF THE U.S. SUPREME COURT

Souter, Justice *There is no support for Atwater's position in this Court's cases. Both the legislative tradition of granting warrantless misdemeanor arrest authority and the judicial tradition of sustaining such statutes against constitutional attack are buttressed by legal commentary that, for more than a century now, has almost uniformly recognized the constitutionality of extending warrantless arrest power to misdemeanors without limitation to breaches of the peace. If an officer has probable cause to believe that an individual has committed even a very minor criminal offense in his presence, he may, without violating the Fourth Amendment, arrest the offender.*

DECISION AND REMEDY

The U.S. Supreme Court held that the Fourth Amendment permits police officers to make a warrantless arrest pursuant to a minor criminal offense. The judgment of the court of appeals is affirmed.

CASE QUESTIONS

Critical Legal Thinking Do you agree with the U.S. Supreme Court's decision in this case? Why or why not?

Business Ethics Did the police officer act ethically in this case? Should he have used more discretion?

Contemporary Business What would be the consequences if the Supreme Court had held in favor of Atwater?

---

plea bargain

When the accused admits to a lesser crime than charged. In return, the government agrees to impose a lesser sentence than might have been obtained had the case gone to trial.

Plea Bargaining Sometimes the accused and the government enter into a **plea bargaining agreement**. The government engages in plea bargaining to save costs, avoid the risks of a trial, and prevent further overcrowding of the prisons. This type of arrangement allows the accused to admit to a lesser crime than charged. In return, the government agrees to impose a lesser penalty or sentence than might have been obtained had the case gone to trial.

The Criminal Trial

At a criminal trial, all jurors must *unanimously* agree before the accused is found *guilty* of the crime charged. If even one juror disagrees (i.e., has reasonable doubt) about the guilt of the accused, the accused is *not guilty* of the crime charged. If all of the jurors agree that the accused did not commit the crime, the accused is *innocent* of the crime charged. After trial, the following rules apply:

hung jury

A jury that cannot come to a unanimous decision about the defendant's guilt. The government may choose to retry the case.

- If the defendant is found guilty, he or she may appeal.
- If the defendant is found innocent, the government cannot appeal.
- If the jury cannot come to a unanimous decision about the defendant's guilt, the jury is considered a **hung jury**. The government may choose to retry the case before a new judge and jury.

Contemporary Business Environment

MONEY LAUNDERING

The term *money laundering* is used to refer to the process by which criminals convert tainted proceeds into apparently legitimate funds or property. It applies equally to an international wire transfer of hundreds of millions of dollars in drug proceeds and the purchase of an automobile with funds robbed from a bank.

Money laundering is a federal crime. The following activities are among those that were criminalized by the Money Laundering Control Act:

- Knowingly engaging in a *financial transaction* involving the proceeds of some form of specified unlawful activity. Transactions covered include the sale of real property, personal property, intangible assets, and anything of value [18 U.S.C. § 1956].

- Knowingly engaging in a *monetary transaction* by, through, or to a financial institution involving property of a value greater than $10,000, which is derived from specified unlawful activity. Money transaction is defined as a deposit, withdrawal, transfer between accounts, and use of a monetary instrument [18 U.S.C. § 1957].

"Specified unlawful activity" includes narcotics activities and virtually any white-collar crime.

Money laundering statutes have been used to go after entities and persons involved in illegal check-cashing schemes, bribery, insurance fraud, Medicaid fraud, bankruptcy fraud, bank fraud, fraudulent transfer of property, criminal conspiracy, environmental crime, and other types of illegal activities.

Conviction for money laundering carries stiff penalties. Persons can be fined up to $500,000 or twice the value of the property involved, whichever is greater, and sentenced to up to 20 years in federal prison. In addition, violation subjects the defendant to provisions that mandate forfeiture to the government of any property involved in or traceable to the offense [18 U.S.C. §§ 981–982]. Any financial institution convicted of money laundering can have its charter revoked or its insurance of deposit accounts terminated.

To avoid running afoul of these increasingly complex statutes, banks and businesses must develop and implement policies and procedures to detect criminal activity and report money laundering by customers to the federal government.

CRIMES AFFECTING BUSINESS

Many crimes are committed against business property. These crimes often involve the theft, misappropriation, or fraudulent taking of property. Many of the most important crimes against business property are discussed in the following paragraphs.

Robbery

At common law, **robbery** is defined as the taking of personal property from another person by the use of fear or force. For example, if a robber threatens to physically harm a storekeeper unless the victim surrenders the contents of the cash register, it is robbery. If a criminal pickpockets somebody's wallet, it is not robbery because there has been no use of force or fear. Robbery with a deadly weapon is generally considered aggravated robbery (or armed robbery) and carries a harsher penalty.

robbery
Taking personal property from another person by use of fear or force.

Burglary

At common law, **burglary** was defined as "breaking and entering a dwelling at night" with the intent to commit a felony. Modern penal codes have broadened this definition to include daytime thefts and thefts from offices and commercial and other buildings. In addition, the "breaking-in" element has been abandoned by most modern definitions of burglary. Thus, unauthorized entering of a building through an unlocked door is sufficient. Aggravated burglary (or armed burglary) carries stiffer penalties.

burglary
Taking personal property from another's home, office, commercial, or other type of building.

Larceny

At common law, **larceny** is defined as the wrongful and fraudulent taking of another person's personal property. Most personal property—including tangible property, trade secrets, computer programs, and other business property—is subject to larceny. The stealing of automobiles and car stereos, pickpocketing, and such are larceny. Neither the use of force nor the entry of a building is required. Some states distinguish between grand larceny and petit larceny. This distinction depends on the value of the property taken.

larceny
Taking another's personal property other than from his or her person or building.

Theft

Some states have dropped the distinction among the crimes of robbery, burglary, and larceny. Instead, these states group these crimes under the general crime of **theft**. Most of these states distinguish between grand theft and petit theft. The distinction depends upon the value of the property taken.

Law cannot persuade, where it cannot punish.

Thomas Fuller
Gnomologia (1732)

Receiving Stolen Property

It is a crime for a person to (1) knowingly receive stolen property and (2) intend to deprive the rightful owner of that property. Knowledge and intent can be inferred from the circumstances. The stolen property can be any tangible property (e.g., personal property, money, negotiable instruments, stock certificates, and such).

receiving stolen property
A person (1) knowingly receives stolen property and (2) intends to deprive the rightful owner of that property.

Arson

At common law, **arson** was defined as the malicious or willful burning of the dwelling of another person. Modern penal codes expanded this definition to include the burning of all types of private, commercial, and public buildings. Thus, in most states, an owner who

arson
Willfully or maliciously burning another's building.

burns his or her own building to collect insurance proceeds can be found liable for arson. If arson is found, the insurance company does not have to pay proceeds of any insurance policy on the burned property.

Forgery

forgery
Fraudulently making or altering a written document that affects the legal liability of another person.

The crime of **forgery** occurs if a written document is fraudulently made or altered and that change affects the legal liability of another person. Counterfeiting, falsifying public records, and the material altering of legal documents are examples of forgery. One of the most common forms of forgery is the signing of another persons signature to a check or changing the amount of a check. Note that signing another person's signature without intent to defraud is not forgery. For example, forgery has not been committed if one spouse signs the other spouse's payroll check for deposit in a joint checking or savings account at the bank.

Extortion

extortion
Threat to expose something about another person unless that other person gives money or property. Often referred to as "blackmail."

The crime of **extortion** means the obtaining of property from another, with his or her consent, induced by wrongful use of actual or threatened force, violence, or fear. For example, extortion occurs when a person threatens to expose something about another person unless that other person gives money or property. The truth or falsity of the information is immaterial. Extortion of private persons is commonly referred to as **blackmail**. Extortion of public officials is called **extortion "under color of official right."**

Credit-Card Crimes

At the present time in this country there is more danger that criminals will escape justice than that they will be subjected to tyranny.

J. Homes
Dissenting
Kepner v. United States (1904)

A substantial number of purchases in this country are made with credit cards. This poses a problem if someone steals and uses another person's credit cards. Many states have enacted statutes that make the misappropriation and use of credit cards a separate crime. In other states, credit-card crimes are prosecuted under the forgery statute.

Bad Check Legislation

Many states have enacted *bad check legislation* that makes it a crime for a person to make, draw, or deliver a check at a time when that person knows that there are insufficient funds in the account to cover the amount of the check. Some states require proof that the accused intended to defraud the payee of the check.

Business Ethics

WHISTLE-BLOWERS SING FOR MILLIONS

The federal government is the largest purchaser of goods and services in the country. As such, it is also the target of substantial fraud by the firms it deals with. If caught, a government contractor who defrauds the government is subject to criminal prosecution. But in addition, the federal government relies on a revamped law that elicits employees of government contractors and others to become modern-day bounty hunters and report anyone who defrauds the government. The law is the **Civil False Claims Act**, commonly known as the **Whistle-blower Statute**. This act was originally enacted in 1863 to protect the federal government from corrupt government contractors after the Civil War. It was strengthened in 1986 to provide a penalty of *treble damages* plus up to $10,000 per false claim against the defendant and allows the court to award between 15 and 30 percent of the

recovery to the whistle-blower, who is now politely called a "relator." These lawsuits are called *qui tam* cases (from the Latin phrase "he who sues as much for the king as for himself").

The procedure for bringing a *qui tam* lawsuit is simple: The relator files the lawsuit, notifies the federal government, and then waits to see if the federal government chooses to intervene in the lawsuit. If the federal government intervenes, it pursues the lawsuit; if not, the relator must pursue the lawsuit alone, which is very costly. The federal government intervenes in only 20 percent of the *qui tam* cases filed, and 95 percent of the recoveries are from these cases. Many cases in which the federal government does not intervene are dropped. There is a strong incentive for a defendant to settle *qui tam* cases that are pursued by the federal government, however. If the defendant loses, it faces the possibility of treble damages, plus a penalty of up to $10,000 per false claim, and a ban on ever doing business with the federal government again.

The greater number of whistle-blower cases have involved hospitals and other medical facilities that have been caught overbilling the federal government under Medicare and other government aid programs. The second greatest number of cases have involved oil and gas companies that have cheated the federal government out of royalty and lease payments due on contracts for drilling on federal land. Other cases have been brought against government contractors who overbill the federal government for other products and services, file false claims to receive government subsidies, and overcharge the government for building and construction contracts. Sometimes a potential relator does not even now he or she has a whistle-blower claim. For example, Evelyn Knoob walked into a lawyer's office to file a worker's compensation claim worth $400 per week when she was placed on leave by her employer, Illinois Blue Cross/Blue Shield. After talking

to her attorney, she filed a *qui tam* case against the Illinois Blues, alleging overbilling of the federal government. Several years later the defendants settled with the federal government for $150 million. Ms. Knoob's share was $29 million.

Proponents of the modern Civil False Claim Act cite that the federal government has recovered over $3 billion from fraudulent government contractors. They also allege that the act deters fraud and saves the federal government over $10 billion per year by making government contractors more honest. Detractors argue that the whistle-blower statute generates frivolous lawsuits by disgruntled employees who are taking a shot at the lottery. Currently, over 600 new *qui tam* cases are filed each year.

1. Do you think there is much fraud in government contracting? Does the Civil False Claims Act make government contractors more honest?
2. Do employees face an ethical dilemma when filing a *qui tam* action against their employer? If so, how do you think most employees solve this dilemma?

White-Collar Crimes

Certain types of crime are prone to be committed by businesspersons. These crimes are often referred to as **white-collar crimes**. These crimes usually involve cunning and deceit rather than physical force. Many of the most important white-collar crimes are discussed in the paragraphs that follow.

white-collar crimes
Crimes usually involving cunning and deceit rather than physical force.

Embezzlement

Unknown at common law, the crime of **embezzlement** is now a statutory crime. Embezzlement is the fraudulent conversion of property by a person to whom that property was entrusted. Typically, embezzlement is committed by an employer's employees, agents, or representatives (e.g., accountants, lawyers, trust officers, and treasurers). Embezzlers often try to cover their tracks by preparing false books, records, or entries.

The key element here is that the stolen property was *entrusted* to the embezzler. This differs from robbery, burglary, and larceny, where property is taken by someone not entrusted with the property. For example, embezzlement has been committed if a bank teller absconds with money that was deposited by depositors. The employer (the bank) entrusted the teller to take deposits from its customers.

embezzlement
The fraudulent conversion of property by a person to whom that property was entrusted.

In our complex society the accountant's certificate and the lawyer's opinion can be instruments for inflicting pecuniary loss more potent than the chisel or the crowbar.

Justice Blackmun
Dissenting Opinion,
Ernst & Ernst v. Hochfelder, 425 U.S. 185 (1976)

Criminal Fraud

Obtaining title to property through deception or trickery constitutes the crime of **false pretenses**. This crime is commonly referred to as **criminal fraud** or **deceit**.

criminal fraud
Obtaining title to property through deception or trickery. Also known as false pretenses or deceit.

Consider This Example Bob Anderson, a stockbroker, promises Mary Greenberg, a prospective investor, that he will use any money she invests to purchase interests in oil wells. Based on this promise, Ms. Greenberg decides to make the investment. Mr. Anderson never intended to invest the money. Instead, he used the money for his personal needs. This is criminal fraud.

Mail and Wire Fraud Federal law prohibits the use of mails or wires (e.g., telegraphs or telephone) to defraud another person. These crimes are called **mail fraud**[3] and **wire fraud**,[4] respectively. The government often prosecutes a suspect under these statutes if there is insufficient evidence to prove the real crime that the criminal was attempting to commit or did commit.

mail fraud
The use of mail to defraud another person.

wire fraud
The use of telephone or telegraph to defraud another person.

@ *E-Commerce & Information Technology*

FEDERAL LAW HELPS VICTIMS OF IDENTITY FRAUD

For centuries, some people—for various purposes, mostly financial in nature—have attempted to take the identity of other persons. Today, taking on the identity of another can be extremely lucrative, earning the spoils of another's credit cards, bank accounts, Social Security benefits, and such. The use of new technology—computers and the Internet—have made such "identity fraud" even easier. But the victim of such fraud is left with funds stolen, a dismantled credit history, and thousands of dollars in costs trying to straighten out the mess. Identity fraud is the fastest-growing financial fraud in America. Credit reporting firms say identity fraud cases have increased from 10,000 in 1990 to over 500,000 cases per year today.

Consider the case of Mari Frank. Her misfortune started late one night in 1996 when she got a telephone call from the Bank of New York, asking why she had not made the monthly payment on her credit card. There was one hitch: Frank did not have a credit card with the bank. But Frank's double—who looked nothing like her but had taken Frank's name, background, Social Security number, credit history, and even her business cards—did. The imposter had bought $50,000 in clothing and luxury items and a Mustang convertible and had charged them to Frank's credit. The imposter had used Frank's identity for a year before the fraud was detected. It then took Frank over 500 hours and thousands of dollars in costs to clean up the situation and clear her credit history of the imposter's spending spree. Luckily, Frank was not responsible for more than $50 on her credit-card debts or for any other debt taken out in her name by the imposter. Several banks, however, had to write off the debts incurred by the imposter in Frank's name as bad debts. Identity fraud costs businesses over $1 billion per year.

To combat such fraud, Congress passed the **Identity Theft and Assumption Deterrence Act of 1998**. This act criminalizes identity fraud, making it a federal felony punishable with prison sentences ranging from 3 to 25 years. The act also appoints a federal administrative agency, the Federal Trade Commission (FTC), to help victims restore their credit and erase the impact of the imposter. Law enforcement officials suggest the following steps to protect against identity fraud: Never put your Social Security number on any document unless it is legally required, obtain and review copies of your credit report at least twice each year, and use passwords other than maiden names and birthdays on bank accounts and other accounts that require personal identification numbers (PINs).

---

bribery

When one person gives another person money, property, favors, or anything else of value for a favor in return. Often referred to as a payoff or "kickback."

Bribery

Bribery is one of the most prevalent forms of white-collar crime. A bribe can be money, property, favors, or anything else of value. The crime of commercial bribery prohibits the payment of bribes to private persons and businesses. This type of bribe is often referred to as a **kickback** or **payoff**. Intent is a necessary element of this crime. The offeror of a bribe commits the crime of bribery when the bribe is tendered. The offeree is guilty of the crime of bribery when he or she accepts the bribe. The offeror can be found liable for the crime of bribery even if the person to whom the bribe is offered rejects the bribe.

Consider This Example   Harriet Landers is the purchasing agent for the ABC Corporation and is in charge of purchasing equipment to be used by the corporation. Neal Brown, the sales representative of a company that makes equipment that can be used by the ABC Corporation, offers to pay her a 10 percent kickback if she buys equipment from him. She accepts the bribe and orders the equipment. Both parties are guilty of bribery.

Business Brief

Bribery is probably the most prevalent form of business crime.

At common law, the crime of bribery was defined as the giving or receiving of anything of value in corrupt payment for an "official act" by a public official. Public officials include legislators, judges, jurors, witnesses at trial, administrative agency personnel, and other government officials. Modern penal codes also make it a crime to bribe public officials. For example, a developer who is constructing an apartment building cannot pay the building inspector to overlook a building code violation.

The Supreme Court Speaks

Federal Bribery Statute Narrowly Interpreted

United States v. Sun-Diamond Growers of California
526 U.S. 397, 119 S.Ct. 1402 (1999)
Supreme Court of the United States

BACKGROUND AND FACTS

The Sun-Diamond Growers of California is a trade association that engages in marketing and lobbying activities on behalf of its 5,000 member-growers of raisins, figs, walnuts, prunes, and hazelnuts. Sun-Diamond gave Michael Epsy, U.S. secretary of agriculture, tickets to sporting events (worth $2,295), luggage ($2,427), meals ($665), and a crystal bowl ($524) while several matters in which Sun-Diamond members had an interest in were pending before the secretary. The two matters were decided in Sun-Diamond's favor. The United States sued Sun-Diamond for making illegal gifts to a public official in violation of the federal antibribery and gratuity statute [18 U.S.C. Section 201(b) and 201(c)]. The jury convicted Sun-Diamond, and the district court ordered it to pay a fine of $400,000. The court of appeals reversed. The U.S. Supreme Court granted certiorari to hear the appeal.

SUPREME COURT ISSUE

Does a conviction under the federal antibribery and gratuity statute require a showing of a direct nexus between the value conferred on the public official and the official act performed by the public official in favor of the giver?

IN THE LANGUAGE OF THE U.S. SUPREME COURT

Scalia, Justice *The solicitor general of the United States contends that the statute requires only a showing that a gift was motivated, at least in part, by the recipient's capacity to exercise governmental power or influence in the donor's favor without necessarily showing that it was connected to a particular official act. We are inclined to*

believe this meaning incorrect because of the peculiar results that the government's reading would produce. It would criminalize, for example, token gifts to the president based on his official position and not linked to any identifiable act—such as the replica jerseys given by championship sports teams each year during ceremonial White House visits. Similarly, it would criminalize a high school principal's gift of a school baseball cap to the secretary of education, by reason of his office, on the occasion of the latter's visit to the school.

DECISION AND REMEDY

The U.S. Supreme Court held that there must be proof of a direct nexus between the gratuity given and the public official's act before the federal antibribery and gratuity statute is violated. Because no such direct nexus was proven in this case, there is no violation of the federal antibribery and gratuity statute. The judgment of the court of appeals is affirmed.

CASE QUESTIONS

Critical Legal Thinking   Do you think the Supreme Court should have read the statute so narrowly? Why or why not?

Business Ethics   Is it ethical for a government official to accept gifts and gratuities from parties who have actions or matters pending before the official? Do you think such gifts and gratuities are given with any return favor in mind?

Contemporary Business   What is "lobbying"? Who are the winners and losers of lobbying?

International Law

THE FOREIGN CORRUPT PRACTICES ACT

During the 1970s, several scandals were uncovered where American companies were found to have bribed foreign government officials to obtain lucrative contracts. Congressional investigations discovered that the making of such payments—or bribes—was pervasive in conducting international business. To prevent American companies from engaging in this type of conduct, the U.S. Congress enacted the **Foreign Corrupt Practices Act of 1977 (FCPA)** [15 U.S.C. § 78m]. Congress amended the FCPA as part of the Omnibus Trade and Competitiveness Act of 1988.

The FCPA attacks the problem in two ways. First, it requires firms to keep accurate books and records of all foreign transactions and to install internal accounting controls to ensure transactions and payments are authorized. Inadvertent or technical errors in maintaining books and records do not violate the FCPA.

Second, the FCPA makes it illegal for American companies, or their officers, directors, agents, or employees, to bribe a foreign official, a foreign political party official, or a candidate for foreign political office. A bribe is illegal only where it is meant to influence the awarding of new business or the retention of a continuing business activity. Payments to secure ministerial, clerical, or routine government action (such as scheduling inspections, signing customs documents, unloading and loading of cargo, and the like) do not violate the FCPA.

The FCPA imposes criminal liability only in circumstances where a person knowingly fails to maintain the proper system of accounting, pays the illegal bribe himself, or supplies a payment to a third party or agent knowing that it will be used as a bribe. A firm can be fined up to $2 million and an individual can be fined up to $100,000 and imprisoned for up to five years for violations of the FCPA.

The 1988 amendments created two defenses. One excuses a firm or person charged with bribery under the FCPA if the firm or person can show that the payment was lawful under the written laws of that country. The other allows a defendant to show that a payment was a reasonable and bona fide expenditure related to the furtherance or execution of a contract.

Some people argue that the FCPA is too soft and permits American firms to engage in the payment of bribes internally that would otherwise be illegal in this country. Others argue that the FCPA is difficult to interpret and apply, and that American companies are placed at a disadvantage in international markets where commercial bribery is commonplace and firms from other countries are not hindered by laws similar to the FCPA.

White lily on pond, Japan
Different countries and cultures have different criminal laws. Some acts that are considered criminal in one country may not be thought so in other countries.

Landmark Law

RACKETEER INFLUENCED AND CORRUPT ORGANIZATIONS ACT (RICO)

Organized crime has a pervasive influence on many parts of the American economy. In 1980, Congress enacted the Organized Crime Control Act. The **Racketeer Influenced and Corrupt Organization Act (RICO)** is part of this act [18 U.S.C. §§ 1961–1968]. Originally, RICO was intended to apply only to organized crime. However, the broad language of the RICO statute has been used against nonorganized crime defendants as well. RICO, which provides for both criminal and civil penalties, is one of the most important laws affecting business today.

RICO makes it a federal crime to acquire or maintain an interest in, use income from, or conduct or participate in the affairs of an "enterprise" through a "pattern" of "racketeering activity." An "enterprise" is defined as a corporation, a partnership, a sole proprietorship, another business or organization, and the government. *Racketeering activity* consists of a number of specifically enumerated federal and state crimes, including such activities as gambling, arson, robbery, coun-

terfeiting, dealing in narcotics, and such. Business-related crimes, such as bribery, embezzlement, mail fraud, wire fraud, and the like, are also considered racketeering.

To prove a *pattern of racketeering*, at least two predicate acts must be committed by the defendant within a 10-year period. For example, committing two different frauds would be considered a pattern. Individual defendants found criminally liable for RICO violations can be fined up to $25,000 per violation, imprisoned for up to 20 years, or both. In addition, RICO provides for the *forfeiture* of any property or business interests (even interests in a legitimate business) that were gained because of RICO violations. This provision allows the government to recover investments made with monies derived from racketeering activities. The government may also seek civil penalties for RICO violations. These include injunctions, orders of dissolution, reorganization of business, and the divestiture of the defendant's interest in an enterprise.

The Supreme Court Speaks

Supreme Court Defines the Required Actors for a Civil RICO Violation

Cedric Kushner Promotions, Ltd. v. Don King
121 S.Ct. 2087 (2001)
Supreme Court of the United States

BACKGROUND AND FACTS
Don King is the president and sole shareholder of Don King Productions, a corporation that promotes boxing matches. Cedric Kushner Promotions, Ltd., a corporation that also promotes boxing matches, sued Don King claiming that King had conducted the boxing-related affairs of Don King Productions through a RICO pattern of illegal fraud and other crimes. The district court dismissed the complaint, holding that Don King was not a separate "person" from Don King Productions, and therefore the civil RICO provisions did not apply. The court of appeals affirmed. The U.S. Supreme Court granted certiorari.

SUPREME COURT ISSUE
Are there two separate entities—a "person" and an "enterprise"—as required for the application of RICO's civil provisions?

IN THE LANGUAGE OF THE U.S. SUPREME COURT
Breyer, Justice *The corporate owner/employee, a natural person, is distinct from the corporation itself, a legally different entity with different rights and responsibilities due to its different legal status. And we can find nothing in the statute that requires more "separateness" than that.*

DECISION AND REMEDY
The U.S. Supreme Court held Don King is a "person" separate from the corporate "enterprise" Don King Productions. The Supreme Court reversed the judgment of the court of appeals and remanded the case for trial.

CASE QUESTIONS
Critical Legal Thinking   What do the civil law provisions of RICO provide? What penalties are available for civil RICO violations?

Business Ethics   Do you think there is much fraud in the promotion and staging of professional boxing matches?

Contemporary Business   Do you think civil RICO is used more against mob or non-mob-related defendants? Why?

E-Commerce & Information Technology

COMPUTER CRIMES

Many business transactions are initiated, processed, and completed through the use of computers. Computers may keep a company's financial records; issue its payroll checks; and store its trade secrets, engineering drawings, databases, and other proprietary information. The potential for the misuse of computers is enormous. Federal and state governments have enacted several laws that address computer crimes. The most important computer crime laws are discussed in the paragraphs that follow.

COUNTERFEIT ACCESS DEVICE AND COMPUTER FRAUD AND ABUSE ACT OF 1984
The **Counterfeit Access Device and Computer Fraud and Abuse Act of 1984**, as amended, makes it a federal crime to access a computer knowingly to obtain (1) restricted federal government information, (2) financial records of financial institutions, and (3) consumer reports of consumer reporting agencies. The act also makes it a crime to use counterfeit or unauthorized access devices, such as cards or code numbers, to obtain things of value or transfer funds or to traffic in such devices [Public Law 98–473, Title II].

ELECTRONIC FUNDS TRANSFER ACT
The **Electronic Funds Transfer Act** regulates the payment and deposit of funds using electronic funds transfers, such as direct deposit of payroll and Social Security checks in financial institutions, transactions using automated teller machines (ATMs), and such. The act makes it a federal crime to use, furnish, sell, or transport a counterfeit, stolen, lost, or fraudulently obtained ATM card, code number, or other device used to conduct electronic funds transfers. The act imposes criminal penalties of up to 10 years' imprisonment and fines up to $10,000 [15 U.S.C. § 1693].

STATE LAWS
Often, larceny statutes cover only the theft of tangible property. Because computer software, programs, and data are intangible property, they are not covered by some existing state criminal statutes. To compensate for this, many states have either modernized existing laws to include computer crime or amended existing penal codes to make certain abuses of computers a criminal offense.

Computer trespass, the unauthorized use of computers, tampering with computers, and the unauthorized duplication of computer-related materials are usually forbidden by these acts [See New York Session Laws, 1986, Chapter 514].

Our growing reliance on computers has made us more aware of the risks associated with losing the data stored on them. As a result, it is likely that the safety of the nation's ever-expanding computer networks will be legislated even more in the future.

INCHOATE CRIMES

In addition to the substantive crimes previously discussed, a person can be held criminally liable for committing an *inchoate crime*. Inchoate crimes include incomplete crimes and crimes committed by nonparticipants. The most important inchoate crimes are discussed in the following paragraphs.

Criminal Conspiracy

criminal conspiracy

When two or more persons enter into an agreement to commit a crime and an overt act is taken to further the crime.

A **criminal conspiracy** occurs when two or more persons enter into an *agreement* to commit a crime. To be liable for a criminal conspiracy, an *overt act* must be taken to further the crime. The crime itself does not have to be committed, however.

Business Brief

The use of computers to commit business crimes is increasing. Businesses must implement safeguards to prevent computer crimes.

Consider This Example   Two securities brokers agree over the telephone to commit a securities fraud. They also obtain a list of potential victims and prepare false financial statements necessary for the fraud. Because they entered into an agreement to commit a crime and took overt action, the brokers are guilty of the crime of criminal conspiracy even if they never carry out the securities fraud. The government usually brings criminal conspiracy charges if (1) the defendants have been thwarted in their efforts to commit the substantive crime or (2) there is insufficient evidence to prove the substantive crime.

Attempt to Commit a Crime

attempt to commit a crime

When a crime is attempted but not completed.

The **attempt to commit a crime** is itself a crime. For example, suppose a person wants to kill his or her neighbor. The person shoots at the neighbor but misses. The perpetrator is not liable for the crime of murder but is liable for the crime of attempted murder.

Aiding and Abetting the Commission of a Crime

aiding and abetting the commission of a crime

Rendering support, assistance, or encouragement to the commission of a crime; harboring a criminal after he or she has committed a crime.

Sometimes persons assist others in the commission of a crime. The act of **aiding and abetting the commission of a crime** is a crime. This concept, which is very broad, includes rendering support, assistance, or encouragement to the commission of a crime. Harboring a criminal after he or she has committed a crime is considered aiding and abetting.

The court addressed the issue of aiding and abetting in the following case.

United States v. Cloud

870 F.2d 594 (1989)

United States Court of Appeals, Ninth Circuit

CASE 5.1

BACKGROUND AND FACTS

In 1980, Ronald V. Cloud purchased the Cal-Neva Lodge, a hotel and casino complex located in the Lake Tahoe area near the California-Nevada border, for $10 million. Cloud is a sophisticated 68-year-old entrepreneur who is experienced in buying and selling real estate and has real estate holdings valued at more than $65 million. He also has experience in banking and finance, having been the founder and chairman of Continental National Bank of Fresno. After two years of mounting operation losses, Cloud closed the Cal-Neva Lodge and actively began seeking a new buyer. In December

1984, Cloud met with Jon Perroton and orally agreed to transfer the lodge to Perroton for approximately $17 million. On January 2, 1985, Perroton met with an executive of Hibernia Bank (Hibernia) to discuss a possible loan to finance the purchase of the lodge. Perroton made multiple false representations and presented false documents to obtain a $20-million loan from Hibernia. In particular, Perroton misrepresented the sale price for the lodge ($27.5 million) and stated that $7.5 million had already been paid to Cloud. An escrow was opened with Transamerica Title Company (Transamerica).

On January 15, 1985, Cloud and his attorney and Perroton met at Transamerica to sign mutual escrow instructions. Cloud reviewed the instructions and noticed that the sale price and down payment figures were incorrectly stated at $27.5 million and $7.5 million, respectively, and that the Hibernia loan was for $20 million, almost $3 million above what he knew to be the true sale price. Cloud signed the escrow instructions. Later, Cloud signed a settlement statement containing the same false figures and signed a grant deed to the property. The sale closed on January 23, 1985, with Hibernia making the $20-million loan to Perroton. Subsequently, when the loan went into default, Continental Insurance Company (Continental) paid Hibernia its loss of $7.5 million on the bank's blanket bond insurance policy. The United States sued Cloud for aiding and abetting a bank fraud in violation of federal law (18 U.S.C. §§ 2 and 1344). The jury convicted Cloud of the crime and ordered him to make restitution of $7.5 million to Continental. Cloud appealed.

ISSUE

Is Cloud guilty of aiding and abetting a bank fraud?

COURT'S REASONING

The court stated that aiding and abetting means to assist the perpetrator of a crime, and that an abettor's criminal intent may be inferred from the attended facts and circumstances and need not be established by direct evidence.

The court noted that the evidence established that sometime in December 1984 or early January 1985, Jon Perroton launched a fraudulent scheme to obtain money from Hibernia Bank by means of false representations. The issue before the court was whether a rational trier of fact could conclude on the basis of all the evidence that Cloud at some point knowingly came aboard and participated in Perroton's bank fraud scheme. The court concluded that a reasonable jury could have found that Cloud came aboard on January 15, 1985, at the meeting to sign the escrow instructions.

DECISION

The court of appeals held that Cloud was guilty of the crime of aiding and abetting a bank fraud in violation of federal law. Affirmed.

Case Questions

Critical Legal Thinking Should the law recognize the crime of aiding and abetting? Why or why not?

Business Ethics Did Cloud act ethically in this case?

Contemporary Business What is the moral of this case? Do you think bank fraud of the type in this case happens very frequently?

 *E-Commerce & Information Technology*

THE INFORMATION INFRASTRUCTURE PROTECTION ACT

The Internet and Information Age ushered in a whole new world for education, business, and consumer transactions. But with it followed a new rash of digital crimes. Prosecutors and courts wrestled over how to apply existing laws written in a nondigital age to new Internet-related abuses. In many instances, criminal cases were dismissed because the statutory language of existing criminal laws could not be stretched to reach unauthorized computer breaches.

In 1996, Congress responded by enacting the **Information Infrastructure Protection Act (IIP Act).** In this new federal law, Congress addressed computer-related crimes as distinct offenses. Previously, the Computer Abuse Act outlawed knowingly damaging federal computers, but this act did not cover nonfederal interest computers owned by businesses and individuals. Also, existing criminal acts required that unauthorized access to computer data had to be for the defendant's commercial benefit before it was illegal. The IIP Act cleared up both of these deficiencies in criminal law in the following ways:

• The IIP applies to all "protected computers" not only to federal computers. By statutory definition, a protected computer includes any computer which is used in inter-

state or foreign commerce. Thus, the IIP Act provides protection for any computer attached to the Internet.
• The IIP Act does not require that the defendant accessed a protected computer for commercial benefit. The act makes it clear that simply accessing and obtaining information from a protected computer in excess of one's authorization is unlawful.

The IIP Act makes it a criminal offense for anyone to intentionally access and obtain information from a protected computer without authorization or access of his or her authorization. Thus, persons who transmit a computer virus over the Internet or hackers who trespass into Internet-connected computers may be criminally prosecuted under the IIP Act. Even merely observing data on a protected computer without authorization is sufficient to meet the requirement that the defendant has accessed a protected computer. Criminal penalties for violating the IIP Act include imprisonment for up to 10 years and fines.

The IIP Act gives the federal government a much needed weapon for directly prosecuting cybercrooks, hackers, and others who enter, steal, destroy, or look at others' computer data without authorization.

CORPORATE CRIMINAL LIABILITY

A corporation is a fictitious legal person that is granted legal existence by the state only after certain requirements are met. A corporation cannot act on its own behalf. Instead, it must act through *agents* such as managers, representatives, and employees.

The question of whether a corporation can be held criminally liable has intrigued legal scholars for some time. Originally, under the common law, it was generally held that corporations lacked the criminal mind (*mens rea*) to be held criminally liable. Modern courts, however, are more pragmatic. These courts have held that corporations are criminally liable for the acts of their managers, agents, and employees. In any event, because corporations cannot be put in prison, they are usually sanctioned with fines, loss of a license or franchise, and the like.

Corporate directors, officers, and employees are individually liable for crimes that they personally commit, whether for personal benefit or on behalf of the corporation. In addition, under certain circumstances a corporate manager can be held criminally liable for the criminal activities of his or her subordinates. To be held criminally liable, the manager must have failed to supervise the subordinate appropriately. This is an evolving area of the law.

Contemporary Business Environment

HUGHES AIRCRAFT DOWNED AS A CRIMINAL CONSPIRATOR

Hughes Aircraft Co., Inc. (Hughes), an aircraft manufacturer, contracted with the U.S. government to manufacture microelectronic circuits, known as "hybrids," which are used as components in weapons defense systems. The contract required Hughes to perform tests on each hybrid. A Hughes's employee, Donald LaRue, was the supervisor responsible for ensuring the accuracy of the hybrid testing process. LaRue falsely reported that all tests had been performed and that each hybrid had passed the test. When LaRue's subordinates called his actions to the attention of LaRue's supervisors, they did nothing about it. Instead, they responded that LaRue's decisions were his own and were not to be questioned. The United States sued Hughes and LaRue, charging criminal conspiracy to defraud the government. At trial, LaRue was acquitted, but Hughes was convicted of criminal conspiracy and fined $3.5 million. Hughes appealed its conviction, asserting that it should not be convicted of criminal conspiracy if its alleged coconspirator, LaRue, was acquitted.

Should Hughes be acquitted as a matter of law because the same jury that convicted Hughes acquitted its alleged coconspirator of the charge of criminal conspiracy? No. The court of appeals held that Hughes may be found guilty of criminal conspiracy even though its coconspirator had been acquitted of the same crime. Affirmed.

The court of appeals, as a matter of law, held that the inconsistency of the jury verdicts of two defendants charged with criminal conspiracy does not mean that the convicted defendant should also be acquitted. The court noted that the jury may have been more lenient with defendant LaRue, an individual, than they were with Hughes, the corporate defendant. Moreover, the court stated that the jury could have found Hughes guilty of the required act of conspiracy based on evidence provided at trial by the other Hughes's employees that were called as witnesses, [*United States v. Hughes Aircraft Company, Inc.*, 20 F.3d 974 (9th Cir. 1994)]

CONSTITUTIONAL SAFEGUARDS

When our forefathers drafted the U.S. Constitution, they included provisions that protect persons from unreasonable government intrusion and provide safeguards for those accused of crimes. Although these safeguards originally applied only to federal cases, the Fourteenth Amendment's Due Process Clause made them applicable to state criminal law cases as well. The most important of these constitutional safeguards are discussed in the following paragraphs.

Fourth Amendment Protection Against Unreasonable Searches and Seizures

The *Fourth Amendment* to the U.S. Constitution protects persons and corporations from overzealous investigative activities by the government. It protects the rights of the people from **unreasonable search and seizure** by the government. It permits people to be secure in their persons, houses, papers, and effects.

"Reasonable" search and seizure by the government is lawful. **Search warrants** based on probable cause are necessary in most cases. Such warrants specifically state the place and scope of the authorized search. General searches beyond the specified area are forbidden. *Warrantless searches* are permitted only (1) incident to arrest, (2) where evidence is in "plain view," or (3) where it is likely that evidence will be destroyed. Warrantless searches are also judged by the probable cause standard.

Evidence obtained from an unreasonable search and seizure is considered tainted evidence ("fruit of a tainted tree"). Under the **exclusionary rule**, such evidence generally can be prohibited from introduction at a trial or administrative proceeding against the person searched. However, this evidence is freely admissible against other persons. The U.S. Supreme Court created a *good faith exception* to the exclusionary rule.[5] This exception allows evidence otherwise obtained illegally to be introduced as evidence against the accused if the police officers who conducted the unreasonable search reasonably believed that they were acting pursuant to a lawful search warrant.

unreasonable search and seizure

Any search and seizure by the government that violates the Fourth Amendment.

search warrant

A warrant issued by a court that authorizes the police to search a designated place for specified contraband, articles, items, or documents. The search warrant must be based on probable cause.

exclusionary rule

A rule that says evidence obtained from an unreasonable search and seizure can generally be prohibited from introduction at a trial or administrative proceeding against the person searched.

The Supreme Court Speaks

Warrantless Search of Automobile Permitted if Based on Probable Cause

Maryland v. Dyson
119 S.Ct. 2013 (2001)
Supreme Court of the United States

BACKGROUND AND FACTS

At 11 A.M. on July 2, 1996, a reliable informant gave a tip to a Maryland county sheriff that Kevin Darnell Dyson had gone to New York to buy drugs and would be returning to Maryland in a rented red Toyota automobile, license number DDY 787, with a large quantity of cocaine. When Dyson returned to Maryland in the rented car at 1 A.M. on July 3, the sheriff's deputies stopped and searched the vehicle, finding 23 grams of crack cocaine in a duffel bag in the trunk. Dyson was arrested, tried, and convicted of conspiracy to possess cocaine with intent to distribute. Dyson appealed, arguing that the cocaine evidence should be suppressed because the sheriff had not obtained a search warrant before searching the car. The appellate court held for Dyson. The U.S. Supreme Court granted certiorari to hear the case.

SUPREME COURT ISSUE

If there is probable cause, must the police first obtain a search warrant before searching an automobile?

IN THE LANGUAGE OF THE U.S. SUPREME COURT

The Fourth Amendment generally requires police to secure a warrant before conducting a search. There is an exception to this requirement for searches of vehicles. If a car is readily mobile and probable cause exists to believe it contains contraband, the Fourth Amendment permits police to search the vehicle without more. In this case, there was abundant probable cause that the car contained contraband.

DECISION AND REMEDY

The U.S. Supreme Court held that under the "automobile exception" to the Fourth Amendment, an automobile can be searched by the police without a search warrant as long as there exists probable cause to conduct the search.

CASE QUESTIONS

Critical Legal Thinking   How would the Supreme Court have decided this case had there been no probable cause to search the vehicle?

Business Ethics   Do defendants act ethically when they petition the court to suppress incriminating evidence?

The Supreme Court Speaks

General Highway Checkpoint to Find Drugs Violates Fourth Amendment

City of Indianapolis v. Edmond
531 U.S. 32, 121 S.Ct. 447 (2000)
Supreme Court of the United States

BACKGROUND AND FACTS

In August 1998, the police of the city of Indianapolis, Indiana, began to operate vehicle roadblock checkpoints on Indianapolis roads in an effort to interdict unlawful drugs. Once cars had been stopped, police questioned the driver and passengers, and conducted an open-view examination of the vehicle from the outside. A narcotics-detection dog walked around outside of each stopped vehicle. The police conducted a search and seizure of the occupants and vehicle only if particular suspicion developed from the initial investigation. The overall "hit rate" of the program was approximately 9 percent.

James Edmond and Joel Palmer, each attorneys who had been stopped at one of Indianapolis's checkpoints, filed a lawsuit on behalf of themselves and the class of all motorists who had been stopped or were subject to being stopped at such checkpoints. They claimed that the roadblocks violated the Fourth Amendment of the Constitution. The district court found for Indianapolis, but the court of appeals reversed. The U.S. Supreme Court granted certiorari to hear the appeal.

SUPREME COURT ISSUE

Do Indianapolis's highway checkpoint programs whereby police, without individualized suspicion, stop vehicles for the primary purpose of discovering and interdicting illegal narcotics, violate the Fourth Amendment of the U.S. Constitution?

IN THE LANGUAGE OF THE U.S. SUPREME COURT

O'Connor, Justice The Fourth Amendment requires that searches and seizures be reasonable. A search or seizure is ordinarily unreasonable in the absence of individualized suspicion of wrongdoing. We have recognized only limited circumstances in which the usual rule does not apply. We have upheld brief, suspicionless seizures of motorists at a fixed border patrol checkpoint designed to intercept illegal aliens, United States v. Martinez-Fuerte, 428 U.S. 543, 96 S.Ct. 3074 (1976), and at a sobriety checkpoint aimed at removing drunk drivers from the road, Michigan Dept. of State Police v. Sitz, 496 U.S. 444, 110 S.Ct. 2481 (1990). In none of these cases, however, did we indicate approval of a checkpoint program whose primary purpose was to detect evidence of ordinary criminal wrongdoing.

In Martinez-Fuerte, we entertained Fourth Amendment challenges to stops at two permanent immigration checkpoints located on major United States highways less than 100 miles from the Mexican border. We noted at the outset the particular context in which the constitutional question arose, describing in some detail the "formidable law enforcement problems" posed by the northbound tide of illegal entrants into the United States. In Martinez-Fuerte,

we found that the balance tipped in favor of the government's interests in policing the nation's borders.

In Sitz, we evaluated the constitutionality of a Michigan highway sobriety checkpoint program. The Sitz checkpoint involved brief suspicionless stops of motorists so that police officers could detect signs of intoxication and remove impaired drivers from the road. Motorists who exhibited signs of intoxication were diverted for a license and registration check and, if warranted, further sobriety tests. This checkpoint program was clearly aimed at reducing the immediate hazard posed by the presence of drunk drivers on the highways, and there was an obvious connection between the imperative of highway safety and the law enforcement practice at issue. The gravity of the drunk driving problem and the magnitude of the state's interest in getting drunk drivers off the road weighed heavily in our determination that the program was constitutional.

We have never approved a checkpoint program whose primary purpose was to detect evidence of ordinary criminal wrongdoing. Because the primary purpose of the Indianapolis narcotics checkpoint program is to uncover evidence of ordinary criminal wrongdoing, the program contravenes the Fourth Amendment. Of course, there are circumstances that may justify a law enforcement checkpoint where the primary purpose would otherwise, but for some emergency, relate to ordinary crime control. For example, the Fourth Amendment would almost certainly permit an appropriately tailored roadblock set up to thwart an imminent terrorist attack or to catch a dangerous criminal who is likely to flee by way of a particular route. The exigencies created by these scenarios are far removed from the circumstances under which authorities might simply stop cars as a matter of course to see if there just happens to be a felon leaving the jurisdiction.

DECISION AND REMEDY

The U.S. Supreme Court held that Indianapolis's general highway checkpoints whereby police, without individualized suspicion, stopped vehicles for the primary purpose of discovering and interdicting narcotics is an unreasonable search and seizure in violation of the Fourth Amendment.

CASE QUESTIONS

Critical Legal Thinking How did the Supreme Court reconcile its decision in this case with its prior decisions in *Martinez-Fuerte* and *Sitz*? Explain.

Business Ethics Should the 9 percent of criminals who were caught by the roadblock get off because of the Fourth Amendment?

Contemporary Business How big of a business is illegal narcotics sales in this country? Should this industry be legalized and taxed? Why or why not?

Searches of Business Premises Generally, the government does not have the right to search business premises without a search warrant.[6] Certain hazardous and regulated industries—such as sellers of firearms and liquor, coal mines, and the like—are subject to warrantless searches if proper statutory procedures are met.

The Supreme Court Speaks

Warrantless Search of Regulated Industry Allowed

New York v. Burger
482 U.S. 691, 107 S.Ct. 2636, 96 L.Ed. 3d 601 (1987)
Supreme Court of the United States

BACKGROUND AND FACTS
Joseph Burger is the owner of a junkyard in Brooklyn, New York. His business consists, in part, of dismantling automobiles and selling their parts. The state of New York enacted a statute that requires automobile junkyards to keep certain records. The statute authorizes warrantless searches of vehicle dismantlers and automobile junkyards without prior notice. At approximately noon on November 17, 1982, five plain-clothes officers of the Auto Crimes Division of the New York City Police Department entered Burger's junkyard to conduct a surprise inspection. Burger did not have either a license to conduct the business or records of the automobiles and vehicle parts on his premises as required by state law. After conducting an inspection of the premises, the officers determined that Burger was in possession of stolen vehicles and parts. He was arrested and charged with criminal possession of stolen property. Burger moved to suppress the evidence. The New York supreme court and appellate division held the search to be constitutional. The New York Court of Appeals reversed. New York appealed.

SUPREME COURT ISSUE
Does the warrantless search of an automobile junkyard pursuant to a state statute that authorizes such search constitute an unreasonable search and seizure in violation of the Fourth Amendment to the U.S. Constitution?

IN THE LANGUAGE OF THE U.S. SUPREME COURT
Blackmun, Justice *The court has long recognized that the Fourth Amendment's prohibition on unreasonable searches and seizures is applicable to commercial premises, as well as to private homes.*

An expectation of privacy in commercial premises, however, is different from, and indeed less than, a similar expectation in an individual's home. This expectation is particularly attenuated in commercial property employed in "closely regulated" industries. Because the owner or operator of commercial premises in a closely regulated industry has a reduced expectation of privacy, the warrant and probable cause requirements—which fulfill the traditional Fourth Amendment standard of reasonableness for a government search—have a lessened application in this context. The nature of the regulatory statute reveals that the operation of a junkyard, part of which is devoted to vehicle dismantling, is a closely regulated business in the state of New York. A warrantless inspection of commercial premises may well be reasonable within the meaning of the Fourth Amendment.

The New York regulatory scheme satisfies the criteria necessary to make reasonable warrantless inspections. The state has substantial interest in regulating the vehicle dismantling and automobile junkyard industry because motor vehicle theft has increased in the state of New York and because the problem of theft is associated with this industry. Regulation of the vehicle dismantling industry reasonably serves the state's substantial interest in eradicating automobile theft. It is well established that the theft problem can be addressed effectively by controlling the receiver of, or market in, stolen property. Automobile junkyards and vehicle dismantlers provide the major market for stolen vehicles and vehicle parts. The New York law provides a constitutionally adequate substitute for a warrant. The statute informs the operator of a vehicle dismantling business that inspections will be made on a regular basis.

DECISION AND REMEDY
The U.S. Supreme Court held that the New York statute that authorizes warrantless searches of vehicle dismantling businesses and automobile junkyards does not constitute an unreasonable search in violation of the Fourth Amendment to the U.S. Constitution. The Supreme Court reversed the judgment of the New York Court of Appeals and remanded the case for further proceedings consistent with its decision.

CASE QUESTIONS
Critical Legal Thinking Should the Fourth Amendment's protection against unreasonable searches and seizures apply to businesses? Why or why not?

Business Ethics Was it ethical for the defendant to assert the Fourth Amendment's prohibition against unreasonable searches and seizures?

Contemporary Business Is auto theft a big business? Will the New York law that regulates vehicle dismantling businesses and junkyards help to alleviate this crime?

Fifth Amendment Privilege Against Self-Incrimination

The *Fifth Amendment* to the U.S. Constitution provides that no person "shall be compelled in any criminal case to be a witness against himself." Thus, a person cannot be compelled to give testimony against him- or herself, although nontestimonial evidence (e.g., fingerprints, body fluids, and the like) may be required. A person who asserts this right is described as having "taken the Fifth." This protection applies to federal cases and is extended to state and local criminal cases through the Due Process Clause of the Fourteenth Amendment.

self-incrimination

The Fifth Amendment states that no person shall be compelled in any criminal case to be a witness against him- or herself.

Business Brief

It is improper for a jury to infer guilt from the defendant's exercise of his or her constitutional right to remain silent.

The protection against **self-incrimination** applies only to natural persons who are accused of crimes. Therefore, artificial persons (such as corporations and partnerships) cannot raise this protection against incriminating testimony.[7] Thus, business records of corporations and partnerships are not generally protected from disclosure, even if they incriminate individuals who work for the business. However, certain "private papers" of businesspersons (such as personal diaries) are protected from disclosure.

Contemporary Business Environment

MIRANDA 2000

Most people have not read and memorized the provisions of the U.S. Constitution. The U.S. Supreme Court recognized this fact when it decided the landmark case, *Miranda v. Arizona*, in 1966 [384 U.S. 436, 86 S.Ct. 1602]. In that case, the Supreme Court held that the Fifth Amendment privilege against self-incrimination is not useful unless a criminal suspect has knowledge of this right. Therefore, the Supreme Court required that the following warning—colloquially called the "*Miranda* rights"—be read to a criminal suspect before he or she is interrogated by the police or other government officials:

- You have the right to remain silent.
- Anything you say can and will be used against you.
- You have the right to consult a lawyer, and to have a lawyer present with you during interrogation.
- If you cannot afford a lawyer, a lawyer will be appointed free of charge to represent you.

Any statements or confessions obtained from a suspect prior to being read his *Miranda* rights can be excluded from evidence at trial. *Miranda* has been criticized for letting guilty defendants go free. To combat this problem, the U.S. Congress enacted a statute, 18 U.S.C. Section 3501, that provided that a statement or confession by a suspect is admissible into evidence if it is "voluntarily" given even if the suspect has not been read his *Miranda* rights. Many courts admitted confessions and other statements by defendants into evidence under this federal statute.

In 2000, the U.S. Supreme Court decided to revisit Miranda in *Dickerson v. United States* [120 S.Ct. 2326] to test

the lawfulness of Section 3501. In that case, the criminal defendant Dickerson was indicted for bank robbery. Before trial, Dickerson moved to suppress an incriminating statement he had made to the Federal Bureau of Investigation (FBI) prior to being read his *Miranda* rights. The court of appeals applied Section 3501 and admitted the statement at trial. Dickerson appealed to the U.S. Supreme Court to keep the statement out of trial. In a closely watched case, the Supreme Court upheld the *Miranda* ruling, finding that the *Miranda* decision was constitutionally based, and that Congress's attempt to lessen it by enacting Section 3501 was unconstitutional. In reaching its decision, the Supreme Court stated:

> *We do not think there is justification for overruling* Miranda. Miranda *has become embedded in routine police practice to the point where the warnings have become part of our national culture. Whether or not we would agree with Miranda's reasoning and its resulting rule, were we addressing the issue in the first instance, the principles of stare decisis weigh heavily against overruling it now. We conclude that* Miranda *announced a constitutional rule that Congress may not supercede legislatively. Following the rule of stare decisis, we decline to overrule* Miranda *ourselves.*

Thus, rather than being overturned or chipped away at, *Miranda* has been resurrected in its strict liability format: Police and government officials must read criminal suspects their *Miranda* rights; otherwise the suspect's statements and confessions are inadmissible at trial.

immunity from prosecution

The government agrees not to use any evidence given by a person granted immunity against that person.

Immunity From Prosecution   On occasion, the government may want to obtain information from a suspect who has asserted his or her Fifth Amendment privilege against self-incrimination. The government can often achieve this by offering the suspect **immunity from prosecution**. Immunity from prosecution means that the government agrees not to use any evidence given by a person granted immunity against that person. Once immunity is granted, the suspect loses the right to assert his or her Fifth Amendment privilege. Grants of immunity are often given when the government wants the suspect to give information that will lead to the prosecution of other more important criminal suspects. Partial grants of immunity are also available. For example, a suspect may be granted immunity from prosecution for a serious crime, but not a lesser crime, in exchange for information. The suspect must agree to a partial grant of immunity.

The Attorney-Client Privilege and Other Privileges   To obtain a proper defense, the accused person must be able to tell his or her attorney facts about the case without fear that the attorney will be called as a witness against the accused. The **attorney-client privilege** is protected by the Fifth Amendment. Either the client or the attorney can raise this privilege. For the privilege to apply, the information must be told to the attorney in his or her capacity as an attorney, and not as a friend or neighbor or such.

The following privileges have also been recognized under the Fifth Amendment: (1) *psychiatrist/psychologist-patient privilege*, (2) *priest/minister/rabbi-penitent privilege*, (3) *spouse-spouse privilege*, and (4) *parent-child privilege*. There are some exceptions. For example, a spouse or child who is beaten by a spouse or parent may testify against the accused.

Contemporary Business Environment

ACCOUNTANT-CLIENT PRIVILEGE?

The common law has long recognized an attorney-client privilege that protects communications between a client and his or her lawyer from discovery in a lawsuit. In other words, lawyers cannot testify against their own clients. The rationale for this rule is that if any attorney could be called to testify against a client, the client might choose to withhold information from the attorney. This might prevent the attorney from preparing the best defense.

Although a similar situation occurs when accountants are supplied with information and documents by their clients,

the U.S. Supreme Court has found that there is no corresponding accountant-client privilege under federal law [*Couch v. U.S.*, 409 U.S. 322, 93 S.Ct. 611 (1973)]. Thus, an accountant could be called as a witness in cases involving federal securities laws, federal mail or wire fraud, or federal RICO. Nevertheless, approximately 20 states have enacted special statutes that create an **accountant-client privilege**. An accountant cannot be called as a witness against a client in a court action in a state where these statutes are in effect. Federal courts do not recognize these laws, however.

Fifth Amendment Protection Against Double Jeopardy

The **double jeopardy clause** of the *Fifth Amendment* protects persons from being tried twice for the same crime. For example, if the state tries a suspect for the crime of murder, and the suspect is found innocent, the state cannot bring another trial against the accused for the same crime. However, if the same criminal act involves several different crimes, the accused may be tried for each of the crimes without violating the double jeopardy clause. Suppose the accused kills two people during a robbery. The accused may be tried for two murders and the robbery.

If the same act violates the laws of two or more jurisdictions, each jurisdiction may try the accused. For example, if any accused kidnaps a person in one state and brings the victim across a state border into another state, the act violates the laws of two states and the federal government. Thus, three jurisdictions can prosecute the accused without violating the double jeopardy clause.

Sixth Amendment Right to a Public Jury Trial

The *Sixth Amendment* guarantees certain rights to criminal defendants. These rights are (1) to be tried by an impartial jury of the state or district in which the accused crime was committed, (2) to confront (cross-examine) the witnesses against the accused, (3) to have the assistance of a lawyer, and (4) to have a speedy trial.[8]

cruel and unusual punishment

A clause of the Eighth Amendment that protects criminal defendants from torture or other abusive punishment.

Eighth Amendment Protection Against Cruel and Unusual Punishment

The *Eighth Amendment* protects criminal defendants from **cruel and unusual punishment**. For example, it prohibits the torture of criminals. However, this clause does not prohibit capital punishment.[9]

E-Commerce & Information Technology

AN OUTLAW IN CYBERSPACE

In "techie" circles, Kevin D. Mitnick became the underground icon of computer hackers. During a decade's reign, Mitnick terrorized the federal government, universities, and such high-tech companies as Sun Microsystems, Novell Corporation, MCI Communications, Digital Equipment Corporation, and others by breaking into their computer systems. Mitnick used his computer skills to penetrate his victim's computer systems to steal secret information and wreak havoc with their software and data.

Mitnick, a self-taught computer user, has a history of computer-related crime. As a 17-year-old, he was placed on probation for stealing computer manuals from a Pacific Bell Telephone switching center in Los Angeles. Mitnick was next accused of breaking into federal government and military computers in the early 1990s. He has also been accused of breaking into the nation's telephone and cellular telephone networks, stealing thousands of data files and trade secrets from corporate targets, obtaining at least 20,000 credit card numbers of some of the country's richest persons, and sabotaging government, university, and private computer systems around the nation. Mitnick was arrested and convicted of computer crimes and served time in prison. Upon release from prison, he was put on probation and placed in a medical program to treat his compulsive addiction to computers, which included a court order to not touch a computer or modem. In 1992, Mitnick dropped out of sight and evaded federal law enforcement officials for several years as he continued a life of computer crime.

Mitnick's undoing came when he broke into the computer of Tsutomu Shimomura, a researcher at the San Diego Supercomputer Center. Shimomura, cybersleuth who advises the FBI and major companies on computer and Internet

security, made it his crusade to catch the hacker who broke into his computer. Shimomura watched electronically as Mitnick invaded other computers across the country, but he could not physically locate Mitnick because he disguised his whereabouts by breaking into telephone company computers and rerouting all his computer calls. Eventually, Shimomura's patient watching paid off as he traced the electronic burglar to Raleigh, North Carolina. Shimomura flew to Raleigh, where he used a cellular-frequency-direction-finding antenna to locate Mitnick's apartment. The FBI was notified and an arrest warrant was obtained from a judge at his home. At 2:00 A.M., on February 15, 1995, the FBI arrested Mitnick at his apartment. Mitnick was placed in jail without bail pending the investigation of his case.

Mitnick's computer crimes spree has been estimated to have cost his victims several hundreds of millions of dollars in losses. Mitnick has not been accused of benefiting financially from his deeds. In 1999, Mitnick entered into a plea agreement with federal prosecutors. U.S. District Court judge Mariana Pfaelzer sentenced Kevin Mitnick to 46 months in prison, including time served, and ordered him to pay $4,125 in restitution to the companies he victimized. The judge called this a token amount but did not order a larger restitution because she believed Mitnick would not be able to pay more. With time served pending trial, Mitnick was released from prison in January 2000. As part of the sentencing, Mitnick cannot use electronic devices, from PCs to cellular telephones, during an additional probationary period following his release from prison. Mitnick is now acting as a consultant to businesses advising them how to protect themselves from computer hackers.

International Law

HIDING MONEY IN OFFSHORE BANKS

Little did Christopher Columbus know in 1503 when he sailed past the Cayman Islands in the Caribbean that these tiny islands would become a bastion of international finance in the late twentieth and early twenty-first century. These tiny islands of 35,000 people host about 600 banks with over $500 million in deposits. Why is so much money being hoarded there? The answer is: bank secrecy laws.

Every nation has banking laws, but all banking laws are not equal. What the Cayman Islands banking law provides is confidentiality. In most instances, no party other than the depositor has the right to know the identity of the depositor, account number, or amount in the account. In fact, most accounts are held in the name of trusts instead of the depositor's actual name. This bank secrecy law has attracted many persons—and in some instances crooks—to part their ill-gotten gains in a Cayman Islands bank. Often the bank is no more than a lawyer's office.

Switzerland was once the primary location for depositing money that did not want to be found. After some pressure from the United States and other countries, however, Switzerland entered into memorandums of understanding agreeing to cooperate with criminal investigations by these countries and to help uncover money deposited in Switzerland made through securities frauds and other crimes.

Therefore, Switzerland has lost some of its luster as an international money hideout.

So Switzerland has been replaced by other places offering even more secret bank secrecy laws. The Cayman Islands is now the "Switzerland of the Caribbean." There are several other bank secrecy hideouts around the world, including the Bahamas in the Caribbean, the country of Liechtenstein in Europe, the Isle of Jersey off of Great Britain, and the micro-island of Niue in the South Pacific. These tiny countries and islands follow the adage: "Write a good law and they will come."

The Bahamas Certain countries provide bank secrecy laws that protect the identity of depositors from disclosure. The Bahamas have such a law where many of its chartered "banks" are no more than a lawyer's office in an office building. Who do you think uses these bank accounts?

Contemporary Business Environment

FEDERAL ANTITERRORISM ACT OF 2001

The devastating suicide attack on the World Trade Center in New York and the Pentagon in Washington, DC, on September 11, 2001 shocked the nation. The attacks were organized and orchestrated by terrorists who crossed nations' borders easily, secretly planned and prepared for the attacks undetected, and financed the attacks using money located in banks in the United States, Great Britain, and other countries.

In response, Congress held hearings investigating how to counter such terrorist activities. Congress enacted a new federal Antiterrorism Act that assists the government in detecting and preventing terrorist activities and investigating and prosecuting terrorists. The bill was signed into law by President Bush on October 26, 2001. The act contains the following main features.

- **Special Intelligence Court** The act authorizes a Special Intelligence Court to issue expanded wiretap

orders and subpoenas to obtain evidence of suspected terrorism.
- **Nationwide Search Warrant** The act creates a nationwide search warrant to obtain evidence of terrorist activities. Previously, search warrants were limited to specific geographical locations.
- **Roving Wiretaps** The act permits "roving wiretaps" on a person suspected of involvement in terrorism so that any telephone or electronic device used by the person may be monitored. Previously, officials needed to obtain separate wiretap orders for each phone used by a suspect, which was ineffective against terrorists who used multiple telephones, including cellular phones.
- **Sharing of Information** The act permits evidence obtained during grand jury proceedings and evidence obtained by government law enforcement and intelligence agencies such as the Federal Bureau of Investigation (FBI), Central Intelligence Agency (CIA),

National Security Administration (NSA), Immigration and Naturalization Service (INS), U.S. Treasury Department, and other government agencies, to be shared among the agencies. Previously, sharing of such information was restricted.

- **Detention of Noncitizens** The act gives the federal government authority to detain a nonresident in the United States for up to seven days without filing charges against that person if he or she is certified by the U.S. attorney general as being under suspicion of involvement in terrorist activities. Nonresidents who are certified by a court as a threat to national security may be held for up to six months without a trial. Aliens who raise funds for terrorist organizations may be deported.
- **Bioterrorism Provision** The act makes it illegal for people or groups to possess substances that can be used as biological or chemical weapons for any purpose besides a "peaceful" one.
- **Anti-Money Laundering Provisions** The act includes several provisions to discover, trace, and impound bank

accounts used to fund terrorist activities. The act requires U.S. banks to determine sources of large overseas private bank accounts. Banks that refuse to disclose information on such accounts to U.S. investigators are subject to sanctions, including loss of its license to conduct banking operations. The U.S. Treasury Department may cut off all dealings in the United States of foreign banking institutions located in nations with bank secrecy laws that refuse to disclose information on bank accounts to U.S. investigators. American banks are barred from doing business with offshore shell banks that have no connection to any regulated banking industry.

Proponents of the federal Antiterrorism Act argue that the new investigative and other powers granted by the act are necessary to give law enforcement and intelligence agencies tools necessary to detect and prevent terrorist activities and to investigate and prosecute terrorists. Critics of the act argue that civil liberties and many constitutional freedoms are trampled on by the provisions of the act.

CHAPTER SUMMARY

Definition of a Crime, p. 122

Specifics of a Criminal Trial	1. The accused is *presumed innocent until proven guilty*. 2. The plaintiff (the government) bears the *burden of proof*. 3. The government must prove *beyond a reasonable doubt* that the accused is guilty of the crime charged. 4. The accused does not have to testify against him- or herself.

Definition of a Crime	1. *Crime.* Any act done by a person in violation of those duties that he or she owes to society and for the breach of which the law provides a penalty.
	2. *Penal codes.* State and federal statutes that define many crimes. Criminal conduct is also defined in many *regulatory statutes*.
	3. Parties to a criminal lawsuit:
	   a. *Plaintiff.* The government, which is represented by the *prosecuting attorney* (or *prosecutor*).
	   b. *Defendant.* The person or business accused of the crime, who is represented by a *defense attorney*.

Classification of Crimes	1. *Felonies.* The most serious kinds of crimes. *Mala in se* (inherently evil). Usually punishable by imprisonment. 2. *Misdemeanors.* Less serious crimes. *Mala prohibita* (prohibited by society). Usually punishable by fine and/or imprisonment for less than one year. 3. *Violations.* Not a felony nor a misdemeanor. Generally punishable by a fine.
Elements of a Crime	Most crimes require that the following two elements be proven: 1. *Actus reus.* Guilty act. 2. *Mens rea.* Evil intent.

Criminal Procedure, p. 124

Pretrial Criminal Procedure	1. *Arrest.* Made pursuant to an *arrest warrant* based upon a showing of "probable cause," or, where permitted, by a *warrantless* arrest. 2. *Indictment or information.* Grand juries issue *indictments*; magistrates (judges) issue *informations*. These formally charge the accused with specific crimes. 3. *Arraignment.* The accused is informed of the charges against him or her and enters a *plea* in court. The plea may be *not guilty, guilty,* or *nolo contendere*. 4. *Plea bargaining.* The government and the accused may negotiate a settlement agreement wherein the accused agrees to admit to a lesser crime than charged.

| **Criminal Trial and Appeal** | 1. Criminal trial
  a. *Conviction.* Requires unanimous vote of the jury.
  b. *Innocent.* Requires unanimous vote of the jury.
  c. *Hung jury.* Nonunanimous vote of the jury. The government may prosecute the case again.
2. Appeal
  a. *Defendant.* May appeal his or her conviction.
  b. *Plaintiff (government).* May not appeal a verdict of innocent. |

Crimes Affecting Business, p. 127

| **Crimes Affecting Business** | 1. *Robbery.* The taking of personal property from another by fear or force.
2. *Burglary.* The unauthorized entering of a building to commit a felony.
3. *Larceny.* The wrongful taking of another's property other than from his person or building.
4. *Theft.* The wrongful taking of another's property, whether by robbery, burglary, or larceny.
5. *Receiving stolen property.* A person knowingly receives stolen property with the intent to deprive the rightful owner of that property.
6. *Arson.* The malicious and willful burning of another's building.
7. *Forgery.* Fraudulently making or altering a written document that affects the legal liability of another person.
8. *Extortion.* Threat to expose something about another person unless that person gives up money or property.
9. *Credit-card crimes.* The misappropriation or use of another person's credit card.
10. *Bad check legislation.* The making, drawing, or delivery of a check by a person when that person knows that there are insufficient funds in the account to cover the check. |

White-Collar Crimes, p. 129

| **White-Collar Crimes** | *White-collar crimes.* Crimes that are prone to be committed by businesspersons that involve cunning and trickery rather than physical force.
1. *Embezzlement.* The fraudulent conversion of property by a person to whom the property was *entrusted*.
2. *Criminal fraud.* Obtaining title to another's property through deception or trickery. Also called *false pretenses* or *deceit*.
3. *Mail fraud.* The use of mail to defraud another person.
4. *Wire fraud.* The use of wire (telephone or telegraph) to defraud another person.
5. *Bribery.* The offer of payment of money or property or something else of value in return for an unwarranted favor. The payor of a bribe is also guilty of the crime of bribery.
  a. *Commercial bribery* is the offer of a payment of a bribe to private persons and business. This is often referred to as a *kickback* or *payoff*.
  b. Bribery of public officials for an "official act" is a crime.
6. *Racketeer Influenced and Corrupt Organizations Act (RICO).* Makes it a federal crime to acquire or maintain an interest in, use income from, or conduct or participate in the affairs of an "enterprise" through a "pattern" of "racketeering activity." Criminal penalties include the *forfeiture* of any property or business interests gained by a RICO violation. |

Inchoate Crimes, p. 134

| **Inchoate Crimes** | *Inchoate crimes.* Crimes that are incomplete or that are committed by nonparticipants.
1. *Criminal conspiracy.* When two or more persons enter into an *agreement* to commit a crime and take some *overt act* to further the crime.
2. *Attempt to commit a crime.* The attempt to commit a crime is a crime even if the commission of the intended crime is unsuccessful.
3. *Aiding and abetting the commission of a crime.* Rendering support, assistance, or encouragement to the commission of a crime, or knowingly harboring a criminal after he or she has committed a crime. |

Corporate Criminal Liability, p. 136

| **Corporate Criminal Liability** | 1. Corporate directors, officers, and employees are criminally liable for crimes they commit for personal benefit or on behalf of the corporation.
2. A corporation is criminally liable for crimes committed by directors, officers, and employees while acting on behalf of the corporation. |

Constitutional Safeguards, p. 136

Fourth Amendment Protection Against Unreasonable Searches and Seizures	Protects persons and corporations from *unreasonable searches and seizures*.
	1. *Reasonable searches and seizures* based on *probable cause* are lawful.
	   a. *Search warrant*. Stipulates the place and scope of the search.
	   b. *Warrantless search*. Permitted only:
	      i. Incident to an arrest.
	      ii. Where evidence is in plain view.
	      iii. Where it is likely that evidence will be destroyed.
	2. *Exclusionary rule*. Evidence obtained from an unreasonable search and seizure is *tainted evidence* that may not be introduced at a government proceeding against the person searched.
	3. *Business premises*. Protected by the Fourth Amendment, except that certain *regulated industries* may be subject to warrantless searches authorized by statute.

Fifth Amendment Privilege Against Self-Incrimination	*Privilege against self-incrimination*. Provides that no person "shall be compelled in any criminal case to be a witness against himself." A person asserting this privilege is said to have taken the Fifth.
	1. *Nontestimonial evidence*. This evidence (e.g., fingerprints, body fluids, etc.) is not protected.
	2. *Businesses*. The privilege applies only to natural persons; businesses cannot assert the privilege.
	3. *Miranda rights*. A criminal suspect must be informed of his or her Fifth Amendment rights before the suspect can be interrogated by the police or government officials.
	4. *Immunity from prosecution*. Granted by the government to obtain otherwise privileged evidence. The government agrees not to use the evidence given against the person who gave it.
	5. *Attorney-client privilege*. An accused's lawyer cannot be called as a witness against the accused.
	6. *Other privileges*. The following privileges have been recognized, with some limitations:
	   a. Psychiatrist/psychologist-patient
	   b. Priest/minister/rabbi-penitent
	   c. Spouse-spouse
	   d. Parent-child
	7. *Accountant-client privilege*. None recognized at the federal level. Some states recognize this privilege in state law actions.

Fifth Amendment Protection Against Double Jeopardy Sixth Amendment Right to a Public Jury Trial	Protects persons from being tried twice by the same jurisdiction for the same crime. If the act violates the laws of two or more jurisdictions, each jurisdiction may try the accused. Guarantees criminal defendants the follwing rights: 1. To be tried by an impartial jury. 2. To confront the witness. 3. To have the assistance of a lawyer. 4. To have a speedy trial.
Eighth Amendment Protection Against Cruel and Unusual Punishment	Protects criminal defendants from cruel and unusual punishment. Capital punishment is permitted.

END-OF-CHAPTER INTERNET EXERCISES AND CASE QUESTIONS

Working the Web Internet Exercises

ACTIVITIES

1. Check on the U.S. Department of Justice web page for information about computer-related crimes **www. usdoj.gov/criminal**.

2. **www.hg.org/crime.html** See this site for a comprehensive list of criminal law resources. Find the listing for your jurisdiction and research state laws relating to white-collar crime.

3. As for international crime, see **www.usinfo.state.gov/ usa/infousa/laws/majorlaw/fcpa.htm** regarding the U.S. Foreign Corrupt Practices Act. Compare that legislation with the OECD approach at **www.law. Vanderbilt.edu/journal/32-5-2.html**.

CRITICAL LEGAL THINKING CASES

5.1 Criminal Liability of Corporations Representatives of hotels, restaurants, hotel and restaurant supply companies, and other businesses located in Portland, Oregon, organized an association to attract conventions to their city. Members were asked to make contributions equal to 1 percent of their sales to finance the association. To aid collections, hotel members, including Hilton Hotels Corporation, agreed to give preferential treatment to suppliers who paid their assessments and to curtail purchases from those who did not. This agreement violated federal antitrust laws. The United States sued the members of the association, including Hilton Hotels, for the crime of violating federal antitrust laws. Can a corporation be held criminally liable for the acts of its representatives? If so, what criminal penalties can be assessed against the corporation? [*United States v. Hilton Hotels Corp.*, 467 F.2d 1000 (9th Cir. 1973)]

5.2 Criminal Liability for Acts of Subordinates Acme Markets, Inc., is a national retail food chain with approximately 36,000 employees working in 874 retail stores and 16 warehouses. Mr. Park is the president and chief executive officer of the corporation. In April 1970, the FDA inspected Acme's Philadelphia warehouse and found unsanitary conditions, including rodent infestation. The FDA advised Mr. Park by letter of these conditions and demanded that they be corrected. In 1971, the FDA found that similar conditions existed at the warehouse. It again notified Park to correct the situation. An FDA inspection in March 1972 still showed unsanitary conditions and rodent infestation at the warehouse. Evidence showed that corporate employees did not take appropriate actions to correct this situation. The federal Food, Drug, and Cosmetic Act makes individuals, as well as corporations, criminally liable for violations of the act. The United States brought a criminal action against Mr. Park for the violations. Can a corporate officer such as Mr. Park be held criminally liable for actions of his subordinates? [*United States v. Park*, 421 U.S. 658, 95 S.Ct. 658, 44 L.Ed.2d 489 (1974)]

5.3 Receiving Stolen Property In December 1982, Whitehead bought a stereo from his friend, Walter Gibbs, for between $10 and $40. When Whitehead first saw the stereo, it was one of three in Gibb's home. Whitehead knew that the stereo was new and was worth between $169 and $189. The stereo system, identified as one stolen in late 1982 from the J. C. Penney Warehouse, was found by police officers in Whitehead's bedroom on January 27, 1983. The serial number on the stereo had been scratched out. Is Whitehead guilty of any crime? Explain. [*Whitehead v. State of Georgia*, 313 S.E.2d 775 (Ga. App. 1984)]

5.4 Forgery Evidence showed that there was a burglary in which a checkbook belonging to Mary J. Harris, doing business as The Report Department, and a check encoder machine were stolen. Two of the checks from that checkbook were cashed at the Citizens & Southern National Bank branch office in Riverdale, Georgia, by Joseph Leon Foster, who was accompanied by a woman identified as Angela Foxworth. The bank teller who cashed the checks testified that the same man and

woman cashed the checks on two different occasions at her drive-up window at the bank and that on both occasions they were in the same car. Each time the teller wrote the license tag number of the car on the back of the check. The teller testified that both times the checks and the driver's license used to identify the woman were passed to her by the man driving, and that the man received the money from her. What crime has been committed? [*Foster v. State of Georgia*, 387 S.E.2d 637 (Ga. App. 1989)]

5.5 Extortion On February 3, 1987, the victim (Mr. X) went to the premises at 42 Taylor Terrace in New Milford, Connecticut, where his daughter and her husband lived. Lisa Percoco, who was Gregory Erhardt's girlfriend, was at the residence. Mr. X and Percoco were in the bedroom, partially dressed, engaging in sexual activity, when Erhardt entered the room and photographed them. He then informed Mr. X that unless he procured $5,000 and placed it in a mailbox at a designated address by 8 P.M. that night, Erhardt would show the photographs to Mr. X's wife. Mr. X proceeded to make telephone arrangements for the procurement and placement of the money according to Erhardt's instructions. If the money were paid, what crime would have been committed? [*State of Connecticut v. Erhardt*, 553 A.2d 188 (Conn. App. 1989)]

5.6 Credit-Card Fraud Remi Olu Abod, a Nigerian national, obtained a VISA credit card that bore the name "Norman Skinner" from a supplier. Abod purchased a counterfeit international driving permit bearing the name Norman Skinner at a passport photo shop in California. On June 27, 1984, Abod traveled from Los Angeles, California, to Corpus Christi, Texas. He first used the credit card to obtain $2,400 in cash from each of two blanks. He next appeared at the jewelry counter at Dillard's Department Store and tried to purchase jewelry worth $2,335 with the credit card. When the store employee telephoned the VISA credit authorization center for approval, he was informed that the card was counterfeit. Corpus Christi police were summoned to the store, where they arrested Abod. What crime did Abod commit? [*United States v. Abod*, 770 F.2d 1293 (5th Cir. 1985)]

5.7 Criminal Fraud In 1978, Miriam Marlowe's husband purchased a life insurance policy on his own life, naming her as the beneficiary. After Marlowe's husband died in a swimming accident in July 1981, she received payment on the policy. Marlowe later met John Walton, a friend of a friend. He convinced her and her representative that he had a friend who worked for the State Department and had access to gold in Brazil, and that the gold could be purchased in Brazil for $100 an ounce and sold in the United States for $300 an ounce. Walton convinced Miriam to invest $25,000. Instead of investing the money in gold in Brazil, Walton opened an account at Tracy Collins Bank in the name of Jeffrey McIntyre Roberts and deposited Miriam's money in that account. He later withdrew the money in cash. What crime is Walton guilty of? [*State of Utah v. Roberts*, 711 P.2d 235 (UT 1985)]

5.8 Embezzlement   Marty W. Orr was employed as a deputy treasurer and bookkeeper in the treasurer's office of Washington County, Virginia. She was responsible for computing each day's revenue and depositing funds received on a daily basis. During the course of her work, she took cash totaling several thousand dollars. What crime has she committed? [*Orr v. Commonwealth of Virginia*, 344 S.E.2d 627 (Va. App. 1986)]

5.9 Bribery   In 1979, the city of Peoria, Illinois, received federal funds from the Department of Housing and Urban Development (HUD) to be used for housing rehabilitation assistance. The city of Peoria designated United Neighborhoods, Inc. (UNI), a corporation, to administer the funds. Arthur Dixon was UNI's executive director and James Lee Hinton was its housing rehabilitation coordinator. In these capacities, they were responsible for contracting with suppliers and tradespeople to provide the necessary goods and services to rehabilitate the houses. Evidence showed that Dixon and Hinton used their positions to extract 10 percent payments back on all contracts they awarded. What crime have they committed? [*Dixon and Hinton v. United States*, 465 U.S. 482, 104 S.Ct. 1172, 79 L.Ed.2d 458 (1984)].

5.10 Attempt to Commit a Crime   Mary G. Smith's MasterCard credit card was in her purse when it was stolen in June 1985. On June 28, 1985, Beulah Houston entered a Ventura store located in Griffith, Indiana, and indicated to the manager of the jewelry department that she wished to purchase a man's watch. After making a selection, Houston handed the manager a MasterCard bearing the name Mary G. Smith. Upon contacting the bank for authorization, the manager was told to hold the card. Houston then left the store and was later arrested. Can Houston be convicted of attempt to commit credit-card fraud? [*Houston v. State of Indiana*, 528 N.E.2d 818 (Ind. App. 1988)]

5.11 Administrative Search   Lee Stuart Paulson owns the liquor license for "My House," a bar in San Francisco. The California Department of Alcoholic Beverage Control is the administrative agency that regulates bars in that state. The California Business and Professions Code, which the department administers, prohibits "any kind of illegal activity on licensed premises." On February 11, 1988, an anonymous informer tipped the department that narcotic sales were occurring on the premises of "My House" and that the narcotics were kept in a safe behind the bar on the premises. A special department investigator entered the bar during its hours of operation, identified himself, and informed Paulson that he was conducting an inspection. The investigator, who did not have a search warrant, opened the safe without seeking Paulson's consent. Twenty-two bundles of cocaine, totaling 5.5 grams, were found in the safe. Paulson was arrested. At his criminal trial, Paulson challenged the lawfulness of the search. Was the warrantless search of the safe a lawful search? [*People v. Paulson*, 216 Cal.App.3d 1480, 265 Cal.Rptr. 579 (Cal. App. 1990)]

5.12 Search Warrant   The Center Art Galleries-Hawaii sells artwork. Approximately 20 percent of its business involves art by Salvador Dali. The federal government, which suspected the center of fraudulently selling forged Dali artwork, obtained identical search warrants for six locations controlled by the center. The warrants commanded the executing officer to seize items which were "evidence of violations of federal criminal law." The warrants did not describe the specific crimes suspected and did not stipulate that only items pertaining to the sale of Dali's work could be seized. There was no evidence of any criminal activity unrelated to that artist. Is the search warrant valid? [*Center Art Galleries-Hawaii, Inc. v. United States*, 875 F.2d 747 (9th Cir. 1989)]

5.13 Fifth Amendment's Privilege Against Self-Incrimination   John Doe is the owner of several sole-proprietorship businesses. In 1980, during the course of an investigation of corruption in awarding county and municipal contracts, a federal grand jury served several subpoenas on John Doe demanding the production of certain business records. The subpoenas demanded the production of the following records: (1) general ledgers and journals, (2) invoices, (3) bank statements and canceled checks, (4) financial statements, (5) telephone-company records, (6) safe-deposit box records, and (7) copies of tax returns. John Doe filed a motion in federal court seeking to quash the subpoenas, alleging that producing these business records would violate his Fifth Amendment privilege of not testifying against himself. Do the records have to be disclosed? [*United States v. John Doe*, 465 U.S. 605, 104 S.Ct. 1237, 79 L.Ed.2d 552 (1984)]

BUSINESS ETHICS CASES

5.14 Business Ethics   R. Foster Winans was a reporter for the *Wall Street Journal* from 1981 through 1984, during which time he wrote a column called "Heard on the Street." In the column, Winans would discuss the future prospects of companies and their securities. Evidence showed that positive comments would make the company's stock increase in value; negative comments would have the opposite result. Winans systematically leaked the contents of his future "Heard" columns prior to publication to Peter Brant, a stockbroker, in exchange for a share of the profits made by Brant. Upon discovery, Winans was convicted of wire and mail fraud, which are federal crimes. The crimes were committed within the state of New York. In September 1985, Winans entered into a book publishing contract with St. Martin's Press, and in 1988, St. Martin's published Winan's book *Trading Secrets*. The book details Winan's own actions that resulted in his federal conviction for insider trading. New York had previously adopted a "Son of Sam" law. The New York State Crimes Victims Board moved for an order directing St. Martin's to turn over the royalties due Winans, which would be deposited in an escrow account and held for the benefit of and payable to any victims of Winans's crimes. Who is legally entitled to the royalties? Is it ethical for a convicted criminal to make money by selling the media rights to the story about the crime? [*St. Martin's Press v. Zweibel, N.Y. Law Journal*, 2/26/90 (N.Y. Sup. 1990)].

5.15 Business Ethics   In 1979, Leo Shaw, an attorney, entered into a partnership agreement with three other persons to build and operate an office building. From the outset, it was agreed that Shaw's role was to manage the operation of the building. Management of the property was Shaw's contribution to the partnership; the other three partners contributed the necessary capital. In January 1989, the other partners discovered that the loan on the building was in default and that foreclosure proceedings were imminent. Upon investigation, they discovered that

Shaw had taken approximately $80,000 from the partnership's checking account. After heated discussions, Shaw repaid $13,000. In May 1989, when no further payment was forthcoming, a partner filed a civil suit against Shaw and notified the police. The state filed a criminal complaint against Shaw on March 15, 1990. On April 3, 1990, Shaw repaid the remaining funds as part of a civil settlement. At his criminal trial in November 1990, Shaw argued that the repayment of the money was a defense to the crime of embezzlement. Did Shaw act ethically in this case? Would your answer be different if he had really only "borrowed" the money and had intended to return it? [*People v. Shaw*, 10 Cal. App.4th 969, 12 Cal.Rptr.2d 665 (Cal. App. 1992)]

BRIEFING THE CASE WRITING ASSIGNMENT

Read the following case, which has been excerpted from the court's opinions. Review and brief the case.

Schalk v. Texas
823 S. W.2d 633 (1991)
Court of Criminal Appeals of Texas

Miller, Judge

Appellants Schalk and Leonard are former employees of Texas Instruments (hereafter TI). Both men have doctoral degrees and specialized in the area of speech research at TI. Schalk resigned his position with TI in April 1983 to join a newly developed company, Voice Control Systems (hereafter VCS). In February 1985, Leonard resigned from TI and joined VCS. Several TI employees eventually joined the ranks of VCS. Speech research was the main thrust of the research and development performed by VCS. In fact, VCS was a competitor of TI in this field. In April 1985 Sam Kuzbary, then employed with VCS and a former TI employee, noticed some information which he believed to be proprietary to TI stored in the memory of the computer he was using at VCS. Kuzbary contacted TI and agreed to serve as an "informant" for them.

He then searched the premises of VCS and photographed materials which he recognized from his employment with TI. A TI internal investigation revealed that a few hours prior to Schalk's and Leonard's departures from TI, each appellant, utilizing TI computers, copied the entire contents of the directories respectively assigned to them. This information included computer programs which TI claimed to be its trade secrets. Officials of TI then contacted the Dallas District Attorney's office. A search of the premises of VCS resulted in the seizure of computer tapes containing the alleged TI trade secret programs from appellants' offices. Appellants were arrested.

We granted review to consider, first, whether the evidence was sufficient to establish that the computer programs named in the indictments were trade secrets, and second, to determine whether the items listed in the search warrant were sufficiently described so as to preclude a general exploratory search.

Having determined that computer programs are proper subjects for trade secret litigation under Texas civil and criminal law, we now look to the case sub judice to determine whether the programs which appellants copied and took with them to VCS are trade secrets as defined by §31.05 of the Penal Code.

§31.05 Theft of trade secrets:
(a) For the purpose of this section:
(4) "Trade secret" means the whole or any part of any scientific or technical information, design, process, procedure, formula, or improvement that has value and that the owner has taken measures to prevent from becoming available to persons other than those selected by the owner to have access for limited purposes.

Appellants claimed on appeal that the programs did not meet the statutory trade secrets criteria because they alleged their former employer TI failed to take "measures to prevent [the information] from becoming available to persons other than those selected by the owner." We note, as did the court of appeals, that the statute sets no standards for degree of sufficiency of the "measures" taken. Specifically, appellants pointed to considerable disclosure of speech research information, citing the "academic environment" of the laboratory in which they worked as encouraging the sharing of information, rather than maintaining secrecy. Appellants also claimed that TI policy favored protection of its research and development efforts through the patent process, as opposed to trade secret designation. Further, appellants allege that the programs that are the subject of the instant case were not listed in the TI register of trade secrets and that TI was lax in implementing its standard procedures with regard to notifying employees of trade secrets within the company. The precise issue before us in the case sub judice is one of the first impression in Texas, to wit: What constitutes requisite "measures" to protect trade secret status?

We now determine whether the information disclosed with TI's permission or encouragement, such as published articles, seminar papers, speeches given at public meetings, information provided to government agencies, etc., was so extensive as to destroy any trade secret status that may have existed regarding the computer software which is the subject of the instant indictments. It is axiomatic that the core element of a trade secret must be that it remain a secret. However, absolute secrecy is not required.

A trade secret can exist in a combination of characteristics and components, each of which, by itself, is in the public domain, but the unified process and operation of which, in unique combination, affords a competitive advantage and is a protectable secret. We find based on the record in this case that the limited disclosure made by TI in regard to the speech research lab activities merely described the application and configuration of the certain elements of the software but did not reveal the actual composition of the programs. The measures used by TI to secure its premises to prevent unauthorized personnel from admission to or exposure to its proprietary research data were reasonable under the circumstances.

We need not decide today whether any one of the preventive measures listed, standing alone, is factually sufficient to support trade secret status. We do find that the combination of employment agreements, strict plant security, restricted computer access, the nonauthorization of disclosure of the subject programs and the general nondisclosure of those programs by TI and its

employees served to support trade secret status of the computer programs that are the subject of the instant indictments. Appellants neither requested nor received permission to copy the files containing these programs. The unauthorized copying of the article representing a trade secret constitutes an offense under V.T.C.A. Penal Code $31.05(b)(2).

Therefore we affirm the court of appeals' ruling that the subject programs are trade secrets.

ENDNOTES

1. Title 18 of the U.S. Code contains the federal criminal code.
2. Sentencing Reform Act of 1984, 18 U.S.C. § 3551 et. seq. The sentencing guidelines for federal crimes, which were promulgated by the U.S. Sentencing Commission, became effective on November 1, 1987.
3. 18 U.S.C. § 1341.
4. 18 U.S.C. § 1343.
5. *United States v. Leon*, 468 U.S. 897, 104 S.Ct. 3405, 82 L.Ed.2d 677 (1984).
6. *Marshall v. Barlow's Inc.*, 436 U.S. 307, 98 S.Ct. 1816, 56 L.Ed.2d 305 (1978).
7. *Bellis v. United States*, 417 U.S. 85, 94 S.Ct. 2179, 40 L.Ed.2d 678 (1974).
8. The Speedy Trial Act requires that a criminal defendant be brought to trial within 70 days after indictment [18 U.S.C. § 3161(c)(1)]. Continuances may be granted by the court to serve the "ends of justice."
9. *Baldwin v. Alabama*, 472 U.S. 372, 105 S.Ct. 2727, 86 L.Ed.2d 300 (1985).

CHAPTER 6

International and Comparative Law

International law, or the law that governs between nations, has at times been like the common law within states, a twilight existence during which it is hardly distinguishable from morality or justice, till at length the imprimatur of a court attests its jural quality.

—Justice Cardozo
New Jersey v. Delaware, 291 U.S. 361, 54 S.Ct. 407, 78 L.Ed. 847 (1934)

Chapter Objectives

After studying this chapter, you should be able to:

1. Describe the federal government's power under the Foreign Commerce and Treaty Clauses of the U.S. Constitution.

2. List and describe the sources of international law.

3. Describe the functions and governance of the United Nations.

4. Describe the North American Free Trade Agreement (NAFTA) and other regional economic organizations.

5. Describe the United States–China trade port.

6. Describe international intellectual property rights provided by Internet treaties.

7. Describe the act of state doctrine and the doctrine of sovereign immunity.

8. Describe the World Trade Organization (WTO) and explain how its dispute resolution procedure works.

9. Describe the arbitration of international disputes.

10. List and describe international e-commerce and Internet laws.

Chapter Contents

international law

Law that governs affairs between nations and that regulates transactions between individuals and businesses of different countries.

International Brief

International trade is increasing in importance for the United States and other countries of the world.

International law, important to both nations and businesses, has many unique features. First, there is no single legislative source of international law. All countries of the world and numerous international organizations are responsible for enacting international laws. Second, there is no single world court that is responsible for interpreting international law. There are, however, several courts or tribunals that hear and decide international legal disputes of parties that agree to appear before them. Third, there is no world executive branch that can enforce international laws. Thus, nations do not have to obey international law enacted by other countries or international organizations. Because of these uncertainties, some commentators question whether international law is really "law."

As technology and transportation bring nations closer together and American and foreign firms increase their global activities, international law will become even more important to governments and businesses. This chapter introduces the main concepts of international law and discusses the sources of international law and the organizations responsible for its administration.

*T*HE UNITED STATES AND FOREIGN AFFAIRS

The U.S. Constitution divides the power to regulate the internal affairs of this country between the federal and state governments. On the international level, however, the Constitution gives most of the power to the federal government. The following two constitutional provisions are the ones that establish this authority.

Foreign Commerce Clause

Clause of the U.S. Constitution that vests Congress with the power "to regulate commerce with foreign nations."

Treaty Clause

Clause of the U.S. Constitution that states the president "shall have the power . . . to make treaties, provided two-thirds of the senators present concur."

- **Foreign Commerce Clause**   Article I, Section 8, clause 3 vests Congress with the power "to regulate commerce with foreign nations."
- **Treaty Clause**   Article II, Section 2, clause 2 states that the president "shall have power, by and with the advice and consent of the Senate, to make treaties, provided two-thirds of the senators present concur."

The Constitution does not vest exclusive power over foreign affairs in the federal government, but any state or local law that unduly burdens foreign commerce is unconstitutional under the Commerce Clause. Under the Treaty Clause, only the federal government may enter into treaties with foreign nations. Under the Supremacy Clause of the Constitution, treaties become part of the "law of the land" and conflicting state or local law is void. The president is the agent of the United States in dealing with foreign countries.

The Supreme Court Speaks

Massachusetts' "Burma" Law Struck Down

Crosby, Secretary of Administration and Finance of Massachusetts v. National Foreign Trade Council
530 U.S. 363, 120 S.Ct. 2288 (2000)
2000 U.S. Lexis 4153
Supreme Court of the United States

BACKGROUND AND FACTS

The military regime of the country of Burma (renamed "Myanmar" in 1989) has been accused of major civil-rights violations, including using forced and child labor, imprisoning and torturing political opponents, and harshly repressing ethnic minorities. These inhuman actions have been condemned by human-rights organizations around the world.

The state legislators in the state of Massachusetts were so appalled at these actions that in June 1996 they enacted a state statute banning the state government from purchasing goods and services from any company that did business with Burma. In the meantime, Congress enacted its own federal statute that delegated power to the president to regulate the United States' dealings with Burma. The federal statute (1) banned all aid to the Burmese government except for humanitarian assistance, (2) authorized the president to impose economic sanctions against Burma, and (3) authorized the president to develop a comprehensive multilateral strategy to bring democracy to Burma. The National Foreign Trade Council (Council)—a powerful Washington, DC–based trade association with over 500 member companies—filed a lawsuit against Massachusetts to have the state law declared unconstitutional. The Council argued that the Massachusetts' "anti-Burma" statute was pre-empted by the Supremacy Clause of the U.S. Constitution that makes federal law the "supreme law of the land" and the federal government's power to regulate foreign affairs. The district court and court of appeals ruled in favor of the Council. The U.S. Supreme Court agreed to hear Massachusetts' appeal.

SUPREME COURT ISSUE

Does the Massachusetts' "anti-Burma" state statute violate the Supremacy Clause of the U.S. Constitution?

IN THE LANGUAGE OF THE U.S. SUPREME COURT

Within the sphere defined by Congress, then, the federal statute has placed the president in a position with as much discretion to exercise economic leverage against Burma, with an eye toward national security, as our law will admit. And it is just this plenitude of executive authority that we think controls the issue of preemption here. The president has been given this authority not merely to make a political statement but to achieve a political result, and the fullness of his authority shows the importance in the congressional mind of reaching that result. It is simply implausible that Congress would have gone to such lengths to empower the president if it had been willing to compromise his effectiveness by deference to every provision of state statute or local ordinance that might, if enforced, blunt the consequences of discretionary presidential action.

We find it unlikely that Congress intended both to enable the president to protect national security by giving him the flexibility to suspend or terminate federal sanctions and simultaneously to allow Massachusetts to act at odds with the president's judgment of what national security requires. And that is just what the Massachusetts Burma law would do in imposing a different, state system of economic pressure against the Burmese political regime. This unyielding application undermines the president's intended statutory authority by making it impossible for him to restrain fully the coercive power of the national economy when he may choose to take the discretionary action open to him, whether he believes that the national interest requires sanctions to be lifted, or believes that the promise of lifting sanctions would move the Burmese regime in the democratic direction. Quite simply, if the Massachusetts law is enforceable the president has less to offer and less economic and diplomatic leverage as a consequence.

DECISION AND REMEDY

The U.S. Supreme Court affirmed the court of appeals, finding that the Massachusetts anti-Burma law conflicted with and was therefore preempted by the Supremacy Clause of the Constitution.

CASE QUESTIONS

Critical Legal Thinking Should the federal government have sole power to regulate the foreign affairs of the United States? Or should the states share in this power?

Business Ethics Do you think companies that have goods manufactured in Burma violate any ethical principles? Explain.

Contemporary Business Did the Massachusetts anti-Burma law have any economic implications for business? What would have been the consequences if the U.S. Supreme Court had held that the Massachusetts anti-Burma statute was lawful?

SOURCES OF INTERNATIONAL LAW

The **sources of international law** are those things that international tribunals rely on in deciding international disputes. **Article 38(1) of the Statute of the International Court of Justice** lists the following four sources of international law: *treaties and conventions, custom, general principles of law,* and *judicial decisions and teachings.* Most courts rely on the hierarchy suggested by this list; that is, treaties and conventions are turned to before custom, and so on. Each of these sources of law is discussed in the following paragraphs.

sources of international law
Those things that international tribunals rely on in settling international disputes.

Indonesia The federal government of the United States has exclusive power to regulate commerce with foreign nations.

treaties

The first source of international law, consisting of agreements or contracts between two or more nations that are formally signed by an authorized representative and ratified by the supreme power of each nation.

convention

Treaty that is sponsored by an international organization.

Treaties and Conventions

Treaties and conventions are the equivalents of legislation at the international level. A **treaty** is an agreement or contract between two or more nations that is formally signed by an authorized representative and ratified by the supreme power of each nation. *Bilateral treaties* are between two nations; *multilateral treaties* involve more than two nations. **Conventions** are treaties that are sponsored by international organizations, such as the United Nations. Conventions normally have many signatories.

Treaties and conventions address such matters as human rights, foreign aid, navigation, commerce, and the settlement of disputes. Most treaties are registered with and published by the United Nations.

E-Commerce & Information Technology

WORLD INTELLECTUAL PROPERTY ORGANIZATION (WIPO) INTERNET TREATIES

In 1967, the United Nations (UN) created the **World Intellectual Property Organization (WIPO)**. WIPO is a special agency of the UN that administers international intellectual property conventions and treaties. Over 160 nations are members of WIPO. WIPO administers over 20 major conventions and treaties affecting intellectual property, including the Paris Convention of 1883 that provides international patent and trademark protection and the Berne Convention of 1886 that provides international copyright protection. The United States is a signatory to both of these conventions. In addition to administering existing conventions and treaties, WIPO develops and adopts new conventions and treaties.

WIPO convened its members in 1996 to address the impact that the new digital technologies and the Internet were having on intellectual property rights. The goal of the delegation was to conclude new conventions that would cover and expand copyright and intellectual property protection in the digital environment. After much negotiation,

WIPO issued two new conventions collectively called the **Internet Treaties**. The two conventions are:

- **Copyright Treaty** This treaty grants copyright protection to computer programs and data compilations, protects the rights of copyright holders to make their works available on the Internet or by any other wire or wireless means, and extends copyright protection to rentals and means of distribution in addition to sale transactions.
- **Phonogram Treaty** This treaty provides protection to performers and producers by giving them exclusive rights to broadcast, reproduce, distribute, and rent copies of their performances using any type of media including video recordings, satellite transmissions, digital sound, and encrypted signals.

These two WIPO treaties go far to create new intellectual property rights and to grant protection to copyright holders over the Internet and in the digital marketplace. The United States signed the final act of the convention.

---

custom

The second source of international law, created through consistent, recurring practices between two or more nations over a period of time that have become recognized as binding.

International Brief

Even customs that have not been elevated to the level of international law are still vitally important to the conduct of transnational business.

general principles of law

The third source of international law, consisting of principles of law recognized by civilized nations. These are principles of law that are common to the national law of the parties to the dispute.

Custom

Custom between nations is an independent source of international law. Custom describes a practice followed by two or more nations when dealing with each other. It may be found in official government statements, diplomatic correspondence, policy statements, press releases, speeches, and the like. Two elements must be established to show that a practice has become a custom:

1. Consistent and recurring action by two or more nations over a considerable period of time.
2. Recognition that the custom is binding—that is, followed because of legal obligation rather than courtesy.

International customs evolve as mores, technology, forms of government, political parties, and other factors change throughout the world. Customs that have been recognized for some period of time are often codified in treaties.

General Principles of Law

Courts and tribunals that decide international disputes frequently rely on **general principles of law** that are recognized by civilized nations. These are principles of law that are common to the *national* law of the parties to the dispute. They may be derived from constitutions, statutes, regulations, common law, or other sources of national law. In some cases, however, the countries' laws may differ concerning the matter in dispute.

Judicial Decisions and Teachings

A fourth source of law to which international tribunals can refer is **judicial decisions and teachings** of the most qualified scholars of the various nations involved in the dispute. Although international courts are not bound by the doctrine of *stare decisis* and may decide each case on its own merits, the courts often refer to their own past decisions for guidance. Court decisions of national courts do not create precedent for international courts.

judicial decisions and teachings

The fourth source of international law, consisting of judicial decisions and writings of the most qualified legal scholars of the various nations involved in the dispute.

International Law

COMITY: THE GOLDEN RULE AMONG NATIONS

Countries often grant courtesies to other countries that are not obligations of law but are based on respect, goodwill, and civility. The extension of such courtesies is referred to as the **principle of comity**. It is not a rule of law, but one of practice. The courts of the United States resort to the comity principle as a rationale for not applying U.S. law to foreign persons or situations where (1) concurrent jurisdiction exists with a foreign country and (2) foreign law is different from U.S. law. The following case is an example of the application of this doctrine.

Lee Wong, a U.S. citizen and California resident, was a produce grower who wanted to set up farming operations in Mexico. The Mexican Constitution, however, prohibited foreign ownership and control of farming operations. Therefore, Wong contracted with several Mexican citizens to act as "front men" for him to own and operate his farming operations in Mexico. Wong provided the money, and the front men acquired farming property in Mexico.

Wong entered into marketing contracts with a subsidiary of Tenneco, Inc. (Tenneco), a California corporation. Tenneco, with full knowledge of the nature of Wong's interest in the Mexican farming operations, purchased farm products from Wong. After several years, the Mexican government discovered Wong's interest and began threatening the front men with foreclosure and government action for nonpayment of taxes on the farming operation. In January 1975, Tenneco bowed to the demands of the front men and severed its ties with Wong. Tenneco began purchasing the farm produce directly from the front men. Wong sued Tenneco in California court to recover damages for breach of contract. The jury awarded Wong $1,691,422 in damages.

Tenneco argued that its contract with Wong violated Mexican law and therefore the United States should not enforce the contract. The California Supreme Court agreed and refused to enforce the jury's verdict. The court stated

A contract with a view of violating the laws of another country, though not otherwise obnoxious to the law of the forum, will not be enforced. Protection of persons, like Wong, who wrongfully seek to circumvent the substantive laws of one jurisdiction by enlisting the aid of the courts in another violates and offends public policy of both jurisdictions. In the interest of comity, our courts must vigilantly resist such recruitment efforts.

Applying principles of comity, we conclude that Wong's failure to comply with the requirements of Mexican law casts a pall of illegality over all of his business transactions tied to the Mexican farming operation, including the marketing arrangement with Tenneco. California public policy dictates that we leave the parties as we found them.

Adherence to the comity principle demonstrates nations' respect for the laws of other nations. It has been characterized as the golden rule among nations, and it will grow in importance as the number of international transactions increases. [*Wong v. Tenneco, Inc.*, 39 Cal.3d 126, 216 Cal.Rptr. 412 (CA 1985)]

The UNITED NATIONS

One of the most important international organizations is the **United Nations**, which was created by a multilateral treaty on October 24, 1945.[1] Most countries of the world are members of the United Nations. The goals of the United Nations (U.N.), which is headquartered in New York City, are to maintain peace and security in the world, promote economic and social cooperation, and protect human rights (see Exhibit 6.1).

United Nations

An international organization created by multilateral treaty in 1945 to promote social and economic cooperation among nations and to protect human rights.

*E*XHIBIT **6.1** *Selected Provisions from the Charter of the United Nations*

Our respective Governments, through representatives assembled in the city of San Francisco, who have exhibited their full powers found to be in good and due form, have agreed to the present Charter of the United Nations and do hereby establish an international organization to be known as the United Nations.

Chapter 1. Purposes and Principles

Article 1 The Purposes of the United Nations are:

(1) To maintain international peace and security, and to that end: to take effective collective measures for the prevention and removal of threats to the peace, and for the suppression of acts of aggression or other breaches of the peace, and to bring about by peaceful means, and in conformity with the principles of justice and international law, adjustment or settlement of international disputes or situations which might lead to a breach of the peace;

(2) To develop friendly relations among nations based on respect for the principle of equal rights and self-determination of peoples, and to take other appropriate measures to strengthen universal peace;

(3) To achieve international co-operation in solving international problems of an economic, social, cultural, or humanitarian character, and in promoting and encouraging respect for human rights and for fundamental freedoms for all without distinction as to race, sex, language, or religion; and

(4) To be a centre for harmonizing the actions of nations in the attainment of these common ends.

Article 2 The Organization and its Members, in pursuit of the Purposes stated in Article 1, shall act in accordance with the following Principles.

(1) The Organization is based on the principle of the sovereign equality of all its Members.

(2) All Members, in order to ensure to all of them the rights and benefits resulting from membership, shall fulfill in good faith the obligations assumed by them in accordance with the present Charter.

(3) All Members shall settle their international disputes by peaceful means in such a manner that international peace and security, and justice, are not endangered.

(4) All Members shall refrain in their international relations from the threat or use of force against the territorial integrity or political independence of any state, or in any other manner inconsistent with the Purposes of the United Nations.

(5) All Members shall give the United Nations every assistance in any action it takes in accordance with the present Charter, and shall refrain from giving assistance to any state against which the United Nations is taking preventive or enforcement action.

(6) The Organization shall ensure that states which are not Members of the United Nations act in accordance with these Principles so far as may be necessary for the maintenance of international peace and security.

Governance of the United Nations

The United Nations is governed by

- **The General Assembly** composed of all member nations. As the legislative body of the United Nations, it adopts resolutions concerning human rights, trade, finance and economics, and other matters within the scope of the U.N. Charter. Although resolutions have limited force, they are usually enforced through persuasion and the use of economic and other sanctions.
- **The Security Council** composed of 15 member nations, five of which are permanent members (China, France, Russia, the United Kingdom, and the United States) and ten other countries chosen by the members of the General Assembly to serve two-year terms. The council is primarily responsible for maintaining international peace and security and has authority to use armed forces.
- **The Secretariat** which administers the day-to-day operations of the United Nations. It is headed by the *Secretary-General*, who is elected by the General Assembly. The Secretary-General may refer matters that threaten international peace and security to the Security Council and use his office to help solve international disputes.

Only when the world is civilized enough to keep promises will we get any kind of international law.

Julius Henry Cohen (1946)

The United Nations is also composed of various autonomous agencies that deal with a wide range of economic and social problems. These include UNESCO (United Nations Educational, Scientific, and Cultural Organization), UNICEF (United Nations International Children's Emergency Fund), the IMF (International Monetary Fund), the World Bank, and IFAD (International Fund for Agricultural Development).

International Court of Justice

The **International Court of Justice** (ICJ), also called the **World Court**, is located in The Hague, the Netherlands. It is the judicial branch of the United Nations. Only nations, not individuals or businesses, may have cases decided by this court. The ICJ may hear cases that nations refer to it as well as cases involving treaties and the U.N. Charter. A nation may seek redress on behalf of an individual or business that has a claim against another country. The ICJ is composed of 15 judges who serve nine-year terms; not more than two judges may be from the same nation. A nation that is a party to a dispute before the ICJ may appoint one judge on an ad hoc basis for that case.

International Court of Justice

The judicial branch of the United Nations that is located in The Hague, the Netherlands. Also called the *World Court*.

Regional Courts

Various treaties have created regional courts to handle disputes among member nations. For example, most regional economic organizations have established courts to enforce provisions of their respective treaties and to solve disputes among member nations. Regional courts, however, usually do not have mechanisms to enforce their judgments.

International Law

HOLOCAUST VICTIMS' ASSET LITIGATION SETTLED

During World War II, the German Nazi regime engaged in years of persecution of Jews, including genocide, slave labor, and a wholesale and systematic looting of personal and business property of the Jewish victims. World War II ended in 1945 when the Allies defeated Germany and its Axis collaborators. During World War II, the European country of Switzerland remained neutral.

Switzerland has been a financial center to Europe for centuries. It is famous for its bank secrecy laws; that is, Swiss law protects the names and other information of depositors. Before and during the war, many Swiss banks held money and other property of Jews throughout Europe. And during the war, the Swiss banks obtained new clients—the Nazis—who stole their Jewish victims' property and placed it with the Swiss banks for safekeeping.

Over 50 years later, beginning in 1996, a series of class-action lawsuits were filed in U.S. district courts by the survivors of the Holocaust and their heirs against Union Bank of Switzerland and many other Swiss banks. The plaintiffs alleged that during World War II the Swiss banks knowingly retained, concealed, and laundered the money and assets of Holocaust victims stolen by the Nazis. The lawsuits also alleged that Swiss banks did not pay money back to the Jewish survivors or to the heirs of the deceased victims that was on deposit at the banks once World War II was over.

After substantial negotiations, the plaintiffs reached a settlement with the defendant Swiss banks. The defendants dropped their defense that the claims were time-barred and agreed to pay $1.25 billion into a Settlement Fund. In exchange, the plaintiffs agreed to release all further claims against the banks. The district court judge approved the Settlement Agreement. Ernest Lobet, a survivor of the Holocaust, commented about the settlement:

> *I have no quarrel with the settlement. I do not say it is fair, because fairness is a relative term. No amount of money can possibly be fair under those circumstances, but I'm quite sure it is the very best that could be done by the groups that negotiated for the settlement. The world is not perfect and the people that negotiated I'm sure tried their very best, and I think they deserve our cooperation and that they be supported and the settlement be approved.*

A procedure was established for the plaintiffs to make claims against the Settlement Fund. [*In re Holocaust Victim Asset Litigation*, 105 F.Supp.2d 139 (E.D.N.Y. 2000)]

INTERNATIONAL REGIONAL ORGANIZATIONS

There are several significant regional organizations whose members have agreed to work together to promote peace and security as well as economic, social, and cultural development. The most important of these organizations are discussed in the following paragraphs.

Islamic Mosque, Uzbekistan
Religious beliefs are often reflected in a nation's laws. For example, the Jewish, Hindu, and Islamic religions provide the basis for many nation's laws, such as those of Israel, India, and Egypt, respectively.

The European Union

European Union (Common Market)

Comprises many countries of Western Europe; created to promote peace and security plus economic, social, and cultural development.

One of the most important international regional organizations is the **European Union** (EU), formerly called the **European Community**, or **Common Market**. The EU was created in 1957. The EU is composed of many countries of Western Europe, including Belgium, France, Italy, Luxembourg, The Netherlands, Germany, Denmark, Ireland, the United Kingdom, Greece, Portugal, and Spain, which represent more than 300 million people and a gross community product that exceeds that of the United States and Canada combined.

The EU's **Council of Ministers** is composed of representatives from each member country who meet periodically to coordinate efforts to fulfill the objectives of the treaty. The council votes on significant issues and changes to the treaty. Some matters require unanimity, whereas others require only a majority vote. The member nations have surrendered substantial sovereignty to the EU. The EU **Commission**, which is independent of member nations, acts in the best interests of the union. The member nations have delegated substantial powers to the commission, including authority to enact legislation and to take enforcement actions to ensure member compliance with the treaty.

When Kansas and Colorado have a quarrel over the water in the Arkansas River they don't call out the National Guard in each state and go to war over it. They bring a suit in the Supreme Court of the United States and abide by the decision. There isn't a reason in the world why we cannot do that internationally.

Harry S. Truman Speech (1945)

The EU treaty creates open borders for trade by providing for the free flow of capital, labor, goods, and services among member nations. Under the EU, customs duties have been eliminated among member nations. Common customs tariffs have been established for EU trade with the rest of the world. A single monetary unit, the Euro, and common monetary policy have been introduced. An EU central bank equivalent to the U.S. Federal Reserve Board has been established.

A unanimous vote of existing EU members is needed to admit a new member. Other Western European and some Eastern European countries are expected to apply for and be admitted as members of the EU.

European Court of Justice

The judicial branch of the European Union, located in Luxembourg. It has jurisdiction to enforce European Union law.

European Court of Justice The **European Court of Justice**, located in Luxembourg, has jurisdiction to enforce European Union law. Each EU member country appoints one judge to the court for a six-year term. The court decides disputes concerning member nations' compliance with EU law. The court follows civil law (rather than common law) traditions. Thus, the court may call witnesses, order documents produced, and hire experts.

Member nations, EU institutions, and interested persons and businesses may bring actions before the court. Although national courts may interpret and enforce EU law, the European Court of Justice is the final arbiter of EU law. National courts are responsible for enforcing judgments of the European Court of Justice. Although the court's decisions are given great respect, the court has no means of enforcing its decisions against member nations.

An amendment to the Treaty of Rome created the **European Court of First Instance** (CFI), which is attached to the European Court. It has jurisdiction to hear actions brought by individuals and businesses. The purpose of the court is to relieve some of the European Court's caseload. The CFI started to hear cases in 1989.

Landmark Law

THE NORTH AMERICAN FREE TRADE AGREEMENT (NAFTA)

Mexico is a poor country with a population of about 90 million people. In the past, Mexico was dominated by government-run industries and protectionist laws. In the late 1980s, however, Mexico began a program to privatize its government-owned industries and to embrace capitalism.

In 1990, Mexican President Carlos Salinas de Gortari asked President George Bush to set up a two-country trade pact. Negotiations between the two countries began. Canada joined the negotiations eight months later, largely to make sure the United States did not undercut the earlier U.S.-Canada trade pact.

On August 12, 1992, after 14 months of arduous negotiations, the **North American Free Trade Agreement (NAFTA)** was signed by the leaders of the three countries. The treaty creates a free-trade zone stretching from the Yukon to the Yucatan, bringing together 360 million consumers in a $6.5-trillion market.

NAFTA eliminates or reduces most of the duties, tariffs, quotas, and other trade barriers between Mexico, the United States, and Canada. Agriculture, automobiles, computers, electronics, energy and petrochemicals, financial services, insurance, telecommunications, and many other industries are affected. The treaty contains a safety valve: A country can reimpose tariffs if an import surge from one of the other nations hurts its economy or workers.

Some of the major features of the treaty are:

- Mexican tariffs on vehicles and light trucks were cut in half immediately. Mexican trade barriers and restrictions on autos and auto parts are to be phased out over 10 years.
- All North American trade restrictions on textiles and apparel will be eliminated within 10 years.
- Banks and securities firms are allowed to establish wholly owned subsidiaries in all three countries.
- Mexican import licenses, which cover about 25 percent of U.S. exports, were dropped immediately, and remaining Mexican tariffs will be phased out over 15 years.
- Tariffs on import-sensitive American industries will be phased out over 15 years.
- Intellectual property rights, such as patents, trademarks, and copyrights, will receive increased protection.

The parties to NAFTA are the United States, Canada and Mexico.

Like other regional trading agreements, NAFTA allows the bloc to discriminate against outsiders and to cut deals among themselves. For example, only automobiles that consist of 62.5 percent North American content benefit from the treaty's tariff cuts.

NAFTA also includes special protection for favored industries with a lot of lobby muscle. For example, Mexico's oil industry, far and away its most lucrative, may keep out U.S. companies except on the most minimal basis. The U.S. sugar industry is protected by a quota system. Thus, many economists assert that NAFTA is not a "free trade" pact, but a *managed* trade agreement.

Proponents allege that NAFTA forms a supranational trading region that can more effectively compete with Japan and the European Community. Consumers in all three countries can expect lower prices on a wide variety of goods and services as trade barriers fall and competition increases.

Critics contend that NAFTA will shift American jobs—particularly blue-collar jobs—south of the border where Mexican wage rates are about one-tenth of those in the United States. Environmentalists criticize the pact for not doing enough to prevent and clean up pollution in Mexico.

International Law

FREE TRADE AREA OF THE AMERICAS (FTAA)

In April 2001, the leaders of 34 Western Hemisphere nations met at the Summit of the Americas in Quebec City, Canada, to discuss future trade opportunities in the hemisphere. The leaders agreed to a *Plan of Action* to create a regional Free Trade Area of the Americas (FTAA). The FTAA would be an extension of the North American Free Trade Agreement (NAFTA) that currently exists between Canada, Mexico, and the United States. The proposed FTAA would include all of the countries of North, Central, and South America and would extend from Alaska in the north to Argentina in the south.

The FTAA would eliminate or reduce trade barriers among its member nations and create a trading zone of over 800 million people where trade of over $12 trillion could flourish between seamless economic borders. The plan is to create the FTAA by the year 2005. Negotiations of the details of the FTAA will be conducted for several years, with the United States and Brazil cochairing the process.

The FTAA is supported by the United States and most large U.S. corporations. The FTAA is not without its critics, however. Labor unions fear loss of jobs, and environmentalists envision more loss of rain forests and further destruction of the environment caused by economic advancement. Brazil and several other nations have also voiced reservations.

My nationalism is intense internationalism. I am sick of the strife between nations or religions.

Gandhi

International Brief

The importance of regional organizations and their mutual agreements is increasing.

International Brief

The development of a uniform body of law and the creation of tribunals to peacefully settle disputes between nations and commercial enterprises are necessary for the further development of international trade.

Asian Economic Communities

Few Asian nations are formally organized into regional economic communities. In 1967, Indonesia, Malaysia, the Philippines, Singapore, and Thailand created the **Association of South East Asian Nations (ASEAN)**. Since then five other countries—Brunei Darussalam, Cambodia, Laos, Myanmar, and Vietnam—have joined the ASEAN. This is a cooperative association of diverse nations.

Two of the world's largest countries, Japan and China, do not belong to any significant economic community. Although not a member of ASEAN, Japan has been instrumental in providing financing for the countries that make up that organization. China is a potential member of ASEAN, particularly after it reacquired jurisdiction over Hong Kong in 1997.

Latin, Central, and South American Economic Communities

Countries of Latin America and the Caribbean have established several regional organizations to promote economic development and cooperation. These include (1) the **Central American Common Market**, compromised of Costa Rica, El Salvador, Guatemala, Honduras, Nicaragua, and Panama; (2) the **MERCOSUR Common Market**, created by Argentina, Brazil, Paraguay, and Uruguay; (3) the **Caribbean Community**, whose member countries are Barbados, Belize, Dominica, Grenada, Jamaica, St. Kitts-Nevis-Anguilla, St. Lucia, St. Vincent, and Trinidad-Tobago; and (4) the **Andean Common Market** (ANCOM), with current members being Bolivia, Colombia, Ecuador, and Venezuela.

Mexico, the largest industrial country in Latin America and the Caribbean, has entered into a free trade agreement with all the countries of Central America as well as Chile, Colombia, and Venezuela.

African Economic Communities

Several regional economic communities have been formed in Africa. They include (1) the **Economic Community of West African States** (ECOWAS), created by Dahomey, Gambia, Ghana, Guinea-Bissau, Ivory Coast, Liberia, Mali, Mauritania, Niger, Nigeria, Senegal, Sierra Leone, Togo, and Upper Volta; (2) the **Economic and Customs Union of Central Africa**, comprised of Cameroon, Central African Republic, Chad, Congo, and Gabon; and (3) the **East African Community (EAC)**, created by Kenya, Tanzania, and Uganda. In 1991, 51 African countries of the **Organization of African Unity** signed a **Treaty Establishing the African Economic Community**. This wide-ranging treaty with its large organization of countries is expected to wield more power than the smaller African regional organizations.

Middle Eastern Economic Communities

The most well-known Middle Eastern economic organization is **OPEC**, the **Organization of Petroleum Exporting Countries**. This organization—which is composed of the Middle Eastern countries of Iraq, Iran, Kuwait, Libya, and Saudi Arabia, as well as Venezuela—sets quotas on the output of oil production by member nations. The **Gulf Cooperation Council** was established by Bahrain, Kuwait, Oman, Qatar, Saudi Arabia, and the United Arab Emirates to establish an economic trade area.

International Brief

By raising prices and restricting output, the OPEC cartel caused the "oil crisis" of the early 1970s in the United States and other countries.

International Law

MEXICO BECOMES AN INTERNATIONAL BUSINESS JUGGERNAUT

For decades the economy of Mexico was stagnant compared to the United States. But in 1992, Mexico joined the United States and Canada to create the North American Free Trade Agreement (NAFTA), effective January 1, 1994. By reducing tariffs and eliminating most protectionism, the Mexican economy improved steadily under the new NAFTA rules.

There was one major problem: As of 1999, 85 percent of Mexico's imports went to the United States. Once Mexico saw that the regional trade pacts were good for its economy, it started seeking out new trading partners to balance its exports and reduce its reliance on the United States. Mexico also feared the consequences of China increasing its exports to the United States under the new China-U.S. trade pact. To boost its export trade, Mexico entered into individual trade treaties with over a dozen Central and South American countries, including Chile and Colombia.

But Mexico decided to exploit its unique position and sought an even bigger deal. After much negotiations, in November 1999 Mexico signed an international trade agreement with the 15-member European Union (EU). This

international trade agreement gave Mexico access to the markets of the United Kingdom, Germany, France, Spain, Greece, and the other European nations that represent over 300 million people. The pact called for Europe to grant duty-free entry to most Mexican products beginning in 2000, and for Mexico to gradually open its markets to EU goods and services by 2007. The pact reduced tariffs and duties from an average of 12 percent to 2 percent or lower, depending on the types of goods and services.

With the creation of this new trade pact, Mexico became the only country other than Israel to have international trade agreements with both the United States, Canada, and the European nations of the EU. This new position encourages European firms to establish factories in Mexico so that they can more cheaply sell goods in the United States, and for U.S. firms to establish factories in Mexico as well so they can directly export goods more cheaply to the EU. The new trade pact with the EU assures that Mexico, already the world's eighth-largest trading country, will continue the growth in its industrial-export economy.

⑦HE WORLD TRADE ORGANIZATION (WTO)

In 1995, the **World Trade Organization (WTO)** was created as part of the Uruguay Round of trade negotiations on the *General Agreement on Tariffs and Trade (GATT)*. GATT is a multilateral treaty that establishes trade agreements and limits tariffs and trade restrictions among its more than 130 member nations.

The WTO is an international organization located in Geneva, Switzerland. WTO members have entered into many trade agreements among themselves, including international agreements on investments, sale of goods, provision of services, intellectual property, licensing, tariffs, subsidies, and the removal of trade barriers.

World Trade Organization (WTO)

An international organization of more than 130 member nations created to promote and enforce trade agreements among member nations.

International Law

CHINA JOINS THE WORLD TRADE ORGANIZATION (WTO)

For the past 50 years, China and the United States have pursued divergent paths. China became the world's largest Communist country and the United States the leading

democracy. China maintained its agricultural base, while the United States pursued industrialization. China's businesses were state-owned, while those in the United States were privately owned under a capitalist system. So what do these countries have in common? A new landmark trade pact. For over a decade, these two countries engaged in on-again, off-again trade negotiations. Then in November 1999 the two countries reached a landmark trade pact.

In exchange for being granted the right to import most goods and services into the United States, China, which had substantially restricted imports into its country, agreed to open its markets to foreign goods and services in the following ways:

- **Telecommunications**   Foreign telephone companies may own up to 50 percent of Chinese telephone companies.
- **Entertainment**   China will double the number of U.S. films that can be imported into the country to 20 annually; the content of these films must be approved by the Chinese government.
- **Banking and Financial Services**   Foreign banks may offer financial services to Chinese customers. China will allow foreign companies to own up to 49 percent of banks, insurance companies, and other financial-service companies.
- **Distribution**   Foreigners may establish their own product distribution systems and sell directly to Chinese customers.
- **Services**   Foreigners may establish their own repair and maintenance service businesses in China.
- **Vehicle Sales**   China will permit foreign automobile manufacturers to sell and finance sales to Chinese customers.
- **Farm Products**   China will eliminate subsidies of Chinese exports.
- **Internet**   Foreign investors may own up to 50 percent of Chinese Internet businesses.

The China-U.S. trade agreement was a prelude to China's application to join the World Trade Organization (WTO). In 2002, China became a member of the WTO. China's entry into the WTO makes China a full partner in the world's trading system. The landmark China-U.S. trade pact is only one of many agreements that underscore the importance that trade and commerce now play in international politics.

The China-U.S. trade agreement is not without its critics. In the United States, labor unions criticize the agreement for its potential to ship U.S. manufacturing jobs to China, while environmentalists complain that little is being done to protect the environment from an industrialized economy the size of China. In China, workers at state-owned enterprises might lose their jobs to foreign capitalist companies that can produce goods and services more efficiently, and China's already impoverished farmers may be harmed by cheap farm products imported from other countries. But leaders from both countries thought the entry of China as a full member of the international trading community was worth these risks.

Advertisement, China *In 2002, China became a member of the World Trade Organization (WTO). By doing so, China opened its markets and became a full member of the international economic community.*

WTO Dispute Resolution

One of the primary functions of the WTO is to hear and decide trade disputes between member nations. Before the creation of the WTO, GATT governed trade disputes between signatory nations. This system was inadequate because any member nation that was found to have violated any GATT trade agreement could itself veto any sanctions imposed by GATT's governing body. The WTO solved this problem by adopting a "judicial" mode of dispute resolution to replace GATT's more politically based one.

A member nation that believes that another member nation has breached one of these agreements can initiate a proceeding to have the WTO hear and decide the dispute.

The dispute is first heard by a three-member **panel** of the WTO, which issues a "panel report." The members of the panel are professional judges from member nations. The report is the decision of the panel and contains its findings of fact and law and orders a remedy if a violation has been found. The report is then referred to a newly created **dispute settlement body** of the WTO. This body is required to adopt the panel report unless the body, by consensus, agrees not to adopt the report. Because each member nation has a representative on this settlement body, it can be presumed that panel reports will automatically be adopted because the winning nation to the dispute will almost assuredly vote to adopt it. This is a radical change from the former GATT settlement procedure. Under GATT, unanimity was required to enforce a panel report, and the losing party usually voted to "block" the implementation of a panel's findings against it. One of the most important features of the WTO is the elimination of this blocking power of member nations.

The WTO creates an **appellate body** to which a party can appeal a decision of the dispute settlement body. This appeals court is comprised of seven professional justices selected from member nations. Appeals are heard by panels composed of three members of the apellate body. Appeals are limited to issues of law, not fact. The entire dispute proceeding is completed within nine months when a panel report is not appealed, and in 12 months when there is an appeal. A shortened period is available if the parties agree or if there is an urgent matter that must be decided quickly.

If a violation of a trade agreement is found, the general report and appellate decision can order the offending nation to cease from engaging in the violating practice and to pay damages to the other party. If the offending nation refuses to abide by the order, the WTO can order retaliatory trade sanctions (e.g., tariffs) by other member nations against the noncomplying nation.

International Brief

One of the primary functions of the WTO is to hear and decide trade dispute between member nations.

panel

A panel of three WTO judges that hears trade disputes between member nations and issues a "panel report."

dispute settlement body

A board comprised of one representative from each WTO member nation that reviews panel reports.

appellate body

A panel of seven judges selected from WTO member nations that hears and decides appeals from decisions by the dispute settlement body.

International Law

WTO TAKES A BITE OUT OF JAPANESE APPLES

Japan produces and sells over $1.6 billion of apples annually, the majority of which are consumed there. The United States, which produces over 100 varieties of apples, would like to export apples to Japan and compete for a share of this market. There's a problem, however. Although Japan has removed tariffs on United States apples, in accordance with WTO rules, the Japanese government has frustrated foreign apple growers with time-consuming apple-testing regulations that have in effect prevented the sale of most varieties of U.S. apples in Japan. Japan insists that these regulations are necessary to ensure the safety of apples imported into their country. U.S. apple growers argue that Japan's complex inspection, fumigation, quarantine, and handling regulations are calculated to accomplish what old tariffs used to do: block another country's goods from entering the market.

After attempts at negotiations failed to resolve the issue, U.S. apple growers took their case to court, the court of the World Trade Organization (WTO). There, the U.S. growers presented evidence that the Japanese rules lacked scientific merit and were blatant protectionist measures designed to shield local farmers from global competition. The Japanese government argued that its rules were required to protect against pests that could travel on the apples.

After hearing presentations by both sides, the Geneva-based WTO concluded that the Japanese apple-testing regulations lacked scientific merit and improperly impeded entry of foreign-grown apples into Japan. The WTO ordered that the apple-testing regulations be disbanded to allow the importation of foreign-grown apples into Japan.

The Future of the WTO

International Brief

By enforcing trade agreements among its more than 130 member nations, the WTO has become the world's most important trade organization.

The WTO, which has been referred to as the "Supreme Court of Trade," has become the world's most important trade organization. The WTO has jurisdiction to enforce the most important and comprehensive trade agreements in the world among its more than 130 member nations. Some critics argue that the WTO has been granted powers too great and will impinge upon the sovereignty of individual nations. Others herald the WTO as a much-needed world court that can peaceably solve trade disputes among nations.

 *International Law*

WTO AUDITS U.S. TAX LAWS

The number-one plaintiff in cases brought before the World Trade Organization (WTO) has been the United States. It has initiated and won cases against Japan, Brazil, and the European Union to knock down subsidies and other measures instituted by these countries to protect their industries from open trade. But in a recent and important case, the tables were turned on the United States, which lost an important case brought against it in the WTO by the European Union.

This was the situation. The U.S. Tax Code provided that if U.S. companies ran the paperwork concerning the export of goods to Europe through the tax-haven countries in the Caribbean, then the goods would not be subject to U.S. export tax. The goods could be shipped directly from the United States to their destination in Europe, however, and still qualify for this tax saving as long as paperwork (which is basically digital) was routed through the Caribbean counties. The European Union (EU) brought an action before the WTO against the United States, alleging that this tax break was an illegal export subsidy that violated WTO free-trade rules. After a hearing, the WTO ruled that the United States had engaged in a subtle and lucrative export subsidy that violated WTO trade laws. The WTO ordered the United States to dismantle this favorable tax subsidy. This ruling by the WTO is its most significant to date, repealing hundreds of millions of dollars of tax breaks sneakily given by the U.S. government to Microsoft Corporation, Boeing Company, and other large U.S. exporters. [World Trade Organization, 2001]

 *International Law*

OLD ENEMIES BECOME ECONOMIC PARTNERS

During the late 1960s and early 1970s, the United States engaged in a military action to aid South Vietnam in its struggle against Communist North Vietnam. The might of the United States was unable to defeat the guerilla warfare of the Communists, and in 1972 the United States abandoned Vietnam. The Communists unified North and South Vietnam into one county. The war left visible scars—millions of Vietnamese soldiers and civilians on both sides died or were wounded, 50,000 U.S. soldiers died, and hundreds of thousands were wounded.

Vietnam and the United States remained enemies for the rest of the century. It was not until 1999 that the two countries opened diplomatic relations. In July 2000, Vietnam and the United States took a historical step and signed a trade pact that opened up each other's borders. The new deal took years to negotiate and had been abandoned several times by the Vietnamese Communist rulers who feared loss of power over Vietnam's economy. But after witnessing the trade deal struck by China and the United States, and fearing the loss of what little trade it did have with the United States to China, the Vietnamese leaders negotiated a final deal with the United States. The deal contains the following features:

- The United States reduces tariffs on Vietnamese imports from the current average of 40 percent to 3 percent.
- Vietnam eliminates the 50 percent surcharge it applies to the importation of American products.
- Vietnam adopts World Trade Organization (WTO) standards for the protection of intellectual property rights (e.g., trademarks, copyrights, and patents).
- Over a five-year period Vietnam will phase in entry of U.S. service industries such as distribution, legal, accounting, and engineering services.

The trade pact still allows many restrictions on U.S. companies doing business in Vietnam. For example, U.S. retailers will only be allowed one store in Vietnam. Also, U.S. companies desiring to do business in Vietnam are required to enter into joint ventures with Vietnamese partners, and U.S. ownership of cellular phone, satellite, and telecommunications companies is limited to 49 percent.

The new trade pact gives Vietnam much easier access to the rich U.S. consumer marketplace, and gives U.S. companies entry into the Vietnamese marketplace, both for the manufacture and sale of goods. The United States has accomplished by an economic trade pact what it could not do through military action: convert a socialist redoubt into the world's newest capitalist recruit. Although not a member of the WTO, the trade pact will move Vietnam to adopt many of the world's global trading standards.

JURISDICTION OF NATIONAL COURTS TO DECIDE INTERNATIONAL DISPUTES

The majority of cases involving international law disputes are heard by **national courts** of individual nations. This is primarily the case for commercial disputes between private litigants that do not qualify to be heard by an international court. Some countries have specialized courts that hear international commercial disputes. Other countries permit such disputes to proceed through their regular court system. In the United States, commercial disputes between U.S. companies and foreign governments or parties may be brought in federal district court.

Judicial Procedure

A party seeking judicial resolution of an international dispute faces several problems, including which nation's courts will hear the case and what law should be applied to the case. Jurisdiction is often a highly contested issue. Absent an agreement providing otherwise, a case involving an international dispute will usually be brought in the national court of the plaintiff's home country.

Many international contracts contain a **choice of forum (or forum-selection) clause** that designates which nation's court has jurisdiction to hear a case arising out of the contract. In addition, many contracts also include a **choice of law clause** that designates which nation's laws will be applied in deciding the case. Absent these two clauses, and without the parties agreeing to these matters, an international dispute may never be resolved.

national courts
The courts of individual nations.

International Brief
The majority of commercial litigation involving international business transactions is heard by national courts.

choice of forum clause
Clause in an international contract that designates which nation's court has jurisdiction to hear a case arising out of the contract. Also known as a *forum-selection clause.*

choice of law clause
Clause in an international contract that designates which nation's laws will be applied in deciding a dispute.

CONCEPT SUMMARY INTERNATIONAL CONTRACT CLAUSES AFFECTING JURISDICTION AND CHOICE OF LAW

Clause	Description
Forum-selection	Designates the judicial or arbitral forum that will hear and decide the case.
Choice of law	Designates the law to be applied by the court or arbitrator in deciding the case.

Business Ethics

JURISDICTION OF COURTS: THE BHOPAL DISASTER

On the night of December 2–3, 1984, the most tragic industrial disaster in history occurred in the city of Bhopal, state of Madhya Pradesh, Union of India. Located there was a chemical plant owned and operated by Union Carbide India Limited (UCIL), an Indian company. Most of UCIL's stock (50.9 percent) was owned by Union Carbide Corporation, a New York corporation; 22 percent was owned by the government of India; and the remainder was held by more than 23,000 Indian citizens.

The plant manufactured the pesticides Sevin and Temik. Methyl isocyanate (MIC), a highly toxic gas, is an ingredient in the production of both pesticides. On the night of the tragedy, MIC leaked from the plant in substantial quantities. The prevailing winds blew the deadly gas into the over-populated residential areas adjacent to the plant and one of the most densely occupied areas of the city. The results were horrendous: More than 3,000 people died and more than 200,000 people suffered injuries—some serious and permanent. Livestock were killed and crops damaged. Businesses were interrupted.

The Union of India filed a consolidated complaint on behalf of all Indian claimants in the U.S. district courts in the United States. Union Carbide filed a motion with the district courts seeking dismissal of the consolidated action on the grounds of *forum non conveniens*. Union Carbide argued that the action should be transferred to a more convenient judicial forum within the Union of India pursuant to this doctrine. India opposed the motion. The court had to decide whether U.S. courts or Indian courts should hear the cases.

After permitting and reviewing extensive discovery on the issue, the district court held that the United States was a *forum non conveniens* for the purpose of suits arising from the Bhopal disaster. The court stated, "This court is firmly convinced that the Indian legal system is in a far better position than the American courts to determine the cause of the tragic event and thereby fix liability."

Litigation continued in India for more than two years. On February 14, 1989, the Supreme Court of India entered an order settling all civil claims and criminal charges arising out of the Bhopal disaster upon payment by UCIL and Union Carbide of $470 million to a fund to be administered on behalf of the claimants. The companies, declaring the settlement "just and reasonable," agreed to the terms. The Indian Parliament established a procedure for claimants to submit their claims for payment. Critics argued that the amount of the settlement was too low—less than $1,000 per claimant. [In re Union Carbide Corporation Gas Plant Disaster at Bhopal, India, in December, 1984, 634 F.Supp. 842 (S.D.N.Y. 1986); 809 F.2d 195 (2d Cir. 1987); cert. denied, 484 U.S. 871 (1987)]

1. Did Union Carbide act responsibly in fighting so hard to get the case removed from the United States?
2. Why did the Indian plaintiffs want their case heard in the United States rather than India? Is "forum-shopping" ethical conduct?

Act of State Doctrine

act of state doctrine

States that judges of one country cannot question the validity of an act committed by another country within that other country's borders. It is based on the principle that a country has absolute authority over what transpires within its own territory.

A general principle of international law is that a country has absolute authority over what transpires *within* its own territory. In furtherance of this principle, the **act of state doctrine** states that judges of one country cannot question the validity of an act committed by another country within that other country's own borders. In *United States v. Belmont*,[2] the U.S. Supreme Court declared, "Every sovereign state must recognize the independence of every other sovereign state; and the courts of one will not sit in judgment upon the acts of the government of another, done within its own territory." This restraint on the judiciary is justified under the doctrine of separation of powers and permits the executive branch of the federal government to arrange affairs with foreign governments.

The Supreme Court Speaks

The Act of State Doctrine

W. S. Kirkpatrick & Co., Inc. v. Environmental Tectonics Corporation, International
493 U.S. 400, 110 S.Ct. 701 (1990)
Supreme Court of the United States

BACKGROUND AND FACTS
In 1981, Harry Carpenter, a U.S. citizen and chairman of the board and chief executive officer of W. S. Kirkpatrick & Co., Inc. (Kirkpatrick), learned that the Republic of Nigeria was interested in contracting for the construction of an aeromedical center at Kaduna Air Force Base in Nigeria. He made arrangements with Benson "Tunde" Akindale, a Nigerian citizen, whereby Akindale would help secure the contract for Kirkpatrick by paying bribes to Nigerian officials. In accordance with the plan, the contract was awarded to a wholly owned subsidiary of Kirkpatrick; Kirkpatrick paid the agreed-upon funds to Akindale, which were dispersed as bribes to Nigerian officials. Environmental Tectonics Corporation, International (Environmental), an unsuccessful bidder for the

Kaduna contract, learned of the bribes and informed the U.S. embassy in Lagos, Nigeria. In a criminal action, Carpenter and Kirkpatrick pleaded guilty to violating the U.S. Foreign Corrupt Practices Act. Environmental then brought this civil action against Carpenter, Kirkpatrick, and Akindale seeking damages under federal and state racketeering and antitrust laws. The district court held that the action was barred by the act of state doctrine and dismissed the complaint. The court of appeals reversed. The defendants appealed to the U.S. Supreme Court.

SUPREME COURT ISSUE
Does the act of state doctrine bar the plaintiff's civil suit against the defendants?

The Doctrine of Sovereign Immunity

One of the oldest principles of international law is the **doctrine of sovereign immunity**. Under this doctrine, *countries* are granted immunity from suits in courts in other countries. For example, if a U.S. citizen wanted to sue the government of China in a U.S. court, he or she could not (subject to the exceptions discussed below).

Originally, the United States granted absolute immunity to foreign governments from suits in U.S. courts. In 1952, the United States switched to the principle of *qualified* or *restricted immunity*, which was eventually codified in the **Foreign Sovereign Immunities Act of 1976 (FSIA).**[3] This act now exclusively governs suits against foreign nations in the United States, whether in federal or state court. Most Western nations have adopted the principle of restricted immunity. Other countries still follow the doctrine of absolute immunity.

Exceptions The FSIA provides that a foreign country is not immune from lawsuits in U.S. courts in the following two situations:

1. The foreign country has waived its immunity, either explicitly or by implication.
2. The action is based upon a *commercial activity* carried on in the United States by the foreign country or carried on outside the United States but causing a direct effect in the United States.

What constitutes "commercial activity" is the most litigated aspect of the FSIA. If it is commercial activity, the foreign sovereign is subject to suit in the United States; if it is not, the foreign sovereign is immune from suit in this country.

doctrine of sovereign immunity
States that countries are granted immunity from suits in courts of other countries.

Foreign Sovereign Immunities Act
Exclusively governs suits against foreign nations that are brought in federal or state courts in the United States; codifies the principle of *qualified* or *restricted immunity*.

International Brief
A foreign nation may be sued in a court in the United States if that nation has engaged in a *commercial activity* that either (1) is carried on in the United States or (2) is carried on outside the United States but causes a direct effect in the United States.

The Supreme Court Speaks

Commercial Exception to the Doctrine of Sovereign Immunity

Republic of Argentina v. Weltover, Inc.
112 S.Ct. 2160 (1992)
Supreme Court of the United States

BACKGROUND AND FACTS
In an attempt to stabilize its currency, Argentina and its central bank, Banco Central (collectively Argentina), issued bonds called "Bonods." The bonds, which were sold to investors worldwide, provided for repayment in U.S. dollars through transfers on the London, Frankfurt, Zurich, and New York markets at the bondholder's election. Argentina lacked sufficient foreign exchange to retire the bonds when they matured.

Argentina unilaterally extended the time for payment and offered bondholders substitute instruments as a means of rescheduling the debts. Two Panamanian corporations and a Swiss bank refused the rescheduling and insisted that full payment be made in New York. When Argentina did not pay, they brought a breach of contract action against Argentina in U.S. district court in New York. Argentina moved to dismiss, alleging that it was not subject to suit in U.S. courts under the federal Foreign Sovereign Immunities Act (FSIA). The plaintiffs asserted that the "commercial activity" exception to the act applied, subjecting Argentina to suit in U.S. court. The district court denied Argentina's motion for dismissal and the court of appeals affirmed. Argentina appealed to the U.S. Supreme Court.

SUPREME COURT ISSUE
Does the doctrine of sovereign immunity prevent the plaintiffs from suing Argentina in a U.S. court?

IN THE LANGUAGE OF THE U.S. SUPREME COURT
Scalia, Justice When a foreign government acts, not as regulator of a market, but in the manner of a private player within it, the foreign sovereign's actions are "commercial" within the meaning of the FSIA. Thus, a foreign government's issuance of regulations limiting foreign currency exchange is a sovereign activity, because such authoritative control of commerce cannot be exercised by a private party; whereas a contract to buy army boots or even bullets is a "commercial" activity, because private companies can similarly use sales contracts to acquire goods.

The commercial character of the Bonods is confirmed by the fact that they are in almost all respects garden-variety debt instruments: They may be held by private parties; they are negotiable and may be traded on the international market; and they promise a future stream of cash income. We conclude that Argentina's issuance of the Bonods was a "commercial activity" under the FSIA. We have little difficulty concluding that Argentina's unilateral rescheduling of the maturity dates on the Bonods had a "direct effect" in the United States.

DECISION AND REMEDY
The Supreme Court held that Argentina's issuance of the bonds was a commercial activity that had a direct effect in the United States. Therefore, the commercial activity exception to the Sovereign Immunities Act applied, which allowed the plaintiffs to sue Argentina in a U.S. court.

CASE QUESTIONS
Critical Legal Thinking Should the United States recognize the doctrine of absolute sovereign immunity or qualified immunity? Explain.

Business Ethics Did the government of Argentina act ethically in not paying the bonds when due and unilaterally rescheduling the debt?

Contemporary Business Is there more risk for investors who invest in obligations of foreign countries than in obligations of the U.S. government?

CONCEPT SUMMARY ACT OF STATE AND SOVEREIGN IMMUNITY DOCTRINES COMPARED

Doctrine	Description
Act of state	Act of a government in its *own country* is not subject to suit in a foreign country's courts.
Sovereign immunity	Act of a government in a *foreign country* is not subject to suit in the foreign country. Some countries provide absolute immunity, whereas other countries (such as the United States) provide limited immunity.

International Law

NATIONALIZATION OF PRIVATELY OWNED PROPERTY BY FOREIGN NATIONS

When a company invests capital in a foreign country in plant, equipment, bank accounts, and such, it runs the risk that that country may **nationalize** (seize) its assets. International law recognizes the right of nations to nationalize private property owned by foreigners if done for a public purpose. Nationalization of assets occurs more often in underdeveloped or developing countries than in developed countries. Nationalization can be classified as

- **Expropriation** The owner of the property is paid just compensation by the government that seized the property.

- **Confiscation** The owner receives no payment or inadequate payment from the government that seized the property.

When a foreign government confiscates property of U.S. firms, there are few legal remedies available to the owners. The U.S. government may try to recover payment for the firms through diplomatic means, but this is often not successful.

The United States has created the **Overseas Private Investment Corporation (OPIC)**, a government agency, which insures U.S. citizens and businesses against losses incurred as a result of the confiscation of their assets by foreign governments. This is often called **political risk insurance**. Low-cost premiums are charged for the insurance. Those insured that receive a payment under this insurance program must assign their claim against the foreign government to OPIC. The **United States Export-Import Bank (Eximbank)** also offers insurance protection against confiscation to U.S. firms engaged in exporting. Political risk insurance is also available through several private insurance companies.

INTERNATIONAL ARBITRATION

As an alternative to litigation, the parties to an international contract may agree that any dispute that arises between them regarding the transaction will be decided by mandatory arbitration. **Arbitration** is a nonjudicial method of dispute resolution whereby a neutral third party decides the case. The parties agree to be bound by the arbitrator's decision. Generally, arbitration is faster, less expensive, less formal, and more private than litigation.

An **arbitration clause** should specify the arbitrator or the means of selecting the arbitrator. Several organizations conduct international arbitrations, including the American Arbitration Association, the International Chamber of Commerce, the International Center for the Settlement of Investment Disputes, and the United Nations Commission on International Trade Law. International arbitrators are usually businesspeople or lawyers experienced in worldwide commercial transactions. An arbitration clause should also specify the law to be applied by the arbitrator. Arbitration clauses are appearing in an increasing number of international contracts.

An arbitrator issues an *award*, not a judgment. An arbitrator does not have the power to enforce the award it renders. Therefore, if the losing party refuses to pay the award, the winning party must petition a court to enforce the award. More than 50 countries that conduct the bulk of worldwide commercial transactions are signatories to the **United Nations Convention on the Recognition and Enforcement of Foreign Arbitral Awards** (Convention).[4] The United States adopted the Convention in 1970 and amended the Federal Arbitration Act to reflect this international law.[5] The recipient of an arbitral award subject to the Convention can attach property of the loser that is located in any country that is a signatory to the Convention.

arbitration

A nonjudicial method of dispute resolution whereby a neutral third party decides the case.

arbitration clause

A clause contained in many international contracts that stipulates that any dispute between the parties concerning the performance of the contract will be submitted to an arbitrator or arbitration panel for resolution.

International Law

ARBITRATION OF INTERNATIONAL BUSINESS DISPUTES

Arbitration clauses often appear in international commercial agreements signed by U.S. companies that designate that a foreign country's arbitration system will hear and decide the dispute. Consider the following case.

Mitsubishi Motors Corporation (Mitsubishi) is a Japanese corporation that manufactures automobiles and has its principal place of business in Tokyo, Japan. Soler Chrysler-Plymouth, Inc. (Soler), is a Puerto Rican corporation with its principal place of business in Puerto Rico. On October 31, 1979, Soler entered into a sales and distributor agreement that gave Soler the right to sell Mitsubishi-manufactured automobiles within a designated area, including metropolitan San Juan. The agreement included an arbitration clause that stipulated, "All disputes, controversies, or differences which may arise between the parties out of this

Agreement or for the breach thereof, shall be finally settled by arbitration in Japan in accordance with the rules and regulations of the Japan Commercial Arbitration Association." Initially, Soler did a brisk business in Mitsubishi-manufactured vehicles. In early 1981, the new-car market slackened, and Soler ran into serious difficulties in meeting the agreed-upon minimum sales volume. Soler repudiated its agreement with Mitsubishi. Mitsubishi requested arbitration before the Japan Commercial Arbitration Association and brought an action in U.S. district court in Puerto Rico for an order compelling arbitration. Soler filed a cross-complaint alleging that Mitsubishi violated U.S. antitrust laws. The district court held that all claims were subject to arbitration. The court of appeals reversed as to the **antitrust claims.** Mitsubishi appealed to the U.S. Supreme Court, arguing that issues involving U.S. antitrust laws are subject to arbitration by an arbitration panel located in a foreign country.

The U.S. Supreme Court agreed with Mitsubishi and held that issues involving U.S. antitrust laws may be arbitrated by a foreign arbitration panel and ordered the arbitration agreement between Soler and Mitsubishi enforced. The Supreme Court noted that by agreeing to arbitrate a statutory claim, a party does not forgo the substantive rights afforded by the statute; it only submits to their resolution in an arbitral, rather than a judicial, forum. It trades the procedures and opportunity for review of the courtroom for the simplicity, informality, and expedition of arbitration. In upholding international arbitration of the antitrust claims, the Supreme Court noted,

"The expansion of American business and industry will hardly be encouraged if, notwithstanding solemn contracts, we insist on a parochial concept that all disputes must be resolved under our laws and in our courts. We cannot have trade and commerce in world markets and international waters exclusively on our terms, governed by our laws, and resolved in our courts. We conclude that concerns of international comity, respect for the capacities of foreign and transnational tribunals, and sensitivity to the need of the international commercial system for predictability in the resolution of disputes require that we enforce the parties' arbitration agreement." [*Mitsubishi Motors Corporation v. Soler Chrysler-Plymouth, Inc.*, 473 U.S. 614, 105 S.Ct. 3346 (1985)]

CRIMINAL PROSECUTIONS IN THE INTERNATIONAL ARENA

extradition

Sending a person back to a country for criminal prosecution.

A nation has authority to criminally prosecute individuals or businesses that commit crimes within its territory or that violate that nation's laws, as well as its citizens (including businesses) that commit crimes elsewhere. One of the main problems of criminal prosecution, however, is that the perpetrator may be taking refuge in another country. In such cases, the person may be **extradited** (sent back) to the country seeking to criminally try him or her. The United States has entered into *extradition treaties* with many countries. If the perpetrator is not extradited the crime may go unpunished.

International Law

JEWISH LAW AND THE TORAH

Jewish law, which has existed for centuries, is a complex legal system based on ideology and theology of the Torah. The Torah prescribes comprehensive and integrated rules of religious, political, and legal life that together form Jewish thought. Jewish law is decided by rabbis who are scholars of the Torah and other Jewish scriptures. Rabbinic jurisprudence, known as *Halakhah*, is administered by rabbi-judges sitting as the *Beis Din*, Hebrew for the "house of judgment." As a court, the Beis Din has roots that go back 3,000 years.

Today, Jews are citizens of countries worldwide. As such, they are subject to the criminal and civil laws of their host countries. But Jews, no matter where they live, abide by the principles of the Torah in many legal matters such as marriage, divorce, inheritance, and other family matters. Thus, the legal principles imbedded in the Torah coexist with the secular laws of Jew's home countries.

The rabbinical judges tend to be more actively involved in the case. True to its roots, the Beis Din is more a search for the truth than it is an adversarial process.

The legal principles in the Torah coexist with the secular laws of many countries.

International Law

ISLAMIC LAW AND THE KORAN

Approximately 20 percent of the world's population is Muslim. Islam is the principal religion of Afghanistan, Algeria, Bangladesh, Egypt, Indonesia, Iran, Iraq, Jordan, Kuwait, Libya, Malaysia, Mali, Mauritania, Morocco, Niger, North Yemen, Oman, Pakistan, Qatar, Saudi Arabia, Somalia, South Yemen, Sudan, Syria, Tunisia, Turkey, and the United Arab Emirates. *Islamic law* (or *Shari'a*) is the only law in Saudi Arabia. In other Islamic countries, the *Shari'a* forms the basis of family law but coexists with other laws.

The Islamic law system is derived from the Koran, the Sunnah (decisions and sayings of the Prophet Muhammad), and reasonings by Islamic scholars. By the tenth century A.D., Islamic scholars decided that no further improvement of the divine law could be made, closed the door of *ijtihad* (indepen-

dent reasoning), and froze the evolution of Islamic law at that point. Islamic law prohibits *riba*, or the making of unearned or unjustified profit. Making a profit from the sale of goods or the provision of services is permitted. The most notable consequence of *riba* is that the payment of interest on loans is forbidden. To circumvent this result, the party with the money is permitted to purchase the item and resell it to the other party at a profit or to advance the money and become a trading partner who shares in the profits of the enterprise.

Today, Islamic law is primarily used in the areas of marriage, divorce, and inheritance and to a limited degree in criminal law. To resolve the tension between *Shari'a* and the practice of modern commercial law, the *Shari'a* is often ignored in commercial transactions.

International Law

HINDU LAW—DHARMASASTRA

Over 20 percent of the world's population is Hindu. Most live in India, where they make up 80 percent of the population. Others live in Burma, Kenya, Malaysia, Pakistan, Singapore, Tanzania, and Uganda. *Hindu law* is a religious law. As such, individual Hindus apply this law to themselves regardless of their nationality or place of domicile.

Classical Hindu law rests neither on civil codes nor on court decisions, but on the works of private scholars that were passed along for centuries by oral tradition and eventually were recorded in the *smitris* (law books). Hindu law—called *dharmasastra* in Sanskrit, that is, the doctrine of proper behavior—is linked to the divine revelation of Veda (the holy

collection of Indian religious songs, prayers, hymns, and sayings written between 2000 and 1000 B.C.). Most Hindu law is concerned with family matters and the law of succession.

After India became a British colony, British judges applied a combination of Hindu law and common law in solving cases. This Anglo–Hindu law, as it was called, was ousted once India gained its independence. In the mid-1950s, India codified Hindu law by enacting the Hindu Marriage Act, the Hindu Minority and Guardianship Act, the Hindu Succession Act, and the Hindu Adoptions and Maintenance Act. Outside of India, Anglo–Hindu law applies in most other countries populated by Hindus.

International Law

THE SOCIALISTIC LAW SYSTEM

The youngest of the major legal systems is the **Sino–Soviet socialist law system**, which applies to over 30 percent of the people of the world. The Sino–Soviet theory of law is based on the philosophy of Karl Marx, which advocated the eradication of capitalism and the elimination of the private ownership of property. After the creation of the Soviet state following the Russian Revolution of 1917, Lenin replaced the old court system

with a system of law meted out by workers, peasants, and the military. This legal nihilism (or absence of law) did not last long, and a formal legal system was restored pursuant to new criminal and civil law codes that promoted the socialist ideal. With its emphasis on codes, the Sino–Soviet legal system is a variant of the civil law.

Because private property in most respects is not permitted under Sino–Soviet law, the legal system comprises mostly public law. Therefore, property law, contract law, and business organization law (e.g., corporation and partnership law) that are prevalent in common law and civil law countries are not as important in Sino–Soviet law. Sino–Soviet public law preserves the authority of the state over property and the means of production.

As the republics of the now dismantled Soviet Union and Eastern bloc countries adopt free market economies, Sino–Soviet public law is being replaced by laws establishing and protecting private property rights. Today, socialist law forms the basis of the legal systems of Angola, Cambodia, China, Cuba, Ethiopia, Guinea, Guyana, Laos, Libya, Mozambique, North Korea, Somalia, and Vietnam. But even Communist China is promoting capitalism and permitting individual ownership of property. This will require the development of business and property laws and the establishment of a court system to decide commercial and property-related disputes.

E-Commerce & Information Technology

GERMANY BECOMES THE WORLD'S E-COMMERCE POLICE

E-commerce—selling of products and services over the Internet—is exploding! American marketeers, who are already used to compiling, maintaining, and selling lists of detailed information about customers and potential customers, welcome the ability not only to sell over the Internet but also to collect more detailed information about customer profiles. Now they can target sales pitches more accurately. Today, soon after a person subscribes to a magazine, he or she is inundated with advertising from myriad companies, often related to the subject of the new magazine. What has happened? The magazine has sold the new subscriber's name to companies, without the subscriber's permission. Compiling and selling customer lists is a very lucrative side business for many retailers. Companies also use "cross-marketing" to reach potential customers. For example, airlines commonly try to sell customers everything from car rentals, hotel services, and even luxury goods.

In the United States, the compilation and selling of customer databases is all very legal. In the European Union, however, as of October 25, 1998, the compilation and selling of consumer databases became highly regulated. Led by Germany, the European Union, the world's largest economy made up of many nations of Europe and surrounding areas, has adopted the **European Union Directive on Data Protection**. This directive, which is law, establishes the following rules.

1. If a company wants personal information on an individual, it must get that person's permission after explaining what the information will be used for. For example, an airline would have to explain why it wants birth dates to distinguish one John Smith from another. A person can refuse to give the data.

2. Companies will have to show customers their complete data profiles on demand, correct a profile if it is wrong, and delete it if it is objectionable.
3. Web site owners will not be able to use "cookies," the data tags that hook into a log-in name, track the Web sites the user has explored, and send back consumer profiles.
4. Companies cannot engage in cross-marketing without customer permission.
5. A company cannot transmit personal data about European Union citizens to users in other countries whose privacy laws do not meet European Union standards.

Any company wanting to do business in any European Union country will have to abide by the law. Police from European Union countries investigate companies to ensure that they abide by the directive, and companies and individuals may be prosecuted criminally for violating it. Companies like Citicorp, which issues credit cards in Europe, permits the Datenschutz—the German data police—to pay regular visits to its giant data-processing center in Sioux City, South Dakota, to ensure compliance with the new law. Other companies that wish to do business in the European Union must do the same or be denied access to do business there.

This concerted directive from the European Union attempts to dictate a norm for protecting privacy and e-commerce on the Internet to the rest of the world. The Germans argue that a global system requires global regualtion to protect privacy rights, and they believe that the new directive accomplishes this goal. Regardless of whether or not the directive establishes a world standard, companies that want to do business in the European Union must abide by its requirements.

CHAPTER SUMMARY

The United States and Foreign Affairs, p. 152

The United States and Foreign Affairs	The following two provisions in the U.S. Constitution establish the federal government's authority to regulate international affairs. 1. *Commerce Clause*. Vests Congress with the power "to regulate commerce with foreign nations." 2. *Treaty Clause*. Gives the president the authority to enter into treaties with foreign nations subject to a two-thirds vote of the Senate.

Sources of International Law, p. 153

Sources of International Law	1. *Treaties and conventions.* Agreements between nations that are formally ratified by the supreme power of each signatory nation. Conventions are treaties that are sponsored by international organizations (e.g., the United Nations). 2. *Custom.* Practices followed by two or more nations over a period of time when dealing with each other. 3. *General principles of law.* Principles of law that are common to the nations of the parties involved in a dispute. 4. *Judicial decisions and teachings.* Judicial decisions of national courts and teachings of the most qualified legal scholars of the nations of the parties involved in a dispute.
Principle of Comity	Courtesies granted by a nation to other nations that are not obligations of law but are based on respect, goodwill, and civility.

The United Nations, p. 155

The United Nations	*Governance of the United Nations.* International organization located in New York City. Most countries of the world are members. Its goals are to maintain peace and security in the world, promote economic and social cooperation, and protect human rights.

International Regional Organizations, p. 157

Regional Economic Organizations	1. European Union (EU) (or Common Market) 2. Central American Common Market 3. MERCOSUR Common Market 4. Caribbean Community 5. Andean Common Market (ANCOM) 6. Economic Community of West African States (ECOWAS) 7. Economic and Customs Union of Central Africa 8. East African Community (EAC) 9. African Economic Community 10. Organization of Petroleum Exporting Countries (OPEC) 11. Gulf Cooperation Council 12. Association of South East Asian Nations (ASEAN) 13. North American Free Trade Agreement (NAFTA)

The World Trade Organization (WTO), p. 161

World Trade Organization	*World Trade Organization.* International organization located in Geneva, Switzerland. Many countries of the world are members. Its goals are to limit tariff and trade restrictions and provide a mechanism for resolving trade disputes among its member nations.

Jurisdiction of National Courts to Decide International Disputes, p. 165

Principles of Judicial Restraint	National courts are limited by the following two principles of judicial restraint:
	1. *Act of state doctrine.* States that judges of one country cannot question the validity of an act committed by another country *within* that other country's borders.
	2. *Doctrine of sovereign immunity.* States that countries are granted immunity from suits in courts in other countries. Some countries provide for *absolute immunity* and other countries (such as the United States) provide *qualified* or *restricted immunity. Exceptions.* The United States provides that a foreign country is not immune from lawsuits in U.S. court if:
	  a. The foreign country has *waived* its immunity.
	  b. The foreign country has engaged in *commercial activity* in the United States or outside the United States that causes a direct effect in the United States.

International Arbitration, p. 169

International Arbitration	1. *Arbitration.* A nonjudicial method of dispute resolution whereby a neutral third party decides the case. 2. *Arbitration clauses.* Clauses included in many international contracts that require arbitration of disputes arising from the contract.

Criminal Prosecutions in the International Arena, p. 170

Criminal Prosecutions in the International Arena	*Extradition treaty.* Treaty between nations that provides a procedure for sending a person located in one country back to another country that seeks to criminally prosecute that person.

END-OF-CHAPTER INTERNET EXERCISES AND CASE QUESTIONS

Working the Web Internet Exercises

ACTIVITIES

1. Go to Hieros Gamos **www.hg.org**. It is a huge international law site. It covers laws of 230 countries in more than 50 languages! Check on the list of countries and review the legal structure of Afghanistan.

2. Go to **travel.state.gov/judicial assistance.html**. Check on the procedures for enforcement of judgments in foreign countries. Why are there no treaties or conventions that make enforcement of US judgments easier?

3. Survey the ADR material at **search.info.usaid.gov**. What are some of the particular advantages to using ADR in other countries?

4. For an outstanding online lecture on many international law topics, visit **www.august1.com/pubs**. It contains outlines and online lectures from Professor Ray August.

CRITICAL LEGAL THINKING CASES

6.1 Act of State Doctrine   Prior to 1918, the Petrograd Metal Works, a Russian corporation, deposited a large sum of money with August Belmont, a private banker doing business in New York City under the name of August Belmont & Co. In 1918, the Soviet government nationalized the corporation and appropriated all of its property and assets wherever situated, including the deposit account with Belmont. As a result, the deposit became the property of the Soviet government. In 1933, the Soviet government and the United States entered into an agreement to settle claims and counterclaims between them. As part of the settlement, it was agreed that the Soviet government would take no steps to enforce claims against American nationals (including Belmont), and assigned all such claims to the United States. The United States brought this action against the executors of Belmont's estate to recover the money originally deposited with Belmont by Petrograd Metal Works. Who owns the money? [*United States v. Belmont*, 301 U.S. 324, 57 S.Ct. 758 (1937)]

6.2 Act of State Doctrine   Banco Nacional de Costa Rica is a bank wholly owned by the government of Costa Rica. It is subject to the rules and regulations adopted by the minister of finance and central bank of Costa Rica. In December 1980, the bank borrowed $40 million from a consortium of private banks located in the United Kingdom and the United States. The bank signed promissory notes agreeing to repay the principal plus interest on the loan in four equal installments due on July 30, August 30, September 30, and October 30, 1981. The money was to be used to provide export financing of sugar and sugar products from Costa Rica. The loan agreements and promissory notes were signed in New York City, and the loan proceeds were tendered to the bank there.

On July 30, 1981, the bank paid the first installment on the loan. The bank did not, however, make the other three installment payments and defaulted on the loan. The lending banks sued the bank in U.S. district court in New York to recover the unpaid principal and interest. The bank alleged in defense that on August 27, 1981, the minister of finance and the central bank of Costa Rica issued a decree forbidding the repayment of loans by the bank to private lenders, including the lending banks in this case. The action was taken because Costa Rica was having trouble servicing debts to foreign creditors. The bank alleged that the act of state doctrine prevented the plaintiffs from recovering on their loans to the bank. Who wins? [*Libra Bank Limited v. Banco Nacional de Costa Rica*, 570 F.Supp. 870 (S.D.N.Y. 1983)]

6.3 Forum-Selection Clause Zapata Off-Shore Company is a Houston, Texas–based American corporation that engages in drilling oil wells throughout the world. Unterweser Reederei, GMBH is a German corporation that provides ocean shipping and towing services. In November 1967, Zapata requested bids from companies to tow its self-elevating drilling rig "Chaparral" from Louisiana to a point off Ravenna, Italy, in the Adriatic Sea, where Zapata had agreed to drill certain wells. Unterweser submitted the lowest bid and was requested to submit a proposed contract to Zapata, which it did. The contract submitted by Unterweser contained the following provision: "Any dispute arising must be treated before the London Court of Justice." Zapata executed the contract without deleting or modifying this provision.

On January 5, 1968, Unterweser's deep-sea tug *Bremen* departed from Venice, Louisiana, with the Chaparral in tow, bound for Italy. On January 9, while the flotilla was in international waters in the middle of the Gulf of Mexico, a severe storm arose. The sharp roll of the Chaparral in Gulf waters caused portions of it to break off and fall into the sea, seriously damaging the rig. Zapata instructed the *Bremen* to tow the Chaparral to Tampa, Florida, the nearest port of refuge, which it did. On January 12, Zapata filed suit against Unterweser and the *Bremen* in U.S. district court in Florida, alleging negligent towing and

breach of contract. The defendants assert that suit can be brought only in the London Court of Justice. Who is correct? [*M/S Bremen and Unterweser Reederei, GMBH v. Zapata Off-Shore Company*, 407 U.S. 1, 92 S.Ct. 1907, 32 L.Ed.2d 513 (1972)].

6.4 International Arbitration Alberto-Culver Company is an American company incorporated in Delaware with its principal office in Illinois. It manufactures and distributes toiletries and hair products in the United States and other countries. Fritz Scherk owned three interrelated businesses organized under the laws of Germany and Liechtenstein that were engaged in the manufacture of toiletries. After substantial negotiations, in February 1969, Alberto-Culver entered into a contract with Scherk to purchase his three companies along with all rights held by these companies to trademarks in cosmetic goods. The contract contained a number of express warranties whereby Scherk guaranteed the sole and unencumbered ownership of these trademarks. The contract also contained a clause that provided that "any controversy or claim that shall arise out of this agreement or breach thereof" was to be referred to arbitration before the International Chamber of Commerce in Paris, France. The transaction closed in June 1969 in Geneva, Switzerland.

Nearly one year later, Alberto-Culver allegedly discovered that the trademark rights purchased under the contract were subject to substantial encumbrances that threatened to give other parties superior rights to the trademarks and to restrict or preclude Alberto-Culver's use of them. Alberto-Culver sued Scherk in U.S. district court in Illinois, alleging fraudulent misrepresentation in violation of Section 10(b) of the federal Securities Exchange Act of 1934. Scherk asserts in defense that the case is subject to mandatory arbitration in Paris. Who is correct? [*Scherk v. Alberto-Culver Co.*, 417 U.S. 506, 94 S.Ct. 2249, 41 L.Ed. 2d 270 (1974)]

BUSINESS ETHICS CASES

6.5 Business Ethics Bank of Jamaica is wholly owned by the government of Jamaica. Chisholm & Co. is a Florida corporation that is owned by James Henry Chisholm, a Florida resident. The Export-Import Bank of the United States (Eximbank) provides financial services and credit insurance to export and import companies. In January 1982, the bank and Chisholm & Co. agreed that Chisholm & Co. would arrange lines of credit from various banks and procure $50 million of credit insurance from Eximbank to be available to aid Jamaican importers. Chisholm & Co. was to be paid commissions for its services.

Chisholm & Co. negotiated and arranged for $50 million of credit insurance from Eximbank and lines of credit from Florida National Bank, Bankers Trust Company, and Irving Trust Company. Chisholm also arranged meetings between the bank and the American banks. Unbeknownst to Chisholm & Co., the bank went directly to Eximbank to exclude Chisholm & Co.

from the Jamaica program, and requested that the credit insurance be issued solely in the name of the bank: As a result, Chisholm & Co.'s Eximbank insurance application was not considered. The bank also obtained lines of credit from other companies and paid them commissions. Chisholm & Co. sued the bank in the U.S. district court in Miami, Florida, alleging breach of contract and seeking damages. The bank filed a motion to dismiss the complaint, alleging that its actions were protected by sovereign immunity. Who wins? Did the Bank of Jamaica act ethically in trying to avoid its contract obligations? [*Chisholm & Co. v. Bank of Jamaica*, 643 F.Supp. 1393 (S.D.Fla. 1986)]

6.6 Business Ethics Nigeria, an African nation, while in the midst of a boom period due to oil exports, entered into $1 billion of contracts with various countries to purchase huge quantities of Portland cement. Nigeria was going to use the cement to build and improve the country's infrastructure. Several of the contracts were with American companies, including Texas Trading & Milling Corporation. Nigeria substantially overbought cement, and the country's docks and harbors became clogged with ships waiting to unload. Unable to accept delivery of the cement it had bought, Nigeria repudiated many of its contracts, including the one with

Texas Trading. When Texas Trading sued Nigeria in a U.S. district court to recover damages for breach of contract, Nigeria asserted in defense that the doctrine of sovereign immunity protected it from liability. Who wins? [*Texas Trading & Milling Corp. v. Federal Republic of Nigeria*, 647 F.2d 300 (2nd Cir. 1981)]

BRIEFING THE CASE WRITING ASSIGNMENT

Read the following case, which has been excerpted from the court's opinion. Review and brief the case.

OHG v. Kolodny
NY County, Supreme Court
1st Jud. Dept., IA Part II (1992)

Baer, Justice

Plaintiff is an auction house dealing in works of art. Defendant is an art dealer. His gallery has purchased fine art from the plaintiff over the years, presumably with happier results than in this case. In 1988, defendant received, in New York, a catalogue sent by plaintiff that described works of art that would be put up for auction by plaintiff. Among these, defendant says, was "a bronze sculpture produced by Hiliare Germain Edgar Degas before 1900," to wit, the "Dancer Gazing." Plaintiff phoned defendant in New York during the auction and solicited a bid for the "Dancer." Without ever having set eyes on the right foot or any other part of the sculpture, plaintiff offered a bid of DM 220,000 and triumphed. Defendant was never told the identity of the consignor of the Degas. Defendant wired to plaintiff the purchase price and a commission.

The "Dancer" arrived shortly thereafter in New York, where she immediately did a pirouette and departed for London. Defendant wished to let no grass grow under either of his feet; he would put the Degas up for resale at Christie's and would, he was confident, earn a great deal of not bronze, but sterling. Eagle eyes at Christie's surveyed the work. Defendant was told, to his horror, that Christie's suspected that the statue was ersatz, in a word, a fake. Defendant contacted Herr Hanstein and advised that his heart was heavy and his wallet, he was afraid, too light. Defendant sought a refund.

Defendant allegedly secured the agreement of plaintiff that the "Dancer" would be given the once or twice over by the world's foremost expert of Degas bronzes, whose determination would be binding. The statue was brought to New York, where the expert, like many another world's foremost experts, resides. His conclusion unfortunately was that the work was not genuine.

A German court decided in favor of plaintiff, rejecting defendant's contention that he was entitled to an offset for the purchase price of the pseudo-Degas. The court held that plaintiff had disclaimed any warranty as to the authenticity of the "Dancer"; that since the job of an auction house is to sell as commission agent many items owned by others, the authenticity of which the auctioneer cannot readily confirm, disclaimers do not violate

the law; and that defendant in his letter on the Riopelle had disavowed any offset.

After plaintiff launched its blitzkrieg here in New York, defendant responded with a lawsuit of his own. Defendant seeks to recover the purchase price of the ill-fated Degas. Defendant, relying inter alia upon Article 15 of the New York Arts and Cultural Affairs Law (the "Art Law"), contends that plaintiff is liable for having provided inaccurate information about the Degas and that the German judgment contravenes New York public policy, as a consequence of which its enforcement in favor of plaintiff is verboten. The argument, while creative and well presented, must fail.

CPLR Sec. 5304(b)(4) provides that a monetary judgment of a foreign country need not be recognized by New York if the cause of action on which the judgment is based "is repugnant to the public policy of this state." Normally, the judgment of a foreign nation will be given effect. Differences between the laws of New York and those of the many sovereign nations of the world are likely to arise often, but such differences alone cannot constitute a violation of public policy. As Judge Cardozo said, "We are not so provincial as to say that every solution of a problem is wrong because we deal with it otherwise at home." Were we New Yorkers to be overly provincial, we might well inspire foreign nations to reject enforcement of New York judgments, precisely the opposite of the purpose Article 53 was created to achieve and an outcome particularly undesirable as the economy of this country grows every day more intertwined with those of other nations.

The German court applied German law in this case. This is not unreasonable since the auction occurred in Germany and defendant placed his bid during a telephone call with the auction house in Germany. In addition, plaintiff's conditions of sale stated that legal relations between plaintiff and the bidder would be governed by German law. Defendant appeared in the German action, defended, and lost. There is, of course, no claim that German law and procedures are unfair and unworthy of respect here.

The Germans are less Bismarckian than defendant contends. German law, as exemplified by the decision of the Cologne court in this case, is not indifferent to the general sale of fakes by art merchants. The court relied upon the warranty exclusion that formed a condition of sale.

Enforcement of the German judgment would not undermine the public interest, public confidence in the law or security for individual rights, nor violate fundamental notions of what is decent and fair. The German judgment is enforceable.

ENDNOTES

1. The Charter of the United Nations was entered into force on October 24, 1945; it was adopted by the United States on October 24, 1945 [59 Stat. 1031, T.S. 993, 3 Bevans 1153, 1976 Y.B.U.N. 1043].

2. 301 U.S. 324, 57 S.Ct. 758 (1937).
3. 28 U.S.C. §§ 1602–1611.
4. 21 U.S.T. 2517, T.I.A.S. 6997.
5. 9 U.S.C. §§ 201–208.

CHAPTER 7

Ethics and Social Responsibility of Business

Ethical considerations can no more be excluded from the administration of justice, which is the end and purpose of all civil laws, than one can exclude the vital air from his room and live.

—John F. Dillon
Laws and Jurisprudence of England and America Lecture 1 (1894)

Chapter Objectives

After studying this chapter, you should be able to:

1. Describe ethical fundamentalism and ethical relativism.

2. Describe utilitarianism as a moral theory.

3. Describe Kantian ethics.

4. Describe Rawls's social justice theory.

5. Describe maximizing profits as a theory of social responsibility.

6. Describe the moral minimum theory of social responsibility.

7. Describe the stakeholder interest and the corporate citizenship theory of social responsibility.

8. Describe corporate social audits.

9. Explain how the Internet has increased the potential for unethical conduct.

10. Examine how international ethical standards differ from country to country.

Chapter Contents

Ethics precede laws as man precedes society.

Jason Alexander
Philosophy for Investors (1979)

Businesses organized in the United States are subject to its laws. They are also subject to the laws of other countries in which they operate. In addition, businesspersons owe a duty to act ethically in the conduct of their affairs, and businesses owe a social responsibility not to harm society.

Although much of the law is based on ethical standards, not all ethical standards have been enacted as law. The law establishes a minimum degree of conduct expected by persons and businesses in society. Ethics demands more. This chapter discusses business ethics and the social responsibility of business.

LAW AND ETHICS

ethics

A set of moral principles or values that governs the conduct of an individual or a group.

Sometimes the rule of law and the golden rule of **ethics** demand the same response by the person confronted with a problem. For example, federal and state laws make bribery unlawful. A person violates the law if he or she bribes a judge for a favorable decision in a case. Ethics would also prohibit this conduct.

The law may permit something that would be ethically wrong.

Business Brief

What is lawful conduct is not always ethical conduct.

Consider This Example   Occupational safety laws set standards for emissions of dust from toxic chemicals in the workplace. Suppose a company can reduce the emissions below the legal standard by spending additional money. The only benefit from the expenditure would be better employee health. Ethics would require the extra expenditure; the law would not.

Another alternative occurs where the law demands certain conduct but a person's ethical standards are contrary.

International Brief

Corruption by government officials and the influence of criminal mafias are the largest impediments to the growth of the economies of several countries. Can such corruption be contained?

Consider This Example   Federal law prohibits employees from hiring certain illegal alien workers. Suppose an employer advertises the availability of a job and receives no responses except from a person who cannot prove he or she is a citizen of this country or does not posses a required visa. The worker and his or her family are destitute. Should the employer hire him or her? The law says no, but ethics says yes (see Exhibit 7.1).

*Ɛ*XHIBIT **7.1** *Law and Ethics*

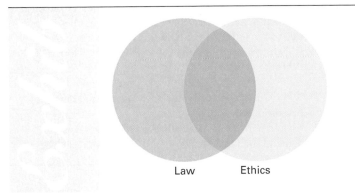

Law   Ethics

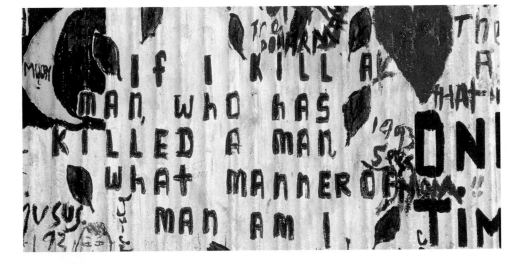

Moral Theory *Should the death penalty be permitted?*

Business Ethics

AN UNLICENSED CONTRACTOR GETS DUNKED

The doctrine of illegality is designed to protect persons from certain types of contracts deemed unfair, unscrupulous, or unconscionable by society. The doctrine denies violators access to taxpayer-supported courts to enforce their illegal contracts. Should parties sometimes be allowed to enforce their otherwise illegal contracts? Consider the following case.

Hydrotech Systems, Ltd. (Hydrotech), is a New York corporation that manufacturers and installs patented equipment to simulate ocean waves. Oasis Waterpark (Oasis) is a California corporation that owns and operates a water-oriented amusement park in Palm Springs, California. Wessman Construction Company, Inc. (Wessman), is Oasis's general contractor at the park.

In July 1985, Wessman contracted with Hydrotech to design and construct a 29,000-square-foot "surfing pool" at the park using Hydrotech's wave equipment. The total con-

tract price was $850,000. Hydrotech was aware of a California law that requires a contractor to have a California contractor's license to provide construction services in California. The statute stipulates that an unlicensed contractor cannot sue in a California court to recover compensation for work requiring a California contractor's license [California Business and Professional Code § 7031].

Because it was concerned with the licensing problem, Hydrotech wished only to sell and deliver the equipment and to avoid involvement in the design or construction of the pool. Oasis, however, insisted that Hydrotech's unique expertise in design and construction was essential. Oasis induced Hydrotech to provide these services by promising to pay Hydrotech even if the law provided otherwise.

In reliance on these promises, Hydrotech furnished equipment and services in full compliance with the contract. Hydrotech had been paid $740,000 during the course of the contract. When it billed Oasis for the remaining $110,000, Oasis refused to pay. Hydrotech sued Oasis and Wessman for damages in a California court for breach of contract and fraud. The defendants moved the court to dismiss the action because Hydrotech did not possess a California contractor's license as required by law.

The California Supreme Court agreed with the defendants and ordered Hydrotech's complaint dismissed. The court found that Hydrotech had violated the licensing statute. The supreme court stated: "The obvious statutory intent is to discourage persons who have failed to comply with the licensing law from offering or providing their unlicensed services for pay. Because of the strength and clarity of this policy, it is well settled that Section 7031 applies despite injustice to the unlicensed contractor." [*Hydrotech Systems, Ltd. v. Oasis Waterpark*, 52 Cal.3d 988, 277 Cal. Rptr. 517 (CA 1991)].

1. Did Oasis act ethically in not paying the full amount it had promised to pay?
2. Should persons act ethically even if the law does not demand such conduct?

*M*ORAL THEORIES AND BUSINESS ETHICS

He who seeks equality must do equity.

Joseph Story
Equity Jurisprudence (1836)

ethical fundamentalism
When a person looks to an outside source for ethical rules or commands.

How can ethics be measured? The answer is very personal: What is considered ethical by one person may be considered unethical by another. However, there do seem to be some universal rules about what conduct is ethical and what conduct is not. The following discussion highlights five major theories of ethics.

Ethical Fundamentalism

Under **ethical fundamentalism**, a person looks to an *outside source* for ethical rules or commands. This may be a book (e.g., the Bible or the Koran) or a person (e.g., Karl Marx). Critics argue that ethical fundamentalism does not permit people to determine right and wrong for themselves. Taken to an extreme, the result could be considered unethical under most other moral theories. For example, a literal interpretation of the maxim "an eye for an eye" would permit retaliation.

*B*usiness *E*thics

SHATTERING THE GLASS CEILING

Females have long been discriminated against in employment. **Title VII of the Civil Rights Act of 1964**, a federal statute, prohibits sex discrimination in employment. Today, the "glass ceiling" may still prevent women from reaching the highest employment positions. The following case demonstrates how blatant this can be.

Ann Hopkins was a senior manager in the Washington, DC, office of Price Waterhouse, a national firm of certified public accountants. In 1982, Hopkins was proposed for partnership in the firm. Of the 88 persons proposed for partnership that year, only one—Hopkins—was a woman. Hopkins was a project leader, worked long hours, met deadlines, and was productive, energetic, and creative. In addition, she had secured a $25-million contract for the firm. No other candidate had a comparable record for securing major contracts for the firm. Evidence did show, however, that Hopkins lacked some interpersonal skills.

All partners of the firm were invited to submit written comments on each candidate. Thirteen partners supported Hopkins's bid for partnership and eight recommended that she be denied partnership. Some of the partners reacted negatively to Hopkins's personality because she was an aggressive woman. One partner described her as "macho," another suggested that she "overcompensated for being a woman," a third advised her to take "a course at charm school," and a fourth objected to her swearing "because it is a lady using foul language."

Price Waterhouse neither offered nor denied her admission to the firm but held her candidacy for reconsideration the following year. The male partner who had the responsibility of telling Hopkins the reasons for the decision told her that she should "walk more femininely, talk more femininely, dress more femininely, wear makeup, have her hair styled, and wear jewelry." When the partners in her office refused to repropose her for partnership the next year, she sued Price Waterhouse for sex discrimination in violation of Title VII. The case went all the way to the U.S. Supreme Court.

The Supreme Court held that Price Waterhouse's action constituted "sex stereotyping" in violation of Title VII. The court stated, "We are beyond the day when an employer could evaluate employees by assuming or insisting that they matched the stereotype associated with their group. An employer who objects to aggressiveness in women but whose positions require this trait places women in a intolerable and impermissible catch-22: out of a job if they behave aggressively and out of a job if they don't. Title VII lifts women out of this bind. We sit not to determine whether Ms. Hopkins is nice, but to decide whether the partners reacted negatively to her personality because she is a woman."

The Supreme Court remanded the case to the district court. On remand, judgment was entered in favor of Ms. Hopkins against Price Waterhouse. The court ordered Price Waterhouse

to admit Ms. Hopkins as a partner retroactively effective July 1, 1983, to pay her back compensation of $371,175, and to pay her costs and attorney's fees of $422,460. [*Price Waterhouse v. Hopkins*, 490 U.S. 228, 109 S.Ct. 1775 (1989)]

1. Do you think the accounting partners who stereotyped Hopkins acted ethically?
2. Do you think that Title VII of the Civil Rights Act of 1964 is based on ethical principles? Explain.
3. Do you think the glass ceiling still exists?

Utilitarianism

Utilitarianism is a moral theory with its origins in the works of Jeremy Bentham (1748–1832) and John Stuart Mill (1806–1873). This moral theory dictates that people must choose the actions or follow the rule that provides the *greatest good to society*. This does not mean the greatest good for the greatest number of people. For instance, if one action would increase the good of 25 people one unit each, and an alternative action would increase the good of one person 26 units, the latter action should be taken.

Consider This Example A company is trying to determine whether it should close an unprofitable plant located in a small community. Utilitarianism would require that the benefits to shareholders from closing the plant be compared to the benefits to employees, their families, and others in the community in keeping it open.

Utilitarianism has been criticized because it is difficult to estimate the "good" that will result from different actions, it is hard to apply in an imperfect world, and it treats morality as if it were an impersonal mathematical calculation.

utilitarianism

A moral theory that dictates that people must choose the action or follow the rule that provides the greatest good to society.

The ultimate justification of the law is to be found, and can only be found, in moral considerations.

Lord MacMillian
Law and Other Things *(1937)*

Business Ethics

GENERAL MOTORS SKIPS TOWN

For decades, job-hungry communities have offered tax abatements, low-interest loans, and other financial inducements to lure companies to locate in their community. Some companies take these incentives but then leave town when they run out. Cities are fighting back, and many are bringing lawsuits.

Consider the case of Ypsilanti, Michigan. From 1984 to 1988, Ypsilanti gave General Motors Corporation (GM) $13 million in tax abatements to keep its Willow Run plant, which produced Chevrolet automobiles, in the city. In 1991, GM announced that it was going to close the Willow Run plant and move the work being done there to its Arlington, Texas, plant. The closure meant the loss of thousands of jobs in a city already suffering severe unemployment and financial difficulties.

Ypsilanti sued GM for reneging on its implied promise to stay put in return for the tax breaks. The trial court judge invoked a doctrine of promissory estoppel and enjoined GM from closing its plant in Ypsilanti.

The trial court judge stated, "There would be a gross inequity and patent unfairness if General Motors, having lulled the people of the Ypsilanti area into giving up millions

of tax dollars which they desperately need to educate their children and provide basic governmental services, is allowed to simply decide it will desert 4,500 workers and their families because it thinks it can make these same cars cheaper somewhere else."

The Michigan court of appeals reversed, however. The appeals court held that GM made no promise to stay put in Ypsilanti as a quid pro quo for the tax abatements. The court held that any statements made by GM concerning maintaining continuous employment at the Willow Run plant were merely expressions of hope or expectation but did not amount to a promise. The court's decision permits GM to transfer production from the Michigan plant to Texas. [*Charter Township of Ypsilanti, Michigan v. General Motors Corporation*, No. 161245 (Mich. App. 1993)]

1. Did GM act ethically by attempting to close its plant in Ypsilanti? Would your answer be different if GM were losing money at the plant?
2. Which court do you think was correct, the trial court or the court of appeals?

Kantian Ethics

Kantian or duty ethics

A moral theory that says that people owe moral duties that are based on universal rules, such as the categorical imperative "do unto others as you would have them do unto you."

Immanuel Kant (1724–1804) is the best-known proponent of **duty ethics**, or **deontology** (from the Greek word *deon*, meaning duty). Kant believed that people owe moral duties that are based on *universal* rules. For example, keeping a promise to abide by a contract is a moral duty even if that contract turns out to be detrimental to the obligated party. Kant's philosophy is based on the premise that people can use reasoning to reach ethical decisions. His ethical theory would have people behave according to the *categorical imperative* "Do unto others as you would have them do unto you."

Deontology's universal rules are based on two important principles: (1) consistency, that is, all cases are treated alike with no exceptions and (2) reversibility, that is, the actor must abide by the rule he or she uses to judge the morality of someone else's conduct. Thus, if you are going to make an exception for yourself, that exception becomes a universal rule that applies to all others. For example, if you rationalize that it is all right for you to engage in deceptive practices, it is all right for competitors to do so also. A criticism of Kantian ethics is that it is hard to reach a consensus as to what the universal rules should be.

Ethical issues are raised in the following case.

Zivich v. Mentor Soccer Club, Inc.
696 N.E.2d 201 (1998)
Supreme Court of Ohio

CASE 7.1

BACKGROUND AND FACTS
In May 1993, Pamela Zivich registered her seven-year old son, Bryan, to play soccer with the Mentor Soccer Club, Inc. (Club), for the 1993-1994 season. The Club is a nonprofit organization composed primarily of volunteers in the Mentor, Ohio, area who provide children with the opportunity to learn and play soccer. The club's registration form, which Mrs. Zivich signed, contained the following language:

Recognizing the possibility of physical injury associated with soccer and for the Mentor Soccer Club, and the USYSA [United States Youth Soccer Association] accepting the registrant for its soccer programs and activities, I hereby release, discharge and/or otherwise indemnify the Mentor Soccer Club and the USYSA, its affiliated organizations and sponsors, their employees, and associated personnel, including the owners of the fields and facilities utilized by the Soccer Club, against any claim by or on behalf of the registrant as a result of the registrant's participation in the Soccer Club.

On October 7, 1993, Bryan attended soccer practice with his father, Philip Zivich. During practice, the team participated in an intrasquad scrimmage. After the scrimmage, Bryan jumped onto the soccer goal and was swinging back and forth on it, but the goal was not anchored down. It tipped backward, and Bryan fell. The goal came down on his chest, breaking three of his ribs and his collarbone and severely bruising his lungs. Bryan's parents sued the club for negligence to recover damages for injuries suffered by Bryan and the loss of consortium for themselves. The club moved for summary judgment, asserting that the exculpatory agreement signed by Bryan's mother barred the claims. The trial court agreed and granted the club's summary judgment motion. The court of appeals affirmed. The plaintiff's appealed to the Supreme Court of Ohio.

ISSUE
Did the exculpatory agreement signed by Mrs. Zivich on behalf of her son release the club from liability for the child's claims and the parents claims?

COURT'S REASONING
The court noted that with respect to adult participants, the general rule is that releases from liability for injuries caused by negligent acts arising in the context of recreational activities are enforceable. Here, however, the exculpatory agreement was executed by a parent on behalf of the minor child. The court stated that the threat of liability strongly deters many individuals from volunteering for nonprofit organizations. The court reasoned that although Bryan, like many children before him, gave up his right to sue for the negligent acts of others, the public as a whole received the benefit of these exculpatory agreements. Because of this agreement, the club was able to offer affordable recreation and to continue to do so without the risks and overwhelming costs of litigation. Bryan's parents agreed to shoulder the risk. The court stated, public policy does not forbid such an agreement. In fact, public policy supports it.

DECISION
A parent's signature on an exculpatory agreement on behalf of his or her child releases the other party from liability to the child, the parent who signed the agreement, and the other parent. Affirmed.

Case Questions

Critical Legal Thinking   Do exculpatory agreements serve any valid purpose? Should exculpatory agreements be enforceable?

Business Ethics   Was it ethical for Mrs. Zivich to sign the exculpatory agreement and then bring this lawsuit?

Contemporary Business   What would have been the consequences if the court had found the exculpatory agreement to be invalid in this case?

Rawls's Social Justice Theory

John Locke (1632–1704) and Jean Jacques Rousseau (1712–1778) proposed a **social contract** theory of morality. Under this theory, each person is presumed to have entered into a social contract with all others in society to obey moral rules that are necessary for people to live in peace and harmony. This implied contract states, "I will keep the rules if everyone else does." These moral rules are then used to solve conflicting interests in society.

The leading proponent of the modern social justice theory is John Rawls, a contemporary philosopher at Harvard University. Under Rawls's *distributive justice theory*, fairness is considered the essence of justice. The principles of justice should be chosen by persons who do not yet know their station in society—thus, their "veil of ignorance" would permit the fairest possible principles to be selected. For example, the principle of equal opportunity would be promulgated by people who would not yet know if they were in a favored class. As a caveat, Rawls also proposes that the least advantaged in society must receive special assistance to allow them to realize their potential.

Rawls's theory of distributive justice is criticized for two reasons. First, establishing the blind "original position" for choosing moral principles is impossible in the real world. Second, many persons in society would choose not to maximize the benefit to the least advantaged persons in society.

In the following case, the court addressed an ethical and law issue.

> **Rawls's social contract**
>
> A moral theory that says each person is presumed to have entered into a social contract with all others in society to obey moral rules that are necessary for people to live in peace and harmony.

Castle Rock Entertainment, Inc. v. Carol Publishing Group, Inc.
150 F.3d 132 (1998)
United States Court of Appeals, Second Circuit

CASE 7.2

BACKGROUND AND FACTS

Castle Rock Entertainment, Inc., is the producer and copyright owner of the successful "Seinfeld" television series. For years, "Seinfeld" was the highest-rated show on television. The series revolved around petty tribulations in the lives of four single, adult friends in New York: Jerry Seinfeld, George Costanza, Elaine Benes, and Cosmo Kramer. To take advantage of the public interest in Seinfeld, Carol Publishing Group, Inc. published a book written by Beth Golub entitled *The Seinfeld Aptitude Test* (SAT). The 132-page book contained 643 questions and answers about events and characters in 84 TV episodes of "Seinfeld." These included 211 multiple-choice questions, 93 matching questions, and a number of short-answer questions. The correct answers to these questions have as their source fictional moments in "Seinfeld" episodes, and 41 questions contain exact dialogue from "Seinfeld." The name "Seinfeld" appears prominently on the front and back covers of the SAT, and pictures of the principal actors in Seinfeld appear on the cover and throughout the book.

In February 1995, Castle Rock filed this action against Carol Publishing and Golub alleging federal copyright infringement. Castle Rock made a motion for summary judgment alleging that no facts were in dispute and that the court could make a decision as a matter of law whether copyright infringement occurred. The trial court agreed that no facts were in dispute that required a jury's determination. The court, therefore, considered the undisputed evidence and found that the defendants had violated Castle Rock's copyrights of "Seinfeld," and awarded damages and issued an injunction enjoining the defendants from publishing the *Seinfeld Aptitude Test* book. The court granted Castle Rock's motion for summary judgment. The defendants appealed.

ISSUE

Is Castle Rock entitle to summary judgment on its copyright infringement claim?

COURT'S REASONING

Walker, Circuit Judge Summary judgment is appropriate if the moving party can show that there is no genuine issue as to any material fact and that the moving party is entitled to judgment as a matter of law. In the instant case, no one disputes that Castle Rock owns valid copyrights in the Seinfeld television programs and that defendants actually copied from those programs in creating the SAT. Golub freely admitted that she created the SAT by taking notes from Seinfeld programs at the time they were aired on television and subsequently reviewing videotapes of several of the episodes that she or her friends recorded.

Each SAT trivia question is based directly upon original, protectable expression in Seinfeld. Each "fact" tested by the SAT is in reality fictitious expression created by Seinfeld authors. The SAT does not quiz such true facts as the identity of the actors in Seinfeld, the number of days it takes to shoot an episode, the biographies of the actors, the location of the Seinfeld set, etc. Rather, the SAT tests whether the reader knows that the character Jerry places a Pez dispenser on Elaine's leg during a piano recital *or that Kramer enjoys going to the airport because he's hypnotized by the baggage carousels. Because these characters and events spring from the imagination of* Seinfeld *authors, the SAT plainly copies copyrightable, creative expression.*

DECISION AND REMEDY

The court of appeals held that the defendants had infringed Castle Rock's copyright and affirmed the district court's grant of summary judgment in Castle Rock's favor.

Case Questions

Critical Legal Thinking What purpose does the legal doctrine of summary judgment serve?

Business Ethics Do you think Carol Publishing and Golub acted unethically in this case?

Contemporary Business If the court had found the defendants' conduct to have been legal, would it lead to more or less ethical conduct in society? Explain.

Ethical Relativism

ethical relativism

A moral theory that holds that individuals must decide what is ethical based on their own feelings as to what is right or wrong.

Ethical relativism holds that *individuals must decide what is ethical based on their own feelings as to what is right or wrong.* Under this moral theory, if a person meets his or her own moral standard in making a decision, no one can criticize him or her for it. Thus, there are no universal ethical rules to guide a person's conduct. This theory has been criticized because action that is usually thought to be unethical (e.g., committing fraud) would not be unethical if the perpetrator thought it was in fact ethical. Few philosophers advocate ethical relativism as an acceptable moral theory.

In the following case, the court found that the defendant company had engaged in unethical and illegal comparative false advertising.

McNeil-P.C.C., Inc. v. Bristol-Meyers Squibb Co.
938 F.2d 1544 (1991)
United States Court of Appeals, Second Circuit

CASE 7.3

BACKGROUND AND FACTS

McNeil-P.C.C., Inc. (McNeil), the leading manufacturer of over-the-counter analgesic pain remedies, markets Extra-Strength Tylenol (Tylenol). A two-tablet dose of Tylenol contains 1,000 milligrams of acetaminophen. In the spring of 1990, Bristol-Meyers Squibb Company (Bristol-Meyers) began marketing a competing analgesic pain remedy called Aspirin-Free Excedrin (Excedrin). A two-tablet dose of Excedrin contains 1,000 milligrams of acetaminophen plus 130 milligrams of caffeine. To market its new Excedrin pain reliever, Bristol-Meyers sent promotional literature to drug retailers and began a television advertising campaign that claimed that Excedrin "works better" than Tylenol. The claim was based on a "crossover" study conducted by Bristol-Meyers. A crossover study has the patients take one drug in period one and another drug in period two and then evaluates the performance of both drugs. Because McNeil believed that the Bristol-Meyers "works better" claim was false, it sued Bristol-Meyers for violating Section 43(a) of the Lanham Act, a federal statute that prohibits false advertising. The district court held in favor of McNeil and permanently enjoined Bristol-Meyers from making its "works better" claims for Excedrin a claim. Bristol-Meyers appealed.

ISSUE

Did defendant Bristol-Meyers make false advertising claims about the superiority of its Excedrin pain-relieving product in violation of the Lanham Act?

COURT'S REASONING

The evidence introduced at court showed that the period one tests showed no statistical difference between the performance of Excedrin and Tylenol. The court found that although period two tests showed a slight difference, the results were tainted because they were distorted by psychological effects. Consequently, the court determined that the Bristol-Meyers tests did not prove the superiority of its Excedrin brand product. McNeil proved that the Bristol-Meyers "works better" than Tylenol claim was false.

DECISION

The court of appeals held that Bristol-Meyers had made false advertising claims and therefore violated the Lanham Act.

Case Questions

Critical Legal Thinking Should false advertising constitute a tort?

Business Ethics Did Bristol-Meyers act ethically in making its "works better" claim?

Contemporary Business Should companies be permitted to engage in comparative advertising? Why or why not?

CONCEPT SUMMARY   THEORIES OF ETHICS

Theory	Description
Ethical fundamentalism	Persons look to an outside source (e.g., Bible or Koran) or central figure for ethical guidelines.
Utilitarianism	Persons choose the alternative that would provide the greatest good to society.
Kantian ethics	A set of universal rules establishes ethical duties. The rules are based on reasoning and require (1) consistency in application and (2) reversibility.
Rawls's social justice theory	Moral duties are based on an implied social contract. Fairness is justice. The rules are established from an original position of a "veil of ignorance."
Ethical relativism	Individuals decide what is ethical based on their own feelings as to what is right or wrong.

E-Commerce & Information Technology

LAWYER'S LEGAL DUTY TO SURF THE NET

Sometimes an injured party has a valid complaint upon which to base a lawsuit but has waited too long to do so. In such a case, the defendant asserts that the relevant statute of limitations has not been met and that the case should be thrown out of court. In lawsuits based on fraud, the statute of limitations does not start to run until the defendant should have been on notice—**inquiry notice**—that he or she has been defrauded. Often there is a battle between the plaintiff and defendant about when this inquiry notice day occurred. Consider the following case.

In July 1991, Whirlpool Financial Corporation (Whirlpool) made a $10 million loan to GN Holdings, Inc. (GN), to help GN acquire another company, Cross Country Healthcare Personnel, Inc., which provided temporary nurses and other health care professionals to hospitals across the United States. GN executed a promissory note agreeing to pay Whirlpool the borrowed money at a 15.5 percent annual interest rate (payable in quarterly installments) with a balloon payment of the principal in 1998. To secure the financing, GN prepared a private placement memorandum that provided financial data, narrative information, and projections about future performance. Whirlpool relied on this information when making the loan to GN.

As happens in many new ventures, the projections painted a much rosier picture than what actually unfolded. In the years 1991 through 1993, net sales were 32 to 48 percent lower than projected, operating profit was 50 to 73 percent lower than projected, pretax profit was 95 to 257 percent lower than projected, and net income was 104 to 283 percent lower than projected. GN defaulted on the interest payment due on April 1,

1994. In July 1994, Whirlpool filed suit against GN for securities fraud, three years after having made the loan to GN. GN asserted even assuming that it committed fraud, that the one-year statute of limitations in federal securities law barred Whirlpool's lawsuit. Whirlpool contended that the one-year period did not begin to run until an inquiry date sometime after July 1993. The federal district court agreed with the defendants and dismissed the lawsuit. The court of appeals affirmed.

The court of appeals analyzed Whirlpool's contention that GN had information that it concealed from Whirlpool, causing the inquiry date to be extended. First, the court dismissed Whirlpool's claim that GN failed to disclose legislation that could affect the provision of temporary medical care personnel. The court stated that Whirlpool could have easily discovered this public information itself. Second, the court ruled against Whirlpool's claim that GN did not disclose economic trends in the temporary nursing care industry. The court noted that with reasonable diligence, which included using the Internet, Whirlpool could have easily discovered the industry trends it alleged GN concealed from it. The court admonished Whirlpool for failing to investigate GN's claims, particularly with the availability of new technology like the Internet to conduct a "due diligence" investigation. The court of appeals held that Whirlpool had not shown any reason to extend the statue of limitations beyond the date the loan was made and held that Whirlpool's claim was time-barred by the statute of limitations. [*Whirlpool Financial Corporation v. GN Holdings, Inc.*, 67 F.3d 605 (1995)]

THE SOCIAL RESPONSIBILITY OF BUSINESS

Business does not operate in a vacuum. Decisions made by businesses have far-reaching effects on society. In the past, many business decisions were made solely on a cost-benefit analysis and how they affected the "bottom line." Such decisions, however, may cause

Ethics Brief

Corporations that conduct social audits will be more apt to prevent unethical and illegal conduct by managers, employees, and agents.

social responsibility

Duty owed by businesses to act socially responsible in producing and selling goods and services.

Ethical standards vary from country to country.

negative externalities for others. For example, the dumping of hazardous wastes from a manufacturing plant into a river affects the homeowners, farmers, and others who use the river's waters. Thus, corporations are considered to owe some degree of **social responsibility** for their actions. Four theories of the social responsibility of business are discussed in the following paragraphs.

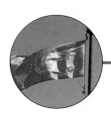

International Law

ETHICAL PRINCIPLES FOR INTERNATIONAL BUSINESS

Ethics is a function of history, culture, religion, and other factors. It differs from culture to culture and person to person. The social responsibility of business also differs considerably, depending on the corporation's philosophy and the influence of the home country's mores.

Recognizing that laws are necessary but insufficient guides for conduct, a group called the Caux Round Table—a collaboration of leaders from various multinational corporations—promulgated an international ethics code called the *Principles for International Business.* These principles are unique because they are based on transnational values from the East and West: the Japanese concept of *kyosei* (living and working together for the common good) and the Western concept of the dignity of the human person. Since they were first introduced in 1994, the *Principles* have been adopted by many multinational corporations around the world.

The Caux Round Table *Principles* that international businesses should take into consideration when making business decisions are:

- **Principle 1**   *The Responsibilities of Businesses: Beyond Shareholders Toward Stakeholders* The value of business to society is the wealth and employment it creates and the marketable products and services it provides to consumers at a reasonable price commensurate with quality. To create such value, a business must maintain its own

economic health and viability, but survival is not a sufficient goal.

Businesses have a role to play in improving the lives of all their customers, employees, and shareholders by sharing with them the wealth they have created. Suppliers and competitors as well should expect businesses to honor their obligations in a spirit of honesty and fairness. As responsible citizens of the local, national, regional, and global communities in which they operate, businesses share a part in shaping the future of those communities.

- **Principle 2**   *The Economic and Social Impact of Business: Toward Innovation, Justice, and World Community* Businesses established in foreign countries to develop, produce, or sell should also contribute to the social advancement of those countries by creating productive employment and helping to raise the purchasing power of their citizens. Businesses also should contribute to human rights, education, welfare, and vitalization of the countries in which they operate.

Businesses should contribute to economic and social development not only in the countries in which they operate but also in the world community at large, through effective and prudent use of resources, free and fair competition, and emphasis upon innovation in technology, production methods, marketing, and communications.

- **Principle 3**   *Business Behavior: Beyond the Letter of Law Toward a Spirit of Trust* While accepting the legitimacy of trade secrets, businesses should recognize that sincerity, candor, truthfulness, the keeping of promises, and transparency contribute not only to their own credibility and stability but also to the smoothness and efficiency of business transactions, particularly on the international level.
- **Principle 4**   *Respect for Rules* To avoid trade frictions and to promote freer trade, equal conditions for competition, and fair and equitable treatment for all participants, businesses should respect international and domestic rules. In addition, they should recognize that some behavior, although legal, may still have adverse consequences.
- **Principle 5**   *Support for Multilateral Trade* Businesses should support the multilateral trade systems of the GATT/World Trade Organization and similar international agreements. They should cooperate in efforts to promote the progressive and judicious liberalization of trade and to relax those domestic measures that unreasonably hinder global commerce, while giving due respect to national policy objectives.
- **Principle 6**   *Respect for the Environment* A business should protect and, where possible, improve the environment, promote sustainable development, and prevent the wasteful use of natural resources.
- **Principle 7**   *Avoidance of Illicit Operations* A business should not participate in or condone bribery, money laundering, or other corrupt practices; indeed, it should seek cooperation with others to eliminate them. It should not trade in arms or other materials used for terrorist activities, drug traffic, or other organized crime.

International Law

ANTIDUMPING LAWS

Dumping is the sale of imported goods at less than fair market value. This usually occurs when a company sells goods in a foreign country at prices lower than the goods are sold for in the producer's domestic market. Dumping usually occurs where the foreign seller wants to increase its share of the other country's market or is being subsidized by its government.

The United States and other countries of the world have tried to control this practice. The **U.S. International Trade Administration (ITA)** of the Department of Commerce and the **U.S. International Trade Commission (ITC)** both have jurisdiction to investigate charges of dumping of foreign goods in the United States. The **U.S. Court of International Trade** located in Washington, D.C., hears cases on dumping, and appeals may be taken to the U.S. Court of Appeals for the Federal Circuit, which is also located in Washington, D.C. Under the **Tariff Act of 1930** [19 U.S.C. § 1673], as amended, a U.S. company that suspects dumping in the United States by a foreign firm may file a complaint with the ITA and the ITC.

If the agencies find that illegal dumping has occurred that has caused material injury to U.S. companies, the agency may assess an *antidumping* or *countervailing duty* (i.e., extra tariff) on the imported goods. This duty may also be assessed retroactively in more severe cases.

Maximizing Profits

The traditional view of the social responsibility of business is that business should **maximize profits** for shareholders. This view, which dominated business and the law during the nineteenth century, holds that the interest of other constituencies (e.g., employees, suppliers, residents of the communities in which businesses are located) are not important in and of themselves.

In the famous case of *Dodge v. Ford Motor Company*[1] a shareholder sued the car company when Henry Ford introduced a plan to reduce the price of cars so that more people would be put to work and more people could own cars. The shareholders alleged that such a plan would not increase dividends. Mr. Ford testified, "My ambition is to employ still more men, to spread the benefits of this industrial system to the greatest number, to help them build up their lives and their homes." The court sided with the shareholders and stated that

> *[Mr. Ford's] testimony creates the impression that he thinks the Ford Motor Company has made too much money, has had too large profits and that, although large profits might still be earned, a sharing of them with the public, by reducing the price of the output of the company, ought to be undertaken.*

maximizing profits

A theory of social responsibility that says a corporation owes a duty to take actions that maximize profits for shareholders.

Public policy: That principle of the law which holds that no subject can lawfully do that which has a tendency to be injurious to the public or against the public good.

Lord Truro
Egerton v. Brownlow *(1853)*

There should be no confusion of the duties which Mr. Ford conceives that he and the stockholders owe to the general public and the duties which in law he and his codirectors owe to protesting, minority stockholders. A business corporation is organized and carried on primarily for the profit of the stockholders. The powers of the directors are to be employed for that end. The discretion of directors is to be exercised in the choice of means to attain that end and does not extend to a change in the end itself, to the reduction of profits, or to the nondistribution of profits among stockholders in order to devote them to other purposes.

Ethics Brief

Patagonia, the Ventura, California-based outdoor apparel company, gives the greater of 10 percent of annual pretax profits or 1 percent of sales to environmental causes.

Milton Friedman, who won the Nobel Prize in economics when he taught at the University of Chicago, advocated this theory. Friedman asserted that in a free society, "there is one and only one social responsibility of business—to use its resources and engage in activities designed to increase its profits as long as it stays within the rules of the game, which is to say, engages in open and free competition without deception and fraud."[2]

Business Ethics

Joe Camel Exhales

Since his introduction in 1988, Joe Camel has become a cartoon icon. R.J. Reynolds Tobacco Company splashed the cool camel on billboards, in magazines, and in other media across the country. Joe Camel could be seen riding motorcycles, playing pool, jamming with a jazz band, and hanging out with his female comrade, Josephine Camel. Joe and his buddies were used to promote R.J. Reynolds's Camel cigarettes.

Why would a cigarette company choose a cartoon character to advertise its cigarettes? In December 1991, San Francisco attorney Janet Mangini thought she knew when she read results of three studies that were published by the *Journal of the American Medical Association (JAMA)*. These studies concluded that the popularity of Camel cigarettes had increased 66-fold with teen smokers in the three years following the introduction of Joe Camel. Joe Camel was right up there with Mickey Mouse in recognition by children. Mangini concluded that R.J. Reynolds had gone after children and teens to promote cigarette smoking, so she decided to go after Joe Camel.

But how do you successfully sue a monolith like R.J. Reynolds? Mangini enlisted the lawyers at the five-attorney firm of Bushnell, Caplan & Fielding in San Francisco to help brainstorm the attack on R.J. Reynolds. They were aware that traditional personal-injury lawsuits against cigarette companies had not been successful, so they turned to California Business and Professional Code Section 17200 et seq., also know as the Unfair Business Practices Act. This act permits any individual to act as a private attorney general for the state of California and to file a suit against a company to halt a harmful or unfair business practice. Mangini and the small law firm knew they were in over their heads in taking on R.J. Reynolds, so they sought the help of Milberg Weiss, a large law firm in San Diego know for filing shareholder class-action lawsuits. Patrick J. Coughlin, a partner at the firm whose father was a smoker who had died of lung cancer,

became interested. Milberg Weiss joined the team and agreed to shoulder 80 percent of the work. Mangini became the plaintiff. The law firms filed an unfair business practices lawsuit against R.J. Reynolds to try to eliminate Joe Camel and his cohorts.

R.J. Reynolds's first action was to try to get the case thrown out of court. The company argued that Joe Camel was protected by the Free Speech Clause of the First Amendment of the U.S. Constitution and that the state law claims were preempted by the Federal Cigarette Labeling and Advertising Act, the act that requires warnings on cigarette packages. The trial court threw the case out of court, but the California Supreme Court reinstated the case stating,

The targeting of minors is oppressive and unscrupulous, in that it exploits minors by luring them into an unhealthy and potentially life-threatening addiction before they have achieved the maturity necessary to make an informed decision whether to take up smoking despite its health risks.

R.J. Reynolds appealed to the U.S. Supreme Court, which declined to hear the case. With the courtroom door finally open, the real work began. The plaintiff's attorneys reviewed more than 30 million pages of documents over a five-year period. The evidence showed that R.J. Reynolds's advertising was aimed at the "youth market." Company reports outlined the importance of attracting "presmokers," aged 12 to 24, and stated that "young adult smokers are the only source of replacement smokers." R.J. Reynolds's market research reported: "Less than one third of smokers start after age 18. Only 5 percent of smokers start after age 24."

Twenty states, the U.S. Surgeon General, the American Lung Association, the American Cancer Society, and the American Heart Association backed Mangini's claim against R.J. Reynolds. Eventually, the parties entered into settlement negotiations. The plaintiff and her lawyers agreed that there was no amount of money they would accept to settle the case; Joe Camel must go! With mounting pressure and facing trial, in July 1997, R.J. Reynolds formally agreed to terminate the Joe Camel campaign across the nation. [*Mangini v. R.J. Reynolds Tobacco Company*].

1. Do you think that the Joe Camel advertising campaign was aimed at children and teenagers? Did R.J. Reynolds make a profit from children and teenage smokers? Explain.

2. Do you believe that there was a link between the advertising campaign and smoking? If there was no link, do you think that R.J. Reynolds would have spent millions of dollars on the advertising campaign?

3. Should R.J. Reynolds have been permitted to continue the Joe Camel advertising campaign under free-speech rights of the First Amendment of the U.S. Constitution? Why or why not?

Business Ethics

SEARS'S AUTO REPAIR CENTERS: WHO GOT THE LUBE JOB?

Sears, Roebuck & Co. is a venerable retailer at which generations of Americans have shopped for clothes, tools, appliances, and other goods and services. For years, the company billed itself as the place "where Americans shop." Today, Sears's auto repair centers, which generate more than $3 billion in annual sales, have been charged with being the place where Americans get robbed.

Spurred by a 50 percent increase in consumer complaints over a three-year period, several states conducted undercover investigations to determine the legitimacy of those complaints. The New Jersey Division of Consumer Affairs found that all six Sears Auto Centers visited by undercover agents recommended unnecessary repairs. The California Department of Consumer Affairs found that Sears—the largest provider of auto services in the state—had systematically overcharged an average of $223 for repairs and routinely billed for work that was not done. Forty-one other states lodged similar complaints.

The "bait and rip off" scheme worked as follows: Sears would send consumers coupons advertising discounts on brake jobs. When consumers came in to redeem their coupons, the sales staff would convince them to authorize additional repairs. Sears also established quotas for repair services that their employees had to meet.

California officials got the company's attention when the state started proceedings to revoke Sears's auto repair license. Sears quickly agreed to settle all lawsuits against it. As part of the settlement, Sears agreed to distribute $50 worth of coupons to almost 1 million customers nationwide who obtained one of five specific repair services from Sears between August 1, 1990, and January 31, 1992. The coupons could be redeemed for merchandise and services at Sears stores. In addition, Sears agreed to pay $3.5 million to cover the costs of various government investigations, to contribute $1.5 million to community colleges to conduct auto mechanic training programs, and to abandon its repair service quotas. The settlement cost Sears $30 million.

In agreeing to the settlement, Sears denied any wrongdoing, simply stating that "mistakes were made." It said that it agreed to the settlement to avoid the burden, expenses, and uncertainty of prolonged litigation.

1. Did Sears act ethically in this case? Should it have admitted culpability?

2. Why do you think Sears chose to settle the cases instead of defending itself in court?

3. Do you think Sears let the "profit motive" overshadow its ethics?

Moral Minimum

Some proponents of corporate social responsibility argue that a corporation's duty is to *make a profit while avoiding causing harm to others*. This theory of social responsibility is called the **moral minimum**. Under this theory, as long as business avoids or corrects the social injury it causes, it has met its duty of social responsibility. For instance, a corporation that pollutes the waters and then compensates those whom it injures has met its moral minimum duty of social responsibility.

The legislative and judicial branches of government have established laws that enforce the moral minimum of social responsibility on corporations. For example, occupational safety laws establish minimum safety standards for protecting employees from injuries in the workplace. Consumer protection laws establish safety requirements for products and make manufacturers and sellers liable for injuries caused by defective products. Other laws establish similar minimum standards for conduct for business in other areas.

moral minimum

A theory of social responsibility that says a corporation's duty is to make a profit while avoiding harm to others.

Ethics Brief

Many people do not buy tuna because the tuna nets also catch dolphins. Is this socially responsible behavior? Should someone care about the tuna?

International Law

PAYMENT OF BRIBES

Universal ethical rules may exist within a country, but they definitely do not exist for the world as a whole. This is because the cultures and laws of countries are different. Thus, what may be unethical in one country may be considered ethical in another. A corporation that operates in many countries—a "transnational company"—is faced with a dilemma: Does it follow the ethical rule of its parent country or its host country?

The Lockheed Corporation (Lockheed), a *Fortune 500* company that manufactures aircraft, faced this problem. In the 1970s, it manufactured the L-1011, or "TriStar," commercial airliner. It competed with McDonnell Douglas and Boeing, both U.S. corporations, as well as other competitors, to sell the aircraft to airline carriers in the United States and other countries.

In 1975, an investigation revealed that Lockheed had paid more than $12 million to the president of All Nippon Airlines (ANA) and several Japanese politicians and government officials in conjunction with its sale of L-1011s to the airline carrier. A. Carl Kotchian, the chairman of Lockheed, authorized the payments. Congressional hearings on the matter reveled that such payments were common in the aircraft industry.

Mr. Kotchian provided several justifications for his actions. First, he cited the fact that such payments by Lockheed in Japan did not at the time violate any U.S. laws. Second, he testified that the payments were "worthwhile from Lockheed's standpoint" because "they would provide Lockheed workers with jobs, and thus redound to the benefit of their dependents, their communities, and stockholders of the corporation."

Concerning one of the payments, Mr. Kotchian wrote:

Soon after landing in Japan, I found myself deep in conversation with Toshiharu Okubo, and official of Marubeni, the trading company that was serving as Lockheed's representative and go-between in the already ongoing TriStar negotiations.

Beaming, Okubo reviewed Marubeni's efforts on behalf of TriStar, then gave me the good news that "tomorrow at

7:30 A.M. we are seeing Prime Minster Tanaka" about the matter. I was quite impressed with and encouraged by the "power of Marubeni"—power that made it possible to make an appointment with the prime minister only 24 hours after I had asked Marubeni to set up such a meeting. Then came an unexpected development: When we began to discuss in detail how to bring about the sale of TriStar, Okubo suddenly suggested that I make a "pledge" to pay money for a major favor like this. Though the proposal did not appall and outrage me, I was nonetheless quite astonished that the question of money had been brought up so abruptly.

"How much money do we have to pledge?" I asked.

"The going rate when asking for a major favor is usually five hundred million yen."

I was now faced with the problem of whether to make a payment to Japan's highest government office. Sensing my hesitation, Okubo reiterated "If you wish to be successful in selling the aircraft, you would do well to pledge five hundred million yen."

Lockheed made this payment and similar payments and was successful in selling planes to the Japanese.

The Lockheed case and similar cases led Congress to enact the **Foreign Corrupt Practices Act of 1977** (15 U.S.C. § 78m). This act, as amended, makes it a crime for U.S. companies to bribe a foreign official, a foreign political party official, or a candidate for foreign political office. The payment of a bribe does not violate the act if the payment was lawful under the written laws of the foreign country in which it was paid, however.

1. Do international ethical standards differ from country to country? Explain.
2. Did the fact that U.S. law did not make the payments unlawful at the time they were made justify them?
3. Should economic factors (e.g., jobs) outweigh ethics? Explain.

Stakeholder Interest

stakeholder interest

A theory of social responsibility that says a corporation must consider the effects its actions have on persons other than its stockholders.

Businesses have relationships with all sorts of people other than their stockholders, including employees, suppliers, customers, creditors, and the local community. Under the **stakeholder interest** theory of social responsibility, a corporation must consider the effects its actions have on these *other stakeholders*. For example, a corporation would violate the stakeholder interest theory if it viewed employees solely as a means of maximizing stockholder wealth.

This theory is criticized because it is difficult to harmonize the conflicting interests of stakeholders. For example, in deciding whether to close a plant, certain stakeholders may benefit (e.g., stockholders and creditors) while other stakeholders may not (e.g., current employees and the local community).

Business Ethics

TOY SALES NOT CHILD'S PLAY

When a child opens a new toy, there is a 30 percent probability that the toy was purchased at a Toys "R" Us retail store; the company controls that much of the retail toy market in the United States. But Toys "R" Us did not gain this 30 percent market share by being a stuffed animal on a shelf. In fact, the Federal Trade Commission (FTC), the federal government agency empowered to protect consumers, decided that Toys "R" Us needed to be disciplined for its unruly behavior on the playground.

Toys "R" Us , the nation's largest toy retailer, built a reputation for being a low-cost toy seller, but it now faces price competition from warehouse clubs such as Costco and Wal-Mart. Not liking this competition, Toys "R" Us decided to bully its suppliers, the toy manufacturers. Toys "R" Us used its dominance as a toy distributor to extract agreements from toy manufacturers to *boycott*—not sell—toys to warehouse clubs. The manufacturers that were "persuaded" to joint the Toys "R" Us-sponsored boycott accounted for 40 percent of the toys sold in the United States. To police its policy, Toys "R" Us threatened to stop buying from any toy manufacturer that violated this vertical boycott. In addition, the company used its muscle to orchestrate a horizontal boycott agreement among most of these manufacturers to adhere to the restriction on toy sales to warehouse clubs and to "tattle" on one another for any violations.

The FTC investigated and found that Toys "R" Us and its reluctant collaborators unfairly stifled competition in the marketplace. The FTC held that the Toys "R" Us boycott was an unreasonable restraint of trade in violation of the federal Sherman Antitrust Act. They also ruled that the boycott caused harmful effects to consumers and to the warehouse clubs and that there was no legal business justification for this conduct. The FTC issued a *cease and desist order* that barred Toys "R" Us from entering into any agreement with toy manufacturers to limit the supply of toys that can be sold to discount warehouse stores and prohibited Toys "R" Us from attempting to facilitate any agreement among its suppliers regarding the sale of toys to any retailer. [*Federal Trade Commission v. Toys "R" Us*]

1. Why did Toys "R" Us engage in such conduct? Explain.
2. Did Toys "R" Us act unfairly, or was this just good, clean competition? Did Toys "R" Us misuse its market power?
3. What would be the consequences if Toys "R" Us got away with what it was doing?

The Supreme Court Speaks

The Imposition of Punitive Damages Punishes Immoral Business Conduct

Copper Industries, Inc. v. Leatherman Tool Group, Inc.
121 S.Ct. 1678 (2001)
Supreme Court of the United States

BACKGROUND AND FACTS
Leatherman Tool Group, Inc. manufactures and sells a multifunctional tool called the PST that improves upon the classic Swiss army knife. Leatherman dominates the market for multifunctional pocket tools. In 1995, Cooper Industries, Inc. decided to design and sell a competing multifunctional tool under the name "ToolZall." Cooper introduced the ToolZall in August 1996 at the National Hardware Show in Chicago. At that show, Cooper used photographs in its posters, packaging, and advertising materials that purported to be a ToolZall but were actually of a modified PST. When those materials were prepared, the first of the ToolZalls had not yet been manufactured. A Cooper employee created a ToolZall "mock-up" by grinding the Leatherman trademark from a PST and substituting the unique fastenings that were to be used on the ToolZall. At least one of the photographs was retouched to remove a curved indention where the Leatherman trademark had been. The photographs were used, not only at the trade show, but also in marketing materials and catalogs used by Cooper's sales force throughout the United States.

Shortly after the trade show, Leatherman sued Cooper in district court for unfair competition. The district court jury found that Cooper had engaged in unfair competition and awarded Leatherman $50,000 in compensatory damages and $4.5 million in punitive damages. Cooper appealed the award of punitive damages, but the court of appeals applied the "abuse of discretion" standard and refused to reduce the award. Cooper appealed to the U.S. Supreme Court, alleging that an appellate court should analyze the size of an award of punitive damages using a *"de novo"* independent review of the facts. The Supreme Court granted certiorari to hear the appeal.

Supreme Court Issue

Should the appellate court analyze the lawfulness of an award of punitive damages using the "abuse of discretion" or *"de novo"* standard of review?

In the Language of the U.S. Supreme Court

Stevens, Justice Although compensatory damages and punitive damages are typically awarded at the same time by the same decision maker, they serve distinct purposes. The former are intended to redress the concrete loss that the plaintiff has suffered by reason of the defendant's wrongful conduct. The latter, which have been described as "quasi-criminal," operate as private fines intended to punish the defendant and to deter future wrongdoing. A jury's assessment of the extent of a plaintiff's injury is essentially a factual determination, whereas its imposition of punitive damages is an expression of its moral condemnation. The question whether a fine is constitutionally excessive calls for the application of a constitutional standard to the facts of a particular case, and in this context de novo *review of that question is appropriate.*

Decision and Remedy

The U.S. Supreme Court held that an appellate court should engage in a *de novo* review of the trial court's decision in awarding punitive damages. Since the court of appeals used the abuse of discretion standard, rather than the *de novo* standard in reviewing the size of the punitive damage award in this case, the Supreme Court reversed and remanded the case for a determination whether the award of $4.5 million of punitive damages against defendant Cooper Industries was lawful.

Case Questions

Critical Legal Thinking What is the difference between the "abuse of discretion" and the *"de novo"* standards of appellate review?

Business Ethics Do you think a jury's ability to award punitive damages makes businesses act more ethically?

Contemporary Business Do you think an award of $4.5 million in punitive damages was warranted in this case?

Corporate Citizenship

corporate citizenship

A theory of responsibility that says a business has a responsibility to do good.

The notion that a business is clothed with a public interest and has been devoted to the public use is little more than a fiction intended to beautify what is disagreeable to the sufferers.

Justice Holmes
Tyson & Bro-United Theatre Ticket Officers v. Banton *(1927).*

The **corporate citizenship** theory of social responsibility argues that business has a *responsibility to do good*. That is, business is responsible for helping to solve social problems that it did little, if anything, to cause. For example, under this theory corporations owe a duty to subsidize schools and help educate children.

This theory contends that corporations owe a duty to promote the same social goals as do individual members of society. Proponents of the "do good" theory argue that corporations owe a debt to society to make it a better place and that this duty arises because of the social power bestowed on them. That is, this social power is a gift from society and should be used to good ends.

A major criticism of this theory is that the duty of a corporation to do good cannot be expanded beyond certain limits. There is always some social problem that needs to be addressed, and corporate funds are limited. Further, if this theory were taken to its maximum limit, potential shareholders might be reluctant to invest in corporations.

Corporate Citizenship *The corporate citizenship theory of social responsibility states that businesses have the responsibility to do good for society.*

Contemporary Business Environment

STATES ENACT CONSTITUENCY STATUTES

Under the traditional *business judgment rule*, directors of a corporation owe a *fiduciary duty* to act on an informed basis, with reasonable care, and in good faith. Historically, this duty has been rigidly and exclusively owed to the corporation and its shareholders and to no others. Under this classical theory of the corporation, the rights of other constituents—such as employees, bondholders, and creditors, suppliers and customers—exists by contract, period.

This view prevailed during the 1980s, when leveraged buyouts and the greed of corporate raiders caused the demise of many venerable companies, dislodged workers, destroyed pension rights and ruined many local economies. In response, more than 30 states have enacted **constituency statutes** that allow directors to consider constituents other than shareholders when making decisions.

For example, Minnesota adopted the following statute:

In discharging the duties of the position of director, a director may, in considering the best interests of the corporation, consider the interest of the corporation's employees, customers, suppliers, and creditors, the economy of the

state and nation, community and societal considerations, and the long-term as well as short-term interests of the corporation and its shareholders, including the possibility that these interests may be best served by the continued independence of the corporation. [Minn. Stat. § 302A.251(5)]

Most constituency statutes are permissive, not mandatory. That is, directors may take into account nonstockholder interests but are not required to do so.

Constituency statutes recognize the complex nature of the modern corporation and the modern view that shareholders are not the only "owners" of corporations. These statutes acknowledge the rights of a variety of participants, including lenders, employees, managers, suppliers, distributors, customers, and the local communities in which corporations are located.

1. Why did state legislatures enact constituency statutes?
2. Do constituency statutes make corporate boards of directors more socially responsible?

Business Ethics

THE CORPORATE SOCIAL AUDIT

It has been suggested that corporate audits should be extended to include not only audits of the financial health of a corporation but also of its moral health. Corporations that conduct social audits will be more apt to prevent unethical and illegal conduct by managers, employees, and agents. The audit would examine how well employees have adhered to the company's code of ethics and how well the corporation has met its duty of social responsibility. Such audits would focus on the corporation's efforts to promote employment opportunities for members of protected classes, worker safety, environmental protection, consumer protection, and the like. Social audits are not easy. First, it may be hard to conceptualize just what is being audited. Second, it may be difficult to measure results. Despite these factors, more companies are expected to undertake social audits.

Companies should institute the following procedures when conducting a social audit:

- An independent outside firm should be hired to conduct the audit. This will ensure autonomy and objectivity in conducting the audit.
- The company's personnel should cooperate fully with the auditing firm while the audit is being conducted.
- The auditing firm should report its findings directly to the company's board of directors.
- The results of the audit should be reviewed by the board of directors.
- The board of directors should determine how the company can better meet its duty of social responsibility and can use the audit to implement a program to correct any deficiencies it finds.

CONCEPT SUMMARY — THEORIES OF SOCIAL RESPONSIBILITY

Theory	Social Responsibility
Maximizing profits	To maximize profits for stockholders.
Moral minimum	To avoid causing harm and to compensate for harm caused.
Stakeholder interest	To consider the interests of all stakeholders, including stockholders, employees, customers, suppliers, creditors, and local community.
Corporate citizenship	To do good and solve social problems.

International Law

UNITED NATIONS CODE OF CONDUCT FOR TRANSNATIONAL CORPORATIONS

RESPECT FOR NATIONAL SOVEREIGNTY

Transnational corporations shall respect the national sovereignty of the countries in which they operate and the right of each state to exercise its permanent sovereignty over its natural wealth and resources. Transnational corporations should carry out their activities in conformity with the development policies, objectives and priorities set out by the governments of the countries in which they operate and work seriously toward making a positive contribution to the achievement of such goals at the national and, as appropriate, the regional level, within the framework of regional integration programs. Transnational corporations should cooperate with the governments of the countries in which they operate with a view to contributing to the development process and should be responsive to requests for consultation in this respect, thereby establishing mutually beneficial relations with these countries.

ADHERENCE TO SOCIO-CULTURAL OBJECTIVES AND VALUES

Transnational corporations should respect the social and cultural objectives, values, and traditions of the countries in which they operate. While economic and technological development is normally accompanied by social change, transnational corporations should avoid practices, products
or services which cause detrimental effects on cultural patterns and socio-cultural objectives as determined by governments. For this purpose, transnational corporations should respond positively to requests for consultations from government concerned.

RESPECT FOR HUMAN RIGHTS AND FUNDAMENTAL FREEDOMS

Transnational corporations shall respect human rights and fundamental freedoms in the countries in which they operate. In their social and industrial relations, transnational corporations shall not discriminate on the basis of race, color, sex, religion, language, social, national and ethnic origin or political or other opinion. Transnational corporations shall conform to government policies designed to extend quality of opportunity and treatment.

ABSTENTION FROM CORRUPT PRACTICES

Transnational corporations shall refrain, in their transactions, from the offering, promising or giving of any payment, gift or other advantage to or for the benefit of a public official as consideration for performing or refraining from the performance of his duties in connection with those transactions.

CHAPTER SUMMARY

Law and Ethics, p. 178
Moral Theories and Business Ethics, p. 180

Moral Theories	
	1. *Ethical fundamentalism.* Persons look to an outside source (e.g., Bible or Koran) or central figure to set ethical guidelines.
	2. *Utilitarianism.* Persons choose the alternative that would provide the greatest good to society.
	3. *Kantian ethics.* A set of universal rules establishes ethical duties. The rules are based on reasoning and require (1) consistency in application and (2) reversibility.

4. *Rawls's social justice theory.* Moral duties are based on an implied social contract. Fairness is justice. The rules are established from an original position of a "veil of ignorance."
5. *Ethical relativism.* Individuals decide what is ethical based on their own feelings of what is right or wrong.

The Social Responsibility of Business, p. 185

Theories of Social Responsibility	1. *Maximizing profits.* To maximize profits for shareholders. 2. *Moral minimum.* To make a profit and avoid harm and to compensate for harm caused. 3. *Stakeholder interests.* To consider the interests of stakeholders other than stockholders, such as employees, suppliers, customers, creditors, and local community. 4. *Corporate citizenship.* To do good and help solve social problems.

The Corporate Social Audit, p. 193

Corporate Social Audit	Audit of a corporation by independent auditors that examines how well employees have adhered to the company's code of ethics and how well the company has met its duty of social responsibility.

END-OF-CHAPTER INTERNET EXERCISES AND CASE QUESTIONS

Working the Web Internet Exercises

ACTIVITIES

1. Review the Codes of Ethics at **www.ethics.ubc.ca/resources/business/codes.html.** How do these compare with your employer's code? If your employer does not have a Code of Ethics, use the examples at this site to draft one.

2. Find the list of Baby Boomer Sports Injuries at **www.cpsc.gov.** What is the ethical duty of the companies who sell sports equipment to consumers in this age bracket?

3. Locate the Drudge Report **www.drudgereport.com.** What is the ethical basis for the press to report on topics such as: consumer fraud, arrests and trials of notorious criminals, questionable tax policies, etc.?

4. Locate and review the story on the use of torture and drugs to interrogate captured suspect terrorists at **www.alchemind.org/news/narcointerrogation1.htm.** Is it constitutional? Is it ethical?

BUSINESS ETHICS CASES

7.1 Business Ethics The A.H. Robins Company manufactured the Dalkon Shield, an intrauterine device used by more than 2 million women for contraception during the early 1970s. The device was defectively designed and caused women problems of infection, pelvic inflammatory disease, infertility, and spontaneous abortion, as well as health defects in their children. Thousands of product liability lawsuits were filed against the company by the women and children who were injured by the Dalkon Shield. The company and its insurers chose to fight these cases aggressively and spent multimillions of dollars in legal fees.

U.S. District Court Judge Miles Lord handled many of these cases. He called the Dalkon Shield an "instrument of death, mutilation, and disease" and chastised the executives of the company for violating "every ethical precept" of the Hippocratic oath, the medical profession's promise to save lives. Judge Lord stated,

> Your company in the face of overwhelming evidence denies its guilt and continues its monstrous mischief. You have taken the bottom line as your guiding beacon and the low road as your route. This is corporate irresponsibility at its meanest.

The company eventually filed for bankruptcy. The U.S. court of appeals censored Judge Lord for being too vocal. Is it ethical for a company to aggressively contest lawsuits that are filed against it even if it knows that it is responsible for the injury?

7.2 Business Ethics The Warner-Lambert Company has manufactured and distributed Listerine antiseptic mouthwash since 1879. Its formula has never changed. Ever since its introduction, the company has represented it as being beneficial in preventing and curing colds and soar throats. Direct advertising of these claims to consumers began in 1921. In 1971, Warner-Lambert spent $10 million advertising these claims in print media and in television commercials.

In 1972, the FTC filed a complaint against Warner-Lambert alleging that the company engaged in false advertising in violation of federal law. Four months of hearings were held before an administrative law judge that produced an evidentiary record of more than 4,000 pages of documents from 46 witnesses. In 1975, after examining the evidence, the FTC issued an opinion that held that the company's representations that Listerine prevented and cured colds and soar throats were false. The U.S. court of appeals affirmed.

Did Warner-Lambert act ethically in making its claims for Listerine? What remedy should the court impose on the company? Would making Warner-Lambert cease such advertising be sufficient? [*Warner-Lambert Company v. Federal Trade Commission*, 562 F.2d 749 D. (C. Cir. 1977)]

7.3 Business Ethics Stanford University is one of the premiere research universities in the country. Stanford has an operating budget of approximately $400 million a year and receives about $175 million a year in direct research funding from the federal government. In addition, the government reimburses the university for certain overhead and indirect costs associated with the research. This amounts to about $85 million a year.

In 1990, a navy accountant took a close look at Stanford's books and alleged that the university may have overstated overhead and indirect costs associated with research by as much as $200 million during the 1980s. The university provides a house for its president, Donald Kennedy. Some of the expenses charged against overhead for research were (a) $3,000 for a cedar-lined closet at the president's home, (b) $4,000 for the president's 1987 wedding reception, (c) $7,000 in bed sheets and table lines, and (d) $184,000 in depreciation on a yacht donated to Stanford's sailing program. Did the administration of Stanford act ethically in charging these expenditures as overhead against research? What penalty should be assessed?

7.4 Social Responsibility The Johns-Manville Corporation was a profitable company that made a variety of building and other products. It was a major producer of asbestos, which was used for insulation in buildings and for a variety of other uses. It has been medically proven that excessive exposure to asbestos causes asbestosis, a fatal lung disease. Thousands of employees of the company and consumers who were exposed to asbestos and contracted this fatal disease sued the company for damages. In 1983, the lawsuits were being filed at the rate of more than 400 per week.

As a response, the company filed for reorganization bankruptcy. It argued that if it did not, an otherwise viable company that provide thousands of jobs and served a useful purpose in this country would be destroyed, and that without the declaration of bankruptcy a few of the plaintiffs who first filed their lawsuits would win awards of hundreds of million of dollars, leaving nothing for the remainder of the plaintiffs. Under the bankruptcy court's protection, the company was restructured to survive. As part of the release from bankruptcy, the company contributed money to a fund to pay current and future claimants. The fund is not large enough to pay all injured persons the full amount of their claims.

Was it ethical for Johns-Manville to declare bankruptcy? Did it meet its duty of social responsibility in this case? If you were a member of the board of directors of the company, would you have voted to place the company in bankruptcy? Why or why not? [*In re Johns-Manville Corporation*, 36 B.R. 727 (B.C. S.D.N.Y. 1984)]

7.5 Social Responsibility In 1977, Reverend Leon H. Sullivan, a Baptist minister from Philadelphia who was also a member of the board of directors of General Motors Corporation, proposed a set of rules to guide American-owned companies doing business in the Republic of South Africa. The **Sullivan Principles**, as they became known, call for the nonsegregation of races in South Africa. They call for employers to (a) provide equal and fair employment practices for all employees and (b) improve the quality of employees' lives outside the work environment in such areas as housing, schooling, transportation, recreation, and health facilities. The principles also require signatory companies to report regularly and be graded on their conduct in South Africa.

Eventually, the Sullivan Principles were subscribed to by several hundred U.S. corporations with affiliates doing business in South Africa. Concerning the companies that have subscribed to the Sullivan Principles, which of the following theories of social responsibility are they following?

1. Maximizing profits
2. Moral minimum
3. Stakeholder interest
4. Corporate citizenship

To put additional pressure on the government of the Republic of South Africa to end apartheid, in 1987 Reverend Sullivan called for the complete withdrawal of all U.S. companies from doing business in or with South Africa. Very few companies have agreed to do so. Do companies owe a social duty to withdraw from South Africa? Should universities divest themselves of investments in companies that do not withdraw from South Africa?

7.6 Social Responsibility In 1974, Kaiser Aluminum & Chemical Corporation entered into a collective bargaining agreement with the United Steelworkers of America, a union that represented employees at Kaiser's plants. The agreement contained an affirmative action program to increase the representation of minorities in craft jobs. To enable plants to meet these goals, on-the-job training programs were established to teach unskilled production workers the skills necessary to become craft workers. Assignment to the training program was based on seniority, except the plan reserved 50 percent of the openings for black employees.

In 1974, 13 craft trainees were selected from Kaiser's Gramercy plant for the training program. Of these, seven were black and six white. The most senior black selected had less seniority than several white production workers who had applied for the positions but were rejected. Brian Webster, one of the white rejected employees, instituted a class action lawsuit alleging that the affirmative action plan violated Title VII of the Civil Rights Act of 1964, which made it "unlawful to discriminate because of race" in hiring and selecting apprentices for training programs. The U.S. Supreme Court upheld the affirmative action plan in this case. The decision stated,

> *We therefore hold that Title VII's prohibition against racial discrimination does not condemn all private, voluntary, race-conscious affirmative action plans. At the same time, the plan does not unnecessarily trammel the interests of the white employees. Moreover, the plan is a temporary measure; it is not intended to maintain racial balance, but simply to eliminate a manifest racial imbalance.*

Do companies owe a duty of social responsibility to provide affirmative action programs? [*Steelworkers v. Weber*, 443 U.S. 193, 99 S.Ct. 2721, 61 L.Ed.2d 480 (1979)]

7.7 Social Responsibility Iroquois Brands, Ltd. is a Delaware corporation that had $78 million in assets, $141 million in sales, and $6 million in profits in 1984. As part of its business, Iroquois imports pâté de foie gras (goose pâté) from France and sells it in the United States. Iroquois derived only $79,000 in revenues from sales of such pâté. The French producer force-feeds the geese from which the pâté is made. Peter C. Lovenheim, who owns 200 shares of Iroquois common stock, proposed to include a shareholder proposal in Iroquois's annual proxy materials to be sent to shareholders. His proposal criticized the company because the force-feeding caused "undue stress, pain and suffering" to the geese and requested that shareholders vote to have Iroquois discontinue importing and selling pâté produced by this method.

Iroquois refused to allow the information to be included in its proxy materials. Iroquois asserted that its refusal was based on the fact that Lovenheim's proposal was "not economically significant" and had only "ethical and social" significance. The company reasoned that because corporations are economic entities, only an economic test applied to its activities and it was not subject to an ethical or social responsibility test. Is the company correct; that is, should only an economic test be applied in judging the activities of a corporation? Or should a corporation also be subject to an ethical or social responsibility test? [*Lovenheim v. Iroquois Brands, Ltd.*, 618 F.Supp. 554 (D.C. 1985)]

BRIEFING THE CASE WRITING ASSIGNMENT

Read the following case, which has been excerpted from the court's opinions. Review and brief the case.

Ramirez v. Plough, Inc.
15 Cal. App. 4th 1110, 12 Cal. RPTR. 2D 423 (1992)
Court of Appeals California

Thaxter, Judge

Jorge Ramierz, a minor, by his guardian ad litem Rosa Rivera, appeals from a summary judgment in favor of Plough, Inc. Appellant sued Plough alleging negligence, product liability, and fraud. The action sought damages for injuries sustained in March of 1986 when Jorge, who was then four months old, contracted Reye's Syndrome after ingesting St. Joseph Aspirin for Children (SJAC). Plough marketed and distributed SJAC.

Reye's Syndrome is a serious disease of unknown cause characterized by severe vomiting, lethargy, or irritability which may progress to delirium or coma. The disease generally strikes children or teenagers who are recovering from a mild respiratory tract infection, influenza, chicken pox, or other viral illnesses. The mortality rate of the disease is high, and permanent brain damage occurs in many cases. As a result of contracting Reye's Syndrome, appellant suffered catastrophic injuries including quadriplegia, blindness, and profound mental retardation.

In early 1980s there was significant scientific debate concerning the cause of Reye's syndrome. Several state studies suggested a statistical association between the ingestion of aspirin and the disease. In December 1982, the federal government acknowledged the debate. After considering the state studies and their critics, the federal government rejected a proposal which would require a warning label and instead, undertook an independent study. Apparently, Plough participated in efforts to influence government officials and agencies to reject the label proposal which Plough considered premature.

In December 1985, the Food and Drug Administration (FDA) requested that aspirin manufacturers voluntarily place a label on aspirin products warning consumers of the possible association between aspirin and Reye's Syndrome. Plough voluntarily complied and began including a warning and insert in SJAC packaging. On June 5, 1986, the Reye's Syndrome warning became mandatory.

In March 1986, SJAC labeling bore the following warning: "Warning: Reye's Syndrome is a rare but serious disease which can follow flu or chicken pox in children and teenagers. While the cause of Reye's Syndrome is unknown, some reports claim that aspirin may increase the risk of developing this disease. Consult a doctor before use in children or teenagers with flu or chicken pox." In addition, the SJAC package insert included the following statement: "The symptoms of Reye's Syndrome can include persistent vomiting, sleepiness, and lethargy, violent headaches, unusual behavior, including disorientation, combativeness, and delirium. If any of these symptoms occur, especially following chicken pox or flu, call your doctor immediately, even if your child has not taken any medication. Reye's Syndrome is Serious, so Early Detection and Treatment are Vital."

Rosa Rivera purchased SJAC on March 12, 1986, and administered it to appellant who was suffering from what appeared to be a cold or upper respiratory infection. She gave appellant the aspirin without reading the directions or warnings appearing on the SJAC packaging. The packaging was in English and Ms. Rivera can speak and understand only Spanish. She did not seek to have the directions or warnings translated from English to Spanish, even though members of her household spoke English.

The trial court granted Plough's motion for summary judgment on the grounds that "there is no duty to warn in a foreign language and there is no casual relationship between plaintiff's injuries and defendant's activities."

It is undisputed that SJAC was marketed and intended for the treatment of minor aches and pains associated with colds, flu, and minor viral illnesses. The SJAC box promised "fast, effective relief of fever and minor aches and pains of colds." Both parties accept the premise that Plough had a duty to warn consumers that the intended use of SJAC after a viral infection or chicken pox could lead to Reye's Syndrome, an illness with serious, possible fatal, consequences. In March 1986, federal regulations requiring a Reye's Syndrome warning had been promulgated and were final, although not yet effective. The FDA had previously solicited voluntary labeling. In response to the request for voluntary labeling, Plough started packaging SJAC with explicit warnings of the risks of Reye's Syndrome. The scientific community had already confirmed and documented the relationship between Reye's Syndrome and the use of aspirin after a viral illness. There is no doubt Plough had a duty to warn of the Reye's Syndrome risk.

The question thus is whether the warning given only in English was adequate under the circumstances. Respondent argues that as a matter of law it has no duty to place foreign-language warnings on products manufactured to be sold in the United States and that holding manufacturers liable for failing to do so would violate public policy.

Although the constitutional, statutory, regulatory, and judicial authorities relied on by respondent may reflect a public policy recognizing the status of English as an official language, nothing compels the conclusion that a manufacturer of a dangerous or defective product is immunized from liability when an English-only warning does not adequately inform non-English literate persons likely to use the product.

Plough's evidence showed that over 148 foreign languages are spoken in the United States and over 23 million Americans speak another language other than English in their homes. That evidence plainly does not prove that Plough used reasonable care in giving an English-only warning. Plough, then, resorts to arguing that the burden on manufacturers and society of requiring additional warnings is so "staggering" that the courts should preclude liability as a matter of law. We are not persuaded.

Certainly the burden and costs of giving foreign-language warnings is one factor for consideration in determining whether a manufacturer acted reasonably in using only English. The importance of that factor may vary from case to case depending upon other circumstances, such as the nature of the product, marketing efforts directed to segments of the population unlikely to be English-literate, and the actual and relative size of the consumer market which could reasonably be expected to speak or read only a certain foreign language. Plough presented no evidence from which we can gauge the extent of the burden under the facts of this case.

Ramirez submitted evidence that Plough knew Hispanics were an important part of the market for SJAC and that Hispanics often maintain their first language rather than learn English. SJAC was advertised in the Spanish media, both radio and television. That evidence raises material questions of fact concerning the foreseeability of purchase by a Hispanic not literate in English and the reasonableness of not giving a Spanish-language warning. If Plough has evidence conclusively showing that it would have been unreasonable to give its label warning in Spanish because of the burden, it did not present that evidence below.

Given the triable issues of material fact, if we accepted Plough's arguments in this case in effect we would be holding that failure to warn in a foreign language is not negligence, regardless of the circumstances. Such a sweeping grant of immunity should come from the legislative branch of the government, not the judicial. In deciding that Plough did not establish its right to judgment as a matter of law, we do not hold that manufacturers are required to warn in languages other than English simply because it may be foreseeable that non-English literate persons are likely to use their products. Our decision merely recognizes that under some circumstances the standard of due care may require such warning.

Because the evidence shows triable issues of material fact and because Plough did not establish its immunity from liability as a matter of law, its motion for summary judgment should have been denied.

ENDNOTES

1. 170 N.W. 668 (MI 1919).
2. Milton Friedman, "The Social Responsibility of Business Is to Increase Its Profits," *New York Times Magazine*, September 13, 1970.

Traditional and E-Commerce Contracts

CHAPTER 8

Nature of Traditional and E-Commerce Contracts

The movement of the progressive societies has hitherto been a movement from status to contract.

—Sir Henry Maine
Ancient Law, Ch. 5

Chapter Objectives

After studying this chapter, you should be able to:

1. Define *contract*.

2. List the elements necessary to form a valid contract.

3. Distinguish between bilateral and unilateral contracts.

4. Describe and distinguish between express and implied-in-fact contracts.

5. Define and distinguish between executed and executory contracts.

6. Describe and distinguish among valid, void, voidable, and unenforceable contracts.

7. Define and describe quasi-contracts.

8. Apply the concept of equity to contracts.

9. Describe how the Uniform Computer Information Transactions Act applies to Internet contracts.

10. Describe the scope of the United Nations Convention on Contracts for the International Sale of Goods.

Chapter Contents

Contracts are the basis of many of our daily activities. They provide the means for individuals and businesses to sell and otherwise transfer property, services, and other rights. The purchase of goods, such as books and automobiles, is based on sales contracts; the hiring of employees is based on service contracts; the lease of an apartment is based on a rental contract; the sale of goods and services over the Internet is based on electronic contracts. The list is almost endless. Without enforceable contracts, commerce would collapse.

Contracts are voluntarily entered into by parties. The terms of the contract become *private law* between the parties. One court has stated that "The contract between parties is the law between them and the courts are obliged to give legal effect to such contracts according to the true interests of the parties."[1]

Nevertheless, most contracts are performed without the aid of the court system. This is usually because the parties feel a moral duty to perform as promised. Although some contracts, such as illegal contracts, are not enforceable, most are **legally enforceable**.[2] This means that if a party fails to perform a contract, the other party may call upon the courts to enforce the contract.

This chapter introduces you to the study of traditional and Internet contract law. Such topics as the definition of a contract, requirements for forming a contract, sources of contract law, and the various classifications of contracts are discussed.

Contracts must not be the sports of an idle hour, mere matters of pleasantry and badinage, never intended by the parties to have any serious effect whatever.

Lord Stowell
Dalrymple v. Dalrymple *(1811)*

legally enforceable contract

If one party fails to perform as promised, the other party can use the court system to enforce the contract and recover damages or other remedy.

DEFINITION OF A CONTRACT

A contract is an agreement that is enforceable by a court of law or equity. A simple and widely recognized definition of a contract is provided by the Restatement (Second) of Contracts: "A contract is a promise or a set of promises for the breach of which the law gives a remedy or the performance of which the law in some way recognizes a duty."[3]

Parties to a Contract

Every contract involves at least two parties. The **offeror** is the party who makes an offer to enter into a contract. The **offeree** is the party to whom the offer is made (see Exhibit 8.1). In making an offer, the offeror promises to do—or to refrain from doing—something. The offeree then has the power to create a contract by accepting the offeror's offer. A contract is created if the offer is accepted. No contract is created if the offer is not accepted.

offeror

The party who makes an offer to enter into a contract.

offeree

The party to whom an offer to enter into a contract is made.

EXHIBIT 8.1 *Parties to a Contract*

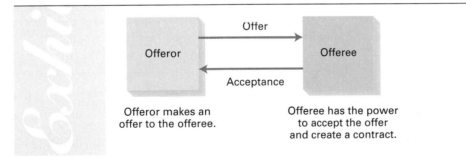

Offeror makes an offer to the offeree.

Offeree has the power to accept the offer and create a contract.

Elements of a Contract

To be an enforceable contract, the following four basic requirements must be met:

1. **Agreement** To have an enforceable contract, there must be an agreement between the parties. This requires an *offer* by the offeror and an *acceptance* of the offer by the offeree. There must be mutual assent by the parties (Chapter 9).
2. **Consideration** The promise must be supported by a bargained-for consideration that is legally sufficient. Gift promises and moral obligations are not considered supported by valid consideration (Chapter 9).

Justice is the end of government. It is the end of civil society. It ever has been, and ever will be pursued, until it be obtained, or until liberty be lost in the pursuit.

James Madison
The Federalist No. 51 *(1788)*

3. **Contractual Capacity**   The parties to a contract must have contractual capacity. Certain parties, such as persons adjudged insane, do not have contractual capacity (Chapter 10).

4. **Lawful Object**   The object of the contract must be lawful. Contracts to accomplish illegal objects or contracts that are against public policy are void (Chapter 10).

Defenses to the Enforcement of a Contract

There are two *defenses* that may be raised to the enforcement of contracts. These defenses are as follows.

1. **Genuineness of Assent**   The consent of the parties to create a contract must be genuine. If the consent is obtained by duress, undue influence, or fraud, there is no real consent (Chapter 11).

2. **Writing and Form**   The law requires that certain contracts be in writing or in a certain form. Failure of these contracts to be in writing or to be in proper form may be raised against the enforcement of the contract (Chapter 11).

Contemporary Business Environment

THE EVOLUTION OF THE MODERN LAW OF CONTRACTS

The use of contracts originally developed in ancient times. The common law of contracts developed in England around the fifteenth century. American contract law evolved from the English common law.

At first, the United States adopted a *laissez-faire* approach to the law of contracts. The central theme of this theory was *freedom of contract*. The parties (such as consumers, shopkeepers, farmers, and traders) generally dealt with one another face-to-face, had equal knowledge and bargaining power, and had the opportunity to inspect the goods prior to sale. Contract terms were openly negotiated. There was little, if any, government regulation of the right to contract. This "pure" or **classical law of contracts** produced objective rules, which, in turn, produced certainty and predictability in the enforcement of contracts. It made sense until the Industrial Revolution.

The Industrial Revolution changed many of the underlying assumptions of pure contract law. For example, as large corporations developed and gained control of crucial resources, the traditional balance of parties' bargaining power shifted: Large corporations now had the most power. The chain of distribution for goods also changed because (1) buyers did not have to deal face-to-face with sellers, and (2) there was not always an opportunity to inspect the goods prior to sale.

Eventually, sellers began using *form contracts* that offered their goods to buyers on a take-it or leave-it basis. The majority of contracts in this country today are form contracts. Automobile contracts, mortgage contracts, sales contracts for consumer goods, and such are examples of form contracts.

Both federal and state governments enacted statutes intended to protect consumers, creditors, and others from unfair contracts. In addition, the courts began to develop certain common law legal theories that allowed some oppressive or otherwise unjust contracts to be avoided. Today, under this **modern law of contracts**, there is substantial government regulation of the right to contract.

ƧOURCES OF CONTRACT LAW

There are several sources of contract law in the United States, including the *common law of contracts*, the *Uniform Commercial Code*, and the *Restatement (Second) of Contracts*. The following paragraphs explain these sources in more detail.

The Common Law of Contracts

common law of contracts

Contract law developed primarily by state courts.

A major source of contract law is the **common law of contracts**. The common law of contracts developed from early court decisions that became precedent for later decisions. There is a limited federal common law of contracts that applies to contracts made by the federal government. The larger and more prevalent body of common law has been developed from state court decisions. Thus, although the general principles remain the same throughout the country, there is some variation from state to state.

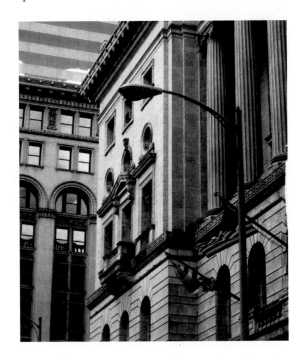

Courthouse, Baltimore, Maryland *Courts are often called upon to enforce contracts between contracting parties.*

The Uniform Commercial Code

Another major source of contract law is the **Uniform Commercial Code (UCC)**. The UCC, which was first drafted by the National Conference of Commissioners on Uniform State Law in 1952, has been amended several times. Its goal is to create a uniform system of commercial law among the 50 states. The provisions of the UCC normally take precedence over the common law of contracts (Chapters 16–18).

The UCC is divided into nine main articles. Every state has adopted at least part of the UCC.

Uniform Commercial Code

Comprehensive statutory scheme that includes laws that cover aspects of commercial transactions.

The Restatement of the Law of Contracts

In 1932, the American Law Institute completed the **Restatement of the Law of Contracts**. The Restatement is a compilation of contract law principles as agreed upon by the drafters. The Restatement, which is currently in its second edition, will be cited in this book as **Restatement (Second) of Contracts**. Note that the Restatement is not law. However, lawyers and judges often refer to it for guidance in contract disputes because of its stature.

Restatement of the Law of Contracts

A compilation of model contract law principles drafted by legal scholars. The Restatement is not law.

 *E-Commerce & Information Technology*

UNIFORM ELECTRONIC COMMERCE ACT ADOPTED

The United States and the global economy have witnessed several major economic shifts in the past centuries. In the nineteenth century, agricultural production dominated the economy. In the Agricultural Age, farms dotted local landscapes. Family farmers in Iowa, ranchers in Nebraska, and fishermen in Washington sold their products locally as well as to faraway markets such as Chicago, New York, and San Francisco. The common law of contracts was sufficient to handle most of these transactions. At the beginning of the twentieth century, the United States and many major coun-

tries of the world moved into the Industrial Age. Manufacturing and the distribution of goods nationally, and eventually internationally, dominated commerce. To handle this goods-oriented economy, Article 2 (Sales) of the Uniform Commercial Code (UCC) was developed. Article 2 prescribes a set of uniform rules for the creation and enforcement of sales of goods contracts. As leasing of goods (e.g., automobiles, equipment) flourished in the later part of the twentieth century, Article 2A (Leases) was added to the UCC to govern the formation and enforcement of lease agreements.

Throughout history, laws have changed to address new commercial situations. The beginning of the twenty-first century saw its own evolution of commerce and contract law. As we entered the new century, a new economic shift brought the United States and the world into the Information Age. Computer technology and the use of the Internet increased dramatically. By the year 2000, a new form of commerce—**electronic commerce**, or **e-commerce**—was flourishing. All sorts of goods and services are now sold over the Internet. You can purchase automobiles and children's toys, participate in auctions, purchase airline tickets, make hotel reservations, and purchase other goods and services over the Internet. In fact, in the early 2000s, the economic value of computer technology and e-commerce exceeded that of the manufacturing sector of the U.S. economy.

A problem that developed was that the common law of contracts and Articles 2 (Sales) and 2A (Leases) of the UCC did not provide adequate rules for contracting over the Internet and in e-commerce. That is because much of the new cyberspace economy is based on electronic contracts and the licensing of computer information. E-commerce created problems for forming contracts over the Internet, enforcing e-commerce contracts, and providing consumer protection. To address these problems, the National Conference of Commissioners on Uniform State Laws (a group of lawyers, judges, and legal scholars) drafted the **Uniform Computer Information Transactions Act (UCITA)**.

The UCITA establishes uniform legal rules for the formation and enforcement of electronic contracts and licenses. The UCITA addresses most of the legal issues that are encountered while conducting e-commerce over the Internet. The UCITA is a model act that does not become law until a state legislature adopts it as a statute for the state. Since its promulgation in July 1999, the UCITA has been adopted in whole or part by many states. Because of the need for uniformity of e-commerce rules, the UCITA is expected to become the basis for the creation and enforcement of cyberspace contracts and licenses. The UCITA is so important that it is covered in Chapter 19 of this book.

CLASSIFICATIONS OF CONTRACTS

There are several types of contracts. Each differs somewhat in formation, enforcement, performance, and discharge. The different types of contracts are discussed in the following paragraphs.

Bilateral and Unilateral Contracts

bilateral contract

A contract entered into by way of exchange of promises of the parties; "a promise for a promise."

unilateral contract

A contract in which the offeror's offer can be accepted only by the performance of an act by the offeree; a "promise for an act."

Contracts are either *bilateral or unilateral*, depending upon what the offeree must do to accept the offeror's offer. The contract is **bilateral** if the offeror's promise is answered with the offeree's promise of acceptance. In other words, a bilateral contract is a "promise for a promise." This exchange of promises creates an enforceable contract. No act of performance is necessary to create a bilateral contract.

A contract is **unilateral** if the offeror's offer can be accepted only by the performance of an act by the offeree. There is no contract until the offeree performs the requested act. An offer to create a unilateral contract cannot be accepted by a promise to perform. It is a "promise for an act."

The language of the offeror's promise must be carefully scrutinized to determine whether it is an offer to create a bilateral or a unilateral contract. If there is any ambiguity as to which it is, it is presumed to be a bilateral contract.

Business Brief

Distinguish bilateral from unilateral contracts according to the number of promises involved. Bilateral is "promise for promise." Unilateral is "promise for act."

Consider This Example   Suppose Mary Douglas, the owner of the Chic Dress Shop, says to Peter Jones, a painter, "If you promise to paint my store by July 1, I will pay you $2,000." Peter promises to do so. A bilateral contract was created at the moment Peter promised to paint the dress shop (a promise for a promise). If Peter fails to paint the store, he can be sued for whatever damages result from his breach of contract. Similarly, Peter can sue Mary if she refuses to pay him after he has performed as promised.

However, if Mary had said, "If you paint my shop by July 1, I will pay you $2,000," the offer would have created a unilateral contract. The offer can be accepted only by the painter's performance of the requested act. If Peter does not paint the shop by July 1, there has been no acceptance and the painter cannot be sued for damages.

Incomplete or Partial Performance   Problems can arise if the offeror of a unilateral contract attempts to revoke an offer after the offeree has begun performance. Generally, an offer to create a unilateral contract can be revoked by the offeror anytime prior to the offeree's performance of the requested act. However, the offer cannot be revoked if the offeree has begun or has substantially completed performance. For example, suppose Alan Mattthews tells Sherry Levine that he will pay her $5,000 if she finishes the Boston Marathon. Alan cannot revoke the offer once Sherry starts running the marathon.

Entreprenuer and the Law

READY FOR LOVE? NOT BEFORE YOU'VE BEEN NDA'D

You're out on a date and your partner whispers sweet nothings in your ear. What's a guy or girl to do? Quick, whip out a **nondisclosure agreement**—or **NDA** as they are called—and have the other side sign it before responding. That is what many entrepreneurs and techies are doing, having their boyfriends, girlfriends, family members, friends, and others sign NDAs before revealing anything about what they are doing.

NDAs have been around for a long time, and traditionally have been used among lawyers, investment bankers, and others involved in secret takeovers and other large corporate deals. NDAs swear the signatory to secrecy about confidential ideas, trade secrets, and other nonpublic information revealed by the party proffering the NDA. But today many entrepreneurs, particularly those in high-tech industries, are handing out NDAs as fast as business cards. An NDA serves a purpose in that it protects a person who has a great idea (or so they think) and wants to share it with a potential partner, investor, lawyer, or investment banker, but wants an assur-

ance that the recipient of the information will not steal or reveal the information to anyone else.

NDAs are enforceable contracts, so if someone violates it the disclosing party can sue the breaching party for damages. Bill Gates of Microsoft has plumbers and other persons who work on his house sign NDAs. Sabeer Bhatia, the founder of Hotmail, collected more then 400 NDAs in two years before selling his company to Microsoft for $400 million.

Although it may not be hard to get some people to sign NDAs, others balk. Some friends and relatives refuse to sign NDAs thrust on them because they present an aura of distrust. And it is particularly insulting to sign an NDA and then to hear a harebrained idea from the disclosing party. Industry bigwigs—venture capitalists, securities analysts, and successful technology companies—routinely refuse to sign NDAs because they see too many similar ideas and do not want their tongues tied by any single one. NDAs will continue to increase in use, however. So the next time you are at a party and you ask someone what they do, don't be surprised if you are NDA'd!

Express and Implied-in-Fact Contracts

An *actual contract* (as distinguished from a quasi-contract, which is discussed later in this chapter) may be either *express* or *implied-in-fact*.

Express contracts are stated in oral or written words. Examples of such contracts include an oral agreement to purchase a neighbor's bicycle and a written agreement to buy an automobile from a dealership.

Implied-in-fact contracts are implied from the conduct of the parties. Implied-in-fact contracts leave more room for questions. The following elements must be established to create an implied-in-fact contract:

1. The plaintiff provided property or services to the defendant.
2. The plaintiff expected to be paid by the defendant for the property or services and did not provide the property or services gratuitously.
3. The defendant was given an opportunity to reject the property or services provided by the plaintiff but failed to do so.

express contract

An agreement that is expressed in written or oral words.

implied-in-fact contract

A contract where agreement between parties has been inferred from their conduct.

Entreprenuer and the Law

OWNER OF SCRABBLE SPELLED "L-O-S-E-R"

Implied-in-fact contracts are implied from the conduct of the parties. Consider the following case.

Selchow & Richter (S&R) owns the trademark to the famous board game *Scrabble*. Mark Landsberg wrote a book

on strategy for winning at *Scrabble* and contracted S&R to request permission to use the Scrabble trademark. In response, S&R requested a copy of Landsberg's manuscript, which he provided. After prolonged negotiations between the parties regarding the possibility of S&R's publication of the manuscript broke off, S&R brought out its own Scrabble strategy book. No express contract was ever entered into between Landsberg and S&R. Landsberg sued S&R and its subsidiary, Scrabble Crossword Game Players, Inc., for damages for breach of an implied contract.

Was there an implied-in-fact contract between the parties?

The district court and appellate court held that an implied-in-fact contract had been formed between the parties and that the contract was breached by the defendants. The court noted

that the law allows for recovery for the breach of an implied-in-fact contract when the recipient of a valuable idea accepts and uses the information without paying for it even though he knows that compensation is expected. Here, the court found (1) that Landsberg's disclosure of his manuscript was confidential and for the limited purpose of obtaining approval for the use of the Scrabble mark, and (2) given Landsberg's express intention to exploit his manuscript commercially, the defendant's use of any portion of it was conditioned on payment. Landsberg was awarded $440,300 damages.

Objective Theory of Contracts

objective theory of contracts

A theory that says the intent to contract is judged by the reasonable person standard and not by the subjective intent of the parties.

The **objective theory of contracts** holds that the intent to enter into an express or implied-in-fact contract is judged by the **reasonable person standard**. Would a hypothetical reasonable person conclude that the parties intended to create a contract after considering (1) the words and conduct of the parties and (2) the surrounding circumstances? For example, no valid contract results from offers that are made in jest, anger, or undue excitement.

Under the objective theory of contracts, the subjective intent of a party to enter into a contract is irrelevant. The following case illustrates the application of the objective theory of contracts.

City of Everett, Washington v. Mitchell

631 P.2d 366 (1981)

Supreme Court of Washington

CASE 8.1

BACKGROUND AND FACTS

Al and Rosemary Mitchell owned a small secondhand store. On August 12, 1978, the Mitchells attended Alexander's Auction, where they frequently shopped to obtain merchandise for their business. While at the auction, they purchased a used safe for $50. They were told by the auctioneer that the inside compartment of the safe was locked and that no key could be found to unlock it. The safe was part of the Sumstad Estate. Several days after the auction, the Mitchells took the safe to a locksmith to have the locked compartment opened. When the locksmith opened the compartment he found $32,207 in cash. The locksmith called the City of Everett Police, who impounded the money. The City of Everett commenced an interpleader action against the Sumstad Estate and the Mitchells. The trial court entered summary judgment in favor of Sumstad Estate. The court of appeals affirmed. The Mitchells appealed.

ISSUE

Was a contract formed between the seller and the buyer of the safe?

COURT'S REASONING

The objective theory of contracts stresses the outward manifestation of assent made by the parties. In the instant case, evidence showed that the rule of the auction was that all sales were final. Furthermore, the auctioneer made no statement

reserving the rights to any contents of the safe. Under these circumstances, the court held that reasonable persons would conclude that the auctioneer manifested an objective intent to sell the safe and its contents, including the contents of the locked compartment. The subjective intention of the parties is irrelevant. The court stated: "If, however, it were proved by twenty bishops that either party, when he used the words, intended something else than the usual meaning which the law imposes upon them, he would still be held."

DECISION

The state supreme court held that under the objective theory of contracts, a contract was formed between the seller and the buyer of the safe. The court reversed the court of appeals's grant of summary judgment to the Sumstad Estate and remanded the case to the trial court for entry of judgment in favor of the Mitchells.

Case Questions

Critical Legal Thinking   Does the objective theory of contracts work? Is it easy to define a "reasonable person"?

Business Ethics   Did the seller of the safe act ethically in alleging that no contract had been made with the Mitchells?

Contemporary Business   What do you think the economic consequences to business would be if the courts recognized a subjective theory of contracts?

Quasi-Contracts (Implied-in-Law Contracts)

The equitable doctrine of **quasi-contract**, also called **implied-in-law contract**, allows a court to award monetary damages to a plaintiff for providing work or services to a defendant even though no actual contract existed between the parties. Recovery generally is based on the reasonable value of the services received by the defendant.

The doctrine is intended to prevent *unjust enrichment* and *unjust detriment*. It does not apply where there is an enforceable contract between the parties.

A quasi-contract is imposed where (1) one person confers a benefit on another who retains the benefit and (2) it would be unjust not to require that person to pay for the benefit received. The following case illustrates the doctrine of quasi-contract.

quasi- or implied-in-law contract

An equitable doctrine whereby a court may award monetary damages to a plaintiff for providing work or services to a defendant even though no actual contract existed. The doctrine is intended to prevent unjust enrichment and unjust detriment.

Dines v. Liberty Mutual Insurance Company
548 N.E.2d 1268 (1990)
Appeals Court of Massachusetts

CASE 8.2

BACKGROUND AND FACTS
Roger J. Dines is engaged in the business of towing and storing vehicles. On October 15, 1985, the state police recovered a stolen trailer and ordered it stored at Dines's facility. The rightful owner of the trailer, the Liberty Mutual Insurance Company (Liberty), learned that the trailer was stored at Dines's facility on January 7, 1986, but it did nothing to recover its property. Dines discovered that Liberty owned the trailer on March 11, 1986. On March 14, 1986, Dines gave written notice to Liberty that its trailer was at his storage facility. He enclosed an invoice for storage fees computed at $20 per day. Liberty refused to pay the charges. On March 11, 1987, Liberty sued to replevy the trailer. Dines released the trailer to Liberty on March 18, 1987, but sued Liberty to recover $10,400 in storage fees. The trial court found an implied-in-law contract and awarded Dines $5,000, which represented the value of the trailer. Both parties appealed.

ISSUE
Do the facts and circumstances justify the imposition of an implied-in-law contract?

COURT'S REASONING
A quasi-contract is an obligation created by law for reasons of justice. The underlying basis for awarding quasi-contract

damages is unjust enrichment of one party and unjust detriment to the other party. Here, the property was stored in a safe facility preventing vandalism. Therefore, Liberty benefited from the storage of its property. The court noted that quasi-contract damages are limited to the amount of benefit bestowed on the defendant. If Dines were permitted to recover the full amount he had billed, he would have recovered more than the benefit conferred on Liberty.

DECISION
The appeals court held that the facts and circumstances of the case justified the imposition of an implied-in-law contract. Affirmed.

Case Questions

Critical Legal Thinking   What public policy underlies the doctrine of implied-in-law contract?

Business Ethics   When should Liberty have notified Dines that he was holding its property? Was it ethical for Liberty to refuse to pay the storage charges?

Contemporary Business   Should a business be made to pay contract damages when it has not entered into an express contract with the plaintiff?

Formal and Informal Contracts

Formal Contracts   Contracts may be classified as either *formal or informal*. **Formal contracts** are contracts that require a special form or method of creation. The Restatement (Second) of Contracts identifies the following types of formal contracts.[4]

- **Contracts Under Seal**   This type of contract is one to which a seal (usually a wax seal) is attached. Although no state currently requires contracts to be under seal, a few states provide that no consideration is necessary if a contract is made under seal.
- **Recognizances**   In a recognizance, a party acknowledges in court that he or she will pay a specified sum of money if a certain event occurs. A bail bond is an example of a recognizance.
- **Negotiable Instruments**   Negotiable instruments, which include checks, drafts, notes, and certificates of deposit, are special forms of contracts recognized by the UCC. They require a special form and language for their creation and must meet certain requirements for their transfer.
- **Letters of Credit**   A letter of credit is an agreement by the issuer of the letter to pay a sum of money upon the receipt of an invoice and bill of lading. Letters of credit are governed by the UCC.

formal contract

A contract that requires a special form or method of creation.

Business Brief

Originally, only contracts under seal were recognized as valid contracts in England. Around 1600, the common law courts of England began to enforce simple contracts that were not made under seal.

informal contract

A contract that is not formal. Valid informal contracts are fully enforceable and may be sued upon if breached.

Informal Contracts   All contracts that do not qualify as formal contracts are called **informal contracts** (or **simple contracts**). The term is a misnomer. Valid informal contracts (e.g., leases, sales contracts, service contracts) are fully enforceable and may be sued upon if breached. They are called informal contracts only because no special form or method is required for their creation.

Valid, Void, Voidable, and Unenforceable Contracts

valid contract

A contract that meets all of the essential elements to establish a contract; a contract that is enforceable by at least one of the parties.

A **valid contract** is one that meets all of the essential elements to establish a contract. In other words, it must (1) consist of an agreement between the parties, (2) be supported by legally sufficient consideration, (3) be between parties with contractual capacity, and (4) accomplish a lawful object. Valid contracts are enforceable by at least one of the parties.

void contract

A contract that has no legal effect; a nullity.

A **void contract** is one that has no legal effect. It is as if no contract had ever been created. For example, a contract to commit a crime is void. If a contract is void, neither party is obligated to perform and neither party can enforce the contract.

voidable contract

A contract where one or both parties have the option to avoid their contractual obligations. If a contract is avoided, both parties are released from their contractual obligations.

A **voidable contract** is one where at least one party has the *option* to avoid his or her contractual obligations. If the contract is avoided, both parties are released from their obligations under the contract. If the party with the option chooses to ratify the contract, both parties must fully perform their obligations. With certain exceptions, contracts may be voided by minors; insane persons; intoxicated persons; persons acting under duress, undue influence, or fraud; and cases involving mutual mistake.

unenforceable contract

A contract where the essential elements to create a valid contract are met, but there is some legal defense to the enforcement of the contract.

An **unenforceable contract** is one where there is some legal defense to the enforcement of the contract. For example, if a contract is required to be in writing under the Statute of Frauds but is not, the contract is unenforceable. The parties may voluntarily perform a contract that is unenforceable.

 *E-Commerce & Information Technology*

CLICK-WRAP LICENSES

In the past, most business and consumer contracts consisted of written agreements signed by both parties. With the advent of the Internet, many online contracts no longer fit this traditional mode. Take **click-wrap licenses**, for example. A click-wrap license is a contract used by many software companies to sell their software over the Internet or in physical packages where the software is later installed on a computer. The software company, called the *licensor*, typically displays a series of dialogue boxes on the computer screen that states the terms of the agreement before the software is downloaded or installed by the potential licensee. The terms of a software click-wrap license are typically not negotiable, and the *licensee* (the person who is granted the license) indicates his or her acceptance by clicking on a prompt button on the screen labeled "I accept" or "I agree." Click-wrap licenses contain terms of the agreement, disclaimers of warranties, guarantees for the protection of trademarks and trade secrets, and other provisions that would normally be contained in a paper license. Click-wrap agreements provide a fast, inexpensive, and convenient way for licensors to mass market their software to users without requiring paper contracts or physical signatures.

A question recently presented to the courts is whether click-wrap licenses are enforceable since they lack paper and signatures of traditional contracts. The courts have applied the general principle of the Uniform Commercial Code Article 2 "Sales" that provides that a contract for the sale of goods may be made in any manner sufficient to show agreement, including conduct by both parties that recognizes the contract's existence. Courts have also referred to the Restatement (Second) of Contracts § 19, which provides that "manifestation of assent may be made by written or spoken words or by other action." The courts reason by analogy that a party is considered to have manifested her consent to enter into a contract by her physical action of using a mouse to click the "I Agree" prompt button for the click-wrap license.

The new **Uniform Computer Information Transactions Act (UCITA)**, which is a proposed model act for conducting e-commerce, specifically provides that a licensee who has the opportunity to review the terms of the license is bound by those terms if the licensee "manifests assent" before or during the party's initial use of or access to the licensor's software [UCITA § 210(a)]. Thus, under the modern e-commerce interpretation of the law of contracts, popular click-wrap licenses are enforceable contracts between software licensors and user licensees.

Executed and Executory Contracts

A completed contract, that is, one that has been fully performed on both sides, is called an **executed contract**. A contract that has not been performed by both sides is called an **executory contract**. Contracts that have been fully performed by one side but not by the other are classified as executory contracts.

executed contract
A contract that has been fully performed on both sides; a completed contract.

executory contract
A contract that has not been fully performed by either or both sides.

Consider This Example   (1) Suppose Elizabeth Andrews signs a contract to purchase a new Jaguar automobile from Ace Motors. She has not yet paid for the car and Ace Motors has not yet delivered it. This is an executory contract. (2) Assume that the car was paid for, but Ace Motors has not yet delivered the car. Here, the contract is executed by Elizabeth but is executory as to Ace Motors. This is an executory contract. (3) Assume that Ace Motors now delivers the car to Elizabeth. The contract has been fully performed by both parties. It is an executed contract.

CONCEPT SUMMARY   CLASSIFICATIONS OF CONTRACTS

Formation	1. **Bilateral contract** A promise for a promise.
	2. **Unilateral contract** A promise for an act.
	3. **Express contract** A contract expressed in oral or written words.
	4. **Implied-in-fact contract** A contract inferred from the conduct of the parties.
	5. **Formal contract** A contract that requires a special form or method of creation.
	6. **Informal contract** A contract that requires no special form or method of creation.
	7. **Quasi-contract** A contract implied by law to prevent unjust enrichment.
Enforceability	1. **Valid contract** A contract that meets all of the essential elements to establish a contract.
	2. **Void contract** No contract exists.
	3. **Voidable contract** A party has the option of voiding or enforcing the contract.
	4. **Unenforceable contract** A contract that cannot be enforced because of a legal defense.
Performance	1. **Executed contract** A contract that is fully performed on both sides.
	2. **Executory contract** A contract that is not fully performed by one or both parties.

EQUITY

Recall that two separate courts developed in England, a court of law and a chancery court (or court of equity). The equity courts developed a set of maxims based on fairness, equality, moral rights, and natural law that were applied in settling disputes. **Equity** was resorted to when (1) an award of money damages "at law" would not be the proper remedy or (2) fairness required the application of equitable principles. Today, in most states of the United States, the courts of law and equity have been merged into one court. In an action " in equity" the judge decides the equitable issue; there is no right to a jury trial in an equitable action. The doctrine of equity is sometimes applied in contract cases.

equity
A doctrine that permits judges to make decisions based on fairness, equality, moral rights, and natural law.

A man must come into a court of equity with clean hands.

C. B. Eyre
Dering v. Earl of Winchelsea
(1787)

Business Ethics

EQUITY SAVES CONTRACTING PARTY

The courts usually interpret a valid contract as a solemn promise to perform. This view of the sanctity of a contract can cause an ethical conflict. Consider the following case.

In 1975, a landlord leased a motel he owned to lessees for a 10-year period. The lessees had an option to extend the lease for an additional 10 years, commencing on March 1, 1985. To do so, they had to give written notice to the landlord on or before December 1, 1984. The lease provided for forfeiture of all furniture, fixtures, and equipment installed by the lessees, free of any liens, upon termination of the lease.

From 1975 to 1985, the lessees devoted most of their assets and a great deal of their energy building up the business. During this time, they transformed a disheveled, unrated motel into a AAA three-star operation. With the landlord's knowledge, the lessees made extensive long-term improvements that greatly increased the value of both the property and the business. The landlord knew that the lessees had obtained long-term financing for the improvements that would extend well beyond the first 10-year term of the lease. The landlord also knew that the only source of income the lessees had to pay for these improvements was the income generated from the motel business. The lessees told the landlord in a conversation that they intended to extend the lease.

The lessees had instructed their accountant to timely exercise the option by December 1, 1984. Despite reminders from the lessees, the accountant failed to give the written notice by December 1, 1984. On December 13, 1984 as soon as they discovered the mistake, the lessees personally delivered written notice of renewal of the option to the landlord, who rejected it as late and instituted a lawsuit for unlawful detainer to evict the lessees.

The trial and appellate courts held in favor of the lessees. They rejected the landlord's argument for the strict adherence to the deadline for giving notice of renewal of the lease. Instead, the courts granted **equitable relief** and permitted the late renewal notice. The court reasoned that "there is only minimal delay in giving notice, the harm to the lessor is slight, and the hardship to the lessee is severe." [*Romasanta v. Mitton*, 234 Cal.Rptr. 729 (Cal.App. 1987)]

1. Did the landlord act ethically in this case?
2. Should the court have applied equity and saved the lessees from their mistake? Or should they have been held to the terms of the lease?

Singapore *The United Nations Convention on Contracts for the International Sale of Goods (CISG) provides rules for the enforcement of contracts for the international sale of goods if (1) the nations of the contracting parties recognize the CISG and (2) the international contract specifies that the CISG has control.*

International Law

THE UNITED NATIONS CONVENTION ON CONTRACTS FOR THE INTERNATIONAL SALE OF GOODS

The United Nations Convention on Contracts for the International Sale of Goods (CISG) came into effect on January 1, 1988, climaxing more than 50 years of negotiations. The CISG supersedes two earlier conventions, the Convention Relative to a Uniform Law on the International Sale of Goods (ULIS) and the Convention Relating to a Uniform Law on the Formation of Contracts for the International Sale of Goods (ULF).

Neither the ULIS nor the ULF was widely adopted because both were drafted without the participation of the Third World or the Eastern bloc. The CISG, on the other hand, is the work of more than 60 countries and several international organizations. Many of its provisions are remarkably similar to the American Uniform Commercial Code, for example. It incorporates rules from all the major legal systems. It has, accordingly, received widespread support from developed, developing, and Communist countries. Countries that have adopted it include Argentina, Austria, China, Egypt, Finland, France, Hungary, Italy, Mexico, Sweden, Syria, and the United States. Because the United States has ratified the CISG, Americans engaged in sales overseas need to be aware of the CISG.

The CISG applies to contracts for the international sale of goods. That is, the buyer and seller must have their places of business in different countries. Additionally, either (1) both of the nations must be parties to the convention, or (2) the contract specifies that the CISG controls. The contracting parties may agree to exclude (i.e., opt out of) or modify its application. In the United States, such a provision would be honored.

Chapter Summary

Definition of a Contract, p. 201

Definition of a Contract	"A promise or a set of promises for the breach of which the law gives a remedy or the performance of which the law in some way recognizes a duty."
Parties to a Contract	1. *Offeror*. Party who makes an offer to enter into a contract. 2. *Offeree*. Party to whom the offer is made.
Elements of a Contract	1. Agreement 2. Consideration 3. Contractual capacity 4. Lawful object
Defenses to the Enforcement of a Contract	1. Genuineness of assent 2. Writing and form

Sources of Contract Law, p. 202

Sources of Contract Law	1. Common law of contracts (law) 2. Uniform Commercial Code (law) 3. Restatement (Second) of Contracts (advisory only, not law)
Theories of Contract Law	1. *Classical law of contracts*. Parties were free to negotiate contract terms without government interference. 2. *Modern law of contracts*. Parties may negotiate contract terms subject to government regulations.

Classifications of Contracts, p. 204

Formation	1. *Bilateral contract*. A promise for a promise. 2. *Unilateral contract*. A promise for an act. 3. *Express contract*. A contract expressed in oral or written words. 4. *Implied-in-fact contract*. A contract implied from the conduct of the parties. 5. *Quasi-contract*. A contract implied by law to prevent unjust enrichment and unjust detriment. 6. *Formal contract*. A contract that requires a special form or method for creation. 7. *Informal contract*. A contract that requires no special form or method for creation.
Enforceability	1. *Valid contract*. Meets all of the essential elements to establish a contract. 2. *Void contract*. No contract exists. 3. *Voidable contract*. One or both parties have the option of avoiding or enforcing the contract. 4. *Unenforceable contract*. A contract that cannot be enforced because of a legal defense.
Performance	1. *Executed contract*. A contract that is fully performed on both sides. 2. *Executory contract*. A contract that is not fully performed by one or both parties.

Equity, p. 209

Equity	A doctrine that permits judges to make decisions based on fairness, equality, moral rights, and natural law.

END-OF-CHAPTER INTERNET EXERCISES AND CASE QUESTIONS

 Working the Web Internet Exercises

ACTIVITIES

1. Try **www.findlaw.com** and review the extensive material on contracts. Determine the statute of limitations on written contracts in your jurisdiction.

2. Review **www.perkinscoie.com** as an example of one law firm's Web site. Examine the materials collected there on contract law by using the search feature for "contracts." How many different kinds can you find?

3. For international sales contracts, compare the CISG and UCC by visiting the Web site **www.cisg.law.pace.edu**. It contains the entire text of the Convention on the International Sale of Goods and related information.

4. What is the rule regarding contractual capacity of minors in your jurisdiction? Use FindLaw again to locate the statute. Hint: Using FindLaw, narrow your search by selecting your state first. Then enter your search terms.

CRITICAL LEGAL THINKING CASES

8.1 Objective Theory of Contracts On January 23, 1974, G. S. Adams, Jr., vice president of the Washington Bank & Trust Co., met with Bruce Bickham. An agreement was reached whereby Bickham agreed to do his personal and corporate banking business with the bank and the bank agreed to loan Bickham money at $7\frac{1}{2}$ percent interest per annum. Bickham would have 10 years to repay the loans. From January 1974 to September 1976, the bank made several loans to Bickham at $7\frac{1}{2}$ percent interest. In September 1976, Adams resigned from the bank. The bank then notified Bickham that general economic changes made it necessary to charge a higher rate of interest on both outstanding and new loans. Bickham sued the bank for breach of contract. Was the contract a bilateral or a unilateral contract? Does Bickham win? [*Bickham v. Washington Bank & Trust Company*, 515 So.2d 457 (La.App. 1987)]

8.2 Implied-in-Fact Contract From October 1964 through May 1970, Lee Marvin, an actor, lived with Michelle Marvin. They were not married. In May 1970, Lee Marvin compelled Michelle Marvin to leave his household. He continued to support her until November 1971 but thereafter refused to provide further support. During their time together, Lee Marvin earned substantial income and acquired property, including motion-picture rights worth over $1 million. Michelle Marvin brought an action against Lee Marvin, alleging that an implied-in-fact contract existed between them and that she was entitled to half of the property that they had acquired while living together. She claimed that she had given up a lucrative career as an entertainer and singer to be a full-time companion, homemaker, housekeeper, and cook. Can an implied-in-fact contract result from the conduct of unmarried persons who live together? [*Marvin v. Marvin*, 557 P.2d 106 (Cal. 1976)]

BUSINESS ETHICS CASES

8.3 Business Ethics On Sunday, October 6, 1974, the Lewiston Lodge of Elks sponsored a golf tournament at the Fairlawn Country Club in Poland, Maine. For promotional purposes, Marcel Motors, an automobile dealership, agreed to give any golfer who shot a hole-in-one a new 1974 Dodge Colt. Fliers advertising the tournament were posted in the Elks Club and sent to potential participants. On the day of the tournament, the 1974 Dodge Colt was parked near the clubhouse with one of the posters conspicuously displayed on the vehicle. Alphee Chenard, Jr., who had seen the promotional literature regarding the hole-in-one offer, registered for the tournament and paid the requisite entrance fee. While playing the thirteenth hole of the golf course, in the pres-

ence of the other members of his foursome, Chenard shot a hole-in-one. When Marcel Motors refused to tender the automobile, Chenard sued for breach of contract. Was the contract a bilateral or a unilateral contract? Does Chenard win? Was it ethical for Marcel Motors to refuse to give the automobile to Chenard? [*Chenard v. Marcel Motors*, 387 A.2d 596 (ME 1978)]

8.4 Business Ethics Loren Vranich, a doctor practicing under the corporate name Family Health Care, P.C., entered into a written employment contract to hire Dennis Winkel. The contract provided for an annual salary, insurance benefits, and other employment benefits. Another doctor, Dr. Quan, also practiced with Dr. Vranich. About nine months later, when Dr.

Quan left the practice, Vranich and Winkel entered into an oral modification of their written contract whereby Winkel was to receive a higher salary and a profit-sharing bonus. During the next year Winkel received the increased salary. However, a disagreement arose, and Winkel sued to recover the profit-sharing bonus. Under Montana law, a written contract can be altered only in writing or by an executed oral agreement. Dr. Vranich argued that the contract could not be enforced because it was not in writing. Does Winkel receive the profit-sharing bonus? Did Dr. Vranich act ethically in raising the defense that the contract was not in writing? [*Winkel v. Family Health Care, P.C.*, 668 P.2d 208 (MT 1983)]

BRIEFING THE CASE WRITING ASSIGNMENT

Read the following case, which has been excerpted from the court's opinion, and brief the case.

Mark Realty, Inc. v. Rogness
418 So.2d 373 (1982)
District Court of Appeals of Florida

Cowart, Judge

Tilman A. Rogness, owner, entered into four separate agreements with Mark Realty, Inc., a real estate broker. They were entitled "exclusive right of sale" and gave the broker, for a stated period of time, the exclusive right to sell the property for a certain stated price and on certain terms. The broker sued on the four agreements for brokerage commissions, alleging that during the time provided in the agreements the owner had conveyed the four properties. The owner's answer alleged affirmative defenses to the effect that the owner had "canceled, revoked, and terminated" the brokerage agreements before the properties were sold and that the broker had never performed under the agreements.

The trial judge construed the brokerage agreements to constitute mere offers to enter into unilateral contracts under which the broker would be entitled to a commission only if he performed by "finding a purchaser of the above property." If the documents in question are merely offers limited to acceptance by performance only, the trial judge's analysis and conclusion would be correct.

We cannot agree that the documents were only offers for a unilateral contract. The documents illustrate what has been termed "the usual practice" in the making of bargains. One party indicates what he will do and what he requires in exchange and the other then agrees. These documents, when first executed by the owner and tendered to the broker, constituted offers which, when accepted by the broker by his execution, constituted contracts. The contract is bilateral because it contains mutual promises made in exchange for each other by each of the two contracting parties.

The most common recurring brokerage transaction is one in which the owner employs a broker to find a purchaser able and willing to buy, on terms stated in advance by the owner, and in which the owner promises to pay a specific commission for the service. Such a transaction as this is an offer by the owner of a unilateral contract, an offered promise to pay by the owner, creating in the broker a power of accepting the offer by actual rendition of the requested services. The only contemplated contract between the owner and broker is a unilateral contract—a promise to pay a commission for services rendered. Such an offer of a promise to pay a commission for services rendered is revocable by the owner by notice before the broker has rendered any part of the requested service.

On the other hand, the transaction between the owner and the broker can be a bilateral contract. An owner who puts his land in the hands of a broker for sale usually clearly promises to pay a commission, but the broker rarely promises in return that he will produce a purchaser, although he often promises, expressly, or impliedly, that he will make certain efforts to do so. If the parties have thus made mutual promises, the transaction no longer has the status of an unaccepted offer—there is an existing bilateral contract and neither party has a power of revocation. During the term of such a contract the owner may withdraw any power the owner has given the broker to contract with a third party in the owner's name, but this is not a revocation of the contract between the owner and the broker and normally such action constitutes a breach of the brokerage contract.

In this case, the broker promised to inspect the property, to list the property with a multiple listing service, to advertise the property in the local newspaper or other media, to furnish information to inquiring cooperating brokers and prospective purchasers, to show the property, to make efforts to find a purchaser, to "make an earnest and continued effort to sell," and to direct the concentrated efforts of his organization in bringing about a sale.

In the instant case, the contract clearly provided that the brokerage commission would be paid "whether the purchaser be secured by you or me, or by any other person." Thus the contract granted the broker an exclusive right of sale and the trial court erred in construing the agreement as an offer of a unilateral contract revocable at will at any time prior to performance.

The final judgment is reversed.

ENDNOTES

1. *Rebstock v. Birthright Oil & Gas Co.*, 406 So.2d 636 (La. App. 1981).
2. Restatement (Second) of Contracts, § 1.
3. Restatement (Second) of Contracts, § 1.
4. Restatement (Second) of Contracts, § 6.

CHAPTER

9

Agreement and Consideration

"When I use a word," Humpty Dumpty said, in rather a scornful tone, "it means just what I choose it to mean—neither more nor less."

"The question is," said Alice, "whether you can make words mean so many different things."

"The question is," said Humpty Dumpty, "which is to be master—that's all."

—Lewis Carroll
Alice's Adventures in Wonderland (1865)

Chapter Contents

Chapter Objectives

After studying this chapter, you should be able to:

1. Define an offer and an acceptance.

2. Identify what terms can be implied in a contract.

3. Describe how offers are terminated by action of the parties.

4. Define a counteroffer and describe its effects.

5. Describe the legal procedure for holding online auctions.

6. Define *consideration*.

7. Identify when there is inadequacy of consideration.

8. Analyze whether contracts are lacking in consideration.

9. Apply the doctrine of promissory estoppel.

10. Describe the enforceability of shrinkwrap licenses used with computer software.

Contracts are voluntary agreements between the parties. One party makes an offer, and the other accepts it. Without mutual assent, there is no contract. Assent may be expressly evidenced by the words of the parties or implied from their conduct.

To be enforceable, a contract must be supported by "consideration," which is broadly defined as something of legal value. It can consist of money, property, the provision of services, the forbearance of a right, or anything else of value. Most contracts that are not supported by consideration are not enforceable. The parties may voluntarily perform a contract that is lacking in consideration, however.

This chapter discusses the primary elements of a contract: agreement (i.e., offer and acceptance) and consideration.

A contract is a mutual promise.
William Paley
The Principles of Moral and
Political Philosophy *(1784)*

AGREEMENT

Agreement is the manifestation by two or more persons of the substance of a contract. It requires an *offer* and an *acceptance*. The process of reaching an agreement usually proceeds as follows. Prior to entering into a contract, the parties may engage in preliminary negotiations about price, time of performance, and such. At some point during these negotiations, one party makes an **offer**. The person who makes the offer is called the **offeror**, and the person to whom the offer is made is called the **offeree**. The offer sets forth the terms under which the offeree is willing to enter into the contract. The offeree has the power to create an agreement by accepting the offer.

agreement

The manifestation by two or more persons of the substance of a contract.

offeror

The party who makes an offer.

offeree

The party to whom an offer has been made.

Kyoto, Japan International trade is often governed by contracts between businesses or parties from different nations.

OFFER

Section 24 of the Restatement (Second) of Contracts defines an **offer** as: "The manifestation of willingness to enter into a bargain, so made as to justify another person in understanding that his assent to that bargain is invited and will conclude it." The following three elements are required for an offer to be effective:

1. The offeror must *objectively intend* to be bound by the offer.
2. The terms of the offer must be definite or reasonably *certain*.
3. The offer must be *communicated* to the offense.

offer

The manifestation of willingness to enter into a bargain, so made as to justify another person in understanding that his assent to that bargain is invited and will conclude it. (Section 24 of Restatement (Second) of Contracts)

Objective Intent

The intent to enter a contract is determined using the **objective theory of contracts**, that is, whether a reasonable person viewing the circumstances would conclude that the parties intended to be legally bound. Subjective intent is irrelevant. Therefore, no valid contract results from preliminary negotiations, offers that are an expression of opinion, or offers made in jest, anger, or undue excitement.

objective theory of contracts

A theory that says that the intent to contract is judged by the reasonable person standard and not by the subjective intent of the parties.

"Your offer's a crumpled little ball in the middle of my desk."

Preliminary Negotiations For example, a question such as "Are you interested in selling your building for $2 million?" is not an offer. It is an invitation to make an offer or an invitation to negotiate. The statement, "I will buy your building for $2 million" is a valid offer, however, because it indicates the offeror's present intent to contract.

Offers That Are Made in Jest, Anger, or Undue Excitement For example, suppose the owner of Company A has lunch with the owner of Company B. In the course of their conversation, Company A's owner exclaims in frustration, "For $2 I'd sell the whole computer division!" An offer such as that cannot result in a valid contract.

Offers That Are an Expression of Opinion A lawyer who tells her client that she thinks the lawsuit will result in an award of $100,000 cannot be sued for the difference if the trial jury awards only $50,000. The lawyer's statement is not an enforceable promise.

There is grim irony in speaking of freedom of contract of those who, because of their economic necessities, give their service for less than is needful to keep body and soul together.

Harlan Fiske Stone
Morehead v. N.Y. ex rel. Tipaldo
(1936)

E-Commerce & Information Technology

CONTRACTING BY FAX

Throughout history, contract law, which dates back thousands of years, has struggled to keep pace with inventions that change the way that we communicate—and hence form contracts—with each other. The latest technological challenge to come down the pike is the fax machine, which has quickly become an indispensable means of business communications. Although faxes have revolutionized communications by enabling the instantaneous exchange of written documents between people in distant corners of the world, they have also caused a variety of problems. For example, amid the flurry of faxes that are sent back and forth during contractual negotiations, it is sometimes difficult to tell exactly if and when the haggling ended and an agreement was reached.

There are several problems that the courts must address concerning faxes as contracts. First, the courts must examine the faxes to determine if an agreement was reached and, if so, the terms of the agreement. Courts examine faxes the same way they examine other documents in determining whether a meeting of the minds was reached. Therefore, it is important for businesses to retain copies of faxes so they can substantiate the contracts they have entered into. Second, to enforce a written contract against a party, his or her signature must appear on the writing. Most court decisions that have addressed the issue have recognized the enforceability of signatures sent by fax. Otherwise, the rules regarding oral contracts apply to faxes.

As faxes are used increasingly to communicate everything from orders for concert tickets to multimillion-dollar orders for equipment, judges and juries will be called upon to read through stacks of faxes to help them decide if disputing parties ever really reached an agreement and, if so, what they really agreed upon.

Definiteness of Terms

The terms of an offer must be clear enough for the offeree to be able to decide whether to accept or reject the terms of the offer. If the terms are indefinite, the courts cannot enforce the contract or determine an appropriate remedy for its breach.

To be considered definite, an offer (and contract) generally must contain the following terms: (1) identification of the parties, (2) identification of the subject matter and quantity, (3) consideration to be paid, and (4) time of performance. Complex contracts usually state additional terms.

Implied Terms   The common law of contracts required an exact specification of contract terms. If one essential term was omitted, the courts would hold that no contract had been made. This rule was inflexible.

The modern law of contracts is more lenient. The Restatement (Second) of Contracts merely requires that the terms of the offer be "reasonably certain."[1] Accordingly, the court can supply a missing term if a reasonable term can be implied.[2] The definition of *reasonable* depends on the circumstances. Terms that are supplied in this way are called **implied terms**.

Generally, time of performance can be implied. Price can be implied if there is market or source from which to determine the price of the item or service, for example, the "blue book" for an automobile price, the New York Stock Exchange for a stock price. The parties or subject matter of the contract usually cannot be implied if an item or service is unique or personal, such as the construction of a house or the performance of a professional sports contract.

Contemporary Business Environment

OWNER OF MIGHTY MORPHIN POWER RANGERS BATTLES LOGO DESIGNER

Mighty Morphin Power Rangers has been a phenomenal success as a television series. The Power Rangers have battled to save the universe from all sorts of diabolical plots and bad guys. They are also featured in a profitable line of toys and garments bearing the Power Rangers' logo. The Power Rangers' name and logo are known to millions of children and their parents worldwide. The claim of ownership of the logo for the Power Rangers ended up in a battle itself, this time in a courtroom.

David Dees is a designer who works as d/b/a David Dees Illustration. Saban Entertainment, Inc. (Saban), which owns the copyright and trademark to Power Ranger figures and the name "Power Ranger," hired Dees as an independent contractor to design a logo for the Power Rangers. The contract signed by the parties was entitled "Work-for-Hire/Independent Contractor Agreement." The contract was drafted by Saban with the help of its attorneys; Dees signed the agreement without the representation of legal counsel.

Dees designed the logo currently used for the Power Rangers and was paid $250 to transfer his copyright ownership in the logo. Subsequently, Dees sued Saban to recover damages for copyright and trademark infringement. Saban defended, arguing that a contract is a contract is a contract, and Dees was bound by the agreement he had signed.

The trial court agreed with Saban, finding that the "Work-for-Hire/Independent Contractor Agreement" was an enforceable contract between the parties and that Dees had transferred his ownership interests in the logo to Saban. Dees appealed. The court of appeals affirmed the judgment for Saban, stating, "The disputed agreement transferred plaintiff's copyright in the Mighty Morphin Power Rangers' logo with as much specificity as the law requires." The court found that a contract is a contract is a contract, at least in this case. Dee's appeal to the U.S. Supreme Court was denied. [*Dees, d/b/a David Dees Illustration v. Saban Entertainment, Inc.*, 131 F.3d 146 (1997)]

Communication

An offer cannot be accepted if it is not communicated to the offeree by the offeror or a representative or agent of the offeror. For example, suppose Mr. Jones, the CEO of Ace Corporation, wants to sell a manufacturing division to Baker Corporation. He puts the offer in writing, but he does not send it. Assume Mr. Griswald, the CEO of Baker Corporation, visits Mr. Jones and sees the written offer lying on Jones's desk. Griswald tells his CEO about the offer. Because Mr. Jones never communicated the offer to the CEO of Baker Corporation, there is no offer to be accepted.

Special Offer Situations

There are several special situations where there is a question whether an offer has been made. Advertisements, rewards, and auctions are examples of such situations.

advertisement

A general advertisement is an invitation to make an offer. A specific advertisement is an offer.

Advertisements Advertisements for the sale of goods, even at specific prices, generally are treated as *invitations to make an offer*. For example, catalogs, price lists, quotation sheets, offering circulars, and other sales materials are viewed in the same way. This rule is intended to protect advertiser-sellers from the unwarranted breach of contract suits for nonperformance that would otherwise arise if the seller ran out of the advertised goods.

There is one exception to this rule: An advertisement is considered an offer if it is so definite or specific that it is apparent that the advertiser has the present intent to bind himself or herself to the terms of the advertisement. For example, an automobile dealer's advertisement to sell a "previously owned maroon 2000 Lexus 400 SC, serial no. 3210674, $25,000" is an offer. Since the advertisement identifies the exact automobile for sale, the first person to accept the offer owns the automobile.

In the following case, the court had to decide whether an advertisement was a solicitation of an offer or an offer.

Mesaros v. United States
845 F.2d 1576 (1988)
United States Court of Appeals, Federal Circuit

CASE 9.1

BACKGROUND AND FACTS
In July 1985, the U.S. Congress directed the Secretary of the Treasury to mint and sell a stated number of specially minted commemorative coins to raise funds to restore and renovate the Statue of Liberty. In November and December 1985, the U.S. Mint mailed advertising materials to persons, including Mary and Anthony C. Mesaros, husband and wife, that described the various types of coins that were to be issued. Payment could be made by check, money order, or credit card. The materials included an order form. Directly above the space provided on this form for the customer's signature was the following: "YES, Please accept my order for the U.S. Liberty Coins I have indicated." On November 26, 1985, Mary Mesaros forwarded to the mint a credit-card order of $1,675 for certain coins, including the $5 gold coin. All credit-card orders were forwarded by the Mint to Mellon Bank in Pittsburgh, Pennsylvania, for verification, which took a period of time. Meanwhile, cash orders were filled immediately, and orders by check were filled as the checks cleared. The issuance of 500,000 gold coins was exhausted before Mesaros's credit-card order could be filled. The Mint sent a letter to the Mesaroses notifying them of this fact. The gold coin increased in value by 200 percent within the first few months of 1986. On May 23, 1986, Mary and Anthony C. Mesaros filed a class action lawsuit against the United States seeking in the alternative either damages for breach of contract or a decree of mandamus ordering the Mint to deliver the gold coins to the plaintiffs. The district court held for the Mint. The Mesaroses appealed.

ISSUE
Was the United States Mint's advertisement a solicitation of an offer or an offer?

COURT'S REASONING
It is well established that materials such as those mailed to prospective customers by the Mint are no more than advertisements or invitations to deal. They are mere solicitations for offers that create no power of acceptance in the recipient. The court stated: "Generally, it is considered unreasonable for a person to believe that advertisements and solicitations are offers that bind the advertiser. Otherwise, the advertiser could be bound by an excessive number of contracts requiring delivery of goods far in excess of amounts available. That is particularly true in the instant case where the gold coins were limited to 500,000 by the Act of Congress. We conclude that a thorough reading, construction, and interpretation of the materials sent to the plaintiffs by the Mint makes clear that the contention of the plaintiffs that they reasonably believed the materials were intended as an offer is unreasonable as a matter of law."

DECISION
The court of appeals held that the advertising materials sent out by the U.S. Mint was a solicitation to make an offer and not an offer. Therefore, the Mint wins.

Case Questions

Critical Legal Thinking Should an advertisement be treated as an offer instead of an invitation to make an offer? Why or why not?

Business Ethics Do you think the Mesaroses acted ethically by suing the Mint?

Contemporary Business Would it cause any problems for businesses if advertisements were considered offers? Explain.

Rewards An offer to pay a **reward** (e.g., for the return of lost property or the capture of a criminal) is an offer to form a unilateral contract. To be entitled to collect the reward, the offeree must (1) have knowledge of the reward offer prior to completing the requested act and (2) perform the requested act.

reward
To collect a reward, the offeree must (1) have knowledge of the reward offer prior to completing the requested act and (2) perform the requested act.

Consider This Example John Anderson accidentally leaves a briefcase containing $500,000 in negotiable bonds on a subway train. He places newspaper ads stating "$5,000 reward for return of briefcase left on a train in Manhattan on January 10, 2002, at approximately 10 A.M. Call 212-555-6789." Helen Smith, who is unaware of the offer, finds the briefcase. She reads the luggage tag containing Anderson's name, address, and telephone number, and she returns the briefcase to him. She is not entitled to the reward money because she did not know about it when she performed the requested act.

Auctions At a auction, the seller offers goods for sale through an auctioneer. Unless otherwise expressly stated, an auction is considered an **auction with reserve**; that is, it is an invitation to make an offer. The seller retains the right to refuse the highest bid and withdraw the goods from sale. A contract is formed only when the auctioneer strikes the gavel down or indicates acceptance by some other means. The bidder may withdraw his or her bid prior to that time.

If an auction is expressly announced to be an **auction without reserve**, the participants reverse the roles: The seller is the offeror and the bidders are the offerees. The seller must accept the highest bid and cannot withdraw the goods from sale. A seller who sets a minimum bid only has to sell the item if the highest bid is equal to or greater than the minimum bid.

auction with reserve
Unless expressly stated otherwise, an auction is an auction with reserve; that is, the seller retains the right to refuse the highest bid and withdraw the goods from sale.

auction without reserve
An auction in which the seller expressly gives up his or her right to withdraw the goods from sale and must accept the highest bid.

CONCEPT SUMMARY TYPES OF AUCTIONS

Type	Offer
Auction with reserve	No. It is an invitation to make an offer. Because the bidder is the offeror, the seller (the offeree) may refuse to sell the goods. An auction is with reserve unless otherwise stated.
Auction without reserve	Yes. The seller is the offeror and must sell the goods to the highest bidder (the offeree). An auction is without reserve only if it is stipulated as such.

E-Commerce & Information Technology

ONLINE AUCTIONS

Auctions have been used traditionally to sell horses, antiques, paintings, and other such one-of-a-kind items. A bidder usually had to be physically present at the auction to bid, although some auctions allow telephone bids from prequalified callers. Because of these restrictions, auctions occupied a small portion of the U.S. economy. But no more, thanks to the advent of the Internet.

Led by the giant online auction house, eBay, online auctions have exploded on the Internet. eBay started as a small online auction house that made a market in such consumer collectibles as Pez dispensers, Beanie Babies, and such. After seeing how successful this mode of business was for these items, eBay expanded into a full-service online auctioneer. By the year 2000, eBay was offering several million items each day for sale over the Internet. The millions of eBay's cyber shoppers are loyal, spending an average of 130 minutes per month at the eBay auction site.

eBay does not own the items it sells. Instead, sellers list the items they want to auction on the eBay site, and buyers bid for the items. The purchase contract is between the cyber seller and the cyber buyer. One of the problems with Internet auctions is that many sellers do not take credit cards, so payment must be made by check or cash. Thus, many transactions take days, if not weeks, to complete. eBay takes a 6 percent commission on items sold by its online auction house. In the beginning of online auctions, most of the goods sold were goods that were customarily sold at flea markets, antique stores, and classified advertisements. Today, many businesses have started using eBay auctions to sell their excess inventory or to sell mainstream consumer and business goods. Business sales through online auctions now exceed nonbusiness sales.

eBay is now receiving stiff competition from many other online auctioneers. The giant e-commerce leader Amazon.com conducts online auctions, and many small online auction houses specialize in selling jewelry, baseball cards, horses, and other items. eBay itself began offering localized auctions in individual cities for such large items as cars and furniture. Even traditional auction houses such as Sotheby's, which auctions pricey items like paintings, jewelry, and antiques, have begun selling through online auctions. As proven by the success of eBay and other online auctioneers, consumers and businesses have embraced the dynamic pricing and fluid give-and-take of Internet auctions. Auctions, which have been around for most of history, are again giving fixed-priced selling, which has only been around for about 100 years, a run for its money.

Termination of an Offer by Action of the Parties

An offer may be terminated by the following actions of the parties.

revocation

Withdrawal of an offer by the offeror terminates the offer.

Business Brief

Generally, an offeror can revoke an offer at any time prior to its acceptance by the offeree.

Revocation of the Offer by the Offeror Under the common law, an offeror may **revoke** (i.e., withdraw) an offer any time prior to its acceptance by the offeree. Generally, an offer can be so revoked even if the offeror promised to keep the offer open for a longer time. The revocation may be communicated to the offeree by the offeror or by a third party and made by (1) the offeror's express statement (for example, "I hereby withdraw my offer") or (2) an act of the offeror that is inconsistent with the offer (for example, selling the goods to another party). Most states provide that the revocation is not effective until it is actually received by the offeree or the offeree's agent.

Offers made to the public may be revoked by communicating the revocation by the same means used to make the offer. For example, if a reward offer for a lost watch was published in two local newspapers each week for four weeks, notice of revocation must be published in the same newspapers for the same length of time. The revocation is effective against all offerees, even those who saw the reward offer but not the notice of revocation.

rejection

Express words or conduct by the offeree that rejects an offer. Rejection terminates the offer.

Rejection of the Offer by the Offeree An offer is terminated if the offeree **rejects** it. Any subsequent attempt by the offeree to accept the offer is ineffective and is construed as a new offer that the original offeror (now the offeree) is free to accept or reject. A rejection may be evidenced by the offeree's express words (oral or written) or conduct. Generally, a rejection is not effective until it is actually received by the offeror.

Consider This Example Harriet Jackson, sales manager of IBM Corporation, offers to sell 1,000 computers to Ted Green, purchasing manager of General Motors Corporation, for $250,000. The offer is made on August 1. Green telephones Jackson to say that he is not interested. This rejection terminates the offer. If Green later decides that he wants to purchase the computers, an entirely new contract must be formed.

counteroffer

A response by an offeree that contains terms and conditions different from or in addition to those of the offer. A counteroffer terminates an offer.

Counteroffer by the Offeree A **counteroffer** by the offeree simultaneously terminates the offeror's offer and creates a new offer. For example, suppose in the prior example Green says, "I think $250,000 is too high for the computers. I will pay you $200,000." He has made a counteroffer. The original offer is terminated, and the counteroffer is a new offer that Jackson is free to accept or reject.

Termination of an Offer by Operation of Law

Offers can be terminated by operation of law in the following situations.

Business Brief

Destruction of the subject matter terminates an offer; it does not terminate the contract if the offer has already been accepted, however.

Destruction of the Subject Matter The offer terminates if the subject matter of the offer is destroyed through no fault of either party prior to its acceptance. For example, if a fire destroys an office building that has been listed for sale, the offer automatically terminates.

Death or Incompetency of the Offeror or Offeree The death or incompetency of either the offeror or the offeree terminates the offer. Notice of the other party's death or incompetence is not a requirement. For example, suppose on June 1 Shari Hunter offers to sell her house to Damian Coe for $100,000, providing he decides on or before June 15. Hunter dies on June 7 before Coe has made up his mind. Since there is no contract prior to her death, the offer automatically terminates on June 7.

Supervening Illegality If the object of an offer is made illegal prior to the acceptance of an offer, the offer terminates. This situation, which usually occurs when a statute is enacted or a court case is announced that makes the object of the offer illegal, is called a **supervening illegality**. For example, suppose City Bank offers to loan ABC Corporation $5 million at an 18 percent interest rate. Prior to ABC's acceptance of the offer, the state legislature enacts a statute that sets a usury interest rate of 12 percent. City Bank's offer to ABC Corporation is automatically terminated when the usury statute became effective.

Lapse of Time The offer may state that it is effective only until a certain date. Unless otherwise stated, the time period begins to run when the offer is actually received by the offeree and terminates when the stated time period expires. Statements such as 'This offer is good for 10 days" or "This offer must be accepted by January 1, 2002" are examples of such notices. If no time is stated in the offer, the offer terminates after a "reasonable time" dictated by the circumstances. Thus, a reasonable time to accept an offer to purchase stock traded on a national stock exchange may be a few moments, but a reasonable time to accept an offer to purchase a house may be a few days. Unless otherwise stated, an offer made face to face or during a telephone call usually expires after the conversation.

supervening illegality

The enactment of a statute, regulation, or court decision that makes the object of an offer illegal. This action terminates the offer.

lapse of time

An offer terminates when a stated time period expires. If no time is stated, an offer terminates after a reasonable time.

Entrepreneur and the Law

OPTION CONTRACTS

An offeree can prevent the offeror from revoking his or her offer by paying the offeror compensation to keep the offer open for an agreed-upon period of time. This payment is called an **option contract**. In other words, the offeror agrees not to sell the property to anyone but the offeree during the option period. The death or incompetency of either party does not terminate an option contract unless it is for the performance of a personal service.

Consider This Example Anne Mason offers to sell a piece of real estate to Harold Greenberg for $1 million. Greenberg wants time to make a decision, so he pays Mason $20,000 to keep her offer open to him for six months. At any time during the option period, Greenberg may exercise his option and pay Mason the $1 million purchase price. If he lets the option expire, however, Mason may keep the $20,000 and sell the property to someone else.

ACCEPTANCE

Acceptance is a manifestation of assent by the offeree to the terms of the offer in a manner invited or required by the offer as measured by the objective theory of contracts.[3] Recall that generally (1) unilateral contracts can be accepted only by the offeree's performance of the required act and (2) a bilateral contract can be accepted by an offeree who promises to perform (or where permitted, by performance of) the requested act.

Who Can Accept the Offer?

Only the offeree has the legal power to accept an offer and create a contract. Third persons usually do not have the power to accept an offer. If an offer is made individually to two or more persons, each has the power to accept the offer. Once one of the offerees accepts the offer, it terminates as to the other offerees. An offer that is made to two or more persons jointly must be accepted jointly.

Unequivocal Acceptance

The offeree's acceptance must be **unequivocal**. The **mirror image rule** requires the offeree to accept the offeror's terms. Generally, a "grumbling acceptance" is a legal acceptance. For example, a response such as "Okay, I'll take the car, but I sure wish you would make me a

acceptance

A manifestation of assent by the offeree to the terms of the offer in a manner invited or required by the offer as measured by the objective theory of contracts. (Section 50 of the Restatement (Second) of Contracts)

mirror image rule

States that for an acceptance to exist, the offeree must accept the terms as stated in the offer.

The law has outgrown its primitive stage of formalism when the precise word was the sovereign talisman, and every slip was fatal. It takes a broader view today. A promise may be lacking, and yet the whole writing may be "instinct with an obligation," imperfectly expressed.

J. Cardozo
Wood v. Duff-Gordon *(1917)*

better deal" creates an enforceable contract. An acceptance is equivocal if certain conditions are added to the acceptance. For example, suppose the offeree had responded, "I accept, but only if you repaint the car red." There is no acceptance in this case.

Trees Reflected in Water *The common law of contracts follows the mirror image rule of contracting. A contract is made if the offeree accepts the terms offered by the offeror.*

Silence as Acceptance

Silence usually is not considered acceptance even if the offeror states that it is. This rule is intended to protect offerees from being legally bound to offers because they failed to respond. Nevertheless, silence *does* constitute acceptance in the following situations:

1. The offeree has indicated that silence means assent. (For example, "If you do not hear from me by Friday, ship the order.")
2. The offeree signed an agreement indicating continuing acceptance of delivery until further notification. Book-of-the-month and CD-of-the-month club memberships are examples of such acceptances.
3. Prior dealings between the parties indicate that silence means acceptance. For example, a fish wholesaler who delivers 30 pounds of fish to a restaurant each Friday for several years and is paid for the fish can continue the deliveries with expectation of payment until notified otherwise by the restaurant.
4. The offeree takes the benefit of goods or services provided by the offeror even though he or she (a) has an opportunity to reject the goods or services but fails to do so and (b) knows the offeror expects to be compensated. For example, a homeowner who stands idly by and watches a painter whom she has not hired mistakenly paint her house owes the painter for the work.

 *E-Commerce & Information Technology*

COMPUTER SHRINKWRAP LICENSES ENFORCEABLE

Although around for centuries, sales of goods through the mail reached new heights with the sale of computer hardware and software through the Internet. One only has to pick up the telephone or log onto the computer to order thousands of dollars of computer hardware and software. Computer hardware usually arrives via mail or overnight carrier (United Parcel Service) within a few days, whereas software can arrive the same way or downloaded from your computer. Also in the box, or on the computer, is the contract, either a license agreement in the case of most software or a sales contract in the case of most computer equipment. These licenses or con-

tracts contain the terms upon which the licensor or seller is willing to license or sell the goods to the user. The user usually has some stated period of time, often 30 days, to accept or reject the goods based on the license or contract terms. One issue has been presented to the courts by these types of licenses and sales: Are the terms of the previously unseen license or sales contract valid and enforceable? This issue was addressed by the court in the following two cases.

In *ProCD, Incorporated v. Ziedenberg*, ProCD had spent over $10 million to develop a database of names called SelectPhone. ProCD sells this database to both commercial and consumer users who are licensed to use the information in seeking customers. Matthew Zeidenberg purchased a version of SelectPhone for $150 but then offered it for sale over the Internet at a lower price than ProCD charged. ProCD sued Ziedenberg for violating its license agreement, which prohibited the resale of the data. Ziedenberg countered that the license agreement did not apply because it was included in the software box and that he had not had the opportunity to read it before buying the software. The trial court sided with Ziedenberg and held that the "shrinkwrap license"—so called because retail software packages are covered in plastic or cellophane—was not enforceable. ProCD appealed.

In the second case, *Hill v. Gateway 2000, Inc.*, Rich and Enza Hill purchased a Gateway computer by telephoning Gateway and ordering the computer. The computer arrived in a box, and the Hills unpacked the computer and began using it. The Hills failed to read the sales contract that was enclosed in the box. This contract contained an arbitration clause stating that customers had 30 days in which to return the computer; if they did not, they therefore accepted the computer and any complaints thereafter would be settled by arbitration. After more than 30 days, the Hills filed a class action lawsuit against Gateway, alleging that Gateway had engaged in wire fraud and mail fraud and had violated federal racketeering laws. Gateway moved for arbitration, but the Hills argued that the sales contract was unenforceable against them because they had not had the opportunity to read it before they purchased the computer. The trial court agreed with the Hills and allowed their lawsuit against Gateway to proceed. Gateway appealed.

In these two decisions, the court of appeals had to address an issue of first impression: Are licenses and contracts inside software boxes and computer equipment boxes enforceable against the purchaser? In each of these two cases the court answered yes. The court noted that modern commercial transactions would be hindered if such contracts and licenses were not recognized as enforceable. The court found that with the "accept-or-return" nature of these agreements, the purchaser or licensee could read and accept the terms of the offer or could return the goods. Therefore, potential licensees or purchasers had adequate protection against contracts they did not want to accept; they could return the goods and not accept them. The court of appeals held that both Ziedenberg and the Hills were bound by the license and sales contract they received in the boxes from ProCD and Gateway, respectively. [*ProCD, Incorporated v. Ziedenberg*, 86 F.3d 1447 (1996); *Hill v. Gateway 2000, Inc.*, 105 F.3d 1147 (1997)]

Time and Mode of Acceptance

Contract law establishes the following rules concerning the time and mode of acceptance.

Acceptance-upon-Dispatch Rule   Under the common law of contracts, acceptance of a bilateral contract occurs when the offeree *dispatches* the acceptance by an authorized means of communication. This rule is called the **acceptance-upon-dispatch rule** or, more commonly, the **mailbox rule**. Under this rule, the acceptance is effective when it is dispatched even if it is lost in transmission. If an offeree first dispatches a rejection and then sends an acceptance, the mailbox rule does not apply to the acceptance.[4]

The problem of lost acceptances can be minimized by expressly altering the mailbox rule. The offeror can do this by stating in the offer that acceptance is effective only upon actual receipt of the acceptance.

Proper Dispatch Rule   The acceptance must be **properly dispatched**. The acceptance must be properly addressed, packaged in an appropriate envelope or container, and have prepaid postage or delivery charges. Under common law, if an acceptance is not properly dispatched, it is not effective until it is actually received by the offeror.

proper dispatch

An acceptance must be properly addressed, packaged, and posted to fall within the mailbox rule.

Mode of Acceptance   Generally, an offeree must accept an offer by an *authorized* means of communication. The offer can stipulate that acceptance must be by a specified means of communication (e.g., registered mail, telegram). Such stipulation is called **express authorization**. If the offeree uses an unauthorized means of communication to transmit the acceptance, the acceptance is not effective even if it is received by the offeror within the allowed time period because the means of communication was a condition of acceptance.

Most offers do not expressly specify the means of communication required for acceptance. The common law recognizes certain implied means of communication. **Implied authorization** may be inferred from what is customary in similar transactions, usage of trade, or prior dealings between the parties. Section 30 of the Restatement (Second) of Contracts permits implied authorization "by any medium reasonable in the circumstances."

express authorization

A stipulation in the offer that says the acceptance must be by a specified means of communication.

implied authorization

Mode of acceptance that is implied from what is customary in similar transactions, usage of trade, or prior dealings between the parties.

CONCEPT SUMMARY OFFER AND ACCEPTANCE

Communication by Offeror	Effective When
Offer	Received by offeree
Revocation of offer	Received by offeree

Communication by Offeree	Effective When
Rejection of offer	Received by offeror
Counteroffer	Received by offeror
Acceptance of offer	Sent by offeree
Acceptance after previous rejection of offer	Received by offeror

CONSIDERATION

consideration

Something of legal value given in exchange for a promise.

Consideration must be given before a contract can exist. **Consideration** is defined as something of legal value given in exchange for a promise. Consideration can come in many forms. The most common types consist of either a tangible payment (e.g., money or property) or the performance of an act (e.g., providing legal services). Less usual forms of consideration include the forbearance of a legal right (e.g., accepting an out-of-court settlement in exchange for dropping a lawsuit) and noneconomic forms of consideration (e.g., refraining from "drinking, using tobacco, swearing, or playing cards or billiards for money" for a specified time period).[5]

Written contracts are presumed to be supported by consideration. This rebuttable presumption, however, may be overcome by sufficient evidence. A few states provide that contracts made under seal cannot be challenged for lack of consideration.

Requirements of Consideration

Consideration consists of two elements: (1) Something of legal value must be given (e.g., either a legal benefit must be received or legal detriment suffered), and (2) there must be a bargained-for exchange. Each of these is discussed in the paragraphs that follow.

Business Brief

The more formal approach to finding consideration has been replaced by a modern definition that considers a contract supported by consideration if either (1) the promisee suffers a legal detriment or (2) the promisor receives a legal benefit.

bargained-for exchange

Exchange that parties engage in that leads to an enforceable contract.

gift promise

An unenforceable promise because it lacks consideration.

Ethics Issue

A "completed gift promise" becomes a true gift, which by definition is irrevocable.

1. **Legal Value** Under the modern law of contracts, a contract is considered supported by **legal value** if (1) the promisee suffers a *legal detriment* or (2) the promisor receives a *legal benefit*. For example, suppose the Dallas Cowboys contract with a tailor to have the tailor make uniforms for the team. The tailor completes the uniforms, but the team manager thinks the color is wrong and refuses to allow the team to wear them. Here, there has been no legal benefit to either the manager or the players. The tailor, however, has suffered a legal detriment (time spent making the uniforms). Under the modern rule of contracts, there is sufficiency of consideration and the contract is enforceable.

2. **Bargained-For Exchange** To be enforceable, a contract must arise from a **bargained-for exchange**. In most business contracts, the parties engage in such exchanges. The commercial setting in which business contracts are formed lead to this conclusion.

   Gift promises, also called **gratuitous promises**, are unenforceable because they lack consideration. To change a gift promise into an enforceable promise, the promisee must offer to do something in exchange—that is, consideration—for the promise. For example, suppose Mrs. Colby promised to give her son $10,000 and then rescinded the promise. The son would have no recourse because it was a gift promise that lacked consideration. If, however, Mrs. Colby promised her son $10,000 for getting an "A" in his business law course and the son performed as required, the contract would be enforceable. A completed gift promise cannot be rescinded for lack of consideration.

   In the following case, the court refused to enforce a gift promise.

Alden v. Presley
637 S.W. 2d 862 (1982)
Supreme Court of Tennessee

CASE 9.2

BACKGROUND AND FACTS
Elvis Presley, a singer of great renown and a man of substantial wealth, became engaged to Ginger Alden. He was generous with the Alden family, paying for landscaping the lawn, installing a swimming pool, and making other gifts. When his fiancée's mother, Jo Laverne Alden, sought to divorce her husband, Presley promised to pay off the remaining mortgage indebtedness on the Alden home, which Mrs. Alden was to receive in the divorce settlement. On August 16, 1977, Presley died suddenly, leaving the mortgage unpaid. When the legal representative of Presley's estate refused to pay the $39,587 mortgage, Mrs. Alden brought an action to enforce Presley's promise. The trial court denied recovery. Mrs. Alden appealed.

ISSUE
Was Presley's promise to pay the mortgage enforceable?

COURT'S REASONING
Under contract law, gift promises are unenforceable because they lack consideration. The court found that plaintiff Alden had not given any consideration in exchange for Presley's promise. The court also found that the gift promise had not been completed by Presley. Therefore, the unexpected gift promise could not be enforced against Presley's estate.

DECISION
The supreme court held that Presley's promise was a gratuitous executory promise that was not supported by consideration. As such, it was unenforceable against Presley's estate. The court dismissed the case and assessed costs against the plaintiff.

Case Questions
Critical Legal Thinking Should gratuitous promises be enforced? Why or why not?

Business Ethics Was it unethical for the representative of Presley's estate to refuse to complete the gift? Did he have any other choice?

Contemporary Business Does it make a difference if a gift promise is executed or executory? Explain.

Best Efforts Contracts
Many business contracts contain a clause that requires one or both of the parties to use their "best efforts" to achieve the objective of the contract. For example, real estate listing contracts often require a real estate broker to use his or her best efforts to find a buyer for the listed real estate. Contracts often require underwriters to use their best efforts to sell securities on behalf of their corporate clients. The courts generally have held that the imposition of the best efforts duty provides sufficient consideration to make a contract enforceable.

Business Brief

Many business contracts require one or both parties to use their "best efforts" to attain the contract's objectives. Such contracts are not illusory and are enforceable.

Entrepreneur and the Law

OUTPUT AND REQUIREMENTS CONTRACTS

Generally, the courts tolerate a greater degree of uncertainty in business contracts than in personal contracts under the premise that sophisticated parties know how to protect themselves when negotiating contracts. The law imposes an obligation of good faith on the performance of the parties to requirements and output contracts.

The following are special types of business contracts that specifically allow a greater degree of uncertainty concerning consideration:

• **Output Contracts** In an **output contract**, the seller agrees to sell all of its production to a single buyer.

Output contracts serve the legitimate business purpose of (1) assuring the seller of a purchaser for all its output and (2) assuring the buyer of a source of supply for the goods it needs.

• **Requirements Contracts** A **requirements contract** is one where a buyer contracts to purchase all of the requirements for an item from one seller. Such contracts serve the legitimate business purposes of (1) assuring the buyer of a uniform source of supply and (2) providing the seller with reduced selling costs.

Contracts Lacking Consideration

Some contracts seem as though they are supported by consideration even though they are not. The following types of contracts fall into this category.

illegal consideration

A promise to refrain from doing an illegal act. Such a promise will not support a contract.

illusory promise

A contract into which parties enter, but one or both of the parties can choose not to perform their contractual obligations. Thus the contract lacks consideration.

Ethics Issue

Promises made out of a sense of moral obligation lack consideration. Such promises are unenforceable in most states.

preexisting duty

A promise lacks consideration if a person promises to perform an act or do something he or she is already under an obligation to do.

Business Brief

If a party runs into substantial unforeseen difficulties while performing his or her contractual duties, the contract can be modified without new consideration being given.

past consideration

A prior act or performance. Past consideration (e.g., prior acts) will not support a new contract. New consideration must be given.

- **Illegal Consideration**   A contract cannot be supported by a promise to refrain from doing an illegal act because that is **illegal consideration**. Contracts based on illegal consideration are void. For example, statements such as, "I will burn your house down unless you agree to pay me $10,000" cannot become enforceable contracts. Even if the threatened party agrees to make the payment, the contract is unenforceable and void because it is supported by illegal consideration (arson is unlawful).

- **Illusory Promises**   If the parties enter into a contract but one or both of the parties can choose not to perform their contractual obligations, the contract lacks consideration. Such promises, which are known as **illusory promises** (or **illusory contracts**), are unenforceable. For example, a contract that provides that one of the parties only has to perform if he or she chooses to do so is an illusory contract.

- **Moral Obligations**   Promises made out of a sense of **moral obligation** or honor are generally not enforceable on the ground that they lack consideration. In other words, moral consideration is not treated as legal consideration. Contracts based on love and affection and deathbed promises are examples of such promises. A minority of states hold that moral obligations are enforceable.

- **Preexisting Duty**   A promise lacks consideration if a person promises to perform an act or do something he or she is already under an obligation to do. This is called a **preexisting duty**. The promise is unenforceable because no new consideration has been given. For example, many states have adopted statutes that prohibit police officers from accepting rewards for apprehending criminals.

  In the private sector, the preexisting duty rule often arises when one of the parties to an existing contract seeks to change the terms of the contract during the course of its performance. Such midstream changes are unenforceable: The parties have a preexisting duty to perform according to the original terms of the contract. Sometimes a party to a contract runs into substantial **unforeseen difficulties** while performing his or her contractual duties. If the parties modify their contract to accommodate these unforeseen difficulties, the modification will be enforced even though it is not supported by new consideration.

  For example, suppose a landowner enters into a contract with a contractor who agrees to excavate the hole for the foundation of a major office building. When the excavation is partially completed, toxic wastes are unexpectedly found at the site. Removal of toxic wastes is highly regulated by law and would substantially increase the cost of the excavation. If the landowner agrees to pay the contractor increased compensation to remove the toxic wastes, this modification of the contract is enforceable even though it is unsupported by new consideration.

- **Past Consideration**   A promise that is based on a party's **past consideration** (i.e., prior act or performance) lacks consideration. Such contracts are unenforceable unless some new consideration is given to support the contract. The following case illustrates this rule.

Dementas v. Estate of Tallas

764 P.2d 628 (1988)
Court of Appeals of Utah

CASE 9.3

BACKGROUND AND FACTS

Jack Tallas emigrated to the United States from Greece in 1914. He lived in Salt Lake City for nearly 70 years, during which time he achieved considerable success in business, primarily as an insurance agent and landlord. Over a period of 14 years, Peter Dementas, a close personal friend of Tallas's, rendered services to Tallas, including picking up his mail, driving him to the grocery store, and assisting with the management of his rental properties. On December 18, 1982, Tallas met with Dementas and dictated a memorandum to him, in Greek, stat-

ing that he owed Dementas $50,000 for his help over the years. Tallas indicated in the memorandum that he would change his will to make Dementas an heir for this amount. Tallas signed the document. Tallas died on February 4, 1983, without changing his will to include Dementas as an heir. He left a substantial estate. Dementas filed a claim for $50,000 with Tallas's estate. When the estate denied the claim, Dementas brought this action to enforce the contract. The trial court dismissed Dementas's claim, stating that his contract with Tallas lacked consideration. Dementas appealed.

ISSUE
Was the contract enforceable?

COURT'S REASONING
A generally accepted definition of consideration is that a legal detriment has been bargained for and exchanged for a promise. The appellate court found no such bargained for exchange in this case. The court stated: "Even though the testimony showed that Dementas rendered at least some services for Tallas, the subsequent promise by Tallas to pay $50,000 for services already performed by Dementas is not a promise supported by legal consideration. Events which occur prior to the making of the promise and not with the purpose of inducing the promise in exchange are viewed as past consideration and are the legal equivalent of no consideration. This is so because the promisor is making his promise because those events occurred, but he is not making his promise in order to get them. "There is . . . no saying that if you will do this for me I will do that for you. A benefit conferred or detriment incurred in the past is not adequate consideration for a present bargain."

DECISION
The appellate court held that Tallas's promise to pay Dementas $50,000 was unenforceable because it was based on past consideration. The court cited the rule of contract law that a promise based on a party's past consideration lacks consideration.

Case Questions

Critical Legal Thinking Should past consideration be considered legal consideration? Why or why not?

Business Ethics Did the executor of Tallas's estate act ethically in failing to pay Dementas the money? Do you think the executor's decision is what Tallas would have wanted?

Contemporary Business Can you think of any situations where a business may be involved in a contract based on past considerations? What is the moral of this case?

CONCEPT SUMMARY PROMISES LACKING CONSIDERATION

Type of Consideration	Description of Promise
Illegal consideration	Promise to refrain from doing an illegal act.
Illusory promise	Promise where one or both parties can choose not to perform their obligation.
Moral obligation	Promise made out of a sense of moral obligation or honor or love or affection. Some states enforce these types of contracts.
Preexisting duty	Promise based on the preexisting duty of the promisee to perform. The promise is enforceable if (1) the parties rescind the contract and enter into a new contract or (2) there are unforeseen difficulties.
Past consideration	Promise based on the past performance of the promisee.

Settlement of Claims

The law promotes the voluntary settlement of disputed claims. Settlement saves judicial resources and serves the interests of the parties entering into the settlement.

In some situations, one of the parties to a contract believes that he or she did not receive what he or she was due. This party may attempt to reach a compromise with the other party (e.g., by paying less consideration than was provided for in the contract). The compromise agreement is called an **accord**. If the accord is performed, it is called the **satisfaction**. This type of settlement is called an **accord and satisfaction** or a **compromise**). If the accord is not satisfied, the other party can sue to enforce either the accord or the original contract.

Consider This Example Suppose that a contract stipulated that the cost of a computer system that keeps track of inventory, accounts receivable, and so on is $100,000. After it is installed, the computer system does not perform as promised. To settle the dispute, the parties agree that $70,000 is to be paid in full and final payment for the computer. This accord is enforceable even though no new consideration is given because reasonable persons would differ as to the worth of the computer system that actually was installed.

Business Brief

Businesses should consider settling potential legal disputes. The law promotes the settlement of disputes because it saves judicial time and resources.

accord

An agreement whereby the parties agree to accept something different in satisfaction of the original contract.

satisfaction

The performance of an accord.

Business Ethics

WHEN IS CONSIDERATION INADEQUATE?

The courts usually do not inquire into the **adequacy of consideration**. Generally, parties are free to agree on the consideration they are willing to pay or receive under a contract. This rule is based on the court's reluctance to inquire into the motives of a party for entering into a contract or to save a party from a "bad deal."

Some states recognize an exception to the general rule that the courts will not examine the sufficiency of consideration. These states permit a party to escape from a contract if the inadequacy of consideration **"shocks the conscience of the court."** This standard, which is applied on a case-by-case basis, considers the value of the item or service contracted for, the amount of consideration paid, the relationship of the parties, and other facts and circumstances of the case.

Consider this situation: Mr. and Mrs. James Paul DeLaney were married in January 1953. A few years later they acquired a painting, allegedly the work of Peter Paul Rubens entitled "Hunting of the Caledonian Boar." In 1966, the DeLaneys moved into an apartment building and became friends with Mr. and Mrs. Nicholas T. O'Neill. Mr. DeLaney and Mr. O'Neill became close friends. On August 18, 1970, Mr. DeLaney purportedly sold the Rubens painting to Mr. O'Neill for $10 and "other good and valuable consideration." A written contract embodying the terms of the agreement was prepared and signed by Mr. DeLaney and Mr. O'Neill. Mrs. DeLaney was not informed of the sale. At the time of the sale, Mr. DeLaney told Mr. O'Neill that the painting was worth at least $100,000. The painting, however, remained with DeLaney and was in storage at the time of this lawsuit. In 1974, Mrs. DeLaney instituted a divorce action against Mr. DeLaney. At that time she learned of the purported sale of the painting to O'Neill. In the divorce action, Mrs.

DeLaney claimed an interest in the painting as marital property. Mr. O'Neill instituted this action seeking a declaratory judgment regarding title to the painting.

The trial court held in favor of Mrs. DeLaney and voided the sales contract between Mr. DeLaney and Mr. O'Neill. The appellate court affirmed. The courts held that the consideration paid by Mr. O'Neill for the painting "shocked the conscience" of the court, and thereby rendered the transfer void. The appellate court stated: "Plaintiff expressly testified that 'other good and valuable consideration' meant the love and affection plaintiff and James Paul DeLaney had for one another. In Illinois, love and affection does not constitute legal consideration. Thus, the only remaining valid consideration for the transaction was the tender of $10. A purchase price of $10 for such a valuable work of art is so grossly inadequate consideration as to shock the conscience of this court, as it did the trial court's. To find $10 valid consideration for this painting would be to reduce the requirement of consideration to a mere formality. This we will not do."

Critics of this case argue that the parties should be free to contract based upon what they feel is adequate consideration in the circumstances. Proponents of this case argue that courts should be allowed to examine the adequacy of consideration underlying a contract to prevent unfair contracts. [*O'Neill v. DeLaney*, 415 N.E.2d 1260 (Ill.App.1980)]

1. Was it ethical for Mr. O'Neill to accept the painting without paying adequate consideration?
2. Should the courts be allowed to examine the adequacy of consideration underlying a contract, or should the parties be free to contract based on what they feel is adequate consideration in the circumstances?

Promissory Estoppel

promissory estoppel

An equitable doctrine that prevents the withdrawal of a promise by a promisor if it will adversely affect a promisee who has adjusted his or her position in justifiable reliance on the promise.

The courts have developed the doctrine of **promissory estoppel** or (**detrimental reliance**) to avoid injustice. This doctrine is a broad policy-based doctrine. It is used to provide a remedy to a person who has relied on another person's promise, but that person withdraws his or her promise and is not subject to a breach of contract action because one of the two elements discussed in this chapter (i.e., agreement or consideration) is lacking. The doctrine of promissory estoppel *estops* (prevents) the promisor from revoking his or her promise. Therefore, the person who has detrimentally relied on the promise for performance may sue the promisor for performance or other remedy the court feels is fair to award in the circumstances.

For the doctrine of promissory estoppel to be applied, the following elements must be shown:

Now equity is no part of the law, but a moral virtue, which qualifies, moderates, and reforms the rigor, hardness, and edge of the law, and is a universal truth.

Lord Cowper
Dudley v. Dudley (1705)

1. The promisor made a promise.
2. The promisor should have reasonably expected to induce the promisee to rely on the promise.
3. The promisee actually relied on the promise and engaged in an action or forbearance of a right of a definite and substantial nature.
4. Injustice would be caused if the promise were not enforced.

Consider This Example XYZ Construction Company, a general contractor, requests bids from subcontractors for work to be done on a hospital building that XYZ plans to submit a bid to build. Bert Plumbing Company submits the lowest bid for the plumbing work, and XYZ incorporates Bert's low bid in its own bid for the general contract. In this example, the doctrine of promissory estoppel prevents Bert from withdrawing its bid. If XYZ is awarded the contract to build the hospital, it could enforce Bert's promise to perform.

CHAPTER SUMMARY

Agreement, p. 215

Offer	1. *Offer.* Manifestation by one party of a willingness to enter into a contract.
	2. *Offeror.* Party who makes an offer.
	3. *Offeree.* Party to whom an offer is made. This party has the power to create an agreement by accepting the terms of the offer.

Offer, p. 215

Requirements of an Offer	1. *Objective intent.* The intent to enter into a contract is determined by the *objective theory of contracts*, that is, whether a reasonable person viewing the circumstances would conclude that the parties intended to be legally bound.
	2. *Definite terms.* The terms of the offer must be definite so that the agreement between the parties can be determined. Reasonable terms (e.g., price, time for performance) may be *implied*.
	3. *Communication.* The offer must be communicated to the offeree by the offeror.
Special Offer Situations	1. *Advertisement*:
	a. *General rule.* An invitation to make an offer.
	b. *Exception.* An offer if it is so definite and specific as to show that the advertiser's intent to be bound to the terms of the advertisement.
	2. *Reward.* An offer to create a unilateral contract.
	3. *Auction*:
	a. *Auction with reserve.* An invitation to make an offer. The seller retains the right to refuse the highest bid and withdraw the good from sale.
	b. *Auction without reserve.* An offer. The seller must accept the highest bid (above the minimum bid). This type of auction must be stipulated.
Termination of an Offer by Action of the Parties	1. *Revocation.* The offeror may *revoke* (withdraw) an offer any time prior to its acceptance by the offeree.
	2. *Rejection.* An offer is terminated if the offeree rejects the offer by his or her words or conduct.
	3. *Counteroffer.* A counteroffer by the offeree terminates the offeror's offer (and creates a new offer).
Termination of an Offer by Operation of Law	1. *Destruction of the subject matter.* An offer terminates if the subject matter of the offer is destroyed prior to acceptance through no fault of either party.
	2. *Death or incompetency.* The death or incompetency of either the offeror or the offeree prior to acceptance terminates the offer.
	3. *Supervening illegality.* If prior to the acceptance of an offer the object of the offer is made illegal by statute, regulation, court decision, or other law, the offer terminates.
	4. *Lapse of time.* An offer terminates upon the expiration of a stated time in the offer. If no time is stated, the offer terminates after a "reasonable time."
Option Contract	If an offeree pays the offeror compensation to keep an offer open for an agreed upon period of time, an *option contract* is created. The offeror cannot sell the property to anyone else during the option period.

Acceptance, p. 221

Acceptance	Manifestation of assent by the offeree to the terms of the offer. Acceptance of the offer by the offeree creates a contract.
Rules for Acceptance	1. *Mirror image rule.* Under the common law of contracts, the offeree must accept the terms offered by the offeror to create a contract. Any change in terms by the offeree constitutes a counteroffer, not an acceptance.
	2. *Acceptance-upon-dispatch rule.* Unless otherwise provided in the offer, acceptance is effective when it is dispatched by the offeree. This rule is often called the *mailbox rule*.

3. *Proper dispatch rule.* An acceptance must be properly addressed, packaged, and have prepaid postage or delivery charges to be effective when dispatched. Generally, improperly dispatched acceptances are not effective until actually received by the offeror.

4. *Mode of acceptance.* Acceptance must be by the express means of communication stipulated in the offer, or, if no means is stipulated, then by reasonable means in the circumstances.

Consideration, p. 224

Consideration	Thing of value given in exchange for a promise. May be tangible or intangible property, performance of a service, forbearance of a legal right, or another thing of value.
Requirements of Consideration	1. *Legal value.* Something of legal value must be given. Either (a) the promisee suffers a *legal detriment* or (b) the promisor receives a *legal benefit*. 2. *Bargained-for-exchange.* A contract must arise from a bargained-for-exchange. *Gift promises* (or *gratuitous promises*) are unenforceable because they lack consideration.
Special Contracts	1. *Requirements contracts.* Contracts where the buyer agrees to purchase all the requirements for an item from a single seller. Such contracts are enforceable if the parties act in good faith. 2. *Output contracts.* Contracts where the seller agrees to sell all its production to a single buyer. Such contracts are enforceable if the parties act in good faith. 3. *Best efforts contracts.* Contracts that require a party to use its best efforts to accomplish the objective of the contract are enforceable.
Contracts Lacking Consideration	The following contracts are unenforceable because they lack consideration: 1. *Illegal consideration.* Promise to refrain from doing an illegal act. 2. *Illusory promise.* If one or both parties to a contract can choose not to perform their contractual duties. 3. *Moral obligation.* Promise made out of a sense of moral obligation, honor, or love and affection. 4. *Preexisting duty.* Promise to perform an act or do something that a person is already under an obligation to do. 5. *Past consideration.* Promise based on a party's past consideration.
Settlement of Claims	*Accord and satisfaction.* Compromise agreement where the parties agree to settle a contract dispute and do so. 1. *Unliquidated debt.* One in which reasonable persons would differ as to the amount owed. It can be compromised without the payment of new consideration. 2. *Liquidated debt.* One that is due and certain. It cannot be compromised unless new consideration is paid.
Adequacy of Consideration	1. *Adequacy of consideration.* Courts usually do not inquire into the adequacy of consideration. Thus, *nominal consideration* (e.g., $1) is usually sufficient. 2. *Inadequacy of consideration.* Some states permit a party to escape from a contract if the consideration received is so inadequate as to "*shock the conscience of the court.*"
Promissory Estoppel	Policy-based equitable doctrine that prevents a promisor from revoking his or her promise even though the promise lacks consideration. The requirements are: 1. The promisor made a promise. 2. The promisor should have reasonably expected to induce the promisee to rely on the promise. 3. The promisee actually relied on the promise and engaged in an action or forbearance of a right of a definite and substantial nature. 4. Injustice would be caused if the promise were not enforced.

*E*ND-OF-*C*HAPTER *I*NTERNET *E*XERCISES AND *C*ASE *Q*UESTIONS

Working the Web Internet Exercises

ACTIVITIES

1. Visit **www.cori.missouri.edu**. Use this site to aid in drafting specific types of contracts and/or clauses. Test your ability by visiting the site and search for employment agreements with noncompetition clauses.

2. To review the basic elements of a contract, visit **www. freeadvice.com/law/518us.htm**.

3. For some tips on entering into contracts, see **www. itslegal. com/infonet/consumer/contracts.html.**

4. An extensive overview of contract law can be found at Contracts Home Page (Craig Smith, Santa Barbara College of Law) **www.west.net/~smith/contracts.htm**. Review the "Offer and Acceptance" page. Do you recognize any of the cases cited there?

CRITICAL LEGAL THINKING CASES

9.1 Essential Terms Ben Hunt and others operated a farm under the name S. B. H. Farms. Hunt went to McIlroy Bank and Trust and requested a loan to build hog houses, buy livestock, and expand farming operations. The bank agreed to loan S. B. H. Farms $175,000, for which short-term promissory notes were signed by Hunt and the other owners of S. B. H. Farms. At that time, oral discussions were held with the bank officer regarding long-term financing of S. B. H.'s farming operations: No dollar amount, interest rate, or repayment terms were discussed. When the owners of S. B. H. Farms defaulted on the promissory notes, the bank filed for foreclosure on the farm and other collateral. S. B. H. Farms counterclaimed for $750,000 in damages, alleging that the bank breached its oral contract to provide long-term financing. Was there an oral contract for long-term financing? [*Hunt v. McIlroy Bank and Trust*, 616 S.W.2d 759 (Ark. App. 1981)]

9.2 Implied Terms MacDonald Group, Ltd. (MacDonald) is the managing general partner of "Fresno Fashion Square," a regional shopping mall in Fresno, California. The mall has several major anchor tenants and numerous smaller stores and shops, including Edmond's of Fresno, a jeweler. In 1969, Edmond's signed a lease with MacDonald that provided that "there shall not be more than two jewelry stores" located in the mall. In 1978, MacDonald sent Edmond's notice that it intended to expand the mall and lease space to other jewelers. The lease was silent as to the coverage of additional mall space. Edmond's sued MacDonald, arguing that the lease applied to mall additions. Who wins? [*Edmond's of Fresno v. MacDonald Group, Ltd.*, 171 Cal.App.3d 598, 217 Cal.Rptr. 375 (Cal.App. 1985)]

9.3 Reward Offer Rudy Turilli operated the "Jesse James Museum" in Stanton, Missouri. He contends the man who was shot, killed, and buried as the notorious desperado Jesse James in 1882 was an impostor and that Jesse James lived for many years thereafter under the alias J. Frank Dalton and last lived with Turilli at this museum until the 1950s. On February 27, 1967, Turilli appeared before a nationwide television audience and stated that he would pay $10,000 to anyone who could prove that his statements were wrong. After hearing this offer, Stella James, a relative of Jesse James, produced affidavits of persons related to and acquainted with the Jesse James family constituting evidence that Jesse James was killed as alleged in song and legend on April 3, 1882. When Turilli refused to pay the reward, James sued for breach of contract. Who wins? [*James v. Turilli*, 473 S.W.2d 757 (Mo.App. 1972)]

9.4 Counteroffer Glende Motor Company (Glende), an automobile dealer that sold new cars, leased premises from certain landlords. In October 1979, fire destroyed part of the leased premises, and Glende restored the leasehold premises. The landlords received payment of insurance proceeds for the fire. Glende sued the landlords to recover the insurance proceeds. On May 7, 1982, 10 days before the trial was to begin, the defen-

dants jointly served on Glende a document entitled "Offer to Compromise Before Trial," which was a settlement of $190,000. On May 16, Glende agreed to the amount of the settlement but made it contingent upon the execution of a new lease. On May 17, the defendants notified Glende that they were revoking the settlement offer. Glende thereafter tried to accept the original settlement offer. Has there been a settlement of the lawsuit? [*Glende Motor Company v. Superior Court*, 159 Cal.App.3d 389, 205 Cal.Rptr. 682 (Cal.App. 1984)]

9.5 Acceptance General Motors Corporation requested bids from contractors to construct a central air-conditioning unit at its Mesa, Arizona, proving grounds. Burr & Sons Construction Co. (Burr) decided to submit a bid to be the general contractor, and itself requested bids from subcontractors to do some of the work. Corbin-Dykes Electric Company submitted a bid to Burr to do the electrical work on the project. Burr incorporated Corbin-Dyke's bid in its own bid to General Motors. When Burr was awarded the General Motors's contract, it hired another subcontractor—not Corbin-Dykes—to do the electrical work. Corbin-Dykes sued Burr for breach of contract. Was a contract formed between Corbin-Dykes and Burr? [*Corbin-Dykes Electric Company v. Burr*, 500 P.2d 632 (Ariz.App. 1972)]

9.6 Silence Peter Andrus owned an apartment building that he had insured under a fire insurance policy sold by J. C. Durick Insurance (Durick). Two months prior to the expiration of the policy, Durick notified Andrus that the building should be insured for $48,000 (or 80 percent of the building's value) required by the insurance company. Andrus replied that (1) he wanted insurance to match the amount of the outstanding mortgage on the building (i.e., $24,000) and (2) if Durick could not sell this insurance, he would go elsewhere. Durick sent a new insurance policy in the face amount of $48,000 with the notation that the policy was automatically accepted unless Andrus notified him to the contrary. Andrus did not reply. He did not, however, pay the premiums on the policy. Durick sued Andrus to recover these premiums. Who wins? [*J. C. Durick Insurance v. Andrus*, 424 A.2d 249 (Vt. 1980)]

9.7 Time for Acceptance Economic Research Properties (ERP), a partnership, owned a tract of land in Florida. Donald R. Sullivan, who became interested in purchasing the property, mailed a written offer and deposit to Dwayne R. Klein, the managing partner of ERP, to purchase the property. The offer stated that it must be accepted by ERP by February 4, 1980, after which time the deposit was to be returned to Sullivan. ERP made several changes to the offer, including changing the time for acceptance from February 4 to February 14 so as to allow sufficient time for its counteroffer to reach Sullivan, and signed it.

Sullivan received the counteroffer several days before February 14. On February 18, 1980, Sullivan signed the counteroffer and mailed it to ERP. On February 19, Klein, having neither received the contract nor been notified of its acceptance, telephoned Sullivan and advised him that the negotiations were terminated. ERP later sold the property to another buyer. Sullivan sued ERP for breach of contract. Was a contract formed between ERP and Sullivan? [*Sullivan v. Economic Research Properties*, 455 So.2d 630 (Fla.App. 1984)]

9.8 The Mailbox Rule William Jenkins and Nathalie Monk owned a building in Sacramento, California. In 1979, they leased the building to Tuneup Masters for five years. The lease provided that Tuneup Masters could extend the lease for an additional five years if it gave written notice of its intention to do so by certified or registered mail at least six months prior to the expiration of the term of the lease, or August 1, 1983.

On July 29, 1983, Larry Selditz, vice president of Tuneup Masters, prepared a letter exercising the option, prepared and sealed an envelope with the letter in it, prepared U.S. Postal Service Form 3800, affixed the certified mail sticker on the envelope, and had his secretary deliver the envelope to the Postal Service annex located on the ground floor of the office building. Postal personnel occupied the annex only between the hours of 9 A.M. and 10 A.M. At the end of each day, between 5 P.M. and 5:15 P.M., a postal employee picked up outgoing mail. The letter to the landlords was lost in the mail. The landlords thereafter refused to renew the lease and brought an unlawful detainer action against Tuneup Masters. Was the notice renewing the option effective? [*Jenkins v. Tuneup Masters*, 190 Cal.App.3d 1, 235 Cal.Rptr. 214 (Cal.App. 1987)]

9.9 Consideration Clyde and Betty Penley were married in 1949. In late 1967, Clyde operated an automotive tire business while Betty owned an interest in a Kentucky Fried Chicken (KFC) franchise. That year, when Betty became ill, she requested that Clyde begin spending additional time at the KFC franchise to ensure its continued operation. Subsequently, Betty agreed that if Clyde would devote full time to the KFC franchise, they would operate the business as a joint enterprise, share equally in the ownership of its assets, and divide its returns equally. Pursuant to this agreement, Clyde terminated his tire business and devoted himself full time to the KFC franchise. On December 31, 1979, Betty abandoned Clyde and denied him any rights in the KFC franchise. Clyde sued to enforce the agreement with Betty. Is the agreement enforceable? [*Penley v. Penley*, 332 S.E.2d 51 (N.C. 1985)]

9.10 Forbearance to Sue When John W. Frasier died, he left a will that devised certain of his community and separate property to his wife, Lena, and their three children. These devises were more valuable to Lena than just her interest in the community property that she would otherwise have received without the will. The devise to her, however, was conditioned upon the filing of a waiver by Lena of her interest in the community property, and if she failed to file the waiver, she would then receive only her interest in the community property and nothing more. Lena hired her brother, D. L. Carter, an attorney, to represent her. Carter failed to file the waiver on Lena's behalf, thus preventing her from receiving her inheritance under the will. Instead, she received her interest in the community property,

which was $19,358 less than she would have received under the will. Carter sent Lena the following letter:

> *This is to advise and confirm our agreement—that in the event the J. W. Frasier estate case now on appeal is not terminated so that you will receive settlement equal to your share of the estate as you would have done if your waiver had been filed in the estate in proper time, I will make up any balance to you in payments as suits my convenience and will pay interest on your loss at 6 percent.*

The appeal was decided against Lena. When she tried to enforce the contract against Carter, he alleged that the contract was not enforceable because it was not supported by valid consideration. Who wins? [*Frasier v. Carter*, 437 P.2d 32 (Idaho 1968)]

9.11 Past Consideration A. J. Whitmire and R. Lee Whitmire were brothers. From 1923 to 1929, A. J. lived with his brother and his brother's wife, Lillie Mae. During this period, A. J. performed various services for his brother and sister-in-law. In 1925, R. Lee and Lillie Mae purchased some land. In 1944, in the presence of Lillie Mae, R. Lee told A. J., "When we're gone, this land is yours." A. J. had not done any work for R. Lee or Lillie Mae since 1929, and none was expected or provided in the future. On May 26, 1977, after both R. Lee and Lillie Mae had died, A. J. filed a claim with the estate of Lillie Mae seeking specific performance of the 1944 promise. Does A. J. get the property? [*Whitmire v. Watkins*, 267 So.2d 6 (Ga. 1980)]

9.12 Preexisting Duty Robert Chuckrow Construction Company (Chuckrow) was employed as the general contractor to build a Kinney Shoe Store. Chuckrow employed Ralph Gough to perform the carpentry work on the store. The contract with Gough stipulated that he was to provide all labor, materials, tools, equipment, scaffolding, and other items necessary to complete the carpentry work. On May 15, 1965, Gough's employees erected 38 trusses at the job site. The next day, 32 of the trusses fell off the building. The reason for the trusses' falling was unexplained, and evidence showed that it was not due to Chuckrow's fault or a deficiency in the building plans. Chuckrow told Gough that he would pay him to reerect the trusses and continue work. When the job was complete, Chuckrow paid Gough the original contract price but refused to pay him for the additional cost of reerecting the trusses. Gough sued Chuckrow for this expense. Can Gough recover? [*Robert Chuckrow Construction Company v. Gough*, 159 S.E.2d 469 (Ga.App.1968)]

9.13 Charitable Pledge Milton Polinger pledged $200,000 as a charitable subscription to the United Jewish Appeal Federation of Greater Washington, Inc. (UJA). The pledge was not for a specific purpose and was not made in consideration of pledges of others, and UJA borrowed no money against this pledge. The pledge was to the UJA generally and to the Israel Emergency Fund. After paying $76,500 toward the pledge, Polinger died and the Maryland National Bank was appointed representative of the Polinger estate. The UJA filed a claim against the estate for the balance of $133,500. The bank, however, denied the claim, alleging that the promise was unenforceable for lack of consideration.

Who wins? [*Maryland National Bank v. United Jewish Appeal Federation of Greater Washington, Inc.*, 407 A.2d 1130 (Md.App. 1979)]

9.14 Promissory Estoppel Nalley's, Inc. (Nalley's), was a major food distributor with its home office in the state of Washington. In 1964, Jacob Aronowicz and Samuel Duncan approached Nalley's about the possibility of their manufacturing a line of sliced meat products to be distributed by Nalley's. When Nalley's showed considerable interest, Aronowicz and Duncan incorporated as Major Food Products, Inc. (Major). Meetings to discuss the proposal continued at length with Charles Gardiner, a vice president and general manager of Nalley's Los Angeles division. On February 5, 1965, Gardiner delivered a letter to Major agreeing to become the exclusive Los Angeles and Orange County distributor for Major's products, but stated in the letter "that should we determine your product line is not representative or is not compatible with our operation we are free to terminate our agreement within 30 days." Nalley's was to distribute the full production of products produced by Major.

Based on Gardiner's assurances, Major leased a plant, built out the plant to its specifications, purchased and installed equipment, signed contracts to obtain meat to be processed, and hired personnel. Both Aronowicz and Duncan resigned from their

positions at other meat processing companies to devote themselves full time to the project. Financing was completed when Aronowicz and Duncan used their personal fortunes to purchase the stock of Major. Gardiner and other representatives of Nalley's visited Major's plant and expressed satisfaction with the premises. Major obtained the necessary government approvals regarding health standards on June 15, 1965, and immediately achieved full production. Because Nalley's was to pick the finished products up at Major's plant, Nalley's drivers visited Major's plant to acquaint themselves with its operations.

Gardiner sent the final proposal regarding the Nalley's–Major relationship to Nalley's home office for final approval. On June 22, 1965, Nalley's home office in Washington made a decision not to distribute Major's products. Nalley's refused to give any reason to Major for its decision. No final agreement was ever executed between the parties. Immediate efforts by Major to secure other distribution for its products proved unsuccessful. Further, because Major owned no trucks itself and had no sales organization, it could not distribute the products itself. In less than six months, Major had failed and Aronowicz's and Duncan's stock in Major was worthless. Major, Aronowicz, and Duncan sued Nalley's for damages under the doctrine of promissory estoppel. Do they win? [*Aronowicz v. Nalley's Inc.*, 30 C.A.3d 27, 106 Cal.Rptr. 424 (Cal.App. 1972)]

BUSINESS ETHICS CASES

9.15 Business Ethics Kortney Dempsey took a cruise on a ship operated by Norwegian Cruise Line (Norwegian). In general, suits for personal injuries arising out of maritime torts are subject to a three-year statute of limitations. Congress permits this period to be reduced to one year by contract, however. The Norwegian passenger ticket limited the period to one year. Evidence showed that the cruise line ticket contained the notation "Important Notice" in a bright red box at the bottom right-hand corner of each of the first four pages of the ticket. The information in the box stated that certain pages of the ticket contain information that "affect[s] important legal rights." In addition, at the top of page 6 of the ticket, where the terms and conditions began, it was stated in bold letters: "Passengers are advised to read the terms and conditions of the Passenger Ticket Contract set forth below." The clause at issue, which appears on page 8, clearly provides that suits must be brought within one year of injury.

More than one year after Dempsey had taken the cruise (but within three years), she filed suit against Norwegian seeking damages for an alleged injury suffered while on the cruise. Dempsey asserted that the one-year limitations period had not been reasonably communicated to her. Did Dempsey act ethically in suing when she did? Did Norwegian act ethically in reducing the limitations period to one year? Who wins the lawsuit? [*Dempsey v. Norwegian Cruise Line*, 972 F.2d 998 (9th Cir. 1992)]

9.16 Business Ethics Ocean Dunes of Hutchinson Island Development Corporation (Ocean Dunes) was a developer of condominium units. Prior to the construction, Albert and Helen Colangelo entered into a purchase agreement to buy one of the units and paid a deposit to Ocean Dunes. A provision in the purchase agreement provided that

If Developer shall default in the performance of its obligations pursuant to this agreement, Purchaser's only remedy shall be to terminate this agreement, whereupon the Deposit shall be refunded to Purchaser and all rights and obligations thereunder shall thereupon become null and void.

The purchase agreement provided that if the buyer defaulted, the developer could retain the buyer's deposit or sue the buyer for damages and any other legal or equitable remedy. When Ocean Dunes refused to sell the unit to the Colangelos, they sued seeking a decree of specific performance to require Ocean Dunes to sell them the unit. Ocean Dunes alleged that the above-quoted provision prevented the plaintiffs from seeking any legal or equitable remedy. Was the defendant's duty under the contract illusory? Was it ethical for Ocean Dunes to place the provision at issue in the contract? [*Ocean Dunes of Hutchinson Island Development Corporation v. Colangelo*, 463 So.2d 437 (Fla.App.1985)]

BRIEFING THE CASE WRITING ASSIGNMENT

Read the following case, which has been excerpted from the court's opinion, and brief the case.

Traco, Inc. v. Arrow Glass Co., Inc.
814 S.W. 2d 186 (1991)
Court of Appeals of Texas

Chapa, Justice

This is a construction dispute stemming from a quotation given by Traco, Inc., a Three Rivers Aluminum Company, a material supplier of pre-engineered aluminum and glass sliding doors and windows, to Arrow Glass Company, Inc., a subcontractor, in connection with the USAA Towers project in San Antonio, Texas. Arrow initially brought suit against Traco on the theories of promissory estoppel and negligence for Traco's failure to supply aluminum and glass sliding doors at the quoted price. After a bench trial, the trial court held for Arrow solely under the theory of promissory estoppel and awarded Arrow judgment against Traco for damages in the amount of $75,843.38, plus attorney's fees and prejudgment interest.

The facts of this case reflect that on October 9, 1986, construction bids were due for the USAA Towers, a $49,000,000 retirement housing project located near Fort Sam Houston, Texas. There were numerous suppliers, subcontractors and general contractors bidding to obtain work on this project, including the appellant, Traco, and the appellee, Arrow.

On bid day, a representative for Arrow received a telephone call from Dale Ferrar of Traco. Mr. Ferrar told Bill Morris, the general manager of Arrow Glass, that Traco was a very large window and sliding glass aluminum door manufacturer in Pennsylvania. Mr. Ferrar offered its A-2 aluminum and glass sliding doors, as an alternate product substitution, to Arrow, which was bidding that portion of the project. However, after some discussion of the required specifications, the parties realized that Traco's doors would have to be modified in order to comply with the project specifications. Arrow declined to use Traco's bid, and instead, submitted its original bid, using a different supplier of doors.

At approximately noon on bid day, Mr. Ferrar phoned Mr. Morris, quoting a new price for the doors which included a modification of the frame depth which, supposedly, enabled the doors to comply with the specifications. At this time, Mr. Morris informed Mr. Ferrar that his bid was low and asked him to recheck his figures. Mr. Ferrar explained that because of Traco's size and the fact that it could manufacture its products under one roof, Traco could sell the project for that amount. Mr. Ferrar also indicated that Traco was seeking a high profile project to represent Traco in the San Antonio area.

After receiving these assurances, Mr. Morris told Mr. Ferrar that he was going to use Traco's bid. Mr. Morris then phoned the contractors to whom he had originally submitted his bid, and deducted $100,000 in reliance upon Traco's bid. Mr. Morris later told Mr. Ferrar that he had received favorable responses from three to four general contractors, and that it appeared Arrow would get the project. Mr. Morris advised Mr. Ferrar that if Arrow obtained the project, then Traco would be awarded the contract on the doors.

The oral quote by Traco was followed with a written bid confirmation on the next day, which reflected the product that would be supplied and the price agreed upon by the parties. The confirmation also included the $1\frac{1}{4}$ inch frame extender at a cost of $27,860, which, allegedly, brought the doors into compliance with the project specifications.

Sometime in November, long after Mr. Morris had relied upon Mr. Ferrar's representations in submitting his bid, Mr. Morris began hearing rumors that there was a problem with the door. Mr. Morris contacted Mr. Ferrar, who admitted that there was a problem with the doors meeting the architect's wind load deflection requirement in the specifications. Shortly after learning of this problem, Mr. Morris received a second quote from Traco, wherein Traco offered its A-3 doors, which were a more expensive, heavy grade commercial door that met the deflection requirement, for a price of $304,300. After receiving this bid, Morris objected to the price and demanded that Traco deliver doors meeting the project specifications at the original price quoted. Traco refused and when it became obvious that Arrow would not be able to use Traco's product, Mr. Morris contracted with another supplier who had bid on the project.

The record clearly reflects the following: that it was Traco that initially contacted Arrow and offered to a certain specific act, i.e., supply the sliding doors required; that Mr. Ferrar phoned Mr. Morris on several occasions and discussed, among other things, the fact that the doors which Traco wished to bid would not comply with the specifications without some modification; and, that Mr. Ferrar assured Mr. Morris that the doors could be modified to comply with the specifications. Thus, under the present facts, Traco's bid gave Arrow "a right to expect or claim the performance of some particular thing"; specifically, Traco's bid constituted a promise to supply sliding doors meeting the project specifications at a specified price.

Appellant initially argues that the trial court erred in rendering judgment for Arrow because Traco's bid was revocable and properly withdrawn 30 days after it was made. Appellant primarily relies upon the argument that its sliding doors are goods as defined by the Texas Business and Commerce Code. Nevertheless, appellant's arguments ignore the appellee's basic contention and legal theory under which this suit was brought. Appellee sought relief under the equitable doctrine of promissory estoppel, on the premise that appellant's promises, by way of its oral bid, caused appellee to substantially rely to its detriment. The appellee relied to its detriment when it reduced its bid based on a telephone conversation with the appellant, prior to the time appellant's confirmation letter was sent or received.

We must now resolve whether the equitable theory of promissory estoppel applies to bid construction cases and, if so, whether this doctrine applies under the specific facts of this case. While no Texas case has previously applied the theory of promissory estoppel in a bid construction case, other jurisdictions have consistently applied this doctrine under similar facts, recognizing the necessity for equity in view of the lack of other remedies.

The Texas Supreme Court, in emphasizing that the underlying function of the theory of promissory estoppel is to promote equity, has stated that: "The vital principle is that he who by his language or conduct leads another to do what he would not otherwise have done shall not subject such person to loss or injury by disappointing the expectations upon which he acted. This remedy is always so applied as to promote the ends of justice." Clearly promissory estoppel is "a rule of equity" applied to prevent injustice. As is true in most, if not all, bid construction cases, this would necessarily mean that, notwithstanding any language or conduct by the subcontractor which leads the general contractor to do that which he would not otherwise have done and, thereby, incur loss or injury, the general contractor would be denied all relief. This proposition is untenable and conflicts with the underlying premise of promissory estoppel.

Section 90 of the Restatement (Second) of Contracts (1981) states the principle of promissory estoppel as follows: "A promise which the promisor should reasonably expect to induce action or forbearance on the part of the promisee or a third person and which does induce such action or forbearance is binding if injustice can be avoided only by enforcement of the promise."

Accordingly, the requirements of promissory estoppel are: "(1) a promise, (2) foreseeability of reliance thereon by the promisor, and (3) substantial reliance by the promisee to his detriment." In order to invoke the doctrine of estoppel, all the necessary elements of estoppel must be present and the failure to establish even one of these elements is fatal to the claimant's cause of action.

Appellant insists, however, that because Traco was not an approved manufacturer and bid its doors as an alternate, that by its nature, Traco's bid was conditional and, therefore, promissory estoppel cannot lie. We fail to see how a bid for a specific door at a specific price, which was submitted in response to solicitations that detailed project specifications, is contingent, or somehow not final, merely because the wrong door was bid upon. The appellant's failure to receive the architect's approval was not due to new specifications originally required when the appellant offered its doors. Appellant's point is rejected.

Notwithstanding the existence of this promise, the appellant argues that appellee could not have justifiably and reasonably relied upon appellant's bid because: Traco was not an approved manufacturer and bid its A-2 doors as an alternate and, further, Traco's bid was lower than the other suppliers who bid upon the contract.

Because of the withdrawal of Traco's bid, Arrow was compelled to seek another supplier of doors at a much greater cost; clearly, this constituted an injustice to the appellee. Additionally, appellee's reliance upon appellant's bid was reasonable in view of the appellant's attempts to modify its doors, and Mr. Ferrar's assurances that the doors, as modified, would meet the project specifications.

We hold that the controlling findings of fact support the promissory estoppel theory.

The judgment is affirmed.

ENDNOTES

1. Restatement (Second) of Contracts, § 33 (1).
2. Ibid. Restatement (Second) of Contracts, § 204.
3. Restatement (Second) of Contracts, § 50(1).
4. Restatement (Second) of Contracts, § 40.
5. *Hamer v. Sidwa*, 27 N.Y. 538, 27 N.E. 256 (NY 1891).

CHAPTER *10*

Capacity and Legality

An unconscionable contract is one which no man in his senses, not under delusion, would make, on the one hand, and which no fair and honest man would accept on the other.

—Hume v. United States,
132 U.S. 406, 10 S.Ct. 134, 33 L.Ed. 393 (1889)

Chapter Objectives

After studying this chapter, you should be able to:

1. Define and describe the infancy doctrine.

2. Identify contracts that may be disaffirmed by minors.

3. Explain a minor's obligation to pay for the necessaries of life.

4. Define legal insanity and explain how it affects contractual capacity.

5. Define intoxication and describe how it affects contractual capacity.

6. Identify illegal contracts that are contrary to statutes.

7. Identify illegal contracts that violate public policy.

8. Describe covenants not to compete and identify when they are lawful.

9. Describe exculpatory clauses and identify when they are lawful.

10. Define *unconscionable contracts* and determine when they are unlawful.

Chapter Contents

Generally, the law presumes that the parties to a contract have the requisite **contractual capacity** to enter into the contract. Certain persons do not have this capacity, however, including minors, insane persons, and intoxicated persons. The common law of contracts and many state statutes protect persons who lack contractual capacity from having contracts enforced against them. The party asserting incapacity, his or her guardian, conservator, or other legal representative bears the burden of proof.

An essential element for the formation of a contract is that the object of the contract be lawful. A contract to perform an illegal act is called an **illegal contract**. Illegal contracts are void. That is, they cannot be enforced by either party to the contract. The term *illegal contract* is a misnomer, however, since no contract exists if the object of the contract is illegal. In addition, courts hold that **unconscionable contracts** are unenforceable. An unconscionable contract is one that is so oppressive or manifestly unfair that it would be unjust to enforce it.

Capacity to contract and the lawfulness of contracts are discussed in this chapter.

> *The right of a minor to disaffirm his contract is based upon sound public policy to protect the minor from his own improvidence and the overreaching of adults.*
>
> *Justice Sullivan*
> Star Chevrolet v. Green *(1985)*

Minors

Minors do not always have the maturity, experience, or sophistication needed to enter into contracts with adults. Common law defines minors as females under the age of 18 and males under the age of 21. In addition, many states have enacted statutes that specify the *age of majority*. The most prevalent age of majority is 18 years of age for both males and females. Any age below the statutory age of majority is called the *period of minority*.

minor

A person who has not reached the age of majority.

The Infancy Doctrine

To protect minors, the law recognizes the **infancy doctrine**, which gives minors the right to *disaffirm* (or *cancel*) most contracts they have entered into with adults. This right is based on public policy that reasons that minors should be protected from the unscrupulous behavior of adults. In most states, the infancy doctrine is an objective standard. If a person's age is below the age of majority, the court will not inquire into his or her knowledge, experience, or sophistication. Generally, contracts for the necessaries of life, which we discuss later in this chapter, are exempted from the scope of this doctrine.

Under the infancy doctrine, a minor has the option of choosing whether to enforce the contract (i.e., the contract is *voidable* by a minor). The adult party is bound to the minor's decision. If both parties to the contract are minors, both parties have the right to disaffirm the contract.

If performance of the contract favors the minor, the minor will probably enforce the contract. Otherwise, the contract probably will be disaffirmed. A minor may not affirm one part of the contract and disaffirm another part.

infancy doctrine

A doctrine that allows minors to disaffirm (cancel) most contracts they have entered into with adults.

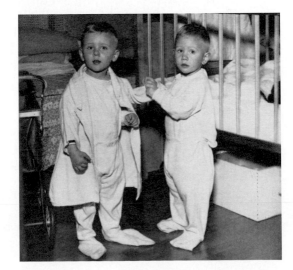

The twins *The Infancy Doctrine protects minors by permitting them to disavow (void) certain contracts. These contracts are voidable because only the minor, and not the adult on the other side of the contract, may disavow the contract.*

disaffirmance

The act of a minor to rescind a contract under the infancy doctrine. Disaffirmance may be done orally, in writing, or by the minor's conduct.

Disaffirmance   A minor can expressly disaffirm a contract orally, in writing, or by the minor's conduct. No special formalities are required. The contract may be disaffirmed at any time prior to reaching the age of majority plus a "reasonable time." The designation of a reasonable time is determined on a case-by-case basis.

Duties of Restoration and Restitution   If the minor's contract is executory and neither party has performed, the minor can simply disaffirm the contract: There is nothing to recover since neither party has given the other party anything of value. If the parties have exchanged consideration and partially or fully performed the contract by the time the minor disaffirms the contract, however, the issue becomes one of what consideration or restitution must be made. The following rules apply.

- **Competent Party's Duty of Restitution**   If the minor has transferred consideration—money, property, or other valuables—to the competent party before disaffirming the contract, that party must place the minor in status quo. That is, the minor must be restored to the same position he or she was in before the minor entered into the contract. This restoration is usually done by returning the consideration to the minor. If the consideration has been sold or has depreciated in value, the competent party must pay the minor the cash equivalent. This action is called the **competent party's duty of restitution**.

competent party's duty of restitution

If a minor has transferred money, property, or other valuables to the competent party before disaffirming the contract, that party must place the minor back into status quo.

minor's duty of restoration

As a general rule, a minor is obligated only to return the goods or property he or she has received from the adult in the condition it is in at the time of disaffirmance.

- **Minor's Duty of Restoration**   Generally, a minor is obligated only to return the goods or property he or she has received from the adult in the condition it is in at the time of disaffirmance (subject to several exceptions discussed later in this chapter), even if the item has been consumed, lost, or destroyed or has depreciated in value at the time of disaffirmance. This rule is called the **minor's duty of restoration**. It is based on the rationale that if a minor had to place the adult in status quo upon disaffirmance of a contract, there would be no incentive for an adult not to deal with a minor.
- **Minor's Duty of Restitution**   Most states provide that the minor must put the adult in status quo upon disaffirmance of the contract if the minor's intentional or grossly negligent conduct caused the loss of value to the adult's property. A few states have enacted statutes that require the minor to make restitution of the reasonable value of the item when disaffirming any contract. This rule is called the **minor's duty of restitution**.

Misrepresentation of Age   On occasion, minors might misrepresent their age to an adult when entering into a contract. Under the common law, such a minor would still have the right to disaffirm the contract. Most states, however, have changed this rule in recognition of its unfairness to adults. The revised rule provides that minors who misrepresent their age must place the adult in status quo if they disaffirm the contract. In other words, a minor who has misrepresented his or her age when entering into a contract owes the duties of restoration and restitution when disaffirming it.

Business Brief

A business should require a customer to prove that he or she is an adult if there is doubt as to age. This practice is extremely important concerning major purchases.

Consider This Example   Sherry McNamara, a minor, misrepresents that she is an adult and enters into a contract to purchase an automobile costing $20,000 from Bruce Ruffino, a competent adult. Ruffino delivers the automobile after he receives payments in full. The automobile later sustains $7,000 worth of damage in an accident which is not McNamara's fault. To disaffirm the contract, McNamara must return the damaged automobile plus $13,000 to Ruffino.

Business Brief

Many businesses, such as car dealerships, require a minor's parent or another competent adult to cosign the contract before they will sell an item to a minor.

ratification

The act of a minor after the minor has reached the age of majority by which he or she accepts a contract entered into when he or she was a minor.

Ratification

If a minor does not disaffirm a contract either during the period of minority or within a reasonable time after reaching the age of majority, the contract is considered ratified (accepted). Hence, the minor (who is now an adult) is bound by the contract: The right to disaffirm the contract has been lost. Note that any attempt by a minor to ratify a contract while still a minor can be disaffirmed just as the original contract can be disaffirmed.

The **ratification**, which relates back to the inception of the contract, can be by express oral or written words or implied from the minor's conduct (e.g., after reaching the age of majority the minor remains silent regarding the contract). The following case presents the issue of whether a minor had ratified a contract when he reached the age of majority.

Jones v. Free Flight Sport Aviation, Inc.
623 P.2d 370 (1981)
Supreme Court of Colorado

CASE 10.1

BACKGROUND AND FACTS
On November 17, 1973, William Michael Jones, a 17-year-old minor, signed a contract with Free Flight Sport Aviation, Inc. (Free Flight), for the use of recreational sky-diving facilities. A covenant not to sue and an exculpatory clause exempting Free Flight from liability were included in the contract. On December 28, 1973, Jones attained the age of majority (18 years of age). Ten months later, while on a Free Flight skydiving operation, the airplane crashed shortly after takeoff from Littleton Airport, causing severe personal injuries to Jones. Jones filed suit against Free Flight alleging negligence and willful and wanton misconduct. The trial court granted summary judgment in favor of Free Flight. The Colorado court of appeals affirmed. Jones appealed.

ISSUE
Did Jones ratify the contract?

COURT'S REASONING
A minor may disaffirm a contract made during his or her minority within a reasonable time after attaining the age of majority or he or she may, after becoming of legal age, by acts recognizing the contract, ratify it. The supreme court stated: "Affirmance is not merely a matter of intent. It may be determined by the actions of a minor who accepts the benefits of a contract after reaching the age of majority, or who is silent or acquiesces in the contract for a considerable length of time. We conclude that the trial court properly determined that Jones ratified the contract, as a matter of law, by accepting the benefits of the contract when he used Free Flight's facilities on October 19, 1974."

DECISION
The supreme court held that Jones had ratified his contract with Free Flight by continuing, for 10 months after reaching the age of majority, to perform under the contract. Therefore, the covenant not to sue and the exculpatory clause exempting Free Flight from liability to Jones are enforceable.

Case Questions

Critical Legal Thinking Should children be allowed to disaffirm a minor's contract after reaching the age of majority? What is a reasonable length of time after reaching the age of majority to permit disaffirmance?

Business Ethics Did Jones act ethically by suing Free Flight Sport Aviation in this case?

Contemporary Business Should the covenant not to sue have been enforced here even though Jones was an adult?

Necessaries of Life

Minors are obligated to pay for the **necessaries of life** that they contract for. Otherwise, many adults would refuse to sell these items to them. There is no standard definition of what is a *necessary of life*, but items such as food, clothing, shelter, and medical services are generally understood to fit this category. Goods and services such as automobiles, tools of trade, education, and vocational training have also been found to be necessaries of life in some situations. The minor's age, lifestyle, and status in life influence what is considered necessary. For example, necessaries for a married minor are greater than for an unmarried minor.

The seller's recovery is based on the equitable doctrine of **quasi-contract** rather than on the contract itself. Under this theory, the minor is obligated only to pay the reasonable value of the goods or services received. Reasonable value is determined on a case-by-case basis.

necessaries of life
A minor must pay the reasonable value of food, clothing, shelter, medical care, and other items considered necessary to the maintenance of life.

Contemporary Business Environment

STATUTES THAT MAKE MINORS LIABLE FOR SPECIAL TYPES OF CONTRACTS

The infancy doctrine of the common law of contracts allows minors to disaffirm many contracts they have entered into with adults. Based on public policy, many states have enacted statutes that make certain specified contracts enforceable against minors—that is, minors cannot assert the infancy doctrine against enforcement for these contracts. These usually include contracts for

• Medical, surgical, and pregnancy care
• Psychological counseling

- Health insurance
- Life insurance
- The performance of duties relating to stock and bond transfers, bank accounts, and the like
- Educational loan agreements
- Contracts to support children

- Contracts to enlist in the military
- Artistic, sports, and entertainment contracts that have been entered into with the approval of the court (many of these statutes require that a certain portion of the wages and fees earned by the minor be put in trust until the minor reaches the age of majority)

Parents' Liability for Their Children's Contracts

Generally, parents owe a legal duty to provide food, clothing, shelter, and other necessaries of life for their minor children. Parents are liable for their children's contracts for necessaries of life if they have not adequately provided such items.

emancipation

When a minor voluntarily leaves home and lives apart from his or her parents.

The parental duty of support terminates if a minor becomes *emancipated*. **Emancipation** occurs when a minor voluntarily leaves home and lives apart from his or her parents. The courts consider factors such as getting married, setting up a separate household, or joining the military service in determining whether a minor is emancipated. Each situation is examined on its merits.

*M*ENTALLY INCOMPETENT PERSONS

Insanity vitiates all acts.

Sir John Nicholl
Countess of Portsmouth v. Earl of
Portsmouth *(1828)*

Mental incapacity may arise because of mental illness, brain damage, mental retardation, senility, and the like. The law protects people suffering from substantial mental incapacity from enforcement of contracts against them because such persons may not understand the consequences of their actions in entering into a contract.

legal insanity

A state of contractual incapacity as determined by law.

To be relieved of his or her duties under a contract, the law requires a person to have been legally insane at the time of entering into the contract. This state is called **legal insanity**. Most states use the *objective cognitive "understanding" test* to determine legal insanity. Under this test, the person's mental incapacity must render that person incapable of understanding or comprehending the nature of the transaction. Mere weakness of intellect, slight psychological or emotional problems, or delusions do not constitute legal insanity. The law has developed the following two standards concerning contracts of mentally incompetent persons:

adjudged insane

A person who has been adjudged insane by a proper court or administrative agency. A contract entered into by such a person is *void*.

1. **Adjudged Insane**　In certain cases, a relative, loved one, or other interested party may institute a legal action to have someone declared legally (i.e., adjudged) insane. If after hearing the evidence at a formal judicial or administrative hearing the person is **adjudged insane**, the court will make that person a ward of the court and appoint a guardian to act on that person's behalf. Any contract entered into by a person who has been adjudged insane is *void*. That is, no contract exists. The court-appointed guardian is the only one who has the legal authority to enter into contracts on behalf of the person.

insane, but not adjudged insane

A person who is insane but has not been adjudged insane by a court or administrative agency. A contract entered into by such person is generally *voidable*. Some states hold that such a contract is void.

2. **Insane, But Not Adjudged Insane**　If no formal ruling has been made, any contracts entered into by a person who suffers from a mental impairment that makes him or her legally insane are voidable by the insane person. Unless the other party does not have contractual capacity, he or she does not have the option to avoid the contract.

Some people have alternating periods of sanity and insanity. Any contracts made by such persons during a lucid interval are enforceable. Contracts made while the person was not legally sane can be disaffirmed.

A person who has dealt with an insane person must place that insane person in status quo if the contract is either void or voided by the insane person. Most states hold that a party who did not know he or she was dealing with an insane person must be placed in status quo upon avoidance of the contract. Insane persons are liable in *quasi-contract* to pay the reasonable value for the necessaries of life they receive.

CONCEPT SUMMARY   DISAFFIRMANCE OF CONTRACTS BASED ON LEGAL INSANITY

Type of Legal Insanity	Disaffirmance Rule
Adjudged insane	Contract is void. Neither party can enforce the contract.
Insane, but not adjudged insane	Contract is voidable by the insane person; the competent party cannot void the contract.

INTOXICATED PERSONS

Most states provide that contracts entered into by certain **intoxicated persons** are voidable by that person. The intoxication may occur because of alcohol or drugs. The contract is not voidable by the other party if that party had contractual capacity.

Under the majority rule, the contract is voidable only if the person was so intoxicated when the contract was entered into that he was incapable of understanding or comprehending the nature of the transaction. In most states, this rule holds even if the intoxication was self-induced. Some states only allow the person to disaffirm the contract if the person was forced to become intoxicated or did so unknowingly.

The amount of alcohol or drugs that is necessary to be consumed for a person to be considered legally intoxicated to disaffirm contracts varies from case to case. The factors that are considered include the user's physical characteristics and his or her ability to "hold" intoxicants.

A person who disaffirms a contract based on intoxication generally must be returned to the status quo. In turn, the intoxicated person generally must return the consideration received under the contract to the other party and make restitution that returns the other party to status quo. After becoming sober, an intoxicated person can ratify the contracts he entered into while intoxicated. Intoxicated persons are liable in *quasi-contract* to pay the reasonable value for necessaries they receive.

In the following case, the court permitted a person to disaffirm the contract because she was intoxicated.

intoxicated person

A person who is under contractual incapacity because of ingestion of alcohol or drugs to the point of incompetence.

Men intoxicated are sometimes stunned into sobriety.

Lord Mansfield
R. v. Wilkes (1770)

Smith v. Williamson
429 So.2d 598 (1983)
Court of Civil Appeals of Alabama

CASE 10.2

BACKGROUND AND FACTS
Carolyn Ann Williamson entered into a contract to sell her house to Mr. and Mrs. Matthews at a time when her house was threatened with foreclosure. Evidence showed that Williamson was an alcoholic. Having read about the threatened foreclosure in the newspaper, attorney Virgil M. Smith appeared at Williamson's home to discuss the matter with her. Williamson told Smith that she expected to receive $17,000 from the sale, but had actually received $1,700. On the following day, after drinking a pint of 100-proof vodka, Williamson and her son went to Smith's office, where Smith prepared a lawsuit to have the sale of the house set aside based on Williamson's lack of capacity due to alcoholism. At that time, Smith loaned Williamson $500 and took back a note and mortgage on her house to secure repayment of this amount and his attorney fees. Evidence showed that Smith

did not allow Williamson's son to read the mortgage. The sale to Mr. and Mrs. Matthews was set aside. Subsequently, Smith began foreclosure proceedings on Williamson's house to recover attorney's fees and advances. Williamson filed this lawsuit to enjoin the foreclosure. The trial court held that Smith's mortgage was void and permanently enjoined him from foreclosing on it. Smith appealed.

ISSUE
Was Williamson's alcoholism a sufficient mental incapacity to void the mortgage?

COURT'S REASONING
In reaching its decision in favor of Williamson, the court stated: "To accept Smith's position would require us to ignore certain subtle ironies arising from the facts of this appeal. The transaction between Ms. Williamson and the

Matthewses was set aside. In overturning the contract and deed to the Matthewses, the court found that Ms. Williamson was incapable of understanding the nature of the transaction and also found that her intoxication, coupled with the gross inadequacy of consideration, supported this result. The record indicates that Ms. Williamson executed the note and mortgage on her home to Smith on October 12, 1978, the following morning. The record further shows that Ms. Williamson had consumed a pint of 100-proof vodka. To hold that Ms. Williamson was incapable of understanding the nature of the transaction with the Matthewses and then to hold that she was able to comprehend the nature of her dealings with Smith would be to reach illogical results, especially in light of the facts presented at trial."

DECISION

The appellate court held that Williamson was not bound to the contract and mortgage with attorney Smith because she was mentally incompetent by reason of intoxication at the time she signed the documents. Affirmed.

Case Questions

Critical Legal Thinking Should the law protect persons who voluntarily become intoxicated from their contracts?

Business Ethics Do you think that attorney Smith acted ethically in this case?

Contemporary Business Do you think many business deals are entered into after the parties have been drinking? Should these deals be allowed to be voided?

ILLEGALITY

One requirement to have an enforceable contract is that the object of the contract must be lawful. Contracts with an illegal object are *void* and therefore unenforceable. The following paragraphs discuss various illegal contracts.

Contracts Contrary to Statutes

Both federal and state legislatures have enacted statutes that prohibit certain types of conduct. For example, penal codes make certain activities crimes, antitrust statutes prohibit certain types of agreements between competitors, and so on. Contracts to perform an activity that is prohibited by statute are illegal contracts.

usury law

A law that sets an upper limit on the interest rate that can be charged on certain types of loans.

Usury Laws State **usury laws** set an upper limit on the annual interest rate that can be charged on certain types of loans. The limits vary from state to state. Lenders who charge a higher rate than the state limit are guilty of usury. These laws are intended to protect unsophisticated borrowers from loan sharks and others who charge exorbitant rates of interest.

Most states provide criminal and civil penalties for making usurious loans. Some states require lenders to remit the difference between the interest rate charged on the loan and the usury rate to the borrower. Other states prohibit lenders from collecting any interest on the loan. Still other states provide that a usurious loan is a void contract, permitting the borrower not to have to pay the interest or the principal of the loan to the lender.

Most usury laws exempt certain types of lenders and loan transactions involving legitimate business transactions from the reach of the law. Often, these exemptions include loans made by banks and other financial institutions, loans above a certain dollar amount, and loans made to corporations and other businesses.

gambling statutes

Statutes that make certain forms of gambling illegal.

Gambling Statutes All states either prohibit or regulate gambling, wagering, lotteries, and games of chance. States provide various criminal and civil penalties for illegal gambling. There is a distinction between lawful risk-shifting contracts and gambling contracts. For example, if property insurance is purchased on one's own car and the car is destroyed in an accident, the insurance company must pay the claim. This agreement is a lawful risk-shifting contract because the purchaser had an "insurable interest" in the car. Insurance purchased on a neighbor's car would be considered to be gambling, however. The purchaser does not have an insurable interest in the car and is betting only on its destruction.

There are many exceptions to wagering laws. For example, many states have enacted statutes that permit games of chance under a certain dollar amount, bingo games, lotteries conducted by religious and charitable organizations, and the like. Many states also permit and regulate horse racing, harness racing, dog racing, and state-operated lotteries.

Business Note

The federal government authorizes Native American Indians to legally operate gambling casinos on Indian reservation property if state law permits such gambling.

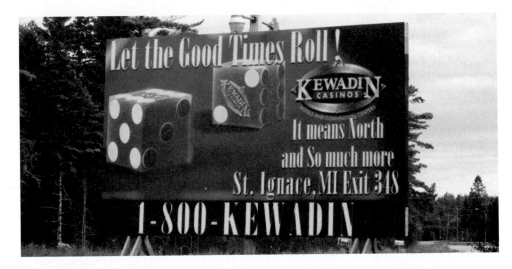

Lawful Gambling *Federal law permits lawful gambling on American Indian reservation land if the state permits such gambling.*

Sabbath Laws   Certain states have enacted laws—called **Sabbath laws**, **Sunday laws**, or **blue laws**—that prohibit or limit the carrying on of certain secular activities on Sundays. Except for contracts for the necessaries of life, charitable donations, and such, these laws generally prohibit or invalidate executory contracts that are entered into on Sunday. Many states do not actively enforce these laws. In some states, they have even been found to be unconstitutional.

Sabbath law
A law that prohibits or limits the carrying on of certain secular activities on Sundays.

Contracts to Commit a Crime   As mentioned previously, contracts to commit criminal acts are void. If the object of a contract became illegal after the contract was entered into because the government enacted a statute that made it unlawful, the parties are discharged from the contract. The contract is not an illegal contract unless the parties agree to go forward and complete it.

Licensing Statutes   All states require members of certain professions and occupations to be licensed by the state in which they practice. Lawyers, doctors, real estate agents, insurance agents, certified public accountants, teachers, contractors, hairdressers, and such are among them. In most instances, a **license** is granted to persons who demonstrate that they have the proper schooling, experience, and moral character required by the relevant statute. Sometimes, a written examination is also required.

licensing statute
Statute that requires a person or business to obtain a license from the government prior to engaging in a specified occupation or activity.

Problems arise if an unlicensed person tries to collect payment for services provided to another under a contract. Some statutes expressly provide that unlicensed persons cannot enforce contracts to provide these services. If the statute is silent on the point, enforcement depends on whether it is a *regulatory statute* or a *revenue-raising statute*.

- **Regulatory Statutes**   Licensing statutes enacted to protect the public are called **regulatory statutes**. Generally, unlicensed persons cannot recover payment for services that a regulatory statute requires a licensed person to provide. For example, state law provides that legal services can be provided only by lawyers who have graduated from law school and passed the appropriate bar exam. Nevertheless, suppose Marie Sweiger, a first-year law student, agrees to draft a will for Randy McCabe for a $150 fee. Since Sweiger is not licensed to provide legal services, she has violated a regulatory statute. She cannot enforce the contract and recover payment from McCabe.

regulatory statute
A licensing statute enacted to protect the public.

- **Revenue-Raising Statutes**   Licensing statutes enacted to raise money for the government are called **revenue-raising statutes**. A person who provides services pursuant to a contract without the appropriate license required by such a statute can enforce the contract and recover payment for services rendered. For example, suppose a state licensing statute requires licensed attorneys to pay an annual $200 license fee without requiring continuing education or other new qualifications. A licensed attorney who forgets to pay the fee can enforce contracts and recover payment for the legal services he or she renders. The statute merely gathers revenue; protection of the public is not a factor.

revenue-raising statute
A licensing statute with the primary purpose of raising revenue for the government.

Contemporary Business Environment

AN UNLICENSED CONTRACTOR GETS DUNKED

The doctrine of illegality is designed to protect persons from certain types of contracts deemed unfair, unscrupulous, or unconscionable by society. The doctrine denies violators access to taxpayer-supported courts to enforce their illegal contracts. Should parties sometimes be allowed to enforce their otherwise illegal contract? Consider the following case.

Hydrotech Systems, Ltd. (Hydrotech), is a New York corporation that manufactures and installs patented equipment to simulate ocean waves. Oasis Waterpark (Oasis) is a California corporation that owns and operates a water-oriented amusement park in Palm Springs, California. Wessman Construction Company, Inc. (Wessman), is Oasis's general contractor at the park.

In July 1985, Wessman contracted with Hydrotech to design and construct a 29,000-square foot "surfing pool" at the park using Hydrotech's wave equipment. The total contract price was $850,000. Hydrotech was aware of a California law that requires a contractor to have a California contractor's license to provide construction services in California. The statute stipulates that an unlicensed contractor cannot sue in a California court to recover compensation for work requiring a California contractor's license [California Business and Professional Code § 7031].

Because it was concerned with the licensing problem, Hydrotech wished only to sell and deliver the equipment and to avoid involvement in the design or construction of the pool. Oasis, however, insisted that Hydrotech's unique expertise in design and construction was essential. Oasis induced Hydrotech to provide these services by promising to pay Hydrotech even if the law provided otherwise.

In reliance on these promises, Hydrotech furnished equipment and services in full compliance with the contract. Hydrotech had been paid $740,000 during the course of the contract. When it billed Oasis for the remaining $110,000, Oasis refused to pay. Hydrotech sued Oasis and Wessman for damages in California court for breach of contract and fraud. The defendants moved the court to dismiss the action because Hydrotech did not possess a California contractor's license as required by law.

The California Supreme Court agreed with the defendants and ordered Hydrotech's complaint dismissed. The court found that Hydrotech had violated the licensing statute. The supreme court stated: "The obvious statutory intent is to discourage persons who have failed to comply with the licensing law from offering or providing their unlicensed services for pay. Because of the strength and clarity of this policy, it is well settled that Section 7031 applies despite injustice to the unlicensed contractor." [*Hydrotech Systems, Ltd. v. Oasis Waterpark*, 52 Cal.3d 988, 277 Cal.Rptr. 517 (CA 1991)]

Contracts Contrary to Public Policy

contracts contrary to public policy

Contracts that have a negative impact on society or that interfere with the public's safety and welfare.

Certain contracts are illegal because they are **contrary to public policy**. Such contracts are void. Although *public policy* eludes a precise definition, the courts have held contracts to be contrary to public policy if they have a negative impact on society or interfere with the public's safety and welfare.

immoral contract

A contract whose objective is the commission of an act that is considered immoral by society.

Immoral Contracts   **Immoral contracts**—that is, contracts whose objective is the commission of an act that is considered immoral by society—may be found to be against public policy. For example, a contract that is based on sexual favors has been held an immoral contract void as against public policy. Judges are not free to define morality based on their individual views. Instead, they must look to the practices and beliefs of society when defining immoral conduct.

The following case raises the issue of whether a contract violates public policy and is therefore illegal.

Flood v. Fidelity & Guaranty Life Insurance Co.
394 So.2d 1311 (1981)
Court of Appeals of Louisiana

CASE 10.3

BACKGROUND AND FACTS

Ellen and Richard Alvin Flood, who were married in 1965, lived in a house trailer in Louisiana. Richard worked as a maintenance man and Ellen was employed at an insurance agency. Evidence at trial showed that Ellen was unhappy with her marriage. Ellen took out a life insurance policy on the life of her husband and named herself as beneficiary. The policy was issued by Fidelity & Guaranty Life Insurance Company

(Fidelity). In June 1972, Richard became unexpectedly ill. He was taken to the hospital, where his condition improved. After a visit at the hospital from his wife, however, Richard died. Ellen was criminally charged with the murder of her husband by poisoning. Evidence showed that six medicine bottles at the couple's home, including Tylenol and paregoric bottles, contained arsenic. The court found that Ellen had fed Richard ice cubes laced with arsenic at the hospital. Ellen was tried and convicted of the murder of her husband. Ellen, as beneficiary of Richard's life insurance policy, requested Fidelity to pay her the benefits. Fidelity refused to pay the benefits and returned all premiums paid on the policy. This suit followed. The district court held in favor of Ellen Flood and awarded her the benefits of the life insurance policy. Fidelity appealed.

ISSUE
Was the life insurance policy an illegal contract that is void?

COURT'S REASONING
Louisiana follows the majority rule that holds, as a matter of public policy, that a beneficiary named in a life insurance policy is not entitled to the proceeds of the insurance if the beneficiary feloniously kills the insured. Applying this rule, the appellate court held that Ellen Flood could not recover the life insurance benefits from the policy she had taken out on her husband's death. The court stated: "Life insurance policies are procured because life is, indeed, precarious and uncertain. Our law does not and cannot sanction any scheme which has as its purpose the certain infliction of death for, inter alia, financial gain through receipt of the proceeds of life insurance. To sanction this policy in any way would surely shackle the spirit of the letter and life of our laws."

DECISION
The appellate court held that the life insurance policy that Ellen Flood had taken out on the life of her husband was void based on public policy. Reversed.

Case Questions

Critical Legal Thinking Should Ellen Flood have been allowed to retain the insurance proceeds in this case?

Business Ethics Did Ellen Flood act unethically in this case? Did she act illegally?

Contemporary Business What would be the economic consequences if persons could recover insurance proceeds for losses caused by their illegal activities (e.g., murder, arson)?

Contracts in Restraint of Trade The general economic policy of this country favors competition. At common law, **contracts in restraint of trade**—that is, contracts which unreasonably restrain trade—were held to be unlawful. For example, it would be an illegal restraint of trade if all the bakers in a neighborhood agreed to fix the prices of the bread they sold. The bakers' contract would be void.

contract in restraint of trade
A contract that unreasonably restrains trade.

Exculpatory Clauses An **exculpatory clause** is a contractual provision that relieves one (or both) parties to the contract from tort liability. Exculpatory clauses can relieve a party of liability for ordinary negligence. They cannot be used in situations involving willful conduct, intentional torts, fraud, recklessness, or gross negligence. Exculpatory clauses are often found in leases, sales contracts, ticket stubs to sporting events, parking lot tickets, service contracts, and the like. Such clauses do not have to be reciprocal (i.e., one party may be relieved of tort liability, whereas the other party is not).

exculpatory clause
A contractual provision that relieves one (or both), parties to the contract from tort liability for ordinary negligence.

Generally, the courts do not favor exculpatory clauses unless both parties have equal bargaining power. The courts are willing to permit competent parties of equal bargaining power to establish which of them bears the risk.

Consider This Example Jim Jackson voluntarily enrolled in a parachute jump course and signed a contract containing an exculpatory clause that relieved the parachute center of liability. After receiving proper instruction, he jumped from an airplane. Unfortunately, Jim was injured when he could not steer his parachute toward the target area. He sued the parachute center for damages, but the court enforced the exculpatory clause, reasoning that parachute jumping did not involve an essential service and that there was no decisive advantage in bargaining power between the parties.

Business Brief

Exculpatory clauses are void as against public policy if they either (1) affect the *public interest* or (2) result from the superior bargaining power of the party asserting the clause.

Exculpatory clauses that either affect the *public interest* or result from superior bargaining power are usually found to be void as against public policy. Although the outcome varies with the circumstances of the case, the greater the degree that the party serves the general public, the greater the chance that the exculpatory clause will be struck down as illegal. The courts will consider such factors as the type of activity involved, the relative bargaining power, knowledge, experience, and sophistication of the parties as well as other relevant factors.

In the following case, the courts had to decide the legality of exculpatory clauses.

Gardner v. Downtown Porsche Audi

180 Cal.App.3d 713, 225 Cal.Rptr. 757 (1986)

Court of Appeals of California

CASE 10.4

BACKGROUND AND FACTS

In late June 1978, Bruce Gardner took his 1976 Porsche 911 automobile to be repaired at Downtown Porsche Audi (Downtown), located in downtown Los Angeles, California. Evidence showed that Gardner signed Downtown's repair-order form contract, which contained the following exculpatory clause disclaiming Downtown from liability. "NOT RESPONSIBLE FOR LOSS OR DAMAGE TO CARS OR ARTICLES LEFT IN CARS IN CASE OF FIRE, THEFT OR ANY OTHER CAUSE BEYOND OUR CONTROL." Someone stole Gardner's Porsche while it was parked at Downtown's repair garage. Gardner sued Downtown for failing to redeliver the car to him. The trial court found in favor of Gardner and awarded him $16,000 plus costs against Downtown. Downtown appealed.

ISSUE

Does the contract involve a "public interest" that would cause the exculpatory clause to be void?

COURT'S REASONING

This case raises an issue common in daily life: Can an automobile repair garage avoid liability for its negligence by having car owners sign a waiver form when they leave their cars with the garage? The appellate court stated: "The modern citizen lives—and all too frequently dies—by the automobile. Members of the general public need cars not merely for dis-cretionary recreational purposes but to get to and from their places of employment, to reach the stores where they can purchase the necessities—as well as the frivolities—of life. An out-of-repair automobile is an unreliable means of transportation. Moreover, it is a dangerous one as well—to pedestrians and other drivers, not just the owner. What is true of modern societies in general is doubly true in Southern California, the capital of the motor vehicle. It follows that clauses which exculpate repair firms for ordinary negligence in handling and securing vehicles under repair are invalid as contrary to public policy."

DECISION

The appellate court held that the car repair contract involved the public's interest and the exculpatory clause was therefore void. Affirmed.

Case Questions

Critical Legal Thinking Should exculpatory clauses that involve the public interest be struck down as void as against public policy? Would an exculpatory clause used by a doctor be valid?

Business Ethics Did Downtown Porsche Audi act ethically in denying liability in this case?

Contemporary Business Why do firms use exculpatory clauses?

Entrepreneur and the Law

USING A COVENANT NOT TO COMPETE WITH A SALE OF A BUSINESS

Entrepreneurs and others often buy and sell businesses. The sale of a business includes its "goodwill" or reputation. To protect this goodwill after the sale, the seller often enters into an agreement with the buyer not engage in a similar business or occupation within a specified geographical area for a specified period of time following the sale. This agreement is called a **covenant not to compete**, or a **noncompete clause**.

Covenants not to compete that are *ancillary* to a legitimate sale of a business or employment contract are lawful if they are reasonable in three aspects: (1) the line of business protected, (2) the geographical area protected, and (3) the duration of the restriction. A covenant that is found to be unreasonable is not enforceable as written. The reasonableness of covenants not to compete are examined on a case-by-case basis. If a covenant not to compete is unreasonable, the courts may either refuse to enforce it or change it so that it is reasonable. Usually, the courts choose the first option.

Consider This Example Suppose Stacy Rogers is a certified public accountant (CPA) with a lucrative practice in San Diego, California. Her business includes a substantial amount of goodwill. When she sells her practice she agrees not to open another accounting practice in the state of California for a 50-year period. This covenant not to compete is reasonable in the line of business protected but is unreasonable in geographical scope and duration. It will not be enforced by the courts as written. The covenant not to compete would be reasonable and enforceable if it prohibited Ms. Rogers only from practicing as a CPA in the city of San Diego for five years.

A covenant not to compete that is not *ancillary* to a legitimate business transaction is void as against public policy because the noncompete clause is not protecting a legitimate business interest. For example, a contract where one lawyer paid another lawyer not to open an office nearby would be void as against public policy because it is not ancillary to a legitimate business transaction.

Employment contracts often contain noncompete clauses that prohibit an employee from competing with his or her employer for a certain time period after leaving the employment.

Effect of Illegality

Since illegal contracts are void, the parties cannot sue for nonperformance. Further, if an illegal contract is executed, the court will generally leave the parties where it finds them.

Exceptions to the General Rule   Certain situations are exempt from the general rule of the effect of finding an illegal contract. If an exception applies, the innocent party may use the court system to sue for damages or to recover consideration paid under the illegal contract. Persons who can assert an exception are:

1. Innocent persons who were justifiably ignorant of the law or fact that made the contract illegal. For example, a person who purchases insurance from an unlicensed insurance company may recover insurance benefits from the unlicensed company.
2. Persons who were induced to enter into an illegal contract by fraud, duress, or undue influence. For example, a shop owner who pays $5,000 "protection money" to a mobster so that his store will not be burned down by the mobster can recover the $5,000.
3. Persons who entered into an illegal contract withdrawn before the illegal act is performed. For example, if the president of New Toy Corporation pays $10,000 to an employee of Old Toy Corporation to steal a trade secret from his employer but reconsiders and tells the employee not to do it before he has done it, the New Toy Corporation may recover the $10,000.
4. Persons who were less at fault than the other party for entering into the illegal contract. At common law, parties to an illegal contract were considered **in pari delicto** (in equal fault). Some states have changed this rule and permit less-at-fault parties to recover restitution of the consideration they paid under an illegal contract from the more-at-fault party.

in pari delicto

When both parties are equally at fault in an illegal contract.

Business Ethics

"HEADS I WIN, TAILS YOU LOSE"

Sometimes courts face a close question of whether a contract is illegal. Consider the following case. R. D. Ryno Jr. owned Bavarian Motors, an automobile dealership in Fort Worth, Texas. On March 5, 1981, Lee Tyra discussed purchasing a 1980 BMW M-1 from Ryno for $125,000. Ryno then suggested a double-or-nothing coin flip, to which Tyra agreed. When Tyra won the coin flip, Ryno said, "It's yours," and handed Tyra the keys and German title to the car. Tyra drove away in the car. This suit ensued as to the ownership of the car. The trial court held in favor of Tyra. Ryno appealed. Who owns the car?

The appellate court held that Tyra, the winner of the coin toss, owned the car. The appellate court reasoned as follows: "Ryno complains that the trial court erred in granting the Tyra judgment because the judgment enforces a gambling contract. We find there was sufficient evidence to sustain the jury finding that Ryno intended to transfer to Tyra

his ownership interest in the BMW at the time he delivered the documents, keys, and possession of the automobile to Tyra. We agree with appellant Ryno that his wager with Tyra was unenforceable. The trial court could not have compelled Ryno to honor his wager by delivering the BMW to Tyra. However, Ryno did deliver the BMW to Tyra and the facts incident to that delivery are sufficient to establish a transfer by gift of the BMW from Ryno to Tyra." The appellate court found that there was an illegal contract and left the parties where it found them. That is, with Tyra in possession of the car. [*Ryno v. Tyra*, 752 S.W.2d 148 (TX, 1988)]

1. Did Ryno act ethically by trying to renege on his promise?
2. What is the moral of this story if you ever win anything in an illegal gambling contract?

Contemporary Business Environment

UNCONSCIONABLE CONTRACTS

The general rule of freedom of contract holds that if (1) the object of a contract is lawful and (2) the other elements for the formation of a contract are met, the courts will enforce a contract according to its terms. Although it is generally presumed that parties are capable of protecting their own interests when contracting, it is a fact of life that dominant parties sometimes take advantage of weaker parties. As a result, some lawful contracts are so oppressive or manifestly unfair that they are unjust. To prevent the enforcement of such contracts, the courts developed the equitable **doctrine of unconscionability**, which is based on public policy. A contract found to be unconscionable under this doctrine is called an **unconscionable contract**, or a **contract of adhesion**.

The courts are given substantial discretion in determining whether a contract or contract clause is unconscionable. There is no single definition of *unconscionability*. The doctrine may not be used merely to save a contracting party from a bad bargain.

The following elements must be shown to prove that a contract or clause in a contract is unconscionable:

1. The parties possessed severely unequal bargaining power.
2. The dominant party unreasonably used its unequal bargaining power to obtain oppressive or manifestly unfair contract terms.
3. The adhering party had no reasonable alternative.

In other words, the dominant party must *misuse* its greater power to obtain oppressive contract terms from the adhering party and the adhering party must prove that it could not reasonably refuse to accept those terms. This situation is often proven by showing that the oppressive terms are contained in standard contracts used industrywide.

If the court finds that a contract or contract clause is unconscionable, it may (1) refuse to enforce the contract, (2) refuse to enforce the unconscionable clause but enforce the remainder of the contract, or (3) limit the applicability of any unconscionable clause so as to avoid any unconscionable result. The appropriate remedy depends on the facts and circumstances of each case. Note that since unconscionability is a matter of law, the judge may opt to decide the case without a jury trial.

Business Ethics

SUPERCUTS GIVEN CREWCUT BY THE COURT

Sometimes contracts favor one party over another party. This unbalance often occurs when the strongest party drafts the contract and presents it to the other party on a take-it-or-leave-it basis. Mere unbalanced contracts are not necessarily illegal, but those that overreach and are too lopsided can be found to be unenforceable under the equitable doctrine of **unconscionability**. Consider the following case.

Supercuts, Inc., a Delaware corporation, conducts a national hair care franchise business. The president of Supercuts is David E. Lipson. From January 1993 until March 1994, Supercuts employed William N. Stirlen as its vice president and chief financial officer. Stirlen signed an employment agreement that was prepared by Supercuts. The contract provided for Stirlen to receive an annual salary of $150,000, stock options, a bonus plan, a supplemental retirement plan, and a $10,000 signing bonus. The contract was an at-will employment contract, meaning that Stirlen could be terminated without cause at any time.

Late in 1993 and early in 1994, Stirlen informed Lipson and other corporate officers of various problems and "accounting irregularities" he feared might be in violation of

state and federal statutes. Stirlen also expressed concern that the company's decline in profits "was being hidden in the books and from public shareholders." At a meeting in November 1993, Stirlen provided senior managers with accounting statements outlining the accounting irregularities. After Stirlen brought these issues to Supercuts's outside auditors, Lipson allegedly reprimanded Stirlen and accused him of being a "troublemaker." Lipson also told him that if Stirlen did not reverse his position on these issues, he would no longer be considered a "member of the team." At the end of February 1994, Lipson suspended Stirlen from his job; Stirlen was fired the following month.

Stirlen sued Supercuts and Lipson for breach of contract, wrongful termination in violation of public policy, and intentional misrepresentation. The defendants made a motion to the court alleging that the arbitration clause in Stirlen's employment contract required the dispute to be arbitrated. Stirlen countered that the arbitration clause, and other clauses in Supercuts' contract, were unconscionable and therefore unenforceable. The challenged clauses provided that (1) Stirlen would have to submit to final and binding arbitration all disputes concerning the contract, but that Supercuts could go to court on most matters if it sued Stirlen, (2) any damages that could be awarded Stirlen could not exceed the actual damages for breach of contract, and (3) any salary or benefits payable to Stirlen would cease pending the outcome of any action between the parties.

Stirlen argued that the employment contract was so one-sided as to be "unconscionable." The court of appeals held that a contract is unconscionable if it "does not fall within the reasonable expectations of the weaker party" or if the contact is "unduly oppressive." Supercuts's attorneys argued that Stirlen was a sophisticated business executive who knew what he was doing when he signed Supercuts's contract.

After weighing all the evidence, the court found that Supercuts's contract was an **unconscionable contract—a contract of adhesion**—that was unenforceable. The court found

Supercuts's contract to be unconscionable in the following ways: Supercuts reserved the right to sue in court but denied this right to Stirlen; Supercuts limited the damages that Stirlen could recover from them in violation of the law; and state law provided that a party could not require another party to waive the ability to sue for fraud, which Supercuts required Stirlen to do. The court also held that Stirlen could proceed with his lawsuit against Supercuts to recover damages. [*Stirlen v. Supercuts, Inc.*, 52 Cal.App.4th 1519, 60 Cal.Rptr.2d 138 (1997)]

1. Is the doctrine of unconscionability supported by ethical principles? Explain.
2. Did Supercuts act ethically in drafting its employment contract? Should it have been more "fair"?
3. Did Stirlen act ethically by refusing to be a "team member"? What would you have done?

International Law

COMITY: THE GOLDEN RULE AMONG NATIONS

The **comity principle** is a rule among nations that each will respect the laws of others. It is not a rule of law, but one of ethics. The courts of the United States resort to the comity principle as a rationale for not applying U.S. law to foreign persons or situations where (1) concurrent jurisdiction exists with a foreign country and (2) foreign law is different from U.S. law. The following case is an example of the application of this doctrine.

Lee Wong, a U.S. citizen and California resident, was a produce grower who wanted to set up farming operations in Mexico. The Mexican Constitution, however, prohibited foreign ownership and control of farming operations. Therefore, Wong contracted with several Mexican citizens to act as "front men" for him to own and operate his farming operations in Mexico. Wong provided the money, and the front men acquired farming property in Mexico.

Wong entered into marketing contracts with a subsidiary of Tenneco, Inc. (Tenneco), a California corporation. Tenneco, with full knowledge of the nature of Wong's interest in the Mexican farming operations, purchased farm products from Wong. After several years, the Mexican government discovered Wong's interest and began threatening the front men with foreclosure and government action for non-payment of taxes on the farming operation. In January 1975, Tenneco bowed to the demands of the front men and severed its ties with Wong. Tenneco began purchasing the farm produce directly from the front men. Wong sued Tenneco in

California court to recover damages for breach of contract. The jury awarded Wong $1,691,422 in damages.

Tenneco argues that its contract with Wong violated Mexican law and therefore the United States should not enforce the contract. The California Supreme Court agreed and refused to enforce the jury's verdict. The court stated:

A contract with a view of violating the laws of another country, though not otherwise obnoxious to the law of the forum, will not be enforced. Protection of persons, like Wong, who wrongfully seek to circumvent the substantive laws of one jurisdiction by enlisting the aid of the courts in another violates and offends public policy of both jurisdictions. In the interest of comity, our courts must vigilantly resist such recruitment efforts.

Applying principles of comity, we conclude that Wong's failure to comply with the requirements of Mexican law casts a pall of illegality over all of his business transactions tied to the Mexican farming operation, including the marketing arrangement with Tenneco. California public policy dictates that we leave the parties as we found them.

Adherence to the comity principle demonstrates nations' respect for the laws of other nations. It has been characterized as the golden rule among nations, and it will grow in importance as the number of international transactions increase. [*Wong v. Tenneco, Inc.*, 39 Cal.3d. 126, 216 Cal.Rptr. 412 (CA 1985)]

CHAPTER SUMMARY

Minors, p. 237

Minors	1. *Infancy doctrine.* Minors under the age of majority may *disaffirm* (cancel) most contracts they have entered into with adults. The contract is *voidable* by the minor but not by the adult.
	2. *Disaffirmance.* Must occur before or within a reasonable time after the minor reaches the age of majority.
	3. *Competent party's duty of restitution.* If a minor disaffirms a contract, the adult must place the minor in status quo by returning the value of the consideration that the minor paid.
	4. *Minor's duty upon disaffirmance:*
	    a. *Minor's duty of restoration.* Generally, upon disaffirmance of a contract, a minor owes a duty to return the consideration to the adult in whatever condition it is in at the time of disaffirmance.
	    b. *Minor's duty of restitution.* A minor's duty to place the adult in status quo by returning the value of the consideration paid by the adult at the time of contracting if the minor (1) misrepresented his or her age or (2) intentionally or with gross negligence caused the loss to the adult's property.
	5. *Ratification.* If a minor does not disaffirm a contract during the period of minority or within a reasonable time after reaching the age of majority, the contract *is ratified* (accepted).
	6. *Necessaries of life.* Minors are obligated to pay the reasonable value for the necessaries of life (e.g., food, clothing, shelter).
	7. *Special contracts.* Many states have enacted statutes that make minors liable on certain types of contracts, such as for medical care, health and life insurance, educational loan agreements, and the like.
	8. *Emancipation.* This occurs when a minor voluntarily leaves home and lives apart from his or her parents. The parent's duty to support the minor terminates upon emancipation.

Mentally Incompetent Persons, p. 240

Mentally Incompetent Persons	1. *Adjudged insane.* Contracts by persons who have been adjudged insane are *void.* That is, the contract cannot be enforced by either the sane or insane party. 2. *Insane, but not adjudged insane.* Contracts by persons who are insane but have not been adjudged insane are *voidable* by the insane person but not by the competent party to the contract. 3. *Duty of restitution.* A person who has dealt with an insane person must place the insane person in status quo by returning the value of the consideration paid by the insane person at the time of contracting. Most states place the same duty on insane persons when they void a contract. 4. *Necessaries of life.* Insane persons are obligated to pay the reasonable value for the necessaries of life.

Intoxicated Persons, p. 241

Intoxicated Persons	1. *Intoxicated persons.* Contracts by intoxicated persons are *voidable* by the intoxicated person but not by the competent party to the contract. 2. *Duty of restitution.* Both parties owe a duty to place the other party in status quo by returning the value of the consideration paid by the other party at the time of contracting. 3. *Necessaries of life.* Intoxicated persons are obliged to pay the reasonable value for the necessaries of life.

Illegality, p. 242

Contracts Contrary to Statutes	Contracts that violate statutes are illegal, void, and unenforceable.
	1. *Usury laws.* These set the upper limit on the annual interest rate that can be charged on certain types of loans by certain lenders.
	2. *Gambling statutes.* These make certain types of gambling illegal.
	3. *Sabbath laws.* These prohibit or limit the carrying on of certain secular activities on Sundays. They are also called *Sunday laws* or *blue laws.*
	4. *Criminal statutes.* Contracts to commit crimes are illegal.
	5. *Licensing statutes:*
	    a. *Regulatory statutes.* Licensing statutes enacted to protect the public. Unlicensed persons cannot recover payment for providing services that a licensed person is required to provide.
	    b. *Revenue raising statutes.* Licensing statutes enacted to raise money for the government. Unlicensed persons can enforce contracts and recover for rendering services.

Contracts Contrary to Public Policy	Contracts that violate public policy are illegal, void, and unenforceable.
	1. *Immoral contracts.* Contracts whose objective is the commission of an act that is considered immoral by society are illegal.
	2. *Contracts in restraint of trade.* Contracts that unreasonably restrain trade are illegal contracts.
	3. *Exculpatory clauses.* Contract clauses that relieve one or both of the parties to the contract from tort liability for ordinary negligence. Exculpatory clauses that affect public interests, that result from superior bargaining power, or that attempt to relieve one of liability for intentional torts, fraud, recklessness, or gross negligence are illegal. Reasonable exculpatory clauses between parties of equal bargaining power are legal.
	4. *Covenants not to compete.* Contracts that provide that a seller of a business or an employee will not engage in a similar business or occupation within a specified geographical area for a specified time following the sale of the business or termination of employment. Also called *noncompete clauses.* They are illegal if they are *unreasonable* in scope, area, or time. Reasonable noncompete clauses are legal and enforceable.
Effect of Illegality	1. *General rule.* An illegal contract *is void.* Therefore, the parties cannot sue for nonperformance. If the contract has been executed, the court will *leave the parties where it finds them.*
	2. *Exceptions to the general rule.* An innocent party can use the courts to recover consideration paid or damages under an illegal contract where the person
	a. Was justifiably ignorant of the law or fact that made the contract illegal.
	b. Was induced to enter into the illegal contract by fraud, duress, or undue influence.
	c. Withdrew from the illegal contract before it was performed.
	d. Was less at fault than the other party to the illegal contract.

Unconscionable Contracts, p. 248

Unconscionable Contracts	Contracts that are oppressively unfair or unjust. Also called *contracts of adhesion.*
	1. *Elements of unconscionable contracts:*
	a. The parties possessed severely unequal bargaining power.
	b. The dominant party unreasonably used its power to obtain oppressive or manifestly unfair contract terms.
	c. The adhering party had no reasonable alternative.
	2. *Remedies for unconscionability:* Where a contract or contract clause is found to be unconscionable, the court may do one of the following:
	a. Refuse to enforce the contract.
	b. Refuse to enforce the unconscionable clause but enforce the remainder of the contract.
	c. Limit the applicability of any unconscionable clause so as to avoid any unconscionable result.

END-OF-CHAPTER INTERNET EXERCISES AND CASE QUESTIONS

Working the Web Internet Exercises

ACTIVITIES

Note: To search for statutory law of the 50 US states, try **www. hg.org/usstates.html**. *A good summary of the rules relating to capacity can be found at* **consumer. pub.findlaw.com/newcontent/consumerlaw/ chp2_a.html**. *Capacity as it relates to other areas of the law is summarized at* **cobrands.consumer.findlaw. com/newcontent/flg/ch15/st7/mc1.html**.

1. Minors. Review the laws of your jurisdiction regarding minors and: purchases of alcohol and tobacco; motor vehicles; renting an apartment.

2. Insane, intoxicated. Find the Web site for your state that explains the requisite level of intoxication for a 'Driving while impaired' traffic citation. Would that minimum amount be sufficient to provide a lack of capacity defense to a contract claim?

3. Illegality. Find your state statutes relating to usury. What is the maximum allowable interest rate?

4. An extensive overview of contract law can be found at Contracts Home Page (Craig Smith, Santa Barbara College of Law) **www.west.net/~smith/contracts. htm**. Review the "Policing the Bargain" page. Note that "capacity" is listed with other problem areas.

CRITICAL LEGAL THINKING CASES

10.1 Infancy Doctrine James Halbman Jr., a minor, entered into a contract to purchase a 1968 Oldsmobile automobile from Michael Lemke. Halbman paid $1,000 cash and agreed to pay $25 per week until the full purchase price was paid. Five weeks later, a connecting rod on the vehicle's engine broke, and Halbman took the car to a garage where it was repaired at a cost of $637.40. Halbman refused to pay for the repairs, disaffirmed the contract with Lemke, and notified Lemke where the car was located. When Lemke refused to pick up the car and pay the repair bill, the garage legally satisfied its garageman's lien by removing the vehicle's engine. It then towed the car to Halbman's residence. Halbman notified Lemke to remove the car, but Lemke refused to do so. The car was subsequently vandalized, making it worthless and unsalvageable. Halbman sued to disaffirm the contract and recover the consideration from Lemke. Lemke argues that Halbman must make full restitution. Who is correct? [*Halbman v. Lemke*, 298 N.W.2d 562 (Wis. 1980)]

10.2 Disaffirmance of a Minor's Contract Steven M. Kiefer purchased an automobile from Fred Howe Motors, Inc. (Howe). At the time of the purchase, Kiefer was 20 years of age, married, the father of a child, and emancipated from his parents. Kiefer then disaffirmed the contract, claiming his rights as a minor. Howe urges that emancipated minors are an exception to this rule and that emancipated minors should be legally responsible for their contracts. Can Kiefer disaffirm the contract? [*Kiefer v. Fred Howe Motors, Inc.*, 158 N.W.2d 288 (Wis. 1968)]

10.3 Ratification of a Minor's Contract Charles Edwards Smith, a minor, purchased an automobile from Bobby Floars Toyota (Toyota) on August 15, 1973. Smith executed a security agreement to finance part of the balance due on the purchase price, agreeing to pay off the balance in 30 monthly installments. On September 25, 1973, Smith turned 18, which was the age of majority in his state. Smith made 10 monthly payments after turning 18. He then decided to disaffirm the contract and stopped making the payments. Smith claims that he may disaffirm the contract entered into when he was a minor. Toyota argues that Smith had ratified the contract since attaining the age of majority. Who is correct? [*Bobby Floars Toyota, Inc. v. Smith*, 269 S.E. 320 (N.C. App. 1980)]

10.4 Necessities of Life Bobby L. Rogers, a 19-year-old emancipated minor, had to quit engineering school and go to work in his state to support his wife and expected baby. Rogers contracted with Gastonia Personnel Corporation (Gastonia), an employment agency, agreeing to pay Gastonia a $295 fee if it found him employment. Soon thereafter, Rogers was employed by a company referred to him by Gastonia. Rogers sought to disaffirm the contract to pay Gastonia the $295 fee. Gastonia sues for the fee, claiming that the contract was for necessaries. Who wins? [*Gastonia Personnel Corporation v. Rogers*, 172 S.E.2d 19 (N.C. 1970)]

10.5 Emancipation Dwaine Ebsen, an 18-year-old minor, lived with his widowed mother, Violet. After numerous arguments with his mother regarding the people he associated with, Dwaine and his mother agreed that he should move out and support himself. Dwaine took his personal belongings and moved to Orchard, Nebraska. After moving out, Dwaine received no further support from his mother. While living in Orchard, Dwaine was shot and taken to a hospital for treatment. He remained in the hospital for two weeks. Thereafter, the hospital sought payment from Violet. When she refused to pay, the hospital turned the matter over to Accent Service Company, a collection agency, who brought this action against Violet. Is Violet liable for her son's medical expenses? [*Accent Service Company v. Ebsen*, 306 N.W.2d 575 (NE 1981)]

10.6 Adjudicated Insane Manzelle Johnson, who had been adjudicated insane, executed a quitclaim and warranty deed conveying real estate she owned to her guardian, Obbie Neal. Neal subsequently conveyed the real estate to James R. Beavers by warranty deed. Charles L. Weatherly, Johnson's present guardian, brought this action seeking a decree of the court that title to the real estate be restored to Johnson because of her inability to contract. Should Johnson be allowed to void the contract? [*Beavers v. Weatherly*, 299 S.E.2d 730 (GA 1983)]

10.7 Intoxication Betty Galloway, an alcoholic, signed a settlement agreement upon her divorce from her husband, Henry Galloway. Henry, in Betty's absence in court, stated that she had lucid intervals from her alcoholism, had been sober for two months, and was lucid when she signed the settlement agreement on September 22, 1978. Betty moved only to vacate the settlement agreement on September 27, 1978, after she had retained present legal counsel. On January 23, 1979, Betty was declared incompetent to handle her person and her affairs, and a guardian and conservator was appointed. Betty, through her guardian, sued to have the settlement agreement voided. Who wins? [*Galloway v. Galloway*, 281 N.W.2d 804 (N.D. 1979)]

10.8 Contract to Commit a Crime In 1972, Jordanos', Inc., suspected and accused one of its employees, Arthur T. Allen, of theft. The union to which Allen belonged negotiated an oral contract with Jordanos' whereby Allen agreed to accept a permanent layoff if Jordanos' would not report the suspected theft to the state's unemployment agency so that Allen could collect unemployment benefits. Jordanos' agreed. It is a crime for an employer and employee to withhold relevant information from the state's unemployment agency. Jordanos' subsequently reported the suspected theft to the state's unemployment agency, and Allen was denied unemployment benefits. Allen sued Jordanos' for damages for breach of contract. Can Allen recover against Jordanos'? [*Allen v. Jordanos', Inc.*, 52 Cal.App.3d 160, 125 Cal. Rptr. 31 (Cal. App. 1975)]

10.9 Effect of an Illegal Contract James L. Strickland paid an unsolicited $2,500 bribe to Judge Sylvania W. Woods so that the judge would be lenient on a friend of Strickland's who had a case pending before Judge Woods. Paying a bribe to a government official is a crime. Judge Woods reported the incident and turned the money over to the state's attorney general. The state of Maryland indicted Strickland for bribery and sentenced him to four years in prison. Strickland filed a motion to recover the $2,500 from the state. Can Strickland recover the money? [*State of Maryland v. Strickland*, 400 A.2d 451 (Md. App. 1979)]

10.10 Licensing or Revenue-Raising Statute The state of Hawaii requires a person who wants to practice architecture to meet certain educational requirements and to pass a written examination before that person is granted a license to practice. After receiving the license, an architect must pay an annual license fee of $15. In 1967, Ben Lee Wilson satisfied the initial requirements and was granted an architecture license. He renewed his license by paying the annual fee up until April 1971, when he failed to pay the annual fee. In February 1972, Wilson contracted with Kealakekua Ranch, Ltd., and Gentry Hawaii (defendants) to provide architectural services for the Kealakekua Ranch Center Project. During the period February 1972 through May 1972, Wilson provided $33,994 of architectural services to the defendants. The defendants refused to pay this fee because Wilson did not have an architectural license. Wilson sued to collect his fees. Who wins? [*Wilson v. Kealakekua Ranch, Ltd., and Gentry Hawaii*, 551 P.2d 525 (HI 1976)]

10.11 Public Policy American Home Enterprises, Inc., was a corporation that made jewelry and drug paraphernalia, such as roach clips and bongs to smoke marijuana and tobacco. Evidence showed that the corporation predominantly produced drug paraphernalia and was not engaged significantly in jewelry production. In 1978, Robert Bovard and James T. Ralph contracted to purchase the corporation and, as part of the purchase price, executed several promissory notes payable to the sellers. Although at the time of the sale the manufacture of drug paraphernalia was not itself illegal, the possession, use, and transfer of marijuana was illegal. When Bovard and Ralph defaulted on the promissory notes, the sellers sued to enforce the notes. Bovard and Ralph allege that the contract is illegal and unenforceable as against public policy. Who wins? [*Bovard v. American Home Enterprises, Inc.*, 201 Cal.App.3d 832, 247 Cal.Rptr. 340 (Cal. App. 1988)]

10.12 Covenant Not to Compete Gerry Morris owned a silk screening and lettering shop in Tucson, Arizona. On April 11, 1974, Morris entered into a contract to sell the business to Alfred and Connie Gann. The contract contained the following covenant not to compete: "Seller agrees not to enter into silk screening or lettering shop business within Tucson and a 100-mile radius of Tucson, a period of ten (10) years from the date of this agreement and will not compete in any manner whatsoever with buyers, and seller further agrees that he will refer all business contracts to buyers." Morris opened a silk screening and lettering business in competition with the Ganns and in violation of the noncompetition clause. The Ganns brought this action

against Morris for breach of contract and to enforce the covenant not to compete. Is the covenant not to compete valid and enforceable in this case? [*Gann v. Morris*, 596 P.2d 43 (Ariz. App. 1979)]

10.13 Exculpatory Clause Grady Perkins owned the Raleigh Institute of Cosmetology (Insitute), and Ray Monk and Rovetta Allen were employed as instructors there. The school trains students to do hair styling and coloring, cosmetology, and other beauty services. The students receive practical training by providing services to members of the public under the supervision of the instructors. On March 28, 1985, Francis I. Alston went to the Institute to have her hair colored and styled by a student who was under the supervision of Monk and Allen. Before receiving any services, Alston signed a written release form that released the Institute and its employees from liability for their negligence. While coloring Alston's hair, the student negligently used a chemical that caused Alston's hair to fall out. Alston sued the Institute, Perkins, Monk, and Allen for damages. The defendants asserted that the release form signed by Alston barred her suit. Is the exculpatory clause valid? [*Alston v. Monk*, 373 S.E.2d 463 (N.C. App. 1988)]

10.14 Exculpatory Clause Wilbur Spaulding owned and operated the Jacksonville racetrack at the Morgan County Fairgrounds, where automobile races were held. Lawrence P. Koch was a flagman at the raceway. On May 28, 1982, when Koch arrived at the pit shack at the raceway, he was handed a clipboard upon which was a track release and waiver of liability form that released the racetrack from liability for negligence. Koch signed the form and took up his position as flagman. During the first race, the last car on the track lost control and slid off the end of the track, striking Koch. Koch suffered a broken leg and other injuries and was unable to work for 14 months. Koch sued Spaulding for damages for negligence. Spaulding asserted that the release form signed by Koch barred his suit. Is the exculpatory clause valid against Koch? [*Koch v. Spaulding*, 529 N.E.2d 19 (Ill. App. 1988)]

10.15 Unconscionable Contract Bill Graham, an experienced promoter and producer of musical concerts, entered into a contract with Leon Russell, a rock singer who did business under the corporate name Scissor-Tail, Inc., whereby Graham would promote several concerts for Russell. Russell belonged to the American Federation of Musicians (AFM), a union that represented most big-name musicians. The contract between Graham and Russell was on a standard, preprinted form required to be used by all AFM members. The contract contained an arbitration clause that required any disputes regarding the contract to be heard and decided by the executive board of the AFM. When a monetary dispute arose between Graham and Russell regarding the division of proceeds from the concerts, Graham sued Russell in court. Russell filed a motion to compel arbitration. Graham asserted that the arbitration clause in the AFM contract is unconscionable. Is it? [*Graham v. Scissor-Tail, Inc.*, 28 Cal. App. 3d 807, 171 Cal. Rptr. 604 (Cal. App. 1981)]

BUSINESS ETHICS CASES

10.16 Business Ethics Joe Plumlee owned and operated an ambulance company. He alleged that the law firm of Paddock, Loveless & Roach agreed to pay him an up-front fee and a percentage of the law firm's fees generated from personal injury case referrals. When the law firm did not pay Plumlee, he sued to recover damages for breach of contract. Texas law prohibits lawyers from sharing fees with laypersons [Tex. Penal Code § 38.12; Supreme Court of Texas]. A disciplinary rule also forbids such activity [State Bar Rules Art. X, § 9]. The law firm asserted that the contract could not be enforced because it would be an illegal contract. Who wins? Did Plumlee act ethically in this case? If the contract existed, did the lawyers act ethically? [*Plumlee v. Paddock, Loveless, and Roach*, 832 S.W.2d 757 (Tex. App. 1992)]

10.17 Business Ethics Richard Zientara was friends with Chester and Bernice Kaszuba. All three were residents of Indiana. Bernice, who was employed in an Illinois tavern where Illinois state lottery tickets were sold, had previously obtained lottery tickets for Zientara because Indiana did not have a state lottery. In early April 1984, Zientara requested that Kaszuba purchase an Illinois lottery ticket for him. He gave Kaszuba the money for the ticket and the numbers 6–15–16–23–24–37. Kaszuba purchased the ticket, but when it turned out to be the winning combination worth $1,696,800 she refused to give the ticket to Zientara and unsuccessfully tried to collect the money. Zientara filed suit against Kaszuba in Indiana, claiming the ticket and proceeds thereof. Was the contract legal? Did the Kaszubas act ethically in this case? [*Kaszuba v. Zientara*, 506 N.E.2d 1 (Ind. 1987)]

10.18 Business Ethics On August 31, 1965, Clifton and Cora Jones, who were welfare recipients, received a visit from a salesman representing You Shop at Home Service, Inc. After a sales presentation, Jones signed a retail installment contract to purchase a home freezer unit for the sale price of $900. With the addition of time credit charges, credit life insurance, and credit property insurance, the contract price totaled $1,234.80. The freezer had a maximum retail value of $300. Evidence showed that the Joneses were unsophisticated and uneducated concerning contracts.

After paying $619.88, Jones brought an action to rescind the contract. Star Credit Corporation, which had come into possession of the credit contract, counterclaimed for $819.81, the amount remaining on the contract plus charges for missed payments. Is the contract unconscionable in the legal sense? If so, what remedy should be awarded? Was it ethical for the sales representative to prey upon ignorant and unsophisticated consumers? Was it ethical for the Joneses to attempt to get out of the contract they signed? [*Jones v. Star Credit Corp.*, 298 N.Y.S.2d 264 (N.Y. Sup. 1969)]

BRIEFING THE CASE WRITING ASSIGNMENT

Read the following case, which has been excerpted from the court's opinion. Review and brief the case.

Carnival Leisure Industries, Ltd. v. Aubin
938 F.2d 624 (1991)
United States Court of Appeals, Fifth Circuit

Garwood, Circuit Judge

During a January 1987 visit to the Bahamas, George J. Aubin, a Texas resident, visited Cable Beach Hotel and Casino (the Casino), which was owned and operated by Carnival Leisure Industries, Ltd. (Carnival Leisure). While gambling at the Casino, Aubin received markers or chips from the Casino and the Casino received drafts drawn on Aubin's bank accounts in Texas. Aubin spent all of the markers provided on gambling, although he could also have spent them on food, beverages, souvenirs, or lodging at the Casino. Aubin ultimately gambled and lost $25,000, leaving the Casino with the same amount in bank drafts.

Carnival Leisure was unable to cash the bank drafts because Aubin had subsequently directed his bank to stop payment. Carnival Leisure sued Aubin in the United States District Court for the Southern District of Texas to enforce the debt. The district court granted Carnival Leisure's motion for summary judgment against Aubin in the amount of $25,000 and attorney's fees and costs. Carnival Leisure claimed that the debt was enforceable under Texas law because public policy had changed and now favored enforcement of gambling debts. The district court agreed. Aubin raises on appeal only the issue of whether public policy in Texas continues to prevent the enforcement of gambling debts.

Carnival Leisure claims, however, that since 1973 the public policy of Texas toward gambling and the legality of gambling debts has changed. Although gambling is generally proscribed in Texas, there has been an exception for the "social" gambler since 1973. The Texas legislature enacted the Bingo Enabling Act in 1981, the Texas Racing Act in 1986, and the Charitable Raffle Enabling Act in 1989. Provisions were added to the Texas Penal Code excepting these three activities from its general proscription against gambling.

The enactment of statutes legalizing some forms of gambling admittedly evidences some dissipation or narrowing of public disapproval of gambling. However, such statutes hardly introduce a judicially cognizable change in public policy with respect to gambling generally. The social gambling permitted is confined to private places where no one receives any benefit other than his personal winnings and all participants are subject to the same risks, a categorically vastly different kind of activity from the sort involved here. The racing, bingo, and raffling exceptions are narrow, strictly regulated exceptions to a broad public policy in Texas against most forms of gambling. Further, the kind of gambling engaged in here is not of the sort permitted by any of these exceptions.

Even if gambling legislation in Texas were evidence sufficient to warrant judicial notice of a shift in public policy with respect to legalized gambling, such a shift would not be inconsistent with a continued public policy disfavoring gambling on credit. Although Aubin could have used the loaned markers for nongambling purposes at the Casino, it is undisputed that they were in fact used exclusively for gambling. Aubin's gambling debt therefore fits squarely within the terms of the public policy of Texas prohibiting enforcement of gambling debts owed to gambling participants incurred for the purpose of gambling.

We hold that the public policy in Texas against gambling on credit prevents enforcement of a debt incurred for the purpose of gambling and provided by a participant in the gambling activity. The district court's grant of summary judgment in favor of Carnival Leisure is accordingly reversed and this case is remanded to the district court for further proceedings consistent with this opinion.

CHAPTER 11

Writing and E-Commerce Signature Law

A verbal contract isn't worth the paper it's written on.

—Samuel Goldwyn

Chapter Objectives

After studying this chapter, you should be able to:

1. Explain genuineness of assent.

2. Distinguish between unilateral and mutual mistakes of fact.

3. Describe fraudulent misrepresentation.

4. Define and describe undue influence.

5. Describe physical and economic duress.

6. List and describe the contracts that must be in writing under the Statute of Frauds.

7. Describe the Statute of Frauds applicable to the sale of goods.

8. Define and apply the doctrine of promissory estoppel.

9. Apply the parol evidence rule.

10. Describe the scope of the Electronic Signatures in Global and National Commerce Act (ESIGN).

Chapter Contents

A contract may not be enforced even if all the required elements of a legal contract are met. This situation happens when the party against whom enforcement is sought raises certain defenses against its enforcement.

There are two primary defenses to the enforcement of a contract. The first is that the assent of one or both of the parties to the contract was not genuine or real. **Genuine assent** may be missing because a party entered into a contract based on mistake, fraudulent misrepresentation, duress, or undue influence. The second defense is that the contract did not meet the requirements of the Statute of Frauds. The Statute of Frauds requires certain contracts to be in writing or in a stipulated form.

Problems concerning genuineness of assent and writing are discussed in this chapter.

> *Most of the disputes in the world arise from words.*
> Lord Mansfield, C. J.
> Morgan v. Jones *(1773)*

genuineness of assent
The requirement that a party's assent to a contract be genuine.

MISTAKES

A **mistake** occurs where one or both of the parties has an erroneous belief about the subject matter, value, or some other aspect of the contract. Mistakes may be either *unilateral* or *mutual*. The law permits **rescission** of some contracts made in mistake.

rescission
An action to undo the contract.

Unilateral Mistakes

Unilateral mistakes occur when only one party is mistaken about a material fact regarding the subject matter of the contract. There are three types of situations where the contract may not be enforced due to such a mistake:

1. One party makes a unilateral mistake of fact and the other party knew (or should have known) that a mistake was made.
2. A unilateral mistake occurs because of a clerical or mathematical error that is not the result of gross negligence.
3. The mistake is so serious that enforcing the contract would be unconscionable.[1]

In most cases, however, the mistaken party will not be permitted to rescind the contract. The contract will be enforced on its terms.

unilateral mistake
When only one party is mistaken about a material fact regarding the subject matter of the contract.

Consider This Example   Suppose Trent Anderson wants to purchase a car from the showroom floor. He looks at several models. Although he decides to purchase a car with a sunroof, he does not tell the salesperson about this preference. The model named in the contract he signs does not have this feature, although he believes it does. Anderson's unilateral mistake will not relieve him of his contractual obligation to purchase the car.

In the following case, the court had to decide whether to allow a party out of a contract because of the party's unilateral mistake.

> *Words are chameleons, which reflect the color of their environment.*
> Justice L. Hand
> Commissioner v. National Carbide Co. *(1948)*

Wells Fargo Credit Corp. v. Martin
650 So.2d 531 (1992)
District Court of Appeals of Florida

CASE 11.1

BACKGROUND AND FACTS
Wells Fargo Credit Corporation (Wells Fargo) obtained a judgment of foreclosure on a house owned by Mr. and Mrs. Clevenger. The total indebtedness stated in the judgment was $207,141. The foreclosure sale was scheduled for 11:00 A.M. on July 12, 1991, at the west front door of the Hillsborough County Courthouse. Wells Fargo was represented by a paralegal, who had attended more than 1,000 similar sales. Wells Fargo's handwritten instruction sheet informed the paralegal to make one bid at $115,000, the tax-appraised value of the property. Because the first "1" in the number was close to the "$," the paralegal misread the bid instruction as $15,000 and opened the bidding at that amount. Harley Martin, who was attending his first judicial sale, bid $20,000. The county clerk

gave ample time for another bid and then announced, "$20,000 going once, $20,000 going twice, sold to Harley . . ." The paralegal screamed, "Stop, I'm sorry, I made a mistake!" The certificate of sale was issued to Martin. Wells Fargo filed suit to set aside the judicial sale based on its unilateral mistake. The trial court held for Martin. Wells Fargo appealed.

ISSUE
Does Wells Fargo's unilateral mistake constitute grounds for setting aside the judicial sale?

COURT'S REASONING
The appellate court held that Martin's right to purchase the property vested at the moment the county clerk announced

"sold." Generally, a unilateral mistake will not permit the mistaken party to rescind a contract. The appellate court held that the trial court had the discretion to place the risk of the mistake on Wells Fargo.

DECISION

The appellate court held that Wells Fargo's unilateral mistake did not entitle it to relief from the judicial sale.

Case Questions

Critical Legal Thinking   Should contracts be allowed to be rescinded because of unilateral mistakes? Why or why not?

Business Ethics   Did Wells Fargo act ethically in trying to set aside the judicial sale?

Contemporary Business   Do you think mistakes such as that made by Wells Fargo happen very often in business?

Mutual Mistakes

mutual mistake of fact

A mistake made by both parties concerning a material fact that is important to the subject matter of the contract.

Either party may rescind the contract if there has been a **mutual mistake of a past or existing material fact**.[2] A material fact is one that is important to the subject matter of the contract. An ambiguity in a contract may constitute a mutual mistake of a material fact. An ambiguity occurs where a word or term in the contract is susceptible to more than one logical interpretation. If there has been a mutual mistake, the contract may be rescinded on the ground that no contract has been formed because there has been no "meeting of the minds" between the parties.

Landmark Law

In *Raffles v. Wichelhaus*, the court held that a mutual mistake of fact excused performance of the contract.

In the celebrated case of *Raffles v. Wichelhaus*,[3] which has become better known as the case of the good ship *Peerless*, the parties agreed on a sale of cotton that was to be delivered from Bombay by the ship. There were two ships named *Peerless*, however, and each party, in agreeing to the sale, was referring to a different ship. Because the sailing time of the two ships was materially different, neither party was willing to agree to shipment by the other *Peerless*. The court ruled that there was no binding contract because each party had a different ship in mind when the contract was entered into.

mutual mistake of value

A mistake that occurs if both parties know the object of the contract but are mistaken as to its value.

The courts must distinguish between *mutual mistakes of fact* and *mutual mistakes of value*. A **mutual mistake of value** exists if both parties know the object of the contract but are mistaken as to its value. Here, the contract remains enforceable by either party because the identity of the subject matter of the contract is not at issue. If the rule were different, almost all contracts could later be rescinded by the party who got the "worst" of the deal.

The meaning of words varies according to the circumstances of and concerning which they are used.

Justice Blackburn
Allgood v. Blake (1873)

Consider This Example   Suppose Eileen Ney cleans her attic and finds a painting of tomato soup cans. She has no use for it, so she offers to sell it to Fred Lee for $100. Fred, who likes the painting, accepts the offer and pays Eileen $100. It is later discovered that the painting is worth $200,000 because it was painted by Andy Warhol. Neither party knew this at the time of contracting. It is a mistake of value. Eileen cannot recover the painting.

The issue of mutual mistake was raised in the following case.

Konic International Corp. v. Spokane Computer Services, Inc.

708 P.2d 932 (1985)
Court of Appeals of Idaho

CASE 11.2

BACKGROUND AND FACTS

David Young, an employee of Spokane Computer Services, Inc. (Spokane Computer), was instructed by his employer to investigate the possibility of purchasing a surge protector, a device that protects computers from damaging surges of electrical current. Although Young's investigation turned up several units priced from $50 to $200, none was appropriate for his employer's needs. Young then contacted Konic International Corporation (Konic) by telephone and was referred to a salesman. The salesman described a unit Young

thought would be good, and Young inquired as to the price. The salesman replied, "Fifty-six twenty." The salesman meant $5,620. Young thought he meant $56.20. Young ordered the unit by telephone, and it was shipped and installed in Spokane Computer's office. The error was not discovered until two weeks later when Konic sent Spokane Computer an invoice for $5,620. Spokane Computer decided to return the unit to Konic. Konic sued Spokane Computer for the purchase price of the unit. The trial court held in favor of Spokane Computer. Konic appealed.

ISSUE

Was there a mutual mistake of fact that permitted Spokane Computer to rescind the contract?

COURT'S REASONING

Both parties attributed different meanings to the same term, "fifty-six twenty." Thus, there was no meeting of the minds of the parties. The vast difference between the two prices made price a material term that was expressed in an ambiguous form. Because two meanings were obviously applied, the court concluded that no contract was ever formed between the parties. The court stated, "The mutual misunderstanding of the parties was so basic and so material that any agreement the parties thought they had reached was merely an illusion."

DECISION

The appellate court held that there was a mutual mistake of material fact that permitted Spokane Computer to rescind its contract with Konic. The appellate court affirmed the trial court's judgment in favor of Spokane Computer.

Case Questions

Critical Legal Thinking Should parties be able to rescind a contract because of mutual mistake of fact? Why or why not?

Business Ethics Did either party act unethically in this case?

Contemporary Business Are there any winners or losers when a contract is rescinded based on mutual mistake of fact?

FRAUDULENT MISREPRESENTATION

A **misrepresentation** occurs when an assertion is made that is not in accord with the facts.[4] An **intentional misrepresentation** occurs when one person consciously decides to induce another person to rely and act on a misrepresentation. Intentional misrepresentation is commonly referred to as **fraudulent misrepresentation**, or **fraud**. When a fraudulent misrepresentation is used to induce another to enter into a contract, the innocent party's assent to the contract is not genuine and the contract is voidable by the innocent party.[5] The innocent party can either rescind the contract and obtain restitution or enforce the contract and sue for contract damages.

intentional misrepresentation

Occurs when one person consciously induces another person to rely and act on a misrepresentation. Also called *fraud*.

Fraud includes the pretense of knowledge when knowledge there is none.

Chief Justice Cardozo
Ultramares Corp. v. Touche
(1931)

Entrepreneur and the Law

DON'T BE TAKEN BY FRAUD

Entrepreneurs and other business persons must be on guard in their commercial dealings not to be taken by fraud. Basically, if it sounds "too good to be true," it is a signal that the situation might be fraudulent. Other frauds are difficult to detect. To prove fraud, the following elements must be shown:

1. The wrongdoer made a false representation of material fact.
2. The wrongdoer intended to deceive the innocent party.
3. The innocent party justifiably relied on the misrepresentation.
4. The innocent party was injured.

Each of these elements is discussed in the following paragraphs.

1. *Material Misrepresentation of Fact* A misrepresentation may occur by words (oral or written) or by the conduct of the party. To be actionable as fraud, the misrepresentation must be of a past or existing *material fact*. This means that the misrepresentation must have been a significant factor in inducing the innocent party to enter into the contract. It does not have to be the sole factor. Statements of opinion or predictions about the future generally do not form the basis for fraud.

2. *Intent to Deceive* To prove fraud, the person making the misrepresentation must have either had knowledge that the representation was false or made it without sufficient knowledge of the truth. This is called **scienter** ("guilty mind"). The misrepresentation must have been made with the intent to deceive the innocent party. Intent can be inferred from the circumstances.

3. *Reliance on the Misrepresentation* A misrepresentation is not actionable unless the innocent party to whom the misrepresentation was directed acted upon it. Further, an innocent party who acts in reliance on the misrepresentation must justify his or her reliance.[6] Justifiable reliance generally is found unless the innocent party knew that the misrepresentation was false or was so extravagant as to be obviously false. For example, reliance on a statement such as "This diamond ring is worth $10,000, but I'll sell it to you for $100" would not be justified.

4. *Injury to the Innocent Party* To recover damages, the innocent party must prove that the fraud caused economic injury. The measure of damages is the difference between the value of the property as represented and the actual value of the property. This measure of damages gives the innocent party the "benefit of the bargain." In the alternative, the buyer can rescind the contract and recover the purchase price.

Types of Fraud

There are various types of fraud. Some of the most common ones follow.

fraud in the inception

Occurs if a person is deceived as to the nature of his or her act and does not know what he or she is signing.

fraud in the inducement

Occurs when the party knows what he or she is signing but has been fraudulently induced to enter into the contract.

fraud by concealment

Occurs when one party takes specific action to conceal a material fact from another party.

Business Brief

Although the law permits a victim of fraud to rescind the contract and recover damages from the wrongdoer, often the wrongdoer cannot be found or the money has been spent. Therefore, it is best to be cautious not to become a victim of fraud by questioning deals that are "too good to be true."

A charge of fraud is such a terrible thing to bring against a man that it cannot be maintained in any court unless it is shown that he had a wicked mind.

M. R. Lord Esher
Le Lievre v. Gould (1732)

innocent misrepresentation

Occurs when a person makes a statement of fact that he or she honestly and reasonably believes to be true, even though it is not.

1. **Fraud in the Inception**   **Fraud in the inception**, or **fraud in the factum**, occurs if a person is deceived as to the nature of his or her act and does not know what he or she is signing. Such contracts are void rather than just voidable. For example, suppose Heather brings her professor a grade card to sign. The professor signs the front of the grade card. On the back, however, are contract terms that transfer all of the professor's property to Heather. Here there is fraud in the inception. The contract is void.

2. **Fraud in the Inducement**   A great many fraud cases concern **fraud in the inducement**. Here, the innocent party knows what he or she is signing but has been fraudulently induced to enter into the contract. Such contracts are voidable by the innocent party. For example, suppose Lyle Green tells Candice Young he is forming a partnership to invest in drilling for oil and invites her to invest in this venture. In reality, though, Green intends to use whatever money he receives for his personal expenses, and he absconds with Young's $30,000 investment. Here, there has been fraud in the inducement. Young can rescind the contract and recover the money from Green, if he can be found.

3. **Fraud by Concealment**   **Fraud by concealment** occurs when one party takes specific action to conceal a material fact from another party.[7] For example, suppose that ABC Blouses, Inc. contracts to buy a used sewing machine from Wear-Well Shirts, Inc. Wear-Well did not show ABC the repair invoices from the sewing machine even though ABC asked to see them. Relying on the knowledge that the machine was in good condition and never had to be repaired, ABC bought the machine. If ABC discovers that a significant repair record has been concealed, it can sue Wear-Well for fraud.

4. **Silence as Misrepresentation**   Generally, neither party to a contract owes a duty to disclose all the facts to the other party. Ordinarily, such silence is not a misrepresentation unless (1) nondisclosure would cause bodily injury or death, (2) there is a fiduciary relationship (i.e., a relationship of trust and confidence) between the contracting parties, or (3) federal and state statutes require disclosure. The Restatement (Second) of Contracts specifies a broader duty of disclosure: Nondisclosure is a misrepresentation if it would constitute a failure to act in "good faith."[8]

5. **Misrepresentation of Law**   Usually, a misrepresentation of law is not actionable as fraud. The innocent party cannot generally rescind the contract, because each person to a contract is assumed to know the law that applies to the transaction either through his own investigation or by hiring a lawyer. There is one major exception to this rule: The misrepresentation will be allowed as a ground for rescission of the contract if one party to a contract is a professional who should know what the law is and intentionally misrepresents the law to a less sophisticated contracting party.[9]

Innocent Misrepresentation

An **innocent misrepresentation** occurs when a person makes a statement of fact that he or she honestly and reasonably believes to be true, even though it is not. Innocent misrepresentation is not fraud. If an innocent misrepresentation has been made, the aggrieved party may rescind the contract but may not sue for damages. Often, innocent misrepresentation is treated as a mutual mistake.

In the following case, the court allowed a contract to be rescinded.

Wilson v. Western National Life Insurance Co.

235 Cal.App.3d 981. 1 Cal.Rptr.2d 157 (1991)
California Court of Appeal

CASE 11.3

BACKGROUND AND FACTS
Daniel and Doris Wilson were husband and wife. On August 13, 1985, Daniel fainted from a narcotics overdose and was rushed unconscious to the hospital. Doris accompanied him. Daniel responded to medication used to counteract a narcotics overdose and recovered. The emergency room physician

noted that Daniel had probably suffered from a heroin overdose and that Daniel had multiple puncture sites on his arms.

On October 8, 1985, an agent for Western National Life Insurance Company (Western) met with the Wilsons in their home for the purpose of taking their application for life insurance. The agent asked questions and recorded the Wilsons' responses on a written application form. Daniel answered the following questions:

| 13. In the past 10 years, have you been treated or joined an organization for alcoholism or drug addiction? If "Yes," explain on the reverse side. | **Yes** | **No** |
| | | X |

| 17. In the past 5 years, have you consulted or been treated or examined by any physician or practitioner? | **Yes** | **No** |
| | | X |

Both of the Wilsons signed the application form and paid the agent the first month's premium. Under insurance law and the application form, the life insurance policy took effect immediately. Daniel Wilson died from a drug overdose two days later. Western rescinded the policy and rejected Doris Wilson's claim to recover the policy's $50,000 death benefit for Daniel's death, alleging failure to disclose the August 13, 1985, incident. Doris sued to recover the death benefits. The trial court granted summary judgment for Western. Doris appealed.

ISSUE

Was there a concealment of a material fact that justified Western's rescission of the life insurance policy?

COURT'S REASONING

A material misrepresentation or concealment, whether intentional or innocent, entitles the injured party to rescind the contract. The court held that the Wilsons had made such a misrepresentation by concealment, that it was material, and that Western had relied on it and had been injured. The court found that Western would not have issued the life insurance policy to Daniel Wilson if it had been informed of his prior drug overdose.

DECISION

The appellate court held that there was a concealment by the Wilsons that warranted rescission of the life insurance policy by Western.

Case Questions

Critical Legal Thinking Should a contract be allowed to be rescinded because of an *innocent* misrepresentation? Why or why not?

Business Ethics Do you think the concealment was intentional or innocent?

Contemporary Business Do you think there is very much insurance fraud in this country? Explain.

𝒞ONCEPT SUMMARY   TYPES OF MISREPRESENTATION

| Type of Misrepresentation | Legal Consequences—Innocent Party May: | |
	Sue for Damages	Rescind Contract
Fraud in the inception	Yes	Yes
Fraud in the inducement	Yes	Yes
Fraud by concealment	Yes	Yes
Silence as a misrepresentation	Yes	Yes
Misrepresentation of law	Usually no	Usually no
Innocent misrepresentation	No	Yes

𝒰NDUE INFLUENCE

The courts may permit the rescission of a contract based on the equitable doctrine of **undue influence**. Undue influence occurs when one person (the dominant party) takes advantage of another person's mental, emotional, or physical weakness and unduly persuades that person (the servient party) to enter into a contract. The persuasion by the wrongdoer must overcome the free will of the innocent party. A contract that is entered

undue influence

Occurs when one person takes advantage of another person's mental, emotional, or physical weakness and unduly persuades that person to enter into a contract; the persuasion by the wrongdoer must overcome the free will of the innocent party.

into because of undue influence is voidable by the innocent party.[10] Wills often are challenged as having been made under undue influence.

The following elements must be shown to prove undue influence:

1. A fiduciary or confidential relationship must have existed between the parties.
2. The dominant party must have unduly used his or her influence to persuade the servient party to enter into a contract.

If there is a confidential relationship between persons—such as a lawyer and client, doctor and patient, psychiatrist and patient—any contract made by the servient party that benefits the dominant party is presumed to be entered into under undue influence. This rebuttable presumption can be overcome by proper evidence.

Business Ethics

UNDUE INFLUENCE: FLEECING THE FLOCK

Religions obviously have an influence on their members. People who belong to religions often donate money and property to their churches and religious causes. Most religious giving (and church asking) is legitimate. Sometimes there are charges of illegal and unethical conduct, however. Sometimes the charge is undue influence. Consider the following case.

Elizabeth Dayton Dovydenas was born in 1952. As an heir to the Dayton-Hudson department store chain fortune she was worth approximately $19 million. She married Jonas Dovydenas.

When Elizabeth was interested in finding a church to attend, the couple's housekeeper suggested her church, The Bible Speaks (TBS). Elizabeth and Jonas went to a TBS service, liked what they saw, and left a $500 check in the collection plate.

After this, pastors from TBS contacted them and set up a tea with Carl Stevens, the founder of TBS. Stevens had been a fundamentalist preacher for 26 years. At the first meeting, Stevens asked Elizabeth for money for a counseling center, and she gave him a check for $2,000.

Elizabeth became a devout member of TBS. Eventually, Elizabeth met with Stevens alone on a daily basis after Bible classes and attended other functions with him. She abandoned her prior friends and saw little of her family.

One day in the fall of 1984, as she was driving with Stevens, Elizabeth heard a voice telling her to give $1 million to TBS. Elizabeth gave $1 million of Dayton-Hudson stock to TBS.

Elizabeth was led to believe that large gifts by her to TBS could affect events on earth. She was also told that she had to obey Stevens because he was the highest authority on earth.

In March 1985, Elizabeth told Stevens that she heard God tell her to give $5 million to TBS in June. Elizabeth had planned a trip to Florida on April 18. Before she left, she was told that a TBS pastor had been detained in Romania and that "they're probably pulling his fingernails out right now." Elizabeth went to Florida but called Stevens on April 21 and told him that she wanted to give the $5 million right away so the pastor would be released. Stevens did not tell her that the pastor had already been released. Elizabeth was cautioned against telling anyone that she had worked a miracle. The gift of $5 million of Dayton-Hudson stock was completed on May 13.

After being tricked away from Stevens by her relatives, Elizabeth was deprogrammed from her "cult" experience. Elizabeth then sued to rescind her gifts to TBS, alleging that Stevens and TBS had engaged in undue influence. The district court agreed and ordered that the gifts be rescinded. The court of appeals reversed as to the $1-million gift, finding no undue influence at the time this gift was made, but affirmed as to the $5-million gift. The court of appeals stated, "Any species, of coercion, whether physical, mental, or moral, which subverts the sound judgment and genuine desire of the individual, is enough to constitute undue influence." [*Dovydenas v. The Bible Speaks*, 869 F.2d 628 (1st Cir. 1989)]

1. Did Stevens and the other members of TBS act ethically in this case?
2. Should the plaintiff have been saved from her folly?

*D*URESS

duress

Occurs when one party threatens to do a wrongful act unless the other party enters into a contract.

Duress occurs where one party threatens to do some wrongful act unless the other party enters into a contract. If a party to a contract has been forced into making the contract, the assent is not voluntary. Such contracts are not enforceable against the innocent party.

The threat to commit physical harm or extortion unless someone enters into a contract constitutes duress. So does a threat to bring (or not drop) a criminal lawsuit. Such threats are duress even if the criminal lawsuit is well founded.[11] A threat to bring (or not drop) a civil lawsuit, however, does not constitute duress unless such a suit is frivolous or brought in bad faith.

The courts have recognized another type of duress, **economic duress**. Economic duress usually occurs when one party to a contract refuses to perform his or her contractual duties unless the other party pays an increased price, enters into a second contract with the threatening party, or the like. The duressed party must prove that he or she had no choice but to give in to the threat.

economic duress

Occurs when one party to a contract refuses to perform his or her contractual duties unless the other party pays an increased price, enters into a second contract with the threatening party, or undertakes a similar action.

Contemporary Business Environment

ECONOMIC DURESS

Economic duress is also called **business compulsion**, **business duress**, and **economic coercion**. The appropriateness of these terms becomes apparent when the facts of the following case are examined.

Ashton Development, Inc. (Ashton), hired Bob Britton, Inc. (Britton), a general contractor, to build a development for it. Britton signed a contract with a subcontractor, Rich & Whillock, Inc. (R & W), to provide grading and excavation work at the project. The contract stated that "any rock encountered will be considered an extra at current rates" and expressly excluded blasting work. The contract price was $112,990. In late March 1981, when R & W encountered rock at the project site, a meeting was held between the parties to discuss the problem. Britton directed R & W to go ahead with the rock work and agreed to pay for the additional work. R & W proceeded with the excavation work and rock removal, which included blasting.

On June 17, 1981, after completing all of the required work and receiving $109,363 in payments to date, R & W submitted a final bill to Britton for $72,286. The total bill was $68,659 above the original contract price.

Ashton and Britton refused to pay this amount. R & W told Britton that it would go "broke" if payment was not received. On July 10, 1981, Britton presented R & W with an agreement whereby Britton would pay $25,000 upon the signing of the agreement and another $25,000 on August 10, 1981. When R & W complained of the financial bind it was in, Britton stated: "I have a check for you, and you just take it

or leave it, this is all you get. If you don't take this you have got to sue me." After claiming that is was "blackmail," R & W accepted the $25,000 check. Britton did not pay the other $25,000 until August 20, 1981, after requiring R & W to sign a release of claims form.

In December 1981, R & W sued Ashton and Britton for breach of contract. The defendants argued that the settlement agreement and release signed by R & W prevented it from collecting. The trial and appellate courts held in favor of R & W, finding that Ashton and Britton's tactics amounted to economic duress. In applying the doctrine of economic duress to the case, the court stated: "The underlying concern of the economic duress doctrine is the enforcement in the marketplace of certain minimal standards of business ethics." The court found that Ashton and Britton had acted in bad faith when they refused to pay R & W's final billing and offered instead to pay a compromise amount of $50,000. At the time of their bad faith breach and settlement offer, Ashton and Britton knew that R & W was a new company overextended to creditors and subcontractors and faced with imminent bankruptcy if not paid its final billing. Under these circumstances, the court found that the July 10 agreement and the August 20 release were products of economic duress and were therefore unenforceable. The court ordered Ashton and Britton to pay the balance due on the contract to R & W. [*Rich & Whillock, Inc. v. Ashton Development, Inc.*, 157 Cal.App.3d 1154, 204 Cal.Rptr. 86 (Cal.App. 1984)]

STATUTE OF FRAUDS: WRITING REQUIREMENT

In 1677, the English Parliament enacted a statute called "An Act for the Prevention of Frauds and Perjuries." This act required that certain types of contracts had to be in writing and signed by the party against whom enforcement was sought. Today, all states have enacted a **Statute of Frauds** that requires certain types of contracts to be in *writing*. This statute is intended to ensure that the terms of important contracts are not forgotten, misunderstood, or fabricated.

Statute of Frauds

State statute that requires certain types of contracts to be in writing.

Although the statutes vary slightly from state to state, most states require the following types of contracts to be in writing.[12]

Statute of Frauds: That unfortunate statute, the misguided application of which has been the cause of so many frauds.

Bacon, V.C.
Morgan v. Worthington (1878)

- Contracts involving interests in land
- Contracts that by their own terms cannot possibly be performed within one year
- Collateral contracts where a person promises to answer for the debt or duty of another
- Promises made in consideration of marriage
- Contracts for the sale of goods for more than $500
- Real estate agents' contracts
- Agents' contracts where the underlying contract must be in writing
- Promises to write a will
- Contracts to pay debts barred by the statute of limitations or discharged in bankruptcy
- Contracts to pay compensation for services rendered in negotiating the purchase of a business
- Finders fee contracts

Business Brief

Although only certain contracts must be in writing under the Statute of Frauds, it is good practice to place other contracts in writing so there is no dispute as to the terms of the contract at a later date.

Generally, an *executory contract* that is not in writing even though the Statute of Frauds requires it to be is unenforceable by either party. (If the contract is valid in all other respects, however, it may be voluntarily performed by the parties.) The Statute of Frauds is usually raised by one party as a defense to the enforcement of the contract by the other party. If an oral contract that should have been in writing under the Statute of Frauds is already executed, neither party can seek to rescind the contract on the ground of noncompliance with the Statute of Frauds.

Entrepreneur and the Law

AN ORAL CONTRACT ISN'T WORTH THE PAPER IT'S WRITTEN ON

The Statute of Frauds, which requires certain contracts to be in writing before they are enforceable, is designed to prevent fraud. Entrepreneurs and other businesspersons should know the requirements of the state's Statute of Frauds; otherwise they may find themselves with an unenforceable oral contract. Consider the following case.

Whitman Heffernan Rhein & Co., Inc. (Whitman) is a company that provides financial advice to firms planning mergers and acquisitions. The Griffin Company (Griffin), which is owned primarily by Merv Griffin, was negotiating to purchase Resorts International, Inc. from Donald Trump. Whitman alleged that it entered into an oral contract to provide the Griffin Company with financial and investment advice in connection with the negotiation of the purchase of Resorts International. Once Griffin completed the acquisition of Resorts International from Trump, Whitman requested payment for its services from Griffin. When Griffin did not pay, Whitman sued Griffin to recover pay-

ment. Griffin asserted the New York Statute of Frauds in defense, arguing that Whitman's alleged contract to provide services in negotiating the purchase of a business had to be in writing to be enforceable, and because Whitman's complaint alleged that it was an oral contract, it was not enforceable.

The New York court agreed with Griffin and held that the alleged contract was oral and therefore barred by the Statute of Frauds. The court stated:

New York General Obligations Law § 5-701(a)(10) provides that an agreement is void, unless evidenced by a writing signed by the party to be charged, if the agreement is a contract to pay compensation for services rendered in negotiating the purchase of a business. The term "negotiating" includes assisting in the consummation of the transaction.

The moral of the story for entrepreneurs and other businesspersons is: Get it in writing! [*Whitman Heffernan Rhein & Co., Inc. v. The Griffin Co.*, 557 N.Y.S.2d 342 (NY 1990)]

real property

The land itself as well as buildings, trees, soil, minerals, timber, plants, crops, and other things permanently affixed to the land.

fixtures

Personal property that is permanently affixed to the real property, such as built-in cabinets in a house.

Contracts Involving Interests in Land

Under the Statutes of Frauds, any contract that transfers an ownership interest in **real property** must be in writing to be enforceable. Real property includes the land itself, buildings, trees, soil, minerals, timber, plants, crops, fixtures, and things permanently affixed to the land or buildings. Certain personal property that is permanently affixed to the real property—for example, built-in cabinets in a house—are **fixtures** that become part of the real property.

Other contracts that transfer an ownership interest in land must be in writing under the Statute of Frauds. These interests include the following:

- **Mortgages**   Borrowers often give a lender an interest in real property as security for the repayment of a loan. This action must be done through the use of a written **mortgage** or **deed of trust**. For example, suppose Procter & Gamble Corporation purchases a factory and borrows part of the purchase price from City Bank. City Bank requires that the factory be used as collateral for the loan and takes a mortgage on the factory. Here, the mortgage must be in writing to be enforceable.
- **Leases**   A **lease** is the transfer of the right to use real property for a specified period of time. Most Statutes of Frauds require leases for a term over one year to be in writing.
- **Life Estates**   On some occasions, a person is given a **life estate** in real property. In other words, the person has an interest in the land for the person's lifetime, and the interest will be transferred to another party on that person's death. A life estate is an ownership interest that must be in writing under the Statute of Frauds.
- **Easements**   An **easement** is a given or required right to use another person's land without owning or leasing it. Easements may be either express or implied. Express easements must be in writing to be enforceable, while implied easements need not be written.

mortgage

An interest in real property given to a lender as security for the repayment of a loan.

Contracts that transfer an ownership interest in real property such as this beachfront must be in writing under the Statute of Frauds.

Part Performance Exception   In an oral contract for the sale of land or transfer of another interest in real property has been partially performed, it may not be possible to return the parties to their *status quo*. To solve this problem, the courts have developed the equitable doctrine of **part performance**. This doctrine allows the court to order such an oral contract to be specifically performed if performance is necessary to avoid injustice. For this performance exception to apply, most courts require that the purchaser either pay part of the purchase price and take possession of the property or make valuable improvements on the land. The following case applies the doctrine of part performance.

part performance

A doctrine that allows the court to order an oral contract for the sale of land or transfer of another interest in real property to be specifically performed if it has been partially performed and performance is necessary to avoid injustice.

Sutton v. Warner
12 Cal.App.4th 415, 15 Cal.Rptr.2d 632 (1993)
California Court of Appeal

CASE 11.4

BACKGROUND AND FACTS
In 1983, Arlene and Donald Warner inherited a one-third interest in a home at 101 Molimo Street in San Francisco. The Warners bought out the other heirs and obtained a $170,000 loan on the property. Donald Warner and Kenneth Sutton were friends. In January 1984, Donald Warner proposed that Sutton and his wife purchase the residence. His proposal included a $15,000 down payment toward the pur-

chase price of $185,000. The Suttons were to pay all the mortgage payments and real estate taxes on the property for five years, and at any time during the five-year period they could purchase the house. All this was agreed to orally. The Suttons paid the down payment and cash payments equal to the monthly mortgage ($1,881) to the Warners. They paid the annual property taxes on the house. The Suttons also made improvement to the property. In July 1988, the Warners reneged on the sales/option agreement. At that time the house had risen in value to between $250,000 and $320,000. The Suttons sued for specific performance of the sales agreement. The Warners defended, alleging that the oral promise to sell real estate had to be in writing under the Statute of Frauds and was therefore unenforceable. The trial court applied the equitable doctrine of part performance and ordered specific performance. The Warners appealed.

ISSUE

Does the equitable doctrine of part performance take this oral contract for the sale of real property out of the Statute of Frauds?

COURT'S REASONING

Normally, a contract to purchase real property must be in writing to satisfy the Statute of Frauds. The court, however, held that part performance by the Suttons—making the down payment, paying the monthly mortgage payments and the annual property tax payment, and making improvements to the property—sufficed to remove the bar of the Statute of Frauds. Therefore, the specific performance of the oral contract to sell real estate is equitable.

DECISION

The appellate court held that the doctrine of part performance applied and that the Statute of Frauds did not prevent the enforcement of the oral contract to sell real estate.

Case Questions

Critical Legal Thinking   What purposes are served by the Statute of Frauds? Explain.

Business Ethics   Did the Warners act ethically in this case? Did the Statute of Frauds give them a justifiable reason not to go through with the deal?

Contemporary Business   Should important business contracts be reduced to writing? Why or why not?

One-Year Rule

one-year rule

An executory contract that cannot be performed by its own terms within one year of its formation must be in writing.

According to the Statute of Frauds, an executory contract that cannot be performed by its own terms within one year of its formation must be in writing.[13] This **one-year rule** is intended to prevent disputes about contract terms that may otherwise occur toward the end of a long-term contract. If the performance of the contract is possible within the one-year period, the contract may be oral.

Business Brief

Employment contracts are often for periods longer than one year. These contracts should be in writing to be enforceable.

The extension of an oral contract might cause the contract to violate the Statute of Frauds. For example, suppose the owner of a Burger King franchise hires Eugene Daly as a manager for six months. This contract may be oral. Assume that after three months the owner and manager agree to extend the contract for an additional 11 months. At the time of the extension, the contract would be for 14 months (the three left on the contract plus 11 added by the extension). The modification would have to be in writing because it exceeds the one-year Statute of Frauds.

Business Ethics

STATUTE OF FRAUDS DOES NOT PREVENT THE ENFORCEMENT OF AN ORAL "LIFETIME" CONTRACT

Most courts strictly construe the Statute of Frauds. Consider the following case. In the mid-1930s, Bill and Jim Doherty, who were brothers, founded an insurance and real estate agency in Andover, Massachusetts. The business was successful. In 1955, Bill discovered that he was seriously ill. Concerned that Jim would be left to run the family business alone, Bill and Jim asked another brother, Joseph, if he was interested in joining the family business. Joseph was apprehensive about doing so because he was superintendent of schools in Easthampton, Connecticut, and was concerned about losing his retirement benefits. Jim (on behalf of the business) orally promised Joe "retirement benefits for his remaining life" equal to his salary at age 65 when he retired. Relying on this promise, Joe quit his job and joined the business. Bill retired on full salary in 1970. Joe retired in 1978 and was paid $2,000 a month in retirement

benefits. Jim retired in 1980 on full salary. The business passed on to the next generation, consisting of Jim's and Joe's children. In 1981, a dispute arose, and Joe's children left the business. Jim's children terminated Joe's retirement payments. Joe sued. The defendants argued that the oral lifetime retirement contract was unenforceable under the Statute of Frauds because it ended up being longer than one year. The trial court held in favor of Joe. The defendants appealed.

The court of appeals held that the Statute of Frauds did not prevent the enforcement of the oral lifetime retirement contract. The court stated:

The fact that the present contract provided for retirement benefits and that the instant dispute, arising during Joe's senior years, pertains to the payment of compensation during retirement, does not indicate that the contract could not have been performed within its initial year, had Joe had the misfortune to die then, while still in his 40s. The jury expressly found that in exchange for Joe's promise to join his brothers in Andover and "work with them for the balance of his working days," Jim (on behalf of Insurance) promised that Joe's "compensation would include retirement benefits for his remaining life." If Joe were to have died within the year, he would have completely fulfilled his promise to work "for the balance of his working days" (because his working days would have been over), and

Insurance would have fulfilled its promise to compensate him for his remaining life.

The court concluded that the oral agreement fell outside the Statute of Frauds and was therefore enforceable [*Doherty v. Doherty Insurance Agency, Inc.*, 878 F.2d 540 (1st Cir. 1989)]

1. Was it ethical for Jim's children to terminate Joe's retirement benefits?
2. Should oral lifetime contracts be enforced? Or should they be required to be in writing?

Collateral Promises

A **collateral** or **guaranty contract** occurs where one person agrees to answer for the debts or duties of another person. Collateral promises are required to be in writing under the Statute of Frauds.[14]

In a guaranty situation, there are at least three parties and two contracts. (See Exhibit 11.1 The *first contract*, which is known as the **original** or **primary contract**, is between the debtor and the creditor. It does not have to be in writing (unless another provision of the Statute of Frauds requires it to be). The *second contract*, called the **guaranty contract**, is between the person who agrees to pay the debt if the primary debtor does not (i.e., the **guarantor**) and the original creditor. The guarantor's liability is secondary because it does not arise unless the party primarily liable fails to perform.

Consider This Example   Jay Hoberman, a recent college graduate, offers to purchase a new automobile on credit from a General Motors dealership. Because the purchaser does not have a credit history, the dealer will agree to sell the car only if there is a guarantor. Jay's mother signs the guaranty contract. She becomes responsible for any payments her son fails to make.

collateral contract

A promise where one person agrees to answer for the debts or duties of another person.

guaranty contract

The contract between the guarantor and the original creditor.

guarantor

The person who agrees to pay the debt if the primary debtor does not.

*𝓔*XHIBIT **11.1**   *Original and Guaranty Contracts*

The "Main Purpose" Exception   If the main purpose of a transaction and an oral collateral contract is to provide pecuniary (i.e., financial) benefit to the guarantor, the collateral contract is treated like an original contract and does not have to be in writing to be enforced.[15] This exception is called the **main purpose** or **leading object exception** to the Statute of Frauds. The exception is intended to ensure that the primary benefactor of the original contract (i.e., the guarantor) is answerable for the debt or duty.

main purpose or leading object exception

If the main purpose of a transaction and an oral collateral contract is to provide pecuniary benefit to the guarantor, the collateral contract does not have to be in writing to be enforced.

Consider This Example Suppose Ethel Brand is president and sole shareholder of Brand Computer Corporation, Inc. Assume that (1) the corporation borrows $100,000 from City Bank for working capital and (2) Ethel orally guarantees to repay the loan if the corporation fails to pay it. City Bank can enforce the oral guaranty contract against Ethel if the corporation does not meet its obligation because the main purpose of the loan was to benefit her as the sole shareholder of the corporation.

Promises Made in Consideration of Marriage

Under the Statute of Frauds, a unilateral promise to pay money or property in consideration for a promise to marry must be in writing. For example, a **prenuptial agreement**, which is a contract entered into by parties prior to marriage that defines their ownership rights in each other's property, must be in writing.

Contracts for the Sale of Goods

Section 201 of the **Uniform Commercial Code (UCC)** is the basic Statute of Frauds provision for sales contracts. It requires that contracts for the sale of goods costing *$500 or more* must be in writing to be enforceable.[16] If the contract price of an original sales contract is below $500, it does not have to be in writing under the UCC Statute of Frauds, but if a modification of the contract increases the sales price to $500 or more, the **modification** has to be in writing to be enforceable.[17]

Agent's Contracts

Many state Statutes of Frauds require that *agent's contracts* to sell real property covered by the Statute of Frauds must be in writing to be enforceable. The requirement is often referred to as the **equal dignity rule**.

Consider This Example Suppose Barney Berkowitz hires Cynthia Lamont, a licensed Century-21 real estate agent, to sell his house. Because a contract to sell real estate must be in writing pursuant to the Statute of Frauds, the equal dignity rule requires the agent's contract to be in writing as well. Some state Statutes of Frauds expressly list the agent's contracts that must be in writing.

Promissory Estoppel

The doctrine of **promissory estoppel** or **equitable estoppel**, is another equitable exception to the strict application of the Statute of Frauds. The Restatement (Second) of Contracts version of promissory estoppel provides that if parties enter into an oral contract that should be in writing under the Statute of Frauds, the oral promise is enforceable against the promisor if these three conditions are met: (1) The promise induces action or forbearance of action by another, (2) the reliance on the oral promise was foreseeable, and (3) injustice can be avoided only by enforcing the oral promise.[18] Where this doctrine applies, the promisor is **estopped** (prevented) from raising the Statute of Frauds as a defense to the enforcement of the oral contract.

prenuptial agreement

A contract entered into by parties prior to marriage that defines their ownership rights in each other's property; must be in writing.

UCC Statute of Frauds

Contracts for the sale of *goods* costing $500 or more must be in writing.

equal dignity rule

A rule that says that agent's contracts to sell property covered by the Statute of Frauds must be in writing to be enforceable.

promissory estoppel

An equitable doctrine that permits enforcement of oral contracts that should have been in writing. It is applied to avoid injustice.

To break an oral agreement which is not legally binding is morally wrong.

Talmud
Bava Metzi'a

Business Ethics

Grape Grower Stomped

Bronco Wine Company (Bronco) crushed grapes and sold them for use in bulk wines. It purchased the grapes it needed from various grape growers. In 1981, Bronco entered into an oral contract with Allied Grape Growers (Allied), a cooperative corporation of many grape growers, to purchase 850 tons of Carnelian grapes for delivery in 1982. Allied had origi-

nally contracted to sell these grapes to United Vintners but received special permission to sell the grapes to Bronco instead.

The 1982 grape crop was the largest to date in California history, and there was a glut of foreign wines on the market. Thus, the price of grapes and wines decreased substantially.

Bronco accepted and paid for one shipment of Carnelian grapes from Allied but refused to accept the rest. By the time Bronco started to reject the highly perishable goods, it was too late for Allied to resell the grapes to United Vintners or others.

Allied sued for breach of contract, and Bronco alleged the Statute of Frauds as its defense. In essence, Bronco argued that it did not have to perform because the contract was not in writing.

The appellate court applied the doctrine of promissory estoppel and prohibited Bronco from raising the Statute of Frauds against enforcement of its oral promise to buy the grapes from Allied. The court stated: "In California, the doctrine of estoppel is proven where one party suffers an uncon-

scionable injury if the Statute of Frauds is asserted to prevent enforcement of oral contracts. There is substantial evidence that Allied's loss was unconscionable given these facts. The Statute of Frauds should not be used in this instance to defeat the oral agreement reached by the parties in this case." The appellate court affirmed the trial court's verdict awarding damages to Allied. [*Allied Grape Growers v. Bronco Wine Company*, 203 Cal.App.3d 432, 249 Cal.Rptr. 872 (Cal.App. 1988)]

1. Is it ever ethical to raise the Statute of Frauds against the enforcement of an oral contract?
2. Should courts apply the equitable doctrine of estoppel to save contracting parties from the Statute of Frauds?

Sufficiency of the Writing

Both the common law of contracts and UCC have adopted several rules regarding the legal sufficiency of written contracts. These rules are discussed in the following paragraphs.

Singing Sand Mountains, Dunhuang, China Styles of contracting vary around the world. In many countries substantial time is necessary to build a relationship of trust before contract negotiations ensue.

Formality of the Writing

Some written commercial contracts are long, detailed documents that have been negotiated by the parties and drafted and reviewed by their lawyers. Others are preprinted forms with blanks that can be filled in to fit the facts of the particular situation.

A written contract does not, however, have to be either drafted by a lawyer or formally typed to be legally binding. Generally, the law only requires a writing containing the essential terms of the parties' agreement. For example, any writing—including letters, telegrams, invoices, sales receipts, checks, and handwritten agreements written on scraps of paper— can be an enforceable contract under this rule.

Required Signature

The Statute of Frauds and the UCC require the written contract, whatever its form, to be signed *by the party against whom enforcement is sought.* The signature of the person who is enforcing the contract is not necessary. Thus, a written contract may be enforceable against one party but not the other party.

Counsel Randle Jackson: In the book of nature, my lords, it is written—Lord Ellenborough: Will you have the goodness to mention the page, sir, if you please.

Lord Campbell
Lives of the Chief Justices
(1857)

Generally, the signature may appear anywhere on the writing. In addition, it does not have to be a person's full legal name. For example, the person's last name, first name, nickname, initials, seal, stamp, engraving, or other symbol or mark (e.g., an *X*) that indicates the person's intent can be binding. The signature may be affixed by an authorized agent.

Contemporary Business Environment

WHAT CONSTITUTES A SIGNATURE?

In the past, courts have accepted nicknames, first names, initials, symbols, and X's as proper signatures of a promisor. But what happens if the promisor does not actually sign the document? Can it be enforced? One court said yes. Consider the following facts.

MRLS Construction Corporation (MRLS), which was the construction manager on a building project, hired a subcontractor, Sime Construction Company (Sime), to work on the project. When Parma Tile, Mosaic & Marble Company, Inc. (Parma), refused to deliver tile to Sime unless MRLS guaranteed payment, MRLS sent the following fax to Parma: "MRLS would guarantee payment for goods delivered to the Nehemiah project in the event Sime Construction does not pay within terms."

The name MRLS was printed across the top of the unsigned fax. Parma delivered the tile to Sime and, when

Sime failed to pay, billed MRLS in reliance on the purported guarantee. MRLS refused to pay. MRLS argued that there was no enforceable contract because the fax was not signed. Parma sued MRLS.

The court rejected this argument and held that the fax constituted an enforceable guarantee because the printed name MRLS appeared across the top of the fax. The court found that this satisfied the signature requirement of the Statute of Frauds. The court stated, "The Statute of Frauds was not meant to be utilized to evade an obligation intentionally incurred. MRLS should not be permitted to evade its obligation because of the current and extensive use of electronic transmissions in modern business transactions." [*Parma Tile, Mosaic & Marble Company, Inc. v. Estate of Short*, New York Law Journal, December 10, 1992]

Integration of Several Writings

integration
The combination of several writings to form a single contract.

Both the common law of contracts and the UCC permit several writings to be **integrated** to form a single written contract. That is, the entire writing does not have to appear in one document to be an enforceable contract.

incorporation by reference
When integration is made by express reference in one document that refers to and incorporates another document within it.

Integration may be by an *express reference* in one document that refers to and incorporates another document within it. This procedure is called **incorporation by reference**. Thus, what may often look like a simple one-page contract may actually be hundreds of pages long. For example, credit cards often incorporate by express reference such documents as the master agreement between the issuer and cardholders, subsequent amendments to the agreement, and such.

Several documents may be integrated to form a single written contract if they are somehow physically attached to each other to indicate a party's intent to show integration. For example, attaching several documents together by a staple, paper clip, or some other means may indicate integration. Placing several documents in the same container (e.g., an envelope) may also indicate integration. This action is called *implied integration*.

Entrepreneur and the Law

INTERPRETING CONTRACT WORDS AND TERMS

When contracts are at issue in a lawsuit, courts are often called upon to interpret the meaning of certain contract words or terms. The parties to a contract may define the words and terms used in their contract. Many written contracts contain a detailed definitional section—usually called a

glossary—that defines many of the words and terms used in the contract. In interpreting the contract, the court is assisted by the glossary's definitions. Businesspersons should consider including a glossary of words and terms in their contracts to make interpretation easier and clearer.

If the parties have not defined the words and terms of a contract, the courts apply the following **standards of interpretation**:

- *Ordinary* words are given their usual meaning according to the dictionary.
- *Technical words* are given their technical meaning, unless a different meaning is clearly intended. Testimony from expert witnesses is often necessary to determine the precise meaning of technical words.
- *Specific terms* are presumed to qualify *general terms*. For example, if a provision in a contract refers to the subject matter as "corn," but a later provision refers to the subject matter as "feed corn" for cattle, this specific term qualifies the general term.

- Where a preprinted form contract is used, typed words in a contract prevail over *preprinted words*. *Handwritten words* prevail over both preprinted and typed words.
- If there is an ambiguity in a contract, the ambiguity will be resolved against the party who drafted the contract.
- If both parties are members of the same trade or profession, words will be given their meaning as used in the trade (i.e., *usage of trade*). If the parties do not want trade usage to apply, the contract must indicate that.
- Words will be interpreted to promote the *principal object* of the contract. For example, if a word is subject to two or more definitions, the court will choose the definition that will advance the principal object of the contract.

The Parol Evidence Rule

By the time a contract is reduced to writing, the parties usually have engaged in prior or contemporaneous discussions and negotiations or exchanged prior writings. Any oral or written words outside of the *four corners* of the written contract are called **parol evidence**. *Parol* means "word."

The **parol evidence rule** was originally developed by courts as part of the common law of contracts. The UCC has adopted the parol evidence rule as part of the law of sales contracts.[19] The parol evidence rule states that if a written contract is a complete and final statement of the parties' agreement (i.e., a **complete integration**), any prior or contemporaneous oral or written statements that alter, contradict, or are in addition to the terms of the written contract are inadmissible in any court proceeding concerning the contract.[20] In other words, a completely integrated contract is viewed as the best evidence of the terms of the parties' agreement.

The parties to a written contract may include a clause stipulating that the contract is a complete integration and the exclusive expression of their agreement and that parol evidence may not be introduced to explain, alter, contradict, or add to the terms of the contract. This type of clause is called a **merger** or **integration clause**. It expressly reiterates the parol evidence rule.

Exceptions to the Parol Evidence Rule There are several major exceptions to the general rule excluding parol evidence. Parol evidence may be admitted in court if it:

- Shows that a contract is void or voidable (e.g., evidence that the contract was induced by fraud, misrepresentation, duress, undue influence, or mistake).
- Explains ambiguous language.
- Concerns *a prior course of dealing or course of performance* between the parties or a *usage of trade*.[21]
- *Fills in the gaps* in the contract (e.g., if a price term or time of performance term is omitted from a written contract, the court can hear parol evidence to imply the reasonable price or time of performance under the contract).
- Corrects an obvious clerical or typographical error. The court can **reform** the contract to reflect the correction.

parol evidence

Any oral or written words outside the four corners of the written contract.

parol evidence rule

A rule that says if a written contract is a complete and final statement of the parties' agreement, any prior or contemporaneous oral or written statements that alter, contradict, or are in addition to the terms of the written contract are inadmissible in court regarding a dispute over the contract.

merger clause

A clause in a contract that stipulates that it is a complete integration and the exclusive expression of the parties' agreement. Parol evidence may not be introduced to explain, alter, contradict, or add to the terms of the contract.

Business Brief

It is good practice to include a merger clause in written contracts to avoid allegations of promises outside the contract.

Contemporary Business Environment

INTEGRATION CLAUSE SUPERSEDES PAROL EVIDENCE

On January 2, 1977, Carl M. Malmstrom applied for a job at Kaiser Aluminum & Chemical Corporation (Kaiser) in its aluminum can division. During the prehiring interviews with Kaiser, Malmstrom questioned his interviewers about the permanency of the position he was offered. Malmstrom testified that at the time he was hired, Mr. Johnson of Kaiser told him "as long as one does a commendable job up to Kaiser's expectations, that you had no fear of being laid off" and that

"Kaiser never laid off anyone unless there was due cause obviously of some nature."

On January 13, 1977, Malmstrom was employed by Kaiser. He signed a one-page agreement with the company concerning his employment. Paragraph 1 provided: "Employer employs and shall continue to employ Employee at such compensation and for such a length of time as shall be mutually agreeable to Employer and Employee." Paragraph 6 of the employment contract was an integration clause that provided "This agreement shall supersede all previous agreements by and between Employer and Employee and shall be retroactive to the date on which Employee commenced his employment."

In April 1981, because of a decrease in business, Kaiser began terminating many employees. On January 5, 1982, Malmstrom was told he was terminated as part of the staff reduction. In the two-year period following Malmstrom's layoff, the number of Kaiser employees declined from 27,000 to 18,000. Malmstrom sued Kaiser for breach of alleged oral contracts to provide permanent employment to him. The trial court granted summary judgment for Kaiser. Malmstrom appealed.

Does the parol evidence rule make the evidence concerning the alleged oral contracts inadmissible? The appellate court held that the written employment agreement between Malmstrom and Kaiser was integrated, and evidence of other alleged oral contracts between the parties was inadmissible, under the parol evidence rule.

Paragraph 6 of the contract provided that the agreement "shall supersede all previous agreements by and between Employer and Employee." The court held that the meaning of this paragraph was clear on its face and Malmstrom offered no alternative meaning. Contrary to Malmstrom's assertion, the alleged oral agreement occurred before he signed the written agreement. The scope of the contract covered the term of employment and the compensation of the employee. It is unlikely that there would be two agreements concerning the term of the employment. The court found that the alleged oral agreement was completely inconsistent with the terms of the written contract.

The court held that the contract was a contract for employment terminable at will and that, because the contract was integrated and provided that it superseded all prior agreements, evidence of an implied agreement that contradicts the terms of the written agreement is not admissible. [*Malmstrom v. Kaiser Aluminum & Chemical Corp.*, 187 Cal.App.3d 299, 231 Cal.Rptr. 820 (Cal.App. 1986)]

International Law

WRITING REQUIREMENT FOR INTERNATIONAL CONTRACTS

Traditionally, many countries require certain contracts to be in writing. In the civil law countries, this requirement generally does not apply to commercial transactions. In Socialist countries, writings usually are required because of the need for certainty both in interpreting and enforcing foreign trade contracts.

Most of the delegates involved in the drafting of the United Nations Convention on Contracts for the International Sale of Goods (CISG) decided that a writing requirement would be inconsistent with modern commercial practice, especially in market economies where speed and informality characterize so many transactions. Some dele-gates, however, insisted that a writing requirement is important for protecting their country's longtime pattern of making foreign trade contracts.

The result of this disagreement was a compromise. Article 11 of the Convention states: "A contract of sale need not be concluded in or evidenced by writing and is not subject to any other requirement as to form. It may be proved by any means, including witnesses." The CISG's Article 96, however, authorizes a contracting nation that requires written sales contracts to stipulate at the time of ratification that Article 11 (and some other provisions of the Convention) does not apply if any party operates a business in that nation.

Chapter Summary

Mistakes, p. 257

Unilateral Mistakes	These occur when only one party is mistaken about a material fact regarding the subject matter of the contract. The legal consequences are:
	1. *General rule.* The mistaken party is not permitted to rescind the contract.
	2. *Exceptions.* The mistaken party can rescind the contract if:
	  a. The other party knew or should have known of the mistake and took advantage of it.
	  b. The mistake occurred because of a clerical or mathematical error that was not the result of gross negligence.
	  c. The mistake is so serious that enforcing the contract would be unconscionable.

Mutual Mistakes	1. *Mutual mistake of fact.* Both parties are mistaken about the essence or object of the contract. Either party may rescind the contract 2. *Mutual mistake of value.* Both parties know the object of the contract but are mistaken as to its value. Neither party may rescind the contract.

Fraudulent Misrepresentation, p. 259

Elements of Fraud	*Fraudulent misrepresentation.* When a person intentionally makes an assertion that is not in accord with the facts. Also called *fraud.*
	1. *Elements of fraud:*
	  a. The wrongdoer made a false representation of material fact.
	  b. The wrongdoer intended to deceive the innocent party.
	  c. The innocent party justifiably relied on the misrepresentation.
	  d. The innocent party was injured.
	2. *Legal consequence if fraudulent misrepresentation is found.* The innocent party may:
	  a. Rescind the contract and obtain restitution, or
	  b. Enforce the contract and sue for damages

Types of Fraud	*Common types of fraud:* 1. *Fraud in the inception.* An innocent person is deceived as to the nature of his or her act. Also called *fraud in the factum.* 2. *Fraud in the inducement.* The wrongdoer fraudulently induces another party to enter into a contract. 3. *Fraud by concealment.* The wrongdoer takes specific action to conceal a material fact from the other party. 4. *Silence as misrepresentation.* The wrongdoer remains silent when he or she is under a legal obligation to disclose a material fact. 5. *Misrepresentation of law.* A professional who should know what the law is intentionally misrepresents the law to a less sophisticated party.
Innocent Misrepresentation	When a person unintentionally makes an assertion that is not in accord with the facts. The innocent party may rescind the contract but cannot recover damages. Innocent misrepresentation is not fraud.

Undue Influence, p. 261

Undue Influence	Occurs when one person takes advantage of another person's mental, emotional, or physical weakness and unduly persuades that person to enter into a contract. A contract entered into under undue influence cannot be enforced.
	1. *Elements of undue influence:*
	  a. A fiduciary or confidential relationship existed between the dominant and servient parties.
	  b. The dominant party unduly used his or her influence to persuade the servient party to enter into a contract.
	2. *Presumption.* If there is a confidential relationship between persons, any contract by the servient party that benefits the dominant party is presumed to be entered into under undue influence. This position is a *rebuttable presumption.*

Duress, p. 262

Duress	Occurs when one party threatens to do some wrongful act unless the other party enters into a contract. A contract entered into under duress cannot be enforced.
	1. *Types of duress:*
	  a. Physical duress
	  b. Extortion
	  c. Economic duress

Statute of Frauds: Writing Requirement, p. 263

Writing Requirement	*Statute of Frauds.* A state statute that requires the following contracts to be in writing: 1. *Contracts involving the transfer of interests in real property.* Includes contracts for the sale of land, buildings and items attached to land, mortgages, leases for a term of more than one year, and express easements. a. *Part performance exception.* Permits the specific enforcement of oral contracts for the sale of land when they have been partially performed to avoid injustice. 2. Contracts that cannot be performed within one year of their formation.

3. Collateral contracts occur where one person promises to answer for the debts or duties of another person. Also called *guaranty contracts*.
   a. *Main purpose exception.* Permits enforcement of oral collateral promises if main or leading purpose of collateral promise is to benefit the guarantor.
4. Promises made in consideration of marriage, such as prenuptial agreements.
5. Agents' contracts to sell real property.
6. Contracts for the sale of goods costing $500 or more. [UCC §201]

Promissory Estoppel   Equitable doctrine that prevents the application of the Statute of Frauds. It permits the enforcement of oral contracts that should otherwise be in writing under the Statute of Frauds to prevent injustice or unjust enrichment.

Sufficiency of the Writing, p. 269

Sufficiency of the Writing
1. *Formality of the writing.* A written contract does not have to be formal or drafted by a lawyer to be enforceable. Informal contracts, such as handwritten notes, letters, and invoices, are enforceable contracts.
2. *Required signature.* The party against whom enforcement of the contract is sought must have signed the contract. The signature may be the person's full legal name, last name, first name, nickname, initials, or other symbol or mark.
3. *Integration of several writings.* Several writings may be integrated to form a contract. Integration may be by:
   a. *Express reference.* One document expressly incorporates another document.
   b. *Implied reference.* Documents are physically attached by staple or by paper clip or are placed in the same envelope.

The Parol Evidence Rule
1. *Parol evidence.* Any oral or written words that are outside of the four corners of a written contract.
2. *Parol evidence rule.* Provides that if a written contract is a complete integration, any prior contemporaneous oral or written statements are inadmissible as evidence to alter or contradict the terms of the written contract.
3. *Exceptions to the parol evidence rule.* Parol evidence may be admitted in court to:
   a. Prove mistake, fraud, misrepresentation, undue influence, or duress.
   b. Explain ambiguous language.
   c. Explain a prior course of dealing or course of performance between the parties or a usage of trade.
   d. Fill in the gaps in a contract.
   e. Correct obvious clerical or typographical errors.

Interpretation of Contracts
The courts have developed the following rules for interpreting contracts:
1. *Ordinary words* are given their usual dictionary meaning.
2. *Technical words* are given their technical meaning, unless a different meaning is clearly intended.
3. *Specific terms* are presumed to qualify *general terms*.
4. *Typed words* prevail over *preprinted words*; *handwritten words* prevail over both preprinted and typed words.
5. Ambiguities in the contract are resolved against the party who drafted the contract.
6. Unless otherwise agreed, words will be given their usual meaning in the trade if both parties are members of the same trade.
7. Words will be interpreted to promote the *principal object* of the contract.

END-OF-CHAPTER INTERNET EXERCISES AND CASE QUESTIONS

Working the Web Internet Exercises

ACTIVITIES

1. For an overview of the developing law of e-commerce and digital signatures see: "Are Online Business Transactions Executed by Electronic Signatures Legally Binding?" at **www.law.duke.edu/journals/ dltr/ARTICLES/2001dltr0005.html**. And Protecting the Digital Consumer: "The Limits of Cyberspace Utopianism" at **www.law.indiana.edu/ilj/v74/no3/rothchil.pdf**.

2. While common law contract principles have general application, many contracts are regulated, on an industry-wide basis, by state statutes. See **www.law.cornell.edu/topics/topic2.html#particular** for examples.

3. For an overview of defenses to contract claims, see **www.west.net/~smith/contracts.htm**.

CRITICAL LEGAL THINKING CASES

11.1 Unilateral Mistake Mrs. Chaney died in 1985, leaving a house in Annapolis, Maryland. The representative of her estate listed the property for sale with a real estate broker, stating that the property was approximately 15,650 square feet. Drs. Steele and Faust made an offer of $300,000 for the property, which was accepted by the estate. A contract for the sale of the property was signed by all of the parties on July 3, 1985. When a subsequent survey done before the deed was transferred showed that the property had an area of 22,047 square feet, the estate requested the buyers to pay more money for the property. When the estate refused to transfer the property to the buyers, they sued for specific performance. Can the estate rescind the contract? [*Steele v. Goettee*, 542 A.2d 847 (Md. App. 1988)]

11.2 Mutual Mistake Ron Boskett, a part-time coin dealer, purchased a dime purportedly minted in 1916 at the Denver Mint for nearly $450. The fact that the *D* on the coin signified Denver mintage made the coin rare and valuable. Boskett sold the coin to Beachcomber Coins, Inc. (Beachcomber), a retail coin dealer, for $500. A principal of Beachcomber examined the coin for 15 to 45 minutes prior to its purchase. Soon thereafter, Beachcomber received an offer of $700 for the coin subject to certification of its genuineness by the American Numismatic Society. When this organization labeled the coin counterfeit, Beachcomber sued Boskett to rescind the purchase of the coin. Can Beachcomber rescind the contract? [*Beachcomber Coins, Inc. v. Boskett*, 400 A.2d 78 (NJ 1979)]

11.3 Fraud Robert McClure owned a vehicle salvage and rebuilding business. He listed the business for sale and had a brochure printed that described the business and stated that during 1981 the business grossed $581,117 and netted $142,727. Fred H. Campbell saw the brochure and inquired about buying the business. Campbell hired a CPA to review McClure's business records and tax returns, but the CPA could not reconcile these with the income claimed for the business in the brochure. When Campbell asked McClure about the discrepancy, McClure stated that the business records did and tax returns did not accurately reflect the cash flow or profits of the business because it was such a high-cash operation with much of the cash not being reported to the Internal Revenue Service on tax returns. McClure signed a warranty that stated the true income of the business was as represented in the brochure. Campbell bought the business based on these representations. The business, however, although operated in substantially the same manner as when owned by McClure, failed to yield a net income similar to that warranted by McClure. Evidence showed that McClure's representations were substantially overstated. Campbell sued McClure for damages for fraud. Who wins? [*Campbell v. McClure*, 182 Cal.App.3d 806, 227 Cal.Rptr. 450 (Cal.App. 1986)]

11.4 Fraud James L. "Skip" Deupree, a developer, was building a development of town houses called Point South in Destin, Florida. All the town houses in the development were to have individual boat slips. Sam and Louise Butner, husband and wife,

bought one of the town houses. The sales contract between Deupree and the Butners provided that a boat slip would be built and included in the price of the town house. The contract stated that permission from the Florida Department of Natural Resources (DNR) had to be obtained to build the boat slips. It is undisputed that a boat slip adds substantially to the value of the property and that the Butners relied on the town house having a boat slip. Prior to the sale of the town house to the Butners, the DNR had informed Deupree that it objected to the plan to build the boat slips and that permission to build them would probably not be forthcoming. Deupree did not tell the Butners this information but instead stated that there would be "no problem" in getting permission from the state to build the boat slips. When the DNR would not approve the building of the boat slips for the Butner's town house, they sued for damages for fraud. Who wins? [*Deupree v. Butner*, 522 So.2d 242 (AL 1988)]

11.5 Economic Duress Mr. Weller, who was in business in Coalinga, California, filed tax returns for 1943, 1944, and 1945 using the cash basis. Weller then hired Mr. Eyman, a CPA, to prepare his 1946 income tax return. While preparing the 1946 return using the accrual basis, Eyman examined the prior years' returns. Based on Eyman's suggestion, Eyman prepared revised tax returns for the prior years and Weller submitted these to the Internal Revenue Service (IRS) claiming a $1,800 refund. Instead of receiving the refund, however, the IRS assessed Weller $118,000 in unpaid taxes and fines. Eyman told Weller that the proposed assessment was asinine, and it was a simple matter to clean up. Weller contracted with Eyman to do the necessary work for $1,000. After obtaining several extensions, the IRS notified Weller and Eyman that Monday, September 18, 1950, was the deadline for filing a protest to the proposed assessment. On Saturday, September 16, Eyman called Weller to his office to sign the protest. When Weller got there, Eyman produced a written contract purporting to be a fee arrangement whereby Eyman was to receive $1,000 plus $7\frac{1}{2}$ percent of any monies saved of the assessment. When Weller refused to sign the new fee agreement, Eyman told him that the protest had to be in the mail that afternoon to reach the IRS on Monday, and that if it were not filed Weller would be liable for the $118,000 assessment. Weller signed the fee agreement and the protest was timely filed with the IRS. Weller filed a complaint to have the new fee agreement rescinded. Who wins? [*Thompson Crane & Trucking Co. v. Eyman*, 267 P.2d 1043, 123 Cal.App.2d 904 (Cal. App. 1954)]

11.6 Undue Influence Conrad Schaneman Sr. had eight sons and five daughters. He owned four 80-acre farms in the Scottsbluff area of Nebraska. Conrad was born in Russia and could not read or write English. Prior to 1974, all his children had frequent contact with Conrad and helped with his needs. In 1974, his eldest son, Lawrence, advised the other children that he would henceforth manage his father's business affairs. On March 18, 1975, after much urging by Lawrence, Conrad deeded the farm to Lawrence for $23,500. Evidence showed that at the time of the sale the reasonable fair market value of the farm was between $145,000 and $160,000. At the time of the conveyance, Conrad was over 80 years old; had deteriorated in health; suffered from heart problems, diabetes, high and uncontrollable blood sugar levels; weighed almost 300 pounds; had difficulty breathing; could not walk more than 15 feet; and had to have a jackhoist lift him in and out of the bathtub. He was for all purposes an invalid, relying on Lawrence for most of his personal needs, transportation, banking, and other business matters. After Conrad died, the conservators of the estate brought this action to cancel the deed transferring the farm to Lawrence. Can the conservators cancel the deed? [*Schaneman v. Schaneman*, 291 N.W.2d 412 (NE 1980)]

11.7 Undue Influence Margaret Delorey was a client of Joseph P. Plonsky, an attorney. In addition, they were friends of long standing. In September 1976, Delorey telephoned Plonsky's office and told him that she wanted him to draft a will for her naming him as executor and leaving everything she owned to him. Plonsky drafted the will and mailed it to her. She had the will executed and witnessed at a bank and mailed the will back to Plonsky. When Delorey died, Plonsky, as the sole legatee, attempted to take control under the will. At the time of her death, Delorey was survived by two nephews, two nieces, two grandnephews, and one grandniece, none of whom were named in the will. Does the doctrine of undue influence apply in this case? [*Matter of Delorey*, 529 N.Y.S.2d 153, 141 A.D.2d 540 (N.Y. App. 1988)]

11.8 Land Contract In 1976, Fritz Hoffman and Fritz Frey contacted the Sun Valley Company (Company) about purchasing a 1.64-acre piece of property known as the "Ruud Mountain Property," located in Sun Valley, Idaho, from the Company. Mr. Conger, a representative of the Company, was authorized to sell the property, subject to the approval of the executive committee of the Company. On January 21, 1977, Conger reached an agreement on the telephone with Hoffman and Frey whereby they would purchase the property for $90,000, payable at 30 percent down, with the balance to be payable quarterly at an annual interest rate of $9\frac{3}{4}$ percent. The next day Hoffman sent Conger a letter confirming the conversation. The executive committee of the Company approved the sale. Sun Valley Realty prepared the deed of trust, note, seller's closing statement, and other loan documents. Before the documents were executed by either side, however, the Company sold all its assets, including the Ruud Mountain Property, to another purchaser. When the new owner refused to sell the Ruud Mountain lot to Hoffman and Frey, they brought this action for specific performance of the oral contract. Do they win? [*Hoffman v. Sun Valley Company*, 628 P.2d 218 (ID 1981)]

11.9 Land Contract In 1955, Robert Briggs and his wife purchased a home located at 167 Lower Orchard Drive, Levittown, Pennsylvania. They made a $100 down payment and borrowed the balance of $11,600 on a 30-year mortgage. In late 1961, when the Briggs were behind on their mortgage payments, they entered into an oral contract to sell the house to Winfield and Emma Sackett if the Sacketts would pay the three months' arrearages on the loan and agree to make future payments on the mortgage. Mrs. Briggs and Mrs. Sackett were sisters. The Sacketts paid the arrearages,

moved into the house, and have lived there to date. In 1976, Robert Briggs filed an action to void the oral contract as in violation of the Statute of Frauds and evict the Sacketts from the house. Who wins? [*Briggs v. Sackett*, 418 A.2d 586 (Pa.App. 1980)]

11.10 One-Year Contract Robert S. Ohanian was vice president of sales for the West Region of Avis Rent a Car System, Inc. (Avis). Officers of Avis testified that Ohanian's performance in the West Region was excellent and, in a depressed economic period, Ohanian's West Region stood out as the one region that was growing and profitable. In the fall of 1980, when Avis's Northeast Region was doing badly, the president of Avis asked Ohanian to take over that region. Ohanian was reluctant to do so, since he and his family liked living in San Francisco, he had developed a good "team" in the West Region, was secure in his position, and feared the politics of the Northeast Region. Ohanian agreed to the transfer only after the general manager of Avis orally told him, "Unless you screw up badly, there is no way you are going to get fired—you will never get hurt here in this company." Ohanian did a commendable job in the Northeast Region. Approximately one year later, on July 27, 1982, at the age of 47, Ohanian was fired without cause by Avis. Ohanian sued Avis for breach of the oral lifetime contract. Avis asserted the Statute of Frauds against this claim. Who wins? [*Ohanian v. Avis Rent a Car System, Inc.*, 779 F.2d 101 (2nd Cir. 1985)]

11.11 Guaranty Contract On May 17, 1979, David Brown met with Stan Steele, a loan officer with the Bank of Idaho (now First Interstate Bank) to discuss borrowing $5,000 from the bank to start a new business. After learning that he did not qualify for the loan on the basis of his own financial strength, Brown told Steele that his former employers, James and Donna West of California, might be willing to guarantee the payment of the loan. On May 18, 1979, Steele talked to Mr. West, who orally stated on the telephone that he would personally guarantee the loan to Brown. Based on this guarantee, the bank loaned Brown $5,000. The bank sent a written guarantee to Mr. and Mrs. West for their signature, but it was never returned to the bank. When Brown defaulted on the loan, the bank filed suit against the Wests to recover on their guarantee contract. Are the Wests liable? [*First Interstate Bank of Idaho, N.A. v. West*, 693 P.2d 1053 (ID 1984)]

11.12 Guaranty Contract Six persons, including Benjamin Rosenbloom and Alfred Feiler, were members of the board of directors of the Togs Corporation. A bank agreed to loan the corporation $250,000 if the members of the board would personally guarantee the payment of the loan. Feiler objected to signing the guarantee to the bank because of other pending personal financial negotiations that the contingent liability of the guarantee might adversely affect. Feiler agreed with Rosenbloom and the other board members that if they were held personally liable on the guarantee, he would pay his one-sixth share of that amount to them directly. Rosenbloom and the other members of the board signed the personal guarantee with the bank, and the bank made the loan to the corporation. When the corporation defaulted on the loan, the five guarantors had to pay the loan amount to the bank. When they attempted to collect a one-sixth share from Feiler, he refused to pay, alleging that his oral promise had to be in writing under the Statute of Frauds. Does Feiler have to pay the one-sixth share to the other board members? [*Feiler v. Rosenbloom*, 416 A.2d 1345 (Md.App. 1980)]

11.13 Promissory Estoppel Natale and Carmela Castiglia were married in 1919 in Colorado. Carmela had a son from a previous marriage, Christie Lo Greco, who lived with them. Natale and Carmela moved to California where they invested their assets of $4,000 in agricultural property. Christie, then in his early teens, moved with them to California. In 1926, Christie, then 18 years old, decided to leave home and seek an independent living. Natale and Carmela, however, wanted him to stay with them and participate in the family venture. They made an oral promise to Christie that if he stayed home and worked they would leave their property to him by will. Christie accepted and remained home and worked the family venture. He received only his room and board and spending money. When Christie married, Natale told him that his wife should move in with the family and that Christie need not worry, for he would receive all the property when Natale and Carmela died. Natale and Carmela entered into identical wills leaving their property to Christie when they died. Natale died in the late 1940s. Shortly before his death, without the knowledge of Christie or Carmela, he had changed his will and left his share of the property to his grandson, Carmen Monarco. Christie sued to enforce Natale's oral promise. Does the doctrine of promissory estoppel prevent the application of the Statute of Frauds in this case? [*Monarco v. Lo Greco*, 220 P.2d 737, 35 Cal.2d 621 (CA 1950)]

11.14 Promissory Estoppel The Atlantic Wholesale Company (Atlantic), which is located in Florence, South Carolina, is in the business of buying and selling gold and silver for customers' accounts. Gary A. Solondz, a New York resident, became a customer of Atlantic's in 1979 and thereafter made several purchases through Atlantic. On January 23, 1980, Solondz telephoned Atlantic and received a quotation on silver bullion. Solondz then bought 300 ounces of silver for a total price of $12,978. Atlantic immediately contacted United Precious Metals in Minneapolis and purchased the silver for Solondz. The silver was shipped to Atlantic, who paid for it. Atlantic placed the silver in its vault while it awaited payment from Solondz. When Atlantic telephoned Solondz about payment, he told Atlantic to continue to hold the silver in its vault until he decided whether to sell it. Meanwhile, the price of silver had fallen substantially and continued to fall. When Solondz refused to pay for the silver, Atlantic sold it for $4,650, sustaining a loss of $8,328. When Atlantic sued Solondz to recover this loss, Solondz asserted that the Statute of Frauds prevented enforcement of his oral promise to buy the silver. Does the doctrine of promissory estoppel prevent the application of the Statute of Frauds in this case? [*Atlantic Wholesale Co., Inc. v. Solondz*, 320 S.E.2d 720 (S.C.App. 1984)]

11.15 Sufficiency of a Writing Irving Levin and Harold Lipton owned the San Diego Clippers Basketball Club, a professional basketball franchise. On December 3, 1980, Levin and Lipton met with Philip Knight to discuss the sale of the Clippers to Knight. After the meeting, they both initialed a three-page handwritten memorandum that Levin had drafted during the meeting. The memorandum outlined the major terms of their discussion, including subject matter, price, and the parties to the agreement. On December 13, 1980, Levin and Lipton forwarded to Knight a letter and proposed sale agreement. Two days later, Knight informed Levin that he had decided not to purchase the Clippers. Levin and Lipton sued Knight for breach of contract. Knight argued in defense that the handwritten memorandum was not enforceable because it did not satisfy the Statute of Frauds. Is he correct? [*Levin v. Knight*, 865 F.2d 1271 (9th Cir. 1989)]

BUSINESS ETHICS CASES

11.16 Business Ethics The First Baptist Church of Moultrie, Georgia, invited bids for the construction of a music, education, and recreation building. The bids, which were to be opened on May 15, 1986, were to be accompanied by a bid bond of 5 percent of the bid amount. Barber Contracting Company (Barber) submitted a bid in the amount of $1,860,000. A bid bond in the amount of 5 percent of the bid—$93,000—was issued by the American Insurance Company. The bids were opened by the church on May 15, 1986, as planned, and Barber's was the lowest bid.

On May 16, 1986, Albert W. Barber, the president of Barber Contracting Company, informed the church that its bid was in error and should have been $143,120 higher. The error was caused in totaling the material costs on Barber's estimate worksheets. The church had not been provided these worksheets. On May 20, 1986, Barber sent a letter to the church stating that it was withdrawing its bid. The next day the church sent a con-

struction contract to Barber containing the original bid amount. When Barber refused to sign the contract and refused to do the work for the original contract price, the church signed a contract with the second lowest bidder, H & H Construction and Supply Company, Inc,. to complete the work for $1,919,272. The church sued Barber Contracting Company and the American Insurance Company seeking to recover the amount of the bid bond. Who wins? Did Barber act ethically in trying to get out of the contract? Did the church act ethically in trying to enforce Barber's bid? [*First Baptist Church of Moultrie v. Barber Contracting Co.*, 377 S.E. 2d 717 (Ga.App. 1989)]

11.17 Business Ethics Adolfo Mozzetti, who owned a construction company, orally promised his son, Remo, that if Remo would manage the family business for their mutual benefit and would take care of him for the rest of his life, he would leave the family home to Remo. Section 2714 of the Delaware Code requires contracts for the transfer of land to be in writing. Section 2715 of the Delaware Code requires testamentary transfers of real property to be in writing. Remo performed as requested: he managed the family business and took care of his father until the father died. When the father died, his will devised the family home to his daughter, Lucia M. Shepard.

Remo brought this action to enforce his father's oral promise that the home belonged to him. The daughter argued that the will should be upheld. Who wins? Did the daughter act ethically in trying to defeat the father's promise to leave the property to the son? Did the son act ethically in trying to defeat his father's will? [*Shepard v. Mozzetti*, 545, A.2d 621 (DE 1988)]

 ## BRIEFING THE CASE WRITING ASSIGNMENT

Read the following case, which has been excerpted from the court's opinion. Review and brief the case.

Continental Airlines, Inc. v. McDonnell Douglas Corporation, 216 Cal.App.3d 388, 264 Cal.Rptr. 779 (1990) Court of Appeals of California

Hoffman, Associate Justice

This action was commenced by plaintiff and respondent Continental Airlines (Continental) in Los Angeles Superior Court on December 3, 1979, and alleged, against defendant and appellant McDonnell Douglas Corporation (Douglas), causes of action for deceit. On January 30, 1986, the jury returned verdicts in favor of Continental for $17 million on its claims for fraud by misrepresentation and fraud by nondisclosure of known facts. The judgment was granted. This appeal is from that judgment. We affirm the judgment as modified.

On March 1, 1978, a Continental DC-10 aircraft, which had been delivered to Continental by Douglas in 1972, was in its takeoff roll at Los Angeles International Airport when two tires burst on the left landing gear. The captain elected to try to stop the plane, but it ran off the end of the runway at 85 miles per hour. The landing gear broke through the tarmac, burrowed into the ground, and was ripped from the wing, making a 3.7 foot hole which allowed fuel to pour from the wing fuel tanks. The plane was severely damaged by the resulting fire and rendered unrepairable.

Douglas had approached Continental in 1968 to sell Continental DC-10 aircraft. Douglas used a series of briefings and sales brochures in its sales campaign. The sales brochures given to Continental consisted of hundreds of pages of technical information drafted by Douglas's engineers, and reviewed by its top management, for the express purpose of explaining the DC-10 design and a "Detail Type Specification" to potential aircraft purchasers. That specification, as its name implies, described the technical details of the DC-10. The Douglas briefings covered the landing gear and wing design, as did many of its brochures. Continental personnel used the brochures to write portions of Continental's "Tri-Jet Evaluation," a comparison between the DC-10 and Lockheed's L-1011, which became a basis for Continental's decision to purchase the DC-10. When Continental decided to purchase the DC-10, instead of the L-1011 aircraft, it finalized a purchase agreement with Douglas which incorporated by reference the Detail Specification for the DC-10.

The brochures contained statements that "the fuel tank will not rupture under crash load conditions"; that the landing gear "are designed for wipe-off

without rupturing the wing fuel tank"; that "the support structure is designed to a higher strength than the gear to prevent fuel tank rupture due to an accidental landing gear overload"; that the DC-10 "is designed and tested for crashworthiness"; that the "landing gear will be tested" to demonstrate the fail safe integrity and wipe-off characteristics of the gear design; and that "good reliability" for the DC-10 landing gear could be predicted with an "usually high degree of confidence" because of its close similarity to the successful design on the DC-8 and DC-9 aircraft.

Douglas argues that "the Uniform Commercial Code and cases interpreting it have recognized that general promotional observations of this type are merely expressions of opinion that are not actionable as fraudulent statements." The alleged false representations in the subject brochures were not statements of "opinion or mere puffing." They were, in essence, representations that the DC-10 was a safe aircraft. Promises of safety are not statements of opinion— they are representations of fact.

Douglas contends in its opening brief that there was no substantial evidence that its pre-contract representations were material or that Continental reasonably relied on them in deciding to purchase the DC-10. The materiality of the representations can hardly be questioned. Any airline shopping for aircraft to service its customers naturally searches for planes that are safe. Where representations have been made in regard to a material matter and action has been taken, in the absence of evidence showing the contrary, reliance on the representations will be presumed. Here, both materiality and reliance are demonstrated by the fact the Continental evaluated the DC-10 breakaway design in its "Tri-Jet Evaluation," which compared the DC-10 with the L-1011 for the purpose of deciding which aircraft to purchase. Douglas was the only possible source for the information; there was no way Continental could independently investigate or analyze the adequacy of that design. The foregoing provides more than substantial evidence that Continental relied on Douglas's representations regarding landing gear breakaway in choosing to purchase the DC-10 and that those representations were material.

False representations made recklessly and without regard for their truth in order to induce action by another are the equivalent of misrepresentations knowingly and intentionally uttered. Therefore, there is substantial evidence of the requisite intent for intentional fraud. For the forgoing reasons we conclude the evidence supports the jury's findings of liability for fraud. The judgment is modified to reflect an award of prejudgment interest in the amount $9,549,750. As so modified, the judgment is affirmed.

ENDNOTES

1. Restatement (Second) of Contracts, § 153.
2. Restatement (Second) of Contracts, § 152.
3. 159 Eng. Rep. 375 (1864).

4. Restatement (Second) of Contracts, § 159.
5. Restatement (Second) of Contracts, §§ 163 and 164.
6. Restatement (Second) of Contracts, § 172.

7. Restatement (Second) of Contracts, § 160.
8. Restatement (Second) of Contracts, § 161.
9. Restatement (Second) of Contracts, § 170.
10. Restatement (Second) of Contracts, § 177.
11. Restatement (Second) of Contracts, § 176.
12. Restatement (Second) of Contracts, § 110.
13. Restatement (Second) of Contracts, § 130.
14. Restatement (Second) of Contracts, § 112.

15. Restatement (Second) of Contracts, § 116.
16. UCC § 2-201(1).
17. UCC § 2-209(3).
18. Restatement (Second) of Contracts, § 139.
19. UCC § 2-202.
20. Restatement (Second) of Contracts, § 213.
21. UCC §§ 1-205, 2-202, and 2-208.

CHAPTER 12

Third-Party Rights and Discharge

An honest man's word is as good as his bond.

—Don Quixote

Chapter Objectives

After studying this chapter, you should be able to:

1. Describe assignment of contracts and what contract rights are assignable.

2. Define anti-assignment and approval clauses and determine their lawfulness.

3. Describe a delegation of duties and explain the liability of the parties to a delegation.

4. Define an intended beneficiary and describe his or her rights under a contract.

5. Define an incidental beneficiary.

6. Define a covenant.

7. Distinguish between conditions precedent, conditions subsequent, and concurrent conditions.

8. Explain when the performance of a contract is excused because of objective impossibility.

9. Define and apply the doctrine of commercial impracticability.

10. Explain how contracts are discharged by operation of law.

The parties to a contract are said to be in **privity of contract**. Contracting parties have a legal obligation to perform the duties specified in their contract. A party's duty of performance may be **discharged** by agreement of the parties, excuse of performance, or operation of law. If one party fails to perform as promised, the other party may enforce the contract and sue for breach.

With two exceptions, third parties do not acquire any rights under other people's contracts. The exceptions are (1) **assignees** to whom rights subsequently are transferred and (2) **intended third-party beneficiaries** to whom the contracting parties intended to give rights under the contract at the time of contracting.

This chapter discusses the rights of third parties under a contract, conditions to performance, and ways of discharging the duty of performance.

privity of contract

The state of two specified parties being in a contract.

Freedom of contracts begins where equality of bargaining power begins.

Oliver Wendell Holmes Jr.
(1928)

$\mathcal{A}$SSIGNMENT OF RIGHTS

In many cases, the parties to a contract can transfer their rights under the contract to other parties. The transfer of contractual rights is called an **assignment of rights** or just an **assignment**.

Form of Assignment

The party who owes the duty of performance is called the *obligor*. The party owed a right under the contract is called the *obligee*. An obligee who transfers the right to receive performance is called an **assignor**. The party to whom the right has been transferred is called the **assignee**. The assignee can assign the right to yet another person (called a **subsequent assignee**, or **subassignee**). Exhibit 12.1 illustrates these relationships.

assignment

The transfer of contractual rights by the obligee to another party.

assignor

The obligee who transfers the right.

assignee

The party to whom the right has been transferred.

$\mathcal{E}$XHIBIT **12.1** *Assignment of a Right*

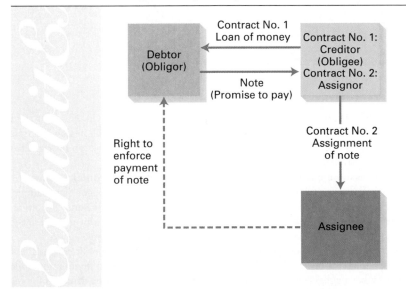

Consider This Example Suppose the owner of a clothing store purchases $5,000 worth of goods on credit from a manufacturer. Payment is due in 120 days. Assume that the manufacturer needs cash before that period expires, so he sells his right to collect the money to a factor for $4,000. If the store owner is given proper notice of the assignment, he must pay $5,000 to the factor. The manufacturer is the assignor and the factor is the assignee.

Generally, no formalities are required for a valid assignment of rights. Although the assignor often uses the word *assign*, other words or terms, such as *sell, transfer, convey,* and *give*, are sufficient to indicate an intent to transfer a contract right.

Business Brief

The word *assignment* does not have to be used to create an assignment.

Rights That Can and Cannot Be Assigned

In the United States, public policy favors a free flow of commerce. Hence, most contract rights are assignable, including sales contracts and contracts for the payment of money.

The types of contracts that present special problems for assignments are discussed below.

Business Brief

Personal service contracts are generally not assignable.

1. **Personal Service Contracts**   Contracts for the provision of personal services are generally not assignable.[1] For example, if an artist contracts to paint someone's portrait, the artist cannot send a different artist to do the painting without the prior approval of the person to be painted. The parties may agree that a personal service contract may be assigned. For example, many professional athletes' contracts contain a clause permitting assignability of the contract.

Many professional athletes' contracts contain a clause that permits the contract to be assigned.

2. **Assignment of Future Rights**   Usually, a person cannot assign a currently nonexistent right that he or she expects to have in the future. For example, suppose a multimillion-dollar heiress signs a will leaving all her property to her grandson. The grandson cannot assign his expected right to receive his inheritance.

Business Brief

Businesses often sell (assign) their accounts receivable to another party called a "factor" for collection. Accounts receivable are usually sold at a discount to reflect risk of noncollection of some accounts.

3. **Contracts Where Assignment Would Materially Alter the Risk**   A contract cannot be assigned if the assignment would materially alter the risk or duties of the obligor. For example, suppose Laura Peters, who has a safe driving record, purchases automobile insurance from an insurance company. Her rights to be insured cannot be assigned to another driver because the assignment would materially alter the risk and duties of the insurance company.

4. **Assignment of Legal Actions**   Legal actions involving personal rights cannot be assigned. For example, suppose Donald Matthews is severely injured by Alice Hollyfield in an automobile accident caused by her negligence. Matthews can sue Hollyfield to recover damages for his injuries. He may not assign his right to sue her to another person.

A legal right that arises out of a breach of contract may be assigned. Fore example, suppose Andrea borrows $10,000 from the bank. If she defaults on the loan, the bank may assign the legal rights to collect the money to a collection agency.

Effect of an Assignment of Rights

Business Brief

Where there has been an assignment of a right the assignee "stands in the shoes of the assignor" and is entitled to performance from the obligor.

Where there has been a valid assignment of rights, the assignee "stands in the shoes of the assignor." That is, the assignor is entitled to performance from the obligor. The unconditional assignment of a contract right extinguishes all the assignor's rights, including the right to sue the obligor directly for nonperformance.[2]

An assignee takes no better rights under the contract than the assignor had. For example, if the assignor has a right to receive $10,000 from a debtor, the right to receive this $10,000 is all that the assignor can assign to the assignee. An obligor can assert any defense he or she had against the assignor or the assignee. For example, an obligor can raise the fraud, duress, undue influence, minority, insanity, illegality of the contract, mutual mistake, or payment by worthless check by the assignor against enforcement of the contract by the assignee. The obligor can also raise any personal defenses (e.g., participation in the assignor's fraudulent scheme) he or she may have directly against the assignee.

Notice of Assignment

When an assignor makes an assignment of a right under a contract, the assignee is under a duty to notify the obligor that (1) the assignment has been made and (2) performance must be rendered to the assignee. If the assignee fails to notify the obligor of the assignment, the obligor may continue to render performance to the assignor, who no longer has a right to it. The assignee cannot sue the obligor to recover payment because the obligor has performed according to the original contract. The assignee's only course of action is to sue the assignor for damages.

The result changes if the obligor is notified of the assignment but continues to render performance to the assignor. In such situations, the assignee can sue the obligor and recover payment. The obligor will then have to pay twice: once wrongfully to the assignor and then rightfully to the assignee. The obligor's only recourse is to sue the assignor for damages.

Anti-Assignment and Approval Clauses

Some contracts contain **anti-assignment clauses** that prohibit the assignment of rights under the contracts. Such clauses may be used if the obligor does not want to deal with or render performance to an unknown third party. Some contracts contain an **approval clause**. Such clauses require the obligor to approve any assignment. Many states prohibit the obligor from unreasonably withholding approval.

Business Brief

To protect his or her rights, an assignee should immediately notify the obligor that (1) the assignment has been made and (2) performance must be rendered to the assignee.

anti-assignment clause

A clause that prohibits the assignment of rights under the contract.

approval clause

A clause that permits the assignment of the contract only upon receipt of an obligor's approval.

Entrepreneur and the Law

SUCCESSIVE ASSIGNMENT OF THE SAME RIGHT

An obligee (the party who is owed a performance, money, right, or other thing of value) has the right to assign a contract right or benefit to another party. If the obligee fraudulently or mistakenly makes successive assignments of the same right to a number of assignees, which assignee has the legal right to the assigned right? To answer this question, the following rules are applied:

- **The American rule** (or New York rule) provides that the first assignment *in time* prevails, regardless of notice. Most states follow this rule.
- **The English rule** provides that the first assignee to *give notice* to the obligor (the person who owes the performance, money, duty, or other thing of value) prevails.

- **The possession of tangible token rule** provides that under either the American or English rule if the assignor makes successive assignments of a contract right that is represented by a tangible token, such as a stock certificate or a savings account passbook, the first assignee who receives delivery of the tangible token prevails over subsequent assignees. However, if the first assignee leaves the tangible token with the assignor, the subsequent assignee prevails. This is because the first assignee could have prevented the problem by having demanded delivery of the tangible token. In other words, physical possession of the tangible token is the pivotal issue.

DELEGATION OF DUTIES

Unless otherwise agreed, the parties to a contract generally can transfer the performance of their duties under the contract to other parties. This transfer is called the **delegation of duties**, or just **delegation**.

delegation of duties

A transfer of contractual duties by the obligor to another party for performance.

delegator

The obligor who transferred his or her duty.

delegatee

The party to whom the duty has been transferred.

An obligor who transfers his or her duty is called a **delegator**. The party to whom the duty has been transferred is the **delegatee**. The party to whom the duty is owed is the *obligee*. Generally, no special words or formalities are required to create a delegation of duties. Exhibit 12.2 illustrates the parties to a delegation of a duty.

*Є*XHIBIT **12.2**   *Delegation of a Duty*

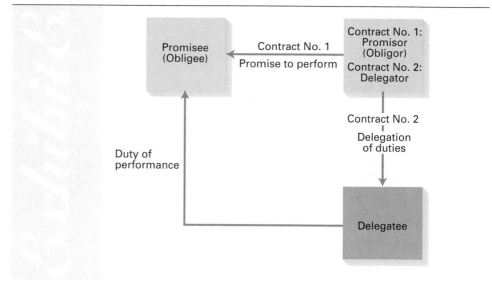

Duties That Can and Cannot Be Delegated

"If there's no meaning in it," said the King, "that saves a world of trouble, you know, we needn't try to find any."

Lewis Carroll
Alice in Wonderland
Chapter 12

Often, contracts are entered into with companies or firms rather than with individuals. In such cases, the firm may designate any of its qualified employees to perform the contract. For example, if a client retains a firm of lawyers to represent her, the firm can **delegate** the duties under the contract to any qualified member of the firm. If the obligee has a substantial interest in having the obligor perform the acts required by the contract, however, duties may not be transferred.[3] This restriction includes obligations under the following types of contracts:

1. **Personal service contracts calling for the exercise of personal skills, discretion, or expertise.** For example, if Dr. Dre is hired to give a concert on campus, the Dixie Chicks cannot appear in his place.
2. **Contracts whose performance would materially vary if the obligor's duties were delegated.** For example, if a person hires an experienced surgeon to perform a complex surgery, a recent medical school graduate cannot be substituted in the operating room.

Effect of Delegation of Duties

assumption of duties

When a delegation of duties contains the term *assumption, I assume the duties,* or other similar language; the delegatee is legally liable to the obligee for nonperformance.

declaration of duties

If the delegatee has not assumed the duties under a contract, the delegatee is not legally liable to the obligee for nonperformance.

If the delegation is valid, the delegator remains legally liable for the performance of the contract. If the delegatee does not perform properly, the obligee can sue the obligor-delegator for any resulting damages.

The question of the delegatee's liability to the obligee depends on whether there has been an *assumption of duties* or a *declaration of duties*. Where a delegation of duties contains the term *assumption* or other similar language, there is an **assumption of duties** by the delegatee. The delegatee is liable to the obligee for nonperformance. The obligee can sue either the delegator or the delegatee.

If the delegatee has not assumed the duties under a contract, the delegation of duties is called a **declaration of duties**. Here, the delegatee is not legally liable to the obligee for nonperformance. The obligee's only recourse is to sue the delegator. A delegatee who fails to perform his or her duties is liable to the delegator for damages arising from this failure to perform.

Anti-Delegation Clause

The parties to a contract can include an **anti-delegation clause** indicating that the duties cannot be delegated. Anti-delegation clauses are usually enforced. Some courts, however, have held that duties that are totally impersonal in nature—such as the payment of money—can be delegated despite such clauses.

anti-delegation clause
A clause that prohibits the delegation of duties under the contract.

An Assignment and Delegation

An **assignment and delegation** occurs where there is a transfer of both rights and duties under a contract. If the transfer of a contract to a third party contains only language of assignment, the modern view holds that there is corresponding delegation of the duties of the contract.[4]

assignment and delegation
Transfer of both rights and duties under the contract.

THIRD-PARTY BENEFICIARIES

Third parties sometimes claim rights under others' contracts. Such third parties are either *intended* or *incidental beneficiaries*. Each of these designations is discussed here.

Intended Beneficiaries

When the parties enter into a contract, they can agree that one of the party's performances should be rendered to or directly benefit a third party. Under such circumstances, the third party is called an **intended third-party beneficiary**. An intended third-party beneficiary can enforce the contract against the party who promised to render performance.[5]

The beneficiary may be expressly named in the contract from which he or she is to benefit or may be identified by another means. For example, there is sufficient identification if a testator of a will leaves his estate to "all my children, equally."

Intended third-party beneficiaries may be classified as either *donee* or *creditor* beneficiaries. These terms are defined below. The Restatement (Second) of Contracts and many state statutes have dropped this distinction, however, and now refer to both collectively as intended beneficiaries.[6]

intended beneficiary
A third party who is not in privity of contract but who has rights under the contract and can enforce the contract against the obligor.

Donee Beneficiaries   When a person enters into a contract with the intent to confer a benefit or gift on an intended third party, the contract is called **donee beneficiary contract**. A life insurance policy with a named beneficiary is an example of such a contract. The three persons involved in such a contract are:

donee beneficiary contract
A contract entered into with the intent to confer a benefit or gift on an intended third party.

1. The **promisee** (the contracting party who directs that the benefit be conferred on another)
2. The **promisor** (the contracting party who agrees to confer performance for the benefit of the third person)
3. The **donee beneficiary** (the third person on whom the benefit is to be conferred)

donee beneficiary
The third party on whom the benefit is to be conferred.

If the promisor fails to perform the contract, the donee beneficiary can sue the promisor directly.

Consider This Example   Brian Peterson hires a lawyer to draft his will. He directs the lawyer to leave all of his property to his best friend, Jeffrey Silverman. Assume that (1) Peterson dies and (2) the lawyer's negligence in drafting the will causes it to be invalid. Consequently, Peterson's distant relatives receive the property under the state's inheritance statute. Silverman can sue the lawyer for damages because he was the intended donee beneficiary of the will (see Exhibit 12.3).

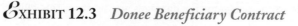

*ℰ*XHIBIT **12.3**   *Donee Beneficiary Contract*

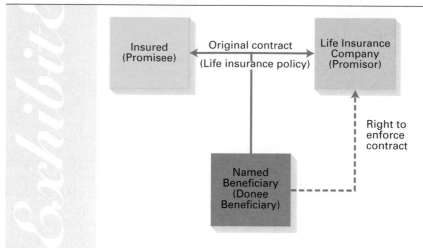

creditor beneficiary contract

A contract that arises in the following situation: (1) a debtor borrows money, (2) the debtor signs an agreement to pay back the money plus interest, (3) the debtor sells the item to a third party before the loan is paid off, and (4) the third party promises the debtor that he or she will pay the remainder of the loan to the creditor.

creditor beneficiary

Original creditor who becomes a beneficiary under the debtor's new contract with another party.

Creditor Beneficiaries   The second type of intended beneficiary is the creditor beneficiary. A **creditor beneficiary contract** usually arises in the following situation:

1. A debtor borrows money from a creditor to purchase some item.
2. The debtor signs an agreement to pay the creditor the amount of the loan plus interest.
3. The debtor sells the item to another party before the loan is paid.
4. The new buyer promises the debtor that he or she will pay the remainder of the loan amount to the creditor.

The creditor is the new intended creditor beneficiary to this second creditor.[7] The parties to the second contract are the original debtor (the promisee), the new party (the promisor), and the original creditor (the **creditor beneficiary**). (See Exhibit 12.4.)

*ℰ*XHIBIT **12.4**   *Creditor Beneficiary Contract*

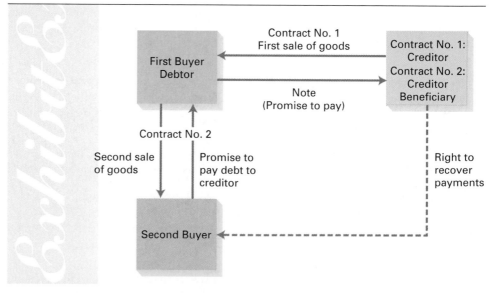

If the promisor fails to perform according to the contract, the creditor beneficiary may either (1) enforce the original contract against the debtor-promisee or (2) enforce the new contract against the promisor. The creditor, however, can collect only once.

Consider This Example Suppose Hilton Hotels, Inc., obtains a loan from City Bank to refurbish a hotel in Atlanta, Georgia. The parties sign a promissory note requiring the loan to be paid off in equal monthly installments over the next 10 years. Before the loan is paid, Hilton sells the hotel to ABC Hotels, another chain of hotels. ABC Hotels agrees with Hilton to complete the payments due on the City Bank loan. The bank has two options if ABC Hotels fails to pay: It can sue Hilton Hotels, Inc., on the promissory note to recover the unpaid loan amount, or it can use its status as a creditor beneficiary to sue ABC Hotels.

Incidental Beneficiaries

In many instances, the parties to a contract unintentionally benefit a third party when the contract is performed. In such situations, the third party is referred to as an **incidental beneficiary**. An incidental beneficiary has no rights to enforce or sue under other people's contracts. Generally, the public and taxpayers are only incidental beneficiaries to contracts entered into by the government on their behalf. As such, they acquire no rights to enforce government contracts or to sue parties who breach these contracts.

Often, the courts are asked to decide whether a third party is an intended or an incidental beneficiary, as in the following case.

incidental beneficiary
A party who is unintentionally benefited by other people's contracts.

Bain v. Gillispie
357 N. W. 2d 47 (1984)
Court of Appeals of Iowa

CASE 12.1

BACKGROUND AND FACTS
James C. Bain, a college basketball referee, had a contract with the Big 10 Basketball Conference (Big 10) to referee various basketball games. During a game that took place on March 6, 1982, Bain called a foul on a University of Iowa player that permitted free throws by a Purdue University player. That player scored the point that gave Purdue a last-minute victory and eliminated Iowa from the Big 10 championship. Some Iowa fans, including John and Karen Gillispie, asserted that the foul call was clearly in error. The Gillispies operated a novelty store in Iowa City that sold University of Iowa sports memorabilia. They filed a complaint against Bain, alleging that his negligent refereeing constituted a breach of his contract with the Big 10 and destroyed a potential market for their products. The Gillispies sought $175,000 compensatory damages plus exemplary damages. The trial court granted Bain's motion for summary judgment. The Gillispies appealed.

ISSUE
Were the Gillispies intended beneficiaries of the contract between Bain and the Big 10 Basketball Conference?

COURT'S REASONING
The Gillispies claimed that they were direct donee beneficiaries. The real test is whether the contracting parties intended that a third person should receive a benefit that might be enforced in the courts. The court stated, "The Gillispies can be considered nothing more than incidental beneficiaries and as such are unable to maintain a cause of action."

DECISION
The appellate court held that the Gillispies were merely incidental beneficiaries of the contract between Bain and the Big 10 Basketball Conference. Therefore, they could not maintain their lawsuit for an alleged breach of that contract. Affirmed.

Case Questions

Critical Legal Thinking Should the law allow incidental beneficiaries to recover damages for the breach of other people's contracts? Why or why not?

Business Ethics Did the Gillispies have a legitimate lawsuit in this case?

Contemporary Business Do third parties have rights under many business contracts? Give some examples.

COVENANTS AND CONDITIONS

In contracts, parties make certain promises to each other. These promises may be classified as *covenants* or *conditions*. The difference between each of these is discussed in the following paragraphs.

covenant

An unconditional promise to perform.

Business Brief

Nonperformance of a covenant is a breach of contract that gives the other party the right to sue.

Buddha Statute, China
International contracts contain covenants and conditions of performance as specified or implied by law.

Covenants

A **covenant** is an unconditional promise to perform. Nonperformance of a covenant is a breach of contract that gives the other party the right to sue. For example, if Medcliff Corporation borrows $100,000 from a bank and signs a promissory note to repay this amount plus 10 percent interest in one year, this promise is a covenant. That is, it is an unconditional promise to perform.

Conditions of Performance

A conditional promise (or qualified promise) is not as definite as a covenant. The promisor's duty to perform (or not perform) arises only if the **condition** does (or does not) occur.[8] It becomes a covenant if the condition is met, however.

Generally, contractual language such as *if, on condition that, provided that, when, after,* and *as soon as* indicate a condition. A single contract may contain numerous conditions that trigger or excuse performance. There are three types of conditions: *conditions precedent, conditions subsequent,* and *concurrent conditions.*

Conditions Precedent   If the contract requires the occurrence (or nonoccurrence) of an event *before* a party is obligated to perform a contractual duty, there is a **condition precedent**. The happening (or nonhappening) of the event triggers the contract or duty of performance. If the event does not occur, no duty to perform arises because there is a failure of condition.

Consider This Example   Suppose E. I. du Pont offers Joan Andrews a job as an industrial engineer upon her graduation from college. If Andrews graduates, the condition has been met. If the employer refuses to hire Andrews at that time, she can sue the employer for breach of contract. If Andrews does not graduate, however, du Pont is not obligated to hire her because there has been a failure of condition.

condition

A qualification of a promise that becomes a covenant if it is met. There are three types of conditions: conditions precedent, conditions subsequent, and concurrent conditions.

condition precedent

A condition that requires the occurrence of an event before a party is obligated to perform a duty under a contract.

Entrepreneur and the Law

CONDITIONS PRECEDENT IN BUSINESS CONTRACTS

Businesses often include conditions precedent in their contracts that must be met before they have any duty to perform under the contract. Consider the following case.

Carley Capital Group (Carley) was the owner of a project in the city of Baltimore known as "Henderson's Wharf." The project was designed to convert warehouses into residential condominiums. On September 4, 1987, Carley hired Gilbane Building Company (Gilbane) to be the general contractor and construction manager for the project. Gilbane hired Architectural Systems, Inc. (ASI), as the subcontractor to perform drywall and acoustical tile work on the project. The subcontract included the following clause: "It is specifically understood and agreed that the payment to the trade contractor is dependent, as a condition precedent, upon the construction manager receiving contract payments from the owner."

Gilbane received periodic payments from Carley and paid ASI as work progressed. By late 1988, ASI had satisfactorily performed all of its obligations under the subcontract and submitted a final bill of $348,155 to Gilbane. Gilbane did not pay this bill because it had not received payment from Carley. On March 10, 1989, Carley filed for bankruptcy. ASI sued Gilbane seeking payment. Must Gilbane pay ASI?

The district court held that Gilbane was not obligated to pay ASI because the condition precedent to this payment—receipt of payment from Carley—had not occurred. The court granted summary judgment to Gilbane. [*Architectural Systems, Inc. v. Gilbane Building Co.*, 760 F.Supp. 79 (D.C.Md. 1991)]

Conditions Precedent Based on Satisfaction   Some contracts reserve the right to a party to pay for services provided by the other only if the services meet the first party's "satisfaction." The courts have developed two tests—the *personal satisfaction test* and the *reasonable person test*—to examine whether this special form of condition precedent has been met.

1. The **personal satisfaction test** is a *subjective* test that applies if the performance involves personal taste and comfort (e.g., contracts for decorating, tailoring, etc.). The only requirement is that the person given the right to reject the contract acts in good faith.

   For example, suppose Gretchen Davidson employs an artist to paint her daughter's portrait. Assume the contract provides that the client does not have to pay for the portrait unless she is satisfied with it. Accordingly, Ms. Davidson may reject the painting if she personally dislikes it, even though a reasonable person would be satisfied with it.

2. The **reasonable person test** is an *objective* test that is used to judge contracts involving mechanical fitness and most commercial contracts. Most contracts that require the work to meet a third person's satisfaction (e.g., an engineer or architect) are judged by this standard.

   For example, suppose Lillian Vernon, Inc., a large mail-order catalog business, hires someone to install a state-of-the-art computer system that will handle its order entry and record-keeping functions. The system is installed and operates to industry standards. According to the reasonable person test, the company cannot reject the contract as not meeting its satisfaction.

Time of Performance as a Condition Precedent   Generally, there is a breach of contract if the contract is not performed when due. Nevertheless, if the other party is not jeopardized by the delay, most courts treat the delay as a minor breach and give the nonperforming party additional time to perform. Conversely, if the contract expressly provides that "*time is of the essence*" or similar language, performance by the stated time is an express condition. There is a breach of contract if the contracting party does not perform by the stated date.

Conditions Subsequent   A **condition subsequent** exists when a contract provides that the occurrence or nonoccurrence of a specific event automatically excuses the performance of an existing duty to perform. For example, many employment contracts include a clause that permits the employer to terminate the contract if the employer fails a drug test.

Note that the Restatement (Second) of Contracts eliminates the distinction between conditions precedent and conditions subsequent. Both are referred to as "conditions."[9]

Concurrent Conditions   **Concurrent conditions** arise when the parties to a contract must render performance simultaneously. That is, when each party's absolute duty to perform is conditioned on the other party's absolute duty to perform.

For example, suppose a contract to purchase goods provides that payment is due upon delivery. In other words, the buyer's duty to pay is conditioned on the seller's duty to deliver the goods, and vice versa. Recovery is available if one party fails to respond to the other party's performance.

Implied Conditions   Any of the previous types of conditions may be further classified as either an express or implied condition. An *express condition* exists if the parties expressly

---

condition precedent based on satisfaction

Clause in a contract that reserves the right to a party to pay for the items or services contracted for only if they meet his or her satisfaction.

personal satisfaction test

Subjective test that applies to contracts involving personal taste and comfort.

reasonable person test

Objective test that applies to commercial contracts and contracts involving mechanical fitness.

Business Brief

If "time is of the essence" is stated in a contract, it is an express condition; failure to perform by the stated date is a material breach of contract.

condition subsequent

A condition, if it occurs or doesn't occur, that automatically excuses the performance of an existing contractual duty to perform.

concurrent condition

A condition that exists when the parties to a contract must render performance simultaneously; each party's absolute duty to perform is conditioned on the other party's absolute duty to perform.

implied-in-fact condition

A condition that can be implied from the circumstances surrounding a contract and the parties' conduct.

agree on it. An **implied in-fact condition** is one that can be implied from the circumstances surrounding a contract and the parties' conduct. For example, a contract in which a buyer agrees to purchase grain from a farmer implies that there is proper street access to the delivery site, proper unloading facilities, and the like.

CONCEPT SUMMARY   TYPES OF CONDITIONS

Type of Condition	Description
Condition precedent	A specified event must occur (or not occur) before a party is obligated to perform contractual duties.
Condition subsequent	The occurrence (or nonoccurence) of a specified event excuses the performance of an existing contractual duty to perform.
Concurrent condition	The parties to a contract are obligated to render performance simultaneously. Each party's duty to perform is conditioned on the other party's duty to perform.
Implied condition	An implied-in-fact condition is implied from the circumstances surrounding the contract and the parties' conduct.

 *Business Ethics*

SATISFACTION CLAUSE: "I DON'T LIKE IT"

Commercial contracts often include "satisfaction clauses" that are designed to ensure that an appropriate quality of performance is received before the promisee is obligated to pay. But how satisfied must the contracting party be before there is an obligation to pay? Consider the following case.

General Motors Corporation hired Baystone Construction, Inc. (Baystone), to build an addition to a Chevrolet plant in Muncie, Indiana. Baystone, in turn, hired Morin Building Products Company (Morin) to supply and erect the aluminum walls for the addition. The contract required that the exterior siding of the walls be of "aluminum with a mill finish and stucco embossed surface texture to match finish and texture of existing metal siding." The contract also included a satisfaction clause. Morin put up the walls. The exterior siding did not give the impression of having uniform finish when viewed in bright sunlight from an acute angle and General Motor's representative rejected it. Baystone removed Morin's siding and hired another subcontractor to replace it. General Motors approved the replacement siding. When Baystone refused to pay Morin the $23,000 balance owing on the contract, Morin brought suit against Baystone to recover this amount.

The trial court held in favor in Morin and permitted it to recover the balance from Baystone. The court of appeals affirmed. The court held that the objective reasonable person standard governed the satisfaction clauses in this commercial dispute.

The reasonable person standard applies to most contracts involving commercial quality, operative fitness, or mechanical utility that other knowledgeable persons can judge. The court of appeals held that Baystone was not justified in rejecting Morin's work under the reasonable person standard. The court stated: "The building for which the aluminum siding was intended was a factory. Aesthetic considerations were decidedly secondary to considerations of function and cost. The parties probably did not intend to subject Morin's rights to aesthetic whims." [*Morin Building Products Co., Inc. v. Baystone Construction, Inc.*, 717 F.2d 413 (7th Cir. 1983)]

1. Do you think General Motors was justified in rejecting Morin's work in this case?
2. Should the law adopt the personal satisfaction test to judge compliance with satisfaction clauses in all instances? Why or why not?

DISCHARGE OF PERFORMANCE

A party's duty to perform under a contract may be discharged by *mutual agreement* of the parties, by *impossibility of performance*, or by *operation of law*. These methods of discharge are discussed in the paragraphs that follow.

Discharge by Agreement

In many situations, the parties to a contract mutually decide to discharge their contractual duties. The different types of mutual agreement are discussed below.

- **Mutual Rescission**   If a contract is wholly or partially executory on both sides, the parties can agree to rescind (i.e., cancel) the contract. **Mutual rescission** requires the parties to enter into a second agreement that expressly terminates the first one. Unilateral rescission of the contract by one of the parties without the other party's consent is not effective. Unilateral rescission of a contract constitutes a breach of that contract.

- **Substituted Contract**   The parties to a contract may enter into a new contract that revokes and discharges a prior contract. The new contract is called a **substituted contract**. If one of the parties fails to perform his or her duties under a substituted contract, the nonbreaching party can sue to enforce its terms against the breaching party. The prior contract cannot be enforced against the breaching party because it has been discharged.

- **Novation**   A **novation agreement** (commonly called **novation**) substitutes a third party for one of the original contracting parties. The new substituted party is obligated to perform the contract. All three parties must agree to the substitution. In a novation, the existing party is relieved of liability on the contract.

- **Accord and Satisfaction**   The parties to a contract may agree to settle a contract dispute by an **accord and satisfaction**. The agreement whereby the parties agree to accept something different in satisfaction of the original contract is called an **accord**.[10] The performance of an accord is called a **satisfaction**.

  An accord does not discharge the original contract. It only suspends it until the accord is performed. Satisfaction of the accord discharges both the original contract and the accord. If an accord is not satisfied when it is due, the aggrieved party may enforce either (1) the accord or (2) the original contract.

Discharge by Impossibility

Under certain circumstances, the nonperformance of contractual duties is excused—discharged—because of *impossibility of performance*. The different doctrines of impossibility are discussed below.

Impossibility of Performance   **Impossibility of performance** (or **objective impossibility**) occurs if the contract becomes impossible to perform.[11] The impossibility must be objective impossibility ("it cannot be done") rather than subjective impossibility ("I cannot do it"). The following types of objective impossibility excuse nonperformance:

1. The death or incapacity of the promisor prior to the performance of a personal service contract.[12] For example, if a professional athlete dies prior to or during a contract period, her contract with the team is discharged.
2. The destruction of the subject matter of a contract prior to performance.[13] For example, if a building is destroyed by fire, the lessees are discharged from further performance unless otherwise provided in the lease.
3. A supervening illegality makes performance of the contract illegal.[14] For example, suppose an art dealer contracts to purchase native art found in a foreign country. The contract is discharged if the foreign country enacts a law forbidding native art from being exported from the country before the contract is performed.

In the following case, the court had to decide whether there was impossibility of performance.

Business Brief

The parties to a contract may mutually agree to discharge or end their contractual duties.

novation

An agreement that substitutes a new party for one of the original contracting parties and relieves the exiting party of liability on the contract.

accord and satisfaction

The settlement of a contract dispute.

impossibility of performance

Nonperformance that is excused if the contract becomes impossible to perform; must be objective impossibility, not subjective.

If a man will improvidently bind himself up by a voluntary deed, and not reserve a liberty to himself by a power of revocation, this court will not loose the fetters he hath put upon himself, but he must lie down under his own folly.

L. C. Lord Nottingham
Villers v. Beaumont
(1682)

Parker v. Arthur Murray, Inc.
295 N.E.2d 487 (1973)
Appellate Court of Illinois

CASE 12.2

BACKGROUND AND FACTS
In November 1959, Ryland S. Parker, a 37-year-old college-educated bachelor, went to the Arthur Murray Studios (Arthur Murray) in Oak Park, Illinois, to redeem a certificate entitling him to three free dancing lessons. At that time he lived alone in a one-room attic apartment. During

the free lessons the instructor told Parker that he had "exceptional potential to be a fine and accomplished dancer." Parker thereupon signed a contract for more lessons. Parker attended lessons regularly and was praised and encouraged by his instructors despite his lack of progress. Contract extensions and new contracts for additional instructional hours were executed, which Parker prepaid. Each written contract contained the bold-type words, "NONCANCELABLE CONTRACT." On September 24, 1961, Parker was severely injured in an automobile accident, rendering him incapable of continuing his dancing lessons. At that time he had contracted for a total of 2,734 hours of dance lessons, for which he had prepaid $24,812. When Arthur Murray refused to refund any of the money, Parker sued to rescind the outstanding contracts. The trial courts held in favor of Parker and ordered Arthur Murray to return the prepaid contract payments. Arthur Murray appealed.

ISSUE

Does the doctrine of impossibility excuse Parker's performance of the personal service contracts?

COURT'S REASONING

In Illinois, impossibility of performance is recognized as a ground for rescission. Arthur Murray contended that the bold-type words "NONCANCELABLE CONTRACT" manifested the parties' mutual intent to waive their respective rights to invoke the doctrine of impossibility. The court replied: "This is a construction that we find unacceptable. We conclude that plaintiff never contemplated that by signing the contracts that he was waiving a remedy expressly recognized by Illinois courts."

DECISION

The appellate court held that the doctrine of impossibility of performance excused Parker's performance of the personal service contracts. Affirmed.

Case Questions

Critical Legal Thinking   Should the doctrine of impossibility excuse parties from performance of their contracts? Why or why not?

Business Ethics   Did Arthur Murray act ethically in not returning Parker's money?

Contemporary Business   Why do you think Arthur Murray fought this case?

 *Entrepreneur and the Law*

FORCE MAJEURE CLAUSES

The parties may agree in their contract that certain events will excuse nonperformance of the contract. These clauses are called **force majeure clauses**.

Usually force majeure clauses excuse nonperformance caused by natural disasters such as floods, tornadoes, earthquakes, and such. Modern clauses often excuse performance due to labor strikes, shortages of raw materials, and the like.

commercial impracticability

Nonperformance that is excused if an extreme or unexpected development or expense makes it impractical for the promisor to perform.

Commercial Impracticability   Many states recognize the doctrine of **commercial impracticability** as an excuse of nonperformance of contracts. Commercial impracticability excuses performance if an unforeseeable event makes it impractical for the promisor to perform. This doctrine has not yet been fully developed by the courts. It is examined on a case-by-case basis.

Consider This Example   A utility company enters into a contract to purchase uranium for its nuclear-powered generator from a uranium supplier at a fixed price of $1 million per year for five years. Suppose a new uranium cartel is formed worldwide and the supplier must pay $3 million for uranium to supply the utility with each year's supply. In this case, the court would likely allow the supplier to rescind its contract with the utility based on commercial impracticability. Note that it is not impossible for the supplier to supply the uranium.

Contemporary Business Environment

THE DOCTRINE OF COMMERCIAL IMPRACTICABILITY

Sometimes, unforeseen circumstances make the performance of a contract highly impracticable or very expensive. Modern contract law, including the Uniform Commercial Code (UCC), recognizes the doctrine of commercial impracticability as excusing nonperformance in certain situations. Consider the following case.

In July 1980, Alimenta (U.S.A.), Inc. (Alimenta), entered into a contract with Cargill, Incorporated (Cargill), under which Cargill agreed to deliver to Alimenta shelled, edible peanuts. The peanut crop had been planted in the fields at the time the contract was entered into. Cargill, which had contracts with other buyers as well, expected to make $3 million in profit from its peanut sales.

Unfortunately, there was a severe drought that year, and the crop yield was substantially reduced. Thus, Cargill could deliver to Alimenta only about 65 percent of the promised peanuts. Cargill delivered the same percentage to all of its customers. Alimenta filed suit against Cargill for breach of contract. Cargill asserted that further performance under the contract was excused by the doctrine of commercial impracticability. At trial the jury rendered a verdict for Cargill. Alimenta Appealed.

Both the trial court and the court of appeals held that the drought in this case was unforeseen. The evidence showed that the shortage of peanuts in 1980 was unprecedented. In fact, there had been a surplusage of domestic peanuts for the preceding 20 years.

The trial court found that it was not impossible for Cargill to fully perform the contract. Cargill could have gone into the market and purchased the peanuts, which were selling at a much higher price than contracted for, and delivered the peanuts to Alimenta. Cargill, however, had already suffered a $47-million loss on its peanut contract even without taking this step.

The court of appeals affirmed the trial court's ruling in favor of Cargill. The court held that Cargill was excused from further performance by the doctrine of commercial impracticability. The court stated that "the focus of impracticability analysis is upon the nature of the agreement and the expectations of the parties" and not on whether it is physically possible for the defendant to perform the contract. [*Alimenta (U.S.A.), Inc. v. Cargill, Incorporated*, 861 F.2d 650 (11th Cir. 1988)]

Frustration of Purpose   The doctrine of **frustration of purpose** excuses the performance of contractual obligations if (1) the object or benefit of the contract is made worthless to a promisor, (2) both parties knew what the purpose was, and (3) the act that frustrated the purpose was reasonably unforeseeable.

Consider This Example   Suppose Eileen Ney leases a piece of property from a landowner for $1,000 to watch the Rose Bowl parade on January 1 in Pasadena, California. If the parade is unexpectedly canceled, Ney is excused from paying the rental fee. Note that the promisor is not prevented from performing, however. Ney could have used the leased land even though there was no parade.

Discharge by Operation of Law

Certain legal rules discharge parties from performing contractual duties. These rules are discussed below.

- **Statutes of Limitations**   Every state has a **statute of limitations** that applies to contract actions. Although the time periods vary from state to state, the usual period for bringing a lawsuit based on breach of contract is one to five years. The UCC proves that a cause of action based on a breach of sales or lease contract must be brought within four years after the cause of action accrues. [UCC §2-725, UCC §2A-506].
- **Bankruptcy**   Bankruptcy, which is governed by federal law, is a means of allocating the debtor's nonexempt property to satisfy his or her debts. Debtors may also reorganize in bankruptcy. In most cases, the debtor's assets are insufficient to pay all the creditors' claims. If so, the debtor receives a **discharge** of the unpaid debts. The debtor is then relieved of legal liability to pay the discharged debts.
- **Alteration of the Contract**   If a party to a contract intentionally alters the contract materially, the innocent party may opt either to discharge the contract or to enforce it. The contract may be enforced either on its original terms or on the altered terms. A material alteration is a change in price, quantity, or some other important term.

frustration of purpose

A doctrine which excuses the performance of contractual obligations if (1) the object or benefit of a contract is made worthless to a promisor, (2) both parties knew what the purpose was, and (3) the act that frustrated the purpose was unforeseeable.

statute of limitations

Statute that establishes the time period during which a lawsuit must be brought; if the lawsuit is not brought within this period, the injured party loses the right to sue.

That what is agreed to be done, must be considered as done.

L. C. Lord Hardwicke
Guidot v. Guidot (1745)

CHAPTER SUMMARY

Assignment of Rights, p. 281

Form of Assignment	1. *Assignment.* Transfer of contractual rights by a party to a contract to a third person. 2. *Assignor.* Contract party who assigns the contractual rights. 3. *Assignee.* Third person to whom contract rights are assigned.
Effect of Assignment	The assignee "stands in the shoes of the assignor" and is entitled to performance of the contract by the obligor.
Notice of Assignment	1. *Duty to notify.* Assignee must notify the obligor that (1) the assignment has been made and (2) performance must be rendered to the assignee. 2. *Failure to give notice.* If the assignee fails to give proper notice to the obligor and the obligor renders performance to the assignor, the assignee's only course of action to recover is from the assignor.
Anti-Assignment and Approval Clauses	1. *Anti-assignment clause.* This prohibits the assignment of rights under a contract. 2. *Approval clause.* This permits assignment of the contract only upon receipt of the obligor's approval.
Successive Assignments	If the obligee makes successive assignments of the same right, one of the following rules (depending on state law) applies: 1. *American rule.* First assignment in time prevails, regardless of notice. Also called the *New York rule.* 2. *English rule.* First assignee to give notice to the obligor prevails.

Delegation of Duties, p. 283

Delegation of Duties	1. *Delegation.* Transfer of contractual duties by a party to a contract to a third person. 2. *Delegator.* Party who transfers his or her contractual duties. 3. *Delegatee.* Third person to whom contractual duties are delegated.
Effect of Delegation	Depends on whether there has been: 1. *Assumption of duties.* Delegatee is liable to obligee for nonperformance. Obligee may sue either the delegatee or the delegator. 2. *Declaration of duties.* Delegatee is not liable to the obligee for nonperformance. Obligee can sue only the delegator. The delegatee is liable to the delegator for any damages suffered by the delegator because of the delegatee's nonperformance.
Anti-Delegation Clause	Prohibits the delegation of duties under a contract.

Third-Party Beneficiaries, p. 285

Intended Beneficiaries	Third person who is owed performance under other parties' contract. There are two types: 1. *Donee beneficiary.* Person who is to be rendered performance gratuitously under a contract. For example, a beneficiary of a life insurance policy. Donee beneficiary may sue the promisor for nonperformance. 2. *Creditor beneficiary.* Creditor who becomes a beneficiary to a contract between the debtor and a third party who agrees to perform the debtor's obligation. If the debt is not paid, the creditor may sue either (1) the debtor under the original contract or (2) the third party as a creditor beneficiary.
Incidental Beneficiaries	A third person who incidentally receives some benefit under other parties' contract but who has no rights to enforce it or to sue for its nonperformance.

Covenants and Conditions, p. 287

Covenants	Unconditional promises to perform. Nonperformance of a covenant is a breach of contract that gives the other party the right to sue.

Conditions of Performance	*Condition.* Promisor's duty to perform or not perform arises only if the *condition* does or does not occur. Also called a *qualified promise.* There are several types:
	1. *Condition precedent.* This requires the occurrence or nonoccurrence of an event before a party is obligated to perform. Conditions precedent based on "satisfaction" are measured by one or two standards:
	a. *Personal satisfaction test.* The subjective intent of the decision maker applies if the performance involves personal taste or comfort.
	b. *Reasonable person test.* The objective intent of a reasonable person in the circumstances applies to contracts involving mechanical fitness or commercial contracts.
	2. *Condition subsequent.* This provides that the occurrence or nonoccurrence of a specific event automatically excuses performance under a contract.
	3. *Concurrent condition.* This arises when the parties to a contract must render performance simultaneously.
	4. *Implied-in-fact condition.* A condition that is implied from the circumstances surrounding a contract and the parties' conduct.

Discharge of Performance, p. 290

Discharge by Agreement	1. *Mutual rescission.* The parties mutually agree to rescind an executory contract.
	2. *Substituted contract.* The parties enter into a new contract that revokes a prior contract.
	3. *Novation.* The parties agree to the substitution of a third party for one of the original parties. The exiting party is relieved of liability, and the entering party is obligated to perform the contract.
	4. *Accord and satisfaction.* The parties agree to settle a contract dispute. The *satisfaction* of the *accord* discharges the original contract.
Discharge by Impossibility	1. *Impossibility of performance.* The contract is objectively impossible to perform because of an event.
	2. *Commercial impracticability.* The contract is impractical for the promisor to perform because of an event.
	3. *Frustration of purpose.* The object of the contract, of which both parties have knowledge, becomes worthless because of an unforeseeable event.
	4. *Force majeure clause.* The parties stipulate in the contract what events will excuse performance.
Discharge by Operation of Law	1. *Statute of limitations.* A contract that is not brought within the stipulated limitations period discharges contractual duties.
	2. *Bankruptcy.* Discharge in bankruptcy relieves the debtor of legal liability to pay the discharged debts.
	3. *Alteration of a contract.* If a party to a contract intentionally alters it materially, the innocent party may opt either to discharge the contract or to enforce it on its original or altered terms.

END-OF-CHAPTER INTERNET EXERCISES AND CASE QUESTIONS

Working the Web Internet Exercises

ACTIVITIES

1. Which provision of the UCC permits assignment and delegation? An extensive overview of contract law can be found at the Contracts Home Page (Craig Smith, Santa Barbara College of Law) **www.west.net/ ~smith/contracts.htm**. Review the "Third Party Rights" page.

2. Why does bankruptcy have the effect of discharging contractual obligations? See **www.nolo.com** and search via *bankruptcy*.

3. A good case can be lost because of a statute of limitations. These statutes vary by state and by type of claim. See **www.nolo.com/encyclopedia/articles/ cm/timely.html** for a summary of the statutes and find your state law.

4. Federal law may limit the ability of certain parties to collect on overdue debts. See the Fair Debt Collection Practices Act—15 U.S.C. § 1692 via the Cornell Web site **www.cornell.edu**.

CRITICAL LEGAL THINKING CASES

12.1 Third-Party Beneficiary Eugene H. Emmick hired L. S. Hamm, an attorney, to draft his will. The will named Robert Lucas and others (Lucas) as beneficiaries. When Emmick died, it was discovered that the will was improperly drafted, violated state law, and was therefore ineffective. Emmick's estate was transferred pursuant to the state's intestate laws. Lucas did not receive the $75,000 he would have otherwise received had the will been valid. Lucas sued Hamm for breach of the Emmick-Hamm contract to recover what he would have received under the will. Who wins? [*Lucas v. Hamm*, 364 P.2d 685, 56 Cal.2d 583, 15 Cal.Rptr. 821 (CA 1961)]

12.2 Third-Party Beneficiary Abrams and others sponsored a condominium project for a luxury condominium building on Manhattan's East Side. Abrams contracted with Lehrer/McGovern, Inc. (L/M), and other contracting companies to construct the building. After the building was completed and the individual condominium units sold, certain defects in construction appeared. Monarch Owners Committee, the condominium association, and individual condominium owners sued L/M and other contracting companies for damages for breach of their contracts with Abrams. Can the condominium association and owners sue the contracting companies? [*Monarch Owners Committee v. Abrams*, 454 N.Y.S.2d 4 (N.Y.Sup. 1982)]

12.3 Third-Party Beneficiary Angelo Boussiacos hired Demetrios Sofias, a general contractor, to build a restaurant for him. Boussiacos entered into a loan agreement with the Bank of America (B of A) whereby the bank would provide the construction financing to build the restaurant. As is normal with most construction loans, the loan agreement provided that loan funds would be periodically disbursed by the bank to Boussiacos at different stages of construction as requested by Boussiacos. Problems arose in the progress of the construction. When Boussiacos did not pay Sofias for certain work that had been done, Sofias sued B of A for breach of contract to collect payment directly from B of A. Can Sofias maintain the lawsuit against B of A? [*Sofias v. Bank of America*, 172 Cal.App.3d. 583, 218 Cal.Rptr 626 (Cal. App. 1985)]

12.4 Third-Party Beneficiary David Seeley owned an apartment building located at 15 East 21st Street in the Gramercy Park area of New York. Seeley contracted with Rem Discount Security Products, Inc. (Rem), to install security locks on the front door of the building. On June 7, 1981, when Lori Einhorn was visiting her fiancé at the building, she was accosted on the second-floor landing, dragged to her fianacé's apartment, and raped. Einhorn sued Rem for breach of contract, alleging that the front-door lock to the building was negligently installed and could be opened by a firm push, even when the door was locked. Can Einhorn sue Rem for breach of contract? [*Einhorn v. Seeley and Rem Discount Security Products, Inc.*, 525 N.Y.S.2d 212 (N.Y.Sup. 1988)]

12.5 Assignment William John Cunningham, a professional basketball player, entered into a contract with Southern Sports Corporation, which owned the Carolina Cougars, a professional basketball team. The contract provided that Cunningham was to play basketball for the Cougars for a three-year period commencing on October 2, 1971. The contract contained a provision that it could not be assigned to any other professional basketball franchise without Cunningham's approval. Subsequently, Southern Sports Corporation sold its assets, including its franchise and Cunningham's contract, to the Munchak Corporation (Munchak). There was no change in the Cougars' location after the purchase. When Cunningham refused to play for the new owners, Munchak sued to enforce Cunningham's contract. Was Cunningham's contract assignable to the new owner? [*Munchak Corporation v. Cunningham*, 457 F.2d 721 (4th Cir. 1972)]

12.6 Assignment In 1974, Berlinger Foods Corporation (Berlinger), pursuant to an oral contract, became a distributor for Häagen-Dazs ice cream. Over the next decade both parties flourished as the marketing of high-quality, high-priced ice cream took hold. Berlinger successfully promoted the sale of Häagen-Dazs to supermarket chains and other retailers in the Baltimore-Washington, D.C., area. In 1983, the Pillsbury Company acquired Häagen-Dazs. Pillsbury adhered to the oral distribution agreement and retained Berlinger as a distributor for Häagen-Dazs ice cream. In December 1985, Berlinger entered into a contract and sold its assets to Dreyers, a manufacturer of premium ice cream that competed with Häagen-Dazs. Dreyers ice cream had previously been sold primarily in the western part of the United States. Dreyers attempted to expand its market to the east by choosing to purchase Berlinger as a means to obtain distribution in the mid-Atlantic region. When Pillsbury learned of the sale, it advised Berlinger that its distributorship for Häagen-Dazs was terminated. Berlinger, which wanted to remain a distributor for Häagen-Dazs, sued Pillsbury for breach of contract, alleging that the oral distribution agreement with Häagen-Dazs and Pillsbury was properly assigned to Dreyers. Who wins? [*Berlinger Foods Corporation v. The Pillsbury Company*, 633 F.Supp. 557 (D.Md. 1986)]

12.7 Right of an Assignee John Handy Jones paid Richard Sullivan, the chief of police of the Addison, Texas, Police Department, a $6,400 bribe in exchange for Sullivan's cooperation in allowing Jones and others to bring marijuana by airplane into the Addison airport without police intervention. Sullivan accepted the money, but rather than perform the requested services, he arrested Jones and turned the money over to the Dallas County District Attorney's Office. The $6,400 was introduced as evidence at Jones' criminal trial, where he was convicted. Subsequent to his conviction, Jones assigned his interest in the money to Melvyn Carson Bruder. The City of Addison brought an action, claiming that the money belonged to the city. Bruder intervened in the suit and claimed that he was entitled to the money because of the assignment from Jones. Who wins? [*Bruder v. State of Texas*, 601 S.W.2d 102 (Tex. App. 1980)]

12.8 Approval Clause Lincoln Plaza Associates owned Lincoln Plaza (1900 Broadway at 64th Street) in New York. Chase Manhattan Bank (Chase) entered into a written lease whereby it leased premises in the building. The lease provided that Chase could not sublease or assign the premises without the landlord's prior approval. After occupying the premises for some time, Chase notified the landlord that it wished to sublease the premises to Bank Leumi, which was the twenty-first largest commercial bank in New York with 20 branches in New York City, assets of more than $3 billion, and a net worth of almost $150 million. The landlord refused to grant approval for the assignment. Chase sued the landlord for breach of contract. Who wins? [*The Chase Manhattan Bank, N.A. v. Lincoln Plaza Associates, N.Y. Law Journal,* 9 Jan. 1989 (N.Y.Sup. 1989)]

12.9 Anti-assignment Clause In 1976, the city of Vancouver, Washington, contracted with B & B Contracting Corporation (B & B) to construct a well pump at a city-owned water station. The contract contained the following anti-assignment clause: "The contractor shall not assign this contract or any part thereof, or any moneys due or to become due thereunder." The work was not completed on time, and the city withheld $6,510 as liquidated damages from the contract price. B & B assigned the claim to this money to Portland Electric and Plumbing Company (PEPCo). PEPCo, as the assignee, filed suit against the City of Vancouver, alleging that the city breached its contract with B & B by wrongfully refusing to pay $6,510 to B & B. Can PEPCo maintain the lawsuit against the City of Vancouver? [*Portland Electric and Plumbing Company v. City of Vancouver,* 627 P.2d 1350 (Wash. App. 1981)]

12.10 Delegation of Duties C. W. Milford owned a registered quarterhorse named Hired Chico. In March 1969, Milford sold the horse to Norman Stewart. Recognizing that Hired Chico was a good stud, Milford included the following provision in the written contract that was signed by both parties: "I, C. W. Milford, reserve 2 breedings each year on Hired Chico registration # 403692 for the life of this stud horse regardless of whom the horse may be sold to." The agreement was filed with the County Court Clerk of Shelby County, Texas. Stewart later sold Hired Chico to Sam McKinnie. Prior to purchasing the horse, McKinnie read the Milford-Stewart contract and testified that he understood the terms of the contract. When McKinnie refused to grant Milford the stud services of Hired Chico, Milford sued McKinnie for breach of contract. Who wins? [*McKinnie v. Milford,* 597 S.W.2d 953 (TX 1980)]

12.11 Condition Shumann Investments, Inc. (Shumann), hired Pace Construction Corporation (Pace), a general contractor, to build "Outlet World of Pasco County." In turn, Pace hired OBS Company, Inc. (OBS), a subcontractor, to perform the framing, dry wall, insulation, and stucco work on the project. The contract between Pace and OBS stipulated: "Final payment shall not become due unless and until the following conditions precedent to final payment have been satisfied . . . (c) receipt of final payment for subcontractor's work by contractor from owner." When Shumann refused to pay Pace, Pace refused to

pay OBS. OBS sued Pace to recover payment. Who wins? [*Pace Construction Corporation v. OBS Company, Inc.,* 531 So.2d 737 (Fla. App. 1988)]

12.12 Excuse of Condition In January 1976, Maco, Inc. (Maco), a roofing contractor, hired Brian Barrows as a salesperson. Barrows was assigned a geographical territory and was responsible for securing contracts for Maco within his territory. The employment contract provided that Barrows was to receive a 26 percent commission on the net profits from roofing contracts that he obtained. The contract contained the following provision: "To qualify for payment of the commission, the salesperson must sell and supervise the job; the job must be completed and paid for; and the salesperson must have been in the continuous employment of Maco, Inc., during the aforementioned period." In July 1977, Barrows obtained a $129,603 contract with the Board of Education of Cook County for Maco to make repairs to the roof of the Hoover School in Evanston, Illinois. During the course of the work, Barrows visited the site more than 60 times. In January 1978, before the work was completed, Maco fired Barrows. Later, Maco refused to pay Barrows the commission when the project was completed and paid for. Barrows sued Maco to recover the commission. Who wins? [*Barrows v. Maco, Inc.,* 419 N.E.2d 634 (Ill. App. 1981)]

12.13 Accord and Satisfaction Eugene and Irene Leonard owned a hardware business, including the building and land, in Humboldt, Iowa. The Leonards listed the business and property for sale with Merlyn J. Pollock, a licensed real estate broker. The asking price was $650,000, and Pollock was to receive a flat fee of $50,000 if he found a buyer. Pollock introduced the Leonards to Vincent Kopacek. After substantial negotiations, the Leonards and Kopacek signed a contract for the sale of the hardware store. Thereafter, Mr. Leonard went to Pollock's office and tried to get him to lower his commission. After much discussion, Leonard told Pollock that if he would reduce his fee to $15,000, he would get two other hardware store owners to list their stores for sale with Pollock. Pollock agreed. Subsequently, the Leonards refused to sell their business to Kopacek, who sued and won a decree of specific performance. Can Pollock recover damages from the Leonards, and if so, how much? [*Sergeant, as Trustee for the Estate of Merlyn J. Pollock v. Leonard,* 312 N.W.2d 541 (IA 1981)]

12.14 Novation On July 21, 1981, Magnum Enterprises, Inc. (Magnum), executed an offer and agreement to purchase the Diamond Ring Ranch in Haakon County, South Dakota, from the Armstrong family for $10,800,000. Donald A. Haggar was the real estate broker on the transaction. The offer included a provision for a $500,000 earnest money deposit by a promissory note that was payable as follows: $50,000 due on August 10, 1981, $25,000 due on August 31, 1981, and $200,000 due on September 11, 1981. The closing date of the sale was set for November 2, 1981. The offer also contained a provision for liquidated damages of $500,000 if the buyer did not perform. Magnum paid the original $50,000 into Haggar's client trust account. On August 31, 1981, Magnum agreed to let Berja, a Montana investment group, purchase the ranch. The Armstrongs agreed to the substitution of Berja as the buyer, and Berja executed an offer and agreement to purchase the ranch on the same terms as Magnum. When Berja failed to close the

sale, Haggar, as trustee, brought an action against Magnum to recover on the promissory note. Magnum counterclaimed to recover the $50,000 it paid into Haggar's client trust account. Who wins? [*Haggar v. Olfert*, 387 N.W.2d 45 (SD 1986)]

BUSINESS ETHICS CASES

12.15 Business Ethics Pabagold, Inc. (Pabagold), a manufacturer and distributor of suntan lotions, hired Mediasmith, an advertising agency, to develop an advertising campaign for Pabagold's Hawaiian Gold Pabatan suntan lotion. In the contract, Pabagold authorized Mediasmith to enter into agreements with third parties to place Pabagold advertisements for the campaign and to make payments to these third parties for the Pabagold account. Pabagold agreed to pay Mediasmith for its services and to reimburse it for expenses incurred on behalf of Pabagold. The Pabagold-Mediasmith contract provided for arbitration of any dispute arising under the contract.

In April 1981, Medismith entered into a contract with Outdoor Services, Inc. (Outdoor Services), an outdoor advertising company to place Pabagold ads on billboards owned by Outdoor Services. Outdoor Services provided the agreed-upon work and billed Mediasmith $8,545 for its services. Mediasmith requested payment of this amount from Pabagold so it could pay Outdoor Services. When Pabagold refused to pay, Outdoor Services filed a demand for arbitration as provided in the Pabagold-Mediasmith contract. Pabagold defended, asserting

that Outdoor Services could not try to recover the money because it was not in privity of contract with Pabagold.

Did Pabagold act ethically in refusing to pay Outdoor Services? From a moral perspective, does it matter that Outdoor Services and Pabagold were not in privity of contract? Who wins? [*Outdoor Services Inc. v. Pabagold, Inc.*, 185 Cal.App.3d 676, 230 Cal.Rptr. 73 (Cal.App. 1986)]

12.16 Business Ethics Indiana Tri-City Plaza Bowl (Tri-City) leased a building from Charles H. Glueck for use as a bowling alley. The lease provided that Glueck was to provide adequate paved parking for the building. The lease gave Tri-City the right to approve the plans for the construction and paving of the parking lot. When Glueck submitted paving plans to Tri-City, it rejected the plans and withheld its approval. Tri-City argues that the plans must meet its personal satisfaction before it has to approve them. Evidence showed that the plans were commercially reasonable in the circumstances. A lawsuit was filed between Tri-City and Glueck. Who wins? Was it ethical for Tri-City to reject the plans? [*Indiana Tri-City Plaza Bowl, Inc. v. Estate of Glueck*, 422 N.E.2d 670 (Ind. App. 1981)]

BRIEFING THE CASE WRITING ASSIGNMENT

Read the following case, which has been excerpted from the court's opinion. Review and brief the case.

Chase Precast Corporation v. John J. Paonessa Co., Inc.
409 Mass. 371, 566 N.E. 2d 603 (1991)
Supreme Judicial Court of Massachusetts

Lynch, Justice

This appeal raises the question whether the doctrine of frustration of purpose may be a defense in a breach of contract action in Massachusetts, and, if so, whether it excuses the defendant John J. Paonessa Company, Inc. (Paonessa) from performance.

The claim of the plaintiff, Chase Precast Corporation (Chase), arises from the cancellation of its contracts with Paonessa to supply median barriers in a highway construction project of the Commonwealth. Chase brought an action to recover its anticipated profit on the amount of the median barriers called for by its supply contracts with Paonessa but not produced. Paonessa brought a cross action against the Commonwealth for indemnification in the event it should be held liable to Chase. After a jury-waived trial, a Supreme Court judge ruled for Paonessa on the basis of impossibility of performance. Chase and Paonessa cross appealed. The Appeals Court affirmed, noting that

the doctrine of frustration of purpose more accurately described the basis of the trial judge's decision than the doctrine of impossibility. We agree. We allowed Chase's application for further appellate review and we now affirm.

The pertinent facts are as follows. In 1982, the Commonwealth, through the Department of Public Works (department), entered into two contracts with Paonessa for resurfacing and improvements to two stretches of Route 128. Part of each contract called for replacing a grass median strip between the north and southbound lanes with concrete resurfacing and precast concrete median barriers. Paonessa entered into two contracts with Chase under which Chase was to supply, in the aggregate, 25,800 linear feet of concrete median barriers according to the specifications of the department for highway construction. The quantity and type of barriers to be supplied were specified in two purchase orders prepared by Chase.

The highway reconstruction began in the spring of 1983. By late May, the department was receiving protests from angry residents who objected to use of the concrete barriers and removal of the grass median strip. Paonessa and Chase became aware of the protest around June 1. On June 6, a group of about 100 citizens filed an action in the Superior Court to stop installation of the concrete barriers and other aspects of the work. On June 7, anticipating modification by the department, Paonessa notified Chase by letter to stop producing concrete barriers for the projects. Chase did so upon receipt of the letter the following day. On June 17, the department and the citizen's group entered into a settlement which provided, in part, that no additional concrete median barriers would be installed. On June 23, the department deleted the permanent concrete median barriers item from its contracts with Paonessa.

Before stopping production on June 8, Chase had produced approximately one-half of the concrete median barriers called for by its contracts with Paonessa, and had delivered most of them to the construction sites. Paonessa paid Chase for all that it had produced, at the contract price. Chase suffered no out-of-pocket expense as a result of cancellation of the remaining portion of barriers.

This court has long recognized and applied the doctrine of impossibility as a defense to an action of breach of contract. Under the doctrine, "where from the nature of the contract it appears that the parties must from the beginning have contemplated the continued existence of some particular specified thing as the foundation of what was to be done, then, in the absence of any warranty that the thing shall exist . . . the parties shall be excused . . . when performance becomes impossible from the accidental perishing of the thing without the fault of either party."

On the other hand, although we have referred to the doctrine of frustration of purpose in a few decisions, we have never clearly defined it. Other jurisdictions have explained the doctrine as follows: When an event neither anticipated nor caused by either party, the risk of which was not allocated by the contract, destroys the object or purpose of the contract, thus destroying the value of performance, the parties are excused from further performance.

In Mishara Construction Co., *we called frustration of purpose a "companion rule" to the doctrine of impossibility. Both doctrines concern the effect of supervening circumstances upon the rights and duties of the parties. The difference lies in the effect of the supervening event.*

Another definition of frustration of purpose is found in the Restatement (Second) of Contracts § 265 (1981). "Where, after a contract is made, a party's principle purpose is substantially frustrated without his fault by the occurrence of an event the nonoccurrence of which was a basic assumption on which the contract was made, his remaining duties to render performance are discharged, unless the language or the circumstances indicate the contrary."

Paonessa bore no responsibility for the department's elimination of the median barriers from the projects. Therefore, whether it can rely on the defense of frustration turns on whether elimination of the barriers was a risk allocated by the contracts to Paonessa. The question is, given the commercial circumstances in which the parties dealt: "Was the contingency which developed one which the parties could reasonably be thought to have foreseen as a real possibility which could affect performance? Was it one of that variety of risks which the parties were tacitly assigning to the promisor by their failure to provide for it explicitly? If it was, performance will be required. If it could not be considered, performance is excused."

The record supports the conclusion that Chase was aware of the department's power to decrease quantities of contract items. The judge found that Chase had been a supplier of median barriers to the department in the past. The provision giving the department the power to eliminate items or portions thereof was standard in its contracts. The judge's finding that all parties were well aware that lost profits were not an element of damage in either of the public works projects in issue further supports the conclusion that Chase was aware of the department's power to decrease quantities, since the term prohibiting claims for anticipated profit is part of the same sentence in the standard provision as that allowing the engineer to eliminate items or portions of work. In this case, even if the parties were aware generally of the department's power to eliminate contract items, the judge could reasonably have concluded that they did not contemplate the cancellation for a major portion of the project of such a widely used item as concrete median barriers, and did not allocate the risk of such cancellations.

Judgment affirmed.

ENDNOTES

1. Restatement (Second) of Contracts, §§ 311 and 318.
2. Restatement (Second) of Contracts, § 317.
3. Restatement (Second) of Contracts, § 318(2).
4. Restatement (Second) of Contracts, § 328.
5. Restatement (Second) of Contracts, § 302.
6. Restatement (Second) of Contracts, § 302(1)(b).
7. Restatement (Second) of Contracts, § 302(1)(a).
8. The Restatement (Second) of Contracts, § 224, defines a *condition* as "An event, not certain to occur, which must occur, unless its nonperformance is excused, before performance under a contract is due."
9. Restatement (Second) of Contracts, § 224.
10. Restatement (Second) of Contracts, § 281.
11. Restatement (Second) of Contracts, § 261.
12. Restatement (Second) of Contracts, § 262.
13. Restatement (Second) of Contracts, § 263.
14. Restatement (Second) of Contracts, § 264.

CHAPTER 13

Remedies for Breach of Traditional and Online Contracts

Contracts must not be sports of an idle hour, mere matters of pleasantry and badinage, never intended by the parties to have any serious effect whatsoever.

—Lord Stowell
Dalrymple v. Dalrymple,
2 Hag.Con. 54, at 105 (1811)

Chapter Objectives

After studying this chapter, you should be able to:

1. Explain how complete performance discharges contractual duties.

2. Identify inferior performance and the material breach of a contract.

3. Describe compensatory, consequential, and nominal damages.

4. Describe liquidated damages and identify when they are a penalty.

5. Explain the duty of mitigation of damages.

6. Describe the remedy of rescission of a contract.

7. Define the equitable remedies of specific performance, quasi contract, and injunction.

8. Describe torts associated with contracts.

9. Define *punitive damages*.

10. Describe breach of Internet contracts.

Chapter Contents

There are three levels of performance of a contract: complete, substantial, and inferior. Complete (or strict) performance by a party discharges that party's duties under the contract. Substantial performance constitutes a minor breach of the contract. Inferior performance constitutes a material breach that impairs or destroys the essence of the contract. Various remedies may be obtained by a nonbreaching party if a **breach of contract** occurs, that is, if a contracting party fails to perform an absolute duty owed under a contract.[1]

The most common remedy for a breach of contract is an award of **monetary damages**, often called the "law remedy." If a monetary award does not provide adequate relief, however, the court may order any one of several **equitable remedies**, including specific performance, reformation, quasi contract, and injunction. Equitable remedies are based on the concept of fairness.

This chapter discusses breach of contracts and the remedies available to the nonbreaching party.

PERFORMANCE AND BREACH

If a contractual duty has not been discharged (i.e., terminated) or excused (i.e., relieved of legal liability), the contracting party owes an absolute duty (i.e., covenant) to perform the duty. As mentioned in the chapter introduction, there are three types of performance of a contract: (1) complete performance, (2) substantial performance (or minor breach), and (3) inferior performance (or material breach). These concepts are discussed in the following paragraphs.

Complete Performance

Most contracts are discharged by the **complete** or **strict performance** of the contracting parties. Complete performance occurs when a party to a contract renders performance exactly as required by the contract. A fully performed contract is called an **executed contract**.

Note that **tender of performance** also discharges a party's contractual obligations. Tender is an unconditional and absolute offer by a contracting party to perform his or her obligations under the contract.

Consider This Example   Suppose Ashley's Dress Shops, Inc., contracts to purchase dresses from a manufacturer for $25,000. Ashley's has performed its obligation under the contract once it tenders the $25,000 to the manufacturer. If the manufacturer fails to deliver the dresses, Ashley's can sue it for breach of contract.

breach of contract
If a contracting party fails to perform an absolute duty owed under a contract.

It is a vain thing to imagine a right without a remedy; for want of right and want of remedy are reciprocal.

C. J. Holt
Ashby v. White *(1703)*

No cause of action arises from a bare promise.

Legal Maxim

complete performance
Occurs when a party to a contract renders performance exactly as required by the contract; discharges that party's obligations under the contract.

tender of performance
Tender is an unconditional and absolute offer by a contracting party to perform his or her obligations under the contract.

Beijing, China *As capitalism increases in China, the performance and judicial enforcement of contracts will become more important.*

Substantial Performance: Minor Breach

Substantial performance occurs when there has been a **minor breach** of contract. In other words, it occurs when a party to a contract renders performance that deviates only slightly from complete performance. The nonbreaching party may (1) convince the breaching party to elevate his or her performance to complete performance, (2) deduct the cost to repair the defect from the contract price and remit the balance to the breaching party, or (3) sue the breaching party to recover the cost to repair the defect if the breaching party has already been paid.

Consider This Example Suppose Donald Trump contracts with Big Apple Construction Co. to have Big Apple construct an office building for $50 million. The architectural plans call for installation of three-ply windows in the building. Big Apple constructs the building exactly to plan except that it installs two-ply windows. There has been substantial performance. It would cost $300,000 to install the correct windows. If Big Apple agrees to replace the windows, its performance is elevated to complete performance, and Trump must remit the entire contract price. However, if Trump has to hire someone else to replace windows, he may deduct this cost of repair from the contract price and remit the difference to Big Apple.

Inferior Performance: Material Breach

A **material breach** of a contract occurs when a party renders inferior performance of his or her contractual obligations that impairs or destroys the essence of the contract. There is no clear line between a minor breach and a material breach. A determination is made on a case-by-case basis.

Where there has been a material breach of contract, the nonbreaching party may *rescind* the contract and seek restitution of any compensation paid under the contract to the breaching party. The nonbreaching party is discharged from any further performance under the contract.[2] Alternatively, the nonbreaching party may treat the contract as being in effect and sue the breaching party to recover *damages*.

Consider This Example Suppose a university contracts with a general contractor to build a new three-story building with classroom space for 1,000 students. However, the completed building can support the weight of only 500 students because the contractor used inferior materials. The defect cannot be repaired without rebuilding the entire structure. Because this is a material breach, the university may rescind the contract and require the removal of the building. The university is discharged of any obligations under the contract and is free to employ another contractor to rebuild the building. Alternatively, the university could accept the building and deduct damages caused by the defect from the contract price.

*C*ONCEPT SUMMARY   TYPES OF PERFORMANCE

Type of Performance	Legal Consequence
Complete performance	The contract is discharged.
Substantial performance (minor breach)	The nonbreaching party may recover damages caused by the breach.
Inferior performance (material breach)	The nonbreaching party may either (1) rescind the contract and recover restitution or (2) affirm the contract and recover damages.

Anticipatory Breach

Anticipatory breach (or **anticipatory repudiation**) of contract occurs when the contracting party informs the other in advance that he or she will not perform his or her contractual duties when due. This type of material breach can be expressly stated or implied from the conduct of the repudiator. Where there is an anticipatory repudiation, the nonbreaching party's obligations under the contract are discharged immediately. The nonbreaching party also has the right to sue the repudiating party when the anticipatory breach occurs; there is no need to wait until performance is due.[3]

E-Commerce & Information Technology

BREACH OF AN INTERNET CONTRACT

A contract is a contract is a contract, even if it is over the Internet. Consider the following case. The Hotmail Corporation (Hotmail) is a Silicon Valley company that provides free e-mail on the Internet. Hotmail's online services allow its millions of registered subscribers to exchange e-mail messages over the Internet. The company registered the name "Hotmail" as a federal trademark and obtained the Internet domain name "hotmail.com." Every e-mail sent by a Hotmail subscriber automatically displays Hotmail's domain name and mark. To become a Hotmail subscriber, one must agree to abide by a Service Agreement by clicking an "accept" prompt on the computer screen. This click-wrap contract expressly prohibits subscribers from using Hotmail's services to send unsolicited commercial bulk e-mail, or "spam," or to send obscene or pornographic messages. The transmission of spam is a practice widely condemned by the Internet community.

In the fall of 1997, Hotmail discovered that defendants Van$ Money Pie Inc., ALS Enterprises, Inc., LCGM, Inc., and the Genesis Network, Inc. created Hotmail accounts that were facilitating their sending spam e-mail to Hotmail subscribers. The spam messages advertised pornography and "get-rich-quick" schemes, among other things. Hotmail was inundated with complaints from its subscribers who had received the spam, and faced the loss of customers as well as an overloading of its services from the spam e-mail.

Hotmail sued the defendants in district court for breach of contract and sought a preliminary injunction to enjoin the defendants from sending spam e-mail using Hotmail accounts, domain name, and mark. This district court agreed with Hotmail on its breach of contract claim stating

The evidence supports a finding that plaintiff Hotmail will likely prevail on its breach of contract claim and that there are at least serious questions going to the merits of this claim in that plaintiff has presented evidence of the following: that defendants obtained a number of Hotmail mailboxes and access to Hotmail's services; that in so doing defendants agreed to abide by Hotmail's Terms of Service which prohibit using a Hotmail account for purposes of sending spam and/or pornography; that defendants breached their contract with Hotmail by using Hotmail's services to facilitate sending spam and/or pornography; that Hotmail complied with the conditions of the contract except those from which its performance was excused; and that if defendants are not enjoined they will continue to create such accounts in violation of the Terms of Service.

The district court enforced the click-wrap contract and held the defendants in breach of Hotmail's Internet contract. The court issued a preliminary injunction prohibiting the defendants from using Hotmail accounts or Hotmail's domain name or mark to send spam. [*Hotmail Corporation v. Van$ Money Pie, Inc.*, 47 U.S.P.Q. 1020 (N.D.Cal. 1998)]

MONETARY DAMAGES

A nonbreaching party may recover **monetary damages** from a breaching party. Monetary damages are available whether the breach was minor or material. Several types of monetary damages may be awarded. These include *compensatory*, *consequential*, *liquidated*, and *nominal damages*.

monetary damages

An award of money.

Compensatory Damages

Compensatory damages are intended to compensate a nonbreaching party for the loss of the bargain. In other words, they place the nonbreaching party in the same position as if the contract had been fully performed by restoring the "benefit of the bargain."

compensatory damages

An award of money intended to compensate a nonbreaching party for the loss of the bargain; they place the nonbreaching party in the same position as if the contract had been fully performed by restoring the "benefit of the bargain."

Consider This Example Suppose Lederle Laboratories enters into a written contract to employ a manager for three years at a salary of $6,000 per month. Before work is to start, the manager is informed that he or she will not be needed. This is a material breach of contract. Assume the manager finds another job, but it pays only $5,000 a month. The manager may recover $1,000 per month for 36 months (total $36,000) from Lederle Laboratories as compensatory damages. These damages place the manager in the same situation as if the contract with Lederle had been performed.

The amount of compensatory damages that will be awarded for breach of contract depends on the type of contract involved and which party breached the contract. The award of compensatory damages in some special types of contracts is discussed in the following paragraphs.

Sale of Goods   Compensatory damages for a breach of a sales contract involving goods are governed by the Uniform Commercial Code (UCC). The usual measure of damages for a breach of a sales contract is the difference between the contract price and the market price of the goods at the time and place the goods were to be delivered.[4]

Consider This Example   Suppose (1) Revlon, Inc., contracted to buy a piece of equipment from Greenway Supply Co. for $20,000 and (2) the equipment is not delivered. Revlon then purchases the equipment from another vendor but has to pay $25,000 because the current market price for the equipment has risen. Revlon can recover $5,000—the difference between the market price paid ($25,000) and the contract price ($20,000)—in compensatory damages.

Construction Contracts   A construction contract arises when the owner of real property contracts to have a contractor build a structure or do other construction work. The compensatory damages recoverable for a breach of a construction contract vary with the stage of completion the project is in when the breach occurs.

The contractor may recover the profits he or she would have made on the contract if the owner breaches the construction contract before construction begins.

Consider This Example   Suppose RXZ Corporation contracts to have the Ace Construction Co. build a factory for $1.2 million. It will cost the contractor $800,000 in materials and labor to build the factory. If RXZ Corporation breaches the contract before construction begins, the contractor can recover $400,000 in "lost profit."

The contractor can recover his or her lost profits plus the cost of construction to date if RXZ Corporation decides not to go ahead with the new factory after construction begins. Assume in the prior example that Ace Construction Co. had spent $300,000 on materials and labor before the contract was breached. Here, the contractor can recover $700,000—$400,000 lost profit plus $300,000 expended on materials and labor. If the owner breaches the contract after the project is completed, the contractor can recover the full contract price ($1.2 million).

If the builder breaches a construction contract, either before or during construction, the owner can recover the increased cost above the contract price that he or she has to pay to have the work completed by another contractor. For example, suppose in the previous instance Ace Construction Co. breached the contract by refusing to build the factory. Assume that RXZ Corporation has to pay $1.5 million to have the same factory built by another contractor. RXZ can recover the increased cost of construction ($300,000) from the contractor as compensatory damages.

Employment Contracts   An employee whose employer breaches an employment contract can recover lost wages or salary as compensatory damages. If the employee breaches the contract, the employer can recover the costs to hire a new employee plus any increase in salary paid to the replacement.

Consequential Damages

In addition to compensatory damages, a nonbreaching party sometimes can recover **special** or **consequential damages** from the breaching party. Consequential damages are *foreseeable* damages that arise from circumstances outside the contract. To be liable for consequential damages, the breaching party must know or have reason to know that the breach will cause special damages to the other party.

Consider This Example   Suppose Soan-Allen Co., a wholesaler, enters into a contract to purchase 1,000 men's suits for $150 each from the Fabric Manufacturing Co., a manu-

Necessitious men are not, truly speaking, free men, but, to answer a present exigency, will submit to any terms that the crafty may impose upon them.

Lord Thomas Henley
Vernon v. Bethell *(1762)*

He who derives the advantage ought to sustain the burden.

Legal Maxim

consequential damages

Foreseeable damages that arise from circumstances outside the contract. To be liable for these damages, the breaching party must know or have reason to know that the breach will cause special damages to the other party.

facturer. Prior to contracting, the wholesaler tells the manufacturer that the suits will be resold to retailers for $225. The manufacturer breaches the contract by failing to manufacture the suits. The wholesaler cannot get the suits manufactured by anyone else in time to meet his contracts. He or she can recover $75,000 of lost profits on the resale contracts (1,000 suits × $75 profit) as consequential damages from the manufacturer because the manufacturer knew of this special damage to Soan-Allen Co. if it breached the contract.

In the following case, the court awarded consequential damages against a breaching party.

Super Valu Stores, Inc. v. Peterson
506 So.2d 317 (1987)
Supreme Court of Alabama

CASE 13.1

BACKGROUND AND FACTS
Super Valu Stores, Inc. (Super Valu), a wholesale operator of supermarkets, developed a new concept for a market called "County Market." The basic concept of the County Market was that it must be the lowest priced store in the marketplace and operate on a high-volume, low-profit margin structure. In 1981, Super Valu purchased a parcel of property in Oxford, Alabama, for the development of a County Market. It planned to lease the store to an independent retailer to operate. Thomas J. Peterson, who was an executive of Super Valu, applied for the operator's position at the proposed store. In January 1984, Peterson was approved as the retail operator of the proposed Oxford County Market. On February 24, 1984, Peterson retired from Super Valu so that he could operate the new store. When Super Valu failed to construct and lease the store to Peterson, he sued Super Valu for breach of contract. The trial court held in favor of Peterson and awarded him $5 million in lost profits that would have been derived by him from the store. Super Valu appealed.

ISSUE
Are lost profits from an unestablished business recoverable as consequential damages even though it can be argued that they are inherently too speculative and conjectural?

COURT'S REASONING
Current Alabama law, like the law of other states, authorizes recovery of anticipated profits of an unestablished business, if

proved with reasonable certainty. The supreme court stated: "The fundamental basis for Peterson's evidence as to damages was Super Valu's own projections of profits, produced in its normal course of business long before this dispute arose. These projections were the product of an intense, exhaustive process involving many different Super Valu personnel. Super Valu's projections resulted from the application of a scientific methodology that for many years had accurately predicted the future performance of stores associated with Super Valu. These projections were also based upon the prior successful performances of the Super Valu business system, of which the Oxford County Market would have become a standardized part."

DECISION
The supreme court held that lost profits from an unestablished business can be recovered as consequential damages if they can be determined with reasonable certainty as in this case and affirmed the trial court's judgment.

Case Questions

Critical Legal Thinking   Are lost profits too speculative to be awarded in breach of contract actions?

Business Ethics   Did Super Valu act ethically by denying liability in this case?

Contemporary Business   If unestablished businesses could not recover lost profits, would there be more or fewer breaches of contract with such businesses?

Liquidated Damages

Under certain circumstances, the parties to a contract may agree in advance to the amount of damages payable upon a breach of contract. These damages are called **liquidated damages**. To be lawful, the actual damages must be difficult or impracticable to determine, and the liquidated amount must be reasonable in the circumstances.[5] An enforceable liquidated damage clause is an exclusive remedy even if actual damages are later determined to be different.

A liquidated damage clause is considered a **penalty** if actual damages are clearly determinable in advance or if the liquidated damages are excessive or unconscionable. If a liquidated damage clause is found to be a penalty, it is unenforceable. The nonbreaching party may then recover actual damages. In the following case, the court had to decide whether a liquidated damage clause was a penalty.

liquidated damages
Damages to which parties to a contract agree in advance if the contract is breached.

Business Brief
Many businesses include liquidated damage clauses in their commercial contracts, which help to provide certainty, avoid lawsuits, and provide an incentive to enter into contracts.

Samarkan, Uzbekistan Many international contracts include liquidated damage clauses.

California and Hawaiian Sugar Co. v. Sun Ship, Inc.
794 F.2d 1433 (1986)
United States Court of Appeals, Ninth Circuit

CASE 13.2

BACKGROUND AND FACTS

The California and Hawaiian Sugar Company (C&H), a California corporation, is an agricultural cooperative owned by 14 sugar plantations in Hawaii. It transports raw sugar to its refinery in Crockett, California. Sugar is a seasonal crop, with about 70 percent of the harvest occurring between April and October. C&H requires reliable seasonal shipping of the raw sugar from Hawaii to California. Sugar stored on the ground or left unharvested suffers a loss of sucrose and goes to waste.

After C&H was notified by its normal shipper that it would be withdrawing its services as of January 1981, C&H commissioned the design of a large hybrid vessel—a tug of a catamaran design consisting of a barge attached to the tug. After substantial negotiation, C&H contracted with Sun Ship, Inc. (Sun Ship), a Pennsylvania corporation, to build the vessel for $25,405,000. The contract, which was signed in the fall of 1979, provided a delivery date of June 30, 1981. The contract also contained a liquidated damage clause calling for a payment of $17,000 per day for each day that the vessel was not delivered to C&H after June 30, 1981. Sun Ship did not complete the vessel until March 16, 1982. The vessel was commissioned in mid-July 1982 and christened the *Moku Pahu*.

During the 1981 season, C&H was able to find other means of shipping the crop from Hawaii to its California refinery. Evidence established that actual damages suffered by C&H because of the nonavailability of the vessel from Sun ship were $368,000. When Sun Ship refused to pay the liquidated damages, C&H filed suit to require payment of $4,413,000 in liquidated damages under the contract. The

district court entered judgment in favor of C&H and awarded the corporation $4,413,000 plus interest. Sun Ship appealed.

ISSUE

Is the liquidated damage clause enforceable, or is it a penalty clause that is not enforceable?

COURT'S REASONING

Contracts are contracts because they contain enforceable promises. Absent some overriding public policy, those promises are to be enforced. Parties who agree to pay damages of a fixed amount normally have a good sense of what damages can occur, and the courts are reluctant to override their judgment. In this case, the court of appeals stated: "Proof of this loss is difficult. Whatever the loss, the parties had promised each other that $17,000 per day was a reasonable measure. When sophisticated parties with bargaining parity have agreed what lack of this prize would mean, and it is now difficult to measure what the lack did mean, the court will uphold the parties' bargain."

DECISION

The court of appeals held that the liquidated damage clause was not a penalty and was therefore enforceable. Affirmed.

Case Questions

Critical Legal Thinking Should liquidated damage clauses be enforced or should nonbreaching parties be allowed to recover only actual damages caused by the breaching party?

Business Ethics Did either party act unethically in this case?

Contemporary Business Do you think many businesses use liquidated damage clauses? Can you give some examples?

Nominal Damages

The nonbreaching party can sue the breaching party for nominal damages even if no financial loss resulted from the breach. **Nominal damages** usually are awarded in a small amount such as $1. Cases involving nominal damages are usually brought on "principle."

nominal damages

Damages awarded when the nonbreaching party sues the breaching party even though no financial loss has resulted from the breach; usually consists of $1 or some other small amount.

CONCEPT SUMMARY   TYPES OF MONETARY DAMAGES

Type of Damage	Description
Compensatory	Compensates a nonbreaching party for the loss of the bargain. It places the nonbreaching party in the same position as if the contract had been fully performed.
Consequential	Compensates a nonbreaching party for foreseeable special damages. The breaching party must have known or should have known that these damages would result from the breach.
Liquidated	Agreement by the parties in advance that sets the amount of damages recoverable in case of breach. These damages are lawful if they do not cause a penalty.
Nominal	Damages awarded against the breaching party even though the nonbreaching party has suffered no actual damages because of the breach. A small amount (e.g., $1) is usually awarded

Mitigation of Damages

If a contract has been breached, the law places a duty on the innocent nonbreaching party of take reasonable efforts to **mitigate** (i.e., avoid and reduce) the resulting damages. The extent of mitigation required depends on the type of contract involved. For example, if an employer breaches an employment contract, the employee owes a duty to mitigate damages by trying to find substitute employment. The employee is only required to accept comparable employment. The courts consider such factors as compensation, rank, status, job description, and geographical location in determining the comparability of jobs.

In the following case, the court had to decide whether a job was comparable.

mitigation

A nonbreaching party is under a legal duty to avoid or reduce damages caused by a breach of contract.

Parker v. Twentieth Century-Fox Film Corp.

3 Cal.3d 176, 89 Cal.Rptr. 737 (1970)

California Supreme Court

CASE 13.3

BACKGROUND AND FACTS

On August 6, 1965, Twentieth Century-Fox Film Corporation (Fox), a major film production studio, entered into an employment contract with Shirley MacLaine Parker (Parker), an actress. Under the contract, Parker was to play the leading female role in a musical production called *Bloomer Girl*, to be filmed in Los Angeles. In the movie, Parker would be able to use her talents as a dancer as well as an actress. The contract provided that Parker was to be paid guaranteed compensation of $53,571.42 per week for 14 weeks commencing on May 23, 1966, for a total $750,000. On April 4, 1966, Fox sent Parker a letter notifying her that it was not going to film *Bloomer Girl*. The letter, however, offered Parker the leading female role in a film tentatively entitled *Big Country*, which was to be a dramatic western to be filmed in Australia. The

compensation Fox offered Parker was identical to that offered for *Bloomer Girl*. Fox gave Parker one week to accept. She did not and the offer expired. Parker sued Fox to recover the guaranteed compensation provided in the *Bloomer Girl* contract. The trial court granted summary judgment to Parker. Fox appealed.

ISSUE

Was the job that Fox offered Parker in *Big Country* comparable employment that Parker was obligated to accept to mitigate damages?

COURT'S REASONING

Before projected earnings from other employment opportunities not sought or accepted by the discharged employee can be applied in mitigation, the employer must show that the other employment was comparable, or substantially similar, to that of which the employee has been deprived. In finding that the offered employment was not comparable, the supreme court stated: "[I]t is clear that the trial court correctly ruled that plaintiff's failure to accept defendant's tendered substitute employment could not be applied in mitigation of damages because the offer of the *Big Country* lead was of employment both different and inferior. The mere circumstances that *Bloomer Girl* was to be a musical review calling upon plaintiff's talents as a dancer as well as an actress, and was to be produced in the City of Los Angeles, whereas *Big Country* was a straight dramatic role in a western-type story taking place in an opal mine in Australia, demonstrates the difference in kind between the two employments: The female lead as a dramatic actress in a western-style motion picture can by no stretch of imagination be considered the equivalent of or substantially similar to the lead in a song-and-dance production."

DECISION

The supreme court held that the job that Fox offered to Parker in *Big Country* was not comparable employment to the role Fox had contracted Parker to play in *Bloomer Girl*. Therefore, Parker did not fail to mitigate damages by refusing to accept such employment. The supreme court affirmed the trial court's summary judgment.

Case Questions

Critical Legal Thinking Should nonbreaching parties be under a duty to mitigate damages caused by the breaching party? Why or why not?

Business Ethics Did Fox act ethically in this case? Did Parker?

Contemporary Business Who is more likely to be able to mitigate damages when there is a breach of an employment contract: (1) the president of a large corporation, (2) a middle manager, or (3) a bank teller?

Contemporary Business Environment

ENFORCEMENT OF REMEDIES

If a nonbreaching party brings a successful lawsuit against a breaching party to a contract, the court will enter a *judgment* in his or her favor. This judgment must then be collected. If the breaching party refuses to pay the judgment, the court may

- **Issue a Writ of Attachment** This writ orders the sheriff to seize property in the possession of the breaching party that he or she owns, and to sell the property at auc-

tion to satisfy the judgment. In all states, certain property is exempt from attachment.

- **Issue a Writ of Garnishment** This writ orders that wages, bank accounts, or other property of the breaching party that is in the hands of third parties be paid over to the nonbreaching party to satisfy the judgment. Federal and state laws limit the amount of the breaching party's wages or salary that can be garnished.

RESCISSION AND RESTITUTION

rescission

An action to rescind (undo) the contract. Rescission is available if there has been a material breach of contract, fraud, duress, undue influence, or mistake.

restitution

Returning of goods or property received from the other party to rescind a contract; if the actual goods or property is not available, a cash equivalent must be made.

Rescission is an action to undo the contract. It is available where there has been a material breach of contract, fraud, duress, undue influence, or mistake. Generally, to rescind a contract, the parties must make **restitution** of the consideration they received under the contract.[6] Restitution consists of returning the goods, property, money, or other consideration received from the other party. If possible, the actual goods or property must be returned. If the goods or property have been consumed or are otherwise unavailable, restitution must be made by conveying a cash equivalent. The rescinding party must give adequate notice of the rescission to the breaching party. Rescission and restitution restore the parties to the position they occupied prior to the contract.

Consider This Example Suppose Filene's Department Store contracts to purchase $100,000 of goods from a sweater manufacturer. The store pays $10,000 as a down payment, and the first $20,000 of goods are delivered. The goods are materially defective, and the defect cannot be cured. This breach is a material breach. Filene's can rescind the contract. The store is entitled to receive its down payment back from the manufacturer, and the manufacturer is entitled to receive the goods back from the store.

Business Ethics

MUST AN ENGAGEMENT RING BE RETURNED IF THE ENGAGEMENT IS BROKEN OFF?

When a man and woman are in love, the man often asks the woman to marry him and presents her with an engagement ring. But engagements do not always lead to weddings and are sometimes broken off by one of the parties. The question then is: Who gets the engagement ring? Does the woman get to keep the ring, or can the man recover it? Consider the following case.

In August 1993, Rodger Lindh (Rodger) proposed marriage to Janis Surman (Janis) and presented her with a diamond ring he purchased for $17,400. She accepted his proposal and ring. Discord developed in their relationship, however, and in March 1994 Rodger called off the engagement. He asked Janis to return the engagement ring, but when she refused, Rodger sued her seeking recovery of the ring. The Pennsylvania trial court and appellate court applied a no-fault rule and held that Janis must return the ring to Rodger. Janis appealed to the Pennsylvania Supreme Court.

The Pennsylvania Supreme Court noted that Janis favored the "fault" rule for deciding who gets the ring in a broken engagement case. Under this rule if "she" breaks off the engagement, "he" gets the ring back, if "he" breaks off the engagement, "she" gets to keep the ring. Although noting that some states still follow this rule, the Pennsylvania Supreme Court stated that Pennsylvania would not follow the fault-rule. The court noted that the process of determining who is "wrong" and who is "right" is difficult in modern relationships and that this would require parties to aim bitter and unpleasant accusations at each other.

Instead, the Pennsylvania Supreme Court decided to follow the modern, objective "no fault" rule that holds that an engagement ring must be returned to the donor no matter who breaks off the engagement. The court stated:

Courts that have applied no-fault principles to engagement ring cases have borrowed from the policies of their respective legislatures that have moved away from the notion of fault in their divorce statutes. We agree with those jurisdictions that have looked toward the development of no-fault divorce law for a principle to decide engagement ring cases, and the inherent weaknesses in any fault-based system lead us to adopt a no-fault approach to resolution of engagement ring disputes. We believe that the benefits from the certainty of our rule outweigh its negatives, and that a strict no-fault approach is less flawed than a fault-based theory.

The Pennsylvania Supreme Court affirmed the judgment of the lower courts awarding the engagement ring to Rodger. [*Lindh v. Surman*, 1999 WL 1073639 (PA 1999)]

EQUITABLE REMEDIES

Equitable remedies are available if there has been a breach of contract that cannot be adequately compensated by a legal remedy. They are also available to prevent unjust enrichment. The most common equitable remedies are specific performance, reformation, quasi contract, and injunction.

Specific Performance

An award of **specific performance** orders the breaching party to perform the acts promised in the contract. The courts have the discretion to award this remedy if the subject matter of the contract is unique.[7] For example, this remedy is available to enforce land contracts since every piece of real property is considered to be unique. Works of art, antiques, items of sentimental value, rare coins, stamps, heirlooms, and such also fit the requirement for uniqueness. Most other personal property does not. Specific performance of personal service contracts is not granted because the courts would find it difficult or impracticable to supervise or monitor performance of the contract.

> *Every unjust decision is a reproach to the law or the judge who administers it. If the law should be in danger of doing injustice, then equity should be called in to remedy it. Equity was introduced to mitigate the rigor of the law.*
>
> Lord Denning, M. R.
> Re Vandervell's Trusts (1974)

specific performance

A remedy that orders the breaching party to perform the acts promised in the contract; usually awarded in cases where the subject matter is unique, such as in contracts involving land, heirlooms, and paintings.

Entrepreneur and the Law

HARD DEALING FOR THE HARD ROCK CAFE

In the 1970s, Peter Morton operated a popular restaurant and tourist attraction in England known as the "Hard Rock Cafe." At that time, Milton Okun of the United States inquired about investing in the business. Morton declined Okun's offer but indicated that if he contemplated expanding the business to the United States, he would contact Okun. In

December 1981, Morton located a site suitable for a Hard Rock Cafe in Los Angeles, California. Morton contacted Okun and offered him stock in the general partnership. An agreement was executed on March 2, 1982, whereby Okun contributed $100,000 in exchange for a 20 percent interest in the general partnership. Paragraph 9 of the agreement gave Okun the option to participate in future Hard Rock Cafes with the same 20 percent interest.

After Morton raised funds from limited partners, the Hard Rock Cafe opened in the Beverly Center in Los Angeles and was a commercial success. As a result, Morton decided to exploit the San Francisco market. Per their agreement, Morton offered Okun a 20 percent interest, which Okun accepted.

In 1984, while Morton was finalizing plans for operating a Hard Rock Cafe in Chicago, Illinois, Morton and Okun had a disagreement. Morton advised Okun that he planned to exclude Okun from participating in the venture. Okun offered to participate on the terms of their 1982 agreement. Morton rejected that offer and proceeded with the development of restaurants in Houston, Honolulu, and Chicago without offering Okun a general partnership interest in these ventures. Okun sued Morton for breach of contract, seeking an order of specific performance of their 1982 agreement. The trial court held in favor of Okun and ordered specific performance of the contract. Morton appealed.

Can the 1982 agreement between Morton and Okun be specifically performed?

The court of appeals noted that as a whole, the terms of the agreement were sufficient to establish from the outset the ways in which future ventures were to be financed, owned, and operated by the parties. The fundamental structure of all such undertakings was to be based on the 20/80 ratio estab-

lished for the creation of the L.A. Hard Rock Cafe. The court stated that although the agreement admittedly does not deal in specifics, neither law nor equity requires that every term and condition be set forth in the contract. In light of the fact that neither defendant nor plaintiff could predict with any degree of certainty the success of the Los Angeles operation, it is not surprising that Paragraph 9 was drafted broadly enough to accommodate changing circumstances and unforeseen developments.

Defendant asserts, however, that specific performance should not have been granted because enforcement of the contract will require continuous and protracted judicial supervision. The courts of this state have generally followed this "archaic" rule. This case merely involves the offering of an opportunity to participate in a business venture and the concomitant payment of capital and expenses for that participation.

The court stated, "We are not here concerned with the day-to-day management of any particular Hard Rock Cafe or related enterprises that would require the close and ongoing cooperation of the parties or the court." The defendant retains the discretion under the terms of the judgment to structure each venture as he pleases so long as he maintains the 20/80 ratio and does nothing to interfere with or burden plaintiff's right to participate in the deal. Under these circumstances, the court concluded that the decree of specific performance is not unduly burdensome nor requires inordinate supervision by the trial court.

The appellate court held that the subject matter of the agreement between Morton and Okun was unique and therefore that the agreement can be specifically enforced. [*Okun v. Morton*, 203 Cal.App.3d, 250 Cal.Rptr. 220 (Cal.App. 1988)]

Reformation

reformation

An equitable doctrine that permits the court to rewrite a contract to express the parties' true intentions.

Reformation is an equitable doctrine that permits the court to rewrite a contract to express the parties' true intentions. For example, suppose a clerical error is made during the typing of the contract and both parties sign the contract without discovering the error. If a dispute later arises, the court can reform the contract to correct the clerical error to read what the parties originally intended.

Quasi Contract

quasi contract

An equitable doctrine that permits the recovery of compensation even though no enforceable contract exists between the parties.

A **quasi contract** (also called **quantrum meruit** or an **implied-in-law contract**) is an equitable doctrine that permits the recovery of compensation even though no enforceable contract exists between the parties because of lack of consideration, the Statue of Frauds has run out, or the like. Such contracts are imposed by law to prevent unjust enrichment. Under quasi contract, a party can recover the reasonable value of the services or materials provided. For example, a physician who stops to render aid to an unconscious victim of an automobile accident may recover the reasonable value of his or her services from that person.

Injunction

injunction

A court order that prohibits a person from doing a certain act.

An **injunction** is a court order that prohibits a person from doing a certain act. To obtain an injunction, the requesting party must show that he or she will suffer irreparable injury unless the injunction is issued.

Consider This Example   Suppose a professional football team enters into a five-year employment contract with a "superstar" quarterback. The quarterback breaches the contract and enters into a contract to play for a competing team. Here, the first team can seek an injunction to prevent the quarterback from playing for the other team.

CONCEPT SUMMARY   TYPES OF EQUITABLE REMEDIES

Type of Equitable Remedy	Description
Specific performance	Court orders the breaching party to perform the acts promised in the contract. The subject matter of the contract must be unique.
Reformation	Court rewrites a contract to express the parties' true intentions. It is usually used to correct clerical errors.
Quasi contract	Permits the recovery of damages for breach of an implied-in-law contract where no actual contract exists between the parties. Only the reasonable value of the services or materials may be recovered.
Injunction	Court order that prohibits a party from doing a certain act. Available in contract actions only in limited circumstances.

TORTS ASSOCIATED WITH CONTRACTS

The recovery for breach of contract usually is limited to contract damages. A party who can prove a contract-related **tort**, however, may also recover tort damages. Tort damages include compensation for personal injury, pain and suffering, emotional distress, and possibly punitive damages. The major torts associated with contracts are (1) *intentional interference with contractual relations* and (2) *breach of the implied covenant of good faith and fair dealing*.

Business Brief

Many breach of contract actions also involve torts. The merging of these two areas has led some commentators to call this area "contorts."

Intentional Interference with Contractual Relations

A party to a contract may sue any third person who intentionally interferes with the contract and causes that party injury. The third party does not have to have acted with malice or bad faith. This tort, which is known as the tort of **intentional interference with contractual relations**, usually arises when a third party induces a contracting party to breach the contract with another party. The following elements must be shown:

1. A valid, enforceable contract between the contracting parties
2. Third-party knowledge of this contract
3. Third-party inducement to breach the contract

A third party can contract with the breaching party without becoming liable for this tort if a contracting party has already breached the contract, because the third party cannot be held to have induced a preexisting breach.

intentional interference with contractual relations

A tort that arises when a third party induces a contracting party to breach the contract with another party.

Contemporary Business Environment

THE MEANING OF A HANDSHAKE

There is a substantial danger of being found liable for tortious conduct and being assessed punitive damages if one intentionally interferes with another's contract. Consider the celebrated case of *Texaco, Inc. v. Pennzoil Company* [729 S.W.2d 768 (Tex.App. 1987)].

The saga began in 1983, when Pennzoil tried to buy up 20 percent of Getty Oil's (Getty) outstanding stock for $100 per share. At that time, about 40 percent of Getty's outstanding stock was owned by the Sarah C. Getty Trust (Trust), 11.8 percent was owned by the J. Paul Getty Museum in Los Angeles (Museum), and the rest was held by other investors.

On January 1, 1984, the head of the Trust met with representatives of Pennzoil. Pennzoil decided to make a play for total control of Getty by offering investors a buyout price of

$110 per share. The Trust accepted a resolution approving Pennzoil's offer on January 3, 1984. Two days later, Getty, Pennzoil, the Trust, and the Museum issued a joint press release announcing that the parties had "agreed in principle" to a merger of Getty with Pennzoil. The parties shook hands and hoisted glasses of champagne to toast the deal. Nothing in writing had yet been signed by the parties, however.

Forty-eight hours later, the party was over. Texaco, Inc. (Texaco), had been tipped that Getty was for sale. Representatives of Texaco met secretly with some trustees of the Trust and officials from the Museum about how Texaco could structure a takeover of Getty. A written deal was reached whereby Texaco would purchase shares held by the Museum and the Trust for $125 per share and thereby acquire more than 50 percent of Getty's outstanding shares in a $10-billion deal. Texaco completed its takeover of Getty.

Not surprisingly, Pennzoil was not pleased with Texaco's maneuver. On February 8, 1985, Pennzoil filed suit in Texas alleging that Texaco had tortiously interfered with its agreement with Getty. Pennzoil argued its handshake deal with Getty was a contract. It cited a Texas oil industry custom according to which handshakes were gentlemen's agreements that were to be honored. Texaco asserted that the argument wouldn't get Pennzoil to first base because the contract had to be formalized in writing to be enforceable.

Before the trial even began, Texaco accused Pennzoil's lawyer of impropriety for having given a $10,000 campaign contribution to the state court judge who was presiding in the case. Another Texas judge found no reason for the trial court judge to withdraw.

After a hard-fought trial, the jury held that the handshake between the Getty and Pennzoil people did count as a contract and that a definitive written agreement was unnecessary to seal the deal. After finding that such an agreement had indeed been reached, the jury moved on to the question of whether the tactics Texaco used to reach its takeover agreement were tortious. The jury found that Texaco had intentionally interfered with Pennzoil's agreement with Getty.

With the issue of liability resolved, the jury awarded a mind-boggling amount of money: $7.53 billion in actual damages. The jury heaped another $3 billion in punitive damages onto Pennzoil's award. This was the largest judgment in history. Texaco's appeals succeeded in getting the punitive damages reduced to $1 billion. Ultimately, to avoid the judgment, Texaco declared bankruptcy. Texaco emerged from bankruptcy one year later after the parties agreed to settle the entire matter for $3 billion. It is estimated that Pennzoil's lawyer, who had taken the case on contingency, earned a fee of approximately $600 million.

Breach of the Implied Covenant of Good Faith and Fair Dealing

covenant of good faith and fair dealing

Under this implied covenant, the parties to a contract not only are held to the express terms of the contract but are also required to act in "good faith" and deal fairly in all respects in obtaining the objective of the contact.

Several states have held that a **covenant of good faith and fair dealing** is implied in certain types of contracts. Under this covenant, the parties to a contract not only are held to the express terms of the contract but are also required to act in "good faith" and deal fairly in all respects in obtaining the objective of the contract. A breach of this implied covenant is a tort for which tort damages are recoverable. This tort, which is sometimes referred to as the **tort of bad faith,** is an evolving area of the law.

Punitive Damages

punitive damages

Damages that are awarded to punish the defendant, to deter the defendant from similar conduct in the future, and to set an example for others.

Generally, **punitive damages** are not recoverable for breach of contract. They are recoverable, however, for certain tortious conduct that may be associated with the nonperformance of a contract. These actions include fraud, intentional conduct, or other egregious conduct. Punitive damages are in addition to actual damages and may be kept by the plaintiff. Punitive damages are awarded to punish the defendant, to deter the defendant from similar conduct in the future, and to set an example for others.

The court found a bad faith tort in the following case and awarded punitive damages.

Gourley v. State Farm Mutual Automobile Insurance Co.
227 Cal.App.3d 1099, 265 Cal.Rptr. 634 (1990)
California Court of Appeals

CASE 13.4

BACKGROUND AND FACTS

In late 1981, Julie Gourley was a passenger in an automobile that was struck by an out-of-control vehicle driven by an uninsured drunk driver. Gourley, who was not wearing a seat belt at the time of the accident, suffered a fractured right shoulder when she struck some portion of her vehicle's interior. Gourley made a claim under the uninsured motorist coverage in her automobile policy with State Farm Mutual Automobile Insurance Company (State Farm). Medical evidence showed that Gourley had some permanent disability and a limited range of motion, suffered residual pain, and might require surgery in the future. She demanded the policy limit of $100,000. In September 1982, State Farm's attorney, Barry Allen, advised Gourley that State Farm would contest the proximate cause of the injuries based on Gourley's failure to wear her seat belt. Evidence showed that under California law the seat belt issue was not a defense. State Farm offered a settlement of $20,000. Gourley refused it. When Gourley reduced her demand to $60,000, State Farm responded with a counteroffer of $25,000. Since the parties could not reach a settlement, the case went to arbitration. In October 1984, the arbitrator awarded Gourley $88,137, which State Farm promptly paid. Gourley sued State Farm for breach of the implied covenant of good faith and fair dealing in handling the claim and sought actual damages for emotional distress and punitive damages. The jury awarded her $15,765 in actual damages and $1,576,000 in punitive damages. State Farm appealed.

ISSUE
Did State Farm's conduct amount to a bad faith tort for which punitive damages could be awarded?

COURT'S REASONING
There is an implied covenant in every insurance contract that the insurer will do nothing to impair the insured's right to receive the benefit of the contractual bargain. That is, the insurer is expected to promptly pay to the insured all sums due under the contract. A major motivation for the purchase of insurance is the peace of mind that claims will be paid promptly. Withholding benefits is unreasonable if it is without proper cause. In reaching its decision, the appellate court stated: "The jury could reasonably find 'intentional' bad faith. . . . Gourley presented substantial evidence that State Farm adopted a 'stonewall' or 'see-you-in-court' attitude as exhibited by grossly insufficient offers to settle. The evidence was sufficient to support the jury's finding of bad faith. . . . State Farm . . . argues the evidence was insufficient as a matter of law to support the award of punitive damages. Not so. To support an award of punitive damages, the plaintiff must show 'oppression, fraud, or malice.' There was ample evidence to support an award of punitive damages."

DECISION
The appellate court held that State Farm's actions in not settling the claim under the policy limits by asserting an illegal defense (failure of Gourley to wear a seat belt) constituted bad faith. Affirmed.

Case Questions

Critical Legal Thinking   Should the law recognize the doctrine of bad faith tort? Why or why not?

Business Ethics   Does an insurer act unethically whenever it refuses to settle a claim under the policy limits? Do you think State Farm acted unethically in this case?

Contemporary Business   What effect will the recognition of bad faith torts associated with contracts have on businesses such as insurance companies? Explain.

Business Ethics

STATE FARM: NOT SUCH A GOOD NEIGHBOR

Most car drivers purchase automobile insurance to cover themselves from liability for accidents. Many drivers also purchase collision insurance, which means that the insurance covers the cost of repairing an insured's damaged automobile. Collision insurance policies routinely provide that replacement parts be of "like kind and quality" to the original damaged parts. But what if the replacement parts are "after-market" parts, that is, parts manufactured by companies other than the original automobile manufacturer. Do these generic parts qualify as "like kind and quality?" Many insureds (and their lawyers, of course) did not think so and sued their insurance company, State Farm Mutual Automobile Insurance Company, the largest insurance company in the United States, for breach of contract for including replacement parts in their vehicles without telling them.

The plaintiff's class-action lawsuit on behalf of all similarly situated insureds of State Farm included all those who had their automobiles repaired by State Farm over the past 10 years. The plaintiffs presented evidence that State Farm required body shops to use replacement parts made by after-market manufacturers and not by the automobile's original manufacturer. State Farm said it did this to save costs. For Example, a replacement hood for a 1995 Pontiac Grand Am cost $307 from General Motors but only $154 from an after-market manufacturer.

The plaintiffs argued that the replacement parts were inferior to original parts, were less safe and had not been crash-tested, and lowered the value of the automobile. The plaintiffs argued that State Farm forced body shops to use after-market parts to save it money at the expense of the insureds, and therefore that State Farm had breached its contract to provide replacement parts of "like kind and quality." The case went to trial in rural Marion, Illinois. After hearing the evidence, the jurors believed the plaintiffs and held that State Farm had breached its contract with the insureds. As a remedy, the jury returned a verdict of $456 million against State Farm. In a further blow, the trial court judge held that State Farm had committed consumer fraud and tacked on an additional $730 million in punitive and other damages, bringing the total award to almost $1.2 billion. State Farm has over $75 billion in assets. Each of the 4.7 million affected insureds would receive on average about $275 from State Farm.

State Farm argues that it did nothing wrong and that because of this judgment consumers will be hurt by higher insurance costs. The plaintiffs argue that State Farm merely got caught cheating its insureds and now must pay for its misbehavior. Lawsuits are pending against other automobile insurance companies based on the same issue.

1. Did State Farm act ethically in this case? Do you think it was acting in the best interests of its insureds?
2. Should it have told its insureds that it was ordering body shops to use after-market rather than original replacement parts? Why do you think State Farm did not tell its insureds this fact?
3. Do you think the amount of the award was justified? Why or why not? Should punitive damages have been assessed?

Chapter Summary

Performance and Breach, p. 301

Levels of Performance	1. *Complete performance.* A party renders performance exactly as required by the contract. That party's contractual duties are discharged. 2. *Substantial performance.* A party renders performance that deviates only slightly from complete performance. There is a *minor breach.* The nonbreaching party may recover damages caused by the breach. 3. *Inferior performance.* A party fails to perform express or implied contractual duties that impair or destroy the essence of the contract. There is a *material breach.* The nonbreaching party may either (1) rescind the contract and recover restitution or (2) affirm the contract and recover damages.
Anticipatory Breach	One contracting party informs the other party—by express words or by conduct—that he or she will not perform his or her contractual duties when due. This gives and immediate cause of action to the nonbreaching party to sue for breach of contract. It is also called *anticipatory repudiation.*

Monetary Damages, p. 303

Monetary Damages	1. *Compensatory damages.* Damages that compensate a nonbreaching party for the loss of the contract. Restores the "benefit of the bargain" to the nonbreaching party as if the contract had been fully performed.
	2. *Consequential damages.* Foreseeable damages that arise from circumstances outside the contract and of which the breaching party either knew or had reason to know of. They are also called *special damages.*
	3. *Nominal damages.* A small amount of damages awarded to a nonbreaching party who has suffered no financial loss because of the defendant's breach of contract. It is usually awarded "on principle."
	4. *Liquidated damages.* Damages payable upon breach of contract that are agreed on in advance by the contracting parties. Liquidated damages substitute for actual damages. For a liquidated damage clause to be lawful, the following two conditions must be met:
	  a. The actual damages must be extremely difficult or impracticable to determine.
	  b. The liquidated amount must be a reasonable estimate of the harm that would result from the breach.
	
	A liquidated damage clause is considered a *penalty* if actual damages are clearly determinable in advance or the liquidated damages are excessive or unconscionable. A penalty is unenforceable and the nonbreaching party may recover actual damages.

Mitigation of Damages	The duty the law places on a nonbreaching party to take reasonable efforts to avoid or reduce the resulting damages from a breach of contract. To mitigate a breach of an employment contract, the nonbreaching party must only accept "comparable" employment.

Rescission and Restitution, p. 308

Rescission and Restitution	*Rescission* is an action by a nonbreaching party to undo the contract. Available upon the material breach of a contract. The parties must make restitution of the consideration they have received from the other party. Rescission and restitution restore the parties to the position they occupied prior to the contract.

Equitable Remedies, p. 309

Equitable Remedies	*Equitable remedies* are available if the nonbreaching party cannot be adequately compensated by a legal remedy or to prevent unjust enrichment. 1. *Specific performance.* Court order that requires the breaching party to perform his or her contractual duties. Only available if the subject matter of the contract is *unique*. 2. *Reformation.* Permits the court to rewrite a contract to express the parties' true intention. Available to correct clerical and mathematical errors. 3. *Quasi contract.* Permits the court to order recovery of compensation even though no enforceable contract exists between the parties. Used to prevent unjust enrichment. Also called an *implied-in-law contract* or *quantum meruit*. 4. *Injunction.* Court order that prohibits a person from doing a certain act. The requesting party must show that he or she will suffer irreparable injury if the injunction is not granted.

Torts Associated With Contracts, p. 311

Types of Torts Associated With Contracts	1. *Intentional interference with contractual relations.* A third party intentionally interferes with another party's contract and induces the other party to that contract to breach it, causing the nonbreaching party injury. 2. *Breach of the implied covenant of good faith and fair dealing.* A party to a contract does not act in good faith or fails to deal fairly in achieving the object of the contract. This duty is only implied in certain contracts (e.g., insurance contracts). Also called the *tort of bad faith*.
Tort Damages	1. *Compensatory damages.* These include compensation for personal injury, pain and suffering, emotional distress, and other injuries caused by the defendant's tortious conduct. 2. *Punitive damages.* These are recoverable against a defendant for intentional or egregious conduct. They are awarded to punish the defendant, to deter the defendant from similar conduct in the future, and to set an example for others. The plaintiff may keep these damages.

END-OF-CHAPTER INTERNET EXERCISES AND CASE QUESTIONS

Working the Web Internet Exercises

ACTIVITIES

1. Use the Cornell Web site **www.law.cornell.edu/topics/injunctions.html** to review U.S. Supreme Court: Recent Injunction Decisions.

2. Visit LII: Law about . . . Remedies **www.law.cornell.edu/topics/remedies.html** and Legal Information Institute (LII) Commercial Law Overview **www.secure.law.cornell.edu/topics/commercial.html**.

Includes information on Consumer Credit, Damages, Debtor and Creditor, Injunctions, and Remedies, under those headings.

Determine whether the following are provided in your jurisdiction. Find a leading case for each:

Punitive damages

Implied covenant of good faith and fair dealing

Intentional interference with contractual relations

CRITICAL LEGAL THINKING CASES

13.1 Performance Louis Haeuser, who owned several small warehouses, contracted with Wallace C. Drennen, Inc. (Drennen), to construct a road to the warehouses. The contract price was $42,324. After Drennen completed the work, some cracks appeared in the road, causing improper drainage. In addition, "birdbaths" that accumulated water appeared in the road. When Haeuser refused to pay, Drennen sued to recover the full contract price. Haeuser filed a cross complaint to recover the cost of repairing the road. Who wins? [*Wallace C. Drennen, Inc. v. Haeuser*, 402 so.2d 771 (La. App. 1979)]

13.2 Anticipatory Repudiation In September 1976, Muhammad Ali (Ali) successfully defended his heavyweight boxing championship of the world by defeating Ken Norton. Shortly after the fight, Ali held a press conference and, as he had done on several occasions before, announced his retirement from boxing. At that time Ali had beaten every challenger except Duane Bobick, whom he had not yet fought. In November 1976, Madison Square Garden Boxing, Inc. (MSGB), a fight promoter, offered Ali $2.5 million if he would fight Bobick. Ali agreed, stating, "We are back in business again." MSGB and Ali signed a Fighters' Agreement and MSGB paid Ali $125,000 advance payment. The fight was to take place in Madison Square Garden on a date in February 1977. On November 30, 1976, Ali told MSGB that he was retiring from boxing and would not fight Bobick in February. Must MSGB wait until the date performance is due to sue Ali for breach of contract? [*Madison Square Garden Boxing, Inc. v. Muhammad Ali*, 430 F.Supp. 679 (N.D.Ill. 1977)]

13.3 Damages In 1978, Hawaiian Telephone Company entered into a contract with Microform Data Systems, Inc. (Microform), for Microform to provide a computerized assistance system that would handle 15,000 calls per hour with a one-second response time and with a "nonstop" feature to allow automatic recovery from any component failure. The contract called for installation of the host computer no later than mid-February 1979. Microform was not able to meet the initial installation date, and at that time it was determined that Microform was at least nine months away from providing a system that met contract specifications. Hawaiian Telephone canceled the contract and sued Microform for damages. Did Microform materially breach the contract to allow recovery of damages? [*Hawaiian Telephone Co. v. Microform Data Systems Inc.*, 829 F.2d 919 (9th Cir. 1987)]

13.4 Damages Raquel Welch was a movie actress who appeared in about 30 films between 1965 and 1980. She was considered a sex symbol, and her only serious dramatic role was a roller derby queen in *Kansas City Bomber*. In about 1980, Michael Phillips and David Ward developed a film package based on the John Steinbeck novella *Cannery Row*. In early 1981, Metro-Goldwyn-Mayer Film Company (MGM) accepted to produce the project and entered into a contract with Welch to play the leading female character, a prostitute named Suzy. At 40 years old, Welch relished the chance to direct her career toward more serious roles. Welch was to receive $250,000 from MGM, with payment being divided into weekly increments during filming. Filming began on December 1, 1980. On December 22, 1980, MGM fired Welch and replaced her with another actress, Debra Winger. Welch sued MGM to recover the balance of $194,444, which remained unpaid under the contract. Who wins? [*Welch v. Metro-Goldwyn-Mayer Film Co.*, 207 Cal.App.3d 164, 254 Cal.Rptr. 645 (Cal.App. 1989)]

13.5 Damages On August 28, 1979, Ptarmigan Investment Company (Ptarmigan), a partnership, entered into a contract with Gundersons, Inc. (Gundersons), a South Dakota corporation in the business of golf course construction. The contract provided that Gundersons would construct a golf course for Ptarmigan for a contract price of $1,294,129. Gundersons immediately started work and completed about one third of the work by late November 1979, when bad weather forced cessation of most work. Ptarmigan paid Gundersons for the work to that date. In the spring of 1980, Ptarmigan ran out of funds and was unable to pay for the completion of the golf course. Gundersons sued Ptarmigan and its individual partners to recover the lost profits that it would have made on the remaining two thirds of the contract. Can Gundersons recover these lost profits as damages? [*Gundersons, Inc. v. Ptarmigan Investment Company*, 678 P.2d 1061 (Colo. App. 1983)]

13.6 Liquidated Damages In December 1974, H. S. Perlin Company, Inc. (Perlin), and Morse Signal Devices of San Diego (Morse) entered into a contract whereby Morse agreed to provide burglar and fire alarm service to Perlin's coin and stamp store. Perlin paid $50 per month for this service. The contract contained a liquidated damage clause limiting Morse's liability to $250 for any losses incurred by Perlin based on Morse's failure of service. During the evening of August 25, 1980, a burglary occurred at Perlin's store. Before entering the store, the burglars cut a telephone line that ran from the burglar system in Perlin's store to Morse's central location. When the line was cut, a signal indicated the interruption of service at Morse's central station. Inexplicably, Morse took no further steps to investigate the interruption of service at Perlin's store. The burglars stole stamps and coins with a wholesale value of $958,000, and Perlin did not have insurance against this loss. Perlin sued Morse to recover damages. Is the liquidated damage clause enforceable? [*H. S. Perlin Company, Inc. v. Morse Signal Devices of San Diego*, 209 Cal.App.3d 1289, 258 Cal.Rptr. 1 (Cal. App. 1989)]

13.7 Liquidated Damages United Mechanical Contractors, Inc. (UMC), an employer, agreed to provide a pension plan for its unionized workers. UMC was to make monthly payments into a pension fund administered by the Idaho Plumbers and Pipefitters Health and Welfare Fund (Fund). Payments were due by the fifteenth of the month. The contract between UMC and the Fund contained a liquidated damage clause that provided if payments due from UMC were received later than the 20th of the month, liquidated damages of 20 percent of the required contribution would be assessed against UMC. In June 1985, the fund received UMC's payment on the 24th. The Fund sued UMC to recover $9,245.23 in liquidated damages. Is the liquidated damage clause enforceable? [*Idaho Plumbers and Pipefitters Health and Welfare Fund v. United Mechanical Contractors, Inc.*, 875 F.2d 212 (9th Cir. 1989)]

13.8 Nominal Damages To boost his career as an actor, John Ericson agreed with Playgirl, Inc. (Playgirl), that it could publish a picture of him posing naked at Lion Country Safari as the centerfold of the January 1974 issue of *Playgirl* magazine without compensation. The magazine was published with Ericson as the centerfold, but no immediate career boost to Ericson resulted from the publication. In April 1974, Playgirl wished to use Ericson's photograph in its annual edition entitled *Best of Playgirl*. Playgirl and Ericson entered into a contract whereby

Ericson's picture was to occupy a quarter of the front cover of the annual edition. Due to an editorial mixup, Ericson's picture did not appear on the cover of the *Best of Playgirl*. Ericson sued Playgirl, seeking damages for breach of contract. How much damages should Ericson recover for Playgirl's breach of contract? [73 Cal.App.3d 850, 140 Cal.Rptr. 921 (Cal.Rptr. 1977)]

13.9 Specific Performance Liz Claiborne, Inc. (Claiborne), is a large maker of women's better sportswear in the United States and a well-know name in fashion, with sales of over $1 billion a year. Claiborne distributes its products through 9,000 retail outlets in the United States. Avon Products, Inc. (Avon), is a major producer of fragrances, toiletries, and cosmetics, with annual sales of more than $3 billion a year. Claiborne, which desired to promote its well-known name on perfumes and cosmetics, entered into a joint venture with Avon whereby Claiborne would make available its names, trademarks, and marketing experience and Avon would engage in the procurement and manufacture of the fragrances, toiletries, and cosmetics. The parties would equally share the financial requirements of the joint venture. In 1986, its first year of operation, the joint venture had sales of more than $16 million. In the second year, sales increased to $26 million, making it one of the fastest growing fragrance and cosmetic lines in the country. In 1987, Avon sought to "uncouple" the joint venture. Avon thereafter refused to procure and manufacture the line of fragrances and cosmetics for the joint venture. When Claiborne could not obtain the necessary fragrances and cosmetics from any other source for the fall/Christmas season, Claiborne sued Avon for breach of contract, seeking specific performance of the contract by Avon. Is specific performance an appropriated remedy in this case? [*Liz Claiborne, Inc. v. Avon Products, Inc.*, 530 N.Y.S.2d 425, 141 A.D.2d 329 (N.Y.Sup.App. 1988)]

13.10 Quasi Contract Wood Dimension, Inc. (Wood), manufactured stereo speakers for resale to other companies. Fisher Corporation, a major customer, accounted for 30 percent to 50 percent of Wood's business. In early 1982, Fisher stopped buying from Wood. To regain Fisher's business, the president of Wood solicited the help of L. Dale Watson, who had known the vice president of Fisher for many years. Wood agreed to pay Watson 5 percent of all Fisher's orders if he succeeded in persuading Fisher to buy at Wood again. They shook hands to seal the agreement. Due to Watson's efforts, Fisher again became a customer of Wood's. In May 1984, Wood terminated Watson.

Between that time and July 1985, Fisher placed orders of almost $10 million with Wood. Although the oral contract between Wood and Watson was terminable at will, Watson sued Wood to recover commissions on Fisher's orders that were placed after he was discharged. Can Watson recover these damages under the theory of quasi contract? [*Watson v. Wood Dimension, Inc.*, 209 Cal.App.3d 1359, 257 Cal.Rptr. 816 (Cal. App. 1989)]

13.11 Injunction In 1982, Anita Baker, a then-unknown singer, signed a multiyear recording contract with Beverly Glen Music, Inc. (Beverly Glen). Baker recorded a record album for Beverly Glen that was moderately successful. After having some difficulties with Beverly Glen, Baker was offered a considerably more lucrative contract by Warner Communications, Inc. (Warner). Baker accepted the Warner offer and informed Beverly Glen that she would not complete her contract because she had entered into an agreement with Warner. Beverly Glen sued Baker and Warner, and sought an injunction to prevent Baker from performing as a singer for Warner. Is an injunction an appropriate remedy in this case? [*Beverly Glen Music, Inc. v. Warner Communications, Inc.*, 178 Cal.App.3d 1142, 224 Cal.Rptr. 260 (Cal.App. 1986)]

13.12 Intentional Interference With Contractual Relations In 1963, Pacific Gas and Electric Company (PG & E) entered into a contract with Placer County Water Agency (Agency) to purchase hydroelectric power generated by the Agency's Middle Fork American River Project. The contract was not terminable until 2013. As energy prices rose during the 1970s, the contract became extremely valuable to PG & E. The price PG & E paid for energy under the contract was much lower than the cost of energy from other sources. In 1982, Bear Stearns & Company (Bear Stearns), an investment bank and securities underwriting firm, learned of the Agency's power contract with PG & E. Bear Stearns offered to assist the Agency in an effort to terminate the power contract with PG & E in exchange for a share of the Agency's subsequent profits and the right to underwrite any new securities issued by the Agency. Bear Stearns also agreed to pay the legal fees incurred by the Agency in litigation concerning their attempt to get out of the PG & E contract. Under what legal theory can PG & E sue Bear Stearns? [*Pacific Gas and Electric Company v. Bear Stearns & Company*, 50 Cal.3d 1118, 270 Cal.Rptr. 1 (Cal. App. 1990)]

BUSINESS ETHICS CASES

13.13 Business Ethics Walgreen Company has operated a pharmacy in the Southgate Mall in Milwaukee since 1951, when the mall opened. Its current lease, signed in 1971 and carrying a 30-year term, contains an exclusivity clause in which the landlord, Sara Creek Property Company (Sara Creek), promises not to lease space in the mall to anyone else who wants to operate a pharmacy or a store containing a pharmacy. In 1990, after its anchor tenant went broke,

Sara Creek informed Walgreen that it intended to lease the anchor tenant space to Phar-Mor Corporation. Phar-Mor, a "deep discount" chain, would occupy 100,000 square feet, of which 12,000 square feet would be occupied by a pharmacy the same size as Walgreen's. The entrances to the two stores would be within a few hundred feet of each other. Walgreen sued Sara Creek for breach of contract and sought a permanent injunction against Sara Creek's leasing the anchor premises to Phar-Mor.

Do the facts of this case justify the issuance of a permanent injunction? Did Sara Creek act ethically in not living up to the contract? [*Walgreen Co. v. Sara Creek Property Co.*, 966 F.2d 273 (7th Cir. 1992)]

13.14 Business Ethics Rosina Crisci owned an apartment building in which Mrs. DiMare was a tenant. One day while DiMare was descending a wooden staircase on the outside of the apartment building she fell through the staircase and was left handing 15 feet above the ground until she was saved. Crisci had a $10,000 liability insurance policy on the building from the Security Insurance Company (Security) of New Haven, Connecticut. DiMare sued Crisci and Security for $400,000 for physical injuries and psychosis suffered from the

fall. Prior to trial, DiMare agreed to take $10,000 in settlement of the case. Security refused this settlement offer. DiMare reduced her settlement offer to $9,000, of which Crisci offered to pay $2,500. Security again refused to settle the case. The case proceeded to trial and the jury awarded DiMare and her husband $110,000. Security paid $10,000 pursuant to the insurance contract, and Crisci had to pay the difference. Crisci, a widow of 70 years of age, had to sell her assets, became dependent on her relatives, declined in physical health, and suffered from hysteria and suicide attempts. Crisci sued Security for tort damages for breach of the implied covenant of good faith and fair dealing. Did Security act in bad faith? [*Crisci v. Security Insurance Company of New Haven, Connecticut*, 426 P. 2d 173,66 Cal.App.2d 425, 58 Cal.Rptr. 13 (Cal. App. 1967)]

BRIEFING THE CASE WRITING ASSIGNMENT

Read the following case, which has been excerpted from the court's opinion. Review and brief the case.

E. B. Harvey & Company, Inc. v. Protective Systems, Inc.
1989 Tenn. App. Lexis 105 (1989)
Court of Appeals of Tennessee

Sanders, Presiding Judge

The plaintiff-appellant, E. B. Harvey & Company, Inc. (Harvey), is engaged in the manufacture and wholesale of fine jewelry in Chattanooga. It has been engaged in this business for about 10 years. It maintains an inventory in excess of $1 million of gold, silver, precious stones, pearls, and other such materials related to the manufacture of jewelry. A considerable amount of its jewelry is on consignment and, by the very nature of its business, it requires a great deal of insurance. However, the insurance companies will not write the insurance unless it maintains an Underwriters Laboratories (U.L.)-approved AA burglary protection alarm system. The defendant-appellee, Protective Systems, Inc. (Protective), is one of two companies in Hamilton County which furnishes and maintains a U.L.-approved AA burglar protection system. In June 1981, Harvey entered into a three-year contract with Protective to install and maintain a burglar protective system. The contract provided:

> *It is agreed that Protective is not an insurer and that the payments hereinbefore named are based solely upon the value of the services herein described and it is not the intention of the parties that Protective assume responsibility for any losses occasioned by malfeasance or misfeasance in the performance of the services under this contract or for any loss or damage sustained through burglary, theft, robbery, fire or other cause or any liability on the part of Protective by virtue of this agreement or because of the relation hereby established.*
>
> *If there shall at any time be or arise any liability on the part of Protective, by virtue of this agreement or because of the relation hereby established, whether due to the negligence of Protective or otherwise, such liability is and shall be limited to a sum total in amount to the rental service charge hereunder for a period of service not to exceed six months, which sum shall be paid and received as liquidated damages.*

The burglary and holdup system provided to Harvey operated by means of Grade AA telephone lines between the central monitoring station of

Protective and Harvey's premises. Said telephone lines were at all times owned and maintained by the South Central Bell Telephone Company. On July 22, 1984, at 11:14 P.M., an outage condition was indicated on the E. B. Harvey & Company account. For a period of two weeks prior to this date, Protective's computer had been registering an inordinate number of outage signals which had all been traced back to problems in telephone company equipment. For this reason, on July 22, 1984, Protective's president, Pendell Meyers, notified the telephone company of this condition and reported a potential problem to the police department but did not contact a representative of Harvey to notify them of the outage condition.

The phone company was unable to locate the exact nature of the problem despite several telephone conversations with Meyers. The Chattanooga Police Department patrolled the premises surrounding Harvey's place of business twice that evening but did not note any unusual activity. The following morning when an employee of Harvey reported to work, it was discovered that a burglary had in fact taken place. Some $200,000 worth of jewelry and inventory was stolen. Harvey sued Protective for damages resulting from the burglary. It alleged that Protective was guilty of negligence for its failure to notify Harvey or its employees of the outage that appeared on the burglary monitoring equipment.

Protective, for answer, denied the allegations of Harvey's complaint and, as an affirmative defense, alleged the contract between the parties with its exculpatory and limitation of liability provisions was enforceable and binding upon Harvey. After hearing testimony, the trial court held the extent of Harvey's recovery against Protective would be 650 percent as liquidated damages. A final judgment was entered and Harvey has appealed.

There is nothing in public policy to render inoperative or nugatory the contractual limitations contained in the agreement. Limitations against liability for negligence or breach of contract have generally been upheld in this state in the absence of fraud or overreaching. Limitations such as those contained in the present contract have generally been deemed reasonable and have been sustained in actions against the providers of burglary and fire alarm systems. Such clauses do not ordinarily protect against liability for fraud or intentional misrepresentation.

We concur with the trial court. The issues are found in favor of the appellees. The judgment of the trial court is affirmed. The cost of this appeal is taxed to the appellant and the case is remanded to the trial court for collection of cost.

ENDNOTES

1. Restatement (Second) of Contracts, § 235(2).
2. Restatement (Second) of Contracts, § 241.
3. Restatement (Second) of Contracts, § 253; UCC § 2-610.
4. UCC §§ 2-708 and 2-713.
5. Restatement (Second) of Contracts, § 356(1).
6. Restatement (Second) of Contracts, § 370.
7. Restatement (Second) of Contracts, § 359.

UNIT III

E-Commerce and Information Technology

CHAPTER 14

Intellectual Property and Internet Law

The Congress shall have the power . . . To promote the Progress of Science and useful Arts, by securing for limited Times to Authors and Inventors the exclusive Right to their respective Writings and Discoveries.

—Article I, Section 8, clause 8 of the U.S. Constitution

Chapter Objectives

After studying this chapter, you should be able to:

1. Describe the business tort of misappropriating a trade secret.

2. Describe the criminal conduct that violates the Economic Espionage Act.

3. Describe how an invention can be patented under federal patent laws and the penalties for patent infringement.

4. Describe how cyber business plans qualify for patent protection.

5. List the writings that can be copyrighted and describe the penalties of copyright infringement.

6. Describe the legal rights that computer and software designers have in their works.

7. Describe the changes made in copyright law by the Digital Millennium Copyright Act.

8. Describe how the NET Act prohibits criminal copyright infringement.

9. Define *trademarks* and *service marks*, and describe the penalties for trademark infringement.

10. Describe international protection of intellectual property rights.

Chapter Contents

The American economy is based on the freedom of ownership of property. In addition to real estate and personal property, **intellectual property rights** have value to both businesses and individuals. This is particularly the case in the modern era of the Information Age, computers, and the Internet.

Trade secrets form the basis of many successful businesses, which are protected from misappropriation. Federal law provides protections for intellectual property rights, such as patents, copyrights, and trademarks. In addition, businesses and individuals may register domain names to use on the Internet. Anyone who infringes on these rights may be stopped from doing so and is liable for damages. Computers and computer software are accorded special protection from infringement.

This chapter discusses trade secrets, patents, copyrights, trademarks, domain names, and computer law.

intellectual property rights

Intellectual property rights, such as patents, copyrights, trademarks, trade secrets, trade names, and domain names are very valuable business assets. Federal and state laws protect intellectual property rights from misappropriation and infringement.

"'How I Spent My Summer Vacation,' by Lilia Anya, all rights reserved, which includes the right to reproduce this essay or portions thereof in any form whatsoever, including, but not limited to, novel, screenplay, musical, television miniseries, home video, and interactive CD–ROM."

Drawing by Mort Gerberg; © 1993 The *New Yorker* Magazine, Inc.

TRADE SECRETS

Many businesses are successful because their **trade secrets** set them apart from their competitors. Trade secrets may be product formulas, patterns, designs, compilations of data, customer lists, or other business secrets. Many trade secrets either do not qualify to be—or simply are not—patented, copyrighted, or trademarked. Many states have adopted the **Uniform Trade Secrets Act** to give statutory protection to trade secrets.

State unfair competition laws allow the owner of a trade secret to bring a lawsuit for *misappropriation* against anyone who steals a trade secret. To be actionable, the defendant (often an employee of the owner or a competitor) must have obtained the trade secret through unlawful means such as theft, bribery, or industrial espionage. No tort has occurred if there is no misappropriation. For example, a competitor can lawfully discover a

trade secret

A product formula, pattern, design, compilation of data, customer list, or other business secret.

trade secret by performing reverse engineering (i.e., taking apart and examining a rival's product).

The owner of a trade secret is obliged to take all reasonable precautions to prevent those secrets from being discovered by others. Such precautions include fencing in buildings, placing locks on doors, hiring security guards, and the like. If the owner fails to take such actions, the secret is no longer subject to protection under state unfair competition laws.

Generally, a successful plaintiff in a trade secret action can (1) recover the profits made by the offender from the use of the trade secret, (2) recover for damages, and (3) obtain an injunction prohibiting the offender from divulging or using the trade secret.

Ethics Brief

Businesses should take all necessary precautions to protect their trade secrets from unwanted discovery.

E-Commerce & Information Technology

THE ECONOMIC ESPIONAGE ACT

Although the stealing of trade secrets exposes the offender to a civil lawsuit by the injured party to recover economic damages, the offender seldom faced criminal charges except under a few state laws. All that changed with the enactment by Congress of the federal **Economic Espionage Act of 1996** [18 U.S.C. 1831–1839]. This act makes it a federal crime to steal another's trade secrets. Previously, no federal statute directly addressed economic espionage and the stealing of trade secrets.

Under the Espionage Act, it is a federal crime for any person to convert a trade secret to his or her benefit or for the benefit of others, knowing or intending that the act would cause injury to the owner of the trade secret. The definition of *trade secret* under the Espionage Act is very broad, and parallels the definition used under the civil laws of misappropriating a trade secret. Under the Espionage Act, a trade secret includes any economic, business, financial, technical, scientific, or engineering information, including processes, software programs, and codes.

One of the major reasons for the passage of the Espionage Act was to address the ease of stealing trade secrets through computer espionage and using the Internet. For example, hundreds of pages of confidential information can be downloaded onto a small computer diskette, placed in a pocket, and taken from the legal owner. In addition, computer hackers can crack into a company's computers and steal customer lists, databases, formulas, and other trade secrets. The Espionage Act is a very important weapon to address and penalize computer and Internet espionage.

The Espionage Act provides for severe criminal penalties. An organization can be fined up to $5 million per criminal act and $10 million if the criminal act was committed to benefit a foreign government. The act imposes prison terms on individuals of up to 15 years per criminal violation, which can be increased to 25 years per violation if the criminal act was done with the intent to benefit a foreign government. By adding criminal penalties, the Espionage Act adds another weapon to safeguard trade secrets and intellectual property in this country.

Landmark Law

FEDERAL PATENT STATUTE

Pursuant to the express authority granted in the U.S. Constitution,[1] Congress enacted the **Federal Patent Statute of 1952**.[2] This law is intended to provide an incentive for inventors to invent and make their inventions public and to protect patented inventions from infringement. Federal patent law is exclusive; there are no state patent laws. The *U.S. Court of Appeals for the Federal Circuit* in Washington, DC, was created in 1982 to hear patent appeals. The court was established to promote uniformity in patent law.

Patent applicants must file a *patent application* containing a written description of the invention with the **U.S. Patent and Trademark Office** in Washington, DC. If a patent is granted, the invention is assigned a patent number. Patent holders usually affix the word *Patent* or *Pat.* and the patent number to the patented article. If a patent application is filed but a patent has not yet been issued, the applicant usually places the words *patent pending* on the article. Any party can challenge either the issuance of a patent or the validity of an existing patent.

PATENTING AN INVENTION

To be patented, the invention must be *novel*, *useful*, and *nonobvious*. In addition, only certain subject matters can be patented. Patentable subject matter includes (1) machines, (2) processes, (3) compositions of matter, (4) improvements to existing machines, processes, or compositions of matter, (5) designs for an article of manufacture, (6) asexually reproduced plants, and (7) living material invented by a person.[3] Abstractions and scientific principle cannot be patented unless they are part of the tangible environment. For example, Einstein's Theory of Relativity ($E = MC^2$) cannot be patented.

In Case 14.1, the court had to decide whether the subject matter was patentable.

Federal Patent Statute of 1952

Federal statute that establishes the requirements for obtaining a patent and protects patented inventions from infringement.

The patent system added the fuel of interest to the fire of genius.

Abraham Lincoln
Lectures on Discoveries, Inventions, and Improvements
(1859)

Lamb-Weston, Inc. v. McCain Foods, Ltd.
78 F.3d 540 (1996)
United States Court of Appeals, Federal Circuit

CASE 14.1

BACKGROUND AND FACTS

Plaintiff Lamb-Weston, Inc., is a food-processing company that sells frozen potato products. The defendant, McCain Foods, Ltd., competes with Lamb-Weston in this industry. Both Lamb-Weston and McCain Foods make partially fried (parfried) and frozen potato products that are distributed to grocery stores, restaurants, and other users.

In October 1979, Mr. Matsler offered to sell the waffle-slicing machine he had invented to Lamb-Weston, but the company turned it down. In February 1980, Lamb-Weston examined a waffle-fry cutting machine invented by Mr. Jayne. Again Lamb-Weston found the machine unacceptable. Eventually, Lamb-Weston developed its own "waffle fry," a potato slice somewhere in size between a potato chip and a french fry with a waffle shape. In 1983, Lamb-Weston began selling waffle fried under the name "CrissCut." Lamb-Weston filed for a patent on its process for making these frozen potato slices. Its claim in the patent application read:

A parfried potato product, suitable for reconstitution by cooking, comprising: a frozen, sliced potato section having a substantially ellipsoidal shape and a variable thickness, including a peak to peak thickness within the range of about 4/16 to 10/16 inch; the section including opposed first and second sides, each side having longitudinal ridges and grooves there-between, the ridges and grooves of the first side extending angularly to the ridges and grooves of the second side; the grooves of the first and second sides having a depth sufficient to intersect one another to form a grid of openings in the potato section; the section, before reconstitution, having an oil content of about 6–20 percent, by weight, and a solids content of about 32–40 percent by weight; whereby the product, upon reconstitution by cooking, is characterized by very thin, crisp portions of locally increased oil flavor adjacent the openings, relatively thick portions defined by intersecting ridges having an internal mealy texture and strong potato flavor similar to thick-cut french fried potato strips, and portions of intermediate thickness whose characteristics are similar to french fried shoe string potato strips.

The Patent Board granted the patent to Lamb-Weston. In 1985, McCain Foods began making and selling a competing parfried waffle fry. Lamb-Weston sued McCain Foods for patent infringement. McCain Foods counterclaimed for a declaratory judgment to have Lamb-Weston's patent declared invalid. The district court held that the patent was invalid and unenforceable. Lamb-Weston appealed.

ISSUE

Was Lamb-Weston's patent for the process of making frozen, partially fried lattice-shaped french fries called "waffle fries" a valid patent?

COURT'S REASONING

The court of appeals determined that the process of making waffle fries was part of "prior art" and, therefore, obvious. The court cited evidence that waffle fries were available as early as 1935 at the Gem Cafe in Plainsville, Texas; in 1979 at the Plaza Restaurant in Quincy, Illinois; and in 1980 at the Dairy Queen Restaurant in Dallas, Oregon. The court of appeals concluded, "Frozen, parfried french fries of various configurations and degrees of thickness were well known in the art at the time of the claimed invention." Thus, the process claimed by Lamb-Weston was in the prior art obvious, and was therefore unpatentable.

DECISION AND REMEDY

The court of appeals ruled that the process of making waffle fries was too obvious to be patentable. The court held that Lamb-Weston's patent was invalid. Affirmed.

Case Questions

Critrical Legal Thinking What is the purpose of the federal government granting patents? What statutory requirements must be made for a patent to be granted?

Business Ethics Was there any unethical conduct by any of the parties in this case? Do you think Lamb-Weston knew its waffle fry process was unpatentable?

Contemporary Business What were the financial consequences of the court's decision in this case? Who were the winners and who were the losers?

International Law

CHANGES IN PATENT LAW MANDATED BY GATT

In 1994, the **General Agreement on Tariffs and Trade (GATT)** established the **World Trade Organization (WTO)**, an international trade organization of which the United States is a member. GATT's intellectual property provisions, and implementing legislation passed by Congress, made the following important changes in U.S. patent law:

1. Patents are valid for *20 years*, instead of the previous term of 17 years.

2. The patent term begins to run from the date the patent application is *filed* instead of when the patent is issued as was previously the case.

These changes, which became effective June 8, 1995, brought the U.S. patent system in harmony with the majority of other developed nations. The United States still follows the first-to-invent rule rather than the first-to-file rule followed by some other countries.

Patent Infringement

patent infringement

Unauthorized use of another's patent. A patent holder may recover damages and other remedies against a patent infringer.

Patent holders own exclusive rights to use and exploit their patent. **Patent infringement** occurs when someone makes unauthorized use of another's patent. In a suit for patent infringement, a successful plaintiff can recover (1) money damages equal to a reasonable royalty rate on the sale of the infringed articles, (2) other damages caused by the infringement (such as loss of customers), (3) an order requiring the destruction of the infringing article, and (4) an injunction preventing the infringer from such action in the future. The court has the discretion to award up to treble damages if the infringement was intentional.

Entrepreneur and the Law

INVENTOR WIPES FORD'S AND CHRYSLER'S WINDSHIELDS CLEAN

In 1967, Robert Kearns, a professor at Wayne State University in Detroit, Michigan, patented his design for the electronic intermittent windshield wiper for automobiles and other vehicles. He peddled his invention around to many automobile manufacturers but never reached a licensing deal with any of them. In 1969, automobile manufacturers began producing cars with Kearns's invention. Virtually all cars sold in the United States today now have these wipers as standard equipment.

Kearns filed patent infringement lawsuits against Ford in 1978 and Chrysler in 1982. He later filed patent infringement cases against virtually all automobile manufacturers. The Ford case went to trial first. Kearns sought $325 million in damages from Ford. Ford alleged that Kearns's patents were not valid because of obviousness and prior art. The jury disagreed with Ford and decided that Kearns's patents were valid. The jury ordered Ford to pay $5.2 million, plus interest. In 1990, Ford settled by paying Kearns $10.2 million and agreeing to drop all appeals. This represented 50¢ per Ford vehicle that used the wiper system.

Kearns sought $468 million in damages from Chrysler. In that case, Kearns fired his lawyers and represented himself. This was at least the fourth law firm hired and fired in the course of Kearns's patent infringement lawsuits. Kearns won

a second victory: In 1991, the jury found that Chrysler had infringed Kearns's patents and awarded him $11.3 million. The court denied Kearns injunctive relief because his 17-year patents had expired years ago. The court of appeals affirmed the judgment and the Supreme Court refused to hear Kearns's appeal. Kearns received over $21 million from Chrysler, which amounted to 90¢ for every vehicle sold by Chrysler with the wiper system.

In 1993 and 1994, courts dismissed Kearns's lawsuits against 23 automobile manufacturers, including General Motors, Porsche, Nissan, Toyota, Honda, and Rolls Royce, among others, because Kearns failed to comply with court orders to disclose documents relevant to the cases. The district court then ordered Kearns to pay his fired lawyers $6.4 million in contingency fees. Thus ended Kearns's over 30-year saga and legal battle with the automobile industry. In an interview Kearns stated, "The patent system is a fraud pure and simple."

1. Did the automobile manufacturers act unethically in these cases? Other than Ford and Chrysler, did the other auto manufacturers get off too easily?
2. Do you think Kearns could have won more money? Explain.

E-Commerce & Information Technology

SAY CHEESE! CAMERA COMPANIES LOSE PATENT INFRINGEMENT CASE

U.S. companies often complain that they spend huge amounts of money on research and development only to find that foreign companies make profits by selling goods that contain the misappropriated technology. The following case demonstrates that the courts may be a good place to begin tackling this problem.

In the early 1970s, researchers at Honeywell, Inc., which is based in Minneapolis, invented autofocus technology for cameras. This technology, which uses computer chips to focus camera lenses automatically, takes over a task previously done manually by photographers. Between 1975 and 1977, Honeywell obtained four patents for the technology, but it left the camera business without ever using the technology. Instead, it tried to market the technology to other manufacturers, most of them in Japan.

The companies Honeywell approached chose not to purchase or license Honeywell's technology. Instead, they developed their own autofocus technology. One such company was Minolta, which introduced the Maxxum camera with autofocus technology in 1985. The Maxxum was a hit with consumers. It sent Minolta into its current position as the leading camera maker in the United States, with annual sales of more than $400 million and 30 percent of the market.

There was only one hitch: Honeywell thought Minolta had infringed on its patented autofocus technology. Honeywell sued Minolta, as well as 14 other camera makers from the Far East, alleging patent infringement.

In 1992, after a four-month trial, a federal jury of nine persons found that Minolta had infringed two of Honeywell's four patents. The jury ordered Minolta to pay Honeywell $96 million in back royalties. Within months, Minolta paid Honeywell $124 million in a settlement in which Honeywell agreed not to seek a ban on the sale of Minolta cameras in the United States. The two patents found to have been infringed expired in late 1992.

Since the jury verdict against Minolta was announced, 14 other camera makers have settled infringement suits with Honeywell. These companies include Canon, Nikon, Pentax, Olympus, Ricoh, Chinon, and Vivitar. The settlements put more than $300 million in Honeywell's coffer.

The Minolta decision and the other settlements should mean that foreign companies will be more apt to license technology from U.S. patent holders legally. Pirating the technology will not be as attractive an option as it once appeared.

Entrepreneur and the Law

PROTECTING A PATENT IS EXPENSIVE BUSINESS

Inventors spend years dreaming up new products and inventions, then file an application with the Patent and Trademark Office and wait to see if their patent is granted. The day the patent is issued is a cause for celebration, or is it? Ask Donald BonAsia. The young entrepreneur invented "forkchops"—two eating utensils with chopsticks on one end and a knife and fork on the other end. He spent two years and $7,500 to receive a patent on his invention.

But his worst fear happened. Other manufacturers began copying his invention and selling them without seeking BonAsia's permission or paying him a royalty fee. BonAsia contacted a patent lawyer and found out the following: The normal cost to pursue a patent infringement case through trial is $1.5 million, and $1 million if it settles near trial.

Attorneys typically want over $100,000 in retainer fees before filing a patent infringement case. BonAsia discovered he had a patent, but not enough money to protect it.

BonAsia's plight is typical for small-time inventors who are under the misconception that a patent gives the holder an exclusive right to make the item. Wrong: What a patent gives the holder is the right to defend the patent and try to stop others from making the patented article. BonAsia learned a valuable lesson: patent law is usually the playing field of big corporations that have deep pockets to protect their patents. It may be that small entrepreneurs have the same legal rights; it is just that as in many areas of the law, justice can only be obtained at a price.

One-Year "On Sale" Doctrine

Under the **one-year "on sale" doctrine**, also called the **public use doctrine**, a patent may not be granted if the invention was used by the public for more than one year prior to the filing of the patent application. This doctrine forces inventors to file their patent applications at the proper time.

one-year "on sale" doctrine

A doctrine that says a patent may not be granted if the invention was used by the public for more than one year prior to the filing of the patent application.

Consider This Example Suppose Cindy Parsons invents a new invention on January 1. She allows the public to use this invention and does not file a patent application until February of the following year. The inventor has lost the right to patent her invention

The Supreme Court Speaks

One-Year "On Sale" Doctrine Invalidates Patent

Pfaff v. Wells Electronics, Inc.
525 U.S. 55, 119 S.Ct. 304 (1998)
Supreme Court of the United States

BACKGROUND AND FACTS

Wayne K. Pfaff commenced work on designing a computer chip socket in November 1980. Pfaff prepared detailed engineering drawings that described the design, dimensions, and materials to be used in making the socket. Prior to March 17, 1981, Pfaff showed a sketch of his design to representatives of Texas Instruments, a large company. On April 8, 1981, Texas Instruments and Pfaff signed a written contract confirming a previously placed verbal purchase order for 30,100 of his new sockets for a total price of $91,000. Pfaff did not make a prototype of the new socket device before offering it for sale to Texas Instruments.

Pfaff filled the order in July 1981. The socket achieved substantial commercial success, as other companies placed orders. On April 19, 1982, Pfaff filed an application for a patent on his computer chip socket, and a patent was issued. When a competitor made a similar socket, Pfaff sued for patent infringement. The competitor countered that Pfaff did not have a valid patent because the one-year "on sale" doctrine of Section 102(b) of the federal patent statute had been violated. The district court held for Pfaff, but the court of appeals reversed. The U.S. Supreme Court granted certiorari to hear the appeal.

SUPREME COURT ISSUE

Was the one-year "on sale" doctrine violated, thus invalidating Pfaff's patent on the computer chip socket?

IN THE LANGUAGE OF THE U.S. SUPREME COURT

Stevens, Justice *The primary meaning of the word* invention *in the Patent Act unquestionably refers to the inventor's conception rather than to a physical embodiment of that idea. The statute does not contain any express requirement that an invention must be reduced to practice before it can be patented.*

It is well settled that an invention may be patented before it is reduced to practice. In 1888, this Court upheld a patent issued to Alexander Graham Bell even though he had filed his application before constructing a working telephone. The Telephone Cases, *126 U.S. 1, 8 S.Ct. 778 (1888). When we apply the reasoning of* The Telephone Cases *to the facts of the case before us today, it is evident that Pfaff could have obtained a patent on his novel socket when he accepted the purchase order from Texas Instruments for 30,100 units.*

DECISION AND REMEDY

The U.S. Supreme Court held that the one-year "on sale" rule started to run on or before April 8, 1981, the date when Pfaff contracted in writing to sell sockets to Texas Instruments. Since the filing of his patent application on April 19, 1982 was more than one year later, his patent was invalidated pursuant to the one-year "on sale" doctrine. The judgment of the court of appeals was affirmed.

CASE QUESTIONS

Critical Legal Thinking What does the one-year "on sale" doctrine provide? What is the public policy behind this rule?

Business Ethics Was it ethical for the competitor to copy and produce Pfaff's computer chip socket?

Contemporary Business How valuable is a patent? What were the economic consequences to Pfaff of the Supreme Court's decision? To others?

E-Commerce & Information Technology

CYBER BUSINESS PLANS ARE PATENTABLE

Federal patent law recognizes four categories of innovation: (1) machines, (2) articles of manufacture, (3) compositions, and (4) processes. For centuries most patents involved tangible inventions, such as the telephone and the light bulb. But the computer and the Internet have changed the traditional view of what can be patented. Consider the case of *State Street Bank & Trust Co. v. Signature Financial Group, Inc.*, 149 F.3d 1368 (Fed. Cir. 1998).

Signature Financial Group, Inc. (Signature), filed for and was granted a patent for a computerized accounting system that determines share prices through a series of mathematical calculations and is then used to manage mutual funds [U.S. Patent No. 5,193,056]. State Street Bank, another financial institution that wanted to offer a similar mutual fund investment program to clients, sued to have Signature's patent declared invalid. Signature defended, arguing that its intangible financial business model was a "process" that was protected under federal patent law. The U.S. Court of Appeals, Federal Circuit, upheld the patent as a "practical application of a mathematical, algorithm, formula, or calculation, because it produces a useful, concrete and tangible result."

Taking the lead from the *State Street* case, many persons and businesses have filed for and received patents for business and financial models that are used over the Internet. Critics contend that Congress did not intend to grant patents for intangible processes when it enacted federal patent law. Business plan patent holders counter that the trend reflects a necessary evolution in patent law and claim that business plan patterns are to the Internet Age what machine patents were to the Industrial Age. These proponents argue that critics had the same complaints when chemicals, polymers, and biotech patents were first granted. One thing is certain: The exponential growth in computer and Internet business plan patents will lead to an avalanche of patent litigation.

E-Commerce & Information Technology

AMAZON.COM FILES FOR "1-CLICK" PATENT

Our forefathers believed that innovation was so important that they provided in the U.S. Constitution, as ratified by the states in 1788, for the protection of inventions. Since then, the U.S. Congress has enacted several patent statutes. The most recent major overhaul of the patent laws was completed in 1952, during the Industrial Age of mechanical devices. But what happens when old laws meet the new technology of the Digital Age? Consider the following case.

Amazon.com, Inc. enables customers to find and purchase books, music, videos, consumer electronics, games, toys, gifts, and other items over the Internet by using its Web site **www.amazon.com**. As an early entrant into this market, Amazon.com became a leader in electronic commerce. Other e-commerce retailers began offering goods and services for sale over the Web.

One problem that most of these e-commerce retailers faced was that over 50 percent of potential customers who went shopping online and selected items for purchase abandoned their transaction before checkout. To address this problem, Amazon.com devised a method that enabled online customers to purchase selected items with a single click of a computer mouse button. Only customers who had previously registered their name, address, and credit card number with Amazon.com could complete purchases by clicking an instant "buy" button. This ordering system was implemented by Amazon.com in September 1997. On September 21, 1997, Amazon.com applied for a patent for its one-click ordering system, and on September 28, 1998, the United States Patent and Trademark office granted patent No. 5,960,411 ('411 patent) to Amazon.com. This was designated the 1-click® ordering system by Amazon.com.

While Amazon.com's patent application was pending, other online retailers began offering similar one-click ordering systems. One was Barnesandnoble.com, which operates a Web site through which it sells books, software, music, videos, and other items. Barnesandnoble.com called its one-click ordering system "Express Lane." On October 21, 1999, Amazon.com sued Barnesandnoble.com alleging patent infringement, and sought an injunction against Barnesandnoble.com from using its one-click ordering system. Barnesandnoble.com defended, asserting that a one-click ordering system was clearly obvious and, therefore, did not meet the required "nonobvious" test of federal patent law for an invention to qualify for a patent.

The court was faced with several novel issues. The first was whether this business model—the one-click ordering system—qualified as patentable subject matter. Following the lead of the U.S. Court of Appeals in *State Street Bank & Trust Co. v. Signature Financial Group, Inc.*, 149 F.3d 1368 (Fed. Cir. 1998), the court acknowledged that business models qualify as a new breed of patentable subject matter. The second issue was whether the one-click ordering system was "nonobvious." After examining the evidence, the court decided that Amazon.com's 1-click system was nonobvious when it was invented in 1997.

Barnesandnoble.com appealed to the federal court of appeals, arguing that Amazon.com's 1-click ordering system was not novel or nonobvious as required by patent law. Barnesandnoble.com cited the following evidence that one-click ordering systems existed in the *prior art* before Amazon.com filed for its patent: (1) since the 1990s the CompuServe Trend System provided for single-click ordering of stock charts over the Internet; (2) another Internet vendor's "WebBasket" allowed one-click ordering; (3) the "Oliver's Market" ordering system of another online vender permitted one-click ordering; and (4) the book *Creating the Virtual Store*, published before Amazon.com filed for its '411 patent, suggested modifying software to provide for one-click ordering online. The federal court of appeals relied on these prior art references and reversed the trial court's grant of an injunction in favor of Amazon.com. The court of appeals allowed Barnesandnoble.com to use its Express Lane one-click ordering system. [*Amazon.com, Inc. v. Barnesandnoble.com, Inc.*, 239 F.3d 1343 (Fed. Cir. 2001)]

@ *E-Commerce & Information Technology*

THE AMERICAN INVENTORS PROTECTION ACT

In 1999, Congress enacted the **American Inventors Protection Act**. This statute, which was a watered-down version of the initial bill that was introduced, still made significant changes in federal patent law. The act reorganized the U.S. Patent and Trademark Office (PTO) and granted the PTO new regulatory powers. The act does the following:

- Establishes "Inventor's Rights" by giving the PTO power to regulate "invention promoters." This part of the statute addresses problems created by unscrupulous invention registration services that took advantage of individual inventors by charging substantial fees for marketing services that generally were unsuccessful. The act provides for penalties and fines for violations of Inventor's Rights.
- Permits an inventor to file a provisional application with the PTO pending the preparation and filing of a final

and complete patent application. This part of the law grants "provisional rights" to an inventor for three months pending the filing of a final application.

- Requires the PTO to issue a patent within three years after the filing of a patent application unless the applicant engages in dilatory activities.
- Provides that non-patent holders may challenge a patent as overly broad by requesting a contested reexamination of the patent application by the PTO. This provides that the reexamination will be within the confines of the PTO; the decision of the PTO can be appealed to the U.S. Court of Appeals for the Federal Circuit in Washington, DC.

The new act also upgrades the PTO Commissioner to an Assistant Secretary of Commerce with authority to advise the U.S. government on intellectual policy.

Landmark Law

FEDERAL COPYRIGHT REVISION ACT

Congress enacted a federal copyright law pursuant to an express grant of authority in the U.S. Constitution.[4] This law protects the work of authors and other creative persons from the unauthorized use of their copyrighted materials and provides a financial incentive for authors to write, thereby increasing the number of creative works available in society. The **Copyright Revision Act of 1976** governs copyright law.[5] Effective March 1, 1989, the United States became a member of the **Berne**

Convention, an international copyright treaty. Federal copyright law is exclusive; there are no state copyright laws.

To be protected under federal copyright law, the work must be the original work of the author. Published and unpublished works may be copyrighted and registered with the **United States Copyright Office** in Washington, DC. Registration is permissive and voluntary and can be effected at any time during the term of the copyright. Registration itself does not create the copyright.

Copyright Revision Act of 1976

Federal statute that (1) establishes the requirements for obtaining a copyright and (2) protects copyrighted works from infringement.

Business Brief

The expression of an idea is copyrightable. The idea itself is not.

*R*EGISTRATION OF COPYRIGHTS

Only *tangible writings*—writings that can be physically seen—are subject to copyright registration and protection. The term *writing* has been broadly defined to include books, periodicals, and newspapers; lectures, sermons, and addresses; musical compositions; plays, motion pictures, radio and television productions; maps; works of art, including paintings, drawings, sculpture, jewelry, glassware, tapestry, and lithographs; architectural drawings and models; photographs, including prints, slides, and filmstrips; greeting cards and picture postcards; photoplays, including feature films, cartoons, newsreels, travelogues, and training films; and sound recordings published in the form of tapes, cassettes, compact discs, and phonograph albums.

International Law

BERNE CONVENTION ELIMINATES NEED FOR COPYRIGHT NOTICE

In 1989, the United States signed the Berne Convention. This international convention provides the copyright law that is now followed by most countries of the world. The

convention made a major change in U.S. copyright law. Prior to 1989, to protect a copyright in a published work in the United States, the copyright holder had to place a copyright notice on the work that contained the following information: (1) the copyright holder's name, (2) a "(c)" or "©" or "Copyright" or "copr.," and (3) the year the material was copyrighted. Under the Berne Convention, however, notice is not required on works entering the public domain on or after March 1, 1989. Although notice is now permissive, it is recommended that notice be placed on copyrighted works to defeat a defendant's claim of innocent infringement.

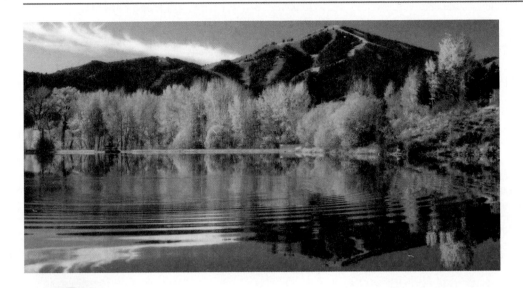

Sun Valley, Idaho *Photographs, such as this one, no longer need the © to be placed on them to be copyrighted.*

Contemporary Business Environment

A MICKEY MOUSE COPYRIGHT LAW

The Founding Fathers decided to provide copyright protection in the U.S. Constitution when they granted Congress authority to secure for "limited times" to authors the exclusive right to their writings. In 1970, copyright law guaranteed 14 years of protection with a 14-year renewal. The period of protection has been extended several times since, and in 1998 stood at the life of the author plus 50 years. A corporation-owned copyright was good for 75 years from the date of publication or 100 years from the date of creation, whichever was shorter.

After the copyright period runs out, the work enters the **public domain**, which means that anyone can publish the work without paying the prior copyright holder. Many small publishers and Internet sites were dedicated to publishing great works—and not-so-great works—only they entered the public domain. These publishers and Internet content providers waited anxiously as such popular works as A. A. Milne's *Winnie the Pooh*, Ernest Hemingway's *Three Stories and Ten Poems*, and the Walt Disney Company's first Mickey Mouse cartoon were set to enter the public domain. Cartoons starring such Disney characters as Donald Duck and Goofy would follow shortly after.

The Walt Disney Company was driven goofy at the prospect of their leading cartoon characters joining the likes of Santa Claus and Uncle Sam (both created by nineteenth century cartoonist Thomas Nast) in the public domain. So the long-arm of Disney went into action, lobbying Congress for a new copyright law that would increase the length of copyright protection for its characters. Disney, joined by the American Society of Composers, Authors, and Publishers, and other publishing and entertainment companies, persuaded Congress to pass the **Sonny Bono Copyright Term Extension Act of 1998 (CTEA)**. Although not restoring copyright protection to works already in the public domain, the act added 20 years to existing copyrighted works and works to be copyrighted in the future. The act grants the following copyright terms to the following copyright holders:

- **Individual Copyright Holder** Life of the author plus 70 years.
- **Corporate Copyright Holder** Ninety-five years from the year of first publication or 120 years from the year of creation, whichever is shorter.

Opponents of the new copyright law argue that it was passed to fill the pockets of large publishers and entertainment companies and the heirs of famous writers. They also argue that the act is unconstitutional because life of the writer plus 70 years and corporate copyrights of 95 or 120 years exceed the constitutional mandate of "limited time" copyrights. Proponents of the new copyright act argue that corporations such as the Walt Disney Company should be rewarded for spending millions of dollars in creating such cartoon icons as Mickey Mouse. Proponents also assert that the law is good for the country because the United States is the world's leading exporter of intellectual property.

@ E-Commerce & Information Technology

COPYRIGHTING SOFTWARE

The advent of new technology challenges the ability of laws to protect it. For example, the invention of computers and the writing of software programs caused problems for existing copyright laws. These laws had to be changed to afford protection to software.

In 1980, Congress enacted the **Computer Software Copyright Act**, which amended the Copyright Act of 1976. The 1980 amendments included computer programs in the list of tangible items protected by copyright law. The amendments define *computer program* broadly as "a set of statements or instructions to be used directly or indirectly in a computer in order to bring about a certain result" [17 U.S.C. § 101].

A computer program is written first in programming language, which is called a *source code*. It is then translated into another language, called an *object code*, which is understood by the computer. In an important decision, *Apple Computer,*

Inc. v. Franklin Computer Corp., 714 F.2d 1240 (3d Cir. 1983), the court held that object codes could be copyrighted.

As with other works, the creator of a copyrightable software program obtains automatic copyright protection. The **Judicial Improvement Act of 1990** authorizes the Register of Copyright to accept and record any document pertaining to computer software, and to issue a **certificate of recordation** to the recorder [P.L. 101–650]. Congress passed the **Semiconductor Chip Protection Act of 1984** to provide greater protection of the hardware components of a computer. This law protects masks that are used to create computer chips. A *mask* is an original layout of software programs that is used to create a semiconductor chip. This act is sometimes referred to as the "Mask Work Act." Notice on the work is optional but when used must contain (1) the words *Mask Work* or the symbol *M* or (M) and (2) the name of the owner [17 U.S.C. §§ 901–914].

Copyright Infringement

copyright infringement

When a party copies a substantial and material part of the plaintiff's copyrighted work without permission. A copyright holder may recover damages and other remedies against the infringer.

Copyright infringement occurs when a party copies a substantial and material part of the plaintiff's copyrighted work without permission. The copying does not have to be either word for word or the entire work. A successful plaintiff can recover (1) the profit made by the infringer from the copyright infringement, (2) damages suffered by the plaintiff, (3) an order requiring the impoundment and destruction of the infringing works, and (4) an injunction preventing the infringer from doing so in the future. The court, in its discretion, can award statutory damages ranging from $200 for innocent infringement up to $100,000 for willful infringement in lieu of actual damages.

The court had to decide whether copyright infringement occurred in Case 14.2

Ty, Inc. v. GMA Accessories, Inc.
132 F.3d 1167 (1997)
United States Court of Appeals, Seventh Circuit

CASE 14.2

BACKGROUND AND FACTS
In 1993, Ty, Inc., began selling the "Beanie Babies" line of small stuffed animals and introduced a new stuffed design each month. Beanie Babies became an immensely popular line of toys. Children, teenagers, and even adults collect some or all of the line of stuffed animals. Beanie Babies are copyrighted as "soft sculpture" under federal copyright law. Ty limits the production of individual Beanie Babies, thus creating a secondary market in them. Some Beanie Babies that originally sold for $5 now have a price as high as $2,000. One Beanie Baby produced by Ty was Squealer the pig. Subsequently, GMA Accessories, Inc. (GMA), a competing toy manufacturer, brought out a line of its own small stuffed animals. One of the GMA's animals was Preston the pig. GMA's Preston the pig was identical to Ty's Squealer. Ty sued GMA for copyright infringement. The district court granted a preliminary injunction against GMA prohibiting the company from producing Preston. GMA appealed.

ISSUE
Did GMA engage in copyright infringement?

COURT'S REASONING
The Copyright Act forbids copying, but if an independent creation results in an identical work, the creator of that work is free to sell it. The court of appeals noted that circumstantial evidence is sufficient to find copyright infringement. After examining the evidence—including samples and photographs of Ty's Daisy and Squealer and GMA's Louie and Preston—the court concluded that GMA had engaged in copyright infringement. The court found that GMA had access to Ty's creations because they were distributed to the public. The court rejected GMA's assertion that Louie and Preston were its independent creations. The court found that GMA's stuffed animals were identical to Ty's Beanie Babies and that such identical design could not have been from independent work. The court stated that the public could be misled into believing that it was buying Beanie Babies rather than

the GMA knockoffs and that Ty would suffer irreparable harm if GMA were allowed to sell the Louie and Preston stuffed animals. The court of appeals affirmed and granted the injunction against GMA's production and sale of these two stuffed animals.

DECISION AND REMEDY

The court of appeals held that GMA engaged in copyright infringement and affirmed the district court's grant of the preliminary injunction against GMA.

Case Questions

Critical Legal Thinking Do copyright laws serve any useful purpose? What would the consequences be if copyright laws did not exist?

Business Ethics Did GMA act unethically in this case? Why do you think GMA fought this case all the way to the court of appeals?

Contemporary Business Did Ty have much to lose if it had not won this case? Explain.

The Supreme Court Speaks

Supreme Court Finds Publishers Engaged in Copyright Infringement

New York Times Company, Inc. v. Tasini
121 S.Ct. 2381 (2001)
Supreme Court of the United States

BACKGROUND AND FACTS

Between 1990 and 1993, Jonathan Tasini and other authors wrote articles that were printed in the *New York Times*, *Sports Illustrated*, and various other newspapers and magazines. The publishers hired the authors as independent contractors (freelancers) under contracts that did not secure consent from the authors to place their articles in electronic databases. At a later date, the publishers placed these articles in computerized databases and made them available to the public through subscription services from electronic publishers such as LEXIS/NEXIS. The publishers did not pay the authors royalties on monies derived from electronic database sales. Tasini and other authors sued the publishers for copyright infringement. The district court granted the publishers summary judgment, but the court of appeals reversed. The U.S. Supreme Court granted certiorari to hear the appeal.

SUPREME COURT ISSUE

Did the publishers engage in copyright infringement when they placed and sold the authors' articles through electronic databases?

IN THE LANGUAGE OF THE U.S. SUPREME COURT

Ginsburg, Justice In the instant case, the Authors wrote several Articles and gave the Print Publishers permission to publish the Articles in certain newspapers and magazines. It is undisputed that the Authors hold copyrights and, therefore, exclusive rights in the Articles. The crucial fact is that the Databases, like the hypothetical library, store and retrieve articles separately within a vast domain of diverse texts. Such a storage and retrieval system effectively overrides the Authors' exclusive right to control the individual reproduction and distribution of each Article. We conclude that the Electronic Publishers infringed the Authors' copyrights by reproducing and distributing the Articles in a manner not authorized by the Authors. We further conclude that the Print Publishers infringed the Authors' copyrights by authorizing the Electronic Publishers to place the Articles in the Databases and by aiding the Electronic Publishers in that endeavor.

DECISION AND REMEDY

The U.S. Supreme Court held that the publishers infringed the authors' copyrights by publishing and selling the authors' articles through electronic databases without the permission of the authors to do so. The judgment of the court of appeals is affirmed.

CASE QUESTIONS

Critical Legal Thinking When the original publisher-author contracts were written, was the placement of articles in electronic databases common?

Business Ethics Did the publishers act ethically in this case? What should they have done?

Contemporary Business After this case has been decided, what contract provision will new publisher agreements with freelancers contain? Explain.

E-Commerce & Information Technology

NAPSTER UNPLUGGED BY THE COURT

In May 1999, 18-year-old Shawn Fanning cofounded Napster, Inc. and instantly created an Internet phenomenon. Using Napster software, Internet users could access digitally-compressed MP3-format music files stored on other users' computers that were connected to the Internet. Although Napster did not actually provide a library of songs itself, it kept a directory available to its users, that listed the names and computer locations of songs on its users' computers. The Napster program made it possible for peer-to-peer swapping of music files, including those that were copyrighted, for free.

There was one major problem. If copyrighted music was being copied for free, the songwriters, artists, and record companies that wrote, sang, and produced the songs were being cut out by the copiers and not paid anything. In December 1999, most of the world's biggest record labels, such as A&M Records, Sony Music, Universal Music, MCA Records, Warner Music, EMI Group, and others sued Napster for contributory copyright infringement. The heavy metal band Metallica and rapper Dr. Dre joined the lawsuit against Napster.

Napster defended, arguing that it did nothing illegal. For one and one-half years Napster continued to operate while the legal maneuverings wound their way through the federal courts. However, in February 2001 (Napster had over 50 million users who were sharing over 3 billion songs each month), the federal court of appeals issued an almost total victory for the record companies. Although the court did not hold that Napster was an actual copyright infringer (the individual computer users who used Napster to copy copyrighted songs were), the court did find Napster liable for *contributory copyright infringement* in violation of federal copyright law.

The court stated that Napster "knowingly encourages and assists in the infringement of copyrights" by others. When Napster tried to argue it did not know of its users infringing conduct, the court cited a document written by Napster Cofounder Sean Parker that mentioned "the need to remain ignorant of users' real names and IP addresses since they are exchanging pirated music." The court of appeals ordered the lower court to fashion an injunction that required Napster to block its users from swapping copyrighted songs, when music companies notify Napster that the songs are copyrighted and should be blocked. The court's decision permits Napster to be used for authorized song swapping—either of nonprotected songs or those songs that artists are willing to share.

Although winning a victory over Napster, the real victor was the new music-swapping technology. Faced with even more potent free music-swapping programs such as the Gnutella system, record companies began negotiating with record-sharing program owners to provide fee-based subscription services whereby users pay a monthly fee to swap copyrighted music and the fees are then split with the record companies, songwriters, and artists. But even now record companies face new free music-swapping technologies and those originating in other countries where U.S. copyright laws do not reach. [*A&M Records v. Napster, Inc.*, 239 F.3d 1004 (9th Cir. 2001]

Contemporary Business Environment

ARTISTS GRANTED "MORAL RIGHTS" IN CREATIVE WORKS

Today, an artist who produces a painting, sculpture, photograph, or other work of art holds a copyright in the work. Prior to 1990, when the artist sold the work, the buyer usually obtained the copyright unless the artist and buyer contracted otherwise.

Things changed when Congress passed the **Visual Artists Rights Act** in 1990. The act gives artists **moral rights** in their creations that continue even after the sale of the artwork. Although long recognized in European countries, the notion of moral rights is new in this country.

The rights granted to artists under the act include

- The artist is given moral right in his or her work that transcends the sale of the artwork and the transfer of the copyright to it.

- Before an owner of the artist's work can change, modify, or tamper with the artwork, reproduce it in any other medium (e.g., produce prints from a painting), or remove certain artwork (e.g., remove a mural from a building wall), the owner must notify the artist.
- The artist has 90 days after notice to respond to the owner. If the artist and owner do not settle the issue, the artist may file a lawsuit that seeks an injunction to prevent the owner from taking the proposed action.
- If the case goes to litigation, the court must decide whether the artist's moral rights have been violated and whether to grant injunctive relief.
- When purchasing a piece of artwork, the buyer can seek a waiver of moral rights from the artist so that the buyer is not restricted in the future use of the artwork.

The Fair Use Doctrine

fair use doctrine

A doctrine that permits certain limited use of a copyright by someone other than the copyright holder without the permission of the copyright holder.

The copyright holder's rights in the work are not absolute. The law permits certain limited unauthorized use of copyrighted materials under the **fair use doctrine**. The following uses are protected under this doctrine: (1) quotation of the copyrighted work for review or criticism or in a scholarly or technical work, (2) use in a parody or satire, (3) brief quotation in a news report, (4) reproduction by a teacher or student of a small part of the work to illustrate a lesson, (5) incidental reproduction of a work in a newsreel or broadcast of an event being reported, and (6) reproduction of a work in a legislative or judicial proceeding. The copyright holder cannot recover for copyright infringement where fair use is found.

The Supreme Court Speaks

Rap Singers' Parody on "Oh, Pretty Woman" Upheld as Fair Use

Campbell v. Acuff-Rose Music, Inc.
510 U.S. 569, 114 S.Ct. 1164 (1994)
Supreme Court of the United States

BACKGROUND AND FACTS

In 1964, Roy Orbison collaborated with another songwriter and wrote a rock ballad called "Oh, Pretty Woman." The song was copyrighted under federal copyright law. Roy Orbison recorded the song, which became a memorable classic from the 1960s. The writers assigned their rights in the song to Acuff-Rose Music, Inc. (Acuff-Rose).

2 Live Crew is a popular rap music group led by Luther R. Campbell. In 1989, Campbell wrote a song called "Pretty Woman" that was a parody of Roy Orbison's original recording. The lyrics of Campbell's version differed from Roy Orbison's version, except for the first line, which was verbatim from the original. 2 Live Crew wrote Acuff-Rose and asked permission to record their rap version of the song and stated that they were willing to pay a fee for the right to do so. When Acuff-Rose refused the permission, 2 Live Crew recorded the song anyway and put it on their rap album "As Clean as They Wanna Be," which sold over 250,000 copies.

The rap version of "Pretty Woman" used the same rhythm as the original, although the rap version included additional sounds such as scraper noises, overlays of different keys, and altered drum beats. The lyrics of the two versions of the song follow.

Acuff-Rose sued 2 Live Crew and their record company, Luke Skyywalker Records, for copyright infringement. The defendants asserted the affirmative defense of fair use based on parody. The district court found fair use, but the court of appeals reversed. The U.S. Supreme Court agreed to hear the case.

SUPREME COURT ISSUE

Can commercial parody be fair use?

IN THE LANGUAGE OF THE U.S. SUPREME COURT

Souter, Justice *It is uncontested here that 2 Live Crew's song would be an infringement of Acuff-Rose's rights in "Oh, Pretty Woman," under the Copyright Act of 1976, but for a finding of fair use through parody. Modern dictionaries describe a parody as a "literary or artistic work that imitates the characteristic style of an author or a work for comic effect or ridicule." [American Heritage Dictionary, 1317 (3d ed. 1992)].*

It is true, of course, that 2 Live Crew copied the characteristic opening bass riff (or musical phrase) of the original, and true that the words of the first line copy the Orbison lyrics. The words of 2 Live Crew's song then quickly degenerate into a play on words, substituting predictable lyrics with shocking ones that derisively demonstrate how bland and banal the Orbison song seems to them. 2 Live Crew juxtaposes the romantic musings of a man whose fantasy comes true, with degrading taunts, a bawdy demand for sex, and a sigh of relief from paternal responsibility. The later words can be taken as a comment on the naivete of the original of an earlier day, as a rejection of its sentiment that ignores the ugliness of street life and the debasement that it signifies. Parody needs to mimic an original to make its point. Suffice it to say here that, as to the lyrics, we think that no more was taken than necessary.

Roy Orbison's Version of "Oh, Pretty Woman"	2 Live Crew's Version of "Pretty Woman"
Pretty Woman, walking down the street,	Pretty woman walkin' down the street
Pretty Woman, the kind I like to meet,	Pretty woman girl you look so sweet
Pretty Woman, I don't believe you, you're not the truth,	Pretty woman you bring me down to that knee
No one could look as good as you	Pretty woman you make me wanna beg please
Mercy	Oh, pretty woman
Pretty Woman, won't you pardon me,	Big hairy woman you need to shave that stuff
Pretty Woman, I couldn't help but see,	Big hairy woman you know I bet it's tough
Are you lonely just like me?	Big hairy woman all that hair it ain't legit'
Pretty Woman, stop a while,	Cause you look like 'Cousin It'
Pretty Woman, talk a while,	Big hairy woman
Pretty Woman give your smile to me	Bald headed woman girl your hair won't grow

Pretty Woman, yeah, yeah, yeah
Pretty Woman, look my way,
Pretty Woman, say you'll stay with me
'Cause I need you, I'll treat you right
Come to me baby, Be mine tonight
Pretty Woman, don't walk on by,
Pretty Woman, don't make me cry,
Pretty Woman, don't walk away
Hey, O.K.
If that's the way it must be, O.K.
I guess I'll go on home, it's late
There'll be tomorrow night, but wait!
What do I see
Is she walking back to me?
Yeah, she's walking back to me!
Oh, Pretty Woman.

Bald headed woman you got a teeny weeny afro
Bald headed woman you know your hair could look nice
Bald headed woman first you got to roll it with rice
Bald headed woman here, let me get this hunk of biz for ya
Ya know what I'm saying you look better than rice a roni
Oh bald headed woman
Big hairy woman come on in
And don't forget your bald headed friend
Hey pretty woman let the boys
Jump in
Two timin' woman girl you know you ain't right
Two timin' woman you's out with my boy last night
Two timin' woman that takes a load off my mind
Two timin' woman now I know the baby ain't mine
Oh, two timin' woman
Oh pretty woman

DECISION AND REMEDY

The U.S. Supreme Court held that commercial parody can qualify as fair use of another's copyrighted work. The Court reversed the judgment of the court of appeals and remanded the case for further proceedings.

CASE QUESTIONS

Critical Legal Thinking   Should there be a fair use exception to copyright infringement? What purpose is served by the fair use doctrine?

Business Ethics   Did 2 Live Crew act ethically in using the "Oh Pretty Woman" song even though the copyright holder denied them permission to do so?

Contemporary Business   Do you think 2 Live Crew's parody version caused any economic loss to the original copyright holder?

Business Ethics

KINKO'S K.O.'D BY COPYRIGHT LAW

Kinko's Graphics Corporation (Kinko's) operates approximately 200 stores, or "copyshops," nationwide. The stores provide photocopying and other services and serve many colleges and universities and millions of students.

Since the mid-1980s, Kinko's has offered a service called "Professor Publishing." Under this program, Kinko's photocopies excerpts from selected materials at the request of college professors for educational use in the classroom. The materials are then bound into packets that contain a cover page printed with Kinko's logo, the name of the course and professor, and a price list. The packets—or "anthologies," as Kinko's calls them—are sold to students at Kinko's stores.

The majority of the materials in the packets are copied from copyrighted books and materials. Many packets contained full chapters from books, and some packets contained up to 100 pages from the same source. In most instances, Kinko's did not obtain permission from the copyright holder to reproduce the materials and did not pay anything to the holder.

Eight major textbook publishing houses brought suit against Kinko's for copyright infringement. The publishers sought an injunction against Kinko's use of their copyrighted materials without permission. They also sought damages. The publishers did not name professors or students as defendants.

Kinko's defense asserted the doctrine of "fair use." Kinko's claimed that the course packets are of tremendous importance to teaching and learning. It argued that an injunction against its educational copying would pose a serious threat to teaching and the welfare of education. The district court responded.

> *Although Kinko's tried to impress this court with its altruistic motives, the facts show that Kinko's copying had the intended purpose of supplanting the copyright holder's commercial valuable rights. The extent of Kinko's insistence that there are educational concerns and not profit-making ones boggles the mind.*

The district court held that Kinko's preparation of the packets violated fair use because (1) there was multiple (as opposed to single) copying of materials, (2) a lot of material was copied (rather than of a selected quote or passage), and

(3) Kinko's was a commercial enterprise, without nonprofit academic purpose. Therefore, the court held that Kinko's had engaged in infringement of the plaintiff's copyrighted materials.

As a remedy, the court granted the plaintiffs' request for an injunction and assessed damages of $510,000 and attorneys' fees and costs against Kinko's. The court also noted that the nature of Kinko's business meant that the threat of continued infringe-

ment remained even after its decision. [*Basic Books, Inc. v. Kinko's Graphics Corporation*, 758 F.Supp. 1522 (S.D.N.Y. 1991)]

1. Did Kinko's act morally in this case?
2. Do you think that the fair use doctrine should have protected Kinko's action?
3. Did the students who purchased the anthologies do anything wrong?

E-Commerce & Information Technology

THE DIGITAL MILLENNIUM COPYRIGHT ACT

The Internet makes it easier for people to illegally copy and distribute copyrighted works. To combat this, software and entertainment companies developed "wrappers" and encryption technology to protect their copyrighted works from unauthorized access. Not to be outdone, software pirates and other Internet users devised ways to crack these wrappers and protection devices. Seeing that they were losing the battle, software companies and the entertainment industry lobbied Congress to enact legislation that made the cracking of their wrappers and selling of technology to do so illegal. In 1998, Congress responded by enacting the **Digital Millennium Copyright Act (DMCA)** [17 U.S.C. 1201], which does the following:

- Prohibits unauthorized *access* to copyrighted digital works by circumventing the wrapper or encryption technology that protects the intellectual property. This "black box" protection prohibits simply accessing the protected information and does not require that the accessed information be misused.
- Prohibits the manufacture and distribution of technologies, products, or services primarily designed for the purpose of circumventing wrappers or encryption protection. Multipurpose devices that can be used in ways other than cracking wrappers or encryption technology can be manufactured and sold without violating the DMCA.

The DMCA changes the traditional fair use doctrine of copyright law. Historically, it has never been a crime to access or make a copy of a copyrighted work; what has been a crime is the misuse of that information. This rule remains valid for the nondigital world of copyrighted works. The DMCA changes this rule for digital protected works, making it illegal to merely access the copyrighted material by breaking through the digital wrapper or encryption technology that protects the work. Thus, a professor who can access and quote a nondigital copyrighted work in a paper he or she is writing pursuant to the fair use doctrine would violate the DMCA by merely accessing a digital work protected by the act.

Congress granted the following exceptions to DMCA liability to

- Software developers to achieve compatibility of their software with the protected work.
- Federal, state, and local law enforcement agencies conducting criminal investigations.
- Parents who are protecting children from pornography or other harmful materials available on the Internet.
- Internet users who are identifying and disabling "cookies" and other identification devices that invade their personal privacy rights.
- Nonprofit libraries, educational institutions, and archives who access a protected work to determine whether to acquire the work.

The DMCA imposes civil and criminal penalties. A successful plaintiff in a civil action can recover actual damages from first-time offenders and treble damages from repeat offenders, costs and attorney's fees, an order for the destruction of illegal product and devices, and an injunction against future violations by the offender. As an alternative to actual damages, a plaintiff can recover statutory damages of not less than $2,500 and up to $25,000 per act of circumvention. The following criminal penalties can be accessed for willful violations committed for "commercial advantage" or "private financial gain": First-time violators can be fined up to $500,000 and imprisoned for up to 5 years; subsequent violators can be fined up to $1 million and imprisoned up to 10 years.

The passage of the DMCA marks a significant victory for the software and entertainment industries, who allege that the new law will allow a huge growth in electronic commerce. Opponents, such as academics, scientists, libraries, and consumers argue that the act restricts access to information that would have previously been available under the fair use doctrine. They also note that the act paves the way for the software and entertainment industries to impose a per-use fee for their works. In the end, the DMCA has elevated the protection of digital copyrighted works above the protection of nondigital copyrighted works.

E-Commerce & Information Technology

THE NET ACT: CRIMINAL COPYRIGHT INFRINGEMENT

A copyright holder owns a valuable right and may sue an infringer in a civil lawsuit to recover damages, injunctions, and other remedies for copyright infringement. In 1997, Congress enacted the **No Electronic Theft Act (NET Act)**, which criminalizes certain copyright infringement as well. The impetus for the passage of this act was the failure of the U.S. government to obtain criminal convictions against copyright infringers under existing, non-Internet specific criminal statutes.

In one notable case, David LaMacchia, a 21-year-old student at the Massachusetts Institute of Technology (MIT), encouraged Internet users to upload computer games and software to a bulletin board. LaMacchia then made this software available free to Internet users without compensating the copyright holders. The worldwide traffic generated by the availability of free software attracted the notice of university and federal authorities. The U.S. government sued LaMacchia, asserting a violation of the federal wire fraud statute, but the federal court judge dismissed the case holding that this statute's language did not prohibit LaMacchia's conduct because he did not recognize financial gain. [*United States v. LaMacchia*, 871 F.Supp. 535 (D. Mass. 1994)]

So Congress passed the NET Act to directly criminalize such copyright infringement. The NET Act prohibits any person from willfully infringing a copyright for either the purpose of commercial advantage or financial gain, or by reproduction or distribution even without commercial advantage or financial gain, including by electronic means, where the retail value of the copyrighted work exceeds $1,000. Criminal penalties for violating the act include imprisonment for up to one year and fines of up to $100,000.

The NET Act has closed the "LaMacchia loophole." For example, Jeffrey Gerald Levy, a 22-year-old University of Oregon senior, pleaded guilty to criminal copyright infringement in violation of the NET Act because he was caught maintaining a Web site on the university's server where the public could make copies of thousands of software programs, movies, and musical recordings [*United States v. Levy* (D. Or. 1999)]. The NET Act adds a new law for the federal government to criminally attack copyright infringement and curb digital piracy.

International Law

INTERNATIONAL PROTECTION OF INTELLECTUAL PROPERTY RIGHTS

For centuries, national patent, copyright, and trademark laws defined the rights of inventors, authors, and businesses. These laws offered protection within a country's borders, but not in other countries. Beginning in the late 1800s, countries began entering into treaties and conventions with other countries that provided international protection of intellectual property rights. The major international agreements protecting intellectual property rights are discussed below.

The major convention that provides international protection to patents is the **1883 Convention of the Union of Paris (Paris Convention)**. The Convention's major purpose is to allow the nationals of each member country to file for patents in all other member nations. The Convention does not, however, eliminate the need to file separate patent applications in each member nation in which the applicant desires protection. The Convention gives an applicant who has filed for a patent in one member country 12 months to submit applications in other member countries.

The **Paris Convention** also allows nationals of each member nation to file for trademarks and service marks in all other member nations on an individual, nondiscriminatory basis, even if the applicant does not own the mark in the country of origin. The applicant has six months after his or her original registration to submit application to other member countries.

The major copyright treaty is the **Berne Convention of 1886**, as revised, to which the United States became a signatory in 1989. The Convention provides for the recognition of a copyright in all member nations. The Convention establishes a minimum copyright term of the life of the author plus 50 years and eliminates the requirement to put a © on copyrighted works.

In 1997, the World Intellectual Property Organization (WIPO), an agency of the United Nations, promulgated two new "**Internet Treaties**." These treaties recognized the importance of new digital technologies and the Internet. The first treaty, the WIPO **Copyright Treaty**, extends copyright protection to computer programs and data compilations and grants copyright holders the exclusive right to make their works available on the Internet as well as by any other wire or wireless means. The second treaty, the WIPO **Phonogram Treaty**, gives performers and producers the exclusive right to broadcast, reproduce, and distribute copies of their performances by any means, including video recording, digital sound, or encryption signal.

Japan *International agreements, such as the Paris Convention, Berne Convention, Phonogram Treaty, and other treaties provide international protection of patents, copyrights, trademarks, domain names, and other intellectual property rights.*

Landmark Law

FEDERAL LANHAM TRADEMARK ACT

Trademark law is intended to (1) protect the owner's investment and goodwill in a **mark** and (2) prevent consumers from being confused as to the origin of goods and services. In 1946, Congress enacted the **Lanham Trademark Act** to provide federal protection to trademarks, service marks, and other marks.[6] Congress passed the **Trademark Law Revision Act of 1988**, which amended trademark law in several respects.[7] The amendments made it easier to register a trademark but harder to maintain it. States may also enact trademark laws.

Trademarks are registered with the **U.S. Patent and Trademark Office** in Washington, DC. The original registration of a mark is valid for 10 years and can be renewed for an unlimited number of 10-year periods.[8] The registration of a trademark, which is given nationwide effect, serves as constructive notice that the mark is the registrant's personal property. The registrant is entitled to use the registered trademark symbol ® in connection with a registered trademark or service mark. Use of the symbol is not mandatory. Note that the frequently used notations "TM" and "SM" have no legal significance.

ℛEGISTRATION OF TRADEMARKS

An applicant can register a mark if (1) it was in use in commerce (e.g., actually used in the sale of goods or services) or (2) the applicant verifies a bona fide intention to use the mark in commerce and actually does so within six months of its registration. Failure to do so during this period causes loss of the mark to the registrant. A party other than the registrant can submit an opposition to a proposed registration of a mark or the cancellation of a previously registered mark.

Lanham Trademark Act (as amended)

Federal statute that (1) establishes the requirements for obtaining a federal mark and (2) protects marks from infringement.

Distinctiveness of a Mark

To qualify for federal protection, a mark must be **distinctive** or have acquired a **"secondary meaning."** For example, marks such as *Acura, Dr. Pepper, Roto Rooter,* and *Apple Computer* are *distinctive*. A term such as *English Leather*, which literally means leather processed in England, has taken on a "secondary meaning" as a trademark for an aftershave lotion. Words that are *descriptive* but have no secondary meaning cannot be trademarked. For example, the word *cola* alone could not be trademarked.

distinctive

A brand name that is unique and fabricated.

"secondary meaning"

When an ordinary term has become a brand name.

mark
The collective name for trademarks, service marks, certification marks, and collective marks that all can be trademarked.

trademark
A distinctive mark, symbol, name, word, motto, or device that identifies the goods of a particular business.

service mark
A mark that distinguishes the services of the holder from those of its competitors.

The law in respect to literature ought to remain upon the same footing as that which regards the profits of mechanical inventions and chemical discoveries.

William Wordsworth
Letter *(1838)*

This certification mark designates California cheese manufactures.

Marks That Can Be Trademarked

The following types of **marks** can be trademarked:

- **Trademarks** A **trademark** is a distinctive mark, symbol, name, word, motto, or device that identifies the *goods* of a particular business. For example, the words *Xerox*, *Coca-Cola*, and *IBM* are trademarks.
- **Service marks** A **service mark** is used to distinguish the *services* of the holder from those of its competitors. The trade names *United Airlines*, *Marriott Hotels*, and *Weight Watchers* are examples of service marks.
- **Certification marks** A **certification mark** is a mark that is used to certify that goods and services are of a certain quality or originate from particular geographical areas; for example, wines from the "Napa Valley" of California or "Florida" oranges. The owner of the mark is usually a nonprofit corporation that licenses producers that meet certain standards or conditions to use the mark.
- **Collective marks** A **collective mark** is a mark used by cooperatives, associations, and fraternal organizations. "Boy Scouts of America" is an example of a collective mark.

Certain marks cannot be registered. They include (1) the flag or coat of arms of the United States, any state, municipality, or foreign nation, (2) marks that are immoral or scandalous, (3) geographical names standing alone (e.g., "South"), (4) surnames standing alone (note that a surname can be registered if it is accompanied by a picture or fanciful name, such as "Smith Brothers' Cough Drops," and (5) any mark that resembles a mark already registered with the federal Patent and Trademark Office.

Contemporary Business Environment

COLOR MAY BE TRADEMARKED

The issue of whether color could be trademarked confused the courts of appeals for years: Some said it could, whereas others said it could not. In 1995, the U.S. Supreme Court ended this division and decided the issue in the following case.

Since the 1950s, Qualitex Company has manufactured and sold dry cleaning pads with a special shade of green-gold color. These pads are used on cleaning presses at dry cleaning firms. Qualitex registered the special green-gold color of its pads with the Patent and Trademark Office as a trademark.

In 1989, Jacobson Products, a Qualitex rival, began to sell its own press pads to dry cleaning firms, and it colored these pads a similar green-gold. Qualitex sued Jacobson for trademark infringement. Qualitex won the lawsuit in the district court, but the court of appeals reversed. Qualitex appealed to the U.S. Supreme Court.

The Supreme Court, in a unanimous decision, held that color qualifies for registration as a trademark when it is associated with a particular good where the color has obtained a secondary meaning that identifies a particular brand and manufacturer as its source. The Court held that Qualitex's special green-gold color on its press pads met this require-ment and could be registered and protected as a trademark. [*Qualitex Company v. Jacobson Products Company, Inc.*, 115 S.Ct. 1300, 131 L.Ed.2d 248 (1995)]

Trademark Infringement

The owner of a mark can sue a third party for the unauthorized use of a mark. To succeed in a **trademark infringement** case, the owner must prove that (1) the defendant infringed the plaintiff's mark by using it in an unauthorized manner and (2) such use is likely to cause confusion, mistake, or deception of the public as to the origin of the goods or services. A successful plaintiff can recover (1) the profits made by the infringer by the unauthorized use of the mark, (2) damages caused to the plaintiff's business and reputation, (3) an order requiring the defendant to destroy all goods containing the unauthorized mark, and (4) an injunction preventing the defendant from such infringement in the future. The court has discretion to award up to *treble* damages where intentional infringement is found.

trademark infringement
Unauthorized use of another's mark. The holder may recover damages and other remedies from the infringer.

Business Brief
An applicant can register a mark six months prior to its proposed use in commerce. If the mark is not used within this period, the applicant loses the mark.

Business Ethics

WAL-MART KNOCKS OFF DESIGNER'S CLOTHES

Fashion designers spend a fortune of money and time in creating unique fashion designs for their clothing. They then produce these clothes and sell them at upscale prices. But what is the designer to do if another manufacturer or retailer copies the original design and sells these "knockoffs" at much lower prices? Sue, that's what! Consider the following case.

Samara Brothers, Inc. (Samara) is a designer and manufacturer of children's clothing. The core of Samara's business is its annual new line of spring and summer children's garments. Wal-Mart Stores, Inc. (Wal-Mart) operates a large chain of budget warehouse stores that sells thousands of items at very low prices. In 1995, Wal-Mart contacted one of its suppliers, Judy-Philippine, Inc. (JPI) about the possibility of making a line of children's clothes just like Samara's successful line. Wal-Mart sent photographs of Samara's children's clothes to JPI (the name "Samara" was readily discernible on the labels of the garments) and directed JPI to produce children's clothes exactly like those in the photographs. JPI produced a line of children's clothes for Wal-Mart that copied the designs, colors, flower patterns, etc. of Samara's clothing. Wal-Mart then sold this line of children's clothing in its stores, making a gross profit of over $1.15 million on these clothes sales during the 1996 selling season.

In June 1996, one of the retailers that purchased Samara's children's clothing complained to Samara that Wal-Mart was selling the knockoff clothes at less than the retailer was paying Samara for its clothes. Samara investigated and discovered Wal-Mart had copied its designs. After sending unsuccessful cease and desist letters to Wal-Mart, Samara sued Wal-Mart, alleging trade dress infringement in violation of the Lanham Act. The U.S. district court held in favor of Samara and awarded damages. Wal-Mart appealed all the way to the U.S. Supreme Court, which granted review.

In a 9–0 decision, the Supreme Court came down on the side of Wal-Mart and held that, in this case, Wal-Mart had not violated the Lanham Act. The Court ruled that Samara's children's clothing had not acquired a "secondary meaning" in the minds of the public—that is, when most people saw Samara's clothing they did not automatically think "that is a Samara design." The Supreme Court established the following legal rule for product design infringement cases under the Lanham Act: If a product design has not acquired a secondary meaning in the minds of the public, it can be knocked off; if a product design has acquired a secondary meaning, then it cannot be knocked off. Thus, designers of nondistinctive goods, such as dresses, shoes, jewelry, golf clubs, and other products that have not acquired a secondary meaning, will find look-alikes being sold at discount stores such as Wal-Mart, Target, and Mervyn's.

There are some limitations to copying, however. Under the Supreme Court's *Wal-Mart* decision, goods that have acquired a secondary meaning—such as Ferrari automobile or Apple Computer's iMac computer—are protected from being copied. Goods that are patented, such as Nike's "air" technology in its athletic shoes, cannot be copied because it would constitute patent infringement. And counterfeiting—selling knockoff goods with a fake original manufacturer's trademarked name or logo on them—is illegal trademark infringement. [*Wal-Mart Stores, Inc. v. Samara Brothers, Inc.*, 2000 WL 293238, U.S. Supreme Court (2000)]

1. Under ethical principles, should Wal-Mart sell knock off goods?
2. What are the economic effects of the U.S. Supreme Court's decision? Who wins? Who loses?

Generic Names

Most companies promote their trademarks and service marks to increase the public's awareness of the availability and quality of their products and services. At some point in time, however, the public may begin to treat the mark as a common name to denote the type of product or service being sold, rather than as the trademark or trade name of an individual seller. A trademark that becomes a common term for a product line or type of service is called a **generic name**. Once that happens, the term loses its protection under federal trademark law because it has become *descriptive* rather than *distinctive* (see Exhibit 14.1).

*E*XHIBIT 14.1   *Reprinted with permission of Xerox Corporation*

E-Commerce & Information Technology

AOL's *You've Got Mail* a Generic Name

America Online, Inc. (AOL), operates one of the world's largest interactive online service. More than 20 million people subscribe to, and are members of, AOL online service. For a basic monthly fee, AOL service enables its members to receive computer information, access the Internet, and receive and send e-mail. For nearly a decade, AOL used the terms *You Have Mail* and *You've Got Mail* in connection with its automatic e-mail notification service. When an AOL member starts online and has e-mail, the cheerful spoken words *You've God Mail* are immediately heard. At the same time this voice sounds, a red signal flag is pictured prominently on the member's computer screen above the phrase *You Have Mail*. AOL applied for service mark protection for the two phrases *You've Got Mail* and *You Have Mail*.

AT&T Corp. (AT&T), a telecommunications company, began offering Internet access to subscribers for a monthly fee that included e-mail services. In December 1998, AT&T added a *You Have Mail!* notification to its e-mail service. AOL sent a letter to AT&T to cease and desist from using *You Have Mail!* When AT&T refused, AOL sued AT&T in federal dis-

trict court for unauthorized appropriation and infringement of AOL's common-law service marks *You Have Mail* and *You've Got Mail*. AT&T argued that these terms were generic and that AOL had no protectable interest in them.

The district court held as a matter of law that the two phrases were generic and thus were not protected marks. The court stated that a mark is generic when it "identifies a class of product or service, regardless of source." The court found that *You Have Mail* and *You've Got Mail* are common words and phrases that are used for their ordinary meaning. The court stated that the phrases *You Have Mail* and *You've Got Mail* indicate to the public at large what the service is, not where it came from. The court cited evidence that many of AOL's competitors used the term *mail* and *e-mail* when delivering e-mail to their subscribers. The court held that a generic term cannot receive service mark protection. The court granted summary judgment to AT&T and allowed it to use the term *You Have Mail!* when delivering e-mail to its subscribers. The court of appeals affirmed the judgment. [*America Online, Incorporated v. AT&T Corporation*, 243 F.3d 812 (4th Cir. 2001)]

CONCEPT SUMMARY   TYPES OF INTELLECTUAL PROPERTY PROTECTED BY FEDERAL LAW

Type	Subject Matter	Term
Patent	Inventions (e.g., machines; processes; compositions of matter; designs for articles of manufacture; and improvements to existing machines, processes). Invention must be 1. Novel 2. Useful 3. Nonobvious Public use doctrine: Patent will not be granted if the invention was used in public for more than one year prior to the filing of the patent application.	Patents on articles of manufacture and processes: 20 years; design patents: 14 years.
Copyright	Tangible writing (e.g., books, magazines, newspapers, lectures, operas, plays, screenplays, musical compositions, maps, works of art, lithographs, photographs, postcards, greeting cards, motion pictures, newsreels, sound recordings, computer programs, and mask works fixed to semiconductor chips). Writing must be the original work of the author. Fair use doctrine: It permits use of copyrighted material without consent for limited uses (e.g., scholarly work, parody or satire, and brief quotation in news reports).	Individual registrant: life of author plus 70 years. Business registrant: for the shorter of either (1) 120 years from the date of creation or (2) 95 years from the date of first publication.
Trademark	Marks (e.g., name, symbol, word, logo, or device). Marks include trademarks, service marks, certification marks, and collective marks. Mark must be distinctive or have acquired a secondary meaning. Generic name: A mark that becomes a common term for a product line or type of service loses its protection under federal trademark law.	Original registration: 10 years. Renewal registration: unlimited number of renewals for 10-year terms.

E-Commerce & Information Technology

FEDERAL DILUTION ACT: TRADEMARKS PREEMPT DOMAIN NAMES

One of the most important assets of many businesses is its name. Companies often trademark their name and then spend millions of dollars each year advertising and promoting the quality of the goods and services sold under the name. Coca-Cola, McDonald's, Microsoft, and others are household names that are recognized by millions of consumers. Once the use of the Internet exploded, and goods and services started to be sold over the Internet, many companies sought to conduct business over the Internet using their famous names. When they got there, many found that certain persons had already registered these famous names as domain names (i.e., ".com"). These domain name holders are called *cybersquatters* because they register domain names with the primary purpose of exacting a ransom payment from the trademark owner to buy the domain name from them.

Traditional trademark law was of little help to the trademark owners in many of these cases because to sue for trademark infringement consumers had to be confused as to the source of the goods or services. In many cases the cybersquatters either did not sell any goods or services or sold goods and services different from those sold by the trademark holder, therefore avoiding the consumer confusion requirement of a trademark infringement case.

To combat this situation, owners of trademarks and service marks lobbied Congress for help. Congress responded by enacting the **Federal Dilution of 1995**. This act protects famous marks from dilution. The Dilution Act provides that owners of marks have a valuable property right in their marks

that should not be eroded, blurred, tarnished, or diluted in any way by another. The Dilution Act does not require consumer confusion before there is a violation of the act. The Federal Dilution Act has three fundamental requirements:

1. The mark must be famous.
2. The use by the other party must be commercial.
3. The use must cause dilution of the distinctive quality of the mark.

In determining the fame of the mark, the court examines such factors as the distinctiveness of the mark, the duration and extent of the use of the mark, the channels of trade it is used in, and such. The second element, the commercial use requirement, is meant to avoid First Amendment free speech concerns. Finally, *dilution* is broadly defined as the lessening of the capacity of a famous mark to identify and distinguish goods and services, regardless of the presence or absence of competition between the owner of the mark and the other party or the likelihood of confusion, mistake, or deception.

The Federal Dilution Act is designed to stop those who attempt to benefit from the time and money spent by a company to develop and promote its famous marks. The act is primarily aimed at unseating cybersquatters who have appropriated famous marks on the Internet. Although most cases brought under the Federal Dilution Act have been domain name cases, the act applied to non-Internet dilution of famous marks as well.

State Antidilution Statutes

antidilution statutes

State laws that allow persons and companies to register trademarks and service marks.

States recognize common law trademarks. In addition, many states have enacted their own trademark statutes. These state laws, which allow persons and companies to register trademarks and service marks, are often called **antidilution statutes**. They prevent others from infringing on and diluting a registrant's mark. Companies that only do business locally sometimes register under these laws.

Contemporary Business Environment

BOOTLEGGING OF LIVE MUSIC OUTLAWED

In 1995, the United States joined over 130 other countries and became a member of the World Trade Organization (WTO). The WTO member nations adopted the international **Agreement on Trade Related Aspects of Intellectual Property (TRIPs)**, which outlawed unauthorized taping of sounds or images of live musical performances. To enforce this agreement in the United States, the U.S. Congress enacted the following federal antibootlegging statutes:

• **18 U.S.C. 2319A** Imposes criminal liability for the unauthorized taping of the sounds and images of live musical performances "knowingly and for purposes of commercial advantage or private financial gain." A first offense carries a prison term of up to five years; subsequent offenses carry prison terms up to 10 years. The court can order unauthorized recordings to be destroyed.

• **17 U.S.C. 1101** Imposes civil liability for similar conduct but without the commercial advantage or private financial gain requirement. A successful plaintiff can recover actual damages and any profits made by the defendant, destruction of any unauthorized recordings, and an injunction against any future violations by the defendant.

It is important to note that both recording the sound of the concert and taking photographs of the performance are conduct that is outlawed by these statutes. The lawfulness of the antibootlegging statute has been upheld as a valid exercise of Congress's power under the Commerce Clause of the U.S. Constitution. [*United States v. Moghadam*, 175 F.3d 1269 (11th Cir. 1999)]

International Law

ENFORCEMENT OF INTELLECTUAL PROPERTY RIGHTS UNDER TRIPS

Since the late 1800s, many countries have entered into treaties and conventions with each other to protect intellectual property rights such as patents, copyrights, and trademarks. However, if a country was not a party to an international treaty, persons and businesses within that country sometimes freely used patents, copyrights, and trademarks of persons and businesses from other countries without penalty or repercussion. And even if the infringer's country was a party to an international treaty, the infringement charge would be heard by a national court whose judgment was not always satisfactory to the intellectual property holder in the other country. This system of having national courts hear intellectual property disputes continued until 1967.

In 1967, the United Nations established the **World Intellectual Property Organization (WIPO)**. This special agency was created to administer intellectual property treaties and conventions that member nations had signed. Although being of some benefit in deciding intellectual property disputes, the WIPO had no means of enforcing its decisions. Therefore, decisions issued by the WIPO against offending countries were often ignored.

The United States, the largest producer of intellectual property rights in the world, lost billions of dollars annually as its patents, copyrights, and trademarks were "knocked off" by infringers in many countries of the world. The development of digital technologies and the Internet increased the United States' concern of how to rein in infringement of intellectual property rights. When the United States

attended the Uruguay Round of the General Agreement on Tariffs and Trade (GATT) in the early 1990s, it not only argued for reductions of tariffs and trade barriers worldwide, but made the international protection of intellectual property rights a major issue of negotiation. In addition to obtaining an agreement for the reduction of tariffs and trade restrictions, the United States, Japan, and other developed nations secured the passage of the **Agreement on Trade-Related Aspects of Intellectual Property Rights (TRIPs)**. TRIPs, which became effective on January 1, 1995, mandates that member nations comply with international treaties and conventions protecting copyrights in traditional works, computer programs, and digital works, and related intellectual property laws.

In order to remedy the enforcement problems of the WIPO, the United States urged, and obtained agreement, that TRIPs would be administered by the **World Trade Organization (WTO)**. What this means is that if one country believes another country is not enforcing international intellectual property laws, a nation can file a charge with the WTO. The dispute is heard by a WTO panel, with an appeal to the WTO court. The WTO has the authority to enforce its decisions by ordering economic sanctions against infringing member nations that do not comply with its decision. Thus, the United States and other developed nations for the first time have an effective mechanism to pursue disputes against rogue nations who either promote infringement or do not protect intellectual property rights within their borders.

Chapter Summary

Trade Secret, p. 323

Trade Secrets	1. *Trade secret.* A *trade secret* is a product formula, pattern, design, compilation of data, customer list, or other business secret that makes a business successful. The owner of a trade secret must take reasonable precautions to prevent its trade secret from being discovered by others.
	2. *Misappropriation of a trade secret.* Obtaining another's trade secret through unlawful means such as theft, bribery, or espionage is a tort. A successful plaintiff can recover profits, damages, and an injunction against the offender.
	3. *The Economic Espionage Act.* A federal statute that makes it a crime for any person to convert a trade secret for his or another's benefit, knowing or intending to cause injury to the owners of the trade secret.

Patenting an Invention, p. 325

Patents

Patent law is exclusively federal law; there are no state patent laws.

1. *Patent.* Patentable subject matter includes inventions such as machines; processes; compositions of matter; improvements to existing machines, processes, or compositions of matter; designs for articles of manufacture; asexually reproduced plants; and living matter invented by man.
   To be patented, an invention must be:
   a. Novel
   b. Useful
   c. Nonobvious
2. *Business plants.* In *State Street Bank & Trust Co. v. Signature Financial Group, Inc.*, the U.S. Court of Appeals held that business plans are patentable.
3. *Patent application.* An application containing a written description of the invention must be filed with the *U.S. Patent and Trademark Office* in Washington, DC.
4. *Term.* Patents are valid for 20 years.
5. *Public use doctrine.* A patent may not be granted if the invention was used by the public for more than one year prior to the filing of the patent application.
6. *Patent infringement.* The unauthorized use of author's patent. The patent holder may recover damages and other remedies against the infringer.
7. *The American Inventors Protection Act.* This federal statute does the following:
   a. Permits an inventor to file a *provisional application* with the U.S. Patent and Trademark Office (PTO) three months pending the filing of a final patent application.
   b. Requires the PTO to issue a patent within three years after the filing of a patent application.
8. *Patent appeals.* These are heard by the *U.S. Court of Appeals for the Federal Circuit* in Washington, DC.

Registration of Copyrights, p. 330

Copyrights

Copyright law is exclusively federal law; there are no state copyright laws.

1. *Copyright.* Only tangible writings can be copyrighted. These include books, newspapers, addresses, musical compositions, motion pictures, works of art, architectural plans, greeting cards, photographs, sound recordings, computer programs, and mask works fixed in semiconductor chips.
2. *Requirements for copyright.* The writing must be the original work of the author.
3. *Copyright registration.* Copyright registration is permissive and voluntary. Published and unpublished works may be registered with the *U.S. Copyright Office* in Washington, DC. Registration itself does not create the copyright.
4. *Term.* Copyrights are for the following terms:
   a. *Individual holder.* Life of the author plus 70 years.
   b. *Corporate holder.* Either (1) 120 years from the date of creation or (2) 95 years from the date of publication, whichever is shorter.
5. *Copyright infringement.* The copying of a substantial and material part of a copyrighted work without the holder's permission. The copyright holder may recover damages and other remedies against the infringer.
6. *Fair use doctrine.* Permits use of copyrighted material without the consent of the copyright holder for limited uses (e.g., scholarly work, parody or satire, and brief quotation in news reports).
7. *Digital Millennium Copyright Act (DMCA).* A federal statute enacted in 1998 that provides civil and criminal penalties that
   a. Prohibits the manufacture and distribution of technologies, products, or services primarily designed for the purpose of circumventing wrappers or encryption protection.
   b. Prohibits unauthorized *access* to copyrighted digital works by circumventing the wrapper or encryption technology that protects the intellectual property.
8. *Visual Artists Rights Act.* A federal statute that gives artists *moral rights* in their creation after the sale of the artwork.
9. *No Electronic Theft Act (NET Act).* A federal statute that makes it a crime for a person to willfully infringe a copyright work exceeding $1,000 in retail value.

Registration of Trademarks, p. 339

Trademarks and Service Marks

1. Mark. Trade name, symbol, word, logo, design, or device that distinguishes the owner's goods or services. Marks are often referred to collectively as trademarks. Types of marks are:
   a. *Trademark.* Identifies goods of a particular business.
   b. *Service mark.* Identifies services of a particular business.
   c. *Certification mark.* Certifies that goods or services are of a certain quality or origin.
   d. *Collective mark.* Used by cooperatives, associations, and fraternal organizations.

2. *Requirements for a trademark.* The mark must either (a) be *distinctive* or (b) have acquired a *secondary meaning.* The mark must have been used in commerce or the holder intends to use the mark in commerce and actually does so within six months after registering the mark.
3. *Trademark registration.* Marks are registered with the *U.S. Patent and Trademark Office* in Washington, DC.
4. *Term.* The original registration of a mark is valid for 10 years and can be renewed for an unlimited number of 10-year periods.
5. *Trademark infringement.* The unauthorized use of another's registered mark. The mark holder may recover damages and other remedies from the infringer.
6. *Generic name.* A mark that becomes a common term for a product line or type of service loses its protection under federal trademark law.
7. *Federal Dilution Act of 1995.* A federal statute that protects famous marks from dilution. A violation of the act requires that the mark be famous, the use by the other party was commercial, and the use caused dilution of the distinctive quality of the mark.

ℰND-OF-ℭHAPTER ℐNTERNET ℰXERCISES AND ℭASE ℚUESTIONS

 Working the Web Internet Exercises

ACTIVITIES

1. Trade Secrets: Research the web to determine if your state has adopted the Uniform Trade Secrets Act. Visit the Trade Secrets Home Page at **www.execpc.com/~mhallign**.

2. Trademarks: **www.uspto.gov** contains information about the federal trademark registration system. Find your analogous state trademark site. See also Marksonline—free trademark search and domain name search—**www.marksonline.com**.

3. Copyrights: **www.uspto.gov** contains information about the federal copyright registration system. Does the most recent copyright law require authors to use the copyright notice on printed material in order to protect it from infringement?

4. What is the current duration of a U.S. Patent? What was the duration of a U.S. Patent under previous law and why was it changed? See Patents: **www.uspto.gov**

5. International protection of intellectual property: Visit **www.wipo.int** and outline the process for international registration of a patent.

 ## CRITICAL LEGAL THINKING CASES

14.1 Trade Secret CRA-MAR Video Center, Inc., sells electronic equipment and videocassettes, as does its competitor, Koach's Sales Corporation. Both CRA-MAR and Koach's purchased computers from Radio Shack. CRA-MAR used the computer to store customer lists, movie lists, personnel files, and financial records. Because the computer was new to CRA-MAR, Randall Youts, Radio Shack's salesman and programmer, agreed to modify CRA-MAR's programs when needed, including the customer list program. At one point, CRA-MAR decided to send a mailing to everyone on its customer list. The computer was unable to perform the function, so Youts took the disks containing the customer lists to the Radio Shack store to work on the program. Somehow Koach's came into possession of CRA-MAR's customer lists and did advertising mailings to the parties on the lists. When CRA-MAR discovered this fact, it sued Koach's, seeking an injunction

against any further use of its customer lists. Is a customer list a trade secret that can be protected from misappropriation? [*Koach's Sales Corp. v. CRA-MAR Video Center, Inc.*, 478 N.E.2d 110 (Ind. App. 1985)]

14.2 Trade Secret Acuson Corporation, a Delaware corporation, and Aloka Co., Ltd., a Japanese company, are competitors who both manufacture ultrasonic imaging equipment, a widely used medical diagnostic tool. The device uses sound waves to produce moving images of the inside of a patient's body, which a computer processes into an image that is displayed on a video monitor. Acuson's unit provides finer resolution than Aloka's unit. Both companies have sold many units to hospitals and medical centers. In November 1985, Aloka decided to purchase an Acuson unit. Aloka had another company make the actual purchase because it was concerned that Acuson would not sell the unit to a competitor. After the unit was shipped to Tokyo, Aloka's engineers partially dismantled the Acuson unit. They recorded their observations in notebooks. When Acuson discovered that Aloka had purchased one of its units, it sued Aloka, seeking an injunction and return of the unit. Is Aloka liable for misappropriation of a trade secret? [*Acuson Corp. v. Aloka Co., Ltd.*, 10 U.S.P.Q.2d 1814, 257 Cal.Rptr. 368 (Cal.App. 1989)]

14.3 Patent In 1968, patent no. 3,397,928 (928) was issued to Edward M. Galle, an executive of Hughes Tool Company. Galle assigned the patent, and other related patents, to Hughes. The patent was for an O-ring rubber seal that was used to seal bearings in the cone of a rock bit that rotated to drill holes in rocks. Rock bits were used to drill oil wells. Hughes did not license its 928 patent, which was a substantial commercial success. Smith International, Inc. was Hughes's major competitor in this industry. Between 1971 and 1984, Smith made more than 460,000 rock bits (reaping sales of about $1.3 billion) that contained rubber seals that infringed on Hughes's patents. Hughes sued Smith for patent infringement and requested $1.2 billion in lost royalties and interest. Smith offered $20 million to $60 million in settlement. The case went to trial, and the court found Smith liable for patent infringement. How much in damages should Hughes be awarded? [*Smith International Inc. v. Hughes Tool Co.*, 229 U.S.P.Q. 81 (Fed. Cir. 1986)]

14.4 Copyright When Spiro Agnew resigned as vice president of the United States, President Richard M. Nixon appointed Gerald R. Ford as vice president. In 1974, amid growing controversy surrounding the Watergate scandal, President Nixon resigned and Vice President Ford acceded to the presidency. As president, Ford pardoned Nixon for any wrongdoing regarding the Watergate affair and related matters. Ford served as president until he was defeated by Jimmy Carter in the 1976 presidential election. In 1973, Ford entered into a contract with Harper & Row, Publishers, Inc. to publish his memoirs in book form. The memoirs were to contain significant unpublished materials concerning the Watergate affair and Ford's personal reflections on that time in history. The publisher instituted security measures to protect the confidentiality of the manuscript. Several weeks before the book was to be released, an unidentified person secretly brought a copy of the manuscript to Victor Navasky, editor of *The Nation*, a weekly political commentary magazine. Navasky, knowing that his possession of the purloined manuscript was not authorized, produced a 2,250-word piece entitled "The Ford Memoirs" and published it in the April 3, 1979, issue of *The Nation*. Verbatim quotes of between 300 and 400 words from Ford's manuscript, including some of the most important parts, appeared in the article. Harper & Row sued the publishers of *The Nation* for copyright infringement. Who wins? [*Harper & Row, Publishers, Inc. v. Nation Enterprises*, 471 U.S. 539, 105 S.Ct. 2218, 85 L.Ed.2d 588 (1985)]

14.5 Copyright The Sony Corporation of America manufactures video-cassette recorders (VCRs) that can be used to videotape programs and films that are shown on television and cable stations. VCRs are used by consumers and others to videotape both copyrighted and uncopyrighted works. The primary use for VCRs is by consumers for "time-shifting"—taping a television program for viewing at a more convenient time. Universal City Studios, Inc. and Walt Disney Productions hold copyrights on a substantial number of motion-picture and audiovisual works that are shown on television and cable stations, which pay them a fee to do so. Some of Universal's and Disney's copyrighted works have been copied by consumers using Sony's VCRs. Universal and Disney sued Sony, seeking an injunction against the sale of VCRs by Sony. Is Sony liable for contributory copyright infringement? [*Sony Corp. of America v. Universal City Studios, Inc.*, 464 U.S. 417, 104 S.Ct. 774, 78 L.Ed.2d 574 (1984)]

14.6 Fair Use Doctrine In the dark days of 1977, when the City of New York teetered on the brink of bankruptcy, on the television screens of America there appeared an image of a top-hatted Broadway showgirl, backed by an advancing phalanx of dancers, chanting: "I-I-I-I-I Love New Yo-o-o-o-o-ork." As an ad campaign for an ailing city, it was an unparalleled success. Crucial to the campaign was a brief but exhilarating musical theme written by Steve Karmin called "I Love New York." Elsmere Music, Inc., owned the copyright to the music. The success of the campaign did not go unnoticed. On May 20, 1978, the popular weekly variety program *Saturday Night Live (SNL)* performed a comedy sketch over National Broadcasting Company's (NBC) network. In the sketch the cast of *SNL*, portraying the mayor and members of the chamber of commerce of the biblical city of Sodom, were seen discussing Sodom's poor public image with out-of-towners, and its effect on the tourist trade. In an attempt to recast Sodom's image in a more positive light, a new advertising campaign was revealed, with the highlight of the campaign being a song "I Love Sodom" sung a cappella by a chorus line of *SNL* regulars to the tune of "I Love New York." Elsmere Music did not see the humor of the sketch and sued NBC for copyright infringement. Who wins? [*Elsmere Music, Inc. v. National Broadcasting Co., Inc.*, 623 F.2d 252 (2d Cir. 1980)]

14.7 Copyright Professional Real Estate Investors, Inc., and Kenneth Irwin own and operate La Mancha, a resort hotel in Palm Springs, California. Guests at La Mancha may rent movie videodiscs from the lobby gift shop for a $5 daily fee per disc, which can be charged on the hotel bill. Each guest room is equipped with a large-screen projection television and videodisc player. Guests view the videodisc movies projected on the television screen in their rooms. After learning of these activities, Columbia Pictures, Inc., and six other motion-picture studios (Columbia) who owned copyrights on films rented on videodisc at La Mancha filed suit to prevent La Mancha from renting videodiscs to its guests, alleging copyright infringement. Is La Mancha liable for copyright infringement? [*Columbia Pictures Industries, Inc. v. Professional Real Estate Investors, Inc.*, 866 F.2d 278 (9th Cir. 1989)]

14.8 Trademark Clairol Incorporated manufactures and distributes hair tinting, dyeing, and coloring preparations. In 1956, Clairol embarked on an extensive advertising campaign to promote the sale of its "Miss Clairol" hair-color preparations that included advertisements in national magazines, on outdoor billboards, on radio and television, in mailing pieces, and on point-of-sale display materials to be used by retailers and beauty salons. The advertisements prominently displayed the slogans "Hair Color So Natural Only Her Hairdresser Knows for Sure" and "Does She or Doesn't She?" Clairol registered these slogans as trademarks. During the next decade Clairol spent more than $22 million for advertising materials resulting in more than a billion separate audio and visual impressions using the slogans. Roux Laboratories, Inc., a manufacturer of hair-coloring products and a competitor of Clairol's, filed an opposition to Clairol's registration of the slogans as trademarks. Do the slogans qualify for trademark protection? [*Roux Laboratories, Inc. v. Clairol Inc.*, 427 F.2d 823 (Cust.Pat.App. 1979)]

14.9 Trademark In 1967, two friends from California designed a sailing surfboard that combined the sports of sailing and surfing. Originally they called it a "sailboard." They filed for and were granted a patent on the sailboard, which was assigned to the company Windsurfing International, Inc. (WSI). In 1968, WSI's Seattle dealer coined the term *windsurfing*. WSI applied for and was granted trademarks for terms using the word *Windsurfer*. Between 1969 and 1976, WSI produced a particular type of board called the Windsurfer. At that time, WSI controlled more than 95 percent of the market. In the early years, there was no generic word for the sport or craft. To promote sales, WSI and its employees continually referred to the sport as windsurfing and individual sportspeople as windsurfers. WSI also engaged in an extensive advertising campaign using the terms *windsurfing* to describe the sport and *windsurfer* to describe individual sportspersons. People who participated in the sport, trade magazines, and the general public used the word *windsurfing* to describe the sport. In 1977, WSI started to police the use of its trademarked term. However, its use remained rather futile, as evidence showed that the general public used the terms *windsurfing* and *windsurfer* in a general, common sense to

mean the sport and its participants. AMF Incorporated (AMF) seeks cancellation of WSI's trademarks containing the term *Windsurfer*. Should the trademark be canceled? [*AMF Inc. v. Windsurfing International, Inc.*, 613 F.Supp. (D.C.N.Y. 1985)]

14.10 Trademark Since 1972, Mead Data Central, Inc. has provided computer-assisted legal research services to lawyers and others under the trademark "LEXIS." LEXIS is based on *lex*, the Latin word for law, and *IS*, for information systems. Through extensive sales and advertising, Mead has made LEXIS a strong mark in the computerized legal research field, particularly among lawyers. However, LEXIS is recognized by only one percent of the general population, with almost half of this one percent being attorneys. Toyota Motor Corporation has for many years manufactured automobiles, which it markets in the United States through its subsidiary Toyota Motor Sales, U.S.A., Inc. On August 24, 1987, Toyota announced a new line of luxury automobiles to be called Lexus. Toyota planned on spending almost $20 million for marketing and advertising Lexus during the first nine months of 1989. Mead filed suit against Toyota, alleging that Toyota's use of the name Lexus violated New York's antidilution statute and would cause injury to the business reputation of Mead and a dilution of the distinctive quality of the LEXIS mark. Who wins? [*Mead Data Central, Inc. v. Toyota Motor Sales, U.S.A., Inc.*, 875 F.2d 1026 (2d Cir. 1989)]

14.11 Generic Name The Miller-Brewing Company, a national brewer, produces a reduced-calorie beer called Miller Lite. Miller began selling beer under this name in the 1970s and has spent millions of dollars promoting the Miller Lite brand name on television, in print, and via other forms of advertising. Since July 11, 1980, Falstaff Brewing Corporation has been brewing and distributing a reduced-calorie beer called Falstaff Lite. Miller brought suit under the Lanham Trademark Act seeking an injunction to prevent Falstaff from using the term *Lite*. Is the term *Lite* a generic name that does not qualify for trademark protection? [*Miller Brewing Co. v. Falstaff Brewing Corp.*, 655 F.2d 5 (1st Cir. 1981)]

BUSINESS ETHICS CASES

14.12 Business Ethics Integrated Cash Management Services, Inc. (ICM) designs and develops computer software programs and systems for banks and corporate financial departments. ICM's computer programs and systems are not copyrighted, but they are secret. After Alfred Sims Newlin and Behrouz Vafa completed graduate school, they were employed by ICM as computer programmers. They worked at ICM for several years writing computer programs. In March 1987, they left ICM to work for Digital Transactions, Inc. (DTI). Before leaving ICM, however, they copied certain ICM files onto personal diskettes. Within two weeks of starting to work at DTI, they created prototype computer programs that operated in substantially the same manner as comparable ICM programs and were designed to compete directly with ICM's programs. ICM sued Newlin, Vafa, and DTI for misappropriation of trade secrets.

Are the defendants liable? Did the defendants act ethically in this case? [*Integrated Cash Management Services, Inc. v. Digital Transactions, Inc.* 920 F.2d 171 (2nd Cir. 1990)]

14.13 Business Ethics John W. Carson was the host and star of *The Tonight Show*, a well-known nightly television talk show broadcast by the National Broadcasting Company (NBC) until he retired in 1992. Carson also appeared as an entertainer in theaters and night clubs around the country. From the time that he began hosting *The Tonight Show* in 1962, he had been introduced on the show each night with the phrase "Here's Johnny." The phrase "Here's Johnny" was generally associated with Carson by a substantial segment of the television viewing public. Carson had licensed the use of the phrase to a chain of restaurants, a line of toiletries, and other business ventures. Johnny

Carson Apparel, Inc., founded in 1970, manufactures and markets men's clothing to retail stores. Carson, president of Apparel and owner of 20 percent of its stock, had licensed Apparel to use the phrase "Here's Johnny" on labels for clothing and in advertising campaigns. The phrase had never been registered by Carson or Apparel as a trademark or service mark.

Earl Broxton was the owner and president of Here's Johnny Portable Toilets, Inc., a Michigan corporation that engages in the business of renting and selling "Here's Johnny" portable toilets. Broxton was aware when he formed the corporation that the phrase "Here's Johnny" was the introductory slogan for Carson on *The Tonight Show*. Broxton indicated that he coupled the phrase "Here's Johnny" with a second one, "The World's Foremost Commodian," to make a good play on the phrase. Shortly after Toilets went into business in 1976, Carson and Apparel sued Toilets, seeking an injunction prohibiting the further use of the phrase "Here's Johnny" as a corporate name for or in connection with the sale or rental of its portable toilets. Who wins? Did Broxton act ethically by appropriating the phrase "Here's Johnny" to promote the sale and rental of portable toilets? [*Carson v. Here's Johnny Portable Toilets, Inc.*, 698 F.2d 831 (6th Cir. 1983)]

14.14 Business Ethics   Master Distributors, Inc. (MDI), manufactures and sells "Blue Max," a blue leader splicing tape that is used to attach undeveloped film to a leader cord for photoprocessing through a minilab machine that develops the film and prints the photographs. Leader tape can be created in any color, and MDI dyed its Blue Max tape aquamarine blue. Blue Max is well-known and enjoys a reputation as the industry standard. Both distributors and customers often order Blue Max by asking for "the blue tape" or simply for "blue." When MDI learned that Pakor, Inc. was manufacturing and selling a brand of aquamarine blue leader splicing tape, "Pakor Blue," it brought suit for trademark infringement. Did Pakor act morally in copying MDI's color for its splicing tape? Why do you think Pakor did this? Was there trademark infringement? [*Master Distributors, Inc. v. Pakor Inc.*, 956 F.2d 219 (8th Cir. 1993)]

BRIEFING THE CASE WRITING ASSIGNMENT

Read the following case, which has been excerpted from the court's opinion, and brief the case.

Feist Publications, Inc. v. Rural Telephone Service Co., Inc.
499 U.S. 340, 111 S.Ct. 1282, 113 L.ED.2D 358 (1991)
U.S. Supreme Court

O'Conner, Justice

Rural Telephone Service Company is a certified public utility that provides telephone service to several communities in northwest Kansas. It is subject to a state regulation that requires all telephone companies operating in Kansas to issue annually an updated telephone directory. Accordingly, as a condition of its monopoly franchise, Rural publishes a typical telephone directory, consisting of white pages and yellow pages. The white pages list in alphabetical order the names of Rural's subscribers, together with their towns and telephone numbers. The yellow pages list Rural's business subscribers alphabetically by category and feature classified advertisements of various sizes. Rural distributes its directory free of charge to its subscribers, but earns revenue by selling yellow pages advertisements.

Feist Publications, Inc., is a publishing company that specializes in area-wide telephone directories. Unlike a typical directory, which covers only a particular calling area, Feist's area-wide directories cover a much larger geographical range, reducing the need to call directory assistance or consult multiple directories. The Feist directory that is the subject of this litigation covers 11 different telephone service areas in 15 countries and contains 46,878 white pages listings—compared to Rural's approximately 7,700 listings.

Of the 11 telephone companies, only Rural refused to license its listings to Feist. Rural's refusal created a problem for Feist, as omitting these listings would have left a gaping hole in its area-wide directory, rendering it less attractive to potential yellow pages advertisers. Unable to license Rural's white pages listings, Feist used them without Rural's consent.

Rural sued for copyright infringement in the District Court for the District of Kansas taking the position that Feist, in compiling its own directory, could not use the information contained in Rural's white pages. The District Court granted summary judgment to Rural, explaining that "courts have consistently held that telephone directories are copyrightable" and citing a string of lower court decisions. In an unpublished opinion, the Court of Appeals for the Tenth Circuit affirmed "for substantially the reasons given by the district court."

This case concerns the interaction of two well-established propositions. The first is that facts are not copyrightable; the other, that compilations of facts generally are. The key to resolving the tension lies in understanding why facts are not copyrightable. The sine qua non of copyright is originality. To qualify for copyright protection, a work must be original to the author. Original, as the term is used in copyright, means only that the work was independently created by the author (as opposed to copied from other works), and that it possesses at least some minimal degree of creativity.

Originality is a constitutional requirement. The source of Congress' power to enact copyright laws is Article I, §8, Cl. 8, of the Constitution, which authorizes Congress to "secure for limited Timers to Authors . . . the exclusive Right to their respective Writings." It is this bedrock principle of copyright that mandates the law's seemingly disparate treatment of facts and factual compilations. No one may claim originality as to facts. This is because facts do not owe their origin to an act of authorship. The distinction is one between creation and discovery: the first person to find and report a particular fact has not created the fact; he or she has merely discovered its existence.

If the selection and arrangement of facts are original, these elements of the work are eligible for copyright protection. No matter how original the format, however, the facts themselves do not become original through association.

There is no doubt that Feist took from the white pages of Rural's directory a substantial amount of factual information. At a minimum, Feist copied the names, towns, and telephone numbers of 1,309 of Rural's subscribers. Not all copying, however, is copyright infringement, two elements must be proven:

(1) ownership of a valid copyright and (2) copying of constituent elements of the work that are original. The first element is not at issue here; Feist appears to concede that Rural's directory, considered as a whole, is subject to a valid copyright because it contains some foreword text, as well as original material in its yellow pages advertisements.

The question is whether Rural has proved the second element. In other words, did Feist, by taking 1,309 names, towns, and telephone numbers from Rural's white pages, copy anything that was "original" to Rural? Certainly, the raw data does not satisfy the originality requirement. Rural may have been the first to discover and report the names, towns, and telephone numbers of its subscribers, but this data does not "owe its origin" to Rural. The question

that remains is whether Rural selected, coordinated, or arranged these copyrightable facts in an original way. The selection, coordination, and arrangement of Rural's white pages do not satisfy the minimum constitutional standards for copyright protection. Rural's selection of listings could not be more obvious: it publishes the most basic information—name, town, and telephone number—about each person who applies to it for telephone service. This is "selection" of a sort, but it lacks the modicum of creativity necessary to transform mere selection into copyrightable expression. Rural expended sufficient effort to make the white pages directory useful, but insufficient creativity to make it original.

The judgment of the Court of Appeals is reversed.

ENDNOTES

1. Article I, Section 8, clause 8 of the U.S. Constitution provides: The Congress shall have the power . . . To promote the Progress of Science and useful Arts, by securing for limited Times to Authors and Inventors the exclusive Right to their respective Writings and Discoveries.
2. 35 U.S.C. § 10 et seq.
3. *Diamond v. Chakrabarry*, 447 U.S. 303, 100 S.Ct. 2204, 65 L.Ed.2d 144 (1980). The U.S. Supreme Court held that genetically engineered bacterium that was capable of breaking up oil spills was patentable subject matter.
4. Article I, Section 8, clause 8 of the U.S. Constitution.
5. 17 U.S.C. §§ 101 et seq.
6. 15 U.S.C. §§ 1114 et seq.
7. Senate Bill 1883, effective November 16, 1989.
8. Prior to the 1988 amendments, original registration of a mark was valid for 20 years and could be renewed for an unlimited number of 20-year periods.

15

Electronic Commerce and Information Technology Licensing

Through the use of chat rooms, any person with a phone line can become a town crier with a voice that resonates farther than it could from any soapbox. Through the use of Web pages, mail exploders, and newsgroups, the same individual can become a pamphleteer.

—Justice Stevens
Reno v. American Civil Liberties Union, 521 U.S. 844 (1977)

Chapter Objectives

After studying this chapter, you should be able to:

1. Describe the free-speech protection granted to the Internet by the U.S. Supreme Court's opinion *Reno v. American Civil Liberties Union.*

2. Describe the process for obtaining Internet domain names.

3. Describe how the Federal Dilution Act prohibits domain names from diluting or tarnishing famous trademarks.

4. Define *license* and the parties to a licensing agreement.

5. Describe the provisions of the Federal Electronics Signatures Act for e-commerce.

6. Describe the Uniform Electronic Transactions Act (UETA).

7. Describe the Uniform Computer Information Transactions Act (UCITA).

8. Describe the informational rights protected by the UCITA.

9. Describe how the UCITA provides comprehensive rules for the creation, performance, and enforcement of licensing agreements.

10. Describe the procedure for arbitrating Internet domain name disputes.

Chapter Contents

In the late 1990s and early 2000s the use of the Internet and the World Wide Web, and the sale of goods and services through **e-commerce**, exploded. Large and small businesses began selling goods and services over the Internet through Web sites and registered domain names. Consumers and businesses can purchase almost any good or service they want over the Internet using such sites as Amazon.com, eBay, and others. In addition, software and information may be licensed either by physically purchasing the software or information and installing it on a computer or by merely downloading the software or information directly into the computer.

Many legal scholars and lawyers argued that traditional rules of contract law do not adequately meet the needs of Internet transactions and software and information licensing. These concerns led to an effort to create a new contract law for electronic transactions. After much debate, the National Conference of Commissioners on Uniform State Laws developed the **Uniform Electronic Transactions Act (UETA)** and the **Uniform Computer Information Transactions Act (UCITA)**. These model acts provide uniform and comprehensive rules for contracts involving computer information transactions and software and information licenses.

This chapter covers the registration of domain names and the operation of Web businesses and explains how the UETA and UCITA and other laws regulate the creation, transfer, and enforcement of e-commerce and informational rights licensing contracts.

*T*HE INTERNET

The **Internet**, or **Net**, is a collection of millions of computers that provide a network of electronic connections between the computers. The Internet began in 1969 by the U.S. Department of Defense to create electronic communications for military and national defense purposes. Building on this start, in the 1980s the National Science Foundation, the federal government's main scientific and technical agency, established the Net to facilitate high-speed communications among research centers at academic and research institutions around the world.

Eventually, individuals and businesses began using the Internet for communication of information and data. In 1980 there were fewer than 250 computers hooked to the Internet. Growth was rapid in the late 1990s and into the early 2000s, and today there are several hundred million computers connected to the Internet. The Internet's evolution helped usher in the Information Age of today.

e-commerce
The sale of goods and services by computer over the Internet.

Business Brief
The use of the Internet and the sale of goods and services through e-commerce has exploded in the United States and worldwide.

Uniform Computer Information Transactions Act (UCITA)
A model act that provides uniform and comprehensive rules for contracts involving computer information transactions and software and information licenses.

Internet
A collection of millions of computers that provide a network of electronic connections between computers.

Our legal system faces no theoretical dilemma but a single continuous problem: how to apply to ever changing conditions the never changing principles of freedom.
Earl Warren (1995)

World Wide Web *The evolution of the World Wide Web and the Internet has changed how business is conducted.*

E-Commerce & Information Technology

RENO V. AMERICAN CIVIL LIBERTIES UNION

In 1997, the U.S. Supreme Court decided *Reno v. American Civil Liberties Union*, a major case involving free-speech rights over the Internet. In this decision, the Supreme Court recognized the importance and uniqueness of the Internet and World Wide Web and issued an opinion guaranteeing the users of the Internet the highest constitutional free-speech protection. This edited decision, in the language of the Supreme Court, follows.

Reno v. American Civil Liberties Union 521 U.S. 844, 117 S.Ct. 2329 (1977) Supreme Court of the United States

FACTS

The Internet is an international network of interconnected computers. The Internet has experienced extraordinary growth. The number of "host" computers—those that store information and relay communications—increased from about 300 in 1981 to approximately 9,400,000 by the time of the trial in 1996. Roughly 60 percent of these hosts are located in the United States. About 40 million people used the Internet at the time of trial, a number that is expected to mushroom to 200 million by 1999. Individuals can obtain access to the Internet from many different sources, generally hosts themselves or entities with a host affiliation. Most colleges and universities provide access for their students and faculty; many corporations provide their employees with access through an office network. Several major national "online services" such as American Online, CompuServe, the Microsoft Network, and Prodigy offer access to their own extensive proprietary networks as well as a link to the much larger resources of the Internet.

Anyone with access to the Internet may take advantage of a wide variety of communication and information retrieval methods. These methods are constantly evolving and difficult to categorize precisely. But, as presently constituted, those most relevant to this case are electronic mail ("e-mail"), automatic mailing list services ("mail exploders," sometimes referred to as "listservs"), "newsgroups," "chat rooms," and the "World Wide Web." All of these methods can be used to transmit text; most can transmit sound, pictures, and moving video images. Taken together, these tools constitute a unique medium—known to its users as "cyberspace"—located in no particular geographical location but available to anyone, anywhere in the world, with access to the Internet.

The best known category of communication over the Internet is the World Wide Web, which allows users to search for and retrieve information stored in remote computers, as well as, in some cases, to communicate back to designated sites. In concrete terms, the Web consists of a vast number of documents stored in different computers all over the world. Some of these documents are simply files containing information. However, more elaborate documents,

commonly known as Web "pages," are also prevalent. Navigating the Web is relatively straightforward. A user may either type the address of a known page or enter one or more keywords into a commercial "search engine" in an effort to locate sites on a subject of interest. Users generally explore a given Web page, or move to another, by clicking a computer "mouse" on one of the page's icons or links. Sexually explicit material on the Internet includes text, pictures, and chat and extends from the modestly titillating to the hardest-core. Some of the communications over the Internet that originate in foreign countries are also sexually explicit.

STATUTE BEING INTERPRETED

The Telecommunications Act of 1996, Pub.L. 104-104, 110 Stat. 56, was an unusually important legislative enactment. Title V—known as the "Communications Decency Act of 1996" (CDA)—contains provisions that were either added in executive committee after congressional hearings were concluded or as amendments offered during floor debate on the legislation. An amendment offered in the Senate was the source of the two statutory provisions challenged in this case. They are informally described as the "indecent transmission" provision and the "patently offensive display" provision. The first, 47 U.S.C.A. Section 223(a), prohibits the knowing transmission of obscene or indecent messages to any recipient under 18 years of age. The second provision, Section 223(d), prohibits the knowing sending or displaying of patently offensive messages in a manner that is available to a person under 18 years of age.

LOWER COURT'S OPINION

On February 8, 1996, immediately after the president signed the statute, 20 plaintiffs filed suit against the Attorney General of the United States and the Department of Justice challenging the constitutionality of Sections 223(a) and 223(d). A second suit was then filed by 27 additional plaintiffs, the two cases were consolidated, and a three-judge District Court was convened pursuant to Section 561 of the Act. After an evidentiary hearing, that Court entered a preliminary injunction against enforcement of both the challenged provisions.

ISSUE

At issue is the constitutionality of two statutory provisions enacted to protect minors from "indecent" and "patently offensive" communications on the Internet.

U.S. SUPREME COURT'S REASONING

Each medium of expression may present its own problems. Thus, some of our cases have recognized special justifica-

tions for regulation of the broadcast media that are not applicable to other speakers. In these cases, the Court relied on the history of extensive government regulation of the broadcast medium, the scarcity of available frequencies at its inception, and its "invasive" nature. Those factors are not present in cyberspace. Neither before nor after the enactment of the CDA have the vast democratic fora of the Internet been subject to the type of government supervision and regulation that has attended the broadcast industry. Moreover, the Internet is not as "invasive" as radio or television. The District Court specifically found that "communications over the Internet do not invade an individual's home or appear on one's computer screen unbidden. Users seldom encounter content by accident." It also found that "almost all sexually explicit images are preceded by warnings as to the content," and cited testimony that "odds are slim that a user would come across a sexually explicit site by accident."

Unlike the conditions that prevailed when Congress first authorized regulation of the broadcast spectrum, the Internet can hardly be considered a "scarce" expressive commodity. It provides relatively unlimited, low-cost capacity for communication of all kinds. This dynamic, multifaceted category of communication includes not only traditional print and news services, but also audio, video, and still images, as well as interactive, real-time dialogue. Through the use of chat rooms, any person with a phone line can become a town crier with a voice that resonates farther than it could from any soapbox. Through the use of Web pages, mail exploders, and newsgroups, the same individual can become a pamphleteer. As the District Court found, "the content on the Internet is as diverse as human thought."

The vagueness of the CDA is a matter of special concern for two reasons. First, the CDA is a content-based regulation of speech. The vagueness of such a regulation raises special First Amendment concerns because of its obvious chilling effect on free speech. Second, the CDA is a criminal statute. In addition to the opprobrium and stigma of a criminal conviction, the CDA threatens violators with penalties including up to two years in prison for each act of violation. The severity of criminal sanctions may well cause speakers to remain silent rather than communicate even arguably unlawful words, ideas, and images. Given the vague contours of the coverage of the statute, it unquestionably silences some speakers whose messages would be entitled to constitutional protection.

Systems have been developed to help parents control the material that may be available on a home computer with Internet access. A system may either limit a computer's access to an approved list of sources that have been identified as containing no adult material, it may block designated inappropriate sites, or it may attempt to block messages containing identifiable objectionable features. Although parental control software currently can screen for certain suggestive words or for known sexually explicit sites, it cannot now screen for sexually explicit images. Nevertheless, the evidence indicates that a reasonably effective method by which parents can prevent their children from accessing sexually explicit and other material which parents may believe is inappropriate for their children will soon be available.

We are persuaded that the CDA lacks the precision that the First Amendment requires when a statute regulates the content of speech. In order to deny minors access to potentially harmful speech, the CDA effectively suppresses a large amount of speech that adults have a constitutional right to receive and to address to one another. In evaluating the free speech rights of adults, we have made it perfectly clear that "sexual expression which is indecent but not obscene is protected by the First Amendment" [Sable Communications of Cal., Inc. v. FCC, 492 U.S. 115 (1989)]. The Government may not reduce the adult population to only what is fit for children. The CDA, casting a far darker shadow over free speech, threatens to torch a large segment of the Internet community.

HOLDING

Notwithstanding the legitimacy and importance of the congressional goal of protecting children from harmful materials, we agree with the three-judge District Court that the statute abridges "the freedom of speech" protected by the First Amendment. For the foregoing reasons, the judgment of the district court is affirmed. It is so ordered.

Electronic Mail

Electronic mail, or e-mail, is one of the most widely used applications for communication over the Internet. Using e-mail, individuals can instantaneously communicate in electronic writing with one another around the world. Each person can have his or her e-mail address, which identifies the user by a unique address. E-mail will continue to grow in use in the future as it replaces some telephone and paper correspondence and increases new communication between persons.

electronic mail (e-mail)
Electronic written communication between individuals using computers connected to the Internet.

E-Commerce & Information Technology

E-MAIL CONTRACTS

E-mail has exploded as a means of personal and business communication. In the business environment, e-mail is sometimes the method used to negotiate and agree on contract terms and to send and agree to the final contract. The question presented is whether an e-mail contract is enforceable. Assuming that all of the elements to establish a contract are present, an e-mail contract is valid and enforceable. The main problem in a lawsuit seeking to enforce an e-mail contract is evidence, but this problem, which exists in almost all lawsuits, can be overcome by printing out the e-mail contract and its prior e-mail negotiations, if necessary.

A further issue arises if the contract is required to be in writing by the state Statute of Frauds. Because the parties to an e-mail contract can print a paper version of the electronic contract, this would meet the writing requirement of the Statute of Frauds. The analogy would be that a contract that is printed from the e-mail message is no different from a contract that is printed on the same printer from a word-processing program. Thus, e-mail contracts meet the writing requirements for enforceable contracts.

E-Commerce & Information Technology

ELECTRONIC COMMUNICATIONS PRIVACY ACT

E-mail, computer data, and other electronic communications are sent daily by millions of people using computers and the Internet. Recognizing how the use of computer and electronic communications raise special issues of privacy, the federal government enacted the **Electronic Communications Privacy Act (ECPA)**. The ECPA makes it a crime to intercept an "electronic communication" at the point of transmission, while in transit, when stored by a router or server, or after receipt by the intended recipient. An electronic communication includes any transfer of signals, writings, images, sounds, data, or intelligence of any nature. The ECPA makes it illegal to access stored e-mail as well as e-mail in transmission.

The ECPA provides that stored electronic communications may be accessed without violating the law by the following:

1. The party or entity providing the electronic communication service. The primary example would be an employer who can access stored e-mail communications of employees using the employer's service.
2. Government and law enforcement entities that are investigating suspected illegal activity. Disclosure would be required only pursuant to a validly issued warrant.

The ECPA provides for criminal penalties. In addition, the ECPA provides that an injured party may sue for civil damages for violations of the act.

The World Wide Web

World Wide Web

An electronic connection of millions of computers that support a standard set of rules for the exchange of information.

Business Brief

E-commerce over the Web has increased dramatically and will continue to grow in the future.

The **World Wide Web** consists of millions of computers that support a standard set of rules for the exchange of information called Hypertext Transfer Protocol (HTTP). Web-based documents are formatted using common coding languages such as Hypertext Markup Language (HTML) and Java. Businesses and individuals can hook up to the Web by registering with a server such as America Online (AOL) or other servers.

Individuals and businesses can have their own Web sites. A Web site is composed of electronic documents known as Web pages. The Web sites and pages are stored on servers throughout the world. They are viewed by using Web browsing software such as Microsoft Internet Browser and Netscape Navigator. Each Web site has a unique online address. Web pages can contain a full range of multimedia content, including text, images, video, sound, and animation. Web pages can include references, called *hyperlinks*, or *links*, to other Web pages or sites.

The Web has made it extremely attractive to conduct commercial activities online. Companies such as Amazon.com and eBay are e-commerce powerhouses that sell all sorts of goods and services. Existing companies, such as Wal-Mart, Merrill Lynch, and Dell Computers, sell their goods and services online as well. E-commerce over the Web will continue to grow dramatically each year.

International Law

CHINA OPENS THE INTERNET

In November 1999, China and the United States entered into a historic trade pact that reduced tariffs and other barriers to entry for selling goods and services between the two countries. Prior to this trade pact, China had announced that it would not allow investment by foreign firms in China's Internet markets. In exchange for the United States opening its borders to more Chinese-made goods, China agreed to allow U.S. firms to invest in China's Internet business.

Although it agreed to open up its Internet markets, China has placed restrictions on foreign investment in Internet businesses. These restrictions include

- Foreign companies cannot own more than 50 percent of any Internet business in China.
- Foreign companies must obtain a special license from the Chinese government for such investments.
- China will regulate the content of Internet Web sites, including advertisements placed on the Web.

Critics of the pact argue that China could use the licensing procedures and content-approval rules to erect bureaucratic nontariff barriers to entry. Proponents argue that China has an incentive not to enforce the restrictions too harshly because strict enforcement would cause China to lose much-needed foreign investment and technological knowledge and to risk retaliatory actions by the United States. Others argue that there are always ways around such restrictions, such as the traditional method of paying the appropriate government officials to get things done. In the borderless world of the Internet, some foreign companies may set up business in countries and areas near China and offer Internet services to China from these locations.

With over 1.2 billion people, China offers a great potential for the growth of the use of the Internet and e-commerce. If foreign companies are allowed up to a 50 percent investment in Internet companies and businesses in China, this is still far better than being shut out of the market altogether.

INTERNET DOMAIN NAMES

Each Web site is identified by a unique Internet **domain name**. For example, the domain name for the publisher of this book is **www.prenhall.com**. The four top-level suffixes for domain names are *com* for commercial use, *net* for networks, *org* for organizations, and *edu* for educational institutions.

Domain names can be registered. The first step in registering a domain name is determining whether any other party already owns the name. For this purpose, InterNIC maintains a "Whois" database that contains the domain names that have been registered. The InterNIC Web site is located online at **internic.net**. Domain names can also be registered at Network Solutions, Inc.'s, Web site, which is located online at **www.networksolutions.com**, as well as at other online sites. An applicant must complete a registration form, which can be done online. It costs less than $50 to register a domain for one year, and the fee may be paid by credit card online.

domain name

A unique name that identifies an individual's or company's Web site.

Business Brief

Domain names may be registered by filing the appropriate form with the domain name registration service and paying the appropriate fee.

Entrepreneur and the Law

WEB DOMAIN NAMES SOLD FOR MILLIONS

What is a name worth? Plenty! It used to be that a person could make money by trademarking a name before a large company wanted to use the name for a product or service or as a new company name. Once in possession of the trademark, the owner could sell it at a profit if some company wanted it desperately enough. But trying to guess what names would be wanted took some work. In addition, trademark law required the name to be used in commerce.

Although trademarking and selling trademark names is still a way to make money, the hottest area for name-selling is registering and selling Internet domain names.

Take the case of the domain name *business.com*. This name, which was originally registered as a domain name for $70, was sold to entrepreneur Marc Ostrofsky for $150,000 in 1996. Many people at the time thought this was an outrageous sum to pay for a domain name—that is, until

Mr. Ostrofsky turned around and resold the name to ECompanies in 1999 for $7,500,000. That was the most ever paid for an Internet domain name. ECompanies thought it was a bargain and plans to use it for its new Web site, where it will offer a form of Internet Yellow Pages.

Other domain names have been sold at high prices too. *Altavista.com* was purchased by Compaq Computer for its Internet search engine. Other domain names sold for high prices include *wine.com* for $3 million, *bingo.com* for $1.1 million, *wallstreet.com* for $1 million, and *drugs.com* for $800,000. As commerce over the Internet increases, and as unregistered memorable names become harder to find, transactions in the sale of domain names are expected to accelerate, with multimillion dollar price tags being paid for the most desirable names—which were originally registered for $70.

E-Commerce & Information Technology

ANTICYBERSQUATTING ACT PASSED BY CONGRESS

When the famous actress Julia Roberts went to register her name as the Internet domain name juliaroberts.com, she discovered that someone else had already registered this domain name. So what's a famous person to do? Rely on Congress to pass a law that helps him or her. And that is exactly what the U.S. Congress did.

In November 1999, the U.S. Congress enacted, and the president signed, the **Anticybersquatting Consumer Protection Act** [15 U.S.C. § 1125(d)]. The act was specifically aimed at cybersquatters who register Internet domain names of famous companies and people and hold them hostage by demanding ransom payments from the famous company or person. In the past, trademark law was of little help, either because the famous person's name was not trademarked or because, even if the name was trademarked, trademark law required distribution of goods or services to find infringement and most cybersquatters did not distribute goods or services but merely sat on the Internet domain name. The new act has two fundamental requirements: (1) The name must be famous and (2) the domain name was registered in bad faith. Thus, the law prohibits the act of cybersquatting itself if it is done in *bad faith*.

The first issue in applying the statute is whether the domain name is someone else's famous name. Trademarked names qualify; nontrademarked names—such as those of famous actors, actresses, singers, sports exhibitures, political exhibitures, and such—also are protected. In determining bad faith, the law provides that courts may consider the extent that the domain name resembles the holder's name or the famous person's name, whether goods or services are sold under the name, the holder's offer to sell or transfer the name, and whether the holder has acquired multiple Internet domain names of famous companies and persons.

The act provides for the issuance of cease-and-desist orders and injunctions by the court. In addition, the law adds monetary penalties: A plaintiff has the option of seeking statutory damages of between $1,000 and $300,000 in lieu of proving damages. The Anticybersquatting Consumer Protection Act gives owners of trademarks and persons with famous names a new weapon to attack the kidnapping of Internet domain names by cyberpirates. Julia Roberts immediately sued the holder of juliaroberts.com for violating the act and won the right to her own domain name. The singer Sting was not so lucky, however, when he found that sting.com was already taken. The court ruled that since the word "sting" is generic and can be found in the dictionary, Sting had no claim under the Anticybersquatting Act to the domain name.

E-Commerce & Information Technology

DOMAIN NAME DISPUTES SET FOR ARBITRATION

Under a contract with the United States government, the **Internet Corporation for Assigned Names and Numbers (ICANN)** is responsible for regulating the issuance of domain names on the Internet. ICANN contracted with Network Solutions, a private company, to register domain names. Until June 1999, Network Solutions was the exclusive registrar for all domain names bearing .com, .net, and .org. Since then, other registrars of domain names have been approved by ICANN.

Domain names are sometimes challenged for infringing on trademarks or service marks owned by businesses and individuals. In addition, the passage of the federal Anticybersquatting Consumer Protection Act of 1999 allows owners of famous names to challenge similar domain names that have been registered in bad faith. Civil lawsuits alleging violations of trademark law or the anticybersquatting law may take years to go to trial and cost a fortune to pursue.

In October 1999, ICANN approved an arbitration procedure for challenging cybersquatting. This procedure, called the **Uniform Dispute Resolution Policy (UDRP)**, requires all ICANN-approved registrars of domain names to agree to use this dispute resolution policy as part of their accreditation. The UDRP requires arbitration of domain name disputes. The dispute is heard by an arbitration panel approved by ICANN. ICANN has approved the World Intellectual Property Organization (WIPO), an agency of the United Nations, as an arbitrator of domain name disputes. ICANN has also approved several private companies, including the National Arbitration Forum and the Disputes.org/eResolution.ca Consortium, to be dispute resolution arbitrators. In a UDRP arbitration hearing, a panel of trademark and intellectual property experts, who usually are scholars, retired judges, or other professionals, hear and decide the dispute. The decision of the arbitration panel can be appealed to the U.S. courts.

In its first ruling under the UDRP, the WIPO held that Michael Bosman, a resident of Redlands, California, had registered the domain name **www.worldwrestling federation.com** in bad faith. The World Wrestling Federation (WWF), a promoter of professional wrestling, had long owned the trademark to its name. Bosman, after registering the domain name, contacted the WWF and offered to sell it to the trademark holder. Instead of buying the name, WWF filed a case with the WIPO. The WIPO arbitrator found that Bosman registered the domain name in bad faith in violation of the law. The arbitrator noted that the domain name was not Bosman's nickname or a name of any family member, and that he had not made any use of the name. The arbitrator concluded that the domain name was identical to the WWF's trademark and that Bosman had no legal rights to the domain name. The arbitrator ordered the domain name transferred to the WWF.

E-Commerce & Information Technology

ARMANI OUTMANEUVERED FOR DOMAIN NAME

G.A. Modefine S.A. is the owner of the famous "Armani" trademark under which it produces and sells upscale and high-priced apparel. The "Armani" label is recognized worldwide. But Modefine was surprised when it tried to register for the domain name "armani.com" and found that it had already been taken. Modefine brought an arbitration action in the World Intellectual Property Organization's Arbitration and Mediation Center against the domain name owner to recover the "armani.com" domain name under the Uniform Domain Name Dispute Resolution Policy. To win, Modefine had to prove that the domain name was identical or confusingly similar to its trademark, the owner who registered the name did not have a legitimate interest in the name, and the owner registered the name in bad faith.

The person who owned the domain name, Anand Ramnath Mani, appeared at the proceeding and defended his ownership rights. The arbitrator found that Modefine's trademark and Mr. Mani's domain name were identical, but held that Mr. Mani had a legitimate claim to the domain name. The arbitrator wrote that it is "common practice for people to register domain names which are based upon initials and a name, acronyms or otherwise variants of their full names." The court rejected Modefine's claim that Mr. Mani's offer to sell the name for $1,935 constituted bad faith. The arbitrator ruled against Modefine and permitted Mr. Mani to own the domain name "armani.com." [*G.A. Modefine S.A. v. A. R. Mani*, WIPO, No. D2001-0537 (2001)]

International Law

GOLD RUSH FOR COUNTRY DOMAIN NAMES

When the domain name system was created, only a handful of high-level generic suffixes were provided for individuals and businesses, such as *.com* and *.net*. The cyber rush for names bearing these suffixes was on and many of the names were quickly claimed. Once all the good names were taken, unsuccessful .com and .net applicants tried to exhibiture out what "dot" names to register. They discovered that in addition to the .com and .net generic suffixes, every country was assigned its own two-letter country code suffix to administer as it wished. Some countries like the United States ("US") decided to use the designation for government offices. Other countries, however, decided that they were sitting on a new gold that they could mine.

One example of a country that has capitalized on its country domain name is Tuvalu, which consists of a small group of islands with just over 10,000 inhabitants located in the South Pacific. Tuvalu was assigned the country code *TV*. Because its country code is so commonly used as a shorthand version for the word *television*, it is easily recognizable. So Tuvalu joined forces with a new entrepreneurial Internet company called Dot-TV and began marketing domain names with the suffix *TV*—at a price. Sales have been brisk as individuals and businesses rush to register domain names bearing the suffix *TV*. Thus, countries can market their country code suffixes as part of domain names as an alternative to .com and .net names that have already been taken. For example, if e-business.com was already registered, why not try e-business.TV? Other countries that have marketed their country names commercially are Tonga, the Coco Islands, and Western Samoa.

*L*ICENSING OF INFORMATIONAL RIGHTS

Business Brief

Intellectual property and information rights are valuable assets of individuals and businesses.

license

A contract that transfers limited rights in intellectual property and informational rights.

Intellectual property and informational rights are an extremely important asset of many individuals and companies. Patent, trademark, copyright, trade secret, and other laws protect intellectual property from misappropriation and infringement (see Chapter 14).

The owners of intellectual property and information rights often wish to transfer limited rights in the property or information to parties for specified purposes and limited duration. The agreement that is used to transfer such limited rights is called a **license**, which is defined as [UCITA § 102(a)(40)]

> *License means a contract that authorizes access to, or use, distribution, performance, modification, or reproduction of, information or informational rights, but expressly limits the access or uses authorized or expressly grants fewer than all rights in the information, whether or not the transferee has title to a licensed copy. The term includes an access contract, a lease of a computer program, and a consignment of a copy.*

licensor

The owner of intellectual property or informational rights who transfers rights in the property or information to the licensee.

licensee

The party who is granted limited rights in or access to intellectual property or informational rights owned by the licensor.

The parties to a license are the licensor and the licensee. The **licensor** is the party who owns the intellectual property or informational rights and obligates him- or herself to transfer rights in the property or information to the licensee. The **licensee** is the party who is granted limited rights in or access to the intellectual property of informational rights [UCITA § 102(a)(41),(42)]. A licensing arrangement is illustrated in Exhibit 15.1.

A license grants the contractual rights expressly described in the license and the right to use any informational rights within the licensor's control that are necessary to exercise the expressly described rights [UCITA § 307(a)].

*E*XHIBIT 15.1   *Licensing Arrangement*

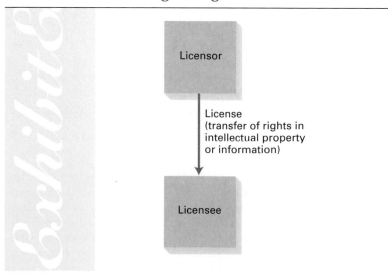

Licensor

License
(transfer of rights in intellectual property or information)

Licensee

Exclusive License   A license can grant the licensee the exclusive rights to use the information. An **exclusive license** means that for the specified duration of the license the licensor will not grant to any other person rights in the same information [UCITA § 307(f)(2)].

exclusive license

A license that grants the licensee exclusive rights to use informational rights for a specified duration.

Licensing Agreement

The licensor and licensee usually enter into a written **licensing agreement** that expressly states the terms of their agreement. Licensing agreements tend to be very detailed and comprehensive contracts. This is primarily because of the nature of the subject matter and the limited uses granted in the intellectual property or informational rights.

licensing agreement

Detailed and comprehensive written agreement between the licensor and licensee that sets forth the express terms of their agreement.

E-Commerce & Information Technology

SOFTWARE AND INFORMATION ACCESS CONTRACTS

Sometimes instead of transferring a copy of information to a licensee, a software license grants the licensee the right to access information in the possession of the licensor. This type of license is called an **access contract**. Access contracts provide for access by the licensee to the information for an agreed-upon time or number of uses. The licensee's access to the information must be available at times and in a manner that complies with the express terms of the license. If such terms are not stated in the agreement, access by the licensee shall be at times and in a manner that is reasonable for the particular type of contract in light of ordinary standards of the business, trade, or industry.

The licensee's right of access is to information as periodically modified and updated by the licensor. A change in the content of the information is not a breach of contract unless the change conflicts with express terms in the license. An occasional failure to have access available is not a breach of contract if it is either (1) normal in the business, trade, or industry or (2) is caused by scheduling downtime; reasonable periods of failure of equipment, communications, or computer programs; or reasonable needs for maintenance [UCITA § 611].

E-Commerce & Information Technology

THE UNIFORM COMPUTER INFORMATION TRANSACTIONS ACT (UCITA)

In July 1999, after years of study and debate, the National Conference of Commissioners on Uniform State Laws (a group of lawyers, judges, and legal scholars) issued the **Uniform Computer Information Transactions Act (UCITA)**. This is a model act that establishes a uniform and comprehensive set of rules that governs the creation, performance, and enforcement of computer information transactions. A computer information transaction is an agreement to create, transfer, or license computer information or informational rights [UCITA § 102(a)(11)].

The UCITA does not become law until a state's legislature enacts it as a state statute. States are expected to adopt the UCITA or laws similar to the UCITA as their law for computer transactions and the licensing of informational rights.

Any provisions of the UCITA that are preempted by federal law are unenforceable to the extent of the preemption [UCITA § 105(a)]. Unless displaced by the UCITA, state law and equity principles, including principal and agent law, fraud, duress, mistake, trade secret law, and other state laws, supplement the UCITA [UCITA § 114].

LICENSING INFORMATION TECHNOLOGY RIGHTS

The **Uniform Computer Information Transactions Act** (UCITA) creates contract law for the licensing of information technology rights. The UCITA will be used for discussing the licensing of information rights in the following paragraphs.

Uniform Computer Information Transactions Act (UCITA)

Model state law that creates contract law for the licensing of information technology rights.

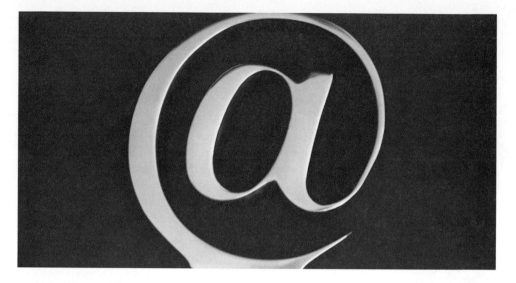

Formation of a Contract

A contract may be formed in any manner that shows agreement, including an offer and acceptance, conduct of both parties, or operation of electronic agents [UCITA § 202(a)]. An offer to make a contract invites acceptance in any manner and by any medium reasonable under the circumstances. If an offer is received, the offer may be accepted by either promptly promising to ship a copy or shipping a copy of it. If an offer in an electronic message evokes an electronic message accepting the offer, a contract is formed when an electronic acceptance is received [UCITA § 203].

A transaction that is covered by the UCITA is not subject to the Statute of Frauds, which requires contracts to be in writing, or by other state laws [UCITA § 201(f)].

Business Brief

States are expected to adopt the UCITA or laws similar to the UCITA as their law for computer transactions and the licensing of informational rights.

Discourage litigation. Persuade your neighbors to compromise whenever you can. Point out to them how the nominal winner is often a real loser—in fees, and expenses, and waste of time. As a peacemaker the lawyer has a superior opportunity of being a good man. There will still be business enough.

Abraham Lincoln
Notes on the Practice of Law
(1850)

Acceptance with Varying Terms   A party can expressly make an offer conditional on agreement by the other party to all the terms of the offer. Acceptance by the other party of all the terms creates a contract, but varying the terms in the purported acceptance does not create a contract [UCITA § 205].

If an offer has not been made conditional on acceptance of all the terms, and the party purporting to accept has varied the terms of the offer in his or her acceptance, the following rules apply: If the transaction is between merchants, the proposed additional nonmaterial terms offered by the offeree become part of the contract unless the original offeror gives notice of objection to these terms within a reasonable time after receiving them. If one of the parties is not a merchant, varying the terms of an offer by the offeree is a rejection of the offer and constitutes a counteroffer. Any material alteration of the terms of the offer by the offeree, even between merchants, rejects the offer and no contract is formed [UCITA § 204].

 *E-Commerce & Information Technology*

COUNTEROFFERS INEFFECTUAL AGAINST ELECTRONIC AGENTS

In today's e-commerce, many sellers use electronic agents to sell goods and services. An electronic agent is any telephonic or computer system that has been established by a seller to accept orders. Voice mail and Web page order systems are examples of electronic agents.

In the past, when humans dealt with each other face to face, by telephone, or in writing, their negotiations might have consisted of an exchange of several offers and coun-

teroffers until agreed-upon terms were reached and a contract was formed. Each new counteroffer extinguished the previous offer and became a new viable offer. Most electronic agents do not have the ability to evaluate and accept counteroffers or to make counteroffers. The Uniform Computer Information Transactions Act (UCITA) recognizes this limitation of e-commerce and provides that a contract is formed if an individual takes action that causes the electronic agent to cause performance or promise benefits to the individual. Thus, counteroffers are not effective against electronic agents [UCITA § 206(a)].

Consider This Example "Birdie" is an electronic ordering system for placing orders for electronic information sold by the Green Company, a producer of computer software and electronic information. Freddie Calloway dials the Green Company's 800 telephone number and orders new software for $1,000 using the Birdie voice mail electronic ordering system. Freddie enters the product code and description, his mailing address and credit card information, and other data needed to complete the transaction, but at the end of the order states "I will accept this software if, after two weeks of use, I am satisfied with the software." Because Freddie has placed the order with an electronic agent, Freddie has ordered the software and his counteroffer is ineffectual.

Title to Copy Title to a copy of the software or electronic information is determined by the license. In many licenses, the licensor reserves title to a copy; in other licenses title to the copy transfers to the licensee. A licensee's right under the license to possess, control, and use a copy is governed by the license [UCITA § 502(a)].

Authenticating the Record

If a contract requires payment of a contract fee of $5,000 or more, the contract is enforceable against a party only if that party authenticated the record [UCITA § 201(a)]. **Authenticate** means either signing the contract or executing an electronic symbol, sound, or message attached to, included in, or linked with the record [UCITA § 102(a)(6)].

An electronic authentication is attributed to a person if it was the act of that person or his or her electronic agent [UCITA § 213]. Authentication may be proven in any manner, including a showing that a party made use of information or access that could have been available only if he or she engaged in operations that authenticated the record [UCITA § 108]. Authentication may be shown by using an **attribution procedure** to verify the electronic authentication and to detect errors or changes in electronic authentication. This procedure requires the use of codes, algorithms, identifying words or numbers, encryption, callback, or other acknowledgment [UCITA § 102(a)(5)].

Consider This Example Yuan uses the Internet and places an order to license software for her computer from License.com, Inc., through its electronic Web site ordering system. The Web page order form asks Yuan to type in her name, address, telephone number, credit card information, computer information, and a personal identification number. The electronic agent requests that Yuan verify this information a second time before accepting the order, which Yuan does. Only after doing so does License.com, Inc.'s, electronic agent place the order and send an electronic copy of the software to Yuan's computer, where she installs the new software program. There has been authentication of Yuan's signature and a proper attribution procedure to verify the authentication.

Confirmation Letter If the parties to a contract are merchants and the contract fee is $5,000 or more, the contract may be enforced even without authentication if one party to the contract sends a record confirming the contract and the other party does not reject the confirmation within 10 days after receiving it [UCITA § 201(d)].

No workman without tools, No lawyer without fools

Benjamin Franklin
Poor Richard's Almanack
(February 1742)

authenticate
Signing the contract or executing an electronic symbol, sound, or message attached to, included in, or linked with the record.

attribution procedure
A procedure using codes, algorithms, identifying words or numbers, encryption, callback, or other acknowledgment to verify an authentication of a record.

People say law, but they mean wealth.

Ralph Waldo Emerson
(1841)

E-Commerce & Information Technology

THE UNIFORM ELECTRONIC TRANSACTIONS ACT (UETA)

To avoid impeding the growth of electronic commerce, there is a substantial need for a uniform law that regulates certain aspects of contracting over the Internet. To this end, the National Conference of Commissioners on Uniform State Laws promulgated the **Uniform Electronic Transactions Act (UETA)**. This model act is designed to create uniform laws for electronic records and electronic signatures. The goal of the act is to place electronic records and signatures on the same level as paper contracts and written signatures. Thus, electronic contracts should be as enforceable, as well as avoidable, as paper contracts.

The UETA applies only to transactions between parties who have agreed to conduct their transaction by electronic means. Whether the parties agree to conduct a transaction by electronic means is determined from the context and surrounding circumstances, including the parties' conduct, customer initiation of Internet communications, and such [UETA § 5].

Once a transaction is determined to be covered by the UETA, the UETA recognizes two main concepts. First, the UETA states that an *electronic record* satisfies the requirement for a contract and also the requirement for writing where the contract is required to be in writing by the Statute of Frauds. Second, the UETA recognizes that an *electronic signature* is a signature that is enforceable equal to a written signature on a

paper contract [UETA § 2]. In addition, the UETA specifies that if a law requires a record or signature to be notarized, acknowledged, or made under oath, the requirement is satisfied by an electronic signature of the authorized person, provided all information required in the notarization, acknowledgment, and so forth, is included [UETA § 11].

The UETA supports the increased use of electronic commerce by assuring that electronic records receive legal recognition on a par with paper contracts and that electronic signatures are treated equally to signatures written on paper. The UETA does not displace existing contract law concerning offer and acceptance, consideration, reliance, mistake, fraud, undue influence, duress, duties of care, and other contract requirements or defenses. The UETA does not become law until a state adopts the model act as its own statute. States are expected to adopt the UETA to provide uniformity of law for enforcing electronic records and signatures as contracts.

Performance

tender of performance
Occurs when a party who has the ability and willingness to perform offers to complete the performance of his or her duties under the contract.

There are times when the national interest is more important than the law.

Henry Kissinger
(1976)

A party to a licensing agreement owes a duty to perform in a manner that conforms to the contract. Each party owes a duty to tender performance when performance is due. **Tender of performance** occurs when a party who has the ability and willingness to perform offers to complete the performance of his or her duties under the contract [UCITA § 601].

A software license requires the delivery of software, information, or data from the licensor to the licensee. The parties may designate in their contract the place for the electronic or physical delivery of a copy of the information. If no place is stated in the contract, the place of delivery is the licensor's place of business [UCITA § 606].

Consider This Example Maria enters into a licensing agreement to license electronic information from DataBase, Inc. DataBase, Inc., notifies Maria that a copy of the electronic information that she has licensed is available for her to download from its Web site; DataBase, Inc., has tendered performance. Maria offers to pay DataBase, Inc., the licensing fee by credit card; Maria has tendered performance.

 *E-Commerce & Information Technology*

THE FEDERAL ELECTRONIC SIGNATURE ACT

In the world of pen-and-paper, it used to be "Sign on the dotted line," "Put your John Hancock right here," or "Sign by the X." No more. In the e-commerce world it is now "What is your mother's maiden name?" "Slide your smart card in the sensor" or "Look into the iris scanner." But are electronic signatures sufficient to form an enforceable contract? The courts and state legislatures of the 50 states have wrestled with this question, often reaching inconsistent decisions on whether electronic contracts meet the writing and signature requirements of the state Statutes of Frauds.

In 2000, the federal government stepped into the breach and enacted the **Electronic Signature in Global and National Commerce Act**. This act is a federal statute enacted by Congress and signed by the president, and therefore has national reach. The act is designed to place the

world of electronic commerce on a par with the world of paper contracts in the United States.

ELECTRONIC SIGNATURE

One of the main features of the federal law is that it recognizes an *electronic signature*, or *e-signature*. The act gives an e-signature the same force and effect as a pen-inscribed signature on paper. The act is technology neutral, however, in that the law does not define or decide which technologies should be used to create a legally binding signature in cyberspace. Loosely defined, a digital signature is some electronic method that identifies an individual. The challenge is making sure that someone who uses a digital signature is the person he or she claims to be. The act provides that a digital signature can basically be verified in one of three ways:

1. By something the signatory knows, such as a secret password, their pet's name, and so forth.
2. By something a person has, such as a smart card, which looks like a credit card and stores personal information.
3. By biometrics, which uses a device that digitally recognizes fingerprints or the retina or iris of the eye.

The verification of electronic signatures will create a need for the use of scanners and methods for verifying personal information.

WRITING REQUIREMENT

Another main feature of the act is that it recognizes electronic contracts as meeting the writing requirement of the Statute of Frauds for most contracts. Statutes of Frauds are state laws that require certain types of contracts to be in writing. The new federal act provides that electronically signed contracts cannot be denied effect because they are in electronic form or delivered electronically. The act also provides that record retention requirements are satisfied if the records are stored electronically.

The federal law was passed with several provisions to protect consumers. First, consumers must consent to receiving electronic records and contracts. Second, to receive electronic records, consumers must be able to demonstrate that they have access to the electronic records. And third, businesses must tell consumers that they have the right to receive hard-copy documents of the transaction.

The new federal act preempts conflicting state law except where states have enacted the e-signature provisions of the model **Uniform Electronic Transactions Act (UETA)**; those states are exempted from this provision. This provision was a conciliation of Congress to tread lightly on states rights and give states an incentive to adopt the more comprehensive UETA for regulating electronic contracts.

One of the shortfalls of the new federal act is that it does not—and cannot—provide a global solution. Some countries have enacted electronic commerce statutes, but with different provisions and requirements than U.S. law. Many other countries do not have e-commerce laws at all. Global contracting requires an international solution, such as an e-commerce treaty signed by the members of the World Trade Organization (WTO).

Risk of Loss of the Copy   When the copy is delivered electronically or is not delivered by a carrier, the risk of loss of the copy passes to the licensee upon its receipt of the copy.

If a copy is delivered from the licensor to the licensee by a carrier, one of two rules apply: (1) If the agreement requires the licensor to deliver the copy to a particular destination, the risk of loss remains with the licensor until the copy is tendered at the designated destination, or (2) if the agreement does not require the licensor to deliver the copy to a particular destination, the risk of loss transfers to the licensees when the licensor delivers the copy to the carrier [UCITA § 614].

Acceptance of a Copy   A licensee who has been tendered a copy by the licensor is deemed to have accepted the copy if the licensee (1) signifies that the tender was conforming, (2) acts with respect to the copy in a manner that signifies that the tender was conforming, (3) retains a copy despite its nonconformity, (4) commingles the copy or information with other copies or information, (5) obtains a substantial benefit from the copy that cannot be returned, or (6) acts in a manner inconsistent with the licensor's ownership of the copy [UCITA § 610].

Excuse of Performance   The UCITA provides that a party's delay in performance or nonperformance under a license agreement is excused if the performance has been made impracticable. The UCITA stipulates that delay or nonperformance is made *impracticable* by (1) the occurrence of a contingency whose nonoccurrence was a basic assumption on which the contract was made or (2) compliance with any domestic or foreign statute or governmental rule. Where there is a delay or nonperformance excused by impracticability, there is no breach of contract.

A party claiming the excuse of impracticability must reasonably notify the other party that there has been a delay in performance. If an excuse affects only part of the party's capacity to perform, the party claiming the excuse shall allocate performance among its customers in any manner that is fair and reasonable and notify the other party of the quota it is to receive. Whenever a party is notified that there is a delay or nonperformance caused by impracticability, that party may terminate the contract and thereby be discharged from the unperformed portion of the contract [UCITA § 615].

Mankind must have laws and conform to them, or their life would be as bad as that of the most savage beast.

Plato
(400 B.C.)

Business Brief

The UCITA excuses performance if performance has been rendered *impracticable* by (1) the occurrence of a contingency whose nonoccurrence was a basic assumption on which the contract was made or (2) compliance with any domestic or foreign statute or governmental rule.

Consider This Example   Zeke, a foreign national and businessperson, enters into a licensing agreement to license certain informational rights from Zendex Corporation, a corporation located in the United States. Zeke is to take possession of the information when it is made available to him on Zendex's Web site, and he will be able to download it to his computer. Prior to the delivery of the informational rights, however, the U.S. Congress enacts a statute restricting the exporting of the type of information that Zeke has contracted to receive. In this instance Zendex's performance is excused because its performance of the contract has been made illegal by government statute.

E-Commerce & Information Technology

CONSUMERS SAVED FROM ELECTRONIC ERRORS

Under the common law of contracts, many parties who make unilateral mistakes while contracting are not relieved of the consequences of their error. The Uniform Computer Information Transactions Act (UCITA), which governs licenses of informational rights, is more lenient. The UCITA provides that consumers are not bound by their unilateral electronic errors if the consumer

1. Promptly upon learning of the error notifies the other party of the error.
2. Does not use or receive any benefit from the information, or make the information or benefit available to a third party.
3. Delivers all copies of the information to the third party or destroys all copies of the information pursuant to reasonable instructions from the other party.
4. Pays all shipping, reshipping, and processing costs of the other party [UCITA § 217].

Section 217 of the UCITA applies only to consumers who make electronic errors in contracting. Electronic errors by nonconsumers are handled under the common law of contracts or Uniform Commercial Code, whichever applies. The UCITA does not relieve a consumer of his or her electronic error if the other party provides a reasonable method to detect and correct or avoid the error.

Thus, many sellers establish methods whereby the buyer must verify the information and purchase order a second time before an electronic order is processed. This procedure strips the consumer of the defense of UCITA Section 217.

Consider This Example   Kai, a consumer, intends to order 10 copies of a video game over the Internet from Cybertendo, a video game producer. In fact, Kai makes an error and orders 110 games. The electronic agent maintaining Cybertendo's Web site's ordering process electronically disburses 110 games. The next morning Kai discovers his mistake and immediately e-mails Cybertendo, describing the mistake and offering to return or destroy the copies at his expense. When Kai receives the games, he returns the 110 copies unused. Under the UCITA, Kai has no contract obligation for 110 copies but bears the cost of returning them to Cybertendo or destroying them if Cybertendo instructs him to do so. If Cybertendo's Web site's electronic ordering system had asked Kai to confirm his order of 110 copies of the purchase order, and Kai confirmed the original order of 110 copies, Kai has to pay for the 110 copies, even if his confirmation was in error.

Warranties

Certain warranties may attach to a license of informational rights because either the licensor has made express warranties or the law has imposed one or more implied warranties. The law, however, permits some of these warranties to be disclaimed if certain requirements are met.

Warranties of Noninterference and Noninfringement   A licensor of information warrants that no third person holds any claim or interest in the information or claim of infringement or misappropriation that would interfere with the licensee's use or enjoyment of the information [UCITA § 401].

Consider This Example   Antoine licenses a certain database from Data.com, Inc., for three years to use in her business. After using the database for a short time, Antoine receives notice from a court to desist from using the database because the data infringes a copyright held by Information.com, Inc. Here, there has been a breach of the warranty of noninfringement by Data.com, Inc.; Antoine can recover damages from Data.com., Inc., for the breach of this warranty.

Express Warranty   Licensors are not required to do so, but they often make express warranties concerning the quality of their software or information. An **express warranty** is any affirmation of fact or promise by the licensor about the quality of its software or information. An express warranty can result from a description of the information, advertising, samples or models, demonstrations of the final product, and such. An express warranty is not created by the licensor's statements of opinion [UCITA § 402].

Consider This Example   Info, Inc., has developed software for the pricing of securities sold on Nasdaq. Info, Inc., warrants that its software is free from defects and will pay $10,000 liquidated damages and replace the software free of charge if the software does not perform correctly within the first year of use. Here, Info, Inc., has made an express warranty about the quality of its information. Financial Times, Inc., a financial services company, licenses the software from Info, Inc., but after three months of use the software fails. Info, Inc., owes Financial Times, Inc., $10,000 and a free replacement copy of the software [UCITA § 406 (a)].

Implied Warranty of Merchantability of the Computer Program   The law implies that a merchant licensor warrants that the computer program is fit for the ordianry purposes for which the computer program is used. This warranty is called the **implied warranty of merchantability of the computer program**. This implied warranty includes a warranty that the copies of the computer program are within the parameters permitted by the licensing agreements, that the computer program has been adequately packaged and labeled, and that the program conforms to any promises or affirmations of fact made on the container or label [UCITA § 403].

Consider This Example   Juan licenses a software program from Medi, Inc., to sort data and information from his extensive databases and to run with other software and database programs used in his medical supplies business. The licensing agreement and label on the Medi software program state that the copy of the licensed program has been tested and will run without error. Juan installs the Medi, Inc., software, but every third or fourth time he runs the software it fails to operate properly and shuts down his computer and other programs. There has been a breach of the implied warranty of the merchantability of the computer program because the Medi software does not fall within the parameters of the licensing agreement or affirmation of fact on the label. Juan can recover remedies from Medi, Inc.

Implied Warranty of Informational Content   A merchant that collects, compiles, processes, provides, or transmits informational content warrants to the licensee that there is no inaccuracy in the informational content caused by the merchant's failure to perform with reasonable care. This warranty is called the **implied warranty of informational content** [UCITA § 404].

Consider This Example   Christine licenses a database of historical and current interest rate information from DataMarket, Inc.; the information is updated daily by DataMarket, Inc. Christine uses the information to make extensive bond investments for her clients. Christine uses the information one day to make certain investments. It turns out, however, that DataMarket, Inc., made several accidental errors in inputting the interest-rate data, thus causing an error in Christine's calculations and decisions. Here there has been a breach of implied warranty of informational content because the licensor, DataMarket, Inc., failed to perform with reasonable care. Christine can seek remedies against DataMarket, Inc.

Implied Warranty of Fitness for a Particular Purpose   A licensor that has a reason to know of any particular purpose for which the computer information is required and knows that the licensee is relying on the licensor's skill or judgment to select or furnish suitable information warrants that the information is fit for the licensee's purpose. This warranty is called the **implied warranty of fitness for a particular purpose** [UCITA § 405].

express warranty

Any affirmation of fact or promise by the licensor about the quality of its software or information.

Business Brief

The UCITA does not require a licensor to make an express warranty about the quality of its software or information.

implied warranty of merchantability of the computer program

An implied warranty that the copies of the computer program are within the parameters permitted by the licensing agreement, that the computer program has been adequately packaged and labeled, and that the program conforms to any promises or affirmations of fact on the container or label.

What the lawyer needs to redeem himself is not more ability, but more courage in the face of financial loss and personal ill will to stand for right and justice.

Louis D. Brandeis (1907)

implied warranty of informational content

An implied warranty that there is no inaccuracy in the informational content caused by the merchant-licensor's failure to perform with reasonable care.

implied warranty of fitness for a particular purpose

An implied warranty that information is fit for the licensee's purpose that applies if the licensor (1) knows of any particular purpose for which the computer information is required and (2) knows that the licensee is relying on the licensor's skill or judgment to select or furnish suitable information.

Consider This Example Ahmad, who operates a large Internet order-taking and delivery business, contacts IMB, Inc., a large software developer, about licensing software to operate his business. Ahmad tells the IMB representative about the volume of his business and his business needs and informs the IMB representative that he is relying on her to select the software that will meet his business needs. The IMB representative selects certain software for Ahmad, which he installs to run his business. The software, however, is inadequate to handle Ahmad's business needs. Here there has been a breach of implied warranty of fitness for a particular purpose. Ahmad may pursue remedies against IMB, Inc.

You must remember that some things that are legally right are not morally right.

Abraham Lincoln
(1840)

General Disclaimer of Warranties The UCITA permits a licensor to disclaim all implied warranties by expressions like "as is" or "with all faults" or other language that in common understanding calls the licensee's attention to the disclaimer and makes plain there are no implied warranties [UCITA § 406(c)]. All of the implied warranties are also disclaimed by stating "Except for express warranties stated in this contract, if any, this 'information' [or 'computer program'] is provided with all faults, and the entire risk as to satisfactory quality, performance, accuracy, and effort is with the user" or by using words of similar import [UCITA § 406(b)(3)]. General disclaimers must be conspicuous.

E-Commerce & Information Technology

ELECTRONIC SELF-HELP

When a licensor licenses its software to a licensee, it expects that the licensee will abide by the terms of the license. This includes protecting the licensor's trade secrets, using the software or information pursuant to the terms of the license, and paying the agreed-upon license fee. Just like normal contracts, however, electronic licenses can be breached by licenses. If such a breach occurs, the licensor can resort to remedies provided in the UCITA. Sections 815 and 816 of the UCITA provide that a licensor can resort to electronic self-help if a breach occurs, for example, if the licensee fails to pay the license fee. Such electronic self-help can consist of activating disabling bugs and time bombs that have been embedded in the software or information that will prevent the licensee from further using the software or information.

Section 816 provides that a licensor is entitled to use electronic self-help only if the following requirements are met:

1. The licensee specifically agrees to the inclusion in the license of self-help as a remedy. General assent to the license is not sufficient; there must be a specific self-help option to which the licensee assents.

2. The licensor must give the licensee at least 15 days notice prior to the disabling action. The notice must contain the name and location of the person to whom the licensee can communicate regarding the issue. The notice period allows the licensee to make lawful adjustments to minimize the effects of the licensor's self-help or to seek a judicial remedy to combat the use of the self-help.

3. The licensor may not use self-help if it would cause a breach of the peace, risk personal injury, cause significant damage or injury to information other than the licensee's information, result in injury to the public health or safety, or cause grave harm to national security.

A licensor who violates these provisions and uses self-help improperly is liable for damages. This liability cannot be disclaimed. The UCITA gives licensees the right to obtain an expedited hearing in court if any of the self-help restrictions are violated. Licensors will continue to install and use such self-help devices, subject to the requirements and restrictions of the UCITA.

It will be of little avail to the people, that the laws are made by men of their own choice, if the laws be so voluminous that they cannot be read, or so incoherent that they cannot be understood.

Alexander Hamilton
The Federalist Papers (1788)

Breach of License Agreements

The parties to a contract for the licensing of information owe a duty to perform the obligations stated in the contract. If a party fails to perform as required, there is a breach of the contract. Breach of contract by one party to a licensing agreement gives the non-breaching party certain rights, including recovering damages or other remedies [UCITA § 701].

Licensee's Refusal of Defective Tender   If the licensor tenders a copy that is a material breach of the contract, the nonbreaching party to whom tender is made may either (1) refuse the tender, (2) accept the tender, (3) accept any commercially reasonable units and refuse the rest [UCITA § 704].

Licensee's Revocation of Acceptance   If a licensee has accepted tender of a copy where the nonconformity is a material breach, the licensee may later revoke his or her acceptance if (1) acceptance was made because discovery was difficult at the time of tender but was then later discovered or (2) the nonconformity was discovered at the time of tender but the licensor agreed to cure the defect, and the defect has not been reasonably cured [UCITA § 707].

Adequate Assurance of Performance   Each party to a license agreement expects to receive due performance from the other party. If any reasonable grounds arise prior to the performance date that make one party think that the other party might not deliver performance when due, the aggrieved party may demand adequate assurance of due performance from the other party. Until such assurance is received, the aggrieved party may, if commercially reasonable, suspend performance until assurance is received. Failure to provide assurance within 30 days permits the aggrieved party to repudiate the contract [UCITA § 708].

Remedies

The UCITA provides certain *remedies* to an aggrieved party upon the breach of a licensing agreement. A party may not recover more than once for the same loss, and his or her remedy (other than liquidated damages) may not exceed the loss caused by the breach [UCITA § 801]. The UCITA provides that a cause of action must be commenced within one year after the breach was or should have been discovered, but not more than five years after the breach actually occurred [UCITA § 805]. Remedies are discussed in the following paragraphs.

Cancellation   If there has been a material breach of the contract that has not been cured or waived, the aggrieved party may cancel the contract. **Cancellation** is effective when the canceling party notifies the breaching party of the cancellation. Upon cancellation, the breaching party in possession or control of copies, information, documentation, or other materials that are the property of the other party must use commercially reasonable efforts to return them or hold them for disposal on instructions from the other party. All obligations that are executory on both sides at the time of cancellation are discharged [UCITA § 802(a),(b)].

Upon cancellation of a license, the licensor has the right to have all copies of the licensed information returned by the licensee and to prevent the licensee from continued use of the licensed information.

Licensor's Damages   If a licensee breaches a contract, the licensor may sue and recover monetary damages from the licensee caused by the breach, plus any consequential and incidental damages [UCITA § 808]. A licensor can recover *lost profits* caused by the licensee's failure to accept or complete performance of the contract. Lost profits is a proper measure of damages in this case because the licensor has effectively unlimited capability to make access available to others so there will be no license to substitute to reduce damages owed by the breaching licensee.

Consider This Example   iSuperSoftware.com licenses a master disk of its software program to Distributors, Inc., to make and distribute 10,000 copies of the software. This is a nonexclusive license and the license fee is $1 million. It costs iSuperSoftware.com $15 to produce the disk. If Distributors, Inc., refuses the disk and breaches the contract, iSuperSoftware.com can recover $1 million less $15 as damages for the profits lost on the transaction.

right to cure

A licensor has the right to cure a contract under certain conditions.

Business Brief

When a licensor breaches a contract, the licensee may sue and recover monetary damages from the licensor.

Licensor's Right to Cure Unlike the common law of contracts, the UCITA provides that a licensor may **cure** a breach of a license in certain circumstances. A breach of contract may be cured if (1) the time of performance of the contract has not expired and the licensor makes conforming performance within the time of performance, (2) the time of performance has expired but the licensor had reasonable grounds to believe the performance would be acceptable, then the licensor has a reasonable time to make conforming performance, or (3) the licensor makes a conforming performance before the licensee cancels the contract. In all three situations the licensor must seasonably notify the licensee of its intent to cure [UCITA § 703(a)].

cover

The licensee's right to engage in a commercially reasonable substitute transaction after the licensor has breached the contract.

There is far too much law for those who can afford it and far too little for those who cannot.

Derek Bo
(1983)

Licensee's Damages When a licensor breaches a contract, the licensee may sue and recover monetary damages from the licensor. The amount of the damages depends on the facts of the situation. Upon the licensor's breach, the licensee may either (1) cover by purchasing other electronic information from another source and recover the difference between the value of the promised performance from the licensor and the cost of cover or (2) not cover and recover the value of the performance from the licensor. **Cover** means engaging in a commercially reasonable substitute transaction. The licensee may obtain an award of consequential and incidental damages in either case. A licensee cannot obtain excessive or double recovery [UCITA § 809].

Consider This Example Auction.com is an Internet company that operates an online auction service. Auction.com enters into a contract with MicroHard, Inc., a software producer, for a site license to use MicroHard, Inc.'s, software. Auction.com agrees to pay $500,000 as an initial license fee and $10,000 per month for the license duration of three years. Before Auction.com pays any money under the license, MicroHard, Inc., breaches the contract and does not deliver the software. Auction.com covers by licensing commercially similar software from another software company for the payment of $600,000 initial licensing fee and $11,000 per month for the license duration of three years. Under the facts of this case, Auction.com can recover $100,000 for the increased initial fee and $36,000 for the increased monthly costs from MicroHard, Inc., for breach of contract.

specific performance

Judgment of the court ordering a licensor to specifically perform the license by making the contracted-for unique information available to the licensee.

Licensee Can Obtain Specific Performance The UCITA provides the remedy of **specific performance** if the parties have agreed to this remedy in their contract or if the agreed-upon performance is unique. The test of uniqueness requires the court to examine the total situation that characterizes the contract [UCITA § 811].

Consider This Example Nedra enters into a licensing agreement to obtain access to certain informational rights from Info, Inc., for a specified monthly license fee. The data are proprietary to Info, Inc., and are not available from any other vendor. If Info, Inc., breaches the license and refuses to give Nedra access to the information, Nedra can sue and obtain an order of specific performance whereby the court orders Info, Inc., to make the contracted-for information available to Nedra for the duration of the license.

Limitations of Remedies

The UCITA provides that the parties to an agreement may limit the remedies available for breach of the contract. This is done by including contract provisions in the contract. Remedies may be restricted to return of copies and repayment of the licensing fee or limiting the remedy to the repair or replacement of the nonconforming copies. Limitation of remedies in licenses subject to the UCITA are enforceable unless they are unconscionable [UCITA § 803].

In the following case, the court upheld a limitation on remedies clause in a software license.

M.A. Mortenson Company, Inc. v. Timberline Software Corporation

970 P. 2d 803 (1999)
Court of Appeals of Washington

CASE 15.1

BACKGROUND AND FACTS

The Timberline Software Corporation (Timberline) produces software programs that are used by contractors to prepare bids to do work on construction projects. The M.A. Mortenson Company (Mortenson), a contractor, had been using Timberline software for some time without any problem. In 1993, Timberline introduced an advanced version of its bidding software program called *Precision*. Mortenson, as the licensee, entered into a license agreement with Timberline, the licensor, to license the use of the Precision software. Timberline delivered the software to Mortenson and a Timberline representative installed the software on Mortenson's computer. The software license agreement contained the following terms, which were printed on the outside of the envelope in which the software disks were packaged and on the inside cover of the user's manual, and they also appear on the introductory computer screen each time the software program is executed:

Carefully read the following terms and conditions before using the programs. Use of the programs indicates your acknowledgement that you have read this license, understand it, and agree to be bound by its terms and conditions. If you do not agree to these terms and conditions, promptly return the programs and user manuals to the place of purchase and your purchase price will be refunded. You agree that your use of the program acknowledges that you have read this license, understand it, and agree to be bound by its terms and conditions.

Limitation of remedies and liability neither Timberline nor anyone else who has been involved in the creation, production or delivery of the programs or user manuals shall be liable to you for any damages of any type, including but not limited to, any lost profits, lost savings, loss of anticipated benefits, or other incidental or consequential damages arising out of the use or inability to use such programs, whether arising out of contract, negligence, strict tort, or under any warranty, or otherwise, even if Timberline has been advised of the possibility of such damages or for any other claim by any other party. Timberline's liability for damages in no event shall exceed the license fee paid for the right to use the programs.

On December 2, 1993, Mortenson used the Precision software and prepared a bid to do contracting work for the Harborview Hospital project. While preparing the bid, the program aborted at least five times before Mortenson's employees finished the bid. Subsequently, Mortenson claimed that its bid was $2 million under what it should have been had the Precision software program worked correctly. Mortenson sued Timberline to recover consequential damages, arguing that the Precision software calculated an inaccurate bid. Timberline defended, alleging that the limitation of remedies clause in the software license prevented Mortenson"s lawsuit. Mortenson countered that the limita-

tions of remedies clause was unconscionable and therefore unenforceable. The trial court granted summary judgment to Timberline and dismissed the lawsuit. Mortenson appealed.

ISSUE

Was the limitation of remedies clause in the Timberline software license unconscionable?

COURT'S REASONING

The court stated that although Mortenson makes much of the fact that Timberline never mentioned the license agreement or any of its terms during the negotiations, the negotiations between the parties involved only the number of copies and the price. The court held that the terms of the present license agreement are part of the contract as formed between the parties. The court further found that Mortenson's installation and use of the software manifested its assent to the terms of the license and that it was bound by all of the terms of that license that were not found to be illegal or unconscionable.

Whether a limitation on consequential damages is unconscionable is a question of law. Considering all the circumstances surrounding the transaction in this case, the court held that the limitations clause was not unconscionable. The introductory screen warned that use of the program was subject to a license. This warning placed Mortenson on notice that use of the software was governed by a license. Mortenson had reasonable opportunity to learn and understand the terms of the agreement. The limitations provision was not hidden in a maze of fine print but appeared in all-capital letters. Finally, the court noted that such limitations provisions are widely used in the computer software industry.

The court found that limitations on consequential damages in commercial transactions are prima facie conscionable. The court stated, "Such clauses are standard in the software industry and do not shock the conscience. Indeed, they are useful in making software affordable. If software developers were prohibited from limiting consequential damages, the significant costs to the industry would be passed on to the consumer." The court held that the limitations of remedies provision was not unconscionable and therefore barred Mortenson's claim for consequential damage.

DECISION AND REMEDY

The court of appeal held that the limitation of remedies clause in the software license was conspicuous and not unconscionable and that it therefore prohibited Mortenson's lawsuit to recover consequential damages from Timberline. The court of appeals affirmed the trial court's grant of summary judgments to Timberline that dismissed the case.

Case Questions

Critical Legal Thinking   What does the doctrine of unconscionability provide? Does the doctrine serve any useful purpose?

Business Ethics   Did Timberline act ethically when it included a limitation of remedies clause in its software license?

Contemporary Business   What would the business consequences be if limitation of remedies clauses in software licenses were all held to be *per se* illegal?

---

liquidated damages

Damages that are specified in the contract rather than determined by the court.

Liquidation of Damages   The parties to a license may provide that damages for breach of contract may be liquidated. **Liquidated damages** are damages that are specified in the contract rather than determined by the court. The amount of liquidated damages must be reasonable in light of the loss anticipated at the time of contracting or the anticipated difficulties of proving loss in the event of breach. The fixing of unreasonably large liquidated damages is void [UCITA § 804].

CHAPTER SUMMARY

The Internet, p. 353

The Internet and World Wide Web	1. *Internet.* A collection of millions of computers that provide a network of electronic connections between computers. 2. *World Wide Web.* An electronic connection of computers that support a standard set of rules for the exchange of information called Hypertext Transfer Protocol (HTTP). 3. *Electronic mail (e-mail).* Electronic written communication between individuals using computers connected to the Internet. 4. *E-mail contracts.* Contracts that are formed electronically over the Internet using e-mail.
Electronic Privacy	1. *Electronic Communications Privacy Act.* A federal statute that makes it a crime to intercept an "electronic communication" at the point of transmission, while in transit, when stored by a router or server, or after receipt by the intended recipient.

Internet Domain Names, p. 357

Domain Name	1. *Domain name.* A unique name that identifies an individual's or company's Web site. 2. *Internet Corporation for Assigned Names and Numbers* (ICANN). ICANN is responsible for regulating the issuance of domain names on the Internet. ICANN approves registrars of domain names. 3. *Domain name registration.* Domain names are registered by filing the appropriate form with a domain name registration service and paying the appropriate fee.
Anticybersquatting Act	1. *Anticybersquatting Consumer Protection Act.* A federal statute that permits a court to issue cease-and-desist orders, injunctions, and to award monetary damages against anyone who has registered a domain name (1) of a famous name (2) in bad faith. 2. *Uniform Dispute Resolution Policy* (UDRP). A policy that requires all ICANN-approved registrars of domain names to agree to use an arbitration procedure for challenging cybersquatting as part of their accreditation.

Licensing of Informational Rights, p. 360

License	1. *License.* A contract that transfers limited rights in intellectual property and informational rights. 2. *Licensor.* The owner of intellectual property or informational rights who transfers rights in the property or information to the licensee. 3. *Licensee.* The party who is granted limited rights or access to intellectual property or informational rights owned by the licensor.

4. *Licensing agreement.* Detailed and comprehensive written agreement between the licensor and the licensee that sets forth the express terms of their agreement.
5. *Access contract.* A type of licensee that grants the license access to the licensed information for an agreed-upon time or number of uses.

The Uniform Computer Information Transactions Act (UCITA), p. 361

The UCITA

1. *The Uniform Computer Information Transactions Act (UCITA).* A model act issued by the National Conference of Commissioners on Uniform State Laws that establishes a uniform and comprehensive set of rules that governs the creation, performance, and enforcement of computer information transactions.
   a. *Adoption of UCITA by states.* The UCITA does not become law until a state's legislature enacts it as a state statute.

Special Provisions of the UCITA

1. *Counteroffer rule.* Counteroffers are not effective against electronic agents. This is because most electronic agents do not have the ability to evaluate and accept counteroffers or make counteroffers.
2. *Authenticating the record.* If a contract requires a payment of a contract fee of $5,000 or more, the contract is enforceable against a party only if that party authenticated the record. *Authentication* means either signing the contract or executing an electronic symbol, sound, or message attached to, included in, or linked with the record.
3. *Electronic errors.* The UCITA provides that *consumers* are not bound by their unilateral electronic errors if the consumer
   a. Promptly upon learning of the error notifies the other party of the error.
   b. Does not use or receive any benefit from the information, or make the information or benefit available to a third party.
   c. Delivers all copies of the information to the third party or destroys all copies of the information pursuant to reasonable instructions from the other party.
   d. Pays all shipping, reshipping, and processing costs of the other party.
4. *Electronic self-help.* If an electronic license has been breached by a licensee, the licensor can resort to electronic self-help such as activating disabling bugs and time bombs that have been embedded in the software or information that will prevent the licensee from further using the software or information. A licensor is entitled to use electronic self-help only if the following requirements are met:
   a. The licensee specifically agrees to the inclusion in the license of self-help as a remedy.
   b. The licensor must give the licensee at least 15 days notice prior to the disabling action.
   c. the licensor may not use self-help if it would cause a breach of the peace, risk personal injury, cause significant damage or injury to information other than the licensee's information, result in injury to the public health or safety, or cause grave harm to national security.

Warranties

1. *Warranty of noninterference and noninfringement.* A licensor of information warrants that no third person holds any claim or interest in the information or claim of infringement or misappropriation that would interfere with the licensee's use or enjoyment of the information.
2. *Express warranty.* Licensors are not required to do so, but they often make express warranties concerning the quality of their software or information. An express warranty is any affirmation of fact or promise by the licensor about the quality of its software or information.
3. *Implied warranty of merchantability of the computer program.* The law implies that a merchant licensor warrants that the computer program is fit for the ordinary purposes for which the computer program is used.
4. *Implied warranty of informational content.* A merchant that collects, compiles, processes, provides, or transmits informational content warrants to the licensee that there is no inaccuracy in the informational content caused by the merchant's failure to perform with reasonable care.
5. *Implied warranty of fitness for a particular purpose.* A licensor that has reason to know of any particular purpose for which the computer information is required and knows that the licensee is relying on the licensor's skill or judgment to select or furnish suitable information warrants that the information is fit for the licensee's purpose.

Electronic Signatures

1. *The Electronic Signature in Global and National Commerce Act (E-Sign Act).* A federal statute that recognizes and gives electronic signatures—e-signatures—the same force and effect as a pen-inscribed signature on paper. The act is technology neutral in that the law does not define or decide which technologies should be used to create a legally binding signature in cyberspace.
   a. *Exemption.* Any state that has enacted the Uniform Electronic Transactions Act (UETA) is exempt from the E-sign act.
2. *The Uniform Electronic Transactions Act (UETA).* A model act issued by the National Conference of Commissioners on Uniform State Laws that establishes a uniform and comprehensive set of rules that governs electronic records and signatures. The act gives electronic records and e-signatures the same force and effect as written contracts and pen-inscribed signatures on paper.
   a. *Adoption of UCITA by states.* The UCITA does not become law until a state's legislature enacts it as a state statute.

*E*ND-OF-*C*HAPTER *I*NTERNET *E*XERCISES AND *C*ASE *Q*UESTIONS

Working the Web Internet Exercises

ACTIVITIES

1. Research the Web to determine if your state has adopted the Uniform Electronic Transactions Act (UETA) or the Uniform Computer Information Transactions Act (UCITA). Start with **www.hg.org. cgi-bin/redir.cgi?url=www.law.cornell.edu/ uniform/vol7.html**.

2. For a discussion of the Federal Dilution Act featuring Barbie, Elvis, and Coca-Cola, see **cyber.law.harvard. edu/property/respect/antibarbie.html**.

3. For an overview of the Federal Electronic Signatures Act, explore the law review article "Are Online Business Transactions Executed by Electronic Signatures Legally Binding?" at **www.law.duke.edu/ journals/dltr/ARTICLES/2001dltr0005.html**.

4. Domain names dispute resolution procedures are presented in great detail at **lweb.law.harvard.edu/ udrp/lobrary/html**. Check this site for everything from an overview to sample pleading forms.

CRITICAL LEGAL THINKING CASES

15.1 Domain Name Francis Net, a freshman in college and computer expert, browses Web sites for hours each day. One day she thinks to herself, "I can make money registering domain names and selling them for a fortune." She has recently seen an advertisement for Classic Coke, a cola drink produced and marketed by the Coca Cola Company. The Coca Cola Company has a famous trademark on the term *Classic Coke* and has spent millions of dollars advertising this brand and making the term famous throughout the United States and the world. Francis goes to the Web site, **www.networksolutions.com**, an Internet domain name registration service, to see if the Internet domain name classiccoke.com has been taken. She discovers that it is available, so she immediately registers the Internet domain name classiccoke.com for herself and pays the $70 registration fee with her credit card. Coca Cola Company decides to register the Internet domain name classiccoke.com but when it checks at Network Solutions, Inc.'s, Web site, it discovers that Francis Net has already registered the Internet domain name. Coca Cola contacts Francis, who demands $500,000 for the name. Coca Cola Company sues Francis to prevent Francis from using the Internet domain name "classiccoke.com" and to recover it from under the federal Anticybersquatting Consumer Protection Act. Who wins?

15.2 Domain Name Francis Net, a freshman in college and computer expert, browses Internet Web sites for hours each day. One day she thinks to herself, "I can make money registering domain names and selling them for a fortune." She has recently seen advertisements for Classic Coke, a cola drink produced and marketed by the Coca Cola Company, and for Pepsi, a cola drink produced and marketed by Pepsi, Inc. The Coca Cola Company has a famous trademark on the term Classic Coke, and Pepsi, Inc., has a famous trademark on Pepsi; both companies have spent millions of dollars advertising their brands and making the

terms famous throughout the United States and the world. Francis, realizing that she cannot trade off the famous names "Classic Coke" or Pepsi, thinks about what terms soda manufacturers might want to use as their domain names. Francis, who has traveled throughout the country, realizes that in some parts of the United States people call soda by the name pop. Francis goes to the Web site, **www.networksolutions.com**, an Internet domain name registration service, to see if the Internet domain name **pop.com** has been taken. She discovers that it is available, so she immediately registers the Internet domain name **pop.com** for herself and pays the $70 registration fee with her credit card. Coca Cola Company decides to register the Internet domain name **pop.com**, but when it checks at Network Solutions, Inc.'s, Web site, it discovers that Francis Net has already registered the Internet domain name **pop.com**. Coca Cola Company contacts Francis, who demands $200,000 for the name. Coca Cola Company sues Francis to prevent Francis from using the Internet domain name **pop.com** and to recover it from her under the federal Anticybersquatting Consumer Protection Act. Who wins?

15.3 E-Mail Contract The Little Steel Company is a small steel fabricator that makes steel parts for various metal machine shop clients. When Little Steel Company receives an order from a client, it must locate and purchase 10 tons of a certain grade of steel to complete the order. The Little Steel Company sends an e-mail to West Coast Steel Company, a large steel company, inquiring about the availability of 10 tons of the described grade of steel. The West Coast Steel Company replies by e-mail that it has available the required 10 tons of steel and quotes $450 per ton. The Little Steel Company's purchasing agent replies by e-mail that the Little Steel Company will purchase the 10 tons of described steel at the quoted price of $450 per ton. The e-mails are signed electronically by the Litle Steel Company's purchasing agent and the selling agent of the West Coast Steel Company. When the steel arrives at the Litle Steel Company's plant, the Litle Steel Company rejects the shipment, claiming the defense of the Statute of Frauds. The West Coast Steel Company sues the Litle Steel Company for damages. Who wins?

15.4 Electronic Contract The Minute Steel Company is a small steel fabricator that makes steel parts for various metal machine shop clients. When Minute Steel Company receives an order from a client, it must locate and purchase 10 tons of a certain grade of steel to complete the order. The Minute Steel Company's purchasing agent opens the Internet and goes to a Web site called **steelauction.com**. This is a Web site where sellers and buyers of steel can locate one another and make deals. On this Web site, the purchasing agent for Minute Steel Company finds that the East Coast Steel Company, a large steel company, has available the required 10 tons of the described steel at $450 per ton. The Minute Steel Company's agent agrees online to purchase the 10 tons of described steel at the quoted price of $450 per ton from East Coast Steel Company. The record and the signatures of both sides agreeing to the transaction are electronic. When the steel arrives at the Minute Steel Company's plant, the Minute Steel Company rejects the shipment, claiming the defense of the Statute of Frauds and invalid signatures. The Uniform Electronic Transactions Act (UETA) applies to the transaction. The East Coast Steel Company sues the Minute Steel Company for damages. Who wins?

15.5 Contract Einstein Financial Analysis, Inc. (EFA), has developed an electronic database that has recorded the number of plastic pails manufactured and sold in the United States since plastic was first invented. Using this data, and a complicated patented software mathematical formula developed by EFA, a user can predict with 100 percent accuracy (historically) how the stock of each of the companies of the Dow Jones Industrial Average will perform on any given day of the year. William Buffet, an astute billionaire investor, wants to increase his wealth, so he enters into an agreement with EFA whereby he is granted the sole right to use the EFA data (updated daily) and its financial model for the next five years. Buffet pays EFA $100 million for the right to the data and mathematical formula. After using the data and software formula for one week, Buffet discovers that EFA has also transferred the right to use the EFA plastic pail database and software formula to his competitor. Buffet sues EFA. What type of arrangement has EFA and Buffet entered into? Who wins?

15.6 Encryption Technology The Silicon Encryption Company, Inc. (SEC), has developed a very powerful encryption technology that permits a user to establish an encryption code that no person or computer program can figure out. Therefore, the encryption code developed by SEC is impenetrable when it is "wrapped" around electronic data. Imports, Inc., a U.S. company organized in the state of Florida, contacts SEC about acquiring the encryption technology. SEC conducts a reasonable investigation and due diligence review of Imports, Inc., and finds that the company is an importer of goods from around the world; SEC discovers no adverse information about Imports,

Inc. SEC decides to deal with Imports, Inc., and Imports, Inc., pays SEC $10 million for the right to use SEC's encryption technology for five years. After one year, the U.S. government believes that Imports, Inc., is engaged in smuggling illegal drugs into the United States and has used SEC's encryption technology to protect any data implicating Imports, Inc., in the illegal activity. The U.S. Department of Justice prosecutes Imports, Inc., for the crime of illegal drug smuggling, but the government loses the case because it cannot produce the necessary evidence that is protected by SEC's encryption technology. The U.S. Department of Justice therefore sues SEC for selling its powerful encryption technology to Imports, Inc. Is SEC guilty?

15.7 License An Internet firm called Info.com, Inc., licenses computer software and electronic information over the Internet. Info.com has a Web site, Info.com, where users can license Info.com software and electronic information. The Web site is operated by an electronics agent; a potential user enters into Info.com's Web site and looks at available software and electronic information that is available from Info.com. Mildred Hayward pulls up the Info.com Web site on her computer screen and decides to order a certain type of Info.com software. Hayward enters the appropriate product code and description; her name, mailing address, and credit card information; and other data needed to complete the order for a three-year license at $300 per month; the electronic agent has Hayward verify all of the information a second time. When Hayward has completed verifying the information, she types at the end of her order, "I accept this electronic software only if after I have used it for two months do I still personally like it." Info.com's electronic agent delivers a copy of the software to Hayward, who downloads the copy of the software onto her computer. Two weeks later Hayward sends the copy of the software back to Info.com stating, "Read our contract: I personally don't like this software, cancel my license." Info.com sues Hayward to recover the license payments for three years. Who wins?

15.8 Electronic Signature David Abacus uses the Internet and places an order to license software for his company from Inet.License, Inc. (Inet), through Inet's electronic Web site ordering system. Inet's Web page order form asks David to type in his name, mailing address, telephone number, e-mail address, credit card information, computer location information, and personal identification number. Inet's electronic agent requests that David verify the information a second time before it accepts the order, which David does. The license duration is two years at a license fee of $300 per month. Only after receiving the verification of information does Inet's electronic agent place the order and send an electronic copy of the software to David's computer, where he installs the new software program. David later refuses to pay the license fee due Inet because he claims his electronic signature and information were not authentic. Inet sues David to recover the license fee. Is David's electronic signature enforceable against him?

15.9 License Tiffany Pan, a consumer, intends to order three copies of a financial software program from iSoftware, Inc. Tiffany, using her computer, enters iSoftware's Web site isoftware.com and places an order with the electronic agent taking orders for the Web site. The license provides for a duration of three years at $300 per month for each copy of the software program. Tiffany enters the necessary product code and description; her name, mailing address, and credit card information; and other data necessary to places the order. When the electronic order form prompts Tiffany to enter the number of copies of the software program she is ordering, Tiffany mistakenly types in "30." Isoftware's electronic agent places the order and ships out 30 copies of the software program to Tiffany. When Tiffany receives the 30 copies of the software program, she ships them back to iSoftware with a note stating, "Sorry, there has been a mistake. I only meant to order three copies of the software, not 30." When iSoftware bills Tiffany for the license fees for the 30 copies, Tiffany refuses to pay. Isoftware sues Tiffany to recover the license fees for 30 copies. Who wins?

15.10 License Silvia Miofsky licenses a software program from Accura.com, Inc., to sort information from a database to be used in Silvia's financial planning business. The license is for three years and the license fee is $500 per month. The new software program from Accura.com will be used to run in conjunction with other software programs and databases used by Silvia in her business. The licensing agreement between Accura.com and Silvia, as well as the label on the software package, state that the copy of the licensed software program has been tested by Accura.com and will run without error. Silvia installs the copy of Accura.com's software, but every fifth or sixth time the program is run it fails to operate properly and shuts down Silvia's computer and other programs. Silvia sends the software back to Accura.com marked *defective*. When Accura.com bills Silvia for the unpaid license fees for the three years of the license, Silvia refuses to pay. Accua.com sues Silvia to recover the license fees under the three-year license. Who wins?

15.11 License Harold Harrington operates a large personal financial planning business. He contacts Hardware/Software,

Inc., a seller of software programs and electronic information, about licensing a software program from Hardware/Software, Inc. Harold tells the Hardware/Software sales representative about the scope and volume of his business and his business needs and informs the Hardware/Software representative that he is relying on her to select the software that will meet his business needs. The Hardware/Software sales representative selects the software program called "PerFinPlan III" for Harold's business. The license is $500 per month for three years. Harold installs the PerFinPlan III software. The software, however, is inadequate to handle Harold's financial planning requirements of his clients. After one month, Harold notifies the sales representative for Hardware/Software that the PerFinPlan III software does not meet his described business needs. Harold returns the copy of the software to Hardware/Software and demands the return of his one month's license fee. Hardware/Software sues Harold to recover the unpaid license fees for the duration of the license. Who wins?

15.12 License Metatag, Inc., is a developer and distributor of software and electronic information rights over the Internet. Metatag produces a software program called Virtual 4-D Links; a user of the program merely types in the name of a city and address anywhere in the world and the computer transports the user there and creates a four-dimensional space and a sixth-sense unknown to the world before. The software license is nonexclusive and Metatag licenses its Virtual 4-D Link to millions of users worldwide. Nolan Bates, who has lived alone with his mother too long, licenses the Virtual 4-D link program for five years at a $350 per month license fee. Bates uses the program for two months before his mother discovers why he has had a smile on his face lately. Bates, upon his mother's urging, returns the Virtual 4-D Link software program to Metatag stating that he is canceling the license. Metatag sues Bates to recover the unpaid license fees. Who wins?

BUSINESS ETHICS CASES

15.13 Business Ethics BluePeace.org is a new environmentalist group that has decided that expounding its environmental causes over the Internet is the best and most efficient way to spend its time and money to advance its environmental causes. To draw attention to its Web sites, BluPeace.org comes up with catchy Internet domain names. One is macyswearus.org, another is exxonvaldezesseals.org, and another is generalmotorscrashesdummies.org. The macyswearus.org Web site first shows beautiful women dressed in mink fur coats sold by Macy's Department Stores and then goes into graphic photos of minks being slaughtered and skinned and made into the coats. The exxonvaldezesseals.org Web site first shows a beautiful pristine bay in Alaska with the Exxon Valdez oil tanker quietly sailing through the waters and then shows photos of the ship breaking open and spewing forth oil and then seals who are gooed with oil suffocating and dying on the shoreline. The Web site generalmo-

torscrashesdummies.org shows a General Motors automobile involved in normal crash tests with dummies followed by photographs of automobile accident scenes where people and children lie bleeding and dying after an accident involving General Motors automobiles. Macy's Department Stores, the Exxon Oil Company, and the General Motors Corporation sue BluePeace.org for violating the federal Anticybersquatting Consumer Protection Act. Who wins? Has BluePeace.org acted unethically in this case?

15.14 Business Ethics Apricot.com is a major software developer that licenses software to be used over the Internet. One of its programs called Match is a search engine that searches personal ads on the Internet and provides a match for users for potential dates and possible marriage partners. Norlan Bates subscribes to the Match software program from Apricot.com. The license duration is five years at a $200 per month license fee. For each subscriber, Apricot.com produces a separate Web page that shows photos of the subscriber and personal data. Bates places a photo of himself with his mother with the caption, "Male, 30 years old, lives with mother, like quiet nights at home." Bates licenses the Apricot.com Match software and uses it 12 hours each day searching for his Internet match. Bates does not pay Apricot.com the required monthly licensing fee for any of the three months he uses the software.

After Bates uses the Match software but refuses to pay Apricot.com its licensing fee, Apricot.com activates the disabling bug in the software and disables the Match software on Bates's computer. Apricot.com did this with no warning to Bates. It then sends a letter to Bates stating, "Loser, the license is canceled!" Bates sues Apricot.com for disabling the Match software program. Who wins? Did Bates act ethically? Did Apricot.com act ethically?

BRIEFING THE CASE WRITING ASSIGNMENT

Read the following case, which has been excerpted from the court's opinion. Review and brief the case.

Toys "R" Us, Inc. v. Abir
1999 WL 61817 (1999)
U.S. District Court, S.D. New York

Koeltl, Judge

In 1997, plaintiff Toys "R" Us, Inc. filed an action alleging violations of federal law related to trademark dilution against the defendants, Eli Abir and Website Management, who had registered the name Toysareus.com as their Internet domain name. The plaintiffs alleged that this domain name diluted the plaintiff's mark TOYS "R" US. In November 1997, this court issued a temporary restraining order enjoining the defendants from "using or inducing others to use the names or marks or any colorable imitation of Plaintiff's TOYS "R" US, KIDS "R" US, BABIES "R" US and/or the family of "R" US marks" pending a decision on the plaintiff's motion for a preliminary injunction.

In December 1997, this court heard argument on the motion for a preliminary injunction. At that time the plaintiffs alleged that the defendants had also registered the domain name Kidsareus.com. This court then issued a preliminary injunction enjoining the defendants from, among other things, using or inducing others to use any colorable imitation of the family of "R" US marks pending final judgment. On August 27, 1998, this court granted the plaintiff's motion for summary judgment on the trademark dilution claims. The following day, this court issued a separate judgment and order permanently enjoining the defendants from further infringement of the family of "R" US marks and ordering the transfer of the Toysareus.com and Kidsareus.com Internet domain names to the plaintiff.

In addition, this court held that because the defendants' conduct in this case was willful, intentional, deliberate, and in bad faith, the plaintiff is entitled to recover attorneys' fees and costs. In order to determine what constitutes "reasonable" attorneys' fees, the starting point is the "lodestar amount," which is the number of hours reasonably expended on the litigation multiplied by a reasonable hourly rate for attorneys and paralegals.

In determining a reasonable hourly rate, courts consider, inter alia, the size and experience of the firm. In this case, Darby & Darby is a well-known New York firm which specializes in intellectual property; the rates charged for its attorneys are comparable to other specialized intellectual property firms in the New York City legal market. The plaintiff's counsel swore in her declaration in support of this application that care was taken to enhance efficiency by assigning, at any one time, only one partner, one mid- to senior-level associate, one to two junior associates, and one to two legal assistants to the prosecution of this case. Having carefully reviewed the itemized request for disbursements, the court finds them neither unnecessary nor excessive for a case of this duration and complexity. The plaintiff is also entitled to costs, as well as those reasonable out-of-pocket expenses incurred by the attorneys and which are normally charged fee-paying clients.

Defendant Eli Abir, who is the owner of defendant Web site Management, does not argue that the award requested by the plaintiffs is excessive. Instead, he argues that due to his business and personal circumstances he has limited financial resources and would be unable to pay more than a "symbolic" amount in attorneys' fees. However, nothing in the record in this case justifies a financially-based reduction in the award of attorneys' fees and costs. For the reasons stated above, the plaintiff's motion for attorneys' fees and costs is granted in the amount of $55,162.76. SO ORDERED.

CHAPTER 16

Formation of Sales, Lease, and Internet Contracts

Commercial law lies within a narrow compass, and is far purer and freer from defects than any other part of the system.

—Henry Peter Brougham
House of Commons
February 7, 1828

Chapter Objectives

After studying this chapter, you should be able to:

1. Define sales contracts governed by Article 2 of the UCC.

2. Define lease contracts governed by Article 2A of the UCC.

3. Describe the formation of sales and lease contracts.

4. Define the UCC's firm offer rule and written confirmation rule.

5. Describe the UCC's additional terms rule and apply it to solve "battles of the forms."

6. Identify when title passes in sales contracts.

7. Describe who bears the risk of loss when goods are lost, damaged, or destroyed.

8. Identify who bears the risk of loss when goods are sold by nonowners such as thieves.

9. Identify unfair and deceptive acts over the Internet.

10. Define letters of credit and describe how Article 5 of the UCC applies to them.

Chapter Contents

Most tangible items—such as books, clothing, and tools—are considered **goods**. In medieval times, merchants gathered at fairs in Europe to exchange such goods. Over time, certain customs and rules evolved for enforcing contracts and resolving disputes. These customs and rules, which were referred to as the "Law Merchant," were enforced by "fair courts" established by the merchants. Eventually, the customs and rules of the Law Merchant were absorbed into the common law.

Toward the end of the 1800s, England enacted a statute (the Sales of Goods Act) that codified the common law rules of commercial transactions. In the United States, laws governing the sale of goods also developed. In 1906, the **Uniform Sales Act** was promulgated in the United States. This act was enacted in many states. It was quickly outdated, however, as mass production and distribution of goods developed in the twentieth century.

In 1952, the Commissioners on Uniform State Laws promulgated a comprehensive statutory scheme called the **Uniform Commercial Code** (the **UCC**). The UCC covers most aspects of commercial transactions.

Article 2 (Sales) and **Article 2A (Leases)** of the UCC govern personal property leases. These articles are intended to provide clear, easy-to-apply rules that place the risk of loss of the goods on the party most able to either bear the risk or insure against it. The common law of contracts governs if either Article 2 or Article 2A is silent on an issue.

This chapter discusses sales and lease contracts. Other articles of the UCC are discussed in subsequent chapters.

goods

Tangible things that are movable at the time of their identification to the contract.

Uniform Commercial Code

Comprehensive statutory scheme that includes laws that cover most aspects of commercial transactions.

*S*COPE OF ARTICLE 2 (SALES)

All states except Louisiana have adopted some version of Article 2 (Sales) of the UCC. Article 2 is also applied by federal courts to sales contracts governed by federal law.

Landmark Law

THE UNIFORM COMMERCIAL CODE (UCC)

One of the major frustrations of businesspersons conducting interstate business is that they are subject to the laws of each of the states in which they operate. To address this problem, in 1949 the National Conference of Commissioners on Uniform State Laws promulgated the **Uniform Commercial Code (UCC)**. The UCC is a **model act** that contains uniform rules that govern commercial transactions. To create this uniformity, individual states needed to enact the UCC as their commercial law statute. They did, and every state (except Louisiana, which has adopted only parts of the UCC) enacted the UCC as a commercial statute.

The UCC is divided into articles, with each article establishing uniform rules for a particular facet of commerce in this country. The articles of the UCC are:

Article 1	General provisions
Article 2	Sales
Article 2A	Leases
Revised	
Article 3	Negotiable instruments
Article 4	Bank deposits and collections
Article 4A	Wire transfers
Article 5	Letter of credit
Article 6	Bulk transfers
Article 7	Documents of title
Article 8	Investment securities
Article 9	Secured transactions

Each of these articles is discussed in the chapters in this section of this book.

The UCC is continually being revised to reflect changes in modern commercial practices and technology. For example, Article 2A was drafted to govern leases of personal property, and Article 4A was added to regulate the use of wire transfers in the banking system. Articles 3 and 4, which cover the creation and transfer of negotiable instruments and the clearing of checks through the banking system, were substantially amended in 1990. Article 2, which covers the sale of goods, currently is in the initial stages of revision.

sale

The passing of title from a seller to a buyer for a price.

Rodeo Drive, Beverly Hills
Businesses offer a variety of goods and services for sale or lease.

What Is a Sale?

Article 2 applies to transactions in goods [UCC 2-102]. All states have held that Article 2 applies to the sale of goods. A **sale** consists of the passing of title from a seller to a buyer for a price [UCC 2-106(1)]. For example, the purchase of a book is a sale subject to Article 2, whether the book was paid for by cash, credit card, or other form of consideration.

What Are Goods?

Goods are defined as tangible things that are movable at the time of their identification to the contract [UCC 2-105(1)]. Specially manufactured goods and the unborn young of animals are examples of goods. Certain items are not considered goods and are not subject to Article 2. They include:

Business Brief

Article 2 applies only to transactions in *goods*. Article 2 does not apply to transactions in intangible items, real estate, or service.

1. Money and intangible items, such as stocks, bonds, and patents, are not tangible goods.
2. Real estate is not a tangible good because it is not movable [UCC 2-105(1)]. Minerals, structures, growing crops, and other things that are severable from real estate may be classified as goods subject to Article 2, however. For example, the sale and removal of a chandelier in a house is a sale of goods subject to Article 2 since its removal would not materially harm the realty. The sale and removal of the furnace, however, would be a sale of real property because its removal would cause material harm [UCC 2-107(2)].

mixed sale

A sale that involves the provision of a service and a good in the same transaction.

Good Versus Services   Contracts for the provision of services—including legal services, medical services, and dental services—are not covered by Article 2. Sometimes, however, a sale involves both the provision of a service and a good in the same transaction. This sale is referred to as a **mixed sale**, Article 2 applies only to mixed sales if the goods are the predominant part of the transaction. The UCC provides no guidance for deciding cases based on mixed sales, therefore, the courts decide these issues on a case-by-case basis.

In the following case, the court had to decide whether a sale was of a good or a service.

Hector v. Cedars-Sinai Medical Center

180 Cal.App. 3d 493, 225 Cal.Rptr. 595 (1986)
California Court of Appeal

CASE 16.1

BACKGROUND AND FACTS
Frances Hector entered Cedars-Sinai Medical Center (Cedars-Sinai), Los Angeles, California, for a surgical operation on her heart. During the operation, a pacemaker was installed in Hector. The pacemaker, which was manufactured

by American Technology, Inc., was installed at Cedars-Sinai by Hector's physician, Dr. Eugene Kompaniez. The pacemaker was defective, causing injury to Hector. Hector sued Cedars-Sinai under Article 2 of the UCC for breach of warranty. The trial court held that the sale was primarily a sale of a service and not of goods, therefore, the UCC did not apply. The court granted Cedars-Sinai motion for summary judgment and dismissed Hector's lawsuit. Hector appealed.

ISSUE
Is the installation of a pacemaker by a hospital a sale of a good subject to Article 2 of the UCC?

COURT'S REASONING
A hospital is not ordinarily engaged in the business of selling any of the products or equipment it uses in providing such services. The essence of the relationship between a hospital and its patients does not relate essentially to any products or piece of equipment it uses but to the professional services it provides. Testimony indicated that Cedars-Sinai does not routinely stock pacemakers, nor is it the business of selling, distributing, or testing pacemakers. The treatment provided by Cedars-Sinai in relation to implantation of pacemakers includes pre- and post-operative care, nursing care, a surgical operating room, and

technicians. As a provider of services rather than a seller of a product, the hospital is not subject to liability for a defective product provided to the patient during the course of his or her treatment.

DECISION
The court of appeal held that Cedars-Sinai was a provider of medical services and not a seller of goods. Therefore, Cedars-Sinai was not liable for breach of warranty under the UCC because the UCC did not apply. Affirmed.

Case Questions

Critical Legal Thinking   Should the UCC be extended to service providers?

Business Ethics   Was it ethical for the hospital to deny liability in this case?

Contemporary Business   Could American Technology, Inc., be held liable to the plaintiff in this case? Why do you think the plaintiff sued Cedars-Sinai in this case?

Who Is a Merchant?

Generally, Article 2 applies to all sales contracts, whether they involve merchants or not. Article 2, however, contains several provisions that either apply only to merchants or impose a greater duty on merchants. UCC 2-104(1) defines a **merchant** as (1) a person who deals in the goods of the kind involved in the transaction or (2) a person who by his or her occupation holds himself or herself out as having knowledge or skill peculiar to the goods involved in the transaction. For example, a sporting goods dealer is a merchant with respect to sporting goods, but is not if he sells his lawn mower to a neighbor. The courts disagree as to whether farmers are merchants within this definition.

merchant

A person who (1) deals in the goods of the kind involved in the transaction or (2) by his or her occupation holds himself or herself out as having knowledge or skill peculiar to the goods involved in the transaction.

SCOPE OF ARTICLE 2A (LEASES)

Personal property leases are a billion-dollar industry. Consumer rentals of automobiles or equipment and commercial leases of such items as aircraft and industrial machinery fall into this category. In the past, these transactions were governed by a combination of common law principles, real estate law, and reference to Article 2. Some of these legal rules and concepts do not quite fit a lease transaction

Article **2A** of the UCC was promulgated in 1987. This article, which is cited as the **Uniform Commercial Code—Leases**, directly addresses personal property leases [UCC 2A-101]. It establishes a comprehensive, uniform law covering the formation, performance, and default of leases in goods [UCC 2A-102, 2A-103(h)].

Article 2A is similar to Article 2. In fact, many Article 2 provisions were changed to reflect leasing terminology and practices that carried over to Article 2A. Many states have adopted Article 2A, and many more are expected to do so in the future.

Business Brief

Article 2A applies only to leases involving *goods*. Article 2A does not apply to real estate or other leases.

Article 2A (Leases)

Article of the UCC that governs lease of goods.

lease

A transfer of the right to the possession and use of the named goods for a set term in return for certain consideration.

Definition of a Lease

A **lease** is a transfer of the right to the possession and use of the named goods for a set term in return for certain consideration [UCC 2A-103(1)(i)(x)]. The leased goods can be anything from a hand tool leased to an individual for a few hours to a complex line of industrial equipment leased to a multinational corporation for a number of years.

In an ordinary lease, the **lessor** is the person who transfers the right of possession and use of goods under the lease [UCC 2A-103(1)(p)]. The **lessee** is the person who acquires the right to possession and use of goods under a lease [UCC 2A-103(1)(n)].

lessor

The person who transfers the right of possession and use of goods under the lease.

lessee

The person who acquires the right to possession and use of goods under a lease.

Finance Lease

A **finance lease** is a three-party transaction consisting of the lessor, the lessee, and the **supplier** (or vendor). The lessor does not select, manufacture, or supply the goods. Instead, the lessor acquires title to the goods or the right to their possession and use in connection with the terms of the lease [UCC 2A-103(1)(g)].

Consider This Example   Dow Chemical Company decides to use robotics to manufacture most of its products. It persuades Ingersoll-Rand to design the robotic equipment that would meet its needs. To finance the purchase of the equipment, Dow Chemical goes to City Bank, which purchases the robotics equipment from Ingersoll-Rand and leases it to Dow Chemical. City bank is the lessor, Dow Chemical is the lessee, and Ingersoll-Rand is the supplier.

FORMATION OF SALES AND LEASE CONTRACTS

Like general contracts, the formation of sales and lease contracts requires an offer, an acceptance, consideration, and so on. The UCC-established rules for each of these elements often differ considerably from common law. Any rules established by Articles 2 and 2A take precedence over the common law of contracts.

Offer

A contract for the sale or lease of goods may be made in any manner sufficient to show agreement, including conduct by both parties that recognizes the existence of a contract [UCC 2-204(1), 2A-204(1)]. Under the UCC, an agreement sufficient to constitute a contract for the sale or lease of goods may be found even though the moment of its making is undetermined [UCC 2-204(2), 2A-204(2)].

Open Terms   Sometimes the parties to a sale or lease contract leave open a major term in the contract. The UCC is tolerant of open terms. According to UCC 2-204(3) and 2A-204(3), the contract does not fail for indefiniteness if (1) the parties intended to make a contract and (2) there is a reasonably certain basis for giving an appropriate remedy. In effect, certain **open terms** are permitted to be "read into" a sales or lease contract. This rule is commonly referred to as **gap-filling rules**.

Some examples of terms that are commonly left open are:

- **Open Price Term**   If a sales contract does not contain a specific price (**open price term**), a "reasonable price" is implied at the time of delivery. The contract may provide that a price is to be fixed by a market rate (e.g., a commodities market), as set or recorded by a third person or agency (e.g., a government agency), or by another standard either upon delivery or on a set date. If the agreed-upon standard is unavailable when the price is to be set, a reasonable price is implied at the time of delivery of the goods [UCC 2-305(1)].

  A seller or buyer who reserves the right to fix a price must do so in good faith [UCC 2-305(2)]. When one of the parties fails to fix an open price term, the other party may opt either (1) to treat the contract as canceled or (2) to fix a reasonable price for the goods [UCC 2-305(3)].

- **Open Payment Term**   If the parties to a sales contract do not agree on payment terms, payment is due at the time and place at which the buyer is to receive the goods. If delivery is authorized and made by way of document of title, payment is due at the time and place at which the buyer is to receive the document of title, regardless of where the goods are to be received [UCC 2-310].

- **Open Delivery Term**   If the parties to a sales contract do not agree to the time, place, and manner of delivery of the goods, the place for delivery is the seller's place of business. If the seller does not have a place of business, delivery is to be made at the seller's residence. If identified goods are located at some other place and both parties know of this fact at the time of contracting, that place is the place of delivery [UCC 2-308].

  Where goods are to be shipped but the shipper is not named, the seller is obligated to make the shipping arrangements. Such arrangements must be made in good faith and within limits of commercial reasonableness [UCC 2-311(2)].

- **Open Time Term**   If the parties to the contract do not set a specific time of performance for any obligation under the contract, the contract must be performed within a reasonable time. If the sales contract provides for successive performance over an unspecified period of time, the contract is valid for a reasonable time [UCC 2-309].
- **Open Assortment Term**   If the assortment of goods to a sales contract is left open, the buyer is given the option of choosing those goods. For example, suppose Macy's contracts to purchase 1,000 dresses from Liz Claiborne, Inc. The contract is silent as to the assortment of colors of the dresses. The buyer may pick the assortment of colors for the dresses from the seller's stock. The buyer must make the selection in good faith and within limits set by commercial reasonableness [UCC 2-311(2)].

Contemporary Business Environment

UCC FIRM OFFER RULE CHANGES THE COMMON LAW OF CONTRACTS

Recall that the common law of contracts allows the offeror to revoke the offer anytime prior to its acceptance. The only exception allowed by the common law is an *option contract* (i.e., where the offeree paid the offeror consideration to keep the offer open).

The UCC recognizes another exception, which is called the **firm offer rule**. This rule states that a merchant who (1) offers to buy, sell, or lease goods and (2) gives a written and signed assurance on a separate form that the offer will be held open cannot revoke the offer for the time stated or, if no time is stated, for a reasonable time. The maximum amount of time permitted under this rule is three months [UCC 2-205, 2A-205].

Consider This Example   On June 1, a merchant-seller offers to sell a Mercedes-Benz to a buyer for $50,000. The merchant-seller signs a written assurance to keep that offer open until August 30. On July 1, the merchant-seller sells the car to another buyer. On August 21, the original offeree tenders $50,000 for the car. The merchant-seller is liable to the original offeree for breach of contract.

Acceptance

Both the common law and the UCC provide that a contract is created when the offeree (i.e., the buyer or lessee) sends an acceptance to the offeror, not when the offeror receives the acceptance. For example, a contract is made when the acceptance letter is delivered to the post office. The contract remains valid even if the post office loses the letter.

Unless otherwise unambiguously indicated by language or circumstance, an offer to make a sales or lease contract may be accepted in any manner and by any reasonable medium of acceptance [UCC 2-206(1)(a), 2A-206(1)]. Applications of this rule are discussed in the following paragraphs.

Methods of Acceptance   The UCC permits acceptance by any reasonable manner or method or communication.

Consider This Example   A seller sends a telegram to a proposed buyer offering to sell the buyer certain goods. The buyer responds by mailing a letter of acceptance to the seller. In most circumstances, mailing the letter of acceptance would be considered reasonable. If the goods were extremely perishable or if the market for the goods were very volatile, however, a faster means of acceptance (such as a telegram) might be warranted.

If an order or other offer to buy goods requires prompt or current shipment, the offer is accepted if the seller (1) promptly promises to ship the goods or (2) promptly ships either conforming or nonconforming goods [UCC 2-206(1)(b)]. The shipment of conforming goods signals acceptance of the buyer's offer.

Acceptance of goods occurs after the buyer or lessee has a reasonable opportunity to inspect them and signifies that (1) the goods are conforming, (2) he or she will take or retain the goods in spite of their nonconformity, or (3) he or she fails to reject the goods within a reasonable time after tender or delivery [UCC 2-513(1), 2A-515(1)].

The foundation of justice is good faith.

Cicero (106–43 B.C.)
De Officiis, *Bk. I, Ch. VII*

accommodation

A shipment that is offered to the buyer as a replacement for the original shipment when the original shipment cannot be filled.

Business Brief

Under certain circumstances the UCC permits an acceptance to contain terms in addition to or different from those in the offer.

Accommodation Shipment   A shipment of nonconforming goods does not constitute an acceptance if the seller reasonably notifies the buyer that the shipment is offered only as an **accommodation** to the buyer [UCC 2-206(1)(b)]. For example, suppose a buyer offers to purchase 500 red candles from a seller. The seller's red candles are temporarily out of stock. The seller sends the buyer 500 green candles and notifies the buyer that these candles are being sent as an accommodation. The seller has not accepted (or breached) the contract. The accommodation is a counteroffer from the seller to the buyer. The buyer is free either to accept or to reject the counteroffer.

Contemporary Business Environment

UCC PERMITS ADDITIONAL TERMS IN SALES AND LEASE CONTRACTS

Under common law's **mirror image rule**, the offeree's acceptance must be on the same terms as the offer. The inclusion of additional terms in the acceptance is considered a **counteroffer** rather than an acceptance. Thus, the offeror's original offer is extinguished.

UCC 2-207(1) is more liberal. It permits definite and timely expressions of acceptance or written confirmations to operate as an acceptance even though they contain terms that are additional to or different from the offered terms unless the acceptance is expressly conditional on assent to such terms. This rule differs for merchants and nonmerchants, as discussed below.

ONE OR BOTH PARTIES ARE NONMERCHANTS

If one or both parties to the sales contract are nonmerchants, any additional terms are considered **proposed additions** to the contract. The proposed additions do not constitute a

counteroffer or extinguish the original offer. If the offeree's proposed additions are accepted by the original offeror, they become part of the contract. If they are not accepted, the sales contract is formed on the basis of the terms of the original offer [UCC 2-207(2)].

Consider This Example   A salesperson at a Lexus dealership offers to sell a top-of-the-line coupe to a buyer for $47,000. The buyer replies, "I accept your offer but I would like to have a CD player in the car." The CD player is a proposed addition to the contract. If the salesperson agrees, the contract between the parties consists of the terms of the original offer plus the additional term regarding the CD player. If the salesperson rejects the proposed addition, the sales contract consists of the terms of the original offer because the buyer made a definite expression of acceptance.

Entrepreneur and the Law

WHO WINS THE "BATTLE OF THE FORMS?"

When merchants negotiate sales contracts, they often exchange preprinted forms. These "boilerplate" forms usually contain terms that favor the drafter. Thus, an offeror who sends a standard form contract as an offer to the offeree may receive an acceptance drafted on the offeree's own form contract. This scenario—commonly called the **battle of the forms**—raises important questions: Is there a contract? If so, what are its terms? The UCC provides guidance in answering these questions.

Under UCC 2-207(2), if both parties are merchants, any additional terms contained in an acceptance become part of the

sales contract unless (1) the offer expressly limits acceptance to the terms of the offer, (2) the additional terms materially alter the terms of the original contract, or (3) the offeror notifies the offeree that he or she objects to the additional terms within a reasonable time after receiving the offeree's modified acceptance.

The most important point in the battle of the forms is that there is no contract if the additional terms so materially alter the terms of the original offer that the parties cannot agree on the contract. This fact-specific determination is made by the courts on a case-by-case basis.

Consideration

The formation of sales and lease contracts requires consideration. The UCC, however, changes the common law rule that requires the modification of a contract to be supported by new consideration. An agreement modifying a sales or lease contract needs no consideration to be binding [UCC 2-209(1), 2A-208(1)].

Modification of a sales or lease contract must be made in good faith [UCC 1-203]. As in the common law of contracts, modifications are not binding if they are obtained through fraud, duress, extortion, and such.

Statute of Frauds

The UCC includes **Statute of Frauds** provisions that apply to all sales and lease contracts. All contracts for the sale of goods costing $500 or more and lease contracts involving payments of $1,000 or more must be in writing [UCC 2-201(1), 2A-201(1)]. The writing must be sufficient to indicate that a contract has been made between the parties. Except as discussed in the paragraphs that follow, the writing must be signed by the party against whom enforcement is sought or by his or her authorized agent or broker. If a contract falling within these parameters is not written, it is unenforceable.

Consider This Example   A seller orally agrees to sell her computer to a buyer for $550. When the buyer tenders the purchase price, the seller asserts the Statute of Frauds and refuses to sell the computer to him. The seller is correct. The contract must be in writing to be enforceable because the contract price for the computer exceeds $499.99.

Exceptions to the Statute of Frauds   The three situations in which a sales or lease contract that would otherwise be required to be in writing is enforceable even if it is not in writing are discussed in the following paragraphs [UCC 2-201(3), UCC 2A-201(4)].

1. **Specially Manufactured Goods**   Buyers and lessees often order specially manufactured goods. If the contract to purchase or lease such goods is oral, the buyer or lessee may not assert the Statute of Frauds against the enforcement of the contract if (1) the goods are not suitable for sale or lease to others in the ordinary course of the seller's or the lessor's business and (2) the seller or lessor has made either a substantial beginning of the manufacture of the goods or commitments for their procurement.
2. **Admissions in Pleadings or Court**   If the party against whom enforcement of an oral sales or lease contract is sought admits in pleadings, testimony, or otherwise in court that a contract for the sale or lease of goods was made, the oral contract is enforceable against that party. However, the contract is only enforceable as to the quantity of goods admitted.
3. **Part Acceptance**   An oral sales or lease contract that should otherwise be in writing is enforceable to the extent to which the goods have been received and accepted by the buyer or lessee.

Consider This Example   A lessor orally contracts to lease 100 personal computers to a lessee. The lessee accepts the first 20 computers tendered by the lessor. This action is part acceptance. The lessee refuses to take delivery of the remaining 80 computers. Here, the lessee must pay for the 20 computers she originally received and accepted. The lessee does not have to accept or pay for the remaining 80 computers.

UCC Statute of Frauds

A rule that requires all contracts for the sale of goods costing $500 or more and lease contracts involving payments of $1,000 or more to be in writing.

Business Brief

Following are exceptions to the writing requirement of the UCC Statute of Frauds: (1) specially manufactured goods, (2) admissions in pleadings or court, and (3) part acceptance.

Business Brief

Note that the written confirmation rule applies to *merchants* only.

Entrepreneur and the Law

UCC WRITTEN CONFIRMATION RULE EXCEPTION TO STATUTE OF FRAUDS

If both parties to an oral sale or lease contract are merchants, the Statute of Frauds requirement can be satisfied if (1) one of the parties to an oral agreement sends a written confirmation of the sale or lease within a reasonable time after contracting and (2) the other merchant does not give written notice of an objection to the contract within 10 days after receiving the confirmation. This situation is true even though the party receiving the written confirmation has not signed it. The only stipulations are that the confirmation is sufficient and that the party to whom it was sent has reason to know its contents [UCC 2-201(2)].

Consider This Example   A merchant-seller in Chicago orally contracts by telephone to sell goods to a merchant-buyer in Phoenix for $25,000. Within a reasonable time after contracting, the merchant-seller sends a sufficient written confirmation to the buyer. The buyer, who has reason to know the contents of the confirmation, fails to object to the contents of the confirmation in writing within 10 days after receiving it. The Statute of Frauds has been met, and the buyer cannot thereafter raise it against enforcement of the contract.

Business Ethics

A CHICKEN FARMER GETS PLUCKED

Sometimes the Statute of Frauds, which was designed to prevent fraud, is used by a party to try to renege on an oral sales contract. Consider the following case.

Perdue Farms, Inc. (Perdue), sells dressed poultry under the brand name "Perdue Roasters." On Octobre 30, 1975, Motts, Inc., of Mississippi (Motts) entered into an oral contract with Perdue to purchase 1,500 boxes of roasters from Perdue at $0.50 per pound. Motts was to pick up the roasters at Perdue's Maryland plant. Motts entered into a contract to resell the roasters to Dairyland, Inc. Motts sent a confirmation letter to Perdue confirming their oral agreement. Perdue received the confirmation and did not object to it. When Motts's truck arrived at Perdue's Maryland plant to pick up the roasters, Perdue informed Motts's drivers that the roasters would not be loaded unless complete payment was made before delivery. Under previous contracts between the parties, payment was due seven days after delivery. Perdue informed Motts that the roasters would not be sold to Motts on credit. Perdue then sold the roasters directly to Dairyland, Inc.

Motts sued Perdue to recover damages for breach of the sales contract. Perdue denied liability, arguing that the contract had to be in writing because it was over $500. Motts argued that the situation fell under the written confirmation rule exception to the UCC Statute of Frauds.

The district court agreed with Motts. UCC 2-201(2) binds merchants to oral sales contracts if one sends the other a confirmation letter that is not objected to within 10 days after its receipt. Both parties in this case were merchants, and Perdue did not object to Motts's confirmation letter within the 10-day period. The court denied Perdue the Statute of Frauds as a defense, thereby making Motts's confirmation letter enforceable against Perdue. [*Perdue Farms, Inc. v. Motts, Inc., of Mississippi*, 25 UCC Rep. Serv. 9 (1978)]

1. Did Perdue act morally in refusing to perform the sales contract?
2. Is it ever ethical to raise the Statute of Frauds in defense to get out of an oral contract?

When Written Modification Is Required

Oral modification of the contract is not enforceable if the parties agree that any modification of the sales or lease contract must be in a signed writing [UCC 2-209(2), 2A-208(2)]. In the absence of such an agreement, oral modifications to sales and lease contracts are binding if they do not violate the Statute of Frauds.

If the oral modification brings the contract within the Statute of Frauds, it must be in writing to be enforceable.

Consider This Example   A lessor and lessee enter into an oral lease contract for the lease of goods at a rent of $450. Subsequently, the contract is modified by raising the rent to $550. Because the modified contract rent is more than $500, the contract comes under the UCC Statute of Frauds, and the modification must be in writing to be enforceable.

Parol Evidence

parol evidence rule

A rule that says that if a written contract is a complete and final statement of the parties' agreement, any prior or contemporaneous oral or written statements that alter, contradict, or are in addition to the terms of the written contract are inadmissible in court regarding a dispute over the contract.

The **parol evidence rule** states that when a sales or lease contract is evidenced by a writing that is intended to be a final expression of the parties' agreement or a confirmatory memorandum, the terms of the writing may not be contradicted by evidence of (1) a prior oral or written agreement or (2) a contemporaneous oral agreement (i.e., parol evidence) [UCC 2-202, 2A-202]. The rule is intended to ensure certainty in written sales and lease contracts.

Occasionally, the express terms of a written contract are not clear on their face and must be interpreted. In such cases, reference may be made to certain sources outside the contract. These sources are construed together when they are consistent with each other. If that is unreasonable, they are considered in descending order of priority [UCC 2-208(2), 2A-207(2)]:

1. **Course of Performance**   The previous conduct of the parties regarding the contract in question
2. **Course of Dealing**   The conduct of the parties in prior transactions and contracts
3. **Usage of Trade**   Any practice or method of dealing that is regularly observed or adhered to in a place, a vocation, a trade, or an industry

Consider This Example A cattle rancher contracts to purchase corn from a farmer. The farmer delivers feed corn to the rancher. The rancher rejects this corn and demands delivery of corn that is fit for human consumption. Ordinarily, usage of trade would be the first source of interpretation of the word *corn*. If the parties had prior dealings, though, the usage of the term in their prior dealings would become the primary source of interpretation.

*C*ONCEPT *S*UMMARY COMPARISON OF CONTRACT LAW AND THE LAW OF SALES

Topic	Common Law of Contracts	UCC Law of Sales
Definiteness	Contract must contain all of the material terms of the parties' agreement.	UCC gap-filling rules permit terms to be implied if the parties intended to make a contract [UCC 2-204].
Irrevocable offers	Option contracts.	Option contracts. Firm offers by merchants to keep an offer open are binding up to three months without any consideration [UCC 2-205].
Counteroffers	Acceptance must be a mirror image of the offer. A counteroffer rejects and terminates the offer.	Additional terms of an acceptance become part of the contract if (1) they do not materially alter the terms of the offer and (2) the offeror does not object within a reasonable time after reviewing the acceptance [UCC 2-207].
Statute of Frauds	Writing must be signed by the party against whom enforcement is sought.	Writing may be enforced against a party who has not signed it if (1) both parties are merchants, (2) one party sends a written confirmation of their oral agreement within a reasonable time after contracting, and (3) the other party does not give written notice of objection within 10 days after receiving the confirmation [UCC 2-201].
Modification	Consideration is required.	Consideration is not required [UCC 2-209].

E-Commerce & Information Technology

UNFAIR AND DECEPTIVE ACTS OVER THE INTERNET

Little did Congress know over 80 years ago when it passed the **Federal Trade Commission Act** that Section 5 of the act would be used to prosecute fraud over the Internet. **Section 5** prohibits "unfair and deceptive" acts affecting commerce. The FTC has demonstrated recently that old laws can learn new tricks. Consider the following case.

Powerful search engines have been developed to allow surfers to browse the Internet and connect to Web sites in which they are interested. Certain scammers came up with a scheme where they would entice unwitting surfers to connect to their porn sites and not be able to get out. The scheme worked as follows. The scammers made fake copies of over 25 million popular Web sites such as the *Harvard Business Review, Japanese Friendship Gardens*, and others. Search engines trolling the Web for new pages found these Web

sites and added them to their listings. The scammers added to the faked Web pages an extra bit of coding so that as soon as surfers found the bogus Web page, it rerouted—"page-jacked"—them to the scammer's porn Web site. Once there, the user was "mouse-trapped" at the porn site and efforts to escape led only to new porn pages. The porn site operators made money by selling advertisements, and ad prices were often based on the number of hits on the site.

The Federal Trade Commission (FTC), a federal government agency, investigated and sued porn site operators in federal court for violating Section 5 of the FTC Act. The court found that the porn site operators had engaged in unfair and deceptive practices in violation of Section 5, issued an injunction to shut down the porn sites, and ordered the operators not to engage in such conduct in the future.

IDENTIFICATION AND PASSAGE OF TITLE

The identification of goods is rather simple. It means distinguishing the goods named in the contract from the seller's or lessor's other goods. The seller or lessor retains the risk of loss of the goods until he or she identifies them to a sales or lease contract. Further, UCC 2-401(1) and 2-501 prevent title to goods from passing from the seller to the buyer unless the goods are identified to the sales contract. In a lease transaction, title to the leased goods remains with the lessor or a third party. It does not pass to the lessee.

The identification of goods and the passage of title are discussed in the following paragraphs.

Identification

identification of goods

Distinguishing the goods named in the contract from the seller's or lessor's other goods.

Identification of goods can be made at any time and in any manner explicitly agreed to by the parties to the contract. In the absence of such an agreement, the UCC mandates when identification occurs [UCC 2-501(1), 2A-217].

Already existing goods are identified when the contract is made and names the specific goods sold or leased. For example, a piece of farm machinery, a car, or a boat is identified when its serial number is listed on the sales or lease contract.

Goods that are part of a larger mass of goods are identified when the specific merchandise is designated. For example, if a food processor contracts to purchase 150 cases of oranges from a farmer who has 1,000 cases of oranges, the buyer's goods are identified when the seller explicitly separates or tags the 150 cases.

future goods

Goods not yet in existence (ungrown crops, unborn stock animals).

Future goods are goods not yet in existence. For example, unborn young animals (such as unborn cattle) are identified when the young are conceived. Crops to be harvested are identified when the crops are planted or otherwise become growing crops. Future goods other than crops and unborn young are identified when the goods are shipped, marked, or otherwise designated by the seller or lessor as the goods to which the contract refers.

Passage of Title

Once the goods exist and have been identified, title to the goods may be transferred from the seller to the buyer. Article 2 of the UCC establishes precise rules for determining the passage of title in sales contracts. (As mentioned earlier, lessees do not acquire title to the goods they lease).

title

Legal, tangible evidence of ownership of goods.

Under UCC 2-401(1), **title** to goods passes from the seller to the buyer in any manner and on any conditions explicitly agreed upon by the parties. If the parties do not agree to a specific time, title passes to the buyer when and where the seller's performance with reference to the physical delivery is completed. This point in time is determined by applying the following rules [UCC 2-401(2)].

shipment contract

A contract that requires the seller to ship the goods to the buyer via a common carrier.

Shipment and Destination Contracts A **shipment contract** requires the seller to ship the goods to the buyer via a common carrier. The seller is required to (1) make proper shipping arrangements and (2) deliver the goods into the carrier's hands. Title passes to the buyer at the time and place of shipment [UCC 2-401(2)(a)].

destination contract

A contract that requires the seller to deliver the goods either to the buyer's place of business or to another destination specified in the sales contract.

A **destination contract** requires the seller to deliver the goods either to the buyer's place of business or to another destination specified in the sales contract. Title passes to the buyer when the seller tenders delivery of the goods at the specified destination [UCC 2-401(2)(b)].

document of title

An actual piece of paper, such as a warehouse receipt or bill of lading, that is required in some transactions of pick up and delivery.

Delivery of Goods Without Moving Them Sometimes a sales contract authorizes the goods to be delivered without requiring the seller to move them. In other words, the buyer might be required to pick up goods from the seller. In such situations, the time and place of the passage of title depends on whether the seller is to deliver a **document of title** (i.e., a warehouse receipt or bill of lading) to the buyer. If a document of title is required, title passes when and where the seller delivers the document to the buyer [UCC 2-401(3)(a)]. For example, if the goods named in the sales contract are located at a warehouse, title passes when the seller delivers a warehouse receipt representing the goods to the buyer.

If (1) no document of title is needed and (2) the goods are identified at the time of contracting, title passes at the time and place of contracting [UCC 2-401(3)(b)]. For example, if the buyer signs a sales contract to purchase bricks from the seller and the contract stipulates that the buyer will pick up the bricks at the seller's place of business, title passes when the contract is signed by both parties. This situation is true even if the bricks are not picked up until a later date.

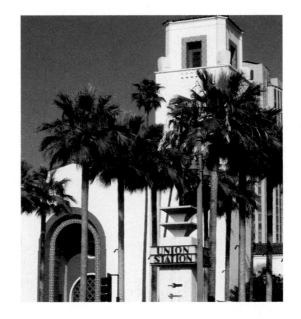

Union Station, Los Angeles
Many goods are shipped from the seller to the buyer via a common carrier, such as a railroad company.

International Law

USE OF LETTERS OF CREDIT IN INTERNATIONAL TRADE

The major risks in any business transaction involving the sale of goods are (1) that the seller will not be paid after delivering the goods and (2) that the buyer will not receive the goods after paying for them. These risks are even more acute in international transactions where the buyer and seller may not know each other, the parties are dealing at long distance, and the judicial system of the parties' countries may not have jurisdiction to decide a dispute if one should arise. The irrevocable **letter of credit** has been developed to manage these risks in international sales. The function of a letter of credit is to substitute the credit of a recognized international bank for that of the buyer.

An irrevocable letter of credit works this way. Suppose a buyer in one country and a seller in another country enter into a contract for the sale of goods. The buyer goes to his or her bank and pays the bank a fee to issue a letter of credit in which the bank agrees to pay the amount of the letter (which is the amount of the purchase price of the goods) to the seller's bank if certain conditions are met. These conditions are usually the delivery of documents indicating that the seller has placed the goods in the hands of a shipper. The buyer is called the **account party**, the bank that issues the

letter of credit is called the **issuing bank**, and the seller is called the **beneficiary** of the letter of credit.

The issuing bank then forwards the letter of credit to a bank that the seller has designated in his or her country. This bank, which is called the **correspondent** or **confirming bank**, relays the letter of credit to the seller. Now that the seller sees that he or she is guaranteed payment, he or she makes arrangements to ship the goods and receives a **bill of lading** from the carrier proving so. The seller then delivers these documents to the confirming bank. The confirming bank will examine the documents and, if it finds them in order, will pay the seller and forward the documents to the issuing bank. By this time, the buyer will usually have paid the amount of the purchase price to the issuing bank (unless an extension of credit has been arranged), and the issuing bank then charges the buyer's account. The issuing bank forwards the bill of lading and other necessary documents to the buyer, who then picks up the goods from the shipper when they arrive.

If the documents (e.g., the bill of lading, proof of insurance) conform to the conditions specified in the letter of credit, the issuing bank must pay the letter of credit. If the account party does not pay the issuing bank, the bank's only recourse is to sue the account party to recover damages.

Article 5 (Letters of Credit) of the Uniform Commercial Code governs letters of credit unless otherwise agreed by the parties. The International Chamber of Commerce has promul-gated the **Uniform Customs and Practices for Documentary Credits (UCP)**, which contains rules governing the formation and performance of letters of credit. Although the UCP is nei-ther a treaty nor a legislative enactment, most banks incorpo-rate the terms of the UCP in letters of credit they issue.

RISK OF LOSS: NO BREACH OF SALES CONTRACT

In the case of sales contracts, the common law placed the risk of loss to goods on the party who had title to the goods. Article 2 rejects this notion and allows the parties to a sales contract to agree among themselves who will bear the risk of loss if the goods subject to the contract are lost or destroyed. If the parties do not have a specific agreement concerning the assessment of the risk of loss, the UCC mandates who will bear the risk.

Carrier Cases: Movement of Goods

Unless otherwise agreed, goods that are shipped via carrier (e.g., railroad, ship, truck) are considered to be sent pursuant to a shipment contract or a destination contract. Absent any indication to the contrary, sales contracts are presumed to be shipment contracts rather than destination contracts.

shipment contract

The buyer bears the risk of loss during transportation.

Shipment Contracts A **shipment contract** requires the seller to ship goods conforming to the contract to a buyer via a carrier. The risk of loss passes to the buyer when the seller delivers the conforming goods to the carrier. The buyer bears the risk of loss of the goods during transportation [UCC 2-509(1)(a)].

Shipment contracts are created in two ways. The first requires the use of the term *shipment contract*. The second requires the use of one of the following delivery terms: F.O.B., F.A.S., C.I.F., or C. & F. (see "Entrepreneur and the Law" box).

destination contract

A sales contract that requires the seller to deliver conforming goods to a specific destination. The seller bears the risk of loss during transportation.

Destination Contracts A sales contract that requires the seller to deliver conforming goods to a specific destination is a **destination contract**. Such contracts require the seller to bear the risk of loss to the goods during their transportation. Thus, with the exception of a no-arrival, no-sale contract, the seller is required to replace any goods lost in transit. The buyer does not have to pay for destroyed goods. The risk of loss does not pass until the goods are tendered to the buyer at the specified destination [UCC 2-509(1)(b)].

Business Brief

The risk of loss of goods while they are being transported depends on what delivery terms are agreed to in the sales contract.

Unless otherwise agreed, destination contracts are created in two ways. The first method requires the use of the term *destination contract*. The alternative method requires use of the following delivery terms: F.O.B. place of destination, ex-ship, or no-arrival, no-sale contract.

 *Entrepreneur and the Law*

SHIPPING TERMS

F.O.B. (free on board) point of shipment (e.g., F.O.B. Anchorage, Alaska) requires the seller to arrange to ship the goods and put the goods in the carrier's possession. The seller bears the expense and risk of loss until this is done [UCC 2-319(1)(a)].

F.A.S. (free alongside) or **F.A.S. (vessel) port of ship-ment** (e.g., *The Gargoyle*, New Orleans) requires the seller to deliver and tender the goods alongside the named vessel or on the dock designated and provided by the buyer. The seller bears the expense and risk of loss until this is done [UCC 2-319(2)(a)].

C.I.F. (cost, insurance, and freight) and **C. & F. (C.F., cost and freight)** are pricing terms that indicate the cost for which the seller is responsible. These terms require the seller to bear the expense and the risk of loss of loading the goods on the carrier [UCC 2-320(1) and (3)].

F.O.B. place of destination (e.g., F.O.B. Miami, Florida) requires the seller to bear the expense and risk of loss until the goods are tendered to the buyer at the place of destination [UCC 2-319(1)(b)].

Ex-ship (from the carrying vessel) requires the seller to bear the expense and risk of loss until the goods are unloaded from the ship at its port of destination [UCC 2-322(1)(b)].

No-arrival, no-sale contracts require the seller to bear the expense and risk of loss of the goods during transportation. However, the seller is under no duty to deliver replacement goods to the buyer because there is no contractual stipulation that the goods will arrive at the appointed destination [UCC 2-324(a)(b)].

International Law

INTERNATIONAL TRADE TERMS

Sales contracts involving transportation customarily contain abbreviated terms describing the time and place where the buyer is to take delivery. These trade terms, such as F.O.B. and C.I.F., may also define other matters, including the time and place of payment, the price, the time the risk of loss shifts from the seller to the buyer, and the costs of freight and insurance.

The same trade abbreviations are widely used in both domestic and international transactions. Unfortunately, they have different meanings depending on the governing law. In the United States, for example, the Uniform Commercial Code (UCC) defines trade terms for domestic sales. In the United Kingdom, the terms are defined by reference to case law. The United Nations Convention on Contracts for the International Sale of Goods (CISG) also allows parties to incorporate trade terms of their choosing.

The most widely used private trade terms are those published by the International Chamber of Commerce. Called *Incoterms*, they are well known throughout the world. Their use in international sales is encouraged by trade councils, courts, and international lawyers. First published in 1936, the current version is *Incoterms 1990*.

Parties who adopt the *Incoterms*, or any other trade terms, should make sure they express their desire clearly. For example, a contract might refer to F.O.B. (*Incoterms 1990*) or C.I.F. (*U.S. Uniform Commercial Code*). Otherwise, the courts will apply the definitions used in their own jurisdiction. Finally, the parties should be wary about making additions or varying the meaning of any particular term, except to the extent that it is allowed by the rules they adopt or by judicial decision. The courts are as apt to ignore a variation, or hold that the entire term is ineffective, as they are to apply it.

Noncarrier Cases: No Movement of Goods

Sometimes a sales contract stipulates that the buyer is to pick up the goods, either at the seller's place of business or another specified location. This type of arrangement raises a question: Who bears the risk of loss if the goods are destroyed or stolen after the contract date and before the buyer picks the goods up from the seller? The UCC provides two different rules for this situation. One applies to merchant-sellers and the other to nonmerchant-sellers [UCC 2-509(3)].

Merchant-Seller If the seller is a merchant, the risk of loss does not pass to the buyer until the goods are received. In other words, a merchant-seller bears the risk of loss between the time of contracting and the time the buyer picks up the goods.

Consider This Example On June 1, Tyus Motors, a merchant, contracts to sell a new automobile to a consumer. Tyus Motors keeps the car for a few days after contracting to prep it. During this period, the car is destroyed by fire. Under the UCC, Tyus Motors bears the risk of loss because of its merchant status.

Nonmerchant-Seller Nonmerchant-sellers pass the risk of loss to the buyer upon "Tender of delivery" of the goods. Tender of delivery occurs when the seller (1) places or holds the goods available for the buyer to take delivery and (2) notifies the buyer of this fact.

Consider This Example On June 1, a nonmerchant contracts to sell his automobile to his next-door neighbor. Delivery of the car is tendered on June 3, and the buyer is notified of this. The buyer tells the seller he will pick the car up "in a few days." The car is destroyed by fire before the buyer picks it up. In this situation, the buyer bears the risk of loss because (1) the seller is a nonmerchant and (2) delivery was tendered on June 3. If the car was destroyed on June 2—that is, before delivery was tendered—he seller would bear the risk of loss.

bailee

A holder of goods who is not a seller or a buyer (e.g., a warehouse).

Goods in the Possession of a Bailee Goods sold by a seller to a buyer are sometimes in the possession of a **bailee** (e.g., a warehouse). If such goods are to be delivered to the buyer without moving them, the risk of loss passes to the buyer when (1) the buyer receives a negotiable document of title (such as a warehouse receipt or bill of lading) covering the goods, (2) the bailee acknowleges the buyer's right to possession of the goods, or (3) the buyer receives a nonnegotiable document of title or other written direction to deliver *and* has a reasonable time to present the document or direction to the bailee and demand the goods. If the bailee refuses to honor the document or direction, the risk of loss remains on the seller [UCC 2-509(2)].

$\mathscr{R}$ISK OF LOSS: CONDITIONAL SALES

Sellers often entrust possession of goods to buyers on a trial basis. These transactions are classified as sales on approval or sales or returns [UCC 2-326].

Sale on Approval

sale on approval

A type of sale in which there is no actual sale unless and until the buyer accepts the goods.

In a **sale on approval**, there is no sale unless and until the buyer accepts the goods. A sale on approval occurs when a merchant (e.g., a computer store) allows a customer to take the goods (e.g., an Apple computer) home for a specified period of time (e.g., three days) to see if it fits the customer's needs. The prospective buyer may use the goods to try them out during this time.

Acceptance of the goods occurs if the buyer (1) expressly indicates acceptance, (2) fails to notify the seller of rejection of the goods within the agreed-upon trial period (or, if no time is agreed upon, a reasonable time), or (3) uses the goods inconsistently with the purpose of the trial (e.g., the customer resells the computer to another person).

Business Brief

In a *sale on approval* the risk of loss and title remain with the seller.

The goods are not subject to the claims of the buyer's creditors until the buyer accepts them. In a sale on approval, the risk of loss and title to the goods remain with seller. They do not pass to the buyer until acceptance [UCC 2-327(1)].

Sale or Return

sale or return

A contract that says that the seller delivers goods to a buyer with the understanding that the buyer may return them if they are not used or resold within a stated or reasonable period of time.

In a **sale or return** contract, the seller delivers goods to a buyer with the understanding that the buyer may return them if they are not used or resold within a stated period of time (or within a reasonable time if no specific time is stated). The sale is considered final if the buyer fails to return the goods within the specified time or reasonable time if no time is specified. The buyer has the option of returning all the goods or any commercial unit of the goods.

Business Brief

In a *sale or return* the risk of loss and title transfer to the buyer when he or she takes possession of the goods.

Consider This Example Suppose a fashion designer delivers 10 dresses to a fashion boutique on a sale or return basis. The boutique pays $10,000 ($1,000 per dress). If the boutique does not resell the dresses within three months, it may return the unsold garments to the designer. At the end of three months, the boutique has sold four of the dresses. The remaining six dresses may be returned to the designer. The boutique can recover the compensation paid for the returned dresses.

In a sale or return contract, the risk of loss and title to the goods pass to the buyer when the buyer takes possession of the goods. In the previous example, if the dresses were destroyed while they were at the boutique, the boutique-owner would be responsible for paying the designer for them [UCC 2-327(2)]. Goods sold pursuant to a sale or return contract are subject to the claims of the buyer's creditors while the goods are in the buyer's possession.

consignment

An arrangement where a seller (the consignor) delivers goods to a buyer (the consignee) for sale.

Consignment

In a **consignment**, a seller (the **consignor**) delivers goods to a buyer (the **consignee**) to sell. The consignee is paid a fee if he or she sells the goods on behalf of the consignor. A consignment is treated as a sale or return under the UCC. Whether the goods are subject to the claims of the buyer's creditors usually depends on whether the seller filed a financing statement as required by Article 9 of the UCC. If the seller files a financing statement, the goods are subject to the claims of the seller's creditors. If the seller fails to file such a statement, the goods are subject to the claims of the buyer's creditors [UCC 2-326(3)].

In the following case, the court had to assess risk of loss in a conditioned sale situation.

Prewitt v. Numismatic Funding Corp.

745 F.2d 1175 (1984)
United States Court of Appeals, Eighth Circuit

CASE 16.2

BACKGROUND AND FACTS

Numismatic Funding Corporation (Numismatic), with its principal place of business in New York, sells rare and collector coins by mail throughout the United States. Frederick R. Prewitt, a resident of St. Louis, Missouri, responded to Numismatic's advertisement in the *Wall Street Journal.* Prewitt received several shipments of coins from Numismatic via the mails. These shipments were "on approval" for 14 days. Numismatic gave no instructions as to the method for returning unwanted coins. Prewitt kept and paid for several coins and returned the others to Numismatic fully insured via FedEx. On February 10, 1982, Numismatic mailed Prewitt 28 gold and silver coins worth over $60,000 on a 14-day approval. On February 23, 1982, Prewitt returned all the coins via certified mail and insured them for the maximum allowed, $400. Numismatic never received the coins. Prewitt brought this action seeking a declaratory judgment as to his nonliability. Numismatic filed a counterclaim. The trial court awarded Prewitt a declaratory judgment of nonliability. Numismatic appealed.

ISSUE

Who bears the risk of loss, Prewitt or Numismatic?

COURT'S REASONING

The court determined that the delivery of coins between seller Numismatic and buyer Prewitt constituted a sale "on approval." Under the provisions of the UCC relating to risk of loss for sale on approval contracts, the risk of loss remains with the seller.

DECISION

The court of appeals held that the transaction in question was a sale on approval and that under UCC 2-327(1) Numismatic, the owner of the coins, bore the risk of their loss during the return shipment from Prewitt. Affirmed.

Case Questions

Critical Legal Thinking   Do you agree with how the UCC assesses risk of loss in sale on approval transactions?

Business Ethics   Should Prewitt have fully insured the coins before sending them back to Numismatic?

Contemporary Business   How could Numismatic have protected its interests in this case?

$\mathscr{R}$ISK OF LOSS: BREACH OF SALES CONTRACT

The risk of loss rules just discussed apply where there is no breach of contract. Separate risk of loss rules apply to situations involving breach of the sales contract [UCC 2-510].

Seller in Breach

A seller breaches a sales contract if he or she tenders or delivers nonconforming goods to the buyer. If the goods are so nonconforming that the buyer has the right to reject them, the risk of loss remains on the seller until (1) the defect or nonconformity is cured or (2) the buyer accepts the nonconforming goods.

Consider This Example   A buyer orders 1,000 talking dolls from a seller. The contract is a shipment contract, which normally places the risk of loss during transportation on the buyer. The seller ships nonconforming dolls that cannot talk. The goods are destroyed in transit. The seller bears the risk of loss because he breached the contract by shipping nonconforming goods.

Buyer in Breach

Buyers breach a sales contract if they (1) refuse to take delivery of conforming goods, (2) repudiate the contract, or (3) otherwise breach the contract. A buyer who breaches a sales contract before the risk of loss would normally pass to him or her bears the risk of loss to any goods identified to the contract. The risk of loss only rests on the buyer for a commercially reasonable time. The buyer is only liable for any loss in excess of insurance recovered by the seller.

Laws are not masters but servants, and he rules them who obeys them.

Henry Ward Beecher
Proverbs from Plymouth Pulpit
(1887)

RISK OF LOSS IN LEASE CONTRACTS

The parties to a lease contract may agree as to who will bear the risk of loss of the goods if they are lost or destroyed. If the parties do not so agree, the UCC supplies the following risk of loss rules:

1. In the case of an ordinary lease, the risk of loss is retained by the lessor. If the lease is a finance lease, the risk of loss passes to the lessee [UCC 2A-219].
2. If a tender of delivery of goods fails to conform to the lease contract, the risk of loss remains with the lessor or supplier until cure or acceptance [UCC 2A-220(1)(a)].

Entrepreneur and the Law

INSURING AGAINST LOSS

To protect against financial loss that would occur if goods are damaged, destroyed, lost, or stolen, the parties to sales and lease contracts should purchase insurance against such loss. If the goods are then lost or damaged, the insured party receives reimbursement from the insurance company for the loss.

To purchase insurance, a party must have an *insurable interest* in the goods. A seller has an insurable interest in goods as long as he or she retains title or has a security interest in the goods. A lessor retains an insurable interest in the goods during the term of the lease. A buyer or lessee obtains an insurable interest in the goods when they are identified to the sales or lease contract. Both the buyer and seller, or lessee and lessor, can have an insurable interest in the goods at the same time [UCC 2-501 and 2A-218].

To obtain and maintain proper insurance coverage on goods, a contacting party should

- Determine the value of goods subject to the sales or lease contract.
- Purchase insurance from a reputable insurance company covering the goods subject to the contract.
- Maintain the insurance by paying the premiums when they are due.
- Immediately file the proper claim and supporting documentation with an insurance company if the goods are damaged, destroyed, lost, or stolen.

SALES BY NONOWNERS

void title

A thief acquires no title to the goods he or she steals.

voidable title

Title that a purchase has if the goods were obtained by (1) fraud, (2) a check that is later dishonored, or (3) impersonating another person.

good faith purchaser for value

A person to whom good title can be transferred from a person with voidable title. The real owner cannot reclaim goods from a good faith purchaser for value.

good faith subsequent lessee

A person to whom a lease interest can be transferred from a person with voidable title. The real owner cannot reclaim the goods from the subsequent lessee until the lease expires.

Sometimes, people sell goods even though they do not hold valid title to them. The UCC anticipated many of the problems this situation could cause and established rules concerning the title, if any, that could be transferred to the purchasers.

Void Title and Lease: Stolen Goods

In a case where a buyer purchases goods or a lessee leases goods from a thief who has stolen them, the purchaser does not acquire title to the goods and the lessee does not acquire any leasehold interest in the goods. The real owner can reclaim the goods from the purchaser or lessee [UCC 2-403(1)]. This is called **void title**.

Consider This Example Suppose someone steals a truckload of Sony television sets that are owned by Sears. The thief resells the televisions to City-Mart, which does not know that the goods were stolen. If Sears finds out where the televisions are, it can reclaim them. Since the thief had no title in the goods, title was not transferred to City-Mart. City-Mart's only recourse is against the thief, if he or she can be found.

Voidable Title: Sales or Lease of Goods to Good Faith Purchasers for Value

A seller or lessor has **voidable title** to goods if the goods were obtained by fraud, a check that is later dishonored, or impersonating another person. A person with voidable title to goods can transfer good title to a **good faith purchaser for value** or a **good faith subsequent lessee**. A good faith purchaser or lessee for value is someone who pays sufficient consideration or rent for the goods to the person he or she honestly believes has good title to those goods [UCC 2-201(1), 1-201(44)(d)]. The real owner cannot reclaim goods from such a purchaser [UCC 2-403(1)].

Consider This Example Suppose a person buys a Rolex watch from his neighbor for near fair market value. It is later discovered that the seller obtained the watch from a jewelry store with a "bounced check." The jewelry store cannot reclaim the watch because the second purchaser purchased the watch in good faith and for value.

Assume instead that the purchaser bought the watch from a stranger for far less than fair market value. It is later discovered that the seller obtained the watch from a jewelry store by fraud. The jewelry store can reclaim the watch because the second purchaser was not a good faith purchaser for value.

Entrustment Rule

The rule found in UCC 2-403(2) holds that if an owner **entrusts** the possession of his or her goods to a merchant who deals in goods of that kind, the merchant has the power to transfer all rights (including title) in the goods to a **buyer in the ordinary course of business**. The real owner cannot reclaim the goods from this buyer.

Consider This Example Kim Jones brings her computer into the Computer Store to be repaired. The Computer Store both sells and services computers. Jones leaves (entrusts) her computer at the store until it is repaired. The Computer Store sells her computer to Harold Green. Green, a buyer in the ordinary course of business, acquires title to the computer. Jones cannot reclaim the computer from Green. Her only recourse is against the Computer Store.

The entrustment rule also applies to leases. If a lessor entrusts the possession of his or her goods to a lessee who is a merchant who deals in goods of that kind, the merchant-lessee has the power to transfer all the lessor's and lessee's rights in the goods to a buyer or sublessee in the ordinary course of business [UCC 2A-305(2)].

> **buyer in the ordinary course of business**
>
> A person who in good faith and without knowledge that the sale violates the ownership or security interests of a third party buys the goods in the ordinary course of business from a person in the business of selling goods of that kind. A buyer in the ordinary course of business takes the goods free of any third-party security interest in the goods.

Business Ethics

CORN FARMERS GET SHUCKED

The entrustment rule is raised in the following case. Robert, David, and Hazel Schluter (Schluters) are grain farmers in Starbuck, Minnesota. They often hired a specific trucker to haul their grain to the public grain elevator, United Farmers Elevator, to whom they would sell their grain. On some occasions, the Schluters would sell their grain to the trucker, who would then resell the grain to the elevator or others. In the case at hand, the Schluters hired the trucker to haul their corn to the elevator. When the trucker got to the elevator, he represented that he owned the corn and sold it to the elevator for $288,000. The trucker absconded with the money.

The Schluters sued the elevator to recover payment for their corn. Who owns the corn, the Schluters or the elevator? The trial court applied the entrustment rule and held that the elevator had title to the corn as a buyer in the ordinary course of business. The appellate court stated:

> *It is undisputed the trucker had for several years bought and sold grain in the farmers' area, and the elevator had done business with the trucker not only as a hauler of grain*

belonging to others but also as a seller of grain belonging to himself. Thus, he was known in the area as a buyer and seller. This combination of the trucker's own conduct over time and his reputation in the area are sufficient to qualify him as a merchant of grain under the UCC, since he dealt in goods of the kind or otherwise held himself out as having knowledge or skill as a grain buyer and seller.

Under these facts, the trucker was a "merchant" and the farmers entrusted their grain to him. The undisputed facts show the farmers entrusted their grain to an independent trucker who was also a merchant, thereby empowering him to transfer ownership to the elevator as a buyer in the ordinary course of business. Under the UCC entrustment rule the elevator owned the corn. [*Schluter v. United Farmers Elevator*, 479 N.W.2d 82 (Minn.App. 1992)].

1. Did the trucker act ethically in this case?
2. Do you think the UCC entrustment rule places loss on the right party? Explain.

CONCEPT SUMMARY PASSAGE OF TITLE IN SALES BY NONOWNER THIRD PARTIES AND SALES OF GOODS SUBJECT TO SECURITY AGREEMENTS

Type of Transaction	Title Possessed by Seller	Innocent Purchaser	Purchaser Acquires Title to Goods
Goods acquired by theft are resold.	Void title.	Good faith purchaser for value.	No. Original owner may reclaim the goods.
Goods acquired by fraud or dishonored check are resold.	Voidable title.	Good faith purchaser for value.	Yes. Purchaser takes free of claim of original owner.
Goods entrusted by owner to merchant who deals in that type of good are resold.	No title.	Buyer in ordinary course of business.	Yes. Purchaser takes free of claim of original owner.
Creditor possesses security interest in goods that are sold.	Good title.	Buyer in ordinary course of business.	Yes. Purchaser takes free of creditor's security interest.

Contemporary Business Environment

BULK SALES LAW DUMPED

Article 6 (Bulk Sales) of the UCC establishes rules that were designed to prevent fraud when there is a bulk transfer of goods. A **bulk transfer** occurs when an owner transfers a major part of a business's material, merchandise, inventory, or equipment not in the ordinary course of business. This usually occurs upon the sale of the assets of a business.

If there is a bulk transfer of assets, Article 6 requires that (1) the seller furnish the buyer with a list of all of the creditors of the business, and (2) the buyer notify all of the listed creditors at least 10 days before taking possession of or paying for the goods, whichever occurs first. The buyer is not responsible for or liable to unlisted creditors [UCC 6-105].

If all of the requirements of Article 6 are met, the buyer receives title to the goods free of all claims of the seller's creditors. If the requirements of Article 6 are not met, the goods in the buyer's possession are subject to the claims of the seller's creditors for six months after the date of the possession [UCC 6-111].

In 1988, after much review, the National Conference of Commissioners on Uniform State Laws (NCCUSL) and the American Law Institute (ALI) reported that the regulation of bulk sales was no longer necessary. Consequently, they withdrew their support for Article 6 and encouraged states that had enacted the Article to repeal it.

The report criticized the bulk transfer law for adding costs—without corresponding benefits—to business transactions. The report claimed that it was unfair to impose liability on an innocent buyer because a dishonest seller failed to pay its creditors. The committee then stated that changing laws and economics, as well as improved communications, made it more difficult for merchants to sell their merchandise and abscond with the proceeds. Further, the report noted that modern jurisdiction laws make it easier to obtain and enforce judgments against debtors who have left the state.

Recognizing that some state legislatures may wish to continue to regulate bulk transfers, the committee also promulgated a revised version of Article 6.

CHAPTER SUMMARY

Scope of Article 2 (Sales), p. 381

Article 2 (Sales)	Article of the UCC that applies to transactions in goods [UCC 2-102]. 1. *Goods.* Tangible things that are movable at the time of their identification to the sales contract [UCC 2-105(1)]. 2. *Scope of Article 2.* Article 2 applies to all sale contracts, whether they involve merchants or not.

Scope of Article 2A (Leases), p. 383

Article 2A, Leases	Article of the UCC that applies to personal property leases of goods [UCC 2A-101].
	1. *Lease.* A transfer of the right to the possession and use of the named goods for a set term in return for certain consideration.
	2. *Parties to a lease*:
	   a. *Lessor.* Person who transfers the right of possession and use of goods [UCC 2A-103(1)(p)].
	   b. *Lessee.* Person who acquires the right to possession and use of the goods [UCC 2A-103(1)(n)].
	3. *Finance lease.* A three-party transaction of the lessor, the lessee, and the supplier of the leased goods. The parties to a finance lease are:
	   a. *Lessor.* Acquires title to the goods from the supplier and leases the goods to the lessee. The lessor is often a bank or other creditor.
	   b. *Lessee.* Person who acquires the right to possession and use of the goods.
	   c. *Supplier.* Third party who supplies the goods. The supplier usually sells the goods to the lessor.

Formation of Sales and Lease Contracts, p. 384

Offer	*Open terms.* If the parties leave open a major term in the sales or lease contract, the UCC permits the following terms to be read into the contract: 1. Price term 4. Time term 2. Payment term 5. Assortment term 3. Delivery term These are commonly called *gap-filling rules* [UCC 2-204(3), 2A-204(3)].
Firm Offer Rule	A UCC rule that says that a merchant who (1) makes an offer to buy, sell, or lease goods and (2) assures the other party in a separate writing that the offer will be held open cannot revoke the offer for the time stated, or if no time is stated, for a reasonable time [UCC 2-205, 2A-205].
Acceptance	*Accommodation shipment.* A shipment that is offered to the buyer by the seller as a replacement for the original shipment when the original shipment cannot be filled. The buyer may either accept or reject this shipment [UCC 2-206(1)(b)].
Additional Terms Permitted	The UCC permits an acceptance of a sales contract to contain additional terms and still to act as an acceptance rather than a counteroffer in certain circumstances. The following UCC rules apply [UCC 2-207(2)]: 1. *One or both parties are nonmerchants.* The additional terms are considered proposed additions to the contract. If the offeree's proposed terms are accepted by the offeror, they become part of the contract. If they are not accepted, the sales contract is formed on the basis of the terms of the original offer. 2. *Both parties are merchants.* The additional terms contained in the acceptance become part of the sales contract *unless* (1) the offer expressly limits the acceptance to the terms of the offer, (2) the additional terms materially alter the original contract, or (3) the offerer notifies the offeree that he or she objects to the additional terms within a reasonable time after receiving the offeree's modified acceptance. There is no contract if the additional terms so materially alter the terms of the original offer that the parties cannot agree on the contract.
Statute of Frauds	The UCC Statute of Frauds requires contracts for the sale of goods costing $500 or more and lease contracts involving payments of $1,000 or more to be in writing [UCC 2-201(1), 2A-201(1)]. *Exceptions to the Statute of Frauds.* The UCC recognizes the following exceptions to the Statute of Frauds where a sales or lease contract that is required to be in writing is enforceable even though it is not in writing: 1. *Specially manufactured goods.* Contracts where the goods are not suitable for sale or lease to others in the ordinary course of business and the seller or lessor has made either a substantial beginning of manufacture of the goods or commitments for their procurement. 2. *Admissions in pleadings or court.* A party admits in pleadings, testimony, or otherwise in court that he or she has entered into a contract. 3. *Part acceptance.* An oral sales or lease contract is enforceable to the extent to which the goods have been received and accepted by the buyer or lessee.
Written Confirmation Rule	If both parties to an oral sales or lease contract are merchants, the Statute of Frauds requirements are satisfied if (1) one of the parties sends a *written confirmation* of the sale to the other within a reasonable time after contracting and (2) the other merchant does not give written notice of an objection to the contract within 10 days after receiving the confirmation [UCC 2-201(2)].

Identification and Passage of Title, p. 390

Identification	Distinguishes the goods named in the contract from the seller's or lessor's other goods [UCC 2-501(1)].
Passage of Title	1. *Passage of title by agreement.* Title to goods of a sales contract passes from the seller to the buyer in any manner and on any conditions explicitly agreed upon by the parties.

2. *Passage of title where there is no agreement.* If the parties have no agreement as to the passage of title, title passes according to the following UCC rules [UCC 2-401(2)]:
   a. *Shipment contract.* Requires the seller to ship the goods to the buyer via a common carrier. Title passes to the buyer at the time and place of shipment.
   b. *Destination contract.* Requires the seller to deliver the goods to the buyer's place of business or other designated destination. Title passes to the buyer when the seller tenders delivery of the goods at the specified destination.
   c. *Goods that do not move.* If a sales contract authorizes the goods to be delivered without requiring the seller to move them, title passes at the time and place of contracting unless a document of title is required, in which case title passes when the seller delivers the document of title to the buyer.
3. *Passage of title in lease contracts.* Title to the leased goods remains with the lessor or a third party. Title does not pass to the lessee.

Article 6 (Bulk Sales)

1. *Bulk Sales.* Occur when an owner/debtor transfers a major part of a business's material, merchandise, inventory, or equipment not in the ordinary course of business.
2. *Article 6 (Bulk Sales).* Establishes rules that require the buyer to notify the creditors of the seller of the proposed sale of assets. If such notice is given, the buyer receives title to the goods free of all claims of the seller's creditors. If the notice is not given, the goods in the buyer's possession are subject to the claims of the seller's creditors for six months after the date of possession.
3. *Amendment.* In 1988, the National Conference of Commissioners on Uniform State Laws (NCCUSL) and the American Law Institute (ALI) recommended that states repeal Article 6. As an alternative, the NCCUSL issued a revised version of Article 6.

Risk of Loss: No Breach of Sales Contract, p. 392

Risk of Loss: No Breach of Sales Contract

1. *Agreement.* The parties to a sales contract may agree among themselves as to who will bear the risk of loss of goods if they are lost or destroyed.
2. *No agreement.* If the parties do not have a specific agreement concerning the assessment of risk of loss, the UCC mandates who will bear the risk [UCC 2-509].

Carrier Cases: Movement of Goods

1. *Shipment contract.* The risk of loss passes to the buyer when the seller delivers conforming goods to a carrier. The buyer bears the risk of loss during transportation.
2. *Destination contract.* The risk of loss does not pass to the buyer until the goods are tendered to the buyer at the designated destination. The seller bears the risk of loss during transportation.

Noncarrier Cases: No Movement of Goods

If the buyer is to pick the goods up from the seller's place of business or other specified location, the following UCC rules apply:
1. *Merchant-seller.* If the seller is a merchant, the risk of loss does not pass to the buyer until the goods are received by the buyer. The merchant-seller bears the risk of loss between the time of contracting and the time the buyer picks up the goods.
2. *Nonmerchant-seller.* If the seller is a nonmerchant, risk of loss passes to the buyer upon tender of delivery of the goods by the seller. (i.e., the seller holds the goods available for the buyer to take delivery).

Risk of Loss: Conditional Sales, p. 394

Conditional Sales

The entrustment of goods by a seller to a buyer on a trial basis. The following UCC rules for risk of loss apply [UCC 2-327]:
1. *Sale on approval.* Occurs when a merchant allows a customer to take the goods for a specified period of time to try the goods. There is no sale unless and until the buyer accepts the goods. The risk of loss remains with the seller and does not transfer to the buyer until acceptance.
2. *Sale or return.* Occurs when a seller delivers goods to a buyer with the understanding that the buyer may return them if they are not used or resold during a stated period of time. The risk of loss passes to the buyer when the buyer takes possession of the goods.
3. *Consignment.* Occurs when a seller (*consignor*) delivers goods to a buyer (*consignee*) to sell. The risk of loss passes to the consignee when the consignee takes possession of the goods.

Risk of Loss: Breach of Sales Contract, p. 395

Risk of Loss: Breach of Sales Contract

If there has been a *breach of the sales contract*, the UCC rules concerning risk of loss apply [UCC 2-510].

Seller in Breach	If a seller breaches the sales contract by tendering or delivering nonconforming goods, the risk of loss to the goods remains with the seller until (1) the defect or nonconformity is cured or (2) the buyer accepts the non-conforming goods.
Buyer in Breach	If a buyer breaches a sales contract by refusing to take delivery of conforming goods or repudiating the contract before the risk of loss would normally transfer to him or her, the buyer bears the risk of loss to any goods identified to the contract for a reasonably commercial time.

Risk of Loss in Lease Contracts, p. 396

Risk of Loss in Lease Contracts	1. *Agreement.* The parties to a lease contract may agree as to who will bear the risk of loss to the goods if they are not lost or destroyed.
	2. *No agreement.* If the parties do not have an agreement concerning the assessment of risk of loss, the following UCC rules for risk of loss apply [UCC 2A-219, 2A-220]:
	  a. *Ordinary lease.* The risk of loss is retained by the lessor.
	  b. *Finance lease.* The risk of loss passes to the lessee.
	  c. *Breach of contract.* If a tender of delivery of goods fails to conform to the lease contract, the risk of loss remains with the lessor or supplier until acceptance or cure.

Sales by Nonowners, p. 396

Sales by Nonowners	If a person sells the goods that he or she does not hold valid title to, the buyer acquires rights in the certain goods under the UCC [UCC 2-403].
Void Title and Lease: Stolen Goods	A thief acquires no title to goods he or she steals. A person who purchases stolen goods does not acquire title to the goods. Any such title is call *void title*. The real owner can reclaim the goods from the purchaser. The purchaser's recourse is to recover from the thief.
Voidable Title: Sale or Lease of Goods to Good Faith Purchasers for Value	If goods are obtained by fraud, by a check that is later dishonored, or by impersonating another person, the perpetrator acquires *voidable title* to the goods. If the perpetrator sells or leases the goods to a *good faith purchaser* or *lessee for value*—a person who pays sufficient consideration or rent for the goods and honestly believes that the seller or lessor has good title to the goods—the buyer or lessee acquires good title to the goods. The real owner's recourse is against the perpetrator who acquired the goods from him or her.
Entrustment Rule	If an owner entrusts possession of his or her goods to a merchant who deals in goods of that kind (e.g., for repair) and the merchant sells those goods to a *buyer in the ordinary course of business* (e.g., a customer of the merchant), the buyer acquires title to the goods. The real owner's recourse is against the merchant who sold his or her goods. This rule is called the *entrustment rule*.

End-of-Chapter Internet Exercises and Case Questions

 ## *Working the Web Internet Exercises*

ACTIVITIES

1. Find the major differences in the rules of contract formation under the common law and the UCC Article 2. Visit the Legal Information Institute (LII) Sales Law Overview at **www.law.cornell.edu/topics/sales.html**.

2. Do the rules change when the parties are both merchants?

3. Can you find the UCC Article 2 version of the Statute of Frauds? **www.law.cornell.edu/ucc/2/overview.html**. See also **www.law.sc.edu/sclr/vol49-4-robertson.pdf** for a law review article, "Electronic Commerce on the Internet and the Statute of Frauds" by R. J. Robertson Jr.

4. Although a contract can be created under UCC Article 2 even when several terms are omitted, there is generally one term that must be included in order for the contract to be deemed valid by a court. Which term is it?

CRITICAL LEGAL THINKING CASES

16.1 Good or Service Gulash lived in Shelton, Connecticut. He wanted an above-ground swimming pool installed in his backyard. Gulash contacted Stylarama, Inc. (Stylarama), a company specializing in the sale and construction of pools. The two parties entered into a contract that called for Stylarama to "furnish all labor and materials to construct a wavecrest brand pool, and furnish and install pool with vinyl liners." The total cost for materials and labor was $3,690. There was no breakdown of costs between labor and materials. After the pool was installed, its sides began bowing out, the two-inch-by-four-inch wooden supports for the pool rotted and misaligned, and the entire pool became tilted. Gulash brought suit alleging that Stylarama had violated several provisions of Article 2 of the UCC. Was this transaction one involving "goods," making it subject to Article 2? [*Gulash v. Stylarama*, 364 A.2d 1221 (CT 1975)]

16.2 Open Terms Alvin Cagle was a potato farmer in Alabama who had had several business dealings with the H. C. Schmieding Produce Co. (Schmieding). Several months before harvest, Cagle entered into an oral sales contract with Schmieding. The contract called for Schmieding to pay the market price at harvest time for all the red potatoes that Cagle grew on his 30-acre farm. Schmieding asked that the potatoes be delivered during normal harvest months. As Cagle began harvesting his red potatoes, he contacted Schmieding to arrange delivery. Schmieding told the farmer that no contract had been formed because the terms of the agreement were too indefinite. Cagle demanded that Schmieding buy his crop. When Schmieding refused, Cagle sued to have the contract enforced. Has a valid sales contract been formed? [*H. C. Schmieding Produce Company v. Cagle*, 529 So.2d 243 (AL 1988)]

16.3 Statute of Frauds Cameron Lawrence lived in Marina Del Rey, California. Lawrence's next-door neighbor, Carey Heyward, owned a 35-foot sailboat. Since Heyward spent most of his time visiting in South America, he seldom used the boat. During one of his rare stays in California, Lawrence asked Heyward about the possibility of buying his sailboat. Heyward did not want to sell but said he would lease the vessel for five years. Lawrence agreed to pay Heyward $2,000 every six months to lease the boat. No written contract was ever signed, and the parties sealed their agreement with a handshake. Lawrence took possession of the boat on June 1 and sailed on it throughout the summer. On August 30, Lawrence decided he did not want the boat anymore and refused to make the required payments. Heyward sued Lawrence. Lawrence claims the lease is unenforceable because it violates the Statute of Frauds. Who wins?

16.4 Firm Offer Gordon Construction Company (Gordon) was a general contractor in the New York area. Gordon planned on bidding for the job of constructing two buildings for the Port Authority of New York. In anticipation of its own bid, Gordon sought bids from subcontractors. On April 22, 1963, E. A. Coronis Associates (Coronis), a fabricator of structured steel, sent a signed letter to Gordon. The letter quoted a price for work on the Port Authority project and stated that the price could change, based on the amount of steel used. The letter contained no information other than the price Coronis would charge for the job. On May 27, Gordon was awarded the Port Authority project. On June 1, Coronis sent Gordon a telegram withdrawing its offer. Gordon replied that it expected Coronis to honor the price quoted in its April 22 letter. When Coronis refused, Gordon sued. Gordon claimed that Coronis was attempting to withdraw a firm offer. Who wins? [*E. A. Coronis Associates v. M. Gordon Construction Co.*, 216 A.2d 246 (N.J.Super, 1966)]

16.5 Battle of the Forms Dan Miller was a commercial photographer who had taken a series of photographs that appeared in the *New York Times*. *Newsweek* magazine wanted to use the photographs. When a *Newsweek* employee named Dwyer phoned Miller, he was told that 72 pages were available. Dwyer said that he wanted to inspect the photographs and offered a certain sum of money for each photo *Newsweek* used. The photos were to remain Miller's property. Miller and Dwyer agreed to the price and the date for delivery. *Newsweek* sent a courier to pick up the photographs. Along with the photos, Miller gave the courier a "Delivery Memo" that set out various conditions for the use of the photographs. The memo included a clause that required *Newsweek* to pay $1,500 each if any of the photos were lost or destroyed. After *Newsweek* received the package, it decided it no longer needed Miller's work. When Miller called to have the photos returned, he was told that they all had been lost. Miller demands that *Newsweek* pay him $1,500 for each of the 72 lost photos. Assuming that the court finds Miller and *Newsweek* to be merchants, were the clauses in the delivery memo part of the sales contract? [*Miller v. Newsweek, Inc.*, 660 F.Supp. 852 (D.Del. 1987)]

16.6 Identification of Goods The Big Knob Volunteer Fire Company (Fire Company) agreed to purchase a fire truck from Hamerly Custom Productions (Hamerly). Hamerly was in the business of assembling various component parts into fire trucks. Fire Company paid Hamerly $10,000 toward the price two days after signing the contract. Two weeks later, it gave Hamerly $38,000 more toward the total purchase price of $53,000. Hamerly bought an engine chassis for the new fire truck on credit from Lowe and Meyer Company. After installing the chassis, Hamerly painted the Big Knob Fire Department's name on the side of the cab. Hamerly never paid for the engine chassis, and the truck was repossessed by Lowe and Meyer. Fire Company seeks to recover the fire truck from Lowe and Meyer. Although Fire Company was the buyer of a fire truck, Louis and Meyer question whether any goods had ever been identified to the contract. Were they? [*Big Knob Volunteer Fire Co. v. Lowe and Meyer Garage*, 487 A.2d 953 (Pa.Super. 1985)]

16.7 Risk of Loss In June 1973, All America Export-Import Corporation (All America) placed an order for several thousand pounds of yarn with A. M. Knitwear Corporation (Knitwear). On June 4, All America sent Knitwear a purchase order. The purchase order stated the terms of the sale, including language that stated that the price was F.O.B. the seller's plant. On Friday, June 22, 1973, a truck hired by All America arrived at Knitwear's plant. On Monday, June 24, Knitwear turned the yarn over to the carrier and notified All America that the goods were now on the truck. The truck left Knitwear's plant and proceeded to a local warehouse. Sometime during the night of June 24, the truck was hijacked and all the yarn was stolen. All America had paid for the yarn by check but stopped payment on it when it learned that the goods had been stolen. Knitwear sued All America, claiming that it must pay for the stolen goods because it bore the risk of loss. Who wins? [*A. M. Knitwear v. All America, Inc.*, 390 N.Y.S.2d 832, 41 N.Y.2d 14 (N.Y.App. 1976)]

16.8 Risk of Loss Mitsubishi International Corporation (Mitsubishi) entered into a contract with the Crown Door Company (Crown). The contract called for Mitsubishi to sell 12 boxcar loads of plywood to Crown. According to the terms of the contract, Mitsubishi would import the wood from Taiwan and deliver it to Crown's plant in Atlanta. Mitsubishi had the wood shipped from Taiwan to Savannah, Georgia. At Savannah, the plywood was loaded onto trains and hauled to Atlanta. When the plywood arrived in Atlanta, it was discovered that the railroad had been negligent in loading the train. The negligent loading had caused the cargo to shift during the trip, and the shifting had caused extensive damage to the wood. Who bore the risk of loss? [*Georgia Ports Authority v. Mitsubishi International Corporation*, 274 S.E.2d 699 (Ga.App. 1980)]

16.9 Risk of Loss In 1982, Martin Silver ordered two rooms of furniture from Wycombe, Meyer & Company Inc. (Wycombe), a manufacturer and seller of custom-made furniture. On February 23, 1982, Wycombe sent invoices to Silver advising him that the furniture was ready for shipment. Silver tendered payment in full for the goods and asked that one room of furniture be shipped immediately and that the other be held for shipment on a later date. Before any instructions were received as to the second room of furniture, it was destroyed in a fire. Silver and his insurance company attempt to recover the money he paid for the destroyed furniture. Wycombe refuses to return the payment, claiming that the risk of loss was upon Silver. Who wins? [*Silver v. Wycombe, Meyer & Co., Inc.*, 477 N.Y.S.2d 288 (N.Y.City Civ.Ct. 1984)]

16.10 Risk of Loss Cal-Ag Corporation (Cal-Ag) needed to lease a new box-sealing machine for its raisin packaging plant. Cal-Ag contacted Uni-Box Company and agreed to lease a Model 3000 Box Sealer from Uni-Box for 10 years. The parties signed a written lease agreement. The box sealer was supposed to be shipped within two weeks. The night before the machine was to be shipped, Uni-Box's employees selected a Model 3000, packaged it for shipping, and placed Cal-Ag's address on the carton. At 4 A.M. fire destroyed the box sealer. Which party bears the risk of loss?

16.11 Stolen Goods John Torniero was employed by Michaels Jewelers, Inc. (Michaels). During the course of his employment, Torniero stole pieces of jewelry, including several diamond rings, a sapphire ring, a gold pendant, and several loose diamonds. Over a period of several months, Torniero sold indi-

vidual pieces of the stolen jewelry to G&W Watch and Jewelry Corporation (G&W). G&W had no knowledge of how Torniero obtained the jewels. Torniero was arrested when Michaels discovered the thefts. After Torniero admitted that he had sold the stolen jewelry to G&W, Michaels attempted to recover it from G&W. G&W claims title to the jewelry as a good faith purchaser for value. Michaels has challenged G&W's claim to title in court. Who wins? [*United States v. Michaels Jewelers, Inc.*, 42 UCCRep.Serv. 141 (D.C.Conn 1985)]

16.12 Passage of Title J. A. Coghill owned a 1979 Rolls Royce Corniche, which he sold to a man claiming to be Daniel Bellman in 1984. Bellman gave Coghill a cashier's check for $94,500. When Coghill tried to cash the check, his bank informed him that the check had been forged. Coghill reported the vehicle as stolen. Early in September 1984, Barry Hyken responded to a newspaper ad listing a 1980 Rolls Royce Corniche for sale. Hyken went to meet the seller of the car, the man who claimed to be Bellman, in a parking lot. When Hyken asked why the car was advertised as a 1980 model when it was in fact a 1979, Bellman replied that it was a newspaper mistake. Hyken agreed to pay $62,000 for the car. When Hyken asked to see Bellman's identification, Bellman provided documents with two different addresses. Bellman explained that he was in the process of moving. Although there seemed to be some irregularities in the title documents to the car, Hyken took possession anyway. Three weeks later, the Rolls was seized by the police. Hyken sued to get it back. Who wins? [*Landshire Food Service, Inc. v. Coghill*, 709 S.W.2d 509 (Mo.App. 1986)]

16.13 Passage of Title On July 19, 1985, Cherry Creek Dodge (Cherry Creek) sold a 1985 Dodge Ramcharger to Executive Leasing of Colorado (Executive Leasing). Executive Leasing, which was in the business of buying and selling cars, paid for the Dodge with a draft. Cherry Creek maintained a security interest in the car until the draft cleared. The same day that Executive Leasing bought the Dodge, it sold the car to Bruce and Peggy Carter. The Carters paid in full for the Dodge with a cashier's check, and the vehicle was delivered to them. The Carters had no knowledge of the financial arrangement between Executive Leasing and Cherry Creek. The draft that Executive Leasing gave Cherry Creek was worthless. Cherry creek attempts to recover the vehicle from the Carters. Who wins? [*Cherry Creek Dodge, Inc. v. Carter*, 733 P.2d 1024 (WY 1987)]

16.14 Insurable Interest On February 7, 1967, Donald Hayward signed a sales contract with Dry Land Marina, Inc. (Dry Land). The contract was for the purchase of a 30-foot Revel Craft Playmate Yacht for $10,000. The contract called for Dry Land to install a number of options on Hayward's yacht and then deliver it to him in April 1967. On March 1, 1967, before taking delivery of the yacht, Hayward signed a security agreement in favor of Dry Land and a promissory note. Several weeks later, a fire swept through Dry Land's showroom. Hayward's yacht was among the goods destroyed in the fire. Who had an insurable interest in the yacht? [*Hayward v. Potsma*, 188 N.W.2d 31 (Mich.App. 1971)]

BUSINESS ETHICS CASES

16.15 Business Ethics Kurt Perschke is a grain dealer in Indiana. In September 1972, he phoned Ken Sebasty, the owner of a large wheat farm, and offered to buy 14,000 bushels of wheat for $1.95 a bushel. Sebasty accepted the offer. Perschke said that he could send a truck for the wheat in March 1973. On the day of the phone call, Perschke's office manager sent a memorandum to Sebasty, stating the price and quantity of wheat that had been contracted for. In February 1973, Perschke called Sebasty to arrange for the loading of the wheat. Sebasty stated that no contract had been made. When Perschke brought suit, Sebasty claimed that the contract was unenforceable because of the Statute of Frauds. Was it ethical for Perschke to raise the Statute of Frauds as a defense? Assuming that both parties are merchants, who wins the suit? [*Sebasty v. Perschke*, 404 N.E.2d 1200 (Ind. App. 1980)]

16.16 Business Ethics In the summer and fall of 1982, Executive Financial Services, Inc. (EFS), purchased three tractors from Tri-County Farm Company (Tri-County), a John Deere dealership owned by Gene Mohr and James Loyd. The tractors cost $48,000, $19,000, and $38,000, respectively. EFS did not take possession of the tractors, but instead left the tractors on Tri-County's lot. EFS leased the tractors to Mohr-Loyd Leasing (Mohr-Loyd), a partnership between Mohr and Loyd, with the understanding and representation by Mohr-Loyd that the tractors would be leased out to farmers. Instead of leasing the tractors, Tri-County sold them to three different farmers. EFS sued and obtained judgment against Tri-County, Mohr-Loyd, and Mohr and Loyd personally for breach of contract. Because that judgment remained unsatisfied, EFS sued the three

farmers who bought the tractors to recover the tractors from them. Did Mohr and Loyd act ethically in this case? Who owns the tractors, EFS or the farmers? [*Executive Financial Services, Inc. v. Pagel*, 715 P.2d 381 (KS 1986)]

16.17 Business Ethics On March 11, 1985, Dugdale of Nebraska, Inc. (Dugdale), purchased a 1985 Ford LTD Crown Victoria automobile from Vannier Ford, an automobile dealership. Dugdale traded in a 1984 vehicle and paid cash for the remaining purchase price of the car. On the day that the vehicle was delivered, the president of Vannier Ford told the representative of Dugdale that the title papers to the vehicles had not yet been received but that they would be given to him as soon as they were received.

Approximately five days before selling the vehicle to Dugdale, Vannier Ford had pledged it as security for a loan from First State Bank, Gothenberg, Nebraska (First State Bank) and had delivered the certificate of title to the bank. This fact was unknown to Dugdale. Vannier Ford did not transmit the proceeds of the sale to First State Bank. After the sale Dugdale made numerous inquiries regarding the title papers and each time was told by Vannier Ford that the papers had not yet arrived. Approximately two months later, after Vannier Ford had defaulted on the loan, First State Bank contacted Dugdale and made demand for possession of the vehicle. Dugdale brought suit seeking a declaratory judgment as to its ownership rights. First State Bank filed a counterclaim. Did Vannier Ford act ethically in this case? Who owns the title to the vehicle, Dugdale or First State Bank? [*Dugdale of Nebraska, Inc. v. First State Bank, Gothenberg, Nebraska*, 420 N.W.2d 273 (NE 1988)]

BRIEFING THE CASE WRITING ASSIGNMENT

Read the following case, which has been excerpted from the court's opinion. Review and brief the case.

Burnett v. Purtell
1992 Ohio App. Lexis 3467 (1992)
Court of Appeals of Ohio

Ford, Presiding Judge

Appellees agreed to purchase a mobile home with shed from appellant. On Saturday, March 3, 1990, appellees paid appellant $6,500 and in return were given the certificate of title to the mobile home as well as a key to the mobile home, but no keys to the shed. At the same time the certificate of title was transferred, the following items remained in the mobile home: The washer and dryer, mattress and box springs, two chairs, items in the refrigerator, and the entire contents of the shed. These items were to be retained by appellant and removed by appellant. To facilitate removal, the estate retained one key to the mobile home and the only keys to the shed.

On Sunday, March 4, 1990, the mobile home was destroyed by fire through the fault of neither party. At the time of the fire, appellant still had a

key to the mobile home as well as the keys to the shed and she had not removed the contents of the mobile home nor the shed. The contents of the shed were not destroyed and have now been removed by appellant. The referee determined that the risk of loss remained with appellant because there was no tender of delivery. Appellant objected to the conclusion of law, but the trial court overruled the objection and entered judgment in favor of appellee.

First, the appellant argues that because the certificate of title was transferred, appellees were given a key to the mobile home and the full purchase price was paid by appellees, that the risk of loss had shifted from appellant to appellees. The risk of loss passes to the buyer on his receipt of goods if the seller is a merchant; otherwise the risk passes to the buyer on tender of delivery.

Analyzing the foregoing elements it is clear that, as the trial court stated, appellant did not tender delivery. The parties agreed that appellees would purchase the mobile home and shed from appellant. The contents of both the shed and the mobile home were to be retained by appellant and removed by appellant. At the time of the fire, appellant had not removed the items that she was required to remove from either the mobile home or the shed. Additionally, all keys to the mobile home were not surrendered and none of the keys to the shed were relinquished. Under this scenario, appellant did not tender con-

forming goods free of items belonging to her which remained in the trailer, nor did she put the mobile home at appellee's disposition without being fettered with the items previously enumerated. Accordingly, the trial court was correct in determining that appellant did not tender delivery within the meaning of the statute, and consequently the risk of loss remained with her.

The trial court was correct in determining that appellant did not tender delivery in a manner sufficient to shift the risk of loss to appellees. Therefore, when it ordered appellant to return appellee's purchase money, it effectually mandated that the contract was "avoided."

Based on the foregoing, the judgment of the trial court is affirmed.

CHAPTER 17

Performance of Sales, Lease, and Internet Contracts

Trade and commerce, if they were not made of Indian rubber, would never manage to bounce over the obstacles which legislators are continually putting in their way.

—Henry D. Thoreau
Resistance to Civil Government (1849)

Chapter Objectives

After studying this chapter, you should be able to:

1. Describe the doctrines of good faith and reasonableness that govern the performance of sales, lease, and Web contracts.

2. Define *perfect tender rule*.

3. Identify when the buyer or lessee has a right to reject nonconforming goods.

4. Identify when the buyer or lessor has a right to cure a nonconforming delivery of goods.

5. Identify when the buyer or lessee has the right to revoke a prior acceptance.

6. List and describe the seller's remedies for the buyer's breach of the sales contract.

7. List and describe the buyer's remedies for the seller's breach of the sales contract.

8. List and describe the lessor's remedies for the lessee's breach of the lease contract.

9. List and describe the lessee's remedies for the lessor's breach of the lease contract.

10. Identify unconscionable sales, lease, and Web contracts.

Chapter Contents

Usually, the parties to a sales or lease contract owe a duty to perform the **obligations** specified in their agreement [UCC 2-301, 2A-301]. The seller's or lessor's general obligation is to transfer and deliver the goods to the buyer or lessee. The buyer's or lessee's general obligation is to accept and pay for the goods.

When one party **breaches** the sales or lease contract, the UCC provides the injured party with a variety of prelitigation and litigation remedies. These remedies are designed to place the injured party in as good a position as if the breaching party's contractual obligations were fully performed [UCC 1-106(1), 2A-401(1)]. The best remedy depends on the circumstances of the particular case.

The performance of obligations and remedies available for breach of sales and lease contracts are discussed in this chapter.

Seller's and Lessor's Obligations

Tender of delivery, or the transfer and delivery of goods to the buyer or lessee in accordance with the sales or lease contract, is the seller's or lessor's basic obligation [UCC 2-301]. Tender of delivery requires the seller or lessor to (1) put and hold conforming goods at the buyer's or lessee's disposition and (2) give the buyer or lessee any notification reasonably necessary to enable delivery of goods. The parties may agree as to the time, place, and manner of delivery. If there is no special agreement, tender must be made at a reasonable hour, and the goods must be kept available for a reasonable period of time. For example, the seller cannot telephone the buyer at 12:01 A.M. and say that the buyer has 15 minutes to accept delivery [UCC 2-503(1), 2A-508(1)].

Unless otherwise agreed or unless the circumstances permit either party to request delivery in lots, the goods named in the contract must be tendered in a single delivery. Payment of a sales contract is due upon tender of delivery unless an extension of credit between the parties has been arranged. If the goods are rightfully delivered in lots, the payment is apportioned for each lot [UCC 2-307]. Lease payments are due in accordance with the terms of the lease contract.

Place of Delivery

Many sales and lease contracts state where the goods are to be delivered. Often, the contract will say that the buyer or lessee must pick up the goods from the seller or lessor. If the contract does not expressly state where the delivery will take place, the UCC will stipulate place of delivery on the basis of whether a carrier is involved.

Noncarrier Cases Unless otherwise agreed, the place of delivery is the seller's or lessor's place of business. If the seller or lessor has no place of business, the place of delivery is the seller's or lessor's residence. If the parties have knowledge at the time of contracting that identified goods are located in some other place, that place is the place of delivery. For example, if the parties contract regarding the sale of wheat located in a silo, the silo is the place of delivery [UCC 2-308].

Sometimes the goods are in the possession of a **bailee** (e.g., a warehouse) and are to be delivered without being moved. In such cases, tender of delivery occurs when the seller either (1) tenders to the buyer a negotiable document of title covering the goods, (2) produces acknowledgment from the bailee of the buyer's right to possession of the goods, or (3) tenders a non-negotiable document of title or a written direction to the bailee to deliver the goods to a buyer. The seller must deliver all such documents in correct form [UCC 2-503(4) and (5)].

Carrier Cases Unless the parties have agreed otherwise, if delivery of the goods to the buyer is to be made by carrier, the UCC establishes different rules for shipment contracts and destination contracts. These rules are described below.

---

obligation

An action a party to a sales or lease contract is required by law to carry out.

breach

Failure of a party to perform an obligation in a sales or lease contract.

tender of delivery

The obligation of the seller to transfer and deliver goods to the buyer in accordance with the sales contract.

The buyer needs a hundred eyes, the seller not one.

George Herbert
Jacula Prudentum *(1651)*

bailee

A holder of goods who is not a seller or a buyer (e.g., a warehouse).

shipment contract

A sales contract that requires the seller to send the goods to the buyer, but not a specifically named destination.

Shipment Contracts Sales contracts that require the seller to send the goods to the buyer, but not to a specifically named destination, are called **shipment contracts**. Under such contracts, the seller must do all the following [UCC 2-504]:

1. Put the goods in the carrier's possession and contract for the proper and safe transportation of the goods.
2. Obtain and promptly deliver or tender in correct form any documents (a) necessary to enable the buyer to obtain possession of the goods, (b) required by the sales contract, or (c) required by usage of trade.
3. Promptly notify the buyer of the shipment.

The buyer may reject the goods if a material delay or loss is caused by the seller's failure to make a proper contract for the shipment of goods or properly notify the buyer of the shipment. For example, if a shipment contract involves perishable goods and the seller fails to ship the goods via a refrigerated carrier, the buyer may rightfully reject the goods if they spoil during transit.

destination contract

A sales contract that requires the seller to deliver the goods to the buyer's place of business or another specified destination.

Destination Contracts A sales contract that requires the seller to deliver the goods to the buyer's place of business or another specified destination is a **destination contract**. Unless otherwise agreed, destination contracts require delivery to be tendered at the buyer's place of business or other location specified in the sales contract. Delivery must be at a reasonable time and in a reasonable manner and with proper notice to the buyer. Appropriate documents of title must be provided by the seller to enable the buyer to obtain the goods from the carrier [UCC 2-503].

Kyrgyzstan Certain shipping terms are used in international contracts to designate pricing terms, insurance requirements, and who bears the risk of loss to the goods.

Perfect Tender Rule

The seller or lessor is under a duty to deliver conforming goods. If the goods or tender of delivery fails in any respect to conform to the contract, the buyer or lessee may opt either (1) to reject the whole shipment, (2) to accept the whole shipment, or (3) to reject part and accept part of the shipment. This option is referred to as the **perfect tender rule** [UCC 2-601, 2A-509].

perfect tender rule

A rule that says if the goods or tender of a delivery fails in any respect to conform to the contract, the buyer may opt either (1) to reject the whole shipment, (2) to accept the whole shipment, or (3) to reject part and accept part of the shipment.

Consider This Example A sales contract requires the seller to deliver 100 shirts to a buyer. When the buyer inspects the delivered goods, it is discovered that 99 shirts conform to the contract and one shirt does not conform. Pursuant to the perfect tender rule, the buyer may reject the entire shipment. If a buyer accepts nonconforming goods, the buyer may seek remedies against the seller.

Exceptions to the Perfect Tender Rule   The UCC alerts the perfect tender rule in the following situations.

1. **Agreement of the Parties**   The parties to the sales or lease contract may agree to limit the effect of the perfect tender rule. For example, they may decide that (1) only the defective or nonconforming goods may be rejected, (2) the seller or lessor may replace nonconforming goods or repair defects, or (3) the buyer or lessee will accept nonconforming goods with appropriate compensation from the seller or lessor.

2. **Substitution of Carriers**   The UCC requires the seller to use a commercially reasonable substitute if (1) the agreed-upon manner of delivery fails or (2) the agreed-upon type of carrier becomes unavailable [UCC 2-614(1)].

Convenience is the basis of mercantile law.

Lord Mansfield
Medcalf v. Hall *(1782)*

Consider This Example   A sales contract specifies delivery of goods by Mac Trucks, Inc., a common carrier, but a labor strike prevents delivery by this carrier. The seller must use any commercially reasonable substitute (such as another truck line or the rails). The buyer cannot reject the delivery because there is a substitute carrier. Unless otherwise agreed, the seller bears any increased cost of the substitute performance.

Cure   The UCC gives a seller or lessor who delivers nonconforming goods an opportunity to **cure** the nonconformity. Although the term *cure* is not defined by the UCC, it generally means an opportunity to repair or replace defective or nonconforming goods [UCC 2-508, 2A-513].

A cure may be attempted if the time for performance has not expired and the seller or lessor notifies the buyer or lessee of his or her intention to make a conforming delivery within the contract time.

cure
An opportunity to repair or replace defective or nonconforming goods.

Consider This Example   A lessee contracts to lease a BMW 850i automobile from a lessor for delivery July 1. On June 15, the lessor delivers a BMW 740i to the lessee, which the lessee rejects as nonconforming. The lessor has until July 1 to cure the nonconformity by delivering the BMW 850i specified in the contract.

A cure may also be attempted if the seller or lessor had reasonable grounds to believe the delivery would be accepted. The seller or lessor may have a further reasonable time to substitute a conforming tender.

Consider This Example   A buyer contracts to purchase 100 red dresses from a seller for delivery July 1. On July 1, the seller delivers 100 blue dresses to the buyer. In the past, the buyer has accepted different-colored dresses than those ordered. This time, though, the buyer rejects the blue dresses as nonconforming. The seller has a reasonable time after July 1 to deliver conforming red dresses to the buyer.

In the following case, a seller attempted to cure a defective delivery.

Joc Oil USA, Inc. v. Consolidated Edison Co. of New York, Inc.

30 UCC Rep.Serv. 426 (1980)
New York Supreme Court, New York County

CASE 17.1

BACKGROUND AND FACTS
Joc Oil USA, Inc. (Joc Oil), contracted to purchase low-sulfur fuel oil from an Italian oil refinery. The Italian refinery issued a certificate to Joc Oil indicating that the sulfur content of the oil was 0.50 percent. Joc Oil entered into a sales contract to sell the oil to Consolidated Edison Company of New York, Inc. (Con Ed). Con Ed agreed to pay $17.875 per barrel for oil not to exceed 0.50 percent sulfur. When the ship delivering the oil arrived, it discharged the oil into three Con Ed storage tanks. On February 20, 1974, a final report issued by Con Ed stated that the sulfur content of the oil was 0.92 percent. At a meeting that day, Joc Oil offered to reduce the price of the oil

by $.50 to $.80 per barrel. Con Ed expressed a willingness to accept the oil at $13 per barrel (the market price of oil at that time). Joc Oil then made an offer to cure the defect by substituting a conforming shipment of oil that was already on a ship that was to arrive within two weeks. Con Ed rejected Joc Oil's offer to cure. Joc Oil sued Con Ed for breach of contract.

ISSUE
Did Joc Oil have a right to cure the defect in the delivery?

COURT'S REASONING
The UCC statutory right to cure is an exception to the precode "perfect tender rule." The UCC cure provision was conceived to protect a seller from surprise rejection by the buyer. In this case, the court held that Joc Oil had reasonable grounds to believe that its original shipment would be acceptable to Con Ed. The court found that Joc Oil made its offer to cure by tendering a new conforming shipment that would arrive within two weeks, a reasonable time in the court's view. Under the circumstances,

Joc Oil had the right to—and did—make a reasonable and timely offer to cure. Con Ed's rejection was improper.

DECISION
The court held that under the circumstances of this case, Joc Oil had the right to cure the defect in delivery and that Con Ed breached the contract by refusing to permit this cure. The court entered judgment against Con Ed and awarded Joc Oil $1,385,512 in damages plus interest and the costs of this action.

Case Questions

Critical Legal Thinking   Should the law recognize the right to cure a defective tender of goods? Why or why not?

Business Ethics   Did Con Ed act ethically in this case? Did Joc Oil?

Contemporary Business   Why do you think Con Ed rejected Joc Oil's offer to cure the defect in delivery? Explain.

---

installment contract

A contract that requires or authorizes the goods to be delivered and accepted in separate lots.

Installment Contracts   An **installment contract** is one that requires or authorizes the goods to be delivered and accepted in separate lots. Such contracts must contain a clause that states "each delivery is a separate contract" or equivalent language. An example of an installment contract is one in which a buyer orders 100 shirts, to be delivered in four equal installments of 25 items.

The UCC alters the perfect tender rule with regard to installment contracts. The buyer or lessee may reject the entire contract only if the nonconformity or default with respect to any installment or installments substantially impairs the value of the entire contract. The buyer or lessee may reject any nonconforming installment if the value of the installment is impaired and the defect cannot be cured. Thus, in each case, the court must determine whether the nonconforming installment impairs the value of the entire contract or only that installment [UCC 2-612, 2A-510].

Destruction of Goods   The UCC provides that if goods identified to a sales or lease contract are totally destroyed without the fault of either party before the risk of loss passes to the buyer or the lessee, the contract is void. Both parties are then excused from performing the contract.

If the goods are only partially destroyed, the buyer or lessee may inspect the goods and then choose either to treat the contract as void or to accept the goods. If the buyer or lessee opts to accept the goods, the purchase price or rent will be reduced in compensation for the damage [UCC 2-613, 2A-221].

Consider This Example   A buyer contracts to purchase a sofa from a seller. The seller agrees to deliver the sofa to the buyer's home. The truck delivering the sofa is hit by an automobile and the sofa is totally destroyed. Since the risk of loss has not passed to the buyer, the contract is voided and the buyer does not have to pay for the sofa.

 ℬ*usiness* ℰ*thics*

GOOD FAITH AND REASONABLENESS GOVERN THE PERFORMANCE OF SALES, LEASE, AND WEB CONTRACTS

Generally, the common law of contracts only obligates the parties to perform according to the terms of their contract. There is no breach of contract unless the parties fail to meet these terms.

Recognizing that certain situations may develop that are not expressly provided for in the contract or that strict adherence to the terms of the contract without doing more may not be sufficient to accomplish the contract's objective, the Uniform Commercial Code (UCC) adopts two broad principles that govern the performance of sales and lease contracts: *good faith* and *reasonableness*.

UCC 1-203 states that "Every contract or duty within this Act imposes an obligation of good faith in its performance or enforcement." Although both parties owe a duty of good faith in the performance of a sales or lease contract, merchants are held to a higher standard of good faith than nonmerchants. Nonmerchants are held to the subjective standard of honesty in fact whereas merchants are held to the objective standard of fair dealing in the trade [UCC 2-103(1)(b)].

The words *reasonable* and *reasonably* are used throughout the UCC to establish the duties of performance by the parties to sales and lease contracts. For example, unless otherwise specified, the parties must act within a "reasonable" time [UCC 1-204(1)(2)]. Another example is if the seller does not deliver the goods as contracted, the buyer may make "reasonable" purchases to cover (i.e., obtain substitute performance) [UCC 2-712(1)]. The term *commercial reasonableness* is used to establish certain duties of merchants under the UCC. Articles 2 and 2A do not specifically define the terms *reasonable* and *commercial reasonableness*. Instead, these terms are defined by reference to the course of performance or the course of dealing between the parties, usage of trade, and such.

Note that the concepts of good faith and reasonableness extend to the "spirit" of the contract as well as the contract terms. The underlying theory is that the parties are more apt to perform properly if their conduct is to be judged against these principles. This is a major advance in the law of contracts. The duties of good faith and reasonableness have been applied to Web contracts.

1. Do the UCC concepts of *good faith* and *reasonableness* enhance ethical conduct?
2. Should the concept of *good faith* be implied in every contract? Why or why not?

Buyer's and Lessee's Obligations

Once the seller or lessor has properly tendered delivery, the buyer or lessee is obligated to accept and pay for the goods in accordance with the sales or lease contract. If there is no agreement, the provisions of the UCC control.

Right of Inspection

Unless otherwise agreed, the buyer or lessee has the right to inspect goods that are tendered, delivered, or identified to the sales contract prior to accepting or paying for them. If the goods are shipped, the inspection may take place after their arrival. If the inspected goods do not conform to the contract, the buyer or lessee may reject them without paying for them [UCC 2-513(1), 2A-515(1)].

The parties may agree as to the time, place, and manner of inspection. If there is no such agreement, the inspection must occur at a reasonable time, place, and manner. Reasonableness depends on the circumstances of the case, common usage of trade, prior course of dealing between the parties, and such. If the goods conform to the contract, the buyer pays for the inspection. If the goods are rejected for nonconformance, the cost of inspection can be recovered from the seller [UCC 2-513(2)].

Buyers who agree to **C.O.D. (cash on delivery)** deliveries are not entitled to inspect the goods before paying for them. In certain sales contracts (e.g., cost, insurance, and freight [or C.I.F.] contracts), payment is due from the buyer upon receipt of documents of title even if the goods have not yet been received. In such cases, the buyer is not entitled to inspect the goods before paying for them [UCC 2-513(3)].

C.O.D. shipment

A type of shipment contract where the buyer agrees to pay the shipper cash upon the delivery of the goods.

Payment

Goods that are accepted must be paid for [UCC 2-607(1)]. Unless the parties agree otherwise, payment is due from a buyer when and where the goods are delivered even if the place of delivery is the same as the place of shipment. Buyers often purchase goods on credit extended by the seller. Unless the parties agree to other terms, the credit period begins to run from the time the goods are shipped [UCC 2-310]. A lessee must pay lease payments in accordance with the lease contract [UCC 2A-516(1)].

The goods can be paid for in any manner currently acceptable in the ordinary course of business (check, credit card, or the like) unless the seller demands payment in cash or unless the contract names a specific form of payment. If the seller requires cash payment, the buyer must be given an extension of time necessary to procure the cash. If the buyer pays by check, payment is conditional on the check being honored (paid) when it is presented to the bank for payment [UCC 2-511].

Acceptance

acceptance

Occurs when a buyer or lessee takes any of the following actions after a reasonable opportunity to inspect the goods: (1) signifies the seller or lessor in words or by conduct that the goods are conforming or that the buyer or lessee will take or retain the goods despite their nonconformity or (2) fails to effectively reject the goods within a reasonable time after their delivery or tender by the seller or lessor. Acceptance also occurs if a buyer acts inconsistently with the seller's ownership rights in the goods.

Acceptance occurs when the buyer or lessee takes any of the following actions after a reasonable opportunity to inspect the goods: (1) signifies to the seller or lessor in words or by conduct that the goods are conforming or that the buyer or lessee will take or retain the goods despite their nonconformity or (2) fails to effectively reject the goods within a reasonable time after their delivery or tender by the seller or lessor. Acceptance also occurs if a buyer acts inconsistently with the seller's ownership rights in the goods. For example, the buyer resells the goods delivered by the seller [UCC 2-606(1), 2A-515(1)].

Buyers and lessees may only accept delivery of a "commercial unit." A commercial unit is a unit of goods that commercial usage deems is a single whole for purpose of sale. Thus, it may be a single article (such as a machine), a set of articles (such as a suite of furniture or an assortment of sizes), a quantity (such as a bale, a gross, or a carload), or any other unit treated in use or in the relevant market as a single whole. Acceptance of a part of any commercial unit is acceptance of the entire unit [UCC 2-606(2), 2A-515(2)].

Revocation of Acceptance

revocation

Reversal of acceptance.

A buyer or lessee who has accepted goods may subsequently **revoke** his or her acceptance if (1) the goods are nonconforming, (2) the nonconformity substantially impairs the value of the goods to the buyer or lessee, and (3) one of the following factors is shown: (a) the seller's or lessor's promise to reasonably cure the nonconformity is not met, (b) the goods were accepted before the nonconformity was discovered and the nonconformity was difficult to discover, or (c) the goods were accepted before the nonconformity was discovered and the seller or lessor assured the buyer or lessee that the goods were conforming.

Revocation is not effective until the seller or lessor is so notified. In addition, the revocation must occur within a reasonable time after the buyer or lessee discovers or should have discovered the grounds for the revocation. The revocation, which must be of a lot or commercial unit, must occur before there is any substantial change in the condition of the goods (e.g., before perishable goods spoil) [UCC 2-608(1), 2A-517(1)].

In the following case, the court had to decide whether to allow revocation of a sales contract.

Fortin v. Ox-Bow Marina, Inc.
557 N.E.2d 1157 (1990)
Supreme Judicial Court of Massachusetts

CASE 17.2

BACKGROUND AND FACTS
In the spring of 1985, Robert and Marie Fortin ordered a 32-foot Bayliner Conquest power boat from Ox-Bow Marina, Inc. (Ox-Bow). In May, on the day of closing, the Fortins checked their boat and found that none of the preparation work had been done, none of the special equipment they had ordered had been installed, and several defects needed to be repaired or corrected, including a nonfunctioning flush mechanism in the marine toilet system, and chips in the wood trim. Ox-Bow's representative assured the Fortins that the problems would be corrected if they closed on the transaction. The Fortins agreed to close. To pay Ox-Bow, they traded in their old boat, paid $6,259 cash, and borrowed $51,500 from Horizon Financial.

In May and June, the Fortins requested Ox-Bow to correct the problems, which Ox-Bow did not do. When the Fortins set out on their maiden voyage on June 22, 1985, they discovered that the depth finder and marine radio did not work and the marine toilets were not functioning properly, and one of the two engines overheated and had to be shut down. Ox-Bow promised to fix these defects but again did not. The Fortins

continued to request Ox-Bow to correct all the defects. Although Ox-Bow always promised to comply, it never did.

Finally, on October 31, 1985, the Fortins notified Ox-Bow that they were revoking their acceptance of the Bayliner and sought a refund of their purchase price, plus damages. The judge ruled that the Fortins had effectively revoked acceptance of the boat and awarded them damages in the amount of $24,364, including sales tax and interest paid on the loan. Ox-Bow appealed.

ISSUE
Was the Fortins' revocation of acceptance effective?

COURT'S REASONING
A buyer may subsequently revoke this or her acceptance of goods if the buyer can show that the nonconformity in the goods substantially impairs its value and that the buyer accepted the goods on the reasonable assumption that the nonconformity would be cured and it has not been reasonably cured. The court ruled that this situation existed in this case. The Fortins accepted the Bayliner on Ox-Bow's assurances

that the defects would be cured. The Fortins had the legal right to revoke their acceptance because the defects were not cured and substantially impaired the value of the boat to them.

DECISION

The appellate court held that the Fortins' revocation of acceptance was effective. Affirmed.

Case Questions

Critical Legal Thinking   Should a buyer be permitted to revoke his or her acceptance once it has been made? Why or why not?

Business Ethics Issue   Did Ox-Bow act ethically in this case?

Contemporary Business   Why do you think Ox-Bow acted as it did in this case? Would it have been cheaper to have fixed the boat in the first place?

ASSURANCE OF PERFORMANCE

Each party to a sales or lease contract expects that every other party will perform their contractual obligations. If one party to the contract has reasonable grounds to believe that the other party either will not or cannot perform his or her contractual obligations, an **adequate assurance** of due performance may be demanded in writing. If it is commercially reasonable, the party making the demand may suspend his or her performance until adequate assurance of due performance is received from the other party [UCC 2-609, 2A-401].

Consider This Example   A buyer contracts to purchase 1,000 bushels of wheat from a farmer. The contract requires delivery on September 1. In July, the buyer learns that floods have caused substantial crop loss in the area of the seller's farm. The farmer receives the buyer's written demand for adequate assurance on July 15. The farmer fails to give adequate assurance of performance. The buyer may suspend performance and treat the sales contract as repudiated.

> **adequate assurance of performance**
>
> A party to a sales or lease contract may demand an adequate assurance of performance from the other party if there is an indication that the contract will be breached by that party.

ANTICIPATORY REPUDIATION

Occasionally, a party to a sales or lease contract repudiates the contract before his or her performance is due under the contract. If the repudiation impairs the value of the contract to the aggrieved party, it is called **anticipatory repudiation**. Mere wavering on performance does not meet the test for anticipatory repudiation.

If an anticipatory repudiation does occur, the aggrieved party can (1) await performance by the repudiating party for a commercially reasonable time (e.g., until the delivery date or shortly thereafter) or (2) treat the contract as breached at the time of the anticipatory repudiation, which gives the aggrieved party an immediate cause of action. In either case, the aggrieved party may suspend performance of his or her obligations under the contract [UCC 2-610, 2A-402].

An anticipatory repudiation may be retracted before the repudiating party's next performance is due if the aggrieved party has not (1) canceled the contract, (2) materially changed his or her position (e.g., purchased goods from another party), or (3) otherwise indicated that the repudiation is considered final. The retraction may be made by any method that clearly indicates the repudiating party's intent to perform the contract [UCC 2-611, 2A-403].

> **anticipatory repudiation**
>
> The repudiation of a sales or lease contract by one of the parties prior to the date set for performance.

Business Ethics

UNCONSCIONABLE SALES, LEASE, AND WEB CONTRACTS

Can a contract term ever be so unfair as to be legally ignored by a party to the contract? After all, law and morality require that contracting parties adhere to the terms of their contract. The doctrine of **unconscionability** says that if a sales, lease, and Web contract (or any clause in it) is unconscionable, the court may either refuse to enforce the contract or limit the application of the unconscionable clause. Consider the following case.

Dynatron, Inc. (Dynatron), executed a lease agreement with Hertz Commercial Leasing Corporation (Hertz) to finance a lease of a Minolta copy machine that was supplied by A-Copy of Glastonbury, Connecticut (A-Copy). The lease agreement, which was prepared by Hertz, designated Dynatron as the lessee and Hertz as the lessor. The vendor was A-Copy. The lease was for a 60-month term, at a monthly rental of $3,720. Paragraph 11 of the lease is a liquidated damage clause that stipulates that in event of default, the lessee is obligated to pay the lessor any arrears of rentals, the entire balance of the rent, the lessor's expenses in retaking possession and removing the equipment, and up to 20 percent of attorney's fees.

Dynatron claimed that almost immediately following delivery, the machine developed operational problems and that its reproduction quantities were defective. Dynatron wrote letters to Hertz and A-Copy demanding repair or replacement of the machine. The machine was not repaired or replaced. Dynatron made no payments on the lease. Finally, Dynatron requested that Hertz repossess the machine. Dynatron then purchased a Xerox copying machine. After the lapse of about one year, or about February 14, 1978, Hertz picked up the machine. In May 1978, Hertz sold the machine for $500. On August 30, 1980, Hertz sued Dynatron to recover a deficiency judgment.

The court held that the terms and conditions of the finance lease agreement in this case were *unconscionable* and that the provisions of the lease are not enforceable against the lessee in any respect whatsoever. Judgment was therefore entered for Dynatron [*Hertz Commercial Leasing Corporation v. Dynatron, Inc.*, 472 A.2d 872 (CT 1980)].

1. Was it ethical for Hertz to include the liquidated damage clause in its form contract?
2. Did Dynatron act morally in signing the lease and then trying to get out from under its provisions?

SELLER'S AND LESSOR'S REMEDIES

Various remedies are available to sellers and lessors if a buyer or lessee breaches the contract. These remedies are discussed in the paragraphs that follow.

Right to Withhold Delivery

Delivery of the goods may be **withheld** if the seller or lessor is in possession of them when the buyer or lessee breaches the contract. This remedy is available if the buyer or lessee wrongfully rejects or revokes acceptance of the goods, fails to make a payment when due, or repudiates the contract. If part of the goods under the contract have been delivered when the buyer or lessee materially breaches the contract, the seller or lessor may withhold delivery of the remainder of the affected goods [UCC 2-703(a), 2A-523(1)(c)].

A seller or lessor who discovers that the buyer or lessee is insolvent before the goods are delivered may refuse to deliver as promised unless the buyer or lessee pays cash for the goods [UCC 2-702(1), 2A-525(1)]. Under the UCC, a person is insolvent when he or she (1) ceases to pay his or her debts in the ordinary course of business, (2) cannot pay his or her debts as they become due, or (3) is insolvent within the meaning of the federal bankruptcy law [UCC 1-201(23)].

Right to Stop Delivery of Goods in Transit

Often, sellers and lessors employ common carriers and other bailees (e.g., warehouses) to hold and deliver goods to buyers and lessees. The goods are considered to be **in transit** while they are in possession of these carriers or bailees. A seller or lessor that learns of the buyer's or lessee's insolvency while the goods are in transit may **stop delivery of the goods** irrespective of the size of the shipment.

Essentially the same remedy is available if the buyer or lessee repudiates the contract, fails to make payment when due, or otherwise gives the seller or lessor some other right to withhold or reclaim the goods. In these circumstances, however, the delivery can be stopped only if it constitutes a carload, a truckload, a planeload, or larger express or freight shipment [UCC 2-705(1), 2A-526(1)].

The seller or lessor must give sufficient notice to allow the bailee, by reasonable diligence, to prevent delivery of the goods. After receipt of notice, the bailee must hold and deliver the goods according to the directions of the seller or lessor. The seller is responsible for all expenses borne by the bailee in stopping the goods [UCC 2-705(3), 2A-526(3)]. Goods may be stopped in transit until the buyer or lessee obtains possession of the goods or the carrier or other bailee acknowledges that it is holding the goods for the buyer or lessee [UCC 2-705(2), 2A-526(2)].

This is the kind of order which makes the administration of justice stink in the nostrils of commercial men.

A. L. Smith,
L. J. Graham v. Sutton,
Carden & Company (1897)

withholding delivery

The act of the seller or lessor purposefully refusing to deliver goods to the buyer or lessee upon breach of the sales or lease contract by the buyer or lessee or the insolvency of the buyer or lessee.

in transit

A state in which goods are in the possession of a bailee or carrier and not in the hands of the buyer, seller, lessee, or lessor.

stopping delivery of goods in transit

A seller or lessor may stop delivery of goods in transit if he or she learns of the buyer's or lessee's insolvency or if the buyer or lessee repudiates the contract, fails to make payment when due, or gives the seller or lessor some other right to withhold the goods.

Right to Reclaim Goods

In certain situations, a seller or lessor may demand the return of the goods it sold or leased that are already in the possession of the buyer or lessee. In a sale transaction, **reclamation** is permitted in two situations. If the goods are delivered in a credit sale and the seller then discovers that the buyer was insolvent, the seller has 10 days within which to demand that the goods be returned [UCC 2-507(2)]. If the buyer misrepresented his or her solvency in writing within three months before delivery [UCC 2-702(2)] or paid for goods in cash sale with a check that bounces [UCC 2-507(2)], the seller may reclaim the goods at any time.

A lessor may reclaim goods in the possession of the lessee if the lessee is in default of the contract [UCC 2A-525(2)].

To exercise a right of reclamation, the seller or lessor must send the buyer or lessee a written notice demanding return of the goods. The seller or lessor may not use self-help to reclaim the goods if the buyer or lessee refuses to honor his or her demand. Instead, appropriate legal proceedings must be instituted.

reclamation

The right of a seller or lessor to demand the return of goods from the buyer or lessee under specified situations.

Right to Dispose of Goods

If the buyer or lessee breaches or repudiates the seller or lease contract before the seller or lessor has delivered the goods, the seller or lessor may resell or release the goods and recover damages from the buyer or lessee [UCC 2-703(d), 2-706(1); UCC 2A-523(1)(e), 2A-527(1)]. This right also arises if the seller or lessor has reacquired the goods after stopping them in transit.

The disposition of the goods by the seller or lessor must be made in good faith and in a commercially reasonable manner. The goods may be disposed of as a unit or in parcels in a public or private transaction. The seller or lessor must give the buyer or lessee reasonable notification of his or her intention to dispose of goods unless the goods threaten to quickly decline in value or are perishable. The party who buys or leases the goods in good faith for value takes the goods free of any rights of the original buyer or lessee [UCC 2-706(5), 2A-527(4)].

The seller or lessor may recover any damages incurred on the disposition of the goods. In the case of a sales contract, damages are defined as the difference between the disposition price and the original contract price. In the case of lease contract, damages are the difference between the disposition price and the rent the original lessee would have paid.

The profit does not revert to the original buyer or lessee if the seller or lessor disposes of the goods at a higher price than the buyer or lessee contracted to pay. The seller or lessor may also recover any **incidental damages** (reasonable expenses incurred in stopping delivery, transportation charges, storage charges, sales commission, and the like [UCC 2-710, 2A-530]) incurred on the disposition of the goods [UCC 2-706(1), 2A-527(2)].

disposition of goods

A seller or lessor who is in possession of goods at the time the buyer or lessee breaches or repudiates the contract may in good faith resell, release, or otherwise dispose of the goods in a commercially reasonable manner and recover damages, including incidental damages, from the buyer or lessee.

incidental damages

When goods are resold or released, incidental damages are reasonable expenses incurred in stopping delivery, transportation charges, storage charges, sales commissions, and so on.

Consider This Example   A buyer contracts to purchase a racehorse for $20,000. When the seller tenders delivery, the buyer refuses to accept the horse or pay for it. The seller, in good faith, and in a commercially reasonable manner, resells the horse to a third party for $17,000. Incidental expenses of $500 are incurred on the resale. The seller can recover $3,500 from the original buyer: The $3,000 difference between the resale price and the contract price and $500 for incidental expenses.

Unfinished Goods   Sometimes the sales or lease contract is breached or repudiated before the goods are finished. In such cases, the seller or lessor may choose either (1) to cease manufacturing the goods and resell them for scrap or salvage value or (2) to complete the manufacture of the goods and resell, release, or otherwise dispose of them to another party [UCC 2-704(2), 2A-524(2)]. The seller or lessor may recover damages from the breaching buyer or lessee.

Right to Recover the Purchase Price or Rent

In certain circumstances, the UCC provides that the seller or lessor may sue the buyer or lessee to **recover the purchase price or rent** stipulated in the sales or lease contract. This remedy is available in the following situations:

1. The buyer or lessee accepts the goods but fails to pay for them when the price or rent is due.

recovery of the purchase price or rent

A seller or lessor may recover the contracted-for purchase price or rent from the buyer or lessee if the buyer or lessee (1) fails to pay for accepted goods, (2) breaches the contract and the seller or lessor cannot dispose of the goods, or if (3) the goods are damaged or lost after the risk of loss passes to the buyer or lessee.

2. The buyer or lessee breaches the contract after the goods have been identified to the contract and the seller or lessor cannot resell or dispose of them.

3. The goods are damaged or lost after the risk of loss passes to the buyer or lessee [UCC 2-709(1), 2A-529(1)].

To recover the purchase price or rent, the seller or lessor must hold the goods for the buyer or lessee. If resale or other disposition of the goods becomes possible prior to the collection of the judgment, however, the seller or lessor may resell or dispose of them. In such situations, the net proceeds of any disposition must be credited against the judgment [UCC 2-709(2), 2A-529(2), (3)]. The seller or lessor may also recover incidental damages from the buyer or lessee.

Right to Recover Damages for Breach of Contract

recovery of damages

A seller or lessor may recover damages measured as the difference between the contract price (or rent) and the market price (or rent) at the time and place the goods were to be delivered, plus incidental damages, from a buyer or lessee who repudiates the contract or wrongfully rejects tendered goods.

recovery of lost profits

If the recovery of damages would be inadequate to put the seller or lessor in as good a position as if the contract had been fully performed by the buyer or lessee, the seller or lessor may recover lost profits, plus an allowance for overhead and incidental damages, from the buyer or lessee.

cancellation

A seller or lessor may cancel a sales or lease contract if the buyer or lessee rejects or revokes acceptance of the goods, fails to pay for the goods, or repudiates the contract in part or in whole.

If a buyer or lessee repudiates a sales or lease contract or wrongfully rejects tendered goods, the seller or lessor may sue to **recover the damages** caused by the buyer's or lessee's breach. Generally, the amount of damages is calculated as the difference between the contract price (or rent) and the market price (or rent) of the goods at the time and place the goods were to be delivered to the buyer or lessee plus incidental damages [UCC 2-708(1), 2A-528(1)].

If the preceding measure of damage will not put the seller or lessor in as good a position as performance of the contract would have, the seller or lessor can seek to **recover any lost profits** that would have resulted from the full performance of the contract plus an allowance for reasonable overhead and incidental damages [UCC 2-708(2), 2A-528(2)].

Right to Cancel the Contract

The seller or lessor may cancel a sales or lease contract if the buyer or lessee breaches that contract by rejecting or revoking acceptance of the goods, failing to pay for the goods, or repudiating all or any part of the contract. The cancellation may refer only to the affected goods or to the entire contract if the breach is material [UCC 2-703(f), 2A-523(1)(a)].

A seller or lessor who rightfully cancels a sales or lease contract by notifying the buyer or lessee is discharged of any further obligations under that contract. The buyer's or lessee's duties are not discharged, however. The seller or lessor retains the right to seek damages for the breach [UCC 2-106(4), 2A-523(3)].

CONCEPT SUMMARY   SELLER'S AND LESSOR'S REMEDIES

Possession of Goods at Time of Buyer's Breach	Seller's or Lessor's Remedies

Goods in the possession of the seller	1. Withhold delivery of the goods [UCC 2-703(a), 2A-523(1)(c)].
	 2. Demand payment in cash if the buyer is insolvent [UCC 2-702(1), 2A-525(1)].
	 3. Resell or re-lease the goods and recover the difference between the contract or lease price and the resale or re-lease price [UCC 2-706, 2A-527].
	 4. Sue for breach of contract and recover as damages either
	   a. Difference between the market price and the contract price [UCC 2-708(1), 2A-528(1)] or
	   b. Lost profits [UCC 2-708(2), 2A-528(2)].
	 5. Cancel the contract [UCC 2-703(f), 2A-523(1)(a)].

Goods in the possession of a carrier or bailee	1. Stop goods in transit [UCC 2-705(1), 2A-526(1)].
	   a. Carload, truckload, planeload, or larger shipment if the buyer is insolvent.
	   b. Any size shipment if the buyer is insolvent.

Goods in the possession of the buyer	1. Sue to recover the purchase price or rent [UCC 2-709(1), 2A-529(1)].
	 2. Reclaim the goods [UCC 2-507(2), 2A-525(2)].
	   a. Seller delivers goods in cash sale and the buyer's check is dishonored.
	   b. Seller delivers goods in a credit sale and the goods are received by an insolvent buyer.

Contemporary Business Environment

LOST VOLUME SELLER

Should a seller be permitted to recover the profits it lost on a sale to a defaulting buyer if the seller sold the goods to another buyer? The answer is, it depends. If the seller had only one item or a limited number of items and could produce no more, the seller cannot recover lost profits from the defaulting buyer. This is because the seller made those profits on the sale of the item to the new buyer. If, however, the seller could have produced more of the item, the seller is a "lost volume seller." In this situation, the seller can make the profit from the sale of the item to the new buyer and sue the defaulting buyer to recover the profit it would have made from this sale. Consider the following case.

National Controls, Inc. (NCI), manufacturers electronic weighing and measuring devices. Among its products is the model 3221 electronic scale that is designed to interface with cash registers at checkout stands. On March 31, 1981, Commodore Business Machines, Inc. (Commodore), placed an order to purchase 900 scales from NCI, 50 to be delivered in May, 150 in June, 300 in July, and 400 in August. The evidence was undisputed that in 1980 and 1981, NCI's manu-facturing plant was operating at approximately 40 percent capacity.

Commodore accepted only the first 50 scales and did not accept or pay for the remaining 850 units. Thereafter, NCI sold all of the 850 units to National Semiconductor. NCI sued Commodore to recover the profits it lost because Commodore did not purchase the scales. Can NCI recover?

The trial court said it could and awarded NCI the $280,000 in lost profits that it would have made had Commodore performed the sales contract. The court of appeals affirmed.

The courts found that NCI was a lost volume seller with excess capacity to make the electronic scales it sold. The courts held that even though NCI resold the scales it would have sold to Commodore, that sale to the new buyer would have been made regardless of Commodore's breach. Thus, if Commodore had performed, NCI would have realized profits from two sales—one to Commodore, and one to the new buyer. [*National Controls, Inc. v. Commodore Business Machines, Inc.*, 163 Cal.App.3d 622, 209 Cal.Rptr. 636 (Cal.App. 1985)]

*B*UYER'S AND LESSEE'S REMEDIES

The UCC provides a variety of remedies to a buyer or lessee upon the seller's or lessor's breach of a sales or lease contract. These remedies are discussed in the following paragraphs.

Right to Reject Nonconforming Goods or Improperly Tendered Goods

If the goods or the seller's or lessor's tender of delivery fails to conform to the sales or lease contract in any way, the buyer or lessee may (1) **reject** the whole, (2) accept the whole, or (3) accept any commercial unit and reject the rest. If the buyer or lessee chooses to reject the goods, he or she must identify defects that are ascertainable by reasonable inspection. Failure to do so prevents the buyer or lessee from relying on those defects to justify the rejection if the defect could have been cured by a seller or lessor who was notified in a timely manner [UCC 2-601, 2A-509]. Nonconforming or improperly tendered goods must be rejected within a reasonable time after their delivery or tender. The seller or lessor must be notified of the rejection. The buyer or lessee must hold any rightfully rejected goods with reasonable care for a reasonable time [UCC 2-602(2), 2A-512(1)].

If the buyer or lessee is a merchant and the seller or lessor has no agent or place of business at the market where the goods are rejected, the merchant-buyer or merchant-lessee must follow any reasonable instructions received from the seller or lessor with respect to the rejected goods [UCC 2-603, 2A-511]. If the seller or lessor gives no instructions and the rejected goods are perishable or will quickly decline in value, the buyer or lessee may make reasonable efforts to sell them on the seller's or lessor's behalf [UCC 2-604, 2A-512].

Any buyer or lessee who rightfully rejects goods is entitled to reimbursement from the seller or lessor for reasonable expenses incurred in holding, storing, reselling, shipping, and otherwise caring for the rejected goods.

rejection of nonconforming goods

If the goods or the seller's or lessor's tender of delivery fails to conform to the contract, the buyer or lessee may (1) reject the whole, (2) accept the whole, or (3) accept any commercial unit and reject the rest.

Lighthouse, Straits of Mackinac
The Uniform Commercial Code (UCC) provides buyers and lessees, and sellers and lessors, certain remedies if the other party breaches the sales or lease contract.

recovery of goods from an insolvent seller or lessor

A buyer or lessee who has wholly or partially paid for goods before they are received may recover the goods from a seller or lessor who becomes insolvent within 10 days after receiving the first payment; the buyer or lessee must tender the remaining purchase price or rent due under the contract.

specific performance

A decree of the court that orders a seller or lessor to perform his or her obligations under the contract; usually occurs when the goods in question are unique, such as art or antiques.

cover

Right of a buyer or lessee to purchase or lease substitute goods if a seller or lessor fails to make delivery of the goods or repudiates the contract or if the buyer or lessee rightfully rejects the goods or justifiably revokes their acceptance.

Right to Recover Goods from an Insolvent Seller or Lessor

If the buyer or lessee makes partial or full payment for the goods before they are received and the seller or lessor becomes insolvent within 10 days after receiving the first payment, the buyer or lessee may **recover the goods** from the seller or lessor. To do so, the buyer or lessee must tender the unpaid portion of the purchase price or rent due under the sales or lease contract. Only conforming goods that are identified to the contract may be recovered [UCC 2-502, 2A-522]. This remedy is often referred to as **capture**.

Right to Obtain Specific Performance

If the goods are unique or the remedy at law is inadequate, a buyer or lessee may obtain **specific performance** of the sales or lease contract. A decree of specific performance orders the seller or lessor to perform the contract. Specific performance is usually used to obtain possession of works of art, antiques, rare coins, and other unique items [UCC 2-716(1), 2A-521(1)].

Consider This Example A buyer enters into a sales contract to purchase a specific Rembrandt painting from a seller for $10 million. When the buyer tenders payment, the seller refuses to sell the painting to the buyer. The buyer may bring an equity action to obtain a decree of specific performance from the court ordering the seller to sell the painting to the buyer.

Right to Cover

The buyer or lessee may **cover** by purchasing or renting substitute goods if the seller or lessor fails to make delivery of the goods or repudiates the contract or if the buyer or lessee rightfully rejects the goods or justifiably revokes their acceptance. The buyer's or lessee's cover must be made in good faith and without unreasonable delay. If the exact commodity is not available, the buyer or lessee may purchase or lease any commercially reasonable substitute.

A buyer or lessee who rightfully covers may sue the seller or lessor to recover as damages the difference between the cost of cover and the contract price or rent. The buyer or lessee may also recover incidental and consequential damages, less expenses saved (such as delivery costs) [UCC 2-712, 2A-518]. The UCC does not require a buyer or lessee to cover when a seller or lessor breaches a sales or lease contract. Failure of the buyer or lessee to cover does not bar the buyer from other remedies against the seller.

The issue of cover is addressed in the following case.

Red River Commodities, Inc. v. Eidsness
459 N.W.2d 811 (1990)
Supreme Court of North Dakota

CASE 17.3

BACKGROUND AND FACTS
In early 1988, George Eidsness, a North Dakota farmer, entered into a contract to grow and sell 229,000 pounds of confection sunflowers to Red River Commodities, Inc. (RRC), at a price of $.1125 per pound. When Eidsness did not deliver any sunflowers to RRC from his 1988 crop, RRC purchased replacement sunflowers from other sellers at $.26 per pound. In mid-December 1988, RRC learned that Eidsness was selling sunflowers to a competitor at $.22 per pound. RRC sued Eidsness to recover damages. The trial court held in favor of RRC and awarded it the difference between the cost of cover at $.26 per pound and the contract price of $.1125 per pound. The award amounted to $3,377,750 ($.1475 × 229,000). Eidsness appealed.

ISSUE
Can RRC recover as damages the difference between the cost of cover and the original contract price?

COURT'S REASONING
The court held that Eidsness had breached the sales contract with RRC by failing to deliver sunflowers at the contract price. RRC had properly covered by purchasing replacement sunflowers from other sellers at $.26 per pound. The $.1475 per pound difference between the contract price and the cover price was recoverable.

DECISION
The appellate court held that RRC properly covered by purchasing replacement goods and was entitled to recover the increased cost of cover from Eidsness.

Case Questions

Critical Legal Thinking Should a buyer be permitted to cover by purchasing replacement goods even if they are more expensive than the contract price? Why or why not?

Business Ethics Did Eidsness act ethically in this case?

Contemporary Business Does the cover and recovery of damages rule make an innocent buyer whole against the defaulting seller? Explain.

Right to Replevy Goods

A buyer or lessee may replevy (recover) goods from a seller or lessor who is wrongfully withholding them. The buyer or lessee must show that he or she was unable to cover or that attempts at cover will be unavailing. Thus, the goods must be scarce, but not unique. **Replevin** actions are available only as to goods identified to the sales or lease contract [UCC 2-716(3), 2A-521(3)].

Consider This Example On January 1, IBM contracts to purchase monitors for computers from a seller for delivery on June 1. IBM intends to attach the monitors to a new computer that will be introduced on June 30. On June 1, the seller refuses to sell the monitors to IBM because it can get a higher price from another buyer. IBM tries to cover but cannot. IBM may successfully replevy the monitors from the seller.

Right to Cancel the Contract

If a seller or lessor fails to deliver conforming goods or repudiates the contract or if the buyer or lessee rightfully rejects the goods or justifiably revokes acceptance of the goods, the buyer or lessee may **cancel** the sales or lease contract. The contract may be canceled with respect to the affected goods or, if there is a material breach, the whole contract. A buyer or lessee who rightfully cancels a contract is discharged from any further obligations on the contract and retains his or her rights to other remedies against the seller or lessor [UCC 2-711(1), 2A-508(1)(a)].

Right to Recover Damages for Nondelivery or Repudiation

If a seller or lessor fails to deliver the goods or repudiates the sales or lease contract, the buyer or lessee may recover **damages**. The measure of damages is the difference between the contract price (or original rent) and the market price (or rent) at the time the buyer or lessee learned of the breach. Incidental and consequential damages, less expenses saved, can also be recovered [UCC 2-713, 2A519].

replevin
An action by a buyer or lessor to recover scarce goods wrongfully withheld by a seller or lessor.

cancellation
A buyer or lessee may cancel a sales or lease contract if the seller or lessor fails to deliver conforming goods or repudiates the contract or if the buyer or lessee rightfully rejects the goods or justifiably revokes acceptance of the goods.

damages
A buyer or lessee may recover damages from a seller or lessor who fails to deliver the goods or repudiates the contract; damages are measured as the difference between the contract price (or original rent) and the market price (or rent) at the time the buyer or lessee learned of the breach.

Consider This Example   Fresh Foods Company contracts to purchase 10,000 bushels of soybeans from Sunshine Farms for $5 per bushel. Delivery is to be on August 1. On August 1 the market price of soybeans is $7 per bushel. Sunshine Farms does not deliver the soybeans. Fresh Foods decides not to cover and to do without the soybeans. Fresh Foods sues Sunshine for market value minus the contract price damages. It can recover $20,000 ($7 market price minus $5 contract price multiplied by 10,000 bushels) plus incidental damages less expenses saved because of Sunshine's breach. Fresh Foods cannot recover consequential damages because it did not attempt to cover.

Right to Recover Damages for Accepted Nonconforming Goods

A buyer or lessee may accept nonconforming goods from a seller or lessor. The acceptance does not prevent the buyer or lessee from suing the seller or lessor to recover as **damages** any loss resulting from the seller's or lessor's breach. Incidental and consequential damages may also be recovered. The buyer or lessee must notify the seller or lessor of the nonconformity within a reasonable time after the breach was or should have been discovered. Failure to do so bars the buyer or lessee from any recovery. If the buyer or lessee accepts nonconforming goods, he or she may deduct all or any part of damages resulting from the breach from any part of the purchase price or rent still due under the contract [UCC 2-714(1), 2A-516(1)].

damages for accepted nonconforming goods

A buyer or lessee may accept nonconforming goods and recover the damages caused by the breach from the seller or lessor or deduct the damages from any part of the purchase price or rent still due under the contract.

Consider This Example   A retail clothing store contracts to purchase 100 designer dresses for $100 per dress from a seller. The buyer pays for the dresses prior to delivery. After the dresses are delivered, the buyer discovers that 10 of the dresses have a flaw in them. The buyer may accept these nonconforming dresses and sue the seller for reasonable damages resulting from the nonconformity.

*C*ONCEPT SUMMARY   BUYER'S AND LESSEE'S REMEDIES

Situation	Buyer's or Lessee's Remedy
Seller or lessor refuses to deliver the goods or delivers nonconforming goods that the buyer or lessee does not want.	1. Reject nonconforming goods [UCC 2-601, 2A-509]. 2. Revoke acceptance of nonconforming goods [UCC 2-608, 2A-517(1)]. 3. Cover [UCC 2-712, 2A-518]. 4. Sue for breach of contract and recover damages [UCC 2-713, 2A-519]. 5. Cancel the contract [UCC 2-711(1), 2A-508(1)(a)].
Seller or lessor tenders nonconforming goods and the buyer or lessee accepts them.	1. Sue for ordinary damages [UCC 2-714(1), 2A-516(1)]. 2. Deduct damages from the unpaid purchase price [UCC 2-714(1), 2A-516(1)].
Seller or lessor refuses to deliver the goods and the buyer or lessee wants them.	1. Sue for specific performance [UCC 2-716(1), 2A-521(1)]. 2. Replevy the goods [UCC 2-716(3), 2A-521(3)]. 3. Recover the goods from an insolvent seller or lessor [UCC 2-502, 2A-522].

*S*TATUTE OF LIMITATIONS

UCC statute of limitations

A rule that provides that an action for breach of any written or oral sales or lease contract must commence within four years after the cause of action accrues. The parties may agree to reduce the limitations period to one year.

The **UCC statute of limitations** provides that an action for breach of any written or oral sales or lease contract must commence within four years after the cause of the action accrues. The parties may agree to reduce the limitations period to one year, but they cannot extend it beyond four years.

A cause of action for breach of a sales contract accrues when the breach occurs, regardless of the aggrieved party's lack of knowledge of the breach. In the case of the default of a lease contract, a cause of action accrues either when the default occurs or when it is or should have been discovered by the aggrieved party, whichever is later. If a warranty explicitly extends to future performance, a cause of action does not accrue until the breach is or should have been discovered.

Consider This Example A buyer purchases a snowmobile at a retailer's April "end of winter" sale. The buyer does not intend to use it until the following winter. In December, when the buyer first uses the snowmobile, it does not work properly. The statute of limitations begins to run in December.

The UCC statute of limitations does not apply if the action concerning the goods is based on legal theory not provided in the UCC (e.g., strict liability, negligence). In such cases, the appropriate state's statute of limitations governs [UCC 2-725, 2A-506].

AGREEMENTS AFFECTING REMEDIES

The parties to a sales or lease contract may agree on remedies in addition to or in substitution for the remedies provided by the UCC. For example, the parties may limit the buyer's or lessee's remedies to repair and replacement of defective goods or parts or to the return of the goods and repayment (refund) of the purchase price or rent. The remedies agreed upon by the parties are in addition to the remedies provided by the UCC unless the parties expressly provide that they are exclusive. If an exclusive remedy fails of its essential purpose (e.g., there is an exclusive remedy of repair but there are no repair parts available), any remedy may be had as provided in the UCC.

Consequential damages for breach of sales or lease contract may be limited or excluded unless the limitation or exclusion is **unconscionable**. With respect to consumer goods, a limitation of consequential damages for personal injuries is prima facie unconscionable. It is not unconscionable to limit consequential damages for a commercial loss [UCC 2-719, 2A-503].

The UCC permits parties to a sales or lease contract to establish in advance the damages that will be paid upon a breach of the contract. Such preestablished damages, called **liquidated damages**, substitute for actual damages. In a sales or lease contract, liquidated damages are valid if they are reasonable in light of the anticipated or actual harm caused by the breach, the difficulties of proof of loss, and the inconvenience or nonfeasibility of otherwise obtaining an adequate remedy [UCC 2-718(1), 2A-504].

A proceeding may be perfectly legal and may yet be opposed to sound commercial principles.

L. J. Lindley
Verner v. General and
Commercial Trust *(1894)*

liquidated damages

Damages that will be paid upon a breach of contract and that are established in advance.

Business Ethics

SALE OF GOODS WITH A DESIGN DEFECT

Manufacturers can often design products to be safer, but at a cost. The extra money or additional time necessary to do so is usually weighed against the benefits of creating a safer product. These cost-benefit decisions often present ethical dilemmas. Consider the following case.

Shortly after midnight on October 21, 1989, Shannon Moseley, age 17, was returning home after bringing his date to her house. He was driving a 1985 GMC Sierra pickup truck that his parents had bought him for his birthday. The truck was manufactured by General Motors Corporation (GM). As Shannon drove his truck through an intersection, David Ruprecht, a drunk driver, ran a red light and rammed into the driver's side of Shannon's truck. Shannon, whose truck immediately burst into flames, died in the accident.

Ruprecht, who was *judgment-proof* (i.e., did not have money to pay a jury award), served jail time for his offense. Shannon's parents also sued GM for product liability. They alleged that Shannon's pickup had dangerous side-saddle gas tanks mounted on the side of the vehicle outside the frame

rail of the truck. Other manufacturers of pickup trucks placed their gas tanks inside the frame so that the vehicles could withstand collisions better. The Moseleys argued that GM's side-saddle gas tank was a design defect that caused Shannon's death.

The Moseley's attorney, through the introduction of evidence, portrayed 20 years of corporate villainy by GM. This included evidence of clandestine crash testing, the results of which were never disclosed to the public, as well as document shredding. This evidence was designed to show not only poor product design but also GM's evil intent in keeping dangerous vehicles on the road. The Moseleys' attorney played to the emotions of the jury, portraying GM as an impersonal giant that ignored the danger to human life when designing its pickup trucks.

GM's counsel presented a very technical defense designed to show that the impact of Reprecht's vehicle—and not the design and placement of the fuel tank—killed Shannon instantly.

The star witness against GM was a disgruntled former employee, Ronald E. Elwell. When he had been employed at GM, Elwell was GM's fuel-tank safety expert who testified in cases on behalf of GM. Elwell testified as to the dangers of mounting gas tanks outside the frame rails on the type of pickup truck Shannon had been driving. He also testified as to secret crash tests that GM conducted on its pickup trucks and had not disclosed to the public or to him.

In the first phase of the trial, the jury returned a verdict of $4.24 million for Shannon's life plus $1 for pain and suffer-ing. In the second phase, the jury returned a punitive damage verdict of *$101 million* against GM.

GM appealed, and the appellate court overturned the decision. The case was later settled for an undisclosed sum of money. [*Moseley v. General Motors Corporation*, (1994)].

1. Did GM act ethically in this case?
2. Do you think an award of punitive damages would be justified in this case?

*C*HAPTER *S*UMMARY

*S*eller's and Lessor's Obligations, p. 407

Tender of Delivery	Requires the seller or lessor to (1) put and hold *conforming goods* at the buyer's or lessee's disposition and (2) give the buyer or lessee any notification reasonably necessary to enable the buyer or lessee to take delivery of the goods [UCC 2-503(1), 2A-508(1)].

Place of Delivery	1. *Agreement.* The parties may agree in the sales or lease contract as to the place of delivery.
	2. *No agreement.* If there is no agreement in the contract as to place of delivery, the following UCC rules apply:
	  a. *Noncarrier cases.* The place of delivery is the seller's or lessor's place of business, unless the seller or lessor has no place of business, in which case the place of delivery is the seller's or lessor's residence.
	  b. *Carrier cases:*
	    i. *Shipment contracts.* A sales contract that requires the seller to send goods to the buyer by carrier. Delivery occurs when the seller puts the goods in the carrier's possession [UCC 2-504].
	    ii. *Destination contracts.* A sales contract that requires the seller to deliver the goods to the buyer's place of business or other destination. Delivery occurs when the goods reach this destination [UCC 2-503].

Perfect Tender Rule	The seller or lessor is under a duty to deliver *conforming goods* to the buyer or lessee. If the goods or tender of delivery fails in any respect to conform to the contract, the buyer or lessee may opt to (1) reject the whole shipment, (2) accept the whole shipment, or (3) reject part and accept part of the shipment [UCC 2-601, 2A-509]. *Exceptions to the perfect tender rule:* 1. *Agreement of the parties.* The parties may agree to limit the effect of the perfect tender rule. 2. *Substitution of carriers.* A seller must use a commercially reasonable substitute if the agreed-upon manner of deliver fails or the agreed-upon type of carrier becomes unavailable [UCC 2-614(1)]. 3. *Cure.* A seller or lessor who delivers nonconforming goods has the opportunity to *cure* the nonconformity by repairing or replacing defective or nonconforming goods if the time for performance has not expired and the seller or lessor notifies the buyer or lessee of his or her intention to make a conforming delivery within the contract time [UCC 2-508, 2A-513]. 4. *Installment contracts.* The buyer or lessee may reject any nonconforming installment if the value of the installment is impaired and the defect cannot be cured. The buyer or lessee may reject the entire contract upon the tender of a nonconforming installment only if the nonconformity substantially impairs the value of the entire contract [UCC 2-612, 2A-510]. 5. *Destruction of goods.* If goods identified to the contract are totally destroyed without fault of either party before the risk of loss passes to the buyer or lessee, the seller or lessor is excused from performance [UCC 2-613].
General Obligations	The UCC has adopted the following broad principles that govern the performance of sales and lease contracts: 1. *Good faith.* Parties to a sales or lease contract must perform their contract obligations in *good faith* [UCC 1-203]. 2. *Reasonableness.* Many UCC provisions require parties to take *reasonable* steps or to act *reasonably* in performing contract obligations. 3. *Commercial reasonableness.* Some provisions of the UCC require merchants to use *commercial reasonableness* in the performance of their contract obligations.

*B*uyer's and Lessee's Obligations, p. 411

Right of Inspection	Unless otherwise agreed, the buyer or lessee has the right to inspect goods that are tendered, delivered, or identified to the sales or lease contract prior to accepting or paying for them [UCC 2-513(1), 2A-515(1)].

Payment	*Duty to pay.* Goods that are accepted by the buyer or lessee must be paid for in accordance with the terms of the sales or lease contract. Unless otherwise agreed, payment or rent is due when and where the goods are delivered [UCC 2-310, 2A-516(1)].
Acceptance	Acceptance occurs when the buyer or lessee takes one of the following actions [UCC 2-606, 2A-515]: 1. Signifies in words or by conduct that the goods are conforming or that the goods will be taken or retained despite their nonconformity 2. Fails to reject the goods within a reasonable time after their delivery by the seller or lessor 3. When a buyer acts inconsistently with the seller's ownership rights in the goods Buyers and lessees may only accept delivery of a *commercial unit*.

Assurance of Performance, p. 413

Assurance of Performance	If one party to a sales or lease contract has reasonable grounds to believe that the other party either will not or cannot perform his or her contractual obligations, he or she may demand in writing an adequate assurance of performance from the other party. The party making the demand may suspend his or her performance until adequate assurance of performance is received [UCC 2-609, 2A-401].

Anticipatory Repudiation, p. 413

Anticipatory Repudiation	Occurs when a party to a sales or lease contract repudiates the contract before his or her performance is due. The aggrieved party can (1) await performance when due or (2) treat the contract as breached at the time of the anticipatory repudiation [UCC 2-610, 2A-402].

Seller's and Lessor's Remedies, p. 414

Right to Withhold Delivery	Delivery of goods may be withheld if the seller or lessor discovers that the buyer or lessee is insolvent before the goods are delivered [UCC 2-703(a), 2A-523(1)(c)]. *Demand payment in cash.* If the seller or lessor discovers that the buyer or lessee is insolvent, he or she may refuse to deliver the goods except for payment of cash [UCC 2-702(1), 2A-525(1)].
Right to Stop Delivery of Goods in Transit	If the goods are in transit or in the bailee's possession, the seller or lessor may stop delivery (1) of a carload, a truckload, or a planeload of goods if the buyer or lessee repudiates the contract, fails to make a payment when due, or otherwise breaches the contract or (2) of any size shipment if the buyer or lessee becomes insolvent [UCC 2-705(1), 2A-526(1)].
Right to Reclaim Goods	A seller or lessor may reclaim goods in the possession of the buyer or lessee if: 1. The goods are delivered in a credit sale and the seller then discovers that the buyer was insolvent [UCC 2-000]. 2. The buyer misrepresented his or her solvency in writing within three months before delivery or paid for goods in a cash sale with a check that bounces [UCC 2-702(2) and 507(2)].
Right to Dispose of Goods	If a buyer or lessee breaches or repudiates the sales or lease contract before the seller or lessor has delivered the goods, the seller or lessor may resell or release the goods and recover damages from the buyer or lessee. Damages are calculated as the difference between the disposition price or rent and the original contract price or rent [UCC 2-706(1), 2A-527(1)].
Right to Recover the Purchase Price or Rent	If the buyer or lessee accepts the goods but fails to pay for them when the contract price or rent is due, the seller or lessor may sue to recover the contracted-for purchase price or rent from the buyer or lessee [UCC 2-709(1), 2A-529(1)].
Payment	*Duty to pay.* Goods that are accepted by the buyer or lessee must be paid for in accordance with the terms of the sales or lease contract. Unless otherwise agreed, payment or rent is due when and where the goods are delivered [UCC 2-310, 2A-516(1)].
Acceptance	Acceptance occurs when the buyer or lessee takes one of the following actions [UCC 2-606, 2A-515]: 1. Signifies in words or by conduct that the goods are conforming or that the goods will be taken or retained despite their nonconformity 2. Fails to reject the goods within a reasonable time after their delivery by the seller or lessor 3. When a buyer acts inconsistently with the seller's ownership rights in the goods Buyers and lesses may only accept delivery of a *commercial unit*.

Buyers and Lessor's Remedies, p. 417

Seller or Lessor Refuses to Deliver the Goods or Delivers Nonconforming Goods Lessee Does Not Want	1. *Reject nonconforming goods.* If the goods or the seller's or lessor's tender of delivery fails to conform to the sales or lease contract in any way, the buyer or lessee may (1) reject the whole, (2) accept the whole, or (3) accept any commercial unit and reject the rest [UCC 2-601, 2A-509].
	2. *Revoke acceptance of nonconforming goods.* A buyer or lessee who has accepted goods may subsequently revoke his or her acceptance if (1) the goods are nonconforming, (2) the nonconformity substantially impairs the value of the goods to the buyer or lessee, and (3) one of the following factors is shown:
	   a. the seller's or lessor's promise to reasonably cure the nonconformity is not met,
	   b. the goods were accepted before the nonconformity was discovered and the nonconformity was difficult to discover, or
	   c. the goods were accepted before the nonconformity was discovered and the seller or lessor assured the buyer or lessee that the goods were conforming [UCC 2-608(1), 2A-517(1)].
	3. *Cover.* If the seller or lessor fails to make delivery of goods or repudiates a sales or lease contract or if the buyer or lessee rightfully rejects the goods or justifiably revokes their acceptance, the buyer or lessee may cover by purchasing or renting substitute goods from another party. The buyer or lessee may recover from the seller or lessor damages calculated as the difference between the cost of cover and the original contract price or rent [UCC 2-712, 2A-518].
	4. *Sue for breach of contact and recover damages.* If a seller or lessor fails to deliver the goods or repudiates the sales or lease contract, the buyer or lessee may recover damages from the seller or lessor. Damages are calculated as the difference between the contract price (or original rent) and the market price (or rent) at the time the buyer or lessee learned of the breach [UCC 2-713, 2A-519].
	5. *Cancel the contract.* A buyer or lessee may cancel a sales or lease contract if the seller or lessor fails to deliver conforming goods or repudiates the contract or if the buyer or lessee rightfully rejects the goods or justifiably revokes acceptance of the goods. The buyer or lessee is discharged from any further obligations under the canceled contract [UCC 2-711(1), 2A-508(1)(a)].

Seller or Lessor Tenders Nonconforming Goods and the Buyer or Lessee Accepts Them	1. *Sue for damages.* If a buyer or lessee accepts nonconforming goods from a seller or lessor, the buyer or lessee may recover as damages any loss resulting from the seller's or lessor's breach [UCC 2-714(1), 2A-516(1)]. 2. *Deduct damages from unpaid purchase price or rent.* If a seller or lessor breaches the sales or lease contract and the buyer or lessee accepts nonconforming goods, the buyer or lessee may deduct all or any part of the damages resulting from the breach from any part of the price or rent still due under the sales or lease contract [UCC 2-714(1), 2A-516(1)].
Seller or Lessor Refuses to Deliver the Goods and the Buyer or Lessee Wants Them	1. *Specific performance.* If the goods are unique or the remedy at law in inadequate, a buyer or lessee may obtain a decree of specific performance that orders the seller or lessor to perform the sales or lease contract [UCC 2-716(1), 2A-521(1)]. 2. *Replevy the goods.* A buyer or lessee may replevy (recover) scarce goods from a seller or lessor who is wrongfully withholding them [UCC 2-716(3), 2A-521(3)]. 3. *Recover the goods from an insolvent seller or lessor.* If the buyer or lessee makes partial or full payment for the goods before they are received and the seller or lessor becomes insolvent within 10 days after receiving the first payment, the buyer or lessee may recover the goods from the seller or lessor [UCC 2-502, 2A522].
Unconscionable Sales and Lease Contracts	If a sales or lease contract or any clause in it is *unconscionable*, the court may either refuse to enforce the contract or limit the application of the unconscionable clause [UCC 2-302, 2A-108].

Statute of Limitations, p. 420

Statute of Limitations	The UCC provides that an action for breach of any written or oral sales or lease contract must commence within four years after the cause of action accrues. The parties may agree to reduce the limitations period to one year, but they cannot extend it beyond four years [UCC 2-725, 2A-506].

Agreements Affecting Remedies, p. 421

Agreements Affecting Remedies	1. *Limitations on remedies.* The parties to a sales or lease contract may agree on remedies in addition to or in substitution for the remedies provided by Article 2 or 2A of the UCC [UCC 2-719(1), 2A-503(1)]. 2. *Unconscionable limitations.* Any agreement concerning the limitation or exclusion of damages that is found to be unconscionable is unenforceable. With respect to consumer goods, a limitation of consequential damages for personal injuries is prima facie unconscionable [UCC 2-719(3), 2A-503(3)]. 3. *Liquidated damages.* The parties to a sales or lease contract may establish in advance the damages that will be paid upon a breach of the contract [UCC 2-718(1), 2A-504].

*E*ND-OF-*C*HAPTER *I*NTERNET *E*XERCISES AND *C*ASE *Q*UESTIONS

Working the Web Internet Exercises

ACTIVITIES

1. Find the UCC Article 2 as adopted in your jurisdiction. Review the seller's remedies under UCC 2-403. See **www.hg.org/cgi-bin/redir.cgi?url=www.law. cornell.edu/uniform/vol7.html**.

2. Find the law of specific performance/replevin for the buyer under UCC 2-716(1). How does this differ from the common law use of the term *replevin*?

3. When may the buyer revoke acceptance? See UCC 2-608(1).

4. Review UCC 2-712. What is the connection between *cover* and *mitigation* of damages?

CRITICAL LEGAL THINKING CASES

17.1 Good Faith Black Butte Coal Company (Coal Company) entered into a contract to supply coal for 20 years to Commonwealth Edison Company (Edison), a utility. The contract called for the two parties to determine each year how much coal was to be delivered during that period. The contract specified a minimum amount of coal that Edison was obligated to buy each year, but allowed Edison to purchase less than that amount if the coal could not be used due to environmental reasons. Several years after the contract was signed, Edison's business began to slump and it was faced with an oversupply of coal. The utility began to reduce the amount of coal it purchased each year. Also, there was an accident at one of Edison's generating plants, which left the plant inoperative for six months. Faced with these problems, the utility ordered less than the minimum amount of coal for the following year. Edison asserted that an "environmental" problem caused it to order less than the minimum amount of coal. The coal company sued Edison. Who wins? [*Big Horn Coal Co. v. Commonwealth Edison Co.*, 852 F.2d 1259 (10th Cir. 1988)]

17.2 Commercial Reasonableness Allsopp Sand and Gravel (Allsopp) and Lincoln Sand and Gravel (Lincoln) both were in the business of supplying sand to construction companies. In March 1986, Lincoln's sand dredge became inoperable. To continue in business, Lincoln negotiated a contract with Allsopp to purchase sand over the course of a year. The contract called for the sand to be loaded on Lincoln's trucks during Allsopp's regular operating season (March through November). Loading at other times was to be done by "special arrangement." By November 1986, Lincoln had taken delivery of one quarter of the sand it had contracted for. At this point, Lincoln requested that several trucks of sand be loaded in December. Allsopp informed Lincoln that it would have to pay extra for this special arrangement. Lincoln refused to pay extra, pointing out that the sand was already stockpiled at Allsopp's facilities. Allsopp also offered to supply an

employee to supervise the loading. Negotiations between the parties broke down, and Lincoln informed Allsopp that it did not intend to honor the remainder of the contract. Allsopp sued Lincoln. Was it commercially reasonable for Lincoln to demand delivery of sand during December? [*Allsopp Sand and Gavel v. Lincoln Sand and Gravel*, 525 N.E.2d 1185 (Ill.App. 1988)]

17.3 Nonconforming Goods The Jacob Hartz Seed Company, Inc. (Hartz), bought soybeans for use as seed from E. R. Coleman. Coleman certified that the seed had an 80 percent germination rate. Hartz paid for the beans an picked them up from a warehouse in Card, Arkansas. After the seed was transported to Georgia, a sample was submitted for testing to the Georgia Department of Agriculture. When the department reported a germination level of only 67 percent, Coleman requested that the seed be retested. The second set of tests reported a germination rate of 65 percent. Hartz canceled the contract after the second test, and Coleman reclaimed the seed. Hartz sought a refund of the money it paid for the seed, claiming that the soybeans were nonconforming goods. Who wins? [*Jacob Hartz Seed Co., v. Coleman*, 612 S.W.2d 91 (AK 1981)]

17.4 Right to Cure On December 21, 1982, Connie R. Grady purchased a new Chevrolet Chevette from Al Thompson Chevrolet (Thompson). Grady gave Thompson a down payment on the car and financed the remainder of the purchase price through General Motors Acceptance Corporation (GMAC). On December 22, 1982, Grady picked up the Chevette. The next day, the car broke down and had to be towed back to Thompson. Grady picked up the repaired car on December 24. The car's performance was still unsatisfactory in that the engine was hard to start, the transmission slipped, and the brakes had to be pushed to the floor to function. Grady again returned the Chevette for servicing on January 6, 1983. When she picked up the car that evening, the engine started, but the engine and brake warning lights came on. This pattern of malfunction and repair continued until March 3, 1983. On that day, Grady wrote a letter to Thompson revoking the sale. Thompson repossessed the Chevette. GMAC sued Grady to recover its money. Grady sued Thompson to recover her down payment. Thompson claimed that Grady's suit is barred because the company was not given adequate opportunity to cure. Who wins? [*General Motors Acceptance Corp. v. Grady*, 2 UCC Rep.Serv.2d 887 (Ohio App. 1985)]

17.5 Revocation of Acceptance Roy E. Farrar Produce Company (Farrar) was a packer and shipper of tomatoes in Rio Arribon County, New Mexico. Farrar contacted Wilson, an agent and salesman for International Paper Company (International), and ordered 21,500 tomato boxes for $.64 per box. The boxes each were to hold between 20 and 30 pounds of tomatoes for shipping. When the boxes arrived at Farrar's plant, 3,624 of them were immediately used to pack tomatoes. When the boxes were stacked, they began to collapse and crush the tomatoes contained within them. The produce company was forced to repackage the tomatoes and store the unused tomato boxes. Farrar contacted International and informed it that it no longer wanted the boxes because they could not perform as promised. International claims that Farrar had accepted the packages and must now pay for them. Who wins? [*International Paper Co. v. Farrar*, 700 P.2d 642 (NM 1985)]

17.6 Adequate Assurance Gal-Tex Oil Corporation owned and operated several oil rigs in the Gulf of Mexico. Gal-Tex provided living quarters for its workers on the oil rigs. These facilities included a small hospital ward. When Gal-Tex needed to lease some medical equipment for the hospital on its newest oil rig, it signed a five-year lease with International Medical Company (International). The contract called for International to provide five specific pieces of equipment. Two weeks after the contract was signed, Gal-Tex executives learned that International was insolvent. Gal-Tex's attorneys wrote to International requesting assurance that the lease would be complied with. International never replied to the letter. Forty-five days later, Gal-Tex enters into a new lease for hospital equipment with a different company. Does Gal-Tex still have any obligation under its lease with International?

17.7 Commercial Impracticability Charles C. Campbell was a farmer who farmed some 600 acres in the vicinity of Hanover, Pennsylvania. In May 1973, Campbell entered into a contract with Hostetter Farms, Inc. (Hostetter), a grain dealer with facilities in Hanover. The sales agreement called for Campbell to sell Hostetter 20,000 bushels of No. 2 yellow corn at $1.70 per bushel. Delivery was made in October 1973. Unfortunately, the summer of 1973 was an unusually rainy one, and Campbell could not plant part of his crop because of the wet ground. After the corn was planted, part of the crop failed due to the excessive rain. As a result, Campbell delivered only 10,417 bushels. Hostetter sued Campbell for breach of contract. Campbell asserted the defense of commercial impracticability. Who wins? [*Campbell v. Hostetter Farms, Inc.*, 380 A.2d 463 (PA 1977)]

17.8 Seller's Right to Stop Goods in Transit Ramco Steel, Inc. (Ramco), was a steel manufacturer located in Buffalo, New York. Ramco made a sales agreement with Murdock Machine and Engineering Company (Murdock) to sell cold drawn steel to Murdock. The steel was to be sold to Murdock on credit. The contract called for the steel to be shipped from Ramco's plant in Buffalo to a warehouse in Indiana for reshipment to Murdock at Clearfield, Utah, the final destination. A shipment of steel bars left Ramco's plant on May 22, 1975. Murdock became insolvent on May 13, and Ramco learned of this fact on May 23. On that same day, Ramco stopped delivery of the steel that was being trucked to the warehouse in Indiana. Murdock had bought the steel to fulfill a government contract to build fins and nozzles for missiles. The government claimed that Ramco had no right to stop delivery of the steel. Did Ramco act properly in stopping delivery? [*In re Murdock Machine & Engineering Company of Utah*, 620 F.2d 767 (10th Cir. 1980)]

17.9 Seller's Right to Reclaim Goods Archer Daniels Midland Company (Archer) sold ethanol for use in gasoline. Between April 11 and April 19, 1984, Archer sold 80,000 gallons of ethanol on credit to Charter International Oil Company (Charter). The ethanol was shipped to Charter's facility in Houston. Charter became insolvent sometime during that period. On April 21, Archer sent a written notice to Charter demanding the return of the ethanol. At the time Charter received the reclamation demand, it had only 12,000 gallons of ethanol remaining at its Houston facility. When Charter refused to return the unused ethanol, Archer sued to recover the ethanol. Who wins? [*Archer Daniels Midland v. Charter International Oil Company*, 60 B.R. 854 (M.D. Fla. 1986)]

17.10 Seller's Right to Resell Goods Meuser Material & Equipment Company (Meuser) was a dealer in construction equipment. On December 13, 1973, Meuser entered into an agreement with Joe McMillan for the sale of a bulldozer to McMillan. The agreement called for Meuser to deliver the bulldozer to McMillan's residence in Greeley, Colorado. McMillan paid Meuser with a check. On December 24, before taking delivery, McMillan stopped payment on the check. Meuser entered into negotiations with McMillan in an attempt to get McMillan to abide by the sales agreement. During this period, Meuser paid for the upkeep of the bulldozer. When it became apparent that further negotiations would be fruitless, Meuser began looking for a new buyer. Fourteen months after the original sale was supposed to have taken place, the bulldozer was resold for less than the original contract price. Meuser sued McMillan to recover the difference between the contract price and the resale price and the cost of upkeep on the bulldozer for 14 months. Who wins? [*McMillan v. Meuser Material & Equipment Company*, 541 S.W.2d (AK 1976)]

17.11 Seller's Right to Recover the Purchase Price C. R. Daniels, Inc. (Daniels) entered into a contract for the design and sale of grass catcher bags for lawn mowers to Yazoo Manufacturing Company, Inc. (Yazoo). Daniels contracted to design grass catcher bags that would fit the "S" Series mower made by Yazoo. Yazoo provided Daniels with a lawn mower to design the bag. After Yazoo approved the design of the bags, it issued a purchase order for 20,000 bags. Daniels began to ship the bags. After accepting 8,000 bags, Yazoo requested that the shipments stop. Officials of Yazoo told Daniels that they would resume accepting shipments in a few months. Despite several attempts, Daniels could not get Yazoo to accept delivery of the remaining 12,000 bags. Daniels sued Yazoo to recover the purchase price of the grass bags still in their inventory. Who wins? [*C. R. Daniels, Inc. v. Yazoo Mfg. Co., Inc.* 641 F.Supp. 205 (S.D. Miss 1986)]

17.12 Seller's Right to Recover Lost Profits Saber Energy, Inc. (Saber), entered into a sales contract with Tri-State Petroleum Corporation (Tri-State). The contract called for Saber to sell Tri-State 110,000 barrels of gasoline per month from July to December 1981. Saber was to deliver the gasoline through the colonial pipeline in Pasadena, Texas. The first 110,000 barrels were delivered on time. On August 1, Saber was informed that Tri-State was canceling the contract. Saber sued Tri-State for breach of contract and sought to recover its lost profits as damages. Tri-State admitted its breach but claimed that lost profits is an inappropriate measure of damages. Who wins? [*Tri-State Petroleum Corporation v. Saber Energy, Inc.* 845 F.2d 575 (5th Cir. 1988)]

17.13 Buyer's Right to Demand Specific Performance Dr. and Mrs. Sedmak (Sedmaks) were collectors of Chevrolet Corvettes. In July 1977, the Sedmaks saw an article in *Vette Vues* magazine concerning a new limited edition Corvette. The limited edition was designed to commemorate the selection of the Corvette as the official pace car of the Indianapolis 500. Chevrolet was manufacturing only 6,000 of these pace cars. The Sedmaks visited Charlie's Chevrolet, Inc. (Charlie's), a local Chevrolet dealer. Charlie's was to receive only one limited edition car, which the sales manager agreed to sell to the Sedmaks for the sticker price of $15,000. When the Sedmaks went to pick up and pay for the car, they were told that because of the great demand for the limited edition, it was going to be auctioned to the highest bidder. The Sedmaks sued the dealership for specific performance. Who wins? [*Sedmak v. Charlie's Chevrolet, Inc.* 622 S.W.2d 694 (Mo. App. 1981)]

17.14 Buyer's Right to Cover and Recover Damages Kent Nowlin Construction, Inc. (Nowlin), was awarded a contract by the state of New Mexico to pave a number of roads. After Nowlin was awarded the contract, it entered into an agreement with Concrete Sales & Equipment Rental Company, Inc.

(C&E). C&E was to supply 20,000 tons of paving material to Nowlin. Nowlin began paving the roads, anticipating C&E's delivery of materials. On the delivery date, however, C&E shipped only 2,099 tons of paving materials. Because Nowlin had a deadline to meet, the company contracted with Gallup Sand and Gravel Company (Gallup) for substitute material. Nowlin sued C&E to recover the difference between the higher price it had to pay Gallup for materials and the contract price C&E had agreed to. C&E claims that it is not responsible for Nowlin's increased costs. Who wins? [*Concrete Sales & Equipment Rental Company, Inc. v. Kent Nowlin Construction, Inc.* 746 P.2d 645 (NM 1987)]

17.15 Buyer's Right to Recover Damages Earl Miller is a well-know sailor and builder of sailboats. Miller operated his own company, Miller Marine, Inc., on Bainbridge Island, Washington. In 1981, Carole Badgley saw an advertisement for a sailboat built by Miller. The advertised sailboat was a lightweight, high-performance racing vessel named *The Bonnie*. Badgley entered into a contract with Miller for the purchase of *The Bonnie* at a price of $135,000. After she took possession of the sailboat, Badgley noticed a steady leak. Badgley had several naval engineers examine the vessel. The engineers attributed the leak to a design defect. Badgley paid $20,000 to have extensive repairs made to stop the leak. She then sued Miller to recover the $20,000. Who wins? [*Miller v. Badgley*, 753 P.2d 530 (Wash. App. 1988)]

17.16 Unconscionable Contract Jane Wilson leased a Toyota pickup truck from World Omni Leasing (Omni). Wilson had experience in business and had signed contracts before. In the past, Wilson had read the contracts before signing them. When signing the contract for the lease of the truck, however, Wilson did not take the opportunity to read the lease. She even signed a statement declaring that she had read and understood the lease. The lease contained a provision that made Wilson responsible for payments on the truck even if the truck was destroyed. Several months after leasing the truck, Wilson was involved in a two-vehicle collision. The pickup was destroyed. Omni demand to be paid for the balance of the lease. Wilson refuses, claiming that the lease was unconscionable. Is the lease unconscionable? [*Wilson v. World Omni Leasing, Inc.* 540 So.2d 713 (AL 1989)]

 BUSINESS ETHICS CASES

17.17 Business Ethics Ruby and Carmen Ybarra purchased a new double-wide mobile home from Modern Trailer Sales, Inc. (Modern). On March 11, 1974, Modern delivered the mobile home to the Ybarras. A few days after delivery, portions of the floor began to rise and bubble, creating an unsightly and troublesome situation for the Ybarras. The Ybarras complained to Modern about the floor as soon as the defects were discovered. Modern sent repairmen to cure the defective floor on at least three occasions, but each

time they were unsuccessful. The Ybarras continued to complain about the defects. The Ybarras continued to rely on Modern's assurances that it was able and willing to repair the floor. After four years of complaints, the Ybarras sued to revoke their acceptance of the sales contract. Did the Ybarras properly revoke their acceptance of the sales contract? Did Modern Trailer Sales act ethically in this case? Did the Ybarras? [*Ybarras v. Modern Trailer Sales, Inc.* 609 P.2d 311 (NM 1980)]

17.18 Business Ethics   In 1974, Alex Abatti was the sole owner of A&M Produce Company (A&M), a small farming company located in California's Imperial Valley. Although Abatti had never grown tomatoes, he decided to do so. He sought the advice of FMC Corporation (FMC), a large diversified manufacturer of farming and other equipment, as to what kind of equipment he would need to process the tomatoes. An FMC representative recommended a certain type of machine, which A&M purchased from FMC pursuant to a form sales contract provided by FMC. Within the fine print, the contract contained one clause that disclaimed any warranty liability by FMC and a second clause that stated that FMC would not be liable for consequential damages if the machine malfunctioned.

A&M paid $10,680 down toward the $32,041 purchase price, and FMC delivered and installed the machine. A&M immediately began experiencing problems with the machine. It did not process the tomatoes quickly enough. Tomatoes began piling up in front of the belt that separated the tomatoes for weight-sizing. Overflow tomatoes had to be sent through the machine at least twice, causing damage to them. Fungus spread through the damaged crop. Because of these problems, the machine had to be continually started and stopped, which significantly reduced processing speed.

A&M tried on several occasions to get additional equipment from FMC, but on each occasion its request was rejected. Because of the problems with the machine, on June 17, 1974, A&M closed its tomato operation. A&M finally stated, "Let's call the whole thing off" and offered to return the machine if FMC would refund A&M's down payment. When FMC rejected this offer and demanded full payment of the balance due, A&M sued to recover its down payment and damages. It alleged breach of warranty caused by defect in the machine. In defense, FMC pointed to the fine print of the sales contract, stating that the buyer waived any rights to sue it for breach of warranty or to recover consequential damages from it.

Was it ethical for FMC to include waiver of liability and waiver of consequential damage clauses in its form contract? Did A&M act morally in signing the contract and then trying to get out from under its provisions? Legally, are the waiver clauses so unconscionable as to not be enforced? [*A&M Produce Company v. FMC Corporation*, 135 Cal.App.3d 473, 186 Cal.Rptr. 114 (Cal.App. 1982)]

BRIEFING THE CASE WRITING ASSIGNMENT

Read the following case, which has been excerpted from the Court's Opinions. Review and brief the case.

LNS Investment Company, Inc. v. Phillips 66 Company
731 F.Supp. 1484 (1990)
United States District Court

O'Connor, Chief Judge

Plaintiff is the successor to a company know as Compu-Blend Corporation (CBC), which blended, labeled, and packaged quart plastic bottles of motor oil for, among others, defendant Phillips 66 Company. On July 29, 1986, W. Peter Buhlinger, defendant's manager of lubricants (Buhlinger), wrote a letter to Dan Tutcher, plaintiff's vice-president of operations (Tucher), which read as follows:

This will confirm our verbal agreement wherein Phillips will purchase additional quantities of plastic bottles from CBC during 1986. CBC, in an effort to increase their packaging capacity has committed to purchase several additional molds to blow the Phillips plastic one-quart container. In order to amortize the cost of the additional equipment Phillips has agreed to take delivery of a maximum of 4,000,000 bottles to be made available by December 31, 1986. This agreement includes the production available now and to be supplemented by the additional equipment. Should CBC not be able to produce the full 4,000,000 quarts by December 31, 1986, this agreement shall be considered satisfied. Phillips' desire is to receive as many bottles packaged with Phillips motor oil in 1986 from CBC as possible.

Plaintiff experienced numerous problems in maintaining even its pre-contract capacity. Moreover, the quality of goods plaintiff was able to deliver was frequently unacceptable to defendant. Laughlin reiterated defendant's dissatisfaction with plaintiff's products by letter dated October 15, 1986. Discussing bottles tendered by Plaintiff, Laughlin stated that, "we definitely do not want bottles on the shelf of the quality submitted." On December 16, 1986, Buhlinger wrote that defendant would not renew any commitments to purchase goods from plaintiff after March 31, 1987, due to plaintiff's poor performance under the July 29 agreement. Plaintiff filed this suit on May 12, 1987, alleging, inter alia, that defendant breached the July 29 agreement by failing to purchase plaintiff's full output of plastic bottles through December 31, 1986.

Plaintiff's failure to provide either the quantity or quality of goods contemplated by the July 29 agreement entitled defendant to suspend its performance. Section 84-2-609 of the Code states as follows: Right to adequate assurance of performance. (1) A contract for sale imposes an obligation on each party that the other's expectation of receiving due performance will not be impaired. When reasonable grounds for insecurity arise with respect to the performance of either party the other may in writing demand adequate assurance of due performance and until he receives such assurance may if commercially reasonable suspend any performance for which he has not already received the agreed return.

It was incumbent upon plaintiff to provide adequate assurance of its future performance to defendant. Plaintiff failed to provide defendant with adequate assurance of its future performance. Official UCC Comment 4 states that what constitutes "adequate" assurance of due performance is subject to the same test of factual conditions as what constitutes "reasonable grounds for insecurity." For example, where the buyer can make use of a defective delivery, a mere promise by a seller of good repute that he is giving the matter his attention and that the defect will not be repeated, is normally sufficient. Under the same circumstances, however, a similar statement by a known corner-cutter might well be considered insufficient without the posting of a guaranty or, if so demanded by the buyer, a speedy replacement of the delivery involved. By the same token where a delivery has defects, even though easily curable, which interfere with easy use by the buyer, no verbal assurance can be deemed adequate which is not accomplished by replacement, repair, money-allowance, or other commercially reasonable cure.

Plaintiff's continual excuses for failing to perform, unaccompanied by corresponding remedial action, cannot be deemed adequate assurance under the Code. Accordingly, defendant was entitled to suspend its own performance

of the contract by refusing to place orders with plaintiff and/or canceling unfilled orders already placed, days after either or both the September 18, 1986, and October 15, 1986, letters. In view of this conclusion, defendant did not breach the contract by suspending performance in December 1986, and judgment will be entered in its favor.

Judgment for defendant.

CHAPTER 18

Product Liability and Warranties

A manufacturer is strictly liable in tort when an article he places on the market, knowing that it is to be used without inspection for defects, proves to have a defect that causes injury to a human being.

—*Greenmun v. Yuba Power Product, Inc.*
59 Cal.2d 57, 27 Cal.Rptr. 697 (1963)

Chapter Objectives

After studying this chapter you should be able to:

1. Identify and describe express warranties.

2. Describe the implied warranties of merchantability and fitness for a particular purpose.

3. Identify warranty disclaimers and determine when they are unlawful.

4. Describe how the Magnuson–Moss Warranty Act affects warranties regarding consumer goods.

5. Define *doctrine of strict liability*.

6. Identify defects in manufacture, design, packaging, failure to warn, and failure to provide adequate instructions.

7. List and describe the damages recoverable in a product liability action.

8. List and describe the defenses to product liability lawsuits.

9. Describe warranty disclaimers contained in software licenses.

10. Describe international product liability laws.

Chapter Contents

The doctrine of *caveat emptor*—let the buyer beware—governed the law of sales and leases for centuries. Finally, the law recognized that consumers and other purchasers and lessees of goods needed greater protection. Article 2 of the Uniform Commercial Code (UCC), which has been adopted in whole or part by all 50 states, establishes certain **warranties** that apply to the sale of goods. Article 2A of the UCC, which many states have adopted, establishes warranties that apply in lease transactions. Consumers and others can sue to recover damages caused by breach of warranty.

In addition, if a product defect causes injury to purchasers, lessees, users, or bystanders, the injured party may be able to recover for his or her injuries under certain tort theories, including negligence, misrepresentation, and the modern theory of strict liability. The liability of manufacturers, sellers, lessors, and others for injuries caused by defective products is commonly referred to as **products liability**.

The various warranty and tort principles that permit injured parties to recover damages caused by defective products are discussed in this chapter.

WARRANTIES OF QUALITY

Warranties are the buyer's or lessee's assurance that the goods they sell or lease meet certain standards of quality. **Warranties of quality**, which are based on contract law, may be either expressly stated or implied by law. If the goods fail to meet a warranty, the buyer or lessee can sue the seller or lessor for breach of warranty. Warranties are discussed in the following paragraphs.

Express Warranties

Express warranties, which are the oldest form of warranty, are created when a seller or lessor affirms that the goods he or she is selling or leasing meet certain standards of quality, description, performance, or condition [UCC 2-313(1); UCC 2A-210(1)]. Express warranties can be either written, oral, or inferred from the seller's conduct.

It is not necessary to use formal words such as warrant or guarantee to create an express warranty. Express warranties can be made by mistake because the seller or lessor does not have to specifically intend to make the warranty [UCC 2-313(2); UCC 2A-210(2)].

Sellers and lessors are not required to make such warranties. Generally, they are made to entice consumers and others to buy or lease their products. That is why these warranties often are in the form of advertisements, brochures, catalogs, pictures, illustrations, diagrams, blueprints, and so on.

Express warranties are created when the seller or lessor indicates that the goods will conform to

1. All *affirmations of fact or promise* made about them (e.g., statements such as "This car will go 100 miles per hour" or "This house paint will last at least five years").
2. Any *description* of them (e.g., terms such as *Idaho potatoes* and *Michigan cherries*).
3. Any *model* or *sample* of them (e.g., a model oil drilling rig or a sample of wheat taken from a silo).

Basis of the Bargain   Buyers and lessees can recover for breach of an express warranty if the warranty was a contributing factor—not necessarily the sole factor—that induced the buyer to purchase the product or the lessee to lease the product. This is known as the **basis of the bargain** [UCC 2-313(1); UCC 2A-210(1)]. The UCC does not define the term basis of the bargain, so this test is broadly applied by the courts. Generally, all statements by the seller or lessor prior to or at the time of contracting are presumed to be part of the basis of the bargain unless good reason is shown to the contrary. Post-sale statements that modify the contract are part of the basis of the bargain.

Generally, a retailer is liable for the express warranties made by manufacturers of goods it sells. Manufacturers are not liable for express warranties made by wholesalers and retailers unless the manufacturer authorizes or ratifies the warranty.

Statements of Opinion   Many express warranties arise during the course of negotiations between the buyer and the seller (or lessor and lessee). The seller's or lessor's **statements of opinion** (i.e., **puffing**) or commendation of the goods do not create an express warranty

---

warranty

A buyer's or lessee's assurance that the goods meet certain standards.

products liability

The liability of manufacturers, sellers, and others for the injuries caused by defective products.

warranties of quality

Seller's or lessor's assurance to buyer or lessee that the goods meet certain standards of quality. Warranties may be expressed or implied.

express warranty

A warranty that is created when a seller or lessor makes an affirmation that the goods he or she is selling or leasing meet certain standards of quality, description, performance, or condition.

When a manufacturer engages in advertising in order to bring his goods and their quality to the attention of the public and thus to create consumer demand, the representations made constitute an express warranty running directly to a buyer who purchases in reliance thereon. The fact that the sale is consummated with an independent dealer does not obviate the warranty.

Justice Francis
Henningsen v. Bloomfield Motors, Inc.,
161 A.2d 69 (NJ 1960)

Ethics Brief

Sellers and lessors of goods do not have to make express warranties concerning the quality of their goods. They often make such warranties to convince people or businesses to purchase or lease goods from them.

Business Brief

Sales "puffing" by salespersons usually does not create a warranty; it is merely a statement of opinion.

[UCC 2-313(2)]. For example, a used car salesperson's statement that "This is the best used car available in town" does not create an express warranty. However, a statement such as "This car has been driven only 20,000 miles" is an express warranty. It is often difficult to determine whether the seller's statement is an affirmation of fact (which creates an express warranty) or statement of opinion (which does not create a warranty).

An affirmation of the *value* of goods does not create an express warranty [UCC 2-313(2)]. For example, statements such as "This painting is worth a fortune" or "Others would gladly pay $20,000 for this car" do not create an express warranty.

In the following case, the court had to decide whether an express warranty had been created.

Daughtrey v. Ashe
413 S.E.2d 336 (1992)
Supreme Court of Virginia

CASE 18.1

BACKGROUND AND FACTS
In October 1985, W. Hayes Daughtrey consulted Sidney Ashe, a jeweler, about the purchase of a diamond bracelet as a Christmas present for his wife. Ashe showed Daughtrey a diamond bracelet that he had for sale for $15,000. When Daughtrey decided to purchase the bracelet, Ashe completed and signed an appraisal form that stated that the diamonds were "H color and v.v.s. quality." (V.v.s. is one of the highest ratings in a quality classification employed by jewelers.) After Daughtrey paid for the bracelet, Ashe put the bracelet and the appraisal form in a box. Daughtrey gave the bracelet to his wife as a Christmas present. In February 1987, when another jeweler looked at the bracelet, Daughtrey discovered that the diamonds were of substantially lower grade than v.v.s. Daughtrey filed a specific performance suit against Ashe to compel him to replace the bracelet with one mounted with v.v.s. diamonds or pay appropriate damages. The trial court denied relief for breach of warranty. Daughtrey appealed.

ISSUE
Was an express warranty made by Ashe regarding the quality of the diamonds in the bracelet?

COURT'S REASONING
Any description of the goods that is made a basis of the bargain creates an express warranty that the goods shall conform to the description. The appellate court found that Ashe's description of the diamonds created an express warranty that became a part of the basis of the bargain between Ashe and Daughtrey. The court noted that it was not necessary for Ashe to have used the word *warrant* or *guarantee* to create an express warranty.

DECISION AND REMEDY
The appellate court held that an express warranty had been created. The trial court's decision was reversed and the case was remanded for determination of appropriate damages to be awarded to Daughtrey.

Case Questions

Critical Legal Thinking   What is the remedy when an express warranty has been breached? Is the remedy sufficient?

Business Ethics   Did Ashe act ethically in denying that his statement created an express warranty?

Contemporary Business   Do businesses have to make express warranties? Why do businesses make warranties about the quality of their products?

Implied Warranty of Merchantability

If the seller or lessor of a good is a merchant with respect to goods of that kind, the sales contract contains an **implied warranty of merchantability** unless it is properly disclaimed [UCC 2-314(1), UCC 2A-212(1)]. This requires the following standards to be met:

implied warranty of merchantability

Unless properly disclosed, a warranty is implied when sold or leased goods are fit for the ordinary purpose for which they are sold or leased, and other assurances.

- **The goods must be fit for the ordinary purposes for which they are used.** For example, a chair must be able to safely perform the function of a chair. For example, if a normal-sized person sits in a chair that has not been tampered with, and the chair collapses, there has been a breach of the implied warranty of merchantability. If however, the same person is injured because he or she used the chair as a ladder and it tips over, there is no breach of implied warranty because serving as a ladder is not the ordinary purpose of a chair.

Business Brief

The implied warranty of merchantability does not apply to sales or leases by nonmerchants or casual sales.

- **The goods must be adequately contained, packaged, and labeled.** The implied warranty of merchantability applies to the milk bottle as well as to the milk inside the bottle.
- **The goods must be of an even kind, quality, and quantity within each unit.** All of the goods in a carton, package, or box must be consistent.

- **The goods must conform to any promise or affirmation of fact made on the container or label.** The goods can be used safely in accordance with the instructions on the package or label.
- **The quality of the goods must pass without objection in the trade.** Other users of the goods would not object to their quality.
- **Fungible goods must meet a fair average or middle range of quality.** To be classified as a certain grade, grain or ore must meet the average range of quality of that grade.

Note that the implied warranty of merchantability does not apply to sales or leases by nonmerchants or casual sales. For example, the implied warranty of merchantability applies to the sale of a lawn mower that is sold by a merchant who is in the business of selling lawn mowers. It does not apply when one neighbor sells a lawn mower to another neighbor. The following case raised the issue of implied warranty of merchantability.

Warranties are favored in law, being a part of a man's assurance.

Coke
First Institute

Denny v. Ford Motor Company
639 N.Y.S.2d 250, 87 N.Y.2d 248 (1995)
Court of Appeals of New York

CASE 18.2

BACKGROUND AND FACTS
Nancy Denny purchased a Bronco II, a small utility vehicle that was manufactured by Ford Motor Company. Denny testified that she purchased the Bronco for use on paved city and suburban streets, and not for off-road use. On June 9, 1986, when Denny was driving the vehicle on a paved road, she slammed on the brakes in an effort to avoid a deer that had walked directly into her motor vehicle's path. The Bronco II rolled over and Denny was severely injured. Denny sued Ford Motor Company to recover damages for breach of the implied warranty of merchantability.

Denny alleged that the Bronco II presented a significantly higher risk of occurrence of rollover accidents than did ordinary passenger vehicles. Denny introduced evidence at trial that showed that the Bronco II had a low stability index because of its high center of gravity, narrow tracks, shorter wheel base, and the design of its suspension system. Ford countered that the Bronco II was intended as an off-road vehicle and was not designed to be used as a conventional passenger automobile on paved streets. The trial court found Ford liable and awarded Denny $1.2 million in damages. Ford appealed.

ISSUE
Did Ford Motor Company breach the implied warranty of merchantability?

COURT'S REASONING
The plaintiff introduced a Ford marketing manual that predicted that many buyers would be attracted to the Bronco II because utility vehicles were suitable to "contemporary lifestyles" in some suburban areas. According to this manual, the sales presentation of the Bronco II should take into account the vehicle's "suitability for commuting and for suburban and city driving." In addition, the vehicle's ability to switch between two-wheel and four-wheel drive would "be particularly appealing to women who may be concerned about driving in snow and ice with their children." Plaintiff testified

that the perceived safety benefits of its four-wheel drive capacity was what attracted her to the Bronco II. She was not at all interested in its off-road use.

The law implies a warranty by a manufacturer that places its product on the market that the product is reasonably fit for the ordinary purpose for which it was intended. If it is, in fact, defective and not reasonably fit to be used for its intended purpose, the warranty is breached. Plaintiff's proof focused on the sale of the Bronco II for suburban driving and everyday road travel. Plaintiff also adduced proof that the Bronco II's design characteristics made it unusually susceptible to rollover accidents when used on paved roads. All this evidence was useful in showing that routine highway and street driving was the "ordinary purpose" for which the Bronco II was sold and that it was not "fit"—or safe—for that purpose. The court concluded that under the evidence in this case, a rational fact finder could have concluded that the vehicle was not safe for the "ordinary purpose" of daily driving for which it was marketed and sold.

DECISION AND REMEDY
The court of appeals held that Ford had breached the implied warranty of merchantability and upheld the jury award for the plaintiff.

Case Questions

Critical Legal Thinking Should the law impose an *implied* warranty of merchantability in the sale of goods? What is the public policy underlying this implied warranty?

Business Ethics Did Ford act ethically in defending that the Bronco II was sold only as an off-road vehicle? Was this argument persuasive?

Contemporary Business What are the business implications of this decision? Do you think that utility vehicles such as the Bronco II have a higher rollover danger than normal passenger automobiles?

Restaurants and other food providers warrant that the food and drink they serve is fit for human consumption. States apply either the foreign substance test or the consumer expectation test in determining whether this implied warranty has been breached.

implied warranty of fitness for human consumption

A warranty that applies to food or drink consumed on or off the premises of restaurants, grocery stores, fast-food outlets, and vending machines.

Business Brief

The consumer expectation test is the modern test adopted by the majority of states to determine merchantability based on what the average consumer would expect to find in food products.

Implied Warranty of Fitness for Human Consumption   The common law implied a special warranty—the **implied warranty of fitness for human consumption**—to food products. The UCC incorporates this warranty, which applies to food and drink consumed on or off the premises, within the implied warranty of merchantability. Restaurants, grocery stores, fast-food outlets, and vending-machine operators all are subject to this warranty.

Some states apply a *foreign substance test* to determine whether food products are unmerchantable. Under this test, a food product is unmerchantable if a foreign object in that product causes injury to a person. For example, the warranty would be breached if an injury were caused by a nail in a cherry pie. If the same injury were caused by a cherry pit in the pie, the pie would not be unmerchantable.

The majority of states have adopted the modern *consumer expectation test* to determine the merchantability of food products. For example, under this implied warranty, if a person is injured by a chicken bone while eating fried chicken, the injury is not actionable. However, the warranty would be breached if a person is injured by a chicken bone while eating a chicken salad sandwich. This is because a consumer would expect that the food preparer would have removed all bones from the chicken.

The following case is a modern implied warranty of fitness for human consumption case.

Goodman v. Wendy's Foods, Inc.

1423 S.E.2d 444 (1992)
Supreme Court of North Carolina

CASE 18.3

BACKGROUND AND FACTS

On October 28, 1983, Fred Goodman purchased a double hamburger sandwich with "everything" on it from a Wendy's Old Fashioned Hamburger restaurant (Wendy's). According to Goodman's testimony, about halfway through the sandwich, he bit a hard substance. He found a bone one-and-one-half inches in length, and the width of one-quarter inch at its widest, from which it narrowed to a point. As a result of biting the bone, Goodman broke three teeth. He incurred substantial dental expenses for root canal surgery, temporary and permanent crowns, and tooth extraction. Goodman sued Wendy's to recover damages for breach of the implied warranty of fitness for human consumption. Wendy's argued that the foreign substance test applied and protected it from liabil-

ity. Goodman alleged that the consumer expectation test applied and that Wendy's was liable. The trial court directed a verdict for Wendy's. Goodman appealed.

ISSUE

Does the foreign substance test or the consumer expectation test apply to a breach of implied warranty of fitness for human consumption case?

COURT'S REASONING

In this era of consumerism and modern technology in food processing, the better test of what is defective appears to be what consumers customarily expect and guard against. The court stated that a "restaurant makes an implied warranty that the food which it serves is fit for human consumption, even though the restaurant in the exercise of all possible care could not have discovered its unwholesome nature."

DECISION AND REMEDY

The state supreme court followed the recent trend and held that the consumer expectation test applied to cases of alleged injuries caused by food products. The supreme court reversed and remanded the case for trial using the consumer expectation test.

Case Questions

Critical Legal Thinking Which do you think is a better test for determining warranty liability of food sellers, the foreign substance test or the consumer expectation test? Explain.

Business Ethics Was it ethical for the defendant to argue against liability in this case?

Contemporary Business On remand, would you find Wendy's liable? If so, what amount of damages would you award?

Implied Warranty of Fitness for a Particular Purpose

The UCC contains an implied **warranty of fitness for a particular purpose**. This implied warranty is breached if the goods do not meet the buyer's or lessee's expressed needs. The warranty applies to both merchant and nonmerchant sellers and lessors.

The warranty of fitness for a particular purpose is implied at the time of contracting if

1. The seller or lessor has reason to know the particular purpose for which the buyer is purchasing the goods or the lessee is leasing the goods.
2. The seller or lessor makes a statement that the goods will serve this purpose.
3. The buyer or lessee relies on the seller's or lessor's skill and judgment and purchases or leases the goods [UCC 2-315, UCC 2A-213].

Consider This Example Susan Logan wants to buy lumber to build a house, so she goes to Winter's lumber yard. Logan describes the house she intends to build to Winter. She also tells Winter that she is relying on him to select the right lumber. Winter selects the lumber, and Logan buys it and builds the house. Unfortunately, the house collapses because the lumber was not strong enough to support it. Logan can sue Winter for breach of the implied warranty of fitness for a particular purpose.

The following case raises the issue of implied warranty of fitness for a particular purpose.

warranty of fitness for a particular purpose

A warranty that arises when a seller or lessor warrants that the goods will meet the buyer's or lessee's expressed needs.

Mack Massey Motors, Inc. v. Garnica

814 S.W.2d 167 (1991)
Court of Appeals of Texas

CASE 18.4

BACKGROUND AND FACTS

Felicitas Garnica sought to purchase a vehicle capable of towing a 23-foot Airstream trailer she had on order. She went to Mack Massey Motors, Inc. (Massey Motors), to inquire about purchasing a Jeep Cherokee that was manufactured by Jeep Eagle. After Garnica explained her requirements to the sales manager, he called the Airstream dealer concerning the specifications of the trailer Garnica was purchasing. The sales manager advised Garnica that the Jeep Cherokee could do the job of pulling the trailer. After purchasing the vehicle, Garnica claimed that it did not have sufficient power to pull the trailer. She brought the Jeep Cherokee back to Massey Motors several times for repairs for a slipping transmission. Eventually, she was told to go to another dealer. The drive shaft on the Jeep Cherokee twisted apart at 7,229 miles. Garnica sued Massey Motors and Jeep Eagle for damages, alleging breach of the implied warranty

of fitness for a particular purpose. The jury returned a verdict in favor of Garnica. Massey Motors and Jeep Eagle appealed.

ISSUE

Did the defendants make and breach an implied warranty of fitness for a particular purpose?

COURT'S REASONING

The appellate court noted that the service provided by Massey Motors's sales staff included undertaking the responsibility of checking with the Airstream dealer and thereafter representing that the Jeep Cherokee, with an automatic transmission, was suitable for pulling the Airstream. Massey Motors's sales manager testified that he knew the intended purpose for the appellee's use of the proposed vehicle and that he undertook to investigate the specifications of the

Airstream. After having undertaken the inquiry, he recommended the Jeep Cherokee as being suitable for the purpose Mrs. Garnica was seeking, that of towing the Airstream trailer she had on order.

A claim of warranty of fitness requires that goods serve their particular purpose. The court concluded that the evidence supported the jury determination that the Jeep Cherokee simply was exceeding its towing capacity and that Massey Motors had misrepresented that this vehicle was suitable for towing the Airstream trailer. In light of Massey Motors' superior knowledge and expertise concerning Garnica's inquiry and reliance, the evidence was sufficient to support the jury's finding.

DECISION AND REMEDY

The appellate court held that Massey Motors had made and breached an implied warranty of fitness for a particular purpose, but that Jeep Eagle had not.

Case Questions

Critical Legal Thinking   Should the law recognize the implied warranty of fitness for a particular purpose? Or should buyers be held to know their own requirements?

Business Ethics   Did Massey Motors act unethically in this case?

Contemporary Business   Do you think damages should have been awarded in this case?

*C*ONCEPT SUMMARY   EXPRESS AND IMPLIED WARRANTIES OF QUALITY

Type of Warranty	How Created	Description
Express warranty	Made by the seller or lessor.	Affirmation that the goods meet certain standards of quality, description, performance, or condition [UCC 2-313(1), UCC 2A-210(1)].
Implied warranty of merchantability	Implied by law if the seller or lessor is a merchant.	Implied that the goods 1. Are fit for the ordinary purposes for which they are used. 2. Are adequately contained, packaged, and labeled. 3. Are of an even kind, quality, and quantity within each unit. 4. Conform to any promise or affirmation of fact made on the container or label. 5. Pass without objection in the trade. 6. Meet a fair, average, or middle range of quality for fungible goods [UCC 2-314(1), UCC 2A-212(1)].
Implied warranty for fitness for a particular purpose	Implied by law.	Implied that the goods are fit for the purpose for which the buyer or lessee acquires the goods if 1. the seller or lessor has reason to know the particular purpose for which the goods will be used, 2. the seller or lessor makes a statement that the goods will serve that purpose, and 3. the buyer or lessee relies on the statement and buys or leases the goods [UCC 2-315, UCC 2A-213].

Overlapping and Inconsistent Warranties

Business Brief

If warranties are inconsistent, some warranties take precedence over other warranties.

Often, two or more warranties are present in the same sales or lease transaction. For example, a transaction may be subject to the seller's or lessor's express warranties with respect to the goods as well as the implied warranties of merchantability and fitness for a particular purpose. In such cases, the UCC provides that the warranties are cumulative if they are consistent with each other.

If the warranties are inconsistent, however, the intention of the parties determines which warranty is dominant. The following rules apply in determining intent [UCC 2-317; UCC 2A-215]:

1. Express warranties displace inconsistent implied warranties other than implied warranties of fitness for a particular purpose.
2. Exact or technical specifications displace inconsistent models or general language of description.
3. A sample from an existing bulk displaces inconsistent general language of description.

Warranty Disclaimers

Subject to other state laws and the Magnuson–Moss Warranty Act (discussed later in this chapter), warranties can be **disclaimed** or limited. The rules for making such disclaimers are

- If an express warranty is made, it can be limited if the disclaimer and the warranty can be reasonably construed with each other. The limitation is inoperative to the extent that such construction is unreasonable [UCC 2-316(1), UCC 2A-214(1)]. For example, if a seller or lessor makes an express warranty in one part of the contract and disclaims the warranty in another part, the courts consider the disclaimer unreasonable and thereby void.
- All implied warranties of quality may be disclaimed by expressions like *as is, with all faults,* or other language that makes it clear to the buyer that there are no implied warranties [UCC 2-316(3)(a), UCC 2A-214(3)(a)]. This type of disclaimer, which is often included in sales contracts for used products, is effective whether it is oral or written.
- If the preceding language is not used, disclaimers of the *implied warranty of merchantability* must specifically mention the term *merchantability*. The disclaimer may be oral or written [UCC 2-316(2), UCC 2A-214(2)].
- The *implied warranty of fitness for a particular purpose* may be disclaimed in general language without specific use of the term *fitness*. For example, language such as "There are no warranties that extend beyond the description on the face hereof" is sufficient to disclaim the fitness warranty. The disclaimer must be in writing [UCC 2-316(2), UCC 2A-214(3)].
- When a buyer or lessee either (1) examines the goods (or sample or model) as fully as he or she desires or (2) refuses to examine the goods after the seller or lessor demands him or her to do so, there are no implied warranties with regard to any defects that such an examination would have revealed [UCC 2-316(3)(b), UCC 2A-214(3)(b)]. Examination only includes obvious defects (e.g., a broken car windshield). Latent (nonobvious) defects (e.g., a problem in the transmission of the car) are not expected to be discovered during such an examination. Note that refusal only occurs if the seller or lessor demands the buyer or lessee to examine the goods and the buyer or lessee refuses to do so.

warranty disclaimer
Statements that negate express and implied warranties.

Business Brief
Read all warranty notices carefully to see if any warranties have been disclaimed.

Conspicuous Display of Disclaimer

Written disclaimers must be conspicuously displayed to be valid. The courts construe **conspicuous** as noticeable to a reasonable person [UCC 2-316, UCC 2A-214]. For example, a heading printed in capitals or typeface that is larger or in a different style than the rest of the body of a sales or lease contract will be considered to be conspicuous. Different-color type is also considered conspicuous.

conspicuous
A requirement that warranty disclaimers be noticeable to the average person.

Unconscionable Disclaimers

As a matter of law, a court may find a warranty disclaimer clause in a sales or lease contract to be **unconscionable.** In such cases, the court may avoid an unconscionable result by (1) refusing to enforce the clause, (2) refusing to enforce the entire contract, or (3) limiting the application of the clause [UCC 2-302(1), UCC 2A-108(1)]. In determining whether warranty disclaimers are unconscionable, the courts generally consider factors such as the sophistication, education, and bargaining power of the parties and whether the sales contract was offered on a take-it-or-leave-it basis.

Ethics Brief
An unconscionable disclaimer is a disclaimer that is so oppressive or manifestly unfair that it will not be enforced by the court.

E-Commerce & Information Technology

WARRANTY DISCLAIMERS IN SOFTWARE LICENSES

Most software companies license their software to users. The software license is a complex contract that contains the terms of the license. Most software licenses contain warranty disclaimer and limitation on liability clauses that limit the licensor's liability if the software malfunctions. Disclaimer of warranty and limitation on liability clauses that are included in a typical software license appear in the following document.

SOFTWARE.COM, INC.
LIMITATION AND WAIVERS OF WARRANTIES,
REMEDIES, AND CONSEQUENTIAL DAMAGES

Limited Warranty. Software.com, Inc. warrants that (a) the software will perform substantially in accordance with the accompanying written materials for a period of 90 days from the date of receipt, and (b) any hardware accompanying the software will be free from defects in materials and workmanship under normal use and service for a period of one year from the date of the receipt. Any implied warranties on the software and hardware are limited to 90 days and one (1) year, respectively. Some states do not allow limitations on duration of an implied warranty, so the above limitation may not apply to you.

Customer Remedies. Software.com, Inc.'s entire liability and your exclusive remedy shall be, at Software.com, Inc.'s option, either (a) return of the price paid or (b) repair or replacement of the software or hardware that does not meet Software.com, Inc.'s Limited Warranty and that is returned to Software.com, Inc. with a copy of your receipt. This Limited Warranty is void if failure of the software or hardware has resulted from accident, abuse, or misapplication. Any replacement software will be warranted for the remainder of the original warranty or 30 days, whichever is longer. These remedies are not available outside the United States of America.

No Other Warranties. Software.com, Inc. disclaims all other warranties, either express or implied, including but not limited to implied warranties of merchantability and fitness for a particular purpose, with respect to the software, the accompanying written materials, and any accompanying hardware. This Limited Warranty gives you specific legal rights. You may have others, which vary from state to state.

No Liability for Consequential Damages. In no event shall Software.com, Inc. or its suppliers be liable for any damages whatsoever (including, without limitation, damages for loss of business profits, business interruption, loss of business information, or other pecuniary loss) arising out of the use of or inability to use this Software.com, Inc. product, even if Software.com, Inc. has been advised of the possibility of such damages. Because some states do not allow the exclusion or limitation of liability for consequential or incidental damages, the above limitation may not apply to you.

Damages Recoverable for Breach of Warranty

Where there has been a breach of warranty, the buyer or lessee may sue the seller or lessor to recover **compensatory damages**. The amount of recoverable compensatory damages is generally equal to the difference between (1) the value of the goods as warranted and (2) the actual value of the goods accepted at the time and place of acceptance [UCC 2-714(2), UCC 2A-508(4)].

compensatory damages

Damages that are generally equal to the difference between the value of the goods as warranted and the actual value of the goods accepted at the time and place of acceptance.

Consider This Example Suppose a used car salesperson warrants that a used car has been driven only 20,000 miles. If true, that would make the car worth $10,000. The salesperson gives the buyer a "good deal" and sells the car for $8,000. Unfortunately, the car was worth only $4,000 because it was actually driven 100,000 miles. The buyer discovers the breach of warranty and sues the salesperson for damages. The buyer can recover $6,000 ($10,000 warranted value minus $4,000 actual value). The contract price ($8,000) is irrelevant to this computation.

A purchaser or lessee can recover for personal injuries that are caused by a breach of warranty.

consequential damages

Foreseeable damages that arise from circumstances outside the contract. To be liable for these damages, the breaching party must know or have reason to know that the breach will cause special damages to the other party.

Consider This Example Suppose Frances Gordon purchases new tires for her car and the manufacturer expressly warrants the tires against blowout for 50,000 miles. Suppose one of the tires blows out after being used only 20,000 miles, causing sever injury to Ms. Gordon. She can recover personal injury damages from the manufacturer because of the breach of warranty.

Unless legally excluded, modified, or otherwise limited by the parties, a buyer or lessee may also recover **consequential damages** from the seller or lessor for breach of warranty.

The same is true of incidental damages [UCC 2-714(3), UCC 2A-519(4)]. Consequential damages may be limited or excluded unless the limitation is unconscionable. Limitation of consequential damages for personal injury with respect to consumer goods is prima facie unconscionable.

Third-Party Beneficiaries of Warranties

Third parties who are injured in their person or property by products may be able to recover from the sellers and lessors of the product for damages caused by breach of warranty. Generally, the common law of contracts only gives the parties to a contract (i.e., those in **privity of contract**) rights under the contract.

In the landmark case, *Henningsen v. Bloomfield Motors, Inc.,*[1] the court held that lack of privity did not prevent a third-party plaintiff from suing for breach of the implied warranty of merchantability. The UCC continued this evolutionary trend by limiting the doctrine of privity. The UCC gives each state the option of choosing between three alternative provisions for liability to third parties [UCC 2-318, UCC 2A-216].

Disclaimers and limitations of liability are ineffective against third parties. This is because they do not have knowledge of and have not agreed to these terms.

Statute of Limitations

The UCC contains a four-year **statute of limitations** that applies to both hidden and obvious defects. The parties may agree to reduce the period of limitation to not less than one year. However, they may not extend it beyond four years. The statute begins to run when the goods are tendered to the buyer or lessee. The only exception is if the warranty extends to the future performance of the goods (such as a "5 years or 50,000 miles" warranty).

privity of contract
The state of two specified parties being in contract.

Landmark Law
In *Henningsen v. Bloomfield Motors, Inc.*, the court held that lack of privity of contract did not prevent a third-party plaintiff from suing for breach of warranty.

UCC statute of limitations
The UCC provides for a four-year statute of limitations for breach of warranty actions. The parties may agree to reduce this period to not less than one year.

Landmark Law

MAGNUSON–MOSS WARRANTY ACT

In 1975, Congress enacted the **Magnuson–Moss Warranty Act** (the Act), which covers written warranties relating to *consumer* products. The Act is administered by the Federal Trade Commission (FTC) [15 U.S.C. § 2301–2312].

Commercial and industrial transactions are not governed by the Act. The Act does not require a seller or lessor to make express written warranties. However, persons who do make such warranties are subject to the provisions of the Act.

FULL AND LIMITED WARRANTIES
If the cost of the good is more than $10 and the warrantor chooses to make an express warranty, the Magnuson–Moss Warranty Act requires that the warranty be labeled as either "full" or "limited."

To qualify as a **full warranty**, the warrantor must guarantee free repair or replacement of the defective product. The warrantor must indicate whether there is a time limit on the full warranty (e.g., "full 36-month warranty").

In a **limited warranty**, the warrantor limits the scope of a full warranty in some way (e.g., a return of the purchase price or replacement or such). The fact that the warranty is full or limited must be conspicuously displayed. The disclosures must be in "understandable language."

A consumer may bring a civil action against a defendant for violating the provisions of the Act. A successful plaintiff can recover damages, attorneys' fees, and other costs incurred in bringing the action. The Act authorizes warrantors to establish an informal dispute resolution procedure. The procedure must be conspicuously described in the written warranty. Aggrieved consumers must assert their claims through this procedure before they can take legal action.

LIMITATION ON DISCLAIMING IMPLIED WARRANTIES
The Act does not create any implied warranties. It does, however, modify the state law of implied warranties in one crucial respect: Sellers or lessors who make express written warranties are forbidden from disclaiming or modifying the implied warranties of merchantability and fitness for a particular purpose. A seller or lessor may set a time limit on implied warranties, but this time limit must correspond to the duration of any express warranty.

$\mathscr{T}$ORT LIABILITY BASED ON FAULT

Depending on the circumstances of the case, persons who are injured by defective products may be able to recover damages under the tort theories of *negligence* and *misrepresentation*. Both theories require the defendant to be *at fault* for causing the plaintiff's injuries. These theories are discussed in the paragraphs that follow.

Negligence

negligence

A tort related to defective products where the defendant has breached a duty of due care and caused harm to the plaintiff.

A person injured by a defective product may bring an action for **negligence** against the negligent party. To be successful, the plaintiff must prove that the defendant breached a duty of due care to the plaintiff that caused the plaintiff's injuries. Failure to exercise due care includes failing to assemble the product carefully, negligent product design, negligent inspection or testing of the product, negligent packaging, failure to warn of the dangerous propensities of the product, and such. It is important to note that in a negligence lawsuit only a party who was actually negligent is liable to the plaintiff.

Landmark Law

In *MacPherson v. Buick Motor Co.*, the court held that an injured consumer could recover damages from the manufacturer of a product even though he or she was only in privity of contract with the retailer from whom he or she had purchased the product.

The plaintiff and the defendant do not have to be in privity of contract.[2] For example, in the landmark case *MacPherson v. Buick Motor Co.*,[3] the court held that an injured consumer could recover damages from the manufacturer of a product even though the consumer was only in privity of the contract with the retailer from whom he had purchased the product. The plaintiff generally bears the difficult burden of proving that the defendant was negligent.

Consider This Example   Assume that the purchaser of a motorcycle is injured in an accident. The accident occurred because a screw was missing from the motorcycle. How does the buyer prove who was negligent? Was it the manufacturer, who left the screw out during the assembly of the motorcycle? Was it the retailer, who negligently failed to discover the missing screw while preparing the motorcycle for sale? Was it the mechanic, who failed to replace the screw after repairing the motorcycle? Negligence remains a viable, yet difficult, theory upon which to base a product liability action.

Misrepresentation

intentional misrepresentation

When a seller or lessor fraudulently misrepresents the quality of a product and a buyer is injured thereby.

A buyer or lessee who is injured because a seller or lessor fraudulently misrepresented the quality of a product can sue the seller for the tort of **intentional misrepresentation** or **fraud**. Recovery is limited to persons who were injured because they relied on the misrepresentation.

Intentional misrepresentation occurs where a seller or lessor either (1) affirmatively misrepresents the quality of a product or (2) conceals a defect in it. Because most reputable manufacturers, sellers, and lessors do not intentionally misrepresent the quality of their products, fraud is not often used as the basis for product liability actions.

In the following case, the court held a defendant manufacturer liable for negligence in a product liability lawsuit.

Benedi v. McNeil-P.P.C., Incorporated

66 F.3d 1378 (1995)

United States Court of Appeals, Fourth Circuit

CASE 18.5

BACKGROUND AND FACTS

Antonio Benedi consumed three to four glasses of wine a night during the week and sometimes more on the weekend. On February 5, 1993, Benedi began taking Extra-Strength Tylenol in normal doses for flu-like aches. On February 10, 1993, Benedi was admitted to the hospital in a coma and near death due to liver and kidney failure. On the night of February 12, 1993, Benedi underwent an emergency liver transplant.

Because of the transplant, Benedi will have to undergo kidney dialysis in the future. Blood tests performed shortly after Benedi's admission to the hospital revealed that he suffered from acetaminophen (Tylenol) toxicity, which is caused by a combination of Tylenol and too much alcohol. The bottle from which Benedi took the Tylenol did not contain a warning of the dangers of the combination of Tylenol and excessive alcohol consumption. Benedi sued McNeil-P.P.C., Incorporated

(McNeil), the manufacturer of Tylenol, for negligent failure to warn. The jury found McNeil negligent and awarded Benedi $7,850,000 in compensatory damages. McNeil appealed.

ISSUE
Is McNeil liable for negligent failure to warn?

COURT'S REASONING
At trial, Benedi called two liver disease specialists who both testified that a warning of the possible danger to heavy drinkers from combining alcohol and acetaminophen should have been placed on the Tylenol label since the mid-1980s. These experts described exactly how the alcohol-acetaminophen mixture can become a toxin in the liver. They cited numerous treatises and articles published in medical journals prior to 1993 that describe the increased risk of liver injury when acetaminophen is combined with alcohol. One of the plaintiff's experts referred to 60 reports that McNeil had received by the end of 1992 documenting cases of liver injury associated with combining therapeutic doses of Tylenol with alcohol. The court of appeals stated that it was the jury's role to assess the weight and credibility of the evidence, and the jury found that Benedi

proved causation. The court concluded that ample evidence existed from which a reasonable jury could find for Benedi.

DECISION AND REMEDY
The court of appeals affirmed the jury's verdict awarding plaintiff Benedi $7,850,000 against McNeil for negligent failure to warn.

Note: In the summer of 1993 (after Benedi's injury), McNeil included a warning on Tylenol that persons who regularly consume three or more alcoholic drinks a day should consult a physician before using Tylenol.

Case Questions

Critical Legal Thinking What elements are necessary to prove negligence? Do you think that McNeil was negligent in this case? Do you think jurors are sophisticated enough to evaluate and judge scientific evidence?

Business Ethics Did McNeil act ethically in failing to put a warning on Tylenol? Do you think a warning was warranted?

Contemporary Business What will be the implication of this case to manufacturers of pain-killing drugs? Will consumers be better off because of this decision? Explain.

THE DOCTRINE OF STRICT LIABILITY

In the landmark case *Greenmun v. Yuba Power Products, Inc.*,[4] the California Supreme Court adopted the **doctrine of strict liability in tort** as a basis for product liability actions. Most states have now adopted this doctrine as a basis for product liability actions. The doctrine of strict liability removes many of the difficulties for the plaintiff associated with other theories of product liability. The remainder of this chapter examines the scope of the strict liability doctrine.

Landmark Law

In *Greenmun v. Yuba Power Products, Inc.*, the California Supreme Court adopted the doctrine of strict liability in tort for product liability actions.

Landmark Law

STRICT LIABILITY IN TORT

The most widely recognized articulation of the doctrine of strict liability is found in **Section 402A** of the **Restatement (Second) of Torts**, which provides

(1) One who sells any product in a defective condition unreasonably dangerous to the user or consumer or to his property is subject to liability for physical harm thereby caused to the ultimate user or consumer, or to his property, if
- *(a) the seller is engaged in the business of selling such a product, and*
- *(b) it is expected to and does reach the user or consumer without substantial change in the condition in which it is sold.*

(2) The rule stated in Subsection (1) applies although
- *(a) the seller has exercised all possible care in the preparation and sale of his product, and*
- *(b) the user or consumer has not bought the product from or entered into any contractual relation with the seller.*

Unlike negligence, strict liability does not require the injured person to prove that the defendant breached a duty of care. *Strict liability is imposed irrespective of fault.* A seller can be found strictly liable even though he or she has exercised all possible care in the preparation and sale of his or her product.

The doctrine of strict liability applies to sellers and lessors of products who are engaged in the business of selling and leasing products. Casual sales and transactions by nonmerchants are not covered. Thus, a person who sells a defective product to a neighbor in a causal sale is not strictly liable if the product causes injury.

Strict liability applies only to products, not services. In hybrid transactions involving both services and products, the dominant element of the transaction dictates whether strict liability applies. For example, in a medial operation that requires a blood transfusion, the operation would be the dominant element and strict liability would not apply.[5] Strict liability may not be disclaimed.

chain of distribution

All manufacturers, distributors, wholesalers, retailers, lessors, and subcomponent manufacturers involved in a transaction.

doctrine of strict liability in tort

A tort doctrine that makes manufacturers, distributors, wholesalers, retailers, and others in the chain of distribution of a defective product liable for the damages caused by the defect *irrespective of fault.*

All in the Chain of Distribution Are Liable

All parties in the **chain of distribution** of a defective product are **strictly liable** for the injuries caused by that product. Thus, all manufacturers, distributors, wholesalers, retailers, lessors, and subcomponent manufacturers may be sued under this doctrine. This view is based on public policy. Lawmakers presume that sellers and lessors will insure against the risk of a strict liability lawsuit and spread the cost to their consumers by raising the price of products.

Consider This Example   Suppose a subcomponent manufacturer produces a defective tire and sells it to a truck manufacturer. The truck manufacturer places the defective tire on one of its new model trucks. The truck is distributed by a distributor to a retail dealer. Ultimately, the retail dealer sells the truck to a buyer. The defective tire causes an accident in which the buyer is injured. All of the parties in the tire's chain of distribution can be sued by the injured party, in this case, the liable parties are the subcomponent manufacturer, the truck manufacturer, the distributor, and the retailer.

A defendant who has not been negligent but who is made to pay a strict liability judgment can bring a separate action against the negligent party in the chain of distribution to recover its losses. In the preceding example, for instance, the retailer could sue the manufacturer to recover the strict liability judgment assessed against it.

Exhibit 18.1 compares the doctrines of negligence and strict liability.

*E*XHIBIT **18.1**   *Doctrines of Negligence and Strict Liability Compared*

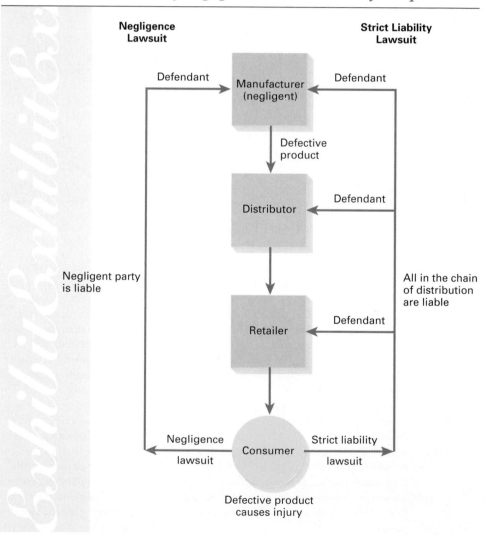

Parties Who Can Recover for Strict Liability

Because strict liability is a tort doctrine, privity of contract between the plaintiff and the defendant is not required. In other words, the doctrine applies even if the injured party had no contractual relations with the defendant. Under strict liability, sellers and lessors are liable to the ultimate user or consumer. Users include the purchaser or lessee, family members, guests, employees, customers, and persons who passively enjoy the benefits of the product (e.g., passengers in automobiles).

Most jurisdictions have judicially or statutorily extended the protection of strict liability to bystanders. The courts have stated that bystanders should be entitled to even greater protection than a consumer or user. This is because consumers and users have the chance to inspect for defects and to limit their purchases to articles manufactured by reputable manufacturers and sold by reputable retailers, whereas bystanders do not have the same opportunity.

Business Brief

Privity of contract is not required for a plaintiff to sue for strict liability.

Business Brief

Strict liability law imposes liability without fault on manufacturers, sellers, and lessors who make and distribute defective products that cause injury to users and others.

Damages Recoverable for Strict Liability

The damages recoverable in a strict liability action vary by jurisdiction. Damages for personal injuries are recoverable in all jurisdictions that have adopted the doctrine of strict liability, although some jurisdictions limit the dollar amount of the award. Property damage is recoverable in most jurisdictions, but economic loss (e.g., lost income) is recoverable in only a few jurisdictions. *Punitive damages* are generally allowed if the plaintiff can prove that the defendant either intentionally injured him or her or acted with reckless disregard for his or her safety.

Business Brief

Punitive damages are often awarded in strict liability lawsuits if the plaintiff proves that the defendant either intentionally injured him or her or acted with reckless disregard for his or her safety.

Entrepreneur and the Law

ENTREPRENEURS LIABLE FOR STRICT LIABILITY

Entrepreneurs often own small and medium-sized retail stores as well as many wholesale and distributor businesses. In this capacity, they distribute and sell products made by manufacturers. Many of these products are sold in their original boxes or are otherwise sold without individual inspection by the retailer, wholesaler, or distributor. But what happens if the product has been produced defectively by the manufacturer and the purchaser or user is injured by the product? Who is liable?

In the past, when negligence was the major legal theory asserted by the injured victim to recover damages, the negligent manufacturer paid, but the retailer, wholesaler, and distributor did not pay because they did nothing wrong. Gone are those days, however. With the advent of the legal theory of **strict liability**, all in the chain of distribution of a defec-

tive product are liable for any injury caused by the product even though some of the parties are not at fault. Today, entrepreneurs and others who sell and distribute products made by others have to worry about being named in a products liability lawsuit and paying for injuries caused by the product.

To protect against such liability, retailers, wholesalers, and distributors should purchase products liability insurance. If the seller is embroiled in a products liability lawsuit, the insurance company will pay the costs of the defenses (e.g., attorney's fees, court costs) as well as any settlement amount or judgment, up to the policy limits. The insured business is liable for any amount beyond the policy limit. Paying for products liability insurance raises the cost of doing business.

The CONCEPT OF DEFECT

To recover for strict liability, the injured party must first show that the product that caused the injury was somehow **defective**. (Remember that the injured party does not have to prove who caused the product to become defective.) Plaintiffs can allege multiple product defects in one lawsuit. A product can be found to be defective in many ways. The most common types of defects are *defects in manufacture, design,* and *packaging* and *failure to warn.* These defects are discussed in the following paragraphs.

defect

Something wrong, inadequate, or improper in manufacture, design, packaging, warning, or safety measures of a product.

defect in manufacture
A defect that occurs when the manufacturer fails to (1) properly assemble a product, (2) properly test a product, or (3) adequately check the quality of the product.

Defect in Manufacture

A **defect in manufacture** occurs when the manufacturer fails to (1) properly assemble a product (2) properly test a product, or (3) adequately check the quality of the product. The following case is a classic example involving a defect in the manufacture.

Shoshone Coca-Cola Bottling Co. v. Dolinski
420 P.2d 855 (1967)
Supreme Court of Nevada

CASE 18.6

BACKGROUND AND FACTS

Leo Dolinski purchased a bottle of "Squirt," a soft drink, from a vending machine at a Sea and Ski plant, his place of employment. Dolinski opened the bottle and consumed part of its contents. He immediately became ill. Upon examination, it was found that the bottle contained the decomposed body of a mouse, mouse hair, and mouse feces. Dolinski visited a doctor and was given medicine to counteract nausea. Dolinski suffered physical and mental distress from consuming the decomposed mouse and possessed an aversion to soft drinks. The Shoshone Coca-Cola Bottling Company (Shoshone) manufactured and distributed the Squirt bottle. Dolinski sued Shoshone, basing his lawsuit on the doctrine of strict liability. The state of Nevada had not previously recognized the doctrine of strict liability. However, the trial court adopted the doctrine of strict liability and the jury returned a verdict in favor of the plaintiff. Shoshone appealed.

ISSUE

Should the state of Nevada judicially adopt the doctrine of strict liability? If so, was there a defect in the manufacture of the Squirt bottle that caused the plaintiff's injuries?

COURT'S REASONING

In adopting the doctrine of strict liability, the court stated, "Public policy demands that one who places upon the market a bottled beverage in a condition dangerous for use must be held strictly liable to the ultimate user for injuries resulting from such use, although the seller has exercised all reasonable care."

DECISION AND REMEDY

The Supreme Court of Nevada adopted the doctrine of strict liability and held that the evidence supported the trial court's finding that there was a defect in manufacture. Affirmed.

Case Questions

Critical Legal Thinking Should the courts adopt the theory of strict liability? Why or why not?

Business Ethics Was it ethical for Shoshone to argue that it was not liable to Dolinski?

Contemporary Business Should all in the chain of distribution of a defective product—even those parties who are not responsible for the defect—be held liable under the doctrine of strict liability? Or should liability be based only on fault?

Defect in Design

defect in design
A defect that occurs when a product is improperly designed.

A **defect in design** can support a strict liability action. Design defects that have supported strict liability awards include toys that are designed with removable parts that could be swallowed by children, machines and appliances designed without proper safeguards, and trucks and other vehicles designed without a warning device to let people know that the vehicle is backing up.

In evaluating the adequacy of a product's design, the courts apply a risk-utility analysis and consider the gravity of the danger posed by the design, the likelihood that injury will occur, the availability and cost of producing a safer alternative design, the social utility of the product, and other factors. The design defect case in the following case demonstrates the application of the risk-utility analysis.

Lakin v. Senco Products, Inc.
925 P.2d 107 (1996)
Court of Appeals of Oregon

CASE 18.7

BACKGROUND AND FACTS

Senco Products, Inc. (Senco), manufactures and markets a variety of pneumatic nail guns, including the SN325 nail gun, which discharges 3.25 inch nails. The SN325 uses special nails designed and sold by Senco. The SN325 will discharge a nail only if two trigger mechanisms are activated; that is, the user must both squeeze the nail gun's finger trigger and press the nail gun's muzzle against a surface, activating the bottom trigger or safety. The SN325 can fire up to nine nails per second if the trigger is continuously depressed and the gun is bounced along the work surface, constantly reactivating the muzzle safety/trigger.

On December 1, 1990, John Lakin was using a Senco SN325 nail gun to help build a new home. When attempting to nail two-by-fours under the eaves of the garage, Lakin stood on tiptoe and raised a two-by-four over his head. As he held the board in position with his left hand and the nail gun in his right hand, he pressed the nose of the SN325 up against the board, depressed the safety, and pulled the finger trigger to fire the nail into the board. The gun fired the first nail and then, in a phenomenon known as "double firing," immediately discharged an unintended second nail that struck the first nail. The gun recoiled violently backward toward Lakin and, with Lakin's finger still on the trigger, came into contact with his cheek. That contact activated the safety/trigger, causing the nail gun to fire a third nail. This third nail went through Lakin's cheekbone and into his brain.

The nail penetrated the frontal lobe of the right hemisphere of Lakin's brain, blocked a major artery, and caused extensive tissue damage. Lakin was unconscious for several days and ultimately underwent multiple surgeries. He suffers permanent brain damage and is unable to perceive information from the left hemisphere of the brain. He also suffers partial paralysis of the left side of his body. Lakin has undergone a radical personality change and is prone to violent outbursts. He is unable to obtain employment. Lakin's previously warm and loving relationship with his wife and four children has been permanently altered. He can no longer live with his family and instead resides in a supervised group home for brain-injured persons. Lakin and his wife sued Senco for strict liability based on design defect. The trial court found Senco liable and awarded $3.6 million to Lakin, $457,000 to his wife, and $4 million in punitive damages against Senco. Senco appealed.

ISSUE

Is Senco liable to Lakin for strict liability based on a design defect in the SN325 that allowed it to double fire?

COURT'S REASONING

Evidence showed that the SN325 double fired once in every 15 firings. The court found that Senco rushed the SN325's production so as to maintain its position in the market. It modified an existing nail gun to shoot the longer 3.25 inch nails without engaging in additional testing to determine if longer nails in that model would increase the prevalence of double fire, which it did. The court found that the SN325 could have been modified with a more restrictive but slower trigger that would have made the nail gun safer. In applying the risk-utility analysis, the court held that the SN325 was defectively designed. The court stated, "Defendant's failure to effectively address the SN325's double firing problem was conscious and was motivated, at least in part, by a profit motive." The court upheld the compensatory and punitive damage award.

DECISION AND REMEDY

The court of appeals applied the risk-utility analysis and held that the SN325 was defectively designed. The court affirmed the award of damages to Lakin and his wife.

Case Questions

Critical Legal Thinking Do you think the utility served by the nine-nail-per-second SN325 outweighed its risk of personal injury?

Business Ethics Did Senco act in a conscious disregard of safety factors when it designed, manufactured, and sold the SN325 nail gun?

Contemporary Business Do you think the award of punitive damages was warranted in this case?

Crashworthiness Doctrine

Often, when an automobile is involved in an accident, the driver or passengers are not injured by the blow itself. Instead, they are injured when their bodies strike something inside their own automobile (e.g., the dashboard or the steering wheel). This is commonly referred to as the "second collision." The courts have held that automobile manufacturers are under a duty to design automobiles to take into account the possibility of this second collision. This is called the **crashworthiness doctrine**. Failure to design an automobile to protect occupants from foreseeable dangers caused by a second collision subjects the manufacturer and dealer to strict liability.

crashworthiness doctrine

A doctrine that says automobile manufacturers are under a duty to design automobiles so they take into account the possibility of harm from a person's body striking something inside the automobile in the case of a car accident.

Contemporary Business Environment

GENERAL MOTORS HIT WITH BILLION DOLLAR JUDGMENT

On Christmas Eve, Patricia Anderson was driving her Chevrolet Malibu automobile, which was manufactured by the General Motors Corporation (GM), home from church. Her four young children, ages one through nine, and a neighbor, were also in the car. The Chevy Malibu was stopped at a stoplight at 89th Place and Figueroa Street in

Los Angeles when a drunken driver plowed his car into the back of the Malibu at 50 to 70 mph. The Malibu burst into flames as its gas tank ruptured and ignited. Although no one died in the crash, the occupants of the Malibu were severely burned. Many required substantial and multiple skin grafts.

The two injured women and four injured children sued GM for product liability. They alleged that the fuel tank of the Chevy Malibu was defectively designed and placed too close to the rear bumper. GM countered that the tragic accident was the fault of the driver who struck the Malibu. The accident victims produced evidence that showed that GM knew that the car's fuel-tank design was unsafe but had not changed the design because of cost. The Chevy Malibu was one of GM's A-Class cars, which also included the Pontiac Grand Am, the Oldsmobile Cutlass, and the Chevrolet Monte Carlo, all of which have similar fuel-tank designs. The plaintiffs produced GM memos that said it would cost GM $8.59 per vehicle to produce and install a safer fuel tank design, but that it would only cost the company an estimated $2.40 per car to not fix the cars and pay damages to injured victims.

After a 10-week trial, the jurors returned a verdict of $107 million in compensatory damages to the plaintiffs for injuries, disfigurement, and pain and suffering caused to them by the accident. The jury then tacked on $4.9 billion as punitive damages to punish GM. This was the largest amount ever awarded in a personal-injury lawsuit. GM, the world's largest automobile company, reported annual earnings of $3 billion in 1998, the year of the verdict. After the trial one juror stated: "We're just like numbers. Statistics. That's something that is wrong."

GM asked the trial judge to throw the trial out. GM claimed that it was not given a fair trail because the trial court judge refused to allow the jury to hear evidence that (1) the driver of the other car was drunk and went to jail and (2) crash-test data that showed the safety history of the vehicle. GM also claimed that the jury was prejudiced by repetitive personal attacks on GM as a "soulless company" and its lawyers as "hired guns" who consumed "cappuccinos and designer muffins." GM did not convince the judge that such animosity influenced the jury. GM also alleged that the jury was allowed to hear evidence that it should not have heard, namely, that GM had lobbied Congress in the 1970s to not adopt tougher standards for protecting fuel tanks in crashes.

In its post-trial motions, GM argued that the award of damages, specifically the $4.8 billion of punitive damages, was the result of bias and prejudice of the jury, and asked the trial court judge to reduce the award of damages. This the trial court judge did do: He let the compensatory damage award stand but reduced the award of punitive damages to $1 billion. The revised award is equivalent to two percent of GM's net worth and 10 times the compensatory damages. GM faces over 30 other lawsuits involving fuel tank explosions in its A-Class cars.

---

defect in packaging

A defect that occurs when a product has been placed in packaging that is insufficiently tamperproof.

Defect in Packaging

Manufacturers owe a duty to design and provide safe packages for their products. This duty requires manufacturers to provide packages and containers that are tamperproof or that clearly indicate if they have been tampered with. Certain manufacturers, such as drug manufacturers, owe a duty to place their products in containers that cannot be opened by children. A manufacturer's failure to meet this duty subjects the manufacturer and others in the chain of distribution of the product to strict liability. In the following case the court had to decide whether there was defective packaging.

Elsroth v. Johnson & Johnson
700 F.Supp. 151 (1988)
United States District Court, S.D. New York

CASE 18.8

BACKGROUND AND FACTS
On February 4, 1986, Harriet Notarnicola purchased a box of Extra-Strength Tylenol capsules from a Bronxville, New York, grocery store owned by The Great Atlantic & Pacific Tea Co. (A&P). The Tylenol was manufactured by McNeil Consumer Products Co., a division of McNeilab, Inc. (McNeil), under the name Johnson & Johnson. Diane Elsroth was visiting her boyfriend, Michael Notarnicola, for a week at the home of Michael's parents. Late on the night of February 7, Diane complained of a headache. Michael went to the kitchen, opened the box and plastic container of Extra-Strength Tylenol purchased by his mother at the A&P store and returned with two capsules and a glass of water for Diane. A short time after ingesting the capsules, Diane retired. Her dead body was found the next day. The medical examiner concluded that the Tylenol capsules ingested by Diane were contaminated by a lethal dose of potassium cyanide. The murder remains unsolved, but evidence shows that the Tylenol bottle had been tampered with after the product left the manufacturer's control. An unknown third party purchased the Tylenol, breached the packaging, substituted cyanide for some of the medicine contained in several of the gelatin capsules,

somehow resealed the container and box in such a way that the tampering was not readily detectable, and placed the contaminated box on the shelf of the A&P store. John Elsroth, administrator of Diane's estate, brought this strict liability action against McNeil and A&P seeking $1 million in compensatory damages and $92 million in punitive damages.

ISSUE
Was there a defect in packaging that would support an action for strict liability?

COURT'S REASONING
The makers of Tylenol have marketed the product in tamper-resistant packaging with the following features: (1) a foil seal glued to the mouth of the container or bottle, (2) a "shrink seal" around the neck and cap of the container, and (3) a sealed box (the end flaps of which are glued shut) in which the product and container are placed.

McNeil, through its research, knew that this packaging could be violated by a determined tamperer using sophisticated means and that no evidence of this kind of sophisticated tampering would be visible to the average consumer. As one McNeil official put it, tampering by "the Rembrandt kind of criminals" could not be prevented by this type of packaging. McNeil was also operating under the constraint, however, as recognized by the FDA that no packaging could prevent this kind of "exotic" tampering; tamper-proof packaging is not possible.

The packaging alternative designed by McNeil employed not one, not two, but three of the taper-resistant features listed as alternatives in the 1982 FDA regulations. When all these factors are thrown into the mix, we find, as a matter of law, that under a risk-utility analysis this packaging was in a condition reasonably contemplated by the ultimate consumer and was not unreasonably dangerous for its intended use. Moreover, plaintiff had presented no evidence of what other steps might feasibly have been taken to ensure a higher degree of safety. If there are better tamper-resistant features available that would be feasible for use, plaintiff did not describe them. We return, however, to the fundamental premise: No packaging can boast of being tamper-proof.

DECISION AND REMEDY
The court held that there was not a defect in packaging. The defendants are not therefore strictly liable for Ms. Elsroth's death.

Case Questions

Critical Legal Thinking Should manufacturers be forced to make tamper-proof packaging for their products? Is this possible? What would be the expense?

Business Ethics Did any of the parties in the case act unethically?

Contemporary Business Do you think the plaintiff's seeking $92 million in punitive damages was warranted?

Failure to Warn

Certain products are inherently dangerous and cannot be made any safer and still accomplish the task for which they are designed. For example, certain useful drugs cause side effects, allergies, and other injuries to some users. Many machines and appliances include dangerous moving parts which, if removed, would defeat the purpose of the machine or appliance. Manufacturers and sellers of such products are under a *duty to warn* users about the product's dangerous propensities. A proper and conspicuous warning placed on the product insulates the manufacturer and others in the chain of distribution from strict liability. **Failure to warn** of these dangerous propensities is a defect that will support a strict liability action.

The court found an inadequate warning in the following case.

failure to warn
A defect that occurs when a manufacturer does not place a warning on the packaging of products that could cause injury if the danger is unknown.

Nowak v. Faberge USA, Inc.
32 F.3d 755 (1994)
United States Court of Appeals, Third Circuit

CASE 18.9

BACKGROUND AND FACTS
Faberge USA Inc. (Faberge) manufactures Aqua Net, a hair spray that is sold in an aerosol can. In addition to the hair-holding spray, Aqua Net contains a mixture of butane or propane as the aerosol propellant and alcohol as a solvent. Alcohol, butane, and propane all are extremely flammable. Aerosol cans of Aqua Net carry a warning on the back stating, "Do not puncture" and "Do not use near fire or flame."

Alison Nowak, a 14-year old girl, tried to spray her hair with a newly purchased can of Aqua Net. The spray valve would not work properly, so she cut open the can with a can opener. She thought she could then pour the contents into an empty aerosol bottle and use it. Nowak was standing in the kitchen near a gas stove when she punctured the can. A cloud of hair spray gushed from the can and the stove's pilot light ignited the spray into a ball of flame. She suffered severe, permanently disfiguring burns over 20 percent of her body. Nowak sued Faberge for damages under strict liability, alleging that Faberge failed to warn her of the dangers of the flammability of Aqua Net. The jury held against Faberge and awarded Nowak $1.5 million. Faberge appealed.

ISSUE
Did Faberge adequately warn the plaintiff of the flammability of Aqua Net?

COURT'S REASONING
A manufacturer owes a duty to adequately warn users of the dangerous propensities of their products. A product is defective if it is distributed without sufficient warnings to notify the ultimate user of the dangers inherent in the product. The trial court properly determined to send the case to the jury for

this determination. The jury's verdict that Faberge's warning was inadequate is upheld.

DECISION AND REMEDY
The court of appeals affirmed the district court's judgment that Faberge had failed to warn the plaintiff of the dangers of flammability of its product and is therefore strictly liable.

Case Questions

Critical Legal Thinking   Should the law recognize a failure to warn as a basis for imposing strict liability on manufacturers and sellers of products? Why or why not?

Business Ethics   Did Faberge violate its duty of social responsibility in this case? Explain.

Contemporary Business   Do you think this case was decided properly? What else could Faberge have done to avoid liability?

Other Product Defects

failure to provide adequate instructions

A defect that occurs when a manufacturer does not provide detailed directions for safe assembly and use of a product.

Other product defects can prove the basis for a strict liability action. **Failure to provide adequate instructions** for either the safe assembly or safe use of a product is a defect that subjects the manufacturer and others in the chain of distribution to strict liability.

Other defects include inadequate testing of products, inadequate selection of component parts or materials, and improper certification of the safety of a product. The concept of "defect" is an expanding area of the law.

DEFENSES TO PRODUCT LIABILITY

Defendants in strict liability or negligence actions may raise several defenses to the imposition of liability. These defenses are discussed in the paragraphs that follow.

Supervening Event

supervening event

An alteration or modification of a product by a party in the chain of distribution that absolves all prior sellers from strict liability.

For a seller to be held strictly liable, the product it sells must reach the consumer or user "without substantial change" in its condition.[6] Under the doctrine of **supervening** or **intervening event**, the original seller is not liable if the product is materially altered or modified after it leaves the seller's possession and the alteration or modification causes an injury. A supervening event absolves all prior sellers in the chain of distribution from strict liability.

Consider This Example   A manufacturer produces a safe piece of equipment. It sells the equipment to a distributor, who removes a safety guard from the equipment. The distributor sells it to a retailer, who sells it to a buyer. The buyer is injured because of the removal of the safety guard. The manufacturer can raise the defense of supervening event against the imposition of liability. However, the distributor and retailer are strictly liable for the buyer's injuries.

Generally Known Dangers

generally known dangers

A defense that acknowledges that certain products are inherently dangerous and are known to the general population to be so.

Certain products are inherently dangerous and are known to the general population to be so. Sellers are not strictly liable for failing to warn of **generally known dangers**. For example, it is a known fact that guns shoot bullets. Manufacturers of guns do not have to place a warning on the barrel of a gun warning of this generally known danger. However, the manufacturer would be under a duty to place a safety lock on the gun.

Government Contractor Defense

Many defense and other contractors manufacture products (e.g., rockets, airplanes, and such) to government specifications. Most jurisdictions recognize a **government contractor defense** to product liability actions. To establish this defense, a government contractor must prove that (1) the precise specifications for the product were provided by the government, (2) the product conformed to those specifications, and (3) the contractor warned the government of any known defects or dangers of the product.

government contractor defense

A defense that says a contractor who was provided specifications by the government is not liable for any defect in the product that occurs as a result of those specifications.

Contemporary Business Environment

CORRECTION OF A PRODUCT DEFECT

A manufacturer that produces a defective product and later discovers said defect must (1) notify purchasers and users of the defect and (2) correct the defect. Most manufacturers faced with this situation recall the defective product and either repair the defect or replace the product.

The seller must make reasonable efforts to notify purchasers and users of the defect and the procedure to correct it.

Reasonable efforts normally consist of sending letters to known purchasers and users and placing notices in newspapers and magazines of general circulation. If a user ignores the notice and fails to have the defect corrected, the seller may raise this as a defense against further liability with respect to the defect. Many courts have held that reasonable notice is effective even against users who did not see the notice.

Assumption of the Risk

Theoretically, the traditional doctrine of **assumption of the risk** is a defense to a product liability action. For this defense to apply, the defendant must prove that (1) the plaintiff knew and appreciated the risk and (2) the plaintiff voluntarily assumed the risk. In practice, the defense assumption of the risk is narrowly applied by the courts.

assumption of the risk

A defense in which the defendant must prove that (1) the plaintiff knew and appreciated the risk and (2) the plaintiff voluntarily assumed the risk.

Misuse of the Product

Sometimes users are injured when they **misuse** a product. If they bring a product liability action, the defendant-seller may be able to assert the misuse as a defense. Whether the defense is effective depends on whether the misuse was foreseeable. The seller is relieved of product liability if the plaintiff has **abnormally misused** the product—that is, there has been an *unforeseeable misuse* of the product. However, the seller is liable if there has been a *foreseeable misuse* of the product. This reasoning is intended to provide an incentive for manufacturers to design and manufacturer safer products.

misuse

A defense that relieves a seller of product liability if the user *abnormally* misused the product. Products must be designed to protect against *foreseeable* misuse.

Statute of Limitations and Statute of Repose

Most states have **statutes of limitations** that require an injured person to bring an action within a certain number of years from the time that he or she was injured by the defective product. This limitation period varies from state to state. Failure to bring an action within the appropriate time relieves the defendant of liability.

In most jurisdictions, the statute of limitations does not begin to run until the plaintiff suffers an injury. This subjects sellers and lessors to exposure for an unspecified period of time because a defective product may not cause an injury for years, or even decades, after it was sold. Because this may be unfair to the seller, some states have enacted **statute of repose**. Statutes of repose limit the seller's liability to a certain number of years from the date when the product was first sold. The period of repose varies from state to state.

statute of limitations

A statute that requires an injured person to bring an action within a certain number of years from the time that he or she was injured by the defective product.

statute of repose

A statute that limits the seller's liability to a certain number of years from the date when the product was first sold.

CONCEPT SUMMARY ... COMPARISON OF STATUTES OF LIMITATION AND STATUTES OF REPOSE

Statute	Begins to Run
Statute of limitations	When the plaintiff suffers injury
Statute of repose	When the product is first sold

Contemporary Business Environment

RESTATEMENT (THIRD) OF TORTS DEFINES *DEFECT* FOR PRODUCT LIABILITY

Soon after Section 402A of the Restatement of Law (Second) of Torts first recognized the doctrine of strict liability in 1965, most states adopted this new doctrine. Section 402A did not define *defect*, however. Courts in each state have wrestled with the issue of what constitutes a defect for product liability purposes, and a substantial body of case law has developed around this definition. In 1997, the American Law Institute (ALI) adopted the **Restatement of the Law (Third) of Torts: Product Liability**. This new Restatement includes the following definition of *defect:*

> *A product is defective when, at the time of sale or distribution, it contains manufacturing defect, is defective in design, or is defective because of inadequate instructions or warnings.*
> *A product:*
> *(a) contains a manufacturing defect when the product departs from its intended design even though all possible care was exercised in the preparation and marketing of the product;*
> *(b) is defective in design when the foreseeable risks of harm posed by the product could have been reduced or avoided by the adoption of a reasonable alternative design by the seller or other distributor, or a predecessor in the commercial chain of distribution, and the omission of the alternative design renders the product not reasonably safe;*
> *(c) is defective because of inadequate instructions or warnings when the foreseeable risks of harm posed by the product could have been reduced or avoided by the provision of reasonable instructions or warnings by the seller or other distributor, or a predecessor in the commercial chain of distribution, and the omission of the instructions or warnings renders the product not reasonably safe.*

Subsection (a) defines a manufacturing defect as one that includes a physical deviation from what the manufacturer intended the product to be. Subsection (b) requires a court to consider any "reasonable alternative design" when determining whether there has been a design defect. In determining whether there has been a failure to warn or failure to provide adequate instructions, subsection (c) looks at the foreseeable risks of harm and whether they could have been reduced or avoided by reasonable warnings or instructions.

There is obviously no easy or bright-line test that can define when a product is defective; however, the new Restatement (Third) definitions of *defect* may be helpful to courts hearing product liability lawsuits.

Contributory and Comparative Negligence

contributory negligence

A defense that says a person who is injured by a defective product but has been negligent and has contributed to his or her own injuries cannot recover from the defendant.

Sometimes a person who is injured by a defective product is negligent and contributes to his or her own injuries. The defense of **contributory negligence** bars an injured plaintiff from recovering from the defendant in a negligence action. However, this doctrine generally does not bar recovery in strict liability actions.

comparative negligence

A doctrine that applies to strict liability actions that says a plaintiff who is contributorily negligent for his or her injuries is responsible for a proportional share of the damages.

Many states have held that the doctrine of **comparative negligence** (or **comparative fault**) applies to strict liability actions. Under this doctrine, a plaintiff who is contributorily negligent for his or her injuries is responsible for a *proportional share* of the damages. In other words, the damages are apportioned between the plaintiff and the defendant.

Consider This Example Suppose an automobile manufacturer produces a car with a hidden defect and a consumer purchases the car from an automobile dealer. Assume that the consumer is injured in an automobile accident in which the defect is found to be 75 percent responsible for the accident and the consumer's own reckless driving is found to be 25 percent responsible. If the plaintiff suffers $1 million worth of injuries, the plaintiff may recover $750,000 from the defendant manufacturer and car dealer.

International Law

PRODUCT LIABILITY LAW IN JAPAN

Japanese manufacturers sell many of the same products in Japan and the United States. In the United States, the products are subject to the same product liability laws as are American companies. In Japan, they enjoy near-immunity from product liability claims. For example, in almost 50 years, consumers have won only 150 product liability cases in Japan and recovered meager damages. In the same period, companies in the United States have lost tens of thousands of such suits and have paid out hundreds of millions of dollars in damages.

Product liability claims are rare in Japan for several reasons:

1. The plaintiff has the difficult burden of proving that the company was negligent. Japan has not adopted the U.S. doctrine of strict liability.
2. Japanese courts do not allow discovery. It is often impossible to prove a product was defective if the plaintiff cannot obtain access to the defendant's files.
3. Win or lose, claimants must pay a percentage of any damages requested (not won) as court fees. This keeps damage requests low.
4. Awards that are granted by courts are small (at least by U.S. standards), and punitive damages are not available.

Consider the case of Japanese chemical maker Showa Denko. The company faces more than 1,000 lawsuits in the United States. The suits allege that the company's food supplement L-typtophan causes injuries. In one of those cases, Showa settled out of court with Randy Simmons, a 43 year-old Wichita, Kansas, resident who alleged that the food supplement caused him to become a quadriplegic. The same company has few Japan-based cases pending against it alleging similar claims. There, the company currently offers only to reimburse Japanese customers the purchase price of the supplement.

The docile attitude of Japanese consumers is changing, and more injured consumers are suing to recover damages for their injuries. There is even a move by the Japanese government to adopt new consumer protection laws. However, the Diet, which has shown a probusiness sentiment in the past, is unlikely to expand the laws to anything near those in the United States.

Critics argue that the Japanese system leaves injured consumers unrecompensed for injuries caused by defective products. Some argue that the near-immunity from product liability claims at home gives Japanese manufacturers an edge in selling goods in international markets. Proponents of the Japanese system argue that it promotes the development and sale of products free from the oppressive liability costs that manufacturers face in the United States. They point to the fact that liability insurance costs are sometimes 20 times higher in the United States than in Japan.

*C*HAPTER *S*UMMARY

*W*arranties of Quality, p. 431

Express Warranty	Affirmation by a seller or lessor that the goods he or she is selling or leasing meet certain standards of quality, description, performance, or condition.
Implied Warranty of Merchantability	1. *Implied warranty of merchantability.* Warranty implied by law in sales and lease transactions that requires that the goods: a. Be fit for the ordinary purposes for which they are used. b. Be adequately contained, packaged, and labeled. c. Be of an even kind, quality, and quantity within each unit. d. Conform to any promise or affirmation of fact made on the container or label. e. Pass without objection in the trade. f. Meet a fair or middle range of quality if the goods are fungible. 2. *Implied warranty of fitness for human consumption.* Warranty implied by law that food products are fit for human consumption. States apply one of the two following tests: a. *Foreign substance test.* A food unmerchantable if a foreign object in the food caused the plaintiff's injury. b. *Consumer expectation test.* A food is unmerchantable if an object in the food that a consumer would not expect to be there caused the plaintiff's injury. The UCC incorporates this warranty within the implied warranty of merchantability.
Implied Warranty of Fitness for a Particular Purpose	*Implied warranty of fitness for a particular purpose.* Warranty by a seller or lessor that the goods will meet the buyer's or lessee's expressed needs.

Overlapping and Inconsistent Warranties	*Priority of inconsistent warranties:* 1. Implied warranty of fitness for a particular purpose 2. Express warranty 3. Implied warranty arising from a course of dealing 4. Implied warranty of custom or usage of trade 5. Implied warranty of merchantability

Warranty Disclaimers	1. *Express warranties.* Can be limited if the warranty and disclaimer can be reasonably construed with each other.
	2. *Implied warranties:*
	  a. *Disclaimer.* Can be disclaimed by expressions like *as is, with all faults,* or such language. If such language is not used, implied warranties are disclaimed.
	    i. *Implied warranty of merchantability.* Oral or written disclaimer that mentions the word merchantability.
	    ii. *Implied warranty of fitness for a particular purpose.* Written disclaimer of general language.
	  b. *Examination of goods.* The buyer or lessor fully examines the goods or refuses to do so. Applies only to obvious defects.
	3. *Conspicuousness.* Written disclaimers must be conspicuously displayed to be enforceable

Magnuson–Moss Warranty Act	Federal statute that covers written warranties that apply to *consumer* products.
	1. *Full and Limited Warranties.* If a good costs more than $10 and the warrantor makes an express warranty, the warranty must be labeled *full* or *limited.*
	  a. *Full warranty:* Guarantees free repair or replacement of a defective product. A time limit may be placed on the warranty.
	  b. *Limited warranty.* Limits the scope of a full warranty in some way (e.g., return of the purchase price).
	2. *Limitation on Disclaiming Implied Warranties.* If a seller or lessor makes an express warranty, he or she cannot disclaim or modify the implied warranties of merchantability and fitness for a particular purpose. A time limit may be placed on implied warranties but must correspond to the duration of the express warranty.

Tort Liability Based on Fault, p. 440

Negligence	Seller or lessor who breached his or her duty of due care by producing a defective product that causes injury to the plaintiff. Privity of contract between the seller or lessor and the plaintiff is not required.
Misrepresentation	Seller or lessor fraudulently misrepresents the quality of a product and the plaintiff relies on the misrepresentation and is injured thereby.

The Doctrine of Strict Liability, p. 441

Strict Liability in Tort	A manufacturer or seller who sells a defective product is liable to the ultimate user who is injured thereby. All in the chain of distribution are liable irrespective of fault. Sometimes called *vertical liability.*

The Concept of Defect, p. 443

The Concept of Defect	1. Defect in manufacture 2. Defect in design 3. Defect in packaging 4. Failure to warn 5. Failure to provide adequate instructions for assembly of a product 6. Other defects

Defenses to Product Liability, p. 448

Defenses to Product Liability	A manufacturer or seller is not liable for damages caused by a product it manufactures or sells if one of the following defenses applies: 1. *Supervening event.* The product was materially altered or modified after it left the seller's possession and the alteration or modification caused an injury. Also called *intervening event.* 2. *Generally known dangers.* A seller is not liable for failing to warn about inherent dangers in products that are know to the general population.

3. *Government contractor defense.* A manufacturer produces a product to government specifications and warns the government of any known defects in the specific design.
4. *Correction of a defect.* A manufacturer or seller who learns about a defect in a product it has sold notifies purchasers and users of the defect and corrects the defect.
5. *Assumption of the risk.* The plaintiff knew and appreciated the risk and voluntarily assumed the risk.
6. *Misuse of the product:*
    a. *Abnormal misuse.* The seller is not liable for injuries caused by the abnormal misuse of the product by the plaintiff. Also called unforeseeable misuse.
    b. *Foreseeable misuse.* The seller is liable for injuries caused by the foreseeable misuse of a product. The manufacturer must design products to be safe for foreseeable misuses.

Statutes of Limitation and Repose

1. *Statute of Limitations.* Requires an injured person to bring a product liability lawsuit within a specified period of time after being injured by a defective product.
2. *Statute of repose.* Requires a person to bring a product liability lawsuit within a specified period of time after a defective product was first purchased or leased.

Contributory and Comparative Negligence

1. *Contributory negligence.* A person who is partially responsible for causing his or her own injuries may not recover anything from the manufacturer or seller of a defective product that caused the remainder or the person's injuries.
2. *Comparative negligence.* A person who is partially responsible for causing his or her own injuries is responsible for a proportional share of the damages. The manufacturer or seller of the defective product is responsible for the remainder of the plaintiff's damages. Also called *comparative fault.*

END-OF-CHAPTER INTERNET EXERCISES AND CASE QUESTIONS

Working the Web Internet Exercises

ACTIVITIES

1. Find statistics on the most frequent type of product liability cases filed in your jurisdiction. Start with Consumer Product Safety Data at **www.cpsc.gov/library/data.html**.

2. What is the statute of limitations on product liability in your jurisdiction? Does it matter if your case is filed under UCC Article 2 warranties, negligence, or strict liability under Section 402A of the Restatement (Second) of Torts? Restatement of Torts, Section 402A **www.ali.org/ali/Tortpl.htm**. See also **www.law.cornell.**

edu/topics/products_liability.html containing an overview of products liability law with links to key primary and secondary sources.

3. Does your state have a statute of repose for product liability cases?

4. The UCC Article 2 provides for disclaimers of warranties. Find the provisions of the Magnuson–Moss Warranty Act and review the various disclaimers. Do you think disclaimers are a good idea? See LII: Law About ... Sales of Goods at **www.law.cornell.edu/topics/sales.html** for a summary of the warranties under the UCC Article 2.

CRITICAL LEGAL THINKING CASES

18.1 Express Warranty The House of Zog manufactures and sells the "Golfing Gizmo," a training device designed to help golfers improve their swing. The device consists of a golf ball attached to one end of a cotton string, the other end of the string being tied to the middle of an elastic cord. The elastic cord is then stretched between two stakes placed in the ground forming a T configuration. This allows the ball to return automatically after it has been struck. The "Golfing Gizmo" is sold in a package that states "COMPLETELY SAFE—BALL WILL NOT HIT PLAYER." In 1966, Louise Hauter gave a Golfing Gizmo to her 13-year old son, Fred, for Christmas. One afternoon, Fred decided to use the device, which had been set up in his front yard. Having used the Gizmo before, Fred felt no apprehension as he took his normal swing at the ball. The last thing he remembered was pain and dizziness. Fred had been hit in the head by the ball and had suffered serious injuries. Fred Hauter sues the House of Zog. Who wins? [*Hauter v. Zogarts*, 13 Cal.3d 104, 120 Cal.Rptr. 681 (CA 1975)]

18.2 Statement of Fact or Opinion? Jack Crothers went to Norm's Auto World to buy a used car. Maurice Boyd, a salesman at Norm's, showed Crothers a 1970 Dodge. While running the car's engine, Boyd told Crothers that the Dodge "had a rebuilt carburetor" and "was a good runner." After listening to the sales pitch, Crothers bought the car. As Crothers was driving the Dodge the next day, the car suddenly went out of control and crashed into a tree. Crothers was seriously injured. The cause of the crash was an obvious defect in the Dodge's accelerator linkage. Crothers sues Norm's Auto World. Who wins? [*Crothers v. Cohen*, 385 N.W.2d 562 (Minn. App. 1986)]

18.3 Implied Warranty of Merchantability Geraldine Maybank took a trip to New York City to visit her son and her two-year-old grandson. She borrowed her daughter's camera for the trip. Two days before leaving for New York, Maybank purchased a package of G.T.E. Sylvania Blue Dot flash cubes at a Kmart store. Kmart is owned by the S. S. Kresge Company. On the carton of the package were words to the effect that each bulb was safety coated. Upon arriving in New York, Maybank decided to take a picture of her grandson. She opened the carton of flash cubes and put one on the camera. When Maybank pushed down the lever to take a picture, the flash cube exploded. The explosion knocked her glasses off and caused cuts to her left eye. Maybank was hospitalized for eight days. Maybank sues S. S. Kresge Company. Who wins? [*Maybank v. S. S. Kresge Company*, 266 S.E.2d 409 (N.C. App. 1980)]

18.4 Implied Warranty of Merchantability Gladys Flippo went to a ladies' clothing store in Baresville, Arkansas, known as Mode O'Day Frock Shops of Hollywood. Flippo tried on two pairs of pants that were shown to her by a saleswoman. The first pair proved to be too small. When Flippo put on the second pair, she suddenly felt a burning sensation in her thigh. Flippo immediately removed the pants, shook them, and a spider fell to the ground. An examination of her thigh revealed a reddened area, which grew progressively worse. Flippo was subsequently hospitalized for 30 days. According to her physician, the injury was caused by the bite of a brown recluse spider. Flippo sues Mode O'Day Frock Shops. Is Mode O'Day Frock Shops liable? [*Flippo v. Mode O'Day Frock Shops of Hollywood*, 449 S.W.2d 692 (AK 1970)]

18.5 Implied Warranty of Fitness for Human Consumption Tina Keperwes went to a Publix Supermarket in Florida and bought a can of Doxsee Brand Clam Chowder. Keperwes opened the can of soup and prepared it at home. While eating the chowder, she bit down on a clam shell and injured one of her molars. Keperwes filed suit against Publix and Doxsee for breach of an implied warranty. In the lawsuit, Keperwes alleged that the clam chowder "was not fit for use as food, but was defective, unwholesome, and unfit for human consumption" and "was in such condition as to be dangerous to life and health." At the trial, Doxsee's general manager testified as to the state-of-the-art methods Doxsee uses in preparing its chowder. Are Publix Supermarkets, Inc., and Doxsee liable for the injury to Keperwes's tooth? [*Keperwes v. Publix Supermarkets, Inc.*, 534 So.2d 872 (Fla. App. 1988)]

18.6 Implied Warranty of Fitness for a Particular Purpose Dennis Walker is the owner of several pizza parlors in Nebraska. The stores operate under the name of El Fredo Pizza Restaurants, Inc. Walker planned to open a new restaurant in 1973. A business associate suggested that Walker purchase an oven from the Roto-Flex Oven Co. Walker contacted an agent of Roto-Flex and negotiated to buy a new oven. Walker told the agent the particular purpose for which he was buying the oven— to cook pizza—and that he was relying on the agent's skill and judgment in selecting a suitable oven. Based on the agent's suggestions, Walker entered into a contract to purchase a custom-built, Roto-Flex "Pizza Oven Special." The oven was installed in the new restaurant and problems immediately ensued. The oven failed to bake pizzas properly because of uneven heating. Constant monitoring of the oven was required, and delays occurred in serving customers. Roto-Flex was notified of the problem and attempted to fix the oven. The oven, however, continued to bake pizzas improperly. El Fredo Pizza, Inc., sues Roto-Flex Oven Company. Was a warranty of fitness for a particular purpose created in this case? [*El Fredo Pizza, Inc. v. Roto-Flex Oven Co.*, 291 N.W.2d 358 (NE 1978)]

18.7 Disclaimer of Warranties Cole Energy Company wanted to lease a gas compressor for use in its business of pumping and selling natural gas. Cole Energy began negotiating with the Ingersoll-Rand Company. On December 5, 1983, the two parties entered into a lease agreement for a KOA gas compressor. The lease agreement contained a section labeled "WARRANTIES." Part of the section read "THERE ARE NO IMPLIED WARRANTIES OF MERCHANTABILITY OR FITNESS FOR A PARTULAR PURPOSE CONTAINED HEREIN." The gas compressor that was installed failed to function properly. As a result, Cole Energy lost business. Cole Energy sued Ingersoll-Rand for the breach of an implied warranty of merchantability. Is Ingersoll-Rand liable? [*Cole Energy Development Company v. Ingersoll-Rand Company*, 678 F.Supp. 208 (C.D. III 1988)]

18.8 Strict Liability Jeppesen and Company produces charts that graphically display approach procedures for airplanes landing at airports. These charts are drafted from tabular data supplied by the Federal Aviation Administration (FAA), a federal agency of the U.S. government. By law, Jeppesen cannot construct charts that include information different from that supplied by the FAA. On September 8, 1973, the pilot of an airplane owned by World Airways was on decent to land at the Cold Bay, Alaska, airport. The pilot was using an instrument approach procedure chart published by Jeppesen. The airplane crashed into a mountain near Cold Bay, killing all six crew members and destroying the aircraft. Evidence showed that the FAA data did not include the mountain. The heirs of the deceased crew members and World Airways brought a strict liability action against Jeppesen. Does the doctrine of strict liability apply to this case? Is Jeppesen liable? [*Brocklesby v. Jeppesen and Company*, 767 F.2d 1288 (9th Cir. 1985)]

18.9 Defect the Emerson Electric Co. manufactures and sells a product called the Weed Eater Model XR-90. The Weed

Eater is a multipurpose weed-trimming and brush-cutting device. It consists of a handheld gasoline-powered engine connected to a long drive shaft, at the end of which can be attached various tools for cutting weeds and brush. One such attachment is a 10-inch circular sawblade capable of cutting through growth up to two inches in diameter. When this sawblade is attached to the Weed Eater, approximately 270 degrees of blade edge are exposed when in use. The owner's manual contained the following warning: "Keep children away. All people and pets should be kept at a safe distance from the work area, at least 30 feet, especially when using the blade." Donald Pearce, a 13-year old boy, was helping his uncle clear an overgrown yard. The uncle was operating a Weed Eater XR-90 with the circular sawblade attachment. When Pearce stooped to pick something up off the ground about 6 to 10 feet behind and slightly to the left of where his uncle was operating the Weed Eater, the sawblade on the Weed Eater struck something near the ground. The Weed Eater kicked back to the left and cut off Pearce's right arm to the elbow. Pearce, through his mother, Charlotte Karns, sued Emerson to recover damages under strict liability. Is Emerson liable? [*Karns v. Emerson Electric Co.*, 817 F.2d 1452 (1987)]

18.10 Crashworthiness Doctrine At 11 P.M. on April 10, 1968, Verne Prior, driving on U.S. 101 under the influence of alcohol and drugs at a speed of 65 to 85 miles per hour, crashed his 1963 Chrysler into the left rear of a 1962 Chevrolet station wagon stopped on the shoulder of the freeway for a flat tire. Christine Smith was sitting in the passenger seat of the parked car when the accident occurred. In the crash, the Chevrolet station wagon was knocked into a gully, where its fuel tank ruptured. The vehicle caught fire and Christine Smith suffered severe burn injuries. The Chevrolet station wagon was manufactured by General Motors Corporation. Evidence showed that the fuel tank was located in a vulnerable position in the back of the station wagon outside of the crossbars of the frame. Evidence further showed that if the fuel tank had been located underneath the body of the station wagon between the crossbars of the frame, it would have been well protected in the collision. Smith sued General Motors for strict liability. Was the Chevrolet station wagon a defective product? [*Self v. General Motors Corporation*, 42 C.A.3d 1, 116 Cal.Rptr. 575 (Cal. App. 1974)]

18.11 Defect Virginia Burke purchased a bottle of Le Domaine champagne that was manufactured by Almaden Vineyards, Inc. At home, she removed the wine seal from the top of the bottle but did not remove the plastic cork. She set the bottle on the counter, intending to serve it in a few minutes. Shortly thereafter, the plastic cork spontaneously ejected from the bottle, ricocheted off the wall, and struck Burke in the left lens of her eyeglasses, shattering the lens, and driving pieces of glass into her eye. The champagne bottle did not contain any warning of this danger. Evidence showed that Almaden had previously been notified of the spontaneous ejection of the cork from its champagne bottles. Burke sued Almaden to recover damages for strict liability. Is Almaden liable? [*Burke v. Almaden Vineyards, Inc.*, 86 C.A.3d 768, 150 Cal.Rptr. 419 (Cal. App. 1978)]

18.12 Assumption of Risk Lillian Horn was driving her Chevrolet station wagon, which was designed and manufactured by General Motors Corporation, down Laurel Canyon Boulevard in Los Angeles, California. Horn swerved to avoid a collision when a car coming toward her crossed the center line and was coming at her. In doing so, her hand knocked the horn cap off the steering wheel, which exposed the area underneath the horn cap, including three sharp prongs that had held the horn cap to the steering wheel. A few seconds later, when her car hit an embankment, Horn's face was impaled on the three sharp exposed prongs, causing her severe facial injuries. Horn sued General Motors for strict liability. General Motors asserted the defense of assumption of the risk against Horn. Who wins? [*Horn v. General Motors Corporation*, 17 C.3d 359, 131 Cal. Rptr. 78 (CA 1976)]

18.13 Misuse On the morning of February 25, 1980, Elizabeth Horton (name changed to Ellsworth) wore a lady's flannelette nightgown inside out. As a result, two pockets on the sides of the nightgown were protruding from the sides of the nightgown. Ellsworth turned on the left front burner of the electric stove to "high" and placed a tea kettle of water on the burner. The kettle only partially covered the burner. As Horton reached above the stove to obtain coffee filters from one of the cupboards, the nightgown came in contact with the exposed portion of the burner and ignited. Ellsworth was severely burned and suffered permanent injuries. Ellsworth sued Sherme Lingerie, the seller of the nightgown, and Cone Mills Corporation, the manufacturer of the textile from which the nightgown was made, for strict liability. Was there a misuse of the product that would relieve the defendant's liability? [*Ellsworth v. Sherme Lingerie and Cone Mills Corporation*, 495 A.2d 348 (Md. App. 1985)]

18.14 Misuse The Wilcox-Crittendon Company manufactured harnesses, saddles, bridles, leads, and other items commonly used for horses, cattle, and other ranch and farm animals. One such item was a stallion or cattle tie, a five-inch-long iron hook with a one-inch ring at one end. The tongue on the ring opened outward to allow the hook to be attached to a rope or other object. In 1964, a purchasing agent for United Airlines, who was familiar with this type of hook because of earlier experiences on a farm, purchased one of these hooks from Keystone Brothers, a harness and saddlery wares outlet located in San Francisco, California. Four years later, on March 28, 1968, Edward Dosier, an employee of United Airlines, was working to install a new grinding machine at a United Airlines maintenance plant. As part of the installation process, Dosier attached the hook to a 1,700-pound counterweight and raised the counterweight into the air. While the counterweight was suspended in the air, Dosier reached under the counterweight to retrieve a missing bolt. The hook broke and the counterweight fell and crushed Dosier's arm. Dosier sued Wilcox-Crittendon for strict liability. Who wins? [*Dosier v. Wilcox-Crittendon Company*, 45 Cal.App.3d 74, 119 Cal.Rptr. 135 (Cal. App. 1975)]

BUSINESS ETHICS CASES

18.15 Business Ethics During October 1978, Brian Keith, an actor, attended a boat show in Long Beach, California. At the boat show Keith obtained sales literature on a sailboat called the Island Trader 41 from a sales representative of James Buchanan, a seller of sailboats. One sales brochure described the vessel as "a picture of sure-footed seaworthiness." Another brochure called the sailboat "a carefully well-equipped and very seaworthy live-aboard vessel." In November 1978, Keith purchased an Island Trader 41 sailboat from Buchanan for a total purchase price of $75,610. After delivery of the sailboat, a dispute arose in regards to the seaworthiness of the vessel. Keith sued Buchanan for breach of warranty. Buchanan defended, arguing that no warranty had been made. Was it ethical for Buchanan to try to avoid being held accountable for statements of quality about its product that were made in the sales brochures given Keith? Should sales "puffing" be considered to create an express warranty? Why or why not? Who wins this case? [*Keith v. Buchanan*, 173 Cal.App.3d 13, 220 Cal.Rptr. 392 (Cal. App. 1985)]

18.16 Business Ethics The Delano Growers' Cooperative Winery, a California winery, produces wine in bulk. Supreme Wine Co., Inc., operated a wine bottling plant in Boston. Since 1968, Supreme purchased finished wine in bulk from Delano and other wine producers, which it then bottled and sold to retailers under the Supreme label. Supreme purchased all its sweet wine from Delano, which was delivered to Supreme's bottling plant in tank cars. Supreme then pumped the wine into redwood vats in its building.

In 1973, Supreme began receiving widespread returns of sweet wine from it customers. All of the returned wine was produced by Delano. The wine was producing sediment, was cloudy, and contained a cottony or hairy substance. Supreme complained to Delano, who promised to correct the situation.

Delano made other shipments of sweet wine to Supreme, but customers continued to return defective wine to Supreme. Evidence showed that the wine contained *lactobacillus trichodes*, also called Fresno mold. More than 8,000 cases of wine were spoiled by the Fresno mold. When Supreme refused to pay an invoice of $25,825 for shipment of wine, Delano sued to collect this amount. Supreme filed a counterclaim to recover damages. Was it ethical for the seller to disavow liability in this case? Who wins? [*Delano Growers' Cooperative Winery v. Supreme Wine Co., Inc.*, 473 N.E.2d 1006 (MA 1985)]

18.17 Business Ethics Celestino Luque lived with his cousins Harry and Laura Dunn in Millbrae, California. The Dunns purchased a rotary lawn mower from Rhoads Hardware. The lawn mower was manufactured by Air Capital Manufacturing Company and was distributed by Garehime Corporation. On December 4, 1965, neighbors asked Luque to mow their lawn. While Luque was cutting the lawn, he noticed a small carton in the path of the lawn mower. Luque left the lawn mower in a stationary position with its motor running and walked around the side of the lawn mower to remove the carton. As he did so, he suddenly slipped on the wet grass and fell backward. Luque's left hand entered the unguarded hole of the lawn mower and was caught in its revolving blade, which turns 175 miles per hour and 100 revolutions per second. Luque's hand was severely mangled and lacerated. The word *Caution* was printed above the unguarded hole on the lawn mower. Luque sued Rhoads Hardware, Air Capital, and Garehime Corporation for strict liability. The defendants argued that strict liability does not apply to *patent* (obvious) defects. Was it ethical for the defendants to argue that they were not liable for patent defects? Would patent defects ever be corrected if the defendants' contention was accepted by the court? Who wins? [*Luque v. McLean, Trustee*, 8 Cal.3d 136, 104 Cal.Rptr. 443 (CA 1972)]

BRIEFING THE CASE WRITING ASSIGNMENT

Read the following case, which has been excerpted from the court's opinions. Review and brief the case.

Johnson v. Chicago Pneumatic Tool Company
607 So.2d 615 (1992)
Court of Appeals of Louisiana

Crain, Judge

This is a products liability action in which William H. Johnson was injured in the course of his employment when a pipejack was accidentally propelled toward Johnson striking him in the back pinning him between the edge of a large diameter pipe which he was grinding and the pipejack. A pipejack is a large mechanical device which is inserted into large pipes which are in the process of being joined together. The pipejack applies pressure forcing the joints into an evenly rounded shape which can then be

welded together. The movement of the pipejack was controlled by an air winch manufactured by Chicago Pneumatic Tool Company (Chicago Pneumatic) which had been utilized and incorporated by McDermott, Inc., Johnson's employer, into a system dedicated to the fitting or joining of large diameter pipe. The accident occurred at the McDermott shipyard when a coemployee either tossed or laid a fifty gallon drum on the ground near the winch in the area where Johnson was working. The drum rolled and toppled over onto the winch throttle pushing the throttle downward which in turn activated the winch and caused the pipejack to move toward Johnson.

Johnson instituted this action against Chicago Pneumatic as manufacturer of the winch, alleging that the winch as designed and manufactured was unreasonably dangerous to normal use. McDermott intervened in this action. After trial on the merits, the jury rendered a special verdict in favor of defendant.

It is uncontroverted that at the time of the accident Johnson was working with his back to the pipejack and the winch; the winch was not being manually operated; and no one was standing at or adjacent to the winch controls. The clutch lever had previously been welded down by McDermott and as a result the clutch remained permanently engaged. Of the other winch controls, the throttle was set in the neutral position and neither the brake nor the safety lock was engaged.

In order to prevail in a products liability action a plaintiff must prove that his damage was a result of a condition of the product which made the product unreasonably dangerous to normal use. The "normal use" of a product encompasses all intended or foreseeable uses and misuses of the product. A manufacturer is obliged to adequately warn the user of any danger inherent in the normal use of the product which is not within the knowledge of or obvious to the normal user. The manufacturer is also required to anticipate the environment in which the product will be used and to notify the user of the potential risks arising from foreseeable use or misuse in the foreseeable environment.

The finding of the jury that the winch was not employed in normal use at the time of the accident is a factual determination which should not be set aside unless clearly wrong. A review of the record reveals that McDermott modified the winch by permanently engaging the clutch; that this modification permanently removed one of the safety and control features designed for its safe and proper operation; the disengagement of the clutch without the engagement of the additional safety features would have prevented the accident; the basic safety mechanisms of the winch were not utilized; the winch was installed backwards thereby requiring the operator to stand away from the controls; and the employees/operators were uninformed regarding familiarity with the controls and the proper operation of the winch. After careful review of the record we conclude that the jury's determination in this matter is not manifestly erroneous.

AFFIRMED.

ENDNOTES

1. 161 A.2d 69 (NJ 1960).
2. Restatement (Second) of Torts, § 395.
3. 111 N.E. 1050, 217 N.Y. 382 (NYApp. 1916).
4. 59 Cal.2d 57, 27 Cal.Rptr. 697, 377 P.2d 897 (1963).
5. Some states have enacted statutes that provide that the doctrine of strict liability does not apply to transactions involving the sale of blood or blood products.
6. Restatement (Second) of Torts, § 402A(1)(b).

19

Creation and Transfer of Negotiable Instruments

The great object of the law is to encourage commerce.

—Judge Chambre
Beale v. Thompson (1803)

Chapter Objectives

After studying this chapter, you should be able to:

1. Distinguish between a negotiable and nonnegotiable instrument.

2. Describe drafts and checks, and identify the parties to these instruments.

3. Describe promissory notes and certificates of deposit, and identify the parties to these instruments.

4. List the formal requirements of a negotiable instrument.

5. Distinguish between orders to pay and promises to pay.

6. Distinguist between instruments payable on demand and payable at a definite time.

7. Distinguish between instruments payable to order and payable to bearer.

8. Describe how negotiable instruments are indorsed and transferred.

9. Distinguish between blank and special indorsements.

10. Define and apply the imposter rule and the fictitious payee rule.

Chapter Contents

Negotiable instruments (or **commercial paper**) are important for the conduct of business and personal affairs. In this country, modern commerce could not continue without them. Examples of negotiable instruments include checks (such as the one that may have been used to pay for this book) and promissory notes (such as the one executed by a borrower of money to pay for tuition).

To qualify as a negotiable instrument, the document must meet certain requirements established by Article 3 of the Uniform Commercial Code (UCC). If these requirements are met, a transferee who qualifies as a *holder in due course* (HDC) takes the instrument free of many defenses that can be asserted against the original payee. In addition, the document is considered an ordinary contract that is subject to contract law.

The concept of *negotiation* is important to the law of negotiable instruments. The primary benefit of a negotiable instrument is that it can be used as a substitute for money. As such, it must be freely transferable to subsequent parties. Technically, a negotiable instrument is negotiated when it is originally issued. The term *negotiation*, however, is usually used to describe the transfer of negotiable instruments to subsequent transferees.

The types, creation, and transfer of negotiable instruments are discussed in this chapter.

negotiable instrument

A special form of contract that satisfies the requirements established by Article 3 of the UCC. Also called *commercial* paper.

Business Brief

If a document qualifies as a negotiable instrument, the terms of Article 3 of the UCC become as much a part of the instrument as if they were written on the instrument itself.

Landmark Law

REVISED ARTICLE 3 (NEGOTIABLE INSTRUMENTS) OF THE UCC

Although negotiable instruments have been used in commerce since medieval times, the English law courts did not immediately recognize their validity. To compensate for this failure, the merchants developed rules governing their use. These rules, which were enforced by local private merchant courts, became part of what was called the **Law Merchant**. Eventually, in 1882, England enacted the Bills of Exchange Act, which codified the rules of the Law Merchant.

In 1886, the National Conference of Commissioners of Uniform Laws promulgated the **Uniform Negotiable Instruments Law (NIL)** in the United States. By 1920, all of the states had enacted the NIL as law, but the rapid development of commercial paper soon made the law obsolete.

Article 3 (Commercial Paper) of the Uniform Commercial Code, which was promulgated in 1952, established rules for the creation of, transfer of, enforcement of, liability on negotiable instruments. All the states and the District of Columbia have replaced the NIL with Article 3.

In 1990, the American Law Institute and the National Conference of Commissioners on Uniform State Laws repealed Article 3 and replaced it with **Revised Article 3**. The new article, which is called "Negotiable Instruments" instead of "Commercial Paper," is a comprehensive revision of Article 3 that reflects modern commercial practices. Individual states are currently replacing Article 3 with Revised Article 3. Revised Article 3 will form the basis of this discussion of negotiable instruments.

FUNCTIONS OF NEGOTIABLE INSTRUMENTS

Negotiable instruments serve the following functions:

1. **Substitute for Money**   Merchants and consumers often do not carry cash for fear of loss or theft. Further, it would be almost impossible to carry enough cash for large purchases (e.g., a car or a house). Thus, certain forms of negotiable instruments—for example, checks—serve as a *substitute for money.*
2. **Credit Device**   Some forms of negotiable instruments extend credit from one party to another. For example, a seller may sell goods to a customer on a customer's promise to pay for the goods at a future time, or a bank may lend money to purchase goods to a buyer who signs a note promising to repay the money. Both these examples represent *extensions of credit.* Without negotiable instruments, the "credit economy" of the United States and other modern industrial countries would not be possible.
3. **Record-Keeping Device**   Negotiable instruments often serve as a *record-keeping device.* For example, banks usually return canceled checks to checking-account customers each month. These act as a record-keeping device for the preparation of financial statements, tax returns, and the like.

Business Brief

Negotiable instruments serve as a substitute for money. Most purchases by businesses and many by individuals are made by negotiable instruments (such as checks) instead of by cash.

International Law

NEGOTIABLE INSTRUMENTS PAYABLE IN FOREIGN CURRENCY

The UCC expressly provides that an instrument may state that it is payable in foreign money [UCC 3-107]. For example, an instrument "payable in 10,000 yen in Japanese currency" is a negotiable instrument that is governed by Article 3 of the UCC.

Unless the instrument states otherwise, an instrument that is payable in foreign currency can be satisfied by the equivalent in U.S. dollars as determined on the due date. The conversion rate is the current bank-offered spot rate at the place of payment on the due date. The instrument can expressly provide that it is payable only in the stated foreign currency. In this case, the instrument cannot be paid in U.S. dollars.

TYPES OF NEGOTIABLE INSTRUMENTS

instrument
Term that means *negotiable instrument*.

The term *instrument* means negotiable instrument [UCC 3-104(b)]. These terms are often used interchangeably.

Revised Article 3 recognizes four kinds of instruments: (1) drafts, (2) checks, (3) promissory notes, and (4) certificates of deposit. Each of these is discussed in the following paragraphs.

Drafts

draft
A three-party instrument that is an unconditional written order by one party that orders the second party to pay money to a third party.

drawer of a draft
The party who writes the order for a draft.

drawee of a draft
The party who must pay the money stated in the draft. Also called the *acceptor* of a draft.

payee of a draft
The party who receives the money from a draft.

A **draft**, which is a three-party instrument, is an unconditional written order by one party (the **drawer**) that orders a second party (the **drawee**) to pay money to a third party (the **payee**) [UCC 3-104(e)]. The drawee must be obligated to pay the drawer money before the drawer can order the drawee to pay this money to a third party (the payee).

For the drawee to be liable on a draft, the drawee must accept the drawer's written order to pay it. Acceptance is usually shown by the written word *accepted* on the face of the draft along with the drawee's signature and the date. The drawee is called the **acceptor** of the draft because it changes his or her obligation from that of having to pay the drawer to that of having to pay the payee. After the drawee accepts the draft, it is returned to the drawer or the payee. The drawer or the payee, in turn, can freely transfer it as a negotiable instrument to another party.

Consider This Example   Mary Owens owes Hector Martinez $1,000. Martinez writes out a draft that orders Owens to pay this $1,000 to Cindy Choy. Owens agrees to this change of obligation and accepts the draft. Martinez is the drawer, Owens is the drawee, and Choy is the payee.

time draft
A draft payable at a designated future date.

sight draft
A draft payable on sight. Also called a *demand draft*.

A draft can be either a time draft or a sight draft. A **time draft** is payable at a designated future date. For example, language such as "pay on January 1, 1994" or "pay 120 days after date" creates a time draft (see Exhibit 19.1). A **sight draft** is payable on sight. A sight draft is also called a **demand draft**. For example, language such as "on demand pay" or "at sight pay" creates a sight draft. A draft can be both a time and a sight draft. Such a draft would provide that it is payable at a stated time after sight. For example, this type of draft is created by language such as "payable 90 days after sight."

trade acceptance
A sight draft that arises when credit is extended (by a seller to a buyer) with the sale of goods. The seller is both the drawer and the payee, and the buyer is the drawee.

A **trade acceptance** is a sight draft that arises when credit is extended with the sale of goods. In this type of draft, the seller is both the drawer and the payee. The buyer to whom credit is extended is the drawee. Even though only two actual parties are involved, it is considered a three-party instrument because three legal positions are involved.

ℰXHIBIT **19.1** *A Time Draft*

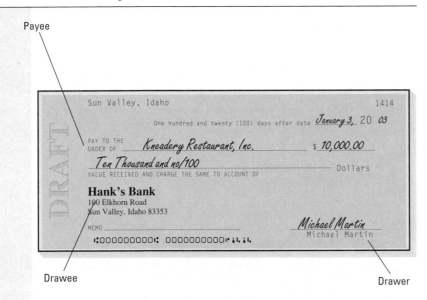

Checks

A **check** is a distinct form of draft. It is unique in that it is drawn on a financial institution (the drawee) and is payable on demand [UCC 3-104(f)]. In other words, a check is an order to pay (see Exhibit 19.2). Most businesses and many individuals have checking accounts at financial institutions.

Like other drafts, a check is a three-party instrument. The customer who has the checking account and writes (draws) the check is the **drawer**. The financial institution upon whom the check is written is the **drawee**. And the party to whom the check is written is the **payee**.

In addition to traditional checks, there are several forms of special checks, including certified checks, cashier's checks, and traveler's checks. These special checks are discussed in Chapter 21.

check

A distinct form of draft drawn on a financial institution and payable on demand.

drawer of a check

The checking account holder and writer of the check.

drawee of a check

The financial institution where the drawer has his or her account.

payee of a check

The party to whom the check is written.

ℰXHIBIT **19.2** *A Check*

Promissory Notes

promissory note

A two-party negotiable instrument that is an unconditional written promise by one party to pay money to another party.

A **promissory note** (or **note**) is an unconditional written promise by one party to pay money to another party [UCC 3-104(e)]. It is a two-party instrument (see Exhibit 19.3), not an order to pay. Promissory notes usually arise when one party borrows money from another. The note is evidence of (1) the extension of credit and (2) the borrower's promise to repay the debt.

*ε*XHIBIT **19.3** *A Promissory Note*

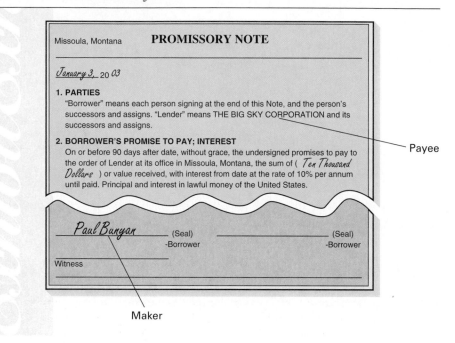

maker of a note

The party who makes the promise to pay (borrower).

payee of a note

The party to whom the promise to pay is made (lender).

time note

A note payable at a specific time.

demand note

A note payable on demand.

Commerce is facilitated by the use of negotiable instruments, such as checks and promissory notes.

The party who makes the promise to pay is the **maker** of the note (i.e., the borrower). The party to whom the promise to pay is made is the **payee** (i.e., the lender). A promissory note is a negotiable instrument that the payee can freely transfer to other parties.

The parties are free to design the terms of the note to fit their needs. For example, notes can be payable at a specific time (**time note**) or on demand (**demand note**). Notes can be made payable to a named payee or to "bearer." They can be payable in a single payment or in installments. The latter are called **installment notes**. Most notes require the borrower to pay interest on the principal.

Lenders sometimes require the maker of a note to post security for the repayment of the note. This security, which is called **collateral**, may be in the form of automobiles, houses, securities, or other property. If the maker fails to repay the note when it is due, the lender can foreclose and take the collateral as payment for the note. Notes are often named after the security that underlies the note. For example, notes that are secured by real estate are called **mortgage notes** and notes that are secured by personal property are called **collateral notes**.

Certificates of Deposit

A **certificate of deposit (CD)** is a special form of note that is created when a depositor deposits money at a financial institution in exchange for the institution's promise to pay back the amount of deposit plus an agreed-upon rate of interest upon the expiration of a set time period agreed upon by the parties [UCC 3-104(j)].

The financial institution is the borrower (the **maker**) and the depositor is the lender (the **payee**). A CD is a two-party instrument (see Exhibit 19.4). Note that a CD is a promise to pay, not an order to pay.

Unlike a regular passbook savings account, a CD is a negotiable instrument. CDs under $100,000 are commonly referred to as **small CDs**. CDs of $100,000 or more are usually called **jumbo CDs**.

collateral

Security against repayment of the note that lenders sometimes require; can be a car, a house, or other property.

certificate of deposit (CD)

A two-party negotiable instrument that is a special form of note created when a depositor deposits money at a financial institution in exchange for the institution's promise to pay back the amount of the deposit plus an agreed-upon rate of interest upon the expiration of a set time period agreed upon by the parties.

maker of a CD

The bank (borrower).

payee of a CD

The depositor (lender).

Exhibit **19.4** *A Certificate of Deposit*

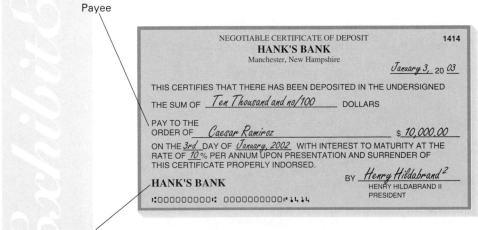

Entrepreneur and the Law

PROMISSORY NOTES AS NEGOTIABLE INSTRUMENTS

People and businesses borrow money from banks and other lenders to purchase automobiles, equipment, real estate, and other items. When people or businesses borrow money from lenders, they usually sign **promissory notes** promising to repay the borrowed money, plus interest, according to the terms of the note. The borrower is the maker of the note and the lender is the payee. The borrower is obligated to make payments (often monthly) until the principal amount borrowed, plus interest, is repaid.

A note that contains an unconditional written promise by one party to pay money to another party qualifies as a promissory note that is subject to the rules of Revised Article 3 of the Uniform Commercial Code. Hence, the promissory note can be negotiated to other parties who can enforce the note according to its terms against the borrower. In essence, the promissory note can be transferred like money, and its enforcement is subject to only a few defenses (these defenses are discussed in Chapter 20).

CONCEPT SUMMARY TYPES OF NEGOTIABLE INSTRUMENTS

Type of Instrument Orders to Pay	Party	Description of Party
Draft	Drawer	Person who issues the draft.
	Drawee	Person who owes money to the drawer; person who is ordered to pay the draft and accepts the draft.
	Payee	Person to whom the draft is made payable.
Check	Drawer	Owner of a checking account at a financial institution; person who issues the check.
	Drawee	Financial institution where drawer's checking account is located; party who is ordered to pay the check.
	Payee	Person to whom the check is made payable.
Promises to Pay		
Promissory note	Maker	Party who issues the promissory note; this is usually the borrower.
	Payee	Party to whom the promissory note is made payable; this is usually the lender.
Certificate of deposit (CD)	Maker	Financial institution that issues the certificate of deposit.
	Payee	Party to whom the certificate of deposit is made payable; this is usually the depositor.

CREATING A NEGOTIABLE INSTRUMENT

negotiable instrument

Commercial paper that must meet these requirements: (1) be in writing, (2) be signed by the maker or drawer, (3) be an unconditional promise or order to pay, (4) state a fixed amount of money, (5) not require any undertaking in addition to the payment of money, (6) be payable on demand or at a definite time, and (7) be payable to order or to bearer.

According to UCC 3-104(a), a **negotiable instrument** must

- Be in writing
- Be signed by the maker or drawer
- Be an unconditional promise or order to pay
- State a fixed amount of money
- Not require any undertaking in addition to the payment of money
- Be payable on demand or at a definite time
- Be payable to order or to bearer

These requirements must appear on the *face* of the instrument. If they do not, the instrument does not qualify as negotiable. Each of these requirements is discussed in the paragraphs that follow. A promise or order that conspicuously states that it is not negotiable or is not subject to Article 3 is not a negotiable instrument [UCC 3-104(d)].

A Writing

Business Brief

A negotiable instrument must be in writing; oral promises or orders do not qualify as negotiable instruments. (They are enforceable, however, under ordinary contract law).

A negotiable instrument must be (1) in writing and (2) *permanent and portable*. Often the requisite writing is on a preprinted form, but typewritten, handwritten, or other tangible agreements are also acceptable [UCC 1-201(46)]. In addition, the instrument can be a combination of different kinds of writing. For example, a check is often a preprinted form on which the drawer hand writes the amount of the check, the name of the payee, and the date of the check. Oral promises do not qualify as negotiable instruments since they are not clearly transferable in a manner that will prevent fraud. Tape recordings and videotapes are not negotiable instruments because they are not considered writings.

permanency requirement

A requirement of negotiable instruments that says they must be in a permanent state, such as written on ordinary paper.

Most writings on paper meet the **permanency requirement**, although a writing on tissue paper does not because of its impermanence. For example, the courts have held that writings on other objects (e.g., baseballs, shirts, and such) meet this requirement. A promise or order to pay that is written in snow or sand is not permanent and, therefore, is not a negotiable instrument. A photograph of such a writing that was signed by the maker or drawer would qualify as a negotiable instrument, however. The picture meets the requirements of permanence.

The **portability requirement** is intended to ensure free transfer of the instrument. For example, a promise to pay chiseled in a California redwood tree would not qualify as a negotiable instrument because the tree is not freely transferable in commerce. Writing the same promise or order to pay on a small block of wood could qualify as a negotiable instrument, however.

The best practice is to place the written promise or order to pay on traditional paper. This method ensures that the permanency and portability requirements are met so that transferees will readily accept the instrument.

Signed by the Maker or the Drawer

A negotiable instrument must be *signed* by the maker if it is a note or certificate of deposit and by the drawer if it is a check or draft. The maker or drawer is not liable on the instrument unless his or her signature appears on it. The signature can be placed on the instrument by the maker or drawer or by an authorized agent [UCC 3-401(a)]. Although the signature of the maker, drawer, or agent can be located anywhere on the face of the negotiable instrument, it is usually placed in the lower right-hand corner.

The UCC broadly defines **signature** as any symbol executed or adopted by a party with a present intent to authenticate a writing [UCC 1-201(39)]. A signature is made by the use of any name, including a trade or assumed name, or by any word or mark used in lieu of a written signature [UCC 3-401(b)]. For example, the requisite signature can be the maker's or drawer's formal name (Henry Richard Cheeseman), informal name (Hank Cheeseman), initials (HRC), or nickname (The Big Cheese). Any other symbol or device (e.g., an *X* or thumbprint) adopted by the signer as his or her signature also qualifies. The signer's intention to use the symbol as his or her signature is controlling. Typed, printed, lithographed, rubber-stamped, or other mechanical means of signing instruments are recognized as valid by the UCC.

portability requirement

A requirement of negotiable instruments that says they must be able to be easily transported between areas.

signature requirement

A negotiable instrument must be signed by the drawer or maker. Any symbol executed or adopted by a party with a present intent to authenticate a writing qualifies as his or her signature.

Business Brief

Companies that are too large to have every check (e.g., payroll checks) individually signed by a corporate officer often use some form of mechanical or computer device to sign payroll and other checks.

Contemporary Business Environment

SIGNATURE BY AN AUTHORIZED REPRESENTATIVE

A maker or drawer can appoint an *agent* to sign a negotiable instrument on his or her behalf. For example, corporations and other organizations use agents, usually corporate officers or employees, to sign the corporation's negotiable instruments. Individuals can also appoint agents to sign their negotiable instruments.

A maker or drawer is liable on a negotiable instrument signed by an authorized agent. The agent is not personally liable on the negotiable instrument if his or her signature properly unambiguously discloses (1) his or her agency status and (2) the identity of the maker or drawer [UCC 3-402(b)]. In the case of an organization, the agent's signature is proper if the organization's name is preceded or followed by the name and office of the authorized agent.

> ENDORSE HERE
>
> *Pay to David Lee*
>
> *without recourse*
>
> *Tiffany Shi*
>
> DO NOT SIGN/ WRITE/ STAMP BELOW THIS LINE
> FOR FINANCIAL INSTITUTION USAGE ONLY

Unconditional Promise or Order to Pay

To be a negotiable instrument under the requirements of UCC 3-104(a), the writing must contain either an **unconditional promise to pay** (note or certificate of deposit) or an **unconditional order to pay** (draft or check). It is the term *unconditional*, which is discussed shortly, that is key.

Promise or Order   To be negotiable, a **promise to pay** must be an unconditional and affirmative undertaking. The mere acknowledgment of a debt is not sufficient to constitute a negotiable instrument. In other words, an implied promise to pay is not negotiable, but an expressly stated promise to pay is negotiable. For example, the statement "I owe you $100" is merely an I.O.U. It acknowledges a debt, but it does not contain an express promise to

unconditional promise or order to pay requirement

A negotiable instrument must contain either an *unconditional promise to pay* (note or CD) or an *unconditional order to pay* (draft or check).

promise to pay

A maker's (borrower's) unconditional and affirmative undertaking to repay a debt to a payee (lender).

repay the money. If the I.O.U. used language such as "I promise to pay" or "the undersigned agrees to pay," however, a negotiable instrument would be created because the note would contain an affirmative obligation to pay.

Certificates of deposit (CDs) are an exception to this rule. CDs do not require an express promise to pay because the bank's acknowledgment of the payee's bank deposit and other terms of the CD clearly indicate the bank's promise to repay the certificate holder. Nevertheless, most CDs contain an express promise to pay.

To be negotiable, a draft or check must contain the drawer's unconditional **order for the drawee to pay** a payee. An order is a direction to pay and must be more than an authorization or request to pay. The language of the order must be precise and contain the word *pay*. For example, the printed word *pay* on a check is a proper order that is sufficient to make a check negotiable. The order can be in a courteous form, such as "please pay" or "kindly pay." A mere request or acknowledgment, such as "I wish you would pay," is not sufficient because it lacks a direction to pay.

An order to pay a draft or check must identify the drawee who is directed to make the payment. The name of the drawee financial institution that is preprinted on a check is sufficient. The order can be directed to one or more parties jointly, such as "to A *and* B," or in the alternative such as "to A *or* B." The order cannot, however, be in succession, such as "to A, and if she does not pay, then to B."

Unconditional Promise or Order To be negotiable, the promise or order must be **unconditional** [UCC 3-104(a)]. A promise or order that is **conditional** on another promise or event is not negotiable because the risk of the other promise or event not occurring would fall on the person who held the instrument. A conditional promise is subject to normal contract law.

Consider This Example Suppose American Airlines buys a $10-million airplane from Boeing Aircraft. American signs a promissory note that promises to pay Boeing if it is "satisfied" with the airplane. This promise is a conditional promise. The condition—that American is satisfied with the airplane—destroys the negotiability of the note.

A promise or order is conditional and, therefore, not negotiable if it states (1) an express condition to payment, (2) that the promise or order is subject to or governed by another writing, or (3) the rights or obligations with respect to the promise or order are stated in another writing. The mere reference to another writing does not make the promise or order conditional [UCC 3-106(a)].

Consider This Example Dow Chemical purchases equipment from Illinois Tool Works and signs a sales contract. Dow Chemical borrows the purchase price from Citibank and executes a promissory note evidencing this debt and promising to repay the borrowed money plus interest. The note contains the following reference, "sales contract—purchase of equipment." This reference does not affect the negotiability of the note. The note would not be negotiable, however, if the reference stated, "This note hereby incorporates by this reference the terms of the sales contract between Dow Chemical and Illinois Tool Works of this date."

A promise or order remains unconditional even though it refers to another writing for rights to collateral, prepayment, or acceleration (e.g., "see collateral agreement dated January 15, 1999"). A promise or order may also stipulate that payment is limited to a particular fund or source (e.g., "payable out of the proceeds of the Tower Construction Contract") [UCC 3-106(b)].

Fixed Amount of Money

To be negotiable, an instrument must contain a promise or order to pay a **fixed amount of money** [UCC 3-104(a)]. This phrase can be analyzed as two promises or orders: (1) to pay a **fixed amount** and (2) to pay in money.

Fixed Amount The **fixed amount** requirement ensures that the value of the instrument can be determined with certainty. The principal amount of the instrument must appear on the face of the instrument.

---

order to pay

A drawer's unconditional order to a drawee to pay a payee.

Business Brief

Notes and CDs contain *promises* to pay; drafts and checks contain *orders* to pay.

unconditional

Promises to pay and orders to pay must be unconditional in order for them to be negotiable.

Business Brief

A negotiable instrument may refer to another writing for rights as to collateral prepayment or acceleration.

One cannot help regretting that where money is concerned it is so much the rule to overlook moral obligations.

Malins, V. C.
Ellis v. Houston *(1878)*

fixed amount of money

A negotiable instrument must contain a promise or order to pay a fixed amount of money.

fixed amount

A requirement of a negotiable instrument that ensures that the value of the instrument can be determined with certainty.

An instrument does not have to be payable with interest, but if it is, the amount of interest being charged may be expressed as either a *fixed* or *variable* rate. The amount or rate of interest may be stated or described in the instrument or may require reference to information not contained in the instrument. If an instrument provides for interest but the amount of interest cannot be determined from the description, interest is payable at the judgment rate (legal rate) in effect at the place of payment of the instrument [UCC 3-112].

For example, a note that contains a promise to pay $10,000 in one year at a stated rate of 10 percent interest is a negotiable instrument because the value of the note can be determined at any time. A note that contains a promise to pay in goods or services is not a negotiable instrument because the value of the note would be difficult to determine at any given time.

Payable in Money UCC 3-104(a) provides that the fixed amount must be payable in "money." The UCC defines **money** as a "medium of exchange authorized or adopted by a domestic or foreign government as part of its currency" [UCC 1-201(24)]. For example, an instrument that is "payable in $10,000 U.S. currency" is a negotiable instrument.

money

A "medium of exchange authorized or adopted by a domestic or foreign government." [UCC 1-201(24)]

Instruments that are fully or partially payable in a medium of exchange other than money are not negotiable. Thus, an instrument that is "payable in $10,000 U.S. gold" is not negotiable. Although the stated amount is a fixed amount, it is not payable in a medium of exchange of the U.S. government. Likewise, instruments that are payable in diamonds, commodities, goods, services, stocks, bonds, and such do not qualify as negotiable instruments.

Contemporary Business Environment

ARE VARIABLE INTEREST RATE NOTES NEGOTIABLE INSTRUMENTS?

Prior to the mid-1970s, most loans that were made in this country were fixed-rate loans, that is, they bore a stated interest rate (e.g., 8 percent) that did not change during the life of the loan. This type of loan was fine for the lender as long as market interest rates did not change considerably. Since the mid-1970s, however, interest rates have become quite volatile.

To compensate for this volatility, many lending institutions began offering *variable interest rate loans*. These loans tied the interest rate to some set measure, such as a major bank's prime rate (e.g., Citibank's prime) or other well-known rate (e.g., Freddie Mac rate). A huge "secondary market" has developed where these loans are brought and sold.

These loans raised one major question: Are variable interest rate notes negotiable instruments? If they are, they are governed by Article 3 of the UCC, which provides certain protection to the holder against third-party claims and defenses. If they are not, they are ordinary contracts that are not subject to the protection of Article 3.

The drafters of Revised Article 3 solved this dilemma. Prior to the revision of Article 3 in 1990, UCC 3-104(1)(b) stipulated that to be a qualified negotiable instrument, a promise or order to pay must state a "sum certain in money." The key legal issue was whether variable interest rate notes were promises to pay a "sum certain in money." The courts were divided on this issue.

The drafters of Revised Article 3 settled the matter by expressly providing that variable interest rate notes are negotiable instruments. UCC 3-112(b) provides: "Interest may be stated in an instrument as a fixed or variable amount of money or it may be expressed as a fixed or variable rate or rates." UCC3-112(b) also provides that the amount or rate of interest may be determined by reference to information not contained in the instrument.

This change in Article 3, which recognizes variable interest rate notes as negotiable instruments, reflects modern commercial and banking practices.

Not Require Any Undertaking in Addition to the Payment of Money

To qualify as a negotiable instrument, a promise or order to pay cannot state any other undertaking by the person promising or ordering payment to do any act in addition to the payment of money [UCC 3-104(a)(3)]. For example, if a note required the maker to pay a stated amount of money *and* perform some type of service, it would not be negotiable.

A promise or order may include authorization or power to protect collateral, dispose of collateral, and waive any law intended to protect the obligee.

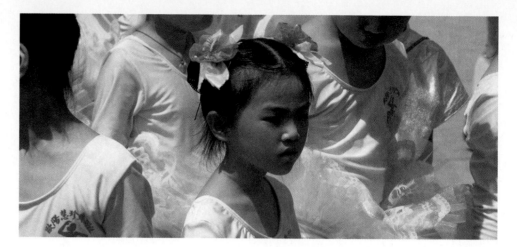

Taipei, Taiwan Negotiable instruments facilitate international commerce.

Payable on Demand or at a Definite Time

For an instrument to be negotiable, it is necessary to know when the maker, drawee, or acceptor is required to pay it. UCC 3-104(a)(2) requires the instrument to be **payable either on demand or at a definite time**, as noted on the face of the instrument.

Payable on Demand   Instruments that are payable on demand are called **demand instruments**. Demand instruments are created by (1) language such as "payable on demand," "payable at sight," or "payable on presentment" or (2) silence regarding when payment is due [UCC 3-108(a)].

By definition, checks are payable on demand [UCC 3-104(f)]. Other instruments, such as notes, certificates of deposit, and drafts can be, but are not always, payable on demand.

Payable at a Definite Time   Instruments that are payable at a definite time are called **time instruments**. UCC 3-108(b) and (c) states that an instrument is payable at a definite time if it is payable:

1. At a fixed date (for example, "payable on January 1, 2004")
2. On or before a stated date (for example, "payable on or before January 1, 2004"). The maker or drawee has the option of paying the note before—but not after—the stated maturity date
3. At a fixed period after sight (for example, "payable 60 days after sight"). Drafts often contain this type of language. The holder must formally present this type of instrument for acceptance so that the date of sight can be established
4. At a time readily ascertainable when the promise or order is issued (for example, "payable 60 days after January 1, 2004")

Instruments that are payable upon an uncertain act or event are not negotiable. For example, suppose Sarah Smith's father executes a promissory note stating, "I promise to pay to the order of my daughter, Sarah, $100,000 on the date she marries Bobby Boggs." This note is nonnegotiable because the act and date of marriage are uncertain.

Prepayment, Acceleration, and Extension Clauses   The inclusion of prepayment, acceleration, or extension clauses in an instrument does not affect its negotiability. Such clauses are commonly found in promissory notes.

A **prepayment clause** permits the maker to pay the amount due prior to the due date of the instrument. An **acceleration clause** allows the payee or holder to accelerate payment of the principal amount of an instrument, plus accrued interest, upon the happening of an event (e.g., default). An **extension clause** is the opposite of an acceleration clause. It allows the date of maturity of an instrument to be extended to some time in the future.

---

payable on demand or at a definite time requirement

A negotiable instrument must be payable either *on demand* or *at a definite time.*

demand instrument

An instrument payable on demand.

time instrument

An instrument payable (1) at a fixed date, (2) on or before a stated date, (3) at a fixed period after sight, or (4) at a time readily ascertainable when the promise or order is issued.

The great source of the flourishing state of this kingdom is its trade, and commerce, and paper currency, guarded by proper regulations and restrictions, is the life of commerce.

Ashhurst, J.
Jordaine v. Lashbrooke *(1798)*

Entrepreneur and the Law

BE CAREFUL WHETHER NEGOTIABLE INSTRUMENTS ARE PAYABLE TO ORDER OR TO BEARER

Because negotiable instruments are primarily intended to act as a substitute for money, they must be freely transferable to other persons or entities. The UCC requires that negotiable instruments be either **payable to order** or **payable to bearer** [UCC 3-104(a)(1)]. Promises or orders to pay that do not meet this requirement are not negotiable. They may, however, be assignable under contract law.

ORDER INSTRUMENTS

An instrument is an **order instrument** if it is payable (1) to the order of an identified person or (2) to an identified person or orders [UCC 3-109(b)]. For example, an instrument that states "payable to the order of IBM" or "payable to IBM or order" is negotiable. It would not be negotiable if is stated either "payable to IBM" or "pay to IBM" because it is not payable to *order*.

An instrument can be payable to the order of the maker, the drawer, the drawee, the payee, two or more payees together, or, alternatively, to an office, an officer by his or her title, a corporation, a partnership, an unincorporated association, a trust, an estate, or another legal entity. A person to whom an instrument is payable may be identified in any way, including by name, identifying number, office, or account number. An instrument is payable to the person intended by the signer of the instrument even if that person is identified in the instrument by a name or other identification that is not that of the intended person [UCC 3-110].

For example, an instrument made "payable to the order of Lovey" is negotiable. The identification of "Lovey" may be determined by evidence. On the other hand, an instrument made "payable to the order of my loved ones" is not negotiable because the payees are not ascertainable with reasonable certainty.

BEARER INSTRUMENTS

A **bearer instrument** is payable to anyone in physical possession of the instrument who presents it for payment when it is due. The person in possession of the instrument is called the **bearer**. Bearer paper results when the drawer or maker does not make the instrument payable to a specific payee.

For example, an instrument is payable to bearer when any of the following language is used: "payable to the order of bearer," "payable to bearer," "payable to Xerox or bearer," "payable to cash," or "payable to the order of cash." In addition, any other indication that does not purport to designate a specific payee creates bearer paper [UCC 3-109(a)]. For example, an instrument "payable to my dog Fido" creates a bearer instrument.

𝒞ONCEPT SUMMARY   FORMAL REQUIREMENTS FOR A NEGOTIABLE INSTRUMENT

Requirement	Description
Writing	Writing must be permanent and portable. Oral or implied instruments are nonnegotiable [UCC 3-104(d)].
Signed by maker or drawer	Signature must appear on the face of the instrument. It may be any mark intended by the signer be his or her signature. Signature may be by an authorized representative [UCC 3-104(a)].
Unconditional promise or order to pay	Instrument must be an unconditional promise or order to pay [UCC 3-104(a)]. Permissible notations listed in UCC 3-106(a) do not affect instrument's negotiability. If payment is conditional on the performance of another agreement, the instrument is nonnegotiable.
Fixed amount of money	Fixed amount: Amount required to discharge the instrument must be on the face of the instrument [UCC 3-104(a). Amount may include payment of interest, discount, and costs of collection. Revised Article 3 provides that variable interest rate notes are negotiable instruments. In money: Amount must be payable in U.S. or foreign country's currency. If payment is to be made in goods, services, or nonmonetary items, the instrument in nonnegotiable [UCC 3-104(a)].
Cannot require any undertaking in addition to the payment of money	A promise or order to pay cannot state any other undertaking to do an act in addition to the payment of money [UCC 3-104(a)(3)]. A promise or order may include authorization or power to protect collateral, dispose of collateral, waive any law intended to protect the obligee, and the like.
Payable on demand or at a definite time	Payable on demand: Payable at sight, upon presentation, or when no time for payment is stated [UCC 3-108(a)]. Payable at a definite time: Payable at a definite date, or before a stated date, a fixed period after a stated date, or at a fixed period after sight [UCC 3-108(b) and (c)]. Instrument payable only upon the occurrence of an uncertain act or event is nonnegotiable.

NONNEGOTIABLE CONTRACTS

nonnegotiable contract

Fails to meet the requirements of a negotiable instrument and, therefore, is not subject to the provisions of UCC Article 3.

If a promise or order to pay does not meet one of the previously discussed requirements of negotiability, it is a **nonnegotiable contract**. As such, it is not subject to the provisions of UCC Article 3. The contract, however, is not rendered either nontransferable or nonenforceable. A nonnegotiable contract can be enforced under normal contract law. If the maker or drawer of a nonnegotiable contract fails to pay it, the holder of the contract can sue the nonperforming party for breach of contract.

TRANSFER BY ASSIGNMENT OR NEGOTIATION

After they have been issued, negotiable instruments can be transferred to subsequent parties by *assignment* or by *negotiation*. The rights acquired by subsequent transferees differ according to the method of transfer. The different methods of transfer are discussed in the following paragraphs.

Transfer by Assignment

assignment

The transfer of rights under a contract.

assignor

The transferor in an assignment situation.

assignee

The transferee in an assignment situation.

An **assignment** is the transfer of rights under a contract. It transfers the rights of the transferor (**assignor**) to the transferee (**assignee**). Because normal contract principles apply, the assignee acquires only the rights that the assignor possessed. Thus, any defenses to the enforcement of the contract that could have been raised against the assignor can also be raised against the assignee.

An assignment occurs when a nonnegotiable contract is transferred. In the case of a negotiable instrument, assignment occurs when the instrument is transferred but the transfer fails to qualify as a negotiation under Article 3. In this case, the transferee is an *assignee* rather than a *holder*.

Transfer by Negotiation

negotiation

Transfer of a negotiable instrument by a person other than the issuer to a person who thereby becomes a *holder*.

holder

What the transferee becomes if a negotiable instrument has been transferred by *negotiation*.

Negotiation is the transfer of a negotiable instrument by a person other than the issuer. The person to whom the instrument is transferred becomes the holder [UCC 3-201(a)]. The **holder** receives at least the rights of the transferor and may acquire even greater rights than the transferor if he or she qualifies as a holder in due course (HDC) [UCC 3-302]. An HDC has greater rights because he or she is not subject to some of the defenses that could otherwise have been raised against the transferor.

The proper method of negotiation depends on whether the instrument is order paper or bearer paper, as discussed next.

order paper

Order paper is negotiated by (1) *delivery* and (2) *indorsement*.

Negotiating Order Paper An instrument that is payable to a specific payee or indorsed to a specific indorsee is **order paper**. Order paper is negotiated by delivery with the necessary indorsement [UCC 3-201(b)]. Thus, for order paper to be negotiated there must be delivery and indorsement.

Business Brief

Bearer paper can be negotiated by delivery alone; indorsement is not required.

Consider This Example Sam Bennett receives a weekly payroll check from his employer, Ace Plumbing Corporation. Bennett takes the check to a local store, signs the back of the check (indorsement), gives the check to the cashier (delivery), and receives cash from the check. Bennett has *negotiated* the check to the store. There has been delivery and indorsement.

bearer paper

Bearer paper is negotiated by *delivery*; indorsement is not necessary.

Negotiating Bearer Paper An instrument that is not payable to a specific payee or indorsee is **bearer paper**. Bearer paper is negotiated by *delivery*; indorsement is not necessary [UCC 3-201(b)]. Substantial risk is associated with the loss or theft of bearer paper.

Business Brief

There is a substantial risk associated with the loss or theft of bearer paper.

Consider This Example Suppose Mary draws a check "pay to cash" and gives it to Peter. There has been a negotiation because Mary delivered a bearer instrument (the check) to Peter. Subsequently, Carmen steals the check from Peter. There has not been a negotiation because the check was not voluntarily delivered. That Carmen physically possess the check is irrelevant. The negotiation is complete, however, if Carmen delivers the check to an innocent third party. The party is a holder and may qualify as an HDC with all the rights in the check [UCC 3-302]. If the holder is an HDC, Peter's only recourse is to recover against Carmen.

Contemporary Business Environment

CONVERTING ORDER AND BEARER PAPER

Instruments can be converted from order paper to bearer paper and vice versa many times until the instrument is paid [UCC 3-109(c)]. The deciding factor is the type of indorsement placed on the instrument at the time of each subsequent transfer. For example, follow the indorsements below to determine whether order or bearer paper has been created.

The front side of the original check, drawn by Henry Cheeseman, was drawn "Pay to the Order of Nikki Nguyen."

Indorsements

First indorsement: creates order paper (Nikki Nguyen transfers the check to Haeran Park)

Second indorsement: converts instrument to bearer paper (Haeran Park transfers the check to Vivian Chou)

Third indorsement: converts instrument to order paper (Vivian Chou transfers the check to Linda Matsubara)

INDORSEMENTS

An **indorsement** is the signature of a signer (other than as a maker, a drawer, or an acceptor) that is placed on an instrument to negotiate it to another person. The signature may (1) appear alone, (2) name an individual to whom the instrument is to be paid, or (3) be accompanied by other words [UCC 3-204(2)]. The person who indorses an instrument is called the **indorser**. If the indorsement names a payee, this person is called the **indorsee**.

Consider This Example Nikki Choy receives a $500 check for her birthday. She can transfer the check to anyone merely by signing her name on the back of the check. Suppose she indorses it "pay to Rob Dewey." Choy is the indorser; Rob Dewey is the indorsee.

Indorsements are usually placed on the reverse side of the instrument, such as on the back of a check (see Exhibit 19.5). If there is no room on the instrument, the indorsement may be written on a separate piece of paper called an **allonge**. The allonge must be affixed (e.g., stapled or taped) to the instrument [UCC 3-204(a)].

Indorsements are required to negotiate order paper, but they are not required to negotiate bearer paper [UCC 3-201(b)]. For identification purposes and to impose liability on the transferor, however, the transferee often requires the transferor to indorse the bearer paper at negotiation.

indorsement

The signature (and other directions) written by or on behalf of the holder somewhere on the instrument.

indorser

The person who indorses a negotiable instrument.

indorsee

The person to whom a negotiable instrument is indorsed.

allonge

A separate piece of paper attached to the instrument on which the indorsement is written.

*Ɛ*XHIBIT **19.5** *Proper Placement of an Indorsement*

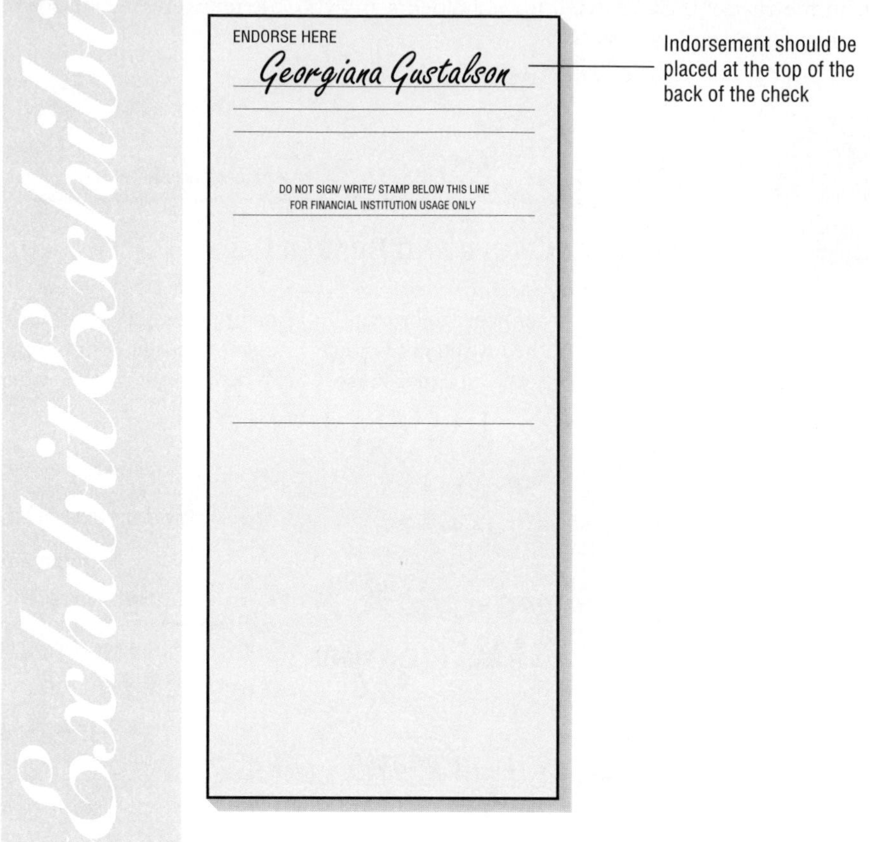

```
ENDORSE HERE
    Georgiana Gustalson ─────────── Indorsement should be
                                    placed at the top of the
                                    back of the check


        DO NOT SIGN/ WRITE/ STAMP BELOW THIS LINE
          FOR FINANCIAL INSTITUTION USAGE ONLY
```

Types of Indorsements

Every indorsement is

1. Blank or special
2. Unqualified or qualified
3. Nonrestrictive or restrictive

These different types of indorsements are discussed in the following paragraphs.

Blank Indorsements

A **blank indorsement** does not specify a particular indorsee. It may consist of a mere signature [UCC 3-205(b)]. For example, suppose Harold Green draws a check "pay to the order of Victoria Rudd" and delivers the check to Victoria. Victoria indorses the check in blank by writing her signature on the back of the check (see Exhibit 19.6).

*Ɛ*XHIBIT **19.6** *A Blank Indorsement*

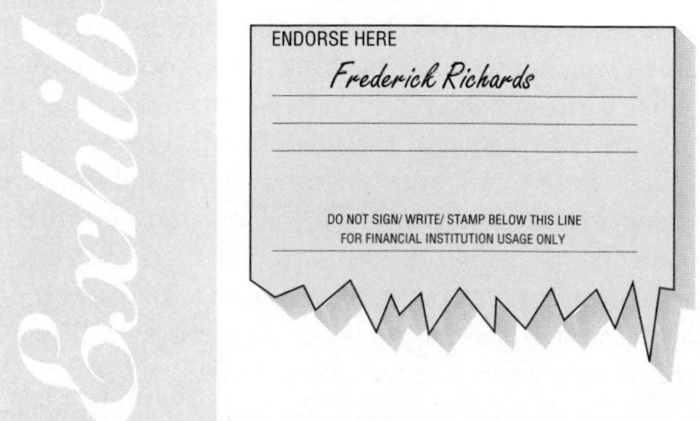

```
ENDORSE HERE
   Frederick Richards


        DO NOT SIGN/ WRITE/ STAMP BELOW THIS LINE
          FOR FINANCIAL INSTITUTION USAGE ONLY
```

Business Brief

An indorsement is necessary to negotiate order paper, but is not required to negotiate bearer paper.

blank indorsement

An indorsement that does not specify a particular indorsee. It creates *bearer paper.*

Order paper that is indorsed in blank becomes bearer paper. As mentioned earlier, bearer paper can be negotiated by delivery; indorsement is not required. For example, if Victoria Rudd loses the check she indorsed in blank and Mary Smith finds it, Mary Smith can deliver it to another person without indorsing it. Thus, the lost check can be presented for payment or negotiated to another holder.

Special Indorsements

A **special indorsement** contains the signature of the indorser and specifies the person (indorsee) to whom the indorser intends the instrument to be payable [UCC 3-205(a)]. Words of negotiation (e.g., "pay to the order of . . . ") are not required for a special indorsement. Words such as "pay Emily Ingman" are sufficient to form a special indorsement. For example, a special indorsement would be created if Betsy McKenny indorsed her check and then wrote "pay to Dan Jones" above her signature (see Exhibit 19.7). The check is negotiated when Betsy gives it to Dan. A special indorsement creates *order paper*. As mentioned earlier, order paper is negotiated by indorsement and delivery.

To prevent the risk of loss from theft, a special indorsement (which creates order paper) is preferred over a blank indorsement (which creates bearer paper). A holder can convert a blank indorsement into a special indorsement by writing any contract consistent with the character of the indorsement over the signature of the indorser in blank [UCC 3-205(c)]. For example, words such as "pay to John Jones" written above the indorser's signature are enough to convert bearer paper to order paper.

> **special indorsement**
> An indorsement that contains the signature of the indorser and specifies the person (indorsee) to whom the indorser intends the instrument to be payable. Creates *order paper*.

ℰXHIBIT 19.7 *A Special Indorsement*

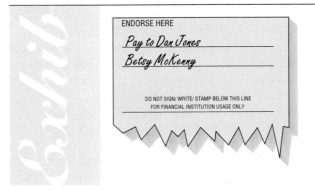

Unqualified and Qualified Indorsements

Generally, an indorsement is a promise by the indorser to pay the holder or any subsequent indorser the amount of the instrument if the maker, drawer, or acceptor defaults on it. This promise is called an **unqualified indorsement**. Unless otherwise agreed, the order and liability of the indorsers are presumed to be the order in which they indorse the instrument [UCC 3-415(a)].

> **unqualified indorsement**
> An indorsement whereby the indorser promises to pay the holder or any subsequent indorser the amount of the instrument if the maker, drawer, or acceptor defaults on it.

Consider This Example Cindy draws a check payable to the order of John. John (indorser) indorses the check and negotiates it to Steve (indorsee). When Steve presents the check for payment, there are insufficient funds in Cindy's account to pay the check. John, as an **unqualified indorser**, is liable on the check. John can recover from Cindy.

The UCC permits **qualified indorsements**, that is, indorsements that disclaim or limit liability on the instrument. A **qualified indorser** does not guarantee payment of the instrument if the maker, drawer, or acceptor defaults on it. A qualified indorsement is created by placing a notation such as "without recourse" or other similar language that disclaims liability as part of the indorsement [UCC 3-415(b)] (see Exhibit 19.8) A qualified indorsement protects only the indorser who wrote it on the instrument. Subsequent indorsers must also place a qualified indorsement on the instrument to be protected from liability. An instrument containing a qualified indorsement can be further negotiated.

> **unqualified indorser**
> An indorser who signs an *unqualified indorsement* to an instrument.

EXHIBIT **19.8**   *A Special Qualified Indorsement*   *A Blank Qualified Indorsement*

> ENDORSE HERE
> *Pay to David Lee*
> *without recourse*
> *Tiffany Shi*
>
> DO NOT SIGN/ WRITE/ STAMP BELOW THIS LINE
> FOR FINANCIAL INSTITUTION USAGE ONLY

> ENDORSE HERE
> *Without recourse*
> *Tiffany Shi*
>
> DO NOT SIGN/ WRITE/ STAMP BELOW THIS LINE
> FOR FINANCIAL INSTITUTION USAGE ONLY

Qualified indorsements are often used by persons signing instruments in a representative capacity. For example, suppose an insurance company that is paying a claim makes out a check payable to the order of the attorney representing the payee. The attorney can indorse the check to his client (the payee) with the notation "without recourse." The notation ensures that the attorney is not liable as an indorser if the insurance company fails to pay the check.

A qualified indorsement can be either a special qualified indorsement or a blank qualified indorsement. A **special qualified indorsement** creates order paper that can be negotiated by indorsement and delivery. A **blank qualified indorsement** creates bearer paper that can be further negotiated by delivery without indorsement.

Nonrestrictive and Restrictive Indorsements

Most indorsements are **nonrestrictive**. Nonrestrictive indorsements do not have any instructions or conditions attached to the payment of the funds. For example, the indorsement is nonrestrictive if the indorsee merely signs his signature to the back of an instrument or includes a notation to pay a specific indorsee ("pay to Sam Smith").

Occasionally, an indorser includes some form of instruction in an indorsement. This instruction is called a **restrictive indorsement**. A restrictive indorsement restricts the indorsee's rights in some manner. An indorsement that purports to prohibit further negotiation of an instrument does not destroy the negotiability of the instrument. For example, a check that is indorsed "pay to Sarah Stein only" can still be negotiated to other transferees. Because of its ineffectiveness, this type of restrictive indorsement is seldom used.

UCC 3-206 recognizes the following types of restrictive indorsements:

- **Conditional Indorsement**   An indorser can condition the guarantee of payment of an instrument dependent on the happening or nonhappening of a specified event. Consider this example: Vincent White, a holder of a check, indorses the check "pay to John Jones if he completes construction of my house by January 1, 1999." This indorsement is a valid conditional indorsement. Neither Jones nor any subsequent holder can require Vincent White to pay the check until this condition is met.
- **Indorsement for Deposit or Collection**   An indorser can indorse an instrument so as to make the indorsee his collecting agent. Such indorsement is often done when an indorser deposits a check or other instrument for collection at a bank. Words such as *for collection, for deposit only,* and *pay any bank* create this type of indorsement. Banks use this type of indorsement in the collection process.
- **Indorsement in Trust**   An indorsement can state that it is for the benefit or use of the indorser or another person. For example, checks are often indorsed to attorneys, executors of estates, real estate agents, and other fiduciaries in their representative capacity for the benefit of clients, heirs or others. These indorsements are called **trust indorsements** or **agency indorsements** (see Exhibit 19.9). The indorser is not personally liable on the instrument if there is a proper trust or agency indorsement.

An indorsee who does not comply with the instructions of a restrictive indorsement is liable to the indorser for all losses that occur because of such noncompliance.

nonrestrictive indorsement

An indorsement that has no instructions or conditions attached to the payment of the funds.

restrictive indorsement

An indorsement that contains some sort of instruction from the indorser.

indorsement for deposit or collection

An indorsement that makes the indorsee the indorser's collecting agent (e.g., "for deposit only").

Consider This Example   Suppose a check is drawn "payable to Anne Spencer, Attorney, in trust for Joseph Watkins." If Spencer indorses the check to an automobile dealer in payment for a car that she purchases personally, the automobile dealer (indorsee) has not followed the instructions of the restrictive indorsement. He is liable to Joseph Watkins for any losses that arise because of his noncompliance with the restrictive indorsement.

*E*XHIBIT 19.9   *A Trust Indorsement*

ENDORSE HERE

Pay to Lana Cheeseman in
trust for Gregory Cheeseman, Jr.
and Nikki Cheeseman
Gregory Cheeseman, Sr.

DO NOT SIGN/ WRITE/ STAMP BELOW THIS LINE
FOR FINANCIAL INSTITUTION USAGE ONLY

Misspelled or Wrong Name

Where the name of the payee or indorsee is misspelled in a negotiable instrument, the payee or indorsee can indorse the instrument in the misspelled name, the correct name, or both. For example, if Susan Worth receives a check payable to "Susan Wirth," she can indorse the check "Susan Wirth," "Susan Worth," or both. A person paying or taking the instrument for value or collection may require signature in both the misspelled and the correct name [UCC3-204(d)].

> *A trader is trusted upon his character, and visible commerce: that credit enables him to acquire wealth. If by secret liens, a few might swallow up all, it would greatly damp that credit.*
>
> Lord Mansfield
> Worseley v. Demattos *(1758)*

*E*ntrepreneur and the *L*aw

MULTIPLE PAYEES OR INDORSEES

Drawers, makers, and indorsers often make checks, promissory notes, and other negotiatable instruments payable to two or more payees or indorsees. The question then arises: Can the instrument be negotiated by the signature of one payee or indorsee, or are all of their signatures required to negotiate the instrument?

UCC 3-110(d) of Revised Article 3 and cases that have interpreted that section establish the following rules:

- If an instrument is *payable jointly* using the word *and* (e.g., pay to Shou-Yi Kang *and* Min-Wer Chen), both persons' indorsement are necessary to negotiate the instrument.

- If the instrument is *payable in the alternative* using the word *or* (e.g., pay to Shou-Yi Kang *or* Min-Wer Chen), either person's indorsement alone is sufficient to negotiate the instrument.

- If a *virgule*—a slash mark—is used, courts have held that the instrument is payable in the alternative. Thus, if a virgule is used (e.g., pay to Shou-Yi Kang/Min-Wer Chen), either person may individually indorse and negotiate the instrument [*Mumma v. Rainer National Bank*, 808 P.2d 767 (Wash.App. 1991)].

*C*ONCEPT SUMMARY TYPES OF INDORSEMENTS

Type of Indorsement	Description
Blank	Does not specify a particular indorsee (e.g., /s/ Mary Jones). This indorsement creates bearer paper.
Special	Specifies the person to whom the indorser intends the instrument to be payable (e.g., "Pay to the order of John Smith" /s/ Mary Jones). This indorsement creates order paper. [If it is not payable to order (e.g., "Pay to John Smith" /s/ Mary Jones), it can be converted to order paper (e.g., "Pay to the order of Fred Roe" /s/ John Smith).]
Unqualified	Does not disclaim or limit liability. The indorsee is liable on the instrument if it is not paid by the maker, acceptor, or drawer.
Qualified	Disclaims or limits the liability of the indorsee. There are two types: 1. Special qualified indorsement (e.g., "Pay to the order of John Smith, without recourse" /s/ Mary Jones). 2. Blank qualified indorsement (e.g., "Without recourse" /s/ Mary Jones).
Nonrestrictive	No instructions or conditions attached to the payment of funds (e.g., "Pay to John Smith or order " /s/ Mary Jones).
Restrictive	Conditions or instructions restrict the indorsee's rights. There are four types: 1. Conditional indorsement (e.g., "Pay to John Smith if he completes construction of my garage by June 1, 2004" /s/ Mary Jones). 2. Indorsement prohibiting further indorsement (e.g., "Pay to John Smith only" /s/ Mary Jones). 3. Indorsement for deposit or collection (e.g., "For deposit only" /s/ Mary Jones). 4. Indorsement in trust (e.g., "Pay to John Smith, trustee" /s/ Mary Jones).

*F*ORGED INDORSEMENT

forged indorsement

The forged signature of a payee or holder on a negotiable instrument.

Article 3 establishes certain rules for assessing liability when a negotiable instrument has been paid over a **forged indorsement**. With few exceptions, unauthorized indorsements are wholly inoperative as the indorsement of the person whose name is signed [UCC 3-401(a)]. Where an indorsement on an instrument has been forged or is unauthorized, the general rule is that the loss falls on the party who first takes the forged instrument after the forgery.

Consider This Example Suppose Andy draws a check payable to the order of Mallory. Leslie steals the check from Mallory, forges Mallory's indorsement, and cashes the check at the Liquor Store. The Liquor Store is liable. Andy, the drawer, is not. The Liquor Store can recover from Leslie, the forger (if she can be found).

There are two exceptions to this rule where a drawer or maker bears the loss where an indorsement is forged. The rules governing these circumstances—the imposter rule and the fictitious payee rule—are discussed in the paragraphs that follow.

The Imposter Rule

imposter

A person who impersonates a payee and induces a maker or drawer to issue an instrument in the payee's name and to give it to the imposter.

imposter rule

A rule that says if an imposter forges the indorsement of the named payee, the drawer or maker is liable on the instrument and bears the loss.

For purposes of the imposter rule, an **imposter** is one who impersonates a payee and induces the maker or drawer to issue an instrument in the payee's name and give the instrument to the imposter. If the imposter forges the indorsement of the named payee, the drawer or maker is liable on the instrument to any person who, in good faith, pays the instrument or takes it for value or for collection [UCC 3-404(a)]. This rule is called the **imposter rule**.

Consider This Example Suppose Fred purchases goods by telephone from Cynthia. Fred has never met Cynthia. Beverly goes to Fred and pretends to be Cynthia. Fred draws a check payable to the order of Cynthia and gives the check to Beverly, believing her to be Cynthia. Beverly forges Cynthia's indorsement and cashes the check at the Liquor Store.

Under the imposter rule, Fred is liable and the Liquor Store is not, because Fred was in the best position to have prevented the forged indorsement.

The imposter rule does not apply if the wrongdoer poses as the agent of the drawer or maker. For example, suppose in the prior example that Beverly lied to Fred and said that she was Cynthia's agent. Believing this, Fred draws the check payable to the order of Cynthia and gives it to Beverly. Beverly forges Cynthia's indorsement and cashes the check at the Liquor Store. Here, the Liquor Store is liable because the imposter rule does not apply. The Liquor Store may recover from Beverly, if she can be found.

The Fictitious Payee Rule

A drawer or maker is liable on a forged or unauthorized indorsement under the **fictitious payee rule**. This rule applies when a person signing as or on behalf of a drawer or maker intends the named payee to have no interest in the instrument or the person identified as the payee is a fictitious person [UCC 3-404(b)].

Consider This Example Marcia is the treasurer of the Weld Corporation. As treasurer, Marcia makes out and signs the payroll checks for the company. Marcia draws a payroll check payable to the order of her neighbor Harold Green, who does not work for the company. Marcia does not intend Harold to receive this money. She indorses Harold's name on the check and names herself as the indorsee. She cashes the check at the Liquor Store. Under the fictitious payee rule, Weld Corporation is liable because it was in a better position to have prevented the fraud.

The fictitious payee rule also applies if an agent or employee of the drawer or maker supplies the drawer or maker with the name of a fictitious payee [UCC 3-405(c)].

Consider This Example Elizabeth is an accountant for the Baldridge Corporation. She is responsible for drawing up a list of employees who are to receive payroll checks. The treasurer of Baldridge Corporation actually signs the checks. Elizabeth places the name "Annabelle Armstrong" (a fictitious person) on the list. Baldridge Corporation issues a payroll check to this fictitious person. Elizabeth indorses the instrument "Annabelle Armstrong" and names herself as indorsee. She cashes the check at the Liquor Store. Under the fictitious payee rule, Baldridge Corporation is liable. The Liquor Store is not.

fictitious payee rule

A rule that says that a drawer or maker is liable on a forged or unauthorized indorsement of a fictitious payee.

Business Ethics

THE FICTITIOUS PAYEE

In the summer of 1981, John Efler, a section manager of Prudential-Bache's dividend department, launched an embezzlement scheme that successfully escaped his employer's notice for nearly two years and netted him a cool $18.9-million profit.

The scheme worked like this: On a regular basis, Efler would order the issuance of Prudential-Bache's dividend checks, which were drawn on the firm's account with Banker's Trust Company and made payable to phony companies with names like those of some of Prudential-Bache's real corporate clients. Because Efler's department was responsible for making dividend payments to customers, Efler was able to create a trail of false records that gave his coworkers the impression that Prudential-Bache procedures were followed and that the checks were requisitioned by one person and approved by

another. In reality, Efler both requested and approved the checks.

Once a check was issued, Lawrence Artese, a friend of Efler's, would deposit it in an account that had been opened in the name of the phony corporations named on the Prudential-Bache check at Citibank. Artese had paid $165,000 in bribes to two Citibank employees. In exchange, the bank employees set up checking accounts without proper records and with fake corporate officers. Additionally, they did not file transaction reports to the Internal Revenue Service. (Such reports are required for cash withdrawals in excess of $10,000.) This enabled Artese to deposit phony checks and leave with a valise full of cash on a nearly daily basis. During one five-month period, for example, Artese deposited $3.7 million in checks at Citibank and withdrew an equal amount in cash.

Eventually, after a tip was received, a Prudential-Bache audit uncovered Elfer's scheme.

In an attempt to recover the laundered funds, Prudential-Bache brought an action against Citibank in a New York State court. The suit involved a variety of civil claims, including conversion and commercial bad faith. Citibank responded by asserting that the action should be dismissed under the fictitious payee rule. The UCC rule passes the burden of the loss to the employer when an employee issues checks to nonexistent (i.e., fictitious) parties.

The New York Court of Appeals held that the fictitious payee rule applied to the fact situation. Therefore, under New York's UCC, the loss occasioned by Prudential-Bache's employee's wrongdoing should fall upon it, rather than upon the depository bank, Citibank. [*Prudential-Bache Securities, Inc. v. Citibank, N.A.*, 539 N.Y.S.2d 699 (NY 1989)]

1. Did Efler act ethically in this case? Did he act illegally?
2. Was it morally right for Prudential-Bache to try to shift liability for its employee's defalcations to Citibank?

*C*HAPTER *S*UMMARY

*R*evised Article 3 (Negotiable Instruments) of the UCC, p. 459

Revised Article 3 (Negotiable Instruments) of the UCC	1. *Article 3 of the UCC.* Article of the Uniform Commercial Code promulgated in 1952 to govern the creation of, transfer of, enforcement of, and liability on negotiable instruments. 2. *Revised Article 3.* In 1990, the American Law Institute and the National Conference of Commissioners on Uniform State Laws approved new *Revised Article 3.* This new article replaces Article 3. It made substantial changes to the law governing negotiable instruments.

*F*unctions of Negotiable Instruments, p. 459

Functions of Negotiable Instruments	1. Substitute for money 2. Credit device 3. Record-keeping device

*T*ypes of Negotiable Instruments, p. 460

Types of Negotiable Instruments	There are four types of negotiable instruments. They are: 1. *Draft.* An order to pay. A three-party instrument. 2. *Check.* An order to pay. A three party-instrument. 3. *Promissory note.* A promise to pay. A two-party instrument. 4. *Certificate of deposit* (CD). A promise to pay. A two-party instrument.

Drafts	An unconditional written order by one party (the *drawer*) that orders a second party (the *drawee*) to pay money to a third party the (*payee*). The drawee must owe money to the drawer for the drawer to issue a draft ordering the money to be paid to the payee.
	1. *Drawer.* The party who writes the order for a draft.
	2. *Drawee.* The party who must pay the money stated in a draft. The drawee is also called the *acceptor.*
	3. *Payee.* The party who receives the money from a draft.
	4. *Types of drafts:*
	   a. *Time draft.* A draft payable at a designated future date.
	   b. *Sight draft.* A draft payable on sight. Also called a *demand draft.*
	   c. *Trade acceptance.* A sight draft that arises when credit is extended (by a seller to a buyer) with the sale of goods. The seller is both the drawer and the payee, and the buyer is the drawee.

Checks	A form of draft drawn on a financial institution (the *drawee*) and payable on demand. The checking account holder (the *drawer*) orders the financial institution (the *drawee*) to pay money to a third party (the *payee*). 1. *Drawer.* The checking account holder and writer of the check. 2. *Drawee.* The financial institution where the drawer has his or her checking account and pays the money to the payee. 3. *Payee.* The party to whom the check is written.

	4. *Types of checks:*
	   a. *Ordinary checks*
	   b. *Special checks:*
	      i. Certified checks
	      ii. Cashier's checks
	      iii. Traveler's checks

Promissory Notes	An unconditional written promise by one party (the *maker*) to pay money to another party (the *payee*). Promissory notes are also called *notes*:
	1. *Maker.* The party who makes the promise to pay (the borrower).
	2. *Payee.* The party to whom the promise to pay is made (the lender).
	3. *Types of promissory notes:*
	   a. *Time note.* A note payable at a specific time.
	   b. *Demand note.* A note payable on demand.
	   c. *Installment note.* A note that is paid in more than one installment.
	   d. *Mortgage note.* A note secured by real estate.
	   e. *Collateral note.* A note secured by personal property.

Certificates of Deposit	A special form of note that is created when a depositor (the *payee*) deposits money at a financial institution (the *maker*) in exchange for the institution's promise to pay back the amount of the deposit plus an agreed-upon rate of interest upon the expiration of a set time period agreed upon by the parties.
	1. *Maker.* The financial institution (the borrower).
	2. *Payee.* The depositor (the lender).
	3. *Types of CDs:*
	   a. *Small CD.* A CD under $100,000.
	   b. *Jumbo CD.* A CD of $100,000 or more.

Creating a Negotiable Instrument, p. 464

Creating a Negotiable Instrument	A negotiable instrument must: 1. Be in writing 2. Be signed by the maker or drawer 3. Be an unconditional promise or order to pay 4. State a fixed amount of money 5. Not require any undertaking in addition to the payment of money 6. Be payable on demand or at a definite time. 7. Be payable to order or to bearer

A Writing	1. *Writing.* A negotiable instrument must be in writing; oral promises or orders do not qualify as negotiable instruments.
	2. *Requirements of the writing:*
	   a. *Permanency requirement.* The writing must be in a permanent state, such as written on ordinary paper.
	   b. *Portability requirement.* The writing must be able to be easily transported between areas.

Signed by the Maker or the Drawer	1. *Signature.* A negotiable instrument must be signed by the *maker* if it is a note or CD and by the *drawer* if it is a draft or check.
	2. *Type of signature.* Any symbol executed or adopted by the maker or drawer with a present intent to authenticate a writing qualifies as his or her signature. This signature can be a formal name, an informal name, initials, a nickname, or any symbol or device.
	3. *Signature of authorized agent.* A maker or drawer can appoint an *agent* to sign a negotiable instrument on his or her behalf. *Liability of the parties:*
	   a. *Maker or drawer.* Liable on a negotiable instrument signed by an authorized agent.
	   b. *Agent.* An agent is not personally liable on the negotiable instrument if his or her signature discloses (i) his or her *agency status* and (ii) the *identity of the maker or drawer.* An agent who fails to meet these requirements is personally liable on the instrument.

Unconditional Promise or Order to Pay	1. *Promise or order.* A *maker's promise to pay* must be an unconditional and affirmative undertaking to repay the debt evidenced by the note or CD. A *drawer's order to pay* must be an unconditional order to a drawee to pay a payee. 2. *Unconditional promise or order.* Promises to pay and orders to pay must be *unconditional* for them to be negotiable.

3. *Conditional promise or order.* A promise or order that is *conditional* on another promise or event is not negotiable. A promise or order is conditional if it states:
   a. An express condition to payment.
   b. That the promise or order is subject to or governed by another writing.
   c. The rights or obligations with respect to the promise or order are stated in another writing.

A promise or order remains *unconditional* if it merely references another writing or refers to another writing for rights as to *collateral*, *prepayment*, or *acceleration*.

Fixed Amount of Money

1. *Fixed amount.* The value of the instrument must be able to be determined with certainty. An instrument does not have to provide for the payment of *interest*, but if it does, interest may be expressed as a *fixed* or *variable* amount or rate. The amount or rate of interest may be determined by reference to information not contained in the instrument (e.g., a bank's prime rate or a government index).
2. *Payable in money.* The fixed amount must be payable in *money*, which is any medium of exchange authorized or adopted by a domestic or foreign government. Instruments that are payable in gold, diamonds, commodities, goods, services, stocks, bonds, and such do not qualify as negotiable instruments.

Not Require Any Undertaking in Addition to the Payment of Money

The promise or order cannot require the person promising or ordering payment to do any act in addition to the payment of money. A note that would require such additional undertaking (e.g., the provision of a service) is not negotiable.

Payable on Demand or at a Definite Time

A negotiable instrument must be payable either on demand or at a definite time.

1. *Payable on demand.* An instrument that is payable on demand, at sight, or on presentment or that is silent regarding when payment is due. Called a *demand instrument*.
2. *Payable at a definite time.* An instrument is payable at a definite time if it is payable:
   a. At a fixed date
   b. On or before a stated date
   c. At a fixed period after sight
   d. At a time readily ascertainable when the promise or order is issued
3. *Prepayment, acceleration, and extension clauses.* The following clauses in an instrument do not affect its negotiability:
   a. *Prepayment clause.* A clause that permits a maker or drawee to pay an instrument prior to its due date.
   b. *Acceleration clause.* A clause that allows the payee or holder to accelerate payment of an instrument upon the happening of an event.
   c. *Extension clause.* A clause that allows the maturity of an instrument to be extended to some time in the future.

Payable to Order or to Bearer

A negotiable instrument must be payable to order or to bearer.

1. *Order instruments.* An instrument payable to the order of an *identified person* or to an identified person or order. The term *order* must be included in the instrument; otherwise, it is not negotiable. For example, an instrument that states "payable to the order of IBM" or "payable to IBM or order" is negotiable; a writing that states "payable to IBM" or "pay to IBM" is not negotiable.
2. *Bearer instruments.* An instrument that is payable to *anyone in physical possession* of the instrument. An instrument is payable to bearer when any of the following language is used: "payable to bearer," "payable to the order of bearer," "payable to IBM or bearer," "payable to cash," or "payable to the order of cash." The person in possession of a bearer instrument is called the *bearer*.

Nonnegotiable Contracts, p. 470

Nonnegotiable Contracts

A writing that fails to qualify as a negotiable instrument is a *nonnegotiable contract*. Nonnegotiable contracts are subject to normal contract law rather than Revised Article 3 of the UCC.

Transfer by Assignment or Negotiation, p. 470

Transfer by Assignment or Negotiation

Once issued, negotiable instruments can be transferred by assignment or negotiation. The rights acquired by transferees differ according to the method of transfer.

Transfer by Assignment

1. *Assignment.* Transfer of rights that the transferor (*assignor*) has in a contract to a transferee (*assignee*). Ordinary contracts, writings that do not qualify as negotiable instruments, and negotiable instruments that are not transferred by negotiation can be transferred by assignment.
2. *Assignor.* The transferor in an assignment situation.
3. *Assignee.* The transferee in an assignment situation.
4. *Rights acquired under an assignment.* The transferee acquires only the rights that the transferor had, and is subject to all of the defenses that can be raised against the transferor.

Transfer by Negotiation	1. *Negotiation.* A transfer of a negotiable instrument by a person other than the issuer to a person who becomes a *holder. Negotiation* is a term signifying that a negotiable instrument has met certain requirements in being transferred.
	2. *Transferor.* Person who transfers a negotiable instrument by negotiation.
	3. *Holder.* Person who receives a negotiable instrument by negotiation.
	4. *Rights acquired under a negotiation.* The holder receives at least the rights of the transferor and may acquire even greater rights than the transferor if he or she qualifies as a *holder in due course (HDC).* Included here is not being subject to some of the defenses that can be raised against the transferor.
	5. *Negotiating order paper.* Order paper (an instrument payable to a specific payee or indorsee) is negotiated by *delivery and indorsement.* That is, the transferor signs (indorses) the instrument, with or without other notation, and delivers the instrument to the holder.
	6. *Negotiating bearer paper.* Bearer paper (an instrument that is not payable to a specific payee) is negotiated by *delivery* (indorsement is not required). There is substantial risk associated with the loss or theft of bearer paper.
	7. *Converting order and bearer paper.* Negotiable instruments can be *converted from order paper to bearer paper* by the holder indorsing the instrument without naming a specific payee. An instrument can be *converted from bearer paper to order paper* by the holder indorsing the instrument and naming a specific payee.

Indorsements, p. 471

Indorsement	An *indorsement* is the signature of the signer (other than as a maker, a drawer, or an acceptor) that is placed on an instrument to negotiate it to another person, for example, a holder singing the back of a check. An indorsement may be a signature alone (creating bearer paper), be accompanied by the name of a specific payee (creating order paper), or be accompanied by other words (e.g., "without recourse").
	1. *Indorser.* The person who indorses a negotiable instrument.
	2. *Indorsee.* The person to whom a negotiable instrument is indorsed.
	3. *Allonge.* Indorsements are usually placed on the reverse side of the negotiable instrument. If there is no room on the instrument, the indorsement may be placed on a separate sheet of paper called an *allonge.* The allonge must be firmly affixed to the instrument.
	4. *Instruments requiring indorsement.* Indorsements are required to negotiate *order paper* (indorsement and delivery required). Indorsements are not required to negotiate *bearer paper* (only delivery is required).
Types of Indorsements	Every indorsement is:
	1. Blank or special
	2. Unqualified or qualified
	3. Nonrestrictive or restrictive
Blank Indorsements	An indorsement that does not specify a particular indorsee, which occurs when an indorser merely signs the instrument without naming a payee. This indorsement creates *bearer* paper.
Special Indorsements	An indorsement that specifies a named payee, which occurs when the indorser signs the instrument and names a particular indorsee. This indorsement creates *order* paper.
Unqualified and Qualified Indorsements	1. *Unqualified indorsement.* An indorsement that does not disclaim or limit the liability of the indorser. An *unqualified indorser* is liable to pay any holder or subsequent indorser if the maker, drawer, or acceptor does not pay the instrument.
	2. *Qualified indorsement.* An indorsement that disclaims or limits the liability of the indorser. A *qualified indorser* is not liable to pay any holder or subsequent indorser if the maker, drawer, or acceptor does not pay the instrument. A qualified endorsement is done by adding the words *without recourse* or similar language that disclaims liability.
Nonrestrictive and Restrictive Indorsements	1. *Nonrestrictive indorsement.* An indorsement that has no instructions or conditions attached to the payment of the funds. This indorsement occurs when the indorser signs his or her signature to the instrument (either naming a specific payee or not), but does not add any specific condition or instruction concerning the payment of the money.
	2. *Restrictive indorsement.* An indorsement that contains some sort of instruction from the indorser. The UCC recognizes the following restrictive indorsements:
	a. *Conditional indorsement.* An indorsement that conditions the payment of an instrument upon the happening or nonhappening of a specified event.
	b. *Indorsement for deposit or collection.* An indorsement that makes the indorsee the indorser's collection agent (e.g., indorsement "for deposit only").
	c. *Indorsement in trust.* An indorsement that states that it is for the benefit or use of the indorser or another person.
	An indorsement that purports to prohibit further negotiation of a negotiable instrument (e.g., "pay to Sarah Smith only") is ineffective and does not destroy the negotiability of the instrument.

Misspelled or Wrong Name	If the name of the payee or indorsee is misspelled or is wrong, the payee or indorsee can indorse the instrument in the misspelled or wrong name, the correct name, or both.
Multiple Payees or Indorsees	1. *Payable jointly.* An instrument that is payable to two or more persons with *and* between their names. All their indorsements are required to negotiate the instrument. 2. *Payable in the alternative.* An instrument that is payable to two or more persons with *or* between their names. Only one of their indorsements is required to negotiate the instrument.

Forged Indorsement, p. 476

Forged Indorsements	1. *Forged indorsement.* The forged signature of a payee or holder on a negotiable instrument. 2. *Liability on a forged indorsement.* Generally, the person who took the check from the forger is liable on a forged indorsement. 3. *Exceptions.* There are two exceptions to the general rule: The imposter rule and the fictitious payee rule.
The Imposter Rule	1. *An imposter.* A person who impersonates a payee and induces a maker or drawer to issue an instrument in the payee's name and give it to the imposter. 2. *The imposter rule.* States that if an imposter forges the indorsement of the named payee, the drawer or maker is liable on the instrument and bears the loss.
The Fictitious Payee Rule	A rule that says a drawer or maker is liable on a forged or unauthorized indorsement of a fictitious payee. This rule applies when a person signing as or on behalf of a drawer or maker intends the named payee to have no interest in the instrument or when the person identified as the payee is a fictitious person.

End-of-Chapter Internet Exercises and Case Questions

Working the Web Internet Exercises

ACTIVITIES

1. Find your state laws on "Financial Institutions" using the Cornell Web site. Notice that the UCC Article 3 is the law of negotiable instruments. Find the imposter rule in your state's version of this section. See LII: Law About . . . Banking at **www.law.cornell. edu./topics/banking.html**.

2. Read the law review article by Winn. What is the function of negotiable instruments?

3. Does your state have special laws covering digital signatures? See **www.law.sc.edu/sclr/vol49-4-winn.pdf** for the law review article, "Couriers Without Luggage: Negotiable Instruments and Digital Signatures" by Jane Kaufman Winn.

CRITICAL LEGAL THINKING CASES

19.1 Indorsement On November 15, 1979, Katherine Warnock purchased a cashier's check in the amount of $53,541, payable to her order and drawn on the Pueblo Bank and Trust Company (Pueblo Bank). At some time between November 15 and November 30, 1979, Warnock indorsed "Katherine Warnock" on the reverse side of the check. Eventually the check came into the hands of Warnock's attorney, Jerry Quick. Quick added the words *for deposit only* under her indorsement and then had the check deposited into his trust account at the La Junta State Bank. Warnock died on November 10, 1981. The executor of her estate suspected that Quick ille-

gally converted Warnock's funds into his own account. The executor claimed that the cashier's check that Quick deposited should have been payable only to Warnock because it was made to a named payee. When the executor discovered that Quick's trust account had been liquidated, the executor sued La Junta State Bank where the deposit had been made. Who wins? [*La Junta Bank v. Travis* 727 P.2d 48 (CO 1986)]

19.2 Time or Demand Instrument Mullins Enterprises, Inc. (Mullins), was a business operating in the state of Kentucky. To raise capital, Mullins obtained loans from Corbin Deposit Bank

& and Trust Company (Corbin Bank). Between 1971 and 1975, Corbin made eight loans to Mullins. Mullins executed a promissory note setting out the amount of the debt, the dates and times of installment payments, and the date of final payment and delivered it to the bank each time a loan was made. The notes were signed by an officer of Mullins. In 1980, a dispute arose between Mullins and Corbin as to the proper interpretation of the language contained in the notes. The bank contended that the notes were demand notes. Mullins claimed that the notes were time instruments. Who wins? [*Corbin Deposit Bank & Trust Co. v. Mullins Enterprises, Inc.* 34 UCC Rptr.Ser. 1201 (Ky. App. 1982)]

19.3 Note On August 17, 1979, Sandra McGuire and her husband entered into a contract to purchase the inventory, equipment, accounts receivable, and name of "Becca's Boutique" from Pascal and Rebecca Tursi. Becca's Boutique was a clothing store that was owned as a sole proprietorship by the Tursis. The McGuires agreed to purchase the store for $75,000, with a down payment of $10,000 and the balance to be paid by October 5, 1979. The promissory note signed by the McGuires read: "For value received, Thomas J. McGuire and Sandra A. McGuire, husband and wife, do promise to pay to the order of Pascal and Rebecca Tursi the sum of $65,000." Is the note an order to pay or a promise to pay? [*P P Inc. v. McGuire*, 509 F.Supp. 1079 (D.N.J. 1981)]

19.4 Bearer or Order Instrument Broadway Management Corporation (Broadway) owned and operated the American Nursing Center. Conan Briggs had received services from the center and had executed an instrument to pay for those services. The instrument reads in relevant part: "Ninety days after date, I, we, or either of us, promises to pay to the order of _____ $3,498.45." Briggs refused to pay on the note. Broadway claims that this note is "bearer paper" and as such is payable to the holder. Briggs claims that the note is "order paper" and is therefore payable only to a named payee. Can Broadway collect on this note as its bearer? [*Broadway Management Corporation v. Briggs*, 332 N.E.2d 131 (Ill. App. 1975)]

19.5 Formal Requirements Mr. Higgins operated a used car dealership in the state of Alabama. In 1978, Higgins purchased a 1977 Chevrolet Corvette for $8,115. He paid for the car with a draft on his account at the First State Bank of Albertville. Soon after, Higgins resold the car to Mr. Holsonback for $8,225. To pay for the car Holsonback signed a check that was printed on a standard-sized envelope. The reason the check was printed on an envelope is that this practice made it easier to transfer title and other documents from the seller to the buyer. The envelope on which the check was written contained a certificate of title, a mileage statement, and a bill of sale. Does a check printed on an envelope meet the formal requirements to be classified as a negotiable instrument under the UCC? [*Holsonback v. First State Bank of Albertville*, 30 UCC Rep.Serv. (AL 1980)]

19.6 Unconditional Promise M. S. Horne executed a $100,000 note in favor of R. C. Clark. The note stipulated that it could not be transferred, pledged, or assigned without Horne's consent. Along with the note, Horne signed a letter authorizing

Clark to use the note as collateral for a loan. Clark pledged the note as collateral for a $50,000 loan from First State Bank of Gallup (First State). First State telephoned Horne to confirm that Clark could pledge the note and Horne indicated that it was okay. Clark eventually defaulted on the loan. First State attempted to collect on the note, but Horne refused to pay. Did the restriction written on Horne's promissory note cause it to be nonnegotiable despite the letter or authorization? [*First State Bank of Gallup v. Clark and Horne*, 570 P.2d 1144 (NM 1977)]

19.7 Negotiable Instrument In 1982, William H. Bailey, M.D., executed a note payable to California Dreamstreet. Dreamstreet is a joint venture that solicits investments for a cattle breeding operation. Bailey's promissory note read: "Dr. William H. Bailey hereby promises to pay to the order of California Dreamstreet the sum of $329,800." In 1986, Dreamstreet negotiated the note to Cooperatieve Centrale Raiffeisen-Boerenleenbank B.A. (Cooperatieve), a foreign bank. A default occurred and Cooperatieve filed suit against Bailey to recover on the note. Was the note executed by Bailey a negotiable instrument? [*Cooperatieve Centrale Raiffeisen-Boerenleenbank B.A. v. Bailey*, 9 UCC Rep Serv 2d 145 (C.D.Cal. 1989)]

19.8 Reference to Another Agreement In 1972, Holly Hill Acres, Ltd. (Holly Hill) purchased land from Rogers and Blythe. As part of its consideration, Holly Hill gave Rogers and Blythe a promissory note and purchase money mortgage. The note, which was executed on April 28, 1972, read in part: "This note with interest is secured by a mortgage on real estate made by the maker in favor of said payee. The terms of said mortgage are by reference made a part hereof." Rogers and Blythe assigned this note and mortgage to Charter Bank of Gainsville (Charter Bank) as security to obtain a loan from the bank. Within a few months, Rogers and Blythe defaulted on their obligation to Charter Bank. Charter Bank sued to recover on Holly Hill's note and mortgage. Did the reference to the mortgage in the note cause it to be nonnegotiable? [*Holly Hill Acres, Ltd. v. Charter Bank of Gainesville*, 314 So.2d 209 (Fla. App. 1975)]

19.9 Demand Instrument In July 1977, Stewart P. Blanchard borrowed $50,000 from Progressive Bank & Trust Company (Progressive) to purchase a home. As part of the transaction, Blanchard signed a note secured by a mortgage. The note provided for a 10 percent annual interest rate. Under the terms of the note, payment was "due on demand, if no demand is made, then $600 monthly beginning 8/1/77." Blanchard testified that he believed Progressive could only demand immediate payment if he failed to make the monthly installments. After one year, Blanchard received notice that the rate of interest on the note would rise to 11 percent. Despite the notice, Blanchard continued to make $600 monthly payments. One year later, Progressive notified Blanchard that the interest rate on the loan would be increased to 12.75 percent. Progressive requested that Blanchard sign a form consenting to the interest-rate adjustment. When Blanchard refused to sign the form, Progressive demanded immediate payment of the note balance. Progressive sued Blanchard to enforce the terms of the note. Was the note a demand instrument?

[*Blanchard v. Progressive Bank & Trust Company*, 413 So.2d 589 (La. App. 1982)]

19.10 Extension Clause Robert and Sandra Evans were stockholders in Traditional Development, Inc. (Traditional). Traditional planned to build townhouses in Arizona. In 1972, the Evanses approached Security Mortgage Company (Security) to obtain financing for the project. Security agreed to make Traditional a $514,000 loan that would be secured by a note. On May 19, 1972, the note was executed, and the Evanses signed as guarantors. The note contained the following language: "The makers and endorsers expressly agree that this note, or any payment thereunder, may be extended from time to time without any way of affecting the liability of the makers and endorsers hereof."

The original maturity date of the note was January 14, 1973, or 245 days after origination. The project was delayed, however, so the note's due date was extended to May 13, 1973, an additional 114 days. The guarantors consented to the extension in writing. Several months later, the note was extended to January 15, 1974. When Traditional realized it was unable to complete the project, it assigned its interest in the note to Union Construction Company, Inc. One final extension of the note was granted, making the maturity date of the loan January 15, 1975. Did the multiple extensions of the note render it nonnegotiable? [*Union Construction Company, Inc. v. Beneficial Standard Mortgage Investors*, 28 UCC Rep.Serv. 711 (Ariz. App. 1980)]

19.11 Order or Bearer Paper Samuel C. Mazilly wrote a personal check that was drawn on Calcasieu-Marine National Bank of Lake Charles, Inc. (CMN Bank). The check was made payable to the order of Lee St. Mary and was delivered to him. St. Mary indorsed the check in blank and delivered it to Leland H. Coltharp Sr. in payment for some livestock. Coltharp accepted the check and took it to the City Savings Bank & Trust Company (City Savings) to deposit it. He indorsed the check as follows: "Pay to the order of City Savings Bank & Trust Company, DeRidder, Louisianna." City Savings accepted the check and forwarded it to CMN Bank for payment. The check never arrived at CMN Bank. Some unknown person stole the check while it was in transit and presented it directly to CMN Bank for payment. The teller at CMN Bank cashed the check without indorsement of the person who presented it. At the time CMN Bank accepted the check, was it order or bearer paper? [*Coltharp v. Calcasieu-Marine National Bank of Lake Charles, Inc.*, 199 So.2d 568 (La. App. 1967)]

19.12 Multiple Payees Murray Walter, Inc. (Walter, Inc.) was the general contractor for the construction of a waste treatment plant in New Hampshire. Walter, Inc., contracted with H. Johnson Electric, Inc. (Johnson Electric), to install the electrical system in the treatment plant. Johnson Electric purchased its supplies for the project from General Electric Supply (G.E. Supply). On May 1, 1980, Walter, Inc. issued a check payable to "Johnson Electric and G.E. Supply" in the amount of $54,900 drawn on its account at Marine Midland Bank (Marine Midland). Walter, Inc., made the check payable to both the subcontractor and its material supplier to be certain that the supplier was paid by Johnson Electric. Despite this precautionary measure, Johnson Electric negotiated the check without G.E. Supply's indorsement, and the check was paid by Marine Midland Bank. Johnson Electric never paid G.E. Supply. G.E. Supply then demanded payment from Walter, Inc. When Walter, Inc., learned that Marine Midland paid the check without G.E. Electric's indorsement, it demanded to be reimbursed. When Marine Midland refused, Walter, Inc., sued Marine Midland to recover for the check. Was Johnson Electric's indorsement sufficient to legally negotiate the check to Marine Midland Bank? [*Murray Walter, Inc. v. Marine Midland Bank*, 39 UCC Rep.Serv. 972 (N.Y.Sup.Ct. 1984)]

19.13 Imposter Rule Allan Q. Mowatt was employed as a bookkeeper at the law firm of McCarthy, Kenney & Reidy, P.C. The law firm maintained a primary checking account at the First National Bank of Boston (Bank of Boston) and two smaller accounts at other banks to pay operating expenses. The law firm's secondary account with the Union Bank of Lowell was under the name Clement McCarthy, the firm's senior partner. It was funded by checks drawn on the Bank of Boston account and payable to "Clement McCarthy." The checks used to fund the secondary accounts were signed by any of four attorneys with check-writing authority. When either of the two accounts was running low, Mowatt would make a check payable to "Clement McCarthy" and have it signed by one of the authorized attorneys. In addition to drawing checks needed to fund the secondary account, Mowatt began making out extra checks on the Bank of Boston account payable to Clement McCarthy. Mowatt would explain that the extra checks were needed to maintain funds in the secondary accounts. Mowatt then forged the indorsement of Clement McCarthy to the extra checks and deposited them into his own bank account. Who is liable for the loss caused by this forgery? [*McCarthy, Kenney & Reidy, P.C. v. First National Bank of Boston*, 2 UCC Rep.Serv. 2d 977 (Ma.Sup.Ct. 1986)]

 BUSINESS ETHICS CASES

19.14 Business Ethics Llobell was the president of Klem Ventures, Ltd. (Klem Ventures). Klem Ventures owed P.J. Panzeca, Inc. (Panzeca), a total of $47,000 for labor and materials used in a construction project. On February 1, 1972, Llobell, acting in his capacity as president, executed two notes to pay the debt owed Klem Ventures to Panzeca. One of the notes was in the amount of $18,000 and

was payable 30 days from the date of making; the other was $29,000 and was payable 60 days from the date of making. Llobell signed both notes on the reverse side. His signature was the only thing written on the back of the notes. When Panzeca presented the notes for payment, they were both dishonored. On September 20, 1974, Panzeca sued Llobell, claiming that he was personally liable for the amount of the notes. Llobell argued he was not personally liable since he signed the notes as an agent for the corporation. Did Llobell act ethically in denying personal liability? Who wins? [*P.J. Panzeca, Inc. v. Llobell*, 19 UCC Rep.Serv. 564 (N.Y.Sup.Ct. 1976)]

19.15 Business Ethics   Samuel K. Yucht was an attorney practicing law in the state of New Jersey. Yucht specialized in personal injury cases. Over the course of a year, Yucht submitted numerous claims on behalf of his clients against the Allstate Insurance Company (Allstate). In each case, Yucht informed Allstate that his client was willing to settle the claim and sub-

mitted a signed release. All the signatures on the releases were forged by Yucht. When Allstate issued settlement checks made payable to the client and Yucht as their attorney, Yucht again forged his clients' indorsements. He added his own indorsement and then deposited the checks into his personal account. Yucht never informed his clients of the settlements he had made on their behalf or of the money he had received in their names. Did Yucht act ethically in this case? Is Allstate liable for the losses caused by Yucht's actions under the imposter rule? [*Client's Security Fund of the Bar of New Jersey v. Allstate Insurance Company*, 5 UCC Rep.Serv. 2d 127 (N.J.Sup.Ct. 1987)]

BRIEFING THE CASE WRITING ASSIGNMENT

Read the following case, which has been excerpted from the court's opinion. Review and brief the case.

Federal Deposit Insurance Corporation v. Woodside Construction, Inc.
979 F.2d 172 (1992)
United States Court of Appeals for the Ninth Circuit

Hug, Circuit Judge

This case arose when Donald Galt signed a deed of trust note twice and signed a contract of guaranty twice. The FDIC claims that Galt is liable for $912,000, first because he signed the note as an indorser or, alternatively, because he signed the contract of guaranty as a guarantor. Galt claims that all of his signatures were in a representative capacity and that he did not sign individually as an indorser or as a guarantor. The FDIC maintains that one of the signatures on the note and one of the signatures on the contract of guaranty were signed in Galt's individual capacity, making him liable as an indorser on the note or, alternatively, as a guarantor on the contract of guaranty. The district court granted summary judgment for Galt on both the indorsement issue and the guaranty issue.

Galt obtained a loan from Alaska Mutual Bank for $912,000 on behalf of Woodside Construction of which he was an officer. The loan was evidenced by a promissory note, a deed of trust, a loan agreement, and a contract of guaranty. The signatures appeared on the note as follows:

(signature of Galt)
 Woodside Construction Inc.
signature(s)
(signature of Galt)
Donald A. Galt, President

The contract of guaranty appears on the form as follows:

Woodside Construction Inc.
(signature of Galt)
by Donald A. Galt
Title Vice President
by (signature of Galt)
Title
Guarantors:
    Guarantor
    Donald A. Galt

As can be seen, the note bore Galt's signature below the name of the corporation, on the line designating his representative capacity as president. It also bore Galt's signature above the name of the corporation with no representative capacity designated.

The contract of guaranty bore Galt's signature below the name of the corporation, on the line designating his representative capacity, and then bore his signature on a line where no representative capacity was indicated. He did not sign on the line designated for his signature as guarantor.

Alaska National Bank merged with two banks and became Alliance Bank, which retained this Woodside obligation. The loan was declared to be in default, and Alliance Bank instituted this action in state court. Alliance Bank was closed by the Alaska Department of Commerce and Economic Development, and the FDIC was appointed receiver. This Woodside obligation was sold by FDIC, as receiver, to FDIC in its corporate capacity. The FDIC then removed this case to federal court. The district court entered summary judgment for the FDIC against Woodside Construction on the note but entered summary judgment for Galt against the FDIC. The FDIC appeals the judgment rendered for Galt.

The manner in which Galt signed the promissory note bound him as an indorser in his individual capacity. He signed the note under the corporate name with the designation of his representative capacity. He also signed the note above the corporate name with no designation of any representative capacity. It is the latter signature that creates Galt's liability.

UCC Sec. 3-403(2) provides:

An authorized representative who signs his own name to an instrument:

(a) is personally obligated if the instrument neither names the person represented nor shows that the representative signed in a representative capacity:

(b) except as otherwise established between the immediate parties, is personally obligated if the instrument names the person represented but does not show that the representative signed in a representative capacity, or if the instrument does not name the person represented but does show that the representative signed in a representative capacity.

Here, the first signature above the principal designation fails to indicate the representative capacity, and the second signature above the representative capacity fails to indicate the principal. Because the FDIC is the holder of the note here, parol evidence of intent is inadmissible, and Galt is personally liable.

The FDIC argues that Galt is liable for attorneys' fees. The note makes the indorser liable for the costs of collection, including attorneys' fees. Because we hold that Galt is the indorser, he is liable for attorneys' fees.

The judgment is REVERSED.

CHAPTER 20

Holder in Due Course and Liability

If one wants to know the real value of money, he needs but to borrow some from his friends.

—Confucius
Analects, c. 500 B.C.

Chapter Objectives

After studying this chapter, you should be able to:

1. Define a holder and a holder in due course.

2. Identify and apply the requirements for becoming a holder in due course.

3. Distinguish between primary and secondary liability on negotiable instruments.

4. Describe the signature liability of makers, drawees, drawers, acceptors, and accommodation parties.

5. List the transfer warranties and describe the liability of parties for breaching them.

6. List the presentment warranties and describe the liabilities of parties for breaching them.

7. Identify real defenses that can be asserted against a holder in due course.

8. Identify personal defenses that cannot be asserted against a holder in due course.

9. Describe the Federal Trade Commission rule that prohibits the holder in due course rule in consumer transactions.

10. Describe how liability on a negotiable instrument is discharged.

Chapter Contents

If payment is not made on a negotiable instrument when it is due, the holder can use the court system to enforce the instrument. Various parties, including both signers and non-signers, may be liable on it. Some parties are primarily liable on the instrument, while others are secondarily liable. Accommodation parties (i.e., guarantors) can also be held liable.

Recall that the primary purpose of commercial paper is to act as a substitute for money. For this to occur, the holder of a negotiable instrument must qualify as a holder in due course (HDC). Commercial paper held by an HDC is virtually as good as money since HDCs take an instrument free of all claims and most defenses that can be asserted by other parties.

This chapter discusses the liability of parties on negotiable instruments, the requirements that must be met to quality as an HDC, the defenses that can be raised against the imposition of liability, and the discharge of liability.

A negotiable bill or note is a courier without luggage.

Chief Justice Gibson
Overton v. Tyler (1846)

HOLDER VERSUS HOLDER IN DUE COURSE

Two of the most important concepts of the law of negotiable instruments are that of "holder" and "holder in due course." A **holder** is a person in possession of an instrument that is payable to bearer or an identified person who is in possession of an instrument payable to that person [UCC 1-201(20)]. The holder of a negotiable instrument has the same rights as an assignee of an ordinary nonnegotiable contract. That is, the holder is subject to all the claims and defenses that can be asserted against the transferor.

The concept of holder in due course is unique to the area of negotiable instruments. A **holder in due course (HDC)** is a holder who takes an instrument for value, in good faith, and without notice that it is defective or is overdue. An HDC takes a negotiable instrument free of all claims and most defenses that can be asserted against the transferor of the instrument. Only real defenses—and not personal defenses—may be asserted against an HDC. (Defenses are discussed later in this chapter.) Thus, an HDC can acquire greater rights from those of the transferor.

The difference between holder and holders in due course is illustrated in this example: John purchases an automobile from Shannen. At the time of sale, Shennen tells John that the car has had only one previous owner and has been driven only 20,000 miles. John, relying on these statements, purchases the car. He pays 10 percent down and signs a promissory note to pay the remainder of the purchase price, with interest, in 12 equal monthly installments. Shannen transfers the note to Patricia. Then John discovers the car has actually had four previous owners and had been drive 100,000 miles. If Patricia were a holder (but not an HDC) of the note, John could assert Shannen's fraudulent representations against enforcement of the note by Patricia. John could rescind the note and refuse to pay Patricia. Patricia's only recourse would be against Shannen.

For example, if Patricia qualified as an HDC, however, the result would be different. John could not assert Shannen's fraudulent conduct against enforcement of the note by Patricia because this type of fraud is a personal defense that cannot be raised against an HDC. Therefore, Patricia could enforce the note against John. John's only recourse would be against Shannen, if she could be found.

holder

A person who is in possession of a negotiable instrument that is drawn, issued, or indorsed to him or his order, or to bearer, or in blank.

holder in due course (HDC)

A holder who takes a negotiable instrument for value, in good faith, and without notice that it is defective or is overdue.

The Federal Trade Commission (FTC), a federal administrative agency, has adopted a rule that eliminates the holder in due course status with regards to consumer credit transactions, such as the purchase of this automobile on credit by a consumer.

*R*EQUIREMENTS FOR HDC STATUS

To qualify as an HDC, the transferee must meet the requirements established by the UCC: The person must be the *holder* of a negotiable instrument that was taken (1) for value; (2) in good faith; (3) without notice that it is overdue, dishonored, or encumbered in any way; and (4) bearing no apparent evidence of forgery, alternations, or irregularity [UCC 3-302]. These requirements are discussed in the paragraphs that follow. Exhibit 20.1 illustrates the holder in due course doctrine.

*E*XHIBIT 20.1   *Holder in Due Course*

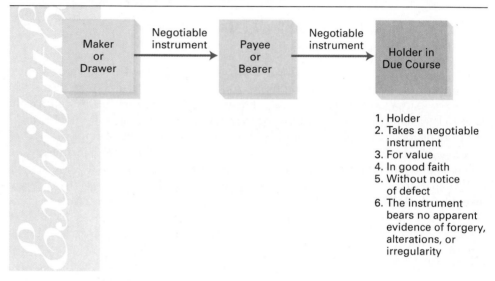

1. Holder
2. Takes a negotiable instrument
3. For value
4. In good faith
5. Without notice of defect
6. The instrument bears no apparent evidence of forgery, alterations, or irregularity

Taking for Value

The holder must have *given value* for the negotiable instrument to qualify as an HDC [UCC 3-302(a)(2)(i)]. For example, suppose Ted draws a check "payable to the order of Mary Smith" and delivers the check to Mary. Mary indorses it and gives it as a gift to her daughter. Mary's daughter cannot qualify as an HDC because she has not given value for it. The purchaser of a limited interest in a negotiable instrument is an HDC only to the extent of the interest purchased.

Under the UCC, value has been given if the holder [UCC 3-303]

1. Performs the agreed-upon promise.
2. Acquires a security interest or lien on the instrument.
3. Takes the instrument in payment of or as security for an antecedent claim.
4. Gives a negotiable instrument as payment.
5. Gives an irrevocable obligation as payment.

If a person promises to perform but has not yet done so, no value has been given and he or she is not an HDC. For example, Karen executes a note payable to Fred for $3,000 for goods she has purchased from him. Fred transfers the note to Amy for her promise to pay the note in 90 days. Before Amy pays for the note, Karen discovers that the goods she purchased from Fred are defective. Karen can raise this defect against enforcement of the note by Amy because no value has yet been given for the note. If Amy had already paid for the note, she would qualify as an HDC and Karen could not raise the issue of defect against enforcement of the note by Amy.

Taking in Good Faith

A holder must **take** the instrument **in good faith** to qualify as an HDC [UCC 3-302(a)(2)(ii)]. **Good faith** means honesty in fact in the conduct or transaction concerned [UCC 1-201(19)]. Honesty in fact is a subjective test that examines the holder's actual belief. A holder's subjective belief can be inferred from the circumstances. For example, if a holder acquires an instrument from a stranger under suspicious circumstances and at a deep discount, it could be inferred that the holder did not take the instrument in good faith. A naive person who acquired the same instrument at the same discount, however, may be found to have acted in good faith and thereby qualify as an HDC. Each case must be reviewed separately.

Note that the good faith test applies only to the holder. It does not apply to the transferor of the instrument. For example, suppose a thief steals a negotiable instrument and transfers it to Harry. Harry does not know that the instrument is stolen. Harry meets the good faith test and qualifies as an HDC.

Taking Without Notice of Defect

Except as allowed under the shelter principle (discussed later in this chapter), a person cannot qualify as an HDC if he or she has notice that the instrument is defective in any of the following ways [UCC 3-302(a)(2)]:

- It is overdue.
- It has been dishonored.
- It contains an unauthorized signature or has been altered.
- There is a claim to it by another person.
- There is a defense against it.

taking without notice of defect requirement

A person cannot qualify as an HDC if he or she has notice that the instrument is defective in certain ways.

Overdue Instruments If a **time instrument** is not paid on its expressed due date, it becomes overdue the next day. An instrument that has not been paid when due indicates that there is some defect to its payment.

For example, suppose a promissory note is due June 15, 1998. To qualify as an HDC, a purchaser must acquire the note before midnight of June 15, 1998. A purchaser who acquires the note on June 16 or later is only a holder, but not an HDC.

Often, a debt is payable in installments or in a series of notes. If a maker misses an installment payment or fails to pay one note in a series of notes, the purchaser of the instrument is on notice that it is overdue [UCC 3-304(b)].

A **demand instrument** is payable on demand. A purchaser cannot be an HDC if the instrument is acquired either (1) after demand or (2) at an unreasonable length of time after its issue. A "reasonable time" for presenting a check for payment is presumed to be 90 days. Business practices and the circumstances of the case determine a reasonable time for the payment of other demand instruments [UCC 3-304(a)].

time instrument

An instrument that specifies a definite date for payment of the instrument.

demand instrument

An instrument payable on demand.

Dishonored Instruments An instrument is **dishonored** when it is presented for payment and payment is refused. A holder who takes the instrument with notice of its dishonor cannot qualify as an HDC. For example, a person who takes a check that has been marked by the payor bank "payment refused—not sufficient funds" cannot qualify as an HDC.

dishonored

Occurs when an instrument has been presented for payment and payment has been refused.

Red Light Doctrine A holder cannot qualify as an HDC if he or she has notice that the instrument contains an unauthorized signature or has been altered or that there is any adverse claim against or defense to its payment. This rule is commonly referred to as the **red light doctrine**.

Notice of a defect is given when the holder has (1) actual knowledge of the defect, (2) received a notice or notification of the defect, or (3) reason to know from the facts and circumstances that the defect exists [UCC 1-201(25)]. The filing of a public notice does not of itself constitute notice unless the person actually reads the public notice [UCC 3-302(b)].

red light doctrine

A doctrine that says a holder cannot qualify as an HDC if he or she has notice of an unauthorized signature or an alteration of the instrument or any adverse claim against or defense to its payment.

no evidence of forgery, alteration, or irregularity requirement

A holder cannot become an HDC to an instrument that is apparently forged or altered or is so otherwise irregular or incomplete as to call into question its authenticity.

No Evidence of Forgery, Alteration, or Irregularity

A holder does not qualify as an HDC if at the time the instrument was issued or negotiated to the holder it bore apparent evidence of forgery or alteration or was otherwise so irregular or incomplete as to call into question its authenticity [UCC 3-302(a)(1)].

Clever and undetectable forgeries and alterations are not classified as obvious irregularities. Determining whether a forgery or alteration is apparent, whether the instrument is so irregular or incomplete that its authenticity should be questioned, are issues of fact that must be decided on a case-by-case basis.

Payee as an HDC

Payees generally do not meet the requirements for being an HDC because they know about any claims or defenses against the instrument. In a few situations, however, a payee who does not have such knowledge would qualify as a HDC.

Consider This Example   Suppose Kate purchases an automobile from Jake for $5,000. Jake owes Sherry Smith $5,000 from another transaction. Jake has Kate make out the $5,000 check for the automobile "payable to the order of Sherry Smith." Jake gives the check to Sherry. The car Jake sold to Kate is defective, and she wants to rescind the purchase. Sherry (payee), who did not have notice of the defect in the car, is an HDC. As such, Sherry can enforce the check against Kate. Kate's only recourse is to recover from Jake.

Contemporary Business Environment

ACQUIRING HDC STATUS UNDER THE SHELTER PRINCIPLE

A holder who does qualify as a holder in due course in his or her own right becomes a holder in due course if he or she acquires the instrument through a holder in due course. This is called the **shelter principle**.

Consider This Example   Jason buys a used car from Debbie. He pays 10 percent down and signs a negotiable promissory note promising to pay Debbie the remainder of the purchase price with interest in 36 equal monthly installments. At the time of sale, Debbie materially misrepresented the mileage of the automobile. Later, Debbie negotiates the note to Eric, who has no notice of the misrepresentation. Eric, a holder in due course, negotiates the note to Jaime. Assume Jaime does not qualify as an HDC in her own right.

She becomes an HDC, however, because she acquired the note through an HDC (Eric). Jaime can enforce the note against Jason.

To qualify as an HDC under the shelter principle, the following rules apply:

- The holder does not have to qualify as an HDC in his or her own right.
- The holder must acquire the instrument from an HDC or be able to trace his or her title back to an HDC.
- The holder must not have been a party to a fraud or illegality affecting the instrument.
- The holder cannot have notice of a defense or claim against the payment of the instrument.

SIGNATURE LIABILITY OF PARTIES

signature liability

A person cannot be held contractually liable on a negotiable instrument unless his or her signature appears on the instrument. Also called contract *liability*.

signer

A person signing an instrument who acts in the capacity of (1) a maker of notes and certificates of deposit, (2) a drawer of drafts and checks, (3) a drawee who certifies or accepts checks and drafts, (4) an indorser who indorses an instrument, (5) an agent who signs on behalf of others, or (6) an accommodation party.

A person cannot be held contractually liable on a negotiable instrument unless his or her signature appears on it [UCC 3-401(a)]. Therefore, this type of liability is often referred to as **signature liability** or **contract liability**. The signatures on a negotiable instrument identify those who are obligated to pay it. If it is unclear who the signer is, parol evidence can identify the signer. This liability does not attach to bearer paper since no indorsement is needed.

Signers of instruments sign in many different capacities, including makers of notes and certificates of deposit, drawers of drafts and checks, drawees who certify or accept checks and drafts, indorsers who indorse an instrument, agents who sign on behalf of others, and accommodation parties. The location of the signature on the instrument generally determines the signer's capacity. For example, a signature in the lower right-hand corner of a check indicates that the signer is the drawer of the check, and a signature in the lower right-hand corner of a promissory note indicates the signer is the maker of the note. The signature of the drawee named in a draft on the face of the draft or other location on the draft indicates that the signer is an acceptor of the draft. Most indorsements appear on the back or reverse side of an instrument. Unless the instrument clearly indicates that such a signature is made in some other capacity, it is presumed to be that of the indorser.

Every party that signs a negotiable instrument (except qualified indorser and agents that properly sign the instrument) is either primarily or secondarily liable on the instrument. The following discussion outlines the particular liability of signers.

Signature Defined

The **signature** on a negotiable instrument can be any name, word, or mark used in lieu of a written signature [UCC 3-401(b)]. In other words, a signature is any symbol that is (1) handwritten, typed, printed, stamped, or made in almost any other manner and (2) executed or adopted by a party to authenticate a writing [UCC 1-201(39)]. This rule permits trade names and other assumed names to be used as signatures on negotiable instruments.

The unauthorized signature of a person on an instrument is ineffective as that person's signature. It is effective as the signature of the unauthorized signer in favor of an HDC, however. For example, a person who forges a signature on a check may be held liable to an HDC. An unauthorized signature may be ratified [UCC 3-403(a)].

Agent's Signatures

A person may either sign a negotiable instrument him- or herself or authorize a representative to sign the instrument on his or her behalf [UCC 3-401(a)]. The representative is the **agent** and the represented person is the **principal**. The authority of an agent to sign an instrument is established under general agency law. No special form of appointment is necessary.

Authorized Signature If an authorized agent signs an instrument by signing either the principal's name or the agent's own name, the principal is bound as if the signature was made on a simple contract. It does not matter whether the principal is identified in the instrument [UCC 3-402(2)].

For example, suppose Anderson was the agent for Puttkammer. The following signatures on a negotiable instrument would bind Puttkammer on the instrument:

1. Puttkammer, by Anderson, agents
2. Puttkammer
3. Puttkammer, Anderson
4. Anderson

An authorized agent's personal liability on an instrument he or she signs on behalf of a principal depends on the information disclosed in the signature. The agent has no liability if the signature shows unambiguously that it is made on behalf of a principal who is identified in the instrument [UCC 3-402(b)(1)]. Signature Number 1 ("Puttkammer, by Anderson, agent") satisfies this requirement.

If the authorized agent's signature does not show unambiguously that the signature was made in a representative capacity and the agent cannot prove the original parties did not intend him or her to be liable, the agent is liable (1) to an HDC who took the instrument without notice that the agent was not intended to be liable on the instrument and (2) to any other person other than an HDC [UCC 3-402(b)(2)]. Signature Number 2 ("Puttkammer") shows such a signature.

Signatures Number 3 ("Puttkammer, Anderson") and 4 ("Anderson") place the agent at risk of personal liability to an HDC that does not have notice that the agent was not intended to be liable on the instrument. To avoid liability to a non-HDC for these signatures, the agent would have to prove that the third-party non-HDC did not intend to hold the agent liable on the instrument.

There is one exception to these rules. If an agent signs his or her name as the drawer of a check without indicating the agent's representative status and the check is payable from the account of the principal who is identified on the check, the agent is not liable on the check [UCC 3-402(c)].

---

signature
Any name, word, or mark used in lieu of a written signature; any symbol that is (1) handwritten, typed, printed, stamped, or made in almost any other manner and (2) executed or adopted by a party to authenticate a writing.

agent
A person who has been authorized to sign a negotiable instrument on behalf of another person.

principal
A person who authorizes an agent to sign a negotiable instrument on his or her behalf.

Business Brief
To avoid personal liability on a negotiable instrument, the agent should properly sign the instrument to indicate his or her agency status and the identify of the principal.

unauthorized signature

A signature made by a purported agent without authority from the purported principal.

Unauthorized Signature An **unauthorized signature** is a signature made by a purported agent without authority from the purported principal. Such a signature arises if (1) a person signs a negotiable instrument on behalf of a person for whom he or she is not an agent or (2) an authorized agent exceeds the scope of his or her authority. An unauthorized signature by a purported agent does not act as the signature of the purported principal. The purported agent is liable to any person who in good faith pays the instrument or takes if for value [UCC 3-403(a)].

The purported principal is liable if he or she ratifies the unauthorized signature [UCC 3-403(a)]. For example, a purported agent signs a contract and promissory note to purchase a building for a purported principal. Suppose that the purported principal likes the deal and accepts it. She has ratified the transaction and is liable on the note.

Business Brief

The unauthorized signature of a person on a negotiable instrument is ineffective as that person's signature unless he or she *ratifies*, the unauthorized signature.

primary liability

Absolute liability to pay a negotiable instrument, subject to certain real defenses.

Primary Liability

Makers of promissory notes and certificates of deposit have **primary liability** for the instrument. Upon signing a promissory note, the maker unconditionally promises to pay the amount stipulated in the note when it is due. Makers are absolutely liable to pay the instrument, subject only to certain real defenses. The holder need not take any action to give rise to this obligation. Generally, the maker is obligated to pay the note according to its original terms. If the note was incomplete when it was issued, the maker is obligated to pay the note as completed as long as he or she authorized the terms as they were filled in [UCC 3-412].

A draft or a check is an order from a drawer to a drawee to pay the instrument to a payee (or other holder) according to its terms. No party is primarily liable when the draft or check is issued since such instruments are merely an order to pay. Thus, a drawee who refuses to pay a draft or a check is not liable to the payee or holder. If there has been a wrongful dishonor of the instrument, the drawee may be liable to the drawer for certain damages.

Business Brief

The following parties are *primarily liable* on negotiable instruments: (1) *makers* of promissory notes and certificates of deposit and (2) *acceptors* of drafts and checks.

On occasion, a drawee is requested to accept a draft or check. Acceptance of a draft occurs when the drawee writes the word *accepted* across the face of the draft. The acceptor—that is, the drawee—is primarily liable on the instrument. A check, which is a special form of draft, is accepted when it is certified by a bank. The bank's certification discharges the drawer and all prior indorsers from liability on the check. Note that the bank may choose to refuse to certify the check without liability. The issuer of a cashier's check also is primarily liable on the instrument [UCC 3-411].

In the following case, the court held that a comaker was primarily liable on a promissory note.

Grand Island Production Credit Assn. v. Humphrey

388 N.W.2d 807 (1986)

Supreme Court of Nebraska

CASE 20.1

BACKGROUND AND FACTS

The Grand Island Production Credit Association (Grand Island) is a federally chartered credit union. On November 25, 1980, Carl M. and Beulah C. Humphrey, husband and wife, entered into a loan arrangement with Grand Island for a $50,000 line of credit. Mr. and Mrs. Humphrey signed a line of credit promissory note that provided in part: "As long as the Borrower is not in default, the Association will lend to the Borrower, and the Borrower may borrow and repay and reborrow at any time from date of said 'Line of Credit' Promissory Note in accordance with the terms thereof and prior to matu-

rity thereof, up to an aggregate maximum amount of principal at any one time outstanding of $50,000."

Mr. Humphrey borrowed money against the line of credit to purchase cattle. In January 1981, Mrs. Humphrey went to Grand Island's office and told the loan officer that she had left Mr. Humphrey and filed for a divorce. She told the loan officer not to advance any more money to Mr. Humphrey for cattle purchases. When the Humphreys failed to pay the outstanding balance on the line of credit, Grand Island sued Mr. and Mrs. Humphrey to recover the unpaid balance of $13,936.71. A default judgment was entered against Mr.

Humphrey. The district court held Mrs. Humphrey not liable for the full outstanding balance. Grand Island appealed.

ISSUE
Was Mrs. Humphrey a comaker of the line of credit promissory note and, therefore, primarily liable for the outstanding principal balance of the note, plus interest?

COURT'S REASONING
The court stated, "Under the provisions of the Nebraska UCC, the maker of a note engages that he or she will pay the instrument according to its tenor at the time of his or her engagement." Mrs. Humphrey admits that she signed the promissory note and the supplemental agreement. Consequently, as a comaker of the note, she is jointly and severally liable for the obligations of the note. If Mrs. Humphrey was to be relieved of this obligation, it was a matter that she needed to arrange and take up with her husband in the divorce action. No such arrangement could, however, be binding upon Grand Island, which entered into this transaction in reliance upon the promise of both Mr. Humphrey and Mrs. Humphrey that they would be liable and would pay the amounts so advanced.

DECISION
The state supreme court held that Mrs. Humphrey was a comaker on the line of credit promissory note and was therefore primarily liable to Grand Island in the amount of $13,936.71 plus interest. Reversed.

Case Questions

Critical Legal Thinking   Should family problems, such as the separation and divorce action in this case, take precedent over the commercial law rules of the UCC? Why or why not?

Business Ethics   Was it ethical for Mrs. Humphrey to deny liability on the promissory note in this case?

Contemporary Business   What would have been the economic effects if the district court's decision had been upheld in this case?

Secondary Liability

Drawers of checks and drafts and unqualified indorsers of negotiable instruments have **secondary liability** on the instrument. This liability is similar to that of a guarantor of a simple contract. It arises when the party primarily liable on the instrument defaults and fails to pay the instrument when due.

If an unaccepted draft or check is dishonored by the drawee or acceptor, the drawer is obliged to pay it according to its terms either when it is issued or, if incomplete when issued, as properly completed [UCC 3-414(a)].

Consider This Example   Elliot draws a check on City Bank "payable to the order of Phyllis Jones." When Phyllis presents the check for payment, City Bank refuses to pay it. Phyllis can collect the amount of the check from Elliot because Elliot—the drawer—is secondarily liable on the check when it is dishonored.

Unqualified indorsers have secondary liability on negotiable instruments. In other words, they must pay any dishonored instrument to the holder or to any subsequent indorser according to its terms, when issued or properly completed. Unless otherwise agreed, indorsers are liable to each other in the order in which they indorsed the instrument [UCC 3-415(a)].

Consider This Example   Dara borrows $10,000 from Todd and signs a promissory note promising to pay Todd this amount plus interest in one year. Todd indorses the note and negotiates it to Frank. Frank indorses the note and negotiates it to Linda. Dara refuses to pay the note when it is presented for payment by Linda. Since Frank became secondarily liable on the note when he indorsed it to Linda, he must pay the note to her. He can then require Todd to pay the note because Todd (as payee) became secondarily liable on the note when he indorsed it to Frank. Todd can then enforce the note against Dara. Linda could have skipped over Frank and required the payee, Todd, to pay the note. In this instance, Frank would have been relieved of any further liability because he indorsed the instrument after the payee.

Qualified indorsers (i.e., indorsers who indorse instruments "without recourse" or similar language that disclaims liability) are not secondarily liable on the instrument because they have expressly disclaimed liability [UCC 3-415(b)]. The drawer can disclaim all liability on a draft (but not a check) by drawing the instrument "without recourse." In this instance, the drawer becomes a qualified drawer [UCC 3-414(e)]. Many payees, however, will not accept a draft or check that has been drawn without recourse.

secondary liability

Liability on a negotiable instrument that is imposed on a party only when the party primarily liable on the instrument defaults and fails to pay the instrument when due.

Business Brief

The following parties are *secondarily liable* on negotiable instruments: (1) *drawers* on unaccepted drafts and checks and (2) *unqualified indorsers*.

indorsers' liability

Unqualified indorsers are secondarily liable on negotiable instruments they indorse; *qualified indorsers* disclaim liability and are not secondarily liable on instruments they indorse.

presentment

A demand for acceptance or payment of an instrument made upon the maker, acceptor, drawee, or other payor by or on behalf of the holder.

notice of dishonor

The formal act of letting the party with secondary liability to pay a negotiable instrument know that the instrument has been dishonored.

Requirements for Imposing Secondary Liability   Parties are secondarily liable on a negotiable instrument only if the following requirements are met:

1. **The instrument is properly presented for payment.**   **Presentment** is a demand for acceptance or payment of an instrument made upon the maker, acceptor, drawee, or other payor by or on behalf of the holder. Presentment may be made by any commercially reasonable means, including oral, written, or electronic communication. Presentment is effective when it is received by the person to whom presentment is made [UCC 3-501].

2. **The instrument is dishonored.**   An instrument is **dishonored** when acceptance or payment of the instrument is refused or cannot be obtained from the party required to accept or pay the instrument within the prescribed time after presentment is duly made [UCC 3-502].

3. **Notice of the dishonor is timely given to the person to be held secondarily liable on the instrument.**   A secondarily liable party cannot be compelled to accept or pay the instrument unless proper **notice of dishonor** has been given. Notice may be given by any commercially reasonable means. The notice must reasonably identify the instrument and indicate that it has been dishonored. Return of an instrument given to a bank for collection is sufficient notice of dishonor. Banks must give notice of dishonor before midnight of the next banking day following the day that presentment is made. Others must give notice of dishonor within 30 days following the day on which the person receives notice of dishonor [UCC 3-503].

In the following case, the court held that an indorser was not secondarily liable on a check because he had not received proper notice of dishonor.

Clements v. Central Bank of Georgia
29 U.C.C. Rep. Serv. 1536 (1980)
Court of Appeals of Georgia

CASE 20.2

BACKGROUND AND FACTS
On September 19, 1978, Mr. Ridley drew a check on a Tennessee bank made payable to the order of Mr. Clements. On September 25, 1978, Clements indorsed the check and negotiated it to Continental Equity Corporation (Continental). Continental indorsed the check and deposited it in the Central Bank of Georgia (Central Bank) for collection. Central Bank sent the check to the Tennessee bank for payment. On September 29, 1978, the branch manager of the Tennessee bank informed Central Bank by telephone that Ridley's check was "no good" because of insufficient funds. Central Bank authorized the Tennessee bank to hold the check. During October, Central Bank made several unsuccessful attempts to collect the check from Ridley. On October 21, 1978, Central Bank requested the Tennessee bank to return the check. On November 3, Central Bank received the check, and on that date it sent written notice to Clements that Ridley's check had been dishonored. Central Bank sued Clements (the indorser) to recover on the check. The court granted summary judgment to Central Bank. Clements appealed.

ISSUE
Did the Central Bank of Georgia give timely notice of dishonor of the check to Clements, the indorser, in order to hold Clements secondarily liable on Ridley's check?

COURT'S REASONING
Every indorser engages that upon dishonor and any necessary notice of dishonor and protest he will pay the instrument according to its tenor at the time of his indorsement to the holder. Unless excused, notice of any dishonor is necessary to charge any indorser. The notice of dishonor to the indorser, Clements, on November 3 came too late as a matter of law. The delay in notice of dishonor to the indorser was not due to circumstances beyond Central Bank's control but simply to the bank's failure to give it once the bank itself had notice of the dishonor and was under obligation to take action.

DECISION
The court of appeals held that Central Bank did not give timely notice to the indorser, Clements. Therefore, he is not secondarily liable on the check he indorsed. Reversed.

Case Questions

Critical Legal Thinking   Should indorsers be held secondarily liable on a negotiable instrument that is drawn or made by another party? Why or why not?

Business Ethics   Was it ethical for central Bank to try to hold the indorser Clements liable on the check?

Contemporary Business   Who bore the loss of the uncollected check in this case?

Accommodation Party

accommodation party

A party who signs an instrument and lends his or her name (and credit) to another party to the instrument.

The party who signs the instrument for the purpose of lending his or her name (and credit) to another party to that instrument is the **accommodation party**. The accommodation party, who may sign the instrument as maker, drawer, acceptor, or indorser, is obliged to pay the instrument in the capacity in which he or she signs [UCC 3-419(a) and 9b)]. An accommodation party who pays an instrument can recover reimbursement from the accommodated party and enforce the instrument against him or her [UCC 3-419(e)].

1. **Guarantee of Payment**   The accommodation party may sign an instrument guaranteeing either payment or collection. An accommodation party who signs an instrument **guaranteeing payment** is *primarily liable* on the instrument. That is, the debtor can seek payment on the instrument directly from the accommodation maker without first seeking payment from the maker.

   Consider This Example   Sonny, a college student, wants to purchase an automobile on credit from ABC Motors. He does not have a sufficient income or credit history to justify the extension of credit to him alone. Sonny asks his mother to cosign the note to ABC Motors, which she does. Mother is an accommodation maker and is primarily liable on the note.

2. **Guarantee of Collection**   An accommodation party may sign an instrument **guaranteeing collection** rather than payment of an instrument. In this situation, the accommodation party is only *secondarily liable* on the instrument. To reserve this type of liability, the signature of the accommodation party must be accompanied by words indicating that he or she is guaranteeing collection rather than payment of the obligation.

   An accommodation party that guarantees collection is obligated to pay the instrument only if (1) execution of judgment against the other party has been returned unsatisfied, (2) the other party is insolvent or in an insolvency proceeding, (3) the other party cannot be served with process, or (4) it is otherwise apparent that payment cannot be obtained from the other party [UCC 3-419(d)].

guaranteeing payment
A form of accommodation where the accommodation party guarantees *payment* of a negotiable instrument; the accommodation party is *primarily liable* on the instrument.

guaranteeing collection
A form of accommodation where the accommodation party guarantees *collection* of a negotiable instrument; the accommodation party is *secondarily liable* on the instrument.

CONCEPT SUMMARY   LIABILITY OF ACCOMMODATION MAKERS AND ACCOMMODATION INDORSERS COMPARED

Accommodation Party	Contract Liability
Accommodation maker	Primarily liable on the instrument
Accommodation indorser	Secondarily liable on the instrument

 *Entrepreneur and the Law*

ACCOMMODATION PARTY FOUND LIABLE

An accommodation party is one who signs a negotiable instrument in any capacity for the purpose of lending his or her name to it. The accommodation party does not have to receive any consideration for signing the instrument and may be bound to pay it even though the accommodation was made gratuitously [UCC 3-419(b)]. Consider the following case.

Michael and Marilu Burke were married in September 1971. Shortly after the marriage, Michael formed a partnership with his cousin to operate an automobile dealership. In 1973, Michael decided to buy his cousin out of the dealership. Michael's father agreed to loan Michael $25,000 for this purpose. However, Michael's father refused to make the loan unless Marilu cosigned the promissory note. Michael's father prepared the promissory note for $25,000 plus interest, and took the note to the home of Michael and Marilu, where they both signed it. Michael's father gave Michael a $25,000 check. The check was payable to Michael Burke

only. Marilu did not receive any of the proceeds herself. Sometime after the note was executed, Michael and Marilu separated. Michael defaulted on the note. Michael's father sued Marilu to recover the amount of the loan. Marilu tried to avoid liability by asserting that the note was unenforceable against her because she received no consideration for signing it.

The trial and appellate courts held that Marilu was an accommodation party and was therefore liable on Michael's note to his father. Marilu was required to pay Michael's father $31,167. The appellate court held that separate consideration is not required to establish primary liability as an accommodation maker. The court stated, "As is true with suretyship in general, the accommodating party is bound by the consideration moving to the primary obligator and the obligation of the accommodation maker need not be supported by separate or additional consideration." [*Burke v. Burke*, 412 N.E.2d 204 (Ill. App. 1980)]

WARRANTY LIABILITY OF PARTIES

In addition to signature liability, transferors can be held liable for breaching certain **implied warranties** when negotiating instruments. Warranty liability is imposed whether or not the transferor signed the instrument. Note that transferors make implied warranties; they are not made when the negotiable instrument is originally issued.

There are two types of implied warranties: transfer warranties and presentment warranties. Transfer and presentment warranties shift the risk of loss to the party who was in the best position to prevent the loss. This party is usually the one who dealt face to face with the wrongdoer. Both of these implied warranties are discussed in the paragraphs that follow.

Transfer Warranties

Any passage of an instrument other than its issuance and presentment for payment is considered a **transfer**. Any person who transfers a negotiable instrument for consideration makes the following five warranties to the transferee. If the transfer is by indorsement, the transferor also makes these **warranties** to any subsequent transferee [UCC 3-416(a)].

1. The transferor has good title to the instrument or is authorized to obtain payment or acceptance on behalf of one who does have good title.
2. All signatures are genuine or authorized.
3. The instrument has not been materially altered.
4. No defenses of any party are good against the transferor.
5. The transferor has no knowledge of any insolvency proceeding against the maker, the acceptor, or the drawer of an unaccepted instrument.

Transfer warranties cannot be disclaimed with respect to checks, but they can be disclaimed with respect to other instruments. An indorsement that states "without recourse" disclaims the transfer warranties [UCC 3-416(c)].

A transferee who took the instrument in good faith may recover damages for breach of transfer warranty from the warrantor equal to the loss suffered. The amount recovered cannot exceed the amount of the instrument plus expenses and interest [UCC 3-416(b)].

Consider This Example   Jill issues a $1,000 note to Adam. Adam cleverly raises the note to $10,000 and negotiates the note to Nick. Nick indorses the note and negotiates it to Matthew. When Matthew presents the note to Jill for payment, she has to pay only the original amount of the note, $1,000. Matthew can collect the remainder of the note ($9,000) from Nick based on a breach of the transfer warranty. If Nick is lucky, he can recover the $9,000 from Adam.

Presentment Warranties

Any person who **presents** a draft or check for payment or acceptance makes the following warranties to a drawee or acceptor who pays or accepts the instrument in good faith [UCC 3-417(a)]:

1. The presenter has good title to the instrument or is authorized to obtain payment or acceptance of the person who has good title.
2. The instrument has not been materially altered.
3. The presenter has no knowledge that the signature of the maker or drawer is unauthorized.

A drawee who pays an instrument may recover damages for breach of presentment warranty from the warrantor. The amount that can be recovered is limited to the amount paid by the drawee less the amount the drawee received or is entitled to receive from the drawer because of the payment plus expenses and interest [UCC 3-417(b)].

Consider This Example   Suppose Maureen draws a $1,000 check on City Bank "payable to the order of Paul." Paul cleverly raises the check to $10,000 and indorses and negotiates the check to Neal. Neal presents the check for payment to City Bank. As the presenter of the check, Neal makes the presentment warranties of UCC 3-417(1) to City Bank. City Bank pays the check as altered ($10,000) and debits Maureen's account. When Maureen discovers

---

implied warranties

The law *implies* certain warranties on transferors of negotiable instruments. There are two types of implied warranties: transfer and presentment.

transfer

Any passage of an instrument other than its issuance and presentment for payment.

transfer warranties

Any of the following five implied warranties: (1) The transferor has good title to the instrument or is authorized to obtain payment or acceptance on behalf of one who does have good title; (2) all signatures are genuine or authorized; (3) the instrument has not been materially altered; (4) no defenses of any party are good against the transferor; and (5) the transferor has no knowledge of any insolvency proceeding against the maker, or acceptor, or the drawer of an unaccepted instrument.

presentment warranties

Any person who presents a draft or check for payment or acceptance makes the following three warranties to a drawee or acceptor who pays or accepts the instrument in good faith: (1) The presenter has good title to the instrument or is authorized to obtain payment or acceptance of the person who has good title, (2) the instrument has not been materially altered, and (3) the presenter has no knowledge that the signature of the maker or drawer is unauthorized.

the alteration, she demands that the bank recredit her account, which the bank does. City Bank can recover against the presenter (Neal) based on breach of the presentment warranty that the instrument was not altered when it was presented. Neal can recover against the wrongdoer (Paul) based on beach of the transfer warranty that the instrument was not altered.

DEFENSES

The creation of negotiable instruments may give rise to a defense against its payment. Many of these defenses arise from the underlying transaction. There are two general types of defenses: real defenses and personal defenses. A **holder in due course** (or a holder through an HDC) takes the instrument free from personal defenses but not real defenses. Personal and real defenses can be raised against a normal holder of a negotiable instrument. Both of these types of defenses are discussed in the paragraphs that follow.

Real Defenses

Real (or universal) defenses can be raised against both holders and HDCs [UCC 3-305(b)]. If a real defense is proven, the holder or HDC cannot recover on the instrument. Real defenses are discussed in the following paragraphs.

- **Minority** Infancy, or **minority**, is a real defense to a negotiable instrument to the extent that it is a defense to a simple contract [UCC 3-305(a)(1)(i)]. In most states, a minor who does not misrepresent his or her age can disaffirm contracts, including negotiable instruments. Usually, minors must pay the reasonable value for necessities of life.
- **Extreme Duress** Ordinary duress is a personal defense (discussed later in this chapter). **Extreme duress** is a real defense against the enforcement of a negotiable instrument by a holder or an HDC [UCC 3-305(a)(1)(ii)]. Extreme duress usually requires some form of force or violence (e.g., a promissory note signed at gunpoint).
- **Mental Incapacity** Adjudicated mental incompetence is a real defense that can be raised against holders and HDCs [UCC 3-305(a)(1)(ii)]. Such a person cannot issue a negotiable instrument; the instrument is void from its inception. Nonadjudicated mental incompetence, which usually is only a personal defense, is discussed later.
- **Illegality** If an instrument arises out of an illegal transaction, the illegality is a real defense if the law declares the instrument void [UCC 3-305(a)(1)(ii)]. For example, assume that a state's law declares gambling to be illegal and gambling contracts to be void. Gordon wins $1,000 from Jerry in an illegal poker game. He signs a promissory note promising to pay Gordon this amount plus interest in 30 days. Gordon negotiates this note to Dawn, an HDC. When Dawn presents the note to Jerry for payment, Jerry can raise the real defense of illegality against the enforcement of the note. Dawn's recourse is against Gordon. If the law makes an illegal contract voidable instead of void, it is only a personal defense. This situation is discussed later in this chapter.)
- **Discharge in Bankruptcy** Bankruptcy law is intended to relieve debtors of burdensome debts, including obligations to pay negotiable instruments. Thus, **discharge in bankruptcy** is a real defense against the enforcement of a negotiable instrument by a holder or an HDC [UCC 3-305(a)(1)(iv)]. For example, suppose Hunt borrows $10,000 from Amy and signs a note promising to pay Amy this amount plus interest in one year. Amy negotiates the note to Richard, an HDC. Before the note is due, Hunt declares bankruptcy and receives a discharge of his unpaid debts. Richard cannot thereafter enforce the note against Hunt, but he can recover against Amy.
- **Fraud in the Inception** Fraud in the inception (also called **fraud in the factum** or **fraud in the execution**) is a real defense against the enforcement of a negotiable instrument by a holder or an HDC [UCC 3-305(a)(1)(iii)]. It occurs when a person is deceived into singing a negotiable instrument thinking that it is something else.

  For example, suppose Sam, a door-to-door salesman, convinces Lance, an illiterate consumer, to sign a document purported to be an agreement to use a set of books on a 90-day trial basis. In actuality, the document is a promissory note in which Lance has agreed to pay $1,000 for the books. Sam negotiates the note to Stephanie, an HDC. Lance can raise the real defense of fraud in the inception against the enforcement of the note by Stephanie. Stephanie, in turn, can recover from Sam.

real defense

A defense that can be raised against both holders and HDCs.

extreme duress

Extreme duress, but not ordinary duress, is a real defense against enforcement of a negotiable instrument.

discharge in bankruptcy

A real defense against the enforcement of a negotiable instrument; bankruptcy law is intended to relieve debtors of burdensome debts, including negotiable instruments.

fraud in the inception

A real defense against the enforcement of a negotiable instrument; a person has been deceived into signing a negotiable instrument thinking that it is something else.

Business Brief

Distinguishing between fraud *in the inception* (real defense) and fraud *in the inducement* (personal defense) can be difficult.

forgery

A real defense against the enforcement of a negotiable instrument; the unauthorized signature of a maker, drawer, or indorser.

material alteration

A partial defense against enforcement of a negotiable instrument by an HDC. An HDC can enforce an altered instrument in the original amount for which the drawer wrote the check.

personal defense

A defense that can be raised against enforcement of a negotiable instrument by an ordinary holder but not against an HDC.

Business Brief

Personal defenses cannot be raised against an HDC.

Business Brief

Breach of the underlying contract cannot be raised as a defense against enforcement of a negotiable instrument by an HDC.

fraud in the inducement

A personal defense against the enforcement of a negotiable instrument; a wrongdoer makes a false statement to another person to lead that person to enter into a contract with the wrongdoer.

Business Brief

These personal defenses can be raised against enforcement of a negotiable instrument by a *holder*, but not against an HDC.

A person is under a duty to use reasonable efforts to ascertain what he or she is signing. The court inquires into a person's age, experience, education, and other factors before allowing fraud in the inception to be asserted as a real defense to defeat an HDC. Fraud in the inducement (discussed later) is only a personal defense.

- **Forgery** Another real defense to the payment of a negotiable instrument is **forgery**. The unauthorized signature of a maker, drawer, or indorser is wholly inoperative as that of the person whose name is signed unless that person either ratifies it or is precluded from denying it. In the latter case, a person can be estopped from raising the defense of forgery if his or her negligence substantially contributes to the forgery. A forged signature operates as the signature of the forger. Thus, the forger is liable on the instrument [UCC 3-403(a)].

- **Material Alteration** An instrument that has been fraudulently and **materially altered** cannot be enforced by an ordinary holder. Material alteration consists of adding to any part of a signed instrument, removing any part of a signed instrument, making changes in the number or relations of the parties, or the unauthorized completion of an incomplete instrument.

  Under the UCC rule that words control figures, correcting the figure on a check to correspond to the written amount on the check is not a material alteration [UCC 3-118(c)]. If an alteration is not material, the instrument can be enforced by any holder in the original amount for which the drawer wrote the check [UCC 3-407(b)].

  Material alteration of a negotiable instrument is only a partial defense against an HDC. Subsequent holders in due course can enforce any instrument, including an altered instrument, according to its original terms if the alteration is not apparent. An obvious change puts the holder on notice of the alteration and disqualifies him or her as an HDC [UCC 3-407(c)].

Personal Defenses

Although **personal defenses** cannot be raised against an HDC, they can be raised against enforcement of a negotiable instrument by an ordinary holder. Personal defenses are discussed in the paragraphs that follow.

- **Breach of Contract** Breach of contract is one of the most common defenses raised by a party to a negotiable instrument. This personal defense is effective only against an ordinary holder. For example, when Brian purchases a used car on credit from Karen, he signs a note promising to pay Karen the $10,000 purchase price plus interest in 36 equal monthly installments. The sales agreement warrants that the car is in perfect working condition. A month later the car's engine fails; the cost of repair is $3,000. Brian, the maker of the note, can raise breach of warranty as a defense against enforcement of the note by Karen.

  The outcome would be different if Karen negotiated the promissory note to Max (an HDC) immediately after the car was sold to Brian. Max would be an HDC and Brian could not raise the breach of warranty defense against him. Max could enforce the note against Brian. Brian's only recourse would be to seek recovery for breach of warranty from Karen.

- **Fraud in the Inducement** **Fraud in the inducement** occurs when a wrongdoer makes a false statement (i.e., a misrepresentation) to another person to lead that person to enter into a contract with the wrongdoer. Negotiable instruments often arise out of such transactions. Fraud in the inducement is a personal defense that is not effective against HDCs. It is effective against ordinary holders, however.

  For example, Morton represents to investors that he will accept funds to drill for oil and that the investors will share in the profits from the oil wells. He plans to use these funds himself, however. Relying on Morton's statements, Mimi draws a $50,000 check payable to him. Morton absconds with the funds. Because Morton is an ordinary holder, Mimi can raise the personal defense of fraud in the inducement and, if she stops payment on the check before Morton receives payment, not pay the check.

  If Morton had negotiated the check to Tim, an HDC, Tim could enforce the check against Mimi. Since personal defenses are not effective against Tim (an HDC), Mimi's only recourse is to recover against the wrongdoer (Morton) if he can be found.

- **Other Personal Defenses** The following personal defenses can be raised against enforcement of a negotiable instrument by an ordinary holder:

  1. Mental illness that makes a contract voidable instead of void (usually a nonadjudicated mental illness)
  2. Illegality of a contract that makes the contract voidable instead of void
  3. Ordinary duress or undue influence [UCC 3-305(a)(1)(ii)]
  4. Discharge of an instrument by payment or cancellation [UCC 3-602 and 3-604]

CONCEPT SUMMARY   REAL AND PERSONAL DEFENSES

Defense	Effect
Real Defenses	Real defenses can be raised against a holder in due course.
1. Minority	
2. Extreme duress	
3. Mental incapacity	
4. Illegality	
5. Discharge in bankruptcy	
6. Fraud in the inception	
7. Forgery	
8. Material alteration	
Personal Defenses	Personal defenses cannot be raised against a holder in due course.
1. Breach of contract	
2. Fraud in the inducement	
3. Mental illness that makes a contract voidable instead of void (usually a nonadjudicated mental illness)	
4. Illegality of a contract that makes the contract voidable instead of void	
5. Ordinary duress or undue influence [UCC 3-305(a)(1)(ii)]	
6. Discharge of an instrument by payment or cancellation [UCC 3-602 and 3-604]	

Business Ethics

THE FTC ELIMINATES HDC STATUS WITH RESPECT TO CONSUMER CREDIT TRANSACTIONS

In certain situations, the HDC rule can cause a hardship for the consumer. To illustrate, Greg, a consumer, purchases a stereo on credit from Lou's Stereo. He signs a note promising to pay the purchase price plus interest to Lou's Stereo in 12 equal monthly installments. Lou's Stereo immediately negotiates the note at a discount to City Bank for cash. City Bank is an HDC. The stereo is defective. Greg would like to stop paying on it, but the HDC rule prevents him from asserting any personal defenses against City Bank. Under the UCC, Greg's only recourse is to sue Lou's Stereo. However, this is often an unsatisfactory result because Greg has no leverage against Lou's Stereo and bringing a court action is expensive and time-consuming.

To correct this harsh result, the Federal Trade Commission (FTC) has adopted a rule that eliminates HDC status with regard to negotiable instruments arising out of certain *consumer* credit transactions [16 C.F.R. 433.2 (1987)]. This federal law takes precedence over state UCCs.

The rule equates the HDC of a consumer credit contract with the assignee of a simple contract. Thus, sellers of goods and services are prevented from separating the consumer's duty to pay the credit and the seller's duty to perform. This subjects the HDC of a consumer credit instrument to *all* of the defenses and claims of the consumer. In the prior example, Greg can raise the defect in the stereo as a defense against enforcement of the promissory note by City Bank, an HDC.

The FTC rules applies to consumer credit transactions in which (1) the buyer signs a sales contract that includes a promissory note, (2) the buyer signs an installment sales contract that contains a waiver of defenses clause, and (3) the seller arranges consumer financing with a third-party lender. Note that payment for goods and services with a check is not covered by this rule because it is not a credit transaction.

The FTC rule requires that the following clause be included in the bold type in covered consumer credit sales and installment contracts:

NOTICE. ANY HOLDER OF THIS CONSUMER CREDIT CONTRACT IS SUBJECT TO ALL CLAIMS AND DEFENSES WHICH THE DEBTOR COULD ASSERT AGAINST THE SELLER OF THE GOODS OR SERVICES OBTAINED PURSUANT HERETO OR WITH THE PROCEEDS HEREOF. RECOVERY HEREUNDER BY THE DEBTOR SHALL NOT EXCEED AMOUNTS PAID BY THE DEBTOR HEREUNDER.

A consumer creditor may assert that the FTC rule to prevent enforcement of a note that arose from a covered transaction. The FTC can impose a fine of $10,000 for each violation.

1. Why do you think the FTC adopted this rule?
2. Do consumers need the protection afforded by this FTC rule?

Business Ethics

MAKER OF PROMISSORY NOTES LIABLE TO HDC

Promissory notes usually arise out of an underlying transaction. That is, a party will sign a promissory note to finance the purchase of goods or services from a seller. In normal contract situations, if there is a problem with the underlying transaction, such as breach of contract or fraud in the inducement by the seller, the buyer can discontinue payments and raise these issues as defenses against the seller's attempt to enforce the contract. This is not so if the note is a negotiable instrument that has been transferred to a holder in due course (HDC). Consider the following case.

In 1983, Leonard Smith was a 22-year-old college senior who was selected in the first round of the National Football League (NFL) draft. He hired an agent, BP&M Sports, Inc. (BP&M), to act as his investment advisor. On BP&M's advice, Smith invested in a cattle-breeding tax-sheltered operation operated by California Dreamstreet (Dreamstreet). Smith signed a promissory note agreeing to pay $490,500 over the next five years. Dreamstreet negotiated the promissory note to Rabobank, a Dutch bank. After paying only $40,336, Smith discovered that Dreamstreet had operated a sham transaction and the sought-after tax benefits would not be forth-

coming. When Smith refused to pay the remaining payments on the note, Rabobank sued to enforce the note against Smith.

Smith countered by asserting that BP&M and Dreamstreet had engaged in fraud in obtaining his signature on the note. The court held that any fraud perpetrated on Smith was fraud in the inducement and that Smith knew what he was signing when he signed the promissory note. Because fraud in the inducement is a personal defense and not a real defense, it cannot be raised against an HDC. The FTC rule excepting consumer credit transactions from the HDC rule did not save Smith because this was not a consumer transaction. The court ordered Smith to pay Rabobank $727,422, representing unpaid principal of $450,163 and interest of $277,259 (at the annual default rate of 10 percent), plus attorneys' fees. [*DH Cattle Holdings Company v. Smith*, 607 N.Y.S.2d 227 (N.Y.App. 1994)]

1. Did Smith act ethically in trying to get out of paying the amount of the promissory note?
2. Do you think the court reached the proper result in this case? Explain.

*D*ISCHARGE

discharge

Actions or events that relieve certain parties from liability on negotiable instruments. There are three methods of discharge: (1) payment of the instrument; (2) cancellation; and (3) impairment of the right of recourse.

The UCC specifies when and how certain parties are **discharged** (relieved) from liability on negotiable instruments. Generally, all parties to a negotiable instrument are discharged from liability if (1) the party primarily liable on the instrument pays it in full to the holder of the instrument or (2) a drawee in good faith pays an unaccepted draft or check in full to the holder. When a party other than a primary obligor (e.g., an indorser) pays a negotiable instrument, that party and all subsequent parties to the instrument are discharged from the liability [UCC 3-602].

The holder of a negotiable instrument can discharge the liability of any party to the instrument by **cancellation** [UCC 3-604]. Cancellation can be accomplished by (1) any manner apparent on the face of the instrument or the indorsement (e.g., writing "canceled" on the instrument) or (2) destroying or mutilating a negotiable instrument with the intent of eliminating the obligation.

Intentionally striking out the signature of an indorser cancels that party's liability on the instrument and the liability of all subsequent indorsers. Prior indorsers are not discharged from liability. The instrument is not canceled if it is destroyed or mutilated by accident or by an unauthorized third party. The holder can bring suit to enforce the destroyed or mutilated instrument.

impairment of right of recourse

Certain parties (holders, indorsers, accommodation parties) are discharged from liability on an instrument if the holder (1) releases an obligor from liability or (2) surrenders collateral without the consent of the parties who would benefit by it.

A party to a negotiable instrument sometimes posts collateral as security for the payment of the obligation. Other parties (e.g., holders, indorsers, accommodation parties) look to the credit standing of the party primarily liable on the instrument, the collateral (if any) that is posted, and the liability of secondary parties for the payment of the instrument when it is due. A holder owes a duty not to impair the rights of others when seeking recourse against the liable parties or the collateral. Thus, a holder who either (1) releases an obligor from liability or (2) surrenders the collateral without the consent of the parties who would benefit thereby discharges those parties from their obligation on the instrument [UCC 3-605(e)]. This discharge is called **impairment of the right of recourse.**

CHAPTER SUMMARY

Holder Versus Holder in Due Course, p. 487

Holder Versus Holder in Due Course	1. *Holder.* A person who is in possession of a negotiable instrument that is drawn, issued, or indorsed to that person or his or her order, or to bearer, or in blank. *Rights of a holder.* A holder has the same rights as the assignee of an ordinary contract. A holder is subject to all claims and defenses that can be asserted against the transferor. 2. *Holder in due course (HDC).* A holder who takes a negotiable instrument for value, in good faith, and without notice that it is defective or is overdue. *Rights of an HDC.* An HDC takes a negotiable instrument free of all claims and most defenses that can be asserted against the transferor. Thus, an HDC can acquire greater rights than those of the transferor.

Requirements for HDC Status, p. 488

Requirements for HDC Status	To quality as an HDC, the transferee must meet the following requirements: 1. Be a holder. 2. Take the negotiable instrument for value. 3. Take the instrument in good faith. 4. Take the instrument without notice that it is overdue, dishonored, or encumbered in any way. 5. The instrument bears no apparent evidence of forgery, alteration, or irregularity.
Taking for Value	Value has been given for a negotiable instrument if the holder: 1. Performs the agreed-upon promise. 2. Acquires a security interest or lien on the instrument. 3. Takes the instrument in payment of or as security for an antecedent claim. 4. Gives a negotiable instrument as payment. 5. Gives an irrevocable obligation as payment.
Taking in Good Faith	A holder must take the instrument in good faith to qualify as an HDC. Good faith means honesty in fact in the conduct or transaction. It is the holder's subjective belief that can be inferred from the circumstances.
Taking without Notice	A person cannot qualify as an HDC if he or she has notice that the instrument is defective in any of the following ways: 1. It is overdue. 2. It has been dishonored. 3. It contains an unauthorized signature or has been altered. 4. There is a claim to it by another person. 5. There is a defense against it.
No Evidence of Forgery, Alteration, or Irregularity	A holder cannot become an HDC to an instrument that is apparently forged or altered or is so otherwise irregular or incomplete as to call into question its authenticity.
The Shelter Principle: Holder through an HDC	1. *Shelter principle.* A rule that says a holder who does not qualify as an HDC in his or her own right becomes an HDC if he or she acquires the instrument through an HDC. 2. *Limitations on the shelter principle.* Persons who participated in the fraud or illegality or have notice of a defense or claim against an instrument cannot improve their position by later acquiring the instrument through an HDC.

Signature Liability of Parties, p. 490

Signature Liability of Parties	1. *Signature liability.* A person cannot be held contractually liable on a negotiable instrument unless his or her signature appears on the instrument. Also called *contract liability.*
	2. *Signers.* Persons can sign an instrument in the capacity of a(n):
	  a. *Maker* of notes and certificates of deposit
	  b. *Drawer* of drafts and checks
	  c. *Drawee* who certifies or accepts checks and drafts
	  d. *Indorser* who indorses an instrument
	  e. *Agent* who signs on behalf of others
	  f. *Accommodation party*
	3. *Liability of signers.* Every party that signs a negotiable instrument (except qualified indorsers and agents that properly sign the instrument) is either *primarily* or *secondarily* liable on the instrument.

Signature Defined

The signature on a negotiable instrument can be any name, word, or mark used in lieu of written signature. A signature may be (a) handwritten, typed, printed, stamped, or made in almost any other manner and (b) executed or adopted by a party to authenticate a writing.

Agent's Signatures

1. *Agent.* A person who has been authorized to sign a negotiable instrument on behalf of another person.
2. *Principal.* A person who authorizes an agent to sign a negotiable instrument on his or her behalf.
3. *Authorized signature.* An agent's signature on a negotiable instrument that is authorized by the principal.
   a. *Principal's liability.* A principal is liable on a negotiable instrument signed on his or her behalf by an authorized agent if either the name of the principal or the name of the agent (or both) appears on the instrument.
   b. *Agent's liability:*
      i. *Unambiguous signature.* An authorized agent is not personally liable on a negotiable instrument he or she signs on behalf of a principal if the signature shows unambiguously that it is made on behalf of a principal who is identified in the instrument.
      ii. *Ambiguous signature.* An authorized agent is personally liable to the following parties on a negotiable instrument if the signature does not show unambiguously that it is made in a representative capacity or the principal is not identified in the instrument:
         a. To a holder in due course (HDC) who took the instrument without notice that the agent was not intended to be liable on the instrument
         b. To any other person other than an HDC unless the agent proves that the original parties did not intend the agent to be liable on the instrument
         c. *Special rule for checks.* An agent who signs a *check* from the account of a principal who is identified on the check without indicating the agent's representative capacity is not personally liable on the check.
4. *Unauthorized signature.* A signature made by a *purported agent* on behalf of a *purported principal* without the purported principal's authority.
   a. *Liability of the purported principal.* An unauthorized signature by a purported agent does not act as the signature of the purported principal. The purported principal is not liable on the instrument.
   b. *Liability of the purported agent.* The purported agent is liable to any person who in good faith pays the instrument or takes it for value.

Primary Liability

Absolute liability of certain signers to pay a negotiable instrument, subject to certain real defenses. *Parties who have primary liability.* The following singers have *primary liability* to pay a negotiable instrument:
1. *Makers* of promissory notes and certificates of deposit
2. *Acceptors* of drafts and checks (e.g., a bank that certifies a check)

Secondary Liability

Liability on a negotiable instrument that is imposed on a party only when the party primarily liable on the instrument defaults and fails to pay the instrument when due.
1. *Parties who have secondary liability.* The following signers have *secondary liability* to pay a negotiable instrument:
   a. *Drawers* of drafts and checks if the check is dishonored by the drawee or acceptor
   b. *Unqualified indorsers* if the primary obligor fails to pay the instrument
2. *Qualified indorsers.* Qualified indorsers (i.e., indorsers who indorse instruments "*without recourse*" or similar language that disclaims liability) are not secondarily liable on the instrument.
3. *Requirements for imposing secondary liability.* Parties are secondarily liable on a negotiable instrument only if the following requirements are met:
   a. The instrument is properly *presented* for payment. *Presentment* is a demand for acceptance or payment of an instrument made upon the maker, acceptor, drawee, or other payor by or on behalf of the holder.
   b. The instrument is *dishonored. Dishonor* occurs when acceptance or payment of the instrument is refused or cannot be obtained from the party required to accept or pay the instrument within the prescribed time after presentment is duly made.
   c. *Notice of dishonor* is timely given to the person to be held secondarily liable on the instrument. *Notice of dishonor* may be given by any commercially reasonable means.

Accommodation Party

1. *Accommodation.* Occurs when a party signs a negotiable instrument to lend his or her name (and credit) to another party to the instrument.
2. *Accommodation party.* The party who signs an instrument and lends his or her name (and credit) to another party to the instrument.
3. *Accommodated party.* The party to whom an accommodation party lends his or her name and credit on a negotiable instrument.
4. *Types of liability.* An accommodation party may sign an instrument guaranteeing either *payment* or *collection*.
   a. *Guaranteeing payment.* A form of accommodation where the accommodation party *guarantees payment* of a negotiable instrument. The accommodation party is *primarily liable* on the instrument with the accommodated party. For example, an *accommodation maker* is primarily liable on a promissory note he or she signs. The debtor can seek payment from the accommodation maker without first seeking payment from the maker.

b. *Guaranteeing collection.* A form of accommodation where the accommodation party *guarantees collection* of a negotiable instrument. The accommodation party is secondarily liable on the instrument. For example, an *accommodation indorser* is secondarily liable on a check he or she indorses. The holder cannot seek payment from the accommodation indorser unless he or she first seeks to recover payment from the primary obligor and is unsuccessful. To reserve this type of liability, the accommodation party's signature must be accompanied by words indicating that he or she is guaranteeing collection rather than payment of the obligation.

Warranty Liability of Parties, p. 496

Warranty Liability of Parties	The law *implies* certain warranties on transferors of negotiable instruments. There are two types of *implied warranties*: 1. Transfer warranties 2. Presentment warranties

Transfer Warranties	1. *Transfer.* Any passage of an instrument other than its issuance and presentment for payment.
	2. *Transfer warranties.* Any person who transfers a negotiable instrument for consideration makes the following five warranties to the transferee:
	  a. The transferor has good title to the instrument or is authorized to obtain payment or acceptance on behalf of one who does have good title.
	  b. All signatures are genuine or authorized.
	  c. The instrument has not been materially altered.
	  d. No defenses of any party are good against the transferor.
	  e. The transferor has no knowledge of any insolvency proceeding against the maker, or acceptor, or the drawer of an unaccepted instrument.
	3. *Breach of transfer warranty.* A transferee who takes an instrument in good faith may recover damages for *breach of transfer warranty* from the warrantor equal to the loss suffered. The amount cannot exceed the amount of the instrument plus expenses and interest.

Presentment Warranties	1. *Presentment.* The demand for acceptance or payment of the instrument made upon the maker, acceptor, drawee, or other party by or on behalf of the holder.
	2. *Presentment warranties.* Any person who presents a draft or check for payment or acceptance makes the following three warranties to a drawee or acceptor who in good faith pays or accepts the instrument:
	  a. The presenter has good title to the instrument or is authorized to obtain payment or acceptance of the person who has good title.
	  b. The instrument has not been materially altered.
	  c. The presenter has no knowledge that the signature of the maker or drawer is unauthorized.
	3. *Breach of presentment warranty.* A drawee who pays an instrument may recover damages for breach of presentment warranty from the warrantor. The amount that can be recovered is limited to the amount paid by the drawee less the amount the drawee received or is entitled to receive from the drawer because of the payment plus expenses and interest.

Defenses, p. 497

Defenses	*Types of defenses.* The creation of negotiable instruments may give rise to a defense against payment of the instrument. There are two types of defenses: 1. *Real defenses.* Defenses that can be raised against holders and holders in due course (HDCs). 2. *Personal defenses.* Defenses that can be raised against holders but not against HDCs.
Real Defenses	Defenses against the enforcement of an negotiable instrument that *can be raised against both holders and HDCs.* Real defenses include: 1. *Minority.* In most states, minors who do not misrepresent their age can disaffirm contracts, including negotiable instruments. 2. *Extreme duress.* A person who has signed a negotiable instrument under *extreme duress* (e.g., because of force or violence or threat of force or violence) may raise this duress as a defense of the enforcement of the instrument. 3. *Mental incapacity.* An instrument that was signed by a person who has been adjudicated mentally incompetent is void. 4. *Illegality.* If an instrument arises out of an illegal transaction, the illegality is a real defense if the law declares the instrument void. 5. *Discharge in bankruptcy.* If an obligor's duty to pay a negotiable instrument has been discharged in bankruptcy, that person is relieved of the obligation to pay the instrument.

6. *Fraud in the inception.* Occurs when a person is deceived into signing a negotiable instrument thinking that it is something else. Fraud in the inception, also called *fraud in the factum* or *fraud in the execution*, is a real defense against enforcement of an instrument.

7. *Forgery.* The unauthorized signature of a maker, drawer, or indorser is wholly inoperative as that of the person whose name is signed. Forgery is a real defense unless the person whose name has been signed ratifies it or is precluded from raising the defense (e.g., his or her negligence substantially contributed to the forgery).

8. *Material alteration.* Material alteration of a negotiable instrument is a partial defense against an HDC. An HDC can enforce an altered instrument according to its original tenor but not to the raised amount.

Personal Defenses

Defenses against the enforcement of a negotiable instrument that can be raised against holders but cannot be raised against HDCs. Personal defenses include:

1. *Breach of contract.* The breach of contract by one of the original parties at the time of contracting can be raised against the enforcement of an instrument by a holder. This defense is not effective against an HDC, however.

2. *Fraud in the inducement.* Occurs when a wrongdoer makes a false representation to another person to lead that person to enter into a contract with the wrongdoer. The type of fraud may be raised as a defense against a holder but not against an HDC.

3. *Other personal defenses.* The following additional personal defenses can be raised against enforcement of a negotiable instrument by an ordinary holder but not against an HDC:
   a. *Mental illness* that makes the contract voidable instead of void (usually a nonadjudicated mental illness)
   b. *Illegality* of a contract that makes the contact voidable instead of void
   c. *Ordinary* duress or undue influence
   d. *Discharge* of an instrument by *payment* or *cancellation*

The FTC Eliminates HDC Status with Respect to Consumer Credit Transactions

1. *Consumer credit transaction.* A transaction whereby a consumer purchases goods or services on credit and signs a negotiable instrument (note) agreeing to pay the remainder of the purchase price.

2. *FTC rule.* The Federal Trade Commission (FTC) has adopted a rule that *eliminates HDC status* with regard to negotiable instruments that arise out of certain consumer credit transactions.

3. *Effect of the rule.* All defenses and claims that can be raised by the consumer purchaser against holders can also be raised against HDCs. Thus, both personal and real defenses can be raised against an HDC in this situation.

Discharge, p. 500

Discharge

Actions or events that relieve certain parties from liability on negotiable instruments. The three methods of discharge are:

1. *Payment.* Generally, all parties to an instrument are discharged from liability if (a) the party primarily liable on the instrument pays it in full to the holder or (b) the drawee pays an unaccepted draft or check in full to the holder.

2. *Cancellation.* Cancellation of the instrument discharges the liability of any party to the instrument. Cancellation can be accomplished by (a) any manner apparent on the face of the instrument or the indorsement (e.g. writing "canceled" on the instrument) or (b) destroying or mutilating the instrument with the intent of eliminating the obligation.

3. *Impairment of the right of recourse.* Certain parties (holders, indorsers, accommodation parties) are discharged from liability on an instrument if the holder (a) releases an obligor from liability or (b) surrenders collateral without the consent of the parties who would benefit by it.

End-of-*Chapter Internet Exercises* and *Case Questions*

Working the Web Internet Exercises

ACTIVITIES

1. Go to the FTC Web site, **www.ftc.gov** and find "Federal Trade Commission Agency: Federal Trade Commission, 16 CFR Part 433 Regulatory Flexibility Act Review of the Trade Regulation Rule concerning Preservation of Consumers' Claims and Defenses." Review this regulation together with the special report on page 499 "FTC Eliminates HDC Status with Respect to Consumer Credit Transactions." Explain.

2. Check your state law version of UCC Article 3 for the rights and remedies available to holders. What is your state rule on duress? Fraud? Illegality? See **www.uchastings.edu/hlj/articles/knapp49_5.6.pdf** "The Perils of Promissory Estoppel" by Charles L. Knapp regarding who qualifies for holder in due course protection. See also a brief overview of negotiable instruments law at **www.secure.law.cornell.edu/topics/negotiable.html**.

CRITICAL LEGAL THINKING CASES

20.1 Holder in Due Course On May 8, 1974, Royal Insurance Company Ltd. (Royal) issued a draft in the amount of $12,000 payable through the Morgan Guaranty Trust Company (Morgan Guaranty). The draft was made payable to Gary E. Terrell in settlement of a claim on an insurance policy for fire damage to premises located at 3031 North 11th Street, Kansas City, Kansas. On May 9, the attorney for Mr. and Mrs. Louis Wexler notified Royal that Terrell's clients had an insurable interest in the damaged property. As a result, Royal immediately stopped payment on the draft. On the same day, the draft was indorsed by Gary E. Terrell and deposited in his account at the UAW-CIO Local #31 Federal Credit Union (Federal). Over the next two days, Terrell withdrew $9,000 from this account. Immediately upon receiving the draft, Federal indorsed it and forwarded it to Morgan Guaranty for payment. The draft was returned to Federal on May 14 with the notation "payment stopped." When Royal refused to pay Federal the amount of the draft, Federal sued. The basis of the suit was whether Federal was a holder in due course. Who wins? [*UAW-CIO Local #31 Federal Credit Union v. Royal Insurance Company, Ltd.*, 594 S.W.2d 276 (MO 1980)]

20.2 Taking for Value On September 30, 1976, Betty Ellis and her then husband W. G Ellis executed and delivered to the Standard Finance Company (Standard) a promissory note in the amount of $2,800. After receiving the note, Standard issued a check to the couple for $2,800. The check was made payable to "W. G. Ellis and Betty Ellis." The check was cashed after both parties indorsed it. Shortly thereafter, the Ellises were divorced. Mrs. Ellis claims that (1) she never saw or used the money and (2) Standard understood that all the money went to her ex-husband. W. G. Ellis was declared bankrupt. When the note became due in 1980, Betty Ellis refused to pay it. Standard sued her, seeking payment as a holder in due course. She claimed that Standard is not a holder in due course in regard to her because she never received consideration for the note and, therefore, Standard did not take the note for value. Who wins? [*Standard Finance Company, Ltd. v. Ellis*, 657 P.2d 1056 (Hawaii App. 1983)]

20.3 Notice of Dishonored Instrument In 1974, William and Eugene Slough executed two notes payable to the order of Quality Mark, Inc. (Quality Mark). The notes were made in payment of the debts of a partnership in which the Sloughs were involved. The aggregate amount of the notes was $42,150. They were due on or before January 1, 1986. On the day the instruments were executed, Quality Mark assigned them for consideration to Philip Baer, Jr. In 1975, Baer sold the notes at discount to the Southtowne Company (Southtowne). On year later, Southtowne resold the notes to Edward Rettig. By this time, the notes had been discounted to the point that Rettig paid only $5,000 for them. Southtowne, however, assured Rettig that the notes had not yet been dishonored. Shortly after Rettig's purchase, the Sloughs announced that they had already defaulted on the notes. Rettig sued all the prior indorsers. Southtowne claimed that the Sloughs had no defenses against Rettig because

he was a holder in due course. The Sloughs claim that because the notes had been discounted to less than 50 percent of their value, Rettig must have taken them with notice of their dishonor. Who wins? [*Rettig v. Slough*, No. 5-82-7, Slip Op. (Ohio App. 1984)]

20.4 Illegality In 1976, Victor Bisharat became a member of the Casanova Club, a British corporation operating a legal casino in London. That year, he purchased £6,350 worth of gambling chips, which he then lost while gambling at the casino. Bisharat paid for the chips with a series of nine bearer checks. Bisharat was the drawer of the checks, all of which were drawn on the Hartford National Bank located in Connecticut. When the Casanova Club presented the checks to the bank for payment, they all were returned to the club with the notation "unpaid for reason: insufficient funds." The Casanova Club then brought suit against Bisharat in a Connecticut state court to recover the amount owed. Bisharat defended the suit by claiming that the checks arose out of a gambling debt and were, therefore, part of an illegal transaction. Except as permitted by law, such as American Indian operated casinos, gambling is otherwise illegal in Connecticut, and gambling debts are not legally enforceable in that state. The Casanova Club claims to be a holder in due course of the checks. Who wins? [*Casanova Club v. Bisharat*, 35 UCC Rep.Serv. 1207 (CT 1983)]

20.5 Fraud in the Factum John Wade was employed by Mike Fazzari. Fazzari was an immigrant who was unable to speak or read English. In December 1957, Wade prepared a promissory note in the amount of $400. The instrument was payable at the Glen National Bank, Watkins Glen, New York. Wade took the note to Fazzari and told him that the document was a statement of wages earned by Wade during the course of his employment. Fazzari signed the instrument after Wade told him it was necessary for income tax purposes. Fazzari was not in debt to Wade and there was no consideration given for the note. On April 10, 1958, the note was presented to the First National Bank of Odessa by Wellington Doane, a customer of the bank and an indorsee of the payee, Wade. Doane indorsed the check in blank and accepted a $400 cashier's check in exchange for the note. Fazzari and Glen National Bank refused payment of the note. Can the First National Bank of Odessa enforce payment of the note as a holder in due course? [*First National Bank of Odessa v. Fazzari*, 179 N.E. 2d 493 (N.Y. App. 1961)]

20.6 Fraud in the Inducement J. H. Thompson went to the Central Motor Company (Central), an automobile dealership, to purchase a car. With the assistance of Central's sales manager, Ed Boles, Thompson selected a 1966 Imperial automobile. Boles drew up a loan agreement that stipulated 35 monthly installments of $125 and a final installment of $5,265. Under this agreement, Thompson would be charged an annual interest rate of 8 percent. Boles assured Thompson that when the $5,265 installment became due he would be allowed to sign a second note to cover that amount. Thompson was told that the interest rate on this second note would also be 8 percent. With this assurance, Thompson signed the original loan agreement and note and made all the payments except the final one. When Thompson went to Central to sign the second note he was told that the interest rate on the second installment note would be 12 percent, not 8 percent. Thompson refused to sign the second note or make the balloon payment on the original note. Instead, he returned the car. Central was able to sell the car, but sued Thompson to recover a deficiency judgment. Who wins? [*Central Motor Company v. J. H. Thompson*, 465 S.W.2d 405 (Tex. App. 1971)]

20.7 Federal Trade Commission Rule Warren and Kristina Mahaffey were approached by a salesman from the Five Star Solar Screens Company (Five Star). The salesman offered to install insulation in their home at a cost of $5,289. After being told that the insulation would reduce their heating bills by 50 percent, the Mahaffeys agreed to the purchase. To pay for the work, the Mahaffeys executed a note promising to pay the purchase price with interest in installments. The note, which was secured by a deed of trust on the Mahaffeys' home, contained the following language: "Notice: Any holder of this consumer credit contract is subject to all claims and defenses which the debtor could assert against the seller of goods or services obtained pursuant hereto or with the proceeds thereof." Several days after Five Star finished working at the Mahaffeys' home, it sold the installment note to Mortgage Finance Corporation (Mortgage Finance).

There were major defects in the way the insulation was installed in the Mahaffey home. Large holes were left in the walls and heater blankets and roof fans were never delivered as called for by the purchase contract. Because of these defects, the Mahaffeys refused to make the payments due on the note. Mortgage Finance instituted foreclosure proceedings to collect the money owed. Can the Mahaffeys successfully assert the defense of breach of contract against the enforcement of the note by Mortgage Finance? [*Mahaffey v. Investor's National Security Company*, 747 P.2d 890 (NV 1987)]

20.8 Transfer Warranties David M. Cox was a distributor of tools manufactured and sold by Matco Tools Corporation (Matco). Cox purchased tools from Matco pursuant to a credit line that he repaid as the tools were sold. The credit line was secured by Cox's Matco tool inventory. To expedite payment on Cox's line of credit, Matco decided to authorize Cox to deposit any customer checks that were made payable to "Matco Tools" or "Matco" into Cox's own account. Matco's controller sent Cox's bank, Pontiac State Bank (Pontiac), a letter stating that Cox was authorized to make such deposits. Several years later, some Matco tools were stolen from Cox's inventory. The Travelers Indemnity Company (Travelers), which insured Cox against such a loss, sent Cox a settlement check in the amount of $24,960. The check was made payable to "David M. Cox and Matco Tool Co." Cox indorsed the check and deposited it in his account at Pontiac. Pontiac forwarded the check through the banking system for payment by the drawee bank. Cox never paid Matco for the destroyed tools. Matco sued Pontiac for accepting the check without the proper indorsements. Is Pontiac liable? [*Matco Tools Corporation v. Pontiac State Bank*, 41 UCC Rep.Serv. 883 (E.D. Mich. 1985)]

20.9 Presentment Warranties John Waddell Construction Company (Waddell) maintained a checking account at the Longview Bank & Trust Company (Longview Bank). Waddell drafted a check from this account made payable to two payees, Engineered Metal Works (Metal Works) and E. G. Smith Construction (Smith Construction). The check was sent to Metal Works, which promptly indorsed the check and presented it to the First National Bank of Azle (Bank of Azle) for payment. The Bank of Azle accepted the check with only Metal Works' indorsement and credited Metal Works's account. The Bank of Azle subsequently presented the check to Longview Bank through the Federal Reserve System. Longview Bank accepted and paid the check. When Waddell received the check along with its monthly checking statements from Longview Bank, a company employee noticed the missing indorsement and notified Longview Bank. Longview Bank returned the check to the Bank of Azle, and the Bank of Azle's account was debited the amount of the check at the Federal Reserve. Did the Bank of Azle breach its warranty of good title? [*Longview Bank & Trust Company v. First National Bank of Azle*, 750 S.W.2d 297 (Tex. App. 1988)]

20.10 Maker's Liability In March 1977, James Wright met with Jones, the president of The Community Bank (Community Bank), to request a loan of $7,500. Because Wright was already obligated on several existing loans, he was informed that his request would have to be reviewed by the bank's loan committee. Jones suggested that this delay could be avoided if the loan were made to Mrs. Wright. Wright asked his wife to go to the bank and "indorse" a note for him. Mrs. Wright went to the bank and spoke to Jones. Although she claims that Jones told her that she was merely indorsing the note, the language of the note clearly indicated that she would be liable in the case of default. Mrs. Wright signed the instrument in its lower right-hand corner. Wright did not sign the instrument. The $7,500 was deposited directly into Wright's business account. The Wrights were subsequently separated. Following the separation, Mrs. Wright received notice that she was in default on the note. The notice indicated that she was solely obligated to repay the instrument. Is Mrs. Wright obligated to repay the note? [*The Community Bank v. Wright*, 267 S.E.2d 159 (VA 1980)]

20.11 Drawer's Liability Carlisle Distributing Company, Inc. (Carlisle), owed William Paladino $10,000. To pay this debt, Carlisle delivered a $10,000 check drawn on an Arkansas bank made payable to Paladino. Paladino indorsed the check and delivered it to Wildman Stores, Inc. (Wildman), as security for an $8,000 loan he had received from that company. Seventeen months after receiving the check, Wildman presented it for payment at the bank upon which it had been drawn. The payor bank dishonored the check due to insufficient funds. Wildman informed Carlisle of the dishonor and demanded payment of the $10,000. Carlisle refused Wildman's demand. Wildman sued Carlisle to collect the $10,000. The statute of limitations for enforcing a negotiable instrument in Arkansas is five years. Who wins? [*Wildman Stores, Inc. v. Carlisle Distributing Co., Inc.*, 688 S.W.2d 748 (Ark. App. 1985)]

20.12 Liability of Accommodation Makers John Valenti wanted to operate an Amoco service station. He contracted with American Oil Company (Amoco), the licensor of Amoco service stations, to lease a service station and become a dealer of Amoco products. The documents that made up the lease agreement included a promissory note and guaranty. Since Valenti had no established credit history, Amoco required that his father be a cosignor. Both Valentis signed the lease and note. After about one year, the younger Valenti abandoned the operation. Amoco sued both Valentis to recover on the note and guaranty. The suit against the son was dropped when Amoco learned that he had no assets from which to satisfy a judgment. The father claimed that Amoco could not go after him because it was not suing his son. Who wins? [*American Oil Company v. Valenti*, 28 UCC Rep. Serv. 118 (Conn.Sup. 1979)]

20.13 Liability of an Accommodation Indorser The Georgia Farm Bureau Mutual Insurance Company (Georgia Farm Bureau) issued a check payable to the order of Willie Mincey, Jr., and MIC for $658. Without indorsing the check, MIC forwarded it to Mincey for his indorsement. Mincey indorsed the check and attempted to cash it at the First National Bank of Allentown (First National). First National would not accept the check since Mincey was not a customer of the bank. Mincey returned to the bank later that day with his uncle, Montgomery, who was a customer of the bank. First National accepted the check after Montgomery added his indorsement to Mincey's. First National forwarded the check to the drawee bank, which dishonored it because it did not bear MIC's indorsement. First National sued Montgomery for the amount of the check as an accommodation indorser. Who wins? [*First National Bank of Allentown v. Montgomery*, 27 UCC Rep.Serv. 164 (Pa.Com.Pl. 1979)]

20.14 Principal's Liability John Smith was the corporate secretary for Carriage House Mobile Homes, Inc. (Carriage House). Beginning on November 9, 1973, Smith signed a series of checks totaling $13,900 made payable to Danube Carpet Mills (Danube). The checks were in payment for carpeting ordered by Carriage House. Each check was signed in the following manner: "Carriage House Mobile Homes, Inc., General Account, By: /s/ John Smith." When Danube presented the checks for payment to the drawee bank, the First State Bank of Phil Campbell, Alabama (First State Bank), payment was refused. The reason for the refusal was that the checks were drawn against uncollected funds. The holder of these checks, Southeastern Financial Corporation, sued Smith and Carriage House to recover the $13,900. Who is liable on the checks? [*Southeastern Financial Corporation v. Smith*, 397 F.Supp. 649 (N.D.Ala. 1975)]

20.15 Authorized Agent's Liability Richard G. Lee was the president of Village Homes, Inc. (Village Homes). Village Homes had several loans from Farmers & Merchants National Bank of Hattan, North Dakota (Farmers Bank) that were in default. Lee and Farmers Bank worked out an arrangement to consolidate the delinquent loans and replace them with a new loan. The new loan would be secured by a promissory note. The parties drafted a note in the amount of $85,000 with a 17 percent annual interest rate. Lee signed the note without indicating that he was signing as an agent of Village Homes. The name "Village Homes, Inc." did not appear on the note. Six months after the note was signed, Village Homes defaulted on it. Farmers Bank sued Lee, seeking to hold him personally liable for the note. Who wins? [*Farmers & Merchants National Bank of Hattan, North Dakota v. Lee*, 333 N.W.2d 792 (ND 1983)]

BUSINESS ETHICS CASES

20.16 Business Ethics Anthony and Dolores Angelini entered into a contract with Lustro Aluminum Products, Inc. (Lustro). Under the contract, Lustro agreed to replace exterior veneer on the Angelini home with Gold Bond Plasticrylic avocado siding. The cash price for the job was $3,600 and the installment plan price was $5,363.40. The Angelinis chose to pay on the installment plan and signed a promissory note as security. The note's language provided that it would not mature until 60 days after a certificate of completion was signed. Ten days after the note was executed, Lustro assigned it for consideration to General Investment Corporation (General), an experienced home improvement lender. General was aware that Lustro (1) was nearly insolvent at the time of the assignment and (2) had engaged in questionable business practices in the past. Lustro never completed the installation of siding at the Angelini home. General demanded payment of the note from the Angelinis as a holder in due course. Did General act morally in this case? Who wins? [*General Investment Corporation v. Angelini*, 278 A.2d 193 (NJ 1971)]

20.17 Business Ethics Marvin Ornstein resides in Pipersville, Pennsylvania. After submitting credit applications, he received a $10,000 line of credit from both the MGM Grand Hotel and Caesar's Palace, in Las Vegas, Nevada. In April 1977, Ornstein traveled to Las Vegas on a gambling junket and borrowed $5,000 at Caesar's Palace. In June 1977, he went to the MGM Grand Hotel and borrowed $10,000. In each instance, the borrowed money was advanced in the form of gambling chips, in exchange for which Ornstein executed counterchecks (i.e., markers) evidencing the debt. Ornstein did not repay the borrowed money. In November 1978, the casinos assigned their claims against Ornstein to National Recovery Systems (NRS) a New York corporation that is a credit and collection agency for casinos. Did Ornstein act ethically in not repaying his gambling markers? Are the notes illegal because they arose from a gambling debt, and, if so, is this illegality a real defense that can be asserted against enforcement of the notes by an HDC? [*National Recovery Systems v. Ornstein*, 541 F.Supp. 1131 (E.D.Pa. 1982)]

20.18 Business Ethics   In 1976, Gerald Tinker purchased for investment purposes a used 1972 Jaguar from De Maria Porsche Audi, Inc. (De Maria). De Maria represented to Tinker, prior to making the sale, that the automobile was in good operating condition, was powered by its original engine, and had never been involved in a major collision. Tinker relied on these representations and executed a retail installment contract and note with De Maria. The contract and note contained the FTC-required notice. De Maria assigned the contract and note to Central Bank of Miami (Central Bank), which provided floor financing for De Maria.

Tinker had problems with the automobile immediately after its purchase. The car operated poorly and Tinker soon discovered that it was not powered by its original engine, had previously been involved in a major collision, and was determined to be a total loss by its previous owner's insurance company. The title held by the owner preceding De Maria stated that it was a "parts car." The title obtained by Tinker from De Maria did not contain this disclaimer. When De Maria failed to replace or successfully repair the automobile after it became totally inoperable, Tinker ceased making payments on the note and sued De Maria and Central Bank for fraud. Central Bank counterclaimed for the amount due on the note. Is it ethical for a third-party lender to assert its HDC status to collect on a note when the seller has engaged in fraud or other misconduct? Does the FTC rule prevent Central Bank from being a holder in due course? [*Tinker v. De Maria Porsche Audi, Inc.*, 459 So.2d 487 (Fla. App. 1984)]

 # BRIEFING THE CASE WRITING ASSIGNMENT

Read the following case, which has been excerpted from the court's opinion. Review and brief the case.

Kedzie & 103rd Currency Exchange, Inc. v. Hodge
601 N.E.2d 803 (Ill. App. 1 Dist. 1992)
Appellate Court of Illinois

Linn, Justice

Plaintiff, Kedzie & 103rd Street Currency Exchange, Inc., cashed a check for defendant Fred Fentress (who is not a party to this appeal). Defendant Beula M. Hodge, drawer of the check, notified her bank to stop payment on the check when Fentress, engaged to perform plumbing services, did not appear at her home to begin work. As a holder in due course, plaintiff sought damages from Hodge. The trial court, however, granted Hodge's motion to dismiss based on the defense of illegality.

Plaintiff states the issue as whether a holder in due course of a check takes the check free from the defense of illegality where the drawer of the check issued it as a partial advance payment for plumbing services to be rendered, but the payee was not licensed as a plumber.

Plaintiff, an Illinois corporation doing business as a currency exchange, filed suit after the $500 check it had cashed for Fentress was returned marked "payment stopped." Hodge had made out the check to "Fred Fentress—A-OK Plumbing" as a partial payment, in advance, for plumbing services at her residence. When he failed to appear on the date work was to begin, Hodge directed her bank to stop payment on the check. Fentress, in the meantime, cashed the check at plaintiff currency exchange, indorsing the back as "Fred Fentress A-OK Plumbing Sole Owner." Plaintiff obtained a default judgment against Fentress.

Hodge filed a motion to dismiss the action as to her, asserting the defense of illegality. She had discovered that Fentress was not a licensed plumber listed with either the State or Chicago. Under An Act in Relation to the Licensing and Regulation of plumbers (Plumber's Licensing Act), plumbers must obtain a license before practicing their trade. A violation of the Act is a Class B misdemeanor for the first offense. According to Hodge, the plumbing contract was illegal and void; therefore, plaintiff took the check subject to the illegality defense. The trial court agreed and entered judgment in favor of Hodge.

Under the Uniform Commercial Code (UCC), commercial instruments including checks are meant to be freely negotiable, and to that end a holder in due course will take the instrument free from "all defenses of any party to the instrument with whom the holder has not dealt except such incapacity, or duress, or illegality of the transaction, as renders the obligation of the party a nullity."

Comment 6 to UCC Sec. 3–305 explains that the question of illegality is a matter of state law and if under the law governing the contract the effect of the illegality is to make the obligation entirely null and void, the defense is good.

The dispositive issue before us, therefore, is whether under Illinois law the contract between Hodge and the plumber was null and void. If so, the defense of illegality was properly asserted and applied in this case. If the underlying obligation was merely voidable, however, the defense fails.

The Illinois legislature, by adopting Sec. 3–305 of the UCC, has expressly declared that illegality is an available defense against a holder in due course, as long as the effect of the illegality is to render the obligation sued upon null and void.

Illinois courts should not apply the illegality defense against holders in due course unless the illegal transaction is of the type that wholly nullifies the contract and thereby renders the instrument subject to the illegality defense.

In this state, the legislature has passed extensive legislation relating to the licensing of many trades and professions, recognizing that the regulation of these professions is essential to the public health, safety, and welfare. In furtherance of the legislative goals of providing standards and protecting the public health, the Plumber's Licensing Act provides that one who attempts to practice plumbing without a license may suffer substantial penalties, including criminal prosecution and fines. By judicial construction, the unlicensed plumber also forfeits his right to compensation for illegal services rendered. The contract in question is not void unless the Plumber's Licensing Act or other legislation expressly declares it to be.

As a matter of policy, plaintiff argues that it is unfair to expect a currency exchange to police the negotiable instruments it receives to ferret out possible illegalities in the underlying contracts. While the argument is reasonable enough, the same could be made for all the defenses which defeat the rights of holders in due course. The currency exchange does not have a way to ascertain if a check has been drafted under duress, if it represents a gambling debt, or if it is the check of one without legal capacity to be bound. The so-called "real" defenses are nonetheless valid and cut off the rights of the innocent holder of the instrument to obtain recourse against makers or endorsers of the instrument in question. Currency exchanges are in the business of cashing checks and undertake the attendant risks.

We conclude that the illegality defense asserted in this case is of the type to render the obligation a nullity under Sec. 3–305 of the Code. Therefore, we affirm the trial court's dismissal of the action against Hodge, as maker of the check.

Affirmed.

CHAPTER 21

Checks and Digital Banking

Bankers have no right to establish a customary law among themselves, at the expense of other men.

—Justice Foster
Hankey v. Trotman, 1 Black. W. 1 (1746)

Chapter Objectives

After studying this chapter, you should be able to:

1. Describe the difference between certified, cashier's, and traveler's checks.

2. Describe the system of processing and collecting checks through the banking system.

3. Define *stale* and *postdated* checks.

4. Identify when a bank engages in a wrongful dishonor of a check.

5. Describe the liability of parties when a signature or indorsement on a check is forged.

6. Describe the liability of parties when a check has been altered.

7. Explain a bank's midnight deadline for determining whether to dishonor a check.

8. Describe the requirements of the Expedited Funds Availability Act.

9. Describe electronic fund transfer systems.

10. Define *wire transfer* and describe the main provisions of Article 4A of the Uniform Commercial Code (UCC).

Chapter Contents

Money speaks sense in a language all nations understand.

Aphra Behn (1640-1689)
The Rover

Checks are the most common form of negotiable instrument used in this country. More than 70 billion checks are written annually. Checks act both as a substitute for money and as a record-keeping device, but they do not serve a credit function. In addition, billions of dollars are transferred each day by **wire transfer** between businesses and banks. This chapter discusses the various forms of checks, the procedure for paying and collecting checks through the banking system, the duties and liabilities of banks and other parties in the collection process, and electronic fund transfers.

𝒯HE BANK–CUSTOMER RELATIONSHIP

creditor–debtor relationship

Created when a customer deposits money into the bank; the customer is the creditor and the bank is the debtor.

When a customer makes a deposit into a bank, a **creditor–debtor relationship** is formed. The customer is the creditor and the bank is the debtor. In effect, the customer is loaning money to the bank.

A **principal–agent relationship** is created if (1) the deposit is a check that the bank must collect for the customer or (2) the customer writes a check against his or her account. The customer is the principal and the bank is the agent. The bank is obligated to follow the customer's order to collect or pay the check. The rights and duties of a bank and a checking account and wire transfer customer are contractual. The signature card and other bank documents signed by the customer form the basis of the contract.

The banking systems of the world make it possible for companies to finance the purchase, sale, and lease of goods and services across country borders.

𝓛andmark 𝓛aw

THE UNIFORM COMMERCIAL CODE BANKING PROVISIONS

Various articles of the Uniform Commercial Code (UCC) establish rules for creating, collecting, and enforcing checks and wire transfers. These articles are

- **Article 3 (Negotiable Instruments)** establishes the requirements for finding a negotiable instrument. Because a check is a negotiable instrument, the provisions of Article 3 apply. **Revised Article 3** was promulgated in 1990. The provisions of Revised Article 3 will serve as the basis of the discussion of Article 3 in this chapter.
- **Article 4 of the UCC (Bank Deposits and Collections)** establishes the rules and principles that regulate bank

deposit and collection procedures for checking accounts offered by commercial banks, NOW accounts, (negotiable orders of withdrawal), and other checklike accounts offered by savings and loan associations, savings banks, credit unions, and other financial institutions. Article 4 controls if the provisions of Articles 3 and 4 conflict [UCC 4-102(a)]. Article 4 was substantially amended in 1990. The amended Article 4 will serve as the basis of the discussion of Article 4 in this chapter.
- **Article 4A (Funds Transfers)** establishes rules that regulate the creation and collection of and liability for wire transfers. Article 4A was added to the UCC in 1989.

ORDINARY CHECKS

Most adults and businesses have at least one checking account at a bank. A customer opens a checking account by going to the bank, completing the necessary forms (including a signature card), and making a **deposit** to the account. The bank issues checks to the customer. The customer then uses the checks to purchase goods and services. When the check is presented for payment, the bank verifies the drawer's signature by matching the signature on the check to the one on the signature card.

Parties to a Check

UCC 3-104(f) defines a **check** as an order by the drawer to the drawee bank to pay a specified sum of money from the drawer's checking account to the named payee (or holder). There are three parties to an ordinary check:

1. **Drawer** The customer who maintains the checking account and writes (draws) checks against the account
2. **Drawee** (or Payor Bank) The bank on which the check is drawn
3. **Payee** The party to whom the check is written

Consider This Example The Kneadery Restaurant has a checking account at Mountain Bank. The Kneadery writes a check for $1,500 from this account to Sun Valley Bakery to pay for food supplies. The Kneadery Restaurant is the drawer, Mountain Bank is the drawee, and Sun Valley Bakery is the payee.

Indorsement of a Check

The payee is a *holder* of the check. As such, the payee has the right to either (1) demand payment of the check or (2) *indorse* the check to another party by signing the back of the check. This latter action is called **indorsement** of a check. The payee is the **indorser** and the person to whom the check is indorsed is the **indorsee**. The indorsee in turn becomes a holder who can either demand payment of the check or indorse it to yet another party. Any subsequent holder can demand payment of the check or further transfer the check [UCC 3-204(a)].

Consider This Example   Referring to the previous example, the Sun Valley Bakery may either present the Kneadery Restaurant's check to Mountain Bank for payment, or it can indorse the check to another party. Assume that Sun Valley Bakery indorses the check to the Flour Company in payment for flour. Sun Valley Bakery is the indorser and the Flour Company is the indorsee. The Flour Company may either present the check for payment or indorse it to another party, and so on.

Article 4 of the UCC

Establishes the rules and principles that regulate bank deposit and collection procedures.

check

An order by the drawer to the drawee bank to pay a specified sum of money from the drawer's checking account to the named payee (or holder).

drawer of a check

The checking account holder and writer of the check.

drawee of a check

The bank where the drawer has his or her account

payee of a check

The party to whom the check is written.

indorsement of a check

Occurs when a payee indorses a check to another party by signing the back of the check.

indorser

The payee who indorses a check to another party.

indorsee

The party to whom a check is indorsed.

 *E-Commerce & Information Technology*

ELECTRONIC FUND TRANSFER SYSTEMS

Computers and electronic technology have made it possible for banks to offer electronic payment and collection systems to bank customers. This technology is collectively referred to as **electronic fund transfer systems (EFTS)**. EFTS are supported by contracts among and between customers, banks, private clearinghouses, and other third parties. The most common forms of EFTS are discussed in the following paragraphs.

AUTOMATED TELLER MACHINES
An **automated teller machine (ATM)** is an electronic machine that is located either on a bank's premises or at some other convenient location, such as a shopping center or supermarket. These devices are connected online to the bank's computers. Bank customers are issued a secret personal identification number (PIN) to access their bank accounts through ATMs.

ATMs are commonly used when the bank is not open. They are also being used as an alternative means of conducting banking when the bank is open. They are used to withdraw cash from bank accounts, cash checks, make deposits to checking or savings accounts, and make payments owed to the bank.

POINT-OF-SALE TERMINALS

Many banks issue *debit cards* to customers. Debit cards replace checks in that customers can use them to make purchases. No credit is extended. Instead, the customer's bank account is immediately debited for the amount of the purchase.

Debit cards can be used only if the merchant has a **point-of-sale (POS) terminal** at the checkout counter. These terminals are connected online to the bank's computers. To make a purchase, the customer inserts the debit card into the terminal for the amount of the purchase. If there are sufficient funds in the customer's account, the transaction will debit the customer's account and credit the merchant's account for the amount of the purchase. If there are insufficient funds in the customer's account, the purchase is rejected unless the customer has overdraft protection. Some POS terminals allow for the extension of credit in the transaction. Gasoline station POS terminals are one example.

DIRECT DEPOSITS AND WITHDRAWALS

Many banks provide the service of paying recurring payments and crediting recurring deposits on behalf of customers. Commonly, payments are for utilities, insurance premiums, mortgage payments, and the like. Social Security checks, wages, and dividend and interest checks are examples of recurring deposits. To provide this service, the customer's bank and the payee's bank must belong to the same clearinghouse.

PAY-BY-INTERNET

Many banks permit customers to pay bills from their bank accounts by use of personal computer by using the Internet. To do so, the customer must enter his or her PIN and account number, the amount of the bill to be paid, and the account number of the payee to whom the funds are to be transferred. Internet banking is expected to increase dramatically in the future.

SPECIAL TYPES OF CHECKS

If a payee fears there may be insufficient funds in the drawer's account to pay the check when it is presented for payment or that the drawer has stopped payment of the check, the payee may be unwilling to accept an ordinary check from the drawer. The payee, however, might be willing to accept a **bank check**; that is, a certified check, a cashier's check, or a traveler's check. These types of checks usually are considered "as good as cash" because the bank is solely or primarily liable for payment. These forms of checks are discussed in the following paragraphs.

Certified Checks

When a bank **certifies a check**, it agrees in advance to (1) accept the check when it is presented for payment and (2) pay the check out of funds set aside from the customer's account and either placed in a special certified check account or held in the customer's account. Certified checks do not become stale. Thus, they are payable at any time from the date they were issued.

The check is **certified** when the bank writes or stamps the word *certified* across the face of an ordinary check. The certification should also contain the date and the amount being certified and the name and title of the person at the bank who certifies the check (see Exhibit 21.1). Note that the bank is not obligated to certify a check. The banks' refusal to do so is not a dishonor of the check [UCC 3-409(d)].

bank check

A certified check, a cashier's check, or a traveler's check, the payment for which the bank is solely or primarily liable.

certified check

A type of check where a bank agrees in advance (*certifies*) to accept the check when it is presented for payment.

process of certification

The accepting bank writes or stamps the word *certified* on the ordinary check of an account holder and sets aside funds from that account to pay the check.

EXHIBIT 21.1 A Certified Check

Liability on a Certified Check Either the drawer or the payee (or holder) can present the check to the drawee bank for certification. If the drawee bank certifies the check, the drawer is discharged from liability on the check, regardless of who obtained the certification [UCC 3-414(c)]. The holder must recover from the certifying bank. The obligated bank can be held liable for the amount of the check, expenses, and loss of interest resulting from non-payment. If the bank refuses to pay after receiving notice of particular circumstances giving rise to such damages, it can also be held liable for consequential damages [UCC 3-411].

Problems may arise if a certified check was altered (e.g., the amount of the check increased). If the alteration occurred before the check was certified, the certifying bank is liable for the certified amount. If the check was altered after certification, the bank is liable for only the certified amount, not the raised amount. The drawer cannot stop payment on a certified check. Since certification constitutes acceptance of the check, the certifying bank can revoke its certification only in limited circumstances [UCC 3-413].

Cashier's Checks

A person can purchase a **cashier's check** from a bank by paying the bank the amount of the check plus a fee for issuing the check. Usually, a specific payee is named. The purchaser does not have to have a checking account at the bank. The check is a noncancellable negotiable instrument upon issue.

A cashier's check is a two-party check for which (1) the issuing bank serves as both the drawer and the drawee and (2) the holder serves as payee [UCC 3-104(g)]. The bank, which has been paid for the check, guarantees its payment. When the check is presented for payment, the bank debits its own account [UCC 3-412]. (See Exhibit 21.2 for a sample cashier's check.)

An obligated bank that wrongfully refuses to pay a cashier's check is liable to the person asserting the right to enforce the check for expenses and loss of interest resulting from nonpayment and consequential damages [UCC 3-411].

𝓔XHIBIT 21.2 *A Cashier's Check*

eCOMMERCE NATIONAL BANK 10341504 16-4/1220
Bank Check Accounting Services
Brea, California 92621-6398 OFFICE NUMBER 142 DATE: August 16, 2003
PAY TO THE ORDER OF ··········· HELEN PITTS ··········· $ 1,000.00
EXACTLY 1,000 AND 00 DOLLARS
($100,000 AND OVER REQUIRES TWO SIGNATURES)
CASHIER'S CHECK
Dg Lotten
AUTHORIZED SIGNATURE AUTHORIZED SIGNATURE
⑆10341504⑆ ⑈122000043⑇928⑈917016⑆

Traveler's Checks

Traveler's checks are so named because individuals often purchase them to use as a safe substitute for cash while on vacations or other trips. They may be issued by banks or by companies other than banks (e.g., American Express). A traveler's check is a two-party instrument, where the issuing bank serves as both the drawer and the drawee. It is drawn by the bank upon itself.

Traveler's checks may be purchased in many denominations, including $10, $20, $50, and $100. Unlike cashier's checks, traveler's checks are issued without a named payee. The checks have two signature blanks. The purchaser signs one blank when the traveler's checks are issued. The purchaser enters the payee's name and signs the second blank when he or she uses the check to purchase goods or services. The traveler's check is not a negotiable instrument until it is signed the second time [UCC 3-104(i)] (see Exhibit 21.3).

Purchasers of traveler's checks do not have to have a checking account at the issuing bank. The purchaser pays the bank the amount of the checks to be issued. When a traveler's check is presented for payment, the bank debits its own account. Most banks charge a fee for this service, but some banks merely earn interest on the "float" while the checks are not written. If a traveler's check is stolen or lost prior to its use, the purchaser can stop payment on the check. Payment cannot be stopped once the check has been negotiated.

*E*XHIBIT 21.3   *A Traveler's Check*

E-Commerce & Information Technology

BANK DEBIT CARDS

The computer has made it much easier and faster for banks and their customers to conduct banking transactions. For example, bank customers can now use **debit cards** to pay for goods and services. When a bank customer uses a debit card to pay, the money is immediately deducted electronically from his or her bank account. There is no extension of credit as there is when a credit card is used; using a debit card is like writing an electronic check.

Congress enacted the **Electronic Fund Transfer Act** [15 U.S.C. §§ 1693 et seq.] to regulate consumer electronic fund transfers. The Federal Reserve Board, which is empowered to enforce the provisions of the act, adopted **Regulation E** to further interpret it. Regulation E has the force of law. The Electronic Fund Transfer Act and Regulation E establish the following consumer rights:

1. **Unsolicited Cards** A bank can send unsolicited EFTS debit cards to a consumer only if the cards are not valid for use. Unsolicited cards can be validated for use by a consumer's specific request.
2. **Lost or Stolen Debit Cards** Debit cards are sometimes lost or stolen. If a customer notifies the issuer bank within two days of learning that his or her debit card has been lost or stolen, the customer is liable for only $50 for unauthorized use. If a customer does not notify the bank within this two-day period, the cus-

tomer's liability increases to $500. If the customer fails to notify the bank within 60 days after an unauthorized use appears on the customer's bank statement, the customer can be held liable for more than $500. Federal law allows states to impose a lesser liability on customers for lost or stolen debit cards.

3. **Evidence of Transaction** Other than for a telephone transaction, a bank must provide a customer with a written receipt of a transaction made through a computer terminal. This receipt is prima facie evidence of the transaction.
4. **Bank Statements** A bank must provide a monthly statement to an electronic funds transfer customer at the end of the month that the customer conducts a transaction. Otherwise, a quarterly statement must be provided to the customer. The statement must include the date and amount of the transfer, the name of the retailer, the location or identification of the terminal, and the fees charged for the transaction. Bank statements must also contain the address and telephone number where inquiries or errors can be reported.

Banks are required to disclose the foregoing information to their customers. A bank is liable for wrongful dishonor when it fails to pay an electronic fund transfer when there are sufficient funds in the customer's account to do so.

Honoring Checks

When a customer opens a checking account at a bank, the customer impliedly agrees to keep sufficient funds in the account to pay any checks written against it. Thus, when the drawee bank receives a properly drawn and payable check, the bank is under a duty to **honor** the check and charge (debit) the drawer's account the amount of the check [UCC 4-401(a)].

honor
Payment of a drawer's properly drawn check by the drawee bank.

Stale Checks

Occasionally, payees or other holders in possession of a check fail to present the check immediately to the payor bank for payment. A check that has been outstanding for more than six months is considered **stale**, and the bank is under no obligation to pay it. A bank that pays a stale check in good faith may charge the drawer's account [UCC 4-404].

stale check
A check that has been outstanding for more than six months.

Incomplete Checks

Drawers sometimes write checks that omit certain information, such as the amount of the check or the payee's name, either on purpose or by mistake. In such cases, the payee or any holder can complete the check, and the payor bank that in good faith makes payment on the completed check can charge the customer's account the amount of the completed check unless it has notice that the completion was improper [UCC 3-407(c) and 4-401(d)(2)]. The UCC places the risk of loss of an incomplete item on the drawer.

Business Brief
A bank may pay an incomplete check as completed by the payee as long as it acts in good faith and without notice that the completion was improper.

Consider This Example   Suppose Richard, who owes Sarah $500, draws a check payable to Sarah on City Bank. Richard signs the check but leaves the amount blank. Sarah fraudulently fills in "$1,000" and presents the check to City Bank, which pays it. City Bank can charge Richard's account $1,000. Richard's only recourse is to sue Sarah. If Richard had telephoned the bank to tell them that he owed Sarah only $500, however, City Bank would be liable for paying any greater amount to Sarah.

Death or Incompetence of a Drawer

Checks may be paid against the accounts of deceased customers or customers who have been adjudicated incompetent until the bank has actual knowledge of such condition and had reasonable opportunity to act on the information. In the case of a deceased customer, the bank may pay or certify checks drawn on the deceased customer's account on or prior to the date of death for 10 days after the date of death. This rule applies unless a person claiming an interest in the account, such as an heir or a taxing authority, orders the bank to stop payment. A bank that pays such a check when it should not have is liable for the amount improperly paid [UCC 4-405].

Business Brief
As a practical matter, banks usually freeze a checking account upon learning of the death of a customer.

Contemporary Business Environment

REQUIREMENTS FOR POSTDATING CHECKS

Prior to a recent revision of Article 4 of the UCC, all a drawer had to do to **postdate** a check was to write the check and date it a date in the future. The bank was then obligated not to pay the check until this later date, and if it did pay the check sooner it was liable for any damages caused to the drawer.

In 1990, Article 4 was amended to make it more difficult to postdate a check. Under new UCC 4-401(c), to require a bank to abide by a postdated check, the drawer must take the following steps:

- The drawer must postdate the check to some date in the future.
- The drawer must give *separate written notice* to the bank describing the check with reasonable certainty and notifying the bank not to pay the check until the date on the check.

If these steps are taken and the bank pays the check before its date, the bank is liable to the drawer for any losses resulting from its act.

stop-payment order

An order by a drawer of a check to the payor bank not to pay or certify a check.

Stop-Payment Orders

A **stop-payment order** is an order by a drawer of a check to the payor bank not to pay or certify a check. Only the drawer can order a stop payment. If the signature of more than one person is required to draw on an account, any of these persons may stop payment on the account. The bank must be given a reasonable opportunity to act on a stop-payment order. The order is ineffectual if the bank has already accepted or certified the check.

The stop-payment order can be given orally or in writing. An **oral order** is binding on the bank for only 14 calendar days, unless confirmed in writing during this time. A **written order** is effective for six months. It can be renewed in writing for additional six-month periods [UCC 4-403].

If the payor bank fails to honor a valid stop-payment order, it must recredit the customer's account. The bank is subrogated to the rights of the drawer. In addition, the bank is liable only for the actual damages suffered by the drawer. The drawer must prove the fact and amount of loss resulting from the payment of a check on which a stop-payment order was issued.

Business Brief

An oral stop-payment order is binding on the bank for only 14 days, unless confirmed in writing during the 14-day period.

written order

A stop-payment order that is good for six months after the date it is written.

Consider This Example Suppose Karen buys a car from Silvio. She pays for the car by drawing a $10,000 check on City Bank payable to the order of Silvio. Karen thinks the car is defective and stops payment on the check. If City Bank mistakenly pays Silvio over the stop-payment order, it is liable and must recredit Karen's account. If it is determined that the car is not defective, however, City Bank does not have to recredit Karen's account because Karen has suffered no actual loss; she owed Silvio for the car.

Overdrafts

If the drawer does not have enough money in his or her account when a properly payable check is presented for payment, the payor bank can either (1) dishonor the check or (2) honor the check and create an overdraft in the drawer's account [UCC 4-401(a)]. The bank notifies the drawer of the dishonor and returns the check to the holder marked "insufficient funds." The holder often resubmits the check to the bank, hoping that the drawer has deposited more money into the account and the check will clear. If the check does not clear, the holder's recourse is against the drawee of the check.

If the bank chooses to pay the check even though there are insufficient funds in the drawer's account, it can later charge the drawer's account for the amount of the **overdraft** [UCC 4-401(a)] because there is an implied promise that the drawer will reimburse the bank for paying checks the drawer orders the bank to pay. If the drawer does not fulfill this commitment, the bank can sue him or her to recover payment for the overdrafts and overdraft fees. A bank cannot charge interest on the amount of the overdraft without the drawer's permission. Therefore, many banks offer optional overdraft protection to their customers.

Business Brief

When a check is dishonored because of insufficient funds, it is said to have "bounced" (i.e., like a rubber check).

overdraft

The amount of money a drawer owes a bank after it has paid a check despite insufficient funds in the drawer's account.

Wrongful Dishonor

If the bank does not honor a check when there are sufficient funds in a drawer's account to pay a properly payable check, it is liable for **wrongful dishonor**. The payor bank is liable to the drawer for damages proximately caused by the wrongful dishonor as well as for consequential damages, damages caused by criminal prosecution, and such. A payee or holder cannot sue the bank for damages caused by the wrongful dishonor of a drawer's check. The only recourse for the payee or holder is to sue the drawer to recover the amount of the check [UCC 4-402].

wrongful dishonor

Occurs when there are sufficient funds in a drawer's account to pay a properly payable check, but the bank does not do so.

Contemporary Business Environment

FEDERAL CURRENCY REPORTING LAW

Federal currency reporting laws require financial institutions and other entities (e.g., retailers, car and boat dealers, antique dealers, jewelers, travel agencies, real estate brokers, and other businesses) to file a **Currency Transaction Report (CTR)** with the Internal Revenue Service (IRS) reporting:

- The receipt in a single transaction or a series of related transactions of cash in an amount greater than $10,000. "Cash" is not limited to currency, but includes cashier's checks, bank drafts, traveler's checks, and money orders (but no ordinary checks) [26 U.S.C. § 60501].
- Suspected criminal activity by bank customers involving a financial transaction of $1,000 or more in funds [12 C.F.R. § 21.11(b)(3)].

The law also stipulates that it is a crime to structure or assist in structuring any transaction for the purpose of evading these reporting requirements [31 U.S.C. § 5324]. Financial institutions and entities may be fined for negligent violations of the currency reporting requirements. A $50,000 fine may be levied for a pattern of negligent violations. Willful failure to file reports may subject the violator to civil money penalties, charges of aiding and abetting the criminal activity, and prosecution for violating the money laundering statutes.

FORGED SIGNATURES AND ALTERED CHECKS

Major problems associated with checks are that (1) certain signatures are sometimes forged and (2) the check itself may have been altered prior to presentment for payment. The UCC rules that apply to these situations are discussed in the following paragraphs. These rules apply to all types of negotiable instruments but are particularly important concerning checks.

> *The love of money is the root of all evil.*
> Bible
> I Timothy *6:10*

Forged Signature of the Drawer

When a check is presented to the payor bank for payment, the bank is under a duty to verify the drawer's signature. This is usually done by matching the signature on the signature card on file at the bank to the signature on the check.

A check with a *forged drawer's signature* is called a **forged instrument**. A forged signature is wholly inoperative as the signature of the drawer. The check is not "properly payable" because it does not contain an order of the drawer. The payor bank cannot charge the customer's account if it pays a check over the forged signature. If the bank has charged the customer's account, it must recredit the account and the forged check must be dishonored [UCC 3-401].

The bank can recover only from the party who presented the check to it for payment if that party had knowledge that the signature of the drawer on the check was unauthorized [UCC 3-417(a)(3)]. The forger is liable on the check because the forged signature acts as the forger's signature [UCC 3-403(a)]. Although the payor bank can sue the forger, the forger usually cannot be found or is judgment-proof.

Consider This Example Suppose Gregory has a checking account at Country Bank. Lana steals a check, completes it, and forges Gregory's signature. She indorses it to Mike, who knows that Gregory's signature has been forged. Mike indorses it to Barbara, who is innocent and does not know of the forgery. She presents it to Country Bank, the payor bank, which pays the check. Country Bank may recover from the original forger, Lana, and from Mike, who knew of the forgery. It cannot recover from Barbara because she did not have knowledge of the forgery.

Altered Checks

Sometimes, a check is altered before it is presented for payment. This is an unauthorized change in the check that modifies the legal obligation of a party [UCC 3-407(a)]. The payor bank can dishonor an **altered check** if it discovers the alteration.

If the payor bank pays the altered check, it can charge the drawer's account for the **original tenor** of the check but not the altered amount [UCC 3-407(c) and UCC 4-401(d)(1)].

If the payor bank has paid the altered amount, it can recover the difference between the altered amount and the original tenor from the party who presented the altered check for payment. This is because the presenter of the check for payment and each prior transferor *warrant* that the check has not been altered [UCC 3-417(a)(2)]. This is called the **presentment warranty**. If there has been an alteration, each party in the chain of collection

forged instrument
A check with a forged drawer's signature on it.

Business Brief
The ultimate loss for the payment of a check over the *forged signature* of the drawer usually falls on the bank that paid the check. The payor bank may recover from the forger, if he or she can be found.

Business Brief
A payor bank that has paid a check over the forged signature of a drawer can recover only from (1) prior transferors who had knowledge that the signature of the drawer was unauthorized or (2) the forger.

altered check
A check that has been altered without authorization that modifies the legal obligation of a party.

original tenor
The original amount for which the drawer wrote the check.

Business Brief
If the payor bank pays the altered check, it can charge the drawer's account the *original tenor* of the check but not the altered amount.

presentment warranty
Each prior transferor warrants that the check has not been altered.

can recover from the preceding transferor based on a breach of this warranty. The ultimate loss usually falls on the party that first paid the altered check because that party was in the best position to identify the alteration. The forger is liable for the altered amount—if he or she can be found and is not judgment-proof.

Consider This Example   Father draws a $100 check on City Bank made payable to his daughter. The daughter alters the check to read "$1,000" and cashes the check at the liquor store. The liquor store presents the check for payment to City Bank. City Bank pays the check. Father is liable only for the original tenor of the check ($100), and City Bank can charge the father's account this amount. City Bank is liable for the $900 difference, but it can recover this amount from the liquor store for breach of presentment warranty. The liquor store can seek to recover the $900 from the daughter.

Business Brief

A checking account customer owes a duty to examine bank statements promptly and with reasonable care to determine if any payment was made because of alteration of a check or forged signature of the customer.

If the same wrongdoer engages in a *series of forgeries* or *alterations* on the same account, the customer must report that to the payor bank within a reasonable period of time, not exceeding 30 calendar days from the date that the bank statement was made available to the customer [UCC 4-406(d)(2)]. The customer's failure to do so discharges the bank from liability on all similar forged or altered checks after this date and prior to notification.

The drawer's failure to report a forged or altered check to the bank within *one year* of receiving the bank statement and canceled checks containing it relieves the bank of any liability for paying the instrument [UCC 4-406(e)]. Thus, the payor bank is not required after this time to recredit the customer's account for the amount of the forged or altered check even if the customer later discovers the forgery or alteration.

International Law

HIDING MONEY IN OFFSHORE BANKS

Little did Christopher Columbus know in 1503 when he sailed past the Cayman Islands in the Caribbean that these tiny islands would become a bastion of international finance in the late twentieth and early twenty-first century. These tiny islands of 35,000 people host about 600 banks with over $500 million in deposits. Why is so much money being hoarded there? The answer is: Bank secrecy laws.

Every nation has banking laws, but all banking laws are not equal. What the Cayman Islands banking law provides is confidentiality. In most instances, no party other than the depositor has the right to know the identity of the depositor, account number, or amount in the account. In fact, most accounts are held in the name of trusts instead of the depositor's actual name. This bank secrecy law has attracted many persons—and in some instances crooks—to park their ill-gotten gains in a Cayman Islands bank. Often the bank is usually no more than a lawyer's office.

Switzerland was once the primary location for depositing money that did not want to be found. After some pressure from the United States and other countries, however, Switzerland entered into memorandums of understanding agreeing to cooperate with criminal investigations by these countries and to help uncover money deposited in Switzerland made through securities frauds and other crimes. Therefore, Switzerland has lost some of its luster as an international money hideout.

So Switzerland has been replaced by other places offering even more secret bank secrecy laws. The Cayman Islands is now the "Switzerland of the Caribbean." There are several other bank secrecy hideouts around the world, including the Bahamas in the Caribbean, the country of Liechtenstein in Europe, the Isle of Jersey off of Great Britain, and the micro-island of Niue in the South Pacific. These tiny countries and islands follow the adage: "Write a good law and they will come."

The COLLECTION PROCESS

payor bank

The bank where the drawer has a checking account and on which the check is drawn.

depository bank

The bank where the payee or holder has an account.

A bank is under a duty to accept deposits into a customer's account. This includes collecting checks that are drawn on other banks and made payable or indorsed to the depositor. The collection process, which may involve several banks, is governed by **Article 4 of the UCC**.

When a payee or holder receives a check, he or she can either go to the drawer's bank (the **payor bank**) and present the check for payment in cash or—as is more common—deposit the check into a bank account at his or her own bank, called the **depository bank**.

(The depository bank may also serve as the payor bank if both parties have accounts at the same bank.)

The depository bank must present the check to the payor bank for collection. At this point in the process, the Federal Reserve System (discussed next) and other banks may be used in the collection of a check. The depository bank and these other banks are called **collecting banks**. Banks in the collection process that are not the depository or payor bank are called **intermediary banks**. A bank can have more than one role during the collection process [UCC 4-105]. The collection process is illustrated in Exhibit 21.4.

collecting bank

The depository bank and other banks in the collection process (other than the payor bank).

intermediary bank

A bank in the collection process that is not the depository or payor bank.

&xhibit 21.4   The Check Collection Process

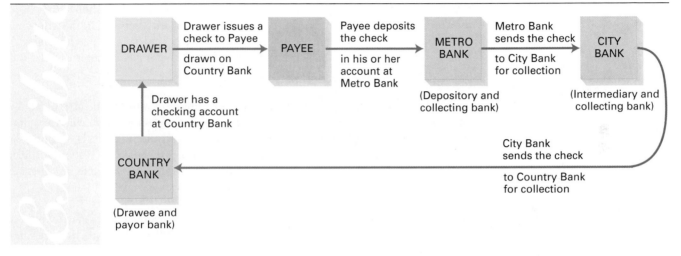

The Federal Reserve System

The **Federal Reserve System**, which consists of 12 regional Federal Reserve banks located in different geographical areas of the country, assists banks in the collection of checks. Rather than send a check directly to another bank for collection, member banks may submit paid checks to the Federal Reserve banks for collection.

Most banks in this country have accounts at the regional Federal Reserve banks. This is usually done by electronic presentment (i.e., by computer). The Federal Reserve banks debit and credit the accounts of these banks daily to reflect the collection and payment of checks. Banks pay the Federal Reserve banks a fee for this service. In large urban areas, private clearinghouses may provide a similar service [UCC 4-110 and 4-213(a)].

Federal Reserve System

A system of 12 regional Federal Reserve banks that assist banks in the collection of checks.

Deferred Posting

The **deferred posting rule** applies to all banks in the collection process. This rule allows banks to fix an afternoon hour of 2:00 P.M. or later as a cutoff hour for the purpose of processing checks. Any check or deposit of money received after this cutoff hour is treated as received on the next banking day [UCC 4-108]. Saturdays, Sundays, and holidays are not *banking days* unless the bank is open to the public for carrying on substantially all banking functions [UCC 4-104(a)(3)].

deferred posting rule

A rule that allows banks to fix an afternoon hour of 2:00 P.M. or later as a cutoff hour for the purpose of processing items.

Provisional Credits

When a customer deposits a check into a checking account for collection, the depository bank does not have to pay the customer the amount of the check until the check "clears"— that is, until final settlement occurs. The depository bank may **provisionally credit** the customer's account. Each bank in the collection process provisionally credits the account of the prior transferor [UCC 4-201(a)]. If the check is dishonored by the payor bank (e.g., insufficient funds, a stop-payment order, or closed account), the check is returned to the

provisional credit

Occurs when a collecting bank gives credit to a check in the collection process prior to its final settlement. Provisional credits may be reversed if the check does not "clear."

payee or holder, and the provisional credits are reversed. The collecting bank must either return the check to the prior transferor or notify that party within a reasonable time that provisional credit is being revoked. If the collecting bank fails to do this, it is liable for any losses caused by its delay [UCC 4-214].

Depository banks often allow their customers to withdraw the funds prior to final settlement. If the bank later learns that the check was dishonored, it can debit the customer's account for the amount withdrawn. If this is not possible (e.g., the payee or holder does not have sufficient funds in his or her account or has closed the account), the depository bank can sue the customer to recover the funds.

Final Settlement

A check is finally paid when the payor bank (1) pays the check in cash, (2) settles for the check without having a right to revoke the settlement, or (3) fails to dishonor the check within certain statutory time periods. These time periods are discussed in the following paragraphs.

When a check is finally settled, the provisional credits along the chain of collecting banks "firm up" and become **final settlements** [UCC 4-215(a)].

"On Us" Checks   If the drawer and the payee or holder have accounts at the *same* bank, the depository bank is also the payor bank. The check is called an **"on us" item** when it is presented for payment by the payee or holder. In this case, the bank has until the opening for business on the second banking day following the receipt of the check to dishonor it. If it fails to do so, the check is considered paid. The payee or holder can withdraw the funds at this time [UCC 4-215(e)(2)].

Consider This Example   Christine and Jim both have checking accounts at Country Bank. On Tuesday morning, Christine deposits a $1,000 check from Jim into her account. Country Bank issues a provisional credit to Christine's account for this amount. On Thursday morning when the bank opens for business, the check is considered honored.

"On Them" Checks   If the drawer and the payee or holder have accounts at *different* banks, the payor and depository bank are not the same bank. In this case, the check is called an **"on them" item**.

Each bank in the collection process, including the payor bank, but excepting the collecting bank, must take proper action on the check prior to its "midnight deadline." The **midnight deadline** is the midnight of the next banking day following the banking day on which the bank received an "on them" check for collection [UCC 4-104(a)(10)]. Collecting banks are permitted to act within a reasonably longer time, but the bank then has the burden of establishing the timeliness of its action [UCC 4-202(b)].

This deadline is of particular importance to the payor bank: If the payor bank does not dishonor a check by its midnight deadline, the bank is *accountable* (liable) for the face amount of the check. It does not matter whether the check is properly payable or not [UCC 4-302(a)].

Consider This Example   If on Wednesday morning a payor bank receives an on them check drawn on an account at the bank, it has until midnight of the next banking day, Thursday, to dishonor the check. If it does not, the check is considered paid by the bank. This deadline does not apply to on us checks, which clear when the bank opens on the second business day following receipt of the checks (unless they are dishonored).

Instead of depositing an on them check for collection, a depositor can physically present the check for payment at the payor bank. This is called **presentment across the counter**. In this case, the payor bank has until the end of that banking day to dishonor the check. If it fails to do so, it must pay the check [UCC 4-301(a)].

Deposit of Money   A deposit of money to an account becomes available for withdrawal at the opening of the next banking day following the deposit [UCC 4-215(a)].

Margin glossary

final settlement

Occurs when the payor bank (1) pays the check in cash, (2) settles for the check without having a right to revoke the settlement, or (3) fails to dishonor the check within certain statutory time periods.

"on us" item

A check that is presented for payment where the depository bank is also the payor bank. That is, the drawer and payee or holder have accounts at the same bank.

"on them" item

A check presented for payment by the payee or holder where the depository bank and the payor bank are not the same bank.

midnight deadline

The midnight of the next banking day following the banking day on which the bank received the on them check for collection.

presentment across the counter

When a depository physically presents the check for payment at the payor bank instead of depositing an on them check for collection.

The "Four Legals" That Prevent Payment of a Check

Sometimes the payor bank will receive some form of notice that affects the payment of a check that has been presented for collection and is in the process of being *posted*. The following types of notices or actions—knows as the **four legals**—effectively prevent payment of the check:

1. Receipt of a notice affecting the account, such as a notice of the customer's death, adjudgment of incompetence, or bankruptcy.
2. Receipt of service of a court order or other legal process that "freezes" the customer's account, such as a writ of garnishment.
3. Receipt of a stop-payment order from the drawer.
4. The payor bank's exercise of its right of setoff against the customer's account.

If one of these four legals is received before the payor bank has finished its process of posting, the check cannot be paid contrary to the legal notice or action. However, the account is not affected if the check was paid or the process of posting was completed before the notice was received. The **process of posting** is considered completed when (1) the responsible bank officer has made a decision to pay the check, and (2) the proper book entry has been made to charge the drawer's account the amount of the check.

Failure to Examine Bank Statements in a Timely Manner

Ordinarily, banks send their checking account customers monthly statements of account. The canceled checks usually accompany the statement, although banks are not required to send them. If the canceled checks are not sent to the customer, the statement of account must provide sufficient information to allow the customer to identify the checks paid (e.g., check number, amount, date of payment) [UCC 4-406(a)]. In addition, if the checks are not returned to the customer, the bank must retain either the original checks or legible copies for seven years. A customer may request the check or a copy of it during this period [UCC 4-406(b)].

The customer owes a duty to examine the statements (and canceled checks, if received) promptly and with reasonable care to determine if any payment was not authorized because of alteration of a check or a forged signature. The customer must promptly notify the bank of unauthorized payments [UCC 4-406(c)]. The customer is liable if the payor bank suffers a loss because of the customer's failure to perform these duties [UCC 4-406(d)(1)].

Liability of Collecting Banks for Their Own Negligence

The collecting bank owes a **duty to use ordinary care** in presenting and sending a check for collection, sending notices of dishonor, and taking other actions in the collection process. Failure to do so constitutes *negligence*. A collecting bank that takes proper action on a check prior to its midnight deadline is deemed to have exercised ordinary care. A bank is liable only for losses caused by its own negligence [UCC 4-202].

four legals

Four notices or actions that prevent the payment of a check if they are received by the payor bank before it has finished its process of posting the check for payment.

A banker so very careful to avoid risk would soon have no risk to avoid.

Lord MacNaghten
Bank of England v. Vaglliano Brothers (1891)

Business Brief

Banks are no longer required to return canceled checks to customers with their monthly statements. Instead, they are required to keep the check or a legible copy for seven years and to provide the check or a copy of it to customers upon request.

duty of ordinary care

Collecting banks are required to exercise ordinary care in presenting and sending checks for collection.

Contemporary Business Environment

MISSING THE "MIDNIGHT DEADLINE"—A BANK TURNS INTO A PUMPKIN

In processing checks for collection, each bank in the collection process must take proper action on the check prior to its "midnight deadline." The midnight deadline is the midnight of the next banking day following the banking day in which the bank received an "on them" item—that is, a check drawn on another bank—for collection. What happens if a bank misses its midnight deadline and the check bounces? The following case answers this question.

Robert Dean Financial (RDF), a mortgage broker, and George I. Benny, one of its clients, used Chicago Title Insurance Company (Title Company) as the escrow agent to close certain real estate transactions in which they were engaged. RDF and Benny wrote checks totaling $17 million drawn on their account at the San Mateo, California, branch office of California Canadian Bank. The checks were payable to the Title Company as payee.

The Title Company deposited the checks from RDF and Benny at its bank, the Bank of San Francisco, for collection. This bank forwarded them to Crocker Bank, which in turn forwarded them to the San Francisco home office of California Canadian Bank for presentment. The next day, the home office of California Canadian Bank sent the checks to its San Mateo branch office for payment. The San Mateo branch dishonored the checks because there were no funds in the drawer's account to pay the checks. The checks left the San Mateo branch by courier for California Canadian Bank's in-house data-processing and computer center prior to the midnight deadline, but the checks were not delivered back to Crocker Bank until the next day—after the midnight deadline.

Unfortunately, RDF and Benny were engaged in a massive check fraud operation, and as a result either the Title Company or California Canadian Bank would end up bearing the loss. Litigation ensued between these two parties. The court held that California Canadian Bank should bear the loss because it failed to return the dishonored checks to Crocker Bank before the midnight deadline prescribed by the UCC. With interest, the judgment against California Canadian Bank totaled $25 million. That is a high price to pay for being one day late in returning bounced checks! [*Chicago Title Insurance Company v. California Canadian Bank*, 1 Cal.App. 4th 798, 2 Cal.Rptr.2d 422 (Cal.App. 1992)]

Beijing, China   The financing of international trade is made easier by the fast same-day use of commercial wire transfers. Trillions of dollars are transferred each day between banks and business in different countries to pay for the sale of goods and services.

ℰ-Commerce & Information Technology

COMMERCIAL WIRE TRANSFERS

Commercial or **wholesale wire transfers** are often used to transfer payments between businesses and financial institutions. Trillions of dollars per day are transferred over the two principal wire payment systems—the **Federal Reserve wire transfer network (Fedwire)** and the **New York Clearing House Interbank Payments System (CHIPS)**. A wire transfer often involves a large amount of money (multimillion-dollar transactions are commonplace). The benefits of using wire transfers are their speed—most transfers are completed in the same day—and low cost. Banks sometimes require a customer to pay for a fund transfer in advance. On other occasions, however, a bank will extend credit to a customer and pay the fund transfer. The customer is liable to pay the bank for any properly paid fund transfer.

Article 4A—Fund Transfers of the UCC, which was promulgated in 1989, governs wholesale wire transfers. Most states have adopted this article. Where adopted, Article 4A governs the rights and obligations between parties to a fund transfer unless they have entered into a contrary agreement. Article 4A applies only to *commercial* electronic fund transfers; consumer electronic fund transfers subject to the Electronic Fund Transfer Act are not subject to Article 4A.

Fund transfers are not complex transactions. For example, suppose Diebold Corporation wants to pay Bethlehem Steel for supplies it purchased. Instead of delivering a negotiable instrument such as a check to Bethlehem, Diebold instructs its bank to wire the funds to Bethlehem's bank with instructions to credit Bethlehem's account. Diebold's order is called a *payment order*. Diebold is the *originator* of the wire transfer and Bethlehem is the *beneficiary*. Diebold's bank is called the *originator's bank* and Bethlehem's bank is called the *beneficiary's bank*. In more complex transactions, there may be one or more additional banks known as *intermediary banks* between the originator's bank and the beneficiary's bank [UCC 4A-103(a)].

If a receiving bank mistakenly pays a greater amount to the beneficiary than ordered, the originator is liable for only the amount he or she instructed to be paid. The receiving bank that erred has the burden of recovering any overpayment from the beneficiary [UCC 4A-303(a)]. If a wrong beneficiary is paid, the originator is not obliged to pay his or her payment order. The bank that issued the erroneous payment order has the burden of recovering the payment from the improper beneficiary [UCC 4A-303(c)].

Banks and customers usually establish security procedures (e.g., codes, identifying numbers, or words) to prevent unauthorized electronic payment orders. To protect the

bank from liability for unauthorized payment orders, the security procedure must be commercially reasonable. If the bank verifies the authenticity of a payment order by complying with such a security procedure and pays the order, the customer is bound to pay the order even if it was not authorized [UCC 4A-202]. The customer is not liable if it can prove that the unauthorized order was not initiated by an employee or other agent or by a person who obtained that information from a source controlled by the customer [UCC 4A-203].

CHAPTER SUMMARY

The Bank–Customer Relationship, p. 510

The Bank–Customer Relationship	1. *Creditor–debtor relationship.* Occurs when a customer (the *depositor*) deposits money into his or her account at a financial institution. In effect, the customer is loaning money to the financial institution. The customer is the *creditor* and the financial institution is the *debtor*. 2. *Principal–agent relationship.* Occurs when a customer writes a check against his or her checking account or deposits a check into his or her account for collection by the financial institution. The customer is the *principal* and the financial institution is the *agent*.

The Uniform Commercial Code, p. 510

The Uniform Commercial Code	The following *articles* of the Uniform Commercial Code (UCC) govern the creation, collection, and enforcement of checks and wire transfers: 1. *Article 3.* Sets forth the requirements for creating a negotiable instrument, including checks. *Revised Article 3* was promulgated in 1990. 2. *Article 4.* Establishes rules and principles that regulate the deposit and collection of *checks* by the banking system. 3. *Article 4A.* Article of the UCC promulgated in 1989 that establishes rules and principles regulating the creation and collection of and liability for *wire transfers*.

Ordinary Checks, p. 511

Ordinary Checks	1. *Check.* An order by a checking account holder (the *drawer*) to the financial institution at which the account is located (the *drawee*) to pay a named person (the *payee*) the amount of the check. 2. *Drawer.* The checking account holder and writer of the check. 3. *Drawee.* The financial institution on which the check is drawn. 4. *Payee.* The party to whom the check is written.

Special Types of Checks, p. 512

Special Types of Checks	*Bank checks.* Special types of checks for which the bank is solely or primarily liable. *Bank checks* include certified checks, cashier's checks, and traveler's checks. These bank checks are considered "as good as cash" because the issuing bank has guaranteed their payment.
Certified Check	A type of check where a bank agrees in advance (*certifies*) to accept and pay the check when it is presented for payment. Occurs when the issuer or holder takes an ordinary check to the bank and the bank writes "certified" on the check. The bank sets aside funds from the issuer's account to pay the check when it is presented for payment.

Cashier's Check	A check issued by a bank where a person pays the bank the amount of the check and a fee, and the bank guarantees that it will pay the check when it is presented for payment. The person purchasing a cashier's check does not have to have a checking account at the bank.
Traveler's Check	A form of check sold by banks and other issuers. The purchaser of the traveler's checks signs them at the time of purchase. When the checks are used to purchase goods or services, the purchaser again signs the check and fills in the payee's name. Purchasers of traveler's checks do not have to have an account at the issuing bank.

Honoring Checks, p. 515

Honoring Checks	*Honor.* When a drawee bank receives a properly drawn check and there are sufficient funds in the drawer's account to pay the check, the bank must *honor* the check and pay it.
Stale Check	A check that has been outstanding for more than six months before it is presented for payment. *Payment of a stale check.* A bank is under no obligation to pay a stale check. A bank that pays a stale check in good faith may charge the drawer's account.
Incomplete Check	A check that omits certain information, such as the amount of the check or the payee's name. *Payment of an incomplete check.* A bank may pay an incomplete check *as completed* by the payee as long as it acts in good faith and without notice that the completion was improper.
Death or Incompetence of a Drawer	1. *Death of drawer.* A bank may pay or certify checks drawn on a deceased customer's account for 10 days after receiving actual notice of the customer's death unless a person claiming an interest in the account (e.g., heir or taxing authority) stops payment on the checks. 2. *Incompetence of drawer.* A bank may pay checks of a customer adjudicated incompetent until the bank has received actual notice of the customer's adjudication of incompetence.
Stop-Payment Orders	An order by a drawer of a check to the payor bank not to pay or certify a check. An oral stop-payment order is binding on the bank for only 14 days; a written stop-payment order is binding for six months and may be renewed for additional six-month periods. *Payment over a stop-payment order.* If the payor bank fails to honor a stop-payment order and pays the check, it must recredit the customer's account the amount paid. The bank is subrogated to the rights of the drawer.
Overdraft	*Insufficient funds.* Occurs when a drawer does not have sufficient funds in his or her account to cover a check the drawer has written. The check is said to have "bounced." *Overdraft.* When a check is presented for payment and there are insufficient funds in the drawer's account to pay the check, the payor bank may either (1) dishonor the check or (2) honor the check and create an *overdraft* in the drawer's account. The bank can later charge the drawer's account the amount of the overdraft or sue the drawer to recover this amount.
Postdated Check	A check that is dated with a date in the future. *Payment of a postdated check.* A bank may pay a postdated check and charge the drawer's account, even though payment is made before the date on the check, *unless* the drawer has given the bank *separate notice* (notice in addition to the date on the check) stating not to pay the postdated check until its date and describing the check with reasonable certainty. Oral notice is good for 14 days and written notice is good for six months, which may be renewed for additional six-month periods. A bank that pays a postdated check over such notice is liable for damages resulting therefrom.
Wrongful Dishonor	Occurs when a payor bank dishonors a drawer's properly payable check when it is presented for payment even though there are sufficient funds in the account to honor the check. *Liability for wrongful dishonor.* The payor bank is liable to the drawer for damages proximately caused by the wrongful dishonor of a check plus consequential damages and damages caused by criminal prosecution.

Forged Signatures and Altered Checks, p. 517

Forged Signature of the Drawer	1. *Forged instrument.* A check on which the *drawer's signature* has been forged.
	 2. *Liability on a forged instrument:*
	   a. *Drawer.* A forged signature is wholly inoperative as the signature of the drawer. Therefore, the drawer is not liable on a forged instrument, and the bank cannot charge the drawer's account the amount paid. If the bank has charged the drawer's account, the account must be recredited.
	   b. *Forger.* The forger is liable on the check because the forged signature acts as the forger's signature.

  c. *Prior transferors.* Prior transferors who had *knowledge* that the signature of the drawer was forged are liable on the forged instrument.

  d. *Payor bank.* A payor bank that has charged the drawer's account for a forged instrument must seek recovery from the forger and prior transferors who had knowledge of the forged signature. The ultimate loss for the payment of a forged check usually falls on the payor bank (unless it can recover from the forger).

Altered Check	A check that has been altered without authorization of the drawer that modifies the legal obligation of a party.

Liability on an altered check:

1. *Drawer.* If a payor bank pays an altered check, it can charge the drawer's account the *original tenor* (original amount) of the check. The drawer is not liable for the altered amount.

2. *Forger.* The person who altered the check is liable on the check for the amount above the original tenor.

3. *Prior transferors.* The presenter of the check for payment and all prior transferors *warrant* that the check has not been altered. This is called a *presentment warranty.* Therefore, the payor bank can recover from the presenter for breach of this warranty, and each party in the chain of collection can recover from the preceding transferor based on the breach of this warranty. The ultimate loss usually falls on the party that first paid the altered check (unless that party can recover from the forger).

4. *Payor bank.* Can recover from the presenter of the altered check, any prior transferor, or the forger.

The Collection Process, p. 518

The Collection Process	1. *Bank's duty to accept deposits.* A bank owes a duty to accept deposits into a customer's account. This includes collecting checks that are drawn on other banks and made payable or indorsed to the customer.

2. *Collection process.* If a customer deposits a check drawn on another bank into his or her account at a bank, his or her bank may send the check directly to the payor bank or through other banks until it is received by the payor bank for payment.

3. *Banks in the collection process.* The *banks* that may be involved in the collection process are:

  a. *Depository bank.* The bank at which the *payee* or *holder* has an account and deposits a check into this account to be collected.

  b. *Payor bank.* The bank where the *drawer* has a checking account and that will pay the check if properly payable. (The payor bank and depository bank will be the same bank if both the drawer and the payee or holder have accounts at the same bank.).

  c. *Collecting bank.* Any bank in the collection process other than the payor bank. The depository bank is also a collecting bank.

  d. *Intermediary bank.* A bank in the collection process other than the depository and payor banks.

The Federal Reserve System	A series of 12 regional Federal Reserve banks that assist banks in the collection of checks. The Federal Reserve banks act as collecting banks by debiting and crediting the accounts of banks at the Federal Reserve banks daily to reflect the collection and payment of checks.

Deferred Posting	1. *Deferred posting rule.* Rule that allows banks to fix an afternoon hour of 2:00 P.M. or later as a *cutoff hour* for the purpose of processing checks. Any check or deposit received after this cutoff hour is treated as received the next banking day.

2. *Banking days.* Days that a bank is open to the public for carrying on substantially all banking functions.

Provisional Credit	Occurs when a bank in the collection process credits a customer's account with the amount of a deposited check before the check has cleared by final settlement.

Reversal of provisional credits. If a deposited check does not clear (e.g., insufficient funds, stop-payment order), all provisional credits may be reversed.

Final Settlement	Occurs when the payor bank either (1) pays the check in cash, (2) settles for the check without having a right to revoke the settlement, or (3) fails to dishonor the check within certain statutory time periods. When a check is finally settled, all provisional credits "firm up" and become final settlements.

Statutory deadlines. Article 4 established the following *statutory deadlines* for collecting and payor banks to act on checks:

a. *"On us" check.* A check that is presented for payment where the drawer and payee or holder have accounts at the *same bank.* That is, the payor bank is also the depository bank. In this case, the bank has until the opening for business on the second banking day following the receipt of the check to dishonor it. If it fails to do so, the check is considered paid.

b. *"On them" check.* A check that is presented for payment where the drawer and payee or holder have accounts at *different banks.* That is, the payor bank and the depository bank are different banks. In this case, each bank in the collection process, including the payor bank, must take proper action on the check (particularly the payor bank to dishonor the check) prior to its "midnight deadline." *Midnight deadline* is the midnight of the next banking day following the banking day on which the bank received the "on them" check for collection.

   c. *Presentment across the counter.* Occurs when a payee or holder physically presents an "on them" check for payment at the payor bank rather than using the collection process. In this case, the payor bank has until the end of that banking day to dishonor the check. If it fails to do so, it must pay the check.

The "Four Legals" That Prevent Payment of a Check	Four notices or actions that prevent the payment of a check if they are received by the payor bank before it has finished its *process of posting* the check for payment. The four legals are: 1. Receipt of a notice affecting the account, such as a notice of the customer's death, adjudgment of incompetence, or bankruptcy 2. Receipt of service of a court order or other legal process that "freezes" the customer's account, such as a writ of garnishment 3. Receipt of a stop-payment order from the drawer 4. The payor bank's exercise of its right of *setoff* against the customer's account
Failure to Examine Bank Statements in a Timely Manner	1. *Duty to examine bank statements.* A bank customer owes a duty to examine bank statements (and canceled checks, if received) *promptly* and with *reasonable care* to determine if any payment was not authorized because of the forged signature of the customer or alteration of a check. The customer must notify the bank of unauthorized payments. 2. *Failure to examine bank statements.* A customer who fails to examine bank statements promptly and reasonably and notify the bank of unauthorized payments is liable for any losses suffered by the bank because of this failure. 3. *Series of forgeries or alterations.* If the *same wrongdoer* engages in a series of forgeries or alterations on the same account, the customer must report that to the payor bank within a reasonable period of time, not exceeding 30 calendar days from the date that the bank statement was made available to the customer. The customer's failure to do so discharges the bank from liability on all similar forged or altered checks after this date and prior to notification.
Liability of Collecting Banks for Their Own Negligence	1. *Duty of ordinary care.* Collecting banks are required to exercise *ordinary care* in presenting for and sending checks for collection. 2. *Liability for negligence.* A collecting bank that fails to exercise ordinary care in the collection of checks is negligent. A collecting bank is liable for losses caused by its *negligence* in the collection process.

Commercial Wire Transfers, p. 522

Commercial Wire Transfers	The transfer of funds electronically by wire between business and financial institutions. 1. *Wire payment systems.* The two principal wire payment systems in this country are the Federal Reserve wire transfer network (*Fedwire*) and the New York Clearing House Interbank Payments Systems (*CHIPS*). 2. *Article 4A of the UCC.* Article of the UCC that governs the creation of, transfer, and collection of and liability for commercial wire transfers.

*E*ND-OF-*C*HAPTER *I*NTERNET *E*XERCISES AND *C*ASE *Q*UESTIONS

Working the Web Internet Exercises

ACTIVITIES

1. Go to the FAQ page of the Federal Reserve site, **www.frbsf.org/tools/faq.html**. Confirm your understanding of how the banking system works.

2. Which article of the UCC provides for provisional credit? See **www.law.cornell.edu/uniform/ucc.html**.

3. Which section of 15 U.S. C. 1693 protects credit card holders with the $50 charge limitation on lost or stolen cards? See "LII: Law About . . . Banking" at **www.law.cornell.edu/topics/banking.html**. For an overview of banking law with links to key primary and secondary sources.

CRITICAL LEGAL THINKING CASES

21.1 Cashier's Check In October 1978, Dr. Graham Wood purchased a cashier's check in the amount of $6,000 from Central Bank of the South (Bank). The check was made payable to Ken Walker and was delivered to him. In September 1979, Bank's branch manager informed Wood that the cashier's check was still outstanding. Wood subsequently signed a form requesting that payment be stopped and a replacement check issued. He also agreed to indemnify Bank for any damages resulting from the issuance of the replacement check. Bank issued a replacement check to Wood. In April 1980, Walker deposited the original cashier's check in his bank, which was paid by Bank. Bank requested that Woods repay the bank $6,000. When he refused, Bank sued Woods to recover this amount. Who wins? [*Wood v. Central Bank of the South*, 435 So.2d 1287 (Ala. App. 1982)]

21.2 Overdraft Louise Kalbe maintained a checking account at the Pulaski State Bank (Bank) in Wisconsin. In December 1981, Kalbe made out a check for $7,260.00 payable in cash. Thereafter, she misplaced it but did not report the missing check to the bank or stop payment on it. In January 1982, some unknown person presented the check to a Florida bank for payment. The Florida bank paid the check and sent it to the Bank for collection. Bank paid the check even though it created a $6,542.12 overdraft in Kalbe's account. Bank requested Kalbe pay this amount. When she refused, Bank sued Kalbe to collect the overdraft. Who wins? [*Pulaski State Bank v. Kalbe* 364 N.W.2d 162 (Wis. App. 1985)]

21.3 Wrongful Dishonor Larry J. Goodwin and his wife maintained a checking and savings account at City National Bank of Fort Smith (Bank). Bank also had a customer named Larry K. Goodwin. In November 1985, two loans of Larry K. Goodwin were in default. Bank mistakenly took money from Larry J. Goodwin's checking account to pay the loans. On Saturday, November 30, 1985, the Goodwins received written notice that four of their checks, which were written to merchants, had been dishonored for insufficient funds. When the Goodwins investigated, they discovered that their checking account balance was zero and the bank had placed their savings account on hold. After being informed of the error, Bank promised to send letters of apology to the four merchants and to correct the error. Bank, however, subsequently "bounced" several other checks of the Goodwins. Eventually, Bank notified all the parties of its error. On January 14, 1986, the Goodwins closed their accounts at Bank and were paid the correct balances due. They sued the bank for consequential and punitive damages for wrongful dishonor. Who wins? [*City National Bank of Fort Smith v. Goodwin*, 783 S.W.2d 335 (AK 1990)]

21.4 Stale Check On June 30, 1972, Charles Ragusa & Son (Ragusa), a partnership consisting of Charles and Michael Ragusa, issued a check in the amount of $5,000 payable to Southern Masonry, Inc. (Southern). The check was drawn on Community State Bank (Bank). Several days later, Southern

informed Ragusa that the check had been lost. Ragusa issued a replacement check for the same amount and sent it to Southern, which was cashed. At the same time, Ragusa gave a verbal stop payment to Bank regarding the original check. In July 1975, the original check was deposited by Southern into its account at the Bank of New Orleans. When the check was presented to Bank, it paid it and charged $5,000 against Ragusa's account. The partnership was not made aware of this transaction until August 4, 1975, when it received its monthly bank statement. Ragusa demanded that Bank recredit its account $5,000. When Bank refused to do so, Ragusa sued. Who wins? [*Charles Ragusa & Son v. Community State Bank*, 360 So.2d 231 (La. App. 1978)]

21.5 Postdated Check David Siegel maintained a checking account with the New England Merchants National Bank (Bank). On September 14, 1973, Siegel drew and delivered a $20,000 check payable to Peter Peters. The check was dated November 14, 1973. Peters immediately deposited the check in his own bank, which forwarded it for collection. On September 17, 1973, Bank paid the check and charged it against Siegel's account. Siegel discovered that the check had been paid when another of his checks was returned for insufficient funds. Siegel informed Bank that the check to Peters was postdated November 14 and requested that the bank return the $20,000 to his account. When Bank refused, Siegel sued for wrongful debit of his account. Must Bank recredit Siegel's account? [*Siegel v. New England Merchants National Bank*, 437 N.E.2d 218 (Mass.Sup. 1982)]

21.6 Stop Payment Dynamite Enterprises, Inc. (Dynamite), a corporation doing business in Florida, maintained a checking account at Eagle National Bank of Miami (Bank). Sometime in 1985, Dynamite drew a check on this account payable to one of its business associates. Before the check had been cashed or deposited, Dynamite issued a written stop-payment order to the Bank. Bank informed Dynamite that it would not place a stop-payment order on the check because there were insufficient funds in the account to pay the check. Several weeks later the check was presented to Bank for payment. By this time, sufficient funds had been deposited in the account to pay the check. Bank paid the check and charged Dynamite's account. When Dynamite learned that the check had been paid, it requested Bank to recredit its account. When Bank refused, Dynamite sued to recover the amount of the check. Who wins? [*Dynamite Enterprises, Inc. v. Eagle National Bank of Miami*, 517 So.2d 112 (Fla. App. 1987)]

21.7 Examining Bank Statements Mr. Gennone maintained a checking account at Peoples National Bank & Trust Company of Pennsylvania (Bank). In June 1965, Gennone noticed that he was not receiving his bank statements and canceled checks. When Gennone contacted Bank, he was informed that the statements had been mailed to him. Bank agreed to hold future statements so that he could pick them up in person. Gennone picked up the statements, but did not reconcile the balance of the account. As a result, it was not until

March 1967 that he discovered that beginning in January 1966 his wife had forged his signature on 25 checks. Gennone requested Bank to reimburse him for the amount of these checks. When Bank refused, Gennone sued Bank to recover. Who wins? [*Gennone v. Peoples National Bank & Trust Co.,* 9 UCC Rep.Serv. 707 (PA 1971)]

21.8 Deferred Posting   Dr. Robert L. Pracht received a check in the amount of $6,571.25 from Northwest Feedyards in payment for three loads of corn. The check was drawn on a checking account at Oklahoma State Bank (Bank). Pracht also maintained an account at the bank. On Friday, January 17, 1975, Pracht indorsed the check and gave it to an associate to deposit to Pracht's account at the bank. When the associate arrived at the bank around 3:00 P.M., he discovered that the bank's doors were locked. After gaining the attention of a bank employee, the associate was allowed into the bank, where he gave the check and deposit slip to a teller. Because the bank's computer had shut down at 3:00 P.M., the teller put the check aside. The associate testified that several bank employees were working at their desks as he left the bank. The bank was not open on Saturday or Sunday. On Monday, January 20, 1975, Bank dishonored the check due to insufficient funds. Pracht sued to recover the amount of the check from Bank. Who wins? [*Pracht v. Oklahoma State Bank,* 26 UCC Rep. Serv. 141 (OK 1979)]

21.9 Right of Setoff   On November 28, 1978, States Steamship Company (States Steamship) drew a check for $35,948 on its checking account at Crocker National Bank (Crocker). The check was made payable to Nautilus Leasing Services, Inc. (Nautilus). Nautilus deposited the check in its account at Chartered Bank of London, which forwarded the check to Crocker for collection. The check was received at Crocker's processing center at 8:00 A.M. on Friday, December 1, 1978.

At the time the check was presented for payment, States Steamship was indebted to Crocker for loans in the amount of $2 million. These loans were payable on demand. During the latter part of 1978, States Steamship was in severe financial difficulty and was conducting merger negotiations with another steamship company. On the morning of Monday, December 4, 1978, Crocker learned that these merger negotiations had broken down and demanded immediate payment of the $2 million. Crocker then seized the $1,726,032 in States Steamship's checking account at the bank. This action left State Steamship's account with a zero balance. State Steamship's check to Nautilus, as well as other checks that had been presented for payment, were returned unpaid. Nautilus sued Crocker to recover the amount of the check. Who wins? [*Nautilus Leasing Services, Inc. v. Crocker National Bank,* 195 Cal.Rptr. 478 (Cal. App. 1983)]

BUSINESS ETHICS CASES

21.10 Business Ethics   In 1982, Actors Equity, a union that represents 37,000 stage actors, sought to hire a new comptroller. A man named Nicholas Scotti applied for the position and submitted an extensive resume showing that he was currently employed by Paris Maintenance Company as its comptroller. Scotti also stated that he had held various financial positions with the Equitable Life Assurance Society and the Investors Funding Corporation. Officers of Actors Equity interviewed Scotti and offered him the job. No attempt was made to verify Scotti's background or prior employment history.

Actors Equity maintained a checking account at the Bank of New York. During the first six months as comptroller, Scotti forged the signature of the appropriate company employee on four Actors Equity checks totaling $100,000. The checks were made payable to N. Piscotti and were cashed by Scotti and paid by the Bank of New York. The forged signatures were of professional quality. After Scotti resigned as comptroller, the forgeries were discovered. Subsequent investigation revealed that Scotti's real name was Piscotti, that the information on his resume was false, and that he had an extensive criminal record. Actors Equity sued the drawee bank to recover the $100,000. Did Scotti act ethically in this case? Should Actors Equity have sued the bank to recover on the forged checks? Who wins? [*Fireman's Fund Insurance Co. v. The Bank of New York,* 539 N.Y.S.2d 339 (N.Y.Sup. 1989)]

21.11 Business Ethics   Golden Gulf, Inc. (Golden Gulf), opened a checking account at AmSouth Bank, N.A. (AmSouth). On August 27, 1988, Golden Gulf entered into a subscription agreement wherein Albert M. Rossini agreed to pay $250,000 for stock in the company. Rossini tendered a check drawn on the Mark Twain Bank in Kansas City, Missouri, to Golden Gulf for that amount. Golden Gulf deposited the check in its checking account at AmSouth on August 30, 1988. On September 2, 1988, Golden Gulf contacted AmSouth and asked if the funds were "available." AmSouth said the funds were available for use. Golden Gulf requested AmSouth to wire transfer the funds to it in New York for use in that state. AmSouth complied with the request. On September 7, 1988, AmSouth received notice from the Mark Twain Bank that Rossini's check would not be paid due to insufficient funds. On September 8, 1988, AmSouth notified Golden Gulf that the check had been dishonored. AmSouth revoked the credit it had given to Golden Gulf's account, resulting in an overdraft of $248,965.69. AmSouth sued to recover this amount. Did Golden Gulf act ethically in this case? Did AmSouth extend a provisional or final settlement to Golden Gulf's account? [*Golden Gulf, Inc. v. AmSouth Bank, N.A.,* 565 So.2d 114 (AL 1990)]

BRIEFING THE CASE WRITING ASSIGNMENT

Read the following case, which has been excerpted from the court's opinion. Review and brief the case.

First American Bank and Trust v. Rishoi
553 So.2d 1387 (Fla. App. 5 Dist. 1990)
District Court of Appeals of Florida

Daniel, Chief Judge

First American Bank and Trust appeals a summary judgment in favor of William M. Rishoi as receiver for Clara Lamstein and the business she operated under the name of Interamerican Business Consultants and Associates, Inc.

In Crosby v. Lewis, *the Crosbys had purchased $180,000 in cashier's checks, payable to Lamstein, from various banks and financial institutions. The checks were all delivered to Lamstein as investments. Lamstein's business was later closed down by the State on the ground that it was an illegal "ponzi" or pyramid scheme. The assets of the business were placed in the control of Rishoi as receiver. Eighty thousand dollars of the cashier's checks from the Crosbys had been cashed and deposited by Lamstein prior to the receivership. However, one hundred thousand dollars in cashier's checks remained uncashed in Lamstein's possession. The Crosbys requested that the banks not pay the cashier's checks. The banks issued stop payment orders on the outstanding cashier's checks and subsequently dishonored the checks when presented by the receiver for payment.*

Although the issuing banks were not parties to that action, this court stated:

The banks which issued the cashier's checks are primarily liable to the receiver, and by refusing to honor the checks, they have prima facie violated the duties imposed on them.

Rishoi thereafter instituted suit against First American Bank and Trust claiming that the bank had improperly refused to honor the cashier's checks.

The court below concluded that the bank had no right to stop payment on the cashier's checks and entered summary judgment in favor of Rishoi.

On appeal, the bank argues that Rishoi is not a holder in due course and therefore it was justified in refusing to honor the cashier's checks. The bank acknowledges that a cashier's check presented by a holder in due course may not be countermanded after issue. It also acknowledges that cashier's checks are treated as the next best thing to cash in the business community. On public policy grounds, however, the bank urges that it should be able to assist its customers by stopping payment on a cashier's check which has been obtained from a customer by a criminal act.

In Warren Finance, Inc. v. Barnett Bank of Jacksonville, N.A., *552 So.2d 194 (FL 1989), the Florida Supreme Court recently held that, in accordance with common commercial practice and the use of a cashier's check as a cash substitute, any defenses which a bank may assert to avoid payment must be narrowly limited. The court concluded that, upon presentment for payment by a holder, a bank may only assert its real and personal defenses in order to refuse payment on a cashier's check issued by the bank. The bank may not, however, rely on a third party's defenses to refuse payment. The only inquiry a bank may make on presentment of a cashier's check is whether the payee or indorsee is in fact a legitimate holder, that is, whether the cashier's check is being presented by a thief or one who simply found a lost check, or whether the check has been materially altered. The court concluded that this approach maintains the validity and use of cashier's checks yet acknowledges the valid concerns of banks.*

In the present case, the receiver was a legitimate holder and the bank had no real or personal defenses to assert against his claim for payment. Thus, the bank wrongfully dishonored its own obligation and is liable for payment. Accordingly, the trial court properly entered summary judgment in favor of the receiver.

AFFIRMED.

Chapter

22

Credit and Secured Transactions

Creditors have better memories than debtors.

—Benjamin Franklin
Poor Richard's Almanack
(1758)

Chapter Objectives

After studying this chapter, you should be able to:

1. Distinguish between unsecured and secured credit.

2. Define a secured transaction in personal property.

3. Describe the scope of Article 9 of the UCC.

4. Define the floating-lien concept.

5. Describe the perfection of a security interest by filing a financing statement.

6. Describe the perfection of a security interest by methods other than by filing a financing statement.

7. Define a purchase money security interest.

8. Identify limits on self-help in repossessing collateral.

9. Define and distinguish between surety and guaranty contracts.

10. Describe how Revised Article 9 recognizes electronic commerce.

Chapter Contents

The American economy is a credit economy. Consumers borrow money to make major purchases (e.g., homes, automobiles, and appliances) and use credit cards (e.g., VISA or MasterCard) to purchase goods and services at restaurants, clothing stores, and the like. Businesses use credit to purchase equipment, supplies, and other goods and services. In a credit transaction, the borrower is the **debtor** and the lender is the **creditor**.

Because lenders are reluctant to loan large sums of money simply on the borrower's promise to repay, many of them take a *security interest* either in the item purchased or some other property of the debtor. The property in which the security interest is taken is called *collateral*. If the debtor does not pay the debt, the creditor can foreclose on and recover the collateral.

A lender who is unsure whether a debtor will have sufficient income or assets to repay a loan may require another person to guarantee payment. If the borrower fails to repay the loan, that person is responsible for paying it. This responsibility is called *suretyship*.

This chapter discusses types of credit, secured transactions in personal property, and suretyship.

Types of Credit

Credit may be extended on either an *unsecured* or *secured* basis. The following paragraphs discuss these types of credit.

Unsecured Credit

Unsecured credit does not require any security (collateral) to protect the payment of the debt. Instead, the creditor relies on the debtor's promise to repay the principal (plus an interest) when it is due. If the debtor fails to make the payments, the creditor may bring legal action and obtain a judgment against him or her. If the debtor is *judgment-proof* (i.e., has little or no property or no income that can be garnished), the creditor may never collect.

Secured Credit

To minimize the risk associated with extending unsecured credit, a creditor may require a security interest in the debtor's property (collateral). The collateral secures payment of the loan. This type of credit is called **secured credit**. Security interests may be taken in real, personal, intangible, and other property.

If the debtor fails to make the payments when due, the collateral may be repossessed to recover the outstanding amount. Generally, if the sale of the collateral is insufficient to repay the amount of the loan (plus any interest), the creditor may bring a lawsuit against the debtor to recover a **deficiency judgment** for the difference. Some states prohibit or limit deficiency judgments with respect to certain types of loans.

---

debtor

The borrower in a credit transaction.

creditor

The lender in a credit transaction.

Business Brief

The United States is a credit economy. Businesses and individuals use credit to purchase many goods and services.

Debt is the prolific mother of folly and of crime.

Benjamin Disraeli
Henrietta Temple *(1837)*

unsecured credit

Credit that does not require any security (collateral) to protect the payment of the debt.

Many consumer purchases are made with credit cards. This creates a debtor–creditor relationship between the consumer–borrower and the issuer of the credit card.

secured credit

Credit that requires security (collateral) that secures payment of the loan.

deficiency judgment

Judgment of a court that permits a secured lender to recover other property or income from a defaulting debtor if the collateral is insufficient to repay the unpaid loan.

Contemporary Business Environment

KLONDIKE BAR'S UNSECURED CLAIM MELTS

Generally, a creditor would rather be a secured creditor than an unsecured creditor because of the extra protection and priority status the secured position gives the creditor. The following case shows why.

Sunstate Dairy & Food Products Co. (Sunstate) distributed dairy products in Florida. It had the following two debts among its other debts:

1. On November 19, 1990, Sunstate borrowed money from Barclays Business Credit, Inc. (Barclays), and signed a security agreement granting Barclays a continuing security interest in and lien upon substantially all of Sunstate's personal property, including all of Sunstate's inventory, equipment, accounts receivable, and general intangibles then existing or thereafter acquired. Barclays perfected its security interest by filing a financing statement with the proper state government authorities.

2. On February 14, 1992, Sunstate purchased $49,512 of Klondike ice cream bars from Isaly Klondike Company

(Klondike) on credit. Klondike did not take a security interest in the ice cream bars.

On February 19, 1992, Sunstate filed for bankruptcy. At that time, Sunstate owed Barclays $10,050,766, and $47,731 of unpaid-for Klondike bars remained in Sunstate's possession. Barclays and Klondike fought over the Klondike bars. Klondike filed a motion with the court seeking to reclaim the Klondike bars. Barclays sought to enforce its security agreement and recover the Klondike bars.

The court sided with Barclays because it was a secured creditor with a perfected security interest. The court found that Klondike, as an unsecured creditor, had no legal right to reclaim the Klondike bars. Klondike was merely one of many unsecured general creditors that would receive but pennies on the dollar in Sunstate's bankruptcy. Klondike learned a costly lesson: It is better to be a secured creditor than an unsecured creditor. [*In the Matter of Sunstate Dairy & Food Products Co.*, 145 Bankr. 341, 19 U.C.C. Rep.Serv.2d 113 (Bk.M.D. Fla.)]

*S*ECURITY INTERESTS IN REAL PROPERTY

A person who owns real property who borrows money from a creditor will often be required to pledge the real property as security for the payment of the loan. Usually, an instrument called a **mortgage** is used to accomplish this. The owner-debtor is the **mortgagor** and the creditor is the **mortgagee**.

Consider This Example Suppose General Electric purchases a manufacturing plant for $10 million, pays $2 million cash as a down payment, and borrows the remaining $8 million from City Bank. To secure the loan, City Bank requires General Electric to give it a mortgage on the plant. If General Electric defaults on the loan, the bank may take action under state law to foreclose on the property.

Some state laws provide for the use of a **note *and* deed of trust** in place of a mortgage. The note is the instrument that evidences the borrower's debt to the lender; the deed of trust is the instrument that gives the creditor a security interest in the debtor's property that is pledged as collateral.

*S*ECURITY INTERESTS IN PERSONAL PROPERTY: ARTICLE 9 OF THE UCC

Article 9 of the UCC governs secured transactions in personal property. Article 9 has been adopted in one form or another by all states except Louisiana. Although there may be some variance between the states, most of the basics of Article 9 are the same.

When a creditor extends credit to a debtor and takes a security interest in some personal property of the debtor, the transaction is called a **secured transaction**. The **secured party** is the seller, lender, or other party in whose favor there is a security interest, including a party to whom accounts or chattel paper have been sold [UCC 9-105(1)].

mortgage

A collateral arrangement where a real property owner borrows money from a creditor who uses a deed as collateral for repayment of the loan.

mortgagor

The owner-debtor in a mortgage transaction.

mortgagee

The creditor in a mortgage transaction.

note and deed of trust

An alternative to a mortgage in some states.

Article 9 of the UCC

An article of the Uniform Commercial Code that governs secured transactions in personal property.

secured transaction

A transaction that is created when a creditor makes a loan to a debtor in exchange for the debtor's pledge of personal property as security.

Secured Transactions

Exhibit 22.1 illustrates a two-party secured transaction. These transactions occur, for example, when a seller sells goods to a buyer on credit and retains a security interest in the goods.

ℰXHIBIT 22.1   *Two-Party Secured Transaction*

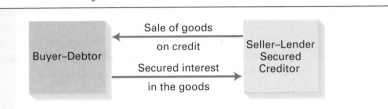

A *three-party secured transaction* is illustrated in Exhibit 22.2. This type of situation occurs where a seller sells goods to a buyer who has obtained financing from a third-party lender (e.g., bank) who takes a security interest in the goods sold.

ℰXHIBIT 22.2   *Three-Party Secured Transaction*

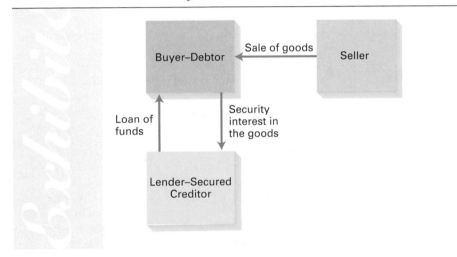

Creating a Security Interest in Personal Property

A secured party must meet the requirements discussed below to have an enforceable secured interest in collateral.

Written Security Agreement   Unless the creditor has possession of the collateral, there must be a written security agreement. To be valid, a written **security agreement** must (1) clearly describe the collateral so that it can be readily identified, (2) contain the debtor's promise to repay the creditor, including terms of repayment (e.g., the interest rate, time of payment), (3) set forth the creditor's rights upon the debtor's default, and (4) be signed by the debtor [UCC 9-203(1)].

security agreement

The agreement between the debtor and the secured party that creates or provides for a security interest.

Consider This Example   Suppose Ashley borrows $1,000 from Chris and gives Chris her gold ring as security for the loan. This agreement does not have to be in writing because the creditor is in possession of the collateral. This oral security agreement is enforceable. If Ashley retained possession of the ring, however, a written security interest describing the collateral (the ring) signed by Ashley would be required.

Value Given to the Debtor   The secured party must give value to the debtor. **Value** is defined as any consideration sufficient to support a simple contract [UCC 1-201(44)]. Normally, a creditor gives value by extending credit to the debtor to buy newly purchased goods. Value can also, however, be given as security for or in total or partial satisfaction of preexisting claims. There is no security agreement if the debtor does not owe a debt to the creditor.

Debtor Has Rights in Collateral   The debtor must have a current or future legal right in or the right to possession of the collateral. For example, a debtor may give a creditor a security interest in goods currently owned or in the possession of the debtor or in goods to be later acquired by the debtor. A debtor who does not have ownership or possessory rights to property cannot give a security interest in that property.

If these requirements are met, the rights of the secured party **attach** to the collateral. **Attachment** means that the creditor has an enforceable security interest against the debtor and can satisfy the debt out of the designated collateral (subject to priority rules discussed later in this chapter) [UCC 9-203(2)].

attachment

The creditor has an enforceable security interest against the debtor and can satisfy the debt out of the designated collateral.

Contemporary Business Environment

PERSONAL PROPERTY SUBJECT TO A SECURITY AGREEMENT

A security interest may be given in various types of **personal property**, including

- **Goods**, including (1) *consumer goods* bought or used primarily for personal, family, or household purposes, (2) *equipment* bought or used primarily for business, (3) *farm products*, including crops, livestock and supplies, used or produced in farming operations, (4) *inventory* held for sale or lease, including work in progress and materials, and (5) *fixtures* affixed to real estate so as to become part thereof.
- **Instruments**, such as checks, notes, stocks, bonds, and other investment securities.
- **Chattel paper** (i.e., a writing or writings that evidence both a monetary obligation and a security interest), such as a conditional sales contract.

- **Documents of title**, including bills of lading, warehouse receipts, and such.
- **Accounts** (i.e., any right of payment not evidenced by an instrument or chattel paper), such as accounts receivable.
- **General intangibles**, such as patents, copyrights, money franchises, royalties, and the like.

Article 9 does not apply to transactions involving real estate mortgages, landlord's liens, artisan's or mechanic's liens, liens on wages, judicial liens, and the like [UCC 9-104]. These types of liens are usually covered by other laws. Further, certain security interests governed by federal statutes are exempt from Article 9. For example, security interests in airplanes are subject to the provisions of the Federal Aviation Act.

personal property

Property that consists of tangible property such as automobiles, furniture, and jewelry; intangible property such as securities, patents, and copyrights; and instruments, chattel paper, documents of title, and accounts.

floating lien

A security interest in property that was not in the possession of the debtor when the security agreement was executed; includes *after-acquired property, future advances,* and *sale proceeds.*

after-acquired property

Property that the debtor acquires after the security agreement is executed.

The Floating-Lien Concept

A security agreement may provide that the security interest attaches to **property** that was not originally in the possession of the debtor when the agreement was executed. This interest is usually referred to as a **floating lien**. A floating lien can attach to the types of property discussed below.

After-Acquired Property   Many security agreements contain a clause that gives the secured party a security interest in **after-acquired property** of the debtor. After-acquired property is property that the debtor acquires after the security agreement is executed [UCC 9-204(1)].

Consider This Example   Manufacturing Corporation borrows $100,000 from First Bank and gives the bank a security interest in both its current and after-acquired inventory. If Manufacturing Corporation defaults on its loan to First Bank, the bank can claim any available original inventory as well as enough after-acquired inventory to satisfy its secured claim.

Sale Proceeds   Unless otherwise stated in the security agreement, if a debtor sells, exchanges, or disposes of collateral subject to such an agreement, the secured party automatically has the right to receive the **proceeds** of the sale, exchange, or disposition [UCC 9-203(3) and 9-306].

sale proceeds

The resulting assets from the sale, exchange, or disposal of collateral subject to a security agreement.

Consider This Example   Zip, Inc., is a retail automobile dealer. To finance its inventory of new automobiles, Zip borrows money from First Bank and gives the bank a security interest in the inventory. Zip sells an automobile subject to the security agreement to Phyllis, who signs an installment sales contract agreeing to pay Zip for the car in 24 equal monthly installments. If Zip defaults on its payment to First Bank, the bank is entitled to receive the remaining payments from Phyllis.

Future Advances   Often, debtors establish a continuing or revolving line of credit at a bank. Certain personal property of the debtor is designated as collateral for future loans from the line of credit. A maximum limit that the debtor may borrow is set, but the debtor can draw against the line of credit at any time. Any **future advances** made against the line of credit are subject to the security interest in the collateral. A new security agreement does not have to be executed each time a future advance is taken against the line of credit [UCC 9-204(3)].

future advances

Personal property of the debtor that is designated as collateral for future loans from a line of credit.

PERFECTING A SECURITY INTEREST

The concept of **perfection of a security interest** establishes the right of a secured creditor against other creditors who claim an interest in the collateral. Perfection is a legal process. The three main methods of perfecting a security interest under the UCC are discussed in the following paragraphs.

perfection of a security interest

Establishes the right of a secured creditor against other creditors who claim an interest in the collateral.

Perfection by Filing a Financing Statement

Often, the creditor's physical possession of the collateral is impractical because it would deprive the debtor of use of the collateral (e.g., farm equipment, industrial machinery, and consumer goods). At other times, it is simply impossible (e.g., accounts receivable). Filing a **financing statement** in the appropriate government office is the most common method of perfecting a creditor's security interest in such collateral. The person who files the financing statement should request the filing officer to note the file number, date, and hour of filing on his or her copy of the document [UCC 9-402(1)]. A financing statement covering fixtures is called a *fixture filing*.

financing statement

A document filed by a secured creditor with the appropriate government office that constructively notifies the world of his or her security interest in personal property.

Financing statements are available for review by the public. They serve as constructive notice to the world that the creditor claims an interest in the property. Financing statements are effective for five years from the date of filing. A *continuation statement* may be filed up to six months prior to the expiration of the financing statement's five-year term. Such statements are effective for a new five-year term. Succeeding continuation statements may be filed [UCC 9-403(2) and (3)].

To be enforceable, the financing statement must contain (1) the debtor's name and mailing address, (2) the name and address of the secured party from whom information concerning the security interest can be obtained, and (3) a statement (preferably exactly as shown in the security agreement) indicating the types, or describing the items, of collateral. The secured party can file the security agreement as a financing statement [UCC 9-402(1)].

State law specifies where the financing statement must be filed. The UCC provides that a state may choose either the secretary of state or the county clerk in the county of the

Business Brief

It is good practice for a creditor who plans on taking a security interest in personal property to check whether any previous financing statements have been filed concerning the property and, if not, to properly file a financing statement covering his or her interest in the property.

debtor's residence or, if the debtor is not a resident of the state, in the county where the goods are kept or other county office or both. Most states require financing statements covering farm equipment, farm products, accounts, and consumer goods to be filed with the county clerk [UCC 9-401].

In the following case, the court found there was a defective filing of the financing statement.

In re Greenbelt Cooperative, Inc.
124 Bankr. 465, 14 U.C.C.R. Serv.2d 920 (1991)
Untied States Bankruptcy Court, Maryland

CASE 22.1

BACKGROUND AND FACTS
Greenbelt Cooperative, Inc. (Greenbelt), was a consumer-owned cooperative engaged in the retail furniture business. It engaged in the business under the trade name SCAN, and it was well known among consumers by that name. On May 4, 1987, Greenbelt executed an Equipment Lease and Security Agreement with Raymond Leasing Corporation (Raymond) to lease forklifts, racking, and other items. At the conclusion of the lease term, Greenbelt could purchase the equipment for $1. On July 6, 1987, Raymond filed a financing statement covering the equipment in the proper state government office. Raymond listed "SCAN Furniture" as the debtor on the financing statement. On December 4, 1988, Greenbelt filed for bankruptcy. The bankruptcy trustee made a motion to avoid Raymond's claimed security interest in the equipment.

ISSUE
Did Raymond properly identify the debtor on the financing statement?

COURT'S REASONING
For a financing statement to be effective, the UCC requires that it be filed under the legal name of the debtor or under a name that is substantially similar to the legal name of the debtor so that it would not mislead a reasonably diligent creditor searching the financing records. The court held that a filing under SCAN Furniture would not be found by those looking for security interests in the assets of Greenbelt Cooperative, Inc. Consequently, Raymond's financing statement was not sufficient to perfect its security interests in Greenbelt's assets.

DECISION
The bankruptcy court held that Raymond failed to identify the actual debtor in its financing statement. The court voided Raymond's lien on the equipment.

Case Questions

Critical Legal Thinking   Should creditors searching financing records be required to search for financing statements filed under the debtor's trade names as well as its legal name?

Business Ethics   Did the bankruptcy trustee act ethically in avoiding the secured creditor's security interest?

Contemporary Business   Was the filing of the financing statement under the wrong name an error that could have easily been prevented?

Perfection by Possession of Collateral

perfection by possession of the collateral

If a secured creditor has physical possession of the collateral, no financing statement has to be filed; the creditor's possession is sufficient to put other potential creditors on notice of his or her secured interest in the property.

No financing statement has to be filed if the creditor has physical **possession of the collateral**. The rationale behind this rule is that if someone other than the debtor is in possession of the property, a potential creditor is on notice that another may claim an interest in the debtor's property. A secured creditor who holds the debtor's property as collateral must use reasonable care in its custody and preservation [UCC 9-207].

Consider This Example   Suppose Karen borrows $3,000 from Alan and gives her motorcycle to him as security for the loan. Another creditor obtains a judgment against Karen. This creditor cannot recover the motorcycle from Alan. Even though Alan has not filed a financing statement, his security interest in the motorcycle is perfected because he has possession of the motorcycle.

Generally, a security interest in money and most negotiable instruments can be perfected only by taking possession of the collateral. A security interest in negotiable documents is temporarily perfected for 21 days without filing a financing statement or taking possession of the documents or instruments [UCC 9-304(4) and (5)].

Businesses often purchase goods on credit from suppliers. A supplier often takes a security interest in personal property to secure the loan, such as the inventory in this store.

Perfection by a Purchase Money Security Interest in Consumer Goods

Sellers and lenders often extend credit to consumers to purchase consumer goods. **Consumer goods** include furniture, television sets, stereos, home appliances, and other goods used primarily for personal, family, or household purposes.

A creditor who extends credit to a consumer to purchase a consumer good under a written security agreement obtains a **purchase money security interest** in the good. This agreement automatically perfects the creditor's security interest at the time of the sale. The creditor does not have to file a financing statement or take possession of the goods to perfect his or her security interest. This interest is called **perfection by attachment** or the **automatic perfection rule**.

Two types of consumer goods are excepted from this rule. Financing statements must be filed to perfect a security interest in motor vehicles and fixtures [UCC 9-302(1)(d)].

purchase money security interest

An interest a creditor automatically obtains when it extends credit to a consumer to purchase consumer goods.

Consider This Example Assume that Marcia buys a $3,000 large-screen television for her home on credit extended by the seller, Circuit City. Circuit City requires Marcia to sign a security agreement. Circuit City has a purchase money security interest in the television that is automatically perfected at the time of the credit sale. Now suppose Marcia borrowed the money from Country Bank to buy the television for cash from Circuit City. If the bank required Marcia to sign a security agreement, its security interest in the television is automatically perfected at the time Marcia buys the television from Circuit City.

In the following case, the court had to decide whether a purchase money security interest had been created.

In re Phillips
55 Bankr. 663 (1985)
Untied States Bankruptcy Court, Western District of Virginia

CASE 22.2

BACKGROUND AND FACTS
Charlene T. Phillips and her husband, Jacob, owned the Village Variety 5 & 10 Store in Bloomfield, Virginia. Charlene was also employed as a computer science teacher at the Wytheville Community College. On December 1, 1984, Charlene entered into a retail installment contract to purchase an IBM computer and other equipment from Holdren's, Inc. (Holdren's). The contract, which was also a security agreement, provided for

total payment of $3,175.68 in equal monthly installments of $132.32. Charlene testified that she told the salesperson at Holdren's that she was purchasing the computer equipment for use in her teaching assignments and for use at the variety store. She received a special discount price given to teachers. Holdren's did not file a financing statement regarding the computer equipment. On December 1, 1984, Holdren's assigned the installment contract to Creditway of America (Creditway). On June 26, 1985, Mr. and Mrs. Phillips filed a petition for Chapter 7 liquidation bankruptcy. The balance due and owing on the computer was $2,597.79. Creditway filed a motion with the bankruptcy court to recover the computer and equipment.

ISSUE

Is the computer and other equipment "consumer goods" in which the secured party obtained a perfected purchase money security interest?

COURT'S REASONING

If the computer goods were classified as "consumer goods," the secured creditor would not have to file a financing statement to have a perfected security interest in the collateral. In this case,

however, the court classified the goods as "equipment" because the goods were purchased for business purposes. Such classification required the secured creditor to file a financing statement to perfect its security interest, which it did not do. The secured creditor holds an unperfected security interest in the collateral.

DECISION

The bankruptcy court held that the secured creditor did not have a perfected purchase money security interest in the collateral because the collateral was equipment, not consumer goods. The court denied the secured creditor's motion to recover the collateral.

Case Questions

Critical Legal Thinking Should purchase money security interests be given priority over other security interests? Why or why not?

Business Ethics Was there any unethical conduct in this case?

Contemporary Business Are secured creditors who perfect their security interests always guaranteed of being able to be paid from the collateral upon default?

CONCEPT SUMMARY   METHODS FOR PERFECTING A SECURITY INTEREST

Perfection Method	How Created
Financing statement	Creditor files a financing statement with the appropriate government office.
Possession of collateral	Creditor obtains physical possession of the collateral.
Purchase money security interest	Creditor extends credit to a debtor to purchase consumer goods and obtains a security interest in the goods.

Contemporary Business Environment

PERFECTION OF SECURITY INTERESTS IN AUTOMOBILES

Automobiles, like many other forms of personal property, are easily movable from state to state. Under the UCC, a secured party who has properly perfected a security interest has either (1) four months after the collateral is moved to another state or (2) the period of time remaining under the perfection in the original state, whichever expires first, to perfect his or her security interest in the property in the new state. Any subsequent perfected security interest in the new state prevails if the secured party does not comply with this rule [UCC 9-103(1)(d) and 9-103(3)(e)].

Most states have enacted *state vehicle licensing statutes* that require security interests in motor vehicles to be noted on *certificates of title* to motor vehicles. In most states, these statutes take precedence over the UCC. If a security interest is not noted on a vehicle's certificate of title, and the buyer does not have knowledge of the defect in title, the buyer is permitted to rely on the ownership and registration certificates without any further inquiry—that is, without having to search for UCC financing statements.

Termination

Once a secured consumer debt is paid, the secured party must file a **termination statement** with each filing officer with whom the financing statement was filed. The termination statement must be filed within one month after the debt is paid or 10 days after receipt of the debtor's written demand, whichever occurs first. In all other cases, the secured party must either file a termination statement with each filing officer with whom the financing statement has been filed or send the termination statement to the debtor within 10 days of receipt of a written demand by the debtor. If the affected secured party fails to file or send the termination statement as required, he or she is liable to the debtor for $100. In addition, the secured party is liable for any other losses caused to the debtor [UCC 9-404(1)].

termination statement

A document filed by the secured party that ends a secured interest because the debt has been paid.

REVISED ARTICLE 9 SECURED TRANSACTIONS

In 1999, the National Conference of Commissioners on Uniform State Laws (Commissioners) promulgated **Revised Article 9 Secured Transactions** of the Uniform Commercial Code (UCC). Revised Article 9, which is the result of almost a decade of study by the Commissioners, is designed to supercede Article 9 of the UCC. Revised Article 9:

- Provides that collateral for secured transactions can include deposit accounts at banks and other financial institutions, promissory notes, permits, franchises, licenses, letters of credit, and payment intangibles where the principal obligation is monetary.
- Clarifies the law and expressly brings agricultural liens within the scope of Article 9.
- Changes the place to file for perfection purposes to the jurisdiction where the debtor is located. For a "registered

organization" such as a corporation or limited liability company (LLC), that location is the state under whose laws the debtor-organization is organized (e.g., a corporation's state of incorporation). For Article 9 purposes, an individual debtor is located at his or her principal residence.
- Allows persons other than the debtor to file a financing statement or any given record as long as the debtor authorizes the filing.

Revised Article 9 is a comprehensive proposed statute that incorporates most of the principles and concepts of the law of Article 9, and it also updates and clarifies many of these principles. The Commissioners recommend that Revised Article 9 be adopted by states to replace existing Article 9. It is expected that states will begin to enact Revised Article 9 as a state statute, either in whole or part, to replace Article 9.

PRIORITY OF CLAIMS

Often, two or more creditors claim an interest in the same collateral or property. The priority of the claims is determined according to (1) whether the claim is unsecured or secured and (2) the time at which secured claims were attached or were perfected.

UCC Rules for Determining Priority

The UCC establishes the following set of rules for determining **priority** among *conflicting claims* of creditors [UCC 9-301(1)(a), UCC 9-312(5), UCC 9-315(2)].

1. **Secured Versus Unsecured Claims** A creditor who has the only secured interest in the debtor's collateral has priority over unsecured interests.
2. **Competing Unperfected Secured Claims** If two or more secured parties claim an interest in the same collateral but neither has a perfected claim, the first to attach has priority.
3. **Perfected Versus Unperfected Claims** If two or more secured parties claim an interest in the same collateral but only one has perfected his or her security interest, the perfected security interest has priority.
4. **Competing Perfected Secured Claims** If two or more secured parties have perfected security interests in the same collateral, the first to perfect (e.g., by filing a financing statement or taking possession of the collateral) has priority.

priority

The order in which conflicting claims of creditors in the same collateral are solved.

Creditor: One of a tribe of savages dwelling beyond the Financial Straits and dreaded for their desolating excursions.

Ambrose Bierce
The Devil's Dictionary
(1911)

Business Brief

Perfection does not always protect a secured party from third-party claims. Consider the following exceptions as discussed: (1) purchase money security interests involving inventory, (2) purchase money security interests involving goods other than inventory, (3) buyers in the ordinary course of business, (4) secondhand consumer goods, (5) artisan's and mechanic's liens.

5. **Perfected Secured Claims in Fungible, Commingled Goods**   If a security interest in goods is perfected but the goods are later commingled with other goods in which there are perfected security interests and the goods become part of a product or mass and lose their identity, the security interests rank equally according to the ratio that the cost of goods to which each interest originally attached bears to the cost of the total product or mass.

Exceptions to the Perfection-Priority Rule

Perfection does not always protect a secured party from third-party claims. As discussed in the paragraphs that follow, the UCC recognizes several exceptions to the perfection-priority rule.

- **Purchase Money Security Interest: Inventory as Collateral**   Under certain circumstances, a perfected purchase money security interest prevails over perfected nonpurchase money security interests in after-acquired property. The order of perfection is irrelevant. If the collateral is inventory, the perfected purchase money security interest prevails if the purchase money secured party gives written notice of the perfection to the perfected nonpurchase money secured party before the debtor receives possession of the inventory [UCC 9-312(3)].

Consider This Example   Toy Shops, Inc., a retailer, borrows money from First Bank for working capital. In return, First Bank gets a security interest in all Toy Shops's current and after-acquired inventory. First Bank perfects its security interest by filing a financing statement. Later, Toy Shops purchases new inventory on credit from Mattel, a toy manufacturer. Mattel perfects its purchase money security interest by filing a financing statement. It notifies First Bank of this fact prior to delivery of the new inventory. Toy Shops defaults on its loans. Mattel's lien has priority.

- **Purchase Money Security Interest: Noninventory as Collateral**   If the collateral is something other than inventory, the perfected purchase money security interest would prevail over a perfected nonpurchase money security interest in after-acquired property if it was perfected before or within 10 days after the debtor receives possession of the collateral [UCC 9-312(4)].

Consider This Example   On September 1, Matco, a manufacturer, borrows money for working capital from First Bank and gives First Bank a security interest in its current and after-acquired equipment. First Bank perfects its security interest by filing a financing statement. On September 20, Matco purchases a new piece of equipment on credit from Allegheny Industries, an equipment manufacturer. On September 30, Allegheny perfects its purchase money security interest by filing a financing statement. Matco defaults on its loans. Here, Allegheny's perfected purchase money security interest prevails because the lien was perfected within 10 days after the debtor received the collateral. If Allegheny had waited until October 1 to perfect its purchase money security interest, First Bank would have prevailed.

- **Buyers in the Ordinary Course of Business**   A **buyer in the ordinary course of business** who purchases goods from a merchant takes the goods free of any perfected or unperfected security interest in the merchant's inventory even if the buyer knows of the existence of the security interest. This rule is necessary because buyers would be reluctant to purchase goods if the merchant's creditors could recover the goods if the merchant defaults on loans owed to secured creditors [UCC 9-307(1)].

Consider This Example   Suppose Central Car Sales, Inc., a new car dealership, finances all its inventory of new automobiles at First Bank. First Bank takes a security interest in Central's inventory of cars and perfects this security interest. Kim, a buyer in the ordinary course of business, purchases a car from Central for cash. The car cannot be recovered from Kim even if Central defaults on its payments to the bank.

- **Secondhand Consumer Goods**   Buyers of secondhand consumer goods take free of security interest if they do not have actual or constructive knowledge about the security interest, give value, and buy the goods for personal, family, or household purposes. The filing of a financing statement by a creditor provides constructive notice of the security interest [UCC 9-307(2)].

Consider This Example   Suppose Anne purchases a microwave oven on credit from Stearns, a retailer, to be used for household purposes. Pursuant to a security agreement, Stearns acquires an automatically perfected purchase money security interest in the oven. Suppose Stearns does not file a financing statement. Anne sells the microwave oven to her neighbor, Jeff, for cash. Anne defaults on her loan payments to Stearns. Stearns cannot recover the microwave oven from Jeff. Note, however, that Stearns could recover the oven from Jeff if it had filed a financing statement prior to the sale to Jeff.

Debt: A rope to your foot, cocklebars in your hair, and a clothespin on your tongue.

Frank McKinney Hubbard
The Roycroft Dictionary
(1923)

---

buyer in the ordinary course of business

A person who in good faith and without knowledge of another's ownership or security interest in goods buys the goods in the ordinary course of business from person in the business of selling goods of that kind [UCC 1-201(9)].

Entrepreneur and the Law

SUPER-PRIORITY LIENS

If a worker in the ordinary course of business furnishes services or materials to someone with respect to goods and receives a lien on the goods by statute or rule of law, this **artisan's** or **mechanic's lien** prevails over all other security interests in the goods unless a statutory lien provides otherwise. Thus, such liens are often called *super-priority liens* [UCC 9-310].

Consider This Example   Suppose Janice borrows money from First Bank to purchase an automobile. First Bank has a purchase money security interest in the car and files a financing statement. The automobile is involved in an accident and Janice takes the car to Joe's Repair Shop (Joe's) to be repaired. Joe's retains a mechanic's lien in the car for the amount of the repair work. When the repair work is completed, Janice refuses to pay. She also defaults on her payments to First Bank. If the car is sold to satisfy the liens, the mechanic's lien is paid in full from the proceeds before First Bank is paid anything.

DEFAULT AND REMEDIES

Article 9 defines the rights, duties, and remedies of the secured party and the debtor in the event of **default**. The term *default* is not defined. Instead, the parties are free to define it in their security agreement. Failure to make scheduled payments when due, bankruptcy of the debtor, breach of the warranty of ownership as to the collateral, and other such events are commonly defined in the security agreement as default [UCC 9-501(1)].

Upon default by the debtor, the secured party may reduce his or her claim to judgment, foreclose, or otherwise enforce his or her security interest by any available judicial procedure [UCC 9-501(1)]. The UCC provides the secured party with the remedies discussed in the following paragraphs.

Taking Possession of the Collateral

Most secured parties seek to cure a default by taking possession of the collateral. This taking is usually done by **repossessing** the goods from the defaulting debtor. After repossessing the goods, the secured party can either (1) retain the collateral or (2) sell or otherwise dispose of it and satisfy the debt from the proceeds of the sale or disposition. There is one caveat: The secured party must act in good faith, with commercial reasonableness, and with reasonable care to preserve the collateral in his or her possession [UCC 9-503].

Consider This Example   Western Drilling, Inc., purchases a piece of oil-drilling equipment on credit from Haliburton, Inc. Haliburton files a financing statement covering its security interest in the equipment. If Western Drilling fails to make the required payments, Haliburton can foreclose on its lien and repossess the equipment.

Retention of Collateral   A secured creditor who repossesses collateral may propose to **retain the collateral** in satisfaction of the debtor's obligation. Notice of the proposal must be sent to the debtor unless he or she has signed a written statement renouncing this right. In the case of consumer goods, no other notice need be given. Otherwise, notice of the proposal must be sent to any other secured party who has given written notice of a claim of interest in the collateral.

A secured creditor may not retain the collateral (and must dispose of the collateral) in the following two situations:

1. **Written Objection**   The secured party receives a written objection to the proposal from a person entitled to receive notice within 21 days after the notice was sent [UCC 9-505(2)].
2. **Consumer Goods**   The debt involves consumer goods and the debtor has paid 60 percent of the cash price or loan. In this case, the secured creditor must dispose of the goods within 90 days after taking possession of them. A consumer may renounce his or her rights under this section [UCC 9-505(1)].

A secured creditor may retain the collateral as satisfaction of the debtor's obligation if neither of the preceding two situations prevents this action.

---

default

Failure to make scheduled payments when due, bankruptcy of the debtor, breach of the warranty of ownership as to the collateral, and other events defined by the parties to constitute default.

Debtors are liars.

George Herbert
Jacula Prudentum (1651)

repossession

A right granted to a secured creditor to take possession of the collateral upon default by the debtor.

retention of collateral

If a secured creditor repossesses collateral upon a debtor's default, he or she may propose to retain the collateral in satisfaction of the debtor's obligation.

We are either debtors or creditors before we have had time to look around.

Johann Wolfgang Von Goethe
Elective Affinities, Bk. II (1808)

disposition of collateral

If a secured creditor repossesses collateral upon a debtor's default, he or she may sell, lease, or otherwise dispose of it in a commercially reasonable manner.

Disposition of Collateral   A secured party who chooses not to retain the collateral may sell, lease, or otherwise **dispose** of it in its then condition or following any commercially reasonable preparation or processing. Disposition of the collateral may be by public or private proceedings. The method, manner, time, place, and terms of the disposition must be commercially reasonable.

The secured party must notify the debtor in writing about the time and place of any public or private sale or any other intended disposition of the collateral unless the debtor has signed a statement renouncing or modifying his rights to receive such notice. In the case of consumer goods, no other notification need be sent. In other cases, the secured party must send notice to any other secured party from whom the secured party has received written notice of a claim of an interest in the collateral. Notice of the sale or disposition is not required if the collateral is perishable or threatens to decline steadily in value or is of a type customarily sold on a recognized market [UCC 9-504(3)]. Disposition discharges the security interest under which it is made as well as any subordinate security interests or liens [UCC 9-504(4)].

Words pay no debts.

William Shakespeare
Troilus and Cressida,
Act III

Proceeds from Disposition   The proceeds from a sale, lease, or other disposition of the collateral must be applied in the following order:

1. Reasonable expenses of retaking, holding, and preparing the collateral for sale, lease, or other disposition are paid first. Attorneys' fees and legal expenses may be paid if provided for in the security agreement and not prohibited by law.
2. Satisfaction of the balance of the indebtedness owed by the debtor to the secured party is next made.
3. Satisfaction of subordinate (junior) security interests whose written notifications of demand have been received before distribution of the proceeds is completed are paid third. The secured party may require subordinate security interests to furnish reasonable proof of his or her interest [UCC 9-504(1)].
4. The debtor is entitled to receive any surplus that remains [UCC 9-504(2)].

deficiency judgment

A judgment that allows a secured creditor to successfully bring a separate legal action to recover a deficiency from the debtor. Entitles the secured creditor to recover the amount of the judgment from the debtor's other property.

Deficiency Judgment   Unless otherwise agreed, if the proceeds from the disposition of the collateral are not sufficient to satisfy the debt to the secured party, the debtor is personally liable to the secured party for the deficiency. The secured party may bring an action to recover a **deficiency judgment** against the debtor. If the underlying transaction was a sale of accounts or chattel paper, the debtor is liable for any deficiency only if the security agreement so provides [UCC 9-504(2)].

Consider This Example   Sean borrows $15,000 from First Bank to purchase a new automobile. He signs a security agreement giving First Bank a purchase money security interest in the automobile. Sean defaults after making payments that reduce the debt to $13,250. First Bank repossesses the automobile and sells it at a public auction for $11,000. The selling expenses and sales commission are $1,250. This amount is deducted from the proceeds. The remaining $9,750 is applied to the $13,250 balance of the debt. Sean remains personally liable to First Bank for the $3,500 deficiency.

right of redemption

A right granted to a defaulting debtor or other secured creditor to recover the collateral from a secured creditor before he or she contracts to dispose of it or exercises his or her right to retain the collateral. Requires the redeeming party to pay the full amount of the debt and expenses caused by the debtor's default.

Redemption Rights   The debtor or another secured party may **redeem** the collateral before the priority lienholder has disposed of it, entered into a contract to dispose of it, or discharged the debtor's obligation by exercising a right to retain the collateral. The **right of redemption** may be accomplished by payment of all obligations secured by the collateral, all expenses reasonably incurred by the secured party in retaking and holding the collateral, and any attorneys' fees and legal expenses provided for in the security agreement and not prohibited by law [UCC 9-506].

Relinquishing the Security Interest and Proceeding to Judgment on the Underlying Debt

judgment on the underlying debt

A right granted to a secured creditor to relinquish his or her security interest in the collateral and sue a defaulting debtor to recover the amount of the underlying debt.

Instead of repossessing the collateral, the secured creditor may relinquish his or her security interest in the collateral and proceed to **judgment** against the debtor to recover the underlying debt. This course of action is rarely chosen unless the value of the collateral has been reduced below the amount of the secured interest and the debtor has other assets from which to satisfy the debt [UCC 9-501(1)].

Consider This Example Suppose Jack borrows $100,000 from First Bank to purchase a piece of equipment, and First Bank perfects its security interest in the equipment for this amount. Jack defaults on the loan. If the equipment has gone down in value to $60,000 at the time of default but Jack has other personal assets to satisfy the debt, it may be in the bank's best interest to relinquish its security interest and proceed to judgment on the underlying debt.

The secured party is not required to elect one of these remedies. Instead, if one remedy is unsuccessful, the secured party can move on to the next. If the collateral is documents, the secured party may proceed either as to the documents or as to the goods covered thereby [UCC 9-501(1)].

Security Agreements Covering Real and Personal Property

If a security agreement covers both real property and personal property (i.e., fixtures), the secured party may either (1) proceed against the personal property under Article 9 or (2) proceed as to both properties in accordance with the rights and remedies provided for real property under state law. If the latter course is chosen, the provisions of Article 9 do not apply [UCC 9-501(4)].

E-Commerce & Information Technology

REVISED ARTICLE 9 RECOGNIZES E-COMMERCE

Revised Article 9, which was promulgated in 1999 as a model act to replace Article 9 Secured Transactions, recognizes many aspects of e-commerce and the digital world. Some of the modern e-commerce features of Revised 9 are:

- Filing of financing statements and other records with the secretary of state, county recorder's office, or other filing office may be made electronically as well as in writing.
- To facilitate electronic filings, the debtor's signature or other authorized signature does not have to appear on the financing statement or other electronic record.
- Electronic chattel paper, which is a record consisting of information stored in an electronic medium (i.e., not

written), can be collateral of Article 9 purposes. Perfection of a security interest in electronic chattel paper may be by filing.

- The seller of software is given a purchase money security interest (PMSI) in its software that has priority over other secured interests. For example, if software with a PMSI is placed on the licensee's computer system that is subject to a security interest itself, the software PMSI takes precedence over the security interest in the computer hardware.

Revised Article 9 reflects the drafters' concern for upgrading commercial law to recognize the increased use of digital information and e-commerce.

SURETY AND GUARANTY ARRANGEMENTS

Sometimes a creditor refuses to extend credit to a debtor unless a third person agrees to become liable on the debt. The third person's credit becomes the security for the credit extended to the debtor. This relationship may be either a surety or guaranty arrangement. Each of these arrangements is discussed in the following paragraphs.

Surety Arrangement

In a strict **surety arrangement**, a third person—known as the **surety** or **codebtor**—promises to be liable for the payment of another person's debt. A person who acts as a surety is commonly called an **accommodation party** or **cosigner**. Along with the principal debtor, the surety is primarily liable for paying the principal debtor's debt when it is due.

surety arrangement

An arrangement where a third party promises to be *primarily* liable with the borrower for the payment of the borrower's debt.

surety

The third person who agrees to be liable in a surety arrangement.

The principal debtor does not have to be in default on the debt, and the creditor does not have to have exhausted all its remedies against the principal debtor before seeking payment from the surety.

Guaranty Arrangement

guaranty arrangement

An arrangement where a third party promises to be *secondarily liable* for the payment of another's debt.

guarantor

The third person who agrees to be liable in a guaranty arrangement.

In a **guaranty arrangement**, a third person (the **guarantor**) agrees to pay the debt of the principal debtor if the debtor defaults and does not pay the debt when it is due. In this type of arrangement, the guarantor is secondarily liable on the debt. In other words, the guarantor is obligated to pay the debt only if the principal debtor defaults and the creditor has attempted unsuccessfully to collect the debt from the debtor.

In the following case, the court had to decide whether there was a surety or guaranty contract.

General Motors Acceptance Corp. v. Daniels
492 A.2d 1306 (1985)
Court of Appeals of Maryland

CASE 22.3

BACKGROUND AND FACTS
In June 1981, John Daniels agreed to purchase a used automobile from Lindsay Cadillac Company (Lindsay Cadillac). Because John had a poor credit rating, his brother, Seymour, agreed to cosign with him. General Motors Acceptance Corporation (GMAC), a company engaged in the business of financing automobiles, agreed to finance the purchase. On June 23, 1981, Seymour accompanied John to Lindsay Cadillac. John signed the contract on the line designated "Buyer." Seymour signed the contract on the line designated "Co-Buyer." In May 1982, GMAC declared the contract in default. After attempting to locate the automobile for several months, GMAC brought this action against the Daniels brothers. Because service of process was never effected upon John, the case proceeded to trial against only Seymour. The trial court found that Seymour had entered into a guaranty contract and that Seymour was not liable because GMAC had not yet proceeded against John. GMAC appealed.

ISSUE
Was the contract Seymour signed a guaranty or surety contract?

COURT'S REASONING
If the contract Seymour signed was a guaranty contract, he would have been only secondarily liable on his brother's loan.

This situation was not true in this case, however, because Seymour signed the contract on the line on the contract designated "Co-Buyer." The contract clearly stated that all buyers agreed to be jointly and severally liable for the purchase of the vehicle. Seymour executed the same contract as his brother, thereby making himself a party to the original contract. These facts establish the existence of a surety contract upon which Seymour became primarily liable.

DECISION
The court of appeals held that Seymour signed a surety contract and thus agreed to be primarily liable with his brother John for the purchase of the automobile. GMAC was therefore not required to proceed against John in the first instance. Reversed.

Case Questions

Critical Legal Thinking What purposes do guaranty and surety contracts serve? Explain.

Business Ethics Did Seymour act ethically in trying to avoid liability for his brother's loan?

Contemporary Business As a lender, would you rather have a third party sign as a surety or guarantor?

Defenses of a Surety or Guarantor

Business Brief

Many businesses will not sell goods and services to minors or persons with a bad credit history unless a competent adult cosigns or guarantees payment.

Generally, the defenses the principal debtor has against the creditor may also be asserted by a surety or guarantor. For example, if credit has been extended for the purchase of a piece of machinery that proves to be defective, the debtor and surety both can assert the defect as a defense to liability. The defenses of fraudulent inducement to enter into the surety or guaranty agreement and duress may also be cited as personal defenses to liability. The surety or guarantor cannot assert the debtor's incapacity (i.e., minority or insanity) or bankruptcy as a defense against liability. The surety's or guarantor's own incapacity or bankruptcy may be asserted, however.

Contemporary Business Environment

COLLECTION REMEDIES

When a debt is past due, the creditor may bring a legal action against the debtor. If the creditor is successful, the court will award a **judgment** against the debtor. The judgment will state that the debtor owes the creditor a specific sum of money. The amount usually consists of principal and interest past due on the debt, other costs resulting from the debtor's default, and court costs.

The most common collection remedies are:

1. **Attachment** A prejudgment court order that permits the seizure of the debtor's property while the lawsuit is pending. To obtain a *writ of attachment*, a creditor must follow the procedures of state law, give the debtor notice, and post a bond with the court.

2. **Execution** A postjudgment court order that permits the seizure of the debtor's property that is in the possession of the debtor. Certain property is exempt from levy (e.g., tools of trade, clothing, homestead exemption). A *writ of execution* is a court order directing the sheriff to seize the debtor's property and authorizing a judicial sale of that property. The proceeds are used to pay the credi-

tor the amount of the final judgment. Any surplus must be paid to the debtor.

3. **Garnishment** A postjudgment court order that permits the seizure of the debtor's property in the possession of third parties. The creditor (also known as the **garnishor**) must go to court to seek a *writ of garnishment*. The third person is called the **garnishee**. Common garnishees are employers who possess wages due a debtor, banks in possession of funds belonging to the debtor, and other third parties in the possession of property of the debtor.

To protect debtors from abusive and excessive garnishment actions by creditors, Congress enacted Title III of the Consumer Credit Protection Act [15 U.S.C.§ 1601 et seq.]. This law allows debtors who are subject to a writ of garnishment to retain the greater of (1) 75 percent of their weekly disposable earnings (after taxes) or (2) an amount equal to 30 hours of work paid at federal minimum wage. State law limitations on garnishment control if they are more stringent than federal law.

International Law

AVAILABILITY OF INTERNATIONAL CREDIT

Commercial banks offer some financing of international and export operations. National governments and international organizations provide credit for international investments as well. Nevertheless, businesses often find it extremely difficult to obtain credit to finance international operations. This is because international ventures and transactions are perceived as riskier than domestic transactions. Third World countries also have a hard time obtaining credit to develop their economies.

The **International Bank for Reconstruction and Development**, commonly called the **World Bank**, is a United Nations agency that finances development projects in member nations. The World Bank is primarily funded by developed nations. Projects include the building of dams, roads, power plants, and other infrastructures. In addition, the World Bank engages in direct investment in private enterprises through a combination of loans and equity investments.

Nations have also created and capitalized regional development banks that extend loans and offer loan guarantees to assist the economic development in member nations.

These include the African Development Bank, the Asian Development Bank, the Arab Fund for Economic and Social Development, the Caribbean Development Bank, the European Investment Bank, and the Inter-American Development Bank (comprised of Latin American countries).

National governments often extend credit to private businesses to stimulate export sales. For example, the **Export-Import Bank (Eximbank)** supports U.S. companies engaged in exporting by loaning overseas buyers funds at below-market rates of interest to purchase U.S.-made goods. The Eximbank also provides loan guarantees and insurance to foreign buyers of U.S. products. Credits have been extended for the purchase of agricultural products, heavy machinery, airplanes, and such. The Eximbank often works closely with commercial banks in structuring credit to foreign buyers.

As international trade continues to develop and become more important to the United States and other countries, credit will become more available to finance international investment and trade.

CHAPTER SUMMARY

Types of Credit, p. 531

Unsecured Credit	Credit that does not require any security (collateral) to protect the payment of the loan. *Recovery of unpaid loan.* If the debtor does not pay the loan, the creditor may bring a legal action and obtain a *judgment* against the debtor. The debtor is called *judgment-proof* if he or she has no money to pay the judgment.
Secured Credit	Credit that requires security (collateral) that secures the payment of the loan. *Collateral.* The property that is pledged as security for the loan.

Security Interests in Real Property, p. 532

Mortgage	1. *Mortgage.* The instrument that represents a security interest in real property. 2. *Mortgagor.* The owner-debtor who pledges his or her real property as security for a loan. 3. *Mortgagee.* The creditor who holds a security interest in the owner-debtor's real property.
Note and Deed of Trust	Some states use a note and deed of trust as an alternative to a mortgage. 1. *Note.* The instrument that evidences the debt. 2. *Deed of trust.* The instrument that gives the creditor a security interest in the owner-debtor's real property.

Security Interests in Personal Property: Article 9 of the UCC, p. 532

Article 9 of the UCC	An article of the Uniform Commercial Code that governs secured transactions in personal property.
Secured Transactions	Transactions that are created when a creditor makes a loan to a debtor in exchange for the debtor's pledge of personal property as security. 1. *Two-party secured transaction.* Where a seller sells goods to a buyer on credit and retains a security interest in the goods. 2. *Three-party secured transaction.* Where a seller sells goods to a buyer who has obtained financing from a third-party lender (e.g., bank) who takes a security interest in the goods sold.
Requirements for Creating a Security Interest	1. *Requirements* a. Written security agreement b. Value given to the debtor c. Debtor has rights in collateral If these requirements are met, the rights of the secured creditor *attach* to the collateral. 2. *Attachment.* The creditor has an enforceable security interest against the debtor and can satisfy the debt out of the designated collateral.
Personal Property Subject to a Security Agreement	1. *Goods* 2. *Instruments* (i.e., checks, notes, stocks, bonds) 3. *Chattel paper* (i.e., conditional sales contracts) 4. *Documents of title* (i.e., bills of lading, warehouse receipts) 5. *Accounts* (i.e., accounts receivable) 6. *General intangibles* (i.e., patents, copyrights, royalties, franchises)
The Floating-Lien Concept	*Floating lien.* Occurs when a security agreement provides that the security interest attaches to personal property that was not originally in the possession of the debtor when the agreement was executed. This property may include: 1. *After-acquired property.* Property acquired after the security agreement is executed. 2. *Sale proceeds.* Proceeds from the sale, exchange, or disposal of collateral subject to the security agreement. 3. *Future advances.* Personal property of the debtor that is designated as collateral for future loans taken against a line of credit.

Perfecting a Security Interest, p. 535

Perfection of a Security Interest	Establishes the right of the secured creditor against other creditors who claim an interest in the collateral. The UCC provides the following three methods of perfecting a security interest. 1. *Perfection by Filing a Financing Statement.* The creditor files a *financing statement* with the appropriate government recording office. This statement puts the world on notice of the creditor's security interest in the property. This method is the most common form of perfecting a security interest.

	2. *Perfection by Possession of Collateral.* If the creditor has physical possession of the collateral, no financing statement has to be filed. This method is the least common form of perfecting a security interest.
	3. *Perfection by a Purchase Money Security Interest in Consumer Goods.* A creditor (seller or lender) who extends credit to a consumer to purchase a *consumer good* under a written security agreement obtains a *purchase money security interest* in the goods. This agreement automatically perfects the creditor's security interest at the time of the sale. The creditor does not have to file a financing statement to perfect his or her security interest. This method is called *perfection by attachment* or the *automatic perfection rule.*
Information Requests and Certificate of Filing	*Certificate of filing.* A document that a person can request of the government filing officer that states (1) whether any presently effective financing statement naming a particular debtor is on file, (2) the date and hour of any such filing, and (3) the names and addresses of the secured parties.
Assignment, Amendment, and Release	1. *Statement of assignment.* A document that shows that the secured party has transferred all or part of his or her rights under a financing statement to another party.
	2. *Amendment.* A writing that is signed by both the debtor and the secured creditor showing that the financing statement has been amended.
	3. *Release.* A document showing that the secured creditor has released all or part of any collateral described in a financing statement.
	All these documents must be filed where the original financing statement has been filed.
Termination	*Termination statement.* A document that must be filed by a secured creditor within a specified number of days after a secured consumer debt has been paid. This statement must be filed where the original financing statement has been filed.

Priority of Claims, p. 539

UCC Rules for Determining Priority	The UCC establishes the following rules for determining *priority* among conflicting claims of creditors to the collateral:
	1. *Secured versus unsecured claims.* Secured claims have priority over unsecured claims.
	2. *Competing unperfected secured claims.* The first claim to attach has priority.
	3. *Perfected versus unperfected claims.* The perfected claim has priority.
	4. *Competing perfected secured claims.* The first to perfect has priority.
	5. *Perfected secured claims in fungible, commingled goods.* The security interests rank equally according to the ratio that the cost of goods to which each interest originally attached bears to the cost of the total product or mass.
Exceptions to the Perfection-Priority Rule	Perfection does not always protect a secured creditor from third-party claims. The UCC recognizes the following *exceptions to the perfection-priority rule.*
	1. *Purchase money security interest—collateral as inventory.* A perfected *purchase* money security interest in *inventory* prevails over a perfected *nonpurchase* money security interest in after-acquired property.
	2. *Purchase money security interest—noninventory as collateral.* A perfected *purchase* money security interest in *noninventory* prevails over a perfected *nonpurchase* money security interest in after-acquired property if it was perfected before or within 10 days after the debtor receives possession of the collateral.
	3. *Buyers in the ordinary course of business.* A buyer in the ordinary course of business who purchases goods from a merchant takes the goods free of any perfected or unperfected security interest in the merchant's inventory, even if the buyer knows of the existence of the security interest.
	4. *Secondhand consumer goods.* Buyers of secondhand consumer goods take free of security interests if they do not have actual or constructive knowledge about the security interest, give value, and buy the goods for personal, family, or household purposes.
	5. *Artisan's and mechanic's liens.* Artisan's and mechanic's liens for services or materials provided prevail over all other security interests in goods unless a statute provides otherwise.

Default and Remedies, p. 541

Default	The parties may define the actions or inactions that cause default under the agreement. These actions usually include failure to make scheduled payments when due, bankruptcy of the debtor, and breach of other terms of the agreement.
Secured Creditor's Remedies	Article 9 of the UCC provides the secured creditor with the following remedies upon the debtor's default:
Taking Possession of the Collateral	*Repossession.* The secured creditor can use self-help to take physical possession of the collateral as long as it does not cause a *breach of peace.*
	1. *Deficiency judgment.* If the proceeds from the disposition of the collateral are not sufficient to satisfy the debt, the secured party may obtain a *deficiency judgment* against the debtor holding the debtor personally liable for the difference.

	2. *Redemption rights.* The debtor may *redeem* the collateral within a statutorily stipulated period of time after repossession by payment of all obligations owed on the debt and all expenses reasonably incurred by the secured creditor in repossessing and holding the collateral.
Relinquishing the Security Interest and Proceeding to Judgment on the Underlying Debt	This course of action is usually taken only when the value of the collateral has been reduced below the amount of the secured interest and the debtor has other assets from which to satisfy the debt.

Surety and Guaranty Arrangements, p. 543

Surety and Guaranty Arrangements	Occur when a creditor refuses to extend credit to a debtor without further security and a third person agrees to provide that security by agreeing to become liable on the debt.
Surety Arrangement	A third party—called the *surety* or *codebtor*—promises to be liable for another person's debt. The surety is *primarily liable* for payment of the debt when it is due, along with the principal debtor. The creditor does not have to attempt to collect the debt from the principal debtor before demanding payment from the surety.
Guaranty Arrangement	A third party—called the *guarantor*—agrees to pay the debt of the principal debtor if the debtor *defaults* and does not pay the debt when it is due. The guarantor is *secondarily liable* and has to pay the debt only if the creditor has attempted unsuccessfully to collect the debt from the debtor.
Right of Subrogation	When a surety or guarantor has been made to pay a debt owed by the principal debtor, the surety or guarantor acquires all the creditor's rights against the debtor and may recover the amount it paid on the debtor's behalf.

Collection Remedies, p. 545

Collection Remedies	If a creditor sues a debtor or obtains a *judgment* against a debtor, the creditor can use the following collection remedies to recover from the debtor:
Attachment	A *prejudgment* court order that permits the seizure of the debtor's property while the lawsuit is pending. The creditor must follow the procedures established by state law, give the debtor notice, and post a bond with the court.
Execution	A *postjudgment* court order that permits the seizure of the debtor's property that is in the *possession of the debtor*. Certain property is exempt from levy (e.g., homestead exemption).
Garnishment	A *postjudgment* court order that permits the seizure of the debtor's property in the *possession of third parties* (e.g., wages to be paid to the debtor by his or her employer). Garnishment is subject to limitations established by federal and state law.

END-OF-CHAPTER INTERNET EXERCISES AND CASE QUESTIONS

Working the Web Internet Exercises

ACTIVITIES

1. Go to the FTC site **www.ftc.gov/bcp/menucredit.htm** and find the "Top Ten Dot Cons."

2. Check your state law. Does your state have "Assignment for the Benefit of Creditors?" See "Legal Information Institute (LII) Secured Transactions Law Overview" at **www.law.cornell.edu/topics/secured_transactions. html**.

3. Using the Cornell site **www.law.cornell.edu/topics/secured_transactions.html**, find the part of the UCC that provides for secured transactions.

4. What is the effect of a creditor having a secured interest when the debtor files for bankruptcy protection? See Secured Debt—Syllabus at **www.scu.edu/law/FacWebPage/Neustadter/courses/SecuredDebt/secureddebt.html**.

CRITICAL LEGAL THINKING CASES

22.1 Financing Statement In 1984, C&H Trucking, Inc. (C&H), borrowed $19,747.56 from S&D Petroleum Company, Inc. (S&D). S&D hired Clifton M. Tamsett to prepare a security agreement naming C&H as the debtor and giving S&D a security interest in a 1984 Mack truck. The security agreement prepared by Tamsett declared that the collateral also secured

any other indebtedness or liability of the debtor to the secured party direct or indirect, absolute or contingent, due or to become due, now existing or hereafter arising, including all future advances or loans which may be made at the option of the secured party.

Tamsett failed to file a financing statement or the executed agreement with the appropriate government office. C&H subsequently paid off the original debt, and S&D continued to extend new credit to C&H. In March 1986, when C&H owed S&D over $17,000, S&D learned that (1) C&H was insolvent, (2) the Mack truck had been sold, and (3) Tamsett had failed to file the security agreement. Does S&D have a security interest in the Mack truck? Is Tamsett liable to S&D? [*S&D Petroleum Company, Inc. v. Tamsett*, 534 N.Y.S.2d 800 (N.Y.Sup.Ct.App. 1988)]

22.2 Priority of Security Agreements On July 15, 1980, World Wide Tracers, Inc. (World Wide), sold certain of its assets and properties, including equipment, furniture, uniforms, accounts receivable, and contract rights, to Metropolitan Protection, Inc. (Metropolitan). To secure payment of the purchase price, Metropolitan executed a security agreement and financing statement in favor of World Wide. The agreement, which stated that "all of the property listed on Exhibit A (equipment, furniture, and fixtures) together with any property of the debtor acquired after July 15, 1980" was collateral, was filed with the Minnesota secretary of state on July 16, 1980.

In February 1982, State Bank (Bank) loaned money to Metropolitan, which executed a security agreement and financing statement in favor of the Bank. The Bank filed the financing statement with the Minnesota secretary of state's office on March 3, 1982. The financing statement contained the following language describing the collateral:

All accounts receivable and contract rights owned or hereafter acquired. All equipment now owned and hereafter acquired, including but not limited to, office furniture and uniforms.

When Metropolitan defaulted on its agreement with World Wide in the fall of 1982, World Wide brought suit asserting its alleged security agreement in Metropolitan's accounts receivable. The Bank filed a counterclaim, asserting its perfected security interest in Metropolitan's accounts receivable. Who wins? [*World Wide Tracers, Inc. v. Metropolitan Protection, Inc.*, 384 N.W.2d 442 (MN 1986)]

22.3 Floating Lien On March 17, 1973, Joseph H. Jones and others (debtors) borrowed money from Columbus Junction State Bank (Bank) and executed a security agreement in favor of the Bank. On March 29, 1973, the Bank perfected its security interest by filing financing statements covering "equipment,

farm products, crops, livestock, supplies, contract rights, and all accounts and proceeds thereof" with the Iowa secretary of state. On January 28, 1978, the Bank filed a continuation statement with the Iowa secretary of state. On February 10, 1983, the Bank filed a second continuation statement with the Iowa secretary of state. On January 31, 1986, the debtors filed for Chapter 7 (liquidation) bankruptcy. The bankruptcy collected $10,073 from the sale of the debtor's 1985 crops and an undetermined amount of soybeans harvested in 1986 on farmland owned by the debtors. The bankruptcy trustee claims the funds and soybeans on behalf of the bankruptcy estate. The Bank claims the funds and soybeans as a perfected secured creditor. Who wins? [*In re Jones*, 79 B.R. 839 (Bk.N.D. Iowa 1987)]

22.4 Sale Proceeds Murphy Oldsmobile, Inc. (Murphy), operated an automobile dealership that sold new and used automobiles. General Motors Acceptance Corporation (GMAC) loaned funds to Murphy to finance the purchase of new automobiles as inventory. The loan was secured by a duly perfected security agreement in all existing and after-acquired inventory and the proceeds therefrom. Section 9-306 of the New York UCC provides that a security interest in collateral continues in "identifiable proceeds." During the first week of May 1980, Murphy received checks and drafts from the sale of the secured inventory in the amount of $97,888, which it deposited in a general business checking account at Norstar Bank (Bank). During that week, Murphy defaulted on certain loans it had received from Bank. Bank exercised its right of setoff and seized the funds on deposit in Murphy's checking account. GMAC sued to enforce its security claim against these funds. Who wins? [*General Motors Acceptance Corporation v. Norstar Bank, N.A.*, 532 N.Y.S.2d 685 (N.Y.Sup.Ct. 1988)]

22.5 Property Subject to a Security Agreement In March 1982, the First National Bank of Chicago (Bank) loaned more than $6 million to J. Catton Farms, Inc. (Catton), a huge farming operation. The loan was secured by "receivables, accounts, inventory, equipment, and fixtures and the proceeds and products thereof" and "all accounts, contract rights including, without limitation, all rights under installment sales contracts and lease rights with respect to rental lands, instruments, documents, chattel paper and general intangibles in which the debtor has or hereafter acquires any right." To perfect its security interest, Bank filed the security agreement in the appropriate state or county recording office in every state in which the Catton's farms were located.

In March 1983, Catton signed a payment in kind (PIK) contract with the U.S. Department of Agriculture whereby it agreed not to plant specific crops (corn) and would receive payment in kind after the growing season. An April 30, 1983, Catton filed for Chapter 11 (reorganization) bankruptcy. Catton assigned its right to receive the payment in kind to Cargill, a large grain elevator company, in exchange for over $200,000 cash. The payment in kind was made to Cargill under the assignment. The corn received by Cargill was estimated to be worth $334,666. Bank filed a motion with the bankruptcy court to enforce its security interest against the payment in kind. Does Bank have a security interest in the payment in kind? [*J. Catton Farms, Inc. v. First National Bank of Chicago*, 779 F.2d 1242 (7th Cir. 1985)]

22.6 Moved Goods   Valley Bank has a general security interest in "all equipment" of a debtor known as Curtis Press. Rockwell International Credit Corporation (Rockwell) has a purchase money security interest in a particular item of equipment acquired by the debtor. Both security interests were duly perfected in Idaho. Generally, the purchase money security interest held by Rockwell has priority over the general security interest held by Valley Bank. A controversy arose after the debtor moved the equipment to Wyoming and then defaulted in the obligations owed to both Rockwell and Valley Bank. UCC 9-103, which has been adopted by both Idaho and Wyoming, provides that the perfection of a security interest follows the collateral into a foreign jurisdiction for a period of four months or the expiration of the perfection period, whichever is less.

Neither Rockwell nor Valley Bank reperfected their security interest in the equipment within the time requirement. Eventually, Valley Bank located the equipment in Wyoming and reperfected its security interest by taking possession of the collateral. Rockwell then belatedly reperfected its security interest by filing a continuation statement with the Wyoming secretary of state. Rockwell brought this action to recover the equipment from Valley Bank, alleging that its purchase money security interest has priority over Valley Bank's general security interest. Who wins? [*Rockwell International Credit Corporation v. Valley Bank*, 707 P.2d 517 (Idaho App. 1985)]

22.7 Priority of Security Interests   Clyde and Marlys Trees, owners of the Wine Shop, Inc., borrowed money from the American Heritage Bank & Trust Company (Bank). They personally and on behalf of the corporation, executed a promissory note, security agreement, and financing statement to Bank. Bank properly filed a security agreement and financing statement naming the Wine Shop's inventory, stock in trade, furniture, fixtures, and equipment "now owned or hereafter to be acquired" as collateral. The Trees also borrowed money from a junior lienholder, whose promissory note was secured by the same collateral. The Wine Shop subsequently defaulted on both notes. Without informing Bank, the junior lienholder took over the assets of the Wine Shop and transferred them to a corporation, O&E, Inc. Fearing that its security interest would not be adequately protected, Bank filed a motion to enforce its security interest. Can Bank enforce its security interest even though the collateral was transferred to another party? [*American Heritage Bank & Trust Company v. O&E, Inc.*, 576 P.2d 566 (Colo. App. 1978)]

22.8 Priority of Security Interests   On October 8, 1980, Paul High purchased various items of personal property and livestock from William and Marilyn McGowen (McGowens). To secure the purchase price, High granted the McGowens a security interest in the personal property and livestock. On December 18, 1980, High borrowed $86,695 from Nebraska State Bank (Bank) and signed a promissory note granting Bank a security

interest in all his farm products, including but not limited to all his livestock. On December 20, 1980, Bank perfected its security agreement by filing a financing statement with the county clerk in Dakota County, Nebraska. The McGowens perfected their security interest by filing a financing statement and security agreement with the county clerk on April 28, 1981. In 1984, High defaulted on the obligations owed to the McGowens and Bank. Whose security interest has priority? [*McGowen v. Nebraska State Bank*, 427 N.W.2d 772 (NE 1988)]

22.9 Purchase Money Security Interest   In 1974, Prior Brothers, Inc. (PBI), began financing its farming operations through Bank of California, N.A. (Bank). Bank's loans were secured by PBI's equipment and after-acquired property. On March 22, 1974, Bank filed a financing statement perfecting its security interest. On April 8, 1976, PBI contacted the International Harvester dealership in Sunnyside, Washington, about the purchase of a new tractor. A retail installment contract for a model 1066 International Harvester tractor was executed. PBI took delivery of the tractor "on approval," agreeing that if it decided to purchase the tractor it would inform the dealership of its intention and send a $6,000 down payment. On April 22, 1976, the dealership received a $6,000 check. The dealership filed a financing statement concerning the tractor on April 27, 1976. Later, when PBI went into receivership, the dealership filed a complaint asking the court to declare that its purchase money security interest in the tractor had priority over Bank's security interest. Did it? [*In the Matter of Prior Brothers, Inc.*, 632 P.2d 522 (Wash. App. 1981)]

22.10 Purchase Money Security Interest   In 1973, Sandwich State Bank (Sandwich) made general farm loans to David Klotz and Hinckley Grain Company. The loan was secured by the assets of Klotz's farm and after-acquired property. Sandwich filed a financing statement with the Kane County Recorder to perfect its security interest. Sandwich filed the necessary continuation statements so its security interest remained in effect up to and during the time of trial. On February 3, 1984, DeKalb Bank (DeKalb) loaned Klotz funds for the particular purpose of purchasing certain cattle. DeKalb filed a financing statement on February 3, 1984 to perfect its security interest in the cattle. The cattle in question all were purchased using funds loaned to Klotz by DeKalb. When Klotz defaulted on its loan to DeKalb, DeKalb sued to enforce its security interest and to recover possession of the cattle. Does DeKalb's security interest have priority over Sandwich's security interest? [*DeKalb Bank v. Klotz*, 502 N.E.2d 1256 (Ill. App. 1987)]

22.11 Buyer in the Ordinary Course of Business   Heritage Ford Lincoln Mercury, Inc. (Heritage), was in the business of selling new cars. In April 1978, Heritage entered into an agreement with Ford Motor Credit Company (Ford) whereby Ford extended a continuing line of credit to Heritage to purchase vehicles. Heritage granted Ford a purchase money security interest in all motor vehicles it owned and thereafter acquired and in all proceeds from the sale of such motor vehicles. Ford filed its financing statement with the secretary of state of Kansas on May 11, 1978. When the dealership experienced financial trouble, two Heritage officers decided to double finance certain new cars by issuing dealer papers to themselves and obtaining financing for two new cars from First National Bank & Trust Company of El Dorado (Bank). The loan proceeds were deposited in the dealership's account to help its financial difficulties. The cars were available for sale. When the dealership closed its doors and turned over the car inventory to Ford, Bank alleged that it had priority over Ford because the Heritage officers were buyers in the ordinary course of business. Who wins? [*First National Bank and Trust Company of El Dorado v. Ford Motor Credit Company*, 646 P.2d 1057 (KS 1982)]

22.12 Artisan's Lien On April 25, 1985, Ozark Financial Services (Ozark) loaned money to Lonnie and Patsy Turner to purchase a tractor truck unit. The Turners signed a security agreement giving Ozark a security interest in the tractor truck. Ozark properly filed a financing statement giving public notice of its security interest. In June 1985, the Turners took the truck to Pete & Sons Garage, Inc. (Pete & Sons), for repairs. When the Turners arrived to pick up the truck, they could not pay for the repairs. Pete & Sons returned the truck to the Turners upon their verbal agreement that if they did not pay for the repairs, they would return the truck to Pete & Sons. The Turners did not pay Pete & Sons for the repair services and defaulted on the loan payments due Ozark. Ozark brought this action to recover the truck under its security agreement. Pete & Sons asserts that it has a common law artisan's lien on the truck for the unpaid repair services that it claims takes priority over Ozark's security interest. Who wins? [*Ozark Financial Services v. Turner*, 735 S.W.2d 374 (Mo. App. 1987)]

22.13 Repossession of Collateral Kent Cobado sold Gerald Hilliman and John Szata a herd of cattle. To secure payment of the purchase price, the buyers granted Cobado a security interest in 66 cows and one bull. Cobado protested when it learned that the buyers had culled a number of cattle from the herd. The buyers gave Cobado 37 replacement cows as additional security. Cobado filed a financing statement with the office of the clerk of county.

Cobado continued to be disturbed by the buyers' continuing practice of culling cattle from the herd. Suddenly, without any prior warning, Cobado, aided by two men, arrived at the buyers' premises. Szata was advised of Cobado's intention to repossess the collateral. Szata replied that all the payments had been made on time. Cobado restated his intent. The county sheriff arrived before the cattle could be loaded onto Cobado's trucks. The sheriff warned Cobado that he would be arrested if he left with the cattle. Cobado ignored the warning, loaded the cattle onto the trucks, and left with the cattle. Was Cobado's repossession of the cattle proper under Article 9 of the UCC? [*Hilliman v. Cobado*, 499 N.Y.S.2d 610 (N.Y.Sup.Ct. 1986)]

 BUSINESS ETHICS CASES

22.14 Business Ethics On February 26, 1982, Jessie Lynch became seriously ill and needed medical attention. Her sister, Ethel Sales, took her to the Forsyth Memorial Hospital in North Carolina for treatment. Lynch was admitted for hospitalization. Sales signed Lynch's admission form, which included the following section:

> *The undersigned, in consideration of hospital services being rendered or to be rendered by Forsyth County Memorial Hospital Authority, Inc., in Winston-Salem, N.C., to the above patient, does hereby guarantee payment to Forsyth County Hospital Authority, Inc., on demand all charges for said services and incidentals incurred on behalf of such patient.*

Lynch received the care and services rendered by the hospital until her discharge over 30 days later. The total bill during her hospitalization amounted to $7,977. When Lynch refused to pay the bill, the hospital instituted an action against Lynch and Sales to recover the unpaid amount. Is Sales liable? Did Sales act ethically in denying liability? Did she have a choice when she signed the contract? [*Forsyth County Memorial Hospital Authority, Inc.*, 346 S.E.2d 212 (N.C. App. 1986)]

22.15 Business Ethics On February 25, 1975, Harder & Sons, Inc., an International Harvester dealership in Ionia, Michigan, sold a used International Harvester 1066 diesel tractor to Terry Blaser on an installment contract. Although the contract listed Blaser's address as Ionia County, Blaser informed Harder at the time of purchase that he was going to work and live in Barry County. Blaser took delivery of the tractor at his Ionia County address on February 28, 1975. On the same day, Harder filed a financing statement, which was executed by Blaser with the installment contract, in Barry County. The state of Michigan UCC requires an Article 9 financing statement to be filed in the debtor's county of the residence. The contract and security agreement were immediately assigned to International Harvester Credit Corporation (International Harvester).

Blaser subsequently moved to Barry County for about three months, then to Ionia County for a few months, then to Kent County for three weeks, and then to Muskegon County, where he sold the tractor to Jay and Dale Vos. At the time of sale, Blaser informed the Vos brothers that he owned the tractor. He did not tell them that it was subject to a lien. The Vos brothers went to First Michigan Bank & Trust Company (Bank) to obtain a loan to help purchase the tractor. When the Bank checked the records of Ionia County and found that no financing statement was filed against the tractor, it made a $7,000 loan to the Vos brothers to purchase the tractor. On May 19, 1977, International Harvester filed suit to recover the tractor from the Vos brothers on the grounds that it had a prior perfected security interest. Did Blaser act ethically in this case? Who wins? [*International Harvester Credit Corporation v. Vos*, 290 N.W.2d 401 (Mich.App. 1980)]

BRIEFING THE CASE WRITING ASSIGNMENT

Read the following case, which has been excerpted from the court's opinion. Review and brief the case.

Davenport v. Chrysler Credit Corporation
818 S.W. 2D 23 (1991)
Court of Appeals of Tennessee

Koch, Judge

Larry and Debbie Davenport purchased a new 1987 Chrysler LeBaron from Gary Mathews Motors on October 28, 1987. They obtained financing through Chrysler Credit Corporation (Chrysler Credit) and signed a retail installment contract requiring them to make the first of 60 monthly payments on or before December 8, 1987.

The automobile developed mechanical problems before the Davenports could drive it off the dealer's lot. Even before their first payment was due, the Davenports had returned the automobile to the dealer seven times for repair. They were extremely dissatisfied and, after consulting a lawyer, decided to withhold their monthly payments until the matter was resolved.

Chrysler Credit sent the Davenports a standard delinquency notice when their first payment was 10 days late. The Davenports did not respond to the notice, and on December 23, 1987, Chrysler Credit telephoned the Davenports to request payment. Mrs. Davenport recounted the problems with the automobile and told Chrysler Credit that she would consult her lawyer and "would let them know about the payment." After consulting the dealer, Chrysler Credit informed Mrs. Davenport that it would repossess the automobile if she did not make the payment.

Employees of American Lender Service arrived at the Davenports' home on the evening of January 14, 1988. They informed the Davenports that they were "two payments in default" and requested the automobile. The Davenports insisted that they were not in default and, after a telephone call to their lawyer, refused to turn over the automobile until Chrysler Credit obtained the "proper paperwork." The American Lender Service employees left without the car.

Before leaving for work the next morning, Mr. Davenport parked the automobile in their enclosed garage and chained its rear end to a post using a logging chain and two padlocks. He also closed the canvas flaps covering the entrance to the garage and secured the flaps with cinder blocks. When the

Davenports returned from work, they discovered that someone had entered the garage, cut one of the padlocks, and removed the automobile.

American Lender Service informed Chrysler Credit on January 18, 1988 that it had repossessed the automobile. On the same day, Chrysler Credit notified the Davenports that they could redeem the car before it was offered for sale. The Davenports never responded to the notice. Instead of selling the automobile immediately, Chrysler Credit held it for more than a year because of the Davenports' allegations that the automobile was defective. In July, 1989, Chrysler Credit informed the Davenports that the automobile had been sold and requested payment of the $6,774.00 deficiency. The proof supports the trial court's conclusion that Chrysler Credit had a legal right to initiate repossession procedures.

The Davenports' dissatisfaction with their automobile did not provide them with a basis to unilaterally refuse to honor their payment obligations in the retail installment contract. At the time the repossession took place, the Davenports had not requested rescission of the contract, attempted to revoke their acceptance of the automobile, pursued their remedies under the "lemon law," or taken any other formal steps to resolve their dispute with the dealer concerning the automobile. The Davenports' conduct gave Chrysler Credit an adequate basis to consider the loan to be in default and to decide to protect its collateral by repossessing the automobile.

The Tennessee General Assembly preserved the secured parties' self-help remedies when it enacted the Uniform Commercial Code in 1963. It also preserved the requirement that repossessions must be accomplished without a breach of the peace. The term "breach of the peace" is a generic term that includes all violations or potential violations of the public peace and order. We can find no support for limiting "breach of the peace" to criminal context.

Secured parties may repossess their collateral at a reasonable time and in a reasonable manner. Self-help procedures such as repossession are the product of a careful balancing of the interests of secured parties and debtors. Chrysler Credit and American Lender Service do not dispute that they obtained the automobile by entering a closed garage and by cutting a lock on a chain that would have prevented them from removing the automobile. The Davenports are only entitled to recover their damages stemming directly from the manner in which American Lender Service repossessed their automobile.

We reverse the trial court's judgment dismissing the Davenports' complaint.

CHAPTER 23

Bankruptcy and Reorganization

A trifling debt makes a man your debtor, a large one makes him your enemy.

—Seneca
Epistulae Morales ad Lucilium, 63–65

Chapter Objectives

After studying this chapter, you should be able to:

1. Describe the procedure for filing for bankruptcy.

2. Define *fresh start* and the discharge of unpaid debts.

3. Describe a Chapter 7 liquidation bankruptcy.

4. Define an automatic stay in bankruptcy.

5. Identify voidable transfers and preferential payments.

6. List the order of priority for paying creditors in Chapter 7 bankruptcy.

7. Define secured and unsecured creditors' rights in bankruptcy.

8. Describe how a business is reorganized in Chapter 11 bankruptcy.

9. Describe a Chapter 13 consumer debt adjustment bankruptcy.

10. Learn about the bankruptcy of Dot-com Companies.

Chapter Contents

Small debts are like small shot; they are rattling on every side, and can scarcely be escaped without a wound; great debts are like cannon; of loud noise, but little danger.

Samuel Johnson
Letter to Joseph Simpson (1759)

The extension of credit from creditors to debtors in commercial and personal transactions is important to the viability of the American and world economics. On occasion, however, borrowers become overextended and are unable to meet their debt obligations.

Years ago in Britain and Europe, persons who could not meet their debts were sentenced to debtors' prisons or indentured to their creditor until the debt was "worked off." To avoid such harsh results, many countries adopted bankruptcy laws that were intended to achieve a better balance between debtors' rights and creditors' rights.

The founders of our country thought the plight of debtors was so important that they included a provision in the U.S. Constitution giving Congress the authority to establish uniform bankruptcy laws. The goal of federal bankruptcy law is to give debtors a "fresh start" by relieving them from legal responsibility for past debts. This chapter discusses federal bankruptcy law, which is the exclusive law that governs throughout this country.

OVERVIEW OF FEDERAL BANKRUPTCY LAW

Business Brief

Bankruptcy law is *federal* law. There are no state bankruptcy laws.

Article I, section 8, clause 4 of the U.S. Constitution provides that "The Congress shall have the power . . . to establish. . . uniform laws on the subject of bankruptcies throughout the United States." Federal bankruptcy law establishes procedures for filing for bankruptcy, resolving creditors' claims, and protecting debtors' rights. Bankruptcy law is exclusively federal law; there are no state bankruptcy laws.

 *Landmark Law*

THE FEDERAL BANKRUPTCY CODE

Congress enacted the original **Bankrutpcy Act** in 1878. It was amended in 1938 by the **Chandler Act**, and that law was completely revised by the **Bankruptcy Reform Act of 1978** [11 U.S.C. §§ 101-1330]. The 1978 act which became effective on October 1, 1979, substantially changed—and eased—the requirements for filing bankruptcy.

Several years later, Congress enacted the **Bankruptcy Amendments and Federal Judgeship Act of 1984**, which made bankruptcy courts part of the federal district court system and attached a bankruptcy court to each district court. Bankruptcy judges are appointed by the President for 14-year terms. Other provisions of the 1984 amendments remedied abuses and misuses of bankruptcy and clarified procedures for filing bankruptcy. The Bankruptcy Reform Act of 1978, as amended, is referred to as the **Bankruptcy Code**.

Jurisdiction of the Bankruptcy Courts

Bankruptcy Code

The name given to the Bankruptcy Reform Act of 1978, as amended.

Bankruptcy judges decide *core proceedings* (e.g., allowing creditor claims, deciding preferences, confirming plans of reorganization) regarding **bankruptcy** cases. *Noncore proceedings* concerning the debtor (e.g., decisions on personal injury, divorce, and other civil proceedings) are resolved in federal or state court. The jurisdiction of the bankruptcy courts became effective on July 10, 1984.

Types of Bankruptcy

Poor bankrupt.

William Shakespeare
Romeo and Juliet (1595)

The Bankruptcy Code is divided into chapters. Chapter 1, 3, and 5 include definitional provisions and provisions for the administration of bankruptcy proceedings. They apply to all forms of bankruptcy. The most common forms of bankruptcy are provided by the following chapters: Chapter 7 (liquidation), Chapter 11 (reorganization), and Chapter 13 (consumer debt adjustment). The remaining chapters of the Bankruptcy Code govern the bankruptcies of municipalities, stockbrokers, and railroads.

The "Fresh Start"

The primary purpose of federal bankruptcy law is to discharge the debtor from burdensome debts. The law gives debtors a **fresh start** by freeing them from legal responsibility for past debts by (1) protecting debtors from abusive activities by creditors in collecting debts, (2) preventing certain creditors from obtaining an unfair advantage over other creditors, (3) protecting creditors from actions of the debtor that would diminish the value of the bankruptcy estate, (4) providing for the speedy, efficient, and equitable distribution of the debtor's nonexempt property to claim holders, and (5) preserving existing business relations.

fresh start

The goal of federal bankruptcy law: To discharge the debtor from burdensome debts and allow him or her to begin again.

CHAPTER 7 LIQUIDATION BANKRUPTCY

Chapter 7 liquidation bankruptcy (also called **straight bankruptcy**) is the most familiar form of bankruptcy. In this type of proceeding, the debtor's nonexempt property is sold for cash, the cash is distributed to the creditors, and any unpaid debts are **discharged**. Any person, including individuals, partnerships, and corporations, may be debtors in a Chapter 7 proceeding. Certain businesses, including banks, savings and loan associations, credit unions, insurance companies, and railroads, are prohibited from filing bankruptcy under Chapter 7.

Chapter 7 liquidation bankruptcy

The most familiar form of bankruptcy; the debtor's nonexempt property is sold for cash, the cash is distributed to the creditors, and any unpaid debts are discharged.

Bankruptcy Procedure

The filing and maintenance of a Chapter 7 case must follow certain procedures. The following paragraphs outline the major steps in the liquidation process.

Business Brief

Approximately 1.5 million personal bankruptcies are filed under Chapter 7 each year.

Filing a Petition   A Chapter 7 bankruptcy is commenced when a **petition** is filed with the bankruptcy court. The petition may be filed by either the debtor (voluntary) or one or more creditors (involuntary).

Voluntary petitions only have to state that the debtor has debts; insolvency (i.e., that debts exceed assets) need not be declared. The petition must include the following schedules: (1) a list of secured and unsecured creditors, including their addresses and the amount of debt owed to each, (2) a list of all property owned by the debtor, including property claimed to be exempt by the debtor, (3) a statement of the financial affairs of the debtor, and (4) a list of the debtor's current income and expenses. The petition must be signed and sworn to under oath. Married couples may file a joint petition.

An **involuntary petition** can be filed against any debtors who can file a voluntary petition under Chapter 7 except farmers, ranchers, and nonprofit organizations. An involuntary petition must allege that the debtor is not paying his or her debts as they become due. If the debtor has more that 12 creditors, the petition must be signed by at least three of them. If there are 12 or fewer creditors, any creditor can sign the petition. The creditor or creditors who sign the petition must have valid unsecured claims of at least $10,000 (in the aggregate).

petition

A document filed with the bankruptcy court that sets the bankruptcy proceedings into motion.

voluntary petition

A petition filed by the debtor; states that the debtor has debts.

involuntary petition

A petition filed by creditors of the debtor; alleges that the debtor is not paying his or her debts as they become due.

Order for Relief   The filing of either a voluntary petition or an unchallenged involuntary petition constitutes an **order for relief**. If the debtor challenges an involuntary petition, a trial will be held to determine whether an order for relief should be granted. If the order is granted, the case is accepted for further bankruptcy proceedings. In the case of an involuntary petition, the debtor must file the same schedules filed by voluntary debtors.

order for relief

The filing of either a voluntary petition, an unchallenged involuntary petition, or a grant of an order after a trial of a challenged involuntary petition.

Meeting of the Creditors   Within a reasonable time (not less than 10 days nor more than 30 days) after the court grants an order for relief, the court must call a **meeting of the creditors** (also called the **the first meeting of the creditors**). The judge cannot attend this meeting. The debtor, however, must appear and submit to questioning by creditors. Creditors may ask questions regarding the debtor's financial affairs, disposition of property prior to bankruptcy, possible concealment of assets, and such. The debtor may have an attorney present at this meeting. A notice of a Chapter 7 bankruptcy case is shown in Exhibit 23.1.

meeting of the creditors

A meeting of the creditors in a bankruptcy case that must occur not less than 10 days nor more than 30 days after the court grants an order for relief.

Exhibit **23.1**   *Notice of Chapter 7 Bankruptcy Case*

FORM B9B (Chapter 7) (1/98)   Case Number: **LA 01-22024-BB**

UNITED STATES BANKRUPTCY COURT	Central District of California

Notice of Chapter 7 Bankruptcy Case, Meeting of Creditors & Deadlines
Corporation/Partnership - No Asset Case

A chapter 7 bankruptcy case concerning the debtor(s) listed below was filed on April 18, 2003.

You may be a creditor of the debtor. **This notice lists important deadlines.** You may want to consult an attorney to protect your rights. All documents filed in the case may be inspected at the bankruptcy clerk's office at the **U.S. Bankruptcy Court, United States Federal Building, 300 North Los Angeles Street, Los Angeles, CA 90012.**

NOTE: The staff of the bankruptcy clerk's office cannot give legal advice.

See Reverse Side For Important Explanations

Debtor(s) (name(s) address)
MARK'S C P A REVIEW COURSE INC
DBA MARK'S NEW C P A REVIEW COURSE

3764 BENEDICT CANYON LANE SHERMAN OAKS, CA 91423

Case Number: LA 01-22024-BB	Taxpayer ID Nos.: 95-4565630
Attorney for Debtor(s) (name, address, telephone) KEITH C OWENS DANNING GILL DIAMOND & KOLLITZ 2029 CENTURY PARK EAST, THIRD FLOOR LOS ANGELES, CA 90067-2904 Telephone number: (310) 277-0077	Bankruptcy Trustee (name, address, telephone) R TODD NEILSON NEILSON, ELGGREN LLP 10100 SANTA MONICA BLVD #410 LOS ANGELES, CA 90067 Telephone number: (310) 282-9911

Meeting of Creditors

Date: **May 23, 2003**   Time: **1:30 P.M.**

Location   **221 N. Figueroa St., Ste. 101, Los Angeles, CA 90012**

Creditors May Not Take Certain Actions

The filing of the bankruptcy case automatically stays certain collection and other actions against the debtor and the debtor's property. If you attempt to collect a debt or take other action in violation of the Bankruptcy Code, you may be penalized.

Please Do Not File A Proof of Claim Unless You Receive a Notice To Do So

Address of the Bankruptcy Clerk's Office:	For the Court:
U.S. Bankruptcy Court 255 East Temple Street Los Angeles, CA 90012 Telephone number: (213) 894-3118	Clerk of the Bankruptcy Court: Jon D. Ceretto
Hours Open: 9:00 A.M. to 4:00 P.M.	Date: April 23, 2003

Appointment of a Trustee A trustee must be appointed in a Chapter 7 proceeding. An interim trustee is appointed by the court when an order for relief is entered. A **permanent trustee** is elected at the first meeting of the creditors. Trustees, who are often lawyers or accountants, are entitled to receive reasonable compensation for their services and reimbursement for expenses. Once appointed, the trustee becomes the legal representative of the bankrupt debtor's estate. Generally, the trustee must

- Take immediate possession of the debtor's property.
- Separate secured and unsecured property.
- Set aside exempt property.
- Investigate the debtor's financial affairs.
- Employ disinterested professionals (e.g., attorneys, accountants, and appraisers) to assist in the administration of the estate.
- Examine proof of claims.
- Defend, bring, and maintain lawsuits on behalf of the estate.
- Invest the property of the estate.
- Sell or otherwise dispose of property of the estate.
- Distribute the proceeds of the estate.
- Make reports to the court, creditors, and debtor regarding the administration of the estate.

permanent trustee

A legal representative of the bankruptcy debtor's estate, usually an accountant or lawyer; elected at the first meeting of the creditors.

Business Brief

Beginning April 1, 1998, the dollar amount stated in the Bankruptcy Code will be adjusted every three years based on changes in Consumer Price Index.

Proof of Claims Unsecured creditors must file a **proof of claim** stating the amount of their claims against the debtor. The form for the statement is provided by the court. The proof of claim must be "timely filed," which generally means within six months of the first meeting of the creditors. Secured creditors are not required to file proof of claim. A secured creditor whose claim exceeds the value of the collateral, however, may submit a proof of claim and become an unsecured claimant as to the difference.

The claim must be allowed by the court before a creditor is permitted to participate in the bankruptcy estate. Any party of interest may object to a claim. If an objection to a claim is raised, the court will hold a hearing to determine the validity and amount of the claim.

proof of claim

A document required to be filed by unsecured creditors that states the amount of their claim against the debtor.

Automatic Stay

The filing of a voluntary or involuntary petition automatically stays—that is, suspends—certain action by creditors against the debtor or the debtor's property.[1] This is called an **automatic stay**. The stay, which applies to collection efforts of both secured and unsecured creditors, is designed to prevent a scramble of the debtor's assets in a variety of court proceedings. The following creditor actions are stayed:

1. Instituting or maintaining legal actions to collect prepetition debts.
2. Enforcing judgments obtained against the debtor.
3. Obtaining, perfecting, or enforcing liens against property of the debtor.
4. Attempting to set off debts owed by the creditor to the debtor against the creditor's claims in bankruptcy.
5. Nonjudicial collection efforts, such as self-help activities (e.g., repossession of a car).

automatic stay

The result of the filing of a voluntary or involuntary petition; the suspension of certain actions by creditors against the debtor or the debtor's property.

The court also has the authority to issue injunctions preventing creditor activity not covered by the automatic stay provision. Actions to recover alimony and child support are not stayed in bankruptcy. The automatic stay does not preclude collection efforts by creditors against codebtors and guarantors of the bankrupt debtor's debts, except (1) in a Chapter 13 bankruptcy (discussed later in this chapter) or (2) if the codebtor is also in bankruptcy.

Business Brief

The importance of the automatic stay in bankruptcy should not be underestimated. For example, in *Pennzoil v. Texaco*, Texaco filed a voluntary petition in bankruptcy to stay any attempt by Pennzoil to perfect its $10 billion judgment against Texaco.

Relief from Stay A secured creditor may petition the court for a **relief from stay**, which usually occurs in situations involving depreciating assets where the secured property is not adequately protected during the bankruptcy proceeding. The court may opt to provide adequate protection rather than granting relief from stay. In such cases, the court may (1) order cash payments equal to the amount of the depreciation, (2) grant an additional or replacement lien, or (3) grant an "indubitable equivalent" (e.g., a guarantee from a solvent party).

relief from stay

May be granted in situations involving depreciating assets where the secured property is not adequately protected during the bankruptcy proceedings; asked for by a secured creditor.

E-Commerce & Information Technology

DOT-COM COMPANY GOES BANKRUPT

Many Internet companies have gone public, making instant millionaires of their founders and employees. Others went public, and then went bust. One such company was eToys.com. The company went public in a much-touted initial public offering (IPO) in 1999 when its shares were sold to the public at $20.00 per share. Less than two years later in 2001, its stock was worthless, the company declared bankruptcy, and shuttered its doors. The bankruptcy of eToys.com is just one example of the many Internet-related companies that failed in the Dot-com "meltdown" of the early 2000s.

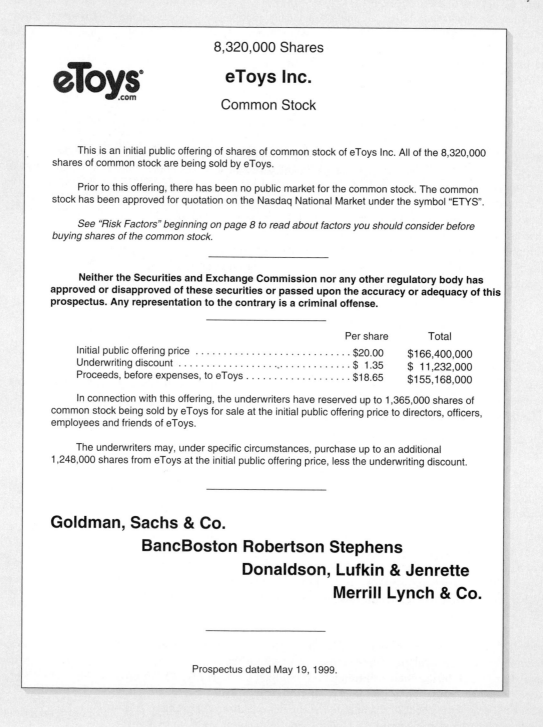

8,320,000 Shares

eToys.com

eToys Inc.

Common Stock

This is an initial public offering of shares of common stock of eToys Inc. All of the 8,320,000 shares of common stock are being sold by eToys.

Prior to this offering, there has been no public market for the common stock. The common stock has been approved for quotation on the Nasdaq National Market under the symbol "ETYS".

See "Risk Factors" beginning on page 8 to read about factors you should consider before buying shares of the common stock.

Neither the Securities and Exchange Commission nor any other regulatory body has approved or disapproved of these securities or passed upon the accuracy or adequacy of this prospectus. Any representation to the contrary is a criminal offense.

	Per share	Total
Initial public offering price	$20.00	$166,400,000
Underwriting discount	$ 1.35	$ 11,232,000
Proceeds, before expenses, to eToys	$18.65	$155,168,000

In connection with this offering, the underwriters have reserved up to 1,365,000 shares of common stock being sold by eToys for sale at the initial public offering price to directors, officers, employees and friends of eToys.

The underwriters may, under specific circumstances, purchase up to an additional 1,248,000 shares from eToys at the initial public offering price, less the underwriting discount.

Goldman, Sachs & Co.
BancBoston Robertson Stephens
Donaldson, Lufkin & Jenrette
Merrill Lynch & Co.

Prospectus dated May 19, 1999.

𝒫ROPERTY OF THE BANKRUPTCY ESTATE

The **bankruptcy estate** is created upon the commencement of a Chapter 7 proceeding. It includes all the debtor's legal and equitable interests in real, personal, tangible, and intangible property, wherever located, that exist when the petition is filed. The debtor's separate and community property are included in the estate.

Property acquired after the petition does not become part of the bankruptcy estate. The only exceptions are gifts, inheritances, life insurance proceeds, and property from divorce settlements that the debtor is entitled to receive within 180 days after the petition if filed. Earnings from property of the estate—such as rents, dividends, and interest payments—are property of the estate.

Exempt Property

Because the Bankruptcy Code is not designed to make the debtor a pauper, certain property is exempt from the bankruptcy estate. The debtor may retain **exempt property**.

The Bankruptcy Code establishes a *federal* exemption scheme (see Exhibit 23.2).

bankruptcy estate

An estate created upon the commencement of a Chapter 7 proceeding that includes all the debtor's legal and equitable interests in real, personal, tangible, and intangible property, wherever located, that exist when the petition is filed, minus exempt property.

exempt property

Property that may be retained by the debtor pursuant to federal or state law; debtor's property that does not become part of the bankruptcy estate.

ℰXHIBIT 23.2   *Federal Exemptions from the Bankruptcy Estate*

1. Interest up to $15,000 in equity in property used as a residence and burial plots. This is called the homestead exemption.
2. Interest up to $2,400 in one motor vehicle.
3. Interest up to $400 per item in household goods and furnishings, wearing apparel, appliances, books, animals, crops, or musical instruments, up to an aggregate value of $8,000 for all items
4. Interest in jewelry up to $1,000 that is held for personal use.
5. Interest in any property the debtor chooses (including cash) up to $800, plus up to $7,500 of any unused portion of the $15,000 homestead exemption.
6. Interest up to $1,500 in value in implements, tools, or professional books used in the debtor's trade.
7. Any unmatured life insurance policy owned by the debtor (other than a credit life insurance contract) and up to $8,000 of any accrued dividends, interest, or cash surrender value of any unmatured life insurance policy.
8. Professionally prescribed health aids.
9. Many government benefits regardless of value, including Social Security benefits, unemployment compensation, veteran's benefits, disability benefits, and public assistance benefits.
10. Certain rights to receive income, including alimony and support payments, pension benefits, profit sharing, and annuity payments, but only to the extent reasonably necessary to support the debtor or his or her dependents.
11. Interests in wrongful death benefits, life insurance proceeds, and personal injury awards (up to $15,000) to the extent reasonably necessary to support the debtor or his or her dependents, and crime victim compensation awards without limit.

State Law Exemptions   The Bankruptcy Code also permits states to enact their own exemptions. States that do so may (1) give debtors the option of choosing between federal and state exemptions or (2) require debtors to follow state law.[2] The exemptions available under state law are often quite liberal. For example, homestead exemptions are often higher under state law than under the federal exemption scheme. Many states require the debtor to file a **Declaration of Homestead** prior to bankruptcy. This document is usually filed in the county recorder's office in the county in which the property is located.

If the debtor's equity in property (above liens and mortgages) exceeds the exemption limits, the trustee may liquidate the property to realize the excess value for the bankruptcy estate.

Business Brief

States that provide liberal exemptions (e.g., California, Florida, Texas) are called "debtors' havens."

Neither a borrower nor a lender be: For loan oft loses both itself and friend. And borrowing dulls the edge of husbandry.

William Shakespeare
Hamlet 1.13 (1600)

Consider This Example Assume that the debtor owns a home worth $100,000 that is subject to a $60,000 mortgage. The trustee may sell the home, pay off the mortgage, pay the debtor $15,000 (applying the federal exemption), and use the remaining proceeds ($25,000) for distribution to the debtor's creditors.

In the following case, the court found that an asset was exempt from the debtor's bankruptcy estate.

In re Witwer
148 Bankr. 930 (1992)
United States Bankruptcy Court, Central District of California

CASE 23.1

BACKGROUND AND FACTS
Dr. James J. Witwer is the sole stockholder, sole employee, and president of James J. Witwer, M.D., Inc., a California corporation under which he practices medicine. He is also the sole beneficiary of the corporation's retirement plan, which was established in 1970. On October 21, 1991, Witwer filed a voluntary petition for relief under Chapter 7 (liquidation). At the time, the value of the assets in his retirement plan was $1.8 million. California law exempted retirement plans from a debtor's bankruptcy estate. When Witwer claimed that his retirement plan was exempt from the bankruptcy estate, several creditors filed objections.

ISSUE
Is Witwer's retirement plan exempt from the bankruptcy estate?

COURT'S REASONING
Under California law, the assets of a retirement plan are entirely exempt if the plan was designed and used for retirement purposes. The bankruptcy court found that the retirement plan established by Witwer fit this exemption. The court stated:

Regardless of the inequities that may result from a debtor's use of the California exemption scheme, this court is constrained by the plain meaning of the statutes in the context of this case. Allowing the debtor to retain over $1.8 million in retirement benefits in bankruptcy while being discharged from debts legitimately owed to creditors seems fundamentally unfair.

The court concluded that under the Bankruptcy Code, the size of a debtor's bankruptcy estate is "subject to the vagaries of state exemption law."

DECISION
The bankruptcy court held that Witwer's retirement plan is fully exempt from his bankruptcy estate.

Case Questions

Critical Legal Thinking Do you think bankruptcy law was intended to reach the result in this case?

Business Ethics Was it ethical for the debtor to declare bankruptcy and wipe out his unsecured creditors while retaining $1.8 million in his retirement account?

Contemporary Business Should businesspeople establish and fund retirement programs?

Contemporary Business Environment

HOMESTEAD EXEMPTIONS: MORE THAN JUST A LOG CABIN

When the term *homestead* is used, many people think of the Wild West, wide-open prairies, and a pioneer's log cabin built with sweat and tears. Long ago, many states enacted laws that protected a debtor's homestead from greedy creditors.

Today, a debtor's homestead may be a condo in a luxury apartment building or a multimillion-dollar split-level home. Depending upon state law, at least a portion of the equity in a debtor's homestead may still be protected from creditors if the owner declares bankruptcy. For example, New York exempts $20,000 of equity in a married couple's home from bankruptcy estate ($10,000 for a single debtor). California exempts $55,000 for a married couple and $35,000 for a single debtor. These exemptions look generous compared to most states except Florida and Texas.

The Florida constitution and statutes give a homestead exemption from bankruptcy without dollar limit. The homestead is 160 acres outside a municipality and one-half acre inside a municipality.

The Texas homestead exemption is even bigger. Texas has an urban homestead of one acre and a rural homestead of up to 200 acres, without any dollar limit.

Florida and Texas are known as "debtors havens" because of their generous homestead exemptions from bankruptcy. In fact, relocating to these states has become attractive to people in financial difficulty, who take what money they have and place it beyond the reach of their creditors in homesteads in these states before declaring bankruptcy. How long a person must reside in the state before declaring bankruptcy is an open question. It is just one factor in deciding whether the debtor has engaged in a bankruptcy fraud that makes the debtor's debts nondischargeable. So far, few bankruptcies have been undone under such a charge.

Proponents of homestead exemptions argue that they are needed to provide a debtor with a fresh start and a roof over his head. Critics argue that debtors are using homestead exemptions to run roughshod over creditors.

Voidable Transfers

The Bankruptcy Code prevents debtors from making unusual payments or **transfers** of property on the eve of bankruptcy that would unfairly benefit the debtor or some creditors at the expense of others. The following paragraphs discuss the transfers that may be avoided by the bankruptcy court.

voidable transfer

An unusual payment or transfer of property by the debtor on the eve of bankruptcy that would unfairly benefit the debtor or some creditors at the expense of other creditors. Such transfer may be avoided by the bankruptcy court.

Preferential Transfers Within 90 Days Before Bankruptcy A **preferential transfer** occurs when (1) a debtor transfers property to a creditor within 90 days before the filing of a petition in bankruptcy, (2) the transfer is made for an antecedent (preexisting) debt, and (3) the creditor would receive more from the transfer than it would from Chapter 7 liquidation. The Bankruptcy Code presumes that the debtor is insolvent during this 90-day period.

preferential transfer

Occurs when (1) a debtor transfers property to a creditor within 90 days before the filing of a petition in bankruptcy, (2) the transfer is made for a preexisting debt, and (3) the creditor would receive more from the transfer than it would from Chapter 7 liquidation.

Consider This Example Assume six months prior to filing bankruptcy that the debtor purchases $10,000 of equipment on credit from a supplier. Within 90 days of filing the petition, the debtor still owes the money to this creditor, which is not due for 120 days. The debtor pays the creditor the $7,000 before filing the petition. In a Chapter 7 liquidation proceeding, the creditor would have received $1,000. This payment is a voidable preference because it was made within 90 days of filing the petition, was made to pay an antecedent debt, and gives the creditor more than he or she would receive in liquidation.

There are exceptions to the 90-day rule. They include (1) transfers for current consideration (e.g., equipment purchased for cash within 90 days of the petition), (2) credit payments made in the ordinary course of the debtor's business (e.g., supplies purchased on credit and paid for within the normal payment term of 30 days after purchase), and (3) payment of up to $600 by a consumer-debtor to a creditor within 90 days of the petition.

Business Brief

Sometimes prior to declaring bankruptcy, debtors transfer property to others as gifts or for less than fair market value, perhaps with a promise that the property will be returned to the debtor after the bankruptcy is over. This is *bankruptcy fraud*.

Preferential Liens Debtors sometimes attempt to favor certain unsecured creditors on the eve of bankruptcy by giving them a secured interest in property. This type of interest is called a **preferential lien**. Preferential liens occur when (1) the debtor gives the creditor a secured interest in property within 90 days of petition, (2) the secured interest is given for an antecedent debt, and (3) the creditor would receive more because of this lien then it would as an unsecured creditor in liquidation.

preferential lien

Occurs when (1) a debtor gives an unsecured creditor a secured interest in property within 90 days before the filing of a petition in bankruptcy, (2) the transfer is made for a preexisting debt, and (3) the creditor would receive more because of this lien than it would as an unsecured creditor.

Preferential Transfers to Insiders The Bankruptcy Code provides that preferential transfers and liens made to "insiders" within one year of the filing of the petition in bankruptcy may be avoided by the court. **Insiders** are defined as relatives, partners, partnerships, officers and directors of a corporation, corporations, and others who have a relationship with the debtor. To avoid a transfer to an insider within one-year period (other than the first 90 days prior to the petition), the trustee must prove that the debtor was insolvent at the time of the transfer.

preferential transfer to an insider

A transfer of property by an insolvent debtor to an "insider" within one year before the filing of a petition in bankruptcy.

Fraudulent Transfers Section 548 of the Bankruptcy Code gives the court the power to avoid **fraudulent transfers** of property that occur within one year of the filing of the petition in bankruptcy. Any transfer of property by the debtor made with actual intent to "hinder, delay, or defraud" creditors is considered a voidable fraudulent transfer. The debtor's actual intent must be proved, although it may be inferred from the circumstances. For example, a transfer of property by an insolvent debtor for substantially less than fair market value would be voidable as a fraudulent transfer. In addition, Section 544(b) of the Bankruptcy Code gives the trustee the power to avoid fraudulent transfers made in violation of state fraudulent conveyances acts. Because these acts usually contain a longer

fraudulent transfer

Occurs when (1) a debtor transfers property to a third person within one year before the filing of a petition in bankruptcy and (2) the transfer was made by the debtor with an intent to hinder, delay, or defraud creditors.

statute of limitations (e.g., six year), a court can avoid any fraudulent transfer made during this period.

If a transfer is voided, a bona fide good faith purchaser must receive the value he or she paid for the property. Thus, if an insolvent debtor sold property worth $50,000 to a bona fide purchaser for $30,000 within the one-year period and the court rescinds the transfer, the trustee must return the $30,000 to the bona fide purchaser.

Business Ethics

Bankruptcy Fraud: Voidable Transfers

Often, a debtor who knows in advance that he or she is heading for bankruptcy will try to get assets out of his or her possession. That way, when bankruptcy comes, the only things left are the debts.

Sometimes the assets are transferred to relatives or friends with a promise to give them back once the bankruptcy is over. Other times, they are transferred to business or entities in which the debtor has a secret interest. Debtors usually rationalize these transfers on the grounds that it does not matter if "faceless" creditors—such as banks and trade creditors—lose out. But are these transfers unethical or illegal? Or both? Consider the following case.

Blair and Marie Woodfield and Parley and Deanna Pearce (Debtors), as partners, operated two "Wendy's Famous Hamburger" restaurants in Washington and Oregon pursuant to a franchise from Wendy's International, Inc. On March 10, 1989, Debtors filed their petitions for bankruptcy under Chapter 7.

Within 10 days prior to filing for bankruptcy, Debtors had formed a new corporation called Quality Foods, Inc. (QFI), in which they each held a 50 percent interest. They then transferred the franchise operating rights, equipment, fixtures, inventory, and restaurant supplies of the two restaurants to QFI. In addition, Woodfield transferred $10,000 cash and Pearce $6,954 cash to QFI within this 10-day period.

Prior to their bankruptcy filings, Debtors somehow ascertained that Wade Bettis, Jr. would be their trustee in bank-

ruptcy. They discussed all the foregoing transactions with him prior to filing bankruptcy. At the creditors' meeting on April 25, 1989, Bettis certified that the Debtors had no assets and had abandoned the assets of the two Wendy's franchises. A creditor, Emmett Valley Associates (EVA), objected. Nevertheless, the bankruptcy court approved the abandonment, and the district court affirmed.

The court of appeals, however, asked, "Where's the beef?" The court stated: " The transaction here carried many badges of fraud. The relationship between the Debtors and QFI could not have been closer, the Debtors created and operated the transferee corporation. The transfer was admittedly made in anticipation of the bankruptcy filing. The partnership was admittedly in poor financial condition at the time, having defaulted on several obligations. Substantially all of the partnership's property relating to the Wendy's franchises was transferred, leaving nothing to satisfy the judgments." The court of appeals held that Debtors transferred property with the intent to hinder, delay, and defraud their creditors. Because of this fraud, the court denied the Debtors' discharge. [*In re Woodfield*, 978 F.2d 516 (9th Cir. 1992)]

1. Did the Debtors act unethically in this case? Did they act legally?
2. Did the trustee act unethically?
3. Do you think many debtors engage in insider and fraudulent transfers prior to declaring bankruptcy?

Distribution of Property and Discharge

Priority of Distribution

Under Chapter 7, the nonexempt property of the bankruptcy estate must be **distributed** to the debtor's secured and unsecured creditors. The statutory priority of distribution is discussed in the following paragraphs.

Secured Creditors   A secured creditor's claim to the debtor's property has priority over the claims of unsecured creditors. The secured creditor may (1) accept the collateral in full satisfaction of the debt, (2) foreclose on the collateral and use the proceeds to pay the debt, or (3) allow the trustee to retain the collateral, dispose of it at a sale, and remit the proceeds of the sale to him or her.

If the value of the collateral exceeds the secured interest, the excess becomes available to satisfy the claims of the debtor's unsecured creditors. Before the excess funds are released, however, the secured creditor is allowed to deduct reasonable fees and costs resulting from the default. If the value of the collateral is less than the secured interest, the secured creditor becomes an unsecured creditor to the difference.

Unsecured Creditors   The Bankruptcy Code stipulates that unsecured claims are to be satisfied out of the bankruptcy estate in the order of their statutory priority.[3] The statutory priority of an unsecured claim is

1. Fees and expenses of administrating the estate, including court costs, trustee fees, attorneys' fees, appraisal fees, and other costs of administration.
2. In an involuntary bankruptcy, secured claims of "gap" creditors who sold goods or services on credit to the debtor in the ordinary course of the debtor's business between the date of the filling of the petition and the date of the appointment of the trustee or issuance of the order for relief (whichever occurred first).
3. Unsecured claims for wages, salary, or commissions earned by the debtor's employees within 90 days immediately preceding the filing of the petition, up to $4,000 per employee; any claim exceeding $4,000 is treated as a claim of a general unsecured creditor (item 9 below).
4. Unsecured claims for contributions to employee benefit plans based on services performed within 180 days immediately preceding the filing of the petition, up to $4,000 per employee.
5. Farm producers and fishermen against debtors who operate grain storage facilities or fish produce storage or processing facilities, up to $4,000 per claim.
6. Unsecured claims for cash deposited by a consumer with the debtor prior to the filing of the petition in connection with either the purchase, lease, or rental of property or the purchase of services that were not delivered or provided by the debtor, up to $1,800 per claim.
7. Debts owed for child support, paternity, alimony, and spousal support.
8. Certain tax obligations owed by the debtor to federal, state, and local governmental units.
9. Claims of general unsecured creditors.
10. If there is any balance remaining after the allowed claims of the creditors are satisfied, it is returned to the debtor.

Each class must be paid in full before any lower class is paid anything. If a class cannot be paid in full, the claims of that class are paid pro rata (proportionately).

Discharge

After the property is distributed to satisfy the allowed claims, the remaining unpaid claims are **discharged** (i.e., the debtor is no longer legally responsible for them). Only individuals may be granted a discharge. Discharge is not available to partnerships and corporations. These entities must liquidate under state law before or upon completion of the Chapter 7 proceeding. A debtor can be granted a discharge in a Chapter 7 proceeding only once every six years.

Consider This Example   Maryjane files for Chapter 7 bankruptcy. At the time of filing, she has many unsecured creditors. Nordstrom's Department Store is one of them. She owes Nordstrom's $3,000. The bankruptcy estate has only enough assets to pay unsecured creditors $.10 on the dollar. Nordstrom's receives $300, the remaining $2,700 is discharged. Nordstrom's cannot thereafter collect this money and will write it off as a bad debt.

Business Brief

Generally, unsecured creditors often receive little if anything in a Chapter 7 bankruptcy.

I will pay you some, and, as most debtors do, promise you infinitely.

William Shakespeare
Henry IV, Pt. II (1597)

discharge

The termination of the legal duty of a debtor to pay debts that remain unpaid upon the completion of a bankruptcy proceeding.

It is the policy of the law that the debtor be just before he be generous.

Finch, J.
Hearn 45 St. Corp. v. Jano
(1940)

ℬ*usiness* ℰ*thics*

ABUSE IN REAFFIRMATION AGREEMENTS PREVENTED

Creditors often attempt to persuade a debtor to agree to pay an unsatisfied debt that is dischargeable in bankruptcy. A debtor may voluntarily choose to enter into a **reaffirmation agreement,** which is a formal agreement that sets out the terms of repayment. Before signing a reaffirmation agreement, the debtor needs to decide if there is an important reason to do so, such as the continuation of a valuable relationship with the creditor.

To prevent abuses, the Bankruptcy Code stipulates that the following requirements must be met before a reaffirmation agreement is legally enforceable:

- The reaffirmation agreement must be made before the debtor is granted a discharge.
- The agreement must be filed with the court.
- If the debtor is not represented by an attorney, court approval of the agreement is necessary.

- The debtor may rescind the agreement at any time prior to discharge or within 60 days after filing the agreement with the court, whichever is later. This right of recission must be conspicuously stated in the reaffirmation agreement.

1. Why would a debtor sign a reaffirmation agreement?
2. Do you think debtors would abuse the use of reaffirmation agreements if it were not for the above protections?

Nondischargeable Debts

The following debts are not dischargeable in a Chapter 7 proceeding:

Business Brief

Not all debts are dischargeable in bankruptcy.

Beggars can never be bankrupts.
Thomas Fuller
Gnomologia (1732)

- Claims for taxes accrued within three years prior to the filing of the petition in bankruptcy.
- Certain fines and penalties payable to federal, state, and local governmental units.
- Claims based on the debtor's liability for causing willful or malicious injury to a person or property.
- Claims arising from the fraud, larceny, or embezzlement by the debtor while acting in a fiduciary capacity.
- Alimony, maintenance, and child support.
- Unscheduled claims.
- Claims based on the consumer-debtor's purchase of luxury goods of more than $1,000 from a single creditor within 60 days of the order for relief.
- Cash advances in excess of $1,000 obtained by a consumer-debtor by use of a revolving line of credit or credit cards within 60 days of the order for relief.
- Judgments and consent decrees against the debtor for liability incurred as a result of the debtor's operation of a motor vehicle while legally intoxicated.

Creditors who have nondischargeable claims against the debtor may participate in the distribution of the bankruptcy estate. The nondischarged balance may be pursued by the creditor against the debtor after bankruptcy.

The Supreme Court Speaks

Malpractice Judgment Discharged in Bankruptcy

118 S. Ct. 974 (1998)
Supreme Court of the United States

BACKGROUND AND FACTS

Margaret Kawaauhau sought treatment from Dr. Paul Geiger for a foot injury. Geiger examined Kawaauhau and admitted her to the hospital to attend to the risks of infection. Although Geiger knew that intravenous penicillin would have been the more effective treatment, he prescribed oral penicillin, explaining that he thought that his patient wished to minimize the cost of her treatment. Geiger then departed on a business trip, leaving Kawaauhau in the care of other physicians. When Geiger returned, he discontinued all antibiotics because he believed that the infection had subsided. Kawaauhau's condition deteriorated over the next few days, requiring the amputation of her right leg below the knee. Kawaauhau and her husband sued Geiger for medical malpractice. The jury found Geiger liable and awarded the Kawaauhaus $355,000 in damages. Geiger, who carried no malpractice insurance, filed for bankruptcy in an attempt to

discharge the judgment. The bankruptcy court denied discharge and the district court agreed. The court of appeals reversed and allowed discharge, and the Kawaauhau appealed to the U.S. Supreme Court.

SUPREME COURT ISSUE

Is a debt arising from a medical malpractice judgment that is attributable to a negligent or reckless conduct dischargeable in bankruptcy?

IN THE LANGUAGE OF THE U.S. SUPREME COURT

Ginsburg, Justice Section 523(a)(6) of the Bankruptcy Code provides that a debt "for willful and malicious injury by the debtor to another" is not dischargeable. The question before us is whether a debt arising from a medical malpractice judgment, attributable to negligent or reckless conduct, falls within this statutory exception. We hold that it does not and that the debt is dischargeable. Had Congress meant to exempt debts resulting from unintentionally *inflicted injuries, it might have selected an additional word or words, i.e., "reckless" or "negligent," to modify "injury."*

The Kawaauhaus maintain that, as a policy matter, malpractice judgments should be excepted from discharge, at least when the debtor acted recklessly or carried no malpractice insurance. Congress, of course, may so decide. But unless and until Congress makes such a decision, we must follow the current direction § 523(a)(6) provides.

DECISION AND REMEDY

The U.S. Supreme Court ruled that a medical malpractice judgment based on negligent or reckless conduct—and not intentional conduct—is dischargeable in bankruptcy. Affirmed.

CASE QUESTIONS

Critical Legal Thinking What public policy is promoted by denying discharge for "willful" injurious conduct? Do you think Geiger's conduct would have been willful?

Business Ethics Was it ethical for Geiger to avoid liability to the Kawaauhaus by declaring bankruptcy?

Contemporary Business What purpose is served by allowing individuals and businesses to declare bankruptcy? What are the business implications of bankruptcy laws?

Acts That Bar Discharge

Any party of interest may file an objection to the discharge of a debt. The court will then hold a hearing. Discharge of the unsatisfied debts will be denied if the debtor:

- Made false representations about his or her financial position when he or she obtained an extension of credit.
- Transferred, concealed, or removed property from the estate with the intent to hinder, delay, or defraud creditors.
- Falsified, destroyed, or concealed records of his or her financial condition.
- Failed to account for any assets.
- Failed to submit to questioning at the meeting of the creditors (unless excused).

Business Brief

Certain acts by the debtor may bar discharge.

If the discharge is obtained through the fraud of the debtor, a party of interest may bring a motion to have the bankruptcy revoked. The bankruptcy court may revoke a discharge within one year after it was granted.

Contemporary Business Environment

DISCHARGE OF STUDENT LOANS

In the past, many students who borrowed a lot of money in student loans sought to avoid paying back their loans by filing a voluntary petition for bankruptcy immediately on leaving college. Section 523(a)(8) of the Bankruptcy Code was enacted to prevent this practice. For any bankruptcy case commenced after October 7, 1998, Section 523 (a)(8)(A) mandates that student loans can only be discharged in bankruptcy if nondischarge would cause an "undue hardship" to the debtor and his or her dependents. [Higher Education Amendments of 1998, P. L. 105-244]. Undue hardships is construed very strictly and would include not being able to pay for food or shelter for the debtor or the debtor's family.

Cosigners (e.g., parents who guarantee their child's student loan) must also meet the heightened undue hardship test to discharge their obligation.

@ E-Commerce & Information Technology

BANKRUPT COMPANY HOLDS DIGITAL GARAGE SALE

When a company files for bankruptcy under Chapter 7 of the Bankruptcy Code, it must liquidate its assets and terminate its existence. In the past, the trustee for a bankrupt company would often advertise and hold a traditional auction to sell the remaining inventory, fixtures, and other assets of the company. The auction would be held by an auction company at the bankrupt company's property, at the auction company, or at some other physical site. This was usually the best method for obtaining the best price for the sale items. There were several problems, however. First, advertising was by mail and print media, which is very costly and limited. Second, the number of persons who showed up in person or bid by telephone at the auction was often quite small.

When Atlantic Rancher, a company that specialized in selling high-end outdoor clothing, filed for Chapter 7 bankruptcy in 1999, it did something very different: It held an online auction over the Internet to get rid of its assets. Online auctions had already proven tremendously successful in consumer-to-consumer transactions. For example, eBay started and grew as the Internet's largest auction portal. It was followed by Priceline.com, uBid, Amazon.com, and other Internet companies offering online auctions. Online auctions are less expensive, reach a greater number of interested parties, and assure competitive bidding.

Atlantic Rancher successfully completed its Internet auction and liquidated its assets. The use of cyberspace auctions by bankrupt companies provides an extremely effective way of liquidating assets quickly and ensuring the highest price possible. Internet auctions are being used by more companies who file and liquidate under Chapter 7 of the Bankruptcy Code. Atlantic Rancher used a Web site to announce its Internet liquidation.

CHAPTER 11 REORGANIZATION BANKRUPTCY

Chapter 11 of the Bankruptcy Code provides a method for reorganizing the debtor's financial affairs under the supervision of the Bankruptcy Court.[4] Its goal is to reorganize the debtor with a new capital structure so that it will emerge from bankruptcy as a viable concern. This option, which is referred to as **reorganization bankruptcy**, is often in the best interests of the debtor and its creditors.

Reorganization Proceeding

Chapter 11 is available to individuals, partnerships, corporations, nonincorporated associations, and railroads. It is not available to banks, savings and loan associations, credit unions, insurance companies, stockbrokers, or commodities brokers. The majority of Chapter 11 proceedings are filed by corporations.

A Chapter 11 petition may be filed voluntarily by the debtor or involuntarily by its creditors. The principles discussed earlier under Chapter 7 regarding the filing of petitions, the first meeting of creditors, the entry of the order for relief, automatic stay, and relief from stay also apply to Chapter 11 proceedings.

Chapter 11

A bankruptcy method that allows reorganization of the debtor's financial affairs under the supervision of the Bankruptcy Court.

Business Brief

Chapter 11 is used primarily by businesses to reorganize their finances under the protection of the bankruptcy court. The debtor usually emerges from bankruptcy a "leaner" business, having restructured and discharged some of its debts.

Federal bankruptcy law provides a method for individuals and businesses to discharge all or a portion of their debt and obtain a "fresh start" free of certain debts.

Debtor-in-Possession

In most Chapter 11 cases, the debtor is left in place to operate the business during the reorganization proceeding. In such cases, the debtor is called a **debtor-in-possession**. The court may appoint a trustee to operate the debtor's business only upon a showing of cause, such as fraud, dishonesty, or gross mismanagement by the debtor or its management. Even if a trustee is not appointed, however, the court may appoint an examiner to investigate the debtor's financial affairs.

debtor-in-possession

A debtor who is left in place to operate the business during the reorganization proceeding.

The debtor-in-possession (or the trustee if one is appointed) has the same powers and duties as a trustee in a Chapter 7 proceeding. In addition, the debtor-in-possession (or trustee) is empowered to operate the debtor's business during the bankruptcy proceeding. This power includes authority to enter into contracts, purchase supplies, incur debts, and so on. Some suppliers will accept only cash for their goods or services during this time, whereas others will extend credit. Credit extended by postpetition unsecured creditors in the ordinary course of business is given automatic priority as an administrative expense in bankruptcy. Further, upon notice and hearing, the court may create a secured interest by granting a postpetition unsecured creditor a lien on the debtor-in-possession's property.

Creditor's Committees

Once an order for relief is granted, the court will appoint a **creditors' committee** composed of representatives of the class of unsecured claims. Generally, the creditors holding the seven largest claims are appointed to the committee. The court may also appoint a committee of secured creditors and a committee of equity holders. Committee members owe a fiduciary duty to represent the interest of the class. Committees may appear at Bankruptcy Court hearings, participate in the negotiation of a plan of reorganization, assert objections to proposed plans, and the like.

> **Business Brief**
>
> Approximately 25,000 U.S. companies file for Chapter 11 protection each year.

> **creditor's committee**
>
> The creditors holding the seven largest unsecured claims are usually appointed to the creditors' committee. Representatives of the committee appear at Bankruptcy Court hearings, participate in the negotiation of a plan of reorganization, assert objections to proposed plans, and so on.

Entrepreneur and the Law

SMALL BUSINESS BANKRUPTCY

Large firms, such as Macy's, Continental Airlines, and Dow Corning have reorganized under Chapter 11 of the Bankruptcy Code. These large firms have resources to hire lawyers, investment bankers, and other professionals to assist them in the time-consuming and expensive Chapter11 reorganization process. Smaller firms often do not have the resources or the luxury of the time necessary to use a Chapter 11 proceeding, however.

To address this problem, Congress enacted the **Bankruptcy Reform Act of 1994**, which amended Chapter 11. **Section 217** of this act permits business with total debts of less than $2 million to elect a "fast-tract" for processing its Chapter 11 case. This procedure makes creditors' committees optional and sets up deadlines aimed at concluding the Chapter 11 case within 160 days of the bankruptcy filing. Section 217 "small business bankruptcy" provides an efficient and cost-saving method for smaller firms to seek bankruptcy protection and reorganize as a going concern using Chapter 11 of the Bankruptcy Code.

*𝒫*LAN OF REORGANIZATION

The debtor has the exclusive right to file a **plan of reorganization** with the Bankruptcy Court within the first 120 days after the date of the order for relief. The debtor also has the right to obtain creditor approval of the plan within the first 180 days after the date of the order. After that, any party of interest (i.e., a trustee, a creditor, or an equity holder) may propose a plan. The court has discretion to extend the 120- and 180-day periods in complex cases.

The plan of reorganization sets forth the debtor's proposed new capital structure. In a Chapter 11 proceeding, creditors have claims and equity holders have interests. The plan must designate the different classes of claims and interests. The reorganization plan may propose altering the rights of creditors and equity holders. For example, it might require claims and interests to be reduced, the conversion of unsecured creditors to equity holders, the sale of assets, or the like.

> **plan of reorganization**
>
> A plan that sets forth a proposed new capital structure for the debtor to have when it emerges from reorganization bankruptcy. The debtor has the exclusive right to file the first plan of reorganization; any party of interest may file a plan thereafter.

> **Business Brief**
>
> In a Chapter 11 proceeding, creditors have *claims* and equity holders have *interests*.

Disclosure Statement

The debtor must supply the creditors and equity holders with a **disclosure statement** that contains adequate information *about the proposed plan of reorganization*. The court must approve the disclosure statement before it is distributed.

> **disclosure statement**
>
> A statement that must contain adequate information about the proposed plan of reorganization that is supplied to the creditors and equity holders.

Executory Contracts

Under the Bankruptcy Code, the debtor-in-possession (or trustee) is given the authority to assume or reject **executory contracts** (i.e., contracts that are not fully performed by both sides). In general, unfavorable executory contracts will be rejected and favorable executory contracts will be assumed. For example, a debtor-in-possession may reject an unfavorable lease. Court approval is necessary to reject an executory contract. Executory contracts may also be rejected in Chapter 7 and Chapter 13 proceedings.

Rejection of Collective Bargaining Agreements   Companies that file for Chapter 11 reorganization sometimes argue that agreements with labor unions that still have years to run are executory contracts that may be rejected in bankruptcy. The U.S. Supreme Court has upheld the right of companies to reject union contracts in bankruptcy.[5] The court held that rejection was permitted if necessary for the successful rehabilitation of the debtor.

Subsequently, *labor unions lobbied Congress* for a change in the law. Congress responded by enacting *Section 1113 of the 1984* amendments to the Bankruptcy Code. Section 1113 established the following multistep process that must be followed before a collective bargaining agreement may be rejected or modified:

1. The debtor must make a proposal to the union regarding the modification of the agreement.
2. The debtor must meet with the union to discuss the proposal.
3. The court must hold a hearing if the union refuses to accept the proposal.

If these requirements are met, the court may order the modification or rejection of the labor agreement if (1) such rejection or modification is necessary to the reorganization, (2) the debtor acted in good faith, and (3) the balance of equities favor rejection or modification of the collective bargaining agreement.

Entrepreneur and the Law

PLANET HOLLYWOOD PLUNGES TO EARTH

When Planet Hollywood International, Inc., opened its first "Planet Hollywood" restaurant in Beverly Hills, it looked like the stars would shine on the company. Entrepreneur-celebrities such as Bruce Willis, Demi Moore, Sylvester Stallone, and Arnold Schwarzennegger—who combined owned about 20 percent of the company's stock—showed up along with a virtual "Who's Who" list of Hollywood for the grand opening. Other major shareholders of Planet Hollywood were Saudi Arabian Prince Alwaleed bin Talal, Singapore billionaire Ong Beng Seng, and cofounder and CEO Robert Earl. Planet Hollywood, a theme restaurant, featured movie memorabilia hanging from the walls and ceiling.

Planet Hollywood enjoyed great early success as a leader in the "eatertainment" industry and went on an expansion spree, opening 48 company-owned restaurants. Planet Hollywood also franchised an additional 32 restaurants worldwide, including outlets in Hong Kong, Rome, and Moscow. The company gave movie stars stock and stock options in exchange for showing up at Planet Hollywood openings. In 1996, the company went public—that is, sold stock to public shareholders—at $18 per share. The price climbed to $32 per share the first day of trading, it highest price ever.

Eventually Planet Hollywood's star crashed, however. Other theme restaurants opened, causing an increase in competition in this niche market. Planet Hollywood restaurants were successful in drawing in first-timers to its outlets, but had trouble luring them back for repeat business. And high prices and a perception of mediocre food stalled sales as well. Profits plunged until the company was bleeding with red ink and could no longer pay interest payments on its crushing debt. Planet Hollywood's share price fell until August 18, 1999, when it reached $.75 per share. On that date the company publicly announced it would seek protection under Chapter 11 of the Bankruptcy Code to financially reorganize itself.

After negotiating with its creditors, Planet Hollywood filed a prepackaged Chapter 11 bankruptcy filing. In a *prepackaged filing,* the creditors and investors have already negotiated and agreed on the terms of the reorganization when the bankruptcy petition is filed. Planet Hollywood's agreed-upon restructuring plan called for the following:

*   There was a dramatic 75 percent reduction of the number of restaurants. The company continues to operate its most successful outlets, such as those in Las Vegas and at Disney World in Orlando but closed many other outlets. The company used the executory contract provision of the Bankruptcy Code to get out of high-cost leases and other money-losing locations.
*   The debt-holders of $250 million in subordinated notes agreed to cancel their debt and the back-interest owed them by Planet Hollywood in exchange for $47.5 million

in cash, $60 million of new notes, and new common stock representing 30 percent of the equity in the new Planet Hollywood.

- Equity holders, including the celebrities and public shareholders alike, were wiped out, that is, their shares were worth nothing in the reorganization. They received warrants to purchase shares in Planet Hollywood in the future at a predetermined price that would not be reached unless Planet Hollywood was successful as a reorganized going concern.

- An investor group led by Prince Alwaleed bin Talal, Ong Beng Seng, and Robert Earl's trust for his children invested $30 million in exchange for 70 percent equity ownership in the new reorganized Planet Hollywood.

The new Planet Hollywood revised its menu and added new merchandise (25 percent of its revenue comes from the sale of T-shirts) with the hope of revitalizing its lost luster. Only time will tell whether Planet Hollywood has staying power or will become a vanishing star.

Confirmation of a Plan of Reorganization

A plan of reorganization must be **confirmed** by the court before it becomes effective. The plan may be confirmed by either (1) the acceptance method or (2) the "cram down" method. These two methods are discussed in the paragraphs that follow. If more than one plan is proposed, the court may confirm only one plan.

confirmation

The bankruptcy court's approval of a plan of reorganization.

Confirmation by the Acceptance Method

Classes of creditors and interests must be given the opportunity to vote to accept or reject the plan before the court considers its confirmation. Under **Section 1129(a)**—that is, the **acceptance method**—the court must confirm a plan of reorganization if the following tests are met:

1. The plan must be in the best interests of each class of claims and interests as indicated by either (a) a unanimous vote of acceptance by the members of the class or (b) the property received by the class members under the plan is worth at least as much as they would receive upon liquidation.
2. The plan must be feasible. That is, the debtor must have a good probability of surviving as a going concern. The court examines the debtor's estimated earnings and expenses as proposed by the plan before making this determination.
3. At least one class of claims must vote to accept the plan. A plan is deemed accepted by a class of claims if at least one-half the number of creditors who vote to accept the plan and the accepting creditors represent two-thirds the dollar amount of allowed claims who vote.
4. Each class of claims and interests is nonimpaired. A class is nonimpaired if (a) its legal, equitable, and contractual rights are unaltered by the plan, or (b) the class votes to accept the plan. A class of claims accepts the plan if one-half the number who vote accept the plan and they represent two-thirds the dollar amount of allowed claims that vote to accept the plan. A class of interests accepts a plan if at least two-thirds of the amount of interests that vote accept the plan.

acceptance method

The bankruptcy court must approve a plan of reorganization if (1) the plan is in the *best interests* of each class of claims and interests, (2) the plan is *feasible*, (3) at least one class of claims *votes to accept the plan*, and (4) each class of claims and interests is *nonimpaired*.

Business Brief

Creditors and equity holders are given the opportunity to vote on the confirmation of a plan of reorganization.

A plan of reorganization cannot discriminate unfairly against members of a class. For example, no member of any class can receive more than any other member of that class. No class of claims or interests may be paid more than the full amount of its claim.

Japan Many other countries do not have the extensive bankruptcy laws like the United States, and in fact discourage companies from declaring bankruptcy.

Confirmation by the Cram Down Method

If a dissenting class of claims is impaired, the plan of reorganization cannot be confirmed using the acceptance method. The court can, however, force an impaired class to participate in a plan of reorganization under the **cram down method** of **Section 1129(b)**. As discussed below, to be crammed down, the plan must be fair and equitable to the impaired class.

Secured Creditors A plan is fair and equitable to an impaired class of secured creditors if the reorganization allows the class to (1) retain its lien on the collateral (whether the property is retained by the debtor or transferred to another party), (2) place a lien on the proceeds from the sale of the collateral, or (3) receive an "indubitable equivalent," such as a lien on other property.

Unsecured Creditors A reorganization plan is fair and equitable to an impaired class of unsecured creditors if (1) that class is paid cash or property that has a discounted present value equal to the allowed amount of the claim or (2) no class below it receives anything in the plan (the **absolute priority rule**).[6]

Consider This Example Assume that in a Chapter 11 case there is a class of secured creditors, a class of unsecured creditors, and a class of equity holders. The secured creditors vote to accept the plan. The unsecured creditors, who are impaired because they are given only 10 percent of their claim, vote to reject the plan. Nevertheless, the plan can be crammed down on the unsecured class under the absolute priority rule if the plan does not give the equity holders anything.

Equity Holders A plan is fair and equitable to an impaired class of equity holders if that class is paid the greater of (1) the fixed liquidation preference (if any), (2) the fixed redemption preference (if any), or (3) the discounted present value of their equity interest. Alternatively, the absolute priority rule can be applied to an impaired equity class if no class below it receives anything.

cram down method
A method of confirmation of a plan of reorganization where the court forces an impaired class to participate in the plan of reorganization.

Business Brief
The term *cram down* derives from the notion that the plan of reorganization is being "crammed down the throats" of the impaired dissenting class.

absolute priority rule
A rule that says a reorganization plan is fair and equitable to an impaired class of unsecured creditors or equity holders if no class below it receives anything in the plan.

The Supreme Court Speaks

"Absolute Priority Rule" Applied in a Cram Down Bankruptcy

Bank of America National Trust and Savings Association v. 203 North LaSalle Street Partnership
526 U.S. 434, 119 S.Ct. 1411 (1999)
Supreme Court of the United States

BACKGROUND AND FACTS

203 North LaSalle Partnership (Partnership) is an Illinois real estate limited partnership that owns 15 floors of an office building in downtown Chicago. The Partnership borrowed $93 million from Bank of America National Trust and Savings Association, giving the bank a mortgage on the real estate to secure the loan. In January 1995, the Partnership defaulted on the loan and filed for Chapter 11 bankruptcy. The Partnership filed a Plan of Reorganization proposing that:

1. The Bank retain a secured claim of $54.5 million on the building, which was the value of the building at the time.
2. The Bank's unsecured deficiency claim of $38.5 million would be discharged.
3. The remaining unsecured trade creditors would be paid their $90,000 of claims in full.

4. The old equity holders of the Partnership would be given the exclusive right to invest $6,125,000 in new capital in the reorganized entity.

The Bank objected to the plan of reorganization, so the Partnership sought to have the Plan "crammed down" on the Bank. The bankruptcy court confirmed the plan of reorganization using the cram down method, and both the district court and the court of appeals affirmed. The Bank appealed to the U.S. Supreme Court.

SUPREME COURT ISSUE

Can a plan of reorganization be crammed down over the objection of a creditor if the old equity holders are given the exclusive authority to invest equity capital in the reorganized debtor?

IN THE LANGUAGE OF THE U.S. SUPREME COURT

Souter, Justice *The absolute priority rule was the basis for the Bank's position that the plan could not be confirmed as a cramdown. As the Bank read the rule, the plan was open to objection simply because certain old equity holders in the Partnership would receive property even though the Bank's unsecured deficiency claim would not be paid in full.*

Given that the opportunity is property of some value, the question arises why old equity alone should obtain it. If the price to be paid for the equity interest is the best obtainable, old equity does not need the protection of exclusiveness; if it is not the best, there is no apparent reason for giving old equity a bargain. There is no reason, that is unless the very purpose of the whole transaction is, at least in part, to do old equity a favor.

DECISION AND REMEDY

The U.S. Supreme Court held that the exclusive right of the old equity holders to invest new equity capital in the reorga-nized debtor violates federal bankruptcy law. The Supreme Court reversed the lower court's order approving the debtor's plan of reorganization and remanded the case for further proceedings.

CASE QUESTIONS

Critical Legal Thinking What does the "absolute priority rule" provide? Explain.

Business Ethics Did the old equity holders act ethically in this case? Why do you think they wanted the exclusive right to be equity investors in the new reorganized entity?

Contemporary Business How much was the Bank's original loan? How much was the Bank's secured interest worth at the time of bankruptcy? What happens to the Bank's deficiency amount in Chapter 11 bankruptcy?

Discharge

Upon confirmation of a plan of reorganization, the debtor is granted a **discharge** of all claims not included in the plan. The plan is binding on all parties once it is confirmed.

discharge
Creditors' claims that are not included in a Chapter 11 reorganization are discharged.

International Law

REORGANIZATION UNDER BRITISH BANKRUPTCY LAW

Many of our country's forefathers were debtors fleeing the harsh laws of Britain and European countries where debtors were often sent to debtors' prisons or were required to work off the debt owed to creditors, When this country was founded, the right to declare bankruptcy was considered just as important as the right to free speech, and both rights were included in the U.S. Constitution.

Even today, U.S. bankruptcy law treats debtors more leniently than the bankruptcy laws of other countries. Consider the case of bankruptcy reorganization laws in Britain versus those of the United States.

In 1987, Britain enacted a new bankruptcy law for handling the reorganization of bankrupt companies. The law banishes lawyers from the reorganization process and puts it in the hands of specially licensed accountants. When a firm files for reorganization bankruptcy in Britain, an administrative order is issued. The order permits the creditors of the troubled company to appoint a team of bankruptcy accountants to handle the company's reorganization.

British law assumes that the company's misfortune is not a result of bad luck but is based on mismanagement by the company's officers and directors. Consequently, the bankruptcy accountants are empowered to remove the firm's existing management and take over control of its operations. The accountants then orchestrate the reorganization and sale of the company's assets.

Many U.S. bankruptcy lawyers allege that British bankruptcy law tramples too hard on debtors' rights. They argue that British law thwarts the fresh start theory underlying American bankruptcy law. Proponents of the British system argue that it is faster, cheaper, and more efficient than a bankruptcy reorganization under Chapter 11 of the U.S. Bankruptcy Code. They assert that the British system does not coddle debtors and make lawyers rich, as the U.S. bankruptcy system does.

CHAPTER 13 CONSUMER DEBT ADJUSTMENT

Chapter 13, which is called a **consumer debt adjustment**, is a rehabilitation form of bankruptcy for natural persons. Chapter 13 permits the court to supervise the debtor's plan for the payment of unpaid debts by installments.

The debtor has several advantages under Chapter 13. They include avoidance of the stigma of Chapter 7 liquidation, retention of more property than is exempt under Chapter 7, and less expense and less compilation than a Chapter 7 proceeding. The creditors have

Chapter 13
A rehabilitation form of bankruptcy that permits the courts to supervise the debtor's plan for the payment of unpaid debts by installments.

advantages, too. They may recover a greater percentage of the debts owed them than they would under a Chapter 7 proceeding.

Filing the Petition

A Chapter 13 proceeding can be initiated only by the voluntary filing of a petition by a debtor who alleges that he or she is (1) insolvent or (2) unable to pay his or her debts when they become due. The petition must state that the debtor desires to effect an extension or composition of debts, or both. An **extension** provides for a longer period of time for the debtor to pay his or her debts. A **composition** provides for a reduction of debts.

Only individuals (including sole proprietors) with regular income who owe individually (or with their spouse) noncontingent, liquidated, unsecured debts of less than $250,000 and secured debts of less than $750,000 may file such a petition. The key is the debtor's regular income, which may be from any source, including wages, salary, commissions, income from investments, Social Security, pension income, or public assistance. The amount of the debtor's assets is irrelevant. Most Chapter 13 petitions are filed by homeowners who want to protect nonexempt equity in their residences.

When (or shortly after) the petition is filed, the debtor must file a list of creditors, assets, and liabilities with the court. The court then schedules a meeting of creditors. The debtor must appear at this meeting. Creditors may submit proof of claims, which will be allowed or disallowed by the court. No creditor committees are appointed, but the court must appoint a trustee upon confirmation of the plan.

Automatic Stay

The filing of a Chapter 13 petition automatically stays (1) liquidation bankruptcy proceedings, (2) judicial and nonjudicial actions by creditors to collect prepetition debts from the debtor, and (3) collection activities against codebtors and guarantors of consumer debts. The automatic stay continues until the Chapter 13 plan is completed or dismissed. The stay does not apply to business debts.

The Plan of Payment

The debtor's plan of payment must be filed within 15 days of filing the petition. The debtor must file information about his or her finances, including a budget of estimated income and expenses during the period of the plan. The plan period cannot exceed three years unless the court approves a longer period (of up to five years). During the plan period, the debtor retains possession of his or her property, may acquire new property and incur debts, and so on.

The debtor must begin making the planned installment payments to the trustee within 30 days after the plan is filed. These interim payments must continue until the plan is confirmed or denied. If the plan is denied, the trustee must return the interim payments to the debtor less any administrative costs. If the plan is converged, the debtor must continue making payments to the trustee. The trustee is responsible for remitting these payments to the creditors. The trustee is paid 10 percent of the debts paid under the plan.

A Chapter 13 plan may be modified if the debtor's circumstances materially change. For example, if the debtor's income subsequently decreases, the court may decrease the debtor's payments under the plan. Request for the modification of a plan may be made by the debtor, the trustee, or a creditor. If an interested party objects to the modification, the court must hold a hearing to determine whether it should be approved.

Confirmation of the Plan

The plan may modify the rights of unsecured creditors and some secured creditors. Any objections they have may be voiced at the confirmation hearing held by the court. The plan must (1) be proposed in good faith, (2) pass the feasibility test (e.g., the debtor must be able to make the proposed payments), and (3) be in the best interests of the creditors (i.e., the present value of the payments must equal or exceed the amount that the creditors would receive in a Chapter 7 liquidation proceeding).

Secured Creditors The plan must be submitted to the secured creditors for acceptance. The plan will be confirmed if the secured creditors unanimously accept it. If a secured creditor does not accept the plan, the court may still confirm the plan if (1) it permits the secured creditor to retain its lien and the value of the plan's distribution to the creditor is more than its secured interest or (2) the debtor surrenders the property securing the claim to the secured creditor.

Unsecured Creditors Although a vote of unsecured creditors is not required for confor-mation of a Chapter 13 plan, their objection to the plan can delay or defeat confirmation. The court cannot confirm the plan unless (1) it proposes to pay the objecting unsecured creditor the present value of his or her claim or (2) the debtor agrees to commit all of his or her disposable income during the plan period to pay his or her creditors. (Disposable income is all income not necessary to maintain the debtor and his or her dependents.)

Law cannot persuade, where it cannot punish.

Thomas Fuller
Gnomologia (1732)

Consider This Example Suppose a debtor earns $1,800 per month, of which $1,200 is reasonably necessary to support the debtor and his or her family. If the $400 per month disposable income is committed to pay prepetition debts, the court may confirm the plan even if the debts of the unsecured creditors are substantially modified or liquidated.

Discharge

The court will grant an order **discharging** the debtor from all unpaid debts covered by the plan after all the payments required under the plan are completed. All debts are discharge-able under Chapter 13 except alimony and child support and priority debts such as trustee fees. Dischargeable debts include student loans, fraudulently incurred debts, and debts arising from malicious or willful injury from drunken driving. Thus, a Chapter 13 discharge may be more beneficial to a debtor than a Chapter 7 liquidation discharge. A discharge can be revoked within one year if it was obtained by fraud. There is a timebar to filing a peti-tion for Chapter 13 proceeding. Thus, a debtor may file successive petitions for Chapter 13 bankruptcy.

discharge

A discharge is granted to a debtor in a Chapter 13 consumer debt adjustment bankruptcy only after all the payments under the plan are completed by the debtor.

Hardship Discharge Even if the debtor does not complete the payments called for in the plan, the court may grant the debtor a **hardship discharge**. Such a discharge will be granted if (1) the debtor fails to complete the payments due to unforeseeable circumstances (e.g., the debtor loses his or her job through no fault of his or her own), (2) the unsecured creditors have been paid as much as they would have been paid in a Chapter 7 liquidation proceeding, and (3) it is not practical to modify the plan.

hardship discharge

A discharge granted if (1) the debtor fails to complete the payments due to unforeseeable circumstances, (2) the unsecured creditors have been paid as much as they would have been paid in a Chapter 7 liquidation proceeding, and (3) it is not practical to modify the plan.

Entrepreneur and the Law

CHAPTER 12 FAMILY FARMER BANKRUPTCY

In the 1980s, farms across the country experienced financial difficulty as farm prices and real estate values fell. Many farmers who found it difficult to meet their financial obligations and faced bankruptcy lobbied Congress for help. In 1986, Congress responded and added **Chapter 12** to the Bankruptcy Code. Chapter 12 gives "family farmers"—defined as farmers whose total debt does not exceed $1.5 million and are at least 80 per-cent farm related—a special form of bankruptcy protection.

Chapter 12 is a reorganization provision that allows fam-ily farmers to reorganize financially. Upon filing, an auto-matic stay goes in place against creditors' actions against the family farmer. The farmer-debtor must file a plan of reorga-nization within 90 days of the order for relief. Creditors can-not vote on the plan of reorganization.

The major provision of Chapter 12 allows family farmers to have mortgage loans rewritten to the fair market value of the property in cases where the value of the farm land has decreased below the value of the loan. For example, assume a farm is worth $1,000,000 at the time a family farmer borrows $800,000 from Rural Bank, which takes back a mortgage on the farm for this amount. After several years the framer suf-fers financial difficulty and files Chapter 12 bankruptcy. At the time of the bankruptcy filing, the farm land is only worth $500,000. Under Chapter 12, the mortgage is reduced to $500,000 under the plan of reorganization.

Chapter 12 allows family farmers to file for a special type of reorganization bankruptcy that gives them added protec-tion not available under Chapter 11 of the Bankruptcy Code.

CHAPTER SUMMARY

Overview of Federal Bankruptcy Law, p. 554

Bankruptcy	1. *Bankruptcy Reform Act of 1978, as amended.* Federal statute that establishes the requirements and procedures for filing bankruptcy. Called the *Bankruptcy Code.* 2. *Bankruptcy courts.* Have exclusive jurisdiction to hear bankruptcy cases. A bankruptcy court is attached to each federal district court. Bankruptcy judges are appointed for 14-year terms.
The "Fresh Start"	The purpose of a bankruptcy is to discharge the debtor from burdensome debts.

Chapter 7 Liquidation Bankruptcy, p. 555

Chapter 7 Bankruptcy	The debtor's nonexempt property is sold for cash, the cash is distributed to the creditors and any unpaid debts are discharged. Also called *liquidation bankruptcy.*

Bankruptcy Procedure	1. *Filing a petition.* The filing of a petition commences a bankruptcy case.
	  a. *Voluntary petition.* Filed by the debtor.
	  b. *Involuntary petition.* Filed by a creditor or creditors.
	2. *Order for relief.* Designates that the bankruptcy court has accepted the case for further proceedings.
	3. *Meeting of the creditors.* The debtor must appear at this meeting and answer questions by the creditors. Also called the *first meeting of the creditors.*
	4. *Appointments of a trustee.* A *permanent trustee* is elected at the first meeting of the creditors in a Chapter 7 case.
	5. *Proof of claims.* Unsecured creditors must file proof of claim stating the amount of their claims against the debtors.

Automatic Stay	The filing of a bankruptcy petition *stays* (suspends) certain legal actions against the debtor or the debtor's property. *Relief from stay.* A secured creditor may petition the court for a relief from stay in situations involving depreciating assets and the creditor is not adequately protected during the bankruptcy proceeding.

Property of the Bankruptcy Estate, p. 559

Property of the Bankruptcy Estate	*Bankruptcy estate.* Includes: 1. All the debtor's legal and equitable interests in real, personal, tangible, and intangible property at the time the petition if filed. 2. Gifts, inheritances, life insurance proceeds, and property from divorce settlements that the debtor is entitled to receive within 180 days after the petition is filed.
Exempt Property	The Bankruptcy Code permits the debtor to retain certain property that does not become part of the bankruptcy estate. Exemptions are stipulated in federal and state law.
Voidable Transfers	The following transfers and preferences are voidable by the trustee: 1. *Preferential transfer within 90 days before bankruptcy.* Transfer must be for an antecedent debt and give the creditor more than he or she would receive in bankruptcy. 2. *Preferential liens within 90 days before bankruptcy.* Transfer must be for an antecedent debt, and the creditor would receive more because of this lien than he or she would as an unsecured creditor in bankruptcy. 3. *Preferential transfer to an insider within one year before bankruptcy.* The transferee must be an "insider" (e.g., relative, business associate) and the creditor insolvent. 4. *Fraudulent transfer within one year before bankruptcy.* Transfer of property by the debtor with the actual intent to hinder, delay, or defraud creditors.

Distribution of Property and Discharge, p. 562

Priority of Distribution	Nonexempt property of the bankruptcy estate is distributed to the creditors in the following statutory priority: 1. *Secured creditors.* A secured creditor either obtains the collateral or the collateral is sold and the secured creditor is paid. If the value of the collateral exceeds the secured interest, the excess becomes available to

	pay other creditors. If the value of the collateral is less than the secured interest, the secured creditor becomes an unsecured creditor to the difference. 2. *Unsecured creditors.* Unsecured creditors are paid in priority established by the Bankruptcy Code. Each class must be paid in full before any lower class is paid anything. If a class cannot be paid in full, the claims of that class are paid pro rata (proportionately).
Discharge	After the nonexempt property is distributed, the remaining unpaid claims of the debtor are *discharged*; the debtor's legal obligation to pay these unpaid debts is terminated. Discharge is available only to individuals.
Nondischargeable Debts	The Bankruptcy Code stipulates that certain debts are not dischargeable.
Acts That Bar Discharge	The bankruptcy court may deny discharge of debts if the debtor has engaged in prohibited conduct.
Discharge of Student Loans	A student loan may be discharged after it is due only if nondischarge would cause an *undue hardship* on the debtor or his or her family.

Chapter 11 Reorganization Bankruptcy, p. 566

Chapter 11 Reorganization Bankruptcy	Provides a method for reorganizing the debtor's financial affairs under the supervision of the bankruptcy court.
Reorganization Proceeding	*Procedure.* The principles discussed earlier under Chapter 7 regarding the filing of petitions, the first meeting of the creditors, the entry for the order of relief, and automatic stay also apply to Chapter 11 proceedings.
Debtor-in-Possession	In most Chapter 11 cases, the debtor is left in place to operate the business during the reorganization proceeding. In such cases, the debtor is called *debtor-in-possession*. *Trustee.* The court may appoint a trustee to operate the debtor's business only upon a showing of cause, such as fraud, dishonesty, or gross mismanagement by the debtor or its management.
Creditors' Committees	The court will appoint a committee of unsecured creditors (usually creditors holding the seven largest claims). The court may also appoint committees of secured creditors and equity holders. Committees participate in the bankruptcy proceeding and in the negotiation of a plan of reorganization.

Plan of Reorganization, p. 567

Plan of Reorganization	Sets forth the debtor's proposed new capital structure. The debtor has the exclusive right to file a plan within the first 120 days after the date of the order for relief.
Disclosure Statement	The debtor must supply the creditors and equity holders with a disclosure statement that contains adequate information about the proposed plan of reorganization.
Executory Contracts	The debtor-in-possession (or trustee) may assume or reject executory contracts. A special procedure has been established for rejecting union collective bargaining agreements.
Confirmation of a Plan of Reorganization	A plan of reorganization must be confirmed by the bankruptcy court before it becomes effective. Confirmation may be by either of the following methods:
Confirmation by the Acceptance Method	As established by Section 1129(a) of the Bankruptcy Code.
Confirmation by the Cram Down Method	As provided for by Section 1129(b) of the Bankruptcy Code.
Discharge	Upon confirmation of a plan of reorganization, the debtor is granted a discharge of all claims not included in the plan. The debtors' legal obligation to pay the discharged debts is terminated.

Chapter 13 Consumer Debt Adjustment, p. 571

Chapter 13 Consumer Debt Adjustment	A rehabilitation form of bankruptcy that permits bankruptcy courts to supervise the debtor's plan for the repayment of unpaid debts by installment. Called *consumer debt adjustment* or *Chapter 13 bankruptcy*.

The Plan of Payment	The debtor must file a plan of payment. The plan period cannot exceed three years unless the court approves a longer period (of up to five years). A plan may be modified if the debtor's circumstances materially change. *Trustee.* A permanent trustee will be appointed by the court. The debtor makes payments to the trustee, who is responsible for remitting payments to the creditors.
Discharge	The court will grant an order discharging the debtor from all unpaid debts covered by the plan only after all the payments required under the plan are completed. *Hardship discharge.* The court can grant the debtor a hardship discharge even if the debtor does not complete the payments called for by the plan if (1) the failure to make the payments was caused by an unforeseeable circumstance, (2) the creditors have been paid as much as they would have been paid in a Chapter 7 liquidation proceeding, and (3) it is not practical to modify the plan.

END-OF-CHAPTER INTERNET EXERCISES AND CASE QUESTIONS

Working the Web Internet Exercises

ACTIVITIES

1. Check on current statistics on the level of bankruptcies filed at **www.abiworld.org/stats/newstatsfront.html** and InterNet Bankruptcy Library—Worldwide Troubled Company Resources and Daily Source of Bankruptcy News—Bankrupt.Com Home Page— **bankrupt.com**.

2. What is the amount of your state's homestead exemption? More theory may be found in "The Outer Boundaries of the Bankruptcy Estate" at **www.law. emory.edu/ELJ/volumes/fall98/plank.html**.

3. The FTC has practical advice for debtors at **www. ftc.gov/bcp/conline/pubs/credit/kneedeep.htm**.

4. See for yourself the plight of commercial debt relief companies who promise more than they can deliver at **www.ftc.gov/os/1998/9803/watson.fin.htm**.

5. Why do we have bankruptcy? Theoretical underpinnings of bankruptcy are explored in **www.law.fsu. edu/journals/lawreview/downloads/263/carl.pdf** "Bankruptcy's Organizing Principle" by David Gray Carlson.

CRITICAL LEGAL THINKING CASES

23.1 Petition In March 1988, Daniel E. Beren, John M. Elliot and Edward F. Mannino formed Walnut Street Four, a general partnership, to purchase and renovate an office building in Harrisburg, Pennsylvania. They borrowed more than $200,000 from Hamilton Bank to purchase the building and begin renovation. Disagreements among the partners arose when the renovation costs exceeded their estimates. When Beren was unable to obtain assistance from Elliot and Mannino regarding obtaining additional financing, the partnership quit paying its debts. Beren filed an involuntary petition to place the partnership into Chapter 7 bankruptcy. The other partners objected to the bankruptcy filing. At the time of the filing, the partnership owed debts of more than $380,000 and had approximately $550 in the partnership bank account. Should the petition for involuntary bankruptcy be granted? [*In re Walnut Street Four*, 106 B.R. 56 (Bk.M.D.Pa. 1989]

23.2 Bankruptcy Estate In 1983, Bill K. and Marilyn E. Hargis, husband and wife, filed a Chapter 11 bankruptcy proceeding. In 1984, more than 120 days after the bankruptcy peti-

tion was filed, Bill died. His life was insured for $700,000. His wife was the beneficiary of the policy. The bankruptcy trustee moved to recover the $700,000 as property of the bankruptcy estate. Who gets the insurance proceeds? [*In re Matter of Hargis*, 887 F.2d 77 (5th Cir. 1989)]

23.3 Automatic Stay In 1985, James F. Kost filed a voluntary petition for relief under Chapter 11 of the Bankruptcy code. First Interstate Bank of Greybull (First Interstate) held a first mortgage on the debtor's residence near Basin, Wyoming. Appraisals and other evidence showed that the house was worth $116,000. The debt owed to First Interstate was almost $103,000 and was increasing at the rate of $32.46 per day. The debtor had only an 11.5 percent equity cushion in the property. Further evidence showed that the (1) Greybull/Basin area was suffering from tough economic times, (2) there were more than 90 homes available for sale in the area, (3) the real estate market in the area was declining, (4) the condition of the house was seriously deteriorating and the debtor was not financially able to make the necessary improvements, and (5) the insurance on the property had lapsed.

First Interstate moved for a relief from stay so that it could fore-close on the property and sell it. Should the motion be granted? [*In re James F. Kost*, 102 B.R. 829 (Bk.D. Wyo. 1989)]

23.4 Fraudulent Transfer In November 1974, Peter and Geraldine Tabala (Debtors), husband and wife, purchased a house in Clarkstown, New York. In November 1976, they pur-chased a Carvel ice cream business for $70,000 with a loan obtained from People's National Bank. In addition, the Carvel Corporation extended trade credit to Debtors. On October 23, 1978, Debtors conveyed their residence to their three daughters, ages 9, 19, and 20, for no consideration. Debtors continued to reside in the house and to pay maintenance expenses and real estate taxes due on the property. On the date of transfer Debtors owed obligations in excess of $100,000. On March 28, 1980, Debtors filed a petition for Chapter 7 bankruptcy. The bank-ruptcy trustee moved to set aside the Debtors' conveyance of their home to their daughters as a fraudulent transfer. Who wins? [*In re Tabala*, 11 B.R. 405 (Bk.S.D.N.Y. 1981)]

23.5 Preferential Payment Air Florida System, Inc. (Air Florida), an airline company, filed a voluntary petition to reor-ganize under Chapter 11 of the Bankruptcy Code. Within 90 days prior to the commencement of the case, Air Florida paid $13,575 to Compania Panamena de Aviacion, S.A. (COPA), in payment of an antecedent debt. This payment enabled COPA to receive more than it would have received if Air Florida were liquidated under Chapter 7. Is the payment to COPA an avoidable preferential transfer? [*In re Jet Florida System, Inc. f/k/a Air Florida System, Inc.*, 105 B.R. 137 (Bk.S.D.Fla. 1989)]

23.6 Executory Contract On October 15, 1980, The Record Company, Inc. (The Record Company), entered into a purchase agreement to buy certain retail record stores from Bummbusiness, Inc. (Bummbusiness). All assets and inventory were included in the deal. The Record Company agreed to pay Bummbusiness $20,000 and to pay the $380,000 of trade debt owed by the stores. In exchange, Bummbusiness agreed not to compete with the new buyer for two years within a 15-mile radius of the stores and to use its best efforts to obtain an extension of the due dates for the trade debt. The Record Company began operating the stores but shortly thereafter filed a petition for Chapter 11 bankruptcy. At the time of the bankruptcy filing (1) The Record Company owed Bummbusiness $10,000 and owed the trade debt of $380,000 and (2) Bummbusiness was obligated not to compete with The Record Company. Can The Record Company reject the purchase agreement? [*In re The Record Company*, 8 B.R. 57 (Bk.S.D.Ind. 1981)]

23.7 Plan of Reorganization Richard P. Friese (Debtor) filed a voluntary petition for Chapter 11 bankruptcy. In May 1989, Debtor filed a plan of reorganization that divided his creditors into three classes. The first class, administrative creditors, were to be paid in full. The second class, unsecured creditors, were to receive 50 percent on their claims. The IRS was the third class. It was to receive $20,000 on confirmation and the balance in future payments. No creditors voted to accept the plan. The unsecured creditors are impaired because their legal, equitable, and contractual rights are being altered. Can the bankruptcy

court confirm Debtors plan of reorganization? [*In re Friese*, 103 B.R. 90 (Bk.S.D.N.Y. 1989)]

23.8 Consumer Debt Adjustment Manuel Guadalupe (Debtor) was a tool and die machinist who was employed at Elco Industries for more than five years. He accumulated more the $19,000 in unsecured debt, including deficiencies owed after secured creditors repossessed a van (leaving a deficiency of $1,066) and a car (leaving a deficiency of $3,130). Shortly after the second automobile was repossessed, Debtor borrowed approximately $19,000 from Elco Credit Union to purchase a 1988 four-wheel-drive Chevrolet Blazer. The $472 monthly payment was to be taken directly from Debtor's earnings.

On February 28, 1989, Debtor filed a voluntary petition for Chapter 13 consumer debt adjustment. The schedule listed total secured debts of $22,132, which included the debt for the Blazer, furniture, and a camcorder. Total unsecured debt was $19,575, which included $2,160 owed to General Finance Corporation (General). Debtor's budget projected $700 per month would be left over for funding the Chapter 13 plan after his monthly expenses were deducted from his $25,000 gross income. Secured creditors were to paid in full; unsecured credi-tors would receive 10 percent of their claims. General objected to the plan. Should Debtor's Chapter 13 plan be confirmed? [*In re Guadalupe*, 106 B.R. 155 (Bk.N.D.Ill. 1989)]

23.9 Student Loan Donald Wayne Doyle (Debtor) obtained a guaranteed student loan to enroll in a school for training truck drivers. Due to his impending divorce, Debtor never attended the program. The first monthly installment of approximately $50 to pay the student loan became due on September 1, 1988. On September 16, 1988, Debtor filed a voluntary petition for Chapter 7 bankruptcy.

Debtor is a 29-year-old man who earns approximately $1,000 per month at an hourly wage of $7.70 as a truck driver, a job that he had held for 10 years. Debtor resided on a farm where he performed work in lieu of paying rent for his quarters. Debtor was paying monthly payments of $89 on a bank loan for his former wife's vehicle, $200 for his truck, $40 for health insurance, $28 for car insurance, $120 for gasoline and vehicular maintenance, $400 for groceries and meals, and $25 for tele-phone charges. In addition, a state court had ordered Debtor to pay $300 per month to support his children, ages four and five. Debtor's parents were assisting him by buying him $130 of gro-ceries per month. Should Debtor's student loan be discharged in bankruptcy? [*In re Doyle*, 106 B.R. 272 (Bk.N.D.Ala. 1989)]

23.10 Preference Rule On December 17, 1986, ZZZZ Best Co., Inc. (Debtor), borrowed $7 million from Union Bank. On July 8, 1987, Debtor filed a voluntary petition under Chapter 7 (liquidation). During the preceding 90-day period, Debtor made two interest payments on its loan to Union Bank totaling $100,000. The trustee of Debtor's estate filed a complaint against Union Bank to recover those interest payments as pref-erential transfers made within 90 days of the bankruptcy filing. Can payments on long-term debt qualify as payments within the ordinary course of business exception to the 90-day preference rule? [*Union Bank v. Wolas*, 112 S.Ct.2d 257 (1991)]

BUSINESS ETHICS CASES

23.11 Business Ethics Scott Greig Keebler (Debtor) became indebted and his debts exceeded his assets. The Internal Revenue Service (IRS) had levied his wages for nonpayment of taxes. Debtor was healthy and capable of earning a substantial income. Evidence showed that Debtor did not try his best to pay his debts, lived an affluent lifestyle, and determined not to pay his principal creditors. Debtor voluntarily quit his job and filed a voluntary petition for Chapter 7 bankruptcy. The petition stated that he was unemployed. Shortly after filing for bankruptcy, the petitioner resumed work. Should Debtor's Chapter 7 case be dismissed because he filed the petition in bad faith? [*In re Scott Greig Keebler*, 106 B.R. 662 (Bk.D. Hawaii 1989]

23.12 Business Ethics On February 3, 1983, Douglas G. and Aleta Brantz (Debtor), husband and wife, borrowed $40,000 from Meritor Financial Services, Inc. (Meritor), and signed a promissory note evidencing the debt. The proceeds of the loan were used in a business operated by Douglas.

After a portion of the debt had been paid, the business began to fail and the Brantzes defaulted on the loan. Debtors made several attempts to cure the default but failed. On August 11, 1988, Meritor filed a collection action and obtained a judgment lien against Debtor's residence.

On August 16, 1988, a $40,000 mortgage on Debtors' home in favor of Aleta's parents, Philip and Sondra Schley, was recorded. The mortgage was dated February 1, 1988. On May 25, 1989, Debtors filed a voluntary petition for bankruptcy. The parties stipulated that Debtor's home was worth $65,000 and was subject to unvoidable mortgages of $38,000. The Schleys asserted their mortgage of $40,000 preceded Meritor's judicial lien of $28,441. Debtors also claimed an exemption of $15,800 in the premises. Who wins? Was Debtors' behavior unethical? [*In re Brantz*, 106 B.R. 62 (Bk.E.D.Pa. 1989)]

23.13 Business Ethics On September 20, 1985, Jane Gnidovec, David Towell, and Robert Dawson (Plaintiffs) obtained a judgment in state court against Alwan Brothers Co., Inc., and Alwan Brothers Partnership and its general partners (jointly Alwans) for $110,059 compensatory damages and $750,000 punitive damages. When the judgment was upheld on appeal, Alwans filed a voluntary petition for Chapter 11 bankruptcy. Is the judgment for compensatory damages and punitive damages dischargeable in bankruptcy? Is it ethical to seek to discharge judgments in bankruptcy? [*In re Alwan Brothers Co., Inc.*, 105 B.R. 886 (Bk.C.D.Ill. 1989)]

BRIEFING THE CASE WRITING ASSIGNMENT

Read the following case, which has been excerpted from the court's opinons. Review and brief the cast.

Dewsnup v. Timm
116 L.Ed. 2D 903
112 S.Ct. 773 (1992)
United States Supreme Court

Blackmun, Justice

We are confronted in this case with an issue concerning §506(d) of the Bankruptcy Code. May a debtor "strip down" a creditor's lien on real property to the value of the collateral, as judicially determined, when that value is less than the amount of the claim secured by the lien?

On June 1, 1978, respondents loaned $119,000 to petitioner Aletha Dewsnup and her husband, T. LaMar Dewsnup, since deceased. The loan was accompanied by a Deed of Trust granting a lien on two parcels of Utah farmland owned by the Dewsnups. Petitioner defaulted the following year. Under the terms of the Deed of Trust, respondents at that point could have proceeded against the real property collateral by accelerating the maturity of the loan, issuing a notice of default, and selling the land at a public foreclosure sale to satisfy the debt.

Respondents did issue a notice of default in 1981. Before the foreclosure sale took place, however, petitioner sought reorganization under Chapter 11 of the Bankruptcy Code. That bankruptcy petition was dismissed, as was a subsequent Chapter 11 petition. In June 1984, petitioner filed a petition seeking

liquidation under Chapter 7 of the Code. Because of the pendency of these bankruptcy proceedings, respondents were not able to proceed to the foreclosure sale.

Petitioner-debtor takes the petition that §506(a) and §506(d) are complementary and to be read together. Because, under §506(a), a claim is secured only to the extent of the judicially determined value of the real property on which the lien is fixed, a debtor can void a lien on the property pursuant to §506(d) to the extent the claim is no longer secured and thus is not "an allowed secured claim." In other words §506(a), bifurcates classes of claims allowed under §502 into secured claims and unsecured claims; any portion of an allowed claim deemed to be unsecured under §506(a) is not an "allowed secured claim" within the lien-voiding scope of §506(d). Petitioner argues that there is no exception for unsecured property abandoned by the trustee.

We conclude that respondent's alternative position, espoused also by the United States, although not without its difficulty, generally is the best of the several approaches. Therefore, we hold that §506(d) does not allow the petitioner to "strip down" respondents' lien, because respondents' claim is secured by a lien and has been fully allowed pursuant to §502.

The practical effect of petitioner's argument is to freeze the creditor's secured interest at the judicially determined valuation. By this approach, the creditor would lose the benefit of any increase in the value of the property by the time of the foreclosure sale. The increase would accrue to the benefit of the debtor, a result some of the parties would describe as a "windfall."

We think however, that the creditor's lien stays with the real property until the foreclosure. That is what was bargained for by the mortgagor and the mort-

gagee. Any increase over the judicially determined valuation during bankruptcy rightly accrues to the benefit of the creditor, not the benefit of the debtor and not to the benefit of other unsecured creditors whose claims have been allowed and who had nothing to do with the mortgagor-mortgagee bargain.

No provision of the pre-Code statute permitted involuntary reduction of the amount of a creditor's lien for any reason other than payment on the debt.

The judgment of the Court of Appeals is affirmed.

Endnotes

1. 11 U.S.C. § 362(a).
2. The following states require debtors to take state law exemptions: Alabama, Alaska, Arizona, Arkansas, California, Colorado, Delaware, Florida, Georgia, Idaho, Illinois, Indiana, Iowa, Kansas, Kentucky, Louisiana, Maine, Maryland, Missouri, Montana, Nebraska, Nevada, New Hampshire, New York, North Carolina, North Dakota, Oklahoma, Oregon, South Carolina, South Dakota, Tennessee, Utah, Virginia, West Virginia, and Wyoming.
3. 11 U.S.C. § 507.
4. 11 U.S.C. §§ 1101-1174.
5. *National Labor Relations Board v. Bildisco and Bildisco*, 465 U.S. 513, 104 S.Ct. 1188 (1984).
6. The absolute priority rule was announced in *Consolidated Rock Products Co. v. Du Bois*, 312 U.S. 510, 61 S.Ct. 675 (1941). The doctrine was codified in the Bankruptcy Reform Act of 1978.

Employment and Equal Opportunity Laws

CHAPTER 24

Agency

Let every eye negotiate for itself, and trust no agent.

—William Shakespeare
Much Ado About Nothing (1598)

Chapter Objectives

After studying this chapter, you should be able to:

1. Define *agency*.

2. Identify and define a principal–independent contractor relationship.

3. Describe how express, implied, and apparent agencies are created.

4. List and describe the agent's duties to the principal and the principal's duties to the agent.

5. Describe the principal's and agent's liability on third-party contracts.

6. Explain the doctrine of *respondeat superior*.

7. Identify and describe the principal's liability for the tortious conduct of an agent.

8. Describe how an agency is terminated by the acts of the parties and by operation of law.

9. Identify a wrongful termination of an agency.

10. Explain the use of representatives, agents, and distributors in foreign commerce.

Chapter Contents

If businesspeople had to personally conduct all of their business, the scope of their activities would be severely curtailed. Partnerships would not be able to operate; corporations could not act through managers and employees; and sole proprietorships would not be able to hire employees. The use of agents (or agency), which allows one person to act on behalf of another, solves this problem.

There are many examples of agency relationships. They include a salesperson who sells goods for a store, an executive who works for a corporation, a partner who acts on behalf of a partnership, an attorney who is hired to represent a client, a real estate broker who is employed to sell a house, and so on. Agency is governed by a large body of common law, known as **agency law**. This law, which is a mixture of contract law and tort law, is discussed in this chapter.

THE NATURE OF AGENCY

Agency relationships are formed by the mutual consent of a principal and an agent. Section 1(1) of the Restatement (Second) of Agency defines *agency* as a *fiduciary relationship* "which results from the manifestation of consent by one person to another that the other shall act in his behalf and subject to his control, and consent by the other so to act." The Restatement (Second) of Agency is the reference source of the rules of agency. A party who employs another person to act on his or her behalf is called a **principal**. A party who agrees to act on behalf of another is called an **agent**. The principal–agent relationship is commonly referred to as an **agency**. This relationship is depicted in Exhibit 24.1.

EXHIBIT 24.1 *The Principal–Agent Relationship*

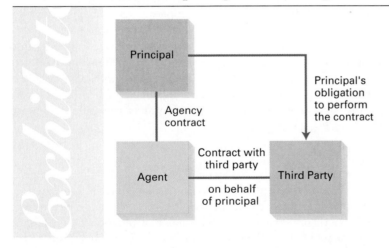

Persons Who Can Initiate an Agency Relationship

Any person who has the capacity to contract can appoint an agent to act on his or her behalf. Generally, persons who lack **contractual capacity**, such as insane persons and minors, cannot appoint an agent. However, the court can appoint a legal guardian or other representative to handle the affairs of insane persons, minors, and others who lack capacity to contract. With court approval, these representatives can enter into enforceable contracts on behalf of the persons they represent.

An agency can be created only to accomplish a lawful purpose. Agency contracts that are created for illegal purposes or are against public policy are void and unenforceable. For example, a principal cannot hire an agent to kill another person. Some agency relationships are prohibited by law. For example, unlicensed agents cannot be hired to perform the duties of certain licensed professionals (e.g., doctors and lawyers).

Hong Kong Multinational companies often use agents to represent them to conduct business in foreign countries.

ℋINDS OF EMPLOYMENT RELATIONSHIPS

employment relationships

(1) Employer-employee. (2) principal-agent, and (3) principal-independent contractor

Businesses usually have three kinds of **employment relationships**: (1) employer–employee relationships; (2) principal–agent relationships; and (3) principal–independent contractor relationships. These relationships are discussed in the following paragraphs.

Employer–Employee Relationship

employer–employee relationship

A relationship that results when an employer hires an employee to perform some form of physical service.

An **employer–employee relationship** exists when an employer hires an employee to perform some form of physical service. For example, a welder on General Motors Corporation's assembly line is employed in an employer–employee relationship because he performs a physical task.

An employee is not an agent unless he or she is specifically empowered to enter into contracts on the principal employer's behalf. Employees may only enter into contracts that are within the scope of their employment. The welder in the previous example is not an agent because he cannot enter into contracts on behalf of General Motors Company. If the company empowered him to enter into contracts, he would become an agent.

Principal–Agent Relationship

principal–agent relationship

An employer hires an employee and gives that employee authority to act and enter into contracts on his or her behalf.

A **principal–agent relationship** is formed when an employer hires an employee and gives that employee authority to act and enter into contracts on his or her behalf. The extent of this authority is governed by any express agreement between the parties and implied from the circumstances of the agency. For example, the president of a corporation usually has the authority to enter into major contracts on the corporation's behalf, but a supervisor on the corporation's assembly line may have the authority only to purchase the supplies necessary to keep the line running.

Principal–Independent Contractor Relationship

independent contractor

A person or business who is not an employee who is employed by a principal to perform a certain task on his behalf.

Principals often employ outsiders–that is, persons and businesses who are not employees—to perform certain tasks on their behalf. These persons and businesses are called **independent contractors**. For example, doctors, dentists, consultants, stockbrokers, architects, certified public accountants, real estate brokers, and plumbers are examples of professions and trades that commonly act as independent contractors. An independent contractor who is a professional, such as a lawyer, is called a professional agent.

A principal can authorize an independent contractor to enter into contracts. Principals are bound by the authorized contracts of their independent contractors. For example, if a client authorizes an attorney to settle a case within a certain dollar amount and the attorney does so, the settlement agreement is binding.

CONCEPT SUMMARY ⋯ KINDS OF EMPLOYMENT RELATIONSHIPS

Type of Relationship	Description
Employer–employee	The employer has the right to control the physical conduct of the employee.
Principal–agent	The agent has authority to act on behalf of the principal as authorized by the principal and implied from the agency. An employee is often the agent of his employer.
Principal–independent contractor	The principal has no control over the details of the independent contractor's conduct. An independent contractor is usually not an agent of the principal.

Contemporary Business Environment

EMPLOYMENT AT WILL

Employees who are offered express employment contracts for a definite term cannot be discharged in violation of the contract. Most employees, however, do not have employment contracts. They are considered **at-will employees**.

Under common law, an at-will employee could be discharged by an employer at any time for any reason. This laissez-faire doctrine gave the employer great flexibility in responding to its changing needs. It also caused unfair results for some employees. Today, there are many statutory, contract, public policy, and tort exceptions to the at-will doctrine. These exceptions are:

- *Statutory Exception*   Federal and state statutes that restrict the employment at-will doctrine include federal labor laws that prohibit employers from discharging employee-members of labor unions in violation of labor laws or collective bargaining agreements. Title VII and other federal and state antidiscrimination laws that prohibit employers from engaging in race, sex, religious, age, handicap, or other forms of discrimination are other examples of such laws.
- *Contract Exception*   The courts have held that an **implied-in-fact contract** can be created between an employer and an employee. Implied-in-fact contracts develop from the conduct of the parties. For example, a company bulletin, handbook, or personnel policy might

mention that employees who do their jobs properly will not be discharged. This can be construed as an implied promise that an employee can only be discharged for good cause. Thus, the employer's ability to discharge an employee at will is removed. An employee who is discharged in violation of an implied-in-fact contract can sue the employer for breach of contract.

- *Public Policy Exception*   The most used common law exception to the employment at-will doctrine is the **public policy exception**. This rule states that an employee cannot be discharged if such discharge violates the public policy of the jurisdiction. For example, discharging an employee for serving as a juror, refusing to do an act in violation of the law (e.g., refusing to engage in dumping of toxic wastes in violation of environmental protection laws), refusing to engage in illegal research (e.g., research that violates patent laws or animal protection laws), refusing to distribute defective products, and the like has been held to violate public policy.

An employee who has been *wrongfully discharged* can sue his or her employer for damages and other remedies (reinstatement, back pay, and such). Punitive damages may be recovered if the employee has engaged in fraud or other intentional conduct.

FORMATION OF THE AGENCY RELATIONSHIP

An agency and the resulting authority of an agent can arise in any of these four ways: (1) express agency, (2) implied agency, (3) apparent agency, and (4) agency by ratification. Each of these types of agencies is discussed in the paragraphs that follow.

Express Agency

Express agency is the most common form of agency. In an express agency, the agent has the authority to contract or otherwise act on the principal's behalf as expressly stated in the agency agreement. In addition, the agent may also possess certain implied or apparent authority to act on the principal's behalf (as discussed later in this chapter).

express agency

An agency that occurs when a principal and an agent expressly agree to enter into an agency agreement with each other

Express agency occurs when a principal and an agent expressly agree to enter into an agency agreement with each other. Express agency contracts can be either oral or written unless the Statute of Frauds stipulates that they must be written. For example, in most states a real estate broker's contract to sell real estate must be in writing.

exclusive agency contract

A contract a principal and agent enter into that says the principal cannot employ any agent other than the exclusive agent.

If the principal and agent enter into an **exclusive agency contract**, the principal cannot employ any agent other than the exclusive agent. If the principal does so, the exclusive agent can recover damages from the principal. If an agency is not an exclusive agency, the principal can employ more than one agent to try to accomplish a stated purpose. When multiple agents are employed, the agencies with all of the agents terminate when any one of the agents accomplishes the stated purpose.

power of attorney

An express agency agreement that is often used to give an agent the power to sign legal documents on behalf of the principal.

Power of Attorney   A **power of attorney** is one of the most formal types of express agency agreements. It is often used to give an agent the power to sign legal documents, such as deeds to real estate, on behalf of the principal. There are two kinds of powers of attorney: *general*, which confers broad powers on the agent to act in any matters on the principal's behalf; and *special*, which limits the agent to those acts specifically enumerated in an agreement. The agent is called an **attorney-in-fact** even though he or she does not have to be a lawyer. Powers of attorney must be written. Usually, they must be notarized. A general power of attorney is shown in Exhibit 24.2.

Implied Agency

implied agency

An agency that occurs when a principal and an agent do not expressly create an agency, but it is inferred from the conduct of the parties.

In many situations, a principal and an agent do not expressly create an agency. Instead, the agency is implied from the conduct of the parties. This type of agency is referred to as **implied agency**. The extent of the agent's authority is determined from the particular facts and circumstances of the particular situation. Implied authority can be conferred by either industry custom, prior dealing between the parties, the agent's position, the acts deemed necessary to carry out the agent's duties, and other factors the court deems relevant. Implied authority cannot conflict with express authority or with stated limitations on express authority.

Incidental Authority   Often, even an express agency agreement does not provide enough detail to cover all contingencies that may arise in the future regarding the performance of the agency. In this case, the agent possesses certain implied authority to act. This implied authority is sometimes referred to as *incidental authority*.

Certain emergency situations may arise in the course of an agency. If the agent cannot contact the principal for instructions, the agent has implied emergency powers to take all actions reasonably necessary to protect the principal's property and rights.

Apparent Agency

apparent agency

Agency that arises when a principal creates the appearance of an agency that in actuality does not exist.

Apparent agency (or **agency by estoppel**) arises when a principal creates the appearance of an agency that in actuality does not exist. Where an apparent agency is established, the principal is estopped from denying the agency relationship and is bound to contracts entered into by the apparent agent while acting within the scope of the apparent agency. Note that it is the principal's actions—not the agent's—that create an apparent agency.

Ethics Brief

Where an apparent agency is established, the principal is *estopped* from denying the agency relationship.

Consider This Example   Suppose Georgia Pacific, Inc., interviews Albert Iorio for a sales representative position. Mr. Iorio, accompanied by Jane Franklin, the national sales manager, visits retail stores located in the open sales territory. While visiting one store, Jane tells the store manager, "I wish I had more sales reps like Albert." Nevertheless, Albert is not hired. If Albert later enters into contracts with the store on behalf of Georgia Pacific and Jane has not controverted the impression of Albert she left with the store manager, the company will be bound to the contract.

ƐXHIBIT **24.2** *A Sample General Power of Attorney*

Power of Attorney

Know All Men by These Presents: That _____

_____

the undersigned (jointly and severally, if more than one) hereby make, constitute and appoint _____

_____

My true and lawful Attorney for me and in my name, place and stead and for my use and benefit:

(a)   To ask, demand, sue for, recover, collect and receive each and every sum of money, debt, account, legacy, bequest, interest, dividend, annuity and demand (which now is or hereafter shall become due, owing or payable) belonging to or claimed by me, and to use and take any lawful means for the recovery thereof by legal process or otherwise, and to execute and deliver a satisfaction or release therefor, together with the right and power to compromise or compound any claim or demand;

(b)   To exercise any or all of the following powers as to real property, any interest therein and/or any building thereon: To contract for, purchase, receive and take possession thereof and of evidence of title thereto; to lease the same for any term or purpose, including leases for business, residence, and oil and/or mineral development; to sell, exchange, grant or convey the same with or without warranty; and to mortgage, transfer in trust, or otherwise encumber or hypothecate the same to secure payment of a negotiable or non-negotiable note or performance of any obligation or agreement;

(c)   To exercise any or all of the following powers as to all kinds of personal property and goods, wares and merchandise, chosen in action and other property in possession or in action: To contract for, buy, sell, exchange, transfer and in any legal manner deal in and with the same and to mortgage, transfer in trust, or otherwise encumber or hypothecate the same to secure payment of a negotiable or non-negotiable note or performance of any obligation or agreement;

(d)   To borrow money and to execute and deliver negotiable or non-negotiable notes therefor with or without security, and to loan money and receive negotiable or non-negotiable notes therefor with such security as said Attorney shall deem proper;

(e)   To create, amend, supplement and terminate any trust and to instruct and advise the trustee of any trust wherein I am or may be trustor or beneficiary; to represent and vote stock, exercise stock rights, accept and deal with any dividend, distribution or bonus, join in any corporate financing reorganization, merger, liquidation, consolidation or other action and the extension, compromise, conversion, adjustment, enforcement or foreclosure, singly or in conjunction with others of any corporate stock, bond, note, debenture or other security; to compound, compromise, adjust, settle and satisfy any obligation, secured or unsecured, owing by or to me and to give or accept any property and/or money whether or not equal to or less in value than the amount owning in payment, settlement or satisfaction thereof;

(f)   To transact business of any kind or class and as my act and deed to sign, execute, acknowledge and deliver any deed, lease, assignment of lease covenant, indenture, indemnity, agreement, mortgage, deed of trust, assignment of mortgage or of the beneficial interest under deed of trust, extension or renewal of any obligation, subordination or waiver or priority, hypothecation, bottomry, charter-party, bill of lading, bill of sale, bill, bond, note, whether negotiable or non-negotiable, receipt, evidence of debt, full or partial release or satisfaction of mortgage, judgment and other debt, request for partial or full reconveyance of deed of trust and such other instruments in writing of any kind or class as may be necessary or proper in the premises.

Giving and Granting unto my said Attorney full power and authority to do and perform all and every act and thing whatsoever, requisite, necessary or appropriate to be done in and about the premises as fully to all intents, and purposes as I might or could do if personally present, hereby ratifying all that my said Attorney shall lawfully do or cause to be done by virtue of these presents. The powers and authority hereby conferred upon my said Attorney shall be applicable to all real and personal property or interests therein now owned or hereafter required by me and whenever situate.

My said Attorney is empowered hereby to determine in said Attorney's sole discretion the time when, purpose for and manner in which any power herein conferred upon said Attorney shall be exercised, and the conditions, provisions and covenants of any instrument or document which may be executed by said Attorney pursuant hereto and in the acquisition or disposition of real or personal property, my said Attorney shall haveexclusive power to fix the terms thereof for cash, credit and/or property, and if on credit with or without security.

The undersigned, if a married person, hereby further authorizes and empowers my said Attorney, as my duly authorized agent, to join in my behalf, in the execution of any instrument by which any community real property or any interest therein, now owned or hereafter acquired by my spouse and myself, or either of us, is sold, leased, encumbered, or conveyed.

When the context to requires, the masculine gender includes the feminine and/or neuter, and the singular number includes the plural.

Witness my hand this _____ **day of** _____ , 20 _____ .

STATE OF CALIFORNIA   } SS
COUNTY OF

On _____ before me, the undersigned,   _____
a Notary Public in and for said State personally appeared _____

_____   _____

_____   _____

_____ personally known
to me (or proved to me on the basis of satisfactory evidence) to be the   _____
person _____ whose name _____
subscribed to the within instrument and acknowledge that _____
_____ executed the same.
WITNESS my hand and official seal.

Signature _____

_____
Name (Typed or Printed)   (This area for official seal)

Contemporary Business Environment

APPARENT AGENCY IN FRANCHISING

Franchising has become a major form of conducting business in the United States. In a franchise agreement, one company (called the franchisor) licenses another company (called the franchisee) to use its trade name, trademarks and service marks, and trade secrets. Many fast-food restaurants, gasoline stations, motels and hotels, and other businesses operate in this fashion.

The franchisor and franchisee are independently owned businesses. A principal–agent relationship usually is not created by the franchise. If no express or implied agency is created, the franchisor would not normally be civilly liable for the tortious conduct (e.g., negligence) of the franchisee. Liability could be imposed on the franchisor, however, if an apparent agency is shown. Consider the following case.

The Howard Johnson Company (HJ) operates a chain of hotels, motels, and restaurants across the United States. Approximately 75 percent of the HJ motor lodges are owned and operated by franchisees that are licensed by HJ to do business under the "Howard Johnson" trade name and trademarks. The rest are company-owned

Orlando Executive Park, Inc. (OEP), is a corporate franchisee that owns and operates an HJ motor lodge franchise in Orlando, Florida. The motor lodge is part of a large complex known as "Howard Johnson's Plaza" located off Interstate 4. The motor lodge contains approximately 300 guest rooms in six separate buildings.

P.D.R. (name withheld by the court), a 35-year-old married woman and mother of a small child, worked as a supervisor for a restaurant chain. Her work occasionally required her to travel and stay overnight in Orlando. On October 22, 1975, P.D.R. stopped to stay at the HJ motor lodge in Orlando. At approximately 9:30 P.M., P.D.R. registered for her previously reserved room at the lodge. The registration form did not inform her that the hotel was an HJ franchisee. P.D.R. parked her car in the motor lodge parking lot and proceeded with her suitcase to her ground-floor room in Building A, which was located directly behind the registration office. P.D.R. then went back to her car to get some papers. After obtaining the papers from her car, P.D.R. returned to Building A. As she proceeded down an interior hallway of the building toward her room, she was accosted by a man she had previously seen standing behind the registration office. The man struck her in the throat and neck and

choked her until she became semiconscious. When P.D.R. fell to the floor, her assailant sat on top of her and stripped her of her jewelry. He then dragged her down the hallway and beneath a secluded stairway where he brutally beat her. The assailant then disappeared into the night and has never been identified.

P.D.R. suffered serious physical and psychological injury, including memory loss, mental confusion, and an inability to tolerate and communicate with people. She lost her job within one year of the assault. P.D.R. suffers permanent injury that requires expensive, long-term medical and psychiatric treatment. P.D.R. brought a tort action against OEP and HJ and sought actual and punitive damages against both of them.

The jury had little trouble finding that OEP had breached its duty of care and was liable. Evidence showed that other criminal activity had occurred previously on the premises, but that OEP failed to warn guests, including P.D.R., of the danger. In fact, OEP management actively discouraged criminal investigations by the sheriff's deputies, thus minimizing any deterrent effect they may have had. Further evidence showed that the dark and secluded stairwell area where P.D.R. was dragged was a security hazard that should have been boarded up or better lit.

The jury also found HJ liable to P.D.R. under the doctrine of apparent agency. The appellate court stated: "While OEP might not be HJ's agent for all purposes, the signs, national advertising, uniformity of building design and color schemes allow the public to assume that this and other similar motor lodges are under the same ownership. An HJ official testified that it was the HJ marketing strategy to appear as a 'chain that sells a product across the nation.'" The court continued, "There was sufficient evidence for the jury to reasonably conclude that HJ represented to the traveling public that it could expect a particular level of service at a Howard Johnson Motor Lodge. The uniformity of signs, design and color schemes easily leads the public to believe that each motor lodge is under common ownership or conforms to common standards, and the jury could find they are intended to do so." The appellate court upheld an award of $750,000 compensatory damages against OEP and HJ jointly. [*Orlando Executive Park, Inc. v. P.D.R.*, 402 So.2d 442 (Fla. App. 1981)]

---

agency by ratification

An agency that occurs when (1) a person misrepresents him- or herself as another's agent when in fact he or she is not and (2) the purported principal ratifies the unauthorized act.

Agency by Ratification

Agency by ratification occurs when (1) a person misrepresents himself or herself as another's agent when in fact he or she is not and (2) the purported principal ratifies (accepts) the unauthorized act. In such cases, the principal is bound to perform and the agent is relieved of any liability for misrepresentation.

Consider This Example   Bill Levine sees a house for sale and thinks his friend Sherry Maxwell would want it. Bill Levine enters into a contract to purchase the house from the seller and signs the contract "Bill Levine, agent for Sherry Maxwell." Because Bill is not Sherry Maxwell's agent, she is not bound to the contract. However, if Sherry agrees to purchase the house, there is an agency by ratification. The ratification "relates back" to the moment Bill Levine entered into the contract. Upon ratification of the contract, Sherry Maxwell is obligated to purchase the house.

CONCEPT SUMMARY   FORMATION OF AGENCY RELATIONSHIPS

Type of Agency	Definition	Enforcement of the Contract
Express	Authority is expressly given to the agent by the principal.	Principal and third party are bound to the contract.
Implied	Authority is implied from the conduct of the parties, custom and usage of trade, or act incidental to carrying out the agent's duties.	Principal and third party acts are bound to the contract.
Apparent	Authority created when the principal leads a third party into believing that the agent has authority.	Principal and third party are bound to the contract.
By ratification	Acts of the agent committed outside the scope of his authority.	Principal and third party are not bound to the contract unless the principal ratifies the contract.

AGENT'S DUTIES

An agent owes certain duties to the principal. These duties may be either set forth in the agency agreement or implied by law. Generally, agents owe the principal the duties of (1) performance, (2) notification, (3) loyalty, and (4) accountability. Each of these duties is discussed in the paragraphs that follow.

Duty of Performance

An agent who enters into a contract with a principal has two distinct obligations: (1) performing the lawful duties expressed in the contract and (2) meeting the standards of reasonable care, skill, and diligence implicit in all contracts. Collectively, these duties are referred to as the agent's **duty of performance**.

Normally, an agent is required to render the same standard of care, skill, and diligence that a fictitious reasonable agent in the same occupation would render in the same locality and under the same circumstances. For example, a general medical practitioner in a rural area would be held to the standard of a reasonable general practitioner in rural areas. That standard might be different for a general medical practitioner in a big city. In some professions, such as accounting, a national standard of performance (called "generally accepted accounting principle") is imposed. If an agent holds himself or herself as possessing higher-than-customary skills, the agent will be held to this higher standard of performance. For example, a lawyer who claims to be a specialist in securities law will be held to a reasonable specialist-in-securities-law standard.

An agent who does not perform his or her express duties or fails to use the standard degree of care, skill, or diligence is liable to the principal for breach of contract. An agent who has negligently (or intentionally) failed to perform properly is also liable in tort.

Duty of Notification

In the course of an agency, the agent usually learns information that is important to the principal. This information may come from third parties or other sources. The agent's duty to notify the principal of such information is called the **duty of notification**. The agent is liable to the principal for any injuries resulting from a breach of this duty.

duty of performance

An agent's duty to a principal that includes (1) performing the lawful duties expressed in the contract and (2) meeting the standards of reasonable care, skill, and diligence implicit in all contracts

duty of notification

An agent's duty to notify the principal of information he or she learns from a third party or other source that is important to the principal.

imputed knowledge

Information that is learned by the agent that is attributed to the principal.

Imputed Knowledge   Most information learned by an agent in the course of the agency is **imputed** to the principal. This means that the principal is assumed to know what the agent knows. This is so even if the agent does not tell the principal certain relevant information.

Business Ethics

AGENT'S DUTY OF LOYALTY

Because the agency relationship is based on trust and confidence, an agent owes the principal a **duty of loyalty** in all agency-related matters. Thus, an agent owes a fiduciary duty not to act adversely to the interests of the principal. If this duty is breached, the agent is liable to the principal. The most common types of breaches of loyalty by an agent are discussed below.

- *Self-Dealing*   Agents generally are prohibited from undisclosed self-dealing with the principal. For example, a real estate agent who is employed to purchase real estate for a principal cannot secretly sell his own property in the transaction. However, the deal is lawful if the principal agrees to buy the property after the agent discloses his or her ownership.
- *Usurping an Opportunity*   An agent cannot usurp an opportunity that belongs to the principal. For example, a third-party offer to an agent must be conveyed to the principal. The agent cannot appropriate the opportunity for himself or herself unless the principal rejects it after due consideration. Opportunities to purchase real estate, businesses, products, ideas, and other property are subject to this rule.
- *Competing with the Principal*   Agents are prohibited from competing with the principal during the course of an agency unless the principal agrees. The reason for this rule is that an agent cannot meet his or her duty of loyalty when his or her personal interests conflict with the

principal's interests. If the parties have not entered into an enforceable covenant-not-to-compete, an agent is free to compete with the principal once the agency has ended.
- *Misuse of Confidential Information*   In the course of an agency, the agent often acquires confidential information about the principal's affairs (e.g., business plans, technological innovations, customer lists, trade secrets, and such). The agent is under a legal duty not to disclose or misuse such information either during or after the course of the agency. There is no prohibition against using general information, knowledge, or experience acquired during the course of the agency.
- *Dual Agency*   An agent cannot meet a duty of loyalty to two parties with conflicting interests. Dual agency occurs when an agent acts for two or more different principals in the same transaction. This practice generally is prohibited unless all of the parties involved in the transaction agree to it. If an agent acts as an undisclosed dual agent, he or she must forfeit all compensation received in the transaction. Some agents, such as middlemen and finders, are not considered dual agents. This is because they only bring interested parties together; they do not take part in any negotiations.

1. Describe an agent's fiduciary duty of loyalty.
2. What remedies should be imposed against an agent who breaches his or her duty of loyalty to the principal?

Duty of Accountability

duty of accountability

A duty that an agent owes to maintain an accurate accounting of all transactions undertaken on the principal's behalf.

Unless otherwise agreed, an agent owes a duty to maintain an accurate accounting of all transactions undertaken on the principal's behalf. This **duty of accountability** includes keeping records of all property and money received and expended during the course of the agency. A principal has a right to demand an accounting from the agent at any time, and the agent owes a legal duty to make the accounting. This duty also requires the agent to (1) maintain a separate account for the principal and (2) use the principal's property in an authorized manner.

Any property, money, or other benefit received by the agent in the course of the agency belongs to the principal. For example, all secret profits received by the agent are the property of the principal. If an agent breaches the agency contract, the principal can

Ethics Brief

A "constructive trust" is created by law, rather than agreement, to impose a duty to transfer property to another.

sue the agent to recover damages caused by breach. The court can impose a *constructive trust* on any secret profits on property purchased with secret profits for the benefit of the principal.

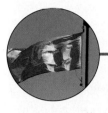

International Law

STRATEGIC ALLIANCES IN FOREIGN COUNTRIES

A **strategic alliance** is an agreement between two or more businesses from different countries to accomplish a specific purpose or function. For example, an agreement between a U.S. automobile company and a Japanese automobile company to jointly produce an automobile to be sold in the United States is a joint venture. A joint venture may also be between a corporation and a foreign government.

Joint ventures are often entered into if it is (1) commercially efficient to do so (e.g., neither party has sufficient capital or expertise to accomplish the objective alone) or (2) required by law (e.g., some countries prohibit a foreign company from owning more than 49 percent of a business that operates in the country).

PRINCIPAL'S DUTIES

The principal owes certain duties to the agent. These duties, which can be expressed in the agency contract or implied by law, include (1) the duty of compensation, (2) the duties of reimbursement and indemnification, and (3) the duty of cooperation.

Duty of Compensation

A principal owes a **duty to compensate** an agent for services provided. Usually, the agency contract (whether written or oral) specifies the compensation to be paid. The principal must pay this amount either upon the completion of the agency or at some other mutually agreeable time.

If there is no agreement as to the amount of compensation, the law implies a promise that the principal will pay the agent the customary fee paid in the industry. If the compensation cannot be established by custom, the principal owes a duty to pay the reasonable value of the agent's services.

There is no duty to compensate a gratuitous agent. However, gratuitous agents who agree to provide their services free of charge may be paid voluntarily.

Certain types of agents traditionally perform their services on a *contingency fee* basis. Under this type of arrangement, the principal owes a duty to pay the agent the agreed-upon contingency fee only if the agency is completed. For example, real estate brokers, finders, lawyers, and salespersons often work on this basis.

duty to compensate

A duty that a principal owes to pay an agreed-upon amount to the agent either upon the completion of the agency or at some other mutually agreeable time.

Business Brief

Many plaintiffs' lawyers agree to take cases on a contingency-fee basis.

Duties of Reimbursement and Indemnification

In carrying out the agency, an agent may spend his or her own money on the principal's behalf. Unless otherwise agreed, the principal owes a **duty to reimburse** the agent for all such expenses if they were (1) authorized by the principal, (2) within the scope of the agency, and (3) necessary to discharge the agent's duties in carrying out the agency. For example, a principal must reimburse an agent for authorized business trips taken on the principal's behalf.

A principal also owes a **duty to indemnify** the agent for any losses the agent suffers because of the principal. This duty usually arises where an agent is held liable for the principal's misconduct. For example, suppose an agent enters into an authorized contract with a third party on the principal's behalf, the principal fails to perform on the contract, and the third party recovers a judgment against the agent. The agent can recover indemnification of this amount from the principal.

duty to reimburse

A duty that a principal owes to repay money to the agent if the agent spent his or her own money during the agency on the principal's behalf.

duty to indemnify

A duty that a principal owes to protect the agent for losses the agent suffered during the agency because of the principal's misconduct.

Basketball players and other professional sports figures usually hire sports agents to represent them in negotiations with owners of the professional teams they are interested in playing for. Professional sports stars also use sports agents to negotiate endorsement contracts with sporting goods companies and other advertisers.

duty to cooperate

A duty that a principal owes to cooperate with and assist the agent in the performance of the agent's duties and the accomplishment of the agency.

Duty of Cooperation

Unless otherwise agreed, the principal owes a **duty to cooperate** with and assist the agent in the performance of the agent's duties and the accomplishment of the agency. For example, unless otherwise agreed, a principal who employs a real estate agent to sell her house owes a duty to allow the agent to show the house to prospective purchasers during reasonable hours.

International Law

INTERNATIONAL LICENSING

A company that owns a valuable property right or expertise—such as a patent or other form of technology—may wish to distribute it or products that contain it in foreign countries without selling it. A method for doing so is the license. In licensing, one party (the *licensor*) sells the right to use its patent or other technology in another country to another company (the *licensee*). The licensor and licensee are independent entities. The licensee is usually granted an exclusive right to sell the technology or product in a specified territory (e.g., a countrywide license). The licensee usually pays royalties or other fees to the licensor.

Consider This Example   The Walt Disney Company, which is a U.S. company, often grants licenses to businesses in other countries to put Mickey Mouse, Mulan, and its other trademarked characters on clothing, toys, and other items sold in other countries. The Walt Disney Company is the licensor and the foreign company is the licensee. Many Internet companies license software and other intellectual property in conducting international e-commerce.

If licensing is used, the exporter (1) does not have to sell its valuable property right, (2) is not subject to the tort or contract liability of the licensee, (3) often avoids any restrictions against foreign entry into a country, (4) does not have to make a substantial investment in foreign country operations, and (5) can control the use of its property right through specific contract provisions (e.g., grant only a limited-time license, impose quality control standards).

*C*ONTRACT LIABILITY TO THIRD PARTIES

A principal who authorizes an agent to enter into a contract with a third party is liable on the contract. Thus, the third party can enforce the contract and recover damages if the principal fails to perform it.

The agent can also be held liable on the contract in certain circumstances. Imposition of such liability depends upon whether the agency is classified as (1) *fully disclosed*, (2) *partially disclosed*, or (3) *undisclosed*.

Fully Disclosed Agency

A **fully disclosed agency** results if the third party entering into the contract knows (1) that the agent is acting as an agent for a principal and (2) the actual identity of the principal.[1] The third party has the requisite knowledge if the principal's identity is disclosed to the third party by either the agent or some other source.

In a fully disclosed agency, the contract is between the principal and the third party. Thus, the principal, who is called a fully disclosed principal, is liable on the contract. The agent, however, is not liable on the contract because the third party relied on the principal's credit and reputation when the contract was made. An agent is liable on the contract if he or she guarantees that the principal will perform the contract.

Business Brief

In a fully disclosed agency, the principal is liable to the third party on the contract; the agent is not liable.

Partially Disclosed Agency

A **partially disclosed agency** occurs if the agent discloses his or her agency status but does not reveal the principal's identity and the third party does not know the principal's identity from another source. The nondisclosure may be because (1) the principal instructs the agent not to disclose his or her identity to the third party or (2) the agent forgets to tell the third party the principal's identity. In this kind of agency, the principal is called a *partially disclosed principal*.

In a partially disclosed agency, both the principal and the agent are liable on third-party contracts.[2] This is because the third party must rely on the agent's reputation, integrity, and credit because the principal is unidentified. If the agent is made to pay the contract, the agent can sue the principal for indemnification. The third party and the agent can agree to relieve the agent's liability.

Business Brief

In a partially disclosed agency, both the principal and the agent are liable to the third party if the principal fails to perform the contract.

Undisclosed Agency

An **undisclosed agency** occurs when the third party is unaware of either the existence of an agency or the principal's identity. The principal is called an **undisclosed principal**. Undisclosed agencies are lawful. They are often used when the principal feels that the terms of the contract would be changed if his or her identity were known. For example, a wealthy person may use an undisclosed agency to purchase property if he thinks that the seller would raise the price of the property if his identity were revealed.

In an undisclosed agency, both the principal and the agent are liable on the contract with the third party. This is because the agent, by not divulging that he or she is acting as an agent, becomes a principal to the contract. The third party relies on the reputation and credit of the agent in entering into the contract. If the principal fails to perform the contract, the third party can recover against the principal of the agent. If the agent is made to pay the contract, he or she can recover indemnification from the principal.

In the following case, the court was presented with the issue of whether an agent was liable on a contract.

Business Brief

In an undisclosed agency, both the principal and the agent are liable to the third party if the principal fails to perform the contract.

You'll See Seafoods, Inc. v. Gravois
520 So.2d 461 (1988)
Court of Appeals of Louisiana

CASE 24.1

BACKGROUND AND FACTS

In 1978, James Gravois purchased a restaurant and named it "The Captain's Raft." The restaurant was actually owned by Computer Tax Services of LA., Inc., a corporation owned by Gravois. Gravois did not inform the managers, employees, or suppliers that the restaurant was owned by a corporation. Further, the menus were printed with the name "The Captain's Raft" with no indication it was a corporate entity. Supplies purchased by the restaurant were paid for by checks signed by Gravois with no indication of his agency capacity.

You'll See Seafoods, Inc. (You'll See), supplied fresh seafood to the restaurant and was paid for the merchandise by checks signed by Gravois. On February 28, 1984, You'll See filed suit against Gravois d.b.a. The Captain's Raft to recover unpaid invoices. Gravois responded by saying that he was merely acting as an agent for a corporate principal. The corporation was in bankruptcy.

ISSUE

Was Gravois liable on the debt owed You'll See Seafoods, Inc.?

COURT'S REASONING

An agent has the burden of proving he or she disclosed his or her capacity and the identity of the principal if he or she wishes to escape personal liability for a contract he or she entered into with a third party on behalf of the principal. Gravois failed to do this.

DECISION

The appellate court held that Gravois was an agent for an undisclosed corporate principal and, therefore, was liable for the debts owed to You'll See Seafoods, Inc.

Case Questions

Critical Legal Thinking   Should agents for undisclosed principals be held personally liable on contracts? Why or why not?

Business Ethics   Did Gravois act ethically in arguing that the debts owed to You'll See belonged to the corporation and not to himself individually?

Contemporary Business   Why do you think Gravois wanted the debts to be placed in the corporation? Why do you think You'll See did not want the debts placed in the corporation?

Agent Exceeding the Scope of Authority

implied warranty of authority

An agent who enters into a contract on behalf of another party impliedly warrants that he or she has the authority to do so.

ratification

When a principal accepts an agent's unauthorized contract.

An agent who enters into a contract on behalf of another party impliedly warrants that he or she has the authority to do so. This is called the agent's **implied warranty of authority**. If the agent exceeds the scope of his or her authority, the principal is not liable on the contract unless the principal **ratifies** it. The agent, however, is liable to the third party for breaching the implied warranty of authority. To recover, the third party must show (1) reliance on the agent's representation and (2) ignorance of the agent's lack of status.

Consider This Example   Suppose Sam, Sara, Satchel, Samantha, and Simone form a rock band called SSSSex. SSSSex is just a voluntary association without any legal status. Sam enters into a contract with Rocky's Musical Instruments to purchase instruments and equipment for the band on credit and signs the contract, "Sam, for SSSSex." When SSSSex fails to pay the debt, Rocky's can sue Sam and recover. Sam must pay the debt because he breached his implied warranty of authority when he acted as an agent for a *nonexistent principal*; that is, the purported principal was not a legal entity upon which liability could be imposed.

CONCEPT SUMMARY   CONTRACT LIABILITY OF PRINCIPALS AND AGENTS TO THIRD PARTIES

Type of Agency	Principal Liable	Agent Liable
Fully disclosed	Yes	No, unless the agent (1) acts as a principal or (2) guarantees the performance of the contract.
Partially disclosed	Yes	Yes, unless the third party relieves the agent's liability.
Undisclosed	Yes	Yes.
Nonexistent	No, unless the principal ratifies the contract	Yes, the agent is liable for breaching the implied warranty of authority.

Entrepreneur and the Law

SIGNING PROPERLY AS AN AGENT

The agent's signature on a contract entered into on the principal's behalf is important. It can establish the agent's status and, therefore, his or her liability. For instance, in a fully disclosed agency the agent's signature must clearly indicate that he or she is acting as an agent for a specifically identified principal. Examples of proper signatures include "Allison Adams, agent for Peter Perceival," "Peter Perceival, by Allison Adams, agent," and "Peter Perceival, by Allison Adams."

An agent who is authorized to sign a contract for a fully disclosed principal but fails to properly do so can be held personally liable on the contract. For example, in the prior example a partially disclosed agency would be created if the contract was signed "Allison Adams, agent." If Adams merely signed the contract "Allison Adams," the agency would be an undisclosed agency. In both these instances the agent is liable on the contract.

*T*ORT LIABILITY TO THIRD PARTIES

The principal and the agent are each personally liable for their own tortious conduct. The principal is liable for the tortious conduct of an agent who is acting within the scope of his or her authority. The agent, however, only is liable for the tortious conduct of the principal if he or she directly or indirectly participates in or aids and abets the principal's conduct.

The courts have applied a broad and flexible standard in interpreting scope of authority in the context of employment. Although other factors may also be considered, the courts rely on the following factors to determine whether an agent's conduct occurred within the scope of his or her employment:

- Was the act specifically requested or authorized by the principal?
- Was it the kind of act that the agent was employed to perform?
- Did the act occur substantially within the time period of employment authorized by the principal?
- Did the act occur substantially within the location of employment authorized by the employer?
- Was the agent advancing the principal's purpose when the act occurred?[3]

Where liability is found, tort remedies are available to the injured party. These remedies include recovery for medical expenses, lost wages, pain and suffering, emotional distress and, in some cases, punitive damages. As discussed in the following paragraphs, the three main sources of tort liability for principals and agents are misrepresentation, negligence, and intentional torts.

An agent's scope of authority was at issue in the following case.

Business Brief

The use of agents creates tort liability exposure for principals. A principal is only liable for the tortious conduct of agents committed within their *scope of employment*, however.

Edgewater Motels, Inc. v. Gatzke and Walgreen Co.
277 N.W.2d 11 (1979)
Supreme Court of Minnesota

CASE 24.2

BACKGROUND AND FACTS
Arlen Gatzke (Gatzke) was a district manager for the Walgreen Company (Walgreen). In August 1979, Gatzke was sent to Duluth, Minnesota, to supervise the opening of a new Walgreen store. In Duluth, Gatzke stayed at the Edgewater Motel (Edgewater). While in Duluth, Gatzke was "on call" 24 hours a day to other Walgreen stores located in his territory. About midnight on the evening of August 23, 1979, Gatzke, after working 17 hours that day, went with several other Walgreen employees to a restaurant and bar to drink. Within one hour's time, Gatzke had consumed three "doubles" and one single brandy Manhattan. About 1:30 A.M., he went back to the Edgewater Motel and filled out his expense report. Soon thereafter a fire broke out in Gatzke's motel room. Gatzke escaped, but the fire spread and caused extensive damage to the motel. Evidence showed that Gatzke smoked two packs of cigarettes a day. An expert fire reconstruction witness testified that the fire started from a lit cigarette in or next to the wastepaper basked in Gatzke's room. Edgewater Motels, Inc., sued Gatzke and Walgreen. The parties stipulated that the damage to the

Edgewater Motel was $330,360. The jury returned a verdict against defendants Gatzke and Walgreen. The court granted Walgreen's posttrial motion for judgment notwithstanding the verdict. Plaintiff Edgewater and defendant Gatzke appealed.

ISSUE
Was Gatzke's act of smoking within his "scope of employment" making his principal, the Walgreen Company, vicariously liable for his negligence?

COURT'S REASONING
In reaching its decision, the supreme court stated: "After careful consideration of the issue we are persuaded that smoking can be an act within an employee's scope of employment. It seems only logical to conclude that an employee does not abandon his employment as a matter of law while temporarily acting for his personal comfort when such activities involve only slight deviations from work that are reasonable under the circumstances, such as eating, drinking, or smoking. The record indicates that Gatzke was an executive type of employee who had no set working

hours. His room at the Edgewater Motel was his 'office away from home.'"

DECISION

The state supreme court held that Gatzke's negligent act of smoking was within the scope of his employment while acting as an employee of the Walgreen Company. The supreme court reinstated the jury's verdict awarding damages to plaintiff Edgewater Motels, Inc.

Case Questions

Critical Legal Thinking   Should smoking cigarettes be held to be within an employee's scope of employment? Why or why not?

Business Ethics   Do employers owe a duty to police the personal habits of their employees?

Contemporary Business   Because of the dangers of smoking, would employers be justified in hiring only nonsmokers as employees?

Misrepresentation

Intentional misrepresentations are also known as **fraud** or **deceit**. They occur when an agent makes statements that he or she knows are not true. An **innocent misrepresentation** occurs when an agent negligently makes a misrepresentation to a third party.

A principal is liable for the intentional and innocent misrepresentations made by an agent acting within the scope of employment. The third party can either (1) rescind the contract with the principal and recover any consideration paid or (2) affirm the contract and recover damages.

Consider This Example   Assume that (1) a car salesman is employed to sell the principal's car and (2) the principal tells the agent that the car was repaired after it was involved in a major accident. If the agent intentionally tells the buyer that the car was never involved in an accident, the agent has made an intentional misrepresentation. Both the principal and the agent are liable for this misrepresentation.

Negligence

Principals are liable for the negligent conduct of agents acting within the scope of their employment. This liability is based on the common law doctrine of ***respondeat superior*** ("let the master answer"), which, in turn, is based on the legal theory of *vicarious liability* (liability without fault). In other words, the principal is liable because of his or her employment contract with the negligent agent, not because the principal was personally at fault.

This doctrine rests on the principle that if someone (i.e., the principal) expects to derive certain benefits from acting through others (i.e., an agent), that person should also bear the liability for injuries caused to third persons by the negligent conduct of an agent who is acting within the scope of his or her employment.

Frolic and Detour   Agents sometimes do things during the course of their employment to further their own interests rather than the principal's. For example, an agent might take a detour to run a personal errand while on assignment for the principal. This is commonly referred to as a **frolic and detour**. Negligence actions stemming from frolic and detour are examined on a case-by-case basis. Agents always are personally liable for their tortious conduct in such situations. Principals generally are relieved of liability if the agent's frolic and detour is substantial. However, if the deviation is minor, the principal is liable for the injuries caused by the agent's tortious conduct.

Consider This Example   A salesperson stops home for lunch while on an assignment for his principal. While leaving his home, the agent hits and injures a pedestrian with his automobile. The principal is liable if the agent's home was not too far out of the way from the agent's assignment. However, the principal would not be liable if an agent who is supposed to be on assignment to Los Angeles flies to San Francisco to meet a friend and is involved in an accident. The facts and circumstances of each case determine its outcome.

intentional misrepresentation

Occurs when an agent makes an untrue statement that he or she knows is not true.

innocent misrepresentation

Occurs when an agent makes an untrue statement that he or she honestly and reasonably believes to be true.

respondeat superior

A rule that says an employer is liable for the tortious conduct of its employees or agents while they are acting within the scope of its authority.

frolic and detour

When an agent does something during the course of his employment to further his own interests rather than the principal's.

The "Coming and Going" Rule   Under the common law, a principal generally is not liable for injuries caused by its agents and employees while they are on their way to or from work. This so-called **"coming and going" rule** applies even if the principal supplies the agent's automobile or other transportation or pays for gasoline, repairs, and other automobile operating expenses. This rule is quite logical. Because principals do not control where their agents and employees live, they should not be held liable for tortious conduct of agents on their way to and from work.

"coming and going" rule

A rule that says a principal is generally not liable for injuries caused by its agents and employees while they are on their way to or from work.

Dual-Purpose Mission   Sometimes, principals request that agents run errands or conduct other acts on their behalf while the agent or employee is on personal business. In this case, the agent is on a **dual-purpose mission**. That is, he or she is acting partly for himself or herself and partly for the principal. Most jurisdictions hold both the principal and the agent liable if the agent injures someone while on such a mission.

dual-purpose mission

An errand or other act that a principal requests of an agent while the agent is on his or her own personal business.

Consider This Example   Suppose a principal asks an employee to drop a package off at a client's office on the employee's way home. If the employee negligently injures a pedestrian while on this dual-purpose mission, the principal is liable to the pedestrian.

Intentional Torts

Intentional torts include such acts as assault, battery, false imprisonment, and other intentional conduct that cause injury to another person. A principal is not liable for the intentional torts of agents and employees that are committed outside the principal's scope of business. For example, if an employee attends a sporting event after working hours and gets into a fight with another spectator at the event, the employer is not liable.

However, a principal is liable under the doctrine of vicarious liability for intentional torts of agents and employees committed within the agent's scope of employment. The courts generally apply one of the tests discussed below in determining whether an agent's intentional torts were committed within the agent's scope of employment.

intentional tort

Occurs when a person has intentionally committed a wrong against (1) another person or his or her character, or (2) another person's property.

1. **The Motivation Test**   Under the **motivation test**, if the agent's motivation in committing the intentional tort is to promote the principal's business, the principal is liable for any injury caused by the tort. However, if the agent's motivation in committing the intentional tort was personal, the principal is not liable even if the tort took place during business hours or on business premises. For example, a principal is not liable if his agent was motivated by jealousy to beat up someone on the job who dated her boyfriend.

motivation test

A test to determine the liability of the principal; if the agent's motivation in committing the intentional tort is to promote the principal's business, then the principal is liable for any injury caused by the tort.

2. **The Work-Related Test**   Some jurisdictions have rejected the motivation test as too narrow. These jurisdictions apply the **work-related test** instead. Under this test, if an agent commits an intentional tort within a work-related time or space—for example, during working hours or on the principal's premises—the principal is liable for any injuries caused by the agent's intentional torts. Under this test, the agent's motivation is immaterial.

work-related test

A test to determine the liability of a principal; if an agent commits an intentional tort within a work-related time or space, the principal is liable for any injury caused by the agent's intentional tort.

In the following case, the court applied the work-related test in determining whether an employer was liable for an agent's intentional tort.

Desert Cab Inc. v. Marino

823 P.2d 898 (1992)

Supreme Court of Nevada

CASE 24.3

BACKGROUND AND FACTS

On October 6, 1986, Maria Marino, a cab driver with Yellow-Checkered Cab Company (Yellow Cab), and James Edwards, a cab driver with Desert Cab Inc. (Desert Cab), parked their cabs at the taxicab stand at the Sundance Hotel and Casino in Las Vegas to await fares. Marino's cab occupied the first position in the line and Edwards occupied the third. As Marino

stood alongside her cab conversing with the driver of another taxi, Edwards began verbally harassing her from inside his cab. When Marino approached Edwards to inquire as to the reason for the harassment, a verbal argument ensued. Edwards jumped from his cab, grabbed Marino by her neck and shoulders, began choking her, and threw her in front of his taxicab. A bystander pulled Edwards off Marino and escorted her back to her cab. Marino sustained injuries that rendered her unable to work for a time. Edwards was convicted of misdemeanor assault and battery. Marino brought a personal injury action against Desert Cab. The jury found Desert Cab liable and awarded Marino $65,000. Desert Cab appealed.

ISSUE
Is Desert Cab liable for the intentional tort of its employee?

COURT'S REASONING
Under the doctrine of *respondeat superior*, an employer is liable for the intentional torts committed by its employees within the scope of their employment. For liability to be imposed on the employer, the intentional tort must be work-related. The court held that Edward's intentional conduct of assault and battery against Marino was work-related, and Desert Cab was, therefore, liable to Marino.

DECISION
The appellate court held that Desert Cab was liable for the intentional tort committed by its employee.

Case Questions

Critical Legal Thinking Should employers be held liable for the intentional torts of their employees?

Business Ethics Did Desert Cab act ethically in denying liability?

Contemporary Business Should employers give prospective employees psychological examinations to determine if they have any dangerous propensities?

𝒞ONCEPT SUMMARY ... TORT LIABILITY OF PRINCIPALS AND AGENTS TO THIRD PARTIES

Agent's Conduct	Agent Liable	Principal Liable
Misrepresentation	Yes	The principal is liable for the intentional and innocent misrepresentations made by an agent acting within the scope of her authority.
Negligence	Yes	The principal is liable under the doctrine of *respondeat superior* if the agent's negligent act was committed within his scope of employment.
Intentional tort	Yes	Motivation test: The principal is liable if the agent's motivation in committing the intentional tort was to promote the principal's business.
	Yes	Work-related test: The principal is liable if the agent committed the intentional tort within work-related time and space.

𝓘NDEPENDENT CONTRACTOR

independent contractor

"A person who contracts with another to do something for him who is not controlled by the other nor subject to the other's right to control with respect to his physical conduct in the performance of the undertaking" [Restatement (Second) of Agency].

Section 2 of the Restatement (Second) of Agency defines an **independent contractor** as "A person who contracts with another to do something for him who is not controlled by the other nor subject to the other's right to control with respect to his physical conduct in the performance of the undertaking."

Independent contractors usually work for a number of clients, have their own offices, hire employees, and control the performance of their work. Merely labeling someone an "independent contractor" is not enough. The crucial factor in determining whether someone is an employee or an independent contractor is the *degree of control* that the employer has over the agent. Critical factors in determining independent contractor status include:

Business Brief

The crucial factor in determining whether a person is an employee or an independent contractor is the *degree of control* that the principal has over that person.

- Whether the worker is engaged in a distinct occupation or an independently established business
- The length of time the agent has been employed by the principal
- The amount of time that the agent works for the principal
- Whether the principal supplies the tools and equipment used in the work
- The method of payment, whether by time or by the job
- The degree of skill necessary to complete the task
- Whether the worker hires employees to assist him
- Whether the employer has the right to control the manner and means of accomplishing the desired result

Business Brief

A principal is generally not liable for the tortious conduct of independent contractors it hires. However, there are several exceptions.

If an examination of these factors shows that the principal asserts little control, the person is an independent contractor. Substantial control indicates an employer–employee relationship.

Independent Contractor *Prentice Hall Publishing's contract with the author of this book creates an independent contractor status between the two parties.*

Contemporary Business Environment

LIABILITY FOR INDEPENDENT CONTRACTOR'S TORTS

Generally, a principal is not liable for the torts of its independent contractors. Independent contractors are personally liable for their own torts. The rationale behind this rule is that principals do not control the means by which the results are accomplished. Nevertheless, there are several exceptions to this rule:

- ***Nondelegable Duties*** Certain duties may not be delegated. For example, railroads owe a duty to maintain safe railroad crossings. They cannot escape this liability by assigning the task to an independent contractor.

- ***Special Risks*** Principals cannot avoid strict liability for dangerous activities assigned to independent contractors. For example, the use of explosives, clearing land by fire, crop dusting, and such involve special risks that are shared by the principal.
- ***Negligence in the Selection of an Independent Contractor*** A principal who hires an unqualified or knowingly dangerous person as an independent contractor is liable if that person injures someone while on the job.

Business Ethics

PRINCIPAL LIABLE FOR REPO MAN'S TORT

Certain duties may not be delegated. For example, railroads owe a duty to maintain safe railroad crossings. They cannot escape this liability by assigning the task to an independent contractor. Consider the following case.

Yvonne Sanchez borrowed money from MBank El Paso (MBank) to purchase an automobile. She gave MBank a security interest in the vehicle to secure the loan. When Sanchez defaulted on the loan, MBank hired El Paso Recovery Service, an independent contractor, to repossess the automobile. The two men who were dispatched to Sanchez's house found the car parked in the driveway, and hooked it to a tow truck. Sanchez demanded that they cease their efforts and leave the premises, but the men nonetheless continued with the repossession. Before the men could tow the automobile into the street, Sanchez jumped into the car, locked the doors, and refused to leave. The men towed the car at a high

rate of speed to the repossession yard. They parked the car in the fenced repossession yard, with Sanchez inside, and padlocked the gate. Sanchez was left in the repossession lot with a Doberman Pinscher guard dog loose in the yard. Later, she was rescued by the police. The law prohibits the repossession of a vehicle if a breach of peace would occur. Sanchez filed suit against MBank, alleging that it was liable for the tortious conduct of El Paso Recovery Service. The trial court granted summary judgment to MBank, but the court of appeals reversed. MBank appealed.

Is the repossession of a vehicle an inherently dangerous activity in which a secured creditor remains liable for the physical harm resulting from the repossessor's tortious conduct?

The Supreme Court of Texas held that MBank, the principal, was liable for the tortious conduct of El Paso Recovery

Service, an independent contractor. The court held that the act of repossessing an automobile from a defaulting debtor is an inherently dangerous activity and a nondelegable duty. The court concluded that El Paso Recovery Service had breached the peace in repossessing the car from Sanchez and caused her physical and emotional harm. The court held that MBank, the principal, could not escape liability by hiring an independent contractor to do this task. The court found MBank liable to Sanches.

1. Did the independent contractor act responsibly in this case?
2. Should the principal bank have been held liable in this case? Why or why not?

TERMINATION OF AN AGENCY AND EMPLOYMENT CONTRACT

An agency contract is similar to other contracts in that it can be terminated either by an act of the parties or by operation of law. These different methods of termination are discussed next. Note that once an agency relationship is terminated, the agent can no longer represent the principal or bind the principal to contracts.

Termination by Acts of the Parties

The parties to an agency contract can terminate an agency contract by agreement or by their actions. The four methods of termination of an agency relationship by **acts of the parties** are:

- **Mutual Agreement** As with any contract, the parties to an agency contract can mutually agree to terminate their agreement. By doing so, the parties relieve each other of any further rights, duties, obligations, or powers provided for in the agency contract. Either party can propose the termination of an agency contract.
- **Lapse of Time** Agency contracts are often written for a specific period of time. The agency terminates when the specified time period elapses. Suppose, for example, that the principal and agent enter into an agency contract "beginning January 1, 2000, and ending December 31, 2003." The agency automatically terminates on December 31, 2003. If the agency contract does not set forth a specific termination date, the agency terminates after a reasonable time has elapsed. The courts often look to the custom of an industry in determining the reasonable time for the termination of the agency.
- **Purpose Achieved** A principal can employ an agent for the time it takes to accomplish a certain task, purpose, or result. Such agencies automatically terminate once they are completed. For example, suppose a principal employs a licensed real estate broker to sell his house. The agency terminates when the house is sold and the principal pays the broker the agreed-upon compensation.
- **Occurrence of a Specified Event** An agency contract can specify that the agency exists until a specified event occurs. The agency terminates when the specified event happens. For example, if a principal employs an agent to take care of her dog until she returns from a trip, the agency terminates when the principal returns from the trip.

termination by acts of the parties

An agency may be terminated by the following acts of the parties: (1) mutual agreement, (2) lapse of time, (3) purpose achieved, and (4) occurrence of a specified event.

Entrepreneur and the Law

NOTIFICATION REQUIRED AT THE TERMINATION OF AN AGENCY

If the agency is terminated by agreement between the parties, the principal is under a duty to give certain third parties notification of the termination. Unless otherwise required, the notice can be from the principal or some other source (e.g., the agent). If an agency terminates by operation of law, there is no duty to notify third parties about the termination, however.

The termination of an agency extinguishes an agent's actual authority to act on the principal's behalf. However, if the principal fails to give the proper notice of termination to a third party, the agent still has apparent authority to bind the principal to contracts with these third parties. If this happens, the contract is enforceable against the principal. The principal's only recourse is against the agent to recover damages caused by these unauthorized contracts.

The following notification requirements must be met:

- *Parties Who Dealt with the Agent* Direct notice of termination must be given to all persons with whom the agent dealt. Although the notice may be either written or oral, it is better practice to give written notice.

- *Parties Who Have Knowledge of the Agency* The principal must give direct or constructive notice to any third party who has knowledge of the agency but with whom the agent has not dealt. Direct notice often is in the form of a letter. Constructive notice usually consists of placing a notice of the termination of the agency in a newspaper serving the relevant community. This notice is effective even against persons who do not see it

- *Parties Who Have No Knowledge of the Agency* Generally, a principal is not obligated to give notice of termination to strangers who have no knowledge of the agency. However, a principal who has given the agent written authority to act but fails to recover the writing upon termination of the agency may be liable to strangers who later rely on this writing and deal with the agent. The laws of most states provide that this liability can be avoided by giving constructive notice (e.g., newspaper announcement) of the termination of the agency.

Termination by Operation of Law

Agency contracts can be terminated by **operation of law** as well as by agreement. The six methods of terminating an agency relationship by operation of law are:

1. **Death** The death of either the principal or the agent terminates the agency relationship. This rule is based on the old legal principle that, because a dead person cannot act, no one can act for him or her. Note that the agency terminates even if one party is unaware of the other party's death. An agent's actions that take place after the principal's death do not bind the principal's estate.
2. **Insanity** The insanity of either the principal or the agent generally terminates the agency relationship. A few states have modified this rule to provide that a contract entered into by an agent on behalf of an insane principal is enforceable if (1) the insane person has not been adjudged insane, (2) the third party does not have knowledge of the principal's insanity at the time of contracting, and (3) the enforcement of the contract will prevent injustice.
3. **Bankruptcy** The agency relationship is terminated if the principal is declared bankrupt. Bankruptcy requires the filing of a petition for bankruptcy under federal bankruptcy law. With few exceptions, neither the appointment of a state court receiver nor the principal's financial difficulties or insolvency terminates the agency relationship. The agent's bankruptcy usually does not terminate an agency unless the agent's credit standing is important to the agency relationship.
4. **Impossibility** The agency relationship terminates if a situation arises that makes its fulfillment impossible. The following circumstances can lead to termination on this ground:
   - **The loss or destruction of the subject matter of the agency.** For example, assume that a principal employs an agent to sell his horse, but the horse dies before it is sold. The agency relationship terminates at the moment the horse dies.
   - The loss of a required qualification. For example, suppose a principal employs a licensed real estate agent to sell her house and the real estate agent's license is revoked. The agency terminates at the moment the license is revoked.
   - **A change in the law.** For example, suppose that a principal employs an agent to trap alligators. If a law is passed that makes trapping alligators illegal, the agency contract terminates when the law becomes effective.
5. **Changed Circumstances** An agency terminates when there is an unusual change in circumstances that would lead the agent to believe that the principal's original instructions should no longer be valid. For example, a principal employs a licensed real estate agent to sell a farm for $100,000. The agent thereafter learns that oil has been discovered on the property that makes it worth $1 million. The agency terminates because of this change in circumstances.
6. **War** The outbreak of a war between the principal's country and the agent's country terminates the agency relationship between the parties. Such an occurrence usually makes the performance of the agency contract impossible.

termination by operation of law

An agency is terminated by operation of law, including: (1) death of the principal or agent, (2) insanity of the principal or agent, (3) bankruptcy of the principal, (4) impossibility of performance, (5) changed circumstances, and (6) war between the principal's and agent's countries.

Contemporary Business Environment

IRREVOCABLE AGENCY

An **agency coupled with an interest** is a special type of agency relationship that is created for the agent's benefit. This type of agency is irrevocable by the principal (e.g., the principal cannot terminate it). An agency coupled with an interest is commonly used in security agreements to secure loans. An agency coupled with an interest is not terminated by the death or incapacity of either the principal or the agent. It terminates only when the agent's obligations are performed. However, the parties can expressly agree that an agency coupled with an interest is terminated.

Consider This Example   Heidi Norville owns a piece of real estate. She goes to Wells Fargo Bank to obtain a loan on the property. The bank makes the loan but requires her to sign a security agreement (e.g., a mortgage) pledging the property as collateral for the loan. The security agreement contains a clause that appoints that bank as Ms. Norville's agent and permits the bank to sell the property and recover the amount of the loan from the sale proceeds if she defaults on her payments. This agency is irrevocable by Ms. Norville, the principal.

Wrongful Termination of an Agency or Employment Contract

Generally, agency and employment contracts that do not specify a definite time for their termination can be terminated at will by either the principal or the agent without liability to the other party. When a principal terminates an agency contract, it is called a **revocation of authority**. When an agent terminates an agency, it is called a **renunciation of authority**.

Unless an agency is irrevocable, both the principal and the agent have an individual power to unilaterally terminate any agency contract. Note that having the power to terminate an agency agreement is not the same as having the right to terminate it. The unilateral termination of an agency contract may be wrongful. If the principal's or agent's termination of an agency contract breaches the contract, the other party can sue for damages for **wrongful termination**.

wrongful termination

The termination of an agency contract in violation of the terms of the agency contract. The nonbreaching party may recover damages from the breaching party.

Business Brief

The distinction between the *power* and the *right* to terminate an agency is critical. Be certain it is clear.

Consider This Example   A principal employs a licensed real estate agent to sell his house. The agency contract gives the agent an exclusive listing for three months. After one month, the principal unilaterally terminates the agency. The principal has the power to do so, and the agent can no longer act on behalf of the principal. However, because the principal did not have the right to terminate the contract, the agent can sue him and recover damages (i.e., lost commission) for wrongful termination.

The Supreme Court Speaks

Public Policy Exception to the At-Will Employment Doctrine Allowed

Haddle v. Garrison
525 U.S. 121, 119 S.Ct. 489 (1998)
Supreme Court of the United States

BACKGROUND AND FACTS

Michael A. Haddle worked as an at-will employee of Healthmaster, Inc. In March 1995, a federal grand jury charged Healthmaster and Jeanette Garrison and Dennis Kelly, two officers of Healthmaster, with Medicare fraud, a federal crime. Haddle cooperated with federal agents in an investigation that led to a criminal indictment against the defendants. Garrison and Kelly, who had been barred by the court from participating in the affairs of Healthmaster, conspired with a remaining officer at Healthmaster to have Haddle fired. Haddle sued Healthmaster, Garrison, and Kelly to recover damages for an alleged violation of Section 1985(2) of the

Civil Rights Act of 1871 that prohibits conspiracies to deter witnesses from testifying in federal court matters. The district court dismissed the case, finding that Haddle was an at-will employee who could be terminated, and the court of appeals affirmed. The U.S. Supreme Court granted certiorari to hear the appeal.

SUPREME COURT ISSUE

Can a terminated at-will employee bring a civil lawsuit for damages against his employer and other conspirators under Section 1985(2) for being dismissed for participating in an investigation of a federal crime?

IN THE LANGUAGE OF THE U.S. SUPREME COURT

Rehnquist, Chief Justice The gist of the wrong at which Section 1985(2) aimed is intimidation or retaliation against witnesses in federal-court proceedings.

We hold that the sort of harm alleged by petitioner here—essentially third-party interference with at-will employment relationships—states a claim for relief under Section 1985(2). Such harm has long been a compensable injury under tort law, and we see no reason to ignore this tradition in this case.

DECISION AND REMEDY

The U.S. Supreme Court held that petitioner Haddle, an at-will employee, could sue the defendants for damages for conspiring to terminate his employment in violation of Section 1985(2) of the federal Civil Rights Act of 1871.

CASE QUESTIONS

Critical Legal Thinking   Should there be a "public policy" exception to the rule that at-will employees may be terminated at will?

Business Ethics   Would you testify against your employer in a federal criminal investigation?

Contemporary Business   What economic effects does the U.S. Supreme Court opinion have for employees? For employers?

CHAPTER SUMMARY

The Nature of Agency, p. 583

The Nature of Agency	1. *Agency.* A fiduciary relationship that results from the manifestation of consent by one person to act on behalf of another person with that person's consent.
	2. *Parties*:
	   a. *Principal.* Party who employs another person to act on his or her behalf.
	   b. *Agent.* Party who agrees to act on behalf of another person.

Kinds of Employment Relationships, p. 584

Employer–Employee Relationship	An employer hires an employee to perform some form of physical service. An employee is not an agent unless the principal authorizes him or her to enter into contracts on the principal's behalf.
Principal–Agent Relationship	An employer hires an employee and authorizes the employee to enter into contracts on the employer's behalf.
Principal–Independent Contractor Relationship	Principal employs a person who is not an employee of the principal. The independent contractor has authority only to enter into contracts authorized by the principal.

Formation of the Agency Relationship, p. 585

Express Agency	Principal and agent expressly agree in words to enter into an agency agreement. The agency contract may be oral or written unless the Statute of Frauds requires it to be in writing.
Implied Agency	An agency is implied (inferred) from the conduct of the parties.
Apparent Agency	Arises when a principal creates an appearance of an agency that in actuality does not exist. Also called *agency by estoppel* or *ostensible agency.*
Agency by Ratification	Occurs when a person misrepresents him- or herself as another's agent when he or she is not and the purported principal ratifies (accepts) the unauthorized act.

Agent's Duties, p. 589

Duty of Performance	Performance of the lawful duties expressed in the agency contract with reasonable care, skill, and diligence.
Duty of Notification	Agent owes duty to notify principal of any information he learns that is important to the agency. Information learned by the agent in the course of the agency is *imputed* to the principal.
Duty of Loyalty	Agent's duty not to act adversely to the interests of the principal. The most common breaches of loyalty are: 1. *Self-dealing.* Agent cannot deal with the principal unless his or her position is disclosed, and the principal agrees to deal with the agent. 2. *Usurping an opportunity.* Agent cannot usurp (take) an opportunity belonging to the principal as his or her own. 3. *Competing with the principal.* Agents are prohibited from competing with the principal during the course of an agency unless the principal agrees. 4. *Misuse of confidential information.* Agent is under a legal duty not to disclose or misuse confidential information learned within the course of an agency. 5. *Dual agency.* Agent cannot act on behalf of two different principals in same transaction unless the principals agree.
Duty of Accountability	Agent must maintain an accurate accounting of all transactions undertaken on the principal's behalf. A principal may demand an accounting from the agent at any time.

Principal's Duties, p. 591

Duty of Compensation	Principal must pay the agent agreed-upon compensation. If there is no agreement, the principal must pay what is customary in the industry, or, if there is no custom, then the reasonable value of the services.
Duties of Reimbursement and Indemnification	Principal must *reimburse* an agent for all expenses paid that were authorized by the principal, within the scope of the agency, and necessary to discharge the agent's duties. The principal must *indemnify* the agent for any losses suffered because of the principal's misconduct.
Duty of Cooperation	The principal must cooperate with and assist the agent in the performance of the agent's duties and the accomplishment of the agency.

Contract Liability to Third Parties, p. 592

Fully Disclosed Agency	The third party entering into the contract knows that the agent is acting for a principal and knows the identity of the principal. The principal is liable on the contract; the agent is not liable on the contract.
Partially Disclosed Agency	The third party knows that the agent is acting for a principal but does not know the identity of the principal. Both the principal and the agent are liable on the contract.
Undisclosed Agency	The third party does not know that the agent is acting for a principal. Both the principal and the agent are liable on the contract.

Tort Liability to Third Parties, p. 595

Tort Liability	Principals are liable for the *tortious conduct* of an agent who is acting within the *scope of his authority*. Liability is imposed for misrepresentation, negligence, and intentional torts.
Misrepresentation	Principals are liable for intentional and innocent misrepresentations made by an agent acting within the scope of his or her employment.
Negligence	Principals are liable for the negligent conduct of agents acting within the scope of their employment. Special negligence doctrines include: 1. *Frolic and detour.* Principals are generally relieved of liability if the agent's negligent act occurred on a substantial frolic and detour from the scope of employment.

	2. *"Coming and going" rule.* Principals are not liable if the agent's tortious conduct occurred while on the way to or from work.
	3. *Dual-purpose mission.* If the agent is acting on his or her own behalf and on behalf of the principal, the principal is generally liable for the agent's tortious conduct.
Intentional Torts	States apply one of the following rules:
	1. *Motivation test.* The principal is liable if the agent's intentional tort was committed to promote the principal's business.
	2. *Work-related test.* The principal is liable if the agent's intentional tort was committed within a work-related time or space.
	Agents are personally liable for their own tortious conduct.

Independent Contractor, p. 598

Liability for Independent Contractor's Torts	Generally, principals are not liable for the tortious conduct of independent contractors. Exceptions to the rule are for:
	1. *Nondelegable duties*
	2. *Special risks*
	3. *Negligence in selecting an independent contractor*
	Independent contractors are personally liable for their own torts.

Termination of an Agency and Employment Contract, p. 600

Termination by Acts of the Parties	The following *acts of the parties* terminate agency contracts:
	1. *Mutual agreement.* Parties mutually agree to terminate an agency contract.
	2. *Lapse of time.* The stipulated time period of the agency expires.
	3. *Purpose achieved.* The stipulated purpose of the agency is achieved.
	4. *Occurrence of a specified event.* The occurrence of a stipulated event happens.
Notification of Termination	If an agency is terminated by agreement between the parties, the principal must notify third parties as follows:
	1. *Parties who dealt with the agent.* Direct notice must be given to these parties.
	2. *Parties who have knowledge of the agency.* Direct or constructive (e.g., public notice in newspapers) notice must be given to these parties.
	3. *Parties who have no knowledge of the agency.* No notice need be given to these parties.
	If the proper notice of the termination of the agency is not given, the agent has *apparent authority* to bind the principal to contracts.
	The principal and agent both have the *power* to terminate an agency at any time. After termination, the agent can no longer act on behalf of the principal. The terminating party may not, however, have had the *right* to terminate the agency, and may be held liable for damages caused by *wrongful termination* of the agency.
Termination by Operation of Law	Agency contracts can be terminated by *operation of law.* This includes the following methods:
	1. *Death.* Death of either the principal or the agent.
	2. *Insanity.* Insanity of either the principal or the agent.
	3. *Bankruptcy.* Bankruptcy of the principal.
	4. *Impossibility.* A situation arises that makes the performance of the agency contract impossible.
	5. *Changed circumstances.* An unusual circumstance would lead the agent to believe that the principal's original instructions are no longer valid.
	6. *War.* Outbreak of war between the principal's country and the agent's country.
Irrevocable Agency	An *agency coupled with an interest* is a special type of agency that is irrevocable by the principal. Commonly used in security interests to secure loans.
Wrongful Termination of an Agency Contract	If an agency is for an agreed-upon term or purpose, the *unilateral termination* of the agency contract by either the principal or the agent constitutes the *wrongful termination* of the agency. The breaching party is liable to the other party for damages caused by the breach.

*E*ND-OF-*C*HAPTER *I*NTERNET *E*XERCISES AND *C*ASE *Q*UESTIONS

Working the Web Internet Exercises

ACTIVITIES

1. Visit Nolo Press at **www.nolo.com/category/ ic_home.html** to find general information regarding the classification of independent contractor versus employee.

2. For the U.S. Department of Labor's view on this question see **www.oshaslc.gov/OshDoc/Interp_data/ I19960326A.html** regarding the relationship between landowners and loggers who are harvesting timber from the land.

3. A quick overview of the topic of agency from a practical business perspective is at **www.consumer.pub. findlaw.com/newcontent/consumerlaw/chp2_h. html**. See also "Law About . . . Agency" at **www. law.cornell.edu/topics/agency.html** and U.S. Department of Labor **www.infoctr.edu/fwl/fedweb. exec.htm#labor**. For an example of a state statute, see **www.lectlaw.com/files/bull6.htm**.

4. One way to create an agency is to execute a power of attorney. See **www.smallbiz.biz.findlaw.com/ bookshelf/sblg/sblgchp13_f.html** for information and **www.consumer.pub.findlaw.com/nllg/forms/ 128.html** for a form.

CRITICAL LEGAL THINKING CASES

24.1 Creation of an Agency Renaldo, Inc., d/b/a Baker Street, owns and operates a nightclub in Georgia. On the evening in question plaintiff Ginn became "silly drunk" at the nightclub and was asked by several patrons and the manager to leave the premises. The police were called and Ginn left the premises. When Ginn realized that his jacket was still in the nightclub, he attempted to reenter the premises. He was met at the door by the manager, who refused him admittance. When Ginn persisted, an unidentified patron, without the approval of the manager, pushed Ginn, who lost his balance and fell backward. To break his fall, Ginn put his hand against the door jamb. The unidentified patron slammed the door on Ginn's hand and held it shut for several minutes. Ginn, who suffered severe injuries to his right hand, sued the nightclub for damages. Was the unidentified patron an agent of the nightclub? [*Ginn v. Renaldo, Inc.*, 359 S.E.2d 390 (Ga. App. 1987)]

24.2 Independent Contractor The Butler Telephone Company, Inc., contracted with the Sandidge Construction Company to lay 18 miles of telephone cable in a rural area. In the contract, Butler reserved the right to inspect the work for compliance with the terms of the contract. Butler did not control how Sandidge performed the work. Johnnie Carl Pugh, an employee of Sandidge, was killed on the job when the sides to an excavation in which he was working caved in on top of him. Evidence disclosed that the excavation was not properly shored or sloped and that it violated general safety standards. Pugh's parents and estate brought a wrongful death action against Butler. Is Butler liable? [*Pugh v. Butler Telephone Company, Inc.*, 512 So.2d 1317 (AL 1987)]

24.3 Independent Contractor Mercedes Connolly and her husband purchased airline tickets and a tour package for a tour

to South Africa from Judy Samuelson, a travel agent doing business as International Tours of Manhattan. Samuelson sold tickets for a variety of airline companies and tour operators, including African Adventurers, which was the tour operator for Connolly's tour. Connolly injured her left ankle and foot on September 27, 1984, while the tour group was on a walking tour to see hippopotami in a river at the Sabi Sabi Game Reserve. Mercedes fell while trying to cross a six-inch-deep stream. She sued Samuelson for damages. Is Samuelson liable? [*Connolly v. Samuelson*, 671 F.Supp. 1312 (D.Kan. 1987)]

24.4 Implied Agency Tom and Judith Sullivan owned real property on which they obtained a loan from the Federal Land Bank of Omaha (FLB). The property secured the loan. The Sullivans defaulted on the loan, and the FLB brought an action to foreclose on the mortgage. The FLB's lawyer wrote a letter to the Sullivans outlining a settlement offer. A copy of the letter was sent to the FLB's regional office located in Yankton, South Dakota. The regional office did not notify the attorney that he did not have authority to offer the settlement without its permission. When the Sullivans accepted the settlement offer, the FLB regional office refused to approve the deal. The Sullivans sued to enforce it. Did the attorney for the FLB have authority to settle the case? [*Federal Land Bank of Omaha v. Sullivan*, 430 N.W.2d 700 (SD 1988)]

24.5 Apparent Agency Gene Mohr and James Loyd both own 50 percent of Tri-County Farm Equipment Company. Tri-County has its depository bank account at First National Bank of Olathe, Kansas. Loyd also personally owns an oil business known as Earthworm Energy, which has its bank account at the State Bank of Stanley. Neither Mohr nor Tri-County has any ownership interest in Earthworm. Mohr did not indicate to the State

Bank of Stanley that Loyd had any authority to personally sign checks on behalf of Tri-County. In 1982, Loyd took eight checks that were payable to Tri-County and endorsed and deposited them into Earthworm's account at the State Bank of Stanley. Mohr brought an action for conversion against the State Bank of Stanley to recover the amount of the checks. The bank argued in defense that Loyd had apparent authority to deposit the checks in his personal business account. Did Loyd possess apparent authority? [*Mohr v. State Bank of Stanley*, 734 P.2d 1071 (KS 1987)]

24.6 Ratification After Francis Pusateri retired, he met with Gilbert J. Johnson, a stockbroker with E. F. Hutton & Co., Inc., and informed Johnson that he wished to invest in tax-free bonds and money market accounts. Pusateri opened an investment account with E. F. Hutton and checked the box stating his objective was "tax-free income and moderate growth." During the course of a year, Johnson churned Pusateri's account to make commissions and invested Pusateri's funds in volatile securities and options. Johnson kept telling Pusateri that his account was making money, and the monthly statement from E. F. Hutton did not indicate otherwise. The manager at E. F. Hutton was aware of Johnson's activities but did nothing to prevent them. When Johnson left E. F. Hutton, Pusateri's account—which had been called the "laughingstock" of the office—had shrunk from $196,000 to $96,880, Pusateri sued E. F. Hutton for damages. Is E. F. Hutton liable? [*Pusateri v. E. F. Hutton & Co., Inc.*, 225 C.R. 526 (Cal. App. 1986)]

24.7 Reasonable Care and Skill Norman R. Barton and his wife decided to vacation in Florida in November 1984. In March 1984, they contacted Wonderful World of Travel, Inc., a travel agency licensed by the state of Ohio, to make the arrangements. They requested a room with a view of the ocean, a kitchenette so they would be saved the expense of dining out, free parking, and a free spa. In August, with the Bartons' approval, the travel agency made reservations at the Beau Rivage motel in Bal Harbour, Florida. The travel agency did not confirm the reservations prior to the Bartons' departure in November. When the Bartons arrived at the motel, they found it closed, chained, and guarded. The only other hotel or motel in the area was a Sheraton, which was almost triple the room cost of the Beau Rivage. The Sheraton overlooked the ocean, but it did not have a kitchenette, free parking, or free spa privileges. The Bartons stayed at the Sheraton. They sued the travel agent upon their return. Is the travel agent liable for the increased costs incurred by the Bartons? [*Barton v. Wonderful World of Travel, Inc.*, 502 N.E.2d 715 (Ohio Mun. 1986)]

24.8 Imputed Knowledge On March 31, 1981, Iota Management Corporation entered into a contract to purchase the Bel Air West Motor Hotel in the City of St. Louis from Boulevard Investment Company. The agreement contained the following warranty: "Seller has no actual notice of any substantial defect in the structure of the Hotel or in any of its plumbing, heating, air-conditioning, electrical, or utility systems."

When the buyer inspected the premises, no leaks in the pipes were visible. Iota purchased the hotel for $2 million. When Iota removed some of the walls and ceilings during remodeling, it found evidence of prior repairs to leaking pipes and ducts, as well

as devices for catching water (e.g., milk cartons, cookie sheets, and buckets). The estimate to repair these leaks was $500,000. Evidence at trial showed that Cecil Lillibridge, who was Boulevard's maintenance supervisor from 1975 until the sale of the hotel in 1981, had actual knowledge of these problems and had repaired some of the pipes. Iota sued Boulevard to rescind the contract. Is Boulevard liable? [*Iota Management Corporation v. Boulevard Investment Company*, 731 S.W.2d 399 (Mo.App. 1987)]

24.9 Dual Agency Chemical Bank is the primary bank for Washington Steel Corporation. As an agent for Washington Steel, Chemical Bank expressly and impliedly promised that it would advance the best interests and welfare of Washington Steel. During the course of the agency, Washington Steel provided the bank with comprehensive and confidential financial information, other data, and future business plans.

At some point during the agency, TW Corporation and others approached Chemical Bank to request a loan of $7 million to make a hostile tender offer for the stock of Washington Steel. Chemical Bank agreed and became an agent for TW. Management at Chemical Bank did not disclose its adverse relationship with TW to Washington Steel, did not request Washington Steel's permission to act as an agent for TW, and directed employees of the bank to conceal the bank's involvement with TW from Washington Steel. After TW commenced its public tender offer, Washington Steel filed suit seeking to obtain an injunction against Chemical Bank and TW. Who wins? [*Washington Steel Corporation v. TW Corporation*, 465 F.Supp. 1100 (W.D.Pa. 1979)]

24.10 Duty of Loyalty Peter Shields was the president and member of the board of directors of Production Finishing Corporation from 1974 through August 1981. The company provided steel polishing services. It did most, if not all, of the polishing work in the Detroit area except for that of the Ford Motor Company. (Ford did its own polishing.) Shields discussed this matter with Ford on behalf of Production Finishing on a number of occasions. When Shields learned that Ford was discontinuing its polishing operation, he incorporated Flat Rock Metal and submitted a confidential proposal to Ford that provided that he would buy Ford's equipment and provide polishing services to Ford. It was not until he resigned from Production Finishing that he informed the boards of directors that he was pursuing the Ford business himself. Production Finishing sued Shields. Did Shields breach his fiduciary duty of loyalty to Production Finishing? [*Production Finishing Corporation v. Shields*, 405 N.W.2d 171 (Mich. App. 1987)]

24.11 Personal Guaranty In May 1978, Sebastian International, Inc., entered into a five-year lease for a building in Chadsworth, California. In September 1980, with the consent of the master lessors, Sebastian sublet the building to West Valley Grinding, Inc. In conjunction with the execution of the sublease, the corporate officers of West Valley, including Kenneth E. Peck, each signed a guaranty of lease personally ensuring the payment of West Valley's rental obligations. The guaranty contract referred to Peck in his individual capacity; however, on the signature line he was identified as "Kenneth Peck, Vice President." In May 1981, West Valley went out of business, leaving 24 months remaining on the sublease. After unsuccessful attempts to secure another sublessee, Sebastian surrendered the leasehold back to the master lessors and brought suit against Peck to recover the unpaid rent. Peck argues he is not personally liable because his signature was that of an agent for a disclosed principal and not that of a principal himself. Who wins? [*Sebastian International, Inc. v. Peck*, 195 C.A.3d 803, 240 C.R. 911 (Cal.App. 1987)]

24.12 Contract Liability G. Elvin Grinder of Marbury, Maryland, was a building contractor who, prior to May 1, 1973, did business as an individual and traded as "Grinder Construction." Grinder maintained an open account, on his individual credit, with Bryans Road Building & Supply Co., Inc. Grinder would purchase materials and supplies from Bryans on credit and later pay the invoices. On May 1, 1973, G. Elvin Grinder Construction, Inc., a Maryland corporation, was formed with Grinder personally owning 52 percent of the stock of the corporation. Grinder did not inform Bryans that he had incorporated and continued to purchase supplies on credit from Bryans under the name "Grinder Construction." In May 1978, after certain invoices were not paid by Grinder, Bryans sued Grinder personally to recover. Grinder asserted that the debts were owed by the corporation. Bryans amended its complaint to include the corporation as a defendant. Who is liable to Bryans? [*Grinder v. Bryans Road Building & Supply Co., Inc.*, 432 A.2d 453 (Md.App. 1981)]

24.13 Contract Liability In the spring of 1974, certain residents of Harrisville, Utah, organized the Golden Spike Little League for the youngsters of the town. This was an unincorporated association. David Anderson and several other organizers contracted with Smith & Edwards, a sporting goods store, that agreed to give them favorable prices on merchandise. During the course of the summer, parents went into Smith & Edwards and picked up uniforms and equipment for their children and other Little Leaguers. At the end of the summer, Smith & Edwards sent them a bill for $3,900. Fund-raising activities produced only $149, and the organizers refused to pay the difference. Smith & Edwards sued Anderson and the other organizers for the unpaid balance. Are the organizers personally liable for the debt? [*Smith & Edwards v. Anderson*, 557 P.2d 132 (UT 1978)]

24.14 Tort Liability Intrastate Radiotelephone, Inc., is a public utility that supplies radiotelephone utility service to the general public for radiotelephones, pocket pagers, and beepers. Robert Kranhold, an employee of Intrastate, was authorized to use his personal vehicle on company business. On the morning of March 9, 1976, when Kranhold was driving his vehicle to Intrastate's main office, he negligently struck a motorcycle being driven by Michael S. Largey, causing severe and permanent injuries to Largey. The accident occurred at the intersection where Intrastate's main office is located. Evidence showed that Kranhold acted as a consultant to Intrastate, worked both in and out of Intrastate's offices, had no set hours of work, often attended meetings at Intrastate's offices, and went to Intrastate's offices to pick things up or drop things off. Largey sued Intrastate for damages. Is Intrastate liable? [*Largey v. Radiotelephone, Inc.*, 136 C.A.3d 660, 186 C.R. 520 (Cal. App. 1982)]

BUSINESS ETHICS CASES

24.15 Business Ethics The Hagues, husband and wife, owned a 160-acre tract that they decided to sell. On March 19, 1976, they entered into a listing agreement with Harvey C. Hilgendorf, a licensed real estate broker, which gave Hilgendorf the exclusive right to sell the property for a period of 12 months. Hague agreed to pay Hilgendorf a commission of six percent of the accepted sale price if a bona fide buyer was found during the listing period.

By letter of August 13, 1976, Hague terminated the listing agreement with Hilgendorf. Hilgendorf did not acquiesce to Hague's termination, however. On September 30, 1976, Hilgendorf presented an offer to the Hagues from a buyer willing to purchase the property at the full listing price. The Hagues ignored the offer and sold the property to another buyer. Hilgendorf sued the Hagues for breach of the agency agreement. Did the Hagues act ethically in this case? Who wins the lawsuit? [*Hilgendorf v. Hague*, 293 N.W.2d 272 (IA 1980)]

24.16 Business Ethics The National Biscuit Company (Nabisco) is a corporation that produces and distributes cookies and other food products to grocery stores and other outlets across the nation. In October 1968, Nabisco hired Ronnell Lynch as a cookie salesman-trainee. On March 1, 1969, Lynch was assigned his own sales territory. Lynch's duties involved making sales calls, taking orders, and making sure that shelves of stores in his territory were stocked with Nabisco products. During the period March 1 to May 1, 1969, Nabisco received numerous complaints from store owners in Lynch's territory that Lynch was overly aggressive and was taking shelf space for Nabisco products that was reserved for competing brands.

On May 1, 1969, Lynch visited a grocery store that was managed by Jerone Lange. Lynch was there to place previously delivered merchandise on the store's shelves. An argument developed between Lynch and Lange. Lynch became very angry and started swearing. Lange, the store manager, told Lynch to stop swearing or leave the store, because children were present. Lynch became uncontrollably angry and went behind the counter and dared Lange to a fight. When Lange refused to fight, Lynch proceeded to viciously assault and batter Lange, causing severe injuries. Lange sued Nabisco. Was it ethical for Nabisco to deny liability in this case? Do you think the prior complaints against Lynch had any effect on the decision reached in this case? Is Nabisco liable for the intentional tort (assault and battery) of its employee, Ronnell Lynch? [*Lange v. National Biscuit Company*, 211 N.W.2d 783 (MN 1983)]

BRIEFING THE CASE WRITING ASSIGNMENT

Read the following case, which has been excerpted from the court's opinion. Review and brief the case.

District of Columbia v. Howell
607 A.2D 501 (D.C. App. 1992)
District of Columbia Court of Appeals

Farrell, Associate Judge

The Murch School Summer Discovery Program was designed to provide hands-on education for gifted and talented eight- and nine-year-old children. The program originated in 1985 when Mrs. Gill, the Murch School principal, attended a reception at Mount Vernon College arranged by Greg Butta, a Ph.D. candidate at The American University, to advertise the success of a summer program he had conducted at Mount Vernon. The program interested Mrs. Gill, and after several discussions, Butta sent her a formal proposal for conducting a similar program at the Murch School. Gill proposed changes to the proposal, then solicited and received approval for the program from the Assistant Superintendent for the District of Columbia Public Schools.

Butta hired the staff for the summer program, including some of the instructors who had taught in the Mount Vernon program. Mrs. Gill, however, reviewed all of the instructors' resumes, had veto authority over their hiring, and interviewed most of the staff, including A. Louis Jagoe, before the hiring was made final. Jagoe, who was hired to teach chemistry to the eight- and nine-year-olds in the program, held a master's degree in chemistry and was a Ph.D. candidate at The American University. Before the first general staff meeting, he told Butta that as part of the class he would do a luminescence experiment and a "cold-pack" experiment and wanted to make sparklers with the children. Jagoe and Butta discussed the safety of the sparkler experiment only in regard to the location where the children would be allowed to light the sparklers.

On August 1, 1985, a staff meeting was held at which Gill, Butta, and all instructors and counselors were present. Each instructor gave a brief talk about what he or she intended to do in class. Several instructors testified that Jagoe told the group, including Mrs. Gill, that he planned to make sparklers as one of the chemistry experiments. Gill, who was in and out of the meeting, did not remember hearing Jagoe discuss the experiment, although notes she took at the meeting reflect that she heard him discuss the luminescence and cold pack experiments and asked him questions about these. Gill spoke and emphasized the "hands-on" nature of the program and her hopes for its success.

One child attending the program was nine-year-old Dedrick Howell, whose parents enrolled him after receiving the school brochure in the mail. The accident occurred on August 12, 1985. At the beginning of the chemistry class, Jagoe distributed his "recipe" for sparklers to the children and also wrote it on the black board. Along with other chemical ingredients, the recipe called for the use of potassium perchlorate as the oxidizing agent. Potassium perchlorate was described at trial as an extremely unstable and highly volatile chemical often used to make rocket fuel. Commercially made sparklers are not made with potassium perchlorate.

The children scooped the chemicals, including the potassium perchlorate, out of jars and, using pestles, ground up the mixture in mortars. While they were combining the chemicals, Jagoe ignited three different chemical mixtures at the front of the room with a butane lighter. Butta was present for one of the ignitions when he entered the room to drop off metal hangers for use in the experiment. Mrs. Gill also entered the room at one point, and saw the children working at tables wearing goggles or glasses. She also saw Jagoe at the front of the room lighting the chemicals with a fire extinguisher on the table next to him.

The children continued to grind the material while a counselor, Rebecca Seashore, distributed pieces of metal hangers to be dipped into the mixture at a later time. Dedrick Howell was specifically told not to dip the hanger into the material until instructed to do so. Moments later the chemicals exploded in front of Dedrick. The chemicals burned at 5000 degrees fahrenheit, and Dedrick was burned over 25 percent of his body including his hands, arms, chest, and face.

An employer generally is not liable for injuries to third parties caused by an independent contractor over whom (or over whose work) the employer has reserved no control. There are exceptions to the rule, however, one of which is that one who employs an independent contractor to do work involving a special danger to others which the employer knows or has reason to know to be inherent in or normal to the work, or which he contemplates or has reason to contemplate when making the contract, is subject to liability for physical harm caused to such others by the contractor's failure to take reasonable precautions against such danger.

It is sufficient that work of any kind involves a risk, recognizable in advance, of physical harm to others which is inherent in the work itself, or normally to be expected in the ordinary course of the usual or prescribed way of doing it, or that the employer has special reason to contemplate such a risk under the particular circumstances under which the work is to be done.

The sparkler experiment combined flammable, combustible chemicals, open flame, and children; for that very reason, presumably, the children had been equipped with goggles. Though sparklers are explosives of a lesser order, conducting controlled explosions is a textbook example of an inherently dangerous activity. It was not unreasonable for the jury to conclude that the manufacture of sparklers by nine-year-old children was an inherently dangerous activity.

Therefore, the jury was well within its authority in finding that Jagoe was an independent contractor performing inherently dangerous work of which the District had actual or constructive knowledge.

The judgment is affirmed as to liability and as to the award of $8 million in damages both for pain and suffering and for past medical expenses.

ENDNOTES

1. Restatement (Second) of Agency, § 4.
2. Restatement (Second) of Agency, § 321.
3. Restatement (Second) of Agency, § 229.

CHAPTER 25

Employment and Labor Law

Strong responsible unions are essential to industrial fair play. Without them the labor bargain is wholly one-sided.

—Louis D. Brandeis
(1935)

Chapter Objectives

After studying this chapter, you should be able to:

1. Describe how a union is organized.

2. Explain the consequences of an employer's illegal interference with a union election.

3. Describe the process of collective bargaining.

4. Describe employees' right to strike and picket.

5. Explain how state workers' compensation programs work and describe the benefits available.

6. Describe employers' duty to provide safe working conditions under the Occupational Safety and Health Act.

7. Explain the rules governing private pensions under the Employment Retirement Income Security Act.

8. Describe how the Immigration Reform and Control Act affects employers and employees.

9. List the benefits provided by unemployment compensation and Social Security laws.

10. Describe the labor laws of Mexico.

Chapter Contents

Before the Industrial Revolution, the doctrine of laissez-faire governed the employment relationship in this country. This meant that employment was subject to the common law of contracts and agency law. In most instances, employees and employers had somewhat equal bargaining power.

This changed dramatically once the country became industrialized in the late 1800s. For one thing, large corporate employers had much more bargaining power than their employees. For another, the use of child labor, unsafe working conditions, long hours, and low pay caused concern. Both federal and state legislation sought to protect workers' rights, and labor unions were made lawful. Today, employment law is a mixture of contract law, agency law, and government regulation.

This chapter discusses employment laws, labor unions, worker safety and security, and immigration laws.

FEDERAL LABOR LAW

In the 1880s, few laws protected workers against employment abuses. The workers reacted by organizing unions in an attempt to gain bargaining strength. Unlike unions in many European countries, unions in the United States did not form their own political party. By the early 1900s, employers used violent tactics against workers who were trying to organize into unions. The courts generally sided with employers in such disputes.

History of American Labor Unions

The **American Federation of Labor (AFL)** was formed in 1886 under the leadership of Samuel Gompers. Only skilled craft workers such as silversmiths and artisans were allowed to belong. Semiskilled and unskilled workers could not become members. In 1935, after an unsuccessful attempt to take over the AFL, John L. Lewis formed the **Congress of Industrial Organizations (CIO)**. The CIO permitted semiskilled and unskilled workers to become members. In 1955, the AFL and CIO combined to form the **AFL-CIO**. Individual unions (such as the United Auto Workers and United Steel Workers) may choose to belong to the AFL-CIO, but not all unions opt to join.

Today, approximately 15 percent of private-sector wage and salary workers belong to labor unions. Many government employees also belong to unions.

Ethics Brief

Prior to this century, the doctrine of *laissez-faire* governed the employment relationship. Since then, federal and state governments have enacted a multitude of statutes that regulate employment.

Business Brief

The right of workers to form, join, and assist labor unions is a statutorily protected right in the United States.

Business Brief

Unions in the United States have not formed their own political party as they have in many other countries.

AFL-CIO

The 1955 combination of the AFL and the CIO.

Management and union may be likened to that serpent of the fables who on one body had two heads that fighting with poisoned fangs, killed themselves.

Peter Drucker
The New Society (1951)

Landmark Law

FEDERAL LABOR UNION STATUTES

In the early 1900s, members of the labor movement lobbied Congress to pass laws to protect their rights to organize and bargain with management. During the Great Depression of the 1930s, several statutes were enacted giving workers certain rights and protections. Other statutes have been added since then. The major federal statutes in this area are:

- **Norris-LaGuardia Act** Enacted in 1932,[1] this act stipulates that it is legal for employees to organize. Thus, it removes the federal courts' power to enjoin peaceful union activity. In response, the courts often ignored the act or found union "violence" to escape their provisions.
- **National Labor Relations Act** This act, also known as the Wagner Act or the NLRA, was enacted in 1935.[2] The NLRA establishes the right of employees to form, join, and assist labor organizations; to bargain collectively

with employers; and to engage in concerted activity to promote these rights. The act places an affirmative duty on employers to bargain and deal in good faith with unions. This act is the heart of American labor law.

- **Labor-Management Relations Act** Industrywide strikes occurred in the rail, maritime, coal, lumber, oil, automobile, and textile industries between 1945 and 1947. As a result, public sympathy for unions waned. In 1947, Congress enacted the Labor-Management Relations Act (the Taft-Hartley Act),[3] which amended the Wagner Act. This act (1) expands the activities that labor unions can engage in, (2) gives employers the right to engage in free-speech efforts against unions prior to a union election, and (3) gives the President the right to seek an injunction (for up to 80 days) against a strike that would create a national emergency.

- **Labor-Management Reporting and Disclosure Act**
  After discovering substantial corruption in labor unions, Congress enacted the Labor-Management Reporting and Disclosure Act of 1959 (the Landrum-Griffin Act).[4] This act regulates internal union affairs and establishes the rights of union members. Specifics of this act include (1) a requirement for regularly scheduled elections for union officials by secret ballot, (2) a prohibition against ex-convicts and communists from holding union office, and (3) a rule that makes union officials accountable for union funds and property.

- **Railway Labor Act** The Railway Labor Act of 1926, as amended in 1934, covers employees of railroad and airline carriers.[5] This act permits self-organization of employees, prohibits interference with this right, and provides for the adjustment of grievances.

National Labor Relations Board (NLRB)

The National Labor Relations Act created the **National Labor Relations Board (NLRB)**. The NLRB is an administrative body comprised of five members appointed by the President and approved by the Senate. The NLRB oversees union elections, prevents employers and unions from engaging in illegal and unfair labor practices, and enforces and interprets certain federal labor laws. The decisions of the NLRB are enforceable in court.

Business Ethics

WORK OR FEATHERBEDDING?

Unions often oppose change that would cause members to lose their jobs. Union workers steadfastly defend their right to preserve their jobs. Others argue that unions sometimes use their economic muscle to preserve jobs that are no longer necessary, an action called *featherbedding*. Featherbedding impedes technological progress and raises the cost of goods and services to consumers. Consider these views in the following case.

Longshoremen are employed by steamship and stevedoring companies to load and unload cargo into and out of oceangoing vessels at the pier. Cargo arriving at the pier on trucks or railroad cars is transferred piece by piece from the truck or railroad car to the ship by the longshoremen. The longshoremen check the cargo, sort it, place it on pallets, move it by forklift to the side of the ship, and lift it by means of a sling or hook into the ship's hold. The process is reversed for cargo taken off ships. The longshoremen are represented by a union, the International Longshoremen's Association, AFL-CIO (ILA).

The introduction of "containerization" revolutionized the transportation of cargo. Containers are large metal boxes that are designed to fit onto trucks and railroad cars and can be removed and placed on ships without unloading and loading their contents. When a ship reaches its destination, the containers are loaded onto trucks or railroad cars for transport to their destination. Containerization eliminates most of the work traditionally performed by longshoremen.

After a prolonged strike, ILA and the steamship and stevedoring companies reached an agreement whereby 80 percent of the containers could pass over the pier intact and be loaded onto the ships. The remaining 20 percent of the containers must be unloaded and reloaded by longshoremen even if this work is unnecessary. This agreement was called the Rules on Containers (Rules). Several transportation companies brought suit challenging the legality of Rules under federal labor law. The National Labor Relations Board (NLRB) held Rules to be unlawful. The court of appeals reversed. NLRB appealed to the U.S. Supreme Court.

The Supreme Court sided with ILA and upheld Rules. The Court concluded that Congress, in enacting federal labor law, had no thought of prohibiting labor agreements directed to work preservation. In essence, that is the purpose of a union. The Supreme Court stated:

> *The question is not whether the Rules represent the most rational or efficient response to innovation, but whether they are a legally permissible effort to preserve jobs. We have often noted that a basic premise of the labor laws is that collective discussions backed by the parties' economic weapons will result in decisions that are better for both management and labor and for society as a whole. The Rules represent a negotiated compromise of a volatile problem bearing directly on the well-being of our national economy.* [National Labor Relations Board v. International Longshoremen's Association, AFL-CIO, 473 U.S. 61, 105 S.Ct. 3045 (1985)]

1. Is it ethical for members of a union to strike to preserve jobs that are no longer needed?
2. Should work preservation be considered a legitimate goal of federal labor policy? Why or why not?
3. Will the decision of the Supreme Court increase or decrease the cost of goods and services to consumers? Explain.

ORGANIZING A UNION

Section 7 of the NLRA gives employees the right to join together and form a union.[6] The group that the union is seeking to represent—called the **appropriate bargaining unit** or **bargaining unit**—must be defined before the union can petition for an election. This group can be the employees of a single company or plant, a group within a single company (e.g., maintenance workers at all of a company's plants), or an entire industry (e.g., nurses at all hospitals in the country). Managers and professional employees may not belong to unions formed by employees whom they manage.

Types of Union Elections

If it can be shown that at least 30 percent of the employees in the bargaining unit are interested in joining or forming a union, the NLRB can be petitioned to investigate and set an election date. Most union elections are contested by the employer. The NLRB is required to supervise all contested elections. A simple majority vote (over 50 percent) wins the election. For example, if 51 of 100 employees vote for the union, the union is certified as the bargaining agent for all 100 employees. If management does not contest the election, a consent election may be held without NLRB supervision.

If employees no longer want to be represented by a union, a decertification election will be held. Such elections must be supervised by the NLRB.

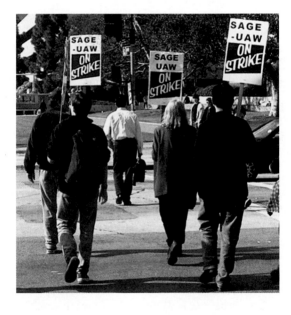

In the United States, federal labor laws protect the rights of workers to form and join unions and to engage in peaceful strikes and picketing. Here, teaching assistants at the University of California picket to have the United Auto Workers recognized as their union.

Union Solicitation on Company Property

If union solicitation is being conducted by fellow employees, an employer may restrict solicitation activities to the employees' free time (e.g., coffee breaks, lunch hours, and before and after work). The activities may also be limited to nonworking areas such as the cafeteria, restroom, or parking lot. Off-duty employees may be barred from union solicitation on company premises, and nonemployees (e.g., union management) may be prohibited from soliciting on behalf of the union anywhere on company property.

An exception to this rule applies if the location of the business and the living quarters of the employees place the employees beyond the reach of reasonable union efforts to communicate with them. This so-called **inaccessibility exception** applies to logging camps, mining towns, company towns, and the like. Employers may dismiss employees who violate these rules.

Section 7 of the NLRA
A law that gives employees the right to join together and form a union.

appropriate bargaining unit
The group that a union seeks to represent.

Business Brief
If a majority of the employees of the appropriate bargaining unit vote to join a union, the union is certified as the bargaining agent of *all* the employees of that unit, even those who did not vote for the union.

Ethics Brief
An employer may restrict union solicitation activities by employees to nonworking areas during employees' free time (e.g., coffee breaks, lunch hours, and before and after work).

inaccessibility exception
A rule that permits employees and union officials to engage in union solicitation on company property if the employees are beyond reach of reasonable union efforts to communicate with them.

The Supreme Court Speaks

Union Solicitation on Private Property Curtailed

Lechmere, Inc. v. National Labor Relations Board
112 S.Ct. 841 (1992)
Supreme Court of the United States

BACKGROUND AND FACTS

Lechmere, Inc. (Lechmere), owns and operates a retail store in the Lechmere Shopping Plaza in Newington, Connecticut. Thirteen smaller stores are located between Lechmere's store and the parking lot, which is owned by Lechmere. In June 1987, the United Food and Commercial Workers Union, AFL-CIO (Union), attempted to organize Lechmere's 200 employees, none of whom belonged to a union. After a full-page advertisement in a local newspaper drew little response, nonemployee Union organizers entered Lechmere's parking lot and began placing handbills on windshields of cars parked in the employee section of the parking lot. Lechmere's manager informed the organizers that Lechmere prohibited solicitation or handbill distribution of any kind on the property and asked them to leave. They did so, and Lechmere personnel removed the handbills. Union organizers renewed their handbill effort in the parking lot on several subsequent occasions, but each time they were asked to leave and the handbills were removed. Union filed a grievance with the National Labor Relations Board (NLRB). The NLRB ruled in favor of Union and ordered Lechmere to allow handbill distribution in the parking lot. The court of appeals affirmed. Lechmere appealed to the U.S. Supreme Court.

SUPREME COURT ISSUE

May a store owner prohibit nonemployee union organizers from distributing leaflets in a shopping mall parking lot owned by the store?

IN THE LANGUAGE OF THE U.S. SUPREME COURT

Thomas, Justice In practice, nonemployee organizational trespassing had generally been prohibited except where "unique obstacles" prevented nontresspassory methods of communication with the employees. The inaccessibility exception is a narrow one. It does not apply wherever nontrespassory access to employees may be cumbersome or less-than-ideally effective, but only where the location of a plant and the living quarters of the employees place the employees beyond the reach of reasonable union efforts to communicate with them.

Although the employees live in a large metropolitan area (Greater Hartford), that fact does not in itself render them "inaccessible." Their accessibility is suggested by the union's success in contacting a substantial percentage of them directly, via mailings, phone calls, and home visits. Such direct contact, of course, is not a necessary element of "reasonably effective" communication; signs or advertising also may suffice. In this case, other alternative means of communication were readily available. Thus, signs (displayed, for example, from the public grassy strip adjoining Lechmere's parking lot) would have informed the employees about the union's organizational efforts. Access to employees, not success in winning them over, is the critical issue.

DECISION AND REMEDY

The U.S. Supreme Court held that under the facts of this case, Lechmere could prohibit nonemployee Union organizers from distributing leaflets to employees in the store's parking lot. Reversed.

CASE QUESTIONS

Critical Legal Thinking   Should property rights take precedence over a union's right to organize employees?

Business Ethics   Is it ethical for an employer to deny union organizers access to company property to conduct their organization efforts? Is it ethical for union organizers to demand this as a right?

Contemporary Business   What implications does this case have for business? Is this a pro- or antibusiness decision?

Illegal Interference with an Election

Section 8(a) of the NLRA

A law that makes it an *unfair labor practice* for an employer to interfere with, coerce, or restrain employees from exercising their statutory right to form and join unions.

Section 8(b) of the NLRA

A law that prohibits *unions* from engaging in unfair labor practices that interfere with a union election.

Section 8(a) of the NLRA makes it an **unfair labor practice** for an employer to interfere with, coerce, or restrain employees from exercising their statutory right to form and join unions. Threats of loss of benefits for joining the union, statements such as "I'll close this plant if a union comes in here," and the like are unfair labor practices. An employer may not form a company union.

Section 8(b) of the NLRA prohibits unions from engaging in unfair labor practices that interfere with a union election. Coercion, physical threats, and such are unfair labor practices. Where an unfair labor practice has been found, the NLRB (or the courts) may issue a cease-and-desist order or an injunction to restrain unfair labor practices, and set aside an election and order a new election.

The Supreme Court Speaks

Employer Found to Have Engaged in an Unfair Labor Practice

National Labor Relations Board v. Exchange Parts Co.
375 U.S. 405, 84 S.Ct. 457 (1964)
Supreme Court of the United States

BACKGROUND AND FACTS

Exchange Parts Co. (Exchange Parts) is engaged in the business of rebuilding automobile parts in Fort Worth, Texas. Prior to November 1959, its employees were not represented by a union. On November 9, 1959, the International Brotherhood of Boilermakers, Iron Shipbuilders, Blacksmiths, Forgers and Helpers, AFL-CIO (Union), advised Exchange Parts that it was going to conduct a campaign to organize the workers at the plant. After obtaining sufficient support from members of the appropriate bargaining unit, Union petitioned the NLRB to set an election date. After completing its investigation on February 19, 1960, the NLRB issued an order setting March 18, 1960, as the election date. On February 25, 1960, Exchange Parts held a dinner for its employees at which management announced a new company benefit allowing employees to have an extra holiday (their birthday). On March 4, Exchange Parts sent a letter to its employees that announced new increased wages for overtime pay and an extended vacation plan for employees. Union subsequently lost the election. Union filed a complaint with the NLRB, which held in favor of Union and ordered a new election. The court of appeals reversed. The NLRB appealed to the U.S. Supreme Court.

SUPREME COURT ISSUE

Is it an unfair practice for an employer to confer new economic benefits on its employees on the eve of a union election?

IN THE LANGUAGE OF THE U.S. SUPREME COURT

Harlan, Justice *The broad purpose of Section 8(a) is to establish the right of employees to organize for mutual aid without employer interference. We have no doubt that it prohibits not only intrusive threats but also conduct immediately favorable to employees that is undertaken with the express purpose of impinging upon their freedom of choice for or against unionization and is reasonably calculated to have that effect. The danger inherent in well-timed increases in benefits is the suggestion of a "fist inside a velvet glove." Employees are not likely to miss the inference that the source of benefits now conferred is also the source from which future benefits must flow and which may dry up if it is not obliged.*

We cannot agree with the court of appeals that enforcement of the NLRB's order will have the ironic result of discouraging benefits for labor. The beneficence of an employer is likely to be ephemeral if prompted by a threat of unionization that is subsequently removed. Insulating the right of collective organization from calculated goodwill of this sort deprives employees of little that has lasting value.

DECISION AND REMEDY

The U.S. Supreme Court held that an employer's conferral of benefits on employees on the eve of a union election, which are designed to affect the outcome of that election, is an unfair labor practice. Reversed.

CASE QUESTIONS

Critical Legal Thinking Should a company be prohibited from taking away (or giving) economic benefits in its fight with a union?

Business Ethics Was it ethical for the employer in this case to increase employee benefits on the eve of the union election?

Contemporary Business Do you think the employer's conduct in this case constituted a "fist in a velvet glove"? Were the benefits conferred in this case likely to be ephemeral?

Contemporary Business Environment

PLANT CLOSING ACT

Often, a company would choose to close a plant without giving its employees prior notice of the closing. To remedy this situation, on August 4, 1988, Congress enacted the **Worker Adjustment and Retraining Notification Act**, also called the **Plant Closing Act** or **WARN Act** [P.L. 100-379, 102 Stat. 840]. The act, which covers employers with 100 or more employees, requires employers to give their employees 60 days' notice before engaging in certain plant closings or layoffs.

If the employees are represented by a union, the notice must be given to the union; if they are not, the notice must be given to the employees individually.

The actions covered by the act are

- **Plant Closings**   A permanent or temporary shutdown of a single site that results in a loss of employment of 50 or more employees during any 30-day period.
- **Mass Layoffs**   A reduction of 33 percent of the employees or at least 50 employees during any 30-day period.

An employer is exempted from having to give such notice if

- The closing or layoff is caused by business circumstances that were not reasonably foreseeable as of the time that the notice would have been required.
- The business was actively seeking capital or business that, if obtained, would have avoided or postponed the shutdown and the employer in good faith believed that giving notice would have precluded it from obtaining the needed capital or business.

COLLECTIVE BARGAINING

collective bargaining

The act of negotiating contract terms between an employer and the members of a union.

collective bargaining agreement

The resulting contract from a collective bargaining procedure.

Ethics Brief

An employer may not sponsor or control a union.

Once a union has been elected, the employer and the union discuss the terms of employment of union members and try to negotiate a contract that embodies these terms. The act of negotiating is called **collective bargaining**, and the resulting contract is called a **collective bargaining agreement**. The employer and the union must negotiate with each other in good faith. Among other things, this prohibits making take-it-or-leave-it proposals.

Subjects of Collective Bargaining

Wages, hours, and other terms and conditions of employment are *compulsory subjects* of collective bargaining. Fringe benefits, health benefits, retirement plans, work assignments, safety rules, and the like are included in this category. *Illegal* subjects (e.g., closed shops and discrimination) may not be negotiated.

Subjects that are not compulsory or illegal are *permissive* subjects of collective bargaining. These include such issues as the size and composition of the supervisory force, location of plants, corporate reorganizations, and the like. These subjects may be bargained for if the company and union agree to do so.

Union Security Agreements

union shop

An establishment where an employee must join the union within a certain number of days after being hired.

agency shop

An establishment where an employee does not have to join the union, but must pay a fee equal to the union dues.

To obtain the greatest power possible, elected unions sometimes try to install a *union security agreement*. The two types of security agreements are

- **Union Shop**   Under a **union shop** agreement, an employee must join the union within a certain number of days (e.g., 30 days) after being hired. Employees who do not join must be discharged by the employer upon notice from the union. Union members pay union dues to the union. Union shops are lawful.
- **Agency Shop**   Under an **agency shop** agreement, employees do not have to become union members, but they do have to pay an agency fee (an amount equal to union dues) to the union. Agency shops are lawful.

Upon proper notification by the union, union and agency shop employers are required to (1) deduct union dues and agency fees from employees' wages and (2) forward these dues to the union. This is called a *check-off provision*.

The Supreme Court Speaks

Union Security Clause Upheld

Marquez v. Screen Actors Guild, Inc.
525 U.S. 33, 119 S.Ct 292 (1998)
Supreme Court of the United States

BACKGROUND AND FACTS
The Screen Actors Guild (SAG) is a labor union that represents performers in the entertainment industry. In 1994,

Lakeside Productions, an entertainment production company, signed a collective bargaining agreement with SAG making SAG the exclusive union for performers that Lakeside hired for its productions. The collective bargaining agreement contained a standard "union security clause" providing that any performer who worked for Lakeside must be a member of SAG. Naomi Marquez, a part-time actress, auditioned for a one-line role in a T.V. episode to be filmed by Lakeside and won the part. When Marquez did not pay the $500 membership fee to SAG, Lakeside hired another actress for the part. Marquez sued SAG and Lakeside, alleging that the union security clause was unlawful. The district court held for the defendants, and the court of appeals affirmed. The U.S. Supreme Court granted certiorari to hear the appeal.

SUPREME COURT ISSUE

Does the union security clause negotiated between Lakeside Productions and the Screen Actors Guild violate federal labor law?

IN THE LANGUAGE OF THE U.S. SUPREME COURT

O'Connor, Justice Section 8(a)(3) of the National Labor Relations Act (NLRA), permits unions and employers to negotiate an agreement that requires union "membership" as a condition of employment for all employees.

The conclusion that Section 8(a)(3) permits union security clauses is not the end of the story. First, in NLRB v. General Motors Corp., 373 U.S. 734, 742, 83 S.Ct. 1453, we held that although Section 8(a)(3) states that unions may negotiate a clause requiring "membership" in the union, an employee can satisfy the membership condition merely by paying to the union an amount equal to the union's initiation fees and dues. In other words, the membership that may be required as a condition of employment is whittled down to its financial core.

Second, in Communications Workers v. Beck, 487 U.S. 735, 108 S.Ct. 2641, we considered whether the employee's "financial core" obligation included a duty to pay for support of union activities beyond those activities undertaken by the union as the exclusive bargaining representative. We held that the language of Section 8(a)(3) does not permit unions to exact dues or fees from employees for activities that are not germane to collective bargaining, grievance adjustment, or contract administration.

As a result of these two conclusions, Section 8(a)(3) permits unions and employers to require only that employees pay the fees and dues necessary to support the union's activities as the employees' exclusive bargaining representative.

DECISION AND REMEDY

The U.S. Supreme Court held that the union security clause negotiated between Lakeside Productions and SAG was lawful under federal labor law. The judgment of the court of appeals is affirmed.

CASE QUESTIONS

Critical Legal Thinking What does an exclusive union security clause provide? Under this agreement, must a worker join a labor union? Explain.

Business Ethics Did SAG and Lakeside act ethically in this case?

Contemporary Business Do the decisions of the U.S. Supreme Court regarding union security agreements prevent the "free rider" problem? Explain.

Contemporary Business Environment

STATE RIGHT-TO-WORK LAWS

In 1947, Congress amended the Taft-Hartley Act by enacting Section 14(b), which provides: "Nothing in this Act shall be construed as authorizing the execution or application of agreements requiring membership in a labor organization as a condition of employment in any State or Territory in which such execution or application is prohibited by State or Territorial Law." In other words, states can enact **right-to-work laws**—either by constitutional amendment or statute—that outlaw union and agency shops.

If a state enacts a right-to-work law, individual employees cannot be forced to join a union or pay union dues and fees even though a union has been elected by other employees. Right-to-work laws are often enacted by states to attract new businesses to a nonunion and low-wage environment. Unions vehemently oppose the enactment of right-to-work laws because they substantially erode union power.

Today, the following 21 states have enacted right-to-work laws:

Alabama	Nevada
Arizona	North Carolina
Arkansas	North Dakota
Florida	South Carolina
Georgia	South Dakota
Idaho	Tennessee
Iowa	Texas
Kansas	Utah
Louisiana	Virginia
Mississippi	Wyoming
Nebraska	

The remedies for violation of right-to-work laws vary from state to state but usually include damages to persons injured by the violation, injunctive relief, and often criminal penalties.

STRIKES AND PICKETING

The NLRA gives union management the right to recommend that the union call a **strike** if a collective bargaining agreement cannot be reached. Before there can be a strike, though, a majority vote of the union's members must agree to the action.

Employer Lockout

It an employer reasonably anticipates a strike by some of its employees, it may prevent those employees from entering the plant or premises. This is called an **employer lockout**.

Crossover and Replacement Workers

Individual members of a union do not have to honor the strike. They may (1) choose not to strike or (2) return to work after joining the strikers for a time. Employees who choose either of these options are known as **crossover workers**.

Once a strike begins, the employer may continue operations by using management personnel and hiring **replacement workers** to take the place of the striking employees. Replacement workers can be hired on either a temporary or permanent status. If replacement workers are given permanent status, they do not have to be dismissed when the strike is over.

Illegal Strikes

Several types of strikes have been held to be illegal and are not protected by federal labor law. Illegal strikes are:

- **Violent Strikes** Striking employees cause substantial damage to property of the employer or a third party. Courts usually tolerate a certain amount of isolated violence before finding that the entire strike is illegal.
- **Sit-Down Strikes** Striking employees continue to occupy the employer's premises. Such strikes are illegal because they deny the employer's statutory right to continue its operations during the strike.
- **Partial or Intermittent Strikes** Employees strike part of the day or workweek and work the other part. This type of strike is illegal because it interferes with the employer's right to operate its facilities at full operation.
- **Wildcat Strikes** Individual union members go out on strike without proper authorization from the union. The courts have recognized that a wildcat strike becomes lawful if it is quickly ratified by the union.
- **Strikes During the 60-day Cooling-Off Period** Strikes begin during the mandatory 60-day **cooling-off period**. This time is designed to give the employer and the union time to negotiate a settlement of the union grievances and avoid a strike. Any strike without a proper 60-day notice is illegal.
- **Strikes in Violation of a No-Strike Clause** Strikes take place in violation of a negotiated no-strike clause, under which an employer gives economic benefits to the union and, in exchange, the union agrees that no strike will be called for a set time.

Illegal strikers may be discharged by the employer with no rights to reinstatement.

Picketing

Striking union members often engage in **picketing** in support of their strike. Picketing usually takes the form of the striking employees and union representatives walking in front of the employer's premises carrying signs announcing their strike. It is used to put pressure on an employer to settle a strike. The right to picket is implied from the NLRA.

Picketing is lawful unless it (1) is accompanied by violence, (2) obstructs customers from entering the employer's place of business, (3) prevents nonstriking employees from entering the employer's premises, or (4) prevents pickups and deliveries at the employer's place of business. An employer may seek an injunction against unlawful picketing.

Secondary Boycott Picketing Unions sometimes try to bring pressure against an employer by picketing his or her suppliers or customers. Such **secondary boycott picketing** is lawful

---

strike

A cessation of work by union members in order to obtain economic benefits or correct an unfair labor practice.

employer lockout

Act of the employer to prevent employees from entering the work premises when the employer reasonably anticipates a strike.

crossover worker

A person who does not honor a strike who either (1) chooses not to strike or (2) returns to work after joining the strikers for a time.

replacement workers

Workers who are hired to take the place of striking workers. They can be hired on either a temporary or permanent basis.

No private business monopoly, producer organization or cartel wields the market (and physical) power or commands the discipline over its members which many unions have achieved.

Gottfried Haberler
Economic Growth and Stability
(1974)

cooling-off period

Requires a union to give an employer at least 60 days' notice before a strike can commence.

picketing

The action of strikers walking in front of the employer's premises carrying signs announcing their strike.

secondary boycott picketing

A type of picketing where unions try to bring pressure against an employer by picketing his or her suppliers or customers.

only if it is product picketing (i.e., if the picketing is against the primary employer's product). The picketing is illegal if it is directed against the neutral employer instead of the struck employer's product.

Consider This Example Suppose the apple pickers' union in the state of Washington goes on strike against its primary employers, the apple growers. Picketing the apple orchards may do little to draw attention of the strike to the public. Therefore, members of the apple pickers union may picket grocery stores in metropolitan areas that sell Washington apples. If the signs the picketers carry ask shoppers at the grocery stores not to buy Washington apples, the secondary boycott is lawful. However, it is unlawful if the signs ask customers not to shop at the grocery stores.

Business Ethics

LABOR UNION VIOLENCE PUNISHED

The primary purpose of a union is to organize employees so that they will have greater bargaining power in negotiating wages and other terms of employment with their employers. If an agreement with an employer is not reached, the union may call a strike of its members and set up picket lines at the employer's place of business to try to bring added pressure on the employer to settle. But when does pressure cross over the ethical line? Consider the following case.

Peter Vargas and Kenneth Henderson owned Chino Farms Market, a grocery store. The employees at the market belonged to the Retail Clerk's Union Local 1428. When the existing collective bargaining agreement expired, the parties began negotiations for a new contract. After several months, the negotiations reached an impasse and the union workers went out on strike. Vargas, Henderson, and workers they hired tried to operate the store.

On the first night of the strike, Henderson voiced concern about the employees' welfare to the union's local agent, who replied, "We don't care about the people. We're going to break you." The union hired professional picketers to join the striking workers on the picket line.

During the course of the picketing, which lasted approximately one year, the picketers

- Blocked the entrances to the store.
- Blocked the driveways leading to the store's parking lot.
- Swore at and threatened customers.
- Scattered nails and carpet tacks over the parking lot.
- Broke windows of delivery trucks trying to make deliveries to the store.

- Spray-painted delivery trucks.
- Painted graffiti on the exterior walls at the store.
- Pushed the store's shopping carts into the street.
- Threw eggs and other food at the store.
- Threw water balloons at customers.
- Placed horse manure in front of the store to offend customers.
- Physically attacked workers at the store and destroyed their vehicles.

The owners of the store obtained court injunctions ordering the picketers from engaging in such conduct. When presented with the injunctions, the picketers tore them up. Customers who complained about the picketers' activities simply stopped shopping at the market. The market was driven out of business.

Vargas and Henderson sued the union for the tort of intentional interference with business relations. The jury found that the striking workers had engaged in illegal activities while picketing the market and that these activities had been condoned by the union. The jury awarded Chino Farms Market $2,602,765 in compensatory damages and $2,602,765 in punitive damages against the union. The court of appeals affirmed the judgment [*Vargas v. Retail Clerk's Union Local 1428*, 212 Cal.App. 2d 287, 260 Cal.Rptr. 650 (Cal. App. 1989)]

1. Were the picketers' activities morally reprehensible?
2. Why did the picketers engage in violent and dangerous activities during their strike?
3. Was the award of damages, particularly punitive damages, warranted in this case?

Internal UNION AFFAIRS

Unions may adopt **internal union rules** to regulate the operation of the union, acquire and maintain union membership, and the like. The undemocratic manner in which many unions were formulating these rules prompted Congress to enact **Title I of the Landrum-Griffin Act**. Title I, which is often referred to as **labor's "bill of rights,"** gives each union member equal rights and privileges to nominate candidates for union office, vote in elections, and

Title I of the Landrum-Griffin Act

Referred to as labor's "bill of rights" that gives each union member equal rights and privileges to nominate candidates for union office, vote in elections, and participate in membership meetings.

participate in membership meetings. It further guarantees union members the right of free speech and assembly, provides for due process (notice and hearing), and permits union members to initiate judicial or administrative action.

A union may discipline members for participating in certain activities, including (1) walking off the job in a nonsanctioned strike, (2) working for wages below union scale, (3) spying for an employer, and (4) any other unauthorized activity that has an adverse economic impact on the union. A union may not punish a union member for participating in a civic duty, such as testifying in court against the union.

Contemporary Business Environment

Drug Testing of Employees

Drug testing of employees or prospective employees by private and public employers has increased dramatically in the last decade. Employers see drug testing as a way to increase productivity and decrease liability exposure. Job applicants and employees often view drug testing as an invasion of privacy. Although the courts have not been totally consistent in deciding drug-testing cases, several trends have emerged.

Generally, pre-employment drug screening has been upheld by the courts. Because job applicants have a lower expectation of privacy than incumbent employees, legal challenges are less likely. Drug testing of incumbent employees by private employers is usually upheld where the employer either has a reasonable suspicion that an employee is impaired or drug testing is required after an accident has occurred.

When the government is the employer, an additional challenge is usually raised against drug testing. Plaintiffs usually say that it constitutes an unreasonable search and seizure by the government in violation of the Fourth Amendment of the U.S. Constitution. This issue was raised in two cases decided by the U.S. Supreme Court.

In *Skinner v. Railway Labor Executives' Association* [489 U.S. 602, 109 S.Ct. 1402, 103 L.Ed.2d 639 (1989)], the Supreme Court upheld the postaccident testing of railway workers even if the employer has no reason to suspect drug use. The Court upheld a Federal Railroad Administration (FRA) rule that regulations require blood and urine tests of every employee involved in a "major accident" and permit testing of any worker who violates certain safety rules. These rules were prompted by an investigation that revealed that alcohol and drug use by railroad employees contributed to a substantial number of train accidents.

After deciding *Skinner*, the Court moved on to consider the case of *National Treasury Employees Union v. Von Raab* [489 U.S. 656, 109 S.Ct. 1384, 103 L.Ed.2d 685 (1989)]. In *Von Raab*, the Supreme Court decided that the U.S. Customs Service, which is responsible for protecting the nation's borders and seizing illegal drugs, could require applicants for jobs that required them to interdict illegal drugs, carry a gun, or handle "classified material" to take a urine test for illegal drugs. The Court stated that even off-duty use of illicit substances can impact on their effectiveness because of the risk of bribery and blackmail.

Workers' Compensation Acts

Many types of employment are dangerous, and each year many workers are injured on the job. At common law, employees who were injured on the job could sue their employer for negligence. This time-consuming process placed the employee at odds with his or her employer. In addition, there was no guarantee that the employee would win the case. Ultimately, many injured workers—or the heirs of deceased workers—were left uncompensated.

Workers' compensation acts were enacted in response to the unfairness of that result. These acts create an administrative procedure for workers to receive compensation for injuries that occur on the job. First, the injured worker files a claim with the appropriate state government agency (often called the workers' compensation board or commission). Next, that entity determines the legitimacy of the claim. If the worker disagrees with the agency's findings, he or she may appeal the decision through the sate court system.

Workers' compensation benefits are paid according to preset limits established by statute or regulation. The amounts that are recoverable vary from state to state.

workers' compensation acts

Acts that compensate workers and their families if workers are injured in connection with their jobs.

Business Brief

Depending on the state, employers are required either to pay for workers' compensation insurance or to self-insure by making payments into a contingency fund. This is a substantial expense for business.

Soo Locks, Michigan Employers are required to cover employees with workers' compensation insurance.

Employment-Related Injury

To be compensable under workers' compensation, the claimant must prove that the injury arose out of and in the course of his or her employment. An accident that occurs while an employee is actively working is clearly within the scope of this rule. Accidents that occur at a company cafeteria or while on a business lunch for an employer are covered. Accidents that happen while the employee is at an off-premises restaurant during his personal lunch hour are not covered. Many workers' compensation acts include stress as a compensable work-related injury.

Business Brief

To recover under workers' compensation, the worker's injuries must have been employment-related.

Exclusive Remedy

Workers' compensation is an exclusive remedy. Thus, workers cannot sue their employers in court for damages. There is one exception to this rule: If an employer intentionally injures a worker, the worker can collect workers' compensation benefits and sue the employer. Workers' compensation acts do not bar injured workers from suing responsible third parties to recover damages.

In the following case, the court had to decide whether an accident was work-related.

Business Brief

Generally, workers' compensation is an *exclusive remedy* for an injured employee. It precludes the injured employee from suing the employer for other damages or remedies. An exception occurs when an employer intentionally injures an employee.

Smith v. Workers' Compensation Appeals Board
191 Cal.App.3d 154, 236 Cal.Rptr. 248 (1987)
Court of Appeals of California

CASE 25.1

BACKGROUND AND FACTS
Ronald Wayne Smith was employed by Modesto High School as a temporary math instructor. In addition, he coached the girls' baseball and basketball teams. The contract under which he was employed stated that he "may be required to devote a reasonable amount of time to other duties" in addition to instructional duties. The teachers in the school system were evaluated once a year regarding both instructional duties and noninstructional duties, including "sponsorship or the supervision of out-of-classroom student activities."

The high school's math club holds an annual end-of-year outing. For the 1983–1984 school year, a picnic was scheduled for June 7, 1984, at the Modesto Reservoir. The students invited their math teachers, including Smith, to attend. The food was paid for by math club members' dues. Smith attended the picnic with his wife and three children. One of the students brought along a windsurfer. Smith watched the students as they used it before and after the picnic. When Smith tried it himself, he fell and was seriously injured. He died shortly thereafter. Mrs. Smith filed a claim for workers' compensation benefits, which was objected to by the employer. The workers' compensation judge denied benefits. The Workers' Compensation Appeals Board affirmed. Mrs. Smith appealed.

ISSUE

Was Smith engaged in employment-related activities when the accident occurred?

COURT'S REASONING

The court of appeal held that the decedent believed that his participation in the math club picnic was expected by his employer and that this belief was objectively reasonable. The court stated, "The school was more than minimally involved in the picnic." Teachers were encouraged to involve themselves in extracurricular activities of the school, thus conferring the benefit of better teacher-student relationships. The court noted that teachers were evaluated on whether they shared equally in the sponsorship or the supervision of out-of-classroom student activities. The court concluded that the decedent's engagement in the recreational activities was causally connected to his employment.

DECISION

The court of appeals held that decedent's accident was causally connected to his employment for purposes of awarding workers' compensation benefits to his heirs. Reversed and remanded.

Case Questions

Critical Legal Thinking Should workers' compensation benefits be awarded only for accidents that occur at the job site? Why or why not?

Business Ethics Did the employer act ethically in objecting to the payment of benefits in this case?

Contemporary Business How costly is workers' compensation for business? Do you think that many fraudulent workers' compensation claims are filed?

Contemporary Business Environment

EMPLOYEE POLYGRAPH PROTECTION ACT

In the past, some employers used polygraph (lie detector) tests to screen job applicants and employees. To correct abuses in this practice and to protect workers' privacy, Congress enacted the **Employee Polygraph Protection Act of 1988** [29 U.S.C. §§ 2001–2009]. The act prohibits most private employers from using polygraph tests. Federal and state governments are not covered by the act. Polygraph tests may also be used by

- Employers in matters dealing with the national defense (e.g., certain defense contractors).
- Security services that hire employees who protect the public health and safety (e.g., guards at electric power plants).
- Drug manufacturers and distributors that hire employees that will have access to the drugs.

- Employers that are investigating incidents of theft, embezzlement, espionage, and the like by current employees. The employer must have a reasonable suspicion that the employee was involved in the incident.

The act requires private employers that are permitted to use polygraph testing to follow certain procedures, including giving notice to the person to be tested, using licensed examiners, and prohibiting certain questions (e.g., those relating to the religion or sexual behavior of the subject).

The act is administered by the Department of Labor, which has the authority to adopt regulations to enforce the act. It can assess civil penalties up to $10,000 and can seek injunctive and legal relief against violators. Employees and job applicants are given a private right of action to sue under the act.

OCCUPATIONAL SAFETY AND HEALTH ACT

Occupational Safety and Health Act

A federal act enacted in 1970 that promotes safety in the workplace.

In 1970, Congress enacted the **Occupational Safety and Health Act**[7] to promote safety in the workplace. Virtually all private employers are within the scope of the act, but federal, state, and local governments are exempted. Industries regulated by other federal safety legislation also are exempt.[8] The act also established the **Occupational Safety and Health Administration (OSHA)**, a federal administrative agency within the Department of Labor. The act imposes recordkeeping and reporting requirements on employers and requires them to post notices in the workplace informing employees of their rights under the act.

The federal Occupational Safety and Health Act establishes certain job safety standards that employers must comply with.

Specific and General Duty Standards

OSHA is empowered to administer the act and adopt rules and regulations to interpret and enforce it. OSHA had adopted thousands of regulations to enforce the safety standards established by the act. These include the following:

- **Specific Duty Standards** Many of the OSHA standards address safety problems of a **specific duty** nature. For example, OSHA standards establish safety requirements for equipment (e.g., safety guards), set maximum exposure levels to hazardous chemicals, regulate the location of machinery, establish safety procedures for employees, and the like.
- **General Duty Standards** The act imposes a **general duty** on an employer to provide a work environment "free from recognized hazards[9] that are causing or are likely to cause death or serious physical harm to his employees." This is so even if no specific regulation applies to the situation.

OSHA is empowered to inspect places of employment for health hazards and safety violations. If a violation is found, OSHA can issue a *written citation* that requires the employer to abate or correct the situation. Contested citations are reviewed by the Occupational Safety and Health Review Commission. Its decision is appealable to the federal circuit court of appeals. Employers who violate the act, OSHA rules and regulations, or OSHA citations are subject to both civil and criminal penalties.

specific duty

An OSHA standard that addresses a safety problem of a specific duty nature (e.g., requirement for a safety guard on a particular type of equipment).

general duty

A duty that an employer has to provide a work environment "free from recognized hazards that are causing or are likely to cause death or serious physical harm to his employees."

Business Ethics

ROOFING COMPANY NAILED BY OSHA

Corbesco, Inc. (Corbesco), an industrial roofing and siding installation company, was hired to put metal roofing and siding over the skeletal structure of five aircraft hangars at Chennault Air Base in Louisiana. In April 1987, Corbesco assigned three of its employees to work on the partially completed flat roof of Hangar B, a large single-story building measuring 60 feet high, 374 feet wide, and 574 feet long. On April 2, 1987, one of the workers, Roger Matthew, who was on his knees installing insulation on the roof, lost his balance and fell 60 feet to the concrete below. He was killed by the fall. The next day, an OSHA compliance officer cited Corbesco for failing to install a safety net under the work site. The officer cited a general industry standard that pro-

vides that safety nets should be provided when workers are more than 25 feet above the ground [25 C.F.R. §1926.105(a)]. The Department of Labor affirmed the citation and assessed a $50 penalty against Corbesco. Corbesco appealed.

Did Corbesco violate the OSHA general industry regulation that required employers to install safety nets below employees working more than 25 feet above the ground?

The court of appeals noted the OSHA rule that stated if a workplace is more than 25 feet above the ground, an employer must furnish some form of fall protection. The language of Section 1926.105(a) gave Corbesco knowledge of this general duty. However, the essence of Corbesco's claim is that it believed that it was complying with the regulation. Corbesco was required to furnish its worker with a safety net only if none of the following safety devices was being used: "Ladders, scaffolds, catch platforms, temporary floors, safety lines, or safety belts." Corbesco argues that the flat roof on which the employees were working served as a "temporary floor" and that the language of the standard is not specific enough to notify it otherwise.

The court held that Corbesco had constructive notice that it was required to install safety nets under its crew while they were working on the edge of a flat roof some 60 feet above a concrete floor. The commission frequently had said that a flat roof cannot serve as a temporary floor if workers must operate along the perimeter of such a roof because it does not provide fall protection; either a safety net or one of the alternate safety devices listed in Section 1926.105(a) must be

used. A reasonable construction company in Corbesco's position would have known about these interpretations of this standard.

The court of appeals held that Corbesco violated 25 C.F.R. Section 1926.105(a) by not providing a safety net below its employees who were working more than 60 feet above the ground. [*Corbesco, Inc. v. Dole, Secretary of Labor*, 926 F.2d 422 (5th Cir. 1991)]

1. Did Corbesco act ethically in arguing that the flat roof created a temporary floor that relieved it of the duty to install a safety net under it?
2. Why are occupational safety laws enacted? Would just letting employees sue their employers for injuries caused by unsafe working conditions accomplish the same result? Explain.

Fair Labor Standards Act (FLSA)

A federal act enacted in 1938 to protect workers; prohibits child labor and establishes minimum wage and overtime pay requirements.

It is difficult to imagine any grounds, other than our own personal economic predilections, for saying that the contract of employment is any the less an appropriate subject of legislation than are scores of others, in dealing with which this Court has held that legislatures may curtail individual freedom in the public interest.

Justice Stone
Dissenting Opinion, Morehead v. New York *(1936)*

FAIR LABOR STANDARDS ACT

In 1938, Congress enacted the **Fair Labor Standards Act (FLSA)** to protect workers.[10] The FLSA applies to private employers and employees engaged in the production of goods for interstate commerce.

Child Labor

The FLSA forbids the use of oppressive child labor and makes it unlawful to ship goods produced by businesses that use oppressive child labor. The Department of Labor has adopted the following regulations that define lawful child labor: (1) children under the age of 14 cannot work except as newspaper deliverers; (2) children ages 14 and 15 may work limited hours in nonhazardous jobs approved by the Department of Labor (e.g., restaurants and gasoline stations); and (3) children ages 16 and 17 may work unlimited hours in nonhazardous jobs. The Department of Labor determines which occupations are hazardous (e.g., mining, roofing, and working with explosives). Children who work in agricultural employment and child actors and performers are exempt from these restrictions. Persons age 18 and older may work at any job whether it is hazardous or not.

 *Entrepreneur and the Law*

MINIMUM WAGE AND OVERTIME PAY REQUIREMENTS

The FLSA establishes minimum wage and overtime pay requirements for workers. Managerial, administrative, and professional employees are exempt from the act's wage and hour provisions. As outlined below, the FLSA requires employers to pay covered workers at least the minimum wage for their regular work hours. Overtime pay is also mandated.

- **Minimum Wage** The minimum wage is set by Congress and can be changed. Currently, it is set at $5.15 per hour. The department of Labor permits employers to pay less than the minimum wage to students and appren-

tices. An employer may reduce minimum wages by an amount equal to the reasonable cost of food and lodging provided to employees.

- **Overtime Pay** Under the FLSA, an employer cannot require nonexempt employees to work more than 40 hours per week unless they are paid one-and-a-half times their regular pay for each hour worked in excess of 40 hours. Each week is treated separately. For example, if an employee works 50 hours one week and 30 hours the next, the employer owes the employee 10 hours of overtime pay.

E-Commerce & Information Technology

MICROSOFT VIOLATES EMPLOYMENT LAW

Microsoft Corporation is the world's largest provider of computer operating systems, software programs, and Internet browsers. The company has grown into a monopoly and made one of its founders, Bill Gates, the richest person in the world. But the company has been caught nickel-and-diming some of its workers out of their stock option benefits. It all started with an Internal Revenue Service (IRS) investigation. Here is the story.

Microsoft is headquartered in the state of Washington. In addition to having regular employees, Microsoft used the services of other workers who are classified as *independent contractors* (called *freelancers*) and temporary agency employees (called *temps*). Most of these special employees worked full time for Microsoft doing jobs that were identical to jobs performed by Microsoft's regular employees. Microsoft paid the special employees by check as outside workers. In 1990, the IRS conducted an employment tax examination and determined that Microsoft had misclassified these special workers as independent contractors and that the workers in these positions should be reclassified as "employees" for federal tax purposes.

The IRS used the following factors to reach the conclusion that the special workers were Microsoft employees rather than independent contractors:

- The party that has the right to control the manner and means by which the service or product is produced
- The skill required
- The source of the instrumentalities and tools
- The location of the work
- The duration of the relationship between the parties
- The extent of the hiring party's discretion over when and how long to work
- The hiring party's role in hiring and paying assistants
- Whether the work is part of the regular business of the hiring party

The IRS applied these factors to both the freelancers and temps who worked at Microsoft and found both to be employees of Microsoft. But that was not the end of the story. Plaintiff Donna Vizcaino and other freelancers sued Microsoft in a class action lawsuit alleging that they were denied employment benefits, especially employee stock options, that were paid to regular employees. Microsoft contributed three percent of an employee's salary to the stock option plan. The court of appeals agreed with the plaintiffs, citing the Internal Revenue Code that requires such stock option plans to be available to all employees. Thus, Microsoft's attempt to define certain full-time employees as freelancers and temps were rebuffed by the courts [*Vizcaino v. United States District Court for the Western District of Washington*, 173 F.3d 713 (9th Cir. 1999)].

*O*THER FEDERAL EMPLOYMENT LAWS

Employee Retirement Income Security Act (ERISA)

Employers are not required to establish pension plans for their employees. If they do, however, they are subject to the recordkeeping, disclosure, and other requirements of the **Employee Retirement Income Security Act (ERISA)**.[11] ERISA is a complex act designed to prevent fraud and other abuses associated with private pension funds. Federal, state, and local government pension funds are exempt from its coverage. ERISA is administered by the Department of Labor and the Internal Revenue Service (IRS).

Among other things, ERISA requires pension plans to be in writing and to name a pension fund manager. The plan manager owes a fiduciary duty to act as a "prudent person" in managing the fund and investing its assets. No more than 10 percent of a pension fund's assets can be invested in the securities of the sponsoring employer.

Vesting occurs when an employee has a nonforfeitable right to receive pension benefits. First, ERISA provides for immediate vesting of each employee's own contributions to the plan. Second, it requires employers' contributions to be either (1) completely forfeitable for a set period of up to five years and totally vested after that (*cliff vesting*) or (2) gradually vested over a seven-year period and completely vested after that time.

Consolidated Omnibus Budget Reconciliation Act (COBRA)

The **Consolidated Omnibus Budget Reconciliation Act of 1985 (COBRA)**[12] provides that an employee of a private employer or the employee's beneficiaries must be offered the opportunity to continue his or her group health insurance after the dismissal or death of

Employee Retirement Income Security Act (ERISA)

A federal act designed to prevent fraud and other abuses associated with private pension funds.

Consolidated Omnibus Budget Reconciliation Act (COBRA)

Federal law that permits employees and their beneficiaries to continue their group health insurance after an employee's employment has ended.

the employee or the loss of coverage due to certain qualifying events defined in the law. The employer must notify covered employees and their beneficiaries of their rights under COBRA. To continue coverage, a person must pay the required group rate premium. Government employees are subject to parallel provisions found in the Public Health Service Act.

Landmark Law

FAMILY AND MEDICAL LEAVE ACT

In February 1993, Congress enacted the **Family and Medical Leave Act**. The act guarantees workers unpaid time off from work for medical emergencies. The act, which applies to companies with 50 or more workers as well as federal, state, and local governments, covers about half of the nation's workforce. To be covered by the act, an employee must have worked for the employer for at least one year and have performed more than 1,250 hours of service during the previous 12-month period.

Covered employers are required to provide up to 12 weeks of unpaid leave during any 12-month period due to the

1. Birth of, and care for, a son or daughter
2. Placement of a child for adoption or in foster care
3. Serious health condition that makes the employee unable to perform his or her duties.

4. Care for a spouse, child, or parent with a serious health problem

Leave because of the birth of a child or the placement of a child for adoption or foster care cannot be taken intermittently unless the employer agrees. Other leaves may be taken on an intermittent basis. The employer may require medical proof of claimed serious health conditions.

An eligible employee who takes leave must, upon returning to work, be restored to either the same or an equivalent position with equivalent employment benefits and pay. The restored employee is not entitled to the accrual of seniority during the leave period, however. A covered employer may deny restoration to a salaried employee who is among the highest-paid 10 percent of that employer's employees if the denial is necessary to prevent "substantial and grievous economic injury" to the employer's operations.

Immigration Reform and Control Act (IRCA)

Immigration Reform and Control Act of 1986 (IRCA)

A federal statute that makes it unlawful for employers to hire illegal immigrants.

INS Form I-9

A form that must be filled out by all U.S. employers for each employee; states that the employer has inspected the employee's legal qualifications to work.

The **Immigration Reform and Control Act of 1986 (IRCA)** is administered by the U.S. Immigration and Naturalization Service (INS).[13] The act makes it unlawful for employers to hire illegal immigrants. As of June 1, 1987, all U.S. employers must complete **INS Form I-9** for each employee. The form attests that the employer has inspected documents of the employee and has determined that he or she is either a U.S. citizen or is otherwise qualified to work in the country (e.g., has a proper work visa). Employers must maintain records and post notices in the workplace of the contents of the law. Violators are subject to both civil and criminal penalties.

In the following case, the court upheld the imposition of fines against an employer for violating the act.

Furr's/Bishop's Cafeterias, L.P. v. U.S. Immigration and Naturalization Service
976 F.2d 1366 (1992)
United States Court of Appeals, Tenth Circuit

CASE 25.2

BACKGROUND AND FACTS
Furr's/Bishop's Cafeterias, L.P. (Furr's) owns and operates more than 150 cafeterias and restaurants located throughout the mid-western United States. Furr's divides its cafeterias into regions. Regional directors have authority to terminate nonmanagement employees at cafeterias located in their

regions. The general manager of each cafeteria is responsible for hiring between 40 and 80 employees for the day-to-day operation of the cafeteria. In August 1988, Furr's was ordered to pay a $5,100 penalty for violating the Immigration Reform and Control Act of 1986 (IRCA) concerning the hiring of undocumented aliens at its Kansas City, Kansas, cafeteria.

The penalty was imposed under the first-time offender provision of the act. In the instant case, Furr's was ordered to pay a $12,000 fine for hiring two undocumented aliens in its Olathe, Kansas, cafeteria. The fine was imposed as a second-time offender because both cafeterias are located in the same region Furr's challenged the assessment of the fine as a repeat offender, arguing that each cafeteria should be considered as a separate employer. The Immigration and Naturalization Service (INS) held that each region should be considered as an employer. Furr's appealed.

ISSUE
Was it lawful for the INS to impose a fine on Furr's as a repeat violator of the Immigration Reform and Control Act of 1986?

COURT'S REASONING
The court of appeals ruled that each region of the Furr's cafeteria chain was a separate employer for purposes of the immigration act. The court noted that each regional director had the authority to discipline cafeteria managers in his region for IRCA violations and to terminate nonmanagement employ-

ees at any cafeteria in his region. Therefore, each region would be considered a separate employer. The court announced that the next IRCA violation in Furr's Kansas region would subject the company to third-level fines.

DECISION
The court of appeals held that the INS had acted properly when it considered each region of Furr's cafeteria chain to be an employer under the IRCA. Affirmed.

Case Questions

Critical Legal Thinking Should the government impose a duty on employers to determine if workers are undocumented aliens? Is this too great a burden to impose on employers?

Business Ethics Is it ethical for employers to hire undocumented aliens as employees? Is it ethical for undocumented aliens to enter this country seeking employment?

Contemporary Business Why do employers hire undocumented aliens? Do you think cases like this one will stop this practice.

UNEMPLOYMENT COMPENSATION AND SOCIAL SECURITY LAWS

In 1935, Congress established an unemployment compensation program to assist workers who were temporarily unemployed. Under the **Federal Unemployment Tax Act (FUTA)**[14] and state laws enacted to implement the program, employers are required to pay unemployment contributions (taxes). The tax rate and unemployment wage level are subject to change. Employees do not pay unemployment taxes.

State governments administer unemployment compensation programs under general guidelines set by the federal government. Each state establishes its own eligibility requirements and the amount and duration of the benefits. To collect benefits, applicants must be able and available for work and seeking employment. Workers who have been let go because of bad conduct (e.g., illegal activity, drug use on the job) or who voluntarily quit work without just cause are not eligible to receive benefits.

Federal Unemployment Tax Act (FUTA)
A federal act that requires employers to pay unemployment taxes; unemployment compensation is paid to workers who are temporarily unemployed.

Social Security

In 1935, Congress established the federal **Social Security** system to provide limited retirement and death benefits to certain employees and their dependents. The Social Security system is administered by the Social Security Administration. The program has expanded greatly since it was first enacted. Today, it provides benefits to approximately 9 out of every 10 workers.[15]

Social Security benefits include (1) retirement benefits, (2) survivors' benefits to family members of deceased workers, (3) disability benefits, and (4) medical and hospitalization benefits (Medicare).

Under the **Federal Insurance Contributions Act (FICA)**,[16] employees and employers must make contributions (pay taxes) into the Social Security fund. The employer must pay a matching amount. Social Security does not operate like a savings account. Instead, current contributions are used to fund current claims. The employer is responsible for deducting employees' portions from their wages and remitting the entire payment to the Internal Revenue Service.

Under the **Self-Employment Contributions Act**,[17] self-employed individuals must pay Social Security, too. The amount of taxes self-employed individuals must pay is equal to the combined employer–employee amount.

Social Security
Federal system that provides limited retirement and death benefits to covered employees and their dependents.

Federal Insurance Contributions Act (FICA)
A federal act that says employees and employers must make contributions into the Social Security fund.

Self-Employment Contributions Act
A federal act that says self-employed persons must pay Social Security taxes equal to the combined employer-employee amount.

Failure to submit Social Security taxes subjects the violator to interest payments, penalties, and possible criminal liability. Social Security taxes may be changed by act of Congress.

International Law

MEXICAN LABOR LAWS

Labor and employment in Mexico are subject to the **Federal Labor Law of Mexico**, which is administered by the **Labor Board of Conciliation and Arbitration**. Because this law promotes unionized labor, labor unions are easy to form. Most collective bargaining agreements are unlimited in duration, although the terms of the agreements are usually revised biannually. Under Mexican law, if there is a strike, the plant will shut down. This will force the parties to settle the strike.

The Mexican government publishes a biannual list of required salaries by occupation. Manual laborers must be paid weekly, whereas other employees must be paid in pay periods not exceeding 15 days. Employees receive an overtime bonus of 25 percent of their wages for working on Sunday. Employees are also paid a bonus equivalent to at least 15 days' pay as a Christmas bonus. Under the law, employers must include workers in profit-sharing programs that distribute 8 percent of earnings, before taxes, to the workers.

Employees who pass a 30-day trial period may not be dismissed for lack of qualification for the job. After one year,

employees can be dismissed only for statutory reasons. An employee who is unjustly dismissed is entitled to recover three months' severance pay plus 20 days' salary for each year of employment.

Another Mexican law establishes a social security system. Both the employer and employee must contribute to this system. Employers must pay fees for workers' compensation, disability, old age, unemployment, death, and maternity leave benefits. In addition, employers are required to contribute an amount equivalent to 5 percent of their employees' wages to the national housing fund, 1 percent to day-care facilities, 1 percent to public education, and 1 percent to payroll taxes.

Although the foregoing employment benefits may seem generous, in reality they are not. There are several reasons for this. First, the cost of a minimum-wage employee in Mexico, including wages, benefits, and taxes, is less than $1 per hour. Second, Mexican labor laws have not been stringently enforced by the government. Many U.S. companies have moved manufacturing plants to Mexico to take advantage of the low wage rates there.

*C*HAPTER *S*UMMARY

*F*ederal Labor Law, p. 611

Federal Labor Statutes	Federal labor statutes include:
	1. *Norris-LaGuardia Act.* Made it legal for employees to organize.
	2. *National Labor Relations Act.* Established the right of employees to form, join, and assist labor unions. Also called the *Wagner Act* or *NLRA*.
	3. *Labor-Management Relations Act.* Expanded the activities labor unions could engage in, gave employers free speech rights to oppose unionization, and gave the President the right to seek injunctions against strikes that would create a national emergency. Also called the *Taft-Harley Act*.
	4. *Labor-Management Reporting and Disclosure Act.* Called labor's "bill of rights," this act gives union members the right to nominate candidates for union offices and vote in union elections. Also called the Landrum-Griffin Act.
	5. *Railway Labor Act.* Governs union rights of railroad and airline employees.
National Labor Relations Board (NLRB)	Federal administrative agency empowered to administer federal labor law, oversee union elections, and decide labor disputes.

*O*rganizing a Union, p. 613

Organizing a Union	1. *Section 7 of the NLRA.* Gives employees the right to join together and form a union.
	2. *Appropriate bargaining union.* Group of employees that a union is seeking to represent.

Types of Union Elections	1. *Contested election.* Management contests the union. The NLRB must supervise the election. 2. *Consent election.* Management does not contest the union election. 3. *Decertification election.* Election to determine if the employees want to reject a union as their representative. The NLRB must supervise the election.
Union Solicitation on Company Property	1. *Employees.* Employer may restrict solicitation activities to the employees' free time (e.g., breaks, lunch hours) and before and after work. 2. *Nonemployee union representatives.* Employer may prohibit solicitation on company property unless the employees cannot otherwise be contacted.
Illegal Interference with an Election	1. *Section 8(a) of the NLRA.* Makes it an *unfair labor practice* for an employer to interfere with, coerce, or restrain employees from exercising their right to form and join unions. 2. *Section 8(b) of the NLRA.* Makes it an unfair labor practice for a *union* to interfere with a union election.

Collective Bargaining, p. 616

Collective Bargaining	Process whereby the union and employer negotiate the terms and conditions of employment for the covered employee union members. 1. *Collective bargaining agreement.* Contract resulting from collective bargaining.
Subjects of Collective Bargaining	1. *Compulsory subjects.* Wages, hours, and other terms and conditions of employment (e.g., vacations, medical benefits, etc.) 2. *Illegal subjects.* Subjects that may not be negotiated (e.g., discrimination). 3. *Permissive subjects.* Subjects that are not compulsory or illegal (e.g., closing of plants).
Union Security Agreements	1. *Union shop.* An establishment where an employee must join a union within a certain number of days after being hired. 2. *Agency shop.* Employees do not have to join the union but must pay an *agency fee* equal to union dues. 3. *Check-off provision.* Requires employers to deduct union and agency dues from employees' wages and remit these payments to the union.
State Right-to-Work Laws	States may enact statutes that make union shops and agency shops illegal. Here, individual employees may choose not to join the union.

Strikes and Picketing, p. 618

Strikes	A strike is a cessation of work by union members in order to obtain economic benefits, to correct an unfair labor practice, or to preserve their work. The NLRA gives union employees the right to strike.
Employer Lockout	An employer may lock employees out of its premises if it reasonably anticipates a strike.
Crossover Workers and Replacement Workers	*Crossover worker.* An employee who does not honor a strike who either (1) chooses not to strike or (2) returns to work after joining strikers for a time. *Replacement worker.* Persons who are hired to take the place of striking workers. The employer may offer these employees permanent positions.
Illegal Strikes	1. *Violent strike.* Striking employees cause substantial damage to the employer's or a third party's property. 2. *Sit-down strike.* Employees occupy and refuse to leave the employer's premises. 3. *Partial or intermittent strike.* Employees strike for only parts of each day or week. 4. *Wildcat strike.* Strike not sanctioned by the union. 5. *Strike during the 60-day cooling-off period.* Strike where the union has not given the employer at lest 60 days' prior notice of the strike. 6. *Strike in violation of a no-strike clause.* Strike that violates a no-strike clause in a collective bargaining agreement.
Picketing	Striking employees and union organizers walking around the employer's premises, usually carrying signs, notifying the public of their grievance against the employer. 1. *Illegal picketing.* Picketing is illegal if it is accompanied by violence or obstructs customers, nonstriking workers, or suppliers from entering the employer's premises. 2. *Secondary boycott.* Picketing conducted at a third party's premises. *Product picketing* against the products of the struck employer is lawful. It is illegal if it is directed against the neutral employer.

Internal Union Affairs, p. 619

Internal Union Rules	*Title I of the Landrum-Griffin Act.* A federal law that gives each union member equal rights and privileges to nominate candidates for union office, vote in union elections, and participate in membership meetings. Commonly called *labor's "bill of rights."*

Workers' Compensation Acts, p. 620

Workers' Compensation Acts	State statutes that create an administrative procedure for workers to receive payments for job-related injuries. 1. *Workers' compensation insurance.* Most states require employers to carry private or government-sponsored workers' compensation insurance. Some states permit employers to self-insure.
Employment-Related Injury	To be compensable under workers' compensation, the claimant must prove that the injury arose out of and in the course of his or her employment.

Exclusive Remedy	Workers' compensation is an exclusive remedy. Thus, workers cannot sue their employers to recover damages for job-related injuries.
	 1. *Exceptions to exclusive-remedy rule.* Workers may recover damages from their employers for job-related injuries if the employer:
	    a. Does not provide workers' compensation.
	    b. Intentionally causes the worker's injuries.
	 2. *Lawsuits against third parties.* Workers' compensation acts do not bar injured workers from suing responsible third parties to recover damages (e.g., manufacturer of a defective machine that caused the worker's injuries).

Occupational Safety and Health Act, p. 622

Occupational Safety and Health Act	Federal statute that requires employers to provide safe working conditions. 1. *Occupational Safety and Health Administration (OSHA).* Federal administrative agency that administers and enforces the Occupational Safety and Health Act.
Specific and General Duty Standards	1. *Specific duty standards.* Safety standards for specific equipment (e.g., lathe) or industry (e.g., mining). 2. *General duty standards.* Impose a general duty on employers to provide safe working conditions.

Fair Labor Standards Act, p. 624

Fair Labor Standards Act (FLSA)	A federal statute that protects workers.
Child Labor	The FLSA forbids the use of illegal child labor. The U.S. Department of Labor defines illegal child labor.
Minimum Wage and Overtime Pay Requirements	1. *Minimum wage.* The minimum wage is set by Congress and can be changed. The minimum wage, as of 1998, is $5.15 per hour. 2. *Overtime pay.* An employer cannot require employees to work more than 40 hours per week unless they are paid 1.5 times their regular pay for each hour worked in excess of 40 hours.

Employee Retirement Income Security Act (ERISA), p. 625

Employee Retirement Income Security Act (ERISA)	Federal statute that governs the establishment and administration of private pension programs to prevent fraud and other abuses.

Consolidated Omnibus Budget Reconciliation Act (COBRA), p. 625

Consolidated Omnibus Budget Reconciliation Act (COBRA)	Federal statute that requires an employer to offer an employee or the employee's beneficiaries the opportunity to continue health benefits (upon payment of the premium) after termination of employment due to dismissal or death.

Immigration Reform and Control Act (IRCA), p. 626

Immigration Reform and Control Act (IRCA)	Federal statute that prohibits employers from employing illegal immigrants, Employers must require workers to prove that they are U.S. citizens or have a proper work visa to work in this country.

Unemployment Compensation, p. 627

Unemployment Compensation	A state and federal program that pays compensation to unemployed persons who meet certain qualifying standards. Employers are required to pay unemployment compensation payments to the government to fund the program. Authorized by the *Federal Unemployment Tax Act (FUTA)* and state laws.

Social Security, p. 627

Social Security	Federal government program that provides limited retirement, disability, and medical and hospitalization to covered employees and their dependents. Employers and employees pay taxes to fund the program.

END-OF-CHAPTER INTERNET EXERCISES AND CASE QUESTIONS

Working the Web Internet Exercises

ACTIVITIES

1. Check the current unemployment rate at the Department of Labor **www.dol.gov**. Is it higher or lower than one year ago?

2. Find the "Major Laws" section of the DOL Web site. Review the provisions of the FLSA and note the year of its enactment. Why is this law becoming important again?

3. Find the section of the DOL site relating to state minimum wage rates and look up the minimum wage for your state.

4. What are the requirements for employment under an H-1B visa? Search the DOL site for the answer.

5. For an overview of Labor Law see Labor and Employment Law at **www.jurist.law.pitt. edu/sg_lab.htm**.

CRITICAL LEGAL THINKING CASES

25.1 Unfair Labor Practice In July 1965, the Teamsters Union began a campaign to organize the employees at a Sinclair Company plant. When the president of Sinclair learned of the Teamsters' drive, he talked with all of his employees and emphasized the results of a long 1952 strike that he claimed "almost put our company out of business" and expressed worry that the employees were forgetting the "lessons of the past." He emphasized that the company was on "thin ice" financially, that the Teamsters' "only weapon is to strike," and that a strike "could lead to the closing of the plant" because the company had manufacturing facilities elsewhere. He also noted that because of the employees' ages and the limited usefulness of their skills, they might not be able to find reemployment if they lost their jobs. Finally, he sent literature to the employees stating that "the Teamsters Union is a strike happy outfit" and that they

were under "hoodlum control," and he included a cartoon showing the preparation of a grave for the Sinclair Company and other headstones containing the names of other plants allegedly victimized by unions. The Teamsters lost the election 7 to 6 and then filed an unfair labor practice charge with the NLRB. Did the company violate labor law? [*N.L.R.B. v. Gissel Packing Co.*, 395 U.S. 575, 89 S.Ct. 1918, 23 L.Ed.2d 547 (1969)]

25.2 Right-to-Work Law Mobil Oil Corporation has its headquarters office in Beaumont, Texas. It operates a fleet of eight oceangoing tankers that transport its petroleum products from Texas to ports on the East Coast. A typical trip on a tanker from Beaumont to New York takes about five days. No more than 10 percent to 20 percent of the seamen's work time is spent in Texas. The 300 or so seamen who are employed to work on the takers belong to the Oil, Chemical & Atomic Workers International Union, AFL-CIO, which has an agency shop agreement with Mobil. The state of Texas enacts a right-to-work law. Mobil sues the union, claiming that the agency shop agreement is unenforceable because it violates the Texas right-to-work law. Who wins? [*Oil, Chemical & Atomic Workers International Union, AFL-CIO v. Mobil Oil Corp.*, 426 U.S. 407, 96 S.Ct. 2140, 48 L.Ed.2d 736 (1976)]

25.3 Work Preservation   The Frouge Corporation was the general contractor on a housing project in Philadelphia. The carpenter-employees of Frouge were represented by the Carpenters' International Union. Traditional jobs of carpenters included taking blank wooden doors and mortising them for doorknobs, routing them for hinges, and beveling them to fit between the door jambs. The union had entered into a collective bargaining agreement with Frouge that provided that no member of the union would handle any doors that had been fitted prior to being furnished to the job site. The housing project called for 3,600 doors. Frouge contracted for the purchase of premachined doors that were already mortised, routed, and beveled. When the union ordered its members not to hang the prefabricated doors, the National Woodwork Manufacturers Association filed an unfair labor practice charge against the union with the NLRB. Was the union's refusal to hang prefabricated doors lawful? [*National Woodwork Manufacturers Association v. N.L.R.B.*, 386 U.S. 612, 87 S.Ct. 1250, 18 L.Ed.2d 357 (1967)]

25.4 Featherbedding   Most local musicians belong to the American Federation of Musicians (Union), which represents more than 200,000 members in the United States. The union was divided into separate local unions that represent the members from a certain geographical area. Gamble Enterprises, Inc., owns and operates the Palace Theater in Akron, Ohio, which stages the performances of local and traveling musicians. The union adopted the following rule: "Traveling members cannot, without the consent of a Local, play any presentation performance unless a local house orchestra is also employed." This meant that the theater owner might have to pay two bands or orchestras. Gamble's refusal to abide by this rule caused the union to block the appearances of traveling bands and orchestras. Gamble filed an unfair labor practice charge with the NLRB. Is the union rule lawful? [*N.L.R.B. v. Gamble Enterprises, Inc.*, 345 U.S. 117, 73 S.Ct. 560, 97 L.Ed.2d 864 (1953)]

25.5 Illegal Strike   In September 1966, the employees of the Shop Rite Foods, Inc.'s warehouse in Lubbock, Texas, elected the United Packinghouse, Food and Allied Workers (Union) as its bargaining agent. Negotiations for a collective bargaining agreement began in late November 1966. In February and March 1967, when an agreement had not yet been reached, the company found excess amounts of damage to merchandise in its warehouse and concluded that it was being intentionally caused by dissident employees as a pressure tactic to secure concessions from the company. The company notified the union representative that employees caught doing such acts would be terminated; the Union representative in turn notified the employees. On

March 31, 1967, a Shop Rite manager observed an employee in the flour section—where he had no business to be—making quick motions with his hands. The manager found several bags of flour had been cut. The employee was immediately fired. Another employee and fellow union member led about 30 other employees in an immediate walkout. The company discharged these employees and refused to rehire them. The employees filed a grievance with the NLRB. Can they get their jobs back? [*N.L.R.B. v. Shop Rite Foods, Inc.*, 430 F.2d 786 (5th Cir. 1970)]

25.6 Employer Lockout   The American Shipbuilding Company operates a shipyard in Chicago, Illinois, where it repairs Great Lakes' ships during the winter months, when freezing on the Great Lakes renders shipping impossible. The workers at the shipyard are represented by several unions. On May 1, 1961, the unions notified the company of their intention to seek modification of the current collective bargaining agreement when it expired on August 1, 1961. On five previous occasions, agreements had been preceded by strikes (including illegal strikes) that were called just after the ships had arrived in the shipyard for repairs so that the unions increased their leverage in negotiations with the company.

Based on this prior history, the company displayed anxiety about the unions' strike plans and possible work stoppage. On August 1, 1961, after extended negotiations, the company and the unions reached an impasse in their collective bargaining. In response, the company decided to lay off most of the workers at the shipyard. It sent them the following notice: "Because of the labor dispute which has been unresolved since August 1, 1961, you are laid off until further notice." The unions filed unfair labor practice charges with the NLRB. Were the company's actions legal? [*American Ship Building Company v. N.L.R.B.*, 380 U.S. 300, 85 S.Ct. 955, 13 L.Ed.2d 855 (1965)]

25.7 Secondary Boycott   Safeco Title Insurance Company is a major insurance company that underwrites title insurance for real estate in the state of Washington. Five local title companies act as insurance brokers who exclusively sell Safeco insurance. In 1972, Local 1001 of the Retail Store Employees Union, AFL-CIO, was elected as the bargaining agent for certain Safeco employees. When negotiations between Safeco and the union reached an impasse, the employees went on strike. The union did not confine its picketing to Safeco's office in Seattle but also picketed each of the five local title companies. The pickets carried signs declaring that Safeco had no contract with the union and distributed handbills asking consumers to support the strike by canceling their Safeco insurance policies. The local title companies filed a complaint with the NLRB. Was the picketing of the neutral title insurance companies lawful? [*N.L.R.B. v. Retail Store Employees Union, Local 1001, Retail Clerks International Association, AFL-CIO*, 447 U.S. 607, 100 S.Ct. 2372, 65 L.Ed.2d 377 (1980)]

25.8 Workers' Compensation   John B. Wilson was employed by the City of Modesto, California, as a police officer. He was a member of the special emergency reaction team (SERT), a tactical unit of the city's police department that is trained and equipped to handle highly dangerous criminal situations. Membership in SERT is voluntary for police officers. No additional pay or benefits are involved. To be a member of SERT, each officer is required to pass physical tests four times a year. One such test requires members to run two miles in 17 minutes. Other tests call for a minimum number of pushups, pullups, and situps. Officers who do not belong to SERT are not required to undergo these physical tests. On June 27, 1984, Wilson completed his patrol shift, changed clothes, and drove to the Modesto Junior College track. While running there, he injured his left ankle. Wilson filed a claim for workers' compensation benefits, which was contested by his employer. Who wins? [*Wilson v. Workers' Compensation Appeals Board*, 196 Cal.App.3d 302, 239 Cal.Rptr. 719 (Cal. App. 1987)]

25.9 Workers' Compensation Joseph Albanese was employed as a working foreman by Atlantic Steel Company, Inc., for approximately 20 years prior to 1970. His duties included the supervision of plant employees. In 1967, the business was sold to a new owner. In 1969, after the employees voted to unionize, friction developed between Albanese and the workers. Part of the problem was caused by management's decision to eliminate overtime work, which required Albanese to go out into the shop and prod the workers to expedite the work. Additional problems resulted from the activities of Albanese's direct supervisor, the plant manager. On one occasion in 1968, the manager informed Albanese that the company practice of distributing Thanksgiving turkeys was to be discontinued. In 1969, the manager told Albanese that the company did not intend to give the workers a Christmas bonus. The plant manager also informed Albanese that he did not intend to pay overtime wages to a worker. On each occasion, after Albanese relayed the information to the workers, the plant manager reversed his own decision. After the last incident, Albanese became distressed and developed chest pains and nausea. When the chest pains became sharper, he went home to bed. Albanese has not worked since. He has experienced continuing pain, sweatiness, shortness of breath, headaches, and depression. Albanese filed a claim for workers' compensation based on stress. The employer contested the claim. Who wins? [*Albanese's Case*, 389 N.E.2d 83 (MA 1979)]

25.10 Occupational Safety Getty Oil Company operates a separation facility where it gathers gas and oil from wells and transmits them to an outgoing pipeline under high pressure. Getty engineers designed and produced a pressure vessel, called a fluid booster, that was to be installed to increase pressure in the system. Robinson, a Getty engineer, was instructed to install the vessel. Robinson picked the vessel up from the welding shop without having it tested. After he completed the installation, the pressure valve was put into operation. When the pressure increased from 300 to 930 pounds per square inch, an explosion occurred. Robinson died from the explosion, and another Getty employee was seriously injured. The secretary of labor issued a citation against Getty for violating the general duty provision for worker safety contained in the Occupational Safety and Health Act. Getty challenged the citation. Who wins? [*Getty Oil Company v. Occupational Safety and Health Review Commission*, 530 F.2d 1143 (5th Cir. 1976)]

25.11 ERISA United Artists is a Maryland corporation doing business in the state of Texas. United Pension Fund (Plan) is a defined-contribution, employee pension-benefit plan sponsored by United Artists for its employees. Each employee has his or her own individual pension account, but Plan assets are pooled for investment purposes. The Plan is administered by a board of trustees. During the period 1977 through 1986, seven of the trustees caused the Plan to make a series of loans to themselves. The trustees did not (1) require the borrowers to submit written applications for the subject loans, (2) assess the prospective borrowers' ability to repay the loans, (3) specify a period in which the loans were to be repaid, or (4) call the loans when they remained unpaid. The trustees also charged less than fair-market-value interest rates for the loans. The secretary of labor sued the trustees, alleging that they breached their fiduciary duty in violation of ERISA. Who wins? [*McLaughlin v. Rowley*, 698 F.Supp. 1333 (N.D.Tex. 1988)]

25.12 Drug Testing Air traffic controllers are federal government employees who are responsible for directing commercial and private air traffic in this country. They are subject to regulation by the secretary of transportation. The secretary adopted a regulation that provides for postaccident urinalysis drug testing of air traffic controllers responsible for the airspace in which an airplane accident has occurred. The National Air Traffic Controllers Association, MEBA/NNU, AFL-CIO sued, alleging that such drug testing was an unreasonable search and seizure in violation of the Fourth Amendment to the U.S. Constitution. Who wins? [*National Air Traffic Controllers Assn., MEBA/NNU, AFL-CIO v. Burnley*, 700 F.Supp. 1043 (N.D.Cal. 1988)]

25.13 Unemployment Benefits Devon Overstreet worked as a bus driver for the Chicago Transit Authority (CTA) for more than six years. She took a sick leave from January 30 to March 15, 1985. Because she had been on sick leave for more than seven days, the CTA required her to take a medical examination. The blood and urine analysis indicated the presence of cocaine. A second test confirmed this finding. On March 20, 1985, the CTA suspended her and placed her in the Employee's Assistance Program for substance abuse for not less than 30 days, with a chance of reassignment to a nonoperating job if she successfully completed the program. The program is an alternative to discharge and is available at the election of the employee. Overstreet filed for unemployment compensation benefits. The CTA contested her claim. Who wins? [*Overstreet v. Illinois Department of Employment Security*, 522 N.E.2d 185 (Ill. App. 1988).

25.14 Plant Closing Act Arrow Automotive Industries, Inc., is engaged in the remanufacture and distribution of automobile and truck parts. All of its operating plants produce identical product lines. Arrow is planning to open a new facility in Santa Maria, California. The employees at the Arrow plant in Hudson, Massachusetts, are represented by the United Automobile, Aerospace, and Agricultural Implement Workers of America (Union). The Hudson plant has a history of unprofitable operations. The union called a strike when the existing collective bargaining agreement expired and a new agreement could not be reached. After several months, the board of directors of the company voted to close the striking plant. The closing gave Arrow a 24-percent increase in gross profits and freed capital and equipment for the new Santa Maria plant. In addition, the existing customers of the Hudson plant could be serviced by the Spartanburg plant, which was currently being underutilized. What would have to be done if the Plant Closing Act applied to this situation? [*Arrow Automotive Industries, Inc., v. N.L.R.B.*, 853 F.2d 223 (4th Cir. 1989)]

BUSINESS ETHICS CASES

25.15 Business Ethics Whirlpool Corporation operates a manufacturing plant in Marion, Ohio, for the production of household appliances. Overhead conveyors transport appliance components throughout the plant. To protect employees from objects that occasionally fall from the conveyers, Whirlpool installed a horizontal wire-mesh guard screen approximately 20 feet above the plant floor. The mesh screen is welded to angle-iron frames suspended from the building's structural steel skeleton.

Maintenance employees spend several hours each week removing objects from the screen, replacing paper spread on the screen to catch grease drippings from the materials on the conveyers, and performing occasional maintenance work on the conveyors. To performs these duties, maintenance employees usually are able to stand on the iron frames, but sometimes they find it necessary to step onto the steel-mesh screen itself. Several employees have fallen partly through the screen. On June 28, 1974, a maintenance employee fell to his death through the guard screen.

On July 7, 1974, two maintenance employees, Virgil Deemer and Thomas Cornwell, met with the plant supervisor to voice their concern about the safety of the screen. Unsatisfied with the supervisor's response, on July 9 they met with the plant safety director and voiced similar concerns. When they asked him for the name, address, and telephone number of the local OSHA office, he told them they "had better stop and think about" what they were doing. The safety director then furnished them with the requested information, and later that day one of the men contacted the regional OSHA office and discussed the guard screen.

The next day, Deemer and Cornwell reported for the night shift at 10:45 P.M. Their foreman directed the two men to perform their usual maintenance duties on a section of the screen. Claiming that the screen was unsafe, they refused to carry out the directive. The foreman sent them to the personnel office, where they were ordered to punch out without working or being paid for the remaining six hours of the shift. The two men subsequently received written reprimands, which were placed in their employment files.

The secretary of labor filed suit, alleging that Whirlpool's actions constituted discrimination against the two men in violation of the Occupational Safety and Health Act. Did Whirlpool act ethically in this case? Can employees engage in self-help under certain circumstances under OSHA regulations? [*Whirlpool Corporation v. Marshall, Secretary of Labor*, 445 U.S. 1, 100 S.Ct. 883, 63 L.Ed.2d 154 (1980)]

25.16 Business Ethics On April 23, 1971, the International Association of Machinists and Aerospace Workers, AFL-CIO (Union), began soliciting the employees of Whitcraft Houseboat Division to organize a union. On April 26, 27, and 28, Whitcraft management dispersed congregating groups of employees. During these three days, production was down almost 50 percent. On April 28, Whitcraft adopted the following no-solicitation rule and mailed a copy to each employee and posted it around the workplace:

> *As you well know working time is for work. No one will be allowed to solicit or distribute literature during our working time, that is, when he or she should be working. Anyone doing so and neglecting his work or interfering with the work of another employee will be subject to discharge.*

On April 30, a manager of Whitcraft found that two employees of the company were engaged in union solicitation during working hours in a working area. The company discharged them for violating the no-solicitation rule. Was their discharge lawful? Did the company act ethically in discharging the employees? [*Whitcraft Houseboat Division, North American Rockwell Corporation v. International Association of Machinists and Aerospace Workers, AFL-CIO*, 195 N.L.R.B. 1046 (1972)]

BRIEFING THE CASE WRITING ASSIGNMENT

Read the following case, which has been excerpted from the court's opinion. Review and brief the case.

Wiljef Transportation, Inc. v. National Labor Relations Board
946 F.2D 1308 (1991)
United States Court of Appeals for the Seventh Circuit

Cudahy, Circuit Judge

This case presents an interesting question concerning the balance between an employer's right of expression and its employees' right of association.

Approximately two months before a vote on unionization, the employer, Wiljef Transportation, Inc. (Wiljef), read to its employees a corporate by-law which states:

> *Section 2—Corporate Dissolution. Wiljef Transportation, Inc. hereby expresses as a matter of corporate policy that operations will cease and the corporation will be dissolved in the event of unionization of its employees. As hereby authorized by the Board of Directors, this by-law may be announced to the employees of Wiljef Transportation, Inc. at any time deemed appropriate by the Board.*

The by-law was adopted in 1979, and the announcement occurred in 1988. In the ensuing union representation election, the employees rejected unionization. The issue in this case is whether the announcement of the by-law constituted a "permitted prediction" of plant closure or a "proscribed threat." The NLRB held that the announcement was a threat in violation of Section 8(a)(1) of the National Labor Relations Act (NLRA), and Wiljef appealed to this court.

An employer's right to communicate its views to its employees is firmly established in the First Amendment and is recognized in Section 8(c) of the NLRA, which provides that "the expressing of any views, argument, or opinion shall not constitute or be evidence of an unfair labor practice if such expression contains no threat of reprisal or force or promise of benefit." On the other hand, the exceptions to the freedom of expression recognized in Section 8(c) reflect the right of employees to associate free of coercion by the employer. Section 8(a)(1) of the NLRA codifies that right by declaring that it is an unfair labor practice to interfere with, restrain or coerce employees exercising their right to organize in unions. The difficulty in cases attempting to relate these two rights is in determining when speech becomes essentially coercive rather than factually informative or predictive so as to fall outside the protection of the First Amendment and violate the NLRA. The real issue, however, remains credibility and bona fides. A by-law purporting to be a management decision to close a business in the event of unionization is not protected expression unless objective factors demonstrate that it is really controlling on the question of closure. This holding preserves the balance between free expression and the right to organize.

Absent some persuasive evidence of other measures indicating that Wiljef intends to implement the corporate policy described in the by-law, the announcement of the by-law to the employees is coercive and in violation of the NLRA. Objective evidence to lend credibility to the by-law need not be based on economics and need not necessarily indicate circumstances beyond the employer's control.

Analytically the line is clear. To predict a consequence that will occur no matter how well disposed the company is toward unions is not to threaten retaliation; to predict a consequence that will occur because the company wants to punish workers for voting for the union—a consequence desired and freely chosen by a company rather than compelled by economic forces over which it has no control—is.

In light of our conclusion that Wiljef used the by-law in an attempt to coerce its employees and that no objective evidence indicated an intent to implement the by-law, the relief granted by the NLRB is proper. The petition for review is denied, and the order of the NLRB requiring Wiljef to expunge the by-law, cease further coercive activity, and post a notice to employees indicating that it had violated the law and will cease such violations is enforced.

ENDNOTES

1. 29 U.S.C. §§ 101-110 and 113–115.
2. 29 U.S.C. §§151 et seq.
3. 29 U.S.C. §§ 141 et seq.
4. 29 U.S.C. §§ 153 and 158–164.
5. 45 U.S.C. §§ 151–162 and 181–188.
6. Section 7 provides that employees shall have the right to self-organization; to form, join, or assist labor organizations; to bargain collectively through representatives of their own choosing; and to engage in other concerted activities for the purpose of collective bargaining or other mutual aid protection.
7. 29 U.S.C. § 651–678.
8. For example, the Railway Safety Act and the Coal Mine Safety Act regulate workplace safety of railway workers and coal miners, respectively.
9. 29 U.S.C. § 654(a)(1).
10. 29 U.S.C. §§ 201 et seq.
11. 29 U.S.C. §§ 1001 et seq.
12. Internal Revenue Code § 4980B(f), 26 U.S.C. § 1161(a).
13. 29 U.S.C. § 1802.
14. 26 U.S.C. §§ 3301–3311.
15. Some federal, state, and local government employees who are covered by comparable legislation are not subject to the Social Security Act.
16. 26 U.S.C. §§ 3101–3126.
17. 26 U.S.C. §§ 1401–1403.

CHAPTER 26

Equal Opportunity in Employment

What people have always sought is equality of rights before the law. For rights that were not open to all equally would not be rights.

—Cicero (106–43 B.C.)
De officiis, Bk. II, Ch. XII

Chapter Objectives

After studying this chapter, you should be able to:

1. Describe the scope of coverage of Title VII of the Civil Rights Act of 1964.

2. Identify race, color, and national origin discrimination that violates Title VII.

3. Identify sex discrimination—including sexual harassment—that violates Title VII.

4. Describe how e-mail messages can be used as evidence in sexual harassment lawsuits.

5. Describe the protections afforded by the Equal Pay Act of 1963.

6. Describe the bona fide occupational qualification (BFOQ) defense.

7. Describe the scope of coverage of the Age Discrimination in Employment Act.

8. Describe the protections afforded by the Americans with Disabilities Act of 1990.

9. Define and apply the doctrine of affirmative action.

10. Examine the scope of Japan's equal opportunity in employment law.

Chapter Contents

At common law, employers could terminate an employee at any time and for whatever reason. In this same vein, employers were free to hire and promote anyone they chose without violating the law. This often created unreasonable hardship on employees and erected employment barriers to certain minority classes.

Starting in the 1960s, Congress began enacting a comprehensive set of federal laws that eliminated major forms of employment discrimination. These laws, which were passed to guarantee **equal employment opportunity** to all employees and job applicants, have been broadly interpreted by the federal courts, particularly the U.S. Supreme Court. States have also enacted antidiscrimination laws.

This chapter discusses federal and state equal opportunity in employment laws.

equal opportunity in employment

The right of all employees and job applicants (1) to be treated without discrimination and (2) to be able to sue employers if they are discriminated against.

EQUAL EMPLOYMENT OPPORTUNITY COMMISSION (EEOC)

The **Equal Employment Opportunity Commission (EEOC)** is the federal agency responsible for enforcing most federal antidiscrimination laws. The members of the EEOC are appointed by the President. The EEOC is empowered to conduct investigations, interpret the statutes, encourage conciliation between employees and employers, and bring suit to enforce the law. The EEOC can also seek injunctive relief.

Equal Employment Opportunity Commission (EEOC)

The federal administrative agency responsible for enforcing most federal antidiscrimination laws.

Landmark Law

TITLE VII OF THE CIVIL RIGHTS ACT OF 1964

After substantial debate, Congress enacted the **Civil Rights Act of 1964**. **Title VII** of the Civil Rights Act of 1964 (entitled the **Fair Employment Practices Act**) was intended to eliminate job discrimination based on the following *protected classes: (1) race, (2) color, (3) religion, (4) sex, or (5) national origin.* As amended by the **Equal Employment Opportunity Act of 1972**, Section 703(a)(2) of the Title VII provides in pertinent part that

It shall be an unlawful employment practice for an employer
(1) to fail or refuse to hire or to discharge any individ-

ual, or otherwise to discriminate against any individual with respect to his compensation, terms, conditions, or privileges of employment, because of such individual's race, color, religion, sex, or national origin; or

(2) to limit, segregate, or classify his employees or applicants for employment in any way which would deprive or tend to deprive any individual of employment opportunities or otherwise adversely affect his status as an employee, because of such individual's race, color, religion, sex, or national origin.

TITLE VII OF THE CIVIL RIGHTS ACT OF 1964

Scope of Coverage of Title VII

Title VII applies to (1) employers with 15 or more employees, (2) all employment agencies, (3) labor unions with 15 or more members, (4) state and local governments and their agencies, and (5) most federal government employment. Indian tribes and tax-exempt private clubs are expressly excluded from coverage.[1]

Title VII prohibits discrimination in hiring, decisions regarding promotion or demotion, payment of compensation and fringe benefits, availability of job training and apprenticeship opportunities, referral systems for employment, decisions regarding dismissal, work rules, and any other *"term, condition, or privilege"* of employment. Any employee of covered employers, including undocumented aliens,[2] may bring actions for employment discrimination under Title VII.

Forms of Title VII Actions

Title VII prohibits the following forms of employment discrimination based on any of the five prohibited factors listed previously.

Title VII of the Civil Rights Act of 1964 (Fair Employment Practices Act)

Intended to eliminate job discrimination based on five protected classes: *race, color, religion, sex,* or *national origin.*

Business Brief

Title VII applies to any term, condition, or privilege of employment including but not limited to hiring, firing, promotion, and payment of fringe benefits decisions.

disparate treatment discrimination

Occurs when an employer discriminates against a specific *individual* because of his or her race, color, national origin, sex, or religion.

Disparate Treatment Discrimination **Disparate treatment discrimination** occurs when an employer treats a specific *individual* less favorably than others because of that person's race, color, national origin, sex, or religion. In such situations, the complainant must prove that (1) he or she belongs to a Title VII protected class, (2) he or she applied for and was qualified for the employment position, (3) he or she was rejected despite this, and (4) the employer kept the position open and sought applicants from persons with the complainant's qualifications.[3]

disparate impact discrimination

Occurs when an employer discriminates against an entire protected *class*. An example would be where a facially neutral employment practice or rule causes an adverse impact on a protected class.

Disparate Impact Discrimination **Disparate impact discrimination** occurs when an employer discriminates against an entire protected *class*. Many disparate impact cases are brought as class action lawsuits. Often, this type of discrimination is proven through statistical data about the employer's employment practices. The plaintiff must demonstrate a *casual link* between the challenged practice and the statistical imbalance. Showing a statistical disparity between the percentage of protected class employees versus the percentage of the population that the protected class makes within the surrounding community is not enough, by itself, to prove discrimination.

Disparate impact discrimination occurs when an employer adopts a work rule that is neutral on its face but is shown to cause an adverse impact on a protected class.

Procedure for Bringing a Title VII Action

God . . . hath made of one blood all nations of men for to dwell on the face of the earth.

Bible, *Acts 17:26*

To bring an action under Title VII, a private complainant must first file a complaint with the EEOC.[4] The EEOC is given the opportunity to sue the employer on the complainant's behalf. If the EEOC chooses not to bring suit, it will issue a *right to sue letter* to the complainant. This gives the complainant the right to sue the employer.

Remedies for Violations of Title VII

A successful plaintiff in a Title VII action can recover up to two years' back pay and reasonable attorney's fees. In cases involving malice or reckless indifference to federally protected rights, the aggrieved party can recover compensatory and punitive damages. The statute caps the amounts that are recoverable on the basis of the size of the employer: (1) 15 to 100 employees, $50,000, (2) 101 to 200 employees, $100,000, (3) 201 to 500 employees, $200,000, (4) more than 500 employees, $300,000.

Ethics Brief

As originally proposed, sex discrimination was not included in Title VII. The amendment (Equal Employment Opportunity Act), designed to kill the entire legislation, backfired when the Civil Rights Act of 1964 passed.

The courts also have broad authority to grant equitable remedies. For instance, the courts can order reinstatement, grant fictional seniority, or issue injunctions to compel the hiring or promotion of protected minorities.

Race, Color, and National Origin Discrimination

Rights matter most when they are claimed by unpopular minorities.

Michael Kirby, J.
Sydney Morning Herald
November 30, 1985

Title VII of the Civil Rights Act of 1964 was primarily enacted to prohibit employment discrimination based on *race, color, and national origin*. Race refers to broad categories such as Black, Caucasian, Asian, and Native American. *Color* refers to the color of a person's skin. *National origin* refers to the country of a person's ancestors or cultural characteristics.

Cases 26.1 and 26.2 demonstrate race and national origin discrimination.

National Association for the Advancement of Colored People, Newark Branch v. Town of Harrison, New Jersey

907 F.2d 1408 (1990)
United States Court of Appeals, Third Circuit

CASE 26.1

BACKGROUND AND FACTS
The town of Harrison, New Jersey (Harrison), followed a policy of hiring only town residents as town employees for as long as any townspeople could remember. In 1978, New Jersey adopted an Act Concerning Residency Requirements for Municipal and County Employees that permitted towns, cities, and counties in the state to require that their employees

be bona fide residents of the local government unit. Pursuant to this statute, Harrison adopted Ordinance 747, which stipulated that "all officers and employees of the Town shall, as a condition of employment, be bona fide residents of the Town."

Although Harrison is a small industrial community located in Hudson County, New Jersey, it is clearly aligned with Essex

County to the west and is considered an extension of the city of Newark, which it abuts. Adjacent counties are within an easy commute of Harrison. Only 0.2 percent of Harrison's population is black. None of the 51 police officers, 55 firefighters, or 80 nonuniformed employees of the town are black. Several blacks who were members of the National Association for the Advancement of Colored People, Newark Branch (NAACP) applied for employment with Harrison but were rejected because they did not meet the residency requirement. The NAACP sued Harrison for employment discrimination.

ISSUE
Does the residency requirement of the town of Harrison violate Title VII of the Civil Rights Act of 1964?

COURT'S REASONING
The district court noted that Harrison's geographical location and transportation facilities allowed the town to be viewed as a functional component of the city of Newark and a part of Essex County. Newark's population is approximately 60 percent Black. Essex County's civilian labor force is 33.3 percent Black. Of the persons employed by private industry, 22.1 per-

cent are Black. Because so few Black persons live in Harrison, most of these persons must have commuted from elsewhere in the labor market that serves Harrison. The court held that the otherwise socially neutral employment rule caused an adverse impact on Blacks.

DECISION
The district court held that the plaintiffs had established that the ordinance constituted disparate impact race discrimination in violation of Title VII of the Civil Rights Act of 1964. The court issued an injunction against enforcement of the ordinance.

Case Questions

Critical Legal Thinking Would the same residency requirement rule cause disparate impact discrimination if it were adopted by New York City or Los Angeles?

Business Ethics Did the town of Harrison act ethically when it adopted the residency requirements?

Contemporary Business Could a private business impose a residency requirement on its employees?

Rivera v. Baccarat, Inc.
10 F.Supp.2d 318 (1998)
United States District Court, S.D. New York

CASE 26.2

BACKGROUND AND FACTS
Irma Rivera is an Hispanic woman who was born in Puerto Rico. In September 1984, she began working for Baccarat, Inc. (Baccarat), a distributor of fine crystal, as a sales representative in its retail store in Manhattan. Rivera was the top sales representative at the Baccarat store from 1992 through 1994. J. D. Watts, the store's manager, stated that Rivera was "one of the best salespeople I have encountered in my 15 years in quality tabletop and gift retailing."

In October 1994, Jean Luc Negre became the new president of Baccarat, with ultimate authority for personnel decisions. Sometime later, Negre angrily told Rivera that he did not like her attitude and that he did not want her to speak Spanish on the job. On July 14, 1995, Dennis Russell, the chief financial officer of Baccarat, notified Rivera that Negre had made a decision to terminate her. Rivera pressed Russell to tell her why she was being fired. According to Rivera, he replied, "Irma, he doesn't want Hispanics." Ivette Brigantty, another Hispanic sales representative, was also terminated by Negre. The non-Hispanic salesperson was retained by the store. Rivera sued Baccarat for national origin discrimination in violation of Title VII of the Civil Rights Act. The jury found Baccarat liable. Baccarat appealed.

ISSUE
Did Baccarat engage in unlawful national origin discrimination?

COURT'S REASONING
The court of appeals held that national origin discrimination includes the denial of employment opportunity because an individual has the linguistic characteristics of a national origin group. The court stated, "Accent and national origin are obviously inextricably intertwined," and continued, "unless an employee's accent materially interferes with her job performance, it cannot legally be the basis for an adverse employment action." The court of appeals found that Baccarat had terminated Rivera on the basis of her national origin in violation of Title VII. The court awarded damages of $50,000 to Rivera.

DECISION
The district court held that Baccarat had engaged in national origin discrimination in violation of Title VII. The court awarded Ms. Rivera $104,373 in damages, attorney's fees of $102,437, and prejudgment interest.

Case Questions

Critical Legal Thinking Why did Congress include national origin discrimination under Title VII? How does it differ from race discrimination?

Business Ethics Did the president of Baccarat act ethically in this case?

Contemporary Business Do you think national origin discrimination is very prevalent in business?

Sex Discrimination

sex discrimination

Discrimination against a person solely because of his or her gender.

Although the prohibition against **sex discrimination** applies equally to men and women, the overwhelming majority of Title VII sex discrimination cases are brought by women. The old airline practice of ignoring the marital status of male flight attendants but hiring only single female flight attendants is an example of such discrimination.

Pregnancy Discrimination Act

Amendment to Title VII that forbids employment discrimination because of "pregnancy, childbirth, or related medical conditions."

In 1978, the **Pregnancy Discrimination Act** was enacted as an amendment to Title VII.[5] This amendment forbids employment discrimination because of "pregnancy, childbirth, or related medical conditions." Thus, a work rule that prohibits the hiring of pregnant women violated Title VII.

In Case 26.3, the court found sex discrimination in violation of Title VII.

Barbano v. Madison County
922 F.2d 139 (1990)
United States Court of Appeals, Second Circuit

CASE 26.3

BACKGROUND AND FACTS

In February 1980, the position of director of the Madison County Veterans Service Agency became vacant. The Madison County Board of Supervisors (Board) appointed a committee of five men to hold interviews. Maureen E. Barbano applied for the position and was interviewed by the committee. Upon entering the interview, Barbano heard someone say, "Oh, another woman." When the interview began, Donald Greene, a committee member, said he would not consider "some woman" for the position. He then asked Barbano personal questions about her plans on having a family and whether her husband would object to her transporting male veterans. When Barbano said the questions were irrelevant and discriminatory, Greene replied that the questions were relevant because he did not want to hire a woman who would get pregnant and quit. Another committee member said the questions were relevant. No committee member said they were not relevant or asked Barbano any substantive questions.

The committee interviewed several other candidates and found them all (including Barbano) to be qualified for the position. Ultimately, the Board acted on the committee's recommendation and hired a male candidate. Barbano sued Madison County for sex discrimination in violation of Title VII. The district court held in favor of Barbano and awarded her $55,000 in back pay, prejudgment interest, and attorneys' fees. Madison County appealed.

ISSUE

Did the defendant engage in sex discrimination in violation of Title VII?

COURT'S REASONING

The court held that the record supported a finding that the committee and Board engaged in sex discrimination against Barbano in making the hiring decision. The court held that the questions asked of Barbano were unrelated to a bona fide occupational qualification and that Greene's questions were discriminatory and tainted the decision process.

DECISION

The court of appeals held that the defendant, Madison County, had engaged in sex discrimination in violation of Title VII. The court affirmed the award of damages to plaintiff Barbano.

Case Questions

Critical Legal Thinking   Why are questions concerning family obligations made illegal by Title VII?

Business Ethics   Was Greene's conduct morally reprehensible?

Contemporary Business   What actions should employers take to make sure their interviewers and other personnel understand Title VII and other antidiscrimination laws?

Sexual Harassment

sexual harassment

Lewd remarks, touching, intimidation, posting pinups, and other verbal or physical conduct of a sexual nature that occur on the job.

In the modern work environment, coworkers sometimes become sexually interested or involved with each other voluntarily. On other occasions, though, a coworker's sexual advances are not welcome.

Refusing to hire or promote someone unless he or she has sex with the manager or supervisor is sex discrimination that violates Title VII. Other forms of conduct, such as lewd remarks, touching, intimidation, posting pinups, and other verbal or physical conduct of a sexual nature, constitute **sexual harassment** and violate Title VII.[6]

To determine what conduct creates a hostile work environment, the Supreme Court stated:

We can say that whether an environment is "hostile" or "abusive" can be determined only by looking at all the circumstances. These may include the frequency of the discriminatory conduct; its severity; whether it is physically threatening or humiliating, or a mere offensive utterance; and whether it unreasonably interferes with an employee's work performance.[7]

Business Brief

To prevent future lawsuits, employers should be fully aware of federal and state equal employment opportunity (EEO) laws and implement policies and procedures to adhere to them.

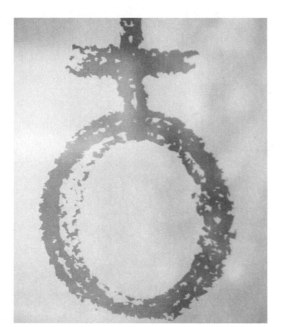

Title VII prohibits sexual harassment that causes a hostile work environment.

The Supreme Court Speaks

Sexual Harassment Violates Title VII

Harris v. Forklift Systems, Inc.
114 S.Ct. 367 (1993)
Supreme Court of the United States

BACKGROUND AND FACTS

Teresa Harris worked as a manager at Forklift Systems, Inc. (Forklift), an equipment rental company, from April 1985 until October 1987. Charles Hardy was Forklift's president. Throughout Harris's time at Forklift, Hardy often insulted her because of her gender and made her the target of unwanted sexual innuendos. Hardy told Harris on several occasions, in the presence of other employees, "You're a woman, what do you know" and "We need a man as the rental manager"; at least once, he told her she was "a dumb ass woman." Again in front of others, he suggested that the two of them "go to the Holiday Inn to negotiate Harris's raise." Hardy occasionally asked Harris and other female employees to get coins from his front pants pocket. He threw objects on the ground in front of Harris and other

women and asked them to pick the objects up. He made sexual innuendos about Harris's and other women's clothing.

In mid-August 1987, Harris complained to Hardy about his conduct. Hardy said he was surprised that Harris was offended, claimed he was only joking, and apologized. He also promised he would stop, and based on this assurance Harris stayed on the job. But in early September, Hardy began anew: While Harris was arranging a deal with one of Forklift's customers, he asked her, again in front of other employees, "What did you do, promise the guy some sex Saturday night?" On October 1, Harris collected her paycheck and quit.

Harris then sued Forklift, claiming that Hardy's conduct had created an abusive work environment for her because of her gender. The district court held that because Harris had not suffered severe psychological injury, she could not recover. The court of appeals affirmed. Harris appealed to the U.S. Supreme Court.

ISSUE

Must conduct, to be actionable as abusive work environment harassment, seriously affect the victim's psychological well-being?

IN THE LANGUAGE OF THE U.S. SUPREME COURT

O'Connor, Justice When the workplace is permeated with discriminatory intimidation, ridicule, and insult, that is sufficiently severe or pervasive to alter the conditions of the victim's employment and create an abusive working environment, Title VII is violated.

A discriminatorily abusive work environment, even one that does not seriously affect employees' psychological well-being, can and often will detract from employee's job performance, discourage employees from remaining on the job, or keep them from advancing in their careers. Moreover, even without regard to these tangible effects, the very fact that the discriminatory conduct was so severe or pervasive that it created a work environment abusive to employees because of their race, gender, religion,

or national origin offends Title VII's broad rule of workplace equality.

Certainly Title VII bars conduct that would seriously affect a reasonable person's psychological well-being, but the statute is not limited to such conduct. So long as the environment would reasonably be perceived, and is perceived, as hostile or abusive, there is no need for it also to be psychologically injurious.

DECISION AND REMEDY

The Supreme Court held that Title VII does not require a victim to prove that the challenged conduct seriously affected her psychological well-being. The case was remanded to the district court for trial.

CASE QUESTIONS

Critical Legal Thinking Should an employer be held liable for sexual harassment committed by one of its employees?

Business Ethics What penalty should be assessed against Hardy for his conduct?

Contemporary Business How can businesses eliminate sexual harassment on the job?

Contemporary Business Environment

THE REASONABLE WOMAN STANDARD

In most cases, the courts use a "reasonable person" standard to determine whether certain conduct violates the norms of society. This traditional standard was used in sexual harassment cases until recently, when several courts held that it was inappropriate. A "reasonable woman" standard was adopted in its place. The following case illustrates how this new standard works.

Kerry Ellison worked as a revenue agent for the Internal Revenue Service. A male coworker, whose desk was 20 feet from Ellison's, wrote her detailed love letters. When Ellison complained, the male employee was transferred to another location for six months, but then he was transferred back. He again wrote love letters to Ellison. The IRS did not take any further action to transfer the male employee elsewhere. Ellison filed a Title VII action against her employer, claiming sexual harassment. The district court granted the defendant's motion for summary judgment.

The court of appeals reversed and remanded the case. In doing so, the court articulated the **reasonable woman stan-**

dard for examining sexual harassment cases brought by females. The court stated

> *We believe that in evaluating the severity and pervasiveness of sexual harassment, we should focus on the perspective of the victim. If we only examined whether a reasonable person would engage in allegedly harassing conduct, we would run the risk of reinforcing the prevailing level of discrimination. We therefore prefer to analyze harassment from the victim's perspective. Conduct that many men consider unobjectionable may offend many women. We hold that a female plaintiff states a prima facie case of hostile environment sexual harassment when she alleges conduct which a reasonable woman would consider sufficiently severe or pervasive to alter the conditions of employment and create an abusive working environment.*

More courts are expected to adopt the reasonable woman standard in analyzing sexual harassment hostile work discrimination cases. [*Ellison v. Brady, Secretary of Treasury*, 924 F.2d 872 (9th Cir. 1991)]

ℰXHIBIT 26.1 *Policies Against Sexual Harassment*

Many businesses have taken steps to prevent sexual harassment in the workplace. For example, some businesses have explicitly adopted policies (see below) forbidding sexual harassment, implemented procedures for reporting incidents of sexual harassment, and conducted training programs to sensitize managers and employees about the issue.

Statement of Prohibited Conduct
The management of Company considers the following conduct to illustrate some of the conduct that violates Company's Sexual Harassment Policy:
A. Physical assaults of a sexual nature, such as
  1. Rape, sexual battery, molestation, or attempts to commit these assaults.
  2. Intentional physical conduct that is sexual in nature, such as touching, pinching, patting, grabbing, brushing against another employee's body, or poking another employee's body.
B. Unwanted sexual advances, propositions or other sexual comments, such as
  1. Sexually oriented gestures, noises, remarks, jokes, or comments about a person's sexuality or sexual experience directed at or made in the presence of any employee who indicates or has indicated in any way that such conduct is unwelcome in his or her presence.
  2. Preferential treatment or promises of preferential treatment to an employee for submitting to sexual conduct, including soliciting or attempting to solicit any employee to engage in sexual activity for compensation or reward.
  3. Subjecting, or threats of subjecting, an employee to unwelcome sexual attention or conduct or intentionally making performance of the employee's job more difficult because of the employee's sex.
C. Sexual or discriminatory displays or publications anywhere in Company's workplace by Company employees, such as
  1. Displaying pictures, posters, calendars, graffiti, objects, promotional materials, reading materials, or other materials that are sexually suggestive, sexually demeaning, or pornographic, or bringing into Company's work environment or possessing any such material to read, display, or view at work.
     A picture will be presumed to be sexually suggestive if it depicts a person of either sex who is not fully clothed or in clothes that are not suited to or ordinarily accepted for the accomplishment of routine work in and around the workplace and who is posed for the obvious purpose of displaying or drawing attention to private portions of his or her body.
  2. Reading or otherwise publicizing in the work environment materials that are in any way sexually revealing, sexually suggestive, sexually demeaning, or pornographic.
  3. Displaying signs or other materials purporting to segregate an employee by sex in any area of the workplace (other than restrooms and similar semi-private lockers/changing rooms).

ℰ-Commerce & Information Technology

E-MAIL'S ROLE IN HOSTILE WORK ENVIRONMENT LAWSUITS

The use of e-mail in business has dramatically increased efficiency and information sharing among employees. Managers and workers alike can communicate with each other, send documents, and keep each other apprised of business developments. In many organizations, e-mail has replaced the telephone as the most used method of communication and has eliminated the need for many meetings. This is a boon for business. But the downside is that e-mail has increased the exposure of businesses to sexual and racial harassment lawsuits. For example, the largest settlement regarding a sex-

ual harassment case arose from e-mail. In 1995, Chevron Corporation paid $2.2 million to settle sexual harassment charges brought by female employees for offensive e-mail messages sent by male coworkers, including one about "25 Reasons Beer is Better Than Women." The employees had signed a complaint letter about the e-mail harassment, but the company had ignored the complaint.

E-mail often sets the social tone of an office and has been permitted to be slightly ribald. At some point, however, e-mail conduct becomes impermissible and crosses the line to actionable sexual or racial harassment. The standard of whether e-mail creates an illegal hostile work environment is the same as that for measuring harassment in any other context: The offensive conduct must be severe and cannot consist of isolated or trivial remarks and incidents. And, as in other harassment cases, an employer may raise the defense that requires two elements: (1) the employer exercised reasonable care to prevent and correct the behavior and (2) the plaintiff employee unreasonably failed to take advantage of any preventive or corrective opportunities provided by the employer or to avoid the harm.

E-mail differs from many other incidents of harassment because it is subtle and insidious. Unlike paper pin-up calendars in plain view, an employer does not readily see e-mail messages. Obscenity pulled off the Internet or scanned into a computer can be sent as a clipping to an e-mail message. Because e-mail is hidden, to detect offensive messages, employers must take affirmative action to review e-mail messages on its network. Courts have generally held that an employee does not have an expectation of privacy of e-mail. Stored e-mail is the property of the employer, which may review it freely. Employers can also use software to scan and filter e-mail messages that contain any of a predefined list of objectionable words or phrases or certain "to" or "from" headers. Employers can also use software programs to scan graphics and block X-rated pictures.

E-mail has not only increased the possibility of there being sexual or racial harassment on the job, but it has also become the smoking gun that undermines a company's attempt to defend such cases. Therefore, employers must adopt policies pertaining to the use of e-mail by its employees and make their employees aware that certain e-mail messages constitute sexual or racial harassment and violate the law. Employers should make periodic inspections and audits of stored e-mail to ensure that employees are complying with the company's antiharassment policies.

Business Brief

Title VII prohibits same-sex employment discrimination.

Same-Sex Discrimination   The U.S. Supreme Court has held that same-sex sexual harassment is actionable under Title VII.[8] State and local laws also prohibit this form of discrimination.

Contemporary Business Environment

EMPLOYERS MAY PROVE AN AFFIRMATIVE DEFENSE IN SOME SEXUAL HARASSMENT CASES

The law of sexual harassment has been evolving since the U.S. Supreme Court first recognized it as a violation of Title VII in *Meritor Savings Bank, FSB v. Vinson*, 477 U.S. 57, 106 S.Ct. 2399 (1986). During the 1997 term, the Supreme Court, in two parallel decisions, again established important rules for sexual harassment cases brought under Title VII.

In *Faragher v. City of Boca Raton* and *Burlington Industries, Inc. v. Ellerth,* female plaintiffs sued their employers, proving that their supervisors had engaged in unconsented physical touching and verbal sexual harassment. In both cases the female employee quit her job and sued her employer for sexual harassment in violation of Title VII. In the first case, the employer had never disseminated a policy against sexual harassment to its employees. In the second case, the employer had disseminated its policy against sexual harassment to its employees and had put into place a complaint system that was not used by the female employee. After trials and appeals, the U.S. Supreme Court accepted these two cases for review to decide the following issue: Are employers strictly liable for the sexual harassment of their employees?

In *Faragher* and *Burlington Industries*, the Supreme Court issued opinions that reject automatic or strict liability. The Court announced that an employer may raise an *affirmative defense* against liability or damages by proving the following two elements:

1. The employer exercised reasonable care to prevent and correct promptly any sexual-harassing behavior
2. The plaintiff employee unreasonably failed to take advantage of any preventive or corrective opportunities provided by the employer or to otherwise avoid harm

The defendant employer has the burden of proving this affirmative defense. Courts should consider the following factors in determining whether such defense has been proven: (1) did the employer have an antiharassing policy, (2) did the employer have a complaint mechanism in place, (3) were employees informed of the antiharassment policy and complaint procedure, and (4) other factors the court deems relevant. Now that the U.S. Supreme Court has announced this rule, it will be the job of lower federal courts to apply the newly announced affirmative defense to specific cases. [*Faragher v. City of Boca Raton*, 118 S.Ct. 2275 (1998); *Burlington Industries, Inc v. Ellerth*, 118 S.Ct. 2257 (1998)]

Forbidden City, Beijing, China
Foreign nationals employed in foreign countries by U.S.-controlled companies are not covered by Title VII; U.S. citizens employed by U.S.-controlled companies in foreign countries are covered by Title VII, however.

Religious Discrimination

Title VII prohibits employment discrimination based on a person's religion. Religions include traditional religions, other religions that recognize a supreme being, and religions based on ethical or spiritual tenets. Many **religious discrimination** cases involve a conflict between an employer's work rule and an employee's religious beliefs (e.g., when an employee is required to work on his or her religious holiday).

The right of an employee to practice his or her religion is not absolute. Under Title VII, an employer is under a duty to *reasonably accommodate* the religious observances, practices, or beliefs of its employees if it does not cause an *undue hardship* on the employer. The courts must apply these general standards to specific fact situations. In making their decisions, the courts must consider such factors as the size of the employer, the importance of the employee's position, and the availability of alternative workers.

Title VII expressly permits religious organizations to give preference in employment to individuals of a particular religion. For example, if a person applies for a job with a religious organization but does not subscribe to its religious tenets, the organization may refuse to hire that person.

religious discrimination

Discrimination against a person solely because of his or her religion or religious practices.

Ethics Brief

Employers owe a duty to *reasonably* accommodate an employee's religious practices, observances, or beliefs if it does not cause *undue hardship* to the employer.

DEFENSES TO A TITLE VII ACTION

Title VII and case law recognize the following defenses to a charge of discrimination under Title VII.

Merit

Employers can select or promote employees based on *merit*. Merit decisions are often based on work, educational experience, and professionally developed ability tests. To be lawful under Title VII, the requirement must be job related. For example, requiring a person to pass a typing test to be hired as a typist would be lawful. Requiring a person to pass a college-level English composition test to be employed as a maintenance worker would violate Title VII.

Business Brief

Employers can select and promote employees based on merit without violating Title VII.

Ethics Brief

An employer may maintain a seniority system that rewards long-term employees. Such systems are lawful if they are not the result of intentional discrimination.

Seniority

Many employers maintain *seniority* systems that reward long-term employees. Higher wages, fringe benefits, and other preferential treatment (e.g., choice of working hours and vacation schedule) are examples of such rewards. Seniority systems provide an incentive for employees to stay with the company. Such systems are lawful if they are not the result of intentional discrimination.

bona fide occupational qualification (BFOQ)

Employment discrimination based on a protected class (other than race or color) is lawful if it is *job related* and a *business necessity*. This exception is narrowly interpreted by the courts.

Bona Fide Occupational Qualification (BFOQ)

Discrimination based on protected classes (other than race or color) is permitted if it is shown to be a **bona fide occupational qualification (BFOQ)**. To be legal, a BFOQ must be both *job related* and a *business necessity*. For example, allowing only women to be locker room attendants in a women's gym is a valid BFOQ, but prohibiting males from being managers or instructors at the same gym would not be a BFOQ.

The Supreme Court Speaks

No Bona Fide Occupational Qualification (BFOQ)

International Union, United Automobile, Aerospace and Agricultural Implement Workers of America, UAW v. Johnson Controls, Inc.
499 U.S. 187, 111 S.Ct. 1196 (1991)
Supreme Court of the United States

BACKGROUND AND FACTS

Johnson Controls, Inc. (Johnson Controls), manufactures batteries. Lead is the primary ingredient in the manufacturing process. Exposure to lead entails health risks, including risk of harm to any fetus carried by a female employee. To protect unborn children from such risk, Johnson Controls adopted an employment rule that prevented pregnant women and women of childbearing age from working at jobs involving lead exposure. Only women who were sterilized or could prove they could not have children were not affected by the rule. Consequently, most female employees were relegated to lower-paying clerical jobs at the company. Several female employees filed a class action suit challenging Johnson Controls's fetal-protection policy as sex discrimination in violation of Title VII. The district court held that the policy was justified as a bona fide occupational qualification (BFOQ) and granted summary judgment to Johnson Controls. The court of appeals affirmed. The plaintiffs appealed to the U.S. Supreme Court.

ISSUE

Is Johnson Controls's fetal-protection policy a BFOQ?

IN THE LANGUAGE OF THE U.S. SUPREME COURT

Blackmun, Justice The bias in Johnson Controls' policy is obvious. Fertile men, but not fertile women, are given a choice as to whether they wish to risk their reproductive health for a particular job. Johnson Controls' fetal-protection policy explicitly discriminates against women on the basis of their sex. The policy excludes women with childbearing capacity from lead-exposed jobs and so creates a facial classification based on gender.

The bona fide occupational qualification's (BFOQ) defense is written narrowly, and this Court has read it narrowly. We have no difficulty concluding that Johnson Controls cannot establish a BFOQ. Fertile women, as far as appears in the record, participate in the manufacture of batteries as efficiently as anyone else. Johnson Controls' professed moral and ethical concerns about the welfare of the next generation do not suffice to establish a BFOQ of female sterility. Decisions about the welfare of future children must be left to the parents who conceive, bear, support, and raise them rather than to the employers who hire those parents.

DECISION AND REMEDY

The U.S. Supreme Court held that Johnson Controls's fetal-protection policy was not a BFOQ. Instead, it was sex discrimination in violation of Title VII. Reversed and remanded.

CASE QUESTIONS

Critical Legal Thinking   Should any BFOQ exceptions to Title VII actions be permitted? Why or why not?

Business Ethics   Should Johnson Controls's moral and ethical concerns about the welfare of the next generation justify its actions?

Contemporary Business   Does Johnson Controls have any tort liability to children who are born injured by exposure to lead? How can Johnson Controls limit such liability?

*C*ONCEPT SUMMARY TITLE VII OF THE CIVIL RIGHTS ACT OF 1964

Covered Employers and Employment Decisions	1. **Employers** Employers with 15 or more employees for 20 weeks in the current or preceding year, all employment agencies, labor unions with 15 or more members, state and local governments, and most federal agencies.
	2. **Employment Decisions** Decisions regarding hiring; promotion; demotion; payment of salaries, wages, and fringe benefits; dismissal; job training and apprenticeships; work rules; or any other *term, condition,* or *privilege* of employment. Decision to admit a partner to a partnership is also covered.
Protected Classes	1. **Race** Broad class of individuals with common characteristics (e.g., Black, Caucasian, Asian, Native American).
	2. **Color** Color of a person's skin (e.g., light-skinned person, dark-skinned person).
	3. **National Origin** A person's country of origin or national heritage (e.g., Italian, Hispanic).
	4. **Sex** A person's sex, whether male or female. Includes sexual harassment and discrimination against females who are pregnant.
	5. **Religion** A person's religious beliefs. An employer has a duty to reasonably accommodate an employee's religious beliefs if it does not cause an undue hardship on the employer.
Types of Discrimination	1. **Disparate Treatment Discrimination** Discrimination against a specific individual because that person belongs to a protected class.
	2. **Disparate Impact Discrimination** Discrimination that occurs where a neutral-looking employment rule causes discrimination against a protected class.
Defenses	1. **Merit** Job-related experience, education, or unbiased employment test.
	2. **Seniority** Length of time an employee has been employed by the employer. Intentional discrimination based on seniority is unlawful.
	3. **Bona Fide Occupational Qualification (BFOQ)** Discrimination based on sex, religion, or national origin is permitted if it is a valid BFOQ for the position. Qualification based on race or color is not a permissible BFOQ.
Remedies	1. The court may order the payment of two years' back pay, issue an injunction awarding reinstatement, grant fictional seniority, or order some other equitable remedy.

*I*nternational *L*aw

INTERNATIONAL REACH OF U.S. ANTIDISCRIMINATION LAWS

Does Title VII extend beyond the territorial reach of the United States? The **Civil Rights Act of 1991** stipulates that it does. The 1991 act expressly protects *U.S. citizens*—but not foreign nationals—employed in a foreign country by U.S.-controlled employers. Foreign operations not controlled by U.S. employers are not covered.

An employer of a U.S. citizen abroad is subject to claims under Title VII in the following two situations:

1. An employer that is incorporated in the United States and operates a branch office in a foreign country is liable for Title VII violations against U.S. citizens that occur in its foreign operation.
2. If a U.S. parent corporation owns a foreign corporation that is incorporated in another country, the foreign-

controlled subsidiary is subject to Title VII because the 1991 act expressly states that discriminatory practices of "controlled foreign corporations" are presumed to be acts engaged in by the parent corporation.

The 1991 act contains an express exception that protects employers from conflicting foreign laws. If required conduct under Title VII would cause the employer to violate the law of a foreign nation (e.g., foreign law does not permit the employment of female workers), compliance with Title VII is excused.

The 1991 act also extends its international reach to the Americans with Disabilities Act (ADA) and the Age Discrimination in Employment Act (ADEA). Both of these acts are discussed later in this chapter.

ℰQUAL PAY ACT OF 1963

Equal Pay Act of 1963

Protects both sexes from pay discrimination based on sex; extends to jobs that require equal skill, equal effort, equal responsibility, and similar working conditions.

By what justice can an association of citizens be held together when there is no equality among the citizens?

Cicero
De Re Publica De Legibus J
XXXII 49

Business Brief

The Equal Pay Act expressly provides four criteria that justify a differential in wages. The employer bears the burden of proving these defenses.

Discrimination often takes the form of different pay scales for men and women performing the same job. The **Equal Pay Act of 1963** protects both sexes from pay discrimination based on sex.[9] This act covers all levels of private sector employees and state and local government employees. Federal workers are not covered, however.

The act prohibits disparity in pay for jobs that require *equal skill* (i.e., equal experience), *equal effort* (i.e., mental and physical exertion), *equal responsibility* (i.e., equal supervision and accountability), or *similar working conditions* (i.e., dangers of injury, exposure to the elements, and the like). To make this determination, the courts examine the actual requirements of jobs to determine whether they are equal and similar. If two jobs are determined to be equal and similar, an employer cannot pay disparate wages to members of different sexes.

Employees can bring a private cause of action against an employer for violating the act. Back pay and liquidated damages are recoverable. In addition, the employer must increase the wages of the discriminated-against employee to eliminate the unlawful disparity of wages. The wages of other employees may not be lowered.

Criteria That Justify a Differential in Wages

The Equal Pay Act expressly provides four criteria that justify a differential in wages. These defenses include payment systems that are based on

- **Seniority**
- **Merit** (as long as there is some identifiable measurement standard)
- **Quantity or quality of product** (commission, piecework, or quality-control-based payment systems are permitted)
- **"Any factor other than sex"** (including shift differentials, i.e., night versus day shifts, and such)

The employer bears the burden of proving these defenses. An employer asserted the "any factor other than sex" defense in Case 26.4.

Glenn v. General Motors Corporation
841 F.2d 567 (1988)
United States Court of Appeals, Eleventh Circuit

CASE 26.4

BACKGROUND AND FACTS
Sheila Ann Glenn, Patricia Johns, and Robbie Nugent, three female employees of General Motors Corporation (GM), sued their employer for violation of the Equal Pay Act. The three females worked in the tools stores department of GM as "Follow Ups." A Follow Up basically ensures that adequate tools are on hand in GM plants to keep the plants running. From 1975 through 1985, the three women were paid less than all their male comparators in the same position, and the most highly paid of the three earned less than the lowest-paid man. When hired, all three women received lower starting salaries than men hired at the same time. The trial court held in favor of the three women and awarded damages against GM. GM appealed.

ISSUE
Did GM violate the Equal Pay Act?

COURT'S REASONING
The court of appeals held that once the appellees established a prima facie case, the burden shifted to GM to prove that the difference in pay was justified by one of the four exceptions in the Equal Pay Act: (1) a seniority system, (2) a merit system, (3) a system that measures earnings by quantity or quality of production, (4) a differential based on any factor other than

sex. GM sought to justify the pay disparity on the fourth ground—a factor other than sex.

The court noted that GM sought to defend the pay disparity as a result of the market force theory. The Supreme Court has long rejected the market force theory as a "factor other than sex." The court reasoned that the argument that supply and demand dictates that women may be paid less is exactly the kind of evil that the Equal Pay Act was designed to eliminate and has been rejected. The market force theory that a woman will work for less than a man is not a valid consideration under the Equal Pay Act.

DECISION
The court of appeals held that GM had violated the Equal Pay Act and affirmed the award of damages to the plaintiffs.

Case Questions

Critical Legal Thinking Do you think the Equal Pay Act was necessary to eliminate pay disparities between men and women?

Business Ethics Was it ethical for GM to pay women less than men for the same job?

Contemporary Business What does the market force theory provide? Does it make economic sense?

Landmark Law

AGE DISCRIMINATION IN EMPLOYMENT ACT OF 1967

In the past, some employers discriminated against employees and prospective employees based on their age. For example, employers often refused to hire older workers. The **Age Discrimination in Employment Act (ADEA)**, which prohibits certain *age discrimination* practices, was enacted in 1967 [29 U.S.C. §§ 621–634].

The ADEA covers nonfederal employers with at least 20 employees, labor unions with at least 25 members, and all employment agencies. State and local government employees except those in policy-making positions are covered, as well as employees of certain sectors of the federal government.

The ADEA prohibits age discrimination in all employment decisions, including hiring, promotions, payment of compensation, and other terms and conditions of employment. The **Older Workers Benefit Protection (OWBPA)** amended the ADEA to prohibit age discrimination with regard to employee benefits. Employers cannot use employment advertisements that discriminate against applicants covered by ADEA. The same defenses that are available in a Title VII action are also available in an ADEA action.

PROTECTED AGE CATEGORIES

Originally, ADEA prohibited employment discrimination against persons between the ages of 40 and 65. In 1978, its coverage was extended to persons up to the age of 70. Further amendments completely eliminated an age ceiling, so ADEA now applies to employees who are 40 and older. As a result, covered employers cannot establish mandatory retirement ages for their employees.

Because persons under 40 are not protected by ADEA, an employer can maintain an employment policy of hiring only workers who are 40 years of age or older without violating the ADEA. However, the employer could not maintain an employment practice whereby it hired only persons 50 years of age and older because it would discriminate against persons aged 40 to 49.

The ADEA is administered by the EEOC. Private plaintiffs can also sue under ADEA. A successful plaintiff in an ADEA action can recover back wages, attorneys' fees, and equitable relief, including hiring, reinstatement, and promotion. Where a violation of ADEA is found, the employer must raise the wages of the discriminated-against employee. It cannot lower the wages of other employees.

Business Ethics

"YOU'RE OVERQUALIFIED FOR THE JOB!"

On October 20, 1982, Preview Subscription Television, Inc. (Preview), a subsidiary of Time Incorporated (Time), hired Thomas Taggart as a print production manager for Preview's magazine *Guide*. Taggart was 58 years old at the time and had more than 30 years' experience in the printing industry. In May 1983, Time notified Preview employees that Preview would be dissolved and, though not guaranteed a job, the employees were told they would receive special consideration for other positions at Time. Time sent weekly job bulletins to former Preview employees, including Taggart.

Taggart applied for 32 positions in various divisions at Time and its subsidiaries, including *Sports Illustrated, People Magazine, Life, Money*, and *Discover* magazines. Although Taggart interviewed for many of these openings, he was not offered employment. Time explained this by saying that Taggart was overqualified for many of the positions. Taggart contends that Time hired less qualified, younger applicants for many of the positions for which he was rejected. Taggart sued Time for age discrimination in violation of the Age Discrimination in Employment Act (ADEA). The district court granted Time's motion for summary judgment. Taggart appealed.

The court of appeals held that an employer's proffered reason for not hiring an applicant for a position because he was overqualified is a circumstance from which a reasonable juror could infer discriminatory animus.

The court noted that Taggart was over 40 years old and belonged to the protected age group. The fact that Taggart was found overqualified for some of the jobs he applied for at Time supported his allegation that he was capable of performing the jobs. Further, Time hired persons younger than he for those jobs. Thus, Taggart established a prima facie case of age discrimination. The court of appeals reversed and remanded the case. Why do businesses tend to want to hire younger workers rather than older ones? [*Taggart v. Time Incorporated*, 924 F.2d 43 (2d Cir. 1991)]

1. Did Time Incorporated act ethically in adopting the "you are overqualified" reason for not hiring Mr. Taggart?
2. Do you think older workers have a harder time finding employment than younger persons and therefore need the protection of the ADEA? Should younger persons be covered by the ADEA, too?

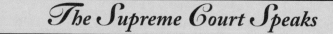

The Supreme Court Speaks

Prima Facie Case of Age Discrimination

Reeves v. Sanderson Plumbing Products, Inc.
530 U.S. 133, 120 S.Ct. 2097 (2000)
Supreme Court of the United States

BACKGROUND AND FACTS

In October 1995, Roger Reeves was 57 years old and spent 40 years employed by Sanderson Plumbing Products, Inc., a manufacturer of toilet seats and covers. Reeves worked as a supervisor of a production line in a department known as the "Hinge Room." Reeves' responsibilities included recording the attendance and hours of those workers under his supervision. In the summer of 1995, the president of Sanderson Plumbing fired Reeves, asserting that Reeves had failed to maintain accurate attendance records. Sanderson Plumbing replaced Reeves with a worker in his thirties. Reeves sued Sanderson Plumbing for violating the Age Discrimination in Employment Act, alleging that Sanderson's stated reason for discharging him was false and the real reason was to discriminate against him because of his age. The jury held in favor of Reeves, but the court of appeals reversed. The U.S. Supreme Court granted certiorari to hear the appeal.

SUPREME COURT ISSUE

Did plaintiff Reeves properly raise the issue to the jury of the falsity of Sanderson Plumbing's claim as to why he had been fired?

IN THE LANGUAGE OF THE U.S. SUPREME COURT

Ginsburg, Justice McDonnell Douglas Corp. v. Green, *411 U.S. 792, 93 S.Ct. 1817 (1973) and subsequent decisions have established an allocation of the burden of production and an order for the presentation of proof in discriminatory-treatment cases. First, the plaintiff must establish a prima facie case of discrimination. It is undisputed that petitioner Reeves satisfied this burden here: (i) at the time he was fired, he was a member of the class protected by the ADEA (individuals who are at least 40 years of age), (ii) he was otherwise qualified for the position of Hinge Room supervisor, (iii) he was discharged by respondent, and (iv) respondent successively hired three persons in their thirties to fill petitioner's position. The burden therefore shifted to respondent to produce evidence that the plaintiff was rejected, or someone else was preferred, for a legitimate, nondiscriminatory reason. Respondent met this burden by offering admissible evidence sufficient for the trier of fact to conclude that petitioner was fired because of his failure to maintain accurate attendance records.*

Although intermediate evidentiary burdens shift back and forth under this framework, the ultimate burden of persuading the trier of fact that the defendant intentionally discriminated against the plaintiff remains at all times with the plaintiff. And in attempting to satisfy this burden, the plaintiff—once the employer produces sufficient evidence to support a nondiscriminatory explanation for its decision—must be afforded the opportunity to prove by a preponderance of the evidence that the legitimate reasons offered by the defendant were not its true reasons, but were a pretext for discrimination. That is, the plaintiff may attempt to establish that he was the victim of intentional discrimination by showing that the employer's proffered explanation is unworthy of credence. Petitioner offered evidence that he had properly maintained the attendance records. It is permissible for the trier of fact to infer the ultimate fact of discrimination from the falsity of the employer's explanation.

DECISION AND REMEDY

The U.S. Supreme Court held that plaintiff Reeves had presented sufficient evidence to the jury that Sanderson Plumbing's asserted justification for dismissing him was false, and thus permitted the jury to conclude that Sanderson Plumbing had unlawfully discriminated against him.

CASE QUESTIONS

Critical Legal Thinking Does the Supreme Court's back-and-forth burden shifting approach in employment discrimination lawsuits work well? Do you think it leads to a fair decision in most cases?

Business Ethics Did Sanderson Plumbing act ethically in this case? Why do you think it used a false pretense to fire Reeves?

Contemporary Business Are there economic reasons for employers to prefer to discharge older employees? Explain.

Landmark Law

AMERICANS WITH DISABILITIES ACT OF 1990

The **Americans with Disabilities Act (ADA)**, which was signed into law on July 26, 1990, is the most comprehensive piece of civil rights legislation since the Civil Rights Act of 1964 [42 U.S.C. §§ 1201 et seq.]. The ADA imposes obligations on employers and providers of public transportation, telecommunications, and public accommodations to accommodate individuals with disabilities.

TITLE I OF THE ADA

Title I of the ADA prohibits employment discrimination against qualified individuals with disabilities in regard to job application procedures, hiring, compensation, training, promotion, and termination. Title I, which became effective July 26, 1992, covers employers with 25 or more employees for two years after the effective date and those with 15 or more employees thereafter. The United States, corporations wholly owned by the United States, and bona fide tax-exempt private membership clubs are exempt from Title I coverage.

Title I requires an employer to make reasonable accommodations to individuals with disabilities that do not cause undue hardship to the employer. *Reasonable accommodations* may include making facilities readily accessible to individuals with disabilities, providing part-time or modified work schedules, acquiring equipment or devices, modifying examination and training materials, and providing qualified readers or interpreters.

Employers are not obligated to provide accommodations that would impose an *undue burden*. This means actions that would require significant difficulty or expense. Factors such as the nature and cost of accommodation, the overall financial resources of the employer, and the employer's type of operation are considered by the EEOC and the courts. Obviously, what may be a significant difficulty or expense for a small employer may not be an undue hardship for a large employer.

Title I of the Americans with Disabilities Act (ADA) requires employers to make reasonable accommodations for individuals with disabilities that do not cause undue hardship to the employer.

AMERICANS WITH DISABILITIES ACT OF 1990

Qualified Individual with a Disability

A **qualified individual with a disability** is a person who, with or without reasonable accommodation, can perform the essential functions of the job that person desires or holds. A disabled person is someone who (1) has a physical or mental impairment that substantially limits one or more of his or her major life activities, (2) has a record of such impairment, or (3) is regarded as having such impairment. Mental retardation, paraplegia, schizophrenia, cerebral palsy, epilepsy, diabetes, muscular dystrophy, multiple sclerosis, cancer, infection with HIV (human immunodeficiency virus), and visual, speech, and hearing impairments are covered under the ADA. A current user of illegal drugs or an alcoholic who uses alcohol or is under the influence of alcohol at the workplace is not covered. However, recovering alcoholics and former users of illegal drugs are protected.

Title I limits an employer's ability to inquire into or test for an applicant's disabilities. Title I forbids an employer from asking a job applicant about the existence, nature, and severity of a disability. An employer may, however, inquire about the applicant's ability to perform job-related functions. Preemployment medical examinations are forbidden before a job offer. Once a job offer has been made, an employer may require a medical examination and may condition the offer on the examination results as long as all entering employees are subject to such an examination. The information must be kept confidential.

Americans with Disabilities Act (ADA) of 1990

Imposes obligations on employers and providers of public transportation, telecommunications, and public accommodations to accommodate individuals with disabilities.

Business Brief

Title I of the ADA requires an employer to make *reasonable accommodations* to employees with disabilities that do not cause *undue hardship* to the employer.

qualified individual with a disability

A person who (1) has a physical or mental impairment that substantially limits one or more of his or her major life activities, (2) has a record of such impairment, or (3) is regarded as having such impairment.

Procedure and Remedies

Title I, which is administered by the EEOC, borrows much of its procedural framework from Title VII of the Civil Rights Act of 1964. An aggrieved individual must first file a charge with the EEOC, which may take action against the employer or permit the individual to pursue a private cause of action.

Relief can take the form of an injunction, hiring or reinstatement (with back pay), payment of attorneys' fees, and recovery of compensatory and punitive damages (subject to the same caps as Title VII damages).

The Supreme Court Speaks

U.S. Supreme Court Defines "Disability"

Sutton v. United Air Lines, Inc.
119 S.Ct. 2139 (1999)
Supreme Court of the United States

BACKGROUND AND FACTS

In 1992, Karen Sutton and Kimberly Hinton (petitioners), twin sisters, applied to United Air Lines, Inc., for employment as commercial airline pilots. They met United's education and experience requirements and the Federal Aviation Administration (FAA) certification qualifications. Both of the petitioners have severe myopia, with uncorrected visual acuity of 20/200 or worse and 20/400 or worse. Each of the petitioners has vision that is 20/20 or better with the use of corrective lens. Without corrective lens, neither of the petitioners can see to conduct activities such as driving a vehicle, watching television, or shopping in public stores, but with corrective lens both function identically to persons without similar impairment. United rejected the petitioners' employment applications because they did not meet United's minimum visual requirement of uncorrected visual acuity of 20/100 or better. Petitioners filed a charge of disability discrimination against United for allegedly violating the Americans with Disabilities Act (ADA). The district court dismissed petitioners' complaint and the circuit court of appeals affirmed. Petitioners appealed to the U.S. Supreme Court, which granted review.

ISSUE

Are the petitioners disabled within the meaning of the ADA?

IN THE LANGUAGE OF THE U.S. SUPREME COURT

O'Connor, Justice With respect to the disability definition, our decision turns on whether disability is to be determined with or without reference to corrective measures. Petitioners maintain that whether an impairment is substantially limiting should be determined without regard to corrective measures. United, in turn, maintains that an impairment does not substantially limit a major life activity if it is corrected. We conclude that United is correct. Looking at ADA as a whole, it is apparent that if a person is taking measures to correct for, or mitigate, a physical or mental impairment, the effects of those measures—both positive and negative—must be taken into account when judging whether that person is "substantially limited" in a major life activity and thus "disabled" under the ADA.

The ADA defines a "disability" as "a physical or mental impairment that substantially limits one or more of the major life activities" of an individual. A person whose physical or mental impairment is corrected by medication or other measures does not have an impairment that presently substantially limits a major life activity. To be sure, a person whose physical or mental impairment is corrected by mitigating measures still has an impairment, but if the impairment is corrected it does not substantially limit a major life activity.

DECISION AND REMEDY

The U.S. Supreme Court held that *disability* under the Americans with Disabilities Act (ADA) does not include persons with corrected conditions, such as petitioners' corrected vision. The Supreme Court concluded that the petitioners' complaint was properly dismissed. Affirmed.

CASE QUESTIONS

Critical Legal Thinking Does the Americans with Disabilities Act promote an important social policy? Do you think a federal law was needed to effectuate this policy?

Business Ethics Did United act ethically in this case? What reasons underlie its decision not to hire the petitioners?

Contemporary Business What is the business implication of the U.S. Supreme Court's decision? What would have been the economic implications for business if the Supreme Court would have held in the petitioners' favor?

The Supreme Court Speaks

PGA Tour Must Allow Disabled Golfer to Use a Golf Cart

PGA Tour, Inc. v. Martin
U.S., 121 S.Ct. 1879 (2001), 2001 U.S. Lexis 415, WL
Supreme Court of the United States

BACKGROUND AND FACTS

The PGA Tour, Inc., is a nonprofit entity that sponsors professional golf tournaments. The PGA has adopted a set of rules that apply to its golf tour. One rule requires golfers to walk the golf course during PGA-sponsored tournaments. Casey Martin is a talented amateur golfer who won many Oregon junior events, and the state championship as a high school senior. He played on the Stanford University golf team and won the 1994 National Collegiate Athletic Association (NCAA) championship.

Martin has been afflicted with Klippel-Trenaunay-Weber Syndrome, a degenerative circulatory disorder that obstructs the flow of blood from his right leg to his heart. The disease is progressive and has atrophied his right leg. Walking causes him pain, fatigue, and anxiety, with significant risk of hemorrhaging. Martin is an individual with a disability as defined by the Americans with Disabilities Act of 1990 (ADA). When Martin turned professional, he qualified for the PGA Tour. He made a request to use a golf cart while playing in PGA tournaments. When the PGA denied his requests, Martin sued the PGA in violation of the ADA for not making reasonable accommodations for his disability. The district court sided with Martin and ordered the PGA to permit Martin to use a golf cart. The court of appeals affirmed. The U.S. Supreme Court agreed to hear the appeal.

SUPREME COURT ISSUE

Does the Americans with Disabilities Act of 1990 require the PGA Tour, Inc. to accommodate Casey Martin, a disabled professional golfer, by permitting him to use a golf cart while playing in PGA sponsored golf tournaments?

IN THE LANGUAGE OF THE U.S. SUPREME COURT

Stevens, Justice In this case, the narrow dispute is whether allowing Martin to use a golf cart, despite the walking requirement that applies to the PGA Tour tournaments, is a modification that would "fundamentally alter the nature" of those events.

As an initial matter, we observe that the use of carts is not itself inconsistent with the fundamental character of the game of golf. From early on, the essence of the game has been shot-making—using clubs to cause a ball to progress from the teeing ground to a hole some distance away with as few strokes as possible. Golf carts

started appearing with increasing regularity on American golf courses in the 1950's. Today they are everywhere. And they are encouraged. For one thing, they often speed up play, and for another, they are great revenue producers.

The force of petitioner PGA Tour's argument is, first of all, mitigated by the fact that golf is a game in which it is impossible to guarantee that all competitors will play under exactly the same conditions or that an individual's ability will be the sole determinant of the outcome. For example, changes in the weather may produce harder greens and more head winds for the tournament leader than for his closest pursuers. A lucky bounce may save a shot or two. Whether such happenstance events are more or less probable than the likelihood that a golfer afflicted with Klippel-Trenaunay-Weber Syndrome would one day qualify for the PGA Tour, they at least demonstrate that pure chance may have a greater impact on the outcome of elite golf tournaments than the fatigue resulting from the enforcement of the walking rule. The District Court credited the testimony of a professor in physiology and expert on fatigue, who calculated the calories expended in walking a golf course (about five miles) to be approximately 500 calories—"nutritionally—less than a Big Mac."

DECISION AND REMEDY

The U.S. Supreme Court held that the Americans with Disabilities Act of 1990 requires that the PGA Tour, Inc. accommodate Casey Martin, a disabled professional golfer, by allowing him to use a golf cart while competing in PGA sponsored professional golf tournaments. The judgment of the court of appeals is affirmed.

CASE QUESTIONS

Critical Legal Thinking   Do you agree with the U.S. Supreme Court's decision? Will the decision open a "floodgate" of similar lawsuits?

Business Ethics   Was Casey Martin just asking for "fairness," or was he asking for an advantage when competing in professional golf tournaments?

Contemporary Business   Is the PGA Tour a lucrative business? Will the Supreme Court's ruling have any effect on the revenues generated by the PGA Tour?

Business Ethics

PERCEIVED DISABILITY

In some circumstances an employer treats prospective or actual employees as if they have a disability when in fact they do not. Consider the following case.

From 1978 to 1986, Bonnie Cook worked as an institutional attendant at the Ladd Center, a residential facility for retarded persons that was operated by the Rhode Island Department of Mental Health, Retardation, and Hospitals (MHRH). Ms. Cook voluntarily left the position for two years, leaving behind a spotless work record. In 1988, Ms. Cook reapplied for the identical position. Despite passing the routine physical examination, the MHRH refused to hire Ms. Cook because she stood 5′2″ but weighed more than 320 pounds. The director of the hospital testified that Ms. Cook was not hired because he believed that her obesity compromised her ability to evacuate patients in case of an emergency and put her at greater risk of being absent and developing serious ailments that would increase her likelihood of filing a workers' compensation claim.

Ms. Cook filed suit against MHRH for violating federal disability law. The district court found that Ms. Cook's obesity did not prevent or impede her from doing the job she applied for. Instead, the court found that MHRH had perceived her to have a disability, when in fact she did not. The district court held that MHRH had violated federal disability law and the court of appeals agreed.

The court of appeals held that obesity is a protected category under federal disability law. The court stated, "In a society that all too often confuses 'slim' with 'beautiful' or 'good,' morbid obesity can present formidable barriers to employment." The court also held that *perceived disability* is covered by the law. The jury award of $100,000 in damages to Ms. Cook was affirmed. [*Cook v. State of Rhode Island, Department of Mental Health, Retardation, and Hospitals,* F.3d (1st Cir. 1993)]

1. What is a perceived disability? Explain.
2. Did MHRH act ethically in this case?

Landmark Law

CIVIL RIGHTS ACT OF 1866

The **Civil Rights Act of 1866** was enacted after the Civil War. *Section 1981* of this act states that all persons "have the same right . . . to make and enforce contracts . . . as is enjoyed by white persons" [42 U.S.C. § 1981]. Employment decisions are covered because the employment relation is contractual. Most employers other than the federal government are subject to this act.

Section 1981 expressly prohibits racial discrimination; it has also been held to forbid discrimination based on national origin. Although most racial and national origin employment discrimination cases are brought under Title VII, there are two reasons that a complainant would bring the action under Section 1981: (1) A private plaintiff can bring an action without going through the procedural requirements of Title VII, and (2) there is no limitations period on the recovery of back pay and no cap on the recovery of compensatory or punitive damages.

Entrepreneur and the Law

SMALL BUSINESSES EXEMPT FROM FEDERAL EQUAL OPPORTUNITY IN EMPLOYMENT LAWS

In passing federal equal opportunity in employment laws, Congress exempted small businesses from the reach of many of these laws. In several of these statutes, Congress set a threshold number of employees that an employer must have to be covered by each act. Some of the threshold requirements are

- **Title VII**   Employers with 15 or more employees
- **Age Discrimination in Employment Act**   Employers with 20 or more employees.
- **Americans with Disabilities Act of 1990**   Employers with 15 or more employees.

The rationale behind these exemptions is that it may be too costly for small employers to comply with the laws and face lawsuits that could arise thereunder. These employers should make every effort to comply with these laws, however.

Affirmative Action

Employers often adopt **affirmative action plans** that provide that certain job preferences will be given to minority or other protected class applicants when an employer makes an employment decision. Such plans can be voluntarily adopted by employers, undertaken to settle a discrimination action, or ordered by the courts. Employee approval is not required.

Affirmative action plans are often controversial. Proponents of such plans argue that the plans are necessary to address imbalances in the workforce and to remedy past discrimination against protected classes. Opponents argue that affirmative action plans actually cause **reverse discrimination**, work hardship on innocent employees, and cause the employment of less qualified individuals.

The Civil Rights Act of 1991 prohibits the practice of "race norming" and other practices that are used to alter or adjust test scores on the basis of race. It does not affect how an employer uses accurately reported test scores or require that test scores be used at all in making employment decisions, however.

affirmative action
Policy that provides that certain job preferences will be given to minority or other protected class applicants when an employer makes an employment decision.

reverse discrimination
Discrimination against a group that is usually thought of as a majority.

Contemporary Business Environment

AFFIRMATIVE ACTION NARROWED

Affirmative action was dealt a severe blow when, in April 1995, the U.S. Supreme Court refused to hear appeals in two cases that gave victories to white men in reverse discrimination lawsuits. These decisions show a willingness by the courts to apply the Equal Protection Clause of the U.S. Constitution and equal opportunity in employment laws to protect white employees as well as minorities from discrimination.

The first case involved an affirmative action plan implemented by the city of Birmingham, Alabama, to ensure the promotion of black firefighters. The case began over 20 years ago when black firefighters sued the city for discrimination because it had only a few black firefighters and none in supervisory positions. After a heated lawsuit, in 1981 the city agreed to promote white and black firefighters to the rank of lieutenant on a 1-to-1 basis until the number of blacks equaled the 28 percent of the surrounding county's workforce that was black. The target was reached in 1989, but the city continued this quota system.

In 1989, several white firefighters challenged the city's affirmative action plan. The white firefighters lost in federal district court, but the court of appeals reversed, finding that the city's affirmative action plan violated the Equal Protection Clause of the Constitution and Title VII. The court of appeals denounced the city's plan as outright racial balancing, stating, "We can imagine nothing less conducive to eliminating the vestiges of past discrimination than a government separating its employees into two categories, black

and nonblack, and allocating a rigid, inflexible number of promotions to each group, year in and year out."

The second case was brought by Frederick Claus, a white engineer with a bachelor's degree in electrical engineering who had worked 29 years for his employer, Duquesne Light Co. Claus, along with four other whites and one black, sought promotion for an open managerial job. The black employee did not have a bachelor's degree or the required seven years' experience for the position. When the company applied its affirmative action plan and chose the black employee for the position, Claus sued under Title VII, claiming that he was a victim of racial discrimination. The jury agreed and awarded him $25,000 in compensatory damages and $400,000 in punitive damages. The court of appeals upheld the verdict.

Without comment, the U.S. Supreme Court turned down appeals in both cases [*Arrington v. Wilks*, 115 S.Ct. 1695(1995); *Duquesne Light Co. v. Claus*, 115 S.Ct. 1700 (1995)].

What is left of affirmative action? For one thing, affirmative action was not held to be per se illegal in either case. Instead, the courts of appeal held that an affirmative action plan, to be legal, must be "narrowly tailored" to achieve some "compelling interest." In these two cases, the courts found that the affirmative action plans were not narrowly tailored but were blatant quotas that were unlawful. Government and private employers must now tailor their affirmative action programs narrowly or face reverse discrimination lawsuits by passed-over nonminority employees.

Racial discrimination in any form and in any degree has no justifiable part whatever in our democratic way of life. It is unattractive in any setting but it is utterly revolting among a free people who have embraced the principles set forth in the Constitution of the United States.

Murphy, J. dissenting
Korematsu v. U.S.
(1944)

STATE AND LOCAL GOVERNMENT ANTIDISCRIMINATION LAWS

Many state and local governments have adopted laws that prevent discrimination in employment. These laws usually include classes protected by federal equal opportunity laws, as well as classes of persons not protected by federal laws, such as homosexuals and other minority groups.

 *International Law*

JAPAN ADOPTS AN EQUAL OPPORTUNITY IN EMPLOYMENT LAW

Prior to April 1, 1999, job openings in Japan were restricted by gender; that is, jobs could be reserved for men only without violating the law. Classified advertisements in major Japanese newspapers typically listed "men only" jobs, which were executive positions and high-paying blue collar jobs. "Women only" listings tended to be for nurses, secretaries, food-service employees, and other low-paying jobs. Japanese women hold only 10 percent of professional positions, as compared to 45 percent in the United States. Only 8 out of every 1,000 factory workers in Japan are women, compared to 160 per 1,000 in the United States. In addition to gender-based discrimination, sexual harassment against females in the workplace was usually ignored.

All this changed with Japan's enactment of the **Equal Employment Opportunity and Labor Standard Law** in 1999. The new statute grants equal opportunity rights to females in being hired for jobs and promoted to higher positions. The law bans the use of gender-specific advertising, so the "men only" and "women only" job listings have disappeared. Women may now compete equally, under the law, for

jobs and promotions. The new law also makes other gender-based discrimination illegal. For example, prior to the new law, women were banned from working after 10:00 P.M. or putting in more than six hours of overtime per week. Both of these restrictions have been removed, allowing females to earn higher wages from working night shifts and overtime. Women are still forbidden from holding positions involving heavy lifting or those involving certain chemicals.

The Equal Opportunity Law prohibits sexual harassment in the workplace. Prior to the passage of the new law, sexual harassment—known in Japan as *seku hara*—was difficult to sue for. Previously, companies could veto any sexual harassment complaint brought against them, which helped explain why fewer than a dozen cases were even ruled on during the 1990s. Under the new law, a woman can file a complaint with the Labor Ministry, a government administrative agency empowered to investigate such charges. So companies are now advising male managers to remove X-rated calendars from offices and to not pressure female employees to accompany them to karaoke, dancing, or other endeavors.

CHAPTER SUMMARY

Equal Employment Opportunity Commission (EEOC), p. 637

Equal Employment Opportunity Commission (EEOC)	Federal administrative agency responsible for administering, interpreting, and enforcing most federal equal employment opportunity (antidiscrimination) laws.

Title VII of the Civil Rights Act of 1964, p. 637

Title VII of the Civil Rights Act of 1964	Federal statute that prohibits job discrimination based on the (1) race, (2) color, (3) religion, (4) sex, or (5) national origin of the job applicant.

Scope of Coverage of Title VII	1. *Employers subject to Title VII.* Employers who had 15 or more employees for at least 20 weeks in the current or preceding year, all employment agencies, labor unions with 15 or more members, state and local governments, and most federal agencies. 2. *Employment decisions subject to Title VII.* Decisions regarding hiring; promotion; demotion; payment of salaries, wages, and fringe benefits; job training and apprenticeships; work rules; or any other "term, condition, or privilege of employment."

Forms of Title VII Actions	1. *Disparate treatment discrimination.* Occurs when an employer treats a specific *individual* less favorably than others because of that person's race, color, national origin, sex, or religion.
	To be successful, the complainant must prove:
	  a. He or she belongs to a Title VII protected class.
	  b. He or she applied for and was qualified for the employment position.
	  c. He or she was rejected despite these qualifications.
	  d. The employer kept the position open and sought applicants from persons with the complainant's qualifications.
	2. *Disparate impact discrimination.* Occurs when an employer discriminates against an entire protected *class*. May be proven by statistical data that demonstrate a causal link between the challenged practice and the statistical imbalance. *Neutral employment rules* that have an adverse impact on a protected class constitute disparate impact discrimination.

Procedure for Bringing a Title VII Action	1. *Complaint.* A private complainant must file a complaint with the EEOC. The EEOC is given the opportunity to sue the employer on the complainant's behalf. 2. *Right to sue letter.* If the EEOC chooses not to bring suit, it will issue a *right to sue letter* that authorizes the complainant to sue the employer.
Remedies for Violations of Title VII	A successful plaintiff in a Title VII action can recover up to two years' back pay, compensatory and punitive damages (subject to certain caps based on the size of the defendant employer), reasonable attorneys' fees, and equitable remedies such as reinstatement, fictional seniority, and injunctions.
Protected Classes	*Protected classes.* Employment discrimination based on the following protected classes is forbidden by Title VII: 1. *Race* 2. *Color* 3. *National origin* 4. *Sex* 5. *Religion*
Race, Color, and National Origin Discrimination	1. *Race.* Broad class of individuals with common physical characteristics (e.g., Black, Caucasian, Asian, Native American). 2. *Color.* Color of a person's skin (e.g., light-skinned person, dark-skinned person). 3. *National origin.* A person's country of origin or national heritage (e.g., Italian, Hispanic).
Sex Discrimination	1. *Sex.* A person's sex, whether male or female. 2. *Pregnancy.* The *Pregnancy Discrimination Act of 1978* amended Title VII to forbid employment discrimination because of "pregnancy, childbirth, or related medical conditions." 3. *Sexual harassment.* Lewd remarks, touching, intimidation, posting pinups, and other verbal or physical conduct of a sexual nature that occurs on the job. Sexual harassment that creates *a hostile work environment* violates Title VII [*Meritor Savings Bank v. Vinson*, 477 U.S. 57 (1986)]. 4. *Sexual preference.* Title VII does not apply to employment discrimination based on sexual preference.
Title VII: Religious Discrimination	Discrimination solely because of a person's religious beliefs or practices. An employer has a duty to *reasonably accommodate* an employee's religious beliefs if it does not cause an *undue hardship* on the employer.

Defenses to a Title VII Action, p. 645

Defenses to a Title VII Action	1. *Merit.* Job-related experiences, education, or unbiased employment test. 2. *Seniority.* Length of time an employee has been employed by the employer. Intentional discrimination based on seniority is unlawful. 3. *Bona fide occupational qualification (BFOQ).* Employment discrimination based on the sex, religion, or national origin of an applicant is permitted if it is a valid *bona fide occupational qualification (BFOQ)* for the position. To be legal, a BFOQ must be *job related* and a *business necessity.* BFOQ exceptions are narrowly interpreted by the courts.

Equal Pay Act of 1963, p. 648

Equal Pay Act	Federal statute that forbids pay discrimination for the same job based on the sex of the employee performing the job. There cannot be pay disparity based on sex for jobs that require equal skill, equal effort, equal responsibility, and similar working conditions.
	1. *Criteria that justify a differential in wages.* The Equal Pay Act stipulates that the following four criteria justify a differential in wages.
	   a. Seniority
	   b. Merit
	   c. Quantity or quality of work (commission, piecework, or quality control-based pay systems)
	   d. Any factor other than sex (e.g., night versus day shifts)

Age Discrimination in Employment Act of 1967, p. 649

Age Discrimination in Employment Act (ADEA)	Federal statute that prohibits employment discrimination against applicants and employees who are 40 years of age or older. 1. *Older Workers Benefit Protection Act (OWBPA).* Federal statute that amended the ADEA to prohibit age discrimination with respect to employment benefits. 2. *Defenses.* The same defenses that are available in a Title VII action are also available in an ADEA action. 3. *Remedies.* A successful plaintiff can recover back wages, attorneys' fees, and equitable relief, including hiring, reinstatement, and promotion.

Americans with Disabilities Act of 1990, p. 651

Americans with Disabilities Act of 1990 (ADA)	Federal statute that imposes obligations on employers and providers of public transportation, telecommunications, and public accommodations to accommodate individuals with disabilities.
Title I of the ADA	Federal law that prohibits employment discrimination against qualified individuals with disabilities. 1. *Reasonable accommodation.* Title I requires employers to make *reasonable accommodations* to accommodate employees with disabilities that do not cause *undue hardship* to the employer.
Qualified Individual with a Disability	A person who has (1) a physical or mental impairment that substantially limits one or more of his or her major life functions, (2) a record of such impairment, or (3) is regarded as having such impairment.
Procedure and Remedies	A successful plaintiff can recover back pay, compensatory and punitive damages (subject to certain caps based on the size of the defendant employer), reasonable attorneys' fees, and equitable remedies such as hiring, reinstatement, or promotion.

Civil Rights Act of 1866, p. 654

Civil Rights Act of 1866	1. *Section 1981 of the Civil Rights Act of 1866.* Federal statute enacted after the Civil War that states that all persons "have the same right" . . . to make and enforce contracts . . . as is enjoyed by white persons." 2. *Protected class.* Section 1981 prohibits *race* and *national origin* discrimination concerning employment contracts. 3. *Remedies.* A successful plaintiff can recover back pay, compensatory and punitive damages, reasonable attorneys' fees, and equitable remedies. There is no limitations period on the recovery of back pay, and there is no cap on the recovery of compensatory or punitive damages.

Affirmative Action, p. 655

Affirmative Action and Reverse Discrimination	A policy that provides that certain job preferences will be given to minority or other protected-class applicants when an employer makes an employment decision. 1. *Lawfulness of affirmative action plans.* An employer may adopt a voluntary affirmative action plan that uses race or other protected-class status as a *"plus factor"* in making employment decisions. *Race norming*—the practice of altering or adjusting test scores on the basis of race—is unlawful. 2. *Reverse discrimination.* Discrimination against a person who is a member of a group that is usually thought of as a majority. Very few reverse discrimination lawsuits are successful.

State and Local Government Antidiscrimination Laws, p. 656

State and Local Government Antidiscrimination Laws	Many state and local governments have adopted laws that prevent discrimination in employment. These laws usually include classes protected by federal equal opportunity laws (e.g., race, color, national origin, sex, religion, age, disability, and such), as well as classes not protected by federal laws (e.g., homosexuals).

END-OF-CHAPTER INTERNET EXERCISES AND CASE QUESTIONS

Working the Web Internet Exercises

ACTIVITIES

1. Review the case *Gupta v. Florida Bd. of Regents* (5/17/2000, No. 98-5392) via the Cornell Discrimination Web site at **www.law.cornell.edu/topics/employment_discrimination.html**. According to the 11th Circuit Court of Appeals, is it considered sexual harassment to make comments to coworkers such as "You are looking very beautiful?"

2. Review Congress' statement of purpose in the ADEA. Has this law served to accomplish that purpose? See U.S. Equal Employment Opportunity Commission Home Page at **www.eeoc.gov/** and "Law About . . . Employment Discrimination" **www.law.cornell.edu/topics/employment_discrimination.html**.

3. For a discussion of the courts' definition of *disability* see *Law Review* article, "The Supreme Court's Definition of Disability Under the ADA: A Return to the Dark Ages," at **www.law.ua.edu/lawreview/tucker521.htm**.

4. Find the case *PGA Tour, Inc. v. Martin* involving the ADA and a professional golfer. Do you agree with the court's decision? Try the Cornell Disability site.

CRITICAL LEGAL THINKING CASES

26.1 Equal Pay Act   For years, certain state laws prevented females from working at night, therefore, Corning Glass Works employed male workers for night inspection jobs and female workers for day inspection jobs. Males working the night shift were paid higher wages than were females who worked the day shift. When the law changed and Corning began hiring females for night shift jobs, it instituted a "red circle" wage rate that permitted previously hired male night shift workers to continue to receive higher wages than newly hired night shift workers. Does this violate the Equal Pay Act? [*Corning Glass Works v. Brennan, Secretary of Labor,* 417 U.S. 188, 94 S.Ct. 2223, 41 L.Ed.2d 1 (1974)]

26.2 Race Discrimination   Winnie Teal is an African-American employee of the Department of Income Maintenance of the State of Connecticut. The first step to being promoted to a supervisor position is to attain a passing score on a written test. When the written test was administered, 54 percent of the African-American candidates passed and 68 percent of the white candidates passed. Teal, who failed the examination, filed a disparate impact Title VII action alleging that the test was biased against African-Americans. To reach a nondiscriminatory bottom-line result, the employer promoted 22.9 percent of the African-American candidates who passed the test but only 13.5 percent of the white candidates who passed. Teal was not promoted because she did not pass the test. Is this result a defense to Teal's Title VII action? [*Connecticut v. Teal,* 457 U.S. 440, 102 S.Ct. 2525, 73 L.Ed.2d 130 (1982)]

26.3 Sex Discrimination   The Los Angeles Department of Water and Power maintains a pension plan for its employees that is funded by both employer and employee contributions. The plan pays men and women retirees pensions with the same monthly benefits. However, because statistically women on average live several years longer than men, female employees are required to make monthly contributions to the pension fund that are 14.84 percent higher than the contributions required of male employees. Because employee contributions are withheld from paychecks, a female employee takes home less pay than a male employee earning the same salary. Does this practice violate Title VII? [*City of Los Angeles Department of Water and Power v. Manhart,* 435 U.S. 702, 98 S.Ct. 1370, 55 L.Ed.2d 657 (1978)]

26.4 Hostile Work Environment Shirley Huddleston became the first female sales representative of Roger Dean Chevrolet, Inc. (RDC) in West Palm Beach, Florida. Shortly after she began working at RDC, Philip Geraci, a fellow sales representative, and other male employees began making derogatory comments to and about her, expelled gas in her presence, called her a bitch and a whore, and such. Many of these remarks were made in front of customers. The sales manager of RDC participated in the harassment. On several occasions, Huddleston complained about this conduct to RDC's general manager. Was Title VII violated? [*Huddleston v. Roger Dean Chevrolet, Inc.,* 845 F.2d 900 (11th Cir. 1988)]

26.5 Pregnancy Discrimination Act The Newport News Shipbuilding and Dry Dock Company provides hospitalization and medical-surgical coverage to its employees and dependents of employees. Under the plan, all covered males, including employees and spouses of female employees, were treated alike for purposes of hospitalization coverage. All covered females, including employees or spouses of male employees, were treated alike except for one major exception: Female employees were provided full hospital coverage for pregnancy whereas female spouses of male employees were provided limited hospital coverage for pregnancy. Does this practice violate Title VII? [*Newport News Shipbuilding and Dry Dock Company v. EEOC,* 462 U.S. 669, 103 S.Ct. 2622, 77 L.Ed.2d 89 (1983)]

26.6 National Origin Discrimination The Federal Bureau of Investigation (FBI) engaged in a pattern and practice of discrimination against Hispanic FBI agents. Job assignments and promotions were areas that were especially affected. Bernardo M. Perez, an Hispanic, brought this Title VII action against the FBI. Did the FBI violate Title VII? [*Perez v. Federal Bureau of Investigation,* 714 F.Supp. 1414 (W.D. Texas 1989)]

26.7 Color Discrimination Walker, a clerk typist with the IRS, is a light-skinned African-American. Her supervisor is a dark-skinned African-American. Walker filed an action alleging that she was terminated by her supervisor in violation of Title VII. Does she have a cause of action under Title VII? [*Walker v. Internal Revenue Service,* 713 F.Supp. 403 (N.D.Ga. 1989)]

26.8 Religious Discrimination Trans World Airlines (TWA), an airline, operates a large maintenance and overhaul base for its airplanes at Kansas City, Missouri. Because of its essential role, the stores department at the base must operate 24 hours per day, 365 days per year. The employees at the base are represented by the International Association of Machinists and Aerospace Workers (Union). TWA and the Union entered into a collective bargaining agreement that includes a seniority system for the assignment of jobs and shifts.

Larry Hardison was hired by TWA to work as a clerk in the stores department. Soon after beginning work, Hardison joined the Worldwide Church of God, which does not allow its members to work from sunset on Friday until sunset on Saturday and on certain religious holidays. Hardison, who had the second lowest seniority within the stores department, did not have enough seniority to observe his Sabbath regularly. When Hardison asked for special consideration, TWA offered to allow him to take his Sabbath off if he could switch shifts with another employee-union member. None of the other employees would do so. TWA refused Hardison's request for a four-day workweek because it would have to either hire and train a part-time worker to work on Saturdays or incur the cost of paying overtime to an existing full-time worker on Saturdays. Hardison sued TWA for religious discrimination in violation of Title VII. Did TWA's actions violate Title VII? [*Trans World Airlines v. Hardison,* 432 U.S. 63, 97 S.Ct. 2264, 53 L.Ed.2d 113 (1977)]

26.9 Bona Fide Occupational Qualification At the age of 60, Manuel Fragante emigrated from the Philippines to Hawaii. In response to a newspaper ad, Fragante applied for an entry-level civil service clerk job with the City of Honolulu's Division of Motor Vehicles and Licensing. The job required constant oral communication with the public either at the information counter or on the telephone. Fragante scored the highest of 731 test takers on a written examination that tested word usage, grammar, and spelling. As part of the application process, two civil service employees who were familiar with the demands of the position interviewed Fragante. They testified that his accent made it difficult to understand him. Fragante was not hired for the position, which was filled by another applicant. Fragante sued, alleging national origin discrimination in violation of Title VII. Who wins? [*Fragante v. City and County of Honolulu,* 888 F.2d 591 (9th Cir. 1989)]

26.10 Age Discrimination Walker Boyd Fite was an employee of First Tennessee Production Credit Association for 19 years. He had attained the position of vice president–credit. During the course of his employment he never received an unsatisfactory review. On December 26, 1983, at the age of 57, Fite was hospitalized with a kidney stone. On January 5, 1984, while Fite was recovering at home, an officer of First Tennessee called to inform him that he had been retired as of December 31, 1983. A few days later, Fite received a letter stating that he had been retired because of poor job performance. Fite sued First Tennessee for age discrimination. Who wins? [*Fite v. First Tennessee Production Credit Association,* 861 F.2d 884 (6th Cir. 1989)]

26.11 Disability Discrimination Woolworth Davis, Salvatore D'Elia, and Herbert Sims, Jr., applied for various jobs with the City of Philadelphia. The City of Philadelphia receives federal government assistance. When Davis reported for a medical examination, scars revealed that he had previously injected illegal drugs intravenously. D'Elia, a former narcotics addict, was enrolled in a methadone program. Sims was a former user of morphine and heroin during his two-year tour of duty with the armed forces. Although the three applicants were rehabilitated and otherwise qualified for the position, the City of Philadelphia refused to hire them because of their past drug use. The three applicants sued the City of Philadelphia, alleging a violation of the Rehabilitation Act of 1973. Are the three applicants protected by the Act? [*Davis v. Bucher,* 451 F.Supp. 791 (E.D.Pa. 1978)]

BUSINESS ETHICS CASES

26.12 Business Ethics Dianne Rawlinson, 22 years old, is a college graduate whose major course of study was correctional psychology. After graduation, she applied for a position as a correctional counselor (prison guard) with the Alabama Board of Corrections. Her application was rejected because she failed to meet the minimum 120-pound weight requirement of an Alabama statute that also established a height minimum of 5 feet 2 inches. In addition, the Alabama Board of Corrections adopted Administrative Regulation 204, which established gender criteria for assigning correctional counselors to maximum-security prisons for "contact positions." These are correctional counselor positions that require continual close physical proximity to inmates. Under this rule, Rawlinson did not qualify for contact positions with male prisoners in Alabama maximum-security prisons. Rawlinson brought this class action lawsuit against Dothard, who was the director of the Department of Public Safety of Alabama. Does either the height-weight requirement or the contact position rule consti-

tute a bona fide occupational qualification that justifies the sexual discrimination in this case? Does society owe a duty of social responsibility to protect women from dangerous job positions? Or is this "romantic paternalism"? [*Dothard, Director, Department of Public Safety of Alabama v. Rawlinson*, 433 U.S. 321, 97 S.Ct. 2720, 53 L.Ed.2d 786 (1977)]

26.13 Business Ethics Rita Machakos, a white female, worked for the Civil Rights Division (CRD) of the Department of Justice. During her employment, she was denied promotion to certain paralegal positions. In each instance, the individual selected was an African-American female. Evidence showed that the CRD maintained an institutional and systematic discrimination policy that favored minority employees over white employees. Machakos sued the CRD for race discrimination under Title VII. Who wins? [*Machakos v. Attorney General of the United States*, 859 F.2d 1487 (D.C.Cir. 1988)]

BRIEFING THE CASE WRITING ASSIGNMENT

Read the following case, which has been excerpted from the court's opinion. Review and brief the case.

Robinson v. Jacksonville Shipyards, Inc.
760 F.Supp. 1486 (1991)
United States District Court

Melton, District Judge

Plaintiff Lois Robinson ("Robinson") is a female employee of Jacksonville Shipyards, Inc. ("JSI"). She has been a welder since September 1977. Robinson is one of a very small number of female skilled craftworkers employed by JSI. Between 1977 and the present, Robinson was promoted from third-class welder to second-class welder and from second-class welder to her present position as a first-class welder.

JSI is a Florida corporation that runs several shipyards engaged in the business of ship repair, including the Commercial Yard and the Mayport Yard. As a federal contractor, JSI has affirmative action and non-discrimination obligations. Defendant Arnold McIlwain ("McIlwain") held the office of President of JSI from the time Robinson was hired by the company through the time of the trial of this case.

In addition to a welding department, JSI's other craft departments included shipfitting, sheetmetal, electrical, transportation, shipping, and receiving (including toolroom), carpenter, boilermaker, inside machine, outside machine, rigging, quality assurance, and pipe. Employees in these craft departments may be assigned to work at either the Mayport Yard, situated at the Mayport Naval Station, or the Commercial Yard, situated at the riverfront site in downtown Jacksonville and sometimes referred to as the downtown yard. Robinson's job assignments at JSI have required her to work at both the Commercial Yard and the Mayport yard. Ship repair work is a dangerous profession; JSI acknowledges the need to "provide a working environment that is safe and healthful."

JSI is, in the words of its employees, "a boys club" and "more or less a man's world." Women craftworkers are an extreme rarity. The company's EEO-1

reports from 1980 to 1987 typically show that women form less than five percent of the skilled crafts.

Pictures of nude and partially nude women appear throughout the JSI work place in the form of magazines, plaques on the wall, photographs torn from magazines and affixed to the wall or attached to calendars supplied by advertising tool supply companies ("vendors' advertising calendars"). JSI has never distributed nor tolerated the distribution of a calendar or calendars with pictures of nude or partially nude men. Management employees from the very top down condoned these displays; often they had their own pictures.

Robinson credibly testified to the extensive, pervasive posting of pictures depicting nude women, partially nude women or sexual conduct and to the occurrence of other forms of harassing behavior perpetrated by her male coworkers and supervisors. Her testimony covered the full term of her employment, from 1977 to 1988.

Reported incidents included the following:

(1) pictures in the fab shop area, in January 1985, including one of a woman wearing black tights, the top pulled down to expose her breasts to view, and one of a nude woman in an outdoor setting apparently playing with a piece of cloth between her legs.

(2) a picture of a nude woman left on the toolbox where Robinson returned her tools in the summer of 1986. The photograph depicted a woman's legs spread apart, knees bent up toward her chest, exposing her breasts and genitals. Several men were present and laughed at Robinson when she appeared upset by the picture.

(3) a drawing on a heater control box, approximately one foot square, of a nude woman with fluid coming from her genital area, in 1987, at the Commercial Yard.

(4) a dart board with a drawing of a woman's breast with her nipple as the bull's eye, in 1987 or 1988, at the Commercial Yard.

Robinson also testified about comments of a sexual nature she recalled hearing at JSI from coworkers. In some instances these comments were made while she also was in the presence of the pictures of nude or partially nude women. Among the remarks Robinson recalled are, "Hey pussycat, come here and give me a whiff," "The more you lick it, the harder it gets," "I'd like to get in bed with that," "I'd like to have some of that," "Black women taste like sardines," 'It doesn't hurt women to have sex right after childbirth," etc. Defendants have admitted that pictures of nude or partially nude women have been posted in the shipfitters' trailer at the Mayport Yard during Robinson's employment at JSI.

Based on the foregoing, the Court finds that sexually harassing behavior occurred throughout the JSI working environment with both frequency and intensity over the relevant time period. Robinson did not welcome such behavior.

In April 1987, during the pendency of this lawsuit, JSI adopted a new sexual harassment policy. It was instituted unilaterally, without consulting or bargaining with the union. The official policy statement, signed by Vice-President for Operations Larry Brown, endorses the following policy:

(1) It is illegal and a violation of Jacksonville Shipyards, Inc., Policy for any employee, male or female, to sexually harass another employee by:

a. making unwelcomed sexual advances or request for sexual favors or other verbal or physical conduct of a sexual nature, a condition of an employee's continued employment, or

b. making submission to or rejection of such conduct the basis for employment decisions affecting the employee, or

c. creating an intimidating, hostile, or offensive working environment by such conduct.

(2) Any employee who believes he or she has been the subject of sexual harassment, should report the alleged act immediately to John Stewart Ext. 3716 in our Industrial Relations Department. An investigation of all complaints will be undertaken immediately. Any supervisor, agent or other employee who has been found by the Company to have sexually harassed another employee will be subject to appropriate sanctions, depending on the circumstances, from a warning in his or her file up to and including termination.

The 1987 policy had little or no impact on the sexually hostile work environment at JSI. Employees and supervisors lacked knowledge and training in the scope of those acts that might constitute sexual harassment.

The Court finds that the policies and procedures at JSI for responding to complaints of sexual harassment are inadequate. The company has done an inadequate job of communicating with employees and supervisors regarding the nature and scope of sexually harassing behavior. This failure is compounded by a pattern of unsympathetic response to complaints by employees who perceive that they are victims of harassment. This pattern includes an unwillingness to believe the accusations, an unwillingness to take prompt and stern remedial action against admitted harassers, and an express condonation of behavior that is and encourages sexually harassing conduct (such as the posting of pictures of nude and partially nude women). In some instances, the process of registering a complaint about sexual harassment became a second episode of harassment.

Ordered and Adjudged

That defendant Jacksonville Shipyards, Inc., is hereby enjoined to cease and desist from the maintenance of a work environment that is hostile to women because of their sex and to remedy the hostile work environment through the implementation, forthwith, of the Sexual Harassment Policy, which consists of the "Statement of Policy," "Statement of Prohibited Conduct," "Schedule of Penalties for Misconduct," "Procedures for Making, Investigating and Resolving Sexual Harassment and Retaliation Complaints," and "Procedures and Rules for Education and Training."

Jacksonville Shipyards, Inc. Sexual Harassment Policy Statement of Policy

Title VII of the Civil Rights Act of 1964 prohibits employment discrimination on the basis of race, color, sex, age, or national origin. Sexual harassment is included among the prohibitions.

Sexual harassment, according to the federal Equal Employment Opportunity Commission (EEOC), consists of unwelcome sexual advances, requests for sexual favors or other verbal or physical acts of a sexual or sex-based nature where (1) submission to such conduct is made either explicitly or implicitly a term or condition of an individual's employment; (2) an employment decision is based on an individual's acceptance or rejection of such conduct; or (3) such conduct interferes with an individual's work performance or creates an intimidating, hostile or offensive working environment.

ENDNOTES

1. 42 U.S.C. §§ 2000e et seq. Other portions of the Civil Rights Act of 1964 prohibit discrimination in housing, education, and other facets of life.
2. *Equal Employment Opportunity Commission v. Tortilleria "La Mejor,"* 758 F.Supp. 585 (E.D.Cal 1991).
3. *McDonnell Douglas v. Green,* 411 U.S. 792, 93 S.Ct. 1817 (1973).
4. In some states, the complaint must be filed with the appropriate state agency rather than the EEOC.
5. 42 U.S.C. §§ 2000e(K).
6. *Meritor Savings Bank v. Vinson,* 477 U.S. 57, 106 S.Ct. 2399 (1986).
7. *Harris v. Forklift Systems, Inc.,* 114 S.Ct. 367 (1993).
8. *Omcale v. Sundowner Offshore Services, Incorporated,* 118 S.Ct. 998 (1998).
9. 29 U.S.C. § 206(d).

Domestic and Multinational Business

CHAPTER 27

Entrepreneurship, Franchising, and Licensing

Commerce never really flourishes so much, as when it is delivered from the guardianship of legislators and ministers.

—William Godwin
Enquiry Concerning Political Justice (1798)

Chapter Objectives

After studying this chapter, you should be able to:

1. Describe the role of entrepreneurs in starting and operating businesses.

2. List and describe the forms of conducting domestic business.

3. Describe sole proprietorships, general partnerships, limited partnerships, limited liability partnerships, limited liability companies, and corporations.

4. Describe the taxation of the major forms of conducting business.

5. Describe the use of agents, representatives, and distributors in conducting international business.

6. Explain the growth of Internet companies.

7. Define *franchise* and identify the parties to a franchise arrangement.

8. Explain how a franchisor licenses its trademarks, service marks, and trade secrets to franchisees.

9. Define a *license* and identify the parties to a *license* arrangement.

10. Describe international franchising and licensing.

Chapter Contents

664

An **entrepreneur** is a person who forms and operates a new business. An entrepreneur may start the business by him- or herself or cofound the business with others. Most businesses started by entrepreneurs are small, although some grow into substantial organizations. For example, Bill Gates started Microsoft Corporation, which grew into the giant software and Internet company. Michael Dell started Dell Computers as a mail-order business; it has become a leader in computer sales. Entrepreneurs in this country and around the world create new businesses daily that hire employees, provide new products and services, and make economies of countries grow.

Franchising is an important method for distributing goods and services to the public. Originally pioneered by the automobile and soft drink industries, franchising today is used in many other forms of business. The 700,000-plus franchise outlets in the United States account for over 25 percent of retail sales and about 15 percent of the gross national product (GNP).

Licensing occurs where one party, by a contract called a **licensing agreement** or **license**, grants another party the right to use its name, trademark, or logo in an agreed-upon manner. For example, the Walt Disney Company licenses the use of the design of many of its characters, such as Mickey Mouse, Moulan, and others, to be placed on clothing, shoes, and other merchandise manufactured and sold by other companies.

This chapter discusses the law of entrepreneurship, franchising, and licensing.

entrepreneur

A person who forms and operates a new business either by him- or herself or with others.

It has been uniformly laid down in this Court, as far back as we can remember, that good faith is the basis of all mercantile transactions.

*Buller, J.
Salomons v. Nissen (1788)*

$\mathcal{E}$NTREPRENEURIAL FORMS OF CONDUCTING BUSINESS

Entrepreneurs who want to conduct domestic or international business must decide whether the business should operate as one of the major forms of business organization—sole proprietorship, general partnership, limited partnership, corporation, and limited liability company—or under some other available legal business form (e.g., franchise, joint venture). The selection depends on many factors, including the ease and cost of formation, the capital requirements of the business, the flexibility of management decisions, the extent of personal liability, tax considerations, and the like.

The primary characteristics of the major types of business organizations are briefly outlined in the paragraphs that follow. Each of these forms of business is discussed in more detail in the chapters that follow.

It is the privilege of a trader in a free country, in all matters not contrary to law, to regulate his own mode of carrying it on according to his own discretion and choice.

*B. Alderson
Hilton v. Eckersly (1855)*

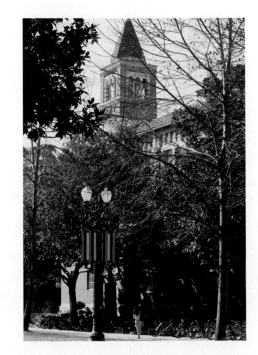

Entrepreneurs Many of today's students will become tomorrow's entrepreneurs.

Entrepreneur and the Law

LAWYERS FOR INTERNET ENTREPRENEURS

Entrepreneurs have been leaders in developing start-up companies that currently dominate the area of e-commerce and the Internet. Entrepreneur Bill Gates created Microsoft Corporation and is now the richest person in the world. The entrepreneurs who started Netscape, Yahoo, AOL, Amazon.com, and eBay are now multimillionaires. Many new entrepreneurs are hatching the successful Internet and e-commerce businesses of the future in their dorm rooms, juice bars, and chat rooms on the Net. These Internet and e-commerce entrepreneurs are a new breed who think big, move fast, and are willing to take risks.

These new cyberspace entrepreneurs need a new type of lawyer who understands their mindset. These lawyers practice "entrepreneur law" in that they must be able to give competent legal and business advice on a moment's notice. Although having to be careful to protect the interests of their clients, and to give correct legal advice, entrepreneurial lawyers must recognize that e-commerce and Internet businesses must sometimes act faster than traditional businesses.

In such cases, the client may be willing to skip some of the minute details that lawyers would insist on for traditional clients. These "techie-owners" often find "Wall Street" lawyers too slow, too expensive, and too risk adverse. The new entrepreneur lawyer is more to their liking.

There is a growing need for lawyers who know e-commerce and Internet law, have specialized skills in handling transactional law, and know small client management. At the start, entrepreneur lawyers need strong skills in finance law, e-commerce contract law, selecting and drafting business entity formation documents, preparing transactional documents of shipping, drawing licensing agreements, drafting shareholder agreements, drafting employment agreements, and protecting trademarks, service marks, and trade secrets. Eventually, the lawyer would be looking at handling the Internet company's initial public offering (IPO) and debt financing. It is hoped that after the Internet company is successful, it will not trade in its entrepreneur lawyer for the "traditional" lawyer.

Sole Proprietorship

sole proprietorship
A noncorporate business that is owned by one person.

A **sole proprietorship** is a noncorporate business that is owned by one person. That person is called a *sole proprietor*. No formalities need be followed to create a sole proprietorship. A sole proprietorship is not a separate taxpaying entity for federal income tax purposes, and a sole proprietor need not even file an informational return with the Internal Revenue Service (IRS). Income and losses are reported on his or her personal income tax return. The sole proprietor is personally liable for the debts and obligations of the business.

General Partnership

general partnership
A voluntary association of two or more persons for the carrying on of a business as co-owners for profit.

A **general partnership** (also called an **ordinary partnership** or **partnership**) is a voluntary association of two or more persons for the carrying on of a business as co-owners for profit. Partners of a general partnership are called either *general partners* or *partners*. No formalities need to be followed to create a general partnership. A general partnership is not a separate taxpaying entity for federal tax purposes. The partnership's income and losses "flow through" to the personal income tax returns of the partners. A general partnership must file an informational return with the IRS. Partners are personally liable for the debts and obligations of the partnership.

Limited Partnership

limited partnership
A special form of partnership that has both limited and general partners.

A **limited partnership** is a special form of partnership that has both limited and general partners. The *limited partners* contribute capital to the business in return for a share of its profits (and losses). They are only liable for the debts and obligations of the limited partnership to the extent of their capital contributions; that is, they are not personally liable beyond their capital contribution. The *general partners* have unlimited personal liability for the debts and obligations of the limited partnership. Every limited partnership must have at least one general partner.

It is when merchants dispute about their own rules that they invoke the law.

Brett, J.
Robinson v. Mollen (1875)

Limited partnerships are created according to statutory requirements. They are not separate taxpaying entities for federal income tax purposes. Although they must file an informational return with the IRS, the income and losses from the limited partnership are reported on the personal income tax returns of the partners.

Limited Liability Partnership (LLP)

Many states have recently enacted legislation that permits the formation of a **limited liability partnership (LLP)**. In an LLP, there does not have to be a general partner. Instead, all partners are limited partners who are not personally liable for the obligations of the partnership. The limited partners may participate in management, however. An LLP is taxed as a partnership. Most LLPs are formed by professionals, such as accountants and lawyers.

limited liability partnership (LLP)

A type of partnership that has only limited partners.

Limited Liability Company (LLC)

In recent years, a majority of states have authorized a form of business called a **limited liability company (LLC)**. An LLC may be formed by two or more persons according to statutory requirements. This form of business combines the most favorable attributes of both partnerships and corporations. Owners of an LLC (called *members*) are not personally liable for the obligations of the LLC. Yet, an LLC is taxed as a partnership.

limited liability company (LLC)

A hybrid form of business that has the attributes of both partnerships and corporations.

Corporation

A **corporation** is a fictitious legal entity that (1) is created according to statutory requirements and (2) is a separate taxpaying entity for federal income tax purposes. The corporation must file a federal income tax return with the IRS and pay the amount of taxes owed on corporate income. Any dividends paid by the corporation are personally taxable to the shareholders. That is why corporations are said to be subject to *double taxation*—once at the corporate level and again at the shareholder level.

Corporations are owned by *shareholders*, whose ownership interests are evidenced by *stock certificates*. Generally, shareholders are not personally liable for the debts and obligations of the corporation except to the extent of their capital contributions. Therefore, shareholders are said to have *limited liability*.

There are several types of for-profit corporations. They range from **close corporations**, owned by one or a few shareholders, to large **public corporations**, which have thousands of shareholders and whose securities are traded on national stock exchanges, to *professional corporations*, formed by lawyers, doctors, and such.

Certain small corporations can elect to be *S Corporations*, which are corporations that are taxed as partnerships. Corporations that do not or cannot elect to be S Corporations are *C Corporations*, which must pay federal income taxes at the corporate level. If dividends are paid to shareholders, they must report these on their individual income tax returns.

Nonprofit corporations can be formed to operate charitable institutions, colleges, and universities.

corporation

A fictitious legal entity that (1) is created according to statutory requirements and (2) is a separate taxpaying entity for federal income tax purposes.

close corporation

A corporation owned by one or a few shareholders.

public corporation

A corporation that has many shareholders and whose securities are traded on national stock exchanges.

*C*ONCEPT SUMMARY — FEDERAL INCOME TAX LIABILITY OF BUSINESS ORGANIZATIONS

Type of Business	Taxpaying Entity	Federal Income Tax Form to Be Filed
Sole proprietorship	No	No separate form. Income and expenses of the business reported on the sole proprietor's individual income tax return.
General partnership	No	Informational form must be filed by the partnership. Each partner's share of the income or loss from the partnership reported on his or her individual income tax return.
Limited partnership	No	Informational form must be filed by the partnership. Each partner's share of the income or loss from the partnership reported on his or her individual income tax return.
Limited liability partnership (LLP)	No	Informational return must be filed by the limited liability partnership. Each partner's share of the income or loss from the partnership is reported on his or her individual income tax return.

Type of Business	Taxpaying Entity	Federal Income Tax Form to Be Filed
Limited liability company (LLC)	No	Taxed as a partnership (unless members elect to be taxed as a corporation). If taxed as a partnership, an informational form must be filed by the limited liability company and each member's share of the income or loss from the company is reported on his or her individual income tax return.
S Corporation	No	An S Corporation must file an informational form. Each shareholder's share of the income or loss from the corporation is reported on his or her individual income tax return.
C Corporation	Yes	A C Corporation must file a separate corporate return and pay the tax owed on corporate income. If the corporation pays dividends, the shareholders must report the dividend income on their separate returns and pay tax on the dividends received.

Entrepreneur and the Law

THE ENTREPRENEURIAL SPIRIT: THE CREATION OF AMAZON.COM

In 1994, Jeff Bezos, the son of a Cuban immigrant to the United States, had made it big. After graduating from Princeton University, he had gone on to Wall Street where he worked for a hedge fund. But Bezos saw an even greater opportunity: online commerce. So he quit his job, jumped in the car with his wife, MacKenzie, and headed west. While she drove, he typed on his laptop computer. Bezos drew up a list of 20 products that he figured he could sell online but then narrowed it to two—books and music. Bezos settled on books for two reasons. First, there are more to sell (about 1.3 million books in print versus 300,000 music titles). Second, the Goliaths of publishing seemed less imposing than the six record companies that dominated music; there were thousands of bookstores, the largest being Barnes & Noble with 12 percent of the industry's $25 billion annual sales.

After checking out Colorado and Oregon, Bezos and his wife settled in Seattle, Washington. They rented a house, hired four employees, and started Amazon.com out of their garage. Bezos and his family incorporated the business, sold some stock to friends and other investors, and kept the rest of the stock for themselves. Bezos took a traditional business—bookselling—online. He reasoned that books were fungible—everyone sold the same product—and that a portion of a traditional bookseller's cost represented the real estate on which the store sat. So Bezos lined up a distribution center in Oregon and began taking orders in cyberspace. Amazon.com sold its first book in July 1995.

Amazon.com became a success, at least at selling books. However, it was not a success at making a profit, losing money for years. But Bezos's business plan called for building a client base and making "Amazon.com" a readily recognized e-commerce name. He accomplished these goals, attracting a client base of over 10 million loyal book-buying

customers and getting the Amazon.com brand name to be recognized by over one-quarter of Americans. Like most start-ups, Amazon.com needed more seed money. Undeterred by the company's unprofitability, the venture capitalist firm Kleiner Perkins Caufield & Byer put up $10 million for preferred stock, which represented a 15 percent stake in Amazon.com

Following on the heels of its book-selling success, Amazon.com began selling other products over the Internet, including CDs, videos, gifts, greeting cards, and thousands of other items. Amazon.com entered the world of online auctions; linked with other companies selling pet supplies, drugstore goods, and more; and agreed to pay fees of 4 to 8 percent to other Web site owners who linked a purchaser to Amazon.com. Purchasers pay Amazon.com by credit card, submitted over the telephone or the Web, and the transaction is guarded by encryption. Amazon.com offers one-click ordering, which lets buyers store credit cards and addresses after their first purchase.

After several years of operation and quick growth, Amazon.com needed more money to reach its goals. In May 1997, Amazon.com went public, raising over $40 million by selling stock for $18 per share. The price of Amazon.com doubled on the first day of trading and reached $200 per share over the next year before retreating. Bezos became a billionaire before the age of 34. Bezos and his family own about 40 percent of Amazon.com. In the span of less than five years, Bezos had taken his business plan and created the largest, most recognized e-commerce company in the world. This entrepreneur's dream became reality. But when asked if he fears Barnes & Noble's entry into online bookselling, Bezos replied that he feared "two guys or girls in a garage" more because they represented the most dangerous of competitors—entrepreneurs.

International Law

CONDUCTING INTERNATIONAL BUSINESS USING AGENTS, REPRESENTATIVES, AND DISTRIBUTORS

A corporation organized in one country may wish to conduct business in other countries. To do so, it has a variety of choices available to it depending on the extent of involvement and market penetration desired, the amount of capital to be invested, the legal and cultural restrictions of the foreign country, and so on. Several major forms of conducting business in a foreign country are by direct selling or by using sales agents, representatives, or distributors.

DIRECT EXPORT AND IMPORT SALES

The simplest form of conducting international business is to engage in *direct export* or *import* sale. For example, if Haliburton Corporation wishes to sell equipment overseas, it can merely enter into a contract with a company in a foreign country that wishes to buy the equipment. Haliburton Corporation is the *exporter* and the firm in the foreign country is the *importer*. If a U.S. company buys goods from a firm in a foreign country, the roles are reversed. The main benefits of conducting international business this way are that (1) it is inexpensive and (2) it usually involves just entering into contracts.

SALES AGENTS, REPRESENTATIVES, AND DISTRIBUTORSHIPS

Companies wishing to do business in a foreign country often appoint a local agent or representative to represent them in that country. A *sales representative* may solicit and take orders for his or her foreign employer but does not have the authority to bind the company contractually. A *sales agent*, on the other hand, may enter into contracts on his or her foreign employer's behalf. The scope of a sales agent's or representative's authority should be explicitly stated in the employment agreement. Sales agents and representatives do not take title to the goods. They are usually paid commissions for business that they generate.

Another commonly used form for engaging in international sales is through a *foreign distributor*. Often, the distributor is a local firm that is separate and independent from the exporter. Distributors are usually given an exclusive territory (e.g., a country or portion of a country). A distributor takes title to the goods and makes a profit on the resale of the goods in the foreign country. A foreign distributor generally is used when a company wants a greater presence in a foreign market than is possible through a sales agent or representative.

Franchise

Franchising is one of the most important forms of business operation in the United States today. Many fast-food restaurants, gasoline stations, hotels and motels, copy centers, real estate brokerage offices, and so on are operated as franchises. In a **franchise**, the owner of a trademark, a trade secret, a patent, or a product (the *franchisor*) licenses another party (the *franchisee*) to sell products or services under the franchisor's name. The franchisee pays a fee to the franchisor (often a royalty) in exchange for such services as design, marketing, and advertising. The franchisor and franchisee are separate legal entities.

franchise

The owner of a trademark, a trade secret, a patent, or a product licenses another party to sell products or services under the franchisor's name.

Joint Venture

A **joint venture** is a voluntary association of two or more parties (natural persons, partnerships, corporations, or other legal entities) to conduct a *single* or *isolated project* with a limited duration. The parties to a joint venture are called *joint adventures*. In most respects (including federal income tax purposes, personal liability for the venture's debts and obligations, right to an accounting, and such), joint ventures are governed by partnership law. They are called *joint venture partnerships*.

joint venture

A voluntary association of two or more parties (natural persons, partnerships, corporations, or other legal entities) to conduct a single or isolated project with a limited duration.

Consider This Example   Suppose that Urban Realty, Inc., and Tri-County Development, Inc., own adjacent pieces of real property. Although the individual properties are too small for the development of a shopping center, together they are well suited for that purpose. Assume that Urban Realty and Tri-County enter into an agreement to sell their properties jointly to the highest bidder and to divide the proceeds in proportion to the size of their properties. Their agreement is a joint venture because their association will end when the properties are sold.

Joint Venture Corporation   Corporation law applies if the joint venture is a corporation. For example, suppose two oil companies form a corporation called Antarctica Drilling, Inc., whose sole purpose is to drill for oil in Antarctica. Suppose both oil companies are shareholders in the new corporation. A *joint venture corporation* has been formed.

Syndicate

syndicate

A group of individuals who join together to finance a project or transaction.

A group of individuals who join together to finance a project or transaction is called a **syndicate** (or an **investment group**). For example, syndicates are often formed to finance real estate developments, to sell new issues of securities, and so on. A syndicate in a non-corporate form is treated as a joint venture. A syndicate in a corporate form is treated as a joint venture corporation.

Business Trust

trust

Established when a person (trustor) transfers title to property to another person (trustee) to be managed for the benefit of specifically named persons (beneficiaries).

Business Brief

Business trusts are often referred to as *Massachusetts Trusts* because they were first used in that state.

A **trust** is established when a person (*trustor*) transfers title to property to another person (*trustee*) to be managed for the benefit of specifically named persons (*beneficiaries*). The trustee is under a duty to manage and invest trust funds and property and to distribute profits to the beneficiaries. Trusts are commonly used to transfer property from one generation to another generation to avoid certain inheritance and other taxes.

In a business context, trusts are sometimes used to conduct commercial enterprises. *Business trusts* resemble a corporation in the following ways: (1) The beneficiaries are not personally liable for the debts and obligations of the trust, and (2) the death or bankruptcy of a beneficiary does not terminate the trust. The trustee's personal liability extends to the contracts of the trust (unless the contracting party agrees to look to the trust estate for satisfaction) and to any torts committed by him- or herself or his or her employees while acting on behalf of the trust. Businesses that pool their assets in a trust are issued *trust certificates*.

Cooperative

cooperative

A voluntary joining together of businesses that provides services to its members.

Businesses often voluntarily join together to create a **cooperative** that provides services to its members. For example, farmers may form a cooperative to provide grain storage facilities, sellers may form a cooperative to market their goods jointly, and consumers may form a cooperative to obtain price advantages from volume purchasing. The profits of a cooperative are distributed to the members on an agreed-upon basis. Unincorporated cooperatives are subject to partnership law, and incorporated cooperatives are subject to corporation law.

Entrepreneur and the Law

VA LINUX IPO SOARS AND SOURS

The exponential growth of the use of computers, the Internet, and the World Wide Web has changed the way people live and businesses work. The Information Age has also created tremendous opportunities for inventors and entrepreneurs to reap the rewards of their intellectual property and informational rights and for investors who believe in them to prosper as well. Take the case of VA Linux, for example.

In 1994, VA Linux began to build computers around the Linux operating system, a free operating system for computers that was designed to compete with Microsoft's dominant operating system. VA Linux was started by engineers and others associated with Stanford University. VA Linux sells what are essentially generic personal computers to compete with the ones sold by PC titan Dell Computer and others that are based on the Microsoft operating system. In 1999, Microsoft had a monopoly of 90 percent of the market for operating systems, with the Linux system and others controlling the rest of the market.

In December 1999, VA Linux decided to "go public" by issuing shares of stock to the public in an **initial public offering (IPO)**. By the time VA Linux decided to go public, many investors were betting that the Linux operating system was a serious contender to Microsoft and that companies building their future around this system were good investments. But no one quite knew how deep this commitment was until December 9, 1999, when VA Linux went public at the initial offering price of $30 per share. By the time the dust settled on its opening day, investors had bid VA Linux to $239 per share, over a 700 percent jump in price for the day. The stock of the president of VA Linux, Larry M. Augustine, was worth over $1.5 billion by the end of the day, and VA Linux's total capitalization reached about $10 billion.

The success of VA Linux follows on the heels of many Internet and Web stocks that had issued IPOs earlier, including Yahoo!, Amazon.com, and Red Hat.

But like many dot-com companies, the success of VA Linux was short lived. In the early 2000s, the stock prices of many tech companies, including VA Linux, soured and fell dramatically. VA Linux survived—unlike some other tech and dot-com companies that went bankrupt.

International Law

CONDUCTING INTERNATIONAL BUSINESS THROUGH A BRANCH OFFICE OR A SUBSIDIARY CORPORATION

A corporation that wants to conduct business in a foreign country has the choice of conducting the business through a branch office or a subsidiary corporation. There are different costs, efficiencies, rules, and liability exposure associated with each of these forms of conducting international business.

BRANCH OFFICE

A company can enter a foreign market by establishing a **branch** in the foreign country. Branches are often used where a corporation wants to enter a foreign market in a substantial way but wants to retain exclusive control over the operation. For example, an American manufacturing company can establish a presence in a foreign country by building a plant there. A branch is not a separate corporation or legal entity (see Exhibit 27.1). It is merely an extension of the corporate owner and is wholly owned by the home corporation.

There are detriments to this form of operation. For instance, it is expensive (because the owner must build or lease plant or office premises), and it exposes the owner to tort and contract liability in the foreign country and to foreign laws.

SUBSIDIARY CORPORATION

A business can enter a foreign market by establishing a separate corporation to conduct business in a foreign country. Such a corporation, which is called a **subsidiary**, must be formed pursuant to the laws of the country in which it is to be located. The **parent corporation** usually owns all or a majority of the subsidiary corporation. The parent corporation and the subsidiary corporation are separate legal entities that are individually capitalized (see Exhibit 27.2).

A foreign subsidiary is usually used where the parent corporation wants to establish a substantial presence in a foreign country. The benefit of using a subsidiary corporation over a branch is that it isolates the parent corporation from the tort and contract liability of the subsidiary corporation (and vice versa), unless the foreign country's laws provide otherwise. On the other hand, establishing and operating a subsidiary corporation in a foreign country is often expensive and complicated. Also, it exposes the subsidiary corporation to the laws of the foreign country.

Consider These Examples Ford Motor Company, Inc., a U.S. corporation organized in the state of Delaware, opens a branch office in India to sell its automobiles there. If an employee at the branch office in India negligently injures an Indian citizen in India while on a test drive, Ford Motor Company, Inc., in the United States is wholly liable for the injured person's damages. Suppose instead that Ford Motor Company, Inc., forms a subsidiary corporation called Ford.India Corporation in India pursuant to Indian law. Ford Motor Company, Inc., is the parent corporation and shareholder of Ford.India Corporation; Ford.India Corporation is the subsidiary corporation. If an employee of Ford.India Corporation negligently injures an Indian citizen in India while on a test drive, only Ford.India Corporation is liable; Ford Motor Company, Inc., in the United States is not liable other than it may lose its capital contribution in Ford.India Corporation if the judgment is large.

Exhibit 27.1 Conducting International Business Using a Branch Office

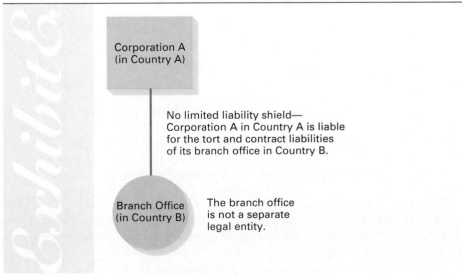

𝓔XHIBIT 27.2 *Conducting International Business Using a Subsidiary Corporation*

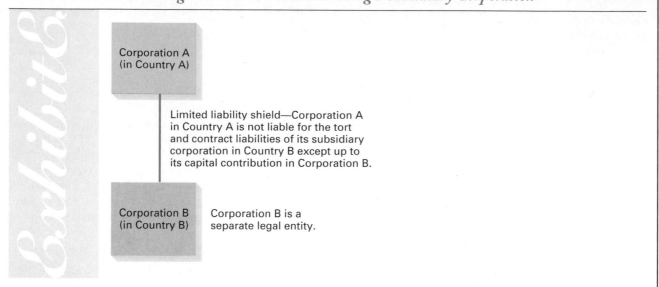

Corporation A
(in Country A)

Limited liability shield—Corporation A
in Country A is not liable for the tort
and contract liabilities of its subsidiary
corporation in Country B except up to
its capital contribution in Corporation B.

Corporation B
(in Country B)

Corporation B is a
separate legal entity.

***Restaurant, Sault Ste. Marie,
Michigan*** *Entrepreneurs have
many choices of legal forms for
conducting their businesses, such as
this restaurant.*

𝓕RANCHISES

franchise

Established when one party licenses
another party to use the franchisor's
trade name, trademarks, commercial
symbols, patents, copyrights, and other
property in the distribution and selling
of goods and services.

A **franchise** is established when one party (the **franchisor** or **licensor**) licenses another
party (the *franchisee* or *licensee*) to use the franchisor's trade name, trademarks, commercial
symbols, patents, copyrights, and other property in the distribution and selling of goods
and services. Generally, the franchisor and the franchisee are established as separate corporations. The term *franchise* refers to both the agreement between the parties and the franchise outlet.

There are several advantages to franchising, including (1) the franchisor can reach lucrative new markets, (2) the franchisee has access to the franchisor's knowledge and resources
while running an independent business, and (3) consumers are assured of uniform product
quality.

A typical franchise arrangement is illustrated in Exhibit 27.3.

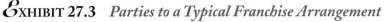

ℰXHIBIT 27.3 *Parties to a Typical Franchise Arrangement*

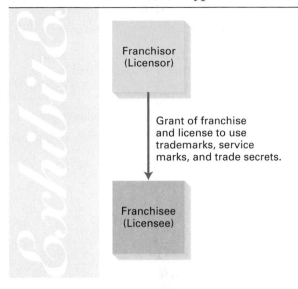

Franchisor
(Licensor)

Grant of franchise
and license to use
trademarks, service
marks, and trade secrets.

Franchisee
(Licensee)

Types of Franchises

There are four basic forms of franchises. They are discussed in the paragraphs that follow.

Distributorship Franchises The franchisor manufactures a product and licenses a retail dealer to distribute the product to the public. For example, the Ford Motor Company manufacturers automobiles and franchises independently owned automobile dealers (franchisees) to sell them to the public.

distributorship franchise

The franchisor manufactures a product and licenses a retail franchisee to distribute the product to the public.

Processing Plant Franchise The franchisor provides a secret formula or the like to the franchisee. The franchisee then manufactures the product at its own location and distributes it to retail dealers. For example, the Coca-Cola Corporation, which owns the secret formulas for making Coca-Cola and other soft drinks, licenses regional bottling companies to manufacture and distribute soft drinks under the "Coca-Cola" and other brand names.

processing plant franchise

The franchisor provides a secret formula or process to the franchisee, and the franchisee manufactures the product and distributes it to retail dealers.

Chain-Style Franchises The franchisor licenses the franchisee to make and sell its products or services to the public from a retail outlet serving an exclusive geographical territory. Most fast-food franchises use this form. For example, the Pizza Hut Corporation franchises independently owned restaurant franchises to make and sell pizzas to the public under the "Pizza Hut" name.

chain-style franchise

The franchisor licenses the franchisee to make and sell its products or distribute services to the public from a retail outlet serving an exclusive territory.

International Law

STARBUCKS INVADES TAIWAN

Starbucks Coffee has been a tremendous success in the Untied States. Beginning with a single outlet in Seattle, Washington, the company has expanded Starbucks Coffee shops across the country. Now even some of the smaller cities in America have a Starbucks Coffee shop. The company expanded in the United States through company-owned

stores; that is, Starbucks has not granted franchises in the United States. When Starbucks wanted to enter overseas markets, however, it realized it could not expand solely through company-owned outlets. This was because (1) government restrictions in some countries prohibit 100 percent ownership of a business by a foreign investor and (2) the company lacked the business expertise and cultural knowledge necessary to enter many foreign markets. To enter foreign markets, Starbucks turned to franchising.

Consider Starbuck's entry into Taiwan, for example. Taiwan is an Asian island with over 20 million people. It has a very successful business climate, and its per capita income is one of the highest in Asia. So the market seemed ripe for entry by Starbucks. After substantial research and investigation, Starbucks decided it would grant an **area franchise** to a local Taiwanese company to develop Starbucks outlets in Taiwan. In an area franchise, the franchisor grants the franchisee a franchise for an agreed-upon geographical area. In this case, Starbucks granted the Taiwanese company an area

franchise for Taiwan. The Taiwanese company could then determine where to locate Starbucks outlets in Taiwan. The Taiwanese company paid Starbucks several million dollars for the area franchise.

Oftentimes, an area franchisee is granted the authority to negotiate and sell franchises in the designated area on behalf of the franchisor. In this arrangement, the franchisee is also called the subfranchisor (see Exhibit 27.4).

Franchising and the use of area franchises allow major U.S. companies, and companies around the world, to enter foreign markets more easily, efficiently, and economically than expanding to many foreign countries through company-owned outlets.

*E*XHIBIT 27.4   *Example of an Area Franchise*

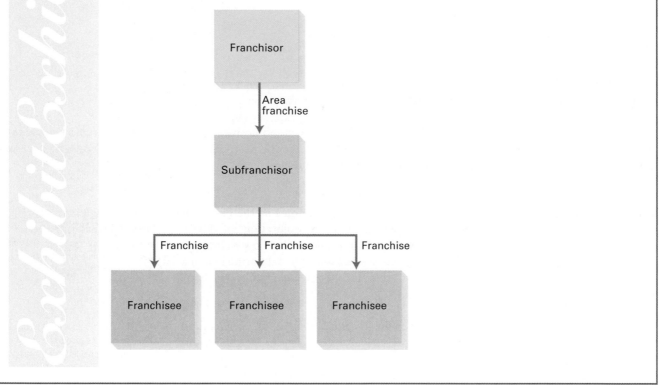

Disclosure Protection

In the past, certain franchisors made material misrepresentations and omissions of facts to potential franchisees concerning the financial future of their franchises. Since then, the **Federal Trade Commission (FTC)** and many states have enacted laws that promote full disclosure to prospective franchisees.

Federal Trade Commission (FTC)

Federal government agency empowered to enforce federal franchising rules.

Uniform Franchise Offering Circular (UFOC)

A uniform disclosure document that requires the franchisor to make specific presale disclosures to prospective franchisees.

State Disclosure Laws   Prior to the 1970s, franchising was not highly regulated by either state or federal governments. In 1971, California enacted its *Franchise Investment Law,*[1] which requires franchisors to register and deliver disclosure documents to prospective franchisees. Since then, many other states have enacted franchise disclosure statutes. For a while, franchisors struggled to comply with the various state statutes. Finally, in the mid-1970s, the state franchise administrators developed a uniform disclosure document called the **Uniform Franchise Offering Circular (UFOC)**.

The UFOC and state laws require the franchisor to make specific presale disclosures to prospective franchisees. Information that must be disclosed includes a description of the franchisor's business, balance sheets and income statements of the franchisor for the preceding three years, material terms of the franchise agreement, any restrictions on the franchisee's territory, grounds for termination of the franchise, and other relevant information.

FTC's Franchise Rule   In 1979, the **FTC franchise rule** became law. The FTC rule requires franchisors to make full presale disclosure nationwide to prospective franchisees.[2] The FTC does not require the registration of the disclosure document prior to its use. The UFOC satisfies both state regulations and the FTC. If a franchisor violates FTC disclosure rules, the wrongdoer is subject to an injunction against further franchise sales, civil fines of up to $10,000 per violation, and an FTC civil action on behalf of injured franchisees to recover damages from the franchisor that were caused by the violation.

> **FTC franchise rule**
>
> A rule set out by the FTC that requires franchisors to make full presale disclosures to prospective franchisees.

Entrepreneur and the Law

REQUIRED DISCLOSURES BY FRANCHISORS TO PROSPECTIVE FRANCISEES

Many potential franchisees are entrepreneurs who want to own and operate their own business. Franchisors, on the other hand, are looking for potential franchisees to whom to sell their franchises. In the past, there has been some fraud by franchisors and failure to disclose important information to prospective franchisees. To remedy this situation, the Federal Trade Commission (FTC) has adopted the following rules.

First, if a franchisor makes sales or earnings projections for a potential franchise location that is based on the actual sales, income, or profit figures of an existing franchise, the franchisor must disclose the following:

- The number and percentage of its actual franchises that have obtained such results; and
- A cautionary statement in at least 12-point boldface type that reads, **"Caution: Some outlets have sold (or earned) this amount. There is no assurance you'll do as well. If you rely upon our figures, you must accept the risk of not doing so well."**

Second, if a franchisor makes sales or earnings projections based on hypothetical examples, the franchisor must disclose the following:

- The assumptions underlying the estimates;
- The number and percentage of actual franchises that have obtained such results; and

- A cautionary statement in at least 12-point boldface print that reads, **"Caution: These figures are only estimates of what we think you may earn. There is no assurance you'll do as well. If you rely upon our figures, you must accept the risk of not doing so well."**

Third, the FTC requires that the following statement appear in at least 12-point boldface type on the cover of a franchisor's required disclosure statement to prospective franchisees:

To protect you, we've required your franchisor to give you this information.

We haven't checked it, and don't know if it's correct. It should help you make up your mind. Study it carefully. While it includes some information about your contract, don't rely on it alone to understand your contract. Read all of your contract carefully. Buying a franchise is a complicated investment. Take your time to decide. If possible, show your contract and this information to an adviser, like a lawyer or an accountant. If you find anything you think may be wrong or anything important that's been left out, you should let us know about it. It may be against the law. There may also be laws on franchising in your state. Ask your state agencies about them.

The FTC hopes that the required disclosures by franchisors will protect prospective entrepreneur-franchisees from fraud and from acting on insufficient information.

THE FRANCHISE AGREEMENT

A prospective franchisee must apply to the franchisor for a franchise. The application often includes detailed information about the applicant's previous employment, financial and educational history, credit status, and so on. If an applicant is approved, the parties enter into a **franchise agreement** that sets forth the terms and conditions of the franchise. Although some states permit oral franchise agreements, most have enacted a Statute of

> **franchise agreement**
>
> An agreement that the franchisor and the franchisee enter into that sets forth the terms and conditions of the franchise.

Frauds that requires franchise agreements to be in writing. To prevent unjust enrichment, the courts will occasionally enforce oral franchise agreements that violate the Statute of Frauds.

Common Terms of a Franchise Agreement

Franchise agreements do not usually have much room for negotiation. Generally, the agreement is a standard form contract prepared by the franchisor. Franchise agreements cover the following topics:

1. **Quality Control Standards**   The franchisor's most important assets are its name and reputation. The quality control standards set out in the franchise agreement—such as the franchisor's right to make periodic inspections of the franchisee's premises and operations—are intended to protect these assets. Failure to meet the proper standards can result in loss of the franchise.
2. **Training Requirements**   Franchisees and their personnel usually are required to attend training programs either on-site or at the franchisor's training facilities.
3. **Covenant Not to Compete**   Covenants not to compete prohibit franchisees from competing with the franchisor during a specific time and in a specified area after the termination of the franchise. Unreasonable (overextensive) covenants not to compete are void.
4. **Arbitration Clause**   Most franchise agreements contain an arbitration clause that provides that any claim or controversy arising from the franchise agreement or an alleged breach thereof is subject to arbitration. The U.S. Supreme Court has held such clauses to be enforceable.[3]
5. **Other Terms and Conditions**   Capital requirements: restrictions on the use of the franchisor's trade name, trademarks, and logo; standards of operation; duration of the franchise; record keeping requirements; sign requirements; hours of operation; prohibition as to the sale or assignment of the franchise; conditions for the termination of the franchise; and other specific terms pertinent to the operation of the franchise and the protection of the parties' rights are included in the agreement.

Japan   The major growth in franchising opportunities for U.S. franchisors, such as McDonald's, is in international markets.

Franchise Fees

Franchise fees payable by the franchisee are usually stipulated in the franchise agreement. The franchisor may require the franchisee to pay any or all of the following fees:

1. **Initial License Fee**   A lump-sum payment for the privilege of being granted a franchise.
2. **Royalty Fee**   A fee for the continued use of the franchisor's trade name, property, and assistance that is often computed as a percentage of the franchisee's gross sales.
3. **Assessment Fee**   A fee for such things as advertising and promotional campaigns and administrative costs, billed either as a flat monthly or annual fee or as a percentage of gross sales.
4. **Lease Fees**   Payment for any land or equipment leased from the franchisor, billed either as a flat monthly or annual fee or as a percentage of gross sales or other agreed-upon amount.
5. **Cost of Supplies**   Payment for supplies purchased from the franchisor.

Sample provisions from a franchise agreement are set forth in Exhibit 27.5.

*℮*XHIBIT 27.5 *Sample Provisions from a Franchise Agreement*

FRANCHISE AGREEMENT

Agreement, this 2nd day of January, 2000, between ALASKA PANCAKE HOUSE, INC., an Alaska corporation located in Anchorage, Alaska (hereinafter called the Company) and PANCAKE SYRUP COMPANY, INC., a Michigan corporation located in Detroit, Michigan (hereinafter called the Franchisee), for one KLONDIKE PANCAKE HOUSE restaurant to be located in the City of Mackinac Island, Michigan.

RECITALS

A.   The Company is the owner of proprietary and other rights and interests in various service marks, trademarks, and trade names used in its business including the trade name and service mark "KLONDIKE PANCAKE HOUSE."

B.   The Company operates and enfranchises others to operate restaurants under the trade name and service mark "KLONDIKE PANCAKE HOUSE" using certain recipes, formulas, food preparation procedures, business methods, business forms, and business policies it has developed. The Company has also developed a body of knowledge pertaining to the establishment and operation of restaurants. The Franchisee acknowledges that he does not presently know these recipes, formulas, food preparation procedures, business methods, or business policies, nor does the Franchisee have these business forms or access to the Company's body of knowledge.

C.   The Franchisee intends to enter the restaurant business and desires access to the Company's recipes, formulas, food preparation procedures, business methods, business forms, business policies, and body of knowledge pertaining to the operation of a restaurant. In addition, the Franchisee desires access to information pertaining to new developments and techniques in the Company's restaurant business.

D.   The Franchisee desires to participate in the use of the Company's rights in its service marks and trademarks in connection with the operation of one restaurant to be located at a site approved by the Company and the Franchisee.

E.   The Franchisee understands that information received from the Company or from any of its officers, employees, agents, or franchisees is confidential and has been developed with a great deal of effort and expense. The Franchisee acknowledges that the information is being made available to him so that he may more effectively establish and operate a restaurant.

F.   The Company has granted, and will continue to grant others, access to its recipes, formulas, food preparation procedures, business methods, business forms, business policies, and body of knowledge pertaining to the operation of restaurants and information pertaining to new developments and techniques in its business.

G.   The Company has and will continue to license others to use its service marks and trademarks in connection with the operation of restaurants at Company-approved locations.

H.   The Franchise Fee and Royalty constitute the sole consideration to the Company for the use by the Franchisee of its body of knowledge, systems, and trademark rights.

I.   The Franchisee acknowledges that he received the Company's franchise offering prospectus at or prior to the first personal meeting with a Company representative and at least ten (10) business days prior to the signing of this Agreement and that he has been given the opportunity to clarify provisions he did not understand and to consult with an attorney or other professional advisor. Franchisee represents he understands and agrees to be bound by the terms, conditions, and obligations of this Agreement.

J.   The Franchisee acknowledges that he understands that the success of the business to be operated by him under this Agreement depends primarily upon his efforts and that neither the Company nor any of its agents or representatives have made any oral, written, or visual representations or projections of actual or potential sales, earnings, or net or gross profits. Franchisee understands that the restaurant operated under this Agreement may lose money or fail.

AGREEMENT

Acknowledging the above recitals, the parties hereto agree as follows:

1.   Upon execution of this Agreement, the Franchisee shall pay to the Company a Franchise Fee of $30,000 that shall not be refunded in any event.

2.   The Franchisee shall also pay to the Company, weekly, a Royalty equal to eight (8%) percent of the gross sales from each restaurant that he operates throughout the term of this Agreement. "Gross sales" means all sales or revenues derived from the Franchisee's location exclusive of sales taxes.

3.   The Company hereby grants to the Franchisee:

   a.   Access to the Company's recipes, formulas, food preparation procedures, business methods, business forms, business policies, and body of knowledge pertaining to the operation of a restaurant.

   b.   Access to information pertaining to new developments and techniques in the Company's restaurant business.

   c.   License to use of the Company's rights in and to its service marks and trademarks in connection with the operation of one restaurant to be located at a site approved by the Company and the Franchisee.

4.   The Company agrees to:

   a.   Provide a training program for the operator of restaurants using the Company's recipes, formulas, food preparation procedures, business methods, business forms, and business policies. The Franchisee shall pay all transportation, lodging, and other expenses incurred in attending the program. The Franchisee must attend the training program before opening his restaurant.

   b.   Provide a Company Representative that the Franchisee may call upon for consultation concerning the operation of his business.

   c.   Provide the Franchise with a program of assistance that shall include periodic consultations with a Company Representative, publish a periodical advising of new developments and techniques in the Company's restaurant business, and grant access to Company personnel for consultations concerning the operation of his business.

5.   The Franchisee agrees to:

   a.   Begin operation of a restaurant within 365 days. The restaurant will be at a location found by the Franchisee and approved by the Company. The Company or one of its designees will lease the premises and sublet them to the Franchisee at cost. The Franchisee will then construct and equip his unit in accordance with Company specifications contained in the Operating Manual. Upon written request from the Franchisee, the Company will grant a 180-day extension that is effective immediately upon receipt of the request. Under certain circumstances, and at the sole discretion of the Company, the Company may grant additional time in which to open the business. In all instances, the location of each unit must be approved by the Company and the Franchisee. If the restaurant is not operating within 365 days, or within any approved extensions, this Agreement will automatically expire.

   b.   Operate his business in compliance with applicable laws and governmental regulations. The Franchisee will obtain at his expense, and keep in force, any permits, licenses, or other consents required for the leasing, construction, or operation of his business. In addition, the Franchisee shall operate his restaurant in accordance with the Company's Operation Manual, which may be amended from time to time as a result of experience, changes in the law, or changes in the marketplace. The Franchisee shall refrain from conducting any business or selling any products other than those approved by the Company at the approved location.

   c.   Be responsible for all costs of operating his unit, including but not limited to, advertising, taxes, insurance, food products, labor, and utilities. Insurance shall include, but not be limited to, comprehensive liability insurance including products liability coverage in the minimum amount of $1,000,000. The Franchisee shall keep these policies in force for the mutual benefit of the parties. In addition, the Franchisee shall save the Company harm from any claim of any type that arises in connection with the operation of his business.

Business Brief

If the franchise agreement is breached, the aggrieved party can sue the breaching party for rescission of the agreement, restitution, and damages.

Breach of the Franchise Agreement

A lawful franchise agreement is an enforceable contract. Each party owes a duty to adhere to and perform under the terms of the franchise agreement. If the agreement is breached, the aggrieved party can sue the breaching party for rescission of the agreement, restitution, and damages.

Business Ethics

HÄAGEN-DAZS ICE CREAM FRANCHISE MELTS

Franchise agreements are detailed documents that are carefully drafted to spell out the rights and duties of the parties. A franchise must be careful to read and understand the terms of the agreement, as the following case demonstrates.

In the late 1950s, Reuben Mattus developed a "super premium" ice cream and named it " Häagen-Dazs" to give the product a Scandinavian flair. Mattus began selling Häagen-Dazs ice cream in prepackaged pints to small stores and delicatessens in the New York metropolitan area. During the 1970s, sales of the product were expanded into some grocery stores and other retail outlets.

In 1976, Mattus's daughter, Doris Mattus-Hurley, opened the first " Häagen-Dazs Shoppe" in Brooklyn Heights, New York. After this shop prospered, Mattus-Hurley began franchising other shops to independent franchisees throughout the country. Häagen-Dazs ice cream is manufactured, distributed, and franchised through a variety of corporate entities (collectively referred to as Häagen-Dazs). The franchise agreement, which has been the same since 1978, grants a limited license to the franchisee to operate a single shop under the Häagen-Dazs trademark at a specific location for a specified term ranging from 5 to 12 years. The franchise agrees to purchase all its ice cream from the franchisor at prices set by Häagen-Dazs.

In 1983, the Pillsbury Company (Pillsbury), a diversified international food and restaurant company headquartered in Minneapolis, Minnesota, purchased the Häagen-Dazs Company, including its franchise operations. The franchise agreements were assigned to Pillsbury as part of the sale. Pillsbury decided that it could maximize sales of Häagen-Dazs ice cream by expanding sales through methods of distribution that did not involve franchisees. Pillsbury substantially increased sales of Häagen-Dazs products to national grocery store chains, convenience stores like 7-Eleven, and other retail outlets.

This change severely harmed sales at existing franchises. Franchisees located in many states sued Pillsbury, alleging breach of the franchise agreement. Plaintiff's claimed that the defendant breached the franchise agreement by distributing Häagen-Dazs ice cream through nonfranchised outlets that were not "upscale" and by mass distribution of prepackaged pints that competed with franchise outlet sales.

The district court held that the express terms of the franchise agreement had not been violated. The franchise agreement expressly reserved the right of the franchisor to distribute Häagen-Dazs products "through not only Häagen-Dazs Shoppes, but through any other distribution method, which may from time to time be established." The court held that this language gave Pillsbury the right to aggressively distribute prepackaged pints of Häagen-Dazs ice cream through nonfranchise outlets even though that distribution adversely affected retail sales by franchisees. The district court granted Pillsbury's motion for summary judgment. [*Carlock v. Pillsbury Company*, 719 F.Supp. 791 (D.Minn. 1989)]

1. Even though the express terms of the franchise agreement allowed Pillsbury to distribute Häagen-Dazs ice cream through nonfranchise outlets, do you think Pillsbury acted ethically in doing so?
2. Should a covenant of good faith and fair dealing be implied in franchise agreements? Why or why not?

Trademark Law, Trade Secrets, and Franchising

A franchisor's ability to maintain the public's perception of the quality of the goods and services associated with its trade name, **trademarks**, and **service marks** is the essence of its success. The size of the advertising budgets of many franchisors supports this view.

trademarks and service marks

A distinctive mark, symbol, name, word, motto, or device that identifies the goods or services of a particular franchisor.

Trademarks The **Lanham Trademark Act**, which was enacted in 1946, provides for the registration of trademarks and service marks with the federal **Patent and Trademark Office** in Washington, DC. Most franchisors license the use of their trade names, trademarks, and service marks and prohibit their franchisees from misusing these marks.

Anyone who uses a mark without authorization may be sued for *trademark infringement*. The trademark holder can see to recover damages and obtain an injunction prohibiting further unauthorized use of the mark.

Misappropriation of Trade Secrets **Trade secrets** are ideas that make a franchise success-ful but that do not qualify for trademark, patent, or copyright protection. Most state laws protect trade secrets.

The misappropriation of a trade secret is called *unfair competition*. The holder of the trade secret can sue the offending party for damages and obtain an injunction to prohibit further unauthorized use of the trade secret.

Business Ethics

FRANCHISEE'S FRAUDULENT SCOUP CAUGHT

Baskin-Robbins Ice Cream Company (Baskin-Robbins) is a franchisor that has established a system of more than 2,700 franchise ice cream retail stores nationwide. The franchisees agree to purchase ice cream in bulk only from Baskin-Robbins or an authorized Baskin-Robbins source, to sell only Baskin-Robbins ice cream under the "Baskin-Robbins" marks, and to keep specific business hours. Franchisees agree to pay ice cream invoices to Baskin-Robbins when due. If ice cream invoices are not paid within seven days of delivery of the ice cream, payment by certified check is required. If such check is not received, prepayment in cash is then required. If Baskin-Robbins must institute a lawsuit for a breach of the franchise agreement, the franchisee is required to pay all costs incurred by Baskin-Robbins if it is successful in the lawsuit.

In 1978, Baskin-Robbins entered into a standard Franchise Agreement with D&L Ice Cream Company, Inc., (D&L), granting it a franchise to operate a retail ice cream store in Brooklyn, New York. During the course of the franchise, D&L consistently failed to maintain proper business hours and failed to satisfy ice cream invoices when due. Baskin-Robbins properly invoked its right to require payment by certified check. When such payment was not received, Baskin-Robbins required prepayment for ice cream deliveries. D&L then purchased bulk ice cream from other manufacturers and sold it in its store, bearing the Baskin-Robbins trademarks. Upon discovering this fact, Baskin-Robbins sent a notice of termination to D&L. D&L ignored the notice and continued to operate the Baskin-Robbins store and sell other brands of ice cream in cups and containers bearing the Baskin-Robbins trademarks. Baskin-Robbins sued D&L for trademark infringement.

The court stated that the sale by a franchised licensee of unauthorized products—that is, products outside the scope of the license—is likely to confuse the public into believing that such products are in fact manufactured or authorized by the trademark owner, when in fact they are not. The court concluded D&L had engaged in trademark infringement. The court held that Baskin-Robbins was entitled to a permanent injunction, to recover outstanding monies owed by D&L, to all profits made by D&L as a result of the trademark infringement, and to full costs and attorneys' fees incurred in connection with this litigation. [*Baskin-Robbins Ice Cream Co. v. D&L Ice Cream Co., Inc.*, 576 F.Supp. 1055 (E.D.N.Y. 1983)]

1. Did D&L act ethically in this case?
2. Do you think there was trademark infringement in this case?

*C*ONTRACT AND TORT LIABILITY OF FRANCHISORS AND FRANCHISEES

Franchisors and franchisees are liable for their own *contracts*. The same is true of *tort liability*. For example, if a person is injured by a franchisee's negligence, the franchisee is liable.

In the following case, the court held that a franchisor was directly liable to the plaintiffs.

Martin v. McDonald's Corporation

572 N.E.2d 1073 (1991)

Appellate Court of Illinois

CASE 27.1

BACKGROUND AND FACTS

McDonald's Corporation (McDonald's) is a franchisor that licenses franchisees to operate fast-food restaurants and to use McDonald's trademarks and service marks. One such fran-chise, which was located in Oak Forest, Illinois, was owned and operated by McDonald's Restaurants of Illinois, the franchisee.

Recognizing the threat of armed robbery at its franchises, especially in the time period immediately after closing,

McDonald's established an entire corporate division to deal with security problems at franchises. McDonald's prepared a manual for restaurant security operations and required its franchisees to adhere to these procedures.

Jim Carlson was McDonald's regional security manager for the area in which the Oak Forest franchise was located. Carlson visited the Oak Forest franchise on October 31, 1979, to inform the manager of security procedures. He specifically mentioned these rules: (1) No one should throw garbage out the backdoor after dark, and (2) trash and grease were to be taken out the side glass door at least one hour prior to closing. During his inspection, Carlson noted that the locks had to be changed at the restaurant and an alarm system needed to be installed for the backdoor. Carlson never followed up to determine whether these security measures had been taken.

On the evening of November 29, 1979, a six-woman crew, all teenagers, was working to clean up and close the Oak Forest restaurant. Laura Martin, Therese Dudek, and Maureen Kincaid were members of that crew. A person later identified as Peter Logan appeared at the back of the restaurant with a gun. He ordered the crew to open the safe and get him the money and then ordered them into the refrigerator. In the course of moving the crew into the refrigerator, Logan shot and killed Martin, and assaulted Dudek and Kincaid. Dudek and Kincaid suffered severe emotional distress from the assault.

Evidence showed that Logan had entered the restaurant through the backdoor. Trial testimony proved that the work crew used the backdoor exclusively, both before and after dark, and emptied garbage and grease through the backdoor all day and all night. In addition, there was evidence that the latch on the backdoor did not work properly. Evidence also showed that the crew had not been instructed about the use of the backdoor after dark and had never received copies of McDonald's security manual, and that the required warning about not using the backdoor after dark had not been posted at the restaurant.

Martin's parents, Dudek, and Kincaid sued McDonald's to recover damages for negligence. The trial court awarded damages of $1,003,445 to the Martins for the wrongful death of their daughter, and awarded $125,000 each to Dudek and Kincaid. McDonald's appealed.

ISSUE
Is McDonald's liable for negligence?

COURT'S REASONING
The appellate court held that McDonald's had voluntarily assumed a duty to the crew at the Oak Forest franchise by establishing and requiring the franchisee to implement certain security measures and by obligating itself to inspect the restaurant to see that the required security measures were implemented. The court held that McDonald's was liable for its own negligence due to the failure of security measures and the failure of its employee, Carlson, to follow up to determine that the security deficiencies at the Oak Forest franchise had been corrected. The appellate court held that there was ample evidence for the jury to determine that McDonald's had breached its assumed duty to the plaintiffs.

DECISION
The appellate court held that McDonald's was negligent for not following up and making sure that the security deficiencies it had found at the Oak Forest franchise had been corrected. Affirmed.

Case Questions

Critical Legal Thinking   Should businesses be held liable for criminal actions of others? Why or why not?

Business Ethics   Should McDonald's have denied liability in this case?

Contemporary Business   What is the benefit to a franchisor to establish and require its franchisees to adhere to security rules? Is there any potential detriment? Explain.

Independent Contractor Status

Business Brief

If properly organized and operated as a separate business, a franchisee is not the agent of the franchisor, and the franchisor is not liable for the franchisee's contracts or torts.

If properly organized and operated, the franchisor and franchisee are separate legal entities. Therefore, the franchisor deals with the franchisee as an *independent contractor*. Because there is no agency relationship, neither party is liable for the contracts or torts of the other.

In the following case, the court applied the independent contractor rule and held that the franchisor was not liable for the tortious conduct of a franchisee.

Cislaw v. Southland Corp.
4 Cal.App.4th 1384, 6 Cal.Rptr.2d 386 (1992)
Court of Appeals of California

CASE 27.2

BACKGROUND AND FACTS
The Southland Corporation (Southland) owns the "7-Eleven" trademark and licenses franchisees to operate convenience stores using this trademark. Each franchise is independently owned and operated. The franchise agreement stipulates that the franchisee is an independent contractor who is authorized

to make all inventory, employment, and operational decisions for the franchise.

Timothy Cislaw, 17 years old, died of respiratory failure on May 10, 1984. His parents filed a wrongful death action against the franchise and Southland, alleging that Timothy's death resulted from his consumption of Djarum Specials (clove cigarettes) sold at a Costa Mesa, California, 7-Eleven franchise store. The Costa Mesa 7-Eleven was franchised to Charles Trujillo and Patricia Colwell-Trujillo. After answering the complaint, Southland moved for summary judgment, arguing that it was not liable for the alleged tortious conduct of its franchisee because the franchisee was an independent contractor. The plaintiffs alleged that the franchisee was Southland's agent, and therefore Southland was liable for its agent's alleged negligence of selling the clove cigarettes to their son. The trial court granted Southland's motion. The Cislaws appealed.

ISSUE
Was the Costa Mesa franchisee an agent of Southland?

COURT'S REASONING
The franchisor–franchisee arrangement does not create a principal–agent relationship unless the franchisor has the right to exercise substantial control over the operations of the franchisee. Although the franchise agreement gave Southland the right to establish the hours of operation of its franchises, to protect its "7-Eleven" trademark from misuse by the franchisee, and to set cleanliness and quality control standards at its franchises, the agreement did not give Southland the right to control the day-to-day operations of its Costa Mesa franchise. The court found that because the franchisee made all inventory, employment, and day-to-day operational decisions, it was an independent contractor.

DECISION
The court of appeals held that the Costa Mesa 7-Eleven franchise was not an agent of Southland, but was an independent contractor. Affirmed.

Case Questions

Critical Legal Thinking Should franchisors be automatically held liable for the tortious conduct of their franchisees? Why or why not?

Business Ethics Did the Cislaws act ethically in suing Southland?

Contemporary Business How careful must a franchisor be to retain enough control to protect the quality of the goods and services sold by its franchisees, but not to retain too much control so as to become liable for the actions of its franchisees?

Agency Status

If the franchisee is the *actual* or *apparent agent* of the franchisor, the franchisor is responsible for the torts and contracts the franchise committed or entered into within the scope of the agency. **Apparent agency** is created when a franchisor leads a third person into believing that the franchisee is its agent. For example, a franchisor and franchisee who use the same trade name and trademarks and make no effort to inform the public of their separate legal status may find themselves in such a situation. However, mere use of the same name does not automatically make the franchisor liable for the franchisee's actions.

apparent agency

Agency that arises when a franchisor creates the appearance that a franchisee is its agent when in fact an actual agency does not exist.

In the following case, the court found that a franchisee was the apparent agent of the franchisor, thereby making the franchisor liable for the tortious conduct of the franchisee.

Holiday Inns, Inc. v. Shelburne
576 So.2d 322 (1991)
District Court of Appeals of Florida

CASE 27.3

BACKGROUND AND FACTS
Holiday Inns, Inc. (Holiday Inns), is a franchisor that licenses franchisees to operate hotels using its trademarks and service marks. Holiday Inns licensed Hospitality Venture to operate a franchised hotel in Fort Pierce, Florida. The Rodeo Bar, which had a reputation as the "hottest bar in town," was located in the hotel.

The Fort Pierce Holiday Inn and Rodeo Bar did not have sufficient parking, so security guards posted in the Holiday Inn parking lot required Rodeo Bar patrons to park in vacant lots that surrounded the hotel but that were not owned by the hotel. The main duty of the guards was to keep the parking lot open for hotel guests. Two unarmed security guards were on duty on the night in question. One guard was drinking on the job, and the other was an untrained temporary fill-in.

The record disclosed that although the Rodeo Bar had a capacity of 240 people, the bar regularly admitted 270 to 300 people with 50 to 75 people waiting outside. Fights occurred all the time in the bar and the parking lots, and often there were three or four fights a night. Police reports involving 58 offenses, including several weapons charges and battery and assault charges, had been filed during the previous 18 months.

On the night in question, the two groups involved in the altercation did not leave the Rodeo Bar until closing time. According to the record, these individuals exchanged remarks as they moved toward their respective vehicles in the vacant parking lots adjacent to the Holiday Inn. Ultimately, a fight erupted. The evidence shows that during the course of physical combat, Mr. Carter shot David Rice, Scott Turner, and Robert Shelburne. Rice died from his injuries.

Rice's heirs, Turner, and Shelburne sued the franchisee, Hospitality Venture, and the franchisor, Holiday Inns, for damages. The trial court found Hospitality Venture negligent for not providing sufficient security to prevent the foreseeable incident that took the life of Rice, and injured Turner and Shelburne. The court also found that Hospitality Venture was the apparent agent of Holiday Inns, and therefore Holiday Inns was vicariously liable for its franchisee's tortious conduct. Turner was awarded $3,825,000 for his injuries, Shelburne received $1 million, and Rice's interests were awarded $1 million. Hospitality Venture and Holiday Inns appealed.

ISSUE
Are the franchisee and the franchisor liable?

COURT'S REASONING
A franchisee is always liable for its own tortioius conduct. A franchisor may be held liable for the tortious conduct of a franchisee if the franchisee is the "apparent agent" of the franchisor. This "apparent agent" occurs when the franchisor mis-

leads the public into believing that the franchise is really owned and operated by the franchisor, even though it is not. Here, the court held that Holiday Inn led the public into believing that its franchisees were part of Holiday Inn's system and not independently owned businesses. The court held that Holiday Inn's reservation system, as well as the signs at the Fort Pierce franchise hotel, gave this appearance to the public. Therefore, Holiday Inns is vicariously liable for the tortious conduct of its franchisee.

DECISION
The court of appeals held that the franchisee was negligent, and that the franchisee was the apparent agent of the franchisor. Affirmed.

Case Questions

Critical Legal Thinking   What does the doctrine of apparent agency provide? How does it differ from actual agency?

Business Ethics   Did Hospitality Venture act ethically in denying liability? Did Holiday Inns act ethically in denying liability?

Contemporary Business   Why do you think the plaintiffs included Holiday Inns as a defendant in their lawsuit? Do you think the damages that were awarded were warranted?

Entrepreneur and the Law

LICENSING: POKÉMON INVADES THE UNITED STATES

In the 1990s, the Japanese company Nintendo's animated Pokémon creatures were a huge hit in Japan. In this role-playing game, children manipulate Pokémon characters with different stated strengths and weaknesses in a variant of the rock, paper, scissors game. The several hundred cute, gender-neutral characters, with such names as Pikachu, Piyo Piyo, Dalki, and Dragon Ball, show up in TV cartoons and Nintendo video games and on playing cards, book bags, and thousands of other items. Japanese children are crazy about acquiring the next Pokémon character. When one new character was introduced at the Nintendo Science World Fair in Japan, over 100,000 kids lined up to get the new character.

But would American children buy into the oddly animated creatures and their interactive games? Nintendo had doubts and did not want to take the exporting risk directly. Up stepped Alfred Kahn and Thomas Kenney, both prior toy company executives, who formed 4Kids Entertainment, Inc., a U.S. Company. They approached Nintendo about bringing the Pokémon games and characters to the United States through the concept of licensing. In 1997, after much negotiation, Nintendo agreed that 4Kids would be its licensing agent in the United States.

4Kids went looking for their first television deal, but the major TV networks turned them down. Not to be deterred, 4Kids syndicated the TV series themselves, dubbed episodes in English, and gave them free to TV stations in exchange for a percentage of advertising revenue. Within four months,

Pokémon was the top-rated syndicated kids program in the United States. After this TV success, Nintendo released the first Pokémon video games in the United States, followed by trading cards, comic books, home videos, and compact disks. 4Kids have signed over 100 licensing deals for Pokémon, including Hasbro toy company as its master toy licensee and Time-Warner for the Pokémon TV series. The first Pokémon movie, *Mewtwo Strikes Back*, was released in 1999 in the United States and was a huge hit. The Pokémon craze reached a fever pitch in the United States as it had in Japan.

The Pokémon invasion of the United States has reaped a plethora of royalties for Nintendo and its local entrepreneurs. Neither Nintendo nor 4Kids will disclose their licensing arrangement or royalty fees. But retailers usually pay a licensing fee between 5 to 15 percent of their retail sales, and 4Kids, as the licensing agent, typically earns commissions from 20 to 50 percent of that royalty. With Pokémon sales exceeding $1 billion in the United States, 4Kids can have earned up to $75 million, making its owners multimillionaires. Nintendo claims that it needs licensing agents such as 4Kids to enter a foreign market because of the expertise they bring in finding hot companies in the foreign country to produce and market T-shirts, school supplies, athletic shoes, and the thousands of other items its Pokémon characters now appear on in the United States. Licensing agents, such as 4Kids, take the ball and run with it, sometimes very successfully.

TERMINATION OF FRANCHISES

The franchise agreement usually contains provisions that permit the franchisor to terminate the franchise if certain events occur. The franchisor's right to terminate a franchise has been the source of litigation.

Termination "For Cause"

Most franchise agreements permit franchisors to terminate the franchise "for cause." For example, the continued failure of a franchisee to meet legitimate quality control standards would be deemed just cause.

Unreasonably strict application of a just cause termination clause constitutes wrongful termination. A single failure to meet a quality control standard, for example, is not cause for termination.

Wrongful Termination

Termination at will clauses in franchise agreements are generally held to be void on the grounds that they are unconscionable. The rationale for this position is that the franchisee has spent time, money, and effort developing the franchise.

If a franchise is terminated without just cause, the franchisee can sue the franchisor for **wrongful termination**. The franchisee can then recover damages caused by the unlawful termination and recover the franchise.

> **Business Brief**
>
> A franchisor can terminate a franchise agreement for "just cause" (e.g., nonpayment of franchise fees by the franchisee or continued failure to meet quality control standards).

> **wrongful termination**
> Termination of a franchise without just cause.

International Law

INTERNATIONAL FRANCHISING

Franchising as a form of business is well established in the United States. Sometimes it seems that certain types of franchises (e.g., gasoline stations) have saturated the market. The international market presently offers the greatest opportunity for U.S. franchisors to expand their businesses. Many U.S. franchisors view international expansion as their number one priority. However, in addition to providing lucrative new markets, international franchising also poses difficulties and risks.

The expansion into other countries through franchising means that U.S. franchisors can expand internationally without the huge capital investments that would be required if they tried to penetrate these markets with company-owned stores or branches. In addition, a foreign franchisee will know things about the cultural and business traditions of the foreign country that the franchisor will not. Consequently, the franchisee will be better able to serve the consumers and customers in the particular market.

Utilizing this foreign expertise probably means that U.S. franchisors will grant area franchises in many foreign countries. The U.S. franchisor will rely on the area franchisee to locate, investigate, and approve individual franchisees.

Foreign franchising is not without its difficulties, however. For example, the host country's laws may differ from U.S. laws. This will have to be taken into consideration in drafting the franchise agreement and operating the franchise. Foreign cultures may also require different advertising, marketing, and promotional approaches. In addition, the franchisor may be subjecting itself to government regulation in the host country. A regional group like the European Union (EU) may possibly become involved. Finally, different dispute settlement procedures may be in place that will have to be used if there is a dispute between the U.S. franchisor and the foreign franchisee.

To aid the development of U.S. franchising abroad, the federal *Agency for International Development (USAID)* guarantees loans to U.S. franchisors' area licensees and franchisees in developing countries. The foreign franchisee would seek financing from its own bank, but the USAID would back 50 percent of the loan through a guarantee. Franchisors must apply and be approved to participate in the program.

In addition to U.S. franchisors' expanding to other countries, foreign franchisors also view the United States as a potential market. This will provide an opportunity for U.S. entrepreneurs to become franchisees for foreign franchisors. As a result, in the future, U.S. consumers will be able to purchase foreign goods and services from franchises located in this country.

CHAPTER SUMMARY

Entrepreneurial Forms of Conducting Business, p. 665

Forms of Conducting Business	Entrepreneurs may choose to conduct business using any of the following forms:
	1. Sole proprietorship.
	2. General partnership.
	3. Limited partnership.
	4. Limited liability partnership (LLP).
	5. Limited liability company (LLC).
	6. Corporation.
	    a. C Corporation.
	    b. S Corporation.

Other Arrangements for Conducting Business	Business may be conducted using any of the following forms of business arrangements:
	1. Franchise.
	2. Joint venture.
	    a. Joint venture partnership.
	    b. Joint venture corporation.
	3. Syndicate.
	4. Business trust.
	5. Cooperative.
	6. Licensing.

Franchises, p. 672

Franchises	Established when one party licenses another party to use the franchisor's trade name, trademarks, commercial symbols, patents, copyrights, and other property in the distribution and selling of goods and services. 1. *Franchisor.* The party who does the licensing in a franchise arrangement. Also called the *licensor.* 2. *Franchisee.* The party who is licensed by the franchisor in a franchise arrangement. Also called the *licensee.*
Types of Franchises	1. *Distributorship franchise.* The franchisor manufactures a product and licenses a retail franchisee to distribute the product to the public. 2. *Processing plant franchise.* The franchisor provides a secret formula or process to the franchisee, and the franchisee manufactures the product and distributes it to retail dealers. 3. *Chain-style franchise.* The franchisor licenses the franchisee to make and sell its products or distribute its services to the public from a retail outlet serving an exclusive territory. 4. *Area franchise.* The franchisor authorizes the franchisee to negotiate and sell franchises on behalf of the franchisor in designated areas. The area franchisee is called a *subfranchisor.*
State Disclosure Laws	Many states have enacted statutes that require franchisors to make specific presale disclosures to prospective franchisees. Some states use a uniform disclosure document called the *Uniform Franchise Offering Circular (UFOC).*
FTC's Franchise Rule	The *FTC* requires franchisors to make presale disclosures to prospective franchisees. If the franchisor uses actual or hypothetical sales or income data in its sales materials, the franchisor must disclose assumptions underlying any estimates and how many franchises have obtained such results, and it must provide a mandated precautionary statement.

The Franchise Agreement, p. 675

The Franchise Agreement	An agreement that the franchisor and franchisee enter into that sets forth the terms and conditions of the franchise (e.g., quality control standards, covenants-not-to-compete, etc.).
Franchise Fees	*Franchise fees.* A franchisee may be required to pay any or all of the following franchise fees to the franchisor: 1. *Initial license fee.* A lump-sum payment for the privilege of being granted a franchise. 2. *Royalty fee.* A fee for the continued use of the franchisor's trade name, property, and assistance that is often computed as a percentage of the franchisee's gross sales. 3. *Assessment fee.* A fee for such things as advertising and promotional campaigns, administrative costs, and the like, billed either as a flat monthly fee or annual fee or as a percentage of gross sales. 4. *Lease fees.* Payment for any land or equipment leased from the franchisor, billed either as a flat monthly or annual fee or as a percentage of gross sales or other agreed-upon amount. 5. *Cost of supplies.* Payment for supplies purchased from the franchisor.

Trademarks	1. *Trademarks and service marks.* A distinctive mark, symbol, name, word, motto, or device that identifies the goods or services of a particular franchisor.
	2. *Licensing of marks.* A franchisor *licenses* the use of its trademarks and service marks to its franchisees in the franchise agreement.
	3. *Trademark infringement.* Anyone who uses a mark without authorization from the franchisor may be sued for *trademark infringement.* The franchisor can recover damages and obtain an injunction prohibiting further unauthorized use of the mark.
Misappropriation of Trade Secrets	1. *Trade secrets.* Ideas, formulas, and methods of doing business that make a franchise successful but do not qualify for trademark, patent, or copyright protection.
	2. *Misappropriation of trade secrets.* Anyone who steals and uses a franchisor's trade secret is liable for misappropriation of a trade secret. The franchisor can recover damages and obtain an injunction prohibiting further unauthorized use of the trade secret.

Contract and Tort Liability of Franchisors and Franchisees, p. 679

Contract and Tort Liability	1. Franchisors and franchisees are liable for their own contracts and torts.
	2. *Independent contractor.* A separately organized and operated business that is not the agent of another party with whom it does business. This is the typical franchisor-franchisee arrangement. There is no agency relationship, so neither party is liable for the other's contracts or torts.
	3. *Actual agency.* An arrangement that occurs where a franchisor expressly or implicitly by its conduct makes a franchisee its agent. The franchisor is liable for the contracts entered into and torts committed by the franchisee while acting within the scope of the agency.
	4. *Apparent agency.* Agency that arises when a franchisor creates the appearance that a franchisee is its agent when in fact an actual agency does not exist. The franchisor is liable for the contracts entered into and torts committed by the franchisee acting as an apparent agent.

Termination of Franchises, p. 683

Termination of Franchises	*Termination "for cause."* Most franchise agreements, and state and federal laws, permit a franchisor to terminate the franchise "for cause" (e.g., nonpayment of franchise fees by the franchisee, continued failure of the franchisee to meet quality control standards).
Wrongful Termination	1. *Termination at will.* Most state and federal laws regulating franchising prohibit franchisors from terminating franchises at will. This is to prevent a franchisor from taking advantage of the good will developed at the franchise location by the franchisee.
	2. *Wrongful termination.* If a franchisor terminates a franchise agreement without just cause, the franchisee can sue the franchisor for *wrongful termination.* The franchisee can recover damages caused by the wrongful termination and recover the franchise.

END-OF-CHAPTER INTERNET EXERCISES AND CASE QUESTIONS

Working the Web Internet Exercises

ACTIVITIES

1. Consider the advantages and disadvantages of doing business as a sole proprietor by surveying the material collected at **www.jurist.law.pitt.edu/sg_bus.htm**. This business association law guide from JURIST: The Legal Education Network contains some basic summaries of the choice of entity question.

2. Review the recent FTC cases of alleged abusive practices of franchisors at **www.ftc.gov/bcp/franchise/1999-2000cases.htm**. How would you advise a franchisee client to protect against such practices? For information on federal law regarding franchising, see **www.ftc.gov/bcp/franchise/netfran.htm**.

3. Find your state law regulating the use of a business trade name, or "doing business as" name.

4. Franchising makes extensive use of licensing of intellectual property, especially trademarks and trade secrets. Use the intellectual property sites listed below to find examples of licensing agreements and the disputes that they can sometimes produce.

- The Trade Secrets Home Page **www.execpc.com/ ~mhallign**

- All About Trademarks **www.ggmark.com**
- Intellectual Property Digital Library **ipdl.wipo.int**
- Intellectual Property Mall **www.fplc.edu/ipmall/ pointbox/pb_copy.htm**
- JurisNotes.Com—Your source for all aspects of intellectual property law **www.jurisnotes.com**
- Marksonline—Free trademark search and domain name search **www.marksonline.com**.
- The Intellectual Property Law Server **www. cybercommercelaw.com**

CRITICAL LEGAL THINKING CASES

27.1 Franchise Agreement H&R Block, Inc. (Block), is a franchisor that licenses franchisees to provide tax preparation services to customers under the "H&R Block" service mark. In 1975, June McCart was granted an H&R Block franchise at 900 Main Street, Rochester, New York. From 1972 to 1979, her husband, Robert, was involved in the operation of an H&R Block franchise in Rensselaer, New York. After that, he assisted June in the operation of her H&R franchise. All the McCarts' income during the time in question came from the H&R Block franchises.

The H&R Block franchise agreement that June signed contained a provision whereby she agreed not to compete (1) in the business of tax preparation (2) within 250 miles of the franchise (3) for a period of two years after the termination of the franchise. Robert did not sign the Rochester franchise agreement. On December 31, 1981, June wrote a letter to H&R Block giving notice that she was terminating the franchise. Shortly thereafter, the McCarts sent a letter to people who had been clients of the Rochester H&R Block office informing them that June was leaving H&R Block and that Robert was opening a tax preparation service in which June would assist him. H&R Block granted a new franchise in Rochester to another franchisee. It sued the McCarts to enforce the covenant not to compete against them. Who wins? [*McCart v. H&R Block, Inc.*, 470 N.E.2d 756 (Ind. App. 1984)]

27.2 Franchise Agreement Libby-Broadway Drive-In, Inc. (Libby), is a corporation licensed to operate a McDonald's fast-food franchise restaurant by the McDonald's System, Inc. (McDonald's). Libby was granted a license to operate a McDonald's in Cleveland, Ohio, and was granted an exclusive territory in which McDonald's could not grant another franchise. The area was described as "bound on the north by the south side of Miles Avenue, on the west and south side by Turney Road, on the east by Warrensville Center Road." In December 1976, McDonald's granted a franchise to another franchisee to operate a McDonald's restaurant on the west side of Turney Road. Libby sued McDonald's, alleging a breach of the franchise agreement. Is McDonald's liable? [*Libby-Broadway Drive-In, Inc. v. McDonald's System, Inc.*, 391 N.E.2d (Ill. App. 1979)]

27.3 Disclosure My Pie International, Inc. (My Pie), an Illinois corporation, is a franchisor that licenses franchisees to open pie shops under its trademark name. My Pie licensed 13 restaurants throughout the country, including one owned by Dowmont, Inc. (Dowmont), in Glen Ellyn, Illinois. The Illinois Franchise Disclosure Act requires a franchisor that desires to issue franchises in the state to register with the state or qualify for an exemption from registration and to make certain disclosures to prospective franchisees. My Pie granted the license to Dowmont without registering with the state of Illinois or qualifying for an exemption from registration and without making the required disclosures to Dowmont. Dowmont operated its restaurant as a "My Pie" franchise between July 1976 and May 1980, and since then has operated it under the name "Arnold's." Dowmont paid franchise royalty fees to My Pie prior to May 1980. My Pie sued Dowmont for breach of the franchise agreement and recover royalties it claimed was due from Dowmont. Dowmont filed a counter claim seeking to rescind the franchise agreement and recover the royalties it had paid to My Pie. Who wins? [*My Pie International, Inc. v. Dowmont, Inc.*, 687 F.2d 919 (7th Cir. 1982)]

27.4 Tort Liability Georgia Girl Fashions, Inc. (Georgia Girl), is a franchisor that licenses franchisees to operate women's retail clothing stores under the "Georgia Girl" trademark. Georgia Girl granted a franchise to a franchisee to operate a store on South Cobb Drive in Smyrna, Georgia. Georgia Girl did not supervise or control the day-to-day operations of the franchisee. Melanie McMullan entered the store to exchange a blouse that she had previously purchased at the store. When she found nothing that she wished to exchange the blouse for, she began to leave the store. At that time, she was physically restrained and accused of shoplifting the blouse. McMullan was taken to the local jail, where she was held until her claim of prior purchase could be verified. The store then dropped the charges against her and she was released from jail. McMullan filed an action against the store owner and Georgia Girl to recover damages for false imprisonment. Is Georgia Girl liable? [*McMullan v. Georgia Girl Fashions, Inc.*, 348 S.E.2d 748 (Ga. App. 1988)]

27.5 Tort Liability The Seven-Up Company (Seven-Up) is a franchisor that licenses local bottling companies to manufacture, bottle, and distribute soft drinks using the "7-Up" trademark.

The Brooks Bottling Company (Brooks) is a Seven-Up franchisee that bottles and sells 7-Up soft drinks to stores in Michigan. Under the franchise agreement, the franchisee is required to purchase the 7-Up syrup from Seven-Up, but it can purchase its bottles, cartons, and other supplies from independent suppliers if Seven-Up approves the design of these articles.

Brooks used cartons designed and manufactured by Olinkraft, Inc., using a design that Seven-Up had approved. Sharon Proos Kosters, a customer at Meijers Thrifty Acre Store in Holland, Michigan, removed a cardboard carton containing six bottles of 7-Up from a grocery store shelf, put it under her arm, and walked toward the checkout counter. As she did so, a bottle slipped out of the carton, fell on the floor, and exploded, causing a piece of glass to strike Kosters in her eye as she looked down; she was blinded in that eye. Evidence showed that the 7-Up carton was designed to be held from the top and was made without a strip on the side of the carton that would prevent a bottle from slipping out if held underneath. Kosters sued Seven-Up to recover damages for her injuries. Is Seven-Up liable? [*Kosters v. Seven-Up Company*, 595 F.2d 347 (6th Cir. 1979)]

27.6 Trademark The Kentucky Fried Chicken Corporation (KFC) is the franchisor of Kentucky Fried Chicken restaurants. Franchisees must purchase equipment and supplies from manufacturers approved in writing by KFC. Equipment includes cookers, fryers, ovens, and the like; supplies include carry-out boxes, napkins, towelettes, and plastic eating utensils known as "sporks." These products are not trade secrets. KFC may not "unreasonably withhold" approval of any suppliers who apply and whose goods are tested and found to meet KFC's quality control standards. The 10 manufacturers who went through KFC's approval process were approved. KFC also sells supplies to franchisees in competition with these independent suppliers. All supplies, whether produced by KFC or the independent suppliers, must contain "Kentucky Fried Chicken" trademarks.

Upon formation in 1972, Diversified Container Corporation (Diversified) began manufacturing and selling supplies to Kentucky Fried Chicken franchisees without applying for or receiving KFC's approval. All the items sold by Diversified contained Kentucky Fried Chicken trademarks. Diversified represented to franchisees that its products met "all standards" of KFC and that it sold "approved supplies." Diversified even affixed Kentucky Fried Chicken trademarks to the shipping boxes in which it delivered supplies to franchisees. Evidence showed that Diversified's products did not meet the quality control standards set by KFC. KFC sued Diversified for trademark infringement. Who wins? [*Kentucky Fried Chicken Corporation v. Diversified Container Corporation*, 549 F.2d 368 (5th Cir. 1977)]

27.7 Trademarks Ramada Inns, Inc. (Ramada Inns), is a franchisor that licenses franchisees to operate motor hotels using the "Ramada Inns" trademarks and service marks. In August 1977, the Gadsden Motor Company (Gadsden), a partnership, purchase a motel in Attalla, Alabama, and entered into a franchise agreement with Ramada Inns to operate it as a Ramada Inns motor hotel. In 1982, the motel began receiving poor ratings from Ramada Inns inspectors, and Gadsden fell behind on its monthly franchise fee payments. Despite proddings from Ramada Inns, the motel never met Ramada Inns' operational standards again. On November 17, 1983, Ramada Inns properly terminated the franchise agreement, citing quality deficiencies and Gadsden's failure to pay past due franchise fees. The termination notice directed Gadsden to remove any materials or signs identifying the motel as a Ramada Inns. Gadsden continued using Ramada Inns' signage, trademarks, and service marks inside and outside the motel. In September 1984, Ramada Inns sued Gadsden for trademark infringement. Who wins? [*Ramada Inns, Inc. v. Gadsden Motel Company*, 804 F.2d 1562 (11th Cir.)]

27.8 Termination of a Franchise In 1976, Amoco Oil Company (Amoco) purchased the land in question and constructed a two-bay gasoline station at a total cost of $125,000. The property was then leased to Robert F. Burns, who operated an Amoco franchise gasoline station. The franchise was maintained through a series of written one-year leases. The leases provided for automatic renewal unless either party gave written notice of cancellation prior to the end of the current term. On June 8, 1977, Amoco gave Burns written notice of nonrenewal and directed Burns to vacate the premises effective September 10, 1977. Evidence showed that the gasoline station had been suffering a steadily decreasing sales volume and that the station was an unprofitable location for Amoco. Evidence further showed that no reasonable steps could be taken to increase the sales volume at the site to make it profitable. Amoco planned on discontinuing the sale of gasoline at the site and selling the property. Burns sued Amoco for wrongful termination? Who wins? [*Amoco Oil Company v. Burns*, 437 A.2d 381 (Pa. 1981)]

27.9 Termination of a Franchise Kawasaki Motors Corporation (Kawasaki), a Japanese corporation, manufactures motorcycles that it distributes in the United States through its subsidiary, Kawasaki Motors Corporation, U.S.A. (Kawasaki USA). Kawasaki USA is a franchisor that grants franchises to dealerships to sell Kawasaki motorcycles. In 1971, Kawasaki USA granted the Kawasaki Shop of Aurora, Inc. (Dealer), a franchise to sell Kawasaki motorcycles in Aurora, Illinois. The franchise changed locations twice. Both moves were within the five-mile exclusive territory granted Dealer in the franchise agreement.

Dealer did not obtain Kawasaki USA's written approval for either move as required by the franchise agreement. Kawasaki USA acquiesced to the first move, but not the second. At the second new location, Dealer also operated Honda and Suzuki motorcycle franchises and was negotiating to operate a Yamaha franchise. The Kawasaki franchise agreement expressly permitted multiline dealerships. Kawasaki USA objected to the second move, asserting that the dealer had not received written approval for the move as required by the franchise agreement. Evidence showed, however, that the real reason Kawasaki objected to the move was because it did not want its motorcycles to be sold at the same location as other manufacturers' motorcycles. Kawasaki terminated the dealer's franchise. The dealer sued Kawasaki USA for wrongful termination. Who wins? [*Kawasaki Shop of Aurora, Inc. v. Kawasaki Motors Corporation, U.S.A.*, 544 N.E.2d 457 (Ill. App. 1989)]

BUSINESS ETHICS CASES

27.10 Business Ethics Southland Corporation (Southland) owned the "7-Eleven" trademark and licenses franchisees throughout the country to operate 7-Eleven stores. The franchise agreement provides for fees to be paid to Southland by each franchisee based on a percentage of gross profits. In return, franchisees receive a lease of premises, a license to use the 7-Eleven trademark and trade secrets, advertising merchandise, and bookkeeping assistance. Vallerie Campbell purchased an existing 7-Eleven store in Fontana, California, and became a Southland franchisee. The franchise was designated #13974 by Southland. As part of the purchase, she applied to the state of California for transfer of the beer and wine license from the prior owner. Southland also executed the application. California approved the transfer and issued the license to "Campbell Vallerie Southland #13974."

On September 9, 1978, an employee of Campbell's store sold beer to Jesse Lewis Cope, a minor who was allegedly intoxicated at the time. After drinking the beer, Cope drove his vehicle and struck another vehicle. Two occupants of the other vehicle, Denise Wickham and Tyrone Crosby, were severely injured, and a third occupant, Cedrick Johnson, was killed. Johnson (through his parents), Wickham, and Crosby sued Southland—but not Campbell—to recover damages. Is Southland legally liable for the tortious acts of its franchisee? Is it morally responsible? [*Wickham v. The Southland Corporation.* 168 Cal.App.3d 49, 213 Cal.Rptr. 825 (Cal. App. 1985)]

27.11 Business Ethics The Kentucky Fried Chicken Corporation (KFC), with its principal place of business in Louisville, Kentucky, is the franchisor of Kentucky Fried Chicken restaurants. KFC's registered trademarks and service marks include "Kentucky Fried Chicken," "It's Finger Lickin' Good," and the portrait of Colonel Harlan Sanders. KFC grants a license to its franchisees to use these marks in connection with the preparation and sale of "Original Recipe Kentucky Fried Chicken." Original Recipe Kentucky Fried Chicken, which is sold only by KFC franchisees, is prepared by a special cooking process featuring the use of a secret recipe seasoning known as "KFC Seasonings." This blend of seasoning was developed by KFC's founder, Colonel Harlan Sanders. As a condition of each franchise agreement, KFC requires that its franchisees use only KFC Seasoning in connection with the preparation and sale of Kentucky Fried Chicken.

KFC Seasoning is a trade secret. To make the seasoning, KFC has entered into contracts with two spice blenders, the John W. Sexton Company, Inc. (Sexton), and Strange Company (Strange). Each of these companies blends approximately one-half the spices of KFC Seasoning; neither has knowledge of the complete formulation of KFC Seasoning, and both entered into secrecy agreements to maintain the confidentiality of their formulation. After the seasoning is blended by Sexton and Strange, it is mixed together and sold directly to all KFC franchisees. KFC does not receive a royalty or other economic benefit from the sale of KFC Seasoning. KFC's relationship with Sexton and Strange has existed for more than 25 years; no other companies are licensed to blend KFC Seasoning.

Marion-Kay Company, Inc. (Marion-Kay), is a spice blender engaged in the manufacture of chicken seasoning known as "Marion-Kay Seasoning." In 1973, Marion-Kay requested permission from KFC to sell its seasoning products to KFC franchisees. KFC refused the request. In 1977, KFC learned that Marion-Kay was supplying some KFC franchisees with Marion-Kay seasoning and demanded it cease this practice. When Marion-Kay refused, KFC sued it for interference with contractual relations. Marion-Kay filed a counterclaim, alleging violation of antitrust law. Who wins? Was KFC justified in preventing Marion-Kay from blending its seasonings? Did Marion-Kay act morally in selling seasoning to KFC franchisees? [*KFC Corporation v. Marion-Kay Company, Inc.* 620 F.Supp. 1160 (S.D.Ind. 1985)]

BRIEFING THE CASE WRITING ASSIGNMENT

Read the following case, which has been excerpted from the court's opinion. Review and brief the case

Little v. Howard Johnson Company
183 Mich.APP.675, 455 N.W. 2D 390 (1990)
Court of Appeals of Michigan

MacKenzie, Judge

Plaintiff Joy Little was injured on January 23, 1982, when she slipped on a walkway which allegedly had not been adequately cleared of ice and snow. The walkway was located on property on which a restaurant business was being operated as a franchise of defendant, Howard Johnson Company. Plaintiff filed suit alleging liability for her injuries. In district court, Howard Johnson moved for summary disposition. The circuit court denied defendant's

subsequent motion for summary disposition and the case proceeded to mediation. When it mediated at less then $10,000, the case was removed to district court for lack of circuit court jurisdiction. The district court found no factual dispute and ruled as a matter of law that defendant was neither directly nor vicariously liable for plaintiff's injuries and, accordingly, granted the motion. The circuit court reversed without elaboration.

Little posited three theories under which she claimed Howard Johnson as a franchisor may be held liable for the injuries she sustained at the franchisee's restaurant: (1) direct liability as a possessor of the land, (2) vicarious liability based on agency principles, and (3) liability based on an apparent agency theory.

1. Direct Liability*—The general rule in Michigan is that invitors are liable for known dangerous conditions of property and for dangerous conditions which might be discovered with reasonable care. However, an invitor's direct liability requires the presence of both possession and control over the land.*

Little contends that defendant should be deemed a "possessor" of the land as a result of the rights of control it retained in its franchise agreement with the restaurant's franchisee. We disagree. The franchise agreement merely provides that the franchisee "at all times will maintain the interior and exterior of the buildings and surrounding premises in a clean, orderly, and sanitary condition satisfactory to Howard Johnson." In short, there is no issue of fact that defendant was a possessor of the premises who could be held directly liable for plaintiff's injuries.

2. Vicarious Liability—Generally, a principal is responsible for the negligence of its agent. In Michigan, the test for a principal-agent relationship is whether the principal has the right to control the agent. The threshold question here is what constitutes "control" sufficient to deem a franchisee to be an agent of a franchisor. Howard Johnson argues that a franchisor must have the right to control the day-to-day operations of a franchisee in order to establish an agency relationship. Little, on the other hand, maintains that an agency relationship is created where the franchisor retains the right to set standards regarding the products and services offered by the franchisee, the right to regulate such items as the furnishings and advertising used by the franchisee, and

the right to inspect for conformance with the agreement. We agree with defendant.

This Court has repeatedly held that in order to establish vicarious liability in such actions, the landowner must have retained some control and direction over the actual day-to-day work. It is not enough that the owner retained mere contractual control, the right to make safety inspections, or general oversight. The franchise agreement in this case primarily insured the uniformity and standardization of products and services offered by a Howard Johnson restaurant. These obligations do not affect the control of daily operations.

3. Apparent Agency—Howard Johnson argues that the district court properly concluded that no genuine issue of fact existed regarding its liability under an agency theory. We agree.

Here, Little has failed to offer any documentary evidence that she was harmed as a result of relying on the perceived fact that the franchise was an agent of Howard Johnson. No evidence was presented which indicated that plaintiff justifiably expected that the walkway would be free of ice and snow because she believed that Howard Johnson operated the restaurant.

Reversed.

ENDNOTES

1. Cal.Corp. Code §§ 31000–31019.
2. 16 CFR Part 436.
3. *Southland Corporation v. Keating*, 465 U.S. 1, 104 S.Ct. 852, 79 L.Ed.2d 1 (1985).

CHAPTER

28

Partnerships and Limited Liability Companies

There are a great many of us who will adhere to that ancient principle that we prefer to be governed by the power of laws, and not by the power of men.

—Woodrow Wilson
Speech, September 25, 1912

Chapter Objectives

After studying this chapter, you should be able to:

1. Define a *sole proprietorship* and the liability of a sole proprietor.

2. Describe how a business files for a d.b.a.—a fictitious business name.

3. Define *general partnership* and describe how general partnerships are formed.

4. Explain the contract and tort liability of partners.

5. Define *limited partnership* and distinguish between limited and general partners.

6. Identify and describe the liability of general and limited partners.

7. Define *limited liability partnership* (*LLP*) and describe the limited liability of partners of an LLP.

8. Define *limited liability company* (*LLC*) and describe the process of organizing an LLC.

9. Describe the limited liability shield provided to members by an LLC.

10. Describe the use of limited liability companies in foreign countries.

Chapter Contents

A person who wants to start a business must decide whether the business should operate as one of the major forms of business organization—*sole proprietorship, general partnership, limited partnership, limited liability partnership, limited liability company,* and *corporation*—or under some other available legal business form. The selection depends on many factors, including the ease and cost of formation, the capital requirements of the business, the flexibility of management decisions, government restrictions, the extent of personal liability, tax considerations, and the like.

This chapter discusses noncorporate forms of business, including sole proprietorships, general partnerships, limited partnerships, limited liability partnerships, and limited liability companies. Corporations are discussed in Chapters 29–31.

> It has been uniformly laid down in this Court, as far back as we can remember, that good faith is the basis of all mercantile transactions.
>
> *Buller, J.*
> Salomons v. Nissen *(1788)*

SOLE PROPRIETORSHIP

Sole proprietorships are the simplest form of business organization. The owner is the business. There is no separate legal entity. Sole proprietorships are the most common form of business organization in the United States. Many small businesses—and a few large ones—operate in this way.

There are several major advantages to operating a business as a sole proprietorship. They include the following:

1. The ease and low cost of formation.
2. The owner's right to make all management decisions concerning the business, including those involving hiring and firing employees.
3. The sole proprietor owns all of the business and has the right to receive all of the business's profits.
4. A sole proprietorship can be easily transferred or sold if and when the owner desires to do so; no other approval (such as from partners or shareholders) is necessary.

There are important disadvantages to this business form, too. For example, (1) the sole proprietor's access to the capital is limited to personal funds plus any loans he or she can obtain, and (2) the sole proprietor is legally responsible for the business's contracts and the torts he/she or any of his or her employees commit in the course of employment.

sole proprietorship

A form of business where the owner is actually the business; the business is not a separate legal entity.

It is the spirit and not the form of law that keeps justice alive.

Earl Warren
The Law and the Future
(1955)

Business Brief

Sole proprietorships are the most common form of business organization in the United States.

Creation of a Sole Proprietorship

It is easy to create a sole proprietorship. There are no formalities, and no federal or state government approval is required. Some local governments require all businesses, including sole proprietorships, to obtain a license to do business within the city. If no other form of business organization is chosen, the business is by default a sole proprietorship.

Business Brief

A sole proprietorship is easy to form and requires no formal filing with state or federal government authorities.

Entrepreneur and the Law

D.B.A.—"DOING BUSINESS AS"

A sole proprietorship can operate under the name of the sole proprietor or a *trade name.* For example, the author of this book can operate a sole proprietorship under the name "Henry R. Cheeseman" or under a trade name such as "The Big Cheese." Operating under a trade name is commonly designated as a **d.b.a. (doing business as)** (e.g., Henry R. Cheeseman, doing business as "The Big Cheese").

Most states require all businesses that operate under a trade name to file a **fictitious business name statement** (or

certificate of trade name) with the appropriate government agency. The statement must contain the name and address of the applicant, the trade name, and the address of the business. Most states also require notice of the trade name to be published in a newspaper of general circulation serving the area in which the applicant does business.

These requirements are intended to disclose the real owner's name to the public. Noncompliance can result in a fine. Some states prohibit violators from maintaining lawsuits in the state's courts.

There shall be one law for the native and for the stranger who sojourns among you.

Moses
Exodus *12:49*

Personal Liability of Sole Proprietors

The sole proprietor bears the risk of loss of the business; that is, the owner will lose his or her entire capital contribution if the business fails. In addition, the sole proprietor has *unlimited personal liability* (see Exhibit 28.1). Therefore, creditors may recover claims against the business from the sole proprietor's personal assets (e.g., home, automobile, and bank accounts).

Consider This Example Suppose Ken Smith opens a clothing store called The Rap Shop and operates it as a sole proprietorship. Smith files the proper statement and publishes the necessary notice of the use of the trade name. He contributes $25,000 of his personal funds to the business and borrows $100,000 in the name of the business from a bank. Assume that after several months Smith closes the business because it was unsuccessful. At the time it is closed, the business has no assets, owes the bank $100,000, and owes rent, trade credit, and other debts of $25,000. Here, Smith is personally liable to pay the bank and all of the debts from his personal assets.

*E*XHIBIT 28.1 *Sole Proprietorship*

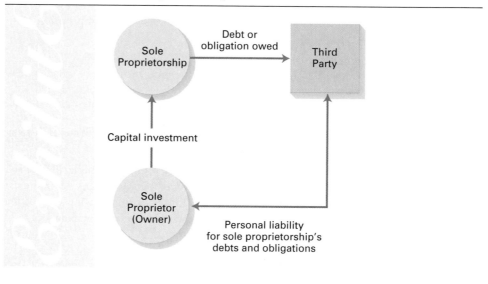

*E*ntrepreneur and the *L*aw

SOLE PROPRIETORSHIP AND SOLE PROPRIETOR ARE ONE AND THE SAME

The law holds that a sole proprietorship is not a distinct legal entity. Instead, the sole proprietorship and the sole proprietor are one and the same. The following case demonstrates this principle.

James Schuster was a sole proprietor doing business as (d.b.a.) "Diversity Heating and Plumbing." Diversity Heating was in the business of selling, installing, and servicing heating and plumbing systems. George Vernon and others (Vernon) owned a building that needed a new boiler. In November 1989, Vernon hired Diversity Heating to install a new boiler in the building. Diversity Heating installed the boiler and gave a warranty that the boiler would not crack for 10 years. On October 20, 1993, James Schuster died. On that date, James's son, Jerry Schuster, inherited his father's business and thereafter ran the business as a sole proprietorship under the d/b/a "Diversity Heating and Plumbing." In February 1994, the boiler installed in Vernon's building broke and could not be repaired. Vernon

demanded that Jerry Schuster honor the warranty and replace the boiler. When Jerry Schuster refused to do so, Vernon had the boiler replaced at the cost of $8,203 and sued Jerry Schuster to recover this amount for breach of warranty. The trial court dismissed Vernon's complaint, but the appellate court reinstated the case. Jerry Schuster appealed to the Supreme Court of Illinois. The issue presented to the supreme court was, Is Jerry Schuster liable for the warranty made by his father?

The supreme court held that Jerry Schuster was not liable for the warranty made by his father. The court stated

Common identity of ownership is lacking when one sole proprietorship succeeds another. It is well settled that a sole proprietorship has no legal identity separate from that of the individual who owns it. The sole proprietor may do business under a fictitious name if he or she chooses. However, doing business under another name does not create an entity distinct from the person operating the business. The individual who does business as a sole proprietor under one or several names remains one person, personally liable for all his or her obligations. There is generally no continuity of existence because on the death of the sole proprietor, the sole proprietorship obviously ends.

In this case, therefore, it must be remembered that "Diversity Heating" has no legal existence. Diversity Heating was only a pseudonym for James Schuster. Once he died, Diversity Heating ceased to exist. Now, Diversity Heating is only a pseudonym for the defendant, Jerry Schuster. Once sole proprietor James Schuster died, he could not be the same sole proprietor as defendant Jerry Schuster who became a sole proprietor after his father's death. James

Schuster and Jerry Schuster, one succeeding the other, cannot be the same entity. Even though defendant Jerry Schuster inherited Diversity Heating from his father, defendant would not have continued his father's sole proprietorship, but rather would have started a new sole proprietorship.

This case demonstrates the legal principle that a sole proprietorship has no legal status separate from its owner. The sole proprietorship and sole proprietor are one and the same. In this case, Vernon should have made a claim against the estate of James Schuster, the sole proprietor who made the warranty, and not against Jerry Schuster. [*Vernon v. Schuster, d/b/a/ Diversity Heating and Plumbing*, 688 N.E.2d 1172 (IL 1997)]

GENERAL PARTNERSHIP

General, or *ordinary*, *partnerships* have been recognized since ancient times. The English common law of partnerships governed early U.S. partnerships. The individual states expanded the body of partnership law.

A **general partnership**, or partnership, is a voluntary association of two or more persons for carrying on a business as co-owners for profit. The formation of a partnership creates certain rights and duties among partners and with third parties. These rights and duties are established in the partnership agreement and by law. **General partners**, or **partners**, are personally liable for the debts and obligations of the partnership (see Exhibit 28.2).

general partnership
A voluntary association of two or more persons for carrying on a business as co-owners for profit. Also called a *partnership*.

EXHIBIT 28.2 *General Partnership*

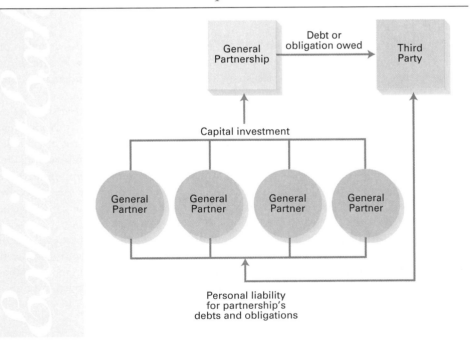

Uniform Partnership Act (UPA)

In 1914, the National Conference of Commissioners on Uniform State Laws (a group of lawyers, judges, and legal scholars) promulgated the **Uniform Partnership Act (UPA)**. The UPA codifies partnership law. Its goal was to establish consistent partnership law that was uniform throughout the United States. The UPA has been adopted in whole or

Uniform Partnership Act (UPA)
Model act that codifies partnership law. Most states have adopted the UPA in whole or part.

One of the most fruitful sources of ruin to men of the world is the recklessness or want of principle of partners, and it is one of the perils to which every man exposes himself who enters into partnership with another.

Malins, V.C.
Mackay v. Douglas, 14 Eq.
106 at 118 (1872)

Business Brief

Partnerships often operate under a fictitious business name. Those that do must file a fictitious business name statement with the appropriate government agency.

Business Brief

A partnership is a *voluntary* association. A person cannot be forced to be a partner or to accept another person as a partner.

The partner of my partner is not my partner.

Legal Maxim

Business Brief

It is compelling evidence of the existence of a partnership if persons are given the right to share in profits, losses, and management of a business.

in part by 48 states,[1] the District of Columbia, Guam, and the Virgin Islands. Because it is so important, the UPA will form the basis of the study of general partnerships in this chapter.

The UPA covers most problems that arise in the formation, operation, and dissolution of ordinary partnerships. Other rules of law or equity govern if there is no applicable provision of the UPA [UPA § 5].

The UPA adopted the **entity theory** of partnership, which considers partnerships as separate legal entities. As such, partnerships can hold title to personal and real property, transact business in the partnership name, and the like.

Partnership Name

An ordinary partnership can operate under the names of any one or more of the partners or under a fictitious business name. If the partnership operates under a fictitious name, it must file a *fictitious business name statement* with the appropriate government agency and publish a notice of the name in a newspaper of general circulation where the partnership does business. The name selected by partnership cannot indicate that it is a corporation (e.g., it cannot contain the term *Inc.*) and cannot be similar to the name used by any existing business entity.

Formation of a Partnership

A business must meet four criteria to qualify as a partnership under the UPA [UPA § 6(1)]. It must be (1) an association of two or more persons (2) carrying on a business (3) as co-owners (4) for profit. Partnerships are voluntary associations of two or more persons. All partners must agree to the participation of each co-partner. A person cannot be forced to be a partner or to accept another person as a partner. The UPA definition of person includes natural persons, partnerships (including limited partnerships), corporations, and other associations. A business—trade, occupation, or profession—must be carried on. The organization or venture must have a profit motive in order to qualify as a partnership, even though the business does not actually have to make a profit.

A general partnership may be formed with little or no formality. Co-ownership of a business is essential to create a partnership. The most important factor in determining co-ownership is whether the parties share the business's profits and management responsibility.

Receipt of a share of business profits is prima facie evidence of a partnership because nonpartners usually are not given the right to share in the business's profits. No inference of the existence of a partnership is drawn if profits are received in payment of (1) a debt owed to a creditor in installments or otherwise, (2) wages owed to an employee, (3) rent owed to a landlord, (4) an annuity owed to a widow, widower, or representative of a deceased partner, (5) interest owed on a loan, or (6) consideration for the sale of goodwill of a business [UPA § 7]. An agreement to share losses of a business is strong evidence of a partnership.

The right to participate in the management of a business is important evidence for determining the existence of a partnership, but it is not conclusive evidence because the right to participate in management is sometimes given to employees, creditors, and others. It is compelling evidence of the existence of a partnership if a person is given the right to share in profits, losses, and management of a business.

The Partnership Agreement

The agreement to form a partnership may be oral, written, or implied from the conduct of the parties. It may even be created inadvertently. No formalities are necessary, although a few states require general partnerships to file certificates of partnership with an appropriate government agency. Partnerships that exist for more than one year or are authorized to deal in real estate must be in writing under the Statute of Frauds.

It is good practice for partners to put their partnership agreement in writing. A written document is important evidence of the terms of the agreement, particularly if a dispute arises among the partners.

A written partnership agreement is called a **partnership agreement** or **articles of partnership**. The partners can agree to almost any terms in their partnership agreement, except terms that are illegal. The articles of partnership can be short and simple or long and complex. If the agreement fails to provide for an essential term or contingency, the provisions of the UPA control. Thus, the UPA acts as a gap-filling device to the partners' agreement.

In the following case, the court had to decide whether a partnership had been created.

It is the privilege of a trader in a free country, in all matters not contrary to law, to regulate his own mode of carrying it on according to his own discretion and choice.

B. Alderson
Hilton v. Eckersley *(1855)*

Vohland v. Sweet
435 N.E. 2d 860 (1982)
Court of Appeals of Indiana

CASE 28.1

BACKGROUND AND FACTS

Norman E. Sweet began working for Charles Vohland as an hourly employee at a garden nursery owned by Vohland in 1956, when he was a youngster. Upon completion of military service (from 1958 to 1960), Sweet resumed his former employment. In 1963, Charles Vohland retired and his son Paul Vohland (Vohland) commenced what became known as Vohland's Nursery, the business of which was landscape gardening. Vohland purchased the interests of his brothers and sisters in the nursery. At that time, Sweet's status changed: He was to receive a 20 percent share of the net profit of the business after all expenses were paid, including labor, supplies, plants, and other expenses. Sweet contributed no capital to the enterprise. The compensation was paid on an irregular basis—every several weeks Vohland and Sweet would sit down, compute the income received and expenses paid, and Sweet would be issued a check for 20 percent of the balance. No Social Security or income taxes were withheld from Sweet's checks.

Vohland and Sweet did not enter into a written agreement. No partnership income tax returns were filed by the business. Sweet's tax returns declared that he was a self-employed salesman. He paid self-employment Social Security taxes. Vohland handled all of the finances and books of the nursery and borrowed money from the bank solely in his own name for business purposes. Vohland made most of the sales for the business. Sweet managed the physical aspects of the nursery, supervised the care of the nursing stock, and oversaw the performance of the contracts for customers. Sweet testified that in the early 1970s, Vohland told him that:

He was going to take me in and that I wouldn't have to punch a time clock anymore, that I would be on a commission basis and that I would be—have more of an interest in the business if I had

an interest in the business. He referred to it as a "piece of the action."

Vohland denied making this statement. Sweet brought this action for dissolution of the alleged partnership and for an accounting. He sought payment for 20 percent of the business's inventory. The trial court held in favor of Sweet and awarded him $58,733. Vohland appealed.

ISSUE

Did Vohland and Sweet enter into a partnership?

COURT'S REASONING

Receipt by a person of a share of the profits is prima facie evidence that he or she is a partner in a business. Here, Sweet shared in the profits of the nursery. Although the parties called Sweet's sharing in the profits a "commission," the court stated that the term "when used by landscape gardeners and not lawyers, should not be restricted to its technical definition." The court found that the absence of a capital contribution by Sweet was not controlling and that his contribution of labor and skill would suffice.

DECISION

The court of appeals held that partnership had been created between Vohland and Sweet. Affirmed.

Case Questions

Critical Legal Thinking Do you think a partnership was formed in this case? Should all partnership agreements be required to be in writing?

Business Ethics Do you think either party acted unethically in this case?

Contemporary Business What are the economic consequences of founding a partnership?

"What happened to our working partnership?"

Right to Participate in Management

Business Brief

Unless otherwise agreed, each partner has a right to participate in the management of the partnership and has an equal vote on partnership matters.

In the absence of an agreement to the contrary, all partners have equal rights in the management and conduct of the partnership business. In other words, each partner has one vote regardless of the proportional size of his or her capital contribution or share in the partnership's profits. Under the UPA, a simple majority decides most ordinary partnership matters [UPA § 18]. If the vote is tied, the action being voted on is considered to be defeated. The partners may agree to modify the majority rule by delegating management responsibility to a committee of partners or to a managing partner.

Right to an Accounting

action for an accounting

A formal judicial proceeding in which the court is authorized to (1) review the partnership and the partners' transactions and (2) award each partner his or her share of the partnership assets.

Partners are not permitted to sue the partnership or other partners at law. Instead, they are given the right to bring an **action for an accounting** against other partners. An accounting is a formal judicial proceeding in which the court is authorized to (1) review the partnership and the partners' transactions and (2) award each partner his or her share of the partnership assets [UPA § 24]. It results in a money judgment for or against partners according to the balance struck.

Entrepreneur and the Law

PARTNERS' RIGHTS TO SHARE IN PROFITS

Unless otherwise agreed, the UPA mandates that a partner has the right to an equal share in the partnership's profits and losses [UPA § 18(a)]. Partnership agreements often provide that profits and losses are to be allocated in proportion to the partners' capital contributions. The right to share in the profits of the partnership is considered to be the right to share in the earnings from the investment of capital.

For example, suppose LeAnn Pearson and Mark Butler form a partnership. Pearson contributes $75,000 capital and Butler contributes $25,000 capital. They do not have an agreement as to how profits or losses are to be shared. Assume the partnership makes $100,000 in profits. Under the UPA, Pearson and Butler share the profits equally— $50,000 each.

Where a partnership agreement provides for the sharing of profits but is silent as to how losses are to be shared, losses are shared in the same proportion as profits. The reverse is not true, however. If a partnership agreement provides for the sharing of losses but is silent as to how profits are to be shared, profits are shared equally.

Expressly providing how profits and losses are to be shared by partners can increase the benefits to partners. For example, partners with high incomes from other sources can benefit most from the losses generated by a partnership.

Contract Liability

As a legal entity, a partnership must act through its agents, that is, its partners. Contracts entered into with suppliers, customers, lenders, or others on the partnership's behalf are binding on the partnership.

Under the UPA, partners are **jointly liable** for the contracts and debts of the partnership [UPA § 15(b)]. This means that a third party who sues to recover on a partnership contract or debt must name all of the partners in the lawsuit. If such a lawsuit is successful, the plaintiff can collect the entire amount of the judgment against any or all of the partners. If the third party's suit does not name all of the partners, the judgment cannot be collected against any of the partners or the partnership assets. Similarly, releasing any partner from the lawsuit releases them all.

A partner who is made to pay more than his or her proportionate share of contract liability may seek **indemnification** from the partnership and from those partners who have not paid their share of the loss.

In the following case, the court found partners jointly liable on a partnership contract.

joint liability

Partners are *jointly liable* for contracts and debts of the partnership. This means that a plaintiff must name the partnership and all of the partners as defendants. If successful, the plaintiff can recover the entire amount of the judgment from any or all of the partners.

Edward A. Kemmler Memorial Foundation v. Mitchell
584 N.E.2d 695 (1992)
Supreme Court of Ohio

CASE 28.2

BACKGROUND AND FACTS
Clifford W. Davis and Dr. William D. Mitchell formed a general partnership to purchase and operate rental properties for investment purposes. The partnership purchased a parcel of real property from the Edward A. Kemmler Memorial Foundation (Foundation) on credit. Davis signed a $150,000 promissory note to the Foundation as "Cliff W. Davis, Partner." Prior to executing the note, Davis and Mitchell entered into an agreement that provided that only Davis, and not Mitchell, would be personally liable on the note to the Foundation. They did not inform the Foundation of this side agreement, however. When the partnership defaulted on the note, the Foundation sued the partnership and both partners to recover on the note. Mitchell asserted in defense that the side agreement with Davis relieved him of personal liability. The trial court found Davis and Mitchell jointly liable. The appellate court reversed, excusing Mitchell from liability. The Foundation appealed.

ISSUE
Are both partners, Davis and Mitchell, jointly liable on the note?

COURT'S REASONING
The court stated the following legal principle: *Every partner is an agent of the partnership for the purpose of its business, and the act of every partner, including the execution in the partnership name of any instrument, for apparently carrying on in the usual way the business of the partnership of which he is a member binds the partnership, unless the partner so acting has in fact no authority to act for the partnership in the particular matter, and the person with whom he is dealing has knowledge of the fact that he has no such authority.*

The court stated that if a promissory note is executed in the name of the partnership, the partnership is bound, unless a contradictory agreement between the partners is known to the parties with whom they are dealing. The trial court found that the Foundation had no knowledge of the agreement between Davis and Mitchell regarding Mitchell's liability for the note.

DECISION
The Supreme Court of Ohio held that both partners were jointly liable on the note. Reversed.

Case Questions

Critical Legal Thinking What is joint liability? Should one general partner be liable to pay a judgment against the partnership?

Business Ethics Should Davis and Mitchell have notified the Foundation of their side agreement?

Contemporary Business Is it financially dangerous to be a partner in a general partnership? Explain.

Tort Liability

While acting on partnership business, a partner or an employee of the partnership may commit a tort that causes injury to a third person. This tort could be caused by a negligent act, a breach of trust (such as embezzlement from a customer's account), a breach of fiduciary duty, defamation, fraud, or other intentional tort. The partnership is liable if the act is committed while the person is acting within the ordinary course of partnership business or with the authority of his or her co-partners.

Under the UPA, partners are **jointly and severally liable** for torts and breaches of trust [UPA § 15(a)]. This is so even if a partner did not participate in the commission of the act. This type of liability permits a third party to sue one or more of the partners separately. Judgment can be collected only against the partners who are sued. The partnership and partners who are made to pay tort liability may seek indemnification from the partner who committed the wrongful act. A release of one partner does not discharge the liability of other partners.

Consider This Example Suppose Nicole, Jim, and Maureen form a partnership. Assume that Jim, while on partnership business, causes an automobile accident that injures Kurt, a pedestrian. Kurt suffers $100,000 in injuries. Kurt, at his option, can sue Nicole, Jim, or Maureen separately, or any two of them, or all of them.

Liability of Incoming Partners A new partner who is admitted to the partnership is liable for the existing debts and obligations (**antecedent debts**) of the partnership only to the extent of his or her capital contribution. The new partner is personally liable for debts and obligations incurred by the partnership after becoming a partner.

joint and several liability

Partners are *joint* and *severally liable* for tort liability of the partnership. This means that the plaintiff can sue one or more of the partners separately. If successful, the plaintiff can recover the entire amount of the judgment from any or all of the defendant-partners.

It is when merchants dispute about their own rules that they invoke the law.

J. Brett
Robinsone v. Mollett (1875)

CONCEPT SUMMARY PERSONAL LIABILITY OF GENERAL PARTNERS

Issue	Joint Liability	Joint and Several Liability
Type of lawsuit	Contract action	Tort action.
Defendants	Plaintiff must name all partners as defendants	Plaintiff can sue partners individually.
Recovery	If successful, the plaintiff can recover the judgment against all or any of the defendants.	If successful, the plaintiff can recover the judgment against all or any of the named defendants.
Indemnification	Partner who pays judgment can recover contribution from other partners for their share of the judgment.	Partner who pays judgment can recover contribution from other partners for their share of the judgment.

Contemporary Business Environment

JOINT AND SEVERAL LIABILITY OF GENERAL PARTNERS

The court applied the doctrine of joint and several liability in the following situation. Jose Pena and Joseph Antenucci were both medical doctors who were partners in a medical practice. Both doctors treated Elaine Zuckerman during her pregnancy. Her son, Daniel Zuckerman, was born with severe physical problems. Elaine, as Daniel's mother and natural guardian, brought this medical practice suit against both doctors. The jury found that Pena was guilty of medical malpractice but that Antenucci was not. The amount of the verdict

totaled $4 million. The trial court entered judgment against Pena but not against Antenucci. The plaintiffs have made a posttrial motion for judgment against both defendants.

Is Antenucci jointly and severally liable for the medical malpractice of his partner, Pena? The court said yes.

The court noted that a partnership is liable for the tortious act of a partner, and a partner is jointly and severally liable for tortious acts chargeable to the partnership. When a tort is committed by the partnership, the wrong is imputable to all of the partners jointly and severally, and an action may be brought against all or any of them in their individual capacities or against the partnership as an entity. Therefore, even though the jury found that defendant Antenucci was not guilty of malpractice in his treatment of the patient, but that defendant Pena, his partner, *wa*s guilty of malpractice in his treatment of the patient, they were then both jointly and severally liable for the malpractice committed by defendant Pena by operation of law. [*Zuckerman v. Antenucci*, 478 N.Y.S.2d 578 (NY 1984)]

Dissolution of Partnerships

The duration of a partnership can be a fixed term (e.g., five years) or until a particular undertaking is accomplished (e.g., until a real estate development is completed) or it can be for an unspecified term. A partnership with a fixed duration is called a **partnership for a term**. A partnership with no fixed duration is called a **partnership at will**.

A partner has the *power* to withdraw and dissolve the partnership at any time, but he or she may not have the *right* to do so. For example, a partner who withdraws from a partnership before the expiration of the term stated in the partnership agreement does not have the right to do so. The partner's actions causes a **wrongful dissolution** of the partnership. The partner is liable for damages caused by the wrongful dissolution of the partnership.

Notice of Dissolution   The dissolution of a partnership terminates the partners' actual authority to enter into contracts or otherwise act on behalf of the partnership. Notice of dissolution must be given to certain third parties. The degree of notice depends on the relationship of the third person with the partnership [UPA § 35].

1. Third parties who have actually dealt with the partnership must be given **actual notice** (verbal or written) of dissolution or have acquired knowledge of the dissolution from another source.
2. Third parties who have not dealt with the partnership but have knowledge of it must be given either actual or **constructive notice** of dissolution. Constructive notice consists of publishing a notice of dissolution in a newspaper of general circulation serving the area where the business of the partnership was regularly conducted.
3. Third parties who have not dealt with the partnership and do not have knowledge of it do not have to be given notice.

If proper notice is not given to a required third party after the dissolution of a partnership, and a partner enters into a contract with the third party, liability may arise on the grounds of *apparent authority*.

Notification of the dissolution of a partnership was not given to a creditor in the following box.

partnership for a term

A partnership with a fixed duration.

partnership at will

A partnership with no fixed duration.

wrongful dissolution

When a partner withdraws from a partnership without having the right to do so at that time.

Business Brief

If a partnership is dissolved, notice of the dissolution must be given to certain third parties. Partners may be liable for debts and obligations incurred on behalf of the partnership after the dissolution if the required notice is not given.

constructive notice

Usually written notice to a third party that is put into general circulation, such as in a newspaper.

Entrepreneur and the Law

CONTINUATION OF A PARTNERSHIP AFTER DISSOLUTION

The surviving or remaining partners are given the right to continue the partnership after dissolution. It is good practice for the partners of a partnership to enter into a *continuation agreement* that expressly sets forth the events that allow for continuation of the partnership, the amount to be paid outgoing partners, and other details.

When a partnership is continued, the old partnership is dissolved and a new partnership is created. The new partnership is composed of the remaining partners and any new partners admitted to the partnership. The creditors of the old partnership become creditors of the new partnership and have equal status with the creditors of the new partnership [UPA § 41].

The dissolution of a partnership does not of itself discharge the liability of outgoing partners for existing partnership debts and obligations. An outgoing partner can be relieved of liability if the outgoing partner, the continuing partners, and the creditor enter into a **novation agreement** that expressly relieves the outgoing partner from liability [UPA § 36].

International Law

PARTNERSHIPS OUTSIDE THE UNITED STATES

The English forms of business organizations are essentially the same as those in the United States. Partnership law, in particular, is virtually identical. Thus, in both countries (and in countries following the English model), a partnership is an association of two or more persons carrying on a business with the intent to make a profit.

In the civil law countries, including France and Germany, every form of business organization, including a partnership, is a "company" (*société* in French, *Gesellschaft* in German). A French partnership, because it is a company, is considered as having separate legal or juridical personality independent from its partners and thus can own property or sue or be sued in its own name. At the election of the partners, it can also opt to be treated as a separate tax entity and pay taxes as if it were a corporation. In Germany, by comparison, a partnership does not have a separate juridical personality. Therefore, even though a German partnership is a company, it is the partners who own the property, and the partners must sue or be sued.

Although partnerships are categorized as companies in both France and Germany, they remain associations of persons who have full individual liability for the actions of their company. Similarly, because they are associations, they must have two or more partners.

Partnerships are supposed to generate profits for the partners. In Germany, however, the partnership agreement may include a "Leonine clause." Such clauses can exclude a particular partner from sharing in either the profits or losses of the company. In France a Leonine clause is void.

A specialized form of partnership, the limited partnership, is recognized in the civil law countries. At least one partner must be a general partner (with personal unlimited liability) and one must be a limited partner. Limited partners have limited liability of the kind that investors in stock companies have. They may invest only cash or property in France, but in Germany services may be fixed and recognized as a contribution. In both countries persons can be either general or limited partners, but they cannot be both. In France, limited partners can participate in the internal administration of the partnership. In Germany, they can participate in internal administration and be given broad powers to deal with third parties on behalf of the partnership.

Germany recognizes another type of partnership, known as the silent partnership. This is a secret relationship between the partners that is unknown to third parties. The active partner conducts the business in his or her name alone, never mentioning the silent partner. So long as the silent partner's participation is not disclosed, the silent partner's risk is limited to the amount he or she invested. Silent partnerships are useful business forms for investment in Germany because the interest paid to the silent partner is treated as interest on a loan and is therefore tax deductible as a business expense from the earnings of the active partner. In France, where partnerships are regarded as separate legal entities, a silent partnership is not recognized as a separate entity and, therefore, is not governed by partnership law.

*L*IMITED PARTNERSHIP

limited partnership

A special form of partnership that is formed only if certain formalities are followed. It has both general and limited partners.

Limited partnerships are statutory creations that have been used since the Middle Ages. They include both general (manager) and limited (investor) partners. Today, all states have enacted statutes that provide for the creation of limited partnerships. In most states these partnerships are called **limited partnerships** or **special partnerships**. Limited partnerships are used for such business ventures as investing in real estate, drilling oil and gas wells, investing in movie productions, and the like.

Revised Uniform Limited Partnership Act (RULPA)

A 1976 revision of the ULPA that provides a more modern, comprehensive law for the formation, operation, and dissolution of limited partnerships.

The great can protect themselves, but the poor and humble require the arm and shield of the law.

Andrew Jackson (1767–1845)

The Revised Uniform Limited Partnership Act

In 1916 the National Conference of Commissioners on Uniform State Laws, a group composed of lawyers, judges, and legal scholars, promulgated the **Uniform Limited Partnership Act (ULPA)**. The ULPA contains a uniform set of provisions for the formation, operation, and dissolution of limited partnerships. Most states originally enacted this law.

In 1976, the National Conference on Uniform State Laws promulgated the **Revised Uniform Limited Partnership Act (RULPA)**, which provides a more modern comprehensive law for the formation, operation, and dissolution of limited partnerships. This law supersedes the ULPA in the states that have adopted it. The RULPA provides the basic foundation for the discussion of limited partnership law in the following materials.

General and Limited Partners

Limited partnerships have two types of partners: (1) **general partners**, who invest capital, manage the business, and are personally liable for partnership debts and (2) **limited partners**, who invest capital but do not participate in management and are not personally liable for partnership debts beyond their capital contribution (see Exhibit 28.3).

A limited partnership must have at least one or more general partners and one or more limited partners [RULPA § 101(7)]. There are no restrictions on the number of general or limited partners allowed in a limited partnership. Any person may be a general or limited partner. This includes natural persons, partnerships, limited partnerships, trusts, estates, associations, and corporations. A person may be both a general and a limited partner in the same limited partnership.

The RULPA permits a corporation to be the sole general partner of a limited partnership. Where this is permissible, it affects the liability of the limited partnership. This is because the limited partners are liable only to the extent of their capital contributions and the corporation acting as general partner is liable only to the extent of its assets.

general partners

Partners in a limited partnership who invest capital, manage the business, and are personally liable for partnership debts.

limited partners

Partners in a limited partnership who invest capital but do not participate in management and are not personally liable for partnership debts beyond their capital contribution.

Exhibit 28.3 Limited Partnership

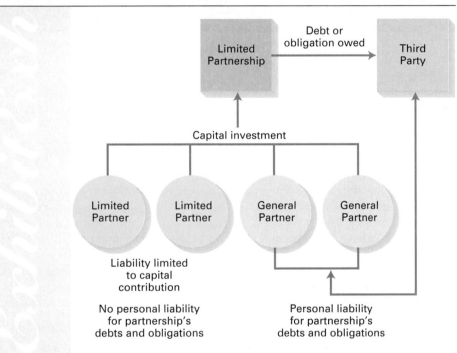

Formation of Limited Partnerships

The creation of a limited partnership is formal and requires public disclosure. The entity must comply with the statutory requirements of the RULPA or other state statutes.

Under the RULPA, two or more persons must execute and sign a **certificate of limited partnership** [RULPA §§ 201 and 206]. The certificate must contain the following information:

1. Name of the limited partnership
2. General character of the business
3. Address of the principal place of business, and the name and address of the agent to receive service of legal process
4. Name and business address of each general and limited partner
5. The latest date upon which the limited partnership is to dissolve
6. Amount of cash, property, or services (and description of property or services) contributed by each partner, and any contributions of cash, property, or services promised to be made in the future
7. Any other matters that the general partners determine to include

certificate of limited partnership

A document that two or more persons must execute and sign that makes the limited partnership legal and binding.

Business Brief

It is good practice to have a written partnership agreement that sets forth in detail the rights and duties of the partners. This will reduce later disputes and lawsuits.

The certificate of limited partnership must be filed with the secretary of state of the appropriate state and, if required by state law, with the county recorder in the county or counties in which the limited partnership carries on business. The limited partnership is formed when the certificate of limited partnership is filed.

Many businesses, such as these windmills near Palm Springs, California, are operated as limited partnerships.

limited partnership agreement

A document that sets forth the rights and duties of the general and limited parties, the terms and conditions regarding the operation, termination, and dissolution of the partnership, and so on.

Morality cannot be legislated, but behavior can be regulated. Judicial decrees may not change the heart, but they can restrain the heartless.

Martin Luther King, Jr.
Strength to Love *(1963)*

Business Brief

A limited partner may be held liable as a general partner if the limited partnership is defectively formed.

Laws too gentle are seldom obeyed; too severe, seldom executed.

Benjamin Franklin
Poor Richard's Almanack *(1756)*

Business Brief

General partners of a limited partnership have unlimited liability for debts and obligations of the partnership. Limited partners are liable only up to their capital contribution.

Business Brief

If a limited partner participates in management, he can become liable as a general partner.

Limited Partnership Agreement

Although not required by law, the partners of a limited partnership often draft and execute a **limited partnership agreement** (also called the **articles of limited partnership**) that sets forth the rights and duties of the general and limited partner, the terms and conditions regarding the operation, termination, and dissolution of the partnership, and so on. Where there is no such agreement, the certificate of limited partnership serves as the articles of limited partnership.

The limited partnership agreement may specify how profits and losses from the limited partnership are to be allocated among the general and limited partners. If there is no such agreement, the RULPA provides that profits and losses from a limited partnership are shared on the basis of the value of the partner's capital contribution [RULPA § 503]. A limited partner is not liable for losses beyond his or her capital contribution.

In addition, it is good practice to establish voting rights in the limited partnership agreement or certificate of limited partnership. The limited partnership agreement can provide which transactions must be approved by which partners (i.e., general, limited, or both). General and limited partners may be given unequal voting rights.

Defective Formation Defective formation occurs when (1) a certificate of limited partnership is not properly filed, (2) there are defects in a certificate that is filed, or (3) some other statutory requirement for the creation of a limited partnership is not met. If there is a substantial defect in the creation of a limited partnership, persons who thought they were limited partners can find themselves liable as general partners. Such partners who erroneously but in good faith believe they have become limited partners can escape liability as general partners by either (1) causing the appropriate certificate of limited partnership (or certificate of amendment) to be filed or (2) withdrawing from any future equity participation in the enterprise and causing a certificate showing this withdrawal to be filed. Nevertheless, the limited partner remains liable to any third party who transacts business with the enterprise before either certificate is filed if the third person believed in good faith that the partner was a general partner at the time of the transaction [RULPA § 304].

Liability of General and Limited Partners

The **general partners** of a limited partnership have unlimited liability for the debts and obligations of the limited partnerships. This liability extends to debts that cannot be satisfied with the existing capital of the limited partnership. Generally **limited partners** are liable only for the debts and obligations of the limited partnership up to their capital contributions.

As a trade-off for limited liability, limited partners give up their right to participate in the control and management of the limited partnership. This means, in part, that limited partners have no right to bind the partnership to contracts or other obligations. Under the RULPA, a limited partner is liable as a general partner if his or her participation in the control of the business is substantially the same as that of a general partner, but the limited partner is liable only to persons who reasonably believed him or her to be a general partner [RULPA § 303(a)].

*C*ONCEPT SUMMARY · LIABILITY OF LIMITED PARTNERS

General rule	Limited partners are not individually liable for the obligations or conduct of the partnership beyond the amount of their capital contribution.
Exceptions to the general rule	Limited partners are individually liable for the debts, obligations, and tortious acts of the partnership in three situations: 1. **Defective Formation** There has not been substantial compliance in good faith with the statutory requirements to create a limited partnership. *Exception:* Persons who erroneously believed themselves to be limited partners either (1) caused the appropriate certificate of limited partnership or amendment thereto to be filed or (2) withdrew from any future equity participation in the profits of the partnership and caused a certificate of withdrawal to be filed. 2. **Participation in Management** The limited partner participated in the management and control of the partnership. *Exception:* The limited partner was properly employed by the partnership as a manager or executive. 3. **Personal Guarantee** The limited partner signed an enforceable personal guarantee that guarantees the performance of the limited partnership.

 *E*ntrepreneur and the *L*aw

LIMITED PARTNER LIABLE ON PERSONAL GUARANTEE

Many small businesses, including limited partnerships, attempt to borrow money from banks or obtain an extension of credit from suppliers. Often these lenders require owners of small businesses to personally guarantee the loan to the business; otherwise the extensions of credit will not be made. Consider the following case.

Linnane Magnavox Home Entertainment Center (Linnane Magnavox) was a limited partnership that was organized under the laws of Kansas. Paul T. Linnane was the sole general partner, and Richard Gale Stover was the limited partner. Stover was the silent partner who provided the capital for the partnership. Stover took no part in the day-to-day management or control of the partnership, employment or discharge of employees, the purchase or sale of inventory, or any other incident of partnership business. In November 1977, Linnane Magnavox entered into a contract with General Electric Credit Corporation (GE Credit) whereby GE credit would provide financing to the partnership. GE Credit refused to grant credit to the undercapitalized partnership unless Stover signed as the guarantor of the credit. It was

not until Stover furnished his personal financial statements to GE Credit and personally signed the credit agreement as a guarantor that it extended credit to the partnership. When Linnane Magnavox defaulted on the debt and Paul Linnane was adjudicated bankrupt, GE Credit sued Stover to recover on the debt. The trial court held in favor of GE Credit. Stover appealed. Is Richard Gale Stover, the limited partner, personally liable for Linnane Magnavox's debt to GE Credit?

The court of appeals held that defendant Stover was liable to pay the debts of Linnane Magnavox to GE Credit. The court stated:

The question for decision was whether, for the purpose of the extension of credit to Linnane Magnavox, Stover put his personal assets at stake and GE Credit was therefore induced to extend its credit to the partnership. The evidence before the trial court was that GE Credit would not have extended credit to Linnane Magnavox had not Stover signed the credit agreement. It was a stipulated fact that prior to the execution of the credit agreement,

GE Credit requested, and Stover furnished, his personal financial statement. In terms of partnership principle, the question is that of holding out: whether the Stover signature induced GE Credit to extend credit on reliance that Stover would be personally bound on those obligations. Stover had every reason to know that his unqualified signature on the documents would bind his personal credit as that of the general partner.

The court held the limited partner Stover to his word. [*General Electric Credit Corporation v. Stover*, 708 S.W.2d 355 (MO 1986)].

Contemporary Business Environment

Master Limited Partnerships

One of the major drawbacks for investors who are limited partners in a limited partnership is that their investment usually is not liquid because there is no readily available market for buying and selling limited partnership interests. The introduction of **master limited partnerships (MLPs)** is changing this situation.

An MLP is a limited partnership whose limited partnership interests are traded on organized securities exchanges such as the New York Stock Exchange. Often, MLPs are created by corporations that transfer certain corporate assets (such as real estate) to an MLP and then sell limited partnership interests to the public. The corporation usually remains as the general partner. Some MLPs are formed to make original investments.

There are tax benefits to owning a limited partnership interest in an MLP rather than corporate stock. MLPs pay no income tax—partnership income and losses flow directly onto the individual partner's income tax return. Profit and other distributions of MLPs also avoid the double taxation of corporate dividends.

The use of master limited partnerships is expected to increase in the future.

Limited Liability Partnership (LLP)

limited liability partnership (LLP)
A special form of partnership where all partners are limited partners and there are no general partners.

Many states have enacted legislation to permit the creation of **limited liability partnerships (LLPs)**. In an LLP, there does not have to be a general partner who is personally liable for the debts and obligations of the partnership. Instead, *all* partners are limited partners who stand to lose only their capital contribution should the partnership fail. None of the partners is personally liable for the debts and obligations of the partnership beyond his or her capital contribution (see Exhibit 28.4).

LLPs enjoy the "flow-through" tax benefit of other types of partnerships, that is, there is no tax paid at the partnership level and all profits and losses are reported on the individual partners' income tax returns.

Articles of Partnership

articles of partnership
Document that must be filed with the secretary of state to form a limited liability partnership.

LLPs must be created formally by filing **articles of partnership** with the secretary of state of the state in which the LLP is organized. This is a public document. The LLP is a **domestic LLP** in the state in which it is organized. The limited liability partnership law of the state governs the operation of the LLP. An LLP may do business in other states, however. To do so, the LLP must register as a **foreign LLP** in any state in which it wants to conduct business.

Liability Insurance Required

Justice is the end of government. It is the end of civil society. It ever has been, and ever will be pursued, until it be obtained, or until liberty be lost in the pursuit.
James Madison
The Federalist No. 51 *(1788)*

In most states limited liability partnership law restricts the use of the LLPs to certain types of professionals, such as accountants and lawyers. Many state laws require LLPs to carry a minimum of $1 million of liability insurance that covers negligence, wrongful acts, and misconduct by partners or employees of the LLP. This requirement guarantees that injured third parties will have compensation to recover for their injuries and is a quid pro quo for permitting partners to have limited liability.

*E*XHIBIT 28.4 *Limited Liability Partnership (LLP)*

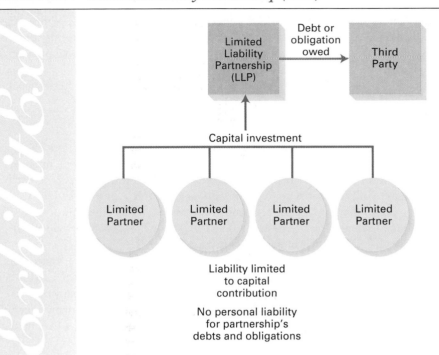

CONTEMPORARY BUSINESS ENVIRONMENT

ACCOUNTING FIRMS OPERATE AS LLPs

Prior to the advent of the limited liability partnership (LLP) form of doing business, accounting firms operated as general partnerships. As such, the general partners were personally liable for the debts and obligations of the general partnership. In large accounting firms, this personal liability was rarely imposed. This was because the general partnership usually carried sufficient liability insurance to cover most awards to third-party plaintiffs in negligence tort actions. Creditors usually extended credit to the large accounting firms based on the reputation of the firms and the fact that these large accounting firms had sufficient capital in the partnership to meet most loan obligations.

Beginning in the early 1980s, large accounting firms were hit with many large court judgments. These cases were brought in conjunction with the failure of large savings banks and commercial banks and the failure of other large firms that accountants had audited. Many of these firms failed because of fraud by their major owners and officers. The shareholders and creditors of these failed companies sued the auditors, alleging that the auditors had been negligent in not catching the fraud. Many juries agreed and awarded large sums against the accounting firms. Sometimes the account-

ing firm's liability insurance was not enough to cover the judgment, thus imposing personal liability on partners. General partners in accounting firms became worried that the inability of the profession to shield itself from such liability jeopardized the profession.

In response, in the 1990s state legislatures created a new form of business, the limited liability partnership (LLP). This entity was particularly created for accountants, lawyers, and other professionals to offer their services under an umbrella of limited liability. The partners of an LLP have limited liability up to their capital contribution; the partners do not have personal liability for the debts and liabilities of the LLP, however.

Once LLPs were permitted by law, all of the Big Five accounting firms changed their status from general partnerships to LLPs. The signs and letterhead of the Big Five accounting firms prominently announce that the accounting firm is an "LLP." Many accounting firms other than the Big Five have also changed over to LLP status, as have many law firms. The LLP form of business has changed how accountants, lawyers, and other professionals offer their services.

LIMITED LIABILITY COMPANY (LLC)

In recent years, a majority of states have approved a new form of business entity called a **limited liability company (LLC)**. An LLC is an unincorporated business entity that combines the most favorable attributes of general partnerships, limited partnerships, and corporations. An LLC may elect to be taxed as a partnership, the owners can manage the business, and the owners have limited liability. Many entrepreneurs who begin new businesses choose the LLC as their legal form for conducting business.

The Uniform Limited Liability Company Act

In 1995, the National Conference of Commissioners on Uniform State Laws (a group of lawyers, judges, and legal scholars) issued the **Uniform Limited Liability Company Act (ULLCA)**. The ULLCA codifies limited liability company law. Its goal is to establish comprehensive LLC law that is uniform throughout the United States. The ULLCA covers most problems that arise in the formation, operation, and termination of LLCs. The ULLCA in not law unless a state adopts it as its LLC statute. Many states have adopted all or part of the ULLCA as their limited liability company law.

Limited liability companies are creatures of state law, not federal law. Limited liability companies can only be created pursuant to the laws of the state in which the LLC is being organized. These statutes, commonly referred to as **limited liability company codes**, regulate the formation, operation, and dissolution of LLCs. The state legislature may amend its LLC statute at any time. The courts interpret state LLC statutes to decide LLC and member disputes.

Entrepreneur and the Law

WHY OPERATE A BUSINESS AS A LIMITED LIABILITY COMPANY (LLC)?

Why should an LLC be used instead of an S Corporation or a partnership? S Corporations and partnerships are subject to many restrictions and adverse consequences that do not exist with an LLC. Some differences are

- S Corporations cannot have shareholders other than estates, certain trusts, and individuals (who cannot be nonresident aliens). S Corporations can have no more than 75 shareholders and one class of stock and may not own more than 80 percent of another corporation. LLCs have no such restrictions.

- In a general partnership, the partners are personally liable for the obligations of the partnership. Members of LLCs have limited liability.
- Limited partnerships must have at least one general partner who is personally liable for the obligations of the partnership (although this partner can be a corporation). Limited partners are precluded from participating in the management of the business. An LLC provides limited liability to all members, even though they participate in management of the business.

Formation of an LLC

Forming an LLC is very similar to organizing a corporation. Two or more persons (which include individuals, partnerships, corporations, and associations) may form an LLC for any lawful purpose. To form an LLC, **articles of organization** must be filed with the appropriate state office, usually the Secretary of State's office (see Exhibit 28.5). The articles of organization must state the LLC's name, duration, and other information required by statute or that the organizers deem important to include. The name of an LLC must contain the words *Limited Liability Company* or the abbreviation *L.L.C.* or *L.C.*

articles of organization
The formal document that must be filed with the Secretary of State to form an LLC.

Conversion of an Existing Business to an LLC Many LLCs are formed by entrepreneurs to start new businesses. In addition, many existing businesses may want to convert to an LLC to obtain its tax benefits and limited liability shield. General partnerships, limited partnerships, and corporations may be converted to an LLC. The conversion takes effect when the articles of organization are filed with the secretary of state.

Business Brief

Some existing businesses, such as general partnerships, limited partnerships, and corporations, may want to convert to an LLC. The law permits such conversions.

Operating Agreement Members of an LLC may enter into an **operating agreement** that regulates the affairs of the company and the conduct of its business and governs relations among the members, managers, and company [ULLCA § 103(a)]. The operating agreement may be amended by the approval of all members unless otherwise provided in the agreement. The operating agreement and amendments may be oral but are usually written.

operating agreement
An agreement entered into among members that governs the affairs and business of the LLC and the relations among members, managers, and the LLC.

Exhibit 28.5 *Sample Articles of Organization*

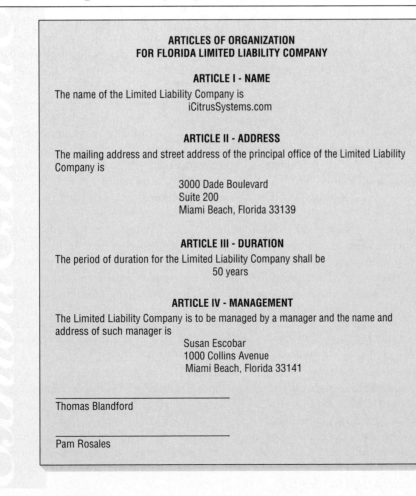

ARTICLES OF ORGANIZATION
FOR FLORIDA LIMITED LIABILITY COMPANY

ARTICLE I - NAME
The name of the Limited Liability Company is
iCitrusSystems.com

ARTICLE II - ADDRESS
The mailing address and street address of the principal office of the Limited Liability Company is

3000 Dade Boulevard
Suite 200
Miami Beach, Florida 33139

ARTICLE III - DURATION
The period of duration for the Limited Liability Company shall be
50 years

ARTICLE IV - MANAGEMENT
The Limited Liability Company is to be managed by a manager and the name and address of such manager is

Susan Escobar
1000 Collins Avenue
Miami Beach, Florida 33141

_____
Thomas Blandford

_____
Pam Rosales

Contemporary Business Environment

"CHECK-THE-BOX" REGULATIONS FOR PARTNERSHIP TAXATION OF LLCs

A limited liability company (LLC) is an unincorporated business entity formed under state law. Because an LLC is neither a partnership nor a corporation, a question arises as to how it should be taxed for federal income tax purposes. Under the Internal Revenue Code, a partnership is not taxed at the entity level, but its income or losses "flow through" to the partners' individual income tax returns. This avoids double taxation. On the other hand, corporations are generally taxed once at the entity level and then again if it pays dividends to shareholders, who must pay tax on these dividends when they file their personal income tax returns. Thus, there is double taxation.

In most cases, an LLC would prefer to be taxed as a partnership than as a corporation. When the first LLC was formed under Wyoming law, the Internal Revenue Service (IRS) issued a Revenue Ruling that classified the LLC as a partnership for federal income tax purposes. After this initial ruling, the IRS issued regulations that provided than an LLC could be taxed as a partnership if it gave up two of the following corporate attributes: (1) associates, (2) objective to carry on the business for a profit, (3) centralized management, (4) limited liability, (5) continuity of life, and (6) free transferability of interests. To obtain partnership taxation, in most instances LLCs gave up continuity of life by stating a term for the LLC (e.g., 50 years) and free transferability of interests by agreeing to buy-and-sell agreements and other restrictions on the sale or transfer of their ownership interests.

This method of obtaining partnership taxation was used by LLCs until 1997. Effective January 1, 1997, the IRS adopted **"Check-the-Box" Regulations** that made it easier for LLCs to be taxed as partnerships. These regulations provide that a business entity falls into one of the following categories:

1. ***Per se* Corporations**   These are defined as corporations incorporated under state law and are taxed as corporations for federal income tax purposes.
2. **Eligible Entities**   These are defined as entities other than *per se* corporations. Eligible entities include unincorporated businesses with two or more owners, such as LLCs, LLPs, limited partnerships, and general partnerships. An eligible entity is taxed as a partnership unless it elects to be taxed as a corporation.
3. **Single-Owner Entity**   A single-owner entity is taxed as a sole proprietorship unless the owner elects to be taxed as a corporation.

The Check-the-Box Regulations have default rules that provide that eligible entities, such as an LLC, are treated as partnerships with flow-through taxation unless an election is made to be taxed as a corporation. This election is made by filing Form 8832 with the IRS and must be signed by all owners or a manager who is given authority to sign such an election. The Check-the-Box Regulations make it easier for LLCs to obtain partnership taxation status for federal income tax purposes. Most states automatically apply the federal classification rules for state income tax purposes, although a few do not.

---

member

An owner of an LLC.

limited liability

Members are liable for the LLC's debts, obligations, and liabilities only to the extent of their capital contributions.

Members' Limited Liability   The owners of LLCs are usually called **members**. The general rule is that members are not personally liable to third parties for the debts, obligations, and liabilities of an LLC beyond their capital contribution. Members are said to have **limited liability** (see Exhibit 28.6). The debts, obligations, and liabilities of an LLC, whether arising from contracts, torts, or otherwise, are solely those of the LLC [ULLCA § 303(a)].

Consider This Example   Jasmin, Shan-Yi, and Vanessa form an LLC and each contributes $25,000 in capital. The LLC operates for a period of time during which it borrows money from banks and purchases goods on credit from suppliers. After some time, the LLC experiences financial difficulty and goes out of business. If the LLC fails with $500,000 in debts, each of the members will lose her capital contribution of $25,000 but will not be personally liable for the rest of the unpaid debts of the LLC.

member-managed LLC

An LLC that has not designated that it is a manager-managed LLC in its articles of organization.

manager-managed LLC

An LLC that has designated in its articles of organization that it is a manager-managed LLC.

Member-Managed and Manager-Managed LLCs   An LLC can be either a **member-managed LLC** or a **manager-managed LLC**. An LLC is a member-managed LLC unless it is designated as a manager-managed LLC in its articles of organization [ULLCA § 203(a)(6)].

The designation of an LLC as a member-managed LLC or manager-managed LLC is important in determining who has the authority to bind the LLC to contracts. In a member-managed LLC, all members have agency authority to bind the LLC to contracts. On the other hand, in a manager-managed LLC, only the designated managers have authority to bind the LLC to contracts; nonmanager members do not have such authority. An LLC is only bound to contracts that are in the ordinary course of business or that the LLC has authorized [ULLCA § 301].

Continuation of an LLC   At the expiration of the term of a term LLC, some of its members may want to continue the LLC. At the expiration of its term, a term LLC can be continued in two situations. First, the members of the LLC may vote prior to the expiration date to continue the LLC for an additional specified term. This requires the unanimous vote of all of the members and the filing of an amendment to the articles of organization with the secretary of state stating this fact. Second, absent the unanimous vote to continue the term LLC, the LLC may be continued as an at-will LLC by a simple majority vote of the members of the LLC [ULLCA § 411(b)].

*Ɛ*XHIBIT 28.6   *Limited Liability Company (LLC)*

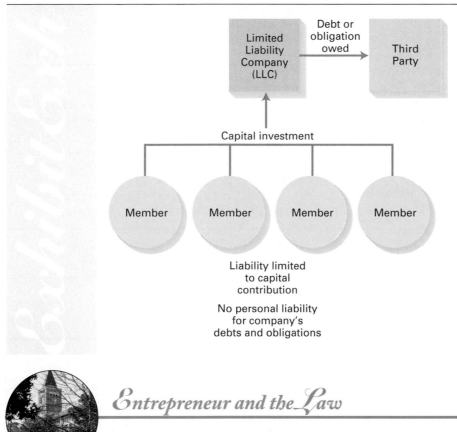

Ɛntrepreneur and the Law

DIVIDING AN LLC'S PROFITS AND LOSSES

Unless otherwise agreed, the ULLCA mandates that a member has the right to an equal share in the LLC's profits [ULLCA § 405(a)]. This is a default rule that the members can override by agreement and is usually a provision in their operating agreement. For example, in many instances the members may not want the profits of the LLC to be shared equally. This would normally occur if the capital contributions of the members were unequal. If the members want the profits divided in the same proportion as their capital contributions, this should be specified in the operating agreement.

Consider This Example   Lilly and Harrison form an LLC. Lilly contributes $75,000 capital and Harrison contributes $25,000 capital. They do not have an agreement as to how profits are to be shared. If the LLC makes $100,000 in profits, under the ULLCA Lilly and Harrison will share

the profits equally—$50,000 each. To avoid this outcome, Lilly and Harrison should agree in their operating agreement how they want the profits to be divided.

Losses from an LLC are shared equally unless otherwise agreed. Sometimes members will not want to divide losses equally and maybe not even in the same way as their capital contributions. If the LLC has chosen to be taxed as a partnership, the losses from an LLC flow to the members' individual income tax returns. Losses from an LLC can sometimes be offset against members' gains from other sources. Therefore, the members may want to agree to divide the losses so that the members who can use them to offset other income will receive a greater share of the losses.

Profits and losses from an LLC do not have to be distributed in the same proportion. For example, a member who has the right to a 10 percent share of profits may be given the right to receive 25 percent of the LLC's losses.

Entrepreneur and the Law

DreamWorks SKG, LLC: Script for a Movie Company

In 1995, Steven Spielberg, Jeffrey Katzenberg, and David Geffen formed DreamWorks SKG, which is a major movie and recording production company. Spielberg's fame and money came from directing such films as *E. T.*, Katzenberg was a leading executive at Disney, and Geffen built and sold Geffen Records. These multimillionaire multimedia giants combined their talents to form a formidable entertainment company.

Interestingly, DreamWorks was hatched as a Delaware limited liability company, or LLC. The organizers chose an LLC because it is taxed as a partnership and the profits (or losses) flow directly to the owners, but like a corporation, the owners are protected from personal liability beyond their capital contributions.

DreamWorks issued several classes of stock, or interests. The three principals put up $100 million ($33.3 million each) for "SKG" stock, which grants the principals 100 percent voting control and 67 percent of the firm's profits. In addition, each principal has a seven-year employment con-

tract that pays them $1 million annually, plus other fringe benefits and perquisites on terms that are customary for similarly situated executives in the entertainment industry.

DreamWorks raised the other $900 million of its $1 billion capital from other investors, who received a third of future profits. The other investors were issued the following classes of stock:

Class	Investment
A	Outside investors. Class A stock was sold to big investors with over $20 million to invest. Microsoft's cofounder, Paul Allen, has purchased $500 million of Class A stock. Class A investors got seats on the board of directors.
S	Outside investors. Class S stock was issued for smallish, "strategic" investments with other companies for cross-marketing purposes.
E	Employees. Employees were granted the right to participate in an employee stock purchase plan.

International Law

Limited Liability Companies in Foreign Countries

The use of the limited liability company (LLC) as a form of conducting business in the United States is of recent origin. In 1977 Wyoming was the first state in the United States to enact legislation creating an LLC as a legal form for conducting business. This new form of business received little attention until the early 1990s when several more states enacted legislation to allow the creation of LLCs. The evolution of LLCs then grew at blinding speed, with all the states having enacted LLC statutes by 1998. Most LLC laws are quite similar, although some differences do exist between these state statutes.

The United States did not invent the LLC as a form of business, however. An LLC form of business has been used in different countries of the world for a long time. The **limitada**, a form of business used in Latin America, has many similarities to the LLC. Limitadas have been used in Argentina, Brazil, Mexico, and other Latin American countries for a century. These entities share the features of limited liability of owners and centralized management with the LLC. In creating its LLC law, the state of Florida noted that its LLC law was necessary to provide a form of business sim-

ilar to Latin limitadas, with which Central and South American investors were familiar.

On the European continent, an equivalent form of business to the LLC has existed for centuries. In Spain it was called the **sociedad de responsibilidades limitada**. Modern continental LLCs provide for limited liability of owners and centralized management. Germany was one of the latest European countries to add the LLC as a form of business— one century ago. In England, an antecedent to the LLC called the **stock company** was developed around 1555. These companies, while technically partnerships, had limited liability of owners, free transferability of ownership interests, and centralized management similar to modern LLCs.

In the United States, the LLC has rapidly become the business of choice for nonpublicly traded business. Although the use of LLCs by entrepreneurs and other business owners has received much attention in this country, it must not be forgotten that the LLC is not a U.S. invention but is an international form of business that has been in use in other countries of the world for centuries.

CHAPTER SUMMARY

Sole Proprietorship, p. 691

Sole Proprietorship	A form of business in which the owner and the business are one. The business is not a separate legal entity.
Business Name	A sole proprietorship can operate under the name of the sole proprietor or a *trade name*. Operating under a trade name is commonly designated as a *d.b.a.* (*doing business as*). If a trade name is used, a *fictitious business name statement* must be filed with the appropriate state government office.
Personal Liability of Sole Proprietors	The sole proprietor is personally liable for the debts and obligations of the sole proprietorship.

General Partnership, p. 693

General Partnerships	1. *Uniform Partnership Act (UPA)*. Model act that codifies partnership law. Most states have adopted all or part of the UPA. 2. *Entity theory of partnerships*. A theory that holds that partnerships are *separate legal entities* that can hold title to personal and real property, transact business in the partnership name, and the like. 3. *Taxation of partnerships*. Partnerships do not pay federal income taxes. The income and losses of partnership flow onto individual partners' federal income tax returns.
Formation of General Partnerships	1. *General Partnership*. An association of two or more persons to carry on as co-owners of a business for profit [UPA § 6(1)]. 2. *Partnership name*. A general partnership can operate under the names of any one or more of the partners or under a fictitious business name.
The Partnership Agreement	Agreement establishing a general partnership. It sets forth the terms of the partnership. It is good practice to have a written partnership agreement that the partners sign. 1. *Certificate of partnership*. A document that general partnerships must file with the appropriate state government agency in some states.
Contract Liability	1. *Partners' contract authority*. A contract entered into by a partner with a third party on behalf of a partnership is binding on the partnership. 2. *Ratification*. The partners can decide to *ratify* an unauthorized contract. The ratification binds the partnership to the contract from the time of execution. 3. *Partnership liability*. A partnership is liable for the contracts entered into on its behalf by partners acting with express, implied, or apparent authority, or where unauthorized contracts have been ratified by the partners.
Tort Liability	1. *Tort*. Occurs when a partner causes injury to a third party by his or her negligent act, breach of trust, breach of fiduciary duty, or intentional tort. 2. *Partnership liability*. The partnership is liable to third persons who are injured by torts committed by a partner while he or she is acting within the ordinary course of partnership business. 3. *Joint and several liability of partners*. Partners are *personally liable* for torts committed by partners acting on partnership business. This liability is *joint and several*. This means that the plaintiff can sue *one or more* of the partners separately. If successful, the plaintiff can recover the entire amount of the judgment from any or all of the defendant-partners.
Liability of Incoming Partners	A new partner who is admitted to the partnership is liable for the existing debts and obligations (*antecedent debts*) of the partnership only to the extent of his or her capital contribution. The new partner is personally liable for debts and obligations incurred by the partnership after becoming a partner.
Dissolution of Partnerships	The change in the relation of the partners caused by any partner ceasing to be associated in the carrying on of the business [UPA § 29].
Wrongful Dissolution	Occurs when a partner withdraws from a partnership without having the *right* to do so at the time. The partner is liable for damages caused by the wrongful dissolution of the partnership.
Notice of Dissolution	1. *Notice of dissolution to partners*. Notice of dissolution must be given to all partners. If a partner who has not received notice of dissolution enters into a contract on behalf of the partnership in the course of partnership business, the contract is binding on all of the partners.

2. _Notice of dissolution to third parties._ The following notice must be given to third parties when a partnership has been dissolved other than by operation of law:
   a. _Actual notice._ Must be given to third parties who have actually dealt with the partnership.
   b. _Constructive notice._ Must be given to third parties who have not dealt with the partnership but have knowledge of it. Constructive notice is given by publishing a notice of dissolution in a newspaper of general circulation serving the area where the business of the partnership is conducted.
   c. _No notice._ Parties who have not dealt with the partnership and do not have knowledge of it do not have to be given notice.

Continuation of the Partnership after Dissolution

The surviving or remaining partners are given the right to continue the partnership after dissolution. When a partnership is continued, the old partnership is dissolved and a new partnership is created.
1. _Continuation agreement._ A document that expressly sets forth the events that allow for continuation of the partnership, the amount to be paid to outgoing partners, and other details.
2. _Creditors' status._ The creditors of the old partnership become creditors of the new partnership and have equal status with the creditors of the new partnership.
3. _Liability of outgoing partners._ An outgoing partner is liable for existing partnership debts unless the creditor, other partners, and the outgoing partner enter into a _novation agreement_ that expressly relieves the outgoing partner of liability to the creditor.

Limited Partnership, p. 700

Uniform Limited Partnership Act

1. _Uniform Limited Partnership Act (ULPA)._ A 1916 model act that contains a uniform set of provisions for the formation, operation, and dissolution of limited partnerships.
2. _Revised Uniform Limited Partnership Act (RULPA)._ A 1976 revision of the ULPA that provides a more modern comprehensive law for the formation, operation, and dissolution of limited partnerships.

Limited Partnerships

1. _Limited partnerships._ A special form of partnership that has both limited and general partners.
   a. _General partners._ Partners in a limited partnership who invest capital, manage the business, and are personally liable for partnership debts.
   b. _Limited partners._ Partners in a limited partnership who invest capital but do not participate in management and are not personally liable for partnership debts beyond their capital contributions.
2. _Corporation as sole general partner._ A corporation may be the sole general partner of a limited partnership. Shareholders of corporations are liable only up to their capital contributions.

Formation of Limited Partnerships

1. _Certificate of limited partnership._ A document that two or more persons must execute and sign that establishes a limited partnership. The certificate of limited partnership must be filed with the Secretary of State of the appropriate state.
2. _Limited partnership agreement._ A document that sets forth the rights and duties of general and limited partners, the terms and conditions regarding the operation, termination, and dissolution of the partnership, and so on.
3. _Offering circular._ Document that is provided to investors of limited partnership interests that describes the issuer, its business, the terms of the partnership agreement, and other relevant information.
4. _Defective formation._ Occurs when (a) a certificate of limited partnership is not properly filed, (b) there are defects in a certificate that is filed, or (c) some other statutory requirement for the creation of a limited partnership is not met. A limited partner may be held liable as a general partner if the limited partnership is defectively formed.

Share of Profits and Losses

Share of profits and losses. Unless otherwise agreed, profits and losses from a limited partnership are shared on the basis of the value of the partner's capital contributions. A limited partner is not liable for losses beyond his or her capital contribution. The limited partnership agreement may specify how profits and losses are to be allocated among the general and limited partners.

Liability of General and Limited Partners

1. _General partners._ General partners of a limited partnership have _unlimited personal liability_ for the debts and obligations of the limited partnership.
2. _Limited partners._ Limited partners of a limited partnership are liable only for the debts and obligations of the limited partnership up to their capital contributions.
3. _Limited partners and management._ Limited partners have no right to participate in the management of the partnership. A limited partner is _liable as a general partner_ if his or her participation in the control of the business is substantially the same as that of a general partner, but the limited partner is liable only to persons who reasonably believed him or her to be a general partner.

Limited Liability Partnership (LLP), p. 704

Limited Liability Partnership	
	1. *Limited liability partnership (LLP).* A new form of business in which there does not have to be a general partner who is personally liable for debts and obligations of the partnership. All partners are limited partners and stand to lose only their capital contribution should the partnership fail. LLPs are formed by accountants and other professionals as allowed by LLP law.
	2. *Partners.* Owners of an LLP.
	3. *Articles of partnership.* A document that the partners of an LLP must execute, sign, and file with the Secretary of State of the appropriate state to form an LLP.
	4. *Taxation.* An LLP does not pay federal income taxes unless it elects to do so. If an LLP is taxed as a partnership, the income and losses of the LLP flow onto individual partners' federal income tax returns.

Limited Liability Company (LLC), p. 706

Limited Liability Company	
	1. *Limited liability company (LLC).* A special form of unincorporated business entity that combines the tax benefits of a partnership with the limited personal liability attribute of a corporation.
	2. *Members.* Owners of an LLC.
	3. *Articles of organization.* A document that owners of an LLC must execute, sign, and file with the Secretary of State of the appropriate state to form an LLC.
	4. *Operating agreement.* An agreement entered into among members that governs the affairs and business of the LLC and the relations among partners, managers, and the LLC.
	5. *Taxation.* An LLC does not pay federal income taxes unless it elects to do so. If an LLC is taxed as a partnership, the income and losses of the LLP flow onto individual members' federal income tax returns.
	6. *Member-managed and manager-managed LLC.* An LLC can be either a *member-managed LLC* or a *manager-managed LLC.* An LLC is a member-managed LLC unless it is designated as a manager-managed LLC.
	a. *Member-managed LLC.* All members of the LLC have agency authority to bind the LLC to contracts.
	b. *Manager-managed LLC.* Only the designated managers have authority to bind the LLC to contracts.

*E*ND-OF-*C*HAPTER *I*NTERNET *E*XERCISES AND *C*ASE *Q*UESTIONS

Working the Web Internet Exercises

ACTIVITIES

1. Review the materials at **smallbiz.biz.findlaw.com/ planning/index.html?planning/wa**. Compare with the text discussion of partnerships. Can you see why lawyers generally advise business clients not to do business in a partnership form?

2. Review business associations at **jurist.law.pitt.edu/ sg_bus.htm** to determine why the LLC is an increasingly popular form of doing business.

3. Check your state statute on LLCs. How many persons are required to form an LLC? See **www.4inc. com/llcfaq.htm**. For an overview of partnerships and LLCs in the context of a state law, see "Florida's New Partnership Law" at **www.law.fsu.edu/journals/ lawreview/issues/232/larson.html**.

4. Check your state statute on LLPs. Are they permitted in your jurisdiction? Any limitations on the type of businesses allowed to operate as an LLP? See "LII: Law About . . . Partnership" at **www.law.cornell.edu/ topics/partnership.html**. A large, rambling, and self-consciously offbeat site, is the "Lectric Law Library," **www.lectlaw.com/bus.html**. There you will find a business law section with numerous items of interest.

CRITICAL LEGAL THINKING CASES

28.1 General Partnership In early 1986, Thomas Smithson, a house builder and small-scale property developer, decided that a certain tract of undeveloped land in Franklin, Tennessee, would be extremely attractive for development into a subdivision. Smithson contacted the owner of the property, Monsanto Chemical Company, and was told that the company would sell the property at the "right price."

Smithson did not have the funds with which to embark unassisted in the endeavor, so he contacted Frank White, a co-owner of the Andrews Realty Company, and two agents of the firm, Dennis Devrow and Temple Ennis. Smithson showed them a sketch map with the proposed layout of the lots, roads, and so forth. Smithson testified that they all orally agreed to develop the property together, and in lieu of a financial investment, Smithson would oversee the engineering of the property. Subsequently, H. R. Morgan was brought into the deal to provide additional financing.

Smithson later discovered that White had contacted Monsanto directly. When challenged about this, White assured Smithson that he was still "part of the deal" but refused to put the agreement in writing. White, Devrow, Ennis, and Morgan purchased the property from Monsanto. They then sold it to H. A. H. Associates, a corporation, for a $184,000 profit. When they refused to pay Smithson, he sued to recover an equal share of the profits. Was a partnership formed between Smithson and the defendants? [*Smithson v. White*, 1988 W. L. 42645 (Tenn. App. 1988)]

28.2 General Partnership Richard Filip owned Trans Texas Properties. Tracy Peoples was an employee of the company. In order to obtain credit to advertise in the *Austin American-Statesman* newspaper, which was owned by Cox Enterprises, Inc., Peoples completed a credit application that listed Jack Elliot as a partner in Trans Texas. Evidence showed that Elliot did not own an interest in Trans Texas and did not consent to or authorize Peoples to make this representation to Cox. Cox made no effort to verify the accuracy of the representation and extended credit to Trans Texas. When Trans Texas defaulted on payments owed Cow, Cox sued both Filip and Elliot to recover the debt. Is Elliot liable? [*Cox Enterprises, Inc. v. Filip and Elliot*, 538 S.W.2d 836 (Tex. App. 1976)]

28.3 Tort Liability In January 1977, Charles Fial and Roger J. Steeby entered into a partnership called "Audit Consultants" to perform auditing services. Pursuant to the agreement, they shared equally the equity, income, and profits of the partnership. Originally, they performed the auditing services themselves, but as business increased, they engaged independent contractors to do some of the audit work. Fial's activities generated approximately 80 percent of the partnership's revenues. Unhappy with their agreement to divide the profits equally, Fial wrote a letter to Steeby on July 11, 1984, dissolving the partnership.

Fial asserted that the clients should be assigned based on who brought them into the business. Fial formed a new business called "Audit Consultants of Colorado, Inc." He then terminated the partnership's contracts with many clients and put them under contract with his new firm. Fial also terminated the partnership's contracts with the independent-contractor auditors and signed many of these auditors with his new firm. The partnership terminated on May 24, 1985. Steeby brought an action against Fial, alleging breach of fiduciary duty and seeking a final accounting. Who wins? [*Steeby v. Fial*, 765 P.2d 1081 (Colo. App. 1988)]

28.4 Fiduciary Duty Edgar and Selwyn Husted, attorneys, formed Husted and Husted, a law partnership. Herman

McCloud, who was the executor of his mother's estate, hired them as attorneys for the estate. When taxes were due on the estate, Edgar told McCloud to make a check for $18,000 payable to the Husted and Husted Trust Account and that he would pay the IRS from this account. There was no Husted and Husted trust account. Instead, Edgar deposited the check into his own personal account and converted the funds to his own personal use. When Edgar's misconduct was uncovered, McCloud sued the law firm for conversion of estate funds. Is the partnership liable for Edgar's actions? [*Husted v. McCloud*, 436 N.E.2d 341 (Ind. App. 1982)]

28.5 Tort Liability Thomas McGrath was a partner in the law firm of Torbenson, Thatcher, McGrath, Treadwell & Schoonmaker. At approximately 4:30 P.M. on February 11, 1980, McGrath went to a restaurant-cocktail establishment in Kirkland, Washington. From that time until about 1:00 P.M. he imbibed considerable alcohol while socializing and discussing personal and firm-related business. After 11:00 P.M., McGrath did not discuss firm business but continued to socialize and drink until approximately 1:45 A.M., when he and Frederick Hayes, another bar patron, exchanged words. Shortly thereafter, the two encountered each other outside, and after another exchange, McGrath shot Hayes. Hayes sued McGrath and the law firm for damages. Who is liable? [*Hayes v. Torbenson, Thatcher, McGrath, Treadwell & Schoonmaker*, 749 P.2d 178 (Wash. App. 1988)]

28.6 Notice of Dissolution In 1976, Leonard Sumter, Sr., entered into a partnership agreement with his son, Michael T. Sumter, to conduct a plumbing business in Shreveport, Louisiana, under the name "Sumter Plumbing Company." On June 18, 1976, the father, on behalf of the partnership, executed a credit application with Thermal Supply of Louisiana, Inc., for an open account to purchase supplies on credit. From that date until the spring of 1980, the Sumters purchased plumbing supplies from Thermal on credit and paid their bills without fail. Both partners and one employee signed for supplies at Thermal. In May 1980, the partnership was dissolved, and all outstanding debts to Thermal were paid in full. The Sumters did not, however, notify Thermal that the partnership had been dissolved.

A year later, the son decided to reenter the plumbing business. He used the name previously used by the former partnership, listed the same post office address for billing purposes, and hired the employee of the former partnership who signed for supplies at Thermal. The father decided not to become involved in this venture. The son began purchasing supplies on credit from Thermal on the open credit account of the former partnership. Thermal was not informed that he was operating a new business. When the son defaulted on payments to Thermal, it sued the original partnership to recover the debt. Is the father liable for these debts? [*Thermal Supply of Louisiana, Inc. v. Sumter*, 452 So.2d 312 (La. App. 1984)]

28.7 Liability of General Partners Pat McGowan, Val Somers, and Brent Robertson were general partners of Vermont Place, a limited partnership formed on January 20, 1984, for the purpose of constructing duplexes on an undeveloped tract of land in Fort Smith, Arkansas. The general partners appointed McGowan and his company, Advance Development Corporation, to develop the project, including contracting with material men, mechanics, and other suppliers. None of the limited partners took part in the management or control of the partnership.

On September 3, 1984, Somers and Robertson discovered that McGowan had not been paying the suppliers. They removed McGowan from the partnership and took over the project. The suppliers sued the partnership to recover the money owed them. The partnership assets were not sufficient to pay all of their claims. Who is liable to the suppliers? [*National Lumber Company v. Advance Development Corporation*, 732 S.W. 2d 840 (AK 1987)]

28.8 Liability of Limited Partners Union Station Associates of New London (USANL) is a limited partnership formed under the laws of Connecticut. Allen M. Schultz, Anderson Notter Associates, and the Lepton Trust were limited partners. The limited partners did not take part in the management of the partnership. The National Railroad Passenger Association (NRPA) entered into an agreement to lease part of a railroad facility from USANL. The NRPA sued the USANL for allegedly breaching the lease and also named the limited partners as defendants. Are the limited partners liable? [*National Railroad Passenger Association v. Union Station Associates of New London*, 643 F.Supp. 192 (D.D.C. 1986)]

28.9 Formation of a Limited Partnership Robert K. Powers and Lee M. Solomon were among other limited partners of the Cosmopolitan Chinook Hotel, a limited partnership. On October 25, 1972, Cosmopolitan entered into a contract to lease and purchase neon signs from Dwinell's Central Neon. The contract identified Cosmopolitan as a "partnership" and was signed on behalf of the partnership, "R. Powers, President." At the time the contract was entered into, Cosmopolitan had taken no steps to file its certificate of limited partnership with the state as required by limited partnership law. The certificate was not filed with the state until several months after the contract was signed. When Cosmopolitan defaulted on payments due under the contract, Dwinell's sued Cosmopolitan and its general and limited partners. Are the limited partners liable? [*Dwinell's Central Neon v. Cosmopolitan Chinook Hotel*, 587 P.2d 191 (Wash. App. 1978)]

28.10 Limited Liability Company Harold, Jasmine, Caesar, and Yuan form "Microhard.com, LLC," a limited liability company, to sell computer hardware and software over the Internet. Microhard.com, LLC, hires Heather, a recent graduate of the University of Chicago and a brilliant software designer, as an employee. Heather's job is to design and develop software that will execute a computer command when the computer user thinks of the next command he or she wants to execute on the computer. Using Heather's research, Microhard.com, LLC, develops the "Third Eye" software program that does this. Microhard.com, LLC, sends Heather to the annual Comdex Computer Show in Las Vegas, Nevada, to unveil this revolutionary software. Heather goes to Las Vegas and while there rents an automobile to get from the hotel to the computer show and to meet interested buyers at different locations in Las Vegas. While Heather is driving from her hotel to the site of the Comdex Computer Show, she negligently causes an accident where she runs over Harold Singer, a pedestrian. Singer, who suffers severe personal injuries, sues Microhard.com, LLC; Heather; Harold; Jasmine; Caesar; and Yuan to recover monetary damages for his injuries. Who is liable?

28.11 Limited Liability Company Juan, Min-Yi, and Chelsea form "Unlimited, LLC," a limited liability company that operates a chain of women's retail clothing stores that sell eclectic women's clothing. The company is a manager-managed LLC, and Min-Yi has been designated in the articles of organization filed with the secretary of state as the manager of Unlimited, LLC. Min-Yi sees a store location on Rodeo Drive in Beverly Hills, California, that she thinks would be an excellent location for an Unlimited store. Min-Yi enters into a five-year lease on behalf of Unlimited, LLC, with Landlord, Inc., the owner of the store building, to lease the store at $100,000 rent per year. While visiting Chicago, Chelsea sees a store location on North Michigan Avenue in Chicago that she thinks is a perfect location for an Unlimited store. Chelsea enters into a five-year lease on behalf of Unlimited, LLC, with Real Estate, Inc., the owner of the store building, to lease the store location at $100,000 rent per year. Is Unlimited, LLC bound to either of these leases?

28.12 Limited Liability Company Donna, Arnold, Jose, and Won-Suk form a limited liability company called "Millennium Foods, LLC," to operate an organic foods grocery store in Portland, Oregon. Donna and Arnold each contribute $25,000 capital, Jose contributes $50,000, and Won-Suk contributes $100,000. The LLC's articles of organization are silent as to how profits and losses of the LLC are to be divided. The organic foods grocery store is an immediate success and Millennium Foods, LLC, makes $200,000 profit the first year. Jose and Won-Suk want the profits distributed based on the amount of the members' capital contribution. Arnold and Donna think the profits should be distributed equally. Who is correct?

BUSINESS ETHICS CASES

28.13 Business Ethics Harriet Hankin, Samuel Hankin, Moe Henry Hankin, Perch P. Hankin, and Pauline Hankin, and their spouses, for many years operated a family partnership composed of vast real estate holdings. Some of the properties included restaurants, industrial buildings, shopping centers, golf courses, a motel chain, and hundreds of acres of developable ground, estimated to be worth $72 million in 1977. In that year, because of family disagreement and discontent, the Hankin family agreed to dissolve the partnership. When they could not agree on how to liquidate the partnership assets, in August 1977, Harriet and Samuel (collectively called Harriet) initiated this equity action.

Based on assurances from Moe and Perch that they would sell the partnership assets as quickly as possible and at the highest possible price, the court appointed them as liquidators of the partnership during the winding-up period. Based on similar assurances, the court again appointed them liquidators for the partnership in 1979. But by 1981, only enough property had been sold to retire the debt of the partnership. Evidence showed that Moe and Perch had not aggressively marketed the remaining properties and that Moe wished to purchase some of the properties for himself at a substantial discount from their estimated value. Six years and three appeals to the superior court later, Harriet brought this action seeking the appointment of a receiver to liquidate the remaining partnership assets.

Did the winding-up partners breach their fiduciary duties? Should the court appoint a receiver to liquidate the remaining partnership assets? Did Moe Henry Hankin act ethically in this case? [*Hankin v. Hankin*, 493 A.2d 675 (PA 1985)]

28.14 Business Ethics   Angela, Yoko, Cherise, and Serena want to start a new business that designs and manufactures toys for children. At a meeting where the owners want to decide what type of legal form to use to operate the business, Cherise states

> *We should use a limited liability company to operate our business because this form of business provides us, the owners, with a limited liability shield, which means that if the business gets sued and loses, we the owners are not personally liable to the injured party except up to our capital contribution in the business.*

The others agree and form a limited liability company called Fuzzy Toys, LLC, to conduct the member-managed business. Each of the four owners contributes $50,000 as their capital contribution to the LLC. Fuzzy Toys, LLC, purchases $800,000 of liability insurance from Allied Insurance Company and starts business. Fuzzy Toys, LLC, designs and produces "Heidi," a new toy doll and female action figure. The new toy doll is an instant success and Fuzzy Toys, LLC, produces and sells millions of these female action figures. After a few months, however, the LLC starts getting complaints that one of the parts of the female action figure is breaking off quite regularly and some children are swallowing the part. The concerned member-managers of Fuzzy Toys, LLC, issue an immediate recall of the female action figure, but before all of the dolls are returned for a refund, Catherine, a seven-year-old child, swallows the toy's part and is severely injured. Catherine, through her mother, sues Fuzzy Toys, LLC, Allied Insurance Company, Angela, Yoko, Cherise, and Serena to recover damages for product liability. At the time of the suit, Fuzzy Toys, LLC, has $200,000 of assets. The jury awards Catherine $10 million for her injuries. Who is liable to Catherine and for how much? How much does Catherine recover? Did Angela, Yoko, Cherise, and Serena act ethically in using an LLC as a form of conducting their toy business? Explain.

BRIEFING THE CASE WRITING ASSIGNMENT

Read the following case, which has been excerpted from the court's opinion. Review and brief the case.

Catalina Mortgage Co., Inc. v. Monier
166 Ariz. 71, 800 P.2D 574 (1990)
Supreme Court of Arizona

Feldman, Vice Chief Judge

In 1984, Michael Monier and Talon Financial Corporation (Talon) formed the Coronado Industrial Investors Limited Partnership (Coronado). Monier and Talon were general partners; other individuals and entities were limited partners in the venture.

Shortly after its formation, Coronado purchased an office and warehouse complex in Tucson. In 1986, the partnership refinanced this property with a loan from Catalina Mortgage Company (Catalina). Talon's president, Roger Howard, executed a promissory note in the amount of $675,000 on behalf of Coronado. In mid-1987, Talon withdrew as a general partner, leaving Monier as the sole general partner in Coronado. The promissory note matured and $687,935.39 plus interest is now due and owing. Coronado filed for protection pursuant to Chapter 11 of the Bankruptcy Code.

In January 1989, Catalina filed a complaint against Monier in United States District Court, seeking judgment for the amount due on the promissory note plus interest, costs, and attorney's fees. Catalina alleged that Monier was jointly and severally liable with the partnership entity for the debt. Monier answered, contending, among other things, that because the note was an

obligation of the partnership, the partnership assets had to be exhausted before the creditor sought recovery from an individual general partner.

If a partnership's debt is contractual in nature, common law requires creditors to resort to and exhaust partnership assets before reaching the partners' individual assets. At common law, a partner is only jointly liable for the partnership's contractual debts, though partners are jointly and severally liable for tort obligations.

As adopted in most states, the Uniform Partnership Act (UPA) preserves this common law rule. The Arizona version of the UPA, however, provides that all partners are liable jointly and severally for everything chargeable to the partnership, and for all other debts and obligations of the partnership; but any partner may enter into a separate obligation to perform a partnership contract.

Catalina maintains that because the statute imposes joint and several liability on all partners, it may proceed against Monier without exhausting partnership assets. Catalina distinguishes cases from other jurisdictions that have considered the issue on the grounds that the applicable law imposed only joint liability as opposed to joint and several liability, that some states specifically provide by statute that partnership assets must be exhausted prior to imposing liability on individual partners for contractual obligations, and that the bankruptcy courts in some instances have misconstrued the state law involved.

Several liability is separate and distinct from liability of another to the extent that an independent action may be brought without joinder of others. The individual liability associated with partners that are jointly liable is not separate and distinct from the liability of all the partners jointly. Rather, that individual liability arises only after it has been shown that the partnership assets are inadequate. No direct cause of action may be maintained against the individual partners until the above condition is met. Several liability, on the other hand, imposes no such conditions precedent before one can be held individually liable.

We hold, therefore, that the scheme imposed by Arizona statutes is simply that a general partner is jointly and severally liable for partnership debts. The partner may be sued severally and his assets reached even though the partnership or other partners are not sued and their assets not applied to the debt. Under Arizona law a creditor may obtain a judgment against an individual general partner on a partnership debt and may reach the partner's assets prior to exhausting partnership assets.

ENDNOTE

1. Georgia and Louisiana have not adopted the UPA. These states enacted their own partnership statutes.

CHAPTER 29

Domestic and Multinational Corporations

A corporation is an artificial being, invisible, intangible, and existing only in the contemplation of law. Being the mere creature of the law, it possesses only those properties which the charter of its creation confers upon it, either expressly or as incidental to its very existence. These are such as supposed best calculated to effect the object for which it was created. Among the most important are immortality, and, if the expression may be allowed, individuality; properties by which a perpetual succession of many persons are considered as the same, and may act as a single individual.

—John Marshall, Chief Justice, U.S. Supreme Court
Dartmouth College v. Woodward
4 Wheaton 518, 636 (1819)

Chapter Objectives

After studying this chapter, you should be able to:

1. Define *corporation* and list the major characteristics of a corporation.

2. Describe the process of forming a corporation.

3. Distinguish between publicly held and closely held corporations.

4. Identify when promoters are liable on preincorporation contracts.

5. Define *S Corporation* and describe its tax benefits.

6. Define *common stock* and distinguish among authorized, issued, treasury, and outstanding shares.

7. Describe the preferences associated with preferred stock.

8. Describe the rights of debenture holders and bondholders.

9. Describe the organization and operation of multinational corporations.

10. Describe Internet corporate alliances in China.

Chapter Contents

Corporations are the most dominant form of business organization in the United States, generating over 85 percent of the country's gross business receipts. Corporations range in size from one owner to thousands of owners. Owners of corporations are called *shareholders*.

Corporations were first formed in medieval Europe. Great Britain granted charters to certain trading companies from the 1500s to the 1700s. The English law of corporations applied in most of the colonies until 1776. After the War of Independence, the states of the United States developed their own corporation law.

Originally, corporate charters were individually granted by state legislatures. In the late 1700s, however, the states began enacting *general corporation statutes* that permitted corporations to be formed without the separate approval of the legislature. Today, most corporations are formed pursuant to general corporation laws of the states.

The formation and financing of corporations are discussed in this chapter.

corporation

A fictitious legal entity that is created according to statutory requirements.

Nature of the Corporation

Corporations can only be created pursuant to the laws of the state of incorporation. These statutes—commonly referred to as **corporations codes**—regulate the formation, operation, and dissolution of corporations. The state legislature may amend its corporate statute at any time. Such changes may require the corporation's articles of incorporation to be amended.

The courts interpret state corporation statutes to decide individual corporate and shareholder disputes. As a result, a body of common law has evolved concerning corporate and shareholder rights and obligations.

corporations codes

State statutes that regulate the formation, operation, and dissolution of corporations.

The Corporation as a Legal "Person"

A corporation is a separate *legal entity* (or *legal person*) for most purposes. Corporations are treated, in effect, as artificial persons created by the state that can sue or be sued in their own names, enter into and enforce contracts, hold title to and transfer property, and be found civilly and criminally liable for violations of law. Because corporations cannot be put in prison, the normal criminal penalty is the assessment of a fine, loss of a license, or other sanction.

Business Brief

A corporation is a separate legal entity—an *artificial person*—that can own property, sue and be sued, enter into contracts, and such.

Characteristics of Corporations

Corporations have the following unique characteristics:

1. **Limited Liability of Shareholders** As separate legal entities, corporations are liable for their own contracts and debts. Generally, the shareholders have only **limited liability**. That is, they are liable only to the extent of their capital contributions.
2. **Free Transferability of Shares** Corporate shares are freely transferable by the shareholder by sale, assignment, pledge, or gift unless they are issued pursuant to certain exemptions from securities registration. Shareholders may agree among themselves on restrictions on the transfer of shares. National securities markets, such as the New York Stock Exchange, the American Stock Exchange, and NASDAQ, have been developed for the organized sale of securities.
3. **Perpetual Existence** Corporations exist in perpetuity unless a specific duration is stated in the corporation's articles of incorporation. The existence of a corporation can be voluntarily terminated by the shareholders. Corporations may be involuntarily terminated by the corporation's creditors if an involuntary petition for bankruptcy against the corporation is granted. The death, insanity, or bankruptcy of a shareholder, a director, or an officer of the corporation does not affect its existence.
4. **Centralized Management** The *board of directors* makes policy decisions concerning the operation of the corporation. The members of the board of directors are elected by the shareholders. The directors, in turn, appoint corporate *officers* to run the corporation's day-to-day operations. Together, the directors and the officers form the corporate "management."

The doctrine of limited liability of shareholders was imposed by the court in the following case.

limited liability

Shareholders are liable for the corporation's debts and obligations only to the extent of their capital contributions.

Joslyn Manufacturing Co. v. T. L. James & Co., Inc.
893 F.2d 80 (1990)
United States Court of Appeals, Fifth Circuit

CASE 29.1

BACKGROUND AND FACTS

The Lincoln Creosoting Company, Inc. (Lincoln), was a Louisiana corporation that was incorporated in 1935. The company operated a wood-treating and creosoting plant on its property. Although the company had a treatment plant, creosoting chemicals dripped into an open pit and were washed away by rain to surrounding land areas and waterways. From 1935 until 1950, Lincoln was 60 percent owned by T. L. James & Company, Inc. (James & Co.). Lincoln maintained separate books and records; held regularly scheduled shareholders' and directors' meetings; owned its own property and equipment; maintained its own employees, payroll, insurance, pension plan, and workers' compensation program; and filed its own tax returns. Thus, Lincoln, the subsidiary corporation, was run separately from its parent corporation, James & Co.

In 1950, Lincoln was sold to Joslyn Manufacturing Company (Joslyn), which in turn sold the plant in 1969. Since that time, the property has passed through six separate owners, the last of which subdivided the property. The current owners of the property and adjacent property owners brought suit under the Comprehensive Environmental Response, Compensation, and Liability Act (CERCLA), a federal environmental statute, to recover damages from Joslyn's and Lincoln's other prior owners for environmental cleanup costs. Joslyn's, which was ordered to clean up the contaminated site, sued James & Co. to recover costs of the cleanup. James & Co. asserted in defense that it was merely a shareholder of Lincoln and was protected by the limited liability doctrine. The district court granted James & Co.'s motion for summary judgment. Joslyn appealed.

ISSUE

Is James & Co. liable for the environmental pollution caused by Lincoln?

COURT'S REASONING

Under corporate law, a shareholder's liability for the debts and obligations of a corporation is limited to his or her capital contribution. In this case, Lincoln was operated as a separate corporation with adequate capital and observed all corporate formalities. Therefore, James & Co., a shareholder of Lincoln, is not liable for environmental pollution caused by Lincoln. The court of appeals noted that Congress is capable of creating statutes that hold shareholders liable for the acts of corporations but held that Congress had not done so in this case.

DECISION

The court of appeals held that the corporate doctrine of limited liability shielded James & Co. from liability for the environmental pollution caused by Lincoln.

Case Questions

Critical Legal Thinking Should parent corporations be held liable for the acts of subsidiary corporations? Or should they be accorded limited liability like other shareholders?

Business Ethics Is it ethical for a shareholder to hide behind the shield of limited liability?

Contemporary Business Should Congress eliminate the concept of limited liability for shareholders of corporations that have caused environmental pollution?

Revised Model Business Corporation Act (RMBCA)

Model Business Corporation Act (MBCA)

A model act drafted in 1950 that was intended to provide a uniform law for regulation of corporations.

Revised Model Business Corporation Act (RMBCA)

A revision of the MBCA in 1984 that arranged the provisions of the act more logically, revised the language to be more consistent, and made substantial changes in the provisions.

The Committee on Corporate Laws of the American Bar Association (the Committee) first drafted the **Model Business Corporation Act (MBCA)** in 1950. The model act was intended to provide a uniform law regulating the formation, operation, and termination of corporations.

In 1984, the Committee completely revised the MBCA and issued the **Revised Model Business Corporation Act (RMBCA)**. Certain provisions of the RMBCA have been amended since 1984. The RMBCA arranged the provisions of the act more logically, revised the language of the act to be more consistent, and made substantial changes in the provisions of the model act. Many states have adopted all or part of the RMBCA. The RMBCA will serve as the basis for the discussion of corporations law of this book.

There is no general federal corporations law governing the formation and operation of private corporations. Many federal laws regulate the operation of private corporations, however. These include federal securities laws, labor laws, antitrust laws, consumer protection laws, environmental protection laws, bankruptcy laws, and the like. These federal statutes are discussed in separate chapters in this book.

Mountain, China   Commercial opportunities for multinational corporations will increase as new markets open up around the world.

CLASSIFICATIONS OF CORPORATIONS

Corporations are classified based on their locations, purpose, or owners. The various classifications of corporations are discussed in the following paragraphs.

Profit and Nonprofit Corporations

Private corporations may be classified as either for profit or nonprofit. **Profit corporations** are created to conduct a business for profit and can distribute profits to shareholders in the form of dividends. Most private corporations fit this definition.

Nonprofit corporations are formed for charitable, educational, religious, or scientific purposes. Although nonprofit corporations may make a profit, they are prohibited by law from distributing this profit to their members, directors, or officers. About a dozen states have enacted the **Model Nonprofit Corporation Act** that governs the formation, operation, and termination of nonprofit corporations. All other states have their own individual statutes that govern the formation, operation, and dissolution of such corporations.

Public and Private Corporations

Government-owned (or **public**) **corporations** are formed to meet a specific governmental or political purpose. For example, most cities and towns are formed as corporations, as are most water, school, sewage, and park districts. Local government corporations are often called *municipal corporations*.

Private corporations are formed to conduct privately owned business. They are owned by private parties, not by the government. Most corporations fall into this category.

Publicly Held and Closely Held Corporations

Publicly held corporations have many shareholders. Often, they are large corporations with hundreds or thousands of shareholders whose shares are traded on organized securities markets. IBM Corporation and General Motors Corporation are examples of publicly held corporations. The shareholders rarely participate in the management of such corporations.

A **closely held** (or **close**) **corporation** is one whose shares are owned by few shareholders who are often family members, relatives, or friends. Frequently, the shareholders are involved in the management of the corporation. The shareholders sometimes enter into buy-and-sell agreements that prevent outsiders from becoming shareholders.

Professional Corporations

Professional corporations are formed by professionals such as lawyers, accountants, physicians, and dentists. The abbreviations *P.C.* (professional corporation), *P.A.* (professional association), and *S.C.* (service corporation) often identify professional corporations.

profit corporation

A corporation created to conduct a business for profit that can distribute profits to shareholders in the form of dividends.

nonprofit corporation

A corporation that is formed to operate charitable institutions, colleges, universities, and other not-for-profit entities.

public corporation

A corporation formed to meet a specific governmental or political purpose.

private corporation

A corporation formed to conduct privately owned business.

publicly held corporation

A corporation that has many shareholders and whose securities are often traded on national stock exchanges.

closely held corporation

A corporation owned by one or a few shareholders.

professional corporation

A corporation formed by lawyers, doctors, or other professionals.

Shareholders of professional corporations are often called *members*. Generally, only licensed professionals may become members.

All states permit the incorporation of professional corporations, although some states allow only designated types of professionals to incorporate. Professional corporations have normal corporate attributes and are formed like other corporations.

Members of the corporation are not usually liable for the torts committed by its agents or employees. Some states impose liability on members for the malpractice of other members of the corporation.

Business Ethics

PROFESSIONALS DODGE CORPORATE LIABILITY

Professionals may form corporations to limit their liability. Consider the following case. Three lawyers, Howard R. Cohen, Richard L. Stracher, and Paul J. Bloom, formed a professional corporation to engage in the practice of law. The three men were the sole shareholders, directors, and officers of the corporation. The corporation entered into an agreement to lease office space from We're Associates Company (We're Associates) in a building in Lake Success, New York. The lease was executed on behalf of the corporation "by Paul J. Bloom, Vice President." We're Associates sued the corporation and its three shareholders to recover $9,000 allegedly due and owing under the lease.

The trial court dismissed the plaintiff's case, and the appellate court affirmed. The appellate court noted that prior to 1970, attorneys, physicians, and other professionals in New York were barred from joining with other members of their respective professions in organizing corporations for the purpose of rendering professional services. In that year, however, with the enactment of Article 15 of the Business Corporation Law, New York joined other states in affording the privilege of incorporation to professionals.

In holding that the three lawyers who formed the professional corporation were not personally liable to We're

Associates on the corporation's lease, the appellate court stated

> It is well established that in the absence of some constitutional, statutory, or charter provision, the shareholders of a corporation are not liable for its contractual obligations and that parties having business dealings with a corporation must look to the corporation itself and not the shareholders for payment of their claims. Indeed, this insulation from individual liability for corporate obligations is one of the fundamental purposes of operating through corporate form. . . . The members of professional corporations are to enjoy the same benefits of limited liability afforded to shareholders of any other form of corporation.

The court concluded: *"Any analysis of the possible ethical considerations or moral obligations of attorneys in this situation is a separate matter and does not bear upon the substantive legal issue of the scope of liability under the statute."* [We're Associates Company v. Cohen, Stracher & Bloom, P.C., 478 N.Y.S.2d 670 (N.Y.App. 1984)]

1. Did the attorneys act ethically in not paying the lease payments themselves?
2. How could We're Associates have protected itself in this case?

Domestic, Foreign, and Alien Corporations

domestic corporation

A corporation in the state in which it was formed.

foreign corporation

A corporation in any state or jurisdiction other than the one in which it was formed.

A corporation is a **domestic corporation** in the state in which it is incorporated. It is a **foreign corporation** in all other states and jurisdictions. For example, suppose a corporation is incorporated in Texas and does business in Montana. The corporation is a domestic corporation in Texas and a foreign corporation in Montana.

A state can require a foreign corporation to *qualify* to conduct intrastate commerce within the state. Where a foreign corporation is required to qualify to do intrastate commerce in a state, it must obtain a *certificate of authority* from the state [RMBCA § 15.01(a)]. This requires the foreign corporation to file certain information with the secretary of state, pay the required fees, and appoint a registered agent for service of process.

Conduct that usually constitutes "doing business" includes maintaining an office to conduct intrastate business, selling personal property in intrastate business, entering into contracts involving intrastate commerce, using real estate for general corporate purposes, and the like. Activities that are generally *not* considered doing business within the state include maintaining, defending, or settling a lawsuit or an administrative proceeding; maintaining bank accounts; effectuating sales thorough independent contractors; soliciting orders through the mail; securing or collecting debts; transacting any business in interstate commerce; and the like [RMBCA § 15.01(b) and (c)].

Conducting intrastate business in a state in which it is not qualified subjects the corporation to fines. In addition, the corporation cannot bring a lawsuit in the state, although it can defend itself against lawsuits and administrative proceedings brought by others [RMBCA § 15.02].

An **alien corporation** is a corporation that is incorporated in another country. In most instances, alien corporations are treated as foreign corporations.

alien corporation

A corporation that is incorporated in another country.

CONCEPT SUMMARY   TYPES OF CORPORATIONS

Type of Corporation	Description
Domestic	A corporation is a domestic corporation in the state in which it is incorporated.
Foreign	A corporation is a foreign corporation in states other than the one in which it is incorporated.
Alien	A corporation is an alien corporation in the Untied States if it is incorporated in another country.

PROMOTERS' ACTIVITIES

The **promoter** is the person or persons who organize and start the corporation, negotiate and enter into contracts in advance of its formation, find the initial investors to finance the corporation, and so on. As discussed shortly, these activities may subject the promoter to personal liability.

Promoters' Liability

Promoters often enter into contracts on behalf of the corporation prior to its actual incorporation. **Promoters' contracts** include leases, sales contracts, contracts to purchase property, employment contracts, and the like. If the corporation never comes into existence, the promoters have joint personal liability on the contract unless the third party specifically exempts them from such liability.

If the corporation is formed, it becomes liable on a promoter's contract only if it agrees to become bound to the contract. This requires a resolution of the board of directors to be bound by the promoter's contract.

The promoter remains liable on the contract unless the parties enter into a novation [RMBCA § 2.04]. A *novation* is a three-party agreement whereby the corporation agrees to assume the contract liability of the promoter with the consent of the third party. After a novation, the corporation is solely liable on the promoter's contract.

In the following case, the court found a promoter liable on a promoter's contract.

promoter

A person or persons who organize and start the corporation, negotiate and enter into contracts in advance of its formation, find the initial investors to finance the corporation, and so forth.

promoter's contracts

A collective term for such things as leases, sales contracts, contracts to purchase property, and employment contracts entered into by promoters on behalf of the proposed corporation prior to its actual incorporation.

Coopers & Lybrand v. Fox

758 P.2d 68 (1988)
Colorado Court of Appeals

CASE 29.2

BACKGROUND AND FACTS
On November 3, 1981, Garry J. Fox met with a representative of Coopers & Lybrand (Coopers), a national accounting firm. Fox informed Coopers that he was acting on behalf of a corporation he was in the process of forming, G. Fox and Partners, Inc., and requested a tax opinion and other accounting services for the corporation. Coopers accepted the engagement with the knowledge that the corporation was not yet in existence. The corporation was

incorporated on December 4, 1981. Coopers completed its work by mid-December and billed the corporation and Fox $10,827 for services rendered. When neither Fox nor the corporation paid the bill, Coopers sued Fox as a promoter to recover the debt. The trial court held in favor of Fox. Coopers appealed.

ISSUE
Is Fox liable on the Coopers & Lybrand contract as a promoter?

COURT'S REASONING

The uncontroverted facts place Fox squarely within the definition of a promoter. As a general rule, promoters are personally liable for the contracts they make, although made on behalf of a corporation to be formed. The well-recognized exception to the general rule of promoter liability is that if the contracting party agrees to look solely to the corporation and not to the promoter for payment, the promoter incurs no personal liability. As the proponent of an alleged agreement to release the promoter from liability, the promoter has the burden of proving the release agreement. Here, Fox did not prove that such an agreement existed.

DECISION

The court of appeals held that Fox was liable, as a matter of law, under the doctrine of promoter liability. Reversed.

Case Questions

Critical Legal Thinking   Should promoters be held liable on their contracts even if the corporation is subsequently formed and accepts the contract as its own?

Business Ethics   Did Fox act ethically in this case?

Contemporary Business   To avoid promoters' liability, when should contracts on behalf of a proposed corporation be executed?

INCORPORATION PROCEDURES

Corporations are creatures of statute. Thus, the organizers of the corporation must comply with the state's incorporation statute to form a corporation. Although relatively similar, the procedure for *incorporating* a corporation varies somewhat from state to state. The procedure for incorporating a corporation is discussed in the following paragraphs.

Contemporary Business Environment

SELECTING A STATE FOR INCORPORATING A CORPORATION

A corporation can be incorporated in only one state even though it can do business in all other states in which it qualifies to do business. In choosing a state for incorporation, the incorporators, directors, and/or shareholders must consider the corporations law of the states under consideration.

For the sake of convenience, most corporations (particularly small ones) choose the state in which the corporation will be doing most of its business as the state for incorporation. Large corporations generally opt to incorporate in the state with the laws that are most favorable to the corporation's internal operations (e.g., Delaware).

Incorporators

One or more persons, partnerships, domestic or foreign corporations, or other associations may act as an **incorporator** of a corporation [RMBCA § 2.01]. The incorporator's primary duty is to sign the articles of incorporation. Incorporators often become shareholders, directors, or officers of the corporation.

Articles of Incorporation

The **articles of incorporation** (or **corporate charter**) are the basic governing documents of the corporation. They must be drafted and filed with, and approved by, the state before the corporation can be officially incorporated. Under the RMBCA, the articles of incorporation must include [RMBCA § 2.02(a)]

1. The name of the corporation
2. The number of shares the corporation is authorized to issue
3. The address of the corporation's initial registered office and the name of the initial registered agent
4. The name and address of each incorporator

The articles of incorporation may also include provisions concerning (1) the period of duration (which may be perpetual), (2) the purpose or purposes for which the corporation is organized, (3) limitation or regulation of the powers of the corporation, (4) regulation of the affairs of the corporation, or (5) any provision that would otherwise be contained in the corporation's bylaws.

Exhibit 29.1 illustrates sample articles of incorporation.

Amending the Articles of Incorporation The articles of incorporation can be amended to contain any provision that could have been lawfully included in the original document [RMBCA § 10.01]. Such an amendment must show that (1) the board of directors adopted a *resolution* recommending the amendment, and (2) the shareholders voted to approve the amendment [RMBCA § 10.03]. The board of directors of a corporation may approve an amendment to the articles of incorporation without shareholder approval if the amendment does not affect rights attached to shares [RMBCA § 10.02]. After the amendment is approved by the shareholders, the corporation must file *articles of amendment* with the secretary of state [RMBCA § 10.06].

> *The corporation is, and must be, the creature of the state, into its nostrils the state must breathe the breath of a fictitious life for otherwise it would be no animated body but individualistic dust.*
>
> Frederic Wm. Maitland
> Introduction to Gierke,
> Political Theories of the
> Middle Ages

EXHIBIT 29.1 *Sample Articles of Incorporation*

ARTICLES OF INCORPORATION
OF
THE BIG CHEESE CORPORATION

ONE: The name of this corporation is:

THE BIG CHEESE CORPORATION

TWO: The purpose of this corporation is to engage in any lawful act or activity for which a corporation may be organized under the General Corporation Law of California other than the banking business, the trust company business, or the practice of a profession permitted to be incorporated by the California Corporations Code.

THREE: The name and address in this state of the corporation's initial agent for service of process is:

Nikki Nguyen, Esq.
1000 Main Street
Suite 800
Los Angeles, California 90010

FOUR: This corporation is authorized to issue only one class of shares which shall be designated common stock. The total number of shares it is authorized to issue is 1,000,000 shares.

FIVE: The names and addresses of the persons who are appointed to act as the initial directors of this corporation are:

Shou-Yi Kang	100 Maple Street Los Angeles, California 90005
Frederick Richards	200 Spruce Road Los Angeles, California 90006
Jessie Qian	300 Palm Drive Los Angeles, California 90007
Richard Eastin	400 Willow Lane Los Angeles, California 90008

SIX: The liability of the directors of the corporation from monetary damages shall be eliminated to the fullest extent possible under California law.

SEVEN: The corporation is authorized to provide indemnification of agents (as defined in Section 317 of the Corporations Code) for breach of duty to the corporation and its stockholders through bylaw provisions or through agreements with the agents, or both, in excess of the indemnification otherwise permitted by Section 317 of the Corporations Code, subject to the limits on such excess indemnification set forth in Section 204 of the Corporations Code.

IN WITNESS WHEREOF, the undersigned, being all the persons named above as the initial directors, have executed these Articles of Incorporation.

Dated: January 1, 2003

Entrepreneur and the Law

SELECTING A CORPORATE NAME

When starting a new corporation, the organizers must choose a name for the entity. To ensure that the name selected is not already being used by another business, the organizers should take the following steps [RMBCA § 4.01]:

- Choose a name (and alternative names) for the corporation. The name must contain the words *corporation, company, incorporated,* or *limited* or an abbreviation of one of these words (i.e., *Corp., Co., Inc., Ltd.*).
- Make sure that the name chosen does not contain any word or phrase that indicates or implies that the corporation is organized for any purpose other than those stated in the articles of incorporation. For example, a corporate name cannot contain the word *Bank* if it is not authorized to conduct the business of banking.

- Determine whether the name selected is federally trademarked by another company and is therefore unavailable for use. Trademark lawyers and specialized firms will conduct trademark searches for a fee.
- Determine whether the chosen name is similar to other nontrademarked names and is therefore unavailable for use. Lawyers and specialized firms will conduct such searches for a fee.
- Determine whether the name selected is available as a domain name on the Internet. If the domain name is already owned by another person or business, the new corporation cannot use this domain name to conduct e-commerce over the Internet. Therefore, it is advisable to select another corporate name.

E-Commerce & Information Technology

DOMAIN NAME REGISTERED IN BAD FAITH

Most large corporations trademark their corporate names as well as the major brand names of their products and services. In addition, since the advent of the Internet, these corporations usually register the domain name of their trademarks and service marks to promote and conduct business over the World Wide Web. One such corporation that did so was Ticketmaster Corporation, which registered the name "Ticketmaster" as a mark with the U.S. Patent and Trademark Office, and also registered the domain name ticketmaster.com.

Subsequently, a person named Brown registered three domain names—urn2ticketmaster.com, urn2ticketmaster.net, and urn2ticketmaster.org. Ticketmaster Corporation brought an arbitration proceeding against Brown in the World Intellectual Property Organization (WIPO) alleging a violation of the Uniform Domain Name Dispute Resolution Procedure (UDRP), to which all domain name registrants agree to abide by. To recover or cancel a domain name under UDRP, the petitioner must prove that (1) the challenged

domain name is identical or confusingly similar to its trademark or service mark, (2) the registrant of the domain name has no legitimate interest in the name, and (3) the domain name was registered in bad faith.

The arbitrator first found that the three domain names registered by Brown were confusingly similar to Ticketmaster's service mark, and that the addition of the prefix "urn2" (pronounced "you are into") did nothing to reduce the domain names' similarity or confusion to Ticketmaster's famous mark. Second, the arbitrator held that Brown had no legitimate interest in the domain names. And third, the arbitrator found that Brown had acted in "bad faith" in registering the domain names. The arbitrator noted that Brown had offered to sell urn2ticketmaster.com to Ticketmaster Corporation for $1,000, and had made no use of any of the names. Accordingly, the arbitrator ordered that the three domain names to be cancelled. [*Ticketmaster Corporation v. Brown*, WIPO, No. D2001-0716 (2001)]

general-purpose clause

A clause often included in the articles of incorporation that authorizes the corporation to engage in any activity permitted corporations by law.

Purpose

A corporation can be formed for "any lawful purpose." Many corporations include a **general-purpose clause** in their articles of incorporation. Such a clause allows the corporation to engage in any activity permitted corporations by law. Corporations may choose to limit the purpose or purposes of the corporation by including a *limited-purpose clause* in the articles of incorporation [RMBCA § 3.01]. For example, a corporation may be organized "to engage in the business of real estate development."

Registered Agent

The articles of incorporation must identify a **registered office** with a designated **registered agent** (either an individual or a corporation) in the state of incorporation [RMBCA § 5.01]. The registered office does not have to be the same as the corporation's place of business. A statement of change must be filed with the secretary of state of the state of incorporation if either the registered office or the registered agent is changed.

The registered agent is empowered to accept service of process on behalf of the corporation. For example, if someone were suing the corporation, the complaint and summons would be served on the registered agent. If no registered agent is named or the registered agent cannot be found at the registered office with reasonable diligence, service may be made by mail or alternative means [RMBCA § 5.04].

registered agent
A person or corporation that is empowered to accept service of process on behalf of the corporation.

Corporate Bylaws

In addition to the articles of incorporation, corporations are governed by their **bylaws**. Either the incorporators or initial directors can adopt the bylaws of the corporation. The bylaws are much more detailed than are the articles of incorporation. Bylaws may contain any provisions for managing the business and affairs of the corporation that are not inconsistent with law or the articles of incorporation [RMBCA § 2.06]. They do not have to be filed with any government official. The bylaws are binding on the directors, officers, and shareholders of the corporation.

The bylaws govern the internal management structure of the corporation. For example, they typically specify the time and place of the annual shareholders' meeting, how special meetings of shareholders are called, the time and place of annual and monthly board of directors' meetings, how special meetings of the board of directors are called, the notice required for meetings, the quorum necessary to hold a shareholders' or board of directors' meeting, the required vote necessary to enact a corporate matter, the corporate officers and their duties, the committees of the board of directors and their duties, where the records of the corporation are kept, directors' and shareholders' inspection rights of corporate records, the procedure for transferring shares of the corporation, and such. Sample provisions of corporate bylaws are set forth in Exhibit 29.2.

The board of directors has the authority to amend the bylaws unless the articles of incorporation reserve that right for the shareholders. The shareholders of the corporation have the absolute right to amend the bylaws even though the bylaws may also be amended by the board of directors [RMBCA § 10.20].

bylaws
A detailed set of rules adopted by the board of directors after the corporation is incorporated that contains provisions for managing the business and the affairs of the corporation.

Business Brief

The bylaws, which are much more detailed than the articles of incorporation, regulate the internal management structure of the corporation.

Organizational Meeting

An **organizational meeting** of the initial directors of the corporation must be held after the articles of incorporation are filed. At this meeting, the directors must adopt the bylaws, elect corporate officers, and transact such other business as may come before the meeting [RMBCA § 2.05]. The last category includes such matters as accepting share subscriptions, approving the form of the stock certificate, authorizing the issuance of the shares, ratifying or adopting promoters' contracts, authorizing the reimbursement of promoters' expenses, selecting a bank, choosing an auditor, forming committees of the board of directors, fixing the salaries of officers, hiring employees, authorizing the filing of applications for government licenses to transact the business of the corporation, and empowering corporate officers to enter into contracts on behalf of the corporation. Exhibit 29.3 contains sample corporate resolutions from an organizational meeting of a corporation.

organizational meeting
A meeting that must be held by the initial directors of the corporation after the articles of incorporation are filed.

EXHIBIT 29.2 *Sample Provisions from Corporate Bylaws*

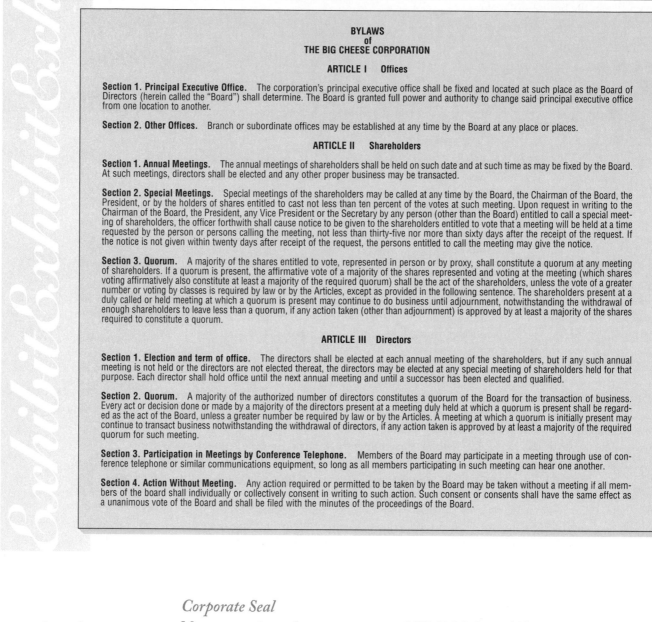

BYLAWS
of
THE BIG CHEESE CORPORATION

ARTICLE I   Offices

Section 1. Principal Executive Office.   The corporation's principal executive office shall be fixed and located at such place as the Board of Directors (herein called the "Board") shall determine. The Board is granted full power and authority to change said principal executive office from one location to another.

Section 2. Other Offices.   Branch or subordinate offices may be established at any time by the Board at any place or places.

ARTICLE II   Shareholders

Section 1. Annual Meetings.   The annual meetings of shareholders shall be held on such date and at such time as may be fixed by the Board. At such meetings, directors shall be elected and any other proper business may be transacted.

Section 2. Special Meetings.   Special meetings of the shareholders may be called at any time by the Board, the Chairman of the Board, the President, or by the holders of shares entitled to cast not less than ten percent of the votes at such meeting. Upon request in writing to the Chairman of the Board, the President, any Vice President or the Secretary by any person (other than the Board) entitled to call a special meeting of shareholders, the officer forthwith shall cause notice to be given to the shareholders entitled to vote that a meeting will be held at a time requested by the person or persons calling the meeting, not less than thirty-five nor more than sixty days after the receipt of the request. If the notice is not given within twenty days after receipt of the request, the persons entitled to call the meeting may give the notice.

Section 3. Quorum.   A majority of the shares entitled to vote, represented in person or by proxy, shall constitute a quorum at any meeting of shareholders. If a quorum is present, the affirmative vote of a majority of the shares represented and voting at the meeting (which shares voting affirmatively also constitute at least a majority of the required quorum) shall be the act of the shareholders, unless the vote of a greater number or voting by classes is required by law or by the Articles, except as provided in the following sentence. The shareholders present at a duly called or held meeting at which a quorum is present may continue to do business until adjournment, notwithstanding the withdrawal of enough shareholders to leave less than a quorum, if any action taken (other than adjournment) is approved by at least a majority of the shares required to constitute a quorum.

ARTICLE III   Directors

Section 1. Election and term of office.   The directors shall be elected at each annual meeting of the shareholders, but if any such annual meeting is not held or the directors are not elected thereat, the directors may be elected at any special meeting of shareholders held for that purpose. Each director shall hold office until the next annual meeting and until a successor has been elected and qualified.

Section 2. Quorum.   A majority of the authorized number of directors constitutes a quorum of the Board for the transaction of business. Every act or decision done or made by a majority of the directors present at a meeting duly held at which a quorum is present shall be regarded as the act of the Board, unless a greater number be required by law or by the Articles. A meeting at which a quorum is initially present may continue to transact business notwithstanding the withdrawal of directors, if any action taken is approved by at least a majority of the required quorum for such meeting.

Section 3. Participation in Meetings by Conference Telephone.   Members of the Board may participate in a meeting through use of conference telephone or similar communications equipment, so long as all members participating in such meeting can hear one another.

Section 4. Action Without Meeting.   Any action required or permitted to be taken by the Board may be taken without a meeting if all members of the board shall individually or collectively consent in writing to such action. Such consent or consents shall have the same effect as a unanimous vote of the Board and shall be filed with the minutes of the proceedings of the Board.

---

corporate seal

A design containing the name of the corporation and the date of incorporation that is imprinted by the corporate secretary using a metal stamp on certain legal documents.

Corporate Seal

Most corporations adopt a **corporate seal** [RMBCA § 3.02(2)]. Generally, the seal is a design that contains the name of the corporation and the date of incorporation. It is imprinted by the corporate secretary on certain legal documents (e.g., real estate deeds and the like) that are signed by corporate officers or directors. The seal is usually affixed by a metal stamp.

Corporate Status

Business Brief

The filing of the articles of incorporation is *conclusive proof* that a corporation exists. After that, only the state can challenge the status of the corporation; third parties cannot.

The RMBCA provides that corporate existence begins when the articles of incorporation are filed. The secretary of state's filing of the articles of incorporation is *conclusive proof* that the incorporators satisfied all conditions of incorporation. After that, only the state can bring a proceeding to cancel or revoke the incorporation or involuntarily dissolve the corporation. Third parties cannot thereafter challenge the existence of the corporation or raise it as a defense against the corporation [RMBCA § 2.03]. The corollary to this rule is: Failure to file articles of incorporation is conclusive proof of the nonexistence of the corporation.

ℰXHIBIT 29.3   *Sample Corporate Resolutions from an Organizational Meeting*

MINUTES OF FIRST MEETING
OF
BOARD OF DIRECTORS
OF
THE BIG CHEESE CORPORATION
January 1, 2003
10:00 A.M.

The Directors of said corporation held their first meeting on the above date and at the above time pursuant to required notice.

The following Directors, constituting a quorum of the Board of Directors, were present at such meeting:

> Shou-Yi Kang
> Frederick Richards
> Jessie Quian
> Richard Eastin

Upon motion duly made and seconded, Show-Yi was unanimously elected Chairman of the meeting and Frederick Richards was unanimously elected Secretary of the meeting.

1.   Articles of Incorporation and Agent for Service of Process

The Chairman stated that the Articles of Incorporation of the Corporation were filed in the office of the California Secretary of State. The Chairman presented to the meeting a certified copy of the Articles of Incorporation. The Secretary was directed to insert the copy in the Minute Book. Upon motion duly made and seconded, the following resolution was unanimously adopted:

> RESOLVED, that the agent named as the initial agent for service of process in the Articles of Incorporation of this corporation is hereby confirmed as this corporation's agent for the purpose of service of process.

2.   Bylaws

The matter of adopting Bylaws for the regulation of the affairs of the corporation was next considered. The Secretary presented to the meeting a form of Bylaws, which was considered and discussed. Upon motion duly made and seconded, the following recitals and resolutions were unanimously adopted:

> WHEREAS, there has been presented to the directors a form of Bylaws for the regulation of the affairs of this corporation; and
>
> WHEREAS, it is deemed to be in the best interests of this corporation that said Bylaws be adopted by this Board of Directors as the Bylaws of this corporation;
>
> NOW, THEREFORE, BE IT RESOLVED, that Bylaws in the form presented to this meeting are adopted and approved as the Bylaws of this corporation until amended or repealed in accordance with applicable law.
>
> RESOLVED FURTHER, that the Secretary of this corporation is authorized and directed to execute a certificate of the adoption of said Bylaws and to enter said Bylaws as so certified in the Minute Book of this corporation, and to see that a copy of said Bylaws is kept at the principal executive or business office of this corporation in California.

3.   Corporate Seal

The secretary presented for approval a proposed seal of the corporation. Upon motion duly made and seconded, the following resolution was unanimously adopted:

> RESOLVED, that a corporate seal is adopted as the seal of this corporation in the form of two concentric circles, with the name of this corporation between the two circles and the state and date of incorporation within the inner circle.

4.   Stock Certificate

The Secretary presented a proposed form of stock certificate for use by the corporation. Upon motion duly made and seconded, the following resolution was unanimously adopted:

> RESOLVED, that the form of stock certificate presented to this meeting is approved and adopted as the stock certificate of this corporation.

The secretary was instructed to insert a sample copy of the stock certificate in the Minute Book immediately following these minutes.

5.   Election of officers

The Chairman announced that it would be in order to elect officers of the corporation. After discussion and upon motion duly made and seconded, the following resolution was unanimously adopted:

> RESOLVED, that the following persons are unanimously elected to the offices indicated opposite their names

Title	Name
Chief Executive Officer	Shou-Yi Kang
President	Frederick Richards
Secretary and Vice President	Jessie Quian
Treasurer	Richard Eastin

There being no further business to come before the meeting, on motion duly made, seconded and unanimously carried, the meeting was adjourned.

Entrepreneur and the Law

S CORPORATIONS

Corporations are separate legal entities. As such, they generally must pay corporate income taxes to federal and state governments. If a corporation distributes its profits to shareholders in the form of dividends, shareholders must pay personal income tax on the dividends. This *double taxation* of corporations is one of the major disadvantages of doing business in the corporate form. Some corporations and their shareholders can avoid double taxation by electing to be an S Corporation.

In 1982, Congress enacted the **Subchapter S Revision Act**. The act divided all corporations into two groups: **S Corporations**, which are those that elect to be taxed under Subchapter S, and **C Corporations**, which are all other corporations [26 U.S.C. §§ 6242 et seq.].

If a corporation elects to be taxed as an S Corporation, it pays no federal income tax at the corporate level. As in a partnership, the corporation's income or loss flows to the shareholders' individual income tax returns. Thus, this election is particularly advantageous if (1) the corporation is expected to have losses that can be offset against other income of the shareholders or (2) the corporation is expected to make profits and the shareholders' income tax brackets are lower than the corporation's. Profits are taxed to the shareholders even if the income is not distributed. The shares

retain other attributes of the corporate form, including limited liability.

Corporations that meet the following criteria can elect to be taxed as S Corporations:

1. The corporation must be a domestic corporation.
2. The corporation cannot be a member of an affiliated group.
3. The corporation can have no more than 75 shareholders.
4. Shareholders must be individuals, estates, or certain trusts. Corporations and partnerships cannot be shareholders.
5. Shareholders must be citizens or residents of the United States. Nonresident aliens cannot be shareholders.
6. The corporation cannot have more than one class of stock. Shareholders do not have to have equal voting rights.
7. No more than 20 percent of the corporation's income can be from passive investment income.

An S Corporation election is made by filing a Form 2553 with the Internal Revenue Service (IRS). The election can be rescinded by shareholders who collectively own at least a majority of the shares of the corporation. However, if the election is rescinded, another S Corporation election cannot be made for five years.

FINANCING THE CORPORATION

A corporation needs to finance the operation of its business. The most common way to do this is by selling *equity securities* and *debt securities*. **Equity securities** (or **stocks**) represent ownership rights in the corporation. Equity securities can be *common stock* and *preferred stock*. These are discussed in the following paragraphs.

equity securities

Representation of ownership rights to the corporation. Also called *stocks*.

Common Stock

common stock

A type of equity security that represents the *residual* value of the corporation.

Common stock is an equity security that represents the residual value of the corporation. Common stock has no preferences. That is, creditors and preferred shareholders must receive their required interest and dividend payments before common shareholders receive anything. Common stock does not have a fixed maturity date. If the corporation is liquidated, the creditors and preferred shareholders are paid the value of their interests first, and the common shareholders are paid the value of their interests (if any) last. Corporations may issue different classes of common stock [RMBCA § 6.01(a) and (b)].

common stockholder

A person who owns common stock.

Persons who own common stock are called **common stockholders**. A common stockholder's investment in the corporation is represented by a **common stock certificate**. Common shareholders have the right to elect directors and to vote on mergers and other important matters. In return for their investment, common shareholders receive *dividends* declared by the board of directors.

common stock certificate

A document that represents the common shareholder's investment in the corporation.

A sample share of common stock is shown in Exhibit 29.4.

Par Value and No Par Shares Common shares are sometimes categorized as either par or no par. *Par share* is a value assigned to common shares by the corporation, usually in the articles of incorporation, which sets the lowest price at which the shares may be issued by the corporation. It does not affect the market value of the shares. Most shares that are issued by corporations are *no par shares*. No par shares are not assigned a par value. The RMBCA has eliminated the concept of par value.

Exhibit 29.4 *Sample Stock Certificate*

Preferred Stock

Preferred stock is an equity security that is given certain *preferences and rights over common stock* [RMBCA § 6.01(c)]. The owners of preferred stock are called **preferred stockholders**. Preferred stockholders are issued a **preferred stock certificate** to evidence their ownership interest in the corporation.

Preferred stock can be issued in classes or series. One class of preferred stock can be given preferences over another class of preferred stock. Like common shareholders, preferred shareholders have limited liability. Preferred shareholders generally are not given the right to vote for the election of directors or such. However, they are often given the right to vote if there is a merger or if the corporation has not made the required dividend payments for a certain period of time (e.g., three years).

preferred stock
A type of equity security that is given certain preferences and rights over common stock.

preferred stockholder
A person who owns preferred stock.

preferred stock certificate
A document that represents a shareholder's investment in preferred stock in the corporation.

Business Brief
Preferred stock is given certain *preferences* and its value is based on these preferences.

dividend preference

The right to receive a fixed dividend at stipulated periods during the year (e.g., quarterly).

liquidation preference

The right to be paid a stated dollar amount if the corporation is dissolved and liquidated.

cumulative preferred stock

Stock that provides any missed dividend payments must be paid in the future to the preferred shareholders before the common shareholders can receive any dividends.

participating preferred stock

Stock that allows the stockholder to participate in the profits of the corporation along with the common stockholders.

convertible preferred stock

Stock that permits the stockholders to convert their shares into common stock.

redeemable preferred stock

Stock that permits the corporation to buy back the preferred stock at some future date.

authorized shares

The number of shares provided for in the articles of incorporation.

issued shares

Shares that have been sold by the corporation.

treasury shares

Shares of stock repurchased by the company itself.

outstanding shares

Shares of stock that are in shareholder hands.

Preferences   Preferences of preferred stock must be set forth in the articles of incorporation. Preferred stock may have any or all of the following preferences or rights.

- **Dividend Preference**   A **dividend preference** is the right to receive a *fixed dividend* at set periods during the year (e.g., quarterly). The dividend rate is usually a set percentage of the initial offering price. For example, suppose a stockholder purchases $10,000 of a preferred stock that pays an 8 percent dividend annually. The stockholder has the right to receive $800 each year as a dividend on the preferred stock.
- **Liquidation Preference**   The right to be paid before common stockholders if the corporation is dissolved and liquidated is called a **liquidation preference**. A liquidation preference is normally a stated dollar amount. For example, a corporation issues a preferred stock that has a liquidation preference of $200. This means that if the corporation is dissolved and liquidated, the holder of each preferred share will receive at least $200 before the common shareholders receive anything. Note that because the corporation must pay its creditors first, there may be insufficient funds to pay this preference.
- **Cumulative Dividend Right**   Corporations must pay a preferred dividend if they have the earnings to do so. **Cumulative preferred stock** provides that any missed dividend payments must be paid in the future to preferred shareholders before the common shareholders can receive any dividends. The amount of unpaid cumulative dividends is called dividend *arrearages*. Usually, arrearages can be accumulated for only a limited period of time (such as three years). If the preferred stock is **noncumulative**, there is no right of accumulation. In other words, the corporation does not have to pay any missed dividends.
- **Right to Participate in Profits**   **Participating preferred stock** allows the stockholder to participate in the profits of the corporation along with the common stockholders. Participation is in addition to the fixed dividend paid on preferred stock. The terms of participation vary widely. Usually, the common stockholders must be paid a certain amount of dividends before participation is allowed. **Nonparticipating preferred stock** does not have a right to participate in the profits of the corporation beyond its fixed dividend rate. Most preferred stock falls into this category.
- **Conversion Right**   **Convertible preferred stock** permits the stockholders to convert their shares into common stock. The terms and exchange rate of the conversion are established when the shares are issued. The holders of the convertible preferred stock usually exercise this option if the corporation's common stock increases significantly in value. Preferred stock without a conversion feature is called **nonconvertible preferred stock**. Nonconvertible stock is more common.

The preceding list of preferences and rights is not exhaustive [RMBCA § 6.01(d)]. Corporations may establish other preferences and rights for preferred stock.

Redeemable Preferred Stock   **Redeemable preferred stock** (or **callable preferred stock**) permits the corporation to redeem (i.e., buy back) the preferred stock at some future date. The terms of the redemption are established when the shares are issued. Corporations usually redeem the shares when the current interest rate falls below the dividend rate of the preferred shares. Preferred stock that is not redeemable is called **nonredeemable preferred stock**. Nonredeemable stock is more common.

Authorized, Issued, and Outstanding Shares

The number of shares provided for in the articles of incorporation is called **authorized shares** [RMBCA § 6.01]. The shareholders may vote to amend the articles of incorporation to increase this amount. Authorized shares that have been sold by the corporation are called **issued shares**. Not all authorized shares have to be issued at the same time. Authorized shares that have not been issued are called *unissued shares*. The board of directors can vote to issue unissued shares at any time without shareholder approval.

A corporation is permitted to repurchase its own shares [RMBCA § 6.31]. Repurchased shares are commonly called **treasury shares**. Treasury shares cannot be voted by the corporation and dividends are not paid on these shares. Treasury shares can be reissued by the corporation. The shares that are in shareholder hands, whether originally issued or reissued treasury shares, are called **outstanding shares**. Only outstanding shares have the right to vote [RMBCA § 6.03].

𝒞ONCEPT SUMMARY   TYPES OF SHARES

Type of Share	Description
Authorized	Shares authorized in the corporation's articles of incorporation.
Issued	Shares sold by the corporation.
Treasury	Shares repurchased by the corporation. They do not have the right to vote.
Outstanding	Issued shares minus treasury shares. These shares have the right to vote.

Consideration to Be Paid for Shares

The RMBCA allows shares to be issued in exchange for any benefit to the corporation, including cash, tangible property, intangible property, promissory notes, services performed, contracts for services performed, or other securities of the corporation. In the absence of fraud, the judgment of the board of directors or shareholders as to the value of consideration received for shares is conclusive [RMBCA § 6.21(b) and (c)].

Business Brief

Shares of a corporation may be sold in exchange for any property or benefit to the corporation as determined by the board of directors.

𝒞ontemporary ℬusiness ℰnvironment

STOCK OPTIONS AND STOCK WARRANTS

A corporation can grant stock options (options) and stock warrants (warrants) that permit parties to purchase common or preferred shares at a certain price for a set time [RMBCA § 6.24].

Corporations commonly grant **stock options** to top-level managers. They are nontransferable. A stock option gives the recipient the right to purchase shares of the corporation from the corporation at a stated price (called the *striking price*) for a specified period of time (called the *option period*). If the profitability of the corporation and the market value of its securities increase during the option period, the holder of the option is likely to *exercise the option*, that is, purchase the shares subject to the option.

A **stock warrant** is a stock option that is evidenced by a certificate. Warrants are commonly issued in conjunction with other securities. A warrant holder can exercise the warrant and purchase the common stock at the strike price anytime during the warrant period. Warrants can be transferable or nontransferable.

Debt Securities

A corporation often raises funds by issuing debt securities [RMBCA 3.02(7)]. **Debt securities** (also called **fixed income securities**) establish a debtor–creditor relationship in which the corporation borrows money from the investor to whom the debt security is issued. The corporation promises to pay interest on the amount borrowed and to repay the principal at some stated maturity date in the future. The corporation is the *debtor* and the holder is the *creditor*. There are three classifications of debt securities: debentures, bonds, and notes.

A **debenture** is a *long-term* (often 30 years or more), *unsecured* debt instrument that is based on the corporation's general credit standing. If the corporation encounters financial difficulty, unsecured debenture holders are treated as general creditors of the corporation (i.e., they are paid only after the secured creditors' claims are met).

A **bond** is a *long-term* debt security that is *secured* by some form of *collateral* (e.g., real estate, personal property, and such). Thus, bonds are the same as debentures except that they are secured. Secured bondholders can foreclose on the collateral in the event of nonpayment of interest, principal, or other specified events.

A **note** is a debt security with a maturity of five years or less. Notes can be either unsecured or secured. They usually do not contain a conversion feature. They are sometimes made redeemable.

debt securities

Securities that establish a debtor–creditor relationship in which the corporation borrows money from the investor to whom the debt security is issued.

debenture

A long-term unsecured debt instrument that is based on the corporation's general credit standing.

bond

A long-term debt security that is secured by some form of collateral.

note

A debt security with a maturity of five years or less.

indenture agreement

A contract between the corporation and the holder that contains the terms of a debt security.

Indenture Agreement The terms of a debt security are commonly contained in a contract between the corporation and the holder known as an **indenture agreement** (or simply **indenture**). The indenture generally contains the maturity date of the debt security, the required interest payment, the collateral (if any), conversion rights into common or preferred stock, call provisions, any restrictions on the corporation's right to incur other indebtedness, the rights of holders upon default, and such. It also establishes the rights and duties of the indenture trustee. Generally, a trustee is appointed to represent the interest of the debt security holders. Bank trust departments often serve in this capacity.

@ *E-Commerce & Information Technology*

INTERNET ALLIANCES IN CHINA

By the year 2005, China will have the largest number of Internet users in the world. Leading Internet companies in the United States have eyed this market for its tremendous growth potential. But China prohibits complete ownership of Internet companies in China by foreigners. In addition, the legendary Chinese "connections" method of conducting business places another hurdle in the way of foreign companies wishing to do business there. So what is the main way to tap into this Internet market? Strategic alliances.

A major strategic alliance by U.S. companies in China was their tie-in and investment in China.com. China.com is a Chinese-language Web portal backed by investments by U.S. companies America Online (AOL), Sun Microsystems, and Bay Networks. China.com became China's largest Internet company when it raised over $84 million in an initial public offering in July 1999. Intel Corp., another major U.S. company, has aligned itself with Sohu.com, a Chinese Internet company located in Beijing. CMGI Inc., a U.S. Internet holding company, has joined with Pacific Century Cyber-Works (PCCW), a Hong Kong company, to sell Web content and e-commerce services to the exploding Chinese Internet market from its base in Hong Kong.

Although the Chinese government has permitted these strategic alliances, it has stated that it will not allow foreign companies to own Internet service providers (ISPs) in China. Some U.S. companies have set up ISPs in countries and areas near China, which will be able to serve the Chinese market. The Information Industries Minister of China has

China's recent entry into the World Trade Organization (WTO) will increase trade between China and other countries.

announced that China will control the content of materials delivered via the Internet in China. Analysts predict that this will be hard to do given the global nature of the Internet.

Based on the communist government's rules in China and a culture that favors business connections, U.S. Internet companies will continue to enter the Chinese Internet market through strategic alliances with Chinese Internet firms. These strategic alliances bring together the expertise of all parties, bring China fully into the information age, and provide Internet users in China the most affordable options.

CORPORATE POWERS

A corporation has the same basic rights to perform acts and enter into contracts as a physical person [RMBCA § 3.02]. The express and implied powers of a corporation are discussed in the following paragraphs.

express powers

Powers given to a corporation by (1) the U.S. Constitution, (2) state constitutions, (3) federal statutes, (4) state statutes, (5) articles of incorporation, (6) bylaws, and (7) resolutions of the board of directors.

Express Powers

A corporation's **express powers** are found in (1) the U.S. Constitution, (2) state constitutions, (3) federal statutes, (4) state statutes, (5) articles of incorporation, (6) bylaws, and (7) resolutions of the board of directors. Corporation statutes normally state the express powers granted to the corporation.

Generally, a corporation has the power to purchase, own, lease, sell, mortgage, or otherwise deal in real and personal property; make contracts; lend money; borrow money; incur liabilities; issue notes, bonds, and other obligations; invest and reinvest funds; sue and be sued in its corporate name; make donations for the public welfare or for charitable, scientific, or educational purposes; and the like. RMBCA § 3.02 provides a list of express corporate powers.

Corporations formed under general incorporation laws cannot engage in certain businesses, such as banking, insurance, or operating public utilities. Corporations must obtain a corporate charter under special incorporation statutes and receive approval of special government administrative agencies before engaging in these businesses.

Implied Powers

Neither the governing laws nor the corporate documents can anticipate every act necessary for a corporation to carry on its business. **Implied powers** allow the corporation to exceed its express powers in order to accomplish its corporate purpose. For instance, a corporation has the implied power to open a bank account, reimburse its employees for expenses, engage in advertising, purchase insurance, and the like.

Ultra Vires *Act*

An act by a corporation that is beyond its express or implied powers is called an ***ultra vires act***. The following remedies are available if an *ultra vires* act is committed:

1. Shareholders can sue for an injunction to prevent the corporation from engaging in the act.
2. The corporation (or the shareholders on behalf of the corporation) can sue the officers or directors who caused the act for damages.
3. The attorney general of the state of incorporation can bring an action to enjoin the act or to dissolve the corporation [RMBCA § 3.04].

implied powers

Powers beyond express powers that allow a corporation to accomplish its corporate purpose.

ultra vires act

An act by a corporation that is beyond its express or implied powers.

Business Brief

Today, the doctrine of *ultra vires* has lost significance because most corporations select general-purpose clauses (making very few acts *ultra vires*).

International Law

ORGANIZATION AND OPERATION OF THE MULTINATIONAL CORPORATION

In the past, the size, power, and range of activities of corporations were limited. This changed at the beginning of the twentieth century, when corporations won the right to own stock in each other. National corporate networks soon followed. Eventually, parent corporations, mostly American, expanded these networks overseas by setting up subsidiary corporations under the laws of other countries. These international networks (or multinational enterprises) are made up of companies of different nationalities that constitute a single economic unit connected by shareholding, managerial control, or contractual agreement. The simplest international operating structure is one that subcontracts with independent firms in the host country to carry out sales or purchases. "National multinational" firms that establish wholly owned branches and subsidiaries overseas are somewhat more complex. "International multinational" firms are even more complicated. They are made up of two or more parents from different countries that co-own operating businesses in two or more countries.

The Ford Motor Company is an example of a national multinational firm. Organized in the United States at the beginning of the 20th century, Ford has always viewed the entire world as its market. The company's policy is for the

American parent to own and control all of its overseas subsidiaries. Ford's 10 European subsidiaries are all owned entirely by the American parent. The Mitsubishi Group is another example of this organizational format. It is actually made up of several Japanese companies that use joint directors' meetings to coordinate their activities in Japan and overseas.

The Royal Dutch/Shell Group is an example of an international multinational corporation. In 1907, the Dutch and British parents each formed a wholly owned holding company in their respective countries. Each then transferred the ownership of the operating subsidiary to the holding company and exchanged shares in the holding companies. The Dutch parent held 60 percent of each holding company, and the British parent held 40 percent. In addition, the management and operation of the two companies were organized to function as a single economic unit. Unilever, Dunlop, Pirelli, and VFW/Fokker also operate under an international multinational umbrella.

There is a special type of international multinational: a publicly owned transnational enterprise. One example is Air Afrique, which was created by several West African countries through the use of a treaty granting each government a voice in the company's operation.

$\mathcal{D}$ISSOLUTION AND TERMINATION OF CORPORATIONS

The life of a corporation may be terminated voluntarily or involuntarily. The methods for dissolving and terminating corporations are discussed in the following paragraphs.

voluntary dissolution

A corporation that has begun business or issued shares can be dissolved upon recommendation of the board of directors and a majority vote of the shares entitled to vote.

1. **Voluntary Dissolution** A corporation can be **voluntarily dissolved**. If the corporation has not commenced business or issued any shares, it may be dissolved by a vote of the majority of the incorporators or initial directors [RMBCA § 14.01]. After that, the corporation can be voluntarily dissolved if the board of directors recommends dissolution and a majority of shares entitled to vote (or a greater number if required by the articles of incorporation or bylaws) votes for dissolution as well [RMBCA § 14.02]. For a voluntary dissolution to be effective, **articles of dissolution** must be filed with the secretary of state of the state of incorporation. A corporation is dissolved upon the effective date of the articles of dissolution [RMBCA § 14.03].

administrative dissolution

Involuntary dissolution of a corporation that is ordered by the secretary of state if the corporation has failed to comply with certain procedures required by law.

2. **Administrative Dissolution** The secretary of state can obtain **administrative dissolution** of a corporation if (1) it failed to file an annual report, (2) it failed for 60 days to maintain a registered agent in the state, (3) it failed, for 60 days after a change of its registered agent, to file a statement of such change with the secretary of state, (4) it did not pay its franchise fee, or (5) the period of duration stated in the corporation's articles of incorporation has expired [RMBCA § 14.20]. Administrative dissolution is simple. If the corporation does not cure the default within 60 days of being notified of it, the secretary of state issues a *certificate of dissolution* that dissolves the corporation [RMBCA § 14.21].

judicial dissolution

Occurs when a corporation is dissolved by a court proceeding instituted by the state.

3. **Judicial Dissolution** A corporation can be involuntarily dissolved by a judicial proceeding. **Judicial dissolution** can be instituted by the attorney general of the state of incorporation if the corporation (1) procured its articles of incorporation through fraud or (2) exceeded or abused the authority conferred upon it by law [RMBCA § 14.30(1)]. If a court judicially dissolves a corporation, it enters a *decree of dissolution* that specifies the date of dissolution [RMBCA § 14.33].

$\mathcal{E}$ntrepreneur and the $\mathcal{L}$aw

JUDICIAL DISSOLUTION OF A CLOSELY HELD CORPORATION

Shareholders and directors of smaller closely held corporations sometimes disagree about management and policy decisions concerning the operation of the business. What happens if there is a deadlock as to the direction the corporation should take, or if damage is being caused to corporate assets? Most corporation statutes solve this problem by providing that a shareholder can go to court and seek judicial dissolution of a corporation if

- The directors are deadlocked in the management of corporate affairs, the shareholders are unable to break the

deadlock, and irreparable injury is being suffered by or threatened to the corporation.
- The shareholders are deadlocked in voting power and have failed for at least two consecutive annual meetings to elect directors whose terms have expired.
- The acts of the directors or those in control of the corporation are illegal, oppressive, or fraudulent.
- The corporate assets are being misapplied or wasted [RMBCA § 14.30(2)].

Winding-Up, Liquidation, and Termination

winding-up and liquidation

The process by which a dissolved corporation's assets are collected, liquidated, and distributed to creditors, shareholders, and other claimants.

A dissolved corporation continues its corporate existence but may not carry on any business except as required to **wind up and liquidate** its business and affairs [RMBCA § 14.05].

In a voluntary dissolution, the liquidation is usually carried out by the board of directors. If (1) the dissolution is involuntary or (2) the dissolution is voluntary but the directors refuse to carry out the liquidation, a court-appointed receiver carriers out the winding-up and liquidation of the corporation [RMBCA § 14.32].

termination

The ending of a corporation that occurs only after the winding-up of the corporation's affairs, the liquidation of its assets, and the distribution of the proceeds to the claimants.

Termination occurs only after the winding-up of the corporation's affairs, the liquidation of its assets, and the distribution of the proceeds to the claimants. The liquidated assets are paid to claimants according to the following priority: (1) expenses of liquidation and creditors according to their respective liens and contract rights, (2) preferred shareholders according to their liquidation preferences and contract rights, and (3) common shareholders.

The dissolution of a corporation does not impair any rights or remedies available against the corporation or its directors, or officers, or shareholders for any right or claim existing or incurred prior to dissolution.

CHAPTER SUMMARY

Nature of the Corporation, p. 719

Name of the Corporation	1. *Corporation.* A legal entity created pursuant to the laws of the state of incorporation. 2. *Corporation codes.* State statutes that govern the formation, operation, and dissolution of corporations.
Public and Private Corporations	1. *Public corporation.* A corporation formed to meet a specific governmental or political purpose. Also called a *government-owned* corporation. *Municipal corporations* (i.e., cities) are an example. 2. *Private corporation.* A corporation formed to conduct privately owned businesses. It may be large or small.
The Corporation as a Legal "Person"	A corporation is a separate legal entity—an *artificial person*—that can own property, sue and be sued, enter into contracts, and such.
Characteristics of Corporations	1. *Limited liability of shareholders.* Shareholders are liable for the debts and obligations of the corporation only to the extent of their capital contributions. 2. *Free transferability of shares.* Shares of a corporation are freely transferable by shareholders unless they are expressly restricted. 3. *Perpetual existence.* Corporations exist in perpetuity unless a specific duration is stated in the corporation's articles of incorporation. 4. *Centralized management.* The *board of directors* of the corporation makes policy decisions of the corporation. Corporate *officers* appointed by the board of directors run the corporation's day-to-day operations. Together, the directors and officers form the corporation's "management."
The Revised Model Business Corporation Act	1. *Model Business Corporation Act (MBCA).* A model act drafted in 1950 that was intended to provide a uniform law for the regulation of corporations. 2. *Revised Model Business Corporation Act (RMBCA).* A revision of the MBCA promulgated in 1984 that arranged the provisions of the model act more logically, revised the language to be more consistent, and made substantial changes that modernized the provisions of the act.

Classifications of Corporations. p. 721

Domestic, Foreign, and Alien Corporations	1. *Domestic corporation.* A corporation in the state in which it is incorporated. 2. *Foreign corporation.* A corporation in any state other than the one in which it is incorporated. A domestic corporation often transacts business in states other than its state of incorporation; hence, it is a foreign corporation in these states. A foreign corporation must obtain a *certificate of authority* from these other states to transact intrastate business in those states. 3. *Alien corporation.* A corporation that is incorporated in another country. Alien corporations are treated as foreign corporations for most purposes.
Profit and Nonprofit Corporations	1. *Profit corporation.* A corporation created to conduct a business for profit that can distribute profits to shareholders in the form of dividends. 2. *Nonprofit corporation.* A corporation that is formed to operate charitable institutions, colleges, universities, and other not-for-profit entities. There are no shareholders of these corporations.
Publicly Held and Closely Held Corporations	1. *Publicly held corporation.* A corporation that has many shareholders and whose securities are often traded on national stock exchanges. General Motors Corporation is an example. 2. *Closely held corporation.* A corporation that is owned by one or a few shareholders. Examples are family-owned corporations. They are also called *close corporations*.
Professional Corporations	Corporations formed by lawyers, doctors, and other professionals. Shareholders of professional corporations are usually called *members*. Members must be licensed to practice the profession for which the corporation is formed.

Promoters' Activities, p. 723

Promoters' Liability	1. *Promoter.* A person or persons who organize and start the corporation, negotiate and enter into contracts in advance of formation, find the initial investors to finance the corporation, and so forth.
	2. *Promoter's contract.* A contract entered into by a promoter on behalf of a proposed corporation prior to its actual incorporation. These contracts often include leases, sales contracts, contracts to purchase property, and so forth.
	3. *Liability of promoters for promoters' contracts.* Promoters are personally liable for promoters' contracts unless (a) the corporation ratifies the contract as its own once it is formed and (b) the corporation, the promoter, and the third party with whom the contract is with enter into a *novation* agreement that expressly releases the promoter from liability.
Subscription for Shares	1. *Subscription agreement.* An agreement by a person to purchase shares of a corporation once the corporation is incorporated.
	2. *Subscriber.* Person who subscribes to purchase shares of a corporation once it is incorporated. Subscription agreements are enforceable against subscribers.

Incorporation Procedures, p. 724

Incorporation Procedures	1. *Incorporation.* The process of incorporating (forming) a new corporation.
	2. *Corporations code.* Corporations are creatures of statute; they can be formed only if certain statutory formalities contained in the state's corporations code are followed.
Selecting a State of Incorporation	A corporation can be incorporated in only one state, although it can conduct business in other states.
Incorporators	The person or persons, partnerships, or corporations who are responsible for incorporating a new corporation.
Articles of Incorporation	The basic governing documents of a corporation. This document must be filed with the secretary of state of the state of incorporation. It is a public document. It is also called the *corporate charter.*
	1. *Information to be set forth in the articles of incorporation.* The corporations code of each state sets out the information that must be included in the articles of incorporation. Additional information may be included in the articles of incorporation as deemed necessary or desirable by the incorporators.
	2. *Amending the articles of incorporation.* The articles of incorporation can be amended to contain any provision that could have been lawfully included in the original articles of incorporation. After an amendment is approved by the shareholders, the corporation must file *articles of amendment* with the secretary of state in the state in which it is incorporated.
Other Issues Concerning Incorporation	1. *Corporate name.* A corporate name selected for a new corporation must be distinguishable from existing corporate names. A corporate name may be reserved for a limited period of time while the corporation is being formed.
	2. *Purpose.* A corporation can be formed for "any lawful purpose." Corporations can limit the purposes of the corporation by including a *limited-purpose clause* in the articles of incorporation that stipulates the purposes and activities the corporation can engage in.
	3. *Registered agent.* A new corporation must designate a person or corporation that is empowered to accept *service of process* on behalf of the corporation. A new designation must be made annually.
Corporate Bylaws	*Bylaws.* A detailed set of rules that are adopted by the board of directors after the corporation is formed that contain provisions for managing the business and affairs of the corporation. This document does not have to be filed with the secretary of state.
Organization Meeting	A meeting that must be held by the initial directors of the corporation after the articles of incorporation are filed. At this meeting, the directors adopt the bylaws, elect corporate officers, ratify promoters' contracts, adopt a corporate seal, and transact such other business as may come before the meeting.
	Minutes. The written recording of the actions taken by the directors at the organizational and other directors' meetings.
Corporate Seal	A design that contains the name of the corporation and the date of incorporation. It is imprinted by the corporate secretary on certain legal documents using a metal stamp containing the design.
Corporate Status	*RMBCA rule.* The filing of the articles of incorporation is *conclusive proof* that a corporation exists. After that, only the state can challenge the status of the corporation; third parties cannot. Failure to file articles of incorporation is conclusive proof that the corporation does not exist. The state and third parties may challenge the existence of the corporation.

Financing the Corporation, p. 730

Financing the Corporation	*Equity securities.* Securities that represent the ownership rights to the corporation. They are also called *stocks*. Equity securities consist of *common stock* and *preferred stock*.
Common Stock	A type of equity security that represents the *residual value* of the corporation. Common stock has no preferences, and its shareholders are paid dividends and assets upon liquidation only after creditors and preferred shareholders have been paid. 1. *Common stockholder.* A person who owns common stock. 2. *Common stock certificate.* A document that represents the common shareholder's investment in the corporation. 3. *Par value.* A value assigned by the corporation to common shares that sets the lowest price at which the shares may be issued by the corporation. *No par shares* are not assigned a par value. The RMBCA has eliminated the concept of par value.

Preferred Stock	A type of equity security that is given certain preferences and rights over common stock.
	1. *Preferred stockholder.* A person who owns preferred stock.
	2. *Preferred stock certificate.* A document that represents the preferred stockholder's investment in the corporation.
	3. *Preferences and rights.* Preferred stock may have any or all of the following preferences or rights:
	  a. *Dividend preference.* The right to receive a fixed dividend at stipulated periods during the year (e.g., quarterly).
	  b. *Liquidation preference.* The right to be paid a stated dollar amount if the corporation is dissolved and liquidated. The corporation must pay its creditors first, however.
	  c. *Cumulative dividend right. Cumulative preferred stock* is stock that provides that any missed dividend payments must be paid in the future to the preferred shareholders before the common shareholders can receive any dividends.
	  d. *Right to participate in profits. Participating preferred stock* is preferred stock that allows the stockholder to participate in the profits of the corporation along with the common stockholders on an expressly stated basis.
	  e. *Conversion right. Convertible preferred stock* is preferred stock that permits stockholders to convert their shares into common stock at a stipulated conversion price.
	4. *Redeemable preferred stock.* Preferred stock that may be bought back by the corporation at a specified price at some future date. This stock is also called *callable preferred stock.*

Consideration to Be Paid for Shares	Shares may be issued in exchange for any benefit to the corporation, including cash, tangible property, intangible property, promissory notes, services performed, contracts for services to be performed, or other securities of the corporation.
Authorized, Issued, and Outstanding Shares	1. *Authorized shares.* The number of shares provided for in the articles of incorporation. The shareholders may amend the articles of incorporation to increase this amount. 2. *Issued shares.* Authorized shares that have been sold by the corporation. 3. *Unissued shares.* Authorized shares that have not been sold by the corporation. 4. *Treasury shares.* Issued shares that have been repurchased by the corporation. They may be resold by the corporation. 5. *Outstanding shares.* Shares that are in shareholder hands, whether originally issued or reissued treasury shares. Only outstanding shares have the right to vote.

Stock Options and Stock Warrants	1. *Stock option.* A nontransferable right to purchase shares of the corporation from the corporation at a stated price for a specific period of time.
	  a. *Striking price.* The stated price at which the stock may be bought at a future date.
	  b. *Option period.* The specified period of time for exercising a stock option.
	  c. *Exercising the option.* The act of purchasing the shares subject to the option by the holder of the option. Stock options are usually granted to the management of a corporation.
	2. *Stock warrant.* A stock option that is represented by a certificate. Stock warrants are commonly issued in conjunction with another security. Warrants may be transferable or nontransferable.

Debt Securities	Securities that establish a *debtor–creditor* relationship in which the corporation borrows money from the investor to whom the debt security is issued. 1. *Debenture.* A *long-term unsecured* debt instrument that is based on the corporation's general credit rating. 2. *Bond.* A *long-term* debt security that is *secured* by some form of property. The property securing the bond is called *collateral.* In the event of nonpayment of interest, principal, or other specified events, bondholders can foreclose on and obtain the collateral. 3. *Note.* A *short-term* debt instrument with a maturity of five years or less. Notes can be either unsecured or secured. 4. *Indenture agreement.* The contract between the corporation and debt security holders that contains the terms of the agreement between the corporation and the holders.

Corporate Powers, p. 734

Corporate Powers	1. *Express powers.* A corporation has the express powers granted to it by the U.S. Constitution, state constitutions, federal statutes, state statutes (particularly the state's corporation code), articles of incorporation, bylaws, and resolutions of the board of directors.
	2. *Implied powers.* Powers that are implied that allow a corporation to accomplish its corporate purpose.
Ultra Vires Acts	Acts by a corporation that are beyond its express or implied powers.
	Remedies. The following remedies are available if an *ultra vires* act is committed:
	a. Shareholders can sue for an *injunction* to prevent the corporation from engaging in the act.
	b. The corporation (or shareholders on behalf of the corporation) can sue the officers and directors who caused the act for *damages.*
	c. The attorney general of the state of incorporation can bring an action to enjoin the act or to dissolve the corporation.

Dissolution and Termination of Corporations, p. 736

Voluntary Dissolution	Dissolution of a corporation by the incorporators or initial directors if the corporation has not begun business or issued shares and by the majority vote of shareholders if the corporation has begun business or issued shares. *Articles of dissolution.* Document filed with the secretary of state of the state of incorporation when a corporation has been voluntarily dissolved.
Administrative Dissolution	Involuntary dissolution of a corporation that is ordered by the secretary of state if the corporation has failed to comply with certain procedures required by law (e.g., failure to pay franchise tax). *Certificate of dissolution.* Document filed by the secretary of state when a corporation is administratively dissolved.
Judicial Dissolution	Dissolution of a corporation by a court proceeding instituted by:
	1. *The state.* If the corporation (a) procured its articles of incorporation through fraud or (b) exceeded or abused the authority conferred upon it by law.
	2. *Decree of dissolution.* Order issued by the court when a corporation has been judicially dissolved.
Winding-Up, Liquidation, and Termination	1. *Winding-up and liquidation.* The process by which a dissolved corporation's assets are collected, liquidated, and distributed to creditors, shareholders and other claimants.
	2. *Termination.* The ending of a corporation that occurs only after the winding up of the corporation's affairs, the liquidation of its assets, and the distribution of the proceeds and property to the claimants.

END-OF-CHAPTER INTERNET EXERCISES AND CASE QUESTIONS

Working the Web Internet Exercises

ACTIVITIES

1. Create a hypothetical corporation by preparing article of incorporation, bylaws, and a shareholder agreement, using forms suitable for your state. For a list of state corporation statutes, see **www.law.cornell.edu/topics/state_statutes.html#corporations**.

2. Prepare minutes of the organizational meeting for your newly formed corporation. See Findlaw's compilation of state corporation and business forms **www.findlaw.com/11stategov/indexcorp.html**.

3. Using your state's database of corporations, find the last field annual report of a local corporation and determine who the officers are, and who is designated as the registered agent for service of process. See the Legal Information Institute's Corporate Law Page **www.law.cornell.edu/topics/corporations.html**. See also The Corporate Library **www.thecorporatelibrary.com**.

4. Assume you have decided to form a nonprofit corporation. What other steps do you need to take to properly create such an entity? See U.S. Incorporation and Nonprofits Online Directory; Charities, Secretary of State, Corporations Division, Foundation Directories, UCC, Trademarks 1996 at **www.internet-prospector.org/secstate.html**.

CRITICAL LEGAL THINKING CASES

29.1 Legal Entity Jeffrey Sammak was the owner of a contracting business known as Senaco. In the early part of 1980, Sammak decided to enter the coal reprocessing business. In April 1980, Sammak attended the "Coal Show" in Chicago, Illinois, at which he met representatives of the Deister Co., Inc., (Deister). Deister was incorporated under the laws of Pennsylvania. Sammak began negotiating with Deister to purchase equipment to be used in his coal reprocessing business. Deister sent Sammak literature guaranteeing a certain level of performance for the equipment. On April 3, 1981, Sammak purchased the equipment. After the equipment was installed, Sammak became dissatisfied with its performance. Sammak believes that Deister breached an express warranty and wants to sue. Can a suit be brought against a corporation such as Deister? [*Blackwood Coal v. Deister Co., Inc.,* 626 F.Supp. 727 (E.D.Pa. 1985)]

29.2 Limited Liability of Shareholders Joseph M. Billy was an employee of the USM Corporation (USM). USM is a publicly held corporation. On October 21, 1976, Billy was at work when a 4,600-pound ram from a vertical boring mill broke loose and crushed him to death. Billy's widow brought suit against USM alleging that the accident was caused by certain defects in the manufacture and design of the vertical boring mill and the two moving parts directly involved in the accident, a metal lifting arm and the 4,600-pound ram. If Mrs. Billy's suit is successful, can the shareholders of USM be held personally liable for any judgment against USM? [*Billy v. Consolidated Mach. Tool. Corp.,* 412 N.E.2d 934, 51 N.Y.2d 152 (N.Y.App. 1980)]

29.3 Type of Corporation William O'Donnel and Vincent Marino worked together as executives of a shipping container repair company known as Marine Trailers. Marine Trailer's largest customer was American Export Lines (American Export). When American Export became unhappy with the owners of Marine Trailers, it let O'Donnel and Marino know that if they formed their own company, American Exports would give them its business. O'Donnel and Marino decided to take American Export's suggestion and bought the majority of shares of a publicly traded corporation known as Marine Repair Service, Inc. (Repair Services). O'Donnel and Marino operated Repair Services as a container repair company at the Port of New York. The company prospered, expanding to five other states and overseas. O'Donnel and Marino's initial $12,000 investment paid off. Ten years after buying the company, both men were earning over $150,000 a year in salary alone. What type of corporation is Repair Service? [*O'Donnel v. Marine Repair Services, Inc.,* 530 F.Supp. 1199 (S.D.N.Y. 1982)]

29.4 Type of Corporation Hutchinson Baseball Enterprises, Inc. (Hutchinson, Inc.) was incorporated under the laws of Kansas on August 31, 1980. Among the purposes of the corporation, according to its bylaws, are to "promote, advance, and sponsor baseball, which shall include Little League and Amateur baseball, in the Hutchinson, Kansas, area." The corporation is involved in a number of activities, including the leasing of a field for American Legion teams, furnishing instructors as coaches for Little League teams, conducting a Little League camp, and the leasing of a baseball field to a local junior college for a nominal fee. Hutchinson, Inc. raises money through ticket sales to amateur baseball games, concessions, and contributions. Any profits are used to improve the playing fields. Profits are never distributed to the corporation's directors or members. What type of corporation is Hutchinson, Inc.? [*Hutchinson Baseball Enterprises, Inc. v. Commissioner of Internal Revenue,* 696 F.2d 757 (10th Cir. 1982)]

29.5 Type of Corporation In November 1979, Elmer Balvik and Thomas Sylvester formed a partnership, named Weldon Electric, for the purpose of engaging in the electrical contracting business. Balvik contributed $8,000 and a vehicle worth $2,000 and Sylvester contributed $25,000 to the partnership's assets. The parties operated the business as a partnership until 1984, when they decided to incorporate. Stock was issued to Balvik and Sylvester in proportion to their partnership ownership interests, with Sylvester receiving 70 percent and Balvik 30 percent of the stock. Balvik and his wife and Sylvester and his wife were the four directors of the corporation. Sylvester was elected president of the corporation. Balvik was vice president. The corporation's bylaws stated that "sales of shares of stock by any shareholder shall be as set forth in a 'Buy Sell Agreement' entered into by the shareholders." What type of corporation is Weldon Electric? [*Balvik v. Sylvester,* 411 N.W.2d 383 (ND 1987)]

29.6 Type of Corporation Leo V. Mysels was the president of Florida Fashions of Interior Design, Inc. (Florida Fashions). Florida Fashions, which was a Pennsylvania corporation, had never registered to do business in the state of Florida. In 1973, while acting in the capacity of a salesman for the corporation, Mysels took an order for goods from Francis E. Barry. The transaction took place in Florida. Barry paid Florida Fashions for the goods ordered. When Florida Fashions failed to perform its obligations under the sales agreement, Barry brought suit in Florida. What type of corporation was Florida Fashions in regards to the state of Pennsylvania and to the state of Florida? Can Florida Fashions defend itself in a lawsuit? [*Mysels v. Barry,* 332 So.2d 38 (Fla.App. 1976)]

29.7 Corporate Name Lippman, Inc. (Lippman), a wholly owned subsidiary of Litton Systems, Inc., was incorporated on September 11, 1973, under the laws of the state of Wisconsin. As a subsidiary, Lippman seldom transacted business under its own name. On October 4, 1976, organizers filed articles of incorporation with the secretary of state of Wisconsin to form a corporation called Lippman-Milwaukee, Inc. (Lippman-Milwaukee). Lippman and the proposed Lippman-Milwaukee were two separate entities with different businesses and different owners. After the secretary of state granted a certificate of incorporation to Lippman-Milwaukee, Lippman sued to prevent Lippman-Milwaukee from using the name. Lippman claimed that the name of the new corporation was too similar and could cause confusion. Who wins? [*Litton Systems, Inc. v. Lippman-Milwaukee, Inc.*, 481 F.Supp. 788 (E.D.Wis. 1979)]

29.8 Promoter's Liability On December 27, 1972, the Homes Corporation (Homes), a closely held corporation whose sole stockholders were Jerry and Beverly Ann Allen, purchased 10 acres of real estate near Kahaluu on the island of Oahu, Hawaii. Homes made a down payment of $50,000. It was the Allens' intention to obtain approval for a planned unit development (PUD) from the city and county of Honolulu and then develop the property with some 60 condominium townhouses. To further this project, the Allens sought an outside investor. Herbert Hadley, a real estate developer from Texas, decided to join the Allens' project. The two parties entered an agreement whereby a new Hawaiian corporation would be formed to build the condominiums, with Handley owning 51 percent of the corporation's stock and the Allen's the remaining 49 percent. The two parties began extensive planning and design of the project. They also took out a $69,500 loan from the Bank of Hawaii. After a year had gone by, Handley informed the Allens that he was no longer able to advance funds to the project. Soon thereafter, the city and county denied their PUD zoning application. The new corporation was never formed. Who is liable for the failed condominium project's contractual obligations? [*Handley v. Ching*, 627 P.2d 1132 (HawaiiApp. 1981)]

29.9 Promoter's Contracts Martin Stern, Jr., was an architect who worked in Nevada. In January 1969, Nathan Jacobson asked Stern to draw plans for Jacobson's new hotel/casino, the Kings Castle at Lake Tahoe. Stern agreed to take on the project and immediately began preliminary work. At this time, Stern dealt directly with Jacobson, who referred to the project as "my hotel." In February 1969, Stern wrote to Jacobson detailing, among other things, the architect's services and fee. Stern's plans were subsequently discussed by the two men and Stern's fee was set at $250,000. On May 9, 1969, Jacobson formed Lake Enterprises, Inc. (Lake Enterprises), a Nevada corporation of which Jacobson was the sole shareholder and president. Lake Enterprises was formed for the purpose of owning the new casino. During this period, Stern was paid monthly by checks drawn on an account belonging to another corporation controlled by Jacobson. Stern never agreed to contract with any of these corporations and always dealt exclusively with Jacobson. When Stern was not paid the full amount of his architectural fee, he sued Jacobson to

recover. Jacobson claims that he is not personally liable for any of Stern's fee because a novation has taken place. Who wins? [*Jacobson v. Stern*, 605 P.2d 198 (NV 1980)]

29.10 Preferred Stock On June 24, 1970, Commonwealth Edison Co. (Commonwealth Edison), through its underwriters, sold one million shares of preferred stock at an offering price of $100 per share. Commonwealth Edison wanted to issue the stock with a dividend rate of 9.26 percent, but its major underwriter, First Boston Corporation (First Boston), advised that a rate of 9.44 percent should be paid. According to First Boston, a shortage of investment funds existed and a higher dividend rate was necessary for a successful stock issue. Commonwealth Edison's management was never happy with the high dividend rate being paid on this preferred stock. On April 2, 1971, Commonwealth Edison's vice chairman was quoted in the report of the annual meeting of the corporation as saying "we were disappointed at the 9.44 percent dividend rate on the preferred stock we sold last August, but we expect to refinance it when market conditions make it feasible." On March 20, 1972, Commonwealth Edison, pursuant to the terms under which the stock was sold, bought back the one million shares of preferred stock at a price of $110 per share. What type of preferred stock is this? [*The Franklin Life Insurance Company v. Commonwealth Edison Company*, 451 F.Supp. 602 (S.D.Ill. 1978)]

29.11 Debt Securities United Financial Corporation of California (United Financial) was incorporated in the state of Delaware on May 8, 1959. United Financial owned the majority of a California savings and loan association as well as three insurance agencies. In 1960, the original investors in United Financial decided to capitalize on an increase in investor interest in savings and loans. In June 1960, the first public offering of United Federal stock was made. The stock was sold as a unit, with 60,000 units being offered. Each unit consisted of two shares of United Financial stock and one $100, five percent interest-bearing debenture bond. This initial offering was a success. It provided $7.2 million to the corporation, of which $6.2 million was distributed as a return of capital to the original investors. What is the difference between the stock offered for sale by United Financial and the debenture bonds? [*Jones v. H.F. Ahmanson & Company*, 1 Cal.3d 93, 81 Cal.Rptr. 592 (CA 1969)]

BUSINESS ETHICS CASES

29.12 Business Ethics John A. Goodman was a real estate salesman in the state of Washington. In 1979, Goodman sold an apartment building that needed extensive renovation to Darden, Doman & Stafford Associates (DDS), a general partnership. Goodman represented that he personally had experience in renovation work. During the course of negotiations on a renovation contract, Goodman informed the managing partner of DDS that

he would be forming a corporation to do the work. A contract was executed in August 1979 between DDS and "Building Design and Development (In Formation), John A. Goodman, President." The contract required the renovation work to be completed by October 15. Goodman immediately subcontracted the work, but the renovation was not completed on time. DDS also found that the work that was completed was of poor quality. Goodman did not file the articles of incorporation for his new corporation until November 1. The partners of DDS sued Goodman to hold him liable for the renovation contracts. Goodman denied personal liability. Was it morally correct for Goodman to deny liability? Is Goodman personally liable? [*Goodman v. Darden, Doman & Stafford Associates*, 670 P.2d 648 (WA 1983)]

29.13 Business Ethics In 1983, pursuant to a public offering, Knoll International, Inc. (Knoll), issued debentures to investors. The debentures bore interest at $8\frac{1}{8}$ percent, matured in 30 years, and were subordinated, convertible into common stock at the rate of each \$19.20 of principal amount for one share of common stock, and redeemable. Section 8.08 of the indenture agreement provided that no debenture holder could sue unless the holders of 35 percent of the debentures requested the trustee to

sue. The indenture also gave the trustee the authority to amend the indenture agreement.

Knoll was controlled through a series of subsidiaries by Knoll International Holdings, Inc. (Holdings), which, in turn, was controlled by Marshall S. Cogan. On January 22, 1987, Knoll merged into Holdings and paid its common shareholders \$12 cash per share. Knoll and the indenture trustee executed a supplemental indenture that provided that each debenture holder would receive \$12 cash for each \$19.20 principal amount of debentures. Simons, a debenture holder who did not own 35 percent of the debentures, brought this suit against Knoll and Cogan. Does Knoll International, Inc., or Cogan owe a fiduciary duty to the debenture holders? Is Cogan breaching an ethical duty to the debenture holders? [*Simons v. Cogan*, 542 A.2d 785 (Del.Ch. 1987)]

 # BRIEFING THE CASE WRITING ASSIGNMENT

Read the following case, which has been excerpted from the court's opinion. Review and brief the case.

Johnson v. Dodgen
451 N.W.2D. 168 (1990)
Supreme Court of Iowa

Lavoranto, Justice

This breach of contract action is the aftermath of a bank failure caused by the embezzlement of \$16.7 million by Des Moines stockbroker Gary Lewellyn. In 1967, Joe W. Dodgen agreed to buy controlling interest in the First National Bank of Humboldt under a stock purchase agreement (agreement) calling for monthly payments. Ben P. and Adeline G. St. John, the sellers, died shortly thereafter. Two trusts were then established to receive payments under the agreement.

Dodgen assigned the agreement to his company, Humboldt Realty Insurance Co., Inc. (Humboldt Realty), which was not in existence at the time the agreement was executed, underwent several name changes until it became known as Iowa Growthland Financial Corporation. After the bank was closed in 1982, Iowa Growthland continued to make payments under the agreement until 1984.

The trusts then sued Dodgen and Iowa Growthland for the payments that were in arrears. Dodgen and Iowa Growthland filed an answer in which they raised failure of consideration as an affirmative defense. Simply put, they were claiming that the consideration for the agreement failed when the bank went out of existence. In addition, Dodgen asserted that he was not personally liable because he signed the agreement as an agent for Humboldt Realty. In its counterclaim, Iowa Growthland sought damages on the theory of unjust enrichment for payments it made after the bank was closed.

The case was tried to a jury. By way of answers to special verdict forms, the jury found that the trustees were not entitled to recover for breach of contract, that Dodgen was indeed acting as an agent when he signed the agreement, and that Iowa Growthland was not entitled to damages for its claim of unjust enrichment.

The district court granted a new trial on all the issues. Dodgen and Iowa Growthland appealed; the trustees cross-appealed.

We reverse and remand with directions to enter judgment in favor of the trustees pursuant to Iowa Rule of Appellate Procedure 26.

I. Failure of Consideration

Dodgen and Iowa Growthland contend that the continued existence of the bank was the essence or root of the agreement—the thing Dodgen really bargained for. They argue that when the bank was closed the consideration for Dodgen's promise to pay failed. This failure of consideration, they assert, excused any future performance on their part.

There is a difference between lack of consideration and failure of consideration. A lack of consideration means no contract is ever formed. In contrast, a failure of consideration means the contract is valid when formed but becomes unenforceable because the performance bargained for has not been rendered.

In our view the potential failure of any business that is being sold is always a risk in the contemplation of the parties. If the buyer wants protection against the risk, the simple solution is to hedge against it in the agreement. That was not done here. Consequently, Dodgen assumed that risk.

What Dodgen bargained for was control of the bank through the stock he purchased; he got it and had it for 15 years. The fact that his investment later turned out worthless does not, in our view, constitute failure of consideration.

A. Essence of the Agreement

Under the agreement here, Dodgen agreed to purchase from St. John 506 shares of capital stock of the bank. The 506 shares represented 50.6 percent of the issued and outstanding stock of the bank. By this purchase, Dodgen was acquiring controlling interest in the bank.

B. The Executory Nature of the Agreement

This issue is inextricably intertwined with the essence of the agreement issue. Dodgen and Iowa Growthland contend that the agreement was still executory when the bank was closed because the trustees had physical possession of the stock. While the trustees are still able to turn over the stock, Dodgen and Iowa Growthland argue such a gesture would be meaningless because the asset that the stock represents is nonexistant. So, they argue, there was a failure of consideration when the bank was closed.

Here we think the parties intended title to the stock to pass to Dodgen once the stock was registered in his name. At this point several things had occurred. Dodgen had made the down payment called for in the agreement and began exercising control of the bank. Likewise, St. John had substantially performed his part of the agreement. Only two promises remained unperformed: Dodgen's full payment of the purchase price and St. John's delivery of the physical possession of the stock.

In these circumstances, we think there was a constructive delivery of the stock to Dodgen. Although the collateral provision of the agreement denied Dodgen physical possession of the stock, it did give him the right to such possession upon full payment. The provision also gave him rights of ownership in all other respects. Risk of loss passed with this constructive delivery. The decline in the stock's value gave Dodgen no greater right to avoid his obligation to pay than an enhanced value would have given St. John an excuse for not delivering the stock.

C. Inability to Pledge the Stock as Security

It is true that under the agreement Dodgen could not borrow against the stock. Dodgen and Iowa Growthland assert this constraint as further evidence that consideration for the agreement failed. The short answer to this argument is that Dodgen should not be allowed to take advantage of a provision he agreed to.

II. Unjust Enrichment

We have already determined that there was not, as a matter of law, a failure of consideration. In view of our holding on the failure of consideration issue, we think the district court should have sustained the trustees' motion for directed verdict on the unjust enrichment counterclaim.

III. Agency

The trustees moved for a directed verdict against Dodgen personally because the record showed he signed the agreement. Dodgen resisted the motion, contending there was enough evidence in the record to generate a jury question on his agency defense. The only evidence on this point was Dodgen's testimony. Dodgen testified that when he signed the agreement St. John agreed that Humboldt Realty—Iowa Growthland's predecessor— would be the responsible party. The district court overruled the motion. The jury then determined that Dodgen was acting as an agent for Humboldt Realty when he signed the agreement. For reasons that follow we think the district court should have sustained the motion for directed verdict.

At the time Dodgen and St. John signed the agreement, Humboldt Realty was not in existence. Ordinarily in these circumstances Dodgen would be per- *sonally liable. The law is clear that an agent who purports to act on behalf of a nonexistent principal is liable as a party to the agreement. The rationale for the rule is simply that in such circumstances there is no agency. This situation frequently happens when a corporate promoter enters into contracts before the corporation is actually incorporated.*

There is, however, an exception to this rule. If the other contracting party knows that the principal does not exist and looks to the principal alone for responsibility, the promoter is relived of personal liability.

Here the pivotal question is whether St. John agreed to look to Humboldt Realty alone for payment. We think reasonable minds would conclude from this record that he did not.

We have substantial evidence that establishes Dodgen was acting in his personal capacity. First, as the district court ruled, the language of the agreement is unequivocal on this point. For example, the opening paragraph states that "This agreement made and entered into by and between B.P. St. John and Joe W. Dodgen said B.P. St. John being hereafter referred to as the seller and the said Joe W. Dodgen being hereafter referred to as the buyer." Moreover, Dodgen ostensibly signed the agreement in his individual capacity.

Second, St. John and Dodgen were, at the time of the agreement, very knowledgeable in financial and legal matters. It is inconceivable to us that St. John would turn over valuable assets and look solely to a nonexistent corporation for payment. It is also equally inconceivable to us that Dodgen would fail to insist on express language in the agreement that would relieve him of personal liability. Simply put, we think reasonable minds would conclude that the absence of such language meant that St. John was looking to Dodgen for payment, and Dodgen knew it.

Last, in 1982 Dodgen acknowledged his personal liability. In a letter to one of the trustees—a letter we previously mentioned—Dodgen said:

> *You are also correct in that the contract between me and Ben and Adeline St. John is a personal obligation even though it was later assigned to First Investors Services, Inc.*

This damaging admission coupled with the other evidence leads us to conclude that the district court should have sustained the motion for directed verdict on the agency issue.

IV. Disposition

We reverse the posttrial ruling of the district court. We remand the case to the district court with directions to enter judgment in favor of the trustees for $160,976.26—the delinquent amount at the time of the trial—together with interest and costs.

CHAPTER 30

Directors, Officers, and Shareholders

Corporation, n. An ingenious device for obtaining individual profit without individual responsibility.

—Ambrose Bierce
The Devil's Dictionary (1911)

Chapter Objectives

After studying this chapter, you should be able to:

1. Describe the function of shareholders, directors, and officers in managing the affairs of a corporation.

2. Describe how shareholders' and directors' meetings are called and conducted.

3. Distinguish between straight and cumulative voting for directors.

4. Describe the agency authority of officers to enter into contracts on behalf of a corporation.

5. Distinguish how the management of close corporations differs from that of publicly held corporations.

6. Describe a director's and officer's duty of care and the business judgment rule.

7. Describe a director's and officer's duty of loyalty and how this duty is breached.

8. Describe directors' and officers' liability insurance and corporate indemnification.

9. Define *piercing of the corporate veil* or *alter ego doctrine.*

10. Describe how Delaware has amended its corporation code to recognize electronic communications.

Chapter Contents

745

To supervise wisely the great corporations is well; but to look backward to the days when business was polite pillage and regard our great business concerns as piratical institutions carrying letters of marque and reprisal is a grave error born in the minds of little men. When these little men legislate they set the brakes going uphill.

Elbert Hubbard
Notebook (1856–1915)

Shareholders, directors, and officers have different rights in managing the corporation. The shareholders elect the directors and vote on other important issues affecting the corporation. The directors are responsible for making policy decisions and employing officers. The officers are responsible for the corporation's day-to-day operations.

As a legal entity, a corporation can be held liable for the acts of its directors and officers and for authorized contracts entered into on its behalf. The directors and officers of a corporation have certain rights and owe certain duties to the corporation and its shareholders. A director or officer who breaches any of these duties can be held personally liable to the corporation, to its shareholders, or to third parties. Insurance is available against certain of these losses. Except in a few circumstances, shareholders do not owe a fiduciary duty to other shareholders or the corporation.

This chapter discusses the rights, duties, and liability of corporate shareholders, directors, and officers.

RIGHTS OF SHAREHOLDERS

A corporation's shareholders own the corporation. Nevertheless, they are not agents of the corporation (i.e., they cannot bind the corporation to any contracts), and the only management duties they have is the right to vote on matters such as the election of directors and the approval of fundamental changes in the corporation.

Business Brief

Shareholders are not agents of the corporation. They cannot bind the corporation to contracts.

Kazakhstan Multinational corporations are entering into partnerships and agreements with the former Soviet Union countries of central Asia to develop substantial oil reserves and engage in other commercial endeavors.

annual shareholders' meeting

Meeting of the shareholders of a corporation that must be held annually by the corporation to elect directors and to vote on other matters.

special shareholders' meetings

Meetings of shareholders that may be called to consider and vote on important or emergency issues, such as a proposed merger or amending the articles of incorporation.

Shareholders' Meetings

Annual shareholders' meetings are held to elect directors, choose an independent auditor, or take other actions. The meeting must be held at the time fixed in the bylaws [RMBCA § 7.01]. If the meeting is not held within either 15 months of the last annual meeting or 6 months after the end of the corporation's fiscal year, whichever is earlier, a shareholder may petition the court to order the meeting held [RMBCA § 7.03].

Special shareholders' meetings may be called by the board of directors, the holders of at least 10 percent of the voting shares of the corporation, or any other person authorized to do so by the articles of incorporation or bylaws (e.g., the president) [RMBCA

§ 7.02]. Special meetings may be held to consider important or emergency issues, such as a merger or consolidation of the corporation with one or more other corporations, the removal of directors, amending the articles of incorporation, or dissolution of the corporation.

Any act that can be taken at a shareholders' meeting can be taken without a meeting if all of the corporate shareholders sign a written consent approving the action [RMBCA § 7.04].

Notice of Meetings The corporation is required to give the shareholders written *notice* of the place, day, and time of annual and special meetings. If the meeting is a special meeting, the purpose of the meeting must also be stated. Only matters stated in the notice of a special meeting can be considered at the meeting. The notice, which must be given not less than 10 days or more than 50 days before the date of the meeting, may be given in person or by mail [RMBCA § 7.05]. If the required notice is not given or is defective, any action taken at the meeting is void.

Proxies

Shareholders do not have to attend the shareholders' meeting to vote. Shareholders may vote by *proxy*; that is they can appoint another person (the proxy) as their agent to vote at the shareholders' meeting. The proxy may be directed exactly how to vote the shares or may be authorized to vote the shares at his or her discretion. Proxies must be in writing. The written document itself is called the **proxy** (or **proxy card**). Unless otherwise stated, a proxy is valid for 11 months [RMBCA § 7.22].

proxy
The written document that a shareholder signs authorizing another person to vote his or her shares at the shareholders' meetings in the event of the shareholder's absence.

Voting Requirements

At least one class of shares of the corporation must have voting rights. The RMBCA permits corporations to grant more than one vote per share to some classes of stock and less than one vote per share to others [RMBCA § 6.01].

Only those shareholders who own stock as of a set date may vote at a shareholders' meeting. This date, which is called the **record date**, is set forth in the corporate bylaws. The record date may not be more than 70 days before the shareholders' meeting [RMBCA § 7.07].

record date
A date specified in the corporate bylaws that determines whether a shareholder may vote at a shareholders' meeting.

The corporation must prepare a *shareholders' list* that contains the names and addresses of the shareholders as of the record date and the class and number of shares owned by each shareholder. This list must be available for inspection at the corporation's main office [RMBCA § 7.20].

Quorum Unless otherwise provided in the articles of incorporation, if a majority of shares entitled to vote are represented at the meeting in person or by proxy, there is a **quorum** to hold the meeting. Once a quorum is present, the withdrawal of shares does not affect the quorum of the meeting [RMBCA § 7.25(a) and (b)].

quorum
The required number of shares that must be represented in person or by proxy to hold a shareholders' meeting. The RMBCA establishes a majority of outstanding shares as a quorum.

Vote Required for Elections Other than for Directors The affirmative **vote** of the majority of the **voting** shares represented at a shareholders' meeting constitutes an act of the shareholders for actions other than for the election of directors [RMBCA § 7.25(c)].

straight voting
Each shareholder votes the number of shares he or she owns on candidates for each of the positions open.

Consider This Example Suppose there are 20,000 shares outstanding of a corporation. Assume that a shareholders' meeting is duly called to amend the articles of incorporation and that 10,001 shares are represented at the meeting. A quorum is present because a majority of the shares entitled to vote are represented. Suppose that 5,001 shares are voted in favor of the amendment. The amendment passes. In this example, just over 25 percent of the shares of the corporation bound the other shareholders to the action taken at the shareholders' meeting.

cumulative voting
A shareholder can accumulate all of his or her votes and vote them all for one candidate or split them among several candidates.

Contemporary Business Environment

ELECTION OF DIRECTORS BY STRAIGHT AND CUMULATIVE VOTING

The election of directors by shareholders may be by one of the following two methods:

STRAIGHT (NONCUMULATIVE) VOTING

Unless otherwise stated in the corporation's articles of incorporation, voting for the election of directors is by the **straight voting** method. This voting method is quite simple: Each shareholder votes the number of shares he or she owns on candidates for each of the positions open for election. Thus, a majority shareholder can elect the entire board of directors.

Consider This Example Assume that a corporation has 10,000 outstanding shares. Erin Caldwell owns 5,100 shares (or 51 percent) and Michael Rhodes owns 4,900 shares (49 percent). Suppose that three directors of the corporation are to be elected. Caldwell casts 5,100 votes each for her chosen candidates. Rhodes votes 4,900 shares for each of his chosen candidates, who are different from those favored by Caldwell. Each of the three candidates whom Caldwell voted for wins with 5,100 votes.

CUMULATIVE VOTING

The articles of incorporation may provide for **cumulative voting** for the election of directors. Under this method, a shareholder can accumulate all of his or her votes and vote them all for one candidate or split them among several candidates. This means that each shareholder is entitled to multiply the number of shares he or she owns by the number of directors to be elected and cast the product for a single candidate or distribute the product among two or more candidates [RMBCA § 7.28]. Cumulative voting gives a minority shareholder a better opportunity to elect someone to the board of directors.

Consider This Example Suppose Lisa Monroe owns 1,000 shares. Assume that four directors are to be elected to the board. Under cumulative voting, Monroe can multiply the number of shares she owns by the number of directors to be elected. She can take the resulting number of votes (4,000) and cast them all for one candidate or split them. Examples of cumulative voting are set forth in Exhibit 30.1

*Ɛ*XHIBIT 30.1 *Examples of Cumulative Voting*

Formula for Cumulative Voting. A shareholder can use the following formula to determine whether or not he or she owns a sufficient number of shares to elect a director to the board of directors using cumulative voting:

$$\frac{S \times T}{D + 1} + 1 = X$$

where X is the number of shares needed by a shareholder to elect a director to the board, S is the number of shares that actually vote at the shareholders' meeting, T is the number of directors the shareholder wants to elect, and D is the number of directors to be elected at the shareholders' meeting.

Example 1 Suppose there are 9,000 outstanding shares of a corporation. Shareholder 1 owns 1,000 shares, shareholder 2 owns 4,000 shares, and shareholder 3 owns 4,000 shares. Assume nine directors are to be elected to the board of directors. All the shares are voted. Under cumulative voting, does shareholder 1 have enough votes to elect a director to the board? The answer is yes:

$$\frac{9,000 \times 1}{9 + 1} + 1 = 901$$

Example 2 If a board of directors is divided into classes and elected by staggered elections, the ability of a minority shareholder to elect a director to the board is diminished. Suppose in Example 1 that the corporation staggered the election of the board of directors so that three directors are elected each year to serve three-year terms. How many shares would a shareholder have to own to elect a director to the board?

$$\frac{9,000 \times 1}{3 + 1} + 1 = 2,251$$

Because of the staggered election of the board of directors, shareholder 1 (who owns 1,000 shares) would not be able to elect a director to the board without the assistance of another shareholder.

Supramajority Voting Requirement   The articles of incorporation or the bylaws of a corporation can require a greater than majority of shares to constitute a quorum or the vote of the shareholders [RMBCA § 7.27]. This is called a **supramajority voting requirement** (or **supermajority**). Such votes are often required to approve mergers, consolidation, the sale of substantially all of the assets of the corporation, and such. To add a supramajority voting requirement, the amendment must be adopted by the number of shares of the proposed increase. For example, to increase a majority voting requirement to an 80 percent supramajority voting requirement would require an 80 percent affirmative vote.

supramajority voting requirement

A requirement that a greater than majority of shares constitutes a quorum of the vote of the shareholders.

Voting Agreements

Sometimes shareholders agree in advance as to how their shares will be voted. The two major forms of shareholder agreements are discussed in the following paragraphs.

1. **Voting Trusts**   A **voting trust** is an arrangement whereby shareholders transfer their stock certificates to a trustee. Legal title to these shares is held in the name of the trustee. In exchange, *voting trust certificates* are issued to the shareholders. The trustee of the voting trust is empowered to vote the shares held by the trust. The trust may either specify how the trustee is to vote the shares or authorize the trustee to vote the shares at his or her discretion. The members of the trust retain all other incidents of ownership of the stock.

   A voting trust agreement must be in writing and cannot exceed 10 years. It must be filed with the corporation and is open to inspection by shareholders of the corporation [RMBCA §7.30].

2. **Shareholder Voting Agreements**   Two or more shareholders may enter into an agreement that stipulates how they will vote their shares for the election of directors or other matters that require shareholder vote. These **voting agreements** are not limited in duration and do not have to be filed with the corporation. They are specifically enforceable [RMBCA § 7.31]. Shareholder voting agreements can be either revocable or irrevocable [RMBCA § 7.22(d)].

voting trust

The shareholders transfer their stock certificates to a trustee who is empowered to vote the shares.

shareholder voting agreements

Agreement between two or more shareholders agreeing on how they will vote their shares.

Right to Transfer Shares

Subject to certain restrictions, shareholders have the right to transfer their shares. The transfer of securities is governed by **Article 8 of the Uniform Commercial Code (UCC)**. Most states have adopted all or part of Article 8. Usually, shares are transferred by indorsement and delivery of the shares to the new owner.

If a stock certificate has been lost, stolen, or destroyed, the corporation is required to issue a *replacement certificate* if the shareholder posts an indemnity bond to protect the corporation from loss for issuing the replacement certificate. If a lost or stolen certificate reappears in the hands of a bona fide purchaser, that certificate must be registered by the corporation. The corporation can recover on the indemnity bond.

Article 8 of the UCC

The article of the UCC that governs transfer of securities.

Transfer Restrictions

Shareholders may enter into agreements with one another to prevent unwanted persons from becoming owners of the corporation [RMBCA § 6.27]. The following are the two most common forms of agreements.

- **Right of First Refusal**   A **right of first refusal** is an **agreement** entered into by shareholders whereby they grant each other the right of first refusal to purchase shares they are going to sell. A selling shareholder must offer his or her shares for sale to the other parties to the agreement before selling them to anyone else. If the shareholders do not exercise their right of first refusal, the selling shareholder is free to sell his or her shares to another party. A right of first refusal may be granted to the corporation as well.

- **Buy-and-Sell Agreement**   A **buy-and-sell agreement** is one entered into by shareholders that requires selling shareholders to sell their shares to the other shareholders or to the corporation at the price specified in the agreement. The price of the shares is normally determined by a formula that considers, among other factors, the profitability of the corporation. The purchase of shares of a deceased shareholder pursuant to a buy-and-sell agreement is often funded by the purchase of life insurance.

right of first refusal agreement

An agreement that requires the selling shareholder to offer his or her shares for sale to the other parties to the agreement before selling them to anyone else.

buy-and-sell agreement

An agreement that requires selling shareholders to sell their shares to the other shareholders or to the corporation at the price specified in the agreement.

Preemptive Rights

preemptive rights

Rights that give existing shareholders the option of subscribing to new shares being issued in proportion to their current ownership interest.

The articles of incorporation can grant shareholders preemptive rights. **Preemptive rights** give existing shareholders the option of subscribing to new shares being issued by the corporation in proportion to their current ownership interest [RMBCA § 6.30]. Such a purchase can prevent a shareholder's interest in the corporation from being *diluted*. Shareholders are given a reasonable period of time (such as 30 days) to exercise their preemptive rights. If the shareholders do not exercise their preemptive rights during this time, shares can then be sold to anyone.

Consider This Example Suppose that the ABC Corporation has 10,000 outstanding shares and that Linda Norton owns 1,000 shares (10 percent). Assume that the corporation plans to raise more capital by issuing another 10,000 shares of stock. With preemptive rights, Norton must be offered the option to purchase 1,000 of the 10,000 new shares before they are offered to the public. If she does not purchase them, her ownership in the corporation will be diluted from 10 percent to 5 percent.

Right to Receive Information and Inspect Books and Records

annual financial statement

A statement provided to the shareholders that contains a balance sheet, an income statement, and a statement of changes in shareholder equity.

right of inspection

A right that shareholders have to inspect the books and records of the corporation.

Shareholders have the right to be informed about the affairs of the corporation. A corporation must furnish its shareholders with an **annual financial statement** containing a balance sheet, an income statement, and a statement of changes in shareholder equity [RMBCA § 16.20].

Shareholders have an absolute **right to inspect** the shareholders' list, the articles of incorporation, the bylaws, and the minutes of shareholders' meetings held within the past three years. To inspect accounting and tax records, minutes of board of directors' and committee meetings, and minutes of shareholders' meetings held more than three years in the past, a shareholder must demonstrate a "proper purpose" [RMBCA § 16.02]. Proper purposes include deciding how to vote in a shareholder election, identifying fellow shareholders to communicate with them regarding corporate matters, investigating the existence of corporate mismanagement or improper action, and the like. A shareholder can employ an agent, such as a lawyer, an accountant, or a business manager, to inspect the books and records of the corporation on his or her behalf [RMBCA § 16.03].

Shareholder Lawsuits

direct lawsuit

A lawsuit that a shareholder can bring against the corporation to enforce his or her personal rights as a shareholder.

derivative lawsuit

A lawsuit a shareholder brings against an offending party on behalf of the corporation when the corporation fails to bring the lawsuit.

Shareholders may bring two types of lawsuits against the corporation to enforce their rights. The difference between these two types of lawsuits are discussed below.

1. **Direct Lawsuits** A shareholder can bring **direct lawsuits** against the corporation for many reasons, including to (1) enforce the right to vote, (2) enforce preemptive rights, (3) compel payment of declared but unpaid dividends, (4) inspect the books and records of the corporation, (5) enjoin the corporation from committing an *ultra vires* act, and (6) compel dissolution of the corporation. If a shareholder is successful in a direct action against the corporation, the award belongs to that shareholder.

2. **Derivative Lawsuit** If a corporation is harmed by someone, the directors of the corporation have the authority to bring an action on behalf of the corporation against the offending party to recover damages or other relief. If the corporation fails to bring the lawsuit, shareholders have the right to bring the lawsuit on behalf of the corporation. This is called a **derivative action** or **derivative lawsuit** [RMBCA § 7.40].

   A shareholder can bring a derivative action if he or she (1) was a shareholder of the corporation at the time of the act complained of, (2) fairly and adequately represents the interests of the corporation [RMBCA § 7.41], and (3) made a written demand upon the corporation to take suitable actions, and the corporation either rejected the demand or 90 days have passed from the date of the demand [RMBCA § 7.42].

   A derivative lawsuit will be dismissed by the court if either a majority of independent directors or a panel of independent persons appointed by the court determines that the lawsuit is not in the best interests of the corporation. This decision must be reached in good faith and only after conducting a reasonable inquiry [RMBCA § 7.44].

   If a shareholder derivative action is successful, any award goes into the corporate treasury. The plaintiff-shareholder is entitled to recover payment for reasonable expenses, including attorneys' fees, incurred in bringing and maintaining the derivative action [RMBCA § 7.46]. Any settlement of a derivative action requires court approval [RMBCA § 7.45].

The Supreme Court Speaks

Shareholder Permitted to Bring Derivative Lawsuit

Kamen v. Kemper Financial Services, Inc.
111 S.Ct. 1711 (1991)
Supreme Court of the United States

BACKGROUND AND FACTS

Jill S. Kamen is a shareholder of Cash Equivalent Fund, Inc. (Fund), a mutual fund that employs Kemper Financial Services, Inc. (Kemper), as its investment advisor. Kamen brought a derivative lawsuit on behalf of Fund against Kemper, alleging that Kemper violated fiduciary duties owed to Fund as imposed by the Investment Company Act of 1940 (Act), a federal statute. Kamen did not make a demand on Fund's board of directors to sue Kemper any earlier. She alleged that it would have been futile to do so because the directors were acting in a conspiracy with Kemper. The Act was silent as to the rule concerning derivative actions under the Act. The trial court granted Kemper's motion to dismiss the lawsuit. The court of appeals adopted a "universal demand rule" as part of the federal common law and affirmed. This rule requires a shareholder always to make a demand on the directors of a corporation before bringing a derivative lawsuit. Kamen appealed to the U.S. Supreme Court.

SUPREME COURT ISSUE

Should federal law adopt the universal demand rule for bringing derivative actions?

IN THE LANGUAGE OF THE U.S. SUPREME COURT

Marshall, Justice *The presumption that state law should be incorporated into federal common law is particularly strong in areas in which private parties have entered legal relationships with the expectation that their rights and obligations would be governed by state law standards. Corporation law is one such area. Corporations are creatures of state law, state law which is the font of corporate directors' powers. Consequently, we conclude that gaps in federal statutes bearing on the allocation of governing power within the corporation should be filled with state law.*

The purpose of requiring a precomplaint demand is to protect the directors' prerogative to take over the litigation or to oppose it. Thus, the demand requirement implements the basic principle of corporate governance that the decisions of a corporation—including the decision to initiate litigation—should be made by the board of directors or the majority of shareholders. To the extent that a jurisdiction recognizes the futility exception to demand, the jurisdiction places a limit upon the directors' usual power to control the initiation of corporate litigation. Demand typically is deemed to be futile when a majority of the directors have participated in or approved the alleged wrongdoing. Superimposing a rule of universal demand over the corporate doctrine of these States would clearly upset the balance that they have struck between the power of the individual shareholder and the power of the directors to control corporate litigation.

DECISION AND REMEDY

The U.S. Supreme Court refused to adopt the universal demand rule as federal common law but instead held that federal law should follow the appropriate state law concerning demands in derivative lawsuits if a federal statute is silent as to this issue. Reversed.

CASE QUESTIONS

Critical Legal Thinking Which do you think is the better rule: (1) the universal demand rule or (2) the futility exception rule? Why?

Business Ethics Should Kamen have given the directors of Fund the opportunity to have sued Kemper before she did?

Contemporary Business Do derivative lawsuits serve any legitimate purposes? Explain.

RIGHTS OF DIRECTORS

The **board of directors** of a corporation is responsible for formulating the *policy decisions* affecting the management, supervision, and control of the operation of the corporation [RMBCA § 8.01]. Such policy decisions include deciding the business or businesses in which the corporation should be engaged, selecting and removing the top officers of the corporation, determining the capital structure of the corporation, declaring dividends, and the like.

The board may initiate certain actions that require shareholders' approval. These actions are initiated when the board of directors adopts a *resolution* that approves a transaction and recommends that it be submitted to the shareholders for a vote. Examples of such transactions include mergers, sale of substantially all of the corporation's assets outside the course of ordinary business operations, amending the articles of incorporation and the voluntary dissolution of the corporation.

board of directors

A panel of decision makers, the members of which are elected by the shareholders.

Business Brief

The directors of a corporation are responsible for formulating the *policy* decisions affecting the corporation.

Members of the board of directors of nonprofit corporations are held to a lesser standard of liability for actions taken on behalf of the corporation than are members of the board of directors of for-profit corporations.

Selecting Directors

Boards of directors are typically composed of inside and outside directors. An **inside director** is a person who is also an officer of the corporation. For example, the president of the corporation often sits as a director of the corporation.

An **outside director** is a person who sits on the board of directors of a corporation but is not an officer of that corporation. Outside directors are often officers and directors of other corporations, bankers, lawyers, professors, and others. Outside directors are often selected for their business knowledge and expertise.

There are no special qualifications that a person must meet to be elected a director of a corporation. A director need not be a resident of the state of incorporation or a shareholder of the corporation. The articles of incorporation or bylaws may prescribe qualifications for directors, however [RMBCA § 8.02].

inside director
A member of the board of directors who is also an officer of the corporation.

outside director
A member of the board of directors who is not an officer of the corporation.

Number of Directors A board of directors can consist of one or more individuals. The number of initial directors is fixed by the articles of incorporation. This number can be amended in the articles of incorporation or the bylaws. The articles of incorporation or bylaws can establish a variable range for the size of the board of directors. The exact number of directors within the range may be changed from time to time by the board of directors or the shareholders [RMBCA § 8.03].

Term of Office

The term of a director's office expires at the next annual shareholders' meeting following his or her election unless terms are staggered [RMBCA § 8.05]. The RMBCA allows boards of directors that consist of nine or more members to be divided into two or three classes (each class to be as nearly equal in number as possible) that are elected to serve *staggered terms* of two or three years [RMBCA § 8.06]. The specifics of such an arrangement must be outlined in the articles of incorporation.

Business Brief
The terms of office of directors may be *staggered* so that only a portion of the board of directors is up for election each year.

Consider This Example Suppose a board of directors consists of nine directors. The board can be divided into three classes of three directors each, each class to be elected to serve a three-year term. Only three directors of the nine-member board would come up for election each year. This nine-member board could also have been divided into two classes of five and four directors, each class to be elected to two-year terms.

Vacancies and Removal of Directors Vacancies on the board of directors can occur because of death, illness, the resignation of a director before the expiration of his or her term, or an increase in the number of positions on the board. Such vacancies can be filled by the shareholders or the remaining directors [RMBCA § 8.10].

The director is really a watch-dog, and the watch-dog has no right, without the knowledge of his master, to take a sop from a possible wolf.

L.J. Bowen
Re The North Australian Territory Co. Ltd. (1891)

Any director—or the entire board of directors—can be removed from office by a vote of the holders of a majority of the shares entitled to vote at the election. The articles of incorporation provide that directors can be removed only for cause, however [RMBCA § 8.08(a)]. Cause might be for defalcation, breach of the duty of loyalty, gross mismanagement, and such.

Meetings of the Board of Directors

The directors can act only as a board. They cannot act individually on the corporation's behalf. Every director has the right to participate in any meeting of the board of directors. Each director has one vote. Directors cannot vote by proxy.

Regular meetings of the board of directors are held at the times and places established in the bylaws. Such meetings can be held without notice. The board can call **special meetings** as provided in the bylaws [RMBCA § 8.20(a)]. They are usually convened for such reasons as issuing new shares, considering proposals to merge with other corporations, adopting maneuvers to defend against hostile takeover attempts, and the like. The directors must be given at least two days' notice of special meetings unless such notice is waived by the director [RMBCA §§ 8.22 and 8.23].

The board of directors may act without a meeting if all of the directors sign written consents that set forth the actions taken. Such consent has the effect of a unanimous vote [RMBCA § 8.21]. The RMBCA permits meetings of the board to be held via conference calls [RMBCA § 8.20(b)].

Quorum and Voting Requirement   A simple majority of the number of directors established in the articles of incorporation or by laws usually constitutes a **quorum** for transacting business. However, the articles of incorporation and the bylaws may increase this number. If a quorum is present, the approval or disapproval of a majority of the quorum binds the entire board. The articles of incorporation or the bylaws can require a greater than majority of directors to constitute a quorum or the vote of the board [RMBCA § 8.24].

regular meeting

A meeting held by the board of directors at the time and place established in the bylaws.

special meeting

A meeting convened by the board of directors to discuss new shares, merger proposals, hostile takeover attempts, and so forth.

Business Brief

To reflect modern technology the RMBCA permits board of directors meetings to be held via conference call.

quorum

The number of directors necessary to hold a board of directors' meeting or transact business of the board.

Contemporary Business Environment

COMMITTEES OF THE BOARD OF DIRECTORS

In the current complex business world, the demands on directors have increased. To help handle this increased workload, boards of directors have turned to creating committees of their members to handle specific duties. Board members with special expertise or interests are appointed to the various committees.

Unless the articles of incorporation or bylaws provide otherwise, the board of directors may create committees of the board and delegate certain powers to those committees [RMBCA § 8.25]. All members of these committees must be directors. An act of a committee pursuant to delegated authority is the act of the board of directors.

Committees commonly appointed by the board of directors include

- **Executive Committee**   Has authority to (1) act on certain matters on behalf of the board during the interim period between board meetings and (2) conduct preliminary investigations of proposals on behalf of the full board. Most members of the committee are inside directors because it is easier for them to meet to address corporate matters.

- **Audit Committee**   Recommends independent public accountants and supervises the audit of the financial records of the corporation by the accountants.
- **Nominating Committee**   Nominates the management slate of directors to be submitted for shareholder vote.
- **Compensation Committee**   Approves management compensation, including salaries, bonuses, stock option plans, fringe benefits, and such.
- **Investment Committee**   Is responsible for investing and reinvesting the funds of the corporation.
- **Litigation Committee**   Reveiws and decides whether to pursue requests by shareholders for the corporation to sue persons who have allegedly harmed the corporation.

The following powers cannot be delegated to committees but must be exercised by the board itself: (1) declaring dividends, (2) initiating actions that require shareholders' approval, (3) appointing members to fill vacancies on the board, (4) amending the bylaws, (5) approving a plan of merger that does not require shareholder approval (short-form merger), and (6) authorizing the issuance of shares.

Compensation of Directors Originally, it was considered an honor to serve as a director. No payment was involved. Today, directors often are paid an annual retainer and an attendance fee for each meeting attended. Unless otherwise provided in the articles of incorporation, the directors are permitted to fix their own compensation [RMBCA § 8.11].

Right of Inspection Corporate directors are required to have access to the corporation's books and records, facilities and premises, as well as any other information affecting the operation of the corporation. This right of inspection is absolute. It cannot be limited by the articles of incorporation, the bylaws, or board resolution.

Directors' Authority to Pay Dividends

For-profit corporations operate to make a profit. The objective of the shareholders is to share in those profits, either through capital appreciation, the receipt of dividends, or both. **Dividends** are paid at the discretion of the board of directors [RMBCA § 6.40]. The directors are responsible for determining when, where, how, and how much will be paid in dividends. This authority cannot be delegated to a committee of the board of directors or to officers of the corporation.

When a corporation declares a dividend, it sets a date, usually a few weeks prior to the actual payment that is called the **record date**. Persons who are shareholders on that date are entitled to receive the dividend even if they sell their shares before the payment date. Once declared, a cash or property dividend cannot be revoked. Shareholders can sue at law to recover declared but unpaid dividends.

The board of directors may opt to retain the profits in the corporation to be used for corporate purposes rather than pay them as dividends. Profits retained by the corporation are called **retained earnings**.

Legal Restrictions on the Payment of Dividends The law imposes certain restrictions on the payment of dividends to common shareholders. Under the RMBCA, a dividend cannot be paid if (1) the corporation would not be able to pay its debts as they became due in the usual course of business, or (2) the corporation's total assets would be less than its total liabilities, and these would be insufficient funds to pay liquidation preferences to preferred shareholders if the corporation were terminated [RMBCA § 6.40(c)].

Directors who vote for or assent to an illegal dividend or distribution are jointly and severally liable to the corporation for that amount [RMBCA § 8.33].

Stock Dividends Corporations may use additional shares of stock as a dividend. **Stock dividends** are not a distribution of corporate assets. They are paid in proportion to the existing ownership interests of shareholders, so they do not increase a shareholder's proportionate ownership interest.

Consider This Example Suppose Betty owns 1,000 shares (10 percent) of the 10,000 outstanding shares of the ABC Corporation. If the ABC Corporation declares a stock dividend of 20 percent, Betty will receive a stock dividend of 200 shares. She now owns 1,200 shares—or 10 percent—of a total of 12,000 outstanding shares.

---

dividend

Distribution of profits of the corporation to shareholders.

Business Brief

Dividends are not automatically paid to shareholders; they are paid at the discretion of the board of directors.

record date

A date that determines whether a shareholder receives payment of a declared dividend.

retained earnings

Profits retained by the corporation and not paid out as dividends.

Business Brief

There are certain legal restrictions on the payment of dividends if the corporation is experiencing financial difficulties.

stock dividend

Additional shares of stock paid as a dividend.

$\mathcal{B}$usiness $\mathcal{E}$thics

STATES ENACT CONSTITUENCY STATUTES

Under the traditional *business judgment rule*, directors of a corporation owe a *fiduciary duty* to act on an informed basis, with reasonable care, and in good faith. Historically, this duty has been rigidly and exclusively owed to the corporation and its shareholders and to no others. Under this classical theory of the corporation, the rights of other constituents—such as employees, bondholders and creditors, suppliers and customers —exist by contract, period.

This view prevailed during the 1980s, when leveraged buyouts and the greed of corporate raiders caused the demise of many venerable companies, dislodged workers, destroyed pension rights, and ruined many local economies. In response, more than 30 states have enacted **constituency statutes** that allow directors to consider constituents other than shareholders when making decisions.

For example, Minnesota adopted the following statute:

In discharging the duties of the position of director, a director may, in considering the best interests of the corporation, consider the interests of the corporation's employees, customers, suppliers, and creditors, the economy of the state and nation, community and societal considerations, and the long-term as well as short-term interests of the corporation and its shareholders, including the possibility that these

interests may be best served by the continued independence of the corporation. [Minn. Stat. § 302A.251(5)]

Most constituency statutes are permissive, not mandatory. That is, directors may take into account nonstockholder interests but are not required to do so.

Constituency statutes recognize the complex nature of the modern corporation and the modern view that shareholders are not the only "owners" of corporations. These statutes acknowledge the rights of a variety of participants, including lenders, employees, managers, suppliers, distributors, customers, and the local communities in which corporations are located.

1. Why did state legislatures enact constituency statutes?
2. Do constituency statutes make corporate boards of directors more socially responsible?

$\mathcal{R}$IGHTS OF OFFICERS

The board of directors has the authority to appoint the **officers** of the corporation. The officers are elected by the board of directors at such time and by such manner as prescribed in the corporation's bylaws. The directors can delegate certain management authority to the officers of the corporation.

At minimum, most corporations have the following officers: (1) a president, (2) one or more vice presidents, (3) a secretary, and (4) a treasurer. The bylaws or the board of directors can authorize duly appointed officers the power to appoint assistant officers. The same individual may simultaneously hold more than one office in the corporation [RMBCA § 8.40]. The duties of each officer are specified in the bylaws of the corporation.

officers

Employees of the corporation who are appointed by the board of directors to manage the day-to-day operations of the corporation.

Agency Authority of Officers

Officers and agents of the corporation have such authority as may be provided in the bylaws of the corporation or as determined by resolution of the board of directors [RMBCA § 8.41]. As agents, the authority of officers to bind a corporation to contracts is derived from express authority, implied authority, and apparent authority.

Ratification of Unauthorized Actions   A corporation can **ratify** an unauthorized act of a corporate officer or agent. For example, suppose an officer acts outside the scope of his or her employment and enters into a contract with a third person. If the corporation accepts the benefits of the contract, it has ratified the contract and is bound by it. The ratification relates back to the moment the unauthorized act was performed. Officers are liable on an unauthorized contract if the corporation does not ratify it.

Removal of Officers   Unless an employment contract provides otherwise, any officer of a corporation may be removed by the board of directors. The board only has to determine that the best interests of the corporation will be served by such removal [RMBCA § 8.43(b)]. Officers who are removed in violation of an employment contract can sue the corporation for damages.

Business Brief

Although theoretically shareholders own the corporation and directors make the policy decisions, officers are often more powerful than the shareholders and the directors. Officers are often criticized for operating corporations for their own self-interest.

ratification

The acceptance by a corporation of an unauthorized act of a corporate officer or agent.

$\mathcal{E}$*ntrepreneur and the* $\mathcal{L}$*aw*

MANAGING CLOSE CORPORATIONS

Many of the formal rules in state corporation statutes are designed to govern the management of large publicly held corporations. These rules may not be relevant for regulating the management of **close corporations**, that is, corporations formed by entrepreneurs with few shareholders who often work for the corporation and manage its day-to-day operations.

To correct this problem, a **Model Statutory Close Corporation Supplement (Supplement)** has been added to the RMBCA. Only corporations with 50 or fewer shareholders may elect statutory close corporation (SCC) status. To choose this status, the following requirements must be met:

1. Two thirds of the shares of each class of shares of the corporation must approve the election [Supp. § 3(b)].
2. The articles of incorporation must contain a statement that the corporation is a statutory close corporation [Supp. § 3(a)].
3. The share certificates must conspicuously state that the shares have been issued by a statutory close corporation [Supp. § 10].

The Supplement permits SCCs to dispense with some of the formalities of operating a corporation. For example, if all of the shareholders approve, an SCC may operate without a board of directors, and the articles of incorporation contain a statement to that effect [Supp. § 21]. The powers and affairs of the corporation are then managed by the shareholders. An SCC need not adopt bylaws if the provisions required by law to be contained in bylaws are contained in the articles of incorporation or a shareholders' agreement [Supp. § 22]. An SCC need not hold annual shareholders' meetings unless one or more shareholders demand in writing that such meetings be held [Supp. § 23]. The shareholders may enter into a shareholders' agreement about how the corporation will be managed [Supp. § 20(a)]. In effect, the shareholders can treat the corporation as a partnership for governance purposes [Supp. § 20(b)(3)].

Selecting statutory close corporation status does not affect the limited liability of shareholders [Supp. § 25].

The Supplement contains a mandatory right of first refusal. A shareholder of an SCC who desires to transfer his or her shares must first offer them to the corporation on the same terms that a third party is willing to pay for them [Supp. § 12]. If the corporation does not purchase the shares, other holders of the same class of shares may purchase them on the offered terms [Supp. § 11]. Only after the shares have been rejected by the corporation and other shareholders can they be sold to nonshareholders. The articles of incorporation of an SCC may include a provision requiring the corporation to purchase a deceased shareholder's shares [Supp. § 14].

The articles of incorporation of an SCC may authorize one or more shareholders to dissolve the corporation at will or upon the occurrence of a specified event or contingency [Supp. § 33]. Judicial dissolution may be ordered by a court if there is an unbreakable deadlock in the management of the corporation; the directors have acted in an illegal, oppressive, or fraudulent manner; or other such statutory grounds [Supp. § 40].

$\mathscr{C}$ONCEPT SUMMARY   MANAGEMENT OF A CORPORATION

Management Group	Function
Shareholders	Owners of the corporation. They vote on the directors and other major actions to be taken by the corporation.
Board of directors	Responsible for making policy decisions and employing the major officers for the corporation. They also make recommendations regarding actions to be taken by the shareholders.
Officers	Responsible for the day-to-day operation of the corporation. Includes acting as agents for the corporation, hiring other officers and employees, and the like.

$\mathscr{E}$-$\mathscr{C}$ommerce & $\mathscr{I}$nformation $\mathscr{T}$echnology

DELAWARE AMENDS CORPORATION CODE TO RECOGNIZE ELECTRONIC COMMUNICATIONS

The state of Delaware leads the nation as the site for incorporation of the United States' largest corporations. This is the result of the Delaware corporation code itself, as well as the expertise of the Delaware courts in resolving corporate disputes. In order to keep this leadership position, in 2000 the state legislature amended the Delaware General Corporation law to recognize evolving electronic technology. The major changes to the law are:

- Delivery of notices to stockholders may be made electronically if the stockholder consents to the delivery of notice in this form.
- Proxy solicitation for shareholder votes may be made by electronic transmission.
- The shareholder list of a corporation that must be made available during the 10 days prior to a stockholder meeting may be made available either at the principal place of

business of the corporation or by posting the list on an electronic network.

- Stockholders who are not physically present at a meeting may be deemed present, participate in, and vote at the meeting by electronic communication; a meeting may be held solely by electronic communication without a physical location.
- The election of directors of the corporation may be held by electronic transmission.

- Directors, actions by unanimous consent may be taken by electronic transmission.

The use of electronic transmissions, electronic networks, and communication by c-mail will make the operation and administration of corporate affairs more efficient in Delaware. Other states are expected to amend their corporation codes to recognize the importance of electronic communications.

LIABILITY OF CORPORATE DIRECTORS AND OFFICERS

A corporation's directors and officers owe the **fiduciary duties** of trust and confidence to the corporation and its shareholders. More specifically, they owe the (1) *duty of obedience*, (2) *duty of care*, and (3) *duty of loyalty*. Each of these is discussed in detail in the paragraphs that follow.

fiduciary duty

Duty of loyalty, honesty, integrity, trust, and confidence owed by directors and officers to their corporate employers.

Duty of Obedience

The directors and officers of a corporation must act within the authority conferred upon them by the state corporation statute, the articles of incorporation, the corporate bylaws, and the resolutions adopted by the board of directors. This duty is called the **duty of obedience**. Directors and officers who either intentionally or negligently act outside their authority are personally liable for any resultant damages caused to the corporation or its shareholders.

duty of obedience

A duty that directors and officers of a corporation have to act within the authority conferred upon them by the state corporation statute, the articles of incorporation, the corporate bylaws, and the resolutions adopted by the board of directors.

Consider This Example   Suppose the articles of incorporation authorize the corporation to invest in real estate only. If a corporate officer invests corporate funds in the commodities markets, the officer is liable to the corporation for any losses suffered.

Contemporary Business Environment

INDEMNIFICATION AND D&O INSURANCE PROTECTION FOR CORPORATE DIRECTORS AND OFFICERS

Directors and officers of corporations are sometimes personally named in lawsuits that involve actions they have taken on behalf of the corporation. Such lawsuits often are brought by disgruntled shareholders or third parties who claim they have suffered damages because of the director's or officer's negligence or other conduct.

Directors and officers can protect themselves against personal liability by making sure the corporation does the following:

- Purchases **directors' and officers' liability insurance (D&O insurance)**. Corporations can purchase D&O insurance from private insurance companies by paying an annual premium for the insurance. The insurance company is required to defend a corporate director or officer who has been sued in his or her corporate capacity. The

insurance company is also required, subject to the terms of the insurance coverage, to pay the litigation costs incurred in defending the lawsuit (e.g., attorneys' fees and court costs) and any judgments or settlement costs. Most D&O policies contain deductible clauses and maximum coverage limits [RMBCA § 8.57].

- Provides **indemnification**. Corporations may provide that directors and officers who are sued in their corporate capacities will be **indemnified** by the corporation for the costs of the litigation as well as any judgments or settlements stemming from the lawsuit. Indemnification means that the corporation—and not the director or officer personally—pays these costs. The RMBCA provides that a court may order indemnification if a director or officer is found to be fairly and reasonably entitled to such indemnification [RMBCA § 8.54 and 8.56(1)].

758   UNIT VI   DOMESTIC AND MULTINATIONAL BUSINESS

Duty of Care

duty of care

A duty that corporate directors and officers have to use care and diligence when acting on behalf of the corporation.

negligence

Failure of a corporate director or officer to exercise the duty of care while conducting the corporation's business.

business judgment rule

A rule that says directors and officers are not liable to the corporation or its shareholders for honest mistakes of judgment.

The **duty of care** requires corporate directors and officers to use *care and diligence* when acting on behalf of the corporation. To meet this duty, the directors and officers must discharge their duties (1) in good faith, (2) with the care that an *ordinary prudent person* in a like position would use under similar circumstances, and (3) in a manner he or she reasonably believes to be in the best interests of the corporation [RMBCA §§ 8.30(a) and 8.42(a)].

A director or officer who breaches this duty of care is personally liable to the corporation and its shareholders for any damages caused by the breach. Such breaches, which are normally caused by **negligence**, often involve a director's or officer's failure to (1) make a reasonable investigation of a corporate matter, (2) attend board meetings on a regular basis, (3) properly supervise a subordinate who causes a loss to the corporation through embezzlement and such, or (4) keep adequately informed about corporate affairs. **Breaches** are examined by the courts on a case-by-case basis.

Contemporary Business Environment

THE BUSINESS JUDGMENT RULE

The determination of whether a corporate director or officer has met his or her duty of care is measured as of the time the decision is made—the benefit of hindsight is not a factor. Therefore, the directors and officers are not liable to the corporation or its shareholders for honest mistakes of judgment. This is called the **business judgment rule**.

Consider This Example   Suppose after conducting considerable research and investigation, the directors of a major auto-

mobile company decide to produce a large and expensive automobile. When the car is introduced to the public for sale, few of the automobiles are sold because of the public's interest in buying smaller, less expensive automobiles. Because this was an honest mistake of judgment on the part of corporate management, their judgment is shielded by the business judgment rule.

Were it not for the protection afforded by the business judgment rule, many high-risk but socially desirable endeavors might not be undertaken.

The court had to decide whether directors were protected by the business judgment rule in the following case.

Smith v. Van Gorkom

488 A.2d 858 (1985)

Supreme Court of Delaware

CASE 30.1

BACKGROUND AND FACTS

Trans Union Corporation (Trans Union) was a publicly traded, diversified holding company that was incorporated in Delaware. Its principal earnings were generated by its railcar leasing business. Jerome W. Van Gorkom was a Trans Union officer for more than 24 years, its chief executive officer for more than 17 years, and the chairman of the board of directors for 2 years. Van Gorkom, a lawyer and certified public accountant, owned 75,000 shares of Trans Union. He was approaching 65 years of age and mandatory retirement. Trans Union's board of directors was composed of 10 members—five inside directors and five outside directors.

In September 1980, Van Gorkom decided to meet with Jay A. Pritzker, a well-known corporate takeover specialist and a social acquaintance of Van Gorkom's, to discuss the possible

sale of Trans Union to Pritzker. Van Gorkom met Pritzker at Pritzker's home on Saturday, September 13, 1980. He did so without consulting Trans Union's board of directors. At this meeting, Van Gorkom proposed a sale of Trans Union to Pritzker at a price of $55 per share. The stock was trading at about $38 in the market. On Monday, September 15, Pritzker notified Van Gorkom that he was interested in the $55 cash-out merger proposal. Van Gorkom, along with two inside directors, privately met with Pritzker on September 16 and 17. After meeting with Van Gorkom on Thursday, September 18, Pritzker notified his attorney to begin drafting the merger documents.

On Friday, September 19, Van Gorkom called a special meeting of Trans Union's board of directors for the following day. The board members were not told the purpose of the meeting. At the meeting, Van Gorkom disclosed the Pritzker offer and described its terms in a 20-minute presentation. Neither the merger agreement nor a written summary of the terms of agreement was furnished to the directors. No valuation study as to the value of Trans Union was prepared for the meeting. After two hours, the board voted in favor of the cash-out merger with Pritzker's company at $55 per share for Trans Union's stock. The board also voted not to solicit other offers. The merger agreement was executed by Van Gorkom during the evening of September 20 at a formal social event he hosted for the opening of the Chicago Lyric Opera's season. Neither he nor any other director read the agreement prior to its signing and delivery to Pritzker.

Trans Union's board of directors recommended the merger be approved by its shareholders and distributed proxy materials to the shareholders stating that the $55 per share price for their stock was fair. In the meantime, Trans Union's board of directors took steps to dissuade two other possible suitors who showed an interest in purchasing Trans Union. On February 10, 1981, 69.9 percent of the shares of Trans Union stock was voted in favor of the merger. The merger was consummated. Alden Smith and other Trans Union shareholders sued Van Gorkom and the other directors for damages. The plaintiffs alleged that the defendants were negligent in their conduct in selling Trans Union to Pritzker. The Delaware Court of Chancery held in favor of the defendants. The plaintiffs appealed.

ISSUE

Did Trans Union's directors breach their duty of care?

COURT'S REASONING

The business judgment rule exists to protect and promote the full and free exercise of the managerial power granted to Delaware directors. The rule itself is a presumption that in making a business decision, the directors of a corporation acted (1) on an informed basis, (2) in good faith, and (3) in the honest belief that the action taken was in the best interests

of the company. Thus, the party attacking a board decision as uninformed must rebut the presumption that its business judgment was an informed one. The determination of whether the directors have informed themselves prior to making a business decision, of all material information available to them. Under the business judgment rule, there is no protection for directors who have made an unintelligent or unadvised judgment.

The supreme court held that the business judgment rule did not protect the director's actions in this case. The court stated, "The directors (1) did not adequately inform themselves as to Van Gorkom's role in forcing the sale of the company and in establishing the per share purchase price; (2) they were uninformed as to the intrinsic value of the company; and (3) given these circumstances, at a minimum, they were grossly negligent in approving the sale of the company upon two hours' consideration, without prior notice, and without the exigency of a crisis or emergency."

DECISION

The Supreme Court of Delaware held that the defendant directors had breached their duty of care. The supreme court remanded the case to the court of chancery to conduct an evidentiary hearing to determine the fair value of the shares represented by the plaintiffs' class. If that value is higher than $55 per share, the difference shall be awarded to the plaintiffs as damages. Reversed and remanded.

Case Questions

Critical Legal Thinking What does the business judgment rule provide? Is this a good rule? Explain.

Business Ethics Do you think Van Gorkom and the other directors had the shareholders' best interests in mind? Were the plaintiff-shareholders being greedy?

Contemporary Business Is there any liability exposure for sitting on a board of directors?

Contemporary Business Environment

DID DISNEY'S BOARD OF DIRECTORS ACT GOOFY?

The business judgment rule was designed to protect corporate officers and directors from being second-guessed by judges and juries for making business decisions they thought were in the best interests of the corporation. How far, however, does the business judgment rule go in protecting board members who make a goofy decision? Consider the following case.

In 1995, Michael D. Eisner was the chairman of the board and chief executive officer of the Walt Disney Company (Disney). In September 1995, in a move to make Disney even more "Hollywood" and more into the digital age, Eisner recruited and hired his friend Michael S. Ovitz to

serve as Disney's president. At the time, Ovitz was head of Creative Artists Agency (CAA), a firm of talent agents, and was notably the "most powerful man in Hollywood." To entice Ovitz away from CAA, Disney's board of directors unanimously approved a five-year employment contract with Ovitz. All parties signed. Ovitz was appointed president and was nominated and elected to Disney's board.

The employment contract provided for Ovitz to receive an annual salary of $1 million, a discretionary bonus determined by the board, and options to purchase (at a discount price) and exercise one million shares of Disney's common stock each year for five years. The contract contained a severance package that included the following provisions: (1) that Disney could terminate Ovitz for "good cause"—which was defined as gross negligence or malfeasance in the execution of his duties—without liability and (2) that if Disney terminated Ovitz without good cause or if Ovitz resigned from Disney with the consent of the board, he would get his remaining salary payments and three million of his options on Disney stock would immediately vest upon his separation from the company. At the time of signing the severance package, no Disney board member bothered to quantify the benefits Ovitz would receive if his employment was terminated before the expiration of the five-year term.

Ovitz began his term as Disney's president amid media hype, but the glamour only lasted about as long as a first-run movie. Within a year, Ovitz was unhappy with his role at Disney and the Disney board of directors did not think Ovitz's employment was working out very well. Ovitz began looking for alternative employment. In September 1996, he sent a letter to Eisner stating his desire to leave Disney. On December 11, 1996, only 14 months after Ovitz joined Disney, Eisner consented to Ovitz's request for a nonfault termination. The next day Disney's board agreed, and Ovitz left Disney. His severance pay package—which included salary, bonus, and three million stock options—was worth $140 million!

Several Disney shareholders brought a derivative lawsuit against the Disney board of directors alleging that they had breached their fiduciary duty to the shareholders by giving away the kingdom. The shareholders argued that the Disney board should have terminated Ovitz for "good cause" instead of agreeing to the nonfault termination and severance pay package. The Disney directors defended, arguing that the business judgment rule protected their largess. Because Disney is incorporated in Delaware, Delaware's chancery court was given the opportunity to write the ending to this script.

The Delaware court, known to favor management over shareholders—why else are so many companies organized there?—decided in favor of the Disney board and dismissed the lawsuit. The judge stated:

> *The Board made a business decision to grant Ovitz a Non-Fault Termination. Plaintiffs may disagree with the Board's judgment as to how this matter should have been handled. But where, as here, there is no reasonable doubt as to the disinterest of or absence of fraud by the Board, mere disagreement cannot serve as grounds for imposing liability based on alleged breaches of fiduciary duty and waste.*

The Delaware judge decided this case in favor of Disney's board of directors and then quickly exclaimed, "I'm going to Disneyland!" [*In re The Walt Disney Company Derivative Litigation*, 1998 WL 731587 (Del.Ch. 1998)]

Business Brief

A corporate director or officer who breaches his or her duty of care is liable to the corporation and its shareholders for any damages caused by the breach.

Business Brief

Corporate directors and officers may rely on information and reports prepared by competent and reliable officers and employees, lawyers, accountants, other professionals, and committees of the board of directors.

Reliance on Others Corporate directors and officers usually are unable to investigate personally every corporate matter brought to their attention. Under the RMBCA, directors and officers are entitled to rely on information, opinions, reports, or statements, including financial statements and other financial data, prepared or presented by [RMBCA §§ 8.30(b) and 8.42(b)]:

- Officers and employees of the corporation whom the director believes are reliable and competent in the matter presented.
- Lawyers, public accountants, and other professionals as to any matters that the director believes to be within their professional or expert competence.
- A committee of the board of directors upon which the director does not serve as to matters within the committee's designated authority and which committee the director reasonably believes to merit confidence.

A director is not liable if such information is false, misleading, or otherwise unreliable unless he or she has knowledge that would cause such reliance to be unwarranted [RMBCA §§ 8.30(c) and 8.42(c)]. The degree of an officer's reliance on such sources is more limited than that given to directors because they are more familiar with corporate operations.

dissension

When an individual director opposes the action taken by the majority of the board of directors.

Dissent to Directors' Action On some occasions, individual directors may oppose the action taken by the majority of the board of directors. To avoid liability for such action, the dissenting director must either resign from the board or register his or her **dissent**. Dissent may be registered by (1) entering it in the minutes of the meeting, (2) filing a written dissent with the secretary before the adjournment of the meeting, or (3) forwarding a written dissent by registered mail to the secretary immediately following the adjournment of the meeting [RMBCA § 8.24(d)]. A dissenting director who has not attended the meeting must follow the latter course of action to register his or her dissent.

Business Ethics

SHOULD DIRECTORS BE LEFT OFF THE HOOK?

In the past, being made a member of a board of directors of a corporation was considered to be an honor. Many persons outside the company, such as lawyers, doctors, businesspeople, professors, and others, were asked to sit on boards because of their knowledge, expertise, or contacts. Meetings were held once a month and usually did not take a lot of time, and votes were often just a formality to "rubber stamp" management's preordained decisions.

In the 1980s, all this changed. The primary cause was the explosion of lawsuits against boards of directors by disgruntled shareholders, bondholders, and others. Under the law, directors are personally liable for their intentional or negligent conduct that causes harm to others. Most of these lawsuits alleged that directors were negligent in one regard or another, and juries often agreed.

Large and mid-sized corporations usually purchased directors' and officers' liability insurance—D&O insurance—that paid any judgments. Many small corporations could not afford to carry such insurance. When D&O carriers were hit with increasing payouts, they did what any good businessperson would do: raised the premiums, increased the deductibles, and reduced the activities covered by the insurance. These changes created a so-called insurance crisis. Many corporations' coverage was severely reduced or they were forced to go "bare" and not carry D&O insurance because of the high expense.

Inside directors—directors who are also executives of the corporation—remained on boards because of their vested interests, and their liability as officers would remain anyway. But "outside directors"— the directors from outside the company—began fleeing from corporations and refusing to accept nominations to boards of directors. The honor of sitting on a board of directors became a liability, and all their personal assets—house, investments, and bank accounts—were at risk.

In response to this situation, in 1985 the Delaware legislature enacted a statute that provided that an outside director of a Delaware corporation could not be held liable for ordinary negligence. Thus, this statute overrode the common law of negligence as it applied to outside directors. The law was hailed as a landmark, and many major corporations who were not already incorporated in Delaware abandoned their current states of incorporation and reincorporated there.

Since then many other states have enacted similar statutes. The Revised Model Business Corporation Act contains a similar provision [RMBCA § 2.02(b)(4)]. The main features of these statutes are that they

- Apply to outside directors but not to inside directors.
- Relieve liability for ordinary negligence but not for intentional conduct, recklessness, or gross negligence.
- Do not apply to violations of federal and state securities law.

Proponents of these laws assert that they are necessary to attract the most qualified individuals to sit on corporate boards of directors. Critics argue that the laws are merely a scam whereby fat-cat directors are favorably treated and relieved of liability for their negligent conduct when no one else in society (e.g., motorists, entrepreneurs) is given the same privilege.

1. Should "outside" directors be relieved of ordinary negligence liability? Why or why not?
2. Do you think outside directors will act more or less carefully because of RMBCA § 2.02(b)(4)?

Duty of Loyalty

The **duty of loyalty** requires directors and officers to subordinate their personal interests to those of the corporation and its shareholders. Justice Benjamin Cardozo defined this duty of loyalty as follows:

> *[A corporate director or officer] owes loyalty and allegiance to the corporation—a loyalty that is undivided and an allegiance that is influenced by no consideration other than the welfare of the corporation. Any adverse interest of a director [or officer] will be subjected to a scrutiny rigid and uncompromising. He may not profit at the expense of his corporation and in conflict with its rights; he may not for personal gain divert unto himself the opportunities that in equity and fairness belong to the corporation.*

> *Many forms of conduct permissible in a workaday world for those acting at arm's length are forbidden to those bound by fiduciary ties. Not honesty alone, but the punctilio of an honor the most sensitive, is then the standard of behavior. As to this there has developed a tradition that is unbending and inveterate.*[1]

If a director or officer breaches his or her duty of loyalty and makes a secret profit on a transaction, the corporation can sue the director or officer to recover the secret profit. Some of the most common breaches of the duty of loyalty are discussed in the following paragraphs.

duty of loyalty

A duty that directors and officers have not to act adversely to the interests of the corporation and to subordinate their personal interests to those of the corporation and its shareholders.

Business Brief

Breach of the *duty of care* usually occurs because of accident or mistake: breach of the *duty of loyalty* usually occurs because of intentional conduct.

usurping a corporate opportunity

A director or officer steals a corporate opportunity for him- or herself.

self-dealing

If the directors or officers engage in purchasing, selling, or leasing of property with the corporation, the contract must be fair to the corporation; otherwise, it is voidable by the corporation. The contract or transaction is enforceable if it has been fully disclosed and approved.

Business Brief

Directors and officers may not compete with their corporation unless the competitive activity has been fully disclosed and approved.

It appears to me that the atmosphere of the temple of Justice is polluted by the presence of such things as companies.

James, L.J.
Wilson v. Church (1879)

Usurping a Corporate Opportunity   Directors and officers may not personally usurp (steal) a corporate opportunity for themselves. **Usurping a corporate opportunity** constitutes a violation of a director's or officer's duty of loyalty. If usurping is proven, the corporation can (1) acquire the opportunity from the director or officer and (2) recover any profits made by the director or officer.

The following elements must be shown to prove usurping:

1. The opportunity was presented to the director or officer in his or her corporate capacity.
2. The opportunity is related to or connected with the corporation's current or proposed business.
3. The corporation has the financial ability to take advantage of the opportunity.
4. The corporate officer or director took the corporate opportunity for him- or herself.

However, the director or officer is free personally to take advantage of a corporate opportunity if it was fully disclosed and presented to the corporation and the corporation rejected it.

Self-Dealing   Under the RMBCA, a contract or transaction with a corporate director or officer is voidable by the corporation if it is unfair to the corporation [RMBCA § 8.31]. Contracts of a corporation to purchase property from, sell property to, or make loans to corporate directors or officers where the directors or officers have not disclosed their interest in the transaction are often voided under this standard. Contract or transactions with corporate directors or officers are enforceable if their interest in the transaction has been disclosed to the corporation and the disinterested directors or the shareholders have approved the transaction.

Competing with the Corporation   Directors and officers cannot engage in activities that *compete* with the corporation unless full disclosure is made and a majority of the disinterested directors or shareholders approve the activity. The corporation can recover any profits made by nonapproved competition and any other damages caused to the corporation.

Disgorgement of Secret Profits   If a director or officer breaches his or her duty of loyalty and makes a secret profit on a transaction, the corporation can sue the director or officer to recover the secret profit. If the corporation does not do so, any shareholder can bring a derivative action and recover the secret profit on behalf of the corporation.

Consider This Example   Suppose Maxine Chambers is the purchasing agent for the Roebolt Corporation. Her duties require her to negotiate and execute contracts to purchase office supplies and equipment for the corporation. Assume Bruce Nevel, a computer salesperson, pays Chambers a $10,000 kickback to purchase typewriters needed by the Roebolt Corporation. The Roebolt Corporation can sue and recover the $10,000 secret profit from Chambers.

CONCEPT SUMMARY   FIDUCIARY DUTIES OF CORPORATION DIRECTORS AND OFFICERS

Duty	Description	Violation
Duty of obedience	Duty to act within the authority conferred by law and the corporation.	Acts outside of corporate officer's or director's authority.
Duty of care	Duty to use care and diligence when acting on behalf of the corporation. This duty is discharged if an officer or director acts: 1. In good faith. 2. With the care that an ordinary prudent person in a like position would use under similar circumstances. 3. In a manner he or she reasonably believes to be in the best interests of the corporation.	Acts of negligence and mismanagement. Such acts include failure to: 1. Make a reasonable investigation of a corporate matter. 2. Attend board meetings on a regular basis. 3. Properly supervise a subordinate who causes a loss to the corporation. 4. Keep adequately informed about corporate matters. 5. Take other actions necessary to discharge duties.

Duty	Description	Violation
Duty of loyalty	Duty to subordinate personal interests to those of the corporation and its shareholders.	Acts of disloyalty. Such acts include unauthorized: 1. Self-dealing with the corporation. 2. Usurping of a corporate opportunity. 3. Competing with the corporation. 4. Making a secret profit that belongs to the corporation.

Liability for Crimes

Corporate directors, officers, employees, and agents are personally liable for the crimes they commit while acting on behalf of the corporation. Criminal law sanctions include fines and imprisonment.

Under the law of agency, a corporation is liable for the crimes committed by its directors, officers, employees, or agents while acting within the scope of their employment. Because a corporation cannot be placed in prison, the criminal penalty imposed on a corporation usually is the assessment of a monetary fine or the loss of some legal privilege (such as a license).

*L*IABILITY OF SHAREHOLDERS

Shareholders of a corporation generally have **limited liability** (i.e., they are liable for the debts and obligations of the corporation only to the extent of their capital contribution). However, shareholders can be found personally liable if (1) the corporate entity is disregarded or (2) a controlling shareholder breaches a fiduciary duty to minority shareholders.

limited liability

Liability that shareholders have only to the extent of their capital contribution. Shareholders are generally not personally liable for debts and obligations of the corporation.

Disregard of the Corporate Entity

If a shareholder or shareholders dominate a corporation and use it for improper purposes, a court of equity can *disregard the corporate entity* and hold the shareholders of a corporation personally liable for the corporation's debts and obligations. This doctrine is commonly referred to as **piercing the corporate veil**. It is often resorted to by unpaid creditors who are trying to collect from shareholders a debt owed by the corporation.

Courts will pierce the corporate veil if (1) the corporation has been formed without sufficient capital (i.e., *thin capitalization*) or (2) separateness has not been maintained between the corporation and its shareholders (e.g., commingling of personal and corporate assets, failure to hold required shareholders' meetings, failure to maintain corporate records and books). The courts examine this doctrine on a case-by-case basis.

The piercing the corporate veil doctrine was raised in the following case.

piercing the corporate veil

A doctrine that says if a shareholder dominates a corporation and uses it for improper purposes, a court of equity can disregard the corporate entity and hold the shareholder personally liable for the corporation's debts and obligations.

Kinney Shoe Corp. v. Polan
939 F.2d 209 (1991)
United States Court of Appeals, Fourth Circuit

CASE 30.2

BACKGROUND AND FACTS
In 1984, Lincoln M. Polan formed Industrial Realty Company (Industrial), a West Virginia corporation. Polan was the sole shareholder of Industrial. Although a certificate of incorporation was issued, no organizational meeting was held and no officers were elected. Industrial issued no stock certificates because nothing was ever paid in to the corporation. Other corporate formalities were not observed. Polan, on behalf of Industrial, signed a lease to sublease commercial space in a building controlled by Kinney Shoe Corporation (Kinney). The first rental payment to Kinney was made out of Polan's personal funds, and no further payments were made

on the lease. Kinney filed suit against Industrial and obtained a judgment of $66,400 for unpaid rent. When the amount was unpaid by Industrial, Kinney sued Polan individually and sought to pierce the corporate veil to collect from Polan. The district court held for Polan. Kinney appealed.

ISSUE
Is Polan personally liable for Industrial's debts?

COURT'S REASONING
The court of appeals found that Industrial's corporate veil should be pierced because the corporation was undercapitalized, corporate formalities were not observed, and Polan com-

mingled his funds with those of the corporation. The court stated that Polan tried to limit his liability by "setting up a paper curtain constructed of nothing more than Industrial's certificate of incorporation." The court allowed Kinney to pierce the corporate veil to reach the responsible party and produce an equitable result.

DECISION

The court of appeals pierced the corporate veil and held Polan personally liable on Industrial's debt to Kinney. Reversed.

Case Questions

Critical Legal Thinking   Is the doctrine of piercing the corporate veil needed? Should parties like Kinney bear the risk of dealing with corporations like Industrial?

Business Ethics   Is it ethical for persons to form corporations to avoid personal liability? Should this be allowed?

Contemporary Business   What is the risk if corporate formalities are not observed? Explain.

Business Ethics

CONTROLLING SHAREHOLDERS' BREACH OF FIDUCIARY DUTY

Shareholders usually do not owe a fiduciary duty to their fellow shareholders. However, many courts have held that a **controlling shareholder** does owe a fiduciary duty to monitor shareholders. A controlling shareholder is one who owns a sufficient number of shares to control the corporation effectively. This may or may not be majority ownership.

The courts have held that controlling shareholders breach their fiduciary duty to minority shareholders if they

• Sell assets of the corporation that cause an unusual loss to the minority shareholders.

• Sell corporate assets to themselves at less than fair market value.
• Sell controlling interest in the corporation to someone who they know intends to loot the corporation, and does.
• Take other action that oppresses the minority shareholders.

This is a developing area of the law. The courts examine each case on its particular facts.

1. Should controlling shareholders be held to a fiduciary duty to other shareholders? Why or why not?
2. Should all shareholders owe a fiduciary duty to each other? Discuss.

International Law

IMPORT AND EXPORT RESTRICTIONS STILL EXIST

Countries impose many restrictions on international trade. They consist of laws restricting imports into a country and exports out of a country. Trade restrictions are imposed for a variety of reasons, including protecting local jobs, national security, and domestically made products and services from foreign competition.

IMPORT RESTRICTIONS

All countries, including the United States, impose restrictions on the importation of certain products or services from some countries. The most common forms of import controls are:

• **Import Quotas**   These either prohibit entirely or restrict the numerical amount of designated goods or services that may be imported.
• **Tariffs**   These are taxes or duties charged on imported goods or services. Tariffs make imported goods or services more expensive to buy.

• **Nontariff Restrictions**   These are requirements that imported goods or services meet certain manufacturing requirements or standards, receive government approval before they are allowed to be imported into the country, or go through time-consuming customs procedures.

The United States has entered into the **North American Free Trade Agreement (NAFTA)** with Canada and Mexico, which is a regional trade treaty that reduces or eliminates many of the tariffs and other trade barriers between these countries. Many other countries of the world have entered into regional trade pacts that reduce tariffs and other import restriction among the member countries. The United States is also a member of the **World Trade Organization (WTO)**, an international convention among over 130 countries to reduce tariffs and other restrictions on international trade. Despite all these trade agreements, most countries still maintain import restrictions on certain types of goods or services or imports from certain countries. Import barriers will continue to be reduced in the future as countries negotiate additional trade agreements.

EXPORT RESTRICTIONS

Although countries usually promote exports, most place restrictions on certain exports. Under the **Export Administration Act of 1979**, as amended [50 U.S.C. §§ 2402 et seq.], the President of the United States may prevent or restrict the export of goods, commodities, and technology that involves (1) national security, (2) foreign policy, (3) nuclear proliferation, or (4) scarce commodities. The U.S. Department of Commerce maintains a list of the goods, commodities, and technology that are subject to export controls. Other countries restrict exports for similar reasons. Cultural property (e.g., artifacts, art) is often subject to export restrictions.

*C*HAPTER *S*UMMARY

Rights of Shareholders, p. 746

Rights of Shareholders	*Ownership rights.* Shareholders of the corporation own the corporation.
Shareholder's Meetings	1. *Annual shareholders' meeting.* Meeting of the shareholders of a corporation that must be held annually by the corporation to elect directors and vote on other matters. 2. *Special shareholders' meeting.* Meetings of shareholders that may be called to consider and vote on important or emergency matters, such as a proposed merger or amending the articles of incorporation. 3. *Notice of shareholders' meetings.* The corporation must notify shareholders of the place, day, and time of annual and special shareholder meetings. If the required notice is not given or is defective, any action taken at the meeting is void.
Proxies	1. *Proxy.* Shareholders may appoint another person (the *proxy*) as their agent to vote their shares at shareholders' meetings. 2. *Proxy card.* Written document that a shareholder signs that authorizes another person to vote his or her shares at a shareholders' meeting.

Voting Requirements	1. *Record date.* A date specified in the corporate bylaws that determines whether a shareholder may vote at a shareholders' meeting. Only persons who are shareholders on the record date are permitted to vote at the meeting.
	2. *Shareholders' list.* A list that contains the names and addresses of the shareholders as of the record date and the class and number of shares owned by each shareholder. This list must be made available to all shareholders.
	3. *Quorum.* The required number of shares that must be represented in person or by proxy to hold a shareholders' meeting. The RMBCA establishes a majority of outstanding shares as a quorum.
	4. *Vote required for elections other than for directors.* The affirmative vote of the *majority* of the voting shares represented at a shareholders' meeting constitutes an act of the shareholders for actions other than for the elections of directors.
	5. *Voting methods for electing directors:*
	  a. *Straight (noncumulative) voting.* Unless otherwise stated, each shareholder votes the number of shares he or she owns on candidates for each of the positions open for election. The candidate or candidates with the most votes win the open position or positions.
	  b. *Cumulative voting.* The articles of incorporation may provide for cumulative voting. Under this method, a shareholder is entitled to multiply the number of shares he or she owns by the number of directors to be elected and cast the product for a single candidate or distribute the product among two or more candidates.
	6. *Supramajority voting requirement.* The articles of incorporation or bylaws can require a greater than majority of shares to constitute quorum or the vote of the shareholders (e.g., 80 percent). Also called *supermajority voting requirement.*

Voting Agreements	1. *Voting trust.* An arrangement whereby participating shareholders transfer their shares to a trustee who is then empowered to vote the shares held by the trust. Shareholders are issued *voting trust certificates* that evidence their interest in the trust. 2. *Voting agreements.* An agreement between two or more shareholders agreeing on how they will vote their shares. Voting agreements are enforceable.
Right to Transfer Shares	1. *Article 8 of the Uniform Commercial Code (UCC).* Shareholders have the right to transfer their nonrestrictive shares. Article 8 of the Uniform Commercial Code governs the transfer of securities. 2. *Lost or stolen stock certificates.* If a stock certificate is lost, stolen, or destroyed, the corporation is required to issue a *replacement certificate* if the shareholder posts an indemnity bond to protect the corporation from loss for issuing the replacement certificate.
Transfer Restrictions	1. *Right of first refusal.* An agreement that requires the selling shareholder to offer his or her shares for sale to the other parties to the agreement before selling them to anyone else. 2. *Buy-and-sell agreement.* An agreement that requires selling shareholders to sell their shares to the other shareholders or to the corporation at the price specified in the agreement.

Preemptive Rights	Rights that give existing shareholders the option of subscribing to new shares being issued by the corporation in proportion to their current ownership interest.
Right to Receive Information and Inspect Books and Records	1. *Annual financial statement.* A corporation must furnish its shareholders with an annual *financial statement* containing a balance sheet, an income statement, and a statement of changes in shareholder equity. 2. *Inspection rights.* Shareholders have the *absolute right to* inspect the shareholders' list, the articles of incorporation, the bylaws, and the minutes of shareholders' meetings held within the past three years. They have the right to inspect accounting and tax records, minutes of board of directors' and committee meetings, and minutes of shareholders' meetings held more than three years in the past if they demonstrate a *proper purpose*.
Derivative Lawsuits	A lawsuit a shareholder brings on behalf of the corporation against an offending party who has injured the corporation when the directors of the corporation fail to bring the suit. The shareholder must make a written *demand* upon the corporation to bring the lawsuit, and the corporation either rejects it or 90 days expire without the corporation bringing the requested lawsuit.

Rights of Directors, p. 751

Rights of Directors	1. *Board of directors.* A panel of decision makers for the corporation, the members of which are elected by the shareholders. 2. *Policy decisions.* The directors of a corporation are responsible for formulating the *policy* decisions affecting the corporation, such as deciding what business to engage in, determining the capital structure of the corporation, and selecting and removing top officers of the corporation. 3. *Resolutions.* The board of directors can adopt a resolution that approves a transaction that requires shareholder vote and recommend it to shareholders.
Selecting Directors	1. *Inside director.* A member of the board of directors who is also an officer of the corporation. 2. *Outside director.* A member of the board of directors who is not an officer of the corporation. 3. *Qualifications.* There are no qualifications to serve as a director unless the articles of incorporation or bylaws prescribe qualifications. 4. *Number of directors.* A board of directors can consist of one or more individuals. The articles of incorporation fix the number of initial directors. This number can be amended by the articles of incorporation or bylaws. 5. *Variable range.* The articles of incorporation or bylaws can establish a *variable range* for the size of the board of directors. The exact number of directors within the range may be changed from time to time by the board or directors or the shareholders.
Term of Office	1. *Annual term.* The term of a director's office expires at the next annual shareholders' meeting following his or her election unless terms are staggered. 2. *Staggered terms.* If a board of directors consists of nine or more members, it may be divided into two or three *classes* (each class to be as nearly equal in number as possible), and classes can be elected to serve *staggered terms* of two or three years. 3. *Vacancies.* Vacancies on the board of directors can be filled by the shareholders or the remaining directors. 4. *Removal of directors.* Any director, or the entire board of directors, can be removed from office by the shareholders. The articles of incorporation provide that directors can be removed only for cause.
Meeting of the Board of Directors	1. *Regular meeting.* A meeting of the board of directors held at the time and place scheduled in the bylaws. 2. *Special meeting.* A meeting of the board of directors convened to discuss an important or emergency matter, such as a proposed merger or a hostile takeover attempt. 3. *Written consents.* The board of directors may act without a meeting if all the directors sign written consents that set forth the action taken. 4. *Conference call.* Board of directors may meet via conference call if all the directors can hear and participate in the call. 5. *Quorum.* A simple *majority* of the number of directors established in the articles of incorporation or bylaws constitutes a quorum for transacting business. 6. *Vote.* The approval or disapproval of a *majority* of the quorum binds the entire board. 7. *Supramajority vote.* The articles of incorporation or bylaws may require a greater then majority of directors to constitute quorum or the vote of the board.
Committees of the Board of Directors	*Committees of the board of directors.* Unless the articles of incorporation or bylaws provide otherwise, the board of directors may create committees of its members and delegate certain powers to those committees. The most common committees are: 1. *Executive committee.* Has authority to (1) act on certain matters during the interim period between board meetings and (2) conduct preliminary investigations of proposals on behalf of the board. 2. *Audit committee.* Recommends independent public accountants and supervises the audit of the financial records of the corporation by the accountants. 3. *Nominating committee.* Nominates the management slate of directors to be submitted for shareholder vote.

4. *Compensation committee.* Approves management compensation, including salaries, bonuses, stock option plans, fringe benefits, and such.
5. *Investment committee.* Responsible for investing and reinvesting the funds of the corporation.
6. *Litigation committee.* Reviews and decides whether to pursue requests by shareholders for the corporation to sue persons who have allegedly harmed the corporation.

Compensation of Directors Directors are usually paid an annual retainer and an attendance fee for each meeting attended.

Right of Inspection Corporate directors have an *absolute right* to have access to the corporation's books, records, facilities, premises, and any other information affecting the operation of the corporation.

Directors' Authority to Pay Dividends
1. *Directors' authority to pay dividends.* The board of directors has the *discretion* to pay *dividends* to shareholders or *retain earnings* for use by the corporation.
2. *Record date.* When a corporation declares a dividend, it sets a date usually a few weeks prior to the actual payment that establishes the *record date* for payment of the dividend. Shareholders as of that date will be paid the dividend.
3. *Legal restrictions on the payment of dividends.* A dividend cannot be paid (a) if the corporation would not be able to pay its debts as they became due in the usual course of business or (b) if the corporation's total assets would be less than its total liabilities and there would be insufficient funds to pay liquidation preferences to preferred shareholders if the corporation were terminated.
4. *Stock dividends.* The issuance of additional shares of stock to the shareholders as a dividend. They are paid in proportion to the existing ownership interests of shareholders, so they do not increase a shareholder's proportionate ownership interest.

Rights of Officers, p. 755

Rights of Officers *Officers.* Employees of the corporation who are appointed by the board of directors to manage the *day-to-day operations* of the corporation.

Agency Authority of Officers Officers and agents of the corporation have express, implied, and apparent authority to bind the corporation to contracts with third parties.

Removal of Officers Unless an employment contract provides otherwise, any officer of a corporation may be removed by the board of directors.

Liability of Corporate Directors and Officers, p. 757

Liability of Corporate Directors and Officers *Fiduciary duties.* Corporate directors and officers owe the fiduciary duties of trust and confidence to the corporation and its shareholders. They owe the duties of *obedience, care,* and *loyalty.*

Duty of Obedience A duty that directors and officers of a corporation have to act within the authority conferred upon them by the state corporation statute, the articles of incorporation, the corporate bylaws, and the resolutions adopted by the board of directors.

Duty of Care A duty that corporate directors and officers have to use care and diligence when acting on behalf of the corporation. This duty is discharged if they perform their duties (a) in good faith, (b) with the care that an *ordinary prudent person* in a like position would use under similar circumstances, and (c) in a manner he or she reasonably believes to be in the best interests of the corporation.
1. *Negligence.* Failure of a corporate director or officer to exercise this duty of care when conducting the corporation's business.
2. *Business judgment rule.* A rule that says directors and officers are not liable to the corporation or its shareholders for honest mistakes of judgment.
3. *Reliance on others.* Directors and officers may rely on information and reports prepared by competent and reliable officers and employees, lawyers, public accountants, and other professionals as well as on committees of the board of directors as long as such reliance is warranted.
4. *Dissent to directors' action.* When an individual director opposes the action taken by the majority of the board of directors, he or she should register his or her dissent by (a) entering it in the minutes of the meeting, (b) filing a written dissent with the secretary before the adjournment of the meeting, or (c) forwarding a written dissent by registered mail to the secretary immediately following the adjournment of the meeting if the director has not attended the meeting.

Indemnification The corporation must indemnify (*pay back*) any director or officer for litigation expenses incurred in a lawsuit won by the director or officer. The corporation may indemnify a director or officer who loses a lawsuit as long as the director or officer was not adjudged liable to the corporation or did not improperly obtain personal

	benefit for himself or herself in the challenged transaction. Directors and officers may not be paid insurance or indemnification for intentional conduct that harmed third parties.
Insurance	Corporations can purchase *directors' and officers' liability insurance (D&O insurance)* that pays the cost to defend litigation against directors and officers and pays any judgment or settlement of the lawsuit.
Duty of Loyalty	A duty that directors and officers have not to act adversely to the interests of the corporation and to subordinate their personal interests to those of the corporation and its shareholders. *Common examples of breaches of the duty of loyalty.* 1. *Usurping a corporate opportunity.* A director or officer may not personally *usurp* (*steal*) an opportunity that belongs to the corporation. The corporation can acquire the opportunity from the director or officer and recover any profits made by the director or officer. 2. *Self-dealing.* The corporation may void any transaction with a director or officer if it is *unfair to the corporation.* Such transactions usually involve undisclosed self-dealing by a director or officer with the corporation. 3. *Competing with the corporation.* Directors and officers may not compete with their corporation unless the competitive activity has been fully disclosed to the corporation and approved by a majority of disinterested directors or shareholders.
Liability for Crimes	1. *Liability of directors and officers.* Corporate directors and officers are *personally liable* for the crimes they commit while acting on behalf of the corporation. Criminal sanctions include fines and imprisonment. 2. *Liability of the corporation.* Under the law of *agency*, corporations are liable for the crimes committed by its directors and officers while acting within the scope of their authority. Criminal sanctions include monetary fines and loss of legal privileges (e.g., loss of a license).

Liability of Shareholders, p. 763

Liability of Shareholders	*Limited liability.* Shareholders of corporations generally have *limited liability*: that is they are liable for the debts and obligations of the corporation only to the *extent of their capital contribution* to the corporation.
Disregard of the Corporate Entity	Shareholders may be found *personally liable* for the debts and obligations of the corporation under the following two doctrines: 1. *Piercing the corporate veil.* Courts can *disregard the corporate entity* and hold shareholders personally liable for the debts and obligations of the corporation if (a) the corporation has been formed without sufficient capital (*thin capitalization*) or (b) separateness has not been maintained between the corporation and its shareholders (e.g., commingling of personal and corporate assets, failure to hold required shareholders' meetings. Also called the *alter ego doctrine.* 2. *Controlling shareholders' breach of fiduciary duty.* As a general rule, shareholders do not owe a fiduciary duty to fellow shareholders or the corporation. Some courts hold that a *controlling shareholder* owes a fiduciary duty to minority shareholders. Controlling shareholders are personally liable to minority shareholders if their actions breach this fiduciary duty and cause injury to the minority shareholders.

*E*ND-OF-*C*HAPTER *I*NTERNET *E*XERCISES AND *C*ASE *Q*UESTIONS

Working the Web Internet Exercises

ACTIVITIES

1. Find your state statute on indemnification for corporate officers and directors. Why do you think that this concept was included in the statute? See **www.law.cornell.edu/topics/corporations.html** for an overview of corporations law with links to key primary and secondary sources.

2. Review the sample indemnification agreement at **www.lawvantage.com/description/corporate_law/director_and_officer_benefits_incentives_and_indemnification/summaries/CODO1000S.shtml**.

3. For more coverage on the background of Directors and Officers Liability see **www.griffincom.com/docont.htm**. For a lengthy list of topics see **guide.lp.findlaw.com/01topics/08corp/index.html**. For a quick overview of corporate law see **www.nolo.com/category/sb_home.html**.

4. Go to **lawcrawler.findlaw.com**. Type in the term *piercing the corporate veil*. Note how many articles are written from the perspective of an attorney representing a small business owner against claims seeking personal assets. For socially responsible investing information see **www.socialinvest.org**.

CRITICAL LEGAL THINKING CASES

30.1 Shareholder Meeting Ocilla Industries, Inc. (Ocilla), owned 40 percent of the stock of Direct Action Marketing, Inc. (Direct Action). Direct Action was a New York corporation that specialized in the marketing of products through billing inserts. In 1985, Ocilla helped place Howard Katz and Joseph Esposito on Direct Action's five-member board of directors. A dispute between Ocilla and the two directors caused Ocilla to claim that Katz and Esposito wanted excess remuneration in exchange for leaving the board at the end of their terms. As a result, no shareholders' meeting was held between September 19, 1986, and January 27, 1988. Under the Model Business Corporations Act, can Ocilla compel Direct Action to hold the meeting earlier? [*Ocilla Industries, Inc. v. Katz*, 677 F.Supp. 1291 (E.D.N.Y. 1987)]

30.2 Special Meeting Jack C. Schoenholtz was a shareholder and member of the board of directors of Rye Psychiatric Hospital Center, Inc. (Rye Hospital). The hospital was incorporated in 1973. By 1977, a split had developed among the board of directors concerning the operation of the facility. Three directors stood on one side of the dispute and three directors on the other. In an attempt to break the deadlock, Schoenholtz, who owned over 10 percent of the corporation's voting stock, asked the corporation's secretary to call a special meeting of the shareholders. In response, the secretary sent a notice to the shareholders stating that a special meeting of the shareholders would be held on November 12, 1982, "for the purpose of electing directors." The meeting was held as scheduled. Some stockholders brought suit claiming that the special shareholders' meeting was not called properly. Who wins? [*Rye Psychiatric Hospital Center, Inc. v. Schoenholtz*, 476 N.Y.S.2d 339 (A.D. 2 Dept. 1984)]

30.3 Irrevocable Proxy George Gibbons, William Smith, and Gerald Zollar were all shareholders in GRG Operating, Inc. (GRG). On May 13, 1983, Zollar contributed $1,000 of his own funds so that the corporation could begin to do business. In exchange for this contribution, Gibbons and Smith both granted Zollar the right to vote their shares of GRG stock. They gave Zollar a signed form that stated that "Gibbons and Smith, for a period of 10 years from the date hereof, appoint Zollar as their proxy. This proxy is solely intended to be an irrevocable proxy." A year after the agreement was signed, Gibbons and Smith wanted to revoke their proxies. Can they? [*Zollar v. Smith*, 710 S.W.2d 155 (Tex. App. 1986)]

30.4 Shareholder Voting Agreement Bookstop, Inc. (Bookstop), was founded in 1982 by Gary Hoover. The corporation met with early and marked success. By 1985, it was one of the largest retail booksellers in Texas and had expanded into California. To finance this rapid growth, Hoover sought outside investors. In 1985, Hoover agreed to sell 18 percent of Bookstop's common stock to H. E. Butt Grocery Company (HEB). As part of the sale of stock, the parties agreed that each had the right to place two nominees on Bookstop's board of directors. For several years, the parties abided by the terms of the agreement. A dispute then arose between Bookstop's shareholders. Can the shareholders' agreement be enforced? [*Crown Books Corporation v. Bookstop, Inc.*, 1990 WL 26166 (Del.Ch. 1990)]

30.5 Transfer Restrictions Stater Brothers Markets (Stater Brothers), a chain of supermarkets located throughout southern California, was a wholly owned subsidiary of Petrolane, Inc. (Petrolane). The company's top executives and an outside investor named Lisa Garrett purchased the chain in a leveraged buyout in March 1983. The executives, known collectively as the la Cadena group, bought 51 percent of Stater Brother's stock; Garrett owned the other 49 percent. In an effort to preserve the continuity of harmonious management, Garrett and the La Cadena group entered into a stockholders' agreement effective March 22, 1983. The agreement prohibited the sale of any Stater Brothers stock without the consent of the other stockholders. Absent such consent, the nonselling stockholders were given the right of first refusal to meet the terms of the proposed sale and be substituted for the outside investor. Is this agreement valid? [*Garrett v. Brown*, 511 A.2d 1044 (Del. Supreme 1986)]

30.6 Right to Inspect Records On July 20, 1983, Helmsman Management Services, Inc. (Helmsman), became a 25 percent stockholder of A&S Consultants, Inc. (A&S), a Delaware corporation. Helmsman paid $50,000 for its interest in A&S. At the time of the stock purchase, Helmsman was also a customer of A&S, paying the company for the use of a computer software program. Since 1983, Helmsman verified A&S's billings by a periodic review of certain of A&S's books and records. In January 1986, Helmsman conducted a review of A&S's records over a six-day period. The review showed that A&S had never paid any dividends on the stock held by Helmsman and that Helmsman had never received notice of A&S's stockholder meetings. Suspecting that A&S was being mismanaged, Helmsman sent a letter to A&S asking to inspect all A&S's records. The letter stated several purposes for the inspection, including to (1) determine the reasons for nonpayment of dividends and (2) gain information to be used in determining how to vote in stockholders' elections. Under the Model Business Corporations Act, should Helmsman's request be honored? [*Helmsman Management Services, Inc. v. A&S Consultants, Inc.*, 525 A.2d 160 (Del.Ch. 1987)]

30.7 Board of Directors Meeting Dick Gregory was chairman of the board of directors of Correction Connection, Inc. (CCI). CCI's bylaws permit special meetings of the board of directors if each board member is given notice of the meeting and informed of the business to be conducted at the meeting. On September 27, 1988, a notice of a special meeting of the board of directors was sent to each director, including Gregory. The notice specified the meeting date of September 30, 1988, and the agenda for the meeting, which included a plan to acquire additional capital. The meeting began as planned on September 30 and reconvened on October 4, October 6, and October 7. Gregory did not attend any of the meetings. In Gregory's absence, the board voted to issue certain authorized but unissued shares of the corporation's stock. Gregory objected to this decision and brought an action to prevent the stock from being issued. Who wins? [*Gregory v. Depte*, 1989 WL 67329 (E.D.Pa. 1989)]

30.8 Dividends   Gay's Super Markets, Inc. (Super Markets) was a corporation formed under the laws of the state of Maine. Hannaford Bros. Company held 51 percent of the corporation's common stock. Lawrence F. Gay and his brother Carrol were both minority shareholders in Super Markets. Lawrence Gay was also the manager of the corporation's store at Machias, Maine. On July 5, 1971, he was dismissed from his job. At the January 1972 meeting of Super Markets's board of directors, a decision was made not to declare a stock dividend for 1971. The directors cited expected losses from increased competition and the expense of opening a new store as reasons for not paying a dividend. Lawrence Gay claims that the reason for not paying a dividend was to force him to sell his shares in Super Markets. Lawrence sued to force the corporation to declare a dividend. Who wins? [*Gay v. Gay's Super Markets, Inc.*, 343 A.2d 577 (Maine Sup. 1975)]

30.9 Duty of Loyalty   Edward Hellenbrand ran a comedy club known as the Comedy Cottage in Rosemont, Illinois. The business was incorporated, with Hellenbrand and his wife as the corporation's sole shareholders. The corporation leased the premises in which the club was located. In 1978, Hellenbrand hired Jay Berk as general manager of the club. In 1980, Berk was made vice president of the corporation and given 10 percent of its stock. Hellenbrand experienced health problems and moved to Nevada, leaving Berk to manage the daily affairs of the business. In June 1984, the ownership of the building where the Comedy Cottage was located changed hands. Shortly thereafter, the club's lease on the premises expired. Hellenbrand instructed Berk to negotiate a new lease. Berk arranged a month-to-month lease but had the lease agreement drawn up in his name instead of that of the corporation. When Hellenbrand learned of Berk's move, he fired him. Berk continued to lease the building in his own name and opened his own club there, known as the Comedy Company, Inc. Hellenbrand sued Berk for an injunction to prevent Berk from leasing the building. Who wins? [*Comedy Cottage, Inc. v. Berk* 495 N.E.2d 1006 (Ill. App. 1986)]

30.10 Duty of Loyalty   Lawrence Gaffney was the president and general manager of Ideal Tape Company (Ideal). Ideal, which was a subsidiary of Chelsea Industries, Inc. (Chelsea), was engaged in the business of manufacturing pressure-sensitive tape. In 1975, Gaffney recruited three other Ideal executives to join him in starting a tape manufacturing business. The four men remained at Ideal for the two years it took them to plan the new enterprise. During this time, they used their positions at Ideal to travel around the country to gather business ideas, recruit potential customers, and purchase equipment for their business. At no time did they reveal to Chelsea their intention to open a competing business. In November 1977, the new business was incorporated as Action Manufacturing Company (Action). When executives at Chelsea discovered the existence

of the new venture, Gaffney and the others resigned from Chelsea. Chelsea sued them for damages. Who wins? [*Chelsea Industries, Inc. v. Gaffney*, 449 N.E.2d 320 (Mass.Sup. 1983)]

30.11 Indemnification   William G. Young was a director of Pool Builders Supply, Inc. (Pool Builders). Pool Builders experienced financial difficulties and was forced to file for bankruptcy. Eddie Lawson was appointed the receiver for the creditors of the corporation. Lawson believed that Young had mismanaged the corporation. Lawson filed a suit against Young and Pool Builders, alleging that Young had used Pool Builders personally to obtain money, goods, and property from creditors on the credit of the corporation. Lawson's suit also alleged that Young attempted to convert corporate assets for his own use. Young defended the suit for himself and the corporation. At trial, the judge found insufficient evidence to support Lawson's charges, and the suit was dismissed. Young now seeks to have Pool Builders pay the legal fees he incurred while defending the suit. Can Young recover this money from the corporation? [*Lawson v. Young*, 486 N.E.2d 1177 (Ohio App. 1984)]

30.12 Derivative Lawsuit   In 1948, four brothers—Monnie, Mechel, Merko, and Sam Dotlich—formed a partnership to run a heavy equipment rental business. By 1957, the company had been incorporated as Dotlich Brothers, Inc. Each brother owned 25 percent of the corporation's stock, and each served on the board of directors. In 1951, the business acquired a 56-acre tract of land in Speedway, Indiana. This land was held in the name of Monnie Dotlich. Each of the brothers was aware of this agreement. By 1976, the corporation had purchased six other pieces of property, all of which were held in Monnie's name. Sam Dotlich was not informed that Monnie was the record owner of these other properties. In 1976, Sam discovered this irregularity and requested the board of directors take action to remedy the situation. When the board refused to do so, Sam initiated a lawsuit on behalf of the corporation. Can Sam bring this lawsuit? [*Dotlich v. Dotlich*, 475 N.E.2d 331 (Ind. App. 1985)]

30.13 Piercing the Corporate Veil   M. R. Watters was the majority shareholder of several closely held corporations, including Wildhorn Ranch Inc. (Wildhorn). All these businesses were run out of Watter's home in Rocky Ford, Colorado. Wildhorn operated a resort called the Wildhorn Ranch Resort in Teller County, Colorado. Although Watters claimed that the ranch was owned by the corporation, the deed for the property listed Watters as the owner. Watters paid little attention to corporate formalities, holding corporate meetings at his house, never taking minutes of these meetings, and paying the debts of one corporation with the assets of another. During August 1986, two guest of Wildhorn Ranch Resort drowned while operating a paddleboat at the ranch. The family of the deceased guests sued for damages. Can Watters be held personally liable? [*Geringer v. Wildhorn Ranch, Inc.*, 760 F.Supp. 1442 (D.Colo. 1988)]

30.14 Shareholder Liability   Robert Orchard and Arthur Covelli owned seven McDonald's franchises in Erie, Pennsylvania. Each individual franchise was owned by a separate corporation. Orchard owned a 27 percent interest in each of these corporations, and Covelli owned 73 percent. Although Orchard and Covelli worked together harmoniously for many years, they eventually became dissatisfied with the relationship. In 1977, they unsuccessfully attempted to have Covelli buy out Orchard's stock. Covelli became angry with Orchard and had him terminated from his position as vice president of the corporations. Six months later, Covelli removed Orchard from the corporations'

boards of directors and replaced him with his own son. Covelli also allowed three of the corporations' franchise agreements with McDonald's to lapse and then resigned them in his own name. Throughout this period, Orchard received no dividends or other compensation from the corporations. Orchard sued Covelli for damages. Who wins? [*Orchard v. Covelli*, 590 F.Supp. 1548 (W.D.Pa. 1984)]

BUSINESS ETHICS CASES

30.15 Business Ethics Alfred S. Johnson, Incorporated (Corporation), was incorporated in 1955 by Alfred S. Johnson, who owned 70 shares of the corporation. Two employees of the corporation, James DeBaun and Walter Stephens, owned 20 and 10 shares, respectively. When Johnson died in 1965, his will created a testamentary trust in which his 70 shares were placed. Johnson's will named First Western Bank and Trust Company (Bank) trustee for the trust. Several years later, Bank decided to sell the 70 shares but did not tell anyone associated with Corporation of its decision. An appraisal was obtained that valued the corporation at $326,000 as a going concern.

On May 27, 1968, Raymond J. Mattison submitted an offer to purchase the 70 shares for $250,000 payable in $50,000 in securities of companies Mattison owned and the $200,000 balance over a five-year period. Bank obtained a Dun & Bradstreet report that showed several outstanding tax liens against Mattison. Bank accepted Mattison's explanation that they were not his fault. At the time, Mattison owed Bank a judgment for fraud. Bank was also aware that Mattison owed unpaid debts and that several entities in which he was involved were insolvent. Bank did not investigate these matters. If it had, the public records of Los Angeles County would have revealed 38 unsatisfied judgments against Mattison and his entities totaling $330,886, 54 pending lawsuits claiming damages of $373,588, and 18 tax liens aggregating $20,327. Bank agreed to sell the 70 shares to Mattison and accepted the assets of Corporation as security for the repayment of the $200,000 balance. As part of the transaction Bank required Mattison to agree to have Corporation give its banking business to Bank.

At the time of sale, Corporation was a successful going business with a bright future. It had cash of $76,000 and other liquid assets of over $120,000. Its net worth was about $220,000. Corporation was profitable, and its trend of earnings indicated a pattern of growth. Mattison immediately implemented a systematic scheme to loot Corporation. He (1) diverted $73,000 in corporate cash to himself and a shell company he owned, (2) caused Corporation to assign all its assets, including accounts receivable, to the shell company, (3) diverted all corporate mail to a post office box and extracted incoming checks to Corporation, (4) refused to pay corporate creditors on time or at all, (5) issued payroll checks without sufficient corporate funds, and (6) removed Corporation's books and records. On June 20,

1969, hopelessly insolvent, Corporation shut down operations and was placed in receivership. At that time, its debts exceeded its assets by over $200,000. DeBaun's and Stephens's shares were worthless. They sued Bank for damages, alleging that Bank, as the majority shareholder of Corporation, breached its fiduciary duty to the minority shareholders.

Did Bank have knowledge of the dangerous situation in which it placed Corporation? Did Bank, as the controlling shareholder of Corporation, breach its fiduciary duty to the minority shareholders? [*DeBaun v. First Western Bank and Trust Co.*, 46 Cal.App.3d 791, 120 Cal.Rptr. 354 (Cal. App. 1975)]

30.16 Business Ethics Jon-T Chemicals, Inc. (Chemicals), was an Oklahoma corporation engaged in the fertilizer and chemicals business. John H. Thomas was its majority shareholder and its president and board chairman. In April 1971, Chemicals incorporated Jon-T Farms, Inc. (Farms), as a wholly owned subsidiary to engage in the farming and land-leasing business. Chemicals invested $10,000 to establish Farms. All the directors and officers of Farms were directors and officers of Chemicals, and Thomas was its president and board chairman. In addition, Farms used officers, computers, and accountants of Chemicals without paying a fee, and Chemicals paid the salary of Farms' only employee. Chemicals made regular informal advances to pay Farms' expenses. These payments reached $7.5 million by January 1975.

Thomas and Farms engaged in a scheme whereby they submitted fraudulent applications for agricultural subsidies from the federal government under the Uplands Cotton Program. As a result of these applications, the Commodity Credit Corporation, a government agency, paid over $2.5 million in subsidies to Thomas and Farms. After discovering the fraud, the federal government obtained criminal convictions against Thomas and Farms. In a separate civil action, the federal government obtained a $4.7 million judgment against Thomas and Farms, finding them jointly and severally liable for the tort of fraud. Farms declared bankruptcy, and Thomas was unable to pay the judgment. Because Thomas and Farms were insolvent, the federal government sued Chemicals to recover the judgment. Was Farms the alter ego of Chemicals, permitting the United States to pierce the corporate veil and recover the judgment from Chemicals? Did Thomas act ethically in this case? [*United States of America v. Jon-T Chemicals, Inc.*, 768 F.2d 868 (5th Cir. 1985)]

BRIEFING THE CASE WRITING ASSIGNMENT

Read the following case, which has been excerpted from the court's opinion. Review and brief the case.

United States v. WRW Corporation
986 F.2d 138 (1993)
United States Court of Appeals for the Sixth Circuit

In 1985, civil penalties totaling $90,350 were assessed against WRW Corporation (WRW), a Kentucky corporation, for serious violations of safety standards under the Federal Mine Safety and Health Act (the Act) which resulted in the deaths of two miners. Following the imposition of civil penalties, WRW liquidated its assets and went out of business.

Three individual defendants, who were the sole shareholders, officers, and directors of WRW, were later indicted and convicted for willful violations of mandatory health and safety standards under the Act. Roger Richardson, Noah Woolum, and William Woolum each served prison sentences and paid criminal fines. After his release from prison, Roger Richardson filed for bankruptcy under Chapter 7 of the Bankruptcy Code.

The United States (the Government) brought this action in May of 1988 against WRW and Roger Richardson, Noah Woolum, and William Woolum to recover the civil penalties previously imposed against WRW. The district court denied the individual defendant's motion to dismiss and granted summary judgment to the Government piercing the corporate veil under state law and holding the individual defendants liable for the civil penalties assessed against WRW. For the reasons discussed herein, we affirm.

Piercing the Corporate Veil.

Having determined that the imposition of $90,350 sanction upon the defendants does not violate principles of double jeopardy, we turn to the defendants' argument that the district court erred in holding the individual defendants liable for the penalty by piercing the corporate veil of WRW under Kentucky law.

The district court held that it was appropriate to pierce WRW's corporate veil under either an equity theory or an alter ego theory, both of which are recognized under Kentucky law. Under either theory, the following factors must be considered when determining whether to pierce the corporate veil: (1) undercapitalization, (2) failure to observe the formalities of corporate existence, (3) nonpayment or overpayment of dividends, (4) a siphoning off of funds by dominant shareholders, and (5) the majority shareholders having guaranteed corporate liabilities in their individual capacities.

The court first found that WRW was undercapitalized because it was incorporated with only $3,000 of capital, which the record indicates was insufficient to pay normal expenses associated with the operation of a coal mine. The district court next found that WRW failed to observe corporate formalities, noting that no bylaws were produced by the defendants, and all corporate actions taken by the individual defendants were without corporation authorization. Finally, although WRW never distributed any dividends to the individual defendants, and there was no evidence that the individual defendants siphoned off corporate funds, these factors alone do not mitigate against piercing the corporate veil in this case because WRW was never sufficiently capitalized and operated at a loss during its two years of active existence.

In addition to holding that the equities of this case support piercing the corporate veil, the district court held that the corporate veil should be pierced under the "alter ego" theory, because WRW and the defendants did not have separate personalities. In light of the lack of observance of corporate formalities or distinction between the individual defendants and the corporation, we agree with the district court's conclusion that "there was a complete merger of ownership and control of WRW with the individual Defendants."

The specific factual findings made by the district court amply support piercing the corporate veil of WRW and holding the individual defendants liable for the penalty assessed against the corporate entity. For all of the foregoing reasons, the judgment of the district court is AFFIRMED.

ENDNOTE

1. *Meinhard v. Salmon*, 164 N.E.2d 545, 546 (N.Y.App. 1928).

CHAPTER 31

Mergers and Takeovers of Corporations

To supervise wisely the great corporations is well; but to look backward to the days when business was polite pillage and regard our great business concerns as piratical institutions carrying letters of marque and reprisal is a grave error born in the minds of little men. When these little men legislate they set the brakes going uphill.

—Elbert Hubbard (1856–1915)
Notebook, p. 16

Chapter Contents

Chapter Objectives

After studying this chapter, you should be able to:

1. Describe the process for soliciting proxies from shareholders.

2. Define *proxy contests*.

3. Identify when a shareholder can include a proposal in proxy materials.

4. Distinguish between a merger and a consolidation.

5. Describe the process for approving a merger or share exchange.

6. Describe dissenting shareholder appraisal rights.

7. Define *tender offer*.

8. Describe poison pills, white knight mergers, greenmail, and other defensive maneuvers to prevent a hostile takeover.

9. Apply the business judgment rule in examining the lawfulness of defensive strategies.

10. Analyze the lawfulness of state antitakeover statutes.

During the course of its existence, a corporation may go through certain *fundamental changes*. A corporation must seek shareholder approval for many changes. This requires the solicitation of votes or proxies from shareholders. Persons who want to take over the management of a corporation often conduct proxy contests to try to win over shareholder votes.

Corporations often engage in acquisitions of other corporations or businesses. This may occur by friendly merger or consolidation or by hostile tender offer. In defense, a corporation may erect certain barriers or impediments to a hostile takeover.

This chapter discusses fundamental changes to a corporation, including the solicitation of proxies, mergers and consolidations, hostile tender offers, and defensive strategies of corporations.

> *The usual trade and commerce is cheating all round by consent.*
>
> *Thomas Fuller*
> Gnomologia (1732)

SOLICITATION OF PROXIES

Corporate shareholders have the right to vote on the election of directors, mergers, charter amendments, and the like. They can exercise their power to vote either in person or by proxy [RMBCA § 7.22]. Voting by proxy is common in large corporations with thousands of shareholders located across the country and the world.

proxy card

A written document signed by a shareholder that authorizes another person to vote the shareholder's shares.

A proxy is a written document (often called a **proxy card**) completed and signed by the shareholder and sent to the corporation. The proxy authorizes another person—the proxy holder—to vote the shares at the shareholders' meeting as directed by the shareholder. The proxy holder is often a director or officer of the corporation. Exhibit 31.1 shows a proxy card.

*E*XHIBIT 31.1   *Proxy: E. I. du Pont de Nemours and Company*

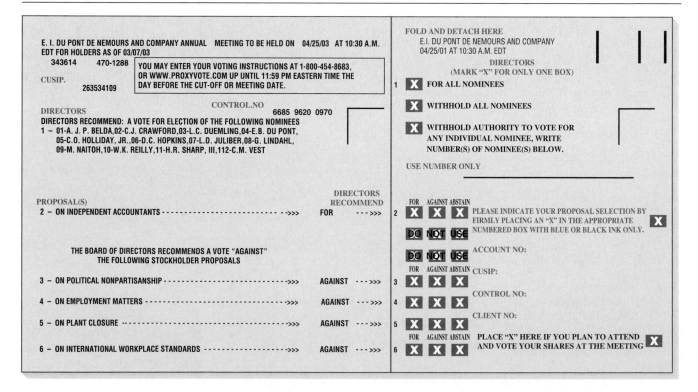

Federal Proxy Rules

Section 14(a) of the Securities Exchange Act of 1934 gives the Securities and Exchange Commission (SEC) the authority to regulate the solicitation of proxies.[1] The federal proxy rules promote full disclosure. In other words, management or any other party soliciting proxies from shareholders must prepare a **proxy statement** that fully describes (1) the matter for which the proxy is being solicited, (2) who is soliciting the proxy, and (3) any other pertinent information.

A copy of the proxy, the proxy statement, and all other solicitation material must be filed with the SEC at least 10 days before the materials are sent to the shareholders. If the SEC requires additional disclosures, the solicitation can be held up until these disclosures are made.

Antifraud Provision

Section 14(a) of the Securities Exchange Act of 1934 prohibits material misrepresentations or omissions of a material fact in the proxy materials. Known false statements of facts, reasons, opinions, or beliefs in proxy solicitation materials are actionable. Violations of this rule can result in civil and criminal actions by the SEC and the Justice Department, respectively. The courts have implied a private cause of action under this provision. Thus, shareholders who are injured by a material misrepresentation or omission in proxy materials can sue the wrongdoer and recover damages. The court can also order a new election if a violation is found.

Proxy Contests

Shareholders sometimes oppose the actions taken by the incumbent directors and management. These shareholders may challenge the incumbent management in a **proxy contest** in which both sides solicit proxies from the other shareholders. The side that receives the greatest number of votes wins the proxy contest. Such contests are usually held with regard to the election of directors.

Management must either (1) provide a list of shareholders to the dissenting group or (2) mail the proxy solicitation materials of the challenging group to the shareholders.

Reimbursement of Expenses

In a proxy contest, both sides usually spend considerable amounts of money on legal expenses, media campaigns, mailers, telephone solicitations, and the like. If a proxy contest involves an issue of policy, the corporation must reimburse the incumbent management for its expenses whether it wins or loses the proxy contest. The expenses of the dissenting group are reimbursed only if it wins the proxy contest. If the proxy contest concerns a personal matter, neither side may recover its expenses from the corporation.

Section 14(a)

Provision of the Securities Exchange Act of 1934 that gives the SEC the authority to regulate the solicitation of proxies.

proxy statement

A document that fully describes (1) the matter for which the proxy is being solicited, (2) who is soliciting the proxy, and (3) any other pertinent information.

Business Brief

Section 14(a) of the 1934 act prohibits misrepresentations or omissions of a material fact in proxy materials. The SEC, U.S. Justice Department, or shareholders who are injured by the misrepresentation or omission may sue the wrongdoer.

proxy contest

When opposing factions of shareholders and managers solicit proxies from other shareholders, the side that receives the greatest number of votes wins the proxy contest.

Contemporary Business Environment

THE SEC'S PROXY RULES

Critics argued for a long time that the SEC's proxy rules did not require sufficient or clear enough disclosures for shareholders to make informed decisions. Finally, in 1992, after three years of study, the SEC adopted new proxy rules. The new rules were designed to allow shareholders to communicate more easily with each other and to give them additional information about management and its compensation.

Prior to the adoption of the 1992 rules, any shareholder who wished to communicate with 10 or more fellow shareholders faced the daunting and expensive task of filing proxy

solicitation materials with the SEC. This tended to thwart shareholder communication and insulate management from shareholder criticism. The 1992 rules exempt from these requirements oral and written communications to shareholders from any shareholder who is not seeking proxy voting authority. For instance, shareholders can now ask each other how the corporation should be run or suggest changes. They have to register with the SEC only if they decide to solicit proxies.

Shareholders who own more than $5 million of the company's securities are not covered by this rule. They must still register any written communication to shareholders with the SEC.

Another 1992 rule change requires companies seeking proxies to "unbundle" the propositions set for shareholder vote so that the shareholders can vote on each separate issue. The old proxy rules allowed companies to bundle the propositions and present them as one package for a single shareholder vote. This tactic prevented shareholders from considering the merits of individual propositions. The 1992 rules also require all companies to include performance charts in their annual reports. These charts must compare the company's stock performance to that of a general index of companies, such as the Standard and Poor's 500, and companies in its peer group index (e.g., retailers).

Finally, the 1992 rules broadened the disclosure requirements concerning executive compensation. The 1992 rules mandate that companies provide tables in their annual reports that succinctly summarize executive compensation for the chief executive officer and its four other most highly compensated executives for the past three years. The tables must disclose salary, stock options, stock appreciation rights, and long-term incentive plans of these executives, including the value of each item. This is the change that generated the most attention.

Proponents of these rule changes assert that shareholders will not get the information they need to make informed decisions. Some argue for disclosure of even more information to shareholders. Some company management, particularly the most highly compensated executives, dislike the new rules.

Business Ethics

SHAREHOLDER RESOLUTIONS: DO THEY PROMOTE SOCIAL RESPONSIBILITY OF BUSINESS?

Shareholders have become more active in corporate governance, as witnessed by the hundreds of shareholder resolutions that are filed each year for vote at annual shareholder meetings.

During the 1980s, apartheid in South Africa was the primary issue of shareholder issues. Prompted by such proposals and the publicity they generated, many U.S. companies left South Africa. The world pressure worked, and South Africa ended apartheid. Free elections were held and new leaders were elected. The United States and other corporations from around the world have returned to do business in South Africa.

In the 1990s, the fastest growth was in shareholder resolutions urging more corporate sensitivity to the environment. The biggest corporate target in this area has been Exxon Corporation, whose March 1989 *Valdez* oil spill fouled the Alaska coastline. Other environmental issues that have appeared as shareholder resolutions address global warming of the ozone layer, overcutting of the rain forests in Brazil, and saving the spotted owl in the Northwest. Shareholder resolutions promoting environmental concerns are expected to continue to increase in the future.

Several new themes have emerged as well. Ever since the Securities and Exchange Commission (SEC), which oversees what resolutions can be included in proxy statements, reversed an earlier position and has now held that cigarette smoking is an area in which shareholders are entitled to vote, resolutions opposing tobacco products are appearing in proxy statements. These resolutions urge cigarette manufacturers, such as Philip

Morris Company and American Brands, to quit producing cigarettes and media companies to quit advertising them. Such resolutions are expected to increase in the future.

Other recent shareholder resolutions deal with proposals to prohibit animal testing by companies, place a moratorium on nuclear weapons and a ban on the use of nuclear power, and dismantle antitakeover devices.

Most shareholder resolutions have a slim chance of being enacted because large-scale investors usually support management. They can, however, cause a corporation to change the way it does business. For example, to avoid the adverse publicity such issues can create, some corporations voluntarily adopt the changes contained in shareholder proposals. Others negotiate settlements with the sponsors of resolutions to get the measures off the agenda before the annual shareholders meetings.

Furthermore, shareholder resolutions are no longer just the bailiwick of individual or eccentric shareholders. Many state, municipal, and private pension funds now advocate socially responsible investing. These funds, which own billions of dollars of stock in American companies, are flexing their muscles and sponsoring shareholder resolutions to protect the environment, promote ethics, and curtail the greed of corporate managers.

1. Do you think shareholder proposals cause companies to act more socially responsible? Explain.
2. Should investors be socially conscious when making investments? Why or why not?

International Law

DU PONT ASKED TO ADOPT INTERNATIONAL WORKPLACE STANDARDS

The E. I. du Pont de Nemours and Company (Du Pont), organized under the laws of the state of Delaware, is one of the largest chemical and consumer products companies in the world. As such, Du Pont has manufacturing and production facilities located in many foreign countries. Several of these countries have been criticized because child labor and

forced labor is alleged to be used to produce goods in those countries.

At its annual meeting in April 2001, the International Brotherhood of Teamsters General Fund, owner of 90 shares of Du Pont common stock, proposed the following shareholder resolution to the shareholders of Du Pont.

Stockholder Proposal on International Workplace Standards

RESOLVED: *That the Board of Directors of E. I. du Pont de Nemours and Company (Du Pont) shall adopt, implement and enforce the workplace Code of Conduct (Code) as based on the International Labor Organization's (ILO) Conventions on workplace human rights, which include:*

- *No use of child labor.*
- *No discrimination or intimidation in employment.*
- *All workers have the right to form and join unions and to bargain collectively.*
- *No use of forced labor.*

Stockholder's (Teamster's) Statement in support of the proposal:
The Teamsters, in support of its proposal, provided the following statement in Du Pont's annual Proxy Statement submitted to Du Pont shareholders.

As a global institution, Du Pont and its international operations and sourcing arrangements are exposed to sundry risks. Adoption of this proposal manages the risk of being a party to serious human rights violations in the workplace. Du Pont operates or has business relationships in a number of countries, including China, Indonesia, and Thailand, where the U.S. State Department, Amnesty International, and Human Rights Watch indicate law and public policy do not adequately protect human rights. To wit: Forced labor, illegal child labor, and violence against women.

The success of Du Pont's operations depends on consumer and governmental good will. Brand name is a significant asset. Du Pont benefits from adopting and enforcing the Code ensuring that it isn't associated with human rights violations. This protects Du Pont's brand names and its relationships with customers and the numerous governments under which Du Pont operates and with which it does business.

Position of the Board of Directors in Opposition to the Proposal

In response, Du Pont included the following statement in the Proxy Statement, recommending that Du Pont shareholders vote against the shareholder resolution.

Du Pont is committed to conducting its business affairs with the highest ethical standards, and works diligently to be a respected corporate citizen throughout the world. The company has had in place for many years an Ethics Policy, Mission Statement and Code of Business Conduct addressing many of the issues covered in the standards proposed for adoption. These corporate policies are applicable to all employees in all Du Pont businesses around the world.

The company is supportive of the general intent of the proposal and similar international workplace standards suggested by other organizations for adoption. The company reviews on an ongoing basis codes offered by other organizations, and examines its own policies and practices in light of the provisions of the proposed codes. The company also meets with advocates of codes to explore issues of mutual concern. These efforts will continue. The company therefore believes adoption of the proposed code is unnecessary.

The shareholder proposal for the adoption of International Workplace Standards was defeated by an overwhelming majority of Du Pont shareholders at the annual meeting. Why do you think the International Brotherhood of Teamsters introduced this shareholder resolution? Do you think the reasons Du Pont asserted for recommending that its shareholders vote against the proposal were legitimate? Would you have voted for the resolution if you were a shareholder of Du Pont? Why or why not?

MERGERS AND ACQUISITIONS

Corporations may agree to friendly acquisitions or combinations of one another. This may be by merger, consolidation, share exchange, or sale of assets. Each of these types of combinations is discussed in the following paragraphs.

Business Brief

Mergers, consolidations, share exchanges, and sale of assets are *friendly* in nature. That is, both corporations have agreed to the combination of corporations or acquisition of assets.

Mergers

merger

Occurs when one corporation is absorbed into another corporation and ceases to exist.

A **merger** occurs when one corporation is absorbed into another corporation and ceases to exist. The corporation that continues to exist is called the *surviving corporation*. The other is called the *merged corporation* [RMBCA § 11.01]. The surviving corporation gains all the rights, privileges, powers, duties, obligations, and liabilities of the merged corporation. Title to property owned by the merged corporation transfers to the surviving corporation without formality or deeds. The shareholders of the merged corporation receive stock or securities of the surviving corporation or other consideration as provided in the plan of merger.

Suppose, for example, that Corporation A and Corporation B merge and it is agreed that Corporation A will absorb Corporation B. Corporation A is the surviving corporation. Corporation B is the merged corporation. A symbolic representation of this merger is A + B = A (see Exhibit 31.2).

*E*XHIBIT **31.2** *Example of a Merger*

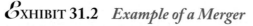

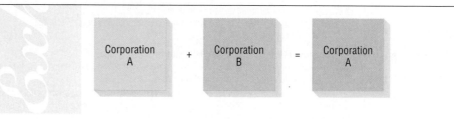

Consolidations

consolidation

Occurs when two or more corporations combine to form an entirely new corporation.

A **consolidation** occurs when two or more corporations combine to form an entirely new corporation (i.e., there is no surviving corporation). The new corporation is called the *consolidated corporation*, and the articles of incorporation of the new corporation replace the articles of incorporation of the component corporations.

Consider This Example Corporation A and Corporation B consolidate to form a new organization called Corporation C. A symbolic representation of this combination is A + B = C (see Exhibit 31.3).

*E*XHIBIT **31.3** *Example of a Consolidation*

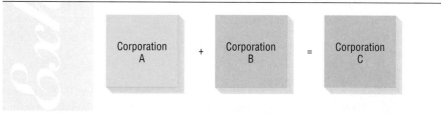

The new corporation accedes to all the rights, privileges, powers, duties, obligations, and liabilities of the constituent corporations. Title to property owned by the component corporations transfers to the new corporation without any formality. The shareholders receive stock of other securities in the consolidated corporation or other agreed-upon consideration.

Today, consolidations are not used very often because it is generally advantageous for one of the corporations to survive. The Revised Model Business Corporation Act (RMBCA) has deleted all references to consolidations.

Share Exchanges

One corporation can also acquire all the shares of another corporation through a **share exchange**. In a share exchange, both corporations retain their separate legal existence. After the exchange, one corporation (*parent corporation*) owns all of the shares of the other corporation (*subsidiary corporation*) [RMBCA § 1102]. (See Exhibit 31.4) Such exchanges are often used to create holding company arrangements (e.g., bank or insurance holding companies).

share exchange

When one corporation acquires all the shares of another corporation and both corporations retain their separate legal existence.

Consider This Example Suppose Corporation H is a bank holding company that wishes to acquire First Bank. Assume that Corporation H offers to exchange its shares for those of First Bank and that First Bank's shareholders approve of the transaction. After the share exchange, Corporation H is the parent corporation, and First Bank is the wholly owned subsidiary of Corporation H.

Exhibit 31.4 *Example of a Share Exchange*

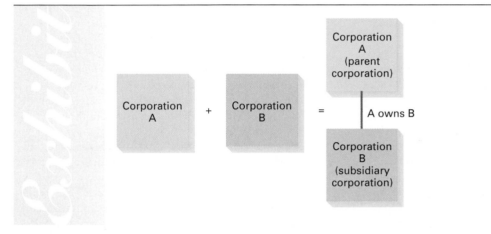

Required Approvals for a Merger

An ordinary merger or share exchange requires (1) the recommendation of the board of directors of each corporation and (2) an affirmative vote of the majority of shares of each corporation that is entitled to vote [RMBCA § 11.03]. The articles of incorporation or corporate bylaws can require the approval of a *supramajority*, such as 80 percent of the voting shares.

The approval of the surviving corporation's shareholders is not required if the merger or share exchange increases the number of voting shares of the surviving corporation by 20 percent or less [RMBCA § 11.03(g)].

The approved *articles of merger or share exchange* must be filed with the secretary of state. The state normally issues a *certificate of merger or share exchange* to the surviving corporation after all the formalities are met and the requisite fees are paid [RMBCA § 11.05].

If one corporation (called the *parent corporation*) owns 90 percent or more of the outstanding stock of another corporation (known as the *subsidiary corporation*), a **short-form merger** procedure may be followed to merge the two corporations. The short-form merger procedure is simpler than an ordinary merger because neither the approval of the shareholders of either corporation nor the approval of the board of directors of the subsidiary corporation is needed. All that is required is the approval of the board of directors of the parent corporation [RMBCA § 11.04].

Business Brief

An ordinary merger or share exchange requires (1) the recommendation of the board of directors of each corporation and (2) an affirmative vote of the majority of shares of each corporation that is entitled to vote.

short-form merger

A merger between a parent corporation and a subsidiary corporation that does not require the vote of the shareholders of either corporation or the board of directors of the subsidiary corporation.

Sale or Lease of Assets

A corporation may sell, lease, or otherwise dispose of all or substantially all of its property in other than the usual and regular course of business. Such a sale or lease transaction requires (1) the recommendation of the board of directors and (2) an affirmative vote of the

Business Brief

Approval of the selling or leasing corporation's shareholders is required for the sale, lease, or disposition of all or substantially all of a corporation's property not in the usual and regular course of business.

majority of the shares of the selling or leasing corporation that is entitled to vote (unless a greater vote is required) [RMBCA § 12.02]. This rule prevents the board of directors from selling all or most of the assets of the corporation without shareholder approval.

E-Commerce & Information Technology

THE TELECOMMUNICATIONS MEGAMERGER: MCI & SPRINT

Move over AT&T. AT&T, the world's largest telecommunications company, has a new challenger—WorldCom—which is the combination of MCI WorldCom and Sprint Corp. In October 1999, the two companies announced their merger, which was the largest corporate merger in history, with MCI paying $115 billion in stock to Sprint shareholders. The merger created the second largest telecommunications company next to AT&T. The new company's stated goal is to unseat AT&T as the largest company.

The MCI and Sprint merger is synergistic. MCI provides a broad base of telecom services, including long-distance, cable, and Internet access. Sprint, on the other hand, is a leader in wireless communications, an area that MCI wanted desperately to be in. The new WorldCom can offer a bundle of telecom services to both businesses and consumers. The vision of the new company is to assemble an unsurpassed digital network of telecommunications services. WorldCom has pinned its hopes on several technologies. The first is providing high-speed digital lines to business and residential users. Another is expanding wireless technology that gives WorldCom a direct link to customers. And finally, the company is banking on the explosion of broadband technology,

called MMDS (for Multichannel Multipoint Distribution Technology). The merged MCI and Sprint have combined to increase technology offerings to customers while saving costs.

The Federal Communications Commission (FCC), a federal administrative agency, must approve all telecommunications mergers, including the MCI Sprint megadeal. After the merger, two companies—AT&T and WorldCom—control 85 percent of the long-distance telephone market in the United States. WorldCom itself controls over 24 percent of the consumer long-distance market, 50 percent of the wholesale telephone market (hawking telephone usage to resellers), and 45 percent of the U.S. access points to the Internet. The FCC's usual approach is to require such large merging companies to shed some of their businesses as part of the approval process.

The colossal MCI and Sprint merger is only the largest of hundreds of combinations of telecommunications, computer software, and Internet companies. MCI itself was an outgrowth of over 60 mergers prior to the Sprint deal. The trend toward technology mergers will continue in the future as the lines between all types of telephone, computer, Internet, and other high-tech industries blur.

DISSENTING SHAREHOLDER APPRAISAL RIGHTS

Specific shareholders sometimes object to a proposed ordinary or short-form merger, share exchange, or sale or lease of all or substantially all of the property of the corporation, even though the transaction received the required approvals. Objecting shareholders are provided a statutory right to dissent and obtain payment of the fair value of their shares [RMBCA § 13.02]. This is referred to as a **dissenting shareholder appraisal right** or **appraisal right**). Shareholders have no other recourse unless the transaction is unlawful or fraudulent.

dissenting shareholder appraisal rights

Shareholders who object to a proposed merger, share exchange, or sale or lease of all or substantially all of the property of a corporation have a right to have their shares valued by the court and receive cash payment of this value from the corporation.

The corporation must notify shareholders of the existence of their appraisal rights before the transaction can be voted on [RMBCA § 13.20]. To obtain appraisal rights, a dissenting shareholder must (1) deliver written notice of his or her intent to demand payment of his or her shares to the corporation before the vote is taken and (2) not vote his or her shares in favor of the proposed action [RMBCA § 13.21]. The shareholder must deposit his or her share certificates with the corporation [RMBCA § 13.23]. Shareholders who fail to comply with these statutory procedures lose their appraisal rights.

As soon as the proposed action is taken, the corporation must pay each dissenting shareholder the amount the corporation estimates to be the fair value of his or her shares, plus accrued interest [RMBCA § 13.25]. If the dissenter is dissatisfied, the corporation must petition the court to determine the fair value of the shares [RMBCA § 13.30].

Business Brief

The court must determine the "fair value" of the shares of dissenting shareholders. Courts usually use appraisers to assist in determining this value.

After a hearing, the court will issue an order declaring the fair value of the shares. Appraisers may be appointed to help in determining this value. Court costs and appraisal fees usually are paid by the corporation. However, the court can assess these costs against the dissenters if they acted arbitrarily, vexatiously, or in bad faith [RMBCA § 13.31].

The court had to determine the appraisal value of a company's shares in the following case.

In the Matter of the Appraisal of Shell Oil Company

607 A.2d 1213 (1992)
Supreme Court of Delaware

CASE 31.1

BACKGROUND AND FACTS

Royal Dutch Petroleum Company (Royal Dutch), a large natural resource conglomerate, owned 94.6 percent of the stock of Shell Oil Company (Shell). The remaining shares of Shell were held by minority, public shareholders. On June 7, 1985, Royal Dutch effectuated a short-form merger with Shell and offered $60 cash per share for the outstanding shares of Shell it did not own. After the merger was complete, 1,005,001 shares had not accepted the offer and qualified for appraisal rights. The Delaware Chancery Court conducted an appraisal hearing. The parties offered extensive evidence through expert witnesses. These experts gave the following estimated per share value for Shell's shares:

Valuation Method	Shell's Expert	Shareholders' Expert
Liquidation value	$57	$100
Comparative value	$60	$106
Market value	$43–$45	$92–$143

Liquidation value was the estimated value if Shell were dissolved and its assets sold. Comparative value was an estimate based on a price reflected by prices in similar transactions in the oil and gas industry. Market value was an estimated price that Shell shares would sell for without the effect of merger speculation.

The chancery court determined that the fair value was $71.20 per share. It further held that the shareholders were entitled to 10 percent interest on that amount from the date

of the merger to the date of payment. Both parties appealed.

ISSUE

What price should Shell be required to pay its minority shareholders who demanded appraisal rights?

COURT'S REASONING

The chancery court assigned little or no weight to the valuations reached by the experts because it found that they lacked objectivity. The court stated: "In this case, each party's valuation evidence was replete with deficiencies and so susceptible to bias that indiscriminate endorsement of either would have been indefensible. The opinions expressed by the expert witnesses significantly reflected the desires of their clients." The chancery court reviewed the evidence and used its broad discretion to arrive at a valuation of $71.20 per share.

DECISION

The Supreme Court of Delaware affirmed the award.

Case Questions

Critical Legal Thinking   Should the law provide dissenting shareholder appraisal rights? Why or why not?

Business Ethics   Do you think expert witnesses act objectively?

Contemporary Business   Is there a temptation for a company to "low-ball" the cash-out price offered to shareholders in a merger? Explain.

TENDER OFFERS

Recall that a merger, a consolidation, a share exchange, and a sale of assets all require the approval of the board of directors of the corporation whose assets or shares are to be acquired. If the board of directors of the target corporation does not agree to the merger or acquisition, the acquiring corporation can make a **tender offer** for the shares directly to the shareholders of the **target corporation**. The shareholders each make an individual decision about whether to sell their shares to the **tender offeror** (see Exhibit 31.5). Such offers are often referred to as *hostile tender offers*.

The tender offeror's board of directors must approve the offer, although the shareholders do not have to approve. The offer can be made for all or a portion of the shares of the target corporation.

In a tender offer, the tendering corporation and the target corporation retain their separate legal status. A successful tender offer is sometimes followed, however, by a merger of the two corporations.

tender offer

An offer that an acquirer makes directly to a target corporation's shareholders in an effort to acquire the target corporation.

target corporation

The corporation that is proposed to be acquired in a tender offer situation.

tender offeror

The party that makes a tender offer.

*E*XHIBIT **31.5** *Illustration of a Tender Offer*

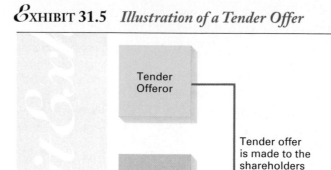

Tender offer is made to the shareholders of the target corporation. The tender offeror offers to purchase their shares in the target corporation.

*L*andmark *L*aw

THE WILLIAMS ACT

Prior to 1968, tender offers were not federally regulated. However, securities that were issued in conjunction with such offers had to be registered with the SEC or qualify for an exemption from registration. Tender offers made with cash were not subject to any federal disclosure requirements

In 1968, Congress enacted the **Williams Act** as an amendment to the Securities Exchange Act of 1934 [15 U.S.C. 78n(d) and (e)]. This act specifically regulates all tender offers, whether they are made with securities, cash, or other consideration, and establishes certain disclosure requirements and antifraud provisions.

*C*ontemporary *B*usiness *E*nvironment

LEVERAGED BUYOUTS

A raider or other party making a tender offer usually does not have the hundreds of millions or billions of dollars necessary to purchase the stock from the shareholders of the target corporation. Instead, a raider relies heavily on the fact that the money can be raised from creditors (e.g., banks). Many tender offers are not possible without such loans. Because of the use of borrowed money, these acquisitions are called **leveraged buyouts** or **LBOs**.

A typical LBO works as follows. The raider identifies a potential target and then contacts a large commercial bank and an investment banker. The commercial bank, for a large fee, agrees to supply some of the funds necessary to make the initial acquisition. The bank will be paid off at a later date,

after the acquisition is successful. The funds to pay back the bank usually come from the raider selling off some of the assets of the target corporation. These bank loans are often referred to as *bridge loans*.

Most of the rest of the purchase price comes from money raised by the investment banker by selling **junk bonds** of the acquiring firm to investors. Junk bonds are nothing more than risky bonds that pay a higher rate of interest than normal corporate bonds. Generally, the buyers are banks, savings and loan associations, pension funds, investment pools, and wealthy individuals. The investment banker is paid a huge fee by the raider for raising this money.

With the money in hand—or at least the pledge that the money will be there when it is needed—the raider commences its hostile tender offer for the shares of the target corporation. When the desired number of shares are tendered, the tender offer is closed using the money borrowed from the bank and raised through the sale of junk bonds. The raider's investment in the tender offer usually amounts to 5 percent or 10 percent of the total.

After the tender offer is completed, the tender offeror—which is usually a shell corporation that is saddled with huge debts (i.e., the bank loans and junk bonds)—merges with the target corporation. The target corporation has all of the assets (e.g., brand names) and income. The resulting entity is a highly leveraged corporation. Its capital structure consists of a low amount of equity and huge amounts of debt.

The raider usually has to sell off some of the assets to pay the bank loans, fees, and other expenses of the takeover. Some LBOs are successful, but others run into problems because the income from the remaining assets is not sufficient to pay the interest on the junk bonds.

Tender Offer Rules

The **Williams Act** does not require the tender offeror to notify either the management of the target company or the SEC until the offer is made.[2] Detailed information regarding the terms, conditions, and other information concerning the tender offer must be disclosed at that time.

Tender offers are governed by the following rules:

1. The offer cannot be closed before 20 business days after the commencement of the tender offer.
2. The offer must be extended for 10 business days if the tender offeror increases the number of shares that it will take or the price that it will pay for the shares.
3. The **fair price rule** stipulates that any increase in price paid for shares tendered must be offered to all shareholders, even those who have previously tendered their shares.
4. The **pro rata rule** holds that the shares must be purchased on a pro rata basis if too many shares are tendered.

A shareholder who tenders his or her shares has the absolute right to withdraw them at any time prior to the closing of the tender offer. The dissenting shareholder appraisal rights are not available.

Williams Act

An amendment to the Securities Exchange Act of 1934 made in 1968 that specifically regulates all tender offers.

fair price rule

A rule that says any increase in price paid for shares tendered must be offered to all shareholders, even those who have previously tendered their shares.

pro rata rule

A rule that says shares must be purchased on a pro rata basis if too many shares are tendered.

Hostile Takeovers *Hostile takeovers are usually not welcomed by the target company. Companies that are possible targets of hostile takeovers often implement antitakeover strategies and tactics, such as adopting "poison pills," to try to thwart any possible takeover.*

Antifraud Provision

Section 14(e) of the Williams Act prohibits fraudulent, deceptive, and manipulative practices in connection with a tender offer.[3] Violations of this section may result in civil charges brought by the SEC or criminal charges brought by the Justice Department. The courts have implied a private civil cause of action under Section 14(e). Therefore, a shareholder who has been injured by a violation of Section 14(e) can sue the wrongdoer for damages.

Section 14(e)

A provision of the Williams Act that prohibits fraudulent, deceptive, and manipulative practices in connection with a tender offer.

Business Ethics

GOLDEN PARACHUTES: WHEN IS THE LANDING TOO CUSHY?

The term *golden parachute* has been coined to describe the large severance payments received by top executives when they leave their employ at a corporation. They are called "golden" because of their lucrative nature. They are called "parachutes" because they are "pulled" when an executive leaves or is fired from a company that has been taken over.

Golden parachutes—formally called change-in-control severance agreement plans—are long-term employment contracts. They usually provide that all cash payments and stock options due under the contract become due and payable immediately upon the occurrence of the trigger—the takeover of the company.

For example, a company enters into a three-year employment contract with its president and agrees to pay a $1-million salary annually and grant options to purchase 10,000 shares of the company stock at $10 per share. The contract includes a golden parachute clause in the event of a takeover. Suppose the company is taken over in a $15-per-share tender offer. The president can "pull" his or her parachute and demand $3 million in salary as well as making $1.5-million profit by exercising his stock options.

Two benefits of golden parachutes are often cited. First, they are necessary to lure talented executives and keep them from looking for other positions when a takeover of the company is pending. Second, they act as an antitakeover device, thus protecting the company from hostile takeovers. Both of

these reasons have been challenged as a coverup for the real reason for golden parachutes: top executives' greed.

Golden parachutes are often criticized by lower-level managers and rank-and-file workers who complain that management can walk away in comfort after a takeover, whereas they are left hanging out to dry. To address these concerns, some companies have added "silver parachutes" to protect lower-level managers and "tin parachutes" to protect wage-earning workers in case of a takeover. As the names indicate, the compensation paid under these plans is much lower than that paid under golden parachutes.

In the past, the SEC has held that golden parachutes need only be approved by a company's outside directors, rather than by a vote of the shareholders. In a recent decision involving a proposed golden parachute to be installed by Transamerica Corporation, the SEC changed its position and ruled that the company must submit the plan for shareholder vote. This decision sends a signal that golden parachutes will receive closer scrutiny in the future than they have in the past.

1. Do you think top executives' compensation is too high? Explain.
2. Are golden parachutes a legitimate compensation scheme? Or are they an egregious example of management greed?

FIGHTING A TENDER OFFER

The incumbent management of many targets of hostile tender offers does not want the corporation taken over by the tender offeror. Therefore, it engages in varied activities to impede and defeat the tender offer.

Contemporary Business Environment

TIME-WARNER-PARAMOUNT: JUST SAY NO!

Time, Inc. (Time), is a publishing company that publishes *People, Money, Sports Illustrated*, and other magazines and newspapers; it owns cable television and pay television channels. Warner Communications, Inc. (Warner), is a communications company that produces and sells movies, television programs, and records, and owns cable stations. In 1989, after years of negotiations, Time and Warner agreed to a merger. Based on the agreed-upon ratio of exchange, Time shareholders were to receive $120 in stock of the new Time/Warner for each share of Time stock they owned. The shareholders meetings to vote on the merger were set.

Paramount Communications, Inc. (Paramount), is a film production and distribution company. For years, it had been looking for an acquisition in the publishing and communications industry. Two weeks before the Time shareholders were to vote on the planned merger with Warner, Paramount announced a hostile tender offer for Time's shares at $175 per share.

Time, which was obviously going to lose the shareholder vote, canceled the proposed merger with Warner and made a friendly tender offer to acquire 50 percent of Warner's stock for $70 per share. This acquisition would make Time too big for Paramount to take over. In addition, the vote of Time shareholders would not be required.

Time had other defensive maneuvers in place as well. These plans consisted of flip-over and flip-in rights plans that would permit Time shareholders to exchange their Time shares for approximately twice the value of the tender offeror's securities if the poison pills were removed by Time's management before the tender offer was completed.

Paramount sued Time, alleging that Time management's refusal to dismantle the poison pills and put Time on the block violated their fiduciary duty. In defense, Time argued that the merger of Time and Warner was in the best interests of Time shareholders over the long run. In other words, the long-term benefits of the combination of Time and Warner and their cultures would create synergism that would pay off

in the future; Paramount's tender offer offered only one-time short-term profits.

The Delaware court, applying the business judgment rule, sided with Time. The court held that the projected long-term benefits to Time shareholders justified Time management's refusal to dismantle the poison pills. The court stated: "The corporation law does not operate on the theory that directors are obligated to follow the wishes of a majority of shares. In fact, directors, not shareholders, are charged with the duty to manage the firm." Thus, incumbent management of a target corporation can "just say no" to a tender offer as long as it can show that it is acting in the long-term interests of the shareholders. [*Paramount Communications, Inc. v. Time, Inc.*, 571 A.2d 1140 (DE 1990)]

Defensive Strategies and Tactics

Some of the strategies and tactics used by incumbent management in defending against hostile tender offers are described as follows:

1. **Persuasion of Shareholders** Media campaigns are organized to convince shareholders that the tender offer is not in their best interests.
2. **Delaying Lawsuits** Lawsuits are filed alleging that the tender offer violates securities laws, antitrust laws, or other laws. The time gained by this tactic gives management the opportunity to erect or implement other defensive maneuvers.
3. **Selling a Crown Jewel** Such assets as profitable divisions or real estate that are particularly attractive to outside interests are sold. This tactic makes the target corporation less attractive to the tender offeror.
4. **Adopting a Poison Pill** Poison pills are defensive strategies that are built into the target corporation's articles of incorporation, corporate bylaws, or contracts and leases. For example, contracts and leases may provide that they will expire if the ownership of the corporation changes hands. These tactics make the target corporation more expensive to the tender offeror.
5. **White Knight Merger** White knight mergers are mergers with friendly parties, that is, parties that promise to leave the target corporation and/or its management intact.
6. **Pac-Man (or Reverse) Tender Offer** The target corporation makes a **tender offer** on the tender offeror. Thus, the target corporation tries to purchase the tender offeror.
7. **Issuing Additional Stock** Placing additional stock on the market increases the number of outstanding shares that the tender offeror must purchase in order to gain control of the target corporation.
8. **Creating an Employee Stock Ownership Plan (ESOP)** A company creates an ESOP and places a certain percentage of the corporation's securities (e.g., 15 percent) in it. The ESOP is then expected to vote the shares it owns against the potential acquirer in a proxy contest or tender offer because the beneficiaries (i.e., the employees) have a vested interest in keeping the company intact.
9. **Flip-over and Flip-in Rights Plans** These plans provide that existing shareholders of the target corporation may convert their shares for a greater amount (e.g., twice the value) of shares of the acquiring corporation (*flip-over rights plan*) or debt securities of the target company (*flip-in rights plan*). Rights plans are triggered if the acquiring firm acquires a certain percentage (e.g., 20 percent) of the shares of the target corporation. They make it more expensive for the acquiring firm to take over the target corporation.
10. **Greenmail and Standstill Agreements** Most tender offerors purchase a block of stock in the target corporation before making an offer. Occasionally, the tender offeror will agree to give up its tender offer and agree not to purchase any further shares if the target corporation agrees to buy back the stock at a premium over fair market value. This payment is called **greenmail**. The agreement of the tender offeror to abandon its tender offer and not purchase any additional stock is called a *standstill agreement*.

There are many other strategies and tactics that target companies initiate and implement in defending against a tender offer.

Business Brief

Target corporations initiate and implement a variety of defensive maneuvers and tactics to defend against unwanted hostile tender offers.

crown jewel

A valuable asset of the target corporation's that the tender offeror particularly wants to acquire in the tender offer.

pac-man tender offer

Occurs when a corporation that is the target of a tender offer makes a *reverse tender offer* for the stock of the tender offeror.

greenmail

The purchase by a target corporation of its stock from an actual or perceived tender offeror at a premium.

Business Judgment Rule

The board of directors of a corporation owes a **fiduciary duty** to the corporation and its shareholders. This duty, which requires the board to act carefully and honestly, is truly tested when a tender offer is made for the stock of the company. That is because shareholders and others then ask whether the board's initiation and implementation or defensive measures were taken in the best interests of the shareholders or to protect the board's own interests and jobs.

The legality of defensive strategies is examined using the **business judgment rule**. This rule protects the decisions of a board of directors that acts on an informed basis, in good faith, and in the honest belief that the action taken was in the best interests of the corporation and its shareholders.[4] In the context of a tender offer, the defensive measures chosen by the board must be reasonable in relation to the threat posed.[5]

Contemporary Business Environment

THE SAGA OF PARAMOUNT-VIACOM-QVC

In the past, the Delaware courts generally sided with the management of target companies in suits involving hostile raids. In most of these cases, the Delaware courts upheld defensive maneuvers taken by target companies to fend off unwanted suitors. This long line of cases ended with a recent Delaware court decision concerning the takeover of Paramount Communications, Inc.

It all started on September 12, 1993, when Viacom, Inc. (Viacom), and Paramount Communications, Inc. (Paramount), announced a friendly merger agreement. Basically, Viacom and its chairman and largest shareholder, billionaire Summer Redstone, were taking over Paramount. Viacom controlled national cable networks, including Showtime and The Movie Channel. Paramount's holdings included Paramount Pictures, the Simon & Schuster publishing house, Madison Square Garden, the New York Knicks basketball team, and the New York Rangers hockey team. Both sides touted the synergism of the marriage of these two companies into a media colossus.

There was only one hitch to this merger: Five days later QVC Network, Inc. (QVC), a rival cable operator led by Barry Diller, made a $90 per share hostile bid for Paramount that topped Viacom's offer. QVC owned the Home Shopping Network. Paramount's board of directors, which was dominated by its chairman, Martin Davis, did not want to be taken over by QVC. Paramount's board adopted the following antitakeover strategies:

1. A **no-shop provision** whereby the Paramount board guaranteed Viacom that it would not investigate QVC's offer or meet with QVC.
2. A **lockup option** that granted Viacom (but not QVC) the right to buy 23.7 million shares of Paramount at $69.14 each if a bidder other than Viacom bought Paramount. (This would cost a competing bidder almost $400 million.)

3. An agreement to drop certain **poison pill** defenses as to Viacom but not as to QVC. (Thus, Viacom could pursue its acquisition of Paramount, but QVC could not.)

QVC sued Paramount in Delaware Chancery Court, alleging that these tactics violated the Paramount board of directors' fiduciary duties to the corporation and its shareholders. To many observers' surprise, the Delaware court agreed with QVC. The court ruled that the "no-shop" provision was unlawful, stating that Paramount directors "had a duty to continue their search for the best value available to shareholders." The court also invalidated the "lockup option" stock purchase plan as being an illegal transfer of corporate wealth to Viacom at the expense of Paramount shareholders.

The chancery court held that the poison pills Paramount had erected must be dismantled for QVC (and any other bidder) as they had been for Viacom. The court also ordered that Paramount be put on the block and auctioned to the highest bidder. The Delaware Supreme Court affirmed this decision.

Both sides lined up their lawyers, investment banks, and commercial banks, as well as enlisting other companies, to assist them in the bidding process. Most significantly, Viacom merged with Blockbuster Entertainment, a national video rental chain, in making its bid. On February 15, 1994, after escalating bids by both sides, the five-month saga ended when Viacom won the right to buy Paramount with a $10-billion-plus bid.

When it was all over, Summer Redstone of Viacom toasted: "Here's to us that won." Barry Diller of QVC tersely concluded: The price of Viacom's stock plummeted on the news of the merger. Redstone has to cope with an unwieldy conglomerate comprised of Viacom, Paramount, and Blockbuster, where the group's combined debt of $10 billion must now be serviced. QVC walks away virtually debt-free and having forced Viacom to pay $2 billion more than its original friendly merger offer for Paramount. QVC will look for other multimedia companies with which to combine. Martin Davis of Paramount walked away from the deal $117 million richer.

STATE ANTITAKEOVER STATUTES

Many states have enacted **antitakeover statutes** that are aimed at protecting corporations that are either incorporated in or do business within the state from hostile takeovers. Many of these state statutes have been challenged as being unconstitutional because they violate the Williams Act and the Commerce and Supremacy clauses of the U.S. Constitution.

state antitakeover statutes

Statutes enacted by state legislatures that protect corporations incorporated in or doing business in the state from hostile takeovers.

The Supreme Court Speaks

Supreme Court Upholds Antitakeover Statute

CTS Corp. v. Dynamics Corp.
481 U.S. 69, 107 S.Ct. 1637 (1987)
Supreme Court of the United States

BACKGROUND AND FACTS

On March 4, 1986, Indiana enacted the Control Share Acquisitions Chapter (Act). The Act covers corporations that (1) are incorporated in Indiana and have at least 100 shareholders, (2) have their primary place of business or substantial assets in Indiana, and (3) have either 10 percent of their shareholders in Indiana or 10 percent of their shares owned by Indiana residents. The Act provides that if any entity acquires 20 percent or more of the voting shares of a covered corporation, the acquirer loses voting rights to these shares unless a majority of the disinterested shareholders of the acquired corporation vote to restore such voting rights. The acquirer can request that such vote be held within 50 days after its acquisition. If the shareholders do not restore the voting rights, the target corporation may redeem the shares from the acquirer at fair market value, but it is not required to do so.

On March 10, 1986, Dynamics Corporation of America (Dynamics), a Delaware corporation, announced a tender offer for 1 million shares of CTS Corporation (CTS), an Indiana corporation covered by the act. The purchase of these shares would have brought Dynamic's voting interest in CTS to 27.5 percent. Dynamics sued in federal court, alleging that Indiana's Control Share Acquisitions Chapter was unconstitutional. The federal district court held for Dynamics. The court of appeals affirmed. CTS appealed.

SUPREME COURT ISSUE

Does the Indiana Control Share Acquisitions Chapter conflict with the Williams Act or violate the Commerce Clause of the U.S. Constitution by unduly burdening interstate commerce?

IN THE LANGUAGE OF THE U.S. SUPREME COURT

Powell, Justice *The first question in this case is whether the Williams Act preempts the Indiana Act. As we have stated frequently, absent an explicit indication by Congress of an intent to preempt state law, a state statute is preempted only where compliance with both federal and state regulations is a physical impossibility or where the state law stands as an obstacle to the accomplishment and execution of the full purposes and objectives of Congress. Because it is entirely possible for entities to comply with both the*

Williams and the Indiana acts, the state statute can be preempted only if it frustrates the purposes of the federal law.

The statute now before the court protects the independent shareholder against both of the contending parties. Thus, the act furthers a basic purpose of the Williams Act, placing investors on an equal footing with the takeover bidder. The Indiana Act operates on the assumption, implicit in the Williams Act, that independent shareholders faced with tender offers often are at a disadvantage. By allowing such shareholders to vote as a group, the act protects them from the coercive aspects of some tender offers. If, for example, shareholders believe that a successful tender offer will be followed by a purchase of nontendering shares at a depressed price [in a second tier merger], individual shareholders may tender their shares—even if they doubt the tender offer is in the corporation's best interest—to protect themselves from being forced to sell their shares at a depressed price. In such a situation under the Indiana Act, the shareholders as a group, acting in the corporation's best interest, could reject the offer although individual shareholders might be inclined to accept it. The desire of the Indiana legislature to protect shareholders of Indiana corporations from this type of coercive offer does not conflict with the Williams Act. Rather, it furthers the federal policy of investor protection.

DECISION AND REMEDY

The U.S. Supreme Court held that the Indiana Control Share Acquisitions Chapter neither conflicted with the Williams Act nor violated the Commerce Clause of the U.S. Constitution. Reversed.

CASE QUESTIONS

Critical Legal Thinking Should states be permitted to adopt antitakeover statutes? Why or why not? Whom do you think these statutes actually protect?

Business Ethics Is it ethical for a target corporation's management to assert a state antitakeover statute?

Contemporary Business What are the economic effects of a state antitakeover statute?

International Law

THE EXON-FLORIO LAW: REGULATING FOREIGN ACQUISITIONS OF U.S. BUSINESSES

Until 1988, foreign investors had virtually the same rights to acquire businesses located in the United States as domestic investors. However, the **Exon-Florio Law** of 1988 [50 U.S.C. 2170], as amended by the **Byrd-Exon amendment** of 1992 [P.L. 102–484, Sec. 837], mandates the President of the United States to suspend, prohibit, or dismantle the acquisition of U.S. businesses by foreign investors if there is credible evidence that the foreign investor might take action that threatens to impair the "national security."

Exon-Florio is administered through the **Committee on Foreign Investment in the United States (CFIUS)**, an interagency committee that is chaired by the U.S. Treasury Department. The provisions apply to mergers, acquisitions, takeovers, stock purchases, asset purchases, joint ventures, and proxy contests that would result in foreign control of U.S. businesses engaged in interstate commerce in the United States. The U.S. business could be a corporation, a partnership, a sole proprietorship, or another business. The size of the U.S. operation is irrelevant.

Exon-Florio and the regulations adopted thereunder do not define the term *national security*. The Treasury Department has interpreted the term broadly to include not only defense contractors but also other businesses. The following factors must be considered in conducting a national security analysis of a proposed foreign U.S. investment:

1. The domestic production needed for defense requirements for national security.

2. The potential effect of a transaction on the international technological leadership of the United States in areas affecting national security.

3. The potential effect of a transaction on sales of military goods to any country that is identified as supporting terrorism.

The term *control* includes any investment exceeding 10 percent ownership in a U.S. business by a foreign investor. The Exon-Florio provision does not apply to "greenfield" investments by foreigners—that is, start-ups of new businesses.

When a foreign investor proposes to acquire an interest in a U.S. business, it may voluntarily notify CFIUS of its intention. CFIUS must commence its investigation within 30 days after receipt of written notification of the transaction. The investigation must be completed within 45 days after receipt of such notice, and the President must announce a decision to take no action no later than 15 days after completion of the investigation. If the President finds a threat to the national security, the acquisition may be prohibited. If the foreign investor chooses not to notify CFIUS and completes the acquisition, it remains indefinitely subject to divestment if the President subsequently determines that the acquisition threatens the national security. The President's decision is not subject to judicial review.

Proponents of Exon-Florio argue that the law is needed to protect U.S. interests in vital industries. Critics allege that the law could discourage foreign investment in the United States.

*C*HAPTER *S*UMMARY

Solicitation of Proxies, p. 774

Solicitation of Proxies	1. *Proxy.* Shareholders can exercise their rights to vote on the election of directors, mergers, charter amendments, and the like either in person or by *proxy*. 2. *Proxy card.* A written document signed by a shareholder that authorizes another person to vote the shareholder's shares.
Federal Proxy Rules	*Section 14(a).* Provision of the Securities Exchange Act of 1934 that authorizes the *Securities and Exchange Commission (SEC)* to regulate the solicitation of proxies. 1. *Solicitation of proxies.* Occurs when management or others seek to obtain proxies from a corporation's shareholders. 2. *Proxy statement.* Written document that must be given to shareholders by management and others who are soliciting shareholder proxies. The statement must fully describe (a) the matter for which the proxy is being solicited, (b) who is soliciting the proxy, and (c) any other pertinent information. 3. *Filing with the SEC.* Proxy statements must be filed with the SEC at least 10 days before the materials are sent to shareholders.
Antifraud Provision	Section 14(a) of the 1934 act prohibits misrepresentations or omissions of a material fact in proxy materials. The SEC, U.S. Justice Department, shareholders, and others may sue the wrongdoer.

Proxy Contests	Occur when opposing factions of shareholders and managers solicit proxies from other shareholders; the side that receives the greatest number of votes wins the proxy contest.
	1. *Opposing groups:*
	  a. *Incumbent group.* Management-sponsored slate of proposed directors.
	  b. *Insurgent group.* Slate of proposed directors sponsored by the group that is challenging the incumbent group.
	2. *Reimbursement of expenses.* In a proxy contest that involves a *policy issue*, the corporation pays the incumbent management's expenses whether they win or lose the proxy contest. If the insurgent group wins the proxy contest, the corporation must reimburse them their expenses, too. If the proxy contest concerned a *personal matter*, neither side may recover its expenses from the corporation.

SEC Proxy Rules	In 1992, the SEC adopted proxy rules that provide: 1. *Shareholder communication.* Shareholders may communicate orally or in writing with other shareholders without filing a proxy statement with the SEC if the shareholder is not seeking proxy voting authority. This rule does not apply to shareholders who own more than $5 million of the company's voting shares; those shareholders must register any written communication to shareholders with the SEC. 2. *Unbundled proposals.* Companies seeking proxies may not bundle propositions for a single shareholder vote. Propositions must be presented separately to shareholders for vote. 3. *Company performance.* Companies must include performance charts in their annual reports comparing the company's stock performance to a general stock index (e.g., Standard and Poor's 500) and that company's peer group index (e.g., retailers). 4. *Executive compensation disclosure.* Companies must provide tables in their annual reports summarizing the compensation for the chief executive officer and their four other most highly compensated executives for the past three years. Compensation includes salary, stock options, stock appreciation rights, and long-term incentive plans.
Shareholder Proposals	Proposal submitted by a shareholder or group of shareholders to be considered and voted by the corporation's shareholders. Most shareholder proposals concern social issues (e.g., protection of the environment, discontinuation of the manufacture and sale of dangerous products). 1. *Inclusion in proxy materials.* If management does not oppose the proposal, it may be included in the proxy materials issued by the corporation. If management opposes the shareholder proposal, the SEC rules on whether the proposal must be submitted to the shareholders in the corporation's proxy materials. 2. *Requirements.* To be included in the corporation's proxy materials, the shareholder proposal must (a) not violate federal or state law, (b) relate to the corporation's business, (c) concern policy issues (and not the day-to-day operations of the corporation), and (d) not concern the payment of dividends.

Mergers and Acquisitions, p. 777

Mergers and Acquisitions	Mergers, consolidations, and share exchanges are *friendly* combinations of corporations. 1. *Merger.* Occurs when one corporation is absorbed into another corporation and ceases to exist. The corporation that continues to exist after a merger is called the *surviving corporation.* The corporation that is absorbed in the merger and ceases to exist as a separate entity is called the *merged corporation.* 2. *Consolidation.* Occurs when two or more corporations combine to form an entirely new corporation. The new corporation is called the *consolidated corporation.* 3. *Share exchange.* Occurs when one corporation acquires all the shares of another corporation while both corporations retain their separate legal existence. The corporation that owns the shares of the other corporation is called the *parent corporation.* The corporation that is owned by the other corporation is called the *subsidiary corporation.*
Required Approvals	1. *Required approvals.* An ordinary merger or share exchange requires (a) the recommendation of the board of directors of each corporation and (b) an affirmative vote of the majority of shares of each corporation that is entitled to vote (unless a greater vote is required). 2. *No shareholder vote required.* The approval of the surviving corporation's shareholders is not required if the merger or share exchange increases the number of voting shares of the surviving corporation by 20 percent or less. 3. *Articles of merger or share exchange.* Document that must be filed with the secretary of state once the merger or share exchange is completed.
Short-Form Mergers	A merger between a *parent corporation* and a *subsidiary corporation* where the parent corporation owns 90 percent or more of the subsidiary corporation. *Required approval.* Only the approval of the board of directors of the parent corporation is required to effectuate a short-form merger. The vote of the shareholders of either corporation and the board of directors of the subsidiary corporation are not required.

| **Sale or Lease of Assets** | 1. *Sale or lease of assets not in the usual and regular course of business.* Sale, lease, or disposition by a corporation of all or substantially all its assets not in the usual and regular course of business.
2. *Required approval.* Requires (a) the recommendation of the board of directors and (b) an affirmative vote of the majority of the shares of the selling or leasing corporation that is entitled to vote (unless a greater vote is required). |

Dissenting Shareholder Appraisal Rights, p. 780

| **Dissenting Shareholder Appraisal Rights** | Statutory right of shareholders who object to a proposed merger, share exchange, or sale or lease of all or substantially all the property of the corporation to have their shares valued by the court and receive cash payment of this value from the corporation.
1. *Procedures.* The corporation must notify shareholders of their appraisal rights. To obtain appraisal rights, the shareholder must (a) deliver written notice to the corporation of his or her intent to demand payment of his or her shares before the vote is taken and (b) not vote his or her shares in favor of the proposed action.
2. *Fair value.* If the shareholder does not accept the value offered by the corporation, the court will determine the *fair value* of the shares. The court may hire appraisers to assist in making this determination. Costs of this proceeding are usually borne by the corporation. |

Tender Offers, p. 781

Tender Offers	An offer that an acquirer makes directly to a *target corporation's shareholders* in an effort to acquire the target corporation or control of the target corporation. 1. *Tender offeror.* The party that makes a tender offer. 2. *Target corporation.* The corporation that is proposed to be acquired in a tender offer situation.
The Williams Act	Federal statute that regulates all tender offers. The Securities and Exchange Commission (SEC) is empowered to administer the Williams Act.
Tender Offer Rules	1. *Notification.* The tender offeror does not have to notify the SEC or the target corporation's management until the tender offer is made. 2. *Completion.* The tender offer cannot be closed before 20 business days after the commencement of the offer. 3. *Extension.* The offer must be extended for 10 business days if the tender offeror increases the number of shares it will take or the price it will pay for the shares. 4. *Fair price rule.* Stipulates that any increase in price paid for shares tendered must be offered to all shareholders, even those who have previously tendered their shares. 5. *Pro rata rule.* Provides that shares must be purchased on a *pro rata basis* if too many shares are tendered. 6. *Withdrawal rights.* Shareholders who tender their shares have an absolute right to withdraw them at any time prior to the closing of the tender offer.
Antifraud Provision	*Section 14(e).* A provision of the Williams Act that prohibits fraudulent, deceptive, and manipulative practices in connection with a tender offer.

Fighting a Tender Offer, p. 784

| **Fighting a Tender Offer** | The management of the target corporation often takes one or more of the following steps to try to defeat a hostile tender offer:
1. Persuade the shareholders not to tender their shares.
2. File delaying lawsuits (e.g., antitrust lawsuits).
3. Sell the *crown jewel* (e.g., a valuable asset that the tender offeror is particularly interested in acquiring).
4. Adopt *poison pills* (e.g., contract provisions that make contracts and leases expire).
5. Find a *white knight* to purchase the corporation in a friendly acquisition.
6. Conduct a *Pac-man tender offer* (i.e., a reverse tender offer to acquire the tender offeror).
7. Issue additional stock to friendly parties.
8. Create an *employee stock ownership plan (ESOP)* and issue stock to the ESOP.
9. Adopt *flip-over* and *flip-in rights plans* that make it more expensive for the tender offeror to acquire shares.
10. Pay *greenmail* by purchasing the shares held by the tender offeror at a premium. Obtain a *standstill agreement* whereby the offeror agrees not to purchase shares of the target corporation for a stipulated period of time.
11. Engage in other strategies and tactics that make it more difficult for a tender offeror to complete its tender offer. |

Business Judgment Rule	A rule that protects the decisions of the board of directors which acts on an *informed basis*, in *good faith*, and in the *honest belief that the action taken was in the best interests of the corporation and its shareholders*. *Tender offers.* The actions of the management of a target corporation in fighting a tender offer are judged by the business judgment rule. The defensive measure must be reasonable in relation to the threat posed.

State Antitakeover Statutes, p. 787

State Antitakeover Statutes	Statutes enacted by state legislatures that are aimed at protecting corporations that are either incorporated in or doing business within the state from hostile takeovers. *Lawfulness.* State antitakeover statutes are lawful if they do not conflict with the federal *Williams Act* or unduly burden interstate commerce in violation of the *Commerce Clause* of the U.S. Constitution.

END-OF-CHAPTER INTERNET EXERCISES AND CASE QUESTIONS

Working the Web Internet Exercises

ACTIVITIES

1. Research your own state law on antitakeover statutes and compile examples. See **www.law.cornell.edu/topics/state_statutes.html#corporations**.

2. What is a *Jennifer Lopez* or a *Phantom Stock*? For a shorthand set of definitions and an example, see **www.morevalue.com/glossary/restrict/White%20KnightWashington%20Mut.html**. An even better and more comprehensive (as well as colorful) list can be found at **www.investopedia.com/categories/buzzwords.asp**.

3. Review your own state statutes on termination of corporations. Why do you think some lawyers advise their corporate clients who are planning to terminate to just allow the secretary of state to cause an *administrative dissolution* for failure to file the annual renewal application? See **www.law.cornell.edu/topics/state_statutes.html#corporations**.

4. Find state statutes that control the distribution of corporate assets at termination for nonprofit corporations. How does this differ from the rules in for-profit corporations? See **www.law.cornell.edu/topics/state_statutes.html#corporations**.

CRITICAL LEGAL THINKING CASES

31.1 Proxy Disclosure Western Maryland Company (Western) was a timbering and mining concern. A substantial portion of its stock was owned by CSX Minerals (CSX), its parent corporation. The remaining shares were owned by several minority shareholders, including Sanford E. Lockspeiser. Western's stock was not publicly traded. In 1983, the board of directors of Western voted to merge the company with CSX. Western distributed a proxy statement to the minority shareholders that stated that CSX would vote for the merger and recommended approval of the merger by the other

shareholders. The proxy materials disclosed Western's natural resource holdings in terms of acreage of minerals and timber. It also stated real property values as carried on the company's books, that is, a book value of $17.04 per share. It included an opinion of the First Boston Corporation, an investment banking firm, that the merger was fair to shareholders; First Boston did not undertake an independent evaluation of Western's physical assets. Lockspeiser sued, alleging that the proxy materials were misleading because they did not state tonnage of Western's coal reserves, timber holdings in board feet, and actual value of

Western's assets. Did Lockspeiser state a claim for relief? [*Lockspeiser v. Western Maryland Company*, 768 F.2d 558 (4th Cir. 1985)]

31.2 Proxy Contest The Medfield Corporation (Medfield) is a publicly held corporation engaged in operating hospitals and other healthcare facilities. Medfield established March 1, 1974, as the date for its annual shareholders' meeting, at which time the board of directors would be elected. In its proxy statement, management proposed the incumbent slate of directors. A group known as the Medfield Shareholders Committee (Committee) nominated a rival slate of candidates and also solicited proxies. Medfield sent proxy solicitation material to shareholders that

1. Failed to disclose that Medfield had been overpaid more than $1.8 million by Blue Cross and this amount was due and owing Blue Cross.
2. Failed to disclose that Medicare funds were being withheld because of Medfield's nonpayment.
3. Failed to adequately disclose self-dealing by one of the directors with Medfield who owned part of a laboratory used by Medfield.
4. Failed to disclose that Medfield was attempting to sell two nursing homes.
5. Impugned the character, integrity, and personal reputation of one of the rival candidates by stating that he had previously been found liable for patent infringement when, in fact, the case had been reversed on appeal.

At the annual meeting, the incumbent slate of directors received 50 percent of the votes cast, against 44 percent of the insurgent slate of directors. The Gladwins, who own voting stock, sued to have the election overturned. Who wins? [*Gladwin v. Medfield Corporation*, 540 F.2d 1266 (5th Cir. 1976)]

31.3 Reimbursement for Expenses Incurred in a Proxy Contest The Fairchild Engine and Airplane Corporation (Fairchild) is a privately held corporation whose management proposed the incumbent slate of directors for election at its annual shareholders' meeting. An insurgent slate of directors challenged the incumbents for election to the board. After the solicitation of proxies and a hard-fought proxy contest, the insurgent slate of directors was elected. Evidence showed the proxy contest was waged over matters of corporate policy and for personal reasons. The old board of directors had spent $134,000 out of corporate funds to wage the proxy contest. The insurgents had spent $127,000 of their personal funds in their successful proxy contest and sought reimbursement from Fairchild for this amount. The payment of these expenses was ratified by a 16-to-1 majority vote of the stockholders. Mr. Rosenfeld, an attorney who owned 25 of the 2,300,000 outstanding shares of the corporation, filed an action to recover the amounts already paid by the corporation and to prevent any further payments of these expenses. Who wins? [*Rosenfeld v. Fairchild Engine and Airplane Corporation*, 128 N.E.2d 291 (N.Y.App. 1955)]

31.4 Shareholder Proposal The Medical Committee for Human Rights (Committee) is a nonprofit corporation orga-

nized to advance concerns for human life. Committee received a gift of shares of Dow Chemical (Dow) stock. Dow manufactured napalm, a chemical defoliant that was used during the Vietnam conflict. Committee objected to the sale of napalm by Dow primarily because of its concerns for human life. Committee owned sufficient shares for a long enough time to propose a shareholders' resolution as long as it met the other requirements to propose such a resolution. Committee proposed that the following resolution be included in the proxy materials circulated by management for the 1969 annual shareholders' meeting:

> RESOLVED, that the shareholders of the Dow Chemical Company request that the Board of Directors, in accordance with the law, consider the advisability of adopting a resolution setting forth an amendment to the composite certificate of incorporation of the Dow Chemical Company that the company shall not make napalm.

Dow's management refused to include the requested resolution in its proxy materials. Committee sued, alleging that its resolution met the requirements to be included in the proxy materials. Who wins? [*Medical Committee for Human Rights v. Securities and Exchange Commission*, 432 F.2d 659 (D.C.Cir. 1970)]

31.5 Merger During the last six months of 1980, the board of directors of Plant Industries, Inc. (Plant), under the guidance of Robert B. Bregman, the chief executive officer of the corporation, embarked on a course of action that resulted in the sale of several unprofitable subsidiaries. Bregman then engaged in a course of action to sell Plant National (Quebec) Ltd., a subsidiary that constituted Plant's entire Canadian operations. This was a profitable subsidiary that comprised over 50 percent of Plant's assets, sales, and profits. Do Plant's shareholders have to be accorded voting and appraisal rights regarding the sale of this subsidiary? [*Katz v. Bregman*, 431 A.2d 1274 (Del.Ch. 1981)]

31.6 Dissenting Shareholder Appraisal Rights Over a period of several years, the Curtiss-Wright Corporation (Curtiss-Wright) purchased 65 percent of the stock of Dorr-Oliver Incorporated (Dorr-Oliver). In early 1979, Curtiss-Wright's board of directors decided that a merger with Dorr-Oliver would be beneficial to Curtiss-Wright. The board voted to approve a merger of the two companies and to pay $23 per share to the stockholders of Dorr-Oliver. The Dorr-Oliver board and 80 percent of Dorr-Oliver's shareholders approved the merger. The merger became effective on May 31, 1979. John Bershad, a minority shareholder of Dorr-Oliver, voted against the merger, but thereafter tendered his 100 shares and received payment of $2,300. Bershad subsequently sued, alleging that the $23 per share paid to Dorr-Oliver shareholders was grossly inadequate. Can Bershad obtain minority shareholder appraisal rights? [*Bershad v. Curtiss-Wright Corporation*, 535 A.2d 840 (DE 1987)]

31.7 Fighting a Tender Offer On October 30, 1981, Mobil Corporation (Mobil) made a tender offer to purchase up to 40 million outstanding common shares of stock in Marathon Oil

Company (Marathon) for $85 per share in cash. It further stated its intentions to follow the purchase with a merger of the two companies. Mobil was primarily interested in acquiring Marathon's oil and mineral interests in certain properties, including the Yates Field. Marathon directors immediately held a board meeting and determined to find a white knight. Negotiations developed between Marathon and Untied States Steel Corporation (U.S. Steel). On November 18, 1981, Marathon and U.S. Steel entered into an agreement whereby U.S. Steel would make a tender offer for 30 million common shares of Marathon stock at $125 per share, to be followed by a merger of the two companies.

The Marathon-U.S. Steel agreement was subject to the following two conditions: (1) U.S. Steel was given an irrevocable option to purchase 10 million authorized but unissued shares of Marathon common stock for $90 per share (or 17 percent of Marthon's outstanding shares), and (2) U.S. Steel was given an option to purchase Marathon's interest in oil and mineral rights in Yates Field for $2.8 billion (Yates Field option). The latter option could be exercised only if U.S. Steel's offer did not succeed and if a third party gained control of Marathon. Evidence showed that Marathon's interest in the Yates Field was worth up to $3.6 billion. Marathon did not give Mobil either of these two options. Mobil sued, alleging that these two options violated Section 14(e) of the Williams Act. Who wins? [*Mobil Corporation v. Marathon Oil Company*, 669 F.2d 366 (6th Cir. 1981)]

31.8 Fighting a Tender Offer The Fruehauf Corporation (Fruehauf) is engaged in the manufacture of large trucks and industrial vehicles. The Edelman group (Edelman) made a cash tender offer for the shares of Fruehauf for $48.50 per share. The stock sold in the low $20-per-share range a few months earlier. Fruehauf's management decided to make a competing management-led leveraged buyout (MBO) tender offer for the company in conjunction with Merrill Lynch. The MBO would be funded using $375 million borrowed from Merrill Lynch, $375 million borrowed from Manufacturers Hanover Bank, and $100 million contributed by Fruehauf. Total equity contribution to the new company under the MBO would be only $25 million: $10 million to $15 million from management and the rest from Merrill Lynch. In return for their equity contributions, management would receive between 40 and 60 percent of the new company.

Fruehauf's management agreed to pay $30 million to Merrill Lynch for brokerage fees that Merrill Lynch could keep even if the deal did not go through. Management also agreed to a no-shop clause whereby they agreed not to seek a better deal with another bidder. Incumbent management received better information about the goings-on. They also gave themselves golden parachutes that would raise the money for management's equity position in the new company.

Edelman informed Fruehauf's management that it could top their bid, but Fruehauf's management did not give them the opportunity to present their offer. Management's offer was accepted. Edelman sued, seeking an injunction. Did Fruehauf's management violate the business judgment rule? [*Edelman v. Fruehauf Corporation*, 798 F.2d 882 (6th Cir. 1986)]

31.9 Poison Pill Defense Household International, Inc. (Household), is a diversified holding company with its principal subsidiaries engaged in financial services, transportation, and merchandising. On August 14, 1984, the board of directors of Household adopted a 48-page "Rights Plan" by a 14-to-2 vote. Basically, the plan provides that Household common stockholders are entitled to the issuance of one irrevocable right per common share if any party acquires 20 percent of Household's shares. The right permits Household shareholders to purchase $200 of the common stock of the tender offeror for $100. In essence, this forces any party interested in taking over Household to negotiate with Household's directors. Dyson-Kissner-Moran Corporation (DKM), which was interested in taking over Household, filed suit alleging that this flip-over rights plan violated the business judgment rule. Who wins? [*Moran v. Household International, Inc.*, 500 Ad.2d 1346 (DE 1985)]

31.10 State Antitakeover Statute The state of Illinois enacted a statute that protects certain defined "target companies" from unwanted takeovers. The protection extends to (1) corporations of which shareholders located in Illinois own 10 percent of a class of equity securities and (2) corporations that are incorporated in Illinois or have their principal place of business in the state. Tender offers for protected companies must be registered with the Illinois secretary of state 20 days before the proposed tender offer is made. The secretary may call a hearing at any time during the 20-day waiting period. The statute does not provide a deadline for when the hearing must be completed. The secretary may deny the tender offer if he finds that it is inequitable.

Chicago Rivet and Machine Co. (Chicago Rivet) is a publicly held Illinois corporation that is covered by the Illinois antitakeover statute. On July 19, 1979, MITE Corporation (MITE), a Delaware corporation, made a cash tender offer for all of the outstanding shares of Chicago Rivet. MITE did not comply with the Illinois Act and brought suit challenging the lawfulness of the state law. Is the Illinois antitakeover statute lawful? [*Edgar, Secretary of State of Illinois v. MITE Corporation*, 457 U.S. 624, 102 S.Ct. 2629 (1982)]

31.11 State Antitakeover Statute The state of Wisconsin enacted an antitakeover statute that protects corporations that are incorporated in Wisconsin and have their headquarters, substantial operations, or 10 percent of their shares of shareholders in the state. The statute prevents any party that acquires a 10 percent interest in a covered corporation from engaging in a business combination (e.g., merger) with the covered corporation for three years unless approval of the management is obtained in advance of the combination. Wisconsin firms cannot opt out of the law. This statute effectively eliminates hostile leveraged buyouts because buyers must rely on the assets and income of the target company to help pay off the debt incurred in effectuating the takeover.

Universal Foods (Universal) is a Wisconsin corporation covered by the statute. On December 1, 1988, Amanda Acquisition Corporation (Amanda) commenced a cash tender offer for up to 75 percent of the stock of Universal. Universal asserted the Wisconsin law. Is Wisconsin's antitakeover statute lawful? [*Amanda Acquisition Corporation v. Universal Foods*, 877 F.2d 496 (7th Cir. 1989), cert. denied 110 S.Ct. 367 (1989)]

BUSINESS ETHICS CASES

31.12 Business Ethics   MCA, Inc. (MCA), a corporate holding company, owned 92 percent of the stock of Universal Pictures Company (Universal) and 100 percent of the stock of Universal City Studios, Inc. (Universal City). On March 25, 1966, these two subsidiaries merged pursuant to Delaware's short-form merger statute. The minority shareholders of Universal were offered $75 per share for their shares. Francis I. Du Pont & Company and other minority shareholders (Plaintiffs) rejected the offer and then perfected their dissenting shareholder appraisal rights. On March 29, 1973, the appraiser filed a final report in which he found the value of Universal stock to be $91.47 per share. Both parties filed exceptions to this report.

The parties' ultimate disagreement is, of course, over the value of the stock. Plaintiffs submit that the true value is $131.89 per share; defendant says it is $52.36. The computations are as follows:

Plaintiffs

Value Factor	Value	Weight	Result
Earnings	$129.12	70%	$90.38
Market	144.36	20	28.87
Assets	126.46	10	12.64
Value per share			**$131.89**

Defendants

Value Factor	Value	Weight	Result
Earnings	$51.93	70%	$36.35
Dividends	41.66	20	8.33
Assets	76.77	10	7.68
Value per share			**$52.36**

Appraiser

Value Factor	Value	Weight	Result
Earnings	$92.89	80%	$74.31
Assets	85.82	20	17.16
Value per share			**$91.47**

Defendant takes exception to the appraiser's failure to find that, in the years prior to merger, the industry was declining and that Universal was ranked near its bottom. And it argues that Universal was in the business of producing and distributing feature motion pictures for theatrical exhibition. It contends that such business, generally, was in a severe decline at the time of merger and that Universal, in particular, was in a vulnerable position because it had failed to diversify, its feature films were of low commercial quality, and, unlike other motion picture companies, substantially all of its film library had already been committed to distributors for television exhibition. In short, defendant pictures Universal as a weak "wasting asset" corporation in a sick industry with poor prospects for revival.

The stockholders see a different company. They say that Universal's business was indeed the production and distribution of feature films, but not merely for theatrical exhibition. They argue that there was a dramatic increase in the television market for such feature films at the time of the merger. This new market, they contend, gave great new value to a fully amortized film library and significantly enhanced the value of Universal's current and future productions. They equate the television market to the acquisition of a new and highly profitable business whose earnings potential was just beginning to be realized at the time of the merger. Finally, say plaintiffs, the theatrical market itself was recovering in 1966. Thus, they paint the portrait of a well-situated corporation in a rejuvenated industry.

Did the parties act ethically arriving at their proposed value of the company? What is the value of the minority shareholders' shares of Universal Pictures Company? [*Francis I. Du Pont & Company v. Universal City Studios, Inc.*, 312 A.2d 344 (Del.Ch. 1973]

31.13 Business Ethics   Realist, Inc. (Realist), is a Delaware corporation that has its principal place of business in Wisconsin. In March 1988, Royal Business Group, Inc. (Royal), a New Hampshire corporation, acquired eight percent of the outstanding voting stock of Realist. Royal sent a series of letters to Realist declaring its intention to acquire all of Realist's outstanding shares at an above-market premium. Realist repulsed Royal's overtures. Unbeknownst to Royal, Realist began negotiations to acquire Ammann Laser Technik AG (Ammann), a Swiss-based company.

Royal instituted a proxy contest and nominated two candidates for the two Realist directorships to be filed at Realist's June 6, 1989, annual shareholders' meeting. Realist and Royal both submitted proxy statements to Realist's shareholders.

The insurgent Royal nominees prevailed. On June 30, 1989, Realist announced that it had acquired Ammann. This acquisition made Realist much less attractive as a takeover target. Royal immediately withdrew its offer to acquire Realist and sued Realist to recover the $350,000 it had spent in connection with the proxy contest. Royal alleged that Realist had engaged in fraud in violation of Section 14(a) of the Securities Exchange Act of 1934 by failing to disclose its secret negotiations with Ammann in its proxy materials. The basis of Royal's complaint was that if Realist had disclosed that it intended to acquire Ammann, Royal would not have engaged in the costly proxy contest. Is Realist liable to Royal? Did Realist act unethically in seeking to acquire Ammann to thwart Royal's takeover attempt? [*Royal Business Group, Inc. v. Realist, Inc.*, 933 F.2d 1056 (1st Cir. 1991)]

BRIEFING THE CASE WRITING ASSIGNMENT

Read the following case, which has been excerpted from the court's opinions. Review and brief the case.

Neal v. Alabama By-Products Corporation
No. 8282, 1990
Del. Ch. Lexis 127 (1990)
Court of Chancery of Delaware

Chandler, Vice Chancellor

Alabama By-Products Corporation (ABC) is a Delaware corporation engaged during the 1970s and 1980s (and for many years before that), primarily in three lines of business. It mined coal on a cost plus basis for Alabama Power Company (a major utility in Alabama); it mined coal for its own account from surface and underground mines that it owned; and it manufactured and sold foundry coke from a plant in Birmingham called the Tarrant plant. To a certain extent ABC was also engaged in the development and sale of timber and forestry products on lands it owned.

ABC's two classes of stock traded in the over-the-counter market and were not listed on an exchange. Trading history in the stock was sporadic, but shows that the average bid price between 1977 and 1984 ranged from $47 to $75 per share. Class A stock had voting rights, while class B stock did not. At all times relevant to this lawsuit, there were about 757,300 class A shares and 1,000,000 class B shares authorized, issued, and outstanding.

Drummond, an Alabama corporation, is also engaged in the mining and sale of coal in the state of Alabama. In 1977 it became interested in acquiring ABC. Between September 1977 and February 1978 Drummond acquired, in privately negotiated transactions, about 75,800 class A shares of ABC stock and 188,167 class B shares. Drummond also obtained a controlling interest in Alabama Chemical Products Company (ACPC), a holding company which at the time held 476,420 class A shares of ABC stock (about 63 percent of those outstanding). Drummond paid the equivalent of $110 per share of ABC stock in these transactions. The book value of ABC's common stock on December 31, 1977, was $55.47 per share. Drummond eventually caused the liquidation of ACPC, with the resulting distribution of the ABC class A stock to Drummond and other ACPC stockholders.

Drummond reconstituted ABC's board of directors in December 1977, replacing five of the nine ABC directors with Drummond designees. At all relevant times for purposes of this litigation, a majority of ABC's directors were also directors or executive officers of Drummond. Around the time that it gained control of ABC's board, Drummond created an executive committee consisting of Gary Neal Drummond, E. A. Drummond and the then current president of ABC. The executive committee had authority to act on behalf of ABC's board of directors. From its controlling position, Drummond caused ABC to lease some of its coal reserves to Drummond. Drummond also purchased ABC mined coal and resold it in certain markets.

In late December 1977 Drummond presented a merger proposal to ABC's board, proposing the acquisition of all outstanding shares not owned by Drummond. This proposal was later withdrawn. Three years later, in 1981, Drummond discussed with Goldman, Sachs, and Company (Goldman Sachs), its investment banker, the possibility of acquiring the remaining equity in ABC. Goldman Sachs recommended at the time that Drummond propose a cash merger at a minimum price of $85 per share. Nevertheless, Drummond decided not to pursue the acquisition at that time.

On March 17, 1983, Drummond again proposed a merger to ABC's board of directors, a proposal by which each share of ABC not owned by Drummond would have been converted into the right to receive $65 in cash and ABC would have become a wholly-owned subsidiary of Drummond. A special committee of ABC's board of directors (consisting of three ABC directors who were not directors or executive officers of Drummond) recommended the retention of the firm of Kidder, Peabody, and Company, Inc. (Kidder Peabody), to evaluate the 1983 merger proposal and to determine whether it was fair from a financial point of view to unaffiliated ABC shareholders. Kidder Peabody's report, submitted in September 1983, concluded that Drummond's $65 cash merger offer was not fair from a financial point of view to unaffiliated ABC shareholders. Drummond's 1983 proposal was later withdrawn.

Drummond acquired additional shares of ABC class A and class B stock in 1984 for $54.40 and $55 per share respectively. Although it was provided, in connection with the 1984 acquisitions, that additional payments would be made by Drummond if its board of directors formally approved a tender offer for shares or a merger with ABC within stipulated time limits, no tender offer or merger proposal was made during the time limits.

In December 1984 Drummond made a tender offer for any and all outstanding shares of class A and class B common stock of ABC at $75 per share. Neither Drummond nor ABC sought a fairness opinion from an independent investment banker or financial adviser with respect to the tender offer. Nor was a committee of outside ABC directors appointed to review or comment upon the fairness of the proposed transaction. ABC's board decided it would take no position with respect to the fairness of the tender offer price, leaving the ultimate determination to the judgment of the individual shareholder.

As a result of the tender offer, Drummond became the holder of more than 90 percent of ABC's outstanding and issued shares. Then, on August 13, 1985, Drummond effected a short-form merger under Delaware law, pursuant to which the minority shareholders were cashed out at $75.60 per share. This amount was determined by adopting the 1984 tender offer price ($75) and adding a $.60 quarterly dividend that had been missed in 1985.

Following the August 13, 1985 merger, certain minority shareholders perfected their appraisal rights pursuant to §262 of Title 8 of the Delaware Code. These minority shareholders own approximately 50,000 class A shares and 75,000 class B shares. Neal characterizes this proceeding as a two-pronged action in which separate claims for appraisal and for unfair dealing have been joined. Drummond, as successor to ABC, is the only necessary and appropriate defendant, say petitioners, as to both the unfair dealing claim and the appraisal claim.

Neal argues they have avoided the risk of double recovery by limiting the relief requested for the unfair dealing claim to (1) costs of the proceeding, (2) reasonable attorneys' fees and disbursements, and (3) expert witness fees incurred by petitioners as part of the appraisals action.

Neal also accuses Drummond of post-merger unfair dealing, complaining that Drummond's defense of the $75.60 merger price is based on contrived liabilities and transparent efforts to ascribe negative values to certain ABC assets, all of which were not disclosed to shareholders at the time of the merger. These allegedly manipulative tactics, added to the unfair dealing associated with the notice of merger and merger price, form the basis for petitioners' unfair dealing claim and, they insist, warrant an award of litigation costs.

Neal challenges the fairness of the merger price, noting that it was fixed unilaterally by Drummond without the benefit of independent expert opinion as to its fairness. They also point out that no committee, special or other-

wise, was appointed to review the fairness of the merger proposal, that the merger notice to stockholders failed to disclose certain allegedly material financial information, causing stockholders to make decisions with regard to accepting the merger price or seeking appraisal on the basis of very limited information about the assets and prospects of ABC.

Neal contends that ABC's fair value was $193.40 per share on August 13, 1985. That conclusion rests upon the testimony of their valuation expert, Mr. Kenneth McGraw, based in an analysis performed by Benchmark Valuation Consultants, a division of the accounting firm Peat Marwick Maine & Co. (Benchmark), which in turn was based in part on an analysis and valuation of ABC's coal reserves and coal mining operations by Dames & Moore, a firm with expertise in geologic, mining, and natural resource engineering.

McGraw testified that Benchmark valued ABC using three alternative methods: historical earnings, net asset value, and discounted cash flow. By the historical earnings approach, Benchmark arrived at a value of $166 per share of ABC stock. The net asset methodology resulted in a value of $205 per share. The discounted cash flow approach resulted in a valuation of $225 per share. Benchmark then applied a weighted average, assigning the greatest weight (40 percent) to the historical earnings and net asset value approaches and the lowest weight (20 percent) to the discounted cash flow methodology, to arrive at a valuation based on all three valuation methodologies, of $193.40 per share.

Respondents assert that the merger price was fair. The merger price, in fact, was extremely generous, because respondents contend that ABC's statutory fair value is only $64 per share, more than $11 less than Drummond paid in the merger. Respondents' valuation is based upon the testimony of their expert trial witnesses, Arnold Spangler, a general partner at Lazard Freres & Co. (Lazard) and Robert Wilken of Paul Weir Company (Weir) who estimated the company's coal reserves.

Lazard's valuation appears to have been based on a hybrid discounted cash flow and net asset methodology. The analysis was designed to predict the value of future cash flows from ABC's continuing operations, including ABC owned mines, power company mines, and the Tarrant coke plant over a 13 year period from 1985 through 1997. This period corresponded to either the life of a variety of ABC's long-term contracts or to the exhaustion of its coal reserves, leaving only its Tarrant coke operation viable in 1997. Lazard arrived at a net after tax cash flow that ABC's continuing operations were expected to generate from 1985 to 1997, to which Lazard applied a multiple of five against the 1997 projected net cash flow (the terminal value) arriving at a value for ABC's activities following the terminal year.

The contrasting opinions regarding ABC's value in August 1985 demonstrate how differently petitioners and respondents view the business prospects and asset valuations of ABC. These starkly contrasting views have been pre-sented to the Court through expert witnesses who have relied on complex business valuation methodologies. Although Benchmark relied on three different methodologies, there has been remarkably little disagreement over the legitimacy of the valuation techniques used by the parties in this case. Dispute has been over the assumptions on which the methodologies have been based as well as the underlying information supplied to the experts. With expert opinions arrayed on each side of widely divergent arguments about the worth of certain assets, or the scope of certain liabilities, the Court is forced to pick and choose among the competing contentions, in search of a reasonable, and fair, value. That is this Court's mandate: determine the fair value of the stock of ABC on August 13, 1985.

Both sides have relied on a discounted future returns model and a net asset model, with petitioners' expert also using a historical earnings analysis. Other valuation approaches, with equivalent theoretical legitimacy, could have been used. But I am satisfied that respondents discounted future cash flow methodology is the appropriate valuation model in this case, especially since it was also used by petitioners' expert.

The more difficult task is to move beyond the analytical framework in order to test the underlying assumptions about ABC that the experts poured into the valuation models. This is the heart of the matter, for, as one commentator has noted, methods of valuation, including a discounted cash flow analysis, are only as good as the inputs to the model. A valuation methodology can produce a correct answer for any type of input. So the relevant question is not how correct the resulting answer is, but how correct was the input or datum that produced the answer? Accordingly this Court must view the assumptions and underlying factual premises for the valuation methodology actually used by both respondents and petitioners. Not every assumption need be scrutinized, however, for the parties have managed to agree, despite their best efforts, on certain assumptions and facts. Serious disputes exist in about eight different areas. The four principal areas of disagreement concern the value of ABC's coal reserves, the value of ABC's investment in the VP-5 mine in Virginia, the amount of ABC's excess working capital and, finally, the EME report on the purported environmental liability at ABC's Tarrant coke plant. The Court is satisfied that respondents discounted future cash flow methodology is the appropriate valuation model in this case, especially since it was also used by petitioner's expert.

The fair value of the petitioners' shares subject to the Court's appraisal was $180.67 per share on August 13, 1985. Petitioners shall be entitled to simple interest upon that amount at a rate of $12\frac{1}{2}$ percent, payable from the date of the merger to the date of payment. The costs of this proceeding, other than expert witness costs and attorneys' fees, shall be assessed against the surviving corporation.

An Order consistent with this Memorandum Opinion has been entered.

ENDNOTES

1. 15 U.S.C. 78n(a).
2. Section 13(d) of the Securities Exchange Act of 1934 requires that any party which acquires 5 percent or more of any equity security of a company registered with the SEC must report the acquisition to the SEC and disclose its intentions regarding the acquisition. This is public information.
3. 15 U.S.C. 78n(e).
4. *Smith v. Van Gorkum*, 488 A.2d 858 (Del. 1985).
5. *Unocal Corporation v. Mesa Petroleum Company*, 493 A.2d 946 (DE 1985).

CHAPTER 32

Investor Protection and Online Securities Transactions

Fraud is infinite in variety; sometimes it is audacious and unblushing; sometimes it pays a sort of homage to virtue, and then it is modest and retiring; it would be honesty itself, if it could only afford it.

—Lord MacNaghten
Reddaway v. Banham (1896)

Chapter Objectives

After studying this chapter, you should be able to:

1. Describe the procedure for "going public" and how securities are registered with the Securities and Exchange Commission (SEC).

2. Describe the requirements for qualifying for private placement, intrastate, and small offering exemptions from registration.

3. Describe how to conduct an initial public offering over the Internet.

4. Define insider trading that violates Section 10(b) of the Securities Exchange Act of 1934.

5. Describe the liability of tippers and tippees for insider trading.

6. Explain how the SEC is prosecuting Internet stock frauds.

7. Describe the criminal liability and penalties for violating federal securities laws.

8. Describe short-swing profits that violate Section 16(b) of the Securities Exchange Act of 1934.

9. Describe the international enforcement of securities laws.

10. Describe commodities trading and apply the antifraud provision of the Commodity Exchange Act.

Chapter Contents

Prior to the 1920s and 1930s, the securities and commodities markets in this country were not regulated by the federal government. Securities and commodities were sold to investors with little, if any, disclosure. Fraud in these transactions was common.

Following the stock market crash of 1929, Congress enacted a series of statutes designed to regulate securities and commodities markets. The *Securities Act of 1933* requires disclosure by companies and others who wish to issue securities to the public. The *Securities Exchange Act of 1934* was enacted to prevent fraud in the subsequent trading of securities, including insider trading.

These federal and state statutes are designed to (1) require disclosure of information to investors and (2) prevent fraud. This chapter discusses federal and state securities laws and regulations that provide investor protection.

THE SECURITIES AND EXCHANGE COMMISSION (SEC)

Securities and Exchange Commission (SEC)

Federal administrative agency that is empowered to administer federal securities laws. The SEC can adopt rules and regulations to interpret and implement federal securities laws.

The Securities Exchange Act of 1934 created the **Securities and Exchange Commission (SEC)** and empowered it to administer federal securities laws. The SEC is an administrative agency composed of five members who are appointed by the President. The major responsibilities of the SEC are:

1. Adopting rules (also called regulations) that further the purpose of the federal securities statutes. These rules have the force of law.
2. Investigating alleged securities violations and bringing enforcement actions against suspected violators. This may include a recommendation of criminal prosecution. Criminal prosecutions of violations of federal securities laws are brought by the U.S. Department of Justice.
3. Regulating the activities of securities brokers and advisors. This includes registering brokers and advisors and taking enforcement action against those who violate securities laws.

DEFINITION OF A SECURITY

security

(1) An interest or instrument that is common stock, preferred stock, a bond, a debenture, or a warrant, (2) an interest or instrument that is expressly mentioned in securities acts, and (3) an investment contract.

A **security** must exist before securities laws apply. Securities are defined as:

1. Interests or instruments that are commonly known as securities (e.g., common stock, preferred stock, bonds, debentures, and warrants).
2. Interests or instruments that are expressly mentioned in securities acts (e.g., preorganization subscription agreements, interests in oil, gas, and mineral rights; and deposit receipts for foreign securities).
3. Investment contracts, that is, any contract whereby an investor invests money or other consideration in a common enterprise and expects to make a profit off the significant efforts of others. Limited partnership interests, pyramid sales schemes, and investments in farm animals accompanied by care agreements have been found to be securities under this test, which is known as the *Howery test*.[1]

 *Landmark Law*

THE SECURITIES ACT OF 1933

The **Securities Act of 1933** primarily regulates the issuance of securities by a corporation, a general or limited partnership, an unincorporated association, or an individual. Unless a security or transaction qualifies for an exemption, Section 5 of the Securities Act of 1933 requires securities offered to the public through the use of the mails or any facility of interstate commerce to be *registered* with the SEC by means of a registration statement and an accompanying prospectus.

*T*HE SECURITIES ACT OF 1933—REGISTRATION OF SECURITIES

Registration Statement

A covered issuer must file a written **registration statement** with the SEC. The issuer's lawyer normally prepares the statement with the help of the issuer's management, accountants, and underwriters.

A registration statement must contain descriptions of (1) the securities being offered for sale, (2) the registrant's business, (3) the management of the registrant, including compensation, stock options and benefits, and material transactions with the registrant, (4) pending litigation, (5) how the proceeds from the offering will be used, (6) government regulation, (7) the degree of competition in the industry, and (8) any special risk factors. In addition, the registration statement must be accompanied by financial statements as certified by certified public accountants.

Registration statements usually become effective 20 business days after they are filed unless the SEC requires additional information to be disclosed. A new 20-day period begins each time the registration statement is amended. At the registrant's request, the SEC may "accelerate" the *effective date* (i.e., not require the registrant to wait 20 days after the last amendment is filed).

The SEC does not pass upon the merits of the securities offered. It decides only whether the issuer has met the disclosure requirements.

Prospectus

The **prospectus** is a written disclosure document that must be submitted to the SEC along with the registration statement. Much of the information included in the prospectus can be found in the registration statement. The prospectus is used as a selling tool by the issuer. It is provided to prospective investors to enable them to evaluate the financial risk of the investment.

A prospectus must contain the following language in capital letters and boldface (usually red) type:

> ***THESE SECURITIES HAVE NOT BEEN APPROVED OR DISAPPROVED BY THE SECURITIES AND EXCHANGE COMMISSION OR ANY STATE SECURITIES COMMISSION NOR HAS THE SECURITIES AND EXCHANGE COMMISSION OR ANY STATE SECURITIES COMMISSION PASSED UPON THE ACCURACY OR ADEQUACY OF THIS PROSPECTUS. ANY REPRESENTATION TO THE CONTRARY IS A CRIMINAL OFFENSE.***

Securities Act of 1933

A federal statute that primarily regulates the issuance of securities by corporations, partnerships, associations, and individuals.

Business Brief

Section 5 of the Securities Act of 1933 requires an issuer to register securities with the SEC before they can be sold to the public.

registration statement

Document that an issuer of securities files with the SEC that contains required information about the issuer, the securities to be issued, and other relevant information.

Business Brief

The SEC does not pass upon the merits of the registered securities

prospectus

A written disclosure document that must be submitted to the SEC along with the registration statement and given to prospective purchasers of the securities.

Business Brief

In 1995, Netscape, Inc., went public by issuing shares of stock to investors after registering the securities with the SEC. Netscape's stock price went from $28 to $75 on its first day of trading as a public company.

Contemporary Business Environment

SECURITIES OFFERINGS MUST BE WRITTEN IN PLAIN ENGLISH

Nonlawyers have always been frustrated by the legalese used by lawyers in contracts, court documents, and regulatory disclosures. No greater place has arcane legal language shown up than in prospectuses offering securities for sale to the public. These documents, which are supposed to provide relevant information to potential investors before they invest in company stock and securities, are usually barely skimmed, let alone read, by potential investors.

The Securities and Exchange Commission (SEC) decided to change this practice in 1998, when it adopted a "plain English" rule for securities offerings. Under this new rule, issuers of securities must use plain English language on the cover page, in the summary, and in the risk factor sections of their prospectuses. Issuers must now use

- Active voice
- Short sentences
- "Everyday" words
- Bullet lists for complex information
- No legal jargon or highly technical terms
- No multiple negatives

The plain English rule will require a major cultural change by issuers, underwriters, and securities lawyers who are used to using long, complicated, and confusing language. The SEC has stated that it will not be the "grammar police," but will instead focus on the clarity of disclosures to potential investors by issuers. The SEC hopes that its new rule will encourage issuers to use plain English throughout the entire prospectus. [Rule 421 (d) of Regulation C].

Limitations on Activities During the Registration Process

Section 5 of the Securities Act of 1933 limits the types of activities that an issuer, an underwriter, and a dealer may engage in during the registration process. These limitations are divided into three time periods: (1) the prefiling period, (2) the waiting period, and (3) the posteffective period.

prefiling period

A period of time that begins when the issuer first contemplates issuing the securities and ends when the registration statement is filed. The issuer may not *condition* the market during this period.

The Prefiling Period The **prefiling period** begins when the issuer first contemplates issuing the securities and ends when the registration statement is filed. During this time, the issuer cannot either sell or offer to sell the securities. The issuer also cannot *condition the market* for the upcoming securities offering. This rule makes it illegal for an issuer to engage in a public relations campaign (e.g., newspaper and magazine articles and advertisements) that touts the prospects of the company and the planned securities issue. However, sending annual reports to shareholders and making public announcements of factual matters (such as the settlement of a strike) are permissible because they are considered normal corporate disclosures.

waiting period

A period of time that begins when the registration statement is filed with the SEC and continues until the registration statement is declared effective. Only certain activities are permissible during the waiting period.

The Waiting Period The **waiting period** begins when the registration statement is filed with the SEC and continues until the registration statement is declared effective.

The issuer is encouraged to condition the market during this time. Thus, the issuer may (1) make oral offers to sell (including face-to-face and telephone conversations), (2) distribute a *preliminary prospectus* (usually called a red herring), which contains most of the information to be contained in the final prospectus except for price, (3) distribute a *summary prospectus*, which is a summary of the important terms contained in the prospectus, and (4) publish *tombstone ads* in newspapers and other publications. Unapproved writings (which are considered illegal offers to sell) as well as actual sales are prohibited during the waiting period.

posteffective period

The period of time that begins when the registration statement becomes effective and runs until the issuer either sells all of the offered securities or withdraws them from sale.

final prospectus

A final version of the prospectus that must be delivered by the issuer to the investor prior to or at the time of confirming a sale or sending a security to a purchaser.

The Posteffective Period The **posteffective period** begins when the registration statement becomes effective and runs until the issuer either sells all of the offered securities or withdraws them from sale. Thus, the issuer and its underwriter and dealers may close the offers received prior to the effective date and solicit new offers and sales.

Prior to or at the time of confirming a sale or sending a security to a purchaser, the issuer (or its representative) must deliver a **final prospectus** (also called a **statutory prospectus**) to the investor. Failure to do so is a violation of Section 5. Tombstone ads are often used during this period.

If an issuer violates any of the prohibitions on activities during these periods, the investor may rescind his or her purchase. If an underwriter or dealer violates any of these prohibitions, the SEC may issue sanctions, including the suspension of securities licenses.

E-Commerce & Information Technology

COMPANY GOES PUBLIC OVER THE INTERNET

The Securities and Exchange (SEC) permits companies to issue securities over the Internet. The same federal securities laws that regulate the traditional issuance of securities also apply to the issuance of securities using the Internet. One such company's Internet IPO appears below.

(Sidebar, rotated text:) The information in this prospectus is not complete and may be changed. We may not sell these securities until the registration statement filed with the Securities and Exchange Commission is effective. This prospectus is not an offer to sell these securities and is not soliciting an offer to buy these securities in any state where the offer or sale is not permitted.

SUBJECT TO COMPLETION, DATED DECEMBER 21, 2000

PEET'S COFFEE & TEA, INC.

3,300,000 Shares
of Common Stock

This is our initial public offering and no public market currently exists for our shares. We expect that the public offering price will be between $10.00 and $14.00 per share. This price may not reflect the market price of our shares after this offering.

THE OFFERING	PER SHARE	TOTAL
Public Offering Price	$	$
Underwriting Discount	$	$
Proceeds to Peet's	$	$
Proceeds to Selling Shareholders	$	$

Of the 3,300,000 shares being offered, we are selling 2,500,000 shares and the selling shareholders identified in this prospectus are selling 800,000 shares. We will not receive any of the proceeds from the sale of shares by the selling shareholders. We have granted the underwriters the right to purchase up to 182,623 additional shares from us and 312,377 additional shares from the selling shareholders within 30 days to cover any over-allotments. The underwriters expect to deliver shares of common stock to purchasers on   , 2001.

Proposed Nasdaq National Market Symbol: PEET

OPENIPO: The method of distribution being used by the underwriters in this offering differs somewhat from that traditionally employed in firm commitment underwritten public offerings. In particular, the public offering price and allocation of shares will be determined primarily by an auction process conducted by the underwriters and other securities dealers participating in this offering. A more detailed description of this process, known as an OpenIPO, is included in "Plan of Distribution."

THIS OFFERING INVOLVES A HIGH DEGREE OF RISK. YOU SHOULD PURCHASE SHARES ONLY IF YOU CAN AFFORD A COMPLETE LOSS OF YOUR INVESTMENT. SEE "RISK FACTORS" BEGINNING ON PAGE 5.

NEITHER THE SECURITIES AND EXCHANGE COMMISSION NOR ANY STATE SECURITIES COMMISSION HAS APPROVED OR DISAPPROVED OF THESE SECURITIES OR DETERMINED IF THIS PROSPECTUS IS TRUTHFUL OR COMPLETE. ANY REPRESENTATION TO THE CONTRARY IS A CRIMINAL OFFENSE.

WR HAMBRECHT + CO

Pacific Growth Equities, Inc.

The date of this prospectus is   , 2001

Regulation A Offerings

Regulation A permits an issuer to sell up to $5 million of securities during a 12-month period pursuant to a simplified registration process. Such offerings may have an unlimited number of purchasers who do not have to be sophisticated investors.

This regulation also stipulates that offerings exceeding $100,000 must file an *offering statement* with the SEC. The offering statement requires less disclosure than does a registration statement and is less costly to prepare. Investors must be provided an offering circular prior to the purchase of securities. There are no resale restrictions on the securities.

Regulation A

A regulation that permits the issuer to sell securities pursuant to a simplified registration process.

SECURITIES EXEMPT FROM REGISTRATION

Certain *securities* are exempt from registration. Once a security is exempt, it is exempt forever. It does not matter how many times the security is transferred. Exempt securities include:

1. Securities issued by any government in the United States (e.g., municipal bonds issued by city governments)
2. Short-term notes and drafts that have a maturity date that does not exceed nine months (e.g., commercial paper issued by corporations)
3. Securities issued by nonprofit issuers, such as religious institutions, charitable institutions, and colleges and universities
4. Securities of financial institutions (e.g., banks and savings associations) that are regulated by the appropriate banking authorities
5. Securities issued by common carriers (railroads and trucking companies) that are regulated by the Interstate Commerce Commission (ICC)
6. Insurance and annuity contracts issued by insurance companies
7. Stock dividends and stock splits
8. Securities issued in a corporate reorganization where one security is exchanged for another security

Contemporary Business Environment

SECURITIES INVESTOR PROTECTION CORPORATION (SIPC)

Millions of investors use securities brokerage firms to buy, sell, and hold their securities in "street name." What happens if a securities firm that holds these securities fails? The securities are insured by the **Securities Investor Protection Corporation (SIPC),** a private insurance company that is funded by annual assessments paid by securities firms.

Some vital statistics and information that investors should know about the SIPC insurance are:

• The SIPC provides insurance coverage of up to $500,000 per customer.

• Of the $500,000 coverage, only $100,000 of cash is covered per customer.
• Unlike deposit insurance for savings and checking accounts at banks, the SIPC is not backed by the full faith and credit of the U.S. government.
• The SIPC currently has under $1 billion in its coffers and an additional $500-million line of credit with banks it can draw on. This is sufficient to cover the failure of many small brokerage firms but is inadequate to cover the failure of large brokerage firms.

TRANSACTIONS EXEMPT FROM REGISTRATION

Certain *transactions* in securities are exempt from registration. Exempt transactions are subject to the antifraud provisions of the federal securities laws. Therefore, the issuer must provide investors with adequate information—including annual reports, quarterly reports, proxy statements, financial statements, and so on—even though a registration statement is not required. The exempt transactions are discussed in the paragraphs that follow.

Nonissuer Exemption

Nonissuers, such as average investors, do not have to file a registration statement prior to reselling securities they have purchased. This is because the Securities Act of 1933 exempts securities transactions not made by an issuer, an underwriter, or a dealer from registration.[2] For example, an investor who owns shares of IBM can resell these shares to another at any time without having to register with the SEC.

Intrastate Offerings

The purpose of the **intrastate offerings exemption** is to permit local business to raise capital from local investors to be used in the local economy without the need to register with the SEC.[3] There is no limit on the dollar amount of capital that can be raised pursuant to an intrastate offering exemption. An issuer can qualify for this exemption in only one state.

Three requirements must be met to qualify for this exemption:[4]

1. The issuer must be a resident of the state for which the exemption is claimed. A corporation is a resident of the state in which it is incorporated.
2. The issuer must be doing business in that state. This requires that 80 percent of the issuer's assets are located in the state, 80 percent of its gross revenues are derived from the state, its principal office is located in the state, and 80 percent of the proceeds of the offering will be used in the state.
3. The purchasers of the securities all must be residents of that state.

Private Placements

An issue of securities that does not involve a public offering is exempt from the registration requirement.[5] This exemption—known as the **private placement exemption**—allows issuers to raise capital from an unlimited number of accredited investors without having to register the offering with the SEC.[6] There is no dollar limit on the amount of securities that can be sold pursuant to this exemption.

An *accredited investor* may be:[7]

1. Any natural person (including spouse) who has a net worth of at least $1 million
2. Any natural person who has had an annual income of at least $200,000 for the previous two years and reasonably expects to make $200,000 income in the current year
3. Any corporation, partnership, or business trust with total assets in excess of $5 million
4. Insiders of the issuers, such as executive officers and directors of corporate issuers and general partners of partnership issuers
5. Certain institutional investors, such as registered investment companies, pension plans, colleges and universities, and the like

No more than 35 *nonaccredited investors* may purchase securities pursuant to a private placement exemption. Nonaccredited investors must be sophisticated investors, however, either through their own experience and education or through representatives (such as accountants, lawyers, and business managers). General selling efforts, such as advertising to the public, are not permitted.

Small Offerings

Securities offerings that do not exceed a certain dollar amount are exempt from registration.[8] Rule 504 exempts the sale of securities not exceeding $1 million during a 12-month period from registration. The securities may be sold to an unlimited number of accredited and unaccredited investors, but general selling efforts to the public are not permitted. This is called the **small offering exemption**.

Resale Restrictions

Certain *resale restrictions* are placed on securities issued pursuant to exemptions from registration. These restrictions are discussed in the following paragraphs.

Restricted Securities   Securities sold pursuant to the intrastate, private placement, or small offering exemptions are called **restricted securities** because they cannot be resold for a limited period of time after their initial issue. The following restrictions apply:

- Rule 147 stipulates that securities sold pursuant to an intrastate offering exemption cannot be sold to nonresidents for a period of nine months.
- Rule 144 provides that securities sold pursuant to the private placement or small offering exemption must be held for one year from the date when the securities are last sold by the issuer. After that time, investors may sell the greater of (1) one percent of the outstanding securities of the issuer or (2) the average weekly volume of trading in the securities (i.e., the four-week moving average) in any three-month period. Information about the issuer must be available to the public. Generally, all restrictions are lifted after two years.

private placement exemption

An exemption from registration that permits issuers to raise capital from an unlimited number of accredited investors and no more than 35 nonaccredited investors without having to register the offering with the SEC.

Business Brief

Up to 35 nonaccredited investors may purchase securities pursuant to a private placement exemption. They must be sophisticated investors through their own experience and education or through representatives.

small offering exemption

For the sale of securities not exceeding $1 million during a 12-month period.

restricted securities

Securities that were issued for investment purposes pursuant to the intrastate, private placement, or small offering exemption.

Ethics Brief

The issuer must take certain actions to ensure that restricted securities are not sold in violation of the restrictions imposed by Rules 144 and 147.

Preventing Transfer of Restricted Securities   To protect the nontransferability of restricted shares, the issuer must

1. Require the investors to sign an *affidavit* stating that they are buying the securities for investment, acknowledging that they are purchasing restricted securities, and promising not to transfer the shares in violation of the restriction.
2. Place a *legend* on the stock certificate describing the restriction.
3. Notify the *transfer agent* not to record a transfer of the securities that would violate the restriction.

If the issuer has taken these precautions, it will not lose its exemption from registration even if isolated transfers of stock occur in violation of the restricted periods. If these precautions are not taken, the issuer may lose its exemption from registration. In that event, it has sold unregistered securities in violation of Section 5, permitting all purchasers to rescind their purchases of the securities.

Rule 144A

Business Brief

To increase the liquidity of the registered securities, the SEC adopted Rule 144A in 1990 that permits "qualified institutional investors" to buy unregistered securities without being subject to the holding periods of Rule 144.

To establish a more liquid and efficient secondary market in unregistered securities, the SEC adopted Rule 144A in 1990. This rule permits "qualified institutional investors"—defined as institutions that own and invest at least $100 million in securities—to buy unregistered securities without being subject to the holding periods of Rule 144. This rule is designed to create an institutional market in unregistered securities as well as to permit foreign issuers to raise capital in this country from sophisticated investors without making registration process disclosures.

Integration of Exempt Offerings

integration of offerings

When separate offerings that might otherwise qualify for individual exemptions are combined if they are really part of one large offering.

Separate offerings that qualify for individual exemptions from registration will be **integrated** if they are really part of one large offering. This larger offering must then be examined to see if it qualifies for an exemption from registration. In deciding whether to integrate offerings, the SEC and the courts examine whether the offerings (1) are part of a single plan of financing, (2) involve the issuance of the same class of securities, (3) are made about the same time, (4) receive the same consideration, and (5) are made for the same general purpose.

Safe harbor rules protect securities offerings made more than six months before or after the current offering from being integrated with the present offering.[9] This creates a 12-month period outside of which none of the securities offering will be integrated with the current offering.

Ethics Brief

If offerings are integrated and the combined offering does not qualify for an exemption, the issuer has illegally sold unregistered securities. This subjects the issuer to certain civil fines and criminal penalties. In addition, purchasers may *rescind* their purchases and recover the price they paid.

Consider This Example   On January 1, the ABC Corporation issued $4 million of common stock for cash to 25 accredited and 15 sophisticated but nonaccredited investors, some of whom are located out of state. The proceeds are to be used for working capital. This offering qualifies for the private placement exemption.

On April 1 of the same year, ABC Corporation issued another $4 million of common stock for cash to 25 accredited and 25 sophisticated but nonaccredited investors, some of whom are located out of state. The proceeds are to be used for working capital. Again, this individual offering qualifies for the private placement exemption.

These offerings must be integrated because they occur within six months of each other, they are the same security, the consideration is the same, and the proceeds from both offerings are used for the same purpose. The integrated offering does not qualify for an exemption from registration. There are 40 nonaccredited investors, too many to qualify for the private placement exemption. The integrated offering does not qualify for the intrastate exemption (there are out-of-state investors) or for the Rule 504 small offering exemption (the securities issued exceed $1 million). As a remedy, the investors can rescind their purchases because there has been a violation of Section 5 of the 1933 act.

Entrepreneur and the Law

SCOR SIMPLIFIES STOCK OFFERINGS BY SMALL COMPANIES

Like large corporations, small businesses often need to raise capital and must find public investors to buy their company's stock. Unlike large corporations, however, small businesses often do not have the money or resources to hire lawyers, investment bankers, CPAs, and other professionals or to pay the printing and other costs associated with an initial public offering (IPO). Also, these small businesses often cannot find enough qualified investors or meet other requirements necessary to qualify for a private placement or other exemptions from registration. And in most cases, the small business only needs to raise a small amount of capital through a public offering.

In 1992, after years of investigation, the Securities and Exchange Commission (SEC) amended its regulations to facilitate capital raising by small businesses. As part of this small business initiative, the SEC amended Regulation A by adopting the **Small Corporate Offering Registration Form (SCOR)**. The SCOR form—Form U-7—is a question-and-answer disclosure form that small businesses can complete and file with the SEC if they plan on raising $1 million or less from the public issue of securities. An issuer must answer the questions on Form U-7, which then becomes the offering circular that must be given to prospective investors.

Form U-7 simplifies and demystifies the registration process. The questions are so clearly and specifically drawn that they can be answered by the issuer without the help of an expensive securities lawyer. The SCOR questions require the issuer to develop a business plan that states specific company goals and how it plans to reach them. An overriding concern of SCOR is uniformity. Form U-7 is designed to replace the myriad of forms previously required by state laws for securities offerings that are exempt from complete SEC registration requirements, but it must comply with state securities laws. Many states have elected to allow SCOR Form U-7 to replace their disclosure requirements. SCOR is limited to domestic businesses and cannot be used by partnerships, foreign corporations, or companies involved in petroleum exploration or mining. The SCOR offering cannot exceed $1 million and the offering price of the common stock or its equivalent may not be less than $5.00 per share. SCOR offerings are a welcomed addition for entrepreneur-owners who want to raise money through a small public offering.

LIABILITY PROVISIONS OF THE SECURITIES ACT OF 1933

Violations of the Securities Act of 1933 may result in various penalties and remedies against the perpetrator. These penalties and remedies are discussed in the following paragraphs.

Criminal Liability

Section 24 of the 1933 act imposes *criminal liability* on any person who *willfully* violates either the act or the rules and regulations adopted thereunder.[10] The maximum penalty is five years' imprisonment. Criminal actions are brought by the Justice Department.

Section 24

A provision of the Securities Act of 1933 that imposes criminal liability on any person who willfully violates the 1933 act or the rules or regulations adopted thereunder.

SEC Actions

The SEC may (1) issue a *consent order* whereby a defendant agrees not to violate securities laws in the future but does not admit to violating securities laws in the past, (2) bring an action in federal district court to obtain an *injunction*, or (3) request the court to grant ancillary relief, such as *disgorgement of profits* by the defendant.

Private Actions

Private parties who have been injured by violations of the 1933 act have recourse against the violator, as discussed in the following paragraphs.

Section 12 **Section 12** of the 1933 act imposes *civil liability* on any person who violates the provisions of Section 5 of the act. Violations include selling securities pursuant to an unwarranted exemption and making misrepresentations concerning the offer or sale of securities. The purchaser's remedy for a violation of Section 12 is either to rescind the purchase or to sue for damages.

Section 12

A provision of the Securities Act of 1933 that imposes civil liability on any person who violates the provisions of Section 5 of the act.

Section 11

A provision of the Securities Act of 1933 that imposes civil liability on persons who intentionally defraud investors by making misrepresentations or omissions of material facts in the registration statement or who are negligent for not discovering the fraud.

due diligence defense

A defense to a Section 11 action that, if proven, makes the defendant not liable.

Section 11   **Section 11** of the 1933 act provides for civil liability for damages when a registration statement on its effective date misstates or omits a material fact. Liability under Section 11 is imposed on those who (1) intentionally defraud investors or (2) are negligent in not discovering the fraud. Thus, the issuer, certain corporate officers (chief executive officer, chief financial officer, chief accounting officer), directors, signers of the registration statement, underwriters, and experts (accountants who certify financial statements and lawyers who issue legal opinions that are included in a registration statement) may be liable.

All defendants except the issuer may assert a **due diligence defense** against the imposition of Section 11 liability. If this defense is proven, the defendant is not liable. To establish a due diligence defense, the defendant must prove that after reasonable investigation, he or she had reasonable grounds to believe and did believe that, at the time the registration statement became effective, the statements contained therein were true and that there was no omission of material facts.

Case 32.1 is a classic case where the court imposed civil liability on defendants who failed to prove their due diligence defense.

Escott v. BarChris Construction Corp.
283 F. Supp. 643 (1968)
United States District Court, Southern District of New York

CASE 32.1

BACKGROUND AND FACTS

In 1961, BarChris Construction Corp. (BarChris), a company primarily engaged in the construction and sale of bowling alleys, was in need of additional financing. To raise working capital, BarChris decided to issue debentures to investors. A registration statement, including a prospectus, was filed with the SEC on March 30, 1961. After two amendments, the registration statement became effective May 16, 1961. Peat, Marwick, Mitchell & Co. (Peat, Marwick) audited the financial statements of the company that were included in the registration statement and prospectus. The debentures were sold by May 24, 1961. Investors were provided a final prospectus concerning the debentures. Unbeknown to the investors, however, the registration statement and prospectus contained the following material misrepresentations and omissions of material fact:

1. Current assets on the 1960 balance sheet were overstated by $609,689 (15 percent)
2. Contingent liabilities of April 30, 1961, were understated by $618,853 (42 percent).
3. Sales for the quarter ending March 31, 1961, were overstated by $519,810 (32 percent).
4. Gross profits for the quarter ending March 31, 1961, were overstated by $230,755 (92 percent).
5. Backlog of orders as of March 31, 1961, was overstated by $4,490,000 (186 percent).
6. Loans to officers of BarChris of $386,615 were not disclosed.
7. Customer delinquencies and BarChris's potential liability thereto of $1,350,000 were not disclosed.
8. The use of the proceeds of the debentures to pay old debts was not disclosed.

In 1962, BarChris was failing financially, and on October 29, 1962, it filed a petition for protection to be reorganized under federal bankruptcy law. On November 1, 1962, BarChris defaulted on interest payments due to be paid on the debentures to investors. Barry Escott and other purchasers of the debentures brought this civil action against executive officers, directors, and the outside accountants of BarChris. The plaintiffs alleged that the defendants had violated Section 11 of the Securities Act of 1933 by submitting misrepresentations and omissions of material facts in the registration statement filed with the SEC.

ISSUE

Are the defendants liable for violating Section 11 or have they proved their due diligence defense?

COURT'S REASONING

The district court addressed the liability of the individual defendants and the accounting firm, as follows.

Russo—Russo was, to all intents and purposes, the chief executive officer of BarChris. He was a member of the executive committee and was familiar with all aspects of the business. He was thoroughly aware of BarChris's stringent financial condition in May 1961. In short, Russo knew all the relevant facts. He could not have believed that there were no untrue statements or material omissions in the prospectus. Russo has no due diligence defenses.

Vitolo and Pugliese—Vitolo and Pugliese were the founders of the business. Vitolo was president and Pugliese was vice president. Vitolo and Pugliese each are men of limited education. It is not hard to believe that for them the prospectus was difficult reading, if indeed they read it at all. But whether it was read or not is irrelevant. The liability of a director who signs a registration statement does not depend on whether or not he or she read it or, if he or she did, whether or not he understood what he or she was reading. And in any case, there is nothing to show that they made any investigation of anything that they may not have known about or understood. They have not proved their due diligence defenses.

Trilling—Trilling was BarChris's controller. He signed the registration statement in that capacity, although he was not a director. He was a comparatively minor figure in BarChris. He was not considered an executive officer. Trilling may well have been unaware of several of the inaccuracies in the prospectus, but he must have known of some of them. As a financial officer, he was familiar with BarChris's finances and with its books of account. Trilling did not sustain the burden of proving his due diligence defenses.

Auslander—Auslander was an "outside" director, that is, one who was not an officer of BarChris. He was chairman of the board of Valley Stream National Bank in Valley Stream, Long Island. In February 1961, Vitolo asked him to become a director of BarChris. Vitolo gave him an enthusiastic account of BarChris's progress and prospects. As an inducement, Vitolo said that when BarChris received the proceeds of a forthcoming issue of securities, it would deposit $1 million in Auslander's bank. Auslander was elected a director on April 17, 1961. The registration statement in its original form had already been filed, of course, without his signature. On May 10, 1961, he signed a signature page for the first amendment to the registration statement that was filed with the SEC on May 11, 1961. This page was a separate sheet without any document attached. Auslander did not know that it was a signature page for a registration statement. He vaguely understood that it was something "for the SEC." Auslander never saw a copy of the registration statement in its final form. Section 11 imposes liability upon a director no matter how new he is. Auslander has not established his due diligence defenses.

Peat, Marwick—Peat, Marwick's work was in general charge of a member of the firm, Cummings, and more immediately in charge of Peat, Marwick's manager, Logan. Most of the actual work was performed by a senior accountant, Berardi, who had junior assistants, one of whom was Kennedy. Berardi was then about 30 years old. He was not yet a CPA. He had had no previous experience with the bowling industry. This work was his first job as a senior accountant. He could hardly have been given a more difficult assignment.

First and foremost is Berardi's failure to discover that Capital Lanes had not been sold. This error affected both the sales figure and the liability side of the balance sheet. Berardi erred in computing the contingent liabilities. Berardi did not make a reasonable investigation in this instance. The purpose of reviewing events subsequent to the date of a certified balance sheet (referred to as an S-1 review when made with reference to a registration statement) is to ascertain whether any material change has occurred in the company's financial position that should be disclosed in order to prevent the balance sheet figures from being misleading. The scope of such a review, under generally accepted auditing standards, is limited. It does not amount to a complete audit. Berardi made the S-1 review in May 1961. He devoted a little over two days to it, a total of $20\frac{1}{2}$ hours. He did not discover any of the errors or omissions pertaining to the state of affairs in 1961, of which all were material. Apparently the only BarChris officer with whom Berardi communicated was Trilling. He could not recall making any inquiries of Russo, Vitolo, or Pugliese. In conducting the S-1 review, Berardi did not examine any important financial records other than the trial balance. As to minutes, he read only the board of directors' minutes of BarChris. He did not read such minutes as there were of the executive committee. He did not read the minutes of any subsidiary. He asked questions, he got answers that he considered satisfactory, and he did nothing to verify them.

Berardi had no conception of how tight the cash position was. He did not discover that BarChris was holding up checks in substantial amounts because there was no money in the bank to cover them. He did not know of the officers' loans. Because he never read the prospectus, he was not even aware that there had ever been any problem about loans. There had been a material change for the worse in BarChris's financial position. That change was sufficiently serious so that the failure to disclose it made the 1960 figures misleading. Berardi did not discover it. As far as results were concerned, his S-1 review was useless.

Accountants should not be held to a standard higher than that recognized in their profession. Berardi's review did not come up to that standard. He did not take some of the steps that Peat, Marwick's written program prescribed. He did not spend an adequate amount of time on a task of this magnitude. Most important of all, he was too easily satisfied with glib answers to his inquiries. There were enough danger signals to require some further investigation on his part. Generally accepted accounting standards required such further investigation under these circumstances. It is not always sufficient merely to ask questions. Here, again, the burden of proof is on Peat, Marwick. That burden has not been satisfied. Peat, Marwick has not established its due diligence defense.

DECISION AND REMEDY

The district court held that the defendants had failed to prove their due diligence defenses.

Case Questions

Critical Legal Thinking Should defendants in a Section 11 lawsuit be permitted to prove a due diligence defense to the imposition of liability? Or should liability be strictly imposed?

Business Ethics Who do you think committed the fraud in this case? Did any of the other defendants act unethically?

Contemporary Business Who do you think bore the burden of paying the judgment in this case?

Entrepreneur and the Law

Two New IPO Billionaires Made on the Same Day

On October 19, 1999, the *Forbes* 400 richest people in the world list had two new members, both the recipients of paper money made when their respective companies went public. The first was Martha Stewart, the "Miss Manners" of the late 1990s and early 2000s, who had propelled herself centerstage into America's conscience as the guru of good taste. The one-time stockbroker, turned catering business owner, turned magazine editor, started her empire by writing the 1982 best-selling book *Entertaining*. She then wrote books on gracious living, cooking, hosting parties, and gardening and created a media empire that includes radio and television shows and a syndicated newspaper column. She has nurtured a superbrand name that now appears on Kmart towels, bedspreads, paints, garden tools, and almost anything used in and around the house. Her company, **Martha Stewart Living Omnimedia**, went public at $18 per share, and on the first day of trading rose to $52 before closing the day at $35. This initial public offering (IPO) of $1.2 billion propelled Stewart into the wealthy elite. Stewart is now one of the richest women in the world.

The second IPO billionaire of the day was Vince McMahon, who took his company, the **World Wrestling Federation (WWF)**, public. The WWF is a company that promotes professional wrestling matches, arranges TV coverage of its fights, and sells wrestling memorabilia. McMahon is a third-generation owner of the company. The wrestlers do not own the WWF but merely contract with the WWF to provide their services. Because you have to tell the truth to the SEC and the investing public, WWF's registration statement filed with the SEC and its prospectus given to investors admitted that professional wrestling is basically entertainment and not truly a sport. The documents also disclosed that there were several substantial lawsuits pending against the company and that it faces competition from World Championship Wrestling (WCW), a company backed by Time Warner. The WWF went public at $16, rose to $34 on the first day of trading, before closing the day at $25. After the IPO, McMahon was worth over $1 billion.

Martha Stewart and Vince McMahon are new entrepreneur-billionaires. Will the public investors who bought their companies' stock recognize similar gains, or have they been made-up by Stewart and put in a head lock by McMahon? Only time will tell.

Landmark Law

The Securities Exchange Act of 1934

Unlike the Securities Act of 1933, which regulates the original issuance of securities, the **Securities Exchange Act of 1934** primarily regulates subsequent trading. (1) It provides for the registration of certain companies with the SEC; continuous filing of periodic reports by these companies to the SEC; and the regulation of securities exchanges, brokers, and dealers. (2) It contains provisions that assess civil and criminal liability on violators of the 1934 act and rules and regulations adopted thereunder.

The Securities Exchange Act of 1934—Trading in Securities

Continuous Reporting Requirements

Securities Exchange Act of 1934

A federal statute that primarily regulates the trading in securities.

The **Securities Exchange Act of 1934** requires issuers (1) with assets of more than $10 million and at least 500 shareholders, (2) whose equity securities are traded on a national securities exchange or (3) who have made a registered offering under the Securities Act of 1933, to file periodic reports with the SEC. These issuers, called *reporting companies*, must file an annual report (*Form 10-K*), quarterly reports (*Form 10-Q*), and monthly reports within 10 days of the end of the month in which a material event (such as a merger) occurs (*Form 8-K*). These reports may be sent to the SEC on computer tapes or disks.

Section 10(b) and Rule 10b-5

Section 10(b)

A provision of the Securities Exchange Act of 1934 that prohibits the use of manipulative and deceptive devices in the purchase or sale of securities in contravention of the rules and regulations prescribed by the SEC.

Section 10(b) is one of the most important sections in the entire 1934 act. It prohibits the use of manipulative and deceptive devices in contravention of the rules and regulations prescribed by the SEC.

Pursuant to its rule-making authority, the SEC has adopted **Rule 10b-5**, which provides that:

It shall be unlawful for any person, directly or indirectly, by use of any means or instrumentality of interstate commerce or of the mails, or of any facility of any national securities exchange,

a. to employ any device, scheme, or artifice to defraud,

b. to make any untrue statement of a material fact or to omit to state a material fact necessary in order to make the statements made, in light of the circumstances under which they were made, not misleading, or

c. to engage in any act, practice, or course of business that operates or would operate as a fraud or deceit upon any person, in connection with the purchase or sale of any security.

Rule 10b-5 is not restricted to purchases and sales of securities of reporting companies.[11] All transfers of securities, whether made on a stock exchange, in the over-the-counter market, in a private sale, or in connection with a merger, are subject to this rule.[12] The U.S. Supreme Court has held that only conduct involving **scienter** (intentional conduct) violates Section 10(b) and Rule 10b-5. Negligent conduct is not a violation.[13]

Section 10(b) and Rule 10b-5 require reliance by the injured party on the misstatement. However, many sales and purchases of securities occur in open market transactions (e.g., over stock exchanges) where there is no direct communication between the buyer and the seller.

Rule 10b-5

A rule adopted by the SEC to clarify the reach of Section 10(b) against deceptive and fraudulent activities in the purchase and sale of securities.

scienter

Means international conduct. Scienter is required for there to be a violation of Section 10(b) and Rule 10b-5.

Business Ethics

REGULATION FD REQUIRES FAIR DISCLOSURE TO ALL

Prior to 2000, publicly-held companies routinely announced crucial earnings and other significant information to securities analysts and other Wall Street insiders before making the information public. This meant that the analysts and others on Wall Street could profit from the information before it was made available to the general public. They did this by purchasing securities of the disclosing companies on good news, and selling securities on bad news, before others could act. The Securities and Exchange Commission (SEC) felt that this so-called "front-running" gave an unfair advantage to the investment professionals.

In 2000, over the objections of Wall Street, the SEC adopted **Regulation Fair Disclosure**, or **Reg FD**, that pro-hibits companies from leaking important information to securities professionals before the information is disclosed to the public. Reg FD forces companies, by law, to reveal sensitive information to the general public at the same time that the information is released to stock analysts. Reg FD has leveled the playing field and taken away a lucrative advantage that the Wall Street professionals had over the general investing public.

1. Was it ethical for securities professionals to "front-run" in the trading of securities?
2. Do you think Reg FD levels the playing field? Do securities professionals still have an advantage over members of the public when investing in securities? Explain.

*I*NSIDER TRADING

One of the most important purposes of Section 10(b) and Rule 10b-5 is to prevent **insider trading**. Insider trading occurs when a company employee or company advisor uses material nonpublic information to make a profit by trading in the securities of the company. This practice is considered illegal because it allows insiders to take advantage of the investing public.

In the **Matter of Cady, Roberts & Co.**,[14] the SEC announced that the duty of an insider who possesses material nonpublic information is to either (1) abstain from trading in the securities of the company or (2) disclose the information to the person on the other side of the transaction before the insider purchases the securities from or sells the securities to him or her.

insider trading

When an insider makes a profit by personally purchasing shares of the corporation prior to public release of favorable information or by selling shares of the corporation prior to the public disclosure of unfavorable information.

Insiders

For purposes of Section 10(b) and Rule 10b-5, *insiders* are defined as (1) officers, directors, and employees at all levels of the company, (2) lawyers, accountants, consultants, and other agents and representatives who are hired by the company on a temporary and non-employee status to provide services or work to the company, and (3) others who owe a fiduciary duty to the company.

Case 32.2 is a classical case of insider trading.

Securities and Exchange Commission v. Texas Gulf Sulphur Co.
401 F.2d 833 (1968)
United States Court of Appeals, Second Circuit

CASE 32.2

BACKGROUND AND FACTS

Texas Gulf Sulphur Co. (TGS) had for several years conducted aerial geophysical surveys in eastern Canada. On November 12, 1963, TGS drilled an exploratory hole—Kidd 55—near Timmins, Ontario. Assay reports showed that the core from this drilling proved to be remarkably high in copper, zinc, and silver. Because TGS did not own the mineral rights to properties surrounding the drill site, TGS kept the discovery secret, camouflaged the drill site, and diverted drilling efforts to another site. This allowed TGS to engage in extensive land acquisition around Kidd 55.

Eventually, rumors of a rich mineral strike began circulating. On Saturday, April 11, 1964, the *New York Times* and the *New York Herald-Tribune* published unauthorized reports of TGS drilling efforts in Canada and its rich mineral strike. On Sunday, April 12, officers of TGS met with a public relations consultant and drafted a press release that was issued that afternoon. The press release appeared in morning newspapers of general circulation on Monday, April 13. It read in pertinent part:

The work done to date has not been sufficient to reach definite conclusions and any statement as to size and grade of ore would be premature and possibly misleading. When we have progressed to the point where reasonable and logical conclusions can be made, TGS will issue a definite statement to its stockholders and to the public in order to clarify the Timmins project.

The rumors persisted. On April 16, 1964, at 10:00 A.M. TGS held a press conference for the financial media. At this conference, which lasted about 10 minutes, TGS disclosed the richness of the Timmins's mineral strike and that the strike would run to at least 25 million tons of ore. In early November 1963, TGS stock was trading at $173 per share. On April 15, 1964, the stock closed at $298. Several officers, directors, and other employees of TGS who had knowledge of the mineral strike at Timmins traded in the stock of TGS during the period November 12, 1963, to April 16, 1964. By May 15, 1964, the stock was selling at 58\frac{1}{4}$.

The SEC brought this action against David M. Crawford and Francis G. Coates, two TGS executives who possessed the nonpublic information about the ore strike and who traded in TGS securities. The SEC sought to rescind their stock purchases. The district court found Crawford liable for insider trading but dismissed the complaint against Coates. Appeals were taken from this judgment.

ISSUE

Are Crawford and Coates liable for trading on material inside information in violation of Section 10(b) and Rule 10b-5?

COURT'S REASONING

The insiders here were not trading on an equal footing with the outside investors. They alone were in a position to evaluate the probability and magnitude of what seemed from the outset to be a major ore strike.

Crawford—Crawford telephoned his orders to his Chicago broker about midnight on April 15 and again at 8:30 on the morning of April 16 with instructions to buy at the opening of the Midwest Stock Exchange that morning. The trial court's finding that "he sought to, and did, 'beat the news,'" is well documented by the record. Before insiders may act upon material information, such information must have been effectively disclosed in a manner sufficient to ensure its availability to the investing public. Particularly here, where a formal announcement to the entire financial news media had been promised in a prior official release known to the media, all insider activity must await dissemination of the promised official announcement.

Coates—Coates was absolved by the court below because his telephone order was placed shortly before 10:20 A.M. on April 16, which was after the announcement had been made even though the news could not be considered already a matter of public information. This result seems to have been predicated upon a misinterpretation of dicta in *Cady, Roberts*, where the SEC instructed insiders to "keep out of the market until the established procedures for public release of the information are carried out instead of hastening to execute transactions in advance of, and in frustration of, the objectives of the release." The reading of a news release, which prompted Coates into action, is merely the first step in the process of dissemination required for compliance with the regulatory objective of providing all investors with an equal opportunity to make informed investment judgments. Assuming that the contents of the official release could instantaneously be acted upon, at the minimum Coates should have waited until the news could reasonably have been expected to appear over the media of widest circulation, the Dow Jones broad tape, rather than hastening to ensure an advantage to himself and his broker son-in-law.

DECISION

The court of appeals held that both executives, Crawford and Coates, had engaged in illegal insider trading.

Case Questions

Critical Legal Thinking Should insider trading be illegal? Why or why not?

Business Ethics Did Crawford and Coates act ethically in this case?

Contemporary Business How can businesses protect against their employees engaging in insider trading? Explain.

The Supreme Court Speaks

U.S. Supreme Court Adopts the "Misappropriation Theory" for Securities Fraud

United States v. O'Hagan
1997 WL 345229 (1997)
Supreme Court of the United States

BACKGROUND AND FACTS

James O'Hagan was a partner in the law firm of Dorsey & Whitney in Minneapolis, Minnesota. In July 1988, Grand Metropolitan PLC (Grand Met), a company based in London, England, hired Dorsey & Whitney to represent it in a secret tender offer for the stock of the Pillsbury Company, headquartered in Minneapolis. On August 18, 1988, O'Hagan began purchasing call options for Pillsbury stock. Each call option gave O'Hagan the right to purchase 100 shares of Pillsbury stock at a specified price. O'Hagan continued to purchase call options in August and September and became the largest holder of call options for Pillsbury stock. In September, O'Hagan also purchased 5,000 shares of Pillsbury common stock at $39 per share. These purchases were all made while Grand Met's proposed tender offer for Pillsbury remained secret to the public. When Grand Met publicly announced its tender offer in October, 1988, Pillsbury call options and common stock, making a profit of more than $4.3 million.

The Securities and Exchange Commission (SEC) investigated, and the Justice Department charged O'Hagan with criminally violating Section 10(b) and Rule 10b-5. Because this was not a case of classical insider trading because O'Hagan did not trade in the stock of his law firm's client, Grand Met, the government alleged that O'Hagan was liable under the "misappropriation theory" for trading in Pillsbury stock by engaging in deceptive conduct by misappropriating the secret information about Grand Met's tender offer from his employer, Dorsey & Whitney, and from its client, Grand Met. The district court found O'Hagan guilty and sentenced him to 41 months in prison. The Eighth Circuit Court of Appeals reversed, finding that liability under Section 10(b) and Rule 10b-5 cannot be based on the misappropriation theory. The government appealed to the U.S. Supreme Court.

SUPREME COURT ISSUE

Can a defendant be criminally convicted of violating Section 10(b) and Rule 10b-5 based on the misappropriation theory?

IN THE LANGUAGE OF THE COURT

Ginsburg, Justice Under the "traditional" or "classical theory" of insider trading liability, Section 10(b) and Rule 10b-5 are violated when a corporate insider trades in the securities of his corporation on the basis of material, nonpublic information. Trading on such information qualifies as a "deceptive device" under Section 10(b) because a relationship of trust and confidence exists between the shareholders of a corporation and those insiders who have obtained confidential information by reason of their position with that corporation.

The "misappropriation theory" holds that a person commits fraud "in connection with" a securities transaction, and thereby violates Section 10(b) and Rule 10b-5, when he misappropriates confidential information for securities trading purposes, in breach of a duty owed to the source of the information. Under this theory, a fiduciary's undisclosed, self-serving use of a principal's information to purchase or sell securities, in breach of a duty of loyalty and confidentiality, defrauds the principal of the exclusive use of that information.

The two theories are complementary, each addressing efforts to capitalize on nonpublic information through the purchase or sale of securities. The classical theory targets a corporate insider's breach of duty to shareholders with whom the insider transacts; the misappropriation theory outlaws trading on the basis of nonpublic information by a corporate "outsider" in breach of a duty owed not to a trading party, but to the source of the information.

The misappropriation theory comports with Section 10(b)'s language, which requires deception "in connection with the purchase or sale of any security," not deception of an identifiable purchaser or seller. In sum, considering the inhibiting impact on market participation of trading on misappropriated information, and the congres-

sional purposes underlying Section 10(b), it makes scant sense to hold a lawyer like O'Hagan a Section 10(b) violator if he works for a law firm representing the target of a tender offer, but not if he works for a law firm representing the bidder. The text of the statute requires no such result. The misappropriation at issue here was properly made the subject of a Section 10(b) charge because it meets the statutory requirement that there be "deceptive" conduct "in connection with" securities transactions.

DECISION AND REMEDY

The Supreme Court held that a defendant can be criminally convicted of violating Section 10(b) and Rule 10b-5 under the misappropriation theory.

CASE QUESTIONS

Critical Legal Thinking   Should the misappropriation theory be recognized as a basis for criminal liability under Section 10(b) and Rule 10b-5? Do you agree with the Supreme Court's decision?

Business Ethics   If the Supreme Court had upheld the Eighth Circuit's decision, would ethics alone be enough to prevent persons like O'Hagan from trading on secret information?

Contemporary Business   Will the securities markets be more or less honest because of the Supreme Court's ruling?

Tipper-Tippee Liability

A person who discloses material nonpublic information to another person is called a **tipper**. The person who receives such information is known as the **tippee**. The tippee is liable for acting on material information that he or she knew or should have known was not public. The tipper is liable for the profits made by the tippee. If the tippee tips other persons, both the tippee (who is now a tipper) and the original tipper are liable for the profits made by these remote tippees. The remote tippees are liable for their own trades if they knew or should have known that they possessed material inside information.

tipper

A person who discloses material nonpublic information to another person.

tippee

The person who receives material nonpublic information from a tipper.

Prior to the enactment of the Securities Act of 1933 and the Securities Exchange Act of 1934, many "stool pigeons" were defrauded by securities schemes. Today there may still be fraud in the purchase and sale of securities, but these federal laws permit the government and the victims of these frauds to sue and recover criminal and civil remedies, respectively.

ℒ̸IABILITY PROVISIONS OF THE SECURITIES EXCHANGE ACT OF 1934

The civil and criminal penalties that may be assessed for violations of the Securities Exchange Act of 1934 are discussed in the following paragraphs.

Criminal Liability

Section 32

A provision of the Securities Exchange Act of 1934 that imposes criminal liability on any person who willfully violates the 1934 act or the rules or regulations adopted thereunder.

Section 32 of the Securities Exchange Act of 1934 makes it a criminal offense to violate willfully the provisions of the act or the rules and regulations adopted thereunder.[15] Upon conviction, a natural person may be fined up to $1 million, imprisoned for up to 10 years, or both. A person cannot be imprisoned unless he or she had knowledge of the rule or regulation violated, however. A corporation or other entity may be fined up to $2.5 million for violating Section 32.

SEC Actions

The SEC may investigate suspected violations of the Securities Exchange Act of 1934 and the rules and regulations adopted thereunder. The SEC may enter into *consent orders* with defendants, seek *injunctions* in federal district court, or seek court orders requiring defendants to *disgorge* illegally gained profits.

In 1984, Congress enacted the **Insider Trading Sanctions Act**,[16] which permits the SEC to obtain a *civil penalty* of up to three times the illegal profits gained or losses avoided on insider trading. The fine is payable to the U.S. Treasury.

Insider Trading Sanctions Act of 1984

A federal statute that permits the SEC to obtain a civil penalty of up to three times the illegal benefits received from insider trading.

Private Actions

Although Section 10(b) and Rule 10b-5 do not expressly provide for a private right of action, courts have implied such a right. Generally, a private plaintiff may seek rescission of the securities contract or recover damages (e.g., disgorgements of the illegal profits by the defendants).

The Supreme Court Speaks

Section 10(b) Applies to Oral Misrepresentations

The Wharf (Holdings) Limited v. United International Holdings, Inc.
U.S. 121 S.Ct. 1776 (2001)
2001 U.S. Lexis 3812
Supreme Court of the United States

BACKGROUND AND FACTS

The Wharf (Holdings) Limited is a Hong Kong firm that was interested in obtaining a license to operate a cable television system in Hong Kong. In 1991, the Hong Kong government announced that it would accept bids for the award of an exclusive license to operate a cable television system in Hong Kong. Wharf decided to find a business partner with cable system experience. Wharf located United International Holdings, Inc., a Colorado-based company with substantial experience in operating cable television systems. Wharf orally agreed to grant United an option to buy 10 percent of the stock of the new Hong Kong cable system if Wharf was awarded the license. United sent several employees to Hong Kong to help prepare Wharf's application for the license, design the cable system, and arrange financing.

In May 1993, Hong Kong awarded the cable franchise to Wharf. When United raised $66 million and tried to exercise its option to invest 10 percent in the new cable company, Wharf refused to permit United to buy any of the new company's stock. Documents and other evidence showed that at the time Wharf granted United the oral 10 percent stock option that it had not intended to ever sell United any stock in the new venture. United sued Wharf in U.S. district court for securities fraud for violating Section 10(b) of the Securities Exchange Act of 1934. The jury held for United and warded it $67 million in compensatory damages and $58.5 million in punitive damages against Wharf. The court of appeals affirmed. The U.S. Supreme Court granted review.

SUPREME COURT ISSUE

Did Wharf's oral stock option to sell United a 10 percent interest in the Hong Kong cable television system, while secretly intending never to do so, violate Section 10(b) of the Securities Exchange Act of 1934?

IN THE LANGUAGE OF THE U.S. SUPREME COURT

Breyer, Justice. Wharf points out that its agreement to grant United an option to purchase shares in the cable system was an oral agreement. And it says that Section 10(b) does not cover oral contracts of sale. There is no convincing reason to interpret the Act to exclude oral contracts as a class. The Act itself says that it applies to "any contract" for the purchase or sale of a security. Oral contracts for the sale of securities are sufficiently common that the Uniform Commercial Code and statutes of frauds in every State now consider them enforceable. To sell an option while secretly intending not to permit the option's exercise is misleading, because a buyer normally presumes good faith. Since Wharf did not intend to honor the option, the option was, unbeknownst to United, valueless.

DECISION AND REMEDY

The U.S. Supreme Court held that an oral contract to sell an option to purchase securities that is not intended to be honored when the promise is made violates Section 10(b) of the Securities Exchange Act of 1934. The judgment of the court of appeals is affirmed.

CASE QUESTIONS

Critical Legal Thinking   Should Section 10(b) apply to oral promises to sell or purchase securities? Why or why not?

Business Ethics   Did Wharf act ethically in this case? Was the award of punitive damages warranted in this case?

Contemporary Business   Should United have obtained a written option contract from Wharf? Why or why not?

*S*HORT-SWING PROFITS

Section 16(a) of the 1934 act defines any person who is an executive officer, a director, or a 10 percent shareholder of an equity security of a reporting company as a *statutory insider* for Section 16 purposes. Statutory insiders must file reports with the SEC disclosing their ownership and trading in the company's securities.[17] These reports must be filed within 10 days after the end of the month in which the trade occurs.

Section 16(b)

Section 16(b) requires that any profits made by a statutory insider on transactions involving so-called *short-swing profits*—that is, trades involving equity securities occurring within six months of each other—belong to the corporation.[18] The corporation may bring a legal action to recover these profits. Involuntary transactions, such as forced redemption of securities by the corporation or an exchange of securities in a bankruptcy proceeding, are exempt. Section 16(b) is a strict liability provision. Generally, no defenses are recognized. Neither intent nor the possession of inside information need be shown.

Consider This Example Rosanne is the president of a corporation and a statutory insider who does not possess any inside information. On February 1, she purchases 1,000 shares of her employer's stock at $10 per share. On June 1, she sells the stock for $14 per share. The corporation can recover the $4,000 profit because the trades occurred within six months of each other. Rosanne would have to wait until after August 1 to sell the securities.

SEC Rules

In 1991, the SEC adopted new rules concerning Section 16.[19] This was the first major change in the rules in 57 years. These rules:

- Clarify the definition of *officer* to include only executive officers who perform policy-making functions. This would include the president, the chief executive officer, the vice presidents in charge of business units or divisions, the principal financial officer, the principal accounting officer, and the like. Officers who run day-to-day operations but are not responsible for policy decisions are not included.
- Create a new *Form 5* report that must be filed by all insiders within 45 days of the end of the company's calendar year.
- Relieve insiders of liability for transactions that occur within six months before becoming an insider. For example, if a noninsider buys shares of his or her company January 15, becomes an insider March 15, and sells the shares May 15, the January 15 purchase is not matched against the May 15 sale.
- Continue the rule that insiders are liable for transactions that occur within six months of the last transaction engaged in while an insider. For example, if an insider buys shares in his or her company April 30 and leaves the company May 15, this purchase must be matched against any sale of the company's shares that occurs on or before October 30.
- Treat derivative securities (e.g., stock options, warrants) as follows: The acquisition or disposition of a derivative security is a Section 16 event; the exercise of the derivative security is a nonevent for Section 16 purposes. For example, suppose a company issues a stock option to its president May 15, who exercises the option June 15 and sells the shares on December 1. There is no violation of Section 16.
- Require companies to disclose delinquent filings of Section 16 forms in their proxy statements.

*C*ONCEPT SUMMARY SECTION 10(B) AND SECTION 16(B) COMPARED

Element	Section 10(b) and Rule 10(b)-5	Section 16(b)
Covered securities	All securities.	Securities required to be registered with the SEC under the 1934 act.
Inside information	Defendant made a misrepresentation or traded on inside (or perhaps misappropriated) information.	Short-swing profits recoverable whether or not they are attributable to misappropriation or inside information.
Recovery	Belongs to the injured purchaser or seller.	Belongs to the corporation.

E-Commerce & Information Technology

ONLINE "FREE" STOCK SCAM DELETED BY SEC

Docs free stock for Internet users sound too good to be true? The Securities and Exchange Commission (SEC), the government agency charged with enforcing federal securities laws, thought so and has launched a crackdown on this recent Internet craze. The scam works as follows: For agreeing to buy certain products or services or for merely agreeing to give some personal information about oneself, the Internet operator gives "free" stock in the company to the buyer or the provider of information. The Internet user is lured into this deal by promises of receiving stock that has value and will become more valuable in the future. These offers are usually made through Internet chat rooms or e-mail messages.

Federal securities laws, which prohibit fraud in the sale or purchase of securities, apply to Internet sales of securities. The SEC applied these antifraud provisions and has sued many Internet companies for "free" stock fraud. The SEC

determined that the person receiving the stock paid something of value, such as buying products or services or by providing valuable personal information that the stock scam operator uses or sells.

One company the SEC brought charges against was Web Works Marketing.com. The company offered shares of its stock to Internet users who registered on its Web site or signed up for long-distance telecommunications services. Investors were told that the shares had a value of $38 and could appreciate to $200 when the company went public and that the company had more than 10,000 customers. In fact, the company had 35 customers, no contract with a long-distance provider, and had taken no steps toward a public offering. The company settled the charges with the SEC. The SEC has targeted many more so-called "free stock" companies for running fraudulent Internet scams.

OTHER FEDERAL SECURITIES LAWS

Racketeer Influenced and Corrupt Organizations Act

The **Racketeer Influenced and Corrupt Organizations Act (RICO)** makes it a federal crime to engage in a pattern of racketeering activity.[20] Because securities fraud falls under the definition of racketeering activity, the government often brings a RICO allegation in conjunction with a securities fraud allegation.

In addition, persons injured by a RICO violation can bring a private civil action against the violator and recover treble (triple) damages but only if the defendant has been criminally convicted in connection with the securities fraud.[21] A third-party independent contractor (e.g., an outside accountant) must have participated in the operation or management of the enterprise to be liable for civil RICO.[22]

> **Racketeer influenced and Corrupt Organizations Act (RICO)**
>
> A federal statute that provides for both criminal and civil penalties.

Private Securities Litigation Reform Act of 1995

Sometimes companies include forward-looking statements about future economic plans and projections of financial data in prospectuses and other documents filed with the SEC and provided to investors. The **Private Securities Litigation Reform Act of 1995** provides a *safe harbor* from liability for companies that make such statements if they are accompanied by meaningful cautionary statements that identify risk factors that could cause actual results to differ from those in the statement.

> **Private Securities Litigation Reform Act of 1995**
>
> Provides a safe harbor from liability for companies that make forward-looking statements that are accompanied by meaningful cautionary statements of risk factors.

STATE SECURITIES LAWS

Most states have enacted securities laws. These laws, which are often called *blue-sky laws*, generally require the registration of certain securities and provide exemptions from registration. They also contain broad antifraud provisions.

The **Uniform Securities Act** has been adopted by many states. This act is drafted to coordinate state securities laws with federal securities laws.

> **Ethics Brief**
>
> State securities laws presumably originated to protect investors from foolishly buying a piece of the blue sky.

Arch, St. Louis, Missouri State securities laws are often referred to as "blue-sky" laws because they help prevent investors from purchasing a piece of the blue sky.

Contemporary Business Environment

COMMODITIES REGULATION

Commodities include grains (e.g., wheat, soybeans, oats), animals (e.g., cattle, hogs), animal products (e.g., pork bellies), foods (e.g., sugar, coffee), metals (e.g., gold, silver), and oil. A *commodities futures contract* is an agreement to buy or sell a specific amount and type of commodity at some future date at a price established at the time of contracting. For example, a futures contract may be to sell 5,000 bushels of oats on July 31 at $2.87 per bushel. Standardized terms are established for futures contracts (e.g., quantity and quality of the commodity, time and place of delivery). Thus, each similar contract is *fungible*. This makes the contracts liquid; that is, they can be bought and sold on the commodities exchanges just as stocks and bonds are bought and sold on securities exchanges. Farmers, ranchers, food processors, milling companies, mineral producers, oil companies, and investors often buy and sell futures contracts

Commodities exchanges have been established at different locations across the country where commodity futures contracts can be bought and sold by food producers, farmers, and speculators. The major commodity exchanges are

- The Chicago Board of Trade (CBOT)
- The Chicago Mercantile Exchange (CME)
- The Commodity Exchange of New York (COMEX)

- Kansas City Board of Trade (KBOT)
- New York Coffee, Sugar, & Cocoa Exchange (NYCSCE)
- New York Cotton Exchange (NYCTN)
- New York Mercantile Exchange (NYME)
- New York Futures Exchange (NYF)

The **Commodity Exchange Act (CEA)** was enacted by Congress in 1936 to regulate the trading of commodity futures contracts. The **Commodity Futures Trading Commission Act**, which was enacted in 1974, significantly amended the prior act [7 U.S.C. § § 1-17a]. **Section 4b** of the CEA prohibits fraudulent conduct in connection with any order or contract of sale of any commodity for future delivery.

The 1974 amendments created the **Commodity Futures Trading Commission (CFTC)** to administer and enforce the CEA. The CFTC is a federal administrative agency consisting of five members appointed by the President. The CFTC has the authority to regulate trading in commodities futures contracts. It has the power to adopt regulations, conduct investigations, bring administrative proceedings against suspected violators, issue cease-and-desist orders and injunctions, and impose civil fines. Suspected criminal violations can be referred to the Justice Department for criminal action.

International Law

ENFORCEMENT OF INTERNATIONAL SECURITIES LAWS

The United States is not the only country in the world that outlaws insider trading and securities fraud. For example, Britain has outlawed insider dealing in securities for years. In

1993, the British government even implemented new legislation to strengthen its insider trading laws. The French insider trading law makes it illegal for a person to trade on nonpublic information received by reason of his or her position or profession. The European Community (EC) has directed all member countries to adopt laws against insider trading. Japan has an insider trading law that is rarely enforced.

Many persons who engage in illegal insider trading in the United States often do so using businesses or "fronts" located in other countries. In addition, these traders often deposit their ill-gotten gains in secret bank accounts located in off-shore bank havens. Can U.S. authorities obtain documents and evidence, as well as information about the location of bank accounts, from other countries? The answer is yes, in many situations.

In 1990, Congress enacted the **International Securities Enforcement Cooperation Act** [P.L. 101-550, 104 Stat.2713]. The act authorizes the SEC to cooperate with foreign securities authorities, to provide records to foreign securities authorities, and to sanction securities professionals in this country who violate foreign securities laws.

The SEC has entered in **memoranda of understandings**, or **MOUs**, with several foreign governments or authorities. As a general rule, the MOUs provide that the SEC and its foreign counterparts will cooperate in the enforcement of each country's securities laws. Thus, the SEC can obtain evidence about the location of bank accounts and other information concerning persons suspected of violating U.S. securities laws from foreign authorities. Currently, the SEC has entered into MOUs with Argentina, Brazil, Canada, France, Great Britain, Italy, Japan, the Netherlands, and Switzerland.

As securities trading becomes more international, it is going to become easier for investors and others to engage in insider trading and securities fraud across national boundaries. The United States and other countries will have to cooperate in finding, prosecuting, and penalizing perpetrators of securities frauds.

CHAPTER SUMMARY

The Securities and Exchange Commission (SEC), p. 798

The Securities and Exchange Commission (SEC)	Created in 1934, it is a federal administrative agency empowered to administer federal securities laws. The SEC can adopt rules and regulations to interpret and implement federal securities.

Definition of a Security, p. 798

Definition of a Security	*Security.* A security must be found before federal securities laws apply. A *security* is defined as: 1. *Common securities.* Interests or instruments that are commonly known as securities, such as common stock, preferred stock, debentures, and warrants. 2. *Statutorily defined securities.* Interests and instruments that are expressly mentioned in securities acts as being securities, such as interests in oil, gas, and mineral rights. 3. *Investment contracts.* A flexible standard for defining a security. Under the *Howey* test, a security exists if (1) an investor invests money (2) in a common enterprise and (3) expects to make a profit off the significant efforts of others.

The Securities Act of 1933—Registration of Securities, p. 799

The Securities Act of 1933	A federal statute that primarily regulates the *issuance* of securities by corporations, partnerships, associations, and individuals.
Registration Statement	1. *Section 5.* A provision of the 1933 act that requires an issuer to register its securities with the SEC prior to selling them to the public if the securities or transaction does not qualify for an exemption from registration. 2. *Registration statement.* Document that an issuer of securities files with the SEC to register its securities. It must contain information about the issuer, the securities to be issued, and other relevant information.
Prospectus	A written disclosure document that is submitted to the SEC with the registration statement. It is distributed to prospective investors to enable them to evaluate the financial risk of the investment.
Limitations on Activities During the Registration Process	1. *Prefiling period.* Begins when the issuer first contemplates issuing securities and ends when the registration statement is filed with the SEC. During this period, the issuer cannot (1) offer to sell securities, (2) sell securities, or (3) *condition the market*. 2. *Waiting period.* Begins when the registration statement is filed with the SEC and ends when the registration statement becomes effective. During this time, the issuer cannot (1) sell securities or (2) use unapproved writing to offer to sell the securities. The issuer may make oral offers, distribute *preliminary* and *summary prospectuses*, and publish *tombstone ads*.

3. *Posteffective period.* Begins when the registration statement becomes effective and runs until the issuer either sells all of the offered securities or withdraws them from sale. The issuer may offer to sell and sell the securities during this period. The issuer must deliver a *final prospectus* (*statutory prospectus*) to a purchaser prior to or at the time of confirming the sale or sending the security to the purchaser.

Regulation A Offerings

Regulation A. A regulation that permits an issuer to sell securities pursuant to a simplified registration process.

Securities Exempt from Registration, p. 802

Securities Exempt from Registration

The following *securities* are exempt from the SEC registration process:
1. Securities issued by any government in the United States (e.g., municipal bonds issued by city governments)
2. Short-term notes and drafts that have a maturity date that does not exceed nine months (e.g., commercial paper issued by corporations)
3. Securities issued by nonprofit issuers, such as religious institutions, charitable institutions, and colleges and universities.
4. Securities of financial institutions (e.g., banks and savings associations) that are regulated by the appropriate banking authorities
5. Securities issued by common carriers (e.g., railroads and trucking companies) that are regulated by the Interstate Commerce Commission (ICC)
6. Insurance and annuity contracts issued by insurance companies
7. Stock dividends and stock splits
8. Securities issued in a corporate reorganization where one security is exchanged for another security

Transactions Exempt from Registration, p. 802

Transactions Exempt from Registration

The following *transactions* are exempt from the SEC registration process: (1) nonissuer transactions, (2) intrastate offerings, (3) private placements, and (4) small offerings.

Nonissuer Exemption

Securities transactions *not* by an issuer, an underwriter, or a dealer are exempt from SEC registration. This covers normal purchases of securities by investors.

Intrastate Offerings

A local business can issue securities without dollar limit without registering with the SEC if the following requirements are met:
1. The issuer is a resident of the state (e.g., the corporation is incorporated in the state).
2. The issuer is doing business in the state. This requires that:
   a. 80 percent of the issuer's assets are located in the state.
   b. 80 percent of the issuer's gross revenues are derived from the state.
   c. The issuer's principal office is located in the state.
   d. 80 percent of the proceeds of the offering will be used in the state.
3. The purchasers of the securities are all residents of the state.

Private Placements

An issue of securities that does not involve a public offering is exempt from SEC registration. There is no dollar limit on the amount of securities that can be issued pursuant to this exemption. Securities can be sold to any number of *accredited investors,* but to no more than 35 *nonaccredited investors.*
1. *Accredited investors.* These include:
   a. Any natural person (including spouse) who has a net worth of at least $1 million.
   b. Any natural person who has had an annual income of at least $200,000 for the previous two years and reasonably expects to make $200,000 income in the current year.
   c. Any corporation, partnership, or business trust with total assets in excess of $5 million.
   d. Insiders of the issuers, such as executive officers and directors of corporate issuers and general partners of partnership issuers.
   e. Certain institutional investors, such as registered investment companies, pension plans, colleges and universities, and the like.

Small Offerings

An offering of securities that does not exceed $1 million during a 12-month period is exempt from SEC registration. The securities may be sold to any number of purchasers.

Resale Restrictions

1. *Restricted securities.* Securities sold pursuant to the intrastate, private placement, or small offering exemptions are called *restricted securities.*
2. *Rule 147.* An SEC rule stipulating that securities sold pursuant to an *intrastate offering exemption* cannot be sold to nonresidents for a period of nine months.

3. *Rule 144.* An SEC rule stipulating that securities sold pursuant to the *private placement or small offering exemption* must be held for two years; limited sales may be made between years two and three; then unlimited sales are permitted.

4. *Preventing transfer of restricted securities.* To prevent the illegal transfer of restricted securities, the issuer must take the following precautions:

   a. *Affidavit.* Require investors to sign an affidavit stating that they are buying the securities for investment, and promising not to transfer the restricted securities until the restrictions no longer apply.

   b. *Legend.* Place a legend on the stock certificate describing the restriction.

   c. *Transfer agent.* Appoint and notify the transfer agent not to record a transfer of the securities that would violate the restriction.

5. *Rule 144A.* An SEC rule that permits *qualified institutional investors*—defined as institutions—that own and invest at least $100 million in securities—to buy unregistered securities without being subject to the holding periods of Rule 144.

Integration of Exempt Offerings	Separate exempt offerings of securities will be *integrated* (added together) if they occur within six months of each other and they are found to be similar and part of the same offering. 1. *Safe harbor rule.* Exempt securities offerings made more than six months before or after the current offering are not integrated with the current offering. 2. *Integrated offering.* If two or more exempt offerings are integrated, they are considered one offering. This *integrated offering* must be examined to determine whether it qualifies for any exemption from SEC registration.

Liability Provisions of the Securities Act of 1933, p. 805

Criminal Liability	*Section 24* of the 1933 act imposes criminal liability on any person who willfully violates either the act or the rules and regulations adopted thereunder. Criminal actions are brought by the U.S. Justice Department.
SEC Actions	The SEC may seek the following remedies: 1. *Consent order.* The SEC may issue a consent order whereby a defendant agrees not to violate securities laws in the future but does not admit to violating securities laws in the past. 2. *Injunction.* The SEC may bring an action in federal district court to obtain an injunction. 3. *Disgorgement of profits.* The SEC may request the court to order the defendant to disgorge illegally gained profits.
Private Actions	Private parties who have been injured by a violation of the 1933 act may sue the violator to rescind the securities contract or recover damages. The plaintiff may sue under: 1. *Section 12.* A provision of the 1933 act that imposes civil liability on any person who violates the provisions of Section 5 of the act (e.g., sells unregistered securities). 2. *Section 11.* A provision of the 1933 act that imposes civil liability on persons who intentionally defraud investors by making misrepresentations or omissions of material facts in the registration statement, or are negligent in not discovering the fraud. a. *Due diligence defense.* A defense to a Section 11 action that, if proven, makes the defendant not liable. This requires the defendant to have made a reasonable investigation and had reasonable grounds to believe and did believe that the statements made in the registration statement were true.

The Securities Exchange Act of 1934—Trading in Securities, p. 808

The Securities Exchange Act of 1934	A federal statute that primarily regulates the *trading* of securities.
Continuous Reporting Requirements	1. *Reporting companies.* Issuers (1) with assets of more than $5 million and at least 500 shareholders, (2) whose equity securities are traded on a national securities exchange, or (3) who have made a registered offering under the Securities Act of 1933. 2. *Reporting requirements.* Reporting companies must file the following reports with the SEC: (1) annual reports (*Form 10-K*), (2) quarterly reports (*Form 10-Q*), and (3) monthly reports (*Form 8-K*) within 10 days of the end of the month in which a material event (e.g., merger) occurs.
Section 10(b) and Rule 10b-5	1. *Section 10(b).* A provision of the 1934 act that prohibits the use of manipulative and deceptive devices in the purchase or sale of securities in contravention of the rules and regulations prescribed by the SEC. 2. *Rule 10b-5.* A rule adopted by the SEC to clarify the reach of Section 10(b) against deceptive and fraudulent activities in the purchase and sale of securities. 3. *Scienter.* Only conduct involving *scienter* (intentional conduct) violates Section 10(b) and Rule 10b-5. Negligent conduct is not a violation.

Insider Trading, p. 809

Insider Trading	Occurs when an insider makes a profit by purchasing shares of the commodity prior to public release of favorable information or selling shares of the corporation prior to public disclosure of unfavorable information. Insider trading violates Section 10(b) and Rule 10b-5. 1. *Cady, Roberts rule.* An insider who possesses material information must either (1) abstain from trading in the securities of the company or (2) disclose the information to the person from whom he or she purchases or to whom he or she sells the securities.
Insiders	Insiders for Section 10(b) and Rule 10b-5 purposes include all employees of the company, independent contractors hired by the company on a temporary basis to provide services or work to the company, and others who owe a fiduciary duty to the company.
Tipper-Tippee Liability	1. *Tipper.* A person who discloses material nonpublic information to another person. 2. *Tippee.* A person who receives material nonpublic information from a tipper. 3. *Tippee's liability.* The tippee is liable for acting on material information received from a tipper if he or she knew or should have known that the information was not public. The tippee must disgorge profits made on the tip. 4. *Tipper's liability.* The tipper is liable for his own profits and the profits made by the tippee.

Liability Provisions of the Securities Exchange Act of 1934, p. 812

Criminal Liability	*Section 32* of the 1934 act imposes criminal liability on any person who willfully violates the 1934 act or the rules and regulations adopted thereunder. Criminal actions are brought by the U.S. Justice Department.
SEC Actions	The SEC may enter into *consent orders* with defendants, seek *injunctions* in federal district court, or seek orders requiring defendants to *disgorge* illegally gained profits. 1. *Treble damages.* The *Insider Trading Sanctions Act of 1984* permits the SEC to obtain a civil penalty of up to three times the illegal benefits received from insider trading.
Private Actions	*Section 10(b).* A private plaintiff has an *implied right* under Section 10(b) and Rule 10b-5 to sue to rescind the securities contract or recover damages from a defendant who has engaged in manipulative and deceptive practices that have caused the plaintiff injury.

Short-Swing Profits, p. 814

Short-Swing Profits	*Statutory insiders. Section 16(a)* of the Securities Exchange Act of the 1934 defines a *statutory insider* for Section 16 purposes as any person who is an executive officer, a director, or a 10-percent shareholder of an equity security of a reporting company.
Section 16(b)	1. *Short-swing profits.* Profits made by statutory insiders on trades involving equity securities that occur within six months of each other. 2. *Section 16(b).* A provision of the 1934 act that requires that any profits made by a statutory insider on transactions involving short-swing profits belong to the corporation.
1991 SEC Rules	Rules issued by the SEC that clarify the persons and transactions subject to Section 16 short-swing profit rules

Other Federal Securities Laws, p. 815

Racketeer influenced and Corrupt Organizations Act (RICO)	Federal statute that provides for both criminal and civil penalties for engaging in a *pattern or practice of racketeering activities.* Sometimes securities fraud qualifies as a RICO violation. *Treble damages* are available in a civil RICO action, but only if the defendant has been criminally convicted of securities fraud.
Private Securities Litigation Reform Act of 1995	Federal statute that provides a *safe harbor* from liability for companies that make forward-looking statements about future economic plans and projections if certain cautionary statements accompany the projections.

State Securities Laws, p. 815

State Securities Laws	Most states have enacted securities laws that regulate the issuance and trading of securities. These acts are often patterned after, and are designed to coordinate with, federal securities laws. The *Uniform Securities Act*, which is a model state securities act, has been adopted by many states.

Commodities Regulation, p. 816

Commodities Regulation	1. *Commodity.* Includes grains, animals, animal products, foods, metals, and oil. 2. A contract to buy or sell a specific amount and type of commodity at some future date at a price established at the time of contracting. 3. A federal statute that, as amended, regulates the trading of commodity futures contracts. 4. *Commodity Futures Trading Commission (CFTC).* Federal administrative agency that administers and enforces the Commodity Exchange Act, as amended. 5. *Section 4b.* A provision of the Commodity Exchange Act that prohibits fraudulent conduct in connection with any order or contract of sale of any commodity for future delivery.

END-OF-CHAPTER INTERNET EXERCISES AND CASE QUESTIONS

WWW Working the Web Internet Exercises

ACTIVITIES

Note: For socially responsible investing information see **www.socialinvest.org**.

1. Using the Stanford Securities Class Action Clearinghouse site, **www.securities.stanford.edu** identify the leading sector, industry, and companies targeted in securities class action litigation.

2. Investigate the modern varieties of fraud by perusing the law review articles listed below.

   "Internet Securities Fraud: Old Trick, New Medium"
   www.law.duke.edu/journals/dltr/ARTICLES/2001dltr0006.html

"Software Disclosure and Liability Under the Securities Act"
www.law.duke.edu/journals/dltr/ARTICLES/2001dltr0016.html

"The Future of Corporate Disclosure: The Internet, Securities Fraud, and Rule 10B-5"
www.law.emory.edu/ELJ/volumes/win98/prentice.html

3. Determine whether an athletic club membership can be a security using the U.S. Securities and Exchange Commission site **www.sec.gov**.

CRITICAL LEGAL THINKING CASES

32.1 Definition of a Security Dare To Be Great, Inc., is a Florida corporation that was wholly owned by Glenn W. Turner Enterprises, Inc. Dare offered self-improvement courses aimed at improving self-motivation and sales ability. In return for an investment of money, the purchaser received certain tapes, records, and written materials. In addition, depending on the level of involvement, the purchaser had the opportunity to help sell the Dare courses to others and to receive part of the purchase price as a commission. There were four different levels of involvement.

The task of salespersons was to bring prospective purchasers to "Adventure Meetings." The meetings, which were conducted by Dare people and not the salespersons, were conducted in a preordained format that included great enthusiasm, cheering and charming, exuberant handshaking, standing on chairs, and shouting. The Dare people and the salespersons dressed in modern, expensive clothes, displayed large sums of cash, drove new and expensive automobiles, and engaged in "hard-sell" tactics to induce prospects to sign their name and part with their money. In actuality, few Dare purchasers ever attained the wealth promised.

The tape recordings and materials distributed by Dare were worthless. Is this sales scheme a "security" that should have been registered with the SEC? [*Securities and Exchange Commission v. Glenn W. Turner Enterprises, Inc.*, 474 F.2d 476 (9th Cir. 1973)]

32.2 Definition of a Security   The Farmer's Cooperative of Arkansas and Oklahoma (Co-Op) was an agricultural cooperative that had approximately 23,000 members. To raise money to support its general business operations, the Co-Op sold promissory notes to investors that were payable upon demand. The Co-Op offered the notes to both members and nonmembers, advertised the notes as an "investment program," and offered an interest rate higher than that available on savings accounts at financial institutions. More than 1,600 people purchased the notes worth a total of $10 million. Subsequently, the Co-Op filed for bankruptcy. A class of holders of the notes filed suit against Ernst & Young, a national firm of certified public accountants that had audited the Co-Op's financial statements, alleging that Ernst & Young had violated Section 10(b) of the Securities Exchange Act of 1934. Are the notes issued by the Co-Op "securities"? [*Reeves v. Ernst & Young*, 495 U.S. 56, 110 S.Ct. 945, 108 L.Ed.2d 47 (1990)]

32.3 Intrastate Offering Exemption   The McDonald Investment Company was a corporation organized and incorporated in the state of Minnesota. The principal and only place of business from which the company conducted operations was located in Rush City, Minnesota. More than 80 percent of the company's assets were located in Minnesota and more than 80 percent of its income was derived from Minnesota. On January 18, 1972, McDonald sold securities to Minnesota residents only. The proceeds from the sale were used entirely to make loans and other investments in real estate and other assets located outside the state of Minnesota. The company did not file a registration statement with the SEC. Does this offering qualify for an intrastate offering exemption from registration? [*Securities and Exchange Commission v. McDonald Investment Company*, 343 F. Supp. 343 (D.Minn. 1972)]

32.4 Transaction Exemption   Continental Enterprises, Inc., had 2,510,000 shares of stock issued and outstanding. Louis E. Wolfson and members of his immediate family and associates owned in excess of 40 percent of those shares. The balance was in the hands of approximately 5,000 outside shareholders. Wolfson was Continental's largest shareholder and the guiding spirit of the corporation who gave direction to and controlled the company's officers. Between August 1, 1960, and January 31, 1962, without public disclosure, Wolfson and his family and associates sold 55 percent of their stock through six brokerage houses. Wolfson and his family and associates did not file a registration statement with the Securities and Exchange Commission with respect to these sales. Do the securities sales by Wolfson and his family and associates qualify for an exemption for registration as a sale "not by an issuer, underwriter, or dealer"? [*United States v. Wolfson*, 405 F.2d 779 (2nd Cir. 1968)]

32.5 Insider Trading   Chiarella worked as a "markup man" in the New York composing room of Pandick Press, a financial printer. Among the documents that Chiarella handled were five secret announcements of corporate takeovers. The tender offer-

ors had hired Pandick Press to print the offers, which would later be made public when the tender offers were made to the shareholders of the target corporations. When the documents were delivered to Pandick Press, the identities of the acquiring and target corporations were concealed by blank space or false names. The true names would not be sent to Pandick Press until the night of the final printing.

Chiarella was able to deduce the names of the target companies before the final printing. Without disclosing this knowledge, he purchased stock in the target companies and sold the shares immediately after the takeover attempts were made public. Chiarella realized a gain of $30,000 in the course of 14 months. The federal government indicted Chiarella for criminal violations of Section 10(b) of the Securities Exchange Act of 1934. Is Chiarella guilty? [*Chiarella v. United States*, 445 U.S. 222, 100 S.Ct. 1108, 63 L.Ed.2d 348 (1980)]

32.6 Section 10(b)   Leslie Neadeau was the president of T.O.N.M. Oil & Gas Exploration Corporation (TONM). Charles Lazzaro was a registered securities broker employed by Bateman Eichler, Hill Richards, Inc. The stock of TONM was traded in the over-the-counter market. Lazzaro made statements to potential investors that he had "inside information" about TONM, including that (1) vast amounts of gold had been discovered in Surinam and that TONM had options on thousands of acres in the gold-producing regions of Surinam; (2) the discovery was "not publicly known, but would be subsequently announced"; and (3) when this information was made public, TONM stock, which was then selling from $1.50 to $3.00 per share, would increase to $10.00 to $15.00 within a short period of time and might increase to $100.00 per share within a year.

The potential investors contacted Neadeau at TONM, who confirmed that the information was not public knowledge. In reliance on Lazzaro's and Neadeau's statements, the investors purchased TONM stock. The so-called "inside information" turned out to be false, and the shares declined substantially below the purchase price. The investors sued Lazzaro, Bateman Eichler, Neadeau, and TONM, alleging violations of Section 10(b) of the Securities Exchange Act of 1934. The defendants asserted that the plaintiffs' complaint should be dismissed because they participated in the fraud. Who wins? [*Bateman Eichler, Hill Richards, Inc. v. Berner*, 472 U.S. 299, 105 S.Ct. 2622, 86 L.Ed.2d 215 (1985)]

32.7 Insider Trading   Donald C. Hoodes was the chief executive officer of the Sullair Corporation. As an officer of the corporation, he was regularly granted stock options to purchase stock of the company at a discount. On July 20, 1982, Hoodes sold 6,000 shares of Sullair common stock for $38,350. On July 31, 1982, Sullair terminated Hoodes as an officer of the corporation. On August 20, 1982, Hoodes exercised options to purchase 6,000 shares of Sullair stock that cost Hoodes $3.01 per share ($18,060) at the time they were trading at $4.50 per share ($27,000). Hoodes did not possess material nonpublic information about Sullair when he sold or purchased the securities of the company. The corporation brought suit against Hoodes to recover the profits Hoodes made on these trades. Who wins? [*Sullair Corporation v. Hoodes*, 672 F.Supp. 337 (N.D.Ill. 1987)]

BUSINESS ETHICS CASES

32.8 Business Ethics Stephen Murphy owned Intertie, a California company that was involved in financing and managing cable television stations. Murphy was both an officer of the corporation and chairman of the board of directors. Intertie would buy a cable television station, make a small cash down payment, and finance the remainder of the purchase price. It would then create a limited partnership and sell the cable station to the partnership for a cash down payment and a promissory note in favor of Intertie. Finally, Intertie would lease the station back from the partnership. Intertie purchased more than 30 stations and created an equal number of limited partnerships, from which it received more than $7.5 million from approximately 400 investors.

Evidence showed that most of the limited partnerships were not self-supporting but that this fact was not disclosed to investors. Intertie commingled partnership funds, taking funds generated from the sale of new partnership offerings to meet debt service obligations of previously sold cable systems; Intertie also used funds from limited partnerships that were formed but that never acquired cable systems. Intertie did not keep any records regarding the qualifications of investors to purchase the securities and also refused to make its financial statements available to investors.

Intertie suffered severe financial difficulties and eventually filed for bankruptcy. The limited partners suffered substantial losses. Did each of the limited partnership offerings alone qualify for the private placement exemption from registration? Should the 30 limited partnership offerings be integrated? [*Securities and Exchange Commission v. Murphy*, 626 F.2d 633 (9th Cir. 1980)]

32.9 Business Ethics R. Foster Winans, a reporter for the *Wall Street Journal*, was one of the writers of the "Heard on the Street" column, a widely read and influential column in the *Journal*. This column frequently included articles that discussed the prospects of companies listed on national and regional stock exchanges and the over-the-counter market. David Carpenter worked as a news clerk at the *Journal*. The *Journal* had a conflict of interest policy that prohibited employees from using nonpublic information learned on the job for their personal benefit. Winans and Carpenter were aware of this policy.

Kenneth P. Felis and Peter Brant were stockbrokers at the brokerage house of Kidder Peabody. Winans agreed to provide Felis and Brant with information that was to appear in the "Heard" column in advance of its publication in the *Journal*. Generally, Winans would provide this information to the brokers the day before it was to appear in the *Journal*. Carpenter served as a messenger between the parties. Based on this advance information, the brokers bought and sold securities of companies discussed in the "Heard" column. During 1983 and 1984, prepublication trades of approximately 27 "Heard" columns netted profits of almost $690,000. The parties used telephones to transfer information. The *Wall Street Journal* is distributed by mail to many of its subscribers.

Eventually, Kidder Peabody noticed a correlation between the "Heard" column and trading by the brokers. After an SEC investigation, criminal charges were brought against defendants Winans, Carpenter, and Felis in U.S. district court. Brant became the government's key witness. Winans and Felis were convicted of conspiracy to commit securities, mail, and wire fraud. Carpenter was convicted of aiding and abetting the commission of securities, mail, and wire fraud. The defendants appealed their convictions. Can the defendants be held criminally liable for conspiring to violate, and aiding and abetting the violation of, Section 10(b) and Rule 10b-5 of securities law? Did Winans act ethically in this case? Did Brant act ethically by turning government's witness? [*United States v. Carpenter*, 484 U.S. 19, 108 S.Ct. 316, 98 L.Ed.2d 275 (1987)]

BRIEFING THE CASE WRITING ASSIGNMENT

Read the following case, which has been excerpted from the court's opinions. Review and brief the case.

Lampf, Pleva, Lipkind, Prupis & Petigrow v. Gilbertson
111 S.Ct. 2773, 115 L.Ed.2D 321 (1991)
United States Supreme Court

Blackmun, Justice

The controversy arises from the sale of seven Connecticut limited partnerships formed for the purpose of purchasing and leasing computer hardware and software. Petitioner Lampf, Pleva, Lipkind, Prupis & Petigrow is a West Orange, New Jersey, law firm that aided in organizing the partnerships and that provided additional legal services, including the preparation of opinion letters addressing the tax consequences of investing in the partnerships. The several plaintiff-respondents purchased units in one or more of the partnerships during the years 1979 through 1981 with the expectation of realizing federal income tax benefits therefrom.

The partnerships failed, due in part to the technological obsolescence of their wares. In late 1982 and early 1983, Gilbertson, et al., received notice that the U.S. Internal Revenue Service was investigating the partnerships. The IRS subsequently disallowed the claimed tax benefits because of overvaluation of partnership assets and lack of profit motive. On November 3, 1986, and June 4, 1987, Gilbertson, et al., filed their respective complaints in the U.S. District Court for the District of Oregon, naming as defendants' petitioner and others involved in the preparation of offering memoranda for the partnerships. The complaints alleged that plaintiff-respondents were induced to invest in the partnerships by misrepresentations in the offering memoranda, in violation of, among other things, § 10(b) of the 1934 Securities Exchange Act and Rule 10b-5. The claimed misrepresentations were said to include assurances that the investments would entitle the purchasers to substantial tax benefits; that the leasing of the hardware and software packages would generate a profit; that the software was readily marketable; and that certain equipment appraisals were accurate and reasonable. Gilbertson, et al., asserted that they became aware of the alleged misrepresentations only in 1985 following the disallowance by the IRS of the tax benefits claimed.

After consolidating the actions for discovery and pretrial proceedings, the District Court granted summary judgment for the defendants on the ground that the complaints were not timely filed. The Court of Appeals for the Ninth Circuit reversed and remanded the cases. In view of the divergence of opinion among the Circuits regarding the proper limitations period for Rule 10b-5 claims, we granted certiorari to address this important issue.

It is the usual rule that when Congress has failed to provide a statute of limitations for a federal cause of action, a court "borrows" or "absorbs" the local time limitation most analogous to the case at hand. This practice, derived from the Rules of Decision Act, has enjoyed sufficient longevity that we may assume that, in enacting remedial legislation, Congress ordinarily "intends by its silence that we borrow state law." The rule, however, is not without exception.

First, the court must determine whether a uniform statute of limitations is to be selected. Where a federal cause of action tends in practice to "encompass numerous and diverse topics and subtopics," such that a single state limitations period may not be consistently applied within a jurisdiction, we have concluded that the federal interests in predictability and judicial economy counsel the adoption of one source, or class of sources, for borrowing purposes.

Second, assuming a uniform limitations period is appropriate, the court must decide whether this period should be derived from a state or federal source. In making this judgment, the court should accord particular weight to the geographic character of the claim.

Finally, even where geographic considerations counsel federal borrowing, the aforementioned presumption of state borrowing that requires that a court determine that an analogous federal source truly affords a "closer fit" with the cause of action at issue than does any available state-law source. Although considerations pertinent to this determination will necessarily vary depending upon the federal cause of action and the available state and federal analogues, such factors as commonality of purpose and similarity of elements will be relevant.

We conclude that where, as here, the claim asserted is one implied under a statute that also contains an express cause of action with its own time limitation, a court should look first to the statute of origin to ascertain the proper limitations period. In the present litigation, there can be no doubt that the contemporaneously enacted express remedial provisions represent "a federal statute of limitations actually designed to accommodate a balance of interests very similar to that at stake here—a statute that is, in fact, an analogy to the present lawsuit more apt than any of the suggested state-law parallels." The 1934 Act contained a number of express causes of action, each with an explicit limitations period. With only one more restrictive exception, each of these includes some variation of a 1-year period after discovery combined with a 3-year period of repose. In adopting the 1934 Act, the 73rd Congress also amended the limitations provision of the 1933 Act, adopting the 1-and-3-year structure for each cause of action contained therein. We therefore conclude that we must reject the Commission's contention that the 5-year period contained in § 20A, added to the 1934 Act in 1988, is more appropriate for § 10(b) actions than is the 1-and-3-year structure in the Act's original remedial provisions.

Litigation instituted pursuant to § 10(b) and Rule 10b-5 therefore must be commenced within one year after the discovery of the facts constituting the violation and within three years after such violation. As there is no dispute that the earliest of plaintiff-respondents' complaints was filed more than three years after petitioner's alleged misrepresentations, Gilbertson et al., claims were untimely.

The judgment of the Court of Appeals is reversed.

ENDNOTES

1. *Securities and Exchange Commission v. W.J. Howey Co.*, 328 U.S. 293, 66 S.Ct. 1100 (1946).
2. Securities Act of 1933, § 4(1).
3. Securities Act of 1933, § 3(a)(11).
4. SEC Rule 147.
5. Securities Act of 1933, § 4(2).
6. SEC Rule 506.
7. SEC Rule 501.
8. Securities Act of 1933, § 3(b).
9. SEC Rules 502(a) and 147(b)(2).
10. 15 U.S.C. § 77x.
11. Litigation instituted pursuant to § 10(b) and Rule 10b-5 must be commenced within one year after the discovery of the violation and within three years after such violation [*Lampf, Pleva, Lipkind, Prupis & Petigrow v. Gilbertson*, 111 S.Ct. 2773 (1991)].
12. The U.S. Supreme Court has held that the sale of a business is a sale of securities that is subject to Section 10(b). See *Gould v. Ruefenacht*, 471 U.S. 701, 105 S.Ct. 2308 (1985) (where 50 percent of a business was sold) and *Landreth Timber Co. v. Landreth*, 471 U.S. 681, 105 S.Ct. 2297 (1985) (where 100 percent of a business was sold).
13. *Ernst & Ernst v. Hochfelder*, 425 U.S. 185, 96 S.Ct. 1375 (1976).
14. 40 SEC 907 (1961).
15. 15 U.S.C. § 78 ff.
16. P.L. 98-376.
17. 15 U.S.C. § 78l.
18. 15 U.S.C. § 78p(b).
19. Ownership Reports and Trading by Officers, Directors and Principal Security Holders, Exchange Act Release No. 28869.
20. 18 U.S.C. §§ 1961 to 1968.
21. Private Securities Litigation Reform Act of 1995.
22. *Reves v. Ernst & Young*, 113 S.Ct. 1163 (1993).

Government Regulation

33

Administrative Law and Consumer Protection

I should regret to find that the law was powerless to enforce the most elementary principles of commercial morality.

—Lord Hershell
Reddaway v. Banham (1896), A.C. 199, at p. 209.

Chapter Objectives

After studying this chapter, you should be able to:

1. Describe government regulation and the functions of administrative agencies.

2. List the responsibilities of the federal Food and Drug Administration.

3. Describe government regulation of food, food additives, drugs, cosmetics, and medicinal devices.

4. Explain the protections provided by United Nations Biosafety Protocol for Genetically Altered Foods.

5. Explain the coverage of consumer product safety acts.

6. Describe the scope of federal laws to childproof containers and packages.

7. Identify unfair and deceptive practices that violate Section 5 of the Federal Trade Commission Act.

8. Describe the coverage of consumer credit protection statutes.

9. Describe the protections of international consumer protection laws.

10. Describe the reach of state "anti-spam" statutes regulating commercial e-mail.

Chapter Contents

Congress and the executive branch of government have created over 100 federal **administrative agencies**. These agencies are intended to provide resources and expertise in dealing with complex commercial organizations and businesses. Additionally, state governments have created many state administrative agencies. Thousands of *rules and regulations* regarding business operations have been adopted and enforced by federal and state administrative agencies. Since the 1960s, the number of administrative agencies, and the regulations they produce, have increased substantially. Because of their importance, administrative agencies are informally referred to as the *fourth branch of government*.

Originally, sales transactions in this country were guided by the principle of ***caveat emptor*** ("let the buyer beware"). To promote product safety and prohibit abusive, unfair, and deceptive selling practices, federal and state governments have enacted a variety of statutes that regulate the behavior of businesses that deal with consumers. These laws are collectively referred to as **consumer protection laws**.

This chapter discusses administrative agencies and consumer protection laws.

GOVERNMENT REGULATION

The government's recordkeeping and reporting requirements form a large part of administrative law. Other government regulations concern proper business purpose and conduct, entry restrictions into an industry, government rate setting, and the like.

Proponents of government regulation argue that it is needed to protect consumers and others from unethical and deceptive business practices. Opponents say that the time and compliance and enforcement costs outweigh the benefits of regulation. The debate rages on, but one fact is certain: Government regulation will continue to affect business operations.

General Government Regulation

Most government regulation applies to many businesses and industries collectively. For example, the National Labor Relations Board (NLRB) is empowered to regulate the formation and operation of labor unions in most industries, the Occupational Safety and Health Administration (OSHA) is authorized to formulate and enact safety and health standards for the workplace, the Consumer Product Safety Commission (CPSC) is empowered to establish mandatory safety standards for products sold in this country, and the Securities and Exchange Commission (SEC) is authorized to enforce federal securities laws that apply to issuers and persons who trade in securities.

administrative agencies

Agencies that the legislative and executive branches of federal and state governments establish.

caveat emptor

"Let the buyer beware," the traditional guideline of sales transactions.

consumer protection laws

Federal and state statutes and regulations that promote product safety and prohibit abusive, unfair, and deceptive business practices.

Business Brief

Businesses spend billions of dollars each year complying with government regulation.

Business Brief

Businesses are subject to *general government regulation* that applies to many businesses and industries collectively (e.g., antidiscrimination laws).

E-Commerce & Information Technology

TELEPHONE CONSUMER PROTECTION ACT

In recent years, telemarketing has become a popular means for advertisers and telemarketers to reach greater numbers of potential consumers. However, many consumers resented receiving these unsolicited calls. In response, Congress enacted the **Telephone Consumer Protection Act of 1991** to address certain telemarketing abuses.

One provision of the act restricts the use of automated devices that dial up to hundreds and thousands of phone numbers an hour and play a prerecorded sales pitch. The act makes it unlawful for phone calls to be initiated by using a prerecorded voice to deliver a message without the prior written consent of the called party. Congress justified the restriction by finding that such calls invaded the privacy of the receiver, cluttered up answering machines, and did not disconnect if the receiver hung up. Under the act, a prerecorded message can be used only if a live person introduces the call and receives the consumer's permission to play the message. The act exempts calls initiated for emergency purposes, calls made to businesses, and calls made by nonprofit organizations. Personal calls are not covered by the act at all.

The trade association representing telemarketer operators challenged the law, claiming that it violated their First Amendment free-speech rights. The court of appeals upheld the law as a valid time, place, and manner restriction on commercial speech. The court reasoned that the law left open ample alternative channels for the communication of information [*Moser v. Federal Communications Commission*, 46 F.3d 970 (9th Cir. 1995)].

Specific Government Regulation

Congress and the executive branch created some administrative agencies to monitor certain regulated industries. For example, the Federal Communications Commission (FCC) regulates the operation of television and radio stations, the Interstate Commerce Commission (ICC) regulates railroads, the Federal Aviation Administration (FAA) regulates commercial airlines, and the Office of the Comptroller of the Currency (OCC) regulates national banks. Although a detailed discussion of these agencies and the laws they administer is beyond the scope of this book, it is important to know that they exist.

Entrepreneur and the Law

U.S. DEPARTMENT OF AGRICULTURE ADMINISTERS FARMING LAWS

In May 1862, Congress created the **U.S. Department of Agriculture (USDA)** to administer the country's farm-oriented programs. The USDA, which is headed by the secretary of agriculture, a cabinet-level post, is composed of several administrative agencies and programs. Other federal administrative agencies (such as the Veterans Administration and the Environmental Protection Agency) and state administrative agencies also have an impact on farming operations. The USDA may affect farmers through (1) rule making, (2) adjudication proceedings, and (3) reparation proceedings that decide disputes between private parties (discussed later).

The federal statutes administered by the USDA include the following:

- Agricultural Marketing Agreement Act
- Animal Quarantine Act
- Animal Welfare Act
- Archaeological Resources Protection Act
- Beef Research and Information Act
- Cotton Research and Promotion Act

- Egg Products Inspection Act
- Egg Research and Consumer Information Act
- Endangered Species Act
- Federal Land Policy and Management Act
- Federal Meat Inspection Act
- Federal Seed Act
- Horse Protection Act
- Meat Inspection Act
- Packers and Stockyards Act
- Perishable Agricultural Commodities Act
- Potato Research and Promotion Act
- Poultry Production Inspection Act
- Poultry Products Protection Act
- Swine Health Protection Act
- United States Cotton Standards Act
- United States Grain Standards Act
- United States Warehouse Act
- Virus-Serum-Toxin Act
- Wheat and Wheat Foods Research and Nutrition Education Act

The U.S. Department of Agriculture, a federal administrative agency, administers and enforces numerous federal statutes that regulate the safety of agricultural and food products.

ADMINISTRATIVE AGENCIES

Administrative agencies are generally established with the goal of creating a body of professionals who are experts in a particular field. These experts have delegated authority to regulate an individual industry or a specific area of commerce.

Administrative agencies are created by federal, state, and local governments. They range from large, complex federal agencies, such as the Department of Health and Human Resources, to local zoning boards. Many administrative agencies are given the authority to adopt **rules and regulations** that enforce and interpret statutory law (the rule-making power of administrative agencies is discussed later in this chapter).

Federal Administrative Agencies

The most pervasive government regulations have developed from the statutes enforced by and the rules and regulations adopted by **federal administrative agencies**. The majority of federal administrative agencies—including the Justice Department, the Department of Housing and Urban Development, the Labor Department, the Transportation Department, and the Commerce Department—are part of the executive branch of government.

Congress has established many federal administrative agencies. These agencies are independent of the executive branch and have broad regulatory powers over key areas of the national economy. Many of these independent agencies are discussed separately in this book.

State Administrative Agencies

All states have created administrative agencies to enforce and interpret state law. For example, most states have a corporations department to enforce state corporations law, a banking department to regulate the operation of banks, fish and game departments, and workers' compensation boards. **State administrative agencies** also have a profound effect on business. Local governments and municipalities create administrative agencies, such as zoning commissions, to administer local law.

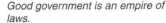

> Good government is an empire of laws.
>
> *John Adams*
> Thoughts on Government
> *(1776)*

rules and regulations
Adopted by administrative agencies to interpret the statutes that they are authorized to enforce.

federal administrative agencies
Administrative agencies that are part of the executive or legislative branch of government.

Administrative Procedure Act (APA)
An act that establishes certain administrative procedures that federal administrative agencies must follow in conducting their affairs.

state administrative agencies
Administrative agencies that states create to enforce and interpret state law.

Landmark Law

ADMINISTRATIVE PROCEDURE ACT

In 1946, Congress enacted the **Administrative Procedure Act (APA)** [5 U.S.C. §§ 551 et seq.]. This act establishes certain administrative procedures that federal administrative agencies must follow in conducting their affairs. For example, the APA establishes notice and hearing requirements, rules for conducting agency adjudicative actions, and procedures for rule making. Most states have enacted administrative procedural acts that govern state administrative agencies.

Administrative law judges (ALJs) preside over administrative proceedings. They decide questions of law and fact concerning the case. There is no jury. The ALJ is an employee of the administrative agency. Both the administrative agency and the respondent may be represented by counsel. Witnesses may be examined and cross-examined, evidence may be introduced, objections may be made, and such.

The ALJ's decision is issued in the form of an **order**. The order must state the reasons for the ALJ's decision. The order becomes final if it is not appealed. An appeal consists of a review by the agency. The agency review can result in new findings of fact and law. Further appeal can be made to the appropriate federal court (in federal agency actions) or state court (in state agency actions).

Administrative Law

Administrative law is a combination of substantive and procedural law. Each federal administrative agency is empowered to administer a particular statute or statutes. For example, the Securities and Exchange Commission (SEC) is authorized to enforce the Securities Act of 1933, the Securities Exchange Act of 1934, and other federal statutes dealing with securities markets. These statutes are the *substantive law* that is enforced by the agency.

Business Brief

Administrative agencies are often criticized for creating too much "red tape" for businesses and individuals.

delegation doctrine

A doctrine that says when an administrative agency is created, it is delegated certain powers; the agency can only use those legislative, judicial, and executive powers that are delegated to it.

substantive rules

Government regulation that has the force of law and must be adhered to by covered persons and businesses.

Because the U.S. Constitution does not stipulate that administrative agencies are a separate branch of the government, they must be created by the legislative or executive branch. When an administrative agency is created, it is delegated certain powers. The agency has only the legislative, judicial, and executive powers that are delegated to it. This is called the **delegation doctrine**.

Legislative Powers of Administrative Agencies

Administrative agencies usually are delegated certain *legislative powers*. Many federal statutes expressly authorize an administrative agency to issue **substantive rules**. A substantive regulation is much like a statute: It has the force of law and must be adhered to by covered persons and businesses. Violators may be held civilly or criminally liable, depending on the rule. All substantive rules are subject to judicial review.

The Supreme Court Speaks

Federal Food and Drug Administration Cannot Regulate Tobacco as a Drug

Food and Drug Administration v. Brown & Williamson Tobacco Corporation
529 U.S. 120, 120 S.Ct. 1291 (2000)
Supreme Court of the United States

BACKGROUND AND FACTS

The Food and Drug Administration (FDA) is a federal administrative agency empowered to administer the Food, Drug, and Cosmetic Act (FDC Act). Pursuant to this act, the FDA can regulate "drugs" and medical "devices." Based on its perceived power under the FDA Act, the FDA enacted a rule regulating tobacco products. The rule:

1. Prohibits the sale of cigarettes and smokeless tobacco to persons younger than 18.
2. Requires retailers to verify through photo identification the age of all purchasers younger than 27.
3. Prohibits the sale of cigarettes in quantities smaller than 20.
4. Prohibits the distribution of free samples.
5. Prohibits sales through self-service displays and vending machines except in adult-only locations.
6. Requires print advertising appear in black-and-white, text-only format.
7. Prohibits outdoor advertising within 1,000 feet of any public school or playground.
8. Prohibits the distribution of any promotional items, such as T-shirts or hats, bearing the manufacturer's brand.
9. Prohibits a manufacturer from sponsoring any athletic, musical, artistic, or other social or cultural event using its brand name.
10. Requires that the statement "A Nicotine-Delivery Device for Persons 18 or Older" appear on all tobacco products.

A group of tobacco manufacturers and advertisers filed a lawsuit in district court, asserting that the FDA did not have authority to regulate tobacco as a "drug" or "device" that delivered nicotine to the body. The district court certified the issue to the court of appeals, which held that the FDC Act did not grant the FDA power to regulate tobacco products. The U.S. Supreme Court granted certiorari to hear the appeal.

SUPREME COURT ISSUE

Does the Food, Drug, and Cosmetics Act grant the Food and Drug Administration authority to regulate tobacco products as a "drug" or "device"?

IN THE LANGUAGE OF THE U.S. SUPREME COURT

O'Connor, Justice Regardless of how serious the problem an administrative agency seeks to address, however, it may not exercise its authority in a manner that is inconsistent with the administrative structure that Congress enacted into law. Congress has foreclosed the removal of tobacco products from the market. A provision of the United States Code currently in force states that "the marketing of tobacco constitutes one of the greatest basic industries of the United States with ramifying activities which directly affect interstate and foreign commerce at every point, and stable conditions therein are necessary to the general welfare." More importantly, Congress has directly addressed the problem of tobacco and health through legislation on six occasions since 1965. See Federal Cigarette Labeling and Advertising Act (FCLAA), Public Health Cigarette Smoking Act of 1969, Alcohol and Drug Abuse Amendments of 1983, Comprehensive Smoking Education Act, Comprehensive Smokeless Tobacco Health Education Act of 1986, and Alcohol, Drug Abuse, and Mental Health Administration Reorganization Act. When Congress enacted these statutes, the adverse health consequences of tobacco use were well known, as were nicotine's pharmacological effects. Nonetheless, Congress stopped well short of ordering a ban. Instead, it has generally regulated the labeling and advertisement of tobacco products.

Considering the FDC Act as a whole, it is clear that Congress intended to exclude tobacco products from the FDA's jurisdiction. A fundamental precept of the FDC Act is that any product regulated by the FDA—but not banned—must be safe for its intended use. Consequently, if tobacco products were within the FDA's jurisdiction, the FDC Act would require the FDA to remove them from the market entirely. But a ban would contradict Congress' clear intent as expressed in its more recent, tobacco-specific legislation. The inescapable conclusion is that there is no room for tobacco products within the FDC Act's regulatory scheme.

By no means do we question the seriousness of the problem that the FDA has sought to address. The agency has amply demonstrated that tobacco use, particularly among children and adolescents, poses perhaps the single most significant threat to public health in the United States. Nonetheless, no matter how important, conspicuous, and controversial the issue, an administrative agency's power to regulate in the public interest must always be grounded in a valid grant of authority from Congress. And, in our anxiety to effectuate the congressional purpose of protecting the public, we must take care not to extend the scope of the statute beyond the point where Congress indicated it would stop. Reading the FDC Act as a whole, as well as in conjunction with Congress' subsequent tobacco-specific

legislation, it is plain that Congress has not given the FDA the authority that it seeks to exercise here.

DECISION AND REMEDY

The U.S. Supreme Court held that the FDA does not have authority under the Food, Drug, and Cosmetics Act to regulate tobacco products as a "drug" or "device." The judgment of the court of appeals is affirmed.

CASE QUESTIONS

Critical Legal Thinking   Did the FDA exceed its delegated authority under the FDC Act by enacting its tobacco products rules?

Business Ethics   Do you think that the cigarette companies have "bought off" Congress? Explain your answer.

Contemporary Business   Do the state and federal governments have a "stake" in cigarette product sales? What economic effects would a ban on cigarette sales cause to state and federal governments?

Entrepreneur and the Law

LICENSING POWERS OF ADMINISTRATIVE AGENCIES

Statutes often require the issuance of a government *license* before a person can enter certain types of industries (e.g., the operation of banks, television and radio stations, and commercial airlines) or professions (e.g., doctors, lawyers, dentists, certified public accountants, and contractors). Most administrative agencies have the power to determine whether to grant licenses to applicants.

Applicants must usually submit detailed applications to the appropriate administrative agency. In addition, the agency usually accepts written comments from interested parties and holds hearings on the matter. The administrative agency's decision is subject to judicial review. However, the courts generally defer to the expertise of administrative agencies in licensing matters.

Executive Powers of Administrative Agencies

Administrative agencies are usually granted **executive powers** such as the investigation and prosecution of possible violations of statutes, administrative rules, and administrative orders. To perform these functions successfully, the agency must often obtain information from the persons and businesses under investigation as well as from other sources.

Administrative Searches   Sometimes a physical inspection of the business premises is crucial to the investigation. Most inspections by administrative agencies are considered "searches" that are subject to the Fourth Amendment of the U.S. Constitution. The Fourth Amendment protects persons (including businesses) from **unreasonable search and seizures**.

Searches by administrative agencies are generally considered to be reasonable within the meaning of the Fourth Amendment if

- The party voluntarily agrees to the search.
- The search is conducted pursuant to a validly issued *search warrant*.
- A warrantless search is conducted in an emergency situation.
- The business is part of a special industry where warrantless searches are automatically considered valid (such as liquor or firearm sales).
- The business is part of a hazardous industry, and a statute expressly provides for nonarbitrary warrantless searches (such as coal mines).

Evidence from an unreasonable search and seizure ("tainted evidence") may be inadmissible in court, depending on the circumstances of the case.

executive powers

Powers that administrative agencies are granted, such as the investigation and prosecution of possible violations of statutes, administrative rules, and administrative orders.

unreasonable search and seizure

Any search and seizure by the government that violates the Fourth Amendment.

The Supreme Court Speaks

Administrative Agency Aerial Search of a Business Found Constitutional

Dow Chemical Company v. United States
476 U.S. 227, 106 S.Ct. 1819 (1986)
Supreme Court of the United States

FACTS AND BACKGROUND

Since the 1890s, Dow Chemical Company (Dow) has manufactured chemicals at a facility in Midland, Michigan. Its complex covers 2,000 acres and contains a number of chemical-processing plants. Many of these are "open-air" plants, with reactor equipment, loading and storage facilities, motors, transfer lines, and piping conduits located in the open areas between the buildings. Dow has undertaken elaborate precautions to secure the facility from unwelcome intrusion: An eight-foot-high chain-link fence completely surrounds the facility, security personnel guard the plant and monitor it by closed-circuit television, unauthorized entry into the facility triggers alarm systems, motion detectors indicate movement of persons within restricted areas, and the use of camera equipment by anyone other than authorized Dow personnel is prohibited. Dow considers its entire facility a trade secret.

The Environmental Protection Agency (EPA) is a federal administrative agency empowered to administer and enforce the federal Clean Air Act. In 1978, Dow denied an EPA request to conduct an on-site inspection of the Midland facility. EPA did not seek an administrative search warrant. Instead, EPA employed a commercial aerial photographer to take photographs of the facility from altitudes of 12,000, 3,000, and 1,200 feet. Using a standard floor-mounted, precision aerial-mapping camera, this firm took approximately 75 color photographs of various parts of the plant. When the photographs taken from 1,200 feet were enlarged, it was possible to discern equipment, pipes, and power lines as small as one-half inch in diameter. Several weeks later, after Dow learned about the EPA-authorized flight from independent sources, it filed suit against EPA. The district court held in favor of Dow and issued an injunction against the EPA's use of the photographs. The court of appeals reversed. Dow appealed.

SUPREME COURT ISSUE

Did EPA's aerial photography of Dow's plant constitute an unreasonable search in violation of the Fourth Amendment to the U.S. Constitution?

IN THE LANGUAGE OF THE U.S. SUPREME COURT

Burger, Chief Justice *We turn to Dow's contention that taking aerial photographs constituted a search without warrant, thereby violating Dow's rights under the Fourth Amendment. Plainly a business establishment or an industrial or commercial facility enjoys certain protections under the Fourth Amendment. Dow plainly has a reasonable, legitimate, and objective expectation of privacy within the interior of its covered buildings, and it is equally clear that expectation is one society is prepared to observe. Dow's inner manufacturing areas are elaborately secured to ensure they are not open or exposed to the public from the ground. Any actual physical entry by EPA into any enclosed area would raise significantly different questions, because the businessman, like the occupant of a residence, has a constitutional right to go about his business free from unreasonable official entries upon his private commercial property.*

The issue raised by Dow's claim of search and seizure, however, concerns aerial observation of a 2,000-acre outdoor manufacturing facility without physical entry. The intimate activities associated with family privacy and the home and its curtilage simply do not reach the outdoor areas or spaces between structures and buildings of a manufacturing plant. The government has greater latitude to conduct warrantless inspections of commercial property because the expectation of privacy that the owner enjoys in such property differs significantly from the sanctity accorded an individual's home. We emphasized that unlike a homeowner's interest in his dwelling, the interest of the owner of commercial property is not one in being free from any inspections. And with regard to regulatory inspections, we have held that what is observable by the public is observable without warrant, by the government inspector as well.

Here, EPA was not employing some unique sensory device that, for example, could penetrate the walls of buildings and record conversations in Dow's plants, offices, or laboratories, but rather a conventional, albeit precise, commercial camera commonly used in map making. It may well be, as the government concedes, that the surveillance of private property by using highly sophisticated surveillance equipment not generally available to the public, such as satellite technology, might be constitutionally proscribed absent warrant. But the photographs here are not so revealing of intimate details as to raise constitutional concerns. Although they undoubtedly give EPA more detailed information than naked-eye views, they remain limited to an outline of the facility's buildings and equipment. The mere fact that human vision is enhanced somewhat, at least to the degree here, does not give rise to constitutional problems.

DECISION AND REMEDY

The Supreme Court held that the taking of photographs of an industrial plant complex from navigable airspace is not a search prohibited by the Fourth Amendment. Affirmed.

CASE QUESTIONS

Critical Legal Thinking Should the government be given greater latitude to conduct warrantless searches of business property than personal homes? Why or why not?

Business Ethics Did EPA act ethically in this case?

Contemporary Business Could Dow have in any way protected itself from the search conducted in this case?

The Supreme Court Speaks

Warrantless Administrative Agency Search of Regulated Business Permitted

New York v. Burger
482 U.S. 691, 107 S.Ct. 2636, 96 L.Ed.2d 601 (1987)
Supreme Court of the United States

BACKGROUND AND FACTS

Joseph Burger is the owner of a junkyard in Brooklyn, New York. His business consists, in part, of dismantling automobiles and selling their parts. The state of New York enacted a statute that requires automobile junkyards to keep certain records. The statute authorizes warrantless searches of vehicle dismantlers and automobile junkyards without prior notice. At approximately noon on November 17, 1982, five plainclothes officers of the Auto Crimes Division of the New York City Police Department entered Burger's junkyard to conduct a surprise inspection. Burger did not have either a license to conduct the business or records of the automobiles and vehicle parts on his premises as required by state law. After conducting an inspection of the premises, the officers determined that Burger was in possession of stolen vehicles and parts. He was arrested and charged with criminal possession of stolen property. Burger moved to suppress the evidence. The New York Supreme Court and appellate division held the search to be constitutional. The New York court of appeals reversed. New York appealed.

SUPREME COURT ISSUE

Does the warrantless search of an automobile junkyard pursuant to a state statute that authorizes such search constitute an unreasonable search and seizure in violation of the Fourth Amendment to the U.S. Constitution?

IN THE LANGUAGE OF THE U.S. SUPREME COURT

Blackmun, Justice The Court has long recognized that the Fourth Amendment's prohibition on unreasonable searches and seizures is applicable to commercial premises, as well as to private homes.

An expectation of privacy in commercial premises, however, is different from, and indeed less than, a similar expectation in an individual's home. This expectation is particularly attenuated in commercial property employed in "closely regulated" industries. Because the owner or operator of commercial premises in a closely regulated industry has a reduced expectation of privacy, the warrant and probable cause requirements—which fulfill the traditional Fourth Amendment standard of reasonableness for a government search—have a lessened application in this context. The nature of the regulatory statute reveals that the operation of a junkyard, part

of which is devoted to vehicle dismantling, is a closely regulated business in the state of New York. A warrantless inspection of commercial premises may well be reasonable within the meaning of the Fourth Amendment.

The New York regulatory scheme satisfies the three criteria necessary to make reasonable warrantless inspections. First, the state has a substantial interest in regulating the vehicle dismantling and automobile junkyard industry because motor vehicle theft has increased in the state of New York and because the problem of theft is associated with this industry. Second, regulation of the vehicle dismantling industry reasonably serves the state's substantial interest in eradicating automobile theft. It is well established that the theft problem can be addressed effectively by controlling the receiver of, or market in, stolen property. Automobile junkyards and vehicle dismantlers provide the major market for stolen vehicles and vehicle parts. Third, the New York law provides a constitutionally adequate substitute for a warrant. The statute informs the operator of a vehicle dismantling business that inspections will be made on a regular basis.

DECISION AND REMEDY

The U.S. Supreme Court held that the New York statute that authorizes warrantless searches of vehicles dismantling businesses and automobile junkyards does not constitute an unreasonable search in violation of the Fourth Amendment to the U.S. Constitution. The Supreme Court reversed the judgment of the New York court of appeals and remanded the case for further proceedings consistent with its decision.

CASE QUESTIONS

Critical Legal Thinking Should the Fourth Amendment's protection against unreasonable searches and seizures apply to businesses? Why or why not?

Business Ethics Was it ethical for the defendant to assert the Fourth Amendment's prohibition against unreasonable searches and seizures?

Contemporary Business Is auto theft a big business? Will the New York law that regulates vehicle dismantling businesses and junkyards help to alleviate this crime?

Judicial Powers of Administrative Agencies

Many administrative agencies have the judicial authority to adjudicate cases through an administrative proceeding. Such a proceeding is initiated when an agency serves a complaint on a party the agency believes has violated a statute or administrative rule or order. The person on whom the complaint is served is called the *respondent*.

In adjudicating cases, an administrative agency must comply with the Due Process Clause of the U.S. Constitution (and state constitution where applicable). *Procedural due process* requires the respondent to be given (1) proper and timely notice of the allegations or charges against him or her and (2) an opportunity to present evidence on the matter. *Substantive due process* requires that the statute or rule that the respondent is charged with violating be clearly stated.

Administrative law judges (ALJs) preside over administrative proceedings. They decide questions of law and fact concerning the case. There is no jury. The ALJ is an employee of the administrative agency. The ALJ's decision is issued in the form of an **order**. The order must state the reasons for the ALJ's decision. The order becomes final if it is not appealed. An appeal consists of a review by the agency. The agency review can result in new findings of fact and law.

An administration agency rule, order, or decision may be appealed to the appropriate court (see Exhibit 33.1).

administrative law judge (ALJ)

A judge, presiding over administrative proceedings, who decides questions of law and fact concerning the case.

order

Decision issued by an administrative law judge.

Business Brief

A party must have exhausted all his or her administrative remedies within the appropriate administrative agency before he or she can seek judicial review of the agency's decision.

𝓔XHIBIT **33.1** *Appeal of a Federal Administrative Agency Rule, Order, or Decision*

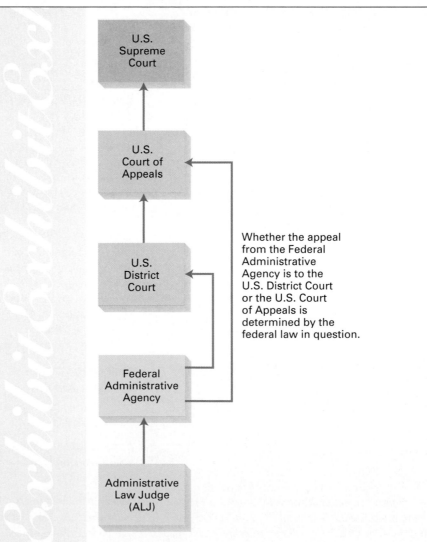

Whether the appeal from the Federal Administrative Agency is to the U.S. District Court or the U.S. Court of Appeals is determined by the federal law in question.

*C*ONCEPT SUMMARY   POWERS OF ADMINISTRATIVE AGENCIES

Power	Description of Power
Legislative Powers	To adopt rules that advance the purpose of the statutes that the agency is empowered to enforce. These rules have the force of law. Public notice and participation are required.
Executive Powers	To prosecute violations of statutes and administrative rules and orders. This includes the power to investigate suspected violations, issue administrative subpoenas, and conduct administrative searches.
Judicial Powers	To adjudicate cases through an administrative proceeding. This includes the power to issue a complaint, hold a hearing by an administrative law judge (ALJ), and issue an order deciding the case and assessing remedies.

*L*andmark *L*aw

FEDERAL FOOD, DRUG, AND COSMETIC ACT

The first federal statute regulating the wholesomeness of food and drug products was enacted in 1906. A much more comprehensive act—the federal **Food, Drug, and Cosmetic Act (FDCA)**—was enacted in 1938 [21 U.S.C. § 301]. This act, as amended, provides the basis for the regulation of much of the testing, manufacture, distribution, and sale of foods, drugs, cosmetics, and medicinal products and devices in the United States. The act is administered by the **Food and Drug Administration (FDA)**.

Before certain food additives, drugs, cosmetics, and medicinal devices can be sold to the public, they must receive FDA approval. An applicant must submit an application to the FDA that contains relevant information about the safety and uses of the product. The FDA, after considering the evidence, will either approve or deny the application.

The FDA can seek search warrants and conduct inspections; obtain orders for the seizure, recall, and condemnation of products, seek injunctions; and suspected criminal violations to the U.S. Department of Justice for prosecution.

*T*HE FDA'S ADMINISTRATION OF THE FEDERAL FOOD, DRUG, AND COSMETIC ACT

The **FDA** is empowered to regulate food, food additives, drugs, cosmetics, and medicinal devices.

Regulation of Food

The **FDCA** prohibits the shipment, distribution, or sale of *adulterated food*. Food is deemed adulterated if it consists in whole or in part of any "filthy, putrid, or decomposed substance" or if it is otherwise "unfit for food." Note that food does not have to be entirely pure to be distributed or sold—it only has to be unadulterated.

The FDCA also prohibits *false and misleading labeling* of food products. In addition, it mandates affirmative disclosure of information on food labels, including the name of the food, the name and place of the manufacturer, and a statement of ingredients. A manufacturer may be held liable for deceptive labeling or packaging.

Food and Drug Administration (FDA)

Federal administrative agency that administers and enforces the federal Food, Drug, and Cosmetic Act (FDCA) and other federal consumer protection laws.

Food, Drug, and Cosmetic Act (FDCA)

A federal statute enacted in 1938 that provides the basis for the regulation of much of the testing, manufacture, distribution, and sale of foods, drugs, cosmetics, and medicinal products.

Contemporary Business Environment

A HIDDEN SOURCE OF PROTEIN IN PEANUT BUTTER

So you take a big bite of a peanut butter sandwich and savor the taste. It has been processed by a food manufacturer and inspected by the federal government, so you think that it is pure peanut butter. Not necessarily. Under federal FDA guidelines, peanut butter may contain up to 30 insect fragments per 3½ ounces and still be considered "safe" for human consumption.

The FDA has set ceilings, or "action levels," for certain contaminants, or "defects," as the FDA likes to call them, for various foods. Several of these action levels are

> *Golden raisins—35 fly eggs per 8 ounces*
> *Popcorn—two rodent hairs per pound*
> *Shelled peanuts—20 insects per 100 pounds*
> *Canned mushrooms—20 maggots per 3½ ounces*
> *Tomato juice—10 fly eggs per 3½ ounces*

The FDA can mount inspections and raids to enforce its action levels. If it finds that the federal tolerance system has been violated, it can seize the offending food and destroy it at the owner's expense. For example, in the Great Peanut Raid of 1991, the FDA seized 8.5 million pounds of peanuts shipped to the United States from foreign countries. The FDA found these peanuts contained illegal levels of contamination and sent them back to their home countries.

The courts have upheld the presence of some contamination in food as lawful under the federal Food, Drug, and Cosmetic Act. For example, in one case the court found that 28 insect parts in nine pounds of butter did not violate the act. The court stated, "Few foods contain no natural or unavoidable defects. Even with modern technology, all defects in foods cannot be eliminated." [*United States v. Capital City Foods, Inc.,* 345 F. Supp. 277 (ND 1972)]

Business Ethics

LESS BALONEY ON THE SHELVES

For much of its existence, the federal FDA has been a paper tiger that was led by wine-and-dine-with-the-industry regulators. In April 1991, the FDA shocked the food industry by having U.S. marshals seize 24,000 half-gallon cartons of "Citrus Hill Fresh Choice" orange juice, which is made by mammoth food processor Procter & Gamble (P&G). After trying for a year to get P&G to remove the word *fresh* from the carton—the product is made from concentrate and is pasteurized—the FDA finally got tough. P&G gave in after two days and agreed to remove the word *fresh* from its Citrus Hill products.

Next on the FDA's hit list were Best Foods, which markets Mazola Corn Oil; Great Foods of America, makers of HeartBeat Canola Oil; and again P&G, manufacturer of Crisco Corn Oil. These companies had prominently advertised their cooking oils as having "no cholesterol," and some even added cute little hearts to the labels. Although the claim was literally true (these oils do not contain cholesterol), they are in fact 100% fat—which is not especially good for the heart. The FDA felt that these companies were hoodwinking the public and ordered the companies to take the "no cholesterol" labels off their vegetable oils.

In late 1990, Congress passed a sweeping truth-in-labeling law called the **Nutrition Labeling and Education Act**. The statute requires food manufacturers and processors to provide more nutritional information on virtually all foods

and bars them from making scientifically unsubstantiated health claims.

The new law requires the more than 20,000 food labels found on grocery store shelves to disclose the number of calories derived from fat and the amount of dietary fiber, saturated fat, cholesterol, and a variety of other substances. The law applies to packaged foods as well as fruit, vegetables, and raw seafood. Meat, poultry, and egg products, which are regulated by the Department of Agriculture, are exempt from the act, as are restaurant food and prepared dishes sold in supermarkets or delicatessens.

In December 1992, the FDA announced final regulations to implement the act. The regulations require food processors to provide uniform information about serving sizes and nutrients on labels of the food products they sell and establish standard definitions for *light, low fat, natural,* and other terms routinely bandied about by food processors.

With the new law on the books and a tough new stand, the FDA is coming out of its corner with its gloves on. The American consumer can only come out a winner.

1. Did Procter & Gamble act ethically when it used the word *fresh* on its orange juice cartons? Why do you think it did this?
2. Do you think labeling laws serve a useful purpose? Explain.

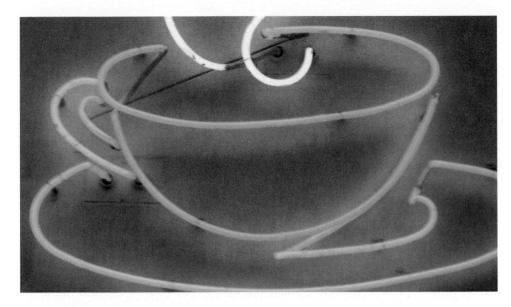

The shipment, distribution, and sale of adulterated food, and false mislabeling of food, is prohibited by the Federal Food, Drug, and Cosmetic Act.

Regulation of Drugs

The FDCA gives the FDA the authority to regulate the testing, manufacture, distribution, and sale of drugs. The **Drug Amendment to the FDCA**,[1] enacted in 1962, gives the FDA broad powers to license new drugs in the United States. After a new drug application is filed, the FDA holds a hearing and investigates the merits of the application. This process can take many years. The FDA may withdraw approval of any previously licensed drug.

This law requires all users of prescription and nonprescription drugs to receive proper directions for use (including the method and duration of use) and adequate warnings about any related side effects. The manufacture, distribution, or sale of adulterated or misbranded drugs is prohibited.

Business Brief

The FDA may speed up the process for experimental drugs that hold promise in treating incurable diseases (e.g., AIDS).

Business Ethics

SOMETIMES VIAGRA STIRS THE HEART TOO QUICKLY

The anti-impotency drug Viagra, introduced in 1997, was heralded as the most important drug to hit the market since the birth control pill. Viagra is prescribed by doctors to male patients who cannot have or have trouble getting erections and helps such men have intercourse. It became wildly successful and is now used by millions of men worldwide. In the United States, the Food and Drug Administration (FDA) approved the drug for use by the general public. A black market for Viagra has developed in countries where the drug has not been given government approval. Pfizer, the manufacturer of the drug, is receiving a financial bounty from its now-famous drug.

It seems that Viagra not only gets men's hearts stirring again, but it may also cause their hearts to explode, literally. After hundreds of deaths of men taking the drug were reported, the FDA investigated and found that men with certain health predispositions may be at risk of death if they take Viagra. Therefore, the FDA now requires Viagra labels to warn individuals with the following conditions to be careful when taking the drug:

- Men who have had a heart attack or an irregular heartbeat in the past six months
- Men who have a history of cardiac failure or coronary artery disease that caused angina
- Men who have significant high or low blood pressure

Viagra causes visual disturbance—particularly the ability to distinguish between blue and green—in about three percent of the men who use it. And Viagra sometimes works too well, causing priapism, or painful erections that last up to four hours. Doctors and consumers must also be warned against these conditions.

Pfizer asserts that its explosively popular drug was not the culprit in the reported deaths, but that the drug was taken by men with health problems who should have not used the drug. By requiring the new warnings, the FDA wants men with the noted risk factors to first ask, "Is sex a good idea for me?" before taking Viagra.

1. Are there risks in taking many of the prescription drugs on the market today?

2. In applying a cost-benefit analysis to the development and marketing of a drug, when is the point reached where the cost (in injuries, side effects, and deaths) exceeds the benefits to society? Discuss.

Regulation of Cosmetics

The FDA's definition of cosmetics includes substances and preparations for cleansing, altering the appearance of, and promoting the attractiveness of a person. For example, eye shadow and other facial makeup are cosmetics subject to FDA regulation. Ordinary household soap is expressly exempted from this definition.

The FDA has issued regulations that require cosmetics to be labeled, to disclose ingredients, and to contain warnings if they are carcinogenic (cancer causing) or otherwise dangerous to a person's health. The manufacture, distribution, or sale of adulterated or misbranded cosmetics is prohibited. The FDA may remove from commerce cosmetics that contain unsubstantiated claims of preserving youth, increasing virility, growing hair, and such.

Ethics Brief

The federal Public Health Cigarette Smoking Act of 1985 requires cigarette manufacturers to place certain warnings on cigarette packages. Do you think these warnings adequately warn consumers of the dangers of cigarette smoking?

Medicinal Device Amendment to the FDCA

An amendment enacted in 1976 that gives the FDA authority to regulate medicinal devices and equipment.

Regulation of Medicinal Devices

In 1976, Congress enacted the **Medicinal Device Amendment to the FDCA**.[2] This amendment gives the FDA authority to regulate medicinal devices, such as heart pacemakers, kidney dialysis machines, defibrillators, surgical equipment, and other diagnostic, therapeutic, and health devices. The mislabeling of such devices is prohibited. The FDA is empowered to remove "quack" devices from the market.

The Supreme Court Speaks

Food, Drug, and Cosmetic Act Provides Consumer Protection

Buckman Company v. Plaintiffs' Legal Committee
531 U.S. 341, 121 S.Ct. 1012 (2001)
Supreme Court of the United States

BACKGROUND AND FACTS

The AcroMed Corporation developed orthopedic bone screws to be placed in the pedicles of patients' spines during surgical operations. With the help of Buckman Company, a consulting service, AcroMed filed applications with the Federal Food and Drug Administration (FDA), a federal administrative agency, for approval to sell this medical device. The Federal Food, Drug, and Cosmetic Act (FDCA) and the Medical Device Amendments of 1976 (MDA), federal statutes, required the FDA's approval before the device could be marketed. After reviewing the information submitted by AcroMed and Buckman, the FDA approved the device for sale. The bone screws have been used in thousands of surgical operations.

However, over 2,000 lawsuits were filed by patients who had the bone screws installed, claiming that they have been injured by the screws. The plaintiffs based their lawsuits on state law tort claims that fraud had been committed on the FDA by AcroMed and Buckman in the information submitted

in the applications filed with the FDA. The defendants brought a motion to have the cases dismissed. alleging that the plaintiffs were prohibited from suing for "fraud on the FDA" because the federal law—the FDCA and MDA—preempted any state law tort claim. The district court dismissed the plaintiffs' cases, but the court of appeals reversed, allowing the plaintiffs to sue. The U.S. Supreme Court granted review.

SUPREME COURT ISSUE

Is the plaintiffs' state law "fraud on the FDA" tort claim preempted by federal law?

IN THE LANGUAGE OF THE U.S. SUPREME COURT

Policing fraud against federal agencies is hardly a field which the States have traditionally occupied. To the contrary, the relationship between a federal agency and the entity it regulates is inherently federal in character because the relationship originates from, is governed by, and terminates according to federal law. Given this analytical framework, we hold that the plaintiffs' state-law fraud-on-

the-FDA claims conflict with, and are therefore impliedly preempted by federal law. The conflict stems from the fact that the federal statutory scheme amply empowers the FDA to punish and deter fraud against the Agency, and that this authority is used by the Agency to achieve a somewhat delicate balance of statutory objectives. The balance sought by the Agency can be skewed by allowing fraud-on-the-FDA claims under state tort law.

DECISION AND REMEDY

The U.S. Supreme Court held that the plaintiffs' state law "fraud on the FDA" tort claim was preempted by valid federal law. The cases against the defendants were dismissed.

CASE QUESTIONS

Critical Legal Thinking   What does the "fraud on the FDA" claim state? Why did the Supreme Court hold that the plaintiffs could not assert this theory?

Business Ethics   Was it ethical for the defendants to try to avoid facing the merits of the lawsuit rather than hiding behind the federal preemption doctrine?

Contemporary Business   Do you think consumers are adequately protected by the Federal Food and Drug Administration? Why or why not?

Other Acts Administered by the FDA

In addition to the FDCA, the FDA administers the following statutes and amendments to the FDCA:

- **Pesticide Amendment of 1954**[3]   Authorizes the FDA to establish tolerances for pesticides used on agricultural products.
- **Food Additives Amendment of 1958**[4]   Requires FDA approval of new food ingredients or articles that come in contact with food, such as wrapping and packaging materials.
- **Color Additives Amendment of 1960**[5]   Requires FDA approval of color additives used in foods, drugs, and cosmetics.
- **Animal Drug Amendment of 1968**[6]   Requires FDA approval of any new animal drug or additive to animal food.
- **Biologies Act of 1902**[7]   Gives the FDA power to regulate biological products, including vaccines, blood, blood components and derivatives, and allergenic products.
- **Section 361 of the Public Health Service Act**[8]   Gives the FDA power to regulate and set standards for sanitation at food service establishments (including colleges and universities) and on interstate carriers (e.g., airlines and railroads).
- **Section 354 of the Public Health Service Act**[9] **and the Radiation for Health and Safety Act of 1968.**[10]   Empower the FDA to regulate the manufacture, distribution, and use of X-ray machines, microwave ovens, ultrasound equipment, and other products that are capable of emitting radiation.

Business Brief

In many FDA actions, the proceeding is brought against the product.

Things are seldom what they seem.

Skim milk masquerades as cream.

Highlows pass as patent leathers.

Jackdaws strut in peacock's feathers

> William S. Gilbert
> H. M. S. Pinafore, *Act II*

Outdoor Market, Kashgar   *Many other countries of the world have different means for distributing and regulating the production and sale of food products than the United States.*

International Law

UNITED NATIONS BIOSAFETY PROTOCOL FOR GENETICALLY ALTERED FOODS

Many food processors in the United States and across the world genetically modify some foods by adding genes from other organisms to help crops grow faster or ward off pests. In the past, food processors did not notify consumers that they were purchasing genetically modified agricultural products. Although the companies insist that genetically altered foods are safe, consumers and many countries began to demand that such foods be clearly labeled so that buyers could decide for themselves. When most large food processors balked at this idea, the consumers went to their lawmakers.

The most concerned countries in the world regarding this issue were in Europe. Led by Germany, many European countries wanted to require genetically engineered food products to be labeled as such and be transported separately from non-altered agricultural products. Some European countries wanted genetically altered foods to be banned completely. The United States, a major exporter of agricultural products and the leader in the development of biotech foods, argued that these countries were using this issue to erect trade barriers to keep U.S. produced food products out of their countries in violation of international trade treaties and conventions administered by the World Trade Organization (WTO) that had reduced or eliminated many international trade restrictions.

In January 2000, a compromise was reached when 138 countries, including the United States, agreed to the United Nations-sponsored **Biosafety Protocol**. After much negotiation, the countries agreed that all genetically engineered foods would be clearly labeled with the phrase "May contain living modified organisms." This allows consumers to decide on their own whether to purchase such altered food products. In addition, the boxes and containers in which such goods are shipped must also be clearly marked as containing genetically altered food products. This compromise assures that new biosafety labeling rules will coexist with the free trade agreements of the WTO.

*R*EGULATION OF PRODUCT SAFETY

To promote product safety, the federal government has enacted several statutes that directly regulate the manufacture and distribution of consumer products.[11] These acts are discussed in the paragraphs that follow.

Consumer Product Safety Act

Consumer Product Safety Act (CPSA)

A federal statute that regulates potentially dangerous consumer products and created the Consumer Product Safety Commission.

Consumer Product Safety Commission (CPSC)

An independent federal regulatory agency empowered to (1) adopt rules and regulations to interpret and enforce the Consumer Product Safety Act, (2) conduct research on safety, and (3) collect data regarding injuries.

In 1972, Congress enacted the **Consumer Product Safety Act (CPSA)**[12] and created the **Consumer Product Safety Commission (CPSC)**. The CPSC is an independent federal regulatory agency empowered to (1) adopt rules and regulations to interpret and enforce the CPSA, (2) conduct research on the safety of consumer products, and (3) collect data regarding injuries caused by consumer products. Certain consumer products, including motor vehicles, boats, aircraft, and firearms, are regulated by other government agencies.

Because the CPSC regulates potentially dangerous consumer products, it issues product safety standards for consumer products that pose an unreasonable risk of injury. If a consumer product is found to be imminently hazardous—that is, its use can cause an unreasonable risk of death or serious injury or illness—the manufacturer can be required to recall, repair, or replace the product or take other corrective action. Alternatively, the CPSC can seek injunctions, bring actions to seize hazardous consumer products, seek civil penalties for knowing violations of the act or of CPSA rules, and seek criminal penalties for knowing and willful violations of the act or of CPSC rules. A private party can sue for an injunction to prevent violations of the act or of CPSC rules and regulations.

*B*usiness *E*thics

SHOULD ALL-TERRAIN VEHICLES BE GROUNDED?

All-terrain vehicles (ATVs) are three- and four-wheeled motorized vehicles generally characterized by large low-pressure tires, a relatively high center of grav-ity, a seat designed to be straddled by the operator, and handlebars for steering. They are sold by a variety of manufacturers.

ATVs are intended for off-road, recreational use over rough roads and various nonpaved terrain. The ATV industry's television and print advertising promotes ATVs as "family fun vehicles" that pose little danger to their operators. The truth is that ATVs are extremely dangerous, particularly when operated by inexperienced youthful riders. The danger of death or serious injury associated with the operation of ATVs has received wide public attention. Both the Senate and the House of Representatives have held hearings concerning the dangers of ATVs.

In December 1986, after receiving substantial public comment, the CPSC filed an emergency action in federal district court against the manufacturers of ATVs. The CPSC formally referred the matter to the U.S. Department of Justice to seek a judicial declaration that ATVs present an "imminent and unreasonable risk of death, serious illness, and severe personal injury."

The case never made it to trial, however. The CPSC and the defendant ATV and manufacturers entered into a settlement whereby the defendants signed a consent decree in which they agreed to discontinue the "family fun" advertising of ATVs, provide warnings of their danger, publish manuals for their safe operation, provide training to ATV buyers, and set age-limit restrictions for the sale and use of certain ATV models. The CPSC agreed to the settlement because it was designed to alert consumers and reduce the hazards of using ATVs.

Several consumer groups thought that the CPSC had sold out and sought to intervene in the action to compel it to get tougher. Some consumer groups wanted an outright ban on the sale of ATVs in this country. The court of appeals rejected the interveners' arguments and upheld the consent decree. The court held that the settlement reached between the CPSC and the ATV industry was "fair, adequate, reasonable, and in the general public interest." The court stated, "No decree designed to protect consumers has ever gone this far in meeting such a massive national consumer problem." [*United States v. American Honda Motor Co., Inc.*, 143 F.R.D. 1 (D.D.C. 1992)]

1. Do you think that the CPSC acted in the public's best interest by entering into the consent decree with the ATV industry?
2. Should the government just "butt out" and let consumers assume the risk of dangerous activities in which they want to participate?

Fair Packaging and Labeling Act

The **Fair Packaging and Labeling Act**[13] requires the labels on consumer goods to identify the product; the manufacturer, processor, or packager of the product and its address; the net quantity of the contents of the package; and the quantity of each serving if the number of servings is stated. The label must use simple and clear language that a consumer can understand. This act is administered by the Federal Trade Commission (FTC) and the Department of Health and Human Services.

Fair Packaging and Labeling Act

A federal statute that requires the labels on consumer goods to identify the product; the manufacturer, processor, or packager of the product and its address; the net quantity of the contents of the package; and the quantity of each serving.

Poison Prevention Packaging Act

Many children suffer serious injury or death when they open household products and inhale, ingest, or otherwise mishandle dangerous products. The **Poison Prevention Packaging Act**[14] is intended to avoid this problem by requiring manufacturers to provide "childproof" containers and packages for all household products.

 *Business Ethics*

LEMON LAWS PROTECT CONSUMERS FROM SOUR DEALS

In the past, consumers who purchased automobiles and other vehicles that developed nagging mechanical problems had to try to convince the dealer or manufacturer to correct the problem. If the problem was not corrected, the consumer's only recourse was to seek redress through costly and time-consuming litigation. Today, most states have enacted **lemon laws**, which give consumers a new weapon in this battle.

Lemon laws provide a procedure for consumers to follow to correct recurring problems in vehicles. Lemon laws establish an administrative procedure that is less formal than a court proceeding. Most of these laws require that an arbitrator decide the dispute between a consumer and car dealer. Lemon laws stipulate that if the dealer or manufacturer does not correct a recurring defect in a vehicle within a specified number of tries (e.g., four tries) within a specified period of time (e.g., two years), the purchaser can rescind the purchase and recover a full refund of the vehicle's purchase price.

To properly invoke a state's lemon law, a consumer should take the following steps:

- Notify the car dealer immediately of any mechanical or other problems that develop in the vehicle.
- Take the vehicle back to the dealer for the statutory number of times to give the dealer the opportunity to correct the defect.
- File a claim with the appropriate state agency seeking arbitration of the claim if the defect is not corrected dur-

ing the number of times and time period established by the state's lemon law.

- Attend the arbitration hearing and present evidence to substantiate the claim that the vehicle suffered from a defect that was not corrected by the dealer or manufacturer within the statutorily prescribed period.

1. In general, do you think automobile dealerships are very scrupulous?
2. Are lemon laws needed to protect consumers?

UNFAIR AND DECEPTIVE PRACTICES

Sellers sometimes engage in unfair, deceptive, or abusive sales techniques. If these practices result in fraud, an injured consumer can bring a civil action to recover damages. Such actions are not always brought, though, because it is difficult, costly, and time-consuming to prove fraud. Therefore, the federal government has enacted statutes to regulate sellers' behavior.

Section 5 of the Federal Trade Commission Act

Federal Trade Commission (FTC)

Federal administrative agency empowered to enforce the Federal Trade Commission Act and other federal consumer protection statutes.

Section 5 of the FTC Act

Prohibits *unfair and deceptive* practices.

Like a gun that fires at the muzzle and kicks over at the breach, a cheating transaction hurts the cheater as much as the man cheated.

Henry Ward Beecher
Proverbs from Plymouth Pulpit
(1887)

The **Federal Trade Commission Act (FTC Act)** was enacted in 1914.[15] The **Federal Trade Commission (FTC)** was created the following year. The FTC is empowered to enforce the FTC Act as well as other federal consumer protection statutes.

Section 5 of the FTC Act, as amended, prohibits *unfair and deceptive practices*. It has been used extensively to regulate business conduct. This section gives the FTC the authority to bring an administrative proceeding to attack a deceptive or unfair practice. If, after a public administrative hearing, the FTC finds a violation of Section 5, it may order a cease-and-desist order, an affirmative disclosure to consumers, corrective advertising, or the like. The FTC may sue in state or federal court to obtain compensation on behalf of consumers. The decision of the FTC may be appealed to federal court.

False and Deceptive Advertising

Advertising is false and deceptive under Section 5 if it (1) contains misinformation or omits important information that is likely to mislead a "reasonable consumer" or (2) makes an unsubstantiated claim (e.g., "This product is 33 percent better than our competitor's"). Proof of actual deception is not required. Statements of opinion and "sales talk" (e.g., "This is a great car") do not constitute deceptive advertising.

The Supreme Court Speaks

Company Found to Have Engaged in Deceptive Advertising

Federal Trade Commission v. Colgate-Palmolive Co.
380 U.S. 374, 85 S.Ct. 1035 (1965)
Supreme Court of the United States

BACKGROUND AND FACTS
The Colgate-Palmolive Co. (Colgate) manufactures and sells a shaving cream called "Rapid Shave." Colgate hired Ted Bates &Company (Bates), an advertising agency, to prepare television commercials designed to show that Rapid Shave could shave the toughest beards. With Colgate's consent, Bates pre-

pared a television commercial that included the sandpaper test. The announcer informed the audience, "To prove Rapid Shave's super-moisturizing power, we put it right from the can onto this tough, dry sandpaper. And off in a stroke."

While the announcer was speaking, Rapid Shave was applied to a substance that appeared to be sandpaper and immediately a razor was shown shaving the substance clean. Evidence showed that the substance resembling sandpaper was in fact a simulated prop or "mock-up" made of Plexiglas to which sand had been glued. The Federal Trade Commission (FTC) issued a complaint against Colgate and Bates, alleging a violation of Section 5 of the Federal Trade Commission Act. The FTC held against the defendants. The court of appeals reversed. The FTC appealed to the U.S. Supreme Court.

SUPREME COURT ISSUE

Did the defendants engage in false and deceptive advertising in violation of Section 5 of the Federal Trade Commission Act?

IN THE LANGUAGE OF THE U.S. SUPREME COURT

Warren, Chief Justice We agree with the FTC that the undisclosed use of Plexiglas in the present commercial was a material deceptive practice. Respondents claim that it will be impractical to inform the viewing public that it is not seeing an actual test, experiment or demonstration, but we think it inconceivable that the ingenious advertising world will be unable, if it so desires, to conform to the FTC's insistence that the public be not misinformed.

If, however, it becomes impossible or impracticable to show simulated demonstrations on television in a truthful manner, this indicates that television is not a medium that lends itself to this type of commercial, not that the commercial must survive at all costs. Similarly unpersuasive is respondents' objection that the FTC's decision discriminates against sellers whose product claims cannot be verified on television without the use of stimulation. All methods of advertising do not equally favor every seller. If the inherent limitations of a method do not permit its use in the way a seller desires, the seller cannot by material misrepresentation compensate for those limitations.

The court of appeals could find no difference between the Rapid Shave commercial and a commercial which extolled the goodness of ice cream while giving viewers a picture of a scoop of mashed potatoes appearing to be ice cream. We do not understand this difficulty. In the ice cream case the mushed potato prop is not being used for additional proof of the product claim, while the purpose of the Rapid Shave commercial is to give the viewer objective proof of the claims made. If in the ice cream hypothetical the focus of the commercial becomes the undisclosed potato prop and the viewer is invited, explicitly or by implication, to see for himself the truth of the claims about the ice cream's rich texture and full color, and perhaps compared to a rival product, then the commercial has become similar to the one now before us. Clearly, however, a commercial which depicts happy actors delightedly eating ice cream that is in fact mashed potatoes or drinking a product appearing to be coffee but which is in fact some other substance is not covered by the present order.

DECISION AND REMEDY

The U.S. Supreme Court held that Colgate and Bates had engaged in false and deceptive advertising. Reversed and remanded.

CASE QUESTIONS

Critical Legal Thinking Does the government owe a duty to protect consumers from false and misleading business practices?

Business Ethics Did Colgate and Bates act ethically in this case? Do you think the viewing public believed the commercial?

Contemporary Business Do you think Colgate needed "some fencing in"?

Bait and Switch

The **bait and switch** is another type of deceptive advertising under Section 5. It occurs when a seller advertises the availability of a low-cost discounted item (the "bait") to attract customers to its store. Once the customers are in the store, however, the seller pressures them to purchase more expensive merchandise (the "switch").

It is often difficult to determine when a seller has engaged in this practice. The FTC states that a bait and switch occurs if the seller refuses to show consumers the advertised merchandise, discourages employees from selling the advertised merchandise, or fails to have adequate quantities of the merchandise available.

bait and switch

A type of deceptive advertising that occurs when a seller advertises the availability of a low-cost discounted item but then pressures the buyer into purchasing more expensive merchandise.

Door-to-Door Sales

Some salespersons sell merchandise and services door-to-door. In some situations, these salespersons use aggressive sales tactics to overcome a consumer's resistance to the sale. To protect consumers from ill-advised decisions, many states have enacted laws that give the consumer a certain number of days to rescind (cancel) a door-to-door sales contract. The usual period is three days. The consumer must send a required notice of cancellation to the seller. An FTC regulation requires the salesperson to permit cancellation of the contract within the stipulated time.

Business Brief

Many states have enacted statutes that permit consumers to rescind contracts made at home with door-to-door sales representatives within a three-day period after signing the contract.

Unsolicited Merchandise

The **Postal Reorganization Act**[16] makes the mailing of unsolicited merchandise an unfair trade practice. The act permits persons who receive unsolicited merchandise through the mail to retain, use, discard, or otherwise dispose of the merchandise without incurring any obligation to pay for it or return it. Unsolicited mailings by charitable organizations and mailings made by mistake are excepted from this rule.

Postal Reorganization Act

An act that makes the mailing of unsolicited merchandise an unfair trade practice.

Business Ethics

KRAFT NO LONGER THE "BIG CHEESE"

Kraft, Inc. (Kraft), the king of cheese producers in the United States, makes and sells Singles American Pasteurized Process Cheese slices (Singles) that can be used on sandwiches and for other purposes. When Kraft's dominant position in this market began to be eroded by imitation cheese slices made from vegetable oil and other products, Kraft designed a new advertising campaign to tout the health benefits of its Singles. In its campaign, Kraft advertised that (1) a slice of its Singles contained the same amount of calcium as five ounces of milk and (2) its Singles contained more calcium than most imitation slices.

The Federal Trade Commission (FTC) filed charges against Kraft claiming that neither of these statements was true. The FTC found that although Kraft uses five ounces of milk in making each Kraft Single, about one-third of the calcium contained in the milk is lost during processing. The FTC also found that most imitation slices sold in the United States contain the same amount of calcium as Kraft Single. The FTC held that Kraft's advertisements constituted unfair and deceptive advertising in violation of Section 5 of the Federal Trade Commission Act because they were likely to mislead consumers. The FTC ordered Kraft to cease and desist from making these misrepresentations. The court of appeals upheld the FTC's order. [*Kraft, Inc. v. Federal Trade Commission,* 970 F.2d 311 (7th Cir. 1992)]

1. Do you think Kraft made untrue statements?
2. Was the punishment sufficient in this case? Why or why not?

E-Commerce & Information Technology

ANTI-SPAM STATUTE UPHELD

As most computer users are aware, when they open up their e-mail account they often find lots of junk spam—unsolicited commercial e-mail messages selling anything from everyday products and services to sexually explicit materials. But spamming—as it is called—can reach outrageous proportions as spammers can send 100,000s, even millions, of messages with a touch of a button. Consider the following case.

The state of Washington enacted an anti-spam statute that prohibits false and misleading commercial e-mail messages. Jason Heckel, an Oregon resident doing business as Natural Instincts, sent 100,000 to 1,000,000 unsolicited commercial e-mail messages per week, many to Washington residents, trying to sell his 46-page booklet "How to Profit from the Internet." The state of Washington sued Heckel for violating its anti-spam statute. Heckel allegedly did what many spammers do to get someone to read their messages, he disguised the message's point of origin and transmission path. The trial court dismissed the lawsuit, finding that

Washington's anti-spam statute caused an undue burden on interstate commerce. The Washington Supreme Court upheld the statute, finding the law to be constitutional. The court stated:

> The Act limits the harm that deceptive commercial e-mail causes Washington businesses and citizens. The Act prohibits e-mail solicitors from using misleading information in the subject line or transmission path of any commercial e-mail message to Washington residents or from a computer located in Washington. We find that the local benefits of the Act outweigh any conceivable burdens the Act places on those sending commercial e-mail messages. Consequently, we hold that the Act does not violate the dormant Commerce Clause of the United States Constitution.

Many other states have enacted similar anti-spam statutes. [*State v. Heckel,* 24 P.3d 404 (WA 2001)]

*F*EDERAL CONSUMER-DEBTOR PROTECTION LAWS

Business Brief

The federal government protects *consumer-debtors* (borrowers) from abusive, deceptive, and unfair practices by *creditors* (lenders).

Creditors have been known to engage in various abusive, deceptive, and unfair practices when dealing with consumer-debtors. To protect consumer-debtors from such practices, the federal government has enacted a comprehensive scheme of laws concerning the extension and collection of credit. These laws are discussed in the following sections.

Landmark Law

TRUTH-IN-LENDING ACT

In 1968, Congress enacted the **Truth-in-Lending Act (TILA)** as part of the Consumer Credit Protection Act (CCPA) [15 U.S.C. §§ 1601 et seq.]. The TILA, as amended, requires creditors to make certain disclosures to debtors in consumer transactions that do not exceed $25,000 (e.g., retail installment sales, automobile loans) and real estate loans of any amount on the debtor's principal dwelling.

The TILA covers only creditors who regularly (1) extend credit for goods or services to consumers or (2) arrange such credit in the ordinary course of their business. Consumer credit is defined as credit extended to natural persons for personal, family, or household purposes.

REGULATION Z

The TILA is administered by the Federal Reserve Board, which has authority to adopt regulations to enforce and interpret the act. **Regulation Z**, which sets forth detailed rules for compliance with the TILA, was adopted under this authority [12 C.F.R. 226]. The uniform disclosures required by the TILA and Regulation Z are intended to help consumers shop for the best credit terms.

The TILA and Regulation Z require the following information to be disclosed by the creditor to the consumer-debtor:

- Cash price of the product or service
- Down payment and trade-in allowance
- Unpaid cash price
- Finance charge, including interest, points, and other fees paid for the extension of credit
- Annual percentage rate (APR) of the finance charges
- Charges not included in the finance charge (such as appraisal fees)
- Total dollar amount financed
- Date the finance charge begins to accrue
- Number, amounts, and due dates of payments
- A description of any security interest
- Penalties to be assessed for delinquent payments and late charges
- Prepayment penalties
- Comparative costs of credit (optional)

Consumer Leasing Act   Consumers often opt to lease consumer products such as automobiles and large appliances rather than purchase them. As originally enacted, the TILA applied only to certain forms of leases. The **Consumer Leasing Act (CLA)** extended the TILA's coverage to lease terms in consumer leases.[17] The CLA applies to lessors who engage in leasing or arranging leases for consumer goods in the ordinary course of their business. Casual leases (such as leases between consumers) and leases of real property (such as lease on an apartment) are not subject to the CLA. Creditors who violate the CLA are subject to the same civil and criminal penalties as those provided in the TILA.

Fair Credit and Charge Card Disclosure Act of 1988   The **Fair Credit and Charge Card Disclosure Act of 1988**[18] amended the TILA to require disclosure of credit terms on credit-and charge-card solicitations and applications.

The regulations adopted under the act require that any direct written solicitation to a consumer display, in tabular form, the following information: (1) the APR, (2) any annual membership fee, (3) any minimum or fixed finance charge, (4) any transaction charge for use of the card for purchases, and (5) a statement that charges are due when the periodic statement is received by the debtor.

Consumer Leasing Act (CLA)

An amendment to the TILA that extends the TILA's coverage to lease terms in consumer leases.

Fair Credit and Charge Card Disclosure Act of 1988

An amendment to the TILA that requires disclosure of certain credit terms on credit-and charge-card solicitations and applications.

Business Brief

Issuers of credit cards are subject to certain rules concerning (1) unsolicited credit cards, (2) faulty products purchased with credit cards, and (3) lost or stolen credit cards.

Contemporary Business Environment

CREDIT-CARD RULES PROTECT CONSUMERS

Many consumer purchases are made with *credit cards.* Cardholders are liable to pay for authorized purchases even if they exceed the established dollar limit of the credit card. The Truth-in-Lending Act (TILA) regulates the issuance and use of credit cards in the following ways:

- **Unsolicited Credit Cards**   Issuers (e.g., VISA, MasterCard) are not prohibited from sending an *unsolicited credit card.* However, the TILA stipulates the addressee is not liable for any charges made on an unsolicited card that is lost or stolen prior to its acceptance by the addressee. Acceptance of the card makes the addressee liable for authorized charges made with it.

- **Faulty Products**   A consumer who unknowingly purchases a faulty product with a credit card may withhold payments to the credit-card issuer until the dispute over the defect is resolved. The cardholder may notify the issuer about the defect immediately or wait until receipt of the billing statement. If the consumer and the seller cannot resolve the dispute (e.g., by replacing or repairing the defective product), the credit-card issuer is under a duty to intervene. If the dispute cannot be settled, a legal action may be necessary to resolve the dispute.
- **Lost or Stolen Credit Cards**   Sometimes credit cards are lost by or stolen from the cardholder. The TILA

limits the cardholder's liability to $50 per card for unauthorized charges made on the card before the issuer is notified that the card is missing. There is no liability if the issuer is notified before the missing card is used.

Consider This Example   Suppose Karen loses her VISA credit card. Before Karen realizes she has lost the card, Michael finds it and charges $750 of goods. When Karen discovers the card is missing, she notifies VISA. Karen is liable for only $50 of the $750 of unauthorized charges. If Karen had notified VISA prior to the charges being made on her card, she would not have been liable for the $50.

Equal Credit Opportunity Act

Equal Credit Opportunity Act (ECOA)

A federal statute that prohibits discrimination in the extension of credit based on sex, marital status, race, color, national origin, religion, age, or receipt of income from public assistance programs.

adverse action

A denial or revocation of credit or a change in the credit terms offered.

The **Equal Credit Opportunity Act (ECOA)** was enacted in 1975.[19] The ECOA, as amended, prohibits discrimination in the extension of credit based on sex, marital status, race, color, national origin, religion, age, or receipt of income from public assistance programs. The ECOA applies to all creditors who extend or arrange credit in the ordinary course of their business, including banks, savings and loan associations, automobile dealers, real estate brokers, credit-card issuers, and the like.

The creditor must notify the applicant within 30 days regarding the action taken on a credit application. If the creditor takes an **adverse action** (i.e., denies, revokes, or changes the credit terms), the creditor must provide the applicant with a statement containing the specific reasons for the action. If a creditor violates the ECOA, the consumer may bring a civil action against the creditor and recover actual damages (including emotional distress and embarrassment).

Fair Credit Reporting Act

Fair Credit Reporting Act (FCRA)

An amendment to the TILA that protects customers who are subjects of a credit report by setting out guidelines for credit bureaus.

credit report

Information about a person's credit history that can be secured from a credit bureau.

He begs of them that borrowed of him.

James Kelly
Scottish Proverbs (1721)

The 1970 Congress enacted the **Fair Credit Reporting Act (FCRA)** as Title VI of the TILA.[20] This act protects consumers who are subjects of a **credit report** by setting out guidelines for consumer reporting agencies, that is, credit bureaus that compile and sell credit reports for a fee.

The consumer may request the following information at any time: (1) the nature and substance of all of the information in the consumer's credit file (except medical information), (2) the sources of this information (except sources of this information (except sources used solely for investigative reports), and (3) the names of recipients of a credit report within the past 6 months, or 10 months if it was used for employment purposes.

Consumer reporting agencies are required to maintain reasonable procedures to ensure the accuracy of their information. If a consumer challenges the accuracy of pertinent information contained in the credit file, the agency may be compelled to reinvestigate. If the agency cannot find an error despite the consumer's complaint, the consumer may file a 100-word written statement of his or her version of the disputed information.

If a consumer reporting agency or user violates the FCRA, the injured consumer may bring a civil action against the violator and recover actual damages. The FCRA also provides for criminal penalties.

Fair Debt Collection Practices Act

Fair Debt Collection Practices Act (FDCPA)

An act enacted in 1977 that protects consumer-debtors from abusive, deceptive, and unfair practices used by debt collectors.

debt collector

An agent who collects debts for other parties.

In 1977, Congress enacted the **Fair Debt Collection Practices Act (FDCPA)**.[21] This act protects consumer-debtors from abusive, deceptive, and unfair practices used by **debt collectors**. The FDCPA expressly prohibits debt collectors from using certain practices. They are (1) harassing, abusive, or intimidating tactics (e.g., threats of violence and obscene or abusive language), (2) false or misleading misrepresentations (e.g., posing as a police officer or attorney), and (3) unfair or unconscionable practices (e.g., threatening the debtor with imprisonment).

In some circumstances, the debt collector may not contact the debtor. These situations include the following:

1. At any inconvenient time. The FDCPA provides that convenient hours are between 8:00 A.M. and 9:00 P.M. unless this time is otherwise inconvenient for the debtor (e.g., the debtor works a night shift and sleeps during the day).
2. At inconvenient places, such as at a place of worship or social events.
3. At the debtor's place of employment if the employer objects to such contact.
4. If the debtor is represented by an attorney.
5. If the debtor gives a written notice to the debt collector that he or she refuses to pay the debt or does not want the debt collector to contact him or her again.

The FDCPA limits the contact that a debtor collector may have with third persons other than the debtor's spouse or parents. Such contacts are strictly limited. Unless the court has given its approval, third parties can be consulted only for the purpose of locating the debtor. They can be contacted only once. The debt collector may not inform the third person that the consumer owes a debt that is in the process of collection. A debtor may bring a civil action against a debt collector for intentionally violating the FDCPA.

Business Brief

The Fair Debt Collection Practices Act prohibits certain contact by the creditor with third parties and the debtor.

To contract new debts is not the way to pay old ones.

George Washington
Letter to James Welch *(1799)*

Contemporary Business Environment

FEDERAL STATUTE OUTLAWS JUNK FAXES

A provision of the Federal **Telephone Consumer Protection Act of 1991** bans unsolicited faxes that contain advertisements. The law was passed to protect owners of fax machines from receiving "junk faxes" for which they were required to pay as the receiver. Unsolicited private and political faxes are exempt from the law. The law gives anyone who gets an unsolicited fax the right to recover $500 in damages from the sender.

This federal law was challenged by a junk advertiser as being an unconstitutional infringement on its First Amendment free-speech rights. The court of appeals upheld the law, finding no free-speech violation. The court stated, "The ban is evenhanded, in that it applies to commercial solicitation by any organization, be it a multinational corporation or the Girl Scouts." [*Destination Ventures Ltd. v. Federal Communications Commission*, 46 F.3d 54 (9th Cir. 1995)]

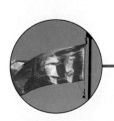

International Law

CONSUMER PROTECTION LAWS IN MEXICO

In the decades following World War II, Mexico developed both an industrial base that created jobs in manufacturing and in service industries and a large consumer base. The ever-growing consumer population gave rise to increased consumer complaints of faulty products, consumer fraud, false advertising, and unfair business practices.

Prior to 1975, the traditional civil remedies provided by mercantile codes in Mexico provided little protection for Mexican consumers because they favored merchants and service providers. In addition, legal cases brought in the civil court system were slow, procedurally complicated, and costly.

In 1975, the Mexican Federal Congress enacted the **Federal Consumer Protection Act (FCPA)** [D.O. Dec. 22, 1975 (Mex.)]. The FCPA was modeled after several U.S. consumer protection statutes. The fact that most consumer transactions are codified and regulated in Mexico in a single

statute is a clear advantage for Mexican consumers. The provisions of the FCPA are granted the highest legal rank in Mexico, second only to constitutional precepts.

The FCPA contains the following legal rules designed to protect consumers:

- The legal relationship between the merchant and the consumer is based on the "principle of truthfulness." This includes advertising, labeling, instructions, and warnings.
- Consumer contracts must be drafted in precise and clear language.
- Warranties of any goods and services are legally enforceable.
- Public authorities have the power to establish maximum interest rates and total expenses associated with consumer credit. Total disclosure is required in consumer credit transactions.

- Consumers have the legal right to modify, through judicial means, clauses included in adhesion or unconscionable contracts.
- Federal authorities have the power to regulate offers, advertising, and conduct of sales by businesses selling goods or services to consumers.
- Consumer protection rules contained in the FCPA may not be legally renounced.

The FCPA also created agencies to enforce its rules. For example, it created the **Federal Attorney General for Consumer Affairs,** an independent agency of the Mexican government that is empowered to represent the interests of consumers in proceedings before federal administrative agencies and federal courts.

The **Consumer Affairs Office** is empowered to settle disputes between suppliers and consumers as a *compositeur amiable.* A consumer may file a complaint with this office, which then acts as a conciliator or arbitrator to try to settle the dispute. Most consumer disputes are settled using the conciliation and arbitration method of the Consumer Affairs Office, even though the parties have the option of using traditional judicial avenues.

The **National Consumer Institute** educates the Mexican population concerning their rights and obligations as consumers. The work of the Institute has established a "consumer protection consciousness" among Mexican consumers and merchants selling goods and services in Mexico.

CHAPTER SUMMARY

Government Regulations, p. 827

Government Regulation of Business	1. *General government regulation.* Government regulation that applies to many industries (e.g., antidiscrimination laws). 2. *Specific government regulation.* Government regulation that applies to a specific industry (e.g., banking laws).

Administrative Agencies, p. 829

Administrative Agencies	1. *Administrative agencies.* Created by federal and state legislative and executive branches. Consist of professionals having an area of expertise in a certain area of commerce, who interpret and apply designated statutes. 2. *Administrative rules and regulations.* Administrative agencies are empowered to adopt rules and regulations that interpret and advance the laws they enforce. 3. *Administrative Procedure Act.* Act that establishes procedures (i.e., notice, hearing, and such) to be followed by federal agencies in conducting their affairs. States have enacted their own procedural acts to govern state agencies.

The FDA's Administration of the Federal Food, Drug, and Cosmetic Act, p. 835

Federal Food, Drug, and Cosmetic Act (FDCA)	Federal statute that regulates the testing, manufacture, distribution, and sale of foods, food additives, drugs, cosmetics, and medicinal products.
Required FDA Approval	1. *Federal Food and Drug Administration (FDA).* Federal administrative agency empowered to interpret and enforce the Federal Food, Drug, and Cosmetic Act and other federal consumer protection laws. 2. *Powers of the FDA.* The FDA has the power to approve or deny applications by private companies to distribute drugs, food additives, and medicinal devices to the public.
Regulation of Food, Drugs, and Cosmetics	*Adulterated food.* The FDA prohibits the shipment, distribution, or sale of *adulterated* or *misbranded* food, drugs, cosmetics, or medicinal devices.
Other Acts Administered by the FDA	The FDA also has authority to administer the following health-related federal statutes and amendments: 1. Pesticide Amendment of 1954 2. Food Additives Amendment of 1958 3. Color Additives Amendment of 1960 4. Animal Drug Amendment of 1968 5. Biologics Act of 1902 6. Public Health Service Act 7. Radiation for Health and Safety Act of 1968

Nutrition Labeling and Education Act of 1990	Federal statute that (1) requires food manufacturers and processors to provide nutritional information on food products and (2) prohibits the making of scientifically unsubstantiated health claims.

Regulation of Product Safety, p. 840

Consumer Product Safety Act (CPSA)	Federal statute that regulates the safety of consumer products. It created the Consumer Product Safety Commission.
	1. *Consumer Product Safety Commission (CPSC).* Federal administrative agency that is empowered to
	   a. interpret and enforce the Consumer Product Safety Act,
	   b. conduct research on safety, and
	   c. collect data regarding injuries.

Consumer Product Safety Statutes Administered by the CPSC	The CPSC also has authority to administer the following federal consumer product safety acts: 1. Consumer Product Safety Act (CPSA) 2. Fair Packaging and Labeling Act 3. Poison Prevention Packaging Act

Unfair and Deceptive Practices, p. 842

Section 5 of the Federal Trade Commission Act (FTC Act)	Federal statute that prohibits unfair and deceptive practices, including false and deceptive advertising, abusive sales tactics, consumer fraud, and other unfair business practices. *Federal Trade Commission (FTC).* Federal administrative agency that is empowered to enforce the Federal Trade Commission Act and other federal consumer protection statutes.

Federal Consumer-Debtor Protection Laws, p. 844

Truth-in-Lending Act (TILA)	Federal statute that requires creditors to make certain disclosures to consumer-debtors in most consumer credit transactions. It mandates disclosure of a single-figure *annual percentage rate (APR)*. *Regulation Z.* Regulation adopted by the Federal Reserve Board to enforce and interpret the TILA.
Consumer Leasing Act	Federal statute that requires lessors to make disclosures to lessees in most consumer lease transactions.
Fair Credit and Charge Card Disclosure Act of 1988	Federal statute that requires disclosure of certain credit terms to credit card holders. The act provides the following protections: 1. *Unsolicited credit cards.* A consumer is not liable for any charges on an unsolicited credit card that is lost or stolen prior to its acceptance by the addressee. 2. *Faulty products.* A consumer who unknowingly purchases a faulty product with a credit card may withhold payment to the credit card issuer until the dispute over the defect is resolved. 3. *Lost or stolen credit cards.* A cardholder's liability for unauthorized charges on a lost or stolen credit card is limited to $50 per card before the issuer is notified that the card is missing. The cardholder has no liability if the issuer is notified before the missing card is used.
Equal Credit Opportunity Act (ECOA)	Federal statute that prohibits discrimination in the extension of credit based on the applicant's sex, marital status, race, color, national origin, religion, age, or receipt of income from public assistance programs. 1. *Notification.* The ECOA requires a creditor to notify a consumer-debtor of the reasons for an *adverse action* on a credit application.
Fair Credit Reporting Act (FCRA)	Federal statute that regulates credit reporting agencies and establishes a procedure for a consumer-debtor to have errors in credit reports corrected. 1. *100-word statement.* The act permits a consumer-debtor to place a 100-word written statement in his or her credit report file concerning any unresolved dispute. This information must be conveyed to anyone seeking a credit report on the debtor.
Fair Debt Collection Practices Act (FDCPA)	Federal statute that protects consumer-debtors from abusive, deceptive, and unfair practices used by debt collectors. 1. *Prohibited contact.* The FDCPA prohibits or limits the creditor from making certain contact with third parties and the debtor concerning a debt it is trying to collect.

END-OF-CHAPTER INTERNET EXERCISES AND CASE QUESTIONS

Working the Web Internet Exercises

ACTIVITIES

1. Check the Consumer Product Safety Commission site for information on window blinds and/or batteries for notebook computers. See the U.S. Consumer Product Safety Commission at **www.cpsc.gov**.

2. Go to the Association of Trial Lawyers of America Web site at **www.atla.org** and find out what the trial lawyers have to say about products liability cases in the "Civil Justice Fact Sheets."

3. Find out what *made in the U.S.A.* means, according to the FTC Web site **www.ftc.gov**.

4. Review the FDA Enforcement Reports for a detailed list of recent violators. Are any of your favorite foods listed? See the U.S. Food and Drug Administration at **www.fda.gov**. See also **www.law.cornell.edu/topics/ consumer_credit.html** for an overview of consumer credit law with links to key primary and secondary sources.

CRITICAL LEGAL THINKING CASES

33.1 Adulterated Food   Barry Engel owned and operated the Gel Spice Co., Inc., which specialized in the importation and packaging of various food spices for resale. All of the spices Gel Spice imported were unloaded at a pier in New York City and taken to a warehouse on McDonald Avenue. Storage and repackaging of the spices took place in the warehouse. Between July 1976 and January 1979, the McDonald Avenue warehouse was inspected four times by investigators from the FDA. The investigators found live rats in bags of basil leaves, rodent droppings in boxes of chili peppers, and mammalian urine in bags of sesame seeds. The investigators produced additional evidence that showed that spices packaged and sold from the warehouse contained insects, rodent excreta pellets, rodent hair, and rodent urine. The FDA brought criminal charges against Engel and Gel Spice. Are they guilty? [*United States v. Gel Spice Co., Inc.,* 601 F.Supp. 1205 (E.D.N.Y. 1984)]

33.2 Food Additive   Coco Rico, Inc., manufactures a coconut concentrate called "Coco Rico" for use as an ingredient in soft drinks. The concentrate that is sold to beverage bottlers in Puerto Rico contains potassium nitrate, which is added for the purpose of developing and fixing a desirable color and flavor. Puerto Rico is subject to U.S. federal laws, including those administered by the FDA. The FDA has not approved the use of potassium nitrate as a food additive in soft drinks. The FDA learned of the use of the Coco Rico concentrate in soft drinks and on March 10, 1982, obtained a warrant from a federal district court to search the premises of a Puerto Rican bottler. On March 24, 1982, government investigators discovered three lots of soft drinks containing Coco Rico on the premises of the bottler and seized them pursuant to the warrant. Coco Rico, Inc., sued to reclaim the soft drinks. Who wins? [*United States v. An Article of Food,* 752 F.2d 11 (1st Cir. 1985)]

33.3 Regulation of Drugs   Dey Laboratories, Inc., is a drug manufacturer operating in the state of Texas. In 1983, Dey scientists created an inhalant know as ASI. The only active ingredient in ASI is atropine sulfate. The inhalant is sold to physicians, who then prescribe the medication for patients suffering from asthma, bronchitis, and other pulmonary diseases. In May 1983, Dey filed a new drug application with the FDA. By September 1983, Dey was advised that its application would not be approved. In spite of the lack of FDA approval, Dey began marketing ASI in November 1983. On August 25, 1985, the United States filed a complaint for forfeiture of all ASI manufactured by Dey. The inhalant was seized and Dey sued to have the FDA's seizure declared illegal. Who wins? [*United States v. Atropine Sulfate 1.0 MG (Article of Drug),* 843 F.2d 860 (5th Cir. 1988)]

33.4 Cosmetics   FBNH Enterprises, Inc., is a distributor of a product know as French Bronze Tablets. The purpose of the tablets is to allow a person to achieve an even tan without exposure to the sun. When ingested, the tablets impart color to the skin through the use of various ingredients, one of which is canthaxanthin, a coloring agent. Canthaxanthin has not been approved for use by the FDA as a coloring additive. The FDA became aware that FBNH was marketing the tablets and that each contains 30 milligrams of canthaxanthin. On June 16, 1988, the FDA filed a lawsuit seeking the forfeiture and condemnation of eight cases of the tablets in the possession of FBNH. FBNH challenged the government's right to seize the tablets. Who wins? [*United States v. Eight Unlabeled Cases of an Article of Cosmetic,* 888 F.2d 945 (2nd Cir 1989)]

33.5 Medicinal Device   General Medical Company manufacturers and markets a product known as the drionic antiperspirant device. The device is designed as a substitute for chemical antiperspirants or for the extensive medical treatment for those who suffer from greatly increased perspiration. The device consists of a housing for two wool felt pads and a battery. The pads are soaked in ordinary tap water and then placed against the treated area, typically the hands, feet, and underarms. An electrical current is passed through the pads and the area of skin between the pads for about 20 minutes. Ions (atoms carrying an electrical charge) are thereby transmitted across the skin. General Medical claims this process works in controlling perspiration in the treated area. The FDA seeks to regulate the device. Does it have authority to do so? [*General Medical Company v. United States Food and Drug Administration*, 770 F.2d 214 (D.C. Cir. 1985)]

33.6 Poison Prevention Packaging Act In June 1980, Joseph Wahba had a prescription filled at Zuckerman's Pharmacy in Brooklyn, New York. The prescription was for Lomotil, a drug used to counteract stomach disorders. The pharmacy dispensed 30 tablets in a small, plastic container unequipped with a "childproof" cap. Joseph took the medicine home, where it was discovered by Wahba's two-year-old son, Mark. Mark opened the container and ingested approximately 20 pills before Mark's mother saw him and stopped him. She rushed him to a hospital but, despite the efforts of the doctors, Mark lapsed into a coma and died. The Wahbas sued H&N Prescription Center, Inc., the company that owns Zuckerman's Pharmacy, for damages. Who wins? [*Wahba v. H&N Prescription Center, Inc.*, 539 F.Supp. 352 (E.D.N.Y. 1982)]

33.7 Truth-in-Lending In June 1979, Elizabeth Valentine purchased a home in Philadelphia, Pennsylvania. In October 1979, she applied for and received a $4,500 home loan from Salmon Building and Loan Association for the purpose of paneling the cellar walls and redecorating the house. Salmon took a security interest in the house as collateral for the loan. Although Valentine was given a disclosure document by Salmon, nowhere on the document were "finance charges" disclosed. The document did notify Valentine that Salmon had a security interest in the house. In May 1982, Valentine sued Salmon (which had since merged with Influential Savings and Loan Association) to rescind the loan. Who wins? [*Valentine v. Influential Savings and Loan Association*, 572 F.Supp. 36 (E.D.Pa. 1983)]

33.8 Consumer Leasing Act In April 1986, Joyce Givens entered into a rental agreement with Rent-A-Center, Inc., whereby she rented a bar and entertainment center. The agreement provided that she must pay in advance to keep the furniture for periods of one week or one month. Givens could terminate the agreement at any time by making arrangements for the furniture's return. Givens made payments between April and August of 1986. After that, she failed to make any further payments but continued to possess the property. When Rent-A-Center became aware that Givens had moved and taken the furniture with her, in violation of the rental agreement, it filed a criminal complaint against her. On January 9, 1988, Givens

agreed to return the furniture and Rent-A-Center dropped the charges. After Rent-A-Center recovered the furniture, Givens sued the company, claiming that the agreement she had signed violated the Consumer Leasing Act. Who wins? [*Givens v. Rent-A-Center, Inc.*, 720 F.Supp. 160 (S.D. Ala 1988)]

33.9 Fair Credit Billing Act Oscar S. Gray had been an American Express cardholder since 1964. In 1980, Gray used his card to purchase airline tickets costing $9,312. American Express agreed that Gray could pay for the tickets in 12 equal monthly installments. In January and February of 1981, Gray made substantial prepayments of $3,500 and $1,156, respectively. When his March bill arrived, Gray was surprised because American Express had converted the deferred payment plan to a currently due charge, making the entire amount for the tickets due and payable. Gray paid the normal monthly charge under the deferred payment plan and informed American Express by letter dated April 22, 1981, of its error. In the letter, Gray identified himself, his card number, and the nature of the error. Gray did not learn of any adverse action by American Express until almost one year later, on the night of his and his wife's anniversary. When he offered his American Express card to pay for their wedding anniversary dinner, the restaurant informed Gray that American Express had canceled his account and had instructed the restaurant to destroy the card. Gray sued American Express. Did American Express violate the Fair Credit Billing Act? [*Gray v. American Express Company*, 743 F.2d 10 (D.C. Cir. 1984)]

33.10 Fair Credit Reporting Act The San Antonio Retail Merchants Association (SARMA) is a business engaged in selling computerized credit reports. In November 1974, William Daniel Thompson, Jr., opened a credit account with Gordon's Jewelers in San Antonio, listing his Social Security number as 457-68-5778. Thompson subsequently ran up a delinquent account of $77.25 at Gordon's that was later charged off as a bad debt. Gordon's reported the bad debt to SARMA, which placed the information and a derogatory credit rating in Thompson's file No. 5867114.

In early 1978, William Douglas Thompson III applied for credit with Gulf Oil and Wards. He listed his Social Security number as 407-86-4065. On February 9, 1978, a worker in the credit department at Gulf accepted file No. 5867114 from SARMA as a credit history of William. Thereafter, SARMA combined the credit reports of the two men. William was denied credit by both Gulf and Wards on the basis of the erroneous information. It was not until June 1979 that William learned of the mistake. After straightening out the facts with Gordon's, William requested SARMA to correct the error. SARMA took no action on William's complaint for four months. William Douglas Thompson III sued SARMA for violating the Fair Credit Reporting Act. Who wins? [*Thompson v. San Antonio Retail Merchants Association*, 682 F.2d 509 (5th Cir. 1982)]

33.11 Fair Debt Collection Practices Act Stanley M. Juras was a student at Montana State University (MSU) from 1972 to 1976. During his years at MSU, Juras took out several student loans from the school under the National Direct Student Loan program. By the time Juras left MSU, he owed the school more than $5,000. Juras defaulted on these loans and MSU assigned the debt to Aman Collection Service, Inc., for purposes of collection. Aman obtained a judgment against Juras in a Montana state court for $5,015 on the debt and $1,920 in interest and attorney's fees. Juras, who now lived in California, still refused to pay these amounts. On May 5, 1982, a vice president of Aman, Mr. Gloss, telephoned

Juras twice in California before 8:00 A.M. Pacific Standard Time. Mr. Gloss told Juras that if he did not pay the debt, he would not receive a college transcript. Juras sued Aman, claiming that the telephone calls violated the Fair Debt Collection Practices Act. Gloss testified at trial that he made the calls before 8:00 A.M. because he had forgotten the difference in time zones between California and Aman's offices in South Dakota. Who wins? [*Juras v. Aman Collection Services, Inc.*, 829 F.2d 739 (9th Cir.) 1987)]

BUSINESS ETHICS CASES

33.12 Business Ethics   Charles of the Ritz Distributors Corporation is a New York corporation engaged in the sale and distribution of a product called Rejuvenescence Cream. The extensive advertising campaign that accompanied the sale of the cream placed emphasis upon the supposed rejuvenating powers of the product. The ads claimed that the cream would bring to the user's "skin quickly the clear radiance" and "the petal-like quality and texture of youth." Another advertisement claimed that the product would "restore natural moisture necessary for a live, healthy skin" with the result that "Your face need not know drought years." The FTC learned of the ads and asked several experts to investigate application of cosmetics to overcome skin conditions that result from physiological changes occurring with the passage of time. The FTC issued a cease-and-desist order in regard to the advertising. Ritz appealed the FTC's decision to a federal court. Did Ritz act ethically in making its advertising claims? Who

wins? [*Charles of the Ritz Distributing Corp. v. FTC*, 143 F.2d 676 (2nd Cir. 1944)]

33.13 Business Ethics   Leon A. Tashof operated a store known as the New York Jewelry Company. The store was located in an area that serves low-income consumers, many of whom have low-paying jobs and have no bank or charge accounts. About 85 percent of the store's sales are made on credit. The store advertised eyeglasses "from $7.50 complete," including "lenses, frames and case." Tashof advertised this sale extensively on radio and in newspapers. Evidence showed that of the 1,400 pairs of eyeglasses sold by the store, fewer than 10 were sold for $7.50; the rest were more-expensive glasses. The Federal Trade Commission sued Tashof for engaging in "bait and switch" marketing. Was Tashof's conduct ethical? Who wins? [*Tashof v. Federal Trade Commission*, 437 F.2d 707 (D.C. Cir. 1970)]

BRIEFING THE CASE WRITING ASSIGNMENT

Read the following case, which has been excerpted from the court's opinion. Review and brief the case.

X-TRA Art, Inc. v. Consumer Product Safety Commission
1991 W.L. 405183 (N.D. Cal.) (1991)
United States District Court

Patel, District Judge

X-TRA Art, Inc. produces Rainbow Foam Paint (Rainbow) a shaving cream-like paint designed for use by children ages three years and up. In December 1990, Consumers Union, a nonprofit organization, published an article in the children's magazine, Zillions, which indicated that Rainbow was an unsafe toy because it could catch fire. Plaintiffs demanded a retraction. Irvin Landau, Consumers Union editorial director, initially sent a letter apologizing for the article and indicating that Consumers Union had made a mistake and would publish a retraction. On December 31, 1990, Landau sent plaintiffs another letter indicating that Consumers Union had conducted additional tests on Rainbow, believed the paint to be in violation of the Federal Hazardous Substances Act (FHSA), and had reported it to the Consumer Product Safety Commission (CPSC). Tests conducted by the CPSC indicated that the Rainbow container, when held upright horizontally, and especially upside down, and exposed to a flame at times produced a flame or flashback (a flame extending back to the dispenser).

On January 17, 1991, Lee Baxter of the CPSC sent plaintiffs a Letter of Advice informing plaintiffs that the CPSC had found Rainbow to be a banned hazardous substance under the FHSA because it was flammable. Baxter requested that X-TRA Art cease distribution and sale of the product and reformulate it. The letter provided plaintiffs with an opportunity to submit opposing views and warned plaintiffs of potential criminal liability if X-TRA Art continued to distribute Rainbow. A copy of the letter was sent to the California Department of Health Services, which subsequently recommended to the California Department of Education that Rainbow not be purchased for use in California public schools.

Plaintiffs sent two letters to the CPSC outlining the objections to the Letter of Advice. The CPSC responded in a letter dated March 18, 1991, which addressed plaintiffs' objections and threatened civil penalties if X-TRA Art did not cease distribution of Rainbow.

As a result of the CPSC findings, on April 26, 1991, the United States Attorney for the Connecticut district secured a warrant authorizing the seizure of Rainbow stored at Early Learning Centre, a toy distribution warehouse in Milford, Connecticut. The warrant was executed on April 29 and the Early Learning Centre instructed its outlets to cease sale of the product. The U.S. Attorney issued a press release detailing the seizure action and CPSC findings regarding Rainbow. Plaintiffs have moved for a preliminary injunction to prevent any further government action against Rainbow.

X-TRA Art brings this action to enjoin the CPSC from taking any action to remove Rainbow Foam Paint from the market pursuant to the Federal Hazardous Substances Act. Plaintiffs argue that: (1) the CPSC has failed to follow statutorily mandated procedural requirements in declaring Rainbow a banned hazardous substance pursuant to the FHSA; (2) the CPSC used invalid and improper testing methods in determining that Rainbow is flammable; (3) the CPSC violated provisions of the Consumer Product Safety Act, governing public disclosure of findings concerning safety hazards posed by products; (4) the CPSC cannot establish that substantial injury or illness can be caused as a proximate result of any customary or reasonably foreseeable use of Rainbow, as required by the FHSA; and (5) plaintiffs' rights to due process and equal protection have been violated.

Following an evidentiary hearing on May 7, 1991, the court ordered the government to desist from taking any action against Rainbow for 10 days and further ordered the parties to file additional briefing on the matter. Having reviewed the parties' papers and held an additional hearing, the court DENIES plaintiffs' motion for a preliminary injunction.

The CPSC argues that under FHSA a product intended for use by children is automatically banned if the CPSC determines said product to be a hazardous substance. Plaintiffs, citing to other provisions of the FHSA, contend that a children's product such as Rainbow may not be banned without notice, comment, and a public hearing. The plain language of the FHSA supports the CPSC's position.

In 1966 Congress amended the FHSLA to authorize the banning of hazardous toys, children's articles and household goods; "Labeling" was deleted from the title of the FHSLA and the Federal Hazardous Substance Act was created. The legislative history of the 1966 amendments makes it clear that, while the banning of hazardous household substances was to occur only after a public hearing, Congress intended that the Secretary (Commission) have the power to ban hazardous toys and children's articles without regulation. There is no question that plaintiffs were provided with notice of the agency action, given the Letter of Advice and the correspondence between the plaintiffs and the CPSC which followed. Moreover, in early 1990 the CPSC determined that foam-like string streamers designed for children and dispensed from self-pressurized containers were flammable and therefore were banned hazardous substances. The manufacturers voluntarily recalled their products and reformulated them with a nonflammable propellant. The agency action against the string streamer products appears to have been well publicized. In light of the similarity between the string streamer products and Rainbow Foam Paint, it is surprising to hear plaintiffs argue that they were caught completely off-guard by the agency action challenged in this case.

The court concludes that X-TRA Art raised serious legal issues with regard to the procedures utilized by the CPSC in declaring Rainbow Foam Paint a "banned hazardous substance" and that plaintiffs are unlikely to prevail on the merits of the issue. This being the case, plaintiffs' motion for a preliminary injunction is DENIED.

ENDNOTES

1. 21 U.S.C. § 321.
2. 21 U.S.C. §§ 360(c) et seq.
3. 21 U.S.C. § 346(a).
4. 21 U.S.C. § 348.
5. 21 U.S.C. § 376(a).
6. 21 U.S.C. § 360(b).
7. 21 U.S.C. § 357.
8. 42 U.S.C. § 264.
9. 42 U.S.C. § 263(b).
10. 42 U.S.C. § 263.
11. A consumer who is injured by a defective product can bring a civil action to recover damages from his or her injuries. Product liability is discussed in Chapter 6.
12. 15 U.S.C. § 2051.
13. 15 U.S.C. § § 1451 et seq.
14. 15 U.S.C. § 1471.
15. 15 U.S.C. § § 41–51.
16. 39 U.S.C. § 3009.
17. 15 U.S.C. §§ 1667 et seq.
18. 15 U.S.C. § 1637.
19. 15 U.S.C. § 1691.
20. 15 U.S.C. § § 1681 et seq.
21. 15 U.S.C. § 1692.

CHAPTER 34

Environmental Protection

All animals are equal but some animals are more equal than others

—George Orwell
Animal Farm, 1945

Chapter Objectives

After studying this chapter, you should be able to:

1. Describe an environmental impact statement and identify when one is needed.

2. Describe the national ambient air quality standards required by the Clean Air Act.

3. Describe the effluent water standards required by the Clean Water Act.

4. Describe the pollution control technologies that must be installed to prevent air and water pollution.

5. Explain how environmental laws regulate the use of toxic substances.

6. Explain how environmental laws regulate the storage, transport, and disposal of hazardous wastes.

7. Describe the government's authority to recover the cost of cleaning up hazardous waste sites pursuant to the Superfund law.

8. Describe how the Endangered Species Act protects endangered and threatened species and their habitats.

9. Describe how environmental laws have criminalized certain polluting activities.

10. Explain how the North American Commission on Environmental Cooperation (CEC) monitors transborder pollution.

Chapter Contents

In producing and consuming products, businesses and consumers generate air pollution, water pollution, and hazardous and toxic wastes that cause harm to the environment and to human health. Although environmental protection has been a concern since medieval England enacted laws regulating the burning of soft coal, pollution has now reached alarming rates in this country and the world.

This chapter is concerned with how the federal and state governments are trying to contain the levels of pollution and to clean up hazardous waste sites in this country. It examines the scope and impact of the major environmental protection laws applicable to businesses and individuals.

*E*NVIRONMENTAL PROTECTION

Under the common law, both individuals and the government could bring a civil suit against the offending party. Individuals could bring a private civil suit based on *private nuisance* to recover damages from the polluting party. The injured party could also sue for an injunction to prevent further pollution by the offending party. The government could bring a lawsuit against a polluter based on the common law theory of *public nuisance*. By the 1950s and 1960s, federal and state governments realized that this approach was not enough to contain the problems caused by pollution and began enacting legislation to protect the environment.

In the 1970s, the federal government began enacting statutes to protect our nation's air and water from pollution. Federal legislation was also enacted to regulate hazardous wastes and to protect wildlife. In many instances, states enacted their own environmental laws that now coexist with federal law as long as they do not directly conflict with the federal law or unduly burden interstate commerce. These laws provide both civil and criminal penalties. The development of such a vast body of law in such a short period of time is unprecedented in U.S. history. Environmental protection is one of the most important, and costly, issues facing business and society today.

Those who hike the Appalachian Trail into Sunfish Pond, New Jersey, and camp or sleep there, or run the Allagash in Maine, or climb the Guadalupes in West Texas, or who canoe and portage the Quentico Superior in Minnesota, certainly should have standing to defend those natural wonders before courts or agencies, though they live 3,000 miles away. Then there will be assurances that all of the forms of life will stand before the court—the pileated woodpecker as well as the coyote and bear, the lemmings as well as the trout in the streams. Those inarticulate members of the ecological group cannot speak. But those people who have so frequented the place as to know its values and wonders will be able to speak for the entire ecological community.

Justice Douglas,
Dissenting Opinion Sierra
Club v. Morton, Secretary of the
Interior *31 L.Ed.2d 636 (1972)*

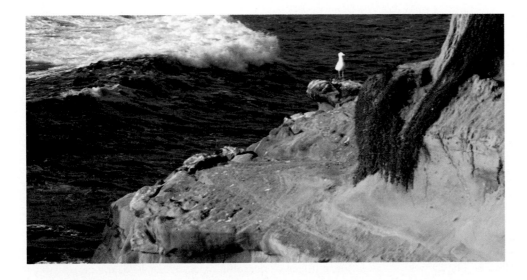

La Jolla, California The federal and state governments have enacted many statutes to protect the environment from pollution.

The Environmental Protection Agency

In 1970, Congress created the **Environmental Protection Agency (EPA)** to coordinate the implementation and enforcement of the federal environmental protection laws. The EPA has broad rule-making powers to adopt regulations to advance the laws that it is empowered to administer. The agency also has adjudicative powers to hold hearings, make decisions, and order remedies for violations of federal environmental laws. In addition, the EPA can initiate judicial proceedings in court against suspected violators of federal environmental laws.

Environmental Protection Agency (EPA)

An administrative agency created by Congress in 1970 to coordinate the implementation and enforcement of the federal environmental protection laws.

Landmark Law

NATIONAL ENVIRONMENTAL POLICY ACT

The **National Environmental Policy Act (NEPA)** which was enacted in 1969, became effective January 1, 1970 [42 U.S.C. §§ 4321 et seq.]. The **Council on Environmental Quality** was created under this act. The NEPA mandates that the federal government consider the "adverse impact" of proposed legislation, rule making, or other federal government action on the environment before the action is implemented.

ENVIRONMENTAL IMPACT STATEMENT
The NEPA and rules adopted thereunder require that an **environmental impact statement (EIS)** must be prepared for all proposed legislation or major federal action that significantly affects the quality of the human environment. The purpose of the EIS is to provide enough information about the environment to enable the federal government to determine the feasibility of the project. The EIS is also used as evidence in court whenever a federal action is challenged as violating the NEPA or other federal environmental protection laws. Examples of actions that require an EIS include proposals to build a new federally funded highway, to license nuclear plants, and the like.

The EIS must (1) describe the affected environment, (2) describe the impact of the proposed federal action on the environment, (3) identify and discuss alternatives to the proposed action, (4) list the resources that will be committed to the action, and (5) contain a cost-benefit analysis of the proposed action and alternative actions. Expert professionals, such as engineers, geologists, and accountants, may be consulted during the preparation of the EIS.

Once an EIS is prepared, it is subject to public review. The public has 30 days in which to submit comments to the EPA. After the comments have been received and reviewed, the EPA will issue an order that states whether the proposed federal action may proceed. Decisions of the EPA are appealable to the appropriate U.S. court of appeals.

The NEPA does not apply to action by state or local governments or private parties. Most states and many local governments have enacted laws that require an environmental impact statement to be prepared regarding proposed state and local government action as well as private development.

$\mathcal{A}$IR POLLUTION

air pollution

Pollution caused by factories, homes, vehicles, and the like that affects the air.

One of the major problems facing this country is **air pollution**. Prior to the advent of the internal combustion engine, most air pollution consisted of smoke from factories and homes. Today, most air pollution is invisible and odorless. The air pollution is caused by both mobile sources (such as automobiles) and stationary sources (such as public utilities, manufacturing facilities, and households).

Landmark Law

THE CLEAN AIR ACT

The federal government's first legislation concerning air pollution came in 1955 when it authorized funds for air pollution research. The **Clean Air Act** was enacted in 1963 to assist states in dealing with air pollution. The act was amended in 1970 and 1977 and, most recently, by the **Clean Air Act Amendments of 1990** [42 U.S.C. §§ 7401 et seq.]. The Clean Air Act, as amended, provides comprehensive regulation of air quality in this country.

NATIONAL AMBIENT AIR QUALITY STANDARDS
The Clean Air Act directs the EPA to establish **national ambient air quality standards (NAAQS)** for certain pollutants. These standards are set at two different levels: pri-

mary (to protect human beings) and secondary (to protect vegetation, matter, climate, visibility, and economic values). Specific standards have been established for carbon monoxide, nitrogen oxide, sulfur oxide, ozone, lead, and particulate matter.

Although the EPA establishes air quality standards, the states are responsible for their enforcement. The federal government has the right to enforce these air pollution standards if the states fail to do so. Each state is required to prepare a *state implementation plan* (SIP) that sets out how the state plans to meet the federal standards. The EPA has divided each state into *air quality control regions (AQCRs)*. Each region is monitored to ensure compliance.

The Supreme Court Speaks

Costs Not Considered When Enforcing the Clean Air Act

Whitman, Administrator of Environmental Protection Agency v. American Trucking Association
531 U.S. 457, 121 S.Ct. 903 (2001)
Supreme Court of the United States

BACKGROUND AND FACTS

Section 109 of the Federal Clean Air Act (CAA) requires the Administrator of the Environmental Protection Agency (EPA), a federal administrative agency, to set national ambient air quality standards (NAAQS) for air pollutants. Section 109 instructs the EPA to set NAAQS at levels "to protect the public health" with "an adequate margin of safety." Pursuant to Section 109, the EPA issued new standards for ozone and particulate matter emitted from the operation of trucks. The American Trucking Association sued the EPA, arguing that the EPA must consider the cost caused to trucking firms before issuing the NAAQS. The EPA argued that it did not have to do so under the statute. The district court held for the American Trucking Association, but the court of appeals held for the EPA on this issue. The U.S. Supreme Court granted review.

SUPREME COURT ISSUE

Under Section 109 of the Federal Clean Air Act, must the Environmental Protection Agency consider the cost imposed on trucking firms before setting NAAQS for ozone and particulate matter emissions from trucks?

IN THE LANGUAGE OF THE U.S. SUPREME COURT

Scalia, Justice Section 109 instructs the EPA to set primary ambient air quality standards "the attainment and maintenance of which are requisite to protect the public health" with "an adequate margin of safety." Were it not for the hundreds of pages of briefing respondent American Trucking Association have submitted on the issue, one would have thought it fairly clear that this text does not permit the EPA to consider costs in setting the standards. The language, as one scholar has noted, "is absolute." The EPA, based on the information about health effects contained in the technical criteria documents is to identify the maximum airborne concentration of a pollutant that the public health can tolerate, decrease the concentration to provide an adequate margin of safety, and set the standard at that level. Nowhere are the costs of achieving such a standard made part of that initial calculation.

Respondent argues many more factors than air pollution affect public health. In particular, the economic cost of implementing a very stringent standard might produce health losses sufficient to offset the health gains achieved in cleaning the air—for example, by closing down whole industries and thereby impoverishing the workers and consumers dependent upon those industries. That is unquestionably true. Accordingly, to prevail in their present challenge, respondent must show a textual commitment of authority to the EPA to consider costs in setting NAAQS under Section 109. Congress does not alter the fundamental details of a regulatory scheme in vague terms or ancillary provisions—it does not, one might say, hide elephants in mouseholes. Respondent's textual arguments ultimately founder upon this principle.

DECISION AND REMEDY

The U.S. Supreme Court held that the statutory language of Section 109 of the Clean Air Act does not require the EPA to consider the cost to trucking firms for implementing the NAAQS set by the EPA. The judgment of the court of appeals is affirmed as to this issue.

CASE QUESTIONS

Critical Legal Thinking Do you think the statutory language of Section 109 was clear in this case?

Business Ethics Would the "public health" be compromised under the trucking firms' argument? Why did the trucking firms resist the NAAQS set by the EPA?

Contemporary Business What are the economic consequences of the Supreme Court's ruling? Explain.

Stationary Sources of Air Pollution

Substantial amounts of air pollution are emitted by **stationary sources** (e.g., industrial plants, oil refineries, public utilities). The Clean Air Act requires states to identify major stationary sources and develop plans to reduce air pollution from these sources.

stationary sources

Sources of air pollution such as industrial plants, oil refineries, and public utilities.

Mobile Sources of Air Pollution

Automobile and other vehicle emissions are one of the major sources of air pollution in this country. In an effort to control emissions from these **mobile sources**, the Clean Air Act requires air pollution controls to be installed on motor vehicles. Emission standards have

mobile sources

Sources of air pollution such as automobiles, trucks, buses, motorcycles, and airplanes.

been set for automobiles, trucks, buses, motorcycles, and airplanes. (The Federal Aviation Administration is responsible for enforcing pollution standards for airplanes.)

The manufacture of automobiles is regulated to ensure compliance with EPA emission standards. The Clean Air Act requires new automobiles and light-duty trucks to meet air quality control standards. The EPA can require automobile manufacturers to recall and repair or replace pollution control equipment that does not meet these requirements. In addition, the Clean Air Act authorizes the EPA to regulate air pollution caused by fuel and fuel additives.

Nonattainment Areas

nonattainment areas

Regions that do not meet air quality standards.

Regions that do not meet the air quality standards are designated **nonattainment areas**. Nonattainment areas are classified into one of five categories—(1) marginal, (2) moderate, (3) serious, (4) severe, and (5) extreme—based on the degree to which they exceed the ozone standard. Deadlines are established for areas to meet the attainment level. States must submit compliance plans that (1) identify major sources of air pollution and require them to install pollution control equipment, (2) institute permit systems for new stationary sources, and (3) implement inspection programs to monitor mobile sources. States that fail to develop or implement an approved plan are subject to the following sanctions: (1) loss of federal highway funds and (2) limitations on new sources of emissions (e.g., the EPA can prohibit the construction of a new pollution-causing industrial plant in the nonattainment area).

Contemporary Business Environment

SMOG SWAPPING

Businesses have long thought that the enforcement of environmental laws was too burdensome and cumbersome, whereas environmentalists argue that current laws have not brought about sufficient reductions in pollution. Today, the "command and control" environmental regulation—the amount of pollution a plant can produce—is giving way to a market-based trading scheme. It is hoped that the new scheme will reduce pollution without unduly burdening businesses.

The **Clean Air Act Amendments of 1990** include a new program that allows companies to trade sulfur dioxide emissions (which are responsible for acid rain). Under this plan, companies still face strict quotas for reducing such emissions, but they are free to satisfy their limits by buying pollution credits from other companies.

Consider This Example Company A uses all of its 2,000-pound limit, and it wants to add equipment that would increase the amount of emissions it produces. Company B also has a 2,000-pound limit, but it uses only 1,500 pounds. Company A can buy pollution credits from Company B. The credits are deducted in pounds of pollution allowed per day. For every 1.2 pounds of pollution eliminated by the selling company, the program allows the creation of only one pound of pollution by the buying company. This system is designed to reduce overall pollution. Trades cannot happen until the EPA certifies the pollution credits for sale.

The Southern California Air Quality Management District (AQMD), where the air pollution levels exceed federal health standards more than 180 days each year, has also adopted an extensive market-based trading program. The program covers the three pollutants most responsible for smog: sulfur oxide, nitrogen oxide, and reactive organic gas.

There is even a movement at the United Nations to create an international market for trading emission credits for carbon dioxide. Carbon dioxide is the main cause of global warming.

Markets are developing for the trading of pollution credits. For example, the Chicago Board of Trade will offer futures contracts on pollution credits. Manufacturers, refiners, utilities, and speculators would buy and sell pollution credits on these markets. Companies that buy credits can lock in pollution rights for the future.

Businesses argue that the market-based trading of pollution credits will work to reduce pollution in this country. They feel that trading is the best way to solve social and environmental problems at the least cost to society. Critics, most notably environmental groups, contend that the system will be hard to monitor. They also assert that it is immoral to allow companies to buy and sell the right to pollute the environment.

Toxic Air Pollutants

Section 112 of the Clean Air Act requires the EPA to identify **toxic air pollutants** that cause serious illness or death to humans.[1] So far, more than 200 chemicals have been listed as toxic, including asbestos, mercury, vinyl chloride, benzene, beryllium, and radionuclides.

The act requires the EPA to establish standards for these chemicals and requires stationary sources to install equipment and technology to control emissions of toxic substances. EPA standards for toxic substances are set without regard to economic or technological feasibility.

The EPA's setting of the level for a toxic pollutant was challenged in the following case.

toxic air pollutants

Air pollutants that cause serious illness or death to humans.

Natural Resources Defense Council, Inc. v. Environmental Protection Agency
824 F.2d 1146 (1987)
United States Court of Appeals, District of Columbia Circuit

CASE 34.1

BACKGROUND AND FACTS
Vinyl chloride, a gaseous synthetic chemical used in the manufacture of plastics, is a strong carcinogen. The EPA issued a notice of proposed rule making to establish emission standards for vinyl chloride as a toxic pollutant under Section 112 of the Clean Air Act. Section 112 stipulates that the EPA must set minimum emission standards for toxic air pollutants at the level that in its judgment "provides an ample margin of safety to protect the public health." The EPA issued a final order that required emissions of vinyl chloride to be set at a level that would provide an ample margin of safety for human beings. The National Resources Defense Council, Inc. (NRDC), an environmental activist organization, sued the EPA, alleging that its final order violated Section 112. The NRDC argued that the EPA must set a zero level of emissions of vinyl chloride.

ISSUE
Must the EPA set a zero level of emissions of the toxic pollutant vinyl chloride?

COURT'S REASONING
The court of appeals stated that to accept the NRDC's zero level of emissions rule: "We would have to conclude that Congress mandated massive economic and social dislocations by shutting down entire industries. That is not a reasonable way to read the legislative history. The EPA has determined that zero-emissions standards for toxic pollutants would

result in the elimination of such activities as the generation of electricity from either coal burning or nuclear energy; the manufacture of steel; the mining, smelting, or refining of virtually any mineral (e.g., copper, iron, lead, zinc, and limestone); the manufacture of synthetic organic chemicals; and the refining, storage, or dispensing of any petroleum product. It is simply not possible that Congress intended such havoc in the American economy, and not a single representative or senator mentioned the fact. Thus, we find no support for the NRDC's extreme position in the language or legislative history of the act."

DECISION
The court of appeals held that the EPA must reach a determination of what amount of vinyl chloride is "safe" and then set emission standards accordingly to provide for an "ample margin of safety."

Case Questions

Critical Legal Thinking   Should emission levels of toxic pollutants be set at "risk-free" levels rather than just "safe" levels? Explain.

Business Ethics   Do environmental activist groups and organizations serve an important public purpose? Explain.

Contemporary Business   Can you think of instances in which environmental laws should be used to shut down whole industries? Explain.

Contemporary Business Environment

INDOOR AIR POLLUTION: A FRONTIER FOR ENVIRONMENTAL LITIGATION

Most people who live or work in our country's urban centers have grown to accept air pollution as an unavoidable peril of modern life. What many of these people do not realize, however, is that they should not breathe a sigh of relief upon entering their offices or homes. According to officials of the

EPA, the air inside some buildings may be 100 times more polluted than outside air.

Indoor air pollution, or "**sick building syndrome**," has two primary causes. In an effort to reduce dependence on foreign oil, many recently constructed office buildings were overly insulated and built with sealed windows and no out-side air ducts. As a result, absolutely no fresh air enters many workplaces. This absence of fresh air can cause headaches, fatigue, and dizziness among workers.

The other chief cause of sick building syndrome, which is believed to affect up to one-third of U.S. office buildings, is hazardous chemicals and construction materials. In the office, these include everything from asbestos to noxious fumes emitted from copy machines, carbonless paper, and cleaning fluids. In the home, radon, an odorless gas that is emitted from the natural breakdown of uranium in soil, poses a partic-ularly widespread danger. Four million to ten million homes in the United States have radon levels in excess of EPA guidelines. Radon gas damages and may destroy lung tissue. It is estimated that radon causes 20,000 deaths each year.

Indoor air pollution has placed businesses between a rock and a hard place. Employer inactivity in the face of this dan-ger will surely result in higher healthcare bills for employee

illnesses as doctors increasingly attribute a wide range of symptoms to sick building syndrome. Indoor air pollution also adversely affects worker productivity and morale and increases absenteeism. On the other hand, the costs of elimi-nating these conditions can be colossal.

Experts predict that sick building syndrome is likely to spawn a flood of litigation, and that a wide range of parties will be sued. Manufacturers, employers, home sellers, builders, engineers, and architects will increasingly be forced to defend themselves against tort and breach of contract actions filed by homeowners, employees, and others affected by indoor air pollution. Federal and state governments may also be dragged into court to pay for defects in their build-ings and to defend their regulatory standards. Insurance companies will undoubtedly be drawn into costly lawsuits stemming from indoor air pollution.

Presently, the government has not adopted any regulations governing indoor air quality.

WATER POLLUTION

water pollution

Pollution of lakes, rivers, oceans, and other bodies of water.

River and Harbor Act

A federal statute enacted in 1886 that established a permit system for the discharge of refuse, wastes, and sewage into U.S. navigable waterways.

Water pollution affects human health, recreation, agriculture, and business. Pollution of waterways by industry and humans has caused severe ecological and environmental prob-lems, including water sources that are unsafe for drinking water, fish, birds, and animals.

The federal government has enacted a comprehensive scheme of statutes and regula-tions to prevent and control water pollution. The first regulation dates back to the **River and Harbor Act**, which was enacted in 1886. This act, as codified in 1899, established a permit system for the discharge of refuse, wastes, and sewage into the nation's navigable waterways. This permit system was replaced in 1972 by the *National Pollutant Discharge Elimination System (NPDES)*, which requires any person who proposes to discharge pollu-tion into the water to obtain a permit from the EPA. The EPA can deny or set restrictions on such permits.

Landmark Law

CLEAN WATER ACT

In 1948, Congress enacted the **Federal Water Pollution Control Act (FWPCA)** to regulate water pollution. This act was amended several times before it was updated by the Clean Water Act of 1972, the Clean Water Act of 1977, and the Water Quality Act of 1987. The FWPCA, as amended, is simply referred to as the **Clean Water Act** [33 U.S.C. §§ 1251 et seq.]. This act is administered by the EPA.

Pursuant to the Clean Water Act, the EPA has estab-

lished water quality standards that define which bodies of water can be used for public drinking water, recreation (such as swimming), propagation of fish and wildlife, and agricul-tural and industrial uses.

States are primarily responsible for enforcing the provi-sions of the Clean Water Act and EPA regulations adopted thereunder. If a state fails to do so, the federal government may enforce the act.

Point Sources of Water Pollution

point sources

Sources of water pollution such as paper mills, manufacturing plants, electric utility plants, and sewage plants.

The Clean Water Act authorizes the EPA to establish water pollution control standards for **point sources** of water pollution (i.e., mines, manufacturing plants, paper mills, elec-tric utility plants, municipal sewage plants, and other stationary sources of water pollu-tion). The EPA issues guidelines as to the best available technologies. Dischargers of pol-lutants are required to keep records, maintain monitoring equipment, and keep samples of discharges.

The Supreme Court Speaks

Civil Lawsuit Allowed Against Water Polluter

Friends of the Earth, Incorporated v. Laidlaw Environmental Services (TOC), Inc.
528 U.S. 167, 120 S.Ct. 693 (2000)
Supreme Court of the United States

BACKGROUND AND FACTS

Laidlaw Environmental Services (TOC), Inc. operated a hazardous waste incinerator facility in Roebuck, South Carolina, where it discharged wastes into the North Tyger River. Between 1987 and 1995, Laidlaw discharged wastes into the river that exceeded the mercury limits allowed at the site. Mercury is a dangerous pollutant. The South Carolina Department of Health and Environmental Control (DHEC) sued Laidlaw. Laidlaw, which had gained an economic benefit of over $1 million by making these illegal discharges, reached a settlement with the DHEC whereby it paid $100,000 in penalties.

The Friends of the Earth, Incorporated (FOE) and other environmental groups brought a lawsuit against Laidlaw seeking to obtain civil penalties permitted in civil-citizen lawsuits under the federal Clean Water Act. Laidlaw argued that FOE could not sue because Laidlaw had already reached a settlement with the state of South Carolina. The district court held for FOE and ordered Laidlaw to pay $405,800 in civil penalties; the court also ordered a hearing to determine the amount of attorneys' fees to be awarded FOE. The court of appeals reversed. The U.S. Supreme Court granted review.

SUPREME COURT ISSUE

Does settlement with a state for environmental violations make moot a civil-citizen lawsuit under the federal Clean Water Act?

IN THE LANGUAGE OF THE U.S. SUPREME COURT

Ginsburg, Justice It can scarcely be doubted that, for a plaintiff who is injured or faces the threat of future injury due to illegal conduct ongoing at the time of suit, a sanction that effectively abates that conduct and prevents its recurrence provides a form of redress. Civil penalties can fit that description. To the extent that they encourage defendants to discontinue current violations and deter them from committing future ones, they afford redress to citizen plaintiffs who are injured or threatened with injury as a consequence of ongoing unlawful conduct.

DECISION AND REMEDY

The U.S. Supreme Court held that defendant Laidlaw was subject to the Friends of the Earth's civil-citizen lawsuit for damages under the Clean Water Act even though Laidlaw had previously been sued and reached a settlement with the state of South Carolina. The Supreme Court remanded the case for a determination of the attorneys' fees to be awarded to Friends of the Earth.

CASE QUESTIONS

Critical Legal Thinking   Should citizens be permitted to bring lawsuits to enforce environmental laws? Or should only the government have this power? Explain.

Business Ethics   Did Laidlaw act ethically in this case?

Contemporary Business   Did Laidlaw come out ahead financially in its settlement with the state of South Carolina?

Thermal Pollution

The Clean Water Act expressly forbids **thermal pollution** because the discharge of heated waters or materials into the nation's waterways may upset the ecological balance; decrease the oxygen content of water; and harm fish, birds, and animals that use the waterways.[2] Sources of thermal pollution (such as electric utility companies and manufacturing plants) are subject to the provisions of the Clean Water act and regulations adopted by the EPA.

thermal pollution
Heated water or material discharged into waterways that upsets the ecological balance and decreases the oxygen content.

Wetlands

Wetlands are defined as areas that are inundated or saturated by surface water or ground water that support vegetation typically adapted for life in saturated soil conditions. Wetlands include swamps, marshes, bogs, and similar areas that support birds, animals, and vegetative life. The Clean Water Act forbids the filling or dredging of wetlands unless a permit has been obtained from the **Army Corps of Engineers (Corps)**. The Corps is empowered to adopt regulations and conduct administrative proceedings to enforce the act.

wetlands
Areas that are inundated or saturated by surface water or ground water that support vegetation typically adapted for life in such conditions.

Safe Drinking Water Act

The **Safe Drinking Water Act**,[3] which was enacted in 1974 and amended in 1986, authorizes the EPA to establish national primary drinking water standards (minimum quality of water for human consumption). The act also prohibits the dumping of wastes into wells

Safe Drinking Water Act
A federal statute enacted in 1974 and amended in 1986 that authorizes the EPA to establish national primary drinking water standards.

used for drinking water. The states are primarily responsible for enforcing the act. If a state fails to do so, the federal government can enforce the act.

Ocean Dumping

Marine Protection, Research, and Sanctuaries Act

A federal statute enacted in 1972 that extends environmental protection to the oceans.

The **Marine Protection, Research, and Sanctuaries Act**,[4] enacted in 1972, extended environmental protection to the oceans. It (1) requires a permit for dumping wastes and other foreign materials into ocean waters and (2) establishes marine sanctuaries in ocean waters as far seaward as the edge of the Continental Shelf and in the Great Lakes and their connecting waters.

Ethics Brief

When the oil tanker *Exxon Valdez* ran aground off Alaska in 1989, the oil industry was not prepared to respond to the emergency.

Oil Spills

The Clean Water Act authorizes the U.S. government to clean up oil spills and spills of other hazardous substances in ocean waters within 12 miles of the shore and on the Continental Shelf and to recover the cleanup costs from responsible parties.

The Supreme Court Speaks

Army Corps of Engineers Lack Power to Regulate Non-Navigable Waters

Solid Waste Agency of Northern Cook County, Illinois v. United States Army Corps of Engineers
531 U.S. 159, 121 S.Ct. 675 (2001)
Supreme Court of the United States

BACKGROUND AND FACTS

Section 404 of the federal Clean Water Act (CWA) regulates the discharge of dredged or fill material into *navigable waters*. The U.S. Army Corps of Engineers (Corps) is authorized to enforce this statute and to issue permits for discharge of dredged or fill material into navigable waters in the United States. The Solid Waste Agency of Northern Cook County, Illinois (Agency), a consortium of 23 suburban Chicago cities and villages, located a 533-acre parcel of real property that was a closed sand and gravel pit mining operation as a proposed disposal site for baled nonhazardous solid waste. Long since abandoned, the old mining site had permanent and seasonal water ponds of varying size and depth that served several species of migrating birds. The ponds were not connected to any water tributary, but were filled by rain water and melting snow. When the Corps refused to issue a permit, the Agency sued the Corps, arguing that the Corps had no jurisdiction over the site because it did not contain any *navigable waters*. The district court held for the Corps, and the court of appeals affirmed. The U.S. Supreme Court granted review.

SUPREME COURT ISSUE

Does the gravel and sand pit contain *navigable waters* that give the Army Corps of Engineers jurisdiction over the site?

IN THE LANGUAGE OF THE U.S. SUPREME COURT

Rehnquist, Chief Justice Congress passed the CWA for the stated purpose of restoring and maintaining the chemical, physical, and biological integrity of the Nation's waters. Relevant here, Section 404 authorizes respondents U.S. Army Corps of Engineers to regulate the discharge of fill material into "navigable waters," which the statute defines as "the waters of the United States, including the territorial seas." Respondents have interpreted these words to cover the abandoned gravel pit at issue here because it is used as habitat for migratory birds. We thus decline respondents' invitation to hold that isolated ponds, some only seasonal, wholly located within Illinois, fall under § 404's definition of "navigable waters" because they serve as habitat for migratory birds. As counsel for respondents conceded at oral argument, such a ruling would assume that the use of the word navigable *in the statute does not have any independent significance.*

DECISION AND REMEDY

The U.S. Supreme Court held that the ponds located on the sand and gravel pit are not *navigable waters* as defined by Section 404 of the Clean Water Act. Therefore, the U.S. Army Corps of Engineers does not have authority or jurisdiction over these ponds. The judgment of the court of appeals is reversed.

CASE QUESTIONS

Critical Legal Thinking Do you think that the U.S. Supreme Court properly interpreted the term *navigable waters* as used in Section 404 of the Clean Water Act?

Business Ethics Did the petitioner Solid Waste Agency act ethically in placing a waste disposal site on an area where the habitat of several migrating birds could be destroyed?

Contemporary Business In the United States, has a proper balance been struck between the protection of the environment and the ability of businesses to operate without too much burden from these laws? Explain.

Contemporary Business Environment

THE OIL POLLUTION ACT

In March 1989, the *Exxon Valdez*, an oil supertanker, ran aground in Prince William Sound in Alaska, spilling millions of gallons of oil into the water. Exxon and the oil industry were not prepared to respond to this emergency. The first cleanup barge did not reach the site until 14 hours after the oil spill. The response was totally inadequate, and the oil eventually contaminated 1,100 miles of shoreline. Tens of thousands of dead animals and birds lay strewn on the shore, and there were unknown numbers of dead fish.

Two factors—the devastation caused by the *Exxon Valdez* catastrophe and the oil industry's illpreparedness to address oil spills—caused Congress to enact the **Oil Pollution Act of 1990 (OPA)**. This act, which is administered by the U.S. Coast Guard, requires the oil industry to adopt procedures that can more readily respond to oil spills.

The OPA contains strict requirements for constructing oil tankers. It requires new ships to have double hulls and phases out single-hull tankers between 1995 to 2010. Barges must be double-hulled by 2015. The tanker industry is upset over the double-hull requirement and is seeking a less expensive means to ensure protection in case of a mishap.

The OPA also requires each tanker owner–operator to establish an oil pollution cleanup contingency plan. The Coast Guard has issued regulations for emergency response plans by tankers operating in U.S. waters. Under the OPA and Coast Guard regulations, tanker owner–operators must have enough personnel and equipment to handle a "worst case" spill of an entire cargo in "adverse" weather conditions. They will also have to contract with an oil-spill response company. In response, 20 major oil companies funded the creation of the Marine Spill Response Corporation. Other response firms are also being set up by other oil companies.

The Coast Guard must issue a certificate to a tanker owner–operator before oil may be brought to the United States. To obtain the certificate, the tanker owner–operator must prove that it is fully insured to cover any liability that may occur from an oil spill.

It is hoped that the emergency response procedures mandated by the OPA will not be needed. But at least this time the mechanism will be in place to respond more quickly and adequately to such a spill so that an environmental catastrophe the size of that caused by the *Exxon Valdez* will never occur again.

International Law

THE LAW OF THE SEA

For centuries, the oceans were considered "high seas" over which no nation had jurisdiction. In the middle of the nineteenth century, coastal nations began claiming exclusive rights to territorial waters and seabeds that bordered their nations. Nations claimed exclusive rights to seas extending anywhere from 12 to 200 miles from the shoreline. Most of these national laws were enacted to protect fishing rights.

In 1971, the United Nations Conference on the Law of the Sea (LOS Convention) established a 200-mile exclusive economic zone (EEZ) for coastal nations. This Convention grants sovereign rights to coastal nations to explore, exploit, conserve, and manage living resources in their EEZs. It also grants these nations sovereign right over nonliving resources of the seabed and subsoil in the EEZs.

The LOS Convention grants all nations the freedom of navigation and overflight over EEZs as well as the right to lay submarine cables and pipelines. In exercising these rights, nations must comply with the lawful and nondiscriminatory laws of the coastal nation. A coastal nation may permit other nations to fish and use the waters and seabeds of its EEZ, subject to conservation and other laws established by the coastal nation.

The LOS Convention gives coastal nations the right to board and inspect ships, arrest a ship and its crew, and institute legal proceedings against violators. Appeals may be made to the International Tribunal for the Law of the Sea.

*T*OXIC SUBSTANCES

The use of chemicals for agricultural, industrial, and mining uses has greatly increased productivity in this country. Unfortunately, many of these chemicals contain **toxic substances** that cause cancer, birth defects, and other health-related problems in human beings, as well as injury or death to birds, animals, fish, and vegetation. Because of these dangers, the federal government has enacted legislation to regulate the use of toxic substances. Two of these statutes are discussed in the following paragraphs.

toxic substances

Chemicals used for agricultural, industrial, and mining uses that cause injury to humans, birds, animals, fish, and vegetation.

Insecticide, Fungicide, and Rodenticide Act

Insecticide, Fungicide, and Rodenticide Act

A federal statute that requires pesticides, herbicides, fungicides, and rodenticides to be registered with the EPA; the EPA may deny, suspend, or cancel registration.

Farmers and ranchers use chemical pesticides, herbicides, fungicides, and rodenticides to kill insects, pests, and weeds. Evidence shows that the use of some of these chemicals on food, and their residual accumulation in soil, poses health hazards. In 1947, Congress enacted the **Insecticide, Fungicide, and Rodenticide Act**, which gave the federal government authority to regulate pesticides and related chemicals. This act, which was substantially amended in 1972,[5] is administered by the EPA.

Under the act, pesticides must be registered with the EPA before they can be sold. The EPA may deny registration, certify either general or restricted use, or set limits on the amount of chemical residue permitted on crops sold for human or animal consumption. The EPA has authority to register and inspect pesticide manufacturing facilities.

The EPA may suspend the registration of a registered pesticide that it finds poses an imminent danger or emergency. If the EPA finds that the use of a registered pesticide poses environmental risks (but not imminent danger), it may initiate a proceeding to cancel the registration of the pesticide. After reviewing the evidence, the EPA may cancel a registration if it finds use of the pesticide would cause unreasonably adverse effects on the environment.

The federal Clean Air Act, Clean Water Act, Toxic Substances Control Act, and other federal statutes protect plant life, animal life, and the environment from pollution.

Toxic Substances Control Act

Toxic Substances Control Act

A federal statute enacted in 1976 that requires manufacturers and processors to test new chemicals to determine their effect on human health and the environment before the EPA will allow them to be marketed.

Many chemical compounds that are used in the manufacture of plastics and products are toxic (e.g., PCBs and asbestos). Hundreds of new chemicals and chemical compounds that may be toxic are discovered each year. In 1976, Congress enacted the **Toxic Substances Control Act**[6] and gave the EPA authority to administer the act.

The act requires manufacturers and processors to test new chemicals to determine the effect on human health and the environment and to report the results to the EPA before they can be marketed. The EPA may limit or prohibit the manufacture and sale of toxic substances, or remove them from commerce, if it finds that they pose an imminent hazard or an unreasonable risk of injury to human health or the environment. The EPA also requires special labeling of toxic substances.

International Law

KYOTO PROTOCOL REDUCES GREENHOUSE GASES

For decades, scientists have been concerned that *greenhouse gases*—particularly from carbon dioxide created by burning coal, oil, and gas—were causing a global warming effect and

creating a hole in the ozone layer around the earth. In 1997, after much debate, the countries of the world met in Kyoto, Japan, and proposed the **Kyoto Protocol**, an international treaty to reduce greenhouse gases. The deal almost fell apart; but in 2001, 178 countries agreed to abide by the rules of the Kyoto Protocol.

The Kyoto Protocol calls for the reduction of greenhouse gases worldwide to 5.2 percent below 1990 levels, with this goal to be reached by 2012. The Protocol originally set targets for 39 industrialized countries, however, developing nations are not covered by the initial emission control standards. The Protocol calls for member nations to create a $400 million fund to help developing nations adopt technology to reduce greenhouse gases. The United States was not a signatory to the Kyoto Protocol, but instead chose to adopt its own laws to control greenhouse gas emissions.

ℋazardous Waste

Wastes, which often contain hazardous substances that can harm the environment or pose a danger to human health, are generated by agriculture, mining, industry, other businesses, and households. Wastes consist of garbage, sewage, industrial discharges, old equipment, and such. The mishandling and disposal of **hazardous wastes** can cause air, water, and **land pollution**.

Prior to the mid-1970s, the disposal of solid wastes was generally regarded as a problem for local governments. However, discovery of thousands of dump sites and landfills containing hazardous wastes caused concern at the federal level. To prevent future problems, and to assist in cleaning up past problems, Congress enacted the statutes discussed in the following paragraphs to deal with hazardous wastes.

Resource Conservation and Recovery Act

In 1976, Congress enacted the **Resource Conservation and Recovery Act (RCRA)**,[7] which regulates the disposal of new hazardous wastes. This act, which has been amended several times, authorizes the EPA to regulate facilities that generate, treat, store, transport, and dispose of hazardous wastes. States have primary responsibility for implementing the standards established by the act and EPA regulations. If states fail to act, the EPA can enforce the act.

The act defines hazardous waste as a solid waste that may cause or significantly contribute to an increase in mortality or serious illness or pose a hazard to human health or the environment if improperly managed. The EPA has designated substances that are toxic, radioactive, or corrosive or that ignite as hazardous and can add to the list of hazardous wastes as needed.

Pursuant to its authority under the act, the EPA has implemented a "cradle to grave" tracking system and regulation of hazardous substances. Under the act, anyone who generates, treats, stores, or transports hazardous wastes must obtain a government permit to do so. It also establishes standards and procedures for the safe treatment, storage, disposal, and transportation of hazardous wastes. Under the act, the EPA is authorized to regulate underground storage facilities, such as underground gasoline tanks.

hazardous waste

Solid waste that may cause or significantly contribute to an increase in mortality or serious illness or pose a hazard to human health or the environment if improperly managed.

land pollution

Pollution of the land that is generally caused by hazardous waste being disposed of in an improper manner.

Resource Conservation and Recovery Act (RCRA)

A federal statute that authorizes the EPA to regulate facilities that generate, treat, store, transport, and dispose of hazardous wastes.

ℬusiness Ethics

ILLEGAL DUMPING OF POLLUTANTS IS A CRIME

Environmental laws establish methods and procedures for treating and disposing of contaminated wastes. Persons and businesses sometimes intentionally violate environmental laws by secretly dumping polluted materials into the environment. Consider the following case:

Mark Irby was plant manager of a waste-water treatment plant. The record shows that Irby ordered employees of the plant to bypass the treatment system after hours and to discharge approximately 500,000 gallons of raw untreated sewage and partially treated sludge sewage at least twice a week for two years into the Reedy River. The court found that these discharges caused environmental damage. Irby was charged with criminal violation of the Clean Water Act. The jury convicted him of six criminal violations of the act, and the district court sentenced him to the maximum allowable jail sentence (33 months). Irby challenged his sentence.

The court of appeals held that Irby exercised decision making authority in directing the employees of the wastewater treatment plant to discharge the untreated sewage into the Reedy River. The court also held that the offense resulted in an ongoing, continuous, and repetitive discharge of pollutants into the environment, thus justifying the imposition of the 33 months of jail time. The court stated, "There was absolutely no acceptance of responsibility in this case. No remorse whatsoever was shown by Irby." [*United States v. Irby*, 944 F.2d 902 (4th Cir. 1991)]

1. Did Irby act ethically in this case?
2. What is the incentive for businesses and organizations to avoid environmental laws?

Landmark Law

COMPREHENSIVE ENVIRONMENTAL RESPONSE, COMPENSATION, AND LIABILITY ACT (SUPERFUND)

In 1980, Congress enacted the **Comprehensive Environmental Response, Compensation, and Liability Act (CERCLA)**, which is commonly called "Superfund" [42 U.S.C. § 9601 et seq.]. The act, which was significantly amended in 1986, is administered by the EPA. The act gave the federal government a mandate to deal with hazardous wastes that have been spilled, stored, or abandoned.

DESIGNATED HAZARDOUS WASTE SITES
The Superfund requires the EPA to (1) identify sites in the United States where hazardous wastes had been disposed, stored, abandoned, or spilled and (2) rank these sites regarding the severity of the risk. More than 25,000 sites have been identified. The EPA considers such factors as the types of hazardous waste, the toxicity of the wastes, the types of pollution (air, water, land, or other pollution) caused by the wastes, the number of people potentially affected by the risk, and other factors when it ranks the sites. The hazardous waste sites with the highest ranking are put on a National Priority List. The sites on this list receive first consideration for cleanup. Before the cleanup can begin, though, engineering and scientific studies are conducted to determine the best method for cleaning up the waste site. The EPA has the authority to clean up hazardous priority or non-priority sites quickly to prevent fire, explosion, contamination of drinking water, or other imminent danger.

The Superfund provides for the creation of a fund to finance the cleanup of hazardous waste sites (hence the name *Superfund*). The fund is financed through taxes on chemicals, feedstocks, motor fuels, and other products that contain hazardous substances.

LIABILITY FOR CLEANUP OF SUPERFUND SITES
The EPA can order a responsible party to clean up a hazardous waste site. If that party fails to do so, the EPA can clean up the site and recover the cost of the cleanup. The Superfund imposes strict liability, that is, liability without fault. The EPA can recover the cost of the cleanup from (1) the generator who deposited the wastes, (2) the transporter of the wastes to the site, (3) the owner of the site at the time of the disposal, and (4) the current owner and operator of the site. Liability is *joint and several*; that is, a person who is responsible for only a fraction of the hazardous waste may be liable for all the cleanup costs. The Superfund permits states and private parties who clean up hazardous waste sites to seek reimbursement from the fund.

The Superfund contains a **right to know provision** that requires businesses to (1) disclose the presence of certain listed chemicals to the community, (2) annually disclose emissions of chemical substances released into the environment, and (3) immediately notify the government of spills, accidents, and other emergencies involving hazardous substances.

Entrepreneur and the Law

SUPERFUND LAW CLEANS CAR WASH OWNER

Jim Wilson nearly forgot that he once owned a car wash in Sherman Oaks, California, 30 years ago until he received a bill in the mail from the Environmental Protection Agency (EPA) for $142,500. The bill was his share of the $600-million cost of cleaning up a toxic waste site in Monterey Park, some 20 miles from the site of his prior car wash. The EPA had designated the Monterey Park location, which had been a waste disposal site, as a "Superfund site" and was now sending bills to about 700 prior users to recover money to clean up the site. By designating a Superfund site, the EPA is responsible by law to clean up the site and seek compensation from "polluters" to pay for the cleanup costs.

What was Jim Wilson's sin? He had sent soapy nontoxic carwash water to the Monterey Park dump site in the 1960s. Wilson correctly argues that what he did was legal under existing laws when he did it. The Superfund law, however, was drafted to apply retroactively; that is, a party can be held liable for violating the law for actions it took before the Superfund law was enacted by Congress. Although the retroactive application of the law has been challenged, the federal courts have held that the Superfund law does not violate the Due Process Clause of the U.S. Constitution.

Superfund is a tort law that imposes *strict liability*, or liability without fault, and *joint and several liability*, which means that each individual defendant is legally liable for the entire cleanup cost no matter how small that defendant's pollution was relative to all the pollution at the site. Thus, under these two legal principles, any defendant could be held liable for the entire cleanup cost of an EPA Superfund site without being found to be at fault. Superfund law also allows liable private parties to sue to recover from other polluters for their share of the cleanup costs. Thus, if a party should decide to ignore the EPA's bill, it can be sued by other polluters.

If a party settles with the EPA by paying the bill sent to it, it generally is not liable beyond this amount. If a party does not pay the bill, it risks lawsuits from the EPA and other polluters and could be assessed liability much greater than the billed amount. Persons who receive EPA Superfund bills claim that this law is unfair because the EPA has a hammer that forces them to pay. In addition, if a party decides to fight the bill, it could pay hundreds of thousands of dollars in legal fees with little probability of winning.

Wilson and others like him claim that they have been steamcleaned by the EPA. The EPA claims that Wilson owes a duty to clean the EPA Superfund site as well as he did cars.

NUCLEAR WASTE

Nuclear-powered fuel plants create radioactive wastes that maintain a high level of *radioactivity*. Radioactivity can cause injury and death to humans and other life and can also cause severe damage to the environment. Accidents, human error, faulty construction, and such, all can be causes of **radiation pollution**.

Regulation of nuclear energy in this country is primarily placed with the following two federal agencies:

1. **Nuclear Regulatory Commission**   The **Nuclear Regulatory Commission (NRC)**, which was created by Congress in 1977, licenses the construction and opening of commercial nuclear power plants. It continually monitors the operation of nuclear power plants and may close a plant if safety violations are found.
2. **EPA**   The EPA is empowered to set standards for radioactivity in the environment and to regulate the disposal of radioactive waste. The EPA also regulates thermal pollution from nuclear power plants and emissions from uranium mines and mills.

Currently, nuclear wastes are stored on an interim basis at the power plants that generated the wastes or other temporary sites. **The Nuclear Waste Policy Act of 1982**[8] mandates that the federal government select and develop a permanent site for the disposal of nuclear wastes.

radiation pollution

Emissions from radioactive wastes that can cause injury and death to humans and other life and can cause severe damage to the environment.

Nuclear Regulatory Commission (NRC)

Federal agency that licenses the construction and opening of commercial nuclear power plants.

Nuclear Waste Policy Act of 1982

A federal statute that says the federal government must select and develop a permanent site for the disposal of nuclear waste.

Business Ethics

DISCLOSING ENVIRONMENTAL LIABILITIES TO SHAREHOLDERS

In the past, most corporations did not disclose environmental liabilities in the financial statements given to shareholders and others. As of 1992, the Securities and Exchange Commission (SEC) adopted rules requiring companies to report their environmental liabilities in their financial statements. The SEC and the EPA share information concerning corporations' compliance with environmental laws. Failure to disclose environmental liabilities under the new rules subjects violators to civil and criminal penalties.

In developing a program to access and report environmental liabilities, companies should take the following steps:

- Designate a senior officer to be responsible for the environmental disclosure process. This environmental officer should report directly to the president and the board of directors.
- Create a committee of the board of directors to oversee the environmental compliance and disclosure process of the company.

- Retain outside environmental consultants, if feasible, to assist in the data gathering, evaluation, and disclosure process. This will lead to a more objective assessment of environmental liabilities.
- Review the company's environmental exposure and make a list of the important environmental problems facing the company.
- Decide which environmental problems are "material" and must be disclosed under SEC rules. Decide whether additional information should be disclosed.

- Document what the company is doing to rectify its environmental problems. Also document why the company thought it was doing the right thing in taking the action it took.
- Prepare the environmental disclosure report as required by the SEC and include the relevant information from this report in the financial statements of the company.
- Monitor new developments and reassess whether additional disclosures have to be periodically made to the SEC, EPA, shareholders, and others.

Landmark Law

THE ENDANGERED SPECIES ACT

Many species of animals are endangered or threatened with extinction. The reduction of certain species of wildlife may be caused by environmental pollution, real estate development, or hunting. The **Endangered Species Act** was enacted in 1973 [16 U.S.C. §§ 1531 et seq.]. The act, as amended, protects *endangered* and *threatened* species of animals. The secretary of the interior is empowered to declare a form of wildlife *endangered* or *threatened*. The act requires the EPA and the Department of Commerce to designate *critical habitats* for each endangered and threatened species. Real estate and other development in these areas is prohibited or severely limited. The secretary of commerce is empowered to enforce the provisions of the act as to marine species.

In addition, the Endangered Species Act, which applies to both government and private persons, prohibits the *taking* of any endangered species. *Taking* is defined as an act intended to "harass, harm, pursue, hunt, shoot, wound, kill, trap, capture, or collect" an endangered animal.

OTHER FEDERAL LAWS THAT PROTECT WILDLIFE
Numerous other federal laws protect wildlife. These include (1) the Migratory Bird Treaty Act, (2) the Bald Eagle Protection Act, (3) the Wild Free-Roaming Horses and Burros Act, (4) the Marine Mammal Protection Act, (5) the Migratory Bird Conservation Act, (6) the Fishery Conservation and Management Act, (7) the Fish and Wildlife Coordination Act, and (8) the National Wildlife Refuge System. Many states have enacted statutes that protect and preserve wildlife.

The Supreme Court Speaks

Snail Darter Protected by Endangered Species Act

Tennessee Valley Authority v. Hill, Secretary of the Interior
437 U.S. 153, 98 S.Ct. 2279 (1978)
Supreme Court of the United States

BACKGROUND AND FACTS
The Tennessee Valley Authority (TVA) is a wholly owned public corporation of the United States that operates a series of dams, reservoirs, and water projects that provide electric power, irrigation, and flood control to areas in several southern states. In 1967, with appropriations from Congress, the TVA began construction of the Tellico Dam on the Little Tennessee River. When completed, the dam would impound water covering 16,500 acres, thereby converting the river's shallow, fast-flowing waters into a deep reservoir over 30 miles in length. Construction of the dam continued until 1977, when it was completed.

In 1973, a University of Tennessee ichthyologist found a previously unknown species of perch called the Percina (Imostoma) Tansai—or "snail darter"—in the Little Tennessee River. After further investigation, it was determined that approximately 10,000 to 15,000 of these 3-inch, tannish-colored fish existed in the river's waters that would be flooded by the operation of the Tellico Dam. The snail darter was not found anywhere else in the world. It feeds exclusively on snails and requires substantial oxygen, both supplied by the fast-moving waters of the Little Tennessee River. The impounding of the water behind the Tellico Dam would destroy the snail darter's food and oxygen supplies, thus causing its extinction. Evidence was introduced showing that the TVA could not, at that time, successfully transplant the snail darter to any other habitat.

Also in 1973, Congress enacted the Endangered Species Act (Act). The Act authorizes the secretary of the interior (Secretary) to declare species of animal life *endangered* and to identify the *critical habitat* of these creatures. When a species or its habitat is so listed, Section 7 of the Act mandates that the Secretary take such action as is necessary to ensure that actions of the federal government do not jeopardize the continued existence of such endangered species. The Secretary declared the snail darter an endangered species and the area that would be affected by the dam its critical habitat.

Congress continued to appropriate funds for the construction of the dam, which was completed at a cost of over $100 million. In 1976, a regional association of biological scientists, a Tennessee conservation group, and several individuals filed an action seeking to enjoin the TVA from closing the gates of the dam and impounding the water in the reservoir on the grounds that those actions would violate Section 7 of the Act by causing the extinction of the snail darter. The district court held in favor of the TVA. The court of appeals reversed and remanded with instructions to the district court to issue a permanent injunction halting the operation of the Tellico Dam. The TVA appealed to the U.S. Supreme Court.

SUPREME COURT ISSUE

Would the TVA be in violation of the Endangered Species Act if it operated the Tellico Dam?

IN THE LANGUAGE OF THE U.S. SUPREME COURT

Burger, Chief Justice *It may seem curious to some that the survival of a relatively small number of 3-inch fish among all the countless millions of species extant would require the permanent halting of a virtually completed dam for which Congress has expended more than $100 million. We conclude, however, that the explicit provisions of the Endangered Species Act required precisely this result.*

One would be hard pressed to find a statutory provision whose terms were any plainer than those in Section 7 of the Endangered Species Act. Its very words affirmatively command all federal agencies to ensure that actions authorized, funded, or carried out by them do not jeopardize the continued existence of an endangered species or result in the destruction or modification of habitat of such species. This language admits no exception. Nonetheless, petitioner TVA urges that the Act cannot reasonably be interpreted as applying to a federal project that was well under way when Congress passed the Endangered Species Act of 1973. To sustain that position, however, we would be forced to ignore the ordinary meaning of plain language.

Examination of the language, history, and structure of the legislation under review here indicates beyond doubt that Congress intended endangered species to be afforded the highest of priorities. As it was passed, the Endangered Species Act of 1973 represented the most comprehensive legislation for the preservation of endangered species ever enacted by any nation. Virtually all dealings with endangered species, including taking, possession, transportation, and sale, were prohibited. Section 7 of the Act, which of course is relied upon by respondents in this case, provides a particularly good gauge of congressional intent.

DECISION AND REMEDY

The Supreme Court held that the Endangered Species Act prohibited the impoundment of the Little Tennessee River by the Tellico Dam. Affirmed.

NOTE

Eventually, after substantial research and investigation, it was determined that the snail darter could live in another habitat that was found for it. After the snail darter was removed, at government expense, to this new location, the TVA was permitted to close the gates of the Tellico Dam and begin its operation.

CASE QUESTIONS

Critical Legal Thinking Should the law protect endangered species? Why or why not?

Business Ethics Did the TVA act ethically in this case by completing construction of the dam?

Contemporary Business Do you think the cost of constructing the Tellico Dam ($100 million) should have been considered by the Court in reaching its decision?

Monterey, California *Greenpeace is an international organization that engages in activism to protect animals, fish, birds, and the environment. Greenpeace members often use physically combative tactics to block hunters from killing seals.*

NOISE POLLUTION

Unwanted sound affects almost every member of society on a daily basis. The sources of **noise pollution** include airplanes, manufacturing plants, motor vehicles, construction equipment, gardeners, radios, toys, automobile alarms, and such. Noise pollution causes hearing loss, loss of sleep, depression, and other emotional and psychological symptoms and injuries.

Noise Control Act

The **Noise Control Act**,[9] enacted in 1972, authorizes the EPA to establish noise standards for products sold in the United States. The EPA, jointly with the Federal Aviation Administration (FAA), establishes noise limitations on new aircraft. The EPA, jointly with the Department of Transportation, regulates noise emissions from trucks, railroads, and interstate carriers. Other federal agencies also regulate noise pollution. For example, the Occupational Safety and Health Administration (OSHA) regulates noise levels in the workplace.

The **Quiet Communities Act**[10] authorizes the federal government to provide financial and technical assistance to state and local governments in controlling noise pollution. The act, which was enacted in 1978, is administered by the EPA.

STATE ENVIRONMENTAL PROTECTION LAWS

Many state and local governments have enacted statutes and ordinances to protect the environment. For example, most states require that an EIS or report be prepared for any proposed state action. In addition, under their police power to protect the "health, safety, and welfare" of their residents, many states require private industry to prepare EISs for proposed developments.

Some states have enacted special environmental statutes to protect unique areas within their boundaries. For example, Florida has enacted laws to protect the Everglades, and California has enacted laws to protect its Pacific Ocean coastline. State environmental protection law must be consulted by businesses before engaging in major developments.

 *International Law*

TRANSBORDER POLLUTION

Countries can adopt laws to govern, prevent, and clean up pollution occurring within their own borders. However, in some instances, another country is the source of the pollution. This is called **transborder pollution**.

Whether the affected country has any recourse against the polluting country depends on whether the two countries have entered into a treaty concerning such an occurrence, and whether the polluting country wants to abide by the provisions of the treaty. For example, the United States has entered into several treaties with Canada and Mexico that coordinate their efforts to control transborder pollution. The countries have agreed to regulate transborder air pollution (particularly acid rain) and water pollution. These three countries have created the North American Commission on Environmental Cooperation (CEC), a regional international agency located in Montreal, Canada, to review and coordinate environmental issues affecting the North American continent.

One of the most important international environmental issues focuses on the rain forests in Brazil and other South American countries. The rain forests are being clear-cut at an alarming rate. Environmental activists are trying to save the rain forests, but to no avail. It is difficult for countries like the United States and those of Western Europe, who have cut down over 90 percent of their own forests, to try to convince Brazil and its neighbors not to cut down the rain forests.

In June 1992, an **Earth Summit** was held in Rio de Janeiro, Brazil. Most countries sent representatives to this conference. The countries at the summit signed the Rio Declaration, which directs signatory nations to enact effective environmental legislation. In addition, two treaties emerged from the summit, the Climate Change Control Convention (CCCC) and the Convention on Biological Diversity (CBD).

The focus of the CCCC is the stabilization of the greenhouse gas concentration in the atmosphere that is causing a hole in the ozone layer. The CBD is directed at ensuring that patents and inventions do not harm the environment.

It is obvious that environmental problems are not confined to individual countries. International cooperation is necessary to protect the environment and prevent global pollution.

CHAPTER SUMMARY

Environmental Protection, p. 855

Environmental Protection	*Environmental protection laws.* Federal and state governments have enacted environmental protection statutes to control pollution and to penalize those who violate these statutes.
The Environmental Protection Agency (EPA)	Federal administrative agency created in 1970 that is empowered to implement and enforce federal environmental protection statutes. The EPA can adopt regulations to interpret and enforce the laws it is authorized to administer.

National Environmental Policy Act, p. 856

National Environmental Policy Act (NEPA)	Federal statute that mandates that the federal government consider the *adverse impact* a federal government action would have on the environment before the action is implemented.
Environmental Impact Statement (EIS)	A document that must be prepared for all proposed legislation or major federal action that significantly affects the quality of the human environment. The EIS must (1) describe the affected environment, (2) describe the impact of the proposed federal action on the environment, (3) identify and discuss alternatives to the proposed action, (4) list the resources that will be committed to the action, and (5) contain a cost-benefit analysis of the proposed action and alternative actions.

Air Pollution, p. 856

Air Pollution	Pollution caused by factories, homes, vehicles, and the like that affects the air.
Clean Air Act	Federal statute enacted in 1963 and amended several times that regulates air pollution.
National Ambient Air Quality Standards (NAAQS)	Standards for certain pollutants set by the EPA that protect (1) human beings (*primary*) and (2) vegetation, matter, climate, visibility, and economic values (*secondary*). 1. *State implementation plan (SIP).* A document issued by each state that explains how the state plans to meet federal air pollution standards. 2. *Air quality control regions (AQCRs).* Divisions by the EPA of each state into geographical areas that are monitored to ensure compliance with federal air pollution standards. 3. *Nonattainment areas.* Regions that do not meet federal air quality standards. They are classified into one of five categories—(1) marginal, (2) moderate, (3) serious, (4) severe, and (5) extreme—based upon the degree to which they exceed federal air quality standards. States that fail to develop or implement an approved plan to correct deficiencies are subject to sanctions.
Stationary Sources of Air Pollution	Sources of air pollution such as industrial plants, oil refineries, and public utilities. 1. *Pollution controller.* Stationary sources are required to install pollution control equipment.
Mobile Sources of Air Pollution	Sources of air pollution such as automobiles, trucks, buses, motorcycles, and airplanes. 1. *Pollution controls.* The Clean Air Act requires air pollution controls to be installed on automobiles and other sources of mobile air pollution.
Toxic Air Pollutants	Pollutants that cause serious illness or death. 1. *Pollution controls.* The Clean Air Act requires stationary sources to install equipment and technology to control emissions of toxic substances.

Water Pollution, p. 860

Water Pollution	Pollution of lakes, rivers, oceans, and other bodies of water. 1. *River and Harbor Act of 1886.* Established a permit system for the discharge of refuse, wastes, and sewage into U.S. navigable waters.
Clean Water Act	*Federal Water Pollution Control Act (FWPCA) of 1948.* Federal statute that regulates water pollution. As amended, called the *Clean Water Act.*
Point Sources of Water Pollution	Sources of water pollution such as paper mills, manufacturing plants, electric utility plants, and sewage plants. 1. *Pollution controls.* Point sources are required to install pollution control equipment.
Thermal Pollution	Heated water or material discharged into waterways that upsets the ecological balance and decreases the oxygen content. Thermal pollution is subject to the provisions of the Clean Water Act.
Wetlands	Areas that are inundated or saturated by surface or groundwater that support vegetation typically adapted for life in such conditions. The Clean Water Act forbids the filling or dredging of wetlands unless a permit has been obtained from the *Army Corps of Engineers.*
Safe Drinking Water	The *Safe Drinking Water Act of 1974* authorizes the EPA to establish national minimum quality of water standards for human consumption. States are primarily responsible for enforcing the act. If a state fails to do so, the federal government can enforce the act.
Ocean Dumping	*Marine Protection, Research, and Sanctuaries Act of 1972.* Federal statute that extends environmental protection to oceans. It requires a permit for dumping wastes and other foreign materials into ocean waters.
Oil Spills	The Clean Water Act authorizes the U.S. government to clean up oil spills and spills of other hazardous substances in ocean waters within 12 miles of the shore and on the Continental Shelf. The act authorizes the federal government to recover the cleanup costs from responsible parties.

Toxic Substances, p. 863

Toxic Substances	Chemicals used for agricultural, industrial, and mining uses that cause injury to humans, birds, animals, fish, and vegetation.
Federal Insecticide, Fungicide, and Rodenticide Act	Federal statute that requires pesticides, herbicides, fungicides, and rodenticides to be registered with the EPA. The EPA may deny, suspend, or cancel registration.
Toxic Substances Control Act	Federal statute that requires manufacturers and processors to test new chemicals to determine their effect on human health and the environment before the EPA will allow them to be marketed. The EPA requires special labeling of toxic substances.

Hazardous Waste, p. 865

Hazardous Waste	Solid waste that may cause or significantly contribute to an increase in mortality or serious illness, or pose a hazard to human health or the environment if improperly managed. 1. *Land pollution.* Pollution of the land that is generally caused by hazardous waste being disposed of in an improper manner.
Resource Conservation and Recovery Act	Federal statute that authorizes the EPA to regulate facilities that generate, treat, store, transport, and dispose of hazardous wastes.

Comprehensive Environmental Response, Compensation, and Liability Act (Superfund), p. 866

Superfund Act	Federal statute that gives the federal government a mandate to deal with hazardous wastes that have been spilled, stored, or abandoned. This act is commonly called *Superfund.* 1. *Hazardous waste sites.* CERCLA requires the EPA to identify sites in the United States where hazardous wastes have been disposed, stored, spilled, or abandoned, and to rank these sites regarding the severity of the risk. The EPA has identified more than 25,000 hazardous waste sites.

2. *Superfund.* CERCLA created a fund to finance the cleanup of hazardous waste sites (hence, the name Superfund). The fund is financed through taxes on chemicals, feedstocks, motor fuels, and other products that contain hazardous substances.
3. *Liability for cleanup costs.* The EPA can order a responsible party to clean up a hazardous waste site. If that party fails to do so, the EPA can clean up the site and recover the cost of the cleanup from the responsible parties. Superfund imposes strict liability (liability without fault). Liability is joint and several (i.e., a party who is only partially responsible may be liable for all the cleanup costs).
4. *Right to know provision.* A provision in Superfund that requires businesses to (1) disclose the presence of certain listed chemicals to the community, (2) annually disclose emissions of chemical substances released into the environment, and (3) immediately notify the government of spills, accidents, and other emergencies involving hazardous substances.

Nuclear Waste, p. 867

Nuclear Waste	Radioactive wastes generated by nuclear-powered fuel plants. 1. *Radioactive pollution.* Emissions from radioactive wastes that can cause injury and death to humans and other life and can cause severe damage to the environment. 2. *Nuclear Regulatory Commission (NRC).* Federal agency that licenses the construction and opening of commercial nuclear power plants. The NRC may deny or revoke a license. 3. *Nuclear Waste Policy Act of 1982.* Federal statute that says the federal government must select and develop a permanent site for the disposal of nuclear wastes.

Preservation of Wildlife, p. 868

Endangered Species Act	Federal statute that protects *endangered* and *threatened* species of animals. 1. *Critical habitat.* The act requires the EPA to designate *critical habits* for each endangered and threatened species. 2. *Taking.* The act prohibits the *taking* (e.g., hunting, trapping, harming) of any endangered species.
Other Federal Laws That Protect Wildlife	Other federal laws that protect wildlife include: 1. Migratory Bird Treaty Act 2. Bald Eagle Protection Act 3. Wild Free-Roaming Horses and Burros Act 4. Marine Mammal Protection Act 5. Migratory Bird Conservation Act 6. Fishery Conservation and Management Act 7. Fish and Wildlife Coordination Act 8. National Wildlife Refuge System

Noise Pollution, p. 870

Noise Pollution	Unwanted sound from planes, manufacturing plants, motor vehicles, construction equipment, stereos, and the like.
Noise Control Act	Federal statute that authorizes the EPA to establish noise standards for products sold in the United States. 1. *Quiet Communities Act.* Federal statute that authorizes the federal government to provide financial and technical assistance to state and local governments in controlling noise pollution.

State Environmental Protection Laws, p. 870

State Environmental Protection Laws	Many state and local governments have enacted statutes and ordinances to protect the environment. States and local governments are entitled to set pollution control standards that are stricter than federal requirements.

ℰND-OF-ℭHAPTER ℐNTERNET ℰXERCISES AND ℭASE ℚUESTIONS

Working the Web Internet Exercises

ACTIVITIES

1. Find the EPA Superfund toxic waste cleanup sites in your state. See the U.S. Environmental Protection Agency at **www/epa/gov/**

2. Compare the position of Greenpeace, the Sierra Club, and others on drilling in the Artic Wildlife Refuge.

   Greenpeace
   www.greenpeace.org

   National Audubon Society
   www.audubon.org

   Natural Resources Defense Council
   www.nrdc.org

   Sierra Club
   www.sierraclub.org

   Earth Watch Institute
   www.earthwatch.org/index.html

   World Environmental Law
   www.hg.org/environ.html

3. Compare your state's environmental laws to the federal controls in the area of water and air pollution. For an overview of land use law with links to key primary and secondary sources, see "Law About . . . Land Use" at **www.law.cornell.edu/topics/land_use.html.**

4. Is your state home to any of the animals protected by the Endangered Species Act? Which ones? See the Earth Justice Legal Defense Fund's Web site at **www.earthjustice.org** and the Environmental Defense Fund's Web site at **www.edf.org**.

CRITICAL LEGAL THINKING CASES

34.1 Environmental Impact Statement   The U.S. Forest Service is responsible for managing the country's national forests for recreational and other purposes. This includes issuing special use permits to private companies to operate ski areas on federal lands. Sandy Butte is a 6,000-foot mountain located in the Okanogan National Forest in Okanogan County, Washington. Sandy Butte, like the Methow Valley it overlooks, is a pristine, unspoiled, sparsely populated area located within the North Cascades National Park. Large populations of mule deer and other animals exist in the park.

In 1978, Methow Recreation, Inc., (MRI) applied to the Forest Service for a special use permit to develop and operate its proposed Early Winters Ski Resort on Sandy Butte and a 1,165-acre parcel of private land it had acquired adjacent to the national forest. The proposed development would make use of approximately 3,900 acres of Sandy Butte to provide up to 16 ski lifts capable of accommodating 10,500 skiers at one time. Is an environmental impact statement required? [*Robertson v. Methow Valley Citizens Council*, 490 U.S. 332, 109 S.Ct. 1835, 104 L.Ed.2d 351 (1989)]

34.2 Clean Air Act   Pursuant to the Clean Air Act, the state of New Mexico divided its territory into eight air quality control regions, one of which consisted of the city of Albuquerque and parts of three counties (AQCR 2). AQCR 2 was a nonattainment area for purposes of carbon monoxide (CO). The act requires states to prepare and submit a state implementation plan showing how they will attain compliance and have the plan approved by the EPA. As part of the plan, the state must implement a vehicle emission control inspection and maintenance program (I/M program). New Mexico filed an SIP but failed to implement an enforceable I/M program. The EPA engaged in formal, public rule making, disapproved New Mexico's SIP, and imposed sanctions by cutting off certain federal funds that New Mexico would have otherwise received. New Mexico challenges the EPA's action. Who wins? [*New Mexico Environmental Improvement Division v. Thomas, Administrator, U.S. Environmental Protection Agency*, 789 F.2d 825 (10th Cir. 1986)]

34.3 Clean Air Act   Pilot Petroleum Associates, Inc., and various affiliated companies distribute gasoline to retail gasoline stations in the state of New York. Pilot owns some of these stations and leases them out to individual operators who are under contract to purchase gasoline from Pilot. At various times during 1984, the EPA took samples of gasoline from five different service stations to which Pilot had sold unleaded gasoline. These samples showed that Pilot had delivered "unleaded gasoline that contained amounts of lead in excess of that permitted by the Clean Air Act and EPA regulations." The United States brought criminal charges against Pilot for violating the act and EPA regulations and sought fines from Pilot. Who wins? [*United States v. Pilot Petroleum Associates, Inc.*, 712 F.Supp. 1077 (E.D.N.Y. 1989)]

34.4 Clean Water Act   Placer mining is a method used to mine for gold in streambeds of Alaska. The miner removes soil, mud, and clay from the streambed, places it in an on-site sluice box, and separates the gold from the other matter by forcing water through the paydirt. The water in the sluice box is discharged into the stream, causing aesthetic and water quality impacts on the water both in the immediate vicinity and downstream. Toxic metals, including arsenic, cadmium, lead, zinc, and copper, are found in higher concentrations in streams where mining occurs than in nonmining streams.

In 1988, after public notice and comment, the EPA issued rules that require placer miners to use the best practical control technology (BPCT) to control discharges of nontoxic pollutants and the best available control technology (BACT) to control discharges of toxic pollutants. The BACT standard requires miners to construct settling ponds and recycle water through these ponds before discharging the water into the streambed. This method requires substantial expenditure. The Alaska Miners Association challenged the EPA's rule making. Who wins? [*Rybachek v. U.S. Environmental Protection Agency*, 904 F.2d 1276 (9th Cir. 1990)]

34.5 Wetlands Leslie Salt Company owns a 153-acre tract of undeveloped land south of San Francisco. The property abuts the San Francisco National Wildlife Refuge and lies approximately one-quarter mile from Newark Slough, a tidal arm of the San Francisco Bay. Originally the property was pasture land. The first change occurred in the early 1900s when Leslie's predecessors constructed facilities to manufacture salt on the property. They excavated pits and created large, shallow, watertight basins on the property. Salt production on the property was stopped in 1959. The construction of a sewer line and public roads on and around the property created ditches and culverts on the property. Newark Slough is connected to the property by these culverts, and tidewaters reach the property. Water accumulates in the ponds, ditches, and culverts, providing wetland vegetation to wildlife and migratory birds. Fish live in the ponds on the property. In 1985, Leslie started to dig a ditch to drain the property and began construction to block the culvert that connected the property to the Newark Slough. The Army Corps of Engineers issued a cease-and-desist order against Leslie. Leslie challenged the order. Who wins? [*Leslie Salt Co. v. United States*, 896 F.2d 354 (9th Cir.)]

34.6 Water Pollution The Reserve Mining Company owns and operates a mine in Minnesota that is located on the shores of Lake Superior and produces hazardous waste. In 1947, Reserve obtained a permit from the state of Minnesota to dump its wastes into Lake Superior. The permits prohibited discharges that would "result in any clouding or discoloration of the water outside the specific discharge zone" or "result in any material adverse affects on public water supplies." Reserve discharged its wastes into Lake Superior for years, until they reached 67,000 tons per day in the early 1970s. Evidence showed that the discharges caused discoloration of surface waters outside the zone of discharge and contained carcinogens that adversely affected public water supplies. The United States sued Reserve for engaging in unlawful water pollution. Who wins? [*United States v. Reserve Mining Co.*, 8 Envir. Rep. Cases 1978 (D.Minn. 1976)]

34.7 Pesticides DDT is a pesticide that is sprayed by farmers on cotton, soybean, peanut, and other crops to control insects and pests. Evidence showed that DDT is an uncontrollable, durable chemical that persists in the aquatic and terrestrial environments. Given its insolubility in water and its propensity to be stored in tissue, it collects in the food chain and is passed up to higher forms of aquatic and terrestrial life. Evidence also shows that DDT can persist in soil for many years and that it will move along with eroding soil. DDT has been found in remote areas and in ocean species, such as whales, far from any known area of application. DDT kills and injures birds, fish, and animals and affects their reproductive capabilities. DDT also poses a threat to human life because it is carcinogenic. The EPA brought a proceeding to cancel all registrations of DDT products and uses. Thirty-one registrants challenged the proposed cancellation. Who wins? [*Consolidated DDT Hearings*, 37 Fed.Reg. 13.369 (EPA 1972)]

34.8 Toxic Substances During the U.S. involvement in the Vietnam conflict, the U.S. military used an herbicide called Agent Orange. It was sprayed from airplanes to defoliate the jungles of Vietnam. People on the ground, including U.S. soldiers, were exposed to the spray. Agent Orange contains dioxin, a poison that causes cancer and other health problems. After returning home from Vietnam, often years later, veterans who had been exposed to Agent Orange began contracting cancer, suffering skin problems, and having children with birth defects. The veterans brought a class action lawsuit against Monsanto Company, Dow Chemical Company, and several other chemical companies that manufactured the Agent Orange used in Vietnam. This action, which would have been the largest, and probably the longest, private toxic injury action in history, was set to go to trial in May 1984 when the defendants offered to establish a $180-million trust fund for the plaintiffs. The settlement would provide each veteran who was exposed to Agent Orange with approximately $2,000 in damages. Should the veterans accept the settlement? [*Agent Orange Settlement* (E.D.N.Y. 1984)]

34.9 Hazardous Waste Douglas Hoflin was the director of the Public Works Department for Ocean Shores, Washington. From 1975 to 1982, the department purchased 3,500 gallons of paint for road maintenance. As painting jobs were finished, the 55-gallon drums that had contained the paint were returned to the department's yard. Paint contains hazardous substances such as lead. When 14 of the drums were discovered to still contain unused paint, Hoflin instructed employees to haul the paint drums to the city's sewage treatment plant and bury them. The employees took the drums, dug a hole on the grounds of the treatment plant, and dumped the drums in. Some of the drums were rusted and leaking. The hole was not deep enough, so the employees crushed the drums with a front-end loader to make them fit. The refuse was then covered with sand. Almost two years later, one of the city's employees reported the incident to state authorities, who referred the matter to the EPA. Investigation showed that the paint had contaminated the soil. The United States brought criminal charges against Hoflin for aiding and abetting the illegal dumping of hazardous waste. Who wins? [*United States v. Hoflin*, 880 F.2d 1033 (9th Cir. 1989)]

34.10 Nuclear Power Metropolitan Edison Company owns and operates two nuclear-fueled power plants at Three Mile Island near Harrisburg, Pennsylvania. Both power plants were licensed by the NRC after extensive proceedings and investigations, including the preparation of the required environmental impact statements. On March 28, 1979, when one of the power plants was shut down for refueling, the other plant suffered a serious accident that damaged the reactor. The governor of Pennsylvania recommended an evacuation of all pregnant women and small children, and many area residents did leave their homes for several days. As it turned out, no dangerous radiation was released.

People Against Nuclear Energy (PANE), an association of area residents who opposed further operation of either nuclear power plant at Three Mile Island, sued to enjoin the plants from reopening. They argued that the reopening of the plants would cause severe psychological health damage to persons living in the vicinity and serious damage to the stability and cohesiveness of the community. Are these reasons sufficient to prevent the reopening of the nuclear power plants? [*Metropolitan Edison Co. v. People Against Nuclear Energy*, 460 U.S. 766, 103 S.Ct. 1556, 75 L.Ed.2d 534 (1983)]

34.11 Endangered Species The red-cockaded woodpecker is a small bird that lives almost exclusively in the old pine forests throughout the southern United States. Its survival depends on a very specialized habitat of pine trees that are at least 30, if not 60, years old in which they build their nests and forage for insects. The population of this bird decreased substantially between 1978 and 1987 as pine forests were destroyed by clear-cutting. The Secretary of the Interior has named the red-cockaded woodpecker as an endangered species.

The Forest Service, which is under the authority of the Secretary of Agriculture, manages federal forests and is charged with duties to provide recreation, protect wildlife, and provide timber. To accomplish the charge of providing timber, the Forest Service leases national forest lands to private companies for lumbering. When the Forest Service proposed to lease several national forests in Texas, where the red-cockaded woodpecker lives, to private companies for lumbering, the Sierra Club sued. The Sierra Club seeks to enjoin the Forest Service from leasing these national forests for lumbering. Who wins? [*Sierra Club v. Lyng, Secretary of Agriculture*, 694 F.Supp. 1260 (E.D.Tex 1990)]

BUSINESS ETHICS CASES

34.12 Business Ethics The state of Michigan owns approximately 57,000 acres of land that comprise the Pigeon River County State Forest in southwestern Michigan. On June 12, 1977, Shell Oil Company applied to the Michigan Department of Natural Resources (DNR) for a permit to drill 10 exploratory oil wells in the forest. Roads had to be constructed to reach the proposed drill sites. Evidence showed that the only sizable elk herd east of the Mississippi River annually use the forest as their habitat and returned to this range every year to breed. Experts testified that elk avoid roads, even when there is no traffic, and that the construction of the roads and wells would destroy the elk's habitat. Michigan law prohibits activities that adversely impact natural resources. The West Michigan Environmental Action Council sued the DNR, seeking to enjoin the DNR from granting the drilling permits to Shell. Who wins?

[*West Michigan Environmental Action Council, Inc. v. Natural Resources Commission*, 275 N.W.2d 538 (MI 1979)]

34.13 Business Ethics Riverside Bayview Homes, Inc., owns 80 acres of low-lying marshland (wetlands) near the shores of Lake St. Clair in Macomb County, Michigan. In 1976, Riverside began to place fill materials on its property as part of its preparations for construction of a housing development. Riverside did not obtain a permit from the Army Corps of Engineers. Upon discovery of Riverside's activities, the Corps sued, seeking to enjoin Riverside from discharging a pollutant (fill) onto wetlands. Is the subject property subject to the Corps of Engineers permit system? Did Riverside Bayview Homes act ethically in this case? [*United States v. Riverside Bayview Homes, Inc.*, 474 U.S. 121, 106 S.Ct. 455, 88 L.Ed.2d 419 (1985)]

BRIEFING THE CASE WRITING ASSIGNMENT

Read the following case, which has been excerpted from the court's opinion. Review and brief the case.

FMC Corp. v. United States Department of Commerce
786 F.Supp. 471 (E.D. PA. 1992)
United States District Court

Newcomer, District Judge

This action is brought pursuant to the Comprehensive Environmental Response, Compensation and Liability Act of 1980, as amended (CERCLA), and the Declaratory Judgment Act. Plaintiff FMC Corporation (FMC) owned

and operated, from 1963 to 1976, the Avtex site in Front Royal, Virginia, ("the Facility"), a site which has been listed on the National Priorities List since 1986. FMC seeks indemnification from the defendants for some portion of its present and future response costs of response in performing removal actions and other response actions at the Facility. FMC bases its claim on the United States Government (Government) activities during the period of January 1942 through 1945 relating to the operation of a rayon manufacturing facility at the Avtex site, and contends that these activities render the Government liable as an "owner," "operator," and/or "arranger" under section 107 of CERCLA.

During World War II, after the bombing of Pearl Harbor and the Japanese conquest of Asia, the United States suffered a loss of 90 percent of its crude rubber supply. An urgent need arose for natural rubber substitute to be used in manufacturing airplane tires, jeep tires, and other war related items. The best rubber substitute available was high tenacity rayon tire cord. The Facility was one of the major producers of high tenacity rayon yarn, which was twisted and woven into high tenacity rayon tire cord. FMC presented evidence at trial showing that during the World War II period, the Government participated in managing and controlling the Facility, which was then owned by American Viscose Corporation (American Viscose), requiring the Facility to manufacture increasing quantities of high tenacity rayon yarn, which involved the treatment of hazardous materials, and necessitated the disposal of hazardous materials. FMC also presented evidence showing that the Government owned "facilities" and equipment at the plant used in the treatment and disposal of hazardous materials.

The evidence included the following:

(1) During World War II, the Government took over numerous plants which, for a multitude of reasons, failed to meet production requirements, including a plant producing high tenacity rayon yarn. Beginning no later than 1943, the rayon tire cord program received constant attention from the highest officials of the War Production Board (WPB), as well as top officials of the War Department and other Government departments and agencies.

(2) Once the WPB determined that there was a need for substantial expansion of the production capabilities at the Facility, Government personnel were assigned to facilitate and expedite construction. The rayon tire cord program, in general, and the implementation of the program at the Facility, in particular, required and received far more involvement, participation, and control by the Government than the vast majority of the production programs implemented during World War II.

(3) The disposal or treatment of hazardous substance is inherent in the production of high tenacity rayon yarn. The Government was familiar with the Facility's process for producing high tenacity rayon yarn. The Government knew or should have known that the disposal or treatment of hazardous substances was inherent in the manufacture of high tenacity rayon yarn and that its production requirements caused a significant increase in the amount of hazardous substances generated and disposed of at the Facility.

The District Court concluded that the United States, through the actions and authority of the WPB and other departments, agencies, and instrumentalities of the United States Government, "operated" the Facility, from approximately January 1942 to at least November 1945, as defined by section 101(20) of CERCLA. During the period the Government operated the Facility, wastes containing "hazardous substances," as defined by section 101 (14) of CERCLA, and as identified in 40 C.F.R. Part 302, Table 302.4 (1990), were "disposed of" at the Facility.

There has been a "release or threatened release" of hazardous substances from facilities which were owned by the United States. Such release or threatened release of hazardous substances has caused and will continue to cause FMC to incur "necessary costs of response" within the meaning of Section 107 of CERCLA, including without limitation the costs which FMC has incurred and will incur in monitoring, assessing, and evaluating the release or threatened release of hazardous substances and performing removal and/or remedial activities and taking other actions required or requested by the EPA, as well as attorneys' fees and expenses associated with this lawsuit.

Liability of an owner or operator of a facility as defined by § 107(a) for the cost of removal "is strict and joint and several." The United States Government as owner is responsible for costs resulting from responses to the release of hazardous substances.

And it is so ordered.

ENDNOTES

1. 42 U.S.C. § 7412(b).
2. 33 U.S.C. § 1254(t).
3. 21 U.S.C. § 349; 42 U.S.C. §§ 201 and 300F et seq.
4. 16 U.S.C. §§ 1431 et seq.; 33 U.S.C. §§ 1407 et seq.
5. 7 U.S.C. §§ 135 et seq.
6. 15 U.S.C. §§ 2601 et seq.
7. 42 U.S.C. § 6901 et seq.
8. 42 U.S.C. §§ 10101 et seq.
9. 42 U.S.C. § 4901.
10. 42 U.S.C. § 4913.

CHAPTER 35

Antitrust Law

While competition cannot be created by statutory enactment, it can in large measure be revived by changing the laws and forbidding the practices that killed it, and by enacting laws that will give it heart and occasion again. We can arrest and prevent monopoly.

—Woodrow Wilson
Speech, August 7, 1912

Chapter Objectives

After studying this chapter, you should be able to:

1. List and describe the enforcement of federal antitrust laws.

2. Apply the rule of reason and the per se rule to identify unreasonable restraints of trade.

3. Describe the horizontal and vertical restraints of trade that violate Section 1 of the Sherman Act.

4. Identify acts of monopolization that violate Section 2 of the Sherman Act.

5. Describe the *United States v. Microsoft Corp.* monopolization antitrust case.

6. Explain how the lawfulness of mergers is examined under Section 7 of the Clayton Act.

7. Describe how Section 7 of the Clayton Act applies to Internet company mergers.

8. Apply Section 5 of the Federal Trade Commission Act to antitrust cases.

9. Describe how antitrust laws prohibit unfair and deceptive conduct over the Internet.

10. Compare U.S. antitrust laws to international antitrust laws of other countries.

Chapter Contents

The American economic system was built on the theory of freedom of competition. After the Civil War, however, the American economy changed from a rural and agricultural economy to an industrialized and urban one. Many large industrial trusts were formed during this period. These arrangements resulted in a series of monopolies in basic industries such as oil and gas, sugar, cotton, and whiskey.

Because the common law could not deal effectively with these monopolies, Congress enacted a comprehensive system of **antitrust laws** to limit anticompetitive behavior. Almost all industries, businesses, and professions operating in the United States were affected. Although many states have also enacted antitrust laws, most actions in this area are brought under federal law.

This chapter discusses federal and state antitrust laws.

FEDERAL ANTITRUST LAWS

The **Sherman Act**, enacted in 1890, made certain restraints of trade and monopolistic acts illegal. Both the **Clayton Act** and the **Federal Trade Commission Act** (FTC Act) were enacted in 1914. The Clayton Act regulates mergers and prohibits certain exclusive dealing arrangements. The FTC Act prohibits unfair methods of competition. The **Robinson-Patman Act**, which prohibits price discrimination, was enacted in 1930.

Antitrust Enforcement

The federal antitrust statutes are broadly drafted to reflect the government's enforcement policy and to allow it to respond to economic, business, and technological changes. Each administration that occupies the White House adopts an enforcement policy for antitrust laws. From the 1940s through the 1970s, antitrust enforcement was quite stringent. During the 1980s, government enforcement of antitrust laws was more relaxed. During the 1990s, antitrust enforcement increased.

Antitrust Penalties

Federal antitrust laws provide for both government and private lawsuits.

Government Actions   The federal government is authorized to bring actions to enforce federal antitrust laws. Government enforcement of the federal antitrust law is divided between the Antitrust Division of the Justice Department and the Bureau of Competition of the Federal Trade Commission (FTC).

The Sherman Act is the only major antitrust act with *criminal* sanctions. Intent is the prerequisite for criminal liability under this act. Penalties for individuals include fines of up to $350,000 per violation and up to three years in prison; corporations may be fined up to $10 million per violation.[1]

The government may seek *civil* damages, including treble damages, for violations of antitrust laws.[2] Broad remedial powers allow the courts to order a number of civil remedies, including orders for divestiture of assets, cancellation of contracts, liquidation of businesses, licensing of patents, and such. Private parties cannot intervene in public antitrust actions brought by the government.

Private Actions   **Section 4** of the **Clayton Act** permits any person who suffers antitrust injury in his or her "business or property" to bring a *private civil action* against the offenders.[3] Consumers who have to pay higher prices because of an antitrust violation have recourse under this provision.[4] To recover damages, plaintiffs must prove that they suffered *antitrust injuries* caused by the prohibited act. The courts have required that consumers must have dealt *directly* with the alleged violators to have standing to sue; indirect injury resulting from higher prices being "passed on" is insufficient.

Successful plaintiffs may recover **treble damages** (i.e., triple the amount of the damages), plus reasonable costs and attorneys' fees. Damages may be calculated as lost profits, an increase in the cost of doing business, or a decrease in the value of tangible or intangible property caused by the antitrust violation. This rule applies to all violations of the Sherman

antitrust laws

A series of laws enacted to limit anticompetitive behavior in almost all industries, businesses, and professions operating in the United States.

The notion that a business is clothed with a public interest and has been devoted to the public use is little more than a fiction intended to beautify what is disagreeable to the sufferers.

Holmes, J.
Tyson & Bro-United Theatre Ticket Offices v. Banton
(1927)

Business Brief

Each administration that occupies the White House adopts an enforcement policy for antitrust laws.

Business Brief

The Sherman Act is the only major federal antitrust act that provides for *criminal* penalties.

Ethics Brief

Businesses or individuals who are found to violate federal antitrust laws may be assessed *treble* (triple) damages in a private civil lawsuit by any person who suffers injury in his or her business or property because of the violation.

Act, the Clayton Act, and the Robinson-Patman Act. Only actual damages—not treble damages—may be recovered for violations of the FTC Act.

A private plaintiff has four years from the date on which an antitrust injury occurred to bring a private civil treble damage action. Only damages incurred during this four-year period are recoverable. This statute is *tolled* (i.e., does not run) during a suit by the government.

Effect of a Government Judgment

A government judgment against a defendant for an antitrust violation may be used as prima facie evidence of liability in a private civil treble damage action. Antitrust defendants often opt to settle government-brought antitrust actions by entering a plea of *nolo contendere* in a criminal action or a *consent decree* in a government civil action. These pleas usually subject the defendant to penalty without an admission of guilt or liability.

Section 16 of the **Clayton Act** permits the government or a private plaintiff to obtain an injunction against anticompetitive behavior that violates antitrust laws.[5] Only the FTC may obtain an injunction under the FTC Act.

Landmark Law

SHERMAN ANTITRUST ACT SECTION 1

Section 1 of the **Sherman Act** is intended to prohibit certain concerted anticompetitive activities. It provides that

> *Every contract, combination in the form of trust or otherwise, or conspiracy, in restraint of trade or commerce along the several states, or with foreign nations, is hereby declared to be illegal. Every person who shall make any contract or*

engage in any combination or conspiracy hereby declared to be illegal shall be deemed guilty of a felony [15 U.S.C. § 1].

In other words, Section 1 outlaws *contracts*, *combinations*, and *conspiracies* in restraint of trade. Thus, it applies to unlawful conduct by *two or more parties*. The agreement may be written, oral, or inferred from the conduct of the parties.

SECTION 1 OF THE SHERMAN ACT—RESTRAINTS OF TRADE

Section 1 of the Sherman Act

Prohibits *contracts*, *combinations*, and *conspiracies* in restraint of trade.

Landmark Law

In *Standard Oil Company of New Jersey v. United States* (1911), the U.S. Supreme Court adopted the "rule of reason" standard for analyzing Sherman Act Section 1 cases.

rule of reason

A rule that holds that only unreasonable restraints of trade violate Section 1 of the Sherman Act. The court must examine the pro- and anticompetitive effects of the challenged restraint.

per se rule

A rule that is applicable to those restraints of trade considered inherently anticompetitive. Once this determination is made, the court will not permit any defenses or justifications to save it.

The **Sherman Act** has been called the "Magna Carta of free enterprise."[6] **Section 1** outlaws certain *restraints of trade*. The two tests the U.S. Supreme Court has developed for determining the lawfulness of a restraint—the *rule of reason* and the *per se rule*—are discussed in the paragraphs that follow.

Rule of Reason

If Section 1 were read literally, it would prohibit almost all contracts. In the landmark case, *Standard Oil Company of New Jersey v. United States*,[7] the Supreme Court adopted the **rule of reason** standard for analyzing Section 1 cases. This rule holds that only *unreasonable restraints of trade* violate Section 1 of the Sherman Act. Reasonable restraints are lawful. The courts examine the following factors in applying the rule of reason:

- The pro- and anticompetitive effects of the challenged restraint
- The competitive structure of the industry
- The firm's market share and power
- The history and duration of the restraint
- Other relevant factors

Per Se Rule

The Supreme Court adopted a **per se rule** that is applicable to those restraints of trade considered inherently anticompetitive. No balancing of pro- and anticompetitive effects is necessary in such cases: The restraint is automatically in violation of Section 1 of the

Sherman Act. Once a restraint is characterized as a per se violation, no defenses or justifications for the restraint will save it, and no further evidence need be considered. Restraints that are not characterized as per se violations are examined under the rule of reason.

ℋORIZONTAL RESTRAINTS OF TRADE

A **horizontal restraint of trade** occurs when two or more competitors at the *same level of distribution* enter into a contract, combination, or conspiracy to restrain trade (see Exhibit 35.1). Many horizontal restraints fall under the per se rule; others are examined under the rule of reason. The most common forms of horizontal restraint are discussed in the following paragraphs.

> **horizontal restraint of trade**
>
> A restraint of trade that occurs when two or more competitors at the same *level of distribution* enter into a contract, combination, or conspiracy to restrain trade.

ℰXHIBIT 35.1 *Horizontal Restraint of Trade*

Competitor No. 1 — Agreement to restrain trade → Competitor No. 2

Price-Fixing

Horizontal **price fixing** occurs where the competitors in the same line of business agree to set the price of goods or services they sell. Price-fixing is defined as raising, depressing, fixing, pegging, or stabilizing the price of a commodity or service. Illegal price-fixing includes setting minimum or maximum prices or fixing the quantity of a product or service to be produced or provided. Although most price-fixing agreements occur between sellers, an agreement among buyers to set the price they will pay for goods or services is also price-fixing. The plaintiff bears the burden of proving a price-fixing agreement.

Price-fixing is a *per se violation* of Section 1 of the Sherman Act. No defenses or justifications of any kind—such as "the price-fixing helps consumers or protects competitors from ruinous competition"—can prevent the per se rule from applying.

> **price-fixing**
>
> Occurs where competitors in the same line of business agree to set the price of the goods or services they sell: raising, depressing, fixing, pegging, or stabilizing the price of a commodity or service.

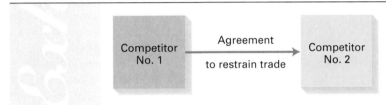

The Supreme Court Speaks

Price Fixing Is a Per Se Violation of Antitrust Law

Federal Trade Commission v. Superior Court Trial Lawyers Association
493 U.S. 411, 110 S.Ct. 768 (1990)
Supreme Court of the United States

BACKGROUND AND FACTS
In the District of Columbia, lawyers in private practice are appointed to represent indigent defendants in less serious felony and misdemeanor cases. These private attorneys are paid pursuant to District's Criminal Justice Act (CJA), which in 1982 provided for fees of $30 per hour for court time and $20 per hour for out-of-court time. Most appointments went to approximately 100 lawyers called "CJA regulars," who handled more than 25,000 cases in 1982. These lawyers derived almost all of their income from representing indigents.

The CJA regulars belonged to the Superior Court Trial Lawyers Association (SCTLA), which was a professional organization and not a labor union. Beginning in 1982,

SCTLA unsuccessfully tried to persuade District to increase CJA rates. In August 1983, about 100 CJA lawyers resolved not to accept any new cases after September 6, 1983, if legislation providing for an increase in fees was not passed by that date. When the legislation was not enacted, on September 6, most CJA regulars refused to accept new assignments. As anticipated, their action had a severe impact on District's criminal justice system. Within 10 days, District's criminal justice system was on the brink of collapse.

The Federal Trade Commission (FTC) filed a complaint against SCTLA, alleging that SCTLA's actions restrained trade in violation of federal antitrust law. FTC held against SCTLA. The court of appeals vacated the FTC order. The U.S. Supreme Court agreed to hear FTC's appeal.

SUPREME COURT ISSUE

Did the actions of SCTLA constitute price-fixing and a per se violation of Section 1 of the Sherman Act?

IN THE LANGUAGE OF THE U.S. SUPREME COURT

Stevens, Justice *Prior to the boycott CJA lawyers were in competition with one another, each deciding independently whether and how often to offer to provide services to the District at CJA rates. The agreement among the CJA lawyers was designed to obtain higher prices for their services and was implemented by a concerted refusal to serve the only customer in the market for the particular services that CJA regulars offered. This constriction of supply is the essence of price-fixing.*

The horizontal arrangement among these competitors was unquestionably a "naked restraint" on price and output. The social justifications preferred for respondents' restraint of trade thus do not make it any less unlawful. The statutory policy underlying the Sherman Act precludes inquiry into the question whether competition is good or bad. No matter how altruistic the motives of respondents may have been, it is undisputed that their immediate objective was to increase the price that they would be paid for their services. The per se rules are, of course, the product of judicial interpretations of the Sherman Act, but the rules nevertheless have the same force and effect as any other statutory commands.

DECISION AND REMEDY

The U.S. Supreme Court held that SCTLA lawyers' horizontal agreement to fix prices was a per se violation of Section 1 of the Sherman Act. Reversed and remanded.

CASE QUESTIONS

Critical Legal Thinking Do you think that per se rules are necessary? Or should the courts be required to examine fully the pro- and anticompetitive effects of an activity to determine whether it violates Section 1 of the Sherman Act?

Business Ethics Do you think CJA lawyers were acting "altruistically"? Did District act ethically by keeping CJA rates low and refusing to increase them?

Contemporary Business Should professionals be subject to antitrust laws? Why or why not?

Division of Markets

division of markets

When competitors agree that each will serve only a designated portion of the market.

Competitors that agree that each will serve only a designated portion of the market are engaging in a **division of markets** (or **market sharing**), which is a *per se violation* of Section 1 of the Sherman Act. Each market segment is considered a small monopoly served only by its designated "owner." Horizontal market-sharing arrangements include division by geographical territory, customers, and products.

The Supreme Court Speaks

Antitrust Law Forbids Division of Markets

Palmer v. BRG of Georgia, Inc.
498 U.S. 46, 111 S.Ct. 401 (1990)
Supreme Court of the United States

BACKGROUND AND FACTS

Harcourt Brace Jovanovich Legal and Professional Publications (HBJ) is the nation's largest provider of bar review materials and lecture services. In 1976, HBJ began offering a Georgia bar review course in direct competition with BRG of Georgia, Inc. (BRG), the only other main provider of bar review services in the state. In 1980, HBJ and BRG entered into an agreement whereby BRG was granted an exclusive license to market HBJ bar review materials in Georgia in exchange for paying HBJ $100 per student enrolled by BRG in the course. HBJ agreed not to compete with BRG in Georgia, and BRG agreed not to compete with HBJ outside of Georgia.

Immediately after the 1980 agreement, the price of BRG's course was increased from $150 to $400. Jay Palmer and other law school graduates who took the BRG bar review course in preparation for the 1985 Georgia bar exam sued BRG and HBJ, alleging a violation of Section 1 of the Sherman Act. The district court held in favor of the defendants. The court of appeals affirmed. The Supreme Court agreed to hear the plaintiffs' appeal.

SUPREME COURT ISSUE

Did the BRG-HBJ agreement constitute a division of markets and a per se violation of Section 1 of the Sherman Act?

IN THE LANGUAGE OF THE U.S. SUPREME COURT

Per Curiam   *The revenue-sharing formula in the 1980 agreement between BRG and HBJ, coupled with the price increase that took place immediately after the parties agreed to cease competing with each other, indicates that this agreement was formed for the purpose and with the effect of raising the price of the bar review course.*

Here, HBJ and BRG had previously competed in the Georgia market; under their allocation agreement, BRG received that mar- *ket, while HBJ received the remainder of the United States. Each agreed not to compete in the other's territories. Such agreements are anticompetitive. Thus, the agreement between HBJ and BRG was unlawful on its face.*

DECISION AND REMEDY

The U.S. Supreme Court held that the agreement between BRG and HBJ constituted a division of markets and as such was a per se violation of Section 1 of the Sherman Act. Reversed and remanded.

CASE QUESTIONS

Critical Legal Thinking   Should the division of markets be considered a per se violation of Section 1 of the Sherman Act? Or should the rule of reason apply?

Business Ethics   Did BRG and HBJ act ethically in this case? Should the defendants, as bar review providers, have been aware of the antitrust law that prohibits division of markets?

Contemporary Business   Why do you think BRG and HBJ entered into the 1980 agreement?

Group Boycotts

A **group boycott** (or **refusal to deal**) occurs when two or more competitors at one level of distribution agree not to deal with others at a different level of distribution. For example, a boycott would occur if a group of television manufacturers agreed not to sell their products to certain discount retailers (See Exhibit 35.2). A boycott would also occur if a group of rental car companies agreed not to purchase Chrysler automobiles for their fleets (see Exhibit 35.3).

Although in the past the U.S. Supreme Court has held that group boycotts were per se illegal, recent Supreme Court decisions have held that only certain group boycotts are per se illegal. Others are to be examined under the rule of reason. Nevertheless, most group boycotts are found to be illegal.

group boycott

When two or more competitors at one level of distribution agree not to deal with others at another level of distribution.

People of the same trade seldom meet together, even for merriment and diversion, but that the conversation ends in a conspiracy against the public, or in some contrivance to raise prices.

Adam Smith
The Wealth of Nations *(1776)*

*E*XHIBIT 35.2   *Group Boycott by Sellers*

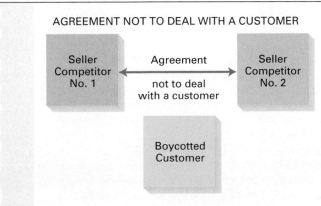

AGREEMENT NOT TO DEAL WITH A CUSTOMER

Seller Competitor No. 1 — Agreement not to deal with a customer → Seller Competitor No. 2

Boycotted Customer

*E*XHIBIT 35.3   *Group Boycott by Purchasers*

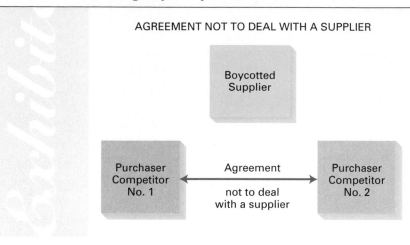

AGREEMENT NOT TO DEAL WITH A SUPPLIER

Boycotted Supplier

Purchaser Competitor No. 1 — Agreement not to deal with a supplier — Purchaser Competitor No. 2

Other Horizontal Agreements

Some agreements entered into by competitors at the same level of distribution—including trade association activities and rules, exchanging nonprice information, participating in joint ventures, and the like—are examined using the *rule of reason.* Reasonable restraints are lawful; unreasonable restraints violate Section 1 of the Sherman Act.

The Supreme Court Speaks

Group Boycott Does Not Exist Without a Horizontal Agreement

NYNEX Corporation v. Discon, Incorporated
525 U.S. 128 (1998)
Supreme Court of the United States

BACKGROUND AND FACTS

The NYNEX Corporation owns New York Telephone, a provider of local telephone services on the east coast of the United States. NYNEX also owns the Material Enterprises Company (Material), an entity that purchases services for the removal of old switching equipment and other obsolete telephone equipment from New York Telephone's physical locations. For years, Material contracted with Discon Incorporated, an independent company, to provide this equipment removal services. After several years, Material did not renew Discon's contract, and instead contracted with AT&T to provide these

removal services. Discon, which went out of business, sued NYNEX, Material, New York Telephone, and AT&T for engaging in a group boycott not to deal with Discon, an alleged *per se* violation of Sherman Act Section 1. The district court dismissed Discon's complaint. The court of appeals affirmed. The U.S. Supreme Court granted review.

SUPREME COURT ISSUE

Did the conduct of the defendants amount to a horizontal agreement necessary to constitute a *per se* group boycott violation of Section 1 of the Sherman Act?

Business Ethics

THE JUSTICE DEPARTMENT FLUNKS THE IVY LEAGUE SCHOOLS

Many college students think that tuition is too high and financial aid too low. After conducting an investigation, the U.S. Justice Department thought so too. It brought an action against the eight Ivy League schools (Brown, Columbia, Cornell, Dartmouth, Harvard, Princeton, the University of Pennsylvania, and Yale) and the Massachusetts Institute of Technology (M.I.T.). The Justice Department alleged that these schools had conspired and engaged in horizontal restraint of trade in violation of Section 1 of the Sherman Act. The facts of the case are as follows.

For years, the administrators of the Ivy League schools met annually to trade information about applicants seeking scholarships. They then agreed to offer scholarships to the students they thought would attend their schools. Scholarships were not offered to those less likely to attend. The schools defended this practice as preventing "overlap"— that is, certain students getting scholarship offers from many schools and other applicants receiving no scholarship offers. The schools figured this would save administrative costs as well as best serve the interests of the students.

The Justice Department did not think so. It felt that this trading of information and agreements to offer scholarships only to specified students constituted price-fixing by explicitly fixing the amount of scholarship money applicants were paid to attend school. The Justice Department lawyers pointed to what they learned in Economics 101 and asserted that this collegiate cartel was no different from any other cartel—it denied customers (students) the right to "comparison shop" just as they would for other services.

After weathering bad publicity, the eight Ivy League schools agreed to settle the case with the Justice Department. Under the terms of the consent decree, the schools agreed to no longer share financial aid information or discuss future tuition levels or faculty salaries with other schools. M.I.T. chose to fight the case in court and lost. The court found M.I.T. guilty of price-fixing and enjoined the challenged practices. [*United States. v. Brown University*, 5 F.3d 658 (3d Cir. 1993)]

1. Do you think the schools acted ethically in this case?
2. Did their "overlap" argument justify their actions?

VERTICAL RESTRAINTS OF TRADE

A **vertical restraint of trade** occurs when two or more parties on *different levels of distribution* enter into a contract, combination, or conspiracy to restrain trade (see Exhibit 35.4). The Supreme Court has applied both the per se rule and the rule of reason in determining the legality of vertical restraints of trade under Section 1 of the Sherman Act. The most common forms of vertical restrain are discussed in the following paragraphs.

vertical restraint of trade

A restraint of trade that occurs when two or more parties on *different levels of distribution* enter into a contract, combination, or conspiracy to restrain trade.

ℰXHIBIT 35.4   *Vertical Restraint of Trade*

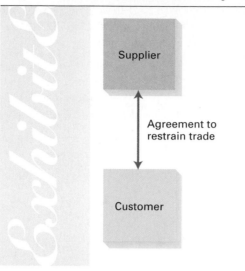

resale price maintenance

A per se violation of Section 1 of the Sherman Act; occurs when a party at one level of distribution enters into an agreement with a party at another level to adhere to a price schedule that either sets or stabilizes prices.

Resale Price Maintenance

Resale pricing maintenance (or **vertical price-fixing**) is a *per se violation* of Section 1 of the Sherman Act. It occurs when a party at one level of distribution enters into an agreement with a party at another level to adhere to a price schedule that either sets or stabilizes prices. For example, a computer manufacturer that sells its computers only to retailers that agree to resell them at the prices set by the manufacturer is enaged in this illegal practice.

The Supreme Court Speaks

Setting of Maximum Resale Price Judged by "Rule of Reason" Standard

State Oil Company v. Khan
522 U.S. 3, 118 S.Ct. 275 (1997)
Supreme Court of the United States

BACKGROUND AND FACTS
Barkat U. Khan and his corporation entered into an agreement with State Oil Company to lease and operate a gas station and convenience store owned by State Oil. The agreement provided that Khan would obtain his station's gasoline supply from State Oil. The agreement also provided that Khan could charge any price for the gasoline he sold to the station's customers, but if the price charged was higher than State Oil's "suggested retail price," the excess was to be rebated to State Oil. Khan could also choose to sell gasoline for less than State Oil's suggested retail price. After operating the station under these terms for about one year, Khan lost the station back to State Oil for falling behind in lease payments. Khan sued State Oil, alleging that the maximum resale price required by State Oil was a per se violation of Section 1 of the Sherman Act. The district court entered summary judgment for State Oil.

The court of appeals reversed and held that the maximum resale price set by State Oil was a per se violation of Section 1. The court of appeals cited a previous U.S. Supreme Court Case—*Albrecht v. Herald Co.*, 390 U.S. 145 (1968)—that held that the setting of maximum resale prices also was a per se violation of Section 1. State Oil appealed to the U.S. Supreme Court.

SUPREME COURT ISSUE
Is the establishment of a maximum resale price by a supplier a per se violation of Section 1 of the Sherman Act?

IN THE LANGUAGE OF THE U.S. SUPREME COURT
O'Connor, Justice Although the Sherman Act, by its terms, prohibits every agreement "in restraint of trade," this Court has long recognized that Congress intended to outlaw only unreasonable restraints. As a consequence, most antitrust claims are analyzed under a rule of rea-

son, according to which the finder of fact must decide whether the questioned practice imposes an unreasonable restraint on competition, taking into account a variety of factors, including specific information about the relevant business, its condition before and after the restraint was imposed, and the restraint's history, nature, and effect. Some types of restraints, however, have such predictable and pernicious anticompetitive effect, and such limited potential for procompetitive benefit, that they are deemed unlawful per se.

We find it difficult to maintain that vertically-imposed maximum prices could harm consumers or competition to the extent necessary to justify their per se invalidation. Although we have acknowledged the possibility that maximum pricing might mask minimum pricing, we believe that such conduct can be appropriately recognized and punished under the rule of reason. Indeed, both courts and antitrust scholars noted that Albrecht's *rule may actually harm consumers and manufacturers. After reconsidering* Albrecht's *rationale and the substantial criticism the decision has received, we conclude that there is insufficient economic justification for per se invalidation of vertical maximum price fixing.*

In overruling Albrecht, we of course do not hold that all vertical maximum price fixing is per se lawful. Instead, vertical maxi-

mum price fixing, like the majority of commercial arrangements subject to the antitrust laws, should be evaluated under the rule of reason. In our view, rule-of-reason analysis will effectively identify those situations in which vertical maximum price fixing amounts to anticompetitive conduct.

DECISION AND REMEDY

The U.S. Supreme Court reversed *Albrecht*. The Supreme Court held that the setting of a maximum resale price is not a per se violation of Section 1 of the Sherman Act. The Court remanded the case for trial using the rule of reason standard.

CASE QUESTIONS

Critical Thinking How often do you think the U.S. Supreme Court reverses itself? Do you think it should have done so in this case?

Business Ethics Was the State Oil contract that set a maximum resale price in this case lawful under the rule of reason standard?

Contemporary Business How will this decision affect suppliers and the retailers they sell to? Explain.

Nonprice Vertical Restraints

The legality of **nonprice vertical restraints** of trade under Section 1 of the Sherman Act is examined using the rule of reaon.[8] Nonprice restraints are unlawful under this analysis if their anticompetitive effects outweigh their procompetitive effects. Nonprice vertical restraints include situations where a manufacturer assigns exclusive territories to retail dealers or limits the number of dealers that may be located in a certain territory.

nonprice vertical restraints
Restaints of trade that are unlawful under Section 1 of the Sherman Act if their anticompetitive effects outweigh their procompetitive effects.

Entrepreneur and the Law

HOW TRADE ASSOCIATION MEMBERS CAN AVOID ANTITRUST LIABILITY

Trade associations are organizations that are formed by industry members to promote the industry, provide education to members, formulate rules for self-regulation of the industry, and conduct lobbying and other activities.

Trade associations usually hold annual and other meetings that industry members attend. To avoid antitrust problems, attendees should avoid sharing and discussing

certain information with each other. Here are some activities to avoid:

- Do not discuss or exchange price information about current or future sales to customers.
- Do not agree to share or split customers or geographical areas.
- Do not agree to operate only during agreed-upon hours.

DEFENSES TO SECTION 1 OF THE SHERMAN ACT

The courts have recognized several defenses to alleged violations of Section 1 of the Sherman Act. These defenses are discussed below.

Unilateral Refusal to Deal

The U.S. Supreme Court has held that a firm can unilaterally choose not to deal with another party without being liable under Section 1 of the Sherman Act. A **unilateral refusal to deal** is not a violation of Section 1 because there is no concerted action with others. This rule was announced in *United States v. Colgate & Co.*, and is therefore often referred to as the **"Colgate doctrine."**[9]

unilateral refusal to deal
A unilateral choice by one party not to deal with another party. This does not violate Section 1 of the Sherman Act because there is not concerted action.

Conscious Parallelism

If two or more firms act the same but no concerted action is shown, there is no violation of Section 1 of the Sherman Act. This doctrine is often referred to as **conscious parallelism**. For example, if two competing manufacturers of a similar product both separately reach an independent decision not to deal with a retailer, there is no violation of Section 1 of the Sherman Act. The key is that each of the manufacturers acted on its own.

Noerr Doctrine

The *Noerr* **doctrine** holds that two or more persons may petition the executive, legislative, or judicial branch of the government or administrative agencies to enact laws or to take other action without violating the antitrust laws. The rationale behind this doctrine is that the right to petition the government has precedence because it is guaranteed by the Bill of Rights.[10] For example, General Motors and Ford could collectively petition Congress to pass a law that would limit the import of foreign automobiles into this country.

There is an exception to this doctrine. Under the *"sham" exception*, petitioners are not protected if their petition or lawsuit is baseless—that is, if a reasonable petitioner or litigant could not realistically expect to succeed on its merits. If the protection of the *Noerr* doctrine is lost, an antitrust action may be maintained against those parties who had asserted its protection.

Landmark Law

SHERMAN ANTITRUST ACT SECTION 2

Section 2 of the Sherman Act prohibits the act of monopolization. It provides that

> *Every person who shall monopolize, or attempt to monopolize, or combine or conspire with any other person or persons, to monopolize any part of the trade or commerce among the several States, or with foreign nations, shall be deemed guilty of a felony* [15 U.S.C. § 2].

Proving that a defendant is in violation of Section 2 means proving that the defendant (1) possesses monopoly power in the relative market and (2) is engaged in a willful act of monopolization to acquire or maintain the power. Each of these elements is discussed in the following paragraphs.

*S*ECTION 2 OF THE SHERMAN ACT—MONOPOLIZATION

Section 2 of the Sherman Act

Prohibits the act of monopolization and attempts or conspiracies to monopolize trade.

By definition, monopolies have the ability to affect the price of goods and services. **Section 2** of the **Sherman Act** was enacted in response to widespread concern about the power generated by this type of anticompetitive activity.

Defining the Relevant Market

relevant product or service market

A relevant market that includes substitute products or services that are reasonably interchangeable with the defendant's products or services.

relevant geographical market

A relevant market that is defined as the area in which the defendant and its competitors sell the product or service.

Identifying the **relevant market** for a Section 2 action requires defining the relevant product or service market and geographical market. The definition of the relevant market often determines whether the defendant has monopoly power. Consequently, this determination is often litigated.

The **relevant product or service market** generally includes substitute products or services that are reasonably interchangeable with the defendant's products or services. Defendants often try to make their market share seem smaller by arguing for a broad definition of the product or service market. Plaintiffs, on the other hand, usually argue for a narrow definition.

The **relevant geographical market** usually is defined as the area in which the defendant and its competitors sell the product or service. This may be a national, regional, state, or local area, depending on the circumstances.

Monopoly Power

For an antitrust action to be sustained, the defendant must possess **monopoly power** in the relevant market. Monopoly power is defined by the courts to be the power to control prices or exclude competition. The courts generally apply the following guidelines: Market share above 70 percent is monopoly power; market share under 20 percent is not monopoly power. Otherwise, the courts generally prefer to examine the facts and circumstances of each case before making this determination.

monopoly power

The power to control prices or exclude competition measured by the market share the defendant possesses in the relevant market.

Willful Act of Monopolizing

Section 2 outlaws the **act of monopolizing**, not monopolies. Any act that otherwise violates any other antitrust law (such as illegal restraints of trade in violation of Section 1 of the Sherman Act) is an act of monopolization that violates Section 2. When coupled with monopoly power, certain otherwise lawful acts have been held to constitute an act of monopolization. For example, *predatory pricing*—that is, pricing below average or marginal cost—that is intended to drive out competition has been held to violate Section 2.[11]

act of monopolizing

A required act for there to be a violation of Section 2 of the Sherman Act. Possession of monopoly power without such act does not violate Section 2.

Defenses to Monopolization

Only two narrow defenses to a charge of monopolizing have been recognized: (1) innocent acquisition (for example, acquisition because of a *superior business acumen*, skill, foresight, or industry) and (2) *natural monopoly* (for example, a small market that can support only one competitor, such as a small-town newspaper). If a monopoly that fits into one of these categories exercises its power in a predatory or exclusionary way, the defense is lost.

Business Brief

Note carefully that, in contrast to Section 1, which requires *concerted action*, Section 2 may apply to individual behavior.

Attempts and Conspiracies to Monopolize

Firms that *attempt* or *conspire* to monopolize a relevant market may be found liable under Section 2 of the Sherman Act. A single firm may be found liable for monopolizing or attempting to monopolize. Two or more firms may be found liable for conspiring to monopolize.

E-Commerce & Information Technology

UNITED STATES V. MICROSOFT CORPORATION

Not since the days of John D. Rockefeller and the Standard Oil trust has the power of one man's company transfixed so many people as Bill Gates' Microsoft Corporation. In less than 25 years, Microsoft has grown from a start-up company into the world's largest software company, whose products touch the lives of virtually everyone who uses a personal computer. Microsoft dominates the software market with its Windows operating system, which is used in most of the world's personal computers.

One market that Microsoft did not dominate was the rapidly growing Internet Web browser market. Netscape developed its Navigator Internet Web browser and by 1994, controlled over 80 percent of the market. This posed a serious threat to Microsoft because not only was Navigator extremely popular, it bypassed Microsoft's operating system altogether. Microsoft called a meeting with Netscape to offer a "special relationship" that meant that Navigator would be absorbed into Microsoft Windows. Netscape refused.

Microsfot began a campaign to defeat Netscape. Microsoft developed its own browser called *Explorer* and attached it to its Windows operating system for free. Microsoft warned Apple, a manufacturer of personal com-

puters, that it would cancel Microsoft's all-important Office software unless Apple used Explorer; Apple capitulated and made Explorer its Web browser. Microsoft muscled AOL into offering Explorer in return for a small placement on the Windows desktop if it would not offer Netscape anywhere on its online service. AOL agreed. Microsoft gave Compaq, a maker of personal computers, a lower price for Windows in return for placing a Microsoft icon for the Explorer Web browser on Compaq's computers. And when Intel developed technology that would set its own software standards in competition with Microsoft's Windows, Microsoft threatened to cut support for Intel PCs. Intel promptly stopped work on its new technology.

After investigating, the United States and 19 states sued Microsoft in a civil antitrust case. After a nine-month trial and four months of failed settlement negotiations, U.S. District Court Judge Thomas Penfield Jackson decided the case, finding that (1) Microsoft used predatory and anticompetitive conduct to illegally maintain its monopoly in the Windows operating system in violation of Section 2 of the Sherman Act, (2) Microsoft illegally attempted to monopolize the market for Internet browsing software in violation of

Section 2 of the Sherman Act, and (2) Microsoft illegally bundled its Web browser Explorer with its successful Windows operating system, thus engaging in a tying arrangement in violation of Section 1 of the Sherman Act.

The district judge rendered a decision that prohibited Microsoft from engaging in such conduct in the future and ordered that Microsoft be split into two separate companies, one company that owns the operating systems such as Windows, and a second company that owns software,

Internet browsers, and other computer applications. On appeal, the court of appeals upheld the finding that Microsoft had engaged in monopolization in violation of Section 2, but reversed the ruling ordering the breakup of the company. The case was remanded for further proceedings.

Microsoft appealed the decision. In the meantime, Microsoft must defend over 100 civil class-action antitrust lawsuits brought against it by competitors and consumers. [*United States v. Microsoft Corporation*, 253 F.3d 34 (2001)].

CONCEPT SUMMARY   THE SHERMAN ACT

Section	Description
1	Prohibits contracts, combinations, and conspiracies in restraint of trade. To violate Section 1, the restraint must be found to be unreasonable under either of two tests: 1. Rule of reason 2. Per se rule Requires the concerted action of two or more parties.
2	Prohibits the act of monopolizing and attempts or conspiracies to monopolize. Can be violated by the conduct of one firm.

Landmark Law

CLAYTON ACT SECTION 7

In the late 1800s and early 1900s, *mergers* led to increased concentration of wealth in the hands of a few wealthy individuals and large corporations. **Section 7 of the Clayton Act** gave the federal government the power to check anticompetitive mergers. Originally, it applied only to stock mergers. The **Celler-Kefauver Act**, which was enacted in 1950, widened Section 7's scope to include asset acquisitions [15 U.S.C. § 18]. Today, Section 7 applies to all methods of external expansion, including technical mergers, consolidations, purchases of assets, subsidiary operations, joint ventures, and other combinations.

Section 7 of the Clayton Act provides that it is unlawful for a person or business to acquire stock or assets of another "where in any line of commerce or in any activity affecting commerce in any section of the country, the effect of such acquisition may be substantially to lessen competition, or to tend to create a monopoly."

SECTION 7 OF THE CLAYTON ACT—MERGERS

In determining whether a merger is lawful under Section 7 of the Clayton Act, the courts must examine the elements discussed in the following paragraphs.

Line of Commerce

line of commerce

Includes products or services that consumers use as substitutes. If an increase in the price of one product or service leads consumers to purchase another product or service, the two products are substitutes for each other.

Determining the **line of commerce** that will be affected by the merger involves defining the relevant *product or service market*. Traditionally, the courts have done this by applying the functional interchangeability test. Under this test, the relevant line of commerce includes products or services that consumers use as substitutes. If two products are substitutes for each other, they are considered as part of the same line of commerce. For example, suppose a price increase for regular coffee causes consumers to switch to Sanka (decaffeinated coffee). The two products are part of the same line of commerce because they are interchangeable.

Section of the Country

Defining the relevant **section of the country** consists of determining the relevant *geographical market*. The courts traditionally identify this market as the geographical area that will feel the direct and immediate effects of the merger. It may be a local, state, or regional market, the entire country, or some other geographical area. For example, Anheuser-Busch and the Miller Brewing Company sell beer nationally, whereas a local brewery, like Anchor Steam, sells beer only in the western states. If Anheuser-Busch and the Miller Brewing Company plan to merge, the relevant section of the country is the nation; if Anheuser-Busch intends to acquire a local brewery that sells beer in the West, the relevant section of the country is the western states.

section of the country

A division of the country that is based on the relevant geographical market; the geographical area that will feel the direct and immediate effects of the merger.

Probability of a Substantial Lessening of Competition

Once the relevant product or service and geographical market have been defined, the court must determine whether the merger or acquisition is **likely to substantially lessen competition or create a monopoly**. If the court feels that the merger is likely to do either, it may prevent the merger. Section 7 tries to prevent potentially anticompetitive mergers before they occur. It details in probabilities; an actual showing of the lessening of competition is not required.

In applying Section 7, mergers are generally classified as one of the following: *horizontal merger, vertical merger, market extension merger, or conglomerate merger.* Each of these is discussed in the paragraphs that follow.

probability of a substantial lessening of competition

If there is a probability that a merger will substantially lessen competition or create a monopoly, the court may prevent the merger under Section 7 of the Clayton Act.

Horizontal Mergers

A **horizontal merger** is a merger between two or more companies that compete in the same business and geographical market. The merger of two grocery store chains that serve the same geographical market fits this definition. Such mergers are subjected to strict review under Section 7 because they clearly result in an increase in concentration in the relevant market. For example, if General Motors Corporation and Ford Motor Company tried to merge, this horizontal merger would clearly violate Section 7.

In the landmark case *United States v. Philadelphia National Bank,*[12] the U.S. Supreme Court adopted the *presumptive illegality test* for determining the lawfulness of horizontal mergers. This test finds horizontal mergers presumptively illegal under Section 7 if (1) the merged firm would have a 30 percent or more market share in the relevant market and (2) the merger would cause an increase in concentration of 33 percent or more in the relevant market. This presumption is rebuttable—that is, the defendants may overcome it by introducing evidence that shows that the merger does not violate Section 7.

This test is not the only criterion for evaluating the lawfulness of a merger. The court must also examine factors such as the trend toward concentration in the relevant market, the past history of the firms involved, the aggressiveness of the merged firms, the economic efficiency of the proposed merger, and consumer welfare.

horizontal merger

A merger between two or more companies that compete in the same business and geographical market.

@ *E-Commerce & Information Technology*

AOL Acquires Time Warner in Megamerger

In 1989, entrepreneur Steve Case introduced a nationwide service called America Online (AOL) that provided Internet access to subscribers. In 1990, this upstart company was in desperate need of cash and offered to sell 11 percent ownership to media giant Time Warner for $5 million. Time Warner rejected the offer. Ten years later AOL made a second offer to Time Warner, this time to buy Time Warner for $180 billion in AOL stock. Time Warner accepted the offer. Although the agreement is called a merger, there is no doubt as to who the buyer is: AOL, the new-kid-on-the-block and member of the high-tech community, is buying the venerable media company Time Warner. The trading symbol for the new company, tellingly, is AOL. When announced in January 2000, the AOL-Time Warner merger was the largest in history.

AOL had only become a public company seven years prior to the merger when it sold stock to the public at $11.

Since that time, its stock had increased 35,000 percent in value. At the time of the merger announcement, AOL was worth more than 2.5 times more than Time Warner on the stock market. With no historical reference to valuing Net companies, AOL and Time Warner negotiated a trade that valued AOL 1.5 times more than Time Warner. This gave a premium of 70 percent to each Time Warner stockholder over the then current stock price per share. After the merger, the AOL stockholders would own 55 percent of the $350 billion merged company. The Time Warner part of the merger, with over 82,000 employees, would provide 80 percent of the profits compared to AOL, with its 12,000 employees.

The merger marries content with the Internet. Time Warner is a media conglomerate that owns Warner Bros. Studios, New Line Cinema, and Castle Rock film companies; Warner Bros. and HBO television companies, Time Warner Cable, TNT, TBS, and CNN cable companies; Warner and Elektra music labels; 33 magazines including *Time*, *People*, and *Sports Illustrated*; and Time Warner and Little Brown book publishers. AOL, on the other hand, is a high-tech Internet company that owns America Online Internet service, AOL sites, MapQuest, MovieFone, CompuServe, Netscape, part of DIRECTV, deals with regional bells for providing DSL service, and strategic alliances with other Internet companies. The merger also combines customer databases. AOL has 25 million Internet subscribers, while Time Warner has 28 million magazine subscribers, 35 million HBO subscribers, and 75 million households that have the TBS and TNT television channels. The merger provides substantial synergies for delivering media content over the Internet and providing opportunities for cross-marketing of products and services to customers.

Before the merger, Time Warner made forays into becoming an Internet company by internal expansion, but failed. It realized it could not get there unless it bought an Internet company, but with large debt and a low stock price it did not have the currency to buy a large Internet company. AOL, on the other hand, had currency to buy in the form of its Net-inflated stock value. So the old-line media giant, with content and wires, sold to the upstart, with a connection to the Internet and the future. The result is a new kind of conglomerate in the digital economy. The merger validates both the Internet and the value of content. The AOL-Time Warner merger may be the first of many that combine entertainment and high-technology, but probably no other merger can match the size and scope of this landmark deal.

The federal government antitrust authorities examined the horizontal merger. The government decided not to challenge it after the parties agreed to divest certain assets.

Vertical Mergers

vertical merger

A merger that integrates the operations of a supplier and a customer.

backward vertical merger

A vertical merger in which the customer acquires the supplier.

forward vertical merger

A vertical merger in which the supplier acquires the customer.

A **vertical merger** is a merger that integrates the operations of a supplier and a customer. For example, if Prentice Hall, Inc., a textbook publisher, acquired a paper mill, it would be a **backward vertical merger**. If a book publisher, such as Doubleday, acquired a retail bookstore chain, such as B. Dalton Bookstores, it would be a **forward vertical merger**. In examining the legality of vertical mergers, the courts usually consider such factors as the past history of the firms, the trend toward concentration in the industries involved, the barriers to entry, the economic efficiencies of the merger, and the elimination of potential competition caused by the merger.

Vertical mergers do not create an increase in market share because the merging firms serve different markets. They may, however, cause anticompetitive effects such as *foreclosing* competitors from either selling goods or services to or buying them from the merged firm.

Consider This Example Assume a furniture manufacturer acquires a chain of retail furniture stores. The merger is unlawful if it is likely that the merged firm will not buy furniture from other manufacturers or sell furniture to other retailers.

Market Extension Mergers

market extension merger

A merger between two companies in similar fields whose sales do not overlap.

A **market extension merger** is a merger between two companies in similar fields whose sales do not overlap. The merger may expand the acquiring firm's geographical or product market. For example, a merger between two regional brewers that do not sell beer in the same geographical area is called a *geographical market extension merger*. A merger between sellers of similar products, such as a soft drink manufacturer and an orange juice producer, is called a *product market extension merger*. The legality of market extension mergers is examined under Section 7 of the Clayton Act. They are treated like conglomerate mergers.

Conglomerate Mergers

Conglomerate mergers are mergers that do not fit into any other category. That is, they are mergers between firms in totally unrelated businesses. For example, if an oil company like Exxon merged with a clothing retailer like Neiman-Marcus, the result would be a conglomerate merger. Section 7 examines the lawfulness of such mergers under the *unfair advantage theory*, the *potential competition theory*, and the *potential reciprocity theory*, which are discussed in the paragraphs that follow.

Unfair Advantage Theory   The **unfair advantage theory** holds that a merger may not give the acquiring firm an unfair advantage over its competitors in finance, marketing, or expertise. This rule is intended to prevent wealthy companies from overwhelming the competition in a given market.

Potential Competition Theory   The **potential competition** (or **waiting-in-the-wings**) **theory** reasons that the real or implied threat of increased competition keeps businesses more competitive. A merger that would eliminate this perception can be enjoined under Section 7. For example, if IBM were perceived as a potential entrant to the fax machine business de novo, it could not merger with a large manufacturer of such machines.

Potential Reciprocity Theory   A merger may be enjoined if **potential reciprocity** can be shown between the merged firms and other firms. For example, suppose The New York Times Company (Company) purchases paper supplies from Hammermill, a paper manufacturer. Hammermill, in turn, purchases the raw materials for its paper from Northwest Logging Company (Northwest). Assume Company proposes to merge with Northwest. In this merger, the potential danger is that Company can threaten not to purchase its paper supplies from Hammermill unless Hammermill agrees to purchase all its logs from Northwest. The potential reciprocity theory is illustrated in Exhibit 35.5.

conglomerate merger

A merger that does not fit into any other category; a merger between firms in totally unrelated businesses.

unfair advantage theory

A theory that holds that a merger may not give the acquiring firm an unfair advantage over its competitors in finance, marketing, or expertise.

potential competition theory

A theory that reasons that the real or implied threat of increased competition keeps businesses more competitive. A merger that would eliminate this perception can be enjoined under Section 7.

potential reciprocity theory

A theory that says if Company A, which supplies materials to Company B, merges with Company C (which in turn gets its supplies from Company B), the newly merged company can coerce Company B into dealing exclusively with it.

ℰXHIBIT 35.5 *Potential Reciprocity Theory*

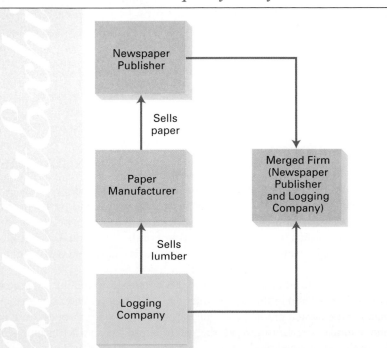

Defenses to Section 7 Actions

The Supreme Court has recognized two defenses to a Section 7 action. These defenses can be raised even if the merger would otherwise violate Section 7. The defenses are

- **The Failing Company Doctrine** According to this defense, a competitor may merge with a failing company if (1) there is no other reasonable alternative for the failing company, (2) no other purchaser is available, and (3) the assets of the failing company would completely disappear from the market if the anticompetitive merger were not allowed to go through.
- **The Small Company Doctrine** The courts have permitted two or more small companies to merge without liability under Section 7 if the merger allows them to compete more effectively with a large company.

Premerger Notification

Hart-Scott-Rodino Antitrust Improvement Act

Requires certain firms to notify the FTC and the Justice Department in advance of a proposed merger. Unless the government challenges the proposed merger within 30 days, the merger may proceed.

In 1976, premerger notification rules were enacted pursuant to the **Hart-Scott-Rodino Antitrust Improvement Act**.[13] These rules require certain firms to notify the FTC and the Justice Department of any proposed merger. This gives those agencies time to investigate and challenge any mergers they deem anticompetitive. If the merger is reportable, the parties must file the notification form and wait 30 days. If within the waiting period the government sues, the suit is entitled to expedited treatment in the courts.

London, England The European Union (EU) has very strict antitrust laws that have recently been enforced to prevent mergers of large multinational companies.

SECTION 3 OF THE CLAYTON ACT—TYING ARRANGEMENTS

Section 3 of the Clayton Act

Prohibits tying arrangements involving sales and leases of goods.

tying arrangement

A restraint of trade where a seller refuses to sell one product to a customer unless the customer agrees to purchase a second product from the seller.

Section 1 of the Sherman Act

Prohibits tying arrangements involving goods, services, intangible property, and real property.

Section 3 of the Clayton Act prohibits tying arrangements involving sales and leases of goods (tangible personal property).[14] **Tying arrangements** are vertical trade restraints that involve the seller's refusal to sell a product (the *tying* item) to a customer unless the customer purchases a second product (the *tied* item). **Section 1 of the Sherman Act** (restraints of trade) forbids tying arrangements involving goods, services, intangible property, and real property.

The defendant must be shown to have had sufficient economic power in the tying product market to restrain competition in the tied product market. Suppose, for example, that a manufacturer makes one patented product and one unpatented product. A tie-in arrangement occurs if the manufacturer refuses to sell the patented product to a buyer unless the buyer also purchases the unpatented product.

A tying arrangement is lawful if there is some justifiable reason for it. For example, the protection of quality control coupled with a trade secret may save a tie-in arrangement.

Consider This Example   Coca-Cola Company owns the right to the formula for the syrup to make Coca-Cola, which is a trade secret. Suppose Coca-Cola requires its distributors to purchase the syrup to make Coca-Cola from it. The tying product is the Coca-Cola franchise distributorship, and the tired product is the syrup. Here, the trying arrangement is lawful because a trade secret is involved and quality control must be preserved.

Contemporary Business Environment

KODAK'S COPIER REPLACEMENT PARTS JAMMED

Tying arrangements require that there be two products—the *tying* product and the *tied* product. A defendant who proves that the products are not separate cannot be held liable for a tying arrangement. Consider the following case.

Eastman Kodak Company (Kodak) manufactures and sells complex high-volume photocopier machines and micrographics equipment, such as microfilmers, scanners, microfilm viewers, and data-processing peripherals. Kodak equipment is unique because its equipment and parts are not compatible with other manufacturers' equipment and parts, and vice versa.

Kodak provides replacement parts and service for its machines. After the initial warranty period, Kodak provides service either through annual service contracts (which include all necessary parts) or on a per-call basis. Kodak manufactures some of the parts itself; the rest are made to order for Kodak by independent original equipment manufacturers (OEMs). Beginning in the early 1980s, independent service organizations (ISOs) began repairing and servicing Kodak equipment at prices substantially lower than Kodak's. ISOs purchased parts from Kodak and OEMs. Kodak customers sometimes purchased parts from Kodak but hired ISO's to do the actual repairs. Some customers found that the ISO service was of higher quality.

In 1985 and 1986, Kodak implemented a policy to limit ISO access to Kodak parts. Kodak also implemented a policy of selling replacement parts only to owners of Kodak equipment who used Kodak to service and repair their machines. Through these policies, Kodak intended to make it difficult for ISOs to sell service for Kodak machines. It succeeded. Many ISOs were forced out of business, and others lost substantial revenue.

In 1987, many ISOs sued Kodak, alleging that Kodak had unlawfully tied the sale of service for Kodak machines to the sale of parts, in violation of Section 1 of the Sherman Act. Kodak moved for summary judgment, alleging that parts and service were only one item—repair. The district court granted Kodak's motion, but the court of appeals reversed. The U.S. Supreme Court granted certiorari.

The Supreme Court held that the sale of replacement parts and the provision of services to install these parts and repair Kodak machines could be found to be two separate and distinct markets that would support a charge of unlawful tying. The Court found that there was sufficient evidence of a tie between service and parts to deny Kodak's motion for summary judgment. The Court held that the ISOs were entitled to a trial on their claim against Kodak and remanded the case for this trial. [*Eastman Kodak Company v. Image Technical Services, Inc.*, 112 S.Ct. 2072 (1992)].

Landmark Law

THE ROBINSON-PATMAN ACT

Businesses in the American economy survive by selling their goods and services at prices that allow them to make a profit. Sellers often offer favorable terms to their preferred customers. **Price discrimination** occurs if the seller does this without just cause. The rules regarding this type of unlawful trade practice are found in **Section 2** of the **Clayton Act**, which is commonly referred to as the **Robinson-Patman Act.** *De minimis* price discrimination is not actionable under the act.

Section 2(a) of the **Robinson-Patman Act** contains the following basic prohibition against price discrimination in the sale of goods [15 U.S.C. § 13(a)]:

It shall be unlawful for any person engaged in commerce, either directly or indirectly, to discriminate in price between different purchases of commodities of like grade and quality, where either or any of the purchases involved in such discrimination are in commerce, where the effect of such discrimination may be substantially to lessen competition or tend to create a monopoly in any line of commerce, or to injure, destroy, or prevent competition with any person who either grants or knowingly receives the benefit of such discrimination, or with customers of either of them.

This section does not apply to the sale of services, real estate, intangible property, securities, leases, consignments, or gifts. Mixed sales (i.e., those involving both services and commodities) are controlled by the dominant nature of the transaction.

SECTION 2 OF THE CLAYTON ACT—PRICE DISCRIMINATION

To prove a violation of **Section 2(a)**, the following elements of price discrimination must be shown:

- **Sales to Two or More Purchasers**   To violate Section 2(a), the price discrimination must involve sales to at least two different purchasers at approximately the same time. It is legal to make two or more sales of the same product to the same purchaser at different prices. The Robinson-Patman Act requires that the discrimination occur "in commerce."
- **Commodities of Like Grade and Quality**   A Section 2(a) violation must involve goods of "like grade and quality." To avoid this rule, sellers sometimes try to differentiate identical or similar products by using brand names. Nevertheless, as one court stated, "Four Roses under any other name would still swill the same."[15]
- **Injury**   To recover damages, the plaintiff must have suffered actual injury because of the price discrimination. The injured party may be the purchaser who did not receive the favored price (*primary line injury*), that party's customers to whom the lower price could not be passed along (*secondary line injury*), and so on down the line (*tertiary line injury*).

A plaintiff who has not suffered injury because of the price discrimination cannot recover. For example, assume that a wholesaler sells cheaper Michelin tires to General Motors than to Ford Motor Company. If Ford could have purchased comparable Michelin tires elsewhere at the lower price, it cannot recover.

Indirect Price Discrimination

Because direct forms of price discrimination are readily apparent, sellers of goods have devised sophisticated ways to provide discriminatory prices to favored customers. Favorable credit terms, freight charges, and such are examples of **indirect price discrimination** that violate the Robinson-Patman Act.

Defenses to Section 2(a) Actions

The Robinson-Patman Act establishes three statutory defenses to Section 2(a) liability: (1) cost justification, (2) changing conditions, and (3) meeting the competition. These defenses are discussed in the following paragraphs.

Cost Justification   Section 2(a) provides that a seller's price discrimination is not unlawful if the price differential is due to "differences in the cost of manufacture, sale, or delivery" of the product. This is called the **cost-justification defense**. For example, quantity or volume discounts are lawful to the extent they are supported by cost savings. Sellers may classify buyers into various broad groups and compute an average cost of selling to the group. The seller may then charge members of different groups different prices without being liable for price discrimination. The seller bears the burden of proving this defense.

Consider This Example   If the Procter & Gamble Company can prove that bulk shipping rates make it less costly to deliver 10,000 boxes of Tide than lesser quantities, it may charge purchasers accordingly. However, Procter & Gamble may not simply lower its price per box because the buyer is a good customer.

Changing Conditions   Price discrimination is not unlawful if it is in response to "changing conditions in the market for or the marketability of the goods." For example, the price of goods can be lowered to subsequent purchasers to reflect the deterioration of perishable goods (e.g., fish), obsolescence of seasonable goods (e.g., winter coats sold in the spring), a distress sale pursuant to court order, or discontinuance of a business. This is called the **changing conditions defense**.

Section 2(a) of the Robinson-Patman Act

Prohibits direct and indirect price discrimination by sellers of a commodity of a like grade and quality where the effect of such discrimination may be to substantially lessen competition or to tend to create a monopoly in any line of commerce.

Business Brief

To prove a violation of Section 2(a), the following elements must be shown: (1) The defendant sold commodities of like grade and quality, (2) to two or more purchasers at different prices at approximately the same time, and (3) the plaintiff suffered injury because of the price discrimination.

indirect price discrimination

A form of price discrimination (e.g., favorable credit terms) that is less readily apparent than direct forms of price discrimination.

cost justification defense

A defense in Section 2(a) action that provides that a seller's price discrimination is not unlawful if the price differential is due to "differences in the cost of manufacture, sale, or delivery" of the product.

changing conditions defense

A price discrimination defense that claims prices were lowered in response to changing conditions in the market for or the marketability of the goods.

meeting the competition defense

A defense provided in Section 2(b) that says a seller may lawfully engage in price discrimination to meet a competitor's price.

Section 2(b) of the Robinson-Patman Act

a defense that provides that a seller may lawfully engage in price discrimination to meet a competitor's price.

Meeting the Competition The **meeting the competition defense** to price discrimination is stipulated in **Section 2(b)** of the **Robinson-Patman Act**.[16] This defense holds that a seller may lawfully engage in price discrimination to meet a competitor's price. For example, assume Rockport sells its "ProWalker" shoe nationally at $100 per pair, while the Great Lakes Shoe Co. (Great Lakes), which produces and sells a comparable walking shoe, sells its product only in Michigan and Wisconsin. If Great Lakes sells its walking shoes at $75 per pair, Rockport can do the same. Rockport does not have to reduce the price of the shoe in the other 48 states. The seller can only meet, not beat, the competitor's price, however.

Landmark Law

SECTION 5 FEDERAL TRADE COMMISSION ACT

In 1914, Congress enacted the **Federal Trade Commission Act** (FTC Act) and created the **Federal Trade Commission (FTC)**. **Section 5** of the **FTC Act** prohibits *unfair methods of competition and unfair or deceptive acts or practices* in or affecting commerce [15 U.S.C. § 45]. Section 5, which is broader than the other antitrust laws, covers conduct that (1) violates any provision of the Sherman Act or the Clayton Act, (2) violates the "spirit" of those acts, (3) fills the gaps of those acts, and (4) offends public policy, or is immoral, oppressive, unscrupulous, or

unethical, or causes substantial injury to competitors or consumers.

The FTC is exclusively empowered to enforce the FTC Act. It can issue interpretative rules, general statements of policy, trade regulation rules, and guidelines that define unfair or deceptive practices, and conduct investigations of suspected antitrust violations. It can also issue cease-and-desist orders against violators. These orders are appealable to federal court. The FTC Act provides for a private civil cause of action for injured parties. Treble damages are not available.

E-Commerce & Information Technology

UNFAIR AND DECEPTIVE ACTS PROHIBITED OVER THE INTERNET

Little did Congress know over 80 years ago when it passed the **Federal Trade Commission Act** that Section 5 of the act would be used to prosecute fraud over the Internet. **Section 5** prohibits "unfair and deceptive" acts affecting commerce. The FTC has demonstrated recently that old laws can learn new tricks. Consider the following case.

Powerful search engines have been developed to allow surfers to browse the Internet and connect to Web sites in which they are interested. Certain scammers came up with a scheme where they would entice unwitting surfers to connect to their porn sites and not be able to get out. The scheme worked as follows. The scammers made fake copies of over 25 million popular Web sites such as the *Harvard Business Review, Japanese Friendship Gardens,* and others. Search engines trolling the Web for new pages found these Web

sites and added them to their listings. The scammers added to the faked Web pages an extra bit of coding so that as soon as surfers found the bogus Web page, it rerouted—"page-jacked"—them to the scammer's porn Web site. Once there, the user was "mouse-trapped" at the porn site and efforts to escape led only to new porn pages. The porn site operators made money by selling advertisements, and ad prices were often based on the number of "hits" on the site.

The Federal Trade Commission (FTC), a federal government agency, investigated and sued porn site operators in federal court for violating Section 5 of the FTC Act. The court found that the porn site operators had engaged in unfair and deceptive practices in violation of Section 5 and issued an injunction to shut down the porn sites and ordered the operators not to engage in such conduct in the future.

*E*XEMPTIONS FROM ANTITRUST LAWS

Certain industries and businesses are exempt from federal antitrust laws. The three categories of exemptions—*statutory, implied,* and *state action*—are discussed in the paragraphs that follow.

statutory exemptions

Exemptions from antitrust laws that are expressly provided in statutes enacted by Congress.

implied exemptions

Exemptions from antitrust laws that are implied by the federal courts.

state action exemptions

Business activities that are mandated by state law are exempt from federal antitrust laws.

Statutory Exemptions

Certain statutes expressly exempt some forms of business and other activities from the reach of antitrust laws. **Statutory exemptions** include labor unions,[17] agricultural cooperatives,[18] export activities of American companies,[19] and insurance business that is regulated by a state.[20] Other statutes exempt railroad, utility, shipping, and securities industries from most of the reach of antitrust laws.

Implied Exemptions

The federal courts have implied several exemptions from antitrust laws. Examples of **implied exemptions** include professional baseball (but not other professional sports) and airlines.[21] The airline exemption was granted on the ground that railroads and other forms of transportation were expressly exempt. The Supreme Court has held that professionals, such as lawyers, do not quality for an implied exemption from antitrust laws.[22] The Supreme Court strictly construes implied exemptions from antitrust laws.

State Action Exemptions

The U.S. Supreme Court has held that economic regulations mandated by state law are exempt from federal antitrust laws. The **state action exemption** extends to businesses that must comply with these regulations.

Consider This Example States may set the rates that public utilities (e.g., gas, electric, and cable television companies) may charge their customers. The states that set these rates and the companies that must abide by them are not liable for price-fixing in violation of federal antitrust law.

Contemporary Business Environment

BASEBALL'S GRAND SLAM AGAINST ANTITRUST LAWS

It was 1922. Babe Ruth was slamming home runs as the New York Yankees of the American League won the World Series of baseball. But that year the most important home run in baseball was hit at the U.S. Supreme Court. The opposing team—the U.S. government—struck out. Here is the story.

The American League and the National League were the dominant professional baseball leagues of the day, with such teams as the New York Giants, Boston Red Sox, and Chicago Cubs drawing millions of fans in various metropolitan markets throughout the country. Seeing these leagues' success, an upstart league called the Federal League began fielding teams in competing and other metropolitan markets.

To eliminate this competition, the National League induced some of the Federal League clubs to leave the league and purchased other Federal League teams. The lone remaining Federal League team sued the National League, alleging that it conspired to wreck the Federal League in violation of federal antitrust laws. The trial court agreed with the plaintiff, but the appeals court and the Supreme Court did not.

The Supreme Court justices held that the "national pastime" was exempt from antitrust laws because there was no interstate commerce involved in the National League's activities. Because of the finding of no interstate commerce, federal antitrust laws did not apply and the merit of the case was never decided [*Federal Baseball Club of Baltimore, Inc. v. National League of Professional Baseball Clubs*, 259 U.S. 200, 42 S.Ct. 465, 66 L.Ed. 898 (1922)]. In 1972, the U.S. Supreme Court refused to overturn its ruling reached in 1922 in the *Federal Baseball* case [*Flood v. Kuhn*, 407 U.S. 258, 92 S.Ct. 2099 (1972)].

Under the modern broad definition of "interstate commerce," the 1922 decision seems clearly wrong. Other sports have not been accorded a similar exemption from antitrust laws. Attempts to statutorily remove baseball's antitrust exemption during the baseball strike of 1995 failed in Congress.

Oriole Stadium, Baltimore, Maryland In 1922, the U.S. Supreme Court held that professional baseball was exempt from federal antitrust law.

$\mathcal{S}$TATE ANTITRUST LAWS

Most states have enacted antitrust statutes. These statutes are usually patterned after the federal antitrust statutes. They often contain the same language as well. State antitrust laws are used to attach anticompetitive activity that occurs in intrastate commerce. When federal antitrust laws are laxly applied, plaintiffs often bring lawsuits under state antitrust laws.[23]

$\mathcal{I}$nternational $\mathcal{L}$aw

JAPANESE *KEIRETSUS* IGNORE ANTITRUST LAWS

The United States has the most stringent antitrust laws in the world, enforces them most diligently, and assesses the greatest penalties for their violation. U.S. antitrust laws have been used to break up monopolies and cartels in many industries, including oil, steel, and telecommunications, to name but a few. These laws have also prevented U.S. companies from growing larger through mergers. Many critics argue that the stringent enforcement of antitrust laws has placed U.S. companies at a disadvantage in the international marketplace where they have to compete against larger foreign firms from countries where antitrust laws do not exist or are not enforced.

Take the case of Japan. In the past 40 or 50 years, Japan has gone from a war-ravaged country to an economic superpower. Much of this success has to do with the cozy relationship between Japan's federal government and the *keiretsu* (industrial groupings). *Keiretsu* cartels are considered a key factor behind the country's economic success.

After World War II, American-style antitrust laws were enacted in Japan; since then, though, they have been virtually ignored. The Japan Fair Trade Commission (JFTC), which is empowered to enforce antitrust laws, is more interested in promoting *keiretsus* than checking them. For example, the JFTC has filed only one antitrust criminal complaint in the past 17 years.

Japan's industry and commerce are rife with cartels—247 were legally permitted as of 1992. These cartels blatantly engage in anticompetitive conduct. Price-fixing permeates the beer, cosmetics, over-the-counter drug, and construction industries, among others. The cartels are politically entrenched because they are the largest contributors to campaigns of Japanese politicians. They use their political muscle to lobby against the passage of laws that would curtail their monopolistic positions.

This protectionist attitude has helped Japanese *keiretsus* become giants that have a substantial advantage in the international marketplace. This has come at the expense of Japanese consumers, however, who have to pay higher than competitive prices for goods and services sold by these cartels. This helps Japanese cartels compete abroad.

As Japanese consumers became more vocal, and as pressure increased from other countries—particularly the United States—the JFTC issued tougher guidelines for the enforcement of antitrust laws. But, if history is any indicator, these moves are probably little more than window dressing, and *keiretsus* will retain their monopolistic positions with little interference from the Japanese government.

CHAPTER SUMMARY

Federal Antitrust Law, p. 879

Federal Antitrust Law	A series of laws enacted by Congress to limit anticompetitive behavior in business. Federal antitrust laws include: 1. *Sherman Act.* An act enacted in 1890 that made certain restraints of trade and monopolistic acts illegal. 2. *Clayton Act.* An act enacted in 1914 that regulates mergers and prohibits certain exclusive dealing arrangements. 3. *Federal Trade Commission (FTC) Act.* An act enacted in 1914 that prohibits unfair methods of competition. 4. *Robinson-Patman Act.* An act enacted in 1930 that prohibits price discrimination.
Antitrust Enforcement	Each administration adopts an enforcement policy for antitrust laws. Antitrust laws are enforced more stringently at some times than at other times.
Antitrust Penalties	Federal antitrust laws provide the following penalties: 1. *Criminal sanctions.* Criminal penalties may be assessed for violations of the Sherman Act. 2. *Civil penalties.* The federal government may seek civil damages, including treble damages, for violations of federal antitrust laws. Courts may issue orders for divestiture of assets, cancellation of contracts, and other remedies. 3. *Private civil actions.* Section 4 of the Clayton Act provides that anyone injured in his or her business or property by the defendant's violation of any federal antitrust law (except the FTC Act) may bring a civil action and recover *treble damages*, plus reasonable costs and attorneys' fees, from the defendant. 4. *Effect of government judgment.* A government judgment against a defendant for an antitrust violation may be used as prima facie evidence of liability in a private, civil treble-damage action. A plea of *nolo contendere* or a *consent decree* cannot be used as evidence in a subsequent private, civil antitrust action.

Section 1 of the Sherman Act—Restraints of Trade, p. 880

Restraints of Trade	*Section 1 of the Sherman Act.* Prohibits contracts, combinations, or conspiracies that cause *unreasonable restraints of trade.* Requires *concerted activity* between two or more parties. The courts apply one of the following two tests in determining the lawfulness of a restraint of trade: 1. *Rule of reason.* Requires a balancing of pro- and anticompetitive effects of the restraint. Restraints found to be unreasonable are unlawful, violating Section 1 of the Sherman Act. 2. *Per se rule.* Applied to restraints that are inherently anticompetitive. No justification for the restraint is permitted.

Horizontal Restraints of Trade, p. 881

Horizontal Restraints of Trade	Occurs when two or more competitors at the *same level of distribution* enter into a contract, combination, or conspiracy to restrain trade. Horizontal restraints include: 1. *Price fixing.* Competitors in the same line of business agree to set the price of the goods or services they sell. A *per se violation.* 2. *Division of markets.* Competitors agree that each will serve only a designated portion of a market. Also called *market sharing.* A *per se violation.* 3. *Group boycott.* Competitors agree not to deal with others at another level of distribution (e.g., customer or supplier). Most examined using the *rule of reason.* 4. *Other horizontal agreements.* Examined using the *rule of reason.*

Vertical Restraints of Trade, p. 885

Vertical Restraints of Trade	Occur when two or more parties on *different levels of distribution* enter into a contract, combination, or conspiracy to restrain trade. Vertical restraints include: 1. *Resale price maintenance.* A party at one level of distribution (e.g., a manufacturer) requires a party at another level of distribution (e.g., a retailer) to sell a good or service at a designated price. Also called *vertical price fixing.* A *per se violation.* 2. *Nonprice vertical restraints.* Examined using the *rule of reason.*

Defenses to Section 1 of the Sherman Act, p. 887

Defenses	The following defenses may be raised against an alleged violation of Section 1 of the Sherman Act:
	1. *Unilateral refusal to deal.* A party may unilaterally refuse to deal with another party. This does not violate Section 1 because there has been no concerted action.
	2. *Conscious parallelism.* Occurs where two or more firms act the same but without concerted action; they all reached their decision independently.
	3. *The Noerr doctrine.* Two or more parties may petition the executive, legislative, or judicial branches of government to enact laws or take other action.
	4. *Sham exception.* The *Noerr* doctrine does not protect petitioners or plaintiffs if their petition or lawsuit is without merit.

Section 2 of the Sherman Act—Monopolization, p. 888

Monopolization	*Section 2 of the Sherman Act.* Prohibits the act of *monopolization* and attempts, combinations, and conspiracies to monopolize trade or commerce in a relevant market. The following elements are necessary to prove a defendant in violation of Section 2 of the Sherman Act:
	1. *Relevant market.* Defined as:
	a. *Relevant product or service market.* Includes substitute products or services that are reasonably interchangeable with the defendant's products or services.
	b. *Relevant geographical market.* Geographical area in which the defendant and its competitors sell the product or service.
	2. *Monopoly power.* The defendant must possess monopoly power in the relevant market. This is defined as the power to control prices or exclude competition.
	3. *Act of monopolizing.* The defendant must have engaged in a willful act of monopolization. Mere possession of a monopoly is not enough.
Defenses to Monopolization	The following defenses may be raised against an alleged violation of Section 2 of the Sherman Act:
	1. *Superior business acumen.* Monopoly that is acquired by superior skill, foresight, or industry.
	2. *Natural monopoly.* Monopoly that is thrust upon the defendant (e.g., only newspaper in a small town).

Section 7 of the Clayton Act—Mergers, p. 890

Elements of a Section 7 Action	*Section 7 of the Clayton Act.* Prohibits acquisitions that may substantially lessen competition in any line of commerce in any section of the country. The following elements are necessary to prove a violation of Section 7 of the Clayton Act:
	1. *Line of commerce.* Defined as the market that will be affected by the merger. Includes products or services that consumers use as substitutes for those produced or sold by the merging firms.
	2. *Section of the country.* Geographical market that will be affected by the merger. Includes the area that will feel the direct and immediate impact of the merger.
	3. *Probability of a substantial lessening of competition.* If the court determines that the merger would have a probability of a substantial lessening of competition, the merger may be prohibited. The statute deals with probabilities: A showing of actual lessening of competition is not required.
Horiztonal Mergers	Merger between two or more firms that compete in the same business and geographical market; a merger between competitors at the same level of distribution.
Vertical Mergers	Merger between firms at different levels of distribution that integrates the operations of a supplier and a customer.
Market Extension Mergers	Merger of two firms in similar fields whose sales do not overlap.
	1. *Geographical market extension merger.* Merger of two firms that sell the same product or service but in different geographical markets.
	2. *Product market extension merger.* A merger of two firms that sell similar products or services in the same geographical market.
Conglomerate Mergers	Merger of firms in totally unrelated businesses. Conglomerate mergers may be challenged under:
	1. *Unfair advantage theory.* A merger may not give the acquiring firm an unfair advantage over its competitors in finance, marketing, or expertise.
	2. *Potential competition theory.* A merger may not remove a competitor that posses a real or implied threat of increased competition that keeps businesses in the market more competitive.

	3. *Potential reciprocity theory.* A merger of Company A and Company C, where Company A supplies materials to Company B and Company C purchases supplies from Company B. The danger is that the newly merged company (Company A and Company C) could coerce Company B into dealing exclusively with it.
Defenses to Section 7 Actions	The following defenses may be raised against a violation of Section 7 of the Clayton Act: 1. *Failing company doctrine.* A competitor may merge with a failing company if (1) there is no other reasonable alternative for the failing company, (2) no other purchaser is available, and (3) the assets of the failing company would completely disappear from the market if the anticompetitive merger were not allowed to go through. 2. *Small company doctrine.* Two or more small companies may merge if the merger allows them to compete more effectively with a large company.
Premerger Notification	1. *Hart-Scott-Rodino Antitrust Improvement Act.* Federal act that requires certain firms to notify the FTC and Justice Department in advance of a proposed merger. Unless the government challenges the proposed merger within 30 days, the merger may proceed.

Section 3 of the Clayton Act—Tying Arrangements, p. 894

Section 3 of the Clayton Act	1. *Tying arrangement.* Occurs when a seller refuses to sell a product (the *tying* product) to a customer unless the customer purchases a second product (the *tied* product). 2. *Section 3 of the Clayton Act.* Prohibits tying arrangements involving sales and leases of *goods*. 3. *Section 1 of the Sherman Act.* Prohibits trying arrangements involving goods, *services*, intangible property and real property

Section 2 of the Clayton Act—Price Discrimination, p. 896

Section 2 of the Clayton Act	Commonly referred to as the *Robinson-Patman Act.* Prohibits price discrimination and discriminatory fees, payments, and services. The act applies only to products, not services.
Price Discrimination	*Section 2(a).* Prohibits a seller from discriminating in price between two or more different purchasers of commodities of *like grade and quality* where the effect may be substantially to lessen competition. *Direct* and *indirect* price discrimination is unlawful.
Defenses to Section 2(a) Actions	A seller's price discrimination is not unlawful if the price differential is due to: 1. *Cost justification.* Differences in the cost of maintenance, sale, or delivery of the product to different purchasers. 2. *Changing conditions.* The seller is responding to changing conditions in the market (e.g., deterioration of perishable goods). 3. *Meeting the competition, Section 2(b)* permits a seller to have a lower price in one market than in another market to meet the price of a competitor in the lower-priced market.

Section 5 of the Federal Trade Commission Act—Unfair Methods of Competition, p. 897

Sections 5 of the FTC Act	Prohibits *unfair methods of competition and unfair or deceptive acts or practices.* Section 5 covers conduct that (1) violates any provision of the Sherman Act or the Clayton Act, (2) violates the "spirit" of those acts; (3) fills the gaps of those acts, and (4) causes substantial injury to competitors or consumers.

Exemptions from Antitrust Laws, p. 897

Statutory Exemptions	Statutes expressly exempt labor unions; agricultural cooperatives; export activities of American companies; insurance business regulated by states; railroad, utility, shipping, and securities industries from federal antitrust laws.
Implied Exemptions	The courts have held that certain industries, including professional baseball and airlines, are implicitly exempt from federal antitrust laws.
State Action Exemptions	Businesses' activities that are mandated by state law are exempt from federal antitrust laws.

State Antitrust Laws	Most states have enacted state antitrust laws that attack anticompetitive activity that occurs in intrastate commerce.

*E*ND-OF-*C*HAPTER *I*NTERNET *E*XERCISES AND *C*ASE *Q*UESTIONS

Working the Web Internet Exercises

ACTIVITIES

1. The largest antitrust case of our times, *United States v. Microsoft*, leaves a long and rich trail of documents for study. See **www.ssrn.com/update/lsn/lsn_microsoft-case.html**, which contains a lengthy list of links to articles about the famous case. List the specific sections of the antitrust laws that Microsoft was alleged to have violated.

2. Find your state's laws relating to unfair competition and restraint of trade. Are they consistent with federal law? See "Law About . . . Antitrust" at **www.law.cornell.edu/topics/antitrust.html** for an overview of

antitrust law with links to key primary and secondary sources.

3. Antitrust is an area of law deeply connected with economic theory. The intent of the law is to protect competition. So how can mergers be permitted under the Clayton Act? See Section 7 of the Clayton Act, 15 U.S.C. § 18.

4. Where does the United States derive its purported authority to enforce its antitrust laws extraterritorially? See **www.usdoj.gov/atr/public/guidelines/internat.htm**.

CRITICAL LEGAL THINKING CASES

35.1 Price Fixing The Maricopa County Medical Society is a professional association that represents doctors of medicine, osteopathy, and podiatry in Maricopa County, Arizona. The society formed the Maricopa Foundation for Medical Care, a nonprofit Arizona corporation. Approximately 1,750 doctors, who represent 70 percent of the practitioners in the county, belong to the foundation. The foundation acts as an insurance administrator between its member doctors and insurance companies that pay patients' medical bills.

The foundation established a maximum fee schedule for various medical services. The member doctors agreed to abide by this fee schedule when providing services to patients. The state of Arizona brought this action against the society, the foundation and its members, alleging price fixing in violation of Section 1 of the Sherman Act. Who wins? [*Arizona v. Maricopa County Medical Society*, 457 U.S. 332, 102 S.Ct. 2466, 73 L.Ed. 2d 48 (1982)]

35.2 Division of Markets Topco Associates, Inc., was founded in the 1940s by a group of small, local grocery store chains to act as a buying cooperative for the member stores. In this capacity, Topco procures and distributes more than 1,000 different food and related items to its members. Topco does not itself own any manufacturing or processing facilities, and the items it procures

are shipped directly from the manufacturer or packer to Topco members. Topco members agree to sell only Topco brand products within an exclusive territory. The United States sued Topco and its members, alleging a violation of Section 1 of the Sherman Act. Who wins? [*United States v. Topco Associates, Inc.*, 405 U.S. 596, 92 S.Ct. 1126, 31 L.Ed.2d 515 (1972)]

35.3 Tying Arrangement Mercedes-Benz of North America (MBNA) is the exclusive franchiser of Mercedes-Benz dealerships in the United States. MBNA's franchise agreements require each dealer to establish a customer service department for the repair of Mercedes-Benz automobiles and for dealers to purchase Mercedes-Benz replacement parts from MBNA. At least eight independent wholesale distributors, including Metrix Warehouse, Inc., sell replacement parts for Mercedes-Benz automobiles. Because they are precluded from selling parts to Mercedes-Benz dealers, these parts distributors sell their replacement parts to independent garages that specialize in the repair of Mercedes-Benz automobiles. Evidence showed that Metrix sold replacement parts for Mercedes-Benz automobiles of equal quality and at a lower price than those sold by MBNA. Metrix sued MBNA, alleging a violation of Section 1 of the Sherman Act. Who wins? [*Metrix Warehouse, Inc. v. Mercedes-Benz of North America, Inc.*, 828 F.2d 1033 (4th Cir. 1987)]

35.4 Conscious Parallelism The Crest Theatre is a movie theater that is located in a neighborhood shopping center in a suburb six miles from downtown Baltimore, Maryland. The owner of the Crest Theatre has repeatedly sought to obtain first-run feature films from Paramount Film Distribution Corporation and other film distributors. Each film distributor has independently rejected the request, stating that they restrict "first-run" movies to theaters located in downtown Baltimore. Each cited the same reasons: First-runs are normally granted to the largest theaters, profits are higher for showing films in downtown theaters, the drawing area around the Crest Theatre was less than one-tenth that of the downtown theaters, and the downtown theaters offered greater opportunities for widespread advertisements and exploitation of newly released feature films. There was no evidence of an agreement between the film producers to restrict the showing of feature films at the Crest Theatre. Evidence showed that each film distributor made an independent decision to show its first-run films in theaters located in downtown Baltimore. Crest Theatre sued Paramount and the other film distributors, alleging a violation of Section 1 of the Sherman Act. Who wins? [*Theatre Enterprises, Inc. v. Paramount Film Distribution Corporation*, 346 U.S. 537, 74 S.Ct. 257, 98 L.Ed.2d 273 (1954)]

35.5 Resale Price Maintenance The Union Oil Company is a major oil company that operates a nationwide network of franchised service station dealers who sell Union Oil gasoline and other products throughout the United States. The franchise dealers lease their stations from Union Oil; they also sign a franchise agreement to purchase gasoline and other products on assignment from Union Oil. Both the lease and the franchise agreement are one-year contracts that may be canceled by Union Oil if a dealer does not adhere to the contract. The franchise agreement provided that all dealers shall adhere to the retail price of gasoline as set by Union Oil. The retail price fixed by Union Oil for gasoline during the period in question was $.299 per gallon. Simpson, a franchised dealer, violated this provision in the franchise agreement and sold gasoline at $.279 per gallon to meet competitive prices. Because of this, Union Oil canceled Simpson's lease and franchise agreement. Simpson sued Union Oil, alleging a violation of Section 1 of the Sherman Act. Who wins? [*Simpson v. Union Oil Company*, 377 U.S. 13, 84 S.Ct. 1051, 12 L.Ed.2d 98 (1964)]

35.6 Nonprice Vertical Restraint GTE Sylvania, Inc., manufactured and sold television sets to independent or company-owned distributors, which in turn resold the sets to a large and diverse group of retailers. Prompted by a decline in its market share, Sylvania instituted a franchise program whereby it phased out its wholesale distribution and began to sell its televisions directly to a smaller and select group of franchised retail dealers. A franchise did not constitute an exclusive territory, and Sylvania retained sole discretion to increase the number of retailers in an area.

In the spring of 1965, Sylvania decided to franchise another outlet in San Francisco that was approximately one mile from a Sylvania retail outlet operated by Continental TV, Inc. Continental protested the location of the new outlet, but to no avail. Continental then proposed to open a new Sylvania store in Sacramento, but Sylvania denied the franchise because it believed the Sacramento area was adequately served. In the face of this denial, Continental advised Sylvania that it was in the process of moving Sylvania merchandise from its warehouse to a new retail location in Sacramento. Shortly thereafter, Sylvania terminated Continental's San Francisco franchise. Continental sued Sylvania, alleging that Sylvania had engaged in unreasonable restraint of trade in violation of Section 1 of the Sherman Act. Does the per se rule or the rule of reason apply? [*Continental TV, Inc. v. GTE Sylvania, Inc.*, 433 U.S. 36, 97 S.Ct. 2549, 56 L.Ed.2d 568 (1977)]

35.7 Monopolization The International Business Machine Corporation (IBM) manufactures entire computer systems, including mainframes and peripherals, and provides software and support services to customers. IBM both sells and leases computers. Greyhound Computer Corporation, Inc., is a computer leasing company that buys older computers from IBM and then leases them to businesses. Thus, Greyhound is both a customer and a competitor of IBM. Prior to 1963, IBM sold its second-generation equipment at a 10 percent discount per year up to a maximum of 75 percent. Thus, equipment on the market for several years could be purchased at a substantial discount from its original cost.

IBM's market share of this leasing market was 82.5 percent. The portion of the leasing market not controlled by IBM was dispersed among many companies, including Greyhound. IBM officials became concerned that the balance between sales and leases was turned too heavily toward sales and that the rapid increase in leasing companies occurred because of their ability to purchase second-generation computers from IBM at a substantial discount. In 1963, IBM reduced the annual discount to 5 percent per year with a maximum of 35 percent. In 1964, the discount was changed to 12 percent after the first year with no further discounts. Greyhound sued IBM, alleging IBM engaged in monopolization in violation of Section 2 of the Sherman Act. Who wins? [*Greyhound v. International Business Machine Corporation*, 559 F.2d 488 (9th Cir. 1977)]

35.8 Superior Business Acumen In the 1970s the Eastman Kodak Company was the dominant and preeminent manufacturer and distributor of cameras and film in the United States. In 1972, Kodak introduced a new instamatic camera called the "110 camera" and a new film called "Kodacolor III" to be used in the cameras. Kodak engineers invented the camera and film with their own ingenuity. Kodak invested substantial money in inventing the new camera and film and held many patents necessary to develop the 110 system. The camera and film were superior to any other on the market and were an instant success. With the introduction of the new camera and film, Kodak obtained a monopoly position in the amateur photography market.

Berkey Photo, Inc., was a small photography company that competed with Kodak. Berkey's attempt to develop and sell its own version of the 110 camera failed. Berkey then brought an antitrust action against Kodak, alleging that Kodak's introduction of the 110 camera and Kodacolor III film was an attempt to monopolize the camera market in violation of Section 2 of the Sherman Act. Who wins? [*Berkey Photo, Inc. v. Eastman Kodak Company*, 603 F.2d 263 (2nd Cir. 1979)]

35.9 Merger The Lipton Tea Co. is the second largest U.S. producer of herbal teas, controlling 32 percent of the national market. Lipton announced that it would acquire Celestial Seasonings, the largest U.S. producer of herbal teas, controlling 52 percent of the national market. R. C. Bigelow, Inc., the third largest producer of herbal teas with 13 percent of the national market brought this action, alleging that the merger would violate Section 7 of the Clayton Act and seeking an injunction against the merger. What type of merger is proposed? What is the relevant market? Should the merger be enjoined? [*R.C. Bigelow, Inc., v. Unilever, N.V.*, 867 F.2d 102 (2nd Cir. 1989)]

35.10 Merger The G. R. Kinney Company, Inc., was the largest independent chain of family-owned shoe stores in the nation. It had assets of $18 million and sold more than 8 million pairs of shoes annually through its 350 retail outlets. Kinney announced that it would merge with the Brown Shoe Company, Inc., which was the fourth largest manufacturer of shoes in the country with assets of more than $72 million and which sold more than 25 million pairs of shoes annually. The United States brought this action, alleging a violation of Clayton Act Section 7 and seeking a preliminary injunction against the merger. What type of merger would this be? What is the relevant market? Does the merger violate Section 7? [*Brown Shoe Company, Inc. v. United States*, 370 U.S. 294, 82 S.Ct. 1502, 8 L.Ed.2d 510 (1962)]

35.11 Reciprocal Buying Consolidated Foods Corporation owns a network of wholesale and retail food stores. Consolidated purchases a substantial amount of products from food processors who use dehydrated onion and garlic in their products. Consolidated acquired Gentry, Inc., a manufacturer of dehydrated onion and garlic. Gentry controlled 32 percent of the market for these products and, with its chief competitor, accounted for 90 percent of total industry sales. Two small competitors accounted for the other 10 percent of sales. Evidence showed that after the acquisition, Consolidated required firms from which it purchased food products to purchase the dehydrated onion and garlic they needed from Gentry. The FTC sued Consolidated, alleging that Consolidated violated Section 7 of the Clayton Act by its acquisition of Gentry. Who wins? [*Federal Trade Commission v. Consolidated Foods Corporation*, 380 U.S. 592, 85 S.Ct. 1220, 14 L.Ed.2d 95 (1965)]

35.12 Antitrust Injury The Brunswick Corporation was the second largest manufacturer of bowling equipment in the United States. In the late 1950s, the bowling industry expanded rapidly. Brunswick's sales of lanes, automatic pinsetters, and ancillary equipment to bowling alley operators rose accordingly. Because the equipment required a major capital expenditure by bowling center operators, Brunswick extended credit for all of the purchase price except a cash down payment. It took a security interest in the equipment.

Brunswick's sales dropped in the early 1960s, when the bowling industry went into a sharp decline. In addition, many of the bowling center operators defaulted on their loans. By the end of 1964, Brunswick was in financial difficulty. It met with limited success when it foreclosed on its security interests and attempted to lease or sell the repossessed equipment and bowling centers. To avoid complete loss, Brunswick started running those that would provide a positive cash flow. This made Brunswick the largest operator of bowling centers in the country, with more than five times as many bowling centers as its next largest competitor. Because the bowling industry was so deconcentrated, however, Brunswick controlled less than 2 percent of the bowling centers in the country.

Pueblo Bowl-O-Mat, Inc., operated three bowling centers in markets where Brunswick had repossessed bowling centers and began operating them. Pueblo Bowl sued Brunswick, alleging that Brunswick had violated Section 7 of the Clayton Act. Pueblo Bowl alleged that it suffered injury in the form of lost profits that it would have made had Brunswick allowed the bowling centers to go bankrupt, and requested treble damages. Is Brunswick liable? [*Brunswick Corporation v. Pueblo Bowl-O-Mat, Inc.*, 429 U.S. 477, 97 S.Ct. 690, 50 L.Ed.2d 701 (1977)]

35.13 Price Discrimination Corn Products Refining Company manufactures corn syrup or glucose at two plants, one located in Chicago, Illinois, and the other in Kansas City, Missouri. Glucose is a principal ingredient of low-priced candy. Corn Products sells glucose at the same retail price to all purchasers, but charges separately for freight charges. Instead of charging actual freight charges, Corn Products charges every purchaser the freight that it would have cost if the glucose were shipped from Chicago, even if the glucose was shipped from its Kansas City plant. This "base point pricing" system created a favored price zone for Chicago-based purchasers. This put them in a better position to compete for business. The FTC sued Corn Products, alleging that it engaged in price discrimination in violation of Section 2(a) of the Robinson-Patman Act. Did it? [*Corn Products Refining Company v. Federal Trade Commission*, 324 U.S. 726, 65 S.Ct. 961, 89 L.Ed.2d 1320 (1945)]

35.14 Defense The Morton Salt Company manufacturers and sells table salt in interstate commerce. Morton Salt manufacturers several different brands of table salt and sells them directly to (1) wholesalers, who in turn resell to retail stores, and (2) large retailers. Morton Salt sells its finest brand of table salt, "Blue Label," based on the following standard-quantity discount system, which is available to all customers:

Price Per Case

Less than carload purchase	$1.60
Carload purchases	1.50
5,000-case purchases	1.40
50,000-case purchases	1.35

The standard-quantity discount pricing schedule was not based on actual costs incurred by Morton Salt in serving its customers; instead, it was designed to give large purchasers an incentive to purchase salt from Morton Salt. Evidence showed that only five large retail chains ever bought Blue Label salt in sufficient quantities to qualify for the $1.35 per case price. Evidence also showed that small retailers who could not qualify for any discount had to pay wholesalers higher prices for salt than the large retailers were selling the salt at retail to their customers. The FTC sued Morton Salt, alleging that it violated Section 2(a) of the Robinson-Patman Act. Is Morton Salt's quantity discount pricing system justified? [*Federal Trade Commission v. Morton Salt Company*, 334 U.S. 37, 68 S.Ct. 822, 92 L.Ed. 1196 (1948)]

35.15 FTC Act   Texaco, Inc, is one of the nation's largest petroleum companies. It sells its products through approximately 30,000 franchised service stations, which constitute about 16 percent of all service stations in the United States. Nearly 40 percent of the Texaco dealers lease their stations from Texaco. This is typically a one-year lease that may be terminated (1) at the end of any year upon proper notice or (2) at any time if in Texaco's judgment any lease provisions relating to the use and appearance of the station are not fulfilled. The franchise agreement under which the dealers received their supply of gasoline

and other petroleum products also is a one-year agreement and is terminable upon 30 days' notice.

Texaco entered into an agreement with the Goodrich Tire Company whereby Texaco agreed to promote the sale of Goodrich tires, batteries, and accessories (TBA) through its franchised dealers. The agreement provided that Goodrich would pay Texaco a 10 percent commission on all TBA purchases by Texaco dealers. During the five-year period 1952–1956, Texaco received commissions of $22 million.

Although Texaco dealers were not forced to carry the TBA, Texaco strongly recommended that they carry the line. In addition, the Texaco representatives who were responsible for recommending the renewal of dealer franchise and lease agreements were told to promote Goodrich products. Texaco also received regular reports on the amount of TBA purchased by its dealers. The FTC brought an action that alleged that Texaco violated Section 5 of the FTC Act. Who wins? [*Federal Trade Commission v. Texaco, Inc.*, 393 U.S. 223, 89 S.Ct. 429, 21 L.ED.2d 394 (1968)]

BUSINESS ETHICS CASES

35.16 Business Ethics   E.I. du Pont de Nemours & Co. is a manufacturer of chemicals, paints, finishes, fabrics, and other products. General Motors Corporation is a major manufacturer of automobiles. During the period 1917–1919, du Pont purchased 23 percent of the stock of General Motors. Du Pont became a major supplier of finishes and fabrics to General Motors.

The du Pont Company's commanding position as a General Motors supplier was not achieved until shortly after its purchase of a sizable block of General Motors stock in 1917. The company's interest in buying into General Motors was stimulated by John J. Raskob, du Pont's treasurer, and Pierre S. du Pont, du Pont's president, who acquired personal holdings of General Motors stock in 1914. General Motors was organized six years earlier by William C. Durant to acquire previously independent automobile manufacturing companies—Buick, Cadillac, Oakland, and Oldsmobile. Durant later brought in Chevrolet, organized by him when he was temporarily out of power, during 1910–1915, and a bankers' group controlled General Motors. In 1915, when Durant and the bankers deadlocked on the choice of a board of directors, they resolved the deadlock by an agreement under which Pierre S. du Pont was named chairman of the General Motors Board, and Pierre S. du Pont, Raskob, and two nominees of Mr. du Pont were named neutral directors. By 1916, Durant settled his differences with the bankers and resumed the presidency and his controlling position in General Motors. He prevailed upon Pierre S. du Pont and Raskob to continue their interest in General Motors' affairs, which both did as members of the Finance Committee, working closely with Durant in matters of finances and operations and plans for future expansion.

Raskob foresaw the success of the automobile industry and the opportunity for great profit in a substantial purchase of General Motors stock. On December 19, 1917, Raskob submitted a treasurer's report to the du Pont Finance Committee recommending a purchase of General Motors stock in the amount

of $25,000,000. That report made it clear that more than just a profitable investment was contemplated. A major consideration was that an expanding General Motors would provide a substantial market needed by the burgeoning du Pont organization. Raskob's summary of reasons in support of the purchase included this statement: "Our interest in the General Motors Company will undoubtedly secure for us the entire Fabrikoid, Pyralin (celluloid), paint and varnish business of those companies, which is a substantial factor."

General Motors was the colossus of the giant automobile industry. It accounted annually for upwards of two-fifths of the total sales of automotive vehicles in the nation. Expressed in percentages, du Pont supplied 67 percent of General Motors' requirements for finishes in 1946 and 68 percent in 1947. In fabrics, du Pont supplied 52.3 percent of requirements in 1946 and 38.5 percent in 1947. Because General Motors accounted for almost one-half of the automobile industry's annual sales, its requirements for automotive finishes and fabrics must have represented approximately one-half of the relevant market for these materials.

In 1949, the United States brought an antitrust action against du Pont, alleging violation of Section 7 of the Clayton Act and seeking the divestiture of du Pont's ownership of stock in General Motors. Did du Pont's ownership of 23 percent of the stock of General Motors constitute a vertical merger that gave du Pont illegal preferences over competitors in the sale of finishes and fabrics to General Motors in violation of Section 7 of the Clayton Act? Did the du Ponts act ethically in this case? [*United States v. E.I. du Pont de Nemours & Co.*, 353 U.S. 586, 77 S.Ct. 872, 1 L.Ed.2d 1057 (1957)]

35.17 Business Ethics   Falls City Industries, Inc., is a regional brewer located in Nebraska. It sells its "Falls City" brand beer in 13 states, including Indiana and Kentucky. In Indiana, Falls City sells its beer to Vanco Beverage, Inc., a beer wholesaler located in Vanderburgh County. In Kentucky, Falls City sells its beer to wholesalers located in Henderson County. The two counties are directly across from each other and are separated only by the Indiana-Kentucky state line. A four-lane interstate highway connects the two counties. When other brewers raised their wholesale prices in Indiana, Falls City also raised its prices. Falls City also raised its wholesale prices in Kentucky, but less than its prices were raised in Indiana. Vanco brought this treble damage action against

Falls City, alleging that Falls City had engaged in price discrimination in violation of Section 2(a) of the Robinson-Patman Act by raising prices less in Kentucky than in Indiana. Does the meeting the competition defense protect Falls City Industries from liability for price discrimination? Did Falls City act unethically in this case? [*Falls City Industries, Inc. v. Vanco Beverage, Inc.*, 460 U.S. 428, 103 S.Ct. 1282, 75 L.Ed.2d 174 (1983)]

BRIEFING THE CASE WRITING ASSIGNMENT

Read the following case, which has been excerpted from the court's opinion. Review and brief the case.

Texaco, Inc. v. Hasbrouck, dba Rick's Texaco
496 U.S. 543, 110 S.Ct. 2535, 110 L.Ed. 2d 492 (1990)
United States Supreme Court

Stevens, Justice

Petitioner (Texaco) sold gasoline directly to respondents and several other retailers in Spokane, Washington, at its retail tank wagon prices (RTW) while it granted substantial discounts to two distributors. During the period between 1972 and 1981, the stations supplied by the two distributors increased their sales volume dramatically, while respondents' sales suffered a corresponding decline. Respondents filed an action against Texaco under the Robinson-Patman Amendment to the Clayton Act (Act), alleging that the distributor discounts violated Section 2(a) of the act. Respondents recovered treble damages, and the Court of Appeals for the Ninth Circuit affirmed the judgment. We grant certiorari, to consider Texaco's contention that legitimate functional discounts do not violate the Act because a seller is not responsible for its customers' independent resale pricing decisions. While we agree with the basic thrust of Texaco's argument, we conclude that in this case it is foreclosed by the facts of record.

Respondents are 12 independent Texaco retailers. They displayed the Texaco trademark, accepted Texaco credit cards, and bought their gasoline products directly from Texaco. Texaco delivered the gasoline to respondents' stations.

The retail gasoline market in Spokane was highly competitive throughout the damages period, which ran from 1972 to 1981. Stations marketing the nationally advertised Texaco gasoline competed with other major brands as well as with stations featuring independent brands. Moreover, although discounted prices at a nearby Texaco station would have the most obvious impact on a respondent's trade, the cross-city traffic patterns and relatively small size of Spokane produced a city-wide competitive market. Texaco's throughput sales in the Spokane market declined from a monthly volume of 569,269 gallons in 1970 to 389,557 gallons in 1975. Texaco's independent retailers' share of the market for Texaco gas declined from 76 percent to 49 percent. Seven of the respondents' stations were out of business by the end of 1978.

The respondents tried unsuccessfully to increase their ability to compete with lower priced stations. Some tried converting from full service to self-service stations. Two of the respondents sought to buy their own tank trucks and haul their gasoline from Texaco's supply point, but Texaco vetoed that proposal.

While the independent retailers struggled, two Spokane gasoline distributors supplied by Texaco prospered. Gull Oil Company (Gull) had its headquarters in Seattle and distributed petroleum products in four western states under its own name. In Spokane it purchased its gas from Texaco at prices that ranged from $.06 to $.04 below Texaco's RTW price. Gull resold that product under its own name; the fact that it was being supplied by Texaco

was not known by either the public or the respondents. In Spokane, Gull supplied about 15 stations; some were "consignment stations" and some were "commission stations." In both situations Gull retained title to the gasoline until it was pumped into a motorist's tank. In the consignment stations, the station operator set the retail prices, but in the commission stations Gull set the prices and paid the operator a commission. Its policy was to price its gasoline at a penny less than the prevailing price for major brands. Gull employed two truck drivers in Spokane who picked up product at Texaco's bulk plant and delivered it to the Gull stations. It also employed one supervisor in Spokane. Apart from it trucks and investment in retail facilities. Gull apparently owned no assets in that market. At least with respect to the commission stations, Gull is fairly characterized as a retailer of gasoline throughout the relevant period.

The Dompier Oil Company (Dompier) started business in 1954 selling Quaker State Motor Oil. In 1960 it became a full line distributor of Texaco products, and by the mid-1970s its sales of gasoline represented over three-quarters of its business. Dompier purchased Texaco gasoline at prices of $0.395 to $0.365 cents below the RTW price. Dompier thus paid a higher price than Gull, but Dompier, unlike Gull, resold its gas under the Texaco brand names. It supplied about 8 to 10 Spokane retail stations. In the period prior to October 1974, 2 of those stations were owned by the president of Dompier but the others were independently operated. In the early 1970s, Texaco representatives encouraged Dompier to enter the retail business directly, and in 1974 and 1975 it acquired 4 stations. Dompier's president estimated at trial that the share of its total gasoline sales made at retail during the middle 1970s was "probably 84 to 90 percent."

Like Gull, Dompier picked up Texaco's product at the Texaco bulk plant and delivered directly to retail outlets. Unlike Gull, Dompier owned a bulk storage facility, but it was seldom used because its capacity was less than that of many retail stations. Again, unlike Gull, Dompier received from Texaco the equivalent of the common carrier rate for delivering the gasoline product to the retail outlets. Thus, in addition to its discount from the RTW price, Dompier made a profit on its hauling function.

The stations supplied by Dompier regularly sold at retail at lower prices than respondents, Even before Dompier directly entered the retail business in 1974, its customers were selling to consumers at prices barely above the RTW price. Dompier's sales volume increased continuously and substantially throughout the relevant period. Between 1970–1975 its monthly sales volume increased from 155,152 gallons to 462,956 gallons; this represented an increase from 20.7 percent to almost 50 percent of Texaco's sales in Spokane.

There was ample evidence that Texaco executives were well aware of Dompier's dramatic growth and believed that it was attributable to "the magnitude of the distributor discount and the hauling allowance." In response to complaints from individual respondents about Dompier's aggressive pricing, however, Texaco representatives professed that they couldn't understand it.

Respondents filed suit against Texaco in July 1976. After a four-week trial, the jury awarded damages measured by the difference between the RTW price and the price paid by Dompier. As we subsequently decided in J. Truett Payne Co. v. Chrysler Motors Corp., this measure of damages was improper. Accordingly, although it rejected Texaco's defenses on the issue of liability, the Court of Appeals for the Ninth Circuit remanded the case for a new trial.

At the second trial, Texaco contended that the special prices to Gull and Dompier were justified by cost savings, were the product of a good faith attempt to meet competition, and were lawful "functional discounts." The District Court withheld the cost justification defense from the jury because it was not supported by the evidence and the jury rejected the other defenses. It awarded the respondents actual damages of $449,900. The jury apparently credited the testimony of the respondents' expert witness who had estimated what the respondents' profits would have been if they had paid the same prices as the four stations owned by Dompier.

In Texaco's motion for judgment notwithstanding the verdict, it claimed as a matter of law that its functional discounts did not adversely affect competition within the meaning of the Act because any injury to respondents was attributable to decisions made independently by Dompier. The District Court denied the motion. In an opinion supplementing its oral ruling denying Texaco's motion for a directed verdict, the Court assumed, arguendo, that Dompier was entitled to a functional discount, even on the gas that was sold at retail, but nevertheless concluded that the "presumed legality of functional discounts" had been rebutted by evidence that the amount of the discounts to Gull and Dompier was not reasonably related to the cost of any function that they performed.

*The Court of Appeals affirmed. It reasoned: "As the Supreme Court long ago made clear, and recently reaffirmed, there may be a Robinson-Patman violation even if the favored and disfavored buyers do not compete, so long as the customers of the favored buyer compete with the disfavored buyer or its customers. Despite the fact that Dompier and Gull, at least in their capacities as wholesalers, did not compete directly with Hasbrouck, a Section 2(a) violation may occur if (1) the discount they received was not cost-based and (2) all or a portion of it was passed on by them to customers of theirs who competed with Hasbrouck. Hasbrouck pre-*sented ample evidence to demonstrate that the services performed by Gull and Dompier were insubstantial and did not justify the functional discount."*

The Court of Appeals concluded its analysis by observing: "To hold that price discrimination between a wholesaler and a retailer could never violate the Robinson-Patman Act would leave immune from antitrust scrutiny a discriminatory pricing procedure that can effectively serve to harm competition. We think such a result would be contrary to the objectives of the Robinson-Patman Act."

In order to establish a violation of the Act, respondent had the burden of proving four facts: (1) that Texaco's sales to Gull and Dompier were made in interstate commerce, (2) that the gasoline sold to them was of the same grade and quality as that sold to respondents, (3) that Texaco discriminated in price as between Gull and Dompier on the one hand and respondents on the other, and (4) that the discrimination had a prohibited effect on competition. Moreover, for each respondent to recover damages, he had the burden of proving the extent of his actual injuries.

The first two elements of respondents' case are not disputed in this Court, and we do not understand Texaco to be challenging the sufficiency of respondents' proof of damages. Texaco does argue, however, that although it charged different prices, it did not "discriminate in price" within the meaning of the Act, and that, at least to the extent that Gull and Dompier acted as wholesalers, the price differentials did not injure competition. We consider the two arguments separately.

A supplier need not satisfy the rigorous requirements of the cost justification defense in order to prove that a particular functional discount is reasonable and accordingly did not cause any substantial lessening of competition between a wholesaler's customers and the supplier's direct customers. The record in this case, however, adequately supports the finding that Texaco violated the Act.

The proof established that Texaco's lower prices to gull and Dompier were discriminatory throughout the entire nine-year period; that at least Gull, and apparently Dompier as well, was selling at retail during that entire period; that the discounts substantially affected competition throughout the entire market; and that they injured each of the respondents. There is no doubt that respondents' proof of a continuing violation of the Act throughout the nine-year period was sufficient.

The judgment is affirmed.

ENDNOTES

1. Antitrust Amendments Act of 1990, P.L. 101–588.
2. Antitrust Amendments Act of 1990, P.L. 101–588.
3. 15 U.S.C. § 15.
4. *Reiter v. Sonotone Corporation*, 442 U.S. 330, 99 S.Ct. 2326 (1979).
5. 15 U.S.C. § 26.
6. Justice Marshall, *United States v. Topco Associates, Inc.*, 405 U.S. 596, 92 S.Ct. 1126 (1972).
7. 221 U.S. 1, 31 S.Ct. 502 (1911). The Court found that Rockefeller's oil trust violated the Sherman Act and ordered the trust broken up into 30 separate companies.
8. *Continental T.V., Inc. v. GTE Sylvania, Inc.*, 433 U.S. 36, 97 S.Ct. 2549 (1977), reversing *United States v. Arnold Schwinn & Co.*, 388 U.S. 365, 87 S.Ct. 1856 (1969).
9. 250 U.S. 300, 39 S.Ct. 465 (1919).
10. This doctrine is the result of two U.S. Supreme Court decisions: *Eastern R.R. President's Conference v. Noerr Motor Freight, Inc.*, 365 U.S. 127, 81 S.Ct. 523 (1961), and *United Mine Workers v. Pennington*, 381 U.S. 657, 85 S.Ct. 1585 (1965).
11. *William Inglis & Sons Baking Company v. ITT Continental Baking Company, Inc.*, 668 F.2d 1014 (9th Cir. 1982).

12. 374 U.S. 321, 83 S.Ct. 1715 (1963).
13. 15 U.S.C. § 18(a).
14. 15 U.S.C. § 14.
15. *Hartley & Parker, Inc. v. Florida Beverage Corp.*, 307 F.2d 916, 923 (5th Cir. 1952).
16. 15 U.S.C. § 13(b).
17. Section 6 of the Clayton Act, 15 U.S.C. § 17; the Norris-LaGuardia Act of 1932, 29 U.S.C. §§ 101–155; and the National Labor Relations Act of 1935, 29 U.S.C. §§ 141 et seq. Labor unions that conspire or combine with nonlabor groups to accomplish a goal prohibited by federal antitrust law lose their exemption.
18. Capper-Volstrand Act of 1922, 7 U.S.C. § 291; Cooperative Marketing Act of 1926, 15 U.S.C. § 521.
19. Webb-Pomerene Act, 15 U.S.C. §§ 61–65.
20. McCarran-Ferguson Act of 1945, 15 U.S.C. §§ 1011–1015.
21. *Community Communications Co., Inc. v. City of Boulder*, 455 U.S. 40, 102 S.Ct. 835 (1982).
22. *Goldfarb v. Virginia State Bar*, 421 U.S. 773, 95 S.Ct. 2004 (1975).
23. For example, see *California v. ARC America Corporation*, 490 U.S. 93, 109 S.Ct. 1661 (1989).

Property and Insurance

Personal Property and Bailments

*P*roperty and law are born and must die together.

—Jeremy Bentham
Principles of the Civil Code, 1 Works 309

Chapter Contents

Chapter Objectives

After studying this chapter, you should be able to:

1. Define *personal property*.

2. Describe the methods for acquiring ownership in personal property.

3. Explain how ownership rights are transferred by gift *inter vivos* and gift *causa mortis*.

4. Describe how title to personal property is acquired by purchase, production, accession, and confusion.

5. Describe and apply rules regarding ownership rights in mislaid, lost, and abandoned property.

6. Define *ordinary bailments*.

7. List and describe the elements for creating a bailment.

8. List and describe the rights and duties of bailors and bailees.

9. Explain the liability of bailees for lost, damaged, or destroyed goods in ordinary bailment situations.

10. Explain the liability of bailees in special bailment situations.

Private ownership of property forms the foundation of our economic system. As such, a comprehensive body of law has been developed to protect property rights. The law protects the rights of property owners to use, sell, dispose of, control, and prevent others from trespassing on their rights.

In this country, property is expressly protected by the U.S. Constitution. The Fifth Amendment provides, "No person shall be . . . deprived of life, liberty, or property, without due process of law; nor shall private property be taken for public use, without just compensation." The Fourteenth Amendment provides, "No State shall . . . deprive any person of life, liberty, or property, without due process of law." These rights are not absolute. The government can acquire private property for public use (e.g., for highways, parks) as long as it pays just compensation for the property.

The first part of this chapter discusses the kinds of personal property, methods of acquiring ownership in personal property, and property rights in mislaid, lost, and abandoned property. The second part of this chapter discusses bailment, situations where possession of (but not title to) personal property is delivered to another party for transfer, safekeeping, or some other purpose.

Property is the most ambiguous of categories. It covers a multitude of rights which have nothing in common except that they are exercised by persons and enforced by the state.

R. H. Tawney
The Acquisitive Society
Ch. V (1921)

$\mathcal{T}$HE NATURE OF PERSONAL PROPERTY

There are two kinds of property: real property and personal property. **Real property** includes land and property that is permanently attached to it. For example, minerals, crops, timber, and buildings that are attached to land are generally considered real property. **Personal property** (sometimes referred to as goods or chattels) consists of everything that is not real property. Real property can become personal property if it is removed from the land. For example, a tree that is part of a forest is real property; a tree that is cut down is personal property.

Personal property that is permanently affixed to land or buildings is called a **fixture**. Such property, which includes things like heating systems and storm windows, is categorized as real property. Unless otherwise agreed, fixtures remain with a building when it is sold. Personal property (e.g., furniture, pictures, other easily portable household items) may be removed by the seller prior to sale.

Personal property can be either tangible or intangible. **Tangible property** includes physically defined property such as goods, animals, and minerals. **Intangible property** represents rights that cannot be reduced to physical form, stock certificates, certificates of deposit, bonds, and copyrights are examples of intangible property.

Real and personal property may be owned by one person or by more than one person. If property is owned concurrently by two or more persons, there is **concurrent ownership**.

real property

The land itself as well as buildings, trees, soil, minerals, timber, plants, and other things permanently affixed to the land.

personal property

Property that consists of tangible property such as automobiles, furniture, and jewelry, and intangible property such as securities, patents, and copyrights.

tangible property

All real property and physically defined personal property such as buildings, goods, animals, and minerals.

intangible property

Rights that cannot be reduced to physical form such as stock certificates, certificates of deposit, bonds, and copyrights.

Spinner Domestic animals are the personal property of their owners. This dog is the author's bearded collie, Moonspinner (a.k.a. Spinner).

*A*CQUIRING OWNERSHIP IN PERSONAL PROPERTY

The right of property enables an industrious man to reap where he has sown.

Anonymous

Personal property may be acquired or transferred with a minimum of formality. Commerce would be severely curtailed if the transfer of such items were difficult. The methods for acquiring ownership in personal property are discussed below.

By Possession

taking possession

A method of acquiring ownership of unowned personal property.

A person can acquire ownership in unowned personal property by **taking possession** of it or **capturing** it. The most notable unowned objects are things in their natural state. For example, people who obtain the proper fishing license acquire ownership of all the fish they catch. This type of property acquisition was important when this country was being developed. In today's urbanized society, however, there are few unowned objects, and this method of acquiring ownership in personal property has become less important.

By Purchase or Production

purchasing property

The most common method of acquiring title to personal property.

The most common method of acquiring title to personal property is by **purchasing** the property from its owner. For example, Urban Concrete Corporation owns a larger piece of equipment. City Builders, Inc., purchases the equipment from Urban Concrete for $50,000. Urban Concrete signs over the title to the equipment to City Builders. City Builders is now the owner of the equipment.

Production is another common method of acquiring ownership in personal property. Thus, a manufacturer who purchases raw materials and produces a finished product owns that product.

*B*usiness *E*thics

WHAT'S MINE IS MINE AND WHAT'S YOURS IS MINE

The Beech Aircraft Corporation (Beech) and Lowell and Aileen Anderson owned adjacent property in Kansas. The Stalmaker gas reserve, which had long ago been drilled and depleted of natural gas, underlies both properties.

Beech purchased natural gas for its own use and for sale. Ground storage of natural gas is almost impossible because it is not economically feasible to build containers large enough to hold the gas, so Beech began storing gas in the Stalmaker reserve. It purchased large quantities of natural gas from interstate pipelines and injected it through wells into the reservoir. There was only one problem: The natural gas flowed into the reservoir and came to rest under both Beech's and the Anderson's property. Beech did not obtain a lease, license, or permit from the Andersons to store the gas under their property.

Avanti Petroleum (Avanti) held an oil and gas lease on the Anderson farm. When it discovered that the natural gas was under the property, it began drilling and extracting the natural gas with full knowledge that Beech had placed it there. A lawsuit between Beech and Avanti ensued. Beech argued that it owned the gas because it had paid for it. Avanti argued that because the gas migrated to its lease field, it could rightfully extract it.

The Kansas Supreme Court decided in favor of Avanti. The court stated

As far as natural gas is concerned, Kansas has long recognized the law of capture, holding that natural gas in the ground is part of the real estate until it is actually produced and severed. At that point, it becomes personalty. The courts have also recognized the nature of oil and gas as being fugitive and migratory, having the power and tendency to escape without the volition of its owner. The courts have analogized oil and gas to wild animals or animals ferae naturale. The ownership of birds and wild animals becomes vested in the person capturing or reducing them to possession. However, when restored to their natural wild and free state, the dominion and individual proprietorship of any person over them is at an end, and they resume their status as common property.

Thus, legally Beech had lost its ownership interest in the natural gas when it flowed under the Andersons' farm. Avanti could drill for the natural gas that Beech had already paid for. [*Anderson v. Beech Aircraft Corp.*, 699 P.2d 1023 (KS 1985)]

1. Did Avanti act ethically when it drilled for and removed the natural gas it knew had been paid for and stored in the underground reserve by Beech?
2. Should Beech have requested and received permission from the Andersons before storing the natural gas beneath the Andersons' property? Did it get what it deserved?

By Gift

A **gift** is a voluntary transfer of property without consideration. The lack of consideration is what distinguishes a gift from a purchase. The person making a gift is called the **donor**. The person who receives the gift is called the **donee**. There are three elements of a valid gift: donative intent, delivery, and acceptance.

1. **Donative Intent** For a gift to be effective, the donor must have intended to make a gift. Donative intent can be inferred from the circumstances or language used by the donor. The courts also consider such factors as the relationship of the parties, the size of the gift, and the mental capacity of the donor.
2. **Delivery** Delivery must occur for there to be a valid gift. Although **physical delivery** is the usual method of transferring personal property, it is sometimes impracticable. In such circumstances, **constructive delivery** (or **symbolic delivery**) is sufficient. For example, if the property being gifted is kept in a safe-deposit box, physically giving the key to the donee is enough to signal the gift. Most intangible property is transferred by written conveyance (e.g., conveying a stock certificate represents a transfer of ownership in a corporation).
3. **Acceptance** Acceptance is usually not a problem because most donees readily accept gifts. In fact, the courts presume acceptance unless there is proof that the gift was refused. Nevertheless, a person cannot be forced to accept an unwanted gift.

Gifts* Inter Vivos *and Gifts* Causa Mortis** A gift made during a person's lifetime which is an irrevocable present transfer of ownership is a **gift *inter vivos*.** A **gift *causa mortis is a gift made in contemplation of death. A gift *causa mortis* is established when (1) the donor makes a gift in anticipation of approaching death from some existing sickness or peril and (2) the donor dies from such sickness or peril without having revoked the gift. Gifts *causa mortis* can be revoked by the donor up until the time he or she dies. A gift *causa mortis* takes precedent over a prior conflicting will.

Consider This Example Suppose Sandy is a patient in the hospital. She is to have a major operation from which she may not recover. Prior to going into surgery, Sandy removes her diamond ring and gives it to her friend Pamela, stating, "In the event of my death, I want you to have this." This gift is a gift *causa mortis*. If Sandy dies from the operation, the gift is effective and Pamela owns the ring. If Sandy lives, the requisite condition for the gift (her death) has not occurred; therefore, the gift is not effective and Sandy can recover the ring from Pamela.

In the following case, the court had to determine whether a gift had been made of a valuable painting.

gift
A voluntary transfer of title to property without payment of consideration by the donee. To be a valid gift, three elements must be shown: (1) *donative intent,* (2) *delivery,* and (3) *acceptance.*

donor
A person who gives a gift.

donee
A person who receives a gift.

Business Brief
The donee must accept the gift for the gift to be effective.

gift *inter vivos*
A gift made during a person's lifetime that is an irrevocable present transfer of ownership.

gift *causa mortis*
A gift that is made in contemplation of death.

Gruen v. Gruen
505 N.Y.S.2d 849 (1986)
Court of Appeals of New York

CASE 36.1

BACKGROUND AND FACTS
Victor Gruen was a successful architect. In 1959, Victor purchased a painting entitled *Schloss Kammer am Attersee II* by a noted Austrian modernist, Gustav Klimt, and paid $8,000 for the painting. In 1963, Victor wrote a letter to his son Michael, then an undergraduate student at Harvard University, giving the painting to Michael but reserving a life estate in the painting. The letter stated

Dear Michael:
The 21st birthday, being an important event in life, should be celebrated accordingly. I therefore wish to give you as a present the oil painting by Gustav Klimt of Schloss Kammer which now hangs in the New York living room.
Happy birthday again.
Love,
s/Victor

Because Victor retained a life interest in the painting, Michael never took possession of the painting. Victor died on February 14, 1980. The painting was appraised at $2.5 million. When Michael requested the painting from his stepmother, Kemija Gruen, she refused to turn it over to him. Michael sued to recover the painting. The trial court held in favor of the stepmother. The appellate division reversed. The stepmother appealed.

ISSUE
Did Victor Gruen make a valid gift *inter vivos* of the Klimt painting to his son Michael?

COURT'S REASONING
The appellate court held that the elements necessary to create a valid gift *inter vivos* had been met. First, the court held

that the evidence was conclusive that Victor had the requisite *donative intent* to transfer ownership of the painting to Michael in 1963. Second, the court stated that physical *delivery* of the painting was not required in this case because Victor intended to retain a life estate in the painting. The court held that Victor's letter constituted constructive delivery of the painting. Third, the court found that Michael had *accepted* the gift. Evidence showed that Michael had told several of his friends and classmates about the gift when it was made in 1963 and that he had retained the letter for more than 17 years to verify the gift after his father died.

DECISION

The appellate court held that Victor Gruen had made a valid gift *inter vivos* of the Klimt painting to his son Michael. The court affirmed the judgment of the appellate division in favor of Michael Gruen.

Case Questions

Critical Legal Thinking   Should donors who make gifts *inter vivos* be required to relinquish physical possession of the property to the donee?

Business Ethics   Did the stepmother act ethically in refusing to turn the painting over to Michael?

Uniform Gift to Minors Act and Revised Uniform Gift to Minors Act

Acts that establish procedures for adults to make gifts of money and securities to minors.

Uniform Gifts to Minor Acts   All states have adopted in whole or part the **Uniform Gift to Minors Act** or the **Revised Uniform Gift to Minors Act**. These laws establish procedures for adults to make irrevocable gifts of money and securities to minors. Gifts of money can be made by depositing the money in an account with a financial institution with the donor or another trustee (such as another adult or bank) as custodian for the minor. Gifts of securities can be made by registering the securities in the name of a trustee as custodian for the minor. The laws give custodians broad discretionary powers to invest the money or securities for the benefit of the minor.

Personal property is often transferred by gift. The person who makes the gift is called the donor, *and the person who receives the gift is called the* donee.

will or inheritance

A way to acquire title to property that is a result of another's death.

By Will or Inheritance

Title to personal property is frequently acquired by **will** or **inheritance**. If the person who dies has a valid will, the property is distributed to the **beneficiaries**, pursuant to the provisions of that will. Otherwise, the property is distributed to the **heirs** as provided in the relevant state's inheritance statute.

accession

Occurs when the value of personal property increases because it is added to or improved by natural or manufactured means.

By Accession

Accession occurs when the value of personal property increases because it is added to or improved by natural or manufactured means. Accession that occurs naturally belongs to the owner (e.g., a colt that is born to a mare belongs to the mare's owner). If accession occurs by manufactured means and the owner consents to the improvement, the owner acquires title to the improvement but must pay the improver for labor and services. For example, a business owner who contracts to have an addition built onto his factory owns the new structure but must pay the contract price to the improver.

Wrongful Improvement If the improvement was made wrongfully, the owner acquires title to the improved property and does not have to pay the improver for the value of the improvements. For example, suppose a thief steals the car and puts a new engine in it. The owner is entitled to recover the car as improved without having to pay the thief for the improvements.

Mistaken Improvement If the improvement was mistakenly made by the improver, the courts generally follow these rules:

1. If the improvements can be easily separated from the original article, the improver must remove the improvements and pay any damages caused by such removal. For example, a builder who puts the wrong door on a house must replace that door with the correct door at his own cost.
2. If the improvements cannot be removed, the owner owns title to the improved property and does not have to pay the improver for the improvements. For example, a builder misreads blueprints and extends an addition to a building too far, the building owner is entitled to keep the improvement at no extra cost. In some cases, if the improvements are substantial and cannot be removed, the court can permit the improver to acquire title to the personal property by paying the owner the value of the original article.

By Confusion

Confusion occurs if two or more persons commingle fungible goods (i.e., goods that are exactly alike, such as the same grade of oil, grains, or cattle). Title to goods can be acquired by confusion.

The owners share ownership in the commingled goods in proportion to the amount of goods contributed. It does not matter whether the goods were commingled by agreement or by accident. For example, if three farmers agree to store the same amount of grade B winter wheat in a silo, each of them owns one third. When the grain is sold, the profits are divided into three parts; if the silo burns to the ground, each suffers one third of the loss. If goods are wrongfully or intentionally commingled without permission, the innocent party acquires title to them.

confusion

Occurs if two or more persons commingle fungible goods; title is then acquired by confusion.

By Divorce

When a marriage is dissolved by a divorce, the parties obtain certain rights in the property of the marital estate. Often, a settlement of property rights is reached. If not, the court must decide the property rights of the spouses. In the following case, the court decided the spouse's ownership right to personal property upon divorce.

Laws are always useful to persons of property, and hurtful to those who have none.

Jean-Jacques Rousseau
Du Contrat Social (1761)

Giha v. Giha
609 A.2d 945 (1992)
Supreme Court of Rhode Island

CASE 36.2

BACKGROUND AND FACTS
On October 7, 1987, Nagib Giha (husband) filed a complaint for divorce from Nelly Giha (wife) on the grounds of irreconcilable differences. On May 20, 1988, the parties reached an agreement for the disposition of their property that provided that they would divide equally the net proceeds from the sale of their marital assets. They had to wait a statutory waiting period before the divorce was final. On December 25, 1988, the husband learned that he had won $2.4 million in the Massachusetts MEGABUCKS state lottery. The husband kept this fact secret. After the waiting period was over, the family court entered its final judgment, severing the parties' marriage on April 27, 1989. The husband claimed his lottery

prize on October 6, 1989. In December 1990, after learning of the lottery winnings, the wife sued to recover the lottery prize. She alleged that the lottery prize was a marital asset because her husband had won it before their divorce was final. The trial court dismissed her complaint. The wife appealed.

ISSUE
Was the $2.4-million lottery prize personal property of the marital estate?

COURT'S REASONING
The court held that the marital agreement did not sever either the matrimonial or economic ties between the husband and

the wife. Because the parties' marriage remained in effect during the statutory waiting period, so did the property rights of each spouse during that period. The court concluded that the lottery prize was a marital asset.

DECISION

The appellate court held that the parties remained as husband and wife until the entry of final judgment of divorce in April 1989. Therefore, the lottery prize was a marital asset. Reversed and remanded.

Case Questions

Critical Legal Thinking   Should a spouse's lottery winnings be considered separate property? Why or why not?

Business Ethics   Did the husband act ethically in this case?

MISLAID, LOST, AND ABANDONED PROPERTY

> *Personal property has no locality.*
>
> C.J. Lord Loughborough
> Sill v. Worswick *(1971)*

Often, people find another person's personal property. Ownership rights to the property differ depending on whether the property is mislaid, lost, or abandoned. The following paragraphs discuss these legal rules.

Mislaid Property

mislaid property
When an owner voluntarily places property somewhere and then inadvertently forgets it.

Property is **mislaid** when its owner voluntarily places the property somewhere and then inadvertently forgets it. It is likely that the owner will return for the property upon realizing that it was misplaced.

The owner of the premises where the property is mislaid is entitled to take possession of the property against all except the rightful owner. This right is superior to the rights of the person who finds it. Such possession does not involve a change of title. Instead, the owner of the premises becomes an involuntary bailee of the property (bailments are discussed later in this chapter) and owes a duty to take reasonable care of the property until it is reclaimed by the owner.

Business Brief
The owner of the premises where personal property is *mislaid* is entitled to take possession of the property against all except the rightful owner.

Lost Property

lost property
When a property owner leaves property somewhere because of negligence, carelessness, or inadvertence.

Property is considered **lost** when its owner negligently, carelessly, or inadvertently leaves it somewhere. The finder obtains title to such property against the whole world except the true owner. The lost property must be returned to its rightful owner whether he or she discovers the loser's identity or the loser finds him or her. A finder who refuses to return the property is liable for the tort of conversion and the crime of larceny. Many states require the finder to conduct a reasonable search (e.g., place advertisements in newspapers) to find the rightful owner.

Business Brief
The finder of *lost property* obtains title to the found property against everyone except the true owner.

Consider This Example   If a commuter finds a diamond ring on the floor of a subway station in New York City, the ring is considered lost property. The finder can claim title to the ring against the whole world except the true owner. If the true owner discovers that the finder has her ring, she may recover it from the finder.

Business Ethics

ESTRAY STATUTES

Most states have enacted **estray statutes** that permit a finder of *mislaid* or *lost* property to clear title to the property if

1. The finder reports the found property to the appropriate government agency and then turns over possession of the property to this agency,

2. Either the finder or the government agency posts notices and publishes advertisements describing the lost property, and

3. A specified time (usually a year or a number of years) has passed without the rightful owner's reclaiming the property.

Many state estray statutes provide that the government receive a portion of the value of the property. Some statutes provide that title cannot be acquired in found property that is the result of illegal activity. For example, title has been denied to finders of property and money deemed to have been used for illegal drug purchases.

Consider the following case. While hunting on unposted and unoccupied property in Oceola Township, Michigan, Duane Willsmore noticed an area with branches arranged in a crisscross pattern. When he kicked aside the branches and sod, he found a watertight suitcase in a freshly dug hole. Willsmore informed the Michigan state police of his find. A state trooper and Willsmore together pried open the suitcase and discovered $383,840 in cash. The state police took custody of the money, which was deposited in an interest-bearing account. Michigan's estray statute provides that the finder and the township in which the property was found must share the value of the property if the finder publishes required notices and the true owner does not claim the property within one year. Willsmore published the required notices and brought a declaratory judgment action seeking a determination of the ownership of the money. After one year had gone by and the rightful owner had not claimed the briefcase, the court ordered that Willsmore and the Township of Oceola were equal one-half owners of the briefcase and its contents. [*Willsmore v. Township of Oceola, Michigan*, 308 N.W.2d 796 (Mich.App. 1981)]

1. Would you have turned the suitcase in to the police?

Abandoned Property

Property is classified as **abandoned** if (1) an owner discards the property with the intent to relinquish his or her rights in it or (2) an owner of mislaid or lost property gives up any further attempts to locate it. Anyone who finds abandoned property acquires title to it. The title is good against the whole world, including the original owner. For example, property left at a garbage dump is abandoned property. It belongs to the first person who claims it.

abandoned property

Property that an owner has discarded with the intent to relinquish his or her rights in it and mislaid or lost property that the owner has given up any further attempts to locate.

Entrepreneur and the Law

WHO OWNS THE TREASURE TROVE ON THE *SS CENTRAL AMERICA*?

On Saturday, September 12, 1857, the *SS Central America*, a luxurious steamship that made frequent trips between New York and Panama, lost a desperate three-day battle to keep itself afloat. It sank 169 miles off the coast of South Carolina. The ship carried 587 passengers, many of whom were returning from California, where they had recovered gold from newly discovered mines. Only 166 passengers survived. Insurance companies paid claims for the $1.2 million (1857 value) of gold coins and bricks that sank with the ship.

For nearly 130 years, the *SS Central America* lay peacefully in the icy waters off the East Coast. While many dreamed of finding the ship and its cargo, which is estimated to be worth up to $1 billion in today's market, no one knew exactly where to look.

In 1981, Thomas G. Thompson, an Ohio-based scientist and entrepreneur, organized an expedition called the Columbus-America Discovery Group to recover the sunken ship by submerging a 5,000-pound robot, with a video camera attached to its arm, into the water. Finally, in 1987, the robot found what Thompson had been tirelessly searching for—the *SS Central America* and its undisturbed cargo of thousands of rare gold coins and even rarer gold bars.

When the jubilant Thompson and crew returned to port, they were greeted by more than just well-wishers. Representatives of several insurance companies immediately claimed that some of the *SS Central America's* loot belonged to them as compensation for the claims they had paid 130 years earlier.

Thompson's group sought to vindicate its exclusive right to the *SS Central America* and her cargo by filing an action in federal court. The U.S. court of appeals applied the maritime **Law of Salvage**. Under the doctrine, original owners retain ownership interest, although the salvager is entitled to a very liberal salvage award.

The district court determined that the salvager was entitled to 90 percent of the gold coins and other treasure trove found on the *SS Central America*. The court of appeals affirmed this award. [*Columbus-America Discovery Group v. Atlantic Mutual Insurance Company*, 56 F.2d 556 (4th Cir. 1995)]

CONCEPT SUMMARY RULES REGARDING OWNERSHIP RIGHTS IN MISLAID, LOST, AND ABANDONED PROPERTY

Common Law Rules

Type of Property	Ownership Rights
Mislaid property	The owner of the premises where property is mislaid is entitled to possession but does not acquire title. He or she holds the property as an involuntary bailee until the owner reclaims it.
Lost property	The finder acquires title to the property against the whole world except the true owner; the owner may reclaim his or her property from the finder.
Abandoned property	The finder acquires title to the property, even against its original owner.

Estray Statutes

Many states have enacted estray statutes that give a finder of mislaid or lost property clear title to the property if certain requirements are met, including (1) reporting the find to an appropriate government agency, (2) advertising the lost property, and (3) the owner not claiming the property within a stated time period (e.g., one year). The finder acquires title to the property and is thereafter not required to return the property if the rightful owner appears to claim it.

BAILMENTS

bailment

A transaction where an owner transfers his or her personal property to another to be held, stored, delivered, or for some other purpose. Title to the property does not transfer.

bailor

The owner of property in a bailment.

bailee

A holder of goods who is not a seller or a buyer (e.g., a warehouse or common carrier).

A **bailment** occurs when the owner of personal property delivers his or her property to another person either to be held, stored, or delivered or for some other purpose. In a bailment, the owner of the property is the **bailor**. The party to whom the property is delivered for safekeeping, storage, or delivery (e.g., warehouse, common carrier) is the **bailee** (see Exhibit 36.1). Almost everyone has been involved in a bailment transaction.

A bailment is different than a sale or a gift because title to the goods does not transfer to the bailee. Instead, the bailee must follow the bailor's directions concerning the goods. For example, suppose Hudson Corporation is relocating offices and hires American Van Lines to move its office furniture and equipment to the new location. American Van Lines (the bailee) must follow Hudson's (the bailor's) instructions regarding delivery. The law of bailments establishes the rights, duties, and liabilities of parties to a bailment.

Bailment A bailment would be created where an owner of an automobile lends it to another person. The owner is the bailor and the borrower is the bailee.

Exhibit **36.1** *Parties to a Bailment*

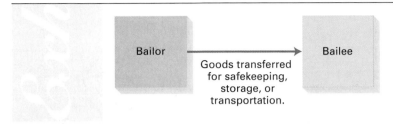

Elements Necessary to Create a Bailment

Three **elements** are necessary **to create a bailment**: personal property, delivery of possession, and a bailment agreement.

1. **Personal Property** Only **personal property** can be bailed. The property can be **tangible** (e.g., automobiles, jewelry, animals) or **intangible** (e.g., stocks, bonds, and promissory notes).
2. **Delivery of Possession** Delivery of possession involves two elements: (1) The bailee has exclusive control over the personal property, and (2) the bailee must knowingly accept the personal property. For example, no bailment is created if a patron goes into a restaurant and hangs her coat on an unattended coat rack because other patrons have access to the coat. A bailment, however, is created if the patron checked her coat with a checkroom attendant because the restaurant has assumed exclusive control over the coat. If valuable property was left in the pocket of the coat, there would be no bailment of that property since the checkroom attendant did not knowingly accept it. Most bailments are created by **physical delivery**. For example, Great Lakes Shipping, Inc., delivers a vessel to Marina Repairs, Inc., for repairs. **Constructive delivery** can create a bailment, too. For example, there has been constructive delivery of an automobile if the owner gives someone the keys and registration to his car.
3. **Bailment Agreement** The creation of a bailment does not require any formality. A bailment may be either express or implied. Most **express bailments** can be either written or oral. Under the Statute of Frauds, however, a bailment must be in writing if it is for more than one year. An example of an **implied bailment** is the finding and safeguarding of lost property.

Bailments generally expire at a specified time or when a certain purpose is accomplished. A **bailment for a fixed term** terminates at the end of the term or sooner by mutual consent of the parties. A party who terminates a bailment in breach of the bailment agreement is liable to the innocent party for damages resulting from the breach. Bailments without a fixed term are called **bailments at will**. A bailment at will can be terminated at any time by either party. Gratuitous bailees can generally be permitted to terminate a fixed-term bailment prior to expiration of the term.

Upon termination of the bailment, the bailee is legally obligated to do as the bailor directs with the property. Unless otherwise agreed, the bailee is obligated to return the identical goods bailed. Where commingled **fungible goods** are involved (e.g., grain), identically equivalent goods may be returned by the bailee.

In the following case, the court had to determine whether a bailment had been created.

elements of a bailment
The following three elements are necessary to create a bailment: (1) personal property, (2) delivery of possession, and (3) a bailment agreement.

bailment for a fixed term
A bailment that terminates at the end of the term or sooner by mutual consent of the parties.

bailment at will
A bailment without a fixed term; can be terminated at any time by either party.

Magliocco v. American Locker Co., Inc.
239 Cal.Rptr. 497 (1987)
Court of Appeals of California

CASE 36.3

BACKGROUND AND FACTS
Richard George Whitehurst told Salvatore Magliocco that he could buy gold that had been smuggled out of Vietnam by American soldiers who now sought to sell it. Magliocco agreed to purchase the gold for $409,000. To pay for the gold, Magliocco placed $409,000 cash in a locked briefcase, which was then placed in a suitcase provided by Whitehurst that had

a combination lock. Both men knew the combination. They then went to the Richmond, California, Greyhound bus station, where Magliocco placed the suitcase in a coin-operated locker owned and operated by American Locker Company, Inc. Magliocco kept the key.

Shortly thereafter, a Whitehurst accomplice told an employee of the Greyhound station that he had lost the key to his locker. The employee opened the locker with a master key. When the man opened the combination lock to the briefcase, the employee released the suitcase to him. When Whitehurst did not contact Magliocco as planned to permit him to inspect the gold, Magliocco discovered the locker was empty. Magliocco sued Greyhound Lines, Inc., and American Locker Company, Inc., for damages. The jury found a bailment and held in favor of Magliocco. The defendants appealed.

ISSUE
Was a bailment created between Magliocco and Greyhound and American Locker?

COURT'S REASONING
The appellate court held that a necessary element of bailment—that possession of the stored goods is given to the bailee—is not established in a case involving use of a coin-operated locker. The court reasoned that no bailment existed because the user who retains a key to the locker never relinquishes primary physical control of the items stored, even if

the person making the lockers available has a master key. Thus, one who stores items in a coin-operated locker does not create a bailment.

DECISION
The court held that a bailment was not created when Magliocco used the coin-operated locker at the Richmond Greyhound bus station. The appellate court reversed the trial court's judgment and ordered Magliocco to pay all costs of the appeal.

Case Questions

Critical Legal Thinking   Do you think the assessment of the loss fell on the proper party? Why or why not?

Business Ethics   Did Magliocco act ethically in suing Greyhound and American Locker? Whose fault was it that the money was stolen?

Contemporary Business   What would be the impact on coin-operated locker businesses if the jury's verdict were allowed to stand?

Ordinary Bailments

ordinary bailments

(1) Bailments for the sole benefit of the bailor, (2) bailments for the sole benefit of the bailee, and (3) bailments for the mutual benefit of the bailor and bailee.

There are three classifications of **ordinary bailments**. The importance of these categories is the degree of care owed by the bailee in protecting the bailed property. The three types of ordinary bailments are bailments for the sole benefit of the bailor, bailments for the sole benefit of the bailee, and mutual benefit bailments.

bailment for the sole benefit of the bailor

A gratuitous bailment that benefits only the bailor. The bailee owes only a *duty of slight care* to protect the bailed property.

Bailments for the sole benefit of the bailor are **gratuitous bailments** that benefit only the bailor. They arise when the bailee is requested to care for the bailor's property as a favor. The bailee owes only a **duty of slight care** to protect the bailed property; that is, he or she owes a duty not to be grossly negligent in caring for the bailed goods.

duty of slight care

A duty not to be grossly negligent in caring for something in one's responsibility.

Consider This Example   The Watkins are going on vacation and ask their neighbors, the Smiths, to feed their dog, which is allowed to run free. The Smiths diligently feed the dog, but the dog runs away and does not return. The Smiths are not liable for the loss of the dog.

An **involuntary bailment** arises when someone finds lost or misplaced property. An involuntary bailee owes a duty of slight care to protect the bailed property.

bailment for the sole benefit of the bailee

A gratuitous bailment that benefits only the bailee. The bailee owes a *duty of utmost care* to protect the bailed property.

Bailments for the sole benefit of the bailee are gratuitous bailments that benefit solely the bailee. They generally arise when a bailee requests to use the bailor's property for personal reasons. In this situation, the bailee owes a **duty of great utmost care** (or **great care**) to protect the bailed property; that is, he or she owes a duty not to be slightly negligent in caring for the bailed goods.

duty of utmost care

A duty of care that goes beyond ordinary care.

Consider This Example   Suppose Mitch borrows Courtney's lawn mower (free of charge) to mow his own lawn. Mitch is the bailee, and Courtney is the bailor. This bailment is for the sole benefit of the bailee. Suppose Mitch, while mowing his lawn, leaves the lawn mower in his front yard when he goes into his house to answer the telephone. While he is gone, the lawn mower is stolen. Here, Mitch will be held liable to Courtney for the loss of the lawn mower because Mitch breached his duty of great care to protect the lawn mower.

mutual benefit bailment

A bailment for the mutual benefit of the bailor and bailee. The bailee owes a *duty of ordinary care* to protect the bailed property.

Mutual benefit bailments are bailments that benefit both parties. The bailee owes a **duty of reasonable care** (or **ordinary care**) to protect the bailed goods. Thus, the bailee is liable for any goods that are lost, damaged, or destroyed because of his or her negligence. The law presumes that if bailed property is lost, damaged, destroyed, or stolen while in the possession of the bailee, it is because of lack of proper care by the bailee; the bailee may rebut this presumption by the introduction of appropriate evidence. Commercial bailments, where the bailor pays the bailee compensation to store, hold, or transport bailed goods, fall into this category.

duty of reasonable care

The duty that a reasonable bailee in like circumstances would owe to protect the bailed property.

Consider This Example   Suppose ABC Garment Company delivers goods to Lowell, Inc., a commercial warehouse, for storage. A fee is charged for this service. ABC Garment Company receives the benefit of having its goods stored, and Lowell, Inc., receives the benefit of being paid compensation for storing the goods. In this example, Lowell, Inc. (the bailee), owes a duty of ordinary care to protect the goods.

Some states have eliminated the above categories of ordinary bailments, ruling that all bailees owe a duty of reasonable care regardless of whether they benefit from the bailment.

*6*ONCEPT SUMMARY   ORDINARY BAILEE'S DUTY OF CARE

Type of Bailment	Duty of Care Owed by Bailee	Bailee Liable to Bailor for
For the sole benefit of the bailor	Slight	Gross negligence
For the sole benefit of the bailee	Great	Slight negligence
For the mutual benefit of the bailor and bailee	Ordinary	Ordinary negligence

Bailee's Rights   During the term of a bailment, the **bailee** has the **right** to exclusive possession of the bailed property. This right is temporary, however, because the property must be returned when the bailment is terminated. If a fixed-term mutual benefit bailment is terminated by the bailor prior to the expiration of its term, the bailee can recover damages for the breach of the bailment contract. Generally, a bailor or bailee can terminate a gratuitous bailment at any time without liability.

In some bailments, the bailee has the right to use the bailed property. This right is determined from the terms of the bailment contract and the facts and circumstances surrounding the bailment. For example, suppose a farmer leases a farm tractor for the summer months. During the course of the bailment, the farmer may use the tractor to plow his fields.

In a mutual benefit bailment, the bailee has a right to be compensated for work done or services provided to the bailor. The amount of compensation is usually stated in the bailment contract. If no specific amount is stated, reasonable compensation is presumed. Bailees usually obtain a **possessory lien** (also called an **artisan's lien**) on the bailed property for compensation owed by the bailor. If the bailee refuses to or cannot fulfill this commitment, most states permit the bailee to foreclose on the lien, sell the bailed property at a judicial sale, and recover the amount of compensation due from the sale proceeds. Any excess proceeds must be returned to the bailor.

Gratuitous bailees are not entitled to compensation for services provided. They are, however, entitled to recover reimbursement for all costs and expenses rendered in protecting the bailed property.

Bailor's Duties   Many of the bailor's duties complement the bailee's rights. The bailor owes the duty to pay the agreed-upon compensation to the bailee and not interfere with the bailee's possessory interest during the term of the bailment.

One of the bailor's primary duties is to notify the bailee of any defects in the bailed property that could cause injury to the bailee or others. The extent of this duty depends on the type of bailment. In a bailment for the sole benefit of the bailee, the bailor must notify the bailee of any known defects in the bailed property. In a bailment for the mutual benefit of both parties, the bailor must notify the bailee of any known defects or defects that could have been discovered through reasonable inspection.

A bailor who fails to fulfill these duties is liable for damages caused by the defects. In addition, bailors can be held liable for breach of any express or implied warranties they make about the bailed property.

bailee's rights

Depending on the type of bailment, bailees may have the right to (1) exclusive possession of the bailed property, (2) use of the bailed property, and (3) compensation for work done or services provided.

possessory lien

Lien obtained by a bailee on bailed property for the compensation owed by the bailor to the bailee.

Only a ghost can exist without material property.

Ayn Rand
Atlas Shrugged (1957)

Entrepreneur and the Law

PARKING LOTS: WHO IS LIABLE IF YOUR CAR IS STOLEN?

Who is liable when a car is stolen while parked in a commercial lot or garage? The answer to this question depends upon whether the parking lot is considered to be a bailee of an automobile or merely a lessor of parking space.

It is clear that parking lots and garages are bailees of automobiles once they assume control and possession of the automobile. Thus, if a valet parking attendant parks the car and keeps the keys, it is relatively certain that a court will recognize the existence of a bailment and hold the garage liable if the vehicle is stolen. Disclaimers to the contrary (either on the ticket or posted at the parking lot) are usually held to be ineffective.

On the other hand, if the owner of a car parks his or her own car in a parking lot and takes the keys, this is considered a lease. The general rule in this case is that the "landlord"—the parking lot—is not responsible for the safety of the car.

SPECIAL BAILMENTS

special bailees

Includes common carriers, warehouse companies, and innkeepers.

Special (or **extraordinary**) **bailees** include common carriers, innkeepers, and warehouse companies. Special bailees must follow most of the rules applicable to ordinary bailees. In addition, they are subject to special liability rules contained in **Article 7 of the Uniform Commercial Code (UCC)**.

Article 7 of the UCC

An article of the Uniform Commercial Code that provides a detailed statutory scheme for the creation, perfection, and foreclosure on common carriers' and warehouse operators' liens.

Common Carriers

Common carriers offer transportation services to the general public. For example, commercial airlines, railroads, public trucking companies, public pipeline companies, and such are common carriers. Many common carriers are regulated by the government.

The delivery of goods to a **common** carrier creates a mutual benefit bailment. The person shipping the goods is the **shipper** or **consignor** (the bailor). The transportation company is called the **common carrier** (the bailee). The person to whom the goods are to be delivered is called the **consignee**.

common carrier

A firm that offers transportation services to the general public. The bailee. Owes a *duty of strict liability* to the bailor.

Common carriers are held to a **duty of strict liability**.[1] Thus, if the goods are lost, damaged, destroyed, or stolen, the common carrier is liable even if it was not at fault for the loss. Common carriers are not liable for the loss, damage, or destruction of goods caused by (1) an act of God (e.g., a tornado), (2) an act of a public enemy (e.g., a terrorist activity), (3) an order of the government (e.g., statutes, court decisions, government regulations), (4) an act of the shipper (e.g., improper packaging), or (5) the inherent nature of the goods (e.g., perishability).

consignor

The person shipping the goods. The bailor.

consignee

The person to whom the bailed goods are to be delivered.

Common carriers can limit their liability to a stated dollar amount by expressly stating that in the bailment agreement. Federal law requires common carriers who take advantage of such limitation to offer shippers the opportunity to pay a premium and declare a higher value for the goods.[2]

duty of strict liability

A duty that common carriers owe that says if the goods are lost, damaged, destroyed, or stolen, the common carrier is liable even if it was not at fault for the loss.

Warehouse Companies

A **warehouser** (or **warehouse company**) is a bailee engaged in the business of storing property for compensation.[3] Warehousers are subject to the rights, duties, and liability of an ordinary bailee. As such, they owe a **duty of reasonable care** to protect the bailed property in its possession from harm or loss.[4] Warehousers are liable only for loss or damage to the bailed property caused by their own negligence. They are not liable for loss or damage caused to bailed goods by another person's negligence or conduct.

warehouse company

A bailee engaged in the business of storing property for compensation. Owes a *duty of reasonable care* to protect the bailed property.

Warehousers can limit the dollar amount of their liability if they offer the bailor the opportunity to increase the liability limit for the payment of an additional charge.[5] Warehouse companies are subject to a comprehensive set of federal and state statutes that govern the operation of warehouse facilities.

duty of strict liability

Common law duty that says innkeepers are liable for lost, damaged, or stolen goods of guests even if they were not at fault for the loss.

Innkeepers

An **innkeeper** is the owner of a facility that provides lodging to the public for compensation (e.g., a hotel or motel). Under the common law, innkeepers are held to a **strict liabil-**

ity standard regarding loss caused to the personal property of transient guests. Permanent lodgers are not subject to this rule.

Almost all states have enacted **innkeepers' statutes** that limit the liability of innkeepers. Most of these statutes allow innkeepers to avoid liability for loss caused to guest's property if (1) a safe is provided in which the guests' valuable property may be kept and (2) the guests are aware of the safe's availability. Most state laws also allow innkeepers to limit the dollar amount of their liability by notifying their guests of this limit (e.g., by posting a notice on each guest room door). This limitation on liability does not apply if the loss is caused by the innkeeper's negligence.

> **innkeepers' statutes**
>
> State statutes that limit an innkeeper's common law liability. An innkeeper can avoid liability for loss caused to a guest's property if (1) a safe is provided in which the guest's valuable property may be kept and (2) the guest is notified of this fact.

Contemporary Business Environment

LOSS OF PROPERTY LAWSUIT LODGED AGAINST INNKEEPER

Marvin J. Frockt, a traveling jewelry salesman, checked into a Comfort Inn (Inn) in North Carolina owned by Max H. Goodloe and others. Frockt had in his possession a jewelry sample case that contained approximately $150,000 worth of gems and jewels. Frockt requested that the desk clerk place the case in the safe provided by Inn, stating that the case was "very valuable." The clerk did not give Frockt a receipt for the case.

North Carolina law states that innkeepers have a duty to safely keep up to $500 worth of money, jewelry, or other valuables for any guest who requests such a service. The innkeeper is required to give the guest a receipt that plainly states this limitation on liability. Innkeepers have no liability for valuables that are not given to them for safekeeping. In addition, the statute requires the following:

> *Every innkeeper shall keep posted in every room of his house occupied by guests, and in the office, a printed copy of this Article and of all regulations relating to the conduct of guests. This Chapter shall not apply to innkeepers, or their guests, where the innkeeper fails to keep such notices posted. [N.C.Gen.Stat. § 72].*

Inn had not posted the required notice. When Frockt called for his case the next day, it could not be located and was never recovered. Frockt sued the owners of Inn for damages. Is Inn's liability limited to $500?

The defendants urged that N.C.Gen.Stat. Section 72 held Inn harmless for loss or damage to plaintiff above the statutory amount of $500. The court noted that the defendants' argument would be persuasive absent two facts: (1) no receipt was given to the plaintiff by Inn—that notified him of Section 72 and (2) the evidence is uncontradicted that Inn did not display in the office a copy of Section 72.

In holding that Inn's liability for the lost case was not limited to $500, the court stated

> *The consequences of failing to post notice as required by Section 72-6 are clear: rather than benefiting from the protection afforded by the statute, the innkeeper must look to the common law to define its duties and liabilities. The common law rule in North Carolina is that the innkeeper is strictly liable for the loss of a guest's property, except in a few rare instances, such as where such loss is occasioned by the guest's own negligence. Had the Inn wished to alleviate the draconian effect of the common law rule, it had only to follow the dictates of the statute by posting the notice required therein. This it did not do; consequently, it will not be heard to complain that the rule is untenable.*

*C*ONCEPT SUMMARY   SPECIAL BAILEES' DUTY OF CARE

Type of Bailee	Liability	Limitation on Liability
Common carrier	Strictly liable except for 1. Act of God 2. Act of a public enemy 3. Order of the government 4. Act of the shipper 5. Inherent nature of the goods	May limit the dollar amount of liability by offering the bailor the right to declare a higher value for the bailed goods for an additional charge.
Warehouse company	Ordinary negligence	May limit the dollar amount of liability by offering the bailor the right to declare a higher value for the bailed goods for an additional charge.
Innkeeper	Strictly liable	State statutes may limit the liability of an innkeeper for others' negligence.

International Law

WHEN AIRLINES LOSE LUGGAGE

Every day, airlines are bailors for hundreds of thousands of pieces of luggage that are checked by domestic and international travelers. As bailors, the common law would impose liability on airlines for the full value of any luggage lost or damaged by their negligence.

Two statutes, however, protect the airlines from the harsh results of the common law of bailments. Under the first statute, the **Civil Aeronautics Act of 1938**, 49 U.S.C. § 646, which applies to domestic flights, airlines can limit their liability for passengers' lost or damaged property to a specific dollar amount per pound or per item by filing tariffs with the Civil Aeronautics Board. The current tariff is $1,250 per piece of luggage.

The only way for passengers to beat the limitations of liability is to declare that the value of their property exceeds the tariffs and then pay a fee for additional coverage.

The second statute is the **Warsaw Convention**, 49 U.S.C. § 1502, which was concluded in 1929. This statute limits recovery for luggage that is lost or damaged on international flights. Passengers can purchase additional coverage upon check-in at the airport.

Undoubtedly, passengers who fail to declare the excess value of their luggage will lose money if their luggage is lost. The limitations of liability contained in both the Civil Aeronautics Act and the Warsaw Convention, however, are widely viewed as necessary protection for airlines.

Chapter Summary

The Nature of Personal Property, p. 911

Personal Property	*Personal property.* Consists of everything that is not real property. Sometimes referred to as goods or *chattels.* Types of personal property: a. *Tangible property.* Physically defined property such as goods, animals, and minerals. b. *Intangible property.* Rights that cannot be reduced to physical form, such as stock certificates, bonds, and copyrights.

Acquiring Ownership in Personal Property, p. 912

Methods of Acquiring Ownership in Personal Property	1. *Possession or capture.* Taking possession of or capturing unowned property, such as wild animals.
	 2. *Purchase.* Purchasing the property from its rightful owner.
	 3. *Production.* Producing a finished product from raw materials and supplies.
	 4. *Gift.* Voluntary transfer of property by its owner to a donee without consideration.
	    a. Three elements necessary to create a valid gift:
	      i. *Donative intent.* The donor must have intended to make a gift. This intent can be inferred from the circumstances.
	      ii. *Delivery.* Delivery of the personal property must be made to the donee by *physical delivery* or, where impracticable, by *constructive* (or *symbolic*) *delivery.*
	      iii. *Acceptance.* The donee must accept the gift. Donees are free to reject gifts that they do not want.
	    b. Types of gifts:
	      i. Gifts *inter vivos.* Gifts made during a donor's lifetime that are irrevocable present transfers of ownership.
	      ii. Gifts *causa mortis.* Gifts that are made in anticipation of death. A gift *causa mortis* is established if
	        a. The donor makes a gift in anticipation of approaching death from an existing illness or peril.
	        b. The donor dies from such illness or peril without having revoked the gift.
	 5. *Will.* Gift to beneficiaries named in a will.
	 6. *Inheritance.* Heirs stipulated in an inheritance statute.
	 7. *Accession.* Occurs when the value of personal property increases because it is added to or improved by natural or manufactured means.
	 8. *Confusion.* Where fungible goods are commingled, the owners share title to the commingled goods in proportion to the amount of goods contributed.
	 9. *Divorce.* When a marriage is dissolved by a divorce, the parties obtain certain rights in the property of the marital estate.

Mislaid, Lost, and Abandoned Property, p. 916

Mislaid, Lost, and Abandoned Property	1. *Mislaid property.* Personal property that an owner voluntarily places somewhere and then inadvertently forgets. The owner of the premises where the property is mislaid does not acquire title to the property but has the right of possession against all except the rightful owner. The rightful owner can reclaim the property.
	2. *Lost property.* Personal property that an owner leaves somewhere because of negligence or carelessness. The finder obtains title to the property against the whole world except the true owner. The rightful owner can reclaim the property.
	  a. *Estray statutes.* State statutes that permit a finder of mislaid or lost property to obtain title to the property. To obtain clear title, the finder must:
	    i. Report the find to the appropriate government agency and turn over possession of the property to the agency.
	    ii. Post and publish required notices.
	    iii. Wait the statutorily required time (e.g., one year) without the rightful owner claiming the property.
	3. *Abandoned property.* Personal property that an owner has discarded, or mislaid or lost property that the owner gives up any further attempt to locate. The finder acquires title to the property. The prior owner cannot reclaim the property.

Bailments, p. 918

Bailment	*Bailment.* Occurs when the owner of personal property delivers the property to another person to be held, stored, or delivered, or for some other purpose.
	1. Parties to a bailment:
	  a. *Bailor.* Owner of the property.
	  b. *Bailee.* Party to whom the property is delivered.
	2. Three elements necessary to create a bailment:
	  a. *Personal property.* Only personal property can be bailed.
	  b. *Delivery of possession.* The bailee must knowingly accept the property and have exclusive control over it.
	  c. *Bailment agreement.* There must be a bailment agreement. *Express bailments* may be oral or written unless required to be in writing by the Statute of Frauds. A bailment may be *implied* from the circumstances.

Types of Bailments	1. *Bailment for a fixed term.* Bailment that terminates at the end of a stipulated term. May be terminated prior to the end of the term by mutual assent of the bailor and bailee. 2. *Bailments at will.* Bailments without a fixed term. May be terminated at any time by either party.

Ordinary Bailments	1. *Bailments for the sole benefit of the bailor.*
	  a. *Gratuitous bailment.* Arises when the bailee is requested to care for the bailor's property as a favor.
	  b. *Involuntary bailment.* Arises when the bailee finds lost or misplaced property and decides to protect it.
	  c. *Duty of care.* The bailee owes a duty of *slight care;* that is, the bailee is liable for *gross negligence.*
	2. *Bailments for the sole benefit of the bailee:*
	  a. *Gratuitous bailment.* A gratuitous bailment that arises when the bailee uses the bailor's property for personal reasons without paying compensation.
	  b. *Duty of care.* The bailee owes a duty of *great care* (or *utmost care*) and is liable for *slight negligence.*
	3. *Bailments for the mutual benefit of the bailor and the bailee.*
	  a. *Mutual benefit bailment.* Arises when both parties benefit from the bailment. This includes commercial bailments.
	  b. *Duty of care.* The bailee owes a duty of *reasonable care* (or *ordinary care*) and is liable for *ordinary negligence.*

Special Bailments, p. 922

Special Bailees	1. *Common carriers.* Companies that offer transportation services to the public, such as airlines, railroads, and trucking firms. The parties are:
	  a. *Consignor or shipper.* The person shipping the goods. The bailor.
	  b. *Common carrier.* The transportation company. The bailee.
	  c. *Consignee.* Party to whom the goods are to be delivered.
	  d. *Duty of care.* Common carriers owe a duty of *strict liability;* that is, if the goods are lost, damaged, destroyed, or stolen, the common carrier is liable even if it was not its fault.
	2. *Warehouse companies.* Companies that engage in the business of storing property for compensation.
	Duty of care. Warehouse companies owe a duty of reasonable care (or ordinary care) to protect the bailed goods from loss or damage.

3. *Innkeepers.* The owner of a facility that provides lodging to the public for compensation (e.g., a hotel or motel).
   a. *Duty of care.* Under the common law, innkeepers owe a duty of *strict liability* regarding loss caused to guests' property.
   b. *Innkeepers' statutes.* Laws that have been enacted to limit the liability of innkeepers for loss or damage to guests' property. The innkeeper must post required notices to be covered by the law.

End-of-Chapter Internet Exercises and Case Questions

Working the Web Internet Exercises

ACTIVITIES

1. Find your state's probate code. Does it follow the Uniform Probate Code? See state laws at **www.law.cornell.edu/statutes.html#state**.

2. Find your state's law on bailments relating to parking lots. See "The Parking Lot Cases Revisited: Confusion at or About the Gate," 40 Santa Clara L. rev. 27 (1999) by William V. Vetter

3. Review your state's laws on innkeeper liability for lost or stolen property of hotel guests. What is the statutory limitation on losses?

4. Many states have statutes regarding lost or abandoned property. For example, see Washington State's statute, Title 63 RCW, Personal Property.

CRITICAL LEGAL THINKING CASES

36.1 Personal Property of Fixture   NYT Cable TV is division of the New York Times Company (NYT) that operates a cable television station in Camden County, New Jersey. NYT has erected a 250-foot-high cable antenna tower on real property to distribute its broadcast signals. The structure is attached to a large concrete foundation in the ground and consists of a large vertical triangular steel superstructure connected by steel cross bars and circular metal ties. The Camden County Board of Taxation assessed a real property tax on the property, including the cable television tower. NYT opposed the tax, alleging that the cable television tower was personal property—not real property—and was exempt from the real property tax. Who wins? [*NYT Cable TV v. Borough of Audubon, New Jersey*, 553 A.2d 1368 (N.J. Sup. 1989)]

36.2 Accession   On June 6, 1983, Mack's Used Cars & Parts, Inc. (Mack's), sold a 1975 model GMC one-ton truck with a 1979 Atlas wrecker assembly attached thereto to Jack W. Weaver on credit. At the time of the purchase, the wrecker assembly was bolted to the frame of the truck, and its hydraulic boom operated off the transmission of the truck. To protect its credit extension to Weaver, Mack's took a security interest in the vehicle and perfected its interest by a notation on the truck's title. Mack's filed a financing statement with the Tennessee secretary of state covering the vehicle. Weaver subsequently sold the vehicle to McCall, who removed the wrecker assembly from the truck and sold the wrecker assembly to the Tennessee Truck & Equipment Company (Tennessee Truck). When the original extension of credit was not paid, Mack's brought this action to repossess the vehicle and also to repossess the wrecker assembly from Tennessee Truck. Who wins? [*Mack's Used Cars & Parts, Inc. v. Tennessee Truck & Equipment Co.*, 694 S.W.2d 323 (Tenn. App. 1985)]

36.3 Gift *Causa Mortis*   Olga V. Watson lived in an apartment building that was managed by Edward P. McCarton. During 1980, Watson's health started to deteriorate, and she eventually began to call on McCarton for assistance in her daily affairs. By 1982, Watson's health had deteriorated to the point where she could no longer take care of herself. McCarton arranged for her to move into his apartment. Except for a brief stay in a nursing home, Watson lived in McCarton's apartment until her death. During her stay, she met many of McCarton's relatives. On July 26, 1981, two days before her death, Watson stated that she realized she was dying and asked McCarton to write down her wishes for the disposition of her assets. She directed that McCarton receive her stocks and bonds, worth $235,000, and that McCarton's relatives receive her bank accounts, worth $354,000. The stock certificates, bonds, and bank statements were located in a dresser in the McCarton apartment. Later, it was discovered that Watson had prepared a will several years earlier in which she left one half of her estate to her sister and the other half to the sister's adopted nephew. Evidence showed that once, when Watson received a letter from the adopted nephew demanding his inheritance, she stared, "He won't get a dime from me." The will was admitted to probate. Which prevails, Watson's gift letter or the old will? [*McCarton v. Estate of Watson*, 693 P.2d 192 (Wash. App. 1984)]

36.4 Uniform Gift to Minors Act   Between 1972 and 1984, Theodore Alexander Buder's father made substantial gifts to his minor grandchildren. The Buders divorced during this period. The cash gifts, typically in the form of checks made directly payable to the children, were given to Buder with the understanding that he would safeguard the money and invest it on behalf of the children. Buder invested various amounts of the children's money in "blue chip" stocks traded over the New York and American stock exchanges. In 1974, he began investing substantial sums of the children's money in speculative penny stocks. The stocks were purchased in Buder's name as custodian for the children, as required by the Uniform Gifts to Minors Act (UGMA). At one point, almost half of the children's money was invested in penny stocks. All the penny stocks except one suffered substantial losses. Buder's ex-wife, Sartore, sued him, alleging that he had breached his fiduciary owed to the children under the UGMA. She sought to recover the funds lost by Buder's investment of the children's funds in penny stocks. Who wins? [*Buder v. Sartore*, 774 P.2d 1383 (CO 1989)]

36.5 Lost Property   In June 1983, Danny Lee Smith and his brother, Jeffrey Allen Smith, found a 16-foot fiberglass boat lying beside the roadway in Mobile County, Alabama. Seeing two sheriff's deputies, they stopped them to discuss the boat. Over the Smith's objections, the deputies impounded the boat. The Smiths made it clear that if the true owner of the boat was not found, they wanted the boat. The true owner did not claim the boat. Mobile County claimed the boat and wanted to auction it off for sale to raise money for county recreational programs. The Smiths claimed the boat as finders. Alabama did not have an estray statute that applied to the situation. Who gets the boat? [*Smith v. Sheriff Purvis*, 474 So.2d 1131 (Ala. App. 1985)]

36.6 Abandoned Property   Late in 1975, police officers of the city of Miami, Florida, responded to reports of a shooting at the apartment of Carlos Fuentes. Fuentes had been shot in the neck and shoulder and, shortly after the police arrived, was removed to a hospital. In an ensuing search of the apartment, the police found assorted drug paraphernalia, a gun, and cash in the amount of $58,591. The property was seized, taken to the police station, and placed in custody. About nine days later, the police learned that Fuentes had been discharged from the hospital. All efforts by police to locate Fuentes and his girlfriend, a co-occupant of Fuentes' apartment, were unsuccessful. Neither Fuentes nor his girlfriend ever came forward to claim any of the items taken by the police from his apartment. About four years later, in 1979, James W. Green and Walter J. Vogel, the owners of the apartment building in which Fuentes was a tenant, sued the city of Miami to recover the cash found in Fuentes' apartment. The state of Florida intervened in the case, also claiming an interest in the money. Who wins? [*State of Florida v. Green*, 456 So.2d 1309 (Fla. App. 1984)]

36.7 Bailment   On February 4, 1976, James D. Merritt leased a storage locker from Nationwide Warehouse Co., Ltd. (Nationwide), and agreed to pay $16 per month lease for the locker. Merritt placed various items in the leased premises but never informed Nationwide as to the nature or quantity of articles stored therein. Merritt was free to store or remove whatever he wished without consultation with, permission from, or notice to, Nationwide. Merritt locked the leased premises with his own lock and key. Nationwide was not furnished with a key. Subsequently, certain personal property belonging to Merritt disappeared from the storage space. Merritt sued Nationwide to recover damages of $5,275. Was a bailment created between Merritt and Nationwide? [*Merritt v. Nationwide Warehouse Co., Ltd.*, 605 S.W. 2d 250 (Tenn. App. 1980)]

36.8 Liability for Lost Goods   On May 14, 1980, Clarence Williams brought his wife's fur coat to Debonair Cleaners for cleaning and storage. The clerk told him that the cleaners was experienced in such matters and that the charge would be 3 percent of the stated value of the coat. Williams stated that the coat was worth $13,000, and the clerk gave Williams a claim check and informed Williams that the total fee for storage would be $390, to be paid when the coat was retrieved. That evening Williams related the substance of his conversation with the clerk to his wife, Armicia, and gave her the claim check. Approximately eight months later, Armicia Williams went to Debonair Cleaners to retrieve her coat. She presented the claim check to the clerk who, after searching the premises for the coat, told her that it could not be located. Williams was informed that the coat had probably been stolen during a break-in and burglary. Williams sued Debonair Cleaners to recover the value of the coat. Who wins? [*Mahallati v. Williams*, 479 A.2d 300 (D.C. App. 1984)]

36.9 Gratuitous Bailment   Marsha Hamilton and Andrea Morris were guests at a dinner party attended by approximately 25 people. The party began about 7:00 P.M. and ended at approximately 1:00 A.M. Alcoholic beverages were served throughout the evening. At approximately 11:30, while working in the kitchen, Hamilton removed her watch and placed it on the counter. About midnight, Hamilton left the kitchen and went outside. After about 15 minutes, she became ill and fled to the bathroom. Shortly after Hamilton left the kitchen, Morris saw the watch on the counter and, fearing for its safety, picked it up and carried it in her hand as she looked for Hamilton. When Hamilton came out of the bathroom, she and her fiancé left the party. Morris was unable to find Hamilton and cannot recall precisely what she did with the watch. She testified that she either gave it to Hamilton's fiancé or put it somewhere in the host's house for safekeeping. Hamilton's fiancé testified that Morris did not give him the watch. The next day Hamilton discovered that she did not have her watch, but in a search of the host's home, the watch was not recovered. Hamilton sued Morris for damages. Who wins? [*Morris v. Hamilton*, 302 S.E.2d 51 (VA 1983)]

36.10 Parking Lot's Liability   Allright, Inc., is a parking lot operator in Houston, Texas. On January 18, 1980, Kirkland Strauder drove his 1978 Buick regal automobile to a Houston Allright parking lot, placed it in a row of cars to be parked by the attendant, handed the attendant his keys, and was given a receipt by the attendant. When Strauder returned two hours later to reclaim his car, it could not be found. Strauder reported the car stolen. Allright could not explain the loss of the car, which was found one and one-half weeks later, wrecked and stripped. Strauder sued Allright, Inc., for damages. Who wins? [*Allright, Inc. v. Strauder*, 679 S.W.2d 81 (Tex. App. 1984)]

36.11 Conversion of Bailed Property Alan Brotman and Prem Sahai were the owners and managers of the Brotman Investment Corporation, which was engaged in the business of selling rare coins. In August 1980, Leonard Fazio purchased silver coins worth $4,998 from the corporation. The coins were to be put into the corporation's vault for safekeeping. It was understood that Fazio could demand the return of the coins at any time. In November 1980, Fazio unsuccessfully demanded that his coins be returned. Evidence showed that the coins never made it into the vault and that the coins had been converted to one of the cobailees' own use. Fazio sued Brotman and Sahai for damages. Who wins? [*Fazio v. Brotman and Sahai*, 371 N.W.2d 842 (Iowa App. 1985)]

36.12 Warehouse Company Vernon Pittman Van Lines (Pittman) is a warehouse company that stores goods for a fee. On May 31, 1977, Trudy Royster hired Pittman to store some of her furniture and household goods. Royster paid Pittman a monthly fee for such services. When Royster decided to remove a few items from storage on September 9, 1979, she found her furniture and cartons in a state of disarray. Several pieces of furniture were substantially damaged, including broken legs, scratches, and so forth. Pittman did not produce any evidence showing how the furniture was damaged. Royster sued Pittman to recover damages. Who wins? [*Royster v. Pittman*, 691 S.W.2d 305 (Mo. App. 1985)]

36.13 Disclaimer of Liability On January 23, 1982, Joseph Conboy, his wife, and a group of friends convened in Manhattan, New York, for a party at Studio 54, a discotheque where patrons dance to recorded music played on high-fidelity sound equipment. The Conboy party checked their coats, 14 in all, with the coatroom attendant. After paying a $0.75 charge per coat, they received seven check stubs. A small sign in the coatroom stated "Liability for lost property in this coat/check room is limited to $100 per loss of misplaced article." Conboy testified that he did not notice it when he checked his coat and that the coatroom attendant did not call his attention to the sign. At the end of the evening, Conboy and the other guests of the party attempted to reclaim their coats. Conboy's one-month-old $1,350 leather coat was missing. Conboy sued Studio 54 for damages. Is the disclaimer of liability enforceable? [*Conboy v. Studio 54, Inc.* 449 N.Y.S.2d 391 (N.Y. Civ. Ct. 1982)]

 BUSINESS ETHICS CASES

36.14 Business Ethics When Dr. Arthur M. Edwards died, leaving a will disposing of this property, he left the villa-type condominium in which he lived, its "contents," and $10,000 to his stepson, Ronald W. Souders. Edwards left the residual of his estate to other named legatees. In administering the estate, certain stock certificates, passbook savings accounts, and other bank statements were found in Edward's condominium. Souders claimed that these items belonged to him because they were "contents" of the condominium. The other legatees opposed Souders's claim, alleging that the disputed property was intangible property and not part of the contents of the condominium. The value of the property was as follows: condominium, $138,000; furniture in condominium, $4,000; stocks, $377,000; and passbook and other bank accounts, $124,000. Who is entitled to the stocks and bank accounts? Do you think Souders acted ethically in this case? [*Souders v. Johnson*, 501 So.2d 745 (Fla. App. 1987)]

36.15 Business Ethics Darryl Kulwin was employed by Nova Stylings, Inc. (Nova), as a jewelry salesman. In that capacity, he traveled throughout the country carrying with him jewelry owned and manufactured by Nova to show to prospective buyers. Kulwin was visiting Panoria Ruston, who was a guest registered with the Red Roof Inn in Overland Park, Kansas. Ruston and Kulwin met at the Red Roof Inn and later made plans to leave to go to dinner. Kulwin asked Ruston to make arrangements with the desk clerk to leave his sample case in the office of the Red Roof Inn while they went out to dinner. Ruston asked the clerk if she could leave the bag in the manager's office of the Red Roof Inn and the clerk agreed. Ruston advised the clerk that the contents of the case were valuable but did not descibe the contents of the bag.

Kansas Statute § 36-402(b) provides:

No hotel or motel keeper in this state shall be liable for the loss of, or damage to, merchandise for sale or samples belonging to a guest, lodger, or boarder unless the guest, lodger, or boarder upon entering the hotel or motel, shall give notice of having merchandise for sale or samples in his possession, together with an itemized list of such property, to the hotel or motel keeper, or his authorized agent or clerk in the registration office of the hotel or motel office.

No hotel or motel keeper shall be liable for any loss of such property designated in this subsection (b), after notice an itemized statement having been given and delivered as aforesaid, in an amount in excess of two hundred fifty dollars ($250), unless such hotel or motel keeper, by specific agreement in writing, individually, or by an authorized agent or clerk in charge of the registration office of the hotel or motel, shall voluntarily assume liability for a larger amount with reference to such property. The hotel or motel keeper shall not be compelled to receive such guests, lodgers, or boarders with merchandise for sale or samples.

The Inn posted the proper notice of the provisions of this act in all of the guests' rooms, including that of Ruston. An unidentified person obtained access to the manager's office and removed the case from the office. Nova sued Red Roof Inns for the alleged value of the jewelry, $650,000. Is Red Roof Inns liable? Did either party act unethically in this case? [*Nova Stylings v. Red Roof Inns, Inc.*, 747 P.2ds 107 (KS 1987)]

BRIEFING THE CASE WRITING ASSIGNMENT

Read the following case, which has been excerpted from the court's opinion. Review and brief the case.

The Wackenhut Corporation and Delta Airlines, Inc. v. Lippert
609 SO.2D 1304 (1992)
Supreme Court of Florida

Grimes, Judge

While on her way to board a Delta Airlines flight from West Palm Beach to New York, Felice Lippert took a handbag containing approximately $431,000 worth of jewelry through a security checkpoint at Palm Beach International Airport. The security checkpoint was operated by The Wackenhut Corporation. The checkpoint consisted of a magnetometer scan of baggage and other carry-on items as well as a scan of the person which occurs as the person walks through a specially designed archway. Mrs Lippert placed her bag on the conveyor belt as required and she walked through the archway. The archway magnetometer alarm sounded and Mrs. Lippert was briefly inspected by Wackenhut personnel. After being cleared by Wackenhut, Mrs. Lippert discovered her handbag with the jewelry was missing.

Mrs. Lippert sued Delta and Wackenhut for the value of her jewelry on a theory of negligence. Delta and Wackenhut asserted Delta's limitations of liability as their affirmative defense. The limitations of liability are expressed by reference on the back of Delta's ticket and in full in a governmentally required tariff which is posted according to federal regulations. The limitation contained in the tariff provides that:

> DL shall be liable for the loss, damage to, or delay in the delivery of a fare paying passenger's baggage, or other property (including carry on baggage, if tendered to DL's in flight personnel for storage during flight or otherwise delivered into the custody of DL). Such liability, if any, for the loss, damage, or delay in the delivery of a fare paying passenger's baggage or other property (whether checked or otherwise delivered into the custody of DL), shall be limited to an amount equal to the value of the property, plus consequential damages, if any, and shall not exceed the maximum limitation of USD $1250 for all liability for each fare paying passenger (unless the passenger elects to pay for higher liability).
> DL is not responsible for jewelry, cash, camera equipment, or other similar valuable items contained in checked or unchecked baggage, unless excess valuation has been purchased. These items should be carried by the passenger.

The trial court initially entered partial summary judgment for Delta and Wackenhut, upholding the limitation on liability to the maximum amount of $1,250. A new judge was assigned to the case by the time of trial. The jury returned a verdict for the plaintiff in the amount of $431,609, apportioning damages with Delta 65 percent liable and Wackenhut 35 percent liable. The trial court vacated the earlier partial summary judgment and entered final

judgment for the plaintiff in the amount of $431,609. Delta and Wackenhut appealed the final judgment arguing that the partial summary judgment should have been given its natural effect in limiting liability to $1,250.

The district court of appeal held that the limitation on liability contained in the ticket and the tariff did not apply under the facts of the case. The court also found that a bailment for the mutual benefit of both the passenger and the airline had been created when Mrs. Lippert relinquished possession of her valuables to go through the X-ray machine. Therefore, the trial court was correct in applying the ordinary negligence standard. However, the court felt that the defendants had been unduly prejudiced by the judge's assurances throughout the pretrial proceedings and the trial that the potential judgment could not exceed $1,250. Thus, the case was remanded for a new trial with the proviso that the limitation of liability would not apply.

On petition for review in this Court, Delta and Wackenhut argue for the $1,250 limitation. In addition, they contend that, because the airport security check was mandated by law, they were gratuitous bailees, who could only be held liable if grossly negligent. Mrs. Lippert cross-petitions to review the granting of a new trial.

Mrs. Lippert seems to argue that under the emphasized portion of section 1 of her ticket, quoted above, an article only becomes baggage, and therefore triggers the limitation on liability, when it reaches the cargo compartment or the cabin of the aircraft. However, this interpretation would lead to the dubious conclusion that passengers' property in transit to the airplane after being delivered to the airline at the check-in point where tickets are purchased should not be considered baggage. The phrase in the ticket's definition of baggage—"whether checked in the cargo compartment or carried in the cabin"—is more realistically construed as emphasizing that, for purposes of Delta's contract with its passengers, there is no difference between "carry-on" and "checked" baggage. Thus, the ticket's references to the cargo compartment and the cabin are merely descriptive of the words "checked" or "carried," and there can be no doubt that Mrs. Lippert's handbag was a passenger's "article or other property acceptable for transportation whether checked or carried." We believe that a ticketed passenger's property, destined for an airplane and in transit between the airport's security checkpoint and the actual airplane, constitutes "baggage" as defined by the ticket.

We hold that the $1,250 baggage limitation of liability was applicable to the loss of Mrs. Lippert's handbag while it was in the possession of Delta's agent at the airport security checkpoint. While we find the $1,250 liability limitation applicable in this case, we decline to answer the certified question because it does not precisely track the language of the tariff. We agree with the district court of appeal that the bailment created when Mrs. Lippert surrendered her handbag for inspection was for the mutual benefit of the passenger and the airline, and we adopt the court's reasoning in this respect. Our disposition of the baggage liability limitation issue renders the cross-petition moot. Because the case was tried under the proper standard of care, there is no need for a retrial. We quash the decision below to the extent that it is inconsistent with our opinion and remand the case for entry of a judgment in favor of Mrs. Lippert for $1,250.

ENDNOTES

1. UCC § 7-301(1).
2. UCC § 7-309(2).
3. UCC § 7-102(h).

4. UCC §§ 7-204(1) and 7-403(1).
5. UCC § 7-204(2).

37

Real Property and Landlord–Tenant Relationship

Without that sense of security which property gives, the land would still be uncultivated.

—Francois Quesnay
(1694–1774)
Maximes, IV

Chapter Objectives

After studying this chapter, you should be able to:

1. List and describe the different types of real property.

2. Describe the different types of freehold estates in land.

3. Describe the different types of future interests in land.

4. List and describe concurrent ownership interests in land.

5. Explain how ownership interests in real property can be transferred.

6. Describe the different nonpossessory interests in land.

7. Explain how a landlord–tenant relationship is created.

8. Identify and describe the various types of tenancy.

9. List and describe the landlords' and tenants' rights and duties.

10. Describe the various forms of private and public land use regulation.

Chapter Contents

Property and ownership rights in **real property** play an important part in this country's society and economy. The concept of real property is concerned with the legal rights to the property rather than the physical attributes of the tangible land. Thus, real property includes some items of personal property that are affixed to real property (e.g., fixtures) and other rights (e.g., minerals, air rights).

The area covered by laws concerning real property is very broad. It includes **landlord–tenant relationships** and **land use control**, among other things.

Individuals and families own or rent houses, farmers and ranchers own farmland and ranches, and businesses own or lease commercial and office buildings. In addition, (1) over half of the population rents their homes and (2) many businesses lease office space, stores, manufacturing facilities, and other commercial property. The parties to a **landlord–tenant** relationship have certain legal rights and duties that are governed by a mixture of real estate and contract law.

Although the United States has the most advanced private property system in the world, the ownership and possession of real estate is not free from government regulation. Pursuant to constitutional authority, federal, state, and local governments have enacted myriad laws that regulate the ownership, possession, and use of real property. These laws, which are collectively referred to as **land use control**, include zoning laws, building codes, antidiscrimination laws, and the like.

This chapter covers the law concerning the ownership and transfer of real property, landlord–tenant relationships, and land use control.

NATURE OF REAL PROPERTY

Property is usually classified as either real or personal property. **Real property** is immovable or attached to immovable land or buildings, whereas personal property is movable. The various types of real property are discussed in the following paragraphs.

Land and Buildings

Land is the most common form of real property. A landowner usually purchases the **surface rights** to the land, that is, the right to occupy the land. The owner may use, enjoy, and develop the property as he or she sees fit, subject to any applicable government regulation.

Buildings constructed on land are real property. For example, houses, apartment buildings, manufacturing plants, and office buildings constructed on land are real property. Such things as radio towers and bridges are usually considered real property as well.

> *Property is an instrument of humanity, Humanity is not an instrument of property.*
>
> Woodrow Wilson
> Speech (1912)

real property
The land itself as well as buildings, trees, soil, minerals, timber, plants, and other things permanently affixed to the land.

land
The most common form of real property. Includes the land and buildings and other structures permanently attached to the land.

surface right
The right of a landowner to use, enjoy, develop, or otherwise occupy the land as he or she sees fit, subject to any applicable government regulation.

Mackinac Island, Michigan *The most valuable asset of many families is the home they own, such as this cottage on Mackinac Island, Michigan.*

Subsurface Rights

subsurface rights

Rights to the earth located beneath the surface of the land.

The owner of land possesses **subsurface rights** or (**mineral rights**) to the earth located beneath the surface of the land. These rights can be very valuable. For example, gold, uranium, oil, or natural gas may lie beneath the surface of land. Theoretically, mineral rights extend to the center of the earth. In reality, mines and oil wells usually extend only several miles into the earth. Subsurface rights may be sold separately from surface rights.

Plant Life and Vegetation

plant life and vegetation

Real property that is growing in or on the surface of the land.

Plant life and vegetation growing on the surface of land is considered real property. Such vegetation includes both natural plant life (e.g., trees) and cultivated plant life (e.g., crops). When land is sold, any plant life growing on the land is included unless the parties agree otherwise. Plant life that is severed from the land is considered personal property.

Fixtures

fixtures

Goods that are affixed to real estate so as to become a part thereof.

Certain personal property is so closely associated with real property that it becomes part of the realty. Such items are called **fixtures**. For example, kitchen cabinets, carpeting, and doorknobs are fixtures, but throw rugs and furniture are personal property.

Unless otherwise provided, if a building is sold, the fixtures are included in the sale. If the sale agreement is silent as to whether an item is a fixture, the courts make their determination on the basis of whether the item can be removed, without causing substantial damage to the realty.

Contemporary Business Environment

AIR RIGHTS: VALUE IN THE HEAVENS

Common law provided that the owners of real property owned that property from the center of the earth to the heavens. This rule has been eroded by modern legal restrictions such as land-use control laws, environmental protection laws, and air navigation requirements. Even today, however, the owners of land may sell or lease air space parcels above their land.

An **air space parcel** is a three-dimensional cube of air above the surface of the earth. Air space parcels are valuable property rights, particularly in densely populated metropolitan areas where building property is scarce. For example, many developments have been built in air space parcels in New York City. The most notable are Madison Square Garden which was built in an air space parcel. More developments are expected to be built in air space parcels in the future.

*E*STATES IN LAND

estate

Ownership rights in real property; the bundle of legal rights that the owner has to possess, use, and enjoy the property.

A person's ownership rights in real property is called an **estate in land** (or **estate**). An estate is defined as the bundle of **legal rights** that the owner has to possess, use, and enjoy the property. The type of estate that an owner possesses is determined from the deed, will, lease, or other document that transferred the ownership rights to him or her.

Freehold Estates

freehold estate

An estate where the owner has a present possessory interest in the real property.

A **freehold estate** is one where the owner has a present possessory interest in the real property; that is, the owner may use and enjoy the property as he or she sees fit, subject to any applicable government regulation or private restraint. The two types of freehold estates are estates in fee and life estates.

fee simple absolute

A type of ownership of real property that grants the owner the fullest bundle of legal rights that a person can hold in real property.

1. ***Estates in Fee***   A **fee simple absolute** (or **fee simple**) is the highest form of ownership of real property because it grants the owner the fullest bundle of legal rights that a person can hold in real property. It is the type of ownership most people connect with "owning" real property. It is also the most common form of real estate ownership in the United States. A fee simple owner

has the right to exclusively possess and use his or her property to the extent that the owner has not transferred any interest in the property (e.g., by lease). If a person owns real property in fee simple, his or her ownership:

- Is infinite in duration (fee)
- Has no limitation on inheritability (simple)
- Does not end upon the happening of any event (absolute)

A **fee simple defeasible** (or **qualified fee**) grants the owner all the incidents of a fee simple absolute except that it may be taken away if a specified condition occurs or does not occur. For example, a conveyance of property to a church "as long as the land is used as a church or for church purposes" creates a qualified fee. The church has all the rights of a fee simple absolute owner except that its ownership rights are terminated if the property is no longer used for church purposes.

2. *Life Estates* A **life estate** is an interest in real property that lasts for the life of a specified person, usually the grantee. For example, a conveyance of real property "to Anna for her life" creates a life estate. A life estate may also be measured by the life of a third party (e.g., "to Anna for the life of Benjamin"), in which case it is called an ***estate pour autre vie***. A life estate may be defeasible (e.g., "to John for his life but only if he continues to occupy this residence"). Upon the death of named person, the life estate terminates and the property reverts back to the grantor or the grantor's estate or other designated person.

A life tenant is treated as the owner of the property during the duration of the life estate. He or she has the right to possess and use the property except to the extent that it would cause permanent **waste** of the property. A life tenant may sell, transfer, or mortgage his or her estate in the land. The mortgage, however, cannot exceed the duration of the life estate. A life tenant is obligated to keep the property in repair and to pay property taxes.

fee simple defeasible

A type of ownership of real property that grants the owner all the incidents of a fee simple absolute except that it may be taken away if a specified condition occurs or does not occur.

life estate

An interest in the land for a person's lifetime; upon that person's death, the interest will be transferred to another party.

estate pour autre vie

A life estate measured in the life of a third party.

CONCEPT SUMMARY   FREEHOLD ESTATES

Estate	Description
Fee simple absolute	Highest form of ownership of real property. Ownership (1) is infinite in duration, (2) has no limitation on inheritability, and (3) does not end upon the occurrence or nonoccurrence of an event.
Fee simple defeasible	Grants owner all of the incidents of a fee simple absolute except that it may be taken away if a specified condition occurs or does not occur.
Life estate	Interest in property that lasts for the life of a specified person. A life estate terminates upon the death of the named person and reverts back to the grantor or his or her estate or other designated person.

Future Interests

A person may be given the right to possess property in the future rather than currently. This right is called a **future interest**. The two forms of future interests are reversion and remainder.

1. *Reversion* A **reversion** is a right of possession that returns to the grantor after the expiration of a limited or contingent estate. Reversions do not have to be expressly stated because they arise automatically by law. For example, if a grantor conveys property "to M.R. Harrington for life," the grantor has retained a reversion to the property. That is, when Harrington dies, the property reverts to the grantor or, if he is not living then, to his estate.

2. *Remainder* If the right of possession returns to a third party upon the expiration of a limited or contingent estate, it is called a **remainder**. The person who is entitled to the future interest is called a **remainderman**. For example, a conveyance of property "to Joe for life, remainder to Meredith" is a vested remainder, the only contingency to Meredith's possessory interest is Joe's death.

future interest

The interest that the grantor retains for himself or herself or for a third party.

reversion

A right of possession that returns to the grantor after the expiration of a limited or contingent estate.

remainder

If the right of possession returns to a third party upon the expiration of a limited or contingent estate.

CONCEPT SUMMARY — FUTURE INTERESTS

Future Interest	Description
Reversion	Right to possession of real property returns to the grantor after the expiration of a limited or contingent estate.
Remainder	Right to possession of real property goes to a third person upon the expiration of a limited or contingent estate.

Concurrent Ownership

co-ownership

When two or more persons own a piece of real property. Also called *concurrent ownership*.

Two or more persons may own a piece of real property. This ownership is called **co-ownership** or **concurrent ownership**. The following forms of co-ownership are recognized: joint tenancy, tenancy in common, tenancy by the entirety, community property, condominium, and cooperative.

joint tenancy

A form of co-ownership that includes the right of survivorship.

joint tenant

co-owner in a joint tenancy.

Joint Tenancy The most distinguishing feature of a **joint tenancy** is the co-owners' **right of survivorship**. Upon the death of one of the co-owners (or **joint tenants**), the deceased person's interest in the property automatically passes to the surviving joint tenants. Any contrary provision in the deceased's will is ineffective.

Business Brief

Upon the death of a joint tenant the deceased's interest in the property automatically passes to the surviving joint tenants, not to the deceased's heirs or beneficiaries.

Consider This Example Jones, one of four people who own a piece of property in joint tenancy, executes a will leaving all of his property to a university. Jones dies. The surviving joint tenants—not the university—acquire his interest in the piece of property.

To create a joint tenancy, words that clearly show a person's intent to create a joint tenancy must be used. Language such as "Marsha Leest and James Leest, as joint tenants" is usually sufficient. Some states specify that particular language must be used. Each joint tenant has a right to sell or transfer his or her interest in the property, but such conveyance terminates the joint tenancy. The parties then become tenants in common.

tenancy in common

A form of co-ownership where the interest of a surviving tenant-in-common passes to the deceased tenant's estate and not to the cotenants.

Tenancy in Common In a **tenancy in common**, the interests of a surviving **tenant in common** pass to the deceased tenant's estate and not to the cotenants.

Consider This Example Lopez, who is one of four tenants in common who own a piece of property, has a will that leaves all his property to his granddaughter. When Lopez dies, the granddaughter receives his interest in the tenancy in common, and the granddaughter becomes a tenant in common with three other owners.

A tenancy in common may be created by express words, such as "Jasmin Huang and Karen Ma, as tenants in common." There is a presumption that co-ownership of real property is a tenancy in common unless another intent is clearly indicated. For example, the words "to Annie Tsui and Min-Wer Chen, as co-owners" create a tenancy in common and not a joint tenancy. Unless otherwise agreed, a tenant in common can sell, give, devise, or otherwise transfer his or her interest in the property without the consent of the other co-owners.

tenancy by the entirety

A form of co-ownership of real property that can be used only by married couples.

The right of property has not made poverty, but it has powerfully contributed to make wealth.

J. R. McCulloch
(1789–1864)
Principles of Political
Economy

Tenancy by the Entirety **Tenancy by the entirety** is a form of co-ownership of real property that can be used only by married couples. This type of tenancy must be created by express words such as, "Harold Jones and Maude Jones, husband and wife, as tenants by the entireties." A surviving spouse has the right of survivorship.

Tenancy by the entirety is distinguished from a joint tenancy because neither spouse may sell or transfer his or her interest in the property without the other spouse's consent. A divorce terminates the tenancy because the marriage has ceased. The tenancy is then transformed into a tenancy in common. Only about half of the states recognize a tenancy by the entirety.

In the following case, the court had to decide how to split the proceeds from the sale of real property owned by co-owners.

Cunningham v. Hastings
556 N.E.2d 12 (1990)
Court of Appeals of Indiana

CASE 37.1

BACKGROUND AND FACTS

On August 30, 1984, Warren R. Hastings and Joan L. Cunningham, who were unmarried, purchased a house together. Hastings paid $45,000 down payment toward the purchase price out of his own funds. The deed referred to Hastings and Cunningham as "joint tenants with the right of survivorship." Hastings and Cunningham occupied the property jointly. After their relationship ended, Hastings took sole possession of the property. Cunningham filed a complaint seeking partition of the real estate. Based on its determination that the property could not be split, the trial court ordered it to be sold. The trial court further ordered that $45,000 of the sale proceeds be paid to Hastings to reimburse him for his down payment and the remainder of the proceeds be divided equally between Hastings and Cunningham. Cunningham appealed, alleging that Hastings should not have been given credit for the down payment.

ISSUE

Is Cunningham entitled to an equal share of the proceeds of the sale of the real estate?

COURT'S REASONING

The court stated:

The determination of the parties' interests in the present case is simple. There are only two parties involved in the joint tenancy. Once a joint tenancy relationship is found to exist between two people in a partition action, it is axiomatic that each person owns a one-half interest . . . regardless of who provided the money to purchase the land, the creation of a joint tenancy relationship entitles each party to an equal share of the proceeds of the sale upon partition.

DECISION

Cunningham is entitled to an equal share of the proceeds of the sale because she and Hastings owned the property as joint tenants. The appellate court reversed the trial court's judgment and remanded the case to the trial court with instructions to order the entire proceeds of the sale be divided equally between Cunningham and Hastings.

Case Questions

Critical Legal Thinking Should the law recognize so many different forms of ownership of real property? Do you think most people understand the legal consequences of taking title in the various forms?

Business Ethics Did Cunningham act ethically in demanding one-half the value of the down payment even though she did not contribute to it?

Contemporary Business Could Hastings have protected the $45,000 he paid for the down payment? If so, how could he have done it?

Contemporary Business Environment

COMMUNITY PROPERTY

Nine states—Arizona, California, Idaho, Louisiana, Nevada, New Mexico, Texas, Washington, and Wisconsin—recognize a form of co-ownership known as **community property**. This method of co-ownership applies only to married couples. It is based on the notion that a husband and wife should share equally in the fruits of the marital partnership. Under these laws, each spouse owns an equal one-half share of the income of both spouses and the assets acquired during the marriage, regardless of who earns the income. Property that is acquired through gift or inheritance either before or during marriage remains separate property.

When a spouse dies, the surviving spouse automatically receives one-half the community property. The other half passes to the heirs of the deceased spouse as directed by will or by state intestate statute if there is no will. For example, a husband and wife have community property

assets of $1.5 million and the wife dies with a will. The husband automatically has a right to receive $750,000 of the community property. The remaining $750,000 passes as directed by the wife's will. Any separate property owned by the wife, such as jewelry she inherited, also passes in accordance with her will. Her husband has no vested interest in that property.

During the marriage, neither spouse can sell, transfer, or gift community property without the consent of the other spouse. Upon a divorce, each spouse has a right to one-half the community property.

The location of the real property determines whether community property law applies. For example, if a married couple who lives in a noncommunity property state purchases real property located in a community property state, community property laws apply to that property.

Cooperative

cooperative

A form of co-ownership of a multiple-dwelling building where a corporation owns the building and the residents own shares in the corporation.

A **cooperative** is a form of co-ownership of a multiple-dwelling building where a corporation owns the building and the residents own shares in the corporation. Each cooperative owner then leases a unit in the building from the corporation under a renewable, long-term, proprietary lease. Individual residents may not secure loans with the units they occupy. The corporation may borrow money on a blanket mortgage, and each shareholder is jointly and severally liable on the loan. Usually, cooperative owners may not sell their shares or sublease their units without the approval of the other owners.

CONCEPT SUMMARY CONCURRENT OWNERSHIP

Form of Ownership	Right of Survivorship	Tenant May Unilaterally Transfer His or Her Interest
Joint tenancy	Yes, deceased tenant's interest automatically passes to co-tenants.	Yes, tenant may transfer his or her interest without the consent of cotenants. Transfer severs joint tenancy.
Tenancy in common	No, deceased tenant's interest passes to his or her estate.	Yes, tenant may transfer his or her interest without the consent of cotenants. Transfer does not sever tenancy in common.
Tenancy by the entirety	Yes, deceased tenant's interest automatically passes to his or her spouse.	No, neither spouse may transfer his or her interest without the other spouse's consent.
Community property	Yes, when a spouse dies the surviving spouse automatically receives one-half of the community property. The other half passes to the heirs of the deceased spouse as directed by a valid will or by state interstate statute if there is no will.	No, neither spouse may transfer his or her interest without the other spouse's consent.

Condominium

condominium

A common form of ownership in a multiple-dwelling building where the purchaser has title to the individual unit and owns the common areas as a tenant in common with the other condominium owners.

Condominiums are a common form of ownership in multiple-dwelling buildings. Purchasers of a condominium (1) have title to their individual units and (2) own the common areas (e.g., hallways, elevators, parking areas, and recreational facilities) as tenants in common with the other owners. Owners may sell or mortgage their units without the permission of the other owners. Owners are assessed monthly fees for the maintenance of common areas. In addition to dwelling units, the condominium form of ownership is offered for office buildings, boat docks, and such.

TRANSFER OF OWNERSHIP OF REAL PROPERTY

Ownership of real property may be transferred from one person to another. Title to real property may be transferred by sale; tax sale; gift, will, or inheritance; and adverse possession. The different methods of transfer provide different degrees of protection to the transferee.

Sale of Real Estate

sale

The passing of title from a seller to a buyer for a price. Also called a *conveyance*.

closing

The finalization of a real estate sales transaction that passes title to the property from the seller to the buyer.

A **sale** or **conveyance** is the most common method for transferring ownership rights in real property. An owner may offer his or her real estate for sale either by himself or herself or by using a real estate broker. Once a buyer has been located and the parties have negotiated the terms of the sale, a **real estate sales contract** is executed by the parties. The Statute of Frauds in most states requires this contract to be in writing.

The seller delivers a deed to the buyer and the buyer pays the purchase price at the **closing** or **settlement**. Unless otherwise agreed, it is implied that the seller is conveying fee simple absolute title to the buyer. If either party fails to perform, the other party may sue for breach of contract and obtain either monetary damages or specific performance.

Tax Sale

If an owner of real property fails to pay property taxes, the government may obtain a **lien** on the property for the amount of the taxes. If the taxes remain unpaid for a statutory period of time, the government may sell the property at a **tax sale** to satisfy the lien. Any excess proceeds arc paid to the taxpayer. The buyer receives title to the property.

Many states provide a **period of redemption** after a tax sale during which the taxpayer may redeem the property by paying the unpaid taxes and penalties. In these states, the buyer at a tax sale does not receive title to the property until the period of redemption has passed.

tax sale

A method of transferring property ownership that involves a lien on property for unpaid property taxes. If the lien remains unpaid after a certain amount of time, a tax sale is held to satisfy the lien.

Gift, Will, or Inheritance

Ownership of real property may be transferred by **gift**. The gift is made when the deed to the property is delivered by the donor to the donee or to a third party to hold for the donee. No consideration is necessary. For example, suppose a grandfather wants to give his farm to his granddaughter. To do so, he only has to execute a deed and give the deed to her or to someone to hold for her, such as her parents.

Real property may also be transferred by **will**. For example, a person may leave a piece of real estate to his best friend by will when he dies. This transfer does not require the transfer of a deed during the testator's lifetime. A deed will be issued to the beneficiary when the will is probated. If a person dies without a valid will, his or her property is distributed to the heirs pursuant to the applicable state intestacy statute.

gift

A transfer of property from one person to another without exchange of money.

will or inheritance

If a person dies with a will, his or her property is distributed to the beneficiaries as designated in the will. If a person dies without a will, his or her property is distributed to the heirs as stipulated in the state's intestacy statute.

Entrepreneur and the Law

WHAT A PURCHASER SHOULD DO WHEN BUYING REAL ESTATE

The most important purchase most people make in their lives is when they buy a place to live or other real estate. A potential homebuyer should spend sufficient time to investigate and analyze this decision. When purchasing a home, a buyer should:

- Employ a reputable real estate broker who will represent the buyer's interests in the transaction. This broker should be someone other than the listing broker hired by the seller. The buyer's broker usually splits the real estate sales commission with the listing broker. The commission is usually paid by the seller from the sales proceeds from the house.
- Request that the seller fully disclose all defects in the property. If the seller refuses to do so, it would probably be wise not to purchase the property. Some states require by law that such disclosure be made by the seller to potential buyers.
- Have the offer agreement prepared by an attorney or the real estate broker if the potential buyer decides to make an offer to purchase the house. Review the offer to make sure it is correct before signing it.
- Make sure the offer contains any necessary contingencies. For example, if the buyer needs bank financing, he or she should make the offer contingent on being approved for such financing at reasonable terms.
- Make the offer contingent on a full inspection and approval of the house. The potential buyer should hire the necessary professionals, such as a general contractor, to

examine the house. It is better to spend money in advance to locate any problems than to purchase the house and discover the defects at a later date.

- Hire a surveyor to conduct a survey to determine the true location of the lot lines and size of the property. Surveys sometimes reveal that a neighboring property owner may be encroaching on the seller's property (e.g., fence line). These problems have to be dealt with on a case-by-case basis.
- Either (1) purchase title insurance if available or (2) hire a lawyer to conduct a title search of the property. The purchase of title insurance is recommended because it warrants that the buyer has "clear title" to the property and, if this is not true, the insurance company will pay the buyer any damages suffered by the buyer.
- Make the offer contingent on an environmental report if there is any concern that there may be environmental pollution on the property. The buyer should employ a reputable and licensed environmental engineer to conduct the proper inspection of the property and prepare the report. If any environmental problems are discovered, it may be best not to purchase the property, because some federal and state environmental laws place cleaning costs on the owner of the property even if that owner did not cause the pollution.
- Either (1) hire a lawyer to represent the buyer at the closing of the transaction or (2) hire an independent escrow service to handle the closing of the transaction, depending on the law of the state.

Business Brief

Owners of property should check their property every so many years to determine if anyone is attempting to acquire title by adverse possession. If anyone is found to be doing so, the owner should take appropriate action to prevent the adverse possession.

Adverse Possession

In most states, a person who wrongfully possesses someone else's real property obtains title to that property if certain statutory requirements are met. This is called **adverse possession**. Property owned by federal and state governments is adverse possession.

Under this doctrine, the transfer of the property is involuntary and does not require the delivery of a deed. To obtain title under adverse possession, the wrongful possession must be

- *For a Statutorily Prescribed Period of Time*   In most states, this period is between 10 and 20 years.
- *Open, Visible, and Notorious*   The adverse possessor must occupy the property so as to put the owner on notice of the possession.
- *Actual and Exclusive*   The adverse possessor must physically occupy the premises. The planting of crops, grazing of animals, or building of a structure on the land constitutes physical occupancy.
- *Continuous and Peaceful*   The occupancy must be continuous and uninterrupted for the required statutory period. Any break in normal occupancy terminates the adverse possession. The adverse possessor may leave the property to go to work, to the store, to take vacations, and such. The adverse possessor cannot take the property by force from an owner.
- *Hostile and Adverse*   The possessor must occupy the property without the express or implied permission of the owner. Thus, a lessee cannot claim title to property under adverse possession.

If the elements of adverse possession are met, the adverse possessor acquires clear title to the land. Title is acquired only as to the property actually possessed and occupied during the statutory period, however, not the entire tract. For example, an adverse possessor who occupies one acre of a 200,000-acre ranch for the statutory period of time acquires title only to that acre.

Business Ethics

MODERN-DAY SQUATTERS

Many parts of this country, particularly the West, were settled by "squatters" who came, staked a claim to open property, farmed or ranched the property, and acquired title to it from the government. The federal government encouraged such activity by holding "land rushes" that awarded title to the first person who staked a claim to the designated lands.

Although the days of the Wild West are past, many states today recognize modern-day squatters' rights under the doctrine of adverse possession. Consider the following case.

Edward and Mary Shaughnessey purchased a 16-acre tract in St. Louis county in 1954. Subsequently, they subdivided 12 acres into 18 lots offered for sale and retained possession of the remaining 4-acre tract. In 1967, Charles and Elaine Witt purchased lot 12, which is adjacent to the 4-acre tract. The Witts constructed and moved into a house on their lot. In 1968, they cleared an area of land that ran the length of their property and extended 40 feet onto the 4-acre tract. The Witts constructed a pool and a deck, planted a garden, made a playground for their children, set up a dog run, and built a fence along the edge of the property line, which included the now-disputed property. Neither the Witts nor the Shaughnesseys realized that the Witts had encroached on the Shaughnesseys' property.

In February 1988, the Shaughnesseys sold the 4-acre tract to Thomas and Rosanne Miller. When a survey showed the encroachment, the Millers demanded that the Witts remove the pool and cease using the property. When the Witts refused to do so, the Millers sued to *quiet title*. The Witts defended, arguing that they had obtained title to the disputed property by adverse possession.

The court of appeals agreed with the Witts. The court held that the Witts had proven the necessary elements for adverse possession under state law. The Witts' occupation of the land was open and notorious, actual and exclusive, hostile and adverse, continuous and peaceful, and had been for over the statutory period of 10 years. The court issued an order quieting title to the disputed property in the Witts' favor. [*Witt v. Miller*, 845 S.W.2d 665 (Mo.App. 1993)].

1. Did the Millers act ethically in trying to eject people who had occupied the land for 20 years?
2. Did the Witts act ethically in claiming title to someone else's land? Should they be allowed to benefit from their own mistake?
3. What should owners of property do to protect themselves from adverse possession claims? Explain.

Deeds

Deeds are used to convey real property by sale or gift. The seller or donor is called the **grantor**. The buyer or recipient is called the **grantee**. A deed may be used to transfer a fee simple absolute interest in real property or any lesser estate (e.g., life estate).

State laws recognize different types of deeds that provide differing degrees of protection to grantees. A **warranty deed** (deed in which the grantor warrants that he or she has sold title to the real property) contains the greatest number of warranties and provides the most protection to grantees. A **quitclaim deed** (deed in which the grantor transfer only whatever interest he or she has in the real property) provides the least amount of protection because only the grantor's interest is conveyed.

Recording Statutes

Every state has a **recording statute** that provides that copies of deeds and other documents concerning interests in real property (e.g., mortgages, liens, easements) may be filed in a government office where they become public records open to viewing by the public. Recording statutes are intended to prevent fraud and to establish certainty in the ownership and transfer of property. Instruments are usually filed in the **county recorder's office** of the county in which the property is located. A fee is charged to record an instrument.

Persons interested in purchasing the property or lending on the property should check these records to determine whether the grantor or borrower actually owns the property and whether any other parties (e.g., lienholders, mortgagees, easement holders) have an interest in the property. The recordation of a deed is not required to pass title from the grantor to the grantee. Recording the deed gives **constructive notice** to the world of the owner's interest in the property.

A party who is concerned about his or her ownership rights in a parcel of real property can bring a **quiet title action** to have a court determine the extent of those rights. Public notice of the hearing must be given so that anyone claiming an interest in the property may appear and be heard. After the hearing, the judge declares who has title to the property; that is, the court "quiets title" by its decision.

Marketable Title

A grantor has the obligation to transfer **marketable title** or **good title** to the grantee. Marketable title means that the title is free from any encumbrances, defects in title, or other defects that are not disclosed but would affect the value of the property. The three most common ways of assuring marketable title are as follows:

- **Attorney's Opinion** An attorney examines an **abstract of title** (i.e., a chronological history of the chain of title and encumbrances affecting the property) and renders an opinion concerning the status of the title. The attorney may be sued for any losses caused by his or her negligence in rendering the opinion.
- **Torrens System** The Torrens system is a method of determining title to real property in a judicial proceeding at which everyone claiming an interest in the property may appear and be heard. After the evidence is heard, the court issues a **certificate of title** to the person who is determined to be the rightful owner.
- **Title Insurance** The best way for a grantee to be sure that he or she has obtained marketable title is to purchase **title insurance** from an insurance company. The title insurer must reimburse the insured for any losses caused by undiscovered defects in the title. Each time a property is transferred a new title insurance policy must be obtained.

deed
A writing that describes a person's ownership interest in a piece of real property.

grantor
The seller or donor who transfers an ownership interest in real property.

grantee
The buyer or recipient to whom an interest in real property is transferred.

recording statute
A state statute that requires the mortgage or deed of trust to be recorded in the county recorder's office of the county in which the real property is located.

Business Brief
Anyone interested in purchasing property or lending on the property should check the county recorder's records of the county in which the real property is located to determine if the grantor or borrower actually owns the property and whether any other parties have an interest in the property.

good title
Title that is free from any encumbrances or other defects that are not disclosed but would affect the value of the property.

Business Brief
Grantees should purchase title insurance on real property they acquire. The title insurer must reimburse the insured for any losses caused by undiscovered defects in title.

Landmark Law

THE CIVIL RIGHTS ACT

Federal and state governments have enacted statutes that prohibit discrimination in the sale and rental of real property. The **Civil Rights Act**, a federal statute, prohibits racial discrimination in all transfer of real property, including housing, commercial, and industrial property [42 U.S.C. §§ 1971 et seq.]. The act prohibits private and public discrimination and permits lawsuits to recover damages and obtain injunctions against offending conduct.

Many states and local communities have also enacted statutes and ordinances that prohibit discrimination in the sale or lease of real property. These laws usually prohibit discrimination based on race, color, national origin, sex, or religion but also often prohibit discrimination based on other protected classes such as age, sexual preference, and persons receiving government assistance.

$\mathcal{N}$ONPOSSESSORY INTERESTS

nonpossessory interest

When a person holds an interest in another person's property without actually owning any part of the property.

A person may own a **nonpossessory interest** in another's real estate. The three nonpossessory interests—easements, licenses, and profits—are discussed in the following paragraphs.

Easements

easement

A given or required right to make limited use of someone else's land without owning or leasing it.

An **easement** is an interest in land that gives the holder the right to make limited use of another's property without taking anything from it. Easements may be expressly created by **grant** (where an owner gives another party an easement across his or her property) or **reservation** (where an owner sells land that he or she owns but reserves an easement on the land). They also may be implied by (1) **implication**, where an owner subdivides a piece of property with a well, path, road, or other beneficial appurtenant that serves the entire parcel or by (2) **necessity**, for example, where "land-locked" property has an implied easement across surrounding property to enter and exit the land-locked property. Easements can also be created by **prescription**, that is, adverse possession.

Typical easements are common driveways, party walls, and rights-of-ways. There are two types of easements: easements appurtenant and easements in gross.

easement appurtenant

A situation created when the owner of one piece of land is given an easement over an adjacent piece of land.

1. **Easements Appurtenant** An **easement appurtenant** is created when the owner of one piece of land is given an easement over an adjacent piece of land. The land over which the easement is granted is called the **servient estate**. The land that benefits from the easement is called the **dominant estate**. Adjacent land is defined as two estates that are in proximity to each other, but do not necessarily abut each other. An appurtenant easement runs with the land. For example, if an owner sells the servient estate, the new owner acquires the benefit of the easement. If an owner sells the dominant estate, the buyer purchases the property subject to the easement.

easement in gross

An easement that authorizes a person who does not own adjacent land the right to use another's land.

2. **Easements in Gross** An **easement in gross** authorizes a person who does not own adjacent land the right to use another's land. An easement in gross is a personal right because it does not depend on the easement holder owning adjacent land. Thus, there is no dominant estate. Examples of easements in gross include those granted to run power, telephone, and cable television lines across an owner's property. Commercial easements in gross are transferable, but ordinary, noncommercial easements in gross are not. For example, that a farmer grants a hunter the right to hunt pheasant on his farm does not mean that other hunters are permitted to hunt on the farmer's property.

The easement holder owes a duty to maintain and repair the easement. The owner of the estate can use the property as long as it does not interfere with the easement. For example, if a piece of property is subject to an easement for an underground pipeline, the owner of the property could graze cattle or plant crops on the land above the easement, subject to the easement holder's right to repair the pipeline.

In the following case, the court had to decide whether an easement had been created.

Walker v. Ayres

1993 Lexis 105 (1993)

Supreme Court of Delaware

CASE 37.2

BACKGROUND AND FACTS

Elizabeth Star Ayres and Clara Louise Quillen own in fee simple absolute a tract of land in Sussex County known as "Bluff Point." The tract is surrounded on three sides by Rehoboth Bay and is landlocked on the fourth side by land owned by Irvin C. Walker. At one time, the two tracts were held by a common owner. In 1878, Bluff Point was sold in fee simple absolute apart from the other holdings, thereby land-locking the parcel. A narrow dirt road, which traverses Walker's land, connects Bluff Point to a public road and is its only means of access. Ayres and Quillen sought an easement to use this road, and Walker objected. This lawsuit ensued. The trial court granted an easement. Walker appealed.

ISSUE

Should Ayres' and Quillen's estate be granted an easement against Walker's estate?

COURT'S REASONING

The supreme court held that an easement appurtenant had been created between two adjacent parcels of property. The court held that the easement was created by implication in 1878 when Bluff Point was separated from the rest of the holdings and landlocked at that time. The court also held that an easement was created by necessity because Bluff Point was

landlocked and its only access was over Walker's property. The court found that water access, even if a reasonable substitute for land access, was not feasible because of the shallowness of the water surrounding Bluff Point.

DECISION

The supreme court held that an easement had been created. Affirmed.

Case Questions

Critical Legal Thinking Should easements be recognized by the law? Why or why not?

Business Ethics Did Walker act ethically in denying the easement? Did Ayres and Quillen act ethically in seeking to use Walker's property?

Contemporary Business Does an easement increase or decrease the value of the servient estate? Of the dominant estate?

Licenses

A **license** grants a person the right to enter upon another's property for a specified and usually short period of time. The person granting the license is called the **licensor**; the person receiving the license is called the **licensee**. For example, a common license is a ticket to a movie theater or sporting event that grants the holder the right to enter the premises for the performance. A license does not transfer any interest in the property. A license is a personal privilege that may be revoked by the licensor at any time.

license
Grants a person the right to enter upon another's property for a specified and usually short period of time.

Profits

A **profit a' pendre** (or **profit**) gives the holder the right to remove something from another's real property. Profits usually involve the right to remove gravel, minerals, grain, or timber from another's property. A *profit appurtenant* grants the owner of one piece of land the right to go onto another's adjacent land and remove things from it. A *profit in gross* authorizes someone who does not own adjacent land the right to go onto another's property and remove things from it.

profit
Grants a person the right to remove something from another's real property.

𝒞ONCEPT SUMMARY NONPOSSESSORY INTERESTS

Nonpossessory Interest	Description
Easement appurtenant	Easement over a servient estate that benefits a dominant estate. The easement runs with the land.
Easement in gross	Easement that grants a person a right to use another's land. It is a personal right that does not run with the land.
License	Grants a person the right to enter upon another's real property for a specified event or time (e.g., for a concert).
Profit	Grants the holder the right to remove something from another's real property (e.g., timber, grain).

Contemporary Business Environment

GOVERNMENT REGULATION VERSUS COMPENSABLE "TAKING" OF REAL PROPERTY

The government may use its power of **eminent domain** to acquire private property for public purposes. However, the Due Process Clause of the U.S. Constitution (and state constitutions where applicable) requires the government to allow the owner to make a case for keeping the property. The **Just Compensation Clause** of the Constitution mandates that the government must compensate the property owner (and possibly others, such as lessees) when it exercises the power of eminent domain. Anyone who is not satisfied with the compensation offered by the government can bring an action to have the court determine the compensation to be paid. Often, the government's action is not considered a "taking" even if it causes economic losses to property owners and others.

Consider This Example Assume that ITT acquired a large piece of property with the intention of erecting a commercial building at some future time. Now suppose the government wants to build a new highway that passes through property owned by ITT. The government can use its power of eminent domain to acquire the property. There has been a "taking," so the government must pay ITT just compensation. Suppose, instead, that the government enacts a zoning law that affects ITT's property by restricting building in the area to single-family housing. Although ITT would suffer a substantial economic loss, the zoning law, nevertheless, would probably not constitute a "taking" that required the payment of compensation.

The Supreme Court Speaks

Designation of the Grand Central Station as a Landmark Building Upheld

Penn Central Transportation Company v. City of New York
438 U.S. 104, 98 S.Ct. 2646 (1978)
Supreme Court of the United States

BACKGROUND AND FACTS

In 1965, the city of New York adopted the Landmark Preservation Law to encourage and require the preservation of buildings and areas with historic and aesthetic importance. The law was adopted to promote civic pride in the beauty and noble accomplishments of the past; protect and enhance the city's attractions to tourists and visitors; and enhance the pleasure, welfare, and quality of life of people. The primary responsibility of administering the law is vested in the Landmark Preservation Commission (Commission). Once a structure is designated a "lankmark" by Commission, no modification or change to the exterior of the building or site can be made without the permission of Commission.

On August 2, 1967, Commission designated the Grand Central Terminal (Terminal) as a landmark building and the city block it occupies as a landmark site. Terminal, which is owned by the Penn Central Transportation Company (Penn Central) is one of New York City's most famous buildings. Opened in 1913, this eight-story structure is a magnificent example of the French Beaux Arts style. Penn Central opposed the designation of Terminal as a landmark, but to no avail.

In January 1968, Penn Central filed an application with Commission to construct a 55-story office building in the airspace above the existing facade of Terminal. Commission denied Penn Central's application. Commission stated

We have no fixed rule against making additions to designated buildings—it all depends on how they are done. But to balance a 55-story office tower above a flamboyant Beaux Arts facade seems nothing more than an aesthetic joke. Quite simply, the tower would overwhelm the Terminal by its sheer mass.

Penn Central filed suit in New York Supreme Court. The trial court held in favor of Penn Central and granted an injunction and declaratory relief. The appellate division reversed. The court of appeals affirmed. Penn Central appealed.

SUPREME COURT ISSUE

Does New York City's Landmark Preservation Law effectuate a taking of Penn Central's property without just compensation in violation of the Fifth and Fourteenth amendments to the U.S. Constitution?

IN THE LANGUAGE OF THE COURT

Brennan, Justice *In contending that the New York City law has "taken" their property in violation of the Fifth and Fourteenth Amendments, appellants make a series of arguments. They first observe that the airspace above the Terminal is a valuable property interest. They urge that the Landmark law has deprived them of any gainful use of their air rights above the Terminal. The submission that appellants may establish a taking simply by showing that they have been denied the ability to exploit a property interest that* *they heretofore had believed was available for development is quite simply untenable.*

Second, appellants, focusing on the character and impact of the New York City law, argue that it effects a taking because its operation has significantly diminished the value of the Terminal site. Stated boldly, appellants' position appears to be that the only means of ensuring that selected owners are not singled out to endure financial hardship for no reason is to hold that any restriction imposed on individual landmarks pursuant to the New York City scheme is a taking requiring the payment of just compensation. Agreement with this argument would, of course, invalidate not just the New York City law, but all comparable landmark legislation in the nation. We find no merit in it.

It is, of course, true that the Landmark law has a more severe impact on some landowners than others, but that in itself does not mean that the law effects a "taking." Legislation designed to promote the general welfare commonly burdens some more than others. In any event, appellants' repeated suggestions that they are solely burdened and unbenefited is factually inaccurate. This contention overlooks the fact that the New York City law applies to vast numbers of structures in the city in addition to the Terminal—all the structures contained in the 31 historic districts and over 400 individual landmarks, many of which are close to the Terminal.

DECISION AND REMEDY

The U.S. Supreme Court held that the application of New York City's Landmark Preservation Law is a permissible government regulation that does not effectuate a taking of Penn Central's property under the Fifth and Fourteenth amendments to the U.S. Constitution.

CASE QUESTIONS

Critical Legal Thinking   Does the government owe a duty of social responsibility to protect historic buildings and districts from destruction? Or should the market be permitted to determine the highest value and best use for property?

Business Ethics   Did Penn Central act ethically in trying to construct a 55-story building above Terminal?

Contemporary Business   Does government regulation help or hurt business? Explain.

The Supreme Court Speaks

City Liable for "Regulatory Taking" of Real Property

City of Monterey v. Del Monte Dunes at Monterey, Ltd.
119 S.Ct. 1624 (1999)
Supreme Court of the United States

BACKGROUND AND FACTS

Del Monte Dunes at Monterey, Ltd. (Del Monte) owned a 37-acre ocean front parcel of real estate located in the City of Monterey, California. The parcel was zoned for multifamily residential use under the city's zoning ordinance. In 1981, Del Monte submitted an application to develop the property in conformity with the city's zoning ordinance and general plan requirements. Although the zoning law permitted up to 1,000 residential units for the entire parcel, Del Monte's proposal was limited to 344 units. In 1982, the city's planning commission denied the application, but stated that a proposal for 264 units would receive favorable consideration. Del Monte submitted a revised proposal for 264 units. In late 1983, the planning commission denied the application. The commission stated a plan for 244 units would be received with favor. When Del Monte submitted a proposal for 244 units, it too was denied.

On appeal, the Monterey city council suggested a 190-unit plan, but when Del Monte submitted this proposal the planning commission rejected it. On appeal, the city council requested that more space be dedicated to public open space. In 1985, Del Monte submitted a new plan devoting 17.9 of the 37.6-acre parcel to public open space, including a public beach. Only 5.1 acres were dedicated to buildings and patios. In 1986, the planning commission rejected the proposal. The city then issued a sewer-system hook-up moratorium that prevented development of the property entirely.

After five years, Del Monte decided that the City of Monterey would not permit the development of the property under any circumstances. Del Monte sued the City of Monterey for an unconstitutional, uncompensated "regulatory taking." During the trial, Del Monte sold the property to the state of California. The district court jury found against the City of Monterey and awarded Del Monte $1.75 million in damages. The court of appeals affirmed. The U.S. Supreme Court granted review.

SUPREME COURT ISSUE

Did the City of Monterey engage in a "regulatory taking" of real property in violation of the U.S. Constitution?

IN THE LANGUAGE OF THE U.S. SUPREME COURT

Kennedy, Justice *Rather, to the extent Del Monte Dunes' challenge was premised on unreasonable governmental action, the theory argued and tried to the jury was that the city's denial of the final development permit was inconsistent not only with the city's general ordinances and policies but even with the shifting ad hoc restrictions previously imposed by the city. Del Monte Dunes' argument, in short, was not that the city had followed its zoning ordinances and policies but rather that it had not done so. As is often* *true in these actions, the disputed questions were whether the government had denied a constitutional right in acting outside the bounds of its authority, and, if so, the extent of any resulting damages. These were questions for the jury.*

DECISION AND REMEDY

The U.S. Supreme Court held that the issue of whether the City of Monterey's repeated rejections of Del Monte's development proposals deprived the owner of all economically viable use of the land was properly submitted to the jury. Affirmed.

CASE QUESTIONS

Critical Legal Thinking   What is a *regulatory taking*? Why does this violate the U.S. Constitution? Explain.

Business Ethics   Did the members of the City of Monterey's planning commission and city council act ethically in this case? What do you think was the city's motive in acting the way it did?

Contemporary Business   Is there government regulation that does not violate the U.S. Constitution? Give an example. Does this regulation have any economic consequences?

LANDLORD–TENANT RELATIONSHIP

landlord–tenant relationship

A relationship created when the owner of a freehold estate (landlord) transfers a right to exclusively and temporarily possess the owner's property to another (tenant).

leasehold

A tenant's interest in the property.

landlord

The owner who transfers the leasehold.

tenant

The party to whom the leasehold is transferred.

lease

A transfer of the right to the possession and use of the real property for a set term in return for certain consideration; the rental agreement between a landlord and a tenant.

tenancy for years

A tenancy created when the landlord and tenant agree on a specific duration for the lease.

periodic tenancy

A tenancy created when a lease specifies intervals at which payments are due but does not specify how long the lease is for.

tenancy at will

A lease that may be terminated at any time by either party.

A **landlord–tenant relationship** is created when the owner of a freehold estate (i.e., an estate in fee or a life estate) transfers a right to exclusively and temporarily possess the owner's property. The tenant receives a **nonfreehold estate** in the property; that is, the tenant has a right to possession of the property but not title to the property.

The tenant's interest in the property is called a **leasehold estate**, or **leasehold**. The owner who transfers the leasehold estate is called the **landlord**, or **lessor**. The party to whom the leasehold estate is transferred is called the **tenant**, or **lessee**.

The Lease

The rental agreement between the landlord and the tenant is called the **lease**. Leases can generally be either oral or written except that most Statutes of Frauds require written leases for periods of time longer than one year. The lease must contain the essential terms of the parties' agreement. The lease is often a form contract that is prepared by the landlord and presented to the tenant. This practice is particularly true of residential leases. Other leases are negotiated between the parties. For example, Bank of America's lease of a branch office would be negotiated with the owner of the building.

Types of Tenancy

There are four types of **tenancies**: (1) tenancy for years, (2) periodic tenancy, (3) tenancy at will, and (4) tenancy at sufferance. Each is described in the following paragraphs.

1. *Tenancy for Years*   A **tenancy for years** is created when the landlord and the tenant agree on a specific duration for the lease. Any lease for a stated period—no matter how long or short—is called a tenancy for years. Examples of such arrangements include office space leased in a high-rise office building on a 30-year lease and a cabin leased for the summer.

    A tenancy for years terminates automatically, without notice, upon the expiration of the stated term. Sometimes, such leases contain renewal or extension clauses. If a tenant dies during the lease term, the lease is personal property which transfers to his or her heirs.

2. *Periodic Tenancy*   A **periodic tenancy** is created when a lease specifies intervals at which payments are due but that does not specify how long the lease is for. A lease that states "Rent is due on the first day of the month" establishes a periodic tenancy. Many such leases are created by implication.

    A periodic tenancy may be terminated by either party at the end of any payment interval, but adequate notice of the termination must be given. At common law, the notice period equaled the length of the payment period. That is, a month-to-month tenancy requires a one-month notice of termination. Most states have enacted statutes that set forth the required notice periods for termination of periodic tenancies. If a tenant dies during a periodic tenancy, the lease transfers to his or her heirs for the remainder of the current payment interval.

3. *Tenancy at Will*   A lease that may be terminated at any time by either party is a **tenancy at will**. A tenancy at will may be created expressly (e.g., "to tenant as long as landlord wishes") but is more likely to be created by implication.

At common law, a tenancy at will could be terminated by either party without advance notice—that is, notice of termination ended the lease the moment it was given. Most states have enacted statutes requiring minimum advance notice for the termination of a tenancy at will. The death of either party terminates a tenancy at will.

4. ***Tenancy at Sufferance*** A **tenancy at sufferance** is created when a tenant retains possession of property after the expiration of another tenancy or a life estate without the owner's consent. That is, the owner suffers the *wrongful possession* of his or her property by the holdover tenant. This situation is not really a true tenancy but merely the possession of property without right. Technically, a tenant at sufferance is a trespasser.

A tenant at sufferance is liable for the payment of rent during the period of sufferance. Most states require an owner to go through certain legal proceedings, called **eviction proceedings** or **unlawful detainer actions**, to evict a holdover tenant. A few states allow owners to use self-help to evict a holdover tenant if force is not used.

tenancy at sufferance

A tenancy created when a tenant retains possession of property after the expiration of another tenancy or a life estate without the owner's consent.

CONCEPT SUMMARY   TYPES OF TENANCIES

Type of Tenancy	Description
Tenancy for years	Continues for the duration of the lease and then terminates automatically without notice. It does not terminate by the death of either party.
Periodic tenancy	Continues from payment interval to payment interval. It may be terminated by either party with adequate notice. It does not terminate upon the death of either party.
Tenancy at will	Continues at the will of the parties and may be terminated by either party at any time with adequate notice. It terminates upon the death of either party.
Tenancy at sufferance	Arises when a tenant wrongfully occupies real property after the expiration of another tenancy or life estate. It continues until the owner either evicts the tenant or holds him or her over for another term. It terminates upon the death of the tenant.

Landmark Law

THE FAIR HOUSING ACT

The **Fair Housing Act**, a federal statute, makes it unlawful for a party to refuse to rent or sell a dwelling to any person because of his or her race, color, national origin, sex, or religion [42 U.S.C. §§ 360 et seq.]. The act also prohibits discrimination by real estate brokers, mortgage lenders, and advertisers concerning the sale or rental of real property. The law does not apply to the following leases: (1) a person who owns a building of four or fewer units and occupies one of the units and leases the others and (2) a person who leases a single-family dwelling and does not own more than three single-family dwellings. To qualify for either exemption, the lessor cannot use a real estate broker or advertise in a discriminating manner.

LANDLORD'S AND TENANT'S DUTIES

The duties a landlord owes a tenant are either expressly provided in the lease, set forth in statute, or implied by law. The landlord's and tenant's duties are discussed in the following paragraphs.

Property has its duties as well as its rights.

Benjamin Disraeli
Sybil, Bk. II, Ch. XI
(1845)

Landlord's Duties

A landlord owes the following duties to the tenant:

- **Duty to Deliver Possession** A lease grants the tenant *exclusive* **possession** of the leased premises until (1) the term of the lease expires or (2) the tenant defaults on the obligations under the lease. The landlord is obligated to deliver possession of the leased premises to the tenant on the date the lease term begins. A landlord may not enter leased premises unless the right is specifically reserved in the lease.

possession

A lease grants the tenant *exclusive possession* of the leased premises for the term of the lease or until the tenant defaults on the obligations under the lease.

covenant of quiet enjoyment

A covenant that says that a landlord may not interfere with the tenant's quiet and peaceful possession, use, and enjoyment of the leased premises.

wrongful eviction

A violation of the covenant of quiet enjoyment.

building codes

State and local statutes that impose specific standards on property owners to maintain and repair leased premises.

implied warranty of habitability

A warranty that provides that the leased premises must be fit, safe, and suitable for ordinary residential use.

Good fences make good neighbors.

Robert Frost
Mending Wall (1914)

- **Duty Not to Interfere with the Tenant's Right to Quiet Enjoyment**   The law implies a **covenant of quiet enjoyment** in all leases. Under this covenant, the landlord may not interfere with the tenant's quiet and peaceful possession, use, and enjoyment of the leased premises. The covenant is breached if the landlord, or anyone acting with the landlord's consent, interferes with the tenant's use and enjoyment of the property. This interference is called **wrongful** or **unlawful eviction**. It may occur if the landlord actually evicts the tenant by physically preventing him or her from possessing or using the leased premises or if the landlord **constructively evicts** the tenant by causing the leased premises to become unfit for their intended use (e.g., by failing to provide electricity). If the landlord refuses to cure the defect after a reasonable time, a tenant who has been constructively evicted may (1) sue for damages and possession of the premises or (2) treat the lease as terminated, vacate the premises, and cease paying rent. The landlord is not responsible for wrongful acts of third persons that were done without his or her authorization.

- **Duty to Maintain the Leased Premises**   At common law, the doctrine of *caveat lessee*—"lessee beware"—applied to leases. The landlord made no warranties about the quality of leased property and had no duty to repair it. The tenant took the property "as is." Modern real estate law, however, imposes certain statutory and judicially implied duties on landlords to repair and maintain leased premises.

  States and local municipalities have enacted statutes called **building** or **housing codes**. These statutes impose specific standards on property owners to maintain and repair leased premises. They often provide certain minimum standards regarding heat, water, light, and other services. Depending on the statute, violators may be subject to fines by the government, loss of their claim for rent, and imprisonment for serious violations.

Implied Warranty of Habitability

The courts of many jurisdictions hold that an **implied warranty of habitability** applies to residential leases for their duration. This warranty provides that the leased premises must be fit, safe, and suitable for ordinary residential use. For example, unchecked rodent infestation, leaking roofs, unworkable bathroom facilities, and the like have been held to breach the implied warranty of habitability. On the other hand, a small crack in the wall or some paint peeling from a door does not breach this warranty.

If the landlord's failure to maintain or repair the leased premises affects the tenant's use or enjoyment of the premises, state statutes and judicial decisions provide various remedies. Generally, the tenant may (1) withhold from his or her rent the amount by which the defect reduced the value of the premises to him or her, (2) repair the defect and deduct the cost of repairs from the rent due for the leased premises, (3) cancel the lease if the failure to repair constitutes constructive eviction, or (4) sue for damages in the amount the landlord's failure to repair the defect reduced the value of the leasehold.

In the following case, the court found a breach of the implied warranty of habitability.

Solow v. Wellner
569 N.Y. Supp.2d 882 (1991)
Civil Court of the City of New York

CASE 37.3

BACKGROUND AND FACTS

The defendants are approximately 80 tenants of a 300-unit luxury apartment building on the upper East Side of Manhattan. The rents in the all-glass-enclosed building, which won several architectural awards, ranged from $1,064 to $5,379. The landlord brought a summary proceeding against the tenants to recover rent when they engaged in a rent strike in protest against what they viewed as deteriorating conditions and services. Among other things, the evidence showed that during the period in question (May 1982 to May 1988), the elevator system made tenants and their guests wait interminable lengths of time, the elevators skipped floors and opened on the wrong floors, a stench emanated from garbage stored near the garage and mice appeared in that area, fixtures were missing in public areas, water seeped into mailboxes, the air conditioning in the lobby was inoperative, and air conditioners in individual units leaked. The defendant-tenants sought abatement of rent for breach of the implied warranty of habitability.

ISSUE

Did the landlord breach the implied warranty of habitability?

COURT'S REASONING

New York recognizes the implied warranty of habitability in residential housing. The court held that this warranty requires a landlord not only to maintain premises free of conditions that threaten the lives, safety, and welfare of the tenants but also to meet the "reasonable expectations" of tenants. The court stated, "Certain amenities not necessarily life threatening, but consistent with the nature of the bargain, fall under the protection of this warranty." The court held that the obvious expectations of the tenants of this uniquely designed apartment building on Manhattan's fashionable upper East Side had not been met.

DECISION

The court held that the landlord had breached the implied warranty of habitability. The court abated the rent of each of the tenants individually, in total allowing the landlord to recover only 22 percent of the amount he sued for. The court ordered the landlord to pay the tenants' attorney's fees.

Case Questions

Critical Legal Thinking Should the law recognize the implied warranty of habitability? Why or why not?

Business Ethics Did the landlord act ethically in not correcting the defects in the building? Did the tenants act ethically in engaging in a rent strike?

Contemporary Business Was the remedy the court ordered appropriate in this case?

Tenant's Duties

The tenant owes the following duties to the landlord:

- **Duty Not to Use Leased Premises for Illegal or Nonstipulated Purposes** A tenant may use the leased property for any lawful purposes permitted by the lease. Leases often stipulate that the leased premises can be used only for specific purposes. If the tenant uses the leased premises for unlawful purposes (e.g., operating an illegal gambling casino) or nonstipulated purposes (e.g., operating a restaurant in a residence), the landlord may terminate the lease, evict the tenant, and sue for damages.
- **Duty Not to Commit Waste** A tenant is under a duty not to commit **waste** to the leasehold. Waste occurs when the tenant causes substantial and permanent damage to the leased premises that decreases the value of the property and the landlord's reversionary interest in it. Waste does not include ordinary wear and tear. For example, it would be waste if the floor of the premises buckled because a tenant permitted heavy equipment to be placed on the premises. It would not be waste if the paint chipped from the walls because of the passage of time. The landlord can recover damages from the tenant for waste.
- **Duty Not to Disturb Other Tenants** A tenant owes a duty not to disturb the use and enjoyment of the leased premises by other tenants in the same building. For example, a tenant in an apartment building breaches this duty if he or she disturbs the sleep of other tenants by playing loud music throughout the night. A landlord may evict the tenant who interferes with the quiet enjoyment of other tenants.

waste

Occurs when a tenant causes substantial and permanent damage to the leased premises that decreases the value of the property and the landlord's reversionary interest in it.

Soho, New York City Many people rent apartments from landlords. The landlord and tenant owe each other certain duties.

Entrepreneur and the Law

DUTY TO PAY RENT

A commercial or residential tenant owes a duty to pay the agreed-upon amount of **rent** for the leased premises to the landlord at the agreed-upon time and terms. Generally, rent is payable in advance (e.g., on the first day of the month for use that month), although the lease may provide for other times and methods for payment. Reasonable late charges may be assessed on rent that is overdue. In a **gross lease** the tenant pays a gross sum to the landlord. The landlord is responsible for paying the property taxes and assessments on the property.

Several of the most common commercial rental arrangements are

- **Net Lease**   The tenant is responsible for paying rent and property taxes.
- **Double Net Lease**   The tenant is responsible for paying rent, property taxes, and utilities.
- **Net, Net, Net Lease (or Triple Net Lease)**   The tenant is responsible for paying rent, property taxes, utilities, and insurance.

Upon nonpayment of rent, the landlord is entitled to recover possession of the leased premises from the tenant. This may require the landlord to *evict* the tenant. Most states provide a summary procedure called **unlawful detainer action** that a landlord can institute to evict a tenant. The landlord may also sue to recover the unpaid rent from the tenant. The more modern rule requires the landlord to make reasonable efforts to *mitigate damages* (i.e., to make reasonable efforts to re-lease the premises).

Tenants often are required to pay a *security deposit* to the landlord. In residential leases, the amount generally is equivalent to one month's rent. The landlord may apply the security deposit against unpaid rent or use it to cover the cost of repairing damages caused by the tenant to the leased premises. Any remaining security must be repaid to the tenant within 14 days after the lease is terminated. Some states require landlords to hold the security deposits in a separate trust account and to pay interest on the deposits.

Transferring Rights to Leased Property

Landlords may sell, gift, devise, or otherwise transfer their interests in the leased property. For example, a landlord can sell either the right to receive rents, his or her reversionary interest, or both. If complete title is transferred, the property is subject to the existing lease. The new landlord cannot alter the terms of the lease (e.g., raise the rent) during the term of the lease unless the lease so provides.

The tenant's right to transfer possession of the leased premises to another depends on the terms of the lease. Many leases permit the leases to *assign* or *sublease* his or her rights in the property.

assignment

A transfer by a tenant of his or her rights under a lease to another.

assignor

The party who transfers the right.

assignee

The party to whom the right has been transferred.

sublease

When a tenant transfers only some of his or her rights under the lease.

sublessor

The original tenant in a sublease situation.

sublessee

The new tenant in a sublease situation.

Business Brief

The landlord cannot sue the sublessee to recover rent payments or enforce the lease. The landlord must look to the original tenant (sublessor) for satisfaction of the terms of the lease.

- **Assignment of the Lease**   If a tenant transfers all his or her interests under a lease, it is an **assignment**. The original tenant is the **assignor** and the new tenant is the **assignee**. Under an assignment, the assignee acquires all the rights that the assignor had under the lease. The assignee is obligated to perform the duties that the assignor had under the lease. That is, the assignee must pay the rent and perform other covenants contained in the original lease. The assignor remains responsible for his or her obligations under the lease unless specifically released to do so by the landlord. If the landlord recovers from the assignor, the assignor has a course of action to recover from the assignee.
- **Sublease**   If a tenant transfers only some of his or her rights under the lease, it is a **sublease**. The original tenant is the **sublessor** and the new tenant is the **sublessee**. The sublessor is not released from his or her obligations under the lease unless specifically released by the landlord. Subleases differ from assignments in important ways. In a sublease, no legal relationship is formed between the landlord and the sublessee. Therefore, the sublessee does not acquire rights under the original lease. For example, a sublessee would not acquire the sublessor's option to renew a lease. Further, the landlord cannot sue the sublessee to recover rent payments or enforce duties under the original lease.

In most cases, tenants cannot assign or sublease their leases without the landlord's consent. This right protects the landlord from the transfer of the leasehold to someone who might damage the property or not have the financial resources to pay the rent. Most states, either by statute or judicial decision, hold that the owner's consent cannot be unreasonably withheld.

Landmark Law

TITLE III OF THE AMERICANS WITH DISABILITIES ACT

On July 26, 1990, the **Americans with Disabilities Act (ADA)** was signed into law [42 U.C.C. §§ 1201 et seq.]. Most of the provisions of the ADA became effective on January 26, 1992. The ADA is a broad civil rights statute that prohibits discrimination against disabled individuals in employment, public services, public accommodations and services, and telecommunications. **Title III** of the ADA prohibits discrimination on the basis of disability in places of public accommodation operated by private entities. The attorney general of the United States is empowered to issue regulations that interpret and enforce the ADA.

Title III of the ADA applies to public accommodations and commercial facilities such as motels, hotels, restaurants, theaters, recreation facilities, colleges and universities, department stores, retail stores, and office buildings. It does not generally apply to residential facilities (single- and multifamily housing).

Title III requires facilities that are covered by the law to be designed, constructed, and altered in compliance with specific accessibility requirements established by regulations issued pursuant to the ADA. In 1991, the attorney general issued final regulations that contain minimum guidelines to make covered facilities accessible to disabled individuals. This includes constructing ramps to accommodate wheelchairs, installing railings next to steps, placing signs written in Braille in elevators and at elevator call buttons, and so on. If both the ADA and state law apply, the more stringent rule must be followed.

New construction must be built in such a manner as to be readily accessible to and usable by disabled individuals. Any alterations made to existing buildings must be made so that the altered portions of the building are readily accessible to disabled individuals to the maximum extent feasible. With respect to existing buildings, architectural barriers must be removed if such removal is readily achievable. In determining when an action is readily achievable, the factors to be considered include the nature and cost of the action, the financial resources of the facility, and the type of operations of the facility.

The ADA provides for both private right of action and enforcement by the attorney general. Individuals may seek injunctive relief and monetary damages, while the attorney general may seek equitable relief and civil fines up to $50,000 for the first violation and $100,000 for any subsequent violation.

Proponents of Title III of the ADA argue that the law is necessary to make public accommodations and commercial facilities accommodate the needs of the disabled. They point out that voluntary efforts to make these accommodations were too few and too late. Critics argue that the ADA creates a quagmire of regulations that are difficult to understand and that will cost landowners billions of dollars to comply with.

Building owners, managers, architects, and others involved in the design, construction, ownership, and management of public accommodations and commercial buildings must be knowledgeable about, and comply with, the provisions of Title III of the ADA.

LAND USE CONTROL

Generally, the ownership of property entitles the owner to use his or her property as the owner wishes. Such use, however, is subject to limitations imposed by either private agreement or government regulation. These limitations are collectively referred to as **land use control** or **land use regulation**.

land use control

The collective term for the laws that regulate the possession, ownership, and use of real property.

Ranch, Idaho *Local zoning laws often restrict the use of real property to certain specified uses, such as ranch or farming, commercial, or residential use.*

restrictive covenant

A private agreement between landowners that restricts the use of their land.

Landmark Law

In *Shelley v. Kraemer*, 334 U.S.A. (1948), the U.S. Supreme Court struck down restrictive covenants in deeds that prohibited minorities from owning residential property in certain neighborhoods.

police power

Constitutional authority of state and local governments to enact laws to protect the public health, safety, morals, and welfare.

zoning ordinance

Local laws that are adopted by municipalities and local governments to regulate land use within their boundaries. Zoning ordinances are adopted and enforced to protect the health, safety, morals, and general welfare of the community.

- **Restrictive Covenants**   A **restrictive covenant** is a private agreement between landowners that restricts the use of their land. Restrictive covenants are commonly called **building restrictions** or **CC&Rs (covenants, conditions, and restrictions)**. They are often used by residential developments and condominium buildings to establish uniform rules for all occupants. For example, restrictive covenants often restrict the height, size, and location of buildings; establish rules for collection of garbage; prohibit or limit the number of pets; and so on.

    Lawful restrictive covenants may be enforced in private lawsuits. For example, if several lot owners have agreed not to build houses over one story high to preserve views, any lot holder can sue another lot owner to enforce this covenant against the building of a two-story house. Restrictive covenants that discriminate based on race, national origin, sex, age, religion, or other protected class are illegal and void.

- **Public Regulation of Land Use**   Pursuant to their constitutional "**police power**," state and local governments may enact laws to protect the public health, safety, morals, and general welfare of the community. Pursuant to this power, most counties and municipalities have enacted **zoning ordinances** to regulate land use. For example, zoning ordinances prohibiting the location of adult bookstores near residential areas have been held to be valid to protect public morals. Zoning is the primary form of land use regulation in this country.

    Zoning ordinances generally (1) establish use districts within the municipality (i.e., areas are generally designated residential, commercial, or industrial), (2) restrict the height, size, and location of buildings on a building site, and (3) establish aesthetic requirements or limitations for the exterior of buildings.

    A **zoning commission** usually formulates zoning ordinances, conducts public hearings, and makes recommendations to the city council, who must vote to enact an ordinance. Once enacted, the zoning ordinance commission enforces the zoning ordinance. If a landowner believes that a zoning ordinance is illegal or that it has been applied unlawfully in this situation, he or she may institute a court proceeding seeking judicial review of the ordinance or its application.

    The following case is concerned with the lawfulness of a zoning ordinance.

Guinnane v. San Francisco City Planning Commission
209 Cal.App.3d. 732, 257 Cal.Rptr. 742 (1989)
California Court of Appeal

CASE 37.4

BACKGROUND AND FACTS
In 1979, Roy Guinnane purchased four vacant lots located in Edgehill Way in San Francisco. In July 1980, the city of San Francisco designated an area as "Edgehill Woods." Guinnane's property was located in that area. In 1982, the city adopted a resolution to exercise its discretionary review power over proposed development in the Edgehill Woods area. Guinnane filed an application for a building permit to construct a four-story, 6,000-square-foot house with five bedrooms, five baths, and parking for two cars on one of his lots. Although the proposed building met the specifications of other zoning laws and building codes, the San Francisco Planning Commission disapproved the application because the proposed structure was "not in character" with other homes in the neighborhood. The board of permit appeals agreed. Guinnane appealed.

ISSUE
Is the aesthetic zoning by the city of San Francisco lawful?

COURT'S REASONING
The appellate court held that the planning commission acted within its discretion in finding that Guinnane's proposed building was "not in character" with other homes in the area. In affirming the planning commission's decision, the court stated:

The basic standard guiding the Planning Commission in discharging its function is the promotion of the public health, safety, peace, morals, comfort, convenience, and general welfare. In particular, the Commission is directed to "protect the character and stability of residential areas." Under the Municipal Code, any city department may exercise its discretion in deciding whether to approve any application; and in doing so, it may consider the effect of the proposed project upon the surrounding properties. We conclude that the Planning Commission is authorized to exercise independent discretionary review of a building permit application.

DECISION
The appellate court held that San Francisco's aesthetic zoning ordinance was lawful. The court found that the ordinance was enacted pursuant to the city's "police power" to protect its residents' health, safety, and welfare. The appellate court affirmed the trial court's judgment.

Case Questions

Critical Legal Thinking   Should a city be given zoning authority over the aesthetics of an area? Why or why not?

Business Ethics   Is it ethical for a property owner to build a structure that does not comport with the character of the area?

Contemporary Business   Are businesses helped or harmed by zoning ordinances?

Variances   An owner who wishes to use his or her property for a use different from that permitted under a current zoning ordinance may seek relief from the ordinance by obtaining a **variance**. To obtain a variance, the landowner must prove that the ordinance causes an undue hardship by preventing him or her from making a reasonable return on the land as zoned. Variances are usually difficult to obtain.

Nonconforming Uses   Zoning laws act prospectively; that is, uses and buildings that already exist in the zoned area are permitted to continue even though they do not fit within new zoning ordinances. Such uses are called **nonconforming uses**. For example, if a new zoning ordinance is enacted making an area a residential zone, an existing funeral parlor is a nonconforming use.

variance

An exception that permits a type of building or use in an area that would not otherwise be allowed by a zoning ordinance.

nonconforming uses

Uses and buildings that already exist in the zoned area that are permitted to continue even though they do not fit within new zoning ordinances.

International Law

SORTING OUT REAL PROPERTY OWNERSHIP RIGHTS IN THE FORMER EAST GERMANY

When the Berlin Wall tumbled in 1989, it allowed for the reunification of East and West Germany into one country. The event was heralded as a triumph for democracy because it meant the return of capitalism and private property rights to East Germany. Only one major question remained: Who owns the real property in the former East Germany?

Germany was under the influence and rule of the Nazi Party from 1933 until May 1945, when Germany surrendered to the Allies after World War II. During that time, the Nazis appropriated private property from owners. After the war, Germany was divided between West Germany, which was allied with Europe and the United States, and East Germany, which was under the Soviet Union's control. The city of Berlin, which was located in East Germany, was also divided in half. The Berlin Wall was erected to prevent East Berliners from defecting to the West through West Berlin. From 1945 to 1949, the Soviets appropriated private property in East Germany. In 1949, the East German government was created. Until 1989, East Germany was a communist state that owned the property of the country.

In 1990, after the reunification of Germany, the German government enacted the **Vermogensgesetz (Statute for the Regulation of Open Property Questions)** and the **Anmeldeverordnung (Regulation on the Filing of Claims)**. Together, the statute and the regulations created a procedure for filing and proving claims to property expropriated by the Nazis before and during World War II, by the Soviets between 1945 and 1949, and by the East German government from 1949 to 1989.

The German property claims law set December 31, 1992, as the final date for the filing of claims for the return of real property. Claimants had to file an application that specified the location, kind, and extent of the property; original ownership; and chain of inheritance. After examining the claims, the German authorities make decisions and award ownership rights. This process will take many years.

In the meantime, the German government enacted a new law that requires a permit for the sale or transfer of real property situated in the former East Germany. The permit will not be issued if a claim for the return of the property has been filed. A claimant can also apply for an injunction in the civil court to prevent the transfer of property until the merits of the claim have been decided.

One provision in the German claims law favors Jewish claimants. There is a presumption in the law that any property sold between January 1933 and May 1945 is considered to be sold under duress, unless the buyer can prove otherwise. This is because during that time period, Nazi officials forced Jews to transfer their property for little or no consideration under threat of harm or death.

Resolving the property claims in the former East Germany will not be an easy task. Any other governments in other socialist or communist countries that change to a democratic, capitalist system will face similar problems. For example, real property rights in the former Union of Soviet Socialist Republics (USSR) and many East European countries probably will be determined using a procedure similar to that used in Germany.

CHAPTER SUMMARY

Nature of Real Property, p. 931

Nature of Real Property	*Real property* is immovable. It includes land, buildings, subsurface rights, air rights, plant life, and fixtures.

Estates in Land, p. 932

Freehold Estates	Estates where the owner has a present possessory interest in the real property. *Estates in Fee* 1. *Fee simple absolute* (or *fee simple*). Highest form of ownership. 2. *Fee simple defeasible* (or *qualified fee*). Estate that ends if a specified condition occurs. *Life Estates.* An interest in real property that lasts for the life of a specified person. Called an *estate pour autre vie* if the time is measured by the life of a third person.
Future Interests	Right to possess real property in the future rather than currently. *Reversion.* Right to possession that returns to the grantor after the expiration of a limited or contingent estate. *Remainder.* Right to possession that goes to a third person after the expiration of a limited or contingent estate. The third person is called a *remainderman*.
Concurrent Ownership	Where two or more persons jointly own real property. *Joint Tenancy.* Owners may transfer their interests without the consent of co-owners. Transfer severs the joint tenancy. Under the *right of survivorship*, the interest of a deceased owner passes to his or her co-owners. *Tenancy in Common.* Owners may transfer their interests without the consent of co-owners. Transfer does not sever the tenancy in common. Interest of a deceased owner passes to his or her estate. *Tenancy by the Entirety.* Form of co-ownership that can be used only by a married couple. Neither spouse may transfer his or her interest without the other spouse's consent. A surviving spouse has the right of survivorship. *Community Property.* Form of co-ownership that applies only to a married couple. Neither spouse may transfer his or her interest without the other spouse's consent. When a spouse dies, the surviving spouse automatically receives one-half the community property. *Cooperative.* A corporation owns the building and the residents own shares of the corporation. Usually, owners may not transfer their shares without the approval of the other owners. *Condominium.* Condominium owners have title to their individual units and own the common areas as tenants in common. Owners may transfer their interest without the consent of other owners.

Transfer of Ownership of Real Property, p. 936

Sale of Real Estate	An owner sells his or her property to another for consideration. Government obtains a lien on property for nonpayment of taxes and sells the property at a tax sale to a buyer. The buyer takes the title subject to the taxpayer's right of redemption.
Gift, Will, or Inheritance	Owners may give their property to another during their lifetime or leave their property by will to a beneficiary when they die. If a person dies without a will, his or her property is distributed to the heirs pursuant to state intestacy statutes.
Adverse Possession	A person who occupies another's property acquires title to the property if the occupation has been: 1. For a statutory period of time (in many states, 10 to 20 years) 2. Open, visible, and notorious 3. Actual and exclusive 4. Continuous and peaceful 5. Hostile and adverse
Deeds	Instrument used to convey real property by sale or gift. 1. *Warranty deed.* Provides the most protection to the grantee because the grantor makes warranties against defect in title. 2. *Quitclaim deed.* Provides least amount of protection to the grantee because the grantor transfers only the interest he or she has in the property.
Recording Statutes	Permits copies of deeds and other documents concerning interests in real property (e.g., mortgages, liens) to be filed in a government office where they become public record. Puts third parties on notice of recorded interests.
Marketable Title	Title is free from any undisclosed encumbrances, defects in title, or other defects. Methods of assuring marketable title: 1. *Attorney's opinion.* Attorney renders opinion concerning status of the title. 2. *Torrens system.* Court issues *certificate of title* to the rightful owner of the property. 3. *Title insurance.* Title insurer agrees to reimburse the insured for losses caused by undiscovered defects in title.

Nonpossessory Interests, p. 940

Easements	An interest in land that gives the holder the right to make limited use of another's property without taking anything from it (e.g., driveways, party walls). 1. *Easement appurtenant.* Owner of land is given an easement over an adjacent piece of land. 2. *Easement in gross.* Authorizes a person who does not own adjacent land the right to use another's land.
Licenses	Right to enter upon another's property for a specified and usually short period of time (e.g., ticket to a sporting event).
Profits	Right of the holder to remove something from another's property (e.g., gravel, minerals).

Landlord–Tenant Relationship, p. 944

Landlord–Tenant Relationship	Created when an owner of a freehold estate transfers a right to another to exclusively and temporarily possess the owner's property.
The Lease	The rental agreement between the landlord and the tenant that contains the essential terms of the parties' agreement.
Types of Tenancy	*Tenancy for Years.* Tenancy for a specified period of time. *Periodic Tenancy.* Tenancy for a period of time determined by the payment interval. *Tenancy at Will.* Tenancy that may be terminated at any time by either party. *Tenancy at Sufferance.* Tenancy created by the wrongful possession of property.
Landlord's Duties	*Duty to Deliver Possession.* Landlord is obligated to deliver possession of the leased premises to the tenant on the date the lease term begins. *Duty Not to Interfere with the Tenant's Right to Quiet Enjoyment.* Landlord may not interfere with the tenant's quiet and peaceful possession, use, and enjoyment of the leased premises. *Duty to Maintain the Leased Premises.* Landlord owes contractual and statutory duties to repair and maintain the leased premises. The *implied warranty of habitability* requires leased premises to be fit, safe, and suitable for ordinary residential use.
Tenant's Duties	*Duty to Pay Rent.* Tenant owes a duty to pay the agreed-upon rent to the landlord. Reasonable late charges may be assessed on overdue rent. Common rental agreements are: 1. *Gross lease.* Requires tenant to pay a stated sum to landlord. Landlord responsible for paying property taxes and assessments on the property. 2. *Net lease.* Tenant responsible for paying rent and property taxes. 3. *Double net lease.* Tenant responsible for paying rent, property taxes, and utilities. 4. *Triple net lease.* Tenant responsible for paying rent, property taxes, utilities, and insurance. *Duty Not to Use Leased Premises for Illegal or Nonstipulated Purposes.* Tenant may not use leased premises for any illegal or nonstipulated uses. *Duty Not to Commit Waste.* Tenant may not commit waste to the leased premises. *Duty Not to Disturb Other Tenants.* Tenant may not disturb the use and enjoyment of the premises by other tenants.
Transferring Rights to Leased Property	*Assignment of the Lease.* Landlords may transfer their ownership interest in leased property. The tenant becomes a tenant of the new owner. *Sublease.* Subject to the terms of the lease, tenants may assign or sublease the leased premises to a third party. The original tenant is not relieved of obligations under the lease.

Land Use Control, p. 949

Restrictive Covenants	Agreement between landowners that restricts the use of their land. These restrictions are called *building restrictions* or *CC&Rs (covenants, conditions, and restrictions)*. Restrictive covenants may not cause unlawful discrimination.
Public Regulation of Land Use	*Zoning ordinances.* Laws adopted by local governments that restrict the use of property, set building standards, and establish architectural requirements. 1. *Variance.* Permits an owner to make a nonzoned use of his or her property. A variance requires permission from a zoning board. 2. *Nonconforming use.* A nonzoned use that is permitted (grandfathered in) when an area is rezoned.

END-OF-CHAPTER INTERNET EXERCISES AND CASE QUESTIONS

Working the Web Internet Exercises

ACTIVITIES

1. Some states have special laws relating to land and Indian tribes. See, for example, Washington state statutes, RCW 64.20—Alienation of land by Indians. Does your state have any similar laws? See "Law About . . . Real Estate Transactions" at **www.law. cornell.edu/topics/real_estate.html** for an overview of real estate law with links to key primary and secondary sources.

2. Although most real estate law is local law, there are important federal controls on certain types of transactions. See 42 U.S.C., Chapter 45—Federal Fair Housing Act.

3. There is an ongoing and vigorous debate about governmental authority to regulate land use without paying compensation to the property owner. Read the cited law review for an overview of the taking clause of the Fifth Amendment and related issues. See the Law Review article, "Windfalls or Windmills: The Right of a Property Owner to Challenge Land Use Regulations" at **www.law.fsu.edu/ journals/landuse/Vol131/ABRA.html**.

4. Is your state one that has adopted the Uniform Landlord–Tenant Act? See **www.law.cornell.edu/ uniform/vol7.html#lndtn**.

CRITICAL LEGAL THINKING CASES

37.1 Subsurface Rights In 1883, Isaac McIlwee owned 100 acres of land in Valley Township, Guernsey County, Ohio. In that year, he sold the property to Akron & Cambridge Coal Company (Akron & Cambridge) in fee simple but reserved in fee simple "the surface of all said lands" to himself. Over the years, the interests in the land were transferred to many different parties. As of 1981, the Mid-Ohio Coal Company owned the rights originally transferred to Akron & Cambridge, and Peter and Irene Minnich owned the rights reserved by Isaac McIlwee in 1883. The Minniches claim they possess subsurface rights to the property except for coal rights. Who wins? [*Minnich v. Guernsey Savings and Loan Company*, 521 N.E.2d 489 (Ohio App. 1987)]

37.2 Life Estate and Remainder Baudilio Bowles died testate. His will devised to his sister, Julianita B. Vigil, "one-half of any income, rents, or profits from any real property located in Bull Creek or Colonias, New Mexico." The will contained another clause that left to his children "My interest in any real property owned by me at the time of my death, located in Bull Creek and/or Colonias, San Miguel County." The property referred to in both devises is the same property. Julianita died before the will was probated. Her heirs claim a one-half ownership interest in the real property. Bowles's children assert that they own all his property. Who wins? [*In the Matter of the Estate of Bowles*, 764 P.2d 510 (N.M. App. 1988)]

37.3 Reversion In 1941, W. E. and Jennie Hutton conveyed land they owned to the Trustees of Schools of District Number One of the Town of Allison, Illinois (School District), by warranty deed "to be used for school purpose only; otherwise to revert to Grantor." The School District built a school on the site, commonly known as Hutton School. The Huttons conveyed the adjoining farmland and their reversionary interest in the school site to the Jacqmains, who in turn conveyed their interest to Herbert and Betty Mahrenholz in 1959. The 1.5-acre site sits in the middle of Mahrenhoz's farmland. In May 1973, the School District discontinued holding regular classes at Hutton School. Instead, it used the school building to warehouse and store miscellaneous school equipment, supplies, unused desks, and the like. In 1974, Mahrenholz filed suit to quiet title to the school property in themselves. Who wins? [*Mahrenholz v. County Board of School Trustees of Lawrence County*, 544 N.E.2d 128 (Ill. App. 1989)]

37.4 Community Property Daniel T. Yu and his wife, Bernice, owned a house and two lots as community property. On January 15, 1985, Yu entered into an agreement with Arch, Ltd. (Arch), whereby he agreed to exchange these properties for two office buildings owned by Arch. Yu signed the agreement but his wife did not. At the date set for closing, Arch performed its obligations under the agreement, executed all documents, and was prepared to transfer title to its properties to Yu. Yu, however, refused to perform his obligations under the agreement. Evidence showed that the office building had decreased in value from $800,000 to $700,000 from the date of the agreement to the date set for closing. Arch sued Yu to recover damages for breach of contract. Who wins? [*Arch, Ltd. v. Yu*, 766 P.2d 911 (NM 1988)]

37.5 Easement in Gross John L. Yutterman died in 1953 and left one piece of property, located in Fort Smith, Arkansas, to his two sons and two daughters. Each child received approximately one fourth of the property in fee simple. A 40-foot driveway divided the property. Concerning the driveway, Yutterman's will provided as follows: "Further, a specific condition of this will and of these devises is that the forty (40) foot driveway from Free Ferry Road, three hundred (300) feet Northward, shall be kept open for the common use of the devisees in this will." In 1982, one of the daughters wanted to sell her property to a third party. If the third party purchases the property, will that party have an easement to use the driveway? [*Merriman v. Yutterman*, 723 S.W.2d 823 (AK 1987)]

37.6 Adverse Possession In 1973, Joseph and Helen Naab purchased a tract of land in a subdivision of Williamstown, West Virginia. At the time of purchase, there was both a house and a small concrete garage on the property. Evidence showed that the garage had been erected sometime prior to 1952 by one of the Naabs' predecessors in title. In 1975, Roger and Cynthia Nolan purchased a lot contiguous to that owned by the Naabs. The following year, the Nolans had their property surveyed. The survey indicated that one corner of the Naabs' garage encroached 1.22 feet onto the Nolans' property and the other corner encroached 0.91 feet over the property line. The Nolans requested that the Naabs remove the garage from their property. When the Naabs refused, this lawsuit ensued. Who wins? [*Naab v. Nolan*, 327 S.E.2d 151 (WV 1985)]

37.7 Recording Statute On October 13, 1972, Johnnie H. Hill and his wife, Clara Mae, entered into an installment sales contract with Pinelawn Memorial Park (Pinelawn) to purchase a mausoleum crypt. They made it clear they wanted to buy crypt "D" that faced eastward toward Kinston. The Hills paid $1,035 down payment and continued to make $33.02 monthly payments. On February 13, 1974, William C. Shackelford and his wife, Jennie L., entered into an agreement with Pinelawn to purchase crypt D. They paid $1,406 down payment and two annual installments of $912. The Hills were first put on notice of the second contract when they visited Pinelawn in February 1977 and saw the Shackelford name on crypt D. The Hills then tendered full payment to Pinelawn for crypt D. On April 25, 1977, the Hills sued Pinelawn and the Shackelfords. They demanded specific performance of the contract and the deed to crypt D. Upon being served with summons, the Shackelfords discovered that they had no deed to the crypt and demanded one from Pinelawn. Pinelawn delivered them a deed dated August 18, 1977, which the Shackelfords recorded in the County Register on September 9, 1977. Who owns crypt D? [*Hill v. Pinelawn Memorial Park, Inc.*, 282 S.E.2d 779 (NC 1981)]

37.8 Security Deposit Community Management Corporation (landlord) entered into a rental agreement with Bowman (tenant) to lease an apartment to the tenant on a month-to-month tenancy commencing on October 1, 1981. The agreement required the tenant to give 30 days' notice before vacating the premises. The agreement also required a security deposit of $215, which would be forfeited if the tenant vacated the apartment prior to the end of a month. On September 21, 1982, the tenant informed the landlord that he was vacating the apartment as of September 30, 1982. Because the landlord had only a nine-day notice, it was unable to relet the apartment for the month of October 1982. The landlord retained the security deposit to cover rent for October. The tenant sued to recover the security deposit. Who wins? [*Bowman v. Community Management Corp.*, 469 N.E.2d 1038 (Ohio App. 1984)]

37.9 Implied Warranty of Habitability Sharon Love entered into a written lease agreement with Monarch Apartments for apartment 4 at 441 Winfield in Topeka, Kansas. Shortly after moving in, she experienced serious problems with termites. Her walls swelled, clouds of dirt came out, and when she checked on her children one night, she saw termites flying around the room. She complained to Monarch, who arranged for the apartment to be fumigated. When the termite problem persisted, Monarch moved Love and her children to apartment 2. Upon moving in, Love noticed that roaches crawled over the walls, ceilings, and floors of the apartment. She complained, and Monarch called an exterminator, who sprayed the apartment. When the roach problem persisted, Love vacated the premises. Did Love lawfully terminate the lease? [*Love v. Monarch Apartments*, 771 P.2d 79 (Kan. App. 1989)]

37.10 Tenant's Breach of Lease Susan Nylen, Elizabeth Lewis, and Julie Reed, students at Indiana University, signed a rental agreement as cosigners to lease an apartment from Park Doral Apartments. The rental term was from August 26, 1986, until August 19, 1987, at a monthly rental of $420. The tenants paid a security deposit of $420, constituting prepayment of rent for the last month of the lease term. At the end of the fall semester, Reed moved out of the apartment, and in February 1987, she refused to pay any further rent. Nylen and Lewis remained in possession of the apartment, paying only two thirds of the total rent due for the month of February. Nylen and Lewis made a payment of $280 for the rent due in March. They vacated the apartment on March 13, 1987. The landlord, who was unable to re-lease the apartment during the lease term, sued Reed, Nylen, and Lewis for the unpaid rent. Who wins? [*Nylen v. Park Doral Apartments*, 535 N.E.2d 178 (Ind. App. 1989)]

37.11 Landlord's Tort Liability William Long, d/b/a Hoosier Homes, owned an apartment building in Indianapolis, Indiana. He rented a second-story apartment to Marvin Tardy. On August 20, 1984, Almedia McLayea visited Tardy with her one-month-old nephew, Garfield Dawson. As McLayea was leaving the apartment, she walked down the stairway carrying Dawson in an infant seat. As she came down four steps to a landing, which led to a flight of 10 stairs, she caught her heel on a stair, slipped, and fell forward. There was no handrail along the stairway (as required by law) by which she could beak her fall. Instead, her shoulder struck a window at the landing, the window broke, the rotted screen behind it collapsed, and Dawson fell through the opening to the ground below. He sustained permanent injuries, including brain damage. Dawson (through his mother) sued the landlord to recover damages for negligence. Who wins? [*Dawson v. Long*, 546 N.E.2d 1265 (Ind. App. 1989)]

37.12 Restrictive Covenants   The Middleton Tract consists of approximately 560 acres of land that is located in the Santa Cruz Mountains in San Mateo County, California. The land, once owned by William H. Middleton, has been subdivided into 80 parcels of various shapes and sizes that are owned by various parties. The original deeds of conveyance from Middleton to purchasers contained certain restrictive covenants. One covenant limits use of the land exclusively for "residential purposes." Most of the land consists of thickly wooded forest with redwood and Douglas fir tress. The Holmeses, who own three parcels totaling 144 acres, propose to engage in commercial logging activities on their land. The plaintiffs, who own other parcels in the track, sued the Holmeses, seeking an injunction against such commercial activities. Who wins? [*Greater Middleton Assn. v. Holmes Lumber Co.*, 222 Cal.App.3d 980, 271 Cal.Rptr. 917 (Cal. App. 1990)]

37.13 Zoning   The city of Ladue is one of the finer suburban residential areas of metropolitan St. Louis. The homes in the city are considerably more expensive than surrounding areas and consist of homes of traditional design such as colonial, French provincial, and English. The city set up an architectural board to approve plans for buildings that "conform to certain minimum architectural standards of appearance and conformity with surrounding structures, and that unsightly, grotesque, and unsuitable structures, detrimental to the stability of value and the welfare of surrounding property, structures, and residents, and to the general welfare and happiness of the community, be avoided." The owner of a lot in the city submitted a plan to build a house of ultramodern design. It was pyramid-shaped, with a flat top and triangular-shaped windows and doors. Although the house plans met other city zoning ordinances and building codes, the architectural board rejected the owner's petition for a building permit based on aesthetic reasons. The owner sued the city. Who wins? [*State of Missouri v. Berkeley*, 458 S.W.2d 305 (MO 1970)]

37.14 Variance   The town of Hempstead, New Hampshire, enacted a zoning ordinance "in order to retain the beauty and countrified atmosphere of the town, and to promote health, safety, morals, order, convenience, peace, prosperity, and general welfare of its inhabitants." To preserve abutting property owners' views and light, the ordinance limits the homes in the town to one and one-half stories. In violation of the ordinance, John M. Alexander built a shell of a second story and a new roof on his house. After the town ordered him to halt construction and denied him permission to occupy the second floor, he applied for a variance. Should the variance be granted? [*Alexander v. Town of Hempstead*, 525 A.2d 276 (NH 1987)]

BUSINESS ETHICS CASES

37.15 Business Ethics   On March 19, 1971, Victor and Phyllis Garber (Garber) acquired a piece of real property by warranty deed. The deed was recorded on December 30, 1971. The property consisted of 80 acres that was enclosed by a fence that had been in place for over 50 years. The enclosed area was used to graze cattle and produce hay. Subsequently, William and Herbert Doenz (Doenz) acquired a piece of real property adjacent to the Garbers'. In March 1981, Doenz employed a surveyor to locate his land's boundaries. As a result of the survey, it was discovered that the shared fence was 20 to 30 feet inside the deed line on Doenz's property. The amount of property between the old fence and the deed line was 3.01 acres. In September 1981, Doenz removed the old fence and constructed a new fence along the deed line. Garber brought suit to quiet title. Did Doenz act ethically in removing the fence? Did the Garbers act ethically in claiming title to property that originally belonged with the adjacent property? Did Garber acquire title to property between the fence and the deed through adverse possession? [*Doenz v. Garber*, 665 P.2d 932 (WY 1983)]

37.16 Business Ethics   Moe and Joe Rappaport (tenants) leased space in a shopping mall owned by Bermuda Avenue Shopping Center Associates, L.P. (landlord) to use as an indoor golf arcade. The lease was signed in May 1987, and the tenants were given possession of the leased premises on July 23, 1987. The tenants were not told by the landlord of the extensive renovations planned for the mall. From July 23 until August 18, the golf arcade was busy and earned a net profit. On August 18, the renovation of the mall began in front of the arcade. According to the tenants, their store sign was taken down, there was debris and dust in front of the store, the sidewalks and parking spaces in front of the store were taken away, and their business "died." The tenants closed their arcade on September 30 and sued the landlord for damages. The landlord counterclaimed, seeking to recover lost rental income. Did the landlord act ethically in not explaining the extent of the planned renovations to the tenants? Did the tenants act ethically in terminating the lease? Were the tenants constructively evicted from the leased premise? [*Bermuda Avenue Shopping Center Associates v. Rappaport*, 565 S.2d 805 (Fla. App. 1990)]

BRIEFING THE CASE WRITING ASSIGNMENT

Read the following case, which has been excerpted from the court's opinion. Review and brief the case.

Nollan v. California Coastal Commission
483 U.S. 825, 107 S.Ct. 3141, 97 L.ED.2D 677 (1987)
Supreme Court of the United States

Scalia, Justice

James and Marilyn Nollan own a beachfront lot in Ventura County, California. A quarter-mile north of their property is Faria County Park, an oceanside public park with a public beach and recreation area. Another public beach area, known locally as "the Cove," lies 1,800 feet south of their lot. The Nollans originally leased their property with an option to buy. The building on the lot was a small bungalow, totaling 504 square feet, which for a time they rented to summer vacationers. After years of rental use, however, the building had fallen into disrepair, and could no longer be rented out.

The Nollans' option to purchase was conditioned on their promise to demolish the bungalow and replace it. In order to do so, they were required to obtain a coastal development permit from the California Coastal Commission. On February 25, 1982, they submitted a permit application to the Commission in which they proposed to demolish the existing structure and replace it with a three-bedroom house in keeping with the rest of the neighborhood.

The Nollans were informed that the Commission staff had recommended that the permit be granted subject to the condition that they allow the public an easement to pass across a portion of their property. This would make it easier for the public to get to Faria County Park and the Cove. The Nollans protested imposition of the condition, but the Commission overruled their objections and granted the permit subject to their recordation of a deed restriction granting the easement.

The Nollans filed a petition for a writ of administrative mandamus with the superior court. The superior court granted the writ of mandamus and directed that the permit condition be struck. The Commission appealed to the California court of appeal. While that appeal was pending, the Nollans satisfied the condition on their option to purchase by tearing down the bungalow and building the new house, and bought the property. They did not notify the

Commission that they were taking that action. The court of appeal reversed the superior court. It ruled that the Nollans' "taking" claim failed because, although the condition diminished the value of the Nollans' lot, it did not deprive them of all reasonable use of their property. The Nollans appealed to this Court, raising only the constitutional "taking" question.

Had California simply required the Nollans to make an easement across their beachfront available to the public on a permanent basis in order to increase public access to the beach, rather than conditioning their permit to rebuild their house on their agreeing to do so, we have no doubt there would have been a taking. To say that the appropriation of a public easement across a landowner's premises does not constitute the taking of a property interest but rather (as Justice Brennan contends) "a mere restriction on its use," is to use words in a manner that deprives them of all their ordinary meaning. Indeed, one of the principal uses of the eminent domain power is to assure that the government be able to require conveyance of just such interests, so long as it pays for them. We have repeatedly held that, as to property reserved by its owner for private use, "the right to exclude others is one of the most essential sticks in the bundle of rights that are commonly characterized as property."

We have long recognized that land-use regulation does not effect a taking if it "substantially advances legitimate state interests" and does not "deny an owner economically viable use of his land." Whatever may be the outer limits of legitimate state interests in the takings and land-use context, this is not one of them. The building restriction is not a valid regulation of land use, but an out-and-out plan of extortion. We therefore find that the Commission's imposition of the permit condition cannot be treated as an exercise of its land-use power. To obtain easements of access private property the State must proceed through its eminent domain power.

The permit condition is simply an expression of the Commission's belief that the public interest will be served by a continuous strip of publicly accessible beach along the coast. The Commission may well be right that it is a good idea, but that does not establish that the Nollans (and other coastal residents) alone can be compelled to contribute to its realization. Rather, California is free to advance its comprehensive program if it wishes, by using its power of eminent domain for this "public purpose," but if it wants an easement across the Nollans' property, it must pay for it. Reversed.

CHAPTER 38

Insurance and Estates

When you have told someone you have left him a legacy, the only decent thing to do is to die at once.

—Samuel Butler
(1835–1902)

Chapter Objectives

After studying this chapter, you should be able to:

1. Describe the parties to an insurance contract.

2. Define an *insurable interest*.

3. List and describe the various types of life, health and disability, fire and homeowner's, and automobile insurance.

4. List and describe special forms of business insurance.

5. Describe the types of insurance offered to cover Internet fraud.

6. Describe the requirements for making a valid will.

7. List and describe special forms of wills.

8. Identify how property is distributed under intestacy statutes if a person dies without a will.

9. Define a *trust* and identify the parties to a trust.

10. Describe the lawfullness of videotaped and electronic wills.

Chapter Contents

Insurance is a means for persons and businesses to protect themselves against the risk of loss. For example, a business may purchase fire insurance to cover its buildings. If there is a fire and the property is damaged, the insurance company will pay for all or part of the loss, depending on the policy. Similarly, an individual who purchases automobile insurance may be reimbursed by the insurer if his or her car is stolen. Insurance is crucial to personal, business, and estate planning.

Wills and trusts are means of transferring property. **Wills** transfer property upon a person's death. They permit people to state exactly where they want their property to go when they die. If a person dies *intestate*—that is, without a will—the deceased's property is distributed to relatives according to state statute. The property escheats (goes) to the state if there are no relatives.

Trusts are used to transfer property that is to be held and managed for the benefit of another person or persons. Although trusts are created during one's lifetime, they may be worded to become effective only upon the trustor's (or grantor's) death.

After discussing how insurance is used to protect against risk of loss, this chapter turns to the use of wills and trusts to transfer property.

*I*NSURANCE

Insurance is defined as a contract whereby one party undertakes to indemnify another against loss, damage, or liability arising from a contingent or unknown event. It is a means of transferring and distributing risk of loss. The risk of loss is *pooled* (i.e., spread) among all the parties (or **insureds**) who pay premiums to a particular insurance company. The insurance company—also called the **insurer** or **underwriter**—is then obligated to pay insurance proceeds to those members of the pool who experience a loss.

The insurance contract is called a **policy**. The money paid to the insurance company is called a **premium**. Premiums are based on an estimate of the number of parties within the pool who will suffer the risks insured against. The estimate is based on past experience.

Sometimes an insurer will spread the risk of loss through **reinsurance**. That is, it will sell a portion of the policy's risk and right to receive premiums to other insurance companies called **reinsurers**.

Insurance policies are often sold by insurance agents or brokers. An **insurance agent** usually works exclusively for one insurance company and is an agent of that company. An **insurance broker** is an independent contractor who represents a number of insurance companies. The broker is the agent of the insured. Some insurance is sold directly by the insurer to the insured (e.g., by direct mail).

Regulation of the Insurance Industry

The **McCarran-Ferguson Act**, which was enacted by the federal government in 1945, gave the regulation of insurance to the states and exempted insurance companies from the federal antitrust laws [5 U.S.C. § 1011–1015]. Accordingly, each state has enacted statutes that regulate domestic and out-of-state insurance companies operating within its borders. State regulations cover the incorporation, licensing, supervision, and liquidation of insurance companies, and the licensing and supervision of insurance agents and brokers.

Insurable Interest

Anyone who would suffer a pecuniary (monetary) loss from the destruction of real or personal property has an **insurance interest** in that property. If the insured does not have an **insurable interest** in the property being insured, the contract is treated as a wager and cannot be enforced.

Ownership creates an insurable interest. In addition, mortgagees, lienholders, and tenants have an insurable interest in property. The insurable interest in property must exist at the time of loss.

---

insurance
A means for persons and businesses to protect themselves against the risk of loss.

will
A way to acquire property as a result of a death.

insured
The party who pays a premium to a particular insurance company for insurance coverage.

insurer
The insurance company.

policy
The insurance contract.

premium
The money paid to the insurance company for insurance coverage.

An insurance policy is like old underwear. The gaps in its cover are only shown by accident.
David Yates (1984)

insurable interest
A person who purchases insurance must have a personal interest in the insured item or person.

In the case of life insurance, a person must have a close family relationship or an economic benefit from the continued life of another to have an insurable interest in that person's life. Thus, spouses, parents, children, and sisters and brothers may insure each others' lives. Other more remote relationships (e.g., aunts, uncles, cousins) require additional proof of an economic interest (e.g., proof of support). The insurable interest must exist when the life insurance policy is issued but need not exist at the time of death.

A person may insure his own life and name anyone as the **beneficiary**. The beneficiary does not have to have an insurable interest in the insured's life.

beneficiary

A person or organization who will receive money from the insurer at the time of the insured's death.

Contemporary Business Environment

TYPES OF INSURANCE CONTRACTS

Types of Insurance	
Life Insurance	
Whole life	Provides coverage during the life of the insured. It involves an element of savings. The premium is set to cover both the death benefit and an amount for investment. The value of savings grows at a fixed interest rate.
Term	Covers a limited period of time (e.g., five years). It involves no savings feature.
Universal life	Combines features of both term and whole life insurance. The value of savings grows at a variable interest rate.
Double indemnity	Provision in many life insurance policies that provides for payment of double the amount of the policy if death is caused by accident.
Key person	Life insurance taken out by businesses which insures the life of key executives. Also taken out by partners to insure the lives of other partners.
Annuity	Payments made to insured before death. For the payment of premiums, an insurance company agrees to make period payments (e.g., monthly) to the insured once he reaches a certain age.
Health and Disability Insurance	
Health	Covers the cost of medical treatment, surgery, and hospital care.
Disability	Provides monthly income to an insured who is disabled and cannot work. Benefits are based on degree of disability.
Dental	Covers the costs of dental care.
Fire and Homeowners Insurance	
Standard fire insurance policy	Protects real and personal property against loss resulting from fire, lightning, smoke, water damage, and related perils. Most policies limit recovery to damage caused by *hostile fires* (i.e., fire caused by faulty electrical wiring) and not *friendly fires* (e.g., damage caused by a fire contained in a fireplace). No personal liability coverage is provided.
Homeowners policy	A comprehensive insurance policy that includes coverage for the risks covered by a standard fire insurance policy as well as personal liability insurance. Includes coverage for property damage, personal injury, and medical expenses of persons injured on the insured's property.
Personal articles	Covers specific valuable items (e.g., jewelry, works of art, furs, and the like) that are usually excluded from standard fire and homeowners policies.
Renters insurance	Covers loss and damage to renter's possessions and provides personal liability coverage. Insures against the same perils as a homeowners policy.
Automobile Insurance	
Collision	Property insurance that covers the insured's vehicle against risk of loss or damage when it is struck by another vehicle.
Comprehensive	Property insurance that covers the insured's vehicle against risk of loss or damage from causes other than collision; namely, fire, theft, explosion, hail, windstorm, falling objects, earthquakes, floods, hurricanes, vandalism, and riots.

Automobile Insurance (*cont.*)

Liability	Covers damage and loss that the insured causes to third parties. This includes both bodily injury and property damage. States often require drivers to carry minimum liability insurance specified by statute. The following additional coverage may be purchased: Other driver coverage—liability coverage that protects the owner of a vehicle when someone else drives his or her vehicle with his or her permission. Drive-other coverage—liability coverage that protects the insured while driving other vehicles.
Medical payment	Covers medical expenses incurred by the owner, passengers, and other authorized driver of his car who are injured in an automobile accident.
Uninsured motorist	Provides coverage to the driver and passengers of a vehicle who are injured by an uninsured motorist or a hit-and-run driver.

Other Types of Insurance

Credit	Pays debtors' debts if they are unable to pay because of some insured peril (e.g., death or disability).
Title	Debtors and creditors may purchase this insurance. Insures that a property owner has clear title to real property. May be purchased by the owner, or mortgagees or lienholders of the property.
Marine	Covers loss or damage to the vessel and its cargo caused by perils at sea. Marine insurance is often comprehensive, covering property damage and liability for personal injury.

Entrepreneur and the Law

BUSINESS OWNERS PURCHASE KEY-PERSON LIFE INSURANCE

Small businesses, such as partnerships, limited liability companies, and close corporations, often purchase key-person life insurance on the owners of the business. The company pays the premiums for the life insurance policies. The life insurance is usually used to fund buy–sell agreements among the owners of the business. Thus, if an insured owner dies, the insurance proceeds are paid to the deceased's beneficiaries. The deceased's interest in the company then reverts to either the other owners or the business, according to the terms of the buy–sell agreement.

The following steps should be followed when purchasing key-person life insurance:

- The owners must agree upon the dollar value of their ownership interests in the business.

- The owners must execute a buy–sell agreement among themselves and the company specifying how a deceased owner's interest will be purchased by the other owners or the company upon his or her death.
- The company should purchase key-person life insurance from a reputable insurance company in an amount necessary to fund the buy–sell agreement.
- The company must pay the premiums for the key-person life insurance policies when due.
- When an owner-insured dies, the other owners and the company must file the claim with the insurance company and take all other steps necessary to ensure that the deceased's beneficiaries are paid the amount specified in the buy–sell agreement in a timely fashion.

E-Commerce & Information Technology

INSURANCE OFFERED TO COVER INTERNET FRAUD

In the past, a person could pose as another person to commit financial and commercial fraud, but it usually required the crook to obtain fake IDs, copies of bank passbooks, and other documents. Today, with the use of computers and the Internet, financial fraud is much easier and quicker for criminals to pull off. Called *identity fraud*, a perpetrator obtains personal information about the victim using the computer and the Internet. The perpetrator can wreak havoc by electronically impersonating the victim to remove money from bank accounts, purchase goods and services using the victim's credit cards, transfer assets from the victim's securities accounts, and the like. Electronic identity fraud is escalating throughout the country and the world. On average, a crook runs up over $30,000 of purchases and removed assets before the victim discovers the fraud.

Once the fraud is discovered and stopped, this does not end the victim's plight. The victim is usually not liable beyond $50 on each credit card, and the banks must make good on the money it paid out over fraudulent signatures. However, the victim must take the time and spend the money to restore the bad credit trail left in his or her name. This can take months, and sometimes years, to correct and cost thousands of dollars in legal and other expenses.

Several insurance companies, including Travelers Property Casualty Corp., now offer identity fraud insurance. Any person who has a homeowner's or tenant's insurance policy with the insurance company may purchase identity fraud insurance for an additional premium of around $25 per year. This new coverage pays the expenses a victim incurs in clearing his or her name and correcting financial records after being victimized by identity fraud. Costs that will be reimbursed include attorney's fees, telephone and certified mailing charges, loan reapplication fees, and lost wages for time taken off from work to deal with the consequences of the fraud. Most identity fraud policies limit recovery to $15,000 to $20,000.

*T*HE INSURANCE CONTRACT

Business Brief

Insureds should read insurance contracts carefully so that they fully understand what risks are covered and what risks are not covered.

Insurance contracts (**policies**) are governed by the law of contracts. Most policies are prepared on standardized forms. Some states even make that a requirement. Often, state statutes mandate that specific language be included in different types of insurance contracts. These statutes concern coverage for certain losses, how limitations on coverage must be stated in the contract, and the like. The insurance coverage is in place once the insurance policy is issued. Insurance policies often contain the clauses discussed below.

Deductible Clause

deductible clause

A clause that stipulates that insurance proceeds are payable only after the insured has paid a certain amount of the damage or loss.

Deductible clauses provide that insurance proceeds are payable only after the insured has paid a certain amount of the damage or loss. Typical deductibles for automotive collision insurance are $100, $250, or $500.

Coinsurance Clause

coinsurance clause

A clause that permits an owner who insures his or her property to a certain percent of its value to recover up to the face value of the policy.

A **coinsurance clause** permits an owner who insures his or her property to a certain percent of its value (e.g., 80 percent) to recover up to the face value of the policy. An owner who insures the property for less than the stated percentage must bear a proportionate share of the loss. Most fire insurance policies contain coinsurance clauses.

Exclusions from Coverage Clause

Business Brief

Insurance contracts cover only certain specified risks. They often contain *exclusions* that identify risks not covered by the policy.

Exclusion clauses stipulate certain exclusions from insurance coverage. For example, standard fire insurance policies often exclude coverage for damage caused by the storage of explosives or flammable liquids unless a special premium is paid for this coverage. Insurance policies should be read carefully to determine the extent of coverage.

 *C*ontemporary *B*usiness *E*nvironment

DO LIFE INSURANCE COMPANIES HAVE TO PAY FOR SUICIDE?

In 1982, Farmers New World Life Insurance Co. (Farmers) issued two $100,000 life insurance policies on Lawrence Malcom's life. His wife, Pamela Malcom, and Medmetric Corporation were the beneficiaries. Each policy contained a suicide provision that stated, "Suicide, whether sane or insane, will not be a risk assumed during the first two policy years. In such a case we will refund the premiums paid." In May 1984, within two years after the policies were issued, Lawrence committed suicide. The beneficiaries filed claims with Farmers seeking each policy's $100,000 benefit. When

Farmers refused to pay the benefits and refunded the premiums, the beneficiaries sued Farmers for breach of the insurance contract. They argued that the suicide provision should not be enforced because it was not plain and clear and conspicuous. The trial court granted Farmers's motion for summary judgment. The beneficiaries appealed.

Is Farmers liable on the two life insurance policies? The court of appeals held that the policies' suicide provision was conspicuous, bold, clear, and unambiguous and was, therefore, enforceable.

The court noted that to be conspicuous, an exclusion must be positioned in a place and printed in a form that will attract the reader's attention. The suicide provision was located on the policy's third page—the first operative page after the cover page and the alphabetical guide—and preceded by the bold-faced capitalized word *SUICIDE*. The suicide provision contained only 27 words and was clearly separated from its neighboring provisions by several blank lines and blank spaces. None of those words was beyond the working vocabulary of laypersons. The provision was neither submerged in "a sea of print" nor "inserted incidentally in a paragraph dealing with promised benefits." The suicide provision clearly and conspicuously conveyed its message in understandable language.

If the suicide in this case had occurred two years or more after the policy had been issued, the insurance would have to pay this claim. [*Malcom v. Farmers New World Life Insurance Co.*, 4 Cal.App.4th 296, 5 Cal.Rptr.2d 584 (Cal.App. 1992)]

Modification of Insurance

If both the insurer and insured agree, an insurance contract may be modified. Modification is usually done either by adding an **endorsement** to the policy or by the execution of a document called a **rider**.

endorsement
An addition to an insurance policy that modifies it.

rider
A separate document that will modify an existing insurance policy.

Cancellation of Insurance

In most instances, an insured can cancel the insurance policy at any time. An insurer may cancel an insurance policy for nonpayment of premiums. Many insurance policies provide a **grace period** during which an insured may pay an overdue premium. The insurance usually remains in effect during the grace period.

grace period
A period of time after the actual expiration date of a payment but during which the insured can still pay an overdue premium without penalty.

Duties of Insured and Insurer

The parties to an insurance contract are obligated to perform the duties imposed by the contract. The insured owes the following duties: (1) to pay the premiums stipulated by the policy, (2) to notify the insurer after the occurrence of an insured event within the time period stated in the policy or within a reasonable time, and (3) to cooperate with the insurer in investigating claims made against the insurer.

The insurer owes two primary duties. First, the insurer owes a **duty to defend** against any suit brought against the insured that involves a claim within the coverage of the policy. Thus, the insurer must provide and pay for the lawyers and court costs necessary to defend the lawsuit. Second, the insurer owes the duty to pay legitimate claims up to the policy limit. Insurers who wrongfully refuse to perform these duties are liable for damages.

duty to defend
An insurer owes a duty to defend an insured against a lawsuit involving a risk covered by the policy. This duty includes providing a lawyer and paying court costs and deposition fees.

Entrepreneur and the Law

UMBRELLA INSURANCE POLICY

Liability coverage under most insurance policies is usually limited to a certain dollar amount. Insureds who want to increase their liability coverage can purchase an **umbrella policy**. Coverage under an umbrella policy usually is at least $1 million and often reaches $5 million. An umbrella policy pays only if the basic policy limits have been exceeded. An insurer will issue an umbrella policy only if a stipulated minimum amount of basic coverage has been purchased by the insured.

Consider This Example Suppose an insured purchases automobile liability insurance that pays up to $500,000 per accident and an umbrella policy with an additional $3 million of coverage. If the insured's negligence causes an automobile accident in which injuries to other persons total $2 million, the basic automobile policy will pay the first $500,000 and the umbrella policy will pay the remaining $1.5 million.

Subrogation

If an insurance company pays a claim to an insured for liability or property damage caused by a third party, the insurer succeeds to the right of the insured to recover from the third party. This right is called **subrogation**. For example, if a third party negligently injures an insured who had hospital and disability insurance, the insurer can sue to recover the insurance proceeds it paid from the party who caused the injury. Subrogation does not apply to life insurance policies. An insurer has no right of subrogation against his or her own insured.

subrogation
If an insurance company pays a claim to an insured for liability or property damage caused by a third party, the insurer succeeds to the right of the insured to recover from the third party.

Contemporary Business Environment

NO-FAULT AUTOMOBILE INSURANCE

Until fairly recently, most automobile insurance coverage in this country was based on the principle of "fault," whereby a party injured in an accident relied on the insurance of the at-fault party to pay for his or her injuries. This system led to substantial litigation, but many accident victims were unable to recover because the at-fault party had either inadequate insurance or no insurance at all.

To remedy this problem, over half of the states have enacted legislation that mandates **no-fault insurance** for automobile accidents. Under this system, a driver's insurance company pays for any injuries he or she suffered in an accident, no matter who caused the accident.

Most no-fault statutes stipulate that claimants may not sue to recover damages from the party who caused the accident unless the injured party suffered serious injury (e.g., dismemberment or disfigurement) or death. If the insured recovers the total amount from the at-fault party, he or she must reimburse his or her own insurer for insurance proceeds paid pursuant to the no-fault policy.

No-fault insurance policies provide coverage for medical expenses and lost wages. Pain and suffering are not always covered. No-fault insurance usually covers the insured, members of the insured's immediate family, authorized drivers of the automobile, and passengers.

No-fault insurance reduces litigation costs, lessens the time for an injured person to be compensated for his or her injuries, and assures the insureds that coverage is available if they are injured in an automobile accident. There is also evidence that no-fault insurance reduces the overall cost of automobile insurance. The trend of the law is to replace at-fault systems of automobile insurance with no-fault insurance.

Entrepreneur and the Law

BUSINESS INSURANCE

Businesses purchase insurance to cover myriad risks, including property and liability insurance on buildings, automobile insurance, key-person life insurance, and risks uniquely applicable to businesses. These types of insurance include:

- **Business Interruption Insurance**   When a business is severely damaged or destroyed by fire or some other peril, it usually takes time to repair or reconstruct the damaged property. During this time, the business is losing money. A business can purchase a **business interruption insurance** policy that will reimburse it for any revenues lost during that period.

- **Workers' Compensation Insurance**   Employees are sometimes injured while working within the scope of their employment. All states have enacted legislation that compensates employees for such injuries. Employers may purchase *workers' compensation insurance* to cover this risk. Many states require companies to purchase this form of insurance.

- **Fidelity Insurance**   An employer can purchase **fidelity insurance** to protect against the dishonesty and defalcation of employees. For example, a bank can purchase fidelity insurance to protect against losses caused by the embezzlement of bank employees.

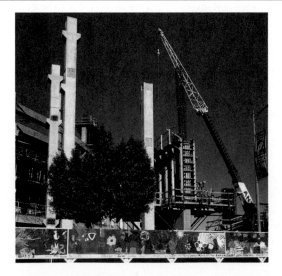

Staples Center, Los Angeles   The owner of real property and a business should purchase liability insurance, fire insurance, workers' compensation insurance, business interruption insurance, and many other forms of insurance to protect against loss.

DEFENSES OF THE INSURER

An insurer may be able to raise certain defenses to the imposition of liability. The most common defenses are discussed in the following paragraphs.

Misrepresentation and Concealment

Insurance companies may require applicants to disclose certain information to help them determine whether they will insure the risk and to calculate the premium. The insurer may avoid liability on the policy (1) if its decision is based on a material misrepresentation on the part of the applicant or (2) if the applicant concealed material information from the insurer. This rule applies whether the misrepresentation was intentional or nonintentional.

Many states have enacted **incontestability clauses** that prevent insurers from contesting statements made by insureds in applications for insurance after the passage of a stipulated number of years (the typical length of time is two to five years). An incontestability clause was at issue in the following case.

The underwriter knows nothing and the man who comes to him to ask him to insure knows everything.

L. Scrutton
Rozanes v. Bowen *(1928)*

incontestability clauses

A clause that prevents insurers from contesting statements made by insureds in applications for insurance after the passage of a stipulated number of years.

Amex Life Assurance Company v. Slome Capital Corp.

60 Cal.Rptr.2d 898 (1997)
Supreme Court of California

CASE 38.1

BACKGROUND AND FACTS

In January 1991, Jose Morales applied for a life insurance policy from Amex Life Assurance Company (Amex). Morales knew he was HIV (human immunodeficiency virus) positive, but he lied on the application form and denied having AIDS (acquired immune deficiency syndrome). As part of the application process, Amex required Morales to have a medical examination. In March 1991, a paramedic working for Amex met a man claiming to be Morales and took blood and urine samples from him. On his application, Morales had listed his height as 5 feet 6 inches and his weight as 147 pounds. The examiner registered the man taking the examination as 5 feet 10 inches tall, weighing 172 pounds, and appearing to be "older than the stated age." The blood samples tested HIV negative. Amex issued Morales a life insurance policy on May 1, 1991; the policy included a two-year incontestability clause as required by state law. All premiums were paid. Morales sold the policy to Slome Capital Corporation (Slome), a viatical company that purchased life insurance policies at a discount from AIDS carriers before their death.

On June 11, 1993, Morales died of AIDS-related causes. When Slome presented Morales's policy to Amex for payment, Amex refused to pay, alleging that Morales had engaged in fraud and had had an imposter take his physical examination for him. The trial court denied Amex's summary judgment motion. The court of appeals held that the incontestability clause prevented Amex from denying coverage. Amex appealed.

ISSUE

Does the two-year incontestability clause prevent Amex from raising the insured's fraud as a reason not to pay the life insurance proceeds?

COURT'S REASONING

Most states, including California, have enacted statutes that require that an incontestability clause be part of a life insurance contract. In California, the statute requires a two-year incontestability clause, which was part of the life insurance contract between Morales and Amex. The court noted that incontestability clauses are designed to require the insurer to investigate and act with reasonable promptness if it wishes to deny liability on the grounds of false representation or warranty by the insured. The facts can best be ascertained and proven early, instead of waiting until the death of the insured, who can no longer give testimony or defend himself or herself. The court stated that incontestability clauses apply to fraud claims as well as to nonfraud claims. Therefore, Morales's fraudulent statements on the life insurance application form and his having an imposter take the physical exam for him does not prohibit payment of life insurance benefits because the two-year incontestability clause had run out on May 1, 1993, and Morales did not die until six weeks later.

DECISION

The California Supreme Court held that the incontestability clause prevented Amex from denying coverage. The court ordered Amex to pay the proceeds of Morales's life insurance policy to Slome.

Case Questions

Critical Legal Thinking   Should the law contain incontestability clauses? What public policy is served by these clauses?

Business Ethics   Did Morales act ethically in this case? Should unethical conduct be rewarded?

Contemporary Business   Who pays the cost of insurance fraud?

Breach of Warranty

A **warranty** is a representation of the insured that is expressly incorporated in the insurance contract:

affirmative warranty

A statement asserting that certain facts are true.

promissory warranty

Stipulates that the facts will continue to be true throughout the duration of the policy.

- An **affirmative warranty** is a statement asserting that certain facts are true (e.g., there are no environmental problems currently existing as to the property the insured is insuring).
- A **promissory warranty** stipulates that facts will continue to be true throughout the duration of the policy (e.g., the insured will not store flammable products in the insured building). An insurer may avoid liability caused by a breach of warranty.

In the following case, the court had to decide whether the insured made a misrepresentation on his application for insurance.

Peckman v. Mutual Life Insurance Company of New York

509 N.Y.S.2d 336 (1986)
New York Supreme Court, Appellate Division

CASE 38.2

BACKGROUND AND FACTS

Alan L. Peckman filed an application with the Mutual Life Insurance Company of New York (MONY) for life insurance in the face amount of $100,000 with double indemnity coverage for accidental death. On the application, Peckman indicated that for the previous six years he had been self-employed in the occupation of "marketing." MONY issued the policy, which named Alan's mother as beneficiary.

On August 5, 1982, within the contestability period of the policy, Alan's body was found in a steamer trunk with a gunshot wound to the head. Alan's mother filed a claim with MONY for the insurance proceeds from Alan's life insurance policy.

MONY denied the claim, asserting that Alan falsely misrepresented his occupation and fraudulently concealed that he was a drug dealer. The company introduced police evidence showing that Alan had been involved in the distribution of drugs for several years. Articles in newspapers stated that Alan ran a million-dollar marijuana distribution ring.

Alan's mother sued MONY to recover the insurance proceeds. The trial court granted summary judgment in favor of Alan's mother and awarded her the double indemnity insurance benefits. MONY appealed.

ISSUE

Did the decedent misrepresent his employment on the life insurance application?

COURT'S REASONING

In reaching its decision, the appellate court stated: "In the instant case the applicant did not misrepresent his occupation. Webster's Dictionary defines *marketing* as 'the act or business of buying or selling in the market.' This definition clearly encompasses the applicant's alleged pursuit of drug dealing."

DECISION

The appellate court held that the insured had not misrepresented his employment on the life insurance application. The appellate court affirmed the trial court's judgment and award of double indemnity life insurance proceeds to the plaintiff-beneficiary.

Case Questions

Critical Legal Thinking   Should insurance companies be permitted to group persons into "risk categories" and charge higher premiums to members of higher risk categories (e.g., smokers, teenage drivers)?

Business Ethics   Do you think the insured acted ethically in disclosing his occupation as marketing?

Contemporary Business   Do you think an insurance company would issue a life insurance policy if it knew the applicant was a drug dealer?

International Law

LLOYD'S OF LONDON

International businesses are often faced with risks that are not a primary concern for domestic businesses. These risks include such things as damage to businesses from military conflict, loss of assets from expropriation by foreign govern- ments, and losses when currency becomes inconvertible. Many domestic insurance companies will not write insurance against such risks. **Lloyd's of London** is one insurer that is famous for insuring unique international risks. The company, which is based in London, England, has been insuring international business risks for over 300 years.

Lloyd's is organized differently from most insurance companies in that it is really an insurance syndicator. That is, it originates insurance business and then seeks a pool of investors to guarantee payment if the risk occurs. A separate partnership of investors is arranged to insure individual risks. For example, if a business wants to insure against the risk of loss to an oil tanker traveling in international waters, Lloyd's would seek investors for that insurance pool. If enough investors agreed to guarantee payment if the risk occurred, Lloyd's would write the policy.

The investors are called "Names." To become a Name, an investor must pledge all of his or her assets to pay any losses incurred for the risk he or she has agreed to guarantee. As one Brit put it, "down to their last pair of cufflinks." For years, a Name was almost guaranteed an annual return of

about 10 percent on the investment without ever having to put up any cash. The affluent grew even more wealthy just by being a Name.

In the last 1980s and early 1990s, things started to go sour. Lloyd's underwriters had failed to charge sufficient premiums to cover many insured risks. With more strife in the world and major natural disasters, insurance payouts soared. The losses wiped out the personal assets of hundreds of wealthy families whose liability as Names was unlimited. Because of the losses, the number of Names dropped from about 32,000 in 1988 to about 20,000 in 1993.

In 1993, Lloyd's of London restructured. It laid off about 20 percent of its staff, courted new Names, including corporations with limited liability, and instituted more cautious underwriting standards. International risk is still difficult to insure, but as long as Lloyd's of London is around, there will be a place to purchase such insurance—at a premium.

$\mathcal{W}$ILLS

A **will** is a declaration of how a person wants his or her property to be distributed upon his or her death. It is a testamentary deposition of property. The person who makes the will is called the **testator** or **testatrix**. The persons designated in the will to receive the testator's property are called **beneficiaries**.

Requirements for Making a Will

Every state has a **Statute of Wills** that establishes the requirements for making a valid will in that state. These requirements are:

- **Testamentary Capacity** The testator must have been of legal age and "sound mind" when the will was made. The courts determine testamentary capacity on a case-by-case basis. The legal age for executing a will is set by state statute.
- **Writing** Wills must be in writing to be valid (except for dying declarations, discussed later in this chapter). The writing may be formal or informal. Although most wills are typewritten, they can be handwritten (see the later discussion of holographic wills). The writing may be on legal paper, other paper, scratch paper, envelopes, napkins, or the like. A will may incorporate other documents by reference.
- **Testator's Signature** Wills must be signed.

Most jurisdictions require the testator's signature to appear at the end of the will. This step is to prevent fraud that could occur if someone added provisions to the will below the testator's signature. For example, courts have held that initials (*R.K.H.*), a nickname (*Buffy*), title (*mother*), and even an *X* is a valid signature on a will if it can be proven that the testator intended it to be his or her signature.

- **Attestation by Witnesses** Wills must be attested to by mentally competent witnesses. Although state law varies, most states require two or three witnesses. The witnesses do not have to reside in the jurisdiction in which the testator is domiciled. Most jurisdictions stipulate that interested parties (e.g., a beneficiary under the will or the testator's attorney) cannot be witnesses. If an interested party has attested to a will, state law either voids any clauses that benefit such person or voids the entire will.

Witnesses usually sign the will following the signature of the testator. These signatures are called the **attestation clause**. Most jurisdictions require that each witness attest to the will in the presence of the other witnesses.

A will that meets the requirements of the Statute of Wills is called a **formal will**. A sample will is shown in Exhibit 38.1.

will
A declaration of how a person wants his or her property distributed upon death.

testator
The person who makes a will.

beneficiary
A person or organization designated in the will who receives all or a portion of the testator's property at the time of the testator's death.

Statute of Wills
A state statute that establishes the requirements for making a valid will.

attestation
The action of a will being witnessed by two or three objective and competent people.

formal will
A will that meets the requirements of the Statute of Wills.

ℰXHIBIT 38.1   A Sample Will

Last Will and Testament of Florence Winthorpe Blueblood

I, **FLORENCE WINTHORPE BLUEBLOOD**, presently residing at Boston, County of Suffolk, Massachusetts, being of sound and disposing mind and memory, hereby make, publish, and declare this to be my Last Will and Testament.

FIRST. I hereby revoke any and all Wills and Codicils previously made by me.

SECOND. I direct that my just debts and funeral expenses be paid out of my Estate as soon as practicable after my death.

THIRD. I am presently married to Theodore Hannah Blueblood III.

FOURTH. I hereby nominate and appoint my husband as the Personal Representative of this my Last Will and Testament. If he is unable to serve as Personal Representative, then I nominate and appoint Mildred Yardly Winthorpe as Personal Representative of this my Last Will and Testament. I direct that no bond or other security be required to be posted by my Personal Representative.

FIFTH. I hereby nominate and appoint my husband as Guardian of the person and property of my minor children. In the event that he is unable to serve as Guardian, then I nominate and appoint Mildred Yardly Winthorpe Guardian of the person and property of my minor children. I direct that no bond or other security be required to be posted by any Guardian herein.

SIXTH. I give my Personal Representative authority to exercise all the powers, rights, duties, and immunities conferred upon fiduciaries under law with full power to sell, mortgage, lease, invest, or reinvest all or any part of my Estate on such terms as he or she deems best.

SEVENTH. I hereby give, devise, and bequeath my entire estate to my husband, except for the following specific bequests:

I give my wedding ring to my daughter, Hillary Smythe Blueblood.
I give my baseball card collection to my son, Theodore Hannah Blueblood IV.
In the event that either my above-named daughter or son predeceases me, then and in that event, I give, devise, and bequeath my deceased daughter's or son's bequest to my husband.

EIGHTH. In the event that my husband shall predecease me, then and in that event, I give, devise and bequeath my entire estate, with the exception of the bequests in paragraph SEVENTH, to my beloved children or grandchildren surviving me, per stirpes.

NINTH. In the event I am not survived by my husband or any children or grandchildren, then and in that event, I give, devise, and bequeath my entire estate to Harvard University.

IN WITNESS WHEREOF, I, Florence Winthorpe Blueblood, the Testatrix, sign my name to this Last Will and Testament this 3rd day of January, 2003.

Florence Winthorpe Blueblood
(Signature)

Signed, sealed, published and declared by the above-named Testatrix, as and for her Last Will and Testament, in the presence of us, who at her request, in her presence, and in the presence of one another, have hereunto subscribed our names as attesting witnesses, the day and year last written above.

Witness	Address
Norm Peterson	*100 Beacon Hill Rd* *Boston, Massachusett*
Clifford Claven	*200 Minute Man Drive* *Boston, Massachusetts*
Rebecca Howe	*300 Charles River Place* *Boston, Massachusett*

Changing a Will

A will cannot be amended by merely striking out existing provisions and adding new ones. **Codicils** are the legal way to change an existing will. A codicil is a separate document that must be executed with the same formalities as a will. In addition, it must incorporate by reference the will it is amending. The codicil and the will are then read as one instrument.

Revoking a Will

A will may be **revoked** by acts of the testator. A will is revoked if the testator intentionally burns, tears, obliterates, or otherwise destroys it. A properly executed **subsequent will** revokes a prior will if it specifically states that it is the testator's intention to do so. If the second will does not expressly revoke the prior will, the wills are read together. If any will provisions are inconsistent, the provision in the second will controls.

Wills can also be revoked by operation of law. For example, divorce or annulment revokes disposition of property to the former spouse under the will. The remainder of the will is valid. The birth of a child after a will has been executed does not revoke the will but does entitle the child to receive his or her share of the parents' estate as determined by state statute.

Simultaneous Deaths

Sometimes people who would inherit property from each other die simultaneously. If it is impossible to determine who died first, the question becomes one of inheritance. The **Uniform Simultaneous Death Act** provides that each deceased person's property is distributed as though he or she survived.

Consider This Example   Suppose a husband and wife make wills that leave their entire estate to each other. Assume that the husband and wife are killed simultaneously in an airplane crash. Here, the husband's property would go to his relatives and the wife's property would go to her relatives.

Undue Influence

A will may be found to be invalid if it was made as a result of **undue influence** on the testator. Undue influence can be inferred from the facts and circumstances surrounding the making of the will. For example, if an 85-year-old woman leaves all her property to the lawyer who drafted her will and ignores her blood relatives, the court is likely to presume undue influence.

---

codicil

A separate document that must be executed to amend a will. It must be executed with the same formalities as a will.

Business Brief

A will cannot be amended or changed by striking out existing provisions and adding new ones on to the will itself.

revocation

Termination of a will.

Uniform Simultaneous Death Act

An act that provides that if people who would inherit property from each other die simultaneously, each person's property is distributed as though he or she survived.

The power of making a will is an instrument placed in the hands of individuals for the prevention of private calamity.

Jeremy Bentham
Principles of the Civil Code
(1748)

Angel Statute *It is wise for a person to have a valid will that designates how his or her property will be distributed upon his or her death.*

undue influence

Occurs where one person takes advantage of another person's mental, emotional, or physical weakness and unduly persuades that person to make a will; the persuasion by the wrongdoer must overcome the free will of the testator.

Undue influence is difficult to prove by direct evidence, but it may be proved by circumstantial evidence. The elements that courts examine to find the presence of undue influence include:

- The benefactor and beneficiary are involved in a relationship of confidence and trust.
- The will contains substantial benefit to the beneficiary.
- The beneficiary caused or assisted in effecting execution of the will.
- There was an opportunity to exert influence.
- The will contains an unnatural disposition of the testator's property.
- The bequests constitute a change from a former will.
- The testator was highly susceptible to the undue influence.

Business Ethics

MURDER, SHE WROTE

Most states, by statute or court decision, provide that a person who murders another person cannot inherit the victim's property. This rule, often called the **murder disqualification doctrine**, is based on the public policy that a person should not benefit from his or her wrong-doing. Consider the following case.

Walter A. Gibbs resided with his mother until 1963, when he hired Delores Christenson to help care for her. He married Delores in 1964. The couple were divorced in 1973. Gibbs married Delores's twin sister, Darlene Wahl. That marriage ended in divorce in 1980.

During the winter of 1988–1989, Delores, Darlene, and Darlene's new husband, Jerry Phillips, who were all living together, experienced difficult times due to lack of money. Delores contacted Gibbs, who was over 80 years old at the time, at the nursing home where he resided and offered to move back into his house and care for him. In February 1989, Delores, Darlene, and Jerry moved Gibbs to his house and moved in with him. The group lived together as a "family" for about one year.

Gibbs had a will that named his first cousin, Bernice Boettner, as sole beneficiary. In January 1990, Delores located an attorney who drafted a new will for Gibbs, and she procured two witnesses for the will's execution. The will disinherited Gibbs's relations and left his entire estate, worth about $175,000, to Delores. Gibbs executed the will on January 5, 1990.

On January 8, 1990, Darlene and Jerry discussed killing Gibbs to "activate the will." A few weeks later, Darlene suggested in the presence of Jerry and Delores that they hasten Gibbs's death by mixing sleeping pills and nitroglycerin in his tea. At one time, when Darlene suggested smothering Gibbs with a pillow, Delores went to the bedroom, returned with a pillow, and handed it to Jerry, who held it over Darlene's face to see if she could breathe. On the morning of April 1, 1990, Darlene got a pillow from her bedroom and gave it to Jerry. Delores sat at the kitchen table approximately 17 feet from Gibbs's bed. Darlene held Gibbs's arms while Jerry smothered him. After Jerry removed the pillow, Delores went over and embraced Jerry.

In January 1991, Delores, Darlene, and Jerry were indicted on charges of murder, conspiracy to commit murder, and aiding and abetting murder. Jerry pleaded guilty to conspiracy to commit second-degree murder. Darlene was convicted of murder and sentenced to life in prison. Delores was acquitted of all charges.

Delores offered Gibbs's will for probate. Boettner filed a petition to revoke the probate of Gibbs's will and an application to disqualify Delores as the beneficiary as a willful slayer of Gibbs. Delores argued in defense that she should be allowed to inherit Gibbs's estate because she had not been criminally convicted.

The trial court held that Delores qualified as a willful slayer under the murder disqualification statute even though she had not been convicted at her criminal trial. The state supreme court affirmed. The supreme court stated,

We are not dealing with criminal responsibility, but with a civil statute which disqualifies a person who procures the death of a testator from reaping the benefits of that death. Moreover, the evidence indicated Delores interjected herself into the conspiracy by voluntarily procuring a pillow to assist Jerry and Darlene in practicing to smother Gibbs. In summation, Delores's claim she was just an innocent bystander and not an accomplice is without merit.

Gibbs's prior will, which left his estate to Boettner, is subject to probate. [*In the Matter of the Estate of Walter A. Gibbs*, 490 N.W.2d 504 (SD 1992)]

1. What could be the consequences if the law did not impose the murder disqualification doctrine?

TYPES OF TESTAMENTARY GIFTS

In a will, a gift of real estate by will is called a **devise**. A gift of personal property by will is called a **bequest** or **legacy**. Gifts in wills can be specific, general, or residuary.

- **Specific Gifts** Gifts of specifically named pieces of property, such as a ring, a boat, or a piece of real estate.
- **General Gifts** Gifts that do not identify the specific property from which the gift is to be made, such as a cash amount that can come from any source in the decedent's estate.
- **Residuary Gifts** Gifts that are established by a **residuary clause** in the will. Such a clause might state that "I give my daughter the rest, remainder, and residual of my estate." Thus, any portion of the estate left after the debts, taxes, and specific and general gifts have been paid belongs to the decedent's daughter.

A person who inherits property under a will or intestacy statute takes the property subject to all the outstanding claims against it (e.g., liens, mortgages). A person can **renounce** an inheritance and often does where the liens or mortgages against the property exceed the value of the property.

Ademption and Abatement

If a testator leaves a specific gift of property to a beneficiary, but the property is no longer in the estate of the testator when he or she dies, the beneficiary receives nothing. This doctrine is called the doctrine of **ademption**.

If the testator's estate is not large enough to pay all the devises and bequests, the doctrine of **abatement** applies. The doctrine works as follows:

- If a will provides for both general and residuary gifts, the residuary gifts are abated first. For example, suppose a testator executes a will when he owns $500,000 of property that leaves (1) $100,000 to the Red Cross, (2) $100,000 to a university, and (3) the residue to his niece. Suppose that when the testator dies his estate is worth only $225,000. Here, the Red Cross and the university each receive $100,000 and the niece receives $25,000.
- If a will provides only for general gifts, the reductions are proportionate. For example, suppose a testator's will leaves $75,000 to two beneficiaries, but the estate is only $100,000. Each beneficiary would receive $50,000.

Per Stirpes and Per Capita Distribution

A testator's will may state that property is to be left to his or her **lineal descendants** (children, grandchildren, great-grandchildren, etc.) either *per stirpes* or *per capita*. The difference between these two methods is as follows:

- **Per Stirpes** The lineal descendants inherit by representation of their parent; that is, they split what their deceased parent would have received. If their parent is not deceased, they receive nothing.
- **Per Capita** The lineal descendants equally share the property of the estate without regard to degree of the relationship to the testator. That is, children of the testator share equally with grandchildren, great-grandchildren, and so forth.

Consider This Example Suppose Anne dies without a surviving spouse, and she had three children, Bart, Beth, and Bruce. Bart, who survives his mother, has no children. Beth has one child, Carla, and they both survive Anne. Bruce, who predeceased his mother, had two children, Clayton and Cathy; and Cathy, who predeceased Anne, had two children, Deborah and Dominic, both of whom survive Anne.

---

devise
A gift of real estate by will.

bequest
A gift of personal property by will.

specific gift
Gift of a specifically named piece of property.

general gift
Gift that does not identify the specific property from which the gift is to be made.

residuary gift
Gift of the estate left after the debts, taxes, and specific and general gifts have been paid.

ademption
A principle that says if a testator leaves a specific devise of property to a beneficiary, but the property is no longer in the estate when the testator dies, the beneficiary receives nothing.

abatement
If the property the testator leaves is not sufficient to satisfy all the beneficiaries named in a will and there are both general and residuary bequests, the residuary bequests are abated first; if a will provides for general bequests, they are reduced proportionately if the residuary bequests are full abated or there are none.

lineal descendants
Children, grandchildren, great grandchildren, and so on of the testator.

per stirpes
A distribution of the estate that makes grandchildren and great grandchildren of the deceased inherit by representation of their parent.

per capita
A distribution of the estate that makes each grandchild and great grandchild of the deceased inherit equally with the children of the deceased.

𝓔XHIBIT 38.2 *Per Stirpes Distribution*

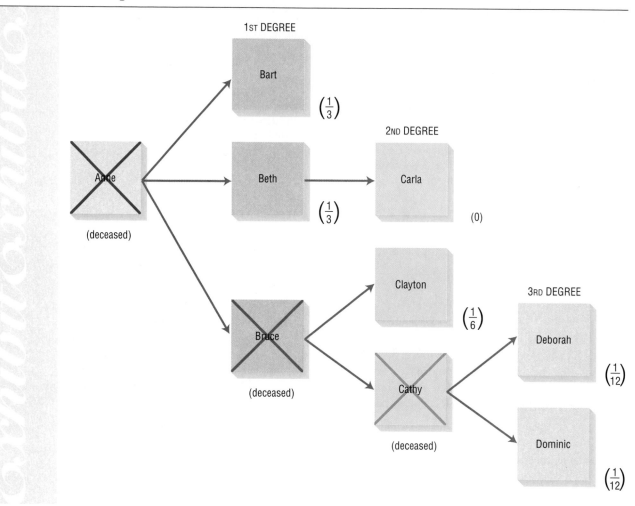

1ST DEGREE

Bart $\left(\frac{1}{3}\right)$

2ND DEGREE

Anne (deceased)

Beth $\left(\frac{1}{3}\right)$

Carla (0)

3RD DEGREE

Clayton $\left(\frac{1}{6}\right)$

Bruce (deceased)

Cathy (deceased)

Deborah $\left(\frac{1}{12}\right)$

Dominic $\left(\frac{1}{12}\right)$

Disinherit: The prankish action of the ghosts in cutting the pockets out of trousers.

Frank McKinney Hubbard
The Roycroft Dictionary
(1923)

If Anne leaves her estate to her lineal descendants *per stirpes*, Bart and Beth each get one third, Carla receives nothing because Beth is alive, Clayton gets one sixth, and Deborah and Dominic each get one twelfth. See Exhibit 38.2.

On the other hand, if Anne leaves her estate to her lineal descendants *per capita*, all of the surviving issue—Bart, Beth, Carla, Clayton, Deborah, and Dominic—share equally in the estate. That is, they each get one sixth of Anne's estate. See Exhibit 38.3.

@ *𝓔-Commerce & Information Technology*

VIDEOTAPED AND ELECTRONIC WILLS

Many acrimonious will contests involve written wills. The contestors allege such things as mental incapacity of the testator at the time the will was made, undue influence, fraud, or duress. Although the written will speaks for itself, the mental capacity of the testator and the voluntariness of his or her actions cannot be determined from the writing alone.

If a challenge to the validity of a will has merit, it, of course, should be resolved. However, some will contests are based on unfounded allegations. After all, the testator is not there to defend his or her testamentary wishes.

To prevent unwarranted will contests, a testator can use a videotaped or electronically recorded will to supplement a written will. Videotaping a will that can withstand challenges by disgruntled relatives and alleged heirs involves a certain amount of planning.

The following procedures should be followed. A written will should be prepared to comply with the state's Statute of Wills. The video session should not begin until after the testator has become familiar with the document. The video should begin with the testator reciting the will verbatim. Next, the lawyer should ask the testator questions to demonstrate the testator's sound mind and understanding of the implications of his or her actions. The execution ceremony—the signing of the will by the testator and the attestation by the witnesses—should be the last segment on the film. The videotape should then be stored in a safe place.

With the testator's actions crystallized on videotape, a judge or jury will be able to determine the testator's mental capacity at the time the will was made and the voluntariness of his or her testamentary gifts. In addition, fraudulent competing wills will crumble in the face of such proof.

In the future, it is likely that videotaped wills will become invaluable evidential tools. Whether such wills alone without a writing will be recognized as testamentary instruments will depend on the development of state laws.

Currently, most electronic signature acts, which recognize electronic signatures for e-commerce and Internet transactions, do not validate electronic wills. Thus, wills must still be in writing in most states.

*Ɛ*XHIBIT **38.3** *Per Capita Distribution*

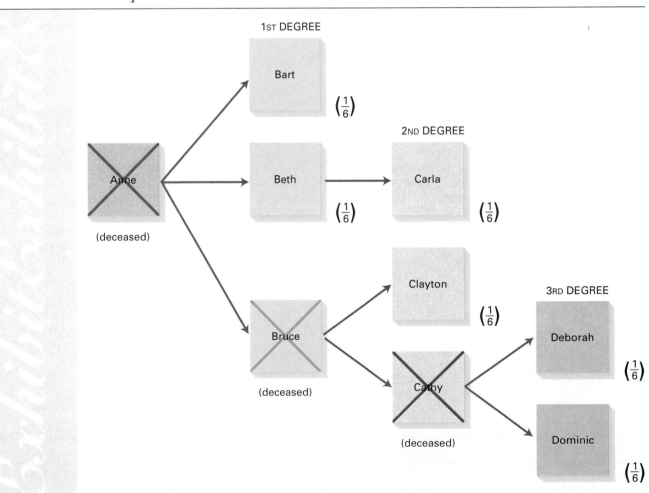

holographic will

Will that is entirely handwritten and signed by the testator.

nuncupative will

Oral will that is made before a witness during the testator's last illness. Also called a *dying declaration* or *deathbed* will.

joint will

A will that is executed by two or more testators.

mutual wills

Occurs where two or more testators execute separate wills that leave their property to each other on the condition that the survivor leave the remaining property on his or her death as agreed by the testators.

Special Types of Wills

The law recognizes several types of wills that do not meet all the requirements discussed above. The special types of wills admitted by the courts include:

- **Holographic Wills** Wills that are entirely handwritten and signed by the testator. The writing may be in ink, pencil, crayon, or some other writing instrument. Many states recognize the validity of such wills even though they are not witnessed.
- **Nuncupative Wills** Oral wills that are made before witnesses. Such wills are usually valid only if they are made during the testator's last illness. They are sometimes called **dying declarations** or **deathbed wills**.

Joint and Mutual Wills

If two or more testators execute the same instrument as their will, the document is called a **joint will**. A joint will may be held invalid as to one testator but not the others.

Mutual or **reciprocal wills** arise where two or more testators execute separate wills that make testamentary dispositions of their property to each other on the condition that the survivor leave the remaining property on his or her death as agreed by the testators. The wills are usually separate instruments with reciprocal terms. Because of their contractual nature, mutual wills cannot be unilaterally revoked after one of the parties has died.

 *Entrepreneur and the Law*

INTESTATE SUCCESSION

Entrepreneurs often accumulate a sizeable estate. They therefore should have a proper will that designates who receives his or her business and other property when he or she dies. If an entrepreneur or other person dies without a will, or his or her will fails for some legal reason, the property is distributed to his or her relatives pursuant to the state's **intestacy statute**.

Relatives who receive property under these statutes are called **heirs**. Although intestacy statutes differ from state to state, the general rule is that the deceased's real property is distributed according to the intestacy statute of the state where the real property is located, and the deceased's personal property is distributed according to the intestacy statute of the state where the deceased had his or her permanent residence.

Intestacy statutes usually leave the deceased's property to his or her heirs in this order: spouse, children, lineal heirs (e.g., grandchildren, parents, brothers and sisters), collateral heirs (e.g., aunts, uncles, nieces, nephews), and other next of kin (e.g., cousins). If the deceased has no surviving relatives, the deceased's property **escheats** (goes) to the state. In-laws do not inherit under most intestacy statutes. If a child dies before his or her parents, the child's spouse does not receive the inheritance.

To avoid the distribution of an estate as provided in an intestacy statute, a person should have a properly written, signed, and witnessed will that distributes the estate property as the testator wishes.

*C*ONCEPT SUMMARY   COMPARISON OF DYING WITH AND WITHOUT A VALID WILL

Situation	Parties Who Receive Deceased's Property
Deceased dies with a valid will	Beneficiaries named in the will.
Deceased dies without a valid will	Heirs set forth in the applicable intestacy statute. If there are no heirs, the deceased's property escheats to the state.

Business Ethics

THE RIGHT TO DIE AND LIVING WILLS

Technological breakthroughs have greatly increased the life span of human beings. This same technology, however, permits life to be sustained long after a person is "brain dead." Some people say they have a right to refuse such treatment. Others argue that human life must be preserved at all costs. The U.S. Supreme Court was called upon to decide the **right to die** issue in the case of Nancy Cruzan.

In 1983, an automobile accident left Cruzan, a 25-year-old Missouri woman, in an irreversible coma. Four years later, Cruzan's parents petitioned a state court judge to permit the hospital to withdraw the artificial feeding tube that had been keeping Cruzan alive. The judge agreed. However, Missouri's attorney general intervened and asked an appellate court to reverse the lower court's decision. The appellate court sided with the attorney general. The appellate court held that the family had not proven with certainty that Cruzan herself would have wanted the treatment stopped.

In reviewing the Missouri court's decision, eight of the nine justices of the U.S. Supreme Court acknowledged that the right to refuse medical treatment is a personal liberty protected by the U.S. Constitution. However, the Court also recognized

that the states have an interest in preserving life. This interest can be expressed through a requirement for clear and convincing proof that the patient did not want to be sustained by artificial means. The Missouri attorney general then withdrew from the case, and a Missouri judge finally permitted the family to have Cruzan's tubes withdrawn. She died shortly afterward.

The clear message of the Supreme Court's opinion is that people who do not want their lives prolonged indefinitely by artificial means should sign a **living will** that stipulates their wishes before catastrophe strikes and they become unable to express it themselves because of an illness or an accident. The living will could state which life-saving measures they do and do not want. Alternatively, they could state that they want any such treatments withdrawn if doctors determine that there is no hope of a meaningful recovery. The living will provides clear and convincing proof of a patient's wishes with respect to medical treatment. [*Cruzan v. Director, Missouri Department of Health*, 497 U.S. 261, 110 S.Ct. 2841 (1990)]

1. Do you have a *living will?*
2. Do you think it is morally right to have a living will?

TRUSTS

A **trust** is a legal arrangement under which one person (the **settlor**, **trustor**, or **transferor**) delivers and transfers legal title to property to another person (the **trustee**) to be held and used for the benefit of a third person (the **beneficiary**). The property held in trust is called the **trust corpus** or **trust res**. The trust has legal title to the trust corpus, and the beneficiary has equitable title. Unlike wills, trusts are not public documents, so property can be transferred in privacy. Exhibit 38.4 shows the parties to a trust.

trust

A legal arrangement established when one person transfers title to property to another person to be held and used for the benefit of a third person.

settlor or trustor

Person who creates a trust.

trustee

Person who holds legal title to the trust corpus and manages the trust for the benefit of the beneficiary or beneficiaries.

beneficiary

Person for whose benefit a trust is created.

trust corpus

The property held in trust.

EXHIBIT 38.4 *Parties to a Trust*

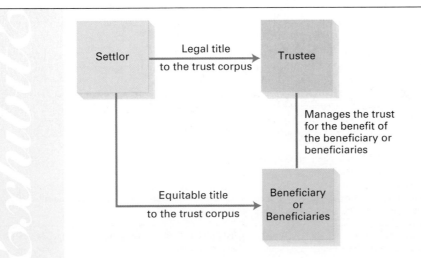

Trusts often provide that any trust income is to be paid to a person called the **income beneficiary**. The person to receive the trust corpus upon the termination of the trust is called the **remainderman**. The income beneficiary and the remainderman can be the same person or different persons. The designated beneficiary can be any identifiable person, animal (such as a pet), charitable organization, or other institution or cause that the settlor chooses. An entire class of persons—for example, "my grandchildren"—can be named.

A trust can allow the trustee to invade (use) the trust corpus for certain purposes. These purposes can be named (e.g., "for the beneficiary's college education"). The trust agreement usually specifies how the receipts and expenses of the trust are to be divided between the income beneficiary and the remainderman.

Generally, the trustee has broad management powers over the trust property. Thus the trustee can invest the trust property to preserve its capital and make it productive. The trustee must follow any restrictions on investments contained in the trust agreement or state statute.

"A grain of sand has been ten thousand mountains. Who are we to hold them?"
In memory of my parents, Henry Benjamin and Florence Lorrain Cheeseman.

*C*HAPTER *S*UMMARY

*I*nsurance, p. 959

Insurance	1. A contract whereby one party (insurer) undertakes to indemnify another party (insured) against loss, damage, or liability arising from a contingent or unknown event.
	2. Insurance is based on the concept of *risk pooling*, that is, transferring and distributing the risk of loss among a large number of persons (insureds).
	3. Parties:
	a. *Insured.* Person who purchases insurance to cover a risk.
	b. *Insurer.* The insurance company (or underwriter) that is obligated to pay insurance proceeds if an insured risk occurs.
	c. *Reinsurer.* An insurance company that purchases insurance contracts from other insurance companies and is obligated to pay insurance proceeds if an insured risk occurs.
	d. *Agent.* Party who sells insurance exclusively for one insurance company.
	e. *Broker.* Party who is an independent contractor and sells insurance for a number of insurance companies.
	f. *Policy.* The insurance contract between the insured and the insurer.
	g. *Premium.* The money the insured is obligated to pay the insurer for insurance coverage.
Insurable Interest	A person must have an insurable interest in anything he or she insures. That is, the person must benefit from the preservation of the life, health, property, or other interest insured.
Regulation of the Insurance Industry	The federal McCarran-Ferguson Act gave the regulation of insurance to the states. States have enacted laws that require the licensing of insurance agents and brokers and regulate insurance companies.

The Insurance Contract, p. 962

The Insurance Contract	Insurance contracts are governed by the law of contracts and statutes enacted to regulate the insurance contract.
Deductible Clause	Requires insureds to pay a certain amount of the loss before the insurer is obligated to pay.
Coinsurance Clause	Requires an owner to insure his or her property to a certain percent of its value to recover the face value of the policy.
Exclusions from Coverage Clause	Stipulates exclusions from insurance coverage (e.g., preexisting conditions).
Modification of Insurance	The insurer and insured may modify an insurance contract by adding an *endorsement* to the policy or executing a document called a *rider*.
Incontestability Statutes	Prohibit insurers from contesting statements made by insureds after the passage of a stipulated number of years.
Cancellation of Insurance	*Grace period*. Time period during which an insured may pay an overdue premium and during which the insurance remains in effect.
Duties of Insured and Insurer	Duties of the insured: 1. Pay premiums stipulated in the policy. 2. Notify the insurer after the occurrence of an insured event. 3. Cooperate with the insurer in the investigation of claims. Duties of the insurer: 1. Defend against suits brought against the insured that involve a claim within the coverage of the policy. 2. Pay legitimate claims up to the policy limit.
Subrogation	If an insurer pays a claim to an insured for liability or property damage caused by a third party, the insurer succeeds to the right of the insured to recover from the third party.

Defenses of the Insurer, p. 965

Misrepresentation and Concealment	Misrepresentation or concealment of material information by the insured prior to the running of the incontestability period.
Breach of Warranty	An *affirmative warranty* is a statement asserting facts to be true. A *promissory warranty* stipulates that facts will continue to be true.

Wills, p. 967

Wills	A declaration of how a person wants his or her property to be distributed upon his or her death.

Requirements for Making a Will	1. *Statute of Wills*. A state statute that establishes the requirements for making a valid will.
	 2. The normal requirements for making a will are:
	   a. *Testamentary capacity*. The testator must have been of legal age and "sound mind" when the will was made.
	   b. *Writing*. A will must be in writing, except for certain special wills.
	   c. *Testator's signature*. A will must be signed by the testator.
	   d. *Attestation by witnesses*. Wills must be attested to by the stipulated number of mentally competent and uninterested witnesses.

Parties to a Will	Parties to a will: 1. *Testator or testatrix*. Person who makes a will. 2. *Beneficiary*. Person designated in the will to receive the testator's property. There may be multiple beneficiaries. 3. *Executor or executrix*. Person named in a will to administer the testator's estate during the settlement of the estate.

Changing a Will	*Codicil.* A legal way to change an existing will. It must be executed with the same formalities as a will.
Simultaneous Deaths	The Uniform Simultaneous Death Act provides that if people who would inherit property from each other die simultaneously, each deceased person's property is distributed as though he or she had survived.
Undue Influence	A will may be found to be invalid if it was made under undue influence, where one person takes advantage of another person's mental, emotional, or physical weakness and unduly persuades that person to make a will. *Murder disqualification.* A person who murders another person cannot inherit the victim's property.

Types of Testamentary Gifts, p. 971

Types of Testamentary Gifts	1. *Specific gift.* Gift of a specifically mentioned piece of property (e.g., a ring). 2. *General gift.* Gift that does not identify the specific property from which the gift is to be made (e.g., gift of cash). 3. *Residuary gift.* Gift of the remainder of the testator's estate after the debts, taxes, and specific and general gifts have been paid.
Ademption and Abatement	1. *Ademption.* If a testator leaves a specific gift but the property is no longer in the estate when the testator dies, the beneficiary of that gift receives nothing. 2. *Abatement.* If the testator's estate is insufficient to pay the stated gifts, the gifts are abated (reduced) in the following order: (1) residuary gifts, then (2) general gifts proportionately.
Per Stirpes and Per Capita Distribution	1. *Per stirpes.* Lineal descendants inherit by representation of their parent; that is, they split what their deceased parent would have received. 2. *Per capita.* Lineal descendants equally share the property of the estate without regard to degree.
Special Types of Wills	1. *Holographic will.* Will that is entirely handwritten and signed by the testator. Most states recognize the validity of these wills even though they are not witnessed. 2. *Nuncupative will.* Oral wills that are made by dying persons before witnesses. Many states recognize these oral wills. Also called a *dying declaration* or a *deathbed will.*
Joint and Mutual Wills	1. *Joint will.* Two or more testators execute the same instrument as their will. 2. *Mutual or reciprocal wills.* Two or more testators execute separate wills that leave property in favor of the other on condition that the survivor leave the remaining property on his or her death as agreed by the testators.
Intestate Succession	1. *Intestacy statute.* State statute that stipulates how a deceased's property will be distributed if he or she dies without leaving a will or if the will fails for some legal reason. 2. *Heirs.* Relatives who receive property under an intestacy statute. 3. *Escheat.* Intestacy statutes provide that if there are no heirs, the deceased's property goes to the state.

Trusts, p. 975

Trusts	A legal arrangement whereby one person delivers and transfers legal title to property to another person to be held and used for the benefit of a third person.
	1. *Trust corpus.* The property that is held in trust. Also called *trust res.*
	2. *Parties:*
	  a. *Settlor.* Person who establishes a trust. Also called a *trustor* or *transferor.*
	  b. *Trustee.* Person to whom *legal title* of the trust assets is transferred. Responsible for managing the trust assets as established by the trust and law.
	  c. *Beneficiary.* Person for whose benefit a trust is created. Holds *equitable title* to the trust assets. There can be multiple beneficiaries, including:
	    i. *Income beneficiary.* Person to whom trust income is to be paid.
	    ii. *Remainderman.* Person who is entitled to receive the trust corpus upon the termination of the trust.

$\mathcal{E}$ND-OF-$\mathcal{C}$HAPTER $\mathcal{I}$NTERNET $\mathcal{E}$XERCISES AND $\mathcal{C}$ASE $\mathcal{Q}$UESTIONS

$\mathcal{W}$orking the Web Internet Exercises

ACTIVITIES

1. Estate Planning is more than just the distribution of decedents' property. Review the issues presented by The Kansas Elder Law Network Aging, Legal, Senior Citizens, Resources, Awards at **www.keln.org**.

2. Review the requirements of Maryland state law with regard to probate at **www.registers.state.md.us/html/pamphlet2.html**. Compare with your state's procedures.

3. For an overview of trusts, including a link to the draft Uniform Trust Act, see **www.law.cornell.edu/topics/estates_trusts.html**. Note the historical purposes of a trust. Why are trusts permitted by law?

4. Review the map of state insurance regulators to find your state's page. What is the commission's position on exclusion of coverage for *terrorist acts*? See Map of Insurance Regulators at **www.naic.org/1regulator/usamap.htm**.

5. Who qualifies as *accredited investors*? See Bloomberg Online Financial Market Information at **www.bloomberg.com**.

6. What is *Rule 144* stock? See The Motley Fool at **www.fool.com**.

7. What constitutes *insider trading*? See Microsoft Investor Version 4.0 at **moneycentral.msn.com/investor/home.asp**.

CRITICAL LEGAL THINKING CASES

38.1 Exclusion Richard Usher's home was protected by a homeowner's policy issued by National American Insurance Company of California. The policy included personal liability insurance. A provision in the policy read: "Personal liability and coverage do not apply to bodily injury or property damage arising out of the ownership, maintenance, use, loading, or unloading of a motor vehicle owned or operated by, or rented or loaned to any insured." On August 24, 1984, Usher parked a Chevrolet van he owned in his driveway. He left the van's side door open while he loaded the van in preparation for a camping trip. While Usher was inside his house, several children, including two-year-old Graham Coburn, began playing near the van. One of the children climbed into the driver's seat and moved the shift lever from *park* to *reverse*. The van rolled backward, crushing Coburn and killing him. Coburn's parents sued Usher for negligence. Is the accident covered by Usher's homeowner's policy? [*National American Insurance Company of California v. Coburn*, 209 Cal.App.3d 914, 257 Cal.Rptr.591 (Cal. App. 1989)]

38.2 Uninsured Motorist Coverage Antonio Munoz and Jacinto Segura won some money from two unidentified men in a craps game in a Los Angeles park. When Munoz and Segura left the park in Segura's car, the two men followed them in another car. After chasing Segura's car for several miles on a freeway, the men in the other car fired several gunshots at Segura's car, killing Munoz. At the time of the shooting, Segura had an automobile insurance policy issued by Nationwide Mutual Insurance Company (Nationwide). Munoz was an addi-tional insured on the policy. A provision in the policy covered damages from "an accident arising out of the use of an uninsured vehicle." Munoz's widow and child filed a claim with Nationwide to recover for Munoz's death. Nationwide rejected the claim. Who wins? [*Nationwide Mutual Insurance Company v. Munoz*, 245 Cal.Rptr. 324 (Cal. App. 1988)]

38.3 Duty to Pay Premiums Mutual Life Insurance Company of New York (Mutual Life) issued a $100,000 life insurance policy on the life of 65-year-old Alex Brecher, effective December 22, 1977. In consideration for the policy, Brecher agreed to pay an annual insurance premium of $7,830 in 12 monthly installments. On July 14, 1983, Brecher made a written request and authorization to have the insurance company with-draw the premiums directly from his checking account at Citibank. The insurance company's first attempt to do so, on July 15, 1983, was returned unpaid. Mutual Life and Brecher were informed that one of Brecher's creditors had placed a restraining order on the bank account. On July 29, 1983, Mutual Life sent Brecher a returned check notice, advising him that the July withdrawal had been dishonored by his bank and that to keep the policy in force both the July and August premiums would have to be paid before August 28. Mutual Life received Brecher's check for the outstanding amounts on August 26. When Mutual Life tried to cash the check, which was drawn on the Citibank account, the bank returned it unpaid, marked "refer to maker." Brecher made no further attempts to pay the insur-ance premiums. He died on September 18, 1983. His widow, the beneficiary of life insurance policy, filed a claim to recover

$100,000 from Mutual Life. When Mutual Life refused to pay, the widow sued. Who wins? [*Brecher v. Mutual Life Insurance Company of New York*, 501 N.Y.S.2d 879 (N.Y. App. 1986)]

38.4 Duty to Defend In February 1983, Judith Isenhart purchased a 1983 Dodge station wagon. She then contacted Ed Carpenter, an agent of the National Automobile and Casualty Insurance Company (National) and told him she was interested in obtaining "full coverage" for the car. The policy that Carpenter provided to Judith provided coverage for bodily injury, property damage, medical costs, and collision damage. The policy specifically exempted coverage for accidents involving "non-owned automobiles." In July 1984, Judith's 16-year-old son Matt purchased a 1969 Volkswagen. Insurance for this car was obtained from Allstate Insurance Company (Allstate). Two months after buying the car, Matt had an accident in which a passenger in the Volkswagen, Thea Stewart, was severely injured. Stewart sued Matt and Judith. Allstate agreed to defend the suit up to the limits of its policy. When National was contacted regarding the accident, the company refused to defend Judith in the suit and denied coverage based on the policy's exclusion. Must National defend Judith? [*National Automobile and Casualty Insurance Company v. Stewart*, 223 Cal.App.3d 452, 272 Cal.Rptr. 625 (Cal. App. 1990)]

38.5 Misrepresentation M&M Restaurant, Inc. (M&M), operated a restaurant in the state of New York. M&M purchased fire insurance for the restaurant from St. Paul Surplus Lines Insurance Company (St. Paul). On July 10, 1984, a fire caused major damage to the restaurant. M&M submitted a claim against St. Paul for losses sustained by the restaurant in the fire. An investigation of the fire by the local police department led to the filing of criminal charges against the owners of M&M. Among the findings of the investigation was that M&M had willfully concealed factual information and had misled St. Paul in obtaining the insurance. On May 25, 1989, the owners of M&M were convicted of insurance fraud, grand larceny, and falsifying business records. St. Paul refused to pay M&M's insurance claim. Who wins? [*M&M Restaurant Inc. v. St. Paul Surplus Lines Insurance Company, N.Y. Law Journal*, June 18, 1990, p. 29 (N.Y. Sup. 1990)]

38.6 Concealment A federal regulation to the Resource Conservation and Discovery Act required certain manufacturers to insure against pollution hazards. The regulation was adopted on January 12, 1981. Early in September 1981, Advanced Micro Devices, Inc. (AMD), a company covered by the regulation, purchased the required insurance from Great American Surplus Lines Insurance Company (Great American). Before issuing the policy, Great American asked AMD to disclose any preexisting conditions that could give rise to a claim retroactive to August 27, 1981. AMD warranted that there were none. AMD made this statement despite the existence of a company memorandum written by AMD's environmental supervisor on July 21, 1981. The memo warned that toxic waste was escaping from an underground steel tank in AMD's acid neutralization system "C" and that AMD was "far from being in compliance" with environmental laws. Great American issued the insurance policy. In 1982, the government ordered AMD to undertake a $1.5-million cleanup of the toxic contaminants surrounding the steel tank in system "C." AMD filed a claim for this amount with Great American, which refused to pay. AMD sued. Who wins? [*Advanced Micro Devices, Inc. v. Great American Surplus Lines Insurance Company*, 199 Cal.App.3d 791, 245 Cal.Rptr. 44 (Cal. App. 1988)]

38.7 Subrogation In 1977, Home Indemnity Company (Home Indemnity) agreed to insure Liberty Savings Association (Liberty), a savings and loan association, for losses that Liberty might incur through the dishonest or fraudulent acts of its employees. In August 1983, Liberty filed a proof of loss with Home Indemnity alleging losses of $579,922. The claim was based on the conversion of $98,372 by Richard Doty, the former president and managing officer of Liberty, and loan losses resulting from four unsecured loans Doty made to friends and relatives. None of the borrowers filed financial statements to qualify for the loans. Home Indemnity paid Liberty for the losses and received a general assignment of Liberty's right to recover against Doty and the borrowers. Home Indemnity then sued Liberty's board of directors, claiming they were negligent in their supervision of Doty. Who wins? [*Home Indemnity Company v. Shaffer*, 860 F.2d 186 (6th Cir. 1988)]

38.8 Formalities of a Will On or about June 10, 1959, Martha Jansa executed a will naming her two sons as executors and leaving all her property to them. The will was properly signed and attested to by witnesses. Thereafter, Martha died. When Martha's safe-deposit box at a bank was opened, the original of this will was discovered along with two other instruments that were dated after the will. One was a handwritten document that left her home to her grandson, with the remainder of her estate to her two sons; this document was not signed. The second document was a typed version of the handwritten one; this document was signed by Martha but was not attested to by witnesses. Which of the three documents should be admitted to probate? [*In re Estate of Jansa*, 670 S.W.2d 767 (Tex. App. 1984)]

38.9 Mental Capacity On March 18, 1987, Everett Clark met with William Wham, an attorney, to discuss the preparation of a will. Clark, who had never married and lived with his sister, was to return the following day to execute his will. Clark was hospitalized that evening with a perforated ulcer. He underwent surgery on March 19. Subsequent to the surgery, and until the time of his death, he was in intensive care and unable to communicate verbally. On March 23, Clark's cousin John Bailey retrieved the will prepared by Wham and took it to attorney Frank Walker to have him finalize it. Walker testified that he took the will to the hospital on March 25. Immediately prior to the execution of the will, Walker asked Clark a few questions. Walker testified that Clark knew what he was doing. Dorothy Smith, an attesting witness, testified that Clark could not talk, but answered her questions by nodding yes or no. She asked Clark "if he knew me and if he knew we were all there and he shook his head yes." She testified that he also shook his head yes to the question "Is this your will and testament?" "Is John Bailey your cousin?" and "Do you want to leave everything to John Bailey?" Clark signed the will with an X. On March 26, Clark passed into a coma and died. Bailey introduced the will into probate, but another relative of Clark's challenged it. Is the will valid? [*Bailey v. Bailey*, 561 N.E.2d 367 (Ill. App. 1990)]

38.10 Inheritance In October 1973, Mr. and Mrs. Pate executed separate wills that followed a common plan in disposing of their respective estates. Each will provided for the establishment of trusts with a life estate to their son Billy, and upon his death, the estate was to be distributed "in equal shares per stirpes to my natural born grandchildren." Mr. and Mrs. Pate had two sons, Billy and Wallace. Billy's first marriage ended in divorce without children. Billy's second marriage also ended in divorce without children, although his second wife had a daughter by her previous marriage. Billy married again, and to date no children have been born to his 32-year-old wife. Wallace first married in 1952. Of that marriage five children were born, each before the time that the Pates made their wills. After that marriage ended in divorce, Wallace married his present wife. There are no children of the second marriage, but there are stepchildren by Wallace's second wife. One of Wallace's daughters has two children by her marriage. Mr. Pate died on November 9, 1979, leaving an estate of $1.6 million. Mrs. Pate died on October 21, 1983, leaving an estate of $6.7 million. Who inherits the estate? [*Pate v. Ford*, 360 S.E.2d 145 (S.C. App. 1987)]

BUSINESS ETHICS CASES

38.11 Business Ethics In 1983, Lewis Coe bought a $500,000 life insurance policy from Farmers New World Life Insurance Company (Farmers) from its authorized agent, Hannify. The policy, which was payable in monthly installments, contained a clause allowing for the insurance to remain in effect for a 31-day grace period if the insured failed to pay a premium by the due date. In February 1984, Lewis informed Hannify that he wanted to cancel the policy. Farmers sent Lewis a cancellation form that he signed and returned on or about March 1, 1984. At the time Farmer received the written cancellation notice, Lewis had paid the monthly premium for February, covering the period ending March 10, 1984. Lewis died on April 8, 1984. His widow sued Farmers for the policy proceeds claiming that Lewis died during the 31-day grace period provided by the policy. Farmers claimed the policy had been canceled and the grace period did not apply. Who wins? Did either party act unethically in this case? [*Coe v. Farmers New World Life Insurance Company*, 209 Cal.App.3d 600, 257 Cal.Rptr. 411 (Cal. App. 1989)]

38.12 Business Ethics In 1967, Homer and Edna Jones, husband and wife, executed a joint will that provided "We will and give to our survivor, whether it be Homer Jones or Edna Jones, all property and estate of which the first of us that dies may be seized and possessed. If we should both die in a common catastrophe, or upon the death of our survivor, we will and give all property and estate then remaining to our children, Leonida Jones Eschman, daughter, Sylvia Marie Jones, daughter, and Grady V. Jones, son, share and share alike."

Homer died in 1975, and Edna Jones received his entire estate under the 1967 will. In 1977, Edna executed a new will that left a substantially larger portion of the estate to her daughter, Sylvia Marie Jones, than to the other two children. Edna Jones died in 1982. Edna's daughter introduced the 1977 will for probate. The other two children introduced the 1967 will for probate. Did Edna act ethically in this case? Who wins? [*Jones v. Jones*, 718 S.W.2d 416 (Tex. App. 1986)]

BRIEFING THE CASE WRITING ASSIGNMENT

Read the following case, which has been excerpted from the court's opinion. Review and brief the case.

Saritejdiam, Inc. v. Excess Insurance Company, Ltd.
971 F.2D 910 (1992)
United States Court of Appeals for the Second Circuit

Oakes, Chief Judge

Saritejdiam, Inc. (Saritejdiam) is a New York corporation involved in the wholesaling of diamonds and other precious and semi-precious stones and jewelry. In June 1988, Excess Insurance Company, Ltd., et al., (the Underwriters), a group of London-based insurance companies, issued an insurance policy to Saritejdiam. The policy is called a Jeweler's Block Policy and it insures against all risks of physical loss or damage to insured interests, unless specifically excluded by the policy. This appeal requires us to analyze whether Saritejdiam satisfied a clause in the policy requiring that insured interests remain in the "close personal custody and control" of the insured or its agent while in transit.

On May 13, 1989, Mr. Robert Danilin, an independent contractor/salesman for Saritejdiam, lost a package of loose diamonds valued by Saritejdiam at $267,514.30. On that day, Danilin, his wife, and stepson were in Tuxedo, New York, visiting a townhouse they had just purchased there. At approximately 5:50 P.M., the Danilins arrived at the Orange Top Diner on Route 17 in Tuxedo for dinner. Danilin brought a camera bag into the diner containing two stiff, black diamond wallets (one of which held Saritejdiam's diamonds), his checkbook, and credit cards. The three were seated at a table. Robert placed the camera bag on top of an empty chair to his left. During dinner, he touched the camera bag to make sure it was still on the chair. When they finished eating, Danilin paid the check with cash out of his pants pocket. The three then left the diner, got into their car, and headed for a golf driving range. When the Danilins reached their destination, they discovered that the camera bag containing the diamond wallets was not in the car. They sped back to the diner. The camera bag, however, was no longer on the chair where it had been previously placed.

Connie Grievas, the daughter of the proprietors of the Orange Top Diner, apparently witnessed the events that transpired after Danilin paid his bill.

Grievas was 11 years old at the time. She told Danilin's stepson and, later on, investigators for the Underwriters, that she went to clear Danilin's table after he paid his check. She noticed that a bag with a handle was left behind. Grievas then went to tell her mother that a customer had left a bag behind. Before she reached her mother, she saw two others customers, a man and a woman, take the bag and walk out. She described the man who picked up the bag as white, approximately 40 years old, with shoulder-length black curly hair, standing 5 feet 7 inches, and wearing dark sunglasses. She described the woman as having blonde, waist-length hair.

On the same day, Saritejdiam reported the loss to the Underwriters. On June 23, 1989, after investigating the claim, the Underwriters refused to cover the lost diamonds. The Underwriters claimed that Saritejdiam had not complied with the Personal Conveyance Clause of the insurance policy. The clause provides:

This policy only covers the insured interest in transit when in the close personal custody and control of the Assured and/or Assured's representative and/or agent at all times whilst in transit subject to hotel/motel clause, excluding all losses due to infidelity.

The denial letter states that "the results of our investigation have revealed that there is no evidence that the theft took place whilst your property was in the close personal custody and control of your salesman, Robert Danilin."

We must decide whether the loss of the diamonds at the Orange Top Diner occurred while they were in the "close personal custody and control" of Danilin, Saritejdiam's salesman/independent contractor. If so, Saritejdiam satisfied the requirements of the Personal Conveyance Clause in the policy, and the Underwriters must cover the loss. The issue traditionally arises in disputes over the rights of the finder against those of the owner of the real property on which the disputed personal property was found. The common law generally distinguished between lost *and* mislaid *property. Property is mislaid when the owner purposely parts with possession of the property, but then unintentionally leaves it behind. We believe that under New York common law the camera bag containing Saritejdiam's diamond wallets would be classified as mislaid property. Saritejdiam's salesman purposely placed the camera bag on the adjacent chair at his table in the Orange Top Diner. He then walked away from the table and forgot to pick up the camera bag. This is a paradigmatic example of mislaid property under New York's common law definition of the term. Accordingly, we believe a New York court would hold that a person simply cannot maintain "close personal custody and control" over mislaid property.*

For the foregoing reasons, we reverse the order of the district court granting summary judgment for Saritejdiam and enter summary judgment for the Underwriters.

Appendix A

Uniform Commercial Code (2000 Official Text), Article 2

ARTICLE 2.   SALES

Part 1.   Short Title, General Construction and Subject Matter

§ 2–101.   Short Title.

This Article shall be known and may be cited as Uniform Commercial Code—Sales.

§ 2–102.   Scope; Certain Security and Other Transactions Excluded From This Article.

Unless the context otherwise requires, this Article applies to transactions in goods; it does not apply to any transaction which although in the form of an unconditional contract to sell or present sale is intended to operate only as a security transaction nor does this Article impair or repeal any statute regulating sales to consumers, farmers or other specified classes of buyers.

§ 2–103.   Definitions and Index of Definitions.

(1) In this Article unless the context otherwise requires
  (a) "Buyer" means a person who buys or contracts to buy goods.
  (b) "Good faith" in the case of a merchant means honesty in fact and the observance of reasonable commercial standards of fair dealing in the trade.
  (c) "Receipt" of goods means taking physical possession of them.
  (d) "Seller" means a person who sells or contracts to sell goods.

(2) Other definitions applying to this Article or to specified Parts thereof, and the sections in which they appear are:

(3)   The following definitions in other Articles apply to this Article:

(4)   In addition Article 1 contains general definitions and principles of construction and interpretation applicable throughout this Article.

§ 2–104.   Definitions: "Merchant"; "Between Merchants"; "Financing Agency".

(1) "Merchant" means a person who deals in goods of the kind or otherwise by his occupation holds himself out as having knowledge or skill peculiar to the practices or goods involved in the transaction or to whom such knowledge or skill may be attributed by his employment of an agent or broker or other intermediary who by his occupation holds himself out as having such knowledge or skill.

(2) "Financing agency" means a bank, finance company or other person who in the ordinary course of business makes advances against goods or documents of title or who by arrangement with either the seller or the buyer intervenes in ordinary course to make or collect payment due or claimed under the contract for sale, as by purchasing or paying the seller's draft or making advances against it or by merely taking it for collection whether or not the documents of title accompany the draft. "Financing agency" includes also a bank or other person who similarly intervenes between persons who are in the position of seller and buyer in respect to the goods (Section 2–707).

(3) "Between merchants" means in any transaction with respect to which both parties are chargeable with the knowledge or skill of merchants.

§ 2–105.   Definitions: Transferability; "Goods"; "Future" Goods; "Lot"; "Commercial Unit".

(1) "Goods" means all things (including specially manufactured goods) which are movable at the time of identification to the contract for sale other than the money in which the price is to be paid, investment securities (Article 8) and things in action. "Goods" also includes the unborn young of animals and growing crops and other identified things attached to realty as described in the section on goods to be severed from realty (Section 2–107).

(2) Goods must be both existing and identified before any interest in them can pass. Goods which are not both existing and identified are "future" goods. A purported present sale of future goods or of any interest therein operates as a contract to sell.

(3) There may be a sale of a part interest in existing identified goods.

(4) An undivided share in an identified bulk of fungible goods is sufficiently identified to be sold although the quantity of the bulk is not determined. Any agreed proportion of such a bulk or any quantity thereof agreed upon by number, weight or other measure may to the extent of the seller's interest in the bulk be sold to the buyer who then becomes an owner in common.

(5) "Lot" means a parcel or a single article which is the subject matter of a separate sale or delivery, whether or not it is sufficient to perform the contract.

(6) "Commercial unit" means such a unit of goods as by commercial usage is a single whole for purposes of sale and division of which materially impairs its character or value on the market or in use. A commercial unit may be a single article (as a machine) or a set of articles (as a suite of furniture or an assortment of sizes) or a quantity (as a bale, gross, or carload) or any other unit treated in use or in the relevant market as a single whole.

§ 2–106.   Definitions: "Contract"; "Agreement"; "Contract for Sale"; "Sale"; "Present Sale"; "Conforming" to Contract; "Termination"; "Cancellation".

(1) In this Article unless the context otherwise requires "contract" and "agreement" are limited to those relating to the present or future sale of

goods. "Contract for sale" includes both a present sale of goods and a contract to sell goods at a future time. A "sale" consists in the passing of title from the seller to the buyer for a price (Section 2–401). A "present sale" means a sale which is accomplished by the making of the contract.

(2) Goods or conduct including any part of a performance are "conforming" or conform to the contract when they are in accordance with the obligations under the contract.

(3) "Termination" occurs when either party pursuant to a power created by agreement or law puts an end to the contract otherwise than for its breach. On "termination" all obligations which are still executory on both sides are discharged but any right based on prior breach or performance survives.

(4) "Cancellation" occurs when either party puts an end to the contract for breach by the other and its effect is the same as that of "termination" except that the cancelling party also retains any remedy for breach of the whole contract or any unperformed balance.

§ 2–107. Goods to Be Severed From Realty: Recording.

(1) A contract for the sale of minerals or the like (including oil and gas) or a structure or its materials to be removed from realty is a contract for the sale of goods within this Article if they are to be severed by the seller but until severance a purported present sale thereof which is not effective as a transfer of an interest in land is effective only as a contract to sell.

(2) A contract for the sale apart from the land of growing crops or other things attached to realty and capable of severance without material harm thereto but not described in subsection (1) or of timber to be cut is a contract for the sale of goods within this Article whether the subject matter is to be severed by the buyer or by the seller even though it forms part of the realty at the time of contracting, and the parties can by identification effect a present sale before severance.

(3) The provisions of this section are subject to any third party rights provided by the law relating to realty records, and the contract for sale may be executed and recorded as a document transferring an interest in land and shall then constitute notice to third parties of the buyer's right under the contract for sale.

Part 2. *Form, Formation and Readjustment of Contra*

§ 2–201. Formal Requirements; Statute of Frauds.

(1) Except as otherwise provided in this section a contract for the sale of goods for the price of $500 or more is not enforceable by way of action or defense unless there is some writing sufficient to indicate that a contract for sale has been made between the parties and signed by the party against whom enforcement is sought or by his authorized agent or broker. A writing is not insufficient because it omits or incorrectly states a term agreed upon but the contract is not enforceable under this paragraph beyond the quantity of goods shown in such writing.

(2) Between merchants if within a reasonable time a writing in confirmation of the contract and sufficient against the sender is received and the party receiving it has reason to know its contents, it satisfies the requirements of subsection (1) against such party unless written notice of objection to its contents is given within 10 days after it is received.

(3) A contract which does not satisfy the requirements of subsection (1) but which is valid in other respects is enforceable

(a) if the goods are to be specially manufactured for the buyer and are not suitable for sale to others in the ordinary course of the seller's business and the seller, before notice of repudiation is received and under circumstances which reasonably indicate that the goods are for the buyer, has made either a substantial beginning of their manufacture or commitments for their procurement; or

(b) if the party against whom enforcement is sought admits in his pleading, testimony or otherwise in court that a contract for sale was made, but the contract is not enforceable under this provision beyond the quantity of goods admitted; or

(c) with respect to goods for which payment has been made and accepted or which have been received and accepted (Section 2–606).

§ 2–202. Final Written Expression: Parol or Extrinsic Evidence.

Terms with respect to which the confirmatory memoranda of the parties agree or which are otherwise set forth in a writing intended by the parties as a final expression of their agreement with respect to such terms as are included therein may not be contradicted by evidence of any prior agreement or of a contemporaneous oral agreement but may be explained or supplemented

(a) by course and dealing or usage of trade (Section 1–205) or by course of performance (Section 2–208); and

(b) by evidence of consistent additional terms unless the court finds the writing to have been intended also as a complete and exclusive statement of the terms of the agreement.

§ 2–203. Seals Inoperative.

The affixing of a seal to a writing evidencing a contract for sale or an offer to buy or sell goods does not constitute the writing a sealed instrument and the law with respect to sealed instruments does not apply to such a contract or offer.

§ 2–204. Formation in General.

(1) A contract for sale of goods may be made in any manner sufficient to show agreement, including conduct by both parties which recognizes the existence of such a contract.

(2) An agreement sufficient to constitute a contract for sale may be found even though the moment of its making is undetermined.

(3) Even though one or more terms are left open a contract for sale does not fail for indefiniteness if the parties have intended to make a contract and there is a reasonably certain basis for giving an appropriate remedy.

§ 2–205. Firm Offers.

An offer by a merchant to buy or sell goods in a signed writing which by its terms gives assurance that it will be held open is not revocable, for lack of consideration, during the time stated or if no time is stated for a reasonable time, but in no event may such period of irrevocability exceed three months; but any such term of assurance on a form supplied by the offeree must be separately signed by the offeror.

§ 2–206. Offer and Acceptance in Formation of Contract.

(1) Unless otherwise unambiguously indicated by the language or circumstances

(a) an offer to make a contract shall be construed as inviting acceptance in any manner and by any medium reasonable in the circumstances;

(b) an order or other offer to buy goods for prompt or current shipment shall be construed as inviting acceptance either by a prompt promise to ship or by the prompt or current shipment of conforming or non-conforming goods, but such a shipment of non-conforming goods does not constitute an acceptance if the seller seasonably notifies the buyer that the shipment is offered only as an accommodation to the buyer.

(2) Where the beginning of a requested performance is a reasonable mode of acceptance an offeror who is not notified of acceptance within a reasonable time may treat the offer as having lapsed before acceptance.

§ 2–207. Additional Terms in Acceptance or Confirmation.

(1) A definite and seasonable expression of acceptance or a written confirmation which is sent within a reasonable time operates as an acceptance even though it states terms additional to or different from those offered or agreed upon, unless acceptance is expressly made conditional on assent to the additional or different terms.

(2) The additional terms are to be construed as proposals for addition to the contract. Between merchants such terms become part of the contract unless:

(a) the offer expressly limits acceptance to the terms of the offer;

(b) they materially alter it; or

(c) notification of objection to them has already been given or is given within a reasonable time after notice of them is received.

(3) Conduct by both parties which recognizes the existence of a contract is sufficient to establish a contract for sale although the writings of the parties do not otherwise establish a contract. In such case the terms of the particular contract consist of those terms on which the writings of the parties agree, together with any supplementary terms incorporated under any other provisions of this Act.

§ 2–208. Course of Performance or Practical Construction.

(1) Where the contract for sale involves repeated occasions for performance by either party with knowledge of the nature of the performance and opportunity for objection to it by the other, any course of performance accepted or acquiesced in without objection shall be relevant to determine the meaning of the agreement.

(2) The express terms of the agreement and any such course of performance, as well as any course of dealing and usage of trade, shall be construed

whenever reasonable as consistent with each other; but when such construction is unreasonable, express terms shall control course of performance and course of performance shall control both course of dealing and usage of trade (Section 1–205).

(3) Subject to the provisions of the next section on modification and waiver, such course of performance shall be relevant to show a waiver or modification of any term inconsistent with such course of performance.

§ 2–209. Modification, Rescission and Waiver.

(1) An agreement modifying a contract within this Article needs no consideration to be binding.

(2) A signed agreement which excludes modification or rescission except by a signed writing cannot be otherwise modified or rescinded, but except as between merchants such a requirement on a form supplied by the merchant must be separately signed by the other party.

(3) The requirements of the statute of frauds section of this Article (Section 2–201) must be satisfied if the contract as modified is within its provisions.

(4) Although an attempt at modification or rescission does not satisfy the requirements of subsection (2) or (3) it can operate as a waiver.

(5) A party who has made a waiver affecting an executory portion of the contract may retract the waiver by reasonable notification received by the other party that strict performance will be required of any term waived, unless the retraction would be unjust in view of a material change of position in reliance on the waiver.

§ 2–210. Delegation of Performance; Assignment of Rights.

(1) A party may perform his duty through a delegate unless otherwise agreed or unless the other party has a substantial interest in having his original promisor perform or control the acts required by the contract. No delegation of performance relieves the party delegating of any duty to perform or any liability for breach.

(2) Except as otherwise provided in Section 9–406, unless otherwise agreed all rights of either seller or buyer can be assigned except where the assignment would materially change the duty of the other party, or increase materially the burden or risk imposed on him by his contract, or impair materially his chance of obtaining return performance. A right to damages for breach of the whole contract or a right arising out of the assignor's due performance of his entire obligation can be assigned despite agreement otherwise.

(3) The creation, attachment, perfection, or enforcement of a security interest in the seller's interest under a contract is not a transfer that materially changes the duty of or increases materially the burden or risk imposed on the buyer or impairs materially the buyer's chance of obtaining return performance within the purview of subsection (2) unless, and then only to the extent that, enforcement actually results in a delegation of material performance of the seller. Even in that event, the creation, attachment, perfection, and enforcement of the security interest remain effective, but (i) the seller is liable to the buyer for damages caused by the delegation to the extent that the damages could not reasonably be prevented by the buyer, and (ii) a court having jurisdiction may grant other appropriate relief, including cancellation of the contract for sale or an injunction against enforcement of the security interest or consummation of the enforcement.

(4) Unless the circumstances indicate the contrary a prohibition of assignment of "the contract" is to be construed as barring only the delegation to the assignee of the assignor's performance.

(5) An assignment of "the contract" or of "all my rights under the contract" or an assignment in similar general terms is an assignment of rights and unless the language or the circumstances (as in an assignment for security) indicate the contrary, it is a delegation of performance of the duties of the assignor and its acceptance by the assignee constitutes a promise by him to perform those duties. This promise is enforceable by either the assignor or the other party to the original contract.

(6) The other party may treat any assignment which delegates performance as creating reasonable grounds for insecurity and may without prejudice to his rights against the assignor demand assurances from the assignee (Section 2–609).

Part 3. *General Obligation and Construction of Contract*

§ 2–301. General Obligations of Parties.

The obligation of the seller is to transfer and deliver and that of the buyer is to accept and pay in accordance with the contract.

§ 2–302. Unconscionable Contract or Clause.

(1) If the court as a matter of law finds the contract or any clause of the contract to have been unconscionable at the time it was made the court may refuse to enforce the contract, or it may enforce the remainder of the contract without the unconscionable clause, or it may so limit the application of any unconscionable clause as to avoid any unconscionable result.

(2) When it is claimed or appears to the court that the contract or any clause thereof may be unconscionable the parties shall be afforded a reasonable opportunity to present evidence as to its commercial setting, purpose and effect to aid the court in making the determination.

§ 2–303. Allocation or Division of Risks.

Where this Article allocates a risk or a burden as between the parties "unless otherwise agreed", the agreement may not only shift the allocation but may also divide the risk or burden.

§ 2–304. Price Payable in Money, Goods, Realty, or Otherwise.

(1) The price can be made payable in money or otherwise. If it is payable in whole or in part in goods each party is a seller of the goods which he is to transfer.

(2) Even though all or part of the price is payable in an interest in realty the transfer of the goods and the seller's obligations with reference to them are subject to this Article, but not the transfer of the interest in realty or the transferor's obligations in connection therewith.

§ 2–305. Open Price Term.

(1) The parties if they so intend can conclude a contract for sale even though the price is not settled. In such a case the price is a reasonable price at the time for delivery if

(a) nothing is said as to price; or

(b) the price is left to be agreed by the parties and they fail to agree; or

(c) the price is to be fixed in terms of some agreed market or other standard as set or recorded by a third person or agency and it is not so set or recorded.

(2) A price to be fixed by the seller or by the buyer means a price for him to fix in good faith.

(3) When a price left to be fixed otherwise than by agreement of the parties fails to be fixed through fault of one party the other may at his option treat the contract as cancelled or himself fix a reasonable price.

(4) Where, however, the parties intend not to be bound unless the price be fixed or agreed and it is not fixed or agreed there is no contract. In such a case the buyer must return any goods already received or if unable so to do must pay their reasonable value at the time of delivery and the seller must return any portion of the price paid on account.

§ 2–306. Output, Requirements and Exclusive Dealings.

(1) A term which measures the quantity by the output of the seller or the requirements of the buyer means such actual output or requirements as may occur in good faith, except that no quantity unreasonably disproportionate to any stated estimate or in the absence of a stated estimate to any normal or otherwise comparable prior output or requirements may be tendered or demanded.

(2) A lawful agreement by either the seller or the buyer for exclusive dealing in the kind of goods concerned imposes unless otherwise agreed an obligation by the seller to use best efforts to supply the goods and by the buyer to use best efforts to promote their sale.

§ 2–307. Delivery in Single Lot or Several Lots.

Unless otherwise agreed all goods called for by a contract for sale must be tendered in a single delivery and payment is due only on such tender but where the circumstances give either party the right to make or demand delivery in lots the price if it can be apportioned may be demanded for each lot.

§ 2–308. Absence of Specified Place for Delivery.

Unless otherwise agreed

(a) the place for delivery of goods is the seller's place of business or if he has none his residence; but

(b) in a contract for sale of identified goods which to the knowledge of the parties at the time of contracting are in some other place, that place is the place for their delivery; and

(c) documents of title may be delivered through customary banking channels.

§ 2–309. Absence of Specific Time Provisions; Notice of Termination.

(1) The time for shipment or delivery or any other action under a contract if not provided in this Article or agreed upon shall be a reasonable time.

(2) Where the contract provides for successive performance but is indefinite in duration it is valid for a reasonable time but unless otherwise agreed may be terminated at any time by either party.

(3) Termination of a contract by one party except on the happening of an agreed event requires that reasonable notification be received by the other party and an agreement dispensing with notification is invalid if its operation would be unconscionable.

§ 2–310. Open Time for Payment or Running of Credit; Authority to Ship Under Reservation.

Unless otherwise agreed

   (a) payment is due at the time and place at which the buyer is to receive the goods even though the place of shipment is the place of delivery; and

   (b) if the seller is authorized to send the goods he may ship them under reservation, and may tender the documents of title, but the buyer may inspect the goods after their arrival before payment is due unless such inspection is inconsistent with the terms of the contract (Section 2–513); and

   (c) if delivery is authorized and made by way of documents of title otherwise than by subsection (b) then payment is due at the time and place at which the buyer is to receive the documents regardless of where the goods are to be received; and

   (d) where the seller is required or authorized to ship the goods on credit the credit period runs from the time of shipment but post-dating the invoice or delaying its dispatch will correspondingly delay the starting of the credit period.

§ 2–311. Options and Cooperation Respecting Performance.

(1) An agreement for sale which is otherwise sufficiently definite (subsection (3) of Section 2–204) to be a contract is not made invalid by the fact that it leaves particulars of performance to be specified by one of the parties. Any such specification must be made in good faith and within limits set by commercial reasonableness.

(2) Unless otherwise agreed specifications relating to assortment of the goods are at the buyer's option and except as otherwise provided in subsections (1) (c) and (3) of Section 2–319 specifications or arrangements relating to shipment are at the seller's option.

(3) Where such specification would materially affect the other party's performance but is not seasonably made or where one party's cooperation is necessary to the agreed performance of the other but is not seasonably forthcoming, the other party in addition to all other remedies

   (a) is excused for any resulting delay in his own performance; and

   (b) may also either proceed to perform in any reasonable manner or after the time for a material part of his own performance treat the failure to specify or to cooperate as a breach by failure to deliver or accept the goods.

§ 2–312. Warranty of Title and Against Infringement; Buyer's Obligation Against Infringement.

(1) Subject to subsection (2) there is in a contract for sale a warranty by the seller that

   (a) the title conveyed shall be good, and its transfer rightful; and

   (b) the goods shall be delivered free from any security interest or other lien or encumbrance of which the buyer at the time of contracting has no knowledge.

(2) A warranty under subsection (1) will be excluded or modified only by specific language or by circumstances which give the buyer reason to know that the person selling does not claim title in himself or that he is purporting to sell only such right or title as he or a third person may have.

(3) Unless otherwise agreed a seller who is a merchant regularly dealing in goods of the kind warrants that the goods shall be delivered free of the rightful claim of any third person by way of infringement or the like but a buyer who furnishes specifications to the seller must hold the seller harmless against any such claim which arises out of compliance with the specifications.

§ 2–313. Express Warranties by Affirmation, Promise, Description, Sample.

(1) Express warranties by the seller are created as follows:

   (a) Any affirmation of fact or promise made by the seller to the buyer which relates to the goods and becomes part of the basis of the bargain creates an express warranty that the goods shall conform to the affirmation or promise.

   (b) Any description of the goods which is made part of the basis of the bargain creates an express warranty that the goods shall conform to the description.

   (c) Any sample or model which is made part of the basis of the bargain creates an express warranty that the whole of the goods shall conform to the sample or model.

(2) It is not necessary to the creation of an express warranty that the seller use formal words such as "warrant" or "guarantee" or that he have a specific intention to make a warranty, but an affirmation merely of the value of the goods or a statement purporting to be merely the seller's opinion or commendation of the goods does not create a warranty.

§ 2–314. Implied Warranty: Merchantability; Usage of Trade.

(1) Unless excluded or modified (Section 2–316), a warranty that the goods shall be merchantable is implied in a contract for their sale if the seller is a merchant with respect to goods of that kind. Under this section the serving for value of food or drink to be consumed either on the premises or elsewhere is a sale.

(2) Goods to be merchantable must be at least such as

   (a) pass without objection in the trade under the contract description; and

   (b) in the case of fungible goods, are of fair average quality within the description; and

   (c) are fit for the ordinary purposes for which such goods are used; and

   (d) run, within the variations permitted by the agreement, of even kind, quality and quantity within each unit and among all units involved; and

   (e) are adequately contained, packaged, and labeled as the agreement may require; and

   (f) conform to the promises or affirmations of fact made on the container or label if any.

(3) Unless excluded or modified (Section 2–316) other implied warranties may arise from course of dealing or usage of trade.

§ 2–315. Implied Warranty: Fitness for Particular Purpose.

Where the seller at the time of contracting has reason to know any particular purpose for which the goods are required and that the buyer is relying on the seller's skill or judgment to select or furnish suitable goods, there is unless excluded or modified under the next section an implied warranty that the goods shall be fit for such purpose.

§ 2–316. Exclusion or Modification of Warranties.

(1) Words or conduct relevant to the creation of an express warranty and words or conduct tending to negate or limit warranty shall be construed wherever reasonable as consistent with each other, but subject to the provisions of this Article on parol or extrinsic evidence (Section 2–202) negation or limitation is inoperative to the extent that such construction is unreasonable.

(2) Subject to subsection (3), to exclude or modify the implied warranty of merchantability or any part of it the language must mention merchantability and in case of a writing must be conspicuous, and to exclude or modify any implied warranty of fitness the exclusion must be by a writing and conspicuous. Language to exclude all implied warranties of fitness is sufficient if it states, for example, that "There are no warranties which extend beyond the description on the face hereof."

(3) Notwithstanding subsection (2)

   (a) unless the circumstances indicate otherwise, all implied warranties are excluded by expression like "as is", "with all faults" or other language which in common understanding calls the buyer's attention to the exclusion of warranties and makes plain that there is no implied warranty; and

   (b) when the buyer before entering into the contract has examined the goods or the sample or model as fully as he desired or has refused to examine the goods there is no implied warranty with regard to defects which an examination ought in the circumstances to have revealed to him; and

   (c) an implied warranty can also be excluded or modified by course of dealing or course of performance or usage of trade.

(4) Remedies for breach of warranty can be limited in accordance with the provisions of this Article on liquidation or limitation of damages and on contractual modification of remedy (Sections 2–718 and 2–719).

§ 2-317. Cumulation and Conflict of Warranties Express or Implied.

Warranties whether express or implied shall be construed as consistent with each other and as cumulative, but if such construction is unreasonable the intention of the parties shall determine which warranty is dominant. In ascertaining that intention the following rules apply:

(a) Exact or technical specifications displace an inconsistent sample or model or general language of description.

(b) A sample from an existing bulk displaces inconsistent general language of description.

(c) Express warranties displace inconsistent implied warranties other than an implied warranty of fitness for a particular purpose.

§ 2-318. Third Party Beneficiaries of Warranties Express or Implied.

Note: *If this Act is introduced in the Congress of the United States this section should be omitted. (States to select one alternative.)*

Alternative A. A seller's warranty whether express or implied extends to any natural person who is in the family or household of his buyer or who is a guest in his home if it is reasonable to expect that such person may use, consume or be affected by the goods and who is injured in person by breach of the warranty. A seller may not exclude or limit the operation of this section.

Alterntive B. A seller's warranty whether express or implied extends to any natural person who may reasonably be expected to use, consume or be affected by the goods and who is injured in person by breach of the warranty. A seller may not exclude or limit the operation of this section.

Alternative C. A seller's warranty whether express or implied extends to any person who may reasonably be expected to use, consume or be affected by the goods and who is injured by breach of the warranty. A seller may not exclude or limit the operation of this section with respect to injury to the person of an individual to whom the warranty extends.

§ 2-319. F.O.B. and F.A.S. Terms.

(1) Unless otherwise agreed the term F.O.B. (which means "free on board") at a named place, even though used only in connection with the stated price, is a delivery term under which

(a) when the term is F.O.B. the place of shipment, the seller must at that place ship the goods in the manner provided in this Article (Section 2-504) and bear the expense and risk of putting them into the possession of the carrier; or

(b) when the term is F.O.B. the place of destination, the seller must at his own expense and risk transport the goods to that place and there tender delivery of them in the manner provided in this Article (Section 2-503);

(c) when under either (a) or (b) the term is also F.O.B. vessel, car or other vehicle, the seller must in addition at his own expense and risk load the goods on board. If the term is F.O.B. vessel the buyer must name the vessel and in an appropriate case the seller must comply with the provisions of this Article on the form of bill of lading (Section 2-323).

(2) Unless otherwise agreed the term F.A.S. vessel (which means "free alongside") at a named port, even though used only in connection with the stated price, is a delivery term under which the seller must

(a) at his own expense and risk deliver the goods alongside the vessel in the manner usual in that port or on a dock designated and provided by the buyer; and

(b) obtain and tender a receipt for the goods in exchange for which the carrier is under a duty to issue a bill of lading.

(3) Unless otherwise agreed in any case falling within subsection (1)(a) or (c) or subsection (2) the buyer must seasonably give any needed instructions for making delivery, including when the term is F.A.S. or F.O.B. the loading berth of the vessel and in an appropriate case its name and sailing date. The seller may treat the failure of needed instructions as a failure of cooperation under this Article (Section 2-311). He may also at his option move the goods in any reasonable manner preparatory to delivery or shipment.

(4) Under the term F.O.B. vessel or F.A.S. unless otherwise agreed the buyer must make payment against tender of the required documents and the seller may not tender nor the buyer demand delivery of the goods in substitution for the documents.

§ 2-320. C.I.F. and C. & F. Terms.

(1) The term C.I.F. means that the price includes in a lump sum the cost of the goods and the insurance and freight to the named destination. The term C. & F. or C.F. means that the price so includes cost and freight to the named destination.

(2) Unless otherwise agreed and even though used only in connection with the stated price and destination, the term C.I.F. destination or its equivalent requires the seller at his own expense and risk to

(a) put the goods into the possession of a carrier at the port for shipment and obtain a negotiable bill or bills of lading covering the entire transportation to the named destination; and

(b) load the goods and obtain a receipt from the carrier (which may be contained in the bill of lading) showing that the freigt has been paid or provided for; and

(c) obtain a policy or certificate of insurance, including any war risk insurance, of a kind and on terms then current at the port of shipment in the usual amount, in the currency of the contract, shown to cover the same goods covered by the bill of lading and providing for payment of loss to the order of the buyer or for the account of whom it may concern; but the seller may add to the price the amount of the premium for any such war risk insurance; and

(d) prepare an invoice of the goods and procure any other documents required to effect shipment or to comply with the contract; and

(e) forward and tender with commercial promptness all the documents in due form and with any indorsement necessary to perfect the buyer's rights.

(3) Unless otherwise agreed the term C. & F. or its equivalent has the same effect and imposes upon the seller the same obligations and risks as a C.I.F. term except the obligation as to insurance.

(4) Under the term C.I.F. or C. & F. unless otherwise agreed the buyer must make payment against tender of the required documents and the seller may not tender nor the buyer demand delivery of the goods in substitution for the documents.

§ 2-321. C.I.F. or C. & F.: "Net Landed Weights"; "Payment on Arrival"; Warranty of Condition on Arrival.

Under a contract containing a term C.I.F. or C. & F.

(1) Where the price is based on or is to be adjusted according to "net landed weights", "delivered weights", "out turn" quantity or quality or the like, unless otherwise agreed the seller must reasonably estimate the price. The payment due on tender of the documents called for by the contract is the amount so estimated, but after final adjustment of the price a settlement must be made with commercial promptness.

(2) An agreement described in subsection (1) or any warranty of quality or condition of the goods on arrival places upon the seller the risk of ordinary deterioration, shrinkage and the like in transportation but has no effect on the place or time of identification to the contract for sale or delivery or on the passing of the risk of loss.

(3) Unless otherwise agreed where the contract provides for payment on or after arrival of the goods the seller must before payment allow such preliminary inspection as is feasible; but if the goods are lost delivery of the documents and payment are due when the goods should have arrived.

§ 2-322. Delivery "Ex-Ship".

(1) Unless otherwise agreed a term for delivery of goods "ex-ship" (which means from the carrying vessel) or in equivalent language is not restricted to a particular ship and requires delivery from a ship which has reached a place at the named port of destination where goods of the kind are usually discharged.

(2) Under such a term unless otherwise agreed

(a) the seller must discharge all liens arising out of the carriage and furnish the buyer with a direction which puts the carrier under a duty to deliver the goods; and

(b) the risk of loss does not pass to the buyer until the goods leave the ship's tackle or are otherwise properly unloaded.

§ 2-323. Form of Bill of Lading Required in Overseas Shipment; "Overseas".

(1) Where the contract contemplates overseas shipment and contains a term C.I.F. or C. & F. or F.O.B. vessel, the seller unless otherwise agreed must obtain a negotiable bill of lading stating that the goods have been loaded on board or, in the case of a term C.I.F. or C. & F., received for shipment.

(2) Where in a case within subsection (1) a bill of lading has been issued in a set of parts, unless otherwise agreed if the documents are not to be sent from abroad the buyer may demand tender of the full set; otherwise only one part of the bill of lading need be tendered. Even if the agreement expressly requires a full set

(a) due tender of a single part is acceptable within the provisions of this Article on cure of improper delivery (subsection (1) of Section 2–508); and

(b) even though the full set is demanded, if the documents are sent from abroad the person tendering an incomplete set may nevertheless require payment upon furnishing an indemnity which the buyer in good faith deems adequate.

(3) A shipment by water or by air or a contract contemplating such shipment is "overseas" insofar as by usage of trade or agreement it is subject to the commercial, financing or shipping practices characteristic of international deep water commerce.

§ 2–324. "No Arrival, No Sale" Term.
Under a term "no arrival, no sale" or terms of like meaning, unless otherwise agreed.

(a) the seller must properly ship conforming goods and if they arrive by any means he must tender them on arrival but he assumes no obligation that the goods will arrive unless he has caused the non-arrival; and

(b) where without fault of the seller the goods are in part lost or have so deteriorated as no longer to conform to the contract or arrive after the contract time, the buyer may proceed as if there had been casualty to identified goods (Section 2–613).

§ 2–325. "Letter of Credit" Term; "Confirmed Credit".
(1) Failure of the buyer seasonably to furnish an agreed letter of credit is a breach of the contract for sale.

(2) The delivery to seller of a proper letter of credit suspends the buyer's obligation to pay. If the letter of credit is dishonored, the seller may on seasonable notification to the buyer require payment directly from him.

(3) Unless otherwise agreed the term "letter of credit" or "banker's credit" in a contract for sale means an irrevocable credit issued by a financing agency of good repute and, where the shipment is overseas, of good international repute. The term "confirmed credit" means that the credit must also carry the direct obligation of such an agency which does business in the seller's financial market.

§ 2–326. Sale on Approval and Sale or Return; Rights of Creditors.
(1) Unless otherwise agreed, if delivered goods may be returned by the buyer even though they conform to the contract, the transaction is

(a) a "sale on approval" if the goods are delivered primarily for use, and

(b) a "sale or return" if the goods are delivered primarily for resale.

(2) Goods held on approval are not subject to the claims of the buyer's creditors until acceptance; goods held on sale or return are subject to such claims while in the buyer's possession.

(3) Any "or return" term of a contract for sale is to be treated as a separate contract for sale within the statute of frauds section of this Article (Section 2–201) and as contradicting the sale aspect of the contract within the provisions of this Article on parol or extrinsic evidence (Section 2–202).

§ 2–327. Special Incidents of Sale on Approval and Sale or Return.
(1) Under a sale on approval unless otherwise agreed

(a) although the goods are identified to the contract the risk of loss and the title do not pass to the buyer until acceptance; and

(b) use of the goods consistent with the purpose of trial is not acceptance but failure seasonably to notify the seller of election to return the goods is acceptance, and if the goods conform to the contract acceptance of any part is acceptance of the whole; and

(c) after due notification of election to return, the return is at the seller's risk and expense but a merchant buyer must follow any reasonable instructions.

(2) Under a sale or return unless otherwise agreed

(a) the option to return extends to the whole or any commercial unit of the goods while in substantially their original condition, but must be exercised seasonably; and

(b) the return is at the buyer's risk and expense.

§ 2–328. Sale by Auction.
(1) In a sale by auction if goods are put up in lots each lot is the subject of a separate sale.

(2) A sale by auction is complete when the auctioneer so announces by the fall of the hammer or in other customary manner. Where a bid is made while the hammer is falling in acceptance of a prior bid the auctioneer may in his discretion reopen the bidding or declare the goods sold under the bid on which the hammer was falling.

(3) Such a sale is with reserve unless the goods are in explicit terms put up without reserve. In an auction with reserve the auctioneer may withdraw the goods at any time until he announces completion of the sale. In an auction without reserve, after the auctioneer calls for bids on an article or lot, that article or lot cannot be withdrawn unless no bid is made within a reasonable time. In either case a bidder may retract his bid until the auctioneer's announcement of completion of the sale, but a bidder's retraction does not revive any previous bid.

(4) If the auctioneer knowingly receives a bid on the seller's behalf or the seller makes or procures such a bid, and notice has not been given that liberty for such bidding is reserved, the buyer may at his option avoid the sale or take the goods at the price of the last good faith bid prior to the completion of the sale. This subsection shall not apply to any bid at a forced sale.

Part 4. *Title, Creditors and Good Faith Purchasers*

§ 2–401. Passing of Title; Reservation for Security; Limited Application of This Section.
Each provision of this Article with regard to the rights, obligations and remedies of the seller, the buyer, purchasers or other third parties applies irrespective of title to the goods except where the provision refers to such title. Insofar as situations are not covered by the other provisions of this Article and matters concerning title become material the following rules apply:

(1) Title to goods cannot pass under a contract for sale prior to their identification to the contract (Section 2–501), and unless otherwise explicitly agreed the buyer acquires by their identification a special property as limited by this Act. Any retention or reservation by the seller of the title (property) in goods shipped or delivered to the buyer is limited in effect to a reservation of a security interest. Subject to these provisions and to the provisions of the Article on Secured Transactions (Article 9), title to goods passes from the seller to the buyer in any manner and on any conditions explicitly agreed on by the parties.

(2) Unless otherwise explicitly agreed title passes to the buyer at the time and place at which the seller completes his performance with reference to the physical delivery of the goods, despite any reservation of a security interest and even though a document of title is to be delivered at a different time or place; and in particular and despite any reservation of a security interest by the bill of lading

(a) if the contract requires or authorizes the seller to send the goods to the buyer but does not require him to deliver them at destination, title passes to the buyer at the time and place of shipment; but

(b) if the contract requires delivery at destination, title passes on tender there.

(3) Unless otherwise explicitly agreed where delivery is to be made without moving the goods.

(a) if the seller is to deliver a document of title, title passes at the time when and the place where he delivers such documents; or

(b) if the goods are at the time of contracting already identified and no documents are to be delivered, title passes at the time and place of contracting.

(4) A rejection or other refusal by the buyer to receive or retain the goods, whether or not justified, or a justified revocation of acceptance revests title to the goods in the seller. Such revesting occurs by operation of law and is not a "sale".

§ 2–402. Rights of Seller's Creditors Against Sold Goods.
(1) Except as provided in subsections (2) and (3), rights of unsecured creditors of the seller with respect to goods which have been identified to a contract for sale are subject to the buyer's rights to recover the goods under this Article (Sections 2–502 and 2–716).

(2) A creditor of the seller may treat a sale or an identification of goods to a contract for sale as void if as against him a retention of possession by the seller is fraudulent under any rule of law of the state where the goods are situated, except that retention of possession in good faith and

current course of trade by a merchant-seller for a commercially reasonable time after a sale or identification is not fraudulent.

(3) Nothing in this Article shall be deemed to impair the rights of creditors of the seller

(a) under the provisions of the Article on Secured Transactions (Article 9); or

(b) where identification to the contract or delivery is made not in current course of trade but in satisfaction of or as security for a pre-existing claim for money, security or the like and is made under circumstances which under any rule of law of the state where the goods are situated would apart from this Article constitute the transaction a fraudulent transfer or voidable preference.

§ 2–403. Power to Transfer; Good Faith Purchase of Goods; "Entrusting".

(1) A purchaser of goods acquires all title which his transferor had or had power to transfer except that a purchaser of a limited interest acquires rights only to the extent of the interest purchased. A person with voidable title has power to transfer a good title to a good faith purchaser for value. When goods have been delivered under a transaction of purchase the purchaser has such power even though

(a) the transferor was deceived as to the identity of the purchaser, or

(b) the delivery was in exchange for a check which is later dishonored, or

(c) it was agreed that the transaction was to be a "cash sale", or

(d) the delivery was procured through fraud punishable as larcenous under the criminal law.

(2) Any entrusting of possession of goods to a merchant who deals in goods of that kind gives him power to transfer all rights of the entruster to a buyer in ordinary course of business.

(3) "Entrusting" includes any delivery and any acquiescence in retention of possession regardless of any condition expressed between the parties to the delivery or acquiescence and regardless of whether the procurement of the entrusting or the possessor's disposition of the goods have been such as to be larcenous under the criminal law.

(4) The rights of other purchasers of goods and of lien creditors are governed by the Articles on Secured Transactions (Article 9). [Bulk Transfers/Sales (Article 6)* and Documents of Title (Article 7)].

Part 5. Performance

§ 2–501. Insurable Interest in Goods; Manner of Identification of Goods.

(1) The buyer obtains a special property and an insurable interest in goods by identification of existing goods as goods to which the contract refers even though the goods so identified are non-conforming and he has an option to return or reject them. Such identification can be made at any time and in any manner explicitly agreed to by the parties. In the absence of explicit agreement identification occurs.

(a) when the contract is made if it is for the sale of goods already existing and identified;

(b) if the contract is for the sale of future goods other than those described in paragraph (c), when goods are shipped, marked or otherwise designated by the seller as goods to which the contract refers;

(c) when the crops are planted or otherwise become growing crops or the young are conceived if the contract is for the sale of unborn young to be born within twelve months after contracting or for the sale of crops to be harvested within twelve months or the next normal harvest season after contracting, whichever is longer.

(2) The seller retains an insurable interest in goods so long as title to or any security interest in the goods remains in him and where the identification is by the seller alone he may until default or insolvency or notification to the buyer that the identification is final substitute other goods for those identified.

(3) Nothing in this section impairs any insurable interest recognized under any other statute or rule of law.

§ 2–502. Buyer's Right to Goods on Seller's Insolvency.

(1) Subject to subsections (2) and (3) and even though the goods have not been shipped a buyer who has paid a part or all of the price of goods in which he has a special property under the provisions of the immediately preceding section may on making and keeping good a tender of any unpaid portion of their price recover them from the seller if:

(a) in the case of goods bought for personal, family, or household purposes, the seller repudiates or fails to deliver as required by the contract; or

(b) in all cases, the seller becomes insolvent within ten days after receipt of the first installment on their price.

(2) The buyer's right to recover the goods under subsection (1)(a) vests upon acquisition of a special property, even if the seller had not then repudiated or failed to deliver.

(3) If the identification creating his special property has been made by the buyer he acquires the right to recover the goods only if they conform to the contract for sale.

§ 2–503. Manner of Seller's Tender of Delivery.

(1) Tender of delivery requires that the seller put and hold conforming goods at the buyer's disposition and give the buyer any notification reasonably necessary to enable him to take delivery. The manner, time and place for tender are determined by the agreement and this Article, and in particular

(a) tender must be at a reasonable hour, and if it is of goods they must be kept available for the period reasonably necessary to enable the buyer to take possession; but

(b) unless otherwise agreed the buyer must furnish facilities reasonably suited to the receipt of the goods.

(2) Where the case is within the next section respecting shipment tender requires that the seller comply with its provisions.

(3) Where the seller is required to deliver at a particular destination tender requires that he comply with subsection (1) and also in any appropriate case tender documents as described in subsections (4) and (5) of this section.

(4) Where goods are in the possession of a bailee and are to be delivered without being moved

(a) tender requires that the seller either tender a negotiable document of title covering such goods or procure acknowledgment by the bailee of the buyer's right to possession of the goods; but

(b) tender to the buyer of a non-negotiable document of title or of a written direction to the bailee to deliver is sufficient tender unless the buyer seasonably objects, and receipt by the bailee of notification of the buyer's rights fixes those rights as against the bailee and all third persons; but risk of loss of the goods and of any failure by the bailee to honor the non-negotiable document of title or to obey the direction remains on the seller until the buyer has had a reasonable time to present the document or direction, and a refusal by the bailee to honor the document or to obey the direction defeats the tender.

(5) Where the contract requires the seller to deliver documents

(a) he must tender all such documents in correct form, except as provided in this Article with respect to bills of lading in a set (subsection (2) of Section 2–323); and

(b) tender through customary banking channels is sufficient and dishonor of a draft accompanying the documents constitutes non-acceptance or rejection.

§ 2–504. Shipment by Seller.

Where the seller is required or authorized to send the goods to the buyer and the contract does not require him to deliver them at a particular destination, then unless otherwise agreed he must

(a) put the goods in the possession of such a carrier and make such a contract for their transportation as may be reasonable having regard to the nature of the goods and other circumstances of the case; and

(b) obtain and promptly deliver or tender in due form any document necessary to enable the buyer to obtain possession of the goods or otherwise required by the agreement or by usage of trade; and

(c) promptly notify the buyer of the shipment.

Failure to notify the buyer under paragraph (c) or to make a proper contract under paragraph (a) is a ground for rejection only if material delay or loss ensues.

§ 2–505. Seller's Shipment Under Reservation.

(1) Where the seller has identified goods to the contract by or before shipment:

(a) his procurement of a negotiable bill of lading to his own order or otherwise reserves in him a security interest in the goods. His procurement of the bill to the order of a financing agency or of the buyer indicates in addition only the seller's expectation of transferring that interest to the person named.

    (b) a non-negotiable bill of lading to himself or his nominee reserves possession of the goods as security but except in a case of conditional delivery (subsection (2) of Section 2–507) a non-negotiable bill of lading naming the buyer as consignee reserves no security interest even though the seller retains possession of the bill of lading.

(2) When shipment by the seller with reservation of a security interest is in violation of the contract for sale it constitutes an improper contract for transportation within the preceding section but impairs neither the rights given to the buyer by shipment and identification of the goods to the contract nor the seller's powers as a holder of a negotiable document.

§ 2–506. Rights of Financing Agency.

(1) A financing agency by paying or purchasing for value a draft which relates to a shipment of goods acquires to the extent of the payment or purchase and in addition to its own rights under the draft and any document of title securing it any rights of the shipper in the goods including the right to stop delivery and the shipper's right to have the draft honored by the buyer.

(2) The right to reimbursement of a financing agency which has in good faith honored or purchased the draft under commitment to or authority from the buyer is not impaired by subsequent discovery of defects with reference to any relevant document which was apparently regular on its face.

§ 2–507. Effect of Seller's Tender; Delivery on Condition.

(1) Tender of delivery is a condition to the buyer's duty to accept the goods and, unless otherwise agreed, to his duty to pay for them. Tender entitles the seller to acceptance of the goods and to payment according to the contract.

(2) Where payment is due and demanded on the delivery to the buyer of goods or documents of title, his right as against the seller to retain or dispose of them is conditional upon his making the payment due.

§ 2–508. Cure by Seller of Improper Tender or Delivery; Replacement.

(1) Where any tender or delivery by the seller is rejected because nonconforming and the time for performance has not yet expired, the seller may seasonably notify the buyer of his intention to cure and may then within the contract time make a conforming delivery.

(2) Where the buyer rejects a non-conforming tender which the seller had reasonable grounds to believe would be acceptable with or without money allowance the seller may if he seasonably notifies the buyer have a further reasonable time to substitute a conforming tender.

§ 2–509. Risk of Loss in the Absence of Breach.

(1) Where the contract requires or authorizes the seller to ship the goods by carrier

    (a) if it does not require him to deliver them at a particular destination, the risk of loss passes to the buyer when the goods are duly delivered to the carrier even though the shipment is under reservation (Section 2–505); but

    (b) if it does require him to deliver them at a particular destination and the goods are there duly tendered while in the possession of the carrier, the risk of loss passes to the buyer when the goods are there duly so tendered as to enable the buyer to take delivery.

(2) Where the goods are held by a bailee to be delivered without being moved, the risk of loss passes to the buyer

    (a) on his receipt of a negotiable document of title covering the goods; or

    (b) on acknowledgment by the bailee of the buyer's right to possession of the goods; or

    (c) after his receipt of a non-negotiable document of title or other written direction to deliver, as provided in subsection (4)(b) of Section 2–503.

(3) In any case not within subsection (1) or (2), the risk of loss passes to the buyer on his receipt of the goods if the seller is a merchant; otherwise the risk passes to the buyer on tender of delivery.

(4) The provisions of this section are subject to contrary agreement of the parties and to the provisions of this Article on sale on approval (Section 2–327) and on effect of breach on risk of loss (Section 2–510).

§ 2–510. Effect of Breach on Risk of Loss.

(1) Where a tender or delivery of goods so fails to conform to the contract as to give a right of rejection the risk of their loss remains on the seller until cure or acceptance.

(2) Where the buyer rightfully revokes acceptance he may to the extent of any deficiency in his effective insurance coverage treat the risk of loss as having rested on the seller from the beginning.

(3) Where the buyer as to conforming goods already identified to the contract for sale repudiates or is otherwise in breach before risk of their loss has passed to him, the seller may to the extent of any deficiency in his effective insurance coverage treat the risk of loss as resting on the buyer for a commercially reasonable time.

§ 2–511. Tender of Payment by Buyer; Payment by Check.

(1) Unless otherwise agreed tender of payment is a condition to the seller's duty to tender and complete any delivery.

(2) Tender of payment is sufficient when made by any means or in any manner current in the ordinary course of business unless the seller demands payment in legal tender and gives any extension of time reasonably necessary to procure it.

(3) Subject to the provisions of this Act on the effect of an instrument on an obligation (Section 3–310), payment by check is conditional and is defeated as between the parties by dishonor of the check on due presentment.

§ 2–512. Payment by Buyer Before Inspection.

(1) Where the contract requires payment before inspection nonconformity of the goods does not excuse the buyer from so making payment unless

    (a) the non-conformity appears without inspection; or

    (b) despite tender of the required documents the circumstances would justify injunction against honor under this Act (Section 5–109(b)).

(2) Payment pursuant to subsection (1) does not constitute an acceptance of goods or impair the buyer's right to inspect or any of his remedies.

§ 2–513. Buyer's Right to Inspection of Goods.

(1) Unless otherwise agreed and subject to subsection (3), where goods are tendered or delivered or identified to the contract for sale, the buyer has a right before payment or acceptance to inspect them at any reasonable place and time and in any reasonable manner. When the seller is required or authorized to send the goods to the buyer, the inspection may be after their arrival.

(2) Expenses of inspection must be borne by the buyer but may be recovered from the seller if the goods do not conform and are rejected.

(3) Unless otherwise agreed and subject to the provisions of this Article on C.I.F. contracts (subsection (3) of Section 2–321), the buyer is not entitled to inspect the goods before payment of the price when the contract provides

    (a) for delivery "C.O.D." or on other like terms; or

    (b) for payment against documents of title, except where such payment is due only after the goods are to become available for inspection.

(4) A place or method of inspection fixed by the parties is presumed to be exclusive but unless otherwise expressly agreed it does not postpone identification or shift the place for delivery or for passing the risk of loss. If compliance becomes impossible, inspection shall be as provided in this section unless the place or method fixed was clearly intended as an indispensable condition failure of which avoids the contract.

§ 2–514. When Documents Deliverable on Acceptance; When on Payment.

Unless otherwise agreed documents against which a draft is drawn are to be delivered to the drawee on acceptance of the draft if it is payable more than three days after presentment; otherwise, only on payment.

§ 2–515. Preserving Evidence of Goods in Dispute.

In furtherance of the adjustment of any claim or dispute

    (a) either party on reasonable notification to the other and for the purpose of ascertaining the facts and preserving evidence has the right to inspect, test and sample the goods including such of them as may be in the possession or control of the other; and

(b) the parties may agree to a third party inspection or survey to determine the conformity or condition of the goods and may agree that the findings shall be binding upon them in any subsequent litigation or adjustment.

Part 6.   Breach, Repudiation and Excuse

§ 2–601.   Buyer's Rights on Improper Delivery.
Subject to the provisions of this Article on breach in installment contracts (Section 2–612) and unless otherwise agreed under the sections on contractual limitations of remedy (Sections 2–718 and 2–719), if the goods or the tender of delivery fail in any respect to conform to the contract, the buyer may
(a) reject the whole; or
(b) accept the whole; or
(c) accept any commercial unit or units and reject the rest.

§ 2–602.   Manner and Effect of Rightful Rejection.
(1) Rejection of goods must be within a reasonable time after their delivery or tender. It is ineffective unless the buyer seasonably notifies the seller.
(2) Subject to the provisions of the two following sections on rejected goods (Sections 2–603 and 2–604),
(a) after rejection any exercise of ownership by the buyer with respect to any commercial unit is wrongful as against the seller; and
(b) if the buyer has before rejection taken physical possession of goods in which he does not have a security interest under the provisions of this Article (subsection (3) of Section 2–711), he is under a duty after rejection to hold them with reasonable care at the seller's disposition for a time sufficient to permit the seller to remove them; but
(c) the buyer has no further obligations with regard to goods rightfully rejected.
(3) The seller's rights with respect to goods wrongfully rejected are governed by the provisions of this Article on Seller's remedies in general (Section 2–703).

§ 2–603.   Merchant Buyer's Duties as to Rightfully Rejected Goods.
(1) Subject to any security interest in the buyer (subsection (3) of Section 2–711), when the seller has no agent or place of business at the market of rejection a merchant buyer is under a duty after rejection of goods in his possession or control to follow any reasonable instructions received from the seller with respect to the goods and in the absence of such instructions to make reasonable efforts to sell them for the seller's account if they are perishable or threaten to decline in value speedily. Instructions are not reasonable if on demand indemnity for expenses is not forthcoming.
(2) When the buyer sells goods under subsection (1), he is entitled to reimbursement from the seller or out of the proceeds for reasonable expenses of caring for and selling them, and if the expenses include no selling commission then to such commission as is usual in the trade or if there is none to a reasonable sum not exceeding ten percent on the gross proceeds.
(3) In complying with this section the buyer is held only to good faith and good faith conduct hereunder is neither acceptance nor conversion nor the basis of an action for damages.

§ 2–604.   Buyer's Options as to Salvage of Rightfully Rejected Goods.
Subject to the provisions of the immediately preceding section on perishables if the seller gives no instructions within a reasonable time after notification of rejection the buyer may store the rejected goods for the seller's account or reship them to him or resell them for the seller's account with reimbursement as provided in the preceding section. Such action is not acceptance or conversion.

§ 2–605.   Waiver of Buyer's Objections by Failure to Particularize.
(1) The buyer's failure to state in connection with rejection a particular defect which is ascertainable by reasonable inspection precludes him from relying on the unstated defect to justify rejection or to establish breach
(a) where the seller could have cured it if stated seasonably; or
(b) between merchants when the seller has after rejection made a request in writing for a full and final written statement of all defects on which the buyer proposes to rely.

(2) Payment against documents made without reservation of rights precludes recovery of the payment for defects apparent on the face of the documents.

§ 2–606.   What Constitutes Acceptance of Goods.
(1) Acceptance of goods occurs when the buyer
(a) after a reasonable opportunity to inspect the goods signifies to the seller that the goods are conforming or that he will take or retain them in spite of their non-conformity; or
(b) fails to make an effective rejection (subsection (1) of Section 2–602), but such acceptance does not occur until the buyer has had a reasonable opportunity to inspect them; or
(c) does any act inconsistent with the seller's ownership; but if such act is wrongful as against the seller it is an acceptance only if ratified by him.
(2) Acceptance of a part of any commercial unit is acceptance of that entire unit.

§ 2–607.   Effect of Acceptance; Notice of Breach; Burden of Establishing Breach After Acceptance; Notice of Claim or Litigation to Person Answerable Over.
(1) The buyer must pay at the contract rate for any goods accepted.
(2) Acceptance of goods by the buyer precludes rejection of the goods accepted and if made with knowledge of a non-conformity cannot be revoked because of it unless the acceptance was on the reasonable assumption that the non-conformity would be seasonably cured but acceptance does not of itself impair any other remedy provided by this Article for non-conformity.
(3) Where a tender has been accepted
(a) the buyer must within a reasonable time after he discovers or should have discovered any breach notify the seller of breach or be barred from any remedy; and
(b) if the claim is one for infringement or the like (subsection (3) of Section 2–312) and the buyer is sued as a result of such a breach he must so notify the seller within a reasonable time after he receives notice of the litigation or be barred from any remedy over for liability established by the litigation.
(4) The burden is on the buyer to establish any breach with respect to the goods accepted.
(5) Where the buyer is sued for breach of a warranty or other obligation for which his seller is answerable over
(a) he may give his seller written notice of the litigation. If the notice states that the seller may come in and defend and that if the seller does not do so he will be bound in any action against him by his buyer by any determination of fact common to the two litigations, then unless the seller after seasonable receipt of the notice does come in and defend he is so bound.
(b) if the claim is one for infringement or the like (subsection (3) of Section 2–312) the original seller may demand in writing that his buyer turn over to him control of the litigation including settlement or else be barred from any remedy over and if he also agrees to bear all expense and to satisfy any adverse judgment, then unless the buyer after seasonable receipt of the demand does turn over control the buyer is so barred.
(6) The provisions of subsection (3), (4) and (5) apply to any obligation of a buyer to hold the seller harmless against infringement or the like (subsection (3) of Section 2–312).

§ 2–608.   Revocation of Acceptance in Whole or in Part.
(1) The buyer may revoke his acceptance of a lot or commercial unit whose non-conformity substantially impairs its value to him if he has accepted it
(a) on the reasonable assumption that its non-conformity would be cured and it has not been seasonably cured; or
(b) without discovery of such non-conformity if his acceptance was reasonably induced either by the difficulty of discovery before acceptance or by the seller's assurances.
(2) Revocation of acceptance must occur within a reasonable time after the buyer discovers or should have discovered the ground for it and before any substantial change in condition of the goods which is not caused by their own defects. It is not effective until the buyer notifies the seller of it.
(3) A buyer who so revokes has the same rights and duties with regard to the goods involved as if he had rejected them.

§ 2–609. Right to Adequate Assurance of Performance.

(1) A contract for sale imposes an obligation on each party that the other's expectation of receiving due performance will not be impaired. When reasonable grounds for insecurity arise with respect to the performance of either party the other may in writing demand adequate assurance of due performance and until he receives such assurance may if commercially reasonable suspend any performance for which he has not already received the agreed return.

(2) Between merchants the reasonableness of grounds for insecurity and the adequacy of any assurance offered shall be determined according to commercial standards.

(3) Acceptance of any improper delivery or payment does not prejudice the aggrieved party's right to demand adequate assurance of future performance.

(4) After receipt of a justified demand failure to provide within a reasonable time not exceeding thirty days such assurance of due performance as is adequate under the circumstances of the particular case is a repudiation of the contract.

§ 2–610. Anticipatory Repudiation.

When either party repudiates the contract with respect to a performance not yet due the loss of which will substantially impair the value of the contract to the other, the aggrieved party may

(a) for a commercially reasonable time await performance by the repudiating party; or

(b) resort to any remedy for breach (Section 2–703 or Section 2–711), even though he has notified the repudiating party that he would await the latter's performance and has urged retraction; and

(c) in either case suspend his own performance or proceed in accordance with the provisions of this Article on the seller's right to identify goods to the contract notwithstanding breach or to salvage unfinished goods (Section 2–704).

§ 2–611. Retraction of Anticipatory Repudiation.

(1) Until the repudiating party's next performance is due he can retract his repudiation unless the aggrieved party has since the repudiation cancelled or materially changed his position or otherwise indicated that he considers the repudiation final.

(2) Retraction may be by any method which clearly indicates to the aggrieved party that the repudiating party intends to perform, but must include any assurance justifiably demanded under the provisions of this Article (Section 2–609).

(3) Retraction reinstates the repudiating party's rights under the contract with due excuse and allowance to the aggrieved party for any delay occasioned by the repudiation.

§ 2–612. "Installment Contract"; Breach.

(1) An "installment contract" is one which requires or authorizes the delivery of goods in separate lots to be separately accepted, even though the contract contains a clause "each delivery is a separate contract" or its equivalent.

(2) The buyer may reject any installment which is non-conforming if the non-conformity substantially impairs the value of that installment and cannot be cured or if the non-conformity is a defect in the required documents; but if the non-conformity does not fall within subsection (3) and the seller gives adequate assurance of its cure the buyer must accept that installment.

(3) Whenever non-conformity or default with respect to one or more installments substantially impairs the value of the whole contract there is a breach of the whole. But the aggrieved party reinstates the contract if he accepts a non-conforming installment without seasonably notifying of cancellation or if he brings an action with respect only to past installments or demands performance as to future installments.

§ 2–613. Casualty to Identified Goods.

Where the contract requires for its performance goods identified when the contract is made, and the goods suffer casualty without fault of either party before the risk of loss passes to the buyer, or in a proper case under a "no arrival, no sale" term (Section 2–324) then

(a) if the loss is total the contract is avoided; and

(b) if the loss is partial or the goods have so deteriorated as no longer to conform to the contract the buyer may nevertheless demand inspection and at his option either treat the contract as avoided or accept the goods with due allowance from

the contract price for the deterioration or the deficiency in quantity but without further right against the seller.

§ 2–614. Substituted Performance.

(1) Where without fault of either party the agreed berthing, loading, or unloading facilities fail or an agreed type of carrier becomes unavailable or the agreed manner of delivery otherwise becomes commercially impracticable but a commercially reasonable substitute is available, such substitute performance must be tendered and accepted.

(2) If the agreed means or manner of payment fails because of domestic or foreign governmental regulation, the seller may withhold or stop delivery unless the buyer provides a means or manner of payment which is commercially a substantial equivalent. If delivery has already been taken, payment by the means or in the manner provided by the regulation discharges the buyers obligation unless the regulation is discriminatory, oppressive or predatory.

§ 2–615. Excuse by Failure of Presupposed Conditions.

Except so far as a seller may have assumed a greater obligation and subject to the preceding section on substituted performance:

(a) Delay in delivery or non-delivery in whole or in part by a seller who complies with paragraphs (b) and (c) is not a breach of his duty under a contract for sale if performance as agreed has been made impracticable by the occurrence of a contingency the non-occurrence of which was a basic assumption on which the contract was made or by compliance in good faith with any applicable foreign or domestic governmental regulation or order whether or not it later proves to be invalid.

(b) Where the causes mentioned in paragraph (a) affect only a part of the seller's capacity to perform, he must allocate production and deliveries among his customers but may at his option include regular customers not then under contract as well as his own requirements for further manufacture. He may so allocate in any manner which is fair and reasonable.

(c) The seller must notify the buyer seasonably that there will be delay or non-delivery and, when allocation is required under paragraph (b), of the estimated quota thus made available for the buyer.

§ 2–616. Procedure on Notice Claiming Excuse.

(1) Where the buyer receives notification of a material or indefinite delay or an allocation justified under the preceding section he may by written notification to the seller as to any delivery concerned, and where the prospective deficiency substantially impairs the value of the whole contract under the provisions of this Article relating to breach of installment contracts (Section 2–612), then also as to the whole,

(a) terminate and thereby discharge any unexecuted portion of the contract; or

(b) modify the contract by agreeing to take his available quota in substitution.

(2) If after receipt of such notification from the seller the buyer fails so to modify the contract within a reasonable time not exceeding thirty days the contract lapses with respect to any deliveries affected.

(3) The provisions of this section may not be negated by agreement except in so far as the seller has assumed a greater obligation under the preceding section.

Part 7. Remedies

§ 2–701. Remedies for Breach of Collateral Contracts Not Impaired.

Remedies for breach of any obligation or promise collateral or ancillary to a contract for sale or not impaired by the provisions of this Article.

§ 2–702. Seller's Remedies on Discovery of Buyer's Insolvency.

(1) Where the seller discovers the buyer to be insolvent he may refuse delivery except for cash including payment for all goods therefore delivered under the contract, and stop delivery under this Article (Section 2–705).

(2) Where the seller discovers that the buyer has received goods on credit while insolvent he may reclaim the goods upon demand made within ten days after the receipt, but if misrepresentation of solvency has been made to the particular seller in writing within three months before delivery the ten day limitation does not apply. Except as provided in this subsection the seller may not base a right to reclaim goods on the buyer's fraudulent or innocent misrepresentation of solvency or of intent to pay.

(3) The seller's right to reclaim under subsection (2) is subject to the rights of a buyer in ordinary course or other good faith purchaser under this Article (Section 2–403). Successful reclamation of goods excludes all other remedies with respect to them.

§ 2–703. Seller's Remedies in General.

Where the buyer wrongfully rejects or revokes acceptance of goods or fails to make a payment due on or before delivery or repudiates with respect to a part or the whole, then with respect to any goods directly affected and, if the breach is of the whole contract (Section 2–612), then also with respect to the whole undelivered balance, the aggrieved seller may

    (a) withhold delivery of such goods;

    (b) stop delivery by any bailee as hereafter provided (Section 2–705);

    (c) proceed under the next section respecting goods still unidentified to the contract;

    (d) resell and recover damages as hereafter provided (Section 2–706);

    (e) recover damages for non-acceptance (Section 2–708) or in a proper case the price (Section 2–709);

    (f) cancel.

§ 2–704. Seller's Right to Identify Goods to the Contract Notwithstanding Breach or to Salvage Unfinished Goods.

(1) An aggrieved seller under the preceding section may

    (a) identify to the contract conforming goods not already identified if at the time he learned of the breach they are in his possession or control;

    (b) treat as the subject of resale goods which have demonstrably been intended for the particular contract even though those goods are unfinished.

(2) Where the goods are unfinished an aggrieved seller may in the exercise of reasonable commercial judgment for the purposes of avoiding loss and of effective realization either complete the manufacture and wholly identify the goods to the contract or cease manufacture and resell for scrap or salvage value or proceed in any other reasonable manner.

§ 2–705. Seller's Stoppage of Delivery in Transit or Otherwise.

(1) The seller may stop delivery of goods in the possession of a carrier or other bailee when he discovers the buyer to be insolvent (Section 2–702) and may stop delivery of carload, truckload, planeload or larger shipments of express or freight when the buyer repudiates or fails to make a payment due before delivery or if for any other reason the seller has a right to withhold or reclaim the goods.

(2) As against such buyer the seller may stop delivery until

    (a) receipt of the goods by the buyer; or

    (b) acknowledgment to the buyer by any bailee of the goods except a carrier that the bailee holds the goods for the buyer; or

    (c) such acknowledgment to the buyer by a carrier by reshipment or as warehouseman; or

    (d) negotiation to the buyer of any negotiable document of title covering the goods.

(3) (a) To stop delivery the seller must so notify as to enable the bailee by reasonable diligence to prevent delivery of the goods.

    (b) After such notification the bailee must hold and deliver the goods according to the directions of the seller but the seller is liable to the bailee for any ensuing charges or damages.

    (c) If a negotiable document of title has been issued for goods the bailee is not obliged to obey a notification to stop until surrender of the document.

    (d) A carrier who has issued a non-negotiable bill of lading is not obliged to obey a notification to stop received from a person other than the consignor.

§ 2–706. Seller's Resale Including Contract for Resale.

(1) Under the conditions stated in Section 2–703 on seller's remedies, the seller may resell the goods concerned or the undelivered balance thereof. Where the resale is made in good faith and in a commercially reasonable manner the seller may recover the difference between the resale price and the contract price together with any incidental damages allowed under the provisions of this Article (Section 2–710), but less expenses saved in consequence of the buyer's breach.

(2) Except as otherwise provided in subsection (3) or unless otherwise agreed resale may be at public or private sale including sale by way of one or more contracts to sell or of identification to an existing contract of the seller. Sale may be as a unit or in parcels and at any time and place and on any terms but every aspect of the sale including the method, manner, time, place and terms must be commercially reasonable. The resale must be reasonably identified as referring to the broken contract, but it is not necessary that the goods be in existence or that any or all of them have been identified to the contract before the breach.

(3) Where the resale is at private sale the seller must give the buyer reasonable notification of his intention to resell.

(4) Where the resale is at public sale

    (a) only identified goods can be sold except where there is a recognized market for a public sale of futures in goods of the kind; and

    (b) it must be made at a usual place or market for public sale if one is reasonably available and except in the case of goods which are perishable or threaten to decline in value speedily the seller must give the buyer reasonable notice of the time and place of the resale; and

    (c) if the goods are not to be within the view of those attending the sale the notification of sale must state the place where the goods are located and provide for their reasonable inspection by prospective bidders; and

    (d) the seller may buy.

(5) A purchaser who buys in good faith at a resale takes the goods free of any rights of the original buyer even though the seller fails to comply with one or more of the requirements of this section.

(6) The seller is not accountable to the buyer for any profit made on any resale. A person in the position of a seller (Section 2–707) or a buyer who has rightfully rejected or justifiably revoked acceptance must account for any excess over the amount of his security interest, as hereinafter defined (subsection (3) of Section 2–711).

§ 2–707. "Person in the Position of a Seller".

(1) A "person in the position of a seller" includes as against a principal an agent who has paid or become responsible for the price of goods on behalf of his principal or anyone who otherwise holds a security interest or other right in goods similar to that of a seller.

(2) A person in the position of a seller may as provided in this Article withhold or stop delivery (Section 2–705) and resell (Section 2–706) and recover incidental damages (Section 2–710).

§ 2–708. Seller's Damages for Non-Acceptance or Repudiation.

(1) Subject to subsection (2) and to the provisions of this Article with respect to proof of market price (Section 2–723), the measure of damages for non-acceptance or repudiation by the buyer is the difference between the market price at the time and place for tender and the unpaid contract price together with any incidental damages provided in this Article (Section 2–710), but less expenses saved in consequence of the buyer's breach.

(2) If the measure of damages provided in subsection (1) is inadequate to put the seller in as good a position as performance would have done then the measure of damages is the profit (including reasonable overhead) which the seller would have made from full performance by the buyer, together with any incidental damages provided in this Article (Section 2–710), due allowance for costs reasonably incurred and due credit for payments or proceeds of resale.

§ 2–709. Action for the Price.

(1) When the buyer fails to pay the price as it becomes due the seller may recover, together with any incidental damages under the next section, the price

    (a) of goods accepted or of conforming goods lost or damaged within a commercially reasonable time after risk of their loss has passed to the buyer; and

    (b) of goods identified to the contract if the seller is unable after reasonable effort to resell them at a reasonable price or the circumstances reasonably indicate that such effort will be unavailing.

(2) Where the seller sues for the price he must hold for the buyer any goods which have been identified to the contract and are still in his control except that if resale becomes possible he may resell them at any time prior to the collection of the judgment. The net proceeds of any such resale must be credited to the buyer and payment of the judgment entitles him to any goods not resold.

(3) After the buyer has wrongfully rejected or revoked acceptance of the goods or has failed to make a payment due or has repudiated (Section 2–610), a seller who is held not entitled to the price under this section shall nevertheless be awarded damages for non-acceptance under the preceding section.

§ 2–710. Seller's Incidental Damages.
Incidental damages to an aggrieved seller include any commercially reasonable charges, expenses or commissions incurred in stopping delivery, in the transportation, care and custody of goods after the buyer's breach, in connection with return or resale of the goods or otherwise resulting from the breach.

§ 2–711. Buyer's Remedies in General; Buyer's Security Interest in Rejected Goods.
(1) Where the seller fails to make delivery or repudiates or the buyer rightfully rejects or justifiably revokes acceptance then with respect to any goods involved, and with respect to the whole if the breach goes to the whole contract (Section 2–612), the buyer may cancel and whether or not he has done so may in addition to recovering so much of the price as has been paid
   (a) "cover" and have damages under the next section as to all the goods affected whether or not they have been identified to the contract; or
   (b) recover damages for non-delivery as provided in this Article (Section 2–713).

(2) Where the seller fails to deliver or repudiates the buyer may also
   (a) if the goods have been identified recover them as provided in this Article (Section 2–502); or
   (b) in a proper case obtain specific performance or replevy the goods as provided in this Article (Section 2–716).

(3) On rightful rejection of justifiable revocation of acceptance a buyer has a security interest in goods in his possession or control for any payments made on their price and any expenses reasonably incurred in their inspection, receipt, transportation, care and custody and may hold such goods and resell them in like manner as an aggrieved seller (Section 2–706).

§ 2–712. "Cover"; Buyer's Procurement of Substitute Goods.
(1) After a breach within the preceding section the buyer may "cover" by making in good faith and without unreasonable delay any reasonable purchase of or contract to purchase goods in substitution for those due from the seller.

(2) The buyer may recover from the seller as damages the difference between the cost of cover and the contract price together with any incidental or consequential damages as hereinafter defined (Section 2–715), but less expenses saved in consequence of the seller's breach.

(3) Failure of the buyer to effect cover within this section does not bar him from any other remedy.

§ 2–713. Buyer's Damages for Non-Delivery or Repudiation.
(1) Subject to the provisions of this Article with respect to proof of market price (Section 2–723), the measure of damages for nondelivery or repudiation by the seller is the difference between the market price at the time when the buyer learned of the breach and the contract price together with any incidental and consequential damages provided in this Article (Section 2–715), but less expenses saved in consequence of the seller's breach.

(2) Market price is to be determined as of the place for tender or, in cases of rejection after arrival or revocation of acceptance, as of the place of arrival.

§ 2–714. Buyer's Damages for Breach in Regard to Accepted Goods.
(1) Where the buyer has accepted goods and given notification (subsection (3) of Section 2–607) he may recover as damages for any non-conformity of tender the loss resulting in the ordinary course of events from the seller's breach as determined in any manner which is reasonable.

(2) The measure of damages for breach of warranty is the difference at the time and place of acceptance between the value of the goods accepted and the value they would have had if they had been as warranted, unless special circumstances show proximate damages of a different amount.

(3) In a proper case any incidental and consequential damages under the next section may also be recovered.

§ 2–715. Buyer's Incidental and Consequential Damages.
(1) Incidental damages resulting from the seller's breach include expenses reasonably incurred in inspection, receipt, transportation and care and custody of goods rightfully rejected, any commercially reasonable charges, expenses or commissions in connection with effecting cover and any other reasonable expense incident to the delay or other breach.

(2) Consequential damages resulting from the seller's breach include
   (a) any loss resulting from general or particular requirements and needs of which the seller at the time of contracting had reason to know and which could not reasonably be prevented by cover or otherwise; and
   (b) injury to person or property proximately resulting from any breach of warranty.

§ 2–716. Buyer's Right to Specific Performance or Replevin.
(1) Specific performance may be decreed where the goods are unique or in other proper circumstances.

(2) The decree for specific performance may include such terms and conditions as to payment of the price, damages, or other relief as the court may deem just.

(3) The buyer has a right of replevin for goods identified to the contract if after reasonable effort he is unable to effect cover for such goods or the circumstances reasonably indicate that such effort will be unvailing or if the goods have been shipped under reservation and satisfaction of the security interest in them has been made or tendered. In the case of goods bought for personal, family, or household purposes, the buyer's right of replevin vests upon acquisition of a special property, even if the seller had not then repudiated or failed to deliver.

§ 2–717. Deduction of Damages From the Price.
The buyer on notifying the seller of his intention to do so may deduct all or any part of the damages resulting from any breach of the contract from any part of the price still due under the same contract.

§ 2–718. Liquidation or Limitation of Damages; Deposits.
(1) Damages for breach by either party may be liquidated in the agreement but only at an amount which is reasonable in the light of the anticipated or actual harm caused by the breach, the difficulties of proof of loss, and the inconvenience of nonfeasibility of otherwise obtaining an adequate remedy. A team fixing unreasonably large liquidated damages is void as a penalty.

(2) Where the seller justifiably withholds delivery of goods because of the buyer's breach, the buyer is entitled to restitution of any amount by which the sum of his payments exceeds
   (a) the amount to which the seller is entitled by virtue of terms liquidating the seller's damages in accordance with subsection (1), or
   (b) in the absence of such terms, twenty percent of the value of the total performance for which the buyer is obligated under the contract or $500, whichever is smaller.

(3) The buyer's right to restitution under subsection (2) is subject to offset to the extent that the seller establishes
   (a) a right to recover damages under the provisions of this Article other than subsection (1), and
   (b) the amount or value of any benefits received by the buyer directly or indirectly by reason of the contract.

(4) Where a seller has received payment in goods their reasonable value or the proceeds of their resale shall be treated as payments for the purposes of subsection (2); but if the seller has notice of the buyer's breach before reselling goods received in part performance, his resale is subject to the conditions laid down in this Article on resale by an aggrieved seller (Section 2–706).

§ 2–719. Contractual Modification or Limitation of Remedy.
(1) Subject to the provisions of subsections (2) and (3) of this section and of the preceding section on liquidation and limitation of damages,
   (a) the agreement may provide for remedies in addition to or in substitution for those provided in this Article and may limit or alter the measure of damages recoverable under this Article, as by limiting the buyer's remedies to return of the goods and repayment of the price or to repair and replacement of non-conforming goods or parts; and
   (b) resort to a remedy as provided is optional unless the remedy is expressly agreed to be exclusive, in which case it is the sole remedy.

(2) Where circumstances cause an exclusive or limited remedy to fail of its essential purpose, remedy may be had as provided in this Act.

(3) Consequential damages may be limited or excluded unless the limitation or exclusion is unconscionable. Limitation of consequential damages for injury to the person in the case of consumer goods is prima facie unconscionable but limitation of damages where the loss is commercial is not.

§ 2-720. Effect of "Cancellation" or "Rescission" on Claims for Antecedent Breach.

Unless the contrary intention clearly appears, expressions of "cancellation" or "rescission" of the contract or the like shall not be construed as a renunciation or discharge of any claim in damages for an antecedent breach.

§ 2-721. Remedies for Fraud.

Remedies for material misrepresentation or fraud include all remedies available under this Article for non-fraudulent breach. Neither rescission or a claim for rescission of the contract for sale nor rejection or return of the goods shall bar or be deemed inconsistent with a claim for damages or other remedy.

§ 2-722. Who Can Sue Third Parties for Injury to Goods.

Where a third party so deals with goods which have been identified to a contract for sale as to cause actionable injury to a party to that contract

(a) a right of action against the third party is in either party to the contract for sale who has title to or a security interest or a special property or an insurable interest in the goods; and if the goods have been destroyed or converted a right of action is also in the party who either bore the risk of loss under the contract for sale or has since the injury assumed that risk as against the other,

(b) if at the time of the injury the party plaintiff did not bear the risk of loss as against the other party to the contract for sale and there is no arrangement between them for disposition of the recovery, his suit or settlement is, subject to his own interest, as a fiduciary for the other party to the contract;

(c) either party may with the consent of the other sue for the benefit of whom it may concern.

§ 2-723. Proof of Market Price: Time and Place.

(1) If an action based on anticipatory repudiation comes to trial before the time for performance with respect to some or all of the goods, any damages based on market price (Section 2-708 or Section 2-713) shall be determined according to the price of such goods prevailing at the time when the aggrieved party learned of the repudiation.

(2) If evidence of a price prevailing at the times or places described in this Article is not readily available the price prevailing within any reasonable time before or after the time described or at any other place which in commercial judgment or under usage of trade would serve as a reasonable substitute for the one described may be used, making any proper allowance for the cost of transporting the goods to or from such other place.

(3) Evidence of a relevant price prevailing at a time or place other than the one described in this Article offered by one party is not admissible unless and until he has given the other party such notice as the court finds sufficient to prevent unfair surprise.

§ 2-724. Admissibility of Market Quotations.

Whenever the prevailing price or value of any goods regularly bought and sold in any established commodity market is in issue, reports in official publications or trade journals or in newspapers or periodicals of general circulation published as the reports of such market shall be admissible in evidence. The circumstances of the preparation of such a report may be shown to affect its weight but not its admissibility.

§ 2-725. Statute of Limitations in Contracts for Sale.

(1) An action for breach of any contract for sale must be commenced within four years after the cause of action has accrued. By the original agreement the parties may reduce the period of limitation to not less than one year but may not extend it.

(2) A cause of action accrues when the breach occurs, regardless of the aggrieved party's lack of knowledge of the breach. A breach of warranty occurs when tender of delivery is made, except that where a warranty explicitly extends to future performance of the goods and discovery of the breach must await the time of such performance the cause of action accrues when the breach is or should have been discovered.

(3) Where an action commenced within the time limited by subsection (1) is so terminated as to leave available a remedy by another action for the same breach such other action may be commenced after the expiration of the time limited and within six months after the termination of the first action unless the termination resulted from voluntary discontinuance or from dismissal for failure or neglect to prosecute.

(4) This section does not alter the law on tolling of the statute of limitations nor does it apply to causes of action which have accrued before this Act becomes effective.

Glossary

abandoned property Property that an owner has discarded with the intent to relinquish his or her rights in it and mislaid or lost property that the owner has given up any further attempts to locate. [917]

abatement If the property the testator leaves is not sufficient to satisfy all the beneficiaries named in a will and there are both general and residuary bequests, the residuary bequests are abated first; if a will provides for general bequests, they are reduced proportionately if the residuary bequests are full abated or there are none. [971]

absolute priority rule A rule that says a reorganization plan is fair and equitable to an impaired class of unsecured creditors or equity holders if no class below it receives anything in the plan. [570]

acceptance A manifestation of assent by the offeree to the terms of the offer in a manner invited or required by the offer as measured by the objective theory of contracts. (Section 50 of the Restatement (Second) of Contracts) [221]; Occurs when a buyer or lessee takes any of the following actions after a reasonable opportunity to inspect the goods: (1) signifies the seller or lessor in words or by conduct that the goods are conforming or that the buyer or lessee will take or retain the goods despite their nonconformity or (2) fails to effectively reject the goods within a reasonable time after their delivery or tender by the seller or lessor. Acceptance also occurs if a buyer acts inconsistently with the seller's ownership rights in the goods. [412]

acceptance method The bankruptcy court must approve a plan of reorganization if (1) the plan is *in the best interests* of each class of claims and interests, (2) the plan is *feasible*, (3) at least one class of claims *votes to accept the plan,* and (4) each class of claims and interests is *nonimpaired.* [569]

accession Occurs when the value of personal property increases because it is added to or improved by natural or manufactured means. [914]

accommodation A shipment that is offered to the buyer as a replacement for the original shipment when the original shipment cannot be filled. [386]

accommodation party A party who signs an instrument and lends his or her name (and credit) to another party to the instrument. [494]

accord An agreement whereby the parties agree to accept something different in satisfaction of the original contract. [227]

accord and satisfaction The settlement of a contract dispute. [291]

action for an accounting A formal judicial proceeding in which the court is authorized to (1) review the partnership and the partners' transactions and (2) award each partner his or her share of the partnership assets. [696]

act of monopolizing A required act for there to be a violation of Section 2 of the Sherman Act. Possession of monopoly power without such act does not violate Section 2. [889]

act of state doctrine States that judges of one country cannot question the validity of an act committed by another country within that other country's borders. It is based on the principle that a country has absolute authority over what transpires within its own territory. [166]

actus reus "Guilty act"—the actual performance of the criminal act. [123]

ademption A principle that says if a testator leaves a specific devise of property to a beneficiary, but the property is no longer in the estate when the testator dies, the beneficiary receives nothing. [971]

adequate assurance of performance A party to a sales or lease contract may demand an adequate assurance of performance from the other party if there is an indication that the contract will be breached by that party. [413]

adjudged insane A person who has been adjudged insane by a proper court or administrative agency. A contract entered into by such a person is *void.* [240]

administrative agencies Agencies that the legislative and executive branches of federal and state governments establish. [827]

administrative dissolution Involuntary dissolution of a corporation that is ordered by the secretary of state if the corporation has failed to comply with certain procedures required by law. [736]

administrative law judge (ALJ) A judge, presiding over administrative proceedings, who decides questions of law and fact concerning the case. [834]

Administrative Procedure Act (APA) An act that establishes certain administrative procedures that federal administrative agencies must follow in conducting their affairs. [829]

adverse action A denial or revocation of credit or a change in the credit terms offered. [846]

adverse possession When a person who wrongfully possesses someone else's real property obtains title to that property if certain statutory requirements are met. [938]

advertisement A general advertisement is an invitation to make an offer. A specific advertisement is an offer. [218]

affirmative action Policy that provides that certain job preferences will be given to minority or other protected class applicants when an employer makes an employment decision. [655]

affirmative warranty A statement asserting that certain facts are true. [966]

AFL-CIO The 1955 combination of the AFL and the CIO. [611]

after-acquired property Property that the debtor acquires after the security agreement is executed. [534]

agency The principal–agent relationship: the fiduciary relationship "which results from the manifestation of consent by one person to another that the other shall act in his behalf and subject to his control, and consent by the other so to act." [583]

agency by ratification An agency that occurs when (1) a person misrepresents him- or herself as another's agent when in fact he or she is not and (2) the purported principal ratifies the unauthorized act. [588]

agency law The large body of common law that governs agency: A mixture of contract law and tort law. [583]

agency shop An establishment where an employee does not have to join the union, but must pay a fee equal to the union dues. [616]

agent A person who has been authorized to sign a negotiable instrument on behalf of another person. [491, 583]

agreement The manifestation by two or more persons of the substance of a contract. [215]

aiding and abetting the commission of a crime Rendering support, assistance, or encouragement to the commission of a crime; harboring a criminal after he or she has committed a crime. [134]

air pollution Pollution caused by factories, homes, vehicles, and the like that affects the air. [856]

alien corporation A corporation that is incorporated in another country. [723]

allonge A separate piece of paper attached to the instrument on which the indorsement is written. [471]

altered check A check that has been altered without authorization that modifies the legal obligation of a party. [517]

alternative dispute resolution (ADR) Methods of resolving disputes other than litigation. [43]

Americans with Disabilities Act (ADA) of 1990 Imposes obligations on employers and providers of public transportation, telecommunications, and public accommodations to accommodate individuals with disabilities. [651]

annual financial statement A statement provided to the shareholders that contains a balance sheet, an income statement, and a statement of changes in shareholder equity. [750]

annual shareholders' meeting Meeting of the shareholders of a corporation that must be held annually by the corporation to elect directors and to vote on other matters. [746]

answer The defendant's written response to the plaintiff's complaint that is filed with the court and served on the plaintiff. [36]

anti-assignment clause A clause that prohibits the assignment of rights under the contract. [283]

anticipatory breach A breach that occurs when one contracting party informs the other that he or she will not perform his or her contractual duties when due. [302]

anticipatory repudiation The repudiation of a sales or lease contract by one of the parties prior to the date set for performance. [413]

anti-delegation clause A clause that prohibits the delegation of duties under the contract. [285]

antidilution statutes State laws that allow persons and companies to register trademarks and service marks. [344]

antitrust laws A series of laws enacted to limit anticompetitive behavior in almost all industries, businesses, and professions operating in the United States. [879]

apparent agency Agency that arises when a principal creates the appearance of an agency that in actuality does not exist. [586]; Agency that arises when a franchisor creates the appearance that a franchisee is its agent when in fact an actual agency does not exist. [681]

appeal The act of asking an appellate court to overturn a decision after the trial court's final judgment has been entered. [42]

appellant The appealing party in an appeal. Also known as petitioner. [42]

appellate body A panel of seven judges selected from WTO member nations that hears and decides appeals from decisions by the dispute settlement body. [163]

appellee The responding party in an appeal. Also known as *respondent*. [42]

appropriate bargaining unit The group that a union seeks to represent. [613]

approval clause A clause that permits the assignment of the contract only upon receipt of an obligor's approval. [283]

arbitration A nonjudicial method of dispute resolution whereby a neutral third party decides the case. [43, 169]

arbitration clause A clause contained in many international contracts that stipulates that any dispute between the parties concerning the performance of the contract will be submitted to an arbitrator or arbitration panel for resolution. [43, 169]

arraignment A hearing during which the accused is brought before a court and is (1) informed of the charges against him or her and (2) asked to enter a plea. [125]

arrest warrant A document for a person's detainment based upon a showing of probable cause that the person committed the crime. [125]

arson Willfully or maliciously burning another's building. [127]

Article 2A (Leases) Article of the UCC that governs lease of goods. [383]

Article 4 of the UCC Establishes the rules and principles that regulate bank deposit and collection procedures. [511]

Article 7 of the UCC An article of the Uniform Commercial Code that provides a detailed statutory scheme for the creation, perfection, and foreclosure on common carriers' and warehouse operators' liens. [922]

Article 8 of the UCC The article of the UCC that governs transfer of securities. [749]

Article 9 of the UCC An article of the Uniform Commercial Code that governs secured transactions in personal property. [532]

articles of incorporation The basic governing documents of the corporation. These documents must be filed with the secretary of state of the state of incorporation. [724]

articles of organization The formal document that must be filed with the Secretary of State to form an LLC. [707]

articles of partnership Document that must be filed with the secretary of state to form a limited liability partnership. [704]

assault (1) The threat of immediate harm or offensive contact or (2) any action that arouses reasonable apprehension of imminent harm. Actual physical contact is unnecessary. [91]

assignee The party to whom the right has been transferred. [281, 948]; The transferee in an assignment situation. [470]

assignment The transfer of contractual rights by the obligee to another party. [281]; The transfer of rights under a contract. [470]; A transfer by a tenant of his or her rights under a lease to another. [948]

assignment and delegation Transfer of both rights and duties under the contract. [285]

assignor The obligee who transfers the right. [281]; The transferor in an assignment situation. [470]; The party who transfers the right. [948]

assumption of duties When a delegation of duties contains the term *assumption, I assume the duties,* or other similar language; the delegatee is legally liable to the obligee for nonperformance. [284]

assumption of the risk A defense a defendant can use against a plaintiff who knowingly and voluntarily enters into or participates in a risky activity that results in injury. [105]; A defense in which the defendant must prove that (1) the plaintiff knew and appreciated the risk and (2) the plaintiff voluntarily assumed the risk. [449]

attachment The creditor has an enforceable security interest against the debtor and can satisfy the debt out of the designated collateral. [534]

attempt to commit a crime When a crime is attempted but not completed. [134]

attestation The action of a will being witnessed by two or three objective and competent people. [967]

attorney–client privilege A rule that says a client can tell his or her lawyer anything about the case without fear that the attorney will be called as a witness against the client. [141]

attribution procedure A procedure using codes, algorithms, identifying words or numbers, encryption, callback, or other acknowledgment to verify an authentication of a record. [363]

auction without reserve An auction in which the seller expressly gives up his or her right to withdraw the goods from sale and must accept the highest bid. [219]

auction with reserve Unless expressly stated otherwise, an auction is an auction with reserve; that is, the seller retains the right to refuse the highest bid and withdraw the goods from sale. [219]

authenticate Signing the contract or executing an electronic symbol, sound, or message attached to, included in, or linked with the record. [363]

authorized shares The number of shares provided for in the articles of incorporation. [732]

automatic stay The result of the filing of a voluntary or involuntary petition; the suspension of certain actions by creditors against the debtor or the debtor's property. [557]

backward vertical merger A vertical merger in which the customer acquires the supplier. [892]

bailee A holder of goods who is not a seller or a buyer (e.g., a warehouse or common carrier). [394, 407, 918]

bailee's rights Depending on the type of bailment, bailees may have the right to (1) exclusive possession of the bailed property, (2) use of the bailed property, and (3) compensation for work done or services provided. [921]

bailment A transaction where an owner transfers his or her personal property to another to be held, stored, delivered, or for some other purpose. Title to the property does not transfer. [918]

bailment at will A bailment without a fixed term; can be terminated at any time by either party. [919]

bailment for a fixed term A bailment that terminates at the end of the term or sooner by mutual consent of the parties. [919]

bailment for the sole benefit of the bailee A gratuitous bailment that benefits only the bailee. The bailee owes a *duty of utmost care* to protect the bailed property. [920]

bailment for the sole benefit of the bailor A gratuitous bailment that benefits only the bailor. The bailee owes only a *duty of slight care* to protect the bailed property. [920]

bailor The owner of property in a bailment. [918]

bait and switch A type of deceptive advertising that occurs when a seller advertises the availability of a low-cost discounted item but then pressures the buyer into purchasing more expensive merchandise. [843]

bank check A certified check, a cashier's check, or a traveler's check, the payment for which the bank is solely or primarily liable. [512]

Bankruptcy Code The name given to the Bankruptcy Reform Act of 1978, as amended. [554]

bankruptcy estate An estate created upon the commencement of a Chapter 7 proceeding that includes all the debtor's legal and equitable interests in real, personal, tangible, and intangible property, wherever located, that exist when the petition is filed, minus exempt property. [559]

bargained-for exchange Exchange that parties engage in that leads to an enforceable contract. [224]

battery Unauthorized and harmful or offensive physical contact with another person. Direct physical contact is not necessary. [91]

bearer paper Bearer paper is negotiated by delivery; indorsement is not necessary. [470]

beneficiary A person or organization who will receive money from the insurer at the time of the insured's death. [960]; A person or organization designated in the will who receives all or a portion of the testator's property at the time of the testator's death. [967]; Person for whose benefit a trust is created. [975]

bequest A gift of personal property by will. [971]

bilateral contract A contract entered into by way of exchange of promises of the parties; "a promise for a promise." [204]

blank indorsement An indorsement that does not specify a particular indorsee. It creates *bearer paper*. [472]

board of directors A panel of decision makers, the members of which are elected by the shareholders. [751]

bona fide occupational qualification (BFOQ) Employment discrimination based on a protected class (other than race or color) is lawful if it is *job related* and a *business necessity*. This exception is narrowly interpreted by the courts. [646]

bond A long-term debt security that is secured by some form of collateral. [733]

breach Failure of a party to perform an obligation in a sales or lease contract. [407]

breach of contract If a contracting party fails to perform an absolute duty owed under a contract. [301]

breach of the duty of care A failure to exercise care or to act as a reasonable person would act. [98]

bribery When one person gives another person money, property, favors, or anything else of value for a favor in return. Often referred to as a payoff or "kickback." [130]

building codes State and local statutes that impose specific standards on property owners to maintain and repair leased premises. [946]

burglary Taking personal property from another's home, office, commercial, or other type of building. [127]

business judgment rule A rule that protects the decisions of the board of directors, who act on an informed basis, in good faith, and in the honest belief that the action taken was in the best interests of the corporation and its shareholders. [758, 786]

buy-and-sell agreement An agreement that requires selling shareholders to sell their shares to the other shareholders or to the corporation at the price specified in the agreement. [749]

buyer in the ordinary course of business A person who in good faith and without knowledge that the sale violates the ownership or security interests of a third party buys the goods in the ordinary course of business from a person in the business of selling goods of that kind. A buyer in the ordinary course of business takes the goods free of any third-party security interest in the goods. [397]; A person who in good faith and without knowledge of another's ownership or security interest in goods buys the goods in the ordinary course of business from a person in the business of selling goods of that kind [UCC 1-201(9)]. [540]

bylaws A detailed set of rules adopted by the board of directors after the corporation is incorporated that contains provisions for managing the business and the affairs of the corporation. [727]

cancellation The termination of a contract by a contracting party upon the material breach of the contract by the other party. [369]; A seller or lessor may cancel a sales or lease contract if the buyer or lessee rejects or revokes acceptance of the goods, fails to pay for the goods, or repudiates the contract in part or in whole. [416]; A buyer or lessee may cancel a sales or lease contract if the seller or lessor fails to deliver conforming goods or repudiates the contract or if the buyer or lessee rightfully rejects the goods or justifiably revokes acceptance of the goods. [419]

case brief A summary of each of the following items of a case: 1. Case name and citation, 2. Key facts, 3. Issue presented, 4. Holding of the court, 5. Court's reasoning. [19]

cashier's check A check issued by a bank where the customer has paid the bank the amount of the check and a fee. The bank guarantees the payment of the check. [513]

causation A person who commits a negligent act is not liable unless his or her act was the cause of the plaintiff's injuries. The two types of causation that must be proven are (1) *causation in fact* (*actual cause*) and (2) *proximate cause* (*legal cause*). [99]

causation in fact or actual cause The actual cause of negligence. A person who commits a negligent act is not liable unless causation in fact can be proven. [99]

caveat emptor "Let the buyer beware," the traditional guideline of sales transactions. [827]

certificate of deposit (CD) A two-party negotiable instrument that is a special form of note created when a depositor deposits money at a financial institution in exchange for the institution's promise to pay back the amount of the deposit plus an agreed-upon rate of interest upon the expiration of a set time period agreed upon by the parties. [463]

certificate of limited partnership A document that two or more persons must execute and sign that makes the limited partnership legal and binding. [701]

certified check A type of check where a bank agrees in advance (*certifies*) to accept the check when it is presented for payment. [512]

chain of distribution All manufacturers, distributors, wholesalers, retailers, lessors, and subcomponent manufacturers involved in a transaction. [442]

chain-style franchise The franchisor licenses the franchisee to make and sell its products or distribute services to the public from a retail outlet serving an exclusive territory. [673]

changing conditions defense A price discrimination defense that claims prices were lowered in response to changing conditions in the market for or the marketability of the goods. [896]

Chapter 11 A bankruptcy method that allows reorganization of the debtor's financial affairs under the supervision of the Bankruptcy Court. [566]

Chapter 13 A rehabilitation form of bankruptcy that permits the courts to supervise the debtor's plan for the payment of unpaid debts by installments. [571]

Chapter 7 liquidation bankruptcy The most familiar form of bankruptcy; the debtor's nonexempt property is sold for cash, the cash is distributed to the creditors, and any unpaid debts are discharged. [555]

check A distinct form of draft drawn on a financial institution and payable on demand. [461]; An order by the drawer to the drawee bank to pay a specified sum of money from the drawer's checking account to the named payee (or holder). [511]

choice of forum clause Clause in an international contract that designates which nation's court has jurisdiction to hear a case arising out of the contract. Also known as a forum-selection clause. [165]

choice of law clause Clause in an international contract that designates which nation's laws will be applied in deciding a dispute. [165]

close corporation A corporation owned by one or a few shareholders. [667]

closing The finalization of a real estate sales transaction that passes title to the property from the seller to the buyer. [936]

codicil A separate document that must be executed to amend a will. It must be executed with the same formalities as a will. [969]

C.O.D. shipment A type of shipment contract where the buyer agrees to pay the shipper cash upon the delivery of the goods. [411]

coinsurance clause A clause that permits an owner who insures his or her property to a certain percent of its value to recover up to the face value of the policy. [962]

collateral Security against repayment of the note that lenders sometimes require; can be a car, a house, or other property. [463]

collateral contract A promise where one person agrees to answer for the debts or duties of another person. [267]

collecting bank The depository bank and other banks in the collection process (other than the payor bank). [519]

collective bargaining The act of negotiating contract terms between an employer and the members of a union. [616]

collective bargaining agreement The resulting contract from a collective bargaining procedure. [616]

"coming and going" rule A rule that says a principal is generally not liable for injuries caused by its agents and employees while they are on their way to or from work. [597]

Commerce Clause A clause of the U.S. Constitution that grants Congress the power "to regulate commerce with foreign nations, and among the several states, and with Indian tribes." [59]

commercial impracticability Non-performance that is excused if an extreme or unexpected development or expense makes it impractical for the promisor to perform. [292]

commercial speech Speech used by businesses, such as advertising. It is subject to time, place, and manner restrictions. [65]

common carrier A firm that offers transportation services to the general public. The bailee. Owes a *duty of strict liability* to the bailor. [922]

common law Developed by judges who issued their opinions when deciding a case. The principles announced in these cases became precedent for later judges deciding similar cases. [7]

common law of contracts Contract law developed primarily by state courts. [202]

common stock A type of equity security that represents the *residual* value of the corporation. [730]

common stock certificate A document that represents the common shareholder's investment in the corporation. [730]

common stockholder A person who owns common stock. [730]

comparative negligence A doctrine under which damages are apportioned according to fault. [106]; A doctrine that applies to strict liability actions that says a plaintiff who is contributorily negligent for his or her injuries is responsible for a proportional share of the damages. [450]

compensatory damages An award of money intended to compensate a non-breaching party for the loss of the bargain; they place the nonbreaching party in the same position as if the contract had been fully performed by restoring the "benefit of the bargain." [303]; Damages that are generally equal to the difference between the value of the goods as warranted and the actual value of the goods accepted at the time and place of acceptance. [438]

competent party's duty of restitution If a minor has transferred money, property, or other valuables to the competent party before disaffirming the contract, that party must place the minor back into status quo. [238]

complaint The document the plaintiff files with the court and serves on the defendant to initiate a lawsuit. [35]

complete performance Occurs when a party to a contract renders performance exactly as required by the contract; discharges that party's obligations under the contract. [301]

conciliation A form of mediation in which the parties choose an interested third party to act as the mediator. [45]

concurrent condition A condition that exists when the parties to a contract must render performance simultaneously; each party's absolute duty to perform is conditioned on the other party's absolute duty to perform. [289]

concurrent jurisdiction Jurisdiction shared by two or more courts. [31]

condition A qualification of a promise that becomes a covenant if it is met. There are three types of conditions: conditions precedent, conditions subsequent, and concurrent conditions. [288]

condition precedent A condition that requires the occurrence of an event before a party is obligated to perform a duty under a contract. [288]

condition precedent based on satisfaction Clause in a contract that reserves the right to a party to pay for the items or services contracted for only if they meet his or her satisfaction. [289]

condition subsequent A condition, if it occurs or doesn't occur, that automatically excuses the performance of an existing contractual duty to perform. [289]

condominium A common form of ownership in a multiple-dwelling building where the purchaser has title to the individual unit and owns the common areas as a tenant in common with the other condominium owners. [936]

confirmation The bankruptcy court's approval of a plan of reorganization. [569]

confusion Occurs if two or more persons commingle fungible goods; title is then acquired by confusion. [915]

conglomerate merger A merger that does not fit into any other category; a merger between firms in totally unrelated businesses. [893]

consequential damages Foreseeable damages that arise from circumstances outside the contract. To be liable for these damages, the breaching party must know or have reason to know that the breach will cause special damages to the other party. [304, 438]

consideration Something of legal value given in exchange for a promise. [224]

consignee The person to whom the bailed goods are to be delivered. [922]

consignment An arrangement where a seller (the consignor) delivers goods to a buyer (the consignee) for sale. [394]

consignor The person shipping the goods. The bailor. [922]

Consolidated Omnibus Budget Reconciliation Act (COBRA) Federal law that permits employees and their beneficiaries to continue their group health insurance after an employee's employment has ended. [625]

consolidation The act of a court to combine two or more separate lawsuits into one lawsuit. [37]; Occurs when two or more corporations combine to form an entirely new corporation. [778]

conspicuous A requirement that warranty disclaimers be noticeable to the average person. [437]

Constitution of the United States of America The supreme law of the United States. [9]

constructive notice Usually written notice to a third party that is put into general circulation, such as in a newspaper. [699]

Consumer Leasing Act (CLA) An amendment to the TILA that extends the TILA's coverage to lease terms in consumer leases. [845]

Consumer Product Safety Act (CPSA) A federal statute that regulates potentially dangerous consumer products and created the Consumer Product Safety Commission. [840]

Consumer Product Safety Commission (CPSC) An independent federal regulatory agency empowered to (1) adopt rules and regulations to interpret and enforce the Consumer Product Safety

Act, (2) conduct research on safety, and (3) collect data regarding injuries. [840]

consumer protection laws Federal and state statutes and regulations that promote product safety and prohibit abusive, unfair, and deceptive business practices. [827]

contract in restraint of trade A contract that unreasonably restrains trade. [245]

contracts contrary to public policy Contracts that have a negative impact on society or that interfere with the public's safety and welfare. [244]

contributory negligence A defense that says a person who is injured by a defective product but has been negligent and has contributed to his or her own injuries cannot recover from the defendant. [106, 450]

controlling shareholder A shareholder that owns a sufficient number of shares to control the corporation effectively. [763]

convention Treaty that is sponsored by an international organization. [154]

conversion of personal property A tort that deprives a true owner of the use and enjoyment of his or her personal property by taking over such property and exercising ownership rights over it. [96]

convertible preferred stock Stock that permits the stockholders to convert their shares into common stock. [732]

cooling-off period Requires a union to give an employer at least 60 days' notice before a strike can commence. [618]

cooperative A voluntary joining together of businesses that provides services to its members. [670]; A form of co-ownership of a multiple-dwelling building where a corporation owns the building and the residents own shares in the corporation. [936]

co-ownership When two or more persons own a piece of real property. Also called *concurrent ownership*. [934]

copyright infringement When a party copies a substantial and material part of the plaintiff's copyrighted work without permission. A copyright holder may recover damages and other remedies against the infringer. [332]

Copyright Revision Act of 1976 Federal statute that (1) establishes the requirements for obtaining a copyright and (2) protects copyrighted works from infringement. [330]

corporate citizenship A theory of responsibility that says a business has a responsibility to do good. [192]

corporate seal A design containing the name of the corporation and the date of incorporation that is imprinted by the corporate secretary using a metal stamp on certain legal documents. [728]

corporation A fictitious legal entity that (1) is created according to statutory requirements and (2) is a separate taxpaying entity for federal income tax purposes. [667, 719]

corporations codes State statutes that regulate the formation, operation, and dissolution of corporations. [719]

cost justification defense A defense in Section 2(a) action that provides that a seller's price discrimination is not unlawful if the price differential is due to "differences in the cost of manufacture, sale, or delivery" of the product. [896]

counteroffer A response by an offeree that contains terms and conditions different from or in addition to those of the offer. A counteroffer terminates an offer. [220]

Court of Appeals for the Federal Circuit A court of appeals in Washington, DC, that has special appellate jurisdiction to review the decisions of the Claims Court, the Patent and Trademark Office, and the Court of International Trade. [28]

Court of Chancery Court that granted relief based on fairness. Also called equity court. [7]

covenant An unconditional promise to perform. [288]

covenant of good faith and fair dealing Under this implied covenant, the parties to a contract not only are held to the express terms of the contract but also are required to act in "good faith" and deal fairly in all respects in obtaining the objective of the contract. [109, 312]

covenant of quiet enjoyment A covenant that says that a landlord may not interfere with the tenant's quiet and peaceful possession, use, and enjoyment of the leased premises. [946]

cover The licensee's right to engage in a commercially reasonable substitute transaction after the licensor has breached the contract. [370]; Right of a buyer or lessee to purchase or lease substitute goods if a seller or lessor fails to make delivery of the goods or repudiates the contract or if the buyer or lessee rightfully rejects the goods or justifiably revokes their acceptance. [418]

cram down method A method of confirmation of a plan of reorganization where the court forces an impaired class to participate in the plan of reorganization. [570]

crashworthiness doctrine A doctrine that says automobile manufacturers are under a duty to design automobiles so they take into account the possibility of harm from a person's body striking something inside the automobile in the case of a car accident. [445]

credit report Information about a person's credit history that can be secured from a credit bureau. [846]

creditor The lender in a credit transaction. [531]

creditor beneficiary Original creditor who becomes a beneficiary under the debtor's new contract with another party. [286]

creditor beneficiary contract A contract that arises in the following situation: (1) a debtor borrows money, (2) the debtor signs an agreement to pay back the money plus interest, (3) the debtor sells the item to a third party before the loan is paid off, and (4) the third party promises the debtor that he or she will pay the remainder of the loan to the creditor. [286]

creditor–debtor relationship Created when a customer deposits money into the bank; the customer is the creditor and the bank is the debtor. [510]

creditor's committee The creditors holding the seven largest unsecured claims are usually appointed to the creditors' committee. Representatives of the committee appear at Bankruptcy Court hearings, participate in the negotiation of a plan of reorganization, assert objections to proposed plans, and so on. [567]

crime A crime is a violation of a statute for which the government imposes a punishment. [122]

criminal conspiracy When two or more persons enter into an agreement to commit a crime and an overt act is taken to further the crime. [134]

criminal fraud Obtaining title to property through deception or trickery. Also known as false pretenses or deceit. [129]

critical legal thinking The process of specifying the issue presented by a case, identifying the key facts in the case and applicable law, and then applying the law to the facts to come to a conclusion that answers the issue presented. [19]

cross-complaint Filed by the defendant against the plaintiff to seek damages or some other remedy. [36]

crossover worker A person who does not honor a strike who either (1) chooses not to strike or (2) returns to work after joining the strikers for a time. [618]

crown jewel A valuable asset of the target corporation's that the tender offeror particularly wants to acquire in the tender offer. [785]

cruel and unusual punishment A clause of the Eighth Amendment that protects criminal defendants from torture or other abusive punishment. [142]

cumulative preferred stock Stock that provides any missed dividend payments must be paid in the future to the preferred shareholders before the common shareholders can receive any dividends. [732]

cumulative voting A shareholder can accumulate all of his or her votes and vote them all for one candidate or split them among several candidates. [747]

cure An opportunity to repair or replace defective or nonconforming goods. [409]

custom The second source of international law, created through consistent, recurring practices between two or more nations over a period of time that have become recognized as binding. [154]

damages A buyer or lessee may recover damages from a seller or lessor who fails to deliver the goods or repudiates the contract; damages are measured as the difference between the contract price (or original rent) and the market price (or rent) at the time the buyer or lessee learned of the breach. [419]

damages for accepted nonconforming goods A buyer or lessee may accept nonconforming goods and recover the damages caused by the breach from the seller or lessor or deduct the damages from any part of the purchase price or rent still due under the contract. [420]

"danger invites rescue" doctrine Doctrine that provides that a rescuer who is injured while going to someone's rescue can sue the person who caused the dangerous situation. [104]

debenture A long-term unsecured debt instrument that is based on the corporation's general credit standing. [733]

debt collector An agent who collects debts for other parties. [846]

debtor The borrower in a credit transaction. [531]

debtor-in-possession A debtor who is left in place to operate the business during the reorganization proceeding. [566]

debt securities Securities that establish a debtor–creditor relationship in which the corporation borrows money from the investor to whom the debt security is issued. [733]

declaration of duties If the delegatee has not assumed the duties under a contract, the delegatee is not legally liable to the obligee for nonperformance. [284]

deductible clause A clause that stipulates that insurance proceeds are payable only after the insured has paid a certain amount of the damage or loss. [962]

deed A writing that describes a person's ownership interest in a piece of real property. [939]

defamation of character False statement(s) made by one person about another. In court, the plaintiff must prove that (1) the defendant made an untrue statement of fact about the plaintiff and (2) the statement was intentionally or accidentally published to a third party. [92]

default Failure to make scheduled payments when due, bankruptcy of the debtor, breach of the warranty of ownership as to the collateral, and other events defined by the parties to constitute default. [541]

defect Something wrong, inadequate, or improper in manufacture, design, packaging, warning, or safety measures of a product. [443]

defect in design A defect that occurs when a product is improperly designed. [444]

defect in manufacture A defect that occurs when the manufacturer fails to (1) properly assemble a product, (2) properly test a product, or (3) adequately check the quality of the product. [444]

defect in packaging A defect that occurs when a product has been placed in packaging that is insufficiently tamper-proof. [446]

deferred posting rule A rule that allows banks to fix an afternoon hour of 2:00 P.M. or later as a cutoff hour for the purpose of processing items. [519]

deficiency judgment A judgment that allows a secured creditor to successfully bring a separate legal action to recover a deficiency from the debtor. Entitles the secured creditor to recover the amount of the judgment from the debtor's other property. [531, 542]

delegatee The party to whom the duty has been transferred. [284]

delegation doctrine A doctrine that says when an administrative agency is created, it is delegated certain powers; the

agency can only use those legislative, judicial, and executive powers that are delegated to it. [830]

delegation of duties A transfer of contractual duties by the obligor to another party for performance. [283]

delegator The obligor who transferred his or her duty. [284]

demand instrument An instrument payable on demand. [468, 489]

demand note A note payable on demand. [462]

deponent Party who gives his or her deposition. [38]

deposition Oral testimony given by a party or witness prior to trial. The testimony is given under oath and is transcribed. [38]

depository bank The bank where the payee or holder has an account. [518]

derivative lawsuit A lawsuit a shareholder brings against an offending party on behalf of the corporation when the corporation fails to bring the lawsuit. [750]

destination contract A contract that requires the seller to deliver the goods either to the buyer's place of business or to another destination specified in the sales contract. The seller bears the risk of loss during transportation. [390, 392, 408]

devise A gift of real estate by will. [971]

direct lawsuit A lawsuit that a shareholder can bring against the corporation to enforce his or her personal rights as a shareholder. [750]

disaffirmance The act of a minor to rescind a contract under the infancy doctrine. Disaffirmance may be done orally, in writing, or by the minor's conduct. [238]

discharge Actions or events that relieve certain parties from liability on negotiable instruments. There are three methods of discharge: (1) payment of the instrument; (2) cancellation; and (3) impairment of the right of recourse. [500]; The termination of the legal duty of a debtor to pay debts that remain unpaid upon the completion of a bankruptcy proceeding. [563]; Creditors' claims that are not included in a Chapter 11 reorganization are discharged. [571]; A discharge is granted to a debtor in a Chapter 13 consumer debt adjustment bankruptcy only after all the payments under the plan are completed by the debtor. [573]

discharge in bankruptcy A real defense against the enforcement of a negotiable

instrument; bankruptcy law is intended to relieve debtors of burdensome debts, including negotiable instruments. [497]

disclosure statement A statement that must contain adequate information about the proposed plan of reorganization that is supplied to the creditors and equity holders. [567]

discovery A legal process during which both parties engage in various activities to discover facts of the case from the other party and witnesses prior to trial. [38]

dishonored Occurs when an instrument has been presented for payment and payment has been refused. [489]

disparate impact discrimination Occurs when an employer discriminates against an entire protected class. An example would be where a facially neutral employment practice or rule causes an adverse impact on a protected class. [638]

disparate treatment discrimination Occurs when an employer discriminates against a specific individual because of his or her race, color, national origin, sex, or religion. [638]

disposition of collateral If a secured creditor repossesses collateral upon a debtor's default, he or she may sell, lease, or otherwise dispose of it in a commercially reasonable manner. [542]

disposition of goods A seller or lessor who is in possession of goods at the time the buyer or lessee breaches or repudiates the contract may in good faith resell, release, or otherwise dispose of the goods in a commercially reasonable manner and recover damages, including incidental damages, from the buyer or lessee. [415]

dispute settlement body A board comprised of one representative from each WTO member nation that reviews panel reports. [163]

dissension When an individual director opposes the action taken by the majority of the board of directors. [760]

dissenting shareholder appraisal rights Shareholders who object to a proposed merger, share exchange, or sale or lease of all or substantially all of the property of a corporation have a right to have their shares valued by the court and receive cash payment of this value from the corporation. [780]

distinctive A brand name that is unique and fabricated. [339]

distribution of property *Nonexempt property* of the bankruptcy estate must be distributed to the debtor's secured and unsecured creditors pursuant to the statutory priority established by the Bankruptcy Code. [562]

distributorship franchise The franchisor manufactures a product and licenses a retail franchisee to distribute the product to the public. [673]

diversity of citizenship A case between (1) citizens of different states, (2) a citizen of a state and a citizen or subject of a foreign country, and (3) a citizen of a state and a foreign country where a foreign country is the plaintiff. [30]

dividend Distribution of profits of the corporation to shareholders. [754]

dividend preference The right to receive a fixed dividend at stipulated periods during the year (e.g., quarterly). [732]

division of markets When competitors agree that each will serve only a designated portion of the market. [882]

doctrine of sovereign immunity States that countries are granted immunity from suits in courts of other countries. [167]

doctrine of strict liability in tort A tort doctrine that makes manufacturers, distributors, wholesalers, retailers, and others in the chain of distribution of a defective product liable for the damages caused by the defect irrespective of fault. [442]

document of title An actual piece of paper, such as a warehouse receipt or bill of lading, that is required in some transactions of pick up and delivery. [390]

domain name A unique name that identifies an individual's or company's Web site. [357]

domestic corporation A corporation in the state in which it was formed. [722]

donee A person who receives a gift. [913]

donee beneficiary The third party on whom the benefit is to be conferred. [285]

donee beneficiary contract A contract entered into with the intent to confer a benefit or gift on an intended third party. [285]

donor A person who gives a gift. [913]

double jeopardy clause A clause of the Fifth Amendment that protects persons from being tried twice for the same crime. [141]

draft A three-party instrument that is an unconditional written order by one party that orders the second party to pay money to a third party. [460]

Dram Shop Act Statute that makes taverns and bartenders liable for injuries caused to or by patrons who are served too much alcohol. [104]

drawee of a check The financial institution where the drawer has his or her account. [461]; The bank where the drawer has his or her account [511]

drawee of a draft The party who must pay the money stated in the draft. Also called the *acceptor* of a draft. [460]

drawer of a check The checking account holder and writer of the check. [461, 511]

drawer of a draft The party who writes the order for a draft. [460]

dual-purpose mission An errand or other act that a principal requests of an agent while the agent is on his or her own personal business. [597]

due diligence defense A defense to a Section 11 action that, if proven, makes the defendant not liable. [806]

Due Process Clause A clause that provides that no person shall be deprived of "life, liberty, or property" without due process of the law. [72]

duress Occurs when one party threatens to do a wrongful act unless the other party enters into a contract. [262]

duty not to willfully or wantonly injure The duty an owner owes a trespasser to prevent intentional injury or harm to the trespasser when the trespasser is on his or her premises. [105]

duty of accountability A duty that an agent owes to maintain an accurate accounting of all transactions undertaken on the principal's behalf. [590]

duty of care The obligation we all owe each other not to cause any unreasonable harm or risk of harm. [97]; A duty that corporate directors and officers have to use care and diligence when acting on behalf of the corporation. [758]

duty of loyalty A duty that directors and officers have not to act adversely to the interests of the corporation and to subordinate their personal interests to those of the corporation and its shareholders. [761]

duty of notification An agent's duty to notify the principal of information he or she learns from a third party or other source that is important to the principal. [589]

duty of obedience A duty that directors and officers of a corporation have to act within the authority conferred upon them by the state corporation statute, the articles of incorporation, the corporate bylaws, and the resolutions adopted by the board of directors. [757]

duty of ordinary care The duty an owner owes an invitee or a licensee to prevent injury or harm when the invitee or licensee steps on the owner's premises. [104]; Collecting banks are required to exercise ordinary care in presenting and sending checks for collection. [521]

duty of performance An agent's duty to a principal that includes (1) performing the lawful duties expressed in the contract and (2) meeting the standards of reasonable care, skill, and diligence implicit in all contracts. [589]

duty of reasonable care The duty that a reasonable bailee in like circumstances would owe to protect the bailed property. [920]

duty of slight care A duty not to be grossly negligent in caring for something in one's responsibility. [920]

duty of strict liability A duty that common carriers owe that says if the goods are lost, damaged, destroyed, or stolen, the common carrier is liable even if it was not at fault for the loss. [922]

duty of utmost care A duty of care that goes beyond ordinary care that says common carriers and innkeepers have a responsibility to provide security to their passengers or guests. [105, 920]

duty to compensate A duty that a principal owes to pay an agreed-upon amount to the agent either upon the completion of the agency or at some other mutually agreeable time. [591]

duty to cooperate A duty that a principal owes to cooperate with and assist the agent in the performance of the agent's duties and the accomplishment of the agency. [592]

duty to defend An insurer owes a duty to defend an insured against a lawsuit involving a risk covered by the policy. This duty includes providing a lawyer and paying court costs and deposition fees. [963]

duty to indemnify A duty that a principal owes to protect the agent for losses the agent suffered during the agency because of the principal's misconduct. [591]

duty to reimburse A duty that a principal owes to repay money to the agent if the agent spent his or her own money during the agency on the principal's behalf. [591]

easement A given or required right to make limited use of someone else's land without owning or leasing it. [940]

easement appurtenant A situation created when the owner of one piece of land is given an easement over an adjacent piece of land. [940]

easement in gross An easement that authorizes a person who does not own adjacent land the right to use another's land. [940]

e-commerce The sale of goods and services by computer over the Internet. [353]

economic duress Occurs when one party to a contract refuses to perform his or her contractual duties unless the other party pays an increased price, enters into a second contract with the threatening party, or undertakes a similar action. [263]

electronic mail (e-mail) Electronic written communication between individuals using computers connected to the Internet. [355]

elements of a bailment The following three elements are necessary to create a bailment: (1) personal property, (2) delivery of possession, and (3) a bailment agreement. [919]

emancipation When a minor voluntarily leaves home and lives apart from his or her parents. [240]

embezzlement The fraudulent conversion of property by a person to whom that property was entrusted. [129]

Employee Retirement Income Security Act (ERISA) A federal act designed to prevent fraud and other abuses associated with private pension funds. [625]

employer–employee relationship A relationship that results when an employer hires an employee to perform some form of physical service. [584]

employer lockout Act of the employer to prevent employees from entering the work premises when the employer reasonably anticipates a strike. [618]

employment relationships (1) Employer–employee, (2) principal–agent, and (3) principal–independent contractor. [584]

endorsement An addition to an insurance policy that modifies it. [963]

entrepreneur A person who forms and operates a new business either by him- or herself or with others. [665]

enumerated powers Certain powers delegated to the federal government by the states. [55]

Environmental Protection Agency (EPA) An administrative agency created by Congress in 1970 to coordinate the implementation and enforcement of the federal environmental protection laws. [855]

Equal Credit Opportunity Act (ECOA) A federal statute that prohibits discrimination in the extension of credit based on sex, marital status, race, color, national origin, religion, age, or receipt of income from public assistance programs. [846]

equal dignity rule A rule that says that agent's contracts to sell property covered by the Statute of Frauds must be in writing to be enforceable. [268]

Equal Employment Opportunity Commission (EEOC) The federal administrative agency responsible for enforcing most federal antidiscrimination laws. [637]

equal opportunity in employment The right of all employees and job applicants (1) to be treated without discrimination and (2) to be able to sue employers if they are discriminated against. [637]

Equal Pay Act of 1963 Protects both sexes from pay discrimination based on sex; extends to jobs that require equal skill, equal effort, equal responsibility, and similar working conditions. [648]

Equal Protection Clause A clause that provides that a state cannot "deny to any person within its jurisdiction the equal protection of the laws." [71]

equity A doctrine that permits judges to make decisions based on fairness, equality, moral rights, and natural law. [209]

equity securities Representation of ownership rights to the corporation. Also called *stocks*. [730]

Establishment Clause A clause to the First Amendment that prohibits the government from either establishing a state religion or promoting one religion over another. [69]

estate Ownership rights in real property; the bundle of legal rights that the owner has to possess, use, and enjoy the property. [932]

estate pour autre vie A life estate measured in the life of a third party. [933]

ethical fundamentalism When a person looks to an outside source for ethical rules or commands. [180]

ethical relativism A moral theory that holds that individuals must decide what is ethical based on their own feelings as to what is right or wrong. [184]

ethics A set of moral principles or values that governs the conduct of an individual or a group. [178]

European Court of Justice The judicial branch of the European Union, located in Luxembourg. It has jurisdiction to enforce European Union law. [158]

European Union (Common Market) Comprises many countries of Western Europe; created to promote peace and security plus economic, social, and cultural development. [158]

exclusionary rule A rule that says evidence obtained from an unreasonable search and seizure can generally be prohibited from introduction at a trial or administrative proceeding against the person searched. [137]

exclusive agency contract A contract a principal and agent enter into that says the principal cannot employ any agent other than the exclusive agent. [586]

exclusive jurisdiction Jurisdiction held by only one court. [31]

exclusive license A license that grants the licensee exclusive rights to use informational rights for a specified duration. [361]

exculpatory clause A contractual provision that relieves one (or both) parties to the contract from tort liability for ordinary negligence. [245]

executed contract A contract that has been fully performed on both sides; a completed contract. [209]

executive branch The part of the government that consists of the President and Vice President. [55]

executive order An order issued by a member of the executive branch of the government. [12]

executive powers Powers that administrative agencies are granted, such as the investigation and prosecution of possible violations of statutes, administrative rules, and administrative orders. [831]

executory contract A contract that has not been fully performed by either or both sides. [209]; Property that may be retained by the debtor pursuant to federal or state law; debtor's property that does not become part of the bankruptcy estate. [559]; With court approval, executory contracts may be rejected by a debtor in bankruptcy. [568]

exempt property express agency An agency that occurs when a principal and an agent expressly agree to enter into an agency agreement with each other. [585]

express authorization A stipulation in the offer that says the acceptance must be by a specified means of communication. [223]

express contract An agreement that is expressed in written or oral words. [205]

express powers Powers given to a corporation by (1) the U.S. Constitution, (2) state constitutions, (3) federal statutes, (4) state statutes, (5) articles of incorporation, (6) bylaws, and (7) resolutions of the board of directors. [734]

express warranty Any affirmation of fact or promise by the licensor about the quality of its software or information. [367]; A warranty that is created when a seller or lessor makes an affirmation that the goods he or she is selling or leasing meet certain standards of quality, description, performance, or condition. [431]

extortion Threat to expose something about another person unless that other person gives money or property. Often referred to as "blackmail." [128]

extradition Sending a person back to a country for criminal prosecution. [170]

extreme duress Extreme duress, but not ordinary duress, is a real defense against enforcement of a negotiable instrument. [497]

failure to provide adequate instructions A defect that occurs when a manufacturer does not provide detailed directions for safe assembly and use of a product. [448]

failure to warn A defect that occurs when a manufacturer does not place a warning on the packaging of products that could cause injury if the danger is unknown. [447]

Fair Credit and Charge Card Disclosure Act of 1988 An amendment to the TILA that requires disclosure of certain credit terms on credit- and charge-card solicitations and applications. [845]

Fair Credit Reporting Act (FCRA) An amendment to the TILA that protects customers who are subjects of a credit report by setting out guidelines for credit bureaus. [846]

Fair Debt Collection Practices Act (FDCPA) An act enacted in 1977 that protects consumer-debtors from abusive, deceptive, and unfair practices used by debt collectors. [846]

Fair Labor Standards Act (FLSA) A federal act enacted in 1938 to protect workers; prohibits child labor and establishes minimum wage and overtime pay requirements. [624]

Fair Packaging and Labeling Act A federal statute that requires the labels on consumer goods to identify the product; the manufacturer, processor, or packager of the product and its address; the net quantity of the contents of the package; and the quantity of each serving. [841]

fair price rule A rule that says any increase in price paid for shares tendered must be offered to all shareholders, even those who have previously tendered their shares. [783]

fair use doctrine A doctrine that permits certain limited use of a copyright by someone other than the copyright holder without the permission of the copyright holder. [334]

false imprisonment The intentional confinement or restraint of another person without authority or justification and without that person's consent. [91]

federal administrative agencies Administrative agencies that are part of the executive or legislative branch of government. [829]

Federal Insurance Contributions Act (FICA) A federal act that says employees and employers must make contributions into the Social Security fund. [627]

Federal Patent Statute of 1952 Federal statute that establishes the requirements for obtaining a patent and protects patented inventions from infringement. [325]

federal question A case arising under the U.S. Constitution, treaties, or federal statutes and regulations. [30]

Federal Reserve System A system of 12 regional Federal Reserve banks that assist banks in the collection of checks. [519]

Federal Trade Commission (FTC) Federal government agency empowered to enforce federal franchising rules. [674]; Federal administrative agency empowered to enforce the Federal Trade Commission Act and other federal consumer protection statutes. [842]

Federal Unemployment Tax Act (FUTA) A federal act that requires employers to pay unemployment taxes; unemployment compensation is paid to workers who are temporarily unemployed. [627]

federalism The U.S. form of government; the federal government and the 50 state governments share powers. [55]

fee simple absolute A type of ownership of real property that grants the owner the fullest bundle of legal rights that a person can hold in real property. [932]

fee simple defeasible A type of ownership of real property that grants the owner all the incidents of a fee simple absolute except that it may be taken away if a specified condition occurs or does not occur. [933]

felony The most serious type of crime; inherently evil crime. Most crimes against the person and some business-related crimes are felonies. [122]

fictitious payee rule A rule that says that a drawer or maker is liable on a forged or unauthorized indorsement of a fictitious payee. [477]

fiduciary duty Duty of loyalty, honesty, integrity, trust, and confidence owed by directors and officers to their corporate employers. [757, 786]

final prospectus A final version of the prospectus that must be delivered by the issuer to the investor prior to or at the time of confirming a sale or sending a security to a purchaser. [800]

final settlement Occurs when the payor bank (1) pays the check in cash, (2) settles for the check without having a right to revoke the settlement, or (3) fails to dishonor the check within certain statutory time periods. [520]

finance lease A three-party transaction consisting of the lessor, the lessee, and the supplier. [384]

financing statement A document filed by a secured creditor with the appropriate government office that constructively notifies the world of his or her security interest in personal property. [535]

fixed amount A requirement of a negotiable instrument that ensures that the value of the instrument can be determined with certainty. [466]

fixed amount of money A negotiable instrument must contain a promise or order to pay a fixed amount of money. [466]

fixtures Personal property that is permanently affixed to the real property, such as built-in cabinets in a house. [264]; Goods that are affixed to real estate so as to become a part thereof. [932]

floating lien A security interest in property that was not in the possession of the debtor when the security agreement was executed; includes *after-acquired property, future advances,* and *sale proceeds.* [534]

Food and Drug Administration (FDA) Federal administrative agency that administers and enforces the federal Food, Drug, and Cosmetic Act (FDCA) and other federal consumer protection laws. [835]

Food, Drug, and Cosmetic Act (FDCA) A federal statute enacted in 1938 that provides the basis for the regulation of much of the testing, manufacture, distribution, and sale of foods, drugs, cosmetics, and medicinal products. [835]

Foreign Commerce Clause Clause of the U.S. Constitution that vests Congress with the power "to regulate commerce with foreign nations." [152]

foreign corporation A corporation in any state or jurisdiction other than the one in which it was formed. [722]

Foreign Sovereign Immunities Act Exclusively governs suits against foreign nations that are brought in federal or state courts in the United States; codifies the principle of qualified or restricted immunity. [167]

forged instrument A check with a forged drawer's signature on it. [476, 517]

forgery Fraudulently making or altering a written document that affects the legal liability of another person. [128]; A real defense against the enforcement of a negotiable instrument; the unauthorized signature of a maker, drawer, or indorser. [498]

formal contract A contract that requires a special form or method of creation. [207]

formal will A will that meets the requirements of the Statute of Wills. [967]

forum-selection clause Contract provision that designates a certain court to hear any dispute concerning nonperformance of the contract. [33]

forward vertical merger A vertical merger in which the supplier acquires the customer. [892]

four legals Four notices or actions that prevent the payment of a check if they are received by the payor bank before it has finished its process of posting the check for payment. [521]

Fourteenth Amendment Amendment that was added to the U.S. Constitution in 1868. It contains the Due Process, Equal Protection, and Privileges and Immunities clauses. [71]

franchise Established when one party licenses another party to use the franchisor's trade name, trademarks, commercial symbols, patents, copyrights, and other property in the distribution and selling of goods and services. [669, 672]

franchise agreement An agreement that the franchisor and the franchisee enter into that sets forth the terms and conditions of the franchise. [675]

fraud by concealment Occurs when one party takes specific action to conceal a material fact from another party. [260]

fraud in the inception A real defense against the enforcement of a negotiable instrument; a person has been deceived into signing a negotiable instrument thinking that it is something else. [260, 497]; A personal defense against the enforcement of a negotiable instrument; a wrongdoer makes a false statement to another person to lead that person to enter into a contract with the wrongdoer. [498]

fraudulent transfer Occurs when (1) a debtor transfers property to a third person within one year before the filing of a petition in bankruptcy and (2) the transfer was made by the debtor with an intent to hinder, delay, or defraud creditors. [561]

Free Exercise Clause A clause to the First Amendment that prohibits the government from interfering with the free exercise of religion in the United States. [69]

freedom of speech The right to engage in oral, written, and symbolic speech protected by the First Amendment. [64]

freehold estate An estate where the owner has a present possessory interest in the real property. [932]

fresh start The goal of federal bankruptcy law: To discharge the debtor from burdensome debts and allow him or her to begin again. [555]

frolic and detour When an agent does something during the course of his employment to further his own interests rather than the principal's. [596]

frustration of purpose A doctrine which excuses the performance of contractual obligations if (1) the object or benefit of a contract is made worthless to a promisor, (2) both parties knew what the purpose was, and (3) the act that frustrated the purpose was unforeseeable. [293]

FTC franchise rule A rule set out by the FTC that requires franchisors to make full presale disclosures to prospective franchisees. [675]

future advances Personal property of the debtor that is designated as collateral for future loans from a line of credit. [535]

future goods Goods not yet in existence (ungrown crops, unborn stock animals). [390]

future interest The interest that the grantor retains for himself or herself or for a third party. [933]

gambling statutes Statutes that make certain forms of gambling illegal. [242]

gap-filling rule A rule that says an open term can be "read into" a contract. [384]

general duty A duty that an employer has to provide a work environment "free from recognized hazards that are causing or are likely to cause death or serious physical harm to his employees." [623]

general gift Gift that does not identify the specific property from which the gift is to be made. [971]

general-jurisdiction trial court A court that hears cases of a general nature that are not within the jurisdiction of limited-jurisdiction trial courts. Testimony and evidence at trial are recorded and stored for future reference. [25]

generally known dangers A defense that acknowledges that certain products are inherently dangerous and are known to the general population to be so. [448]

general partners Partners in a limited partnership who invest capital, manage the business, and are personally liable for partnership debts. [701]

general partnership A voluntary association of two or more persons for the carrying on of a business as co-owners for profit. [666]; Also called a *partnership*. [693]

general principles of law The third source of international law, consisting of principles of law recognized by civilized nations. These are principles of law that are common to the national law of the parties to the dispute. [154]

general-purpose clause A clause often included in the articles of incorporation that authorizes the corporation to engage in any activity permitted corporations by law. [726]

generic name A term for a mark that has become a common term for a product line or type of service and therefore has lost its trademark protection. [342]

genuineness of assent The requirement that a party's assent to a contract be genuine. [257]

gift A voluntary transfer of title to property without payment of consideration by the donee. To be a valid gift, three elements must be shown: (1) *donative intent*, (2) *delivery*, and (3) *acceptance*. [913]; A transfer of property from one person to another without exchange of money. [937]

gift *causa mortis* A gift that is made in contemplation of death. [913]

gift *inter vivos* A gift made during a person's lifetime that is an irrevocable present transfer of ownership. [913]

gift promise An unenforceable promise because it lacks consideration. [224]

good faith Honesty in fact in the conduct or transaction concerned. The good faith test is subjective. [488]

good faith purchaser for value A person to whom good title can be transferred from a person with voidable title. The real owner cannot reclaim goods from a good faith purchaser for value. [396]

good faith subsequent lessee   A person to whom a lease interest can be transferred from a person with voidable title. The real owner cannot reclaim the goods from the subsequent lessee until the lease expires. [396]

Good Samaritan law   Statute that relieves medical professionals from liability for ordinary negligence when they stop and render aid to victims in emergency situations. [103]

goods   Tangible things that are movable at the time of their identification to the contract. [381]

good title   Title that is free from any encumbrances or other defects that are not disclosed but would affect the value of the property. [939]

government contractor defense   A defense that says a contractor who was provided specifications by the government is not liable for any defect in the product that occurs as a result of those specifications. [449]

grace period   A period of time after the actual expiration date of a payment but during which the insured can still pay an overdue premium without penalty. [963]

grantee   The buyer or recipient to whom an interest in real property is transferred. [939]

grantor   The seller or donor who transfers an ownership interest in real property. [939]

greenmail   The purchase by a target corporation of its stock from an actual or perceived tender offeror at a premium. [785]

group boycott   When two or more competitors at one level of distribution agree not to deal with others at another level of distribution. [883]

guaranteeing collection   A form of accommodation where the accommodation party guarantees *collection* of a negotiable instrument; the accommodation party is *secondarily liable* on the instrument. [495]

guaranteeing payment   A form of accommodation where the accommodation party guarantees *payment* of a negotiable instrument; the accommodation party is *primarily liable* on the instrument. [495]

guarantor   The person who agrees to pay the debt if the primary debtor does not. [267]; The third person who agrees to be liable in a guaranty arrangement. [544]

guaranty arrangement   An arrangement where a third party promises to be *secondarily liable* for the payment of another's debt. [544]

guaranty contract   The contract between the guarantor and the original creditor. [267]

guest statute   Statute that provides that if a driver of a vehicle voluntarily and without compensation gives a ride to another person, the driver is not liable to the passenger for injuries caused by the driver's ordinary negligence. [104]

hardship discharge   A discharge granted if (1) the debtor fails to complete the payments due to unforeseeable circumstances, (2) the unsecured creditors have been paid as much as they would have been paid in a Chapter 7 liquidation proceeding, and (3) it is not practical to modify the plan. [573]

Hart-Scott-Rodino Antitrust Improvement Act   Requires certain firms to notify the FTC and the Justice Department in advance of a proposed merger. Unless the government challenges the proposed merger within 30 days, the merger may proceed. [894]

hazardous waste   Solid waste that may cause or significantly contribute to an increase in mortality or serious illness or pose a hazard to human health or the environment if improperly managed. [865]

holder   What the transferee becomes if a negotiable instrument has been transferred by negotiation. [470]; A person who is in possession of a negotiable instrument that is drawn, issued, or indorsed to him or his order, or to bearer, or in blank. [487]

holder in due course (HDC)   A holder who takes a negotiable instrument for value, in good faith, and without notice that it is defective or is overdue. [487]

holographic will   Will that is entirely handwritten and signed by the testator. [974]

honor   Payment of a drawer's properly drawn check by the drawee bank. [515]

horizontal merger   A merger between two or more companies that compete in the same business and geographical market. [891]

horizontal restraint of trade   A restraint of trade that occurs when two or more competitors at the same *level of distribution* enter into a contract, combination, or conspiracy to restrain trade. [881]

hung jury   A jury that cannot come to a unanimous decision about the defendant's guilt. The government may choose to retry the case. [126]

identification of goods   Distinguishing the goods named in the contract from the seller's or lessor's other goods. [390]

illegal consideration   A promise to refrain from doing an illegal act. Such a promise will not support a contract. [226]

illusory promise   A contract into which parties enter, but one or both of the parties can choose not to perform their contractual obligations. Thus the contract lacks consideration. [226]

Immigration Reform and Control Act of 1986 (IRCA)   A federal statute that makes it unlawful for employers to hire illegal immigrants. [626]

immoral contract   A contract whose objective is the commission of an act that is considered immoral by society. [244]

immunity from prosecution   The government agrees not to use any evidence given by a person granted immunity against that person. [140]

impairment of right of recourse   Certain parties (holders, indorsers, accommodation parties) are discharged from liability on an instrument if the holder (1) releases an obligor from liability or (2) surrenders collateral without the consent of the parties who would benefit by it. [500]

implied agency   An agency that occurs when a principal and an agent do not expressly create an agency, but it is inferred from the conduct of the parties. [586]

implied authorization   Mode of acceptance that is implied from what is customary in similar transactions, usage of trade, or prior dealings between the parties. [223]

implied exemptions   Exemptions from antitrust laws that are implied by the federal courts. [898]

implied powers   Powers beyond express powers that allow a corporation to accomplish its corporate purpose. [735]

implied term   A term in a contract that can reasonably be supplied by the courts. [217]

implied warranties   The law *implies* certain warranties on transferors of negotiable instruments. There are two types of implied warranties: transfer and presentment. [496]

implied warranty of authority   An agent who enters into a contract on behalf of another party impliedly warrants that he or she has the authority to do so. [594]

implied warranty of fitness for a particular purpose   An implied warranty that information is fit for the licensee's purpose that applies if the licensor (1) knows of any particular purpose for which the computer information is required and (2) knows that the licensee is relying on the licensor's skill or judgment to select or furnish suitable information. [367]

implied warranty of fitness for human consumption A warranty that applies to food or drink consumed on or off the premises of restaurants, grocery stores, fast-food outlets, and vending machines. [434]

implied warranty of habitability A warranty that provides that the leased premises must be fit, safe, and suitable for ordinary residential use. [946]

implied warranty of informational content An implied warranty that there is no inaccuracy in the informational content caused by the merchant-licensor's failure to perform with reasonable care. [367]

implied warranty of merchantability Unless properly disclosed, a warranty is implied when sold or leased goods are fit for the ordinary purpose for which they are sold or leased, and other assurances. [432]

implied warranty of merchantability of the computer program An implied warranty that the copies of the computer program are within the parameters permitted by the licensing agreement, that the computer program has been adequately packaged and labeled, and that the program conforms to any promises or affirmations of fact on the container or label. [367]

implied-in-fact condition A condition that can be implied from the circumstances surrounding a contract and the parties' conduct. [290]

implied-in-fact contract A contract where agreement between parties has been inferred from their conduct. [205]

impossibility of performance Nonperformance that is excused if the contract becomes impossible to perform; must be objective impossibility, not subjective. [291]

imposter A person who impersonates a payee and induces a maker or drawer to issue an instrument in the payee's name and to give it to the imposter. [476]

imposter rule A rule that says if an imposter forges the indorsement of the named payee, the drawer or maker is liable on the instrument and bears the loss. [476]

imputed knowledge Information that is learned by the agent that is attributed to the principal. [590]

inaccessibility exception A rule that permits employees and union officials to engage in union solicitation on company property if the employees are beyond reach of reasonable union efforts to communicate with them. [613]

incidental beneficiary A party who is unintentionally benefited by other people's contracts. [287]

incidental damages When goods are resold or released, incidental damages are reasonable expenses incurred in stopping delivery, transportation charges, storage charges, sales commissions, and so on. [415]

incontestability clauses A clause that prevents insurers from contesting statements made by insureds in applications for insurance after the passage of a stipulated number of years. [965]

incorporation by reference When integration is made by express reference in one document that refers to and incorporates another document within it. [270]

incorporator The person or persons, partnerships, or corporations that are responsible for incorporation of a corporation. [724]

indenture agreement A contract between the corporation and the holder that contains the terms of a debt security. [734]

independent contractor A person or business who is not an employee who is employed by a principal to perform a certain task on his behalf. [584]; "A person who contracts with another to do something for him who is not controlled by the other nor subject to the other's right to control with respect to his physical conduct in the performance of the undertaking" [Restatement (Second) of Agency]. [598]

indictment The charge of having committed a crime (usually a felony), based on the judgment of a grand jury. [125]

indirect price discrimination A form of price discrimination (e.g., favorable credit terms) that is less readily apparent than direct forms of price discrimination. [896]

indorsee The person to whom a negotiable instrument is indorsed. [471]; A person who is in possession of a negotiable instrument that is drawn, issued, or indorsed to him or his order, or to bearer, or in blank. [487]

indorsement The signature (and other directions) written by or on behalf of the holder somewhere on the instrument. [471]

indorsement for deposit or collection An indorsement that makes the indorsee the indorser's collecting agent (e.g., "for deposit only"). [474]

indorsement of a check Occurs when a payee indorses a check to another party by signing the back of the check. [511]

indorser The person who indorses a negotiable instrument. [471]; The payee who indorses a check to another party. [511]

indorsers' liability *Unqualified indorsers* are secondarily liable on negotiable instruments they indorse; *qualified indorsers* disclaim liability and are not secondarily liable on instruments they indorse. [493]

infancy doctrine A doctrine that allows minors to disaffirm (cancel) most contracts they have entered into with adults. [237]

inferior performance Occurs when a party fails to perform express or implied contractual obligations that impair or destroy the essence of the contract. [302]

informal contract A contract that is not formal. Valid informal contracts are fully enforceable and may be sued upon if breached. [208]

information The charge of having committed a crime (usually a misdemeanor), based on the judgment of a judge (magistrate). [125]

injunction A court order that prohibits a person from doing a certain act. [310]

injury The plaintiff must suffer personal injury or damage to his or her property to recover monetary damages for the defendant's negligence. [98]

innkeepers' statutes State statutes that limit an innkeeper's common law liability. An innkeeper can avoid liability for loss caused to a guest's property if (1) a safe is provided in which the guest's valuable property may be kept and (2) the guest is notified of this fact. [923]

innocent misrepresentation Occurs when a person makes a statement of fact that he or she honestly and reasonably believes to be true, even though it is not. [260]; Occurs when an agent makes an untrue statement that he or she honestly and reasonably believes to be true. [596]

in pari delicto When both parties are equally at fault in an illegal contract. [247]

in personam jurisdiction Jurisdiction over the parties to a lawsuit. [32]

in rem jurisdiction Jurisdiction to hear a case because of jurisdiction over the property of the lawsuit. [32]

insane, but not adjudged insane   A person who is insane but has not been adjudged insane by a court or administrative agency. A contract entered into by such person is generally voidable. Some states hold that such a contract is void. [240]

Insecticide, Fungicide, and Rodenticide Act   A federal statute that requires pesticides, herbicides, fungicides, and rodenticides to be registered with the EPA; the EPA may deny, suspend, or cancel registration. [864]

INS Form I-9   A form that must be filled out by all U.S. employers for each employee; states that the employer has inspected the employee's legal qualifications to work. [626]

inside director   A member of the board of directors who is also an officer of the corporation. [752]

insider trading   When an insider makes a profit by personally purchasing shares of the corporation prior to public release of favorable information or by selling shares of the corporation prior to the public disclosure of unfavorable information. [809]

Insider Trading Sanctions Act of 1984   A federal statute that permits the SEC to obtain a civil penalty of up to three times the illegal benefits received from insider trading. [813]

installment contract   A contract that requires or authorizes the goods to be delivered and accepted in separate lots. [410]

instrument   Term that means *negotiable instrument*. [460]

insurable interest   A person who purchases insurance must have a personal interest in the insured item or person. [959]

insurance   A means for persons and businesses to protect themselves against the risk of loss. [959]

insured   The party who pays a premium to a particular insurance company for insurance coverage. [959]

insurer   The insurance company. [959]

intangible property   Rights that cannot be reduced to physical form such as stock certificates, certificates of deposit, bonds, and copyrights. [911]

integration   The combination of several writings to form a single contract. [270]

integration of offerings   When separate offerings that might otherwise qualify for individual exemptions are combined if they are really part of one large offering. [804]

intellectual property rights   Intellectual property rights, such as patents, copyrights, trademarks, trade secrets, trade names, and domain names are very valuable business assets. Federal and state laws protect intellectual property rights from misappropriation and infringement. [323]

intended beneficiary   A third party who is not in privity of contract but who has rights under the contract and can enforce the contract against the obligor. [285]

intentional infliction of emotional distress   A tort that says a person whose extreme and outrageous conduct intentionally or recklessly causes severe emotional distress to another person is liable for that emotional distress. Also known as the *tort of outrage*. [95]

intentional interference with contractual relations   A tort that arises when a third party induces a contracting party to breach the contract with another party. [109, 311]

intentional misrepresentation   Intentionally defrauding another person out of money, property, or something else of value. [108]; Occurs when one person consciously induces another person to rely and act on a misrepresentation. Also called *fraud*. [259]; When a seller or lessor fraudulently misrepresents the quality of a product and a buyer is injured thereby. [440]; Occurs when an agent makes an untrue statement that he or she knows is not true. [596]

intentional tort   A category of torts that requires that the defendant possessed the intent to do the act that caused the plaintiff's injuries. [91]; Occurs when a person has intentionally committed a wrong against (1) another person or his or her character, or (2) another person's property. [597]

intermediary bank   A bank in the collection process that is not the depository or payor bank. [519]

intermediate appellate court   An intermediate court that hears appeals from trial courts. [26]

intermediate scrutiny test   Test that is applied to classifications based on protected classes other than race (e.g., sex or age). [71]

International Court of Justice   The judicial branch of the United Nations that is located in The Hague, the Netherlands. Also called the *World Court*. [157]

international law   Law that governs affairs between nations and that regulates transactions between individuals and businesses of different countries. [152]

Internet   A collection of millions of computers that provide a network of electronic connections between computers [353]

interrogatories   Written questions submitted by one party to another party. The questions must be answered in writing within a stipulated time. [38]

interstate commerce   Commerce that moves between states or that affects commerce between states. [59]

intervention   The act of others to join as parties to an existing lawsuit. [36]

intoxicated person   A person who is under contractual incapacity because of ingestion of alcohol or drugs to the point of incompetence. [241]

in transit   A state in which goods are in the possession of a bailee or carrier and not in the hands of the buyer, seller, lessee, or lessor. [414]

intrastate offering exemption   An exemption from registration that permits local businesses to raise capital from local investors to be used in the local economy without the need to register with the SEC. [802]

invasion of the right to privacy   A tort that constitutes the violation of a person's right to live his or her life without being subjected to unwarranted and undesired publicity. [95]

involuntary petition   A petition filed by creditors of the debtor; alleges that the debtor is not paying his or her debts as they become due. [555]

issued shares   Shares that have been sold by the corporation. [732]

joint and several liability   Partners are *joint* and *severally liable* for tort liability of the partnership. This means that the plaintiff can sue one or more of the partners separately. If successful, the plaintiff can recover the entire amount of the judgment from any or all of the defendant-partners. [698]

joint liability   Partners are *jointly liable* for contracts and debts of the partnership. This means that a plaintiff must name the partnership and all of the partners as defendants. If successful, the plaintiff can recover the entire amount of the judgment from any or all of the partners. [697]

joint tenancy   A form of co-ownership that includes the right of survivorship. [934]

joint tenant   Co-owner in a joint tenancy. [934]

joint venture A voluntary association of two or more parties (natural persons, partnerships, corporations, or other legal entities) to conduct a single or isolated project with a limited duration. [669]

joint will A will that is executed by two or more testators. [974]

judgment on the underlying debt A right granted to a secured creditor to relinquish his or her security interest in the collateral and sue a defaulting debtor to recover the amount of the underlying debt. [542]

judicial branch The part of the government that consists of the Supreme Court and other federal courts. [55]

judicial decision A decision about an individual lawsuit issued by federal and state courts. [12]

judicial decisions and teachings The fourth source of international law, consisting of judicial decisions and writings of the most qualified legal scholars of the various nations involved in the dispute. [155]

judicial dissolution Occurs when a corporation is dissolved by a court proceeding instituted by the state. [736]

jurisdiction The authority of a court to hear a case. [32]

jurisprudence The philosophy or science of law. [5]

Kantian or duty ethics A moral theory that says that people owe moral duties that are based on universal rules, such as the categorical imperative "do unto others as you would have them do unto you." [182]

land The most common form of real property. Includes the land and buildings and other structures permanently attached to the land. [931]

land pollution Pollution of the land that is generally caused by hazardous waste being disposed of in an improper manner. [865]

land use control The collective term for the laws that regulate the possession, ownership, and use of real property. [949]

landlord The owner who transfers the leasehold. [944]

landlord–tenant relationship A relationship created when the owner of a freehold estate (landlord) transfers a right to exclusively and temporarily possess the owner's property to another (tenant). [944]

Lanham Trademark Act (as amended) Federal statute that (1) establishes the requirements for obtaining a federal mark and (2) protects marks from infringement. [339]

lapse of time An offer terminates when a stated time period expires. If no time is stated, an offer terminates after a reasonable time. [221]

larceny Taking another's personal property other than from his or her person or building. [127]

law That which must be obeyed and followed by citizens subject to sanctions or legal consequences; a body of rules of action or conduct prescribed by controlling authority, and having binding legal force. [4]

law court A court that developed and administered a uniform set of laws decreed by the kings and queens after William the Conqueror; legal procedure was emphasized over merits at this time. [7]

lease A transfer of the right to the possession and use of the named goods for a set term in return for certain consideration. [383]; A transfer of the right to the possession and use of the real property for a set term in return for certain consideration; the rental agreement between a landlord and a tenant. [944]

leasehold A tenant's interest in the property. [944]

legal insanity A state of contractual incapacity as determined by law. [240]

legally enforceable contract If one party fails to perform as promised, the other party can use the court system to enforce the contract and recover damages or other remedy. [201]

legislative branch The part of the government that consists of Congress (the Senate and the House of Representatives). [55]

lessee The person who acquires the right to possession and use of goods under a lease. [383]

lessor The person who transfers the right of possession and use of goods under the lease. [383]

libel A false statement that appears in a letter, newspaper, magazine, book, photograph, movie, video, and so on. [92]

license A contract that transfers limited rights in intellectual property and informational rights. [360]; Grants a person the right to enter upon another's property for a specified and usually short period of time. [941]

licensee The party who is granted limited rights in or access to intellectual property or informational rights owned by the licensor. [360]

licensing agreement Detailed and comprehensive written agreement

between the licensor and licensee that sets forth the express terms of their agreement. [361]

licensing statute Statute that requires a person or business to obtain a license from the government prior to engaging in a specified occupation or activity. [243]

licensor The owner of intellectual property or informational rights who transfers rights in the property or information to the licensee. [360]

licensor's damages If a licensee breaches a contract, the licensor may sue and recover monetary damages from the licensee caused by the breach. [369]

life estate An interest in the land for a person's lifetime; upon that person's death, the interest will be transferred to another party. [933]

limited-jurisdiction trial court A court that hears matters of a specialized or limited nature. [25]

limited liability Members are liable for the LLC's debts, obligations, and liabilities only to the extent of their capital contributions. [708]; Liability that shareholders have only to the extent of their capital contribution. Shareholders are generally not personally liable for debts and obligations of the corporation. [719, 763]

limited liability company (LLC) A hybrid form of business that has the attributes of both partnerships and corporations. [667, 706]

limited liability partnership (LLP) A special form of partnership where all partners are limited partners and there are no general partners. [667, 704]

limited partners Partners in a limited partnership who invest capital but do not participate in management and are not personally liable for partnership debts beyond their capital contribution. [701]

limited partnership A special form of partnership that is formed only if certain formalities are followed. It has both general and limited partners. [666, 700]

limited partnership agreement A document that sets forth the rights and duties of the general and limited parties, the terms and conditions regarding the operation, termination, and dissolution of the partnership, and so on. [702]

line of commerce Includes products or services that consumers use as substitutes. If an increase in the price of one product or service leads consumers to purchase another product or service, the two products are substitutes for each other. [890]

lineal descendants Children, grandchildren, great grandchildren, and so on of the testator. [971]

liquidated damages Damages that are specified in the contract rather than determined by the court. [305, 372]; Damages that will be paid upon a breach of contract and that are established in advance. [421]

liquidation preference The right to be paid a stated dollar amount if the corporation is dissolved and liquidated. [732]

litigation The process of bringing, maintaining, and defending a lawsuit. [35]

long-arm statute A statute that extends a state's jurisdiction to nonresidents who were not served a summons within the state. [33]

lost property When a property owner leaves property somewhere because of negligence, carelessness, or inadvertence. [916]

mail fraud The use of mail to defraud another person. [129]

main purpose or leading object exception If the main purpose of a transaction and an oral collateral contract is to provide pecuniary benefit to the guarantor, the collateral contract does not have to be in writing to be enforced. [267]

maker of a CD The bank (borrower). [463]

maker of a note The party who makes the promise to pay (borrower). [462]

manager-managed LLC An LLC that has designated in its articles of organization that it is a manager-managed LLC. [708]

Marine Protection, Research, and Sanctuaries Act A federal statute enacted in 1972 that extends environmental protection to the oceans. [862]

mark The collective name for trademarks, service marks, certification marks, and collective marks that all can be trademarked. [340]

market extension merger A merger between two companies in similar fields whose sales do not overlap. [892]

material alteration A partial defense against enforcement of a negotiable instrument by an HDC. An HDC can enforce an altered instrument in the original amount for which the drawer wrote the check. [498]

material breach A breach that occurs when a party renders inferior performance of his or her contractual duties. [302]

maximizing profits A theory of social responsibility that says a corporation owes

a duty to take actions that maximize profits for shareholders. [187]

mediation A form of ADR in which the parties choose a neutral third party to act as the mediator of the dispute. [45]

Medicinal Device Amendment to the FDCA An amendment enacted in 1976 that gives the FDA authority to regulate medicinal devices and equipment. [838]

meeting of the creditors A meeting of the creditors in a bankruptcy case that must occur not less than 10 days nor more than 30 days after the court grants an order for relief. [555]

meeting the competition defense A defense provided in Section 2(b) that says a seller may lawfully engage in price discrimination to meet a competitor's price. [896]

member An owner of an LLC. [708]

member-managed LLC An LLC that has not designated that it is a manager-managed LLC in its articles of organization. [708]

mens rea "Evil intent"—the possession of the requisite state of mind to commit a prohibited act. [123]

merchant A person who (1) deals in the goods of the kind involved in the transaction or (2) by his or her occupation holds himself or herself out as having knowledge or skill peculiar to the goods involved in the transaction. [383]

Merchant Court The separate set of courts established to administer the "law of merchants." [8]

merger Occurs when one corporation is absorbed into another corporation and ceases to exist. [778]

merger clause A clause in a contract that stipulates that it is a complete integration and the exclusive expression of the parties' agreement. Parol evidence may not be introduced to explain, alter, contradict, or add to the terms of the contract. [271]

midnight deadline The midnight of the next banking day following the banking day on which the bank received the on them check for collection. [520]

minor A person who has not reached the age of majority. [237]

minor breach A breach that occurs when a party renders substantial performance of his or her contractual duties. [302]

minor's duty of restoration As a general rule, a minor is obligated only to return the goods or property he or she has received from the adult in the condition it is in at the time of disaffirmance. [238]

mirror image rule States that for an acceptance to exist, the offeree must accept the terms as stated in the offer. [221]

misdemeanor A less serious crime; not inherently evil but prohibited by society. Many crimes against property are misdemeanors. [123]

mislaid property When an owner voluntarily places property somewhere and then inadvertently forgets it. [916]

misuse A defense that relieves a seller of product liability if the user abnormally misused the product. Products must be designed to protect against foreseeable misuse. [449]

mitigation A nonbreaching party is under a legal duty to avoid or reduce damages caused by a breach of contract. [307]

mixed sale A sale that involves the provision of a service and a good in the same transaction. [382]

mobile sources Sources of air pollution such as automobiles, trucks, buses, motorcycles, and airplanes. [857]

Model Business Corporation Act (MBCA) A model act drafted in 1950 that was intended to provide a uniform law for regulation of corporations. [720]

monetary damages An award of money. [303]

money A "medium of exchange authorized or adopted by a domestic or foreign government." [UCC 1-201(24)] [467]

monopoly power The power to control prices or exclude competition measured by the market share the defendant possesses in the relevant market. [889]

moral minimum A theory of social responsibility that says a corporation's duty is to make a profit while avoiding harm to others. [189]

mortgage An interest in real property given to a lender as security for the repayment of a loan. [265]; A collateral arrangement where a real property owner borrows money from a creditor who uses a deed as collateral for repayment of the loan. [532]

mortgagee The creditor in a mortgage transaction. [532]

mortgagor The owner-debtor in a mortgage transaction. [532]

motion for judgment on the pleadings Motion that alleges that if all the facts presented in the pleadings are taken as true, the party making the motion would win the lawsuit when the proper law is applied to these asserted facts. [39]

motion for summary judgment Motion that asserts that there are no factual disputes to be decided by the jury; if so, the judge can apply the proper law to the undisputed facts and decide the case without a jury. These motions are supported by affidavits, documents, and deposition testimony. [39]

motivation test A test to determine the liability of the principal; if the agent's motivation in committing the intentional tort is to promote the principal's business, then the principal is liable for any injury caused by the tort. [597]

mutual benefit bailment A bailment for the mutual benefit of the bailor and bailee. The bailee owes a *duty of ordinary care* to protect the bailed property. [920]

mutual mistake of fact A mistake made by both parties concerning a material fact that is important to the subject matter of the contract. [258]

mutual mistake of value A mistake that occurs if both parties know the object of the contract but are mistaken as to its value. [258]

mutual wills Occurs where two or more testators execute separate wills that leave their property to each other on the condition that the survivor leave the remaining property on his or her death as agreed by the testators. [974]

national courts The courts of individual nations. [165]

National Labor Relations Board (NLRB) A federal administrative agency that oversees union elections, prevents employers and unions from engaging in illegal and unfair labor practices, and enforces and interprets certain federal labor laws. [612]

necessaries of life A minor must pay the reasonable value of food, clothing, shelter, medical care, and other items considered necessary to the maintenance of life. [239]

negligence A tort related to defective products where the defendant has breached a duty of due care and caused harm to the plaintiff. [440]; Failure of a corporate director or officer to exercise the duty of care while conducting the corporation's business. [758]

negligence per se Tort where the violation of a statute or ordinance constitutes the breach of the duty of care. [102]

negligent infliction of emotional distress A tort that permits a person to recover for emotional distress caused by the defendant's negligent conduct. [101]

negotiable instrument A special form of contract that satisfies the requirements established by Article 3 of the UCC. Also

called commercial paper. [459]; Commercial paper that must meet these requirements: (1) be in writing, (2) be signed by the maker or drawer, (3) be an unconditional promise or order to pay, (4) state a fixed amount of money, (5) not require any undertaking in addition to the payment of money, (6) be payable on demand or at a definite time, and (7) be payable to order or to bearer. [464]

negotiation Transfer of a negotiable instrument by a person other than the issuer to a person who thereby becomes a *holder*. [470]

no evidence of forgery, alteration, or irregularity requirement A holder cannot become an HDC to an instrument that is apparently forged or altered or is so otherwise irregular or incomplete as to call into question its authenticity. [489]

Noise Control Act A federal statute enacted in 1972 that authorizes the EPA to establish noise standards for products sold in the United States. [870]

noise pollution Unwanted sound from planes, manufacturing plants, motor vehicles, construction equipment, stereos, and the like. [870]

nominal damages Damages awarded when the nonbreaching party sues the breaching party even though no financial loss has resulted from the breach; usually consists of $1 or some other small amount. [307]

nonattainment areas Regions that do not meet air quality standards. [858]

nonconforming uses Uses and buildings that already exist in the zoned area that are permitted to continue even though they do not fit within new zoning ordinances. [951]

nonnegotiable contract Fails to meet the requirements of a negotiable instrument and, therefore, is not subject to the provisions of UCC Article 3. [470]

nonpossessory interest When a person holds an interest in another person's property without actually owning any part of the property. [940]

nonprice vertical restraints Restraints of trade that are unlawful under Section 1 of the Sherman Act if their anticompetitive effects outweigh their procompetitive effects. [887]

nonprofit corporation A corporation that is formed to operate charitable institutions, colleges, universities, and other not-for-profit entities. [721]

nonrestrictive indorsement An indorsement that has no instructions or

conditions attached to the payment of the funds. [474]

note A debt security with a maturity of five years or less. [733]

note and deed of trust An alternative to a mortgage in some states. [532]

notice of dishonor The formal act of letting the party with secondary liability to pay a negotiable instrument know that the instrument has been dishonored. [494]

novation An agreement that substitutes a new party for one of the original contracting parties and relieves the exiting party of liability on the contract. [291]

Nuclear Regulatory Commission (NRC) Federal agency that licenses the construction and opening of commercial nuclear power plants. [867]

Nuclear Waste Policy Act of 1982 A federal statute that says the federal government must select and develop a permanent site for the disposal of nuclear waste. [867]

nuncupative will Oral will that is made before a witness during the testator's last illness. Also called a dying declaration or deathbed will. [974]

objective theory of contracts A theory that says the intent to contract is judged by the reasonable person standard and not by the subjective intent of the parties. [206, 215]

obligation An action a party to a sales or lease contract is required by law to carry out. [407]

obscene speech Speech that (1) appeals to the prurient interest, (2) depicts sexual conduct in a patently offensive way, and (3) lacks serious literary, artistic, political, or scientific value. [67]

Occupational Safety and Health Act A federal act enacted in 1970 that promotes safety in the workplace. [622]

offensive speech Speech that is offensive to many members of society. It is subject to time, place, and manner restrictions. [65]

offer The manifestation of willingness to enter into a bargain, so made as to justify another person in understanding that his assent to that bargain is invited and will conclude it. (Section 24 of Restatement (Second) of Contracts) [215]

offeree The party to whom an offer to enter into a contract is made. [201, 215]

offeror The party who makes an offer to enter into a contract. [201, 215]

officers Employees of the corporation who are appointed by the board of directors to manage the day-to-day operations of the corporation. [755]

"on them" item A check presented for payment by the payee or holder where the depository bank and the payor bank are not the same bank. [520]

"on us" item A check that is presented for payment where the depository bank is also the payor bank. That is, the drawer and payee or holder have accounts at the same bank. [520]

one-year "on sale" doctrine A doctrine that says a patent may not be granted if the invention was used by the public for more than one year prior to the filing of the patent application. [327]

one-year rule An executory contract that cannot be performed by its own terms within one year of its formation must be in writing. [266]

operating agreement An agreement entered into among members that governs the affairs and business of the LLC and the relations among members, managers, and the LLC. [707]

order Decision issued by an administrative law judge. [834]

order for relief The filing of either a voluntary petition, an unchallenged involuntary petition, or a grant of an order after a trial of a challenged involuntary petition. [555]

order paper Order paper is negotiated by (1) *delivery* and (2) *indorsement*. [470]

order to pay A drawer's unconditional order to a drawee to pay a payee. [466]

ordinances Laws enacted by local government bodies such as cities and municipalities, counties, school districts, and water districts. [11]

ordinary bailments (1) Bailments for the sole benefit of the bailor, (2) bailments for the sole benefit of the bailee, and (3) bailments for the mutual benefit of the bailor and bailee. [920]

organizational meeting A meeting that must be held by the initial directors of the corporation after the articles of incorporation are filed. [727]

original tenor The original amount for which the drawer wrote the check. [517]

outside director A member of the board of directors who is not an officer of the corporation. [752]

outstanding shares Shares of stock that are in shareholder hands. [732]

overdraft The amount of money a drawer owes a bank after it has paid a check despite insufficient funds in the drawer's account. [516]

pac-man tender offer Occurs when a corporation that is the target of a tender offer makes a *reverse tender offer* for the stock of the tender offeror. [785]

palming off Unfair competition that occurs when a company tries to pass one of its products as that of a rival. [107]

panel A panel of three WTO judges that hears trade disputes between member nations and issues a "panel report." [163]

parol evidence Any oral or written words outside the four corners of the written contract. [271]

parol evidence rule A rule that says if a written contract is a complete and final statement of the parties' agreement, any prior or contemporaneous oral or written statements that alter, contradict, or are in addition to the terms of the written contract are inadmissible in court regarding a dispute over the contract. [271, 388]

participating preferred stock Stock that allows the stockholder to participate in the profits of the corporation along with the common stockholders. [732]

partnership at will A partnership with no fixed duration. [699]

partnership for a term A partnership with a fixed duration. [699]

part performance A doctrine that allows the court to order an oral contract for the sale of land or transfer of another interest in real property to be specifically performed if it has been partially performed and performance is necessary to avoid injustice. [165]

past consideration A prior act or performance. Past consideration (e.g., prior acts) will not support a new contract. New consideration must be given. [226]

patent infringement Unauthorized use of another's patent. A patent holder may recover damages and other remedies against a patent infringer. [326]

payable on demand or at a definite time requirement A negotiable instrument must be payable either *on demand or at a definite time.* [468]

payee of a CD The depositor (lender). [463]

payee of a check The party to whom the check is written. [461]

payee of a draft The party who receives the money from a draft. [460]

payee of a note The party to whom the promise to pay is made (lender). [462]

payor bank The bank where the drawer has a checking account and on which the check is drawn. [518]

penal codes A collection of criminal statutes. [122]

per capita A distribution of the estate that makes each grandchild and great grandchild of the deceased inherit equally with the children of the deceased. [971]

perfect tender rule A rule that says if the goods or tender of a delivery fails in any respect to conform to the contract, the buyer may opt either (1) to reject the whole shipment, (2) to accept the whole shipment, or (3) to reject part and accept part of the shipment. [408]

perfection by possession of the collateral If a secured creditor has physical possession of the collateral, no financing statement has to be filed; the creditor's possession is sufficient to put other potential creditors on notice of his or her secured interest in the property. [536]

perfection of a security interest Establishes the right of a secured creditor against other creditors who claim an interest in the collateral. [535]

periodic tenancy A tenancy created when a lease specifies intervals at which payments are due but does not specify how long the lease is for. [944]

permanency requirement A requirement of negotiable instruments that says they must be in a permanent state, such as written on ordinary paper. [464]

permanent trustee A legal representative of the bankruptcy debtor's estate, usually an accountant or lawyer; elected at the first meeting of the creditors. [557]

per se rule A rule that is applicable to those restraints of trade considered inherently anticompetitive. Once this determination is made, the court will not permit any defenses or justifications to save it. [880]

personal defense A defense that can be raised against enforcement of a negotiable instrument by an ordinary holder but not against an HDC. [498]

personal property Property that consists of tangible property such as automobiles, furniture, and jewelry; intangible property such as securities, patents, and copyrights; and instruments, chattel paper, documents of title, and accounts. [534]; Property that consists of tangible property such as automobiles, furniture, and jewelry, and intangible property such as securities, patents, and copyrights. [911]

personal satisfaction test Subjective test that applies to contracts involving personal taste and comfort. [289]

per stirpes A distribution of the estate that makes grandchildren and great grandchildren of the deceased inherit by representation of their parent. [971]

petition A document filed with the bankruptcy court that sets the bankruptcy proceedings into motion. [555]

petition for certiorari A petition asking the Supreme Court to hear one's case. [29]

physical or mental examination A court may order another party to submit to a physical or mental examination prior to trial. [38]

picketing The action of strikers walking in front of the employer's premises carrying signs announcing their strike. [618]

piercing the corporate veil A doctrine that says if a shareholder dominates a corporation and uses it for improper purposes, a court of equity can disregard the corporate entity and hold the shareholder personally liable for the corporation's debts and obligations. [763]

plaintiff The party who files the complaint. [35]

plan of reorganization A plan that sets forth a proposed new capital structure for the debtor to have when it emerges from reorganization bankruptcy. The debtor has the exclusive right to file the first plan of reorganization; any party of interest may file a plan thereafter. [567]

plant life and vegetation Real property that is growing in or on the surface of the land. [932]

pleadings The paperwork that is filed with the court to initiate and respond to a lawsuit. [35]

plea bargain When the accused admits to a lesser crime than charged. In return, the government agrees to impose a lesser sentence than might have been obtained had the case gone to trial. [126]

point sources Sources of water pollution such as paper mills, manufacturing plants, electric utility plants, and sewage plants. [860]

police power The power of states to regulate private and business activity within their borders. [61]; Constitutional authority of state and local governments to enact laws to protect the public health, safety, morals, and welfare. [950]

policy The insurance contract. [959]

portability requirement A requirement of negotiable instruments that says they must be able to be easily transported between areas. [465]

possession A lease grants the tenant *exclusive possession* of the leased premises for the term of the lease or until the tenant defaults on the obligations under the lease. [945]

possessory lien Lien obtained by a bailee on bailed property for the compensation owed by the bailor to the bailee. [921]

Postal Reorganization Act An act that makes the mailing of unsolicited merchandise an unfair trade practice. [843]

posteffective period The period of time that begins when the registration statement becomes effective and runs until the issuer either sells all of the offered securities or withdraws them from sale. [800]

potential competition theory A theory that reasons that the real or implied threat of increased competition keeps businesses more competitive. A merger that would eliminate this perception can be enjoined under Section 7. [893]

potential reciprocity theory A theory that says if Company A, which supplies materials to Company B, merges with Company C (which in turn gets its supplies from Company B), the newly merged company can coerce Company B into dealing exclusively with it. [893]

power of attorney An express agency agreement that is often used to give an agent the power to sign legal documents on behalf of the principal. [586]

precedent A rule of law established in a court decision. Lower courts must follow the precedent established by higher courts. [12]

preemption doctrine The concept that federal law takes precedence over state or local law. [56]

preemptive rights Rights that give existing shareholders the option of subscribing to new shares being issued in proportion to their current ownership interest. [750]

preexisting duty A promise lacks consideration if a person promises to perform an act or do something he or she is already under an obligation to do. [226]

preferential lien Occurs when (1) a debtor gives an unsecured creditor a secured interest in property within 90 days before the filing of a petition in bankruptcy, (2) the transfer is made for a preexisting debt, and (3) the creditor would receive more because of this lien than it would as an unsecured creditor. [561]

preferential transfer Occurs when (1) a debtor transfers property to a creditor within 90 days before the filing of a petition in bankruptcy, (2) the transfer is made for a preexisting debt, and (3) the creditor would receive more from the

transfer than it would from Chapter 7 liquidation. [561]

preferential transfer to an insider A transfer of property by an insolvent debtor to an "insider" within one year before the filing of a petition in bankruptcy. [561]

preferred stock A type of equity security that is given certain preferences and rights over common stock. [731]

preferred stock certificate A document that represents a shareholder's investment in preferred stock in the corporation. [731]

preferred stockholder A person who owns preferred stock. [731]

prefiling period A period of time that begins when the issuer first contemplates issuing the securities and ends when the registration statement is filed. The issuer may not condition the market during this period. [800]

Pregnancy Discrimination Act Amendment to Title VII that forbids employment discrimination because of "pregnancy, childbirth, or related medical conditions." [640]

premium The money paid to the insurance company for insurance coverage. [959]

prenuptial agreement A contract entered into by parties prior to marriage that defines their ownership rights in each other's property; must be in writing. [268]

presentment A demand for acceptance or payment of an instrument made upon the maker, acceptor, drawee, or other payor by or on behalf of the holder. [494]

presentment across the counter When a depository physically presents the check for payment at the payor bank instead of depositing an on them check for collection. [520]

presentment warranties Any person who presents a draft or check for payment or acceptance makes the following three warranties to a drawee or acceptor who pays or accepts the instrument in good faith: (1) The presenter has good title to the instrument or is authorized to obtain payment or acceptance of the person who has good title, (2) the instrument has not been materially altered, and (3) the presenter has no knowledge that the signature of the maker or drawer is unauthorized. [496]

presentment warranty Each prior transferor warrants that the check has not been altered. [517]

pretrial hearing   A hearing before the trial in order to facilitate the settlement of a case. Also called a settlement conference. [39]

pretrial motion   A motion a party can make to try to dispose of all or part of a lawsuit prior to trial. [39]

price-fixing   Occurs where competitors in the same line of business agree to set the price of the goods or services they sell: raising, depressing, fixing, pegging, or stabilizing the price of a commodity or service. [881]

primary liability   Absolute liability to pay a negotiable instrument, subject to certain real defenses. [492]

principal   A person who authorizes an agent to sign a negotiable instrument on his or her behalf. [491]; The party who employs another person to act on his or her behalf. [583]

principal–agent relationship   An employer hires an employee and gives that employee authority to act and enter into contracts on his or her behalf. [584]

priority   The order in which conflicting claims of creditors in the same collateral are solved. [539]

private corporation   A corporation formed to conduct privately owned business. [721]

private placement exemption   An exemption from registration that permits issuers to raise capital from an unlimited number of accredited investors and no more than 35 nonaccredited investors without having to register the offering with the SEC. [803]

Private Securities Litigation Reform Act of 1995   Provides a safe harbor from liability for companies that make forward-looking statements that are accompanied by meaningful cautionary statements of risk factors. [815]

Privileges and Immunities Clause   A clause that prohibits states from enacting laws that unduly discriminate in favor of their residents. [74]

privity of contract   The state of two specified parties being in contract. [281, 439]

probability of a substantial lessening of competition   If there is a probability that a merger will substantially lessen competition or create a monopoly, the court may prevent the merger under Section 7 of the Clayton Act. [891]

procedural due process   Requires that the government must give a person proper notice and hearing of the legal action before that person is deprived of his or her life, liberty, or property. [73]

process of certification   The accepting bank writes or stamps the word certified on the ordinary check of an account holder and sets aside funds from that account to pay the check. [512]

processing plant franchise   The franchisor provides a secret formula or process to the franchisee, and the franchisee manufactures the product and distributes it to retail dealers. [673]

production of documents   Request by one party to another party to produce all documents relevant to the case prior to the trial. [38]

products liability   The liability of manufacturers, sellers, and others for the injuries caused by defective products. [431]

professional corporation   A corporation formed by lawyers, doctors, or other professionals. [721]

professional malpractice   The liability of a professional who breaches his or her duty of ordinary care. [102]

profit   Grants a person the right to remove something from another's real property. [941]

profit corporation   A corporation created to conduct a business for profit that can distribute profits to shareholders in the form of dividends. [721]

promise to pay   A maker's (borrower's) unconditional and affirmative undertaking to repay a debt to a payee (lender). [465]

promissory estoppel   An equitable doctrine that prevents the withdrawal of a promise by a promisor if it will adversely affect a promisee who has adjusted his or her position in justifiable reliance on the promise. [228]; An equitable doctrine that permits enforcement of oral contracts that should have been in writing. It is applied to avoid injustice. [268]

promissory note   A two-party negotiable instrument that is an unconditional written promise by one party to pay money to another party. [462]

promissory warranty   Stipulates that the facts will continue to be true throughout the duration of the policy. [966]

promoter   A person or persons who organize and start the corporation, negotiate and enter into contracts in advance of its formation, find the initial investors to finance the corporation, and so forth. [723]

promoter's contracts   A collective term for such things as leases, sales contracts, contracts to purchase property, and employment contracts entered into by promoters on behalf of the proposed corporation prior to its actual incorporation. [723]

proof of claim   A document required to be filed by unsecured creditors that states the amount of their claim against the debtor. [557]

proper dispatch   An acceptance must be properly addressed, packaged, and posted to fall within the mailbox rule. [223]

pro rata rule   A rule that says shares must be purchased on a pro rata basis if too many shares are tendered. [783]

prospectus   A written disclosure document that must be submitted to the SEC along with the registration statement and given to prospective purchasers of the securities. [799]

provisional credit   Occurs when a collecting bank gives credit to a check in the collection process prior to its final settlement. Provisional credits may be reversed if the check does not "clear." [519]

proximate cause or legal cause   A point along a chain of events caused by a negligent party after which this party is no longer legally responsible for the consequences of his or her actions. [100]

proxy   The written document that a shareholder signs authorizing another person to vote his or her shares at the shareholders' meetings in the event of the shareholder's absence. [747]

proxy card   A written document signed by a shareholder that authorizes another person to vote the shareholder's shares. [774]

proxy contest   When opposing factions of shareholders and managers solicit proxies from other shareholders, the side that receives the greatest number of votes wins the proxy contest. [775]

proxy statement   A document that fully describes (1) the matter for which the proxy is being solicited, (2) who is soliciting the proxy, and (3) any other pertinent information. [775]

public corporation   A corporation that has many shareholders and whose securities are traded on national stock exchanges. [667]; A corporation formed to meet a specific governmental or political purpose. [721]

publicly held corporation   A corporation that has many shareholders and whose securities are often traded on national stock exchanges. [721]

punitive damages   Damages that are awarded to punish the defendant, to deter the defendant from similar conduct in the future, and to set an example for others. [110, 312]

purchase money security interest An interest a creditor automatically obtains when it extends credit to a consumer to purchase consumer goods. [537]

purchasing property The most common method of acquiring title to personal property. [912]

qualified individual with a disability A person who (1) has a physical or mental impairment that substantially limits one or more of his or her major life activities, (2) has a record of such impairment, or (3) is regarded as having such impairment. [651]

quasi contract An equitable doctrine that permits the recovery of compensation even though no enforceable contract exists between the parties. [310]

quasi in rem jurisdiction Jurisdiction allowed a plaintiff who obtains a judgment in one state to try to collect the judgment by attaching property of the defendant located in another state. [33]

quasi- or implied-in-law contract An equitable doctrine whereby a court may award monetary damages to a plaintiff for providing work or services to a defendant even though no actual contract existed. The doctrine is intended to prevent unjust enrichment and unjust detriment. [207]

quorum The required number of shares that must be represented in person or by proxy to hold a shareholders' meeting. The RMBCA establishes a majority of outstanding shares as a quorum. [747]; The number of directors necessary to hold a board of directors' meeting or transact business of the board. [753]

Racketeer Influenced and Corrupt Organizations Act (RICO) Federal statute that authorizes civil lawsuits against defendants for engaging in a pattern of racketeering activities. [111]; A federal statute that provides for both criminal and civil penalties. [815]

radiation pollution Emissions from radioactive wastes that can cause injury and death to humans and other life and can cause severe damage to the environment. [867]

ratification The act of a minor after the minor has reached the age of majority by which he or she accepts a contract entered into when he or she was a minor. [238]; When a principal accepts an agent's unauthorized contract. [594]; The acceptance by a corporation of an unauthorized act of a corporate officer or agent. [755]

rational basis test Test that is applied to classifications not involving a suspect or protected class. [71]

Rawls's social contract A moral theory that says each person is presumed to have entered into a social contract with all others in society to obey moral rules that are necessary for people to live in peace and harmony. [183]

real defense A defense that can be raised against both holders and HDCs. [497]

real property The land itself as well as buildings, trees, soil, minerals, timber, plants, crops, and other things permanently affixed to the land. [264, 911, 931]

reasonable person test Objective test that applies to commercial contracts and contracts involving mechanical fitness. [289]

receiving stolen property A person (1) knowingly receives stolen property and (2) intends to deprive the rightful owner of that property. [127]

reclamation The right of a seller or lessor to demand the return of goods from the buyer or lessee under specified situations. [415]

record date A date specified in the corporate bylaws that determines whether a shareholder may vote at a shareholders' meeting. [747]; A date that determines whether a shareholder receives payment of a declared dividend. [754]

recording statute A state statute that requires the mortgage or deed of trust to be recorded in the county recorder's office of the county in which the real property is located. [939]

recovery of damages A seller or lessor may recover damages measured as the difference between the contract price (or rent) and the market price (or rent) at the time and place the goods were to be delivered, plus incidental damages, from a buyer or lessee who repudiates the contract or wrongfully rejects tendered goods. [416]

recovery of goods from an insolvent seller or lessor A buyer or lessee who has wholly or partially paid for goods before they are received may recover the goods from a seller or lessor who becomes insolvent within 10 days after receiving the first payment; the buyer or lessee must tender the remaining purchase price or rent due under the contract. [418]

recovery of lost profits If the recovery of damages would be inadequate to put the seller or lessor in as good a position as if the contract had been fully performed

by the buyer or lessee, the seller or lessor may recover lost profits, plus an allowance for overhead and incidental damages, from the buyer or lessee. [416]

recovery of the purchase price or rent A seller or lessor may recover the contracted-for purchase price or rent from the buyer or lessee if the buyer or lessee (1) fails to pay for accepted goods, (2) breaches the contract and the seller or lessor cannot dispose of the goods, or if (3) the goods are damaged or lost after the risk of loss passes to the buyer or lessee. [415]

red light doctrine A doctrine that says a holder cannot qualify as an HDC if he or she has notice of an unauthorized signature or an alteration of the instrument or any adverse claim against or defense to its payment. [489]

redeemable preferred stock Stock that permits the corporation to buy back the preferred stock at some future date. [732]

reformation An equitable doctrine that permits the court to rewrite a contract to express the parties' true intentions. [310]

registered agent A person or corporation that is empowered to accept service of process on behalf of the corporation. [727]

registration statement Document that an issuer of securities files with the SEC that contains required information about the issuer, the securities to be issued, and other relevant information. [799]

regular meeting A meeting held by the board of directors at the time and place established in the bylaws. [753]

Regulation A A regulation that permits the issuer to sell securities pursuant to a simplified registration process. [801]

regulatory statute A licensing statute enacted to protect the public. [243]

rejection Express words or conduct by the offeree that rejects an offer. Rejection terminates the offer. [220]

rejection of nonconforming goods If the goods or the seller's or lessor's tender of delivery fails to conform to the contract, the buyer or lessee may (1) reject the whole, (2) accept the whole, or (3) accept any commercial unit and reject the rest. [417]

relevant geographical market A relevant market that is defined as the area in which the defendant and its competitors sell the product or service. [888]

relevant product or service market A relevant market that includes substitute products or services that are reasonably interchangeable with the defendant's products or services. [888]

relief from stay   May be granted in situations involving depreciating assets where the secured property is not adequately protected during the bankruptcy proceedings; asked for by a secured creditor. [557]

religious discrimination   Discrimination against a person solely because of his or her religion or religious practices. [645]

remainder   If the right of possession returns to a third party upon the expiration of a limited or contingent estate. [933]

replacement workers   Workers who are hired to take the place of striking workers. They can be hired on either a temporary or permanent basis. [618]

replevin   An action by a buyer or lessor to recover scarce goods wrongfully withheld by a seller or lessor. [419]

reply   Filed by the original plaintiff to answer the defendant's cross-complaint. [36]

repossession   A right granted to a secured creditor to take possession of the collateral upon default by the debtor. [541]

res ipsa loquitur   Tort where the presumption of negligence arises because (1) the defendant was in exclusive control of the situation and (2) the plaintiff would not have suffered injury but for someone's negligence. The burden switches to the defendant(s) to prove they were not negligent. [103]

resale price maintenance   A *per se violation* of Section 1 of the Sherman Act; occurs when a party at one level of distribution enters into an agreement with a party at another level to adhere to a price schedule that either sets or stabilizes prices. [886]

rescission   An action to rescind (undo) the contract. Rescission is available if there has been a material breach of contract, fraud, duress, undue influence, or mistake. [257, 308]

residuary gift   Gift of the estate left after the debts, taxes, and specific and general gifts have been paid. [971]

Resource Conservation and Recovery Act (RCRA)   A federal statute that authorizes the EPA to regulate facilities that generate, treat, store, transport, and dispose of hazardous wastes. [865]

respondeat superior   A rule that says an employer is liable for the tortious conduct of its employees or agents while they are acting within the scope of its authority. [596]

Restatement of the Law of Contracts   A compilation of model contract law principles drafted by legal scholars. The Restatement is not law. [203]

restitution   Returning of goods or property received from the other party to rescind a contract; if the actual goods or property is not available, a cash equivalent must be made. [308]

restricted securities   Securities that were issued for investment purposes pursuant to the intrastate, private placement, or small offering exemption. [803]

restrictive covenant   A private agreement between landowners that restricts the use of their land. [950]

restrictive indorsement   An indorsement that contains some sort of instruction from the indorser. [474]

retained earnings   Profits retained by the corporation and not paid out as dividends. [754]

retention of collateral   If a secured creditor repossesses collateral upon a debtor's default, he or she may propose to retain the collateral in satisfaction of the debtor's obligation. [541]

revenue-raising statute   A licensing statute with the primary purpose of raising revenue for the government. [243]

reverse discrimination   Discrimination against a group that is usually thought of as a majority. [655]

reversion   A right of possession that returns to the grantor after the expiration of a limited or contingent estate. [933]

Revised Model Business Corporation Act (RMBCA)   A revision of the MBCA in 1984 that arranged the provisions of the act more logically, revised the language to be more consistent, and made substantial changes in the provisions. [720]

Revised Uniform Limited Partnership Act (RULPA)   A 1976 revision of the ULPA that provides a more modern, comprehensive law for the formation, operation, and dissolution of limited partnerships. [700]

revocation   Withdrawal of an offer by the offeror terminates the offer. [220]; Reversal of acceptance. [412]; Termination of a will. [969]

reward   To collect a reward, the offeree must (1) have knowledge of the reward offer prior to completing the requested act and (2) perform the requested act. [219]

rider   A separate document that will modify an existing insurance policy. [963]

right of first refusal agreement   An agreement that requires the selling shareholder to offer his or her shares for sale to the other parties to the agreement before selling them to anyone else. [749]

right of inspection   A right that shareholders have to inspect the books and records of the corporation. [750]

right of redemption   A right granted to a defaulting debtor or other secured creditor to recover the collateral from a secured creditor before he or she contracts to dispose of it or exercises his or her right to retain the collateral. Requires the redeeming party to pay the full amount of the debt and expenses caused by the debtor's default. [542]

right to cure   A licensor has the right to cure a contract under certain conditions. [370]

River and Harbor Act   A federal statute enacted in 1886 that established a permit system for the discharge of refuse, wastes, and sewage into U.S. navigable waterways. [860]

robbery   Taking personal property from another person by use of fear or force. [127]

rule of reason   A rule that holds that only unreasonable restraints of trade violate Section 1 of the Sherman Act. The court must examine the pro- and anticompetitive effects of the challenged restraint. [880]

rules and regulations   Adopted by administrative agencies to interpret the statutes that they are authorized to enforce. [829]

Rule 10b-5   A rule adopted by the SEC to clarify the reach of Section 10(b) against deceptive and fraudulent activities in the purchase and sale of securities. [809]

Sabbath law   A law that prohibits or limits the carrying on of certain secular activities on Sundays. [243]

Safe Drinking Water Act   A federal statute enacted in 1974 and amended in 1986 that authorizes the EPA to establish national primary drinking water standards. [861]

sale   The passing of title from a seller to a buyer for a price. [382]; Also called a *conveyance*. [936]

sale on approval   A type of sale in which there is no actual sale unless and until the buyer accepts the goods. [394]

sale or return   A contract that says that the seller delivers goods to a buyer with the understanding that the buyer may return them if they are not used or resold within a stated or reasonable period of time. [394]

sale proceeds The resulting assets from the sale, exchange, or disposal of collateral subject to a security agreement. [535]

satisfaction The performance of an accord. [227]

scienter Means international conduct. Scienter is required for there to be a violation of Section 10(b) and Rule 10b-5. [809]

search warrant A warrant issued by a court that authorizes the police to search a designated place for specified contraband, articles, items, or documents. The search warrant must be based on probable cause. [137]

secondary boycott picketing A type of picketing where unions try to bring pressure against an employer by picketing his or her suppliers or customers. [618]

secondary liability Liability on a negotiable instrument that is imposed on a party only when the party primarily liable on the instrument defaults and fails to pay the instrument when due. [493]

"secondary meaning" When an ordinary term has become a brand name. [339]

Section 1 of the Sherman Act Prohibits *contracts*, *combinations*, and *conspiracies* in restraint of trade. [880]; Prohibits tying arrangements involving goods, services, intangible property, and real property. [894]

Section 2 of the Sherman Act Prohibits the act of monopolization and attempts or conspiracies to monopolize trade. [888]

Section 2(a) of the Robinson-Patman Act Prohibits direct and indirect price discrimination by sellers of a commodity of a like grade and quality where the effect of such discrimination may be to substantially lessen competition or to tend to create a monopoly in any line of commerce. [896]

Section 2(b) of the Robinson-Patman Act A defense that provides that a seller may lawfully engage in price discrimination to meet a competitor's price. [896]

Section 3 of the Clayton Act Prohibits tying arrangements involving sales and leases of goods. [894]

Section 5 of the FTC Act Prohibits *unfair and deceptive* practices. [842]

Section 7 of the NLRA A law that gives employees the right to join together and form a union. [613]

Section 8(a) of the NLRA A law that makes it an unfair labor practice for an employer to interfere with, coerce, or restrain employees from exercising their statutory right to form and join unions. [614]

Section 8(b) of the NLRA A law that prohibits unions from engaging in unfair labor practices that interfere with a union election. [614]

Section 10(b) A provision of the Securities Exchange Act of 1934 that prohibits the use of manipulative and deceptive devices in the purchase or sale of securities in contravention of the rules and regulations prescribed by the SEC. [808]

Section 11 A provision of the Securities Act of 1933 that imposes civil liability on persons who intentionally defraud investors by making misrepresentations or omissions of material facts in the registration statement or who are negligent for not discovering the fraud. [806]

Section 12 A provision of the Securities Act of 1933 that imposes civil liability on any person who violates the provisions of Section 5 of the act. [805]

Section 14(a) Provision of the Securities Exchange Act of 1934 that gives the SEC the authority to regulate the solicitation of proxies. [775]

Section 14(e) A provision of the Williams Act that prohibits fraudulent, deceptive, and manipulative practices in connection with a tender offer. [783]

Section 16(a) A section of the Securities Exchange Act of 1934 that defines any person who is an executive officer, a director, or a 10 percent shareholder of an equity security of a reporting company as a *statutory insider* for Section 16 purposes. [814]

Section 16(b) A section of the Securities Exchange Act of 1934 that requires that any profits made by a statutory insider on transactions involving *short-swing profits* belong to the corporation. [814]

Section 24 A provision of the Securities Act of 1933 that imposes criminal liability on any person who willfully violates the 1933 act or the rules or regulations adopted thereunder. [805]

Section 32 A provision of the Securities Exchange Act of 1934 that imposes criminal liability on any person who willfully violates the 1934 act or the rules or regulations adopted thereunder. [812]

section of the country A division of the country that is based on the relevant geographical market; the geographical area that will feel the direct and immediate effects of the merger. [891]

secured credit Credit that requires security (collateral) that secures payment of the loan. [531]

secured transaction A transaction that is created when a creditor makes a loan to a debtor in exchange for the debtor's pledge of personal property as security. [532]

Securities Act of 1933 A federal statute that primarily regulates the issuance of securities by corporations, partnerships, associations, and individuals. [799]

Securities and Exchange Commission (SEC) Federal administrative agency that is empowered to administer federal securities laws. The SEC can adopt rules and regulations to interpret and implement federal securities laws. [798]

Securities Exchange Act of 1934 A federal statute that primarily regulates the trading in securities. [808]

security (1) An interest or instrument that is common stock, preferred stock, a bond, a debenture, or a warrant, (2) an interest or instrument that is expressly mentioned in securities acts, and (3) an investment contract. [798]

security agreement The agreement between the debtor and the secured party that creates or provides for a security interest. [533]

self-dealing If the directors or officers engage in purchasing, selling, or leasing of property with the corporation, the contract must be fair to the corporation; otherwise, it is voidable by the corporation. The contract or transaction is enforceable if it has been fully disclosed and approved. [762]

Self-Employment Contributions Act A federal act that says self-employed persons must pay Social Security taxes equal to the combined employer-employee amount. [627]

self-incrimination The Fifth Amendment states that no person shall be compelled in any criminal case to be a witness against him- or herself. [140]

service mark A mark that distinguishes the services of the holder from those of its competitors. [340]

service of process A summons is served on the defendant to obtain personal jurisdiction over him or her. [32]

settlor or trustor Person who creates a trust. [975]

sex discrimination Discrimination against a person solely because of his or her gender. [640]

sexual harassment Lewd remarks, touching, intimidation, posting pinups, and other verbal or physical conduct of a sexual nature that occur on the job. [640]

share exchange When one corporation acquires all the shares of another corporation and both corporations retain their separate legal existence. [779]

shareholder voting agreements Agreement between two or more shareholders agreeing on how they will vote their shares. [749]

shipment contract A contract that requires the seller to ship the goods to the buyer via a common carrier. [390]; The buyer bears the risk of loss during transportation. [392]; A sales contract that requires the seller to send the goods to the buyer, but not a specifically named destination. [408]

short-form merger A merger between a parent corporation and a subsidiary corporation that does not require the vote of the shareholders of either corporation or the board of directors of the subsidiary corporation. [779]

sight draft A draft payable on sight. Also called a *demand draft*. [460]

signature Any name, word, or mark used in lieu of a written signature; any symbol that is (1) handwritten, typed, printed, stamped, or made in almost any other manner and (2) executed or adopted by a party to authenticate a writing. [491]

signature liability A person cannot be held contractually liable on a negotiable instrument unless his or her signature appears on the instrument. Also called contract *liability*. [490]

signature requirement A negotiable instrument must be signed by the drawer or maker. Any symbol executed or adopted by a party with a present intent to authenticate a writing qualifies as his or her signature. [465]

signer A person signing an instrument who acts in the capacity of (1) a maker of notes and certificates of deposit, (2) a drawer of drafts and checks, (3) a drawee who certifies or accepts checks and drafts, (4) an indorser who indorses an instrument, (5) an agent who signs on behalf of others, or (6) an accommodation party. [490]

slander Oral defamation of character. [92]

small claims court A court that hears civil cases involving small dollar amounts. [25]

small offering exemption For the sale of securities not exceeding $1 million during a 12-month period. [803]

social host liability Rule that provides that social hosts are liable for injuries caused by guests who become intoxicated at a social function. States vary as to whether they have this rule in effect. [104]

social responsibility Duty owed by businesses to act socially responsible in producing and selling goods and services. [186]

Social Security Federal system that provides limited retirement and death benefits to covered employees and their dependents. [627]

sole proprietorship A form of business where the owner is actually the business; the business is not a separate legal entity. [666, 691]

sources of international law Those things that international tribunals rely on in settling international disputes. [153]

special bailees Includes common carriers, warehouse companies, and innkeepers. [922]

special federal courts Federal courts that hear matters of specialized or limited jurisdiction. [27]

special indorsement An indorsement that contains the signature of the indorser and specifies the person (indorsee) to whom the indorser intends the instrument to be payable. Creates *order paper*. [473]

special meeting A meeting convened by the board of directors to discuss new shares, merger proposals, hostile takeover attempts, and so forth. [753]

special shareholders' meetings Meetings of shareholders that may be called to consider and vote on important or emergency issues, such as a proposed merger or amending the articles of incorporation. [746]

specific duty An OSHA standard that addresses a safety problem of a specific duty nature (e.g., requirement for a safety guard on a particular type of equipment). [623]

specific performance A remedy that orders the breaching party to perform the acts promised in the contract; usually awarded in cases where the subject matter is unique, such as in contracts involving land, heirlooms, and paintings. [309]; Judgment of the court ordering a licensor to specifically perform the license by making the contracted-for unique information available to the licensee. [370]; A decree of the court that orders a seller or lessor to perform his or her obligations under the contract;

usually occurs when the goods in question are unique, such as art or antiques. [418]

stakeholder interest A theory of social responsibility that says a corporation must consider the effects its actions have on persons other than its stockholders. [190]

stale check A check that has been outstanding for more than six months. [515]

standing to sue The plaintiff must have some stake in the outcome of the lawsuit. [32]

stare decisis Latin: "To stand by the decision." Adherence to precedent. [12]

state action exemptions Business activities that are mandated by state law are exempt from federal antitrust laws. [898]

state administrative agencies Administrative agencies that states create to enforce and interpret state law. [829]

state antitakeover statutes Statutes enacted by state legislatures that protect corporations incorporated in or doing business in the state from hostile takeovers. [787]

state supreme court The highest court in a state court system; it hears appeals from intermediate state courts and certain trail courts. [26]

stationary sources Sources of air pollution such as industrial plants, oil refineries, and public utilities. [857]

statute Written law enacted by the legislative branch of the federal and state governments that establishes certain courses of conduct that must be adhered to by covered parties. [10]

Statute of Frauds State statute that requires certain types of contracts to be in writing. [263]

statute of limitations A statute that establishes the period during which a plaintiff must bring a lawsuit against a defendant. [37]; Statute that establishes the time period during which a lawsuit must be brought; if the lawsuit is not brought within this period, the injured party loses the right to sue. [293]; A statute that requires an injured person to bring an action within a certain number of years from the time that he or she was injured by the defective product. [449]

statute of repose A statute that limits the seller's liability to a certain number of years from the date when the product was first sold. [449]

Statute of Wills A state statute that establishes the requirements for making a valid will. [967]

statutory exemptions Exemptions from antitrust laws that are expressly provided in statutes enacted by Congress. [897]

stock dividend Additional shares of stock paid as a dividend. [754]

stop-payment order An order by a drawer of a check to the payor bank not to pay or certify a check. [516]

stopping delivery of goods in transit A seller or lessor may stop delivery of goods in transit if he or she learns of the buyer's or lessee's insolvency or if the buyer or lessee repudiates the contract, fails to make payment when due, or gives the seller or lessor some other right to withhold the goods. [414]

straight voting Each shareholder votes the number of shares he or she owns on candidates for each of the positions open. [747]

strict liability Liability without fault. [111]

strict or absolute liability Standard for imposing criminal liability without a finding of *mens rea* (intent). [123]

strict scrutiny test Test that is applied to classifications based on race. [71]

strike A cessation of work by union members in order to obtain economic benefits or correct an unfair labor practice. [618]

subject matter jurisdiction Jurisdiction over the subject matter of a lawsuit. [32]

sublease When a tenant transfers only some of his or her rights under the lease. [948]

sublessee The new tenant in a sublease situation. [948]

sublessor The original tenant in a sublease situation. [948]

subrogation If an insurance company pays a claim to an insured for liability or property damage caused by a third party, the insurer succeeds to the right of the insured to recover from the third party. [963]

substantial performance Performance by a contracting party that deviates only slightly from complete performance. [302]

substantive due process Requires that government statutes, ordinances, regulations, or other laws be clear on their face and not overly broad in scope. [72]

substantive rules Government regulation that has the force of law and must be adhered to by covered persons and businesses. [830]

subsurface rights Rights to the earth located beneath the surface of the land. [932]

summons A court order directing the defendant to appear in court and answer the complaint. [35]

superseding event A defendant is not liable for injuries caused by a superseding or intervening event for which he or she is not responsible. [105]

supervening event An alteration or modification of a product by a party in the chain of distribution that absolves all prior sellers from strict liability. [448]

supervening illegality The enactment of a statute, regulation, or court decision that makes the object of an offer illegal. This action terminates the offer. [221]

supramajority voting requirement A requirement that a greater than majority of shares constitutes a quorum of the vote of the shareholders. [749]

Supremacy Clause A clause of the U.S. Constitution that establishes that the federal Constitution, treaties, federal laws, and federal regulations are the supreme law of the land. [56]

surety The third person who agrees to be liable in a surety arrangement. [543]

surety arrangement An arrangement where a third party promises to be *primarily* liable with the borrower for the payment of the borrower's debt. [543]

surface right The right of a landowner to use, enjoy, develop, or otherwise occupy the land as he or she sees fit, subject to any applicable government regulation. [931]

syndicate A group of individuals who join together to finance a project or transaction. [670]

taking for value requirement A holder must *give value* for the negotiable instrument to qualify as an HDC. [488]

taking in good faith requirement A holder must take the instrument in good faith to qualify as an HDC. [488]

taking possession A method of acquiring ownership of unowned personal property. [912]

taking without notice of defect requirement A person cannot qualify as an HDC if he or she has notice that the instrument is defective in certain ways. [489]

tangible property All real property and physically defined personal property such as buildings, goods, animals, and minerals. [911]

target corporation The corporation that is proposed to be acquired in a tender offer situation. [781]

tax sale A method of transferring property ownership that involves a lien on

property for unpaid property taxes. If the lien remains unpaid after a certain amount of time, a tax sale is held to satisfy the lien. [937]

tenancy at sufferance A tenancy created when a tenant retains possession of property after the expiration of another tenancy or a life estate without the owner's consent. [945]

tenancy at will A lease that may be terminated at any time by either party. [944]

tenancy by the entirety A form of co-ownership of real property that can be used only by married couples. [934]

tenancy for years A tenancy created when the landlord and tenant agree on a specific duration for the lease. [944]

tenancy in common A form of co-ownership where the interest of a surviving tenant-in-common passes to the deceased tenant's estate and not to the cotenants. [934]

tenant The party to whom the leasehold is transferred. [944]

tender of delivery The obligation of the seller to transfer and deliver goods to the buyer in accordance with the sales contract. [407]

tender offer An offer that an acquirer makes directly to a target corporation's shareholders in an effort to acquire the target corporation. [781]

tender offeror The party that makes a tender offer. [781]

tender of performance Tender is an unconditional and absolute offer by a contracting party to perform his or her obligations under the contract. [301]; Occurs when a party who has the ability and willingness to perform offers to complete the performance of his or her duties under the contract. [364]

termination The ending of a corporation that occurs only after the winding-up of the corporation's affairs, the liquidation of its assets, and the distribution of the proceeds to the claimants. [736]

termination by acts of the parties An agency may be terminated by the following acts of the parties: (1) mutual agreement, (2) lapse of time, (3) purpose achieved, and (4) occurrence of a specified event. [600]

termination by operation of law An agency is terminated by operation of law, including: (1) death of the principal or agent, (2) insanity of the principal or agent, (3) bankruptcy of the principal, (4) impossibility of performance, (5) changed circumstances, and (6) war between the principal's and agent's countries. [601]

termination statement   A document filed by the secured party that ends a secured interest because the debt has been paid. [539]

testator   The person who makes a will. [967]

thermal pollution   Heated water or material discharged into waterways that upsets the ecological balance and decreases the oxygen content. [861]

time draft   A draft payable at a designated future date. [460]

time instrument   An instrument payable (1) at a fixed date, (2) on or before a stated date, (3) at a fixed period after sight, or (4) at a time readily ascertainable when the promise or order is issued. [468, 489]

time note   A note payable at a specific time. [462]

tippee   The person who receives material nonpublic information from a tipper. [812]

tipper   A person who discloses material nonpublic information to another person. [812]

title   Legal, tangible evidence of ownership of goods. [390]

Title I of the Landrum-Griffin Act   Referred to as labor's "bill of rights" that gives each union member equal rights and privileges to nominate candidates for union office, vote in elections, and participate in membership meetings. [619]

Title VII of the Civil Rights Act of 1964 (Fair Employment Practices Act)   Intended to eliminate job discrimination based on five protected classes: *race, color, religion, sex,* or *national origin.* [637]

tort   A wrong. There are three categories: (1) intentional torts, (2) unintentional torts (negligence), and (3) strict liability. [91]

tort of misappropriation of the right to publicity   An attempt by another person to appropriate a living person's name or identity for commercial purposes. [93]

toxic air pollutants   Air pollutants that cause serious illness or death to humans. [859]

toxic substances   Chemicals used for agricultural, industrial, and mining uses that cause injury to humans, birds, animals, fish, and vegetation. [863]

Toxic Substances Control Act   A federal statute enacted in 1976 that requires manufacturers and processors to test new chemicals to determine their effect on human health and the environment before the EPA will allow them to be marketed. [864]

trade acceptance   A sight draft that arises when credit is extended (by a seller to a buyer) with the sale of goods. The seller is both the drawer and the payee, and the buyer is the drawee. [460]

trademark   A distinctive mark, symbol, name, word, motto, or device that identifies the goods of a particular business. [340]

trademark infringement   Unauthorized use of another's mark. The holder may recover damages and other remedies from the infringer. [341]

trademarks and service marks   A distinctive mark, symbol, name, word, motto, or device that identifies the goods or services of a particular franchisor. [678]

trade secret   A product formula, pattern, design, compilation of data, customer list, or other business secret. [323]; An idea that makes a franchise successful but that does not qualify for trademark, patent, or copyright protection. [679]

transfer   Any passage of an instrument other than its issuance and presentment for payment. [496]

transfer warranties   Any of the following five implied warranties: (1) The transferor has good title to the instrument or is authorized to obtain payment or acceptance on behalf of one who does have good title; (2) all signatures are genuine or authorized; (3) the instrument has not been materially altered; (4) no defenses of any party are good against the transferor; and (5) the transferor has no knowledge of any insolvency proceeding against the maker, or acceptor, or the drawer of an unaccepted instrument. [496]

treasury shares   Shares of stock repurchased by the company itself. [513, 732]

treaties   The first source of international law, consisting of agreements or contracts between two or more nations that are formally signed by an authorized representative and ratified by the supreme power of each nation. [154]

treaty   A compact made between two or more nations. [10]

Treaty Clause   Clause of the U.S. Constitution that states the president "shall have the power ... to make treaties, provided two-thirds of the senators present concur." [152]

treble damages   Civil damages three times actual damages may be awarded to persons whose business or property is injured by a RICO violation. [111]

trespass to land   A tort that interferes with an owner's right to exclusive possession of land. [96]

trespass to personal property   A tort that occurs whenever one person injures another person's personal property or interferes with that person's enjoyment of his or her personal property. [96]

trial briefs   Documents submitted by the parties' attorneys to the judge that contain legal support for their side of the case. [40]

trier of fact   The jury in a jury trial; the judge where there is not a jury trial. [40]

trust   Established when a person (trustor) transfers title to property to another person (trustee) to be managed for the benefit of specifically named persons (beneficiaries). [670]; A legal arrangement established when one person transfers title to property to another person to be held and used for the benefit of a third person. [975]

trust corpus   The property held in trust. [975]

trustee   Person who holds legal title to the trust corpus and manages the trust for the benefit of the beneficiary or beneficiaries. [975]

tying arrangement   A restraint of trade where a seller refuses to sell one product to a customer unless the customer agrees to purchase a second product from the seller. [894]

UCC Statute of Frauds   A rule that requires all contracts for the sale of goods costing $500 or more and lease contracts involving payments of $1,000 or more to be in writing. [268, 387]

UCC statute of limitations   A rule that provides that an action for breach of any written or oral sales or lease contract must commence within four years after the cause of action accrues. The parties may agree to reduce the limitations period to one year. [420, 439]

***ultra vires* act**   An act by a corporation that is beyond its express or implied powers. [735]

unauthorized signature   A signature made by a purported agent without authority from the purported principal. [492]

unconditional   Promises to pay and orders to pay must be unconditional in order for them to be negotiable. [466]

unconditional promise or order to pay requirement   A negotiable instrument must contain either an *unconditional promise to pay* (note or CD) or an *unconditional order to pay* (draft or check). [465]

undue influence   Occurs when one person takes advantage of another person's mental, emotional, or physical weakness and unduly persuades that person to enter into a contract; the persuasion by the wrongdoer must overcome the free will of the innocent party or testator. [261, 969]

unenforceable contract A contract where the essential elements to create a valid contract are met, but there is some legal defense to the enforcement of the contract. [208]

unfair advantage theory A theory that holds that a merger may not give the acquiring firm an unfair advantage over its competitors in finance, marketing, or expertise. [893]

unfair competition Competition that violates the law. [107]

Uniform Commercial Code Comprehensive statutory scheme that includes laws that cover aspects of commercial transactions. [203, 381]

Uniform Computer Information Transactions Act (UCITA) Model state law that creates contract law for the licensing of information technology rights. [353, 361]

Uniform Franchise Offering Circular (UFOC) A uniform disclosure document that requires the franchisor to make specific presale disclosures to prospective franchisees. [674]

Uniform Gift to Minors Act and Revised Uniform Gift to Minors Act Acts that establish procedures for adults to make gifts of money and securities to minors. [914]

Uniform Limited Liability Company Act (ULLCA) A model act that provides comprehensive and uniform laws for the formation, operation, and dissolution of LLCs. [706]

Uniform Partnership Act (UPA) Model act that codifies partnership law. Most states have adopted the UPA in whole or part. [693]

Uniform Simultaneous Death Act An act that provides that if people who would inherit property from each other die simultaneously, each person's property is distributed as though he or she survived. [969]

unilateral contract A contract in which the offeror's offer can be accepted only by the performance of an act by the offeree; a "promise for an act." [204]

unilateral mistake When only one party is mistaken about a material fact regarding the subject matter of the contract. [257]

unilateral refusal to deal A unilateral choice by one party not to deal with

another party. This does not violate Section 1 of the Sherman Act because there is not concerted action. [887]

unintentional tort or negligence A doctrine that says a person is liable for harm that is the foreseeable consequence of his or her actions. [97]

union shop An establishment where an employee must join the union within a certain number of days after being hired. [616]

United Nations An international organization created by multilateral treaty in 1945 to promote social and economic cooperation among nations and to protect human rights. [155]

unprotected speech Speech that is not protected by the First Amendment and may be forbidden by the government. [67]

unqualified indorsement An indorsement whereby the indorser promises to pay the holder or any subsequent indorser the amount of the instrument if the maker, drawer, or acceptor defaults on it. [473]

unqualified indorser An indorser who signs an *unqualified indorsement* to an instrument. [473]

unreasonable search and seizure Any search and seizure by the government that violates the Fourth Amendment. [137, 831]

unsecured credit Credit that does not require any security (collateral) to protect the payment of the debt. [531]

U.S. Constitution The fundamental law of the United States of America. It was ratified by the states in 1788. [55]

U.S. courts of appeals The federal court system's intermediate appellate courts. [27]

U.S. district courts The federal court system's trial courts of general jurisdiction. [27]

U.S. Supreme Court The Supreme Court was created by Article III of the U.S. Constitution. The Supreme Court is the highest court in the land. It is located in Washington, DC. [28]

usurping a corporate opportunity A director or officer steals a corporate opportunity for him- or herself. [762]

usury law A law that sets an upper limit on the interest rate that can be charged on certain types of loans. [242]

utilitarianism A moral theory that dictates that people must choose the action or follow the rule that provides the greatest good to society. [181]

valid contract A contract that meets all of the essential elements to establish a

contract; a contract that is enforceable by at least one of the parties. [208]

variance An exception that permits a type of building or use in an area that would not otherwise be allowed by a zoning ordinance. [951]

venue A concept that requires lawsuits to be heard by the court with jurisdiction that is nearest the location in which the incident occurred or where the parties reside. [34]

vertical merger A merger that integrates the operations of a supplier and a customer. [892]

vertical restraint of trade A restraint of trade that occurs when two or more parties on *different levels of distribution* enter into a contract, combination, or conspiracy to restrain trade. [885]

violation A crime that is neither a felony nor a misdemeanor that is usually punishable by a fine. [123]

voidable contract A contract where one or both parties have the option to avoid their contractual obligations. If a contract is avoided, both parties are released from their contractual obligations. [208]

voidable title Title that a purchase has if the goods were obtained by (1) fraud, (2) a check that is later dishonored, or (3) impersonating another person. [396]

voidable transfer An unusual payment or transfer of property by the debtor on the eve of bankruptcy that would unfairly benefit the debtor or some creditors at the expense of other creditors. Such transfer may be avoided by the bankruptcy court. [561]

void contract A contract that has no legal effect; a nullity. [208]

void title A thief acquires no title to the goods he or she steals. [396]

voluntary dissolution A corporation that has begun business or issued shares can be dissolved upon recommendation of the board of directors and a majority vote of the shares entitled to vote. [736]

voluntary petition A petition filed by the debtor; states that the debtor has debts. [555]

voting trust The shareholders transfer their stock certificates to a trustee who is empowered to vote the shares. [749]

waiting period A period of time that begins when the registration statement is filed with the SEC and continues until the registration statement is declared effective. Only certain activities are permissible during the waiting period. [800]

warehouse company A bailee engaged in the business of storing property for compensation. Owes a *duty of reasonable care* to protect the bailed property. [922]

warranties of quality   Seller's or lessor's assurance to buyer or lessee that the goods meet certain standards of quality. Warranties may be expressed or implied. [431]

warranty   A buyer's or lessee's assurance that the goods meet certain standards. [431]

warranty disclaimer   Statements that negate express and implied warranties. [437]

warranty of fitness for a particular purpose   A warranty that arises when a seller or lessor warrants that the goods will meet the buyer's or lessee's expressed needs. [435]

waste   Occurs when a tenant causes substantial and permanent damage to the leased premises that decreases the value of the property and the landlord's reversionary interest in it. [947]

water pollution   Pollution of lakes, rivers, oceans, and other bodies of water. [860]

wetlands   Areas that are inundated or saturated by surface water or ground water that support vegetation typically adapted for life in such conditions. [861]

white-collar crimes   Crimes usually involving cunning and deceit rather than physical force. [129]

will   A declaration of how a person wants his or her property distributed upon death. [959, 967]

will or inheritance   A way to acquire title to property that is a result of another's death. [914]; If a person dies with a will, his or her property is distributed to the beneficiaries as designated in the will. If a person dies without a will, his or her property is distributed to the heirs as stipulated in the state's intestacy statute. [937]

Williams Act   An amendment to the Securities Exchange Act of 1934 made in 1968 that specifically regulates all tender offers. [783]

winding-up and liquidation   The process by which a dissolved corporation's assets are collected, liquidated, and distributed to creditors, shareholders, and other claimants. [736]

wire fraud   The use of telephone or telegraph to defraud another person. [129]

withholding delivery   The act of the seller or lessor purposefully refusing to deliver goods to the buyer or lessee upon breach of the sales or lease contract by the buyer or lessee or the insolvency of the buyer or lessee. [414]

workers' compensation acts   Acts that compensate workers and their families if workers are injured in connection with their jobs. [620]

work-related test   A test to determine the liability of a principal; if an agent commits an intentional tort within a work-related time or space, the principal is liable for any injury caused by the agent's intentional tort. [597]

World Trade Organization (WTO)   An international organization of more than 130 member nations created to promote and enforce trade agreements among member nations. [161]

World Wide Web   An electronic connection of millions of computers that support a standard set of rules for the exchange of information. [356]

writ of certiorari   An official notice that the Supreme Court will review one's case. [29]

written order   A stop-payment order that is good for six months after the date it is written. [516]

wrongful dishonor   Occurs when there are sufficient funds in a drawer's account to pay a properly payable check, but the bank does not do so. [516]

wrongful dissolution   When a partner withdraws from a partnership without having the right to do so at that time. [699]

wrongful eviction   A violation of the covenant of quiet enjoyment. [946]

wrongful termination   The termination of an agency contract in violation of the terms of the agency contract. The non-breaching party may recover damages from the breaching party. [602]; Termination of a franchise without just cause. [683]

zoning ordinance   Local laws that are adopted by municipalities and local governments to regulate land use within their boundaries. Zoning ordinances are adopted and enforced to protect the health, safety, morals, and general welfare of the community. [950]

Case Index

Cases cited or discussed are in roman type. Principal cases are in **bold type**.

Subject Index

Contemporary Business Environment